BROOKS MEMORIAL

CHARLES A. BROOKS

ANNA CLOYDE BROOKS

CONGRESSIONAL QUARTERLY'S

Guide to Congress

SECOND EDITION

Congressional Quarterly Inc.

Congressional Quarterly Inc., an editorial research service and publishing company, serves clients in the fields of news, education, business and government. It combines specific coverage of Congress, government and politics by Congressional Quarterly with the more general subject range of an affiliated service, Editorial Research Reports.

Congressional Quarterly was founded in 1945 by Henrietta and Nelson Poynter. Its basic periodical publication was and still is the CQ *Weekly Report,* mailed to clients every Saturday. A cumulative index is published quarterly.

The CQ *Almanac,* a compendium of legislation for one session of Congress, is published every spring. *Congress and the Nation* is published every four years as a record of government for one presidential term. Congressional Quarterly also publishes paperback books on public affairs.

CQ Direct Research is a consulting service which performs contract research and maintains a reference library and query desk for the convenience of clients.

Editorial Research Reports covers subjects beyond the specialized scope of Congressional Quarterly. It publishes reference material on foreign affairs, business, education, cultural affairs, national security, science and other topics of news interest. Service to clients includes a 6,000-word report four times a month bound and indexed semi-annually. Editorial Research Reports publishes paperback books in its fields of coverage. Founded in 1923, the service merged with Congressional Quarterly in 1956.

Copyright 1976 by Congressional Quarterly Inc.
1414 22nd St. N.W., Washington, D.C. 20037

Library of Congress Cataloging in Publication Data

Congressional Quarterly Inc.
  Congressional Quarterly's Guide to Congress.
Second Edition.

  Bibliography.
  Includes index.
  1. United States. Congress. I. Title. II. Title: Guide to the Congress of the United States.
JK1021.C56   1976a   328.73   76-41925
ISBN 0-87187-100-9

Contributors to the *Guide to Congress*

Editors: Robert A. Diamond, Patricia Ann O'Connor

Associate Editor: David Tarr

Major Contributors: Margaret C. Thompson, James R. Wagner

Editorial Coordinator: Robert E. Healy

Contributors: Michael Carson, Prentice Bowsher, Martha V. Gottron, Ed Johnson, Elder Witt.
Barbara Cornell, Mary Cohn, Edna Frazier, William Gerber, Susan B. Jenkins, William Korns, Karen Landis, Warden Moxley, James Phillips, Georgiana Rathbun, Joan Szabo, Park Teter, Paula Walker, Laura Weiss.

Index: Mary Neumann, Jeanne D. Heise
Art and Graphics: Howard Chapman (Director), Richard A. Pottern.

Proofreaders: Eugene J. Gabler, Sumie Kinoshita, Lynda McNeil.

Congressional Quarterly Inc.

Executive Editor: Wayne Kelley
General Manager: Paul Massa
Production Manager: I. D. Fuller
Assistant Production Manager: Kathleen E. Walsh

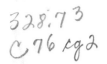

Introduction

The Congress of the United States is, as David Truman once wrote, a "well known stranger." Few symbols are better known than the Capitol building, few public officials receive more publicity than the 535 men and women who work there. Compared to our other political institutions—the presidency, the bureaucracy, the courts—Congress conducts its business in full view. And yet Congress remains a dimly perceived and confusing institution to most Americans.

Understanding Congress is not easy. Its size, decentralized complexity, lack of hierarchy and changefulness see to that. For a quarter of a century, Congressional Quarterly Inc. has specialized in providing thoroughly factual, authoritative and non-partisan reports on Congress. The various CQ publications have become indispensable aids to journalists, scholars, politicians, bureaucrats, lobbyists and everyone else (including members of Congress) who want to know what is happening on Capitol Hill.

This *Guide to Congress* was first published in 1971 and quickly recognized as the best general reference work on our fascinating and frustrating national legislature. The rush of important events and spate of congressional reforms of the last five years have outdated this admirable work; hence this extensively revised second edition was prepared.

Among the more important new developments treated in this edition are: Watergate and its consequences, the struggle between the White House and Congress for control of foreign policy, efforts to reform campaign finance and the federal budgetary process and the "democratization" of Congress.

Watergate and Its Aftermath

The crimes and wrongdoings of the Nixon Administration did far more than lead to the first presidential resignation in American history; Watergate profoundly altered the political and moral context within which Congress operates. Popular confidence in all our political institutions was badly shaken but most especially and appropriately in the presidency. Congress' role in uncovering the scandals may have been limited, but the Watergate hearings of the Ervin Committee in the Senate and the House Judiciary Committee's hearings on impeachment led many Americans to a new-found appreciation of a strong, competent and in-

dependent national legislature. Whether this mood will last is unclear, but the Congress has been far more assertive in dealing with the President, far more sensitive to charges of misused or arbitrary power within its own ranks, than ever before in recent times. The indirect effects of Watergate on Congress are writ large on many of the pages which follow.

Foreign Affairs

Nowhere has the struggle between President and Congress for control over public policy been more one-sided than in the area of foreign policy. The unpopularity of the Vietnam War, along with Watergate, has emboldened Congress to seek to recapture at least some of its constitutional authority over foreign policy. The War Powers Act of 1973, which limits presidential power to commit American combat forces abroad without congressional approval, is the high water mark of this thrust. Presidents will find it more difficult to dominate the making of foreign and defense policy in the future.

Campaign Finance

In the wake of Watergate, Congress enacted drastic reforms in the nation's electoral system. While the legislators' devotion to civic rectitude has proven more thoroughgoing in regulating presidential elections than their own, new limits on expenditures and contributions in congressional races have been written into law, along with new public disclosure provisions. Outright public financing of presidential campaigns has also been legislated and is undergoing its first test as I write. It seems almost certain that these fruits of Watergate will require revision in the future if they are to achieve their manifest objectives. But experimentation has begun to brighten one of the darkest corners of American politics.

The Federal Budget

Perhaps the most important congressional reform in recent times seems the most technical and dull. And yet the Congressional Budget and Impoundment Control Act of 1974 is a potentially momentous step toward coordinated congressional control over the federal government's $350-billion budget. If this statute works as intended—or comes even close to doing so—the relationships between President and Congress, and the internal distribution of power within both House and Senate will be basically altered. No student of American government can afford to ignore the action here. The origins, promise and pitfalls of the new congressional machinery and procedures are fully described in this volume.

"Democratization" of the House and Senate

Both houses of the Congress (but especially the House of Representatives) have made a number of changes in their internal organization and procedures which seem to make them more "open" and "democratic" institutions. The power of committee chairmen has been diluted significantly and their selection made subject to the votes of their fellow party members—that the latter reform was not merely symbolic was underscored when the House Democrats proceeded to defeat three incumbent chairmen in 1975. Committee sessions, including the all-important mark-up and conference committee sessions, have been opened to the public and the press. Non-recorded floor votes have become a rarity on matters of significance. The Congress has shown a willingness to face up to the problem of disciplining its own members when their conduct has fallen well beyond the bounds of conventional morality.

Whether all these changes will endure is problematical. Whether the further dispersion of power in an institution already suffering from weak central leadership is really "democratic" can be argued at length. Whether these and other changes of the last five to six years will result in a national legislature better able to cope with the problems of the late 1970s remains to be seen. But one thing is certain; the Congress has changed more rapidly and basically in the 1970s than at any other time in recent memory. The story of these changes, and an early look at their probable consequences, is fully treated here.

Those who create something excellent are captured and controlled by it to a surprising degree. The original *Guide to Congress* was an excellent work. It is not surprising therefore that this edition contains no radical departures in subject, organization or style. But there are a few changes from the first edition which should make it an even better research tool. The work has been fully footnoted, thereby leading readers to additional, more specialized sources of information if needed. The bibliographies at the end of each chapter have been updated. And the index has been expanded and revised. Otherwise the Congressional Quarterly has merely done its thing once again.

All Congress watchers, from neophytes to grizzled old-timers, can learn much from this volume.

Donald R. Matthews
University of Washington
August 1976

How to Use
the *Guide to Congress*

In his introduction to this volume, Professor Matthews has outlined the major congressional developments of the past five years which have warranted a new edition of the *Guide to Congress*. This note offers suggestions to assist users of the *Guide* in locating material of interest to them.

Research Aids

There are two key aids to locating information in the *Guide*—the Table of Contents and the Index. The Table of Contents offers an overall view of the scope of the book and allows quick access to major sections. The Index pinpoints references to the broad range of subjects appearing throughout the book.

Table of Contents

The Summary Table of Contents *(p. vii)* indicates the organization of the volume. The detailed Table of Contents *(p. xiii)* shows the outline and contents of the seven major parts of the *Guide*—Part I: Origins and Development of Congress; Part II: Powers of Congress; Part III: Congressional Procedures; Part IV: Housing and Support of Congress; Part V: Congress and the Electorate; Part VI: Pressures on Congress; and Part VII: Qualifications and Conduct of Members.

The 34 chapters comprising Parts I through VII contain primarily narrative material designed to be read as concise historical summaries of the subjects covered. For example, the reader interested in the history of the House of Representatives will find it on pages 35 to 67. The history of congressional investigations is covered on pages 141 to 173. And the development of the committee system and seniority is covered on pages 365 to 407.

Supplementing the narrative chapters of the *Guide* is an Appendix containing information relevant to many of the chapters. The detailed contents of the Appendix appear on pages xxi to xxii. Major items in the Appendix include a Biographical Index of every member of Congress since 1789, the texts of key historical documents, the Standing Rules of the Senate and the Rules of the House of Representatives and compilations of such key facts as party control of Congress and sessions of Congress since 1789. Pages in the Appendix are numbered 1-A, 2-A, 3-A, etc.

Index

The Index *(p. 253-A)* is designed for the user seeking quick reference to the many subjects, charts, tables, summaries, individuals and compilations of facts appearing throughout the book. For example, the researcher seeking a brief identification of the Bricker amendment, the number of times the Vice President has voted in the Senate, a complete list of congressional votes on impeachment, the definition of an executive agreement or a complete list of cloture votes in the Senate should consult the Index.

In the Index, the term "box" will frequently appear. This term indicates that there will be detailed background information on the page the "box" appears.

Footnotes and Selected Bibliographies

At the end of each chapter is a list of footnotes indicating sources used throughout the chapter. A Selected Bibliography is also included at the end of each chapter; it includes sources used in preparing the chapter as well as additional sources for the reader who may wish to do further research.

The Congressional Quarterly *Weekly Reports, Almanacs* and the *Congress and the Nation* series should also be consulted for additional information on material covered in the *Guide to Congress.*

Summary Table of Contents

Table of Contents

Part I

Origins and Development of Congress

Part II

Powers of Congress

Part III

Congressional Procedures

Part IV

Housing and Support of Congress

Part V

Congress and the Electorate

Part VI

Pressures on Congress

Part VII

Qualifications and Conduct of Members

APPENDIX

Reorganization Provisions

GLOSSARY OF CONGRESSIONAL TERMS

Act—The term for legislation which has passed both houses of Congress and has been signed by the President or passed over his veto, thus becoming law.

Also used technically for a bill that has been passed by one house and engrossed. *(See Engrossed.)*

Adjournment sine die—Adjournment without definitely fixing a day for reconvening; literally "adjournment without a day." Usually used to connote the final adjournment of a session of Congress. A session can continue until noon, Jan. 3, of the following year, when a new session usually begins.

Adjournment to a Day Certain—Adjournment under a motion or resolution which fixes the next time of meeting. Neither house can adjourn for more than three days without the concurrence of the other. A session of Congress is not ended by adjournment to a day certain.

Amendment—Proposal of a congressman to alter the language or stipulations in a bill or act. It is usually printed, debated, and voted upon in the same manner as a bill.

Appeal—A senator's challenge of a ruling or decision made by the presiding officer of the Senate. The senator appeals to members of the chamber to override the decision. If carried by a majority vote, the appeal nullifies the chair's ruling. In the House the decision of the Speaker traditionally has been final, with no appeal to the members to reverse his stand. To appeal a ruling would be considered an attack on the Speaker.

Appropriation Bill—Grants the actual monies approved by authorization bills, but not necessarily to the total permissible under the authorization bill. An appropriation bill originates in the House, and normally is not acted on until its authorization measure is enacted. General appropriations bills are supposed to be enacted before the start of the fiscal year to which they apply, but in recent years this has rarely happened. *(See Continuing Appropriations.)* In addition to general appropriations bills, there are two specialized types. *(See Deficiency and Supplemental.)*

Authorization Bill—Authorizes a program, specifies its general aim and conduct, and, unless "open-ended," puts a ceiling on monies that can be used to finance it. Usually enacted before appropriation bill is passed. *(See Contract Authorization.)*

Bills—Most legislative proposals before Congress are in the form of bills, and are designated as HR (House of Representatives) or S (Senate) according to the house in which they originate and by a number assigned in the order in which they were introduced, from the beginning of each two-year congressional term. "Public bills" deal with general questions, and become Public Laws if approved by Congress and signed by the President. "Private bills" deal with individual matters such as claims against the government, immigration and naturalization cases, land titles, etc., and become Private Laws if approved and signed.

The introduction of a bill, and its referral to an appropriate committee for action, follows the process given in "How A Bill Becomes Law." *(See also Concurrent Resolution, Joint Resolution, Resolution, in this Glossary.)*

Bills Introduced—In the Senate, any number of senators may join in introducing a single bill. In the House, until 1967, only one members's name could appear on a single bill. But the House April 25, 1967, voted to allow cosponsorship of bills, setting a limit of 25 cosponsors on any one bill.

Many bills in reality are committee bills and are introduced under the name of the chairman of the committee or subcommittee as a formality. All appropriation bills fall into this category, as do many other bills, particularly those dealing with complicated, technical subjects. A committee frequently holds hearings on a number of related bills, and may agree on one of them or on an entirely new bill. *(See Clean Bill and By Request.)*

Bills Referred—When introduced a bill is referred to the committee which has jurisdiction over the subject with which the bill is concerned. The appropriate reference for bills is spelled out in Senate and House rules. Committee jurisdictions in the House were reorganized in 1974. Bills are referred by the Speaker in the House and the presiding officer in the Senate. Appeals may be made from their decisions.

Budget—The document sent to Congress by the President in January of each year's estimated government revenue and expenditures for the ensuing fiscal year and recommending appropriations in detail. The President's budget message forms the basis for congressional hearings and legislation on the year's appropriations.

By Request—A phrase used when a senator or representative introduces a bill at the request of an executive agency or private organization but does not necessarily endorse the legislation.

Calendar—An agenda or list of pending business before committees or either chamber. The House uses five legislative calendars. *(See Consent, Discharge, House, Private and Union Calendar.)*

In the Senate, all legislative matters reported from committee go on a single calendar. They are listed there in order, but may be called up irregularly by the majority leader either by a motion to do so, or by obtaining the unanimous consent of the Senate. Frequently the minority leader is consulted to assure unanimous consent. Only cloture can limit debate on bills thus called up. *(See Call of the Calendar.)*

The Senate also uses one nonlegislative calendar, for treaties, etc. *(See Executive Calendar.)*

Calendar Wednesday—In the House on Wednesdays, committees may be called in the order in which they appear in Rule X of the House Manual, for the purpose of bringing up any of their bills from the House or the Union Calendars, except bills which are privileged. General debate is limited to two hours. Bills called up from the Union Calendar are considered in Committee of the Whole. Calendar Wednesday is not observed during the last two weeks of a session, and may be dispensed with at other times—by a two-thirds vote. It usually is dispensed with.

Call of the Calendar—Senate bills which are not brought up for debate by a motion or a unanimous consent agreement are brought before the Senate for action when the calendar listing them in order is "called." Bills considered in this fashion are usually noncontroversial, and debate is limited to five minutes for each senator on a bill or on amendments to it.

Chamber—Meeting place for the total membership of either the House or the Senate, as distinguished from the respective committee rooms.

Clean Bill—Frequently after a committee has finished a major revision of a bill, one of the committee members, usually the chairman, will assemble the changes plus what is left of the original bill into a new measure and introduce it as a "clean bill." The new measure, which carries a new number, is then sent to the floor for consideration. This often is a timesaver, as committee-recommended changes do not have to be considered one at a time by the chamber.

Clerk of the House—Chief administrative officer of the House of Representatives with duties corresponding to those of the Secretary of the Senate. *(See Secretary of the Senate.)*

Cloture—The process by which a filibuster can be ended in the Senate, other than by unanimous consent. A motion for cloture can apply to any measure before the Senate, including a proposal to change the chamber's rules. It requires 16 senators' signatures for introduction and the votes of three-fifths of the entire Senate membership (60 if there are no vacancies), except that to end a filibuster against a proposal to amend the Standing Rules of the Senate a two-thirds vote of senators present and voting is required. It is put to a roll-call vote one hour after the Senate meets on the second day following introduction of the motion. If voted, cloture limits each senator to one hour of debate.

Committee—A subdivision of the House or Senate which prepares legislation for action by the parent chamber, or makes investigations as directed by the parent chamber. There are several types of committees. *(See Standing, and Select or Special.)* Most standing committees are divided into subcommittees, which study legislation, hold hearings, and report their recommendations to the full committee. Only the full committee can report legislation for action by the House or Senate.

Committee of the Whole—The working title of what is formally "The Committee of the Whole House [of Representatives] on the State of the Union." Unlike other committees, it has no fixed membership. It is comprised of any 100 or more House members who participate—on the floor of the chamber—in debating or altering legislation before the body. Such measures, however, must first have passed through the regular committees and be on the calendar.

Technically, the Committee of the Whole considers only bills directly or indirectly appropriating money, authorizing appropriations, or involving taxes or charges on the public. Actually, the Committee of the Whole often considers other types of legislation. Because the Committee of the Whole need number only 100 representatives, a quorum is more readily attained, and business is expedited. Prior to 1971, members' positions were not individually recorded on votes taken in Committee of the Whole except for automatic roll calls in the absence of a quorum.

When the full House resolves itself into the Committee of the Whole, it supplants the Speaker with a "chairman." The measure is debated or amended, with votes on amendments as needed. When the committee completes its action on the measure, it dissolves itself by "rising." The Speaker returns, and the full House hears the erstwhile chairman of the committee report that group's recommendations. The full House then acts upon them.

At this time members may demand a roll-call vote on any amendment *adopted* in the Committee of the Whole.

Concurrent Resolution—A concurrent resolution, designated H Con Res or S Con Res, must be passed by both houses but does not require the signature of the President and does not have the force of law. Concurrent resolutions generally are used to make or amend rules applicable to both houses or to express the sentiment of the two houses. A concurrent resolution, for example, is used to fix the time for adjournment of a Congress. It might also be used to convey the congratulations of Congress to another country on the anniversary of its independence.

Conference—A meeting between the representatives of the House and Senate to reconcile differences between the two houses over provisions of a bill. Members of the conference committee are appointed by the Speaker and the president of the Senate and are called "managers" for their respective chambers. A majority of the managers for each house must reach agreement on the provisions of the bill (often a compromise between the versions of the two chambers) before it can be sent up for floor action in the form of a "conference report." There it cannot be amended, and if not approved by both chambers, the bill goes back to conference. Elaborate rules govern the conduct of the conferences. All bills which are passed by House and Senate in slightly different form need not be sent to conference; either chamber may "concur" in the other's amendments. *(See Custody of the Papers.)*

Congressional Record—The daily, printed account of proceedings in both House and Senate chambers, with debate, statements and the like reported verbatim. Committee activities are not covered, except that their reports to the parent body are noted. Highlights of legislative and committee action are embodied in a Digest section of the Record, and congressmen are entitled to have their extraneous remarks printed in an appendix known as "Extension of Remarks." They may edit and revise remarks made on the floor, and frequently do, so that quotations reported by the press are not always found in the Record.

Congressional Terms of Office—Begin on Jan. 3 of the year following the general election.

Consent Calendar—Members of the House may place on this calendar any bill on the Union or House Calendar which is considered to be noncontroversial. Bills on the Consent Calendar are normally called on the first and third Mondays of each month. On the first occasion when a bill is called in this manner, consideration may be blocked by the objection of any member. On the second time, if there are three objections, the bill is stricken from the Consent Calendar. If less than three members object, the bill is given immediate consideration.

A bill on the Consent Calendar may be postponed in another way. A member may ask that the measure be passed over "without prejudice." In that case, no objection is recorded against the bill, and its status on the Consent Calendar remains unchanged.

A bill stricken from the Consent Calendar remains on the Union or House Calendar.

Continuing Appropriation—When a fiscal year begins and Congress has not yet enacted all the regular appropriation bills for that year, it passes a joint resolution "continuing appropriations" for government agencies at rates generally based on their previous year's appropriations.

Contract Authorizations—Found in both authorization and appropriation bills, these authorizations are stopgap provisions which permit the federal government to let contracts or obligate itself for future payments from funds not yet appropriated. The assumption is that funds will be available for payment when contracted debts come due.

Correcting the Record—Rules prohibit members from changing their votes after the result has been announced. But frequently, hours, days, or months after a vote has been taken, a member announces that he was "incorrectly recorded." In the Senate, a request to change one's vote almost always receives unanimous consent. In the House, members are prohibited from changing their votes if tallied by the electronic voting system installed in 1973. If taken by roll call, it is permissible if consent is granted. Errors in the text of the Record may be corrected by unanimous consent.

Custody of the Papers—To reconcile differences between the House and Senate versions of a bill, a conference may be arranged. The chamber with "custody of the papers"—the engrossed bill, engrossed amendments, messages of transmittal—is the only body empowered to request the conference. That body then has the advantage of acting last on the conference report when it is submitted.

Deficiency Appropriation—An appropriation to cover the difference between an agency's regular appropriation and the amount deemed necessary for it to operate for the full fiscal year. In recent years deficiency bills have usually been called supplemental appropriations.

Dilatory Motion—A motion, usually made upon a technical point, for the purpose of killing time and preventing action on a bill. The rules outlaw dilatory motions, but enforcement is largely within the discretion of the presiding officer.

Discharge a Committee—Relieve a committee from jurisdiction over a measure before it. This is rarely a successful procedure, attempted more often in the House than in the Senate.

In the House, if a committee does not report a bill within 30 days after the bill was referred to it, any member may file a discharge motion. This motion, treated as a petition, needs the signatures of 218 members (a majority of the House). After the required signatures have been obtained, there is a delay of seven days. Then, on the second and fourth Mondays of each month, except during the last six days of a session, any member who has signed the petition may be recognized to move that the committee be dis-

charged. Debate on the motion to discharge is limited to 20 minutes, and, if the motion is carried, consideration of the bill becomes a matter of high privilege.

If a resolution to consider a bill *(see Rule)* is held up in the Rules Committee for more than seven legislative days, any member may enter a motion to discharge the committee. The motion is handled like any other discharge petition in the House.

Occasionally, to expedite noncontroversial legislative business, a committee is discharged upon unanimous consent of the House, and a petition is not required. *(For Senate procedure, see Discharge Resolution.)*

Discharge Calendar—The House calendar to which motions to discharge committees are referred when they have the necessary 218 signatures and are awaiting action.

Discharge Petition—In the House, a motion to discharge a committee from considering a bill. The motion, or petition, requires signatures of 218 House members.

Discharge Resolution—In the Senate, a special motion any senator may introduce to relieve a committee from consideration of a bill before it. The resolution can be called up on motion for approval or disapproval, in the same manner as other matters of Senate business. *(For House procedure, see Discharge a Committee.)*

Division Vote—Same as Standing Vote. *(See below.)*

Enacting Clause—Key phrase in bills saying, "Be it enacted by the Senate and House of Representatives...." A successful motion to strike it from legislation kills the measure.

Engrossed Bill—The final copy of a bill as passed by one chamber, with the text as amended by floor action and certified to by the Clerk of the House or the Secretary of the Senate.

Enrolled Bill—The final copy of a bill which has been passed in identical form by both chambers. It is certified to by an officer of the house of origin (House clerk or Senate secretary) and then sent on for signatures of the House Speaker, the Senate president, and the U.S. President. An enrolled bill is printed on parchment.

Executive Calendar—This is an additional, non-legislative calendar, in the Senate, on which presidential documents such as treaties and nominations are listed.

Executive Document—A document, usually a treaty, sent to the Senate by the President for consideration or ratification. These are identified for each session of Congress as Executive A, 90th Congress, 1st Session; Executive B, etc. They are referred to committee in the same manner as other measures. Unlike legislative documents, however, treaties do not die at the end of a Congress, but remain "live" proposals until acted on by the Senate or withdrawn by the President.

Executive Session—Meeting of a Senate or a House committee (or, occasionally, of the entire chamber) which only the group's members are privileged to attend. Frequently witnesses appear before committees meeting in executive session, and other congressmen may be invited, but the public and press are not allowed.

Expenditures—The actual spending of money as distinguished from the appropriation of it. Expenditures are made by the disbursing officers of the administration; appropriations are made only by Congress. The two are rarely identical in any fiscal year; expenditures may represent money appropriated one, two or more years previously.

Filibuster—A time-delaying tactic used by a minority in an effort to prevent a vote on a bill which probably would pass if brought to a vote. The most common method is to take advantage of the Senate's rules permitting unlimited debate, but other forms of parliamentary maneuvering may be used. The stricter rules in the House make filibusters more difficult, but they are attempted from time to time through various delaying tactics arising from loopholes in House rules.

Fiscal Year—Financial operations of the government are carried out in a 12-month fiscal year, beginning on July 1 and ending on June 30. The fiscal year carries the date of the calendar year in which it ends. Beginning with fiscal 1977, the fiscal year will run from Oct. 1 through Sept. 30.

Floor Manager—A member, usually representing sponsors of a bill, who attempts to steer it through debate and revision to a final vote in the chamber. Floor managers are frequently chairmen or ranking members of the committee that reported the bill. Managers are responsible for apportioning the time granted supporters of the bill for debating it. The minority leader or the ranking minority member of the committee often apportions time for the opposition.

Frank—A congressman's facsimile signature on envelopes, used in lieu of stamps for his official outgoing mail, thus postage-free. Also the privilege of sending mail postage-free.

Germane—Pertaining to the subject matter of the measure at hand. All House amendments must be germane to the bill. The Senate requires that amendments be germane only when they are proposed to general appropriation bills, bills being considered under cloture, or, often, when proceeding under an agreement to limit debate.

Grants-in-Aid—Payments by the federal government which aid the recipient state, local government or individual in administering specified programs, services or activities.

Hearings—Committee sessions for hearing witnesses. At hearings on legislation, witnesses usually include specialists, government officials and spokesmen for persons affected by the bills under study. Hearings related to special investigations bring forth a variety of witnesses. Committees sometimes use their subpoena power to summon reluctant witnesses. The public and press may attend "open" hearings, but are barred from "closed" or "executive" hearings.

The committee announces its hearings, from one day to many weeks in advance, and may invite certain persons to testify. Persons who request time to testify may be turned down by the committee, but most requests are honored.

Both houses have rules against conducting committee hearings in secret, but the House's are much more stringent.

Hopper—Box on House clerk's desk where bills are deposited on introduction.

House—The House of Representatives, as distinct from the Senate, although each body is a "house" of Congress.

House Calendar—Listing for action by the House of Representatives of public bills which do not directly or indirectly appropriate money or raise revenue.

Immunity—Constitutional privilege of congressmen to make verbal statements on the floor and in committee for which they cannot be sued or arrested for slander or libel. Also, freedom from arrest while traveling to or from sessions of Congress or on official business. Congressmen in this status may be arrested only for treason, felonies or a breach of the peace, as defined by congressional manuals.

Joint Committee—A committee composed of a specified number of members of both House and Senate. Usually a joint committee is investigative in nature. There are a few standing joint committees, such as the Joint Committee on Atomic Energy and the Joint Economic Committee.

Joint Resolution—A joint resolution, designated H J Res or S J Res, requires the approval of both houses and the signature of the President, just as a bill does, and has the force of law if approved. There is no real difference between a bill and a joint resolution. The latter is generally used in dealing with limited matters, such as a single appropriation for a specific purpose.

Joint resolutions also are used to propose amendments to the Constitution. They do not require presidential signature, but become a part of the Constitution when three-fourths of the states have ratified them.

Journal—The official record of the proceedings of the House and Senate. The Journal records the actions taken in each chamber, but unlike the *Congressional Record,* it does not include the verbatim report of speeches, debate, etc.

Law—An act of Congress which has been signed by the President, or passed over his veto by the Congress. Laws are listed numerically by Congress; for example, the Civil Rights Act of 1964 (HR 7152) became Public Law 88-352 during the 88th Congress.

Legislative Day—The "day" extending from the time either house meets after an adjournment until the time it next adjourns. Because the House normally adjourns from day to day, legislative days and calendar days usually coincide. But in the Senate, a legislative day may, and frequently does, extend over several calendar days. *(See Recess.)*

Lobby—A group seeking to influence the passage or defeat of legislation. Originally the term referred to persons frequenting the lobbies or corridors of legislative chambers in order to speak to lawmakers.

The exact definition of a lobby and the activity of lobbying is a matter of opinion. By some definitions, lobbying is limited to attempts at direct influence by personal interview and persuasion. Under other definitions, lobbying includes attempts at indirect influence, such as stirring members of a group to write or visit congressmen, or attempting to create a climate of opinion favorable to a desired legislative action.

The right to attempt to influence legislation is based on the First Amendment to the Constitution, which says Congress shall make no law abridging the right of the people "to petition the government for a redress of grievances."

Majority Leader—Chief strategist and floor spokesman for the party in nominal control in either chamber. He is elected by his party colleagues and is virtually program director for his chamber, since he usually speaks for its majority.

Majority Whip—In effect, the assistant majority leader, in House or Senate. His job is to help marshal majority forces in support of party strategy.

Manual—The official handbook in each house prescribing its organization, procedures and operations in detail. The Senate manual contains standing rules, orders, laws and resolutions affecting Senate business; the House manual is the equivalent for that chamber. Both volumes contain previous codes under which Congress functioned and from which it continues to derive precedents. Committee powers are outlined. The rules set forth in the manuals may be changed by elaborate chamber actions also specified by the manuals.

Marking Up a Bill—Going through a measure, usually in committee, taking it section by section, revising language, penciling in new phrases, etc. If the bill is extensively revised, the new version may be introduced as a separate bill, with a new number. *(See Clean Bill.)*

Memorial—A request for congressional opposition or an objection from an organization or citizens' group to particular legislation or government practice under the purview of Congress. All communications, both supporting and opposing legislation, from state legislatures are embodied in memorials. They are referred to appropriate committees unless the legislation dealt with in the memorial has been reported to the Senate, in which case the memorial is placed on the table. It can be called up for consideration at the time the bill is read for amendments. *(See Petition.)*

Minority Leader—Floor leader for the minority party. *(See Majority Leader.)*

Minority Whip—Performs duties of whip for the minority party. *(See Majority Whip.)*

Morning Hour—The time set aside at the beginning of each legislative day for the consideration of regular routine business. The "hour" is of indefinite duration in the House, where it is rarely used. In the Senate it is the first two hours of a session following an adjournment, as distinguished from a recess. The morning hour can be terminated earlier if the morning business has been completed. This business includes such matters as messages from the President, communications from the heads of departments, messages from the House, the presentation of petitions and memorials, reports of standing and select committees, and the introduction of bills and resolutions.

During the first hour of the morning hour in the Senate, no motion to proceed to the consideration of any bill on the calendar is in order except by unanimous consent. During the second hour, motions can be made but must be decided without debate. Senate committees may meet while the Senate is in the morning hour.

Motion—Request by a congressman for any one of a wide array of parliamentary actions. He "moves" for a certain procedure, or the consideration of a measure or a vote, etc. The precedence of motions, and whether they are debatable, is set forth in the House and Senate manuals.

Nominations—Appointments to office by the executive branch of the government, subject to Senate confirmation. Although most nominations win quick Senate approval, some are controversial and become the topic of hearings and debate. Sometimes senators object to appointees for patronage reasons—for example, when a nomination to a local federal job is made without consulting the senators of the state concerned. Then a senator may use the stock objection that the nominee is "personally obnoxious" to him. Usually other senators join in blocking such an appointment out of courtesy to their colleague.

One Minute Speeches—Addresses by House members at the beginning of a legislative day. The speeches may cover any subject, but are limited strictly to one minute's duration. By unanimous consent, members may also be recognized to address the House for longer periods after completion of all legislative business for the day. Senators, by unanimous consent, are permitted to make speeches of a predetermined length during Morning Hour.

Override a Veto—If the President disapproves a bill and sends it back to Congress with his objections, Congress may override his veto by a two-thirds vote in each chamber. The Constitution requires a yea-and-nay roll call. The question put to each house is: "Shall the bill pass, the objections of the President to the contrary notwithstanding?" *(See also Pocket Veto and Veto.)*

Pair—A "gentlemen's agreement" between two lawmakers on opposite sides to withhold their votes on roll calls so their absence from Congress will not affect the outcome of a recorded vote. If passage of the measure requires a two-thirds majority, a pair would require two members favoring the action to one opposed to it.

Two kinds of pairs—special and general—are used; neither is counted in vote totals. The names of lawmakers pairing on a given vote and their stands, if known, are printed in the *Congressional Record*.

The special pair applies to one or a series of roll-call votes on the same subject. On special pairs, lawmakers usually specify how they would have voted.

A general pair in the Senate, now rarely used in the chamber, applies to all votes on which the members pairing are on opposite sides, and it lasts for the length of time pairing senators agree on. It usually does not specify a senator's stand on a given vote.

The general pair in the House differs from the other pairs. No agreement is involved and the pair does not tie up votes. A representative expecting to be absent may notify the House clerk he wishes to make a "general" pair. His name then is paired arbitrarily with that of another member desiring a general pair, and the list is printed in the

Congressional Record. He may or may not be paired with a member taking the opposite position. General pairs in the House give no indication of how a congressman would have voted. *(See Record Vote and Stand.)*

Petition—A request or plea sent to one or both chambers from an organization or private citizens group asking support of particular legislation or favorable consideration of a matter not yet receiving congressional attention. They are referred to appropriate committees and are considered or not, according to committee decision. *(See Memorial.)*

Pocket Veto—The act of the President in withholding his approval of a bill after Congress has adjourned—either for the year or for a specified period. However, the U.S. District Court of Appeals for the District of Columbia on Aug. 14, 1974, upheld a congressional challenge to a pocket veto used by former President Nixon during a six-day congressional recess in 1970, declaring that it was an improper use of the pocket veto power. When Congress is in session, a bill becomes law without the President's signature if he does not act upon it within 10 days, excluding Sundays, from the time he gets it. But if Congress adjourns within that 10-day period, the bill is killed without the President's formal veto.

Point of Order—An objection raised by a congressman that the chamber is departing from rules governing its conduct of business. The objector cites the rule violated, the chair sustaining his objection if correctly made. Order is restored by the chair's suspending proceedings of the chamber until it conforms to the prescribed "order of business." Members sometimes raise a "point of no order"—when there is noise and disorderly conduct in the chamber.

President of the Senate—Presiding officer of the upper chamber, normally the Vice President of the United States. In his absence, a president pro tempore (president for the time being) presides.

President pro tempore—The chief officer of the Senate in the absence of the Vice President. He is elected by his fellow senators. The recent practice has been to elect to the office the senator of the majority party with longest continuous service.

Previous Question—In this sense, a "question" is an "issue" before the House for a vote and the issue is "previous" when some other topic has superseded it in the attention of the chamber. A motion for the previous question, when carried, has the effect of cutting off all debate and forcing a vote on the subject originally at hand. If, however, the previous question is moved and carried before there has been any debate on the subject at hand and the subject is debatable, then 40 minutes of debate is allowed before the vote. The previous question is sometimes moved in order to prevent amendments from being introduced and voted on. The motion for the previous question is a debate-limiting device and is not in order in the Senate.

Private Calendar—Private House bills dealing with individual matters such as claims against the government, immigration, land titles, etc., are put on this calendar.

When it is before the chamber, two members may block a private bill, which then is recommitted to committee.

Backers of a private bill thus recommitted have another recourse. The measure can be put into an "omnibus claims bill"—several private bills rolled into one. As with any bill, no part of an omnibus claims bill may be deleted without a vote. When a private bill goes back to the floor in this form, it can be defeated only by a majority of those present. The private calendar can be called on the first and third Tuesdays of each month.

Privilege—Privilege relates to the rights of congressmen and to the relative priority of the motions and actions they may make in their respective chambers. The two are distinct. "Privileged questions" concern legislative business. "Questions of privilege" concern legislators themselves. *(See below.)*

Privileged Questions—The order in which bills, motions and other legislative measures may be considered by Congress is governed by strict priorities. A motion to table, for instance, is more privileged than a motion to recommit. Thus, a motion to recommit can be superseded by a motion to table, and a vote would be forced on the latter motion only. A motion to adjourn, however, would take precedence over this one, and is thus considered of the "highest privilege."

Pro Forma Amendment—*See Strike Out the Last Word.*

Questions of Privilege—These are matters affecting members of Congress individually or collectively.

Questions affecting the rights, safety, dignity and integrity of proceedings of the House or Senate as a whole are questions of privilege of the House or Senate, as the case may be.

Congressmen singly involve questions of "personal privilege." A member's rising to a question of personal privilege is given precedence over almost all other proceedings. An annotation in the House rules points out that the privilege of the member rests primarily on the Constitution, which gives him a conditional immunity from arrest and an unconditional freedom to speak in the House.

Quorum—The number of members whose presence is necessary for the transaction of business. In the Senate and House, it is a majority of the membership (when there are no vacancies, this is 51 in the Senate and 218 in the House). A quorum is 100 in the Committee of the Whole House. If a point of order is made that a quorum is not present, the only business in order is either a motion to adjourn or a motion to direct the sergeant-at-arms to request the attendance of absentees.

Readings of Bills—Traditional parliamentary law required bills to be read three times before they were passed. This custom is of little modern significance except in rare instances. Normally the bill is considered to have its first reading when it is introduced and printed, by title, in the *Congressional Record.* Its second reading comes when floor consideration begins. (This is the most likely point at which there is an actual reading of the bill, if there is any.) The third reading (usually by title) takes place when action has been completed on amendments.

Recess—Distinguished from adjournment in that a recess does not end a legislative day and therefore does not interfere with unfinished business. The rules in each house set forth certain matters to be taken up and disposed of at the beginning of each legislative day. The House, which operates under much stricter rules than the Senate, usually adjourns from day to day. The Senate often recesses.

Recommit to Committee—A simple motion, made on the floor after deliberation on a bill, to return it to the committee which reported it. If approved, recommittal usually is considered a death blow to the bill. In the House a motion to recommit can be made only by a member opposed to the bill, and in recognizing a member to make the motion, the Speaker gives the minority party preference over the majority.

A motion to recommit may include instructions to the committee to report the bill again with specific amendments or by a certain date. Or the instructions may be to make a particular study, with no definite deadline for final action.

Reconsider a Vote—A motion to reconsider the vote by which an action was taken has, until it is disposed of, the effect of suspending the action. In the Senate the motion can be made only by a member who voted on the prevailing side of the original question, or by a member who did not vote at all. In the House it can be made only by a member on the prevailing side.

A common practice after close votes in the Senate is a motion to reconsider, followed by a motion to table the motion to reconsider. On this motion to table, senators vote as they voted on the original question, to enable the motion to table to prevail. The matter is then finally closed and further motions to reconsider are not entertained. In the House, as a routine precaution, a motion to reconsider usually is made every time a measure is passed. Such a motion almost always is tabled immediately, thus shutting off the possibility of future reconsideration except by unanimous consent.

Motions to reconsider must be entered in the Senate within the next two days of actual session after the original vote has been taken. In the House they must be entered either on the same day or on the next succeeding day the House is in session.

Recorded Vote—A vote upon which each member's stand is individually made known. In the Senate, this is accomplished through a roll call of the entire membership, to which each senator on the floor must answer "yea," "nay" or, if he does not wish to vote, "present." Since January 1973, the House has used an electronic voting system both for yeas and nays and other recorded votes in the Committee of the Whole. *(See Teller Vote.)*

The Constitution requires yea-and-nay votes on the question of overriding a veto. In other cases, a recorded vote can be obtained by the demand of one-fifth of the members present.

Report—Both a verb and a noun, as a congressional term. A committee which has been examining a bill referred to it by the parent chamber "reports" its findings and recommendations to the chamber when the committee returns the measure. The process is called "reporting" a bill.

A "report" is the document setting forth the committee's explanation of its action. House and Senate reports are numbered separately and are designated S Rept. or H Rept. Conference reports are numbered and designated in the same way as regular committee reports.

Most reports favor a bill's passage. Adverse reports are occasionally submitted, but more often, when a committee disapproves a bill, it simply fails to report it at all. When a committee report is not unanimous, the dissenting committeemen may file a statement of their views, called minority views and referred to as a minority report. Sometimes a bill is reported without recommendation.

Rescission—An item in an appropriation bill rescinding, or cancelling, funds previously appropriated but not spent. Also, the repeal of a previous appropriation by the President to cut spending, if approved by Congress under procedures in the Budget and Impoundment Control Act of 1974.

Resolution—A simple resolution, designated H Res or S Res, deals with matters entirely within the prerogatives of one house or the other. It requires neither passage by the other chamber nor approval by the President, and does not have the force of law. Most resolutions deal with the rules of one house. They also are used to express the sentiments of a single house, as condolences to the family of a deceased member or to give "advice" on foreign policy or other executive business. *(Also see Concurrent and Joint Resolutions.)*

Rider—A provision, usually not germane, tacked on to a bill which its sponsor hopes to get through more easily by including in other legislation. Riders become law if the bills embodying them do. Riders providing for legislation in appropriations bills are outstanding examples, though technically they are banned. The House, unlike the Senate, has a strict germaneness rule; thus riders are usually Senate devices to get legislation enacted quickly or to bypass lengthy House consideration.

Rule—The term has two specific congressional meanings. A rule may be a standing order governing the conduct of House or Senate business and listed in the chamber's book of rules. The rules deal with duties of officers, order of business, admission to the floor, voting procedures, etc.

In the House, a rule also may be a decision made by its Rules Committee about the handling of a particular bill on the floor. The committee may determine under which standing rule a bill shall be considered, or it may provide a "special rule" in the form of a resolution. If the resolution is adopted by the House, the temporary rule becomes as valid as any standing rule, and lapses only after action has been completed on the measure to which it pertains.

A special rule sets the time limit on general debate. It may also waive points of order against provisions of the bill in question or against specified amendments intended to be proposed to the bill. It may even forbid all amendments or all amendments except, in some cases, those proposed by the legislative committee which handled the bill. In this instance it is known as a "closed" or "gag" rule as opposed to an "open" rule which puts no limitation on floor action, thus leaving the bill completed open to alteration. *(See Suspend the Rules.)*

Secretary of the Senate—Chief administrative officer of the Senate, responsible for direction of duties of Senate employees, education of pages, administration of oaths, receipt of registration of lobbyists and other activities necessary for the continuing operation of the Senate.

Select or Special Committee—A committee set up for a special purpose and a limited time by resolution of either House or Senate. Most special committees are investigative in nature.

Senatorial Courtesy—Sometimes referred to as "the courtesy of the Senate," it is a general practice without written rule applied to consideration of executive nominations. In practice, generally it means nominations from a state are not to be confirmed unless they have been approved by the senators of the President's party of that state, with other senators following their lead in the attitude they take toward such nominations.

Sine Die—See Adjournment sine die.

Slip Laws—The first official publication of a bill that has been enacted into law. Each is published separately in unbound single-sheet or pamphlet form. It usually takes two to three days from the date of presidential approval to the time when slip laws become available.

Speaker—The presiding officer of the House of Representatives, elected by its members.

Special Session—A session of Congress after it has adjourned sine die, completing its regular session. Special sessions are convened by the President of the United States under his constitutional powers.

Stand—A lawmaker's position, for or against, on a given issue or vote. He can make known his stand on a roll-call vote by answering "yea" or "nay," by "pairing" for or against, or by "announcing" his position to the House or Senate. Members also may go on record by answering the Congressional Quarterly poll of unrecorded congressmen on roll calls. *(See Pair, and Recorded Vote, above. See also Teller Vote, below.)*

Standing Committees—A group permanently provided for by House and Senate rules. The standing committees of the House were last reorganized by the committee reorganization act of 1974. The last major reorganization of Senate committees was in the Legislative Reorganization Act of 1946.

Standing Vote—A nonrecorded vote used in both House and Senate. A standing vote, also called a division vote, is taken as follows: Members in favor of a proposal stand and are counted by the presiding officer. Then members opposed stand and are counted. There is no record of how individual members voted. In the House, the presiding officer announces the number for and against. In the Senate, usually only the result is announced.

Statutes-at-Large—A chronological arrangement of the laws enacted in each session of Congress. Though indexed, the laws are not arranged by subject matter nor is there an indication of how they affect previous law. *(See U.S. Code.)*

Strike from the Record—Remarks made on the House floor may offend some member, who moves that the offending words be "taken down" for the Speaker's cognizance, and then expunged from the verbatim report to be carried in the *Congressional Record.*

Strike Out the Last Word—A move whereby House members are entitled to speak for a fixed time on a measure then being debated by the chamber. A member gains recognition from the chair by moving to strike out the last word of the amendment or section of the bill then under consideration. The motion is pro forma, and customarily requires no vote.

Substitute—A motion, an amendment, or an entire bill introduced in place of pending business. Passage of a substitute measure kills the original measure by supplanting it. A substitute may be amended.

Supplemental Appropriations—Normally are passed after the regular (annual) appropriations bills, but before the end of fiscal year to which they apply. Also referred to as "deficiencies."

Suspend the Rules—Often a time-saving procedure for passing bills in the House. The wording of the motion, which may be made by any member recognized by the Speaker, is: "I move to suspend the rules and pass the bill...." A favorable vote by two-thirds of those present is required for passage. Debate is limited to 40 minutes and no amendments from the floor are permitted. If a two-thirds favorable vote is not attained, the bill may be considered later under regular procedures. The suspension procedure is in order on the first and third Mondays and Tuesdays of each month.

Table a Bill—The motion to "lay on the table" is not debatable in either house, and is usually a method of making a final, adverse disposition of a matter. In the Senate, however, different language is sometimes used. The motion is worded to let a bill "lie on the table," perhaps for subsequent "picking up." This motion is more flexible, merely keeping the bill pending for later action, if desired.

Teller Vote—In the House, members file past tellers and are counted as for or against a measure, but they are not recorded individually. The teller vote is not used in the Senate. In the House, tellers are ordered upon demand of one-fifth of a quorum. This is 44 in the House, 20 in Committee of the Whole.

The House also has a recorded teller vote procedure, now largely supplanted by electronic voting, under which the individual votes of members are made public just as they would be on a yea-and-nay vote. This procedure, introduced in 1971, has forced members to take a public position on amendments to bills considered in Committee of the Whole. *(See Recorded Vote.)*

Treaties—Executive proposals which must be submitted to the Senate for approval by two-thirds of the senators present. Before they act on such foreign policy matters, senators usually send them to committee for scrutiny. Treaties are read three times and debated in the chamber much as are legislative proposals, but are rarely amended. After approval by the Senate, they are ratified by the President.

Unanimous Consent—Synonymous with Without Objection. *(See below.)*

Union Calendar—Bills which directly or indirectly appropriate money or raise revenue are placed on this House calendar according to the date reported from committee.

U.S. Code—A consolidation and codification of the general and permanent laws of the United States arranged by subject under 50 titles, the first six dealing with general or political subjects, and the other 44 alphabetically arranged from agriculture to war and national defense. The code is now revised every six years and a supplement is published after each session of Congress.

Veto—Disapproval by the President of a bill or joint resolution, other than one proposing an amendment to the Constitution. When Congress is in session, the President must veto a bill within 10 days, excluding Sundays, after he has received it; otherwise it becomes law with or without his signature. When the President vetoes a bill, he returns it to the house of its origin with a message stating his objections. The veto then becomes a question of high privilege. *(See Override a Veto.)*

When Congress has adjourned, the President may pocket veto a bill by failing to sign it. *(See Pocket Veto)*

Voice Vote—In either House or Senate, members answer "aye" or "no" in chorus and the presiding officer decides the result. The term also is used loosely to indicate action by unanimous consent or without objection.

Whip—See Majority Whip.

Without Objection—Used in lieu of a vote on non-controversial motions, amendments or bills, which may be passed in either the House or the Senate if no member voices an objection.

ORIGINS AND DEVELOPMENT OF CONGRESS

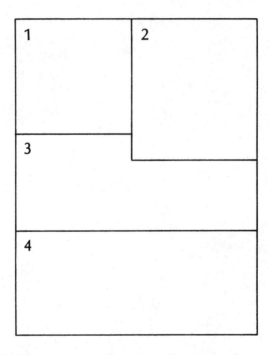

1. Committee drafting the Declaration of Independence: Benjamin Franklin, Thomas Jefferson, John Adams, Robert Livingston and Roger Sherman. Engraving by Johnson, Fry and Co. from original painting by Chappel. (Library of Congress photo no. LC-USZ62-2062.)

2. Delegates leaving Carpenter's Hall. From an original drawing by H. A. Ogden. (Library of Congress photo no. LC-USZ62-49980.)

3. Patrick Henry addressing the First Continental Congress in Carpenter's Hall, Philadelphia, 1774. Painting by Clyde O. De Land. (Library of Congress photo no. LC-USZ62-17110.)

4. Signing of the Declaration of Independence. Painting by John Trumbull in rotunda of U.S. Capitol Building; collection of the Architect of the Capitol. (Library of Congress photo no. LC-USA7-12762.)

The Origins and Development of Congress

The 55 delegates who gathered in Philadelphia in the summer of 1787 faced a challenge of no mean proportions: how were they to devise a system of government that would bind 13 sovereign and rival states into one firm union without threatening the traditional freedoms for which the American colonists so recently had fought?

Americans, with their predominantly English heritage, were wedded to the principles of representative government and personal freedom that had developed in England from the time of Magna Carta. They had gone to war against the mother country to preserve their freedoms from the encroachments of centralized power.

But independence had brought new problems. Men's allegiance still was directed toward the states, and most were reluctant to yield state sovereignty to any superior governmental power. The Articles of Confederation, the first basic law of the new nation, reflected this widespread distrust of centralized power. Under the Articles the United States was little more than a league of sovereign states, bickering and feuding among themselves. The states retained control over most essential governmental functions, and Congress—in which each state had one vote—was the sole organ of central government. So limited were its powers that it could not levy taxes or regulate trade, and it had no sanction to enforce any of its decisions.

The inadequacies of the Articles of Confederation, brought into sharp focus by Shays' Rebellion in 1786, gave impetus to a growing movement for governmental reform that culminated in the Philadelphia convention the following year. There the delegates voted to create a new national government consisting of supreme legislative, judicial and executive branches of government.[1]

In the Constitution that emerged from these deliberations, the concept of government by consent of the governed formed the basic principle; accountability was the watchword. The rights of the people were to be protected by diffusing power among rival interests.

The Constitution strengthened central authority, but national powers were carefully enumerated and other powers were reserved to the states and the people. The Constitution provided for a President, to be chosen by electors in each state, a national judiciary and a legislature of two chambers. The House of Representatives was to be popularly elected, while the Senate which shared certain executive powers with the President, was to be chosen by the state legislatures. Under the terms of the Great Compromise between the large and small states, representation in the House was to be proportional to a state's population and each state was to have two votes in the Senate. The national plan chosen by the delegates along with the separation of powers between the three branches of government created a system of checks and balances.

Writing in *The Federalist,* James Madison explained the delicate relationship between the federal and state governments and the division of power within the system. He stated: "In the compound republic of America, the power surrendered by the people is first divided between two distinct governments, and then the portion allotted to each subdivided among distinct and separate departments. Hence a double security arises to the rights of people. The different governments will control each other, at the same time that each will be controlled by itself."[2]

The final draft of the Constitution provided a broad framework for the new government. Thus for nearly 200 years the document has proved flexible enough to meet the nation's changing needs without extensive formal revision. Although many modern governmental practices would seem alien to the authors of the Constitution, the basic structure continues to operate in much the way they planned it. Madison realized the importance of "maintaining in practice the necessary partition of power among the several departments." He wrote that this could best be done "by so contriving the interior structure of the government as that

Madison on the Constitution

"If men were angels, no government would be necessary. If angels were to govern men, neither external nor internal controls on government would be necessary. In framing a government which is to be administered by men over men, the great difficulty lies in this: you must first enable the government to control the governed; and in the next place oblige it to control itself. A dependence on the people is, no doubt, the primary control on the government; but experience has taught mankind the necessity of auxiliary precautions."

—James Madison, *The Federalist,* No. 51

its several constituent parts may by their mutual relations, be the means of keeping each other in their proper places."[3]

Separate Roles of House and Senate

The House because of its popularity with the people was expected by Alexander Hamilton to be "a full match if not an overmatch for every other member of the government."[4] The Senate was originally designed to serve as a restraining influence on the House. But each chamber was given special power not shared by the other. The Senate's special authority over appointments and treaties was counterbalanced by the right of the House to originate all revenue bills.

At first the House, under the leadership of Madison and later under Henry Clay, was the preeminent chamber of Congress, but the Senate quickly emerged as a powerful legislative force. In the years preceding the Civil War it was the chief forum for the discussion of national issues, and in the post-Reconstruction era it became the dominant arm of the government. The House, as its membership increased, was compelled to adopt a variety of procedures that diminished the power of individual representatives but assured its ability to act when action was desired. The Senate remained a comparatively small body which found elaborate institutional structures unnecessary for the deliberation that it saw as its paramount function.

In his book, *Congressional Government*, written in 1885, Woodrow Wilson stated: "It is indispensable that besides the House of Representatives which runs on all fours with popular sentiment, we should have a body like the Senate which may refuse to run with it at all when it seems to be wrong—a body which has time and security enough to keep its head, if only now and then and but for a little while, till other people have had time to think. The Senate is fitted to do deliberately and well the revising which is its properest function, because its position as a representative of state sovereignty is one of eminent dignity, securing for it ready and sincere respect, and because popular demands, ere they reach it with definite and authoritative suggestion, are diluted by passage through the feelings and conclusions of the state legislatures, which are the Senate's only immediate constituents."[5]

Wilson's concept of the Senate might have been satisfactory to the framers of the Constitution, but in the 20th century it would no longer serve. As the Progressive era advanced, an increasingly restive public demanded more genuinely popular government, and in 1912 the Senate reluctantly agreed to a constitutional amendment providing for the direct election of senators. The House, too, felt the pressures of the times: the power of the Speaker which "Czar" Thomas B. Reed had established in the name of party responsibility in 1890 was dismantled under the banner of popular rule in 1910.

The Seventeenth Amendment, by taking senatorial elections out of the hands of the state governments, blurred the constitutional distinction between the Senate and House, and from the time of its adoption in 1913 the Senate came more and more to resemble the lower chamber. At times it, rather than the House, would appear to be the more representative legislative body. Both chambers, however, were subject to continuing charges that they failed to represent the will of the electorate. Although members of Congress ran for office as Republicans or Democrats, the absence of unity within the national parties precluded party responsibility in legislative action. Moreover, the in-stitutional characteristics of Congress itself often prevented a legislative majority from working its will. Campaigns against the seniority system, under which senators and representatives rose to power within their respective chambers, the Senate filibuster and secrecy in congressional activities all represented attempts to make Congress more accountable to the people. The same goal prompted demands for reapportionment of the House of Representatives to make congressional districts more nearly equal in population.

Congress and Presidential Power

The growth of presidential power in the 20th century, spurred by a major economic depression, two world wars, the Korean and Indochina conflicts, posed a threat to the viability of Congress as a coequal branch of government. As the volume and complexity of government business increased, legislative initiative shifted from the Capitol to the White House, and Congress with its antiquated procedures often found that it was no match for the tremendous resources of the executive branch. By passing reorganization acts in 1946 and 1970 and a congressional budget law in 1974, Congress sought to restore its equality in the three-branch federal partnership. But repeated clashes over spending, war and treaty powers marked congressional resistance to executive encroachment upon the powers delegated to Congress by the Constitution. One peak was Congress' overriding of President Nixon's veto of the War Powers Act of 1973, the first legislation ever to define the President's constitutional role in making war.

Then, all that went before was eclipsed by the most momentous constitutional confrontation since the Civil War—Watergate. Before expiring abruptly after some two years of mounting national agony, the great scandal had ultimately tested the powers of executive, legislative and judicial. A mesmerized nation and world watched the events in Washington from the Watergate burglary on June 17, 1972, until Nixon's resignation on Aug. 9, 1974.

The Supreme Court played a crucial role when it ruled unanimously that the President had no power to withhold evidence in a criminal trial. Nixon obeyed the court and surrendered the evidence, certain White House tape recordings. In quick order, the House Judiciary Committee approved three articles of impeachment against Nixon, the new evidence further gravely incriminated him, and 16 days after the court decision, he became the first President in history to resign the office.

In his brief inaugural address, President Ford proclaimed, "Our Constitution works." But others were not so convinced. Rep. John Conyers Jr. (D Mich.) foresaw a future Congress recoiling from the agony of exercise of the impeachment power and concluded "that impeachment can never again succeed unless another President demonstrated the same, almost uncanny ability to impeach himself."[6]

1. Carl Van Doren, *The Great Rehearsal: The Story of the Making and Ratifying of the Constitution of the United States* (New York: The Viking Press, 1948), p. 35.

2. *The Federalist Papers*, with an Introduction by Clinton Rossiter (New York: Mentor, 1961), p. 323.

3. *Ibid.*, p. 320.

4. *Ibid.*, p. 403.

5. Woodrow Wilson, *Congressional Government* (Cleveland: Meridian, 1956) (Reprint of 1885 ed.), pp. 154-155.

6. Congressional Quarterly, *Watergate: Chronology of a Crisis* (Washington, D.C., 1975), *pp. xv-xix.*

Constitutional Beginnings

When the Federal Convention met in Philadelphia in 1787 to consider revising the Articles of Confederation, the reasons for seeking a more effective form of national government for the newly independent United States of America seemed manifest and pressing. The exact form that government should take was by no means clear, however, and substantial compromise was required before agreement could be reached.

What finally emerged as the Constitution of the United States nevertheless reflected in good measure the shared experience of men who had grown up in a colonial America that was predominantly English in origin, and who had finally rebelled against English sovereignty when that seemed the only way to preserve the freedom they had come to expect as a part of their English heritage.

Colonial Background

Almost a century passed between Columbus' voyage of discovery in 1492 and Sir Walter Raleigh's attempt in 1587 to plant the first English settlement in the New World—the ill-fated "Lost Colony" on Roanoke Island in what is now North Carolina.[1] By then, Spain had seized the Caribbean and much of South and Central America (with its gold and silver) and had placed outposts in Florida. But at the beginning of the 17th century, most of North America was still unexplored, Spain's power was on the wane, and England was primed for colonial venture.

English Dominance

Private initiative was the prime mover behind settlement of America by the English during the 17th century, when all of the 13 colonies except one were founded. Several were started by promoters with an eye to profits or the creation of new feudal domains. Religious strife underlay the "Great Migration" of Puritans to New England (and the West Indies) during the repressive reign of Charles I (1625-49).[2] Poverty drove many others to take a chance on America. Whatever the motive for settlement, though, it was entirely a private undertaking, receiving little more help from the state than a charter to the land to be settled.

The English achieved their dominant position along the Atlantic seaboard in two waves of colonization. Virginia, Maryland and the New England colonies were founded before 1642, when the outbreak of civil war in England absorbed English energies. After restoration of the monarchy in 1660, the English added New York, New Jersey, Pennsylvania, Delaware and the Carolinas. Georgia, the 13th colony, was founded in 1733. By 1700, the colonies had a population of 200,000—largely of English origin—stretched along a thousand miles of coast from Maine to the Carolinas.

Roots of Self-Government

By the time Jamestown was founded in 1607, Englishmen had already attained significant rights and privileges. English justice was grounded on a solid body of common law that included the right to trial by jury, and no Englishman could be deprived of life, liberty or property without due process in the courts. The first colonists brought with them the models of English courts and other organs of local government.

The long English struggle for the right of self-government was also well-advanced by the beginning of the 17th century. The Crown was still supreme, and it would take the beheading of Charles I in 1649 and the dethroning of James II in 1688 to assure Parliament ascendancy over the King. Already, though, the two houses of Parliament—the Lords and the Commons—symbolized the principle of government by law and representative assembly, and this principle too was soon transplanted to America. In 1619, the Virginians (then about 1,000 in number) elected 22 "burgesses" to a General Assembly.[3] After Virginia became a royal colony in 1624, the governor and council were appointed by the King, but popular representation in the assembly was retained.

The organizers of the Massachusetts Bay Company carried matters considerably further when they voted to transfer the entire enterprise and its charter as "one body

---

Reference

See Appendix table of contents for texts of the Declaration of Independence, the Articles of Confederation, the Constitution and other documents relating to the origins of Congress.

Colonial Beginnings in the 17th and 18th Centuries

Virginia. The Virginia Company of London, a joint stock company with a charter from James I, founded the first permanent English settlement in America at Jamestown in 1607. After severe setbacks, the company found tobacco to be a thriving crop and profitable export and began to attract new settlers with "head rights" to 50 acres of land. The company was dissolved in 1624, when Virginia became a royal colony whose population reached 15,000 in 1648.

Maryland. In 1632 Charles I gave a proprietary charter to Maryland (originally a part of Virginia) to Sir George Calvert, who wanted a feudal domain for his family that would serve also as a refuge for English Catholics. Settlement began at St. Mary's in 1634. Protestants soon outnumbered Catholics, leading to continuing friction between settlers and proprietor. Maryland became a royal colony in 1692 but was restored to the Calvert family in 1715.

Massachusetts. A small band of Pilgrims founded Plymouth in 1620. Few others came until 1630, when John Winthrop and other Puritan organizers of the Massachusetts Bay Company arrived with 1,000 colonists to settle Boston and nearby towns. The Bay Colony (which attained a population of 16,000 by 1643) remained a self-governing Puritan commonwealth until its charter was annulled in 1684. In 1691 Massachusetts became a royal colony, incorporating Plymouth and Maine as well.

Connecticut. Thomas Hooker led a group of Puritans from the Bay Colony to found Hartford in 1636. About the same time other groups of Puritans settled Saybrook and New Haven. Modeled along the theocratic lines of Massachusetts, these and other settlements were joined when Connecticut in 1662 obtained from Charles II its own charter as a self-governing colony. The colony retained this status until 1776.

Rhode Island. Providence was founded in 1636 by Roger Williams, a strong believer in religious freedom who had been banished from the Bay Colony for opposing the intolerant and conformist rule of Governor Winthrop and the Puritans. The area drew other free thinkers and nonconformists, and in 1644 the settlements federated as Rhode Island and Providence Plantations. They obtained a royal charter of their own in 1663 and remained a self-governing colony until the Revolution.

New Hampshire. Various groups of Antinomians, Puritans and Anglicans began a number of settlements between 1623 and 1640 on land granted to John Mason by Charles I. Massachusetts annexed these settlements briefly, and border disputes between the two continued even after New Hampshire became a royal colony in 1679. The governor of Massachusetts served also as governor of New Hampshire from 1699 to 1741.

New York. The Dutch West Indies Company founded New Netherland with posts at Albany (1624) and on the island of Manhattan (1626). Confined largely to the Hudson River Valley, the Dutch colony had a population of about 10,000 when it was seized by the English in 1664 and renamed New York as part of a grant by Charles II to his brother, the Duke of York, of all land between the Connecticut and Delaware Rivers. The Duke attempted to run the colony without an assembly until 1683; as James II, he made it a royal colony in 1685.

New Jersey. In 1665, the Duke of York gave the land between the Hudson and Delaware Rivers to Lord John Berkeley and Sir George Carteret (former governor of the Isle of Jersey), who named the area New Jersey. The two proprietors later sold East and West Jersey separately, and although the two were reunited as a royal colony in 1702, confusion of land titles continued to plague New Jersey. The colony had the same governor as New York until 1738.

Pennsylvania. William Penn, a Quaker convert, received proprietary title to Pennsylvania from the Duke of York in 1681. Penn attracted settlers from the Continent as well as England with promises of political and religious liberty and the offer of land on generous terms. German Mennonites were among the first to come, settling Germantown in 1683. Pennsylvania prospered under Penn's tolerant rule, and it remained a proprietary colony until the Revolution.

Delaware. Lewes on Delaware Bay was settled by the Dutch in 1631. They were followed by Swedes, who held forth as New Sweden until overcome by Dutch forces in 1655. The area was conquered by the English in 1664 and was included in the grant to the Duke of York, who sold it to William Penn in 1682. Known as the "Lower Counties," Delaware had its own assembly after 1704 but had the same proprietary governor as Pennsylvania until 1776.

Carolinas. In 1663 Charles II gave proprietary title to all land between Virginia and Florida to the Carolina Proprietors, a group of promoters led by Sir John Colleton and the Earl of Shaftesbury. Charleston, the first settlement, was founded in 1670 by settlers from England and Barbados; later, French Huguenots and Scots came to settle. South Carolina became a plantation colony like Virginia. North Carolina became an area of small farms. The two became royal colonies in 1729.

Georgia. Gen. James Oglethorpe and other English philanthropists envisioned Georgia as a refuge for debtors. They founded Savannah in 1733, and in the next eight years brought over about 1,800 charity colonists. Many of these colonists moved on to South Carolina, however, and Georgia had a population of little more than 2,000 when it became a royal colony in 1752.

politique and corporate" to New England.[4] On their arrival in 1630, the officers promptly established themselves as the government of the Bay Colony, subject only to annual election thereafter by the stockholder-colonists. The founders of Massachusetts thereby asserted a right to full self-government that neither the King nor Parliament had con-

templated or would be prepared to challenge for another 50 years.

The great distance that separated England from America was itself a major factor in promoting a spirit of independence and self-reliance among the early colonists. Many of those drawn to America were predisposed to resist authority in any event, and this attitude was reinforced by the free availability of land and the harshness of frontier living. In New England, where entire congregations of Puritans had often emigrated and settled together in a town of their own, the town meeting became a unique instrument of self-government that was exceptionally democratic for the times.

Origins of Conflict with England

England left the colonies pretty much to themselves initially, but it was not for lack of a concept of the role they would be expected to play. Under the prevailing economic doctrine of the times—mercantilism—the central goal of any nation-state was self-sufficiency, and it was taken for granted that all profits of empire should accrue to the benefit of the mother country. Thus the English were quick to try to monopolize the trade in Virginia tobacco, the first American product to find a wide market. And in 1660 they began systematic efforts to exploit colonial trade, with the first of a series of Acts of Trade and Navigation.

These laws were designed to maximize English profits on the transport of colonial imports and exports and the marketing of major colonial products. They required all trade between England and the colonies to be carried by English or colonial-built ships manned by English subjects; stipulated that colonial imports from other countries in Europe first be landed and reloaded at English ports; and prohibited exports of specified colonial products to countries other than England. Tobacco was the first of these enumerated items, and eventually every important American export except salt fish was added to the list.

The trade acts were not without some benefit to the colonies. But in exchanging their raw products for English manufactures, the colonists rarely found the terms of trade to their advantage. When tobacco prices collapsed in the 1660s, for example, Virginians had no recourse against the English merchants who raised the prices of goods sent in exchange. This situation was aggravated by England's continuing refusal to permit its coins to circulate in the colonies. To get specie (gold or silver), the colonists had to sell their products in the West Indies or other markets.

The trade acts were met with widespread evasion in the colonies; smuggling, bribery and the use of false documents were commonplace. New Englanders, who ran a chronic deficit in their balance of trade with England, were especially resourceful in evading the trade acts. Massachusetts went so far as to refuse to obey them, asserting that the laws of England "do not reach America" because the colonies were unrepresented in Parliament. For this and similar acts of defiance against English authority, the Bay Colony's charter was annulled in 1684.[5]

When James II came to the throne in 1685, England moved to strengthen colonial administration by consolidating the New England colonies, New York and the Jerseys into one Dominion of New England; for three years these colonies were ruled by Sir Edmund Andros as Governor-general with the aid of an appointed council but no representative assembly. The colonists bridled at being taxed without their consent and were quick to overthrow Andros and other dominion officials as soon as they received word of the Glorious Revolution of 1688 and the expulsion of James from England. The concept of the Dominion was promptly abandoned.

The accession of William and Mary in 1689 marked the beginning of a transfer of power from the Crown to Parliament and of a series of colonial wars that ended in 1763 with the English in control of all of America east of the Mississippi. Mercantilist aims continued to dominate English colonial policy throughout this period, and new restrictions were placed on colonial trade. But the American colonists went on growing in numbers, economic strength and political assertiveness.

Growth of the Colonies

Between 1700 and 1760, large families and new immigrants boosted the colonial population from 200,000 to about 1,700,000. Persons of English stock were in the majority over-all and among colonial leaders; the first Adams came in 1636, the first Washington in 1656, the first Franklin in 1685. Other major ethnic groups in 1760 were the Scotch-Irish (estimated to number 280,000) and the Germans (170,000), whose forebears had started coming to America toward the end of the 17th century. Finding the best land along the seaboard already taken, most had moved on to settle the back country.

Even more numerous in the American population of 1760 were an estimated 310,000 black slaves. The Spaniards brought the first African slaves to the New World in the 16th century; a Dutch ship brought the first 20 to Virginia in 1619. The English saw nothing wrong in slavery, and the Puritans regularly took Indians as slaves and sold them in the West Indies.

Slaves helped to meet a chronic shortage of labor in colonial America at a time when most colonists wanted and could easily get their own land. Slavery eventually declined in the North, where it became unprofitable, but it flourished in the plantation economy of the South; the number of slaves in Virginia, the Carolinas and Georgia grew rapidly during the 18th century. Americans vied with the English slave traders in meeting the demand. Yankee slavers were especially successful in trading New England rum for Africans, who were then sold in the West Indies for sugar and molasses with which to make more rum.

Profits from slave labor and the slave trade thus added to a prosperity that was sustained by a rise in prices for colonial produce in England and the rest of Europe. In 1731 exports leaving Charleston included 42,000 barrels of rice, 14,000 barrels of pitch, tar and turpentine, and 250,000 deerskins. Virginia and Maryland shipped more tobacco, while Pennsylvania found a growing market for its wheat and flour. The fur trade was centered in New York. The New England colonies exported large quantities of ship timber and lumber of all types along with fish and meat.

Most of the colonial products were not competitive with those of England, but when competition did appear, restrictions followed. The Woolens Act of 1699 barred sale of colonial cloth outside the place where it was woven. Parliament in 1732 banned the export of hats from one colony to another. To protect English exports of iron and steel products, the colonies in 1750 were ordered to stop building various kinds of mills. After the British West Indies complained that the Americans were buying cheaper sugar and molasses from the French, Parliament passed the Molasses Act of 1733, placing a stiff duty on imports from the French islands. For the most part, however, these restrictions were poorly enforced and easily evaded by the Americans.

Governors vs. Assemblies

As the American population and economy grew, so did the problems of English colonial administration. All of the colonies were permitted to elect their own assemblies after the Dominion of New England collapsed in 1689, but only Connecticut and Rhode Island kept the right to elect their governors as well. The governors of the eight royal colonies were appointed by the King and those of the five proprietary colonies with the King's approval. And it was these royal and proprietary governors who had primary responsibility for enforcing English laws and regulations in America.

The governors were armed with great legal authority. They had the right of absolute veto over colonial legislation, the authority to terminate and dissolve assemblies, and the power to dismiss judges and create courts, long after the Crown had been stripped of these prerogatives in England. But the real power of the governors was effectively limited by their dependence on the colonial assemblies (in almost all cases) for their salaries and operating revenues. "In this situation, many governors chose simply not to 'consider anything further than how to sit easy,' and to be careful 'to do nothing, which upon a fair hearing...can be blamed.' Because the surest way to 'sit easy' was to reach a political accommodation with local interests, they very frequently aligned themselves with dominant political factions in the colonies. Such governors sought to avoid disputes with the lower houses by taking especial care not to challenge their customary privileges and, if necessary, even quietly giving way before their demands."[6]

The powers of the assemblies, though nowhere carefully defined by charter or statute, grew steadily. In time they claimed and exercised the right to lay taxes, raise troops, incur debts, issue currency, and otherwise initiate all legislation. They commonly passed only short-term revenue bills, stipulated in detail how appropriations were to be spent, tacked riders on essential money bills, and vied with the governors for control of patronage.

Claiming prerogatives similar to those of the British House of Commons, the assemblies made the most of their power of the purse to extract concessions from the governors. When one governor asked for a fixed revenue for five years, the assembly demanded the right to appoint every official to be paid from the grant.

Some governors came to feel "impotent to carry out either imperial directions or their own projects against the exorbitant power" of the assemblies. "The too great and unwarrantable encroachments of the assemblies," declared Governor Lewis Morris of New Jersey, "make it necessary that a stop some way or other should be put to them, and they reduced to such proper and legal bounds as is consistent with his majesty's prerogative and their dependence."[7]

If the governors found it impolitic to veto some colonial legislation, it could still be killed by the royal disallowance. Acts so vetoed included ones that discriminated against religious minorities, assessed duties on the products of neighboring colonies, authorized unbacked issues of paper currency, and restricted the slave trade. But preventing the assemblies from taking unwanted action was not the same as winning their support for imperial projects, as the English found out during their wars with the French. *(See box p. 9)*

During these wars English requisitions on the colonies for men, money and supplies were honored by the assemblies slowly, in part or not at all, especially in those colonies that were not under fire. New York and Pennsylvania were notorious for continuing to trade with the French in time of war. But all of the colonies resisted imperial direction in some degree and cherished their independence one from another. Not one of the assemblies ratified the Albany Plan of Union of 1754, although it had been drafted primarily by Benjamin Franklin with the approval of representatives from seven of the 13 colonies. The Plan was designed to create "one general government" in America.

Growth of Colonial Indignation

The French and Indian War (1754-63) doubled the national debt of England (to 130 million pounds), quadrupled the prospective costs of administering the greatly enlarged empire in America (to 300,000 pounds a year), and helped thereby to put the government of George III, crowned in 1760, on a collision course with the colonists. To the mercantilists in Parliament, it now seemed logical to plug the loopholes in trade controls and to make the colonies pay a share of the costs of imperial overhead. The shift in English colonial policy began in 1763 when George Grenville became prime minister.

Grenville's first step was to set aside the claims of Virginia and other colonies to portions of the vast lands taken from the French. By the Proclamation of 1763, the entire region between the Appalachians and the Mississippi, south of Quebec and north of Florida, was reserved for the Indians. And the English adhered to this policy despite strong pressures from highly placed speculators (including Benjamin Franklin) who promoted the settlement of such proposed inland colonies as Vandalia, Charlotiana and Transylvania.

At the same time, Parliament began to strengthen enforcement of trade controls. Admiralty courts, which tried smuggling cases without juries, could now move such trials to Halifax in Nova Scotia at considerable cost to those whose goods and ships were detained. Colonial issues of paper money, which had been permitted during the war, were banned by the Currency Act of 1764. And to lighten the British tax load, Grenville pushed three other laws through Parliament.

● The Revenue Act of 1764, to defray the expenses of defending, protecting and securing the colonies, cut in half the widely evaded duty laid on foreign molasses in 1733 but placed new duties on such colonial imports as wine, silk and linen. It also enumerated more colonial products, including hides and skins, that could be exported only to England.

● The Quartering Act of 1765 required the colonies to contribute to the upkeep of the 10,000 troops England planned to station in America. The colonies were to supply them with barracks or other quarters and with some of their provisions and were to pay a part of the money costs.

● The Stamp Act of 1765 required that revenue stamps costing up to 20 shillings be affixed to all licenses, legal documents, leases, notes and bonds, newspapers, pamphlets, almanacs, advertisements and other documents issued in the colonies. Passed on March 22, the law was to take effect Nov. 1 and was expected to yield 60,000 pounds a year.

None of these measures sat well with the Americans, but opposition focused on the Stamp Act as the first direct tax ever laid on the colonies by Parliament. Americans believed they could be taxed only by their own assemblies and that the Stamp Act, which was taxation without representation, was unconstitutional. The Virginia House of Burgesses so resolved at the urging of Patrick Henry, while the Massachusetts House of Representatives called for an intercolonial meeting to be held in New York in October.

The Stamp Act Congress was attended by 28 delegates from nine colonies. They affirmed their allegiance to the

Colonial Wars from 1689 to 1763

Between 1689 and 1763, the American colonies were involved in four wars born of European conflicts and the imperial rivalries of England, France and Spain. At the outset French Canada was only sparsely settled and Spanish Florida not at all, but the French had built a lucrative fur trade with Indians throughout the Great Lakes region while La Salle had sailed down the Mississippi in 1682 and claimed Louisiana. Most of the fighting that ensued, however, involved New England and New York.

King William's War: 1689-97 (called War of the League of Augsburg in Europe). When William of Orange became King of England, the English joined a continental alliance against Louis XIV of France. In America, French and Indians raided English settlements in New York, New Hampshire and Maine. New Englanders captured the French base at Port Royal, Nova Scotia, but an English attempt to take Quebec failed. The Treaty of Ryswick restored Port Royal to the French.

Queen Anne's War: 1702-13 (War of the Spanish Succession). In America, French and Indians burned Deerfield and raided most of the frontier settlements of Massachusetts and New Hampshire. The French captured the English post of St. John's, Newfoundland, while the English and colonials retook Port Royal. But expeditions against Quebec and Montreal again failed. By the Treaty of Utrecht the French accepted British sovereignty over Nova Scotia and Hudson's Bay and the English inherited Spain's monopoly over the slave trade with its colonies.

King George's War: 1745-48 (War of the Austrian Succession). The major military event in America was the capture of Louisbourg, a French fortress on Cape Breton Island, by an army of 4,000 colonial militiamen led by William Pepperell, a Maine merchant. By the Treaty of Aachen, England restored Louisbourg to France in exchange for Madras in India but paid the cost of the colonial campaign.

French and Indian War: 1754-63 (the Seven Years War). In America, this world-wide conflict focused on upper New York and western Pennsylvania where the French built several forts. The English fared badly until William Pitt came to power in 1758 and reorganized the war effort under new and younger generals. The French were dislodged from Fort Duquesne (renamed Pittsburgh), Fort Niagara and Fort Ticonderoga, and in 1759 the English took Quebec, then Montreal the next year. The English also defeated the French in India and the West Indies and, after Spain entered the war in 1762, took Havana and Manila.

The Peace of Paris (1763) left England dominant in North America. France ceded Canada and all claims east of the Mississippi to England and gave Louisiana to Spain. England also got Spanish Florida in exchange for Havana, and Manila reverted to Spain.

Crown, asserted their right as Englishmen not to be taxed without their consent, noted that the colonists were not represented in the House of Commons, and concluded that "no taxes ever have been or can be constitutionally imposed on them, but by their respective legislatures." The delegates urged Parliament to repeal the Stamp Act and other recent laws that had "a manifest tendency to subvert the rights and liberties of the colonists."

The English insisted that Parliament represented and acted in behalf of all Englishmen. But they could not ignore the sharp drop in exports that followed a colonial boycott of English goods or the attacks on royal officials by colonial mobs calling themselves "Sons of Liberty." When it became clear in 1766 that the Stamp Act could not be enforced, it was repealed. But Parliament, through a Declaratory Act, asserted its authority to legislate for the colonies "in all cases whatsoever" and declared colonial resolves to the contrary to be "utterly null and void."[8]

The Intolerable Acts

Following repeal of the Stamp Act, Chancellor of the Exchequer Charles Townshend proposed an increase of customs receipts to get the needed revenue. Parliament passed laws in 1767 laying new duties on imports by the colonies of paper, lead, glass, paint and tea; reorganizing the customs service in America; and authorizing broad use of general search warrants known as Writs of Assistance to ferret out violations. The Townshend Acts were greeted by a new outbreak of protests, colonial merchants revived their nonimportation agreements, and the adverse effects on English business again persuaded Parliament to retreat.

When Lord North came to power in 1770, all of the Townshend duties except the one on tea were repealed. Most of the colonists were appeased, trade revived, and for three quiet years England and the colonies lived in relative harmony.

To American radicals like Samuel Adams of Massachusetts, this period of calm foreshadowed a further attack on colonial liberties, for the English had begun to pay the salaries of the royal governors and other officials from their increased customs receipts, thus freeing them from the hold of the assemblies. Adams, Patrick Henry, Thomas Jefferson and others, who now questioned the right of Parliament to legislate for the colonies in any respect, formed committees of correspondence that became the underground of the resistance movement.

The quiet years ended abruptly in 1773 when the faltering East India Company was authorized to dump a surplus of tea on the American colonies by undercutting the price of tea smuggled in from Holland. Colonial merchants, foreseeing ruinous competition, joined the radicals in protesting the Tea Act, and everywhere the colonists prepared to boycott the first shipments. In Boston, however, Adams and John Hancock urged direct action, and on Dec. 16, 1773, a mob disguised as Indians boarded three tea ships and dumped their cargoes into the harbor.

The Boston Tea Party alarmed many Americans who opposed British policy, but it also provoked the English government into a series of coercive acts that drove the colonists together. On March 25, 1774, the House of Commons ordered the Port of Boston closed until the city paid for the tea thrown into the harbor. That order was followed

Albany Plan of Union

The Albany Congress of 1754 was initiated by the British in an effort to nail down the wavering friendship of their long-time allies, the six Indian nations of the Iroquois Confederacy, which had come under increasing French pressure on the western frontier. The Americans who represented the seven colonies that took part—Massachusetts, New Hampshire, Connecticut, Rhode Island, New York, Pennsylvania and Maryland—were more ambitious and adopted a Plan of Union drafted largely by Benjamin Franklin of Pennsylvania.

JOIN, or DIE.

Wood engraving in the "Pennsylvania Gazette," 1754.

The plan called on Parliament to create "one general government" in America to be administered by a president-general appointed by the Crown and a grand council of representatives from all of the colonies (in proportion to their financial contributions) elected by the assemblies. This government would have sole authority to regulate Indian affairs and the purchase and sale of new lands, as well as the power to raise troops for the common defense and to levy "such general duties, imposts or taxes...as may be collected with the least inconvenience to the people."

Both the British government and the colonial assemblies opposed the Albany Plan as involving too large a grant of power. The English were not prepared to give the colonies so much autonomy, while the assemblies were not ready to share their power to tax. "The different and contrary reasons of dislike to my plan made me suspect that it was really the true medium," Franklin later wrote, "and I am still of the opinion it would have been happy for both sides of the water if it had been adopted."*

As it was, the Albany Plan reflected a growing awareness of the need for a common approach to administration of the far-flung and expanding American colonies. Rejection of the plan was a major landmark on the road that led to the Constitutional Convention of 1787.

*Carl Van Doren, Benjamin Franklin (Greenwood Press, 1973), p. 223.

by laws revising the Massachusetts charter to strengthen royal control and transferring to England the trials of colonists charged with murder.

To these Intolerable Acts Parliament added one that alienated most of Protestant America by giving to the French-Canadian—and Catholic—royal province of Quebec all of the land west of the Appalachians lying north of the Ohio River and east of the Mississippi. The Quebec Act of June 22 was regarded as another punitive measure by most colonists and helped to muster broad support for a "general congress of all the colonies" proposed by the Virginia and Massachusetts assemblies.[9]

First Continental Congress

Every colony except Georgia (whose governor blocked the selection of delegates) was represented at the First Continental Congress, which met in Philadelphia on Sept. 5, 1774. Describing the Congress in a letter to his wife, John Adams wrote: "The business of the Congress is tedious beyond expression. This assembly is like no other that ever existed.... Every man upon every question must show his oratory, his criticism and his political abilities."[10] Conservative Joseph Galloway of Pennsylvania hoped to conciliate the English, while radical Samuel Adams wanted to defy all British controls. As the session continued, more and more delegates joined in the movement to protest and repudiate British policies toward the colonies.

The turning point came when Paul Revere arrived with the Suffolk Resolves, adopted by a convention of towns around Boston, which called on Massachusetts to arm itself against efforts to "enslave America" and urged Congress to adopt economic sanctions against England. To Galloway, these "inflammatory resolves...contained a complete declaration of war against Great Britain," and many others agreed. But most delegates felt compelled to register their support of Massachusetts. By a vote of six colonies to five they set aside Galloway's plan (based on the Albany Plan of Union of 1754) to give Parliament and a colonial legislature joint control over American affairs, and endorsed the Suffolk Resolves.[11]

The Congress then adopted a Declaration of Rights and Grievances against all British acts to which "Americans cannot submit" and approved a wide-ranging nonimportation, nonconsumption and nonexportation agreement or "Association" as "the most speedy, effectual and peaceable" means of swaying England. Locally elected committees were directed to enforce this commercial boycott by publicizing violations so that "all such foes to the rights of British-America may be publicly known and universally condemned as the enemies of American liberty." On Oct. 22, 1774, the Continental Congress adjourned, after agreeing to meet again the following May if necessary.

King George III declared that the colonies were "now in a state of rebellion; blows must decide whether they are to be subject to this country or independent." While the Earl of Chatham and Edmund Burke hoped conciliation was possible, they held firmly to "the view that the British Parliament was supreme over the colonies, that the authority of the empire could not be surrendered."[12] In the colonies patriot forces began to gather arms and supplies to train militia, and in Massachusetts they soon controlled all of the colony outside of Boston where the Governor, Gen. Thomas Gage, was installed with 5,000 troops.

On April 19, 1775, Gage sent 1,000 of these men to destroy patriot stores in Lexington and Concord. They were met by Minutemen, firing broke out, and the British lost 247 in dead and wounded before getting back to Boston. These turned out to be the opening shots of the Revolutionary War, although more than a year was to pass before the Americans were sufficiently united to declare their independence.

Revolution and Confederation

When the Second Continental Congress met on May 10, 1775, in Philadelphia, most of the delegates still hoped to avoid both war and independence. Faced with pleas for help from Massachusetts, the delegates agreed in mid-June to raise a Continental Army of 20,000 men, to ask the colonies for $2-million (in proportion to their population) for the army's support, and to make George Washington (a delegate from Virginia) the army's commander-in-chief.

Soon afterward, however, the Congress approved a petition to George III (drafted by John Dickinson) asking for "a happy and permanent reconciliation" between the colonies and England. The delegates also adopted a Declaration of the Causes of Necessity of Taking up Arms (drafted by Dickinson and Jefferson) in which they disavowed any desire for independence but resolved "to die free men rather than live slaves."[13]

The King's response, on Aug. 23, was to proclaim a state of rebellion in America. The British began to hire mercenaries in Germany and to incite the Iroquois against the colonials, while Congress authorized an expedition against Canada and efforts to contact other nations for aid. Yet the legislatures of five colonies took positions against independence that autumn. Pennsylvania's delegation to the Congress was told to "utterly reject any proposition...that may cause or lead to a separation from our mother country or a change in the form of this government."[14]

The British gave no signs of retreating, however, and the appearance in January 1776 of Thomas Paine's pamphlet "Common Sense" marked the beginning of what was to be a rising demand for independence. Paine argued that it was time for Americans to stand on their own feet, for there was "something absurd in supposing a continent to be perpetually governed by an island" and "it is evident that they belong to different systems: England to Europe, America to itself." Paine also put the onus for the colonies' troubles on the King rather than Parliament.[15]

Declaration of Independence

Pressure on the Congress to act reached a climax when, on June 7, 1776, Richard Henry Lee of Virginia introduced a resolution stating that "these United Colonies are, and of right ought to be, free and independent States."[16] Jefferson, John Adams, Franklin, Roger Sherman and Robert Livingston were named to draw up a declaration, but it was largely Jefferson's draft that was presented on June 28. Lee's resolution was adopted July 2; Jefferson's Declaration was then debated and slightly amended (to strike out an indictment of the British slave trade, for example) before it was approved July 4 by all of the delegations except New York's, which later voted for it after receiving new instructions.

The greater part of the Declaration—and the most important to Americans at that time—consisted of a recitation of every grievance against English colonial policy that had emerged since 1763. The grievances were presented as facts to prove that George III was seeking "the establishment of

Benjamin Franklin

Thomas Jefferson

an absolute Tyranny over these States" and to justify their decision to dissolve "all political connection" with Britain. But it was the preamble that was to exert the greatest influence on others as a statement of political philosophy with universal appeal. Rooted in the concept of natural rights as developed by such philosophers as Thomas Hooker and John Locke, the preamble made these assertions:

"We hold these truths to be self-evident, that all men are created equal, that they are endowed by their Creator with certain unalienable Rights, that among these are Life, Liberty and the pursuit of Happiness. That to secure these rights, Governments are instituted among Men, deriving their just powers from the consent of the governed. That whenever any Form of Government becomes destructive of these ends it is the Right of the People to alter or to abolish it, and to institute new Government, laying its foundation on such principles and organizing its powers in such form, as to them shall seem most likely to effect their Safety and Happiness."

In conclusion, the signers, who styled themselves "the Representatives of the united States of America, in General Congress, Assembled," declared that "these United Colonies are, and of Right ought to be Free and Independent States," that as such "they have full Power to levy War, conclude Peace, contract Alliances, establish Commerce, and to do all other Acts and Things which Independent States may of right do," and that in support of this stand "we mutually pledge to each other our Lives, our Fortunes and our Sacred Honor."

Formation of State Governments

The Declaration of Independence committed the colonies to wage a war that was already under way and that would drag on for more than five years before England gave up the struggle. The Declaration also put an end to tolerance of the many Americans who remained loyal to the King; Tories who refused to sign an oath of allegiance to the United States suffered imprisonment and confiscation of property; as many as 80,000 fled to Canada and England. At home, the Declaration put to immediate test the capacity of the patriots to govern.

As early as the fall of 1774, Massachusetts had set up a provisional government in response to the Coercive Acts. As revolutionary sentiment grew, patriots took control of provincial assemblies and conventions, and the royal governors and judges began to leave. New Hampshire adopted a constitution in January 1776, South Carolina followed suit in March, and on May 10 the Continental Congress advised all of the colonies to form new governments. All except Massachusetts and the self-governing charter colonies of

(Continued on p. 13)

Chronology of the Revolutionary War

Those Americans who waged and won the Revolutionary War did so under severe handicaps. Many others (one-third, said Patriot John Adams; four-fifths, said Loyalist Joseph Galloway) were opposed to the cause of independence to the end, and more than a few collaborated openly with the British. Apathy was widespread and parochialism common; as in earlier times of trouble, those who were not in the direct line of fire were often unwilling either to fight the war or to help pay for it.

As commander-in-chief, George Washington was plagued by problems of raising and maintaining effective military forces. At no time did he have many more than 30,000 men under arms, less than half of whom were regulars enlisted for three years. The balance were militia, signed up for as little as three months.

The Continental Congress assumed responsibility for prosecuting the war, but it had no power to tax or to compel actions by the states, and its requisitions for money and supplies were no better honored than those of the British had been. The war was largely financed by paper money—some $240 million in national bills and $210 million in state bills—which depreciated to the point of being worthless. Without subsidies and loans of about $8 million from France, and that country's military intervention in 1778, the war might have been lost.

However, England also was sharply divided by the war, and the opposition increased in Parliament as time went on. For lack of recruits at home, the government was forced to hire 30,000 mercenaries in Germany to supplement the 15,000 regulars sent to America. The transport, supply and direction of those forces over a distance of 3,000 miles was even more difficult after France entered the war as America's ally.

Major developments in the war were as follows:

1775. Washington took command after Battle of Bunker Hill (June 17), and British were holed up in Boston until they evacuated the city March 17, 1776. Meanwhile, Americans under Ethan Allen and Benedict Arnold had marched on Canada, taken Montreal (Nov. 13), been badly beaten at Quebec (Dec. 31) and had withdrawn.

1776. After buildup of forces at Halifax and in Quebec, the British launched three campaigns. Gen. Henry Clinton sailed for the Carolinas, was beaten off at Charleston June 28 and withdrew. Gens. Guy Carleton and John Burgoyne marched for Albany, but were stopped at Ticonderoga in October. Howe sailed for New York, inflicted heavy losses on Washington in several battles, and occupied the city Sept. 15 (until the end of the war). Washington retreated into New Jersey and across the Delaware, then recrossed it the night of Dec. 25 to surprise and capture 1,000 Hessians at Trenton. He then went into winter quarters at Morristown with fewer than 5,000 men.

1777. In August Sir William Howe sailed up Chesapeake Bay with 15,000 men, defeated Washington at Brandywine Creek, and occupied Philadelphia Sept.

25. Washington set up winter quarters at Valley Forge. Meanwhile, Burgoyne launched a two-pronged attack on Albany, suffered a series of reverses in August and September in battles with Arnold and others, and surrendered Oct. 17 at Saratoga with 5,000 men. Burgoyne's defeat led to a French-American treaty of alliance, signed Feb. 6, 1778.

1778. The British offered wide concessions to end the war short of independence, but Congress rejected the offer June 17. Clinton (Howe's successor) evacuated Philadelphia, moving back to New York. The British raided coastal towns, while George Rogers Clark seized British posts north of the Ohio, but no decisive battles were fought.

1779. The British captured Savannah Dec. 29, 1778, and took control of Georgia, but Americans under Benjamin Lincoln successfully defended Charleston. However, Lincoln's attempt to retake Savannah (with help of French fleet) failed Oct. 9. Spain joined the war against England June 21 but did not enter alliance with Americans.

1780. The war went badly for the Americans. Long unpaid and underfed, troops in Morristown mutinied. On May 12 the British captured Charleston and 5,000 troops—the worst American defeat of the war. Benedict Arnold defected to the British in September.

1781. The South was the major fighting arena. Americans under Nathaniel Greene beat Lord Charles Cornwallis at Cowpens, South Carolina (Jan. 17). In July Cornwallis moved north with 7,000 men to fortify Yorktown, Virginia. More than 15,000 American and French troops converged there in September; surrounded on land and sea, Cornwallis surrendered his army Oct. 17.

1782. The House of Commons resolved, March 4, to give up the struggle, Lord North resigned, and a new government asked for peace talks. Congress named John Adams (envoy to the Netherlands), John Jay (envoy to Spain), Benjamin Franklin (envoy to Paris) and Henry Laurens to negotiate jointly with the French. Jay, suspicious of the French (who supported Spanish claims in America), persuaded the others to enter separate negotiations with the British in September. A preliminary treaty was signed Nov. 30 pending Anglo-French accord.

1783. The Treaty of Paris, signed Sept. 3 (ratified by Congress Jan. 14, 1784), was a triumph for Americans. It validated independence and claims to the West, fixing the boundary with Canada along the St. Lawrence and the Great Lakes, and retained American fishing rights around Newfoundland. It also validated American private debts to England and stated that Congress would "earnestly recommend" to the states that they restore property confiscated from the Tories. At the same time, England gave West and East Florida back to Spain. The last British troops left New York Nov. 25. Washington resigned Dec. 23 to take "leave of all the employments of public life."

(Continued from p. 11)

Connecticut and Rhode Island had done so by July 4, 1777, first anniversary of the signing of the Declaration of Independence. Four days later, Vermont, not previously a separate colony, declared its independence and adopted a constitution. Connecticut and Rhode Island did not get around to replacing their colonial charters by state constitutions until 1818 and 1842, respectively.

The new state constitutions of the Revolutionary period emerged in various ways. Those of South Carolina, Virginia and New Jersey were drafted by legislative bodies without explicit authorization and put into effect without popular consent. Those of New Hampshire, Georgia, Delaware, New York and Vermont were authorized but were not submitted to the voters for approval. In Maryland, Pennsylvania and North Carolina the constitutions were authorized and ratified by the voters. Only Massachusetts and New Hampshire (which wrote a new constitution in 1784 to replace the one adopted in 1776) employed what was to become the standard method of electing a constitutional convention and putting the product to a vote of the people.

Although they varied in detail, the new constitutions reflected a number of concepts held in common by Americans of the period. All were written, because the unwritten British constitution had been a source of such contention between the colonists and England. All included or were accompanied by some kind of "Bill of Rights" to secure those English liberties that George III had violated, such as freedom of speech, press and petition and the rights of habeas corpus and trial by jury. All paid tribute to the doctrine of separation of powers between the legislative, executive and judiciary, as it had been developed in England after the revolution of 1688 and expounded by Montesquieu's *Spirit of Laws*, published in 1748.

Separation did not mean balance, however, and most of the constitutions betrayed the colonists' great fear of executive authority, born of their many conflicts with the Crown and the royal governors. Executive power was weakened in every state except New York, Massachusetts and New Hampshire, and the governors of only two states were given the power of veto. In most cases the state legislature appointed the judiciary, although efforts were made to protect the independence of judges by preventing their arbitrary removal.

Power under most state constitutions was lodged in their legislatures. Ten of these were bicameral (Pennsylvania, Georgia and Vermont had one house), with the lower house predominant. Virginia's constitution provided, for example, that: "All laws shall originate in the House of Delegates, to be approved of or rejected by the Senate, or to be amended, with consent of the House of Delegates; except money bills, which in no instance shall be altered by the Senate, but wholly approved or rejected."[17]

All of the constitutions recognized the people as sovereign, but few entrusted them with much power. The Pennsylvania constitution (copied by Vermont), written by radicals who came to power early in 1776 after a major reapportionment of the colonial assembly, was the most democratic. It replaced governor and upper chamber with an executive council from whose ranks a president was chosen. Its members could serve no more than three years in seven while assemblymen were limited to four years in seven, to guard against establishing an aristocracy. There were no property qualifications for voting or for holding office.

Most other states adhered to prerevolutionary limits on suffrage. Ownership of some amount of property was

First State Constitutions

	Date Adopted
New Hampshire (1st)	Jan. 6, 1776
South Carolina (1st)	March 26, 1776
Virginia	June 29, 1776
New Jersey	July 2, 1776
Delaware	Aug. 22, 1776
Pennsylvania	Sept. 28, 1776
Maryland	Nov. 11, 1776
North Carolina	Dec. 18, 1776
Georgia	Feb. 5, 1777
New York	April 20, 1777
Vermont*	July 8, 1777
South Carolina (2nd)	March 19, 1778
Massachusetts	June 15, 1780
New Hampshire (2nd)	June 13, 1784

* Vermont became a state in 1791.

generally required as a qualification to vote, and more was required to hold office. The property qualification for state senator in New Jersey and Maryland was 1,000 pounds, in South Carolina 2,000 pounds. Most states also imposed religious qualifications for public office.

Articles of Confederation

When Richard Henry Lee called for a declaration of independence on June 7, 1776, he proposed also that "a plan of confederation be prepared and transmitted to the respective Colonies for their consideration and approbation."[18] On June 11 Congress agreed and named a committee of 13 (one from each colony) to undertake the task. The plan recommended, based on a draft by John Dickinson, was presented July 12, but it was not until Nov. 15, 1777, that Congress, after much debate and some revision, adopted the Articles of Confederation and Perpetual Union.

The Articles reflected the dominant motive of Americans who were rebelling against British rule—to preserve their freedoms from the encroachments of centralized power. Even as Congress was struggling with tenuous authority to prosecute the war (and it gave Washington dictatorial powers over the army in December 1776), few of the delegates or other American leaders were prepared to entrust a national government with any power that would diminish the sovereignty and independence of the states. Thus the scope of federal authority was not a central issue in the design of the confederation.

What was at issue was the relative standing of 13 rival and jealous states. Would they be represented equally in the national legislature (as they were in the Continental Congress and as the smaller states desired) or in proportion to their population (as the larger states wished)? Cost of a national government would have to be shared, but on what basis—wealth, population or (as the southerners insisted) the white population only? States without claims to lands west of the Appalachians thought Congress should control the area; those with claims were reluctant to give them up.

As finally adopted, the Articles conferred less authority on the national government than had been proposed in the Albany Plan of Union of 1754. They did little more than legalize what Congress was already doing by sufferance of the states. Congress remained the sole organ of government;

the states retained their equality in Congress, having one vote each; and of the specific powers delegated to Congress the most important could not be exercised without the assent of nine of the 13 states.

The delegated authority included the power to declare war, enter treaties and alliances, raise an army and a navy, regulate coinage and borrow money. Congress was empowered also to regulate Indian affairs, establish a postal service, and adjudicate disputes between the states. But it had no power to tax (other than to charge postage); the costs of government would be allocated to the states in proportion to the value of their land and improvements as determined by Congress. The states were also to be assigned quotas for troops in proportion to the number of white inhabitants. But in no case did Congress have any power to compel the states to comply.

The Articles provided that Congress be composed of from two to seven delegates from each state (and from Canada if it chose to join). The delegates were to be selected annually and paid by the states, and they could serve no more than three years in any six. Members of Congress were barred from holding any federal post for pay and were immune from arrest while in attendance and from action for anything said in debate—provisions that were later incorporated in the Constitution. A Committee of the States (with one delegate from each) was authorized to act for Congress during a recess on such matters as did not require the assent of nine states.

Congress was authorized to appoint committees and civil officers necessary for managing the affairs of the United States. Following ratification, Robert Livingston was named as Secretary of Foreign Affairs, Robert Morris as Superintendent of Finance, and Gen. Benjamin Lincoln as Secretary of War. But the Articles made no provision for a federal executive or judiciary, gave Congress no sanction by which to enforce any of its decisions, left control of taxation and tariffs with the states, and required the unanimous consent of the states to adopt any amendment.

Final ratification was delayed by the reluctance of Maryland, New Jersey and Delaware to act until the states with western claims agreed to cede them to the national government. Cession of state claims did not actually begin until 1784, but it was clear by the start of 1781 that the states would cede, and Maryland, the last holdout, ratified the Articles March 1, 1781. Congress proclaimed them to be in effect the same day.

Trials of the Confederation

Adoption of the Articles of Confederation did nothing to relieve the chaotic state of federal finances. Of $10-million requisitioned by Congress in the first two years, the states paid in less than $1.5-million. From 1781 to 1786, federal collections averaged half a million a year, which was barely enough to meet current expenses. After two years as Superintendent of Finance, Robert Morris resigned in 1783, saying "our public credit is gone."[19] The foreign debt of the United States increased from less than $8-million in 1783 to more than $10-million in 1789, plus almost $1.8-million in unpaid interest.

Congress recognized the need for some independent financial authority even before the Articles took effect. A month earlier, it had asked the states for authority to levy a duty of 5 per cent on all imports. But it took unanimous agreement to amend the Articles, and the proposal died in 1782 when Rhode Island rejected it. In 1783 Congress again asked for the power to levy import duties, and this time New York refused approval.

Peace put an end to the destruction and drain of war, but it also underscored the weakness and disunity of the now sovereign and independent American states. As agreed in the peace treaty with England, Congress in 1783 recommended that the states restore property confiscated from the Loyalists, but few of them took any steps to do so. And instead of helping British merchants to recover their prewar debts (as the treaty obligated them to do), many of the states enacted laws to make recovery more difficult. The British, in turn, refused to evacuate several posts on the American side of the border with Canada.

The inability of Congress to force the states to comply with terms of the peace treaty contributed to the refusal of England, France and Spain to enter commercial treaties with the Confederation. Lacking any authority over trade, Congress was unable to retaliate when the British in 1783 closed Canada and the British West Indies to American shipping, and the attempts of the states to retaliate individually failed completely. The weakness of the Confederation also encouraged Spain to close the Mississippi to American ships in 1784 and to intrigue for the secession of frontier areas north of the Floridas.

Congress was equally powerless to help resolve a postwar conflict between debtors and creditors that was aggravated by a depression and a shortage of currency. Most of the states stopped issuing paper money and set out to pay off their war debts by raising taxes. At the same time, merchants and other creditors began to press for the collection of private debts. Squeezed on all sides, debtors (who were mostly farmers) clamored for relief through state laws to put off the collection of debts and to provide cheap money.

In response to this pressure, seven of the states resorted to paper money issues in 1786 during the worst of the depression. Debtors put over their entire program in Rhode Island where creditors, compelled by law to accept repayment in highly depreciated paper money, fled the state to avoid doing so. But in Massachusetts, where the commercial class was in power, the state government refused to issue paper money and pressed forward with a deflationary program of high taxes; cattle and land were seized for debts, debtors crowded the jails, and all petitions for relief were ignored.

Out of this turmoil came Shays' Rebellion of 1786, an uprising of distressed farmers in central Massachusetts led by Daniel Shays. Although the rebellion was put down by state militia in fairly short order, there was a good deal of sympathy for the rebels. Their leaders were treated leniently, and a newly elected legislature acted to meet some of their demands. But the rebellion aroused the fears of many Americans for the future, pointed up another weakness of the Confederation (for Congress had been unable to give Massachusetts any help), and gave a strong push to the gathering movement for governmental reform.

The Constitution

The state of the union under the Articles of Confederation had become a source of growing concern to leading Americans well before Shays' Rebellion shook the confidence of a wider public. In voluminous correspondence beginning as early as 1780, George Washington, John Jay, Thomas Jefferson, James Madison, James Monroe and many others expressed their fear that the union forged in blood could not survive the strains of internal dissension and external weakness without some strengthening of central authority.

To Washington, writing in 1783, it was clear "that the honor, power and true interest of this country must be measured by a Continental scale, and that every departure therefrom weakens the Union, and may ultimately break the band which holds us together. To avert these evils, to form a Constitution that will give consistency, stability, and dignity to the Union and sufficient powers to the great Council of the Nation for general purposes" was a challenge to every patriot.[20]

How to form such a constitution was not yet clear. Opinions varied widely as to what would be "sufficient powers...for general purposes." Alexander Hamilton, in 1780 (when he was only 23), thought Congress should be given "complete sovereignty" over all but a few matters.[21] But Congress had ignored proposals of its own committees in 1781 that it seek authority to use troops "to compel any delinquent State to fulfill its Federal engagement" and to seize "the property of a State delinquent in its assigned proportion of men and money."[22] And when there was wide agreement on giving Congress authority to levy a federal import duty, the effort to amend the Articles foundered on the rule of unanimity.

At Hamilton's urging, the New York assembly asked Congress in 1782 to call a general convention of the states to revise the Articles. The Massachusetts Legislature seconded the request in 1785. Congress studied the proposal but was unable to reach agreement. Then, in 1785, Virginia and Maryland worked out a plan to resolve conflicts of those two states over navigation and commercial regulations. This gave Madison the idea of calling a general meeting on commercial problems. In January 1786 the Virginia Assembly issued the call for a meeting in Annapolis in September.

Nine states named delegates to the Annapolis Convention, but the dozen who assembled represented only five states—New York, New Jersey, Pennsylvania, Delaware and Virginia. Rather than seek a commercial agreement from so small a group, Madison and Hamilton persuaded the delegates to adopt a report, Sept. 14, that described the state of the Union as "delicate and critical." The report recommended that the states appoint commissioners to meet the next May in Philadelphia "to devise such further provisions as shall appear to them necessary to render the constitution of the Federal Government adequate to the exigencies of the Union."[23]

The proposal was deliberately vague. Madison and Hamilton knew that many others would oppose giving the central government much more power. And some, they knew, preferred the alternative of dividing the union into two or more confederations of states with closer economic and political ties. Southerners were convinced that this was the ultimate objective of John Jay's offer to Spain to give up free navigation of the Mississippi in return for trading concessions of interest to New England. Monroe (a Virginia delegate to Congress) saw it as part of a scheme "for dismembering the Confederacy and throwing the states eastward of the Hudson into one government."[24]

The Virginia Assembly, prodded by Madison and Washington, agreed on Oct. 16, 1786, to send delegates to Philadelphia, and six other states took similar action before Congress, on Feb. 21, 1787, moved to retain control of the situation. Its resolution endorsed the proposed convention for the purpose of reporting to Congress and the several legislatures its recommendations. Officially, therefore, the convention was to be no more than advisory to Congress.

Soon after the Philadelphia Convention opened on May 25, 1787, the delegates were asked to decide whether to try to patch up the Articles of Confederation or to ignore them and draw up a new plan of government. Congress, the state legislatures and many of the delegates expected no more than a revision of the Articles that would somehow strengthen the Confederation without altering the system of state sovereignty. But Madison and others who had worked to bring about a convention were convinced of the need for fundamental reform.

The Virginia Plan

These nationalists had come prepared, and on May 29 they seized the initiative. Edmund Randolph, acting for the Virginians, introduced 15 resolutions that added up to a plan for a new "National Government" of broad powers. The Virginia Plan called for a "National Legislature" of two houses, one to be elected by the people and the other by members of the first; a "National Executive" to be chosen by the Legislature; and a "National Judiciary." The legislature would have power to legislate in all cases where the states were "incompetent" or would interrupt "the harmony of the United States," and to "negative" state laws contrary to the articles of union. And the states would be represented in both chambers in proportion to their wealth or white population.[25]

The Convention moved at once into Committee of the Whole to consider the Randolph resolutions. They clearly envisaged a central government that, unlike that of the Confederation, would operate directly upon the people and independently of the states. It was to be a "national government" in contrast to the "merely federal" system that had been tried and found wanting. What the Virginians had in mind, though, was a system in which national and state governments would exercise dual sovereignty over the people within separate and prescribed fields. Randolph said that his plan "only means to give the national government power to defend and protect itself—to take, therefore, from the respective legislatures of states no more sovereignty than is competent to this end."[26]

Such a dual system was unknown in 1787. To many delegates the term "national government" implied a unitary or consolidated regime of potentially unlimited powers that would extinguish the independence of the states. However, on May 30, with only Connecticut opposed and New York divided, they adopted Randolph's proposition "that a National Government ought to be established consisting of a supreme Legislative, Executive and Judiciary."

(Continued on p. 17)

John Adams

James Monroe

Details of the Constitutional Convention

All of the 13 states except Rhode Island (whose upper house balked) were represented at the Federal Convention of 1787. They appointed 74 delegates in all, but only 55 attended. On May 14, when the Convention was scheduled to open at the State House in Philadelphia, only the Virginia and Pennsylvania delegates were on hand. It was May 25 before delegates from a majority of the states (seven) had arrived and the 29 present could organize. From then until the Convention finished its work on Sept. 17, the comings and goings of delegates held the average attendance to little more than 30.

Delegates. The 55 delegates who took part included many of the most distinguished men in America. Eight had signed the Declaration of Independence, seven had been governors of their states, 39 had served in Congress. More than half were college graduates, and at least 33 had been lawyers. Most of them had held prominent posts in the Revolution, and all were men of position and substance in their states. A majority were under 50 (five were under 30), and only four were over 60 years of age.

George Washington (then 55) and Benjamin Franklin (the oldest at 81) were the most influential Americans of the time. Washington, who had not wanted to be a delegate but had yielded for fear that his absence might be taken for indifference to the outcome, was the unanimous choice on May 25 to preside over the Convention, in which role he took a limited but effective part in the deliberations.

Those credited with influencing most the decision of the Convention were Gouverneur Morris and James Wilson of Pennsylvania, James Madison of Virginia and Roger Sherman of Connecticut, each of whom spoke well over 100 times. Others who took leading roles were George Mason and Edmund Randolph of Virginia, Oliver Ellsworth of Connecticut, Rufus King and Elbridge Gerry of Massachusetts, John Rutledge and Charles Pinckney of South Carolina, Alexander Hamilton of New York, John Dickinson of Delaware and William Paterson of New Jersey.

Not among the delegates were John Jay, busy as Secretary of Foreign Affairs, and America's envoys to France and England—Thomas Jefferson and John Adams. Also missing were such Revolutionary leaders as Samuel Adams, Patrick Henry, John Hancock, Christopher Gadsden, and Richard Henry Lee.

Rules. The Convention adopted rules May 28 and 29. There was some talk of the larger states getting more votes than the smaller, but the Convention followed the Articles of Confederation in giving one vote to each state. The rule provided that seven states would constitute a quorum and that "all questions should be decided by a majority of the states which shall be fully represented." This rule was amended to permit reconsideration of any vote—a step taken many times during the Convention.

Reconsideration was made easier by a rule of secrecy providing that "nothing spoken in the House be printed or otherwise published or communicated without leave."

Most delegates agreed with Madison who wrote to Thomas Jefferson that secrecy was needed "to secure unbiased discussion within doors and to prevent misconceptions and misconstructions without."* The press was critical, but the delegates abided by the rule. The official journal, limited to a report of formal motions and votes, was closed until 1819. Madison's shorthand notes, withheld until 1840, provided the fullest account.

Procedure. The Convention began by moving into committee of the whole to debate the Virginia resolutions, which called for a new national government composed of a bicameral legislature, an executive and a judiciary. The smaller states then rallied behind a New Jersey Plan for a modest revision of the Articles of Confederation. After that plan was defeated June 19, the members reverted to convention, and a threatened deadlock was broken by the "Great Compromise" of July 16 giving to each state an equal vote in the Senate.

On July 24 a Committee of Detail (Nathaniel Gorham of Massachusetts, Ellsworth, Wilson, Randolph and Rutledge) was appointed to draft a constitution based on agreements already reached. The Convention took a ten-day recess during which Washington went fishing near Valley Forge. The draft presented Aug. 6 included changes and additions which were discussed and refined through the following month. On Sept. 8 another committee (William S. Johnson of Connecticut, Hamilton, Gouverneur Morris, Madison and King) was named to revise the style and arrange the articles agreed to by the House. The final document (polished by Morris) was put before the Convention on Sept. 17.

The Signing. At this point Dr. Franklin said: "There are several parts of this Constitution which I do not at present approve, but I am not sure I shall never approve them." He would accept the Constitution, however, "because I expect no better and because I am not sure that it is not the best." And he hoped that "every member of the Convention who may still have objections to it, would, with me, on this occasion doubt a little of his own infallibility, and to make manifest our unanimity, put his name to this instrument."**

Franklin then moved that the Constitution be signed by the unanimous consent of the States present. The motion was approved as was one final change to increase representation in the House from one member for every 40,000 inhabitants to one for every 30,000—a change supported by Washington, in his only speech of the Convention. The Constitution was then signed by all except three of the 42 delegates present—Mason and Randolph of Virginia and Gerry of Massachusetts. After resolving that it should be submitted to special conventions of the states for ratification, the Convention adjourned.

---

* Charles Warren, *The Making of the Constitution* (Boston: Little, Brown, 1928), p. 135.
** *Ibid.*, p. 709.

(Continued from p. 15)

This opening commitment by most of the delegates then present reflected the air of crisis in which they met.[27]

The next step of the Committee of the Whole was to take up and approve several of the specific proposals of the Virginia Plan. As the debate proceeded, some members from smaller states became alarmed by the insistence of the larger states on proportional representation in both houses of the proposed Legislature. Under one formula, this would have given Virginia, Pennsylvania and Massachusetts—the three most populous states—13 of 28 seats in the Senate as well as a similar share of seats in the House. This spelled domination to those accustomed to the equality of states which prevailed in the Congress of the Confederation, and in the Convention as well.

To Luther Martin of Maryland, such a plan meant "a system of slavery which bound hand and foot ten states of the Union and placed them at the mercy of the other three." John Dickinson of Delaware declared that "we would rather submit to a foreign power than submit to be deprived of an equality of suffrage in both branches of the Legislature, and thereby be thrown under the domination of the large states." New Jersey would "never confederate" on such a basis, said William Paterson, for "she would be swallowed up" and he would "rather submit to a monarch, to a despot, than to such a fate."[28]

The New Jersey Plan

On June 11 the committee voted, six states to five, to constitute the Senate on the same proportional basis as the House. That decision led Paterson and others to draft a purely federal alternative to the Virginia Plan. The New Jersey Plan, presented June 15, proposed amending the Articles of Confederation to give Congress authority to levy import duties and to regulate trade. It would have provided also for a plural executive to be chosen by Congress and for a federal judiciary. It proposed that treaties and acts of Congress "shall be the supreme law," and that the executive be authorized to "call forth the power of the Confederated States" to enforce the laws if necessary. But the plan would have left each state with an equal voice in Congress and most of the attributes of sovereignty.

Paterson argued that his plan "accorded first with the powers of the Convention, and second with the sentiments of the people.... Our object is not such a Government as may be best in itself, but such a one as our constituents have authorized us to prepare and as they will approve." The nationalists rejected this concept of their responsibility; as Hamilton put it, the Union was in peril, and "to rely on and propose any plan not adequate to these exigencies, merely because it was not clearly within our powers, would be to sacrifice the means to the end."[29]

Madison was the last to speak against the New Jersey Plan, pointing up serious problems of the Confederation for which it offered no solution. On June 19 the delegates were asked to decide whether the Randolph resolutions "should be adhered to as preferable to those of Mr. Paterson."[30] Seven states voted yes and only three states no. That settled the issue of partial versus total reform; a clear majority of the delegates were now committed to abandoning the Articles and to drafting a new constitution.

The Great Compromise

The task was to take three months. There were few points of unanimity among the 55 men participating. Delegates from the same state were frequently divided and,

Gouverneur Morris

Roger Sherman

as a result, occasionally unable to vote. The records of the Convention also reveal that, although the nationalists won over a majority to their cause at an early stage, the original Virginia Plan was unacceptable in many of its details. The Constitution could not have been written without some degree of willingness on all sides to compromise in the interests of designing a workable and acceptable plan.

This became evident soon after defeat of the New Jersey Plan when the small states continued to demand and the large states to oppose equal representation in the Senate. On July 2 the Convention split five to five on this issue, with Georgia divided. Faced with a deadlock, the Convention named a committee to seek a compromise. It proposed on July 5 that, in return for equality of state representation in the Senate, the House be given sole power to originate money bills, which the Senate could accept or reject but not modify. This formula was finally approved July 16, five states to four, with Massachusetts divided and New York not voting because two of its three delegates had departed never to return. On July 24 a Committee of Detail was appointed to draft the Constitution according to the resolutions adopted by the Convention.

Without the Great Compromise the Convention would have collapsed. As Madison pointed out, however, "the great division of interests" in America was not between the large and small but between the northern and southern states, partly because of climate but "principally from the effects of having or not having slaves."[31] Although the southerners were for the most part supporters of a strong central government, they were determined to limit its power to discriminate against the South's special interests in slavery, agricultural exports and western expansion. This stand necessitated other compromises that accounted for some of the key provisions of the new plan of government.

What finally emerged Sept. 17 as the Constitution of the United States was a unique blend of national and federal systems based on republican principles of representative and limited government. It met the basic objective of the nationalists by providing for a central government of ample powers that could function independently of the states. It also met the concerns of states' rights supporters by surrounding that government with checks and balances to prevent the tyranny of any one branch.

The text of the Constitution does not follow the order in which the separate provisions were developed. The Convention moved generally from decisions on broad principles to questions of detail and precision. But the interdependent nature of the various parts of the plan made for frequent reconsideration of decisions in one area to take account of subsequent decisions in another but related area. As a result, many of the provisions were altered or added in the

Legislative Nomenclature, 1787

The Constitutional Convention continued to speak of the "Legislature of the United States" and its "first branch" and "second branch" until these terms were changed, in the Aug. 6 report of the Committee of Detail, to "Congress of the United States," "House of Representatives," and "Senate." The term "Congress" was taken from the Articles of Confederation. "House of Representatives" was the name of the first branch in five states (others being called Assembly, House of Delegates and House of Commons), while the second branch was called "Senate" in all but two states.*

Provisions of the Constitution relating to both House and Senate referred to "each House" in keeping with English usage. But the terms "upper house" and "lower house," also taken from English usage to denote the Senate and the House, were not included in the Constitution.

* Charles Warren, *The Making of the Constitution* (Boston: Little, Brown, 1928), p. 388.

---

final weeks of the Convention. How the major provisions were developed is described in the following sections.

The Structure of Congress

The Convention's early decision that a national government, if formed, should consist of three branches—legislative, executive and judicial—was undisputed. This division of governmental functions had been recognized from early colonial times and was reflected in most of the state constitutions. The failure of the Articles of Confederation to separate the functions was generally recognized as a serious mistake. The decision as to three branches also implied broad acceptance of the principle of separation of powers, although most of the provisions of the Constitution that gave effect to the principle were adopted on practical rather than theoretical grounds.

The Virginia Plan called for a legislature of two houses, according to a practice initiated by Parliament, followed by most of the colonial governments and retained by 10 of the 13 states. The Continental Congress and the Congress of the Confederation were unicameral, but once the Convention had decided to abandon the Articles there was little question that the new Congress should be bicameral. As George Mason saw it, the minds of Americans were settled on two points—"an attachment to republican government (and) an attachment to more than one branch in the Legislature."[32] Only Pennsylvania dissented when the Committee of the Whole voted for two houses, and the Convention confirmed the committee's decision, June 21, by a vote of seven states to three.

Election of the House

The nationalists insisted that the new government rest on the consent of the people rather than the state legislatures. So they held it essential that at least "the first branch" or House be elected "by the people immediately," as Madison put it. The government "ought to possess...the mind or sense of the people at large," said James Wilson, and for that reason "the Legislature ought to be the most ex-

act transcript of the whole society." The House "was to be the grand depository of the democratic principles of the government," said Mason.[33]

Those who were suspicious of a national government preferred election of the House by the state legislatures. "The people immediately should have as little to do" with electing the government as possible, said Roger Sherman, because "they want information and are constantly liable to be misled." Elbridge Gerry was convinced that "the evils we experience flow from the excess of democracy," while Charles Pinckney thought "the people were less fit judges"[34] than the legislatures to choose members of the House. Election by the legislatures was twice defeated, however, and popular election of the House was confirmed June 21 by a vote of nine states to one.

Election of the Senate

The Virginia Plan proposed that the House elect the "second branch" or Senate from persons nominated by the state legislatures. There was little support for this plan because it would have made the Senate subservient to the House. Most delegates agreed with Gouverneur Morris that it was to be the Senate's role "to check the precipitation, changeableness and excesses of the first branch."[35] (The role of representing the states emerged later, after the decision for equal representation.) Neither was there any support for the view of Madison and Wilson that the people should elect the Senate as well as the House. Election of the Senate by the state legislatures was carried unanimously in Committee of the Whole, June 7, and confirmed June 25 by a Convention vote of nine states to two.

Basis of Representation

The Virginia Plan called for representation of the states in both House and Senate in proportion to their wealth or free population. This proposal led to the revolt of the small states, which was ended by the vote of July 16 for equal representation of the states in the Senate. But while the principle of proportional representation in the House was never seriously challenged, the idea of basing it on wealth or the free population raised questions that led to adoption of important qualifications.

To retain southern support for proportional representation in the Senate, Wilson had proposed on June 11 that the House be apportioned according to a count of the whole number of free citizens and three-fifths of all others (meaning slaves) except Indians not paying taxes. This formula (first proposed in Congress in 1783) was adopted with only New Jersey and Delaware opposed. Then on July 9 the Convention decided that the new Congress should have power "to regulate the number of representatives upon the principles of wealth and number of inhabitants."[36] Since southerners regarded slaves as property, this led northerners who wanted representation to be based on population alone to ask why slaves should be counted at all.

As a result, on July 11 the Convention voted, six states to four, to exclude blacks from the formula of June 11. At this point Gouverneur Morris proposed that the power of Congress to apportion the House according to wealth and numbers be subject to a proviso "that direct taxation shall be in proportion to representation,"[37] and the proviso was adopted without debate. The slave issue now appeared in a different light, for it seemed that the South must pay for any increases in representation it would gain by counting slaves. So the northerners dropped the opposition to the three-fifths count demanded by the southerners, and on July 13 the Convention restored that provision.

Because it was now agreed that representation was to be based solely on population (counting all whites and three-fifths of blacks), the word "wealth" was deleted from the provision adopted July 9. This resolution of the question gave five free voters in a slave state a voice in the House equivalent to that of seven free voters in a non-slave state, according to Rufus King, but it was "a necessary sacrifice to the establishment of the Constitution."[38]

Size of Congress

The committee that recommended equal representation in the Senate on July 5 also proposed that each state have one vote in the House for every 40,000 inhabitants. This proposal precipitated the debate on representation discussed above, during which it was decided to let Congress regulate the future size of the House to allow for population changes and the admission of new states. Upon reflection, however, it was seen that under this arrangement a majority in Congress would be able to block a reapportionment and even to change the basis of representation for slaves. Northerners and southerners now agreed that the periods and rules of revising the representation ought to be fixed by the Constitution.

Randolph was the first to propose a regular census, and on July 13 the Convention adopted the plan, finally incorporated in Article I, Section 2, linking the apportionment of representatives to an "enumeration" every 10 years of the "whole number of free persons...and three fifths of all others." On Aug. 8 it was decided that the number of representatives "shall not exceed one for every 40,000," a figure that was lowered to 30,000 on the last day of the Convention. Until the first census should be taken, the size of the House was fixed at 65 representatives allotted as set forth in Article I.[39]

The size of the Senate was fixed on July 23 when the Convention considered and adopted (with Maryland alone voting against it) a proposal that the body should "consist of two members from each state, who shall vote per capita." A proposal to allow each state three senators had been turned down on the ground that it would penalize poorer and more distant states, and that "a small number was most convenient for deciding on peace and war," as Nathaniel Gorham put it. The idea that senators should vote individually rather than as a delegation came from Gerry, who wanted to "prevent the delays and inconveniences" that had occurred in Congress under the unit rule for voting.[40] Although this provision was at odds with the decision that the states should be equally represented in the Senate, it was accepted with little objection and included in Article I, Section 3.

Terms of Office

There was strong attachment in the Convention to the tradition of annual elections—"the only defense of the people against tyranny," according to Gerry. But Madison argued that representatives would need more than one year to become informed about the interests of other states, and his proposal of a three-year term for the House was adopted June 12. Many delegates still wanted more frequent elections. "The Representatives ought to return home and mix with the people," said Sherman, for "by remaining at the seat of Government they would acquire the habits of the place which might differ from those of their constituents."

On reconsideration June 21, the Convention compromised on biennial elections and a two-year term for representatives.[41]

The delegates also changed their minds about the Senate, agreeing first to a term of seven years although the terms of state senators varied from two to a maximum of five. When this decision was reviewed, alternatives of four, six and nine years were considered. Charles Pinckney opposed six years because senators would be "too long separated from their constituents, and will imbibe attachments different from that of the state." But having decided in biennial elections for the House, the Convention voted June 26 to make it a six-year term in the Senate with one-third of the members to be elected every two years.[42]

Qualifications of Voters

The report of the Committee of Detail, Aug. 6, provided that the qualifications of electors for the House should be the same as those required by the states for "the most numerous branch" of their own legislatures. Because property and other voting qualifications varied widely from state to state, no uniform standard seemed feasible. When Gouverneur Morris proposed giving Congress power to alter the qualifications, Oliver Ellsworth replied: "The clause is safe as it is—the states have staked their liberties on the qualifications which we have proposed to confirm."[43] A proposal by Morris and others to limit the franchise to those who owned land was rejected, and on Aug. 8 the Convention adopted the committee proposal without dissent.

Regulation of Elections

The Committee of Detail also proposed that the states regulate the times and places of electing senators and representatives, but that Congress retain the power to change the regulations. The states should not have the last word in this regard, said Madison, since "it was impossible to foresee all the abuses that might be made of the discretionary power." The Convention adopted this provision Aug. 9 but amended it Sept. 14 by adding "except as to the places of choosing Senators," who were to be elected by the state legislatures. The purpose of the change was to "exempt the seats of government in the states from the power of Congress."[44]

Qualifications of Members

The Convention decided in June on a minimum age of 30 for senators and 25 for representatives. The Committee of Detail added two more qualifications: United States citizenship (three years for the House, four for the Senate)

Oliver Ellsworth   **Elbridge Gerry**

and residence within the state to be represented. Fearful of making it too easy for foreigners to be elected, the Convention lengthened the citizenship requirement to seven years for representatives and nine years for senators, after voting down 14 years as likely (in Ellsworth's view) to discourage "meritorious aliens from emigrating to this country."[45]

Some delegates wanted to require residence in a state for a minimum time, from one to seven years. Mason feared that "rich men of neighboring states may employ with success the means of corruption in some particular district and thereby get into the public councils after having failed in their own state."[46] But these proposals were voted down, and it was left that "no person shall be a representative (or senator) who shall not, when elected, be an inhabitant of that state in which he shall be chosen."[47]

The Convention debated the desirability of a property qualification. Most of the state constitutions required members of their legislatures to own certain amounts of property. Dickinson doubted "the policy of interweaving into a Republican Constitution a veneration of wealth."[48] But on July 26, by a vote of eight states to three, the Convention instructed the Committee of Detail to draft a property qualification. As reported, this would have given Congress authority to establish "uniform qualifications...with regard to property." But when the provision was debated on Aug. 10, it was rejected and there was no further effort to include a property qualification.[49]

There was even less disposition to include a religious qualification, although all of the states except New York and Virginia imposed such a qualification on state representatives. The Convention's outlook on this point was made clear when, in debating an oath of office on Aug. 30, the delegates adopted without dissent Charles Pinckney's proviso (which became a part of Article VI) that "no religious test shall ever be required as a qualification to any office or public trust under the United States."[50] The only qualifications established by the Constitution for election to Congress, therefore, related to age, citizenship and residence.

Pay of Members

The Virginia Plan wanted members of the National Legislature to be paid "liberal stipends" without saying who should pay them. To the nationalists, however, one of the weaknesses of the Confederation was that members of Congress were paid by their states. So on June 12, after submitting "fixt" for "liberal," the Committee of the Whole agreed that in the case of representatives "the wages should be paid out of the National Treasury." But on June 22 Ellsworth moved that the states pay. Randolph opposed the change, saying it would create a dependence that "would vitiate the whole system." Hamilton agreed, saying "those who pay are the masters of those who are paid." The motion was rejected, four states to five.

When the pay of senators was discussed on June 26, Ellsworth again moved that the states pay. Madison argued that this would make senators "the mere agents and advocates of state interests and views, instead of being the impartial umpires and guardians of justice and general good." Ellsworth's motion was again defeated, five states to six. Despite this, the Aug. 6 report of the Committee of Detail provided that the pay of senators and representatives should be "ascertained and paid" by the states. But Ellsworth and others had now changed their minds, and on Aug. 14 the Convention voted, nine to two, to pay members out of the national treasury.

Whether the amount of pay should be fixed in the Constitution was another matter. To let Congress set its own wages, said Madison, "was an indecent thing and might, in time, prove a dangerous one." Ellsworth proposed five dollars a day. Others thought the decision should be left to Congress, although Sherman was afraid the members would pay themselves too little rather than too much, "so that men ever so fit could not serve unless they were at the same time rich." On Aug. 14, however, the Convention voted to give Congress full authority to fix its own pay by law.[51]

Eligibility to Office

Because of the attachment of several states to the theory of rotation in office, the Articles of Confederation had provided that "no person shall be capable of being a delegate for more than three years in any term of six years."[52] This rule had forced out of Congress some of its better members and was widely criticized. The Virginia Plan proposed, nevertheless, that members ought to be incapable of re-election for an unspecified period after the expiration of their term of service, and to be subject to recall. But this provision was eliminated in Committee of the Whole, without debate or dissent, and no further effort was made to qualify the eligibility of representatives or senators for re-election.

Whether members of Congress should be eligible to hold other office was debated at much greater length. Under the Articles, a delegate was not "capable of holding any office under the United States for which he, or another for his benefit, receives any salary, fees or emolument of any kind."[53] But the Congress had appointed many delegates to diplomatic and other jobs, and the practice had created much resentment. There was also a general concern over the office-seeking propensities of state legislators. So the Virginia Plan proposed making any member of Congress ineligible to any office established by a particular state, or under the authority of the United States during the term of service and for an unspecified period after its expiration.

Although this provision—with the time of one year inserted in the blank—was adopted in Committee of the Whole, June 12, the Convention reconsidered and modified it several times before the final form was approved on Sept. 3. Delegates who wanted to shut the door on appointments saw them as a source of corruption. "What led to the appointment of this Convention?" asked John Mercer, and answered: "The corruption and mutability of the legislative councils of the states."[54] Those opposed to too many strictures feared they would discourage good men from running for Congress. "The legislature would cease to be a magnet to the first talents and abilities," said Charles Pinckney.[55]

The compromise that emerged was a twofold disqualification. Members could not be appointed during their terms to federal offices created during those terms or for which the pay was increased, and no one holding federal office could be a member at the same time. The provision, incorporated in Section 6 of Article I, made no reference to state office or to ineligibility following expiration of a member's term.

Regulation of Congress

Article I included four provisions for the regulation of House and Senate that originated with the Committee of Detail and were only slightly modified in Convention.

● The provision that "Each House shall be the Judge of the Elections, Returns and Qualifications of its own

Members..." was found in the constitutions of eight states and was agreed to without debate.

● The provision that "Each House may determine the Rules of its Proceedings, punish its Members for disorderly Behaviour, and, with the Concurrence of two-thirds, expel a Member" was amended to require a two-thirds vote for expulsion. The change, proposed by Madison because "the right of expulsion was too important to be exercised by a bare majority of a quorum," was approved by a unanimous vote.

● The provision that "Each House shall keep a Journal, and from time to time publish the same..." stemmed from a similar provision in the Articles. When Madison proposed giving the Senate some discretion in the matter, Wilson objected that "the people have a right to know what their agents are doing or have done, and it should not be in the option of the legislature to conceal their proceedings."[56] The Convention voted to require publication of the Journals of each House, but with the proviso "excepting such parts as may in their judgment require secrecy." The clause also provided for recording the "yea" and "nay" votes of members, although some delegates objected that "the reasons governing the votes never appear along with them."

● The provision that "Neither House, during the Session of Congress, shall, without the Consent of the other, adjourn for more than three days, nor to any other Place than that in which the two Houses shall be sitting," was agreed to after brief debate. Most of the state constitutions had similar provisions, reflecting a common commitment to legislative independence born of colonial experience with the right of royal governors to suspend and dissolve the assemblies.

Powers of Congress

The Virginia resolutions proposed that the National Legislature be empowered—

"to enjoy the Legislative Rights vested in Congress by the Confederation and moreover to legislate in all cases to which the separate States are incompetent, or in which the harmony of the United States may be interrupted by the exercise of individual Legislation;

"to negative all laws passed by the several States, contravening in the opinion of the National Legislature the articles of Union; and

"to call forth the force of the Union against any member of the Union failing in its duty under the articles thereof."

These proposals reflected the great concern of the nationalists with the powerlessness of Congress under the Confederation to protect the interests of the United States at large against the "prejudices, passions and improper views of the state legislatures,"[57] in the words of Dickinson. Madison deplored "a constant tendency in the states to encroach on the federal authority, to violate national treaties, to infringe the rights and interests of each other, to oppress the weaker party within their respective jurisdiction."[58] So it seemed essential that, in addition to adequate authority to legislate for the general interests of the Union, the new national government should possess the power to restrain the states and to compel their obedience.

When these proposals were first discussed May 31, some delegates wanted an exact enumeration of powers before voting, but the first of the Virginia resolutions was approved after brief debate without dissent. The second, granting a power to negate state laws akin to the royal disallowance of colonial laws, was also approved without

George Mason   **Edmund Randolph**

debate or dissent. When the third resolution was called up, however, Madison moved to set it aside because he feared that "the use of force against a state would look more like a declaration of war than an infliction of punishment."[59] Although the New Jersey Plan contained a similar provision, there was no further consideration of this power by the Convention.

On June 8, Charles Pinckney proposed that the power to nullify state laws be extended to all such laws Congress should judge to be improper. Such an expansion would enslave the states, said Gerry, and the motion was rejected, seven states to three. Strong opposition now developed to any power to negate state laws. Madison continued to defend it as the most certain means of preserving the system, but Gouverneur Morris concluded that it would disgust all the states. On July 17 the Convention reversed its earlier action by voting seven to three against the power to negative. The problem of securing conformity of states to national law was finally resolved by adoption of a "supremacy" clause and the specific prohibition of certain state laws.

The Convention on July 17 also reconsidered the first of the Virginia resolutions. Sherman proposed as a substitute that Congress be empowered "to make laws binding on the people of the United States in all cases which may concern the common interests of the Union; but not to interfere with the Government of the individual States in any matters of internal police which respect the Government of such States only, and wherein the general welfare of the United States is not concerned." This formulation (in which the term "general welfare" made its first appearance in the Convention) seemed too restrictive to most delegates and it was rejected, eight to two. Then, by a vote of six states to four, the Convention inserted in the resolution approved May 31 the additional power to legislate "in all cases for the general interests of the Union."[60]

When this broad grant of legislative authority was examined by the Committee of Detail it seemed so vague and unlimited that the committee decided to replace it with an enumeration of specified powers. Eighteen of these powers were listed in the report of Aug. 6, which also contained, for the first time, lists of powers to be denied to Congress and to the states. The various lists formed the basis for the powers and prohibitions that were finally incorporated in Sections 8, 9 and 10 of Article I of the Constitution, of which the major provisions were developed as explained in the following pages.

Power to Tax

The committee's first proposal—that Congress "shall have the power to lay and collect taxes, duties, imposts and excises"—was adopted Aug. 16 without dissent. The Convention then became embroiled in the issue of paying off the public debt and soon amended the tax clause to provide that Congress "shall fulfill the engagements and discharge the debts of the United States and shall have the power to lay and collect taxes...." Pierce Butler objected that this provision would require Congress to redeem at face value all government paper, including that held by "bloodsuckers who had speculated on the distresses of others and bought up securities at heavy discounts."[61] They thought Congress should be free to buy up such holdings at less than full value.

As a result, the Convention dropped the language added to the tax clause and adopted in its place the declaration found in Article VI that "All debts contracted and engagements entered into before the adoption of this Constitution shall be as valid against the United States under this Constitution as under the Confederation." This declaration left open the question of full or partial redemption, which was to become a major issue in the First Congress.

But some delegates now thought that the power to tax should be linked explicitly to the purpose of paying the debt. Their position led to further amendment of the tax clause on Sept. 4 to provide that Congress "shall have power to lay and collect taxes, duties, imposts and excises, to pay the debts and provide for the common defense and general welfare of the United States." The further proviso in the first clause of Section 8 of Article I that "all duties, imposts and excises shall be uniform throughout the United States" had been approved earlier as a part of the effort to prevent Congress from discriminating against the commerce of any one state.

It was to be argued later that inclusion of the words "general welfare" was intended to confer an additional and unlimited power on Congress. The records of the Convention indicate, however, that when it was decided to qualify the power to tax "to pay the debts," it became necessary to make it clear that this was not the only purpose for which taxes could be levied. "To provide for the common defense and general welfare" was taken from the Articles of Confederation and used to encompass all of the other specific and limited powers vested by the Constitution in Congress.[62]

Direct Taxes. As already noted, in settling the basis for representation in the House, the Convention had linked the apportionment of "direct taxes" as well as representatives to a count of all whites and three-fifths of blacks. When this provision was reconsidered Aug. 20, King asked "what was the precise meaning of direct taxation" but, according to Madison, "no one answered."[63] The only direct taxes in use at that time were land taxes and capitation or poll taxes. Because southerners feared that Congress might seek to levy a special tax on slaves, the Committee of Detail recommended and the Convention later adopted a further provision, incorporated in Section 9 of Article I, that "No Capitation, or other direct, Tax shall be laid, unless in Proportion" to the count required by Section 2. Another limitation on the power to tax—also adopted as a concession to the South—prohibited levies on exports.

Power to Regulate Commerce

Trade among the states and with other countries was severely handicapped under the Confederation by a lack of uniformity in duties and commercial regulations. The states commonly discriminated against the products of neighboring states, incurring retaliation in kind that added to the divisiveness and suspicions of the times. To Madison and many others, it was as essential to the new plan of government that Congress have the power to regulate commerce as it was that it have the power to tax. It soon became clear, however, that the southern states would not accept a Constitution that failed to protect their vested interest in slave

As a result, the Committee of Detail proposed that Congress have the power to regulate commerce with foreign nations and among the several states subject to two limitations—a ban on export taxes and a prohibition against any effort to tax or outlaw the slave trade. The general power to regulate commerce was approved on Aug. 16 without dissent. (The words "and with the Indian Tribes" were added Sept. 4.) But the proposed limitations met with considerable opposition.

In keeping with mercantilist doctrines, it was common practice at that time for governments to tax exports; the idea of prohibiting such action was novel. "To deny this power is to take from the common government half the regulation of trade," said Wilson.[64] It was also to deny Congress the power to menace the livelihood of the South by taxing the exports of rice, tobacco and indigo on which its economy was largely dependent. Other northerners considered this concession to the South as wise as it was necessary; Gerry said the Convention had already given Congress "more power than we know how will be exercised."[65] On Aug. 21, by a vote of seven states to four, the Convention agreed that "No Tax or Duty shall be laid on Articles exported from any State." This provision was placed in Section 9 of Article I in the final draft.

The second limitation on the power to regulate commerce provided that no tax or duty was to be laid on the migration or importation of such persons as the several States shall think proper to admit; nor shall such migration or importation be prohibited. The limitation was designed to meet the South's objection to any interference with the slave trade, although those words were carefully avoided. Luther Martin thought it was "inconsistent with the principles of the Revolution and dishonorable to the American character to have such a feature in the Constitution."[66] But most other delegates, including those opposed to slavery, argued that it was a political rather than a moral issue.

Some northerners, as well as southerners, agreed with Ellsworth that "the morality or wisdom of slavery" should be left to the states to determine. "Let us not intermeddle," he said, predicting that "slavery, in time, will not be a speck in our country."[67] Many others agreed with Mason that the labor and agricultural exports from the burdensome restrictions that a Congress controlled by northerners might seek. "infernal traffic" in slaves was holding back the economic development of the country, and that for this reason the national government "should have power to prevent the increase of slavery."[68] Since the provision reported by the Committee of Detail was clearly unacceptable to many delegates, a committee was named to seek a compromise.

It now proposed that Congress be barred from prohibiting the slave trade until 1800, but that it have power to levy a duty on slaves as on other imports. Both provisions were approved Aug. 25, the first by a vote of seven states to four after the year 1800 had been changed to 1808, and the second after limiting the duty to $10. So the power of Congress to regulate commerce was further limited by these provisions respecting slaves, which became the first clause of Section 9 of Article I.

Still another limit on the commerce power, sought by the South and recommended by the Committee of Detail, would have required a two-thirds vote of both House and Senate to pass a navigation act. England had used such laws to channel colonial imports and exports into British ships and ports, and southerners now feared that the North, where shipping was a major interest, might try to monopolize the transport of their exports by a law requiring them to be carried aboard American ships.

Northern delegates were strongly opposed to the two-thirds proposal, and in working out the compromise on the slave trade succeeded in having it dropped. As a result, Charles Pinckney moved to require a two-thirds vote of both houses to enact any commercial regulation. This motion was rejected Aug. 29, seven states to four, and the Convention confirmed the decision to drop the proposed two-thirds rule for navigation acts. Mason (one of three who refused to sign the Constitution) later argued that a bare majority of Congress should not have the power to "enable a few rich merchants in Philadelphia, New York and Boston to monopolize the staples of the Southern States."[69]

A relatively minor limitation on the power to regulate commerce was adopted to allay the fear of Maryland that Congress might require ships traversing Chesapeake Bay to enter or clear at Norfolk or another Virginia port in order to simplify the collection of duties. As approved Aug. 31 and added to Section 9 of Article I, it provided that "No Preference shall be given by any Regulation of Commerce or Revenue to the Ports of one State over those of another; nor shall Vessels bound to or from one State be obliged to enter, clear or pay Duties in another."

War and Treaty Power

The Articles of Confederation had given Congress the exclusive right and power of determining on peace and war. The Committee of Detail proposed giving to the new Congress as a whole the power to make war and to the Senate alone the power to make treaties. The treaty power was later divided between the President and the Senate. But in discussing the war power, Aug. 17, Charles Pinckney was for giving it to the Senate since "it would be singular for one authority to make war, and another peace." On the other hand, Butler thought the war power should rest with the President, "who will have all the requisite qualities and will not make war but when the Nation will support it." Neither view drew any support, and the Convention voted to give Congress the power "to declare war." The word "declare" had been substituted for "make" to leave the President free to repel a sudden attack. Sherman said, "The Executive should be able to repel, and not commence war."[70]

On Aug. 18, the Convention agreed to give Congress the power "to raise and support Armies," "to provide and maintain a Navy," and "to make Rules for the Government and Regulation of the land and naval Forces." All were taken from the Articles of Confederation. Gerry, voicing the old colonial fears of a standing army, wanted a proviso that "in time of peace" the army should consist of no more than two or three thousand men, but his motion was unanimously rejected.[71] On Sept. 5, however, the Convention added to the power to "raise and support Armies" the proviso "but no Appropriation of Money to that Use shall be for a longer Term than two Years."[72] This was intended to quiet fears similar to those that had led the British to require annual appropriations for the army.

The Convention approved without dissent the power, proposed by the Committee of Detail and included in Section 8 of Article I, "to provide for calling forth the Militia to execute the Laws of the Union, suppress Insurrections and repel Invasions." But a further proposal by Mason that Congress have power to regulate the militia alarmed the defenders of state sovereignty. To Gerry, this was the last point remaining to be surrendered. Others argued that the states would never allow control of the militia to get out of their hands.

The shortcomings of the militia during the Revolutionary War were a bitter memory to most of the delegates, however, and they shared the practical view of Madison that "as the greatest danger to liberty is from large standing armies, it is best to prevent them by an effectual provision for a good militia."[73] So on Aug. 23 the Convention adopted the provision, as later incorporated in Section 8, giving Congress power "to provide for organizing, arming, and disciplining the Militia, and for governing such Part of them as may be employed in the Service of the United States...."

Special Case of Money Bills

The committee named to resolve the issue of equal or proportional representation in the Senate proposed as a compromise that each state have one vote in the Senate, but that the House originate all bills for raising and appropriating money and paying government salaries, and that the Senate be denied the right to amend such bills. Included in the proposal was the phrase that "No money shall be drawn from the public Treasury, but in pursuance of appropriations to be originated in the first branch." Seven states at this time required that money bills originate in the lower house, but only four of those states forbade amendment by the upper house. Some delegates objected that such a provision would be degrading to the Senate, but it was approved July 6, five states to three.

The Committee of Detail phrased the provision as follows: "All bills for raising or appropriating money, and for fixing the salaries of the officers of Government, shall originate in the House of Representatives, and shall not be altered or amended by the Senate." Madison was for striking the entire provision as likely to promote "injurious altercations" between House and Senate; others insisted that it was necessary because the people "will not agree that any but their immediate representatives shall meddle with their purse."[74] The Convention's division on the question reflected contrasting concepts of the Senate as likely to be the most responsible branch or the most aristocratic one, to be strengthened or checked accordingly.

James Madison   **Alexander Hamilton**

On Aug. 8 the Convention reversed itself, voting seven states to four to drop the provision. Further debate, however, underscored the importance of reaching a compromise, and the one finally proposed was adopted Sept. 8, nine to two. It provided that "All bills for raising revenue shall originate in the House of Representatives, and shall be subject to alterations and amendments by the Senate; no money shall be drawn from the Treasury but in consequence of appropriations made by law." The first sentence, slightly revised, was incorporated in the final draft as the first clause of Section 7, while the second sentence was made one of the limitations on the powers of Congress listed in Section 9 of Article I.

The Constitution thus gave the House exclusive power to originate any bill involving taxes or tariffs of any kind, but it did not extend that power to appropriation bills. However, the House assumed the additional power, on the basis of the consideration it had received in the Convention, and it became the recognized prerogative of the House to originate spending as well as revenue bills.

Admission of New States

As early as 1780, the Continental Congress had resolved that lands ceded to the United States "shall be disposed of for the common benefit of the United States, and be settled and formed into distinct republican States, which shall become members of the Federal Union, and have the same rights of sovereignty, freedom and independence as the other States." By 1786 the Congress of the Confederation was in possession of all land south of Canada, north of the Ohio, west of the Alleghenies and east of the Mississippi. Provisions for governing this great territory were laid down by Congress in the Northwest Ordinance of July 13, 1787.

The Ordinance provided that, upon attaining a population of 5,000 free male inhabitants of voting age, the territory would be entitled to elect a legislature and send a nonvoting delegate to Congress. It provided also that no less than three nor more than five states were to be formed out of the territory. Each state was to have at least 60,000 free inhabitants to qualify for admission to the Union "on an equal footing with the original States in all respects whatever." And the Ordinance declared that "there shall be neither slavery nor involuntary servitude in the said territory....."[75]

As this far-sighted plan was being approved in New York by the Congress of the Confederation, Gouverneur Morris and other eastern delegates to the Constitutional Convention in Philadelphia were arguing strongly against equality for the new states. "The busy haunts of men, not the remote wilderness, are the proper school of political talents," said Morris. "If the western people get the power into their hands, they will ruin the Atlantic interests. The back members are always most adverse to the best measures."[76]

Among those of an opposing view were the delegates of Virginia and North Carolina, whose western lands were to become Kentucky and Tennessee. Mason argued that the western territories "will either not unite with or will speedily revolt from the Union, if they are not in all respects placed on an equal footing." In time, he thought, they might well be "both more numerous and more wealthy" than the seaboard states. Madison was certain that "no unfavorable distinctions were admissible, either in point of justice or policy."[77]

In the light of this debate, the Committee of Detail proposed on Aug. 6 that Congress have the power to admit new states with the consent of two-thirds of the members present in each House (the Articles of Confederation required the consent of nine states) and, in the case of a state formed from an existing state, the consent of the legislature of that state. New states were to be admitted on the same terms with the original states. But when this proposal was considered Aug. 29, the Convention adopted a motion by Morris to strike out the provision for equality.

Morris and Dickinson then offered a new draft, eliminating the condition of a two-thirds vote, which was adopted and became the first clause of Section 3 of Article IV. It provided simply that new states could be admitted by Congress, subject to the consent of the state legislatures where concerned. Although this provision of the Constitution was silent as to the status of the new states, Congress was to adhere to the principle of equality in admitting them.

The Convention then adopted the provision governing territories set out in the second clause of Section 3 of Article IV. Madison had first proposed adding such a provision to the Constitution to give a legal foundation to the Northwest Ordinance, since the Articles of Confederation had given Congress no explicit power to legislate for territories. A proviso ruling out prejudice to any claims of the United States or of any particular state was added because some delegates feared that, without it, the terms on which new states were admitted might favor the claims of some state to vacant lands ceded by Britain.

Power of Impeachment

It was decided early in the Convention that the Executive should be "removable on impeachment and conviction of malpractice or neglect of duty."[78] Who should impeach and try him, however, depended on how he was to be chosen. So long as Congress was to elect the President—and that decision stood until Sept. 4—few delegates were willing to give Congress the additional power to remove him. The final decision to have the President chosen by presidential electors helped to resolve the problem.

The Virginia Plan called for the national judiciary to try "impeachments of any National officers," without specifying which branch of government would impeach. Because all the state constitutions vested that power in the lower house of the assembly, the Committee of Detail proposed removal of the President on impeachment by the House and conviction by the Supreme Court "of treason, bribery or corruption." No action was taken on this proposal until the special committee, in advancing the plan for presidential electors, suggested that the Senate try all impeachments and that conviction require the concurrence of two-thirds of the members present.

When this plan was debated Sept. 8, Charles Pinckney opposed trial by the Senate on the ground that if the President "opposes a favorite law, the two Houses will combine against him, and under the influence of heat and faction throw him out of office."[79] But the Convention adopted the formula for impeachment by the House, trial by the Senate, and conviction by a two-thirds vote. It also extended the grounds for impeachment from treason and bribery to "other high crimes and other misdemeanors" and made the Vice President and other civil officers similarly impeachable and removable.. These provisions were incorporated in Section 2 and 3 of Article I and in Section 4 of Article II.

Miscellaneous Powers

The Committee of Detail proposed that Congress retain the power granted in the Articles "to borrow money and emit bills on the credit of the United States." But state emissions of paper money in 1786 had contributed greatly to the alarms that had led to the calling of the Convention, and most delegates agreed with Ellsworth that this was a "favorable moment to shut and bar the door against paper money."[80] So the words "and emit bills" were struck out, with only two states dissenting, before this provision was approved Aug. 16.

Most of the other powers of Congress specified in Section 8 of Article I were derived from the Articles of Confederation or included as appropriate to the new plan of government, and were approved with little debate or dissent. This was true of provisions respecting naturalization and bankruptcy, coinage, counterfeiting, post offices, copyrights, inferior tribunals, piracies, and the seat of government. It was true also of the final provision of Section 8—proposed by the Committee of Detail and adopted Aug. 20 without debate—which was to be named the "sweeping clause" of the Constitution.

That clause authorized Congress "to make all Laws which shall be necessary and proper for carrying into Execution the foregoing Powers, and all other Powers vested by this Constitution in the Government of the United States, or in any Department or Officer thereof." The intent of this grant was simply to enable Congress to enact legislation giving effect to the specified powers. No member of the Convention suggested that it was meant to confer some power in addition to those previously specified. But the meaning of the clause and of the words "necessary and proper" was to become the focus of the continuing controversy between broad and strict constructionists of the Constitution that began with passage by the First Congress of a law to create a national bank.

Limits on Powers of Congress

Section 9 of Article I as finally adopted imposed eight specific limitations on the powers of Congress. Five of the limitations—those relating to the slave trade, capitation taxes, sport taxes, preference among ports, and appropriations—have been discussed in connection with the powers to tax, to regulate commerce and to originate money bills. The others were adopted as follows:

• On Aug. 28, Charles Pinckney moved to adopt a provision of the Massachusetts Constitution that barred suspension of the writ of habeas corpus except on the most urgent occasions and then for a period not to exceed one year. This was amended and adopted to provide that "the Privilege of the Writ of Habeas Corpus shall not be suspended, unless when in Cases of Rebellion or Invasion the public Safety may require it."

• On Aug. 22, Gerry proposed a prohibition on the passage of bills of attainder and ex post facto laws. Some delegates objected that such a provision would imply an improper suspicion of Congress and was an unnecessary guard. The Convention agreed, however, that "No Bill of Attainder or ex post facto Law shall be passed." A later motion by Mason to strike out ex post facto laws (on the ground that the ban might prevent Congress from redeeming the debt at less than face value) was unanimously rejected.

• On Aug. 23 the Convention adopted the two provisions that make up the final clause of Section 9 of Article I, both of which were taken from the Articles of Confederation. The bar to titles of nobility was proposed by the Committee of Detail. The bar to acceptance of emolument, office or title from foreign governments without the consent of Congress

John Jay

George Washington

was urged by Pinckney to help keep American officials independent of external influence.

Pinckney and others proposed adding to the Constitution a number of provisions similar to those contained in the Bills of Rights of the various states. On Sept. 12, Gerry moved to appoint a committee to draft a Bill of Rights, but 10 states voted No. Anxious to complete their work and return home, the delegates were in no mood to spend additional time on something most of them believed to be unnecessary, since none of the powers to be vested in Congress seemed to countenance legislation that might violate individual rights. However, omission of a Bill of Rights became a major issue in seeking ratification of the Constitution and led to assurances that it would be amended promptly to include the missing guarantees.

Executive and Judiciary

No question troubled the Convention more than the place to give the executive in the new plan of government. The office did not exist under the Articles of Confederation, which placed the executive function in Congress. A long-standing fear of executive authority had led Americans "to throw all power into the Legislative vortex," as Madison put it, and under most of the state constitutions the executives were indeed "little more than cyphers, the Legislatures omnipotent."[81] How much more authority and independence to give the National Executive remained in dispute until the very end of the Convention.

The Virginia Plan had in view a national executive chosen by the national legislature for a fixed term, ineligible for reappointment, and empowered with "a general authority to execute the National laws" as well as "the Executive rights vested in Congress by the Confederation." Debate on these proposals disclosed a spectrum of views ranging from that of Sherman, who thought the executive should be "nothing more than an institution for carrying the will of the Legislative into effect," to that of Gouverneur Morris, who felt the Executive should be "the guardian of the people" against legislative tyranny.[82]

Until September, the Convention favored a single executive chosen by Congress for one term of seven years, whose powers would be limited by the fact that Congress would appoint judges and ambassadors and make treaties. This plan for legislative supremacy was then abandoned for the more balanced one that was finally adopted and incorporated in Article II of the Constitution. The President would be chosen by electors for a four-year term without limit as to re-election, and he would have the power to make all appointments subject to confirmation by the Senate and to make treaties subject to approval by two-thirds of the Senate. Major provisions of Article II were developed as related below.

A Single Executive

Randolph, who presented the Virginia Plan, opposed a single executive as "the foetus of monarchy" and proposed three persons, who, Mason thought, should be chosen from the northern, middle and southern states. But Wilson foresaw "nothing but uncontrolled, continued and violent animosities" among three persons; a single executive, he said, would give "most energy, dispatch and responsibility to the office."[83] On June 4, the delegates voted for a single executive, seven states to four, and the Convention confirmed the decision July 17 without dissent.

The Committee of Detail then proposed that "the Executive Power of the United States shall be vested in a single person" to be called the President and to have the title of "His Excellency." These provisions were adopted Aug. 24 without debate, but in drafting the final document the Committee of Style dropped the title and provided simply that "the Executive Power shall be vested in a President of the United States of America." The omission from the Constitution of any title other than President helped to defeat a proposal in the First Congress that he be addressed as "His Highness."[84]

Method of Election, Term of Office

The method of election and term of office were closely related issues. If Congress were to choose the President, most delegates thought he should have a fairly long term and be ineligible for reappointment. For as Randolph put it, "if he should be reappointable by the Legislature, he will be no check on it."[85] But if the President was to be chosen in some other manner, a shorter term with re-eligibility was generally acceptable. Thus the method of election was the key question.

The Convention first decided that Congress should choose the President for a single seven-year term. On reflection, however, some delegates thought this would not leave him sufficiently independent. Wilson proposed election by electors chosen by the people, but Gerry considered the people "too little informed of personal characters" to choose electors, and the proposal was rejected, eight to two. Gerry himself proposed that the governors of the states pick the President to avoid the corruption he foresaw in having Congress choose him, but this plan also was rejected.[86]

Several other methods were proposed, and at one point the delegates agreed on choice by electors chosen by the state legislatures. But this decision was soon reversed. However, when Morris on Aug. 24 renewed Wilson's original proposal for electors chosen by the people, only six states were opposed and five were in favor. Three of the latter were smaller states that had opposed an earlier decision to have the Senate and the House ballot jointly when electing a President, thereby giving the large states a bigger voice in making the selection.

All of the questions concerning the President were then reconsidered by a special committee on postponed matters, whose report of Sept. 4 recommended most of the provisions that were finally adopted. According to Morris, the committee rejected choice of the President by Congress because of "the danger of intrigue and faction" and "the opportunity for cabal."[87] Instead, it proposed that he be chosen by electors equal in number to the senators and representatives

from each state, who would be chosen as each state decided. They would vote by ballot for two persons, at least one of whom could not be an inhabitant of their state. The one receiving a majority of the electoral votes would become President, the one with the next largest vote would become Vice President. In the event of a tie, or if no one received a majority, the Senate would decide.

The plan provided for a four-year term with no restriction as to re-election; shifted from the Senate to the President the power to appoint ambassadors and judges and to make treaties subject to Senate approval, and gave the Senate instead of the Supreme Court the power to try impeachments. This realignment of powers between the President and the Senate appealed to the small states because it was generally assumed that the Senate (in which each state was to be represented equally) would have the final say in choosing the President in most cases.

For the same reason, however, some delegates now feared that the combination of powers to be vested in the Senate would (in Randolph's words) "convert that body into a real and dangerous aristocracy."[88] Sherman thereupon proposed moving the final election of the President from the Senate to the House, with the proviso that each state have one vote. The change, which preserved the influence of the small states while easing the fears expressed about the Senate, was quickly adopted, as was the rest of the electoral plan and the four-year term without limit as to re-eligibility.

Qualifications

The Committee of Detail first proposed that a President be at least 35 years of age, a citizen, and an inhabitant of the United States for 21 years, just as age, citizenship and minimum period of residence were the only qualifications stipulated for senators and representatives. The committee added the qualification that the President must be a natural born citizen or a citizen at the time of the adoption of the Constitution, and it reduced the time of residence within the United States to at least 14 years "in the whole." The phrase "in the whole" was dropped in drafting the final provision in Section 1 of Article II, which was also adjusted to make it clear that the qualifications for President applied equally to the Vice President.

The Vice President

The office of the vice presidency was not considered by the Convention until Sept. 4, when a special committee proposed that a Vice President, chosen for the same term as the President, serve as ex officio President of the Senate. (A Vice President or lieutenant governor served in a similar capacity in four of the 13 states.) The proposal was designed to provide a position for the runner-up in the electoral vote, and to give the Senate an impartial presiding officer without depriving any state of one of its two votes.

When this proposal was debated Sept. 7, Mason objected that "it mixed too much the Legislative and the Executive." Gerry thought it tantamount to putting the President himself at the head of the Senate because of "the close intimacy that must subsist between the President and the Vice President." But Sherman noted that "if the Vice President were not to be President of the Senate, he would be without employment."[89] The Convention then adopted the proposal with only Massachusetts opposed. The provision that the Vice President "shall be President of the Senate, but shall have no Vote unless they be equally divided," was placed in Section 3 of Article I.

The Convention never discussed the role of the Vice President as successor to the President in the event of the latter's removal by death or otherwise. It seems to have contemplated that he would merely perform the duties of President until another was elected. Thus the special committee proposed that in case of the President's removal (by impeachment), "death, absence, resignation or inability to discharge the powers or duties of his office, the Vice President shall exercise those powers and duties until another President be chosen, or until the inability of the President be removed."

This language was revised to provide that "in case of the removal of the President from office, or of his death, resignation, or inability to discharge the powers and duties of the said office, the same shall devolve on the Vice President." The revised wording, incorporated in Article II, left it unclear as to whether it was the "said office" or the "powers and duties" that were to "devolve" on the Vice President. The right of the Vice President to assume the office of President was first asserted by John Tyler in 1841 and became the established practice.[90]

There remained the question of providing for the office in the event both men were removed. Randolph proposed that Congress designate an officer to "act accordingly until the time of electing a President shall arrive." Madison objected that this would prevent an earlier election, so it was agreed to substitute "until such disability be removed, or a President shall be elected." The Committee of Style ignored this change, so the Convention voted on Sept. 15 to restore it. The final provision, authorizing Congress to designate by law an officer to "act as President" until "a President shall be elected," was joined to the earlier provision concerning the Vice President in Article II.[91]

Presidential Powers

Initially, the Convention conferred only three powers on the President—"to carry into effect the National laws," "to appoint to offices in cases not otherwise provided for," and to veto bills. The Committee of Detail proposed a number of additional powers drawn from the state constitutions, most of which were adopted with little discussion or change. This was true of provisions (placed in Section 3 of Article II) for informing Congress "of the State of the Union" and recommending legislation, for convening and adjourning Congress, for receiving ambassadors, and for seeing "that the Laws be faithfully executed."

The Convention also agreed without debate that "the President shall be Commander in Chief of the Army and Navy" and of the militia when called into national service; almost all of the state constitutions vested a similar power in the state executives. The power of the President "to grant reprieves and pardons except in cases of impeachment" was likewise approved, although Mason argued that Congress should have this power while Randolph wanted to bar pardons for treason as "too great a trust" to place in the President.[92] These two provisions were included in Section 2 of Article II.

Power to Appoint. The appointive powers of the President were limited until September to "cases not otherwise provided for." The Virginia Plan had proposed that judges be appointed by the legislature (a practice followed in all except three states), but the Convention voted to give the power to the Senate alone as the "less numerous and more

---

The Cabinet

In 1787 eight states had a Privy Council to advise the governor, and the idea of providing for a similar body to advise the President was discussed at length in the Convention. Elbridge Gerry and others thought it would "give weight and inspire confidence" in the executive. To Benjamin Franklin, "a Council would not only be a check on a bad President, but be a relief to a good one." But Gouverneur Morris saw it in a different light: "Give him an able Council and it will thwart him; a weak one, and he will shelter himself under their sanction."* On Aug. 22 the Committee of Detail submitted the following proposal (first offered by Morris and Charles Pinckney) to the Convention:

"The President of the United States shall have a Privy Council which shall consist of the President of the Senate, the Speaker of the House of Representatives, the Chief Justice of the Supreme Court, and the principal officer in the respective departments of Foreign Affairs, Domestic Affairs, War, Marine, and Finance, as such departments of office shall from time to time be established, whose duty it shall be to advise him in matters respecting the execution of his office, which he shall think proper to lay before them; but their advice shall not conclude him, nor affect his responsibility for the measures which he shall adopt."**

The Convention did not vote on the foregoing proposal. The Sept. 4 report of the special committee proposed only that the President "may require the Opinion in writing of the principal Officer in each of the executive Departments, upon any Subject relating to the Duties of their respective Offices." This provision, adopted Sept. 7 (after the Convention had rejected, eight states to three, a proposal by Mason for an executive council to be appointed by Congress), was included among the powers of the President set out in Section 2 of Article II.

The word "Cabinet" was not used in the Convention or the Constitution. But as that institution developed under Washington and later Presidents, it conformed to the limited role that had been envisioned in the Morris-Pinckney proposal for a Privy Council.

* Charles Warren, *The Making of the Constitution* (Boston: Little, Brown, 1928), p. 646.
** *Ibid.*, pp. 646-47.

---

select body." In July the delegates considered and rejected alternative proposals that judges be appointed by the President alone, by the President with the advice and consent of the Senate, and by the President unless two-thirds of the Senate should disagree.

All this was changed when, on Sept. 7, the Convention adopted the proposal of the special committee that the President appoint ambassadors and other public ministers, justices of the Supreme Court and all other officers of the United States "by and with the Advice and Consent of the Senate." This power (incorporated in Section 2) was further qualified Sept. 15 by requiring that offices not otherwise provided for "be established by law" and by authorizing Congress to vest appointment of inferior officers in the President, the courts or the heads of departments. Nothing was said of a power of removal from office—a power that was to become a much-argued issue.

Treaty Power. The proposal that the Senate alone have the power to make treaties (first put forward by the Committee of Detail) drew considerable opposition. Mason said it would enable the Senate to "sell the whole country by means of treaties." Madison thought the President, representing the whole people, should have the power. Morris argued for a provision that "no treaty shall be binding...which is not ratified by a law."[93] Southern delegates were especially concerned to prevent abandonment by treaty of free navigation of the Mississippi.

The issue was referred to a special committee on postponed matters, which recommended vesting the President with the power to make treaties subject to the advice and consent of two-thirds of the senators present. The latter provision provoked extended debate. Motions were made and rejected to strike out the two-thirds requirement, to require consent of two-thirds of all members of the Senate, to require a majority of the whole number of senators and to provide that no treaty should be made without previous notice to the members.

On Sept. 7 the Convention voted to except peace treaties from the two-thirds rule. Madison then moved to authorize two-thirds of the Senate alone to make a peace treaty, arguing that the President "would necessarily derive so much power and importance from a state of war that he might be tempted, if authorized to impede a treaty of peace."[94] The motion was rejected, but after further debate on the advantages and disadvantages of permitting a majority of the Senate to approve a peace treaty, the Convention reversed itself and made all treaties subject to the concurrence of two-thirds of the senators present.

Veto Power. The Virginia Plan had proposed joining the judiciary with the executive in exercising the power to veto acts of the legislature, subject to repassage. Because it was expected that the judiciary might have to pass on the constitutionality of legislation, most delegates thought it improper to give the judiciary a share of the veto power, and the proposal was rejected. Wilson and Hamilton favored giving the executive an absolute veto, but on June 4 the delegates voted for Gerry's motion (based on the Massachusetts constitution) for a veto that could be overridden by two-thirds of each branch of the legislature.

When this provision was reconsidered on Aug. 15, it was in the context of a plan to lodge in Congress the power to elect the President, to impeach him, and to appoint judges. Many delegates then agreed with Wilson that such an arrangement would not give "a sufficient self-defensive power either to the Executive or Judiciary Department," and the Convention voted to require a vote of three-fourths of each House to override a veto.[95] But on Sept. 12, after having adopted the presidential elector plan and other changes proposed by the special committee, the Convention restored the two-thirds provision.

The veto power was incorporated in Section 7 of Article I, setting out the procedure for the enactment of a bill with or without the President's signature. This section also made provision for the "pocket veto" of a bill when "the Congress by their Adjournment prevent its return, in which Case it shall not become Law." Although some delegates indicated a belief that the two-thirds provision was intended to apply to the entire membership of the House and Senate, a two-thirds vote of those present came to be accepted in practice.

The Judiciary

Article III of the Constitution, relating to "the judicial Power of the United States," was developed in the Convention with relative ease. The Virginia Plan called for "one or more supreme tribunals" and inferior tribunals to be appointed by the national legislature and to try all cases involving crimes at sea, foreigners and citizens of different states, "collection of the National revenue," impeachments, and "questions which may involve the national peace and harmony." The Convention went on to spell out the jurisdiction of these courts in greater detail, but the only basic changes made in the plan were to vest the Senate and finally the President with the power to appoint judges, and to transfer the trial of impeachments from the Supreme Court to the Senate.

Lower Courts and Appointment of Judges

The delegates agreed to one Supreme Court without debate, but some objected to establishing any lower courts. John Rutledge thought the state courts should hear all cases in the first instance, "the right of appeal to the Supreme National Tribunal being sufficient to secure the National rights and uniformity of judgments." Sherman deplored the expense. But Madison argued that without lower courts "dispersed throughout the Republic, with final jurisdiction in many cases, appeals would be multiplied to an oppressive degree." Randolph said the state courts "cannot be trusted with the administration of the National laws."[96] As a compromise, the Convention agreed to permit Congress to decide whether to "ordain and establish" inferior courts.

The proposal that the national legislature appoint the judiciary was based on similar provisions in most of the state constitutions. Wilson, arguing that "intrigue, partiality and concealment" would result from such a method, proposed appointment by the President. Madison urged appointment by the Senate as "a less numerous and more select body," and this plan was approved June 13.[97] A proposal that the President appoint judges "by and with the advice and consent of the Senate" was defeated by a tie vote July 18, but that was the method finally adopted in September as a part of the compromise that also moved the trial of impeachments from the Supreme Court to the Senate.

Tenure and Jurisdiction

Both the Virginia Plan and the New Jersey Plan provided that judges would hold office "during good behaviour"—a rule long considered essential to maintaining the independence of the judiciary. When this provision was considered Aug. 27, Dickinson proposed that judges "may be removed by the Executive on the application by the Senate and the House of Representatives." Others objected strongly, Wilson contending that "the Judges would be in a bad situation, if made to depend on every gust of faction which might prevail in two branches of our Government."[98] Only Connecticut voted for the proposal, and the Convention agreed to tenure during good behavior.

Most of the provisions embodied in Section 2 of Article III specifying the cases to which "the judicial Power shall extend," and in which cases the Supreme Court would have original and in which cases appellate jurisdiction, were set out in the Aug. 6 report of the Committee of Detail and adopted by the Convention on Aug. 27 with little change or debate. The most important change was made in the committee's first provision, extending jurisdiction to "all cases arising under the laws" of the United States, when the Convention voted to insert the words "the Constitution and" before "the laws." This made it clear that the

---

The Two-Thirds Rule

To the men who drafted the Constitution, a major weakness of the Articles of Confederation was the rule that nine (or two-thirds) of the 13 states must concur in all important decisions. So there was broad agreement on the general principle (embodied in Article I, Section 5) that in the two Houses of Congress "a Majority of each shall constitute a Quorum to do Business." With respect to certain powers, however, a requirement for something greater than a majority seemed essential to a balanced design of government.

As finally approved, the Constitution imposed a two-thirds requirement in six instances. No one was to be convicted on impeachment nor could a treaty be made without the concurrence of two-thirds of the senators "present." Neither House could expel a member without "the concurrence of two-thirds." If vetoed, a bill could be enacted by the votes of two-thirds of both Houses. Congress could propose amendments to the Constitution "whenever two-thirds of both Houses shall deem it necessary." And if the House was called on to ballot for President, a quorum was to "consist of a Member or Members from two-thirds of the States...."

The Convention also considered but rejected proposals to require the consent of two-thirds of both Houses to the admission of new states and to the enactment of laws to regulate foreign commerce (leaving these matters to be decided by majority vote), and to permit export taxes to be levied by a two-thirds vote of both Houses (leaving a flat prohibition on such taxes).

Of the provisions included in the Constitution, only those relating to the Senate's role in trying impeachments and approving treaties made it clear that the decision rested with two-thirds of the members "present," not with two-thirds of the entire membership. There is persuasive evidence that the latter interpretation was intended by the delegates for the provisions relating to vetoes, expulsion of members, and constitutional amendments. However, in the absence of an explicit requirement to that effect, Congress assumed that two-thirds of members "present" was likewise sufficient for a decision in those cases—an assumption sustained by the Supreme Court in 1919 (*Missouri Pac. R.R. Co. v. Kansas*, 248 U.S. 276) and 1920 (*Rhode Island v. Palmer*, 253 U.S. 350).

Supreme Court was ultimately to decide all questions of constitutionality, whether arising in state or federal courts.

Article III did not explicitly authorize the court to pass on the constitutionality of acts of Congress, but the Convention clearly anticipated the exercise of that power as one of the acknowledged functions of the courts. Several delegates noted that state courts had "set aside" laws in conflict with the state constitutions. The Convention debated at great length (and rejected four times) a proposal to join the court with the President in the veto power; Wilson favored it because "laws may be unjust, may be unwise, may be dangerous, may be destructive, and yet may not be so unconstitutional as to justify the judges in refusing to give them effect." Mason agreed that the court "could declare an unconstitutional law void."[99]

Supremacy Clause

The role of the judiciary in determining the constitutionality of laws was also implicit in the provision, incorporated in Article VI, which asserted that the Constitution, the laws and the treaties of the United States "shall be the supreme Law of the Land." This provision first appeared on July 17 after the Convention had reversed itself and voted to deny Congress the proposed power. Anxious to place some restraint on the free-wheeling state legislatures, the Convention adopted instead and without dissent a substitute offered by Luther Martin and drawn directly from the New Jersey Plan of June 14.

The substitute provided that the laws and treaties of the United States "shall be the supreme law of the respective States, as far as those acts or treaties shall relate to the said States, or their citizens and inhabitants—and that the Judiciaries of the several States shall be bound thereby in their decisions, anything in the respective laws of the individual States to the contrary notwithstanding." In its report of Aug. 6, the Committee of Detail dropped the qualifying phrase "as far as those acts or treaties shall relate to the said States," substituted the word "Judges" for "Judiciaries" in the next clause and the words "Constitutions or laws" for "laws" in the final proviso, and made a few other word changes.

The Convention agreed to these changes Aug. 23 and to another prefacing the entire provision with "This Constitution." Further revision by the Committee of Style changed "supreme law of the several States" to "supreme law of the land," in what became the final phrasing of the provision in Article VI. The effect of the various changes was to make it clear that all judges, state and federal, were bound to uphold the supremacy of the Constitution over all other acts.

The "supremacy" clause was reinforced by the further provision in Article VI that all members of Congress and of the state legislatures, as well as all executive and judicial officers of the national and state governments "shall be bound by Oath or Affirmation to support this Constitution."[100]

Limits on Powers of the States

The "supremacy" clause was designed to prevent the states from passing laws contrary to the Constitution. Since the Constitution was also to specify the powers granted to Congress, those powers were denied by implication to the states. By the same reasoning, however, any powers not granted to Congress remained with the states. To eliminate any doubt of their intention to put an end to irresponsible acts of the individual states, the delegates decided to specify what the states could not or must do. Acts prohibited to the states were placed in Section 10 of Article I, while those required of them were placed in Sections 1 and 2 of Article IV.

Most of these provisions (many of which were taken from the Articles of Confederation) were proposed by the Committee of Detail and adopted by the Convention Aug. 28 with little debate or change. The committee had proposed that no state be allowed to make anything but gold or silver legal tender without the consent of Congress, but the Convention voted for an absolute prohibition on such laws, Sherman saying this was "a favorable crisis for crushing paper money."[101] The Convention also added a provision, drawn from the Northwest Ordinance, aimed at the welter of state laws favoring debtors over creditors: no state was to pass any ex post facto law or law impairing the obligation of contracts.

The provisions of Article IV requiring each state to give "full faith and credit" to the acts of other states, to respect "all Privileges and Immunities" of all citizens, and to deliver up fugitives from justice were derived from the Articles. To these the Convention added the provision, requested by southerners, that became known as the "fugitive slave" clause, requiring such persons to be "delivered up on Claim of the Party to whom such Service or Labour may be due." As with the rest of the Constitution, the enforcement of these provisions was assigned, by the "supremacy" clause, to the courts.

Amendment and Ratification

A major reason for calling the Convention of 1787 had been the impossibility of obtaining the unanimous approval of the states that was required to amend the Articles of Confederation. So there was general agreement that it was better to provide for amending the Constitution "in an easy, regular and constitutional way, than to trust to chance and violence," as Mason put it.[102] But the method for doing so received little consideration until the final days of the Convention.

The Committee of Detail was the first to propose that the legislatures of two-thirds of the states have the sole power to initiate amendments by petitioning Congress to call a convention for that purpose. This provision was adopted Aug. 30 after a brief debate during which no one supported the argument of Gouverneur Morris that Congress also should have the power to call a convention on its own. But, on reconsideration Sept. 10, Hamilton asserted that Congress "will be the first to perceive and will be the most sensible to the necessity of amendments," and he proposed that two-thirds of the Senate and House also have the power to call a convention."[103]

Wilson moved that amendments be adopted when ratified by two-thirds of the states. When that proposal was defeated, six states to five, Wilson moved to substitute ratification by three-fourths of the states, which was approved without dissent. The Convention then adopted a new formula, providing that Congress "shall" propose amendments "whenever two-thirds of both Houses shall deem necessary or on the application of two-thirds" of the state legislatures, and that such amendments would become valid when ratified by the legislatures or conventions of three-fourths of the states as Congress might direct.

Under this formula, any amendment requested by two-thirds of the states would be submitted directly to the states for ratification. As modified Sept. 15, on the motion of Morris, the formula provided instead that on the application of two-thirds of the states, Congress "shall call a Convention for proposing Amendments." Thus, as finally drafted, Article V provided that, in proposing amendments to the Constitution, Congress would act directly while the states would act indirectly. In either case, however, amendments would take effect when approved by three-fourths of the states.

While working out these terms, the Convention also adopted two restrictions on the amending power. As a concession to the southern states, the Convention had already agreed (in Section 9 of Article I) to prohibit Congress from outlawing the slave trade before 1808 or levying any direct tax unless in proportion to a count of all whites and three-fifths of blacks. On Sept. 10, Rutledge noted that unless a similar limit were placed on the amending power, the

provisions "relating to slaves might be altered by the States not interested in that property and prejudiced against them."[104] So it was agreed, without debate, to add the proviso that no amendment adopted before 1808 "shall in any manner affect" those two provisions of Article I.

Sherman now worried that "three fourths of the States might be brought to do things fatal to particular States, as abolishing them altogether or depriving them of their equality in the Senate." He proposed, as a further proviso to the amending power, that "No state shall without its consent be affected in its internal police, or deprived of its equal suffrage in the Senate."[105] The term "internal police" covered much more than most delegates were prepared to exclude, and only three states supported Sherman. But the more limited proviso that "no State, without its Consent, shall be deprived of its equal suffrage in the Senate" was accepted without debate and added to Article V.

Campaign for Ratification

According to the resolution of Congress, the Philadelphia Convention was to meet for the "sole and express purpose of revising the Articles of Confederation and reporting to Congress and the several legislatures" its recommendations. But the nationalists who organized the Convention and persuaded it to ignore these narrow instructions were determined that the fate of the new Constitution should not be entrusted to the state legislatures, but that the instrument should be ratified "by the supreme authority of the people themselves," as Madison put it. The legislatures, he pointed out, were in any event without power to consent to changes that "would make essential inroads on the State Constitutions."[106]

By "the people themselves" the nationalists meant special conventions elected for the purpose. Conventions would be more representative than the legislatures, which excluded "many of the ablest men," and they would be more likely to favor the Constitution than would be legislatures that (as King said) "being to lose power will be most likely to raise objections." Opposed to this view were delegates like Ellsworth, who thought conventions were "better fitted to pull down than to build up Constitutions," and Gerry, who said the people "would never agree on anything."[107] But the Convention rejected Ellsworth's motion for ratification by the legislatures and agreed July 23, nine states to one, that the Constitution should be submitted to popularly elected conventions.

This decision was followed, on Aug. 31, by the key decision that the Constitution should enter into force when approved by the conventions of no more than nine of the 13 states. By this time, only a few of the delegates still felt as Martin did that "unanimity was necessary to dissolve the existing Confederacy."[108] Seven and ten were also proposed as minimums, but nine was chosen as the more familiar figure, being the number required to act on important matters under the Articles. It was also clearly impractical to require (as the Committee of Detail had proposed) that the Constitution be submitted to the Congress "for their approbation," so it was agreed to strike out that provision.

Randolph and Mason (two of the three delegates who finally refused to sign the Constitution) continued to argue that it should be submitted to another General Convention, along with any amendments proposed by the state conventions, before it was finally acted on. Few others believed another such gathering could improve the product significantly, and their proposal was unanimously rejected

Sept. 13. As finally drafted, Article VII provided simply that "the Ratifications of the Conventions of nine States shall be sufficient for the Establishment of this Constitution between the States so ratifying the Same."

By a separate resolution adopted Sept. 17, it was agreed that the Constitution should "be laid before the United States in Congress assembled," and that in the opinion of the Convention it should then be submitted to "a Convention of Delegates, chosen in each State by the People thereof." As soon as nine states had ratified, the resolution continued, the Congress should set a day for the election of Presidential electors, Senators and Representatives, and "the Time and Place for commencing Proceedings under this Constitution."[109]

Ten days after the Philadelphia Convention had adjourned on Sept. 17, 1787, the Congress of the Confederation submitted the Constitution to the states for their consideration and the struggle for ratification began. In that contest, ironically, those who had argued successfully in the Convention for a national rather than a merely federal plan and who now took the lead in urging ratification, called themselves Federalists (although there was no reference to anything federal in the Constitution). Those who opposed the Constitution became the Anti-Federalists.

These two factions, out of which the first political parties were formed, tended to reflect long-standing divisions among Americans between commercial and agrarian interests, creditors and debtors, men of great or little property, tidewater planters and the small farmers of the interior. But there were important and numerous exceptions to the tendency of Federalists and Anti-Federalists to divide along class, sectional and economic lines. Among the Anti-Federalists were some of the wealthiest and most influential men of the times, including George Mason, Patrick Henry, Richard Henry Lee, George Clinton, James Winthrop and many others.

As in drafting the Constitution, the Federalists seized the initiative in seeking speedy ratification. The ensuing campaign of political maneuver, persuasion and propaganda was intense and bitter. Both sides questioned the motives of the other and exaggerated the dire consequences of one or the other course. All Anti-Federalists, wrote Ellsworth, were either "men who have lucrative and influential State offices" or "tories, debtors in desperate circumstances, or insurgents."[110] To Luther Martin, the object of the Federalists was "the total abolition of all State Governments and the erection on their ruins of one great and extreme empire."[111]

All of the newspapers of the day published extensive correspondence on the virtues and vices of the new plan of government. The fullest and strongest case for the Constitution was put in a series of letters written by Madison, Hamilton and Jay under the name of "Publius." Seventy-seven of the letters were published in New York City newspapers between Oct. 27 and April 4, 1788, and in book form (along with eight additional letters) as *The Federalist* on May 28, 1788. These letters probably had only small influence on ratification, but *The Federalist* came to be regarded as the classic exposition of the Constitution.

Political maneuvers were common in both camps. In Pennsylvania, Federalists moved to call a convention before Congress had officially submitted the Constitution. Nineteen Anti-Federalists thereupon withdrew from the assembly, depriving it of a quorum until a mob seized two of them and dragged them back. When the Massachusetts Convention met, the Anti-Federalists were in the majority

---

The Federalist

The Federalist is a collection of 85 letters to the public signed with a pseudonym, Publius, that appeared at short intervals in the newspapers of New York City beginning on Oct. 27, 1787. The identity of Publius was a secret until several years after publication. In March 1788, the first 36 letters were issued in a collected edition. A second volume containing numbers 37-85 was published in May 1788.

The idea for publication of *The Federalist* came from Alexander Hamilton who wanted to wage a literary campaign to explain the proposed Constitution and build support for it. James Madison and John Jay agreed to work with him.

Of the 85 letters, Hamilton wrote 56; Madison, 21; and Jay, five. Hamilton and Madison collaborated on three. Jay's low productivity was due to a serious illness in the fall of 1787.

The essays probably had only a small impact on the ratification of the Constitution. Even the most widely circulated newspapers did not travel far in 1788. But they gained importance later as a classic exposition of the Constitution.

Prof. Clinton Rossiter wrote in a 1961 introduction to the papers: *"The Federalist* is the most important work in political science that has ever been written, or is likely ever to be written, in the United States. It is, indeed, the one product of the American mind that is rightly counted among the classics of political theory.... *The Federalist* stands third only to the Declaration of Independence and the Constitution itself among all the sacred writings of American political history."*

The Federalist Papers, with an Introduction by Clinton Rossiter (New York: Mentor, 1961), p. vii.

---

until John Hancock, the president, was won over to the Federalist side by promises of support for the new post of Vice President of the United States.

Among the major arguments advanced against the Constitution were the failure to include a Bill of Rights and the fear that the presidency would tend toward monarchy through endless re-election. Federalists met the first argument by pledging the early enactment of amendments, which Massachusetts and Virginia were particularly determined should be included. The fear of monarchy was mitigated by a widespread assumption (held also in the Convention) that George Washington would become the first President. This assumption, together with the fact that most Americans knew Washington and Benjamin Franklin supported the Constitution, contributed as much as anything to the success of the ratification campaign.

The Delaware Convention was the first to ratify, unanimously, on Dec. 7, 1787. Then came Pennsylvania, by a vote of 46 to 23, Dec. 12; New Jersey, unanimously, Dec. 19; Georgia, unanimously Jan. 2, 1788; Connecticut, 128 to 40, January 9; Massachusetts, 187 to 168, Feb. 6; Maryland, 63 to 11, April 26; South Carolina, 149 to 73, May 23; and New Hampshire, 57 to 46, June 21. This met the requirement for approval by nine states, but it was clear that without the approval of Virginia and New York the Constitution would stand on shaky ground.

In Virginia, according to Ellsworth, "the opposition wholly originated in two principles: the madness of Mason, and enmity of the Lee faction to Gen. Washington."[112] But Randolph, who had refused with Mason and Gerry to sign the Constitution, was brought over to its support, and on June 25 the Federalists prevailed, by a vote of 89 to 79. New York, where Governor Clinton led the Anti-Federalists, finally ratified on July 26 by an even narrower margin of 30 to 27, after Hamilton and Jay had threatened that otherwise New York City would secede and join the Union as a separate state. North Carolina ratified on Nov. 21, 1789, and Rhode Island (which had not taken part in the Philadelphia Convention) became the last of the 13 states to ratify, on May 29, 1790.

In accord with the request of the Philadelphia Convention, the Congress of the Confederation on Sept. 13, 1788, fixed New York City (where it sat) as the seat of the new government, the first Wednesday of January 1789 as the day for choosing presidential electors, the first Wednesday of February for the meeting of electors, and the first Wednesday of March for the opening session of the new Congress.

The First Elections

The Constitution empowered the state legislatures to prescribe the method of choosing their presidential electors as well as the time, place and manner of electing their representatives and senators. Virginia and Maryland put the choice of electors directly to the people; in Massachusetts, two were chosen at large while the other eight were picked by the legislature from 24 names submitted by the voters of the eight congressional districts. Elsewhere, all electors were chosen by the legislature. But in New York, where Federalists controlled the senate and Anti-Federalists dominated the assembly, the two houses became deadlocked on the question of acting by joint or concurrent vote, and the legislature adjourned without choosing electors.

Elections to the House also involved a number of spirited contests between Federalists and Anti-Federalists, although the total vote cast (estimated between 75,000 and 125,000) amounted to a small fraction of the free population of 3,200,000. In Massachusetts and Connecticut, several elections were required in some districts before one candidate obtained a majority. Elbridge Gerry, who had refused to sign the Constitution, finally beat Nathaniel Gorham (also a delegate to the Philadelphia Convention) after saying he no longer opposed it. In New Jersey the law did not fix a time for closing the polls and they stayed open for three weeks; the elections of all four New Jersey representatives were contested when the House was finally organized.

Although March 4, 1789, had been fixed as the day for commencing proceedings of the new government, only 13 of the 59 representatives and eight of the 22 senators had arrived in New York City by then. (Seats allotted to North Carolina and Rhode Island were not filled until 1790, after those states had ratified the Constitution.) It was not until April 1 that a 30th representative arrived to make a quorum of the House, while the Senate attained its quorum of 12 on April 6. The two houses then met jointly, for the first time, to count the electoral vote.

As everyone had assumed, each of the 69 electors had cast one vote for George Washington, who thus became President by unanimous choice. (Four additional electors—two from Maryland and two from Virginia—had failed to show up on Feb. 4 to vote.) Of 11 other men among whom the electors distributed their second vote, John Adams received the highest number—34—and was declared Vice President.

Adams arrived in New York on April 21, Washington on the 23rd, and the inaugural took place on the 30th. Washington took the oath of office prescribed by the Constitution on the balcony of Federal Hall (New York's former City Hall that housed the President and both houses of Congress until all moved to Philadelphia in 1790). The President then went to the Senate chamber to deliver a brief inaugural address, in the course of which he declined to accept whatever salary Congress might confer on the office. Thus, by April 30, 1789, the long task of designing and installing a new government had been completed.

Footnotes

1. Charles M. Andrews, *The Colonial Period of American History*, Vol. 1: *The Settlements* (New Haven: Yale University Press, 1934), p. 23.
2. *Ibid.*, p. 375.
3. *Ibid.*, p. 185.
4. *Ibid.*, p. 368.
5. Andrews, *The Colonial Period of American History*, Vol. 4: *England's Commercial and Colonial Policy*, p. 150.
6. Jack P. Greene, ed., *Great Britain and the American Colonies, 1606-1763* (New York: Harper Paperbacks, 1970), p. xxxix.
7. *Ibid.*, p. xli.
8. Edmund S. Morgan, *The Birth of the Republic 1763-89* (Chicago: University of Chicago Press, 1956), p. 31.
9. *Ibid.*, pp. 60-61.
10. L. H. Butterfield, ed., *Adams Family Correspondence*, Vol. 1: *December 1761-May 1776* (Cambridge, Mass.: The Belknap Press of Harvard University, 1963), p. 166.
11. Edmund Cody Burnett, *The Continental Congress* (New York: Norton, 1964), pp. 42-50.
12. *Ibid.*, p. 61.
13. Burnett, *The Continental Congress*, pp. 85-87.
14. *Ibid.*, p. 127.
15. *Ibid.*, pp. 131-137.
16. *Ibid.*, p. 171.

17. Charles Ramsdell Lingley, *The Transition In Virginia From Colony to Commonwealth* (New York: Columbia University, 1910), p. 172.
18. Burnett, *The Continental Congress*, p. 171.
19. Andrew C. McLaughlin, *The Confederation and the Constitution 1783-1789*, with a Foreword by Henry Steele Commager (New York: Collier Books, 1962), p. 51.
20. Charles Warren, *The Making of the Constitution* (Boston: Little, Brown, 1928), p. 12.
21. *Ibid.*, pp. 6-7.
22. *Ibid.*, p. 8.
23. *Ibid.*, p. 23.
24. *Ibid.*, p. 25.
25. James Madison, *Notes of Debates in the Federal Convention of 1787*, with an Introduction by Adrienne Koch (Athens, Ohio: Ohio University Press, 1966), p. 30.
26. Warren, *The Making of the Constitution*, p. 150.
27. Madison, *Notes of Debates in the Federal Convention*, p. 36.
28. Warren, *The Making of the Constitution*, pp. 216-218. McLaughlin, *The Confederation and the Constitution 1783-1789*, p. 144.
29. Warren, *The Making of the Constitution*, p. 223.
30. *Ibid.*, p. 232.

31. *Ibid.,* p. 257.
32. *Ibid.,* p. 159.
33. *Ibid.,* pp. 160, 162.
34. *Ibid.,* p. 161.
35. *Ibid.,* p. 195.
36. **Madison, *Notes of Debates in the Federal Convention,* p. 257.**
37. Warren, *The Making of the Constitution,* p. 290.
38. *Ibid.,* p. 292.
39. *Ibid.,* pp. 294-298.
40. *Ibid.,* p. 345.
41. *Ibid.,* p. 242.
42. *Ibid.,* p. 243
43. *Ibid.,* p. 401.
44. *Ibid.,* p. 409
45. *Ibid.,* pp. 415-416.
46. *Ibid.,* p. 414.
47. *Ibid.,* p. 415.
48. *Ibid.,* p. 417.
49. *Ibid.,* pp. 418-419.
50. *Ibid.,* p. 426.
51. *Ibid.,* pp. 445-451.
52. Merrill Jensen, *The Articles of Confederation* (Madison: University of Wisconsin Press, 1940), p. 264.
53. *Ibid.*
54. Warren, *The Making of the Constitution,* p. 616.
55. *Ibid.,* pp. 615-616.
56. *Ibid.,* p. 431.
57. *Ibid.,* p. 166.
58. *Ibid.,* p. 316.
59. Madison, *Notes of Debates in the Federal Convention,* p. 45.
60. Warren, *The Making of the Constitution,* pp. 314-315.
61. *Ibid.,* p. 469.
62. *Ibid.,* pp. 473-475.
63. *Ibid.,* p. 497.
64. *Ibid.,* p. 574.
65. *Ibid.,* p. 573.
66. *Ibid.,* p. 575.
67. *Ibid.*
68. *Ibid.,* p. 576.
69. *Ibid.,* p. 583.
70. Madison, *Notes of Debates in the Federal Convention,* pp. 475-477.
71. *Ibid.,* p. 482.

72. *Ibid.,* p. 580.
73. *Ibid.,* p. 516.
74. Warren, *The Making of the Constitution,* pp. 665-666.
75. Henry Steele Commager, ed., *Documents of American History,* Vol. 1: *To 1898* (Englewood Cliffs, N.J.: Prentice-Hall, 1973), p. 128.
76. Warren, *The Making of the Constitution,* p. 594.
77. *Ibid.,* pp. 594-595.
78. *Ibid.,* p. 661.
79. *Ibid.,* p. 662.
80. Madison, *Notes of Debates in the Federal Convention,* p. 471.
81. Warren, *The Making of the Constitution,* p. 359.
82. *Ibid.,* pp. 174, 360.
83. *Ibid.,* pp. 174-175.
84. *Ibid.,* p. 525.
85. *Ibid.,* p. 360.
86. *Ibid.,* p. 358.
87. *Ibid.,* p. 623.
88. *Ibid.,* pp. 628-629.
89. Madison, *Notes of Debates in the Federal Convention,* p. 596.
90. Warren, *The Making of the Constitution,* pp. 635-638.
91. *Ibid.,* p. 638.
92. *Ibid.,* p. 530.
93. *Ibid.,* pp. 651-652.
94. *Ibid.,* p. 656.
95. *Ibid.,* p. 456.
96. *Ibid.,* pp. 326-327.
97. *Ibid.,* pp. 327-328.
98. Madison, *Notes of Debates in the Federal Convention,* pp. 536-537.
99. Warren, *The Making of the Constitution,* pp. 333-334.
100. *Ibid.,* p. 650.
101. *Ibid.,* p. 552.
102. *Ibid.,* p. 673.
103. *Ibid.,* p. 675.
104. *Ibid.,* p. 679.
105. *Ibid.,* pp. 679-680.
106. *Ibid.,* pp. 348-350.
107. *Ibid.*
108. *Ibid.,* p. 607.
109. *Ibid.,* p. 717.
110. *Ibid.,* p. 746.
111. *Ibid.,* p. 754.
112. *Ibid.,* p. 749.

Selected Bibliography

Andrews, Charles M. *The Colonial Period of American History.* 4 vols. New Haven: Yale University Press, 1934.

Beard, Charles A. *An Economic Interpretation of the Constitution of the United States.* New York: Macmillan, 1935.

Beard, Charles A., ed. *The Enduring Federalist.* Garden City, N.Y.: Doubleday, 1948.

Brant, Irving. *James Madison: Father of the Constitution, 1787-1800.* Indianapolis: Bobbs-Merrill, 1950.

Burnett, Edmund C. *The Continental Congress.* New York: Macmillan, 1941.

Butterfield, L.H., ed. *Adams Family Correspondence.* Vol. 1: *December 1761-May 1776.* Cambridge, Mass.: The Belknap Press of Harvard University Press, 1963.

Commager, Henry Steele, ed. *Documents of American History.* Vol. 1: *To 1898.* Englewood Cliffs, N.J.: Prentice-Hall, 1973.

Elliot, Jonathan, ed. *The Debates in the Several State Conventions on the Adoption of the Federal Constitution.* 5 vols. Philadelphia: J.B. Lippincott, 1937.

Farrand, Max. *The Framing of the Constitution of the United States.* New Haven: Yale University Press, 1913.

————, ed. *The Records of the Federal Convention of 1787.* 4 vols. New Haven: Yale University Press, 1973.

Greene, Jack P., ed. *Great Britain and the American Colonies, 1606-1763.* New York: Harper Paperbacks, 1970.

Jensen, Merrill. *The Articles of Confederation.* Madison, Wis.: University of Wisconsin Press, 1940.

Kelly, Alfred H. and Harbison, Winfred A. *The American Constitution: Its Origins and Development.* New York: Norton, 1955.

Lingley, Charles Ramsdell. *The Transition in Virginia From Colony to Commonwealth.* New York: Columbia University, 1910.

McLaughlin, Andrew C. *The Confederation and the Constitution, 1783-1789.* Foreword by Henry Steele Commager. New York: Collier Books, 1962.

Madison, James; Hamilton, Alexander; and Jay, John. *The Federalist Papers.* Introduction by Clinton Rossiter. New York: Mentor, 1961.

Madison, James. *Notes of Debates in the Federal Convention of 1787.* Introduction by Adrienne Koch. Athens, Ohio: Ohio University Press, 1966.

Morgan, Edmund S. *The Birth of the Republic.* Chicago: University of Chicago Press, 1956.

Nevins, Allan. *The American States During and After the Revolution, 1775-1789.* New York: Macmillan, 1924.

Rossiter, Clinton. *1787: The Grand Convention.* New York: Macmillan, 1966.

Smith, David G. *The Convention and the Constitution.* New York: St. Martin's Press, 1965.

Van Doren, Carl. *Benjamin Franklin.* Westport, Conn.: Greenwood Press, 1973.

_____. *The Great Rehearsal: The Story of the Making and Ratifying of the Constitution of the United States.* New York: Viking, 1948.

Warren, Charles. *The Making of the Constitution.* Boston: Little, Brown, 1928.

Wilson, Woodrow. *Congressional Government.* Introduction by Walter Lippmann. Cleveland: Meridian Books, **1956. (Reprint of 1885 ed.)**

Wright, Benjamin F. *Consensus and Continuity, 1776-1787.* Boston: Boston University Press, 1958.

History of the

House of Representatives

When the 30th of the 59 representatives elected to the First Congress reached New York on April 1, 1789, the assembled quorum promptly chose as Speaker of the House Frederick A. C. Muhlenberg of Pennsylvania. Next day, Muhlenberg named a committee of 11 to draw up the first rules of procedure, which the House adopted April 7. The first standing committee of the House—a seven-member Committee on Elections—was chosen April 13, and its report accepting the credentials of 49 members was approved April 18. By then, the House was already debating the first tariff bill.

By contrast, it took five years of study and negotiation to produce agreement in the 91st Congress on a limited revision of House rules. The House had long since become a highly structured institution governed by an elaborate set of rules, precedents and customs, all closely guarded by its most senior, privileged and influential members. Since its founding, however, the House had often adapted its procedures to the needs of the times, and its continuing ability to do so seemed to be confirmed by the passage of the Legislative Reorganization Act of 1970.

From the beginning, politics and personalities have played their part in influencing the timing and direction of changes in House procedure and organization. But it was the rapid increase in the size of its membership in the 19th century and of its workload in the 20th century that compelled development of what became the major features of the legislative process in the House—strict limitations on floor debate, a heavy reliance on the committee system and techniques for channeling the flow of business.

It was Speaker Thomas B. Reed who told the House, in 1890, that "the object of a parliamentary body is action, and not stoppage of action."[1] But how to insure the right of a majority to work its will has been a perennial challenge in the House, conceived by George Mason in 1787 to become "the grand depository of the democratic principles of the government."[2] The men, parties and events that contributed to the evolution of the House as a legislative body are the focus of this account.

Formative Years: 1789-1809

The great majority of the representatives elected to the First Congress had served in the Continental Congress or in their state legislatures, and the procedures followed in those bodies (which were derived in large part from English parliamentary practice) formed the basis for the first rules of the House. Those rules included provisions that:

● The Speaker was to preside over the House, preserve decorum and order, put questions and decide all points of order. He was to announce the results of votes and to vote in all cases of ballot by the House.

● Committees of three or fewer members were to be appointed by the Speaker, while larger ones were to be chosen by ballot.

● Members could not introduce bills or speak more than twice to the same question without leave of the House. They were required to vote if present, unless excused, and barred from voting if not present or if they had a direct personal interest in the outcome.

The first rules also set forth legislative procedure. As in the Continental Congress, the principal forum for considering and perfecting legislation was to be the Committee of the Whole House—the House itself under another name. When sitting in Committee of the Whole, a member other than the Speaker occupied the chair and certain motions permitted in the House—such as the previous question and the motion to adjourn—were not in order, nor were roll-call votes taken. Amendments rejected in committee could not be offered again in the House except as part of a motion to recommit. As in the House, it took a majority of the members to make a quorum in the Committee of the Whole.

Early House Procedure

In the early years of the House, it was the practice to begin discussion of all major legislative proposals in Committee of the Whole House on the State of the Union. After broad agreement had been reached on the principles involved, a select committee was named to draft a bill. When this committee reported back to the House, the bill itself was referred to a Committee of the Whole for section-by-section debate and approval or amendment. Its work completed, the committee rose, the Speaker resumed the chair, and the House either accepted or rejected the amendments agreed to in Committee of the Whole. This was followed by a third and final reading of the engrossed or complete bill and passage by the House.

Since there were no time limits as yet on the right of members to speak, even the small membership of the First and Second Congresses found this procedure cumbersome. Rep. James Madison blamed the "delays and perplexities" of the House on "the want of precedents."[3] But Rep. Fisher Ames of Massachusetts saw the problem as an excessive concern with detail in the "unwieldy" Committee of the Whole, for "a great, clumsy machine is applied to the slightest and most delicate operations—the hoof of an elephant to the strokes of mezzotinto."[4]

A small time-saver was introduced in 1790, when the House amended its rules to permit the Speaker to appoint all committees unless otherwise specially directed by the House. Similarly, in 1794, the House empowered the Speaker to name the chairman of the Committee of the Whole, who had been elected each time theretofore. But the practice of hammering out the broad terms of major legislation in Committee of the Whole before naming a select committee to draft a bill (more than 350 select committees were formed during the Third Congress) prevailed into the 1800s.

By confiding each proposal to a special committee that ceased to exist when a bill was reported, the House kept effective control over the legislation. But as its business multiplied and its membership increased (to 106 after the census of 1790 and to 142 after that of 1800), the House began to delegate increasing responsibility for initiating legislation to standing or permanent committees. Four were established by 1795; between 1802 and 1809, six were added. Among the more important were the Committees on Interstate and Foreign Commerce, created in 1795; Ways and Means, a select committee made permanent in 1802; and Public Lands, whose establishment in 1805 was prompted by the Louisiana Purchase.

Emergence of Parties

Neither the Constitution nor the first rules of the House envisioned a role for political parties in the legislative process. The triumph of Federalists over Anti-Federalists in winning ratification of the Constitution, the unanimous and nonpartisan choice of Washington as the first President, and the great preponderance of nominal Federalists elected to the First Congress tended to obscure the underlying economic, sectional and philosophic differences of the times. But these differences were not long in surfacing after Alexander Hamilton took office as the first Secretary of the Treasury. The statute creating the department required the Treasury "to digest and prepare plans for the improvement and management of the revenue and for the support of the public credit."[5]

Hamilton, a skilled financier, administrator and political organizer at 34, quickly responded with proposals for paying off the national and state debts at par and for creating a Bank of the United States. Designed to establish confidence in the new federal government, these proposals also appealed to the mercantile and moneyed interests to whom Hamilton looked for support in his desire to strengthen central authority. Since most of those elected to the First Congress shared his outlook (and some members stood to profit from his proposals), he soon emerged as the effective leader of a new Federalist party, meeting frequently with its adherents in caucus to plan legislative strategy.

Madison was the first to take issue with the substance of Hamilton's program as well as the dominance of the executive branch in guiding the decisions of the House. He was joined by his close friend and fellow Virginian, Thomas

Jefferson, who became Secretary of State in 1790. Jefferson strongly opposed Hamilton from within the Cabinet. In a letter to President Washington, Jefferson criticized his colleague for attempting to exert undue influence upon Congress. He wrote that Hamilton's "system flowed from principles adverse to liberty, and was calculated to undermine and demolish the republic, by creating an influence of his department over the members of the legislature."[6] The cleavage was reinforced by the French Revolution and the wars that followed in its wake; Hamilton and the Federalists, with strong commercial and other ties to England, urged American neutrality, while Jefferson and his followers looked on the French as democratic allies to be helped.

By 1792, Madison and Jefferson were the recognized leaders of a nascent Republican Party of opposition, rooted in southern fears of Federalist economic policies and rising agrarian antagonism to the aristocratic views of Hamilton, Vice President John Adams and other prominent Federalists. In the Third through the Sixth Congresses, spanning Washington's second term and Adams' single term as President, the House was closely divided between Republicans and Federalists. But in 1800 Jefferson's party emerged with a clear majority, and during his two terms as President the Republicans outnumbered the Federalists in the House two and three to one.

Leadership in the House

With the early emergence of two parties, choice of a Speaker soon fell to the party with a majority in the House. Thus in 1799, Theodore Sedgwick of Massachusetts was elected Speaker over Nathaniel Macon of North Carolina by a vote of 44 to 38, a margin that approximated that of Federalists over Republicans in the Sixth Congress. Two years later, Macon was elected Speaker by the heavy Republican majority in the Seventh Congress.

As party choices, the early Speakers were not unwilling to use their powers in support of party policies. In 1796, when House Republicans mounted an attack on Jay's treaty with Britain, Speaker Jonathan Dayton, a Federalist, twice voted to produce ties that resulted in the defeat of anti-treaty motions. Republicans in the Sixth Congress found the rulings of Sedgwick so partisan that they refused to join in the by-then customary vote of thanks to the Speaker at adjournment.

But these early Speakers were not the actual political or legislative leaders of the House. Until he left the Treasury in 1795, Hamilton—operating through members of his own choice—dominated the Federalist majority—an "all-powerful" leader, according to one Republican, who "fails in nothing, he attempts."[7] As the leader of House Republicans until he left Congress in 1797, Madison was seen in much the same light by Federalist Fisher Ames, who wrote: "Virginia moves in a solid column and the discipline of the party is as severe as the Prussian. Deserters are not spared."[8]

As Republicans (or Democrats, as the Federalists soon took to calling them), Jefferson and Madison were opposed in principle to the concept of executive supremacy embraced by Hamilton and the early Federalists. When he became President in 1801, Jefferson promptly discarded a favored symbol of Federalist theory—the personal appearance of the President before a joint session of Congress to read his annual State of the Union message and instituted the practice (followed by all Presidents until

Woodrow Wilson) of sending up the message to be read by a clerk. But Jefferson also took steps to assert his leadership over the new Republican majority in the House.

Jefferson's Secretary of the Treasury, Swiss-born Albert Gallatin (who had succeeded Madison as leader of House Republicans) soon became as adept as Hamilton had been in guiding administration measures through the party caucus and the House. Moreover, Jefferson picked his own floor leader, who was named chairman of the Committee on Ways and Means at the same time. The men who held the posts of floor leader and Ways and Means chairman during Jefferson's tenure were known as the President's spokesmen in establishing party policy. When one of these leaders, the tempestuous John Randolph, broke with Jefferson over a plan to acquire Florida, the President had him deposed as the committee chairman.

Randolph, meanwhile, had already affronted some members of the House by his conduct as Ways and Means chairman. Representative James Sloan complained in 1805 that he had tied up committee business "by going to Baltimore or elsewhere, without leave of absence" and by keeping appropriations' estimates "in his pockets or locked up in his drawer," and that he had rushed out important bills at the end of the session "when many members are gone home."[9] Sloan proposed that all standing committees be elected by ballot and choose their own chairmen. Committees were given the choice of selecting their own chairmen under a rule adopted in the Eighth Congress, but selection of chairmen (as well as committee members) reverted to the Speaker at the beginning of the 11th Congress.

In sum, the first 20 years of the House saw the beginnings of the standing committee system and the emergence of a floor leader and committee chairmen as key men in the legislative process. But that process was dominated, by and large, by the executive branch, and the effective decisions on legislative issues were reached behind the scenes in closed caucuses of the majority party. As Federalist Josiah Quincy lamented in 1809, the House "acts and reasons and votes, and performs all the operations of an animated being, and yet, judging from my own perceptions, I cannot refrain from concluding that all great political questions are settled somewhere else than on this floor."[10]

Congressional Ascendancy: 1809-1829

The era of executive supremacy over Congress came to an end under Jefferson's successor, James Madison, whose strong performance in the Constitutional Convention, in the House and as Secretary of State for eight years was not matched in the presidency. Although he was nominally backed by Republican majorities during his two terms in office, Madison soon lost control of his party to a group of young "war hawks" (as John Randolph called them) first elected to the 12th Congress, who pushed the President into the War of 1812 against England. Led in the House by Henry Clay and John C. Calhoun, these men capitalized on Madison's weakness and a rising resistance to executive control to effect a shift of power to Congress that was not reversed until Jackson became President in 1829.

Clay as Speaker

Henry Clay first came to national attention while serving briefly as a senator from Kentucky in 1810-11. He then

spoke eloquently of the need for "a new race of heroes" to preserve the achievements of America's founders. He proposed the conquest of Canada, asserting that "the militia of Kentucky are alone competent to place Montreal and Upper Canada at your feet."[11] It was as spokesman for a new nationalism, affronted by British interference with American trade and shipping, that Clay entered the House in 1811 and—although only 34 and a newcomer—was promptly elected Speaker by like-minded Republicans. Using to the full his power to appoint committees and their chairmen, Clay put his fellow war hawks in all of the key positions. Together they took control of the House.

Clay greatly enhanced the power and prestige of the Speaker. In addition to presiding over the House as his predecessors had, he took over leadership of the majority party. This made him the leader of the House in fact as well as name. A forceful presiding officer, Clay was also an accomplished debater who frequently used his right to speak in the House as in Committee of the Whole. Gifted with great charm and tact, Clay remained Speaker as long as he was in the House. Although he resigned his seat twice—in 1814 (to help negotiate an end to the War of 1812) and in 1820—he was again elected Speaker as soon as he returned to the House in 1815 and in 1823.

It was the job of the Speaker, Clay said in his 1823 inaugural speech, to be prompt and impartial in deciding questions of order, to display "patience, good temper, and courtesy" to every member, and to make "the best arrangement and distribution of the talent of the House" for the dispatch of public business. Above all, he said, the Speaker must "remain cool and unshaken amidst all the storms of debate, carefully guarding the preservation of the permanent laws and rules of the House from being sacrificed to temporary passions, prejudices or interests."[12]

This was no easy job in Clay's time, when political passions were strong, the size of House membership continued to increase (to 186 after the census of 1810 and to 213 after that of 1820), and the right of debate was essentially unlimited. It is true that the House (after becoming exasperated with the unyielding tactics of Barent Gardenier, a New Yorker who once held the floor for 24 hours) had decided in 1811 that a majority could shut off further debate by calling for the previous question—the device which in time became the normal means of closing debate in the House. But in this period John Randolph was not alone in regarding this as a gag rule, and it was not easily invoked. Under the existing rules, moreover, those skilled in parliamentary tactics (as Randolph was) could and frequently did succeed in tying up House proceedings.

Clay once outwitted Randolph. It was after the House in 1820 had finally passed the hotly disputed Missouri

Frederick Muhlenberg

Henry Clay

Compromise bill to admit Missouri as a slave state but to bar slavery in any future state north of 36°30' north latitude. When Randolph, who opposed the bill, moved the next day to reconsider the vote, the Speaker held the motion to be out of order pending completion of the prescribed order of business. Clay then proceeded to sign the bill and send it to the Senate before Randolph could renew his motion. The Speaker's action was upheld, in effect, when the House refused, 61-71, to consider Randolph's subsequent motion to censure the clerk for having removed the bill.

Growth of Standing Committees

Efforts to refine House procedures continued in the period 1809-1829. The first rule to establish a daily order of business was adopted in 1811. In 1812 the Committee on Enrolled Bills was given leave to report at any time—a privilege later granted to certain other committees in order to expedite consideration of important bills. A rule adopted in 1817 enabled the House to protect itself against business it did not wish to consider. In 1820 the House created by rule the first calendars of the Committee of the Whole. And in 1822 it was decided that no rule should be suspended except by a two-thirds vote.

But the chief development in House procedures during this period was the proliferation of standing committees and their emergence as the principal forums for the initial consideration of proposed legislation—a practice recognized in 1822 by a rule giving standing committees leave to report by bill or otherwise. The number of select committees created to draft bills had dropped from 350 in the Third Congress (1793-95) to 70 in the 13th Congress (1813-15). And the number of standing committees grew from 10 in 1809 to 28 in 1825.

Among the standing committees were the Committee on the Judiciary, made permanent in 1813, and the Committees on Military Affairs, Naval Affairs and Foreign Affairs, all created in 1822. Six Committees on Expenditures in as many executive departments were established by Clay in 1816 to check up on economy and efficiency in the administration. Between 1816 and 1826 these and other House committees conducted at least 20 major investigations. The inquiries included such matters as the conduct of General Andrew Jackson in the Seminole War, charges against Secretary of the Treasury William Crawford, and the conduct of John Calhoun as Secretary of War.

Decline of King Caucus

In Clay's time as Speaker, the party caucus still afforded House Republicans an important means of reaching legislative decisions. It took Federalist Daniel Webster less than two weeks after being seated in 1813 to conclude that "the time for us to be put on the stage and moved by the wires has not yet come," since "before anything is attempted to be done here, it must be arranged elsewhere."[13] And Webster soon noted that the caucus worked "because it was attended with a severe and efficacious discipline, by which those who went astray were to be brought to repentance."[14] But the extent of party unity among Republicans had already started to decline under Jefferson as a result of sectional rivalries, and while the Federalists continued to lose ground as a national party, factionalism increased among the Republicans in Congress.

The change was reflected also in the rise and fall of the congressional caucus as the agency for selecting party nominees for President and Vice President. The practice began in 1800, when both Federalist and Republican members of the House and Senate met secretly to pick running mates for Jefferson and Adams. In 1804, Jefferson was renominated unanimously and openly by a caucus of 108 Republican senators and representatives. Four years later, a caucus of 94 Republicans nominated Madison for President over the protests of others who preferred James Monroe. But only 83 of the 133 Republicans in Congress attended the caucus that renominated Madison in 1812, just before he asked Congress for the declaration of war against England that Clay and others had been urging.

The Republican caucus of 1816 drew 119 of the party's 141 members in the House and Senate. Madison favored the nomination of Secretary of State Monroe for President, but there was rising opposition to continuation of the Virginia "dynasty" in the White House, and Monroe was nominated by only 65 votes to 54 for Secretary of War William Crawford of Georgia. By 1820, however, there was no real opposition in either party to Monroe, who was credited with bringing about "the era of good feelings" and had kept clear of the controversy over the Missouri Compromise. Fewer than 50 members showed up for the caucus that found it inexpedient to make any nomination, and Monroe was reelected with every electoral vote but one.

The race to succeed Monroe began almost at once and included three members of his Cabinet—Crawford, Calhoun and John Quincy Adams—as well as Henry Clay and Andrew Jackson, hero of the Battle of New Orleans. When it appeared that Crawford would get a majority in a caucus, supporters of the other candidates began to denounce the caucus system. As a result, only 66 of the 261 senators and representatives then seated in Congress attended the caucus that nominated Crawford early in 1824. The election that fall gave Jackson a plurality but not a majority of the popular and electoral votes, and the choice went to the House, which picked Adams.

The presidential contest of 1824 marked the end of the old party system and the congressional nominating caucus. Helping to kill the caucus were changes in voting procedures and an expansion of the suffrage. Between 1800 and 1824, the number of states in which the electors were chosen by popular vote instead of by the legislature increased from five out of 16 to 18 out of 24. Four years later, in 1828, the electors were popularly chosen in all except two of the 24 states, and the popular vote jumped from less than 400,000 in 1824 to more than 1.1 million. With the emergence of a mass electorate, aspirants for the presidency were forced to seek a much broader base of support than the congressional caucus.

A House Divided: 1829-1861

National politics entered a period of increasing turmoil, lasting until the Civil War, during the presidency of Andrew Jackson. Jackson made unprecedented use of the veto and of the removal and patronage powers of his office to establish primacy over Congress. Two new parties emerged during his presidency (1829-37): the Jacksonian Democrats, heirs to the agrarian and states' rights philosophy of the Jeffersonian Republicans, and the Whigs, spokesmen for the commercial and industrial interests once represented by the Federalists. But the Democrats now embraced the Federalist principle of executive leadership, while the Whigs extolled the Republican doctrine of legislative supremacy and tried thereafter to weaken the presidency.

The power and influence of the House began to decline under Jackson, when the size of the membership was increased to 242. Such former luminaries of the House as Henry Clay, Daniel Webster and John Calhoun moved to the Senate, which now became the major arena of debate on national policy. Party control of the presidency, the House and the Senate fluctuated considerably after Jackson. Increasingly, however, both Democrats and Whigs found themselves divided by the issue of slavery and its extension to the new territories and states beyond the Mississippi. The issue was reflected in the bitter election battles for the speakership that occurred in 1839, 1849, 1855 and 1859.

Contests to Elect the Speaker

Intra-party contests for Speaker were not new in the House. In 1805, when Republicans outnumbered Federalists almost four to one, it took four ballots to re-elect Macon, a southerner, over Joseph B. Varnum, the northern candidate. Two years later, when there were five candidates, Varnum won on the second ballot after Macon withdrew. By 1820—the year of the Missouri Compromise—the issue of slavery was an explicit part of the sectional contest for Speaker; to replace Clay, who had resigned, the House cast 22 ballots before electing John W. Taylor of New York, the antislavery candidate, over William Lowndes of South Carolina, a compromiser.

Next year, Taylor was one of five candidates in a contest that underscored the breakup of the Republicans and foreshadowed the presidential race of 1824. Taylor lost on the 12th ballot to Philip C. Barbour of Virginia, a Crawford supporter. And in 1834, when Andrew Stevenson resigned in his fourth term as Speaker (only to see the Senate reject his nomination as Minister to Great Britain), it took 10 ballots to elect John Bell over his fellow Tennessean, James K. Polk.

Contest of 1839. Martin Van Buren, Jackson's hand-picked successor, was elected President in 1836, but Democrats barely won control of the House in the 25th Congress (1837-39). When it adjourned, Whigs deplored the "most partial and unjust rulings" of Speaker Polk, who then left the House to become Governor of Tennessee. At the opening of the 26th Congress on Dec. 2, 1839, the House found itself with 120 Democrats, 118 Whigs, and five contested seats in New Jersey. Control of the House rested on the decision of these contests, but the clerk (who presided under House practice pending election of a Speaker) refused to choose between the claimants or to bring up the question until the House was organized.

After four days of bitter debate, the members elected a temporary chairman—the venerable John Quincy Adams, who had returned to the House in 1831. But it was Dec. 14 before it was decided to elect a Speaker without the New Jersey votes. There were six candidates to start, and John W. Jones of Virginia led on the first five ballots. But Robert M. T. Hunter—also of Virginia—was elected Dec. 16 on the 11th ballot (when there were 13 candidates) because he "finally united all the Whig votes and all the malcontents of the administration," according to Adams.[15]

Contest of 1849. Control of the House passed to the Whigs in the 27th Congress (1841-43), then to the Democrats in the 28th and 29th, then back to the Whigs in the 30th (1847-49) during the last two years of the Polk administration. Zachary Taylor, the Whig candidate, was elected President in 1848, but neither party had a majority in the House when the 31st Congress met on Dec. 3, 1849,

because a number of Free-Soil Whigs and Democrats refused to support the leading candidates for Speaker—Robert C. Winthrop of Massachusetts, Whig Speaker in the previous Congress, and Howell Cobb, a Democrat from Georgia. The pending issue was what to do about slavery in the territory won in the war against Mexico, and the Free Soilers were determined to prevent the election of a Speaker who would appoint pro-slavery majorities to the Committees on Territories and the District of Columbia.

Cobb led 11 candidates on the first ballot with 103 votes. But there were five recognized factions in the House—Whigs, Democrats, Free Soilers, Native Americans and Taylor Democrats—and neither Cobb nor Winthrop, who alternated in the lead for 60 ballots, could get a majority. Finally, on Dec. 22, the House voted, 113 to 106, to elect a Speaker by a plurality, so long as it was a majority of a quorum. Cobb, the pro-slavery candidate, was elected on the 63rd ballot when he received 102 votes to 100 for Winthrop, with 20 votes spread among eight other candidates. This decision was then confirmed by a majority vote of the House.

Contest of 1855. Pro-slavery Democrats held firm control of the House in the 32nd and 33rd Congresses (1851-55), when Linn Boyd of Kentucky was Speaker. But their attempt to extend slavery into the Kansas and Nebraska Territories produced a large turnout of anti-slavery forces in the elections of 1854—the first in which a new Republican party, successor to the Whigs, participated. When the 34th Congress convened on Dec. 3, 1855, the House membership was divided among 108 Republicans or Whigs, 83 Democrats and 43 members of minor parties that sprang up in the 1850s. Although the so-called "Anti-Nebraska men" were in the majority, they were unable to unite behind any candidate for Speaker; two months passed and 133 ballots were taken before a choice was made.

The 21 candidates on the first ballot were led by William A. Richardson of Illinois with 74 votes. As in previous contests, various motions to help resolve the deadlock—including one to drop the low man on each ballot until only two remained—were made and tabled as the voting continued. After a series of votes in which Nathaniel P. Banks of Massachusetts fell only a few votes short of a majority, the House finally agreed to follow the plurality rule of 1849. On Feb. 2, 1856, Banks was declared Speaker. On the 133rd ballot he had received 103 votes to 100 for William Aiken of South Carolina. Banks, who had been elected to the 33rd Congress as a Coalition Democrat and to the 34th as a candidate of the nativist American Party of Know Nothings, fulfilled the expectations of the anti-slavery forces by his committee appointments.

Contest of 1859. Democrats won the presidency in 1856 with James Buchanan, last of the "northern men with southern principles." They also gained control of the House in the 35th Congress (1857-59). But the 36th opened on Dec. 5, 1859, with no party in control of the House, which was composed of 109 Republicans, 101 Democrats and 27 Know Nothings. Pro- and anti-slavery blocs were again deadlocked over the choice of a Speaker. With passions running high and debate unchecked by a presiding clerk who refused to decide any points of order, the struggle continued for two months.

John Sherman of Ohio, the Republican choice, led the early balloting, receiving at one point 110 votes, just six short of a majority. But Sherman had become anathema to the pro-slavery camp, and the Republicans finally concluded that he couldn't be elected. So Sherman withdrew on the 39th ballot, and the Republicans switched their support to William Pennington of New Jersey, a new member of the House and politically unknown. Pennington received 115 votes on the 40th ballot (compared to one on the 38th) and was elected on the 44th, on Feb. 1, 1860, by a bare majority of 117 votes out of 233. Pennington's distinction (shared with Clay) of being Speaker in his first term ended there, for he was defeated at the polls the next year and served only the one term in the House.

Changes in House Rules

Agitation over the issue of slavery was not confined to the contests over the choice of a Speaker. In 1836, John Quincy Adams challenged a House practice (begun in 1792) of refusing to receive petitions and memorials on the subject of slavery. Adams offered a petition from citizens of Massachusetts for the abolition of slavery in the District of Columbia. His action led to protracted debate and the adoption of a resolution (by a vote of 117 to 68) that any papers dealing with slavery "shall, without being either printed or referred, be laid upon the table and that no further action whatever shall be had thereon."[16]

Adams, who considered adoption of the resolution to be a violation of the Constitution and of the rules of the House reopened the issue in 1837 by asking the Speaker how to dispose of a petition he had received from 22 slaves. Southerners moved at once to censure Adams. The move failed, but the House agreed, 163-18, that "slaves do not possess the right of petition secured to the people of the United States by the Constitution."[17] Further agitation led the House in 1840 to adopt (by a vote of 114-108) a rule that no papers "praying the abolition of slavery...shall be received by this House or entertained· in any way whatever."[18] Four years later, however, the rule was rescinded by a vote of 108-80.

Other rules adopted in this period were more significant to the long-range development of House procedures. In 1837, for example, precedence was given to floor consideration of revenue and appropriation bills, and the inclusion of legislation in an appropriation bill (which had led the Senate to kill a number of such bills) was barred. In 1841, the House finally agreed to limit to one hour the time allowed any member in a debate—a proposal made first in 1820 after John Randolph had spoken for more than four hours against the Missouri Compromise. At the same time, to prevent indefinite debate in Committee of the Whole, a rule was adopted providing that the House by majority vote could discharge the committee from consideration of a bill after pending amendments were disposed of without debate.

Objection to the latter provision led in 1847 to adoption of the five-minute rule, giving any member that much time to explain his amendment. But this rule encouraged a practice of offering and then withdrawing scores of amendments in an effort to delay action on controversial bills. So the rule was amended in 1850 to prohibit the withdrawal of any amendment without unanimous consent. But the House was still at the mercy of a determined minority; during debate on the Kansas-Nebraska bill in 1854, according to Asher Hinds (R Maine), opponents engaged in "prolonged dilatory operations, such as the alternation of the motions to lay on the table, for a call of the House, to excuse individual members from voting, to adjourn, to reconsider votes whereby individual members were excused from voting, to adjourn, to fix the day to which the House should adjourn, and, after calls of the House had

been ordered, to excuse individual absentees,"[19] all of which required 109 roll calls and consumed many days.

In 1858, the House agreed to set up a select committee to revise the accumulation of more than 150 rules. The committee included the Speaker—the first time that officer had served on any committee of the House. While its report was not acted on, most of its recommendations were repeated in 1860 by another committee named the day Pennington was finally chosen Speaker. As approved by the House in March, this first general revision of the rules was largely of a technical nature, although it included important changes affecting use of the previous question and the motion to strike the enacting clause. On balance, however, the revised rules of 1860 left ample opportunity for a resolute minority to keep a closely divided House tied up in parliamentary knots for days at a time.

Apart from the adoption of the first limitations on debate—the hour rule and the five-minute rule in the 1840s—there was little significant change in House procedures in the period 1829-1860. The system of standing committees that had been established by 1825 (when there were 28) was expanded by the addition of eight more. The Committee on Ways and Means continued to handle both appropriations and revenue bills, and while its chairman was not always the designated floor leader of the majority party, he was always among the most influential members. The Speaker continued to appoint members to committees and to designate their chairmen.

But none of the Speakers who followed Clay achieved his stature or influence. Of the 14 who were elected between 1825 and 1860, only three—Stevenson, Polk and Boyd—served for more than one Congress. In only one respect was the job of leading the House made, not easier, but at least no more difficult: the size of the membership increased to 242 in 1833 and was kept about the same for the next 40 years. Otherwise, the rising passions of the country doomed the House to increasing turmoil as America moved toward internecine conflict.

New Complexities: 1861-1890

The Civil War all but eliminated the South from national politics and representation in Congress for eight years. Most of the 66 House seats held by the 11 secessionist states in 1860 remained vacant from 1861 to 1869. The war also greatly weakened the Democratic Party outside the South; as in the War of 1812, when the Federalists were criticized for their pro-British sympathies, the Democrats suffered from their identification with the southern cause. And Democratic weakness helped the Republicans to keep control of the presidency until 1885, of the Senate until 1879, and of the House until 1875.

At the same time, the war and its aftermath gave rise to bitter conflict between Congress and the President leading to the impeachment of Andrew Johnson in 1868 and to a prolonged period of legislative dominance thereafter. The years from 1860 to 1890 saw a further expansion of House membership, an intensification of House efforts to control government spending, an increase in the number and power of House committees, and a continuing struggle to adapt the rules of the House to its legislative purposes.

Congress Is Paramount

President Lincoln assumed unprecedented powers during the Civil War, at a time when the Republican majorities in Congress were dominated by Radicals committed to the Whig doctrine of legislative supremacy. The conflict between Lincoln and Congress was sharpest over the issue of Reconstruction. Lincoln, who held that the Confederate states had never left the Union, was prepared to restore their political rights as quickly as possible. But the Radicals were determined to reshape the power structure of the South before readmitting the secessionists and insisted that the decision rested with Congress.

When Lincoln set up new governments in Louisiana and Arkansas in 1863, the Radicals passed a bill to place all Reconstruction authority under the direct control of Congress. Lincoln pocket-vetoed the bill after Congress had adjourned in 1864, whereupon the Radicals issued the Wade-David Manifesto asserting that "the authority of Congress is paramount and must be respected." If the President wanted their support, said the Radicals, "he must confine himself to his executive duties—to obey and execute, not make the laws—to suppress by arms armed rebellion, and leave political reorganization to Congress."[20]

The Radicals proceeded to put their views into effect with a vengeance under Andrew Johnson, the Tennessee Democrat who became President when Lincoln was assassinated in 1865 and whose views were openly sympathetic to the established order in the South. Passed over Johnson's veto were numerous bills the effects of which were to give Congress full control over Reconstruction and to strip the President of much of his authority.

One of these measures was the Tenure of Office Act of 1867, passed on the suspicion that Johnson intended to fire Secretary of War Edwin Stanton. The law made it a high misdemeanor to remove without the Senate's approval any official whose nomination had been confirmed by the Senate. After Johnson—holding the law to be unconstitutional—had suspended Stanton from office, the House voted, 126-47, to impeach him. Tried by the Senate, Johnson was acquitted May 16, 1868, when a vote of 35 to 19 for conviction fell one short of the two-thirds required by the Constitution.

Power of the Purse

The Civil War led to renewed efforts by the House to control federal expenditures (which climbed from $63 million in 1860 to $1.3 billion in 1865) by a more careful exercise of its power over appropriations. Until then, the Committee on Ways and Means had handled all supply as well as revenue bills, in addition to bills on monetary matters. But in 1865 the House agreed with little opposition to transfer some of these responsibilities to two new standing committees—a Committee on Appropriations and a Committee on Banking and Currency. Speaking of the former, the sponsor of the change declared that "we require of this new committee their whole labor in the restraint of extravagant and illegal appropriations."[21]

Congress now began to tighten controls on spending. Wartime authority to transfer funds from one account to another was repealed, agencies were required to return unexpended funds to the Treasury, and obligation of funds in excess of appropriations was prohibited. Although Congress continued to make lump-sum appropriations to the Army and the Navy, it specified in great detail the amounts and purposes for which money could be spent by the civilian departments and agencies. These efforts helped to keep federal expenditures below $300 million in every year except one from 1871 to 1890.

The House's "power of the purse" was exercised to another end during the administration of Rutherford B. Hayes (1877-81), the Republican successor to Ulysses S. Grant (1869-77). Democrats were again in the majority in the House in the 45th Congress (1877-79) and won control of both chambers in the 46th, but by margins too small to be able to override a veto. So in their attempts to repeal certain Reconstruction laws, the Democrats revived the practice of adding legislative riders to appropriation bills in the hope of forcing the President to accept them. But Hayes vetoed a series of such bills, rejecting the tactic as an attempt at coercive dictation by the House. When they were unable to override his vetoes, the Democrats finally passed the appropriation bills without the riders.

During the height of the dispute in 1879, Hayes wrote in his diary: "This is a controversy which cannot and ought not to be compromised. The Revolutionists claim that a bare majority in the House of Representatives shall control all legislation, by tacking the measures they can't pass through the Senate, or over the President's objections, to the appropriation bills which are required to carry on the government.... [I]t is idle to talk of compromises as to the particular measures which are used as riders on the appropriation bills. These measures may be wise or unwise. It is easy enough to say in regard to them, that used as they are to establish a doctrine which overthrows the Constitutional distribution of power between the different departments of the government, and consolidates in the House of Representatives, the whole law making power of the government...we will not discuss or consider them when they are so presented....

"To tack political legislation to appropriation bills and to threaten that no appropriations will be made unless the political measures are approved is not in my judgment constitutional conduct."[22]

Meanwhile, House members of both parties were becoming concerned over a concentration of power in the Appropriations Committee itself. In 1877, the committee was deprived of its jurisdiction over appropriations for rivers and harbors—the "pork barrel" on which members relied to finance projects of interest to their districts. The agriculture appropriation was taken from the committee in 1880, and in 1885, it was stripped of authority over six other supply bills—Army, Navy, Military Academy, Consular and Diplomatic Affairs, Post Office and Post Roads, and Indian Affairs—all of which were transferred to the appropriate legislative committees.

In taking from the Appropriations Committee control over bills comprising almost one-half of the federal budget, the House was apparently moved by hostility to Chairman Samuel J. Randall (D Pa.) and what was considered to be the committee's excessive concern for economy under his leadership. The feeling was widespread and bipartisan; three-fourths of the Democrats and of the Republicans joined in the vote of 227 to 70 to strip the committee of a giant share of its jurisdiction. They were led, moreover, by the senior members of most of the other important committees, underscoring the rivalry that had developed among House committees.

The effect of this decision in 1885 was to reinforce the decentralization of power in the House and to give added weight to the criticism of Congress voiced by Woodrow Wilson that year in his book *Congressional Government.* According to Wilson, power in the House was scattered among "47 seigniories, in each of which a standing committee is the court-baron and its chairman lord-proprietor."[23] Wilson noted that, "by custom, seniority in congressional service determines the bestowal of the principal chairmanships," and that on the House floor "chairman fights against chairman for use of the time of the assembly."[24]

Wilson attributed the lack of strong party control in the House to the fact that committees were not composed entirely of members of the majority, as he believed they should be. "The legislation of a session does not represent the policy of either [party]," he wrote; "it is simply an aggregate of the bills recommended by committees composed of members from both sides of the House, and it is known to be usually, not the work of the majority men upon the committees, but compromise conclusions...of the committeemen of both parties."[25]

Speakers and the Rules

If power in the House was not dispersed among the standing committees and their chairmen, it was also true (as Wilson noted) that "he who appoints those committees is an autocrat of the first magnitude."[26] While Speakers had held that authority since the earliest days of the House, its exercise had assumed new importance with the broadening legislative interests of the country and of the House.

Schuyler Colfax, first elected to the House from Indiana in 1854, served as Republican Speaker from 1863 to 1869, when he left the House to become Vice President during the first term of President Grant. Although Colfax enjoyed as much personal popularity as had Henry Clay, he was not a forceful Speaker and was regarded as a figurehead in a House dominated by Thaddeus Stevens (R Pa.), who became chairman of the Ways and Means Committee in 1861 and of the newly created Appropriations Committee in 1865. Stevens, who engineered the impeachment of President Johnson, was described by George Boutwell, a fellow Republican, as "a tyrant" in his rule as leader of the House who was "at once able, bold and unscrupulous."[27]

Colfax's successor as Speaker was James G. Blaine of Maine, one of the founders of the Republican Party, who entered the House in 1863. As Speaker from 1869 to 1875, Blaine was an avowed partisan of Republican principles and successfully manipulated committee assignments to produce majorities favorable to legislation he desired. Like Clay, Blaine aspired to become President. But after losing the Republican nomination to Rutherford B. Hayes in 1876 and to James A. Garfield in 1880, he was nominated in 1884 only to lose the election to Democrat Grover Cleveland.

Democrats won control of the House in 1875. After the death in 1876 of their first choice for Speaker, Michael C. Kerr of Indiana, they elected Samuel J. Randall of Pennsylvania, who had entered the House with Blaine and Garfield in 1863. Randall, who was Speaker until 1881, initiated a thorough revision of House rules in 1880 designed "to secure accuracy in business, economy in time, order, uniformity and impartiality."[28] The net effect of these changes was to increase to some extent the ability of floor leaders and committee chairmen to expedite legislation on the floor. The Committee on Rules, which had been a select committee since 1789 and had been chaired by the Speaker since 1858, was made a standing committee, and it soon began to make systematic use of special orders or rules which, when adopted by majority vote of the House, governed the amount of time to be allowed for debate on major bills and the extent to which members might offer amendments.

The Democrats lost control of the House in the 47th Congress (1881-83) but regained it in the 48th Congress (1883-85). They then passed over Randall (because he had opposed the party's low-tariff policy) and elected John G. Carlisle of Kentucky as Speaker. Carlisle, a member since 1877 who remained Speaker from 1883 to 1889, made notable use of his power of recognition to forestall motions he opposed. By the device of asking "For what purpose does the gentleman rise?"[29] Carlisle was able to withhold recognition from any member whose purpose he did not share. But Carlisle did not lead a united party; in 1884, for example, the Democrats lost a tariff reduction bill through the defection of Randall and 40 other party members.

Blaine, Randall and Carlisle all contributed importantly to the body of precedents by which Speakers were guided under the House rules. But none was able or willing to prevent determined minorities from obstructing the business of the House. Under Carlisle, in particular, the House was frequently subjected to organized filibusters and such dilatory tactics as the "disappearing quorum" which was likely to result in endless roll calls to no purpose but delay. These displays, coupled with a disappointing legislative output, led to increasing public criticism of the House and to demands that the rules be modified "to permit the majority to control the business for which it is responsible," as the *New York Tribune* put it.[30]

The Reed Rules

The opportunity for reform came when Republicans took control of the House in 1889 and elected Thomas B. Reed of Maine as Speaker. First elected to the House in 1876, Reed had been a leader of House Republicans since 1882 when he became a member of the Rules Committee and an increasingly outspoken critic of the rules. He once said, "The only way to do business inside the rules is to suspend the rules."[31]

When the 51st Congress convened on Dec. 2, 1889, the House was composed of 330 members, with Republicans in a small majority. Reed was elected Speaker over Carlisle on a party-line vote, and in keeping with long-standing practice the rules of the 50th Congress were referred to the five-member Rules Committee (of which the Speaker was chairman) while the House proceeded under general parliamentary procedure. With several election contests pending, it was expected that the Republicans would settle them in their favor (as party majorities had always done) in order to increase their majority, before adopting new rules.

On Jan. 29, 1890, the Republicans called up the West Virginia election case of Smith vs. Jackson. Charles F. Crisp of Georgia, the Democratic leader, immediately raised the question of consideration, to be decided by majority vote. The roll call produced 161 "yeas," two "nays" and 165 not voting—mostly Democrats who, although present, were using the device of the "disappearing quorum" to block action. But when the point of "no quorum" was made (since less than one-half of the members had voted), Speaker Reed ordered the clerk to enter the names of those present and refusing to vote; he then ruled that a quorum was present and consideration in order.[32]

In the ensuing uproar, Reed was denounced as a "tyrant" and a "czar" but held to his ground. An appeal from his ruling was tabled by a majority of a quorum. When next day, in order to make a quorum, he again counted nonvoting Democrats who were present, he refused to allow another appeal on the ground that the House had already decided the question. Reed went on to declare that he would refuse to recognize any member rising to make a dilatory motion, saying:

"There is no possible way by which the orderly methods of parliamentary procedure can be used to stop legislation. The object of a parliamentary body is action, and not stoppage of action. Hence, if any member or set of members undertakes to oppose the orderly progress of business, even by the use of the ordinarily recognized parliamentary motions, it is the right of the majority to refuse to have those motions entertained...."[33]

Reed's rulings on dilatory motions and the counting of a quorum were incorporated in the revised rules reported by the Rules Committee, Feb. 6, 1890, and adopted by the House after four days of debate by a vote of 161 to 144. Of the rule that "no dilatory motion shall be entertained by the speaker," the committee report said: "There are no words which can be framed which will limit members to the proper use of proper motions. Any motion the most conducive to progress in the public business...may be used for purposes of unjust and oppressive delay.... Why should an assembly be kept from its work by motions made only to delay and to weary, even if the original design of the motion was salutary and sensible?"[34]

In addition to these changes in the rules, the revision of 1890 reduced the size of the quorum required in the Committee of the Whole from one-half of the membership of the House to 100 members—a change that facilitated floor action as the size of the House continued to grow. The revised rules also took account of the fact that the House had long since abandoned its original requirement that members obtain leave to introduce bills; the practice of introducing bills simply by filing them with the clerk was now made a rule.

Coincidentally, the number of bills introduced, which had first passed the 1,000 mark in the 24th Congress (1835-37) and had not exceeded 2,000 until the 40th Congress (1867-69), reached a new peak of more than 19,000 in the 51st Congress (1889-91). But the fate of most of these bills continued to be as described by Woodrow Wilson in 1885: "As a rule, a bill committed [to committee] is a bill doomed. When it goes from the clerk's desk to a committee room, it crosses a parliamentary bridge of sighs to dim dungeons of silence whence it will never return."[35]

Under the Reed Rules of 1890, the Speaker was enabled to take effective command of the House. By his authority to name the members and chairmen of all committees, he had the power to reward or to punish his fellow members. As chairman of the Rules Committee (which now shared with Ways and Means and Appropriations the right to report at any time and thereby get immediate access to the floor), he could control the timing and content of bills to be brought before the House. And now, with unlimited power of recognition, he could determine in large measure what was to be taken up on the floor.

Tyranny and Reaction: 1890-1919

Although the Democrats dropped the rule against the "disappearing quorum" when they took control of the House in the 52nd Congress (1891-93), they restored it in the 53rd (1893-95), and Charles F. Crisp of Georgia, the Democratic Speaker in both Congresses, made just as full use of his powers as had Reed in the 51st. Crisp (who persuaded two rivals to withdraw from the party contest for Speaker by

Thaddeus Stevens   **Thomas B. Reed**

promising them the chairmanships of Appropriations and Ways and Means) once refused to entertain an appeal by Reed from a ruling, refused to let Reed speak any further, and directed the Sergeant at Arms to see that he took his seat.

Reed, who served as minority leader during these four years and as Speaker again for the next two Congresses (1895-99), was able by his forceful leadership of House Republicans to restore the concept of party responsibility within the House. His chief aides in the 51st Congress included William McKinley (R Ohio), as chairman of the Ways and Means Committee, and Joseph G. Cannon (R Ill.), as chairman of the Appropriations Committee. McKinley left the House in 1891 (to become governor, then President in 1897), and when Reed resumed the speakership in 1895 he named Nelson Dingley (R Maine) to head Ways and Means. Cannon again became chairman of the Appropriations Committee in 1897, when Reed also named James A. Tawney (R Minn.) as the first Republican whip, charged with keeping party members on the floor and voting with the leadership. Under Reed, House Republicans achieved an exceptional degree of party unity during the 1890s, occasionally voting solidly for measures on which they had been sharply divided in caucus.

The centralization of power in the House during this period coincided with another, less visible change of significance. Until the Civil War, few members had chosen—or had been enabled by the voters—to make a career of service in the House. As late as the 1870s, more than half of the 293 Representatives then elected to the House every two years were freshmen, and the mean length of service for all members was barely two terms. Thus, although Speakers for some time had followed seniority to a degree in appointing members to committees of their choice and in advancing them to chairmanships, it was not a matter of great importance to most members when they failed to do so.

By 1899, however, the proportion of newcomers among the 357 members entering the House had fallen to 30 per cent, while the mean period of service had increased to more than three terms. As more members sought to stay in the House for longer periods, it became of increasing importance to them that they have the opportunity to gain political recognition through specialization and rising influence within the committee structure. There was thus a growing demand among members of both parties for assurance that their seniority would be respected in assigning them rank on committees of their choice. The resulting new expectations contributed to the reaction against centralization that began under Speaker Cannon.

Revolt Against 'Cannonism'

Speaker Reed resigned from the House in 1899, having broken with President McKinley over American intervention in Cuba and the annexation of Hawaii. The Republican majority in the 56th Congress (1899-1901) replaced Reed with David B. Henderson of Iowa, who served two ineffective terms as Speaker (1899-1903) before retiring from the House. In 1903, when Joseph G. Cannon was finally elected Speaker by the Republicans (having been an unsuccessful candidate in 1881, 1889 and 1899), he was the oldest representative in age (67) and service (28 years) ever to have headed the House.

Like Reed, Cannon set out to rule the House and its Republican majority through his control of the Rules Committee and the key chairmen. He kept Sereno E. Payne (R N.Y.) as majority leader and chairman of the Ways and Means Committee (positions to which Payne was first appointed by Henderson in 1899). He also retained Tawney as majority whip until 1905, when he named him chairman of Appropriations. Cannon turned over the committee assignments of Democrats to their leader, John Sharp Williams of Mississippi, subject to his veto. But Williams used his authority to build party unity among the Democrats, and Cannon took back the privilege in 1908 when James Beauchamp (Champ) Clark (D Mo.) succeeded Williams as minority leader.

As a strong conservative, Cannon was out of sympathy with much of the progressive legislation sought by President Theodore Roosevelt (1901-1909) and by a growing number of liberal Republicans and Democrats in the House. To maintain control, therefore, he made increasing use of his powers as Speaker to block legislation that he opposed and to thwart and punish members who opposed him. In a period of rising public interest in political reform, "Cannonism" came to be a synonym for the arbitrary use of the Speaker's powers to obstruct the legislative will, not of the majority party, but of a new majority of House members of both parties.

The movement to curb Cannon got under way during the last session of the 60th Congress when, just before final adjournment on March 3, 1909, the House adopted the Calendar Wednesday rule. This set aside Wednesday of each week for calling the roll of committees, whose chairmen or other authorized members could then call up bills that their committees had reported without getting clearance from the Rules Committee. At the time, progressives considered this a major reform because it seemed to insure the House a chance to act on measures favored in committee but opposed by the leadership. In practice, however, the procedure proved ineffective and in later years the House commonly agreed to dispense with Calendar Wednesday by unanimous consent.

Joseph G. Cannon

Nicholas Longworth

When the 61st Congress first met, in special session, on March 15, 1909, the House was composed of 219 Republicans and 172 Democrats. But the Republicans included about 30 insurgents led by George W. Norris of Nebraska and John M. Nelson of Wisconsin. After helping to elect Cannon to a fourth term as Speaker, the Republican insurgents joined with the Democrats to defeat the usual motion to adopt the rules of the preceding Congress. Clark, the Democratic leader, then offered a resolution to take from the Speaker his existing authority to appoint all committees, to limit that authority to only five committees (of which the only important one would be Ways and Means), to remove the Speaker from the Rules Committee, and to enlarge that body from five to 15 members.

Although 28 Republicans joined in supporting the Clark resolution, 22 Democrats led by Rep. John J. Fitzgerald (N.Y.) voted with the majority of Republicans to defeat it. The House thereupon adopted a compromise resolution, offered by Fitzgerald, which passed over the principal abuses complained of and only slightly curtailed the Speaker's authority. The main change was to establish a Consent Calendar for minor bills of particular interest to individual members and to set aside two days each month when bills on this Calendar could be called up without the prior approval of the Speaker and passed by unanimous consent. (Adoption of this rule led both parties to designate certain members as official "objectors," to prevent passage of bills opposed for any reason within the party. But the Consent Calendar became a useful device for processing minor bills.)

Agitation against "Cannonism" nevertheless continued, and the coalition of Democrats and progressive Republicans finally prevailed in 1910. Taking advantage of a parliamentary opening on March 16, Rep. Norris asked for immediate consideration of a reform resolution modeled on Clark's that had been bottled up in the Rules Committee. When Cannon held the motion out of order, the House overruled him by a decisive vote. Debate then began on the Norris resolution, which stripped the Speaker of all authority to appoint committees and their chairmen, removed him from the Rules Committee, and expanded that committee to 10 members who would choose their own chairman.

Rep. Nelson expressed the feelings of the insurgents in these terms: "Have we not been punished by every means at the disposal of the powerful House organization? Members long chairmen of important committees, others holding high rank—all with records of faithful and efficient party service to their credit—have been ruthlessly removed, deposed and humiliated before their constituents and the country because, forsooth, they would not cringe or crawl before the arbitrary power of the Speaker and his House machine.... We are fighting with our Democratic brethren for the common right of equal representation in this House, and for the right of way of progressive legislation in Congress."[36]

The House finally adopted the Norris resolution on March 19, by a vote of 191 to 156, after a continuous session of 29 hours during which Cannon had done his best to round up absentees among his supporters. Recognizing the nature of his defeat, Cannon invited a motion to declare the chair vacant so that the House might elect a new Speaker. Rep. A. S. Burleson (D Texas) made the motion, but it was quickly tabled; Cannon, known to the House as "Uncle Joe," was personally popular with many members, and the Republican insurgents were unwilling to help elect a Democrat. Cannon remained Speaker until the end of the 61st Congress in 1911 and a member of the House (except in the 63rd Congress) until 1923, by which time he had completed 46 years of service.

The revolt against "Cannonism" was consolidated in 1911, when the Democrats took control of the House, elected Champ Clark as Speaker, and adopted a revised body of rules that incorporated most of the changes agreed to in 1909-10. The new rules provided that all members of the standing committees, including their chairmen, would be "elected by the House, at the commencement of each Congress."[37] The rules of 1911 included the Calendar Wednesday and Consent Calendar innovations of 1909, as well as a discharge rule (adopted in 1910) by which a petition signed by a majority of House members could be used to free a bill locked up in any committee. Also established at this time was a special calendar for private bills, which could be called up two days each month.

Return of the Caucus

No less important than the rules of 1911 were the procedures adopted by the Democratic majority for organizing their control of the House. At the party caucus of Jan. 19 that nominated Clark for Speaker, it was also agreed that Oscar W. Underwood of Alabama would be majority leader and chairman of the Ways and Means Committee. And it was decided that the Democratic members of Ways and Means would constitute the party's Committee on Committees to draw up the committee assignments of all Democrats, leaving to the Republicans (who first established their own Committee on Committees in 1917) the selection of their own committeemen. In practice, therefore, the election of committees and their chairmen now took the form of a perfunctory vote to approve the slates drawn up by key members of the majority and minority parties and endorsed by the party caucus.

Underwood rather than Speaker Clark became the recognized leader of House Democrats from 1911 to 1915 (when he moved to the Senate), and he made frequent use of the party caucus to develop unity on legislative issues. Democratic caucus rules at this time provided that "in deciding upon action in the House involving party policy or principle, a two-thirds vote of those present and voting at a caucus meeting shall bind all members of the caucus" so long as the vote represented a majority of the Democrats in the House. But no member could be bound "upon questions involving a construction of the Constitution of the United States or upon which he made contrary pledges to his constituents prior to his election or received contrary instructions by resolution or platform from his nominating authority."[38]

A typical caucus resolution of 1911 bound Democrats to vote for certain bills reported by the Ways and Means Committee and "to vote against all amendments, except formal committee amendments, to said bills and motions to recommit, changing their text from the language agreed upon in this conference."[39] Underwood also used the caucus to develop legislative proposals which would then be referred to committees for formal approval, to instruct committees as to which bills they might or might not report, and to instruct the Rules Committee on the terms to be included in its special orders governing floor consideration of major bills.

Thus the power once concentrated in the hands of Speaker Cannon now passed to the Democratic Caucus, which was dominated by Underwood as majority leader. Historian George B. Galloway described Underwood's power: "As floor leader, Underwood was supreme, the Speaker a figurehead. The main cogs in the machine were the caucus, the floor leadership, the Rules Committee, the standing committees, and special rules. Oscar Underwood became the real leader of the House. He dominated the party caucus, influenced the rules, and as chairman of Ways and Means chose the committees. Clark was given the shadow, Underwood the substance of power. As floor leader, he could ask and obtain recognition at any time to make motions, restrict debate or preclude amendments or both."[40]

Wilson and Congress

As President, Wilson revived the custom of Washington and Adams (abandoned since the Jefferson presidency) of addressing Congress in person. He worked closely with the Democratic leaders in both houses and conferred frequently with committees and individual members to solicit support for his legislative program. With Wilson's help, Underwood and the Democrats were able to effect House passage of four major pieces of legislation in the 63rd Congress—the Underwood Tariff Act, the Federal Reserve Act, the Clayton Antitrust Act, and the Federal Trade Commission Act.

The Democrats were not so united on foreign policy, however. Both Speaker Clark and Majority Leader Underwood disagreed with Wilson over repeal of the exemption from Panama Canal tolls originally accorded to American coastal shipping. Claude Kitchin (D N.C.), who had become second-ranking Democrat on Ways and Means in 1913 and who succeeded Underwood as chairman and majority leader in 1915, openly challenged the President on several issues, notably when Wilson asked for a declaration of war against Germany in 1917. Clark later denounced the President's military conscription program.

Reflecting these disagreements, the strong party unity displayed by House Democrats during Wilson's first term began to fracture in his second. When the party lost control of the House at the mid-term elections of 1918, the binding party caucus had ceased to be an effective instrument in the hands of the leadership. The Republican minority, meanwhile, had all but abandoned use of the binding caucus in 1911, erecting in its place a non-binding "conference" used for little more than to choose the party's nominee for Speaker and to ratify committee slates. By 1919, the House was no longer willing to accept the centralization of power that had developed under Speakers Reed, Crisp and Cannon and Majority Leader Underwood. Party leaders thus were faced with the task of finding new ways to build and maintain consensus.

Accompanying this change—and helping to account for it—was a hardening of the unwritten rule of seniority that virtually guaranteed succession to committee chairmanships by the next-ranking majority members on the committees. Democrats violated the rule three times in 1911 and on a few occasions thereafter, as did the Republicans. But representatives could now fairly count on rising in the ranks of their committees (so long as they were re-elected) upon the retirement or death of the more senior members of those committees. Such assurance gave to sitting chairmen and ranking members a degree of independence from dictation that put a new premium on the persuasive skills of party leaders.

Recognition of seniority in the advancement of committee members still left the party committees on committees with the job of assigning vacancies to newcomers and to representatives seeking to switch from one committee to another. The task of filling vacancies was complicated by keen competition among individuals and among state and regional delegations for the right to places on such choice committees as Ways and Means and Appropriations; in the inevitable bargaining, the political loyalties of the competitors weighed as much as their interests and capabilities. The filling of important committee vacancies was to remain a significant tool in the hands of party leaders.

Republican Years: 1919-1931

By the end of the First World War in 1918, a majority of American voters were already anxious for the return to normalcy promised to them two years later by Warren G. Harding as the Republican nominee for President. The midterm elections of 1918 replaced Democratic with Republican majorities in both houses of the 66th Congress (1919-21), during which President Wilson lost his historic battle with the Senate over the Treaty of Versailles. With the election of Harding in 1920 began a decade of undivided Republican control of the executive and legislative branches of the federal government, lasting until Democrats recaptured the House in 1931.

These were not years of presidential leadership or strong party government. Harding's administration was marked by widespread corruption, brought to light by Senate investigators after his death in 1923. As Harding's successor, Calvin Coolidge (1923-29) did little to push his legislative program through Congress. President Herbert Hoover (1929-33) was unable to deal effectively with the economic depression that began soon after he took office. Meanwhile, Republican control of the Senate was occasionally nominal, and a minority of party progressives often held the balance of power. Party conservatives were more successful in keeping control of the House during the 1920s, and legislative conflicts between the Senate and the House were common. A notable case in point involved the Senate-approved "lame duck" amendment to the Constitution, which House leaders managed to block until 1932.

There were some important changes in the organization and procedures of the House in this period. Full authority over money bills was reconcentrated in the Appropriations Committee in 1920, and some minor committees were abolished in 1927. Republican leaders introduced, then abandoned, use of a party Steering Committee to guide their legislative program. Under pressure from progressives, House rules were modified in 1924, but the Rules Committee continued to exercise tight control over the legislative options of members. Meanwhile, the representative nature of the chamber declined as the House put off until 1931 the reapportionment of seats that should have followed the census of 1920.

New Budget System

Until 1920, there was no central system for drawing up the federal budget or for its consideration in Congress. The Secretary of the Treasury did no more than compile the estimates of the various departments, which in the House were referred to eight different committees, each of which would report an appropriation bill with no reference to total expenditures or revenues. Nor were all of the requests of a department considered by one committee and appropriated

in one bill; other committees commonly reported bills that included appropriations. This process, which was repeated in the Senate, led to rising criticism; as Rep. Alvan T. Fuller (R Mass.) put it in 1918: "The President is asking our business men to economize and become more efficient while we continue to be the most inefficient and expensive barnacle that ever attached itself to the ship of state."[41]

To improve control over expenditures within the executive branch, President Wilson in 1919 proposed a new budget system. Although he vetoed the first bill passed by Congress in 1920 (because it placed the comptroller general beyond his power of removal), a second bill, signed by President Harding, became the Budget and Accounting Act of 1921. This measure directed the President to prepare and transmit to Congress each year a budget showing federal revenues and expenditures for the previous and current years and estimated for the ensuing year. It set up a Bureau of the Budget as his agency to do the work, and it created a General Accounting Office under the comptroller general to assist Congress in exercising oversight of the administration of federal funds.

Anticipating the passage of this bill, the House on June 1, 1920, voted to restore to the Committee on Appropriations the jurisdiction over all supply bills granted to it originally in 1865. A sizable number of senior House Republicans and Democrats opposed the move, and the House barely agreed to the special rule bringing the resolution to the floor, which was adopted by a vote of 158 to 154. The resolution, which was then approved by a vote of 200 to 117, provided for an increase in the size of the Appropriations Committee from 21 to 35 members. At the same time, the House barred its conferees on appropriation bills from accepting Senate amendments that contravened the rules of the House unless so authorized by a separate House vote on each such amendment.

Most of the responsibility for reviewing budget estimates was now lodged in 10 five-member subcommittees of the House Appropriations Committee, each of which passed on the requests of one or more agencies. Parallel subcommittees were set up by the Senate Appropriations Committee, and in 1922 it, like the House, was given exclusive authority over money bills. These steps toward a more systematic approach to federal expenditures came at a time of general concern for greater economy in government and helped to hold outgo to little more than $3 billion a year from 1922 to 1930. With revenues of close to $4 billion each year, the public debt was reduced from $25 billion in 1919 to $16 billion in 1930.

Additional House Changes

When the Republicans regained control of the House in 1919, their leading contender for Speaker was Rep. James R. Mann (R Ill.), who had been minority leader since 1911. But Mann had offended many of his party colleagues by objecting to passage of their private bills, while others feared that he would seek to recentralize power in the manner of his mentor and close friend, former Speaker Cannon. So the Republican conference, looking for more of a figurehead as Speaker, nominated the respected but less forceful Frederick H. Gillett (R Mass.), a member of the House since 1893. Mann refused the title of majority leader, which went to Frank W. Mondell (R Wyo.), and for the first time this position was divorced from the chairmanship of the Ways and Means Committee.

In a further effort to decentralize power, the Republicans created a five-member Steering Committee chaired by the majority leader and barred both the Speaker and the chairman of the Rules Committee from sitting on it. Complaints about the narrow range of views and states represented on the Steering Committee led to expansion of its membership to eight in the 67th Congress (1921-23), when Mondell also took to inviting the Speaker, the chairman of Rules and others to sit with the committee, which met almost daily and served as the major organ of party leadership from 1919 to 1925.

With a Republican majority of 300 in the 67th Congress, party leaders nevertheless came in for growing criticism for blocking action on measures with wide support in the House. Rules Chairman Philip P. Campbell (R Kan.), for one, simply refused to report a number of resolutions approved by a majority of his committee to authorize certain investigations. He once told the committee: "You can go to hell. It makes no difference what a majority of you decide. If it meets with my disapproval, it shall not be done. I am the committee. In me repose absolute obstructive powers."[42] And Campbell's right to pocket a resolution was upheld by Speaker Gillett and, on appeal, by the House.

But Campbell and many other Republicans were defeated in the elections of 1922, and when the 68th Congress met in December of 1923 the House consisted of 225 Republicans and 207 Democrats. Lack of a larger majority enabled a group of about 20 reform-minded Republican progressives to hold up the election of a Speaker in an effort to bring about some liberalization of the rules. For two days and eight ballots the two party nominees—Speaker Gillett and Minority Leader Finis J. Garrett (D Tenn.)—received about 195 votes each, while the progressives cast 17 votes for Rep. Henry A. Cooper (R Wis.).

Then Nicholas Longworth (R Ohio), who had succeeded Mondell as majority leader, persuaded the insurgents to support the election of Gillett in return for a promise to allow full debate on revision of the rules in January; Gillett was re-elected Speaker on the ninth ballot. Democrat Henry T. Rainey (Ill.) congratulated Longworth for having steered safely "between the Scylla of progressive Republicanism...and the Charybdis of conservative Republicanism.... There is not a scratch on the ship. The paint is absolutely intact."[43]

The promised debate lasted five days and led to a number of changes in House rules. One, designed to outlaw the "pocket veto" exercised by Chairman Campbell, required the Rules Committee to "present to the House reports concerning rules, joint rules, and order of business within three legislative days of the time when ordered reported by the Committee."[44] The new rule provided also that if the member making the report failed to call it up within the next nine days, any other member designated by the Committee could do so.

The House also agreed at this time, by a vote of 253 to 114, to amend the discharge rule first adopted in 1910. The amended rule reduced from 218 (or a majority of members) to 150 the number required to sign a motion to discharge a committee from further consideration of a bill. Once signed, however, such a motion could be called up only on the first and third Mondays of the month and was subject to other constraints. The single attempt (led by Democrats) to use the new rule in the 68th Congress was successfully thwarted by the Republican leadership.

Disciplining of Progressives

President Coolidge won an easy victory in the election of 1924, when he received 15.7 million votes to 8.4 million for Democrat John W. Davis and 4.8 million for the Progressive candidate, Sen. Robert M. La Follette (R Wis.). At the same time, the Republican majority of 225 in the House was increased to 247 in the 69th Congress. This gain wiped out the leverage that Republican Party Progressives had been able to exert at the beginning of the 68th Congress and opened the way for party leaders to discipline those—including most of the Wisconsin delegation—who had supported La Follette in the 1924 campaign.

By the time the new Congress met on Dec. 7, 1925, the Republican Conference had agreed to nominate Majority Leader Longworth for Speaker (Gillett having been elected to the Senate), to oust Progressive leaders, John M. Nelson and Florian Lampert, both of Wisconsin, from their positions as chairmen of the Committee of Elections and the Committee on Patents, and to let the other insurgents know that their committee assignments would depend on how they voted for Speaker and for a new and tougher discharge rule. The insurgents responded by again nominating and voting for Cooper. As Progressive James A. Frear put it:

"The Wisconsin delegation in Congress today finds itself challenged by those assuming to be in control of the Republican party by threats and intimidation on the one hand and by the offer of party recognition with its favors and patronage on the other. We refuse to compromise, or to bargain with Mr. Longworth or with any other Member of the House on an issue affecting our rights as Representatives in Congress to vote our convictions.... Neither flattery nor suggestions concerning committee assignments nor threats will cause the Wisconsin delegation in the House to deviate...."[45]

Longworth was easily elected Speaker on the first ballot, receiving 229 votes to 173 for Democratic Leader Garrett and 13 for Cooper. By a vote of 210 to 192, the House then agreed to substitute for the discharge rule of 1924 a new rule described by Rep. Charles R. Crisp (D Ga. and son of the one-time Speaker) as one that "hermetically seals the door against any bill ever coming out of a committee when the Steering Committee or the majority leaders desire to kill the bill without putting the members of this House on record on the measure."[46]

The new rule to instruct committees not only required that a majority of the membership (or 218 instead of 150) sign the motion to discharge, but also stipulated that a similar majority second its consideration by a teller vote, for which most members would rarely show up. Moreover, the motion could be called up only on the third Monday of the month, and if it then failed to be seconded as prescribed, it could not be brought up again during the same Congress. (Not surprisingly, the rule was never invoked during its life, which ended when Democrats revived the old discharge rule in 1931.)

Ten days later, when the Republican slate of committee assignments was submitted to the House, those Progressives who had voted for Cooper and against the new rule found themselves demoted to the bottom of their committees. (Senate Progressives who had supported La Follette were also dropped to the foot of their committees.) Other Republicans had apparently been brought into line by threats of similar action, according to Minority Leader Garrett, who said "it was demanded that 71 gentlemen who at the beginning of the 68th Congress thought a discharge

Terms and Sessions of Congress

Under the Constitution, representatives were to be elected "every second year" and Congress was to meet at least once each year "on the first Monday in December, unless they shall by law appoint a different day." But the Continental Congress, which had been asked by the Federal Convention to fix "the time and place for commencing proceedings" of the new Government, told the First Congress to meet on the first Wednesday of March 1789, which happened to be the 4th. Soon afterward, Congress decided that the terms of office of the President, senators and representatives would begin on March 4 of the year following their election and expire, in the case of representatives, two years later.

Out of these decisions developed the practice of long and short sessions. The Fourth Congress, for example, met for the first time on Dec. 7, 1795, and remained in session until June 1, 1796. A second session, beginning Dec. 5 of that year, lasted until March 3, 1797, when by law the terms of the representatives elected in 1794 expired. Congresses thereafter were often called into special session by the President, or themselves fixed earlier dates for meeting. But for more than 140 years Congress stuck closely to the basic pattern of two sessions—the first a long one of six months or so that began in December more than a year after the elections, and the second a short one that met from December to March after the next elections.

The political consequences of this schedule became apparent in short order. Presidents inaugurated on March 4 were generally free to make recess appointments and take other actions without consulting Congress until the following December. The short sessions became prey to filibusters and other delaying tactics by members determined to block legislation that would die upon the automatic adjournment of Congress on March 3. Moreover, the Congresses that met in short session always included a substantial number of "lame-duck" members who had been defeated at the polls, yet were able quite often to determine the legislative outcome of the session.

Dissatisfaction with the short session began to mount after 1900. During the Wilson administration, each of four such sessions ended with a Senate filibuster and the loss of important bills including one or more appropriation bills.

Sen. George W. Norris (R Neb.) became the leading advocate of a constitutional amendment to abolish the short session by starting the terms of Congress and the President in January instead of March. The Senate approved the Norris amendment five times during the 1920s, only to see it blocked in the House each time. It was finally approved by both chambers in 1932, and became the Twentieth Amendment upon ratification by the 36th state in 1933.

The amendment established Jan. 3 of the year following election as the day on which the terms of senators and representatives would begin and end, and Jan. 20 as the day on which the President and Vice President would take office.

The Twentieth Amendment provided also that Congress should meet annually on Jan. 3 "unless they shall by law appoint a different day." The second session of the 73rd Congress was the first to convene on the new date, Jan. 3, 1934, while Franklin D. Roosevelt was the first President to be inaugurated on Jan. 20, at the start of his second term in 1937.

The amendment was intended to permit Congress to extend its first session for as long as necessary and to complete the work of its second session before the next election, thereby obviating legislation by a "lame-duck" body. Congress met in almost continuous session during World War II, however, and the 81st Congress met after the elections of 1950 to deal with the Korean War. The Senate alone met after the 1954 elections to act on the censure of Sen. Joseph R. McCarthy (R Wis.). And in 1970 the 91st Congress resumed work after the midterm elections. By the mid-1970s, the average Congress was in session for more than 20 months of its 24-month tenure, and its workload was still mounting. *(Sessions of Congress, Appendix)*

---

rule was proper should change their votes, demanded that they should eat the bravest word that many of them ever spoke in order to maintain their standing with the party."[47]

These developments at the beginning of the 69th Congress reflected Longworth's determination to play the role of party leader in the House. He had already stated his belief that it was the duty of the Speaker, "standing squarely on the platform of his party, to assist in so far as he properly can the enactment of legislation in accordance with the declared principles and policies of his party and by the same token resist the enactment of legislation in violation thereof...."[48] As Speaker, Longworth ignored the party Steering Committee and for six years (1925-31) personally took charge of the House with the aid of Majority Leader John Q. Tilson (R Conn.) and Rules Committee Chairman Bertrand H. Snell (R N.Y.).

Norris Amendment Blocked

The power of House Republican leaders during the 1920s was illustrated by their success in blocking an amendment to the Constitution designed to abolish the regular "short" session of every Congress by advancing from March to January the time when the life of the previous Congress would expire and that of the new one begin. House leaders liked the short session because its automatic termination on March 3 strengthened their ability to control the legislative output of the House. Sponsored by Sen. George W. Norris (R Neb.), the progressive who had helped to curb the powers of Speaker Cannon in 1910, the proposed abolition of the short session was approved six times by the Senate before the House in 1932, finally consented to what became the Twentieth Amendment.

The effort to adopt what was popularly called the "lame duck" amendment began during the 67th Congress in 1922. Sen. Thaddeus H. Caraway (D Ark.) offered a resolution "that all members defeated at the recent polls abstain from voting on any but routine legislation." When his request that the resolution be referred to the Agriculture Committee, chaired by Sen. Norris, was greeted by laughter from his colleagues, he explained: "I presume that by ordinary parliamentary procedure the concurrent resolution would go to the Committee on the Judiciary but...I have every reason to believe that it will slumber there, as some other resolutions that I introduced found a morgue there; and I should like to have the Senate itself pass upon this one."[49]

The Agriculture Committee reported instead a joint resolution embodying the "lame duck" amendment, and the Senate endorsed it on Feb. 13 by a vote of 63 to 6—well over the two-thirds majority required by the Constitution.

The Norris resolution was approved a week later by the House Election Committee, and a special rule for its consideration was ordered reported by majority vote of the Rules Committee. But the chairman of the Rules Committee, Rep. Philip P. Campbell, pocketed the rule, refusing to report it. Then, while sitting as Speaker for the ailing Gillett during the last few days of the session, Campbell (who was himself a "lame duck," having been defeated the previous November) refused to recognize members who were seeking recognition for the purpose of appealing to the House to override his refusal to report the rule.

On March 18, 1924, in the first session of the 68th Congress, the Senate again adopted the Norris resolution, by a vote of 63 to 7, and three days later it was again reported to the House by the Election Committee. This time, however, it was blocked in the Rules Committee, leading Norris to accuse House leaders of "killing it, not directly but smothering it without giving the House of Representatives an opportunity to vote." Norris added that the resolution was "being held up because machine politicans can get more out of this [legislative] jam than the people's representatives can get."[50] The resolution died with the adjournment of the 68th Congress on March 3, 1925.

The Senate approved the proposed amendment for a third time on Feb. 15, 1926, in the first session of the 69th Congress, by a vote of 73 to 2, and on Feb. 24 it was again reported to the House by a unanimous vote of the Election Committee. Chairman Hays B. White (R Kan.) then discussed the problem he faced under the rules: "Gentlemen, realize how meager is the chance to reach the resolution under the Calendar Wednesday rule. That is the logical and proper rule under which it should be considered.... I cannot get unanimous consent...nor can I hope to pass a measure as fundamental as this under a motion to suspend the rules.... The last alternative is for the Rules Committee to grant a special rule for its early consideration."[51] But the rule was not forthcoming before the final adjournment of the 69th Congress on March 3, 1927.

On Jan. 4, 1928, in the first session of the 70th Congress, the Senate again adopted the Norris resolution, by a vote of 65 to 6, and this time its supporters in the House brought it to the floor. Rep. Ole J. Kvale (Farmer-Labor Minn.), said the leaders who had kept the House from voting on it for so long "did not dare block it any longer."[52] Rules Committee Chairman Snell acknowledged that "if it had not been for the significant application of these two words, lame duck, the propaganda that has been spread throughout this country would never have been one-half as effective as it has been, and if it had not been for that propaganda I doubt whether this proposition would be on the floor at this time."[53] The amendment was endorsed by a majority on March 9, 1928, but the vote of 209 to 157 fell 35 short of the two-thirds required for approval.

The Senate approved the Norris resolution for a fifth time on June 7, 1929, by a vote of 64 to 9. A slightly amended version was reported in the House on April 8, 1930,

but was not taken up on the floor until Feb. 24, 1931, a week before adjournment. Speaker Longworth then offered a further amendment, to provide that the second session of each Congress should expire automatically on May 4. The Longworth amendment was adopted by a vote of 230 to 148 before the resolution itself was approved, 290 to 93. But the measure was locked in conference when Congress adjourned on March 3.

When the 72nd Congress convened in December 1931, however, Democrats took control of the House, and after the Senate had adopted the resolution for the sixth time on Jan. 6, 1932, 63 to 7, the House quickly followed suit by a vote of 335 to 56 on Feb. 16. Within less than a year, the Twentieth Amendment had been ratified by three-fourths of the states.

Struggle Over Reapportionment

By 1920, no state had lost a seat in the House through reapportionment since Maine and New Hampshire were deprived of one each after the census of 1880. The reason was that Congress had regularly agreed to increase the total membership by a sufficient number to prevent such a loss. Thus the House was enlarged to 357 members after the census of 1890, to 391 after that of 1900 and to 435 after that of 1910.

The 1920 census showed that unless the size of the House were again increased, 11 states would lose seats through reapportionment while eight would gain. One argument against such a shift was that voiced by Rep. John E. Rankin (D Miss.) in 1921: "The census was taken at a time when we were just emerging from the World War, and when so many thousands of people had left the farms and the small towns temporarily and gone to the large cities of the North and East that a reapportionment under that census would necessarily take from Mississippi and other agricultural states their just representation and place it to the credit of the congested centers."[54]

Limit on Size of House. To avoid reducing the representation of any state, the House Census Committee early in 1921 reported a bill that would have increased the membership to 483, with the additional seats going to 25 states whose population relative to that of the others had grown the most. But the House proceeded to reverse the committee, voting 267 to 76 to keep the membership at 435. Proponents of that limit argued that the great size of the membership had already resulted in serious limitations on the right to debate and an overconcentration of power in the hands of the leadership. Much was also made of the increased costs of a larger membership.

The bill passed by the House on Jan. 19, 1921, therefore, provided for reapportionment on the basis of the existing membership and would have taken 12 seats from 11 states. But the Senate failed to act on the measure before the 66th Congress adjourned on March 3. When the 67th Congress was called into special session a month later, the House Census Committee, by a vote of 9 to 7, reported a new bill that would have fixed the membership at 460 and cost only two states—Maine and Missouri—one seat each. But on Oct. 14, 1921, the House voted 146 to 142 to recommit the bill to committee, and no further action was taken.

By 1925, it was clear that the wartime shift of population from rural to urban areas was not to be reversed. Such rapidly growing cities as Los Angeles and Detroit began to clamor for the increased representation in the House to which they were entitled. When the House Census Committee still refused to report a new bill, Rep. Henry E. Barbour (R Calif.) moved, April 8, 1926, to discharge the committee from further consideration of a bill similar to that passed in 1921. Barbour argued that the bill was privileged under the Constitution, while Rules Committee Chairman Snell, raising a point of order, denied that reapportionment was mandatory under the Constitution.

Speaker Longworth found that three of his predecessors—Keifer, Reed and Henderson had ruled, to the contrary, that Congress was required to order a new apportionment after each census. But Longworth said he doubted whether such a ruling was correct, and he put to the House this question: "Is the consideration of the bill called up by the motion of the gentleman from California in order as a question of constitutional privilege, the rule prescribing the order of business to the contrary notwithstanding?"[55] By a vote of 87 yeas to 265 nays, the House decided the question in the negative.

Coolidge for Reapportionment. In January 1927, President Coolidge made it known for the first time that he favored enactment of a reapportionment bill. When the House Census Committee refused to act, its chairman, E. Hart Fenn (R Conn.), moved on March 2, the day before adjournment, to suspend the rules and pass his bill to authorize a reapportionment of the House by the Secretary of Commerce on the basis of the 1930 census. With only 40 minutes of debate allowed under the rule (which also required a two-thirds vote) and a filibuster under way in the Senate, the House rejected the Fenn motion by a vote of 183 to 197.

The Fenn bill was rewritten early in the 70th Congress, but on May 18, 1928, the House voted 186 to 165 to recommit it to committee. After further revision, the measure was passed by voice vote on Jan. 11, 1929. Reported to the Senate four days later, it was finally abandoned by its supporters on Feb. 27—five days before the end of the session—in the face of a threatened filibuster by senators from states that were destined to lose seats in the House.

President Hoover called the 71st Congress into special session on April 15, 1929, and listed provision for the 1930 census and for reapportionment as matters of emergency legislation. On June 13, 1929, the Senate passed, 48 to 37, a combined census-reapportionment bill that had been approved by voice vote of the House two days earlier.

Automatic Reapportionment. The 1929 law established a permanent system for reapportioning the 435 seats in the House following each census. It provided that immediately after the convening of the 71st Congress in December 1930, the President should transmit to Congress a statement of the apportionment of representatives to each state according to the existing size of the House. Failing enactment of new apportionment legislation by Congress, that apportionment would go into effect for ensuing elections without further action and would remain in effect until another census had been taken. Reapportionment would be effected in the same manner after each decennial count of the population.

The reapportionment based on the 1930 census resulted in a major reshuffling of House seats in the 73rd Congress, which was elected in 1932. Twenty-one states lost a total of 27 seats; Missouri alone lost three, and Georgia, Iowa, Kentucky and Pennsylvania two each. Among the 11 states to which these seats were transferred, California alone gained nine, increasing the size of its delegation from 11 to 20. Other states to win more than one additional seat were Michigan (four), Texas (three), and New Jersey, New York and Ohio (two each).

Democratic Years: 1931-1945

The Great Depression that began in 1929 foreshadowed the end of Republican rule in Washington. The party's majority of 267 in the House of the 71st Congress (1929-31) evaporated in the mid-term elections of 1930, when the returns indicated that the next House would be composed of 218 Republicans, 216 Democrats and one independent. By the time the 72nd Congress met on Dec. 7, 1931, however, 14 representatives-elect (including Speaker Longworth) had died, and special elections to fill the vacancies had resulted in a net gain of four seats for the Democrats, giving them control of the House.

With 12 million Americans unemployed by 1932, Democrat Franklin D. Roosevelt was elected President along with commanding Democratic majorities in both houses of Congress. A strong party leader, Roosevelt in his first term (1933-37) obtained the enactment of a broad range of New Deal economic and social measures. He was less successful in dealing with Congress in his second term (1937-41), when he came into conflict with a conservative coalition opposed to his domestic programs. Germany's attack on Poland in 1939, followed by the fall of France in 1940, helped to re-elect Roosevelt to an unprecedented third term (1941-45) that was largely devoted to waging and winning World War II. But legislative-executive relations deteriorated during the war and when Roosevelt died at the beginning of a fourth term in 1945, Congress was in open rebellion against his plans for postwar reconstruction.

The Democrats who led the House during these years worked closely with the President and did their best, by and large, to marshal support for administration requests. But their power to shape the legislative output of the House was sharply curtailed after 1937, when a coalition of southern Democrats and Republicans gained effective control of the Rules Committee, which had been a key arm of House leaders since 1880. The focus of reformers became much broader during the war, however, when the capacity of Congress as a whole to function effectively as a co-equal branch came under attack. This situation led to passage of the Legislative Reorganization Act of 1946.

Party Leaders

The long tenure of southern Democrats commenced when the party took control of the House in 1931. John Nance Garner of Texas, who had become minority leader on the retirement of Rep. Finis J. Garrett of Tennessee in 1929, was elected Speaker. A member since 1903, Garner was then the second-ranking Democrat in the House. Third-ranking Henry T. Rainey (Ill.) was named majority leader. But southerners became chairmen of 28 of the 47 standing committees of the House. Among them were Edward W. Pou (N.C., since 1901), chairman of Rules; Joseph W. Byrns (Tenn., since 1909), Appropriations; James W. Collier (Miss., since 1909), Ways and Means; and Sam Rayburn (Texas, since 1913), Interstate and Foreign Commerce.

When Garner became Vice President in 1933, House Democrats elevated Rainey to Speaker and made Byrns the new majority leader. Rainey died in 1934 and Byrns was elected Speaker at the beginning of the 74th Congress in 1935, to be succeeded as majority leader by William B. Bankhead (Ala.), who had become chairman of the Rules Committee on the death of Pou in 1934. When Byrns died in 1936, Bankhead became Speaker and the Democrats chose Rayburn as majority leader. Bankhead remained Speaker until his death in 1940, when he was succeeded by Rayburn, and a northern Democrat—John W. McCormack of Massachusetts—became majority leader. Rayburn and McCormack remained in these posts until Republicans took control of the House in 1947.

While the Democrats had been in the minority during the 1920s, southerners had constituted more than one-half of their ranks and there was little occasion for complaint about an unwarranted influence in party councils. But when the party won control of the House in 1931, northern and western Democrats pressed for a larger voice in committee assignments. They proposed entrusting the assignments to a new committee on committees (in place of the one composed of Democratic members of the Ways and Means Committee) to be made up of one member from each state having Democratic representation in the House. This committee would also choose a nine-member steering committee to be in charge of the legislative program.

Steering Committee. These steps were not agreed to in 1931, although additions to the Ways and Means Committee (including McCormack) brought about a better balance of geographical representation. By 1933, however, the Democratic majority in the House had been increased to 313 members, nearly two-thirds of whom were from states outside the South. So it was agreed to set up a Steering Committee composed of the Speaker, majority leader and whip, chairmen of the Appropriations, Ways and Means and Rules Committees and of the party caucus, plus 15 representatives from as many zones to be chosen by Democratic members within those areas. The Steering Committee operated with some success during the 73rd Congress (1933-35), but fell into disuse thereafter.

Gag Rules. The Rules Committee itself was the major tool of House Democratic leaders during the 73rd Congress, which was called into special session by President Roosevelt on March 9, 1933, and asked to pass a series of emergency recovery measures almost sight unseen. Ten of the measures were brought to the House floor under special "closed" rules—drafted by the Rules Committee and adopted by majority vote—that barred all except committee amendments, waived points of order, and sharply limited debate. Among the laws enacted at this session of 100 days with the help of these "gag" rules were the Emergency Banking Act, the Economy Act, the Emergency Relief Act, the first Agricultural Adjustment Act, the Tennessee Valley Authority Act, and the National Industrial Recovery Act.

Faced with mounting opposition to cuts in veterans' benefits and government salaries ordered under the Economy Act, the Rules Committee at the opening of the second session on Jan. 3, 1934, brought in a rule to bar amendments to any appropriation bill for the remainder of the session that would conflict with the economy program of 1933. The purpose, said Rep. Bankhead, was to have the House "deliberately determine for today and hereafter...whether they are going to follow the President's recommendations or not."[56]

Minority Leader Bertrand H. Snell (R N.Y.), saying that he had never been opposed to special rules so long as they were "fairly fair," called this "the most vicious, the most far-reaching special rule" ever proposed. No majority, he said, had "ever dared bring in a rule that not only hog-tied and prohibited the members from expressing themselves on the legislation in hand but even extended through the entire session of Congress." The real purpose, said Snell, was that "you think it will be easier to hog-tie your own men today than it will after we have been in ses-

sion for five months."[57] Snell was joined by all of the Republicans, 84 Democrats and five Farmer-Labor members in voting against the rule, which was barely adopted, 197 to 192.

The only major change in the standing rules of the House in this period involved the discharge rule. When the Democrats took control of the House in 1931, they replaced the unworkable rule of 1925 with that of 1924, which was altered slightly to reduce from 150 to 145 the number of signatures needed to place a discharge motion on the calendar. But that number was increased to 218 or a majority of the House (as it had been from 1910 to 1924) at the beginning of the 74th Congress in 1935, when Democrats in the House numbered 322 and the leadership was finding it difficult to maintain party unity.

The Conservative Coalition

Party unity was badly shaken at the beginning of the 75th Congress in 1937 when President Roosevelt submitted a plan to reorganize the Supreme Court, through the appointment of additional justices, in order to get a majority that could be counted on to uphold the constitutionality of New Deal measures, of which several had been overturned. This plan to "pack" the Court (which died in the Senate) created a furor in the country and led to a new alignment of conservative Democrats and Republicans in Congress generally and on the House Rules Committee in particular.

The "conservative coalition" first appeared in August of 1937, when the Rules Committee voted 10 to 4 against granting a special rule for floor consideration of an administration bill that eventually became the Fair Labor Standards Act. The committee was then chaired by Rep. John O'Connor (D N.Y.) and was composed of five northern Democrats, five southern Democrats, and four Republicans. After its refusal to grant the special rule, House leaders obtained 218 signatures on a discharge petition, but when they brought the bill to the floor in December the House voted 216 to 198 to recommit it to the Labor Committee.

When the Rules Committee in 1938 again refused to clear the wage-hour bill, House leaders once again resorted to the discharge rule to bring the bill to a vote, obtaining passage this time by a margin of 314 to 97. (Although the House had occasionally passed a bill by use of the discharge rule, the Fair Labor Standards Act of 1938 was the first such measure to become law.) Chairman O'Connor's defection in this case made him one of the targets of President Roosevelt's attempted purge of anti-New Deal Democrats in the 1938 primaries. At a press conference, Aug. 16, 1938, Mr. Roosevelt denounced the Rules chairman as "one of the most effective obstructionists in the lower house."[58] O'Connor, unlike other prominent targets of the purge effort, lost his bid for renomination.

O'Connor was succeeded as chairman of the Rules Committee in 1939 by Rep. Adolph J. Sabath of Illinois, the senior House Democrat by then and an ardent New Dealer. But Sabath continued to be outvoted in the committee by a coalition of Republicans and southern Democrats led by Reps. E. E. Cox (D Ga.) and Howard W. Smith (D Va.). During the 76th Congress (1939-40), the committee began the practice of demanding, as the price of sending administration bills to the floor, substantive changes in these bills to accord with the views of conservatives.

Not only did the coalition use its power on the Rules Committee to block or water down administration

Growth of the Congressional Workload, 1789-1974

	First Congress (1789-91)	80th Congress (1947-49)	86th Congress (1959-61)	93rd Congress (1973-74)
Measures introduced:	——*	12,090	20,164	26,222
House	——	8,561	15,506	21,095
Senate	——	3,529	4,658	5,127
Laws Enacted:	118	1,363	1,292	772
Public	108	906	800	649
Private	10	457	492	123
Nominations Confirmed	——	54,796	89,900	131,254

*No figures available for bills introduced in 1st Congress.

Source: Library of Congress, Congressional Research Service; *Congressional Record.*

measures; it was also in a position to clear measures opposed by the administration. Thus the committee in 1939 authorized an investigation of the National Labor Relations Board; in 1943, an investigation of activities of executive agencies; and in 1944, an investigation of the government's seizure of properties of Montgomery Ward & Co. All were intended to embarrass the administration. Also in 1944, the committee reported a rule to bring to the floor a price control bill that had been rejected by the Banking and Currency Committee and never reported to the House. Speaker Rayburn took the floor to denounce the rule, saying the Rules Committee "was never set up to be a legislative committee," and the House voted it down.[59]

At the beginning of the 79th Congress in 1945, the size of the Rules Committee was reduced from 14 to 12 members consisting of eight Democrats and four Republicans. Sabath was still chairman, but whenever Reps. Cox and Smith decided to vote with the Republicans they could produce a tie that would block committee action. In 1945, for example, the committee by a vote of six to six refused a direct request by President Truman for a rule that would permit the House to vote on a bill to establish a permanent Fair Employment Practices Commission. The coalition also blocked a rule to permit consideration of an administration bill to raise the minimum wage from 40 to 65 cents an hour.

In 1946, when the Rules Committee was asked to clear an administration-backed labor relations bill reported by the House Labor Committee, it reported instead a rule to permit substitution of a more drastic measure sponsored by Francis H. Case (R S.D.), which had just been introduced. Chairman Sabath denounced the action as arbitrary and undemocratic, but in this case a majority of House members upheld the committee majority by adopting the rule and passing the Case substitute, which was later vetoed.

The Rules Committee thus ceased to be a dependable arm of the Democratic leadership after 1937, when the coalition of conservative Democrats and Republicans took control. While the views of members of the coalition on social and economic issues were in conflict with those of most Democrats in the House, they frequently reflected the legislative preferences of a bipartisan majority, and it was the support of this broader conservative coalition that enabled those who controlled the Rules Committee to make the most effective use of its powers.

1946 Legislative Reorganization Act

Talk of the need for congressional reform mounted during World War II, when the powers of the executive branch were vastly enlarged. A report of the American Political Science Association asserted in 1945: "Congress must modernize its machinery and methods to fit modern conditions if it is to keep pace with a greatly enlarged and active executive branch. This is a better approach than that which seeks to meet the problem by reducing and hamstringing the executive. A strong and more representative legislature, in closer touch with and better informed about the administration, is the antidote to bureaucracy."[60]

Responding to such criticisms, the House and Senate agreed early in 1945 to establish a Joint Committee on the Organization of Congress composed of six members from each house equally divided among Democrats and Republicans. Sen. Robert M. La Follette Jr. (Prog Wis.) was named chairman with Rep. A. S. Mike Monroney (D Okla.) as vice chairman. From March 13 through June 29, 1945, the group took extensive testimony from more than 100 witnesses, including many members of Congress.

Among the proposals heard were several to restrict the power of the House Rules Committee. Rep. Christian A. Herter (R Mass.) thought the committee should be required to grant, within a specified time, requests for special orders on bills favorably reported by the legislative committees. Herter said: "The House Committee on Rules should not have the power of deciding which committee reports shall be considered by the whole House, but should be confined merely to determining the order of their consideration. The Rules Committee ought not to be permitted to prevent the submission of favorable committee reports to the whole House."[61] Rep. Sherman Adams (R N.H.) thought a unanimous report from a legislative committee should automatically give a bill the right of way without reference to Rules.

But in its final report on March 4, 1946, the La Follette-Monroney committee made no recommendations concerning Rules "because of a lack of agreement within the committee as to workable changes in existing practices."[62] Nor did the committee recommend any of the various proposals it had received to select committee chairmen on some other basis than seniority, or proposals to make it easier to limit debate in the Senate. The report nevertheless included a broad range of proposals designed to streamline the committee structure, strengthen congressional control over the budget, reduce the workload of Congress, and improve staff assistance, and most of these reforms were incorporated in the Legislative Reorganization Act of 1946 that was signed by President Truman on Aug. 2. The major provisions of the act dealt with committees, the legislative budget, the congressional workload, staff and salaries.

Committees. The law reduced the number of standing committees from 33 to 15 in the Senate and from 48 to 19 in the House, dropping inactive committees and merging others with related functions. The House committees were: Agriculture, Appropriations, Armed Services, Banking and Currency (name changed to Banking, Currency and Housing in 1975), District of Columbia, Education and Labor, Expenditures in the Executive Departments (name changed to Government Operations in 1952), Foreign Affairs (name changed to International Relations in 1975), House Administration, Interior and Insular Affairs, Interstate and Foreign Commerce, Judiciary, Merchant Marine and Fisheries, Post Office and Civil Service, Public Works (name changed to Public Works and Transportation in 1975), Rules, Un-American Activities (name changed to Internal Security in 1969), Veterans' Affairs, and Ways and Means. (Un-American Activities, a select committee before and during World War II, had been made a standing committee by a 208-186 vote of the House on Jan. 3, 1945. The committee was abolished in 1975.)

All standing committees (except Appropriations) were directed to fix regular days for meeting, keep complete records of committee action including votes, and open all hearings to the public except executive sessions for marking up the bills or for voting, or where the committee by a majority vote orders an executive session. The act made it the duty of each committee chairman to report or cause to be reported promptly to the House any measure approved by his committee and to take or cause to be taken necessary steps to bring the matter to a vote. But no measure was to be reported from any committee unless a majority of the members were actually present.

Legislative Budget. The act directed the House Ways and Means, the Senate Finance, and the Appropriations Committees of both houses, acting as a Joint Budget Committee, to prepare each year a legislative budget, including estimates of total receipts and expenditures. The Budget Committee's report was to be accompanied by a concurrent resolution for adopting the budget and fixing the amount to be appropriated. Congress was prohibited from appropriating more than estimated receipts without at the same time authorizing an increase in the public debt. The act did not include a proposal that the President be required to reduce all appropriations by a uniform percentage if expenditures were later found to be exceeding receipts.

Workload. The act prohibited the introduction of private bills for the payment of pensions or tort claims, the construction of bridges, or the correction of military records—categories of legislation that at one time consumed much time. But Congress did not accept the Joint Committee's proposal that the District of Columbia be given home rule, a step that would have eliminated the District Committees in both houses and a considerable amount of legislative work.

Staff. The act authorized each standing committee to appoint four professional and six clerical staff members, although no limit was placed on the number that could be hired by the Appropriations Committees. It also made the Legislative Reference Service, which provided information for committees and members requesting it, a separate department of the Library of Congress. The Joint Committee had recommended the appointment of a director of personnel, authorized to establish the equivalent of a Civil Service for legislative employees, but this proposal was eliminated in the Senate.

Salaries. The act increased the salaries of senators and representatives from $10,000 to $12,500, effective in 1947, and retained an existing $2,500 non-taxable expense allowance for all members. The salaries of the Vice President and the Speaker were raised to $20,000. The Act also brought members of Congress under the Civil Service Retirement Act and made them eligible for benefits at age 62 after at least six years of service.

The Legislative Reorganization Act also included, as Title III, the Federal Regulation of Lobbying Act which for the first time required lobbyists to register with and report their expenditures to the clerk of the House. But it did not include a provision, recommended by the La Follette-Monroney committee, that both parties establish seven-member policy committees in each chamber, with the majority policy committees to "serve as a formal council to meet regularly with the executive, to facilitate the formulation and carrying out of national policy and to improve relationships between the executive and legislative branches of government."[63] (The Senate, but not the House, agreed later in 1946 to set up party Policy Committees.)

Despite its shortcomings, the 1946 act was regarded at the time as a major achievement. But its provisions for a legislative budget soon proved to be unworkable, while the Regulation of Lobbying Act was too weak to shed much light on the purposes and activities of pressure groups. In reducing the number of standing committees, it was hoped to limit representatives to serving on one committee (and senators on two) in order to make more efficient use of their time. But this practice broke down in later years with the establishment in both chambers of numerous subcommittees and several select committees. The reform of 1946 skirted the issue of the distribution of power within Congress and did not resolve the question of the balance of power between Congress and the executive; these remained troublesome issues throughout the postwar years.

Postwar Developments: 1945-1969

The Democrats lost control of the House and Senate to the Republicans in the 80th Congress (1947-48) and the 83rd (1953-54) but won majorities in all of the other Congresses from 1949 through 1975. Meanwhile, the presidency passed from Democrat Harry S Truman (1945-52) to Republican Dwight D. Eisenhower (1953-60), who was followed by Democrats John F. Kennedy (1961-63) and Lyndon B. Johnson (1963-68) and Republicans Richard M. Nixon (1969-74) and Gerald R. Ford (1974—). Thus during two years under Truman, six under Eisenhower, five under Nixon and the first two years of the Ford administration, the President was faced with a Congress controlled by the other party.

These periods of divided government tended to emphasize the partisan aspects of conflict between the President and Congress over public policy. But none of the postwar Presidents was in full command of his own party in Congress, whether it was in the majority or minority, and all were forced at times to seek bipartisan support to get their programs enacted. House Democrats always included 60 or more southern conservatives who were opposed to many of their party's economic and social programs, while a score of moderate to liberal Republicans were frequently at odds with the party's conservative majority.

Leadership in the House was relatively stable in this period. As after the Civil War and World War I, the control of federal expenditures became a central issue after World War II, and attempts by Congress generally and the House Appropriations Committee in particular to exercise the power of the purse were matters of controversy. There was continuing agitation over the power of the House Rules Committee to block or reshape major legislation, leading to several efforts to restrict the powers of the committee. Talk of the need for broad-scale congressional reform increased in the 1960s, and in 1970 the House finally agreed to a reorganization bill that had cleared the Senate in 1967.

Party Leaders

Sam Rayburn of Texas was the unrivaled leader of House Democrats from 1940 until his death in 1961, serving as Speaker in all but the Republican-controlled 80th and 83rd Congresses, when he acted as minority leader. Rayburn was a strong Speaker whose influence was enhanced by his veneration of the House as an institution and his high personal standing with most of his colleagues. Faced with a divided party on many issues, he relied heavily on his personal friendships with key members on both sides of the aisle to attain his ends. And younger Democrats who followed his advice—"to get along, go along"—could expect to be rewarded with preferment of some kind, especially if they could demonstrate talent and a capacity for hard work.[64]

Rayburn's preferences were controlling when it came to Democratic committee assignments. In 1948 he obtained the removal from the Un-American Activities Committee of three Democrats who had supported Dixiecrat Strom Thurmond in the 1948 presidential campaign. He saw to it that Democrats named to vacancies on the Ways and Means Committee were favorable to reciprocal trade bills and opposed to reductions in the oil depletion allowance. And he turned the Education and Labor Committee from a predominantly conservative into a liberal body during the 1950s by an infusion of younger Democrats. But Rayburn resisted pressure from party liberals to restructure the Rules Committee until 1961, when he reluctantly agreed to go along.

When Rayburn died late that year after 49 years in the House, Democrats chose John W. McCormack of

Sam Rayburn

Massachusetts, who had served as majority leader during Rayburn's entire tenure as Speaker. Carl Albert (D Okla.) was named majority leader at the same time. McCormack's performance as Speaker suffered by comparison with that of Rayburn. Criticism of his weakness as a party leader culminated at the beginning of the 91st Congress in 1969, when 58 Democrats voted for Morris K. Udall (D Ariz.) for Speaker in the party caucus.

Although easily re-elected Speaker, McCormack decided in 1970 to retire at the end of his term, after 42 years in the House, and Carl Albert was designated to succeed him as Speaker. Hale Boggs (D La.) became majority leader when Albert moved up. Albert was re-elected Speaker for the 93rd and 94th Congresses. Thomas P. O'Neill Jr. (D Mass.) succeeded Boggs, who died in an airplane accident, as majority leader in 1972.

House Republicans were led from 1939 to 1959 by Joseph W. Martin Jr. (R Mass.), who also served as Speaker in the 80th and 83rd Congresses, when Charles A. Halleck (R Ind.) held the post of majority leader. Martin, a close friend of Rayburn's, was considered by more conservative House Republicans to be too accommodating to the Democratic leadership during the 1950s, and in 1959 he lost his post as minority leader to Halleck, an outspoken partisan. In time, Halleck incurred the opposition of younger Republicans seeking a more forceful and positive style of leadership, and in 1965 he was himself ousted when the Republican Conference, by a 73-67 vote, named Gerald R. Ford (R Mich.) as minority leader. John J. Rhodes (R Ariz.) became minority leader in 1973 when Ford assumed the vice presidency.

Efforts to Control Spending

In 1947, pursuant to the requirement of the Legislative Reorganization Act of 1946, the Republican-controlled 80th Congress formed a Joint Committee on the Legislative Budget which quickly agreed to ceilings on appropriations and expenditures that were substantially under the amounts projected in President Truman's budget. The House approved these ceilings, but the Senate increased them and insisted that any budget surplus be used to reduce the public debt rather than to provide a tax cut desired by House leaders. As a result, the resolution embodying the legislative budget died in conference.

In 1948, both chambers reached quick agreement on a legislative budget that projected a surplus of $10 billion (or more than twice the President's estimate) and paved the way for passage of a tax cut over the President's veto. But Republican leaders expressed doubt about the efficacy of the legislative budget as a device for reducing expenditures. Rep. John Taber (N.Y.), then chairman of the House Appropriations Committee, called it "a stab in the dark."[65] His Senate counterpart, H. Styles Bridges (N.H.) said it was "a pre-game guess at the final score."[66] In fact, the projected surplus vanished in fiscal 1949, which ended with a deficit of $1.8 billion.

When the Democrats took control of the 81st Congress, Rep. Clarence Cannon (D Mo.) again became chairman of the House Appropriations Committee. In his view, the legislative budget was "unworkable and impracticable." He told the House: "We have tried it [legislative budget]. We gave it every opportunity. It cannot be made effective. We can no more expect success...with this well-meant but hopeless proposal than we can expect a verdict from the jury before it has heard the evidence."[67] Congress put off a decision by voting to postpone until May 1 the deadline for the Joint Committee's recommendations, but these were never forthcoming. The provisions of the 1946 act for a legislative budget remained a part of the law, but Congress made no further effort to comply with them.

In 1950 Cannon tried another approach to expenditure control by having his committee draft a single omnibus appropriations bill that carried almost $37 billion in spending authority as finally enacted. But this bill was quickly outdated by the Korean War and the need for large supplemental appropriations. More important, the omnibus approach had the effect of reducing the authority of the Appropriations Committee's subcommittees and their chairmen. Cannon asserted that "every predatory lobbyist, every pressure group seeking to get its hands into the U.S. Treasury, every bureaucrat seeking to extend his empire downtown is opposed to the consolidated bill."[68] But in 1951 the committee voted 31 to 18 to return to the traditional method of separate appropriation bills.

Cannon and his committee were in full agreement, however, in opposing the concept of a Joint Budget Committee, to be composed of several members of the Senate and House Appropriations Committees. Bills to create such a group were passed by the Senate eight times between 1952 and 1967 but were never accepted by the House. Rep. George H. Mahon (D Texas), who succeeded Cannon as chairman of the House Committee in 1964, summed up the prevailing view of the House on this proposal in 1965 when he said that "every key provision of the bill...is, in my judgment, either unsound, unworkable, or unnecessary."[69]

House-Senate Feud. Behind Mahon's statement lay a long history of resentment over the Senate's claim to co-equal status in the appropriations process, where the House had always asserted its primacy. The issue boiled over in 1962 when the House Appropriations Committee demanded that conference meetings (traditionally held on the Senate side) be rotated between the Senate and House sides of the Capitol. The Senate Appropriations Committee countered by proposing that it initiate one-half of all appropriation bills. The ensuing deadlock froze action for months.

The House committee complained at one point that "in the past 10 years the Senate conferees have been able to retain $22 billion of the $32 billion in increases which the Senate added to House appropriations—a 2 to 1 ratio in favor of the body consistently advocating larger appropriations, increased spending, and corresponding deficits."[70] Sen. A. Willis Robertson (D Va.) called the communication in which this complaint was voiced "the most insulting document that one body has ever sent to another."[71] When the Senate adopted a continuing resolution (to let federal agencies keep on spending at the old rate until appropriations for the new fiscal year had been approved), the House went on record, 245-1, that the Senate action was "an infringement on the privileges" of the House.[72] The Senate resolved, in turn, that "the acquiescence of the Senate in permitting the House to first consider appropriation bills cannot change the clear language of the Constitution nor affect the Senate's co-equal power to originate any bill not expressly 'raising revenue.' "[73]

The feud was allowed to die without resolution. While it was true that the Senate had consistently voted for larger expenditures than the House, it was also true that Congress had managed generally to authorize less spending than was proposed by the postwar Presidents. Yet the amounts authorized grew more or less steadily after 1947, and it became increasingly apparent that the capacity of Congress to control expenditures through its power of the purse was quite limited. Congress did not pass legislation to reform its budget procedures until 1974.

Checking the Rules Committee

The negative power of the House Rules Committee was forcefully displayed during the Republican 80th Congress in connection with efforts to enact a major housing bill. The committee insisted that the Banking and Currency Committee delete provisions for public housing and slum clearance before it would agree to release the bill. The committee also refused to allow the House to vote on a universal military training bill reported by the Armed Services Committee, and it was only under strong pressure from Speaker Martin that the committee cleared a bill to revive the lapsed Selective Service System.

Liberals dominated the Democratic majority of 263 elected to the House in 1948, but they were again faced with the prospect that the 12-member Rules Committee would be controlled by a conservative coalition of four Republicans and three southern Democrats—Reps. E. E. Cox (Ga.), Howard W. Smith (Va.) and William M. Colmer (Miss.). So with the backing of Speaker Rayburn the party caucus voted 176 to 48 for a "21-day rule" proposed by Rules Committee Chairman Adolph J. Sabath (D Ill.). The rule authorized the chairman of any legislative committee which had reported a bill favorably, and requested a special rule from the Rules Committee, to bring the matter to the House floor if the committee failed to act within 21 calendar days of the request.

Adopted by the House on Jan. 3, 1949, by a procedural vote of 275 to 143, the 21-day rule was used eight times during the 81st Congress to obtain House passage of bills blocked in the Rules Committee, such as an anti-poll tax bill and statehood measures for Alaska and Hawaii. An effort to repeal the new rule in 1950, led by Rep. Cox, was rejected by the House by a vote of 183 to 236.

The Democrats lost 29 seats in the 1950 elections and when the 82nd Congress met on Jan. 3, 1951, Cox again moved to drop the rule. It had been adopted in 1949, he said, because the Rules Committee had "refused to stampede under the lash of the whip applied by strong unofficial minority groups."[74] Rep. Charles A. Halleck (R Ind.) supported repeal because it was the job of the Rules Committee to screen "unwise, unsound, ill-timed, spendthrift and socialistic measures."[75] Sabath protested that repeal would permit an "unholy alliance" of southern Democrats and Republicans to "tear down the rights of every member of the House."[76] But 91 Democrats joined 152 Republicans to repeal the 21-day rule by a vote of 243 to 180.

Smith's Reign. Control of the Rules Committee by a conservative coalition was virtually unchallenged for the next decade. Rep. Smith, who became chairman in 1955, made the most of his power to censor the legislative program of the House. Because the committee had no regular meeting day and could be called together only by the chairman, it was sometimes unable to clear any bills during the final days of a session when Smith simply disappeared to his Virginia farm.

In 1958, 283 Democrats were elected to the House—their largest majority since 1936—and party liberals again talked of curbing the Rules Committee. They proposed changing the ratio of Democrats to Republicans on the committee from 8-4 to 9-3 and reinstituting the 21-day rule. Speaker Rayburn was opposed to any changes, however, and the liberals called off their drive when he "offered his personal assurance" that housing, civil rights, labor and other social welfare legislation "would not be bottled up in the committee."[77]

Rayburn however, was unable to fulfill his pledge during the 86th Congress (1959-60). When Democrat John F. Kennedy was elected President in 1960 (along with a reduced Democratic majority of 263 in the House), it was clear that much of his program might be stymied unless administration Democrats gained control of the Rules Committee when the 87th Congress convened in 1961. Rayburn decided to try to enlarge the committee from 12 to 15 members to make room for the addition of two loyal Democrats and thus create an 8 to 7 majority that would act favorably on administration bills. But his plan was stoutly opposed by Chairman Smith and Republican Leader Halleck, and it took Rayburn and his lieutenants a month of maneuvering and lobbying to round up enough votes to win.

Enlargment of the Rules Committee. The House finally adopted the rule to increase the size of the committee from 12 to 15 on Jan. 31, 1961, by a vote of 217 to 212. Voting for the change were 195 Democrats, including 47 southerners led by Rep. Carl Vinson (Ga.), and 22 Republicans, including former Speaker Martin. Opposed were 64 Democrats—all except one of them southerners—and 148 Republicans. The new balance thus achieved on the Rules Committee proved to be precarious. A major school aid bill was effectively killed by the committee in 1961 when James J. Delaney (D N.Y.), a Catholic from a heavily Catholic district, joined the conservative coalition in voting against it because no provision was made for aid to parochial schools. Two pro-administration southern Democrats on the committee helped to kill a bill to create a department of urban affairs in 1962, after Robert C. Weaver, a black, was designated to become the new secretary.

Terms of the resolution adopted in 1961 limited the enlargement of the committee to the life of the 87th Congress. But the House on Jan. 9, 1963, at the beginning of the 88th Congress, agreed by a vote of 235 to 196 to make the change permanent. Although party ratios had scarcely changed, the resolution was supported this time by 207 Democrats, 59 of them southerners, and 28 Republicans, and opposed by 148 Republicans and 48 Democrats, all except three of them southerners.

New Rules. Democratic leaders nevertheless continued to have problems with the Rules Committee. But the election of President Johnson in 1964, together with a Democratic majority of 295 in the House, paved the way for three further changes in the House rules at the beginning of the 89th Congress in 1965, again over the opposition of a bipartisan coalition. The new rules were adopted Jan. 4 by voice vote after a motion for the previous question ending all debate had been approved by a roll-call vote of 224 to 202. Only 16 Republicans voted with 208 Democrats for the motion, while 79 Democrats (all except four of them southerners) and 123 Republicans were opposed.

The first of the new rules revived, with one change, was the 21-day rule that had been in force during the 81st Congress. Under the 1949 rule the Speaker had been required to recognize the chairman or other member of the committee seeking to bring before the House a bill that had been denied a rule by the Rules Committee for 21 days. The 1965 rule left the question of recognition to the discretion of the Speaker, thereby ensuring that no bill opposed by the leadership could be brought up under the rule.

The second new rule permitted the Speaker to recognize a member to offer a motion that would permit the House to send a bill to conference with the Senate by majority vote, provided that this action was approved by the committee with jurisdiction over the bill. Previously, it had been necessary to obtain unanimous consent or approval of a special rule from the Rules Committee to send a bill to conference, or to suspend the rules by a two-thirds vote.

The third change agreed to in 1965 repealed a rule dating from 1789 that had permitted any member to demand the reading in full of the engrossed (or final) copy of a House bill. Members opposed to legislation had frequently used this privilege to delay final passage of a bill until it could be printed.

The 21-day rule was employed successfully eight times during the 89th Congress, and the threat of its use persuaded the Rules Committee to send several other controversial measures to the floor. As in 1951, however, Republican gains in the 1966 elections opened the way to repeal of the rule at the beginning of the 90th Congress; the vote on Jan. 10, 1967, was 233 to 185. The prevailing coalition included 157 Republicans and 69 southern Democrats. The two other rules adopted in 1965 were retained.

Repeal of the 21-day rule in 1967 proved to be of little consequence during the 90th Congress, largely because of two other developments affecting the Rules Committee. Chairman Smith had been defeated in a primary election in 1966, as had another committee Democrat, and these vacancies were filled by administration supporters. Smith's successor as chairman, Rep. Colmer of Mississippi, was no less strong a conservative, but he was now outvoted on the committee. This became apparent on Feb. 28, 1967, when for the first time in its history the committee adopted a set of rules to govern its procedures. These rules took from the chairman his exclusive power to set meeting dates, required the consent of a committee majority to table a bill, and set limits on proxy voting by members. The net effect of these changes was substantial cooperation with the Democratic leadership in 1967-68 and the end of a decade of agitation for reform of the committee. The situation remained substantially the same during the 91st Congress (1969-70).

Pressures for Reform

Efforts to modify the organization and procedures of the House after 1946 were not confined to the protracted struggle for control of the Rules Committee. Both the Senate and the House came under pressure to curb the free-wheeling activities of their investigating committees in the early 1950s. The questionable conduct of some senators and representatives raised new doubts about congressional ethics in the 1960s to which both chambers were forced to respond. Mounting criticism of the methods and operations of Congress as a whole led both chambers to begin a re-examination in 1965 that finally produced a second reorganization act in 1970. These developments are discussed below.

Fair Play for Committee Witnesses. The efforts of the House Un-American Activities Committee to expose subversion and disloyalty through public hearings became a subject of great controversy in the early 1950s. The committee's access to television was cut off in 1952 when Speaker Rayburn effectively banned radio, television or film coverage of any House committee hearings by holding that there was no authority for such coverage in the rules of the House. But criticism increased in the Republican-controlled 83rd Congress when Chairman Harold H. Velde (R Ill.) of the Un-American Activities Committee and Sen. Joseph R. McCarthy (R Wis.), head of the Senate Permanent Investigations Subcommittee, were accused of conducting one-man investigations and mistreating witnesses. McCarthy was eventually censured by the Senate in 1954 for contemptuous treatment of two Senate committees.

The Rules Committees of both chambers held hearings in 1954 on proposals to reform committee procedures. On

March 23, 1955, the House adopted 10 new rules respecting committee conduct which—

• Required a quorum of not less than two committee members for taking testimony and receiving evidence.

• Allowed witnesses at investigative hearings to be accompanied by counsel for the purpose of advising them concerning their constitutional rights.

• Stipulated that if a committee found that evidence may tend to defame, degrade, or incriminate any person, it receive such evidence in executive (closed) session and allow such person to appear as a witness and request the subpoena of others.

• Barred the release or use in public sessions of evidence or testimony received in executive session without the consent of the committee.

The Senate Rules Committee recommended a similar set of standards in 1955, but the Senate left it to individual committees to draw up their own rules of conduct. Those adopted by the Permanent Investigations Subcommittee in 1955, when Sen. John L. McClellan (D Ark.) became chairman, incorporated provisions similar to those approved by the House. Although the investigative practices of congressional committees continued to vary considerably thereafter, the question of the fair treatment of witnesses declined in importance as a public issue.

Congressional Ethics. Although members of Congress were never immune to the temptations of using public office for private gain, the ethics of Congress as a whole did not begin to stir broad public interest until the years following World War II. Contributing to this interest were the rising costs of political campaigns and an increasing concern with conflicts of interest at all levels of government. The fact that some members of Congress continued to engage in private law practice or other business activities, and to hold a financial interest in such government-regulated businesses as banks and television stations, added to the concern.

Pressure to do something about congressional ethics was intensified in 1963 by charges that Robert G. (Bobby) Baker had used his office as secretary to the Senate majority to promote his outside business interests. The Senate responded by establishing in 1964 a six-member bipartisan Select Committee on Standards and Conduct empowered to investigate allegations of improper conduct by senators and Senate employees, to recommend disciplinary action, and to draw up a code of ethical conduct. Its first inquiry led to the Senate's censure of Sen. Thomas J. Dodd (D Conn.) in 1967 by a vote of 92 to 5, for misuse of political campaign contributions.

In 1968 the Select Committee recommended and the Senate adopted new rules aimed at the practices disclosed in the Baker and Dodd cases. Included were provisions to regulate the outside employment of Senate employees, to require a full accounting of campaign contributions and limit the uses to which they could be put, and to require senators and higher-ranking employees to file copies of their tax returns and some other financial data with the comptroller general each year. But this information was to remain confidential (although accessible to the Select Committee) and the only public accounting required under the new rules was of gifts of $50 or more and honoraria of $300 or more. The Senate, by a vote of 40 to 44, had rejected a proposal for full public disclosure of the finances of its members.

The House, meanwhile, had become embroiled in attempts to discipline Rep. Adam Clayton Powell (D N.Y.), a member since 1945, chairman of the Education and Labor Committee since 1961, and one of the few blacks in the House. Powell was indicted for tax evasion in 1958 and eventually paid $28,000 in back taxes and penalties. He was sued for libel in 1960 and held in contempt of court in the case on several occasions. He kept his wife on his payroll at $20,000 a year although she lived in Puerto Rico. But it was his extensive travels at public expense, his prolonged absences from Congress and his high-handed actions as a committee chairman that turned most of his colleagues against him.

At the beginning of the 90th Congress in 1967, the Democratic Caucus removed Powell as chairman of the Education and Labor Committee, and the House voted 365-65 to deny him his seat pending an investigation by a special committee. Its report recommended that Powell be seated but that he be censured for "gross misconduct," stripped of his seniority and fined $40,000 for misuse of public funds."[78] But on March 1 the House rejected these proposals and voted instead to exclude Powell from the 90th Congress and declare his seat vacant.

Powell promptly filed suit in a federal court to regain his seat on the grounds that he met the constitutional qualifications for membership and that the House had no authority to exclude him. A district court dismissed the case for lack of jurisdiction, and the court of appeals affirmed the finding, noting that the case involved a political question which, if decided by the courts, would constitute a violation of the separation of power. On June 16, 1969, however, the Supreme Court reversed the lower courts by a vote of 7 to 1; the opinion by Chief Justice Earl Warren held that Powell had been improperly excluded by the House.

Powell had been overwhelmingly re-elected following his exclusion in 1967, but he had made no effort to take his seat during the remainder of the 90th Congress. Re-elected in 1968, he presented himself at the opening of the 91st Congress in 1969. By this time tempers had cooled. The House by a vote of 254-158 adopted a resolution that permitted him to take his seat but fined him $25,000 as punishment and "stripped him of his seniority."[79] Powell accepted the judgment, but his career in the House was ended in 1970 when he was defeated in the primary election.

The Powell case, together with the Senate's actions, helped to persuade the House in 1967 to establish its own 12-member, bipartisan Committee on Standards of Official Conduct. In 1968 the committee recommended and the House adopted (as Rule 43) a Code of Official Conduct which included provisions that—

• Forbade a member or employee to use his official position improperly to receive compensation.

• Prohibited the acceptance of gifts of substantial value from an individual or group with a direct interest in legislation before Congress.

• Prohibited acceptance of honoraria of more than the usual and customary value for speeches and articles.

• Required representatives to keep campaign funds separate from personal funds and not to convert campaign funds to personal use.

• Required that, unless some other purpose was made clear in advance, all funds raised at testimonial events must be treated as campaign contributions subject to the reporting requirements and spending limits of the Corrupt Practices Act of 1925.

• Required that employees of a member perform the work for which they were paid.

The House also adopted at the same time a new rule (Rule 44) that required members and officers of the House, their principal assistants, and professional staff members of committees to file with the Committee on Standards of Official Conduct each year a report disclosing certain financial interests—which were to be available to the public—and a sealed report on the amount of income from those interests. As under the Senate rules, the sealed report could be opened by the committee only if it determined that it was essential to an investigation, while the data that might be made public were extremely limited.

The new rules adopted by the Senate and House in 1968 did not put an end to the questioning of congressional ethics. The practice of certain senators in introducing hundreds of private immigration bills for Chinese ship-jumpers came under fire in 1969 and an aide to Speaker McCormack was indicted for influence peddling in 1970. When Supreme Court Justice Abe Fortas resigned in 1969 following disclosures of certain financial activities, Sen. Clifford P. Case (R N.J.) renewed his argument that public confidence in the government would not be restored until Congress made it mandatory for Supreme Court justices and all other members of the federal judiciary, as well as members of Congress and high officials in the executive branch, to make full, regular and, most importantly, public reports of their income and financial activities.[80] But when or whether a majority of senators and representatives would agree to make a full public disclosure of their finances was left an open question until the 1970s.

Reorganization Bill. The efficiency and equity of congressional procedures also were questioned with increasing frequency in the 1960s, and in 1965 the Senate and the House agreed to set up a new Joint Committee on the Organization of the Congress modeled on the committee headed by Sen. Robert M. La Follette Jr. (Prog. Wis.) and Rep. A. S. Mike Monroney (D Okla.) that had put through the Legislative Reorganization Act of 1946. A senator since 1951, Monroney was named co-chairman of the new committee along with Rep. Ray J. Madden (D Ind.). After extensive hearings in 1965, the committee in 1966 issued a long list of recommendations most of which were incorporated in a bill passed by the Senate in 1967. But the bill met with strong opposition from committee chairmen and other senior members of the House and remained bottled up in the Rules Committee until the end of the 90th Congress.

Reform Years: 1970-76

By the end of the 1960s, Americans had been through a tumultuous period during which the nation was torn by a costly and unpopular war in Indochina, by civil disturbances and urban riots and by a rapid inflation.

Congress passed much social legislation during this decade, including major civil rights bills. But the efforts of the legislators did not end the unrest in the country and left many persons convinced that Congress was too hamstrung by ancient rules, outdated procedures and unaccountable use of power to deal effectively with America's complex social and economic problems.

The procedural and other internal problems of Congress and the calls for reform were not new to the 1960s. However, the magnitude of the problems that confronted the members brought new urgency to the calls and cast them in a different light than in the past. Congress was losing its influence over even the fundamental powers of war and spending.

The war in Indochina and the rising costs of the federal government were critical events that compelled Congress to examine the way that legislative business was conducted and power distributed within its chambers. This examination, pushed throughout the 1960s and into the 1970s by junior members aided by some senior colleagues, led to the reforms passed after 1970.

The Indochina war and its cost affected everything that Congress did in the latter half of the 1960s. Until virtually the end of American involvement and the war itself in 1975, Congress always approved military funds requested by the Johnson, Nixon and Ford administrations. This reflected public willingness to go along with the war for a long time. But from about 1968 on, the war became increasingly unpopular with the public, a change in attitude that was slow to be seen in Congress; and even when it was, members conceded that they had no adequate way to force administration officials to end American involvement.

At first, President Johnson believed the nation could both wage the war and fund the substantial domestic programs he advocated—the nation could afford both "guns and butter," commentators observed—without increasing taxes. This proved not to be the case; inflationary pressures built and spending for social programs suffered.

Johnson was followed by Republican Richard Nixon who continued to pursue the war but had a different view of spending for social programs. Much of his first term from 1968-72 was spent battling the Democratic Congress over spending for this or that domestic social program, most of them devised by Democratic Congresses and administrations. Unable to prevent Congress from appropriating funds for these efforts, Nixon attempted to prevent the expenditures by impounding the funds—that is, by administratively deciding simply not to spend the money. Legal challenges to this practice had considerable success, and Congress enacted laws to circumscribe the asserted power of Nixon, and other Presidents, to refuse to spend money appropriated by Congress.

These disputes over the war and spending demonstrated that Congress was poorly equipped to handle the most difficult issues that had faced it in a generation. By implication, the internal difficulties also were obstacles to Congress' dealing with less serious issues.

Even those members who supported the war and cuts in social programs conceded that control of the war-making power and of federal spending had slipped so far from Congress and to the executive that Congress was no longer a partner in these decisions. This realization created a determination among a continually growing number of members during the 1960s to correct this imbalance and restore to Congress the influence that the Founding Fathers had intended for it.

Changing Membership

The need for Congress to change its operations—increasingly evident from the war and spending issues—came at the time of substantial turnover in the membership of the House.

About half of the House membership at the beginning of the 1970s had been elected during the 1960s. By the 94th Congress in 1975-76, 82 per cent of the members had been elected since 1960 and almost a third—61 per cent—had come in since 1967.

This meant that a substantial majority of the House during the 1970-76 period was relatively new to the system and had less interest in maintaining existing methods of operation than more senior members. In fact, a sizeable number of the newer members—particularly those who were elected in the late 1960s and the 1970s—had a personal interest in changing the system because they were excluded from exercising much influence by the rules and folkways that existed when they took their seats. The principal folkway that rendered these junior members to the lowly status of backbenchers was the inflexible seniority system.

Thus, by 1970, the events and the people were in place in the House to launch the most significant reforms in half a century.

Thrust of the Reforms

The center of the reform movement was in the House, but the spirit carried over to the Senate where some important changes were made.

As a result, over the six-year period from 1970 to 1976, Congress ended or revised long-established practices that had made it a junior partner in the federal government.

The reform effort was directed at the institutional structure that determines how Congress conducted its business. These were the major problems:

● The seniority system guaranteed that members rose to power through longevity. It was essentially scrapped in the House when Democrats decided to require committee chairmen to stand for election in the party caucus. (A similar but weaker system was adopted in the Senate.)

● Accountability and Secrecy. Through various measures, the House made members more accountable for their actions. The House did away with unrecorded teller votes on the floor. Committee meetings were open to the public and press so that representatives' actions were observable first hand. Chairmen of committees and subcommittees were required to answer to their colleagues for their actions and were subject to having their decisions reversed.

Leadership. In the House, the Democratic leadership was strengthened by giving it the power to name Rules Committee members and an important role in the naming of Democrats to various other committees.

The upshot of these and other changes was to fundamentally alter the manner that power is held and exercised in the House. Almost absolute authority had been vested through the seniority system in representatives who had served longest. Their power was exercised primarily through the committee system and rarely was challenged successfully.

The 1970-76 revisions weakened these traditional power preserves. By the end of the first session of the 94th Congress in December 1975, the rigid seniority system was in shambles as the sole method by which members rose to power. The system still functioned as a useful device for ordering the hierarchy on committees, but it no longer was the dominant force which gave all power to the most senior members.

The attack on the seniority system was the fundamental battle fought during the period, but other changes—open meetings, better committee rules, strengthened leadership—complemented this reform. Together they helped re-establish Congress' ability to function as an effective and equal branch of government. Whether these mechanisms would be used in the years after the 94th Congress would depend on the will of Congress to use them and on the strength of the congressional leadership.

Changes Not Made

Not all of the changes urged upon Congress by reformers were adopted.

Committee jurisdictions remained a jumble of conflicts and contradictions based on the 1946 Legislative Reorganization Act—a plan drawn up when many 1970s problems, such as energy use and environmental protection, were unknown.

The House made an attempt at reform in 1974 when a special committee headed by Rep. Richard Bolling (D Mo.) suggested sweeping changes. But vested interests, both in and out of the House, killed that plan and only modest changes were adopted. The Senate had not gone even that far by the end of 1976.

In addition, other problems that Congress had not dealt with included scheduling of activities to speed and ease the growing legislative workload, the proliferation of subcommittees and ethical issues (such as conflicts of interests, outside earnings and abuses of congressional prerogatives).

Foreign Policy

The Indochina crisis presented Congress with a special challenge to participate in foreign policy. Congress was initially criticized for being slow to act, but ultimately it did respond. Over presidential veto, Congress enacted the War Powers Act of 1973, marking the first time in history that Congress had defined and limited the President's power to make war.

After the withdrawal of all U.S. combat forces from Indochina, Congress in 1975 refused President Ford further military aid for South Vietnam and Cambodia. Members expressed fears that more aid might mean a never-ending U.S. involvement.

Elsewhere in foreign affairs, Congress clashed with the Ford administration over arms to Turkey in the wake of that country's invasion of Cyprus in July 1974. Turkey had used U.S.-supplied weapons in that invasion in violation of U.S. foreign aid laws. In opposition to President Ford in February 1975, Congress put an embargo on arms aid to Turkey. In October, the lawmakers partially lifted the ban as a result of intensive White House lobbying.

In another clash with the President, the House on Jan. 27, 1976, approved a Senate-sponsored amendment to the defense appropriations bill which barred all further U.S. aid to factions fighting Communist groups in the civil war in Angola. President Ford had publicly called upon the House to reject the amendment, passed by the Senate Dec. 19, 1975, but the House approved it 323-99. President Ford did not veto the bill, and the ban on aid to Angola became law.

Watergate and Impeachment

A second crisis, the Watergate scandal, began with the burglary of the Democratic National Party headquarters in the Watergate building in Washington, D.C., on June 17, 1972. It ended Aug. 9, 1974, when President Nixon resigned in the face of certain impeachment by the House. *(Senate Watergate Committee p. 103)*

Only once before in American history had the House set in motion the machinery of impeachment of a President of the United States. The impeachment power, the most crucial congressional check upon presidential abuse of power, had been used against President Andrew Johnson more than a century earlier.

When President Nixon fired Special Prosecutor Archibald Cox over access to the Watergate tapes in October 1973, several House members introduced impeachment resolutions. In November, the House voted $1-million for an investigation, and its Judiciary Committee, chaired by Rep. Peter W. Rodino Jr. (D N.J.), began assembling an investigative staff that numbered 100 persons, including 45 attorneys. On Feb. 6, 1974, the House, on a 410-4 vote, formally charged the Judiciary Committee with determining whether there were grounds to impeach Nixon, and granting the committee special subpoena power.

Throughout many weeks, the committee took testimony from witnesses and clashed with the President over access to the White House tape recordings. Nixon, who had promised to cooperate with the impeachment inquiry, in May refused to honor two Judiciary Committee subpoenas for tapes, adding he would not surrender any more Watergate evidence to the committee. That prompted Rodino to say the President's defiance could ultimately be considered grounds for impeachment.

At the end of July, before a national television audience, the Judiciary Committee voted three articles of impeachment against Nixon—obstruction of justice, abuse of presidential powers and contempt of Congress. In the case of the first article, Rodino noted it would be reported to the House, stating on television that "Richard M. Nixon has prevented, obstructed, and impeded the administration of justice...has acted in a manner contrary to his trust as President and subversive of constitutional government, to the great prejudice of the cause of law and justice, and to the manifest injury of the people of the United States...[and] warrants impeachment and trial and removal from office."

On Aug. 2, 1974, under Supreme Court order, Nixon surrendered to U.S. District Court Judge John J. Sirica three recorded conversations of June 23, 1972, six days after the burglary of Democratic National Headquarters in Watergate. On Aug. 5, Nixon released transcripts of those conversations to the press. The transcripts showed Nixon's participation in the Watergate coverup and approval of CIA involvement as a means of obstructing the FBI investigation of the Watergate break-in. What support Nixon had left in Congress evaporated; he resigned Aug. 9, 1974, nine days before the House was to begin debate on impeachment.[81]

Reorganization Act of 1970

The legislative reorganization bill, proposed in 1966 by the joint committee chaired by Sen. A. S. Mike Monroney (D Okla.) and Rep. Ray J. Madden (D Ind.) died in the House Rules Committee in 1968. The reform effort was renewed in the 91st Congress. In the final weeks of the Congress, the House acted on a bill of its own, a more modest reform bill than that recommended by the 1966 report of the joint committee. The House passed its bill Sept. 17, 1970, and the Senate approved it Oct. 6.

The Legislative Reorganization Act of 1970, the first such law passed since 1946, ignored the seniority system, the power of the House Rules Committee and the two-thirds rule for cutting off Senate debate. But it did include a number of important provisions designed to give both chambers more information on government finances, to guarantee minority party rights and to maintain a continuing review of legislative needs through a Joint Committee on Congressional Operations.

One of the act's most important items affecting the House required that teller votes on the floor be recorded. Previously, teller votes had only been tabulated in total without recording members' votes. Thus, members had often employed the teller method to elude accountability. The reform put voting in the House on a par with the Senate where teller votes did not exist and where all important floor votes are usually recorded by name.

The 1970 act required committees to have written rules, a check on the arbitrary use of power by committee chairmen, and to make public roll-call votes taken in closed committee sessions, a step toward holding members accountable for their actions in committee as well as on the floor. Other features were designed to give members more information and expedite congressional business. For example, committee reports had to be available at least three days before floor consideration and House quorum calls were shortened.[82]

New Leadership

House Democratic liberals hoped that the retirement of 79-year-old Speaker John W. McCormack (Mass.) in 1971 would result in a new leadership team supportive of their cause. The House chose Carl Albert (Okla.), who had served as majority leader since 1962. In 24 years in the House, Albert had traveled a careful political road along which he had made few enemies. He was acceptable to most factions of the Democratic Party. He was elected Speaker with only token, last-minute opposition.

By contrast, Hale Boggs (La.) had to overcome strong reformist opposition to advance from Democratic whip to majority leader. Boggs rankled the liberals because he made no commitment during the leadership race to a reform of procedures or a new distribution of power. But traditionalists prevailed in the Democratic Caucus, giving Boggs 140 votes to 88 for Morris K. Udall (Ariz.), principal candidate of the reformers, and 17 for B. F. Sisk (Calif.). After Boggs died in an Alaskan airplane crash, the Democrats chose Thomas P. O'Neill Jr. (Mass.) for majority leader in January 1973. Although he was representative of the traditional system of promotion up the leadership ladder (he had been whip under Boggs), O'Neill sided sometimes with the reformers.

Albert's passive style as Speaker drew mounting criticism, especially in the 94th Congress where the Democrats held a 2-to-1 majority in the House with the election of 75 freshmen in November 1974. That largely liberal class, disdaining the backbencher-role expected of freshmen, joined in the outcry against the leadership's inability to muster the two-thirds vote needed to override much Democratic legislation vetoed by President Ford. For example, the House on June 4, 1975, sustained the veto of a Democratic-sponsored appropriations bill aimed at creating more than one million jobs in the public and private sectors. Consideration of the bill came as the national unemployment level was climbing to the May high of 9.2 per cent. Ford held the measure to be inflationary.

On the Republican side, Rep. John J. Rhodes (Ariz.) was elected minority leader in December 1973 when Gerald Ford was appointed vice president by Nixon. Rhodes, a conservative, generally supported Republican White House foreign and domestic policies, and enjoyed the conservative coalition votes of Southern Democrats in sustaining many presidential vetoes.[83]

Democratic Caucus

A major instrument of reform during the 1970s was a rejuvenated House Democratic Caucus. Once a powerful instrument in implementing Woodrow Wilson's domestic program, the caucus had fallen into disuse, meeting only at the beginning of a new Congress for the pro forma election of House Democratic leaders.

The move to revitalize the caucus was led by the House Democratic Study Group (DSG), an organization of moderate and liberal Democrats forming the largest reform bloc in the House. The opening came in 1969 when Speaker McCormack, in a move to appease the reformers, agreed to regular monthly meetings of the caucus.

The membership of the DSG was dominated by junior members of the House in the 1960s—representatives who had come to Congress recently enough to have little seniority and therefore little influence in House affairs. They saw the caucus as an appropriate vehicle to attack what they considered the imbalance in power between junior and senior members and to make changes in House rules and procedures.

In 1970, the caucus created a Committee on Study, Organization and Review headed by Rep. Julia Butler Hansen (D Wash.) to study changes in the seniority system. The committee was seen by some members as a ploy by senior members to head off changes, and in fact it was not controlled by the younger members who were pressing most vigorously for reform. The committee's report proposed only modest seniority changes: seniority need not be followed by the Democratic Committee on Committees in selecting chairmen and a vote on any recommendation could be forced in the caucus by 10 members. It was the beginning of an inexorable trek in the following five years toward making chairmen fully accountable to the caucus.

From 1970 on, the caucus played a key role in pushing procedural and rules reform in the House. On occasion during the period, it became involved in substantive issues, also. The principal incidents were in 1972 and in 1975 on proposals to end U.S. involvement in the Vietnam War. But these and other forays into substantive areas aroused much controversy in the Democratic Party and caused caucus leaders to back away from using the organization as a major force to determine party policy on legislative issues. *(See next section.)*

Thus, by the end of the 94th Congress the caucus had become a primary force for internal House procedural reform, but had not developed equal influence on legislative issues. Many of the reforms that the caucus did help promote are discussed in the following sections.

Legislative Strategy

Although the House Democratic Caucus was credited with accomplishing significant reforms of procedures, its role as a vehicle of legislative strategy remained questionable. And in 1975 a quiet debate took place in the caucus as to its role setting party policy on legislation, an area of limited success since caucus revival.

In 1975, the caucus did instruct Democratic members of the Rules Committee to bring to the House floor two amendments relating to oil depletion, and passed a "sense of the caucus" resolution opposing more U.S. military aid to Indochina.

These actions caused a furor among some Democrats who felt the caucus was usurping the powers of the committees. The caucus was more restrained from then on until later in the year when conservatives attempted to have it order the Judiciary Committee to report a constitutional amendment to prevent court-ordered school busing—exactly the sort of legislative involvement that many conservatives had complained about at the beginning of the year. But the caucus rejected the proposal even though it was done on a public, recorded vote on a volatile issue.

The anti-busing action was on the record because conservatives had persuaded the caucus to open its meetings to the public. This was one part of the effort by some Democrats, mostly conservatives, to make the caucus less active. "We don't really like sunshine for the caucus, but we've got to stop this damn caucus from legislating," said Rep. Joe D. Waggonner Jr. (La.), a leader of the conservative faction. [84]

Reforms of 1973

Directed by the 150-member DSG with outside help from Common Cause, the public interest lobby, and Americans for Democratic Action, reform forces pushed through three new policies at the beginning of the 93rd Congress.

In a move toward more open government, the House adopted a caucus-inspired reform to curb committee secrecy. All committees and subcommittees were required to open to the public most bill-drafting sessions and other business meetings unless a majority voted at an open session to bar the public. Hearings had been open, but sessions where bills were marked up were usually closed. The reform allowed reporters and the public to witness the performance of committee members in shaping bills.

Two years later, first the House, then the Senate adopted rules opening conference committees to the press and public. Conferences, called to iron out differences in each chamber's version of a bill, were one of the last and most traditional vestiges of secrecy in Congress.

Conferences had become the quiet preserves of senior members who exercised great powers over the final form of bills as compromises were worked out behind closed doors.

But a chief advocate of institutional reform in the House, Rep. Richard Bolling (D Mo.) was skeptical about the effectiveness of the new conference rules, saying, "Sunshine laws kid the public. They imply a total openness and there never will be." He cautioned that some accommodations and compromises would still have to be made in secret.

A second major 1973 reform was aimed at the Ways and Means Committee, which held jurisdiction over key legislative areas—taxes, foreign trade, Social Security, Medicare and others. Chairman Wilbur D. Mills (D Ark.) had long been successful in bringing Ways and Means legislation to the House floor under a closed rule, making amendments impossible. Mills, a skilled parliamentarian and an authoritarian chairman, argued that his legislation was so complex that amendments by individual members would twist the bills out of shape and the broader goals would be lost.

The Democratic Caucus struck a compromise between the Mills position and unlimited floor amendments: a minimum of 50 Democrats could propose an amendment to the caucus, and if a majority of the caucus approved the amendment, Democratic members of the Rules Committee would be instructed to write a rule allowing the amendment to be taken up on the House floor. The author of the plan, Rep. Phillip Burton (D Calif.), explained that he was not trying to load every bill down with amendments. Mills, not present during the caucus action, did not oppose the Burton proposal.

Finally in 1973, the Democratic Caucus created a new Steering and Policy Committee to assist the Speaker in developing party and legislative priorities.

Subcommittees Strengthened

The caucus-led attack on the seniority system struck out at the dominance of subcommittees by the full committee chairman. Through rigid control of all levels of major committees, a few chairmen, operating individually and collectively, held much House business in their grip during the 1950s and 1960s.

In 1971, the caucus adopted a rule that no Democratic committee member could be chairman of more than one legislative subcommittee. Two years later, the Democratic Caucus instituted a series of changes, known as the "bill of rights," which gave the subcommittees greater autonomy from control by the chairmen of the full committees. The changes, which affected the Democrats alone and were not made part of the House rules, included:

● Establishment of a Democratic caucus on each full committee, forcing chairmen to share authority with other Democrats. The committee caucus was granted authority to select subcommittee chairmen, to establish subcommittee jurisdictions, to provide adequate subcommittee budgets, and to guarantee all members a major subcommittee assignment as vacancies opened up.

● Requirement that committee chairmen refer legislation to appropriate subcommittees within two weeks, thus preventing chairmen from killing bills by not scheduling them for committee action.

● The right of subcommittee chairmen and ranking minority members to hire one staff member each to work for them on the subcommittee. The purpose of this staff assistance was to help keep the subcommittees independent of the chairman of the full committee.

The diffusion of power to the subcommittees was solidified in 1975 when the Democratic Caucus voted to require all committees having more than 20 members to establish at least four subcommittees and to restrict committee members to positions on no more than two subcommittees. These requirements were designed to correct what the caucus regarded as abuses in the running of the two most powerful committees in the House—Ways and Means and Appropriations.

Ways and Means Chairman Wilbur D. Mills (D Ark.) had operated without subcommittees during most of his 16-year reign (1958-74). In the Appropriations Committee, senior conservative Democrats had dominated important subcommittees handling defense, agriculture, health, education and welfare funding.

In another move designed to curb the Appropriations Committee, the caucus decided that starting with the 94th Congress in 1975, all subcommittee chairmen of the Appropriations Committee had to be approved by the caucus.

Committee Assignments

In 1973, House Democrats adopted a party rule guaranteeing each Democrat a major committee assignment, ending the old system of assigning newcomers to one or more minor committees.

At the December 1974 caucus another blow was struck at Ways and Means which had served since 1911 as the Democratic Committee on Committees. That power to assign Democrats to committees was switched to the party's Steering and Policy Committee, composed of House leaders, their nominees and members elected by the caucus on a regional basis.

Beginning in 1975, a new rule allowed each member of a full committee to choose a subcommittee position before any member could select a second subcommittee slot—a further step in breaking up the conservative monopoly over Appropriations subcommittees.

Seniority System Crippled

Although reforms had rolled on at a rapid pace, the same chairmen—though with reduced powers—were presiding over the same committees in 1974 as at the opening of the decade, unless their House service had been ended by voluntary retirement, re-election defeat or death.

But the Democratic Caucus was at work on its challenge to the seniority system. It began readying itself in 1971 with a modest policy change which allowed 10 or more Democrats to demand a separate vote on any chairman nominee. It was known as the "kamikaze rule" because challengers had to stand up publicly in caucus to demand the vote, risking retribution from unforgiving chairmen. The caucus also stated that seniority need not be considered in recommendations for chairmen, underlining the fact that advancement on the basis of congressional longevity was a custom, not a rule.

In 1973, the caucus passed a rule requiring that each Democratic committee chairman be elected by mandatory secret ballot, but then the caucus went on to award all chairmanships, on 21 separate votes, to the same members who would have received them if the seniority system had gone untouched.

When the 94th Congress convened in January 1975, the 2-to-1 House Democratic majority included the newly elected freshmen who owed no favors to the chamber's senior establishment. When the caucus had finished its work, the seniority system was no longer the sole route by which members became chairmen.

Three chairmen were deposed: Wright Patman (Texas) of the Banking, Currency and Housing Committee; F. Edward Hebert (La.) of the Armed Services Committee; and W. R. Poage (Texas) of the Agriculture Committee. Various reasons were given for their ouster, but there was little doubt the trio made a poor impression on the freshmen Democrats who had interviewed all three before deciding whom they would support in caucus. In addition, each of the three was accused of autocratic actions denying equitable treatment to their committee members. Ideology was thought to have played a role, but not a major one. Hebert was identified as a conservative who gave unflinching support to the military and who voted with Republicans on many issues. Patman, was a Southern populist with a long record of opposing tight money policies and high bank interest rates. At the age of 82, he had had trouble controlling his fractious committee colleagues.

The deposing of the three chairmen encompassed several maneuvers in the Democratic Steering Committee, which recommended chairmen nominees, and the caucus. In Patman's case, the independent-minded caucus ousted him in spite of Steering Committee support. The three chairmen were replaced with a senior member of each committee. The caucus also refined the method of nominating chairmen by allowing competitive contests and nominations from the caucus floor.

The removal of the three broke the system that for decades had governed representatives' progression to House power. In 1967, Rep. Adam Clayton Powell (D N.Y.) was removed from the chairmanship of the Education and Labor

Committee following allegations of misconduct, including payroll padding, extensive travels at public expense and tax evasion. Before Powell, the last time the House had ousted a chairman was in 1925 when two Republican chairmen were removed for campaigning in 1924 for Progressive presidential candidate Robert LaFollette.

Budget Control

For years the House and Senate were plagued by a disjointed appropriations process that gave no overall control of funding to any congressional unit, nor even to the entire Congress itself. To remedy the chaotic situation, the Congressional Budget and Impoundment Control Act was passed in 1974, setting up House and Senate Budget Committees and a Congressional Budget Office. The act's goals were to focus congressional attention in a systematic way on two broad budgetary concerns: national fiscal policy and national priorities.

The sweeping reform required Congress to vote for the first time on a budget deficit. The process forced Congress to compare total spending and total receipts, instead of treating appropriations and tax measures as mutually-exclusive budget items.

In doing so, Congress was required to confront such fiscal policy issues as the effect of the budget on inflation, unemployment and economic growth.

Congress also had to decide on budget priorities. For example, if Congress called for more spending for health purposes, it had to increase revenues through higher taxes, accept a large deficit or balance the addition by cutting other programs.

The law also created a complicated set of deadlines for congressional action on the budget. The key dates each year are May 15, when Congress is supposed to complete action on a first concurrent resolution containing budget targets to guide committees as they process fiscal legislation during the summer months, and Sept. 15, when Congress is to replace the targets with spending ceilings and a floor on revenues in a second concurrent resolution. If the amounts adopted in the fall differ from those adopted during the summer in actual spending and tax bills, Congress must reconcile the amounts before adjourning.

Once this reconciliation process is completed, the limits in the second resolution become binding. Accordingly, the date of the beginning of the fiscal year was changed from July 1 to Oct. 1 to allow Congress time to complete the entire budget process before the fiscal year began.

Moving quickly, Congress in 1975 implemented some of the budget act mechanisms as a trial run. The timetable proved difficult. Congress did not complete action on the second resolution until three months after the Sept. 15 deadline, which indicated trouble on the full set of deadlines which were to be operating in 1976.

The limited implementation of the Budget Act in 1975 did give the new system some credibility. For one thing, the positions of the House and Senate budget committees on the child nutrition and education appropriations bills did help both chambers override vetoes by President Ford in 1975. In the education measure, the spending ceiling was well below the first resolution target, but higher than the amount Ford had requested. The Budget Committees prevailed when they argued that, if the veto were allowed to stand, the priorities set by Congress in the first resolution would be repealed.

Other Reforms

During the first half of the 1970s other changes were instituted aimed at making the operation of the House more open, accountable and efficient. The steps included:

● **Rules Committee.** In a move to strengthen the party's leadership, the caucus gave the Speaker power to nominate Democratic members of Rules, subject to caucus ratification.

● **Proxy voting.** The practice of proxy voting in committee was banned in 1974 and partially restored in 1975 by allowing committees to decide if proxy voting could be used. If proxies were allowed, they could be used only on a specific amendment or on procedural matters, and they had to be in writing and given to a specific person. The practice of one member giving a proxy to another for use as the recipient saw fit was banned.

● **Electronic Voting.** The House in January 1973 started using an electronic system making the recording of the 435 members on roll call and teller votes and quorum calls easier and speedier. Members had 15 minutes to answer calls, and could vote at any of 48 consoles in the House chamber. As they voted, boards installed on the walls showed how they voted and provided a running breakdown of the votes cast.

● **Oversight Function.** Over the years, Congress has usually paid scant attention to the operations of agencies it has created or the administration of programs it had enacted. In 1974, the House approved a plan requiring committees with more than 20 members to set up oversight subcommittees and defining jurisdictional lines for investigations.

Televised Hearings

Although the Senate had a long tradition of permitting television and radio to cover committee hearings, the House did not amend its rules to permit the broadcast coverage of committee hearings until 1970. While the Senate left broadcast decisions to its committees, the House adopted a stringent set of standards for use by committees that did admit television cameras. Among them were requirements that broadcast coverage not distort the purposes of hearings, or cast discredit upon the House, committee or any member.

Television or radio were seldom allowed in the Ways and Means Committee and Rules Committees. The Armed Services Committee flatly prohibited broadcast coverage, a staff member said, simply "because the committee doesn't want it."

In general, House committees seemed to be moving toward more open acceptance of broadcasting. In 1974, in order to permit television coverage of the Judiciary Committee sessions on impeachment, including discussion and votes on the articles of impeachment, the House amended its rules to allow broadcasting of mark-up meetings as well as hearings: The Appropriations Committee, which in the past had permitted telecasting only of its formal budget hearings at the beginning of each year, opened its doors early in 1975 for coverage of testimony on Central Intelligence Agency activities by Defense Secretary James R. Schlesinger and CIA Director William E. Colby.

In 1975, the Joint Committee on Congressional Operations held hearings on the feasibility of live television coverage of Senate and House floor deliberations. The issue sparked lively discussion, and was continued into the 1976 session. In an interim report the committee noted the conclusion of pollster George Gallup that telecasts of the impeachment hearings were largely responsible for the improved public rating of Congress after they ended.

Campaign Finance

In 1971 Congress passed a campaign spending law tightening disclosure requirements on sources of campaign contributions and other income, strengthening reporting requirements of a candidate's expenditures and defining more strictly the roles unions and corporations could play in political campaigns.

The 1971 campaign act played a role in Watergate when the General Accounting Office (GAO), charged with administering the act, investigated press reports of a $25,000 contribution to President Nixon's re-election finance committee. The GAO uncovered key violations which it reported on Aug. 26, 1972. This discovery was a crucial link in the chain of events that opened up the whole Watergate scandal.

Congress followed with another campaign finance law that was even more significant. This legislation, passed in 1974, provided government financing of presidential election campaigns from tax dollars, set campaign contribution and spending limits for candidates in federal elections and required disclosure of the sources of contributions and the purposes of expenditures above $100.

The law was the most important revision of campaign financing requirements since the 1920s and it was promptly challenged in court. In January 1976, the Supreme Court upheld basic parts of the law—federal funds for presidential candidates, contribution limits and disclosure—but declared unconstitutional other important sections. The court rejected limits imposed on spending by candidates (except those presidential candidates accepting federal funds) and on independent spending by individuals, as an infringement on First Amendment freedom-of-expression rights. The court also declared unconstitutional the composition of the Federal Election Commission created to enforce the requirements of the law and to distribute federal funds to candidates. The problem with the commission was that some of the members were named by congressional leaders, a violation of the Constitution's separation-of-powers requirements.

In May Congress sent to the White House legislation to correct the problems and re-establish the commission and thereby the flow of federal funds to presidential candidates. President Ford approved the bill with some misgivings.

The commission problem was corrected by giving the President the power to name all commission members. The independent spending situation could not be altered but Congress wrote a tight definition of such outlays to prevent collusion between an individual and a candidate.

Congress went beyond these matters to correct some other problems in the 1974 law, most importantly by tightening contribution limits to prevent political action committees from proliferating and thereby defeating the ceilings.

Significantly, Congress refused—in spite of considerable urging from many members and some outside groups—to create government financing for congressional campaigns.

Ethics

The House had never spent much time policing the ethical conduct of its members or staffs; only when pressed by the most serious circumstances had it done so.

By the end of 1975, the House Committee on Standards of Official Conduct—created in 1967 after the Powell scandal—had made no formal investigations of any House member, although several members had been convicted of crimes in court during the committee's nine-year existence. But in 1976, the ethics committee, as the panel was commonly known, was forced into action by several cases that it could not ignore.

The most spectacular controversy surrounded sex and payroll scandals that erupted on Capitol Hill in the spring of that year.

In the principal scandal, a woman employee of the House Administration Committee, Elizabeth Ray, asserted that she had been put on the payroll solely to be the mistress of Chairman Wayne L. Hays (D Ohio) and that she did no work and possessed no office skills. Hays admitted a "relationship" with her but denied that she did no work and was paid with public funds simply to be his mistress.

The resulting brouhaha forced Hays to resign as committee chairman and as head of the Democratic Congressional Campaign Committee, the group that gives campaign donations to party candidates. Hays resigned from Congress Sept. 1, 1976.

The scandal also set in motion efforts to revise many of the prerogatives benefiting members, such as stationery funds, mailing allowances, travel privileges and the like, which Hays had used to build a huge power base in the House. A principal change was to place clearly and frequently in public documents substantial amounts of information about congressional employees, including salaries, and the use of various prerogatives by House members. The ethics committee launched a major investigation of the Ray claims soon after they were made.

The newspaper ink on the Hays-Ray matter was hardly dry before similar claims about other members appeared in the press, sometimes without identifying the woman making the claim.

The sex scandal was not the only matter that intruded into the previously placid existence of the ethics committee. A self-styled citizens' lobbying group, Common Cause, brought a complaint against Rep. Robert L. F. Sikes (D Fla.) in early 1976, charging that he had improperly used his official position in Congress for personal gain. He was chairman of the Appropriations Military Construction Subcommittee. Common Cause said he voted on military proposals affecting private firms, including defense contractors, in which he held a financial interest, failed to disclose interests in firms doing federal business and used his House position to advance commercial development of Florida land. The Sikes charges were under investigation by the panel in 1976.

Third, the ethics committee in 1976 was looking into the sources of a leak to a CBS television reporter of a House document on CIA television reporter of a House document on CIA activities. The House had voted not to make the document public but someone turned it over to Daniel Schorr; eventually substantial portions were published in a New York newspaper.

Committee Jurisdiction

In 1974, the House defeated an ambitious plan for reorganization of its committees. The rejected plan had been drafted and unanimously approved by a bipartisan select committee headed by Rep. Richard Bolling (D Mo.). By proposing a wholesale realignment of committee jurisdictions and a limitation of one major committee per member, the Bolling Committee alienated many chairmen and other senior members whose power centers would have been diminished—a sign that veteran members still wielded considerable weight in blocking liberal reformers.

Instead of the Bolling plan, the House passed on Oct. 8, 1974, a much less drastic proposal that left committee jurisdictions largely unchanged. That plan, adopting some Bolling proposals, was drawn up by the Democratic Committee on Organization, Study and Review, chaired by Rep. Julia Butler Hansen (D Wash.).

The Hansen plan as passed did make some jurisdictional shifts, such as giving the Public Works Committee control over most transportation matters, but mainly it kept the existing committee structure. Hansen also included procedural changes. It directed the House to organize itself in December of election years for the next Congress, and gave the Speaker wider latitude in referring bills to committees.

In January 1975, the Democratic caucus voted to abolish the House Internal Security Committee, which was known before 1969 as the House Committee on Un-American Activities. The action ended 30 years of controversy during which the committee zealously pursued subversives in every segment of American society.[85]

Conflicts With the President

The end of 1976 would mark the first time in American history that one party controlled Congress while the opposition party occupied the White House for eight years in succession. The government divided between four Democratic Congresses and Republican Presidents Nixon and Ford was replete with many confrontations on legislation, and extensive use of the presidential veto. Congress often proved unable to override bills the Presidents refused to sign.

Some of the conflicts involved institutional issues, including the impoundment of funds appropriated by Congress. When in 1972, Congress denied Nixon authority

he demanded to limit federal spending to $250-billion in fiscal 1973, the President responded by impounding funds. He also vetoed a $30.5-billion funding bill for labor and health, education and welfare programs for fiscal 1973, and 15 other bills, most of them on budgetary grounds, in 1972.

Nixon provided Congress with a detailed list of impoundments in 1972, the largest single item being $2.5-billion in federal aid funds for highway construction. Nixon also refused to spend $1.9-billion on defense funds and $1.5-billion for such Agriculture Department programs as food stamps, rural water and waste disposal grants and rural electrification loans. The administration argued that the President had "an implied constitutional right" to impound funds.

Congress asserted that impoundment was used by Nixon as an instrument for thwarting the will of Congress and threatening its constitutional control of the purse strings. The lawmakers proposed various measures aimed at releasing impounded funds, and finally wrote anti-impoundment features into the Congressional Budget Act of 1974. However, the act permitted the President to withhold funds temporarily or to cancel their spending under certain conditions, provided Congress approved the non-spending within a 45-day period. On the other side of the issues, the anti-impoundment provisions coupled with other features of the budget law were seen as having the potential to erode the President's fundamental power to direct and control federal spending.[86]

President Ford's Vetoes. The Democratic Congress, counting its biggest majority in 10 years, experienced a disappointing year in 1975. During the year, President Ford vetoed 17 major bills, and four were overridden. Seven bills involved major economic and energy legislation; none of the seven was overridden.

Bills that succumbed to the presidential veto included a measure to regulate strip mining, a bill to restrict the President's authority to impose increased import fees on foreign oil, and an emergency farm bill that would have raised price supports for certain 1975 crops.[87]

Footnotes

1. George B. Galloway, *History of the House of Representatives* (New York: Crowell, 1969), p. 135.
2. *Ibid.*, p. 2.
3. *Ibid.*, p. 10.
4. *Ibid.*, p. 12.
5. *Ibid.*, p. 18.
6. Paul Leicester Ford, ed., *The Writings of Thomas Jefferson*, Vol. 6 (New York: G. P. Putnam's, 1895), p. 102.
7. Galloway, *History of the House of Representatives*, p. 18.
8. *Ibid.*, p. 129.
9. *Ibid.*, p. 71.
10. *Ibid.*, pp. 129-130.
11. Bernard Mayo, *Henry Clay: Spokesman of the New West* (Boston: Houghton Mifflin, 1937), pp. 346-347.
12. *Annals of the Congress of the United States*, 18th Congress, 1st Session, Dec. 1, 1823, p. 795.
13. Galloway, *History of the House of Representatives*, p. 130.
14. *Ibid.*
15. *Ibid.*, p. 43.
16. Marie B. Hecht, *John Quincy Adams: A Personal History of an Independent Man* (New York: Macmillan, 1972), p. 545.
17. *Ibid.*, p. 547.
18. Asher C. Hinds, *Hinds' Precedents of the House of Representatives*, Vol. 4 (Washington: U.S. Government Printing Office, 1907), p. 278.
19. *Ibid.*, Vol. 5, pp. 354-355.

20. Galloway, *History of the House of Representatives*, pp. 245-246.
21. Richard F. Fenno, Jr., *The Power of the Purse: Appropriations Politics in Congress* (Boston: Little, Brown, 1966), p. 8.
22. T. Harry Williams, *Hayes: The Diary of a President 1875-1881* (New York: David McKay Company, 1964), p. 206.
23. Woodrow Wilson, *Congressional Government* (Cleveland: Meridian, 1956), p. 76.
24. *Ibid.*, p. 82.
25. *Ibid.*, p. 80.
26. *Ibid.*, p. 85.
27. Neil MacNeil, *Forge of Democracy: The House of Representatives* (New York: David McKay Company, 1963), p. 185.
28. Galloway, *History of the House of Representatives*, p. 51.
29. MacNeil, *Forge of Democracy*, p. 76.
30. Galloway, *History of the House of Representatives*, p. 132.
31. *Ibid.*, p. 251.
32. *Ibid.*, p. 52.
33. *Ibid.*, p. 135.
34. *Congressional Record*, 51st Congress, 1st Session, Feb. 10, 1890, pp. 1172-1173.
35. Woodrow Wilson, *Congressional Government*, p. 63.
36. Galloway, *History of the House of Representatives*, pp. 54-55.
37. *Ibid.*, p. 55.
38. *Ibid.*, p. 139.
39. *Ibid.*, p. 140.

41. Paul DeWitt Hasbrouck, *Party Government in the House of Representatives* (New York: Macmillan, 1927), p. 15.

42. Floyd M. Riddick, *The United States Congress: Organization and Procedure* (Manassas, Va.: National Capitol Publishers, 1949), p. 123.

43. Hasbrouck, *Party Government in the House of Representatives,* p. 20.

44. *Ibid.,* p. 99.

45. *Congressional Record,* 69th Congress, 1st Session, Dec. 7, 1925, p. 380.

46. Hasbrouck, *Party Government in the House of Representatives,* p. 164.

47. *Congressional Record,* 69th Congress, 1st Session, Dec. 16, 1925, p. 933.

48. Hasbrouck, *Party Government in the House of Representatives,* p. 23.

49. *Congressional Record,* 67th Congress, 3rd Session, Nov. 22, 1922, p. 26.

50. *Congressional Record,* 68th Congress, 2nd Session, Feb. 18, 1925, pp. 4009-4010.

51. *Congressional Record,* 69th Congress, 1st Session, March 25, 1926, p. 6313.

52. Galloway, *History of the House of Representatives,* p. 145.

53. *Ibid.*

54. *Congressional Record,* 67th Congress, 1st Session, Oct. 14, 1921, p. 6315.

55. *Congressional Record,* 69th Congress, 1st Session, April 8, 1926, p. 7148.

56. *Congressional Record,* 73rd Congress, 2nd Session, Jan. 11, 1934, p. 481.

57. *Ibid.,* p. 485.

58. *The Public Papers and Addresses of Franklin D. Roosevelt,* Vol. 7 (New York: Macmillan, 1941), p. 489.

59. Richard Bolling, *Power in the House: A History of the Leadership of the House of Representatives* (New York: Dutton, 1968), p. 164.

60. *The Reorganization of Congress,* A Report of the Committee of Congress of the American Political Science Association (Washington: Public Affairs Press, 1945), pp. 80-81.

61. *Hearings Before the Joint Committee on the Organization of Congress,* 79th Congress, 1st Session, March 19, 1945, p. 109.

62. *Organization of the Congress,* Report of the Joint Committee on the Organization of Congress, 79th Congress, 2nd Session (Washington: U.S. Government Printing Office, 1946), p. 35.

63. *Ibid.,* p. 13.

64. MacNeil, *Forge of Democracy,* p. 129.

65. *Congressional Record,* 80th Congress, 2nd Session, Feb. 27, 1948, p. 1878.

66. *Ibid.,* Feb. 18, 1948, p. 1400.

67. *Congressional Record,* 81st Congress, 1st Session, Feb. 7, 1949, p. 880.

68. George B. Galloway, *The Legislative Process in Congress* (New York: Crowell, 1953), p. 659.

69. Fenno, *The Power of the Purse,* p. 629.

70. *Congressional Record,* 87th Congress, 2nd Session, July 9, 1962, p. 12899.

71. *Ibid.,* p. 12900.

72. *Ibid.,* Oct. 10, 1962, pp. 23014-23015.

73. *Ibid.,* Oct. 13, 1962, p. 23470.

74. *Congressional Record,* 82nd Congress, 1st Session, Jan. 3, 1951, p. 18.

75. *Ibid.,* p. 12.

76. *Ibid.,* p. 10.

77. James A. Robinson, *The House Rules Committee* (Indianapolis: Bobbs-Merrill, 1963), p. 72.

78. *Congress and the Nation, 1965-1968,* Vol. II, p. 897.

79. *Ibid.,* p. 900.

80. Congressional Quarterly, *Congress and the Nation, 1969-1972,* Vol. III, p. 429.

81. Congressional Quarterly, *1973 Almanac,* pp. 905-917, 1007-1010; *1974 Almanac,* pp. 867-902; *1975 Almanac,* pp. 327-331, 801, 885-887.

82. *Congress and the Nation, 1969-1972,* Vol. III, pp. 382-396.

83. Congressional Quarterly, *1971 Almanac,* pp. 9-11; *1975 Almanac,* pp. 3-5.

84. Congressional Quarterly, *Inside Congress* (1976), pp. 1-16, 67-70, 74-91, 99-112, 127-133; *1971 Almanac,* pp. 723-724; *1974 Almanac,* p. 612.

85. *Inside Congress,* pp. 6-7; *1974 Almanac,* pp. 634-640.

86. Congressional Quarterly, *1972 Almanac,* pp. 419-442; *1973 Almanac,* pp. 243-256.

87. *1975 Almanac,* pp. 3-23.

Selected Bibliography

Bolling, Richard H. *House Out of Order.* New York: Dutton, 1965.

————. *Power in the House.* New York: Dutton, 1968.

Brown, George Rothwell. *The Leadership of Congress.* New York: Arno Press, 1974.

Burns, James MacGregor. *Congress on Trial.* New York: Harper & Brothers, 1949.

Carroll, Holbert N. *The House of Representatives and Foreign Affairs.* Pittsburgh: University of Pittsburgh Press, 1958.

Chiu, Chang-Wei. *The Speaker of the House of Representatives Since 1896.* New York: Columbia University Press, 1928.

Clapp, Charles L. *The Congressman: His Work as He Sees It.* Washington: The Brookings Institution, 1963.

Congress and the Nation, 1945-1964. Vol. I. Washington: Congressional Quarterly Inc., 1965.

Congress and the Nation, 1965-1968. Vol. II. Washington: Congressional Quarterly Inc., 1969.

Congress and the Nation, 1969-1972. Vol. III. Washington: Congressional Quarterly Inc., 1973.

Congressional Record. Washington: U.S. Government Printing Office.

Fenno, Richard F. Jr. *The Power of the Purse: Appropriations Politics in Congress.* Boston: Little, Brown, 1966.

Follett, Mary P. *The Speaker of the House of Representatives.* New York: Burt Franklin Reprints, 1974.

Ford, Paul Leicester, ed. *The Writings of Thomas Jefferson.* Vol. 6. New York: G. P. Putnam's, 1895.

Froman, Lewis A., Jr. *Congressmen and their Constituencies.* Chicago: Rand McNally, 1963.

Galloway, George B. *History of the House of Representatives.* New York: Crowell, 1961.

————. *The Legislative Process in Congress.* New York: Crowell, 1953.

————. *Congress at the Crossroads.* New York: Crowell, 1946.

Griffith, Ernest S. *Congress: Its Contemporary Role.* New York: New York University Press, 1951.

Hasbrouck, Paul DeWitt. *Party Government in the House House of Representatives.* New York: Macmillan, 1927.

Hecht, Marie B. *John Quincy Adams: A Personal History of an Independent Man.* New York: Macmillan, 1972.

Hinds, Asher C. *Precedents of the House of Representatives of the United States.* 8 vols. Washington. U.S. Government Printing Office, 1907.

Huitt, Ralph K., and Peabody, Robert L. *Congress: Two Decades of Analysis.* New York: Harper & Row, 1972.

MacNeil, Neil. *Forge of Democracy: The House of Representatives.* New York: David McKay Company, 1963.

McConachie, Lauros G. *Congressional Committees: A Study of the Origins and Development of Our National and Local Legislative Methods.* New York: Burt Franklin Reprints, 1973.

Mayo, Bernard. *Henry Clay: Spokesman of the New West.* Boston: Houghton Mifflin, 1937.

Riddick, Floyd M. *The United States Congress: Organization and Procedure.* Manassas, Va.: National Capitol Publishers, 1949.

Ripley, Randall B. *Party Leaders in the House of Representatives.* Washington: The Brookings Institution, 1967.

Robinson, James A. *The House Rules Committee.* Indianapolis: Bobbs-Merrill, 1963.

Williams, T. Harry. *Hayes: The Diary of a President 1875-1881.* New York: David McKay Company, 1964.

Wilson, Woodrow. *Congressional Government.* Cleveland: Meridian, 1956.

Young, Roland. *The American Congress.* New York: Harper & Brothers, 1958.

History of the Senate

To English Prime Minister William Gladstone it was "the most remarkable of all the inventions of modern politics."[1] To Viscount James Bryce, a British ambassador to the United States, it was the "masterpiece of the constitution makers." Prominent British political analyst Walter Bagehot disagreed. "It may be necessary to have the blemish, but it is a blemish just as much," he wrote.[2] Whether effusively praised or vigorously condemned, the United States Senate clearly ranks as the most powerful upper legislative chamber in the world.

It is not, however, precisely what its creators had in mind. Edmund Randolph said its purpose was to provide a cure for the "turbulence and follies of democracy,"[3] and James Madison asserted that "the use of the Senate is to consist in its proceeding with more coolness, with more system, and with more wisdom, than the popular branch."[4] In the Constitutional Convention, Madison maintained that the purpose of the Senate was first "to protect the people against their rulers; secondly to protect the people against the transient impressions into which they themselves might be led.... They themselves, as well as a numerous body of Representatives, were liable to err also, from fickleness and passion. A necessary fence against this danger would be to select a portion of enlightened citizens, whose limited number, and firmness might seasonably interpose against impetuous councils...."[5] Gouverneur Morris hoped simply "that the Senate will show us the might of aristocracy."[6] Opponents feared it might become an American House of Lords.

Formative Years: 1789-1809

Under the Great Compromise of 1787, the House of Representatives was to represent the "national principle," while the Senate was to be an expression of the "federal principle." Not only would each state have two votes in the Senate, but the election of senators by the state legislatures was thought to be a means of making the states a constituent part of the national establishment. However, although the basis of representation assured each state an equal voice, senators voted as individuals, they were paid by the federal government rather than the states, and the legislatures that elected them had no power to recall them.

Thus it is not surprising that most senators refused to consider themselves merely the agents of the state governments. Efforts by state legislatures to instruct their senators had only mixed success, but the practice did not die out entirely until 1913, when the adoption of the Seventeenth Amendment took the election of senators out of legislative hands.

The framers of the Constitution left unsettled many questions concerning the relationships among the branches of government, and it remained for the Senate—born of compromise and fashioned after no serviceable model—to seek its own place in the governmental structure. In the unending competition for a meaningful share of power, the Senate for nearly two centuries has been trying to define its role, and the history of the Senate is in large part the story of this quest.

Early Conceptions of Senate Role

It had been confidently predicted that the popularly elected House of Representatives would be the predominant chamber in the national legislature, with the Senate acting chiefly as a revisory body. At first the House did overshadow the Senate, both in power and prestige, but within a few decades the Senate—endowed with executive functions which the House did not share and blessed with a smaller and more stable membership—had achieved primacy over the lower chamber. Later the balance of power shifted from time to time, but the Senate never followed the British House of Lords into decline.

As the nation's population expanded, the size of the House mushroomed, while the Senate, in which the large and small states were equally represented, remained a comparatively small body. Growth compelled the House to impose stringent limitations on floor debate, to rely heavily on its committee system and to develop elaborate techniques to channel the flow of business—all steps that diminished the power of individual representatives. Such restrictions were not considered necessary in the Senate, where in any case members tended to view themselves as ambassadors of sovereign states, and the right of unlimited debate became the most cherished tradition of the upper chamber. To the House, action was the primary object; in the Senate, deliberation was paramount.

It had also been expected that the Senate would serve as an advisory council to the President, but natural friction between the two, aggravated by the rise of the party system, made such a relationship impracticable. As time passed, the Senate was far more likely to try to manage the President than to advise him. In the 19th century the Senate was often the dominant force in the government, but the rapid expansion of presidential power in the 20th century was accompanied by a corresponding decline in the power of the legislative branch, and the Senate increasingly felt that its existence as a viable legislative institution was threatened.

Insulation From Popular Pressure

The framers had expressed their distrust of democracy by providing for election of senators by the state legislatures rather than directly by the people. In "refining the popular appointment by successive filtrations," they hoped to assure excellence, guard against "mutability" and incidentally protect the interests of the propertied classes.[7] Under this system, which Madison in *The Federalist* described as "probably the most congenial with public opinion," the Senate enjoyed its periods of greatest prestige.[8] But as suffrage expanded and the democratization of government increased, pressure arose for direct election of senators. At length, the Senate was forced to participate in its own reform, and in 1912 Congress approved a proposed constitutional amendment providing for direct election. The Seventeenth Amendment, ratified in 1913, curtailed the abuses that so frequently had been associated with legislative election, but its other effects were difficult to measure. At any rate, no revolutionary change in the overall character of the institution could be discerned.

So successful were the framers in insulating the Senate from popular pressure that the body often seemed to care more for what Bryce called its "collective self-esteem" than it did for public opinion.[9] Sometimes it could be forced to act—as in the case of the Seventeenth Amendment and the adoption of the cloture rule in 1917—but its resistance to impetuous action was for the most part all its creators could have wished.

Only eight senators had reached New York City by March 4, 1789, the date fixed for the first meeting of Congress, and a quorum of the 22-member Senate—two of the 13 states had not yet ratified the Constitution—did not appear until April 6, five days after the House had organized. Crucial questions concerning the nature of the Senate and its proper role in the new government remained to be worked out.

Was the upper chamber to be principally a council to revise and review House measures, or a fully coequal legislative body? Should it also serve in a quasi-executive capacity as an advisory council to the President, particularly with respect to appointments and treaties? Was the Senate primarily the bastion of state sovereignty, the defender of propertied interests, a necessary check on the popularly elected House, or was it, as its opponents charged, a threat to republican principles and an incipient American House of Lords? Even the method of electing senators was in dispute: Were they to be chosen by joint or concurrent vote of bicameral state legislatures? This issue, which was not resolved until 1866, cost New York its Senate representation during most of the first session of Congress. The terms of individual senators were also in doubt. Under the Constitution, the first senators were to be divided into three classes—with terms of two, four and six years respectively—so that one-third of the Senate might be chosen every second year. To avoid charges of favoritism, the Senate resorted to choice by lot in making the division.

The first Senate, preoccupied with questions of form and precedence, was quick to claim for itself superiority over the House, but the lower chamber initially was the more important legislative body. James Madison stated in a letter to Virginia Governor Edmund Randolph that he would prefer serving in the House to the Senate. He wrote: "...I prefer the House of Representatives, chiefly because, if I can render any service there, it can only be to the public, and, not even in imputation, to myself."[10] (Madison was subsequently elected to the House of Representatives in the First Congress after being defeated for a Senate seat.)

In the earliest days of the first session, while the House was addressing itself to the financial problems of the infant nation, the Senate devoted three weeks to the consuming problem of an appropriate title of dignity for the President. The debate apparently was instigated by Vice President John Adams, whose penchant for ceremony earned him the mocking title of "His Rotundity."

The Senate's early insistence on form and its claim to deference from the House led to disputes over such matters as the method of transmitting communications between the two chambers, wording of the enacting clause in proposed legislation and proposals (briefly accepted) for differential pay for senators. With a mixture of resentment and amusement, the House rebuffed most Senate efforts to enhance its own prestige, the Senate soon abandoned its aristocratic claims, and relations between the two chambers became generally cordial.

Although the Senate initiated bills from the very beginning, in the earliest years most laws originated in the House (78 per cent from 1789 to 1809) with the Senate acting as a revisory body. During the first session of the First Congress only five bills were introduced in the Senate, of which four—including the important Judiciary Act, which established the framework of the judicial system—were passed. During the same period, the House originated and passed 26 bills; two of these were rejected by the Senate, one was lost in conference, and the Senate modified at least 20 of the remaining 23.[11]

Relations With the President

The concept of the Senate as an advisory council to the President never was realized. President Washington took informal advice, not from the Senate as a body, but from Alexander Hamilton, Madison (a House member) and others. The constitutional role of the Senate in the appointment process also fell short of the consultative role that some framers of the Constitution had envisioned. Washington's exercise of the appointment power carefully stressed the separate natures of the nomination and confirmation processes, a point underscored by his decision to submit nominations to the Senate in writing rather than in person. The Senate's role as an advisory council was further restricted in 1789, when the Senate narrowly accepted House-passed language vesting in the President alone the power to remove executive officers. Under Washington's successors, members of Congress had greater influence over appointments, but the principle of executive initiative remained firmly established.

In 1789 Washington attempted to put into practice his early view that "in all matters respecting treaties, oral communications [with the Senate] seem indispensably necessary."[12] On Aug. 22 and 24, he appeared in the Senate chamber to consult with the Senate concerning a treaty with southern Indians. His presence during Senate proceedings, however, created a "tense" atmosphere which was uncomfortable for the senators and the President.[13] It was an experience Washington did not wish to repeat. The result was that Senate participation in the early stages of treaty-making declined. This development made possible greater freedom of action when the time came to vote on ratification of treaties.

Indeed, in 1795 when the treaty with Great Britain negotiated in 1794 by Chief Justice John Jay was brought before the Senate for ratification, a bitter dispute occurred. The controversial treaty secured American frontier posts in the Northwest but permitted Britain to search American merchant ships and confiscate provisions destined for Britain's enemy, France. Ultimately, the treaty was ratified by a bare two-thirds majority June 24, 1795, but not before the Senate deleted a clause limiting U.S. trading rights in the British West Indies.

Relations With the States

The concept of senators as agents of state sovereignty led to repeated but largely unsuccessful efforts to make senators accountable to their state legislatures. Some members of Congress, representatives as well as senators, felt an obligation to make periodic reports on their activities to the state governments, and a continuing controversy raged over the right of state legislatures to instruct their senators. Instruction was more general in the South than in the North, but there was no unanimity of opinion on the question. However, with the emergence of political parties, party loyalty gradually took the place of the expected state allegiance.

Early Senate Procedure

Courtesy, dignity and informality marked the proceedings of the early Senate. A body that on a chill morning might leave its seats to gather around the fireplace had no need for an elaborate system of regulation. At the first session in 1789 the Senate adopted only 20 short rules, a number deemed sufficient to control the proceedings of a Senate no larger than some modern-day congressional committees. In 1806, the number of rules rose to 40; most of the new ones dealt with nominations and treaties.[14]

The rules left a wide area of decision to the Senate president, particularly Rule 16 which gave him sole authority to decide points of order. Vice President Adams presided over the Senate (1789-97) with no specific guides on procedure, but his successor, Thomas Jefferson (1797-1801), felt the need of referring "to some known system of rules, that he may neither leave himself free to indulge caprice or passion nor open to the imputation of them."[15] The result was Jefferson's *Manual of Parliamentary Procedure*, which was also adopted by the House in 1837.

Closed Sessions

Following the practice of the Congress of the Confederation, the Senate originally met behind closed doors. Total secrecy was not maintained, however, since senators often freely discussed their activities outside the chamber, and the Senate *Journal* and sketchy reports of Senate action appeared in print from time to time. The principal result of the closed-door policy was to focus public

---

Washington in the Senate

President Washington's early view was that "in all matters respecting treaties, oral communications [with the Senate] seem indispensably necessary."[1] Accordingly, on Aug. 22, 1789, the President and his Secretary of War, Gen. Henry Knox, appeared in the Senate chamber to consult with the Senate about a treaty with southern Indians. Sen. William Maclay of Pennsylvania gave an account of the proceedings in his *Journal*.

A paper containing the President's proposal was hurriedly read to the Senate by the Vice President, but members were not able to hear because of the noise of carriages passing in the street outside. The windows were closed and the proposals read again. In the silence that followed, the Vice President began to put the first question, but Maclay, fearing "that we should have these advices and consents ravished in a degree from us," rose and called for reading of the treaties and supporting documents alluded to in the President's paper. The President "wore an aspect of stern displeasure." Maclay "saw no chance of a fair investigation of subjects while the President of the United States sat there, with his Secretary of War, to support his opinions and over-awe the timid and neutral part of the Senate." Therefore, he backed a move to refer the entire subject to a committee. At this suggestion, the President "started up in a violent fret," exclaiming "This defeats every purpose of my coming here." After he had "cooled down, by degrees," the President agreed to a two-day postponement, then withdrew from the chamber "with a discontented air."

On his return to the Senate two days later, Washington was "placid and serene, and manifested a spirit of accommodation," but the atmosphere was still tense, and "a shamefacedness, or I know not what, flowing from the presence of the President, kept everybody silent."[2] At length, the business was concluded and the President departed. The experience was not one that he cared to repeat.

Footnotes

1. George H. Haynes, *The Senate of the United States: Its History and Practice,* Vol. 1 (Boston: Houghton Mifflin, 1938), p. 62.
2. *Ibid.,* pp. 63, 68.

---

attention on the widely reported debates of the House and to encourage suspicion of the aristocratic Senate. Beginning in 1790, various state legislatures determined to press for open sessions of the Senate, in part as a means of enforcing accountability from their senators.

After four defeats in four years, the Senate in 1794 finally voted to open its sessions "after the end of the present session of Congress, and, so soon as suitable galleries shall be provided for the Senate chamber."[16] Almost two years went by before the galleries were erected and the rule put into effect, but at the beginning of the first session of the Fourth Congress, in December 1795, the Senate's doors were finally opened to the public. The immediate effects of this action were not great, since the Senate sessions were too

Rules of the First Senate

I. The President having taken the chair, and a quorum being present, the journal of the preceding day shall be read, to the end that any mistakes may be corrected that shall have been made in the entries.

II. No member shall speak to another, or otherwise interrupt the business of the Senate, or read any printed paper while the journals or public papers are reading, or when any member is speaking in any debate.

III. Every member, when he speaks, shall address the chair, standing in his place, and when he has finished shall sit down.

IV. No member shall speak more than twice in any one debate on the same day, without leave of the Senate.

V. When two members shall rise at the same time, the President shall name the person to speak; but in all cases the person first rising shall speak first.

VI. No motion shall be debated until...seconded.

VII. When a motion shall be made and seconded, it shall be reduced to writing, if desired by the President, or any member, delivered in at the table, and read by the President before the same shall be debated.

VIII. While a question is before the Senate, no motion shall be received unless for an amendment, for the previous question, or for postponing the main question, or to commit, or to adjourn.

IX. The previous question being moved and seconded, the question for the chair shall be: "Shall the main question now be put?" and if the nays prevail, the main question shall not then be put.

X. If a question in a debate include several points, any member may have the same divided.

XI. When the yeas and nays shall be called for by one-fifth of the members present, each member called upon shall, unless for special reasons he be excused by the Senate, declare, openly and without debate, his assent or dissent to the question. In taking the yeas and nays, and upon the call of the House, the names of the members shall be taken alphabetically.

XII. One day's notice at least shall be given of an intended motion for leave to bring in a bill.

XIII. Every bill shall receive three readings previous to its being passed; and the President shall give notice at each, whether it be the first, second, or third; which readings shall be on three different days, unless the Senate unanimously direct otherwise.

XIV. No bill shall be committed or amended until it shall have been twice read, after which it may be referred to a committee.

XV. All committees shall be elected by ballot, and a plurality of votes shall make a choice.

XVI. When a member shall be called to order, he shall sit down until the President shall have determined whether he is in order or not; and every question of order shall be decided by the President, without debate; but, if there be a doubt in his mind, he may call for the sense of the Senate.

XVII. If a member be called to order for words spoken, the exceptionable words shall be immediately taken down in writing, that the President may be better enabled to judge the matter.

XVIII. When a blank is to be filled, and different sums shall be proposed, the question shall be taken on the highest sum first.

XIX. No member shall absent himself from the service of the Senate without leave of the Senate first obtained.

XX. Before any petition or memorial, addressed to the Senate, shall be received and read at the table, whether the same shall be introduced by the President or a member, a brief statement of the contents of the petition or memorial shall verbally be made by the introducer.

Source: Roy Swanstrom, *The United States Senate, 1787-1801.*

decorous to attract widespread attention, and the more spirited House remained the center of public interest. Furthermore, there were no official reporters of debates, and no accommodation for newspaper reporters was made in the Senate until 1802, after the government had moved to Washington.

Light Workload

The demands upon early senators do not appear to have been unduly burdensome. Ordinarily the Senate met at 11 a.m., except near the end of the session when the press of business was great, and 3 p.m. adjournments were common. Sen. William Maclay of Pennsylvania, whose *Journal* provides a prejudiced but invaluable record of the Senate in the First Congress, frequently noted that the Senate adjourned its own tedious debates so that members could go and listen to the livelier ones in the House. Absenteeism, a continuing problem, was only in part attributable to the difficulties of travel at this period. Accordingly, in 1798 the Senate finally added enforcement machinery to its rule prohibiting absence without leave.

Because most legislation originated in the House, the Senate had little to do early in the session; under the so-called *de novo* rule of 1790, all bills died at the end of each session of Congress, so the Senate did not have House-passed bills from a previous session on which to work. The House scornfully rejected Senate proposals that the two chambers jointly prepare a legislative program for an entire session; however, joint committees often were appointed near the end of sessions to determine what business had to be completed before adjournment. Much of the legislative output of each session was pushed through in the closing days. In the second session of the Sixth Congress, for example, the Senate passed 35 bills, one-third of them on the final day.

Presidential messages provided a partial agenda for each session. Washington and Adams delivered their messages in person annually, and each chamber prepared a reply which was delivered orally with great ceremony. Since these replies were carefully debated and amended, they provided a valuable opportunity for consideration of the overall legislative situation. Jefferson abandoned his predecessors' practice and delivered his messages in writing; such messages were not thought to require a reply.

Rules on Debate

Dilatory tactics occasionally appeared in the early Senate, but apparently they did not present a serious problem. Only three of the 1789 rules had any direct bearing on limitation of debate: Rule 4, providing that no member should speak more than twice in any one debate on the same day without permission of the Senate; Rule 6, providing that no motion should be debated until seconded; and Rule 16, providing that every question of order should be decided by the president without debate. The previous question, authorized under Rule 9, was not then used to close debate but rather to remove a question from further consideration by reverting to a previous one. The previous question was dropped when the rules were revised in 1806. At the same time, a motion to adjourn was made undebatable.

Although bills could be introduced by individual members with the permission of the majority after one day's notice, the more common practice was to move the appointment of a committee to report a bill. Thus only a limited number of bills were introduced and most of those introduced were passed.

Committee System

Standing committees as they are known today did not exist in the early Senate. Legislation was handled by ad hoc committees, which were appointed to consider a particular issue and disbanded once their work was finished, with the full Senate maintaining firm control over their activities. Membership was flexible, although the same senators were frequently assigned to committees dealing with a particular field of legislation. Following British precedent, opponents of a measure were excluded from the committee that considered it, and the Federalist majority frequently excluded Republicans from committees that were to consider bills involving party issues.

Membership and Turnover

In terms of previous experience, members of the early Senate were well qualified to serve in the national legislature. Of the 94 men in the Senate between 1789 and 1801, 18 had served in the Constitutional Convention, 42 in the Continental Congress or the Congress of the Confederation, and 84 in their state or provincial legislatures. Only one or two were without experience in some governmental capacity. A majority were men of wealth and social prominence, but they were a young "council of elders"—the average age in 1799 was only 45 years.[17]

Experience did not bear out the warnings of those who feared that senators would entrench themselves in office for life. Of the 94 senators who served between 1789 and 1801, 33 resigned within that period before completing their terms, and only six did so in order to take other federal posts. Frequent resignations continued for many years—35 in the period 1801-13—and the rate of re-election also was low.[18]

Emergence of Parties

Political parties had no place in the constitutional framework, and early Senate voting indicated chiefly sectional or economic divisions within the chamber. But upon the presentation of Alexander Hamilton's financial measures, the Senate—like the House—began to exhibit a spirit of partisanship. Supporters of a strong central government, chiefly representatives of mercantile and financial interests, banded together as Federalists under the leadership of Hamilton, while exponents of agrarian democracy, led by Madison and Jefferson, became known as Republicans. Party alignments, still quite fluid in 1791, gradually hardened in the next two years as they were inflamed by the excesses of the French Revolution and troubled relations with Great Britain. By 1794 Sen. John Taylor of Virginia wrote:

"The existence of two parties in Congress is apparent. The fact is disclosed almost upon every important question. Whether the subject be foreign or domestic—relative to war or peace—navigation or commerce—the magnetism of opposite views draws them wide as the poles asunder."[19]

The Federalists held the Senate until 1801, but in 1794 the Republicans came close to overturning that control. The Federalists succeeded in unseating Albert Gallatin on the charge that he had not been a citizen of the United States for the number of years required to be a senator. He was deprived of his seat on a 14-12 party-line vote, but on six

Secret Sessions

Even after the Senate in 1795 opened its doors for regular legislative sessions, it continued to hold closed (secret) executive sessions for the consideration of treaties and nominations. Under a rule of 1800, all confidential documents from the President and all treaties laid before the Senate were to be kept secret until the injunction of secrecy was removed. In 1820 a similar restriction was adopted for nominations, and in 1844 penalties were provided for violations of these rules.

In practice, however, secrecy was difficult to maintain, and repeated efforts to abolish the secret sessions finally bore fruit. In 1888, the Senate for the first time kept its doors open during the consideration of a treaty, and thereafter treaties increasingly came to be considered in open sessions. With few exceptions, nominations were considered in secret session until 1929. The Senate then, by a vote of 69-5, amended Rule 38 to provide for open sessions for the consideration of all Senate business, including treaties and nominations, unless the Senate in closed session decided by majority vote to consider a particular matter in closed session.

Although treaties and nominations are no longer considered in secret sessions, the Senate still goes into closed session from time to time, usually for the discussion of classified information. In such sessions, the public, the press and most Senate aides are required to leave the chamber and galleries. Frequently a censored transcript of the discussion is released later.

From the end of World War II to the close of the first session of the 94th Congress in 1975, the Senate held 17 secret sessions[1]: April 11, 1963, to discuss classified information concerning missile defenses; July 14, 1966, to consider establishment of a special committee to oversee the Central Intelligence Agency; Oct. 2, 1968, and again July 17, 1969, to consider classified material connected with the antiballistic missile program; Dec. 15, 1969, to discuss U.S. activities in Laos and Thailand; Sept. 10 and Dec. 18, 1970, to discuss legislative impasses; June 7, 1971, to discuss a report on U.S. military and related activities in Laos; twice May 2, 1972,[2] and once May 4, 1972, to consider action on a request to print classified National Security Council documents in the *Congressional Record;* Sept. 25, 1973, to debate the need for an accelerated Trident submarine program; June 10, 1974, to consider development of new strategic missiles; June 4, 1975, again to discuss strategic missiles; Nov. 20, 1975, to consider releasing a study on the Central Intelligence Agency and political assassinations; and Dec. 17 and 18, 1975, to consider U.S. activities in Angola.

1. Source for dates: United States Senate, Office of the Secretary, Historical Office.
2. Technically there were two separate secret meetings of the Senate on May 2, 1972, although the period of time between them was less than a minute.

other occasions during the session they needed the vote of Vice President Adams to carry their program.

Approval of the Jay Treaty in 1795 united the Federalists and firmly identified the Senate in the public mind as the focus of the Federalist Party. From that time on, both Federalists and Republicans voted with a high degree of party regularity. During the Fourth, Fifth and Sixth Congresses, the Federalists enjoyed a roughly 2-1 edge over the Republicans in the Senate, while the House was closely divided between the two parties. But the rapprochement with France, engineered by President Adams, deprived the Federalists of their principal issue, and this development, combined with invasion of the chamber by members from newly admitted southern and western states, broke the power of the Federalists in the Senate. In the elections of 1800, Jefferson's Republicans won the presidency and both houses of Congress. When the Seventh Congress convened in December 1801, the Republicans held a narrow Senate majority. Federalist strength in the Senate continued to decline throughout Jefferson's term of office.

Leadership in the Senate

The Constitution solved the problem of a job for the Vice President by making him president of the Senate and it directed the Senate to choose a president pro tempore to act for him in his absence. But there were good reasons why neither of these officers could supply effective legislative leadership.

The Vice President was not chosen by the Senate but imposed upon it from outside, and there was no necessity for him to be sympathetic to its aims. Precedent was set by John Adams who, although clearly in general agreement with the majority of the Senate during his term as Vice President, perceived his role as simply that of presiding officer and made little effort to guide Senate action. His successor, Republican leader Thomas Jefferson, could not have steered the Federalist-controlled Senate even if he had wished to do so, although he did maintain a watching brief for the Republican Party in the upper chamber.

The president pro tempore was elected by the Senate from among its own members, but he could not supply legislative leadership because his term was too random and temporary. By custom a president pro tempore was elected

---

The Early Senate

This eyewitness description of the Senate in session about 1796 was offered by William McKoy in a series of articles in Poulson's American Daily Advertiser *in 1828-29:*

Among the Thirty Senators of that day there was observed constantly during the debate the most delightful silence, the most beautiful order, gravity, and personal dignity of manner. They all appeared every morning full-powdered and dressed, as age or fancy might suggest, in the richest material. The very atmosphere of the place seemed to inspire wisdom, mildness, and condescension. Should any of them so far forget for a moment as to be the cause of a protracted whisper while another was addressing the Vice President, three gentle taps with his silver pencilcase upon the table by Mr. Adams immediately restored everything to repose and the most respectful attention, presenting in their courtesy a most striking contrast to the independent loquacity of the Representatives below stairs, some few of whom persisted in wearing, while in their seats and during the debate, their ample cocked hats, placed "fore and aft" upon their heads....

---

only for the current absence of the Vice President, and his term ended with the reappearance of the Vice President. From the First through the Sixth Congresses (1789-1801), 15 senators served as president pro tempore.[20]

Thus the mantle of legislative leadership soon fell upon individual senators—Oliver Ellsworth, Rufus King and others—and more importantly upon the executive branch. Presidents Washington and Adams shared a strong belief in the separation of powers. Neither was willing to take upon himself the role of legislative leader, but Alexander Hamilton had no such qualms. As Secretary of the Treasury until 1795—and even after his retirement to private life—Hamilton not only developed a broad legislative program but functioned, in the words of one historian, "as a sort of absentee floor leader," in almost daily contact with his friends in the Senate.[21]

Under Jefferson and his Secretary of the Treasury, Albert Gallatin, legislative leadership continued to emanate from the executive branch. Jefferson, wrote Sen. Timothy Pickering of Massachusetts, tried "to screen himself from all responsibility by calling upon Congress for advice and direction.... Yet with affected modesty and deference he secretly dictates every measure which is seriously proposed."[22]

By the end of Jefferson's administration, the Senate had established internal procedures and sampled its various functions. It had both initiated and revised proposed legislation, given its advice and consent to treaties and nominations, conducted its first investigations and held two impeachment trials—the first resulting in the removal from office of a federal judge and the second in the acquittal of Supreme Court Justice Samuel Chase. But the breadth of its powers was not yet clear; relations with the House, the executive branch and the state governments were still only tentatively charted and awaited further tests.

Emerging Senate: 1809-1829

Two decades of legislative supremacy began with the administration of Jefferson's successor, James Madison, for the "Father of the Constitution" proved himself incapable of presidential leadership. He soon lost control of his party to the young "war hawks" of the House, who succeeded in forcing him into the War of 1812, and thereafter he suffered repeated defeats at the hands of Congress.

James Monroe was no more fortunate in his relations with Congress than Madison had been. At the time of his second inauguration Henry Clay commented that "Mr. Monroe has just been re-elected with apparent unanimity, but he had not the slightest influence on Congress."[23]

Neither Madison nor Monroe was temperamentally fit for legislative leadership, and both were further handicapped by their obligation to the congressional caucus that had nominated them for the presidency. The situation of John Quincy Adams was even more difficult, since he owed his very election to the House of Representatives.

Rising Senate Influence

Under the speakership of Henry Clay, the House took a commanding role in government, but the influence of the Senate was on the rise. The trend toward Senate dictation of executive appointments, which had begun late in Jefferson's term of office, continued and increased under Madison. When he sought to make Gallatin Secretary of

State, the Senate blocked his choice and forced him to accept a secretary of its own choosing.

The importance of the Senate's treaty and appointment powers, in which the House had no share, was only one factor in the Senate's rise. The rapidly expanding size of the House soon suggested the advantages of serving in a smaller body; in 1820, there were still only 46 senators.[24] The Senate's longer term and more stable membership also made it seem a more desirable place in which to serve. Henry Clay moved from the Senate to the House in 1811, but by 1823 Martin Van Buren was able to claim that the Senate, more than any other branch, controlled all the efficient power of government. Clay returned to the Senate in 1831.

The Senate's legislative importance increased only gradually. In the early years, most proposed legislation originated in the House, and the great debates surrounding the War of 1812 occurred there. But the Senate took a leading role in the struggle over the Missouri Compromise of 1820 and succeeded in imposing upon the House an amendment barring slavery in any future state north of 36°30' north latitude. Since this was the part of the country in which the population was expanding most rapidly, proponents of slavery could no longer hope to uphold the cause of states' rights in the House. The Senate—where the two sides were more evenly matched—inevitably became the forum for the great anti-slavery debates of the following decades.

Change of Party Alignments

Party alignments changed during the 1809-29 period. The withering Federalist Party ceased to be a factor in national politics after the election of 1816, but Republican supremacy was marred by increasing factionalism. Suffrage expanded, and the newly enfranchised small farmers of the South and West had little in common with the landed aristocracy that was the backbone of the Republican Party. Thus the democratic masses turned from slave-holding planters to the leadership of Andrew Jackson of Tennessee, an exponent of their fiercely egalitarian philosophy. In 1825 when the House of Representatives made Adams President, although Jackson had led in popular voting, the Republican Party split and a new Democratic Party was organized by Jackson's lieutenants. In 1826, the Democrats won control of both houses of Congress, and in 1828 they placed Jackson in the presidency of which they thought he had been defrauded four years earlier.

Growth of Standing Committees

The Senate lagged behind the House in establishing a formal committee structure. In its first quarter century it created only four standing committees, all chiefly administrative in nature: the Joint Standing Committee on Enrolled Bills, the Senate Committee on Engrossed Bills, the Joint Standing Committee for the Library, and the Senate Committee to Audit and Control the Contingent Expenses of the Senate.

During this period most of the legislative committee work fell to ad hoc select committees, usually of three members, appointed as the occasion demanded.[25] But eventually the need to appoint so many committees (between 90 and 100 in the session of 1815-16) exhausted the patience of the Senate, and in 1816 it added 11 standing committees to the existing four: Foreign Relations, Finance, Commerce

and Manufactures, Military Affairs, the Militia, Naval Affairs, Public Lands, Claims, the Judiciary, the Post Office and Post Roads, and Pensions. Most of the new committees were parallel in function to previously created committees of the House. The usual membership was five; this number would rise to seven by mid-century and to nine by 1900.[26]

Senate committees were chosen by ballot until 1823, but in that year the Senate adopted an amendment to its rules giving the presiding officer authority to name committees, unless otherwise ordered by the Senate. At first this power was exercised by the president pro tempore, an officer of the Senate's own choosing, but early in the 19th Congress (1825-27) Vice President John C. Calhoun assumed the appointment power and used it to place Jackson supporters in key committee posts. In the face of this patent effort to embarrass the Adams administration, the Senate quickly returned to the rule of choice by ballot. In 1828 the rule was changed again, this time to give appointment power to the president pro tempore, but in 1833 the Senate once more reverted to choice by ballot.

A general revision of the Senate rules in 1820, bringing the total number of rules to 45, was remarkable chiefly for incorporating the provisions relating to standing committees that the Senate had adopted four years earlier. No great spirit of reform was involved; as in the case of other general revisions of Senate rules, the 1820 revision represented chiefly an attempt to codify changes that had accumulated over a number of years.

'A Senate of Equals'

Daniel Webster was to describe the upper chamber in 1830 as a "Senate of equals, of men of individual honor and personal character, and of absolute independence," who knew no master and acknowledged no dictation.[27] In such a body it is not surprising that no single leader had emerged to parallel the rise of Henry Clay in the House.

Statesmen of prominence served in the Senate during the 1809-29 period. The roster included four future Presidents—Andrew Jackson, Martin Van Buren, William Henry Harrison and John Tyler—and a number of presidential hopefuls. By the close of the period, the great figures of the ensuing "Golden Age" were beginning to gather in the chamber: Thomas Hart Benton of Missouri arrived in 1821, Robert Y. Hayne of South Carolina in 1823 and Daniel Webster of Massachusetts in 1827. Henry Clay of Kentucky, after serving briefly in the Senate in 1810-11, went to the House; he was to return to the Senate in 1831. Calhoun would resign as Vice President in 1832 to succeed Hayne as senator from South Carolina.

Until Calhoun took office in 1825, the Vice Presidents of the period did not play significant roles. Madison's first Vice President, George Clinton, was old and feeble and died in office, as did his successor, Elbridge Gerry. Monroe's Vice President, Daniel D. Tompkins, hardly ever entered the Senate chamber.

Vice President Calhoun, hostile to the Adams administration and harboring presidential ambitions of his own, had no desire to alienate the Senate by exercising undue authority, but he was a commanding figure and his influence was felt. Hayne generally served as his spokesman on the floor.

Calhoun took advantage of his position to make obviously biased committee appointments, but in other respects he assumed as little authority as possible. Although all of his predecessors in the chair had assumed direct

(Continued on p. 77)

Senate Votes by Vice Presidents

From the beginning of the American republic, the executive branch has put to good use the authority granted the Vice President under the Constitution to vote in the Senate in the event of a tie. Through 1975, Vice Presidents had cast Senate votes on 215 occasions. Some of those votes were recorded against questions that would have failed of approval even if the Vice President had not voted, because a question on which the Senate is evenly divided automatically falls by the wayside. In such cases the Vice President's negative vote was superfluous; the only purpose it served was to make known his own opposition to the proposal. Records are not available to show exactly how many of the 215 votes cast by Vice Presidents were in the affirmative and thus decisive.

The first recorded vote by a Vice President was a negative vote cast by John Adams on July 18, 1789, the effect of which was to support the President's right to remove an appointed official without consulting the chamber of Congress which had given original consent to the appointment. The House had included in a bill establishing the Department of Foreign Affairs language that implied recognition of the President's sole power of removal. When the bill reached the upper chamber, the Senate—sitting "as in Committee of the Whole"—first rejected a motion to strike out this language on a 10-10 tie vote.

This action is not recorded in the Senate *Journal,* but Sen. William Maclay's *Journal* for July 16, 1789, describes the scene: "After all the arguments were ended and the question taken, the Senate was ten to ten, and the Vice President with joy cried out, 'It is not a vote,' without giving himself time to declare the division of the House and give his vote in order."* Two days later, when the bill came up for final action, a roll call was demanded on the same question. One senator was absent and another senator on the opposing side withheld his vote, so the Senate was divided 9-9 when the Senate secretary called for the Vice President's vote. Adams voted nay.

The vote was one of 29 cast by Adams—a record approached only by John C. Calhoun, who cast 28 votes as Vice President. Although the Adams vote had no effect on determination of the question at issue, he considered his stand in support of the President's removal power one of his most important acts in public life.

One important vote by a Vice President was cast on July 28, 1846, when George M. Dallas broke a tie in favor of the Polk administration's tariff reform bill.

Among other important vice presidential votes were two cast by Thomas R. Marshall on foreign policy issues. On Feb. 2, 1916, his vote carried an amendment to a Philippines bill pledging full independence to the islands by March 4, 1921. (The amendment was modified in conference to provide for independence as soon as a stable government could be established.) On April 4, 1919, Marshall cast the deciding vote to table a resolution calling for withdrawal of American troops from Russia as soon as practicable.

Two tie-breaking Senate votes of importance were cast by Richard M. Nixon. On April 22, 1959, Nixon voted to table a motion to reconsider the Senate's acceptance of an amendment to a labor reform bill; the amendment aimed to protect union members from coercion and arbitrary actions by union leaders. On Feb. 3, 1960, Nixon broke a tie by voting to table a motion to reconsider the Senate's rejection of an education bill amendment to authorize annual appropriations of $1.1-billion for an indefinite period for school construction and teachers' salaries.

Following is a list of the number of votes cast by each Vice President through 1975:

Period	Vice President	Number of Votes Cast
1789-1797	John Adams	29
1797-1801	Thomas Jefferson	3
1801-1805	Aaron Burr	3
1805-1812	George Clinton	11
1813-1814	Elbridge Gerry	8
1817-1825	Daniel D. Tompkins	5
1825-1832	John C. Calhoun	28
1833-1837	Martin Van Buren	4
1837-1841	Richard M. Johnson	14
1841	John Tyler	0
1845-1849	George M. Dallas	19
1849-1850	Millard Fillmore	3
1853	William R. King	0
1857-1861	John C. Breckinridge	10
1861-1865	Hannibal Hamlin	7
1865	Andrew Johnson	0
1869-1873	Schuyler Colfax	13
1873-1875	Henry Wilson	1
1877-1881	William A. Wheeler	5
1881	Chester A. Arthur	3
1885	Thomas A. Hendricks	0
1889-1893	Levi P. Morton	4
1893-1897	Adlai E. Stevenson	2
1897-1899	Garret A. Hobart	1
1901	Theodore Roosevelt	0
1905-1909	Charles W. Fairbanks	0
1909-1912	James S. Sherman	4
1913-1921	Thomas R. Marshall	4
1921-1923	Calvin Coolidge	0
1925-1929	Charles G. Dawes	2
1929-1933	Charles Curtis	3
1933-1941	John N. Garner	3
1941-1945	Henry A. Wallace	4
1945	Harry S Truman	1
1949-1953	Alben W. Barkley	7
1953-1961	Richard M. Nixon	8
1961-1963	Lyndon B. Johnson	0
1965-1969	Hubert H. Humphrey	4
1969-1973	Spiro T. Agnew	2
1973-1974	Gerald R. Ford	0
1974-1975	Nelson A. Rockefeller	0
TOTAL		215

* George H. Haynes, *The Senate of the United States: Its History and Practice,* Vol. I (Boston: Houghton Mifflin, 1938), pp. 58-62.

Source: Library of Congress, Congressional Research Service.

(Continued from p. 75)
authority to call senators to order for words used in debate, Calhoun contended that his power was appellate only and refused to act unless an offending senator was first called to order by another senator. He would not "for ten thousand worlds look like a usurper," Calhoun declared.[28] His refusal to act on his own initiative led the Senate in 1828 to amend its rules; henceforth the chair would have the power to call a senator to order, but for the first time in Senate history the rule permitted an appeal from the chair's decision on a question of order.

During the 1809-29 period, greater continuity of service developed in the office of president pro tempore. John Gaillard occupied the post for most of the period between 1814 and 1825 and presided over the Senate almost continuously during the five years when Tompkins was Vice President. Elected by the Senate and thus considering himself entitled to its support, Gaillard enforced the rules rigidly but did not exercise a true leadership role.

The Golden Age: 1829-1861

In the years leading up to the Civil War, the Senate became the chief forum for the discussion of national policy. The preeminent national issue in the period between the Missouri Compromise of 1820 and the outbreak of war in 1861 was the struggle between North and South over slavery. The Senate, where the two sides were equally matched due to the system of representation, inevitably became the principal battleground.

Sectional interests were more important than party during these years preceding the Civil War, and party divisions were often blurred. The Jacksonian Democrats adopted the agrarian and states' rights philosophy of the Jeffersonian Republicans, but their concept of strong executive leadership was at odds with Jeffersonian views. Meanwhile, the Whig Party was formed of the coalition of eastern financial and business interests that had once constituted the strength of the Federalists, but the Whigs were committed to a doctrine of legislative supremacy that was alien to Federalist thought.

The Democratic Party split over the question of slavery, and many southern Democrats allied themselves with the Whigs, in the hope of finding protection for states' rights and the institution of slavery under the Whig banner of legislative supremacy. However, the Whig Party had no answer to the slavery question, and in the 1850s it gave way to the new Republican Party, an alliance of northern interests dedicated to preventing the spread of slavery into the territories. Mounting southern defiance of northern opinion led to a North-South split in the Democratic Party, and secession and war soon followed.

In this age of giants three men dominated the Senate chamber. All were former representatives, and all suffered from presidential aspirations that were to influence the shifting coalitions of a turbulent era. Daniel Webster of Massachusetts—Whig, spokesman for eastern moneyed interests, sectionalist turned nationalist, supreme orator—entered the Senate in 1827 and remained there for most of the period until 1850. Henry Clay of Kentucky—Whig, westerner, brilliant tactician and compromiser—returned to the Senate to serve between 1831 and 1842 and again in 1849-52. John C. Calhoun of South Carolina—outstanding logician, devoted son of the South and champion of the right of secession—stepped down from the vice presidency in 1832 to defend his nullification

John Calhoun   **Daniel Webster**

doctrine on the Senate floor and remained a senator for most of the period until his death in 1850. (Nullification was the refusal of a state to recognize or enforce a federal law it regarded as an infringement on its rights.)

French historian and politician Alexis de Tocqueville in 1834 contrasted the "vulgarity" of the House with the nobility of the Senate, where "scarcely an individual is to be found...who does not recall the idea of an active and illustrious career." The Senate, "is composed of eloquent advocates, distinguished generals, wise magistrates, and statesmen of note, whose language would, at all times, do honor to the most remarkable parliamentary debates of Europe."[29]

Senate's Preeminence Over House

De Tocqueville could think of only one explanation for the Senate's superiority: its members were elected by elected bodies, whereas representatives were elected by the people directly. Thomas Hart Benton disputed this analysis. Not only did the Senate enjoy advantages of smaller membership, longer term and greater age and experience on the part of its members, he said, but it was composed of "the pick of the House of Representatives, and thereby gains doubly—by brilliant accession to itself and abstraction from the other."[30]

Undoubtedly the Senate's greater stability of membership contributed to its preeminence over the House, where the Jacksonian concept of rotation in office led to great turnover. More significant, perhaps, was the introduction of the spoils system and the Senate's increasing domination of the appointment process. Finally, growth had strengthened the Senate by turning it from a small intimate body into one large enough for oratory and the exercise of brilliant parliamentary skills. With the addition of two senators from every new state, the Senate increased from 48 members at the beginning of Jackson's administration to 66 in Buchanan's. Its roster included such luminaries as Benton of Missouri, Lewis Cass of Michigan, Sam Houston of Texas, Jefferson Davis and Henry S. Foote of Mississippi, William H. Seward of New York, Stephen A. Douglas of Illinois and Charles Sumner of Massachusetts.

Quarrel With President Jackson

The eclipse of presidential power that had begun under Madison came to an end when Andrew Jackson became President in 1829. Backed by strong popular majorities and skilled in the use of patronage, Jackson was able to dominate the House, but in the Senate he met vigorous opposition from the new Whig Party, a combination of commercial and industrial interests dedicated to the principle of legislative supremacy. The Whigs were quick to challenge Jackson on questions of policy and executive prerogative, and his term was marked by repeated and acrimonious contests with the Senate over legislation and appointments.

These disputes reached a peak in 1834 when the Senate, outraged by Jackson's removal of deposits from the Bank of the United States and his refusal to hand over communications to his Cabinet relating to that subject, adopted a resolution censuring the President for his actions. The resolution, pushed through by Clay, charged "that the President, in the late executive proceedings in relation to the public revenue, has assumed upon himself authority and power not conferred by the Constitution and laws and in derogation of both."[31]

Jackson countered with a message, which the Senate refused to receive, declaring that so serious a charge as that contained in the censure resolution called for impeachment. Because impeachment could originate only in the House, he protested the Senate's action as a violation of the Constitution.

Benton, Jackson's leader in the Senate, promptly undertook a campaign to vindicate Jackson by expunging the censure resolution from the Senate *Journal.* Under pressure from the President, some state legislatures instructed their senators to support Benton's efforts, while others forced anti-Jackson senators into retirement. By the time Jackson's second term was drawing to a close in 1837, the Jacksonian Democrats had gained control of the Senate, and the expunging resolution finally was adopted by a 24-19 vote.

In one of the most dramatic scenes of Senate history the terms of the resolution were carried out: "[T]he Secretary of the Senate...shall bring the manuscript journal of the session of 1833-34 into the Senate, and, in the presence of the Senate, draw black lines round the said resolve, and write across the face thereof, in strong letters, the following words: 'Expunged by order of the Senate, the 16th day of January, in the year of our Lord 1837.' "[32]

Whigs vs. President Tyler

Undeterred by their failure to dominate Jackson, the Whigs persisted in their efforts to establish the doctrine of legislative supremacy. With the election of Whig President William Henry Harrison, they thought their moment had come. Daniel Webster was named Secretary of State, Clay supporters were put in other Cabinet positions, and Harrison's inaugural address—revised by Webster—was a model statement of Whig doctrine. But Harrison died after only one month in office, to be succeeded by John Tyler, a states' rights Virginian who had been elected Vice President on the Whig ticket.

Thomas Benton

Charles Sumner

At first Clay, as the leading Whig member of Congress, thought he could assume effective leadership of the government, and he even introduced a set of resolutions that were designed to be the party's legislative program. But Tyler, it turned out, was determined to be President in fact as well as title, and the two men soon clashed head-on. Tyler's exercise of the veto power drove the Whigs to threats of impeachment and abortive efforts to force his resignation, but Clay was unable to push through his own legislative program. Although all Presidents had trouble with appointments during this period, Tyler, who lacked support in either party, was more unfortunate than most. Many of his nominations, including four to the Cabinet, were rejected by the Senate.

After Tyler's presidency the Whigs were never again able to muster a majority in the Senate that would permit them to put their doctrine of legislative supremacy to a test. Difficulties with nominations continued, for this was the height of the spoils system, but a succession of strong Presidents established a pattern of executive leadership that even the weakness of Pierce and Buchanan could not entirely destroy.

Great Debates Over Slavery

Oratory in the Senate reached its peak in the years leading up to the Civil War, and visitors often thronged the galleries to hear the great debates over slavery. Never had the Senate seemed so splendid as in this period when it served as the forum for the nation.

But the courtesy and decorum of the early Senate gradually began to crumble under the mounting pressures of the time. Although debates were for the most part still close and brief, passions sometimes ran high and legislative obstruction became increasingly common. Filibusters were now often threatened and occasionally undertaken, but they were not yet fully exploited as a means of paralyzing the Senate, and senators seldom admitted that they were employing dilatory tactics.

The first notable Senate filibuster occurred in 1841, when dissident senators held the floor for 10 days in opposition to a bill to remove the Senate printers. Later in the same year a Whig move to re-establish the Bank of the United States was subject to an unsuccessful two-week filibuster. Henry Clay said the tactics of the minority would "lead to the inference that embarrassment and delay were the objects aimed at," and he threatened to introduce a rule to limit debate. Unabashed, the filibusterers invited Clay to "make his arrangements at his boarding house for the winter" and warned that they would resort to "any possible extremity" to prevent restriction of debate. Unable to obtain majority support for his "gag rule," Clay never carried out his threat, and the bank bill eventually passed, only to be vetoed by President Tyler.[33]

In 1846 a bill providing for U.S.-British joint occupancy of Oregon was filibustered for two months. The measure was finally brought to a vote through use, apparently for the first time, of the unanimous consent agreement—a device still employed to speed action in the Senate. Later in 1846 the Wilmot Proviso was talked to death in the closing hours of the session. The proviso, which the House had attached as a rider to an appropriation bill in the early months of the Mexican War, stipulated that slavery be excluded from any territory that might be acquired from Mexico.

Slavery was again the issue in the extended debates over the Compromise of 1850, Clay's valiant attempt to resolve the sectional controversies that were tearing the nation apart. In a crowded chamber, the great triumvirate—Webster, Clay and Calhoun—made their last joint appearance in the Senate. The dying Calhoun dragged himself into the chamber to hear his final speech read by his colleague James Murray Mason of Virginia.

Violence in the Senate. Violence threatened when Sen. Henry S. ("Hangman") Foote of Mississippi brandished a pistol at Missouri's Benton, who was well known as a deadly duelist. Only the intervention of other senators prevented bloodshed.

Greater violence marked the 1856 debate on the Kansas statehood bill. Two South Carolina representatives attacked Charles Sumner while he sat at his desk in the Senate chamber and bludgeoned him so severely that the Massachusetts senator was unable to resume his seat until 1859.

In the next few years, as the nation drifted toward war, debates continued to reflect the rancor of the period. Oratory had little place in a chamber where all members were said to carry arms, and by the time the Senate moved into its present quarters in 1859 the great epoch of Senate debate was at an end. Oratory had flourished in the intimate grandeur of the old hall; in the new chamber—vast and acoustically poor—a new style of debate emerged.

The Committee System

The most important procedural development of the 1829-61 period occurred in 1846 when the Senate transferred responsibility for making committee assignments to the party organizations in the chamber. As long as committee assignments were determined by ballot, majority party control of the committees could not be assured, and, although by 1829 the majority usually controlled the working committees, the opposition party still held important chairmanships.

When the second session of the 29th Congress met in December 1846, the Senate first rejected a proposal to let the Vice President name the committees and then, in accordance with the regular rule, began balloting for chairmen. Midway through this process the balloting rule was suspended, and the Senate proceeded to elect on one ballot a list of candidates for all of the remaining committee vacancies that had been agreed upon by the majority and minority. From that time on, the choice of committees has usually amounted to a routine acceptance by the Senate of lists agreed upon by representatives of the caucus or conference of the two major parties.

The fact that the party organizations did not become the standard instrument of committee selection until 1846 gives some indication of the limited use of party discipline in the early years of the Senate. During this period, party authority was confined to organizational questions; when it came to substantive issues, senators voted as individuals rather than as Democrats or Whigs.

Party influence in the Senate was enhanced by the new method of committee selection, but rank within committees was thereafter increasingly determined by seniority, thus making chairmanships less subject to party control. Experience had always played a major role in making committee assignments, but as long as committees were elected by ballot, rigid adherence to seniority was impossible. However, with the introduction of party lists in 1846 strict compliance with seniority began to be enforced. The bitter sectional disputes leading up to the Civil War may well have

encouraged the use of seniority to avoid fierce inter-party struggles for committee control.

The system was not, of course, impartial in distributing its favors. In 1859 a northern Democrat called the seniority usage "intolerably bad" and complained that it had "operated to give to senators from slave-holding states the chairmanship of every single committee that controls the public business of this government. There is not one exception."[34]

There had been one exception earlier in the same year; Stephen A. Douglas of Illinois was chairman of the Committee on Territories. But the Democratic Caucus had removed him from the chairmanship, in spite of his seniority, because he refused to go along with President James Buchanan and the southern wing of the party on the question of slavery in the territories.

By the time of the Civil War the committee structure of the Senate had changed from a loose aggregation of ad hoc committees appointed for the occasion to a formal system of standing committees, whose members owed their appointments to the party organization and their advancement within committees to the seniority system.

Party Government: 1861-1901

During the Civil War and Reconstruction periods, the Republicans controlled the presidency, the Senate and the House throughout seven consecutive Congresses, ending in 1875. Not only did the Democrats lose the southern seats in Congress, most of which were vacant from 1861 to 1869, but many northern Democrats defected to the Republicans rather than remain in a party so closely tied to the southern cause.

This period of Republican hegemony was marked by a power struggle between Congress and the White House. During the war Congress sought to assert its authority through such mechanisms as the Joint Committee on the Conduct of the War, consisting of three senators and four representatives, which exercised a wide range of authority. Yet President Lincoln managed not only to retain his independence of Congress, but also to increase the armed forces, call for volunteers, spend money on defense, issue a code of regulations for the armed forces, suspend the writ of habeas corpus, and even emancipate the slaves in the states in rebellion without waiting for authority from Congress.

When the President issued a proclamation of Reconstruction in December 1863, Congress passed the Wade-Davis bill transferring Reconstruction powers to itself. In response to the President's pocket veto of this measure, the Radical Republicans in Congress issued the Wade-Davis Manifesto, which declared: "[T]he authority of Congress is paramount and must be respected; that the body of Union men in Congress will not submit to be impeached by him [the President] of rash and unconstitutional legislation; and if he wishes our support he must confine himself to his executive duties—to obey and execute, not to make the laws—to suppress by arms and armed rebellion, and leave political reorganization to Congress."[35]

Era of Radical Republicans

The Republican Congress achieved its aims after Lincoln was assassinated. It passed its own Reconstruction Act, overrode President Andrew Johnson's veto of a civil rights bill and set up Gen. Ulysses S. Grant as General of the Army in Washington, requiring all Army orders to be issued through him (thus bypassing the President as commander in chief) and forbidding the President to remove or transfer the general without prior consent of the Senate. Over Johnson's veto, Congress passed the Tenure of Office Act which required approval by the Senate of the removal of officials appointed with its advice and consent. When Johnson dismissed his Secretary of War to test in the courts the constitutionality of the act, the House impeached him, and the Senate came within one vote of removing him from office. Congress had broken the authority of the executive. Under a compliant President Grant, the Republican Congress governed.

In this period of one-party government, the House, led by Radical Republican Thaddeus Stevens of Pennsylvania, overshadowed the Senate. But following the failure of the effort to impeach Johnson and the death of Stevens, House prestige declined, and the Senate rapidly became the dominant arm of the national legislature. During the remainder of the 19th century, while control of the House shifted back and forth between the two parties, the Republicans managed to maintain control of the Senate in all except two Congresses, and during this period modern party government developed in the upper chamber.

Meanwhile, later Presidents were able to recoup some of the power lost under Grant. With public support, Rutherford B. Hayes refused to let the Republican Senate dictate his Cabinet and customs appointments, and Grover Cleveland's defense of the presidential appointment power led to repeal of the Tenure of Office Act, but on the whole the Senate remained the most powerful force in the government. When William McKinley became President in 1897, Congress and the White House entered a period of almost unprecedented harmony. "We never had a President who had more influence with Congress than McKinley," said Sen. Shelby M. Cullom (R Ill.). "I have never heard of even the slightest friction between him and the party leaders in Senate and House."[36]

Power of Party Bosses in Senate

The character of the Senate underwent a marked change in the post-Civil-War era. Its membership grew from 74 in 1871 to 90 in 1901, and, as state politics became more centralized, a new breed of senator entered the chamber. The great constitutional orators of the pre-war period were succeeded by "party bosses"—professional politicians who had risen through the ranks of their state party organizations and who came to Washington only after they had consolidated their power over the state party structure. As long as they maintained state control, they were immune from external political reprisal, but their dedication to party and their acceptance of the need for discipline made them good "party senators," willing to compromise their differences in order to maintain harmony within the party. To these men the Senate was a career, and a striking increase in average length of Senate service occurred during this period.

The public viewed the Senate's changing character with grave suspicion, and the growing power of party organizations was widely attributed to the "trusts." Political analyst Moisei Ostrogorski charged in 1902 that the economic interests "equipped and kept up political organizations for their own use, and ran them as they pleased, like their trains."[37] Other observers held that political centralization and business concentration were

parallel developments, not directly related, but they agreed that the corporations contributed to the power of the party chiefs.

Loss of Public Esteem

Lobbying by business groups became a vital element in government during the last part of the 19th century, but business itself was not unified and its efforts were too haphazard for it to attain great political control. Still, some of the lobbying practices of the period—ranging from wholesale distribution of railroad passes to loans and sales of stock at attractive prices to members of Congress—fostered the impression of Senate corruption.

The Senate's "usurpation" of executive power, its failure to impose limitations on debate and the undoubted existence of corruption all contributed to the chamber's loss of public esteem. By the close of the 19th century, the Senate was described in derogatory—and somewhat unfair—fashion as a "Millionaires' Club," and it was without question the most unpopular branch of the national government. Dissatisfaction with the Senate led to the movement for direct election of senators, through which reformers hoped to curtail both the power of political parties and the political influence of the corporations. By 1900, it had become clear that a constitutional amendment providing for direct election would eventually be enacted.

Development of Party Leadership

Political parties assumed responsibility for organizational matters in the pre-Civil-War Senate, and party authority was extended during the war to substantive questions as well. However, the Senate had no strong tradition of leadership and party discipline was expected to lapse after the war ended. Indeed, the Republican and Democratic Parties themselves were expected to disintegrate, as other parties had done before them, once the issues that had brought them together were resolved.

Although the parties failed to dissolve, party influence in the upper chamber did decline for a time; when Grant's administration began in 1869, political parties compelled unity only on organizational questions. Disputes over committee assignments were settled in the caucus, and pressing issues were discussed there, but caucus decisions could hardly be considered binding as long as there was no leader to enforce discipline or exact reprisals. The Republican caucus did remove Charles Sumner of Massachusetts from the chairmanship of the Foreign Relations Committee in 1871 when his differences with President Grant had become so extreme that he would communicate neither with the President nor the Secretary of State.

Conkling's Influence. The possibilities of party leadership first became apparent in the Senate career of Roscoe Conkling of New York in the 1870s. Conkling gathered around him a loyal following, and after 1873 his faction usually controlled the Committee on Committees and thus was able to reward his supporters with valuable committee posts. But the Conkling forces stood together only on organizational questions; their influence on substantive legislation was not great. When Conkling resigned his Senate seat in 1881, following an altercation with President Garfield over appointments, the Senate reverted to its old independent ways. "No one," wrote Woodrow Wilson in 1885, "is *the* Senator. No one may speak for his party as well as for himself; no one exercises the special trust of acknowledged leadership. The Senate is merely a body of individual critics...."[38]

William Allison   **Nelson Aldrich**

Modern Party Discipline

Republican Leadership. Modern party discipline made its appearance in the Senate in the 1890s under the leadership of William B. Allison of Iowa, Nelson W. Aldrich of Rhode Island and their fellow members of the School of Philosophy Club, an informal group that met regularly for poker at the home of Joseph McMillan of Michigan. When Allison, because he had served in the Senate longer than any other member of his party, was elected chairman of the Republican Caucus in March 1897, this group assumed control of the Senate. Previous caucus chairmen had not viewed the office as a vehicle for concentrating party authority, but Allison was quick to see the possibilities of his new position. Holding that "both in the committees and in the offices, we should use the machinery for our own benefit and not let other men have it," Allison took advantage of his appointment powers to monopolize party offices.[39]

Since the mid-1880s, a Republican Steering Committee had been appointed biennially to help schedule legislative business. Unlike previous caucus leaders, Allison determined to chair this committee himself, and he filled the committee with other members of his group. Under Allison's guidance, the Steering Committee arranged the order of committee with other members of his group. Under Allison, the Steering Committee arranged the order of business in minute detail and also managed proceedings on the floor.

Allison likewise dominated the Committee on Committees, which had responsibility for assignments to the working committees. The caucus chairman had great leeway in making appointments to this group, and Allison was able to staff it with a majority that would be receptive to his wishes; its chairman was always a member of the ruling faction. Committee chairmanships were by this time invariably filled through seniority, and Allison and Aldrich made no attempt to overturn the seniority rule, to which they owed their own committee chairmanships (Allison on Appropriations and Aldrich on Finance). But seniority did not apply to the filling of committee vacancies, and here the party leaders found an opportunity to reward their supporters and punish dissidents. Access to positions of influence soon depended on the favor and support of the party leaders. When Albert J. Beveridge of Indiana entered the Senate in 1899, he directed his appeal for committee preferment to Allison, in shrewd recognition of the existing order. "I feel that the greatest single point is gained in the possession of your friendship," Beveridge said. "I will labor very hard, strive very earnestly to deserve your consideration."[40]

Caucus approval of the committee slates and order of business became a mere formality, but the caucus still met to consider important issues. Through the caucus mechanism divisive questions were compromised in

privacy, and the party was enabled to speak with a united voice on the floor. Caucus decisions were not formally binding ("We can get along without that," Allison remarked), but once the party leadership was capable of enforcing discipline on those who broke ranks, party solidarity became the norm. "Senators willing to abandon the opportunity to increase their authority could act freely, following their own inclinations," historian David Rothman noted. "The country might honor their names but the Senate barely felt their presence."[41]

Democratic Leadership. Under the leadership of Arthur P. Gorman of Maryland, Senate Democrats developed a power structure similar to that devised by the Republicans. As chairman of the Democratic Caucus in the 1890s, Gorman chaired not only the Steering Committee but the Committee on Committees as well, and in some ways his control over his party was greater than that of Allison and Aldrich over the Republicans. But the Democrats were in the minority most of the time, they often split on substantive issues, and Gorman never attained the power that his Republican counterpart achieved. The lack of harmony within Democratic ranks led, in 1903, to the adoption of a rule making the decisions of the Democratic Caucus binding upon a two-thirds vote. Allison had considered such a rule unnecessary for the Republicans, but Gorman enthusiastically supported it.

Attitude Toward Party Control

The growth of party government was viewed with grave misgivings by the country at large and was by no means always popular in the Senate itself. As early as 1872 the Liberal Republicans (dissident Republicans opposed to the Grant administration) were protesting efforts by "a few Members of the Senate" to use the party organization to "seek to control first a majority of the members belonging to that organization and then of the Senate."[42] Similar complaints came from the Mugwumps (Republicans opposed to the party leadership) in the 1880s and from the Populist Party in the 1890s. The Senate in 1899 took one step toward dispersing authority within the chamber when it transferred responsibility for major appropriations bills from the Appropriations Committee to various legislative committees. The change was pressed, not in caucus, but on the floor where dissidents within both parties were able to carry it over the combined opposition of the Republican and Democratic leaders.

By the end of the 19th century, political parties had assumed a decisive role in the legislative process. The parties named the committees which made the first tentative decisions on proposed legislation, and they also determined what bills would be considered on the floor. When divisive legislative questions arose, party members resolved their differences within the caucus and went forth in disciplined ranks to ratify caucus decisions on the floor, often acting without debate or the formality of a roll-call vote.

The Republicans had a plurality, but not a majority, of the Senate when a bill proposed by representative Nelson Dingley raising tariffs to a new high came from the House in April 1897. Allison, with only the help of the Republican members of the Finance Committee, framed the schedules, which all but three of the Republicans agreed in advance to support. After limited debate in the caucus, the bill went to the Senate floor where united Republican support passed it over solid Democratic opposition. The Republicans, said Benjamin R. Tillman of South Carolina, "under the stress of party orders, I suppose, given by the caucus, sit by quietly and vote. They say nothing...and every schedule prepared by the party caucus is voted by them unanimously."[43] Tillman was wrong in only one particular; he credited the caucus with more influence than it actually had.

Election Law of 1866

For more than 75 years after the adoption of the Constitution, Congress took no advantage of its constitutional power to regulate congressional elections, and the method of electing senators was left to the states. At first, senators generally were chosen by concurrent vote of the two houses of the state legislature, each sitting separately. Later, in about half the states it became common for the two houses to elect senators by per capita voting in joint session.

The election system had serious flaws. Insistence on a majority vote in each house caused frequent deadlocks, which not only kept the legislature from handling other business but also caused the state to lose its representation in the Senate. Irregular practices abounded, and the Senate itself was forced to decide many election contests resulting from the lack of a uniform election law.

Accordingly, Congress in 1866 enacted legislation designed to correct these problems. The 1866 law provided that on the second Tuesday after the organization of a legislature when a senator was to be elected, the two houses should meet separately and by voice vote name a person for senator. On the following day the results of the voting were to be canvassed at a joint session of the two houses. If one candidate had won a majority of both houses, he was to be declared elected, but if this was not the case, "the joint assembly shall meet at twelve o'clock, meridian, of each succeeding day during the session of the legislature, and take at least one vote until a senator shall be elected."[44]

Senatorial elections were regulated by this law for almost half a century, until the adoption of the Seventeenth Amendment in 1913, but the measure was not a success. Deadlocks continued to occur, and irregularities increased. George H. Haynes summarized the problems of legislative election that led to the direct election movement: "...not a few, but nearly half the states of the Union suffered from serious deadlocks. These contests, the outcome of which was often as much a matter of chance as would be the throw of dice, aroused men's worst passions and gave rise now to insistent charges of bribery, now to riot, to assault and to threats of bloodshed, such that legislative sessions had to be held under protection of martial law. Fourteen contests lasted throughout an entire session of the legislature without effecting an election. Four states submitted to the heavy cost and inconvenience of special sessions to elect senators. Six states preferred to accept vacancies, thus losing their 'equal suffrage in the Senate,' while the country was deprived of a Senate constituted as the fathers had intended. At times legislative election led to positive and flagrant misrepresentation of the state in the Senate. To the individual state it brought a domination of state and local politics by the fierce fight for a single federal office, and interference with the work of lawmaking, ranging all the way from the exaction of a few hours of the legislators' time to the virtual annihilation of the legislature, which had been constituted to care for the interests of the state."[45]

Rise of the Filibuster

The oratorical splendor that had brought renown to the Senate in the years preceding the Civil War disappeared with the settlement of the slavery question, and for the remainder of the 19th century Senate debate was not noted for its brilliance. As crucial legislative decisions came to be made in party councils, few floor speeches were delivered for the purpose of swaying votes, and attendance at formal sessions of the Senate became a tedious duty. "It would be a capital thing," wrote George F. Hoar in 1897, "to attend Unitarian conventions if there were not Unitarians there, so too it would be a delightful thing to be a United States Senator if you did not have to attend the sessions of the Senate."[46]

Filibusters, increasingly common as the century advanced, became virtually an epidemic in the 1880s and 1890s. As a result, the Senate suffered a marked loss of public esteem for its failure to impose stringent curbs on debate. Cloture proposals were introduced from time to time, but the Senate held fast to its cherished tradition of unlimited speech.

Wartime pressures had produced two notable filibusters during the 1860s. In 1863 the conference report on a bill to secure the President against loss in any action brought against him for having suspended the writ of habeus corpus sparked an intense filibuster in the closing hours of the session. But the filibuster failed when the presiding officer, in the face of obvious obstruction, called for a vote and refused to entertain an appeal. The tactics of the filibusters were described by Sen. Lyman Trumbull (R Ill.): "Motion after motion was made here last night to lay on the table, to postpone indefinitely, to adjourn, to adjourn, to adjourn and to adjourn again, and the yeas and nays called on each occasion."[47] Similar tactics were employed by Charles Sumner in 1865 to postpone the readmission of Louisiana. He felt so strong on the issue that he declared himself "justified in employing all the instruments that I find in the arsenal of parliamentary warfare."[48]

Democratic proposals to suspend or repeal statutes allowing the use of federal troops in state elections were the subject of the next great filibusters, in 1876 and 1879. In the 1879 filibuster Republicans relied on dilatory motions, roll-call votes and refusal to answer quorum calls, whereupon the president pro tempore ruled that he could determine whether enough senators were present to constitute a quorum.

Famous Filibusters

In a famous filibuster of 1881, the Democratic minority prevented the Republicans from organizing the Senate until the resignations of two senators (Roscoe Conkling and Thomas C. Platt of New York) had given the Democrats numerical control. The filibuster made it impossible for the upper chamber to take action on any legislation from March 24 to May 16 of that year.

In 1890 a bill to provide federal aid to education sponsored by Henry W. Blair (R N.H.) was filibustered from Feb. 26 to March 20 by Blair himself in an effort to get sufficient support for passage. Believing he had won the requisite strength, Blair permitted the bill to come to a vote, but two senators at the last minute decided to vote against it. The bill was defeated, 31-37, with Blair himself voting nay in order to be eligible to move reconsideration. The measure was never revived.

A filibuster against the "Force Bill," sponsored by Rep. Henry Cabot Lodge (R Mass.), lasted from Dec. 2, 1890, to Jan. 26, 1891. The measure would have established federal supervision over polling places at national elections in order to prevent exclusion of black voters in southern states. After seven weeks of debate, the bill's supporters tried to put through a rule for majority cloture. When this failed, the Senate was held in continuous session for four days and nights in an effort to exhaust filibusters. Eventually, after 33 days of actual obstruction, the bill was dropped to permit the enactment of vital appropriation bills before the 51st Congress expired in March 1891. During the debate, West Virginia Democrat C. J. Faulkner nominally held the floor for 11½ hours, although for nearly eight hours of that time he was relieved of the necessity of speaking through the absence of a quorum.

In 1893, a filibuster against repeal of the 1890 Silver Purchase Act lasted from Aug. 29 to Oct. 24. After 46 days of actual filibuster and 13 continuous day-and-night sittings, the repeal was passed Oct. 30 and sent to the President. The minority made use of every weapon in the filibuster arsenal—dilatory motions, roll-call votes and quorum calls, in addition to talk. A new record was set by Nebraska Populist William V. Allen who held the floor, with interruptions, for 14 hours.

This filibuster aroused widespread public concern over the conduct and future of the Senate. "To vote without debating is perilous, but to debate and never vote is imbecile," wrote Sen. Henry Cabot Lodge (R Mass.) shortly after the struggle ended. "As it is, there must be a change, for the delays which now take place are discrediting the Senate.... A body which cannot govern itself will not long hold the respect of the people who have chosen it to govern the country...."[49]

In 1897, during a mild filibuster on a naval appropriation bill, the chair ruled that a quorum call could not be ordered unless business had intervened since the last quorum call. However, since there was as yet no suggestion that debate was not business, this ruling had only limited value in curbing the excesses of the filibuster.

In 1901, Montana Republican Thomas H. Carter, who was retiring from the Senate in a few hours, filibustered against a "pork-barrel" rivers and harbors bill from the night of March 3 until the Senate adjourned *sine die* at noon March 4 (legislative day of March 3). The bill was a raid on the Treasury, Carter said, and he was performing a "public service" in preventing it from becoming law. He readily yielded for other business but resumed his item-by-item denunciation of the bill whenever necessary. No determined attempt was made to stop him, and the bill died.[50]

Early filibusters had not been notably successful, but as obstructionists gradually shifted to bolder techniques the Senate was unable to restrain them, and by the beginning of the 20th century the filibuster had assumed scandalous proportions. This was, says Franklin Burdette, "the heyday of brazen and unblushing aggressors. The power of the Senate lay not in votes but in sturdy tongues and iron wills. The premium rested not upon ability and statesmanship but upon effrontery and audacity."[51]

Senate Rules on Debate

The House of Representatives, whose entire membership is elected anew every two years, must adopt its rules at the beginning of each new Congress. But the Senate, as a continuing body, faces no such task; its rules remain in force from Congress to Congress unless the Senate decides to change them. Several revisions of the Senate rules have occurred since the first rules were adopted in 1789, but these revisions have been chiefly codifications of changes that had accumulated over a number of years.

Two such codifications occurred in the 1861-1901 period. The first, in 1868, increased the number of rules to an all-time maximum of 53, and it reflected some wartime strains. Another codification, in 1884, brought the number of rules down to 40. Although many changes in Senate rules have been adopted since that time, no further codification has taken place.

"Rules are never observed in this body; they are only made to be broken. We are a law unto ourselves," said John J. Ingalls (R Kan.) in 1876.[52] His comment may explain why rules reform has not played as significant a role in the history of the Senate as it has in the House.

Efforts to limit Senate debate provide a notable exception. In the last half of the 19th century, many proposals were offered to curtail debate either through the use of the previous question or some other means. Most of the proposals were simply ignored, but a few minor changes affecting debate were agreed to.

In 1862, the Senate adopted a resolution stating that "in consideration in secret session of subjects relating to the rebellion, debate should be confined to the subject matter and limited to five minutes, except that five minutes be allowed any Member to explain or oppose a pertinent amendment."[53] Adoption of this resolution was attributable to the exigencies of wartime. In later years it also became customary for the Senate, in the closing days of a session when the need for haste was great, to apply a five-minute limit on debate on appropriations bills.

Anthony Rule. In 1870, the Senate first adopted the Anthony Rule named after its originator Sen. Henry B. Anthony (R R.I.). The rule was the most important limitation of debate it had yet agreed to as a means of expediting its business. The rule was so successful in speeding action on noncontroversial bills that in 1880 it became part of the Standing Rules, where it now appears as Rule VIII:

"At the conclusion of the morning business for each day, unless upon motion the Senate shall at any time otherwise order, the Senate will proceed to the consideration of the Calendar of Bills and Resolutions, and continue such consideration until 2 o'clock; and bills and resolutions that are not objected to shall be taken up in their order, and each senator shall be entitled to speak once and for five minutes only upon any question; and the objection may be interposed at any stage of the proceedings, but upon motion the Senate may continue such consideration; and this order shall commence immediately after the call for 'concurrent and other resolutions,' and shall take precedence of the unfinished business and other special orders. But if the Senate shall proceed with the consideration of any matter notwithstanding an objection, the foregoing provisions touching debate shall not apply."[54]

The Anthony Rule greatly speeded the handling of routine measures without prejudice to the right of senators to demand longer debate on controversial bills. Another change that helped to facilitate the business of the Senate was the decision in 1875 that action on an amendment to an appropriation bill could be postponed without prejudice to the bill itself. This rule was so successful that its application was later extended to amendments to any bill.

Era of Reform: 1901-1921

The "Progressive Era," which had begun with movements for economic reform in the 1880s and 1890s, gathered momentum and a radical democratic character after the turn of the century and gradually faded into the background during World War I. The progressive program was foreshadowed in the platform of the Populist Party, which in 1892 polled over a million votes for its presidential candidate, James B. Weaver. Though the party, centered in the agrarian Midwest and West, soon declined, many of its programs were gradually adopted by the two major parties.

Early Progressive Legislation. Under popular pressure, Congress had enacted such early "progressive" legislation as civil service reform (1883), the Interstate Commerce Act (1887), the Sherman Antitrust Act (1890), conservation legislation (1891) and an income tax law (1894). But the income tax was invalidated by the Supreme Court, and the other measures were rendered ineffective by their vagueness and their loopholes, by court rulings and by unenthusiastic administration.

Finding themselves thus frustrated, and laying the blame on the supposed sinister influence of vested interests, reformers concluded that more democratic control of the government was necessary to secure the laws they sought. Accordingly, the reform movement turned increasingly toward such measures as direct election of senators, direct primaries, women's suffrage and laws against corrupt election practices. In the House, the reformers were determined to break the power of the Speaker.

The power of the Senate declined after Theodore Roosevelt became President in 1901. Roosevelt was an aggressive leader who took an active role in promoting legislation. Concentration of authority in the House Speaker had brought cohesion to the lower chamber, which was now prepared to challenge senatorial leadership, and Roosevelt worked mainly through informal contacts with the Speaker of the House to advance his legislative program.

Insurgent Movement in Congress

Congress went along, somewhat reluctantly, with Roosevelt's progressive program, passing such measures as the Hepburn Act, which strengthened the Interstate Commerce Commission, pure food and drug laws and a workmen's compensation act. But William Howard Taft, who was elected in 1908, failed to press Roosevelt's policies in the face of Old Guard opposition, and the defeat of legislation sought by progressives in both parties led to the development of an insurgent movement among western Republicans in Congress.

In the House, Republican insurgents led the revolt against Speaker Joseph G. Cannon, while in the Senate the "Band of Six"—Robert M. La Follette of Wisconsin, Albert J. Beveridge of Indiana, Jonathan P. Dolliver and Albert B. Cummins of Iowa, Francis Bristow of Kansas and Edwin Clapp of Minnesota—unsuccessfully challenged the Nelson W. Aldrich machine on a tariff bill sponsored by Aldrich. Enactment of this distinctly protectionist measure led to resounding Republican defeats in the congressional elections of 1910 and the formation of the Progressive ("Bull Moose") Party which nominated Roosevelt for President in 1912. The split between the Roosevelt and Taft wings of the Republican Party gave an easy victory to the Democrats, and under President Woodrow Wilson the government entered a period of progressive rule that lasted through most of Wilson's first term.

Wilson Reforms. The President's early relations with Congress were easy. He returned to the pre-Jeffersonian practice of addressing the Congress in person and frequently went to the President's room in the Capitol to confer with committees or individual members. Under his leadership a caucus of Democratic senators was proposed in 1913, to marshal party support for a tariff-cutting bill sponsored by Oscar W. Underwood. Other legislative victories included the income tax (made valid by a constitutional amendment submitted to the states in 1909 and belatedly ratified on the eve of Wilson's inauguration), direct election of senators, the Clayton Antitrust Act and the Federal Reserve and Federal Trade Commission Acts.

This flow of progressive legislation ended when the United States entered World War I in 1917. During the war, Wilson assumed almost dictatorial powers, and criticism of his policies was silenced, but with the President's ill-timed appeal for election of a Democratic Congress in the fall of 1918, the opposition surfaced. In the ensuing election, Republicans captured control of both houses of Congress, and the President went off to the Paris Peace Conference a rejected hero. Wilson's health broke in his futile efforts to enlist support for the League of Nations, and the Republican Senate first emasculated, then rejected the Treaty of Versailles in which the League Covenant was embedded. With the election of a Republican Congress in 1918, a new period of congressional hegemony was at hand.

The Seventeenth Amendment, providing for direct election of senators, was undoubtedly the most important development in the evolution of the Senate during the Progressive Era, but other significant changes also occurred. Political parties were beginning to assume their modern place in the legislative structure, and as party leadership roles became institutionalized during the early years of the century, formally identifiable majority and minority leaders emerged. With the admission of Arizona to statehood in 1912, the membership of the Senate increased to 96; no further changes in size would occur for nearly half a century. Finally, in 1917 the Senate was driven by the excesses of filibustering to adopt its first cloture rule, permitting two-thirds of those present and voting to bring debate to a close.

Direct Election of Senators

The Constitution provided for the election of senators by the state legislatures. But the Seventeenth Amendment, ratified in 1913, changed the Constitution to provide for direct election of senators. The change was part of the Progressive Era's movement toward more democratic control of government. Being less immediately dependent on popular sentiment than the House, the Senate did not seek to reform itself. Only strong pressure from the public, expressed through the House of Representatives, the state governments, pressure groups, petitions, referenda and other means, convinced the Senate that it must reform.

It was common in the Progressive Era to attribute legislative disappointments to the dealings of vested interests operating behind the scenes. A Senate chosen by state legislatures, whose decisions were often made in closed-door party caucuses, could not easily escape suspicion. Moreover, the high-tariff views of the Senate served to link this body in the public mind with the great corporations that were widely accused of improper influence on politics. The popular image of the Senate in the Progressive Era was a far cry from the picture presented by de Tocqueville in an earlier age.

Pressures on the Senate. Andrew Johnson, who as President subsequently came within one vote of removal from office at the hands of the Senate, was an early advocate of Senate reform. Twice as representative, once as a senator, and again as President in 1868, Johnson presented resolutions calling for direct election of senators. But in the first 80 years of Congress, a total of only nine resolutions proposing a constitutional amendment to that effect were introduced in Congress. In the 1870s and 1880s the number increased, and by 1912 a total of not less than 287 such joint resolutions had been introduced. Not until 1892 was a resolution reported favorably from committee in the House. In the next decade such a resolution was carried five times in the House with only a handful in opposition. But the proposed amendment to the Constitution was not allowed to reach a vote in the Senate until 1911.

Petitions from farmers' associations and other organizations, particularly in the West, and party platforms in state elections pressed the issue until the national parties took it up. Direct election of senators was a plank in the Populist program at every election, beginning in 1892, and in the Democratic platform in each presidential election year from 1900 to 1912. Starting in California and Iowa in 1894, state legislatures addressed Congress in favor of a direct election amendment, until by 1905 the legislatures in 31 of the 45 states had taken this step, many of them repeatedly. Referenda held in three states showed approval of the amendment by votes of 14 to 1 in California, 8 to 1 in Nevada, and 6 to 1 in Illinois. Support was strongest in the West and North Central states, where every legislature petitioned Congress at least once, and weakest in the Northeast, where only Pennsylvania's legislature voted to address Congress in support of direct election.

In 1900, when the House voted 240-15 in favor of submitting an amendment for direct election of senators, it was favored by a majority of the representatives from every state except Maine and Connecticut.[55]

Other Tactics. Still the Senate did not act. Since the senators would not even consider a change in the method of electing them, other tactics were adopted. Between 1902 and 1911 even the House did not vote on any resolution for direct election of senators. But the states were finding ways to achieve the same results without a constitutional amendment.

The spread of direct primaries in the 1890s led in many states to expressions of popular choice of senator on the primary ballot. Though not legally binding on the legislatures, this choice was likely to be ratified. In the South, the primary winners were soon being "elected" by the one-party legislatures almost as a matter of course. But in states that did not have a one-party system, especially those lacking clear party lines, primaries were less effective in guaranteeing that the popular choice would be ratified by the legislature.

Oregon led the way in devising a system to guarantee popular choice of senators in spite of the Constitution's assignment of this task to the legislatures. In 1901 an Oregon law was enacted enabling voters to express their choice for senator in the same manner as they voted for governor, except that the vote for senator had no legal force. But the law specified that when the legislature assembled to elect a senator, "it shall be the duty of each house to count the votes and announce the candidate having the highest number, and thereupon the houses shall proceed to the election of a senator." In the first test of this system, the man who led the field with 37 per cent of the popular vote for senator secured scant support from the legislators, who scattered their votes among 14 candidates. After a five-week deadlock, the legislature chose a man who had not received a single vote in the popular election.

Far from being discouraged at this mockery of "the people's choice," the people of Oregon in 1904 used their new initiative and referendum powers to petition for and approve a new law. Henceforth each candidate for senator was to be nominated by petition, and allowed to include on the petition a 100-word statement of principles, and on the ballot a 12-word statement to be printed after his name. The legislators, who could not be denied their constitutional power to name senators, were permitted to include in their nomination petitions their signatures to either "Statement No. 1" or "Statement No. 2." The former pledged the signer always to vote "for that candidate for United States Senator in Congress who has received the highest number of the people's votes...without regard to my individual preference." The second statement was a pledge to regard the popular vote "as nothing more than a recommendation, which I shall be at liberty to wholly disregard...." Meanwhile, citizen groups circulated pledges, which were widely subscribed to, that the signer would not support or vote for any candidate to the legislature who did not endorse "Statement No. 1."

The first legislature elected after enactment of this law promptly ratified the "people's choice" for senator. And two years later, when 83 of the 90 members of the legislature were Republicans, the Democratic popular choice was elected. He received 53 votes, including all 52 who had endorsed "Statement No. 1."

The "Oregon System" was adopted in other states in modified forms. By December 1910 it was estimated that 14 of the 30 senators about to be named by state legislatures had already been designated by popular vote.[56]

The Issue in the Senate. Gradually the mounting external pressures began to be felt within the Senate. Some of the senators were themselves products of the new systems of popular election. In fact, the leader in the fight for the Seventeenth Amendment, Sen. William E. Borah (R Idaho), had entered the Senate through a popular mandate after an earlier defeat at the hands of the Idaho legislature.

Beginning in 1901, some of the legislatures were no longer content to request Congress to submit a constitutional amendment to the states. They called for a convention to amend the Constitution, a method as yet untried but obligatory once two-thirds of the states so petition Congress. Some senators, though they opposed popular election, feared that such a convention, like the original Constitutional Convention, might exceed its original mandate and preferred to submit to the states a specific amendment for direct election of senators.

When a resolution for the constitutional amendment was referred to the Senate Judiciary Committee, rather than to the more hostile Committee on Privileges and Elections that had considered it on previous occasions, a favorable report was at last obtained on Jan. 1, 1911. However, a committee amendment, supported by southern senators, which would have modified Congress' power under Article I, Section 4 of the Constitution to control state regulation of Senate and House elections, provoked such a storm of controversy that at times it overshadowed the popular election itself. The amendment would have transferred to the states exclusive power to regulate the election of senators; it would have left unchanged Congress' power to regulate House elections. Once on the floor, the northern opposition prevailed and the committee amendment was removed by a vote of 50-37. But on Feb. 28, 1911, the resolution itself failed, 54-33, to secure the necessary two-thirds majority.[57]

In a special session later that year, the House passed 296-16 the direct election resolution. But the House version was the same as that reported by the Senate committee, giving the states exclusive power to regulate Senate elections. The Senate, on a 45-44 roll call decided by Vice President James S. Sherman's tie-breaking vote, again rejected the committee amendment, and adopted the original resolution, 64-24. A deadlock between the two houses was broken in the next session when on May 13, 1912, the House, 238-39, finally concurred in the Senate version. By May 31, 1913, three-fourths of the states had ratified.[58]

The immediate effects of the Seventeenth Amendment were difficult to assess. Even before its adoption, the direct primary movement had diminished the power of the legislatures, and by 1913 three-fourths of the candidates for the Senate were being nominated in direct primaries. The terms of the senators in office at the time the amendment was ratified ended variously in 1915, 1917 and 1919, so the 66th Congress (1919-21) was the first in which all members of the Senate were the products of direct election. "By that time," George B. Galloway pointed out, "56 of the senators who owed their togas originally to state legislatures had been re-elected by the people, three had died, and 37 had disappeared from the scene either voluntarily or by popular verdict. In other words, more than half of those last chosen by legislative caucus were subsequently approved by the people."[59]

Restraining the Filibuster

In the early years of the 20th century, filibusters continued to be undertaken with frequency and a high degree of success. But mounting opposition to the practice led, in 1908, to efforts to curb obstruction through interpretation of existing rules and, in 1917, to the Senate's first cloture rule.

Meanwhile, 1903 proved to be a vintage year for the filibuster. Democratic Sen. Benjamin R. ("Pitchfork Ben") Tillman of South Carolina filibustered against an appropriation bill until an item for payment of war claims to his state was restored. The item was put back in the bill after Tillman threatened to read Byron's "Childe Harold" and other poems into the record until his colleagues surrendered from boredom.

While Tillman resorted to "legislative blackmail," in the words of House Speaker Joseph G. Cannon (R Ill.), Republican Sen. Albert J. Beveridge of Indiana chose a different method. Beveridge, chairman of the Territories Committee and an opponent of statehood for Arizona and New Mexico, led a filibuster against an omnibus statehood bill. Taking advantage of a custom that no vote should be taken on a measure in the absence of the chairman of the committee that had handled it, Beveridge hid for days in Washington and finally slipped away to Atlantic City. The bill ultimately was dropped.

In 1908, a bitter two-day filibuster against the conference report on an emergency currency measure sponsored by Aldrich and Rep. Edward B. Vreeland (R N.Y.) brought the first significant steps to curb obstruction. Republican Sen. Robert M. La Follette Sr. of Wisconsin held the floor for 18 hours and 23 minutes, a record that stood until 1938, but he was interrupted by 29 quorum calls and three roll calls on questions of order. La Follette fortified himself periodically with eggnogs from the Senate restaurant. According to one account, he rejected one of these eggnogs as doped, and it later was found to contain a fatal dose of ptomaine. No charge of a deliberate poisoning attempt was made.

The filibusterers' cause finally was lost when blind Sen. Thomas P. Gore (D Okla.) yielded the floor after learning that Sen. William J. Stone (D Mo.), who was scheduled to relieve him, was in the chamber. But Stone had been called to the cloakroom, and the blind Gore surrendered the floor. The conference report was approved on a hastily demanded roll call.

First Curbs on Obstruction

Three important curbs on obstruction resulted from the 1908 filibuster. They were rulings that: (1) the chair could count a quorum if enough senators were present, even on a vote, whether or not they answered to their names; (2) debate did not count as intervening business for the purpose of deciding if a quorum call was in order; and (3) senators could by enforcement of existing rules be prevented from speaking more than twice on the same subject in one day.

During a 1914 Republican filibuster against a rivers and harbors bill, the chair ruled that senators could not yield for any purpose, even for a question, without unanimous consent. The Senate tabled an appeal from this ruling, 28-24, but reversed itself the next day and the rules remained unchanged.

In 1915, a successful filibuster was organized against President Wilson's Ship Purchase bill. Republican Sen. Reed Smoot of Utah spoke for 11 hours and 35 minutes without relief and without deviating from the subject. After almost a month of obstruction, seven Democrats who thought the filibuster should give way to other important legislation joined the Republicans to move that the bill be recommitted. Other Democrats supporting the bill then staged a five-day reverse filibuster until they regained control of the chamber. The Republican filibuster then was renewed. A Democratic motion to close the debate was blocked, and the bill finally was dropped, but as a result of the filibuster three important appropriation bills failed.

Eleven Willful Men

The public was disgusted by this episode, but it took one more great filibuster to force the Senate into action. The occasion came in 1917 when the administration's Armed Neutrality bill was talked to death by an 11-man bloc in the closing days of the 64th Congress. Seventy-five senators who signed a statement in support of the measure asked that it be entered in the record "to establish that the Senate favors the legislation and would pass it, if a vote could be had."[60] Not all of the obstruction came from the Republican side of the aisle. On the last day of the session, when it was clear that the bill was doomed, the Democrats staged their own filibuster to keep an outraged La Follette from being able to speak against the measure before crowded Senate galleries.

No sooner had the session ended than President Wilson issued an angry statement: "The Senate of the United States is the only legislative body in the world which cannot act when its majority is ready for action. A little group of willful men, representing no opinion but their own, have rendered the great government of the United States helpless and contemptible...." Wilson immediately called the Senate into special session and demanded that it amend its rules so that it could act and "save the country from disaster."[61]

The Senate yielded, and a conference of Republican and Democratic leaders hastily drew up the Senate's first cloture rule. After only six hours of debate, Rule 22 was adopted by the chamber March 8, 1917, by a vote of 76-3.

Rule 22's Limits on Debate

The new rule provided for limitation of debate upon any pending measure by vote of two-thirds of the senators present and voting, two days after a cloture motion had been submitted by 16 senators. Thereafter, debate was limited to one hour for each senator on the bill itself and all amendments and motions affecting it. No new amendments could be offered except by unanimous consent. Amendments that were not germane to the pending business, and amendments and motions clearly designed to delay action, were out of order.

An amendment was offered to authorize cloture by majority instead of two-thirds vote. The amendment was attacked as a breach of faith and was withdrawn before a vote could be taken. And in 1918 the Senate rejected, 34-41, a proposal to allow use of the previous question to limit debate during the war period.

For a time it looked as if the Senate would never make use of its new tool against obstruction, but the interminable debates on the Treaty of Versailles in 1919 finally provided an occasion. The Senate adopted its first cloture motion Nov. 15, 1919, on a 78-16 roll call, and four days later the treaty itself was brought to a vote, after 55 days of debate.

Party Leadership

The system of party leadership that had evolved in the Senate in the closing years of the 19th century became institutionalized in the early years of the 20th with the creation of formally designated majority and minority leadership positions.

Both Republicans and Democrats for many years had elected chairmen of the party caucuses, but the caucus chairman was not necessarily the effective leader of his party in the Senate. William B. Allison (R Iowa) and Arthur P. Gorman (D Md.) served as chairmen of their respective caucuses, but the position was not essential to their control; Nelson W. Aldrich (R R.I.), the most powerful member of the Senate until his retirement in 1911, never held any official position other than the chairmanship of the Finance Committee.

With the departure of these dynamic leaders from the chamber, power was fragmented within the parties. It became common for both Republicans and Democrats to elect a different floor leader in each session, and the floor leadership did not necessarily correspond with the caucus chairmanship. Under these conditions party unity was hard to maintain.

In 1911, the Democrats—already in control of the House and looking forward to the election of a Democratic Senate two years later—instituted the practice of electing a single, readily identifiable leader, who held the dual posts of floor leader and chairman of the party caucus. The Republicans, threatened by insurgents within their ranks, took a similar course in 1913. Subsequently party whips (assistant floor leaders) were added to the leadership structure—in 1913 by the Democrats and in 1915 by the Republicans. Since this period, the majority and minority leaders have usually been the acknowledged spokesmen for their parties in the Senate.

The importance of the leadership role was underscored in 1913, when progressive Senate Democrats deposed conservative leader Thomas S. Martin (Va.) and engineered the election as majority leader of John W. Kern (Ind.), who had served in the Senate only two years. The Steering Committee, appointed by Kern and dominated by progressives, made committee assignments in such a way as to assure administration control of major committees; seniority was ignored when necessary. The Steering Committee also recommended rules, later adopted by the caucus, that permitted a majority of committee members to call meetings, elect subcommittees and appoint conferees. Thus party authority was augmented and the power of committee chairmen curbed in a movement that somewhat paralleled the revolt against Cannonism in the House.

Early in the 20th century, both parties replaced the title "caucus" with "conference," in formal recognition of the non-binding nature of thse party meetings. The Democratic Caucus in 1903 adopted a binding caucus rule, but there is no evidence that it was ever used, and when Kern in 1913 proposed holding a binding caucus on the tariff bill, opposition was so vigorous that the idea had to be dropped. The compromise finally achieved preserved the appearance of a non-binding "conference," though Democratic senators were under such strong pressure to support caucus decisions that the effect of a binding caucus was maintained.

Republican Stalemate: 1921-1933

After its victory over Woodrow Wilson on the League of Nations, the Senate was in no mood to submit to presidential leadership. It expected to assume control of the government in the Republican administrations that followed Wilson, but after the House revamped its appropriations procedures in 1920 the lower chamber increasingly challenged Senate primacy.

Wilson's three Republican successors, faithful to the GOP doctrine of legislative independence, made little effort to direct Congress in legislative matters. Wilson's immediate successor, Warren G. Harding, promised prior to his election that he would take a hands-off approach with respect to legislation and that the Senate would "have something to say about the foreign relations as the Constitution contemplates." Harding added, "I had rather have the counsel of the Senate than all the political bosses in any party."[62] Harding, who was an ex-senator, appeared before his former colleagues on several occasions. In an unprecedented move in 1921, he personally delivered his nominations for Cabinet positions to the Senate. But he came to regret his promise not to intervene in legislative matters. When he appeared before the Senate in 1921 to urge a balanced budget, the Senate berated him for interfering in its business and the House was offended that the issue had not been raised in the chamber where money bills must originate. Harding's subsequent feeble efforts to exert leadership were rebuffed by Congress, and his administration tarnished by scandals that were exposed by Senate investigators after his death in 1923.

Harding's successor, Calvin Coolidge, was even less inclined to leadership than Harding had been. "I have never felt that it was my duty to attempt to coerce senators or representatives, or to make reprisals," Coolidge wrote. "The people sent them to Washington. I felt I had discharged my duty when I had done the best I could with them."[63] The Senate rejected Coolidge's nomination of Charles Beecher Warren as Attorney General, the first rejection of a Cabinet nomination since 1868, but in other respects it largely ignored the passive President.

More aggressive leadership was expected of Herbert Hoover, but he lacked political experience and, as a recent convert to Republicanism, was distrusted by many members of his own party. Friction with the legislative branch thwarted his efforts to deal with the economic depression that engulfed the nation early in his single term of office.

If the Presidents of the 1920s were unable to lead the government, Congress itself was not much more successful. Although Republicans controlled the White House from 1921 to 1933, the House from 1919 to 1931 and the Senate from 1919 to 1933, the party solidarity that had characterized the McKinley era no longer existed. Throughout the 1920s a "progressive" farm bloc dominated by western Republicans held the balance of power in Congress, and the decade was marked by persistent deadlocks on major issues.

Meanwhile, significant internal developments took place in the chamber. A major consolidation of the committee system occurred in 1921, and exclusive authority over spending was restored to the Appropriations Committee in 1922 after introduction of the new budget system. In 1932, the Senate finally succeeded in winning House concurrence to the Lame-Duck Amendment, which altered the terms and sessions of Congress. But experience did not bear out the hope of Sen. George W. Norris (R Neb.), sponsor of the amendment, that it would end the filibusters that continued to plague the Senate in the 1920s. Of the nine cloture votes taken during that decade, only three succeeded, and opponents of the filibuster continued to seek new ways to halt obstruction.

Republican Insurgency

Agriculture did not share in the prosperity of the 1920s, and efforts to relieve the farmers' plight led to a breakdown of party government and the development of legislative blocs representing sectional and economic interests. Efforts to enact agricultural relief legislation brought a split between eastern and western Republicans and the establishment of a powerful bipartisan farm bloc within Congress. Insurgent Republicans, mostly from the Great Plains and Rocky Mountain areas, usually kept their formal ties to the Republican Party but cooperated with the Democrats on sectional economic legislation. In the House, Republican regulars for the most part kept the upper hand. In the Senate, Republican control was often only nominal. Insurgents frequently succeeded in blocking administration legislation although they lacked the strength to carry their own legislative program. The divisions of the period extended to organizational matters within the chamber.

The congressional elections of 1922 were a disaster for the regular Republicans. Not only did the Republican majority decline from 167 to 15 in the House and from 22 to 6 in the Senate, but throughout the farm states progressive Republicans won over regulars. When the 68th Congress met in December 1923, the insurgents challenged the regulars' control.

The insurgent Republicans and the two Farmer-Labor senators from Minnesota accepted committee assignments from the Republicans but did not attend the Republican conference. When the committee lists came to the floor, Robert M. La Follette (R Wis.) led an effort to remove Albert B. Cummins of Iowa from the chairmanship of the Interstate Commerce Committee. A month-long deadlock ensued. La Follette was the second-ranking Republican on the committee, and the regular Republicans, unable to elect Cummins, had no intention of letting La Follette succeed to

the chairmanship. Finally, on the 32nd ballot, the regulars threw their support to the committee's ranking Democrat, Ellison D. Smith of South Carolina, and Smith was elected chairman although he was of the minority party. Cummins continued as a member of the committee and also retained his office as president pro tempore.

In 1924, La Follette ran for President under the Progressive banner, polling 16 per cent of the vote but carrying only his own state of Wisconsin. The Republicans gained five seats in the Senate, and party leaders felt strong enough to retaliate against the irregulars who had supported the Progressive ticket. Thus the Republican Conference adopted a resolution that the disloyal senators "be not invited to future Republican conferences and be not named to fill any Republican vacancies on Senate committees."[64] The irregulars were permitted to keep the committee assignments they then held, but in many instances they were placed at the bottom of the list. In the Senate reorganization two years later, however, they were welcomed back into the Republican fold.

The Progressives continued to be a thorn in the side of the regular Republicans. In his last two years in office, Hoover had to contend with a Democratic House in which the Republican Progressives regularly sided with the opposition. The situation in the Senate was not much better. The Senate of the 72nd Congress consisted of 48 Republicans, 47 Democrats and one Farmer-Labor. Since some Progressive Republicans continually voted with the Democrats, President Hoover advised James Watson, the Republican leader, to let the Democrats organize the Senate "to convert their sabotage into responsibility." Hoover said he "could deal more constructively with the Democratic leaders if they held full responsibility in both houses, than with an opposition in the Senate conspiring in the cloakrooms to use every proposal of his for demagoguery."[65] Watson, who wanted to be majority leader, and his Republican colleagues, who wanted to be committee chairmen, rejected Hoover's proposal.

Cloture in Practice

Early experience with the Senate cloture rule bore out the predictions of those who expected it to be used only sparingly. Between 1917, when the rule was adopted, and the end of the Hoover administration in 1933, the Senate took only 11 cloture votes, of which five occurred in one two-week period in 1927.

Four of the 11 votes were successful. In addition to the 1919 vote on the Treaty of Versailles, the Senate in 1926 ended a 10-day filibuster against the World Court Protocol by adopting cloture on a 68-26 vote, and in 1927 it voted cloture twice—on a branch banking bill, 65-18, and on a prohibition reorganization measure, 55-27. The seven measures on which cloture failed included two tariff bills, a bill for development of the Lower Colorado River Basin and a banking bill against which Huey Long (D La.) staged his first filibuster early in 1933. On this occasion cloture failed by a single vote.

Some issues were too touchy for cloture even to be attempted. During the third session of the 67th Congress in 1922, a group of southern senators mounted a filibuster against an anti-lynching bill. On behalf of the obstructionists, Oscar W. Underwood (D Ala.) said: "It is perfectly apparent that you are not going to get an agreement to vote on this bill.... I want to say right now to the Senate that if the majority party insist on this procedure, they are not going to pass the bill and they are not going to do any other business.... We are going to transact no other business until we have an understanding about this bill.... We are willing to take the responsibility, and we are going to do it."[66] The obstructionists were as good as their word: the Senate was unable to transact any legislative business until the anti-lynching bill was formally put aside on the last day of the session, but no cloture vote was ever taken.

Similarly, in 1927 no attempt was made to invoke cloture on a filibuster against extending the life of a special campaign-investigating committee headed by James A. Reed (D Mo.). A small group of senators succeeded in killing the committee, which had exposed corruption in the 1926 election victories of Frank L. Smith (R Ill.) and William S. Vare (R Pa.), although a majority of the Senate clearly favored its extension.

As it became apparent that Rule 22 was not an effective weapon against the filibuster, new curbs on obstruction were proposed. During the 1922 filibuster on an anti-lynching bill, Republican Whip Charles Curtis (R Kan.) asked the chair to follow the precedent of Speaker Reed that, notwithstanding the absence of a specific rule on the question, dilatory motions could be ruled out of order under general parliamentary law. Such a precedent would have established a significant tool against obstruction, but Vice President Coolidge declined to rule.

The next Vice President, however, was made of sterner stuff. When Charles G. Dawes made his inaugural address to the Senate in 1925, he coupled a scathing denunciation of the existing Senate rules with a call for new curbs on debate. Not content with attacking the Senate on its own turf, Dawes took his campaign to the country, where he encountered the rather surprising opposition of the American Federation of Labor. The Dawes scheme, said the AFL ominously, "emanates from the secret chambers of the predatory interests."[67] Although Dawes aroused widespread public interest in the problem, the Senate took no action on rules reform proposals.

The Lame-Duck Amendment

One member of the Senate thought he saw a way to end the filibuster. George W. Norris (R Neb.), a progressive who earlier had participated in the House revolt against Speaker Cannon, proposed a constitutional amendment that would eliminate the short, post-election sessions of Congress in which so many filibusters occurred.

Under the Constitution and existing law, a Congress that was elected in November of an even-numbered year did not take office until March 4 of the following odd-numbered year and did not meet in its first regular session until December of that year, 13 months after its election. Meanwhile, the old Congress regularly met in December following the election of its successor and remained in session until the term of the new Congress began in March. This was known as the short session, in which "lame-duck" members who had been repudiated at the polls often determined the course of legislation. The fixed adjournment date was an invitation to filibusters, because merely by talking long enough members could block action until the old Congress expired; it was hardly surprising that the short sessions were seldom productive.

Accordingly, Norris proposed an amendment to the Constitution to abolish the short session by starting the terms of Congress and the President in January instead of March and providing that Congress should meet annually in January rather than December. The Senate approved the change six times before the House agreed to it in 1932. The Twentieth Amendment became part of the Constitution in 1933.

The first Senate vote on the Norris amendment came early in 1923, during the short session of the 67th Congress. Reported from the Senate Agriculture Committee, of which Norris was chairman, the resolution proposing the amendment was adopted by the Senate Feb. 13 on a 63-6 vote. In the House the amendment was reported by the Election Committee and approved by a majority of the Rules Committee, but Rules Chairman Philip P. Campbell (R Kan.), himself a lame duck, managed to keep it from the floor.

In 1924, the Norris amendment was again approved by the Senate, 63-7, and again reported by the House Election Committee, but this time it was blocked in the Rules Committee. The same thing happened in 1926, when the Senate approved the amendment by a vote of 73-2.

The Norris amendment finally reached the House floor in 1928, after the Senate had approved it for a fourth time, 65-6. However, the House vote of 209-157 fell 35 short of the two-thirds required for approval under the Constitution.

In the next Congress, the 71st, the Senate approved the Norris resolution for a fifth time, 64-9. The House adopted a different version, 290-93, and the measure died in conference.

Final action came in the following Congress, when the Democrats had won control of the House. Early in 1932, the Senate adopted the Norris resolution for a sixth time, 63-7, and the House quickly cleared it, 335-56. It became the Twentieth Amendment upon ratification by the 36th state early in 1933.

The amendment established Jan. 3 of the year following election as the day on which the terms of senators and representatives would begin and end, and Jan. 20 as the day on which the President and Vice President would take office. It provided also that Congress should meet annually on Jan. 3 "unless they shall by law appoint a different day."

The second session of the 73rd Congress was the first to convene on the new date, Jan. 3, 1934. And the first President to take office on Jan. 20 was Franklin D. Roosevelt at the beginning of his second term in 1937. It quickly became clear, however, that the amendment would not eliminate the filibuster, as Norris had hoped. The final sessions of the 73rd and 74th Congresses, the first to function under it, both ended in filibusters.

Committee Reorganization

The Senate's standing committee system had expanded fantastically since the middle of the 19th century, and by 1921 it was ripe for pruning. The 25 standing committees of 1853 increased to 42 by 1889, and in the next quarter-century this number almost doubled. Five select committees graduated to standing-committee status in 1884, three more did so in 1896, and all of the remaining select committees were made standing committees in 1909. At the same time, nine new standing committees were created, followed by three more in 1913, bringing the total number to an all-time high of 74.

The expansion of the committee system was only in part a reflection of the increasing complexity of Senate business; committees also provided welcome clerical service and office space for their chairmen in the days before such assistance was available to all members. Thus "sinecure committees" had a way of surviving long after any need for them was gone. (Benefits did not go only to the party in power; in 1907, the Republicans took 61 chairmanships but assigned 10 others to the minority, and several committees were established solely for the purpose of creating chairmanships.)

When the 67th Congress convened in April 1921, the Senate effected a major consolidation of its committee system by reducing the number of committees from 74 to 34 and abolishing a number of long-defunct bodies such as the Committee on Revolutionary Claims.

The revision of the committee system was initiated by the Republican Committee on Committees, which at the same time proposed to increase the Republican margin on each of the major committees to reflect Republican gains in the Senate. To Democratic protests against "steam roller" tactics, Sen. Frank B. Brandegee (R Conn.), the committee chairman, replied: "Criticisms are purely professional. The Republicans are responsible to the country for legislation and must have control of committees. That's not tyranny; that's representative government—the rule of the majority."[68] The Republican proposal was adopted, 45-25, without substantial change.

A further modification of the committee system occurred in 1922 when the Senate, following the lead of the House, restored exclusive spending powers to the Appropriations Committee (from which they had been taken in 1899). When the eight appropriation bills previously considered by other Senate committees were taken up, three ad hoc members (one in the case of a conference) from the committee which previously had considered the bill were to serve with the Appropriations Committee. At the same time, Appropriations was deprived of its power to report amendments proposing new or general legislation.

The change in appropriations procedure was part of a larger effort to develop a more systematic approach to federal expenditures in both the executive and legislative branches. The Budget and Accounting Act of 1921 set up a Bureau of the Budget to assist the President in preparing an annual budget that reconciled federal revenues and expenditures; it also created a General Accounting Office to strengthen congressional surveillance over government spending.

Democratic Leadership: 1933-1945

The United States was in the depths of a great economic depression when Franklin D. Roosevelt entered the White House in 1933 with overwhelming popular support and commanding majorities in both houses of Congress. Asked prior to his election what authority he would seek from Congress, Roosevelt had answered, "Plenty," and he was as good as his word.

Called into special session March 9, 1933, Congress in the next "hundred days" embarked on a whirlwind legislative course dictated by the President. The House on March 9 passed an emergency banking bill, which had not then even been printed, in 38 minutes; the Senate took a little longer, two hours and 15 minutes, but the measure was ready for the President's signature before the day ended.

With time the pace slackened somewhat, but the pattern of action remained the same. The President would send a brief message to Congress, accompanied by a detailed draft of the legislation he proposed. Congress had been outraged when President Lincoln dared to submit his own draft bills, but it readily accepted such action from Roosevelt and the practice became routine. Given the President's popularity and the prevailing economic conditions, opposi-

tion was futile and often nonexistent, and the President's proposals were promptly enacted. Congress did not long continue to be a rubber stamp, but throughout his first term (1933-37) Roosevelt was able—through negotiation, compromise and the exercise of his patronage powers—to obtain the enactment of a broad range of New Deal social and economic programs.

In his second term (1937-41), a conservative coalition of Republicans and southern Democrats frequently opposed Roosevelt on domestic issues. The coalition thwarted his plan to enlarge the Supreme Court and successfully opposed him on other measures. During the President's unprecedented third term (1941-45), wartime issues were paramount. As in previous wars, the executive branch assumed extraordinary powers, and Congress became increasingly restive under executive domination. As the war drew to a close, opposition to Roosevelt's domestic policies mounted, and by the time the President died shortly after the start of his fourth term in 1945, Congress was in open revolt. His successor, Harry S Truman, won broad congressional support for his foreign policy measures, but his domestic programs were largely ignored.

Even before the war ended, Congress began to consider ways of modernizing its machinery so that it would be able to handle its mounting volume of business and regain some of the initiative it had lost to the executive branch. The resulting Legislative Reorganization Act of 1946 was only partially successful in meeting these goals. In the Senate no action was taken to strengthen the cloture rule; filibusters were used repeatedly to defeat civil rights legislation.

President and Senate

President Roosevelt, at times assisted by Vice President Garner, was his own legislative leader in the Senate during his first term, and Senate Democratic leaders viewed themselves as the loyal lieutenants of the President. Senate rules and procedures precluded the close control exercised by party leaders in the House, but the Senate leaders were more experienced than their House counterparts and they were often more successful in advancing administration programs.

Roosevelt in Control. When Sen. Joseph T. Robinson (D Ark.) became majority leader in 1933, he revived the Democratic Caucus and won from Democratic senators an agreement, adopted by a vote of 50-3, to make caucus decisions on administration bills binding by majority vote. The rule read:

"Resolved, That until further order the chairman [Robinson] is authorized to convene Democratic senators in caucus for the purpose of considering any measure recommended by the President; and that all Democratic senators shall be bound by the vote of the majority of the conference; provided, that any senator may be excused from voting for any such measure upon his expressed statement to the caucus that said measure is contrary to his conscientious judgment or that said measure is in violation of pledges made to his constituents as a candidate."[69]

Although there is no evidence that Robinson ever made use of the binding caucus rule, non-binding caucuses frequently were held to mobilize party support. In the House the majority leadership worked through the Steering Committee and the whip organization, but in the Senate the Steering Committee served only as a committee on committees, while it is doubtful if the Policy Committee ever even met.

The Senate had more potential dissidents than the House, among them many southern Democrats who had risen to key committee chairmanships through the seniority system, but Roosevelt was remarkably successful at keeping them in line. Agriculture Chairman Ellison D. Smith (S.C.) was not sympathetic to the proposed Agricultural Adjustment Act of 1933, but after a conference at the White House his committee reported the measure with this comment: "This bill...was drafted by the Department of Agriculture and is practically unchanged from the bill as presented to Congress. Considerable hearings were had by the Senate committee, but on account of the desire of the administration that no change be made the bill is presented to the Senate in practically an unchanged form...."[70]

As long as the Democrats maintained their tremendous margins in Congress and were able to curb the dissidents within their own party, the leadership could afford to ignore the minority—especially since many Republicans supported early New Deal proposals. But by the beginning of Roosevelt's second term in 1937, these conditions no longer prevailed, and a conservative coalition of Republicans and southern Democrats emerged opposed to the New Deal.

Failure of Court Packing

Stung by the Supreme Court's invalidation of major administration acts, Roosevelt sent to the Senate, Feb. 5, 1937, a proposal to enlarge the court by providing for the appointment of additional justices, up to a total of six, to assist those who did not retire within six months after reaching the age of 70. For once, public opinion was not with the President, and Senate Republicans sat on their hands while conservative and New Deal Democrats contested the issue. A series of court decisions favorable to New Deal programs weakened support, as did the sudden death of Sen. Robinson, the administration floor leader, on July 13.

In the leadership contest that followed, Alben W. Barkley (D Ky.), with Roosevelt's implied support, defeated Pat Harrison (D Miss.) for the majority leadership in a fight that brought to the surface the deep split in Democratic ranks. It also cost Roosevelt his court plan, which was rejected shortly thereafter.

Struggling to reassert his party leadership, Roosevelt decided to intervene in Democratic primaries in 1938 in an effort to block the renomination of conservative Democrats in Congress. The "purge" was notably unsuccessful; senators on the purge list were triumphantly returned to office, and the President's only victory was in unseating Rep. John J. O'Connor (D N.Y.), chairman of the House Rules Committee. As a further embarrassment, Republicans gained eight seats in the November election.

Growing Opposition to Roosevelt

With the onset of World War II, opposition to Roosevelt was muted. Wartime supplies were freely voted, and in the Senate the Special Committee to Investigate the National Defense Program, set up in 1941 under the chairmanship of Harry S Truman (D Mo.), earned the President's gratitude for serving as a "friendly watchdog" over defense spending without embarrassing the administration. However, as the war went on, it became apparent that opposition to the President on domestic issues was rising.

The antagonism between Roosevelt and Congress came to the surface in February 1944, when the President against the advice of party leaders vetoed a revenue bill, the first veto of such a measure by any President. The action was denounced by Barkley on the floor of the Senate, Feb. 23, as "a calculated and deliberate assault upon the legislative integrity of every member of Congress." Barkley said: "Other members of Congress may do as they please, but as for me I do not propose to take this unjustifiable assault lying down.... I dare say that, during the last seven years of tenure of majority leader, I have carried the flag over rougher territory than ever traversed by any previous majority leader. Sometimes I have carried it with little help from the other end of Pennsylvania Avenue."[71] The following day Barkley's resignation as floor leader was accepted, but he was at once re-elected by unanimous vote of the Democratic Caucus.

Roosevelt's problems with Congress increased after his election to a fourth term in 1944. His proposals for postwar economic and social legislation were ignored, and his nomination of Henry A. Wallace as Secretary of Commerce was confirmed only after the Reconstruction Finance Corporation had been removed from Commerce Department control. By the time of his death in April 1945, Congress was in open revolt.

When Truman succeeded Roosevelt, many observers predicted a renewal of the happy relationship between Congress and the Executive that had prevailed in the McKinley administration. Like McKinley, Truman was a former member of Congress who enjoyed the goodwill of his colleagues, but his honeymoon with Congress did not last long. Although he was markedly successful in pushing his foreign policy programs, the old conservative coalition stood ready to oppose him on domestic issues. With the election of a Republican House and Senate in 1946, the Democrats' 14-year leadership of Congress came to an end.

Reorganization Act of 1946

Even before World War II ended, the tremendous expansion of the size and the authority of the government, especially the executive branch, led to a debate on reform of Congress. Proposals ranged from granting the President constitutional power to dissolve Congress to limiting selection of page boys to residents of the District of Columbia.

But two themes dominated the debate—the relationship between the organization of Congress and its increased workload, and the relations between Congress and the executive branch.

The feeling of many members of Congress was expressed by Rep. Jerry Voorhis (D Calif.) when he urged approval of a concurrent resolution to set up the Joint Committee on the Organization of Congress. Voorhis on Jan. 18, 1945, said, "[I]n the midst of this war we have to grant executive power...of the most sweeping nature." But he wanted the groundwork laid "in order that this Congress may perform its functions efficiently, effectively, and in accord with the needs of the people of this nation and so that it will become not merely an agency that says yes or no to executive proposals, but an agency capable of, and actually performing the function of bringing forth its own constructive program for the needs of the people of this nation. Thus it will take its place and keep its place as an altogether coequal branch of our government."[72]

In February 1945, Congress set up a Joint Committee on the Organization of Congress, with Sen. Robert M. La Follette Jr. (Prog. Wis.) as chairman, and Rep. A. S. Mike Monroney (D Okla.) as vice chairman. After extensive hearings the committee submitted a detailed report that formed the basis of the Legislative Reorganization Act of

1946 (PL 79-601). Passed with bipartisan support in both houses, the most important provisions of the act concerned congressional salaries, the number of standing committees, committee staffs and the legislative budget. *(See pp. 52-53)*

Filibusters and Civil Rights

Obstruction continued to plague the Senate throughout the New Deal era, but no significant new curbs on the filibuster were imposed. The Senate took no cloture votes in the 73rd and 74th Congresses, but in the years 1938-46 it took eight such votes—four in 1946 alone. None of the eight votes came close to the required two-thirds majority.

The most notorious filibusterer of the early New Deal period was Huey P. Long (D La.), who was at odds with the Roosevelt administration over patronage in Louisiana and other matters. Long staged his most famous filibuster in 1935, during debate on a proposed extension of the National Industrial Recovery Act. The "Kingfish" spoke for 15½ hours, a record for the time, filling 85 pages of the *Congressional Record* with remarks that ranged from commentaries on the Constitution to recipes for southern "potlikker," turnip greens and corn bread. His avowed intent was "to save to the sovereign states their rights and prerogatives" and "to preserve the right and prerogative of the Senate as to the qualifications of important officers."[73] Long conducted his last filibuster, against a deficiency appropriation bill, less than two weeks before his assassination in the summer of 1935.

As time went by, the filibuster increasingly came to be associated with civil rights legislation. Southern senators might lack the votes to defeat civil rights measures outright, but they found they could accomplish the same objective through obstruction. Proponents of civil rights legislation could not muster the requisite two-thirds majority to invoke cloture on a southern filibuster even if they had the simple majority needed for action on substantive issues. Accordingly, the southerners used the filibuster to keep civil rights bills from coming to a vote.

Most of the great filibusters of the period involved civil rights. Anti-lynching bills were filibustered in 1935 and 1938, and anti-poll-tax measures were filibustered in 1942, 1944 and 1946. Fair employment practices legislation was filibustered in 1946.

It was hard to keep senators in the chamber during these exhibitions. At one point during the 1942 debate when a quorum could not be mustered and the business of the Senate halted, the sergeant at arms was directed to "request the attendance" of absent senators, and at length 44 senators—five short of a quorum—appeared. He was then directed to "compel the attendance" of absent members. After some delay, he reported that 43 senators were out of town and eight others were in Washington but could not be located. The exasperated Senate finally ordered him to "execute warrants of arrest" upon absent senators. He was saved from this embarrassing duty by the timely appearance of five senators to complete the quorum. (The sergeant at arms had not always been so fortunate; during debate on the Lower Colorado River project in 1927, several infuriated senators actually were brought into the chamber under arrest.)

Rule 22 proved totally ineffectual against these sustained and organized southern filibusters. Six of the eight unsuccessful cloture votes in the years 1938-46 dealt with civil rights issues; on four of the six votes, cloture did not win even a simply majority.

Two minor curbs on obstruction were imposed during the period. The first dealt with the quorum call, a favorite obstructionist tool. During a 1935 filibuster by Long, the chair ruled that a quorum call constitutes business and that senators who yield for a quorum call lose the floor. Under this ruling a senator who yields twice for a quorum call while the same question is before the Senate may be denied the right to speak again on that question during the same legislative day. The second curb, contained in the Reorganization Acts of 1939 and 1945, limited debate on presidential reorganization plans.

The Legislative Reorganization Act of 1946 contained no provisions on debate limitation, since that subject was outside the purview of the Joint Committee on the Organization of Congress, but by 1946 many senators were convinced that further debate curbs were needed if the Senate was to meet its postwar responsibilities.

Postwar Developments: 1945-1969

The election of a Republican Congress in 1946 marked the beginning of a period of divided government in which the White House and Congress were often in the hands of opposing political parties. From 1947 through 1976, Congress was controlled for 16 of the 30 years by the party in opposition to the President.

Democratic President Harry S Truman (1945-53) faced a Republican House and Senate in the 80th Congress (1947-49). His successor, Republican Dwight D. Eisenhower (1953-61) had a Republican Congress only in his first two years in office (1953-55). The Democrats controlled Congress throughout the terms of Democratic Presidents John F. Kennedy (1961-63) and Lyndon B. Johnson (1963-69), but when Republican Richard M. Nixon was elected in 1968, he became the first President since Zachary Taylor to fail to win control of at least one house of the new Congress in his initial election. The House and Senate remained in Democratic hands for the duration of the Nixon presidency and the term completed by Gerald R. Ford after Nixon resigned.

In only two Congresses did Republicans organize the Senate. In the 80th Congress (1947-49) they enjoyed a 51-45 margin, but in the 83rd (1953-55) their margin was so narrow that the death of Majority Leader Robert A. Taft (R Ohio) gave temporary numerical superiority to the Democrats. In the 82nd, 84th and 85th Congresses, the Democratic margin of control was also razor-thin, but after the Democratic sweep in the 1958 elections the Democrats had comfortable majorities.

Need of Presidents for Bipartisan Support

Throughout the postwar period the parties themselves were often badly split, and both Republican and Democratic Presidents were forced to seek bipartisan support to get their programs enacted. Although Truman and the Republicans were often at loggerheads on domestic issues, Sen. Arthur H. Vandenberg (R Mich.) led his once-isolationist party colleagues into a new bipartisan foreign policy in cooperation with the Democratic administration. President Eisenhower often received more support from Democrats than he did from members of his own party, particularly on foreign policy questions in the early years of his administration, but partisanship increased as the 1960 elections approached, and many domestic bills were not enacted.

President Kennedy's relations with Congress were far from ideal, although the Senate was generally more responsive to his proposals than the House, but much of Kennedy's program was enacted after Johnson succeeded him in November 1963. Early in his administration, Johnson won spectacular legislative victories, but with the escalation of the war in Vietnam and the rise of disorder at home he lost his influence over Congress and was forced into retirement in 1968. During the Nixon administration, as well as the term completed by Ford, Congress and the White House were repeatedly in conflict.

Congress and the Public

Throughout the postwar period, the Senate—like Congress as a whole—was preoccupied with the problem of preserving for itself a viable role in the governmental process. The rapid expansion of the power of the executive branch in the 20th century had seriously weakened legislative authority, but at the same time the volume and complexity of legislative business continued to mount. Meanwhile, Congress as an institution suffered increasing public disfavor.

In an effort to reassert its eroded prerogatives and improve its legislative machinery, Congress in 1946 and 1970 enacted major legislative reorganization bills. In an effort to improve its public image, both chambers in 1968 adopted codes of ethics and rules requiring limited financial disclosure. But sensitive internal matters, such as the seniority system and limitation of Senate debate, remained vexing problems.

Party Leadership

Senate leadership in both parties was fairly stable during the years following World War II.

Barkley. On the Democratic side, Alben W. Barkley (Ky.) retained the floor leadership until his resignation in 1949 to become Vice President. The Democrats then had two majority leaders in as many Congresses—Scott W. Lucas (Ill.) in the 81st and Ernest W. McFarland (Ariz.) in the 82nd, both of whom lost their Senate seats after two years in the leadership post.

Johnson. When the 83rd Congress met in January 1953, with the Republicans in control, the Democrats chose as their minority leader Lyndon B. Johnson (Texas), a former House member who had served only four years in the Senate. Johnson was close to House Speaker Sam Rayburn (D Texas) and had the backing of powerful Senate conservatives, notably Robert S. Kerr (D Okla.) and Richard B. Russell (D Ga.), but he promptly built bridges to the liberal Democratic faction in the Senate in an effort to heal the deep liberal-conservative split within the party. Johnson soon became one of the most powerful leaders in Senate history, serving as minority leader in 1953-54 and as majority leader from 1955 until his resignation to become Vice President in 1961.

As a leader, Johnson was celebrated for his powers of persuasion and his manipulative skills. He revitalized the Democratic Policy Committee, saw to it that liberals won seats both on it and on the Steering Committee (committee on committees) and modified the seniority system to assure freshman senators at least one major committee assignment (a practice later adopted by the Republicans as well). On the floor, efficiency was promoted through the use of such devices as unanimous consent agreements, aborted quorum calls and night sessions. Through an active in-

Lyndon Johnson   **Mike Mansfield**

telligence operation headed by Robert G. (Bobby) Baker, secretary to the senate majority, Johnson kept himself informed about what the Senate was really thinking, and he was adept at rounding up votes for acceptable compromises. A system of rewards and punishments supplemented the famous Johnson "treatment." An apostle of "moderation" and "consensus government," Johnson supported the Eisenhower administration on many major questions and frequently solicited Republican support in the Senate. Such was his skill that in 1957 he was able to bring about passage of the first civil rights bill since Reconstruction without a filibuster and without splitting the Democratic Party.

Mansfield. Johnson's successor as majority leader was Mike Mansfield (D Mont.). Mansfield had served as party whip under Johnson, but his permissive style of leadership was in sharp contrast to the Johnson methods. Mansfield held the respect of his colleagues, but he was not an aggressive leader, and under him the Johnson system gave way to a collegial leadership pattern in which the Policy Committee and the legislative committees played important roles. Mansfield was to retire from Congress in 1977 at the end of his term.

Republican Leaders

On the Republican side, party authority was less concentrated than under the Democrats. Robert A. Taft Sr. (Ohio) had been the de facto Republican power in the Senate since the early 1940s and chairman of the Policy Committee from the time it was created in 1947, but he did not feel it necessary to assume the floor leadership of his party until the Eisenhower administration took office in 1953.

After Taft's death in July 1953, the floor leadership went to William F. Knowland (Calif.), a conservative who frequently split with the Eisenhower administration on major issues, but H. Styles Bridges (N.H.) often spoke for the Republicans as chairman of the Policy Committee. Knowland was succeeded as minority leader in 1959 by Everett McKinley Dirksen (Ill.), one of the most colorful party leaders in recent history. His style, noted one observer, was "one of remaining vague on an issue, or taking an initial position from which he could negotiate: bargaining with the majority party, the President and his own colleagues, and eventually accepting a compromise."[74] When Dirksen died in 1969, he was succeeded as minority leader by Hugh Scott (Pa.), a liberal Republican who sometimes found it difficult to serve as spokesman for the Nixon and Ford administrations in the Senate. Scott was to retire from Congress in 1977 at the end of his term.

Use of Cloture to Pass Civil Rights Acts

As filibusters continued to block civil rights legislation in the years following World War II, liberal senators made persistent efforts to revise the Senate cloture rule to make it easier to cut off debate. Amendments to Rule 22 in 1949 and 1959 did not bring an end to obstruction in the Senate, and during the 1960s cloture votes were taken with increasing frequency.

Four such votes were successful. In 1962 the Senate voted 63-27 for a Mansfield-Dirksen motion to invoke cloture on a liberal filibuster against the administration's communications satellite bill. This was the first successful cloture vote since 1927 and only the fifth since the adoption of Rule 22 in 1917. In 1964, the Senate for the first time in its history invoked cloture, by a 71-29 vote, on a southern filibuster against civil rights legislation. This action was followed by successful cloture votes on two other civil rights measures—the voting rights bill of 1965 and, on the fourth try, the open housing bill of 1968.

The discovery that it was possible to impose cloture on civil rights bills under the existing rule took some of the steam out of liberal efforts to reform Rule 22. But in the closing days of the 91st Congress in 1970, the Senate became embroiled in a confusion of filibusters on a variety of major questions. Although this spectacle led to soul-searching within the Senate and to calls from President Nixon for procedural reform, when the 92nd Congress met a few weeks later the Senate once again declined to strengthen its curbs on the filibuster.

Revision of Cloture Rule in 1949

In its original form, Rule 22 required the votes of two-thirds of the Senators present and voting to invoke cloture. Over the years, however, a series of rulings and precedents rendered Rule 22 virtually inoperative by holding that it could not be applied to debate on procedural questions. By 1948 such were the precedents that President Pro Tempore Arthur H. Vandenberg (R Mich.) ruled, during a filibuster against an attempt to bring up an anti-poll-tax bill, that cloture could not be used on a motion to proceed to consideration of a bill. In making his ruling, Vandenberg conceded that "in the final analysis, the Senate has no effective cloture rule at all."[75]

In 1949, the Truman administration, desiring to clear the way for a broad civil rights program, backed a change in the cloture rule. After a long and bitter floor fight, the Senate adopted a proposal, backed by conservative Republicans and southern Democrats, that was actually more restrictive than the rule it replaced. The new rule required the votes of two-thirds of the entire Senate membership (instead of two-thirds of those present and voting) to invoke cloture, but allowed cloture to operate on any pending business or motion with the exception of debate on motions to change the Senate rules themselves (on which cloture previously had operated).

Because under this rule cloture could not be used to cut off a filibuster against a change in the rules, and because any attempt to change Rule 22 while operating under this rule appeared hopeless, Senate liberals devised a new approach. Senate rules had always continued from one Congress to the next in accordance with the theory that the Senate was a continuing body, but the liberals now challenged this conception, arguing that the Senate had a **right to adopt new rules by majority vote at the beginning of a new Congress.**

Accordingly, in 1953 and 1957, at the opening of the 83rd and 85th Congresses, respectively, Sen. Clinton P. Anderson (D N.M.) moved that the Senate consider the adoption of new rules. On both occasions his motion was tabled, but during the 1957 debate Vice President Richard M. Nixon offered a significant "advisory opinion" on how the Senate could proceed to change its rules. Citing the section of the Constitution which provides that "each house may determine the rules of its proceedings," Nixon said he believed the Senate could adopt new rules "under whatever procedures the majority of the Senate approves."[76]

Although each incoming Senate had traditionally operated under existing rules, Nixon said that in his opinion the Senate could not be bound by any previous rule "which denies the membership of the Senate the power to exercise its constitutional right to make its own rules."[77] In this light he said he regarded as unconstitutional the section of Rule 22 banning any limitation of debate on proposals to change the rules. The Vice President explained that he was stating his personal opinion and that the question of constitutionality of the rule could be decided only by the Senate itself. The Senate did not take a vote on the question.

Change in Cloture in 1959

A modest revision of Rule 22 was accomplished in 1959. Senate liberals hoped to make it possible to invoke cloture by a simple majority or by a three-fifths vote, but they were defeated in their efforts to bring about such a substantial change. Instead, a bipartisan leadership group engineered a slight revision of the rule which the southern bloc opposed but did not really fight. The changes were basically designed and put through by Johnson, who seized the initiative from the liberals, and were adopted on a 72-22 roll call.

The 1959 revision permitted cloture to be invoked by two-thirds of those present and voting (rather than two-thirds of the full membership as the 1949 rule had required) and also applied the cloture rule to debate on motions to change the Senate rules. At the same time the Senate added a new provision to Rule 32, the rule concerning the continuation of Senate business from the first session of a Congress to the second session. The new language stated: "The rules of the Senate shall continue from one Congress to the next unless they are changes as provided in these rules."[78] This language buttressed the position of those who maintained that the Senate was a continuing body, but liberal opponents of the filibuster never conceded the point.

Later Efforts at Revision

In 1969, liberal strategy focused on obtaining a ruling from Vice President Hubert H. Humphrey, who was about to retire as presiding officer of the Senate, that a simple majority could invoke cloture on rules debates at the start of a new Congress. After a cloture motion was filed on a liberal proposal to reduce the requirement for cloture from two-thirds to three-fifths of those present and voting, Humphrey announced, in answer to a parliamentary inquiry, that if a majority, but less than two-thirds, of those present and voting voted for cloture he would rule that the majority prevailed. He said that such a ruling, because it could be appealed by the Senate, would enable the Senate to decide the constitutional issue by a simple majority vote, without debate. Humphrey added that if he held that the cloture motion had failed because of the lack of a two-thirds vote, he would be inhibiting the Senate from deciding the constitutional question.

In explaining the ruling he proposed to make, Humphrey said: "On a par with the right of the Senate to determine its rules, though perhaps not set forth so specifically in the Constitution, is the right of the Senate, a simple majority of the Senate, to decide constitutional questions."[79]

When the cloture motion came to a vote Jan. 16, 1969, a slim majority (51-47) voted for cloture, and Humphrey ruled that debate would proceed under the limitations of Rule 22. Opponents of the rules change immediately appealed his decision, and Humphrey's ruling was reversed, 45-53. The vote on the appeal meant that cloture was not invoked and left the Senate to continue the debate on the motion to consider the rules change proposal. Proponents of the change did not have enough support to limit debate under the two-thirds rule, and so ended another round in the rules reform fight.

The real breakthrough for senators seeking changes in the filibuster rule came in 1975.

Other Rules Changes

Two minor changes in Senate rules were adopted in 1964. The first amended Rule 8 to provide for a three-hour period after the morning hour when debate on a pending measure, or amendments to that measure, must be germane. The period could be waived by unanimous consent or motion without debate. The intent of the proposal was to speed passage of pending bills by preventing speeches on irrelevant matters until late in each day's session, and it was adopted over proposals for more stringent germaneness rules. Senators immediately found one loophole: a nongermane amendment could be offered (and later withdrawn), and debate on that amendment would be in order. The rule was seldom applied in practice.

In the second change, the Senate amended Rule 25 to permit Senate standing committees to meet until completion of the morning hour—a period of up to two hours at the beginning of each legislative day when routine business is conducted. Previously unanimous consent had been required for committees to meet at any time when the Senate was in session.

Integrity of the Senate

To much of the American public the Senate did not present a favorable image in the years following World War II. Not only did it often seem unable, by virtue of its antiquated procedures, to do the work the public expected it to do, but the integrity of its personnel was frequently under attack. The Senate is not a body to be stampeded by public opinion, and it approached this problem in its own way.

McCarthy. From 1950 until 1954, Sen. Joseph R. McCarthy (R Wis.) was by all odds the most controversial member of the Senate. McCarthy's career as a Communist-hunter began with a speech in Wheeling, W.Va., in February 1950 in which he charged that 205 Communists were working in the State Department with the knowledge of the Secretary of State. From that time until his formal censure by the Senate in 1954, McCarthy and his freewheeling accusations of Communist sympathies among high and low-placed government officials absorbed much of the public's attention. The phenomenon of "McCarthyism" had a major impact on the psychological climate of the early 1950s. Taking over the chairmanship of the Senate Govern-

ment Operations Committee in 1953, McCarthy investigated the State Department, the Voice of America, the Department of the Army and other agencies. An opinion-stifling climate of fear was said to be one of the results of his probes.

For several years McCarthy's colleagues showed no disposition to tangle with him, but the Army-McCarthy hearings, televised in the spring of 1954, led finally to his censure by the Senate in a special session following the midterm election of 1954. In the end McCarthy was censured, by a vote of 67-22, not for his "habitual contempt of people" as Sen. Ralph E. Flanders (R Vt.) had originally proposed, but for contemptuous treatment of the Senate itself—for his failure to cooperate with the Subcommittee on Privileges and Elections in 1952 and for his abuse of the select committee that had considered the censure charges against him. The censure resolution asserted that McCarthy had "acted contrary to senatorial ethics and tended to bring the Senate into dishonor and disrepute, to obstruct the constitutional processes of the Senate, and to impair its dignity. And such conduct is hereby condemned."[80]

McCarthy remained in the Senate until his death in 1957, but he lost his committee and subcommittee chairmanships in the next, Democratic-controlled Congress, and his activities no longer attracted much attention in the Senate, the press or elsewhere.

Meanwhile, alleged excesses in treatment of witnesses by congressional committees led in 1954 to an extensive search for a "fair-play" code to govern congressional investigations. Most criticism was directed at the Senate Permanent Investigations Subcommittee, headed by McCarthy, and at the House Un-American Activities Committee. In 1955, the House amended its rules to provide a minimum standard of conduct for House committees. The Senate adopted no general rules on the subject, but the Permanent Investigations Subcommittee under the chairmanship of John L. McClellan (D Ark.) adopted new safeguards for the protection of witnesses.

Bobby Baker. In 1963, the Senate was shaken by charges that Robert G. (Bobby) Baker had used his position as secretary to the Senate majority to promote outside business interests. Baker, who served as secretary from 1955 until his resignation under fire in August 1963, was no ordinary Senate functionary. Exposure of his numerous "improprieties" led to criticism of the Senate as a whole and prompted a review of congressional ethics.

A protégé of Lyndon B. Johnson, to whom the case was particularly embarrassing, Baker had access to leadership councils and was known as the Senate's "most powerful employee." He headed Johnson's intelligence network in the

Joseph McCarthy

Thomas Dodd

Senate and was celebrated for his ability to forecast the outcome of close votes. Johnson once hailed "his tremendous fund of knowledge about the Senate, which is almost appalling in one so young."[81]

In the wake of disclosures about Baker's wide-ranging business ventures, the Senate instructed its Rules and Administration Committee to investigate his activities from the standpoint of congressional ethics. The committee's Democratic majority, in reports issued in 1964 and 1965, accused Baker of "many gross improprieties" but cited no actual violations of law. Committee Republicans charged that the investigation was incomplete and a "whitewash." Both Republicans and Democrats called for rules requiring financial-disclosure statements by members of Congress and their employees.

Baker ultimately was convicted in court and imprisoned for income tax evasion, theft and conspiracy to defraud the government. Meanwhile, largely because of embarrassments caused by the Baker scandal, the Senate in 1964 created a Select Committee on Standards and Conduct to investigate allegations of improper conduct by senators and Senate employees, to recommend disciplinary action and to draw up a code of ethical conduct. The House established a similar committee in 1967.

Dodd. The Select Committee's first investigation began in 1966. It involved charges by syndicated columnists Drew Pearson and Jack Anderson that Sen. Thomas J. Dodd (D Conn.) had misused political campaign funds contributed to him and had committed other offenses. The committee in April 1967 recommended that the Senate censure Dodd for misuse of political funds and for double-billing for official and private travel. The Senate on June 23 censured Dodd on the first charge by a 92-5 roll-call vote but refused, on a 45-51 vote, to censure him on the second charge. The action marked the seventh time in its history that the Senate had censured one of its members. After the vote was taken, the issue was closed, and Dodd continued to serve in the Senate until he was defeated for re-election in 1970.

Adoption of Ethics Codes

Concern over conflicts of interest at all levels of government had been rising since World War II, but Congress showed no inclination to adopt self-policing measures. Pressures generated by the Baker and Dodd cases in the Senate and by investigation of the activities of Rep. Adam C. Powell (D N.Y.) in the House were largely responsible for the adoption of limited financial-disclosure rules in both chambers in 1968.

In the Senate, a code of conduct proposed by the Select Committee on Standards and Conduct was adopted without substantial change on March 22, 1968, by a 67-1 vote. Included were provisions to regulate the outside employment of Senate employees, to require a full accounting of campaign contributions and limit the uses to which they could be put, and to require senators and top employees to file detailed financial reports each year. However, these reports were to be available only to the Select Committee, and the only public accounting required was of gifts of $50 or more and honoraria of $300 or more. The Senate rejected, 40-44, a proposal for full public disclosure of members' finances. The proposal had been pressed by Sen. Joseph S. Clark (D Pa.), who was a persistent advocate of congressional reform.

The code of conduct was embodied in four additions to the Senate Rules:

Rule 41. Stipulated that no officer or employee of the Senate might engage in any other employment or paid activity unless it was not inconsistent with his duties in the Senate. Directed employees to report their outside employment to specified supervisors, including senators, who were to take such action as they considered necessary to avoid a conflict of interest by the employee.

Rule 42. Directed that a senator or a declared candidate for the Senate might accept a contribution from a fund-raising event for his benefit only if he had given express approval before funds were raised and if he received a full accounting of the sources and amounts of each contribution. Official events of his party were exempted from these restrictions.

Permitted a senator or candidate to accept contributions from an individual or an organization provided that a complete accounting of the sources and amounts were made by the recipient.

Specified that a senator or candidate might use such contributions for the expenses of his nomination and election and for the following purposes: travel expenses to and from the senator's home state; printing and other expenses of sending speeches, newsletters and reports to his constituents; expenses of radio, television and other media reports to constituents; telephone, postage and stationery expenses not covered by Senate allowances; and subscriptions to home-state newspapers.

Required disclosure of gifts, from a single, non-family source, of $50 or more under the provisions of Rule 44.

Rule 43. Prohibited employees of the Senate from receiving, soliciting or distributing funds collected in connection with a campaign for the Senate or any other federal office. Exempted from the rule senators' assistants who were designated to engage in such activity and who earned more than $10,000 a year. Required that the senator file the names of such designated aides with the secretary of the Senate, as public information.

Rule 44. Required each senator, declared candidate and Senate employee earning more than $15,000 a year to file with the U.S. Comptroller General, by May 15 each year, a sealed envelope containing the following reports:

● A copy of his U.S. income tax returns and declarations, including joint statements.

● The amount and source of each fee of $1,000 or more received from a client.

● The name and address of each corporation, business or professional enterprise in which he was an officer, director, manager, partner or employee, and the amount of compensation received.

● The identity of real or personal property worth $10,000 or more that he owned.

● The identity of each trust or fiduciary relation in which he held a beneficial interest worth $10,000 or more and the identity, if known, of any interest the trust held in real or personal property over $10,000.

● The identity of each liability of $5,000 or more owed by him or his spouse jointly.

● The source and value of all gifts worth $50 or more received from a single source.

Specified that the information filed with the Comptroller General would be kept confidential for seven years and then returned to the filer or his legal representative. If the filer died or left the Senate, his reports would be returned within a year.

Provided that the Select Committee on Standards and Conduct might, by a majority vote, examine the contents of a confidential filing and make the file available for investigation to the committee staff. Required that due notice be given to an individual under investigation and an opportunity provided for him to be heard by the committee in closed session.

Required each senator, candidate and employee earning more than $15,000 a year to file with the secretary of the Senate by May 15 each year the following information, which was to be kept for three years and made available for public inspection:

• The accounting required under Rule 42 of all contributions received in the previous year (amounts under $50 might be totaled and not itemized).

• The amount, value and source of any honorarium of $300 or more.

Senate-Executive Contests for Power

One of the principal purposes of the Legislative Reorganization Act of 1946 was to help Congress hold its own against the rapidly expanding power of the executive branch. In this it was only partly successful. By the end of World War II it seemed clear that legislative initiative had shifted, apparently irretrievably, from Congress to the President, and during the postwar era Congress was for the most part concerned with preserving its powers to approve, revise or reject presidential programs.

In these years the Senate's sense of itself was frequently offended by what it viewed as presidential encroachments on its constitutional functions. In 1954 the Senate came within one vote of approving a proposed constitutional amendment—the so-called Bricker Amendment—to restrict the President's power to negotiate treaties and other international agreements. Other conflicts arose over the spending power, the war power and to a lesser extent, the appointment power. Frequently the Senate was in contention with the House as well as the executive branch.

Disputes Over Spending Power

In the 1946 act Congress tried to assert new and meaningful control over the budget process through the creation of a legislative budget. After three unsuccessful attempts to use this device, it was abandoned as an unqualified failure.

In 1947, the Joint Committee on the Legislative Budget, composed of members of the House Ways and Means and Appropriations Committees and the Senate Finance and Appropriations Committees, agreed to ceilings on appropriations and expenditures that were substantially lower than the amounts projected in President Truman's budget. The House approved the ceilings, but the Senate increased them and insisted that an expected budget surplus be applied to debt retirement rather than to reduction of taxes as House leaders proposed. As a result, the budget resolution died in conference.

In 1948, both houses adopted the same legislative budget, but Congress appropriated $6 billion more than the agreed-upon ceiling. In 1949, the process broke down entirely when the deadline for a budget was moved from Feb. 15 to May 1. By that date 11 appropriation bills had passed the House and nine had passed the Senate; the legislative budget was never produced.

Failure of the legislative budget prompted a serious effort in Congress in 1950 to combine the numerous separate appropriation bills into one omnibus measure. The omnibus measure was approved by Congress about two months

earlier than the last of the separate measures in 1949. In addition, the appropriations total was about $2.3 billion less than the President's combined budget requests. Chairman Clarence Cannon (D Mo.) of the House Appropriations Committee hailed the omnibus approach as "the most practical and efficient method of handling the annual budget."[82] In spite of his support the House Appropriations Committee in 1951 voted 31-18 to return to the traditional method of separate handling of appropriation bills; the omnibus approach had undercut the authority of subcommittees and their chairmen. Following the vote, Cannon charged that "every predatory lobbyist, every pressure group seeking to get its hands into the U.S. Treasury, every bureaucrat seeking to extend his empire downtown is opposed to the consolidated bill."[83]

The Senate in 1953 voted to make another attempt at an omnibus bill and to place limitations on various forms of spending, but the proposal was not acted on in the House. Another Senate proposal, for the creation of a Joint Budget Committee to provide Congress with meaningful fiscal information, was approved by the Senate eight times between 1952 and 1967 but was never accepted by the House.

As years went by, Congress discovered that the "power of the purse," long considered one of its principal sources of power over the executive branch, was not the bulwark of legislative authority it had thought. Congress generally managed to authorize less spending than was proposed by postwar Presidents, but it proved unable to consider the budget as a whole and it lacked effective control over actual expenditures. This point was underscored by repeated conflicts with the White House over "backdoor spending" and the impounding by executive agencies of funds appropriated by Congress. Congressional frustration found expression in the frequent enactment of spending ceilings not to be exceeded by the executive branch.

Meanwhile, long-standing disagreement between the Senate and House over their respective roles in the appropriations process caused a rift between the two chambers. In 1962 this issue produced a Senate-House feud that delayed final action on appropriation bills and kept Congress in turmoil through much of the session. The feud started as a spat over the physical location of conference committee meetings and quickly moved on to the larger issues of whether the Senate could (1) initiate its own appropriation bills and (2) add to House-passed appropriation bills funds for items either not previously considered by the House or considered and rejected.

When the Senate passed a continuing resolution to provide temporary financing for federal agencies pending final congressional action on their regular appropriations, the House called the action an infringement on its "immemorial" right to initiate appropriation bills. In retaliation, the Senate adopted a resolution stating that "the acquiescence of the Senate in permitting the House to first consider appropriation bills cannot change the clear language of the Constitution nor affect the Senate's co-equal power to originate any bill not expressly 'raising revenue.' "[84] Although the two chambers eventually reached a truce, the basic issues were not resolved. It was not until a decade later that the House and Senate agreed on a new congressional budget control system.

Exercise of the War Power

Events of the post-World-War-II era frequently reminded Congress that its constitutional power to declare war counted for little in the modern world. But in the late 1960s the Senate began to mount a substantial challenge to the President's authority over military involvement.

Truman. Congress did not seriously challenge President Truman's war powers until 1951. At issue then was the President's authority to dispatch troops to Korea and to Western Europe. Sen. Robert A. Taft Sr. (R Ohio) opened a three-month-long debate on Jan. 5, 1951, by asserting that Truman had "no authority whatever to commit American troops to Korea without consulting Congress and without Congressional approval." Moreover, he said, the President had "no power to agree to send American troops to fight in Europe in a war between members of the Atlantic Pact and Soviet Russia."[85]

The debate revolved principally around the troops-to-Europe issue. It came to an end April 4, when the Senate adopted two resolutions approving the dispatch of four divisions to Europe. One of the resolutions stated that it was the sense of the Senate that "no ground troops in addition to such four divisions should be sent to Western Europe...without further Congressional approval."[86] But neither resolution gained the force of law because the House took no action.

Truman never asked Congress for a declaration of war in Korea, and he waited until Dec. 16, 1950—six months after the outbreak of hostilities—to proclaim the existence of a national emergency. In defense of this course, it was argued that the Russians or Chinese or both had violated post-World-War-II agreements on Korea and that emergency powers authorized during World War II could still be applied.

The Korean conflict provided two further tests of presidential powers. In 1951, the nation was split when Truman dismissed Gen. Douglas A. MacArthur from his command of United Nations and U.S. forces in the Far East because of a dispute over policy. The Senate Foreign Relations and Armed Services Committees reviewed the ouster, and their joint hearings were credited with cooling the atmosphere throughout the country. So bitter was the controversy that the committees refrained from making any formal report, but the President's right to remove MacArthur was conceded and the principle of civilian control over the military upheld. In 1952, Congress ignored Truman's request for approval of his seizure of the nation's steel mills, an action taken under his war powers, and the Supreme Court later ruled that the seizure was without statutory authority and constituted a usurpation of the powers of Congress.

Eisenhower. Presidents who followed Truman made frequent use of their war powers, sometimes in cooperation with Congress. For example, President Eisenhower asked Congress in 1955 for advance approval of the use of American armed force in the event of a Communist attack on Formosa or the Pescadores Islands. A resolution to that effect was adopted within a week. However, Eisenhower landed troops in Lebanon in July 1958 strictly on his own authority. In a special message to Congress, July 15, he said the action was designed to protect American lives and "to assist the Government of Lebanon in the preservation of Lebanon's territorial integrity and independence, which have been deemed vital to U.S. national interests and world peace."[87]

Kennedy. President Kennedy, responding to Soviet threats to Allied rights in West Berlin, asked Congress on July 16, 1961, for authority to call up ready reservists and to extend the enlistments of men already on active duty. Such authority was granted in a joint resolution signed by the President Aug. 1. Kennedy did not wait for congressional approval of his actions in the Cuban missile crisis of October 1962. Confronted with a buildup of Soviet missile bases in Cuba, he ordered an immediate "naval quarantine" of Cuba to prevent delivery of additional Russian missiles. More than any other crisis of the post-war period, the Cuban episode illustrated the vast sweep of presidential power in times of great emergency.[88]

Johnson. Congress virtually abdicated its power to declare war in Vietnam when it adopted, in August 1964, the Gulf of Tonkin resolution authorizing the President to "take all necessary measures" to stop aggression in Southeast Asia.[89] The resolution was requested by President Johnson and adopted by a vote of 88-2 in the Senate and 414-0 in the House. The President considered the resolution adequate authority for expanding U.S. involvement in the Vietnam War, but in following years, as public support for the war deteriorated, Congress was to have second thoughts about its 1964 action; the Tonkin Gulf resolution was repealed in January 1971.

Liberal Advances: 1970-1976

While the House was initiating many procedural reforms in the first half of the 1970s, the Senate was making a parallel effort on its side of the Capitol.

Senate reforms were not as broad as those in the House mainly because the 100-member Senate was already a more open body than the 435-member House. The Senate—unlike the House—did not use a closed rule. This difference meant any senator could propose floor amendments. Similarly, the Senate did not have a system of unrecorded teller votes; thus each senator could be held more closely accountable for his actions. And the Senate had admitted television and radio coverage of Senate committees, sanctioned in the Legislative Reorganization Act of 1946, long before the House generally ended its broadcast bans on committee hearings through enactment of the Legislative Reorganization Act of 1970.

The principal obstacle to a more democratic Senate, in the view of reformers, was unlimited debate, the minority's use of the filibuster to obstruct the majority. After years of trying, the reformers succeeded in 1975 in reducing the number of votes needed to invoke cloture. The modification did not destroy the power of a minority from talking legislation to death; but it significantly modified that power by lowering the vote needed to end debate from two-thirds of those present and voting to three-fifths of the 100-member Senate.

By 1973, Congress was able to muster its strength to win enactment of the historic Senate-inspired War Powers Act despite White House lobbying against it and a presidential veto. Principal sponsors of the war powers legislation, which sought to delineate the extent of presidential war powers, were Sens. Jacob K. Javits (R N.Y.), John C. Stennis (D Miss.) and Thomas F. Eagleton (D Mo.). And in 1975, Congress defeated President Ford's proposals for supplementary military aid funds to South Vietnam and Cambodia as they were collapsing before a Communist military offensive; put restrictions on his request for similar funds to Turkey; and legislated against his proposals to provide military aid funds to anticommunist factions in Angola.[90]

The Senate also played an important role in reforming the federal campaign laws, instituting a congressional budgetary control system and exposing the crimes of Watergate. Congress had long been faulted for ignoring its oversight function, unless embarked upon a publicity-laden probe. The Watergate investigation, however, rated as a high point of publicly-aired investigations. It was the Senate Watergate Committee which discovered the existence of the tape recordings that ultimately brought about President Nixon's resignation.

Party Leaders

Majority Leader Mike Mansfield (D Mont.) and Minority Leader Hugh Scott (R Pa.), leaders respectively since 1961 and 1971, announced their retirements from Congress effective at the conclusion of the 94th Congress. Mansfield was called "the gentle persuader" because he held that each senator should conduct his affairs with minimal pressure from the leadership. Despite his reticence on the national stage, Mansfield was a strong defender of Senate prerogatives during the Johnson and Nixon administrations, and differed openly with Democrat Johnson on the Vietnam war. His 16-year tenure (1961-1976) as leader was the longest in Senate history.

Scott defended U.S. actions in Indochina long after much of his Pennsylvania constituency had turned against them. He promised that White House tapes would exonerate President Nixon and suffered embarrassment when the Watergate evidence indicated Nixon's guilt.[91]

Legislative Reorganization

The Legislative Reorganization Act of 1970 was designed to improve the floor and committee operations of Congress, by providing better means to evaluate the federal budget and by increasing congressional resources for research and information. Rules changes, applying to the Senate only and aiming at accountability, openness and efficiency, focused primarily on the operations of committees.

Changes affecting committee operations included allowing a committee majority to call a meeting when the chairman does not do so on request, requiring committees to adopt and publish rules of procedure, and guaranteeing that a majority of minority members of a committee be allowed to call witnesses during hearings.

Rules governing committee assignments and seniority were changed so that senators could be members of only two major committees and one minor, select or joint committee; so that no senator could serve on more than one of the Armed Services, Appropriations, Finance or Foreign Relations Committees; and so that no senator could hold the chairmanship of more than one full committee and one subcommittee of a major committee.

In a move to give senators more information on committee actions, the new rules prohibited Senate consideration of any bill (exceptions included declarations of war and emergency) unless the committee report was available three days prior to floor action, and required conference committees to explain conference action.[92]

Filibuster Reform

Rule 22, which prescribed the way to terminate filibusters, was modified in 1975 after years of battle. The existing rule required two-thirds of senators present and voting to invoke cloture and bring a proposal to a vote. The 1975 change set the number of votes required at three-fifths of the full Senate, or 60 if there were no vacancies. Advocates believed the change would ease the task of ending filibusters.

The change was accomplished after a three-week struggle. Senate liberals had attempted filibuster modification every two years since 1959, with the exception of 1973.

The 1975 reformers wanted a simple majority or a three-fifths majority of senators present and voting to cut off debate, but had to settle for the compromise that set the necessary figure at three-fifths of all 100 members, called "a constitutional majority." The new rule to invoke cloture would apply to any matter except a proposed change in the Standing Rules of the Senate, for which the old two-thirds rule to end debate would still hold.

The limited nature of the filibuster change left it unclear as to how major a victory had been won.

In practical terms, the two-thirds majority rule generally meant that between 61 and 67 senators had to support cloture. This was because most issues that were controversial enough to draw a filibuster also were important enough to prompt many of the 100 senators to vote on a cloture motion.

For example, between 1960, when frequent use of the filibuster and cloture began, and 1975 there were 79 cloture votes. Only a handful of the 79 cloture votes—18—succeeded during this 15-year period under the two-thirds requirement. Moreover, of the 79 cloture votes, only 22—or 28 per cent—recorded at least 60 senators supporting an end to debate.

In addition, the record showed that the three-fifths "constitutional" majority rule would have made almost no difference in the actual outcome of legislation on which filibusters and cloture votes occurred. During the entire history of the two-thirds cloture rule from 1917 to 1975, only one additional cloture vote would have been successful had the three-fifths rule been in effect. This is because 60 votes or more, but not a two-thirds majority, were obtained on several bills, but in each case cloture was reached on subsequent votes under the two-thirds rule.

However, reformers saw the new rule speeding up the Senate's work as well as enhancing the chance of success for senators seeking cloture. In addition, the importance of the filibuster appeared diminished in view of the fact that this tactic was basically a weapon of southern senators to block civil rights legislation in the 1960s and that by 1975 civil rights legislative issues—except for busing—were largely settled.

In April 1976, Senate liberals and conservatives joined forces to persuade the Senate to amend the cloture rule by allowing the introduction of amendments to pending legislation up until the announcement of the outcome of a cloture vote.

Under the existing rule for ending a filibuster, no amendment could be considered after cloture was invoked, unless it had been formally read or considered read before the cloture vote was taken. In practice, the Senate routinely granted unanimous consent to consider read all amendments at the Senate desk at the time of the vote so that they could be eligible for consideration in compliance with Rule 22. The rules change had no effect on the three-fifths voting requirement for ending filibusters. But it could delay bringing an amendment or bill to a final vote after cloture had been invoked.[93]

Seniority System

In 1971, Sens. Fred R. Harris (D Okla.) and Charles McC. Mathias Jr. (R Md.) led an unsuccessful move to scrap

(Continued on p. 102)

Filibusters and the Senate . . .

Filibustering is the practice by which a minority of a legislative body employs extended debate and dilatory tactics to delay or block action favored by the majority.

The word filibuster is derived from the Dutch word *Vrijbuiter,* meaning freebooter. Passing into Spanish as *filibustero,* it was used to describe military adventurers from the United States who in the mid-1800s fomented insurrections against various Latin American governments.[1]

The first legislative use of the word is said to have occurred in the House in 1853, when a representative accused his opponents of "filibustering against the United States."[2] By 1863, filibuster had come to mean delaying action on the floor, but the term did not gain wide currency until the 1880s.

Although the word filibuster as applied to legislative obstruction is relatively new, the tactics it describes are as old as parliamentary government. What are now called filibusters occurred in the colonial assemblies, and obstructive tactics were a feature of Congress from its earliest days. A bill to establish a "permanent residence" for the national government was subjected to a House filibuster early in the First Congress. When the same bill reached the Senate, Pennsylvania's Sen. William Maclay complained that "the design of the Virginians and the South Carolina gentlemen was to talk away the time so that we could not get the bill passed."[3]

Obstruction in the House

Legislative obstruction was characteristic of the House long before it became common in the Senate. But the unwieldy size of the lower chamber's membership soon led to various curbs on debate. The previous-question motion, first adopted in 1789, has been used since 1811 to close debate and bring the matter under consideration to an immediate vote. Under a rule adopted in 1798, House members are permitted to speak only once on a subject in general debate; since 1841, they have been limited to one hour. Since 1847, debate on amendments has been limited to five minutes for each side, and since 1880, a rule of relevancy has been enforced by the Speaker. These limitations on debate curbed the practice of filibustering in the House, although delaying tactics continued to be used from time to time.

Obstruction in the Senate

The Senate, with its cherished tradition of unlimited debate, offered a more favorable climate for obstruction. By the end of the 19th century the upper chamber had become notorious as the home of the filibuster.

The first notable Senate filibuster occurred in 1841, when dissident senators held the floor for 10 days in opposition to a bill to shift the Senate's printing to new contractors. In the next 40 years filibusters were undertaken with increasing frequency and boisterousness, but they were not usually successful. In the last two decades of the 19th century, the practice assumed almost epidemic proportions, and as filibusterers used more daring techniques their rate of success increased. Efforts to curb obstruction in the 20th century had only limited effec-

tiveness. The filibuster came to be identified with southern efforts to block civil rights legislation (although northern liberals occasionally found it a useful device as well); until 1964 the Senate was never able to invoke cloture on a civil rights filibuster.

Filibustering Techniques

The most important tool of the filibusterers is long-continued talk, for which a strong physical constitution is a prerequisite. Other techniques are dilatory motions, roll-call votes, quorum calls, points of order and appeals, and the interjection of other business. Successful use of these devices calls for deft use of parliamentary procedure; senators with less than expert knowledge are likely to rely on talk, because a parliamentary blunder could spell defeat for their cause.

The longest speech in the history of the Senate was made by Strom Thurmond (R S.C.). During a filibuster against passage of the Civil Rights Act of 1957, Thurmond spoke for 24 hours and 18 minutes in a round-the-clock session Aug. 28-29, 1957. Second place goes to Wayne Morse (D Ore.), who in April 1953 spoke for 22 hours and 26 minutes on the tidelands oil bill. The third-place record was set in 1908 by Robert M. La Follette Sr. (R Wis.), who held the floor for 18 hours and 23 minutes in a fight over the Aldrich-Vreeland currency bill. In fourth place is Huey P. Long (D La.), who in June 1935 spoke for 15 hours and 30 minutes on an extension of the National Industrial Recovery Act.

Because the Senate has no germaneness rule, speakers do not always confine themselves to the subject under consideration. Long in 1935 entertained his colleagues with recipes for southern "potlikker," and Glen H. Taylor (D Idaho), a former tent show performer, spent eight and one-half hours in 1947 expounding on fishing, baptism, Wall Street and his children in an effort to delay a vote on overriding President Truman's veto of the Taft-Hartley Act. In this connection, special credit perhaps is due to Reed Smoot (R Utah), who during a successful 1915 filibuster against President Wilson's Ship Purchase bill spoke for 11 hours and 35 minutes without relief and without deviating from the subject.

As a rule, a filibuster is most likely to succeed near the end of a session, when comparatively brief obstruction can imperil all pending legislation. Before the adoption of the Twentieth ("Lame Duck") Amendment to the Constitution in 1933, Congress was required to meet annually in December. When Congress met in December of an even-numbered year, following the election of its successor, it could remain in session only until March 4 of the following year, when the term of the new Congress began. During this short, or lame-duck, session—in which members who had been repudiated at the polls participated—filibusters were an almost routine occurrence. In mid-session, a filibuster may be successful if urgent legislation is delayed or if the filibuster has a large number of senators participating.

Anti-Filibuster Techniques

Several techniques can be employed against the filibuster. The most spectacular, and probably least

. . . Cloture Rule: A Recapitulation

effective, is the use of prolonged sessions to break the strength of the obstructionists. A second technique is strict observance of existing Senate rules. Widely ignored rules provide that a speaker must stand, rather than sit or walk about; permit the presiding officer to take a senator "off his feet" for using unparliamentary language; require that business intervene between quorum calls; and prohibit the reading of speeches or other material by a clerk without Senate consent. Finally, a senator may be refused an opportunity to speak more than twice on a subject in any one day (a legislative day may spread over several calendar days if the Senate recesses rather than adjourns) "without leave of the Senate."

Senate Cloture Rule

The Senate's ultimate check on the filibuster is the provision for cloture, or limitation of debate, contained in Rule 22 of its Standing Rules. The original Rule 22 was adopted in 1917 following a furor over the "talking to death" in the Senate of a proposal by President Wilson for arming American merchant ships before U.S. entry into World War I. The 1917 rule required the votes of two-thirds of the senators present and voting to invoke cloture. In 1949, during a parliamentary battle preceding scheduled consideration of a Fair Employment Practices Commission bill, the requirement was raised to two-thirds of the entire Senate membership.

A revision of the rule in 1959 provided for limitation of debate by a vote of two-thirds of the senators present and voting, two days after a cloture petition was submitted by 16 senators. Thereafter, debate was limited to one hour for each senator on the bill itself and on all amendments and motions affecting it. No new amendments could be offered except by unanimous consent. Amendments that were not germane to the pending business, and amendments and motions clearly designed to delay action, were out of order. The rule applied both to regular legislative business and to motions to change the Senate rules.

Rule 22 was revised significantly in 1975. Under the rule modification, a vote of three-fifths of the entire Senate membership (a "constitutional majority") was required to end a filibuster on any matter except a proposed change in the standing rules of the Senate. With no vacancies in the Senate, 60 votes were required to invoke cloture under this new rule.

The old requirement of a two-thirds majority of senators present and voting would still apply to efforts to end debate on a rules change proposal. The 1975 change did not alter Rule 22's ban on non-germane amendments once cloture was invoked.

Fight for Reform

Advocates of Rule 22 revision began their 1975 campaign for reform as soon as the 94th Congress convened on Jan. 14. The changes were finally adopted on March 7 after a divisive three-week debate in which opponents of the reforms used a number of dilatory tactics.

Reformers began their final drive on Feb. 20. Over the next two and a half weeks, 37 votes were taken on Rule 22, but only a handful were critical votes and most of those were on seemingly arcane parliamentary maneuvers. The original proposal made by reformers was to permit three-fifths of those senators present and voting to end debate.

Opponents of the proposal led by Sen. James B. Allen (D Ala.) began a filibuster against the proposal. Allen and his conservative colleagues suffered a parliamentary setback on Feb. 20 when Vice President Nelson Rockefeller ruled that a simple Senate majority was sufficient to end a filibuster. As debate dragged on and bitterness intensified, Sen. Russell B. Long (D La.) proposed a compromise that was endorsed by Majority Leader Mike Mansfield (D Mont.). Long's plan was to change Rule 22 for the 94th Congress by allowing a three-fifths majority of the full Senate to end debate. In future Congresses, the rule would revert to the old two-thirds requirement.

Under pressure from the Senate leadership, Long's proposal was altered to make the three-fifths majority of the full Senate change permanent. Long's compromise proposal was adopted by a 56-27 vote on March 7.

Effect of Rule 22 Change

The modification of Rule 22 made it appear unlikely that the filibuster would ever again assume the importance that it had in previous years. The two-thirds majority rule generally had meant that between 61 and 67 senators had to support cloture. This was because most issues that were controversial enough to draw a filibuster also were important enough to prompt most of the 100 senators to vote on a cloture motion.

Between 1960 when frequent use of the filibuster and cloture began and 1975, there were 79 cloture votes. Only a handful of the 79 votes—18—succeeded during this 15-year period. (For a complete list of cloture votes since 1917, when Rule 22 was adopted, through 1975, see box on p. 352)

However, of the 79 cloture votes, only 22—or 28 per cent—recorded at least 60 senators supporting an end to debate. The record showed that the requirement for a three-fifths "constitutional" majority would have made almost no difference in the actual outcome of legislation on which filibusters and cloture votes occurred. During the entire history of the two-thirds cloture rule from 1917 to 1975, only one additional cloture vote would have been successful had the three-fifths rule been in effect; the last in a series of cloture votes on a bill to set up a federal agency to represent consumer interests. Sixty votes or more, but not a two-thirds majority, were obtained on three bills, but in each case cloture was reached on subsequent votes.

Footnotes

1. Robert Luce, *Legislative Procedure: Parliamentary Practices and the Course of Business in the Framing of Statutes* (New York: Da Capo Press, 1972), p. 283.

2. George B. Galloway, *The Legislative Process in Congress*, (New York: Crowell, 1953), pp. 559-560.

3. Franklin L. Burdette, *Filibustering in the Senate*, (New York: Russell & Russell, 1965), p. 14.

(Continued from p. 99)

the seniority system, a custom, in the selection of committee chairmen in favor of what they called "a standard of merit" in making the top choices. Their plan would have amended Rule 24 to require that committee chairmen and ranking minority members be nominated individually by a majority vote of the party caucuses and elected individually by majority vote of the full Senate at the beginning of each new Congress. The proposal failed when it was adversely reported by the Senate Rules and Administration Committee. (Rule 24 merely stated that the Senate "shall proceed by ballot to appoint severally the chairmen of each committee, and then, by one ballot, the other members necessary to complete the same.")

Democratic reformers were more successful in January 1975 when they revised party rules to establish a method by which committee chairmen would have to face an election every two years, but the vote was not mandatory as it was in the House. The Democratic caucus voted to require selection of chairmen by secret ballot whenever one-fifth of the caucus requested it. The modification did not affect chairmen in the 94th Congress.

The rule change was intended to make it easier for senators to depose a chairman without fear of retribution. Under the procedure, a list of senators nominated by the Democratic Steering Committee to be committee chairmen would be distributed to all Democrats. The Democrats would check off the names of the nominees they wished to subject to a secret ballot and would submit the list without signing it. If at least 20 per cent of the caucus members wanted a secret vote on a nominee it would be held automatically two days later.

Open Committees, Staffing

Almost three years after the House in March 1973 voted to open up its committee bill-drafting sessions to the public and press, the Senate in November 1975 adopted a similar rule that would require most of its committees to work in public. At the same time, the Senate approved open conference committee sessions as the House had done in January, thereby opening up one of the last bastions of congressional committee secrecy. The new rules included these features:

• All meetings were to be public unless a majority of a committee voted in open session to close a meeting or series of meetings on the same subject for not to exceed 14 days.

• A meeting could be closed only for action on the following matters: 1) national security; 2) committee staff personnel or internal staff management or procedures; 3) criminal or other charges against a person that might harm him or her professionally or otherwise or represent an invasion of privacy; 4) disclosure of the identity of an informer or law enforcement agent or a criminal investigation that should be kept secret to assist the investigation; 5) disclosure of trade secrets or financial or commercial information required by law to be kept secret or obtained by the government on a confidential basis; 6) disclosure of "matters required to be kept confidential under other provisions of law or government regulation."

• A committee on the motion of one member and a second could go into secret session to discuss whether a meeting should be closed under these standards, but required the vote to close be taken in public session.

• Every committee was required to prepare a transcript or electronic record of each meeting, including conference committees, unless a majority of the committee voted to forgo it.

• A chairman was allowed to clear a committee meeting of spectators when there was disorder or a demonstration by the audience, and to continue the meeting in secret.

In another 1975 reform, junior senators obtained committee staff assistance to aid them on legislative issues. In the past, committee staff members were controlled by chairmen and other senior members. Few junior members had regular and dependable access to staff personnel.[94]

Budget Control

The Senate worked closely with the House on the Congressional Budget Act of 1974, setting the foundation for reasserting congressional control over government spending. If faithfully implemented when all of its provisions were to take effect for fiscal year 1977, beginning Oct. 1, 1976, the reform bill would force Congress into more measured and timely action on budgetary legislation, tying its separate spending decisions together with fiscal policy objectives in a congressionally determined budget package. *(For provisions of the budget act, see p. 130)*

Among other items, the budget measure moved back the beginning of the federal fiscal year from July 1 to Oct. 1 and mandated a series of deadlines imposing changes in Congress' appropriations schedule. This was to allow Congress time to complete the entire budget process before the fiscal year began. It had been decades since Congress enacted its appropriations by July 1. Also, the act contained provisions seeking to curb presidential impoundment of funds as a means of cutting government spending.[95]

Campaign Finance

Long criticized for doing little to control the use of money in federal election campaigns, Congress responded by passing the Federal Election Campaign Acts of 1971 and 1974.

Until passage of the 1971 act, the entire history of campaign finance laws was one of non-enforcement. No candidate for Congress was ever prosecuted under the 1925 Corrupt Practices Act, which the 1971 Act repealed.

The new law, actually enacted in 1972, strengthened the requirements for reporting to the public how much a candidate spent on his campaign and his sources of contributions and other income. Also, all candidates and political committees were required to report names and addresses of all persons who made contributions and loans in excess of $100 and to all persons to whom expenditures of $100 were made. Disclosure was viewed by many as the most useful feature of the 1971 Act since it enabled scholars, journalists and investigators to obtain a better picture of patterns of spending and to uncover formerly concealed contributions.

The 1971 Act placed spending limits on communications media campaign spending in an effort to curb the most rapidly escalating cost of political campaigns. Also, the law defined more strictly the roles unions and corporations could play in political campaigns, but was criticized by some reformers for permitting unions and corporations having government contracts to participate in the same political activities as those not doing business with the government.

The 1974 Act provided for public financing of presidential campaigns, including provisions for primary campaigns as well as general elections. Originally, the Senate version of the bill included public financing of congressional campaign costs, but the provision was dropped in conference committee where House members strongly opposed it. Senate reformers had held that public financing would remove the influence of big money in congressional elections as well as presidential races.

The 1974 Act established the first spending limits ever for candidates in presidential primary and general elections and in primary campaigns for the House and Senate. It also set up new expenditure ceilings for general election campaigns for Congress.[96] *(For discussion of Supreme Court decision on the law and subsequent congressional action, see p. 547)*

CIA, FBI Probe

Legislative review or congressional oversight of federal agencies and legislation was another area in which Congress drew heavy criticism. Reformers regularly charged that Congress was reluctant to pursue that function unless there was beneficial publicity attached to an investigation or some other political advantage.

Until 1975, the Central Intelligence Agency and the Federal Bureau of Investigation were almost privileged from any congressional probing. After a series of hearings, the Senate Select Intelligence Committee, in several reports issued in the spring of 1976, aired abuses committed by the two agencies. One stated that since World War II Republican and Democratic administrations alike had used the FBI for secret surveillance of citizens. The report prompted FBI Director Clarence M. Kelley, in a May 1976 speech, to place the blame for FBI wrongdoing on his predecessor, J. Edgar Hoover.[97]

Watergate

The Senate launched its inquiry into Watergate Feb. 7, 1973, when it approved by a 77-0 vote a resolution creating a Select Committee on Presidential Campaign Activities (known as the Senate Watergate Committee), to investigate and study "the extent...to which illegal, improper, or unethical activities" occurred in the 1972 presidential campaign and election. The nationally-televised committee hearings were the major focus of Watergate developments during the summer of 1973.

Several former Committee to Re-Elect the President (which directed Nixon's 1972 campaign) staffers and former White House aides appeared, some to admit perjury during earlier investigations. They drew a picture of political sabotage that went far beyond Watergate, motivated by extreme loyalty to Nixon and by a belief that any tactics against people who had supported anti-Vietnam war demonstrations were acceptable.

The hearings brought forth details of a special White House investigative unit known as the "plumbers" which had been responsible for acts such as harassment of Daniel Ellsberg, who had released the classified Pentagon Papers on the Vietnam war to the press. Among the other highlights was the four-day appearance of former White House counsel John Dean in June. Dean turned over about 50 documents to the Senate committee. Included were a memorandum written by Dean on "dealing with our political enemies" (White House lists named about 200 important "enemies") and a memorandum commenting on 20 persons, including members of Congress, lobbyists, reporters and motion picture personalities, who were to be given priority in that White House "dealing." Dean was the only witness to implicate the President directly in the Watergate cover-up.

The most important revelation of the committee hearings came as a result of questioning of Federal Aviation Administration chief Alexander P. Butterfield, a former White House aide. He testified publicly July 16 that the President's offices were equipped with a special voice-activated system which recorded all conversations. The existence of the tapes entirely changed the Watergate case, for the evidence existed to prove or disprove Dean's allegations.

President Nixon had fought to retain possession of the tapes while the federal trial courts, Congress and Nixon's own special prosecutors sought to obtain them as evidence. The Supreme Court ruled that Nixon on the grounds of executive privilege could not keep the recordings from the trial courts, and on Aug. 2, 1974, he surrendered three critical recordings. The recordings were made June 23, 1972, six days after the Watergate burglary, and proved Nixon's early participation in the Watergate coverup. Meanwhile, the House Judiciary Committee had voted three articles of impeachment against Nixon. He resigned Aug. 9, 1974.[98]

Foreign Policy

Concerted Senate efforts to reassert its voice in the conduct of foreign affairs and decisions to go to war dated back to the late 1960s, spurred by growing congressional and popular opposition to a widening Indochina conflict. Those efforts led to the first law ever passed by Congress defining and limiting presidential war powers. President Nixon suffered a major setback on Nov. 7, 1973, when both houses voted to override his veto. Congressional determination on having a foreign policy role perhaps was reflected in the fact that the War Powers Act of 1973 was the first successful veto override in the 93rd Congress. Previously, eight other vetoes had been sustained in 1973:—five in the House and three in the Senate.

Although the final version of the act was closer to the House-passed bill, the real victory belonged to the Senate. The conference agreement culminated several years of Senate attempts to place substantive limits on executive war powers.

As enacted into law, the act:

● Stated that the President could commit U.S. armed forces to hostilities or situations where hostilities might be imminent, only pursuant to a declaration of war, specific statutory authorization or a national emergency created by an attack upon the United States, its territories or possessions, or its armed forces.

● Urged the President "in every possible instance" to consult with Congress before committing U.S. forces to hostilities or to situations where hostilities might be imminent, and to consult Congress regularly after such a commitment.

● Required the President to report in writing within 48 hours to the Speaker of the House and president pro tempore of the Senate on any commitment or substantial enlargement of U.S. combat forces abroad, except for deployments related solely to supply, replacement, repair or training; required supplementary reports at least every six months while such forces were being engaged.

● Authorized the Speaker of the House and the president pro tempore of the Senate to reconvene Congress if it was not in session to consider the President's report.

● Required the termination of a troop commitment within 60 days after the President's initial report was submitted, unless Congress declared war, specifically authorized continuation of the commitment, or was physically unable to convene as a result of an armed attack upon the United States; allowed the 60-day period to be extended for up to 30 days if the President determined and certified to Congress that unavoidable military necessity respecting the safety of U.S. forces required their continued use in bringing about a prompt disengagement.

● Allowed Congress, at any time U.S. forces were engaged in hostilities without a declaration of war or specific congressional authorization, by concurrent resolution to direct the President to disengage such troops.

● Set up congressional priority procedures for consideration of any resolution or bill introduced pursuant to the provisions of the resolution.

In 1975, Congress demonstrated to President Ford that it was opposed to further military aid to Indochina. As Communist forces were overrunning South Vietnam and Cambodia, the Senate Armed Services Committee, in a series of votes, refused to approve $722-million, in whole or in part, in extra aid that Ford wanted for South Vietnam.

Within weeks after total Communist conquest of the Indochina peninsula, an incident in nearby waters marked usage of the War Powers Act. On May 12, Cambodian communist forces captured the American merchant ship Mayaguez and its crew of 39. President Ford ordered combined Navy, Air Force and Marine units to retake the ship and crew. Ford's action in using force was questioned in Congress, but there was general agreement that he had authority to commit U.S. troops without regard to the War Powers Act even though the President complied with the law by issuing a report to Congress May 15 on his actions.

During 1975, Congress consistently clashed with Ford, questioning and resisting further U.S. involvements in other trouble spots around the world.

● A congressionally imposed ban on arms shipments to Turkey took effect in February despite White House efforts to persuade Congress to reverse it. After intensive and lengthy lobbying, it was only partially lifted in October.

● Secretary of State Henry A. Kissinger's inability to negotiate an interim peace accord between Israel and Egypt early in the year led to the Ford administration's "total reassessment" of its Middle East policy. Many on Capitol Hill viewed it as a thinly disguised attempt to pressure Israel into making concessions for a new settlement, and Congress in turn pressured the White House to continue its traditional support for Israel. One response was a letter to Ford signed by 76 senators urging sufficient financial support for Israel to enable the country to defend itself against any aggression. After Kissinger succeeded in formulating a pact acceptable to Israel and Egypt in August, Congress ultimately gave its approval to a controversial provision calling for the stationing of American technicians in the Sinai to monitor the truce. The acceptance came only after lengthy deliberations that revealed deep suspicion of Kissinger's role.

● As the session came to a close in December 1975, the Senate voted to block the channeling of U.S. funds to two of three factions engaged in a civil war in Angola despite the objections of Ford and Kissinger. The disclosures of the secret U.S. support had aroused fears in Congress of another Vietnam-type involvement and raised anew doubts about the success of the policy of detente with the Soviet Union, which was supporting the third faction. The Angola ban was written into the defense spending bill by the Senate. The House followed the Senate lead by accepting the Senate amendment Jan. 27, 1976.[99]

Footnotes

1. George H. Haynes, *The Senate of the United States: Its History and Practice*, vol. 1 (Boston: Houghton Mifflin, 1938), p. vii.

2. Lindsay Rogers, *The American Senate* (New York, Knopf, 1926), pp. 9, 90.

3. James Madison, *Notes on Debates in the Federal Convention of 1787*, with an Introduction by Adrienne Koch (Athens, Ohio: Ohio University Press, 1966), p. 42.

4. Charles Warren, *The Making of the Constitution* (Boston: Little, Brown, 1929), p. 195.

5. *Ibid.*

6. Rogers, *The American Senate*, p. 18.

7. Haynes, *The Senate of the United States*, vol. 1, p. 11.

8. *The Federalist Papers*, with an Introduction by Clinton Rossiter (New York: Mentor, 1961), p. 377.

9. Rogers, *The American Senate*, p. 21.

10. Gaillard Hunt, ed., *The Writings of James Madison, 1787-1790*, vol. 5 (New York: G. P. Putnam's Sons, 1904), p. 276.

11. Roy Swanstrom, *The United States Senate, 1787-1801*, Senate Document No. 64, 87th Congress, 1st Session (Washington: U.S. Government Printing Office, 1962), p. 86.

12. Haynes, *The Senate of the United States*, vol. 1, p. 62.

13. *Ibid.*, pp. 63, 68.

14. *Ibid.*, pp. 192-194.

15. Swanstrom, *The United States Senate, 1787-1801*, pp. 192-194.

16. *Ibid.*, p. 247.

17. *Ibid.*, pp. 36-37.

18. *Ibid.*, p. 80.

19. *Ibid.*, p. 283.

20. *Congressional Directory*, Washington, D.C.: U.S. Government Printing Office, 1976); p. 404.

21. Swanstrom, *The United States Senate, 1787-1801*, p. 271.

22. W. E. Binkley, *The Powers of the President* (New York: Russell & Russell, 1973), p. 52.

23. *Ibid.*, pp. 60-61.

24. Lauros G. McConachie, *Congressional Committees: A Study of the Origins and Development of our National and Local Legislative Methods* (New York: Burt Franklin Reprints, 1973), p. 312.

25. Haynes, *The Senate of the United States*, vol. 1, pp. 272-278.

26. *Ibid.*

27. *Ibid.*, vol. 2, p. 1003.

28. *Ibid.*, vol. 1, pp. 212-214.

29. Alexis de Tocqueville, *Democracy in America*, vol. 1 (New York: Shocken Books, 1967), pp. 233-234.

30. Haynes, *The Senate of the United States*, vol. 2, p. 1002.

31. Binkley, *The Powers of the President*, p. 81.

32. *Ibid.*, p. 86.

33. Franklin L. Burdette, *Filibustering in the Senate* (New York: Russell & Russell, 1965), pp. 22-25.

34. Haynes, *The Senate of the United States*, vol. 1, p. 298.

35. Binkley, *The Powers of the President*, pp. 130-133.

36. *Ibid.*, p. 207.

37. David J. Rothman, *Politics and Power: The United States Senate 1869-1901* (Cambridge, Mass.: Harvard University Press), p. 188.

38. Woodrow Wilson, *Congressional Government* (Cleveland: Meridian, 1956), p. 147.

39. Rothman, *Politics and Power,* p. 44.
40. *Ibid.,* pp. 56-57.
41. *Ibid.,* p. 60.
42. *Ibid.,* pp. 24-25.
43. *Ibid.,* p. 97.
44. Haynes, *The Senate of the United States,* vol. 1, p. 85.
45. *Ibid.,* p. 95.
46. Rothman, *Politics and Power,* p. 146.
47. *Congressional Globe,* 37th Congress, 3rd Session, Mar. 3, 1863, p. 1491.
48. *Congressional Globe,* 38th Congress, 2nd Session, Feb. 25, 1865, p. 1108.
49. Haynes, *The Senate of the United States,* vol. 1, pp. 398-399.
50. *Ibid.,* p. 400.
51. Burdette, *Filibustering in the Senate,* p. 80.
52. George B. Galloway, *The Legislative Process in Congress* (New York: Crowell, 1953), p. 542.
53. Haynes, *The Senate of the United States,* vol. 1, p. 395.
54. *Ibid.,* pp. 395-396.
55. *Ibid.,* pp. 96-98.
56. *Ibid.,* pp. 100-104.
57. *Ibid.,* pp. 111-112.
58. *Ibid.,* pp. 112-115.
59. George B. Galloway, *Congress at the Crossroads* (New York: Crowell, 1946), p. 38.
60. Haynes, *The Senate of the United States,* vol. 1, p. 402
61. *Ibid.,* pp. 402-403.
62. *Ibid.,* vol. 2, p. 973.
63. Binkley, *The Powers of the President,* p. 243.
64. Haynes, *The Senate of the United States,* vol. 1, p. 291.
65. Charles O. Jones, *The Minority Party in Congress* (Boston: Little, Brown, 1970), p. 144.
66. Haynes, *The Senate of the United States,* vol. 1, p. 411.
67. *Ibid.,* p. 416.
68. Haynes, *The Senate of the United States,* vol. 1, p. 286.
69. Randall B. Ripley, *Majority Party Leadership in Congress* (Boston: Little, Brown, 1969), p. 81.
70. *Ibid.,* p. 77.
71. *Congressional Record,* 78th Congress, 2nd Session, Feb. 23, 1944, p. 1966.
72. *Congressional Record,* 79th Congress, 1st Session, Jan. 18, 1945, p. 349.

73. Haynes, *The Senate of the United States,* vol. 1, p. 413.
74. Jones, *The Minority Party in Congress,* p. 168.
75. *Congress and the Nation, 1945-1964,* vol. I, (Washington: Congressional Quarterly Inc., 1965), p. 1426.
76. *Ibid.,* p. 1427.
77. *Ibid.*
78. *Ibid.*
79. *Congress and the Nation, 1969-1972,* vol. III (Washington: Congressional Quarterly, Inc., 1973), p. 357.
80. *Congress and the Nation, 1945-1964,* vol. I, p. 1726.
81. *Ibid.,* p. 1774.
82. Galloway, *The Legislative Process in Congress,* p. 659.
83. *Ibid.*
84. *Congressional Record,* 87th Congress, 2nd Session, Oct. 13, 1962, p. 23470.
85. *Congress and the Nation, 1945-1964,* vol. I, p. 264.
86. *Ibid.,* p. 265.
87. *Ibid.,* p. 122.
88. *Ibid.,* pp. 132-133.
89. *Ibid.,* pp. 138-139.
90. Arthur M. Schlesinger Jr., *The Imperial Presidency* (Boston: Houghton Mifflin Company, 1973), p. 201; *Congressional Record,* 90th Congress, 1st Session, July 31, 1967, pp. 20706, 20718; Congressional Quarterly, *1972 Almanac,* pp. 905-917; *1975 Almanac,* p. 5.
91. Congressional Quarterly, *1975 Weekly Report,* p. 2657; *1976 Weekly Report,* p. 507.
92. *Congress and the Nation, 1969-1972,* pp. 382-396.
93. Congressional Quarterly, *Inside Congress* (1976), pp. 11-14; *1976 Weekly Report,* pp. 838-839.
94. *Inside Congress,* p. 15.
95. *Ibid.,* pp. 127-133; Congressional Quarterly, *1974 Almanac,* pp. 145-153.
96. Congressional Quarterly, *1971 Almanac,* pp. 875-896; *1974 Almanac,* pp. 611-633.
97. *The Washington Post,* 10 May 1976.
98. Congressional Quarterly, *1973 Almanac,* p. 1008; Congressional Quarterly, *Watergate: Chronology of a Crisis* (1975), pp. 192, 620.
99. *1973 Almanac,* pp. 905-917; *1975 Almanac,* pp. 291, 306-311, 344-349, 885-887.

Selected Bibliography

Bates, Ernest Sutherland. *The Story of Congress, 1789-1935.* New York: Harper & Brothers, 1936.

Benton, Thomas Hart. *Thirty Years' View.* 2 vols. New York: Greenwood Press, 1968.

Binkley, Wilfred E. *The Powers of the President.* New York: Russell & Russell, 1973.

Burdette, Franklin L. *Filibustering in the Senate.* New York: Russell & Russell, 1965.

Clark, Joseph S. *Congress: The Sapless Branch.* New York: Harper and Row, 1964.

————. *The Senate Establishment.* New York: Hill and Wang, 1963.

Galloway, George B. *Congress at the Crossroads.* New York: Crowell, 1946.

————. *The Legislative Process in Congress.* New York: Crowell, 1953.

Harris, Joseph P. *The Advice and Consent of the Senate.* New York: Greenwood Press, 1968.

Haynes, George H. *The Senate of the United States: Its History and Practice.* 2 vols. Boston: Houghton Mifflin, 1938.

Huitt, Ralph K., and Peabody, Robert L. *Congress: Two Decades of Analysis.* New York: Harper & Row, 1972.

Jones, Charles O. *The Minority Party in Congress.* Boston: Little, Brown, 1970.

Luce, Robert. *Legislative Procedure: Parliamentary Practices and the Course of Business in the Framing of Statutes.* New York: Da Capo Press, 1972.

Madison, James; Hamilton, Alexander; and Jay, John. *The Federalist Papers.* Introduction by Clinton Rossiter. New York: Mentor, 1961.

Madison, James. *Notes of Debates in the Federal Convention of 1787.* Introduction by Adrienne Koch. Athens, Ohio: Ohio University Press, 1966.

Matthews, Donald R. *U.S. Senators and Their World.* Chapel Hill, N.C.: University of North Carolina Press, 1960.

McConachie, Lauros G. *Congressional Committees: A Study of the Origins and Development of Our National and Local Legislative Methods.* New York: Burt Franklin Reprints, 1973.

Price, David E. *Who Makes the Laws? Creativity and Power in Senate Committees.* Cambridge, Mass.: Schenkman Publishing Co., 1972.

Ripley, Randall B. *Majority Party Leadership in Congress.* Boston: Little, Brown, 1969.

Ripley, Randall B. *Power in the Senate.* New York: St. Martin's Press, 1969.

Rogers, Lindsay. *The American Senate.* New York: Knopf, 1926.

Rothman, David J. *Politics and Power: The United States Senate, 1869-1901.* Cambridge, Mass.: Harvard University Press, 1966.

Swanstrom, Roy. *The United States Senate, 1787-1801.* Senate Document 64, 87th Congress, 1st Session. Washington: U.S. Government Printing Office, 1962.

Tocqueville, Alexis de. *Democracy in America.* 2 vols. New York: Schocken Books, 1967.

Warren, Charles. *The Making of the Constitution.* Boston: Little, Brown, 1929.

Wilson, Woodrow. *Congressional Government.* Introduction by Walter Lippmann. Cleveland: Meridian, 1956.

POWERS
OF CONGRESS

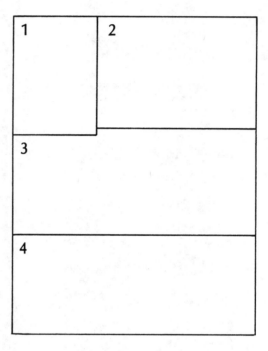

1. Sen. Joseph McCarthy (R Wis.) during the Senate Investigations Subcommittee hearing on the senator's dispute with the Army, April 26, 1954. (Wide World Photos)

2. President Franklin D. Roosevelt signing Declaration of War, December 1941. (Library of Congress photo no. LC-USZ62-32722.)

3. Rep. Thaddeus Stevens (R Pa.) closing the House debate on impeachment of President Andrew Johnson. Wood engraving in *Harper's Weekly,* March 21, 1868, after a sketch by T. R. Davis. (Library of Congress photo no. LC-USZ62-22081.)

4. House Budget Committee working on the first budget resolution, March 26, 1975.

Fiscal Powers: To Tax, Spend, Borrow

Of the numerous powers of Congress, the "power of the purse" is the most important. All of the other powers—such as regulating commerce, conducting investigations, even declaring war—are as nothing without the power to finance the business of government. As George Galloway has remarked, "Perhaps nine-tenths of the work of Congress is concerned, directly or indirectly, with the spending of public money. The spending power is the constitutional birthright of Congress, for that document provides that 'no money shall be drawn from the Treasury, but in consequence of appropriations made by law' and that 'all bills for raising revenue shall originate in the House of Representatives; but the Senate may propose or concur with amendments as on other bills.' "[1]

The "power of the purse" includes both the raising of revenue through taxes, tariffs and other levies, and direction through the appropriations process of the spending of the funds raised. They are opposite sides of the same coin, although until 1975, Congress rarely considered them as an entity.

The taxing and appropriating powers are granted to Congress by various provisions of the Constitution. Over the years, Congress has jealously guarded these powers with the relatively recent exception of the tariff power, the exercise of which was delegated to the executive branch nearly 40 years ago. Occasional proposals that Congress also delegate to the President limited authority to alter tax rates have been ignored by the legislators. While Congress has always been dedicated to preserving its authority over spending, it has had difficulty in maintaining close control over government outlays since President Franklin D. Roosevelt launched the New Deal. In spite of an apparent desire on the part of many members of Congress—particularly those handling appropriations bills—to hold down government spending, it has continued to rise. From an outlay of $567-million in fiscal year 1900, federal expenditures have grown to an estimated outlay of $349.4-billion in fiscal 1976—21.9 per cent of the gross national product.

Along with this rise in outlays, there developed in the late 1960s and the 1970s an intense dispute between Congress and the Nixon administration over spending of funds already appropriated. The Constitution had left vague whether a President was required to spend funds appropriated by Congress or whether he could make independent judgments on the timing and need for outlays.

The issue had been a nettlesome one throughout the nation's history, but became a major dispute only when President Nixon began to impound and refuse to spend appropriated funds running into the billions of dollars.

President Nixon argued that he was withholding funds only as a financial management technique, usually for the purpose of combatting inflation by at least temporarily reducing federal spending. Opposition Democrats in Congress contended that Nixon was using impoundment primarily to assert his own priorities about federal spending over those of Congress.

The issue thus became one of Congress and the President struggling to assert final authority on federal spending. The dispute led to dozens of lawsuits brought by private interest groups against the government to force expenditure of impounded funds. Most of these suits eventually were won by the groups, a result that seemed to support the congressional view of the matter.

Congress, however, did not leave the issue there. The impoundment dispute was one aspect of a struggle over federal spending that characterized the Nixon years and convinced Congress that it was losing to the executive branch most of its influence over federal expenditures. This realization led to passage of a congressional budget control law *(see next section)* that included provisions delineating the conditions under which funds could be impounded. *(See pp. 129-136)*

Separation of Taxing and Spending

Until 1975, Congress rarely considered the two parts of government financing as an integrated whole. An effort in the late 1940s to tie spending and taxing together was unsuccessful, in large part because the resulting bill—and the committee formed to handle it—proved unwieldy.

The task of relating spending to revenue thus fell to the executive branch, which attempted to accomplish it through preparation of the federal budget.

A major reason for the difficulty in obtaining an overview of the budget in Congress is the fact that tax bills and appropriations bills are referred to different committees and are taken up and acted upon separately, even though the level of spending (without deficit financing) is dependent on the amount of revenue raised.

With passage of the 1974 Congressional Budget and Impoundment Control Act (PL 93-344), however, Congress took a potentially momentous step toward more coordinated action on federal economic policy by revising the procedures it uses to handle the government's budget.

The measure, which was to be fully implemented in 1976, established a framework for more timely and better-considered congressional action on legislation approving or amending the appropriations, spending, revenue and debt figures set out in the President's annual budget message to Congress.

In doing so, the measure spelled out a timetable for congressional actions affecting the federal budget and required that those decisions be reviewed in light of their impact on overall fiscal policy. It created House and Senate Budget Committees to supervise the new process. *(Details, p. 129)*

Taxes and Tariffs

Financing of the federal government is carried out under authority granted to Congress in the first article of the Constitution. That authority is specific with regard to raising money, somewhat vague but nevertheless sweeping with regard to spending it. Article I, Section 8, Clause 1 reads:

> The Congress shall have power to lay and collect taxes, duties, imposts and excises, to pay the debts and provide for the common defense and general welfare of the United States....

Under this basic authorization, with a monumental assist from the Sixteenth Amendment (income tax), Congress over the years has devised a taxing system that produced in fiscal 1976 an estimated total revenue of no less than $297.5-billion. Generally, the taxing power has been liberally construed by both Congress and the courts (the most important exception being a Supreme Court decision in 1895 that overturned an attempt by Congress to impose an income tax and which led finally to adoption of the Sixteenth Amendment). The constitutional historian C. H. Pritchett, in his book *The American Constitution,* noted that adequate sources of funds and broad authority to use them were "essential conditions for carrying on an effective government." "Consequently," he observed, "the first rule for judicial review of tax statutes is that a heavy burden of proof lies on anyone who would challenge any congressional exercise of fiscal power. In almost every decision touching the constitutionality of federal taxation, the Supreme Court has stressed the breadth of congressional power and the limits of its own reviewing powers."[2]

The terms used in Article I, Section 8 granting the taxing power were broad enough to include all known forms of taxation. Customs levies, or tariffs, on goods imported from abroad were covered by "duties" and "imposts." "Excises" covered taxes on the manufacture, sale, use or transfer of property within the United States.

Congress and the Taxing Power

Limitations. Although the power of Congress to tax is broad, it is not unlimited. There are constitutional provisions, for example, on direct and indirect taxation.

Article I, Section 9, Clause 4 states: "No capitation, or other direct, tax shall be laid, unless in proportion to the census or enumeration hereinbefore directed to be taken." And Article I, Section 8, Clause 1 states: "...all duties, imposts and excises shall be uniform throughout the United States." The Supreme Court in 1895 laid out a rule to distinguish between these taxes. It said a tax "which cannot be avoided, is a direct tax, while a tax paid primarily by persons who can shift the burden upon others...is an indirect tax."

This rule came in the case which overturned the attempt by Congress to impose a personal income tax. *Pollock v. Farmers' Loan and Trust Co.,* 157 U.S. 429, 158 U.S. 601 (1895). The decision led to the Sixteenth Amendment to the Constitution which says: "The Congress shall have power to lay and collect taxes on incomes, from whatever source derived, without apportionment among the several States, and without regard to any census or enumeration." The amendment, ratified in 1913, opened up a revenue source that has since become the principal one for the government by eliminating the requirement that an income tax be apportioned among the states by population. Wealth is not distributed the same as population. As a result, an apportioned income tax—with high population states paying a larger share than less populated but perhaps richer ones—would be virtually impossible to obtain because of the political opposition that could be expected.

The other provision, dealing with uniformity, concerned the type of tax that is now considered indirect. The language means that the tax must apply equally—with the same force—in any location that the item to be taxed is located. Thus, the provision has come to mean geographical uniformity and has guided Congress in its passage of customs and excise levies that were the primary source of revenue for the national government until World War I.[3]

These constitutional provisions, including the Sixteenth Amendment, give Congress the right to enact virtually any taxes except for export duties, which are specifically prohibited (Article I, Section 9, Clause 5), and direct taxes not covered by the Sixteenth Amendment such as poll or property taxes which are still subject to the apportionment requirement.

Implied Limitations. In addition to specific restrictions, there are implied limitations on the taxing power of Congress. A major limitation extends immunity from federal taxation to state and local governments, their property and activities. A second limitation has exempted from federal taxation the income from state and municipal bonds. These limitations are based on the doctrine of intergovernmental tax immunity laid down in 1819 by Chief Justice Marshall in the Supreme Court's opinion in the case of *McCulloch v. Maryland.*[4] (4 Wheat. 316) That doctrine rested on the theory of state sovereignty and on the belief that, because "the power to tax involves the power to destroy," neither the federal nor a state government could tax the property or instrumentalities of the other without infringing on its sovereignty. The doctrine was applied even to the salaries of public employees.

Taxing Public Salaries, Federal Bonds

It was long assumed that the tax immunity thus decreed could not be terminated other than by a constitutional amendment. However, in decisions handed down in 1938 and 1939, the Supreme Court sustained, respectively, the levying of a federal income tax on the salary of an employee of the Port of New York Authority and the levying of the New York State income tax on the salary of a federal employee. A week after the second decision, Congress completed action on the Public Salary Tax Act of 1939, which provided for federal taxation of state and local governmental salaries and gave the federal government's consent to state taxation of federal salaries.[5]

The Supreme Court decisions of 1938 and 1939 were widely interpreted as removing constitutional objections to intergovernmental taxation of state and municipal bonds as well as public salaries.

However, the question of the federal government's power to tax the interest on government securities has not been definitively resolved. President Roosevelt in 1938 and again in 1939 advocated abolition by statute of the tax exemption on income from future issues of all public securities. Congress went part way in the Public Debt Act of 1941, which provided that interest on federal securities issued after its enactment should have no exemption as such, thus authorizing issuance of wholly taxable obligations by the federal government. Congress refused, however, to act on a Treasury recommendation that interest on future issues of state and municipal securities be subjected to the federal income tax. Subsequent proposals along that line have made no headway. State and local officials, supported by municipal bond dealers, always have contended that they would have trouble borrowing money if those securities were deprived of their special tax status.

Regulation Through Taxation

Congress has the power, confirmed by use over the years, to impose taxes for regulatory rather than revenue purposes. The leading example is the imposition of tariffs not for revenue only but also for the protection of domestic industries against competition from imports. Although the first tariff law was enacted in 1789, the Supreme Court did not have occasion to consider (and uphold) the constitutionality of this form of taxation until 1928.

Regulation through taxation has been employed in other situations even to the extent of destroying a business enterprise. In 1863, Congress enacted a National Banking Act providing for the incorporation of national banks with authority to issue currency notes. In 1866, it imposed a 10-per cent tax on new state bank notes with the avowed purpose of driving such notes out of existence—which it did.[6] There were numerous laws of this kind in ensuing years. Among the best known were: a stiff excise tax on oleomargarine colored to resemble butter; a tax on the manufacture of poisonous white phosphorous matches (which virtually killed the industry); taxes on registered dealers in narcotic drugs; and a special tax (later overturned by the Supreme Court) on the profits of companies employing children under 16 years of age.[7]

Uses of the Tariff

Tariffs for Revenue. The first congressional measure to raise revenue was a tariff act approved July 4, 1789.[8] The revenue from customs duties proved adequate to meet most of the fiscal needs of the federal government until the Civil War. A wartime income tax and numerous excises were then imposed to help defray war costs. However, the pattern of substantial dependence on customs receipts, supplemented increasingly by excise taxes, continued up to World War I, when income and profits taxes became the mainstay of federal revenue. Customs receipts accounted for more than 90 per cent of total federal revenue until the Civil War. Their importance declined gradually after that, but in 1910

they still made up 49 per cent of the federal government's revenue. In contrast, by the late 1960s, the revenue from import duties had shrunk to little more than 1 per cent of the total.

Customs receipts reached a pre-Civil-War peak of $64.2-million in the fiscal year 1854, exceeded $100-million for the first time in fiscal 1864 and $200-million in fiscal 1871, and reached $300-million in fiscal 1906. Although a much-reduced fraction of federal revenue, customs receipts passed the $1-billion mark in fiscal 1960 and the $2-billion mark in fiscal 1968.[9]

Tariffs for Protection. As long as customs receipts were sufficient to meet government needs, the tariff in effect killed two birds with one stone. It supplied a large part of federal revenue while in the process of carrying out its principal purpose, which was to protect domestic producers, especially of manufactured goods, from a flood of foreign imports. Many of the so-called infant industries grew strong as they matured, but few reached the point of considering themselves able to get along without tariff protection. Thus, revenue considerations aside, the duties in numerous cases did more than put domestic producers on a basis of equality with foreign producers; they gave the American producers a competitive advantage.[10]

Conflicts of Interest Over Tariffs

During the first half of the 19th century, the tariff laws offered protection mainly to manufactured goods. Western and northern farmers supported a protectionist policy for manufacturers on the assumption that industrial development, aided by high tariffs, would create a profitable home market for their products.

The Republican Party, founded in the West in 1854, lined up behind the protectionist principle on the eve of the Civil War, thereby availing itself of a policy which was to ensure it the enduring adherence of northern and eastern industrial elements after settlement of the slavery issue. The Democratic Party, on the other hand, generally favored a moderate-or-low tariff policy which helped it to retain the solid support of the agricultural South for years.

William Starr Myers wrote in *The Republican Party: A History* in 1928: "The industrial and business East wants a high protective tariff and has persuaded the agricultural West that the same policy of protection would apply to them. The latter has suffered continually from 'hard times,' and yet has always seemed to be impervious to the fact that it is practically impossible, under present conditions in the United States, to protect the farming interests by a high tariff. It is the play of these two forces, often cut athwart and disturbed by other issues..., that has deferred the inevitable day of some solution or compromise beneficial to both interests."[11]

The fact that the tariff picture was not all black or white—that high tariffs were helpful to certain interests and low tariffs helpful to others—did not lower the voices of extreme protectionists or extreme free traders. But because both sides were represented in each of the major political parties, action at the showdown was sometimes surprising. In 1894, for example, when the Democrats controlled both houses of Congress, the Senate made so many upward changes in a House-passed low-tariff bill that President Cleveland refused to sign the measure, though he let it become law without his signature.[12]

As a member of Congress, President McKinley had been a staunch high-protectionist, but in his last public utterance he entered a strong plea for support of tariff reciprocity. In an address at Buffalo on Sept. 5, 1901, the day before he was assassinated, he said: "The period of exclusiveness is past. The expansion of our trade and commerce is the pressing problem. Commercial wars are unprofitable. A policy of good-will and friendly trade relations will prevent reprisals. Reciprocity treaties are in harmony with the spirit of the times; measures of retaliation are not.... If perchance some of our tariffs are no longer needed for revenue or to encourage and protect our industries at home, why should they not be employed to extend and promote our markets abroad?"[13]

President Taft negotiated a reciprocity agreement with Canada in 1911 which, though accepted by Congress over considerable opposition, was not carried through by Canada. The Democrats, originally opposed to tariff reciprocity, nevertheless included in the Underwood Tariff Act of 1913 a provision specifically authorizing the President to negotiate reciprocity agreements subject to the approval of Congress. The provision was not utilized, however, and no more was heard of the subject until the Democrats revived it 20 years later.[14]

Tariff-Making by Congress

Tariff policy occupied a place of great prominence in American politics during the long period from shortly after the Civil War to the early years of the Great Depression of the 1930s. It was the leading issue in numerous presidential and congressional elections. Before World War I, a change of administrations often meant passage of a new tariff act. The McKinley tariff of 1890 (Republican) was followed by the Wilson-Gorman tariff of 1894 (Democratic) and then by the Dingley tariff of 1897 (Republican). The last-named act had a long life—12 years—but it gave way in 1909 to the Payne-Aldrich tariff (also Republican) and then in 1913 to the Underwood tariff (Democratic).

Congress devoted an inordinate amount of its time to tariff-making, not only because the tariff was made and remade so frequently but also because the process was complex and the subject all-embracing. Affecting, actually or potentially, the varied interests of many segments of the commercial life of the country, a general revision of the tariff inevitably involved a great amount of political pulling and hauling. Tariff bills, like tax bills, originated in the House and, when reported by the Ways and Means Committee, followed the usual legislative course through the House itself, the Senate Finance Committee and the Senate, with final reconciliation of House and Senate differences by a conference committee. At each stage, the treatment of important items was apt to provoke protracted discussion. General tariff bills were so complicated and so full of special-interest provisions that few members, other than those on the Ways and Means or Finance Committees, understood their true effect.

Drastic revision in the Senate was the usual fate of tariff bills passed by the House. The Senate made nearly 500 amendments to the McKinley bill in 1890. Its amendments to the Payne-Aldrich bill of 1909 numbered 847. And Senate amendments to the Fordney-McCumber tariff bill of 1922 reached the unprecedented total of more than 2,400. That bill, moreover, was before Congress for 20 months prior to enactment, a longer period than any tariff bill since the Civil War.[15]

The Fordney-McCumber bill was noteworthy also for taking the first substantial step toward reform of the tariff-making process. It empowered the President, upon recommendation of the U.S. Tariff Commission (a fact-finding body created by the Revenue Act of 1916 to advise Congress on tariff matters), to alter existing rates of duty (1) by changing the tariff classification of an article to make it dutiable under a different rate; (2) by increasing or decreasing the rate by not more than 50 per cent; or (3) by substituting the American selling price for the foreign valuation as the basis for assessment of duties. The act stated that readjustments were to be made only to carry out a policy of "equalizing" foreign and American production costs.

This was the so-called flexible tariff. By mid-May 1929, more than six and one-half years after approval of the Fordney-McCumber Act in September 1922, only 36 changes of duties had been made under the flexible-tariff provision and in only five of the 36 cases had the duties been reduced. The flexible tariff provision was soon challenged on the ground that it amounted to a delegation of legislative and taxing powers to the President. The issue came before the Supreme Court which unanimously upheld the flexible tariff in 1928.[16] (*J. W. Hampton Jr. & Co. v. United States,* 276 U.S. 394). By that time, Congress was already at work on what turned out to be another general tariff revision.

Last Made-by-Congress Tariff

Soon after President Hoover took office on March 4, 1929, he called Congress into special session. A presidential message read at the opening of the session, April 16, assigned the lawmakers the task of redeeming "two pledges given in the last election—farm relief and limited changes in the tariff."[17] Changes in tariff rates, Hoover said, should provide an effective tariff on agricultural products "that will compensate the farmer's higher costs and higher standards of living," and should also afford additional protection to industries suffering from "insurmountable competition from abroad."

The "limited changes" asked by President Hoover became a full-blown tariff act as Congress worked its way through more than 1,800 rate paragraphs in 15 tariff schedules from "Chemicals, Oils and Paint" to "Papers and Books" and, finally, "Sundries." The House Ways and Means Committee had opened hearings on rate schedules three months before the special session began and so was able to report its bill early in May 1929, and the House passed it on May 28. A long contest in the Senate delayed passage there until March 24, 1930. It took weeks longer to resolve in conference the wide differences between the House and Senate versions of the bill. The Hawley-Smoot tariff, finally approved by President Hoover on June 17, 1930, raised tariff duties, on average, to a new peak estimated to exceed the 1922 level by 20 per cent.

In addition to raising rates, the Hawley-Smoot Act made changes in the flexible-tariff provision aimed to speed up Tariff Commission investigations of production costs. The new act also shifted major responsibility for duty changes under that provision from the President to the commission by requiring the President to accept or reject the specific rates which the commission found necessary to equalize production costs.

Shift to Executive Tariff-Making

President Hoover, in a public statement on June 15, 1930, two days before he signed the Hawley-Smoot bill, observed that "Congressional (tariff) revisions are not only disturbing to business but, with all their necessary collateral surroundings in lobbies, logrolling and the activities of group interests, are disturbing to public confidence." He added that, "particularly after the record of the last 15 months, there is a growing and widespread realization that in this highly complicated and intricately organized and rapidly shifting modern economic world the time has come when a more scientific and businesslike method of tariff revision must be devised." It was Hoover's opinion that the revised flexible-tariff provision of the new law represented a long step toward that end and gave "great hope of taking the tariff away from politics, lobbying and logrolling."

Deepening depression and a worldwide collapse of international trade in the period immediately following passage of the Hawley-Smoot act contributed indirectly to forwarding reform in the process of tariff-making. Results of the midterm elections of 1930 enabled the Democrats to organize the House of Representatives in the 72nd Congress and almost wiped out the Republican majority in the Senate. Early in 1932 both houses approved a bill of Democratic origin requesting the President to negotiate reciprocal trade agreements with other nations "under a policy of mutual tariff concessions." Such agreements were to be subject to congressional approval. President Hoover vetoed the bill, May 11, 1932, on the grounds that it would undermine the system of agricultural protection, "make us large importers of food products" and "drive our farmers into the towns and factories and thus demoralize our whole national economic and social stability." In the party platforms of 1932 the Republicans commended Hoover's veto and the Democrats repeated their advocacy of "reciprocal tariff agreements with other nations."[18]

On March 2, 1934, one year almost to the day after President Roosevelt took office, he asked Congress for authority to "enter into executive commercial agreements with foreign nations" for reciprocal reductions of tariffs. The President said: "If American agricultural and industrial interests are to retain their deserved place in this (international) trade, the American government must be in a position to bargain for that place with other governments by rapid and decisive negotiation, based upon a carefully considered program, and to grant with discernment corresponding opportunities in the American market for foreign products supplementary to our own."[19]

Delegation of Power by 1934 Act

The Reciprocal Trade Agreements Act, one of whose principal advocates was Secretary of State Cordell Hull, became law on June 12, 1934. Enacted as an amendment to the Hawley-Smoot Act of 1930, it empowered the President, without reference to the Tariff Commission or the Congress, to lower or raise existing duties by as much as 50 per cent in return for equivalent concessions by a foreign nation. Although the Hoover-vetoed Democratic tariff bill of 1932 had provided for congressional approval of reciprocal trade agreements, a Republican-sponsored amendment to that effect offered in the Senate in 1934 was decisively rejected.

Renewals of Authority. This historic transfer of tariff-making authority from Congress to the President was almost total. The delegation of power was limited initially to three years, but it was periodically renewed for similar (or shorter or longer) periods. And the limitation on the extent of duty increases or reductions was periodically modified as

additional bargaining authority was needed by American tariff negotiators.

The bilateral trade agreements concluded in the early years gave way after World War II to a network of multilateral agreements under GATT, the General Agreement on Tariffs and Trade.

On the basis of their authority under the Trade Agreements act, Presidents participated in several GATT conferences to lower tariffs. A new GATT conference began in 1960, but by then Congress had restricted the President's authority to negotiate tariff reductions by enacting "peril point" and escape-clause provisions to protect American industries from foreign competition.

With the Reciprocal Trade Agreements Act about to expire, President Kennedy in January 1962 asked Congress for new authority to reduce tariffs. Congress responded by passing the Trade Expansion Act of 1962 in October. The act gave the President authority until June 30, 1967, to cut tariffs by as much as 50 per cent. Moreover, he was authorized to negotiate the reductions by broad categories of goods instead of by individual articles. During the next four years, Kennedy Round negotiators concluded what Louis Fisher has described as "the most ambitious effort ever made to liberalize international trade."[20] Agreements in May 1967 granted concessions on trade valued at close to $40-billion.

By 1967, however, protectionist sentiment in Congress, nurtured in part by development of the European Common Market as a powerful trade competitor, had grown so strong that President Johnson delayed asking for renewal of the authority. When he did made the request in 1968, Congress took no action.

Nixon Trade Policy. Administration signals on a trade policy were conflicting during the period 1969-72. This was apparently a result of disagreement among high administration officials. In addition, the President, who had supported freer trade during his election campaign, was indebted to southern protectionists for substantial help during that campaign.

Nixon sent Congress late in 1969 a "modest" omnibus bill which would have permitted him to reduce tariffs and increase assistance to U.S. businesses harmed by imports. During long and complicated action on that bill in 1970, conservatives succeeded in amending it to create strong protectionist legislation. Senate liberals managed a successful filibuster against the measure at the session's end, and it died at the finish of the 91st Congress. It was unclear whether the President would have vetoed the bill if it had reached his desk. He did not resubmit a trade bill to the 92nd Congress.[21]

Although Congress and the administration could not decide on omnibus trade legislation, Congress passed several other bills designed to improve the U.S. balance of trade by increasing exports. In 1969 it replaced the Export Control Act, which had hindered the sale of U.S. goods to Communist countries, with a less restrictive measure. The new bill, the Export Administration Act, was extended and liberalized in 1972. Congress also raised the limit on Export-Import Bank loans and removed some restrictions on its operations in order to increase U.S. trade.

1974 Trade Bill. Nixon renewed his request for trade legislation in 1973. On April 10, he asked Congress to give him broad authority to raise, lower or eliminate tariff barriers to strengthen the bargaining position of U.S. representatives at upcoming international trade negotiations. The President also called for authority to work out agreements on nontariff barriers, subject to a 90-day congressional veto procedure.

The bill became stalled, however, by heated debate over the peripheral issue of Jewish emigration from the Soviet Union. A provision linking trade concessions for Communist countries, including government credits and most-favored-nation (MFN) status, to their emigration policies had been included in the House version of the bill, passed Dec. 11, 1973. The bill then languished for months in the Senate Finance Committee while the President and members of Congress wrangled over the issue. A compromise was finally reached, and the bill—containing broad authority for the President to act on trade matters, as well as a compromise provision on the Soviet emigration and trade issue—cleared Congress Dec. 20, 1974, the last day of the session.[22]

Components of Federal Tax System

Taxes on the income and profits of individuals and corporations have become the federal government's basic source of revenue.[23] Such taxes yielded only modest amounts of revenue before American entry into World War I. Sharply increased rates then pushed up the yield from $360-million in fiscal 1917 to $2.3-billion in fiscal 1918. Since that time, income and profits taxes have produced annually more revenue than all excise and other internal revenue taxes combined except in the nine fiscal years from 1933 through 1941. During those years the Depression was holding down incomes and numerous new excise taxes were levied to bolster federal revenues.

In World War II, high rates and a broadened tax base doubled and redoubled the receipts from income and profits taxes. Following a downward movement after World War II and again after the Korean War, these receipts climbed year by year almost uninterruptedly to the huge net (minus refunds) total of $154-billion projected for fiscal 1976. That sum accounted for about 51.8 per cent of the government's net budget receipts of an estimated $297.5-billion in fiscal 1976. Social Security taxes and contributions of an estimated $91.6-billion made up the next largest share of net budget receipts. Net excise taxes were projected to yield $32.1-billion; estate and gift taxes, $3.6-billion; customs receipts, $4.3-billion; and miscellaneous receipts, $10.9-billion.

Individual Income Tax

A federal tax on personal income was first imposed during the Civil War. Pressed by the wartime need for additional funds, Congress in 1862 levied a tax on individual incomes in excess of $600. The personal exemption was raised to $1,000 in 1867, two years after the war ended, and then to $2,000 in 1870. At one point the tax was graduated up to a rate of 10 per cent. Total revenues under this tax amounted to $376-million. At its peak in 1866, it accounted for almost 25 per cent of internal revenue collections. The law imposing the tax expired by limitation in 1872.[24] The levy had been challenged as violative of the constitutional requirement that direct taxes be apportioned among the states according to population, but the Supreme Court of that day ruled that it was not a direct tax.

During the 1870s and 1880s, little interest was shown in enactment of a new income-tax law. But growth of the country and accumulation of large fortunes began in the 1890s to generate pressure for a return to income taxation.

After the depression of 1893 had reduced federal revenues, Congress yielded and in 1894 levied a tax of 2 per cent on personal incomes in excess of $3,000. Before the new tax law became operative, it was challenged, and this time the Supreme Court held that an income tax was a direct tax and therefore unconstitutional without apportionment *(Pollock v. Farmers' Loan & Trust Co.,* 1895).

The decision was a major defeat for the populist movement of the times and made the court a distinctly unpopular institution. Pritchett in *The American Constitution* notes: "This surrender of the court to entrenched wealth, in the same year that it refused to apply the Sherman Act against the sugar trust and upheld the conviction of Eugene V. Debs for violating an injunction during the Pullman strike, revealed only too clearly the judiciary's alignment on the side of capital, and earned the court a popular reputation as a tool of special privilege which was not dispelled for forty years."[25]

Although the court had blocked the road to this attempted expansion of the tax system, a solution was afforded by the power of Congress and the states to revise the Constitution. A campaign to do so was begun immediately, and on Feb. 25, 1913, the Sixteenth Amendment was officially declared ratified. The one-sentence amendment stated tersely: "The Congress shall have power to lay and collect taxes on incomes from whatever source derived, without apportionment among the several states, and without regard to any census or enumeration."

Thus the problem of apportioning income taxes was swept away and Congress was left free to do what it had tried to do two decades earlier. The new grant of power came at a providential time, for the great expansion of federal revenue soon required by World War I would have been difficult, if not impossible, to achieve by any other means.

Congress instituted the income tax in the year the Sixteenth Amendment was ratified. The new levy applied to wages, salaries, interest, dividends, rents, entrepreneurial income and capital gains. The law contained certain exemptions (such as interest on federal, state and municipal bonds and salaries of state and local government employees) and allowed deductions for personal interest and tax payments and business expenses. Taxes were collected at the source on incomes in excess of $3,000. A personal exemption of $3,000 for a single person and $4,000 for a married couple was allowed. Rates were set initially at only 1 per cent for the normal tax plus 1- to 6-per cent surtax on larger incomes.

In the following half-century, Congress made numerous changes in the income-tax law. Joseph A. Pechman, one of the nation's leading tax authorities, cites in his book *Federal Tax Policy* the following "most significant changes" since the original 1913 act: allowance of a credit for dependents and a deduction for charitable contributions in 1917; elimination of collection at the source in 1916 and its reinstatement in 1943 for wages and salaries of state and local government employees and discontinuance of the sale of tax-exempt federal securities in 1941; adoption of the standard deduction in 1944; enactment of the principle of "income-splitting" for married couples in 1948; introduction of an average plan for certain taxpayers and a minimum standard deduction in 1964; and in the 1969 act, the minimum standard deduction was replaced by a low-income allowance, and a minimum tax on selected preference incomes and a top marginal rate on earned income of 50 per cent were adopted.[26]

Rates and exemptions have changed frequently. According to Pechman, maximum marginal rates reached 77 per cent during World War I, 94 per cent during World War II, and 92 per cent during the Korean War. They declined to 24 per cent in the 1920s and rose to 79 per cent in the 1930s. In the late 1950s and early 1960s, the maximum rate was 91 per cent.[27] At present (1976), the maximum rate is 70 per cent.

Corporation Income and Profits Taxes

Congress did not encounter with a corporation income tax the constitutional difficulty that it had experienced with the tax on individual income. A corporation income tax was levied in 1909 in the guise of "a special excise tax" at a rate of 1 per cent of net income in excess of $5,000. That tax, like the 1894 individual income tax, was challenged in the courts, but the Supreme Court let it stand as an excise on the privilege of doing business as a corporation.[28]

Following ratification of the Sixteenth Amendment, an outright corporation income tax at the same rate was made a part of the Revenue Act of 1913 alongside the individual income tax. The two taxes together, broadened and modified through the years as circumstances required, became basic elements of the nation's revenue system.

During World War I, World War II, and the Korean War, the corporation income tax was supplemented by an excess profits tax. In most other years, revenue from taxation of corporation income has been less than that from taxation of individual income. Particularly in the past decade, the individual income tax has been far and away the greater revenue producer. In fiscal 1974, the individual tax yielded $119-billion, the corporation tax only $38.6-billion.

Excise and Other Taxes

Excise taxes have always been a part of the federal tax system; they were mentioned specifically in Article I, Section 8 of the Constitution among the various levies that Congress was authorized to impose. The excises levied upon ratification of the Constitution included taxes on carriages, liquor, snuff, sugar and auction sales. These and similar taxes have been controversial throughout the republic's history, in important part because they were considerd unfair and burdensome to the poor. Over the years, excises have been imposed and repealed or lowered; during every major war, the perennial liquor and tobacco taxes were supplemented by taxes on manufactured goods, licenses, financial transactions, services, luxury articles and dozens of other items that lent themselves to this form of taxation.[29]

Congress considerably expanded the excise-tax structure during World Wars I and II and the Korean War. The present system was enacted in 1965, when Congress scaled down the Korean War excises to all but a few major taxes. The law (PL 89-44) called for a staged reduction in excise levies that would terminate Jan. 1, 1969. As the Vietnam War grew in scale, however, President Johnson asked for and received extensions on excise items scheduled for repeal.

President Nixon in 1969 asked, and Congress provided, for extension through calendar 1970 of the 7 per cent excise tax on automobiles. At his request, the tax was repealed in 1971.[30]

The power of Congress to tax in other areas has become well established over the years. One of the most important areas has been payroll taxes, which financially underpin the old-age insurance and unemployment compensation systems.[31] Estate taxes date from the Civil War period, and have been a permanent part of the national tax structure since 1916. The gift tax, levied to check avoidance of the estate tax, has been permanent since 1932.[32]

Tax Bills in Congress

Because tax proposals are among the most complicated pieces of legislation considered by Congress, close cooperation between the executive branch and Congress is always required when a tax bill is being drafted. Generally, the initiative on taxes in the post-World-War-II period has been taken by the administration; it has prepared the basic proposals and Congress has acted on them.[33] There is no legal or other requirement that this be the case. Congress itself initiated a major tax-reform bill in 1969. In December 1975, the House passed comprehensive tax revision legislation, the product of several years' study by the House Ways and Means Committee, but the Senate Finance Committee deferred action on the 674-page bill until 1976.

Constitutional Requirement. Tax legislation must, under a constitutional provision (Article I, Section 7, Clause 1), originate in the House of Representatives. Tax bills and bills having to do with tariffs are handled there by the Ways and Means Committee. After House passage, such bills go to the Senate and are referred to that chamber's Finance Committee, where amendments may be proposed. Amendments adopted by the Senate may be far-reaching. As in the case of all legislation, Senate-House differences over tax bills or measures involving tariff matters have to be resolved in conference. The final version, when agreed to by both houses, must then be approved by the President.

House Action

Ways and Means Committee. This committee, one of the most powerful and prestigious in the House, handles tax matters. It was created in 1802 with responsibility for both taxing and spending. Its authority over spending was gradually diminished over the years until an Appropriations Committee was created in 1865. Today the Ways and Means Committee has jurisdiction over revenue, debt, customs, trade and Social Security legislation. In addition, between 1911 and 1975, the Democratic members served as a committee on committees; they decided committee assignments for House Democrats.

The committee has had six chairmen since 1947, four Democrats and two Republicans. Of these, one—Wilbur D. Mills (D Ark.)—gained extraordinary authority over tax legislation. This was because of his length of service (he became chairman in 1958 and served until late 1974), his vast knowledge of the tax laws, his position as head of the committee which considered all tax bills as a whole (until 1975, the committee did not operate through subcommittees, although there were rare exceptions in the postwar years when special subcommittees were created to study a specific problem and then disbanded), and his renowned ability to sense the sentiment of the House and the committee and to draft tax and other measures to suit the sentiment.

The committee was traditionally composed of rather senior House members and was generally considered to be a conservative group that moved with caution after long deliberation. It was usually not a fiery advocate of tax reform, but this attitude was considered to reflect the feeling of the entire House as much as that of the committee itself.

Ways and Means has prided itself on its careful and professional work on tax legislation. This helped to earn it a favorable reputation in the House and resulted in House passage of almost all of the bills it has brought to the floor in the decade prior to 1975.

By 1974, however, there was growing dissatisfaction with the power of the committee and its chairman. This, coupled with disclosures concerning Mills' personal and health problems, prompted House Democrats in October and December of that year to institute far-reaching changes in the complexion and operations of the committee. Subsequently, Mills resigned the chairmanship and was succeeded by Rep. Al Ullman (D Ore.).

The changes included:

● Enlarging the committee to 37 from 25 members, bringing 12 middle-level and freshman Democrats onto the panel.

● Requiring the establishment of subcommittees, and giving members of the committee the power to determine the number and jurisdiction of its subcommittees. Subcommittee chairmen and ranking minority members were allowed to hire one staff person to work on their subcommittees.

● Providing that senior members of the committee would be allowed first choice for only one subcommittee slot and could not make a second choice until the junior members had each made one.

● Stripping Ways and Means of its Democratic committee assignment power and transferring it to the Democratic Steering and Policy Committee.

● Transferring revenue sharing from Ways and Means to the Government Operations Committee and export control legislation to the Foreign Affairs Committee (renamed the International Relations Committee).

As a consequence, the committee was in a great state of flux in 1975, with the "new subcommittee structure having a dramatic impact," according to Barber B. Conable Jr. (R N.Y.), a committee member.[34]

The full committee continued to handle tax legislation, but welfare, trade, Social Security, unemployment compensation and health legislation in 1975 was being written by the panel's six subcommittees. The new setup has increased the workload of committee members. Subcommittees in 1975 met on Monday and Friday and the full committee met Tuesday through Thursday. "The subcommittees are generating more legislation, which would not have been achieved without subcommittees," Conable said. The new subcommittee structure also has let Ways and Means engage in its first oversight of the Social Security program and the Internal Revenue Service.

Hearings. A bill starts on its way through Ways and Means in the normal congressional manner: testimony is collected from interested witnesses, usually leading off with the Secretary of the Treasury as the prime administration witness (although in 1969, when the committee took the initiative on tax legislation, the administration witnesses did not appear until several months after the hearings began). Hearings often are lengthy: they consumed almost eight weeks on the controversial Revenue Act of 1964. Sometimes, however, the group will act without hearings on relatively noncontroversial bills or on questions that were the subject of previous hearings; there were no hearings, for example, on the Excise Tax Reduction Act of 1965.

After hearings, the committee normally will begin mark-up sessions to draft the bill. The Treasury Department may have submitted its own bill, but preparation of legal language often is left to congressional and Treasury experts working together after the hearings have delineated the general scope of the proposals to be put into a bill. Until 1973, mark-ups generally were held in executive (closed) session, but following House passage of new rules on committee secrecy in March of that year, most of the mark-up sessions have been open. (In 1974, the committee opened all but four of its 98 mark-up sessions.)

Floor Action. Once a tax bill has been drafted, approved and reported by the Ways and Means Committee, it is brought to the floor for consideration by the House. However, prior to 1973, it was taken up under special procedures which had become traditional for Ways and Means bills and all but guaranteed acceptance of the committee's work without change. Technically, under House rules, revenue legislation was "privileged" business, which meant that it could be brought up for consideration on the floor ahead of other measures and without a rule. In practice, the committee did not take advantage of this privilege because its bill would then be open to amendment. Instead, the committee obtained from the Rules Committee a "closed rule" for floor action. Under this procedure, the bill was not open to amendment in the course of House debate; essentially, the House had to accept or reject the bill as a whole. The minority party had one opportunity, at the end of debate, to try to make changes in the bill, but significant revisions seldom resulted.

There was one exception to the prohibition against floor amendments. Amendments which were approved by the Ways and Means Committee (separately from the bill) could be offered on the floor by a committee member and voted on. This gave the committee an opportunity to backtrack on any provision which appeared to be in danger of drawing unusual House opposition.

Use of a closed rule was justified on the ground that tax, trade and other Ways and Means bills were too complicated to be opened to revision on the floor, particularly because many of the proposed changes probably would be special-interest provisions designed to favor a small number of persons or groups; such floor proposals, it was argued, might upset carefully drafted legislation approved by the committee.

Nonetheless, the closed rule tradition came under attack as members of the House began to criticize the powers of the Ways and Means Committee. Finally in 1973, Democrats modified the closed rule by adopting a proposal that allowed 50 or more Democrats to bring amendments to Ways and Means bills to the party caucus for debate. If the caucus voted to approve them, the Rules Committee was instructed to write a rule permitting the amendments to be offered on the floor. In 1975, the House went a step further by changing its rules to require that all Ways and Means revenue bills must receive a rule prior to floor action and no longer had "privileged" status. *(Closed rule reform, p. 342)*

The impact of these reforms was vividly demonstrated in 1975 during consideration of two tax bills. The House Feb. 27 passed a Ways and Means Committee tax cut bill, but tacked on a provision repealing the oil depletion allowance, despite Chairman Ullman's objections. The issue was forced by the House Democratic Caucus which voted to allow a floor vote on amendments repealing the depletion allowance offered by dissident Ways and Means members. In a long-sought victory for tax revision advocates, the full House accepted the amendment by a 248-163 vote.[35]

Later that year, to assure committee approval of a tax revision package, Ways and Means Democrats agreed on floor procedures allowing their liberal members to offer floor amendments to tighten some provisions as written by the full panel. The House accepted three proposals, which further tightened the minimum tax provisions, deleted repeal of a withholding tax on foreigners' portfolio investments and removed a controversial provision allowing capital loss carrybacks worth $167-million to wealthy investors.[36]

Senate Action

Finance Committee. A House-passed tax bill is referred to the Senate Finance Committee. This committee, created in 1816, in 1975 had a membership of 18 senators. It has the same jurisdiction as the House Ways and Means Committee. The Finance Committee—like its House counterpart—until 1970 did not operate through subcommittees. In 1975, there were nine subcommittees.

Compared to Ways and Means, the Finance Committee's power and influence on revenue and related matters are limited. Moreover, the committee, through the years, has acquired something of a reputation as a haven for special-interest tax schemes. The primary reason for this trait is found in the second part of the Constitution's Article I, Section 7 on revenue matters: "...but the Senate may propose...amendments...." Because the major work on a tax bill normally is done by the House, the Finance Committee of the Senate is left with relatively little to do (compared to Ways and Means) except to tinker with the House's work and add provisions of special interest to individual senators. As a result of the Senate's power to amend House bills, the committee takes on something of a review or appellate role.

The Finance Committee holds hearings on bills sent to it by the House. As a rule, the first witnesses are administration officials led by the Secretary of the Treasury. The principal testimony of these officials and witnesses who follow after is directed to specific parts of the House bill. In addition, they may repeat much of the testimony they gave to House taxwriters. Administration witnesses of both parties who have gone through the complete tax process say that it is a grueling experience, the more so when it has to be done twice.

The committee eventually will go into mark-up session and make changes it deems necessary in the House bill. It may, and sometimes does, write basic changes into the measure sent to it by the House, but its revisions often will be primarily addition of new material. The committee, like Ways and Means, is assisted in its work by congressional tax experts (many of the same ones who assist Ways and Means) and by Treasury Department experts. Thus, the bill reported by the Finance Committee can be expected to have the characteristics of a professionally prepared tax measure which has been written after due deliberation (even though it may differ in important respects from the House bill).

Finance Committee mark-up sessions generally have been closed (in 1974, 37 per cent of 90 committee sessions were closed); but Senate approval of new open-committee rules in 1975 could change this in the future. *(Details, pp. 370-71)*

Floor Action. When the tax bill reaches the floor of the Senate for debate, there may be a radical departure from the careful consideration given the measure during the three previous steps. The Senate has no applicable procedures or rules to ward off amendment of a tax bill on the floor. Considering the number of tax and other financial bills that go through Congress, the Senate does not often use its amendment prerogative to basically rewrite House bills or load them with unrelated provisions. But when it does so, the event may be spectacular.

A striking example of what can happen occurred in 1966 on a bill called the Foreign Investors Tax Act.[37] It was one of the gems of legislative logrolling and mutual accommoda-

tion among members of Congress. The bill started out as a measure ostensibly intended to help the United States solve its balance-of-payments problems. But after the Finance Committee and the Senate itself had finished adding amendments, the bill contained provisions to help presidential candidates, self-employed individuals, persons in the mineral ore business, big-time investors, an aluminum company and even hearse owners. These amendments, called riders because they were germane to the purpose of the bill only to the extent that they would amend the Internal Revenue Code, earned the measure the appellation of the "Christmas-tree bill" in recognition of the numerous special tax benefits it would bestow on various groups. Many of the amendments were the product of intensive lobbying by individual groups and were attached to this particular bill because it was the last measure of the session—"the last train out of the station," as one senator put it.

One of the key provisions would have established a Presidential Election Campaign Fund in the Treasury to subsidize the costs of presidential election campaigns; the fund was to be financed by taxpayers who voluntarily designated $1 or $2 of their income-tax payments for that purpose. President Johnson called the proposal "precedent-setting." The plan was rendered inoperative in 1967 but was re-enacted in slightly different form in 1972.

The fund was a pet project of Finance Committee Chairman Russell B. Long (D La.), who worked diligently to get it added to the House bill. Efforts such as this, particularly by powerful senior senators, suggest one reason why special provisions may be added by the Senate to a tax bill. Senate riders sometimes are the result of simple logrolling, sometimes are accepted simply out of courtesy to the sponsoring senator who has a strong interest in the proposal, and sometimes are approved only because they have popular appeal and it is certain that they will be quietly dropped later in conference.

All of these reasons, especially the last-mentioned, were evident in Senate action on the tax-reform bill in 1969. The House-passed measure had emerged from the Finance Committee relatively intact, but when it reached the floor, amendments began to be proposed and accepted in considerable number. Among the more popular were: an amendment to liberalize medical deductions for elderly persons; an amendment to increase minimum Social Security payments; an amendment to allow parents a tax credit for college expenses of their children; an amendment to continue for small business the benefits of the investment tax credit (which the bill repealed); and an amendment by a senator from Alaska to retain the investment tax credit for economically depressed areas (which included all of Alaska).

This performance represented an exercise of the time-honored practice of going on record for an amendment which has considerable constituent appeal but which, many senators know, will be killed in conference. Few will publicly admit to such conduct. However, Sen. John J. Williams (R Del.), who was the senior GOP tax expert at the time and who had always taken a dim view of such activity, sharply criticized senators "who can vote for (amendments) and then go home and tell their constituents how much they wanted to help them" but who knew all the time that the proposals would be scrapped in the end. Williams said he had already been approached by a number of senators who wanted him, as a conferee on the bill, to help kill amendments they voted for on the floor. "This is nothing but sheer political hypocrisy," he said. Williams refused to serve as a conferee on the tax-reform bill because he said he could not defend the Senate bill (as expected of a conferee); as it turned out, virtually all of the foregoing and other special-interest amendments were dropped from the final bill.[38]

The length of time the Senate may spend debating a tax bill is governed by the amount of interest in the measure and the number of amendments to be disposed of. The Senate spent more than five weeks debating a 1967 tax bill which dealt with a temporary suspension of the investment tax credit (which was repealed outright in 1969). Senate action generally runs only a few days except on tax bills of the first importance.

Conference Action

The final step in the process is a conference between senior members of the House Ways and Means Committee and of the Senate Finance Committee to resolve differences between the House- and Senate-approved versions of the bill. The conference sessions have usually been held in a small room maintained in the Capitol off the House floor by the Ways and Means Committee. The committee is presided over by the Ways and Means chairman. As a rule, there are three members from the majority and two members from the minority of the Ways and Means and the Finance Committees. The number may be enlarged for major bills, but a larger number for one side or the other makes no difference because each side votes as a unit with the majority vote controlling each group.

The conference may last from a day or two to several weeks on major or controversial bills. Congressional and Treasury tax experts are present to assist the conferees. Once all differences are resolved, the bill is sent back to each chamber for approval of the conference agreement. The House files a conference report (for both chambers) listing the differences and their resolution; it is a rather technical document and of most use to an expert; simpler explanations of conference decisions are given by senior committee members during floor discussion of the bill in both houses. If the conference agreement is approved by both, the bill is sent to the President to be signed into law. *(Details on conference procedure, p. 371)*

Joint Internal Revenue Committee

One of the most important actions taken to improve the handling of tax matters by the legislative branch was the creation in 1926 of the Joint Committee on Internal Revenue Taxation.

The committee itself has only 10 members—the senior members of the Ways and Means and Finance Committees. However, this is of no importance because the Joint Committee's purpose is to maintain a staff to study tax policies and problems and make recommendations to the two tax-writing committees.

The Joint Committee does not have power to report bills. Over the years, it has developed a professional and highly competent staff, which in 1975, according to the *Congressional Staff Directory*, consisted of some 47 attorneys, economists and clerical assistants, who provided much of the expert knowledge needed by the House and Senate committees in formulating tax legislation.

The joint committee's staff engages in all aspects of tax work from making revenue estimates to drafting tax-bill language. Members of the staff normally are present throughout the consideration of tax bills by both committees.

Tax Policy Since World War II

Congressional Initiative. Although in most years since World War II, the administration has taken the initiative in setting tax policy, there were two major exceptions when Congress used its constitutional power to originate tax legislation. The first instance was in 1948 when a Republican Congress passed over President Truman's veto a bill reducing individual income-tax rates, increasing the personal exemption and allowing income-splitting for married couples. The second instance was in 1969 when a Democratic Congress seized the initiative on tax reform and reduction from the newly elected Republican Nixon administration, which did not have tax revision at the top of its list of priorities.

As time passed, the Nixon administration gave its support to the tax-reform bill and made recommendations of its own (many of which were adopted), but it labored under the image of being a few steps behind Congress. This was particularly true of actions in the House. The Ways and Means Committee opened tax-reform hearings at the beginning of the session, several months before the new administration was able to prepare its own proposals. In early summer the committee reported a bill with both revenue-raising reforms and revenue-losing tax cuts that went far beyond the Treasury Department's expectations. Later in the year, the administration brought itself more or less in line with the action of the Congress, but when the tax bill became law, most of the credit for its enactment (and the credit due was substantial because it was the most far-reaching tax-reform bill in decades) rested with Congress and especially the Ways and Means Committee.[39]

Revenue Priority. Except in the two foregoing cases, tax policy in the period after 1945 was largely shaped by Secretaries of the Treasury Vinson, Snyder, Humphrey, Anderson and Dillon in turn, with the emphasis on revenue considerations. It was not until around 1963 that considerations of economic growth began to take precedence.

The earlier policy of revenue priority resulted in tax proposals that tended to be conservative in orientation. The most important consideration usually was to raise enough money to meet government expenses. This view fitted the predilections of many members of tax-writing committees, particularly Ways and Means Chairman Mills. He frequently said publicly that he favored tax reduction as a means of reducing federal revenues and forcing the government to economize.

But the continued growth of federal programs and overall government spending made tax cuts a will-o'-the-wisp goal throughout much of the period.

Congress, as a result, could do little more than comply with the administration's requests to extend (and sometimes hike) corporation and excise taxes. Its authority over taxes did not enable it to go much beyond tinkering with the basic administration recommendations. However, the tinkering often was extensive and the Revenue Acts of 1945, 1950, 1951, 1954, 1962 and 1964 all varied in important respects from the initial Treasury proposals.[40] Typically, the tax law that emerged effected either a greater reduction of revenue or less of a gain than had been recommended.

Tax Policy in the 1960s

An economic philosophy popularized during the Kennedy administration was based on the theory that the federal government's fiscal powers (taxing and spending) could be deliberately used to effect changes in the country's economy. President Kennedy and his economic advisers persuaded Congress to accept this philosophy. Kennedy and his successor, Lyndon B. Johnson, prevailed upon Congress to reduce taxes, and thereby reduce federal revenues, at a time when the budget was already in deficit. The tax cut of $11.6-billion, carried in the Revenue Act of 1964, was designed to stimulate the economy by adding to the spending power of consumers and business.

It is widely agreed that the 1964 tax cut was an important factor in continuing the economic expansion that had begun in 1961 after the most recent recession. The other side of the coin was to use a tax increase to reduce inflationary pressures when they developed. When this was tried later, the effects were much less clear.

Congress in 1968 increased taxes by placing a 10-per cent surcharge on personal and corporation income tax liabilities. The purpose was to draw spendable income away from consumers and business and thereby dampen inflationary pressures.[41]

The effectiveness of this tax action was blurred by several considerations. First, the action came late in the inflationary cycle; many economists agreed that Congress should have enacted a tax hike in 1966, when the budgetary impact of escalating Vietnam War costs became an important influence on the economy.

President Johnson had concluded, however, that Congress would not agree to a tax increase that year, so he did not seek one (other than a few half-hearted measures that raised no new revenue). By 1967, the stark economic fact which the administration had been trying to ignore for two years had to be faced. Inflation was in evidence throughout the economy, and the administration had to acknowledge that higher taxes were necessary. Johnson advanced the surtax proposal in January, but he did not push it seriously with detailed recommendations, until August. The bill got no further than hearings in the Ways and Means Committee, where Chairman Mills demanded satisfactory budget reductions before he would act on the tax request (again demonstrating the power of the committee and its chairman).

In 1968, however, there was an interesting variation on the normal power relationships in Congress which proved the potency of the constitutional power of the Senate to amend House tax bills. The Senate unexpectedly bypassed the tax-writing Ways and Means Committee, in the early spring of 1968, by adding the surcharge and a $6-billion spending cut to a comparatively innocuous House-passed bill extending certain soon-to-expire excise taxes. This action was widely viewed as an exercise in futility because Mills was not expected to agree to so important a tax provision which had originated in the Senate. But—after much political negotiation during which spring turned into summer—Mills did accept the Senate amendment. Although the bill became law, it was some two years past the time when economists believed a tax increase was most needed. This experience again raised the question of whether Congress could exercise its taxing powers swiftly enough to have the desired impact on the economy.

Tax Cuts in the 1970s

Tax policy, like other tools for manipulating the economy, underwent marked change during the first four Nixon years. At the outset of his administration, Nixon

sought and won continuation of the 1968 income tax surcharge as a means of curbing economic activity that was contributing to runaway inflation. But by 1971, when Nixon's concern over recession overshadowed his worries over inflation, the President turned to tax cuts to get the economy moving again. Congress responded by enacting the 1971 Revenue Act, cutting individual and business taxes by an average of $8.6-billion a year over the 1971-73 period.

By mid-1972, however, the administration's priorities had shifted once more: the President decided that stimulation of the economy had gone far enough and that funds added to his budget by Congress were threatening a new inflationary spiral. The term ended with the President warning Congress that further hikes in government spending would necessitate a tax increase.

Faced with continuing recession, Congress in March 1975 cleared a $22.8-billion emergency tax cut to bolster consumer and business purchasing power. President Ford signed the measure, although he protested that the act went far beyond his own $16-billion tax cut proposal in both size and scope. Then, on the day of adjournment (Dec. 19), Congress cleared a six-month tax cut extension that continued 1975 reductions at an $8.4-billion level through June 30, 1976. Final passage came after three months of maneuvering with Ford over federal spending curbs. The President had demanded a flat $395-billion spending ceiling, but acquiesced to a compromise after House and Senate Democrats agreed to a closely hedged commitment to cut fiscal 1977 outlays to offset further revenue losses if the tax reductions were continued beyond the first half of 1976.[42] (Spending ceilings, p. 128)

Proposals for Tax Rate Changes by President

The experience Congress has had so far in use of its taxing and spending powers to influence the course of the economy has been less than satisfactory. Most observers, even many conservatives in Congress, have come to the conclusion that the fiscal powers of the legislative branch can be so employed as to have substantial economic impact. The difficult question is how to use the powers to best advantage. There have been attempts in Congress in the past to relate tax revenues to planned appropriations. These efforts have ended in dismal failure. The task of budgeting, therefore, has been left to the executive branch, and its record of correlating expenditures and revenues has been uneven at best.

Joseph A. Pechman has pointed out that the "most serious drawback of the tax legislative process is that it cannot be used to raise or lower taxes quickly."[43] Indeed, a key to the problem is timing. President Kennedy said that the necessary precise timing could be achieved if Congress would delegate to the President standby power to change tax rates, either upward or downward. "This approach, Pechman asserted, "would emphasize changes which are neutral in their impact on the existing tax structure, as opposed to changes which would alter the distribution of the tax burden."[44]

President Kennedy in 1962 specifically asked for standby authority to lower individual income tax rates temporarily by 5 percentage points, subject to congressional veto, and standby authority to initiate up to $2-billion in public works spending. Kennedy asked for the power again in 1963, and President Johnson renewed the request in 1964. But the tax committees showed no interest in the proposal.[45]

To allay fears of executive usurpation of congressional tax powers, President Johnson in 1965 urged improvement of procedures to speed tax action, but he did not request standby authority. Congress again took no action. In 1966, Johnson proposed "background tax studies" to permit "quick decisions and prompt action to accommodate short-run cyclical changes." A Joint Economic Committee subcommittee in 1966 advocated standby authority for quick changes, and once again the proposal was ignored by the tax-writing committees.

Little more was heard of the idea except for a last-minute suggestion by President Johnson just before he left office in January 1969. In his budget message, the outgoing President asked Congress not only to extend the surcharge but also to give the new President authority to remove it entirely or in part "if warranted by developments," subject to congressional veto. For the long term, Mr. Johnson suggested that Congress delegate to the President limited authority to raise or lower income taxes within a specified range to meet economic conditions.

"As a result of the long delays on the tax proposals made by Presidents Johnson and Nixon during the Vietnam war, experts believe that the only practical way to speed congressional action on changes in tax rates is for the President to establish the practice of formally recommending at the beginning of each year a positive or negative surtax (of the type enacted during the Vietnam War) or no tax change at all," noted Pechman. "If the Congress acted promptly on this recommendation, other tax changes would be needed during the year only in wartime or other emergencies. Adoption of this practice would go a long way toward increasing the speed and flexibility of the tax legislative process."[46]

Proposals to Limit Taxing Power

As government spending increased during the 1930s and 1940s, proposals were advanced to limit the power of Congress to disburse public funds.[47] These proposals came primarily from conservatives, both in and out of government, who were opposed to most government spending and particularly to the social-welfare outlays that had begun to make up an increasing share of the federal budget.

The efforts were directed to limiting the government's power to spend. They reached a peak in the late 1940s and early 1950s but never were successful. The Eisenhower administration's acceptance of New Deal type programs and the concomitant "big government" essentially ended efforts in this direction.

The proposals were numerous. One was a simple joint resolution of Congress that would have forbidden action on any new tax legislation, except to raise revenue to meet war costs, until a special study had been made of the tax system with emphasis on simplification. A proposed constitutional amendment would have banned federal taxes on income except in periods of grave national emergency or, at other times, for the sole purpose of obtaining revenue to pay interest on and reduce the national debt. Another proposed constitutional amendment would have limited the total of all federal taxes to a sum equal to 14 per cent of the national income for the preceding year and would have required that 5 per cent of the total amount collected be set aside for retirement of the national debt. An even stricter variation on this theme would have limited annual federal tax collections used for nonmilitary expenditures to 5 per cent of the national income.

The proposal which probably gained the most support would have limited, not the total tax take, but the rates of particular taxes, primarily individual and corporation income taxes. The limitation would have been imposed by a constitutional amendment.

Power Over Spending

Revenue raised through the taxing system is not available in the Treasury to be disbursed by the administration to meet governmental needs simply as agency officials deem proper. The Constitution gives to Congress the basic authority to determine how monies collected by the government shall be expended. Control of government spending is one of the most important powers of Congress. It is protected in the Constitution by Article I, Section 9, Clause 7, which states: "No money shall be drawn from the Treasury, but in consequence of appropriations made by law; and a regular statement and account of the receipts and expenditures of all public money shall be published from time to time."

Elsewhere in the Constitution (Article I, Section 8, Clause 12) a prohibition is laid down against appropriating money "to raise and support armies" for a period longer than two years. But this limitation and the Section 9 requirement of a "regular" accounting of public funds constitutes the specific authority for and limitations on spending. However, much more is implied. The Constitution directs the government to do various things, such as establish post offices, roads, armed forces and courts and take a decennial census, none of which could be done without expenditures of money. But until fairly recently there was always deep disagreement about the extent of the spending power of Congress. Only in the past few decades has Congress used that power to finance a vast array of activities touching most aspects of the nation's life.

Welfare Clause Meaning

The constitutional provision, Article I, Section 8, Clause 1, which grants the taxing authority, ties the "power to lay and collect taxes" to the need to "pay the debts and provide for the common defense and general welfare of the United States." From the beginning, there were differences over what spending for the general welfare meant. One view was that it was limited to spending for purposes connected with the powers specifically mentioned in the Constitution; this was the strict interpretation and was associated with Madison. "Nothing is more natural nor common," he wrote in No. 41 of *The Federalist*, "than first to use a general phrase, and then to explain and qualify it by recital of particulars." The other view, associated with loose constructionists like Hamilton, was that the general welfare clause conferred upon the government powers separate and different from those specifically enumerated in the Constitution. Under the latter interpretation the federal government was potentially far more powerful than the strict constructionists intended; in fact, it was something more than a government of delegated powers.[48]

The broad interpretation came to be the generally accepted view, but it was not until 1936 that the Supreme Court had an opportunity to give its opinion on the meaning of the controversial wording. In a decision that year *(United States v. Butler,* 297 U.S. 1) the court invalidated the Agricultural Adjustment Act of 1933, which had provided federal payments to farmers who participated in a program of production control for the purposes of price stabilization. Although this law was held unconstitutional, the court construed the general welfare clause to mean that the congressional power to spend was not limited by the direct grants of legislative power found in the Constitution.

Rather, an expenditure was constitutional "so long as the welfare at which it is aimed can be plausibly represented as national rather than local." The 1933 law was overturned on other grounds but was later re-enacted on a different constitutional basis and was sustained by the court. Decisions in the immediately following years upheld the tax provisions of the Social Security Act, thus confirming the broad scope of the general welfare clause.[49]

Appropriations Process Before 1921

The Constitution gives the House power to originate tax bills, but it contains no specific provision to that effect concerning appropriations (this is true also of tariff policy). However, the House has traditionally assumed the responsibility for initiating all appropriations, as well as tariff, bills and has jealously guarded this self-assumed prerogative whenever the Senate (as it has from time to time) has attempted to encroach upon it. The practical result, as far as appropriations are concerned, is that the House Appropriations Committee is more powerful than its counterpart on the Senate side. The bulk of basic appropriations decisions are made in the House committee. The general shape of any appropriations bill is derived from House consideration of the measure; what the Senate does in effect is to review the House action and hear appeals from agencies seeking changes in the allotments accorded them by the House. The Senate is free to make alterations as it deems necessary, but important changes usually are limited to revisions in the financing for a relatively small number of significant or controversial government programs.[50]

Prior to World War I, neither the expenditures nor the revenues of the federal government exceeded $800-million a year. No comprehensive system of budgeting had been developed, although the methods of handling funds had undergone various shifts within Congress. During the pre-Civil-War period, both taxing and spending bills were handled in the House by the Ways and Means Committee. That eventually proved too difficult a task for a single committee, and in 1865 the House Appropriations Committee was created. A similar situation existed in the Senate, where an Appropriations Committee was created in 1867.

In neither chamber did the appropriations power remain exclusively in the hands of these two committees. Between 1877 and 1885, the House removed from the Appropriations Committee jurisdiction over 8 of 14 annual appropriations bills. These bills were placed with the substantive legislative committees. The action was taken, at least in part, to deal with what was considered an excessively independent Appropriations Committee. The Senate eventually followed the House's lead and dispersed the appropriation bills among the legislative committees. Though this division of labor allowed committees most familiar with a subject to consider the pertinent appropriations, it resulted in a division of responsibility that prevented any unified consideration or control of financial policy as a whole.[51]

Budget Policy Before 1921

The federal government has operated under a budget only since 1921—a period embracing only about one-fifth of the nation's history. However, as Lewis Kimmel has noted, "The budget idea...was clearly in the minds of leading political and financial leaders as early as the Revolutionary

---

Appropriations Feud

Many senators have disputed the exclusive right of the House to originate money bills. In 1962, the dispute produced a Senate-House stalemate that put off the enactment of such bills for months.

The controversy centered on whether the Senate could (1) originate its own appropriations bills and (2) add to House-passed appropriations bills funds for items either not previously considered by the House or considered and rejected.

The dispute, which started as a spat over the physical location of conference committee meetings, became increasingly farcical as it continued into the summer and fall with two octogenarian members of Congress as the central antagonists: 83-year-old Rep. Clarence Cannon (D Mo.), chairman of the House Appropriations Committee, and 84-year-old Sen. Carl Hayden (D Ariz.), chairman of the Senate Appropriations Committee. The feud held up final action on appropriations bills for three months until a temporary accord, reached in July, broke the stalemate. Late in the session, however, a Senate-House disagreement over agricultural research funds resulted in a three-week deadlock on the agriculture appropriations bill. The disagreement was resolved only after a bitter exchange between the Senate and House.

Further bitterness resulted when Cannon blocked action, Oct. 12, on the first fiscal 1963 supplemental appropriations bill because the Senate had added "unwarranted sums" to the measure. The response of the Senate was to adopt a resolution, Oct. 13, asserting its "coequal power" with the House to originate appropriation bills—a resolution and an assertion of power which the House ignored.

Although the 1962 dispute was serious and could happen again, long-time students of Congress pointed out that the two houses had been arguing throughout their existence about which one has the right to originate appropriations bills.

Source: Jeffrey L. Pressman, *House vs. Senate, Conflict in the Appropriations Process* (Yale University Press, 1966), pp. 1-11.

---

and formative periods. The absence of logical or systematic budget methods during the early years and throughout the nineteenth century should not be construed as a lack of appreciation of the role of public finance."[52]

Ratification of the Constitution cleared the path toward establishment of a government financial system. In September 1789, Congress enacted a law establishing the Treasury Department and requiring the Secretary of the Treasury "to prepare and report estimates of the public revenues, and the public expenditures." However, according to Kimmel, "Alexander Hamilton's efforts in the direction of an executive budget were unsuccessful, mainly because of congressional jealousy and existing party divisions."[53]

Because the federal government relied on customs duties for the bulk of its revenues throughout the 19th century, and because there was an abundance of these revenues, there was no need to weigh expenditures against revenues. Consequently, the budget-making process underwent a progressive deterioration.[54]

Budget Terminology

The federal budget, like any budget, is a schedule of expected receipts and expenditures. The document is prepared annually by the administration and purports to show, as nearly as can be reliably estimated, what the government will receive and spend in the coming fiscal year.

Congress at one time or another must approve all spending, but some spending scheduled for a given year may have been approved by Congress in a previous year. The following description applies to the federal budget structure put into use by President Johnson in his last two years in office and used subsequently. The structure, called the unified budget, was based on recommendations of a study commission and differed in various respects from that of previous years.

What Congress acts upon is not proposed expenditures—as such—but requests for new budget authority. Government agencies are permitted to enter into obligations, requiring immediate or future payments of money (expenditures), only when they have been granted budget authority by congressional action.

Budget authority is divided into new obligational authority (NOA) and loan authority (LA), and it usually takes the form of appropriations, which permit obligations to be incurred and payments to be made. Some budget authority is in the form of contract authorizations, which permit obligations but require later appropriations. There are several other less important forms of budget authority.

Thus, in any given year the administration in its budget asks for specific amounts of budget authority in the form of NOA or LA. Congress, through the appropriations process, grants all, a part, or none of the authority requested.

Once NOA or LA has been approved by Congress, agencies may enter into obligations. The obligations may be immediate obligations, such as the purchase of office supplies or payment of salaries to federal workers. Most appropriations are for obligation within the year (one-year appropriations). Some congressional appropriations are for specified longer periods (multi-year appropriations), while other appropriations for large projects—construction or research, for example—are made available until expended (no-year appropriations).

As a result, a change in requested NOA or LA for a particular year does not necessarily change either the obligations incurred or the actual expenditures in that year by an equal amount. A change requested in NOA or LA in one year may be reflected in obligations in subsequent years and expenditures in even later years. Obligations are eliminated, or "liquidated" as budget officials put it, by issuing checks, by disbursement of cash or by several other methods. These are the government's expenditures, a main part of the budget.

According to Kimmel, the first important step toward establishing a federal executive budget was taken in 1910, when President Taft appointed a Commission on Economy and Efficiency to study the need for a federal budget. The commission concluded that a restructuring of the system for determining and providing for the financial needs of the government was of paramount importance. But Congress resented the commission's proposed system, and its report was not even considered by the House Appropriations Committee to which it was referred.[55]

Modern Budgeting Procedure

The diffuse appropriations system that had grown up in the first 130 years of the nation's life could no longer meet the financial needs of an increasingly complex government after World War I. Federal receipts exceeded $4-billion in all except two years in the 1920s, and expenditures dropped only to about $3-billion at the lowest point (fiscal 1927). Having seen the government spend $18.5-billion in fiscal 1919, which included the last 4½ months of the war, and having appropriated $6.5-billion for fiscal 1920, the first full postwar year, Congress decided it must reorganize its financial machinery, both to retrench on expenditures and to tighten control over the execution of fiscal policy.[56]

The reorganization was accomplished through enactment of the Budget and Accounting Act of 1921. First, however, the House on June 1, 1920, restored exclusive spending powers to its Appropriations Committee and enlarged the committee from 21 to 35 members (55 in 1975). The Senate on March 6, 1922, similarly concentrated spending powers in its Appropriations Committee but left the membership at 16 (in 1975 it was 26).

In the Budget and Accounting Act, Congress sought also to reform the financial machinery of the executive branch. The 1921 act established two important offices—the Bureau of the Budget and the General Accounting Office (GAO). The former was created to centralize fiscal management of the administration directly under the President; the latter was designed to strengthen the oversight of spending.

Bureau of the Budget. With passage of the 1921 act, Congress ended the right of federal agencies to decide for themselves what appropriations levels to ask of Congress; the Budget Bureau, serving under the President's direction, was to act as a central clearinghouse for budget requests.

Budget Circular 49, approved by President Harding on Dec. 19, 1921, required that all agency proposals for appropriations be submitted to the President prior to presentation to Congress. Agency proposals were to be studied for their relationship to "the President's financial program" and were to be sent on to Capitol Hill only if approved by the President. The bureau, though placed in the Treasury, was kept under the supervision of the President.[57]

In 1935, President Roosevelt broadened the clearance function to include other legislation as well as the appropriations requests.

According to political scientist Richard E. Neustadt, writing in the *American Political Science Review* for September 1954, Roosevelt's new clearance system was not a mere extension of the budget process. "On the contrary...this was Roosevelt's creation, intended to protect not just his budget, but his prerogatives, his freedom of action, and his choice of policies in an era of fast-growing government and of determined presidential leadership."[58]

(Continued on p. 126)

Congress and Backdoor Spending

One form of spending authority was particularly controversial in the 1950s and 1960s. It went under the general name of "backdoor spending," a label applied by its opponents, but it included different types of authority.

In general, backdoor spending reduced the control of Congress over government spending, and it virtually wiped out the authority of the Appropriations Committees over the programs which it covered. Because of the latter consideration, the committees were strongly opposed to this method of financing.

By 1974 only about 60 per cent of federal spending was subject to annual appropriations. The rest either did not require yearly appropriations or created obligations that Congress had no choice but to meet through appropriations. This "backdoor spending" authority was provided through such devices as the following:

- *Borrowing authority,* which permits an agency to borrow either from the Treasury or the public.
- *Contract authority,* which allows agencies to enter into contracts that require future appropriations.
- *Permanent appropriations,* in which funds are made available under basic legislation and no further appropriations action is required. Authority to pay interest on the public debt is one example.
- *Mandatory spending (entitlement programs),* in which basic legislation requires payments—such as Social Security, welfare or veterans' benefits—and forces the enactment of appropriations.

Background. During President Eisenhower's second term, backdoor spending meant for the most part the authority of certain agencies to borrow funds from the Treasury to finance their operations without going to Congress for appropriations. Beginning with the Reconstruction Finance Corp. in 1932, such authority to "expend from public debt receipts" was extended to the Commodity Credit Corp., the Export-Import Bank, and the Federal National Mortgage Assn., among others.

Under this method, the legislative committee (not the Appropriations Committee) responsible for a program would sponsor legislation authorizing an agency to borrow its funds directly from the Treasury, which in turn would be authorized to sell notes to obtain the money; the programs usually provided for repayment, but in practice Congress canceled large amounts of the debt owed by various agencies.

Objections to backdoor spending came to a head in 1961. After Congress had authorized financing of this kind for the new Area Redevelopment Administration, the House Appropriations Committee managed to undo the action and require the ARA to seek appropriations for all of its activities.

A second form of backdoor spending is contract authorization. Once again the legislative committees sponsor the grants of spending authority. In this case, a bill authorizes an agency or department to enter into contracts and to incur obligations prior to approval of appropriations. Contract authorization must be followed by appropriations to meet the obligations incurred. Once an agency has contract authority and has incurred obligations for a project (such as building a subway), the Appropriations Committee and Congress have no alternative but to cough up the money to pay the bills.

Under either approach the basic issue is who will control the financing of government programs. Legislative committees normally only authorize and outline the scope of programs; the Appropriations Committees provide the money. Some programs—over the years—have been vulnerable to attack by a conservative majority on the House Appropriations Committee. Backdoor financing shortcircuited the appropriations process and removed the programs from the financial control of the Appropriations Committees.

Use of Backdoor Financing. Backdoor financing through funds borrowed from the Treasury ended in the early 1960s. Use of contract authorization has tended to increase as legislative committees of Congress and government agencies have become frustrated with spending cuts by the Appropriations Committees.

Backdoor spending began to creep back in the mid-1960s but in a form that differed in an important respect from that formerly used. In earlier periods, the legislative committees would attempt to gain approval of backdoor spending, in the form of either Treasury loans or contract authority that would in effect insulate the program from the budget knife of the Appropriations Committees. From about 1965 on, the programs financed through backdoor spending—invariably in the form of contract authority—have allowed the Appropriations Committees the final say as to the maximum amount of spending permitted for the undertaking. These maximum amounts usually have been written into annual appropriations bills.

However, the contracts for many of the social programs financed by this method run for 30 to 40 years. As a result, once the Appropriations Committees set maximum contract authority and government agencies enter into the contracts, Congress (and the Appropriations Committees) are committed to provide funds for the programs for a long period of time. Thus the Appropriations Committee have regained some, but by no means all, of their former control over spending.

Important programs financed in this manner have included rent supplements, home ownership assistance and rental assistance. All date from the 1965-68 period when President Johnson was in office. A program for federal aid to development of urban mass transit systems, approved by Congress in 1970, carried contract authority of $3.1-billion for the first five years.

The 1974 Congressional Budget and Impoundment Control Act gave Congress more control over backdoor spending beginning in 1975. New borrowing authority and contract authority must be approved by the Appropriations Committees and entitlement programs are subject to tighter Appropriations Committee review. *(1974 Budget Act, p. 129)*

Sources: Congressional Quarterly, *Congress and the Nation,* vol. 1, p. 389; Louis Fisher, *Presidential Spending Power* (Princeton University Press, 1975).

(Continued from p. 124)

Roosevelt in 1939 issued, and Congress approved, Reorganization Plan No. 1, creating the executive office of the President and transferring the Budget Bureau from the Treasury to the new office. By presidential directive, Roosevelt also broadened the bureau's clearance function by making it responsible for coordination of department views on all measures sent to the White House for the President's signature or veto. That responsibility had been limited previously to views on appropriations bills. Any recommendation that the President withhold his approval of a bill was required to have to be accompanied by a draft veto message or, in the case of a pocket veto, a memorandum of disapproval. These procedures were further strengthened by later Presidents.[59]

In 1970, President Nixon streamlined the budget process by restructuring the Bureau of the Budget.[60] The new office, called the Office of Management and Budget (OMB), was given sweeping authority to coordinate the execution of government programs as well as the Budget Bureau's old role of advising the President on agency funding requests. In 1974, Congress enacted legislation making future OMB directors and deputy directors subject to Senate confirmation.

The General Accounting Office. Congress, in setting up the GAO, was attempting to strengthen its surveillance of spending. The GAO is headed by the comptroller general and assistant comptroller general, appointed by the President with the advice and consent of the Senate, for a period of 15 years. They can be removed only by joint resolution of Congress, thus making the agency responsible to Congress rather than the administration. The comptroller general was granted wide powers to investigate all matters relating to the use of public funds and was required to report annually to Congress, including in his report recommendations for greater economy and efficiency.

Many of the auditing powers and duties of the comptroller general had already been established by the Dockery Act of 1894, which assigned them to the new office of the comptroller of the Treasury. But under that act the comptroller and his staff remained executive branch officers, and Congress lacked its own agency for independent review of executive expenditures.

In their book, *Federal Budget Policy*, David J. Ott and Attiat F. Ott describe the three major types of audits made by the GAO. "Recently, the *comprehensive audit* has become the most important. This audit concentrates on the accounting and reporting system used by a particular agency and checks transactions selectively. The *general audit* examines the accounts of agency disbursing and certifying officers to determine the legality of each transaction. If illegal or improper handling of receipts or expenditures is discovered, recovery procedures are instituted against the responsible officer. The *commercial audit* is applied to government corporations and enterprises. No recovery is possible in this case, but Congress is informed of questionable or improper practices."[61]

The results of GAO audits are transmitted to Congress by the comptroller general. The results of special investigations of particular agencies and the annual report are referred to the House and Senate Committees on Government Operations. *(Discussion of GAO functions, p. 488)*

Appropriations Procedures

The complex budgetary process begins in the various agencies of the executive branch as estimates are made of

Sources of Spending Power

The amount of money the federal government spends in a fiscal year is only partly related to actions that Congress takes in that year. At one time or another, Congress must grant the authority to spend money to the federal agencies that make the actual outlays. Some of that authority comes in the year the outlays are made, but much of it originates in earlier years. The illustration below shows the sources of planned fiscal 1976 outlays.

The illustration shows that the budget authority appropriated by Congress for a fiscal year is more than the obligations or outlays within that year for the following reasons:

● Budget authority for some major procurement and construction covers the estimated full cost at the time programs are started, even though outlays take place over a number of years as the programs move toward completion.

● Budget authority for many loan and guarantee or insurance programs also provides financing for a period of years or represents a contingency backup.

● Budget authority for trust funds represents mainly receipts from special taxes, which are used as needed over a period of years for purposes specified in the law.

As a result, substantial unspent budget authority is always carried over from prior years. Most of it is earmarked for specified purposes, and is not available for new programs.

Relation of Budget Authority to Outlays — 1976 Budget
Figures in brackets represent Federal funds only

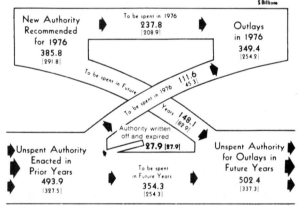

NOTE: The difference between the total budget figures and federal funds shown in brackets consists of trust funds and interfund transactions between fund groups

Source: *The Budget of the U.S. Government, fiscal year 1976* (U.S. Government Printing Office, Washington, 1975).

the funds needed to carry out government programs. All of the estimates are brought together in the White House (previously by the Budget Bureau but under the 1970 reorganization by the Office of Management and Budget). At this point, the requests of the agencies are coordinated with presidential policies and expected revenues.

The President presents his budget to Congress in January. The estimates and requests that it contains are for the fiscal year which will begin the following July 1. (In 1976, the government changed from a fiscal year of July through June to one beginning Oct. 1 and ending the following Sept. 30.)

The expenditure of money by a government agency is the last of three main steps: Congress first authorizes a program of activity for which funds will be needed and sets a ceiling on the amount of these funds. Second, Congress provides the authority to spend money, usually through appropriations but sometimes through other means; the amount of money provided often is less than the maximum amount specified in the authorization for the program. Third, the agency in the government spends the money.

Once funds have been appropriated or otherwise made available, their expenditure is under the control of the departments and agencies in the executive branch, although the congressional committees—particularly the Appropriations Committees—generally keep close track of how the officials are using the funds.

Authorization Requirement

The congressional procedure which leads to the expenditure of funds is a multi-step process. The substantive legislative committees of each chamber of Congress consider the proposed programs; this is the start of the authorizing step. Once the respective programs have been authorized by vote of the two houses and the President's approval, it is up to the Appropriations Committees of each chamber to recommend appropriations for the programs. Passage of the appropriations bills follows. Each step, first as to authorization and then as to appropriation of funds, is an essential part of the congressional process.[62]

The Appropriations Committees cannot act until the authorization has been signed into law. The House has had a rule since 1837 which provides that "No appropriation shall be reported in any general appropriation bill, or be in order as an amendment thereto, for any expenditure not previously authorized by law...." The Senate had a similar rule, but because appropriations bills originate in the House, the House rule is governing. There are some exceptions, such as a portion of the annual military spending that is authorized by the Constitution, but generally appropriations must await authorizations.

This requirement has led to conflict in Congress on numerous occasions. In the 1950-70 period, Congress required to be authorized annually more and more programs that previously had permanent or multi-year authorization. The trend to annual authorizations represented a victory for the legislative committees—such as the Committee on Education and Labor in the House for matters under its jurisdiction—which felt that they had lost effective control over their programs to the Appropriations Committees. The Appropriations Committees, particularly in the House, took a dim view of the annual authorizations, in part because they tended in some degree to diminish their power.

The annual authorization trend contributed importantly to delaying the enactment of appropriations bills beyond the July 1 beginning of the new fiscal year. Rarely since the late 1950s has Congress completed action on more than one or two appropriations bills by July 1. This was due in part to the prohibition against appropriations action before an authorization bill is enacted. Another factor was the increasing number and complexity of government programs that required more time for congressional review.

The result has been to force the government to go into its new financial year without most of its regular funding bills enacted into law. Congress has got around the problem by adopting continuing resolutions that allow agencies to spend at certain levels (usually that of the previous fiscal year) for a specified time, which often has to be extended. This practice pleased hardly anyone. In an attempt to rectify the situation, Congress in the 1974 Congressional Budget and Impoundment Control Act established deadlines for clearing authorization and appropriations bills. It also changed the date on which the new fiscal year begins to Oct. 1. *(See below, p. 129)*

House Appropriations Action

Although the President's budget is sent to Congress at the beginning of each regular session in massively detailed form (the President also submits an economic report at the beginning of each session), until 1975 it was seldom debated or considered as a whole. The detailed business of studying the budget proposals and preparing the appropriations bills was done piecemeal in subcommittees.

The House Appropriations Committee, like the Ways and Means Committee, is one of the most powerful and prestigious. It has been composed in large part of senior members of the House elected from safe congressional districts. It is a conservative body which believes it has a duty to reduce the budget requests submitted to it. This, it usually does—at least overall.

The true power of the committee resides in its 13 (in 1975) subcommittees. When the President's budget reaches Congress, it is divided among the subcommittees which function largely as independent kingdoms. The subcommittees are set up along functional lines: Agriculture, Defense, Interior, Labor-HEW and so on, roughly paralleling the 14 (in 1975) regular appropriations bills cleared by Congress. Generally, the members of the subcommittees become very knowledgeable and often expert in their assigned areas. The subcommittees, and particularly their chairmen, consequently wield substantial power over spending.

House Appropriations subcommittee hearings were traditionally closed, with testimony almost always restricted to that given by agency officials. A voluminous record of the hearings, along with the parent committee's report, usually was not made public until shortly before House floor action on an appropriation bill. As a result, few if any members not on the subcommittee were prepared to challenge the bill. The Legislative Reorganization Act of 1970 provided that all House committee and subcommittee hearings must be open, but not if a majority determines otherwise. In 1974, the Appropriations Committee opened 90 per cent of its hearings, but closed almost half of its mark-ups. Nine of the panel's 13 subcommittees opened all of their mark-ups in 1974, compared with only two in 1973.[63]

The 1970 act provided also that the House Appropriations Committee hold hearings on the President's budget as a whole within 30 days of its receipt; directed the setting up of a standardized data processing system for federal budgetary and fiscal data; and directed the President to send Congress five-year forecasts of the fiscal impact of all federal programs.

As a result of congressional reform efforts, the House Appropriations Committee underwent substantial changes in 1974-75. As of the beginning of the 94th Congress, chairmen of all the appropriations subcommittees had to be approved by the House Democratic Caucus. The caucus

(Continued on p. 129)

Spending Ceilings: A Controversial Tactic

By demanding that Congress link 1976 tax cuts to a $395-billion fiscal 1977 spending ceiling—Congress refused to do so—President Ford resorted to a frequently used tactic in past budget battles between the White House and Capitol Hill.

Congress could "learn from history and from precedent that it had been done," Ford declared in an Oct. 9, 1975, press conference, recalling spending limits that congressional fiscal conservatives exacted from President Johnson in 1967-68.

Those and subsequent ceilings enacted by Congress proved ineffective in restraining spending growth, however. And other requests for spending limits—notably President Nixon's 1972 election-year proposal for a $250-billion ceiling—"have led to nothing but divisiveness and argument," House Ways and Means Committee Chairman Al Ullman (D Ore.) noted Oct. 7, 1975.

Congress denied the 1972 request, provoking further impoundment and veto fights with Nixon, then set about strengthening its own budget-making procedures to take the economic policy initiative back from the executive branch.

Johnson Ceilings

In 1967-68, when Ford was House Republican leader, Congress demanded spending cuts as fiscal conservatives' price for supporting continued government funding and a 10 per cent tax surcharge proposed by President Johnson.

Opposing the growth of federal spending on the Vietnam War and Great Society programs, House Republicans in 1966 had launched an economy drive to curb outlays. Efforts to cut several annual appropriations bills by 5 per cent were frustrated, so they resorted to proposing spending limits that would force government agencies to hold down outlays.

In an amendment tacked on to a routine continuing appropriations measure after months of controversy, Congress in December 1967 directed federal agencies to cut fiscal 1968 spending on "controllable" programs by $4-billion. But outlays for exempted "uncontrollable" programs rose about $5-billion, leaving a net spending increase of $1-billion.

Fiscal conservatives found a better handle for insisting on spending curbs when Johnson in 1967 proposed the 10 per cent surcharge. The Ways and Means Committee refused to act on the proposal, however, as Chairman Wilbur D. Mills (D Ark.) held out for expenditure control commitments from the administration before action on raising taxes.

That deadlock finally was broken in June 1968, after the Senate added the surcharge and a $108.1-billion spending ceiling to House-passed excise tax legislation. After lengthy conference deliberations, the House gave in and the measure was enacted into law.

Nixon Confrontations

With Republican President Richard M. Nixon in the White House, Congress enacted spending ceilings in both 1969 and 1970. A $191.9-billion fiscal 1970 ceiling was tacked on to a supplemental appropriations bill in 1969, with provisions adjusting the ceiling to accommodate any congressional action increasing or decreasing spending and allowing the President himself to raise the limit by up to $2-billion to accommodate uncontrollable expenditures.

That cushion proved insufficient, so Congress in 1970 simply raised the fiscal 1970 ceiling to $197.9-billion, again with allowance for another $2-billion in uncontrollable outlays. In the same bill, Congress set a $200.8-billion fiscal 1971 limit with a cushion for uncontrollables and unlimited additions for spending increases by congressional action.

No spending ceiling was enacted in fiscal 1972, but Nixon's request for a $250-billion limit on fiscal 1973 spending provoked a dispute with Congress that was thrashed out amid the 1972 presidential election campaign.

In what Democrats conceded was a masterful political stroke, Nixon in July 1972 asked Congress for authority to trim federal spending as he saw fit to meet a $250-billion ceiling on fiscal 1973 outlays. If such power were denied, Nixon warned, Congress would be responsible for tax increases in 1973.

The House complied by writing the ceiling into a debt limit extension bill. But the Senate balked at giving the President unlimited discretion to cut federal outlays, adding strict guidelines on the size and nature of spending reductions.

The Senate subsequently rejected a White House-backed compromise circumscribing the President's authority to dictate the reductions, and the provision was dropped. In response to President Nixon's pressure on the spending issue, Congress wrote into the debt ceiling legislation a provision setting up a joint congressional committee to study changes in its budget procedures.

Nixon thereafter waged his war on spending increases through vetoes and impoundments. Congress for its part followed up in 1974 by passing legislation creating House and Senate Budget Committees and establishing a congressional budget-making process for setting spending totals.

The House and Senate in 1973 approved different ceilings on fiscal 1974 outlays as part of anti-impoundment bills, but those measures died in conference as Congress restricted impoundments as part of the budget revision measure. The Senate twice in 1974 defeated floor amendments by Sen. William Proxmire (D Wis.) to impose a $295-billion ceiling for fiscal 1975.

Ford's Proposal

After succeeding Nixon as President, Ford asked Congress to set a $300-billion target for fiscal 1975 outlays as part of an Oct. 8, 1974, economic program featuring a 5 per cent income tax surcharge. While setting a goal for spending reductions, Ford's proposal was not a firm ceiling on outlays.

The House endorsed the Ford target by a 329-20 roll-call vote, but the Senate took no action on the proposal.

(Continued from p. 127)
also voted in late 1974 to restrict senior Democrats to membership on only two of a committee's subcommittees. This was aimed mainly at the Appropriations Committee, where senior conservative Democrats dominated important subcommittees handling defense, agriculture, and labor, health, education and welfare appropriations.

Instead of fragmenting the committee, the strengthening of subcommittees in 1975 made the committee much more active by giving committee liberals a greater voice in the panel's work. Rep. David R. Obey (D Wis.), an Appropriations member who was a prime mover in reforming the panel, called the subcommittee changes "absolutely crucial" to loosening the control of conservative Chairman George Mahon (D Texas) "and the college of cardinals [the conservative subcommittee chairmen]" over the committee.[64]

House procedure on appropriation bills permits amendments from the floor. However, the prestige of the Appropriations Committee is such that few major changes are ever made. By and large, the amounts endorsed by the Appropriations Committee during the post-World-War-II period have been accepted by the House; administration efforts to win "restoration" of cuts in the budget estimates have been concentrated on the Senate.

Senate Appropriations Action

Once an appropriations bill has passed the House, it is sent to the Senate and referred to the Appropriations Committee where a parallel system of subcommittees exists. The Senate subcommittees review the work of the House at hearings which are open to the public. The Senate subcommittees do not attempt to do the same amount of work on a bill that the House has already done; the time required (often it is getting late in the year by the time the Senate receives appropriations bills) and the heavy workload of most senators preclude the same detailed consideration that is given in the House. The Senate subcommittees are viewed more as appellate groups which listen to administration witnesses requesting the restoration of funds cut by the House.

The Senate subcommittees normally will restore some of the funds denied by the House, although it may make cuts in other places. The Senate itself may add or restore more when the bill reaches the floor. Most appropriations bills carry larger total amounts when they pass the Senate than when they passed the House. The differences are resolved in conference, generally by splitting the difference between the two chambers.

Congress and Spending: The 1974 Budget Act

The "power of the purse"—defined broadly to include both receipts through taxes and outlays through appropriations—clearly is a basic power which the framers of the Constitution intended to impart to Congress. Over the years, Congress has jealously and successfully guarded its powers of taxation from encroachment by the executive branch; as noted, this is the basic reason why Presidents Kennedy and Johnson were unsuccessful in obtaining standby authority to alter tax rates for economic purposes.

However, Congress has been much less successful, at least since New Deal days, in retaining control over government expenditures. And, until 1975, it was totally unsuccessful in relating expenditures to revenues even though the two are intrinsically linked. The responsibility for doing so thus fell to the administration.[65]

Prior to 1974, efforts had been made in Congress to exert overall control over appropriations (and in turn, therefore, government spending)—basically with the intention of holding appropriations to a minimal level. Attempts were made also to use the tax system to hold down government outlays and to tie the two together in Congress. But none of these undertakings met with great success, and most were dismal failures. *(See proposals for tax change, p. 121)*

Well aware of the unfortunate record and the need to do something about it, Congress in 1974 enacted legislation to reform its budget procedures. At the end of its first year of (partial) operation in 1975, the new federal budget system appeared to be working.

Background and Provisions of Act

Setting the framework for reasserting congressional control over government spending, Congress June 21, 1974, completed action on legislation (HR 7130—PL 93-344) that revised and elaborated the procedures by which Congress considers the federal budget.

As written, the Congressional Budget and Impoundment Control Act would force Congress into more measured and timely action on budgetary legislation, tying its separate spending decisions together with fiscal policy objectives in a congressionally determined budget package.

Following a budget reform format prepared in 1973 by a joint study committee, the law required Congress before acting on appropriations and spending measures to adopt a budget resolution setting target figures for total appropriations, total spending and appropriate tax and debt levels. The measure created new House and Senate Budget Committees to analyze budget options and prepare the budget resolutions. The committees are assisted by a new Congressional Budget Office (CBO).

While building on the existing committee structure in considering authorization and appropriations bills, the act established a detailed timetable setting deadlines for floor action on various spending measures. To fit the expanded budget-making procedures into the yearly congressional session schedule, the act shifted the federal government onto an Oct. 1-Sept. 30 fiscal year, giving Congress an additional three months to wrap up its budget review. Before the fiscal year begins, Congress must reconsider its budget targets and reconcile its spending actions. *(Timetables, p. 131)*

Correcting existing practices that foiled congressional control over federal spending levels, the law provided procedures for putting limits on backdoor spending programs and for forcing the President to spend impounded funds. *(Box on backdoor spending, p. 125; impoundment, pp. 111, 133)*

However, the act allowed a waiver of its procedural and deadline requirements at several stages. Thus, the success of the new budget process depended on Congress' determination to discipline its spending decisions.

The process was a sweeping reform designed to focus Congress' attention in a systematic way on two broad budgetary concerns: national fiscal policy and national priorities.

The process requires members of Congress for the first time to vote on a deficit. Instead of treating spending and tax measures individually and separately, Congress is forced to compare total spending with total receipts. In doing so, Congress must confront such fiscal policy issues as the effect of the budget on inflation, unemployment and economic growth.

The Budget Act also required members for the first time to make choices and thereby set priorities. For example, if Congress calls for more spending for health programs, it now must increase revenues through higher taxes, accept a larger deficit, or balance the addition by cutting other programs.

So Congress in 1975 began viewing the federal budget as a balloon, which when squeezed in one place would pop up in another. "People are seeing for the first time where all the money is going, and I'm not sure they like it," said House Budget Committee Chairman Brock Adams (D Wash.).

Background

In reforming its budget procedures, Congress in 1974 undertook a task that it tried and abandoned nearly 25 years before.

In three years of trying, the House and Senate never got together to fully implement a legislative budget created by the Legislative Reorganization Act of 1946 (PL 79-601). After unsuccessful attempts in 1947, 1948 and 1949, Congress abandoned the experiment as an unqualified failure.

Similar in some respects to the reform procedures adopted by Congress in 1974, the 1946 act required that Congress set by concurrent resolution a maximum amount to be appropriated for each fiscal year.

That appropriations ceiling was part of a legislative budget based on revenue and spending estimates prepared by a massive Joint Budget Committee composed of all members of the House and Senate Appropriations Committees and of the tax-writing House Ways and Means and Senate Finance Committees.

In 1947, conferees failed to agree on Senate amendments to the budget resolution providing for use of an expected federal surplus for tax reductions and debt retirement. In 1948, Congress appropriated $6-billion more than its own legislative budget ceiling, and in 1949 the legislative budget never was produced as the process broke down completely.

One of the principal reasons the legislative budget failed was the inability of the Joint Budget Committee to make accurate estimates of spending so early in the session and before individual agency requests had been considered in detail. In addition, the committee was said to be inadequately staffed and, with more than 100 members, to be much too unwieldy for effective operation.[66]

Failure of the legislative budget prompted a serious effort in Congress in 1950 to combine the numerous separate appropriations bills into one omnibus measure.

The traditional practice of acting on the separate bills one by one made it difficult to hold total outlays in check. In 1950, the House Appropriations Committee agreed to give the omnibus-bill plan a trial. The overall bill was passed by Congress about two months earlier than the last of the separate bills had been passed in 1949. The appropriations totaled about $2.3-billion less than the President's budget requests. The omnibus approach was praised by many

observers. It was particularly well received by persons or groups seeking reductions in federal spending.

Nevertheless, the House Appropriations Committee in January 1951 voted 31 to 18 to return to the traditional method of handling appropriations bills separately. Two years later, in 1953, the Senate proposed a return to the omnibus plan, but the House did not respond. The plan was dead. Opponents said the omnibus bill required more time and effort than separate bills. Equally important was the opposition of the House Appropriations subcommittee chairmen, who feared that some of their power would be eroded away under the omnibus-bill plan.[67]

In addition to the legislative budget and omnibus appropriations efforts, other proposals to control federal spending were made during the post-war period. Among them were a mandatory balanced budget; a separate budget session of Congress during which all appropriations bills, and no other legislation, would be handled; creation of a Joint Budget Committee (this idea originated in the Senate and was approved by that body on seven occasions between 1952 and 1965, but the House took no action on the Senate bills); and establishment of spending limits.

None of these proposals were enacted; and Congress generally had to fall back on its traditional practice of adding to appropriations bills specific restrictions on how the money provided in the bills could be spent.

Congress began another effort to strengthen its control over the budget process in 1972 when it established a Joint Study Committee on Budget Control. The 32-man committee held hearings and in 1973 made recommendations which were incorporated in the 1974 act. Impetus for action was provided by struggles between Congress and the Nixon administration over presidential impoundment of funds.

Major Provisions of the 1974 Act

The final version of the 1974 Budget Act was the product of intense staff negotiations both during Senate consideration and in conference. As it emerged from conference, the bill tended to follow more detailed Senate provisions where the two versions differed. Following is a summary of the major provisions of the act.[68]

Budget Committees. To give Congress a more expert perspective on budget totals and on fiscal policy requirements, the budget reform act established House and Senate Budget Committees to study and recommend changes in the President's budget.

Assuring that existing House committees concerned with budgetary matters would be represented on the 23-member House Budget Committee, the act assigned five seats to Ways and Means Committee members and five to Appropriations Committee members. The remaining seats are occupied by one member from each of the 11 legislative committees, and by one member from the majority leadership and one from the minority leadership.

The act rotated House Budget Committee membership by prohibiting any member from serving for more than four years out of a 10-year period. Members on the committee must serve for a full Congress.

The 15-member Senate Budget Committee is picked by normal Senate committee selection procedures. No rotation is required, but after 1976, any member holding seats on two other major committees must drop one.

Budget Submission. In moving to an Oct. 1-Sept. 30 fiscal year, the act established a timetable to assure orderly action on spending measures before the fiscal year began.

Congressional Budget Deadlines

October-December: Congressional Budget Office submits five-year projection of current spending as soon as possible after Oct. 1.

Nov. 10: President submits current services budget.

Dec. 31: Joint Economic Committee reports analysis of current services budget to budget committees.

Late January: President submits budget (15 days after Congress convenes).

Late January-March: Budget committees hold hearings and begin work on first budget resolution.

March 15: All legislative committees submit estimates and views to budget committees.

April 15: Budget committees report first resolution.

May 15: Committees must report authorization bills by this date.

May 15: Congress completes action on first resolution. Before adoption of the first resolution, neither house may consider new budget authority or spending authority bills, revenue changes, or debt limit changes.

May 15 through the 7th day after Labor Day: Congress completes action on all budget and spending authority bills.

● Before reporting first regular appropriations bill, the House Appropriations Committee, "to extent practicable," marks up all regular appropriations bills and submits a summary report to House, comparing proposed outlays and budget authority levels with first resolution targets.

● CBO issues periodic scorekeeping reports comparing congressional action with first resolution.

● Reports on new budget authority and tax expenditure bills must contain comparisons with first resolution, and five-year projections.

● "As possible," a CBO cost analysis and five-year projection will accompany all reported public bills, except appropriation bills.

August: Budget committees prepare second budget resolution and report.

Sept. 15: Congress completes action on second resolution. Thereafter, neither house may consider any bill or amendment, or conference report, that results in an increase over outlay or budget authority figures, or a reduction in revenues, beyond the amounts in the second resolution.

Sept. 25: Congress completes action on reconciliation bill or another resolution. Congress may not adjourn until it completes action on the second resolution and reconciliation measure, if any.

Oct. 1: Fiscal year begins.

To give Congress a quicker start in shaping the budget, the act required the executive branch to submit a "current services" budget by Nov. 10 for the fiscal year that would start the following Oct. 1.

Building on the programs and funding levels in effect for the ongoing fiscal year that had started the month before, the November current services budget projects the spending required to maintain those programs at existing commitment levels without policy changes through the following fiscal year. The Joint Economic Committee reviews the current services budget outlook and reports its evaluation to Congress by Dec. 31.

As under existing law, the President submits his revised federal budget to Congress about Jan. 20. In addition to the customary budget totals and breakdowns, however, the act required the budget document to include a list of existing tax expenditures—revenues lost to the Treasury through preferential tax treatment of certain activities and income—as well as any proposed changes.

The measure also required that the budget include estimates of costs for programs whose funds were required to be appropriated one year in advance before they were obligated. Thus the budget would include projections for spending during fiscal 1980, for example, of funds provided under an advance appropriation requested from Congress for fiscal 1979.

Other provisions directed that the budget figures be presented in terms of national needs, agency missions and basic federal programs. The budget also has to include five-year projections of expected spending under federal programs.

Budget Office. The act established an office within Congress to provide the experts and the computers needed to absorb and analyze information that accompanied the President's budget. The act required the Congressional Budget Office to make its staff and resources available to all congressional committees and members, but with priority given to work for the House and Senate Budget Committees. (The CBO also assumed the functions and staff of the Joint Committee on Reduction of Federal Expenditures, which was abolished.)

The office is run by a director appointed for a four-year term by the Speaker of the House and the president pro tempore of the Senate. The director is paid $42,000 annually.

Budget Resolution. After reviewing the President's budget proposals—and considering the advice of the budget office and other committees—the House and Senate Budget Committees draw up a concurrent resolution outlining a tentative alternative congressional budget.

Under the law's timetable, congressional committees have until March 15 to report their budget recommendations to the budget committees. The budget office report is due on April 1.

By April 15, the budget committees must report concurrent resolutions to the House and Senate floors. By May 15, Congress must clear the initial budget resolution.

The initial resolution, a tentative budget, sets target totals for appropriation, spending, taxes, the budget surplus or deficit and the federal debt.

Within those overall targets, the resolution breaks down appropriations and spending among the functional categories—defense, health, income security and so forth—used in the President's budget document.

The resolution also includes any recommended changes in tax revenues and in the level of the federal debt ceiling. If Congress so chooses, the first resolution also could direct that appropriations bills and bills creating federal entitlement programs when cleared by Congress be withheld from the President until Congress had completed its budget reconciliation process in September.

The budget targets are broken down in another way reflecting the congressional committee structure once House and Senate conferees reach agreement on the final version of the first budget resolution. In their statement on the conference agreement, the conferees allocate the targets among committees in Congress that would consider legislation providing the funds to be spent within the total and functional category targets.

The Appropriations Committees, which would be considering the bulk of spending proposals requiring appropriations, would further subdivide their allocations among the 13 subcommittees that handle appropriations for different departments and agencies.

Each committee also would allocate its share of the spending targets between controllable spending and spending that was beyond immediate congressional control.

Appropriations Process. Once enacted, the budget resolution guides but does not bind Congress as it acts on appropriations bills and other measures providing budget authority for spending on federal programs.

No measure appropriating funds, changing taxes or the public debt level or creating a new entitlement program committing the government to pay certain benefits may be considered on the floor before adoption of the first budget resolution. In the Senate, however, that prohibition may be waived by majority vote.

To clear the way for prompt action on appropriations before the fiscal year begins, the law requires that all bills authorizing appropriations be reported by May 15, the deadline for enactment of the budget resolution. That requirement may be waived, however, by majority vote in both the House and the Senate.

There are two exemptions from the May 15 deadline for reporting authorizing legislation: for Social Security legislation, dealing with a variety of trust funds and welfare programs, and for entitlement legislation that could not be considered on the floor until the budget resolution had been cleared.

Starting with programs for fiscal 1977, the law requires the administration to make requests for authorizing legislation a year in advance.

Under its terms, the administration would have to submit its requests by May 15 for the fiscal year following the fiscal year that would start on Oct. 1. That would give congressional committees a full year to study the requests before the following May 15 deadline for reporting authorization bills for the fiscal year in question.

For example, for fiscal 1977, which would start on Oct. 1, 1976, authorization requests would be submitted by May 15, 1975, and authorization bills reported by May 15, 1976.

After enactment of the budget resolution, Congress begins processing the 13 regular appropriations bills for the upcoming fiscal year through its customary appropriations process: House Appropriations subcommittee and full committee action, House floor action, Senate Appropriations subcommittee and full committee action, Senate floor action and conference action.

The law directed the House Appropriations Committee to try to complete action on all appropriations measures and submit a report summarizing its decisions before reporting the first bill for floor action.

All appropriations bills have to be cleared by the middle of September—no later than the seventh day after Labor Day. That deadline also applies to final action on entitlement bills. The deadline may be waived, however, for any appropriation bill whose consideration was delayed because Congress had not acted promptly on necessary authorizing legislation.

If Congress so provides in its initial budget resolution, appropriations and entitlement bills may be held up after final action on conference reports. Under that procedure, no appropriations bills would be sent to the President until Congress had completed a September reconciliation of its initial budget targets with its separate spending measures.

Reconciliation. In mid-September, after finishing action on all appropriations and other spending bills, Congress takes another overall look at its work on the budget.

By Sept. 15, Congress must adopt a second budget resolution that could either affirm or revise the budget targets set by the initial resolution. If separate congressional decisions taken during the appropriations process do not fit the final budget resolution totals, the resolution may dictate changes in appropriations (both for the upcoming fiscal year or carried over from previous fiscal years), entitlements, revenues and the debt limit.

The resolution would direct the committees that had jurisdiction over those matters to report legislation making the required changes.

If all the required changes fell within the jurisdiction of one committee in each house—appropriations changes that the Appropriations Committees would consider, for example—those committees then would report a reconciliation bill to the floor.

If the changes involved two committees—appropriations changes by the Appropriations Committees and tax changes by the House Ways and Means and Senate Finance Committees, for example—those committees would submit recommendations to the Budget Committees. The Budget Committees then would combine the recommendations without substantial change and report them to the floor as a reconciliation bill.

If Congress withholds all appropriations and entitlement bills from the President, reconciliation may be accomplished by passage of a resolution directing the House clerk and secretary of the Senate to make necessary changes in the bills previously cleared. A reconciliation bill still could be needed, however, to change tax levels or other provisions already enacted into law.

Backdoor Spending. The law attempted to bring most forms of new backdoor spending programs under the appropriations process, but existing backdoor programs remained outside that process. The bill required annual appropriations of funds for spending from new contract authority or borrowing authority programs. *(See box, p. 125)*

Contract authority permits federal officials to enter into contracts obligating the federal government to make certain payments before the money is appropriated; borrowing authority permits federal officials to incur indebtedness in advance of appropriations to pay back the money.

Entitlement programs commit the federal government to pay benefits to all eligible recipients. Because the government can not control the number of eligible recipients—at least without tinkering with eligibility standards—it has little control under existing procedures over total spending on these programs. Congress has no choice but to appropriate the funds required to meet the obligations.

In devising special procedures for entitlement programs, the act relied on the initial budget resolution's allocations of spending limits for guidelines on how much spending would be permissible on new programs.

Under the new procedures, a bill reported by an authorizing committee to establish a new entitlement program would be referred to the Appropriations Committee if the amount of the appropriations authorized by the

Impoundment Law Creates New Headaches in Congress

One part of the new congressional budget law was a direct product of former President Nixon's repeated attempts not to spend money Congress had appropriated. That effort—Title X of PL 93-344—may have produced even more headaches for Congress.

There is disagreement, even within Congress, about exactly what Title X was intended to accomplish and did accomplish. But there is considerable agreement that it created additional paperwork that often unnecessarily consumes staff time. Congressional and executive branch employees who must deal with Title X generally agree that the compromise language in the title is vague in many respects and is without sufficient legislative history to explain Congress' intent.

Rescissions and Deferrals

Under current interpretation of the law, there are two methods for Congress to review the President's proposal to delay or cancel spending—actions that were called impoundment during President Nixon's days but were given other designations under the 1974 budget law.

If the President wants to withhold funds temporarily, perhaps because immediate expenditure would be impractical, he can propose to defer their spending until a later time. The President's deferral stands unless overturned by a resolution of either the Senate or House.

If the President believes money should not be spent at all, he may propose a rescission. In this case, both the House and Senate must approve the action within 45 days. If the two houses do not act, the President must release the funds at the end of the 45 days. Some congressional critics see this as one fault in Title X because the President can block spending for almost seven weeks; Congress cannot force the expenditures to be made during that period.

Other Criticisms

But the criticisms and the questions go far beyond that. A basic one is whether Title X created new authority—that is, gave the President new powers—to withhold funds and cancel or greatly delay congressionally approved spending. The other side of this issue is whether Title X and other parts of the new congressional budget law are eroding the President's fundamental power to direct and control federal spending.

The genesis of these disputes was in the various anti-impoundment proposals in Congress in 1973 and 1974 that led to a hybrid compromise in Title X. The House asserted that Title X created new authority for fund withholding and allowed the President to propose deferrals for reasons other than administrative housekeeping, but gave Congress the mechanisms to overturn these actions. Deferring spending for purely managerial reasons was allowed under the old government budgeting procedures that PL 93-344 replaced.

The Senate, on the other hand, argued that Title X did not allow the President to defer spending for policy reasons. The new law gave the General Accounting Office, an arm of Congress, the power to review presidential proposals and rule on their appropriateness. After studying this dispute, the GAO's Comptroller General, Elmer B. Staats, in late 1974 supported the House view of the matter. The Senate, however, was unconvinced and the issue continued.

The alternative argument was that the President's basic budgetary powers were being whittled away. The criticism was that under Title X previously hidden budget juggling maneuvers of the executive branch were now exposed to public and congressional view and therefore to scrutiny. This exposure, along with Congress' power to block presidential anti-spending proposals, worried some observers—generally officials in the executive branch. They feared that Title X, along with other new congressional authority provided in PL 93-344, might tip spending power toward Congress by destroying presidential control over the federal budget. The changes, these critics argued, encourage executive agencies and departments to develop close ties with congressional appropriations subcommittees that had the power to overturn presidential decisions on spending. "What we're talking about here is congressional government—and chaos," one executive branch budget official said.

Another criticism, probably the complaint most often heard in the first year of Title X operation, was that the requirements of the law were generating a mountain of paperwork. The complaint was that Title X requires formal action on administrative matters and other minutiae that were never brought through the system in the past. For example, Title X requires executive branch budget officials to report to Congress many comparatively trivial amounts of money, some totaling only a few thousand dollars, that are withheld purely for reasons of managerial efficiency. A GAO spokesman estimated that as much as 50 per cent of all deferrals fell into this category.

---

bill exceeded the authorizing committee's allocation set out after adoption of the congressional budget resolution.

The Appropriations Committee then would have 15 days to consider the measure and report an amendment putting a limit on appropriations for the new program. If the Appropriations Committee did not act within 15 days, the measure would go on the calendar as reported.

To tie consideration of entitlement bills closely to the budget-making process, the act prohibited floor action on entitlement bills before adoption of the first budget resolution. And no entitlement legislation could go into effect before the start of the fiscal year, making the spending it provided subject to revision in the reconciliation stage.

Exempted from the act's backdoor spending procedures were all Social Security trust funds, all trust funds that received 90 per cent or more of their financing from designated taxes rather than from general revenues, general revenue sharing funds, insured and guaranteed loans, federal government and independent corporations and gifts to the government.

Impoundment. The act prescribed two different procedures for Congress to deal with impoundments (a tactic used by Presidents to withhold expenditures of previously appropriated funds): one for impoundments that simply delayed the spending of funds and a tougher procedure for impoundments made to cut total spending or to terminate programs.

For impoundments that merely deferred spending, Congress could force the President to release the funds if either the House or the Senate passed a resolution calling for their expenditure. No time limit for congressional action was set.

For impoundments that terminate programs or cut total spending for fiscal policy reasons, the act requires congressional action to rescind the previous appropriations action providing the funds. Unless both the House and Senate pass a rescission bill within 45 days, the President must spend the money.

To remove language in existing law that had been cited as justification for presidential impoundments, the act repeals a clause in the Anti-Deficiency Act of 1950 allowing the executive branch to withhold funds from obligation because of "other developments" as well as to save money or take account of changing requirements or improved efficiency.

To keep Congress informed on impoundment actions, the bill requires the President to report deferrals or to request rescissions. If the comptroller general finds that impoundments have been made without reports to Congress, he may report the impoundments himself and Congress then may act to force release of the funds.

If a President refuses to comply with a congressional action overruling an impoundment, the comptroller general may go to court for an order requiring spending of the funds.

Operation of the System

At the beginning of 1975, many observers predicted that the system would collapse under the weight of congressional power rivalries and political logrolling. By the end of the year, however, it appeared that the doubters had misjudged the determination of key members of Congress to make the system work.[69] Among those key players were Sens. Edmund S. Muskie (D Maine) and Henry Bellmon (R Okla.) and Reps. Brock Adams (D Wash.) and Parren J. Mitchell (D Md.). Muskie and Adams were chairmen of the Senate and House Budget Committees.

As a result of their determination, Congress in December cleared H Con Res 466, which specified for the first time the total size of the federal budget. Passage of the measure, called the second concurrent resolution on the budget, limited future congressional action on spending and revenue bills. Subsequent legislation that punctures the spending limits, creates new future spending authority beyond that authorized in the resolution or violates the revenue requirements could be ruled out of order in either chamber and thus be killed.

The resolution was an act of self-discipline. It took effect without the President's signature and could be revised at any time Congress saw fit.

The resolution did not include use of all the budget control devices Congress created in 1974. But it invoked the basic ones. It put into effect binding spending and revenue controls that had not been scheduled to take effect until a year later.

The resolution passed by Congress Dec. 12 set a ceiling of $374.9-billion on spending and a floor of $300.8-billion under revenues in fiscal 1976. The resulting deficit of $74.1-billion was the largest in history. It astounded fiscal conservatives and displeased some pro-spending liberals who believed Congress should do more to pump up the economy and reduce unemployment. In spite of these differences, key conservatives and liberals in both houses came to the rescue of the new budgeting system at critical points and prevented it from being wrecked the first year in operation.

Problems Ahead. Although the system appeared to work the first year, there remained pitfalls for the future that could wreck it.

Probably the most serious was the reluctance of ideological and political blocs in Congress to accept the discipline of budget controls when that interfered with their own goals.

The ceilings themselves contained a large hole. Spending could exceed the limits because of unforeseen rises in the "uncontrollable" parts of the federal budget such as Social Security and unemployment payments.

In 1975, Congress enacted the ceiling almost three months after the deadline that had been set for approval of the resolution. That slippage raised doubts about whether Congress could stay on schedule in the future when the entire system would be in operation.

Nevertheless, participants in the process were pleased. Muskie described the $300.8-billion ceiling as an "historic leap forward." He added, "This congressional budget control is in force a full year earlier than contemplated. What was intended as a trial year has turned out to be a meaningful implementation of the Budget Act."

Operation in 1975. The Budget Act did not make the new process mandatory until fiscal year 1977, beginning Oct. 1, 1976. But it did permit earlier use of the mechanism for the fiscal 1976 budget.

In order to acquaint Congress with the procedures, the budget committees and the congressional leadership decided to implement major parts of the Budget Act for fiscal 1976. But they feared that the new timetable would be disruptive enough in itself, without the added burden of expected heated disputes over division of spending among various budget programs.

Thus, the most significant part of the 1975 implementation plan, announced March 3, involved the 16 individual areas of the budget, called "functional categories." Under the plan, the first budget resolution, setting targets, was to be enacted as provided in the law. But it was to contain only the five total budget figures: outlays, budget authority, revenue, deficit and the amount of the public debt. Spending targets for the 16 individual categories, such as defense and health, were to be left out of the resolution.

The March plan also called for adoption of the second resolution no later than Sept. 15 "if practicable." The second measure was to replace the budget targets with binding limits. But it was not to contain ceilings for the individual categories. Later, in July, the Budget Committees announced that they had decided to proceed with the second resolution.

Deadlines the committees decided to omit included the April 1 CBO submission to the panels of a report on fiscal policy and budget alternatives; the May 15 deadline by which time the legislative committees had to report all program authorizations for the upcoming year; and the deadline for Congress to complete action on all spending bills seven days after Labor Day.

All these deadlines were important to bringing appropriations and authorization activities in line with the new budget mechanism. But the committees were afraid of imposing too much reform too quickly. "We want flexibility as we come to the first political crunch in this process, to avoid creating abrasions or brittleness," one Senate staffer said. The committees decided to omit the functional category ceilings from the resolutions for practical as well as political reasons. The budget process gave rise to a technical problem that Congress had never before had to concern itself with: the different ways in which the President and Congress traditionally viewed the budget.

The Office of Management and Budget (OMB) groups government spending programs into the 16 functional categories. These include, for example, "Income Security," which comprises such programs as Social Security and unemployment benefits; "Community and Regional Development," including urban renewal, housing and some rural development programs; and "General Government," a catch-all category that contains the legislative and executive branch budgets.

Congress appropriates funds through 15 spending bills, most of which also cover a variety of programs. But the appropriations bills and the functional categories do not match. One of OMB's categories may include all or parts of four or five different appropriations bills, while any single appropriations bill may comprise parts of six or seven of the OMB categories.

The tedious job of matching bills with categories is called "crosswalking." It is necessary if the targets and ceilings Congress imposes on the categories are to be split into targets for individual bills.

Budget Committee Chairmen Muskie and Adams attributed their decision not to include the functional categories in the fiscal 1976 resolutions primarily to this crosswalk problem. They noted that the process would be easier the following year, since they then would have a list of how the bills fit into the functional categories.

In deciding to make 1975 more than just a trial run of the procedures, the budget committees began work on the fiscal 1976 budget with several other big handicaps. They were operating without benefit of the current services budget and without a functioning Congressional Budget Office (the agency did not begin providing useful information until well into the year). Still another problem was that by early spring the traditional appropriations process had already begun functioning without the Budget Committees—or the new budget process.

The most threatening problem the process faced in 1975, however, and the one that nearly torpedoed it, was the state of the economy. Congress had to vote on a budget deficit while the nation was in a deep recession. "They were required to vote on the largest deficit in history," CBO Director Alice M. Rivlin said. "They had never voted on a deficit before."

Functional Categories. While leaving the functional categories out of the resolutions on which Congress voted, the Budget Committees decided to include targets for each category in the reports accompanying the resolutions. The category targets were not binding but showed how the committees arrived at the spending totals. They also were starting points for the task of setting guidelines for individual spending bills.

After passage of the first resolution, the functional targets became a key element in the appropriations process. The House Appropriations Committee turned repeatedly to the conference report on the first resolution for guidance as it processed individual spending bills. "The question of whether a bill is above or below the resolution" came up "all the time," according to Adams. "The chairmen call me up and ask me."

Muskie kept the report's figures constantly before the Senate when bills reached the floor for votes. "We treat the resolution as if it did have functional categories," a Senate aide said.

Timetables. Congress adopted the first resolution May 14—one day ahead of schedule. The measure (H Con Res 218) set targets of $367-billion for total spending, and $298.2-billion for revenues, with a resulting deficit of $68.8-billion.

On March 29, Ford had announced on nationwide television that he was determined to adhere to a $60-billion deficit. But the Budget Committees insisted that their higher deficit was due almost entirely to more realistic spending estimates. Although the resolution passed the Senate by a comfortable margin, it ran up against considerable opposition in the House, where it squeaked through on a 200-196 vote.

The two Budget Committees, along with the Congressional Budget Office, spent the interim period between the first and second resolutions tracking various spending measures.

CBO and the Senate Budget Committee issued separate scorekeeping reports showing how congressional action compared with the first resolution. Most bills came in at or below the targets.

During the same period, the Budget Committees divided into "task forces," which essentially served as subcommittees. The House's seven panels and the Senate's four reflected the larger House membership as well as the House committee's somewhat more detailed approach to functional categories. Muskie had maintained that the committees should not deal too explicitly with the categories so as not to preempt the appropriations subcommittees in recommending individual pieces of legislation.

The task force system produced some uncongressional terminology and protocols, particularly in the Senate. Instead of hearings, the Senate task forces called their sessions "seminars." In order to avoid the atmosphere of confrontation that often accompanies hearings, members of the committee and witnesses shared long tables arranged more like conferences. The members' regular platform seats were taken over by staff members and the press.

The Senate adopted the final version of the second resolution containing the firm spending ceiling Dec. 11 by a comfortable 74-19 margin.

In the House, the coalition of Republicans, and conservative Democrats opposed to the size of the deficit combined with liberal Democrats who wanted the budget to reflect more stimulus to come within two votes of defeating the resolution, 189-187.

Spending in almost all categories in the second resolution rose over the first-resolution targets, adding up to a total increase of $7.9-billion in outlays. Again, the committees attributed the rises almost entirely to re-estimates of "uncontrollable" budget items. "This is why we met all the targets and the outlay figure went up," Adams explained.

As approved, the resolution contained non-binding targets for spending, revenue, budget authority, deficit and the public debt for the transition quarter. That was the period between July 1 and Sept. 30, 1976, when the government switches to a new fiscal year beginning Oct. 1. As part of a key compromise between the House and Senate versions of the resolution, Congress agreed to replace these targets with binding limits during the spring of 1976.

Outlook. The budget mechanism's worst enemy in 1976 might be Congress itself. Political battles were sure to take place over setting budget priorities in the 16 functional categories. And, having missed the Sept. 15 deadline for action on the second resolution in 1975 by three months, Congress seemed headed for trouble in meeting the full set of deadlines that would be operating in 1976.

"What we've got here is a kind of timetable that nobody's ever lived by before, the kind of process that was never created before, and an attempt to impose this on an institution that's almost 200 years old and that's generated considerable momentum and habits over those years," Muskie told Congressional Quarterly.

The National Debt: A Way To Attack Spending

Through the years, and particularly since the New Deal days of the 1930s, the national debt and congressional control over it have been controversial subjects. The debt has become increasingly a political issue as compensatory fiscal policies and budget deficits have gained popular acceptance. Growth of the national debt gave legislators and other public officials a convenient opening to express their views on government spending; but expansion of the debt had little effect in curbing the spending.

Constitutional Authority. The Constitution, in Article I, Section 8, Clause 2, gives Congress the power "to borrow money on the credit of the United States." This is a very broad power.[70] Ogg and Ray's *Introduction to American Government* noted that the "power to borrow not only is expressly conferred in the Constitution, but is one of the very few federal powers entirely unencumbered by restrictions—with the result that Congress may borrow from any lenders, for any purposes, in any amounts, on any terms, and with or without provision for the repayment of loans, with or without interest."[71] Ogg and Ray noted also that the United States has no constitutional debt limit, whereas many state constitutions and state charters for counties and local governments impose debt ceilings. The United States has had a statutory debt ceiling for many decades *(see below)*, but the ceiling can be easily altered by Congress and, in fact, has been raised repeatedly—although seldom without an intense political fight in Congress.

Composition of the Debt

Debt has been incurred by the federal government when it has found it necessary to spend more than it has collected in tax and other forms of revenue. When expenditures outstrip revenues, the deficit must be made up by borrowing. Through much of the nation's history, a surplus resulting from an excess of revenues over expenditures has been used, at least in part, to reduce outstanding debt. Since the long string of federal budget deficits began in fiscal 1931, there have been budget surpluses in only seven years. It was during this period that the bulk of the national debt (estimated to reach $605.9-billion by the end of fiscal 1976) was incurred.

The debt consists of various types of obligations. David J. Ott and Attiat F. Ott in *Federal Budget Policy* gave the following definitions: "The federal debt consists of direct obligations or debts of the U.S. Treasury and obligations of federal government enterprises or agencies. It is...broken down into 'public debt'—that part issued by the Treasury—and 'agency debt'—that part issued by federal agencies. The public debt consists of issues (that is, bonds, notes and bills), which are generally sold to the public (some are held by federal agencies and trust funds), and 'special issues,' which are held only by government agencies and trust funds. Of the issues sold to the public, some are 'marketable,' that is, they are traded on securities markets, and some are 'nonmarketable' and cannot be traded (for example, U.S. savings bonds). The latter may, however, be redeemed in cash or converted into another issue."[72]

Philosophy Prior to 1930s

Throughout most of the nation's history, the principal concern of government in regard to budget policy was to assure that revenues were sufficient to meet expenditure requirements. This philosophy, which in application meant an approximate balance between receipts and outlays, was generally accepted from the beginning until the early 1930s.

Lewis H. Kimmel wrote in *Federal Budget and Fiscal Policy, 1789-1958:* "From the beginning of our national history, ideas in public finance have been influenced by the unfolding of events. At the outset acceptance of the balanced budget philosophy was facilitated by the adverse financial experience during the Revolutionary War and under the Articles of Confederation. There was an awareness that the public credit is a valuable resource, especially in an emergency. The experience of the preceding fifteen years suggested to Hamilton and others that the preservation of the public credit depended on the consolidation of existing indebtedness and the provision of adequate revenues for debt service. The thought that the interests of the new nation would be best served if Hamilton's ideas were adopted was soon translated into policy."[73]

Kimmel pointed out that three key ideas were generally accepted by federal officials and economists alike during the period leading up to the Civil War: (1) a low level of public expenditures was desirable; (2) the federal budget should be balanced in time of peace; and (3) the federal debt should be reduced and eventually extinguished. "These ideas," he observed, "were a reflection of views that were deeply rooted in the social fabric."[74]

The Civil War, like other major wars of modern times, resulted in a much enlarged national debt. The reported debt in 1866 amounted to almost $2.8-billion in contrast to less than $90.6-million in 1861. The debt was gradually

(Continued on p. 138)

Federal Receipts and Outlays

(Selected Fiscal Years, 1792-1976*)

Fiscal Year	Receipts	Outlays	Surplus or Deficit
1792	$ 3,669,960	$ 5,079,532	$ − 1,409,572
1800	10,848,749	10,786,075	62,674
1810	9,384,215	8,156,510	1,227,705
1815	15,729,024	32,708,139	− 16,979,115
1816	47,677,671	30,586,691	17,090,980
1820	17,880,670	18,260,627	− 379,957
1830	24,844,116	15,143,066	9,701,050
1835	35,430,087	17,572,813	17,857,274
1840	19,480,115	24,317,579	− 4,837,464
1850	43,603,439	39,543,492	4,059,947
1860	56,064,608	63,130,598	− 7,065,990
1865	333,714,605	1,297,555,224	− 963,840,619
1866	558,032,620	520,809,417	37,223,203
1870	411,255,477	309,653,561	101,601,916
1880	333,526,611	267,642,958	65,883,653
1890	403,080,984	318,040,711	85,040,273
1900	567,240,852	520,860,847	46,380,005
1910	675,511,715	693,617,065	− 18,105,350
1915	683,417,319**	746,093,294	− 62,675,975
1917	1,100,500,109	1,953,857,065	− 853,356,956
1918	3,645,239,790	12,677,359,396	− 9,032,119,606
1919	5,130,042,438	18,492,665,257	− 13,362,622,819
1920	6,648,898,325	6,357,676,777	291,221,548
1930	4,057,884,142	3,320,211,324	737,672,818
1932	1,923,891,824	4,659,181,532	− 2,735,289,708
1940	5,137,249,771	9,055,268,931	− 3,918,019,161
1943	21,947,283,157	79,367,713,522	− 57,420,430,365
1945	44,362,020,944	98,302,937,069	− 53,940,916,126
1946	39,649,870,986	60,326,041,595	− 20,676,170,609
1950	36,421,934,577	39,544,036,935	− 3,122,102,357
1955	65,468,612,716	68,509,184,178**	− 3,040,571,462
1960	92,492,109,550	92,223,353,625	268,755,925
1965	116,833,423,592	118,429,745,187	− 1,596,321,595
1967	149,552,405,078	158,254,256,640	− 8,701,851,561
1968	153,671,422,120	178,832,655,042	− 25,161,232,923
1969	187,792,336,889	184,548,168,542	3,236,294,206
1970	193,743,250,789	196,587,785,632	− 2,844,534,843
1971	188,391,860,086	211,425,028,212	− 23,033,168,126
1972	208,648,558,730	231,875,854,081	− 23,227,295,351
1973	232,225,471,658	246,525,985,309	− 14,300,513,651
1974	264,932,400,526	268,391,983,133	− 3,459,582,607
1975 est.#	278,750,000,000	313,446,000,000	− 34,696,000,000
1976 est.#	297,520,000,000	349,372,000,000	− 51,852,000,000

*Fiscal years ending Dec. 31, 1790-1842; June 30 since 1843.
**Figures from these dates on are for net, rather than total, receipts and outlays.
#1975 and 1976 estimates are from the Budget of the U.S. Government for fiscal 1976.

Source: *Statistical Appendix to Report of the Secretary of the Treasury for Fiscal Year 1974.*

Public Debt of the United States

(Selected Fiscal Years, 1790-1974*)

Fiscal Year	Total Gross Public Debt	Fiscal Year	Total Gross Public Debt	Gross Debt Per Capita
1790	$ 75,463,477	1915	$ 1,191,264,068	$ 11.85
1800	83,038,051	1918	12,455,225,365	119.13
1810	48,005,588	1919	25,484,506,160	242.56
1815	127,334,934	1920	24,299,321,467	228.23
1820	89,987,428	1930	16,185,309,831	131.51
1830	39,123,192	1935	28,700,892,625	225.55
1835	37,513	1940	42,967,531,038	325.23
1840	5,250,876	1945	258,682,187,410	1,848.60
1850	63,452,774	1946	269,422,099,173	1,905.42
1860	64,843,831	1948	252,292,246,513	1,720.71
1865	2,677,929,012	1950	257,357,352,351	1,696.67
1866	2,755,763,929	1955	274,374,222,803	1,660.11
1870	2,436,453,269	1960	286,330,760,848	1,584.70
1880	2,090,908,872	1965	317,273,898,984	1,630.46
1890	1,122,396,584	1967	326,220,937,795	1,638.33
1900	1,263,416,913	1969	353,720,253,841	1,740.61
1910	1,146,939,969	1970	370,918,706,950	1,805.89
		1971	398,129,744,456	1,922.78
		1972	427,260,460,940	2,045.86
		1973	458,141,605,312	2,177.52
		1974	475,059,815,732	2,241.81

*Fiscal years ending Dec. 31, 1790-1842; June 30 since 1843.

Source: Statistical Appendix to Report of the Secretary of the Treasury for Fiscal Year 1974.

(Continued from p. 136)

reduced after the war to a low of $961-million in 1893. However, after the Civil War, there was less concern about eliminating the outstanding debt; increasingly, the emphasis was on servicing the debt in an orderly manner. Proposals to liquidate it became fewer and fewer.

From the post-Civil-War low point in 1893, the debt increased very slowly for half a dozen years and then hovered between $1.1-billion and $1.2-billion until 1917, when the United States entered World War I. The debt jumped from just under $3-billion in fiscal 1917 to a peak of $25.5-billion at the end of fiscal 1919. In the 1920s the debt receded steadily, year by year, down to $16.2-billion at the end of fiscal 1930.

Rise of Debt

In 1930 and following years, the nation was faced with the problems of the Great Depression. Kimmel noted of the early years of the Depression: "A concerted effort was made by the President and the leadership of both parties in Congress to adhere to the balanced-budget philosophy. Yet a balanced federal budget was almost impossible to attain—the annually balanced-budget dogma in effect gave way to necessity. Alternatives were soon suggested, and within a few years what came to be known as compensatory fiscal theory gained numerous adherents."[75]

The practice of using the federal budget to help solve national economic problems was increasingly accepted. Budget deficits and a rapidly increasing national debt were the result. The debt rose to nearly $50-billion—almost twice the World War I peak—at the end of fiscal 1941. Then came Pearl Harbor. The debt passed the $100-billion mark in fiscal 1943 and exceeded $269-billion in fiscal 1946. No steady reduction followed World War II. The debt total fluctuated for a few years but then began a new rise which took it past the World War II peak in fiscal 1954, past $300-billion in fiscal 1963 and all the way to $475-billion at the end of fiscal 1974.

Congress and the Debt

The first overall debt ceiling was established Sept. 25, 1917, by the Second Liberty Bond Act, which fixed a limit of $11.5-billion. By 1945, Congress had amended the act 16 times, and the ceiling had been lifted to $300-billion. In June 1946, the high World War II limit was reduced to a "permanent" $275-billion ceiling. However, as Congress continued to vote more appropriations than taxes, and the executive branch to spend more than it took in, budget deficits resulted and the debt continued to rise. There followed perforce repeated ceiling increases, almost all of which were accompanied by strong partisan activity in

Congress and much sermonizing on the evils of federal expenditures and indebtedness.[76]

Although Congress actually had little choice but to increase the statutory debt limit, the heated debates—primarily in the House—suggested that the events were milestones in public financial affairs. The controversy over rising debt ceilings flowed essentially from the broader issue of government spending. The proponents of a statutory debt ceiling saw the ceiling as a form of expenditure control. They believed that a firm commitment by Congress not to increase the debt limit would force a halt in spending, especially spending that exceeded the tax revenues.

Officials in the executive branch responsible for paying the government's bills, as well as many members—indeed, a majority—of Congress, were convinced that a debt ceiling could not control expenditures. Throughout the postwar period, Secretaries of the Treasury expressed their opposition to use of the debt ceiling for that purpose.

One characteristic aspect of the debt-limit debate in postwar years was that the opposition to raising the limit was led by conservatives who sought to reduce government spending. But expenditures during these years—even during the Republican Eisenhower administration—showed a steady increase. The increase reflected not only the adoption of new government programs but also a buildup of political pressures on Congress that made it difficult to cut and relatively easy to add to existing levels of expenditures.

When it came down to the actual voting, Congress always raised the debt ceiling enough to enable the government to meet its financial obligations. But the attendant congressional debate gave members so inclined an excellent opportunity to throw the spotlight on the public indebtedness and government spending.

Footnotes

1. George B. Galloway, *The Legislative Process in Congress* (Thomas Y. Crowell Co., 1955), p. 91.
2. C. Herman Pritchett, *The American Constitution* (McGraw-Hill Book Co. Inc., 1959), p. 233.
3. For a discussion, see Daniel T. Selko, *The Federal Financial System* (The Brookings Institution, 1940), pp. 30-37.
4. See Pritchett, *The American Constitution*, pp. 420-42.
5. Selko, *The Federal Financial System*, pp. 38-41.
6. Lewis H. Kimmel, *Federal Budget and Fiscal Policy 1789-1958* (Brookings Institution, 1959), p. 63.
7. Frederic A. Ogg and P. Orman Ray, *Introduction to American Government* (Appleton-Century-Crofts Inc., 1951), p. 518.
8. For a history of tariff legislation, see Selko, *The Federal Financial System*, pp. 60, 557-72.
9. Statistical Appendix to the Annual Report of the Secretary of the Treasury for fiscal 1974 (Government Printing Office, 1975).
10. For a discussion of tariff protection, see Ogg and Ray, *Introduction to American Government*, p. 518.
11. William Starr Myers, *The Republican Party: A History* (Century Co., 1928), p. 358.
12. See Paul Webbink, "Deadlocks in Tariff Legislation," *Editorial Research Reports*, Nov. 1, 1929, p. 876.
13. Myers, *The Republican Party*, p. 359.
14. See Webbink, "Deadlocks in Tariff Legislation."
15. *Ibid.*, p. 873.
16. Louis Fisher, *President and Congress* (The Free Press, 1972), pp. 140, 142.
17. Webbink, "Deadlocks in Tariff Legislation," p. 867.
18. Kirk H. Porter and Donald Bruce Johnson, *National Party Platforms 1890-1968* (University of Illinois Press, 1970), pp. 331, 344.
19. *The Public Papers and Addresses of Franklin D. Roosevelt*, Vol. III (Random House, 1938), p. 114.
20. Louis Fisher, *President and Congress*, p. 152. For background, see Congressional Quarterly, *Congress and the Nation*, Vol. 1 (1965), pp. 187-92, 203-05.
21. For details, see Congressional Quarterly, *Congress and the Nation*, Vol. III (1973), pp. 119 ff.
22. Congressional Quarterly, 1974 *Almanac*, pp. 553-62.
23. For a concise summary of tax policy, see Ogg and Ray, *Introduction to American Government*, pp. 514-26.
24. For background, see Joseph A. Pechman, *Federal Tax Policy* (The Brookings Institution, 1966), pp. 247-52.
25. Pritchett, *The American Constitution*, p. 235.
26. Pechman, *Federal Tax Policy*, p. 248.
27. *Ibid.*
28. For background, see Pechman, pp. 249-50.
29. *Ibid.*, pp. 250-52.
30. Congressional Quarterly, *Congress and the Nation*, Vol. III, p. 79.

31. Pechman, *Federal Tax Policy*, pp. 252-54.
32. *Ibid.*, p. 254.
33. Background on tax bills in Congress, see Ray Blough, *The Federal Taxing Process* (Prentice-Hall Inc., 1952), pp. 61-91, and Pechman, *Federal Tax Policy*, pp. 32-50.
34. Congressional Quarterly, 1975 *Weekly Report*, p. 2410.
35. *Ibid.*, p. 419.
36. *Ibid.*, p. 2440.
37. For background, see Congressional Quarterly, *Congress and the Nation*, Vol. II (1969), pp. 149-53.
38. Congressional Quarterly, 1969 *Almanac*, pp. 589-649.
39. Congressional Quarterly, *Congress and the Nation*, Vol. III, pp. 78-85.
40. For details, see Congressional Quarterly, *Congress and the Nation*, Vol. I, pp. 397-442.
41. For background on tax policy 1965-68 and details on the surcharge, see Congressional Quarterly, *Congress and the Nation*, Vol. II, pp. 141-79.
42. For a summary, see Congressional Quarterly, 1975 *Almanac*, pp. 95, 133.
43. Pechman, *Federal Tax Policy*, p. 49.
44. *Ibid.*
45. *Ibid.*, p. 50.
46. *Ibid.*
47. For proposals to limit taxing power, see Blough, *The Federal Taxing Process*, pp. 12, 22-27.
48. Pritchett, *The American Constitution*, p. 246.
49. On spending power limits, general welfare, see Selko, *The Federal Financial System*, pp. 36-37; Ogg and Ray, *Introduction to American Government*, pp. 518-19; Pritchett, *The American Constitution*, pp. 245-48.
50. See Stephen Horn, *Unused Power: The Work of the Senate Committee on Appropriations* (Brookings Institution, 1970); and Jeffrey L. Pressman, *House vs. Senate* (Yale University Press, 1966).
51. Fisher, *President and Congress*, pp. 92-93.
52. Kimmel, *Federal Budget and Fiscal Policy*, p. 2.
53. *Ibid.*, p. 3.
54. *Ibid.*, p. 4.
55. *Ibid.* For additional background on spending powers, see Fisher, *President and Congress*, pp. 85-100; and *Presidential Spending Power*, pp. 9-35; Selko, *The Federal Financial System*, pp. 77-102.
56. On growth of expenditures, see Kimmel, *Federal Budget and Fiscal Policy*, pp. 4-5; and Ogg and Ray, *Introduction to American Government*, pp. 512-14.
57. Fisher, *Presidential Spending Power*, p. 39.
58. Richard E. Neustadt, "Presidency and Legislation: The Growth of Central Clearance," 48 *American Political Science Review*, 1954, pp. 641 ff.
59. For background on 1921 act and developments, see Kimmel, *Federal Budget and Fiscal Policy*; Ogg and Ray, *Introduction to*

American Government, pp. 505-12; Fisher, *Presidential Spending Power,* pp. 36-58; and Selko, *The Federal Financial System,* pp. 101-31. For modern procedures, see David J. Ott and Attiat F. Ott, *Federal Budget Policy,* revised edition (Brookings Institution, 1969).

60. On Nixon changes, see Fisher, *Presidential Spending Power,* pp. 46-59.

61. Ott and Ott, *Federal Budget Policy,* p. 41. See also Richard E. Brown, *The GAO* (University of Tennessee Press, 1970).

62. For a thorough discussion of the process, see Richard F. Fenno Jr., *The Power of the Purse* (Little, Brown and Co. Inc., 1966), Pressman, *House vs. Senate;* Robert Ash Wallace, *Congressional Control of Federal Spending* (Wayne State University Press, 1960); and Horn, *Unused Power.*

63. Congressional Quarterly, 1974 *Almanac,* pp. 961-63.

64. Congressional Quarterly, 1975 *Weekly Report,* p. 2410.

65. For a discussion of current powers, see Louis Fisher, *Presidential Spending Power* (Princeton University Press, 1975).

66. For background, see Congressional Quarterly, *Congress and the Nation,* Vol. I, pp. 349, 352, 354.

67. For background, see Galloway, *The Legislative Process,* pp. 123-24; Wallace, *Congressional Control of Federal Spending,* pp. 131-36.

68. Congressional Quarterly, 1974 *Almanac,* p. 145-53.

69. The following discussion is taken from articles in Congressional Quarterly, 1975 *Almanac,* p. 916.

70. For a discussion of constitutional debt powers, see Pritchett, *The American Constitution,* pp. 248-51.

71. Ogg and Ray, *Introduction to American Government,* p. 527.

72. Ott and Ott, *Federal Budget Policy,* p. 110.

73. Kimmel, *Federal Budget and Fiscal Policy,* p. 305.

74. *Ibid.,* p. 55.

75. *Ibid.,* p. 306.

76. For background, see Congressional Quarterly, *Congress and the Nation,* Vol. I, pp. 393-5.

Selected Bibliography

Books

Blough, Ray. *The Federal Taxing Process.* Englewood Cliffs, N.J.: Prentice-Hall Inc., 1952.

Can Congress Control Spending? Proceedings of the Town Meeting on Domestic Affairs. Washington: American Enterprise Institute for Public Policy Research, 1973.

Fenno, Richard F. Jr. *The Power of the Purse: Appropriation Politics in Congress.* Boston: Little, Brown and Co. Inc., 1973.

Findley, William. *Review of the Revenue System Adopted by the First Congress.* Philadelphia: T. Dobson, 1794; reprint ed., New York: A. M. Kelley, 1971.

Fisher, Louis. *President and Congress.* New York: Free Press, 1972.

———. *Presidential Spending Power.* Princeton: Princeton University Press, 1975.

Galloway, George B. *The Legislative Process in Congress.* New York: Thomas Y. Crowell Co., 1955.

Harris, Joseph P. *Congressional Control of Administration.* Washington: Brookings Institution, 1964.

Horn, Stephen. *Unused Power: The Work of the Senate Committee on Appropriations.* Washington: Brookings Institution, 1970.

Kimmel, Lewis H. *Federal Budget and Fiscal Policy 1789-1958.* Washington: Brookings Institution, 1959.

Kirst, Michael W. *Government Without Passing Laws.* Chapel Hill: University of North Carolina Press, 1969.

MacLean, Joan C. *President and Congress: The Conflict of Powers.* Bronx: H. W. Wilson, 1955.

Manley, John F. *The Politics of Finance: The House Committee on Ways and Means.* Boston: Little, Brown & Co., 1970.

Myers, William Starr. *The Republican Party: A History.* New York: Century Co., 1928.

Ogg, Frederic A., and Ray, P. Orman. *Introduction to American Government.* New York: Appleton-Century-Crofts Inc., 1951.

Ott, David J. and Ott, Attiat F. *Federal Budget Policy.* rev. ed. Washington: Brookings Institution, 1969.

Pechman, Joseph A. *Federal Tax Policy.* rev. ed. Washington: Brookings Institution, 1971.

Pressman, Jeffrey L. *House vs. Senate: Conflict in the Appropriation Process.* New Haven: Yale University Press, 1966.

Pritchett, C. Herman. *The American Constitution.* New York: McGraw-Hill Book Co. Inc., 1959.

Saloma, John S. III. *The Responsible Use of Power.* Washington: American Enterprise Institute, 1964.

Schick, Allen. "The Battle of the Budget." In *Congress Against the President,* pp. 51-70. Edited by Harvey C. Mansfield Sr. New York: Praeger, 1975.

Selko, Daniel T. *The Federal Financial System.* Washington: Brookings Institution, 1940.

Sharkansky, Ira. *The Politics of Taxing and Spending.* New York: Bobbs-Merrill Co. Inc., 1969.

Smithies, Arthur. *The Budgeting Process in the United States.* New York: McGraw-Hill Book Co. Inc., 1955.

Wallace, Robert Ash. *Congressional Control of Federal Spending.* Detroit: Wayne State University Press, 1960.

Weidenbaum, Murray L. *Federal Budgeting, The Choice of Government Programs.* Washington: American Enterprise Institute, 1964.

Wilmerding, Lucius Jr. *The Spending Power: A History of the Efforts of Congress to Control Expenditures.* New Haven: Yale University Press, 1943.

Government Publications

President's Commission on Budget Concepts. *Report of the President's Commission on Budget Concepts.* Washington: Government Printing Office, 1967.

U.S. Congress. House. Committee on the Budget. *Congressional Budget Reform, Committee Print, July 12, 1974.* Washington: Government Printing Office, 1975.

U.S. Congress. Joint Study Committee on Budget Control. *Improving Congressional Control Over Budgetary Outlay and Receipt Totals, Report, February 7, 1973.* Washington: Government Printing Office, 1973.

U.S. Congress. Senate. *The Authority of the Senate to Originate Appropriations Bills.* S. Doc. 17, 88th Cong., 1st sess., 1963.

U.S. Congress. Senate. Committee on Government Operations. *Financial Management in the Federal Government.* S. Doc. 11, 87th Cong., 1st sess., 1961.

Congressional Investigations

The first congressional investigation, a House inquiry into an Army disaster in Indian territory, was conducted in 1792. The hearings staked out a major new area of activity that was to become one of the most controversial and highly publicized powers of Congress.

Since 1792, investigating committees of the House and the Senate have left an erratic trail, marked by some of the brightest and darkest moments in congressional annals. Investigations have led Congress into repeated confrontations with the executive and judicial branches over the constitutional separation of powers. They have elevated comparatively minor political figures to presidential status, broken the careers of important public men and captured the attention of millions of newspaper readers and, in later years, radio listeners and television viewers. *(Box on personalities and investigations p. 147)*

Based on the constitutional assignment of "all legislative powers herein granted" to Congress, investigations have served as the eyes and ears of the two chambers. Investigations have gathered information on the need for possible future legislation, tested the effectiveness of past legislative action, inquired into the qualifications and performance of members and laid the groundwork for impeachment proceedings. The congressional power of investigation has long been regarded as one of the essential functions of the national legislature. The practices of some committees, however, have led critics to brand investigations as political vehicles for personal publicity and as an extravagant waste of time and money, producing few, if any useful legislative results. *(Box on definition of investigations, next page.)*

Woodrow Wilson, writing on congressional government as a Johns Hopkins University graduate student in 1884, asserted that "The informing function of Congress should be preferred even to its legislative function."[1] Sen. Gerald P. Nye (R N.D.), chairman of the controversial Senate Special Committee Investigating the Munitions Industry (Nye Committee), told a radio audience in 1933: "Out of practically every investigation there comes legislation improving the security of the government and the people against selfishness and greed."[2] And President Truman, who achieved national fame as chairman of the World War II Senate Special Committee to Investigate the National Defense Program (Truman Committee), said in the Senate in 1944: "In my opinion, the power of investigation is one of the most important powers of Congress. The manner in which that power is exercised will largely determine the position and prestige of the Congress in the future."[3]

Others, however, have disagreed with this assessment of the value of congressional investigations. "In my opinion, 95 per cent of these investigations are absolutely worthless and nothing has been accomplished by them," remarked Rep. Lindsay C. Warren (D N.C.) in 1935.[4] And Walter Lippmann once spoke of "that legalized atrocity, the congressional investigation, in which congressmen, starved of their legitimate food for thought, go on a wild and feverish manhunt, and do not stop at cannibalism."[5]

No period of American history has been without investigations. Only the Spanish-American War in 1898, of all major U.S. military engagements, escaped congressional scrutiny. President McKinley forestalled legislative inquiry into that conflict by appointing the Dodge Commission.[6]

Many early investigations involved traditional legislative privileges, such as charges against a senator or representative or trials of members accused of libels, assaults or bribery attempts. Until toward the end of the 19th century, however, most of the investigations concerned the civil and military activities of the executive branch. For example, the Post Office Department was the target of

---

References

For a discussion of investigations concerning members of Congress, see chapters on *Seating and Disciplining, p. 681*, and *Ethics and Criminal Prosecutions, p. 703.* For impeachment investigations and powers, see p. 203. On use of the General Accounting Office for oversight, see *p. 485.* For a discussion of oversight committees, see chapter on *Evolution of Committees, p. 365.* On use of committee staff, see chapter on *Development of Committee Staffs, p. 389.* For investigation of lobbies, see p. 667. For discussion of investigations related to war powers, see p. 265.

Definition and Functions of Congressional Investigations

For purposes of this section, "investigation" has been defined as an inquiry by any congressional committee or subcommittee that used investigative procedures (examining records, summoning and questioning witnesses) for one or more of the following reasons:

- Fact-finding for possible special and remedial legislation.
- Fulfilling Congress' function as a "watchdog" over government operations and programs.
- Informing the public.
- Resolving questions concerning membership or procedure such as conduct of elections or fitness of members of Congress. *(These investigations are discussed in the Seating and Disciplining chapter, p. 681, and Ethics and Criminal Prosecutions chapter, p. 703.)*

Among committee activities not included in the definition: inquiries conducted by staff members without participation by members of Congress in formal hearings; routine hearings; and action on bills and resolutions.

In his book, *Congressional Investigating Committees,* Marshall E. Dimock outlines three functions of congressional investigating committees:

- Inquiries about members.
- Investigations to assist law-making.
- Inquiries to assure that the executive branch carries out the legislative will.

M. Nelson McGeary has classified congressional investigations according to four general categories.

(1) Investigations to assist Congress in legislating. The presence of a specific legislative intent at the beginning of an investigation is not essential to the inclusion of the inquiry in this category; the investigation may be made for the purpose of determining whether any legislation is desirable.

(2) Supervisory investigations. This includes both investigations of specific accusations of misfeasance or maladministration as well as inquiries sponsored by legislators who disagree with the policy of the administration or who allege general administrative inefficiency. Also included are a limited number of investigations, readily classifiable as aids to law-making, which, because they aim to weigh proposals by administrators for congressional assistance in improving the execution of the existing law, may also be catalogued as supervisory inquiries. The examinations of charges of misconduct where impeachment is being considered also may be included as supervisory investigations.

(3) Informational inquiries designed to influence public opinion. This is closely related to the first two categories and generally is collateral to the enactment of law or supervision.

(4) Membership investigations. Both chambers conduct investigations in pursuance of the three expressed or implied powers relating to their own members: judging the "elections, returns and qualifications"; punishing for disorderly behavior; and protecting against breaches of immunity or of the dignity of either house. The inquiries in this category form only a fraction of the total.

Concluding his discussion of types of investigations, McGeary notes that most inquiries serve more than one purpose: "It is impracticable, therefore, to attempt a rigid segregation of all investigations into the four categories suggested. Moreover, the underlying purposes of investigations complicate any precise classification. An inquiry may, for example, be principally motivated by personal considerations."

Sources: Marshall E. Dimock, *Congressional Investigating Committees* (Johns Hopkins University Press, 1929, reprinted by the AMS Press Inc., 1971); M. Nelson McGeary, *The Developments of Congressional Investigative Power* (Columbia University Press, 1940, reprinted by Octagon Books Inc., 1966).

---

probes in 1820, 1822 and 1830, the Bank of the United States in 1832 and 1834, the Smithsonian Institution in 1855 and the General Land Office in 1897.[7]

By 1880 a new field for congressional investigation was emerging—economic and social problems across the nation. There were studies of black migration from South to North (1880), strikebreaking by the railroads (1892) and the concentration of wealth in the "money trust" (1912-13).[8]

Government operations and social conditions served as the principal subjects of congressional investigation until the period between World Wars I and II, when the fear of subversion from foreign ideologies led to inquiries of a different sort. Investigations of social conditions and government operations continued but for a time lost much of their former glamor. Meanwhile, probes into possible subversion expanded rapidly, developing new and harsh methods of inquiry. Hearings involved broadscale intrusions into the thoughts, actions and associations of all manner of persons and institutions, and raised searching legal and moral questions about the power and procedures

of congressional inquiry. *(Box on Investigations of Un-Americanism, p. 166)*

The expanded use of investigations made Congress' investigating power itself a major political issue. To some, the threat to national security posed by Communist subversion was so great as to justify exceptional procedures. To others, the threat to individual liberties from the behavior and authority of some committees appeared a more real danger than that of communism. The conflict over the powers of the committees and the rights of witnesses continued, with shifting results and varying intensity, throughout the pre-World-War-II and the postwar period. It was waged in Congress, in the courts, in the executive branch, in the councils of both parties and in public debates and election campaigns.

Power of Congress to Investigate

Congress received its power to investigate from the Constitution.[9] The investigative power of a legislative body had been established as early as the 16th century by the British House of Commons. The Commons first used its investigative power in determining its membership. It then made increasing use of investigations to assist it in performing its lawmaking functions and in overseeing officials responsible for executing laws and spending the funds made available by Parliament. Investigating committees of the House of Commons had authority to summon witnesses and to examine documents, and the Commons could support its committees by punishing uncooperative witnesses for contempt. American colonial legislatures, the Continental Congress and state legislatures relied on these parliamentary precedents in carrying out their own investigations. Thus the power to investigate, to compel the attendance of witnesses and to demand the production of documents was regarded by most members of the early Congresses as an intrinsic part of the power to legislate.

Uncertainty arose, despite the precedents, because of the constitutional assignment to Congress of "all legislative powers herein granted." Strict constructionists asserted that limitation of the authority of Congress to specifically granted powers restricted investigations to clearly defined judicial functions, such as election disputes, impeachment proceedings or cases involving congressional privileges. Broad constructionists argued that the precedents supported an inherent investigative power in the legislative function. The broad constructionists prevailed, and won approval of the Army investigation in 1792. That first investigation served as a precedent for others. Since then, no serious challenge of the basic authority of Congress to investigate has ever been mounted. However, specific investigations have been challenged, with mixed results; opposition has arisen mainly in the case of investigations that have pried into private affairs, infringed on personal liberties or conflicted with executive branch prerogatives.

Power to Punish for Contempt

Like the investigative power which it reinforced, the congressional power to punish for contempt was based on parliamentary precedents dating from Elizabethan times.[10] No express power to punish for contempt, except in the case of a member, was granted Congress in the Constitution. But Congress assumed that it had inherent power to send persons in contempt to jail without a court order because it regarded such power as necessary for its own protection and for the integrity of its proceedings.[11]

The first use of the congressional power to punish a non-member for contempt was on Dec. 28, 1795, when Robert Randall was summoned to the bar of the House on a charge of having tried to bribe a member. Following debate, the House on Jan. 4, 1796, voted 78-17 to jail Randall for a week. Both chambers drew on precedents established in the Randall case to punish other non-members for contemptuous acts. The first committee witness cited for contempt was Nathaniel Rounsavell, editor of the Alexandria, Va., *Herald*, who refused in 1812 to answer questions before a House committee investigating a breach in the security of a secret House session. After a day's confinement in the custody of the House sergeant at arms, Rounsavell apologized for his behavior and was discharged.[12]

The Senate first voted a contempt of Congress citation on March 20, 1800, when William Duane was ordered arrested for libeling a member. On May 14, the Senate by a 13-4 vote sentenced him to 30 days in jail and ordered him to pay costs. The first Senate committee witness to be cited was Thaddeus Hyatt, who had refused a summons by a committee investigating John Brown's raid on Harpers Ferry in 1859. The Senate March 12, 1860, by a 44-10 vote ordered Hyatt jailed. He was released June 15.[13]

Constitutionality of the Power. In 1821 *(Anderson v. Dunn, 6 Wheat. 204)*, the Supreme Court upheld the constitutionality of summary use of the contempt power by Congress. The court declared that the power to punish contempts was assumed to be inherent in each chamber because without it, Congress would be "exposed to every indignity and interruption that rudeness, caprice, or even conspiracy may mediate against it." The power was limited, however, by the court "to the least possible power adequate to the end proposed," and imprisonment could not extend beyond the adjournment of Congress.[14]

The case grew out of an attempt by John Anderson to bribe a House member to help push a land claim through Congress. Anderson was given a summary trial at the bar of the House, at the end of which the Speaker reprimanded Anderson and then freed him. After his release, Anderson brought charges against Sergeant at Arms Thomas Dunn for assault and battery and for false arrest. A lower court ruled against Anderson, and he appealed. The Supreme Court likewise ruled against Anderson, but most of its decision was devoted to upholding the constitutionality of the summary contempt power of Congress.[15]

Passage of Criminal Statute. Considering the limitation of imprisonment only to the end of a legislative session inadequate, Congress in 1857 passed a law, still in effect in amended form (2 U.S.C. 192), making it a criminal offense to refuse information demanded by either chamber.[16] Even after passage of the 1857 law, Congress preferred to punish persons in contempt itself, reasoning that a few days of confinement might induce a witness to cooperate, while turning him over to a court would put him out of reach of the inquiring committee. Later, however, as the press of legislative business mounted and as court review of summary congressional punishment became more frequent, Congress increasingly relied on criminal prosecution for contempt under the 1857 law. Since 1945, all contempt citations have been prosecuted under the criminal statute.

The congressional power of investigation was further strengthened in 1862 by an amendment to the 1857 law providing that no witness could refuse to testify or to produce documents on the ground that doing so would "tend to disgrace him or otherwise render him infamous."

Use of Contempt Power. Between 1789 and 1976, Congress voted 384 contempt citations in cases where a witness refused to appear before a committee, refused to answer questions before a committee, or refused to produce documents for a committee. Most of these citations have occurred since 1945, primarily as the result of activities by the House Un-American Activities Committee. As Ronald L. Goldfarb and Carl Beck have noted in their studies of the contempt power, in the period from 1792 until 1942, there were only 600 congressional investigations and only 108 contempt citations.[17]

Moreover, until 1945, Congress frequently overruled the recommendations of its committees on contempt citations. From 1796 to 1945, the House or Senate reversed the actions of committees in 34 cases.[18] But after 1945, when Congress ended the tradition of deciding both guilt and punishment in contempt cases and began referring its contempt citations to the Justice Department for prosecution, the record was drastically altered.

According to Beck, of 226 contempt citations presented to both houses by 14 committees between 1945 and 1957, few cases were debated, few were discussed and none was defeated. After 1945, Beck wrote, the courts determined guilt or innocence, and approval of a committee's contempt citation by the full House or Senate was "almost automatic."[19] *(For an exception, see box on CBS contempt citation, this page.)*

Use of the contempt power in congressional cases has fallen into two general classes: (1) those involving positive acts, such as bribery or libel, which directly or indirectly obstruct the legislature in carrying out its functions, and (2) those involving refusal to perform acts which the legislature claims authority to compel, such as testifying or producing documents. Few cases of the first type have occurred in recent years, and the courts have had little opportunity to define positive acts of contempt. The second type, while giving rise to much more extensive judicial interpretation, continues to raise many legal questions because of its greater complexity.

Resorting to the inherent power of Congress to punish for contempt, a committee may introduce a resolution directing the presiding officer of the chamber to issue a warrant for arrest of the witness in contempt by the chamber's sergeant at arms. The witness is brought before the bar of the House, or Senate, and questioned. Subsequently, the full chamber may adopt a resolution ordering the confinement of the witness or his discharge, or the witness simply may be reprimanded by the chamber's presiding officer.

When a committee in either chamber wishes to institute criminal proceedings against a contumacious witness, it introduces a resolution in the parent body citing him for contempt. Only a simple majority vote is necessary for approval; there seldom is opposition to such a resolution. The matter is then referred to a U.S. attorney for presentation to a grand jury.

A recent case of contempt of Congress occurred in 1973 as a result of the Watergate and related probes. The House Sept. 10, 1972, voted 334-11 to cite Watergate conspirator G. Gordon Liddy for contempt of Congress. The case was turned over to the U.S. attorney in the District of Columbia for presentation to a grand jury.

Liddy, a former member of the "plumbers" special investigative unit at the White House, was cited for his refusal to be sworn in to testify before the House Armed Services Committee's Special Intelligence Subcommittee July 20. The subcommittee and then the full committee approved the resolution citing him for contempt.

Ordinarily, witnesses reluctant to testify before congressional committees take the oath and then refuse to testify on constitutional grounds such as the Fifth Amendment. Liddy, already serving an eight-month contempt of court sentence in the District of Columbia jail for refusing to testify before a federal grand jury, was summoned before the subcommittee in connection with the 1971 burglary of the office of Pentagon Papers defendant Daniel Ellsberg's former psychiatrist. He was one of four men indicted for the burglary by a California grand jury.

Besides the eight-month contempt sentence, Liddy was sentenced to six to 20 years for his part in planning the June 17, 1972, break-in at Democratic national headquarters in the Watergate building. He was counsel to the Nixon reelection finance committee at that time.

Liddy was found guilty of contempt of Congress May 10, 1974. U.S. District Judge John H. Pratt, who heard the case without a jury in Washington, gave Liddy a suspended six-month sentence.[20] *(Kissinger contempt citation, p. 158)*

CBS Contempt Citation

One exception to the general rule that the House and Senate normally support a committee's contempt citation resolution occurred on July 13, 1971. On that day, the House, by a 226-181 roll-call vote, recommitted—and thus killed—a House Interstate and Foreign Commerce Committee resolution (H Res 534) recommending that the Columbia Broadcasting System (CBS) and its president, Frank Stanton, be cited for contempt of Congress.

On June 24, Stanton had refused to comply with a subpoena issued by the committee's Investigations Subcommittee for film and sound recordings prepared for but not used in the network's controversial documentary, "The Selling of the Pentagon."

Appearing before the subcommittee that day, Stanton invoked the First Amendment guarantee of freedom of the press when he refused to supply the requested material. "If broadcast journalism must comply with subpoenas such as this," he argued, "it can never perform the independent role in preserving those freedoms which the Constitution intended for American journalism." Rep. Harley O. Staggers (D W.Va.), chairman of both the full committee and the subcommittee, replied: "The issue here today is not the First Amendment. It is the willful deception of the public." Staggers also said, "This subcommittee... has sought to protect the public interest by demanding full disclosure. And public disclosure is all we advocate today." Critics of the program had asserted that CBS's editing of film had distorted the meaning of statements made by persons who were interviewed.

The subcommittee June 29 recommended that CBS and Stanton be cited for contempt, and the full committee endorsed the proposal July 1.

During House floor debate on the resolution July 12 and 13, members who supported the citation presented their arguments in moral and pragmatic terms. They said the public must be protected from broadcast media "deception" and the subcommittee needed the CBS film to conduct a study of the network's editing practices. Opponents of the resolution stressed that the measure conflicted with the First Amendment.

"We have come upon dark days when a television network can determine what is, and what is not, the legitimate business of Congress," said Rep. William L. Springer (R Ill.), ranking minority members of Staggers' committee. Rep. Richard H. Poff (R Va.) replied: "The collision here is between the privilege of the press to edit for journalistic purposes and the privilege of the Congress to investigate for legislative purposes. The collision is between the government and the governed.... Whenever two great constitutional privileges collide, one must yield.... I will prefer the governed. I will choose freedom."

Although most members of Congress usually support a committee's contempt recommendation, in this case the House leadership of both parties, committee chairmen, liberal Democrats, freshmen representatives and some conservatives backed away from Staggers' request and recommitted the resolution to the committee.

Investigative Practices

From the beginning, Congress has delegated its power to investigate to committees.

Prior to passage of the Legislative Reorganization Act of 1946 (PL 79-601), the majority of investigations were carried out by special or select committees, with subpoena power, established to conduct the inquiry. When an investigation was concluded, the committee went out of existence and the subpoena power ended. The first attempt to give subpoena power to a standing committee—the House Committee on Manufactures, for tariff investigation—was strongly opposed but was approved Dec. 31, 1827, by a 102-88 vote. Opponents said the proposal was unheard of because subpoena power previously had been used only by committees acting as judicial bodies.[21]

At first, House committees dominated congressional investigations. The House, for example, conducted 27 of the 30 inquiries between 1789 and 1814. But as time passed, the Senate pulled in front of the House, conducting about 40 of the 60 investigations between 1900 and 1925.[22] (The Senate first granted subpoena power to a special investigating committee during an 1818 study of the Seminole war.)[23]

In the meantime, as the number of standing committees increased in both chambers, it became common practice for them to conduct investigations on their own initiative, without a special authorizing resolution, although specific House or Senate approval was still required to compel testimony and to provide funds. Of the 146 investigations between 1929 and 1938, 89 were made by standing committees and 57 by select committees.[24]

The spectacular growth of the executive branch during the New Deal and World War II years led to a proliferation of congressional investigating committees as Congress struggled to fulfill its traditional function of overseeing the administration of laws and the spending of appropriations. By 1945, the House had a total of 111 committees and the Senate, a total of 75; between 1945 and passage of the Reorganization Act in 1946, at least 50 investigations had been voted.[25]

Subpoena Powers in Senate

The 1946 Act attempted to restore the balance by strengthening the congressional investigative procedures and expanding committee staffs. The act reduced the number of standing committees from 48 to 19 in the House and from 33 to 15 in the Senate. It authorized standing committees of both chambers to "exercise continuous watchfulness of the execution by the administrative agencies concerned of any laws, the subject matter of which is within the jurisdiction" of the respective committees. Further, the act extended permanent subpoena power to all standing committees of the Senate and authorized $10,000 in investigating funds for each committee during each Congress. The act also authorized professional staff members for all standing committees.

Subpoena Powers in House

General subpoena power for House committees was blocked for many years by the leadership of Speaker Sam Rayburn (D Texas) and Minority Leader Joseph W. Martin (R Mass.), who feared that such power would make the committees uncontrollable and lead to sensational inquiries motivated by political ambitions. (It was granted in 1974. *See below.*) The only exception was the Un-American Ac-

tivities Committee, which was authorized to issue subpoenas. Subsequently, general subpoena power was granted to the House Committee on Expenditures in the Executive Departments (Government Operations) in 1947 and to the House Appropriations Committee in 1953. When the Un-American Activities Committee was re-named the House Committee on Internal Security, on Feb. 18, 1969, the new committee also was given subpoena power. As a result of Rayburn's and Martin's opposition to general subpoena power for House committees, the panels had to seek specific House approval for authority to compel testimony and documents. In practice, the House normally authorized broad committee investigatory power and use of the subpoena.

When the 93rd Congress began in 1973, for example, the House on one day adopted resolutions authorizing eight standing committees to investigate subjects within their legislative jurisdictions and to issue subpoenas.

One of those committees was Banking and Currency, which issued more than 300 subpoenas between 1965 and 1974, according to staff counsel Benet D. Gellman. All subpoenas the committee issued must specify exactly what was requested and how the documents or testimony related to the committee's jurisdictional mandate, Gellman explained. And because the investigative resolution granted authority to the committee as a whole and not just to its chairman, Gellman said, all members must approve a subpoena before the chairman signed it.[26]

Gellman based what he described as his "conservative view" of the subpoena power on a 1966 Supreme Court decision—*Gojack v. U.S.* (384 U.S. 702). Gojack was convicted of contempt of Congress for refusing to answer certain questions while testifying before a subcommittee of the House Un-American Activities Committee in 1955. The court reversed his conviction on grounds that the committee had not specified the subject of the inquiry or authorized the subcommittee to conduct it.

General Subpoena Power Granted. The House in 1974 gave its committees and subcommittees general subpoena power to compel the attendance and testimony of witnesses and the production of books, records and any other documents considered necessary to an investigation. Specific subpoena authority no longer had to be given to each committee. However, the 1974 change required that a majority of a committee or subcommittee approve a subpoena before it is issued. In addition, compliance with a subpoena may be enforced only by action of the full House.

The general subpoena power was given in a House resolution (H Res 988) dealing with committee jurisdictions, procedures and activities (known informally as the Hansen committee proposals). The provisions granting the authority became part of the House rules.

Watergate Subpoenas. The Senate Select Committee on Presidential Campaign Activities (Watergate Committee) construed its subpoena power more broadly, many thought, when it sought a large but unspecified number of White House tapes and documents Dec. 18, 1973. (The committee had issued earlier subpoenas in July.)[27]

House Banking was the first congressional committee to attempt to use its subpoena power to investigate the Watergate break-in. On Oct. 3, 1972, the committee rejected, 20-15, a resolution backed by Chairman Wright Patman (D Texas) to call 40 individuals and organizations to testify about possible violations of banking laws and irregularities in Republican campaign financing suggested by the break-in.[28]

Impeachment Investigation. The House Judiciary Committee, responsible for conducting the inquiry into charges against President Nixon, was one of the standing committees granted general subpoena power by resolution at the beginning of the 93rd Congress in 1973. At that time, however, the official list of subjects under the committee's jurisdiction did not include impeachment.

But on Feb. 6, 1974, with only four members voting "nay," the House formally granted the committee power to investigate the conduct of President Nixon to determine whether there were grounds for his impeachment.[29] The resolution gave explicit authorization for the committee to conduct the investigation—already under way—and granted it special subpoena power during the inquiry.

The committee's issuance of subpoenas to Nixon in the spring and summer of 1974 was an unprecedented action. In the only other impeachment proceedings against a President—Andrew Johnson in 1867-68—Johnson himself was not subpoenaed.[30] *(For details, see Power of Impeachment, p. 203)*

Before Nixon was served with subpoenas for tapes and documents July 23, 1973—two from the Senate Watergate investigating committee and one from the Watergate special prosecutor—the only President in office to be subpoenaed was Thomas Jefferson in 1807, when former Vice President Aaron Burr was on trial for treason. Burr asked Chief Justice John Marshall, who was presiding over the trial at the circuit level, to subpoena the President, contending that he had a letter which would contradict testimony that had been given against Burr.

Marshall found that without doubt the court could issue a subpoena to the President. He said the only question was whether or not the subpoena could require the President to produce the letter referred to. Eventually, Marshall ruled that the subpoena requiring the letter from the President could be issued. Jefferson did not testify in person, but he said he would—and in fact did—produce the letter without the compulsion of a subpoena.[31] *(Former President Truman's refusal to testify, box, p. 158)*

Cost of Investigation

The combined effect of the 1946 Legislative Reorganization Act and executive branch expansion beginning with the New Deal period in the 1930s was an explosion of investigative activity following World War II. Compared to approximately 500 investigations in almost 150 years from 1789 to 1938, the 90th Congress (1967-68) alone authorized 496 investigations. The cost of investigations paralleled the rising number of inquiries. From 1910 to 1919 the Senate spent approximately $330,000 on investigative activities, compared to $2.9-million in the two years 1951 and 1952.[32] In the two years of the 90th Congress the Senate and House together spent $21,994,843 on investigations. The number and cost of the studies rapidly outdistanced the $10,000 per committee authorized in the 1946 Act, and the committees in most cases were again required to seek special funds for investigative activities.

In 1975, the Senate authorized an investigative budget of $19.4-million for 22 standing committees, and the House authorized $21.2-million for 21 committees.[33]

In 1973, the Senate Watergate investigating committee alone was authorized $2-million to conduct its inquiry.[34]

Although Congress continued to establish special investigating committees in postwar years, most major investigations were carried on by a handful of standing committees or their subcommittees: the House and Senate Committees on Government Operations, the Internal Security Subcommittee of the Senate Judiciary Committee, the Senate Government Operations Permanent Investigations Subcommittee and the (now-defunct) House Internal Security Committee.

Procedural Stages

Congressional investigations undergo three stages of development: authorization, staff preparation and public hearings.[35]

Authorization

Many reasons may cause a senator or representative to propose an investigation. He may seek to gather facts on widely known public occurrences such as an airline crash; he may attempt to confirm reports of improper conduct in the government, labor unions or business; or he may pursue a personal interest such as government monetary policy or fees charged ranchers for grazing cattle on federal range land.

Whatever the reason, the authority and scope of the inquiry are incorporated in a resolution for introduction in the House or Senate. Once introduced, the resolution is referred to a committee. In the Senate, resolutions to authorize and fund investigations are considered by the Rules and Administration Committee and by the standing legislative committee having jurisdiction over the subject to be studied. In the House, the Administration Committee considers the funding of investigations. Prior to January 1975, House resolutions for investigations also had to be considered by the Rules Committee before being sent to the floor. However, this requirement has been eliminated, and in 1975 all standing committees were given direct authority to conduct investigations.

After being reported by the committees, a resolution is voted on by the full chamber. Joint House-Senate investigating committees are authorized by a concurrent resolution adopted by both chambers.

Many resolutions to authorize investigations, like bills and resolutions on other matters, are never acted upon by a committee and die. But if a resolution authorizing an investigation is approved by a committee and adopted on the floor, an investigation almost always follows. One exception occurred in 1933 when an authorized investigation of the Reconstruction Finance Corporation by the Senate Banking and Currency Committee did not occur; the committee reported later that it had had no specific inquiry in mind and had asked for the investigatory power only as a precautionary step.[36]

It has long been a matter of courtesy in both House and Senate that the sponsor of the resolution for an investigation shall preside over the inquiry. When the study is to be made by a standing committee, a subcommittee generally is appointed by the chairman of the full committee, with the sponsor of the resolution being named subcommittee chairman. When a select committee is authorized, the members are chosen by consultation between the Vice President, or the Speaker of the House and the majority and minority leaders.

The life of a special House investigation committee expires with a Congress, but that of a Senate committee depends upon its authorization.

Personalities and Investigations

Several leading persons in congressional investigations became figures of great influence. Sen. Gerald P. Nye (R N.D.) was considered a possible Republican presidential or vice presidential nominee in 1936, after heading the Senate Special Committee Investigating the Munitions Industry.

Harry S Truman achieved national prominence as chairman of the World War II Senate Special Committee to Investigate the National Defense Program.

Richard M. Nixon first won recognition through his activities on the House Un-American Activities Committee, particularly in its investigation of Alger Hiss.

Sen. Estes Kefauver (D Tenn.) became a leading presidential contender after the widely viewed televised hearings of his Senate Special Committee to Investigate Organized Crime in Interstate Commerce. In 1956, Kefauver was the Democratic nominee for vice president. Sen. Robert F. Kennedy (D N.Y.) first achieved a measure of popular recognition while chief counsel of the Senate Select Committee on Improper Activities in the Labor or Management Field.

None of these, however, derived as much authority from congressional investigations as Sen. Joseph R. McCarthy (R Wis.), whose power was felt—and feared—in Congress, in two administrations, in the State Department, in the armed forces, in universities, and in many other public and private institutions throughout the country.

Not only the investigators achieved fame from committee hearings. Leaders in every segment of the community, from the academic world to the underworld, were thrust into the national spotlight. Though public attention was focused on such varied figures as Gen. Douglas A. MacArthur, teamster boss James R. Hoffa, or ex-Communist Whittaker Chambers, the investigations also paved the way for important legislation, much of which will remain on the statute books when personalities are gone and forgotten.

Staff Preparation

Early congressional investigative committees had no staff and inquiries were undertaken informally. The investigating committee frequently knew little about the subject under study and simply struck out blindly, asking questions and considering evidence, hoping that something might be found that would be useful to the investigation.[37]

Committee staffs first came into use by investigating committees in the late 1800s and early 1900s. By the 1920s and 1930s the practice of relying on staff members to gather information was firmly established. Trained investigators, poring over files and records before the start of public hearings, generally have accumulated most of the information produced by investigations. Occasionally an investigating committee has been authorized access to income tax returns, customarily by executive order. *(See discussion of committee staffs, p. 389)*

The Nye Committee's staff investigating the munitions industry in the 1930s consisted of three lawyers, two accountants, a specialist in international law, a financial writer, two free-lance newspapermen, and five persons who were doing or had done graduate work in the social sciences.[38] On the staff of the Truman Committee during World War II were a chief counsel, an associate counsel, an assistant counsel, a chief investigator, 12-18 investigators, a committee clerk, an editor and clerical personnel.[39] In 1975, the staff of the Senate Government Operations Permanent Investigations Subcommittee included a chief counsel, a minority chief counsel, a special counsel, a professional staff director, two assistant counsels, seven professional staff members, two research assistants, one executive assistant, seven investigators, a staff editor, a chief clerk and 11 clerical assistants.[40]

At its peak in 1973, the Senate Watergate committee had a total staff of 64, including 17 attorneys; the House Judiciary Committee's impeachment inquiry staff in 1974 numbered close to 100 and included 43 attorneys.[41]

Until the Legislative Reorganization Act of 1946 authorized professional committee staffs, investigating committees frequently borrowed personnel from the administrative agencies. Persons on relief were lent to some investigating committees during the depression. Trained investigators from government agencies still are used by many committees. For the 12 months ended June 1974, the General Accounting Office reported assigning 98 staff members to 29 congressional committees or subcommittees at a total cost of $788,163.[42]

The activities of an investigating committee's staff in a major inquiry are suggested by the scope of the committee's work. The Truman Committee, active from 1941 to 1948, issued 51 reports totaling 1,946 pages and held 432 public hearings at which 1,798 witnesses appeared, filing 27,568 pages of testimony. In addition, the transcript of about 300 private sessions held by the committee covered 25,000 pages.[43] From 1957 to 1959, the Senate Select Committee on Improper Activities in the Labor or Management Field heard 1,726 witnesses (343 of whom took the Fifth Amendment), whose testimony filled 46,150 pages. Staff members traveled nearly 2.5 million miles, forwarded 128,-204 documents to the committee (not counting photostats), conducted 253 active investigations, served more than 8,000 subpoenas in staff investigations and filed more than 19,000 investigative field reports. At its peak, in 1958, the staff numbered 104.[44]

Hearing

Public hearings have been the most visible and controversial element of investigations, but as a rule they have brought forth little material not already uncovered or suggested by staff work.[45] Hearings have helped to act as a check on staff investigators by giving the investigated person a chance to present his case. Procedures have varied from committee to committee, but a witness usually has been allowed to present a prepared statement and to be accompanied by and to consult with a lawyer. Questioning of witnesses has been conducted by members of the committee, frequently the chairman, and by the committee's staff. In some instances, galley proofs of the testimony have been sent to the witness for corrections; this was the practice of the Truman Committee.

Public hearings have provided a method of presenting facts dramatically to the public and a means of influencing public opinion. Public opinion, in turn, has been affected by methods used in the conduct of hearings, particularly when the procedures appeared to infringe on the rights of witnesses. *(See next page)*

The widespread television and radio coverage afforded the Senate Watergate Committee during its first phase of hearings in the summer of 1973 provides a dramatic example of the controversial impact of publicity. The committee's live audience was strongly anti-Nixon, and in the early months of the hearings made its feelings known with laughter and applause. Chairman Sam J. Ervin Jr. (D N.C.) received a standing ovation when he entered the room. Finally, during the testimony of John D. Erlichman in July, the audience became so abusive that the chairman put an end to demonstrations of opinion.

The publicity led the first Watergate special prosecutor, Archibald Cox, on June 4, 1973, to urge the committee to call off its public hearings for one to three months. One of his reasons for doing so was that witnesses might be less likely to make full disclosures before television cameras than privately to prosecutors. "The continuation of hearings at this time would create grave danger that the full facts about the Watergate case and related matters will never come to light and that many of those who are guilty of serious wrong-doing will never be brought to justice," Cox said.[46]

However, Chief Judge John J. Sirica of the U.S. District Court in Washington, June 12 denied Cox's request that the hearings be delayed or, if continued, be held without radio and television coverage, arguing that "the court lacks completely any power of intervention."

Rights of Witnesses

Not until the late 1930s did the rights of a witness in a congressional investigation become a serious issue.

The potential conflict between the right of Congress to seek information and the right of a witness to protect his privacy always was present; but early legislative investigations were conducted in a comparatively low-key atmosphere, free from the instant mass publicity of television. Witnesses often were allowed to call their own witnesses and to cross-examine hostile witnesses.[47]

The advent in the 1930s of the inquisitorial congressional panel, typified by the House Special Committee to Investigate Un-American Activities (Dies Committee) aroused new concern. The low-key atmosphere had vanished, replaced by relentless probing questions before massed newsmen and newsreel cameras. Complaints mounted that the procedures of congressional investigators were exceeding their powers and violating the rights of witnesses.

In fact, as witnesses—and the courts—discovered, investigating committees had virtually free rein to determine their procedures. Challenges of the legality of committee procedures raised sensitive questions. They loomed as a potentially divisive force between two co-equal branches of the government, the legislative and the judicial, and the courts studiously sought to avoid the issue. They attempted to rule on narrow points of law rather than on the central point, which was the power of a committee to set its own procedures.

The result of the courts' evasiveness was that a witness in essence was at the mercy of the investigating committee, protected only by the general constitutional limitations on congressional authority and by the Bill of Rights. A 1954 study of congressional investigative power by the Legislative Reference Service of the Library of Congress concluded: "There are few safeguards for the protection of a witness before a congressional committee.... In committee, his treatment usually depends upon the skill and attitude of the chairman and the members."[48] That conclusion was foreshadowed clearly by a 1948 comment by House Un-American Activities Committee Chairman J. Parnell Thomas (R N.J.): "The rights you have are the rights given you by this committee. We will determine what rights you have and what rights you have not got before the committee."[49]

During the postwar era, the rights of witnesses before congressional investigating committees became a bitter issue. The growing number and broadened scope of investigations, and the increasing use of committee hearings for the purpose of edifying the public rather than informing the legislature, led to pressure for more precise definitions of committee powers. The advent of television coverage of hearings, first used spectacularly during House Un-American Activities Committee investigations of communism in 1948, exposed witnesses to vast publicity. The publicity, jeopardizing the privacy of witnesses, their reputations and often their careers, provoked demands for safeguards for those testifying.

In search of protection, witnesses turned repeatedly to the Constitution. Despite the constitutional assignment of only specified powers to Congress, the courts repeatedly had shown reluctance to limit congressional investigating power. The new search for safeguards led to tests of the effectiveness of the Bill of Rights in protecting the rights of witnesses.

Most frequently cited were the First, Fourth and Fifth Amendments. Efforts by witnesses to invoke the First Amendment in refusing to provide committees with information, on the ground that Congress had no right to probe their private convictions or their political views or propaganda activities, had mixed results. The Fourth Amendment guarantee against unreasonable search and seizure likewise offered uncertain protection. The arbitrary power of committees to demand the production of documents was the most used—and disputed—authority through the history of congressional investigations.

Once the courts upheld the right of congressional committee witnesses to invoke the Fifth Amendment's protection against self-incrimination, use of the amendment to avoid answering questions became highly controversial. The Fifth Amendment generally stood up as a defense against prosecution for contempt of Congress. However, witnesses could not invoke the privilege partially, answering as to incriminating facts and then refusing further explanation. For this reason, some witnesses repeatedly pleaded the Fifth Amendment in refusing to answer apparently innocuous questions. *(See p. 150)*

Because of the uncertainty and delay in attempting to establish constitutional safeguards for witnesses, pressures mounted both in and out of Congress for reform of committee procedures to protect the rights of witnesses and to give greater assurance that the purposes for which the investigations were instituted would, in fact, be accomplished.

Rules Reforms

Proposals for "fair play" rules for investigations were numerous in the 83rd Congress.[50] Both the House Rules Committee and the Senate Rules and Administration Committee in 1954 held hearings on a variety of proposed codes of committee procedure sponsored by members of both parties.

House. The House March 23, 1955, adopted by voice vote a resolution (H Res 151) amending House Rules to establish a minimum standard of conduct for House committees. The resolution:

● Required a quorum of at least two members when committees take testimony and receive evidence.

● Allowed witnesses at investigations to be accompanied by counsel.

● Required a committee, if it found that evidence "may tend to defame, degrade, or incriminate any person," to receive the evidence in secret session and to allow the person injured to appear as a witness and to request subpoenas of other witnesses.

● Required committee consent for release of evidence taken in secret session.

Senate. The Senate prescribed no "fair play" code for its committees. However, the Senate Republican Policy Committee on March 10, 1954, offered as "suggestions" a set of rules for investigations and sent the proposals to all Senate committee chairmen. The Republican proposals would have allowed counsel for witnesses, prohibited release of executive testimony except by majority vote, and strengthened the control of investigations by the majority of the committee.

The Rules Subcommittee of the Senate Rules and Administration Committee on Jan. 6, 1955, issued a unanimous report recommending 12 rules to protect witnesses and to ensure greater majority control of investigations. Among the recommendations were those to:

● Allow a person who felt his reputation had been damaged by other testimony to testify in his own behalf or file a sworn statement.

● Ban public release of testimony given in closed session, except by authorization of the committee.

● Advise each witness, in advance, of the subject of the investigation.

● Allow witnesses to request that television and other cameras and lights not be directed at him during his testimony, and have committee members present at the time to rule on the request.

The report said "elaborate procedural devices" would be unnecessary if there were "courtesy and understanding on the part of committee members and staff," and ineffective if those qualities were lacking. The subcommittee reported, "What might have been classified decades ago as private opinion of no concern to Congress, takes on a different connotation in the light of world events whose impact Congress may not disregard."

The Senate left investigative procedures to the discretion of individual committees, whose practices varied considerably. The Permanent Investigations Subcommittee of the Senate Government Operations Committee, after Sen. John L. McClellan (D Ark.) replaced McCarthy as chairman, Jan. 18, 1955, adopted rules requiring the presence of two committee members when testimony was being taken, permitted anyone who was the subject of an investigation to submit questions in writing for cross-examination of other witnesses, and allowed any person adversely affected by testimony to request an appearance or file a statement.

Not only do rules vary from one committee to another in the Senate and, except for the minimum code, in the House, but the strictness with which committees adhere to their own rules is not uniform.

Dilemmas of Control. "It would be an unwarranted act of judicial usurpation...to assume for the courts the function of supervising congressional committees," wrote Justice Robert Jackson in 1949. "I should...leave the responsibility for the behavior of its committees squarely on the shoulders of Congress."[51]

Unfortunately, however, as Pritchett noted, "Congress has been too often remiss in assuming this responsibility.... Committee rules of procedure, though generally much improved in recent years, still leave something to be desired. Unfairness may result from limiting the right of representation by counsel, or permitting witnesses to make defamatory charges about persons who have had no advance warning that they are to be named, or holding one-man subcommittee sessions, or denying requests for closed (or sometimes open) hearings. Rules which exist may not be enforced."[52]

In 1965, the American Civil Liberties Union prepared an eleven-point proposal for fair investigatory procedures. Under this plan, committees would be required to hold executive sessions to screen defamatory, prejudicial, or adverse information. The affected individuals would be given adequate notice and the opportunity to appear at the executive session to present their defense. The ACLU also proposed that each house establish supervisory committees to screen investigating committee recommendations for contempt citations.[53]

Although various codes and rules have been proposed for improving congressional investigatory procedures, in the last analysis the actions of committees are determined by its members. For as Sen. J.W. Fulbright (D Ark.) pointed out in 1951: "In order to investigate effectively, a congressional committee must have within the field of inquiry assigned to it a virtually unrestrained delegation of this vast congressional power. As a practical matter, this means that the power to investigate is wielded by individuals, not by institutions.... This is...at once both the weakness and the strength of our legislative processes."[54]

Immunity Statute

The need for immunity statutes first became apparent in the United States in the mid-19th century. In passing the federal statute providing for punishment of recalcitrant witnesses before congressional committees, Congress in 1857 added a second section that contained an automatic and sweeping grant of immunity to witnesses testifying under the compulsion of congressional power. As enacted, the law provided that "no person examined and testifying before either House of Congress or any committee of either House, shall be held to answer criminally in any court of justice, or subject to any penalty or forfeiture, for any fact or act touching which he shall be required to testify before either House of Congress, or any committee of either House, as to which he shall have testified, whether before or after this act;.... Provided, that nothing in this act shall be construed to exempt any witness from prosecution and punishment for perjury committed by him in testifying as aforesaid."[55]

In 1862, however, when it was revealed that embezzlers of millions of dollars in Indian trust bonds had escaped prosecution by appearing before an investigating committee, Congress repealed the 1857 immunity law and replaced it with a provision stating: "No testimony given by a witness before either House, or before any committee of either House...shall be used as evidence in any criminal proceeding against him in any court, except in a prosecution for perjury committed in giving such testimony." Thus, although witnesses' own testimony could not be used as evidence to convict them, there was nothing to prevent its being used as a lead in discovering other evidence of crime.[56]

Congress inserted a similar provision in the 1887 act creating the Interstate Commerce Commission (ICC) and **delegating investigatory powers to it. (Subsequently** Congress delegated powers of investigation to other independent regulatory commissions.) The act authorized the ICC to require witnesses before it to testify despite any claim of privilege against self-incrimination, but provided that such testimony "shall not be used against such person on the trial of any criminal proceeding." (This provision was somewhat modified in 1893.) The constitutionality of the ICC's use of immunity was upheld by the Supreme Court in **1896.[57]** *(Brown v. Walker,* 161 U.S. 591)

The 1862 law regarding immunity before congressional committees remained unchanged until 1954, when the Eisenhower administration proposed, and Congress adopted, the Immunity Act of 1954. The bill (PL 83-600) permitted either chamber of Congress by majority vote, or a congressional committee by two-thirds vote, to grant immunity to witnesses in national security investigations, provided an order was first obtained from a U.S. district court judge and also provided the Attorney General was notified in advance and given an opportunity to offer objections. The bill also permitted the U.S. district courts to grant immunity to witnesses before the court or grand juries. The bill was aimed at witnesses invoking the Fifth Amendment privilege against self-incrimination. Immunity would have the effect of compelling them to testify or go to jail.[58]

The Supreme Court upheld the act in *Ullmann v. United States* (350 U.S. 422, 1956). Dissenting from the majority opinion, however, Justice Douglas argued that the 1954 statute protected individuals from criminal punishment but exposed them to the punishment of infamy and disgrace. Moreover, he declared, "My view is that the **Framers put it beyond the power of Congress to** *compel* any-one to confess his crimes. The evil to be guarded against **was partly self-accusation under legal compulsion. But that was only a part of the evil. The conscience and dignity of man were also involved."[59]**

Watergate and Immunity

Congressional grants of immunity became an issue during the hearings of the Senate Select Committee on **Presidential Campaign Activities (the Watergate Com-**mittee). In one of his first moves as Watergate special prosecutor, Archibald Cox June 4, 1973, urged the committee to delay its public hearings. One of his arguments for postponement was that a grant of partial immunity for certain witnesses before the committee might prevent them from being convicted later.[60]

The Senate committee's lawyers went to work immediately, preparing a 15-page legal brief opposing Cox's request. Filed with the court June 7, it argued that under the doctrine of separation of powers the court had no jurisdiction over the committee's action.

U.S. District Judge John J. Sirica heard arguments June 8 on his power to deny the Senate committee's request for immunity for John W. Dean III and Jeb Stuart Magruder. The two were known to be under consideration for indictment in connection with the Watergate scandal and were reportedly prepared to offer evidence of the involvement of top White House officials, including the President.

Sirica denied Cox's request for postponement of the hearings, ruling June 12 that the court lacked any power of intervention. The judge granted limited—or "use"—immunity to Dean and Magruder, thus clearing them to appear before the committee.[61] (Dean later received a prison sentence of one to four years and Magruder, 10 months to four years.)

Investigations and the Courts

During the greater part of the 19th century, congressional investigations were not subjected to judicial review. The Supreme Court ruling in the 1821 case of *Anderson v. Dunn* (6 Wheat. 204), that the action of the House must be "presumed" to be in accordance with law, warded off legal challenges to the power of Congress to punish for contempt.[62]

This precedent was set aside in 1881 by the court's decision in the important case of *Kilbourn v. Thompson* (103 U.S. 168), which established the principle of judicial review of the investigative activities of Congress. Other cases were to follow. Emerging from the series of judicial decisions since *Kilbourn* was a broad outline of congressional investigative power:

● The power to conduct investigations and to compel the attendance of witnesses and the production of evidence, under the threat of citation for contempt of Congress, was accepted as a necessary corollary of the power to legislate.

● The investigative power was to be connected with a legislative power authorized by the Constitution; before a committee could compel a witness to testify, it had to inform the witness of the connection between the questions and the legislative purpose of the inquiry.

● Investigations were subject in varying degrees to constitutional protection of individual rights and the Constitution's division of powers among three separate and equal branches of government.

● The courts had authority to review investigative activities, although committees were allowed to determine their procedures virtually without restraint.[63]

Kilbourn v. Thompson. The *Kilbourn* case originated with the refusal of a witness, Hallett Kilbourn, to produce papers demanded by the House Select Committee on the Real Estate Pool and Jay Cooke Indebtedness, which was investigating the failure of the banking firm of Jay Cooke.[64] Kilbourn, manager of the real estate pool, said he would not acknowledge "the naked, arbitrary power of the House to investigate private business in which nobody but me and my customers have concern." The House ordered that he be jailed for contempt. Released on a writ of habeas corpus, Kilbourn sued the Speaker, members of the investigating committee and Sergeant at Arms John G. Thompson for false arrest. The Supreme Court heard the case and sustained Kilbourn's claim. In its decision, the court held that the houses of Congress did not have a general power to punish for contempt. A reluctant committee witness could be punished for contempt, the court ruled, only if the inquiry for which the witness had been called was within the "legitimate cognizance" of Congress.

The *Kilbourn* decision appeared to restrict the congressional power to investigate to "legitimate" inquiries, without specifying what they were. In deciding the case, the court declared that investigations of the private affairs of a citizen were not legitimate, but that those made in connection with some specifically granted constitutional power, such as impeachment or the election and qualification of members, were proper. Later court decisions have largely removed the limitations imposed in *Kilbourn;* its value has stemmed from the principle of judicial review of congressional contempt action, which it established.

In re Chapman. Seventeen years after *Kilbourn,* in 1897, the Supreme Court held *(In re Chapman,* 166 U.S. 661) that investigations were "legitimate" inquiries when they involved the conduct of members of Congress. [65] This unanimously upheld the constitutionality of the 1857 contempt of Congress statute. Elverton R. Chapman was a New York stockbroker who had refused to answer an investigating committee's questions about senators' trading in sugar stocks during action on a sugar tariff measure.

McGrain v. Daugherty. In 1927, the court issued a landmark decision *(McGrain v. Daugherty,* 273 U.S. 135) that swept away nearly all the restrictions on the investigating power of Congress left over from the *Kilbourn* decision. [66] The effect of *McGrain v. Daugherty* was to uphold the power of Congress to conduct legislative and oversight investigations. These two types of investigations, together with membership inquiries, have comprised the vast majority of congressional investigations since 1789. Thus, in a broad sense, *McGrain v. Daugherty* firmly established the existence of the congressional power to investigate.

The *Daugherty* decision grew out of a refusal by Mally S. Daugherty, brother of Attorney General Harry M. Daugherty (1921-24), to testify before a Senate committee investigating the Justice Department. The Senate issued a warrant ordering Deputy Sergeant at Arms John J. McGrain to arrest Mally Daugherty, who had challenged the Senate's power to compel him to testify. The Supreme Court sustained the Senate action.

The court held that the Senate or the House had power to compel private persons to appear before committees and to answer pertinent questions in aid of the legislative function. "The power of inquiry—with process to enforce it—is an essential and appropriate auxiliary to the legislative function," the court said. It continued: "A legislative body cannot legislate wisely or effectively in the absence of information respecting the condition which the legislation is intended to affect or change, and where the legislative body does not itself possess the requisite information...recourse must be had to others who possess it. Experience has taught that mere requests for information are often unavailing, and also that information which is volunteered is not always accurate or complete, so some means of compulsion is necessary to obtain what is needed."

The court indicated further that it would presume a legislative purpose lay behind the authorization of a congressional investigation, whether indeed that was the purpose of the inquiry or not. "The only legitimate object the Senate could have in ordering the investigation was to aid in legislating; and we think the subject matter was such that the presumption should be indulged that this was the real object," the court said. "An express avowal of the object would have been better; but in view of the particular subject matter was not indispensable," the court added.

To this sweeping approval of congressional investigations, the court appended two reservations. It cautioned, first, that "Neither house is invested with general power to inquire into private affairs and compel disclosures" and second, that "A witness may rightfully refuse to answer where the bounds of inquiry are exceeded or the questions are not pertinent to the matter under scrutiny."

Sinclair v. United States. In 1929 *(Sinclair v. United States,* 279 U.S. 263) the Supreme Court held that a witness who refused to answer questions asked by a congressional committee could be punished if he were mistaken as to the law on which he based his refusal. [67] The fact that a witness acted in good faith on the advice of counsel was no defense, the court held. This precedent made any challenge of committee powers a risky proposition, with the possibility of a jail sentence for any witness seeking to test his rights in court.

The case grew out of an investigation of the Teapot Dome scandals. The Interior Department had leased public lands, containing oil, to the Mammoth Oil Co., the president and sole stockholder of which was Harry F. Sinclair. Sinclair had refused to answer questions of a Senate investigating committee on the ground that the whole matter was of exclusively judicial concern and therefore beyond the Senate's legitimate range of inquiry. He was convicted and sentenced under the 1857 statute. In upholding the conviction, the Supreme Court declared that the naval oil reserves and their disposition were clearly a proper matter for congressional scrutiny. However, Justice Pierce Butler at the same time emphasized the duty of the courts to protect individuals against "all unauthorized, arbitrary or unreasonable inquiries and disclosures in respect of their personal and private affairs."

Jurney v. MacCracken. In 1935, the court ruled *(Jurney v. MacCracken,* 294 U.S. 125) that an investigating committee had authority to punish for contempt a witness who destroyed papers after the service of a subpoena for them. [68] Several letters had been removed from the office of William P. MacCracken, a Washington lawyer, during a Senate committee investigation of airmail contracts.

United States v. Rumely. Following World War II, the Supreme Court was far more protective of the rights of witnesses than of the rights of congressional committees. [69] In the 1953 case of *United States v. Rumely,* (345 U.S. 41, 1953), the Supreme Court upheld a Court of Appeals decision reversing the conviction for contempt of Congress of Edward A. Rumely. Rumely had refused to tell the House Select Committee on Lobbying Activities the names of individuals making bulk purchases of books distributed by the Committee for Constitutional Government, an archconservative organization. He had asserted to the committee that "under the Bill of Rights, that is beyond the power of your committee to investigate."

A majority of the court avoided the constitutional questions by narrowly construing the authority granted by the resolution establishing the committee. It held that the mandate to investigate "lobbying activities" was limited to "representations made directly to the Congress, its members, or its committees," and excluded attempts to influence Congress indirectly through public dissemination of literature. Otherwise, the court said, it would be confronted by "grave constitutional questions." Interpreting the authorizing resolution to include attempts to influence Congress indirectly, Justice William O. Douglas and Hugo L. Black contended that the requirement that a publisher disclose the identity of purchasers would violate the First Amendment guarantees of freedom of speech and the press.

Subversive and Fifth Amendment Cases

The wartime and postwar quest to uncover subversion in the United States produced a new style of investigation. The overriding purpose of the anti-subversion hearings was exposure, as was indicated in the comments by Rep. Martin

(Continued on p. 153)

Should Congress Legislate on Executive Privilege?

Should Congress set up a statutory mechanism for dealing with claims of executive privilege and thereby implicitly recognize that privilege in law?

This was a recurring issue in the early 1970s. In December 1973, the Senate passed a bill to establish procedures for judicial enforcement of congressional efforts to obtain information from federal officials, but the legislation died in 1974 when the House failed to act.

Extensive hearings on the problem of obtaining information from an unwilling executive branch were held by several congressional subcommittees between 1971 and 1973. Some members of Congress, upset by executive denial of data about foreign affairs, attempted in 1973 to terminate funds for any foreign policy agency that refused to provide requested information. None of the efforts succeeded.

Following hearings by two subcommittees in the spring of 1973, the Senate Government Operations Committee reported a bill to require that all requested information must be provided unless the President in writing ordered the information withheld. The bill also established procedures for Congress to override a claim of privilege, to subpoena the information and to seek court enforcement of subpoenas.

During a hearing on April 10, 1973, Attorney General Richard G. Kleindienst contended, "Your power to get what the President knows is in the President's hands." Congress, he said, does not have power to compel anyone in the executive branch to testify or produce documents if the President forbids it.

In its report endorsing the bill, the committee took issue with this sweeping assertion. If the absolute privilege claimed by Kleindienst exists, the report stated, "the power of the executive branch to screen the conduct of its officials from inquiry would overwhelm and invalidate the power of Congress to make those inquiries." Therefore, legislation was needed to make clear that "the executive may seek to deny information to the legislative branch; that the legislative branch may seek to compel the production of the information despite a claim of privilege; and that the judiciary, in the event the other two branches fail to resolve their disagreement, should be called upon to decide the outcome."

Following Senate passage, the bill was reported by the House Government Operations Committee April 11, 1974. But the committee was seriously divided over the wisdom of legislating procedures to deal with the privilege because it would thereby implicitly acknowledge the existence of that privilege in law. The committee split 24-16 in favor of reporting the bill, which was never brought up on the House floor.

Following are arguments favoring and opposing such legislation.

Support

The proposed legislation would establish congressional access to information "in a way which balances the needs of the executive...with the needs of the Congress in exercising its legislative and in-vestigative functions," the House committee report said. "It gives neither branch a veto over the desires of the other, but places the burden of justifying any denials of information on the President."

By its inaction, the committee report continued, "the Congress has, in effect, acquiesced to the executive's power to restrict the flow of information to the legislative branch.... The committee believes that enactment of [the bill] would remedy this situation in an equitable manner...establishing a procedure for case-by-case determination of when information may be withheld, based on the guiding principle of the Freedom of Information Act: that access to material should be the rule, with exemptions provided only in the specific instances where a compelling national interest so dictates."

Material classified for national security purposes also should be available to Congress, the report said, unless the President claimed executive privilege in a detailed written statement. "Because the Congress must legislate for all the people of this country, it must have access to more information than any one of them. The material may be made available on a confidential basis," it said.

Opposition

Two points of view, diametrically opposed, were expressed by those who opposed the bill. The Justice Department found it too restrictive: "A claim of executive privilege...is essentially a presidential constitutional responsibility; the form in which it is to be exercised therefore is to be determined by the President and not by the Congress."

On the other hand, the committee members who opposed the bill saw it as recognizing—not restricting—executive privilege.

"This would be the first time," wrote House committee chairman Chet Holifield (D Calif.), "that the [executive privilege] doctrine would find its way into the statute books." In views concurred in by nine of the dissenting Democrats, Rep. Jack Brooks (D Texas) agreed. The bill, Brooks wrote, "would enscribe into law the concept of executive privilege and give to every agency...as well as the President, the appearance of legitimacy in denying certain information to Congress."

Furthermore, Brooks objected to the fact that "this bill would confer upon...the judiciary the power to determine what information the Congress has a right to obtain. To give any judge...such authority is an abdication of congressional responsibility.... Congress has adequate authority now to get the information it needs. We should concentrate upon exercising that authority."

"It is just conceivable," warned Rep. Jim Wright (D Texas), that this bill "might inadvertently offer tempting loopholes for federal bureaucrats...and be subject to an unintended interpretation of giving some heretofore nonexistent legal standing to some presumed constitutional privilege of the President to withhold information from Congress."

(Continued from p. 151)

Dies (D Texas), chairman of the House Special Committee to Investigate Un-American Activities: "I am not in a position to say whether we can legislate effectively in reference to this matter, but I do know that exposure in a democracy of subversive activities is the most effective weapon that we have in our possession."[70]

Committee witnesses balked at the new investigative tactics, and the number of contempt of Congress citations grew, leading to new court tests. To meet the new legal issues raised by the anti-subversive inquiries, the courts handed down a number of decisions further defining the rights of witnesses and the powers of investigating committees. Nearly all of the cases originated in hearings by the House Un-American Activities Committee. *(Box, p. 166)*

In *Blau v. United States* (340 U.S. 332, 1950), the Supreme Court reversed the conviction of Mrs. Patricia Blau, who had pleaded the Fifth Amendment in refusing to **answer questions about Communist affiliation before a** federal grand jury in Denver. The court ruled that to support the claim of privilege it was not necessary that the answers sought would support a conviction of crime. It was sufficient that the answers "would have furnished a link in the chain of evidence needed in a prosecution of petitioner for violation of (or conspiracy to violate) the Smith Act." (This act prohibited teaching or advocacy of violent overthrow of the government.) In effect, the court's decision acknowledged that admission of Communist activity might be incriminating.[71]

In a 1951 decision, however, the Supreme Court ruled *(Rogers v. United States,* 340 U.S. 367) that a witness could not invoke the Fifth Amendment privilege after once having answered about materially incriminating facts.[72] The case arose after Jane Rogers, subpoenaed by a federal grand jury, testified that she had been treasurer of the Communist Party in Denver. Having made this admission, she then sought to end her testimony and refused to give the name of the person to whom she had turned over the party's books. A divided Supreme Court ruled that she had waived the privilege of silence by her initial testimony, and that the further questions she had refused to answer did not involve a "reasonable danger of further crimination."

The Supreme Court did not consider any contempt of Congress cases in which a witness had pleaded the Fifth Amendment until 1955. That year, in two decisions decided on the same day *(Emspak v. United States,* 349 U.S. 190 and *Quinn v. United States,* 349 U.S. 155), in a spirited defense of the controversial right, the court laid down general guidelines for the use of the privilege.[73] No special combination of words or "ritualistic formula" was required of a witness wishing to claim the privilege, the court said. If the investigating committee had been in any doubt as to the ground on which refusal to testify was based, it should have asked the witness whether he was in fact relying on the Fifth Amendment.

In the late 1950s, the court handed down a pair of decisions which attempted to establish limits to the "exposure power" of a committee. The court declared in a 1957 case *(Watkins v. United States,* 354 U.S. 178, 1957), that "there is no congressional power to expose for the sake of exposure." Conceding that the public was entitled to be informed of the workings of the government, the court said: "That cannot be inflated into a general power to expose where the predominant result can only be an invasion of the **private rights of individuals." The ruling was praised by** many as an important restriction on the procedures of committees investigating subversion.[74]

But two years later, in 1959 *(Barenblatt v. United States,* 360 U.S. 109), the court backed away from the *Watkins* declaration. A challenged Un-American Activities Committee hearing was not unlawful on the ground that its purpose was "exposure," the court said in the 1959 case. "So long as Congress acts in pursuance of its constitutional power, the judiciary lacks authority to intervene on the **basis of the motives which spurred the exercise of that** power," the court said. In addition, the court made clear **that it would broadly interpret the power of Congress.**[75] *(Excerpts from texts of opinions, pp. 154-155)*

In two 1961 decisions *(Wilkinson v. United States,* 365 U.S. 399, and *Braden v. United States,* 365 U.S. 431), the court went a step beyond the *Barenblatt* decision, affirming the convictions of the defendants, who contended they had been subpoenaed simply because of their criticisms of the Un-American Activities Committee. [76]

Although it thus appeared that the court had recognized a practically unlimited power of congressional inquiry, from 1961 to 1966, it reversed almost every contempt conviction which came before it. According to scholar Pritchett, "These reversals were accomplished for the most part without challenging the scope of investigatory power or querying the motives of the investigators. They were achieved primarily by strict judicial enforcement of the rules on pertinency, authorization, and procedure, plus strict observance of the constitutional standards governing criminal prosecutions."[77]

Investigations and Executive Branch

Investigations have often led Congress into conflict with the executive branch. The most frequent cause of contention has been refusal by the President to comply with congressional demands for information.

Practically every administration since 1792 has clashed with Congress over the question of "executive privilege," although the term was first used only in 1958,[78] and the issue has yet to be resolved. Some experts have asserted that executive departments, having been established by Congress and maintained by its appropriations, are the creatures of the legislature and cannot deny it information regarding their activities. Congress may seek to back up its demands by arousing public support for disclosure, especially if there is any suspicion that an administration is seeking to protect its political reputation by hiding mistakes or malfeasance. However, the long list of precedents in which Presidents have successfully defied congressional demands for infor**mation, and Congress' reluctance to settle the issue by** legislation forcing it into the courts, support claims that the constitutional separation of powers permits the President, at his discretion, to withhold information sought by Congress.

A variety of reasons has been used to justify denying information to Congress. Perhaps the most common has been the need for secrecy in military and diplomatic activities. Presidents have also sought to avoid unwarranted exposure of individuals to unfavorable publicity, especially when documents or files requested contain incomplete, distorted, inaccurate, misleading or unsubstantiated information. The need for confidential exchange of ideas between members of an administration has been cited as justifying refusal to provide records or describe conversations in the executive branch. Fears that disclosures would interfere with criminal or security investigations sometimes have prompted administrative secrecy. Critics of an administration have fre-

Supreme Court 'Balances' Rights of Witnesses . . .

The leading Supreme Court decisions regarding the question of the First Amendment rights of witnesses and the investigating powers of Congress were Watkins v. United States *(354 U.S. 178, 1957) and* Barenblatt v. United States *(360 U.S. 109, 1959). A central issue in both cases was that section of House Rule XI defining the powers and duties of the House Un-American Activities Committee. Following are excerpts from Supreme Court opinions in these two cases:*

Watkins Case

(Majority opinion by Chief Justice Earl Warren)

"The controversy thus rests upon fundamental principles of the power of the Congress and the limitations upon that power. We approach the questions presented with conscious awareness of the far-reaching ramifications that can follow from a decision of this nature....

"We start with several basic premises on which there is general agreement. The power of the Congress to conduct investigations is inherent in the legislative process. That power is broad. It encompasses inquiries concerning the administration of existing laws as well as proposed or possibly needed statutes. It includes surveys of defects in our social, economic or political system for the purpose of enabling the Congress to remedy them. It comprehends probes into departments of the federal government to expose corruption, inefficiency or waste. But, broad as is this power of inquiry, it is not unlimited. There is no general authority to expose the private affairs of individuals without justification in terms of the functions of the Congress. This was freely conceded by the solicitor general in his argument of this case. Nor is the Congress a law enforcement or trial agency. These are functions of the executive and judicial departments of government. No inquiry is an end in itself; it must be related to, and in furtherance of, a legitimate task of the Congress. Investigations conducted solely for the personal aggrandizement of the investigators or to punish those investigated are indefensible....

"Clearly, an investigation is subject to the command that the Congress shall make no law abridging freedom of speech or press or assembly. While it is true that there is no statute to be reviewed, and that an investigation is not a law, nevertheless an investigation is part of lawmaking. It is justified solely as an adjunct to the legislative process. The First Amendment may be invoked against infringement of the protected freedoms by law or by law-making.

"Abuses of the investigative process may imperceptibly lead to abridgment of protected freedoms. The mere summoning of a witness and compelling him to testify, against his will, about his beliefs, expressions or associations is a measure of governmental interference. And when those forced revelations concern matters that are unorthodox, unpopular, or even hateful to the general public, the reaction in the life of the witness may be disastrous. This effect is even more harsh when it is past beliefs, expressions or associations that are disclosed and judged by current standards rather than those contemporary with the matters exposed. Nor does the witness alone suffer the consequences. Those who are identified by witnesses and thereby placed in the same glare of publicity are equally subject to public stigma, scorn and obloquy. Beyond that, there is the more subtle and immeasurable effect upon those who tend to adhere to the most orthodox and uncontroversial views and associations in order to avoid a similar fate at some future time. That this impact is partly the result of nongovernmental activity by private persons cannot relieve the investigators of their responsibility for initiating the reaction....

"Accommodation of the congressional need for particular information with the individual and personal interest in privacy is an arduous and delicate task for any court.... The critical element is the existence of, and the weight to be ascribed to, the interest of the Congress in demanding disclosures from an unwilling witness. We cannot simply assume, however, that every congressional investigation is justified by a public need that overbalances any private rights to be affected. To do so would be to abdicate the responsibility placed by the Constitution upon the judiciary to insure that the Congress does not unjustifiably encroach upon an individual's right to privacy nor abridge his liberty of speech, press, religion, or assembly....

"We have no doubt that there is no congressional power to expose for the sake of exposure. The public is, of course, entitled to be informed concerning the workings of its government. That cannot be inflated into a general power to expose where the predominant result can only be an invasion of the private rights of individuals. But a solution to our problem is not to be found in testing the motives of committee members for this purpose. Such is not our function. Their motives alone would not vitiate an investigation which had been instituted by a house of Congress if that assembly's legislative purpose is being served....

(The court took note of House Rule XI, which incorporated the resolution establishing the Un-American Activities Committee and authorizing it to investigate: "(1) the extent, character, and objects of un-American propaganda activities in the United States, (2) the diffusion within the United States of subversive and un-

quently charged that its real motive for refusing to divulge information was to escape criticism or scandal.

"Clearly, the President cannot turn over documents to Congress so that Congress can then decide whether or not they should have been turned over," wrote Telford Taylor in his 1955 study of investigations. "If there is an executive privilege to withhold information when disclosures would not be 'in the public interest,' then the President must be the one to determine in any particular case whether the public interest permits disclosure or requires nondisclosure. Just as clearly, this leaves open the possibility that the President may abuse his prerogative, especially in

. . . and Congressional Investigating Power

American propaganda that is instigated from foreign countries or of a domestic origin and attacks the principle of the form of government as guaranteed by our Constitution, and (3) all other questions in relation thereto that would aid Congress in any necessary remedial legislation.")

"It would be difficult to imagine a less explicit authorizing resolution. Who can define the meaning of 'un-American?' What is that single, solitary 'principle of the form of government as guaranteed by our Constitution'?...

"An excessively broad charter, like that of the House Un-American Activities Committee, places the courts in an untenable position if they are to strike a balance between the public need for a particular interrogation and the right of citizens to carry on their affairs free from unnecessary governmental interference. It is impossible in such a situation to ascertain whether any legislative purpose justifies the disclosure sought and, if so, the importance of that information to the Congress in furtherance of its legislative function. The reason no court can make this critical judgment is that the House of Representatives itself has never made it."

Barenblatt Case

(Majority opinion by Justice John Marshall Harlan)

"...Granting the vagueness of the Rule (House Rule XI), we may not read it in isolation from its long history in the House of Representatives. Just as legislation is often given meaning by the gloss of legislative reports, administrative interpretation, and long usage, so the proper meaning of an authorization to a congressional committee is not to be derived alone from its abstract terms unrelated to the definite content furnished them by the course of congressional actions. The rule comes to us with a 'persuasive gloss of legislative history,'...which shows beyond doubt that in pursuance of its legislative concerns in the domain of 'national security' the House has clothed the Un-American Activities Committee with pervasive authority to investigate Communist activities in this country....

"The precise constitutional issue confronting us is whether the subcommittee's inquiry into petitioner's past or present membership in the Communist Party transgressed the provisions of the First Amendment, which of course reach and limit congressional investigations.

"The court's past cases establish sure guides to decision. Undeniably, the First Amendment in some circumstances protects an individual from being compelled to disclose his associational relationships. However, the

protections of the First Amendment, unlike a proper claim of the privilege against self-incrimination under the Fifth Amendment, do not afford a witness the right to resist inquiry in all circumstances. Where First Amendment rights are asserted to bar governmental interrogation, resolution of the issue always involves a balancing by the courts of the competing private and public interests at stake in the particular circumstances shown. These principles were recognized in the Watkins case, where, in speaking of the First Amendment in relation to congressional inquiries, we said: 'It is manifest that despite the adverse effects which follow upon compelled disclosure of private matters, not all such inquiries are barred.... The critical element is the existence of, and the weight to be ascribed to, the interest of the Congress in demanding disclosures from an unwilling witness....'

"That Congress has wide power to legislate in the field of Communist activity in this country, and to conduct appropriate investigations in aid thereof, is hardly debatable. The existence of such power has never been questioned by this court, and it is sufficient to say, without particularization, that Congress has enacted or considered in this field a wide range of legislative measures, not a few of which have stemmed from recommendations of the very committee whose actions have been drawn in question here. In the last analysis this power rests on the right of self-preservation, 'the ultimate value of any society.' Justification for its exercise in turn rests on the long and widely accepted view that the tenets of the Communist Party include the ultimate overthrow of the government of the United States by force and violence, a view which has been given formal expression by the Congress. On these premises, this court in its constitutional adjudications has consistently refused to view the Communist Party as an ordinary political party, and has upheld federal legislation aimed at the Communist problem which in a different context would certainly have raised constitutional issues of the gravest character....

"To suggest that because the Communist Party may also sponsor peaceable political reforms the constitutional issues before us should now be judged as if that party were just an ordinary political party from the standpoint of national security, is to ask this court to blind itself to world affairs which have determined the whole course of our national policy since the close of World War II, and to the vast burdens which these conditions have entailed for the entire nation....

"We conclude that the balance between the individual and governmental interests here at stake must be struck in favor of the latter, and that therefore the provisions of the First Amendment have not been offended."

instances where the information would reflect unfavorably on him or his administration of the nation's affairs."[79]

Taylor was writing during a period when critics of the congressional investigating power were pointing to what they considered abuses of the power by the McCarthy panel in excessive demands for information from the ad-

ministration. Twenty years later, however, following clashes between President Johnson and Congress over Vietnam War information and between President Nixon and Congress over Watergate documents and testimony by members of the administration, the weight of opinion had seemed to shift against use of the "privilege." Harvard Professor

Raoul Berger, writing in 1974, offered a detailed critique of the use of "executive privilege," terming it a "constitutional myth"[80]—"a product of the nineteenth century, fashioned by a succession of Presidents who created 'precedents' to suit the occasion.... At bottom, the issue concerns the right of Congress and the people to participate in making the fateful decisions that affect the fortunes of the nation. Claims of presidential power to bar such participation or to withhold on one ground or another the information that is indispensable for intelligent participation undermine this right and sap the very foundations of democratic government. More than extravagant legend is required to sustain such claims, nothing less than demonstrable constitutional sanction, and, even then, proof that a presidential iron curtain is demanded by the highest wisdom."[81]

Presidents who refused demands from investigating committees have included Washington, Jefferson, Monroe, Jackson, Tyler, Polk, Fillmore, Lincoln, Grant, Hayes, Cleveland, Theodore Roosevelt, Coolidge, Hoover and all subsequent Presidents or members of their administrations.[82] In some cases committees have accepted the President's refusal without comment. Other times, the refusal has led to a full-scale constitutional confrontation. A series of selected cases follows.

Early Refusals to Give Information

Washington. The "precedent" of executive privilege was first established in 1792 when a select House committee, conducting the first congressional inquiry, investigated an Indian victory over Maj. Gen. Arthur St. Clair and his men in the Northwest Territory. The committee wrote to War Secretary Henry Knox and asked him to turn over all the documents relating to the St. Clair expedition. Knox asked President Washington for advice; the President raised the subject at a Cabinet meeting. The Cabinet agreed that the House could conduct such an investigation and could call for such papers. It decided, according to the report of Thomas Jefferson, "that the executive ought to communicate such papers as the public good would permit, and ought to refuse those, the disclosure of which would endanger the public." As it developed, none of the St. Clair papers were regarded as confidential, and the President on April 4 directed Knox to make the papers available to the committee.[83]

(Four years later, in 1796, Washington claimed executive privilege when he refused a House request for correspondence relating to the intensely controversial Jay Treaty with Great Britain. The House was debating a bill to implement portions of the treaty; the bill eventually was passed.)

Jackson. A House committee appointed "to examine into the conditions of the executive departments" adopted on Jan. 23, 1837, a series of resolutions that directed President Jackson and members of his Cabinet to furnish lists of federal appointments made without the concurrence of the Senate, along with information as to the salaries of the appointees and as to whether they were being paid without having taken office. Jackson, backed by a large majority in the House, categorically refused, in what was to become one of the most successful efforts of a President to resist congressional investigators.[84]

"According to the established rules of law," Jackson replied on Jan. 27, "you request myself and the heads of departments to become our own accusers, and to furnish the evidence to convict ourselves." The President continued: "If you either will not make specific accusations, or

if, when made, you attempt to establish them by making free men their own accusers, you will not expect me to countenance your proceedings."[85] He then invoked "the principles of justice" as well as the Constitution in refusing the congressional request.[86]

After three months of fruitless questioning of some Cabinet officers and others, the committee concluded that it had overstepped its authority in submitting a blanket request for documents, and dropped the inquiry. The Jackson majority on the committee explained that it had gone along with the requests of Chairman Henry A. Wise (D Va.) to avoid charges of protecting the administration. In a report on March 3, 1837, the committee said: "The condition of the various executive departments is prosperous, and...they have been conducted with ability and industry."

Tyler. The House on May 18, 1842, adopted a resolution requesting War Secretary J. C. Spencer to make available to the Indian Affairs Committee reports on the Cherokee Indians and alleged frauds committed against them. After consulting with President Tyler, Spencer on June 3 refused, asserting that negotiations to settle claims with the Indians still were in progress. The committee persisted in its request, and on Aug. 13 the House by an 83-60 vote adopted a committee resolution requesting the information from Tyler. Tyler took no action on the request. On Dec. 30, the House adopted another resolution asking when the President was going to act.[87]

Tyler replied, Jan. 31, 1843, that the claims negotiations had been concluded in the meantime, and information dealing with the alleged frauds would be submitted. However, the President withheld portions of the reports containing personal comments about Indian negotiators and about recommendations for future action. In doing so, the President argued that the House could not demand information, even if relevant to a House debate, if the information would interfere with the discretion of the executive branch. "It cannot be that the only test is whether the information relates to a legitimate subject of deliberation," Tyler said. Also to be considered, he added, were the protection of confidential sources of government officials and the protection of officials from malicious publicity. The President's message was referred to the Indian Affairs Committee, which submitted a report, Feb. 25, criticizing the President's position but recommending no action.

Cleveland. President Cleveland in 1885 was the first Democrat in the White House since Buchanan in 1861.[88] Democrats also controlled the House, but Republicans had a majority in the Senate. As the new President began replacing holdover Republican officeholders with Democrats, the Senate committees to which the nominations were referred repeatedly requested the information that had led to removal of the Republican incumbents. The standard department reply was that at the direction of the President it refused, on the ground that the public interest would not be served or that the removal had been a purely executive action.

Some 650 Republican officeholders were replaced. Finally, on Dec. 26, 1885, the Senate Judiciary Committee asked Attorney General A.H. Garland for information on the dismissal of George N. Durskin, U.S. district attorney for the southern district of Alabama. There being no response from Garland, the Senate on Jan. 26, 1886, adopted a committee resolution directing the Attorney General to furnish the papers. In his reply, Feb. 1, Garland said the President had directed him to report that "the public interest would not be promoted by compliance with the resolution." The Senate responded, Feb. 18, by adopting a resolution refusing to concur in the removal of officeholders when the documents on which the removal was based were withheld.

In a message to the Senate, March 1, Cleveland disclaimed any intent to withhold official papers and asserted that the letters and reports leading to the dismissals were inherently private and confidential. He continued: "I do not suppose that the public offices of the United States are regulated or controlled in their relations to either house of Congress by the fact that they were created by laws enacted by" Congress.[89] Cleveland's argument raised the recurring question of whether government departments are creatures of the executive branch, because they carry out executive functions, or creatures of the legislative branch, because they are established and financed through congressional action. From March 9 to 26 the Senate debated the issue. It concluded by adopting a resolution citing the Attorney General for being "in violation of his official duty and subversive of the fundamental principles of the government...." President Cleveland stood his ground, however, and the Senate ultimately confirmed his nominee to replace Durskin, John D. Burnett.

Continued Insistence on Executive Privilege

Hoover. During Senate consideration of the London Naval Treaty of 1930, the Foreign Relations Committee asked for the papers relating to the London Conference at which the treaty had been negotiated. Secretary of State Henry L. Stimson submitted some of the papers but withheld others, explaining June 6, 1930, that he had been "directed by the President to say" that their production "would not in his opinion be compatible with the public interest." The committee adopted a resolution, June 12, asserting that the documents were "relevant and pertinent when the Senate is considering a treaty for the purpose of ratification." On July 10, the Senate, supporting the committee, adopted by a 53-4 vote a resolution requesting the President to submit the material, "if not incompatible with the public interest." Pleading the next day that the papers were confidential, Hoover again declined to produce them. The Senate on July 21 consented to ratification of the treaty, with "the distinct and explicit understanding" that it contained no secret agreements.[90]

Truman. President Truman in 1948 became involved in a head-on clash between the executive branch and an investigating committee of Congress. On March 1 the House Un-American Activities Special Subcommittee on National Security issued a report that called Dr. Edward U. Condon, director of the Bureau of Standards, "one of the weakest links in our national security." The subcommittee promptly subpoenaed Commerce Department records of loyalty investigations of Condon, but Secretary of Commerce W. Averell Harriman refused to release them on the ground that their publication would be "prejudicial to the public interest."[91]

President Truman took a direct hand in the controversy on March 13 when he issued a directive barring disclosure of any loyalty files to Congress. The President said: "Any subpoena or demand or request for information, reports or files of the nature described, received from sources other than those persons in the executive branch...who are entitled thereto by reason of their special duties, shall be respectfully declined on the basis of this directive, and the subpoena or demand or other request shall be referred to the office of the President for such response as the President may determine to be in the public interest in the particular case. There shall be no relaxation of this directive except with my express authority."[92]

On April 22 the House by a 302-29 vote adopted a resolution (H Res 522) demanding that Harriman surrender an FBI report on Condon. The disputed documents were transferred to the White House, and the President refused to release them—despite Condon's request that they be made public. The House on May 12 passed by a 219-152 vote a bill (H J Res 342) "directing all executive departments and agencies of the federal government to make available to any and all standing, special or select committees of the House of Representatives and the Senate, information which may be deemed necessary to enable them to properly perform the duties delegated to them by Congress." Refusal to comply was to be considered a misdemeanor, punishable by a fine of up to $1,000 or imprisonment for up to one year, or both. In the Senate, the bill was referred to the Committee on Expenditures in the Executive Departments (Government Operations), where it died upon expiration of the 80th Congress.[93]

Eisenhower. During the Army-McCarthy hearings before the Senate Government Operations Permanent Investigations Subcommittee, President Eisenhower on May 17, 1954, forbade testimony about a Jan. 12 meeting between Attorney General Herbert Brownell Jr. and Army Counsel John Adams. Developments in the aggressively anti-Communist hearings being conducted by Subcommittee Chairman Joseph R. McCarthy (R Wis.) had been discussed at the meeting. In a letter to Defense Secretary Charles E. Wilson imposing the ban on testimony about the meeting, Eisenhower stressed the importance of candid, private communication within the executive branch and the "proper separation of power between the executive and legislative branches." When Adams cited the President's order in refusing to answer a question on May 24, McCarthy accused him of using "a type of Fifth Amendment privilege."[94]

McCarthy said three days later that he wanted all federal workers to know "that I feel it's their duty to give us any information which they have about graft, corruption, Communists, treason, and that there is no loyalty to a superior officer which can tower above and beyond their loyalty to their country." The senator promised to shield the identity of informants. The Democrats on the subcommittee protested McCarthy's call for informers, and Brownell on May 28, with the President's approval, issued a statement: "The executive branch...has the sole and fundamental responsibility under the Constitution for the enforcement of our laws and presidential orders.... That responsibility cannot be usurped by an individual who may seek to set himself above the laws of our land or to override orders of the President of the United States to federal employees of the executive branch."

Kennedy Limitations. President Eisenhower's May 17, 1954, letter and accompanying memorandum soon became the basis for an extension of the claim of "executive privilege" far down the administrative line from the President. After that time, according to a 1973 report prepared by the Government and General Research Division of the Library of Congress, "the executive branch answer to nearly every question about the authority to withhold information from the Congress was 'yes,' they had the authority."[95]

The pattern of invoking the "privilege" by executive branch officials far down the administrative line from the President was somewhat altered, but not broken, by President Kennedy in 1962. The previous year, a special Senate subcommittee had opened hearings on the Pentagon's system for editing speeches of military leaders. When the panel asked the identity of the editors, the President directed the Secretary of Defense, in a Feb. 8, 1962, letter, "not to give any testimony or produce any documents which would disclose such information." He added, however: "The principle which is at stake here cannot be automatically applied to every request for information. Each case must be judged on its own merits." And on March 7, 1962, the President wrote, "Executive privilege can be invoked only by the President and will not be used without specific presidential approval."[96]

Nonetheless, after the Kennedy directive, executive branch officials in his administration refused to provide information to congressional committees three times, apparently without presidential authority.[97]

President Johnson continued this trend, despite a letter of April 2, 1965, in which he stated that "the claim of 'executive privilege' will continue to be made only by the President." Although he personally did not invoke the privilege, there were two refusals by appointees in his administration to provide information to congressional committees.

Nixon Assertions. In addition to Watergate-related information, President Nixon personally and formally invoked the claim of "executive privilege" against congressional committees four times after issuing a memorandum on March 24, 1969, stating that the privilege would not be used without specific presidential approval. Between 1969 and 1973, moreover, there were at least 15 other instances (most of them related to defense or foreign policy) in which documents or testimony were refused to congressional committees without direct presidential approval.[98] "In fact, the presidential statements [on executive privilege] have been limitations in name only," concluded the Library of Congress report.[99]

Watergate and Executive Privilege

The most dramatic clash over use of executive privilege was bound up with Watergate and pitted Nixon against two congressional committees, the special prosecutor (both Archibald Cox and his successor, Leon Jaworski) and a grand jury.

The confrontation began with establishment of the Senate Watergate Committee in February 1973. At first, Nixon pleaded executive privilege, refusing to allow his aides to appear before the panel. But in April he reversed himself, stating that government employees and particularly White House employees "are expected fully to cooperate in this matter. I condemn any attempts to cover up in this case, no matter who is involved."

On May 3, the White House issued new guidelines on the privilege: "The President desires that the invocation of executive privilege be held to a minimum." The privilege should be invoked only in connection with conversations with the President, conversations among aides involving communications with the President, and with regard to presidential papers and national security.[100]

On May 29, Nixon said he would refuse to provide information through oral or written testimony to the Watergate

---

Extent of Executive Privilege

In a July 6, 1973, letter to Sam J. Ervin Jr. (D N.C.), chairman of the Senate Watergate investigating committee, President Nixon cited a 1953 case as a partial justification for his refusal to testify before the panel or to turn over requested presidential papers. He referred to a letter written Nov. 12, 1953, by former President Truman to Rep. Harold H. Velde (R Ill.), chairman of the House Un-American Activities Committee. That committee had issued a subpoena to the former President on Nov. 9.

In refusing to comply with the subpoena, Truman wrote: "It must be obvious to you that if the doctrine of separation of powers and the independence of the presidency is to have any validity at all, it must be equally applicable to a President after his term of office has expired when he is sought to be examined with respect to any acts occurring while he is President." The committee subsequently dropped the subpoena.

Another aspect of the issue surfaced in November 1975 when the House Intelligence Committee issued three subpoenas for information concerning national security affairs. Secretary of State Henry A. Kissinger refused to turn over the State Department documents on the orders of President Ford, who cited executive privilege. The material requested involved "highly sensitive military and foreign affairs assessments and evaluations" as well as consultations and advice to former Presidents Kennedy, Johnson and Nixon, according to the White House letter to Kissinger ordering withholding of the material. Committee Chairman Otis G. Pike (D N.Y.) countered that executive privilege could not be invoked by Ford for the documents of previous administrations. The committee voted to cite Kissinger in contempt, but subsequently dropped the action after receiving "substantial compliance" with two of the subpoenas when the White House agreed to turn over documents dating back to 1961.

The extent of executive privilege also figured in a court decision regarding custody of Nixon administration papers. U.S. District Court Judge Charles C. Richey ruled Jan. 31, 1975, that the Nixon documents were the property of the government and not the former President, arguing that executive privilege applied only to a President in office, not to an ex-President.

---

grand jury or to the Senate committee. For him to do so would be "constitutionally inappropriate" and a violation of the separation of powers.[101]

Nixon repeated his refusal to appear before the committee or to hand over presidential papers in a letter to Chairman Sam J. Ervin Jr. (D N.C.) July 6.[102] "No President could function if the private papers of his office, prepared by his personal staff, were open to public scrutiny," he said. "Formulation of sound public policy requires that the President and his personal staff be able to communicate among themselves in complete candor.... If I were to testify before the committee irreparable damage would be done to the constitutional principle of separation of powers."

Thus the limits of inquiry were apparently set, both for the co-equal judicial branch within which the grand jury investigation was continuing and for the co-equal legislative branch within which the Senate committee was working.

The executive privilege issue assumed new dimensions in July, however, with revelation that tape recordings had been made of many presidential conversations in the White House during the period in which the break-in occurred and the cover-up began. Immediately, a struggle for the tapes began. The legal battle would last almost exactly a year, from July 23, 1973, when the Senate committee and the Watergate grand jury subpoenaed the first group of tapes, to July 24, 1974, when the Supreme Court ruled against Nixon. But the Senate investigating committee never obtained the tapes it sought. The administration's argument against relinquishing the tapes to the Senate committee prevailed in the courts.

In refusing to relinquish the tapes, Nixon repeated his arguments that to do so would be "inconsistent with the public interest and with the constitutional position of the presidency." On Aug. 29, U.S. District Court Judge John J. Sirica ruled that the President should give him the tapes so that he could review them. On Oct. 12, the U.S. Court of Appeals for the District of Columbia Circuit upheld Sirica's decision. In a 44-page majority opinion, the court viewed executive privilege as a qualified privilege to be weighed by courts against competing public interests. On the other hand, a view of executive privilege as absolute and exercised at the sole discretion of the President marked the two lengthy dissenting opinions.[103]

Five days later, Oct. 17, Sirica ruled on the Senate Watergate Committee's request for the same tapes. In this decision the judge ruled that he had no jurisdiction to consider the committee's effort to force Nixon to give up the tapes. In dismissing the case, Sirica said Congress had never enacted any law giving federal courts jurisdiction in such a case.

Moving quickly to rectify the situation, Congress by Dec. 3 had sent to the White House legislation specifically granting the federal district court in the District of Columbia jurisdiction over suits brought by the Senate Watergate Committee to enforce subpoenas. The bill became law (PL 93-190) without Nixon's signature. The Senate committee Dec. 19 approved new subpoenas for nearly 500 presidential tapes and documents; Nixon Jan. 4 refused to comply.[104]

Deciding to seek enforcement of the original subpoenas before litigating Nixon's refusal to comply with the more recent demands, the committee Jan. 7, 1974, renewed its original suit and asked Sirica to reconsider it in light of PL 93-190. Sirica referred the case to U.S. District Court Judge Gerhard A. Gesell. Again, the White House asked the court to dismiss the suit.

On Jan. 25 Gesell issued his ruling, quashing the July 23 subpoena for documents, but directing Nixon to respond more directly to the July 23 subpoena for the five tapes. The judge asked Nixon to provide a detailed statement explaining what parts of the subpoenaed tapes he considered covered by executive privilege. "This statement must be signed by the President," wrote Gesell, "for only he can invoke the [executive] privilege at issue."[105]

In quashing the broader July 23 committee request for documents, Gesell described the subpoena as too broad and too vague, disregarding "the restraints of specificity and reasonableness which derive from the Fourth Amendment," which guarantees citizens protection against unreasonable search and seizure.[106] On Feb. 6, Nixon sent Gesell a letter stating simply that disclosure of the tapes "would not be in the public interest."[107]

On Feb. 8, the Senate Watergate Committee suffered another defeat in court, when Gesell refused to require the White House to turn over the five tapes to the panel, citing the risk that the committee's use of the tapes might make it difficult to obtain an unbiased jury for the trials arising out of the Watergate matter.[108]

"The committee's role as a 'grand inquest' into governmental misconduct is limited," wrote Gesell. "It may only proceed in aid of Congress' legislative function...the time has come to question whether it is in the public interest for the criminal investigative aspects of its work to go forward in the blazing atmosphere of...publicity."

Neither side had argued convincingly, wrote Gesell. "It has not been demonstrated to the court's satisfaction," he wrote, "that the committee has a pressing need for the subpoenaed tapes.... Conversely, the court rejects the President's assertion that the public interest is best served by a blanket, unreviewable claim of confidentiality over presidential communications...."[109]

The Senate Watergate Committee Feb. 19 agreed to terminate its public hearings, but also decided to appeal the Feb. 8 ruling. The bid was lost May 23, when a U.S. Court of Appeals rejected the request on grounds that the committee had failed to show a pressing enough need for the tapes.[110]

Meanwhile, Cox's successor, Leon Jaworski, and the House Judiciary Committee (which was authorized to begin an impeachment inquiry in February 1974) issued their subpoenas for tapes and documents. Again, Nixon and his lawyers, arguing presidential confidentiality, refused to comply. However, Nixon modified his position and announced April 29, 1974—the day before the deadline set by the Judiciary Committee subpoena—that he would make public the transcripts of 46 tapes the next day. Still the committee was not satisfied. Divided closely along party lines, the committee voted May 1 to inform the President that "you have failed to comply with the committee's subpoena...." Jaworski—whose subpoena for evidence Nixon had also rejected—took his case to the Supreme Court late in May.

"Inherent in the executive power vested in the President under Article II of the Constitution is executive privilege, generally recognized as a derivative of the separation of powers doctrine," argued Nixon's lawyer James D. St. Clair June 21. "The President is not subject to the criminal process whether that process is invoked directly or indirectly. The only constitutional recourse against the President is by impeachment and through the electoral process."[111]

"The qualified executive privilege for confidential intra-governmental deliberations, designed to promote the candid interchange between officials and their aides, exists only to protect the legitimate functioning of the government," said Jaworski. "Thus, the privilege must give way where, as here, it has been abused. There has been a *prima facie* showing that each of the participants in the subpoenaed conversations, including the President, was a member of the conspiracy to defraud the United States and to obstruct justice.... The public purpose underlying the executive privilege for governmental deliberations precludes its application to shield alleged criminality."[112]

On July 24, hours before the Judiciary Committee began public debate on impeachment, the Supreme Court ruled unanimously against the President and ordered him to give up the tapes. *(United States v. Nixon)* Reaffirming its 1803 decision, *Marbury v. Madison* (1 Cranch. 137), establishing the power of the courts to review the actions of the other two branches, Chief Justice Warren E. Burger wrote: "We therefore reaffirm that it is 'emphatically the province and the duty' of this court 'to say what the law is' with respect to the claim of privilege presented in this case."

"...[N]either the doctrine of separation of powers, nor the need for confidentiality of high-level communications, without more, can sustain an absolute, unqualified presidential privilege of immunity from judicial process under all circumstances."[113]

Quickly following the Supreme Court's decision, the Judiciary Committee adopted three articles of impeachment, among them contempt of Congress for failing to comply with subpoenas authorized by the panel.

Nixon began surrendering the tapes to Sirica on July 30. On Aug. 2, Nixon made public the transcript of some of the tapes which showed his participation in a coverup after the Watergate break-in and his approval of the use of the CIA to block an FBI investigation of the event. These revelations wiped out almost all of Nixon's remaining support in Congress and led to his resignation Aug. 9.

Politics of Investigations

"Large-scale investigations of alleged mismanagement or improper activities on the part of executive officers are likely to be greatly influenced by partisan considerations," Joseph P. Harris said in his book, *Congressional Control of Administration.*[114] "It is not uncommon for such an inquiry to result in reports that divide along party lines, with pro-administration members of the committee absolving the officers of blame, and anti-administration members finding the charges sustained. Partisanship is also often responsible for the initiation of investigations and greatly affects the manner in which they are conducted.... That an investigation can be conducted in a nonpartisan manner was notably proved by the Truman Committee during World War II and by its successor, the Senate Preparedness Subcommittee, but it must be said that these constitute somewhat exceptional examples."

President Truman was a Democrat and the House was controlled by Republicans during the 1948 fight over the loyalty file of Dr. Edward U. Condon, director of the Bureau of Standards. Similar conflicting political forces, at countless other times, have had a profound impact on congressional investigations. By their very nature, investigating committees have become focal points of partisan political strife.

As an illustration, the three most intensive periods of congressional investigative activities—the last years of the Grant administration and the periods immediately following World Wars I and II—coincided with shifts of congressional majorities that transferred power to a party long in the minority. Grant, a Republican, was President from 1869 to 1877; and when the Democrats in the 1874 election recaptured control of the House for the first time since 1859, the number of investigations soared. In the 1918 election, Republicans gained control of the House and set off on a series of studies of World War I mobilization under President Wilson, a Democrat. In similar fashion, World War II mobilization, and reported infiltration of the government by Communists during the administrations of Democratic Presidents Roosevelt and Truman, were studied closely by committees of the Republican 80th Congress, elected in 1946.

Personal motives have also figured significantly in the inauguration and conduct of congressional investigations. Hopes for favorable publicity or the desire to win popularity have frequently spurred members of Congress to propose and undertake investigations, although Senate munitions probe chairman Gerald P. Nye maintained in 1933: "I have yet to meet the member of Congress who has enjoyed the tremendous responsibility accompanying appointment to such a committee."[115] A further stimulus to inquiry is bound up in the pet hobbies or hates of individual members. A study of nine major investigations of foreign affairs between 1919 and 1940 indicated that "five...grew out of the personal predilections of certain congressmen."[116] Sen. Key Pittman (D Nev.), for example, on behalf of the silver mining interests, conducted an investigation in 1930 of the reduced trade between the United States and China, believing that it was due to the depreciated price of silver in relation to gold.[117]

Maneuvering for Committee Control

A subtler, and potentially far more important form of investigation politics, has taken place in the maneuvering for control of a particular inquiry. The conduct of investigations has depended substantially on the attitude of the investigating committees and of their chairmen. Thus Radical Republicans, gaining control of the joint committee investigating the conduct of the Civil War, used the committee as a platform from which to criticize the moderate policies of President Lincoln and to force more vigorous prosecution of the war.

A similar example, with quite different results, occurred after World War II. The release by President Truman on Aug. 29, 1945, of Army and Navy reports on the Pearl Harbor disaster, brought numerous Republican demands for a congressional investigation. Through quick maneuvering, the Democrats initiated action. Taking advantage of his right to be recognized first, Senate Majority Leader Alben W. Barkley (D Ky.) obtained unanimous consent, Aug. 29, for consideration of a concurrent resolution to appoint a joint House-Senate committee which, with the Democrats in control of Congress, would have a Democratic majority. The resolution was adopted by both chambers without opposition, though House Republicans made an effort, defeated on a party-line vote, to gain equal membership on the committee. Barkley was named chairman, and the committee conducted hearings. The committee's final report, filed July 20, 1946, absolved President Roosevelt of blame for the Pearl Harbor disaster but held Adm. Harold B. Sark, Chief of Naval Operations, and Maj. Gen. Walter C. Short, Army commander in Hawaii, primarily responsible. A Republican minority report laid the primary blame on Roosevelt, suggesting what might have been the majority view if Republicans had been in command of the inquiry.[118]

When controversy over the Vietnam War was building in Congress during the late 1960s, war-related investigations divided more along committee jurisdiction than party lines. The Senate Foreign Relations Committee was critical of the Vietnam policies of the administration, while House and Senate Armed Services Committee inquiries supported the policies or urged stronger war efforts. The positions of the committees reflected the opposing interests of their chairmen. Sen. J.W. Fulbright (D Ark.) of the Foreign Relations panel opposed the war. Sen. John C. Stennis (D Miss.) and Rep. L. Mendel Rivers (D S.C.) of the Armed Services groups favored strong military action.

Resort to Select Committees

Occasionally, a proposed investigation has overlapped the jurisdictions of different committees. When, in addition, the committees have held conflicting views on the subject, the impending impasse has been resolved by formation of a select committee, whose members have been drawn from the opposed standing committees. In 1957, for example, both the Labor and Public Welfare Committee and the Government Operations Permanent Investigations Subcommittee of the Senate claimed jurisdiction to investigate labor racketeering and management malpractices uncovered during a Permanent Investigations Subcommittee study of Defense Department procurement. The issue was resolved by the creation of a Select Committee on Improper Activities in the Labor or Management Field. Four members from each party and from each of the two committees were named to the newly formed group.[119]

A decade later, in 1968, a similar dispute over investigation of reports of hunger and malnutrition in the United States involved the Agriculture and Forestry Committee and the Labor and Public Welfare Committee of the Senate. Government food assistance programs were operated by the Agriculture Department but benefited welfare recipients. Once again, the dispute was resolved by creating a select committee, the Select Committee on Nutrition and Human Needs, comprised of members of both committees plus other senators not on either panel.

The jurisdictional lines, however, often reflect only the surface differences between conflicting claims of committees to conduct an investigation. More fundamental is the conflicting philosophical views of committees that flow from the constituencies represented on the panels.

In the case of food assistance programs, for example, the congressional Agriculture Committees, reflecting the views of the Agriculture Department and farmers and food processors, have never been overly sympathetic to government attempts to provide food for low-income persons. These committees and the groups they represent traditionally have viewed their job as promoting the interest of agriculture—which often has meant keeping farm incomes up and preventing boom and bust in agricultural prices. Members of the committees generally have come from conservative farm states not known for their sympathy to welfare problems that tend to be concentrated in large urban-industrialized states.

The Labor and Public Welfare Committee, on the other hand, traditionally has been concerned about providing government aid to low-income workers and persons on welfare. Committee members tend to be allied with organized labor and other liberal organizations more concerned about urban than rural farm (agricultural) problems. Their preference normally is to keep food prices down in order to benefit not only welfare clients and poor people but average working persons who are their constituents, rather than to keep farm prices high.

This traditional tension between these committees had a concrete focus in the 1960s and 1970s when the food stamp program was created and grew into a multibillion-dollar government effort to provide extra food-purchasing power for low-income and impoverished Americans. The food stamp program was financed out of the Agriculture Department budget, a source of continuing annoyance to the department and to Agriculture Committee members who argued that the funds should go directly to agriculture programs and welfare (food stamp) program money should come from the government's welfare budget.

Consequently, committees with fundamentally different views of a problem, and of their responsibility for a solution, will want to control any congressional investigation that might affect the interest of their constituents. The conclusions from a study of food assistance programs, which could directly affect congressional policy, probably would be quite different depending on whether the Agriculture Committee or Labor Committee was in charge. For this reason, the tug-of-war between competing committees over investigations often is resolved by creation of a new select committee.

Watergate Committee. Controversy accompanied formation of the Senate Select Committee on Presidential Campaign Activities—the Watergate panel—established Feb. 7, 1973, as well as the creation in 1975 of House and Senate select committees to investigate operations of U.S. intelligence and law enforcement agencies, particularly the Central Intelligence Agency (CIA) and Federal Bureau of Investigation (FBI).

Since the CIA was created in 1947, detailed reports on its activities traditionally had been provided by the agency only to intelligence subcommittees of the House and Senate Armed Services and Appropriations Committees. The subcommittees' oversight had long been criticized as inadequate, and their members were said to be too sympathetic to the military and intelligence establishments.

During debate in both chambers on resolutions creating the select committees, divisions were apparent between more conservative members who wanted the existing standing committees to retain their jurisdiction and conduct the investigation, on the one hand, and liberal critics of those panels, on the other. The composition of the select committees also was an issue, with members urging that appointment of pro- or anti-CIA "extremists" be avoided.[120]

Once established, moreover, the House Select Committee on Intelligence was torn by internal dissension, which finally caused its chairman to offer his resignation and immobilized the investigation until a new panel was formed in its place.[121] *(Details, p. 169)*

Major Investigations

Following are summaries of selected major congressional investigations conducted since 1789.

St. Clair Inquiry

The House approved the first congressional investigation in American history when it adopted on March 27, 1792, by a 44-10 vote, a resolution authorizing a select committee to investigate an Indian victory the previous year over troops commanded by Maj. Gen. Arthur St. Clair.[122] The action came after the House, also on March 27, had rejected, 21-35, a resolution calling upon President Washington to carry out the investigation.

Setting precedents along the way, the committee, headed by Chairman Thomas Fitzsimmons (Fed Pa.), asked for and received War Department papers on the expedition that had sent St. Clair and about 1,500 soldiers on a road- and fort-building trip through the Northwest Territory. An Indian attack had killed about 600 men and wounded some 300. Witnesses called by the committee included St. Clair, Secretary of War Henry Knox and Secretary of the Treasury Alexander Hamilton.

The report of the committee, filed May 8, 1792, completely absolved St. Clair, a former president of the Continental Congress. Blame for the disaster was placed on the War Department, particularly the quartermaster and supply contractors, who were accused of mismanagement, neglect and delay in supplying necessary equipment, clothing and munitions. The House took no action on the report, and Federalists prevented its publication because of its reflections on Knox and Hamilton. Early in 1818, Congress approved a $60 monthly pension for the elderly and by then impoverished St. Clair, who died a few months later. Nearly 40 years later, in 1857, Congress appropriated a substantial sum to be paid to his heirs.

Civil War Study

The Joint Committee on the Conduct of the [Civil] War compiled what was widely considered—at least until the McCarthy era of the 1950s—the worst record of any congressional investigating unit.[123] It was a political vehicle for Radical Republicans opposed to President Lincoln, and its far-ranging inquiries were used for intensely partisan purposes.

The Senate on Dec. 9, 1861, by a 33-3 vote, and the House on Dec. 10 by a voice vote authorized appointment of the joint committee simply "to inquire into the conduct of the present war." It was the first time a joint House-Senate panel had been created to conduct a congressional inquiry. The committee was set up in the aftermath of the Union defeats at Bull Run in July and Ball's Bluff in October. At first, it was thought the panel would investigate those defeats, but the Radical majority on the committee, with the leading Senate Radical, Benjamin F. Wade (R Ohio), as chairman, had more ambitious ideas.

In hearings that began Dec. 24, 1861, and continued until early 1865, the committee examined past and future battle plans, disloyal employees, Navy installations, naval engagements, war supplies and war contracts. It filed its final report May 22, 1865.

In a sense, the committee took over partial control of Union operations. It harassed conservative and Democratic generals, particularly Gen. George B. McClellan. Typically, when investigating a general, the committee first would interrogate his subordinate officers, searching for adverse information. With such information in hand, the committee would summon the general for interrogation, frequently without informing him of the accusations against him or the disclosures made by his subordinates. The committee's next step would be a meeting with President Lincoln at which the general's resignation or reassignment would be demanded.

Committee sessions were supposed to be closed to the press, but information often would be made public if it suited the purpose of the Radicals. As a result, Confederate Gen. Robert E. Lee was moved to observe that the committee was worth about two divisions of Confederate troops.[124]

Crédit Mobilier

The number of congressional investigations soared during Grant's eight years as President. According to Joseph Harris, author of *Congressional Control of Administration,* between 1869 and 1877 Congress undertook 37 inquiries into charges of maladministration.[125] Although the investigations were a response to well-founded dissatisfaction with the practices of the executive branch, the Crédit Mobilier scandal touched on some outstanding members of Congress and tarnished the legislative branch as well.[126]

Two committees in the House and one in the Senate investigated charges that arose during the 1872 presidential campaign of wholesale corruption in connection with construction by the Crédit Mobilier of America of the last 667 miles of the Union Pacific Railroad, which had been completed three years earlier. The inquiries disclosed perhaps the most serious legislative scandal in the country's history.

The charges first appeared when the New York *Sun* of Sept. 4, 1872, reported that Rep. Oakes Ames (R Mass.), a principal stockholder in both the Union Pacific and the Crédit Mobilier construction company, had used Crédit Mobilier stock to bribe Vice President Schuyler Colfax, Sen. Henry Wilson (R Mass.), Speaker James G. Blaine (R Maine), Sen. James W. Patterson (R N.H.), Rep. James Brooks (D N.Y.) and Rep. James A. Garfield (R Ohio). The reported bribes represented an attempt to head off a congressional investigation of railroad transportation rates.

Blaine proposed the first House inquiry, and the House on Dec. 2, 1872, appointed a select committee headed by Rep. Luke P. Poland (R Vt.) "to investigate and ascertain whether any member of this House was bribed by Oakes Ames, or any other person or corporation, in any manner touching his legislative duty." A month later, Jan. 6, 1873, the House appointed another select committee, headed by Rep. Jeremiah M. Wilson (R Ind.), to investigate the financial arrangement between the Union Pacific and the Crédit Mobilier.

As the House investigations proceeded simultaneously, the Poland committee discovered evidence implicating members of the Senate, and the information was forwarded to the Senate.

The result was that the Senate on Feb. 4, 1873, established a select committee of its own to look into the alleged bribery. The committee was headed by Sen. Lot M. Morrill (R Maine).

The Poland committee's report filed Feb. 18, 1873, cleared Blaine but recommended that both Ames and Brooks be expelled from the House. The committee said Ames had been "guilty of selling to members of Congress shares of stock in the Credit Mobilier of America, for prices much below the true value of such stock, with intent thereby to influence the votes and decisions of such members in matters to be brought before Congress for action."

Brooks, according to the committee, had purchased stock in his son-in-law's name that was intended for Brooks' own benefit. The House ultimately censured the two representatives but did not expel them.

In a March 3, 1873, report, the Wilson committee said the Crédit Mobilier had been making exorbitant profits, and that some persons connected with it were holding bonds illegally. In addition, the committee recommended that court action be undertaken to eliminate the financial irregularities.

The Senate's committee reported March 1, 1873, that Sen. Patterson had bought Crédit Mobilier stock from Ames at below-market prices. The committee recommended Patterson's expulsion, but his term was to expire March 3, and he retired without Senate action to expel him.

Colfax, whose relation to the matter was not satisfactorily explained, had had a falling out with the regular Republicans before the scandal broke and was not renominated in June 1872 for a second term on the Grant ticket. Henry Wilson, who replaced Colfax as Vice President, and Garfield, elected President in 1880, never were able to explain away their connection with the affair.

Study of the Money Trust

The House on Feb. 24, 1912, authorized its Banking and Currency Committee to investigate the concentration of money and credit in the nation. [127] Conducted at a time when the national interest already was turned to such industrial concentrations as the sugar trust, the meat trust and the steel trust, the new inquiry soon became known as the money trust investigation.

Conducted by a Banking and Currency subcommittee headed by Committee Chairman Arsène P. Pujo (D La.), the inquiry brought to light previously unknown interlocking directorates among two sets of New York banks, controlled by Morgan and Rockefeller interests, and 112 of the country's largest corporations in the fields of banking, public utilities, transportation, insurance, manufacturing and trading.

Witnesses called by committee counsel Samuel Untermyer, the real director and principal actor in the hearings, included such financial giants as J.P. Morgan Sr., George F. Baker of the First National Bank of New York, James Stillman of the National City Bank of New York, Jacob H. Schiff of Kuhn, Loeb & Co., and James J. Hill, the railroad magnate. The range of activities investigated by the subcommittee turned the hearings into the most ambitious and far-flung inquiry to date.

The subcommittee filed its report Feb. 28, 1913, summarizing its findings and calling for corrective legislation. Within two years, Congress, prodded by President Wilson, enacted the Federal Reserve Act of 1913, the Clayton Antitrust Act of 1914 and the Federal Trade Commission Act of 1914. Each of these major measures was based on information developed during the investigation.

Teapot Dome

President Harding was inaugurated in 1921 and suspicions of wrongdoing grew and flourished in the first year of his administration. [128] Oil figured importantly in many rumors. Congress in 1920 had enacted the General Leasing Act, which authorized the Secretary of the Navy under certain conditions to lease naval oil reserves on public lands to private oil operators, and oil interests had been influential at the 1920 Republican convention. Harding on May 31, 1921, signed an executive order transferring jurisdiction over the naval oil reserves to the Interior Department. Early in 1922, Interior leased the Elk Hills reserve in California to Edward L. Doheny of the Pan-American Petroleum and Transport Co. and the Teapot Dome reserve in Wyoming to Harry F. Sinclair's Mammoth Oil Co.

Pressure mounted for a congressional investigation of the transactions. Tight Republican control blocked action in the House. But Senate Democrats and insurgent Republicans succeeded on April 29, 1922, in pushing through a resolution that authorized the Senate Committee on Public Lands and Surveys (renamed in 1948 the Interior and Insular Affairs Committee) "to investigate this entire subject of leases upon naval oil reserves...." The committee was headed by a series of Republican chairmen, but a Democrat on the panel, Thomas J. Walsh (Mont.), took charge of the inquiry. All during the remainder of 1922 and into the fall of 1923, Walsh studied the lease arrangements and gathered information. When the hearings opened on Oct. 25, 1923, they concentrated at first on the legality and expediency of the two leases. Then Walsh began probing the sudden wealth of Secretary of the Interior Albert B. Fall. In a sensational national scandal, rivaling the Crédit Mobilier,

it was developed that Fall had accepted bribes from Doheny and Sinclair. Doheny had given Fall at least $100,000, and Sinclair had given the Interior Secretary at least $300,000. Both Fall and Navy Secretary Edwin Denby resigned. Fall was later convicted of accepting a bribe in connection with the Elk Hills lease and was sentenced to prison and fined $100,000.

By the time the committee filed its report, June 6, 1924, Congress already had adopted a joint resolution declaring the leases contrary to the public interest and ordering the President to initiate court action to cancel them. The courts subsequently did cancel the leases and declared invalid Harding's executive order transferring jurisdiction over the naval oil reserves from the Navy to the Interior Department.

Acting on information developed in the Teapot Dome inquiry, the Senate on March 4, 1924, created a Select Committee to Investigate the Justice Department. The committee was headed by Sen. Smith W. Brookhart (R Iowa). Attorney General Harry M. Daugherty's failure to prosecute Fall, Sinclair, Doheny and others led President Coolidge on March 28, 1924, to demand Daugherty's resignation.

Pecora Stock Exchange Probe

The Senate Banking and Currency Committee from 1932 to 1934 conducted an important investigation of the stock exchange and Wall Street financial manipulations, reminiscent of the Pujo hearings 20 years earlier. [129]

Authorized March 4, 1932, while Sen. Peter Norbeck (R S.D.) was chairman of the committee, the hearings concentrated initially on stock exchanges practices. The 1929 stock market collapse had plunged the nation into a severe depression and a congressional examination of exchange operations became a political necessity. The hearings began rather inconspicuously, and some observers expected them to become a "whitewash."

Then in January 1933, the committee hired Ferdinand Pecora as chief counsel. As the country's banking system headed for collapse, the committee broadened its investigation to include a study of the financial dealings of New York's major banking houses. When the Democrats took over control of the Senate, Sen. Duncan U. Fletcher (D Fla.) became chairman of the committee.

Chief Counsel Pecora demanded careful research and thorough investigation by the committee staff. Pecora, in turn, relied on evidence gathered by the staff as he conducted the interrogation of committee witnesses. Committee members normally listened in silence, asking few questions of their own. Pecora came to dominate the hearings, far overshadowing Fletcher, to the extent that the inquiry was to become known as the Pecora investigation.

As the 1933 hearings progressed under Pecora, they produced spectacular accounts of dubious financial actions. The salary of Charles E. Mitchell, president of the National City Bank of New York, had doubled from $100,000 to $200,000 as the breadlines of the unemployed had lengthened. Albert H. Wiggin, president of the Chase National Bank of New York, had sold short the stock of his own bank. J.P. Morgan Jr. had paid no income tax for several years because his losses offset his gains. Other witnesses recounted the operation of security flotation syndicates and stock market pools. It developed that friends of Morgan, including Cabinet officers, former President Coolidge and top Republican and Democratic party officials, had been profitably let in on the inside of some security flotations.

Practices disclosed in the hearings paved the way for such major Roosevelt administration measures as the Banking Acts of 1933 and 1935, the Securities Act of 1933 and the Securities Exchange Act of 1934.

By the time the committee filed its final report, June 16, 1934, the investigation had compiled an unmatchable record for sustained, sensational publicity, for economically significant disclosures and for important resulting regulatory legislation.

Nye Munitions Inquiry

Riding a wave of public sentiment for a congressional investigation of the munitions industry, the Senate on April 12, 1934, established the Senate Special Committee **Investigating the Munitions Industry.**[130] The public was firmly convinced before the committee began hearings that the country's munitions makers were merchants of death, and the committee accepted the public's verdict and set out to find the proof.

The chief sponsor of the panel had been Sen. Gerald P. Nye (R N.D.). Despite solid Democratic control of the Senate, and a Democratic majority on the committee, Nye was picked as chairman. A Progressive Republican, he had been appointed to the Senate in 1925. He had earned a measure of public prominence as chairman of a special Senate campaign expenditures committee to scrutinize spending in the 1930 election contests. The munitions inquiry made Nye a national figure, a leader of the movement to curb the arms traffic and the nation's most eloquent isolationist.

The Nye Committee, as it soon was called, opened hearings on Sept. 4, 1934. The committee investigated the munitions industry, the shipbuilding industry, and business profits during World War I. Witnesses included leading businessmen, financiers and their associates. Committee investigators gathered documents from government and diplomatic files and from private corporations. Worldwide attention, carefully cultivated by Nye, focused on the committee's efforts to prove that arms makers were merchants of death, linked together in a global ring, opposed to disarmament, promoting armed conflicts and reaping enormous profits along the way. The evidence, however, was thin and failed to support general conclusions. Instead of concentrating on a single allegation at a time, the committee examined separately company after company, thus diffusing its energy. The hearings continued until mid-1935 and were resumed briefly in early 1936.

Controversy was inevitably stirred up by the investigation. Committee disclosures of bribery and arms deals brought sharp responses in Latin America and Great Britain, where the incidents had occurred, and created trouble for the State Department. Some of the disclosures embarrassed President Roosevelt. The committee was criticized for using as staff aides workers on relief in New York.

In the meantime, public sentiment had shifted from control of the munitions industry to support of U.S. neutrality. The result was that the Senate in 1936 refused to provide the committee with any more funds than were needed to conclude its activities. In its final report, filed April 20, 1936, the committee criticized American loans to belligerents during World War I. It recommended a definition of armed merchantmen, a ceiling on wartime exports to belligerents, and restrictions on loans to belligerents. The committee agreed on the need of strictly controlling the munitions industry but divided on the methods by which control could best be exercised.

World War II Truman Committee

The World War II Senate Special Committee to Investigate the National Defense Program came to be widely regarded as the most effective investigating group in the history of Congress.[131] Created March 1, 1941, nine months before the Japanese attack on Pearl Harbor plunged the United States into the war, the committee sought to uncover and to halt wasteful practices in war preparations. Its studies were broadened to cover the entire war mobilization effort, once the country entered the conflict.

Closely identified with its first chairman, Sen. Harry S Truman (D Mo.), the committee had the broadest possible investigating authority. The Truman Committee was "to make a full and complete study and investigation of the operation of the program for the procurement and construction of supplies, materials, vessels, plants, camps and other articles and facilities in connection with the national defense." The group was comprised largely of freshman senators, able to devote much of their time to inquiries.

Confusion in the construction program for training camps, and concentration of war contracts in a few areas of the country and among a few businesses, had led Truman to propose the investigating committee. But the committee's first hearings, which began April 15, 1941, were devoted to a general investigation of the status of the national defense program. Later studies explored camp construction and other problems of war mobilization; shortages of critical war materials, such as aluminum, rubber, petroleum products, housing and steel; the quality of materials supplied under defense contracts and the distribution of the contracts; and war frauds among contractors, lobbyists and government officials.

Aware of the excesses of the Civil War investigating committee, Truman scrupulously avoided any attempt to judge military policy or operations. Hearings of the Truman Committee were conducted in a restrained, thoughtful manner, after careful and thorough preparation. Frequently, private meetings or correspondence with contractors or federal officials led to corrective action, and no public hearings were held. Occasionally, a previously disregarded request of the committee suddenly would be complied with, once a hearing was scheduled.

The committee worked closely with executive branch departments and agencies. Special liaison officers were assigned to it in the War Department, the Navy Department, the War Production Board, the Maritime Commission and the War Shipping Administration. Reports of committee findings and recommendations were supported unanimously by committee members, and most recommendations were put into effect before the findings were published. The record of unanimity on reports was not broken until 1947.

The Truman Committee was not the only congressional group studying national mobilization, but it was the only one to make a systematic effort to survey the entire war program on a continuing basis. Succeeding Congresses continued the committee throughout the war and into the early postwar years. Its final report was submitted April 28, 1948.

Truman resigned as chairman Aug. 3, 1944, after receiving the Democratic vice presidential nomination. The war was nearing an end when he left the committee, and its studies turned more and more to problems of reconverting from war to peace. Truman was succeeded as chairman by James M. Mead (D N.Y.) on Aug. 11, 1944, and Mead, in turn, was succeeded on Oct. 1, 1946, by Harley M. Kilgore (D W.Va.). Owen Brewster (R Maine) became committee chairman on Jan. 6, 1947, when the Republican-controlled 80th Congress took control on Capitol Hill.

Kefauver Crime Hearings

In 1950 and 1951, the Senate Special Committee to Investigate Organized Crime in Interstate Commerce held hearings around the country, many of which were televised. The TV broadcasts created wide interest and were estimated to have been viewed by 20 million persons.[132]

The special committee, approved by the Senate on May 3, 1950, represented a compromise. It grew out of a jurisdictional dispute between the Judiciary Committee and the Interstate and Foreign Commerce Committee over which group should conduct an investigation of organized crime. Sen. Estes Kefauver (D Tenn.), who first proposed the investigation and supported the Judiciary Committee's jurisdictional claim was made chairman. Hearings began May 26.

The committee questioned governors, mayors, sheriffs, and policemen and turned the spotlight on gangsters, gamblers, racketeers and narcotics peddlers. The hearings were full of names of prominent alleged racketeers, including reputed heirs of the Chicago Capone gang and leaders of the Mafia. Many of the alleged criminals proved difficult to locate. Hearings were followed by scores of citations for contempt of Congress and many local indictments for criminal activities.

Kefauver continued as chairman until May 1, 1951, when Sen. Herbert R. O'Conor (D Md.) took the reins. The investigation had been scheduled to end Feb. 28, 1951, but the committee's life was extended to Aug. 31. The group's records and recommendations then were turned over to the Interstate and Foreign Commerce Committee for further action. The latter committee decided not to conduct a further crime probe, but various local investigations continued where the Kefauver committee had left off.

Use of Television. One of the highlights of the hearings was the appearance before the committee of Frank Costello, reputed underworld king. He refused to have his face televised, so TV audiences viewed only his hands. Many other witnesses likewise complained about testifying before television cameras. Some who refused were cited for contempt, in order to get a court ruling on the use of television and radio by committees. The U.S. District Court for the District of Columbia ruled on Oct. 6, 1952, that two of the contemptuous witnesses, Morris Kleinman and Louis Rothkopf, were "justified" in refusing to testify while television and newsreel cameras were in operation. They were freed of the contempt of Congress charges.

Reports. In a series of reports issued in 1951, the committee said crime syndicates were operating with the connivance and protection of law enforcement officials, and that the two major syndicates were centered in Chicago and New York. "Shocking" corruption existed, according to one report, "at all levels of government." The committee recommended creation of a private financed National Crime Coordinating Committee, a thorough overhauling of state and local laws, a stronger attack on narcotics traffic, legalization of wiretapping, and the adoption by Congress of a code or procedure for the broadcasting or televising of committee hearings.

McCarthy's Investigations

Under the chairmanship of Sen. Joseph R. McCarthy (R Wis.), the Permanent Investigations Subcommittee of the Senate Government Operations Committee conducted a series of wide-ranging and controversial hearings in 1953 and 1954.[133] The hearings were the highwater mark of the McCarthy era and bore the unmistakable scars of the senator's abrasive and aggressive character. The subcommittee's activities varied from hearings on Korean War atrocities to investigation of a deal with Greek shipowners, but the State Department and the armed services were the prime targets of the probes.

The subcommittee also investigated the Government Printing Office, Communist infiltration of the United Nations, and the transfer to Russians of currency plates. In 1954, the subcommittee in an unprecedented move in effect undertook an investigation of itself.

McCarthy tangled with the press, Harvard University and other senators. The three Democratic members of the subcommittee—Sens. Henry M. Jackson (Wash.), John L. McClellan (Ark.) and Stuart Symington (Mo.)—resigned July 10, 1953, in protest against the chairman's handling of the group's hired personnel. But after McCarthy on Jan. 25, 1954, announced certain changes in subcommittee procedure, the three Democrats resumed their places on the panel.

Advent of McCarthy Era.[134] Long before the stormy McCarthy hearings got under way, the senator himself had become a controversial public figure. The period that was later dubbed the McCarthy era—one of the most controversial periods in American history—began in 1950. On Feb. 9 of that year, McCarthy delivered a speech before the Ohio County Women's Republican Club in Wheeling, W.Va. According to the Wheeling *News Register* and the Wheeling *Intelligencer,* the senator said at one point: "While I cannot take the time to name all the men in the State Department who have been named as members of the Communist Party and members of a spy ring, I have here in my hand a list of 205 that were known to the Secretary of State as being members of the Communist Party and who, nevertheless, are still working and shaping policy in the State Department." The number varied in later versions of the speech, and the text that was read into the *Congressional Record* omitted the paragraph referring to the list of 205 Communists.

A special subcommittee of the Senate Foreign Relations Committee was set up under the chairmanship of **Millard E. Tydings (D Md.) to investigate McCarthy's** charges. The subcommittee, in one of the most bitterly controversial investigations in the history of Congress, held 31 days of hearings between March 8 and June 28, 1950. During the course of the hearings McCarthy charged 10 individuals by name with varying degrees of Communist activity. One of the persons named was Prof. Owen J. Lattimore of Johns Hopkins University, who in the summer of 1950 published a book, *Ordeal by Slander* defending his record against McCarthy's accusations of disloyalty.

The investigation was a major issue in the 1950 elections. Charges of "softness" toward communism were widely credited with the defeat of Tydings in the Maryland senatorial contest. On Aug. 6, 1951, after a Senate Rules and Administration Committee report had criticized McCarthy's part in the Maryland election, Sen. William Benton (D Conn.) demanded his expulsion from the Senate. McCarthy on April 10, 1952, demanded an investigation of Benton. The result was a simultaneous investigation of both men by the Privileges and Elections Subcommittee of the Senate Rules and Administration Committee.

(Continued on p. 167)

Investigations of 'Un-Americanism'

Perhaps the most significant expansion of the investigative function of Congress was the study of subversive movements and other activities alleged to be detrimental to the interests of the United States. Instead of pursuing traditional lines of congressional inquiry—operations of the government and national social and economic problems—the committee members probed into the thoughts, actions and associations of persons and institutions.

The death in January 1975 of the House Committee on Un-American Activities (HUAC), renamed the Internal Security Committee in 1969, ended 30 years of controversy over the committee's zealous pursuit of subversives.

While its investigations of communism earned the committee a permanent place in 20th century American history—and launched the national political career of one of its early members, Richard M. Nixon—the committee's most amazing achievement was its survival for so many years after the cold-war era ended. From the outset the committee had faced attacks by liberals and civil libertarians. Throughout the 1960s it withstood court suits challenging the constitutionality of its mandate and attempts in the House to end its funding.

Even in 1974 it appeared that the committee was still invincible. On Oct. 2 the House voted by a margin of 246-164 to retain the committee under a new reorganization plan. A little more than a year later, however, the committee's life ended when the House Democratic Caucus, by voice vote, transferred the panel's functions and jurisdiction to the Judiciary Committee.

Postwar Developments. The Dies Committee was reconstituted in succeeding Congresses until 1945. At the beginning of the 79th Congress, Jan. 3, 1945, Rep. John E. Rankin (D Miss.) offered an amendment to the House rules to make the Dies Committee a standing committee and to rename it the House Committee on Un-American Activities. Opponents of the committee, caught unprepared by this strategy, failed to muster their forces, and the Rankin proposal carried, 208-186.

The next five years marked the peak of the committee's influence. In 1947 the committee launched an investigation into communism in the motion picture industry, with repercussions which lasted almost a decade. Its hearings resulted in the Hollywood blacklist, which kept many writers and actors suspected of Communist leanings out of work.

But it was the committee's investigation in 1948 of State Department official Alger Hiss, and Hiss' subsequent conviction for perjury, which established internal communism as a leading political issue and the committee as an important political force. The case against Hiss, which at one point appeared flimsy to other committee members, was vigorously developed by a young member of the committee, Richard M. Nixon.

The committee's tactics during this period included liberal use of contempt citations against unfriendly witnesses, some of whom pleaded the Fifth Amendment right against self-incrimination. In 1950, for instance, the House voted 59 contempt citations, 56 of them recommended by the committee.

The Internal Security Subcommittee of the Senate Judiciary Committee, set up in 1951, also regularly conducted probes of Communist activities. Many state legislatures emulated Congress by undertaking investigations of subversion within their respective domains. The most famous investigations of communism were conducted by Sen. Joseph R. McCarthy (R Wis.) as chairman (1953-54) of the Permanent Investigations Subcommittee of the Senate Government Operations Committee. His behavior in this role intensified concern over the use by Congress of its investigating powers and led in 1954 to his censure by the Senate. After McCarthy's censure, investigations of communism attracted less public attention.

In the 1960s and 1970s, the House committee turned its attention to black militant groups such as the Black Panthers and anti-war and radical youth groups.

Early History. The first congressional investigation of un-American activities was authorized Sept. 19, 1918, two months prior to the armistice in World War I. Its aim was to investigate the activities of German brewing interests. The investigation conducted by the Senate Judiciary Committee was expanded in 1919 to cover "any efforts being made to propagate in this country the principles of any party exercising...authority in Russia...and...to incite the overthrow of the government of this country...."

The House on May 12, 1930, set up a Special Committee to Investigate Communist Activities in the United States—the Fish Committee, so-called after its chairman, Rep. Hamilton Fish Jr. (R N.Y.). On March 20, 1934, the House created a Special Committee on Un-American Activities, under Chairman John W. McCormack (D Mass.). On May 26, 1938, three years after the McCormack Committee submitted its report, which covered Nazi as well as Communist activities in the United States, the House set up another Special Committee on Un-American Activities, under Chairman Martin Dies (D Texas). The committee, whose chairman was avowedly anti-Communist and anti-New Deal, was given a broad mandate to investigate subversion.

Dies focused his early investigations on organized labor groups, especially the Congress of Industrial Organizations, and set a tactical pattern which would guide the permanent Un-American Activities Committee, which was created in 1945. Friendly witnesses, who often met in secret with Dies as a one-man subcommittee, accused hundreds of persons of supporting Communist activities, but few of the accused were permitted to testify in rebuttal. The press treated Dies' charges sensationally, a practice which was to continue after World War II.

Sources: August R. Ogden, *The Dies Committee* (The Catholic University of America Press, 1945); Walter Goodman, *The Committee* (Farrar, Straus and Giroux, 1968); Congressional Quarterly, *Congress and the Nation, 1945-1964*, Vol. I, pp. 1679-80.

(Continued from p. 165)

The subcommittee's report on Jan. 2, 1953, asserted that McCarthy had "deliberately set out to thwart" the investigation.[135] Although it did not accuse him of any specific wrongdoing, the report raised a series of questions such as whether McCarthy had diverted to his "personal advantage" funds collected to fight communism. Benton was criticized for accepting a campaign contribution from a former director of the Reconstruction Finance Corporation. By the time the subcommittee reported, Benton had been defeated in the 1952 Connecticut senatorial election; his defeat was widely attributed to his feud with McCarthy.

The 1952 elections gave Republicans a majority in both chambers of the 83rd Congress. Accordingly, at the start of its first session in January 1953, McCarthy, who had been ranking Republican on the Senate Government Operations Committee, became its chairman and chairman of the Permanent Investigations Subcommittee.

1953 Activities. The subcommittee on Jan. 25, 1954, filed its annual report summarizing its activities in 1953. The report listed "various actions taken as a result" of its investigations, including: the saving of $18-million through exposure of inefficiency in the International Information Administration and its Voice of America programs; removal of a number of "Fifth Amendment Communists" from federal jobs and defense plants; removal of incompetent and undesirable persons from federal employment; and indictment of several witnesses. The report was not signed by the three Democratic members of the subcommittee who had resigned in July.

Army-McCarthy Dispute.[136] During most of the first half of 1954, McCarthy was involved in controversy with high officials of the Army and, by extension, with the Eisenhower administration itself. The Permanent Investigations Subcommittee continued its investigation of the armed services, begun in 1953, and the investigation led to a series of charges and countercharges by the Army and McCarthy. At issue was the question of whether or not McCarthy and his staff had used improper means to secure preferential treatment for a former subcommittee consultant, Private G. David Schine. Also involved was a charge that the Army had tried to pressure McCarthy into calling off his investigation of alleged Communists in the Army.

The Army on April 14, 1954, filed a formal "bill of particulars" detailing charges against McCarthy, subcommittee chief counsel Roy M. Cohn and subcommittee staff director Francis P. Carr. The subcommittee reciprocated April 20 by filing charges against Army Secretary Robert T. Stevens, Army counsel John G. Adams and Assistant Defense Secretary H. Struve Hensel. To investigate the charges, the subcommittee held hearings, with Sen. Karl E. Mundt (R S.D.) as acting chairman. McCarthy resigned temporarily from subcommittee membership. The subcommittee in effect began an investigation of its own activities.

The 35 days of hearings from April 22 to June 17 attracted, during 187 hours of television coverage, audiences as large as 20 million persons at a time. In addition to the principals charged in the case and the subcommittee members, the drama featured, as the main interrogators, special Army counsel Joseph N. Welch and special subcommittee counsel Ray H. Jenkins. Several Army officers testified. In its Aug. 31 report, the subcommittee's Republican majority concluded that the charge of "improper influence" by McCarthy on behalf of Schine "was not established," but that Cohn had been "unduly aggressive and persistent" on Schine's behalf. The

Republicans said also that Stevens and Adams had tried "to terminate or influence" investigations of the Army. The Democratic minority asserted that McCarthy had "fully acquiesced in and condoned" the "improper actions" of Cohn, who in turn had "misused and abused the powers of his office and brought disrepute to the committee." The minority report said also that Stevens "merits severe criticism" for "an inexcusable indecisiveness and lack of sound administrative judgment."

Censure of McCarthy.[137] On June 11, 1954, while the Army-McCarthy hearings were in progress, Sen. Ralph E. Flanders (R Vt.) initiated what was to develop into a six-month controversy over what official attitude the Senate should adopt toward certain of McCarthy's actions.

Flanders introduced a resolution to remove McCarthy from the chairmanship of the Government Operations Committee and any of its subcommittees, and to prohibit him from reassuming such posts unless he answered questions raised in 1952 by the Privileges and Elections Subcommittee of the Senate Rules and Administration Committee. After Senate Majority Leader William F. Knowland (R Calif.) had voiced opposition, Flanders on July 30 introduced a substitute resolution, charging McCarthy with "personal contempt" of the Senate. The Flanders and other resolutions were referred to a Select Committee to Study Censure Charges. Following hearings from Aug. 31 to Sept. 13, the committee on Sept. 27 unanimously recommended adoption of a resolution censuring McCarthy for his attitude toward the Privileges and Elections Subcommittee's Benton-McCarthy investigation in 1952 and toward Army Brig. Gen. Ralph W. Zwicker. At a Permanent Investigations Subcommittee hearing in 1954, McCarthy had told Zwicker that he was "not fit to wear that uniform" and implied that Zwicker did not have "the brains of a five-year-old."

The Senate on Dec. 2, 1954, adopted the resolution censuring McCarthy by a vote of 67 to 22. The resolution condemned McCarthy's abuse of the Privileges and Elections Subcommittee in 1952 and several of his statements about the Select Censure Committee and the special post-election Senate session that had been called to consider the committee's recommendations. Condemnation of McCarthy's comments on the censure move itself had been substituted, during preliminary action on the final resolution, for condemnation of McCarthy's abuse of Zwicker. *(Text p. 697)*

McCarthy lost his committee and subcommittee chairmanships when control of Congress passed to the Democrats in January 1955. His activities no longer attracted any notable attention. He died May 2, 1957.

TFX Plane Contract

The Permanent Investigations Subcommittee of the Senate Government Operations Committee in 1963 launched a major investigation of the Defense Department's November 1962 award of a multibillion-dollar TFX fighter plane contract to the General Dynamics Corp., which was in competition with the Boeing Co.[138] The controversial decision by Pentagon civilian officials to award the contract to General Dynamics was made despite the almost unanimous endorsement of the Boeing bid by military technical advisers.

At stake was an aircraft program for which production orders were estimated eventually to total more than $6.5-billion and involve 20,000 jobs and 1,700 planes—the largest tactical airplane contract since World War II. The initial $28-million contract, for which Boeing and General

Dynamics were bidding, involved 22 developmental planes for testing, to be delivered within two and one-half years.

Subcommittee hearings were initiated in response to allegations that the contract might have been awarded as a result of political or regional pressure—possibly in conflict with national security and economy interests. General Dynamics planned to build the aircraft at its Convair plant in Fort Worth, Texas, and at the Grumman Aircraft Engineering Corp. plant in Bethpage, Long Island, N.Y. Boeing, whose headquarters is in Seattle, Wash., planned to build the aircraft at its Wichita, Kan., plant.

Sen. Henry M. Jackson (D Wash.), a member of the subcommittee, proposed that it look into the circumstances of the award, and Chairman John L. McClellan (D Ark.) decided on a full-scale investigation.

During the long investigation suggestions of political pressure were made concerning Jackson, Rep. K. William Stinson (R Wash.) of Seattle, Rep. Jim Wright (D Texas) of Fort Worth, the Kansas congressional delegation and then-Vice President Lyndon B. Johnson, among others.

Hearings began Feb. 26, were suspended Nov. 20 and, contrary to expectations, did not resume in 1964. Meanwhile, General Dynamics proceeded with its development of the TFX under a Dec. 21, 1962, "letter contract." Such a contract was common Defense Department procedure for permitting the contractor to get work under way, leaving the details of the more complex, formal contract to be settled later.

Unforeseen obstacles hindered development of the aircraft. Development of the Navy version (F-111B) lagged far behind schedule, and the Defense Department on April 18, 1968, canceled the Navy program. Although the Air Force officially expressed satisfaction with its version of the plane (F-111A), loss of three of the first six F-111As sent to Vietnam in 1968 cast serious doubt on the future of the Air Force's F-111 program. President Nixon in 1969 canceled the Air Force's strategic bomber version of the plane (FB-111).

The Watergate Hearings

Between 1955 and 1973, congressional investigations were generally low-key and attracted little public attention. But this was changed dramatically when the Senate Select Committee on Presidential Campaign Activities (the Watergate Committee) began its investigations into illegal campaign practices.[139] Disclosures before that committee created shock waves that reverberated through all three branches of government, creating one of the most serious constitutional crises in the nation's two-century history. *(Discussion of House Judiciary impeachment proceedings, p. 214)*

The committee was established by a unanimous vote of the Senate Feb. 7, 1973. The resolution establishing the committee provided subpoena powers and authorized $500,000 (the total eventually authorized amounted to $2-million) for completion of the investigation and preparation of a report by Feb. 28, 1974.

The hearings, which began in May, were held in the ornate Caucus Room of the Old Senate Office Building, the site of earlier famous hearings, including the McCarthy and Kefauver investigations. There, in the glare of television klieg lights, the Senate Watergate Committee held forth from May until August 1973.

Bushy-browed, Bible-quoting Sam J. Ervin Jr., a North Carolina Democrat serving his last term, was chairman of the seven-member committee. He opened the hearings May

17. "If the allegations that have been made in the wake of the Watergate affair are substantiated," he said, "there has been a very serious subversion of the integrity of the electoral process, and the committee will be obliged to consider the manner in which such a subversion affects the continued existence of this nation as a representative democracy, and how, if we are to survive, such subversions may be prevented in the future."

The committee decided to divide its investigation into three parts: the break-in and coverup, campaign sabotage and espionage—"dirty tricks"—and campaign financing. Its mandate, once it had disclosed the facts, was to make recommendations for legislation that would prevent recurrences of such abuses of the political system.

The Watergate Committee hearings had their moments of high drama as men near the top of the White House hierarchy gave their detailed versions of the byzantine workings of Nixon's executive branch and re-election committee. There was occasional partisan bickering among committee members and staff. Now and then, a witness' testimony drew laughs from the crowd of spectators that filled the room to overflowing each day.

The viewing public would not soon forget this most extensive look at a congressional hearing. The personal qualities and interrogation techniques of the seven senators left their lasting impressions. So did the style and mannerisms of the nearly three dozen men and women who testified during the first phase of the hearings.

The man who, more than any other witness, left his mark on later developments in the Watergate scandal was Alexander P. Butterfield, then head of the Federal Aviation Administration and a former assistant to key Nixon adviser H.R. Haldeman at the White House. On July 16, 1973, Butterfield described the system that had been installed in the White House and Executive Office Building to tape-record the President's conversations.

The key to unlocking Watergate secrets had been found.

The committee recessed for vacation Aug. 7. By the time the hearings resumed Sept. 24, much of the public fascination had evaporated. The big witnesses had testified and the excitement the hearings had generated seemed to vanish. The commercial networks dropped their coverage after a few September sessions. The "dirty tricks" phase two hearings were held intermittently between Oct. 3 and Nov. 15, but public interest in Watergate turned away from the Senate investigation to such other elements of the case as the missing presidential tapes, the firing of special Watergate prosecutor Archibald Cox and, finally, the House Judiciary Committee's impeachment proceedings.

The Senate Watergate Committee released its 2,217-page final report on July 13, 1974. The report contained 35 recommendations for preventing abuses of government power. Some were contained in an election reform bill passed in October. *(Details, p. 546)*

The committee said that its recommendations "relate to the creation of new institutions necessary to safeguard the electoral process, to provide the requisite checks against the abuse of executive power and to ensure the prompt and just enforcement of laws that already exist."[140]

CIA Investigation

Early in 1975, both the House and Senate set in motion the first major investigation and review of the Central Intelligence Agency (CIA) since its creation in 1947. (Between 1947 and 1975, Congress had either rejected or ignored nearly 200 legislative proposals to strengthen its oversight of the agency.)

The probes attracted widespread public attention, provided newspaper headlines of intelligence agency abuses and nearly resulted in an historic contempt-of-Congress citation against a Secretary of State. But by 1976, one of the committees itself (the House panel) faced criticism of its operations and leaks to the press.

Senate Action. The first step was taken by the Senate on Jan. 27, 1975, when it voted 82-4 to establish a Select Committee to Study Government Operations with Respect to Intelligence Activities.[141] The 11-member panel was given broad authority to conduct a comprehensive examination of all federal agencies (totaling 58) having responsibility for federal law enforcement of intelligence activities.

The committee, which was given an authorization of $750,000 to conduct its inquiry, also was expected to detemine 1) whether existing laws governing intelligence and law enforcement operations were adequate; 2) whether present congressional oversight of the agencies was satisfactory and 3) the extent to which overt and covert intelligence activities in the United States and abroad were necessary.

The Senate's decision to establish a select committee was prompted by newspaper reports that the CIA had violated its charter and spied on U.S. citizens during the 1960s—at the height of the Vietnam War—and that the Federal Bureau of Investigation maintained derogatory files on members of Congress.

Appointed to chair the panel was Sen. Frank Church (D Idaho), chairman of the Foreign Relations Subcommittee on Multinational Corporations which in 1973 conducted widely publicized hearings into the role of the CIA in efforts to block the 1970 election of Marxist candidate Salvador Allende Gossens as president of Chile.[142]

By the time it issued its final report, April 26, 1976, the select committee had a staff of 100, including 60 professionals, to assist the panel's members in the inquiry. The committee's work involved more than 800 interviews, over 250 executive hearings, and 110,000 pages of documentation, according to the final report. Throughout the year, the committee was virtually "leakproof," in contrast to the Senate Watergate Committee, which drew criticism throughout its investigation for divulging information to the press and public. One reason for the intelligence committee's lack of leaks was that it adopted stringent rules and procedures governing its staff, investigations, meetings and use of classified materials.[143]

Throughout the year, in both closed and open hearings, the Senate committee probed alleged CIA involvement in foreign assassination plots, receiving testimony June 24 from underworld figure John Roselli, who said he was recruited in late 1960 by the CIA to kill Cuban Premier Fidel Castro.

Rockefeller Report. Meanwhile, President Ford June 10 released the findings of the Rockefeller Commission that the CIA had engaged in widespread illegal activities in the United States. The eight-man commission, established Jan. 5, 1975, had compiled 2,900 pages of sworn testimony from 51 witnesses and took depositions and affidavits from many others. In its 299-page report, the commission noted that although "the great majority of the CIA's domestic activities comply with its statutory authority," some were "plainly unlawful and constituted improper invasions upon the rights of Americans." Among the activities that "should be criticized and not permitted to happen again," the report said, were some "initiated or ordered by Presidents, either

directly or indirectly." The report disclosed that the CIA had intercepted mail between the United States and Soviet Union, infiltrated dissident groups, set up a computerized index with the names of more than 300,000 persons and organizations, compiled files on 7,200 American citizens, conducted unlawful bugging and wiretaps and monitored overseas telephone calls.[144]

House Probe Problems. While the Senate committee was conducting its probe, a similar House panel was beset with internal wrangling. The 10-member House Select Committee on Intelligence, created Feb. 19 by a 286-120 vote, was chaired by Lucien N. Nedzi (D Mich.), who also headed the House Armed Services Intelligence Subcommittee.[145]

The committee was unable to get a full-scale investigation underway because of what Nedzi called the "chemistry that exists within the committee." He pointed out it had taken the seven Democrats and three Republicans nearly three months to agree on a staff director.

Dissension within the committee came to a head June 5 when it was learned that Nedzi had received secret briefings in 1974 about illegal activities of the CIA. But he did not inform the panel of these briefings, and Democrats on the committee felt he could not conduct a full and impartial investigation of the CIA. They then called for his resignation, but on June 11 agreed to place all members of the full select committee on a separate CIA subcommittee which would not be chaired by Nedzi.

This action led to Nedzi's resignation June 12. He charged that it had left him with nothing but a "gavel and a title" as head of the full committee.

The House, however, voted 64-290 on June 16 to reject the resignation. After the vote, Nedzi said he would not call another meeting of the full committee but would await the outcome of attempts in the House to resolve the internal dispute.

The deadlock was broken on July 10, when the Rules Committee voted to abolish the Nedzi committee and replace it with a panel of 13 that would have an identical oversight mandate. After three sessions of often acrimonious debate, the House July 17 accepted the Rules Committee proposal and established a new committee, chaired by Otis G. Pike (D N.Y.), a member of the Ways and Means Committee and formerly on the Armed Services Committee. Eight of the members of the new committee had served on the old panel.

Scarcely had the intra-committee dispute been settled than the panel locked horns with the executive branch. A confrontation arose Sept. 11, when the panel, without first seeking approval from the White House, divulged secret information about the failure of U.S. intelligence efforts during the 1973 Mideast war.

The following day, President Ford cut off the panel's access to additional classified material it had subpoenaed. He said all such documents would be withheld until the committee agreed to observe the administration's controls on the release of the data. Ford also insisted that the White House could delete sensitive information from classified documents before submitting them to the committee. The problem was resolved for the time being on Oct. 1, when the committee agreed to accept certain classified documents with the promise not to publicly disclose the material without White House approval.[146]

Tension flared up again, however, on Nov. 14, when the committee, in an unprecedented move, voted 10-2 to cite a Secretary of State—Henry A. Kissinger—for contempt of

Congress. Kissinger had refused to turn over eight documents relating to overseas covert intelligence operations that the panel had subpoenaed Nov. 5. He did so on the orders of Ford, who cited executive privilege. A floor vote was finally avoided when the committee dropped the contempt action and Pike announced that the panel had received "substantial compliance" with its subpoena.[147]

The committee suffered a major rebuff by its own chamber on Jan. 29, 1976, when the House, by a decisive 246-124 vote, blocked the panel from releasing its 338-page investigative report on the CIA and other intelligence agencies. At issue was the committee's decision to publish classified material in its final report over the objections of the executive branch. The vote followed publication Jan. 26 of sections of the report leaked to the press.[148]

Despite the House action, the leaks continued. On Feb. 11, the day the House panel filed its recommendations for intelligence reform, a New York-based magazine published excerpts of the panel's report in a 24-page supplement. Pike denied that the committee had been the source of the leaks and the House March 3 approved a resolution giving the Committee on Standards of Official Conduct far-reaching subpoena power to investigate the leak. An investigating committee was now itself the subject of a probe.[149]

Senate Committee Report. Wrapping up its 15-month investigation, the Senate Select Intelligence Committee April 26, 1976, recommended that Congress enact new charters for the CIA and other intelligence agencies to prevent the "abuses that have occurred in the past from occurring again."

In a 651-page final report, signed by nine of the committee's 11 members, the panel called for the creation of a new Senate intelligence oversight committee with power to authorize spending by the intelligence community annually.

On April 28, the select committee issued a second intelligence report, pinpointing domestic spying abuses by the FBI, the Internal Revenue Service and other agencies over a 40-year period. "Intelligence agencies have served the political and personal objectives of Presidents and other high officials," the report stated.

The committee's 396-page second report tracked a pattern of FBI misdeeds—beginning with the Roosevelt administration, when the agency was ordered by the President to compile lists of citizens who cabled the White House protesting FDR's war policies.

The committee made its report two months after President Ford, on Feb. 18, had issued his own intelligence reorganization plan. By executive order, rather than through legislation, Ford had spelled out the missions of the CIA and related agencies. The select committee insisted that this should be written into law to prevent alteration by a future President.

Describing the final report as the "most detailed, complete and unprecedented ever conducted" of the intelligence community, panel member Walter F. Mondale (D Minn.) declared that if Congress failed to set up a permanent oversight committee, the nation would again have problems with its intelligence agencies.

But Sens. John G. Tower (R Texas) and Barry Goldwater (R Ariz.), the two members who refused to sign the final report, disagreed. Tower called the recommendations an "overreaction" by the majority and said they were "potentially dangerous" to the nation's security.

The Senate committee's report on foreign and military intelligence pinpointed the following problem areas that it said needed "urgent" attention:

- Congress has failed to provide the necessary statutory guidelines to ensure that intelligence agencies carry out their missions within the framework of the Constitution. Congressional oversight procedures have not been effective, and Congress has not found effective ways to use the valuable data developed by the intelligence agencies.

- Presidents and administrations have made excessive, and at times, self-defeating use of covert action. In addition, covert action has become a routine program with a bureaucratic momentum of its own.

- Congress' failure to monitor the intelligence agencies' expenditures has been a major element in the ineffective oversight of the intelligence community. Without the power to authorize the budgets of the agencies, an oversight committee may find itself in possession of important secret information, but unable to act effectively to protect the principles, integrity and reputation of the United States.

- The operation of an extensive and necessarily secret intelligence system places severe strains on the nation's constitutional system; means must be provided for lawful disclosure of unneeded or unlawful secrets.

- Intelligence activities should not be regarded as ends in themselves.

The fundamental issue the committee said it faced during the investigation was how the requirements of American democracy could be balanced in intelligence matters against the need for secrecy.

In trying to reconcile the two, the panel said it found itself in a "difficult dilemma": As an investigating committee, it could not recommend legislation on some of the matters that came to its attention. On the other hand, because of the secrecy required, the committee could not "publicly present the full case as to why its recommendations are essential."

The experience, the panel concluded, underscored the need for an effective legislative oversight committee that would have sufficient power to resolve these fundamental conflicts.

The committee's 87 proposals covering foreign and military intelligence operations fell into four categories: 1) new laws to define the activities and organization of the intelligence community, 2) reviews of intelligence operations by the executive branch, 3) restrictions on certain intelligence activities and 4) congressional oversight procedures.

The committee proposed that the executive branch review and approve all covert action projects, "however small," before they were put into operation. The panel said it had "given serious consideration" to banning all forms of covert activity, but that this was discarded. Instead, it offered several proposals for better control of covert operations. It recommended prohibiting by statute 1) political assassinations, 2) efforts to subvert democratic governments and 3) U.S. government support for police or other internal security forces that engaged in systematic violation of human rights. (President Ford's Feb. 18 executive order did not prohibit covert operations other than assassinations.)

Eighteen of the committee's recommendations dealt specifically with the CIA. To clear up ambiguities in the 1947 act establishing the agency, the committee proposed that a new charter be established "which makes clear that (CIA) activities must be related to foreign intelligence."

As the centerpiece of its recommendations, the committee proposed that a new congressional oversight panel be given authority to consider and approve a "national intelligence budget" each year. The total amount then would be made public.

In issuing the final report, the select committee complained that despite its legal mandate and its subpoena power to investigate the intelligence agencies, "in no instance has the committee been able to examine the agencies' files on its own. In all the agencies...documents and evidence have been presented through the filter of the agency itself." In some cases, the committee said it was denied data by the executive branch.

In its companion report on domestic spying abuses issued April 28, the committee concluded that domestic intelligence activity, which had become increasingly unchecked in recent years, had threatened and undermined Americans' constitutional rights of free speech. The report stated, "Too many people have been spied upon by too many government agencies and too much information has been collected." It said the FBI, CIA, National Security Agency (NSA) and Defense Department intelligence agencies had engaged in improper domestic intelligence and that the Internal Revenue Service (IRS) and U.S. Postal Service had been involved.

After stating its findings, the committee delineated 96 recommendations, most of which were designed to be included in legislation intended to improve control over domestic intelligence apparatus.

Acting quickly on the Senate investigating committee's recommendation, the Senate May 19 voted 77-22, to establish a permanent Select Committee on Intelligence with legislative and budgetary authority over the CIA and other federal intelligence agencies.

In the key vote on the resolution, the Senate turned down an amendment drafted by John G. Tower (R Texas) and John C. Stennis (D Miss.), chairman of the Armed Services Committee, that would have stripped the new committee of its legislative and budgetary authority over intelligence components of the Defense Department.

A compromise was worked out that gave the committee exclusive legislative and budget authorization authority over the CIA; but jurisdiction over the intelligence components of the FBI and the Defense Department would be shared with the Judiciary and Armed Services Committees respectively.

In the case of shared jurisdiction, legislation approved by one panel would have to be referred to the other and then reported to the Senate floor within 30 days.

The new committee also was given subpoena power and authority to declassify sensitive information; but if the President objected to any disclosure, the matter would be referred to the full Senate for its decision.

The 15 members of the new committee included eight Democrats and seven Republicans selected by the Senate majority and minority leaders. The resolution establishing the panel required that two members be chosen from each of four committees—Appropriations, Armed Services, Judiciary and Foreign Relations; the remaining seven members were to be selected at large. Members' terms of service on the select committee were limited to eight years.

Daniel K. Inouye (D Hawaii) was chosen chairman of the Select Committee on Intelligence, and Howard H. Baker Jr. (R Tenn.) was selected to be ranking minority member.

Footnotes

1. Woodrow Wilson, *Congressional Government* (World Publishing Co., 1967), p. 303.

2. Quoted in M. Nelson McGeary, *The Development of Congressional Investigative Power* (Octagon Books, Inc., 1966), p. 7. Also in the *Congressional Record*, 73rd Congress, 1st session, May 25, 1933, p. 4182.

3. Quoted in Donald H. Riddle, *The Truman Committee* (Rutgers University Press, 1964), p. 12. Also in the *Congressional Record*, 78th Congress, 2nd session, Aug. 7, 1944, p. 6747.

4. McGeary, *Investigative Power*, p. 7.

5. C. Herman Pritchett, *The American Constitution* (McGraw-Hill Inc., 1968), p. 214, quoting Lippmann's *Public Opinion* (Harcourt, Brace and World Inc., 1922), p. 289.

6. Joseph P. Harris, *Congressional Control of Administration* (Doubleday and Co., 1964), p. 253; and Marshall E. Dimock, *Congressional Investigating Committees* (Johns Hopkins Press, 1929), p. 87.

7. Dimock, p. 104; and Telford Taylor, *Grand Inquest* (Simon and Schuster Inc., 1955), p. 33.

8. Taylor, p. 51. For a summary, see Congressional Quarterly, *Congress and the Nation, 1945-1964*, Vol. I, p. 1679.

9. For a discussion of development of the power and controversy surrounding it, see Dimock, *Investigating Committees*, pp. 46, 117-21, and Taylor, *Grand Inquest*, pp. 5-16.

10. For background, see Carl Beck, *Contempt of Congress* (Hauser Press, 1959); and Ronald L. Goldfarb, *The Contempt Power* (Columbia University Press, 1963).

11. Goldfarb, p. 25.

12. *Ibid.*, p. 30; Beck, *Contempt*, p. 3; Ernest J. Eberling, *Congressional Investigations* (Columbia University Press, 1928), pp. 37-42, 66-85.

13. Eberling, pp. 161-67; Beck, p. 191.

14. Dimock, *Investigating Committees*, pp. 121-23; Pritchett, *The American Constitution*, p. 217.

15. Goldfarb, *The Contempt Power*, p. 163.

16. Taylor, *Grand Inquest*, p. 35; *Congress and the Nation*, Vol. I, p. 1783.

17. Goldfarb, *The Contempt Power*, p. 196; Beck, *Contempt*, appendix.

18. Beck, p. 185.

19. *Ibid.*, pp. 185-86, 189.

20. Congressional Quarterly, *Watergate: Chronology of a Crisis*, pp. 311, 637.

21. Dimock, *Investigating Committees*, pp. 73-74.

22. *Ibid.*, p. 58.

23. *Ibid.*, p. 102.

24. McGeary, *Investigative Power*, p. 8.

25. Harris, *Congressional Control*, p. 264.

26. Congressional Quarterly, *Watergate*, p. 514.

27. *Ibid.*, p. 467.

28. *Ibid.*, p. 514.

29. *Ibid.*, p. 518, for text of resolution.

30. *Ibid.*, p. 356.

31. *Ibid.*, p. 103; Raoul Berger, *Executive Privilege* (Harvard University Press, 1974), p. 187-94.

32. Harris, *Congressional Control*, pp. 264-65.

33. Congressional Quarterly, 1975 *Weekly Report*, pp. 496, 627.

34. Congressional Quarterly, *Watergate*, p. 652.

35. For a good discussion of procedure, see McGeary, *Investigative Power*, Chapter III; and Riddle, *The Truman Committee*.

36. McGeary, pp. 51-52.

37. Background on staff, *ibid.*, pp. 59-66.

38. See John E. Wiltz, *In Search of Peace* (Louisiana State University Press, 1963), a book about the Nye committee.

39. Riddle, *The Truman Committee*.

40. According to the Charles B. Brownson, *1975 Congressional Staff Directory.*

41. Congressional Quarterly, *Watergate,* p. 543.

42. *Annual Report of the Comptroller General of the United States for 1974* (Washington: U.S. Government Printing Office, 1975), p. 3.

43. Riddle, *The Truman Committee,* p. 142.

44. *Congress and the Nation,* Vol. I, p. 1746.

45. For a discussion of hearings, see McGeary, *Investigative Power,* pp. 73-81.

46. Congressional Quarterly, *Watergate,* p. 111.

47. For background on rights of witnesses, see Taylor, *Grand Inquest,* Chapter VI; and Library of Congress, Legislative Reference Service, *Congressional Power of Investigation* (Washington: U.S. Government Printing Office, 1954), pp. 15-20.

48. *Ibid.,* p. 15.

49. Quoted in Taylor, *Grand Inquest,* p. 240.

50. *Congress and the Nation,* Vol. I, pp. 1683-85.

51. Quoted in Pritchett, *The American Constitution,* p. 230, from *Eisler v. United States,* 338 U.S. 189 (1949).

52. *Ibid.*

53. *Ibid.,* p. 231.

54. J. W. Fulbright, "Congressional Investigations: Significance for the Legislative Processes," *University of Chicago Law Review,* 1951, p. 442.

55. Taylor, *Grand Inquest,* pp. 215-16.

56. *Ibid.*

57. Pritchett, *The American Constitution,* p. 618.

58. *Congress and the Nation,* Vol. I, pp. 1658, 1685. For a critique see Taylor, *Grand Inquest,* pp. 218-21.

59. Pritchett, *The American Constitution,* p. 619.

60. Congressional Quarterly, *Watergate,* p. 111.

61. *Ibid.,* p. 138.

62. For a summary, see Taylor, *Grand Inquest;* and *Congress and the Nation,* Vol. I, pp. 1680-81, 1684.

63. Riddle, *The Truman Committee,* pp. 4-5.

64. Dimock, *Investigating Committees,* pp. 131-36; and Pritchett, *The American Constitution,* p. 215.

65. Dimock, pp. 126-28.

66. *Ibid.,* pp. 137-45, Pritchett, p. 216.

67. McGeary, *Investigative Power,* pp. 97-100; Taylor, *Grand Inquest,* pp. 56-57.

68. Legislative Reference Service, *Congressional Power of Investigation,* p. 48.

69. *Congress and the Nation,* Vol. I, p. 1686; Pritchett, *The American Constitution,* p. 220; Taylor, *Grand Inquest,* pp. 140-46.

70. Quoted in August Raymond Ogden, *The Dies Committee* (The Catholic University of America Press, 1945), p. 44.

71. *Congress and the Nation,* Vol. I, p. 1686.

72. *Ibid.,* p. 1686; Pritchett, *The American Constitution,* p. 219; Walter Goodman, *The Committee* (Farrar, Straus and Giroux, 1968), p. 284.

73. Pritchett, p. 219.

74. Pritchett, p. 220; *Congress and the Nation,* Vol. I, p. 1684.

75. *Ibid.,* p. 1685; and Pritchett, pp. 222-23.

76. *Ibid.,* p. 226; and *Congress and the Nation,* Vol. I, p. 1686.

77. Pritchett, p. 227.

78. Berger, *Executive Privilege,* p. 1.

79. Taylor, *Grand Inquest,* p. 101.

80. Berger, *Executive Privilege,* p. 1.

81. *Ibid.,* p. 14.

82. *Congress and the Nation,* Vol. I, p. 1681; Taylor, *Grand Inquest,* pp. 99-100.

83. *Ibid.,* p. 99; Berger, *Executive Privilege,* pp. 166-79.

84. Dimock, pp. 105-07; Legislative Reference Service, *Congressional Power of Investigation,* p. 51.

85. Taylor, *Grand Inquest,* p. 193.

86. Eberling, *Congressional Investigations,* p. 135.

87. Berger, *Executive Privilege,* pp. 183-85; Asher C. Hinds, *Hinds' Precedents of the House of Representatives of the United States,* Vol. 3 (Washington: U.S. Government Printing Office, 1907), pp. 181-86.

88. Taylor, *Grand Inquest,* p. 101; Eberling, *Congressional Investigations,* pp. 256-58; *Hinds' Precedents,* Vol. 3, pp. 190-92.

89. Eberling, p. 258.

90. Clarence Cannon, *Cannon's Precedents of the House of Representatives of the United States,* Vol. 6 (Washington: U.S. Government Printing Office, 1935), pp. 597-99.

91. Taylor, *Grand Inquest,* p. 102; Goodman, *The Committee,* pp. 226-37.

92. Taylor, p. 102; *Federal Register,* March 16, 1948.

93. *Congress and the Nation,* Vol. I, p. 1693.

94. Taylor, *Grand Inquest,* p. 133.

95. Reprinted in Berger, *Executive Privilege,* p. 373-86.

96. *Ibid.,* p. 377.

97. *Ibid.,* p. 381.

98. *Ibid.,* p. 382.

99. *Ibid.,* p. 384.

100. Congressional Quarterly, *Watergate,* p. 47. For a good discussion of the Senate committee, see James Hamilton, *The Power to Probe* (Random House, 1975).

101. *Ibid.,* p. 103.

102. *Ibid.,* p. 189.

103. *Ibid.,* pp. 341-44.

104. *Ibid.,* p. 513.

105. *Ibid.*

106. *Ibid.*

107. *Ibid.,* p. 523.

108. *Ibid.*

109. *Ibid.*

110. *Ibid.,* p. 640.

111. *Ibid,* p. 680.

112. *Ibid.,* pp. 678-79.

113. *Ibid.,* pp. 718 ff, for discussion and text of decision.

114. Harris, *Congressional Control,* p. 271.

115. May 25, 1933; quoted in McGeary, *Investigative Power,* p. 45.

116. James A. Perkins, "Congressional Investigation of Matters of International Import," *American Political Science Review,* Vol. 39, 1940, pp. 285-87; quoted in Harris, p. 272.

117. *Ibid.*

118. *Congress and the Nation,* Vol. I, pp. 1687-88.

119. *Ibid.,* p. 1745.

120. Congressional Quarterly, 1975 *Weekly Report,* pp. 180, 240, 367.

121. *Ibid.,* pp. 1285, 1480, 1551.

122. Taylor, *Grand Inquest,* Chapter III; Dimock, *Investigating Committees,* pp. 87-88; Harris, *Congressional Control,* p. 251.

123. Dimock, pp. 111-12; Harris, pp. 253-54.

124. An observation attributed to Truman, quoted in Taylor, p. 109.

125. Harris, *Congressional Control,* p. 255.

126. Background, Dimock, *Investigating Committees,* pp. 115-16.

127. Taylor, *Grand Inquest,* p. 63.

128. Harris, *Congressional Control,* p. 259.

129. Taylor, *Grand Inquest,* pp. 65-67.

130. Wiltz, *In Search of Peace.*

131. Riddle, *The Truman Committee.*

132. *Congress and the Nation,* Vol. I, pp. 1700-01, 1706-07.

133. *Ibid.,* pp. 1718-27.

134. *Ibid.,* pp. 1701-03.

135. *Ibid.,* p. 1714.

136. *Ibid.,* pp. 1720 ff.

137. *Ibid.,* pp. 1720-27.

138. *Ibid.,* p. 1766; and Congressional Quarterly, *Congress and the Nation, 1965-1968,* Vol. II, pp. 875 ff.

139. Congressional Quarterly, *Watergate.*

140. Details of recommendations, *ibid.,* pp. 705-09, 730-33.

141. Background, Congressional Quarterly, *1975 Almanac,* p. 387.

142. Congressional Quarterly, 1973 *Almanac,* p. 845.

143. Congressional Quarterly, 1975 *Almanac,* p. 396.

144. For summary of report, see *ibid.,* p. 392.

145. *Ibid.,* p. 399.

146. *Ibid.,* p. 404.

147. *Ibid.,* p. 406.

148. Congressional Quarterly, 1976 *Weekly Report,* p. 203.

149. *Ibid.,* p. 419.

Selected Bibliography

Books

Barth, Alan. *Government by Investigation.* New York: Viking Press, 1955.

Beck, Carl. *Contempt of Congress: A Study of the Prosecutions Initiated by the Committee on Un-American Activities, 1945-1957.* New Orleans: Hauser Press, 1959.

Bentley, Eric, ed. *Thirty Years of Treason: Excerpts from Hearings before the House Un-American Activities Committee, 1938-1968.* New York: Viking Press, 1971.

Berger, Raoul. *Executive Privilege.* Cambridge: Harvard University Press, 1974.

Carr, Robert K. *The House Committee on Un-American Activities, 1945-1950.* Ithaca: Cornell University Press, 1952.

Chambers, Whittaker. *Witness.* New York: Random House, 1952.

Congressional Quarterly. *Watergate: Chronology of a Crisis.* Washington: Congressional Quarterly Inc., 1975.

Dimock, Marshall E. *Congressional Investigating Committees.* Baltimore: Johns Hopkins Press, 1929.

Eberling, Ernest J. *Congressional Investigations: A Study of the Origin and Development of the Power of Congress to Investigate and Punish for Contempt.* New York: Columbia University Press, 1928.

Galloway, George B. *History of the House of Representatives.* New York: Thomas Y. Crowell Co., 1969.

Goldfarb, Ronald L. *The Contempt Power.* New York: Columbia University Press, 1963.

Goodman, Walter. *The Committee: The Extraordinary Career of the House Committee on Un-American Activities.* New York: Farrar, Straus and Giroux, 1968.

Hamilton, James. *The Power to Probe: A Study of Congressional Investigations.* New York: Random House, 1976.

Harris, Joseph P. *Congressional Control of Administration.* Washington: Brookings Institution, 1964.

McGeary, M. Nelson. *The Development of Congressional Investigative Power.* New York: Octagon Books Inc., 1966.

Ogden, August Raymond. *The Dies Committee: A Study of the Special House Committees for Investigation of Un-American Activities, 1938-1944.* Washington: Catholic University of America Press, 1945.

Pritchett, C. Herman. *The American Constitution.* New York: McGraw-Hill, 1968.

Riddle, Donald H. *The Truman Committee: A Study in Congressional Responsibility.* New Brunswick: Rutgers University Press, 1964.

Rovere, Richard H. *Senator Joe McCarthy.* Cleveland: World Publishing Co., 1968.

Schlesinger, Arthur M. Jr., and Burns, Roger, eds. *Congress Investigates: A Documentary History 1792-1974.* 5 vols. New York: Bowker, 1975.

Taylor, Telford. *Grand Inquest.* New York: Simon & Schuster Inc., 1955.

Wilson, Woodrow. *Congressional Government.* Cleveland: World Publishing Co., 1967 ed.

Wiltz, John E. *In Search of Peace: The Senate Munitions Inquiry, 1934-1936.* Baton Rouge: Louisiana State University Press, 1963.

Articles

"The Application of the Fourth Amendment to Congressional Investigations." *Minnesota Law Review,* January 1968, pp. 665-97.

"Congressional Investigations." *University of Chicago Law Review,* vol. 18, no. 3, 1951.

Cousens, Theodore W. "The Purpose and Scope of Investigation Under Legislative Authority." *Georgetown Law Journal,* vol. 26, 1938, p. 905.

Dilliard, Irving. "Congressional Investigations: The Role of the Press." *University of Chicago Law Review,* vol. 18, 1951, pp. 585-90.

Galloway, George. "Congressional Investigation: Proposed Reforms." *University of Chicago Law Review,* vol. 18, 1951, pp. 478-502.

Galloway, George B. "The Investigative Function of Congress." *American Political Science Review,* February 1927, pp. 47-70.

Kaplan, Lewis A. "The House Un-American Activities Committee and Its Opponents: A Study in Congressional Dissonance." *Journal of Politics,* August 1968, pp. 647-71.

McGeary, M. Nelson "Congressional Investigations: Historical Development." *University of Chicago Law Review,* vol. 18, 1951, pp. 425-39.

McGeary, M. Nelson "Congressional Power of Investigation." *Nebraska Law Review,* vol. 28, 1949, pp. 516-29.

Government Publication

U.S. Congress. Library of Congress. Legislative Research Service. *Congressional Power of Investigation.* Washington: Government Printing Office, 1954.

Senate Confirmation of Nominations

Senatorial confirmation of executive appointments is a distinctly American political and legislative phenomenon. The authors of the Constitution spent considerable time debating how appointments should be made before agreeing to a compromise proposal that the President appoint governmental officers with the advice and consent of the Senate.

If the Founding Fathers were alive today, one of the features of the contemporary political system that probably would much surprise them would be nominations. Although the mechanics of the confirmation system have remained much the same, the growth of the federal government has dramatically increased the number of nominations.

In the last 20 Congresses spanning 40 years, the number of nominations received by the Senate has grown sixfold—from 22,487 in the 74th Congress (1935-36) to 134,-384 in the 93rd (1973-74). *(Boxscore of Nominations, p. 176)*

Routine Confirmation or Detailed Inquiry

Numbers alone do not give an accurate picture of the nominations process. The vast majority of nominations sent annually to the Senate involve the routine confirmation of appointments and promotions for military officers and officers of specialized services such as the Foreign Service and Public Health Service. These nominations are usually passed en bloc and confirmation is a formality. In his book, *The Advice and Consent of the Senate,* Joseph P. Harris placed 99 per cent of the nominations in this category.

It is the remaining 1 per cent of nominations, involving people who will occupy top policy-making positions in government, that sometimes locks the President and Senate in battle. These include nominations to cabinet and sub-cabinet posts, the federal judiciary, major diplomatic and military positions and top positions on independent boards and regulatory agencies. Although most nominations are confirmed by the Senate, pro forma approval is not always certain. Political considerations always have been a part of the nomination and confirmation process. But in recent years, the Senate often has carefully examined a nominee's economic views, social philosophy and personal finances.

Cabinet Nominations

By contrast, cabinet nominations usually are confirmed with little difficulty, on the theory that the President should have great leeway in selecting the members of his official "family." Since 1789, only eight men nominated to the cabinet have been rejected by the Senate.

Nominations to sub-cabinet positions, which have multiplied phenomenally in the 20th century, are treated much like cabinet nominations, although the President is expected to consult in advance with key members of Congress on appointments in which they have a particular interest, and sub-cabinet posts frequently are used to reward various party factions. Since 1933 few such nominations have been withdrawn and none rejected.

Appointments to independent boards and commissions offer a somewhat different situation. Usually created by act of Congress and not subordinate to any executive department, they frequently are viewed as an arm of Congress rather than the executive branch, and members of Congress expect to play a larger role in the selection process. Typically, the act of Congress creating an independent agency may require a bipartisan membership or impose geographical or other limitations on the President's selection power. Contests with the Senate over these nominations have been frequent, although few nominees actually have been rejected. Independent agencies with single administrators have fewer problems—these

---

The Constitutional Mandate

"The President...shall nominate, and by and with the Advice and Consent of the Senate shall appoint Ambassadors, other public Ministers and Consuls, Judges of the Supreme Court, and all other Officers of the United States, whose appointments are not herein otherwise provided for, and which shall be established by Law; but the Congress may by law vest the appointment of such inferior officers, as they think proper, in the President alone, in the courts of law, or in the heads of departments.

"The President shall have power to fill up all vacancies that may happen during the recess of the Senate, by granting commissions which shall expire at the end of their next session." *(Constitution of the United States, Article II, Section 2)*

---

nominations tend to be treated more like cabinet nominations.

Diplomatic and Other Nominations

Major diplomatic nominations usually encounter little opposition. Although in the early days of the Republic the Senate attempted to exercise extensive authority over diplomatic appointments, in modern practice the President has been allowed wide discretion in his selection of ambassadors and other persons to assist him in the conduct of foreign relations.

Appointments to lower federal courts are another matter. By 1840 it had become customary for district court judges to be selected by the senators from the state in which the district was located, provided the senators were of the same party as the President. If they were not, the President was expected to consult with state party leaders before making a selection. Senatorial dictation of judicial appointments was reinforced by the institution of senatorial courtesy; under this unwritten custom, the Senate generally will refuse to confirm a nomination to an office situated within a particular state if the senators of the President's party from that state oppose it. The President has wider discretion in making appointments to circuit court judgeships because these jurisdictions embrace several states, and to other specialized courts such as the tax and customs.

Appointees in one other broad classification historically were selected by the legislative branch. Postmasters of the first, second and third classes constituted the largest group of civilian employees appointed with Senate confirmation. Although it was the Senate that gave its advice and consent, custom decreed that members of the House—if they were of the same party as the President—made the actual selection of appointees in their districts.

This patronage system survived until 1970 when Congress created an independent U.S. Postal Service. The postal reorganization set up an independent government agency, the Postal Service, to take over operations of the Post Office Department. The legislation ended congressional influence over appointment of postmasters.

U.S. attorneys and marshals continue as patronage appointments. Appointed with Senate confirmation for four-year terms, they serve at the pleasure of the President.

History of Appointments

The President "shall nominate, and by and with the Advice and Consent of the Senate, shall appoint...."[1]

Boxscore of Nominations, 1929-74

	Received	Confirmed	Withdrawn	*Rejected	Unconfirmed
71st (1929-31)	17,508	16,905	68	5	530
72nd (1931-33)	12,716	10,909	19	1	1,787
73rd (1933-34)	9,094	9,027	17	3	47
74th (1935-36)	22,487	22,286	51	15	135
75th (1937-38)	15,330	15,193	20	27	90
76th (1939-40)	29,072	28,939	16	21	96
77th (1941-42)	24,344	24,137	33	5	169
78th (1943-44)	21,775	21,371	31	6	367
79th (1945-46)	37,022	36,550	17	3	452
80th (1947-48)	66,641	54,796	153	0	11,692
81st (1949-50)	87,266	86,562	45	6	653
82nd (1951-52)	46,920	46,504	45	2	369
83rd (1953-54)	69,458	68,563	43	0	852
84th (1955-56)	84,173	82,694	38	3	1,438
85th (1957-58)	104,193	103,311	54	0	828
86th (1959-60)	91,476	89,900	30	1	1,545
87th (1961-62)	102,849	100,741	1,279	0	829
88th (1963-64)	122,190	120,201	36	0	1,953
89th (1965-66)	123,019	120,865	173	0	1,981
90th (1967-68)	120,231	118,231	34	0	1,966
91st (1969-71)	134,464	133,797	487	2	178
92nd (1971-72)	117,053	114,909	11	0	2,133
93rd (1973-74)**	134,384	131,254	15	0	3,069

*Category includes only those nominations rejected outright by a vote on the Senate floor. Most nominations that fail to win approval of the Senate are unfavorably reported by committees and never reach the Senate floor. In some cases, the full Senate may vote to recommit a nomination to committee.

**Forty-six nominations were returned to the President during the October-November 1974 recess in accordance with Senate Rule 38 which states: "...if the Senate shall adjourn or take a recess for more than thirty days, all nominations pending and not finally acted upon at the time of taking such adjournment or recess shall be returned by the Secretary to the President, and shall not again be considered unless they shall again be made to the Senate by the President.

Sources: Floyd M. Riddick, *The United States Congress: Organization and Procedures,* 71st-80th Congresses. *Congressional Record,* 81st-93rd Congresses.

The constitutional language governing the appointment power, hammered out in the final weeks of the Constitutional Convention of 1787, represented a compromise between those delegates who favored vesting in the Senate sole authority for appointing principal officers of the government and those who held that the President alone should control appointments as an executive function.

As finally adopted, the Constitution required Senate confirmation of principal officers of the government—"Ambassadors, other public Ministers and Consuls, Judges of the Supreme Court" were mentioned specifically—but provided that Congress could "by law vest the appointment of such inferior officers, as they think proper, in the President alone, in the courts of law, or in the heads of departments."

Approval of the compromise language did not, however, settle the controversy over the Senate's role in the appointment process.

To Hamilton, writing in *The Federalist* (No. 66), the Senate's function did not appear significant: "It will be the office of the President to *nominate,* and with the advice and consent of the Senate to *appoint.* There will, of course, be no exertion of *choice* on the part of the Senate. They may defeat one choice of the Executive and oblige him to make another; but they cannot themselves *choose*—they can only ratify or reject the choice he may have made."[2]

John Adams saw it differently. "Faction and distraction," he wrote, "are the sure and certain consequences of giving to the Senate a vote on the distribution of offices."[3] Looking ahead to the emergence of political parties, Adams foresaw the rise of the spoils system and the use of the appointive power as a senatorial patronage tool.

President Washington regarded the appointment power as "the most irksome part of the executive trust,"[4] but his exercise of that power was widely acclaimed and the Senate withheld its consent only five times during his administration.

Precedents Established by Washington

Methods of handling presidential nominations had to be established early in the new government. Washington established the precedent of submitting nominations to the Senate in writing, and the Senate after debate on the propriety of the secret ballot determined to take voice votes on nominations. The President rejected suggestions that he be present during Senate consideration of appointments: "It could be no pleasing thing, I conceive, for the President, on the one hand to be present and hear the propriety of his nominations questioned; nor for the Senate on the other hand to be under the smallest restraint from his presence from the fullest and freest inquiry into the character of the person nominated."[5]

Uncertainty over the extent of the Senate's powers with respect to appointments surfaced early in the administration. Could the Senate only give its consent to the person named, or could it also rule on the necessity for the post and the grade of the appointee? Washington's nominations of ministers to Paris, London and The Hague in December 1791 were blocked for weeks by Senate debate on a resolution opposing the appointment of "ministers plenipotentiary to reside permanently at foreign courts."[6] Washington's nominations finally were approved, by narrow votes, on the ground of special need for representation at the three capitals.

Washington maintained high standards for selection of appointees, and although he consulted widely both with members of Congress and others, he rebuffed all attempts at encroachment on his prerogatives. Thus he refused to appoint Aaron Burr as minister to France in 1794, despite the recommendation of a caucus of Republican senators and representatives, because he questioned Burr's integrity.

Washington was not always successful in resisting senatorial pressure. Early in the First Congress, the Senate rejected his nomination of Benjamin Fishbourn to the post of naval officer (a customs official handling manifests, clearances, etc.) of the Port of Savannah as a courtesy to the two Georgia Senators, who had a candidate of their own. Washington yielded; he nominated the senators' choice, and senatorial courtesy was born.

The practice of inquiring into the political views of a presidential nominee also had its beginning in the Washington administration. John Rutledge of South Carolina, nominated in 1795 to succeed John Jay as Chief Justice of the United States, was rejected by the Senate on a 10-14 vote, primarily because of his opposition to the Jay Treaty with Great Britain. Rutledge, one of the original six Supreme Court Justices (1789-91), was already serving as Chief Justice on a recess appointment.

Injection of Politics

John Adams, that vigorous critic of the appointment provisions of the Constitution, found nothing in his experience as President to make him change his views. The Federalist Senate cleared his appointments with Federalist leader Alexander Hamilton (then a private citizen), and Adams later complained that he "soon found that if I had not the previous consent of the heads of departments, and the approbation of Mr. Hamilton, I ran the utmost risk of a dead negative in the Senate."[7]

During Adams' tenure, appointments became increasingly subject to political considerations. The practice of consulting, and bowing to the wishes of, state delegations in Congress upon appointments in their states also grew.

Jefferson had far less trouble with appointments than his predecessor. He was the acknowledged leader of his party, and for most of his term that party was in control of Congress. Perhaps his most embarrassing failure was the unanimous rejection of his final nomination, that of William Short as minister to Russia. However, the opposition apparently was directed more against the establishment of the mission than against Short himself.

Unlike Jefferson, Madison soon found that he had to submit to Senate dictation in the matter of appointments. Thus a small clique of Senators was able to force the appointment of Robert Smith as Secretary of State, although Madison had wanted to give the post to his Secretary of the Treasury, Albert Gallatin.

Gallatin's subsequent appointment as envoy to negotiate a peace treaty with Great Britain also met with difficulty in the Senate. Gallatin was already in Europe when the Senate adopted a resolution declaring that the duties of envoy and Secretary of the Treasury were incompatible. Subsequently, Gallatin resigned his Treasury post and was confirmed as envoy.

This nomination led to a controversy over the propriety of consultation between the President and a Senate committee on pending nominations. Although previous Presidents had so consulted with committees appointed by the party caucus or by the Senate itself, Madison decided to put an end to the practice. In a message to the Senate, he insisted that if the Senate wanted information on nominations, the correct procedure was to confer with appropriate department heads, not the President. "The appointment of a committee of the Senate to confer immediately with the executive himself," he said, "appears to lose sight of the coordinate relation between the executive and the Senate, which the Constitution has established, and which ought therefore to be maintained."[8] In spite of this message, the President received a special committee appointed by the Senate to confer with him about the Gallatin nomination, but he refused to discuss the nomination with them.

Madison in 1811 suffered the second outright rejection of a Supreme Court nomination. Alexander Wolcott was opposed by the Federalists because as collector of customs in Connecticut he had vigorously enforced the unpopular embargo acts passed prior to the War of 1812. He was rejected, 9-24, following charges by the press that he lacked the requisite legal qualifications for service on the court.

Growth of Spoils System

The administrations of James Monroe and John Quincy Adams were marked by the growth of the spoils system, as members of the Senate increasingly insisted on control of federal appointments in their states.

The "Four Years" law, enacted in 1820, greatly increased the number of appointments available. This law provided fixed four-year terms for many federal officers who previously had served at the pleasure of the President. Although its ostensible purpose was to ensure the accountability of appointees, its value as a patronage tool soon became clear. Commented Adams: "The Senate was conciliated by the permanent increase of their power, which was the principal ultimate effect of the act, and every senator was flattered by the power conferred upon himself of multiplying chances to provide for his friends and dependents....."[9]

Both Monroe and Adams resisted pressure to use the "Four Years" law as a means of introducing rotation in office; they followed the policy of renominating officers upon expiration of their terms, unless they had been guilty of misconduct. Upon taking office as President in 1825, Adams resubmitted all of Monroe's nominations on which the Senate had failed to act; by contrast, Jackson withdrew all of Adams' nominations.

One of Adams' Supreme Court nominations was blocked by the Senate. The name of John J. Crittenden, a Kentucky Whig, had been sent up shortly before Adams' administration ended in 1829. Jacksonians, who wished to allow the newly elected Democratic President to make the appointment, blocked Senate action on confirmation of Crittenden by a vote of 23-17. Jackson later filled the seat with a man of his choice.

Jackson, to whom rotation in office was a leading principle, made full use of the "Four Years" law to find places for his supporters. Although he was in constant conflict with the Senate over appointments, such was his popularity in the country that relatively few were rejected.

One of the most significant of the rejections was the appointment of Martin Van Buren as minister to England. Van Buren in 1831 resigned his post as Secretary of State in a cabinet reorganization, and President Jackson then gave him a recess appointment to the Court of St. James. He was already in London when the Senate met in December. Clay, Webster and Calhoun, all aspirants for the presidency who looked on Van Buren as a likely opponent, led the opposition to his appointment. When the nomination came to a vote in January 1832, a tie was contrived so that Vice Presi-

Courtesy of the Senate

Under the unwritten custom of senatorial courtesy, the Senate generally will refuse to confirm a nomination to an office situated within a particular state unless the nominee has been approved by the senators of the President's party from that state. The rule is not ordinarily applied to nominations to national office.

A senator typically invokes the rule of courtesy by stating that the nominee is "personally obnoxious" to him; this may mean that the senator and the nominee are personal or political foes, or simply that the senator has another candidate for the post. In effect, the custom permits the senators of the party in office to control selection of local federal officials—district court judges, U.S. attorneys, marshals and the like. In states where neither senator belongs to the President's party, the President has greater freedom of choice, although state party leaders usually make recommendations to him.

Background. The custom of senatorial courtesy had its beginnings in the Washington administration.* In 1789 President Washington nominated Benjamin Fishbourn to the post of naval officer of the port of Savannah, Ga. Fishbourn appeared to be well qualified. He had led a distinguished military career and was elected to several terms in the Georgia assembly. He served as president of Georgia's executive council and was appointed by that body to be collector of the port of Savannah.

Fishbourn lacked one important credential, however—he did not possess the favor of Georgia's two senators. The pair, William Few and James Gunn, supported a candidate of their own, Lachlan McIntosh. Few and Gunn opposed Fishbourn, and the Senate followed their lead and rejected Washington's nomination.

The President acknowledged the Senate's rejection in a letter dated Aug. 6, 1789. In it he announced he would nominate another candidate for the post—Lachlan McIntosh, the Georgia senators' favorite. A precedent had been set.

The custom of senatorial courtesy, however, did not become firmly established until many years later. Under early practice, the objecting senator had only to voice the customary formula, but since 1930 he has been expected to explain the reasons for his opposition to the nominee.

The Senate does not invariably sustain appeals to the rule of courtesy. It depends on whether the objecting senator is in good standing with his colleagues, the nature of his objection and whether the nomination is to a local or national office.

A specialized form of senatorial courtesy decrees that the nomination of a senator or former senator will be confirmed at once, without even being referred to committee. This tradition is not always honored, however. The Supreme Court nominations of Sen. Hugo L. Black in 1937 and of former Sen. Sherman Minton in 1949 were both referred to committee.

*Joseph P. Harris, The Advice and Consent of the Senate (New York: Greenwood Press, Publishers 1968), pp. 40-41, 216-17; James D. Richardson, ed., A Compilation of the Messages and Papers of the Presidents (New York: Bureau of National Literature, 1897), Vol. 1, pp. 50-51.

dent Calhoun could vote against Van Buren. Although his opponents thought a Senate rejection would end Van Buren's political career, he returned home a martyr and was soon elected Vice President of the United States.

The Senate twice rejected Jackson's renomination of four incumbent directors of the Bank of the United States. Senate opposition stemmed from reports critical of the bank that had been submitted to the President by the directors. Efforts to recommit the nominations having failed, the Senate rejected them, 20-24. Jackson renominated the same persons, and they again were rejected.

The Bank of the United States also figured in rejection of the nomination of Roger B. Taney as Secretary of the Treasury in 1834. Taney was rejected on an 18-28 vote after having served for nine months under a recess appointment. Opposition rested on his withdrawal of federal funds from the bank, an action which he had recommended as Attorney General and which he had been appointed Secretary of the Treasury to carry out. This was the first outright Senate rejection of a cabinet appointee in U.S. history, although Madison had been prevented from appointing Gallatin as Secretary of State in 1809 because he feared Gallatin would be rejected.

Early in 1835 Jackson nominated Taney to the Supreme Court. The Senate did not take up that nomination until the closing days of its session, when it voted, 24-21, for an indefinite postponement. Undaunted, the President in December 1835 named Taney to be Chief Justice, a position made vacant by the death of John Marshall. Notwithstanding charges that the selection was an insult to the Senate, because it had twice rejected the nominee, Taney's appointment was confirmed by a vote of 29-15.

Patronage at a Peak

The 40-year period from 1837 to 1877 marked the high point of Senate efforts to control appointments. During this period, the spoils system reached its peak and all Presidents were subject to intense pressure for patronage appointments. Senatorial courtesy—the practice of permitting senators of the President's party to control appointments to federal offices within their states—was firmly entrenched.

President Tyler, a dissident Democrat who had accepted the Whig nomination for Vice President in 1840 and then repudiated the Whigs upon succeeding William Henry Harrison as President, was peculiarly unfortunate in his relations with the Senate. Since he was without a following in either party, both Whigs and Democrats were anxious to embarrass him, and many of his nominees—including four to the cabinet and four to the Supreme Court—were rejected. In 1843, his nomination of Caleb Cushing as Secretary of the Treasury was rejected three times in one day. Tyler's first Supreme Court rejection came in 1844, when the Senate turned down John C. Spencer, 21-26. Two subsequent Court nominations, of Reuben H. Walworth and Edward King, were postponed and later withdrawn. On a final effort to fill the two court vacancies, Tyler won approval of one nominee, Samuel Nelson, but the Senate adjourned without acting on the second nominee, John Meredith Read.

Nine months afted succeeding Tyler in 1845, President Polk offered the still vacant Supreme Court seat to Secretary of State James Buchanan. Buchanan declined, and Polk then named to the court an obscure but able Pennsylvania judge, George W. Woodward. Polk interpreted the Senate's rejection of the nomination by a vote of 20-29 as an attempt to weaken his administration.

In the tension-filled decade of the 1850s, President Fillmore was unable to persuade the Senate to approve his southern nominees to the court. In 1852, the Senate refused to act upon the nomination of Edward A. Bradford of Louisiana. In 1853, Democratic opposition brought postponement, by a 26-25 vote, of action on the nomination of Sen. George E. Badger of North Carolina. Also in 1853, the Democratic Senate failed to act on the Whig President's nomination of William C. Micou of Louisiana.

Weakened by resignations of senators from seceding states, the Senate in 1861, by a 25-26 vote, rejected President Buchanan's nomination of Jeremiah S. Black of Pennsylvania to the Supreme Court. Black, former Attorney General and Secretary of State, was opposed by Republicans who wished the newly elected President Lincoln to fill the court seat with his nominee.

Lincoln, a shrewd politician, made masterful use of the appointment power to hold the divided factions of his party together and to advance his legislative goals. Early in his administration he devoted much of his time to patronage. Most officers subject to presidential appointment had been removed following the 1860 election, and Lincoln tried to distribute these offices equitably among his various supporters. Only for major posts was a high standard of qualification deemed essential.

Andrew Johnson's bitter struggle with the Senate over appointments, a byproduct of the fight over Reconstruction policy, led to curbs on the President's removal powers in the Tenure of Office Act of 1867 and to Johnson's impeachment trial. *(p. 188)*

Senate hostility to Johnson blocked the elevation in 1866 of Attorney General Henry Stanbery of Ohio to the Supreme Court. The Senate never acted directly on the nomination but instead passed a bill to reduce the size of the court to eight from 10 justices. The purpose of the bill was to kill the Stanbery nomination by abolishing the seat to which he was named. Stanbery resigned as Attorney General in 1868 to serve as Johnson's chief counsel during the impeachment proceedings. When Johnson subsequently renominated him to the post of Attorney General, the Senate refused, 11-29, to confirm the appointment.

Pressure for Civil Service Reform

Senatorial ascendancy over the President in the matter of appointments and the excesses of the spoils system led, under Grant, to public pressure for civil service reform. In response to this pressure, Congress in 1871 enacted a civil service law but failed to appropriate funds to implement it.

Three of Grant's appointments to the Supreme Court failed to win Senate approval. The first was his Attorney General, Ebenezer Rockwood Hoar, who had earned the enmity of the Senate by refusing to bow to political pressure in the filling of new judgeships created under an 1869 law. Following Hoar's rejection, 24-33, Sen. Simon Cameron of Pennsylvania exclaimed: "What could you expect for a man who has snubbed 70 senators!"[10] In 1874, Grant was forced to withdraw two successive nominations for Chief Justice, Attorney General George H. Williams and former Attorney General Caleb Cushing. Cushing had been rejected also for the post of Secretary of the Treasury in the Tyler administration.

The accession to the presidency of Rutherford B. Hayes in 1877 marked the beginning of presidential efforts to curb senatorial control over nominations. Hayes' selection of his own cabinet members without consulting Senate leaders was viewed as presumptuous by them, and they countered with unprecedented delay in acting upon nominations. However, when public opinion came to the aid of the President, the nominations were rushed to confirmation.

Unable to obtain from Congress the civil service reform legislation he recommended, Hayes nevertheless attempted throughout his one term of office to curb patronage abuses.

The Senate did not consider Hayes' nomination of former Republican Sen. Stanley Matthews of Ohio to the Supreme Court in 1881. There was some feeling that Hayes was rewarding Matthews for his support in the Hayes-Tilden contest in 1876 and for his service as counsel before the commission which dealt with disputed returns from that election. Garfield later resubmitted Matthews' name and he was confirmed by a one-vote margin.

A protracted conflict over the corruption-ridden New York customhouse led to a showdown between Hayes and Sen. Roscoe Conkling of New York over the right of senators to control nominations. When two Conkling proteges—Chester A. Arthur, the customs collector, and Alonzo B. Cornell, the naval officer of the customhouse—refused to comply with a presidential order prohibiting federal employees from actively engaging in partisan politics, Hayes asked for their resignations. When they refused to resign, he nominated two other persons to replace them. Conkling appealed to senatorial courtesy, and the President's nominees were rejected, 25-31. After Congress adjourned, Hayes suspended Arthur and Cornell and made two more appointments to the posts. Despite Conkling's opposition, the Senate in the following session confirmed the President's choices by wide margins.

Conkling was the loser in another showdown, in 1881, with Hayes' successor, James A. Garfield. Garfield's nomination of one of his own supporters, Judge W. H. Robertson, as collector of the New York port infuriated the senator, who wanted to maintain control of all New York patronage. Conkling invoked the rule of courtesy in his effort to block Robertson's confirmation, and the Republican caucus supported him. However, the Democrats would not agree to vote against the nominee, and Conkling feared a rebuff on the floor. Asserting that they had been humiliated, he and his New York colleague, Sen. Thomas C. Platt, then took the extraordinary step of resigning from the Senate as a rebuke to the President for his presumption in making his own appointment. They expected to be re-elected by the

state legislature as a vindication of their position, but they were disappointed. Conkling's political career was at an end, but Platt later returned to the Senate and to leadership of the Republican party in New York.

Meanwhile, the heyday of the spoils system was drawing to a close. Previous efforts at meaningful civil service reform had ended in failure, but public revulsion over Garfield's assassination by a disappointed office-seeker in 1881 provided new impetus for reform. With the rather surprising endorsement of President Chester A. Arthur, a civil service system was established by the Pendleton Act of 1883.

Resistance to Patronage Demands

A test of the President's right to suspend federal officers, which occurred during Grover Cleveland's first term, was followed by repeal of the Tenure of Office Acts. *(See Power of Removal, p. 187)*

Few Cleveland nominations were rejected thereafter. However, in his second term, two conservative appointees to the Supreme Court were rejected upon appeal to the rule of courtesy by Sen. David B. Hill of New York. William B. Hornblower and Wheeler H. Peckham, respected New York attorneys but of a political faction opposed to Hill, were rejected by votes of 24-30 and 32-41, respectively. Cleveland then nominated Sen. Edward Douglas White of Louisiana, who was confirmed immediately—an example of the courtesy traditionally accorded by the Senate to one of its own members.

Theodore Roosevelt, like William McKinley before him, tried to avoid patronage fights with Congress. However, Roosevelt, an advocate of civil service reform, insisted on qualification standards for federal office. Members of Congress, he said, "may ordinarily name the man, but I shall name the standard and the men have got to come up to it."[11] His care in the matter of judicial appointments twice led him to refuse to nominate candidates recommended by Sen. Platt of New York. On one of these occasions he wrote to Platt, "It is, I trust, needless to say that I fully appreciate the right and duty of the Senate to reject or to confirm any appointment according to what its members conscientiously deem their duty to be; just as it is my business to make an appointment which I conscientiously think is a good one."[12]

President William H. Taft recommended a massive extension of the civil service, to include postmasters and other

Senate Rejections of Cabinet Nominations

Nominee	Position	President	Date	Vote
Roger B. Taney	Secretary of Treasury	Jackson	6/23/1834	18-28
Caleb Cushing	Secretary of Treasury	Tyler	3/3/1843	19-27
Caleb Cushing	Secretary of Treasury	Tyler	3/3/1843	10-27
Caleb Cushing	Secretary of Treasury	Tyler	3/3/1843	2-29
David Henshaw	Secretary of Navy	Tyler	1/15/1844	6-34
James M. Porter	Secretary of War	Tyler	1/30/1844	3-38
James S. Green	Secretary of Treasury	Tyler	6/15/1844	Not recorded
Henry Stanbery	Attorney General	Johnson	6/2/1868	11-29
Charles B. Warren	Attorney General	Coolidge	3/10/1925	39-41
Charles B. Warren	Attorney General	Coolidge	3/16/1925	39-46
Lewis L. Strauss	Secretary of Commerce	Eisenhower	6/19/1959	46-49

Source: George H. Haynes, *The Senate of the United States.* 2 vols. (Russell & Russell, 1960).

field officers then subject to Senate confirmation, but Congress did not enact the necessary legislation.

Woodrow Wilson accepted William G. McAdoo's suggestion that he let his department heads handle distribution of patronage, a chore that traditionally had been undertaken by the President himself. Wilson generally tried to get along with the Senate and on occasion yielded to it in the interests of party harmony, but he suffered several notable rejections in contests over local offices.

Noteworthy Nomination Contests

The two most significant nomination contests during Wilson's administration resulted in the Senate's rejection of the appointment of George Rublee to the Federal Trade Commission and its confirmation of the nomination of Louis D. Brandeis as an associate justice of the Supreme Court.

Rublee was rejected in 1916, following a two-year fight led by Sen. Jacob H. Gallinger of New Hampshire, who opposed the nomination on the ground that it was "personally obnoxious" to him. Sen. Robert M. La Follette of Wisconsin deplored Gallinger's use of the "personally obnoxious" formula against a national appointment; it was the first such application of the rule, he said, since he had been in the Senate. Meanwhile, Rublee actually served on the FTC for a year and a half on a recess appointment.

The confirmation of Brandeis, also in 1916, ended one of the most dramatic appointment contests in the nation's history. The opposition to Brandeis, led by New England business groups that considered him a radical and a crusader because of his unpaid public activities, charged that he was untrustworthy and guilty of unethical conduct. After four months of unusual open hearings by a Senate Judiciary subcommittee—hearings which were twice reopened—and with adjournment of Congress and the national political convention fast approaching, the full committee still had not acted on the nomination. Finally, after personal appeals by Brandeis and the President to doubtful members, the committee cleared the nomination by a 10-8 party-line vote. When the Senate voted June 1, Brandeis was confirmed, 47-22, the vote following party lines.

Early in the administration of Warren G. Harding, the White House announced that Republican senators would select nominees for local offices and that the President "will hold Republican senators to account for appointments made by him on their recommendations." Should the appointees prove unworthy or incompetent, he said, the senators wold bear "the responsibility for whatever trouble arises through this means."[13]

Probably to his detriment, few of Harding's nominees were rejected. Three of his cabinet members later became involved in scandals, and his Veterans administrator was convicted of fraud.

Although Calvin Coolidge had few contests with the Senate over appointments, he became the first President since 1868 to have a cabinet nominee rejected. Coolidge in 1925 nominated Charles Beecher Warren, a prominent Michigan attorney, to be his attorney general. Little opposition was expected. However, when the nomination reached the Senate floor, where it was considered in unusual open session (until 1929, most nominations were considered in closed session), opponents attacked Warren for association with the "Sugar Trust." Such a man, they said, could not be relied upon to enforce the antitrust laws.

The first vote on Warren was a 40-40 tie, and Vice President Charles G. Dawes—napping at his hotel—was not present to cast the deciding vote. While efforts were being made to get Dawes to the floor, a Republican senator changed his vote so that he could offer a motion to reconsider the nomination. This motion was tabled, 41-39, and Warren was rejected. A furious Coolidge promptly renominated Warren, who was again defeated, 39-46. A contributing factor to the second defeat was the President's announcement as debate was in progress that if Warren was not confirmed, he would be given a recess appointment. Warren declined that honor.

President Herbert Hoover took a firm line on patronage abuses and refused to nominate candidates simply because they were recommended by party organizations. Hoover also instituted the practice, not followed by his successors, of making public the endorsers of judicial nominees.

Hoover met one notable nomination defeat. The rejection of Judge John J. Parker's nomination to the Supreme Court in 1930 was the first such rejection in 36 years. The Parker case marked the third effort in five years by Senate liberals to block appointments to the court of persons they thought to be conservative. They had failed to block confirmation of Harlan Fiske Stone in 1925 and of Charles Evans Hughes as Chief Justice earlier in 1930. But, with the aid of a campaign mounted by organized labor and the National Association for the Advancement of Colored People, they were able to defeat Parker, 39-41.

Controversial Roosevelt Appointments

Franklin D. Roosevelt had few problems with appointments in his first years in office, but following the defeat of his court-packing plan and his unsuccessful effort to purge Democratic opponents in the 1938 primaries, difficulties increased.

The only major appointment controversy of his first term involved Rexford G. Tugwell, a member of the President's "brain trust" who was nominated in 1934 to the newly created post of under secretary of agriculture. Despite opposition based on his liberal philosophy, Tugwell was confirmed, 53-24. In Roosevelt's second term, many more appointees came under attack because of their allegedly radical views. Perhaps the most notable of the second-term contests involved Harry Hopkins, who won confirmation as Secretary of Commerce in 1939 only after a fight in which politics in the Works Progress Administration was the central issue. Hopkins was confirmed, 58-27, but a number of Democrats abstained.

Roosevelt's efforts to cut off patronage of Democratic senators who opposed his program had mixed success. He succeeded in disciplining Sens. Huey P. Long of Louisiana and Rush D. Holt of West Virginia but failed with Sens. Harry F. Byrd and Carter Glass of Virginia, Pat McCarran of Nevada and W. Lee O'Daniel of Texas—all of whom successfully invoked senatorial courtesy to defeat nominations they had not approved.

Of Roosevelt's eight nominees to the Supreme Court, only one—Hugo L. Black—faced serious opposition. Roosevelt appointed Black, a senator from Alabama who had vigorously supported New Deal programs, in 1937 following the defeat of the President's court-packing plan. Although it was traditional for the Senate to confirm one of its own members immediately without reference to committee, the Black nomination was sent to the Judiciary Committee—the first such action in 50 years. The nomination was cleared by the committee, 13-4, and the Senate, 66-15, after a debate punctuated by charges that Black had been a member of the Ku Klux Klan and had received Klan support in his 1926 election campaign. Black's confirmation did not end this controversy, and he finally made a public statement that he had once been a member of the Klan but had resigned and severed all ties with the organization.

Partisanship declined during World War II, and the President in the interests of national unity tried to avoid controversial nominations. Most of the emergency agencies were created by executive order, and their heads did not require Senate confirmation.

However, controversy erupted anew in 1945 with the appointment of Henry A. Wallace as Secretary of Commerce to succeed Jesse Jones. Wallace had been dumped from the Democratic ticket in 1944 because of conservative opposition to his "radical" economic views, but he had participated vigorously in the fall campaign and was expected to be rewarded with a cabinet post. On Inauguration Day 1945, Roosevelt wrote to Jones asking him to step aside for Wallace. "Henry Wallace deserves almost any service which he believes he can satisfactorily perform," the letter said.[14]

Wallace's chief reason for wanting the commerce post was that it would give him control of the vast lending powers of the Reconstruction Finance Corporation. However, before acting on the Wallace nomination, Congress passed legislation to remove the RFC from the Commerce Department and give it independent status. Jones, testifying on the bill, said the RFC should not be directed by a man who was "willing to jeopardize the country's future with untried ideas and idealistic schemes."[15] Wallace, replying to charges that he was not qualified to supervise the RFC, said: "...it is not a question of my lack of experience. Rather, it is a case of not liking the experience I have."[16]

Following enactment of the RFC removal bill, the Senate on March 1 confirmed Wallace as Secretary of Commerce by a 56-32 vote. Ten Republicans joined 45 Democrats and one independent in voting for confirmation; five Democrats and 27 Republicans were opposed.

Three weeks later the Senate rejected another Roosevelt appointee charged with radical views. Aubrey W. Williams, nominated to be Rural Electrification Administrator, had a background as social worker, administrator of the National Youth Administration and organization director of the National Farmers' Union. Opposition was based on his liberal racial views and on charges that he was an atheist and a Communist sympathizer. Nineteen Democrats joined 33 Republicans to defeat Williams, 36-52.

Truman's Battles With the Senate

President Harry S Truman engaged in a number of noteworthy contests with the Senate over appointments. Early in his administration he was widely criticized for appointing "cronies" to important offices. The 1946 appointments of George E. Allen to the RFC and James K. Vardaman to the Federal Reserve Board were subject to this charge, as was the 1949 appointment of Monrad C. Wallgren to the Federal Trade Commission. All three men were confirmed.

In 1946, Truman was forced, after a two-month fight, to withdraw the nomination of Edwin W. Pauley to be under secretary of the Navy. Pauley was a California oil man and former treasurer of the Democratic National Committee. In hearings before the Senate Naval Affairs Committee, the opposition, led by Sen. Charles W. Tobey of New Hampshire, presented witnesses who accused Pauley of having used political influence to protect his oil interests. Secretary of the Interior Harold L. Ickes said Pauley had

told him, during the 1944 Presidential campaign, that $300,000 in campaign contributions from California oil men could be raised if the government would drop its suit to establish federal title to the tidewater oil lands. When Truman said at a press conference that Ickes might be mistaken, Ickes resigned his post, accusing the President of wanting him to commit perjury for the sake of the Democratic Party. Pauley denied categorically all the charges made against him and then asked the President to withdraw his nomination. The committee was reported to be divided 10-8 against him.

After the 1946 mid-term election, in which the Republicans won control of Congress, Truman tried to avoid controversy by nominating men who would be acceptable to the Senate. The Republican 80th Congress did not actually reject any of Truman's nominees, although 153 names were withdrawn. However, in 1948 the Senate took no action on 11,122 nominations—apparently in the expectation that a Republican President would be able to fill the vacancies with Republican nominees in 1949.

The two most explosive contests that did occur in the 80th Congress concerned nominees who had been named before the 1946 election, David E. Lilienthal and Gordon R. Clapp. In the autumn of 1946, Truman gave Lilienthal, chairman of the Tennessee Valley Authority, a recess appointment to the chairmanship of the newly created Atomic Energy Commission. He appointed Clapp, who had served under Lilienthal, to replace him as TVA chairman.

The opposition to both nominations was led by Sen. Kenneth McKellar (D) of Tennessee, who for years had been engaged in a patronage dispute with the TVA management. During the mid-1940s, McKellar had made several unsuccessful efforts to require Senate confirmation of all TVA employees earning $4,500 a year or more, and he resented TVA's insistence on a merit employment policy. Further, he had locked horns with TVA in 1941 over the location of a dam to be constructed in his state. Although he was not a member of the committees that considered the two nominations, McKellar conducted lengthy interrogations of witnesses and accused both Lilienthal and Clapp of having Communist sympathies. When the nominations finally reached the floor in April 1947, Lilienthal was confirmed, 50-31, and Clapp, 36-31. During the debate on Clapp, McKellar complained that the President had appointed him "without saying beans to me" and declared that he was "hurt beyond expression" that his colleagues should vote for nominees he opposed.[17]

In 1949, President Truman met two outright defeats at the hands of the Senate. Leland Olds, nominated to a third term as member of the Federal Power Commission, was rejected, 15-53, in the face of opposition by oil and natural gas interests. Opponents, led by Sen. Lyndon B. Johnson of Texas, cited articles Olds had written in the 1920s for the labor press as evidence of Communist leanings. As a member of the FPC, Olds had played a key role in the development of federal regulation of the natural gas industry.

The other 1949 rejection was that of Carl A. Ilgenfritz, who refused to take the chairmanship of the Munitions Board (salary: $14,000) unless he could retain his $70,000 annual salary as a steel executive. The Senate rejected him, 28-40.

Senatorial courtesy played a role in several Truman defeats at the hands of the Senate. In 1950 the Senate rejected, 14-59, the nomination of Martin A. Hutchinson as a member of the Federal Trade Commission. Hutchinson, a foe of Virginia's Byrd machine, was opposed by Sens. Byrd and A. Willis Robertson of that state. In 1951 Sen. Paul H. Douglas of Illinois successfully appealed to the courtesy of the Senate to defeat two of President Truman's choices for federal district judgeships in Illinois. Douglas said the President should have nominated two candidates recommended by him.

One of the plums of Congressional patronage came to an end in 1952. President Truman proposed, and Congress accepted, a reorganization plan putting all Internal Revenue Bureau jobs except that of commissioner under civil service. The action followed 1951 Congressional hearings on scandals in the bureau. The Senate, however, defeated other reorganization plans to put postmasters, customs officials and U.S. marshals under civil service.

Eisenhower, Kennedy Appointments

At the outset of his administration in 1953, President Eisenhower was criticized by conservative Republicans who contended that his cabinet selections failed to give appropriate recognition to the Taft wing of the party. The President also gave his department and agency heads free rein to select their own subordinates, but when Republican leaders in the Senate complained that their suggestions were being ignored and that even the customary clearances were not being obtained, the senators were invited to take their recommendations directly to the department heads. Subsequently, more appointments went to Taft supporters.

Several of Eisenhower's early nominations were opposed on conflict-of-interest grounds. The most celebrated of these cases was the nomination of Charles E. Wilson as Secretary of Defense. Wilson, former president of General Motors, was required to divest himself of all GM stock before the Senate Armed Services Committee consented to recommend his confirmation. Wilson had not planned to give up his stock. Similar issues arose with the nominations of Harold E. Talbott as secretary of the Air Force and Robert T. Stevens as secretary of the Army. From this time on, the Senate showed a continuing preoccupation with conflict-of-interest issues in the consideration of presidential nominations.

One of Eisenhower's subsequent cabinet nominations was defeated in the Senate in 1959—the first such rejection since 1925. Lewis L. Strauss already was serving under a recess appointment when, after months of hearings, the Senate rejected his nomination as Secretary of Commerce by a 46-49 vote. Opponents accused Strauss of lack of integrity and criticized his conservative approach to government. Specific issues raised against him included his role in the Dixon-Yates power contract, viewed by public power advocates as an attempt to undermine the Tennessee Valley Authority; his actions in the J. Robert Oppenheimer security case; and his alleged withholding of information, while chairman of the Atomic Energy Commission, from Congress and the public.

Of President Eisenhower's five appointees to the Supreme Court, three took their seats on the Court under recess appointments before they had been confirmed by the Senate. Chief Justice Earl Warren was unanimously confirmed in 1954 after publication of a 10-point summary of charges against him, including allegations that he was at one time connected with a liquor lobbyist and that he lacked judicial experience. William J. Brennan Jr. was confirmed by voice vote in 1957 after Sen. Joseph R. McCarthy protested that Brennan had compared congressional investigations of communism to Salem witch hunts. Potter Stewart was confirmed in 1959, on a 70-17 vote; all opponents were southern Democrats, who criticized Stewart's concurrence in the Supreme Court's 1954 school desegregation decision.

In 1960, the Senate adopted, 48-37, a Democratic resolution expressing the sense of the Senate that the President should not make recess appointments to the Supreme Court, except to prevent or end a breakdown in the administration of the court's business; and that a recess appointee should not take his seat on the court until the Senate had "advised and consented" to the nomination. Proponents claimed it was difficult to investigate the qualifications of a person already sitting on the court; opponents charged that the Democrats hoped for a victory in the 1960 Presidential election and feared that a vacancy might occur on the court before January, enabling the Republican President to give a recess appointment to a Republican.

Efforts of the Democratic-controlled Congress to keep judicial appointments out of the hands of the Republican President also led to a four-year delay in enacting legislation to create an unprecedented number of new circuit and district court judgeships. Proposed by Eisenhower in 1957, the bill did not become law until after President Kennedy took office in 1961. The 73 judgeships created by this law, plus 42 judgeship vacancies created by death or resignation, gave Kennedy in his first year in office the largest number of judicial appointments ever available to a President in a single year.

Kennedy participated far more actively than Eisenhower had done in the selection of appointees. Although recruitment of candidates for federal office was carried out by a well publicized talent hunt, some care was taken to clear appointments with appropriate members of Congress.

None of Kennedy's nominations was rejected by the Senate, and few were contested. His two nominees to the Supreme Court—Byron R. White and Arthur J. Goldberg in 1962—were confirmed without difficulty.

Racial issues figured in several confirmation contests. Despite southern opposition, Robert C. Weaver was confirmed in 1961 by voice vote as administrator of the Housing and Home Finance Agency. Weaver, a black, had been national chairman of the National Association for the Advancement of Colored People. Similarly, Spottswood W. Robinson III, dean of the Howard University Law School, and a black, was confirmed as a member of the Civil Rights Commission. (He was named a U.S. district court judge in 1964 and a member of the U.S. Court of Appeals for the District of Columbia Circuit in 1966.) But Kennedy's nomination of Thurgood Marshall, a civil rights lawyer, to the Second Circuit Court of Appeals was held up by the Senate Judiciary Committee for a year. Marshall was confirmed in 1962, 54-16, with all the dissenting votes cast by southern Democrats. (Marshall in 1967 became the first black member of the Supreme Court.)

Fight Over Fortas

Lyndon B. Johnson, with one dramatic exception, had very little trouble with the Senate over nominations. His cabinet appointees were confirmed without difficulty, and his first two Supreme Court appointments encountered only routine opposition.

The nomination of Abe Fortas to be an associate justice was confirmed by voice vote in 1965, although three Republicans raised objections on the floor that he had

Judgeships

The prestige of a federal judgeship is high, and appointment to the judiciary is considered by most attorneys and politicians to be the apex of a legal and public career.

Federal judgeships are lifetime appointments and pay $44,600 in the circuit court and $42,000 in the district court annually. There is no mandatory retirement age, but judges may retire at full salary at age 65 after 15 years or at 70 after 10 years on the bench.

The following list gives the number of confirmed federal circuit and district court judges appointed by President Ford in 1975 and by his six immediate predecessors:

	Democrats	Republicans
Roosevelt	188	6
Truman	116	9
Eisenhower	9	165
Kennedy†	111	11
Johnson	159	9
Nixon‡	15	198
Ford (1974)	3	14
Ford (1975)	2	14

†One New York liberal also was appointed.
‡No party affiliation was available for one judge from Puerto Rico, and one independent was chosen.

reportedly asked Washington newspaper editors to delay release of a story that Presidential aide Walter W. Jenkins had been arrested on a morals charge shortly before the 1964 Presidential election.

In 1967, President Johnson nominated Thurgood Marshall, then Solicitor General, to be the first black associate justice of the Supreme Court. Despite criticism from some senators of Marshall's stated belief in an activist judiciary, his nomination was confirmed 69-11. Ten southern Democrats and one northern Democrat voted against him.

However, in 1968 Johnson was unsuccessful in his effort to elevate Fortas to Chief Justice in place of Earl Warren who sought to retire. The Fortas nomination finally was withdrawn in the face of a Senate filibuster, and Warren agreed to remain on the court through the 1968-69 term—thus assuring that his successor would be appointed by the incoming President. Johnson's nomination of Judge Homer Thornberry of the Fifth Circuit Court of Appeals to replace Fortas as associate justice was not acted on.

The fight against Fortas was led by Sen. Robert P. Griffin of Michigan. He charged that the appointment was based on "cronyism" and that Warren had timed his retirement to assure appointment of his successor by a Democratic President. The "lame duck" charge gave way to more serious questions of propriety in the course of hearings held by the Judiciary Committee between July 11 and Sept. 16. One was the question of Fortas' continued involvement in White House affairs after he went on the court in 1965, an involvement that Fortas admitted but played down in his testimony before the committee. Toward the end of the hearings, it was disclosed that Fortas had received a fee of $15,000 for conducting a nine-week law seminar at American University in the summer of 1968. The money for

the fee and other seminar expenses had come from five former business associates, one of whom had a son who was involved in a federal criminal case. During the hearings, as in the subsequent floor debate, attacks were made on the court in general and on Fortas in particular for decisions on criminal procedural law and obscenity.

By an 11-6 vote, Sept. 17, 1968, the Judiciary Committee ordered the Fortas nomination reported to the Senate with the recommendation that it be confirmed. The majority, made up of eight Democrats and three Republicans, described Fortas as "extraordinarily well qualified for the post "[18] of Chief Justice. His acceptance of a fee for teaching at American University and his participation in White House discussions, the report said, were within his rights and in line with what other justices had done over the years. Three dissenting Democrats contended that Fortas had shown poor judgment in advising the President on legislative matters and in accepting the $15,000 teaching fee, and that the positions he had taken in court decisions on crime, obscenity and other matters had been too liberal. One of the three dissenting Republicans (Strom Thurmond of South Carolina) submitted individual views in which he criticized Fortas' positions in decisions on criminal procedure, pornography, federal-state relations and subversive activities.

In the floor debate, which began Sept. 25, Sen. Griffin pressed the attack relentlessly, and as his following grew, the chances of confirmation became more remote. They virtually vanished Sept. 27 when Minority Leader Everett McKinley Dirksen reversed his position and announced that he was officially neutral. Majority Leader Mike Mansfield moved to end what was plainly a filibuster by reading to the Senate, Sept. 29, a cloture motion signed by 26 Senators. The motion was rejected Oct. 1 by a roll-call vote of 45-43, which was 14 votes short of the 59 needed for cloture. The next day Fortas asked the President to withdraw his name. Terming the action of the Senate "tragic," Johnson consented. Renewed controversy over Fortas' extra-judicial activities led to his resignation from the court in 1969. He was the first justice in history to step down under threat of impeachment.

A further diminution of senatorial patronage occurred during the Johnson administration, when Congress acceded to a Presidential reorganization plan placing the Customs Bureau on a career, civil service basis. Previously, appointments of customs collectors and other officers had been made by the President, generally on senators' recommendations. President Johnson submitted the reorganization plan in 1965, and it was allowed to go into effect. A Senate resolution disapproving the plan was rejected, 17-64.

Nixon's Appointments

Early in his first year in office, President Nixon cut off another source of congressional patronage. He said he was ending the patronage system of appointing postmasters and rural letter carriers, and that henceforth high scores on competitive examinations would be the sole criterion for filling the posts.

The system of choosing postmasters from among the three highest scorers on competitive examinations already was in effect. However, under past practice, the preferred candidate of a member of Congress or party official was allowed to repeat the test until he gained a place among the top three. Under the new system, the test would be given only once, and the postmaster general would select from among the three leading scorers. Members of Congress would still be consulted, but their recommendations would not necessarily be followed.

Nixon also sought congressional approval of legislation to end Presidential appointment and senatorial confirmation of first, second and third-class postmasters. The Senate passed the bill in 1969, but the House did not act. This goal was achieved in the Postal Reorganization Act of 1970, which eliminated all political influence in the selection of postal employees, including postmasters.

President Nixon's early appointments to major policy posts were confirmed with little difficulty, although Interior Secretary Walter J. Hickel's confirmation was delayed briefly in the face of opposition from conservation groups and Deputy Defense Secretary David Packard's confirmation raised conflict-of-interest questions.

Appointments that were never made also generated controversy. Dr. John H. Knowles was slated to get the job of assistant secretary of Health, Education and Welfare for health and scientific affairs, but the proposed nomination was blocked after opposition was voiced by Senate Minority Leader Dirksen and the American Medical Association. Franklin Long was rejected for appointment to head the National Science Foundation because of his opposition to the ABM nuclear defense system.

Nixon Court Nominees

These controversies paled by comparison with the struggles that arose over President Nixon's efforts to fill one of two vacancies on the Supreme Court. His first court nomination, that of Warren E. Burger to replace retiring Chief Justice Warren, was confirmed quickly by a 74-3 vote of the Senate. Burger, a judge of the Court of Appeals for the District of Columbia Circuit, was little known outside of legal circles at the time of his nomination, but he appeared to meet Nixon's standard of judicial conservatism.

It was with his next court nomination that Nixon ran into a confrontation with the Senate. In May 1969, Associate Justice Fortas resigned under fire for accepting an outside fee from the family foundation of a convicted stock manipulator. To fill the vacancy, Nixon in August nominated Clement F. Haynsworth Jr. of South Carolina, chief judge of the Fourth Circuit Court of Appeals.

Haynsworth was opposed by labor and civil rights leaders, the same combination that had defeated the Parker nomination in 1930, but as in the Fortas case the debate centered on judicial ethics. Foes of the nomination, led by Democratic Sen. Birch Bayh of Indiana, repeatedly said they did not question Haynsworth's honesty or integrity. But they did question his sensitivity to the appearance of ethical impropriety and his judgment regarding participation in cases in which his financial interests could be said to be involved, if only indirectly.

During committee hearings in September, Haynsworth, his financial affairs and his judicial record were scrutinized more thoroughly and extensively than those of any other court nominee before him. The Judiciary Committee approved the nomination, Oct. 9 by a 10-7 vote. The 10-man majority asserted that Haynsworth was "extraordinarily well qualified" for the court post and that the objections raised to his nomination were without substance.[19]

Notwithstanding growing opposition, the President remained steadfast in his refusal to withdraw the nomination. Political pressure to influence the final vote was exerted by both sides. After a week's debate, the Senate on Nov. 21 rejected the Haynsworth nomination by a 45-55 roll-call vote. Republican defections played a decisive role in the outcome. Seventeen Republicans, including the three top GOP leaders in the Senate, joined 38 Democrats in voting against confirmation. Twenty-six Republicans and 19 Democrats—16 of them from the South—voted for it.

Early in 1970, President Nixon tried once more to fill the Supreme Court vacancy. This time he nominated another southerner, G. Harrold Carswell of Florida, a judge of the Fifth Circuit Court of Appeals. Few senators wanted a repetition of the Haynsworth fight, and opposition to Carswell developed slowly. However, when it came to light that Carswell in a 1948 campaign speech had pledged himself to the principle of white supremacy, resistance to the nomination began to build. Carswell repudiated the views he had expressed more than 20 years earlier, but further charges of a continuing racist attitude were raised against him. Other critics, including many within his own profession, contended that Carswell was a man of mediocre abilities who lacked the judicial competence requisite for service on the high court.

Carswell won the Judiciary Committee's approval, Feb. 16, 1970, by a vote of 13-4. But when the nomination moved to the Senate floor in March, opponents succeeded in delaying the final vote until after the Easter recess. When the Senate returned to consideration of the nomination at the beginning of April, the opposing sides remained closely matched and the outcome was in doubt.

In this atmosphere, Nixon wrote a letter to a pro-Carswell Republican senator declaring that rejection of the nomination would impair his constitutional responsibility and the constitutional relationship of the President to Congress.

"What is centrally at issue in this nomination," he said, "is the constitutional responsibility of the President to appoint members of the court—and whether this responsibility can be frustrated by those who wish to substitute their own philosophy or their own subjective judgment for that of the one person entrusted by the Constitution with the power of appointment. The question arises whether I, as President of the United States, shall be accorded the same right of choice in naming Supreme Court Justices which has been freely accorded to my predecessors of both parties."[20]

Nixon said he respected the right of any senator to differ with his selection. However, he continued: "The fact remains, under the Constitution, it is the duty of the President to appoint and of the Senate to advise and consent. But if the Senate attempts to substitute its judgment as to who should be appointed, the traditional constitutional balance is in jeopardy and the duty of the President under the Constitution impaired."[21]

By agreement, the first Senate vote on Carswell came April 6, on a motion to recommit the nomination to the Judiciary Committee. Opponents had hoped originally to defeat the appointment indirectly by burying the matter in committee, but the recommittal effort became instead a diversionary tactic, a preliminary skirmish that was won by the administration. The recommittal move was rejected, 44-52.

After two days of intensive lobbying, the final vote on Carswell was taken April 8, and the nomination was rejected 45-51. Thirteen Republicans joined 38 Democrats, five of them from the South, in opposition. Not since 1894 had a President suffered similar consecutive rejections of two nominees to a Supreme Court seat.

Nixon responded to the Senate's action with an angry statement that he had "reluctantly" decided that the Senate "as presently constituted" would not confirm a judicial conservative from the South. Thus, he said, he would go elsewhere for his next nominee.[22]

Less than a week later, on April 14, the President nominated Harry A. Blackmun of Minnesota, a judge of the Eighth Circuit Court of Appeals, to fill the Supreme Court vacancy. Blackmun had a reputation as a moderate and scholarly judge, and both liberals and conservatives praised the President's selection. The Senate Judiciary Committee unanimously reported the nomination May 9, and the Senate confirmed it May 12 by a 94-0 vote.

In 1971, President Nixon nominated and the Senate confirmed Lewis F. Powell Jr. and William H. Rehnquist as associate justices of the Supreme Court. Powell acceded to the seat left vacant by the resignation of Hugo Black. Rehnquist took the seat vacated by the resignation of John Marshall Harlan. Both men retired because of poor health. Not since Warren G. Harding had one President, in his first term, had the opportunity to appoint so many members of the Supreme Court. Nixon's four appointees put a decidedly more conservative stamp on the court.

The impact of Nixon's appointments to the courts and regulatory agencies was expected to be felt for many years after the Watergate crisis forced him to resign the

presidency on Aug. 9, 1974. In addition to his Supreme Court appointments, he named 215 judges to the lower courts of the federal judicial system. Nixon appointees (or persons named by previous presidents whom he reappointed) dominated the twelve regulatory agencies.

By the day of his resignation, Nixon had nominated every member of eight regulatory agencies: the five members of the Civil Aeronautics Board, the seven members of the Federal Communications Commission, the five members of the Federal Maritime Commission, the five members of the Federal Power Commission, the five members of the National Labor Relations Board, the three members of the National Mediation Board, the five members of the Securities and Exchange Commission and the five members of the Consumer Product Safety Commission.

Ford's Appointments

President Ford encountered no opposition strong enough to lead to the rejection of his cabinet appointees and nominee to the Supreme Court in 1975. However, three of his appointments to government boards were rejected by Senate committees within two weeks in late 1975. The rejec-

---

Supreme Court Nominations Rejected, Dropped

Nominee	Year Nominated	Nominated By	Actions[5]
William Paterson[1]	1793	Washington	Withdrawn (for technical reasons)
John Rutledge[2]	1795	Washington	Rejected
Alexander Wolcott	1811	Madison	Rejected
John J. Crittenden	1828	J. Q. Adams	Postponed, 1829
Roger B. Taney[1]	1835	Jackson	Postponed
John C. Spencer	1844	Tyler	Rejected
Reuben H. Walworth	1844	Tyler	Withdrawn
Edward King	1844	Tyler	Postponed
Edward King[3]	1844	Tyler	Withdrawn, 1845
John M. Read	1845	Tyler	No action
George W. Woodward	1845	Polk	Rejected, 1846
Edward A. Bradford	1852	Fillmore	No action
George E. Badger	1853	Fillmore	Postponed
William C. Micou	1853	Fillmore	No action
Jeremiah S. Black	1861	Buchanan	Rejected
Henry Stanbery	1866	Johnson	No action
Ebenezer R. Hoar	1869	Grant	Rejected, 1870
George H. Williams[2]	1873	Grant	Withdrawn, 1874
Caleb Cushing[2]	1874	Grant	Withdrawn
Stanley Matthews[1]	1881	Hayes	No action
William B. Hornblower	1893	Cleveland	Rejected, 1894
Wheeler H. Peckham	1894	Cleveland	Rejected
John J. Parker	1930	Hoover	Rejected
Abe Fortas[4]	1968	Johnson	Withdrawn
Homer Thornberry	1968	Johnson	No action
Clement F. Haynsworth Jr.	1969	Nixon	Rejected
G. Harrold Carswell	1970	Nixon	Rejected

1. *Reappointed and confirmed. Taney was confirmed as Chief Justice.*
2. *Nominated for Chief Justice.*
3. *Second appointment.*

4. *Associate justice nominated for Chief Justice.*
5. *A year is given if different from the year of nomination.*

Source: Library of Congress, Congressional Research Service.

tions in two cases were based upon objections to the nominee's social philosophy and in another to a conflict-of-interest.

A number of cabinet changes were made during President Ford's first fifteen months in office until only Agriculture Secretary Earl L. Butz, Secretary of State Henry A. Kissinger and Treasury Secretary William E. Simon remained from the Nixon Administration.

Only one of Ford's cabinet nominations was highly controversial. Stanley K. Hathaway, who was appointed Secretary of the Interior, was attacked by liberal senators and environmental groups for what they considered a pro-development and anti-conservation record as governor of Wyoming. Hathaway was confirmed in June of 1975 by a 60-36 vote after five days of hearings by the Senate Interior Committee. But he resigned July 25 "for reasons of personal health."

Ford's selection for the Supreme Court, Federal Appeals Judge John Paul Stevens, was speedily confirmed Dec. 17 after his nomination Nov. 28, 1975, to fill the seat left vacant by the retirement of William O. Douglas.

The Senate Commerce Committee Nov. 13, 1975, killed the renomination of Isabel A. Burgess to a second five-year term on the National Transportation Safety Board. Opposition to her developed when a committee staff report showed that she had purchased stock in an airline regulated by the board and accepted free transportation, meals and lodging from other regulated companies. She also had unusually high travel expenses and absenteeism.

One day earlier, the Senate Banking, Housing and Urban Affairs Committee rejected the nomination of former Rep. Ben B. Blackburn (R Ga. 1967-75) to be chairman of the Federal Home Loan Bank Board. Foes of the nomination objected to his negative attitude toward blacks and public housing tenants and his opposition to civil rights legislation during his years in the House. The Senate Commerce Committee Oct. 30 tabled, and thus killed, the nomination of Colorado beer executive Joseph Coors to the board of the Corporation for Public Broadcasting (CPB). The question of a possible conflict of interest based upon Coor's membership on the board of Television News, Inc. (TVN) and his conservative political philosophy led to the committee's action.

In 1974, President Ford withdrew four controversial nominations. Two were holdovers from the Nixon administration. Ford withdrew his nomination of Andrew E. Gibson to be federal energy administrator following the publication of reports that he had been promised $880,000 in severance pay from his former employer, an oil shipping company with interests related to matters he would have to monitor. He also did not resubmit three other controversial nominations after the October-November congressional election recess. Under Senate Rule 38, any nomination must be resubmitted when the Senate adjourns or is in recess for more than 30 days. The nominations not resubmitted were those of Peter M. Flanigan to be ambassador to Spain, Stanton B. Anderson to be ambassador to Costa Rica, and Daniel T. Kingsley to be a member of the Federal Power Commission. Anderson and Kingsley had been nominated by Nixon.

Power of Removal

Controversy over the role of the Senate in the removal of public officers began in the early days of the Republic and continued intermittently into the 20th century.

The Constitution contained no language governing removals except for the impeachment provisions of Article II, Section 4. Hamilton, writing in *The Federalist* (No. 77), contended that the consent of the Senate "would be necessary to displace as well as to appoint," but this view was soon challenged and rejected by Congress.[23]

Debate over the power of removal began in the First Congress, during consideration of a bill to establish the Department of Foreign Affairs. Two principal theories were advanced. One group insisted that since the Constitution gave the Senate a share in the appointment power, the Senate must also give its advice and consent to removals. The other group, led by Madison, maintained that the power of removal was an executive function, necessarily implied in the power to nominate, and that Senate participation would violate the principle of separation of powers.

Madison's view prevailed in the House, which passed the bill by a 29-22 vote after striking out language specifically vesting removal power in the President and substituting a provision that deliberately implied recognition of the President's exclusive power of removal under the Constitution.

After a lengthy and spirited debate in closed session, the Senate narrowly acceded to the House interpretation. A motion to strike out the House language recognizing the President's sole power of removal was rejected on a tie vote, with Vice President Adams—voting for the first time—recorded in opposition. The fact that the Senate agreed to limit its own powers was widely attributed to senatorial respect for President Washington.

Early Presidents exercised great restraint in use of the removal power, even after the enactment in 1820 of the "Four Years" law. This law, ostensibly designed to ensure accountability of federal officers, established a fixed four-year term for district attorneys, customs collectors and many other officers who previously had served at the pleasure of the President.

Presidents James Monroe and John Quincy Adams followed a policy of renominating all such persons when their terms expired unless they had been guilty of misconduct. However, senatorial pressure for patronage was on the rise, and Adams' self-restraint was met by Senate demands for a broader role in appointments and removals.

Jackson's Clashes With Senate

Andrew Jackson's sweeping and partisan use of the removal power soon brought renewed Senate demands for an increased share in the patronage pie. Controversy over the issue led to a series of Senate resolutions requesting the President to inform the Senate of his reasons for removing various officials. Jackson complied with several of these requests, but by 1835 he had had enough. A Senate resolution, adopted by a 23-22 vote, requesting information on the "charges, if any," against the recently removed surveyor general of South Tennessee brought the following response:

"It is now, however, my solemn conviction that I ought no longer, from any motive, nor in any degree, to yield to these unconstitutional demands. Their continued repetition imposes on me, as the representative and trustee of the American people, the painful but imperious duty of resisting to the utmost any further encroachment on the rights of the Executive.... The President in cases of this nature possesses the exclusive power of removal from office; and under the sanctions of his official oath, and of his liability to impeachment, he is bound to exercise it whenever the public welfare shall require. On no principle known to our institutions can he be required to account for the manner in which he discharges this portion of his public duties, save only in the mode and under the forms prescribed by the Constitution."[24]

Meanwhile, the Senate had appointed a committee "to inquire into the extent of Executive patronage; the circumstances which contributed to its increase of late; the expediency and practicability of reducing the same, and the means of such reduction."[25] The committee reported a bill to repeal the first two sections of the Four Years Law and to require the President to submit to the Senate the reasons for each removal. John Quincy Adams called this an effort "to cut down the executive power of the president and to grasp it for the Senate."[26] Supported by Calhoun, Webster and Clay, the measure won Senate approval, 31-16, but was never taken up in the House. Webster and Clay disputed the interpretation of the removal power established by the First Congress. Attributing that interpretation largely to congressional confidence in President Washington, Clay said it had not been reconsidered only because prior to Jackson's administration it had not been abused.

Presidential Opposition to Tenure Acts

The next great clash between Senate and President over the removal power occurred in the administration of Andrew Johnson. Among its consequences were the Tenure of Office Act of 1867 and Johnson's impeachment trial.

The conflict grew out of Johnson's fight with the radical Republican leaders of Congress over reconstruction policy and his use of the removal power to make places for his own followers.

As passed by the Senate, the Tenure of Office bill enabled civil officers, excluding members of the cabinet, appointed by and with the advice and consent of the Senate, to remain in office until their successors were appointed by the President and confirmed by the Senate. It permitted the President to suspend an officer during a recess of the Senate and appoint a temporary successor but provided that the suspended officer should resume his post if the Senate failed to approve the suspension. The Senate rejected an amendment to delete the clause excluding cabinet members, as well as one to require Senate confirmation of the appointment of all officers with salaries exceeding $1,000. However, the House deleted the exclusion for cabinet members, and in conference it was agreed that cabinet members should hold office for the term of the President who appointed them and for one month thereafter, subject to removal by and with the advice and consent of the Senate.

President Johnson vetoed the bill on the ground that it would unconstitutionally restrict the President's power of removal, but Congress enacted the measure over the veto—by a 35-11 vote in the Senate and a 133-37 vote in the House.

Johnson promptly put the Tenure of Office Act to the test. First, he suspended Secretary of War Stanton, but the Senate refused to concur in the suspension. Johnson then attempted to dismiss Stanton and make another appointment to the post. The House immediately initiated impeachment proceedings, the principal charge being that Johnson had violated the new law by dismissing Stanton. On this charge, the Senate failed to convict by only one vote; seven Republicans and 12 Democrats voted for acquittal, while 35 Republicans voted for conviction. A two-thirds majority was required to convict.

Early in Grant's administration in 1869, Congress amended the Tenure of Office Act by repealing its provisions regulating suspensions. The new law provided that the President might suspend officers "in his discretion"—without, as before, reporting to the Senate the reasons for his action—but required prompt nomination of successors.[27] A further dispute between President Cleveland and the Republican-controlled Senate finally led to repeal of what was left of the Tenure of Office Act of 1867 and of the amended 1869 version.

While Congress was in recess in the summer of 1885, Cleveland suspended 643 officers subject to senatorial confirmation. When Congress reconvened, he submitted to the Senate the names of their replacements to whom he had given recess appointments. The committees handling these nominations then called upon the executive departments for information concerning the reasons for the suspensions, information which the departments refused to give. Action on the nominations was stalled by the dispute.

The climax to the controversy came over the nomination of a U.S. attorney in Alabama. The Justice Department refused demands by the Senate Judiciary Committee for information concerning the reasons for removal of his predecessor. The Senate responded with a resolution, adopted on a party-line vote, censuring the Attorney General for his refusal to transmit the desired papers. A second resolution, adopted by a one-vote margin, said it was "the duty of the Senate to refuse its advice and consent to proposed removals of officers" in cases where information requested by the Senate was withheld.[28]

The Senate debated the resolutions heatedly over a two-week period. While they were pending, Cleveland sent a special message to the Senate reasserting the President's authority:

"The requests and demands which by the score have for nearly three months been presented to the different departments of the government, whatever their form, have but one complexion. They assume the right of the Senate to sit in judgment upon the exercise of my exclusive function, for which I am solely responsible to the people from whom I have so lately received the sacred trust of office....

"The pledges I have made were made to the people, and to them I am responsible. I am not responsible to the Senate, and I am unwilling to submit my actions and official conduct to them for judgment...."[29]

Public opinion responded to the President's message, and the nomination logjam was broken. The following year Sen. E. R. Hoar (R Mass.) introduced legislation to repeal the Tenure of Office Acts, and the bill was speedily enacted into law.

Wilson and Coolidge on Removals

Another big controversy over the removal power occurred in 1920, when President Wilson vetoed the forerunner of the Budget and Accounting Act of 1921. That measure, as transmitted to Wilson, provided that the comptroller general and assistant comptroller general were to be appointed by the President subject to Senate confirmation, but were to be subject to removal by concurrent resolution of Congress. A concurrent resolution does not require the President's approval; thus the President would have had no control over the removal of these officers. Wilson's veto message was emphatic:

"I am convinced that the Congress is without constitutional power to limit the appointing power and its incident power of removal derived from the Constitution."[30]

The following year, the Budget and Accounting Act of 1921 became law with the signature of President Harding.

The final legislation, however, differed from the 1920 version in providing for removal of the comptroller general and assistant comptroller general by joint resolution, which requires the signature of the President, or passage over his veto, to go into effect.

Senate pressure for a role in removals does not always take the form of resistance to removals desired by the President. The Senate also has attempted to force removals, although without notable success. President Lincoln was able to head off efforts by a caucus of Republican senators to force the resignation of Secretary of State Seward in 1862. More recently, in 1924, the Senate adopted a resolution "that it is the sense of the United States Senate that the President of the United States immediately request the resignation of Edwin Denby as secretary of the Navy."[31] Denby had been implicated in the naval oil lease scandals, and Senate Democrats hoped to press similar resolutions against other members of President Coolidge's cabinet. The Denby resolution was adopted on a 47-34 roll call and a copy was sent to the President. Coolidge promptly issued a statement:

"No official recognition can be given to the passage of the Senate resolution relative to their opinion concerning members of the cabinet or other officers under executive control....

"...The dismissal of an officer of the government, such as is involved in this case, other than by impeachment, is exclusively an executive function."[32]

A few days later Denby resigned.

Another Senate removal effort, with a different twist, involved appointees to the newly created Federal Power Commission during the 71st Congress. Dissatisfied with the actions of FPC members it had confirmed shortly before the Christmas recess, the Senate in January 1931 tried to recall the nominations for reconsideration. President Hoover refused, saying:

"I am advised that these appointments were constitutionally made, with the consent of the Senate, formally communicated to me, and that the return of the documents by me and reconsideration by the Senate would be ineffective to disturb the appointees in their offices."[33]

Court Decisions on Removal Power

The courts upheld the President. After nearly 140 years of controversy over the President's power of removal, the Supreme Court had finally met the issue head on in 1926. In the words of Chief Justice Taft, the court had "studiously avoided deciding the issue until it was presented in such a way that it could not be avoided."[34]

The case involved a postmaster who had been removed from office by President Wilson in 1920, without consultation with the Senate, although the 1876 law under which the man had been appointed stipulated: "Postmasters of the first, second and third classes shall be appointed and may be removed by the President, by and with the advice and consent of the Senate, and shall hold their offices for four years, unless sooner removed or suspended according to law."[35]

In a 6-3 decision, the court upheld the President's unrestricted power of removal as inherent in the executive power invested in him by the Constitution. The court concluded: "It therefore follows that the Tenure of Office Act of 1867, in so far as it attempted to prevent the President from removing executive officers who had been appointed by him by and with the consent of the Senate was invalid, and that subsequent legislation of the same effect was equally so....

The provision of the law of 1876, by which the unrestricted power of removal of first-class postmasters is denied to the President, is in violation of the Constitution and invalid."[36] (*Myers v. U.S.*, 272 U.S. 52, 1926)

In a unanimous 1935 decision, the court modified this position. The 1935 case involved a Federal Trade Commissioner whom President Roosevelt had tried to remove because "I do not feel that your mind and my mind go along together on either the policies or the administration"[37] of the FTC. The court held that the FTC was "an administrative body created by Congress to carry into effect legislative policies" and thus could not "in any proper sense be characterized as an arm or an eye of the Executive." It continued:

"Whether the power of the President to remove an officer shall prevail over the authority of Congress to condition the power by fixing a definite term and precluding a removal except for cause will depend upon the character of the office; the Myers decision, affirming the power of the President alone to make the removal, is confined to purely executive officers, and as to officers of the kind here under consideration, we hold that no removal can be made during the prescribed term for which the officer is appointed, except for one or more of the causes named in the applicable statute.[38] (*Humphrey's Executor v. U.S.*, 295 U.S. 602)

In ruling that Roosevelt had exceeded his authority in removing Humphrey, the court indicated that except for certain types of officials (such as those immediately responsible to the President and those exercising non-discretionary or ministerial functions), Congress could apply such limitations on removal as it chose.

In a later decision (*Wiener v. U.S.*, 357 U.S. 349, 1958), the court built on the *Humphrey's* decision. That case involved the refusal of a member of the War Claims Commission, named by President Truman, to resign when the Eisenhower administration came to power so that a Republican could be named to the position.

Congress created the commission with "jurisdiction to receive and adjudicate according to law" certain damage claims resulting from World War II. The law made no provision for removal of commissioners.

Wiener was removed by the new President and sought his pay in court. The Supreme Court agreed with him. It noted the similarity between the *Weiner* and *Humphrey's* cases: in both situations, Presidents had removed persons from quasi-judicial agencies without showing cause for the sole purpose of naming persons of their own choosing. The court said it understood the *Humphrey's* decision to "draw a sharp line of cleavage between officials who were part of the executive establishment and were thus removable by virtue of the President's constitutional powers, and those who are members of a body 'to exercise its judgment without the leave or hindrance of any other official or any department of the government,'...as to whom a power of removal exists only if Congress may fairly be said to have conferred it. This sharp differentiation derives from the difference in functions between those who are part of the executive establishment and those whose tasks require absolute freedom from executive interference." The court also noted the "intrinsic judicial character" of the commission.

As a result of the case and the *Myers* and *Humphrey's* cases, the rule has developed that a President can remove a member of a quasi-judicial agency only for cause, even if Congress has not so provided. This is a major limitation on a President's normal power of removal that may be exercised at his discretion.

Nomination Procedures

It has been customary since the time of Washington for the President to submit nominations to the Senate in written form. By exception, Harding in 1921 proceeded directly from the inaugural ceremonies to the Senate chamber to present his cabinet nominations in person.

Before submitting a nomination the President normally consults with key members of Congress, political organizations and special interest groups in an effort to obtain informal clearance for his candidate. Because the President usually wants to avoid a confirmation fight, serious opposition at this stage may lead him to choose another person for the post.

In recent years the Federal Bureau of Investigation has conducted investigations of potential candidates, and there have been frequent controversies between the President and the Senate over access to FBI reports. Potential Supreme Court nominees have been evaluated by a committee of the American Bar Association. President Nixon abandoned this procedure in 1969 but returned to it in 1970, after the Haynsworth and Carswell defeats.

Committee Hearings

Since 1868, most nominations have been referred to committee. The committee, or a subcommittee, may hold hearings at which the nominee and others may testify. Most such hearings are purely routine, although some turn into grueling inquisitions. Nominees have been known to ask the President to withdraw their names rather than face such an ordeal.

Until 30 years or so ago, it was unusual for Supreme Court nominees to be invited to appear before the Judiciary Committee. Felix Frankfurter, who received such an invitation in 1939, noted that on only one previous occasion had a Supreme Court nominee testified before the committee. Frankfurter originally declined the committee's invitation but later appeared at the committee's request. Ten years later the committee by a 5-4 vote invited court nominee Sherman Minton to appear before it, but when Minton questioned the propriety of such an appearance, the committee reversed itself and reported the nomination favorably to the Senate. These precedents notwithstanding, in recent years Supreme Court nominees have been expected to testify at hearings on their nominations. Justice Abe Fortas in 1968 became the first nominee for chief justice ever to appear before the committee and the first sitting justice, except for recess appointees, ever to do so.

When hearings on a nomination have been completed, the subcommittee votes and sends the nomination to the full committee. The committee may report the nomination favorably, unfavorably or without recommendation, or it may simply take no action at all. Nominations that fail to gain approval usually meet defeat at this stage.

Floor Action. Nominations that reach the floor are called up on the executive calendar, frequently en bloc, and usually are approved without objection. The question takes the following form: "Will the Senate advise and consent to this nomination?"[39] Controversial nominations may be debated at length, but few nominations are brought to the floor unless sufficient votes for confirmation can be mustered.

Since 1929, Senate rules (Rule 38) have provided that nominations shall be considered in open session unless the Senate, in closed session and by majority vote, decides to consider a particular nomination in closed session. In such a case any senator is permitted to make public his own vote.

Prior to 1929, the customary practice was to consider nominations in closed executive session, and the votes taken were not supposed to be made public.

Nominations may not be put to a vote on the day they are received or on the day they are reported from committee, except by unanimous consent. They may be approved, rejected or returned to committee.

All nominations still pending at the end of the session in which they are made die with that session. If the Senate recesses or adjourns for more than 30 days, all pending nominations must be returned to the President; they cannot be considered again unless he resubmits them.

When a nomination has been confirmed or rejected, a motion to reconsider may be made on the day the vote is taken or on either of the next two days of actual executive session.

Recess Appointments

Recess appointments present special problems. The Constitution provides that "the President shall have power to fill up all vacancies that may happen during the recess of the Senate, by granting commissions which shall expire at the end of their next session." *(Article II, Section 2)*

The ambiguities of this section have produced repeated controversies between the President and the Senate. Chief point at issue is the constitutional meaning of the word "happen." If it means "happen to occur," then the President can only fill offices that become vacant after the Senate adjourns. If it means "happen to exist," he can fill any vacancy, whatever the cause.[40]

President Washington, taking a strict view of his powers, sought specific Senate authorization to make recess appointments of military officers created by a bill enacted near the end of a session. Madison opted for a broad construction. His recess appointment of envoys to negotiate a peace treaty with Great Britain brought outcries from the Senate that a recess appointment could not be made to an office never before filled. However, resolutions protesting Madison's action never came to a vote, and the appointments ultimately were confirmed.

Although the recess appointment debate continued for years, it gradually became accepted that the President could make recess appointments to fill any vacancies, no matter how they arose. However, federal law prohibits payment of salary to any person appointed during a recess of the Senate to fill an existing vacancy, if the vacancy existed while the Senate was in session, until the appointee has been confirmed by the Senate. This prohibition does not apply if the vacancy occurred during the last 30 days of the session, or if the Senate failed to act on a nomination submitted to it before adjournment.

Footnotes

1. For a comprehensive discussion of appointments *see* Joseph P. Harris, *The Advice and Consent of the Senate: A Study of the Confirmation of Appointments By The United States Senate* (Greenwood Press, 1968).

2. *The Federalist Papers,* With an Introduction by Clinton Rossiter (Mentor, 1961), No. 66, p. 405.

3. Harris, *The Advice and Consent of the Senate,* p. 29.

4. George H. Haynes, *The Senate of the United States: Its History and Practice* (Houghton Mifflin, 1938), p. 724.

5. Harris, *The Advice and Consent of the Senate*, p. 39.
6. Haynes, *The Senate*, p. 727.
7. Harris, *The Advice and Consent of the Senate*, p. 45.
8. *Ibid.*, p. 50.
9. *Ibid.*, p. 51.
10. *Ibid.*, p. 75.
11. *Ibid.*, p. 91.
12. *Ibid.*
13. *Ibid.*, p. 116.
14. *Ibid.*, p. 146.
15. *Ibid.*, p. 148.
16. *Ibid.*
17. *Ibid.*, p. 176.
18. Congressional Quarterly, 1968 *Almanac*, p. 536.
19. Congressional Quarterly, *Congress and the Nation, 1969-1972*, Vol. III, p. 294.
20. Congressional Quarterly, 1970 *Almanac*, p. 160.
21. *Ibid.*
22. *Ibid.*, p. 154.
23. *The Federalist Papers*, No. 77, p. 459.
24. Haynes, *The Senate*, p. 796.
25. *Ibid.*, p. 797.
26. *Ibid.*
27. *Ibid.*, p. 805.
28. *Ibid.*, pp. 807-808.
29. *Ibid.*, p. 808.
30. *Ibid.*, p. 810.
31. *Ibid.*, p. 817.
32. *Ibid.*, p. 819.
33. *Ibid.*, p. 826.
34. *Ibid.*, p. 828.
35. *Ibid.*
36. *Ibid.*, p. 829.
37. *Ibid.*, p. 831.
38. *Ibid.*, p. 832.
39. Floyd M. Riddick, *The United States Congress: Organization and Procedure* (National Capitol Publishers, 1949), p. 335.
40. Haynes, *The Senate*, p. 774.

Selected Bibliography

Books

The Federalist Papers. Introduction by Clinton Rossiter. New York: Mentor, 1961.
Freidin, Seymour K. *A Sense of the Senate.* New York: Dodd, Mead and Co., 1972.
Harris, Joseph P. *The Advice and Consent of the Senate: A Study of the Confirmation of Appointments by the United States Senate.* New York: Greenwood Press, 1968.
Harris, Richard. *Decision.* New York: E. P. Dutton, 1971.
Haynes, George H. *The Senate of the United States: Its History and Practice.* 2 vols. Boston: Houghton Mifflin, 1938.
Mann, Dean E. *The Assistant Secretaries: Problems and Processes of Appointment.* Washington: Brookings Institution, 1965.
Riddick, Floyd M. *The United States Congress: Organization and Procedure.* Manassas, Va.: National Capitol Publishers, 1949.
Rogers, Lindsay. *The American Senate.* New York: Alfred A. Knopf, 1926.
Rothman, David J. *Politics and Power: The United States Senate, 1869-1901.* New York: Atheneum, 1969.
Warren, Charles. *The Supreme Court in United States History.* Boston: Little, Brown and Co., 1926.

Articles

Bickel, Alexander M. "The Making of Supreme Court Justices." *New Leader,* May 25, 1970, pp. 14-18.
Black, Charles L. Jr. "A Note on Senatorial Consideration of Supreme Court Nominees." *Yale Law Journal,* March 1970, pp. 657-64.
Carmen, Ira H. "The President, Politics and the Power of Appointment: Hoover's Nomination of Mr. Justice Cardozo." *Virginia Law Review,* May 1969, pp. 616-59.
Gimlin, Hoyt. "Challenging of Supreme Court." *Editorial Research Reports,* Oct. 9, 1968, pp. 741-60.
Griffin, Robert P. and Hart, Philip A. "The Fortas Controversy: The Senate's Role of Advice and Consent to Judicial Nominations ['The Broad Role' by Griffin and 'The Discriminating Role' by Hart]." *Prospectus,* April 1969, pp. 238-310.
McConnell, A. Mitchell Jr. "Haynsworth and Carswell: A New Senate Standard of Excellence." *Kentucky Law Journal,* Fall 1970, pp. 7-34.
Mendelsohn, Rona Hirsch. "Senate Confirmation of Supreme Court Appointments: the Nomination and Rejection of John J. Parker." *Howard Law Journal,* Winter 1967, pp. 105-48.
Rodell, Fred. "The Complexities of Mr. Justice Fortas." *New York Times Magazine,* July 28, 1968, pp. 67-68.
Steele, John L. "Haynsworth v. the U.S. Senate (1969)." *Fortune,* March 1970, pp. 90-93.
Swindler, William F. "The Politics of 'Advice and Consent:' The Senate's Role in Selection of Supreme Court Justices." *American Bar Association Journal,* June 1970, pp. 533-42.
Wukasch, Barry C. "The Abe Fortas Controversy: A Research Note on the Senate's Role in Judicial Selection." *Western Political Quarterly,* March 1971, pp. 24-27.

Government Publications

U.S. Congress. House. Committee on Government Operations. *Confirmation of the Director and Deputy Director of the Office of Management and Budget, Hearings, March 5, 9, 1973.* 93rd Cong., 1st sess., 1973.
U.S. Congress. Senate. Committee on Foreign Relations. *The Senate Role in Foreign Affairs Appointments, Committee Print.* 92nd Cong., 1st sess., 1971.
U.S. Congress. Senate. Committee on the Judiciary. *Nomination of Clement F. Haynsworth, Jr., of South Carolina, to be Associate Justice of the Supreme Court, Hearings, September 16-26, 1969.* 91st Cong., 1st sess., 1969.
U.S. Congress. Senate. Committee on the Judiciary. *Nomination of George Harrold Carswell, of Florida, to be Associate Justice of the Supreme Court, Hearings, January 27-February 3, 1970.* 91st Cong., 2nd sess, 1970.
U.S. Congress. Senate. Committee on the Judiciary. *Nomination of Harry A. Blackmun, of Minnesota, to be Associate Justice of the Supreme Court, Hearings, April 29, 1970.* 91st Cong., 2nd sess., 1970.

Power to Regulate Commerce

"The Congress shall have Power...To regulate Commerce with foreign Nations, and among the several States, and with the Indian Tribes." (Article I, Section 8, Clause 3)

With this simple grant of authority the Constitution attempted to remedy one of the basic weaknesses of the federal government under the Articles of Confederation. The lack of a national power over commerce had been in large part responsible for the drafting of a new Constitution, and the need for such a power was widely accepted.

The constitutional formula is a broad and general one: the positive grant of power to Congress is not coupled with a statement of the powers, if any, reserved to the states, and no definition of terms is offered. Four express limitations on the commerce power are contained in Article I, Section 9, but only one—forbidding Congress to lay a tax or duty on articles exported from any state—has had much practical significance. Thus the extent of federal power over commerce has been established largely by experience and judicial determination.

The basic Supreme Court decision involving the scope of the commerce clause was *Gibbons v. Ogden* in 1824. In a landmark opinion, Chief Justice John Marshall opted for a broad construction of the term "commerce" and emphatically asserted the supremacy of the federal power over it.[1] But he rejected the argument—advanced by Daniel Webster, counsel for Gibbons—that the congressional power over commerce was "complete and entire," holding instead that "the completely internal commerce of a state...may be considered as reserved for the state itself."[2] From this acceptance of a divided authority over commerce has stemmed the concept of interstate as opposed to intrastate commerce, with movement across state lines as the basic test of the distinction.

Although Congress exercised its authority over foreign commerce from its earliest days, for nearly a century it failed to exploit its powers over commerce among the states. Thus most early Supreme Court decisions in the field dealt with state regulations that were challenged as infringements on the constitutional powers of Congress. The limits of state regulatory authority are still a problem for the courts today.

With enactment of the Interstate Commerce Act in 1887, Congress moved decisively into the domestic regulatory field, and in the 20th century the scope of the commerce clause has expanded steadily. For years the

Supreme Court held to the view that manufacturing and production were not a part of commerce and that the commerce power extended only to activities that affected commerce directly. Eventually, however, the court came round to the view that the commerce power embraced activities that had an "effect upon commerce," however indirectly. Application of this doctrine led to a substantial expansion of congressional authority, and in 1946 the court concluded that "the federal commerce power is as broad as the economic needs of the nation."[3]

Early History of Commerce Clause

The necessity for national control over interstate and foreign commerce was the immediate occasion for the calling of the Constitutional Convention in 1787. "Most of our political evils," Madison had written to Jefferson the previous year, "may be traced to our commercial ones."[4] Under the Articles of Confederation, adopted during the Revolutionary War, Congress had power to regulate trade only with the Indians, the control of interstate and foreign commerce having been left to the states. This defect in the Articles was universally recognized. Even those who, like Samuel Adams and Patrick Henry, feared that a federal government would be tyrannical, favored more comprehensive regulation of commerce by Congress.

The conditions under which commerce was carried on became increasingly chaotic after the Revolutionary War. Each state attempted to build up its own prosperity at the expense of its neighbors. Justice William Johnson, in a concurring opinion in *Gibbons v. Ogden*, thus described the situation that had developed:

"For a century the states had submitted, with murmurs, to the commercial restrictions imposed by the parent state; and now, finding themselves in the unlimited possession of those powers over their own commerce, which they had so long been deprived of and so earnestly coveted, that selfish principle which, well controlled, is so salutary, and which, unrestricted, is so unjust and tyrannical, guided by inexperience and jealousy, began to show itself in iniquitous laws and impolitic measures, from which grew up a conflict of commercial regulations, destructive to the harmony of the states, and fatal to their commercial interests abroad."[5]

State legislatures imposed tariffs upon goods coming in from other states as well as from foreign countries. Thus, New York levied duties on firewood from Connecticut and cabbages from New Jersey. "The commerce which Massachusetts found it to her interest to encourage," says J. B. McMaster, "Virginia found it to hers to restrict. New York would not protect the trade in indigo and pitch. South Carolina cared nothing for the success of the fur interests."[6]

Seaport states financed their governments through imposts on European goods passing through their harbors but destined for consumption in neighboring states. Madison described the plight of those states not having seaports: "New Jersey placed between Philadelphia and New York was likened to a cask tapped at both ends; and North Carolina, between Virginia and South Carolina, to a patient bleeding at both arms."[7]

Different currencies in each of the 13 states likewise hampered commercial intercourse. And if a merchant were able to carry on an interstate business in spite of tariff and currency difficulties, he often had trouble in collecting his bills. Local courts and juries were less zealous in protecting the rights of distant creditors than those of their neighbors and friends.

The chaotic condition of interstate trade prompted the General Assembly of Virginia, in 1786, to adopt a resolution proposing a joint meeting of commissioners appointed by each of the states "to take into consideration the trade of the United States; to examine the relative situations and trade of the said states; (and) to consider how far a uniform system in their commercial regulations may be necessary to their common interest and their permanent harmony." The action of the Virginia Assembly led to a meeting at Annapolis later in the year of commissioners from five states: Delaware, New Jersey, New York, Pennsylvania and Virginia.[8]

The members of the Annapolis convention, however, "did not conceive it advisable to proceed on the business of their mission, under the circumstance of so partial and defective a representation." They recommended a general meeting of all the states at Philadelphia in 1787 "for the same, and such other purposes, as the situation may be found to require." It was the judgment of the convention that "the power of regulating trade is of such comprehensive extent and will enter so far into the general system of the federal government, that to give it efficacy and to obviate questions and doubts concerning its precise nature and limits, may require a correspondent adjustment of other parts of the federal system."

Adoption of the Commerce Clause

The desirability of uniform regulation of interstate and foreign commerce was so generally recognized that the proposal to give Congress blanket authority in this field occasioned comparatively little discussion at the Philadelphia convention. Some controversy did arise over an attempt by the South to limit the power of a congressional majority in regulating commerce. The southern states feared that the North might seek to dominate their commerce. Charles Pinckney of South Carolina proposed, therefore, that "all laws regulating commerce shall require the assent of two-thirds of the members present in each house," but this proposal was defeated by a vote of seven states to four, Maryland, Virginia, North Carolina and Georgia voting in the affirmative.

"Had Pinckney's proposal been adopted," says Charles Warren, "the course of American history would have been vitally changed. Enactment of protective tariffs might have been practically impossible. The whole political relations between the South and North growing out of commercial

legislation would have been changed. The Nullification movement in the 1830s, which arose out of opposition to a northern tariff, might not have occurred."[9]

In return for the South's acceptance of the unlimited power of the majority in regulation of commerce, the northern states agreed to a ban on export taxes and to a provision that importation of slaves would not be prohibited before the year 1808. This was one of the important compromises reached at Philadelphia.

Many persons consider it remarkable that so important a part of the Constitution as the commerce clause should be so briefly expressed and should leave so much to future determination. "At that time, at least," Warren remarks, "there seems to have been no doubt as to its meaning. The violent differences of opinion which arose during the first half of the 19th century as to what the term 'commerce' included, and as to whether the power to 'regulate' was exclusive in Congress or exercisable by the states until Congress should act, were apparently not in the least foreseen by the members of the Convention." It is generally agreed that nothing more was immediately intended than that Congress should be empowered to prevent commercial wars among the states. Yet it is not to be doubted that the framers were aware of the scope of the power granted to Congress. Monroe pointed out that the commerce clause involved "a radical change in the whole system of our government."[10]

Other Federal Commerce Powers

In addition to general regulatory power over interstate commerce, the convention reposed in the federal government the admiralty jurisdiction and the powers to coin money, establish uniform laws of bankruptcy, establish post offices and post roads, regulate weights and measures and grant patents and copyrights. That the taxing power was recognized as an instrument of commercial regulation is indicated by the clause of the Constitution (Article I, Section 9) which forbids the federal government to give preference to the ports of one state over those of another "by any regulation of commerce or revenue." The importance of these federal powers was enhanced by provisions expressly forbidding the states to coin money, enact laws impairing the obligation of contracts, lay duties of tonnage or tax exports or imports.

Other specific grants of commercial power were discussed in the convention. Benjamin Franklin proposed that Congress be given power "to provide for cutting canals," and James Wilson expressed the belief that such power was necessary in order to prevent a single state from obstructing the general welfare. But Franklin's motion was lost because of the sentiment of the convention that the expense thereby incurred would be a general burden, while the benefit would be local. It was proposed also to give Congress power to grant charters of incorporation in cases where the public good might require them, and where the authority of a single state might be incompetent; to regulate stages on the post roads; to establish institutions for the promotion of agriculture, commerce, trade and manufactures; to make internal improvements, and to charter a national bank. All motions to make these grants in express terms were lost.[11]

Supreme Court Interpretation

Although the federal government's power over interstate commerce now appears as one of the most important and conspicuous it possesses, no case involving the extent of this power arose in the Supreme Court until 1824, 35 years after the adoption of the Constitution. By 1840, only five cases involving the commerce clause had reached the court, and only 30 had been settled by 1870. Moreover, these cases for the most part did not concern the affirmative power of Congress to regulate interstate commerce, but rather the question whether state laws infringed upon the federal power.

After about 1870, however, the commerce clause began to be used as the constitutional basis for the extension of federal authority over constantly larger areas of American economic life, and, as the federal commercial power was transformed from a negative into a positive one, the amount of litigation increased. From 1870 to 1900, about 185 cases involving the commerce clause were decided by the court.

Marshall's Definition

The first case involving the scope of the commerce power to reach the Supreme Court was *Gibbons v. Ogden* 9 Wheat. 1 (1824).[12] In this case, a New York law granting an exclusive privilege of navigation by steamboat on all waters within the state was held void as repugnant to the commerce clause, so far as the law prohibited vessels licensed by the United States from navigating the same waters. The court's decision, written by Chief Justice John Marshall, assumed great importance both because of the broad construction of the term "commerce" and because of the court's assertion of the supremacy of the federal power in this field.

"The subject to be regulated is commerce," Marshall said. "To ascertain the extent of the power, it becomes necessary to settle the meaning of the word.

"The counsel for the appellee would limit it to traffic, to buying and selling, or the interchange of commodities, and do not admit that it comprehends navigation. This would restrict a general term, applicable to many objects, to one of its significations. Commerce, undoubtedly, is traffic, but it is something more—it is intercourse. It describes the commercial intercourse between nations, and parts of nations, in all its branches.... All America understands...the word 'commerce' to comprehend navigation...."

The federal power over commerce, Marshall said, comprehended navigation within the limits of every state, so far as navigation might be in any manner connected with foreign nations, or among the states, and therefore it passed beyond the jurisdiction of New York and included the public waters of the state which were connected with such foreign or interstate commerce.

"The subject to which the power is next applied," Marshall continued, "is to commerce 'among the several states.' The word 'among' means intermingled with.... Commerce among the states cannot stop at the external boundary lines of each state, but may be introduced into the interior. It is not intended to say that these words comprehend that commerce which is completely internal, which is carried on between man and man in a state, or between different parts of the same state and which does not extend to or affect other states. Such a power would be inconvenient and is certainly unnecessary. Comprehensive as the word 'among' is, it may very properly be restricted to that commerce which concerns more states than one.... The completely internal commerce of a state, then, may be considered as reserved for the state itself."

With regard to the supremacy of the federal power, the Chief Justice said: "This power, like all others vested in

Congress, is complete in itself, may be exercised to its utmost extent and acknowledges no limitations other than are prescribed in the Constitution.... If, as has always been understood, the sovereignty of Congress, though limited to specified objects, is plenary as to those objects, the power over commerce with foreign nations and among the several states is vested in Congress as absolutely as it would be in a single government, having in its constitution the same restrictions on the exercise of the power as are found in the Constitution of the United States."

Justice Johnson's concurring opinion expressed similar conclusions in even more vigorous language. Emphasizing the fact that the necessity for regulation of commerce had been the moving purpose behind the Constitution, Johnson asserted that the power of Congress in this matter "must be exclusive; it can reside but in one potentate; and hence, the grant of this power carries with it the whole subject, leaving nothing for the states to act upon."

Reactions to Court's Opinion

The decision in *Gibbons v. Ogden* was popular. "At the time of its delivery," according to Albert J. Beveridge, "nobody complained of Marshall's opinion except the agents of the steamboat monopoly, the theorists of localism and the slave autocracy. All these influences beheld, in Marshall's statesmanship, their inevitable extinction." Jefferson was "horrified." In 1825 he wrote that he viewed "with the deepest affliction, the rapid strides with which the federal branch of our government is advancing towards the usurpation of all the rights reserved to the states.

"Take together the decision of the federal court, the doctrines of the President, and the misconstructions of the Constitutional Compact acted on by the legislature of the federal branch, and it is too evident that the three ruling branches of that department are in combination to strip their colleagues, the state authorities, of the powers reserved by them, and to exercise themselves all functions, foreign and domestic. Under the power to regulate commerce, they assume indefinitely that also over agriculture and manufactures, and call it regulation to take the earnings of one of these branches of industry...and put them in the pocket of the other."[13]

Political scientists Ogg and Ray wrote: "Marshall not only affirmed full authority of Congress to maintain the free flow of interstate and foreign commerce within the individual states, but declared commerce to consist not only of *traffic* (buying, selling and transporting commodities), but of *intercourse* as well, thereby giving it an entirely new content and meaning. ...Immediately, the carrying of persons (not simply goods) from one state to another, or to a foreign country, became 'commerce,' subject to congressional regulation; and as forms and methods of intercourse later multiplied, the field for control correspondingly expanded. In time came the steamboat; then the railroad; then the telegraph; then the telephone; then the motor vehicle; then 'wireless'; then radio-broadcasting; then the airplane; finally television.... And to all of these the regulative authority of Congress was progressively extended, with the Supreme Court...sometimes hinting at even broader ones that might be assumed."[14]

Regulation of Interstate Commerce

In its first century, Congress made little use of its power to regulate interstate commerce. Before the Civil War, it did so in only two classes of subjects—construction of interstate bridges and extension of the admiralty jurisdiction. But with the passage of the Interstate Commerce Act of 1887, Congress moved into regulation of the domestic economy.

Both before and after the Civil War, the states attempted in various ways to curb increasing abuses by the railroads. These efforts were generally ineffective. Then, in 1886, the Supreme Court ruled in *Wabash, St. Louis & Pacific Ry. Co. v. Illinois* (118 U.S. 557) that any enterprise engaged in interstate commerce could not be regulated by the states through which it passed. Such regulation, the court held, was barred by the commerce clause of the Constitution. The scope of the decision not only nullified state regulation of railroads but also precluded state action in such fields as the curbing of monopolies.[15]

Interstate Commerce Act. Inability of the states to regulate the railroads led directly to the passage in 1887 of the Interstate Commerce Act, which established the Interstate Commerce Commission. In 1894, the Supreme Court upheld the act as a necessary and proper means of enforcing congressional authority.[16] The ICC has served as the prototype for the other regulatory commissions created by Congress.

Under the original law, the ICC did not have power to make or revise rates; ultimately, however, the necessity of conferring extensive rate-making power was brought home to the national mind; and under the transportation acts of 1906 and 1920, the ICC (as an agent of Congress for the purpose) was authorized, on complaint and after hearing, not only to fix "just and reasonable" rates, regulations and practices, but also to prescribe definite maximum or minimum (or both) charges.[17]

In time the ICC's jurisdiction was broadened to include all interstate commerce carried on by railroads, trucking companies, bus lines, freight forwarders, water carriers, oil pipelines, transportation brokers and express agencies.

Antitrust Legislation. In 1890, Congress moved into federal regulation of commercial enterprise with enactment of the Sherman Antitrust Act, "to protect commerce against unlawful restraints and monopolies." The act imposed a general prohibition upon "every contract, combination in the form of trust or otherwise, or conspiracy in restraint of trade or commerce." Federal regulation of commerce was further strengthened in 1914 by passage of the Clayton Act and the Federal Trade Commission Act.[18]

Areas Related to Commerce. An activity which does not itself involve movement across state lines may be regarded as interstate commerce because of the use of the instrumentalities of such commerce. The classic case is that of the correspondence schools which are interstate commerce because of their reliance on the U.S. mails. Regulation of public utility holding companies under the federal act of 1935 was upheld on the ground that their subsidiaries usually operate on an interstate basis, and that the services which the holding company performs for its subsidiaries involve continuous and extensive use of the mails and other facilities of interstate commerce.[19]

Police Power. Congress entered still another field of regulation in 1895 when it enacted a law prohibiting transportation of lottery tickets in interstate commerce. The Supreme Court upheld this law in 1903 with a decision that, in the words of Charles Warren, "disclosed the existence of a hitherto unsuspected field of national power." Warren said: "The practical result of the case was the creation of a federal police power—the right to regulate the manner of produc-tion, manufacture, sale and transportation of articles and the transportation of persons, through the medium of legislation professing to regulate commerce between the states. Congress took very swift advantage of the new field thus opened to it."[20]

Between 1903 and 1917, Congress enacted laws prohibiting the interstate transportation of explosives, diseased livestock, insect pests, falsely stamped gold and silver articles, narcotics, prostitutes and adulterated or misbranded foods and drugs. Interstate transportation of stolen automobiles was made unlawful in 1925, under the Dyer Act, and the so-called "Lindbergh law" of 1932 made interstate transportation of abducted persons a federal offense.

The 1910 Mann Act, forbidding the transportation of women in interstate commerce for the purpose of prostitution and debauchery, was upheld by the Supreme Court in 1913. The court held "that Congress has power over transportation 'among the several States'; that the power is complete in itself, and that Congress, as an incident to it, may adopt not only means necessary but convenient to its exercise, and the means may have the quality of police regulations."

In 1925 (*Brooks v. United States*, 267 U.S. 432), the Supreme Court laid down the following principle: "Congress can certainly regulate interstate commerce to the extent of forbidding and punishing the use of such commerce as an agency to promote immorality, dishonesty, or the spread of any evil or harm to the people of other states from the state of origin. In doing this, it is merely exercising the police power, for the benefit of the public, within the field of interstate commerce."[21]

Child Labor Decision. The same technique of closing the channels of interstate commerce was employed by Congress in enacting the Federal Child Labor Act of 1916. The 1916 act prohibited the shipment in interstate commerce of the products of factories, mines or quarries employing children below specified ages. In a historic 5-4 decision in *Hammer v. Dagenhart* (247 U.S. 251) the court ruled in 1918 that Congress had the power "to control the means by which commerce is carried on," but not the power "to forbid commerce from moving."[22]

Speaking for the majority, Justice William R. Day said: "The thing intended to be accomplished by this statute is the denial of the facilities of interstate commerce to those manufacturers in the states who employ children within the prohibited ages. The act in its effect does not regulate transportation among the states, but aims to standardize the ages at which children may be employed in mining and manufacturing within the states. The goods shipped are of themselves harmless.... Over interstate transportation, or its incidents, the regulatory power of Congress is ample, but the production of articles, intended for interstate commerce, is a matter of local regulation."[23]

In a classic dissent, Justice Holmes challenged the majority view. Congress clearly had the express power under the commerce clause, he said, to forbid the transportation of goods in interstate commerce. Therefore, if the law was to be declared unconstitutional, it would have to be because of its indirect effects on the states. "But if an act is within the powers specifically conferred upon Congress, it seems to me that it is not made any less constitutional because of the indirect effects that it may have, however obvious it may be that it will have those effects, and that we are not at liberty upon such grounds to hold it void."[24]

The court overruled the Hammer decision in 1941 as "a departure from the principles which have prevailed in the interpretation of the commerce clause both before and since" the 1918 decision.

"Influential as it may have been," wrote scholar C. Herman Pritchett, the decision "was never anything but an exception to the general rule, which as stated by Harlan in The Lottery Case (1903) is that the power to regulate commerce 'is plenary, is complete in itself, and is subject to no limitations except such as may be found in the Constitution.' It was the general rule, not the exception, which the court followed in upholding the power of Congress over interstate commerce in stolen motor vehicles in 1925 and kidnapped persons in 1936."[25]

Expansion of Power after 1900

Since 1900, Congress has expanded its regulatory authority over commerce into almost every area of the commercial and industrial life of the nation. For the most part, the Supreme Court has gone along with this expansion and even, on occasion, hinted at broader federal powers than Congress itself claimed.

Many of the New Deal economic recovery programs were launched under the commerce clause. Until 1937, the Supreme Court tended to view the authorizing laws as unconstitutional, either because the programs were considered to range beyond the bounds of the commerce power or because they were thought to involve too broad a delegation of congressional authority. These decisions led to President Roosevelt's plan to enlarge the court.

Two months after the President sent his court-packing plan to Congress, the court altered its stance. In a 5-4 decision in 1937, it upheld the constitutionality of the National Labor Relations (Wagner) Act of 1935 and at the same time clarified the scope of the commerce power. The 1935 act had established the National Labor Relations Board and given it authority to forbid any person from engaging in any unfair labor practice "affecting commerce." The case involved charges of unfair labor practices in one of the Pennsylvania plants of the Jones & Laughlin Corporation, a major steel producer with operations in several states.

Speaking for the court, Chief Justice Hughes said: "Although activities may be intrastate in character when separately considered, if they have such a close and substantial relation to interstate commerce that their control is essential or appropriate to protect that commerce from burdens and obstructions, Congress cannot be denied the power to exercise that control.... When industries organize themselves on a national scale, making their relation to interstate commerce the dominant factor in their activities, how can it be maintained that their industrial relations constitute a forbidden field into which Congress may not enter when it is necessary to protect interstate commerce from the paralyzing consequences of industrial war?" *(NLRB v. Jones & Laughlin Corp.,* 301 U.S. 1).[26]

In a 1941 decision upholding the Fair Labor Standards (Wages and Hours) Act of 1938, the court reversed its earlier decision in the *Hammer* case. The 1938 act banned the shipment in interstate commerce of goods produced in violation of the wage-and-hour standards set by the legislation, which included restrictions on child labor. The law was applicable to employees "engaged in commerce or in the production of goods for commerce." Justice Stone, delivering the opinion of the court, said: "The power of Congress under the commerce clause is plenary to exclude any article from interstate commerce subject only to the specific prohibitions of the Constitution." *(U.S. v. Darby Lumber Co.,* 312 U.S. 100).[27]

(In 1976, however, the court in a decision limiting Congress' power under the commerce clause, struck down a 1974 law which had extended the minimum wage and overtime provisions of the Fair Labor Standards Act to state and municipal employees.) *(National League of Cities v. Usery, California v. Usery,* 44 U.S. Law Week 4974).

In other decisions the court upheld application of the commerce clause to such matters as agricultural marketing controls, regulation of the insurance industry and control over navigable waters (including irrigation and flood control) and the hydroelectric power derived from them. In a decision in 1946 upholding the "death sentence" provision of the Public Utility Holding Company Act, the court concluded: "The federal commerce power is as broad as the economic needs of the nation." *(American Power & Light Co. v. SEC,* 329 U.S. 90).[28]

More recently, the scope of the commerce clause has been enlarged to include civil rights. In the Civil Rights Act of 1964, Congress found sanction in the commerce clause and the "equal protection" clause of the Fourteenth Amendment for a ban on racial discrimination in most public accommodations. In two test cases in 1964, the court upheld the law under the commerce power alone.[29]

In 1968, Congress used the commerce clause as the basis for legislation making it a federal crime to travel in interstate commerce or use the facilities of interstate commerce to incite or participate in a riot. The measure, prompted by rioting in black ghettos, was later used to prosecute some of the demonstrators against the Vietnam War.[30]

Federal Regulatory Agencies

Since the establishment of the Interstate Commerce Commission in 1887, federal regulatory agencies have come to play a major role in the American economy.[31]

Although the *United States Government Organization Manual* lists almost 50 independent federal agencies, many of which perform regulatory functions, discussion of federal regulation usually centers on activities of the so-called "Big Seven." In addition to the ICC, these are the Federal Trade Commission, organized in 1915; the Federal Power Commission, established in 1920; and four agencies established during the administration of President Franklin D. Roosevelt—the Federal Communications Commission (1934), the Securities and Exchange Commission (1934), the National Labor Relations Board (1935) and the Civil Aeronautics Board (1938).

Members of all seven agencies are appointed by the President for fixed terms. Membership ranges from five to 11, and no political party may have more than a one-member majority on any of the Big Seven. The agencies derive their powers from acts of Congress that delegate to them certain regulatory functions that have become too complex for Congress to handle by legislation.

They also have quasi-judicial functions. When the Civil Aeronautics Board promulgates a rule asserting its primary jurisdiction over airspace for both civil and military purposes, it is exercising its quasi-legislative (or rule-making) power. When it decides which of several commercial airlines shall be awarded a specific airline route, it is exercising quasi-judicial (or adjudicatory) power. Similarly, the FCC is making rules when it sets up criteria for evaluating competing claims for a television license, adjudicating when it awards a license.

Regulatory commissions, therefore, exercise a blend of the legislative, executive and judicial powers. They were established by Congress to make the bulk of complicated regulations for industry that Congress had neither the time nor the expertise to do itself. They then enforce the rules they promulgate (although court review of their actions is possible). The President appoints commission members and reviews their budgets. The Senate approves the nominees, and Congress appropriates operative funds and defines in legislation the agencies' responsibilities.

"Big Seven" Powers

The powers and influence of the Big Seven regulatory agencies, reaching into virtually every corner of the American economy, give some indication of the scope of the federal commerce power. The principal functions of these agencies are as follows:

Interstate Commerce Commission. Jurisdiction covers railroads and related carriers, common and contract motor carriers, certain domestic water carriers, pipelines and freight forwarders. ICC fixes rates; sets standards for reasonable service; issues permits or certificates required to engage in interstate transportation; controls consolidations and mergers of carriers, issuance of securities and the accounting systems and records kept by carriers; regulates safety devices and standards.

Federal Trade Commission. FTC may act to prevent practices leading to monopoly or restraint of trade, such as unfair methods of competition (e.g., false and misleading advertising), stock acquisitions of competing enterprises and price discrimination. It has power also to investigate and to issue cease-and-desist orders, and it shares antimonopoly responsibility with the Justice Department.

Federal Power Commission. FPC grants licenses to private power projects on navigable waters subject to federal jurisdiction; fixes rates on interstate sale of electric energy; prescribes uniform accounting methods; and regulates (1) mergers and security issues of electric utilities, (2) most federal power projects and (3) interstate sales of natural gas.

Federal Communications Commission. FCC regulates telephone and telegraph common carriers, including their interstate rates; allocates radio frequencies; licenses radio and television stations; licenses radio operators; monitors broadcasts; administers international communications treaties.

Securities and Exchange Commission. SEC regulates security issues; supervises the stock exchanges; regulates holding companies and investment companies.

National Labor Relations Board. NLRB adjudicates charges of unfair labor practices on the part of employers or unions; enforces requirements for collective bargaining; supervises election of bargaining representatives; decides jurisdictional disputes.

Civil Aeronautics Board. CAB licenses domestic air carriers; issues permits to foreign air carriers landing in the United States; fixes passenger, freight and mail rates; controls mergers, pooling and other arrangements between carriers.

Delegation of Power

All of the commissions exercise, to greater or lesser degree, some executive, legislative and judicial power. By the same token, control over the commissions is shared by the President, Congress and the courts, in a system of checks and balances. The President's power to control the regulatory agencies rests largely in his appointive power,

while that of Congress rests in its responsibility for appropriations.

Members of the legislative branch nevertheless have insisted periodically that the power of Congress has been delegated, not abdicated, and that in the last analysis the commissions are "creatures of Congress." The classic view of the commissions held by federal legislators was expressed in 1931 by the late Speaker of the House, Sam Rayburn (D Texas):

"Far from undermining the constitutional authority of Congress, delegation of authority to administrative agencies is one of the surest safeguards to effective legislative action. It is a procedure which conserves the vital power of Congress for vital matters.... (A commission) does not perform any act that Congress has not the authority to perform itself.... Congress...delegated responsibility to a commission of...trained experts to work out the details for them."[32]

This view has not gone unchallenged. C. Herman Pritchett, a member of the Hoover Commission, wrote in the *American Political Science Review* in October 1949 that "The spurious nature of this 'arm of Congress' claim has long been evident." Pritchett added: "The fact is that Congress has not a single control over any of the regulatory commissions that it does not possess over executive agencies generally.... (The Hoover Commission) wanted to have non-political regulation and at the same time provide for presidential control."[33]

It has been asserted that every President of the United States from Woodrow Wilson on has tried in one way or another to influence commission activity and has succeeded in doing so. For example, "President Hoover made public statements indicating how he thought the Interstate Commerce Commission ought to exercise certain of its powers, and the commission somewhat reluctantly yielded," wrote Robert E. Cushman.[34] President Roosevelt obtained the resignation of Hoover's chairman of the Federal Power Commission and added two appointees of his own. Four days after his inauguration, President Nixon recalled from the Civil Aeronautics Board "for further review and decision" the awards of new Pacific routes which President Johnson had made to five airlines on Dec. 18, 1968. (Although CAB makes final decisions in domestic route cases, the President has statutory authority to approve or reject CAB recommendations on foreign routes.)

1961 Reorganization Proposal

Regulatory commissions have found it difficult to please simultaneously the executive branch, the legislative branch and the regulated industry. Commission actions often are criticized as restrictive or permissive, and commission procedures frequently are attacked.

Numerous plans for improving the performance of federal regulatory agencies have been put forward since World War II, yet few have been adopted. Most reform proposals have foundered because of opposition in Congress. The legislative branch tends to be suspicious of any reorganization that might weaken its influence on regulatory agencies. Moreover, the regulated industries evidently prefer a sometimes uncomfortable status quo to a new regulatory environment that might be less to their liking.

The most ambitious attempt to reshape the regulatory agencies took place shortly after John F. Kennedy became President in 1961. Kennedy had asked James M. Landis, a former chairman of the Securities and Exchange Commission, to study the agencies and submit proposals for improving them. Landis' report, which noted the familiar problems of delay, ethical conduct and quality of personnel, made 16 broad recommendations. Among other things, he called for:

• Extensive reorganization of most of the agencies.

• Establishment of special offices in the White House to develop national transportation policy, telecommunications policy and energy resources policy.

• Establishment by executive order of a federal employee code of ethics and limitation of off-the-record presentation in regulatory agency cases.

• Creation of a special Office for the Oversight of Regulatory Agencies.

In a special message to Congress on regulatory agencies, April 13, 1961, Kennedy proposed to give agency chairmen "broad managerial powers" to correct the existing, diffused authority of the commissions; provide that all agency chairmen serve in that capacity at the President's pleasure; and authorize delegation of a large proportion of agency responsibilities to inter-agency boards and hearing examiners to eliminate needless work on "unimportant details" at the top level. Congress responded by reviving the Reorganization Act of 1949, which had expired two years earlier, so that the President could submit reorganization plans for the agencies.

Seven such plans were submitted, all of which had the basic aim of speeding up and streamlining agency procedures. The first four plans—those for SEC, FCC, CAB and FTC—contained three basically identical steps. They authorized the agency to delegate some of its functions to certain employees; they empowered the chairman to assign the delegated functions; and they made review of certain lower-level decisions discretionary.

The plan for the National Labor Relations Board was the same as the first four but omitted the chairman's power of assignment; the plan for the Federal Home Loan Bank Board (FHLBB) only restored some hiring and firing powers formerly held by the chairman; and in the seventh plan, the Federal Maritime Board (FMB) was abolished and its functions assigned to other agencies.

Jealous as ever of its authority over the agencies, Congress charged that the administration planned to create a White House "czar" and establish a "direct chain of political command" over the regulatory agencies. When the smoke of battle cleared, the final score stood: three plans killed, with one replaced by a more limited version; four plans approved. Congress vetoed the reorganization plans for FCC, SEC and NLRB. It upheld those for CAB, FTC, FMB and FHLBB. A scaled-down reorganization bill for FCC allowed the commission to delegate minor functions to employees, but it did not provide the authority requested by the administration to enable the chairman to make specific work assignments to employees and commissioners. The bill also expedited action by putting oral arguments on exceptions to agency decisions on a discretionary instead of required basis and by giving the commission authority to either accept or deny appeals for overall review without giving a reason.

Challenge in the 1970s

Fearing that the agencies were becoming increasingly more responsive to the White House and industry, Congress in 1973 took several steps to free the commissions from some executive branch controls and moved more forcefully to scrutinize the composition of commission membership.

For the first time since 1950,[35] the Senate refused to confirm a presidential nomination to a regulatory agency. And, refusing to buckle under strong pressure from the Nixon administration, Congress took two steps to free the agencies from executive branch dependence: agencies no longer had to submit information questionnaires to the Office of Management and Budget (the power was transferred to the General Accounting Office from OMB), and the Federal Trade Commission would argue its own civil cases.

The implementation of tougher standards for commission nominees was the product of the Senate Commerce Committee, which approves nominees for the FCC, FTC, ICC, CAB, Federal Maritime Commission, FPC, National Transportation Safety Board and Consumer Product Safety Commission. The first test of the committee's new policy came in January 1973, when President Nixon named Robert H. Morris, a San Francisco lawyer, to a seat on the Federal Power Commission. During his confirmation hearings, Morris acknowledged that from 1956 to 1971, approximately half of his legal work involved representation of the Standard Oil Company of California, a company whose activities are regulated by FPC.

During floor debate on the nomination in June, Commerce Committee Chairman Warren G. Magnuson (D Wash.) said, "The opposition to Mr. Morris stems from the fact that the Senate is again asked to accept, for an independent regulatory agency with vast powers over an industry which affects vital national interest, yet one more nominee whose professional career has been dedicated to the furtherance of the private interests of that industry." Magnuson also warned the White House: "The Senate should serve notice on the President that it expects revision of his criteria for the selection of nominees to all regulatory agencies. Now, more than ever, the Senate should not be asked to confirm appointments...which appear to have been designed as rewards for politically supportive industries or other special interests. Instead, the Senate should be asked to confirm nominees who have demonstrated competence and commitment to the public interest."

The Senate voted, 50-42, to recommit Morris' nomination to the Commerce Committee.

Magnuson's message was apparently not lost on the President. On Nov. 2, he nominated to what would have been Morris' FPC seat Don S. Smith, a member of the Arkansas Public Service Commission with good marks from the state's consumer organizations. In contrast to the delays that marked Morris' confirmation proceedings, the Commerce Committee approved Smith's nomination Nov. 28. The full Senate followed suit later in the same day, confirming Smith by voice vote.

In May 1974, however, Nixon nominated Daniel T. Kingsley, of the White House staff, to another seat on the FPC—but a committee investigation uncovered Kingsley's involvement in the administration's "responsiveness program" designed to make the supposedly nonpolitical Civil Service more responsive to White House wishes. The committee refused to act on the selection, and the name was withdrawn six months later.[36]

Regulation of Foreign Commerce

The power to regulate commerce with foreign nations extends to all transportation or communication that crosses the national boundaries. It is inextricably tied to the powers over foreign relations and fiscal affairs. The commerce power may be used to promote, inhibit or simply make rules for trade with other nations. It may be implemented by treaty or international agreement, as well as by acts of Congress. Such is the breadth of this power that only a suggestion of it can be offered here.[37]

Promotion of Trade. Encouragement of foreign trade may take the form of opening up new markets for American goods in other countries or of securing favorable conditions for American traders abroad. The earliest actions in this field were efforts to replace markets lost when the nation won its independence from England. Modern laws have ranged from antitrust exemptions for exporters to use of tariff reductions to stimulate trade.

Efforts to encourage American shipping have ranged from preferential duties for goods imported in American ships (first enacted in 1789) to federal subsidies for the construction and operation of merchant ships, designed to equalize competition with foreign shipping (since 1936).

Trade Restrictions. The authority to limit or even prohibit foreign trade rests with Congress, although the Legislative Branch frequently delegates this power to the President or executive agencies.

Tariffs. Historically, the predominant mechanism to restrict foreign trade has been the protective tariff. The first major business of the House of Representatives in 1789 was to devise a tariff schedule; unlike many later tariff laws, this one had as its chief object the raising of revenue to finance the new government. But Congress was not four days old when a Philadelphia representative offered an amendment proposing additional duties on manufactured articles "to encourage the productions of our country and to protect our infant manufactures." Congress continued to legislate tariffs until 1930, and the pleas of special interests were frequently reflected in the tariff schedules.

The system also had other pitfalls. Members of Congress could hardly hope to master the intricacies of complicated tariff schedules, and tariffs embodied in the statutes could not readily be adapted to changing conditions. A measure of flexibility was introduced in 1922, when the Fordney-McCumber Tariff Act gave the President authority to adjust tariff rates on the basis of recommendations by the U.S. Tariff Commission, which previously had had only investigative authority.

Reciprocal Trade Agreements Act. Finally, in 1934, the Roosevelt administration—hoping to assist economic recovery at home by expanding American exports—proposed that Congress delegate some of its constitutional power to the President by authorizing him to negotiate trade agreements with other nations. The administration asked authority to cut tariffs by as much as 50 per cent in return for equivalent concessions from other nations. Prodded and persuaded by Secretary of State Cordell Hull, the Democratic-controlled 73rd Congress—over the nearly unanimous opposition of Republicans—made this grant of authority in the Trade Agreements Act of 1934. Thereafter, no serious effort was made to restore congressional tariff-making in place of the method of presidential negotiation of bilateral and, after World War II, multilateral trade agreements.

Non-tariff Barriers. Non-tariff barriers to the free flow of trade range from import quotas to embargoes. Although export taxes are forbidden under the Constitution, Congress can control export trade through licensing or other means. Thus it may bar shipment of strategic materials to hostile countries or restrict exports that would deplete essential domestic supplies. Congress has curbed imports that would interfere with domestic regulatory programs (such as agricultural commodities under production-control and price-support programs). It has also enacted "Anti-Dumping," "Buy American" and "Ship American" legislation.

The ultimate restraint on foreign commerce is the embargo, which suspends commerce completely with all or with specified countries. The United States has used the embargo on a number of occasions, beginning in 1794. Trade with mainland China was completely embargoed after that country entered the Korean War. Exports of strategic goods to other Communist countries have long been subject to embargoes of varying severity.

Other Trade Laws. Laws relating to navigation and ship inspection go back to the First Congress. Since 1798, Congress has assumed responsibility for the health care of American merchant seamen; in the La Follette Seamen's Act of 1915, it undertook to safeguard their rights on shipboard as well. Congress also imposes safety regulations on ships using American ports and requires ship owners to prove financial responsibility as a means of protecting passengers from losses.

Footnotes

1. C. Herman Pritchett, *The American Constitution* (McGraw-Hill Book Co., 1968), p. 253.

2. *Ibid.*, p. 254.

3. *Ibid.*, p. 277. For a concise description of the commerce power, see Frederic A. Ogg and P. Orman Ray, *Introduction to American Government* (Appleton-Century-Crofts Inc., 1951), pp. 549-72.

4. Charles Warren, *The Making of the Constitution* (Little, Brown and Co., 1928), p. 16.

5. Bryant Putney, "Federal Powers under the Commerce Clause," *Editorial Research Reports*, Oct. 4, 1935, p. 292.

6. J. B. McMaster, *History of the People of the United States* (1893), p. 206; quoted in Putney, "Federal Powers," p. 293.

7. *Ibid.*

8. *Ibid.*

9. Warren, *The Making of the Constitution*, pp. 585-86.

10. *Ibid.*, p. 570.

11. *Ibid.*, p. 699-702.

12. Background on the case, see Putney, "Federal Powers," pp. 295-97; Pritchett, *The American Constitution*, pp. 253-55; and Charles Warren, *The Supreme Court in United States History* (Little, Brown and Co., 1926), pp. 587-632.

13. Albert J. Beveridge, *The Life of John Marshall* (Houghton-Mifflin Co., 1919), Vol. 4, pp. 429-30.

14. Ogg and Ray, *Introduction to American Government*, p. 550.

15. *Ibid.*, p. 563.

16. Pritchett, *The American Constitution*, p. 260.

17. Ogg and Ray, *Introduction to American Government*, p. 565.

18. Pritchett, *The American Constitution*, p. 276.

19. *Ibid.*, p. 256.

20. Warren, *The Supreme Court*, pp. 735-36; see also Pritchett, p. 260.

21. Ogg and Ray, *Introduction to American Government*, p. 560.

22. Pritchett, *The American Constitution*, p. 261.

23. Quoted in Putney, "Federal Powers," p. 302.

24. Pritchett, *The American Constitution*, p. 262.

25. *Ibid.*, pp. 262-63.

26. *Ibid.*, p. 270.

27. *Ibid.*, p. 272.

28. *Ibid.*, p. 277.

29. *Ibid.*, p. 278. The cases were *Heart of Atlanta Motel Inc. v. United States* (379 U.S. 241) and *Katzenbach v. McClung* (379 U.S. 294).

30. Congressional Quarterly, *1968 Almanac* (Washington, 1969), p. 152.

31. The following discussion of federal regulatory agencies relies on Richard L. Worsnop, "Federal Regulatory Agencies: Fourth Branch of Government," *Editorial Research Reports,* Feb. 5, 1969, pp. 83-102; and Congressional Quarterly, "Regulatory Agencies: Congress Taking a Fresh Look," 1973 *Weekly Report,* pp. 3447-52.

32. M. H. Bernstein, *Regulating Business by Independent Commission* (Princeton University Press, 1955), p. 67.

33. C. Herman Pritchett, "The Regulatory Commissions Revisited," *American Political Science Review* 43 (October 1949): 988-89.

34. Robert E. Cushman, *The Independent Regulatory Commissions* (Oxford University Press, 1941), pp. 681-82.

35. In 1949, the Senate, by a 15-53 vote, rejected President Truman's nomination of Leland Olds for a third term as a member of the FPC. Olds, who had played a key role in the development of federal regulation of the natural gas industry, was opposed by oil and natural gas interests who blamed him for the commission's "discriminatory and socialistic" attitude toward private power and fuel companies. The following year, the Senate, by a 59-14 vote, rejected Martin A. Hutchinson, a lawyer and political opponent of Sen. Harry Flood Byrd (D Va.) for a seat on the FTC. Hutchinson, who had run unsuccessfully in 1946 against Byrd, was opposed by the Virginia senator.

36. Congressional Quarterly, 1974 *Weekly Report,* pp. 3161, 3255.

37. Background on foreign commerce, see Ogg and Ray, *Introduction to American Government,* pp. 553-58.

Selected Bibliography

Books

Beard, Charles A. *Economic Interpretation of the Constitution of the United States.* New York: Macmillan, 1935.

Benson, Paul R. *Supreme Court and the Commerce Clause, 1937-1970.* Port Washington, N.Y.: Dunellen Publishing Co., 1971.

Bernstein, M. H. *Regulating Business by Independent Commission.* Princeton: Princeton University Press, 1955.

Beveridge, Albert J. *The Life of John Marshall.* 4 vols. Boston: Houghton Mifflin Co., 1919.

Bogart, Ernest L. *Economic History of the American People.* New York: Longmans, Green, 1942.

Corwin, Edward S. *The Commerce Power versus States Rights.* Princeton: Princeton University Press, 1936.

Crosskey, William W. *Politics and the Constitution in the History of the United States.* Chicago: University of Chicago Press, 1953.

Cushman, Robert E. *The Independent Regulatory Commissions.* New York: Oxford University Press, 1941.

Frankfurter, Felix. *The Commerce Clause under Marshall, Taney and Waite.* Chapel Hill: University of North Carolina Press, 1937.

Gavit, Bernard C. *Commerce Clause of the United States Constitution.* New York: AMS Press, 1970.

Haines, Charles Grove, and Sherwood, Foster H. *The Role of the Supreme Court in American Government and Politics, 1835-1864.* Berkeley: University of California Press, 1957.

Hamilton, Walton H. and Adair, Douglas. *The Power to Govern: The Constitution—Then and Now.* New York: W. W. Norton & Co. Inc., 1937.

Kallenbach, Joseph E. *Federal Cooperation with the States under the Commerce Clause.* Ann Arbor: University of Michigan Press, 1942.

Kelly, Alfred H. and Harbison, Winfred A. *The American Constitution: Its Origins and Development.* 3rd ed. New York: W. W. Norton & Co. Inc., 1963.

Liebhafsky, H. H. *American Government and Business.* New York: John Wiley & Sons, 1971.

Ogg, Frederick A. and Ray, P. Orman. *Introduction to American Government.* New York: Appleton-Century-Crofts Inc., 1951.

Pritchett, C. Herman. *The American Constitution.* 2nd ed. New York: McGraw-Hill Book Co., 1968.

———. *The Roosevelt Court: A Study in Judicial Politics and Values, 1937-1947.* New York: Macmillan Co., 1948.

Reynolds, George G. *Distribution of Power to Regulate Interstate Carriers Between the Nation and the States.* New York: AMS Press, 1928.

Warren, Charles. *The Making of the Constitution.* Boston: Little, Brown and Co., 1928.

———. *The Supreme Court in United States History.* rev. ed. 2 vols. Boston: Little, Brown and Co., 1926.

Articles

Apraia, Anthony F. "The Brass Tacks of the ICC Administration Problems." *Public Utilities Fortnightly,* March 31, 1960, pp. 433-42.

"Congressional Supervision of Interstate Commerce." *Yale Law Journal,* July 1966, pp. 1416-33.

Ely, Robert B. "Free Trade, American Style." *American Bar Association Journal,* May 1970, pp. 470-74.

Pritchett, C. Herman. "The Hoover Commission: A Symposium, Part VI. The Regulatory Commissions Revisited." *American Political Science Review,* vol. 43, 1949, pp. 978-1000.

Putney, Bryant. "Federal Powers Under the Commerce Clause." *Editorial Research Reports,* Oct. 4, 1935, pp. 289-304.

Worsnop, Richard L. "Federal Regulatory Agencies: Fourth Branch of Government." *Editorial Research Reports,* Feb. 5, 1969, pp. 83-102.

Government Publication

Udell, Gilman, comp. *Laws Relating to Interstate Commerce and Transportation.* Washington: Government Printing Office, 1966.

Power of Impeachment

Impeachment is perhaps the most awesome though the least used power of Congress. In essence, it is a political action, couched in legal terminology, directed against a ranking official of the federal government. The House of Representatives is the prosecutor. The Senate chamber is the courtroom; and the Senate is the judge and jury. The final penalty is removal from office and disqualification from further office. There is no appeal.

Impeachment proceedings have been initiated in the House more than 60 times since 1789, but only thirteen officers have been impeached: one President, one Cabinet officer, one senator and 10 federal judges.[1] Of these 13, 12 cases reached the Senate. Of the 12 cases reaching the Senate, two were dismissed before trial after the person impeached left office, six resulted in acquittal and four ended in conviction. (In the thirteenth case, Federal Judge Mark H. Delahay was impeached in 1873, but resigned before the House sent the matter to the Senate.)[2]

All of the convictions involved federal judges: John Pickering of the district court for New Hampshire, in 1804; West H. Humphreys of the eastern, middle and western districts of Tennessee, in 1862; Robert W. Archbald of the Commerce Court, in 1913; and Halsted L. Ritter of the southern district of Florida, in 1936.

Two of the impeachments traditionally have stood out from all the rest. They involved Justice Samuel Chase of the Supreme Court in 1805 and President Andrew Johnson in 1868, the two most powerful and important federal officials ever subjected to the process. Both were impeached by the House—Chase for partisan conduct on the bench; Johnson for violating the Tenure of Office Act—and both were acquitted by the Senate after sensational trials. Behind both impeachments lay intensely partisan politics. Chase, a Federalist, was a victim of attacks on the Supreme Court by Jeffersonian Democrats, who had planned to impeach Chief Justice John Marshall if Chase was convicted. President Johnson was a victim of Radical Republicans opposed to his reconstruction policies after the Civil War.

The power of the impeachment process was dramatically demonstrated in 1974 when the House of Representatives initiated an inquiry into the conduct of President Richard Nixon as a result of charges arising out of a 1972 break-in at Democratic National Headquarters in the Watergate Office Building in Washington. The House Judiciary Committee adopted three articles of impeachment against Nixon late in July 1974. The articles charged him with abuse of his presidential powers, obstruction of justice and contempt of Congress. Before the full House voted on these articles, Nixon resigned on Aug. 9—after being told by Republican House and Senate leaders that the evidence against him virtually assured that he would be impeached, convicted and removed from office.[3]

Purpose of Impeachment

Based on specific constitutional authority, the impeachment process was designed "as a method of national inquest into the conduct of public men," according to Alexander Hamilton in *Federalist* No. 65.[4] The Constitution

---

The Constitution on Impeachment

Article I, Section 2. "The House of Representatives...shall have the sole Power of Impeachment."

Article I, Section 3. "The Senate shall have the sole Power to try all Impeachments. When sitting for that Purpose, they shall be on Oath or Affirmation. When the President of the United States is tried, the Chief Justice shall preside: And no Person shall be convicted without the Concurrence of two-thirds of the Members present.

"Judgment in Cases of Impeachment shall not extend further than to removal from Office, and disqualification to hold and enjoy any Office of honor, Trust or Profit under the United States: but the Party convicted shall nevertheless be liable and subject to Indictment, Trial, Judgment and Punishment, according to Law."

Article II, Section 2. "The President...shall have Power to grant Reprieves and Pardons for Offenses against the United States, except in Cases of Impeachment."

Article II, Section 4. "The President, Vice President and all civil Officers of the United States, shall be removed from Office on Impeachment for, and Conviction of, Treason, Bribery, or other high Crimes and Misdemeanors."

Article III, Section 2. "The Trial of all Crimes, except in Cases of Impeachment, shall be by Jury;..."

declares that impeachment proceedings may be brought against "the President, Vice President and all civil officers of the United States," without explaining who is, or is not, a "civil officer." In practice, however, the overwhelming majority of impeachment proceedings have been directed against federal judges, who hold lifetime appointments "during good behavior," and cannot be removed by any other method. Nine of the 12 impeachment cases that have reached the Senate have involved federal judges. Federal judges have also been the subject of most of the resolutions and investigations in the House that have failed to result in impeachment.[5]

In 1953 and again in 1970, attempts were made to impeach Supreme Court Justice William O. Douglas, one after he granted a stay of execution to convicted spies Julius and Ethel Rosenberg, the other after the Senate rejected two of President Nixon's conservative Supreme Court nominees. Neither attempt moved beyond the committee stage.[6]

Others whose impeachment has been sought include Cabinet members, diplomats, customs collectors, a senator and a U.S. district attorney. These officials are subject to removal by dismissal or expulsion as well as by impeachment, and it seldom has been necessary to resort to full-scale impeachment proceedings to bring about their removal. Proceedings against the only senator to be impeached, William Blount of Tennessee, were dismissed in 1799 after Blount had been expelled from the Senate in 1797. War Secretary William W. Belknap, the only Cabinet member to be tried by the Senate, was acquitted in 1876 largely because senators questioned their authority to try Belknap, who had resigned as Secretary several months before the trial.

The House Judiciary Committee twice has ruled that certain federal officials were not subject to impeachment. In 1833, the committee determined that a territorial judge was not a civil officer within the meaning of the Constitution because he held office for only four years and could be removed at any time by the President.[7] In 1926, the committee said that a commissioner of the District of Columbia was immune from impeachment because he was an officer of the District and not a civil officer of the United States.[8]

History: Curbing the Executive

Impeachment as a constitutional process dates from 14th century England when the fledgling Parliament sought to make the King's advisers accountable. The monarch, who was considered incapable of wrongdoing, was immune. Impeachment was used against ministers and judges whom the legislature believed guilty of breaking the law or carrying out the unpopular orders of the King. The system was based on the common law and the House of Lords could inflict the death penalty on those it found guilty.

Grounds for impeachment included both criminal and noncriminal activity. Joseph Story, in his *Commentaries on the Constitution of the United States* (1905), wrote: "Lord chancellors and judges and other magistrates have not only been impeached for bribery and acting grossly contrary to the duties of their office, but for misleading their sovereign by unconstitutional opinions and for attempts to subvert the fundamental laws and introduce arbitrary power."[9]

In the mid-15th century, after the conviction of the Duke of Suffolk, impeachment fell into disuse. This was in large measure due to the ability of the Tudor monarchs to force Parliament to remove unwanted officials by bills of at-

tainder or pains and penalties. In the early 17th century, the excesses and absolutist tendencies of the Stuart kings prompted Parliament to revive its impeachment power to curb the monarch by removing his favorite aides.

The struggle between the King and the Commons came to a head with the impeachment of Charles the First's minister, the Earl of Strafford, in 1642. The Earl was impeached by the House of Commons for subverting the fundamental law and introducing an arbitrary and tyrannical government. While the charge was changed to a bill of attainder in the House of Lords, Raoul Berger writes that "his impeachment may be regarded as the opening gun in the struggle whereby the Long Parliament 'prevented the English monarchy from hardening into an absolutism of the type then becoming general in Europe.' "[10]

More than 50 impeachments were brought to the House of Lords for trial between 1620 and 1787 when the American Constitution was being written. As the framers toiled in Philadelphia, the long impeachment and trial of Warren Hastings was in progress in London. Hastings was charged with oppression, cruelty, bribery and fraud as colonial administrator and first governor general in India. The trial before the House of Lords lasted from Feb. 13, 1788, to April 23, 1795. Hastings was acquitted, but by that time, impeachment was widely regarded as unnecessary—because of ministerial responsibility to Parliament—and overly cumbersome. The last impeachment trial in Britain occurred in 1806.

Debate in Constitutional Convention

Under the English system, an impeachment (indictment) was preferred by the House of Commons and decided by the House of Lords. In America, colonial governments and early state constitutions followed the British pattern of trial before the upper legislative body on charges brought by the lower house.

Despite these precedents, a major controversy arose over the impeachment process in the Constitutional Convention. The issue was whether the Senate should try impeachments. Opposing that role for the Senate, Madison and Pinckney asserted that it would make the President too dependent on the legislative branch. Suggested alternative trial bodies included the "national judiciary," the Supreme Court or the assembled chief justices of state supreme courts. It was argued, however, that such bodies would be too small and perhaps even susceptible to corruption. In the end, the Senate was agreed to. Hamilton (a Senate opponent during the Convention) asked later in *The Federalist*: "Where else than in the Senate could have been found a tribunal sufficiently dignified, or sufficiently independent?"[11]

A lesser issue was the definition of impeachable crimes. In the original proposals, the President was to be removed on impeachment and conviction "for mal or corrupt conduct," or for "malpractice or neglect of duty." Later, the wording was changed to "treason, bribery or corruption," and then to "treason or bribery" alone. Contending that "treason or bribery" were too narrow, George Mason proposed adding "mal-administration," but switched to "other high crimes and misdemeanors against the state" when Madison said that "mal-administration" was too broad. A final revision made impeachable crimes "treason, bribery or other high crimes and misdemeanors."[12] Debate over the meaning of this phrase resumes during every serious impeachment inquiry.

The provisions of the Constitution on impeachment are scattered through the first three articles. To the House is given the "sole power of impeachment." The Senate is given "the sole power to try all impeachments." Impeachments may be brought against "the President, Vice President, and all civil officers of the United States" for "treason, bribery or other high crimes or misdemeanors." Conviction is automatically followed by "removal from office" and possibly by "disqualification to hold" further public office. (Box, p. 203)

The first attempt to use the impeachment power was made in 1796. A petition from residents of the Northwest Territory, submitted to the House on April 25, accused Judge George Turner of the territorial supreme court of arbitrary conduct. The petition was referred briefly to a special House committee and then was referred to Attorney General Charles Lee. Impeachment proceedings were dropped after Lee said, May 9, that the territorial government would prosecute Turner in the territorial courts.[13]

Procedures in Impeachment

The first impeachment proceedings, against Turner, provided no precedents for later impeachments. In fact, the process has been used so infrequently and under such widely varying circumstances that no uniform practice has emerged.

The House has no standing rules dealing with its role in the impeachment process, a role which the Constitution describes in fewer than a dozen words.

At various times impeachment proceedings have been initiated by the introduction of a resolution by a member, by a letter or message from the President, by a grand jury action forwarded to the House from a territorial legislature, by a memorial setting forth charges, by a resolution authorizing a general investigation, or by a resolution reported by the House Judiciary Committee. The five cases to reach the Senate since 1900 were based on Judiciary Committee resolutions.[14]

Before creation of the Judiciary Committee in 1813, the matter was referred to a special committee created for that purpose. This was the case in the first three impeachments which moved to the Senate, those of Sen. William Blount, Judge John Pickering and Justice Samuel Chase. The impeachment of Judge James H. Peck in 1830 was the first referred to the Judiciary Committee.[15]

After submission of the charges, a committee investigation is begun. The committee decides in each case whether the subject of the inquiry has the right to be present at committee proceedings, to be represented by counsel, to present and question witnesses.[16]

If the charges are supported by the investigation, the committee reports an impeachment resolution. Since 1912, articles of impeachment have been reported by the committee simultaneously with the resolution. Before that time, the articles were drawn up after the House had approved the resolution of impeachment.[17]

The House is no more bound by a committee's recommendation on impeachment than it is by a committee recommendation and action on any legislative matter. In 1933, the House Judiciary Committee found insufficient grounds to recommend impeachment of Judge Harold Louderback, but the House impeached the judge anyway.[18] The target of an impeachment resolution is impeached if the House adopts a resolution of impeachment by majority vote. The articles of impeachment may be approved by a simple majority, and may be amended on the House floor. When the articles of impeachment against President Andrew Johnson were considered by the full House in 1868, two additional articles were adopted along with those recommended by the committee.[19]

After the resolution and the articles have been adopted by the House, the House managers are selected to present the case for impeachment to the Senate, acting as prosecutors in the Senate trial. An odd number—ranging from five to 11—has traditionally been selected, including members from both parties who voted in favor of impeachment. They have been selected in various ways—by ballot, with a majority vote necessary for election; by resolution naming the slate; or by the Speaker.[20] The full House may attend the trial, but the House managers are its official representatives in the Senate proceedings.

The Senate

In 1868, for the impeachment trial of President Johnson, the Senate adopted a set of 25 rules for those proceedings. One new rule was added in 1935. (Text of rules, pp. 206-207)

The trial is conducted in a fashion similar to a criminal trial. Both sides may present witnesses and evidence, and the defendant is allowed counsel, the right to testify in his own behalf and the right of cross-examination. If the President or the Vice President is on trial, the Constitution requires the Chief Justice of the Supreme Court to preside. The Constitution is silent on a presiding officer for lesser defendants, but Senate practice has been for the Vice President or the president pro tempore to preside.

The presiding officer can issue all orders needed to compel witnesses to appear or to enforce obedience to Senate orders. The presiding officer administers the oath to all the senators before they take part in the trial. The presiding officer rules on all questions of evidence and his ruling stands unless he decides to submit the question to a vote of the Senate or unless a senator requests such a vote. Custom dictates that most questions concerning the admissibility of evidence are submitted to the Senate for decision. The presiding officer questions witnesses, and asks questions submitted to him in writing by various senators, who do not directly question witnesses themselves.

All of the Senate's orders and decisions during an impeachment trial are made by roll-call vote, and without debate—unless in secret session. On the final question—guilt or innocence—each senator is limited to 15 minutes of debate in secret session. The Senate votes separately on each article of impeachment; the Constitution requires a two-thirds vote for conviction. If no article is approved by two-thirds of the senators present, the impeached official is acquitted. If any article receives two-thirds approval, he is convicted. The Senate then votes to remove him from office. If desired, the Senate may also vote to disqualify him from holding future federal offices. Disqualification is not mandatory; only two of the four convictions have been accompanied by disqualification, which is decided by a majority vote. (Congressional votes on impeachment p. 208)

Records, Resignations and Recesses

The shortest time from House impeachment to Senate verdict was one month—in the impeachment of federal Judge Halsted Ritter in 1936. The longest time was one year—in the early impeachments of Pickering and Chase. The impeachment of Andrew Johnson took three months from House action to Senate judgment.

(Continued on p. 208)

Senate Rules of Procedure and Practice...

Following are the major provisions of rules used by the Senate during impeachment trials. With the exception of Rule XI, which was adopted May 28, 1935, the rules have remained unchanged since their adoption March 2, 1868, for the trial of President Andrew Johnson.

I. Whensoever the Senate shall receive notice from the House of Representatives that managers are appointed on their part to conduct an impeachment against any person and are directed to carry articles of impeachment to the Senate, the Secretary of the Senate shall immediately inform the House of Representatives that the Senate is ready to receive the managers for the purpose of exhibiting such articles of impeachment, agreeably to such notice.

II. When the managers of an impeachment shall be introduced at the bar of the Senate and shall signify that they are ready to exhibit articles of impeachment against any person, the Presiding Officer of the Senate shall direct the Sergeant at Arms to make proclamation,...after which the articles shall be exhibited, and then the Presiding Officer of the Senate shall inform the managers that the Senate will take proper order on the subject of the impeachment, of which due notice shall be given to the House of Representatives.

III. Upon such articles being presented to the Senate, the Senate shall, at 1 o'clock afternoon of the day (Sunday excepted) following such presentation, or sooner if ordered by the Senate, proceed to the consideration of such articles and shall continue in session from day to day (Sundays excepted) after the trial shall commence (unless otherwise ordered by the Senate) until final judgment shall be rendered, and so much longer as may, in its judgment, be needful. Before proceeding to the consideration of the articles of impeachment, the Presiding Officer shall administer the oath hereinafter provided to the members of the Senate then present and to the other members of the Senate as they shall appear, whose duty it shall be to take the same.

IV. When the President of the United States or the Vice President of the United States, upon whom the powers and duties of the office of President shall have devolved, shall be impeached, the Chief Justice of the Supreme Court of the United States shall preside; and in a case requiring the said Chief Justice to preside notice shall be given to him by the Presiding Officer of the Senate of the time and place fixed for the consideration of the articles of impeachment, as aforesaid, with a request to attend; and the said Chief Justice shall preside over the Senate during the consideration of said articles and upon the trial of the person impeached therein.

V. The Presiding Officer shall have power to make and issue, by himself or by the Secretary of the Senate, all orders, mandates, writs, and precepts authorized by these rules or by the Senate, and to make and enforce such other regulations and orders in the premises as the Senate may authorize or provide.

VI. The Senate shall have power to compel the attendance of witnesses, to enforce obedience to its orders, mandates, writs, precepts, and judgments, to preserve order, and to punish in a summary way contempts of, and disobedience to, its authority, orders, mandates, writs, precepts, or judgments, and to make all lawful orders, rules, and regulations which it may deem essential or conducive to the ends of justice. And the Sergeant at Arms, under the direction of the Senate, may employ such aid and assistance as may be necessary to enforce, execute, and carry into effect the lawful orders, mandates, writs, and precepts of the Senate.

VII. The Presiding Officer of the Senate shall direct all necessary preparations in the Senate Chamber, and the Presiding Officer on the trial shall direct all the forms of proceedings while the Senate is sitting for the purpose of trying an impeachment, and all forms during the trial not otherwise specially provided for. And the Presiding Officer on the trial may rule all questions of evidence and incidental questions, which ruling shall stand as the judgment of the Senate, unless some member of the Senate shall ask that a formal vote be taken thereon, in which case it shall be submitted to the Senate for decision; or he may at his option, in the first instance, submit any such question to a vote of the members of the Senate. Upon all such questions the vote shall be without a division, unless the yeas and nays be demanded by one-fifth of the members present, when the same shall be taken.

VIII. Upon the presentation of articles of impeachment and the organization of the Senate as hereinbefore provided, a writ of summons shall issue to the accused, reciting said articles, and notifying him to appear before the Senate upon a day and at a place to be fixed by the Senate and named in such writ, and file his answer to said articles of impeachment, and to stand to and abide the orders and judgments of the Senate thereon; which writ shall be served by such officer or person as shall be named in the precept thereof, such number of days prior to the day fixed for such appearance as shall be named in such precept, either by the delivery of an attested copy thereof to the person accused, or if that can not conveniently be done, by leaving such copy at the last known place of abode of such person, or at his usual place of business in some conspicuous place therein; or if such service shall be, in the judgment of the Senate, impracticable, notice to the accused to appear shall be given in such other manner, by publication or otherwise, as shall be deemed just; and if the writ aforesaid shall fail of service in the manner aforesaid, the proceedings shall not thereby abate, but further service may be made in such manner as the Senate shall direct. If the accused, after service, shall fail to appear, either in person or by attorney, on the day so fixed therefor as aforesaid, or, appearing, shall fail to file his answer to such articles of impeachment, the trial shall proceed, nevertheless, as upon a plea of not guilty. If a plea of guilty shall be entered, judgment may be entered thereon without further proceedings.

IX. At 12:30 o'clock afternoon of the day appointed for the return of the summons against the person impeached, the legislative and executive business of the Senate shall be suspended, and the Secretary of the Senate shall administer an oath to the returning officer.... Which oath shall be entered at large on the records.

X. The person impeached shall then be called to appear and answer the articles of impeachment against him. If he appear, or any person for him, the appearance shall be recorded, stating particularly if by himself, or by agent or attorney, naming the person appearing and the capacity in which he appears.

...When Sitting for Impeachment Trials

If he does not appear, either personally or by agent or attorney, the same shall be recorded.

XI. That in the trial of any impeachment the Presiding Officer of the Senate, upon the order of the Senate, shall appoint a committee of twelve Senators to receive evidence and take testimony at such times and places as the committee may determine, and for such purpose the committee so appointed and the chairman thereof, to be elected by the committee, shall (unless otherwise ordered by the Senate) exercise all the powers and functions conferred upon the Senate and the Presiding Officer of the Senate, respectively, under the rules of procedure and practice in the Senate when sitting on impeachment trials.

Unless otherwise ordered by the Senate, the rules of procedure and practice in the Senate when sitting on impeachment trials shall govern the procedure and practice of the committee so appointed. The committee so appointed shall report to the Senate in writing a certified copy of the transcript of the proceedings and testimony had and given before such committee, and such report shall be received by the Senate and the evidence so received and the testimony so taken shall be considered to all intents and purposes, subject to the right of the Senate to determine competency, relevancy, and materiality, as having been received and taken before the Senate, but nothing herein shall prevent the Senate from sending for any witness and hearing his testimony in open Senate, or by order of the Senate having the entire trial in open Senate.

XII. At 12:30 o'clock afternoon of the day appointed for the trial of an impeachment, the legislative and executive business of the Senate shall be suspended, and the Secretary shall give notice to the House of Representatives that the Senate is ready to proceed upon the impeachment of, in the Senate Chamber, which chamber is prepared with accommodations for the reception of the House of Representatives.

XIII. The hour of the day at which the Senate shall sit upon the trial of an impeachment shall be (unless otherwise ordered) 12 o'clock m.; and when the hour for such thing shall arrive, the Presiding Officer of the Senate shall so announce; and thereupon the Presiding Officer upon such trial shall cause proclamation to be made, and the business of the trial shall proceed. The adjournment of the Senate sitting in said trial shall not operate as an adjournment of the Senate; but on such adjournment the Senate shall resume the consideration of its legislative and executive business.

XIV. The Secretary of the Senate shall record the proceedings in cases of impeachment as in the case of legislative proceedings, and the same shall be reported in the same manner as the legislative proceedings of the Senate.

XV. Counsel for the parties shall be admitted to appear and be heard upon an impeachment.

XVI. All motions made by the parties or their counsel shall be addressed to the Presiding Officer, and if he, or any Senator, shall require it, they shall be committed to writing, and read at the Secretary's table.

XVII. Witnesses shall be examined by one person on behalf of the party producing them, and then cross-examined by one person on the other side.

XVIII. If a Senator is called as a witness, he shall be sworn, and give his testimony standing in his place.

XIX. If a Senator wishes a question to be put to a witness, or to offer a motion or order (except a motion to adjourn), it shall be reduced to writing, and put by the Presiding Officer.

XX. At all times while the Senate is sitting upon the trial of an impeachment the doors of the Senate shall be kept open, unless the Senate shall direct the doors to be closed while deliberating upon its decisions.

XXI. All preliminary or interlocutory questions, and all motions, shall be argued for not exceeding one hour on each side, unless the Senate shall, by order, extend the time.

XXII. The case, on each side, shall be opened by one person. The final argument on the merits may be made by two persons on each side (unless otherwise ordered by the Senate upon application for that purpose), and the argument shall be opened and closed on the part of the House of Representatives.

XXIII. On the final question whether the impeachment is sustained, the yeas and nays shall be taken on each article of impeachment separately; and if the impeachment shall not, upon any of the articles presented, be sustained by the votes of two-thirds of the members present, a judgment of acquittal shall be entered; but if the person accused in such articles of impeachment shall be convicted upon any of said articles by the votes of two-thirds of the members present, the Senate shall proceed to pronounce judgment, and a certified copy of such judgment shall be deposited in the office of the Secretary of State.

XXIV. All the orders and decisions shall be made and had by yeas and nays, which shall be entered on the record, and without debate, subject, however, to the operation of Rule VII, except when the doors shall be closed for deliberation, and in that case no member shall speak more than once on one question, and for not more than ten minutes on an interlocutory question, and for not more than fifteen minutes on the final question, unless by consent of the Senate, to be had without debate; but a motion to adjourn may be decided without the yeas and nays, unless they be demanded by one-fifth of the members present. The fifteen minutes herein allowed shall be for the whole deliberation on the final question, and not on the final question on each article of impeachment.

XXV. Witness shall be sworn.... Which oath shall be administered by the Secretary, or any other duly authorized person....

All process shall be served by the Sergeant at Arms of the Senate, unless otherwise ordered by the court.

XXVI. If the Senate shall at any time fail to sit for the consideration of articles of impeachment on the day or hour fixed therefor, the Senate may, by an order to be adopted without debate, fix a day and hour for resuming such consideration.

The shortest Senate trial on record is that of Judge West H. Humphreys—which took only one day; the longest was the two months consumed in the Senate trial of President Johnson.

In general, the resignation of the official about to be impeached puts an end to impeachment proceedings since the primary objective, removal from office, has been accomplished. This was the case in the impeachment proceedings begun against two federal judges—Mark H. Delahay, impeached by voice vote Feb. 28, 1873, and George W. English, impeached by a 306-62 vote April 1, 1926—and in the case of President Nixon.[21]

However, resignation is not a foolproof way of precluding impeachment. Secretary of War William W. Belknap, aware of the findings of a congressional committee implicating him in the acceptance of bribes, resigned at 10 o'clock on the morning of March 2, 1876. Sometime after 3 o'clock that afternoon, the House impeached him by voice vote. The Senate debated the question of its jurisdiction, in light of his resignation, and decided by a vote of 37-29 that he could be impeached and tried despite his no longer being in office. He was found not guilty of the charges.[22]

Historical precedent indicates that an impeachment proceeding does not die with adjournment. In 1890-91 the Judiciary Committee investigated the conduct of a federal judge and decided that he should be impeached; a resolution to that effect was reported in 1891 and the House began debate, but did not conclude it before adjournment. In the new Congress in 1892, the evidence taken in the first investigation was referred to the committee again, a second investigation was conducted and the committee decided against impeachment.[23]

Congressional Votes on Impeachment, 1797-1936

The following table shows the votes by which the 13 federal officials impeached prior to 1976 were impeached by the House, and the subsequent Senate votes on their cases. The dates in parentheses are the dates on which the votes were taken.

The **series of votes** following some of the "guilty" or "not guilty" verdicts of the Senate are the **votes on each article of impeachment.** Although only a majority vote by the House is required to impeach, a two-thirds vote by the Senate is required to convict on any article of impeachment. After a man is found guilty on any of the articles, the Senate votes on whether to remove him from office—that vote is carried by a majority. Sometimes the Senate goes beyond that vote and votes on disqualifying the man from any future federal office; that vote too requires only majority approval.

	House	Senate		House	Senate
Blount	Voice (July 7, 1797)	Dismissed, 14-11 (Jan. 11, 1799)	Belknap	Voice (March 2, 1876)	Not guilty, 35-25, 36-25, 36-25, 36-25. 37-25. (Aug. 1, 1876)
Pickering	45-8 (March 2, 1803)	Guilty, 19-7, 19-7, 19-7, 19-7 Removed from office, 20-6 (March 12, 1804)	Swayne	Voice (Dec. 13, 1904)	Not guilty, 33-49, 32-50, 32-50, 13-69, 13-69, 31-51, 19-63, 31-51, 31-51, 31-51, 35-47. (Feb. 27, 1905)
Chase	73-32 (March 12, 1804)	Not guilty, 16-18, 10-24, 18-16, 18-16, 0-34 4-30, 10-24, 19-15 (March 1, 1805)			
Peck	123-49 (April 24, 1830)	Not guilty, 21-22 (Jan. 31, 1831)	Archbald	223-1 (July 11, 1912)	Guilty, 68-5, 46-25, 60-11, 52-20, 66-6, 24-45, 29-36, 22-42, 23-39, 1-65, 11-51, 19-46, 42-20.
Humphreys	Voice (May 6, 1862)	Guilty, 39-0, 36-1, 33-4, 28-10, 39-0, 36-1 12-24, 35-1, 35-1 Removed from office, 38-0 Disqualified from future office, 36-0 (June 26, 1862)			Removed, voice. Disqualified, 39-35 (Jan. 13, 1913)
			English	306-62 (April 1, 1926)	Dismissed, 70-9 (Dec. 13, 1926)
			Louderback	183-142 (Feb. 24, 1933)	Not guilty, 34-42, 23-47, 11-63, 30-47, 45-34 (May 24, 1933)
Johnson	57-108 against impeachment (Dec. 6, 1867)		Ritter	181-146 (March 2, 1936)	Guilty, 55-29, 52-32, 44-39, 36-48, 36-48 46-37, 56-28.
	126-47 for impeachment (Feb. 24, 1868)	Not Guilty, 35-19, 35-19, 35-19 (May 16, 26, 1868)			
Delahay	Voice (Feb. 28, 1873)	None			Removed, voice. Not disqualified, 0-76 against. (April 17, 1936)

Sources: *Impeachment: Selected Materials on Procedure,* House Committee on the Judiciary, January 1974; *Congressional Globe* 1868; Ritter data, *Congressional Record,* Vol. 80, April 17, 1936.

In the case of the impeachment of Judge Pickering, the House impeached him, but adjourned before drawing up articles of impeachment, which a committee appointed in the next Congress did do.[24]

Whether impeachment would have to begin again if the House impeached a man in one Congress, but the Senate trial could not begin until the next is unclear—although the view of the Senate as a continuing body according to custom, would indicate that the trial could begin in the new Congress without a repetition of the House procedures. The Senate did decide in 1876 that a trial of impeachment could proceed only when Congress was in session. The vote was 21-19.[25]

Controversial Questions

Three major questions have dominated the history of impeachment in the United States:

- What is an impeachable offense?
- Can senators serve as impartial jurors?
- Are there ways other than impeachment to remove a federal judge from office?

Impeachable Offenses

"Treason" and "bribery," as constitutionally designated impeachable crimes, have raised little debate, for treason is defined elsewhere in the Constitution and bribery is a well-defined act. "High crimes and misdemeanors," however, have been anything that the prosecution has wanted to make them. (In the 1970 attempt to impeach Supreme Court Justice William O. Douglas, then Rep. Gerald R. Ford (R Mich.) declared: "An impeachable offense is whatever a majority of the House of Representatives considers it to be at a given moment in history.")[26] An endless debate has surrounded the phrase, pitting broad constructionists, who have viewed impeachment as a political weapon, against narrow constructionists, who have regarded impeachment as being limited to offenses indictable at common law.

The constitutional debates seemed to indicate that impeachment was to be regarded as a political weapon. Narrow constructionists quickly won a major victory, though, when Supreme Court Justice Samuel Chase was acquitted, using as a defense the argument that the charges against him were not an indictable offense. President Johnson also won acquittal using a similar defense. His lawyers argued that conviction could result only from commission of high criminal offenses against the United States.[27]

The only two convictions to date in the 20th century suggest that the arguments of the broad constructionists still carry considerable weight. The 20th century convictions removed Robert W. Archbald, associate judge of the U.S. Commerce Court, in 1913, and Halsted L. Ritter, U.S. judge for the southern district of Florida, in 1936. Archbald was convicted of soliciting for himself and for friends valuable favors from railroad companies, some of which were litigants in his court. It was conceded, however, that he had committed no indictable offense.[28] Ritter was convicted for conduct in a receivership case which raised serious doubts about his integrity.[29]

This debate resumed in 1974 with the impeachment inquiry into the conduct of President Nixon. The impeachment inquiry staff of the House Judiciary Committee argued for a broad view of "high crimes and misdemeanors"

while Nixon's defense attorneys argued for a narrow view. *(Debate, p. 210)*

As adopted by the House Judiciary Committee, Article I charged the President with obstruction of justice, a charge falling within the narrow view of impeachable offenses. Articles II and III reflected the broader interpretation, charging Nixon with abuse of his presidential powers and contempt of Congress. *(Text of articles, appendix)*

Conflicts of Interest

An equally controversial issue, particularly in earlier impeachment trials, concerned the partisan political interests of senators, which raised serious doubt about their ability to sit as impartial jurors.

President Johnson's potential successor, for example, was the president pro tempore of the Senate, since there was a vacancy in the vice presidency. Sen. Benjamin F. Wade (R Ohio), president pro tempore, took part in the trial and voted—for conviction. On the other hand, Andrew Johnson's son-in-law, Sen. David T. Patterson (D Tenn.), also took part in the trial and voted—for acquittal.

In the Johnson trial and in others, senators have been outspoken critics or supporters of the defendant, yet have participated in the trial and have voted on the articles. Some senators who had held seats in the House when the articles of impeachment first came up, and had voted on them there, have failed to disqualify themselves during the trial. On occasion, intense outside lobbying for, and against, the defendant has been aimed at senators. Senators have testified as witnesses at some trials and then voted on the articles.

Senators may request to be excused from the trial, and in recent cases senators have disqualified themselves when possible conflicts of interest arose.

Removal of Judges

Two forces have encouraged a continuing search for an alternative method of removing federal judges. One force has been led by members of Congress anxious to free the Senate, faced by an enormous legislative workload, from the time consuming process of sitting as a court of impeachment. The other force has been led by members anxious to restrict judicial power by providing a simpler and swifter means of removal than the cumbersome and unwieldy impeachment process.

The search to date has been unsuccessful. Efforts to revise and accelerate the impeachment process have failed. So, too, have attempts to amend the Constitution to limit the tenure of federal judges to a definite term of years. A more recent approach has been to seek legislation providing for a judicial trial and judgment of removal for federal judges violating "good-behavior" standards. The House passed such a bill on Oct. 22, 1941, by a 124-122 vote, but it died in the Senate.

Attempted Impeachments

Several proposed impeachments have failed to come to a vote in the House because the defendant died or because he resigned or received another appointment, removing him from the disputed office. Among the unsuccessful impeachment attempts have been moves against two Presidents, a Vice President, two Cabinet officers, and a Supreme Court justice.[30]

(Continued on p. 211)

Constitutional Grounds for Presidential Impeachment

The debate over the meaning of "high crimes and misdemeanors" resumed with vigor in early 1974. The broad interpretation of this phrase was endorsed in a memorandum prepared by members of the House Judiciary Committee impeachment inquiry staff; the narrow interpretation in an analysis by members of President Nixon's defense team. Excerpts from both documents follow:

Official Misconduct*

"The framers intended impeachment to be a constitutional safeguard of the public trust, the powers of government conferred upon the President...and the division of powers....

"Each of the thirteen American impeachments involved charges of misconduct incompatible with the official position of the officeholder. This conduct falls into three broad categories: 1) exceeding the constitutional bounds of the powers of the office in derogation of the powers of another branch of government; 2) behaving in a manner grossly incompatible with the proper function and purpose of the office; and 3) employing the power of the office for an improper purpose or for personal gain....

"In drawing up articles of impeachment, the House has placed little emphasis on criminal conduct....

"All have involved charges of conduct incompatible with continued performance of the office; some have explicitly rested upon a 'course of conduct'.... Some of the individual articles seem to have alleged conduct that, taken alone, would not have been considered serious....

"Impeachment and the criminal law serve fundamentally different purposes. Impeachment is the first step in a remedial process.... The purpose...is not personal punishment; its function is primarily to maintain constitutional government....

"The general applicability of the criminal law also makes it inappropriate as the standard.... In an impeachment proceeding a President is called to account for abusing powers which only a President possesses.

"Impeachable conduct...may include the serious failure to discharge the affirmative duties imposed on the President by the Constitution. Unlike a criminal case, the cause for removal...may be based on his entire course of conduct in office.... It may be a course of conduct more than individual acts that has a tendency to subvert constitutional government.

"To confine impeachable conduct to indictable offenses may well be to set a standard so restrictive as not to reach conduct that might adversely affect the system of government. Some of the most grievous offenses against our constitutional form of government may not entail violations of the criminal law....

"To limit impeachable conduct to criminal offenses would be incompatible with the evidence...and would frustrate the purpose that the framers intended....

"In the English practice and in several of the American impeachments, the criminality issue was not raised at all. The emphasis has been on the significant effect of the conduct.... Impeachment was evolved...to cope with both the inadequacy of criminal standards and the impotence of the courts to deal with the conduct of great public figures. It would be anomalous if the framers, having barred criminal sanctions from the impeachment remedy...intended to restrict the grounds for impeachment to conduct that was criminal."

Crimes Against the State**

"To argue that the President may be impeached for something less than a criminal offense, with all the safeguards that definition implies, would be a monumental step backwards into all those old English practices that our Constitution sought to eliminate. American impeachment was not designed to force a President into surrendering executive authority...but to check overtly criminal actions as they are defined by law....

"The terminology 'high crimes and misdemeanors' should create no confusion or ambiguity.... It was a unitary phrase meaning crimes against the state, as opposed to those against individuals.... It is as ridiculous to say that 'misdemeanor' must mean something beyond 'crime' as it is to suggest that in the phrase 'bread and butter issues' butter issues must be different from bread issues....

"The acquittal of President Johnson over a century ago strongly indicates that the Senate has refused to adopt a broad view of 'other high crimes and misdemeanors'.... Impeachment of a President should be resorted to only for cases of the gravest kind—the commission of a crime named in the Constitution or a criminal offense against the laws of the United States. If there is any doubt as to the gravity of an offense or as to a President's conduct or motives, the doubt should be resolved in his favor. This is the necessary price for having an independent executive....

"Any analysis that broadly construes the power to impeach and convict can be reached only...by placing a subjective gloss on the history of impeachment that results in permitting the Congress to do whatever it deems most politic. The intent of the Framers, who witnessed episode after episode of outrageous abuse of the impeachment power by the self-righteous English Parliament, was to restrict the *political* reach of the impeachment power.

"Those who seek to broaden the impeachment power invite the use of power 'as a means of crushing political adversaries or ejecting them from office.'.... The acceptance of such an invitation would be destructive to our system of government and to the fundamental principle of separation of powers.... The Framers never intended that the impeachment clause serve to dominate or destroy the executive branch of the government...."

Sources: *U.S. Congress, House, Committee on the Judiciary, *Constitutional Grounds for Presidential Impeachment*, 93rd Cong., 2nd sess., 1974. **"An Analysis of the Constitutional Standards for Presidential Impeachment," February 1974, prepared by James D. St. Clair, John J. Chester, Michael A. Sterlacci, Jerome J. Murphy and Loren A. Smith, attorneys for President Nixon.

Tyler. The House on Jan. 10, 1843, rejected by an 84-127 vote a resolution by Rep. John M. Botts to investigate the possibility of initiating impeachment proceedings against President Tyler. Tyler had become a political outcast, ostracized by both Democrats and Whigs, but impeachment apparently was too strong a measure to take against him.

Colfax. A move developed in 1873 to impeach Vice President Schuyler Colfax because of his involvement in the Crédit Mobilier scandal. The matter was dropped when the Judiciary Committee recommended against impeachment on the ground that Colfax had purchased his Crédit Mobilier stock before becoming Vice President.

Daugherty. A similar move to impeach Attorney General Harry M. Daugherty in 1922 on account of his action, or lack of action, in the Teapot Dome affair was dropped in 1923 when a congressional investigation of the scandal got under way. Daugherty was forced by President Coolidge to tender his resignation, March 28, 1924.

Mellon. A running fight between Rep. Wright Patman (D Texas) and Secretary of the Treasury Andrew W. Mellon over federal economic policy in the depression came to a head in 1932. Patman on Jan. 6 demanded Mellon's impeachment on the ground of conflicting financial interests. To put an end to that move, President Hoover on Feb. 5 nominated Mellon to be ambassador to Great Britain and the Senate confirmed the nomination the same day. Mellon resigned his Treasury post a week later to take on his new duties.

Hoover. Two depression-era attempts by Rep. Louis T. McFadden (R Pa.) to impeach President Hoover on general charges of usurping legislative powers and violating constitutional and statutory law were rejected by the House. The first attempt was tabled Dec. 13, 1932, by a 361-8 vote; the second attempt was tabled Jan. 17, 1933, by a 344-11 vote.

Douglas. Associate Justice William O. Douglas of the Supreme Court was subjected to several impeachment attempts. The day after Douglas granted a stay of execution to Soviet spies Julius and Ethel Rosenberg in June 1953, Rep. W. M. Wheeler (D Ga.) introduced a resolution to impeach the justice. The resolution was unanimously tabled by the Judiciary Committee in July, after a one-day hearing at which Wheeler had been the sole witness. In April 1970 two resolutions for Douglas' impeachment were introduced in the midst of a bitter conflict between President Nixon and the Senate over Senate rejection of two Supreme Court nominations. Among the charges cited were possible financial conflicts similar to those that had led to Senate rejection of the Nixon nominees for the Court. A special House Judiciary Subcommittee on Dec. 3 voted 3-1 that no grounds existed for impeachment.

Officials Impeached

The House has impeached 13 federal officers.[31]

1. Name: William Blount (1797-99). **Position:** Senator. **Charge:** Conspiring to carry on a military expedition for the purpose of conquering Spanish territory for Great Britain. **Decision:** Senate dismissed impeachment proceedings after voting to expel Blount.

On July 3, 1797, President John Adams sent to the House and Senate a letter from Sen. William Blount (Tenn.) to James Carey, a U.S. interpreter to the Cherokee Nation of Indians. The letter told of Blount's plans to launch an attack by Indians and frontiersmen, aided by a British fleet, against Louisiana and Spanish Florida to achieve their transfer to British control. Adams' action initiated the first proceedings to result in impeachment by the House and consideration by the Senate.

In the Senate, Blount's letter was referred to a select committee, which recommended his expulsion for "a high misdemeanor, entirely inconsistent with his public trust and duty as a Senator." The Senate expelled Blount on July 8 by a 25-1 vote.

The House, meanwhile, July 7 adopted a committee resolution impeaching Blount, and on the same day it appointed a committee to prepare articles of impeachment. On Jan. 29, 1798, the House adopted five articles accusing Blount of attempting to influence the Indians for the benefit of the British.

Senate proceedings did not begin until Dec. 17, 1798. Blount challenged the proceedings, contending that they violated his right to a trial by jury, that he was not a civil officer within the meaning of the Constitution, that he was not charged with a crime committed while a civil officer, and that courts of common law were competent to try him on the charges. On Jan. 11, 1799, the Senate by a 14-11 vote dismissed the charges for lack of jurisdiction. Citing the Senate vote, Vice President Thomas Jefferson ruled Jan. 14, that the Senate was without jurisdiction in the case, thus ending the proceedings.

2. Name: John Pickering (1803-04). **Position:** Federal judge. **Charge:** Misconduct in a trial and being intoxicated. **Decision:** Removal from office.

In a partisan move to oust a Federalist judge, President Jefferson on Feb. 4, 1803, sent a complaint to the House citing John Pickering, U.S. judge for the district of New Hampshire. The complaint was referred to a special committee, and on March 2 the House adopted a committee resolution impeaching the judge. A committee was appointed Oct. 20 to prepare articles of impeachment, and the House on Dec. 30 by voice vote agreed to four articles charging Pickering with irregular judicial procedures, loose morals and drunkenness. The judge, who was known to be insane at the time, did not attend the Senate trial, which began March 8, 1804, and ended March 12, with votes of 19-7 for conviction on each of the four articles. The Senate then voted 20-6 to remove Pickering from office, but it declined to consider disqualifying him from further office.

3. Name: Samuel Chase (1804-05). **Position:** Associate Justice of the Supreme Court. **Charge:** Misconduct in trials impairing the court's respect. **Decision:** Acquitted.

In an equally partisan attack on another Federalist judge, the House on Jan. 7, 1804, by an 81-40 vote adopted a resolution for an investigation of Chase and of Richard Peters, a U.S. district court judge in Pennsylvania. Ostensibly, the investigation was to study their conduct during a recent treason trial. The House dropped further action against Peters by voice vote on March 12. On the same day, by a 73-32 vote, it adopted a committee resolution to impeach Chase. A committee was appointed to draw up articles, and the House in a series of votes on Dec. 4, 1804, agreed to the eight articles, charging Chase with harsh and partisan conduct on the bench and with unfairness to litigants.

The trial began Feb. 9, 1805; Chase appeared in person. The Senate voting on March 1 failed to produce the two-thirds majority required for conviction on any of the eight articles; "not guilty" votes outnumbered the "guilty" votes on five of the articles.

President Andrew Johnson's Impeachment in 1868:...

Impeachment is the ultimate limitation on the power of the President. The only presidential impeachment occurred in 1868. President Andrew Johnson was charged with violation of a federal statute, the Tenure of Office Act. But, in addition, the procedure was a profoundly political struggle.

Questions such as control of the Republican Party, how to deal with the South in a state of chaos following the Civil War, and monetary and economic policy all had an effect on the process.

Johnson as President was an anomaly. Lincoln's running mate in 1864, he was a southerner at a time when the South was out of the Union; a Jacksonian Democrat who believed in states' rights, hard money, and minimal federal government activity running with an administration pursuing a policy of expansion both in the money supply and the role of government.

Johnson had been the only member of the U.S. Senate from a seceding southern state (Tennessee) to remain loyal to the Union in 1861. Lincoln later made him military governor of Tennessee and chose him as his running mate in 1864.

On Lincoln's death in 1865, this outsider without allies or connections in the Republican Party succeeded to the presidency. Johnson's ideas on what should have been done to reconstruct and readmit the southern states to representation clashed with the wishes of a majority of Congress, overwhelmingly controlled by the Republicans.

Congress was divided into roughly three groups. The small minority of Democrats supported the President. About half the Republicans were known as "radicals" because they favored strong action to revolutionize southern society, by harsh military means if necessary. The other half of the Republicans were more conservative; while unwilling to go as far as the radicals, they wanted to make sure the South did not return to the unquestioned control of those who ruled it before the Civil War.

Upon taking office, Johnson began to pursue Lincoln's mild and tolerant reconstruction plans. The new President felt that a few basics were all that needed to be secured: abolition of slavery; ratification of the Thirteenth Amendment, which abolished slavery in all states; repudiation of all state debts contracted by the Confederate governments; nullification of secession. When the southern states had done these things, Johnson felt they should be readmitted.

But Republicans wanted more: a Freedmen's Bureau, to protect and provide services for the ex-slaves, a civil rights bill guaranteeing blacks their rights, and an overall plan of reconstruction providing for temporary military governments in the South. Throughout 1866, Johnson and Congress battled over these issues.

The Tenure of Office Act, the violation of which was to be the legal basis for Johnson's impeachment, was passed over his veto March 2, 1867. The act forbade the President to remove civil officers (appointed with the consent of the Senate) without the approval of the Senate. Its purpose was to protect incumbent Republican officeholders from executive retaliation if they did not support the President.

Unsuccessful Ashley Resolution

About the time the Tenure of Office Act was being debated, the first moves toward impeachment began. On Jan. 7, 1867, Rep. James M. Ashley (R Ohio 1859-69) rose on a question of privilege and formally charged the President with high crimes and misdemeanors.

Ashley made general charges, and no specific violations of law were mentioned. Most members recognized the charges as basically political grievances rather than illegal acts. The matter was referred to the House Judiciary Committee, which reported on March 2, 1867, two days before the expiration of the 39th Congress, that the committee had reached no conclusion.

On March 7, 1867, the third day of the 40th Congress, Ashley again introduced his resolution, and it was referred to the Judiciary Committee for further investigation. The committee studied the matter throughout the year and on Nov. 25, 1867, reported an impeachment resolution. When the House voted on the matter on Dec. 7, the radicals suffered a crushing defeat. The resolution calling for impeachment was turned down, 57 to 108.

4. Name: James H. Peck (1830-31). **Position:** Federal judge. **Charge:** Misconduct in office by misuse of contempt power. **Decision:** Acquitted.

On Jan. 7, 1830, the House adopted a resolution authorizing an investigation of Peck's conduct. On April 24, the House by a 123-49 vote adopted a Judiciary Committee resolution impeaching Peck, and later the same day it appointed a committee to prepare articles of impeachment. A single article was adopted May 1 by voice vote charging Peck with setting an unreasonable and oppressive penalty for contempt of court. The trial stretched from Dec. 20, 1830, to Jan. 31, 1831, when 21 senators voted for conviction and 22 for acquittal.

5. Name: West H. Humphreys (1862). **Position:** Federal judge. **Charge:** Supported secession and held Confederate office. **Decision:** Removed from office.

During the Civil War, Humphreys, a U.S. judge for the east, middle and west districts of Tennessee, accepted an appointment as a Confederate judge, without resigning from his Union judicial assignment. Aware of the situation the House on Jan. 8, 1862, by voice vote adopted a resolution authorizing an inquiry. On May 6, the House, also by voice vote, adopted a Judiciary Committee resolution impeaching Humphreys. On May 19, seven articles of impeachment were adopted.

Humphreys could not be personally served with the impeachment summons because he had fled Union territory. He neither appeared at the trial nor contested the charges. In a one-day trial June 26, the Senate convicted Humphreys on all except one charge, removed him from office by a 38-0 vote and disqualified him from further office on a 36-0 vote.

...An Inevitable Clash With an Unpopular President

Successful Second Try

Johnson had long wanted to rid himself of Secretary of War Edwin M. Stanton. Stanton was a close ally of the radical Republicans. After repeatedly trying to get him to resign, Johnson suspended him on Dec. 12, 1867. On Jan. 13, 1868, the Senate refused to concur, thus, under the terms of the Tenure of Office Act, reinstating Stanton.

Apparently flushed by his recent victory on the impeachment issue in the House, Johnson decided to force the issue. He dismissed Stanton on Feb. 21, citing the power and authority vested in him by the Constitution.

This action enraged Congress, driving conservative Republicans into alliance with the radicals on impeachment. A House resolution on impeachment was immediately offered and was referred to the Committee on Reconstruction, headed by Rep. Thaddeus Stevens of Pennsylvania, one of the radical Republican leaders. The next day, Feb. 22, the committee reported a resolution favoring impeachment. The House vote, taken two days later, was 126 to 47 in favor, on a strict party-line basis.

Trial in the Senate

The House March 2-3 approved specific articles of impeachment and appointed managers to present and argue the charges before the Senate. There were 11 articles in all, the main one concerning Johnson's removal of Stanton in contravention of the Tenure of Office Act. *(Text of articles, appendix)*

Between the time of the House action and the beginning of the trial in the Seante, the conservative Republicans had time to reflect. One of the main objects of their reflection was fiery Ben Wade of Ohio. Wade was president pro tempore of the Senate and, under the succession law then in effect, was next in line for the presidency. He was also one of the most radical of the radical Republicans, a hard-liner on southern reconstruction and a monetary expansionist.

The impeachment trial opened March 30, 1868. The managers for the House were John A. Bingham (R Ohio), George S. Boutwell (R Mass.), James F. Wilson (R Iowa), Benjamin F. Butler (R Mass.), Thomas Williams (R Pa.), John A. Logan (R Ill.) and Stevens. The President did not appear at the trial. He was represented by a team of lawyers headed by Henry Stanbery, who had resigned as Attorney General to lead the defense. Associated with Stanbery were Benjamin R. Curtis, Jeremiah S. Black, William M. Evarts, Thomas A. R. Nelson and William S. Groesbeck.

After weeks of argument and testimony, the Senate on May 16 took a test vote on Article XI, a general, catch-all charge, thought by the House managers most likely to produce a vote for conviction. The drama of the vote has become legendary. With 36 "guiltys" needed for conviction, the final count was guilty, 35, not guilty, 19.

Seven Republicans joined the 12 Democrats in supporting Johnson. Stunned by the setback, Senate opponents of the President postponed further voting until May 26. Votes were taken then on Article II and Article III. By identical 35-19 votes Johnson was acquitted also on these articles. To head off further defeats for Johnson opponents, Sen. George H. Williams (Union Republican Ore.) moved to adjourn *sine die,* and the motion was adopted 34-16, abruptly ending the trial.

The Tenure of Office Act was virtually repealed early in Grant's administration, once the Republicans had control of the appointing power, and was entirely repealed in 1887. And in 1926, the Supreme Court declared, "The power to remove...executive officers...is an incident of the power to appoint them, and is in its nature an executive power" *(Myers v. United States,* 272 U.S. 52). The opinion, written by Chief Justice William Howard Taft, himself a former President, referred to the Tenure of Office Act and declared that it had been unconstitutional.

Sources: Michael Les Benedict, *The Impeachment and Trial of Andrew Johnson* (New York: W. W. Norton and Co. Inc., 1973). Raoul Berger, *Impeachment: The Constitutional Problems* (Cambridge: Harvard University Press, 1973). James G. Blaine, *Twenty Years of Congress, 1861-1881* (Norwich, Conn.: The Henry Hill Publishing Co., 1886).

6. Name: Andrew Johnson (1867-68). **Position:** President of the United States. **Charge:** That he removed the Secretary of War contrary to an act of Congress and criticized Congress. **Decision:** Acquitted.

The House adopted a resolution in 1867 authorizing the Judiciary Committee to inquire into the conduct of President Johnson. A majority of the committee recommended impeachment, but the House voted against the resolution 57-108. In January 1868, however, the House authorized an inquiry by the Committee on Reconstruction, which on Feb. 22 reported an impeachment resolution the day after President Johnson had removed Secretary of War Edwin M. Stanton from office. The House Feb. 24 voted to impeach Johnson, 126-47.

Nine of the 11 articles drawn by a select committee and adopted by the House on March 2 and 3 related solely to the President's removal of Stanton; articles 10 and 11 were broader in scope. The trial began March 30, 1868. When voting began in mid-May, the Senate voted only on three of the articles. Johnson was acquitted on each, 35 "guilty" to 19 "not guilty," one vote short of the two-thirds required to convict. *(Details above)*

7. Name: Mark H. Delahay (1873). **Position:** Federal judge. **Charge:** Misconduct in office, unsuitable personal habits, including intoxication. **Decision:** Resigned before articles of impeachment prepared, hence no Senate action.

In 1872 the House adopted a resolution authorizing an investigation of district Judge Delahay. The Judiciary Committee in 1873 proposed a resolution of impeachment, which the House adopted. Delahay resigned before the articles of impeachment were prepared, and the matter was not pursued further by the House.

(Continued on p. 215)

Example of Nixon (handwritten annotation)

President Nixon Resigns in Face of Impeachment

In the case of President Richard Nixon, the process of impeachment did not move beyond its first stage—and yet it realized its purpose. Ten days after the House Judiciary Committee recommended that Nixon be impeached for obstruction of justice, abuse of power and contempt of Congress, Nixon resigned. In the face of certain impeachment by the House and removal by the Senate, he chose to leave the White House voluntarily.

The impeachment inquiry was but one in the chain of events which brought about Nixon's premature departure from the presidency—a chain which began on June 17, 1972, with a burglary at Democratic National Headquarters in the Watergate Office Building in Washington, D.C.

But the work of the House Judiciary Committee and its dramatic conclusion—a televised debate involving all 38 members—were crucial in preparing the nation to accept the resignation of the man elected President by an overwhelming vote less than two years earlier.

Nixon precipitated the inquiry with the "Saturday night massacre"—his firing on Oct. 20, 1973, of the first Watergate Special Prosecutor, Archibald Cox. Cox was persisting in his effort to force Nixon to release tapes of certain of his conversations following—and, Cox suspected, concerning—the Watergate break-in.

On the Monday following the Cox firing a flurry of impeachment resolutions were introduced in the House and referred to the House Judiciary Committee. On Feb. 6, 1974, the House formally authorized the committee "to investigate fully and completely whether sufficient grounds exist for the House of Representatives to exercise its constitutional power to impeach Richard M. Nixon, President...." The vote was 410-4.

"We cannot turn away, out of partisanship or convenience, from problems that are now...our inescapable responsibility to consider," said Judiciary Committee Chairman Peter W. Rodino Jr. (D N.J.). "It would be a violation of our own public trust if we...chose not to inquire, not to consult, not even to deliberate...."

Aware of the import of their task, the committee approached it deliberately. From February to May, the staff, led by former Assistant Attorney General John M. Doar, assembled evidence related to the various charges against the President, which ranged from Watergate-related matters to questions of his personal finances. The committee subpoenaed the President for additional material. Nixon refused to comply, although he did release edited transcripts of a number of the tapes of the conversations the committee sought.

On May 9, the committee began considering the evidence in executive session, a process which continued until mid-July. President Nixon was represented at the proceedings by James D. St. Clair, his chief defense counsel and a noted Boston trial attorney.

On July 18-19, the committee heard Doar and St. Clair summarize the arguments. Doar advocated impeachment, telling the committee that "reasonable men acting reasonably would find the President guilty" of abusing his presidential powers. Defending the President, St. Clair argued that there was a "complete absence of any conclusive evidence demonstrating Presidential wrongdoing sufficient to justify the grave action of impeachment."

On July 24 a unanimous Supreme Court rejected Nixon's claim of executive privilege to withhold evidence sought by the Watergate Special Prosecutor. Nixon, the court ruled, must comply with subpoenas for the tapes of certain of his conversations.

Hours later, on the evening of July 24, before blazing lights and whirring television cameras, the Judiciary Committee began the final phase of its inquiry. For the first time, each of its 38 members spoke publicly to the nation to give his views on the evidence.

By the end of the evening the outcome was clear. Seven of the 17 Republicans indicated that they would support impeachment. All of the Democrats agreed. The vote would be bipartisan—recommending impeachment.

Paramount in the minds of some who spoke was the question of the historical impact of a decision against impeachment. "What if we fail to impeach?" asked Rep. Walter Flowers (D Ala.). "Do we ingrain forever in the very fabric of our Constitution a standard of conduct in our highest office that in the least is deplorable, and at worst is impeachable?"

Four days after the debate began, on the evening of Saturday, July 27, the decisive roll-call came. By a vote of 27-11, the committee approved the first article of impeachment, charging Nixon with obstructing justice, primarily in the Watergate investigation. Six Republicans joined all 21 Democrats to approve it.

The second article, charging abuse of power, was approved July 29, by the even wider margin of 28-10. The third, charging contempt of Congress, was approved July 30, 21-17. Two other proposed articles were rejected. Its work completed, the committee adjourned late on the evening of July 30. *(Text of articles, appendix)*

House debate on impeachment was to begin Aug. 19; the outcome was considered a certainty. The Senate began preparing for a trial. Public opinion swung heavily in favor of impeachment and, for the first time, polls showed a majority of the American people in favor of conviction and removal as well.

But the process of impeachment would not continue. On Aug. 5, Nixon released transcripts of three of the taped conversations that the Supreme Court ruling forced him to turn over to the special prosecutor. These made clear his knowing participation in the coverup of White House involvement in the Watergate burglary.

Faced with this new evidence, even the members of the Judiciary Committee who had continued to defend Nixon called for his resignation or impeachment. On Aug. 7 Republican leaders told him he had no more than 10 supporters in the House and 15 in the Senate.

On Aug. 8, Nixon told the nation he would resign. He made no mention of impeachment. On Aug. 9, his resignation effective, he left the White House. The House Aug. 20 accepted the report of the committee inquiry, 412-3, formally concluding the matter.

Sources: Congressional Quarterly, *1974 Almanac*, pp. 867-902. Congressional Quarterly, *Watergate: Chronology of a Crisis*. U.S. Congress. House. Committee on the Judiciary, *Hearings pursuant to H. Res. 803*, 93rd Cong., 2d sess., 1974.

(Continued from p. 213)

8. Name: William W. Belknap (1876). **Position:** Secretary of War (resigned). **Charge:** That he received money for appointing and continuing in office a post trader at Ft. Sill, Okla. **Decision:** Acquitted.

Faced with widespread corruption and incompetence among high officers of the Grant administration, the House in 1876 initiated a number of general investigations of government departments. On March 2, 1876, the House adopted a resolution from the Committee on Expenditures in the War Department impeaching Belknap. Belknap resigned, but the Judiciary Committee continued work on impeachment articles, and the House April 3 agreed to five articles of impeachment.

As pre-trial manuevering proceeded, the Senate on May 29 declared by a vote of 37-29 that it had jurisdiction over Belknap regardless of his resignation. The trial, which n from July 6 to Aug. 1, 1876, ended in acquittal, with a bstantial number of senators indicating that they had voted against conviction on the ground that the Senate lacked jurisdiction.

9. Name: Charles Swayne (1903-05). **Position:** Federal judge. **Charge:** Padding expense accounts; using railroad property in receivership for his personal benefit; misusing contempt power. **Decision:** Acquitted.

On Dec. 10, 1903, the House adopted a resolution for a Judiciary Committee investigation of Swayne, U.S. judge for the northern district of Florida. Months later, the committee recommended impeachment, and the House adopted the resolution by voice vote on Dec. 13, 1904. After the vote to impeach, 13 articles were drafted and approved by the House in 1905; however, only the first 12 articles were presented to the Senate. The Senate trial opened Feb. 10 and ended Feb. 27, when the Senate voted acquittal on all 12 articles.

10. Name: Robert W. Archbald (1912-13). **Position:** Associate judge, U.S. Commerce Court. **Charge:** Misconduct including personal profits, free trips to Europe, improper appointment of jury commissioner. **Decision:** Removed from office.

On May 4, 1912, the House adopted a Judiciary Committee resolution authorizing an investigation of Archbald, associate judge of the U.S. Commerce Court. A committee resolution impeaching Archbald and setting forth 13 articles of impeachment was adopted by the House July 11 by a 223-1 vote. The trial, which began Dec. 3, ended Jan. 13, 1913, with Archbald convicted on five of the 13 articles. The Senate on the same day removed him from office by voice vote and, by a 39-35 vote, disqualified him from further office.

11. Name: George W. English (1925-26). **Position:** Federal judge. **Charge:** Partiality, tyranny and oppression. **Decision:** Senate dismissed charges at request of House managers following judge's resignation.

A resolution asking for an investigation of English, U.S. judge for the eastern district of Illinois, was introduced Jan. 13, 1925. The House on April 1, 1926, adopted by a 306-62 vote a Judiciary Committee resolution to impeach English. The resolution also set forth five articles of impeachment. The trial was set to begin Nov. 10, but on Nov. 4 English resigned and, at the request of House managers the Senate dismissed the charges Dec. 13 by a vote of 70 to 9.

12. Name: Harold Louderback (1932-33). **Position:** Federal judge. **Charge:** Appointing incompetent receivers and allowing them excessive fees. **Decision:** Acquitted.

On June 9, 1932, the House by voice vote adopted a resolution for an investigation of Louderback, U.S. judge for the northern district of California. The Judiciary Committee's study produced mixed results. The majority recommended censuring but not impeaching Louderback. However, the House on Feb. 24, 1933, by a 183-142 vote adopted a minority resolution impeaching the judge and specifying five articles. They accused Louderback of favoritism and conspiracy in the appointment of bankruptcy receivers. A trial that lasted from May 15 to May 24 ended in acquittal, with the "not guilty" votes outnumbering the "guilty" votes on all except one of the five articles.

13. Name: Halsted L. Ritter (1933-36). **Position:** Federal judge. **Charge:** A variety of judicial improprieties, including receiving corrupt payments; practicing law while serving as a federal judge; preparing and filing false income tax returns. **Decision:** Removed from office.

On June 1, 1933, the House by voice vote adopted a resolution for an investigation of Ritter, U.S. judge for the southern district of Florida. A long delay followed. Then on March 2, 1936, the House by a 181-146 vote adopted a Judiciary Committee impeachment resolution, with four articles of impeachment (the four original articles were subsequently replaced with seven amended ones). The trial lasted from April 6 to April 17. Although there were more "guilty" than "not guilty" votes on all except two of the first six articles, the majorities fell short of the two-thirds required for conviction. However, on the seventh article, with 56 votes necessary for conviction, the vote was 56 guilty and 28 not guilty. Thus, Ritter was convicted. He was ordered removed from office by voice vote. An order to disqualify him from further office was defeated, 0-76.

Footnotes

1. Paul S. Fenton, "The Scope of the Impeachment Power," *Northwestern University Law Review*, Vol. 65, No. 5 (1970), pp. 719-58, reprinted in U.S. Congress, House, Committee on the Judiciary, *Impeachment: Selected Materials*, 93d Cong., 1st sess., October 1973, pp. 663-88.

2. Asher C. Hinds, *Hinds' Precedents of the House of Representatives of the United States*, Vol. 4 (Washington: U.S. Government Printing Office, 1907), pp. 1008-11.

3. For further detail, see Congressional Quarterly, *1974 Almanac*, pp. 867-902; Congressional Quarterly, *Watergate: Chronology of a Crisis*, in particular Part III.

4. *The Federalist Papers*, with an Introduction by Clinton Rossiter (New York: Mentor, 1961), No. 65, p. 397.

5. U.S. Congress, House, Committee on the Judiciary, *Impeachment: Selected Materials on Procedure*, 93d Cong., 2d sess., January 1974, pp. 687-740, 851-900.

6. For further detail, see Congressional Quarterly, *1953 Almanac*, p. 311; *1970 Almanac*, p. 1025.

7. *Impeachment: Selected Materials on Procedure*, p. 697.

8. *Ibid.*, p. 892.

9. Joseph Story, *Commentaries on the Constitution of the United States* (Boston: Hilliard Gray and Co., 1833), Vol. 2, section 798.

10. Raoul Berger, *Impeachment: The Constitutional Problems* (Cambridge: Harvard University Press, 1973), p. 31, quoting G. M. Trevelyan's *Illustrated History of England* (London: Longmans Green, 1956), p. 391.

11. *The Federalist Papers*, No. 65, p. 398.

12. Max Farrand (ed.), *The Records of the Federal Convention of 1787* (New Haven: 1911), Vol. 1, p. 78; Vol. 2, pp. 116, 185-86, 292, 495, 545, 550-52.

13. *Impeachment: Selected Materials on Procedure*, pp. 687-89, citing *Hinds' Precedents*, Vol. 3, p. 981.

14. *Jefferson's Manual of Parliamentary Practice and Rules of the House of Representatives*, Section LIII, 603, reprinted in *Impeachment: Selected Materials*, pp. 21-22; also Clarence Cannon, *Cannon's Precedents of the House of Representatives of the United States*, Vol. 6 (Washington: U.S. Government Printing Office, 1935), p. 657.

15. *Impeachment: Selected Materials on Procedure*, pp. 343ff, 381ff, 411ff, 475ff, citing *Hinds' Precedents*, Vol. 3, pp. 644, 681, 711, 772.

16. *Impeachment: Selected Materials on Procedure*, pp. 477-78, 509-10, 609, 655, 795, 821.

17. *Ibid.*, pp. 345-47, 382-83, 416-17, 483-84, 511, 555, 607-09, 658-59, 797.

18. *Ibid.*, pp. 821-22, citing *Cannon's Precedents*, Vol. 6, p. 709.

19. *Ibid.*, pp. 563-65.

20. *Ibid.*, pp. 765-67, citing *Cannon's Precedents*, Vol. 6, p. 657.

21. *Ibid.*, pp. 716, 890.

22. *Ibid.*, pp. 4-15, 607-52.

23. *Ibid.*, pp. 733-37.

24. *Ibid.*, p. 383.

25. *Ibid.*, p. 2-3.

26. *Congressional Record*, 91st Cong., 2d sess., April 15, 1970, p. 11913.

27. *Impeachment: Selected Materials on Procedure*, p. 456-71, 597.

28. *Ibid.*, pp. 795-818.

29. *Impeachment: Selected Materials*, p. 688, citing *Proceedings of the United States Senate in the Trial of Impeachment of Halsted L. Ritter*, S. Doc. No. 200, 74th Cong., 2d sess., 1936.

30. Background, *Impeachment: Selected Materials on Procedure*, pp. 525, 722-24, 876-82; Congressional Quarterly, *1953 Almanac*, p. 311; *1970 Almanac*, p. 1025.

31. Background, *Impeachment: Selected Materials*, pp. 682-88, citing *Senate Journal*, No. 2, 435-37 (1798), *Hinds' Precedents*, Vol. 3, pp. 644-980, *Cannon's Precedents*, Vol. 6, pp. 684-742, 778-86, and *Proceedings in Ritter Trial. Impeachment: Selected Materials on Procedure*, pp. 343-524, 549-685, 795-850, 884-92.

Selected Bibliography

Books

The Association of the Bar of the City of New York. *The Law of Presidential Impeachment and Removal*. 1974.

Benedict, Michael L. *The Impeachment and Trial of Andrew Johnson*. New York: W. W. Norton & Co., 1973.

Berger, Raoul. *Impeachment: The Constitutional Problem*. Cambridge: Harvard University Press, 1973.

Black, Charles L. *Impeachment: A Handbook*. New Haven: Yale University Press, 1974.

Brant, Irving. *Impeachment: Trials and Errors*. New York: Alfred A. Knopf, 1972.

Dewitt, David M. *Impeachment and Trial of Andrew Johnson*. New York: Russell & Russell, 1967.

Farrand, Max, ed. *The Records of the Federal Convention of 1787*. 4 vols. New Haven: Yale University Press, 1966.

The Federalist Papers. Introduction by Clinton Rossiter. New York: Mentor, 1961.

Haynes, George H. *The Senate of the United States: Its History and Practice*. 2 vols. Boston: Houghton Mifflin, 1938.

Riddick, Floyd M. *The United States Congress: Organization and Procedure*. Manassas, Va.: National Capitol Publishers Inc., 1949.

Simpson, Alexander Jr. *A Treatise of Federal Impeachments*. Philadelphia: 1916; reprint ed., Wilmington, Del.: Scholarly Resources Inc., 1974.

Articles

Bates, William. "Vagueness in the Constitution: The Impeachment Power." *Stanford Law Journal*, June 1973, pp. 908-26.

Berger, Raoul. "Executive Privilege vs. Congressional Inquiry." *UCLA Law Review*, vol. 12, 1965, p. 104.

Berger, Raoul. "Impeachment for 'High Crimes and Misdemeanors.' " *Southern California Law Review*, vol. 44, 1971, pp. 395-460.

Bishop, J. W. "The Executive's Right to Privacy: An Unresolved Constitutional Question." *Yale Law Journal*, vol. 66, 1957, p. 477.

Collins, P. R. "Power of Congressional Committees of Investigations to Obtain Information from the Executive Branch." *Georgia Law Journal*, vol. 39, 1951, p. 563.

Dougherty, J. H. "Inherent Limitations Upon Impeachment." *Yale Law Journal*, vol. 23, 1913, pp. 60-69.

Fenton, Paul S. "The Scope of the Impeachment Power." *Northwestern University Law Review*, November/December 1970, pp. 719-58.

"The Impeachment of Andrew Johnson." *Annals of the American Academy of Political and Social Science*, vol. 10, 1968, pp. 126-33.

"President and Congress: Power of the President to Refuse Congressional Demand for Information." *Stanford Law Review*, vol. 1, 1949, p. 256.

Government Publications

Cannon, Clarence. *Cannon's Precedents of the House of Representatives*. Washington: Government Printing Office, 1935.

Hinds, Asher C. *Hinds' Precedents of the House of Representatives*. Washington, D.C.: Government Printing Office, 1907.

U.S. Congress. House. Committee on the Judiciary. *Constitutional Grounds for Presidential Impeachment*. 93rd Cong., 2nd sess., 1974.

U.S. Congress. House. Committee on the Judiciary. *Impeachment: Selected Materials*. 93rd Cong., 1st sess., 1973.

U.S. Congress. House. Committee on the Judiciary. *Impeachment: Selected Materials on Procedure*. 93rd Cong., 2nd sess., 1974.

U.S. Congress. Senate. Committee on the Judiciary. *Removal Power of Congress With Respect to the Supreme Court*. 80th Cong., 1st sess., 1947.

U.S. Department of Justice. Office of Legal Counsel. "Legal Aspects of Impeachment: An Overview." February 1974.

U.S. President. "An Analysis of the Constitutional Standard for Presidential Impeachment." Prepared by the attorneys for the President, The White House, February 1974.

Power to Amend

It was the difficulty of adapting the Articles of Confederation to changing conditions—a process which required unanimous approval of amendments by the states, as well as the consent of the Continental Congress—which led to the framing of the Constitution. In drafting the amending provision, the delegates to the Philadelphia Convention of 1787 had little to serve as a guide. Six of the 13 early state constitutions had been drawn up as "perpetual charters" and made no provision for amendment. In only three states were the legislatures empowered to propose changes. In four, the amending power was vested solely in popular conventions.

The unwritten British constitution, by contrast, could be effectively amended by act of Parliament. Although the fundamentals of British government were understood as constitutional, and functioned in practice to contain and guide the operation of governing institutions, there was neither a document to define nor an agency to declare what was "unconstitutional." Whatever was enacted in Parliament was the supreme law of the land.

For a variety of reasons the Founding Fathers were unwilling to rely on so flexible a base for their new nation. The 13 independent states could not be expected to resign a part of their newly won sovereignty without a clear, written understanding of what kind of union they were joining. Furthermore, they would need substantial guarantees that the new national government would not unilaterally alter the terms of the agreement, in particular by reducing the sovereignty retained by the states. The reliance on separation of powers, and on checks and balances, for protection against arbitrary government required that the arrangement not be subject to easy alteration, lest the separation and the balance be destroyed. Experience with arbitrary acts of Parliament convinced the former colonists that certain rights must be declared inviolable by any agency of government, and must be controlled by a law which no one of those agencies could itself change.

These and other reasons prompted the Constitutional Convention to write a document that was expected to endure as the fundamental law of the land. And yet those assembled in Philadelphia realized that they could not foresee all the future needs of the new nation, nor regard their labors as perfect. They devised, therefore, a Constitution which would be easier to amend than the Articles of Confederation, but more difficult to revise than the British constitution. They built into the amendment process the principle of checks and balances basic to the Constitution

itself, and they reserved to the states the ultimate power to alter the agreement into which they had originally entered.

The Constitutional Convention

The plan for a national government presented by Edmund Randolph of Virginia on May 29, 1787, the fourth day of the Convention, set forth that "provision ought to be made for the amendment of the Articles of Union whensoever it shall seem necessary" and that "the assent of the National Legislature ought not to be required thereto." A plan proposed by Charles Pinckney of South Carolina on the same day provided that amendments "to invest future additional Powers in the United States" should be proposed by conventions and ratified by an unspecified percentage of the state legislatures.[1]

When Randolph's proposal was brought forward in the convention on June 5, Pinckney expressed doubt as to its "propriety or necessity," while Elbridge Gerry of Massachusetts favored it. "The novelty and difficulty of the experiment requires periodical revision," Gerry said. "The prospect of such a revision would also give intermediate stability to the Government." George Mason of Virginia supported the Randolph proposal, holding that:

"The plan now to be formed will certainly be defective, as the Confederation has been found, on trial, to be. Amendments, therefore, will be necessary and it will be better to provide for them in an easy, regular and constitutional way, than to trust to chance and violence. It would be improper to require the consent of the National Legislature, because they may abuse their power and refuse their consent on that very account."

On June 20, Mason said that "the Convention, though comprising so many distinguished characters, could not be expected to make a faultless government," and that he would prefer "trusting to posterity the amendment of its defects, rather than to push the experiment too far." The Convention agreed, on July 23, that "provisions ought to be made for future amendments...whensoever it shall seem necessary" and referred the matter to the Committee of Detail. In its report of Aug. 6, the committee recommended the provision that: "On the application of the legislatures of two-thirds of the states in the Union, for an amendment of this Constitution, the Legislature of the United States shall call a convention for that purpose." This recommendation was adopted by the Convention on Aug. 30, in spite of the contention of Gouverneur Morris of Pennsylvania that "the

217

Legislature should be left at liberty to call a convention, whenever they please."

Reconsideration of the amendment provision was voted by the Convention on Sept. 10, on the motion of Gerry, who objected to it on the ground that, since the Constitution was to be paramount to the state constitutions, "two-thirds of the states can bind the Union to innovations that may subvert the state constitutions altogether." Alexander Hamilton of New York likewise favored reconsideration, although he "did not object to the consequence stated by Mr. Gerry."

"There was no greater evil in subjecting the people of the United States to the major voice than the people of a particular state (Hamilton said). It had been wished by many and was much to have been desired that an easier mode for introducing amendments had been provided by the Articles of Confederation. It was equally desirable now that an easy mode should be established for supplying defects which will probably appear in the new system. The mode proposed was not adequate. The state legislatures will not apply for alterations but with a view to increase their own powers. The national Legislature will be most sensible to the necessity of amendments, and ought also to be empowered, whenever two-thirds of each branch should concur, to call a convention." This was one of the few suggestions made by Hamilton which found a place in the finished Constitution.

Roger Sherman of Connecticut moved to add to the provision the following clause: "or the Legislature may propose amendments to the several states for their approbation, but no amendments shall be binding until consented to by the several states." James Wilson of Pennsylvania moved to reduce the requirement of unanimous consent of the states to a two-thirds majority. Six states—Connecticut, Georgia, Massachusetts, New Jersey, North Carolina and South Carolina—voted against this motion and five states—Delaware, Maryland, New Hampshire, Pennsylvania and Virginia—in favor of it, but a later motion by Wilson to permit three-fourths of the states to make an amendment effective was adopted without dissent.

Madison then proposed a substitute for the entire article, and this was adopted with only one state dissenting. Madison's plan provided that amendments should be proposed by Congress whenever two-thirds of both houses considered it necessary or when two-thirds of the state legislatures made application, such amendments to be valid when ratified by three-fourths of the state legislatures or three-fourths of the state conventions, as Congress might designate.

When this provision was reported by the Committee on Style, Sept. 15, Morris and Gerry objected that both methods of amendment depended upon Congress. They urged a provision requiring Congress, when requested by two-thirds of the states, to call a convention to propose amendments. This provision was accepted without dissent.

John Rutledge of South Carolina protested that he "could never agree to give a power by which the articles relating to slaves might be altered by the states not interested in that property and prejudiced against it." The Convention consequently agreed to a provision prohibiting amendment before 1808 of the clauses concerned with slavery (the counting of slaves as three-fifths of the population for assessment of direct taxes and authorization of the slave trade). At the last minute, Sherman voiced the fear that "three-fourths of the states might be brought to do things fatal to particular states, as abolishing them altogether or depriving them of their equality in the

Senate." He sought another proviso prohibiting any amendment by which any state would "be affected in its internal policy, or deprived of its equal suffrage in the Senate." Madison warned against adding special provisos restricting the amending power, lest every state insist on protecting its boundaries or exports. However, "the circulating murmurs of the small states" prompted Morris to propose protecting equal representation in the Senate from amendment, a proviso adopted unanimously. These were the only two limitations on the substance of amendments which could be adopted.

Constitutional Provision

As finally agreed upon, Article V of the Constitution provided that: "The Congress, whenever two-thirds of both Houses shall deem it necessary, shall propose Amendments to this Constitution, or, on the Application of the Legislatures of two-thirds of the several States, shall call a Convention for proposing Amendments, which, in either Case, shall be valid to all Intents and Purposes, as Part of this Constitution, when ratified by the Legislatures of three-fourths of the several States, or by Conventions in three-fourths thereof, as the one or the other Mode of Ratification may be proposed by the Congress; Provided that no Amendment which may be made prior to the Year One thousand eight hundred and eight shall in any Manner affect the first and fourth Clauses in the Ninth Section of the first Article; and that no State, without its Consent, shall be deprived of its equal Suffrage in the Senate."

Thus, the Constitution allows either Congress or the state legislatures to initiate the amending process, either Congress or a general convention to propose amendments, and either state legislatures or state conventions to ratify amendments. Congress determines which method of ratification will be employed, and what form a general convention would take if requested by the state legislatures.

The President has no formal authority over constitutional amendments (his veto power does not extend to them); nor can governors veto approval of amendments by their respective legislatures.

Ratification. Notification of state ratification is transmitted by the states to the head of the General Services Administration. (Until 1950, the Secretary of State performed this function.) His action in proclaiming the adoption of an amendment on receipt is purely ministerial; the amendment is brought into effect by the ratifying action of the necessary number of states on the day when the required number of ratifications is reached. (However, the Eighteenth Amendment had an unusual provision postponing its effectiveness for one year after ratification was completed.)

Ratification of the Constitution

Omission of a Bill of Rights constituted the principal source of dissatisfaction with the new Constitution in the state ratifying conventions held in 1788. The demand for amendments to establish these rights, and to effect various other changes in the Constitution, made the provisions of Article V an issue in the struggle for ratification. In the Virginia convention, Patrick Henry and George Mason raised vehement objections to the amending process prescribed in Article V.

"When I come to contemplate this part (Henry said), I suppose that I am mad or that my countrymen are so. The way to amendment is, in my conception, shut.... Two-thirds

Application of Fourteenth Amendment

In the years following World War II, the Supreme Court generally left Congress free to determine the boundaries of federal economic and social powers, and it increasingly restricted state action in the area of civil and political rights. Relying largely on the Fourteenth Amendment's ban against state denial of "equal protection of the laws," the court attacked state policies of racial segregation and legislative malapportionment with sweeping changes in constitutional doctrine. Under the amendment's due process clause, the court also applied many of the Bill of Rights guarantees of civil liberties to state action.

Undoubtedly the most controversial of the Supreme Court's postwar decisions was its 1954 9-0 ruling in *Brown v. Board of Education of Topeka, Kansas* (347 U.S. 483) that racial segregation in public schools constituted denial of equal protection of the laws. Later, refusing to review lower court opinions, the Supreme Court gave effect to decisions prohibiting segregation in other public facilities. In other decisions, segregation in interstate transportation was prohibited under the commerce clause and the Interstate Commerce Act.

Between 1962 and 1964 the Supreme Court in a series of decisions [*Baker v. Carr* (369 U.S. 186), 1962; *Gray v. Sanders* (372 U.S. 368), 1963; *Reynolds v. Sims* (377 U.S. 533) and related cases, 1964] held that unequal apportionment for state legislatures violated the equal protection clause of the Fourteenth Amendment. The effect of these decisions, especially in view of the extent of malapportionment in most states, promised to alter profoundly the character and policies of the state legislatures. In a similar ruling in 1964 in *Wesberry v. Sanders* (376 U.S. 1) the court required that U.S. House of Representatives' districts have approximately equal population, but in this case it did not invoke the Fourteenth Amendment.

The apportionment rulings were criticized as usurpation by federal authority of states' rights. In a vehement dissent from the 1964 state legislative apportionment decisions, Justice John Marshall Harlan said: "...the aftermath of these cases, however desirable it may be thought in itself, will have been achieved at the cost of a radical alteration in the relationship between the states and the federal government, more particularly the federal judiciary. Only one who has an overbearing impatience with the federal system and its political processes will believe that cost was not too high or was inevitable."

The Supreme Court in the postwar years continued a trend of interpreting the due process clause of the Fourteenth Amendment to extend to the states the guarantees of civil liberties contained in the first eight amendments to the Constitution. Reversing earlier doctrine, the Court in 1925 in *Gitlow v. New York* (260 U.S. 703) had initiated a series of decisions whose effect was to hold immune from state invasion the First Amendment's freedoms of speech, press, religion, assembly, association and petition for redress of grievances. Decisions culminating in *Mapp v. Ohio* (367 U.S. 643) prohibited admission in state courts of evidence obtained in violation of the Fourth Amendment. The Eighth Amendment's prohibition of cruel and unusual punishment [*Robinson v. California* (370 U.S. 660), 1962], the Sixth Amendment's provision of counsel in criminal cases [*Gideon v. Wainwright* (372 U.S. 335), 1963] and the Fifth Amendment's protection against compulsory self-incrimination [*Malloy v. Hogan* (378 U.S. 1), 1964] were similarly held applicable to state action, though a blanket application of the Bill of Rights to the states was not undertaken by the Court.

Source: C. Herman Pritchett, *The American Constitution* (McGraw-Hill Book Company, 1968).

---

of Congress or of the state legislatures are necessary even to propose amendments. If one-third of these be unworthy men, they may prevent the application for amendments; but what is destructive and mischievous is that three-fourths of the state legislatures, or of the state conventions, must concur in the amendments when proposed.... A bare majority in four small states may hinder the adoption of amendments.... Is this an easy mode of securing the public liberty? It is, sir, a most fearful situation, when the most contemptible minority could prevent the alteration of the most oppressive government, for it may in many respects prove to be such."[2]

Washington admitted that there were defects in the Constitution, but observed that "As a constitutional door is opened for future amendments and alterations, I think it would be wise in the people to accept what is offered to them...." Jefferson, at first hostile, came to support the Constitution, "contented to travel on towards perfection, step by step."[3]

The Federalist expressed the view that: "The mode (of amendment) preferred by the convention seems to be stamped with every mark of propriety. It guards equally

against that extreme facility, which would render the Constitution too mutable; and that extreme difficulty which might perpetuate its discovered faults. It moreover equally enables the general and the state governments to originate the amendment of errors, as they may be pointed out by the experience on one side or the other."[4]

Change Without Amendment

Since the Constitution was drafted, the United States has been transformed beyond recognition. And yet this document remains the fundamental law of the land. The amending process has contributed to the remarkable durability of the Constitution. But basic changes in the nature of the Constitution are by no means limited to those achieved through the amendment process. Each branch of the national government has contributed to transformation of the arrangement created at the Constitutional Convention.

The interpretation of the Constitution by the Supreme Court has been a major source of change. The principle of judicial review of legislation established the high court as the authoritative interpreter of the Constitution.

In 1803 Chief Justice Marshall, in *Marbury v. Madison* (5 U.S. 137), first asserted the Supreme Court's power to declare acts of Congress unconstitutional. In an *obiter dictum*, Marshall said: "The powers of the Legislature are defined and limited; and that those limits may not be mistaken, or forgotten, the Constitution is written. To what purpose are powers limited, and to what purpose is that limitation committed to writing, if these limits may at any time be passed by those intended to be restrained?"

"It is a proposition too plain to be contested," the Chief Justice continued, "that the Constitution controls any legislative act repugnant to it, or that the Legislature may alter the Constitution by an ordinary act. Between these alternatives there is no middle ground. The Constitution is either a superior paramount law, unchangeable by ordinary means, or it is on a level with ordinary legislative acts, and, like other acts, is alterable when the Legislature shall please to alter it.... If an act of the Legislature, repugnant to the Constitution, is void, does it, notwithstanding its invalidity, bind the courts, and oblige them to give it effect? ...It is emphatically the province and duty of the judicial department to say what the law is.... So if a law be in opposition to the Constitution; if both the law and the Constitution apply to a particular case, so that the Court must either decide that case conformably to the law, disregarding the Constitution; or conformably to the Constitution, disregarding the law; the Court must determine which of these conflicting rules governs the case. This is of the very essence of judicial duty."[5] *(Further excerpts from case, appendix)*

The Constitution has also been affected by the growth in this century of the President's powers during national emergencies. *(p. 273)*

Use of Amending Process

While profound changes in the foundations of American government have been wrought by Congress, the judiciary and the executive, formal amendments also have contributed to the process of constitutional transformation. Indeed, some of the amendments, such as the Eleventh and the Sixteenth, reversed judicial interpretations of the Constitution.

A number of the 26 amendments made only technical adjustments in the mechanisms of government. For example, the Twelfth Amendment provided for separate balloting for President and Vice President in the electoral college, and the Twentieth Amendment revised the dates for the beginning of presidential terms and the convening of Congress. Other amendments advanced the course of democracy by extending the vote to blacks (Fifteenth) and women (Nineteenth), lowering the voting age from 21 to 18 (Twenty-sixth) and providing for the direct election of senators (Seventeenth). The economy was profoundly affected by the Income Tax Amendment (Sixteenth) and social mores by the Prohibition Amendment (Eighteenth, repealed by the Twenty-first). The relationship between the national and state governments was altered by the Fourteenth Amendment, the most fundamental formal revision of the Constitution; its consequences are still unfolding in Supreme Court decisions based on the amendment. *(Box p. 219)*

The constitutional amendments have come in clusters. The first ten, the Bill of Rights, were practically a part of the original Constitution. Two amendments designed to correct the functioning of the Constitution were soon precipitated by a Supreme Court decision and by a crisis arising from a flaw in the procedure for electing the President and Vice President.

The Civil War prompted the Thirteenth, Fourteenth and Fifteenth Amendments. Apart from those three, which grew out of the nation's gravest crisis, more than a century elapsed between constitutional amendments. From 1913 to 1920, largely as the culmination of the progressive movement, four amendments of fundamental importance were ratified—giving the United States the income tax, direct election of senators, Prohibition, and woman suffrage.

The next two amendments, rescinding Prohibition and altering the dates for the beginning of a new Congress and of the presidential term, went into effect in 1933. There have been five amendments since the Second World War, none of them profoundly revising the system of government.

The best known amendment unsuccessfully pressed during the 1940s and 1950s was the so-called Bricker Amendment that would have limited the treaty-making power and the President's authority to enter into executive agreements. The amendment came within one vote of securing the necessary two-thirds Senate majority in 1950. *(See Foreign Affairs p. 245)*

Another goal persistently sought by constitutional amendment has been reform of the system for electing the President by abolishing or revising the electoral college and providing for direct popular elections. *(See Power to Elect the President p. 233)*

Anti-abortion and anti-busing amendments have been other controversial proposals put forward in the 1970s by segments of Congress and outside pressure groups.

Leadership of Congress

Although the Constitutional Convention envisioned a substantial role for the states in the amendment process, Congress has dominated the rewriting of the Constitution. Not once have the states been successful in calling for a convention to propose an amendment, as they are authorized to do by petitions to Congress from two-thirds of the legislatures. During the first 100 years of its existence, Congress received only 10 such petitions from state legislatures, but between 1893 and 1974, more than 300 such petitions were received.[6] The states, while approving 26 amendments proposed by Congress, by mid-1976 had failed to ratify only five. *(Box, p. 225)*

Undoubtedly, the need to obtain the approval of as many as three-fourths of the states has served as a brake on congressional inclinations to alter the Constitution. On at least one occasion, the prospect that the states might take the initiative drove Congress to act. The Seventeenth Amendment, providing for direct election of senators, was continually blocked in the Senate until the state legislatures were on the verge of requiring a convention. Even in this case, however, Congress had for years provided the principal public arena for debate of the issue.

Congress has the power to determine by which of the two procedures the states shall ratify a proposed amendment. In every case except one, approval by the state legislatures has been prescribed. Only for the Twenty-first Amendment, the repeal of Prohibition, did Congress call for ratification by state conventions. The provision for ratification by conventions in that instance was primarily the result of three factors: (1) a desire for speedy ratification; (2) the contention of advocates of repeal that the state legislatures ratifying the Eighteenth Amendment had yielded to the pressure tactics of Prohibition forces, had overrepresented rural areas favoring Prohibition and had not represented the views of the majority of the people; and (3) the desire to remove permanently from the political arena a question which had divided states, regions and political parties. Submitted to the states in February 1933, the Twenty-first Amendment was ratified by conventions in 36 of the then total of 48 states by December of the same year.

The Supreme Court and Procedural Questions. As Pritchett has noted, the Supreme Court generally has regarded the amending process as "almost entirely a concern of Congress."[7] Until 1939, however, the court did rule on procedural questions relating to the adoption of amendments. In 1920 in the *National Prohibition Cases* (253 U.S. 350), it ruled that the two-thirds vote in each house required to propose an amendment meant two-thirds of the members present—assuming the presence of a quorum—and not a vote of two-thirds of the entire membership.[8]

The Supreme Court has ruled that Congress has the power to set a "reasonable" time limit on the period for ratification of constitutional amendments. *(Time for Ratification, below)*

Proposing and Ratifying: Undecided Questions

Convention Formula. Of the two methods of proposing amendments—via a convention called by Congress at the request of the legislatures of two-thirds of the states, or by a two-thirds majority of each house of Congress—only the latter has been employed. State legislatures have petitioned Congress to call a convention on numerous occasions, but all efforts have been unsuccessful.

In the 1960s, however, the Council of State Governments mounted a campaign to secure a constitutional amendment that would allow one house of a state legislature to be apportioned on some basis other than population. *(Box, this page)* Although the effort died out, it pointed to the many uncertainties surrounding use of the convention formula for proposing amendments—questions that have not yet been resolved. *(Box p. 224)*

Ratification Procedures. There are also undecided questions concerning ratification of amendments. Constitutional authorities have disagreed on whether Congress or the state legislatures should determine the procedures for ratification by state conventions.

Bills have been introduced in Congress to spell out procedures, but none of them have passed. State legislatures have been divided on this question. At least 21 of them provided by statute that state officials were to follow the procedures specified in a federal law if Congress should enact one. Sixteen legislatures, assuming that the procedural question was within their jurisdiction, passed laws applicable not merely to the convention summoned for the Twenty-first Amendment, but for all future conventions called to ratify amendments to the U.S. Constitution. One state, New Mexico, claimed exclusive authority on the matter and directed its officials to resist any attempt at congressional encroachment on that authority.

Time for Ratification. Another uncertainty concerning ratification concerns the definition of a "reasonable" time period for ratification, a question which the Supreme Court has left to Congress.

The Eighteenth Amendment (Prohibition) was the first to specify a period of years—in this case, seven—within which ratification had to be effected. In 1921 in *Dillon v. Gloss* (256 U.S. 368), the court held that Congress had the power to fix a definite ratification period "within reasonable limits." In 1939 in *Coleman v. Miller* (307 U.S. 433), the

33 States Call for Convention

The Constitution's provision for amendment by a convention requested by two-thirds of the states has never been successfully invoked. A movement in behalf of an amendment that would limit the maximum rate of federal income, death and gift taxes to 25 per cent was actively promoted among state legislatures before and after World War II. More than a score of state legislatures petitioned Congress to call a convention to propose such an amendment to the states for ratification, but a number of the states subsequently rescinded the resolutions and the movement died out.

Petitions to Congress for a convention to propose an amendment in a different field had been made, by 1969, by 33 state legislatures, only one short of the required number. The proposed amendment—to authorize states to apportion one house of a bicameral legislature on a basis of geography or political subdivisions, as well as population—had been prompted by Supreme Court decisions applying the one-man, one-vote rule to state legislatures.

Background. A revolution in the apportionment of state legislatures was precipitated by the Supreme Court in 1962 when it held in *Baker v. Carr* (369 U.S. 186) that the judiciary could entertain suits challenging malapportionment. The decision overturned a line of legal precedent holding that the makeup of state legislatures was not a justiciable matter, but was political in nature, and that citizens had no standing to sue to effect a change.

In subsequent decisions, the Court elaborated on *Baker* and in 1964 in *Reynolds v. Sims* (377 U.S. 533) applied its "one-man, one-vote" dictum, holding that both houses of a state legislature must be apportioned on a basis of substantial equality of population. That decision struck not only at malapportioned state legislatures, but also at those apportioned—sometimes by terms of the state constitution—on the basis of one state senator for each city, town or county, for example.

A substantial element in Congress opposed the Court's interpretation of the Constitution. In 1964 the House passed a bill which denied federal courts jurisdiction over state reapportionment. In the Senate, Everett McKinley Dirksen (R Ill.) led an unsuccessful move to attach to the foreign aid bill a rider requiring courts to delay reapportionment orders until Congress submitted a proposed constitutional amendment on apportionment. Dirksen tried in 1965 to secure a constitutional amendment but failed.

Despairing of congressional initiatives, supporters of the Dirksen proposal placed their hopes on constitutional amendment via a convention summoned by Congress upon petition by two-thirds of the states.

In December 1964, the General Assembly of the Council of State Governments published a guide for petitions to Congress by state legislatures. By the end of the 89th Congress in 1966, 28 states had petitioned Congress for a convention. During the 90th Congress (1967-68), four more states joined the list, bringing the total to 32. Iowa, the 33rd, was the only one to do so during the 91st Congress.

Court held that the decision as to what was a "reasonable" period was an essentially political one which Congress—and not the Court—had to determine.

The Child Labor Amendment proposed in 1924, with no time limit, might technically still be open for ratification. To date, 28 states have ratified the amendment. Even if 10 more states were to ratify (the three-fourths applies to the number of states presently in the Union, not the number at the time the amendment was proposed), it seems unlikely that Congress would consider this a "reasonable" time period. *(Amendments That Failed p. 225)*

In March of 1976, Kentucky ratified the Thirteenth, Fourteenth and Fifteenth Amendments—more than 100 years after they became part of the Constitution.

A state which has refused to ratify a proposed amendment may later change its mind and vote affirmatively. However, the weight of opinion is that once a state has approved a proposed amendment, it cannot reverse its decision and "unratify." This question could become an issue in the ratification campaign for the Equal Rights Amendment. *(Box, p. 227)*

Appraisal of the Amending Process. As Burns, Peltason and Cronin have noted in their book, *Government by the People,* "The entire amending procedure has been criticized because neither a majority of the voters at large nor even a majority of the voters in a majority of the states can formally alter the Constitution. But when a majority of the people are serious in their desire to bring about changes in our constitutional system, their wishes are usually implemented either by formal amendment or by the more subtle methods of interpretation and adaptation."[9]

Pritchett has commented, "The adoption of three amendments in six years—the Twenty-third, Twenty-fourth and Twenty-fifth—is evidence that the amending machinery is not hard to operate if there is a genuine consensus on the need, and may even lead to some concern that amendments are too easy to achieve.... It is of prime importance that the Constitution retain its brevity and be limited to basic structural arrangements and the protection of individual liberties. It would be disastrous if it became, through the amending power, a vehicle by which pressure groups and crackpots could impose their nostrums on the nation."[10]

The 26 Amendments

The Bill of Rights. Important guarantees of civil liberties were written into the main body of the Constitution. Ex post facto laws and bills of attainder were forbidden, as was suspension of the writ of habeas corpus. A religious test as a qualification for office was prohibited and trial by jury for criminal offenses was guaranteed. Little was said at the Constitutional Convention in favor of a bill of rights. Most delegates were satisfied that the fundamental liberties they cherished would be safe because the federal government was limited to powers explicitly granted in the Constitution and thus was denied any authority that could be used against citizens' rights.[11]

But during the campaign for ratification it became clear that many were not content to leave basic rights protected only by inference. The colonists had long claimed the rights guaranteed Englishmen by precedents going back as far as the *Magna Carta* (1215), and civil liberties had been included in colonial charters. Since independence, six states had adopted bills of rights and others had incorporated similar guarantees into their state constitutions.

When Massachusetts ratified the new Constitution of the United States, its convention recommended that it be amended to protect basic rights. The Virginia ratifying convention chose a committee to report on amendments for submission in the First Congress. New York attached a bill of rights to its ratification. There was no doubt that action had to be taken at once to gain support for the Constitution by adding explicit guarantees of fundamental liberties.

Madison yielded in his view that the grant of only specified powers to the federal government was sufficient protection of civil liberties. He proposed amendments to be fitted into the Constitution at appropriate points within the document. But the House of Representatives, after a committee had considered and revised Madison's proposals, decided to append the amendments as a supplement to the Constitution. Twelve amendments were finally approved by Congress and submitted to the states. The first two, which dealt with apportionment of representatives and compensation of members of Congress, were not ratified. The others became the first 10 amendments to the Constitution when Virginia, the 11th state to ratify, approved them on Dec. 15, 1791.

The Supreme Court in 1833 ruled in *Barron v. Baltimore* (32 U.S. 243) that the Bill of Rights was not applicable to the states. However, the Fourteenth Amendment's due process clause was later held to prohibit the states from denying at least some of the freedoms protected by the Bill of Rights.[12]

The First Amendment's guarantee of freedoms of religion, speech, press and assembly has proved the cornerstone of a free society and government. It has also been a source of great controversies. In the last decade, the Supreme Court has outraged segments of American opinion by interpreting the First Amendment to prohibit prayers in public schools and to permit the publication of literature and the showing of films widely viewed as obscene.

Even more controversial have been decisions prompted by efforts to suppress communism. Justice Oliver Wendell Holmes in 1919 in *Schenck v. United States* (249 U.S. 47) had first formulated the doctrine that freedom of speech could not be abridged except when "the words are used in such circumstances and are of such a nature as to create a clear and present danger that they will bring about the substantive evils that Congress has a right to prevent."[13] This "clear and present danger" doctrine was modified when the Court in 1951 in *Dennis v. United States* (341 U.S. 494) upheld the Smith Act of 1940, which made it a crime to advocate violent overthrow of the government. The Court then ruled that freedom of speech must at times give way to other social values, with the courts determining in each case "whether the gravity of the 'evil,' discounted by its improbability, justifies such invasion of free speech as is necessary to avoid the danger."[14] The Court has also ruled against witnesses who have cited the First Amendment in refusing to testify before congressional investigating committees, balancing their rights to freedom of speech and association against the need of Congress for information. However, the Fifth Amendment's protection against compulsory self-incrimination has consistently been upheld as constitutional justification for refusing to answer questions in congressional investigations. *(Details, p. 148)*

The question of First Amendment freedoms figured significantly in the legal test of the 1974 Federal Election Campaign Act Amendments *(Buckley v. Valeo).* On Jan. 30, 1976, the Supreme Court upheld several provisions of the law, but declared that the campaign spending limits established therein were unconstitutional violations of the First Amendment's guarantee of free expression. The Court stated, "A restriction on the amount of money a person or group can spend on political communication during a campaign necessarily reduces the quantity of expression...." (Campaign Financing, p. 531)

The complex history of judicial interpretations of the first 10 amendments gives an incomplete picture of the role the Bill of Rights has played in the character and development of the United States. It embodies freedoms won through generations of struggle in England and America, and it remains a rallying cry for protecting and extending those freedoms.

Early Amendments After Bill of Rights

Eleventh Amendment. The principle that a sovereign state could not be sued by a private individual, except with its consent, was complicated by the establishment of a federal union. While state governments might refuse suits in their own courts, the Constitution did not indicate whether or not they could similarly refuse to be sued in a federal court. Article III of the Constitution gave jurisdiction to federal courts in cases "between a state and citizens of another state." Although no one doubted that a state could bring a suit against an individual, Article III had not been interpreted in state ratifying conventions as permitting an individual to sue a state without its consent. But the Supreme Court in 1793 in *Chisholm v. Georgia* (2 U.S. 419) upheld the suit of executors of a British creditor against the state of Georgia, which refused to participate in the case.[15]

The ruling gave rise to vigorous agitation on the part of those who opposed a strong federal government. The Massachusetts legislature declared that the power exercised by the Supreme Court was "dangerous to the peace, safety, and independence of the several states and repugnant to the first principles of a federal government." The Georgia house of representatives passed a bill providing that any official who attempted to enforce the Court's decision should be declared guilty of a felony and be hanged, without benefit of clergy. Congress immediately proposed an amendment providing that the power of the federal judiciary "shall not be construed to extend" to private suits against states. Ratification was completed in February 1795.

Twelfth Amendment. The Constitution provided that presidential electors chosen in each state were to cast two votes, with no distinction between the votes for President and Vice President. The candidate receiving the highest number of votes, provided they constituted a majority, would be named President. In the absence of a majority, the House of Representatives would choose among the five candidates with the highest number of electoral votes. After selection of the President, the candidate with the next highest number of electoral votes would, in any case, be named Vice President.[16]

The Constitutional Convention had not anticipated the development of political parties, whose candidates for the electoral college would be pledged to register the party choice for President. In 1800 the Republican Party won a clear majority, with 73 electors as against 65 Federalist electors. But a deadlock resulted because all the Republicans cast one vote for Jefferson, and one vote for Aaron Burr. They had intended that Jefferson would be President and Burr Vice President, but there was no way of distinguishing the votes cast. Because no candidate had a majority, the election was thrown into the House of Representatives. There many of the Federalists voted for

Burr and a deadlock persisted until the 36th ballot. *(Power to Elect the President p. 233)*

A proposed amendment, providing for separate votes by the electors for President and Vice President, was rejected by the Senate in 1802 after having received the necessary two-thirds majority in the House. In 1803, however, the proposed amendment was approved by both houses. Ratification was probably completed on June 15, 1804, when the legislature of the 13th state (New Hampshire) approved the amendment. However, the governor of New Hampshire vetoed the act on June 20, and the amendment failed to pass again by the two-thirds vote then required by the state constitution. However, because Article V provides for ratification by state legislatures or conventions, it has generally been thought that approval or veto by a governor is without significance. If the ratification by New Hampshire is deemed ineffective, then the amendment became operative by Tennessee's ratification on July 27, 1804.

In any event, ratification was completed in time for the elections of 1804. Once this adjustment in electoral machinery was made, the two-party system kept election of the President out of the House of Representatives in every election except that of 1824.

One consequence of the change in the manner of choosing the Vice President was to reduce the prestige of that office. When filled by the man with next to the strongest support for the presidency, the post of Vice President might serve as a platform for national leadership. After the election of 1796, Jefferson, the head of the opposition Republicans, held the office under President Adams, a Federalist. Since ratification of the Twelfth Amendment, the vice presidency has been a singularly powerless position. Statesmen of presidential caliber often decline to run for the office, while political leaders may seek to get rid of an embarrassing party figure by placing him in the obscurity of the vice presidency, as in the case of Theodore Roosevelt.

Post-Civil War Amendments

Thirteenth Amendment. Anxious to preserve the Union, most northerners were not demanding abolition of slavery when the South seceded. As the Civil War progressed, however, abolition increasingly became part of the program of the federal government. President Lincoln and many members of Congress at first favored proposals to compensate slave owners for their property loss. In 1862 Congress provided for release of slaves in the District of Columbia, and owners loyal to the government received up to $300 for each slave freed. Later in the same year, the President recommended a constitutional amendment to authorize federal aid to states that abolished slavery and provided for compensation to owners.[17]

On Jan. 1, 1863, Lincoln issued his Emancipation Proclamation, which stated that "all persons held as slaves within any state or designated part of a state, the people whereof shall be in rebellion against the United States, shall be then, thenceforward, and forever free...." The proclamation was issued without authorization by Congress, and it had no constitutional basis other than the war powers of the President. Although the legality of the action has been much disputed, subsequent constitutional sanction was provided by the Thirteenth Amendment. The resolution proposing this amendment, which was to abolish slavery throughout the United States, was approved by the Senate on April 8, 1864, but it failed to receive the requisite two-thirds vote in the House. The proposed amendment was an

Uncertainties About a Convention

Because Congress never has been required, by petitions from two-thirds of the state legislatures, to call a convention for "proposing amendments" to the Constitution, a number of important questions on the procedures to be followed in that event have not been answered. The close call in the 1960s—when 33 states petitioned Congress for a convention to propose a reapportionment amendment—resulted in pleas by constitutional law experts for procedural guidelines to avoid chaos should a convention be held. *(33 States Call for Convention box p. 221)*

As a result, Sen. Sam J. Ervin Jr. (D N.C.), chairman of the Senate Judiciary Subcommittee on Separation of Powers, introduced a bill to establish procedures relating to constitutional conventions. It called for giving to each state in such a convention as many delegates as it had members in the House and Senate, provided for delegates to be elected, prohibited such conventions from considering any except the amendments referred to it, allowed Congress to determine the method of ratification, and set a seven-year limit on the validity of petitions for a convention. The bill passed the Senate both in 1971 and 1973, but died when the House did not act on it. Subsequently, interest in the matter waned when no more petitions from the states for a convention were forthcoming.

Thus a number of uncertainties remain:

● What constitutes a valid call of two-thirds of the legislatures? Must their resolutions to Congress be identical in all details or simply relate to one general subject?

● In what time span must the required two-thirds of the states submit their resolutions? The Constitution is silent on this point. In resolutions submitting proposed amendments to the states Congress in recent years has stipulated a seven-year maximum period for ratification.

● Can a state rescind a previous call for a convention? The Constitution says nothing about the legality of a rescinding action. But in 1868, when New Jersey and Ohio attempted to withdraw their ratifications of the Fourteenth Amendment, Congress refused to accept the withdrawals.

● If the required two-thirds of the legislatures issue a convention call, is Congress obligated to call the convention? By the letter of the Constitution, it would appear to have no choice. But Congress might find pretexts for invalidating individual state petitions, and the Supreme Court might consider Congress the final judge of those petitions (see *Coleman v. Miller*, 63 U.S. 87, 1939).

● How would Congress act to call a convention? If there were no dispute, the Judiciary Committees of the two houses probably would report appropriate resolutions which the two houses would approve. But what would happen if one of the committees refused to report such a resolution? The resolution might be considered a privileged proposition which could either be referred to committee or considered directly without committee action or recommendation. But what if opponents of the resolution in the Senate blocked action with a filibuster?

● How should a congressional resolution calling a convention be worded? Should it—or could it—limit the convention to proposing an amendment on the subject named in the petitions from the states? Could it narrowly define that subject? The performance of state constitutional conventions raises serious doubts that a national convention to amend the Constitution could be bound in advance. Moreover, the convention that wrote the U.S. Constitution ignored its original mandate merely to amend the Articles of Confederation. But if amendments were submitted on subjects not specified in the summoning of a convention, they might be subjected to political attack on the ground that the convention had not been authorized, or its members elected, to act in other areas. Many members of Congress are known to be concerned by the kind of amendments that a "runaway convention" might submit.

● What would be the apportionment of a constitutional convention? The Constitution is also silent on this point. The Constitutional Convention of 1787 had different numbers of delegates from different states but accorded only one vote to each state. Congress presumably could require that a new constitutional convention be apportioned on the same basis as the existing U.S. House, or the House and Senate combined.

● How would delegates be chosen? That question could be left to the discretion of the state legislatures, or Congress might attempt to lay down ground rules requiring the election either by congressional districts or by statewide balloting, or by a combination of the two.

---

issue in the 1864 election. A Republican victory led in January 1865 to House approval by a vote of 119 to 56; a switch of only three votes would have prevented approval. Ratification was completed in December of the same year.

Fourteenth Amendment. "Black codes" adopted by southern state legislatures at the end of the war to limit the civil rights of freed slaves were among the factors leading Congress to propose the Fourteenth Amendment. It was feared that black rights established by the Thirteenth Amendment would prove hollow unless further action were taken. The Freedmen's Bureau Act and the Civil Rights Act of 1866 sought to protect basic rights, and the latter attempted to void by legislation the famous *Dred Scott* decision of 1857 by which the Supreme Court had denied that a free black, let alone a slave, could be considered a citizen of the United States. Although the Civil Rights Act was passed by two-thirds votes in both houses to override President Johnson's veto, its constitutionality remained in doubt. The Fourteenth Amendment was intended, among other things, to give the act constitutional support and accord permanence to the basic rights the act was intended to guarantee.[18]

The third and fourth sections of the amendment were of only temporary significance. They prohibited anyone from holding state or federal office (unless authorized by Congress) who had participated in rebellion after taking an oath to support the U.S. Constitution, and denied the responsibility of federal or state governments for debts incurred in aid of rebellion. The second section of the amendment in effect eliminated the clause of Article I, Section 2, of the Constitution, which directed that three-fourths of the slave population of a state was to be counted in apportioning the House of Representatives. This provision had been rendered obsolete by the Thirteenth Amendment, but the Fourteenth did not stop at basing apportionment on total population (exclusive of Indians not taxed). It further provided that if any state abridged the right of its citizens to vote for federal or state offices, the number of its representatives in the House should be decreased in proportion to the number of adult male citizens denied the vote. Thaddeus Stevens, leader of the Radicals in the House of Representatives, expected this provision to be the most effective instrument for securing black rights, but its inadequacy in guaranteeing the right to vote led later to the Fifteenth Amendment.

The first section of the Fourteenth Amendment declared that all persons born or naturalized in the United States (except those, such as diplomats, not subject to U.S. jurisdiction) were citizens of the United States and of the state in which they resided, thereby nullifying the *Dred Scott* decision. More importantly, it forbade states to deprive any person of life, liberty or property without due process of law, or to deny anyone equal protection of the laws.

The due process and equal protection clauses, both open to wide differences of interpretation, have served as the basis of controversial shifts in the foundations of American government. The Supreme Court at first frustrated the hopes of those backers of the Fourteenth Amendment who expected to see the federal government assume large responsibilities for civil rights. Next, the Court employed the due process clause to frustrate state interference with the principles of laissez faire economics, an approach not abandoned until the New Deal era. Gradually, freedoms guaranteed by the Bill of Rights were extended, by invoking the due process clause, to cover actions by state governments. After the Second World War, the Supreme Court ruled that the equal protection clause prohibited racial segregation in schools, and Congress enacted civil rights legislation sanctioned in part by this section of the Fourteenth Amendment. *(Box p. 219)*

The Fourteenth Amendment was submitted to the states in June 1866. Ratification was refused by nine of the former Confederate states until after Congress had enacted a law making such ratification a condition of their restoration to the Union. In announcing adoption of the amendment in July 1868, Secretary of State Seward declared it had been ratified by the legislatures of 23 states and "by newly constituted and newly established bodies avowing themselves to be and acting as the legislatures" of six southern states.

Fifteenth Amendment. When it became apparent that the Fourteenth Amendment's threat of reduced representation in the House had failed to prompt southern states to extend the franchise to blacks, Congress proposed a more direct approach. The Fifteenth Amendment, submitted to the states in February 1869, prohibited denial of the right to vote on the basis of race, color, or previous condition of servitude. Ratification was completed in February 1870.[19]

Congress in the same year passed an "Enforcement Act" designed to make the amendment effective. This statute sought to prevent the use of technicalities of registration and voting procedures to confuse and intimidate black voters. Heavy penalties were prescribed for

---

Amendments That Failed

By the end of 1974, more than 8,600 proposed amendments to the Constitution had been introduced in Congress. Many of them, of course, were identical or similar proposals; some were introduced repeatedly in successive Congresses. Almost one-third of all the amendments offered since 1789 were introduced in the past 15 years.

Congress has submitted only 32 amendments to the states for ratification; only five (excluding the pending Equal Rights Amendment) were not ratified. Two of the latter were proposed in September 1789, along with the Bill of Rights. The first, which concerned the apportionment of representatives, was ratified by 10 states—one less than the required number. The second, which provided that no law varying the compensation of members of Congress should be operative until after the next national election, was ratified by six states and rejected by five, with three states taking no action.

In 1810, an amendment providing for revocation of the citizenship of any American accepting a gift or title of nobility from any foreign power, without the consent of Congress, was submitted to the states for ratification. The amendment was ratified by 12 states and by the senate of the South Carolina legislature; had it been approved by that legislature's lower house, it would have become a part of the Constitution. The impression prevailed for nearly a generation that the amendment had been adopted.

A proposed amendment to prohibit interference by Congress with the institution of slavery in the states, offered in 1861 as a last effort to ward off the impending conflict between North and South, was ratified by the legislatures of only two states—Ohio and Maryland. A convention called in Illinois in 1862 to revise the state constitution also ratified the amendment, but since Congress had designated state legislatures as the ratifying bodies, this ratification was manifestly invalid.

A more recent amendment proposed by Congress but not ratified by the states was the Child Labor Amendment. It would have empowered Congress to "limit, regulate, and prohibit the labor of persons under 18 years of age." The amendment sought to reverse rulings by the Supreme Court in 1918 in *Hammer v. Dagenhart* (247 U.S. 251) and in 1922 in *Bailey v. Drexel Furniture Co.* (259 U.S. 20), which had struck down child labor laws enacted by Congress.

Submitted to the states June 4, 1924, the amendment had been ratified by 28 of the 48 states by 1938. In that year Congress again enacted a child labor law utilizing its constitutional power to regulate interstate commerce. In 1941 the Supreme Court in *U.S. v. Darby Lumber Co.* (312 U.S. 100) upheld the law, specifically reversing its 1918 decision. Since then, there have been no further ratifications of the proposed amendment.

Source: Congressional Research Service, *The Constitution of the United States of America: Analysis and Interpretation* (Government Printing Office, 1973) pp. 51-52.

state officials convicted of violating the act. Interference with voting rights by bribery or by threats of violence or economic discrimination was outlawed. Enforcement was to be in federal courts, and the President was authorized to use military force as necessary to support the judicial process. The Supreme Court in 1876 in *United States v. Reese* (92 U.S. 214) held portions of this act unconstitutional and in so doing limited the effectiveness of the Fifteenth Amendment. The authority of Congress to enact "appropriate legislation" to enforce the amendment was construed as limited to legislation to combat outright discrimination on the basis of race; the authority, it was ruled, did not extend to the whole field of obstructions of the right to vote. Nearly a century passed before Congress, in the sweeping Voting Rights Act of 1965, made available effective means for federal enforcement of the Fifteenth Amendment's attempt to bar racial discrimination in connection with the right to vote.

Income Tax and Election of Senators

Sixteenth Amendment. Although the federal government had levied an income tax during the Civil War, a similar tax imposed in 1894 was held unconstitutional by the Supreme Court in 1895 in *Pollock v. Farmers' Loan and Trust Co.* (157 U.S. 429). Failure of Congress to submit a remedial amendment during subsequent years was due in part to a belief that such an amendment was unnecessary and that it would be possible to draft an income tax law that would be held constitutional.[20]

Pressure to impose another income tax grew, but President Taft and others opposed action without an authorizing amendment. They feared that to enact a statute similar to one previously declared unconstitutional, in the expectation that the Supreme Court would reverse its earlier decision, would undermine confidence in the Constitution and would subject the court to the pressures of a public campaign. The amendment to empower Congress to levy taxes on incomes "from whatever source derived" was approved by both houses in 1909, but ratification was not completed until early in 1913. At a special session that year, Congress enacted a graduated personal income tax and converted into a direct income tax a levy on corporation income imposed since 1909 in the guise of an excise tax. *(Fiscal Powers p. 111)*

Seventeenth Amendment. The Seventeenth Amendment is of particular interest because it clearly was forced on Congress, or rather on the Senate, by popular pressure. The Constitution provided for the election of senators by the state legislatures. But the Seventeenth Amendment, ratified in 1913, changed the Constitution to provide for direct election of senators. The change was a part of the progressive era's movement toward more democratic control of government. Being less immediately dependent on popular sentiment than the House, the Senate did not seek to reform itself. Only persistent pressure from the public, expressed through the House of Representatives, the state governments, pressure groups, petitions, referenda and other means, convinced the Senate that it must participate in its own reform.[21]

In the first 80 years of Congress, only nine resolutions proposing a constitutional amendment for direct election of senators were introduced in Congress. In the 1870s and 1880s the number increased, and by 1912 a total of not less than 287 such joint resolutions had been introduced. Not until 1892 was a resolution reported favorably from committee in the House. In the next decade such a resolution was carried five times in the House.

Petitions from farmers' associations and other organizations, particularly in the West, and party platforms in state elections pressed the issue until the national parties took it up. Direct election of senators was a plank in the Populist program at every election, beginning in 1892, and in the Democratic platform in each presidential election year from 1900 to 1912. Starting in California and Iowa in 1894, state legislatures addressed Congress in favor of a direct election amendment, until by 1905 the legislatures in 31 of the 45 states had taken this step, many of them repeatedly. In 1900, when the House voted 240-15 in favor of submitting such an amendment to the states, it was supported by a majority of the representatives from every state except Maine and Connecticut. Still the Senate would not act.

The spread of direct primaries in the 1890s led in many states to expressions of a popular choice for senator on the primary ballot. One-party legislatures in the South generally ratified the popular choice, though the primary was less effective in putting over the popular choice in other states. Oregon in 1901 adopted a plan under which voters could express their preferences for senator, though their expression of a preference carried no binding legal force. When the Oregon legislature nevertheless ignored the popular preference in its next election of a senator, voters used their new powers of initiative and referendum to approve a new law. Henceforth candidates for the legislature could indicate on the ballot whether or not they would vote for the Senate candidate with the highest popular vote total. This "Oregon system'" proved effective and was adopted in other states in modified forms. By December 1910 it was estimated that 14 of the 30 senators about to be named by state legislatures had already been designated by popular vote.

In 1901 some of the legislatures, no longer content to request Congress to submit a constitutional amendment to the states, began calling for a convention to amend the Constitution. Some senators, though they opposed a popular election, feared that such a convention, like the original Constitutional Convention, might exceed its original mandate; they preferred to submit to the states a specific amendment for direct election of senators. A resolution was finally brought to the Senate floor in 1911, but it failed, 54-33, to gain the two-thirds support required. In a special session later that year, the House passed, 296-16, a different version of the resolution. The Senate this time approved its original resolution, 64-24. A deadlock was broken at the next session when the House on May 13, 1912, concurred in the Senate version. By April 1913, three-fourths of the states had ratified the Seventeenth Amendment.

Prohibition and Woman Suffrage

Eighteenth Amendment. Prohibition and woman suffrage amendments were first proposed in the platform of the Prohibition Party in 1872. Favorable Senate action on the Prohibition Amendment was taken in the special session called in 1917 to declare war on Germany; House approval of the joint resolution followed in December 1917. The vigorous campaign carried on by the Anti-Saloon League had already resulted in the enactment of Prohibition laws in about half of the states. The war gave impetus to the movement by identifying the attack on alcoholic beverages with patriotism. The effectiveness of the armed forces and the defense industries, it was argued, would be impaired by drunkenness, and the production of alcoholic drinks would divert resources from the war effort. Under war powers granted in the Constitution, Congress enacted legislation to restrict production of liquor and its sale to members of the armed forces.[22]

While the Eighteenth Amendment was before the states, the Wartime Prohibition Act, approved 10 days after the armistice was signed, prohibited sale of distilled spirits, wine, or beer in the United States from June 30, 1919, until the end of the war. The Eighteenth Amendment was ratified in January 1919, only 13 months after its approval by Congress. Power to enforce the amendment's prohibition of the manufacture, sale or transportation of intoxicating liquors was granted concurrently to Congress and the states, a provision which hindered enforcement by dividing responsibility. The Volstead Act, which Congress passed on Oct. 28, 1919, over President Wilson's veto, was intended not only to enforce the amendment but also to strengthen the Wartime Prohibition Act (which continued in effect because the country was still technically at war) until the amendment went into force Jan. 16, 1920, one year after its ratification.

Before Prohibition was abandoned in 1933, it profoundly affected the mores of the American people in ways not anticipated by its advocates. Widespread violation of the amendment and the Volstead Act seriously undermined respect for the law and buttressed the foundations of organized crime.

Nineteenth Amendment. Because the Constitution left qualifications for voting in federal elections to determination by the states, early attempts to authorize woman suffrage focused on the state legislatures. At the time the Fourteenth and Fifteenth Amendments were considered, efforts were made to have their guarantees of voting rights for blacks extended to women as well. These efforts having proved unsuccessful, a resolution proposing an additional amendment granting the vote to women was introduced in the Senate in 1878. The resolution was reintroduced regularly thereafter until it was finally adopted more than 40 years later.[23]

Meanwhile, some of the states went ahead and gave the vote to women within their jurisdiction. Wyoming, which became a state in 1890, had started blazing the trail toward woman suffrage when it accorded women the right to vote for territorial officials in 1869. By 1914, equal suffrage had been granted in 11 states; New York, considered a center of opposition, joined the procession in 1917.

World War I added impetus to the suffrage movement because it was viewed as a crusade for democracy. President Wilson, who had previously favored attainment of woman suffrage by state action, explained his conversion to the amendment route in terms of the war. The House adopted the resolution proposing the Woman Suffrage Amendment in 1918 by a vote of 274-136, a bare two-thirds majority. Wilson, in a surprise visit to the Senate on Sept. 30, urged adoption of the resolution as "vitally essential to the successful prosecution of the great war of humanity in which we are engaged." The next day, however, the Senate failed, in a 62-34 vote, to supply the necessary margin.

When the Republicans won the November election, Wilson pleaded for approval by the lame-duck Democratic Congress, but a Senate vote of 55-29 in February again fell short of the required two-thirds majority. But at a special session of the new Congress the proposed amendment was approved within three weeks. Submitted to the states in June 1919, it was ratified in August 1920. An amendment to guarantee equal rights to women, proposed in every Congress since 1923, was finally passed and sent to the states in 1972. *(Box, this page)*

Equal Rights Amendment

Forty-nine years after it was first introduced, a constitutional amendment guaranteeing equal rights for men and women was approved by the Senate March 22, 1972, and sent to the states for ratification.

The Senate vote was 84-8—22 more than the two-thirds majority required to adopt a proposed constitutional amendment. The House had approved it by a 354-24 roll-call vote on Oct. 12, 1971. The House margin was 102 more than was necessary.

As sent to the states, the amendment provides that "Equality of rights under the law shall not be denied or abridged by the United States or by any state on account of sex," and provides that Congress has the power to enforce the provision by "appropriate legislation." The amendment would take effect two years after ratification. A resolution proposing such an amendment had been introduced in every Congress since 1923. In 1950 and 1953, the Senate had approved the proposed amendment but the House took no action.

If ratified by three-fourths (38) of the states, the Equal Rights Amendment would become the Twenty-seventh Amendment to the Constitution. Less than two hours after the Senate acted on March 22, Hawaii became the first state to ratify the measure. In the six months following congressional passage, 20 other states followed suit. Nine states endorsed the amendment in 1973, three in 1974, and only one—North Dakota—in 1975. At the beginning of 1976, a total of 34 states had ratified the amendment, four short of the requisite number; but several state legislatures had either shelved or flatly rejected the amendment. Moreover, two states that had ratified it—Nebraska and Tennessee—attempted to rescind their approval. The validity of this action would not be tested in court until the amendment had been approved by 38 states, including those two. In sending the amendment to the states, Congress provided that the legislatures had seven years—until 1979—to approve. If it is not ratified by then, proponents of the measure would have to start the entire process all over.

Opposition and Support

Despite official endorsements from a wide spectrum of women's groups, labor unions and political and civic organizations of every stripe, the drive for passage of the Equal Rights Amendment (ERA) encountered vigorous opposition. It was argued that passage of the ERA would subject women to the draft; abolish protections women had from dangerous and unpleasant jobs; wipe out women's rights to privacy in public facilities (hospital facilities, rest rooms and so forth); and adversely affect marriage laws, property and divorce rights. Supporters have responded that the ERA would not affect constitutional privacy rights, but would put an end to unlawful discrimination, ensuring equal treatment for both women and men in such areas as employment, pay, benefits and criminal trials and sentences. According to the American Bar Association, the amendment would not occasion any change in allocation of family-support responsibilities unwanted by the individuals who compose the family unit.

Lame-Duck Amendment

Twentieth Amendment. Like the Twelfth Amendment, the Twentieth Amendment effected a mechanical change in the Constitution. It abolished "lame-duck" sessions of Congress and advanced the date of the inauguration of the President from March 4 to Jan. 20. Under the terms of the amendment, Congress was to convene annually at noon on Jan. 3 unless it "shall by law appoint a different day."[24]

Prior to this change, the Constitution provided that the terms of representatives and outgoing senators were not to end until March 4, four months after the election of a new Congress. While the terms of members of the new Congress began on March 4, the first regular session did not commence until the first Monday of the following December, 13 months after the election.

Although the President often called Congress into special session in the interim, the long wait between the election and the first regular session of a new Congress, and the potential inequity inherent in actions of a lame-duck Congress at the "short session" (December-March), had drawn criticism for at least a century. Finally, in 1922, a resolution proposing an amendment to correct the situation was taken up on the floor of the Senate. The proposed amendment was approved by the Senate no less than six times between 1923 and 1932, when the House at last took favorable action.

The Twentieth Amendment also gives Congress power to act in the event a President-elect or a Vice President-elect dies or fails to qualify for office by the date their terms are to commence. *(See pp. 223, 235)*

Repeal of Prohibition

Twenty-first Amendment. Between 1921 and 1933 more than 130 amendments were proposed in Congress to repeal or modify the Eighteenth Amendment. Prohibition had become so discredited by 1932 that the platforms of both parties favored constitutional revision. The Democrats proposed repeal of the Eighteenth Amendment; the Republicans favored retaining some authority for the federal government to control liquor traffic and to protect those states that chose to continue Prohibition.[25]

The landslide victory at the polls of Franklin D. Roosevelt, who unequivocally supported repeal, probably contributed to the decision of the lame-duck Congress at the session convened in December 1932. A joint resolution proposing an amendment to repeal the Eighteenth Amendment was submitted to the states in February 1933 and, following ratification by the necessary 36 states, went into effect on Dec. 5 of the same year.

The Twenty-first was the only amendment to be ratified by state conventions rather than by the legislatures. Because delegates to these conventions were clearly identified as favoring or opposing repeal of Prohibition, they did not meet to deliberate the issues but simply to execute the will of the voters. The elections to the conventions thus amounted to a national referendum on Prohibition. The result justified the expectations of those who had proposed ratification by conventions; they sought to remove the issue from partisan politics and from organized pressures on rural-dominated legislatures, and to achieve speedy action.

Presidential Tenure and D.C. Vote

Twenty-second Amendment. The first Republican Congress after President Roosevelt's election to four terms quickly approved and sent to the states a proposed amendment to limit presidential tenure to two terms. The amendment provided that no one might be elected President more than twice; and no one who had served as President for more than two years of a term for which someone else had been elected President was to be elected more than once. The President serving when the amendment was proposed (Truman) was exempted from its provisions, and no one serving on the effective date of ratification was to be prevented from completing his term.[26]

During House floor debate, Republicans insisted that the proposal had nothing to do with politics. The purpose, they said, was merely to incorporate in the Constitution the two-term tradition set by George Washington and maintained until 1940, when Roosevelt was elected to a third term. They urged limitation of tenure as a means of warding off any tendency toward dictatorship.

Democrats contended that the resolution would impose "a limitation upon the people," who had a right to make their own choice of President. Rep. John W. McCormack (D Mass.) declared that Washington, Jefferson and Theodore Roosevelt had stated that an emergency—such as that in 1940 and 1944—might make it advisable for a person to accept more than two terms as President.

The Twenty-second Amendment, submitted to the states March 24, 1947, was not ratified by the required three-fourths of the state legislatures until Feb. 27, 1951, nearly four years after its submission by Congress. In 1959 a Senate subcommittee approved a proposal to repeal the amendment, but no further action was taken. At that time, former President Truman said he "never thought well" of the Twenty-second Amendment. President Eisenhower initially called it "unwise," but he later opposed repeal efforts, saying Congress should "see how it works" for a few years.

Twenty-third Amendment. The Twenty-third Amendment, giving the citizens of the District of Columbia the right to vote in presidential elections, was cleared by Congress June 16, 1960. The last time that residents of the District had voted for President was in 1800. The D.C. Suffrage Amendment, as originally introduced, would have allowed residents of Washington to vote for President and Vice President by giving them three representatives in the electoral college, and also would have given the District a nonvoting delegate in the House of Representatives. In order to ensure House approval and to expedite ratification of the amendment, however, Congress agreed to drop the latter provision, limiting the amendment to national suffrage.[27]

As approved by Congress, the proposed amendment authorized the District of Columbia to appoint a number of electors for President and Vice President equal to the number of senators and representatives to which the District would have been entitled if it had been a state (in effect, three electors). It also authorized Congress to prescribe the qualifications of the District's electors and voters. The proposed amendment was submitted to the states in June. Ratification was completed in less than a year, on March 29, 1961.

Most of the opposition to the D.C. Suffrage Amendment came from the South and was apparently motivated by the race issue. (The District's population was then more than 50 per cent black.) Not a single state of the deep South was among the ratifying states. Some Republican state legislatures were also reportedly apprehensive about the amendment because they feared the District would automatically vote Democratic. District Republican leaders sought to allay these fears, however, and it was a GOP-controlled legislature (Kansas) which gave the amendment its needed 38th ratification.

In 1961, Congress implemented the Twenty-third Amendment by enacting legislation spelling out the regulations under which District residents might participate in presidential elections. Principal discussion on the bill centered on voting age and residence requirements. President Kennedy submitted draft legislation which provided for a 90-day residence requirement and an 18-year-old minimum voting age in the District, but the bill, as enacted, established a one-year residence requirement and a minimum voting age of 21. *(See also Control of the Seat of Government chapter p. 287)*

Poll Taxes and Presidential Disability

Twenty-fourth Amendment. Poll taxes were introduced in some states during the early days of the Republic as a substitute for property qualifications for voting. The intent of the early levies was to enlarge the electorate. These taxes had been eliminated in most states before the Civil War, but between 1889 and 1908 poll taxes were instituted in 11 southern states. Though ostensibly adopted to "cleanse" elections of mass abuse, the taxes were approved in the South as a means of keeping blacks and poor whites from the polls. By 1953, however, only five southern states still required payment of a poll tax as a prerequisite for voting.[28]

Bills to ban such poll taxes by statute, rather than by constitutional amendment, were approved five times between 1942 and 1949 by the House, but died each time in the Senate, with filibusters in 1942, 1944 and 1946. Beginning in 1949, Sen. Spessard L. Holland (D Fla.) introduced a proposed anti-poll tax amendment in every Congress, but it was never reported by the Senate Judiciary Committee. Those who preferred action by legislation feared that reliance on amendment of the Constitution to effect the desired reform would set a precedent that would make other civil rights measures more difficult to enact.

On the theory that poll taxes were not specifically designed to keep blacks from voting, Holland and most of his supporters argued that there was no language in the Constitution that barred a poll tax and therefore it had to be achieved by the amendment process. To do otherwise, they said, would open the states' control over election machinery to attack by federal legislation. (Language in Article I, Section 2, and in the Seventeenth Amendment to the Constitution set the "qualifications" for voters in federal elections as those "requisite" for the electors of the most numerous branch of the state legislature.)

Offered by Holland as a substitute for a minor measure in 1962, the joint resolution proposing the poll tax amendment was approved by the Senate in a 77-16 roll call. The House adopted the resolution, 295-86, on Aug. 27, 1962, and ratification was completed Jan. 23, 1964. The amendment outlawed payment of "any poll tax or other tax" as a voter qualification only in federal elections. A move to extend the ban to state and local elections before the Voting Rights Act of 1965 was not successful, but the final compromise version of the act contained a finding that poll taxes in certain states denied or abridged the right to vote. The act directed the Attorney General to challenge those taxes in the courts "forthwith." The Supreme Court in 1966 [*Harper v. Virginia State Board of Elections* and *Butts v. Harrison*, decided as one case (383 U.S. 663)] struck down Virginia's

---

Time Taken to Ratify Amendments

The time elapsing between the submission by Congress of a constitutional amendment and its ratification by the requisite number of states has averaged about one and one-half years. The first 10 amendments were proposed and ratified as a group, the process taking two years and 81 days. The longest time of all—three years and 340 days—was needed to complete ratification of the Twenty-second Amendment. In contrast, the Twenty-sixth Amendment was ratified in 100 days, and eight other amendments were ratified in less than one year. The detailed record follows:

Amendment	Passed Congress	Ratified	Time Elapsed Years	Days
1-10 (Bill of Rights)	Sept. 25, 1789	Dec. 15, 1791	2	81
11 (Suits Against States)	Mar. 4, 1794	Feb. 7, 1795		340
12 (Presidential Electors)	Dec. 9, 1803	June 15, 1804		189
13 (Abolition of Slavery)	Jan. 31, 1865	Dec. 6, 1865		309
14 (Civil Rights: Due Process)	June 13, 1866	July 9, 1868	2*	26
15 (Black Suffrage)	Feb. 26, 1869	Feb. 3, 1870		342
16 (Income Tax)	July 12, 1909	Feb. 3, 1913	3*	206
17 (Direct Election of Senators)	May 13, 1912	April 8, 1913		330
18 (Prohibition)	Dec. 18, 1917	Jan. 16, 1919	1	29
19 (Woman Suffrage)	June 4, 1919	Aug. 18, 1920	1*	75
20 ("Lame Duck")	Mar. 2, 1932	Jan. 23, 1933		327
21 (Prohibition Repeal)	Feb. 20, 1933	Dec. 5, 1933		288
22 (Presidential Tenure)	Mar. 24, 1947	Feb. 27, 1951	3*	340
23 (D.C. Vote)	June 16, 1960	Mar. 29, 1961		286
24 (Poll Tax)	Sept. 14, 1962	Jan. 23, 1964	1	131
25 (Presidential Disability)	July 6, 1965	Feb. 10, 1967	1	219
26 (18-Year Vote)	Mar. 23, 1971	July 1, 1971		100

* Includes a leap year.

Source: Congressional Research Service, Library of Congress, *The Constitution of the United States of America: Analysis and Interpretation* (Government Printing Office, 1973).

---

poll-tax requirement for state elections as a violation of the equal protection clause of the Fourteenth Amendment.[29]

Twenty-fifth Amendment. Congressional consideration of the question of presidential disability was prompted by President Eisenhower's heart attack in 1955. But ambiguity in the language of the disability clause, Article II, Section I, Clause 6 of the Constitution, had provoked occasional debate ever since the Constitutional Convention of 1787. It had never been agreed how far the term "disability" extended or who was to be the judge of it.[30]

Clause 6 provided that Congress should decide who was to succeed to the presidency in the event that both the President and the Vice President died, resigned, or became disabled. Congress enacted succession laws three times, but the procedures to follow in the event of presidential incapacity had not been laid down by statute. Two Presidents had become seriously disabled in office—President Garfield, who lived for 11 weeks after he was shot in 1881, and President Wilson, who suffered a severe stroke in 1919. In each case the Vice President did not assume any duties of the presidency for fear he would appear to be usurping the powers of that office. After President Eisenhower's series of illnesses in 1955, 1956 and 1957, the President and Vice

President Nixon entered into an agreement for an orderly, temporary transfer of power should the President again become incapacitated. Nixon would have become Acting President after "such consultation as it seems to him appropriate under the circumstances." Presidents Kennedy and Johnson made the same agreements with their respective Vice Presidents, but the legality of these informal arrangements was questioned by some.

The joint resolution proposing the Twenty-fifth Amendment was introduced in January 1965 and approved by Congress, with scarcely any opposition, six months later. Ratification was completed Feb. 10, 1967. The amendment provided that the Vice President should become Acting President under either one of two circumstances. If the President informed Congress that he was unable to perform his duties, the Vice President would become Acting President until the President could resume his responsibilities.

If the Vice President and a majority of the Cabinet, or other body designated by Congress, found the President to be incapacitated, the Vice President would become Acting President until the President informed Congress that his disability had ended. Congress was given 21 days to resolve any dispute over the President's disability.

Whenever a vacancy occurred in the office of Vice President, either by death, succession to the presidency or resignation, the President was to nominate a Vice President to be confirmed by a majority vote of both houses of Congress. *(Further discussion of amendment and proposals for change, p. 242)*

18-Year-Old Vote

Twenty-sixth Amendment. Congress in 1970 enacted legislation lowering the voting age to 18 beginning Jan. 1, 1971. Although President Nixon signed the measure in June 1970 (PL 91-285), he stated that he believed the law was unconstitutional because Congress had no power to extend the suffrage by simple statute. It should initiate such action by constitutional amendment, he said.[31]

At the time of enactment, voters in three states—New Jersey, Ohio and Oregon—already had rejected proposals to lower voter ages in 1969 and 1970. Fifteen more states had scheduled referenda on the issue in the November elections. Only four states allowed persons to vote under the age of 21. They were Georgia and Kentucky, 18; Alaska, 19; and Hawaii, 20.

On Dec. 21, 1970, the Supreme Court, by a 5-to-4 decision in *Oregon v. Mitchell* (400 U.S. 112), upheld the new law lowering the voting age to 18 in presidential and congressional elections, but ruled the change unconstitutional as it applied to state and local elections.

The 92nd Congress wasted little time early in 1971 in approving and sending to the states a proposed Twenty-sixth Amendment lowering the voting age in all elections. Final congressional action was taken on March 23 by a 401-19 roll-call vote in the House. The Senate had approved the measure March 10 by a 94-0 roll call.

The Twenty-sixth Amendment was ratified by the required number of states by July 1, a record time for approval of a constitutional amendment. The speed of ratification was due in part to the fact that without the amendment, many states would have been faced with the cost and administrative difficulty of keeping separate registration books, ballots and voting apparatus for federal and for state and local elections. *(Time Taken to Ratify Amendments, p. 229)*

Footnotes

1. Background on the Constitutional Convention, see Bryant Putney, "Revision of the Constitution," *Editorial Research Reports,* April 21, 1937, pp. 285-303; Charles Warren, *The Making of the Constitution* (Little, Brown and Co., 1928), pp. 672-84.

2. Putney, "Revision of the Constitution," p. 293.

3. Warren, *The Making of the Constitution,* p. 735.

4. *The Federalist Papers,* with an Introduction by Clinton Rossiter (Mentor, 1961), p. 278.

5. Wallace Mendelson, *The Constitution and the Supreme Court* (Dodd, Mead and Company, 1965), pp. 6-9.

6. James MacGregor Burns and J. W. Pelatson, with Thomas E. Cronin, *Government by the People,* 9th edition (Prentice-Hall Inc., 1975), p. 64.

7. C. Herman Pritchett, *The American Constitution* (McGraw-Hill Company, 1968), p. 35.

8. *Ibid.,* p. 36.

9. Burns, et al., *Government by the People,* p. 67.

10. Pritchett, *The American Constitution,* p. 42.

11. Background, see Pritchett, pp. 395-98; and Alfred H. Kelly and Winfred A. Harbison, *The American Constitution* (W.W. Norton and Co. Inc., 1955), pp. 174-76.

12. Pritchett, *The American Constitution,* pp. 399-400.

13. *Ibid.,* p. 416.

14. *Ibid.,* pp. 529-30.

15. Burns et al., *Government by the People,* p. 68.

16. Pritchett, *The American Constitution,* pp. 309-12; Putney, "Revision of the Constitution," p. 294.

17. Burns et al., *Government by the People,* pp. 204-05.

18. Pritchett, *The American Constitution,* pp. 404-10.

19. *Ibid.,* pp. 746-47.

20. *Ibid.,* p. 235; Frederic A. Ogg and P. Orman Ray, *Introduction to American Government* (Appleton-Century-Crofts Inc., 1951), p. 36.

21. Ogg and Ray, pp. 270-73; Congressional Quarterly, *Congress and the Nation,* Vol. I (1965), p. 1415-17.

22. Putney, "Revision of the Constitution," p. 296.

23. Ogg and Ray, *Introduction to American Government,* pp. 152-54.

24. Burns, et al., *Government by the People,* p. 73.

25. Ogg and Ray, *Introduction to American Government,* p. 38; Putney, "Revision of the Constitution," p. 296.

26. *Congress and the Nation,* Vol. I, pp. 1434-35.

27. *Ibid.,* pp. 1514-16.

28. *Ibid.,* pp. 1615-17, 1625, 1627, 1631-32, 1641.

29. Congressional Quarterly, *Congress and the Nation,* Vol. II (1969), p. 353; Pritchett, *The American Constitution,* p. 754.

30. *Congress and the Nation,* Vol. II, pp. 645-48.

31. Congressional Quarterly, *Congress and the Nation,* Vol. III (1973), pp. 1003-06.

Selected Bibliography

Books

Boorstin, Daniel J. *An American Primer.* Chicago: University of Chicago Press, 1966.

Burns, James MacGregor, and Peltason, Jack Walter, with Cronin, Thomas E. *Government by the People. 9th* ed. Englewood Cliffs, N.J.: Prentice-Hall, 1975.

Crosskey, William W. *Politics and the Constitution in the History of the United States.* 2 vols. Chicago: University of Chicago Press, 1953.

Gillette, William. *Right to Vote: Politics and the Passage of the Fifteenth Amendment.* Baltimore: Johns Hopkins University Press, 1970.

Haynes, George H. *The Senate of the United States: Its History and Practice.* 2 vols. Boston: Houghton Mifflin Co., 1938.

Katz, William L. *Constitutional Amendments.* New York: Franklin Watts, 1974.

Kelly, Alfred H., and Harbison, Winfred A. *The American Constitution.* New York: W. W. Norton and Co., 1955.

Lasson, Nelson B. *History and Development of the Fourth Amendment to the United States Constitution.* New York: Plenum, 1970.

Mathews, John M. *Legislative and Judicial History of the Fifteenth Amendment.* New York: Da Capo Press, 1971.

Mendelson, Wallace. *The Constitution and the Supreme Court.* New York: Dodd, Mead and Co., 1965.

Morgan, Donald G. *Congress and the Constitution: A Study of Responsibility.* Cambridge: Harvard University Press, 1966.

Munro, William B., ed. *Initiative, Referendum and Recall.* New York: D. Appleton, 1912.

Oberholtzer, Ellis P. *Referendum in America.* New York: Da Capo Press, 1971.

Ogg, Frederic A., and Ray, P. Orman. *Introduction to American Government.* New York: Appleton-Century-Crofts Inc., 1951.

Orfield, Lester B. *Amending of the Federal Constitution.* New York: Da Capo Press, 1971.

Pritchett, C. Herman. *The American Constitution.* 2nd ed. New York: McGraw-Hill, 1968.

Vose, Clement E. *Constitutional Change: Amendment Politics and Supreme Court Litigation Since 1900.* Lexington, Mass.: Lexington Books, 1972.

Warren, Charles. *The Making of the Constitution.* Boston: Little, Brown and Co., 1928.

Articles

Feerick, John D. "Amending the Constitution Through a Convention." *American Bar Association Journal,* March 1974, pp. 258-88.

Forbush, Emory. "The Poll Tax." *Editorial Research Reports,* July 3, 1941, pp. 1-18.

Lacy, Donald P., and Martin, Philip L. "Amending the Constitution: The Bottleneck in the Judiciary Committees." *Harvard Journal on Legislation,* May 1972, pp. 666-93.

Martin, Philip L. "The Application Clause of Article Five." *Political Science Quarterly,* December 1970, pp. 616-28.

Patch, Buel W. "Tax and Debt Limitation." *Editorial Research Reports,* Feb. 13, 1952, pp. 121-40.

"Proposed Legislation on the Convention Method of Amending the United States Constitution." *Harvard Law Review,* June 1972, pp. 1612-48.

Putney, Bryant. "Revision of the Constitution." *Editorial Research Reports,* April 21, 1937, pp. 285-303.

Government Publications

U.S. Congress. Library of Congress. Congressional Research Service. *The Constitution of the United States: Analysis and Interpretation.* Washington, D.C.: Government Printing Office, 1973.

U.S. Congress. *The Proposed Amendments to the Constitution of the United States During the First Century of Its History,* by Herman V. Ames. H. Doc. 353, pt. 2, 54th Cong., 2nd sess., 1896.

U.S. Congress. *Proposed Amendments to the Constitution of the United States, 1889-1928,* by Michael A. Musmanno. H. Doc. 551, 70th Cong., 2nd sess., 1929.

U.S. Congress. Senate Library. *Proposed Amendments to the Constitution of the United States, 1926-1963.* S. Doc. 163, 87th Cong., 2nd sess., 1963.

U.S. Congress. Senate Library. *Proposed Amendments to the Constitution of the United States of America, 1963-1969.* S. Doc. 91-38, 91st Cong., 1st sess., 1969.

Power to Elect the President

Congress under the Constitution has two key responsibilities relating to the election of the President and Vice President of the United States. First, it is directed to receive and in joint session count the electoral votes certified by the states. Second, if no candidate has a majority of the electoral vote, the House of Representatives must elect the President and the Senate the Vice President.

Although many of the framers of the Constitution apparently thought that most elections would be decided by Congress, the House actually has chosen a President only twice, in 1801 and 1825. But in the course of the nation's history a number of campaigns have been deliberately designed to throw elections into the House, where each state has one vote and a majority of states is needed to elect; apprehension over such an outcome has nurtured electoral reform efforts over the years.

In modern times the formal counting of electoral votes has been largely a ceremonial function, but the congressional role can be decisive when votes are contested. The preeminent example is the Hayes-Tilden contest of 1876, when congressional decisions on disputed electoral votes from four states gave the election to Republican Rutherford B. Hayes despite the fact that Democrat Samuel J. Tilden had a majority of the popular vote. From the very beginning, the constitutional provisions governing the selection of the President have had few defenders, and many efforts at electoral-college reform have been undertaken.

In addition to its role in electing the President, Congress bears responsibility in the related areas of presidential succession and disability. The Twentieth Amendment empowers Congress to decide what to do if the President-elect and the Vice President-elect both fail to qualify by the date prescribed for commencement of their terms; it also gives Congress authority to settle problems arising from the death of candidates in cases where the election devolves upon Congress. Under the Twenty-fifth Amendment, Congress has ultimate responsibility for resolving disputes over presidential disability. It also must confirm presidential nominations to fill a vacancy in the vice presidency.

The power of the President to appoint a new Vice President under the terms of the Twenty-fifth Amendment has been used twice since the amendment was ratified on Feb. 10, 1967. It was used for the first time in 1973 when Vice President Spiro T. Agnew resigned and President Richard M. Nixon nominated Gerald R. Ford as the new Vice President. It was used again in 1974 after Nixon resigned and Ford succeeded to the presidency and chose former New York Gov. Nelson A. Rockefeller as Vice President.

Constitutional Background

The method of selecting a President was the subject of long debate at the Constitutional Convention of 1787. Several plans were proposed and rejected before a compromise solution, which was modified only slightly in future years, was adopted (Article II, Section 1, Clause 2).[1]

Facing the Convention when it convened May 25 was the question of whether the chief executive should be chosen by direct popular election, by the Congress, by state legislatures or by intermediate electors. Direct election was opposed because it was generally felt that the people lacked sufficient knowledge of the character and qualifications of possible candidates to make an intelligent choice. Many delegates also feared that the people of the various states would be unlikely to agree on a single person, usually casting their votes for favorite-son candidates well-known to them. Southerners opposed direct election for the additional reason that suffrage was more widespread in the North than in the South, where black slaves did not vote.

The possibility of giving Congress the power to pick the President also received consideration. However, this plan also was rejected, largely because of fear that it would jeopardize the principle of executive independence. Similarly, a plan favored by many delegates, to let state legislatures choose the President, was turned down because it was feared that the President might feel so indebted to the states as to allow them to encroach on federal authority.

Unable to agree on a plan, the Convention on Aug. 31 appointed a "Committee of Eleven" to propose a solution to the problem. The committee on Sept. 4 suggested a compromise under which each state would appoint presidential electors (known as the electoral college), equal to the total number of its representatives and senators. The electors, chosen in a manner set forth by each state legislature, would meet in their own states and each cast votes for two persons. The votes would be counted in Congress, with the candidate receiving a majority elected President, and the second highest candidate becoming Vice President.

No distinction was made between ballots for President and Vice President. The development of national political parties and the nomination of tickets for President and Vice

President caused confusion in the electoral system. All the electors of one party would tend to cast ballots for their two party nominees. But with no distinction between the presidential and vice presidential nominees, the danger arose of a tie vote between the two. This actually happened in 1800, leading to a change in the original electoral system with the Twelfth Amendment.

The committee plan constituted a great concession to the less populous states, since they were assured two extra votes (corresponding to their senators) regardless of how small their populations might be. The plan also left important powers with the states by giving complete discretion to state legislatures to determine the method of choosing electors.

Only one provision of the committee's plan aroused serious opposition—that giving the Senate the right to decide elections in which no candidate received a majority of electoral votes. Some delegates feared that the Senate, which already had been given treaty ratification powers and the responsibility to "advise and consent" to all important executive appointments, might become too powerful. Therefore, a counterproposal was made, and accepted, to let the House decide in instances when the electors failed to give a majority of their votes to a single candidate. The interests of the small states were preserved by giving each delegation only one vote in the House on roll calls to elect a President.

The system adopted by the Constitutional Convention was a compromise born out of problems involved in diverse state voting requirements, the slavery problem, big- versus small-state rivalries and the complexities of the balance of power among different branches of the government. It also was apparently as close to a direct popular election as the men who wrote the Constitution thought possible and appropriate at the time. Some scholars have suggested that the electoral college, as it came to be called, was a "jerry-rigged improvisation" which really left to future generations to work out the best form of presidential election.[2]

Changes in System

Only once since ratification of the Constitution has an amendment been adopted which substantially altered the method of electing the President. In the 1800 presidential election, the Republican (anti-Federalist) electors inadvertently caused a tie in the electoral college by casting equal numbers of votes for Thomas Jefferson, whom they wished to be elected President, and Aaron Burr, whom they wished to elect Vice President. The election was thrown into the House of Representatives and 36 ballots were required before Jefferson was finally elected President. The Twelfth Amendment, ratified in 1804, sought to prevent a recurrence of this incident by providing that the electors should vote separately for President and Vice President.[3]

Other changes in the system evolved over the years.[4] The authors of the Constitution, for example, had intended that each state should choose its most distinguished citizens as electors and that they would deliberate and vote as individuals in electing the President. But as strong political parties began to appear, the electors came to be chosen merely as representatives of the parties; independent voting by electors almost disappeared.

However, sometimes in American political history an elector has broken ranks to vote for a candidate other than his party's. In 1796, a Pennsylvania Federalist elector voted for Democratic-Republican Thomas Jefferson instead of Federalist John Adams. And in 1820, the New Hampshire

Democratic-Republican elector voted for John Quincy Adams instead of the party nominee, James Monroe.

There was no further occurrence until 1948, when Preston Parks, a Truman elector in Tennessee, voted for Gov. Strom Thurmond of South Carolina, the State Rights Democratic Party (Dixiecrat) presidential nominee. Since then, there have been the following additional instances:

● In 1956, when W.F. Turner, an Adlai E. Stevenson II elector in Alabama, voted for a local judge, Walter E. Jones.

● In 1960 when Henry D. Irwin, a Nixon elector in Oklahoma, voted for Sen. Harry F. Byrd (D Va.).

● In 1968, when Dr. Lloyd W. Bailey, a Nixon elector in North Carolina, voted for George C. Wallace, the American Independent Party candidate.

● In 1972, when Roger L. McBride, a Nixon elector in Virginia, voted for John Hospers, the Libertarian Party candidate.

The original system underwent further change as democratic sentiment mounted early in the 19th century, bringing with it the demand that electors should be chosen by direct popular vote of the people, instead of by the state legislatures. By 1804, the majority of state legislatures had adopted popular-vote provisions.

Initially, most "popular-election" states provided that electors should be chosen from districts similar to congressional districts, with the electoral votes of a state split if the various districts differed in their political sentiment. This "district plan" of choosing electors was supported by the leading statesmen of both parties, including Thomas Jefferson, Alexander Hamilton, James Madison, John Quincy Adams, Andrew Jackson and Daniel Webster.[5]

The district plan, however, tended to dilute the power of political bosses and dominant majorities in state legislatures, who found themselves unable to "deliver" their states for one candidate or another. These groups brought pressure for a change and the states moved toward a winner-take-all popular ballot. Under this system, all of a state's electoral votes went to the party which won a plurality of popular votes statewide.

By 1804, six of the 11 "popular-election" states cast their electoral votes under the statewide popular ballot; by 1824, 12 out of 18. By 1836 all states except South Carolina had adopted the system of choosing electors statewide by popular vote. (After the Civil War, South Carolina switched from the practice of selecting its electors through the state legislature to a system of statewide, popular vote selection.)

However, since no mention of the statewide, popular election system was ever written into the Constitution, the state legislatures retained the power to specify any method of choosing presidential electors and to determine how their votes would be divided. In 1969, for example, Maine adopted a partial district system for use in the 1972 presidential election.

Election by Congress

The election of 1800 was the first in which the contingent election procedures of the Constitution were put to the test and the President was elected by the House of Representatives.[6]

The Federalists, a declining but still potent political force, nominated John Adams for a second term and chose Charles Cotesworth Pinckney as his running mate. A Republican congressional caucus chose Vice President Thomas Jefferson for President and Aaron Burr, who had

(Continued on p. 236)

Constitutional Provisions for Presidential Selection

Article II

Section 1. The executive Power shall be vested in a President of the United States of America. He shall hold his Office during the Term of four Years, and, together with the Vice President, chosen for the same Term, be elected, as follows

Each State shall appoint, in such Manner as the Legislature thereof may direct, a Number of Electors, equal to the whole Number of Senators and Representatives to which the State may be entitled in the Congress: but no Senator or Representative, or Person holding an Office of Trust or Profit under the United States, shall be appointed an Elector.

[The Electors shall meet in their respective States, and vote by Ballot for two Persons, of whom one at least shall not be an Inhabitant of the same State with themselves. And they shall make a List of all the Persons voted for, and of the Number of Votes for each; which List they shall sign and certify, and transmit sealed to the Seat of the Government of the United States, directed to the President of the Senate. The President of the Senate shall, in the Presence of the Senate and House of Representatives, open all the Certificates, and the Votes shall then be counted. The Person having the greatest Number of Votes shall be the President, if such Number be a Majority of the whole Number of Electors appointed; and if there be more than one who have such Majority; and have an equal Number of Votes, then the House of Representatives shall immediately chuse by Ballot one of them for President; and if no Person have a Majority, then from the five highest on the List the said House shall in like Manner chuse the President. But in chusing the President, the Votes shall be taken by States, the Representation from each State having one Vote; A quorum for this Purpose shall consist of a Member or Members from two thirds of the States, and a Majority of all the States shall be necessary to a Choice. In every Case, after the Choice of the President, the Person having the greatest Number of Votes of the Electors shall be the Vice President. But if there should remain two or more who have equal Votes, the Senate shall chuse from them by Ballot the Vice President.].*

The Congress may determine the Time of chusing the Electors, and the Day on which they shall give their Votes; which Day shall be the same throughout the United States.

No Person except a natural born Citizen, or a Citizen of the United States, at the time of the Adoption of this Constitution, shall be eligible to the Office of President; neither shall any Person be eligible to that Office who shall not have attained to the Age of thirty five Years, and been fourteen Years a Resident within the United States....

Amendment XII *(Ratified June 15, 1804)*

The Electors shall meet in their respective states and vote by ballot for President and Vice-President, one of whom, at least, shall not be an inhabitant of the same state with themselves; they shall name in their ballots the person voted for as President, and in distinct ballots the person voted for as Vice-President, and they shall make distinct lists of all persons voted for as President, and of all persons voted for as Vice-President, and of the number of votes for each, which lists they shall sign and certify, and transmit sealed to the seat of the government of the United States, directed to the President of the Senate;—The President of the Senate shall, in the presence of the Senate and House of Representatives, open all the certificates and the votes shall then be counted;—The person having the greatest number of votes for President, shall be the President, if such number be a majority of the whole number of Electors appointed; and if no persons have such majority, then from the persons having the highest numbers not exceeding three on the list of those voted for as President, the House of Representatives shall choose immediately, by ballot, the President. But in choosing the President, the votes shall be taken by states, the representation from each state having one vote; a quorum for this purpose shall consist of a member or members from two-thirds of the states, and a majority of all the states shall be necessary to a choice. [And if the House of Representatives shall not choose a President whenever the right of choice shall devolve upon them, before the fourth day of March next following, then the Vice-President shall act as President, as in the case of the death or other constitutional disability of the President.—]† The person having the greatest number of votes as Vice-President, shall be the Vice-President, if such number be a majority of the whole number of Electors appointed, and if no person have a majority, then from the two highest numbers on the list, the Senate shall choose the Vice-President; a quorum for the purpose shall consist of two-thirds of the whole number of Senators, and a majority of the whole number shall be necessary to a choice. But no person constitutionally ineligible to the office of President shall be eligible to that of Vice-President of the United States.

Amendment XX *(Ratified Jan. 23, 1933)*

Section 1. The terms of the President and Vice President shall end at noon on the 20th day of January,....

Section 3.# If, at the time fixed for the beginning of the term of the President, the President elect shall have died, the Vice President elect shall become President. If a President shall not have been chosen before the time fixed for the beginning of his term, or if the President elect shall have failed to qualify, then the Vice President elect shall act as President until a President shall have qualified; and the Congress may by law provide for the case wherein neither a President elect nor a Vice President elect shall have qualified, declaring who shall then act as President, or the manner in which one who is to act shall be selected, and such person shall act accordingly until a President or Vice President shall have qualified.

Section 4. The Congress may by law provide for the case of the death of any of the persons from whom the House of Representatives may choose a President whenever the right of choice shall have devolved upon them, and for the case of the death of any of the persons from whom the Senate may choose a Vice President whenever the right of choice shall have devolved upon them....

*Superseded by the Twelfth Amendment.
†.Changed by the Twentieth Amendment.
See Twenty-fifth Amendment. (Text, p. 242)

Contingent Election Critics

Except for the Founding Fathers, few Americans have ever found much to commend in the system of contingent election of a President by the House. Some comments:

Thomas Jefferson, 1823: "I have ever considered the constitutional mode of election ultimately by the Legislature voting by states as the most dangerous blot on our Constitution, and one which some unlucky chance will some day hit."

Martin Van Buren, 1826: "There is no point on which the people of the United States (are) more perfectly united than upon the propriety, not to say the absolute necessity, of taking the election away from the House of Representatives."

Sen. Oliver P. Morton of Indiana, a leading reform advocate, 1873: "The objections to this constitutional provision for the election of the President need only to be stated, not argued. First, its manifest injustice. In such an election each state is to have but one vote. Nevada, with its 42,000 population, has an equal vote with New York, having 104 times as great a population. It is a mockery to call such an election just, fair or republican."

Source: Neal Peirce, *The People's President: The Electoral College and the Emerging Consensus for a Direct Vote* (Simon & Schuster, 1968), p. 132.

been instrumental in winning the New York legislature for the Republicans earlier in 1800, for Vice President.

The bitterly fought campaign was marked by efforts in several state to change for partisan advantage the methods of selecting electors. In New York, where electors previously had been chosen by the legislature, Hamilton proposed that Governor John Jay call the lame-duck Federalist legislature into special session to adopt a proposal for popular election of electors under a district system, thus denying the incoming Republicans an opportunity to appoint electors. Jay declined, and in the end the new Republican legislature cast all 12 New York electoral votes for Jefferson and Burr.

The Federalists were more successful in Pennsylvania, another critical state. The state senate, where holdover members maintained Federalist control, refused to renew legislation providing for selection of electors by statewide popular vote. The Republican house of representatives was forced to accept a compromise that gave the Federalists seven electors and the Republicans eight.

Jefferson-Burr Deadlock

The electors met in each state on Dec. 4, and the results gradually became known throughout the country: Jefferson and Burr, 73 electoral votes each; Adams, 65; Pinckney, 64; John Jay, 1. The Federalists had lost, but because the Republicans had neglected to withhold one electoral vote from Burr, their presidential and vice presidential candidates were tied and the election was thrown into the House.

The lame-duck Congress, with a strong Federalist majority, would still be in office for the electoral count, and the possibilities for intrigue were only too apparent. After toying with and rejecting a proposal to block any election until March 4 when Adams' term expired, the Federalists decided

to throw their support to Burr and thus elect a cynical and pliant politician over a man they considered a "dangerous radical." Alexander Hamilton opposed this move: "I trust the Federalists will not finally be so mad as to vote for Burr," he wrote. "I speak with intimate and accurate knowledge of his character. His elevation can only promote the purposes of the desperate and the profligate. If there be a man in the world I ought to hate, it is Jefferson. With Burr I have always been personally well. But the public good must be paramount to every private consideration."[7]

On Feb. 11, 1801, Congress met in joint session—with Jefferson in the chair—to count the electoral vote. This ritual ended, the House retired to its own chamber to elect a President. When the House met, it became apparent that the advice of Hamilton had been rejected. A majority of Federalists in the House insisted on backing Burr over Jefferson, the man they despised more. Indeed, if Burr had given clear assurances he would run the country as a Federalist, he might well have been elected. But Burr was unwilling to make those assurances; and, as one chronicler put it, "no one knows whether it was honor or a wretched indecision which gagged Burr's lips."[8]

In all, there were 106 members of the House at the time, consisting of 58 Federalists and 48 Republicans. If the ballots had been cast per capita, Burr would have been elected, but the Constitution provided that each state cast one vote and a majority was necessary for election.

On the first ballot, Jefferson received the votes of eight states, one short of a majority of the 16 states then in the Union. Six states backed Burr, while the representatives of Vermont and of Maryland were equally divided, so they lost their votes.

In all, 36 ballots were taken before the House came to a decision on Feb. 17. Predictably, there were men who sought to exploit the situation for personal gain. Jefferson wrote on Feb. 15: "Many attempts have been made to obtain terms and promises from me. I have declared to them unequivocally that I would not receive the Government on capitulation; that I would not go in with my hands tied."[9]

The impasse was finally broken when Vermont and Maryland switched to support of Jefferson. Delaware and South Carolina also withdrew their support from Burr by casting blank ballots. The final vote: 10 states for Jefferson, 4 (all New England) for Burr. Thus Jefferson became President, and Burr automatically became Vice President.

Federalist James A. Bayard of Delaware, who had played a key role in breaking the deadlock, wrote to Hamilton: "The means existed of electing Burr, but this required his cooperation. By deceiving one man (a great blockhead) and tempting two (not incorruptible), he might have secured a majority of the states. He will never have another chance of being President of the United States; and the little use he has made of the one which has occurred gives me but an humble opinion of the talents of an unprincipled man."[10]

The Jefferson-Burr contest clearly illustrated the dangers of the double-balloting system established by the original Constitution, and pressure began to build for an amendment requiring separate votes for President and Vice President. Congress approved the Twelfth Amendment in December 1803, and the states—acting with unexpected speed—ratified it in time for the 1804 election.

John Quincy Adams' Election

The only other time a President was elected by the House of Representatives was in 1825. There were many

Presidential Election by the House

The following rules, reprinted from Hinds' Precedents of the House of Representatives, *were adopted by the House in 1825 for use in deciding the presidential election of 1824. They would provide a precedent for any future House election of a President, although the House could change them at will. On February 9, 1825, the election of John Quincy Adams took place in accordance with these rules.*

1. In the event of its appearing, on opening all the certificates, and counting the votes given by the electors of the several States for President, that no person has a majority of the votes of the whole number of electors appointed, the same shall be entered on the Journals of this House.

2. The roll of the House shall then be called by States; and, on its appearing that a Member or Members from two-thirds of the States are present, the House shall immediately proceed, by ballot, to choose a President from the persons having the highest numbers, not exceeding three, on the list of those voted for as President; and, in case neither of those persons shall receive the votes of a majority of all the States on the first ballot, the House shall continue to ballot for a President, without interruption by other business, until a President be chosen.

3. The doors of the Hall shall be closed during the balloting, except against the Members of the Senate, stenographers, and the officers of the House.

4. From the commencement of the balloting until an election is made no proposition to adjourn shall be received, unless on the motion of one State, seconded by another State, and the question shall be decided by States. The same rule shall be observed in regard to any motion to change the usual hour for the meeting of the House.

5. In balloting the following mode shall be observed, to wit:

The Representatives of each State shall be arranged and seated together, beginning with the seats at the right hand of the Speaker's chair, with the Members from the State of Maine; thence, proceeding with the Members from the States, in the order the States are usually named for receiving petitions,* around the Hall of the House, until all are seated.

A ballot box shall be provided for each State.

The Representatives of each State shall, in the first instance, ballot among themselves, in order to ascertain the vote of their State; and they may, if necessary, appoint tellers of their ballots.

After the vote of each State is ascertained, duplicates thereof shall be made out; and in case any one of the persons from whom the choice is to be made shall receive a majority of the votes given, on any one balloting by the Representatives of a State, the name of that

person shall be written on each of the duplicates; and in case the votes so given shall be divided so that neither of said persons shall have a majority of the whole number of votes given by such State, on any one balloting, then the word "divided" shall be written on each duplicate.

After the delegation from each State shall have ascertained the vote of their State, the Clerk shall name the States in the order they are usually named for receiving petitions; and as the name of each is called the Sergeant-at-Arms shall present to the delegation of each two ballot boxes, in each of which shall be deposited, by some Representative of the State, one of the duplicates made as aforesaid of the vote of said State, in the presence and subject to the examination of all the Members from said State then present; and where there is more than one Representative from a State, the duplicates shall not both be deposited by the same person.

When the votes of the States are thus all taken in, the Sergeant-at-Arms shall carry one of said ballot boxes to one table and the other to a separate and distinct table.

One person from each State represented in the balloting shall be appointed by the Representatives to tell off said ballots; but, in case the Representatives fail to appoint a teller, the Speaker shall appoint.

The said tellers shall divide themselves into two sets, as nearly equal in number as can be, and one of the said sets of tellers shall proceed to count the votes in one of said boxes, and the other set the votes in the other box.

When the votes are counted by the different sets of tellers, the result shall be reported to the House; and if the reports agree, the same shall be accepted as the true votes of the States; but if the reports disagree, the States shall proceed, in the same manner as before, to a new ballot.

6. All questions arising after the balloting commences, requiring the decision of the House, which shall be decided by the House, voting per capita, to be incidental to the power of choosing a President, shall be decided by States without debate; and in case of an equal division of the votes of States, the question shall be lost.

7. When either of the persons from whom the choice is to be made shall have received a majority of all the States, the Speaker shall declare the same, and that that person is elected President of the United States.

8. The result shall be immediately communicated to the Senate by message, and a committee of three persons shall be appointed to inform the President of the United States and the President-elect of said election.

Petitions are no longer introduced in this way. This old order of calling the states began with Maine and proceeded through the original 13 states and then through the remaining states in the order of their admission.

contenders for the presidency in the 1824 election, but four predominated: John Quincy Adams, Henry Clay, William H. Crawford and Andrew Jackson. Crawford, Secretary of the Treasury under Monroe, was the early front-runner, but his candidacy faltered after he suffered a paralytic stroke in 1823.[11]

When the electoral votes were counted, Jackson had 99, Adams 84, Crawford 41 and Clay 37. With 18 of the 24 states choosing their electors by popular vote, Jackson also led in the popular voting, although the significance of the popular vote was open to challenge. Under the Twelfth Amendment, the names of the three top contenders—Jackson, Adams

Law for Counting Electoral Votes in Congress

Following is the complete text of Title 3, section 15 of the U.S. Code, enacted originally in 1887, governing the counting of electoral votes in Congress:

Congress shall be in session on the sixth day of January succeeding every meeting of the electors. The Senate and House of Representatives shall meet in the Hall of the House of Representatives at the hour of 1 o'clock in the afternoon on that day, and the President of the Senate shall be their presiding officer. Two tellers shall be previously appointed on the part of the Senate and two on the part of the House of Representatives, to whom shall be handed, as they are opened by the President of the Senate, all the certificates and papers purporting to be certificates of the electoral votes, which certificates and papers shall be opened, presented, and acted upon in the alphabetical order of the States, beginning with the letter A; and said tellers, having then read the same in the presence and hearing of the two Houses, shall make a list of the votes as they shall appear from the said certificates; and the votes having been ascertained and counted according to the rules in this subchapter provided, the result of the same shall be delivered to the President of the Senate, who shall thereupon announce the state of the vote, which announcement shall be deemed a sufficient declaration of the persons, if any, elected President and Vice President of the United States, and, together with a list of the votes, be entered on the Journals of the two Houses. Upon such reading of any such certificate or paper, the President of the Senate shall call for objections, if any. Every objection shall be made in writing, and shall state clearly and concisely, and without argument, the ground thereof, and shall be signed by at least one Senator and one Member of the House of Representatives before the same shall be received. When all objections so made to any vote or paper from a State shall have been received and read, the Senate shall thereupon withdraw, and such objections shall be submitted to the Senate for its decision; and the Speaker of the House of Representatives shall, in like manner, submit such objections to the House of Representatives for its decision; and no electoral vote or votes from any State which shall have been regularly given by electors whose appointment has been lawfully certified to according to section 6* of this title from which but one return has been received shall be rejected, but the two Houses concurrently may reject the vote or votes when they agree that such vote or votes have not been so regularly given by electors whose appointment has been so certified. If more than one return or paper purporting to be a return from a State shall have been received by the President of the Senate, those votes, and those only, shall be counted which shall have been regularly given by the electors who are shown by the determination mentioned in section 5† of this title to have been appointed, if the determination in said section provided for shall have been made, or by such successors or substitutes, in case of a vacancy in the board of electors so ascertained, as have been appointed to fill such vacancy in the mode provided by the laws of the State; but in case there shall arise the question which of two or more of such State authorities determining what electors have been appointed, as mentioned in section 5 of this title, is the lawful tribunal of such State, the votes regularly given of those electors, and those only, of such State shall be counted whose title as electors the two Houses, acting separately, shall concurrently decide is supported by the decision of such State so authorized by its law; and in such case of more than one return or paper purporting to be a return from a State, if there shall have been no such determination of the question in the State aforesaid, then those votes, and those only, shall be counted which the two Houses shall concurrently decide were cast by lawful electors appointed in accordance with the laws of the State, unless the two Houses, acting separately, shall concurrently decide such votes not to be the lawful votes of the legally appointed electors of such State. But if the two Houses shall disagree in respect of the counting of such votes, then, and in that case, the votes of the electors whose appointment shall have been certified by the executive of the State, under the seal thereof, shall be counted. When the two Houses have voted, they shall immediately again meet, and the presiding officer shall then announce the decision of the questions submitted. No votes or papers from any other State shall be acted upon until the objections previously made to the votes or papers from any State shall have been finally disposed of.

* Section 6 provides for certification of votes by electors by state Governors.

† Section 5 provides that if state law specifies a method for resolving disputes concerning the vote for presidential electors, Congress must respect any determination so made by a state.

and the ailing Crawford—were placed before the House. Clay's support was vital to the two front-runners.

From the start, Clay apparently intended to support Adams as the lesser of two evils. But before the House voted, a great scandal erupted. A Philadelphia newspaper printed an anonymous letter alleging that Clay had agreed to support Adams in return for being made Secretary of State. The letter alleged also that Clay would have been willing to make the same deal with Jackson. Clay immediately denied the charge and pronounced the writer of the letter "a base and infamous calumniator, a dastard and a liar."[12] But Jackson believed the charges and found his suspicions vindicated when Adams, after the election, did appoint Clay as Secretary of State. "Was there ever witnessed such a bare-faced corruption in any country before?" Jackson wrote to a friend.[13]

When the House met to vote, Adams was supported by the six New England states and New York and, in large part through Clay's backing, by Maryland, Ohio, Kentucky, Illinois, Missouri and Louisiana. Thus a majority of 13 delegations voted for him—the bare minimum he needed for election, since there were 24 states in the Union at the time. The election was accomplished on the first ballot, but Adams took office under a cloud from which his administration never recovered.

Jackson's successful 1828 campaign made much of his contention that the House of Representatives had thwarted the will of the people by denying him the presidency in 1825 even though he had been the leader in popular and electoral votes.

On only one occasion has the Senate had to decide a vice presidential contest. That was in 1837, when Van Buren was elected President with 170 of the 294 electoral votes while his vice presidential running mate, Richard M. Johnson, received only 147 electoral votes—one less than a majority. This discrepancy occurred because Van Buren electors from Virginia boycotted Johnson. (Johnson's nomination had been opposed by southern Democrats because of his longstanding involvement with a mulatto woman.)[14] The Senate elected Johnson, 33-16, over Francis Granger of New York, the runner-up in the electoral vote for Vice President.

Threat of Election by House

Although only two presidential elections actually have been decided by the House, a number of others—including those of 1836, 1856, 1860, 1892, 1948, 1960 and 1968—could have been thrown into the House by only a small shift in the popular vote.

The threat of House election was clearly evident in 1968, when George C. Wallace of Alabama ran as a third-party candidate.[15] For the record, Wallace frequently asserted that he could win an outright majority in the electoral college by the addition of key midwestern and mountain states to his hoped-for base in the Deep South and border states. In reality, the Wallace campaign had a narrower goal: to win the balance of power in electoral college voting, thus depriving either major party of the clear electoral majority required for election. Wallace made it clear that he would then expect one of the major party candidates to make concessions in return for enough votes from Wallace electors to win the election. Wallace indicated that he expected the election to be settled in the electoral college and not in the House of Representatives. At the end of the campaign it was disclosed that Wallace had obtained written affidavits from all of his electors in which they promised to vote for Wallace "or whomsoever he may direct" in the electoral college.

In response to the Wallace challenge, both major party candidates, Republican Richard M. Nixon and Democrat Hubert H. Humphrey, maintained that they would refuse to bargain with Wallace for his electoral votes. Nixon asserted that the House, if the decision rested there, should elect the popular-vote winner. Humphrey said the representatives should select "the President they believe would be best for the country." Bipartisan efforts to obtain advance agreements from House candidates to vote for the national popular-vote winner if the election should go to the House ended in failure. Neither Nixon nor Humphrey replied to suggestions that they pledge before the election to swing enough electoral votes to the popular-vote winner to assure his election without help from Wallace.

In the end, Wallace received only 13.5 per cent of the popular vote and 46 electoral votes (including the vote of one Republican defector), all from southern states. He failed to win the balance of power in the electoral college which he had hoped to use to wring policy concessions from one of the major party candidates. If Wallace had won a few border states, or if a few thousand more Democratic votes had been cast in northern states barely carried by Nixon, **thus reducing Nixon's electoral vote below 270, Wallace** would have been in a position to bargain off his electoral votes or to throw the election into the House for final settlement.

The near-success of the Wallace strategy provided dramatic impetus for electoral reform efforts. *(p. 241)*

Counting the Electoral Vote

Congress has mandated a variety of dates for the casting of popular votes, the meeting of the electors to cast ballots in the various states and the official counting of the electoral votes before both houses of Congress.[16]

The Continental Congress made the provisions for the first election. On Sept. 13, 1788, the Congress directed that each state choose its electors on the first Wednesday in January 1789. It further directed these electors to cast their ballots on the first Wednesday in February 1789.

In 1792, the Second Congress passed legislation setting up a permanent calendar for choosing electors. Allowing some flexibility in dates, the law directed that states choose their electors within the 34 days preceding the first Wednesday in December of each presidential election year. Then the electors would meet in their various states and cast their ballots on the first Wednesday in December. On the second Wednesday of the following February, the votes were to be opened and counted before a joint session of Congress. Provision also was made for a special presidential election in case of the removal, death, resignation or disability of both the President and Vice President.

Under this system, states chose presidential electors at various times. For instance, in 1840 the popular balloting for electors began in Pennsylvania and Ohio on Oct. 30 and ended in North Carolina on Nov. 12. South Carolina, the only state still choosing presidential electors through the state legislature, appointed its electors on Nov. 26.

Congress modified the system in 1845, providing that each state choose its electors on the same day—the Tuesday next after the first Monday in November—a provision that still remains in force.

The next change occurred in 1887, when Congress provided that electors were to meet and cast their ballots on the second Monday in January instead of the first Wednesday in December. Congress also dropped the provision for a special presidential election.

In 1934, Congress again revised the law. The new arrangements, still in force, directed the electors to meet on the first Monday after the second Wednesday in December. The ballots are opened and counted before Congress on Jan. 6 (the next day if Jan. 6 falls on a Sunday).

The Constitution provides that "The President of the Senate shall, in the presence of the Senate and House of Representatives, open all the certificates, and the votes shall then be counted...." It offers no guidance on handling disputed ballots.

Before counting the electoral votes in 1865, Congress adopted the Twenty-second Joint Rule, which provided that no electoral votes objected to in joint session could be counted except by concurrent votes of both the Senate and House. The rule was pushed by congressional Republicans to ensure rejection of the electoral votes from the newly reconstructed states of Louisiana and Tennessee. Under this rule Congress in 1873 also threw out the electoral votes of Louisiana and Arkansas and three from Georgia.

However, the rule lapsed at the beginning of 1876 when the Senate refused to readopt it because the House was in Democratic control. Thus, following the 1876 election, when it became apparent that for the first time the outcome of an election would be determined by decisions on disputed electoral votes, Congress had no rules to guide it.

Hayes-Tilden Contest

The 1876 campaign pitted Republican Rutherford B. Hayes against Democrat Samuel J. Tilden. Early election night returns indicated that Tilden had been elected. He had won normally Republican Indiana, New York, Connecticut and New Jersey; those states plus his expected southern support would give him the election. However, by the following morning it became apparent that if the Republicans could hold South Carolina, Florida and Louisiana, Hayes would be elected with 185 electoral votes to 184 for Tilden. But if a single elector in any of these states voted for Tilden, he would throw the election to the Democrats. Tilden led in the popular-vote count by more than a quarter of a million votes.[17]

The situation was much the same in each of the three contested states. Historian Eugene H. Roseboom described it as follows: "The Republicans controlled the state governments and the election machinery, had relied upon the Negro masses for votes, and had practiced frauds as in the past. The Democrats used threats, intimidation, and even violence when necessary, to keep Negroes from the polls; and where they were in a position to do so they resorted to fraud also. The firm determination of the whites to overthrow carpetbag rule contributed to make a full and fair vote impossible; carpetbag hold on the state governments made a fair count impossible. Radical reconstruction was reaping its final harvest."[18]

Both parties pursued the votes of the three states with a fine disregard for propriety or legality, and in the end double sets of elector returns were sent to Congress from all three. Oregon also sent two sets of returns. Although Hayes carried that state, the Democratic governor discovered that one of the Hayes electors was a postmaster and therefore ineligible to be an elector under the Constitution, so he certified the election of the top-polling Democratic elector. However, the Republican electors met, received the resignation of their ineligible colleague, then reappointed him to the vacancy since he had in the meantime resigned his postmastership.

Had the Twenty-second Joint Rule remained in effect, the Democratic House of Representatives could have ensured Tilden's election by objecting to any of Hayes' disputed votes. But, since the rule had lapsed, Congress had to find some new method of resolving electoral disputes. A joint committee was created to work out a plan, and the resulting Electoral Commission Law was approved by large majorities and signed into law Jan. 29, 1877—only two days before the date scheduled for counting the electoral votes.

The law, which applied only to the 1876 electoral vote count, established a 15-member Electoral Commission which was to have final authority over disputed electoral votes, unless both houses of Congress agreed to overrule it. The commission was to consist of five senators, five representatives and five Supreme Court justices. Each chamber was to select its own members of the commission, with the understanding that the majority party would have three members and the minority two. Four justices, two from each party, were named in the bill, and these four were to select the fifth. It was expected that they would pick Justice David Davis, who was considered a political independent, but he was disqualified when the Illinois legislature named him to a seat in the Senate. Justice Joseph P. Bradley, a Republican, then was named to the 15th seat on the commission. The Democrats supported his selection, because they considered him the most independent of the remaining justices, all of whom were Republicans. However, he was to vote with the Republicans on every dispute and thus assure the victory of Hayes.

The electoral vote count began in Congress Feb. 1, and the proceedings continued until March 2. States were called in alphabetical order, and as each disputed state was reached, objections were raised to both the Hayes and Tilden electors. The question was then referred to the Electoral Commission, which in every case voted 8-7 for Hayes. In each case, the Democratic House rejected the commission's decision, but the Republican Senate upheld it, so the decision stood.

As the count went on, Democrats in the House threatened to launch a filibuster to block resumption of joint sessions so that the count could not be completed before Inauguration Day. The threat was never carried out, because of an agreement reached between the Hayes forces and southern conservatives. The southerners agreed to let the electoral count continue without obstruction. In return Hayes agreed that, as President, he would withdraw federal troops from the South, end Reconstruction and make other concessions. The southerners, for their part, pledged to respect the rights of blacks, a pledge they proved unable to carry out.

Thus, at 4 a.m., March 2, 1877, the president of the Senate was able to announce that Hayes had been elected President with 185 electoral votes, as against 184 for Tilden. Later that day Hayes arrived in Washington. The following evening he took the oath of office privately at the White House because March 4 fell on a Sunday. His formal inauguration followed on Monday. The country acquiesced. Thus ended a crisis that easily could have resulted in civil war.

Not until 1887 did Congress enact permanent legislation on the handling of disputed electoral votes. The Electoral Count Act of that year gave each state final authority in determining the legality of its choice of electors and required a concurrent majority of both the Senate and House to reject any electoral votes. It also established procedures for counting electoral votes in Congress.

Application of 1887 Law in 1969

The procedures relating to disputed electoral votes were utilized for the first time following the election of 1968. When Congress met in joint session Jan. 6, 1969, to count the electoral votes, Sen. Edmund S. Muskie (D Maine) and Rep. James G. O'Hara (D Mich.), joined by six other senators and 37 other representatives, filed a written objection to the vote cast by a North Carolina elector, Dr. Lloyd W. Bailey of Rocky Mount, who had been elected as a Republican but chose to vote for Wallace and Curtis E. LeMay instead of Nixon and Agnew.

Acting under the 1887 law, Muskie and O'Hara objected to Bailey's vote on the grounds that it was "not properly given" because a plurality of the popular votes in North Carolina was cast for Nixon-Agnew, and the state's voters had chosen electors to vote for Nixon and Agnew only. Muskie and O'Hara asked that Bailey's vote not be counted at all by Congress.

The 1887 statute, currently incorporated in the U.S. Code, Title 3, Section 15, stipulated that "no electoral vote or votes from any state which shall have been regularly given by electors whose appointment has been lawfully certified...from which but one return has been received shall be rejected, but the two Houses concurrently may reject the vote or votes when they agree that such vote or votes have not been so regularly given...." The statute did not define the term "regularly given," though at the time of its adoption chief concern centered on problems of dual sets of electoral vote returns from a state, votes cast on an improper day or votes disputed because of uncertainty about whether a state lawfully was in the Union on the day that the electoral vote was cast.

The 1887 statute provided that if written objection to any state's vote was received from at least one member of both the Senate and House, the two legislative bodies were to retire immediately to separate sessions, debate for two hours with a five-minute limitation on speeches, and that each chamber was to decide the issue by vote before resuming the joint session. The statute made clear that both the Senate and House had to reject a challenged electoral vote (or votes) for such action to prevail. *(Text p. 238)*

At the Jan. 6 joint session, convened at 1 p.m. in the House chamber with Senate President Pro Tempore Richard B. Russell (D Ga.) presiding, the counting of the electoral vote proceeded smoothly through the alphabetical order of states until the North Carolina result was announced, at which time O'Hara rose to announce filing of the complaint. The two houses then proceeded to separate sessions, at the end of which the Senate, by 33-58 roll-call vote, and the House, by a 170-228 roll-call vote, refused to sustain the challenge to Bailey's vote. The two houses then reassembled in joint session at which the results of the separate deliberations were announced and the count of the electoral vote by state proceeded without event. At the conclusion, Russell announced the vote and declared Nixon and Agnew elected.

Although Congress did not sustain the challenge to Bailey's vote, the case of the "faithless" elector led to in-creased pressure for electoral reform. *(Independent voting by electors p. 234)*

Electoral Reform Proposals

Since Jan. 6, 1797, when Rep. William L. Smith (S.C.) introduced in Congress the first proposed constitutional amendment for reform of the electoral college system, hardly a session of Congress has passed without the introduction of one or more resolutions of this nature. But only one—the Twelfth Amendment, ratified in 1804—ever has been approved.

In recent years, public interest in a change in the electoral college system was spurred by the close 1960 and 1968 elections, by a series of Supreme Court rulings relating to apportionment and districting and by introduction of un-pledged elector systems in the southern states.

Early in 1969, President Nixon asked Congress to take prompt action on electoral college reform. He said he would support any plan that would eliminate individual electors and distribute among the presidential candidates the electoral vote of every state and the District of Columbia in a manner more closely approximating the popular vote.[19]

Later that year the House approved, 338-70, a resolution proposing a constitutional amendment to eliminate the electoral college and to provide instead for direct popular election of the President and Vice President. The measure set a minimum of 40 per cent of the popular vote as sufficient for election and provided for a runoff election between the two top candidates for the presidency if no candidate received 40 per cent of the vote. Under this plan the House of Representatives could no longer be called upon to

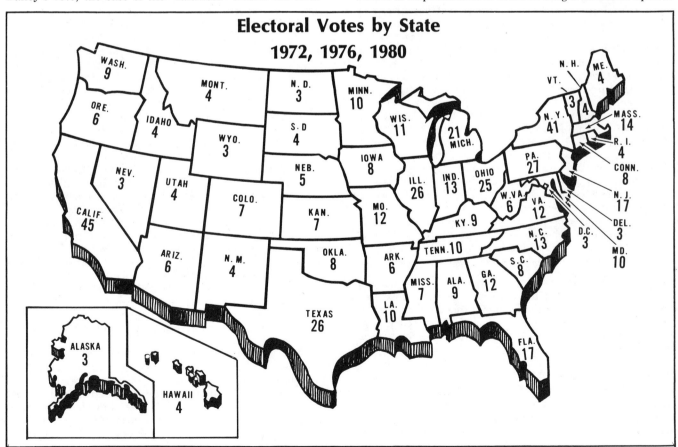

Electoral Votes by State
1972, 1976, 1980

WASH. 9 — ORE. 6 — IDAHO 4 — MONT. 4 — N.D. 3 — MINN. 10 — WIS. 11 — N.H. — VT. — ME. 4 — N.Y. 41 — MASS. 14 — NEV. 3 — UTAH 4 — WYO. 3 — S.D. 4 — IOWA 8 — MICH. 21 — PA. 27 — R.I. 4 — CONN. 8 — CALIF. 45 — ARIZ. 6 — N.M. 4 — COLO. 7 — NEB. 5 — KAN. 7 — MO. 12 — ILL. 26 — IND. 13 — OHIO 25 — W.VA. 6 — VA. 12 — N.J. 17 — DEL. 3 — KY. 9 — OKLA. 8 — ARK. 6 — TENN. 10 — N.C. 13 — D.C. 3 — MD. 10 — S.C. 8 — MISS. 7 — ALA. 9 — GA. 12 — LA. 10 — TEXAS 26 — FLA. 17 — ALASKA 3 — HAWAII 4

Twenty-fifth Amendment

(Ratified Feb. 10, 1967)

Section 1. In case of the removal of the President from office or of his death or resignation, the Vice President shall become President.

Section 2. Whenever there is a vacancy in the office of the Vice President, the President shall nominate a Vice President who shall take office upon confirmation by a majority vote of both Houses of Congress.

Section 3. Whenever the President transmits to the President pro tempore of the Senate and the Speaker of the House of Representatives his written declaration that he is unable to discharge the powers and duties of his office, and until he transmits to them a written declaration to the contrary, such powers and duties shall be discharged by the Vice President as Acting President.

Section 4. Whenever the Vice President and a majority of either the principal officers of the executive departments or of such other body as Congress may by law provide, transmit to the President pro tempore of the Senate and the Speaker of the House of Representatives their written declaration that the President is unable to discharge the powers and duties of his office, the Vice President shall immediately assume the powers and duties of the office as Acting President.

Thereafter, when the President transmits to the President pro tempore of the Senate and the Speaker of the House of Representatives his written declaration that no inability exists, he shall resume the powers and duties of his office unless the Vice President and a majority of either the principal officers of the executive departments or of such other body as Congress may by law provide, transmit within four days to the President pro tempore of the Senate and the Speaker of the House of Representatives their written declaration that the President is unable to discharge the powers and duties of his office. Thereupon Congress shall decide the issue, assembling within forty-eight hours for that purpose if not in session. If the Congress, within twenty-one days after receipt of the latter written declaration, or, if Congress is not in session, within twenty-one days after Congress is required to assemble, determines by two-thirds vote of both houses that the President is unable to discharge the powers and duties of his office, the Vice President shall continue to discharge the same as Acting President; otherwise, the President shall resume the powers and duties of his office.

select a President. The proposed amendment also authorized Congress to provide a method of filling vacancies caused by the death, resignation or inability of presidential nominees before the election and a method of filling post-election vacancies caused by the death of the President-elect or Vice President-elect.

Blocking of Proposed Amendment

President Nixon, who previously had favored a proportional plan of allocating each state's electoral votes, endorsed the House resolution and urged the Senate to adopt it. To become effective, the proposed amendment had to be approved by a two-thirds majority in both the Senate and House and be ratified by the legislatures of three-fourths of the states.

When the proposal reached the Senate floor in September 1970, small-state and southern senators succeeded in blocking final action on it. The resolution was laid aside Oct. 5, following two unsuccessful efforts to cut off debate by invoking cloture.

Presidential Disability

A decade of congressional concern over the question of presidential disability was eased in 1967 by ratification of the Twenty-fifth Amendment to the Constitution. The amendment for the first time provided for continuity in carrying out the functions of the presidency in the event of presidential disability and for filling a vacancy in the vice presidency.[20]

Congressional consideration of the problem of presidential disability had been prompted by President Dwight D. Eisenhower's heart attack in 1955. The ambiguity of the language of the disability clause (Article II, Section 1, Clause 5) of the Constitution had provoked occasional debate ever since the Constitutional Convention of 1787. But it had never been decided how far the term "disability" extended or who would be the judge of it.

Clause 5 provided that Congress should decide who was to succeed to the presidency in the event that both the President and the Vice President died, resigned or became disabled. Congress enacted succession laws three times. By the Act of March 1, 1792, it provided for succession (after the Vice President) of the president pro tempore of the Senate, then of the House Speaker; if those offices were vacant, states were to send electors to choose a new President.

That law stood until passage of the Presidential Succession Act of Jan. 19, 1886, which changed the line of succession to run from the Vice President to the Secretary of State, Secretary of the Treasury and so on through the Cabinet in order of rank. Sixty-one years later, the Act of July 18, 1947 (still in force), placed the Speaker of the House and the president pro tempore of the Senate ahead of Cabinet officers in succession after the Vice President.

Prior to ratification of the Twenty-fifth Amendment in 1967, no procedures had been laid down to govern situations arising in the event of presidential incapacity or of a vacancy in the office of the Vice President. Two Presidents had sustained serious disabilities—President James A. Garfield, who was shot in 1881 and was confined to his bed until he died two and one-half months later, and President Woodrow Wilson, who suffered a stroke in 1919. In each case the Vice President did not assume any duties of the presidency for fear he would appear to be usurping the power of that office. As for a vice presidential vacancy, the United States has been without a Vice President 18 times, for a total of 40 years through 1974, after the elected Vice President either succeeded to the presidency, died or on two occasions resigned. (John C. Calhoun resigned as Vice President Dec. 28, 1832, to become a U.S. senator and Agnew resigned Oct. 10, 1973.)

Ratification of the Twenty-fifth Amendment established procedures that clarified these areas of uncertainty in the Constitution. The amendment provided that the Vice President should become Acting President under either one of two circumstances. If the President informed Congress that he was unable to perform his duties, the Vice President would become Acting President until the President could resume his responsibilities. *(Text this page)*

If the Vice President and a majority of the Cabinet, or other body designated by Congress, found the President to be incapacitated, the Vice President would become Acting President until the President informed Congress that his disability had ended. Congress was given 21 days to resolve any dispute over the President's disability; a two-thirds vote of both chambers was required to overrule the President's declaration that he was no longer incapacitated.

Whenever a vacancy occurred in the office of Vice President, either by death, succession to the presidency or resignation, the President was to nominate a Vice President and the nomination was to be confirmed by a majority vote of both houses of Congress.

The proposed Twenty-fifth Amendment was approved by the Senate and House in 1965. It took effect Feb. 10, 1967, following ratification by 38 states.

Amendment Used Twice

Since its ratification in 1967, the Twenty-fifth Amendment has been used twice to fill a vacancy in the office of the Vice President.[21] The first time was in 1973 after Vice President Agnew's resignation. Agnew—under investigation for multiple charges of alleged conspiracy, extortion and bribery—agreed to resign and avoided imprisonment by pleading *nolo contendere* (no contest) to a single charge of federal income tax evasion.

On Oct. 12, President Nixon nominated House Minority Leader Gerald R. Ford (R Mich.) for Vice President. Ford became the 40th Vice President of the United States Dec. 6,

an hour after the House of Representatives voted 387-5 to confirm him. The Senate had approved the nomination Nov. 27 by a 92-3 vote. Ford's confirmation followed hearings and approval by the House Judiciary and Senate Rules Committees.

The Twenty-fifth Amendment was used a second time in 1974 when Nixon resigned as President Aug. 9, 1974, to avoid impeachment because of the Watergate scandal. Ford succeeded to the presidency, becoming the first unelected President in American history, and on Aug. 20 nominated former Gov. Nelson A. Rockefeller of New York as the new Vice President.

Rockefeller became the 41st Vice President of the United States Dec. 19, 1974, after the House confirmed his nomination, 287-128. The Senate had given its approval to the nomination Dec. 10, on a 90-7 vote. Rockefeller's nomination had been approved by the House Judiciary and Senate Rules Committees after several days of hearings.

With both the President and Vice President holding office through appointment rather than election, members of Congress and the public expressed concern about the power of a President to, in effect, appoint his own successor. Among those proposing change was Sen. John O. Pastore (D R.I.) who sponsored a resolution for a constitutional amendment to provide for a special national election for President whenever an appointed Vice President became President with more than one year remaining in a presidential term. Hearings on proposed changes were held in February 1975 by the Senate Judiciary Subcommittee on Constitutional Amendments.

Footnotes

1. Background, Edward Stanwood, *A History of the Presidency from 1788 to 1897* (Boston: Houghton Mifflin Co., 1898), pp. 1-9.
2. Neal R. Peirce, *The People's President: The Electoral College and the Emerging Consensus for a Direct Vote,* (New York: Simon & Schuster, 1968), p. 52.
3. Background, Stanwood, *History of Presidency*, pp. 11-13, 77-82.
4. Background, Congressional Quarterly, *Guide to U.S. Elections*, pp. 202-05, 948-49.
5. Peirce, *People's President*, p. 76, citing Lucius Wilmerding, *The Electoral College*, (New Brunswick, N.J.: Rutgers University Press, 1958), p. 58.
6. Stanwood, *History of Presidency*, pp. 54-73.
7. *Ibid.*, p. 70.
8. Peirce, *People's President*, p. 69, citing Sidney Hyman, *The American President* (New York, 1954), p. 128.
9. Arthur M. Schlesinger Jr., ed. *History of American Presidential Elections 1789-1968*, 4 Vols. (New York: Chelsea House Publishers and McGraw-Hill Book Co., 1971), Vol. I, p. 133.

10. Eugene H. Roseboom, *A History of Presidential Elections* (New York: Macmillan Co., 1959), p. 47.
11. Background, Stanwood, *History of Presidency*, pp. 123-41.
12. *Ibid.*, p. 138.
13. Roseboom, *History of Presidential Elections*, p. 88.
14. Schlesinger, *History of American Presidential Elections*, Vol. 1, pp. 584, 596.
15. Background, Congressional Quarterly, *1968 Weekly Report*, pp. 1811-23, 2955-56, 3171.
16. Background, Stanwood, *History of Presidency*, pp. 20, 38, 203-04, 242, 452; Roseboom, *History of Presidential Elections*, pp.246-47.
17. Background, Stanwood, *History of Presidency*, pp. 356-93.
18. Roseboom, *History of Presidential Elections*, pp. 243-44.
19. Congressional Quarterly, *Congress and the Nation, 1969-1972*, Vol. III, pp. 1012-19.
20. Congressional Quarterly, *Congress and the Nation, 1965-1968*, Vol. II, pp. 645-48.
21. Background, Congressional Quarterly, *1973 Almanac*, pp. 1061-68; *1974 Almanac*, pp. 917-35.

Selected Bibliography

Books

American Bar Association. *Electing the President: A Report of the Commission on Electoral Reform.* Chicago: 1967.

Association of the Bar of the City of New York. *Report of the Committee on Federal Legislation: Proposed Constitutional Amendment Abolishing the Electoral College and Making Other Changes in the Election of the President and Vice-President.* New York: 1969.

Beman, L. T. *Abolishment of the Electoral College.* New York: H. W. Wilson, 1926.

Best, Judith. *The Case Against Direct Election of the President: A Defense of the Electoral College.* Ithaca, N.Y.: Cornell University Press, 1975.

Bickel, Alexander M. *The New Age of Political Reform: The Electoral College, the Convention and the Party System.* New York: Harper & Row, 1968.

Bickel, Alexander M. *Reform and Continuity: The Electoral College, the Convention and the Party System.* New York: Harper & Row, 1971.

Burnham, Walter D. *Presidential Ballots, 1836-1892.* Baltimore: Johns Hopkins Press, 1955.

Congressional Quarterly. *Guide to U.S. Elections.* Washington, D.C.: 1975.

Daniels, Walter M., ed. *Presidential Election Reforms.* New York: H. W. Wilson, 1953.

David, Paul T., ed. *The Presidential Election and Transition, 1960-1961.* Washington, D.C.: Brookings Institution, 1961.

Feerick, John D. *From Failing Hands: The Story of Presidential Succession.* Bronx, N.Y.: Fordham University Press, 1965.

Feerick, John D. *The Twenty-Fifth Amendment: Its Complete History and Earliest Applications.* Bronx, N.Y.: Fordham University Press, 1976.

Haworth, Paul L. *The Hayes-Tilden Disputed Presidential Election of 1876.* Cleveland: Burrows Bros., 1906.

Knoles, George H. *The Presidential Campaign and Election of 1892.* Stanford: Stanford University Press, 1942.

League of Women Voters. "Who Should Elect the President?" Washington, D.C.: 1969.

Longely, Lawrence D. *The Politics of Electoral College Reform.* New Haven: Yale University Press, 1972.

MacBride, Roger L. *The American Electoral College.* Caldwell, Idaho: Caxton Printers, 1953.

O'Neil, Charles A. *The American Electoral System.* New York: Putnam, 1887.

Peirce, Neal. *The People's President: The Electoral College and the Emerging Consensus for a Direct Vote.* New York: Simon & Schuster, 1968.

Polsby, Nelson. *Presidential Elections: Strategies of American Electoral Politics.* New York: Scribner, 1964.

Roseboom, Eugene H. *A History of Presidential Elections.* New York: Macmillan, 1957.

Sayre, Wallace S. *Voting for President: The Electoral College and the American Political System.* Washington, D.C.: Brookings Institution, 1970.

Schlesinger, Arthur M. Jr., ed. *The Coming to Power: Critical Presidential Elections in American History.* New York: McGraw-Hill, 1972.

Schlesinger, Arthur M. Jr., ed. *History of American Presidential Elections.* 4 vols. New York: McGraw-Hill, 1971.

Stanwood, Edward. *A History of the Presidency, 1788-1916.* 2 vols. Boston: Houghton Mifflin, 1889, 1916.

White, Theodore H. *The Making of the President, 1960.* New York: Atheneum Publishers, 1961.

White, Theodore H. *The Making of the President, 1968.* New York: Atheneum Publishers, 1969.

Wilmerding, Lucius Jr. *The Electoral College.* New Brunswick, N.J.: Rutgers University Press, 1958.

Zeidenstein, Harvey. *Direct Election of the President.* Lexington, Mass.: D. C. Heath, 1973.

Articles

Bayh, Birch. "Electing a President: The Case for Direct Popular Election." *Harvard Journal on Legislation,* January 1969, pp. 1-12.

Eshelman, Edwin D. "Congress and Electoral Reform: An Analysis of Proposals for Changing Our Method of Selecting a President." *Christian Century,* Feb. 5, 1969, pp. 178-81.

Feerick, John D. "The Electoral College: Why It Ought to Be Abolished." *Fordham Law Review,* October 1968, p. 43.

Freund, Paul A. "Direct Election of the President: Issues and Answers." *American Bar Association Journal,* August 1970, p. 733.

Gossett, William T. "Direct Popular Election of the President." *American Bar Association Journal,* March 1970, p. 230.

Huddle, F. P. "Electoral College: Historical Review and Proposals for Reforms." *Editorial Research Reports,* Aug. 18, 1944, vol. 2, pp. 99-114.

Lechner, Alfred J. "Direct Election of the President: The Final Step in the Constitutional Evolution of the Right to Vote." *Notre Dame Lawyer,* October 1971, pp. 122-52.

"Proposals to Change the Method of Electing the President: A Pro and Con Discussion on the Various Proposals for Change." *Congressional Digest,* November 1967, pp. 257-88.

Wildavsky, Aaron. "Choosing the Lesser Evils: The Policy-Maker and the Problem of Presidential Disability." *Parliamentary Affairs,* Winter 1959-1960, pp. 25-37.

Foreign Affairs

Historical practice and the rush of world developments have broadened immensely the late 18th century American attitudes which limited foreign policy to the making of treaties and, if necessary, the waging of war. As a consequence, the division of foreign policy power between the President and Congress, as laid down in 1787 by the framers of the Constitution, has been severely strained.

The Constitution assigned to Congress the powers "to...provide for the common defense and general welfare of the United States; ...to regulate commerce with foreign nations; ...to define and punish piracies and felonies committed on the high seas and offenses against the law of nations; to declare war...and make rules concerning captures on land and water; to raise and support armies; ...to provide and maintain a navy; ...to make all laws which shall be necessary and proper for carrying into execution the foregoing powers...."

The Constitution also stated: "The President shall be Commander-in-Chief of the Army and Navy.... He shall have power, by and with the advice and consent of the Senate, to make treaties, provided two-thirds of the senators present concur; and he shall nominate and, by and with the advice and consent of the Senate, shall appoint ambassadors, other public ministers, and consuls.... He shall receive ambassadors and other public ministers; he shall take care that the laws be faithfully executed...."

Legislative-Executive Antagonism

The division of power over foreign affairs has stirred up antagonism between the legislative and executive branches of government on numerous occasions.[1] Two outstanding facts have emerged from the resulting picture of alternate tension and cooperation: first, the overwhelming importance of presidential initiative in this area of power; and second, the ever-increasing dependence of foreign policy on congressional cooperation and support.

Issuance of a Proclamation of Neutrality by President Washington in 1793, upon the outbreak of war between France and Great Britain, marked the start of the continuing struggle between the President and Congress for control of the nation's foreign policy. The proclamation was attacked by the pro-French Jeffersonian Republicans as a usurpation by the President of authority granted to Congress. In a series of articles published in a Philadelphia newspaper under the pseudonym "Pacificus," Alexander Hamilton defended Washington's action. He argued that the conduct of foreign relations was in its nature an executive function and therefore, except where the Constitution provided otherwise, belonged to the President upon whom was bestowed "the executive power." Possession by Congress of the power to declare war, as well as other powers affecting foreign relations, did not diminish the discretion of the President in the exercise of the powers constitutionally belonging to him, Hamilton said.[2]

This view was disputed by James Madison, writing as "Helvidius." Emphasizing that the vital power to declare war was vested in Congress, Madison took the position that the powers of the executive in foreign relations were to be strictly construed. Doubt as to the exact location of any power in this field was to be resolved in favor of the legislature. Madison attempted to bolster his argument by pointing to the confusion likely to ensue if concurrent discretionary powers were exercised by different branches of the government. "A concurrent authority in two independent departments, to perform the same function with respect to the same thing," he declared, "would be as awkward in practice as it is unnatural in theory." Over time, however, Hamilton's view has prevailed.

Despite the widely recognized prerogatives of the President in foreign relations, the fact is that Congress has enormous powers which are indispensable to the support of any foreign policy. Moreover, congressional laws made in pursuance of these powers are the "supreme law of the land," according to the Constitution, and the President is bound constitutionally to "take care that" they "be faithfully executed."

As Louis Henkin has pointed out in his book, *Foreign Affairs and the Constitution,* "The vast legislative powers of Congress that relate particularly to foreign affairs do not begin to exhaust its authority to make law affecting foreign relations. Congress has general powers that, taken together, enable it to reach virtually where it will in foreign as in

References

For further discussion of the congressional role in overseeing the intelligence community, as well as the congressional investigative process in general and use of executive privilege, see Congressional Investigations, p. 141. On the commerce power, see p. 193. For a discussion of fiscal power in general, including appropriations procedures and trade and tariff policy, see p. 111. Further historical background on the Constitutional Convention and early Congresses is to be found in Part I, pp. 3-34.

domestic affairs, subject only to constitutional prohibitions protecting human rights. The power to tax (Article I, Section 8, Clause 1) has long been a power to regulate through taxation, and could be used to control, say, foreign travel.... Major programs depend wholly on the "spending power"...—to 'provide for the common Defence and general Welfare of the United States'—and it has been used in our day for billions of dollars in foreign aid.

"Other, specialized powers also have their international uses: Congress has authorized a network of international agreements under its postal power (Article I, Section 8, Clause 7), and there are international elements in the regulation of patents and copyrights. The express power to govern territory (Article IV, Section 3) may imply authority to acquire territory, and Congress determines whether territory acquired shall be incorporated into the United States. Congress can exercise 'exclusive legislation' in the nation's capital, its diplomatic headquarters (Article I, Section 8, Clause 17). The power to acquire and dispose of property has supported lend-lease and other arms programs, and sales or gifts of nuclear reactors or fissionable materials.... By implication in the Constitution's grant of maritime jurisdiction to the federal judiciary (Article III, Section 2), Congress can legislate maritime law."[3] In addition, the fact that the appointment of ambassadors, public ministers and other diplomatic officers requires the advice and consent of the Senate gives that body a considerable degree of control over foreign relations.[4] Finally, the power to appropriate funds—for defense, war and general execution of foreign policy—rests solely with Congress.[5]

President's Foreign Policy Leadership

Early Presidents—Washington, Adams, Jefferson, Madison and Monroe—exercised dominant influence in determining the country's relations with other nations. Washington's Neutrality Proclamation and his Farewell Address, and Monroe's warning against foreign intervention in the Western Hemisphere, laid the basis for American foreign policy.[6]

Much of the 19th century was dominated by the twin domestic issues of slavery and development of the American West, which shifted national attention away from foreign affairs. Presidential authority in that field was somewhat less effective, and the executive branch suffered a number of serious setbacks. A major turn in foreign policy, strongly supported by Congress, was taken in 1898. The country dropped its traditional policy of nonintervention, went to war to rid Cuba of Spanish rule, and emerged from the conflict with overseas outposts as far distant as the Philippines in the western Pacific.

During most of the present century, particularly in the years since World War II, the President has been the leader in foreign affairs. An important exception was the 15-year period of commanding congressional influence following Senate rejection of the Treaty of Versailles after World War I. But on the eve of the next great conflict, the country's overseas interests as interpreted by the President began to dominate American foreign policy.

On balance, until the mid-1970s, the foreign affairs legislation enacted by Congress operated to increase presidential powers much more frequently than it operated to curtail them. A classic example of this tendency was the passage of the lend-lease act in the spring of 1941. It authorized the President to "sell, transfer title to, exchange, lease, lend, or otherwise dispose of" defense articles to any country "whose defense the President deems vital to the defense of the United States."

Changes in Role of Congress

As American policies toward other nations have evolved, the role of Congress in foreign affairs has shifted. The Senate, which once claimed dominant influence because of its part in treaty making, plays no part in the making of the increasingly popular executive agreements with foreign countries; executive agreements do not require Senate approval. In addition, it has been argued that the power of Congress to declare war has lost significance as modern weapons have made surprise attack more and more advantageous, if not a matter of necessity, for an aggressor nation. The war power of Congress has been eroded also by actions taken under the constitutional authority claimed by the President as commander-in-chief.

At the same time, congressional influence over other aspects of foreign affairs has greatly expanded. Legislative authority over the massive, post-World-War II foreign aid, defense and military assistance programs is an example. The programs have required specific congressional authorizations and repeated congressional appropriations. Furthermore, foreign policy implications surround much other legislation, such as Food for Peace, regulation of immigration, shipping subsidies, space exploration, the Peace Corps and import quotas. Meanwhile, the fundamental constitutional authority for a share of the treaty-making power and the war power continues to underlie this sweeping congressional involvement in foreign affairs.

The period spanning the late 1940s and early 1950s was characterized by what Francis O. Wilcox, in his book *Congress, the Executive and Foreign Policy,* has called "extraordinary executive-legislative cooperation." "During this period," he said, "the bipartisan approach to foreign policy reached its zenith."[7] The Senate approved, by overwhelming votes, the United Nations Charter, the peace treaty with Italy and the whole network of regional security treaties—the Rio Treaty, NATO, SEATO, and other collective and mutual security arrangements. Congress approved the Marshall Plan, aid to Greece and Turkey, and U.S. participation in a wide variety of U.N. specialized agencies.

By the late 1960s, however, Congress was increasingly restive with what many members considered the aggrandizement of presidential foreign policy power. Critics usually cited these examples of presidential actions: waging costly undeclared wars in Korea and Vietnam, sending troops to other parts of the world without first securing congressional consent and negotiating an array of international commitments through executive agreements not subject to congressional approval. As a result, Congress made several attempts to limit the President's power to send troops abroad, make defense commitments and wage war without legislative approval.

A first indication of congressional discontent occurred in 1951. During the "great debate" concerning Truman's authority to send troops to Europe, two resolutions were introduced to require congressional authorization for sending military forces abroad. Neither measure cleared Congress. Two years later, Sen. John W. Bricker (R Ohio) proposed a constitutional amendment intended to restrain the President's power to make executive agreements. The amendment was rejected in 1954.

Disillusionment with the Vietnam War in the 1960s prompted Congress to make new efforts to regain influence in foreign affairs. In June 1969, by an overwhelming 70-16 vote, the Senate adopted a "national commitments" resolution which declared the sense of the Senate that a national commitment by the United States results "only from affirmative action taken by the executive and legislative branches of the United States government by means of a treaty, statute, or concurrent resolution of both houses of Congress specifically providing for such commitment." In 1969 and 1970, Congress repeatedly attempted to terminate funds for U.S. military activities in Indochina. During that period, Congress used its investigative powers to probe the extent of American commitments abroad—particularly through a series of hearings conducted by the Senate Foreign Relations Subcommittee on United States Security Agreements and Commitments Abroad, chaired by Stuart Symington (D Mo.).[8]

Congressional action in the early 1970s was highlighted by passage of a tough war powers measure over the President's veto in July 1973. The measure set a 60-day limit on any presidential commitment of U.S. troops to hostilities abroad, or to situations where hostilities might be imminent, without specific congressional authorization. *(Discussion, p. 279)*

Congress also began to assert a more decisive voice in the making of foreign policy. For example, Sen. Alan Cranston (D Calif.) introduced a resolution in 1969 on U.S. recognition policy which stated the sense of the Senate that recognition of a foreign government did not imply that the United States necessarily approved of the form, ideology, or policy of that government. The resolution passed the Senate on Sept. 25, 1969, by a 77-3 vote.

In 1974, Congress passed a major trade reform bill only after approving an amendment linking trade concessions for Communist countries to their emigration policies. And throughout the 1970s, Congress played an important role in shaping U.S. policy in the Middle East by repeated calls for continued military support for Israel. In 1974, in reaction to the Turkish invasion of Cyprus, Congress imposed a ban on military aid and arms shipments to Turkey (the ban was partially lifted in October 1975). Congress in 1975 also began weighing new controls on the sale of U.S. weapons abroad.[9]

In 1975, committees in both chambers conducted a major probe of the American intelligence community—the first such investigation since establishment of the Central Intelligence Agency in 1947. The investigations brought to light numerous abuses of power by intelligence and law enforcement agencies and resulted in recommendations for structural changes in both Congress and the agencies so as to improve congressional oversight in the future. *(Further discussion, Congressional Investigations, pp. 141-173)*

These are but a few examples of congressional attempts to fashion for itself a more influential role in foreign policy; they seem to indicate, as Wilcox has phrased it, that "a tide has clearly been running toward a larger congressional role in foreign policy and, perhaps more importantly, toward a new conception of that role."[10]

The impact of Congress on foreign policy in the 1970s has been described by Prof. Edward A. Kolodziej in his article, "Congress and Foreign Policy: The Nixon Years." "The increased congressional influence on American foreign policy has led to the amendment but by no means the abandonment of the U.S. global role in world politics," he wrote. "American military-political obligations, other than those in Southeast Asia, have received sustained congressional support despite vocal opposition to some of them.... In the case of Israel, American commitments have been reinforced through sizable military and economic assistance and diplomatic support. Congress continued to underwrite administration requests for increased defense spending while evidencing an interest, through its budgetary decisions, in defining weapons systems, force levels and troop deployments."[11]

The Treaty Power

The whole of the treaty-making power is contained in a single clause of the Constitution. Spelling out presidential authority, Article II, Section 2, Clause 2 declares: "He shall have power, by and with the advice and consent of the Senate, to make treaties, provided two-thirds of the senators present concur...."

For years this clause served as a cornerstone of American foreign policy. It brought peace with other nations, supported American territorial expansion, established national boundaries, protected U.S. commerce and regulated government affairs with Indian tribes.[12]

Ambiguities in Treaty Clause

Despite its importance, the clause was ambiguous on some points, and the ambiguities led from the beginning to conflicts between the executive and legislative branches. Neither the Senate procedure for advising the President nor the stage of treaty making at which the Senate was to act in an advisory capacity was defined. And, the role of the House of Representatives in treaty making, to the extent that legislation or appropriations were needed to make a treaty effective, was ignored. The Constitution was silent on all of these points.

It is generally agreed that the main purpose of the advice-and-consent formula was to provide for democratic control of foreign policy. In the early years of the nation, the executive branch sought to incorporate Senate advice into the process of treaty negotiation by such means as presidential meetings with senators, Senate confirmation of negotiators, and special presidential messages. But as international relations became more complicated, the early administrations abandoned, one after the other, the various devices by which the Senate's advice had been obtained.

Deprived of opportunities to make its influence felt in treaty negotiations, the Senate resorted to advising the President through drastic amendment—or outright rejection—of completed treaties. The historically dramatic climax of senatorial dissatisfaction came in 1919 and 1920 with the prolonged debate on, and ultimate rejection of, the Treaty of Versailles, which embodied not only the World War I treaty of peace with Germany but also the Covenant of the League of Nations.

Senate's Ratification Record

Despite the shock caused by rejection of the Versailles pact, and consequent reinforcement of the Senate's popular reputation as a graveyard of treaties, its overall record on ratification has been overwhelmingly favorable. Between 1789 and 1976, only 11 treaties were rejected through failure to receive a two-thirds majority in the Senate.[13] The last treaty rejected was an optional protocol to the law-of-the-sea conventions, concerning compulsory settlement of disputes (Exec N, 86th Congress, 1st Session). The May 26, 1960, vote was 49-30 for the protocol, four votes short of the two-thirds required for consent to ratification. *(See box on rejected treaties, p. 252)*

(Continued on p. 249)

Role of Congressional Committees in Foreign Affairs

In dealing with international relations, the Senate Foreign Relations Committee and the House International Relations Committee hold the key roles. The Senate committee's exclusive responsibility for treaties and for diplomatic nominations has made it traditionally the chief congressional voice in foreign affairs.

The increasing use of executive agreements rather than treaties and the growing impact of foreign-aid and military-assistance legislation since the end of World War II have tended to draw additional congressional committees into consideration of foreign-policy matters, but the Foreign Relations and International Relations panels have continued to exert the most influence.

Foreign Relations Committee

Created Dec. 10, 1816, the Senate Foreign Relations Committee rapidly became one of the most prestigious groups on Capitol Hill, primarily because of its jurisdiction over treaties. All treaties, regardless of their subject matter, are referred to the committee, making it the bridge between the executive and legislative branches in the joint process of approval required constitutionally for formal ratification. In addition, the committee has jurisdiction over a broad variety of legislation dealing with international affairs, and over State Department and diplomatic nominations.

The committee has attracted as members some of the most illustrious men to serve in the Senate. Among its members have been ex-President Andrew Johnson, Daniel Webster, John C. Calhoun, Roscoe Conkling and Robert A. Taft. Among its chairmen have been Charles Sumner, Henry Cabot Lodge, William E. Borah, Arthur H. Vandenberg and J. William Fulbright.

The committee frequently has been a center of controversy, typically over an issue that has deeply divided the nation as well. In 1871, President Grant forced Sumner's removal as chairman because of a bitter dispute involving Grant's desire to annex Santo Domingo; Sumner strongly opposed annexation.[1] During the prolonged debate over the Vietnam War in the 1960s, the committee was dominated by opponents of the war.[2]

As a rule, the committee's recommendations on legislation have been decisive; they are not usually overruled by the full Senate. According to James A. Robinson, in *Congress and Foreign Policy Making,* once the committee reports a bill or resolution, the chances are higher than nine out of 10 that the Senate will pass it. From 1949-58, the Senate upheld the committee's position on 201 of the 219 bills which reached the floor. And although the full Senate amended the committee's recommendations in about 20 per cent of the cases, most bills were passed without a roll-call vote.[3]

The Senate also generally follows the committee's recommendations on treaties. During the 93rd Congress, 37 were submitted and 31 approved by the committee, and then by the full Senate; one was reported favorably by the committee but was not approved by the Senate.[4]

International Relations Committee

The House International Relations Committee, which changed its name from the Foreign Affairs Committee on March 19, 1975, was created on March 13, 1822. The committee has broad responsibility for the relations of the United States with other countries; its jurisdiction covers a variety of foreign policy areas, including fostering international trade, economic policy, foreign loans, foreign military aid, trading with the enemy, export controls, neutrality and international commodity agreements (except sugar).

Because it lacked authority over either treaties or nominations, the committee languished in the shadow of its Senate counterpart for more than 100 years. Membership on the House committee was considered a routine assignment. The panel acquired a measure of prestige only when the rapid expansion of American involvement abroad after World War II frequently demanded the House committee's action.[5]

During the Vietnam War, the committee consistently backed the policies of Presidents Johnson and Nixon and was reluctant to challenge either man on other foreign policy issues, including military assistance requests.[6] But with the addition of several liberal members to the committee in the mid-1970s, the committee began to challenge the administrations' requests on matters such as aid to Turkey and foreign military aid.

The historically secondary role of the committee has not prevented its involvement in controversy, however. During the Civil War, it became embroiled in a classic legislative-executive dispute over the making of foreign policy.

Other Committees

Numerous other committees of Congress have some impact currently on foreign policy. The requirement of vast sums for foreign aid and military assistance has given the Appropriations Committees a powerful lever. The Armed Services Committees have a controlling influence over defense policy and its impact abroad. Congressional oversight of foreign policy is maintained through hearings by the House Government Operations Subcommittee on Legislation and National Security and the Senate Government Operations Permanent Investigations Subcommittee. Immigration policies are reviewed by the Judiciary Committees. And trade and import quota bills are referred to the House Ways and Means and the Senate Finance Committees.

Footnotes

1. Samuel Flagg Bemis, *A Diplomatic History of the United States* (Henry Holt and Co., 1936), p. 404.

2. Congressional Quarterly, *The Power of the Pentagon*, p. 15.

3. James A. Robinson, *Congress and Foreign Policy-Making*, (Dorsey Press, 1962), p. 16.

4. Senate Foreign Relations Committee, *Legislative History of the Committee on Foreign Relations United States Senate, 93rd Congress, January 3, 1973-December 20, 1974*. S Rept. 94-37, 94th Congress, 1st session, 1975, p. 1.

5. Holbert N. Carroll, *The House of Representatives and Foreign Affairs* (Little Brown and Co., 1966), pp. 31, 90-93, 110-38, 274-75.

6. *The Power of the Pentagon*, p. 14.

Presidential reaction to rejection of the Treaty of Versailles took two forms. On the one hand, the White House made renewed efforts to court Senate support of proposed treaties by reinstituting some of the old, and developing some new, methods of associating senators with the treaty-making process. On the other hand, there was a growing tendency to rely on the executive agreement as a vehicle of international accords, thus eliminating altogether the need for Senate approval. There was reaction also in Congress, where various constitutional amendments were proposed to curtail the power of the Senate in the making of treaties.

New Importance of Treaty Power

In the years following World War II, the treaty-making power took on added importance. Membership in the United Nations was accomplished by Senate consent to ratification of the U.N. Charter, while membership in an expanding number of international organizations was brought about either by treaty or by both House and Senate approval of appropriate legislation. Treaties were used to conclude the widening circle of U.S. mutual security agreements designed to provide collective defense against aggression. (By the mid-1970s, the United States was committed to the defense of 42 countries through eight mutual security treaties.)[14] Agreements aimed to guide the peaceful and restrict the military use of atomic energy were incorporated in treaties, as were agreements intended to curtail the spread and production of nuclear armaments. And as man opened new frontiers in space and under the oceans, additional treaties were concluded or proposed to govern his behavior there.

Old conflicts over treaty making were renewed in the postwar years. It was a time of strong executive branch leadership, producing congressional reaction which came to a head in 1953-54 with consideration of the Bricker amendment, a proposal to limit presidential treaty power.

Ironically, in view of the Bricker amendment controversy, the postwar development and expansion of foreign aid as an aspect of U.S. foreign policy gave the legislative branch an unprecedented role in international relations. Foreign aid has been the subject of more than 100 enactments since 1945. Requiring in almost every instance the assent of Congress to expenditures, foreign aid proposals afforded senators and representatives their most consistent opportunity to support or to oppose the conduct of foreign relations by the executive branch. Inevitably, aid programs and policies were modified in the process, typically through lower-than-asked-for appropriations.

Action of Constitutional Convention

At the root of the recurring conflict between the President and Congress over the treaty-making power has been the doctrine of separation of powers that is so basic to the governmental structure of the United States.

During the Constitutional Convention, the treaty power came up for discussion repeatedly. At first, it was assumed that the existing power of the Continental Congress to make treaties by a two-thirds majority would be transferred intact to the legislative branch of the new government. Continued legislative control of treaty making was taken for granted despite the fact that it was then the exclusive prerogative of the executive in all other governments at that time.

The first suggestion that the treaty power should be divided between the legislative and executive branches seems to have been made in the convention on June 18, 1787. Hamilton proposed an executive elected for life, who, along with many other powers, would have "with the advice and approbation of the Senate, the power of making all treaties."[15] There was no discussion of Hamilton's suggestion, and it appeared dead when the Aug. 6 report of the Committee of Detail proposed that "the Senate shall have power to make treaties." Debate on the committee's report failed to resolve the issue of who was to exercise the treaty power. The section was referred back to the committee. On Sept. 4, the report of the Committee of Eleven recommended that "the President, by and with the advice and consent of the Senate," would have the power to make treaties, and that no treaty could be made "without the consent of two-thirds of the members present." Several attempts were made to alter the proportion of the Senate whose consent would be required, and to add House participation in treaty making, but on Sept. 8 the provision as proposed in the report was finally agreed to.[16]

There was nearly unanimous support in the convention for some means of enabling the new government to require the states to honor treaty provisions. Although the Articles of Confederation entrusted the treaty-making power to Congress, fulfillment of Congress' promises to other nations was dependent on the state legislatures. Inaction, or adverse action, by certain states had led to violation of some articles of the Peace Treaty of 1783 with Great Britain. A solution was provided in the declaration of Article VI, Clause 2 of the Constitution that "all treaties made, or which shall be made, under the authority of the United States shall be the supreme law of the land...."

The meaning of the declaration was explained by Chief Justice John Marshall in 1829 (*Foster v. Neilson*, 2 Pet. 253): "Our Constitution declares a treaty to be the supreme law of the land. It is, consequently, to be regarded in courts of justice as equivalent to an act of the legislature, whenever it operates of itself, without the aid of any legislative provision. But when the terms of the stipulation import a contract—when neither of the parties engages to perform a particular act, the treaty addresses itself to the political, not the judicial department; and the legislature must execute the contract, before it can become a rule for the Court."[17] Hence, although Congress may have to enact legislation to carry out acts stipulated by a treaty, any self-executing treaty or part of a treaty automatically attains the status of a statute, enforceable by the courts. Provisions of various treaties periodically have been the target of legal challenges, but the Supreme Court never has ruled unconstitutional a treaty of the United States or any provision of a treaty.[18]

Exclusion of the House from the treaty-making process was defended by Hamilton and Jay in *The Federalist*. Using similar arguments, they contended that the legislative role in treaty making should be limited to the Senate because decisions on treaties would thus be placed in the hands of persons chosen by the "select assemblies" of the states instead of by the rank and file, because the longer and overlapping Senate terms would provide relatively greater continuity, because the smaller size of the Senate would aid "secrecy and dispatch," and because agreement among the President, the Senate and the House would be more difficult to obtain.[19]

Final adoption of the two-thirds rule reflected the special concern of certain states over Newfoundland fishing rights and the right of navigation on the Mississippi River.[20]

Form of Senate Consent. In performing its constitutional treaty-making functions, the Senate merely con-

---

Foreign Policy and the House

Deprived by the Constitutional Convention of a share in the treaty-making power, the House has held a less significant role than the Senate in U.S. foreign policy. Nevertheless, the revenue power of the House, including that chamber's dominance of the appropriations process, have given representatives an indirect but important role in policy making. The role has come primarily since World War II as U.S. economic commitments abroad have grown.

In the first administration, when the Senate agreed to a treaty with the Dey of Algiers for release of American captives "provided the expense [sic] do not exceed $40,000,))[1] President Washington announced that he would wait to conclude negotiations until the money had been appropriated by Congress. The Senate objected, urging that the money be taken from the Treasury or raised by borrowing. As reported in *Jefferson's Writings*, the senators feared that "to consult the representatives on one occasion would give them a handle always to claim it."[2] The House then passed a bill, in 1792, appropriating a stated sum to cover the expenses involved and the Senate consented to ratification of a treaty specifying the sum appropriated.

In considering appropriations for the Jay treaty, the House called for all documents in the case. Washington refused this request on the ground that "the assent of the House of Representatives is not necessary to the validity of a treaty."[3] The House made the necessary appropriation in 1796 after long debate, but at the same time it adopted a resolution which said "it is the constitutional right and duty of the House of Representatives in all such cases to deliberate on the expediency or inexpediency of carrying such treaty into effect and to determine and act thereon as in their judgment may be most conducive to the public good."[4]

Submission of commercial and reciprocity treaties has led to repeated assertions of authority by the House, frequently with support in the Senate. The reciprocity treaty with Great Britain in 1854 made its effectiveness dependent upon passage of the laws necessary to put it into operation.[5] In 1883 the Senate amended a reciprocity convention with Mexico to provide that it should not come into force until the legislation called for had been passed by Congress, and this treaty never took effect for lack of action by the House.[6] The House participated in the annexation of Texas and of Hawaii, which was accomplished by joint resolution—in the first case after a treaty of annexation had been defeated in the Senate, and in the second case when a two-thirds vote in the Senate seemed doubtful. *(Box on joint resolutions, p. 251)*

In at least one case, House opposition prevented ratification of a treaty necessitating an appropriation. Shortly before the original treaty for the purchase of the Danish West Indies was submitted in 1867, the House resolved that "in the present financial condition of the country, any further purchases of territory are inexpedient, and this House will hold itself under no obligation to vote money for any such purpose unless there is greater necessity than now exists." In the debate it was said that this resolution was intended to serve notice on the King of Denmark that "this House will not pay for that purchase." When the treaty was sent to the Senate, no action was taken. When the islands were finally acquired 50 years later, the price had risen from $7,500,000 to $25,000,000.[8]

Despite frequent assertions by the House of its right to refuse appropriations pledged in a treaty, it never fas failed to make such appropriations once the treaty has been ratified by the Senate.[9]

Footnotes

1. George H. Haynes, *The Senate of the United States*, (Houghton-Mifflin Co., 1938), Vol. 2, p. 686.
  2. *Ibid.*, p. 686.
  3. *Ibid.*, p. 687.
  4. *Ibid.*, p. 688.
  5. *Ibid.*, p. 691, n.
  6. *Ibid.*, p. 691.
  7. F. M. Brewer, "The Treaty Power," *Editorial Research Reports*, Jan. 18, 1943, p. 53.
  8. *Ibid.*, pp. 53-54.
  9. Haynes, *The Senate*, p. 689.

---

sents to the ratification of a treaty; ratification itself is subject to executive action. Normally, the Senate considers a resolution of advice and consent to ratification of a pending treaty. In the case of the nuclear test-ban treaty, approved by the Senate on Sept. 24, 1963, the resolution of ratification read as follows:

"Be it resolved (two-thirds of the senators present concurring therein), that the Senate advise and consent to the ratification of the treaty banning nuclear weapons tests in the atmosphere, in outer space, and under water, which was signed at Moscow on Aug. 5, 1963, on behalf of the United States of America, the United Kingdom of Great Britain and Northern Ireland and the Union of Soviet Socialist Republics."

Consideration of First Treaties, 1789

The first treaties to be laid before the Senate under the Constitution were submitted on May 25, 1789.[21] They were a pair of treaties with Indian tribes negotiated and signed under the authority of the Continental Congress. It was not until June 12 that the two treaties were referred to a committee for study; in the meantime, the President had submitted another treaty, a consular convention with France, concluded under the Articles of Confederation. After a series of meetings with, and reports from John Jay, secretary of foreign affairs, an office held over from the Confederation, the Senate on July 29, 1789, unanimously consented to ratification of the consular treaty.[22] This was the first time the Senate had given its advice and consent to ratification of a treaty.

The committee studying the two Indian treaties finally reported on Aug. 12. Instead of recommending that the Senate advise and consent to ratification (as had been done with the consular treaty with France), the committee recommended that the President "be advised to execute and enjoin an observance" of the agreements. The Senate on Sept. 8 approved the committee recommendation for one of the treaties (that with the Wyandot, Delaware, Ottawa, Chippewa, Pattawattima and Sacs nations) but took no action on the other (that with the Six Nations, except the Mohawks).

The Senate action confused President Washington. He was not certain whether the Senate meant that he should merely see that the approved treaty went into operation or that he should proceed with a formal ratification. In a message to the Senate, Sept. 17, the President asked for a clarification. His own opinion, he said, was that treaties with Indian tribes should be ratified in the same way as treaties with European nations. The Senate disagreed. A committee that studied the President's messaged reported, Sept. 18, that since past Indian treaties never had been solemnly ratified, it was not "expedient or necessary" to ratify the present treaties. The committee proposed a resolution to advise the President "to enjoin a due observance" of the Wyandot treaty, passing over the treaty with the Six Nations. But on Sept. 22 the Senate substituted a resolution of advice and consent to the Wyandot treaty. No action was taken on the other agreement. Senate consent to ratification of the Wyandot treaty set a precedent that endured until 1871, when a rider to the Indian Appropriations Act of 1871 provided that in the future no American Indian nation or tribe was to be considered an independent nation with which the United States could conclude a treaty. Indian affairs were handled subsequently by statute.[23]

Advice of the Senate

The first treaties considered by the Senate had been negotiated under instructions from the Continental Congress because there was no executive in the confederation government. Although the new Constitution provided for an executive and authorized him to make treaties, with advice from the Senate, it failed to explain what kind of advice was appropriate or how it was to be offered. To be effective the advice would have to be given before the end of negotiations.

In practice, procedures developed by Washington and the first Senate established precedents which have exerted varying degrees of influence. After an abortive attempt at personal consultation with the Senate as an executive council, Washington's usual practice, at least up to the Jay treaty negotiations with Great Britain in 1794, was to ask for advice about opening negotiations; to transmit the full instructions to be given to the negotiators; to submit their names for confirmation; and to keep the Senate fully informed of the progress of negotiations. If matters came up which were not covered in the original instructions, Washington again would call for Senate advice.[24] When treaties would require appropriations, he reported the proceedings to the House as well as to the Senate.

Additional procedures adopted by early administrations included requests for advance appropriations to cover the cost of negotiating, naming of senators and representatives to the negotiating team and consulting personally with key members of the Senate, and, after its establishment in 1816, with the Foreign Relations Committee. At times Congress took the initiative by considering resolutions to suggest or to oppose negotiations.

Consultation With the Senate

While the Senate was considering the first treaties, it named a committee of three senators, Aug. 6, 1789, to meet with the President to establish ground rules for consultation on the making of treaties. Washington favored oral communications rather than written exchanges, and, following a committee recommendation, the Senate on Aug. 21 adopted a rule providing for meetings with the President either in the Senate chamber or elsewhere. Later the same day, the Senate received a message announcing that Washington was coming to the Senate chamber the next day "at half past 11 o'clock" to discuss proposed terms for a treaty with the southern Indians.

Unfamiliar with the background of the situation or with the proposed treaty terms, the Senate sought to refer the papers to a committee for study. Washington, who had hoped for prompt action, objected strenuously. He finally agreed to defer action to Aug. 24. The second meeting went more smoothly; the Senate agreed to vote its advice on each of the points raised by the President.[25] However, Washington never again went before the Senate to consult on treaty terms or discuss foreign policy, nor did any other President until Woodrow Wilson appeared on Jan. 22, 1917, to call for "peace without victory" and propose a League for Peace. President Truman also went to the Senate in person, July 2, 1945, to ask its early consent to ratification of the United Nations Charter. President Nixon appeared before Congress June 1, 1972, to urge approval of the U.S.-Soviet strategic arms limitation talks (SALT) accords.

President Washington, after his initial venture in direct consultation, relied on special messages in seeking the advice of the Senate. Tradition says that the chilling reception which he had met in the Senate chamber led him to swear that he would never go there again.[26]

Although Washington's general position was that he considered it advisable to postpone negotiations until he

Joint Resolutions

From an early date, treaties have not been the sole means of concluding an agreement between the United States and a foreign country.

International accords have been arranged through executive agreements, independently concluded by the executive branch. *(See p. 256)*

On occasion, Presidents have resorted to a joint resolution—the functional equivalent of an act of Congress—when there was fear that a treaty would not command a two-thirds majority in the Senate. A joint resolution requires only a simple majority for approval, but it must be adopted by both Houses of Congress.

After Senate rejection of a treaty for the annexation of Texas in 1844, annexation was accomplished through a joint resolution approved March 1, 1845. Hawaii was annexed as a territory by a joint resolution approved July 7, 1898. Following Senate rejection of the Treaty of Versailles, President Wilson in 1920 vetoed a joint resolution "declaring peace," but President Harding on July 2, 1921, signed a similar resolution. A separate peace treaty with Germany also was concluded in 1921.

Sources: Library of Congress, *Constitution of the United States of America, Analysis and Interpretation* (Government Printing Office, 1973), pp. 505-19; George H. Haynes, *The Senate of the United States* (Houghton-Mifflin Co., 1938), vol. 2, pp. 633-36; Bryant Putney, "Participation by Congress in Control of Foreign Policy," *Editorial Research Reports*, Nov. 9, 1939, pp. 337-55.

had received the advice of the Senate as to the propositions to be offered, he did not follow this course in the case of the Jay treaty. He submitted Jay's name as a negotiator for confirmation by the Senate but withheld the instructions to be given him.[27] The same procedure was adopted by Washington's immediate successors, Adams and Madison, and has been followed by some other Presidents.

Polk returned to the earlier practice when in 1846 he asked the Senate's advice as to whether negotiations should be undertaken with Great Britain on the basis of proposals submitted from London for the settlement of the Oregon boundary question.[28] Similar requests for preliminary advice were sent to the Senate by Buchanan, Lincoln, Johnson, Grant and Cleveland. Harding, in 1922, asked advice as to revival of a patents treaty with Germany.

The right of the Senate to direct treaty making by proposing negotiations has been vigorously debated on the Senate floor. Proponents have defended such initiative as the right and duty of the Senate under the Constitution, and as helpful in showing the United States to be a unit in its demands. Opposition senators have contended that for the Senate to make the first move was "officious and disrespectful," and that it tended to "shelter" the President from responsibility in treaty making. In 1902 a report by the Committee on Foreign Relations declared: "The initiative lies with the President.... Whether he will negotiate a treaty, and when, and what its terms shall be are matters committed by the Constitution to the discretion of the President."[29]

Today the right of either house of Congress to offer advice about negotiations is not questioned, but the advice of the legislative branch is merely persuasive, and not compelling. In its landmark decision in the Curtiss-Wright case in 1936 (*U.S. v. Curtiss-Wright Export Corp.*, 299 U.S. 305) the Supreme Court ruled: "The President...alone negotiates. Into the field of negotiation the Senate cannot intrude, and Congress itself is powerless to invade it."[30]

The reaction of different administrations to Senate advice to negotiate has varied. President Jackson acted on a Senate resolution in opening negotiations with Central American governments for an interoceanic canal. Cleveland replied with some asperity to a similar Senate suggestion for negotiations to limit Chinese labor. Harding refused to recognize that the Borah resolution for agreement with Great Britain and Japan on reduction of naval expenditures was responsible for the calling of the Washington Conference on the Limitation of Armament. Sponsored by Sen. William E. Borah (R Idaho), the resolution was adopted by the Senate May 26, 1921, and by the House on June 29. Formal invitations to the conference were issued Aug. 11, 1921.[31]

Confirmation of Negotiators

Up to the end of Madison's administration, the names of treaty negotiators were referred to the Senate for confirmation. Subsequent neglect of the practice was repeatedly protested in the Senate. In 1883, the Senate attempted in ratifying a treaty with Korea to revive the earlier practice by adopting a resolution which stipulated that the consent given to ratification did not "admit or acquiesce in any right or constitutional power in the President to employ any person to negotiate treaties...unless such person shall have been appointed...with the advice and consent of the Senate."[32] Cleveland's appointment of a special commissioner with "paramount authority" to negotiate with Hawaii was declared by the Republican members of the Foreign Relations Committee to be "an unconstitutional act in that such appointee was never nominated to the Senate.[33]

That confirmation of negotiators gave the Senate an important power was recognized by both the Senate and the executive branch. Commenting on the situation when one of Adams' nominations was under attack, Jefferson wrote that, were a large opposition vote registered, even if confirmation resulted, "it is supposed the President would perhaps not act under it, on the probability that more than a third would be against ratification."[34]

Abandonment of the practice of Senate confirmation of negotiators appears to have been due to the need for secrecy which led to employment of special agents whose appointment was recognized as the right of the executive in carrying out his constitutional duties, and to acceptance of the principle—in Jefferson's words to Citizen Genet, envoy to the United States from the first French Republic—that the President is "the only channel of communication between this country and foreign nations."[35]

Treaties Killed by Lack of Two-Thirds Majority

Date of vote	Country	Vote Yea	:	Nay	Subject
April 17, 1844	German Zollverein	26	:	18	Reciprocity
June 27, 1860	Spain	26	:	17	Cuban Claims Convention
June 1, 1870	Hawaii	20	:	19	Reciprocity
Jan. 5, 1883	Mexico	33	:	20	Claims Convention
April 20, 1886	Mexico	32	:	26	Claims Convention
May 5, 1897	Great Britain	43	:	26	Arbitration
March 19, 1920	Multilateral	49	:	35	Treaty of Versailles
Jan. 18, 1927	Turkey	50	:	34	Amity and Commerce
March 14, 1934	Canada	46	:	42	St. Lawrence Waterway
Jan. 29, 1935	Multilateral	52	:	36	Adherence to World Court
May 26, 1960	Multilateral	49	:	30	Sea Law Convention Protocol

Sources: George H. Haynes, *The Senate of the United States* (Houghton-Mifflin Co., 1938), vol. 2, p. 659; U.S. Congress, Senate, Committee on Foreign Relations, *Background Information on the Committee on Foreign Relations, U.S. Senate*, 3rd rev. ed., 94th Cong., 1st sess., 1975, pp. 25-26.

In later years, on various occasions, the executive sought Senate confirmation of treaty negotiators. Polk submitted the names of his appointees to negotiate a treaty with Mexico. Grant nominated to the Senate the commissioners who negotiated the Treaty of Washington with Great Britain. Harding submitted the names of his appointees to the World War Foreign Debt Commission in 1922, but such submission was required by a provision of the act creating the commission, which stipulated that its members be appointed by the President, "by and with the advice and consent of the Senate."[36]

The United Nations Participation Act of 1945 provided for Senate confirmation of the United States representatives to the United Nations, of members of the U.S. delegation to the General Assembly, and of delegates to various U.N. agencies.

Submission of Negotiators' Instructions

Submission of their instructions along with the names of negotiators, amounted, while Washington was President, to an opportunity for the Senate to advise on treaty proposals. No opportunity to consider the terms of a treaty not yet agreed upon was provided during ensuing administrations until Polk submitted the skeleton of a treaty ending the war with Mexico in 1846. Preliminary drafts of treaties were sent to the Senate in a few instances by four other Presidents—Buchanan, Lincoln, Johnson and Grant. In 1919, the Senate requested a copy of the Treaty of Versailles as presented to the representatives of Germany. The secretary of state replied: "The President feels it would not be in the public interest to communicate to the Senate a text that is provisional and not definite, and finds no precedent for such a procedure."[37]

In at least two instances, the Senate (with the concurrence of the House) has "advised" the executive by specifying the limits within which negotiators of international agreements were to operate. In the act of February 9, 1922, creating the Foreign Debt Commission it was provided that "nothing contained in this act shall be construed to authorize...the commission to extend the time of maturity of...obligations due the United States...beyond June 15, 1947, or to fix the rate of interest at less than 4¼ per centum per annum."[38] In a joint resolution making funds available to send a delegation to the Opium Conference of 1924, Congress specified certain results to be obtained by the negotiators.

Members of Congress as Negotiators

The first two members of Congress to be selected to negotiate a treaty were Sen. James A. Bayard (Federalist Del.) and House Speaker Henry Clay (Ky.). Madison named them to help negotiate a treaty of peace with Great Britain in 1814.[39] Both resigned their places in Congress on the ground that the two offices were not compatible. On at least three occasions resolutions have been introduced in the Senate to prohibit members of that body from serving as treaty negotiators.[40] The first, in 1870, was defeated after a heated all-night debate, when it was turned into a question of confidence in President Grant. The second was occasioned by McKinley's appointment, following a series of such congressional appointments by himself and his predecessors, of three members of the Committee on Foreign Relations on the commission to negotiate the Treaty of Paris in 1898. The Committee on Foreign Relations, to which a resolution of protest was referred, hesitated to make a report that might appear to censure its own members, but

---

Lobbying on Treaties

Treaties periodically are subject to much the same forms of lobbying as regular legislative measures. Consideration of the U.S.-Soviet Consular Convention of 1964 was marked by one of the largest mail and pressure campaigns in recent years. Despite the largely hostile lobbying, the Senate consented to ratification on March 16, 1967, by a 66-28 vote.

The intense "grassroots lobbying" campaign against the convention was led by the ultra-conservative, Washington-based Liberty Lobby, an organization set up in 1955 "for the purpose of reversing the dangerous trend toward socialization internally and to defeat the insidious effort to weaken our resistance to international Communism."

Other conservative groups working against the treaty included the Manion Forum, the Dan Smoot Report, the United Republicans of America, the National Review and the Mothers of American Servicemen of South Pasadena, Calif.

Senators complained that they were swamped by mail which was, to a large extent, generated by these organizations. Opposition to the treaty far outweighed support for it.

The Liberty Lobby used its large mailing list, claimed to include more than 170,000 names, for its campaign. Much of the Liberty Lobby support was attributed to a 16-panel comic strip entitled, "The Communist Next Door." The comic strip was described by Liberty Lobby as "a new technique to reach the voters...clear, direct, motivational." The strip included such statements as: "The most obvious danger from the treaty is provision for 'diplomatic immunity'.... To give Soviet personnel complete immunity is to invite an increase in Red espionage...even sabotage...since the treaty forbids any inspection of any baggage or equipment brought in as 'diplomatic pouch.' " The strip showed a conspirator assembling a suitcase-size A-bomb and ended with the appeal: "How about it, folks? Help your two senators by letting them know how you feel about the Soviet Consular Treaty. There isn't much time left, so write today." The appeal was so successful that even House members, who do not vote on treaties, received numerous letters.

The Liberty Lobby also purchased advertising space in 27 newspapers around the country to reproduce the comic strip. At least 17 additional papers carried the ad placed by other individuals or groups. The Liberty Lobby ads were placed in newspapers in states where at least one senator was already opposed to the treaty or where there was a good possibility to swing an uncommitted vote, according to a Lobby spokesman. The ads appeared for the most part in newspapers in the traditionally conservative Midwest and the South. They also appeared in states or cities with large populations that had close ties to the so-called "captive" nations of Eastern Europe.

---

it directed its chairman to visit the President and express the Senate's strong disapproval.[41] Theodore Roosevelt's selection of Sen. Henry Cabot Lodge (R Mass.) for the Alaskan boundary tribunal led to the third attempt of the Senate to prohibit such service by senators. The resolution introduced at that time was not acted upon.

Senate resentment of Wilson's failure to include any senators on the 1919 peace commission came as a sharp contrast to its previous position. To compensate for lack of representation on the commission, a resolution calling for the appointment of a bipartisan committee of eight senators to visit Paris during the sittings of the Peace Conference, to "make itself familiar with all facts" and report to the Senate "as often as it deemed desirable," was introduced but not acted upon.[42] Senate attempts to advise as to negotiations through debate on the floor and through a round-robin warning against inclusion of provisions for a League of Nations in the peace treaty proved to be without effect.

As a result of Wilson's experience, the appointment of senators to important international conferences has since been frequent. President Harding in 1921 chose the chairman of the Senate Committee on Foreign Relations, Sen. Henry Cabot Lodge (R Mass.), and the minority leader, Sen. Oscar W. Underwood (D Ala.), as delegates to the Conference on the Limitation of Armament, and members of both houses were appointed by Hoover to the American delegation to the London Naval Conference in 1930. President Roosevelt recognized Congress in his selection of commissioners to the World Monetary and Economic Conference, in 1933 and to the International Refugee Conference in 1943.

In 1945, the eight-member U.S. delegation to the United Nations founding conference at San Francisco included four members of Congress: Foreign Relations Committee Chairman Tom Connally (D Texas), Sen. Arthur H. Vandenberg (R Mich.), a committee member, and Reps. Sol Bloom (D N.Y.) and Charles A. Eaton (R N.J.), chairman and ranking minority member of the House Foreign Affairs Committee. Since organization of the United Nations, two senators and two representatives have alternated as members of the U.S. delegation.

During the postwar period, successive administrations have followed the practice of including members of Congress on delegations to international conferences. Wilcox offers this assessment of the practice: "On balance, congressional participation in international conferences seems to have done very little harm and some good. In a few cases...congressional cooperation has been of inestimable value, not only in the drafting process but in securing Senate approval of the finished product. Measured quantitatively over the years, it has most often simply been neutral, having no results commensurate with the time, trouble and money required."[43]

Consent of the Senate

Over the years, Senate action on treaties has led to recurring rounds of controversy. At issue traditionally have been rival claims by the President and the Senate with respect to the treaty power.

The Senate has adopted a simple resolution of consent to ratification on a vast majority of treaties submitted to it. It has modified or rejected relatively few.[44] But the significance of some of the rejected treaties has prompted criticism of the Senate's treaty-making role, as well as the two-thirds rule, and has spawned a variety of proposed constitutional amendments designed to modify the Senate's power.

Treaties are transmitted to the Senate by the President under an injunction of secrecy which normally is removed shortly after the Senate receives the treaty. Once a treaty is submitted, it remains before the Senate until it is disposed of favorably, or until the President requests its return and the Senate agrees.[45]

Senate Procedure

Senate consideration of a treaty is open to presidential discretion at a number of points. The President may refuse to submit a treaty; he may withdraw it after submission; or he may refuse to ratify it even after the Senate has given its consent.[46]

Within the Senate, treaties are subject to the jurisdiction of the Foreign Relations Committee whether or not they involve subjects that usually require consideration by another committee. The Foreign Relations Committee considers a treaty in much the same way that it considers proposed legislation. It may hold open or closed hearings and may recommend adoption or rejection, with or without modifications. Committee actions require a majority vote of the members present; to act, according to the Legislative Reorganization Act of 1946, a committee majority must be "actually present."[47]

After action by the Foreign Relations Committee, treaties are considered by the full Senate. The Senate used to debate treaties in closed executive session, preserving the cloak of secrecy. Pressures later developed to make public the Senate treaty debates. A fisheries treaty with Great Britain was considered—and defeated—in the first open executive session in 1888. Other public treaty debates followed, and the Senate on June 18, 1929, amended its rules to provide that all Senate business, including action on treaties, would be conducted in open session unless a Senate majority decided in a closed session to consider a particular matter in secret.[48]

After a brief experiment (1801 to 1803) with a rule requiring a two-thirds vote on all treaty action, the Senate limited the two-thirds rule to the final question of advice and consent and to a motion for indefinite postponement. All other questions are decided by majority vote.[49]

A separate vote normally is taken on each treaty. But that procedure is sometimes departed from when a large number of similar treaties, or a variety of noncontroversial treaties, is to be considered. It has become the practice in these cases to consider the group of treaties en bloc (taking one vote on several resolutions of consent) or to take a single vote, which by unanimous consent is shown separately in the *Congressional Record* for each resolution. Although Senate rules do not require roll-call votes on treaties, that practice has become customary. It grew out of a 1952 incident in which three noncontroversial consular conventions were approved, on June 13, when only two senators were present in the chamber. On July 20, 1953, acting Majority Leader William F. Knowland (R Calif.) announced that "as a matter of standard operating procedure in the future, we intend, in connection with all treaties...not only to ask for a quorum call, but to ask for a yea-and-nay vote...."[50]

Modification of Treaties

In the Constitution, there is no provision for or against amendment of treaties by the Senate. But since the time of the Jay treaty with Great Britain, the Senate has claimed authority to modify treaties after the completion of negotiations. The Senate on June 24, 1795, by a 20-10 vote consented to ratification of the Jay treaty on condition that an additional article be negotiated to suspend portions of the treaty's 12th article that related to trade between the United States and the British West Indies. Scores of later treaties have been subjected to amendments, reservations, conditions and qualifications, some of them added at the request of the President.[51]

The wisdom of the Senate practice of amending treaties was questioned as early as 1805 by John Quincy Adams. In a Senate debate, Adams said, "I think amendments to treaties imprudent. By making them you agree to all the treaty except the particular you amend, and at the same time you leave it optional with the other party to reject the whole."[52] A later opinion was voiced by Secretary of State Richard Olney, after Senate rejection of an Anglo-American arbitration treaty in 1897: "...Senators have exhausted their ingenuity in devising amendments to the treaty. Before the treaty came to a final vote, the Senate brand had been put upon every part of it, and the original instrument had been mutilated and distorted beyond all possibility of recognition."[53]

On two occasions the Supreme Court has sustained the power of the Senate to amend treaties. In 1869, in the case of *Haver v. Yaker* (9 Wall. 34), the court stated: "In this country a treaty is something more than a contract, for the federal Constitution declared it to be the law of the land. If so, before it can become a law, the Senate in whom rests the power to ratify it, must agree to it. But the Senate are not required to adopt or reject it as a whole, but may modify or amend it."[54] And in a 1901 opinion *(Fourteen Diamond Rings v. U.S.,* 183 U.S. 183) the court said: "The Senate may refuse its ratification or make it conditional upon adoption of amendments to the treaty."[55]

Probably the best known of recent Senate qualifications of U.S. international obligations is the Connally reservation to the compulsory jurisdiction clause of the statute of the International Court of Justice. In adhering to the U.N. Charter in 1945, the United States accepted membership in the court. President Truman contended that the country should also accept compulsory jurisdiction under terms of the court's statute, which excluded matters deemed to be within the domestic jurisdiction of any nation; and on July 31, 1946, the Senate took up a resolution to that effect.

Recalling fears which led to Senate refusal in 1935, after a decade of discussion, to approve adherence to the earlier World Court, some senators objected to letting the International Court of Justice determine what matters might or might not be within U.S. jurisdiction. To obviate this possibility, Sen. Tom Connally (D Texas) proposed adding after a clause excluding "Matters which are essentially within the domestic jurisdiction of the United States" the words "as determined by the United States." The Senate agreed to the Connally reservation on Aug. 2, 1946, by a 51-12 vote, in effect negating the U.S. commitment in principle; it then adopted the amended resolution by a 60-2 vote. Subsequent attempts to repeal the reservation have been unsuccessful.[56]

When the Senate adopts a treaty amendment, the amendment, if it is accepted by the President and the other parties to the treaty, changes it for all parties. A Senate reservation limits only the treaty obligation of the United States, although a reservation may be so significant that the other treaty parties may file similar reservations or refuse to ratify the treaty.

The Senate Foreign Relations Committee has identified four major forms which a treaty qualification may take.

● The Senate may consent to ratification and include its views or interpretations in a committee report accompanying the treaty.

● Senate "understandings" or "interpretations" may be included in the resolution of consent. Such language would have no legal effect on the treaty if it did not substantially affect the treaty's terms or U.S. obligations. Under normal practice, the executive branch would inform the other treaty parties of the interpretations or understandings.

● The Senate may add a "reservation" to the resolution of consent, involving some change in obligations under the treaty. Again, other parties would be informed of the reservation.

● The Senate may amend the terms of the treaty itself, requiring new negotiations with the other parties.[57]

From the point of view of the executive branch, Senate alteration of treaties has become an increasingly serious problem in view of a growing tendency to adjust international relations through multilateral treaties. Resubmission of an amended treaty to a number of foreign governments—any one of which may wish to alter other provisions of the treaty in view of U.S. changes—presents almost insuperable obstacles to final agreement. The substitution of reservations for amendments in recent years has not lessened the difficulty, for the Senate has demanded more and more formal recognition of such reservations.

Proposed Changes in Treaty Power

For more than 70 years attempts have been made to alter the treaty-making provisions of the Constitution.[58] Most of the proposals have been to eliminate the two-thirds rule governing Senate action on treaties or to require consent to ratification by the House as well as the Senate. The Bricker amendment of the 1950s, which sought to curtail the President's treaty power, was a marked exception to the pattern.

Following the war with Spain, two resolutions were introduced in the House of Representatives proposing a constitutional amendment giving the power of consent to a majority of the whole Senate. In 1920, amendments were offered in both houses stipulating that consent to ratification should be by majority vote of members present in the Senate.[59]

Between 1919 and 1928, five resolutions were introduced in the House to let that body participate in giving "advice and consent" in the making of treaties. As Democratic candidate for President in 1924, John W. Davis endorsed the plan to substitute a majority for a two-thirds vote. William Jennings Bryan, in a Jackson day address in 1920, advocated associating the House with the Senate. An even more fundamental change was proposed in Congress in 1921 whereby certain treaties would have to be approved by popular vote.[60]

During World War II, recollection of Senate rejection of the Treaty of Versailles and the League of Nations prompted a number of proposals to change the provisions for treaty ratification so as to reduce the possibility that new postwar arrangements for enforcement of world peace would be rejected. Josephus Daniels, Navy secretary in the cabinet of Woodrow Wilson, suggested in a 1942 speech that the Constitution be amended to provide for consent to ratification by majority vote of both chambers. Proposed amendments to carry out his suggestion were introduced the following year in the House. In the Senate in 1943 a proposed amendment was introduced to allow Senate consent by a simple majority.[61]

In 1945, while the San Francisco conference was debating the charter of the United Nations, destined for consideration by the Senate alone, the House took up a resolution (H J Res 60) by Hatton Sumners (D Texas) to amend the Constitution to require that "Treaties shall be made by the President by and with the advice and consent of both houses of Congress." Despite general agreement that the Senate never would agree to share its treaty power, the House on May 9 adopted the resolution by a 288-88 vote.[62]

Bricker Amendment

During 1953 and 1954 (and briefly in 1956), Congress engaged in a heated debate on an amendment to the Constitution proposed by Sen. John W. Bricker (R Ohio) which would curb the executive's foreign-policy powers.[63] The Bricker amendment reflected fears that American adherence to various United Nations covenants and conventions, such as the genocide convention (which had not been ratified, as of 1976) would enhance federal powers and possibly interfere with enforcement of state laws by reason of the constitutional provision making treaties the "supreme law of the land." The proposed amendment stemmed also from resentment at the tendency to substitute executive agreements, not subject to ratification, for treaties requiring Senate consent. The controversy surrounding the amendment pitted a majority in Congress against the President and turned a highly technical legal question into a wide-ranging debate between "isolationists" and "one-worlders."

On Jan. 7, 1953, Sen. Bricker and 63 cosponsors (45 Republicans and 19 Democrats) introduced S J Res 1, the revised version of a proposed constitutional amendment introduced by Bricker and 58 cosponsors on Feb. 7, 1952. As revised, the proposed amendment read:

"1. A provision of a treaty which denies or abridges any right enumerated in this Constitution shall not be of any force or effect.

"2. No treaty shall authorize or permit any foreign power or any international organization to supervise, control, or adjudicate rights of citizens of the United States within the United States enumerated in this Constitution or any other matter essentially within the domestic jurisdiction of the United States.

3. A treaty shall become effective as internal law in the United States only through the enactment of appropriate legislation by the Congress.

"4. All executive or other agreements between the President and any international organization, foreign power, or official thereof shall be made only in the manner and to the extent to be prescribed by law. Such agreements shall be subject to the limitations imposed on treaties or the making of treaties in this article.

"5. The Congress shall have power to enforce this article by appropriate legislation."

On Feb. 16, Sen. Arthur V. Watkins (R Utah) introduced a variation of Bricker's amendments as S J Res 43, which had been drafted by the American Bar Association. Its two sections covered all except the second of Bricker's provisions.

The crux of the case for a constitutional amendment, as put by ABA spokesmen, was that some 200 treaties proposed or in preparation by U.N. agencies and covering a wide range of political, social and economic matters contained provisions at variance with federal or state law.

On June 15, the full Judiciary Committee, by a 9-5 vote, reported an amended version of S J Res 1 that, except for a slight change of wording, following the text of S J Res 43. Its key provision still declared that "a treaty shall become effective as internal law only through legislation which would be valid in the absence of a treaty."

No further action was taken before Congress adjourned. Senate debate on S J Res 1 was resumed Jan. 27, 1954, and continued through Feb. 26. A final tally that day fell one vote short (60-31) of the two-thirds majority required for Senate approval. Before the next (84th) Congress adjourned July 27, 1956, it considered briefly the question of revising the Constitution's treaty provisions along the lines advocated by Bricker. But, faced with the absence of administration support and the prospect of a long debate, Democratic leaders refused to call up Bricker's latest proposal (again designated S J Res 1), and it died without coming to a vote.

Executive Agreements

Controversy over the extensive use in the post-war period of executive agreements as an alternative to treaties surfaced again in the 1970s, when Congress began to press for legislation that would afford it a voice in the making of such agreements.[64]

The courts repeatedly have upheld the authority of the President to enter into agreements or compacts with other governments without consulting the Senate.[65] The vast majority of executive agreements have concerned such routine

---

Defining an Agreement

American constitutional law recognizes three basic types of international agreements and leaves it up to the executive branch which type to use in international situations, said the Senate Judiciary Subcommittee on Separation of Powers in a 1973 report on executive agreements. The report listed the three types:

● First in importance is the treaty, which the report defines as an international—bilateral or multilateral—compact that requires consent by a two-thirds vote of the Senate.

● Second, the congressional-executive international agreement, entered into under a statute or an existing treaty. Examples of this type include presidential agreements with foreign countries for the distribution of U.S. funds, based upon the foreign aid laws and the 1946 executive agreement providing for the establishment of the United Nations Headquarters District in New York, after appropriate action by Congress.

● Third is what the subcommittee called the "pure" or "true" executive agreement, negotiated by the President entirely on his constitutional authority as 1) commander in chief, 2) chief executive, which the courts have interpreted to include foreign relations, and 3) in his other roles as delineated in Article II of the Constitution; the State Department estimated that this kind of agreement may constitute no more than 3 per cent of all U.S. international agreements.

Source: U.S. Congress, Senate, Committee on the Judiciary, *Congressional Oversight of Executive Agreements*, committee print, 93rd Cong., 1st sess., 1973, p. 4.

Agreements and Treaties Entered into by U.S.

Following is a list of the number of published treaties and executive agreements entered into by the United States. Varying definitions of what comprises an executive agreement make all numbers approximate.

State Department compilations are for all international agreements, loosely defined as those negotiated pursuant to the President's authority under previous legislation, treaties or the Constitution.

Year[1]	Treaties	Executive Agreements	Year[1]	Treaties	Executive Agreements
1789-1839	60	27	1954	17	206
1839-1889	215	238	1955	7	297
1889-1929	382	763	1956	15	233
1930	25	11	1957	9	222
1931	13	14	1958	10	197
1932	11	16	1959	12	250
1933	9	11	1960	5	266
1934	14	16	1961	9	260
1935	25	10	1962	10	319
1936	8	16	1963	17	234
1937	15	10	1964	3	222
1938	12	24	1965	14	204
1939	10	26	1966	14	237
1940	12	20	1967	18	223
1941	15	39	1968	18	197
1942	6	52	1969	6	162
1943	4	71	1970	20	183
1944	1	74	1971	17	214
1945	6[2]	54	1972	20	287
1946	19	139	1973	17	241
1947	15	144	1974	13	230
1948	16	178	Total	1,254	7,809
1949	22	148			
1950	11	157			
1951	21	213			
1952	22	291			
1953	14	163			

1. Year published
2. Includes unpublished water treaty with Mexico, in force since Nov. 18, 1945

Sources: 1789-1929: Rep. Emanuel Celler (D N.Y., 1923-1973), *Congressional Record*, May 2, 1945, p. 4049.
1930-1945: Borchard, Edwin M., "Treaties and Executive Agreements," *American Political Science Review*, vol. 40, no. 4, August 1946, p. 735.
1946-1974: Department of State, Treaty Affairs Staff, Office of the Legal Adviser.

matters as the regulation of fishing rights, private claims against another government and postal agreements. In other cases, however, major U.S. diplomatic policies have been carried out by executive agreements, sometimes with controversial results—as in the case of the World War II summit conference agreements at Cairo, Teheran, Yalta and Potsdam.[66] Still other executive agreements have been concluded under specific delegations of power by Congress, such as tariff agreements under the Reciprocal Trade Agreements Act of 1934.

Executive agreements have been recognized as distinct from treaties since the presidency of George Washington. The Post Office Act of 1792 authorized the postmaster general to "make arrangements with postmasters in any foreign country for the reciprocal receipt and delivery of letters and packets, through the post offices."

But it was not until World War II that the executive agreement assumed a major role as a foreign policy tool. The number of international agreements increased dramatically in the late 1930s, according to statistics provided by the Senate Judiciary Subcommittee on Separation of Powers.[67]

The growth of executive agreements alarmed many members of Congress, who felt that some agreements involved major commitments of U.S. resources or represented significant policy decisions that were made

without the consultation of Congress. As a result of this concern, members of both the House and Senate introduced various bills during the 1970-75 period to give Congress a veto over executive agreements. Foreign policy officials in the Ford administration in 1975 vigorously opposed such legislation on constitutional, foreign policy and pragmatic grounds. They suggested instead a more informal cooperative relationship between the two branches. But that approach failed to satisfy many members who pointed to what they considered were abuses of the use of executive agreements.

Legislative History

Under a law enacted in 1950 (PL 81-821), the secretary of state was directed to compile and publish annually the contents of all treaties and executive agreements entered into the previous year. In practice, however, agreements considered sensitive to national security were withheld from Congress by the executive branch, even from the relevant committees on a classified basis.

Two years after rejecting the Bricker amendment, the Senate in 1956 passed by unanimous voice vote over the objections of the Eisenhower administration a bill requiring the submission of all executive agreements to the Senate within 60 days, but the House took no action on it.

Types of Commitments

In his book, *American Military Commitments Abroad,* Roland A. Paul, who served as counsel to the Senate Foreign Relations Subcommittee on U.S. Security Agreements and Commitments Abroad, lists seven types of commitments. They may be summarized as follows:

1. Formal written treaties (the United States has eight security treaties).

2. Several security agreements that have never been ratified as treaties. (Most notable are agreements of cooperation signed in 1959 with the parties to the CENTO—Central Treaty Organization—and successive defense agreements signed with Spain.)

3. Unilateral government declarations in the form of congressional resolutions or statements by senior American officials.

4. Stationing U.S. troops in another country. (General Earle Wheeler, then chairman of the Joint Chiefs of Staff, informed the Spanish in November 1968: "By the presence of U.S. forces in Spain, the United States gives Spain a far more visible and credible security guarantee than any written document.")

5. Moral commitments arising from past sacrifices made or risks incurred by other countries on behalf of the United States or from reliance placed upon its apparent intentions. (President Johnson, for example, privately informed the Israelis in May 1967 that "Israel will not be alone unless it decides to go alone.")

6. Obligations arising from a general identification between this country and the governing order, broad political programs or society of another country.

7. Commitments arising over time as a result of the accumulation of many small contributions to the defense, survival or well-being of another country.

Sources: Roland A. Paul, *American Military Commitments Abroad* (Rutgers University Press, 1973), pp. 8-11; for an analysis of commitments, see also, Congressional Quarterly, *Global Defense,* pp. 15-21.

In 1972 the issue of executive agreements arose again, this time in reaction to secret agreements uncovered by the Senate Foreign Relations Subcommittee on Security Agreements and Commitments Abroad. The subcommittee study, chaired by Stuart Symington (D Mo.) and conducted in 1969-70, found that commitments and secret conditions had been made throughout the 1960s to such countries as Ethiopia, Laos, Thailand, South Korea and Spain. Causing particular controversy was an agreement permitting U.S. use of Spanish bases in return for American grants, loans and improvements.[68]

Adding to congressional frustrations were agreements with Portugal made in 1971 by the Nixon administration on the use of an airbase in the Azores and with Bahrain for naval base facilities in the Persian Gulf. The two agreements raised important foreign policy questions and should have been submitted as treaties, argued members of the Senate Foreign Relations Committee. The Senate passed a sense of the Senate resolution to that effect.

A result of the controversy was congressional passage, over the initial opposition of the Nixon administration, of a measure (PL 92-403) introduced by Sen. Clifford P. Case (R N.J.) requiring the secretary of state to submit to Congress within 60 days the final text of any international agreement made by the executive branch. Those having national security implications were to be submitted on a classified basis to the House and Senate foreign affairs committees.

Case argued that Congress could not adequately perform its foreign policy role without knowledge of commitments made by the executive branch. The Senate passed the bill by a unanimous 81-0 vote and the House by voice vote.[69]

Although the 1972 act dealt with the problem of secrecy, it was a first step only and did not provide for any congressional response to executive agreements. The Senate in 1974 passed a bill introduced by Sam J. Ervin Jr. (D N.C.) to establish a congressional procedure for disapproving executive agreements, but the House did not act.

Checks and Balances. In 1975, members pressed once again for legislation that would give Congress an opportunity to disapprove executive agreements.

"Circumvention of the treaty-making powers by the executive branch deprives the Congress of its advice and consent responsibilities under the Constitution and fosters secrecy in government," said Sen. James Abourezk (D S.D.) at the opening hearing of his Judiciary Subcommittee on Separation of Powers May 13 on two bills to give Congress a disapproval role. Abourezk said "even a cursory glance at constitutional history" revealed that it was not the intention to allow the President to make "substantive" foreign policy without the advice and consent of the Senate.

Sponsors of legislation took different approaches to the problem of giving Congress a voice without infringing on the President's constitutional authority to execute foreign policy and conclude agreements with foreign countries. All of the bills, however, would provide that executive agreements would take effect 60 days after they were submitted to Congress unless both chambers (or, in some proposals, only the Senate) disapproved them.

Executive Branch Opposition. By attempting to subject all executive agreements to congressional approval, Congress was going beyond its "proper function of making laws" and taking on the role of executing them, argued Antonin Scalia, assistant attorney general, during hearings on the legislation in May 1975.

He said all executive agreements were based upon the President's constitutional authority to make agreements with foreign nations. Additionally, he argued, many treaties and laws specifically authorized the President to enter into follow-up agreements to carry out their provisions, such as the PL 480 (food aid) program.

But under the proposed legislation, Scalia added, "Congress would seek to control executive actions not by passing laws before the fact, but by requiring authorized actions under existing law to be submitted for its approval."

The framers of the Constitution, Scalia maintained, clearly never contemplated such a situation. Neither did they intend that Congress should amend or restrict the President's powers by resolution, since that would distort the legislative process by avoiding a veto. Scalia also pointed out that proponents of the legislation faced the problem of passing a restrictive bill over a presidential veto.

Monroe Leigh, legal adviser of the State Department, testified on May 13 that the bills would result in a "substantial interference" with the President's negotiating ability with foreign governments and introduce an element of uncertainty of authority that would "clearly not be conducive to the effective conduct of U.S. foreign policy."

The potential of congressional veto of an executive agreement also raises national security problems, argued Leigh and Robert Ellsworth, assistant secretary of defense.

Interference with the President's ability to make executive agreements as commander in chief would be "unacceptable," said Leigh.

Major Treaties: 1919-75

League of Nations

Senate opposition to ratification of the Treaty of Versailles was directed principally at the League Covenant, which formed an integral part of the treaty, although other provisions, especially the Shantung settlement which favored Japan at the expense of China, also aroused strong objections. It was upon the League issue, however, that ratification hinged.[70]

The treaty was lost in the irreconcilable conflict that developed between a large group of Republicans led by Henry Cabot Lodge of Massachusetts, chairman of the Foreign Relations Committee, who refused to accept the treaty without drastic reservations, and a group of Democratic followers of President Wilson, who in turn would not accept the Lodge reservations.

On more than one occasion during the war Lodge had publicly advocated an international league for the maintenance of international peace, but his final position was that this proposal should be postponed, in order to give opportunity for adequate study, and that to attempt to make it a part of the treaty of peace with Germany would only lead to prolonged discussion. This viewpoint was given support by 39 Republican senators and senators-elect who signed a proposal, drafted by Sen. Philander C. Knox (R Pa.), which was offered by Lodge in the form of a Senate resolution on March 3, 1919, the closing day of the 65th Congress. The proposed resolution declared that "the constitution of the League of Nations in the form now proposed to the Peace Conference should not be accepted by the United States" and "that the negotiations on the part of the United States should immediately be directed to the utmost expedition of the urgent business of negotiating peace terms with Germany, ...and that the proposal for a League of Nations to insure the permanent peace of the world should be then taken up for careful and serious consideration."

The resolution received an immediate reply from President Wilson. On the evening of March 4, the day before he sailed the second time for France, he told a large audience in the Metropolitan Opera House in New York City that when he finally returned with a completed treaty, that instrument would contain not only the League Covenant but "so many threads of the treaty tied to the Covenant that you cannot dissect the Covenant from the treaty without destroying the whole vital structure. The structure of peace will not be vital without the League of Nations, and no man is going to bring back a cadaver with him."

The Committee on Foreign Relations, composed of 10 Republicans and seven Democrats, held public hearings on the treaty from July 31 to Sept. 12, 1919. The majority report, written by Lodge, recommended ratification but proposed 45 amendments and four reservations. The minority report, signed by Sen. Gilbert M. Hitchcock of Nebraska and five other Democrats, declared against any amendments and deprecated reservations.

Even before the Foreign Relations Committee submitted its reports, a division of the Senate into a number of factional groups was becoming apparent. At one extreme stood the group of "irreconcilables" or bitterenders," led by Sens. William E. Borah (R Idaho), Hiram W. Johnson (R Calif.) and James A. Reed (D Mo.). They were opposed to the treaty with or without reservations. Borah contended that "it really incorporates a scheme which, either directly or indirectly, greatly modifies our governmental powers." At the other extreme were the administration Democrats led by Hitchcock, who lined up with the President in favoring unconditional ratification. Between these two extremes was the important group of "reservationists," which included Lodge. There were also the "mild reservationists," who wanted the treaty accepted with slight alterations.

By the end of October the friends of the treaty, as represented by the Democrats and mild reservationists, had succeeded in defeating all amendments proposed by the Foreign Relations Committee. Amendments were opposed not only for their content but also because they would have required approval by all other signatories of the treaty—a virtually impossible accomplishment—whereas reservations applied only to the power which made them. It was after defeat of the amendments that the struggle for reservations was seriously begun. Inability to reach a compromise there defeated the treaty.

Opposition to the League Covenant centered on Article 10, of which President Wilson himself was the author. This article read as follows:

"The members of the League undertake to respect and preserve as against external aggression the territorial integrity and existing political independence of all members of the League. In case of any such aggression or in case of any threat or danger of such aggression the Council shall advise upon the means by which this obligation shall be fulfilled."

The irreconcilables feared that Article 10 would draw the United States into foreign wars at the bidding of the League of Nations. Another fear raised by the League of Nations proposal was that it would deprive the United States of full liberty of action under the Monroe Doctrine.

Lodge Reservations. The apprehension aroused by the League Covenant and the objections to that instrument and to other parts of the treaty were reflected in the 14 reservations finally incorporated in the Lodge resolution for consent to ratification. The resolution stipulated that ratification by the United States should not become effective until the reservations had been accepted, through an exchange of notes, by three of the four following powers: Great Britain, France, Italy and Japan.

The reservations disclosed a determination on the part of their authors to prevent any encroachment on the powers of Congress, as well as any encroachment on the sovereignty of the United States. In carrying out that purpose, in the view of proponents of American membership in the League, the reservations went far beyond any necessary precautions. They were so distasteful to President Wilson that he wrote to Sen. Hitchcock on Nov. 18, 1919, that in his opinion the Lodge resolution "does not provide for ratification but rather for nullification of the treaty."

Ratification Votes. The Lodge resolution was finally brought to a vote during the evening of Nov. 19, 1919, and twice defeated. On the first vote there were 39 yeas and 55 nays. On a reconsidered vote ratification again failed with only 41 yeas as against 51 nays. Without further debate the Senate proceeded to vote on a separate resolution for simple approval of the treaty without reservations of any kind. Consent to ratification was then withheld for the third time by a vote of 38 yeas to 53 nays. In this last count the 13

Congress Uses Resolutions to Influence Foreign Policy

On numerous occasions, Congress has attempted to influence the course of foreign policy by adopting resolutions. In some cases, the President has followed the advice of Congress, in others, not.

In 1836, President Jackson received separate resolutions from both chambers favoring the acknowledgment of the independence of Texas by the United States; the preamble of the House resolutions intimated that the expediency of recognizing the independence of Texas should be left to the decision of Congress. On Dec. 21, 1838, Jackson replied: "In this view, on the ground of expediency, I am disposed to concur, and do not, therefore, consider it necessary to express my opinion as to the strict constitutional right of the executive, either apart from or in conjunction with the Senate, over the subject."[1]

While the Civil War was in progress, there was universal resentment at the French interference in Mexico. In the Senate, numerous resolutions were introduced condemning the French action, but all were tabled. The House, however, by unanimous vote adopted a resolution on April 4, 1864, declaring: "It does not accord with the policy of the United States to acknowledge a monarchical government erected on the ruins of any republican government in America, under the auspices of any European power."[2]

Secretary of State Seward responded by instructing the U.S. minister to France to inform the French government that "the decision of such questions of policy constitutionally belongs, not to the House of Representatives nor even to Congress, but to the President...." When the House learned of this, it passed by an almost unanimous vote a resolution "that Congress has the constitutional right to an authoritative voice in declaring and prescribing the foreign policy of the United States as well as the recognizing of new powers as in other matters; and it is the constitutional duty of the President to respect that policy...."[3]

Beginning in the Civil War period, there were repeated instances of the Senate attempting to control, by resolution, U.S. relations with Mexico. In addition, resolutions have been introduced from time to time for the recognition of new foreign governments. However, the power of recognition constitutionally lies with the President, through his role of sending and receiving foreign diplomats and ministers. (Washington established a controlling precedent when he received Citizen Genet and then demanded his recall by France without consulting Congress.)[4] On the other hand, the Senate, through its role of advice and consent to ambassadorial nominations, has considerable influence over the nation's foreign relations.

In his book, *Congress and Foreign Policy-Making*, James A. Robinson, discusses congressional involvement in foreign policy decisions in the period 1933-61, concluding that in the vast majority of cases, congressional resolutions or authorizations were in fact measures legitimizing the executive's proposals and amending them, rather than representing a congressional initiative in recommending major policies.[5] A case in point is the Vandenberg Resolution of 1948, named after Senate Foreign Relations Committee Chairman Arthur H. Vandenberg (R Mich.), whose support the Truman administration had particularly sought out for bipartisan cooperation. The resolution, noted Robinson, provided "the legitimization for the origins of United States participation in the development of the North Atlantic Treaty." Adoption of the resolution, he concluded, was an example of the "executive's primacy in the identification and selection of problems which occupy the foreign policy agency of Congress and the executive...."[6] The resolution, "usually regarded as a case of senatorial initiative, was in fact a response to an appeal from the executive."[7]

One clear example of congressional initiative in post-war foreign policy, according to Robinson, was S Res 264 of the 85th Congress, suggesting that the administration study the possibility of proposing to other governments the establishment of an international development association (IDA) as an affiliate of the World Bank. The resolution, introduced by Sen. A. S. Mike Monroney (D Okla.), was at first opposed by the State Department, but it was approved by the Senate July 23, 1958, by a 62-25 vote. "It is not too much to say that the idea of such an organization occurred independently to Senator Monroney," says Robinson. "It is highly unlikely that the executive branch would have taken the initiative of this sort."[8]

Promptly after the Senate passed the resolution, the administration initiated discussions with other governments about the feasibility of attaching an IDA to the World Bank. In late January 1960, the Articles of Agreement on IDA approved by the executive directors of the World Bank were released to the press. Senate Foreign Relations Committee hearings on a proposal for U.S. participation in IDA opened in March 1960. The bill passed both chambers that year.

Footnotes

1. George H. Haynes, *The Senate of the United States* (Houghton-Mifflin Co., 1938), p. 673.
2. *Ibid.,* p. 674.
3. *Ibid.,* p. 675.
4. C. Herman Pritchett, *The American Constitution* (McGraw-Hill Book Co. Inc., 1959), p. 357.
5. James A. Robinson, *Congress and Foreign Policy-Making* (Dorsey Press, 1962), Chapter 2.
6. *Ibid.,* p. 46.
7. *Ibid.,* p. 66.
8. *Ibid.,* p. 62; see also pp. 70-92.

Republican irreconcilables, who in the two previous votes had opposed ratification even with the Lodge reservations, were joined by the whole body of reservationists. McCumber was the sole Republican to favor unconditional consent to ratification.

The treaty issue was revived in the second session of the 66th Congress, and another vote was taken on March 19, 1920. On this occasion there was no question of unconditional approval. The resolution before the Senate contained the original Lodge reservations, slightly revised but with no essential change. President Wilson still characterized them as amounting to a "sweeping nullification of the terms of the treaty," but shortly before the vote was taken Thomas J. Walsh (D Mont.), who had opposed the Lodge resolution in the preceding November, appealed to his colleagues to accept the reservations, since the treaty was too important to be lost. Although more than a dozen Democrats responded to this plea, consent to ratification was once more denied, this time by a vote of 49 yeas to 35 nays, seven votes short of the two-thirds required.

United Nations

Mindful of the Senate's rejection of the League of Nations in 1919, the Roosevelt administration had begun to court bipartisan support for the United Nations long before the Dumbarton Oaks meetings of August-October 1944 at which a draft charter was drawn up; Secretary of State Cordell Hull had assured congressional leaders of both parties in 1943 that Congress would have the final say on U.S. participation in any world security organization.[71] The eight-member delegation to the San Francisco conference, announced Feb. 13, 1945, was picked with an eye to the widest public support. Headed by Secretary of State Edward R. Stettinius Jr. (who had succeeded Hull Dec. 1, 1944), it included Hull; Sens. Tom Connally (D Texas), chairman of the Foreign Relations Committee, and Arthur H. Vandenberg (R Mich.), a committee member; Reps. Sol Bloom (D N.Y.) and Charles A. Eaton (R N.J.), chairman and ranking minority member of the House Foreign Affairs Committee; former Gov. Harold E. Stassen (R Minn.) and Virginia Gildersleeve, dean of Barnard College. John Foster Dulles, foreign policy adviser to Gov. Thomas E. Dewey of New York during the 1944 presidential campaign, was named a principal adviser to the delegation.

Public discussion of the charter was intense and widespread before and during the two-month conference, at which Vandenberg and Dulles played leading roles. In San Francisco on the day the conference ended, June 26, President Truman acclaimed the charter as a declaration of "faith that war is not inevitable." In a personal appearance before the Senate July 2, he called for prompt ratification of the charter and the annexed statute of the International Court of Justice. Said Truman: "The choice before the Senate is now clear. The choice is not between this charter and something else. It is between this charter and no charter at all."

Following a week of hearings, the Senate Foreign Relations Committee on July 13 voted 21-1 to approve the charter (Exec. F, 79th Cong., 1st Session)—the lone dissenter being Hiram W. Johnson (R Calif.), ranking minority member. During Senate debate July 23-28, most of the discussion centering on Article 43, pledging members to "make available to the security council, on its call and in accordance with a special agreement or agreements, armed forces, assistance and facilities, including rights of passage, necessary for the purpose of maintaining international peace and security." Burton K. Wheeler (D Mont.) and others feared this would give the U.S. delegate "the war-making power," but the President assured the Senate on July 27 that any agreements under Article 43 would be sent to Congress for "appropriate legislation to approve them." Next day the Senate gave assent to the establishment of the United Nations, by the overwhelming margin of 89-2. Opposed were GOP Sens. William Langer (N.D.) and Henrik Shipstead (Minn.). Hiram Johnson (who died Aug. 6) announced his opposition.

NATO

Following passage of the Vandenberg Resolution in 1948, which declared U.S. determination to exercise the right of individual or collective self-defense, President Truman directed the State Department to explore the question of regional security with Canada, Britain, France, Belgium, the Netherlands and Luxembourg.[72] By October, these seven countries had reached tentative agreement on a collective defense arrangement and had invited Norway, Denmark, Iceland, Italy and Portugal to join them. Negotiations were concluded April 4, 1949, when representatives of the 12 nations signed the North Atlantic Treaty in Washington "to unite their efforts for collective defense and for the preservation of peace and security."

The text reaffirmed support for the United Nations and for the peaceful settlement of disputes. It also pledged the signatories to work jointly for political, economic and social stability within the North Atlantic area, defined to extend from Alaska through the North Atlantic to the three French departments in Algeria. But its key provisions called for intensified self-help and mutual aid measures to defend the area and pledged that, in the event of an armed attack against one of the members, each of the others would come to its aid by taking "such action as it deems necessary, including the use of armed force, to restore and maintain the security of the North Atlantic area." The treaty also provided for establishment of a North Atlantic Council to draw up plans for concerted action, for the admission of other nations by unanimous invitation, and for the right of members to withdraw after 20 years.

President Truman sent the treaty (Exec L, 81st Cong., 1st Session) to the Senate April 12 and urged prompt approval. The key question that arose at once concerned the relationship between the treaty and the not-yet submitted military assistance program: would approval of the treaty commit Congress to vote for the latter? To clarify the matter, several senators called for consideration of the two together. But the administration refused, withholding its military aid proposals until action on the treaty had been completed.

Hearings by the Senate Foreign Relations Committee, beginning April 27, produced strong backing for the treaty by Secretary of State Dean Acheson and other administration officials. Former Vice President Wallace denounced the pact, saying it would destroy the chances for European recovery and entail costs of $20-billion for military aid. On June 6, the committee voted unanimously to approve the treaty. Its report asserted that approval would not commit the Senate to approve the arms aid request and that the treaty did not give the President any powers "to take any action, without specific congressional authorization," which he could not already take.

The Senate debated the treaty from July 5 to 20, with Sens. Tom Connally (D Texas) and Arthur H. Vandenberg (R Mich.) carrying the burden of the defense. Sen. Robert A. Taft (R Ohio) announced that he would oppose ratification without a reservation disclaiming any obligation to arm Western Europe—a step he said would "promote war." Answering Taft was Sen. John Foster Dulles (R N.Y.), sworn in July 8 as the appointed successor to Sen. Robert F. Wagner (D N.Y.): "If the impression became prevalent that this country was turning its back on international cooperation, the results would be disastrous. Other free countries...would almost certainly fall. We would be encircled and, eventually, strangled ourselves."

On July 21, 1949, the Senate proceeded to vote, rejecting three reservations by large margins before approving the treaty. The first reservation—sponsored by Sens. Kenneth S. Wherry (R Neb.), Taft and Arthur V. Watkins (R Utah)—stated that nothing in the treaty would commit the signatories "morally or legally to furnish or supply arms" to the others. It was rejected, 21-74. Watkins then proposed two other reservations, both of which disclaimed any intention to employ U.S. armed forces without the express approval of Congress. These were rejected, 11-84 and 8-87. The Senate then approved ratification of the North Atlantic Treaty, 82-13 (D 50-2; R 32-11). The only senator not present was Allen J. Ellender (D La.), who supported ratification.

Ban on Nuclear Tests

The world's close brush with nuclear war in the 1962 Cuban missile crisis gave impetus to the continuing search for an agreement to stop nuclear testing.[73] Such a step, it was generally believed, would help to stabilize the nuclear balance between the United States and the Soviet Union, discourage the proliferation of nuclear arsenals among other countries, and furnish a critical turning point in the arms race. Through four years of negotiations, however, the same stumbling block had prevented agreement: America's insistence on on-site inspection of suspected violations involving hard-to-detect underground tests, and the Soviet Union's refusal to accept such inspection on Russian soil by foreign observers. Late in 1962, however, the Soviets said they might accept two or three inspections a year, in addition to several unmanned "black-box" seismic detection stations.

The Americans, British and Soviets resumed private talks in January 1963 but soon reached an impasse regarding the number of on-site inspections to be permitted. The Soviets refused to accept more than three a year, while the United States insisted on a minimum of seven. Attention then shifted to the broader 17-nation disarmament negotiations in Geneva. There, on April 5, American and Soviet delegates agreed to establish a direct telegraphic "hot line" between the White House and the Kremlin as a precaution against the kind of accident or miscalculation that might have touched off a nuclear exchange during the Cuban missile crisis. Symbolizing a mutual concern for the prevention of nuclear war, the "hot-line" agreement was formally signed June 20.

In Washington, meanwhile, Sens. Hubert H. Humphrey (D Minn.) and Thomas J. Dodd (D Conn.), together with 32 cosponsors, had introduced a resolution (S Res 148) May 27 urging the United States to seek agreement on a treaty banning atmospheric and underwater tests but not those conducted underground. Their proposal sidestepped the inspection issue, since it was generally believed that any clandestine tests in the other environments could be detected by national systems without the need for on-site verification. Two weeks later, in a June 10 speech at American University calling for re-examination of attitudes toward the Soviet Union and the Cold War, President Kennedy announced that "high-level discussions will shortly begin in Moscow looking toward early agreement on a comprehensive test ban treaty."

Under Secretary of State Averell Harriman represented the United States in the negotiations that began July 15 and led, with surprising swiftness, to the initialing on July 25 of a treaty banning all except underground tests. The text bound the signatories "to prohibit, to prevent, and not to carry out any nuclear weapon test explosion, or any other nuclear explosion at any place under its jurisdiction or control (a) in the atmosphere, beyond its limits including outer space, or under water including territorial water or high seas, or (b) in any other environment if such explosion causes radioactive debris to be present outside the territorial limits of the state under whose jurisdiction or control such explosion is conducted."

The treaty also pledged the parties "to refrain from causing, encouraging, or in any way participating in" any nuclear tests anywhere else. It provided that amendments could be submitted by any signatory subject to the approval of each of the three original signatories and a majority of all parties to the treaty. It declared that the treaty would be of unlimited duration, but that any party could withdraw on three months' notice if it decided that its supreme interests were being jeopardized.

President Kennedy sent the treaty (Exec M, 88th Cong., 1st Session) to the Senate Aug. 8, following its formal signature in Moscow Aug. 5 by the United States, Great Britain and the Soviet Union, with a message designed to answer the various arguments being voiced by certain political and military leaders against the treaty.

Key administration officials supported ratification before the Foreign Relations Committee Aug. 12-17. Secretary of State Dean Rusk said there were no "side arrangements, understandings or conditions of any kind" to the treaty, and he stressed that it did not affect the use of nuclear weapons in the event of war. Secretary of Defense Robert S. McNamara said the treaty would "at least retard Soviet progress and prolong the duration of our technological superiority" in nuclear weapons. Speaking for the Joint Chiefs of Staff, Chairman Maxwell D. Taylor said they had conditioned their approval on four "safeguards" agreed to by the administration: continued underground testing, maintenance of weapon research facilities and programs, preparation for prompt resumption of atmospheric tests should the Soviets violate the treaty, and improvement of detection methods and intelligence on Sino-Soviet nuclear activities.

The burden of the case against the treaty was stated by Dr. Edward Teller, the physicist credited with development of the H-bomb. Teller called the treaty a "step away from safety and possibly...toward war." He argued that it would retard U.S. development of an anti-ballistic missile defense; block development of high-yield bombs (where the Soviets were conceded to be ahead); inhibit checks on the vulnerability of U.S. missile systems to communications and radar "black-out" caused by atmospheric explosions; make it difficult to verify the "hardness" or invulnerability of American Minuteman missile sites; and do little to prevent the proliferation of nuclear capabilities. But several other scientists disputed Teller's views.

On Sept. 3, the Foreign Relations Committee reported favorably on ratification, having found "the balance of risks weighted in favor" of the pact. But as Senate debate began Sept. 9, the Preparedness Investigating Subcommittee of the Senate Armed Services Committee issued a report based on secret hearings at which Dr. Teller and Gen. Thomas S. Power, chief of the Strategic Air Command, had persuaded the group that the treaty involved "serious—perhaps formidable—military and technical disadvantages to the United States."

Senate debate focused on a series of proposed reservations to the treaty, all of which came to a vote Sept. 23. By heavy bipartisan majorities, the Senate rejected several moves to add restrictions to ratification. There was little opposition, however, to adding a preamble to the resolution of approval reasserting the Senate's right to pass on any future amendments to the treaty. On Sept. 24 the Senate consented to ratification of the Treaty of Moscow by a vote of 80-19 (D 55-11; R 25-8), or 14 more than the required two-thirds majority.

The Soviet Union ratified the pact the next day, and it went into effect Oct. 10, 1963; in short order, more than 100 additional nations signed the treaty. But two major powers refused to do so: France, which had opposed any test ban because of its determination to achieve full status as an independent nuclear power; and Communist China, which was bent on the same goal and coincidentally locked in dispute with the Soviets under Khrushchev's policy of "peaceful coexistence" with the West. On Oct. 16, 1964, the Chinese entered the nuclear "club" by setting off their first fission explosion just as Khrushchev was being ousted from power in Moscow. Although anticipated by the United States and discounted in advance, the Chinese event was viewed by President Johnson as a "sad and serious" fact that would tempt other states "to equal folly."

Nuclear Nonproliferation Treaty

The Soviet occupation of Czechoslovakia in August 1968 was a mortal blow to President Johnson's hope of ratifying a nuclear nonproliferation treaty before leaving office. Johnson continued to press vigorously for Senate action on the treaty, even to the point of considering recalling Congress after the elections, but to no avail.[74]

On June 12, 1968, the United Nations General Assembly voted 95-4, with 21 abstentions, to approve a draft treaty banning the spread of nuclear weapons to states not already possessing them. The product of more than four years of negotiations at the 18-Nation Disarmament Conference in Geneva, the treaty was signed July 1 by the United States, the Soviet Union and 60 other nations. Shortly thereafter, on July 9, it was submitted to the Senate for approval by President Johnson.

The treaty consisted of a preamble and 11 articles, the most important of which were those banning the spread of nuclear weapons, providing for safeguards arrangements and ensuring nondiscriminatory access to the peaceful uses of nuclear energy. Johnson called it "the most important international agreement in the field of disarmament since the nuclear age began."

The Senate Foreign Relations Committee took the unprecedented step of beginning consideration of the treaty less than 24 hours after its submission by the President. Members of the Joint Committee on Atomic Energy joined with the Foreign Relations Committee to question to administration witnesses about the treaty. A principal concern of the senators, particularly those on the Foreign Relations Committee, was whether the treaty would impose any new obligation on the United States to defend any non-nuclear nation threatened with or actually experiencing a nuclear attack. While the testimony of Secretary of State Dean Rusk and U.S. Arms Control and Disarmament Director William C. Foster contained no direct reference to this point, Rusk said repeatedly under questioning that the treaty would in no way add to current U.S. military commitments abroad.

After three unsuccessful attempts to obtain a quorum, the committee Sept. 17 by a 13-3 vote (with three abstentions) ordered the treaty reported favorably and recommended ratification. In its report, the committee

recommended that after the Senate acted, the President delay formal ratification (that is, depositing the actual instruments of ratification) until a majority of nations "nearest to a nuclear weapons capability" promised to honor the agreement.

On Oct. 11, Senate Majority Leader Mike Mansfield (D Mont.) said he would not call up the treaty because "the leadership will not be a party to a partisan treatment of a matter which by its very nature is and must remain nonpartisan." The treaty had become involved in the presidential election campaign. Vice President Hubert H. Humphrey, the Democratic candidate, urged quick ratification of the agreement. Richard M. Nixon, the Republican candidate, said that going ahead with the treaty might appear to be "condoning" the Soviet invasion of Czechoslovakia. He said that could have "a tremendously bad moral effect, detrimental moral effect, all over the world." He said he supported the treaty but believed it desirable to delay ratification until a later date. After Nixon won the election, his views favoring delay took on increased importance. There was no further action in 1968, but on Feb. 5, 1969, President Nixon called for the Senate's "prompt consideration and positive action" on the treaty. Approval of the treaty at this time, he said, "would advance this administration's policy of negotiation rather than confrontation with the U.S.S.R." On March 13, 1969, the Senate by an 83-15 roll-call vote consented to the ratification of the treaty.

SALT Accords

Following ratification of the nuclear nonproliferation treaty, the two superpowers initiated a series of strategic arms limitation talks (SALT) on Nov. 17, 1969. The first round of SALT culminated in the signing of two agreements in Moscow on May 26, 1972.[75] One pact limited strategic missile defense systems, the other restricted offensive nuclear weapons.

The first agreement was a treaty limiting both the United States and the Soviet Union to two ABM (antiballistic missile) sites: one for the defense of each nation's capital and another for the defense of an ICBM (intercontinental ballistic missile) installation in each country.

In 1973, however, Congress prohibited the Defense Department from beginning work on the ABM site to defend Washington; a 1974 protocol between the two nations restricting each nation to one site was approved by the Senate Nov. 10.[76]

The second pact was a five-year interim agreement limiting offensive missile launchers—land-based silos and submarine missile tubes—to those under construction or deployed at the time of the signing. The United States had a total of 1,710 launchers, including 1,054 ICBMs and 656 SLBMs (submarine-launched ballistic missiles).

The Soviet Union was estimated to have a total strategic missile launcher strength of 2,358—1,618 ICBM launchers and 740 SLBM launchers.

In addition to the numerical edge, the Soviets also had the advantage in throw weight, estimated at several times that of the United States' capacity. (Throw weight is the measure of a missile's lift potential and ultimately of the number and size of warheads a missile can carry.)

The United States had a numerical advantage in warheads, as well as superiority in strategic bombers—460 at that time, compared to a Soviet total of 140—and aircraft that could strike the Soviet Union on one-way missions from European arsenals.

Reacting to criticism that the United States was shortchanged by the agreement, the Nixon administration stressed that the Russians had a numerical edge that would have continued to grow in the absence of an agreement because the Soviets had an on-going ICBM development program and the United States did not.

Debate in Congress. President Nixon presented the two pacts to Congress June 1, 1972, less than half an hour after returning from an eight-day trip to the Soviet Union, where he and Soviet Communist Party General Secretary Leonid I. Brezhnev May 26 had signed the ABM treaty and offensive strategic missile limitation agreement.

For both Nixon and Brezhnev, the road from the conference table promised several obstacles. Brezhnev had to contend with some of the more reluctant members of the Soviet hierarchy. President Nixon had to face the Congress.

The offensive arms agreement required approval by simple majorities in both the House and Senate; the ABM treaty had to be ratified by a two-thirds majority in the Senate. *(Box, this page)*

President Nixon had several advantages going into congressional hearings in the summer of 1972 on the nuclear arms pacts he negotiated with the Soviet Union. Though sentiment was mixed, the President hoped to avert an all-out battle like the one when the Senate ratified the 1963 nuclear test ban treaty.

By contrast with 1963, the 1972 agreements:

● Were produced by a President with a long record of militant anti-communism.

● Received early approval of the Joint Chiefs of Staff. In 1963 the joint chiefs qualified their endorsement with insistence on four safeguards eventually incorporated. In 1972 they insisted on weapons progress.

● Were supported by a Secretary of Defense (Melvin R. Laird) with a congressional record of backing a strong military posture. In 1963 Secretary of Defense Robert S. McNamara was widely criticized by proponents of a strong defense policy.

● Were negotiated in a period of comparatively relaxed tensions between the United States and Soviet Union. In 1963 the memory of the 1962 Cuban missile crisis was fresh in congressional minds.

On the other hand, Congress had not abandoned support for a strong military defense. Sen. William Proxmire (D Wis.) and others succeeded in trimming military funds by several billion dollars in 1969, but Congress in 1971 resisted defense-cutting attempts.

Many members of Congress who voiced basic approval of the 1972 pacts, as well as some who criticized them, emphasized they would be influenced by disclosures at committee hearings. A chief complaint by critics was the lack of details on complex technical questions.

In his June 1 appearance before Congress, Nixon urged the assembled lawmakers to "seize the moment so that our children and the world's children live free of the fears and free of the hatreds that have been the lot of mankind through the centuries."

Partisan feelings were evident in the House chamber as the President spoke. The American success in the strategic arms and other negotiations, the President said, "came about because, over the past three years we have consistently refused proposals for unilaterally abandoning the ABM (antiballistic missile), unilaterally pulling back our forces from Europe and drastically cutting the defense budget."

Nixon said Congress deserved "the appreciation of the American people for having the courage to vote such

---

Nuclear Pacts and Congress

Congressional approval was required on both the offensive and defensive aspects of agreements on nuclear arms reached by President Nixon with the Soviets.

A provision in the 1961 law establishing the Arms Control and Disarmament Agency, which negotiated the pacts, specifies that any agreement to limit U.S. armed forces or armaments must be approved by legislation or treaty.

President Nixon in June 1972 submitted the two accords to Congress together with documents explaining U.S.-Soviet agreements and disagreements on interpretations of the accords.

The disagreements concerned mainly the ultimate size of nuclear submarine fleets and the size of certain offensive weapons. The explanation of the differences was designed to head off Senate reservations.

The President urged approval "without delay" promising that U.S. defense capabilities would remain "second to none." He called for "a sound strategic modernization program" as the nation moved to negotiate further arms accords.

The explanatory statements, drawn up in Moscow by U.S.-Soviet negotiators, emphasized U.S. concern over development of large Soviet missiles and envisaged future negotiations on nuclear limitations.

The document recorded a unilateral Soviet statement, not agreed to by the United States, that the Soviets would increase the number of their nuclear submarines, if Washington's NATO allies increased theirs.

The President said the two Moscow agreements were "a significant step into a new era of mutually agreed restraint and arms limitation between the two principal nuclear powers." The agreements did not, he said, "close off all avenues of strategic competition." They "open[ed] up the opportunity for a new and more constructive U.S.-Soviet relationship, characterized by negotiated settlement of differences, rather than by the hostility and confrontation of decades past."

---

proposals down and to maintain the strength America needs to protect its interests."

The Senate Aug. 3 gave its approval to ratification of the ABM treaty by a key roll-call vote of 88-2, after the Foreign Relations Committee unanimously approved both the treaty and the interim agreements. In urging Senate support for the accords, however, the committee made clear that a majority of its members questioned the need for an ABM site to protect Washington, D.C., and for accelerated development of offensive weapons as requested by the administration.

James B. Allen (D Ala.) and James L. Buckley (Cons-R N.Y.) cast the only votes against approval of the ABM treaty. Both argued that the treaty, by limiting each nation to two ABM sites, would expose their civilian populations to destruction in the event of nuclear war.

Allen also questioned whether the United States could trust the Soviet Union to live up to the treaty and the agreement.

While the ABM treaty sailed smoothly through the Senate, the interim agreement had some rough moments on Capitol Hill before it was passed Sept. 25.

The House had given routine consideration to the resolution (H J Res 1227) authorizing approval of the five-year U.S.-Soviet pact. The resolution was passed Aug. 18, by a 329-7 roll-call vote, after about one hour of debate. No changes were made on the floor.

But when the measure reached the Senate the going was rougher. Breaking a six-week deadlock, the Senate Sept. 14 demanded a stiff U.S. bargaining stance in upcoming nuclear arms talks with the Soviet Union when it passed H J Res 1227 by an 88-2 roll-call vote.

The hard-line instructions for negotiators in the strategic arms limitation talks (SALT) were contained in an amendment sponsored by Sen. Henry M. Jackson (D Wash.) which requested that any future permanent treaty on offensive nuclear arms "not limit the United States to levels of intercontinental strategic forces inferior to" those of the Soviet Union, but rather be based on "the principle of equality." The amendment stipulated that failure to negotiate a permanent treaty limiting offensive arms would be grounds to abrogate the U.S.-Soviet ABM agreement. It also endorsed the maintenance of a vigorous research, development and modernization program.

The Jackson amendment was adopted by a 56-35 roll-call vote after its supporters had beaten back several attempts to weaken it.

The White House Aug. 7 endorsed Jackson's effort after he modified his proposal by dropping a stipulation that any Soviet action or deployment that threatened U.S. deterrent capability would be grounds for repudiating the interim agreement.

In its place, Jackson and the White House agreed on the statement that failure to negotiate an offensive arms treaty by 1977 would be grounds for repudiating the ABM treaty—a position taken previously by the administration.

Controversy over the Jackson proposal had threatened to delay the resumption of strategic arms control talks, formerly scheduled to begin in Geneva in mid-October. The House accepted the Senate changes rather than risk further delay.

The Jackson and other amendments added to the bill had no effect on the accord itself as signed in Moscow. But they served to emphasize the disquiet of many members of Congress—and a majority of the Senate, which had to ratify any permanent treaty—concerning the terms of the interim agreement.

Final action came Sept. 25 when the House, by a 308-4 roll-call vote, approved a resolution (H Res 1133) concurring with Senate amendments.

The War Power

The war power—like the treaty power—is divided between the Congress and the President. And, no less than the treaty power, it has been the subject of recurring controversy and debate involving rival claims by the executive and legislative branches.

Article II, Section 2 of the Constitution provides: "The President shall be Commander-in-Chief of the Army and Navy of the United States, and of the militia of the several states, when called into the actual service of the United States."

Article I, Section 8, provides: "The Congress shall have power...to declare war, grant letters of marque and reprisal, and make rules concerning captures on land and water; to raise and support armies...; to provide and maintain a navy; to make rules for the government and regulation of the land

and naval forces; to provide for calling forth the militia to execute the laws of the Union, suppress insurrections and repeal invasions"; and "to provide for organizing, arming and disciplining the militia, and for governing such part of them as may be employed in the service of the United States, reserving to the states respectively, the appointment of the officers and the authority of training the militia according to the discipline prescribed by Congress."

At the time the American Constitution was framed, the war-making power in all other countries was vested in the executive. When the Convention at Philadelphia took up this question, at the session of Aug. 17, 1787, Pierce Butler, a delegate of South Carolina, proposed that the power to make war be granted to the President, "who will have all the requisite qualities and will not make war but when the nation will support it." Elbridge Gerry of Massachusetts thereupon objected that he "never expected to hear in a republic a motion to empower the executive alone to declare war." George Mason of Virginia also opposed "giving the power of war to the executive, because he is not safely to be trusted with it." He was "for clogging rather than facilitating war."[77]

Charles Pinckney of South Carolina contended that the proceedings of the House of Representatives were too slow and that it would be "too numerous for such deliberations." He accordingly suggested that the war power be placed in the Senate, which would be "more acquainted with foreign affairs and most capable of proper resolutions." The Convention nevertheless conferred the power on Congress as a whole. It changed the phrase "to make war," as reported by the Committee of Detail, to "to declare war," so as to leave the President the power to repel sudden attacks but not to commence war.[78]

The innovation of placing the war power in the legislative rather than the executive branch of the government was hailed by Jefferson as a valuable restraint upon exercise of the power. He wrote to Madison, Sept. 6, 1789: "We have already given, in example, one effectual check to the dog of war, by transferring the power of letting him loose from the executive to the legislative body, from those who are to spend to those who are to pay." Madison himself wrote: "The Constitution supposes what the history of all governments demonstrates, that the executive is the branch of power most interested in war and most prone to it. It has accordingly, with studied care, vested the question of war in the legislature."[79]

Writing in *The Federalist* (No. 69), Hamilton noted that the powers of the President as commander in chief would be "much inferior" to that of the British King; "it would amount to nothing more than the supreme command and direction of the military and naval forces, as first general and admiral...while that of the British King extends to the declaring of war and to the raising and regulating of fleets and armies—all which, by the Constitution...would appertain to the legislature."[80]

"Those who are to conduct a war cannot in the nature of things be proper or safe judges whether a war ought to be commenced, continued or concluded," wrote Madison. "They are barred from the latter functions by a great principle in free government, analogous to that which separates the sword from the purse, or the power of executing from the power of enacting laws."[81]

Thus was viewed the system of checks and balances on the war power at the founding of the republic. Writing nearly two centuries later, Prof. Raoul Berger noted: "The commander in chief, as conceived by the Framers, bears slight

(Continued on p. 267)

Congress, Appropriations and Foreign Policy

Development of massive foreign-aid spending—starting with World War II lend-lease—gave Congress a power in foreign affairs not anticipated by the framers of the Constitution.

In almost every instance, the proposals for aid to other countries required consent of Congress to the expenditures, thus involving the House of Representatives in an area of foreign policy that it did not enjoy in the treaty-making and nominations process.

Foreign and military aid programs have generally been proposed on the initiative of the executive branch; and in the early post-war period, Congress generally supported massive aid programs. By the 1970s, however, disenchantment had set in, and Congress repeatedly slashed the administration's request for such funds.

Congress on numerous occasions has used the appropriations weapon as a means to influence U.S. policy. Thus, it repeatedly has pressed the administration to continue U.S. military and economic support for Israel and has complied with executive branch requests for assistance to that country. On the other hand, in reaction against Turkish policy in Cyprus, Congress in 1974 enacted a ban on military aid and arms shipments to Turkey (the ban was partially lifted in 1975). A provision in the economic aid bill for fiscal years 1976 and 1977 stated that no funds in the bill could be used to support authoritarian regimes. In 1975, Congress began weighing proposals for new controls on arms sales, which amounted to $9-billion in fiscal 1975. Members expressed unease over the long-term effects of concentrating sales in sensitive areas of the world, where conflicts could erupt eventually involving the United States.[1]

A major aspect of foreign policy and national security which Congress may control through appropriations is defense spending. Congress, however, has generally acceded to administration requests, although in a few instances (such as the antiballistic missile controversy in 1969 and 1970), it has questioned or cut back spending for particular controversial weapons systems.[2]

Included in the area of defense are congressional appropriations to support overseas military installations (there are approximately 384 major and 3,000 minor American military installations abroad) and the approximately 511,000 U.S. troops stationed abroad.[3] The Constitution requires that "no appropriation of funds [to raise and support armies]...shall be for a longer term than two years." Writing in *The Federalist* (No. 26), Hamilton noted: "The legislature of the United States will be obliged, by this provision, once at least in every two years, to deliberate upon the propriety of keeping a military force on foot; to come to a new resolution on the point; and to declare their sense of the matter, by a formal vote in the face of their constituents."[4]

Congress, however, has found it difficult to exercise this power—as seen in repeated and unsuccessful attempts to reduce substantially the number of American troops in Western Europe.[5] And once American forces have been committed to battle, Congress has been reluctant to cut off funds for their support.

Numerous attempts during 1969-72 to cut off funds for U.S. combat activities in Indochina provide examples. Congress attached funds cutoffs to defense procurement, foreign aid, defense appropriations and military sales bills, but was not successful in actually cutting off funds or setting a specific deadline for withdrawal until 1973. On the other hand, in 1969 Congress approved an amendment to a defense appropriations bill prohibiting use of any funds in the bill to finance *introduction* of U.S. ground combat troops in Laos or Thailand. A similar prohibition on introducing U.S. ground troops into Cambodia was passed in 1970 (air activity was not barred).[6]

In 1973, Congress succeeded in passing legislation barring all U.S. combat activities in the Indochina area as of Aug. 15, 1973. Six other bills enacted that year contained similar prohibitions.[7]

During the early 1970s, Congress attempted to limit the American commitment in Indochina in another way: by setting ceilings on military aid to countries in the area. Use of this weapon was demonstrated in 1975, when Congress refused to appropriate Ford's request for $522-million in additional military aid for Cambodia and South Vietnam. With the U.S. decision not to become further involved, the Communists overran the countries in April 1975, thus ending 25 years of American economic and military involvement in Indochina.

Use of the appropriations process to slash executive funds requests has been termed by Prof. Louis Fisher "essentially a negative" tool. Although Congress could have used the power of the purse successfully during the early stages of involvement in Vietnam, he said, "the long prevailing faith in executive 'expertise' in the field of national security, combined with the postwar tradition of 'bipartisan' foreign policy, had accustomed the legislature to accept rather uncritically most presidential definitions of military need."[8]

Footnotes

1. See Congressional Quarterly, 1975 *Weekly Report*, pp. 2817-19.

2. Louis Fisher, *President and Congress* (The Free Press, 1972), pp. 212-25; and Edward A. Kolodziej, "Congress and Foreign Policy: The Nixon Years," in Harvey C. Mansfield Sr., ed., *Congress Against the President* (Praeger Publishers, 1975), pp. 167-79.

3. The tabulation appears in Arthur M. Schlesinger Jr., *The Imperial Presidency* (Houghton-Mifflin Co., 1973), p. 312. On types of military aid, overseas strength, and leading military aid recipients, see Congressional Quarterly, *Global Defense.*

4. Quoted in House Foreign Affairs Subcommittee on National Security Policy and Scientific Developments, *Hearings on Congress, the President and War Powers*, 91st Congress, 1st session, 1970 (U.S. Government Printing Office, 1970), p. 137.

5. Congressional Quarterly, *Congress and the Nation, 1969-1972*, Vol. III, pp. 214-15.

6. *Ibid.,* pp. 899-946; and Thomas F. Eagleton, *War and Presidential Power* (Liveright, 1974), Chapter 9.

7. For a listing, see Congressional Quarterly, *1975 Almanac*, p. 309.

8. Fisher, *President and Congress*, p. 229.

(Continued from p. 265)

resemblance to the role played by the President today, when, in the words of [Supreme Court] Justice [Robert H.] Jackson, the clause is invoked for the 'power to do anything, anywhere, that can be done with an army or navy,' From history, the Framers had learned of the dangers of entrusting control of the military establishment to a single man who could commit the nation to war."[82]

"With few exceptions, the power to initiate and wage war has shifted to the executive branch," wrote Louis Fisher in his book, *President and Congress.* "The President's power as commander in chief has grown in response to three major developments. First, the President acquired the responsibility to protect American life and property abroad. He has invoked that vague prerogative on numerous occasions to satisfy much larger objectives of the executive branch. Second, the time boundaries of the 'war period' have become increasingly elastic. The President may initiate military operations before congressional action, and he retains wartime powers long after hostilities have ceased. Third, the postwar period, which has been marked by nuclear weapons, the cold war, intercontinental missiles, military alliances, and greater U.S. world responsibilities, has accelerated the growth of presidential power."[83]

Concluded C. Herman Pritchett, in *The American Constitution:* presidential powers are of "tremendous impact—so great in fact that to a considerable degree they cancel out the most important grant of external authority to Congress, the power to declare war."[84] Throughout the nation's history, only two major conflicts—the War of 1812 and the Spanish-American War—were clearly the product of congressional policy.

Declared and Undeclared War

Beginning in 1950, a new dimension was injected into the question of congressional and presidential war powers: presidential commitments of American forces to combat without a declaration of war. U.S. combat troops were involved in full-scale war in Korea from 1950 to 1953 and in Indochina from 1965-73 without declaration of war. In two other instances, Lebanon in 1958 and the Dominican Republic in 1965, U.S. combat troops were used to help maintain conditions of political stability in countries threatened by or undergoing civil strife.

Justifying the absence of a declaration of war, administration spokesmen have pointed to numerous historical "precedents" which involved U.S. forces abroad without such declaration. Indeed, Congress has declared war in only five conflicts: the War of 1812, the Mexican War, the Spanish-American War, World War I and World War II. No declaration was made or requested in the Naval War with France (1798-1800), the First Barbary War (1801-05), the Second Barbary War (1815), or the various Mexican-American clashes of 1914-17.[85]

A 1966 State Department memorandum noted "at least 125 instances in which the President has ordered the armed forces to take action or maintain positions abroad without obtaining prior congressional authorization."[86] A 1970 Library of Congress study cited 160 instances in which U.S. armed forces were used abroad; most of the actions were taken in the name of protecting life and property.[87]

Both Berger and historian Arthur M. Schlesinger Jr. (in his book, *The Imperial Presidency),* have contended, however, that these incidents were relatively minor and could not be used as "precedents" for Korea or Vietnam, as claimed.[88] They have also noted that categorizing the war

with France as "undeclared" may be disputed because President Adams took no independent action before Congress passed a series of acts which amounted, according to the Supreme Court, to a declaration of "imperfect war."[89]

The nineteenth century, noted Berger, offers no example of a President who plunged the nation into war in order to repel an attack on some *foreign* nation. Indeed, this did not occur until the Korean War, as both Wilson and Roosevelt obtained a declaration of war before sending troops to engage in hostilities on foreign soil.[90]

During debate on presidential war powers in the 1960s and 1970s, it was contended that declarations of war were outmoded, given the existence of nuclear weapons and the need to commit troops overseas in emergencies on a limited war basis. Testifying before the Senate Foreign Relations Committee in 1971, Professor Alpheus T. Mason of Princeton University, commented: "The Framers, with deliberate care, made war-making a joint enterprise. Congress is authorized to 'declare war'; the President is designated 'commander in chief.' Technology has expanded the President's role and correspondingly curtailed the power of the Congress. Unchanged are the joint responsibilities of the President and Congress. The fact that a congressional declaration of war is no longer practical does not deprive Congress of constitutionally imposed authority in war-making. On the contrary, it is under obligation to readjust its power position."[91]

Congress attempted to do just that in enacting the 1973 war powers bill, discussed below. *(p. 279)*

Early Use of the War Power

The early Presidents made little use of such war powers as they had received. John Adams went so far in 1798, at the time of the undeclared naval war with France, as to divest himself of the title of commander-in-chief and confer it upon George Washington. The Senate approved that action unanimously. Three years later, President Jefferson forbade the Navy to attack the Tripoli pirates on the ground that Congress had not declared war.[92] Alexander Hamilton ridiculed Jefferson for inaction. He said the Constitution meant that it was "the peculiar and exclusive province of Congress, when the nation is at peace, to change that state into a state of war." But "when a foreign nation declares or openly and avowedly makes war upon the United States, they are then by the very fact already at war and any declaration on the part of Congress is nugatory: it is at least unnecessary."

First Declaration of War, 1812

During the War of 1812, the first declared war in which the United States engaged after the formation of the federal union, Congress made no attempt to usurp any of the functions of the President as commander-in-chief. On the contrary, the legislative branch failed so completely to carry out even its own assigned functions that the successful waging of hostilities was made almost impossible.[93]

President Madison's annual message of 1811 listed the familiar trade grievances against Great Britain and called upon Congress to "put the United States into an armor and an attitude demanded by the crisis...." Congress agreed on a bill for raising 25,000 regular soldiers in January 1812, but debate on a militia bill, authorizing the President to accept the services of 50,000 volunteers, bogged down on constitutional issues. Under the Constitution, the President could call such men into service for any one of three purposes—to execute the laws, to put down insurrection, or to repel invasion. It was well understood, however, that the proposed volunteers were to accompany the regulars on an invasion of Canada, and most members felt that it would be unconstitutional to use them outside the limits of the United States. The question was never settled, and the bill, as approved by Madison in February, said nothing about use of the volunteers beyond the national boundaries—which proved a disastrous mistake.

Although the intention to invade Canada was openly proclaimed—and despite the fact that 25,000 regular troops probably could not be raised in time to render service for at least a year and the 50,000 volunteers probably could not be used in Canada—legislation looking to the organization of a provisional army of 20,000 men for immediate service was voted down in the House.

The nation, as a whole, remained apathetic toward the idea of actual hostilities. By June 1, 1812, when Madison asked for a declaration of war, less than half of the hoped-for 25,000 regulars had enlisted and adequate equipment was available for only 10,000 soldiers. Nevertheless, on June 3 the House voted, 79 to 49 for war; the Senate took similar action on June 18 by a vote of 19 to 13.

In accordance with the law, the secretary of war issued a call for the militia, but the governors of Massachusetts, Rhode Island and Connecticut refused to authorize use of their troops. On July 6, 1812, Congress adjourned. Federalist members now openly denounced the war as being against the wishes of the people. Within a month the American army under General Hull had surrendered at Detroit, almost without firing a shot. The garrison at Fort Dearborn had been massacred by Indians. A large part of Van Rensselaer's force of New York militia had been slaughtered on the Canadian side of the Niagara River, within sight of other militiamen who remained on the United States side and refused to move into foreign territory.

The 13th Congress met in special session in May 1813, and opposition to the administration was immediately evident in the Senate. Daniel Webster offered a series of resolutions designed to embarrass Madison; numerous appointments by the President were rejected; and Josiah Quincy reported a resolution of the Massachusetts legislature characterizing the war as one "waged without justifiable cause...."

Congress reassembled in temporary quarters in the burned city of Washington in September 1814. Little hope was held that success would attend the negotiations then being carried on by peace commissioners at London. Yet with the Army still at only about half its paper strength, and with enlistments falling off, Congress failed to agree to a conscription bill proposed by James Monroe, then secretary of war as well as secretary of state. The welcome Treaty of Ghent was signed by the American commissioners on Dec. 24, 1814, and was consented to by a unanimous Senate on Feb. 16, 1815.

Unpopular Mexican War, 1846

The War with Mexico was distinctly unpopular among large numbers of the people, particularly in the North. Recurring expressions in Congress of opposition to the prosecution of the war were in part a reflection of that antiwar sentiment.[94]

President Tyler had long desired annexation of Texas but was balked by the Senate until after the 1844 presidential election in which Henry Clay, who opposed annexation

without the consent of Mexico, was defeated by James Polk, an ardent expansionist. On March 1, 1845, three days before Polk was inaugurated, annexation was accomplished by adoption of a joint resolution in the 28th Congress.

In the spring of 1846, Gen. Zachary Taylor led his army into a disputed strip of territory claimed by Texas but occupied exclusively by Mexicans. A clash between Mexican soldiers and a reconnoitering party of Americans occurred on April 25, but it was uncertain whether the scene of the skirmish was on Texan or Mexican soil. A few American soldiers were killed. On May 11, two days after the news of the fighting reached Polk, he sent a war message to Congress declaring that Mexico had passed the boundary of the United States, had invaded American territory and had shed American blood upon American soil. "War exists," he said, "and notwithstanding all our efforts to avoid it, exists by the act of Mexico herself."

The House at once adopted, 173 to 14, a joint resolution declaring that war existed by the act of Mexico, appropriating $10-million, and authorizing a call for 50,000 volunteers. Some opposition, in part sincere and in part partisan, was offered by northern Whigs. Somewhat stronger opposition was voiced in the Senate, but the resolution was adopted there, May 12, by a 40-2 vote.

In the elections of 1846, the Democrats retained control of the Senate, but the House was lost to the Whigs. Moreover, as General Taylor marched victoriously through Mexico, the war was being widely denounced in the North and was proving far from universally popular in the South. By the time Congress met in December 1846, members had gathered new courage to question the war's justification and purpose. Polk's annual message, devoted almost wholly to a defense of the war, was deeply resented by the Whigs for in it the President charged that those opposing his policies were giving aid and comfort to the enemy. Thereafter, although the necessary military measures were passed as they came up, debate was concerned less with the merits of particular measures than with the causes, the justice, and the necessity of war itself.

The House was especially sensitive to the growing discontent. Abraham Lincoln offered his "Spot Resolutions," all of which ignored the current status of the war and were intended to probe the original causes of the conflict. A resolution presented in the House late in 1847 stated that the war should not be further prosecuted for any purpose. Another member moved that a committee of five from the Senate and five from the House consult with the President as to the best method of ending the war. Numerous other resolutions of similar purport were introduced, though most of them did not come to a vote. However, a resolution offered in January 1848, by George Ashmun of Massachusetts, which declared the war to have been "unnecessarily and unconstitutionally begun by the President of the United States," was adopted in the House by a margin of four votes. The House adopted also a resolution calling upon the President for information as to the objectives of the war and the exact nature of the proposed terms of peace. This request was refused by Polk. On Feb. 23, the President sent the peace treaty with Mexico to the Senate, which consented to ratification March 10, 1848, by a vote of 38 to 14.

Neither the opposition of a considerable section of the population, nor the resultant "obstructionist tactics" of certain members of Congress hampered the war effort; all necessary war measures survived the opposition. The enemy forces were so inconsiderable that no extraordinary requests

Lincoln's Improvised War Powers

In the early days of the Civil War, Lincoln used not only the war powers at his disposal but also some of the powers reserved to Congress. Without congressional authorization, he issued a proclamation, May 3, 1861, increasing the size of the regular Army and the Navy and calling for 80,000 volunteers. Moreover, he ordered 19 vessels added to the Navy and directed the Secretary of the Treasury to advance $2-million to unauthorized persons to cover military and naval requisitions. When Congress convened July 4, 1861, the President declared that some of his emergency measures, "whether strictly legal or not, were ventured upon under what appeared to be a popular demand and a public necessity, trusting then, as now, Congress would readily ratify them."

Congress validated Lincoln's actions by adopting a resolution Aug. 6, 1861, providing that "All the acts, proclamations, and orders of the President respecting the Army and Navy of the United States, and calling out or relating to the militia or volunteers...are hereby approved and in all respects made valid...as if they had been issued and done under the previous express authority and direction of the Congress of the United States."

The Supreme Court, in a group of rulings involving the *Prize Cases* (67 U.S. 635, 1862), gave its blessing to another of Lincoln's improvised war powers. Early in the war, the President had proclaimed a blockade of Confederate ports to prevent the South from selling cotton to England and importing supplies. Vessels attempting to run the blockade were seized and condemned as "prizes"—that is, they were confiscated for having defied the President's order. The owners sued for redress on the ground that no war had ever been declared between North and South.

The court observed that declarations of war were almost unknown in rebellions and insurrections. The President, charged with seeing that the laws be faithfully executed and armed with the powers of commander-in-chief, was entitled to treat the rebellious states as belligerents, to attack them and to blockade them. The court said:

"By the Constitution, Congress alone had the power to declare a national or foreign war.... [The President] has no power to initiate or declare a war either against a foreign nation or a domestic state.... If a war be made by invasion of a foreign nation, the President is not only authorized but is bound to accept the challenge without any legislative act. And whether the hostile party be a foreign invader or states organized in rebellion, it is none the less a war although the declaration be 'unilateral.' "

On the other hand, the court took a dim view of Lincoln's order authorizing various military commanders to suspend the writ of habeas corpus. Chief Justice Roger Brooke Taney, sitting as a federal circuit judge at Baltimore in 1861, ordered John Merryman released from military detention to stand trial in civil court. If the President had the power to suspend habeas corpus, Taney argued, "the people of the United States are no longer living under a government of laws, but every citizen holds life, liberty and property at the will and pleasure of the army officer in whose military district he may happen to be found." The Supreme Court supported Taney in *Ex parte Milligan,* a case decided in 1866 (71 U.S. 22). It ruled that civilians might be tried by military tribunal only where civil courts could not function because of invasion or disorder.

Sources: Richard L. Worsnop, "War Powers of the President," *Editorial Research Reports,* March 14, 1966, pp. 192-93; Arthur M. Schlesinger Jr., *The Imperial Presidency* (Houghton-Mifflin Co., 1973), pp. 58 ff; Rexford G. Tugwell, *The Enlargement of the Presidency* (Doubleday & Co. Inc., 1960), pp. 150-64; Edward S. Corwin, *The President, Office and Powers* (New York University Press, 1957), pp. 228-34; C. Herman Pritchett, *The American Constitution* (McGraw-Hill, 1968), p. 376.

---

had to be made of the legislative branch. If the United States had suffered military reverses comparable to those in the War of 1812, and requiring the passage of drastic measures by Congress, it is possible that the Whig opposition might have forced far-reaching alterations in the war plans of the advocates of expansion.

War with Spain, 1898

War with Spain over the independence of Cuba was forced on President McKinley in 1898 by the strong expansionist sentiment in Congress and in certain sections of the press.[95] Two years earlier, McKinley's predecessor, Grover Cleveland, had succeeded in averting a similar result only by defying Congress. Early in 1896, a concurrent resolution according belligerent rights to the Cuban insurgents had been adopted in both houses by large majorities. After the presidential election in November, won by McKinley on a platform calling for the independence of Cuba, a resolution granting recognition was offered in Congress. Secretary of State Olney at once declared to the press that the resolution, if adopted, "can probably be regarded only as an expression of opinion by the eminent gentlemen who vote for it." He added:

"The power to recognize the so-called Republic of Cuba as an independent state rests exclusively with the executive. A resolution on the subject...is inoperative as legislation, and is important only as advice of great weight voluntarily tendered to the executive regarding the manner in which he shall exercise his constitutional functions.... The resolution will be without effect and will leave unaltered the attitude of this government toward the two contending parties in Cuba."

A few days later, Cleveland reportedly told a congressional delegation that if the Congress declared war on Spain he would refuse to mobilize the Army. In view of Cleveland's intransigent attitude, Congress took no action on the resolution recognizing Cuba's independence.

After McKinley's inauguration, relations with Spain steadily worsened in spite of a series of diplomatic concessions by that country. Following the sinking of the *Maine* in the harbor of Havana in February 1898, it became clear that nothing short of war would satisfy congressional belligerence. On April 11, McKinley submitted a message to Congress proposing forcible intervention in Cuba. Although Spain had already capitulated to American demands for Cuban autonomy, a resolution declaring that the people of the island "are and of right ought to be free and independent," and authorizing the President to employ the land and naval forces of the United States to expel Spain from Cuba, was adopted in the Senate by a vote of 42 to 35 and in the House, 310 to 6, on April 25, McKinley immediately ordered a blockade of Havana, and the war had begun.

The brevity of the war, the ease with which victory was won and the relatively popular nature of the conflict, both among members of Congress and among the public, worked to insure a satisfied and wholly cooperative attitude by Congress toward the executive branch of the government. However, opposition to the acquisition of the Philippines led to a month's debate on the treaty of peace, which was consented to April 6, 1899, by the Senate, 57-27, with only one vote to spare.

Congress and the World Wars

Once Congress has declared war and voted the necessary funds, Presidents have vastly enlarged the scope of their authority, both in domestic and foreign affairs. During the Civil War, Congress delegated sweeping power to Lincoln to enable him to prosecute the war. Several months after he issued proclamations calling up the state militias and ordering the blockade, Congress passed an act "approving, legalizing, and making valid all the acts, proclamations, and orders of the President, etc., as if they had been issued and done under the previous express authority and direction of the Congress of the United States."[96] *(See box, p. 269)*

By the turn of the century, the government had become increasingly active in regulating the economy, and when the United States entered World War I, Congress delegated extensive and far-reaching powers to President Wilson over the economy and domestic affairs.

The powers exercised by President Roosevelt during World War II were even more considerable, as the concept of a national emergency expanded. As Edward S. Corwin noted in his book, *The President: Office and Powers* (1787-1957), "In the First World War, as in the Civil War, the emergency that constitutional interpretation set itself to meet was a *war* emergency in the narrow, palpable sense. In the Second World War the emergency preceded the war and continued beyond it—a fact of special significance when it is considered in relation to the effect of wartime practices on the constitutional law of peacetime."[97]

"No more sweeping delegation of legislative power has ever been made to an American President than that represented in the enactment of...the Lend-Lease Act of March 11, 1941, nearly nine months before our actual entry into a 'shooting war.' "[98] The act authorized the President to manufacture any defense article and to "sell, transfer title to, exchange, lease, lend or otherwise dispose of" the defense articles to any country whose defense he deemed vital to the defense of the United States.

After Congress declared war, mobilization authority was extended to the control of facilities and the operation of plants closed by strikes. Under the Emergency Price Control Act of 1942, the President appointed a price administrator who was authorized to set maximum rents.[99] According to Corwin, by April 1942, 42 new agencies had been created to oversee the war effort, 35 of which were of "purely presidential creation," and whose constitutional and legal status became a source of controversy.[100]

Both world wars, as well as the Civil War, highlighted the problems of ending the "national emergency." Commented Fisher: "The change-over from emergency war powers to normal executive responsibilities is by no means a rapid process. Long after hostilities have ended, many economic controls remain in force."[101]

On July 25, 1947, Congress terminated certain temporary emergency and war powers, involving about 175 statutory provisions some of which dated back to World War I. Nonetheless, 103 war or emergency statutes remained in effect.[102]

1973 National Emergency Study

Congressional concern with the continuing existence of national emergencies and concomitant delegation of power to the President led to creation of a Special Senate Committee on the Termination of the National Emergency in 1973. At the outset of the study it was thought that the state of national emergency dated back to President Truman's December 1950 proclamation of an emergency in response to China's invasion of South Korea. However, research by the committee showed that the United States had been living in a state of declared national emergency since March 1933, when Congress ratified President Roosevelt's declaration of an emergency resulting from the Depression.

The discovery pointed up the lack of knowledge in the area of emergency powers. In a Sept. 30, 1973, report, the committee stated, "Because Congress and the public are unaware of the extent of emergency powers, there has never been any notable congressional or public objection made to this state of affairs. Nor have the courts imposed significant limitations."[103] The committee listed four existing states of national emergency that should be ended and released a catalogue of some 470 existing emergency statutes which remained "a potential source of virtually unlimited power for a President should he choose to activate them."[104]

As a result, Congress in 1976 cleared a bill ending the four emergency conditions and specifying procedures for the declaration and termination of future national emergencies. The four were the 1933 declaration, one by Truman in 1950 when the Korean War began, and two by Nixon—one in 1970 as a result of a national postal strike and one in 1971 because of an international monetary crisis.

Congress and World War I

Following the outbreak of war in Europe in August 1914, President Wilson urged a policy of neutrality.

Commencement of German submarine warfare in February 1915, and the sinking of the *Lusitania* the following May 7 with the loss of 124 American lives, fanned public debate over the twin issues of neutrality and belligerency. Later in 1915 Wilson swung toward limited preparedness—not far enough to satisfy Secretary of War Lindley M. Garrison, yet too far for Secretary of State William Jennings Bryan, both of whom resigned.

Wilson's re-election in 1916 was due at least in part to his having kept the country out of war, but the situation changed early in 1917. Two days after Germany resumed unrestricted submarine warfare on Feb. 1, the United States broke off diplomatic relations. Publication of the intercepted Zimmermann telegram, offering pledges of German alliance with Mexico in return for slices of U.S. territory after a German victory, followed on March 1.

While pressure mounted in Congress to require a national referendum before a declaration of war, Wilson ordered the arming of American merchant ships. On April 2, addressing a joint session of Congress, he asked for a declaration of war. Despite objections, on April 6 the House by a 373-50 vote and the Senate by an 82-6 vote adopted a resolution providing "that the state of war between the United States and the Imperial German Government which has been thrust upon the United States is hereby formally declared."

Wilson's War Powers

Woodrow Wilson had no need during World War I to resort to actions beyond the law, but he amassed greater powers than those employed by any previous war President. Many of the extraordinary powers exercised by President Wilson came by delegation from Congress. However, he drew also upon his constitutional powers to implement plans for which Congress denied or delayed legislative authorization.[105]

A week after war was declared, the President used his authority as commander-in-chief to create by executive order the Committee on Public Information, under whose direction a system of voluntary news censorship was established and various government publicity services were organized. On April 28, 1917, again acting as commander-in-chief, he imposed stringent cable censorship, which was later extended to other forms of communication with foreign countries under authority of the Trading With the Enemy Act of Oct. 6, 1917.

Wilson appointed Herbert Hoover as Food Administrator on May 19, 1917. Then, on June 12, two months before passage of the Food and Fuel Control Act of Aug. 10, 1917, the President gave Hoover "full authority to undertake any steps necessary" for the conservation of food resources. The functions of the War Industries Board, created originally by the Council of National Defense, were expanded and vested almost exclusively in its chairman, Bernard M. Baruch, by a letter of the President to Baruch on March 4, 1918. By an executive order of May 28, 1918, Wilson formally established the War Industries Board "as a separate administrative agency to act for me and under my direction." Although created without statutory authority, the board was able to exert wide control over industry; behind its "requests" stood the President's power to commandeer factories or withhold fuel and transportation priorities.

The sweeping control of the economy acquired by Wilson during the war constituted, in the opinion of Rexford G. Tugwell, "the most fantastic expansion of the executive known to American experience."[106] The numerous powers conferred upon the President by Congress included power:

To take over and operate enemy vessels for use in war.
To regulate and prohibit exports.
To take over and operate the railroads.
To regulate priorities in transportation.
To regulate by a licensing system the importation, manufacture, storage, mining or distribution of any necessaries.
To requisition foods, fuels, and other supplies necessary for any public use connected with national defense.
To fix a reasonable guaranteed price for wheat based upon a statutory minimum.
To fix the price of coal and regulate the method of its production, sale, shipment, distribution and storage.
To prohibit or license transactions in the United States by foreign insurance companies.

Congress was willing to delegate the foregoing powers to the President because it recognized that modern warfare required singleness of direction, unity of command, and coordination of vital resources.[107] After the war ended, new Republican majorities in Congress reasserted the prerogatives of the legislative branch. Feelings on Capitol Hill were ruffled by Wilson's failure to include senators in the American delegation to the Paris Peace Conference. The Senate twice refused, in 1919 and again in 1920, to consent to ratification of the Treaty of Versailles. *(For details, see Treaty Power above.)*

Roosevelt and World War II

The prevailing mood of isolationism in Congress and the country during the later 1930s sharply limited President Roosevelt's freedom of action in foreign affairs. This mood found expression in such laws as the Neutrality Acts of 1935 and 1937, which prohibited shipments of arms, ammunition or implements of war to belligerent nations.[108] A resolution introduced by Rep. Louis L. Ludlow (D Ind.) in 1935 and again in 1937 would have restricted the war powers of Congress as well as of the President. The resolution proposed a constitutional amendment to require submission of a declaration of war to a popular referendum. Although the Ludlow resolution was pried from committee by a discharge petition, Dec. 14, 1937, a motion to bring it to the House floor for a vote failed to carry.[109]

Following Roosevelt's proclamation of a limited national emergency on Sept. 8, 1939, a week after the outbreak of war in Europe, the United States began to drift from neutrality to engagement. At a special session, Sept. 21-Nov. 3, 1939, Congress revised the Neutrality Act to repeal the arms embargo and allow sale of munitions to belligerents on a cash-and-carry basis. An act of June 15, 1940, authorized military assistance to any Latin American republic that requested it. Almost three months later, on Sept. 3, 1940, the President announced that the United States had entered into an agreement under which Great Britain would receive 50 "over-age" (but reconditioned and recommissioned) destroyers in return for the right to lease certain sites for U.S. naval and air bases on British territory in the western Atlantic. The attorney general defended the constitutionality of the transaction on the ground that the President's power as commander-in-chief enabled him to "dispose" the armed forces of the United States.

Roosevelt cited the same power in 1941 as his authority for ordering American troops to Greenland and Iceland; Congress was not consulted on either occasion. In a special message to Congress, July 7, 1941, the President asserted that the occupation of Iceland by Germany would constitute a serious threat against Greenland and North America, against North Atlantic shipping and against the steady flow of munitions to Britain. While the establishment of bases in Greenland and Iceland was not an act of war, it reflected this nation's hostility toward Germany, which declared war on the United States four days after Japan's attack on Pearl Harbor on Dec. 7, 1941.[110]

Existence of a state of war with Japan was formally declared by Congress on Dec. 8. Existence of a state of war with Germany and Italy was declared on Dec. 11. The resolution declaring war against Japan (S J Res 116) was adopted by the Senate 82 to 0 and by the House 388 to 1. The one negative vote was cast by Jeannette Rankin (R Mont.), who had given a similar vote on the declaration of war against Germany in 1917.

The war declaration against Germany (S J Res 119) was adopted by the Senate 88 to 0 and by the House 393 to 0; the declaration against Italy (S J Res 120) by the Senate 90 to 0 and by the House 399 to 0. Rankin voted "present" on these declarations.

Entry of this country into World War II was accompanied by concentration of virtually all war power in the President's hands. Under his power as commander-in-chief and using powers delegated by Congress, Roosevelt created many new emergency agencies and made them responsible to him rather than to existing departments or independent regulatory agencies. By V-J Day, no fewer than 29 war agencies were grouped under the Office for Emergency Management, which had been created by an administrative order of May 25, 1940.

Congress and Undeclared War

In his book, *President and Congress*, Louis Fisher noted: "The President's warmaking powers were drawn originally from (1) his responsibilities as commander-in-chief, (2) his oath to preserve, protect and defend the Constitution, (3) his duty to protect the nation from sudden attack, and (4) the inherent powers derived from the general heading 'executive power.'" However, "in recent decades, the definition of inherent and implied powers has become increasingly generous because of treaty commitments, vaguely worded congressional resolutions, and an accumulation of emergency statutes. Moreover, the President's constitutional responsibility for repelling sudden attacks and waging defensive war has expanded in scope until it is now used to justify involvement in full-scale wars without legislative approval."[111]

The Korean experience, wrote historian Arthur M. Schlesinger Jr., "beguiled the American government first into an unprecedented claim for inherent presidential power to go to war and then into ill-advised resentment against those who dared bring up the constitutional issue.... By insisting that the presidential prerogative alone sufficed to meet the requirements of the Constitution, Truman did a good deal more than pass on his sacred trust unimpaired. He dramatically and dangerously enlarged the power of future Presidents to take the nation into major war."[112]

The constitutional system of checks and balances in the war power was further eroded with the steady increase of U.S. involvement in Indochina, starting in the mid-1960s. Both Johnson and Nixon substantially enlarged the theory that actions undertaken by the President in defensive wars need not be accompanied by prior approval by the legislative branch. "The role of Congress under the Johnson theory of the war-making power," commented Schlesinger, "was not to sanction but to support the war"—and for the most part, the majority of members of Congress acquiesced in this role.[113] "Johnson and Nixon had surpassed all their predecessors in claiming that inherent and exclusive presidential authority, unaccompanied by emergencies threatening the life of the nation, unaccompanied by the authorization of Congress or the blessing of an international organization, permitted a President to order troops into battle at his unilateral pleasure."[114]

Korean War

The war in Korea began with a massive attack on South Korea by North Koreans on June 25 (Korean time), 1950, and continued for three years at a cost of more than 150,000 U.S. casualties. Late on June 26 (U.S. time) President

Truman ordered American air and sea forces in the Far East to aid South Korea, a day before the U.N. Security Council called on U.N. members for help in repelling the attack. The President on June 30 ordered ground troops into Korea and sent the 7th Fleet to act as a buffer between China and Formosa.[115]

Secretary of State Dean Acheson recommended to Truman that he "should not ask (Congress) for a resolution of approval, but rest on his constitutional authority as commander-in-chief."[116] In fact, Truman never asked Congress for a declaration of war in Korea, and he waited until Dec. 16, 1950—six months after the outbreak of hostilities—to proclaim the existence of a national emergency. In defense of this course, it was argued that the Russians or Chinese or both had violated post-World War II agreements on Korea and that emergency powers authorized during World War II could still be applied.

Provisions in the United Nations Charter were also used to justify Truman's action. A legal memorandum by the State Department in 1950 offered this defense: "Both traditional international law and article 39 of the U.N. Charter and the resolution pursuant thereto authorize the United States to repel the armed aggression against the Republic of Korea."[117] However, the legality of this argument was questioned, on the ground that U.S. armed forces were ordered to Korea before the U.N. Security Council authorized the action.[118]

Although there was never a formal declaration of war or congressional resolution supporting Truman's decision, Congress implicitly ratified the action by consistently appropriating the requested funds for the war.

Congress did not mount a serious challenge to Truman's war powers until 1951. At issue then was the President's authority to dispatch troops to Korea and to Western Europe. Sen. Robert A. Taft (R Ohio) opened a three-month-long "great debate" on Jan. 5, 1951, by asserting that Truman had "no authority whatever to commit American troops to Korea without consulting Congress and without congressional approval." Moreover, Taft said, the President had "no power to agree to send American troops to fight in Europe in a war between the members of the Atlantic Pact and Soviet Russia."[119]

The debate revolved principally around the troops-to-Europe issue. It came to an end on April 4, when the Senate adopted two resolutions approving the dispatch of four divisions to Europe. One of the resolutions stated that it was the sense of the Senate that "no ground troops in addition to such four divisions should be sent to Western Europe...without further congressional approval."

President Truman hailed the action as a "clear endorsement" of his troop plans, saying "there has never been any real questions" about the United States doing its part in the defense of Europe. But he ignored the Senate's claim to a voice in future troop commitments; neither resolution had the force of law.

In essence, the "great debate" had confirmed both the President's power to commit U.S. forces without prior congressional approval and the decision to defend Western Europe on the ground.

Testifying in 1951 on the plan to station American soldiers in Europe, Acheson asserted: "Not only has the President the authority to use the armed forces in carrying out the broad foreign policy of the United States and implementing treaties, but it is equally clear that this authority may not be interfered with by Congress in the exercise of powers which it has under the Constitution."[120]

Travel Restrictions Based on War, National Emergency

Although freedom of travel was not restricted by the Constitution, Congress in 1856 gave the Secretary of State exclusive control over the issuance of passports.

The 1856 Passport Act, which was reenacted in 1926, gives the Secretary certain discretionary powers in the granting of passports. He may refuse a passport to anyone who is not an American citizen; he may also deny issuance to persons engaged in illegal conduct.

Until a 1918 law was passed making it unlawful for a U.S. citizen to leave or enter the country during war time upon a presidential proclamation, passports were rarely needed for international travel. Since then, a series of statutes and State Department actions have sought to restrict freedom of travel. Supreme Court rulings—some asserting the right to freedom of travel, others supporting the government's right to apply area restrictions—have only partially resolved the issue.[1]

The 1918 act, which was in abeyance through the 1920s and 1930s, was amended in 1941 to include national emergencies, short of war. The 1941 law was technically repealed by the Immigration and Nationality Act of 1952; the latter, however, incorporated the provisions of the earlier law. War or continuing national emergency has kept the passport requirement in effect up to the present time.

Early Passport Denials

The first major attempt to deny passports to persons because of their political beliefs came in 1950 with the passage of the Internal Security Act. The act gave statutory authority to the State Department's already existing practice of denying passports to Communist Party members or to others whose travel would "be prejudicial to the interests of the United States."[2] Under the act, passports were forbidden to members of Communist organizations ordered to register with the Attorney General.

Denial of passports to Communists appeared to end in 1958 with the Supreme Court's ruling in *Kent v. Dulles,* (357 U.S. 116), which based the right to travel on the due process clause of the Fifth Amendment. That decision voided all restrictions on issuance of passports to Communists. It also stated that a denial of passports could not be based on the Internal Security Act; however, that act was not being enforced because by 1958 no registration proceedings had been instituted and the constitutionality of the registration provision had not been decided.[3]

A 1961 Supreme Court decision, *The Communist Party of the United States v. Subversive Activities*

Control Board (367 U.S. 1), upholding the registration provision of the Internal Security Act appeared to contradict the *Kent* ruling and to put the passport provisions of the 1950 Internal Security Act back into effect. The decision thus allowed the State Department to again deny passports to members of the Communist Party.

The issue was finally resolved in 1964 in *Aptheker v. Secretary of State* (378 U.S. 500) when the court ruled the passport provision of the 1950 act unconstitutional. The effect was to remove for the second time all restrictions on the issuance of passports to Communists.

The court did not say in *Aptheker* that the right to travel was absolute. In a 1965 case, *Zemel v. Rusk* (381 U.S. 1), the court held that while the broad language of the Passport Act of 1926 did not include denial of passports to Communists, it did sanction area restrictions.[4] Subsequent federal and Supreme Court decisions have tended to circumscribe enforcement efforts for violations of area restrictions.

The Supreme Court held unanimously in *United States v. Laub* (385 U.S. 475) that criminal penalties could not be applied to persons who traveled, with otherwise valid passports, to restricted areas, even if those passports had not been specifically validated for travel to the restricted area. Also in 1967, the United States Court of Appeals for the District of Columbia Circuit ruled in *Lynd v. Rusk* (389 F.2d 940) that the State Department did not have the authority to prevent a person's right to travel to a restricted area, but only as to where he might take his passport. Finally, in 1967, in *Woodward v. Rogers* (344 F. Supp. 974) the United States District Court for the District of Columbia held that the Secretary of State could not require that U.S. citizens swear to or affirm an oath of allegiance as a prerequisite to issuance of a passport.

Area restrictions in 1976 applied to travel in Cuba, Cambodia, North Korea and North and South Vietnam.

Footnotes

1. Jeanne Kuebler, "Freedom of Travel," *Editorial Research Reports*, Feb. 16, 1966, p. 126.
2. C. Herman Pritchett, *The American Constitution*, (McGraw-Hill Book Company, 1968), p. 367.
3. The party registration provision of the Internal Security Act was conclusively overturned in 1967 in *The Communist Party of the United States v. U.S.* (384 F.2d 957). See Congressional Quarterly, *Congress and the Nation, 1965-1968*, Vol. II, p. 418.
4. Pritchett, *The American Constitution*, pp. 369-70.

Truman overstepped his powers as commander-in-chief when he relied on them, April 8, 1952, to take possession and control of all facilities, plants and properties of 86 steel companies involved in a dispute with the United Steelworkers. Congress ignored the President's request to approve the seizure order. Then on June 2, the Supreme Court ruled (*Youngstown Sheet & Tube Co. v. Sawyer*, 343 U.S. 579) that his action was without statutory authority and that it violated the concept of separation of powers by usurping functions of Congress.

Indochina War

U.S. military aid to Vietnam was initiated by the Truman administration. By 1951 military aid to that country amounted to more than $500-million. Although President Eisenhower barred a U.S. combat role in Vietnam, in 1954 the United States sent 200 Air Force technicians to aid the French in their fight against the Viet Minh. The Senate Foreign Relations Committee subsequently expressed concern at the lack of congressional approval for this action, and the State Department pledged to consult with Congress before taking any additional steps in Vietnam.[121]

In March 1954—at the beginning of the 56-day battle at Dienbienphu that was disastrous for the French—the White House tentatively approved a plan for immediate U.S. air intervention, but Sens. Lyndon B. Johnson (D Texas) minority leader, and Richard B. Russell (D Ga.), ranking Democrat on the Armed Services Committee, and others rejected the proposal.

As U.S. involvement increased in Indochina during the Kennedy administration—there were about 15,000 advisers in Vietnam in early 1964—criticism intensified. On March 10, 1964, Sens. Wayne Morse (D Ore.) and Ernest Gruening (D Alaska) demanded total U.S. withdrawal.

Despite the growing criticism of the war, however, Congress during the period spanning the Tonkin Gulf resolution of 1964 and the 1973 Vietnam ceasefire agreement was never united or successful in its attempts to bring U.S. involvement to an end.

This was particularly true in the House, where many members consistently were unwilling to challenge the President's pre-eminence in the conduct of the war or related diplomacy, despite their complaints about aggrandizement of presidential war powers.

At the peak of anti-war strength in Congress only one out of three House members voted to back end-the-war proposals. Of 94 recorded votes on the war between 1966 and 1972, only a few were taken by the House, and House conferees almost invariably were responsible for deleting or emasculating Senate anti-war amendments.

The attitude in the Senate was different, but the result was similar. There was a great deal of complicated legislative action in the Senate on proposals to control or end the war, but most of the plans were deleted in conference or did not carry the force of law. Those restrictions that did become law were largely moot because they affected military activity the executive branch no longer intended to pursue.

Thirteen days before the Jan. 27, 1973, signing of the Vietnam peace agreement, Senate Majority Leader Mike Mansfield (D Mont.) insisted that Congress "can't end the war." "It's really up to the President," Mansfield said. "We shouldn't fool ourselves in that respect."

A revealing picture of congressional impotence on the war was provided by the adoption of the 1964 Tonkin Gulf resolution. The resolution affirmed congressional support for "all necessary measures to repel any armed attack against the forces of the United States...[and] to assist any member or protocol state of the Southeast Asia Collective Defense Treaty requesting assistance...." *(Details, p. 278)*

Initially approved overwhelmingly on the basis of what later emerged as a distorted account of a minor naval engagement, the resolution became the primary legal justification for the Johnson administration's prosecution of the war.

Congress learned subsequently that the naval incident had been misrepresented; it repealed the resolution in 1970. But the Nixon administration already had shifted to another legal rationale for its Vietnam policies. Nixon maintained that his authority to pursue policies and military actions in Vietnam derived from his constitutional prerogatives and obligations as commander-in-chief.

Following adoption of the Tonkin Gulf resolution, neither the Johnson nor Nixon administrations returned to Congress to seek specific legislative consent or additional authority for stepped-up military activity. President Nixon ordered U.S. troops into Cambodia in 1970, provided air support for South Vietnam's 1971 invasion of Laos, ordered Haiphong harbor mined in 1972 and launched the heaviest bombing of North Vietnam in December 1972—all without seeking congressional consent.

Anti-Indochina War Proposals

President Nixon's 1970 decision to send U.S. forces into Cambodia to clean out Communist sanctuaries provoked a six-week Senate debate in May and June on an amendment sponsored by Sens. John Sherman Cooper (R Ky.) and Frank Church (D Idaho) to bar use of U.S. funds for military operations in Cambodia.[122] A weakened version of the amendment—barring use of ground forces but not aircraft—was passed in December, months after Nixon had removed the U.S. troops from Cambodia.

Other action on anti-war proposals in 1970 included repeal of the 1964 Tonkin Gulf resolution and defeat of two "end-the-war" amendments sponsored by Sens. Mark O. Hatfield (R Ore.) and George McGovern (D S.D.).

In 1971, the Senate adopted amendments to three bills introduced by Mansfield calling for withdrawal of troops from Indochina by a certain deadline. Two of these survived House-Senate conference with the withdrawal deadline deleted—the first time the House had gone on record urging an end to the war. The President, however, said the provision was not binding and that he would not follow it. A new Cooper-Church amendment, limiting use of U.S. military funds in Indochina to troop withdrawal, was defeated on the Senate floor in a series of close votes.

Congress in 1972 enacted no legislation restricting U.S. military involvement in Southeast Asia, although the Senate took its toughest stand on terminating U.S. involvement. But continued House support for the President's policies forestalled congressional action to set a date for withdrawal.

The Senate Aug. 2 posed its most serious challenge to the President's Vietnam policy by adopting on a 49-47 roll-call vote an amendment cutting off funds for U.S. participation in the war. The amendment barred use of funds for U.S. participation in the war four months after enactment. All U.S. ground, naval and air forces would have to be out of Indochina by that date if North Vietnam and its allies had released all American prisoners of war. House conferees refused to accept the amendment.

Funding the Indochina War

The picture of the Johnson and Nixon administrations carrying on military activities in Indochina without congressional consent often has been overdrawn by critics of the war. They tended to overlook the frequent votes in Congress for appropriations to support the war. And while they often spoke of a constitutional crisis over war powers, they usually did not consider that throughout the war there was never a constitutional confrontation between a President determined to pursue the war and a Congress unwilling to appropriate the necessary funds.

Yet, from another viewpoint, the increasing number of anti-war votes in Congress—from five roll-call votes in 1969 to 35 in 1972—may well have served to reinforce President Nixon's decision to continue the policy of troop withdrawals from Indochina. The roll-call votes were a constant signal to the administration that slowing down—or even reversing—the troop withdrawal program would carry heavy political costs.

Indochina Postscript

In the spring of 1973, there was an important postscript to the congressional action on the Vietnam war. Although it had pulled out of Vietnam two months after the Jan. 27 peace agreement, the United States had continued bombing in Cambodia and Laos in support of anti-Communist activities there. In action on a supplemental appropriations bill in May, the House for the first time voted to cut off funds for military activity in Laos and Cambodia. Final language adopted by both chambers and signed by President Nixon barred the use of any past or existing appropriations for financing directly or indirectly U.S. combat activities in, over or off the shores of North Vietnam, South Vietnam, Laos or Cambodia.

Congress did not stop with a Cambodia bombing ban in its challenge to presidential power, however. In July, Congress passed a tough war powers measure that set a 60-day limit on any presidential commitment of U.S. troops to hostilities abroad or to situations where hostilities might be imminent unless Congress declared war, specifically authorized continuation of that commitment or was unable to meet the requirements because of an armed attack upon the United States. *(p. 279)*

Policy Resolutions Since 1945

Since 1945, Congress on five occasions has passed a joint resolution authorizing or approving the President's determination to use such armed forces as he deemed necessary to repel armed attacks or threats against the nations or geographical areas covered by the resolution. Four of the resolutions were initiated by the President, who sought congressional approval for military actions either contemplated or already undertaken. The five resolutions are:

1. **Formosa** resolution (H J Res 159), signed into law Jan. 29, 1955, authorizing the President to use U.S. forces to protect Formosa (Nationalist China) and the Pescadores Islands against "armed attack" from Communist China.

2. **Middle East** resolution (H J Res 117), signed into law March 9, 1957, proclaiming U.S. policy to defend Middle East countries "against aggression from any country controlled by international communism."

3. **Cuban** resolution (S J Res 230), signed into law Oct. 3, 1962, authorizing the President to take whatever steps were necessary to defend Latin America against Cuban aggression or subversion and to oppose the deployment of Soviet weapons in Cuba capable of endangering U.S. security.

4. **Berlin** resolution (H Con Res 570), adopted by the House and Senate in October 1962, reaffirming U.S. determination to use armed force, if necessary, to defend West Berlin and the access rights of the Western powers to West Berlin.

5. **Vietnam** resolution (H J Res 1145), signed into law Aug. 10, 1964, known as the **Tonkin Gulf** resolution, authorizing the President to use armed forces to repel attacks against U.S. forces and affirming U.S. determination to defend any SEATO treaty member or protocol state (this included Vietnam) requesting assistance.

The most controversial of the resolutions was the Tonkin Gulf Resolution of 1964—repealed by Congress in 1970—which gave rise to criticism that such resolutions in effect have acted as blank checks to support presidential war-making. In its 1967 report on the "national com-mitments resolution," the Senate Foreign Relations Committee concluded that the "Gulf of Tonkin resolution represents the extreme point in the process of constitutional erosion."[123]

Adoption of the Tonkin resolution and the subsequent expansion of U.S. involvement in Indochina gave rise to heated debate over whether the measure was in fact what Under Secretary of State Nicholas deB. Katzenbach claimed in 1967 to be the "functional equivalent" of a declaration of war. On the one hand, administration spokesmen cited the resolution as providing authority for executive actions; but at the same time, both Presidents Johnson and Nixon claimed they did not really need congressional approval because in any case the authority to act rested on their constitutional powers as commander-in-chief.

Indeed, throughout the post-war period, Presidents have committed troops abroad without first consulting Congress or later obtaining explicit approval: Truman in 1950 (Korea); Eisenhower in 1958 (Lebanon); Johnson in 1964 and 1967 (Congo) and 1965 (Dominican Republic) and Nixon in 1970 (Cambodia).

Commitment to Defend Formosa

Mounting tensions in the Formosa Strait prompted the United States to sign a mutual defense treaty with Nationalist China on Dec. 2, 1954.[124] While the treaty was before the Senate for ratification, Communist China stepped up pressure against Formosa Jan. 18, 1955, by seizing the island of Ichiang, just off the mainland coast, 210 miles north of Formosa. At the same time Peking increased pressure on two other offshore islands, Quemoy and Matsu.

The situation led President Eisenhower to ask Congress, in a special message Jan. 24, for explicit authority to use American armed forces to protect Formosa, the Pescadores Islands and "related positions and territories." It was essential to U.S. security that Formosa "should remain in friendly hands," the President asserted. While "authority for some of the actions which might be required" was clearly his as commander-in-chief, he said, Congress should "make clear the unified and serious intentions" of the nation "to fight if necessary." Enactment of the proposed resolution, he added, would "clarify present policy" and help prevent the Communists from "misjudging our firm purpose and national unity."

Quemoy, Matsu Status

What neither the President nor Secretary of State Dulles attempted to clarify was their intent regarding Quemoy, Matsu and the other offshore islands. The President said that "we must be alert to any concentration or employment of Chinese Communist forces obviously undertaken to facilitate attack upon Formosa, and be prepared to take appropriate military action." This implied that the President might commit American forces to repel an invasion of Quemoy—the message, essentially, that the administration wished to give Peking. To a number of Democrats, however, the offshore islands—unlike Formosa—clearly belonged to mainland China, and the question of their disposition, they believed, was beyond the scope of legitimate U.S. security interests. They feared that the Nationalists, in their efforts to regain the mainland, would use this "fatal ambiguity" over the offshore islands to maneuver the United States into a war with mainland China.

But Democratic leaders in Congress hastened to comply with the President's request despite some misgivings. H J Res 159, authorizing him to "employ the armed forces of the United States as he deems necessary" in the defense of Formosa, was reported by the House Foreign Affairs Committee the same day, unanimously and without amendment. The House adopted it Jan. 25, 1955, 410-3, after hearing Speaker Rayburn say that the resolution added nothing to the constitutional powers of the President and should not be taken as a precedent.

On Jan. 26 the Senate Foreign Relations and Armed Services Committees, sitting jointly, voted 27-2 to report the resolution, after rejecting amendments to limit the President's authority. The Senate passed H J Res 159, Jan. 28, 85-3.

Less than two weeks after passing the resolution, the Senate Feb. 9 ratified the mutual defense pact by a 65-6 roll-call vote.

Resolution Repeal Effort

Both the Eisenhower and Kennedy administrations reaffirmed the U.S. commitment to defend Formosa when tensions flared up again in 1958 and 1962. By the late 1960s and early 1970s, however, the situation had evolved considerably as the Nixon administration, supported by a majority in Congress, dropped its two-decade-old policy of isolating Communist China from the world community of nations.[125] In 1971, the Senate mounted an effort to repeal the 1955 Formosa resolution as Congress grew increasingly wary of presidential use of the war power. The repeal measure, S J Res 48, was attached to the 1972 foreign aid authorization bill. The Senate voted Oct. 28 to delete the repeal resolution from the aid bill, itself later defeated, on a 43-40 roll-call vote. Some saw the resolution as a victim of poor timing, for its defeat came three days after the United Nations voted to expel Nationalist China and to seat the People's Republic as a member of the organization. Though the early 1970s saw the United States quietly phasing out aid to Formosa, the mutual defense treaty and the Formosa resolution were still on the books when nationalist president Chiang Kai-shek died at age 87 on April 5, 1975.

Eisenhower Doctrine in Middle East

At the end of 1956, Secretary of State Dulles was convinced that the Suez crisis had left a dangerous power vacuum in the Middle East into which the Soviets would move unless deterred by the United States. As author of the 1955 Formosa resolution, Dulles believed that a similar expression of congressional support for presidential discretion was needed to convince the Soviets of U.S. determination to block any advance into the Middle East. On Jan. 5, 1957, the President appeared before a joint session of Congress to urge support for a declaration promptly dubbed the Eisenhower Doctrine.[126] The President said:

"In the situation now existing, the greatest risk, as is often the case, is that ambitious despots may miscalculate. If power-hungry Communists should either falsely or correctly estimate that the Middle East is inadequately defended, they might be tempted to use open measures of armed attack. If so, that would start a chain of circumstances which would almost surely involve the United States in military action. I am convinced that the best insurance against this dangerous contingency is to make clear now our readiness to cooperate fully and freely with our

friends of the Middle East in ways consonant with the purposes and principles of the United Nations."[127]

To accomplish this, Eisenhower asked that he be authorized to extend economic aid to nations in the area "dedicated to the maintenance of national independence," to give military aid to nations requesting it and "employ the armed forces of the United States as he deems necessary" to protect the area against "overt armed aggression from any nation controlled by international communism," and to spend for these purposes $200-million in previously appropriated funds.

The Eisenhower Doctrine was greeted with little enthusiasm by Republicans and with some asperity by Democrats, who decried the President's request for a "blank check" and complained that it skirted the basic issues of Arab-Israeli hostility and control over the Suez Canal. Former Secretary of State Dean Acheson called the Eisenhower Doctrine "vague, inadequate and not very useful." It was "not a statement of policy," he said, "but an invitation to devise one."

In hearings before the House Foreign Affairs Committee and the combined Senate Foreign Relations and Armed Services Committees during January, Secretary Dulles defended the administration's draft resolution and urged quick action. Unless the United States moved promptly, he said, "it is our definite belief that this area is very likely to be lost." He defined the Middle East as the area between Libya and Pakistan, Turkey and the Sudan. To the complaints of Senate Majority Leader Lyndon B. Johnson (D Texas) and others that his case rested on generalities with little specific information, Dulles replied: "If we have to pinpoint everything we propose to do, this program will not serve its purpose. If Congress is not willing to trust the President to the extent he asks, we can't win this battle."

Faced with this argument, most members were unwilling to withhold a vote of confidence. The House committee on Jan. 25 reported the requested bill with minor amendments. Fearing more substantive amendments from the floor, the committee insisted on a closed rule which the House adopted Jan. 30 over strong protests from both sides of the aisle, 262-146. Then, bearing out the comment of Rep. James Roosevelt (D Calif.) that rarely had there been a bill "which has so few friends that will get so many votes," the House passed H J Res 117, 355-61.

The Senate debated the measure sporadically for 12 days, rejecting a number of amendments but adding an amendment by Mansfield (D Mont.) directing the President to support the U.N. Emergency Force in maintaining the Suez truce. On March 5 the Senate adopted the amended version of H J Res 117, 72-19. Action was completed when the House on March 7 agreed to the Senate's amendments, 350-60.

First Test of Doctrine

The first test of the Eisenhower Doctrine and resolution came in 1958 following a coup in Iraq, which overthrew the pro-Western government, replacing it with a regime favorable to the Soviet Union and the United Arab Republic (U.A.R.). The United States refrained from military action in this case.

When the government of Lebanon came under similar pressure and its president requested U.S. assistance, Eisenhower ordered U.S. Marines from the 6th Fleet in the Mediterranean to land in Lebanon. Justifying his action on the ground that American lives were endangered, as well as referring indirectly to the Eisenhower Doctrine, the President said in a July 15, 1958, message to Congress that the forces had been sent to Lebanon "to protect American lives and by their presence to assist the government of Lebanon in the preservation of Lebanon's territorial integrity and independence, which have been deemed vital to United States national interests and world peace."[128]

Resolution on Berlin

Unlike other postwar resolutions authorizing the President's use of armed forces to defend certain nations or geographical areas, the Berlin Resolution of 1962 (H Con Res 570) originated in Congress instead of the administration.[129] Also, unlike the others, it merely expressed the sense of the Congress and did not have the force of law. The resolution was an outgrowth of the 1961 Berlin crisis, which followed erection of the Berlin Wall and led President Kennedy to call up reservists.

H Con Res 570 expressed the sense of Congress that the United States was determined to prevent by whatever means might be necessary, including the use of arms, any Soviet violation of Allied rights in Berlin, "including those of ingress and egress." It affirmed the continued right of the United States to remain in Berlin, pursuant to agreements on four-power rights entered into at the end of World War II. The resolution said it was the purpose of the United States to encourage and support the unification of a democratic Germany.

Congressional objection to the resolution came chiefly from Republicans, who criticized it for failing to mention the Berlin Wall and for not delineating Allied rights in Berlin.

The resolution was adopted Oct. 5 by a 312-0 roll-call vote of the House. During the House debate Clement J. Zablocki (D Wis.), sponsor of the resolution, said the executive branch had stood up firmly to the Soviet Union on Berlin, and "the only voice that has not been officially heard on this issue is the voice of the U.S. Congress." He said the resolution was designed to let the Soviet Union "know that our nation stands united behind the administration's firm policy on Berlin."

The Senate Foreign Relations Committee reported an almost identical resolution, but the Senate substituted the House resolution and adopted it by voice vote on Oct. 10.

Definition of Policy on Cuba, 1962

Fidel Castro's open avowal of his attachment to communism, late in 1961, set the stage for a meeting of the Organization of American States Jan. 31, 1962, at which resolutions were adopted expelling Cuba from the OAS and the Inter-American Defense Board, suspending all arms trade with Cuba, and pledging cooperation in countering Communist subversion in the hemisphere. But the U.S.-led effort to isolate Cuba was paralleled by an increasing flow of Soviet-bloc military as well as economic aid to Castro, and by midsummer political pressure was mounting in Washington for a blockade, an invasion or some other form of direct action against Cuba.[130]

At issue were the kinds and quantities of Soviet military deliveries. Sen. Kenneth B. Keating (R N.Y.) and other Republicans, citing Cuban refugee sources, asserted the presence of Soviet missiles and troops. President Kennedy acknowledged, Sept. 4, that missiles had been delivered, but he said they were short-range weapons of a defensive character. On Sept. 13, the President declared that Soviet arms shipments to Castro "do not constitute a serious threat to any other part of this hemisphere" and that "unilateral military intervention on the part of the United States cannot currently be either required or justified." But he added that "if at any time the Communist buildup in Cuba were to endanger or interfere with our security in any way...or if Cuba should ever attempt to export its aggressive purposes by force or the threat of force against any nation in this hemisphere or become an offensive military base of significant capacity for the Soviet Union, then this country will do whatever must be done to protect its own security and that of its allies."

With a mid-term election approaching, the administration's wait-and-see attitude became a campaign issue. On Sept. 7 Minority Leaders Sen. Everett McKinley Dirksen (R Ill.) and Rep. Charles A. Halleck (R Ind.) proposed authorizing the President to use the armed forces to "meet the Cuban problem." Kennedy swiftly asked for more general authority—similar to that granted after the 1961 Berlin crisis—to call up reservists during the congressional recess to deal with challenges "in any part of the free world," and the request was quickly granted. But other moves were afoot to commit the United States to some specific course of action against Cuba, and to head off such moves the administration endorsed a joint resolution modeled on the President's Sept. 13 statement.

Resolution Provisions

As reported Sept. 19, S J Res 230 declared U.S. determination to prevent—with arms if necessary—the Marxist-Leninist regime in Cuba from extending its subversive activities to any part of the hemisphere or the creation in Cuba of an externally supported military capability endangering U.S. security. The Senate adopted the resolution next day, 86-1, with Sen. Winston L. Prouty (R Vt.) opposed on the ground that it was not strong enough. House Republicans voiced the same complaint and moved to insert a provision urging the President to "implement and enforce the Monroe Doctrine"—a euphemism meaning that the Soviet presence in Cuba was already such as to justify direct action. But the motion was rejected on a party-line vote of 140-251, and the House adopted S J Res 230 on Sept. 26 without change, 384-7, with Republicans voicing all the "nays."

Congress adjourned Oct. 13. Three days later—as the President revealed the next week—he was shown aerial photos providing the first "hard" evidence that the Soviets were secretly building launching sites in Cuba for ballistic missiles capable of reaching many U.S. cities. Kennedy responded swiftly; on Oct. 22, he summoned 17 congressional leaders to the White House before addressing the nation that evening on a matter "of the highest national urgency." He announced that he was imposing a U.S. Navy quarantine on Cuba. The fleet was ordered to turn back any ships laden with cargoes of offensive weapons. He called on Soviet Premier Nikita Khrushchev to "halt and eliminate this...threat to world peace" and said that the premier "has an opportunity now to move the world back from the abyss of destruction." Kennedy used the congressional resolution to justify his actions but also invoked his constitutional authority to act as commander-in-chief.[131]

A head-on clash was avoided when the Soviets diverted several ships moving toward Cuba that might have been challenged by U.S. warships; and on Nov. 20, the President stated that "all known offensive missile sites in Cuba have been dismantled."

Dominican Republic Action, 1965

The 1962 Cuban resolution was not cited by President Johnson when in 1965 he ordered 19,000 U.S. troops to the Dominican Republic on the outbreak of civil strife in that country. Johnson said he had sent the troops "to help prevent another Communist state in this hemisphere" (later, he claimed that "99 per cent of our reason for going in there was to try to provide protection for these American lives and for the lives of other nationals").[132]

The administration's actions came under fire from numerous members of Congress, among them Senate Foreign Relations Committee Chairman J. W. Fulbright (D Ark.), who charged that the United States had intervened "forcibly and illegally" and that the administration had acted on the basis of poor advice "based on a misjudgment of the facts."

Tonkin Gulf Resolution

Following reported torpedo attacks by North Vietnam PT boats on American destroyers patrolling the Gulf of Tonkin on Aug. 2 and Aug. 4, 1964, President Johnson ordered a retaliatory air strike on their bases that destroyed or damaged 25 boats. On Aug. 5 the President asked Congress to adopt a resolution to "give convincing evidene to the aggressive Communist nations, and to the world as a whole, that our policy in Southeast Asia will be carried forward, and that the peace and security of the area will be preserved."[133]

On Aug. 7, both chambers adopted the resolution (H J Res 1145) by overwhelming majorities—414 to 0 in the House and 88 to 2 in the Senate. The resolution (Joint Resolution To Promote the Maintenance of International Peace and Security in Southeast Asia) recorded congressional support and approval of the "determination of the President...to take all necessary measures to repel any armed attack against the forces of the United States and to prevent further aggression." The resolution went on to say: "Consonant with the Constitution and the Charter of the United Nations and in accordance with its obligations under the Southeast Asia Collective Defense Treaty, the United States is,therefore, prepared, as the President determines, to take all necessary steps, including the use of armed force, to assist any member or protocol state of...(SEATO) requesting assistance in defense of its freedom."

Disagreement Over Meaning

The meaning of the Tonkin Gulf resolution became a source of intense debate as the Vietnam War grew in scope and as members of Congress who had supported the resolution became increasingly disillusioned with the progress of the war. Many urged that the resolution did not commit the United States to massive participation in the war. Sen. John C. Stennis (D Miss.) rejected Secretary of State Rusk's defense of the resolution in 1966 as a grant of authority for U.S. action in the war. During hearings before the Preparedness Investigating Subcommittee, Stennis declared: "...you stand on mighty thin ice if you rely on the Tonkin Gulf resolution as a constitutional basis for this war."[134]

Disagreement over the meaning of the resolution surfaced again in 1967 during hearings on U.S. commitments before the Senate Foreign Relations Committee. Under Secretary of State Nicholas deB. Katzenbach described the resolution as the "functional equivalent" of a declaration of war. "What could a declaration of war have done that would

have given the President more authority and a clearer voice of the Congress than that did?" Katzenbach asked rhetorically. Katzenbach also maintained that in "limited wars," such as Vietnam, a declaration of war was "inappropriate."[135]

Sen. Albert Gore (D Tenn.) rejected Katzenbach's view. "I did not vote for the resolution with any understanding that it was tantamount to a declaration of war," he said. Sen. Charles H. Percy (R Ill.) and Bourke B. Hickenlooper (R Iowa) expressed doubt that the resolution would have been adopted if it had been known that it would lead to large-scale U.S. military action.

(After leaving office, Katzenbach testified July 28, 1970, that "the constitutional authority to use our armed forces in Vietnam rests squarely on Tonkin and cannot otherwise be constitutionally justified.")[136]

"We stated then, and we repeat now, we did not think the resolution was necessary to do what we did and what we're doing," said President Johnson at an April 1967 news conference. "But we thought it was desirable, and we thought if we were going to ask them (Congress) to stay the whole route and if we expected them to be there on the landing, we ought to ask them to be there on the takeoff."[137]

In the Foreign Relations Committee's 1967 report accompanying the National Commitments Resolution, Chairman J. W. Fulbright (D Ark.) said that "in adopting the [Tonkin Gulf] resolution Congress was closer to believing that it was helping to prevent a large-scale war by taking a firm stand than that it was laying down the legal basis for the conduct of such a war."[138] Taking issue with Katzenbach's description of the resolution as a "functional equivalent" of a declaration of war, Fulbright concluded: "The burden of the under secretary's remarks seems to have been first, that the Gulf of Tonkin resolution was not a declaration of war but its 'functional equivalent,' and, second, that declarations of war are inappropriate when the nation's purposes are 'limited' and in any case are 'outmoded in the international arena.' The committee has difficulty reconciling these various observations with each other, much less divining their basis in the Constitution.... It is obvious that the question of authority to commit the United States to war is in need of clarification."

Resolution Repealed

In the summer of 1970 the Senate twice voted to repeal the Gulf of Tonkin resolution—on June 24 by attaching a repeal amendment, by a roll-call vote of 81-10, to the so-called Military Sales bill (HR 15628), and a second time on July 10, by adopting a separate repealer, in the form of a Senate concurrent resolution (S Con Res 64), by a roll-call vote of 57-5. Congress on Jan. 2, 1971, cleared HR 15628, with the repeal provision intact, thus enacting it into law. S Con Res 64 never was reported from the House Foreign Affairs Committee.

At first, the Nixon administration had objected to repeal, but in early 1970—with increasing numbers of members in both chambers favoring repeal—it modified its opposition and maintained that the authority for pursuing the war rested on the President's constitutional power as commander-in-chief.

A postscript to the Tonkin issue was added in June 1971, with publication of the Defense Department's secret history of the Vietnam War (Pentagon Papers). The study raised questions about the scope of the 1964 destroyer attack and strongly suggested that Congress had been manipulated into granting the authorization.[139]

The War Powers Act

Increasingly frustrated with its ineffectual influence on American involvement in Indochina and on the scope of U.S. military commitments abroad, Congress in 1973 reacted by passing—over President Nixon's veto—a bill designed to limit the President's powers to commit U.S. forces abroad without congressional approval.[140]

The legislation, which came to be known as the "war powers bill" (H J Res 542—PL 93-148), was the product of three years of effort by most liberals and many conservatives in both chambers. The basic and most controversial of the legislation's provisions were those delineating the situations under which the President could commit troops, requiring the President to terminate any troop commitment within 60 days unless Congress specifically authorized its continuation and permitting Congress at any time by concurrent resolution to direct the President to disengage troops involved in an undeclared war. *(Provisions, box)*

Passage of the bill was heralded by its supporters as a major step in reasserting Congress' war-making powers. Said Jacob K. Javits (R N.Y.), chief architect of the Senate version of the legislation: "With the war powers resolution's passage, after 200 years, at last something will have been done about codifying the implementation of the most awesome power in the possession of any sovereignty and giving the broad representation of the people in Congress a voice in it. This is critically important, for we have just learned the hard lesson that wars cannot be successfully fought except with the consent of the people and with their support."

In vetoing the legislation, President Nixon declared that the resolution would impose restrictions on the authority of the President that would be "both unconstitutional and dangerous to the best interests of our nation." The major provisions of the bill, he contended, would "purport to take away, by a mere legislative act, authorities which the President has properly exercised under the Constitution for almost 200 years." They were unconstitutional, he asserted, because "the only way in which the constitutional powers of a branch of the government can be altered is by amending the Constitution—and any attempt to make such alterations by legislation alone is clearly without force."

The President's position was argued by some conservatives and administration supporters during debate on the bill in both chambers. In their assertions that the bill was unconstitutional they were joined by a small group of liberals who agreed that the measure was unconstitutional, but for different reasons. Thus Thomas F. Eagleton (D Mo.), an author of the Senate's original war powers bill, branded the final version as "the most dangerous piece of legislation" he had seen in his five years in the Senate. Eagleton warned his colleagues: "We are going to give him [Nixon] more authority, and legalize it, than perhaps he ever dreamed he had. Not only President Nixon, but every President of the United States will have at least the color of legal authority, the advance blessing of Congress, given on an open, blank-check basis, to take us to war. It is a horrible mistake."

Prelude: The 1969 Commitments Resolution

Congress took a first step in attempting to reassert its voice in decisions committing the United States to the defense of foreign nations by passing a "national commitments" resolution (S Res 85) in 1969.[141]

Provisions of 1973 War Powers Act

As enacted into law, H J Res 542 (PL 93-148):
- Stated that the President could commit U.S. armed forces to hostilities or situations where hostilities might be imminent, only pursuant to a declaration of war, specific statutory authorization or a national emergency created by an attack upon the United States, its territories or possessions, or its armed forces.
- Urged the President "in every possible instance" to consult with Congress before committing U.S. forces to hostilities or to situations where hostilities might be imminent, and to consult Congress regularly after such a commitment.
- Required the President to report in writing within 48 hours to the Speaker of the House and president pro tempore of the Senate on any commitment or substantial enlargement of U.S. combat forces abroad, except for deployments related solely to supply, replacement, repair or training; required supplementary reports at least every six months while such forces were being engaged.
- Authorized the Speaker of the House and the president pro tempore of the Senate to reconvene Congress if it was not in session to consider the President's report.
- Required the termination of a troop commitment within 60 days after the President's initial report was submitted, unless Congress declared war, specifically authorized continuation of the commitment, or was physically unable to convene as a result of an armed attack upon the United States; allowed the 60-day period to be extended for up to 30 days if the President determined and certified to Congress that unavoidable military necessity respecting the safety of U.S. forces required their continued use in bringing about a prompt disengagement.
- Allowed Congress, at any time U.S. forces were engaged in hostilities without a declaration of war or specific congressional authorization, by concurrent resolution to direct the President to disengage such troops.
- Set up congressional priority procedures for consideration of any resolution or bill introduced pursuant to the provisions of the resolution.
- Provided that if any provision of the resolution was declared invalid, the remainder of the resolution would not be affected.

The original version of the resolution had been introduced in 1967 by Foreign Relations Committee Chairman J. W. Fulbright (D Ark.). Fulbright's resolution stated it to be the sense of the Senate that a national commitment by the United States to a foreign war "necessarily and exclusively results from affirmative action" taken by Congress and the President by means of a treaty, convention, or other legislative instrumentality specifically intended to give effect to such a commitment.

By the time the resolution emerged from committee that November, it contained a number of escape clauses for the President. The resolution would pertain to future situations, not those in which the United States was already involved; it recognized the President's power to repel an attack on the country and to protect U.S. citizens or property. It ended rather obscurely by stating that a commitment would result from decisions "made in accordance with constitutional processes, which, in addition to appropriate executive action," would require "affirmative action" by Congress.

The Senate did not vote on the resolution in 1967 or 1968. In February 1969, Fulbright reintroduced his original version, and it was reported out of committee without cumbersome amendments. The Senate passed the measure June 25, after five days of debate, during which almost all members spoke in support of the move. Opinion divided concerning the scope of the resolution and the definition of "national commitments," however.

The actual impact of the resolution on the nature of U.S. foreign commitments was limited by the fact that the measure did not alter existing arrangements, such as treaties. Moreover, the resolution was only an admonition to the President to consult with Congress; he still was not bound to do so. (And in fact, Nixon did not consult Congress in 1970, when he ordered the Cambodian incursion.)

In its final form, S Res 85 stated it to be the sense of the Senate that a national commitment "results only from affirmative action taken by the legislative and executive branches...by means of a treaty, statute, or concurrent resolution of both houses of Congress specifically providing for such commitment."

It defined a commitment as "the use of the armed forces on foreign territory, or a promise to assist a foreign country, government or people by the use of the armed forces or financial resources of the United States, either immediately or upon the happening of certain events."

Shaping the War Powers Bill

After three years of effort, agreement on a bill to limit presidential power to wage undeclared war was reached by a House-Senate conference Oct. 4, 1973. As sent to conference, the Senate-passed bill's delineation of circumstances in which the President could act without specific authority had been the biggest stumbling block in reaching an accord, but the Senate agreed to delete that from the bill and insert a far more general policy statement.

Although the final version of the measure was closer to the House-passed bill, the real victory belonged to the Senate. The conference agreement culminated several years of Senate attempts to place substantive limits on executive war powers.

In 1972 the Senate had approved a bill which was nearly identical to the one it sent to conference in 1973.[142] However, the 1972 bill died in conference with a much weaker House version which only urged the President to consult with Congress prior to an unauthorized commitment and required him to issue reports after a commitment was made; it did not give Congress any authority to terminate a commitment. The 1972 House version was similar to measures passed by that chamber in 1970 and 1971.

Action on a war powers bill in 1973 got underway on March 7, when a House Foreign Affairs subcommittee opened hearings, with House and Senate sponsors of various war power proposals as the lead-off witnesses. The necessity of learning from the Vietnam experience was a dominant theme among those members of Congress who appeared to outline their legislative proposals for curbing executive powers in committing U.S. forces to combat.

On May 2, the subcommittee approved a tough war powers bill—one that was considerably stronger than the 1972 House-passed measure. The new bill would require

that, in the absence of a declaration of war, the President could commit U.S. troops to hostilities for only 120 days without further congressional approval. Congress could order the President to stop operations before the 120-day period if both chambers approved a concurrent resolution to that effect. (Concurrent resolutions, which have the force of law, require no presidential signature and therefore skirt the possibility of a veto and the need to muster support for override.) The bill was approved by the full committee June 7, with an amendment making all ongoing hostilities subject to the measure's provisions.

The bill passed the House July 18, after the amendment relating to current hostilities and another section permitting the President to determine when an emergency existed were dropped.

Meanwhile, the Senate Foreign Relations Committee held two days of hearings in April on a war powers bill sponsored by Sens. Eagleton, Javits and John C. Stennis (D Miss.) and cosponsored by 58 other senators. It was almost identical to the bill passed by the Senate, by a 68-16 vote, in 1972.

The "heart and core" of the bill (S 440), according to the committee in its June 14 report on the bill, were the sections spelling out the emergency circumstances under which the President could commit U.S. forces and providing for a termination of that authorization within 30 days, unless Congress specifically approved continued use of armed forces.

The bill permitted the President, in the absence of a congressional declaration of war, to commit U.S. forces to repel an armed attack on the United States or to forestall the "direct and imminent threat" of such an attack; to repel an armed attack on U.S. forces abroad or to forestall such an attack; to protect while evacuating U.S. citizens and nationals in another country if their lives were threatened. In addition to these emergency situations, the President could commit forces "pursuant to specific statutory authorization."

To avoid resolutions such as the Tonkin Gulf resolution which might be open to wide interpretation, the committee included a requirement that such resolutions or statutes contain a specific authorization for the introduction of U.S. forces or a specific exemption from compliance with the war powers legislation. Specific authority would also be required for assignment of U.S. military personnel to assist a foreign nation's forces in hostilities or situations where hostilities were imminent.

Compromise and Final Action

After being reported favorably by the Foreign Relations Committee, the bill passed the Senate July 20 on a 72-18 roll-call vote. It then was sent to conference with the House-passed version.

There, Senate conferees made several key concessions to the House, agreeing to strike the delineation of circumstances under which the President could commit U.S. troops abroad without a declaration of war and accepting instead a more general policy statement. Some members had argued that any attempt to specifically define the President's emergency powers might have the effect of expanding executive powers and providing the President with a basis for justifying military initiatives.

Conferees also settled on a 60-day deadline on the committment of U.S. troops without congressional authorization, rather than the 30 days provided in the Senate bill or the 120 days in the House bill.

Contrasting Views on War Powers Legislation

"...In my view, Congress has broad authority over matters integrally related to the exercise of war-making authority. If, in any given case, Congress is desirous of asserting itself, it has all the tools at its command. I think it derogates the congressional role for Congress to feel the need to assert itself through the rather artificial means embodied in the legislative proposals which would codify what is conceived to be the constitutional allocation of authority. Such a step would be wholly inconsistent with our historical constitutional traditions, and would in no significant way aid in assuring a meaningful role in war-making for Congress."

> —Thomas E. Kauper, deputy assistant attorney general, Office of Legal Counsel, in testimony before the House Foreign Affairs National Security Policy and Scientific Developments Subcommittee hearing, June 2, 1971.

"I am opposed to the legislation before you as a way to achieve these objectives because 1) it attempts to fix in detail, and to freeze, the allocation of the war power between the President and Congress—a step which the framers in their wisdom quite deliberately decided against and 2) it attempts in a number of respects to narrow the power given the President by the Constitution....

"It appears, for example, that...[the legislation does] not cover situations like that of the Cuban missile crisis. In failing to recognize the need for immediate action and the propriety of a presidential response to such situations, the bills are unduly restrictive....

"...[The legislation] would also seek to restrict the President's authority to deploy forces abroad short of hostilities.... For example, such a restriction could seriously limit the ability of the President to make a demonstration of force to back up the exercise of our rights and responsibilities in Berlin or to deploy elements of the Sixth Fleet in the Mediterranean in connection with the Middle East situation...."

> —Secretary of State William P. Rogers, before Senate Foreign Relations Committee, May 14, 1971.

"The war powers bill is not the correct way to tackle this issue. To my mind, the bill is improper, unwise, and perhaps illegal. It would leave the United States helpless to prevent the annihilation of Israel. It would emasculate NATO. It would unwittingly allow a militant Congress to initiate a nuclear holocaust. And it may incite one of the gravest constitutional crises in American history....

> —Sen. Barry Goldwater (R Ariz.), before House Foreign Affairs Subcommittee, April 23, 1971.

"...This proposal strikes the best balance I have yet seen between the national need for certain powers of immediate presidential action and the national need to in-

sure that in any sustained hostilities the executive branch must act only in partnership with Congress—a partnership in which the President does not act beyond authority explicitly granted by Congress.

"The need for the right of rapid presidential action is clear from our present history.... But it is equally plain that there is a great difference between these immediate executive powers and the power to make war without any limit of time or size. It is clear in the Constitution, as it is in our political history, that war, in this larger sense, should have both popular support and explicit congressional authorization....

"[The legislation] also provides that Congress, if it chooses, can authorize the conduct of hostilities by other means than a formal declaration of war. I believe this provision...is a most important advance in the process of properly engaging Congress in decisions about the use of force...[T]he traditional declaration of war has many dangers, both in its internal and foreign effects.... One special weakness of the declaration of war is that by our whole tradition it transfers unfettered direction over the conduct of war to the Commander-in-Chief."

> —McGeorge Bundy, president, Ford Foundation, testifying before the Senate Foreign Relations Committee, April 26, 1971.

"...[I]n the very difficult and threatening time that we live in—in this particular era where we have confrontations throughout the world...I think it would be advisable for the President to let Congress share the blame, so to speak, if it's necessary to commit troops abroad."

> —Rep. Clement J. Zablocki (D Wis.), floor leader of the House war powers bill, in an Oct. 11, 1973, interview with Congressional Quarterly.

"A war-powers bill requiring the executive branch to testify before Congress on the reasons for and status of presidentially initiated hostilities and giving Congress the right to terminate such hostilities through concurrent or simple resolution would serve a valuable purpose. To this might be added a positive and absolute statutory obligation on Presidents to seek congressional consent when hostilities seemed likely to pass beyond a certain degree of magnitude.... Such a bill could accomplish everything that needed to be accomplished...without the impossible attempt to codify all future contingencies, without the delegation of congressional war-making power to the President, without bestowing congressional approval on pre-emptive war, without the 30-day or 120-day rigmarole."

> —Arthur M. Schlesinger Jr., commenting on the original 1973 House and Senate versions of the bill, in *The Imperial Presidency* (Houghton-Mifflin Co., 1973), pp. 306-07.

One of the most controversial provisions of the House version was incorporated without change in the conference compromise. It permitted Congress to terminate—through passage by majority vote of a concurrent resolution, an ac-

tion that does not require presidential approval—any commitment of troops abroad without a declaration of war or specific congressional authorization. House opponents had argued that the use of a concurrent resolution was unconstitutional and would not be binding on the President. However, proponents insisted that there was precedent for its use and that it would eliminate the possibility of a presidential veto. Their thinking prevailed among conferees who agreed to include the concurrent resolution concept as the vehicle for congressional action rather than the Senate-approved provision requiring enactment into law of either a bill or a joint resolution.

The Senate approved the conference version of H J Res 542 Oct. 10, by a vote of 75-20; the House did the same two days later, by a vote of 238-123. The President, as expected, vetoed the bill Oct. 24. Acting first, the House Nov. 7 overrode the veto by a close vote of 284-135—four votes over the two-thirds majority necessary under the Constitution to override. Four hours later, the Senate completed the process with a 75-18 vote to override—a comfortable 13-vote margin over the two-thirds requirement.

Postscript: The Mayaguez Incident

The war powers bill was put to a test in 1975, when President Ford ordered the use of U.S. troops to free the American merchant ship *Mayaguez* and its crew of 39, seized May 12 by Cambodian Communist troops off the disputed island of Poulo Wai in the Gulf of Siam. In this case, there was general agreement that the President had the authority to commit U.S. troops without regard to the war powers law, even though the President complied with it by issuing a report on his action to Congress May 15 in accordance with the bill's 48-hour reporting requirement.[143]

Congressional reaction to Ford's use of force was generally favorable, but some members were critical of the way Congress had been consulted. Senate Majority Leader Mike Mansfield (D Mont.) said, "I did not give my approval or disapproval because the decision had already been made." He said he had questions about the whole affair and called for greater consultation, as did other congressional leaders.

Problems of Secrecy

"A popular government without popular information, or the means of acquiring it, is but a prologue to a farce or a tragedy; or, perhaps, both," wrote Madison in 1822. "Knowledge will forever govern ignorance; and a people who mean to be their own governors must arm themselves with the power which knowledge gives."[144]

In the post-war period, the executive branch secrecy system has become a major obstacle to Congress'—and the public's—ability to share a role in foreign policy-making. This has been particularly true of the activities of the intelligence community; many of its activities—some of which were illegal—were only brought to light before Congress and the public in 1975 and 1976 as a result of committee investigations. *(CIA Investigation p. 168)*

In his discussion of "the secrecy system," Arthur M. Schlesinger Jr. notes that during the 19th century, information concerning government diplomatic activities generally was made available to Congress and the public. "Even the Civil War was fought to a remarkable degree in the open...there was no effective censorship, no Sedition Act, no Espionage Act."[145] World War I saw the growth of the system of classifying documents; the system was considerably strengthened during World War II. On March 22, 1940, President Roosevelt by executive order conferred presidential recognition for the first time on the military classification system.[146] The system rapidly spread to the

State Department and other executive branch agencies until, in Schlesinger's words, "a legitimate system of restriction grew...into an extravagant and indefensible system of denial."[147]

At the start of the post-war period, the secrecy system was still relatively unsophisticated. Nonetheless, Sen. Robert A. Taft (R Ohio) told the Senate in 1951, "The result of a general practice of secrecy...has been to deprive the Senate and Congress of the substance of the powers conferred on them by the Constitution."[148]

By the 1970s, Congress and the public had begun to lose confidence in the integrity of the secrecy system. "Illegitimate secrecy," said Schlesinger, "had corrupted the conduct of foreign affairs and had on occasion deprived voters of information necessary for democratic control of foreign policy."[149] In Congress, committees in both chambers held hearings on government secrecy.[150] In August 1972, the Senate established a special 10-member Committee to Study Questions related to Secret and Confidential Government Documents, co-chaired by the majority and minority leaders. In its report, filed in October 1973, the committee stated that Congress should take a second look at the broad grant of power it had given Presidents to classify government documents and thus put them beyond the reach even of members of Congress.[151]

The secrecy issue was dramatically highlighted with publication of the Pentagon Papers by *The New York Times* in June 1971—two years after the administration had denied them to the Senate Foreign Relations Committee—and the reading of the classified documents by Sen. Mike Gravel (D Alaska) during a special subcommittee meeting June 29.

The issue not only involved the propriety of the Times' publication and Gravel's action; disclosures in the Pentagon Papers raised serious questions about the propriety of the secrecy system itself.

Commenting on the revelations concerning the administration's Vietnam policy contained in the Pentagon Papers, Prof. Raoul Berger wrote: "We can only conjecture whether the course of events would have been changed had the...facts [disclosed in the papers] been spread before Congress and the people. But undeniably they were deprived of the choice which was theirs to make."[152]

"However the impact on the national interest of disclosure to the *public* may be viewed," Berger continued, "withholdings of the Pentagon Papers from the Senate Foreign Relations Committee and from Congress is something else again. Congress...was intended to be the senior partner in the new federal government, the chief agent in waging, continuing and terminating war. It was therefore entitled to be advised of all the relevant facts.... It is a measure of executive arrogance that refusal of this study to Congress was made in the name of the 'national interest.' Nowhere in the Constitution...does it appear that the Founders looked to the President to protect the 'national interest' against the Congress."[153]

Testifying before the Senate Foreign Relations Committee during its 1971 hearings on war powers legislation, historian Henry Steele Commager said: "If the executive branch is going to conduct foreign relations under cover of secrecy, it is, of course, quite likely that it can obtain from the Congress what it asks for at a time of alleged emergency.... What is needed...is a far fuller disclosure of the facts of the case.... Had the Senate been in possession of everything we now know about the situation in Southeast Asia in 1964, I think it is highly questionable whether they would have passed the Tonkin resolution, and highly doubtful whether you could have gotten a sufficient vote for a declaration of war."[154]

In his book, *Congress, the Executive, and Foreign Policy*, Francis O. Wilcox discusses the "crucial" need for Congress to obtain adequate information—much of which is available only from the executive—if it is to have a voice in foreign policy-making. "Intelligence was crucial to the policy-making process in both the Cuban missile crisis and the Dominican intervention. In the former case, the intelligence was clear and unambiguous; in the latter, almost everything depended on how it was interpreted. What was initially given to Congress and the public was the administration's interpretation.... It was not until the press and Congress examined what lay behind this interpretation that it appeared to some critics to be exaggerated and unjustified.... The executive branch has...traditionally been reluctant to give Congress access to its policy-planning documents at an early enough stage to be significant.... The result is virtually to deny Congress effective access to the policy-making process until it has been completed."[155]

Use of its own professional staff is one method whereby Congress can obtain information. In 1969 and 1970, the newly created Senate Foreign Relations Subcommittee on U.S. Security Agreements and Commitments Abroad sent a two-man team on fact-finding missions to 25 countries. The staff

investigations, followed by detailed, closed-door hearings, revealed a host of U.S. commitments—some express, some implied, some secret, some not—which might lead, in Wilcox's words, to U.S. involvement "in a thousand ways in countries around the world."[156] The committee's probe revealed that the Johnson administration had agreed to special payments for Filipino, Thai and Korean troops in Vietnam. There also were secret military contingency plans with Thailand and previously undisclosed U.S. participation in the war in Laos.[157] (The hearings on Laos were published in heavily censored form.)

Concluding his discussion of "the cost of secrecy," Berger commented: "With all its shortcomings...Congress yet has one great redeeming feature: it is the national forum of debate.... Whether the people will be swayed is not so important as that they should have the opportunity to hear opposition views, to have an informed choice of options, to be alerted to possible consequences of massive commitments rather than to have commitments saddled on them by secret one-man decisions."[158]

"Restraining the secrecy system would not automatically restore a congressional voice in foreign policy," wrote Schlesinger. "But it would at least deprive Congress of a favorite alibi: that, because it did not have the facts, it had no choice but to let Presidents make the decisions."[159]

Footnotes

1. For a general discussion of legislative-executive antagonism, see Edward S. Corwin, *The President: Office and Powers, 1787-1957* (New York, 1957), Chapter V.
2. On the views of Madison and Hamilton, see Arthur M. Schlesinger Jr., *The Imperial Presidency* (Houghton-Mifflin Co., 1973), pp. 18-20; Louis Fisher, *President and Congress* (The Free Press, 1972), pp. 32-33; Raoul Berger, *Executive Privilege* (Harvard University Press, 1974), pp. 135-38; Bryant Putney, "Participation by Congress in Control of Foreign Policy," *Editorial Research Reports*, Nov. 9, 1939, pp. 342-43; and Corwin, *The President: Office and Powers*, pp. 178-84.
3. Louis Henkin, *Foreign Affairs and the Constitution* (W. W. Norton & Co. Inc., 1972), pp. 76-80.
4. See Joseph P. Harris, *The Advice and Consent of the Senate* (Greenwood Press, 1968), Chapter XVI.
5. For a general discussion, see C. Herman Pritchett, *The American Constitution* (McGraw-Hill Book Co. Inc., 1959), pp. 360-62.
6. For an account of the historical development, see Schlesinger, *The Imperial Presidency*; Rexford G. Tugwell, *The Enlargement of the Presidency* (Doubleday and Co. Inc., 1960), and Corwin, *The President: Office and Powers*.
7. Francis O. Wilcox, *Congress, the Executive and Foreign Policy* (Harper and Row, 1971), p. 8.
8. Congressional Quarterly, *Congress and the Nation, 1969-1972*, Vol. III, pp. 857-59, 866-68; and Fisher, *President and Congress*, pp. 199-200.
9. For details on military sales controls, see Congressional Quarterly, 1975 *Weekly Report*, pp. 2817-19.
10. Wilcox, *Congress, the Executive and Foreign Policy*, p. 5. Writing in 1973, however, Schlesinger questions this assertion; following the Vietnam War, he said, "The assertions of sweeping and unilateral presidential authority remained official doctrine in foreign affairs." (*The Imperial Presidency*, p. ix).
11. Edward A. Kolodziej, "Congress and Foreign Policy: The Nixon Years," in Harvey C. Mansfield Sr., ed., *Congress Against the President* (Praeger Publishers, 1975), p. 168.
12. For a general discussion of the treaty power, see Schlesinger, *The Imperial Presidency*, pp. 79-85; Henkin, *Foreign Affairs and the Constitution*, pp. 130-73; George H. Haynes, *The Senate of the United States* (Houghton-Mifflin Co., 1938), Chapter XII.

13. Haynes, *The Senate,* pp. 629-33; Daniel S. Cheever and H. Field Haviland Jr., *American Foreign Policy and the Separation of Powers* (Harvard University Press, 1952).
14. On the range of commitments, see Roland A. Paul, *American Military Commitments Abroad* (Rutgers University Press, 1973); and Congressional Quarterly, *Global Defense*.
15. Haynes, *The Senate,* p. 574.
16. *Ibid.,* pp. 573-75; and Charles Warren, *The Making of the Constitution* (Little-Brown, 1928), pp. 651-58.
17. Buel W. Patch, "Treaties and Domestic Law," *Editorial Research Reports*, March 28, 1952, p. 247.
18. *Ibid.,* p. 241; and Henkin, *Foreign Affairs and the Constitution,* pp. 156-62.
19. Haynes, *The Senate,* p. 575.
20. *Ibid.,* p. 574; and Warren, *The Making of the Constitution,* p. 658.
21. Haynes, *The Senate,* pp. 62-66.
22. *Ibid.,* pp. 583-84.
23. *Ibid.,* p. 692.
24. Harris, *The Advice and Consent of the Senate,* p. 282.
25. Background, see Haynes, *The Senate,* p. 583.
26. *Ibid.,* p. 584.
27. *Ibid.,* p. 591; and F. M. Brewer, "Advice and Consent of the Senate," *Editorial Research Reports*, June 1, 1943, p. 348.
28. Haynes, *The Senate,* pp. 586-87, 600.
29. Quoted in Haynes, *The Senate,* p. 581.
30. For a discussion of the decision, see Schlesinger, *The Imperial Presidency*, pp. 100-4; Pritchett, *The American Constitution*, pp. 356-57; and Louis W. Koenig, *The Chief Executive* (Harcourt, Brace and World Inc., 1964), Chapter 9, for a discussion of the Prrresident as "chief diplomat."
31. Haynes, *The Senate,* p. 529.
32. *Ibid.,* p. 593.
33. *Ibid.,* p. 595; Harris, *The Advice and Consent of the Senate,* p. 285; and Brewer, "Advice and Consent of the Senate," p. 350.
34. Jefferson to Madison, March 15, 1798; quoted in Brewer, "Advice and Consent of the Senate," p. 350.
35. Jefferson to Genet, Nov. 22, 1793; quoted in Brewer, "Advice and Consent of the Senate," p. 350.
36. *Ibid.*
37. *Ibid.,* p. 352.

38. *Ibid.*

39. Haynes, *The Senate*, p. 596.

40. Brewer, "Advice and Consent of the Senate," p. 353.

41. Haynes, *The Senate*, p. 597.

42. Brewer, "Advice and Consent of the Sente," p. 354.

43. Wilcox, *Congress, The Executive and Foreign Policy*, p. 55.

44. See Haynes, *The Senate*, pp. 602 ff. for a discussion.

45. *Ibid.*, p. 666.

46. *Ibid.*, pp. 636-39.

47. Senate Foreign Relations Committee, *Background Information on the Committee on Foreign Relations*, U.S. Senate (U.S. Government Printing Office, 1975), p. 24.

48. Haynes, *The Senate*, pp. 665-70.

49. *Ibid.*, pp. 663-64.

50. Senate Foreign Relations Committee, *Background Information*, pp. 24-25.

51. Haynes, *The Senate*, pp. 604-6.

52. *Ibid.*, p. 608.

53. *Ibid.*, p. 657.

54. *Ibid.*, p. 609.

55. *Ibid.*

56. For a discussion of the Connally reservation, see Congressional Quarterly, *Congress and the Nation, 1945-1964*, Vol. I, pp. 98, 126.

57. Senate Foreign Relations Committee, *Background Information*, p. 24.

58. On proposed changes, see Brewer, "Advice and Consent of the Senate," and "The Treaty Power," *Editorial Research Reports*, Jan. 18, 1943; and Cheever and Haviland, *American Foreign Policy*, pp. 178-85.

59. Brewer, "The Treaty Power," p. 44.

60. *Ibid.*

61. *Ibid.*, pp. 40-41.

62. *Congress and the Nation*, Vol. I, p. 98.

63. On the Bricker Amendment, see *ibid.*, pp. 110-12, 119.

64. For a general discussion of executive agreements, see Corwin, *The President: Office and Powers*, pp. 204-17; Schlesinger, *The Imperial Presidency*, pp. 86-88; Berger, *Executive Privilege*, pp. 140-62; Henkin, *Foreign Affairs and the Constitution*, pp. 176-86. For legislative proposals, see Congressional Quarterly, *1975 Weekly Report*, pp. 1712 ff.

65. Haynes, *The Senate*, pp. 639-51; Henkin, p. 428; Schlesinger, p. 103.

66. The Rush-Bagot Agreement, which limited arms on the Great Lakes, the Boxer rebellion settlements, and the open door policy were executive agreements. See Haynes, *The Senate*, p. 644 and Henkin, *Foreign Affairs and the Constitution*, pp. 179, 428.

67. Senate Judiciary Subcommittee on the Separation of Powers, *Congressional Oversight of Executive Agreements* (U.S. Government Printing Office, 1973), p. 3.

68. Congressional Quarterly, *1970 Almanac*, p. 1008; Paul, *American Military Commitments Abroad.*

69. Congressional Quarterly, *1972 Almanac*, p. 619.

70. For Senate action on the League, see Haynes, *The Senate*, pp. 694-703; Cheever and Haviland, *American Foreign Policy*, Chapter 7; Buel W. Patch, "American Policy on the League of Nations and the World Court," *Editorial Research Reports*, Jan. 2, 1935; and Bryant Putney, "Participation by Congress in Control of Foreign Policy," *Editorial Research Reports*, Nov. 9, 1939.

71. On the United Nations, see Cheever and Haviland, *American Foreign Policy*, p. 97; *Congress and the Nation*, Vol. I, pp. 93-98; and Corwin, *The President: Office and Powers*, pp. 217-26.

72. For background, see Cheever and Haviland, Chapter 11, *Congress and the Nation*, Vol. I, p. 103; and Congressional Quarterly, *Global Defense*, pp. 29-32.

73. *Congress and the Nation*, Vol. I, pp. 134-36.

74. Congressional Quarterly, *Congress and the Nation, 1965-1968*, Vol. II, pp. 104-6.

75. Congressional Quarterly, *Congress and the Nation*, Vol. III, pp. 893-97; *1972 Almanac*, pp. 622-27; *1975 Weekly Report*, pp. 2583-88.

76. Congressional Quarterly, *1974 Weekly Report*, p. 2506.

77. For a discussion of convention proceedings, see Corwin, *The President: Office and Powers*, pp. 194 ff; and Berger, *Executive Privilege*, pp. 65 ff.

78. *Ibid.*

79. *Ibid.*, p. 64.

80. *Ibid.*, p. 63.

81. *Ibid.*, p. 64.

82. *Ibid.*, p. 60.

83. Fisher, *President and Congress*, p. 175.

84. Pritchett, *The American Constitution*, pp. 357-58.

85. Fisher, *President and Congress*, p. 179.

86. Cited in Berger, *Executive Privilege*, p. 75.

87. Cited in Fisher, *President and Congress*, p. 177.

88. Berger, *Executive Privilege*, pp. 76-77; Schlesinger, *The Imperial Presidency*, p. 51.

89. Berger, *Executive Privilege*, p. 75; Schlesinger, *The Imperial Presidency*, p. 21.

90. Berger, *Executive Privilege*, p. 82.

91. Senate Foreign Relations Committee, *Hearings on War Powers Legislation*, 91st Congress, 1st session, 1971 (U.S. Government Printing Office, 1972), p. 254.

92. Berger, *Executive Privilege*, p. 92.

93. On the War of 1812, see Kendrick Lee, "Congress and the Conduct of War," *Editorial Research Reports*, Aug. 24, 1942; and Thomas F. Eagleton, *War and Presidential Power* (Liveright, 1974), pp. 22-24.

94. On the Mexican War, see Lee, "Congress and the Conduct of War," pp. 131-33; Bryant Putney, "Participation by Congress in Control of Foreign Policy," *Editorial Research Reports*, Nov. 9, 1939, pp. 343-44; Tugwell, *The Enlargement of the Presidency*, pp. 119-22, 125-30; and Schlesinger, *The Imperial Pressidency*, pp. 39-43.

95. Onthe Spanish-American War, see Putney, "Participation by Congress," p. 346; Haynes, *The Senate*, pp. 673-674.

96. Fisher, *President and Congress*, p. 187.

97. Corwin, *The President: Office and Powers*, p. 237.

98. *Ibid.*

99. Fisher, *President and Congress*, p. 189.

100. Corwin, *The President: Office and Powers*, p. 242.

101. Fisher, *President and Congress*, p. 190.

102. *Ibid.*, p. 193.

103. Congressional Quarterly, *1973 Almanac*, p. 779.

104. *Ibid.*, p. 778. The Senate in 1974 passed a bill terminating four emergencies. The House passed a similar bill in 1975.

105. For a discussion of Wilson's war powers, see Tugwell, *The Enlargement of the Presidency*, pp. 382-86; Schlesinger, *The Imperial Presidency*, pp. 92 ff; Corwin, *The President: Office and Powers*, pp. 234-37; and Richard L. Worsnop, "War Powers of the President," *Editorial Research Reports*, March 14, 1966.

106. Tugwell, *The Enlargement of the Presidency*, p. 194.

107. *Ibid.*, pp. 362-66; Fisher, *President and Congress*, p. 188; Worsnop, "War Powers of the President," p. 194.

108. For a discussion of Roosevelt's powers, see Schlesinger, *The Imperial Presidency*, Chapter 5; Worsnop, pp. 195-96; Tugwell, *The Enlargement of the Presidency*, pp. 439-56; and Corwin, *The President: Office and Powers*, pp. 234 ff.

109. On the Ludlow amendment, see Buel W. Patch, "The Power to Declare War," *Editorial Research Reports*, Jan. 6, 1938, pp. 1-18, and pp. 398-99.

110. Schlesinger, *The Imperial Presidency*, p.111.

111. Fisher, *President and Congress*, p. 193.

112. Schlesinger, *The Imperial Presidency*, p. 135.

113. *Ibid.*, p. 181.

114. *Ibid.*, p. 193.

115. For a discussion of the Korean War, see Schlesinger, Chapter 6; and James A. Robinson, *Congress and Foreign Policy Making* (Dorsey Press, 1962), pp. 48-50.

116. Berger, *Executive Privilege*, p. 76.

117. Fisher, *President and Congress*, p. 194.

118. *Ibid.*; and Eagleton, *War and Presidential Power*, pp. 70-72.

119. Congressional Quarterly, *Global Defense*, pp. 72-73.

120. Berger *Executive Privilege*, p. 111.

121. For discussion of Vietnam and additional references, see

Congressional Quarterly, 1975 *Weekly Report*, pp. 842-46.

122. For a discussion of anti-war proposals, see Eagleton, *War and Presidential Power*, pp. 107 ff.

123. Quoted in Berger, *Executive Privilege*, p. 87.

124. On the Formosa resolution, see *Congress and the Nation*, Vol. I, p. 114; *Global Defense*, pp. 3, 27, 49.

125. Congressional Quarterly, 1971 *Almanac*, p. 366.

126. On the Middle East doctrine, see Congressional Quarterly, *The Middle East*.

127. *Congress and the Nation*, Vol. I, pp. 120 ff.

128. Fisher, *President and Congress*, p. 179; text of message, 1958 *Almanac*, p. 600.

129. Congressional Quarterly, 1962 *Almanac*, p. 346.

130. On Cuban policy, see *Congress and the Nation*, Vol. I, pp. 132-34; *Global Defense*, pp. 24, 51, 74; Congressional Quarterly, 1962 *Almanac*, pp. 331-40.

131. Eagleton, *War and Presidential Power*, p. 78.

132. Cited in Fisher, *President and Congress*, p. 179. For a discussion, see Wilcox, *Congress, the Executive and Foreign Policy*, pp. 22-24.

133. For a discussion of the resolution, see *ibid.*, pp. 25-32; Eagleton, *War and Presidential Power*, pp. 80-103; Congressional Quarterly, 1964 *Almanac*, pp. 331-32; 1970 *Almanac*, pp. 941, 948-53.

134. Congressional Quarterly, 1966 *Almanac*, p. 388; Joseph C. Goulden, *Truth is the First Casualty* (Rand McNally and Co., 1969), p. 178.

135. *Ibid.*, pp. 190-91.

136. Berger, *Executive Privilege*, p. 85.

137. *Congress and the Nation*, Vol. III, p. 947.

138. Congressional Quarterly, 1967 *Almanac*, p. 949.

139. *Congress and the Nation*, Vol. III, pp. 946-48.

140. On the war powers bill, see Congressional Quarterly, 1973 *Almanac*, pp. 905-17; Schlesinger, *The Imperial Presidency*, pp. 301-07; Eagleton, *War and Presidential Power*.

141. On the national commitments resolution, see *Global Defense*, pp. 79-84; Fisher, *President and Congress*, pp. 225-27.

142. Congressional Quarterly, 1971 *Almanac*, p. 380; 1972 *Almanac*, p. 842.

143. Congressional Quarterly, 1975 *Almanac*, pp. 310-11.

144. Quoted in Schlesinger, *The Imperial Presidency*, p. 332.

145. *Ibid.*, p. 335.

146. *Ibid.*, p. 339.

147. *Ibid.*, p. 338.

148. Quoted in Schlesinger, p. 354.

149. *Ibid.*, p. 359.

150. For details, see Congressional Quarterly, 1972 *Almanac*, pp. 858-62.

151. Congressional Quarterly, 1973 *Almanac*, p. 787.

152. Berger, *Executive Privilege*, pp. 279-80.

153. *Ibid.*, p. 284.

154. Senate Foreign Relations Committee, *Hearings on War Powers Legislation*, 1971, p. 43.

155. Wilcox, *Congress, the Executive and Foreign Policy*, pp. 48-49.

156. *Ibid.*, p. 136.

157. See Paul, *American Military Commitments Abroad*.

158. Berger, *Executive Privilege*, p. 158.

159. Schlesinger, *The Imperial Presidency*, p. 372.

Selected Bibliography

Books

Berger, Raoul. *Executive Privilege*. Cambridge: Harvard University Press, 1974. (Extensive bibliography.)

Butler, Charles H. *The Treaty Making Power of the United States*. New York: Banks Law Publishing Co., 1902.

Carroll, Holbert N. *The House of Representatives and Foreign Affairs*. Boston: Little, Brown & Co., 1966.

Cheever, Daniel S. and Haviland, H. Field Jr. *American Foreign Policy and the Separation of Powers*. Cambridge: Harvard University Press, 1952.

Congressional Quarterly. *Global Defense*. Washington, D.C.: September 1969.

Corwin, Edward S. *The President: Office and Powers, 1787-1957*. New York: New York University Press, 1957.

Crandall, Samuel B. *Treaties, Their Making and Enforcement*. New York: Columbia University Press, 1904.

Dahl, Robert A. *Congress and Foreign Policy*. New York: Harcourt, Brace & Co., 1950.

Dangerfield, Royden J. *In Defense of the Senate*. Norman, Okla.: University of Oklahoma Press, 1933.

Dennison, Eleanor E. *The Senate Foreign Relations Committee*. Stanford: Stanford University Press, 1942.

Eagleton, Thomas J. *War and Presidential Power*. New York: Liveright, 1974. (Extensive bibliography.)

Farnsworth, David N. *The Senate Committee on Foreign Relations*. Urbana: University of Illinois Press, 1961.

The Federalist Papers. Introduction by Clinton Rossiter. New York: Mentor, 1961.

Fisher, Louis. *President and Congress*. New York: The Free Press, 1972.

Fleming, Denna F. *The Treaty Veto of the American Senate*. New York: G. P. Putnam's Sons, 1930.

Harden, Ralston. *The Senate and Treaties 1789-1817*. New York: Macmillan Co., 1920.

Harris, Joseph P. *The Advice and Consent of the Senate*. Westport, Conn.: Greenwood Press, 1968.

Haynes, George H. *The Senate of the United States: Its History and Practice*. 2 vols. Boston: Houghton, Mifflin Co., 1938.

Henkin, Louis. *Foreign Affairs and the Constitution*. New York: W. W. Norton & Co., 1972.

Kolodziej, Edward A. "Congress and Foreign Policy: The Nixon Years." In *Congress Against the President*. Edited by Harvey C. Mansfield Sr. New York: Praeger Publishers, 1975.

Lehman, John. *The Executive, Congress, and Foreign Policy*. New York: Praeger Publishers, 1976.

Paul, Roland A. *American Military Commitments Abroad*. New Brunswick, N.J.: Rutgers University Press, 1973. (Extensive bibliography.)

Pritchett, C. Herman. *The American Constitution*. New York: McGraw-Hill Book Co. Inc., 1959.

Robinson, James A. *Congress and Foreign Policy Making*. Homewood, Ill.: Dorsey Press, 1962.

Schlesinger, Arthur M. Jr. *The Imperial Presidency*. Boston: Houghton, Mifflin Co., 1973.

Stennis, John C. *The Role of Congress in Foreign Policy*. Washington, D.C.: American Enterprise Institute for Public Policy Research, 1971.

Tugwell, Rexford G. *The Enlargement of the Presidency*. New York: Doubleday and Co. Inc., 1960.

Warren, Charles. *The Making of the Constitution*. Boston: Little, Brown & Co., 1928.

Westphal, C. F. *The House Committee on Foreign Affairs*. New York: Columbia University Press, 1942.

Wilcox, Francis O. *Congress, The Executive and Foreign Policy*. New York: Harper and Row, 1971.

Articles

Berry, John M. "Foreign Policy Making and the Congress." *Editorial Research Reports,* April 19, 1967, pp. 281-300.

Brewer, F. M. "Advice and Consent of the Senate." *Editorial Research Reports,* June 1, 1943, pp. 341-56; "The Treaty Power." *Editorial Research Reports,* Jan. 18, 1943, pp. 37-54.

"Congress and Foreign Relations." *Annals of the American Academy of Political and Social Science,* September 1953.

"Congress, the President and the Power to Commit Forces to Combat." *Harvard Law Review,* June 1968, pp. 1771-805.

Eagleton, Thomas F. "Congress and the War Power." *Missouri Law Review,* Winter 1972, pp. 1-32.

Gould, James W. "The Origins of the Senate Committee on Foreign Relations, 1789-1816." *Western Political Quarterly,* September 1959, pp. 670-82.

Humphrey, Hubert H. "The Senate in Foreign Policy." *Foreign Affairs,* July 1959.

Lee, Kendrick. "Congress and the Conduct of War." *Editorial Research Reports,* Aug. 24, 1942, pp. 125-40.

Manley, John F. "The Rise of Congress in Foreign Policy-Making." *Annals of the American Academy of Political and Social Science,* September 1971, pp. 60-70.

Patch, Buel W. "American Policy on the League of Nations and the World Court." *Editorial Research Reports,* Jan. 2, 1935, pp. 1-24; "The Power to Declare War." *Editorial Research Reports,* Jan. 6, 1938, pp. 1-18; "Treaties and Domestic Law." *Editorial Research Reports,* March 28, 1952, pp. 239-56.

"Presidential vs. Congressional War-Making Powers." *Boston University Law Review,* Special Issue, 1970, pp. 5-116.

Putney, Bryant. "Participation by Congress in Control of Foreign Policy." *Editorial Research Reports,* Nov. 9, 1939, pp. 337-55.

Reed, R. P. "Foreign Policy and the Initiation of War: The Congress and the Presidency in the Dispute Over War Powers." *Potomac Review,* Winter 1973, pp. 1-29.

Schlesinger, Arthur M. Jr. "Congress and the Making of American Foreign Policy." *Foreign Affairs,* October 1972, pp. 78-113.

Worsnop, Richard L. "War Powers of the President." *Editorial Research Reports,* March 14, 1966, pp. 181-200.

Government Publications

U.S. Congress. House. Committee on Foreign Affairs. *Background Information on the Use of United States Armed Forces in Foreign Countries.* (1970 revision by the Foreign Affairs Division, Legislative Reference Service, Library of Congress), 91st Cong., 2nd sess., 1970.

——. *Concerning the War Powers of Congress and the President.* H. Rept. 91-1547 to Accompany H. J. Res. 1355, 91st Cong., 2nd sess., 1970.

——. *Concerning the War Powers of Congress and the President.* H. Rept. 92-1302 to Accompany S. 2956, 92nd Cong., 2nd sess., 1972.

——. *Congress, the President and the War Powers: Hearings.* 91st Cong., 2nd sess., 1970.

——. *War Powers Legislation. Hearings before the Subcommittee on National Security Policy and Scientific Developments.* 93rd Cong., 1st sess., 1973.

U.S. Congress. Senate. Committee on Foreign Relations. *Background Information on the Committee on Foreign Relations, United States Senate.* 3rd rev. ed., 94th Cong., 1st sess., 1975.

——. *Documents Relating to the War Power of Congress, the President's Authority as Commander-in-Chief and the War in Indochina.* 91st Cong., 2nd sess., 1970.

——. *Hearings before the Subcommittee on U.S. Security Agreements and Commitments Abroad.* 91st Cong., 1969-1970.

——. *National Commitments.* S. Rept. 90-797 to Accompany S. Res. 187, 90th Cong., 1st sess., 1967.

——. *National Commitments.* S. Rept., 91-129 to Accompany S. Res. 85, 91st Cong., 1st sess., April 16, 1969.

——. *Termination of Southeast Asia Resolution.* S. Rept. 91-872 to Accompany S. Con. Res. 64, 91st Cong., 2nd sess., May 15, 1970.

——. *War Powers.* S. Rept. 92-606 to Accompany S. 2956, 92nd Cong., 2nd sess., 1972.

——. *War Powers Legislation: Hearings.* 92nd Cong., 1st sess., 1971.

——. *War Powers Legislation: Hearings.* 93rd Cong., 1st sess., April 11-12, 1973.

U.S. Congress. Senate. Committee on the Judiciary. Subcommittee on Separation of Powers. *Congressional Oversight of Executive Agreements.* S. Rept. to Accompany S. 1472, committee print, 93rd Cong., 1st sess., 1973.

Control of the
Seat of Government

The Founding Fathers included among the powers of Congress the exclusive right to legislate for the nation's capital. But striking the appropriate balance between federal and local interests has been the continuing dilemma for the residents of the seat of government. Should the government exercise direct control over municipal affairs in the District of Columbia or should it allow a locally elected government to handle purely local matters?

The Constitution is silent on the matter. Article I, Section 8 reads, in part: "The Congress shall have Power...To exercise exclusive Legislation in all Cases whatsoever, over such District (not exceeding 10 Miles square), as may, by Cession of particular States, and the Acceptance of Congress, become the Seat of Government of the United States...."

The phrase "exclusive Legislation" has been used by self-government opponents to justify continued congressional control over the government.

But home rule supporters argue that the framers of the Constitution did not mean to preclude self-government. They point to James Madison's writings in No. 43 of *The Federalist* to illustrate their contention that the drafters took self-government as a matter of course.

"The indispensable necessity of complete authority at the seat of Government carries its own evidence with it.... Without it not only the public authority might be insulted and its proceedings interrupted with impunity, but a dependence of the members of the general government on the state comprehending the seat of the Government for protection in the exercise of their duty might bring on the national councils as imputation of awe or influence...dishonorable to the Government...." Later in the essay Madison wrote: "A municipal legislature for local purposes, derived from their own suffrages, will of course be allowed them...."[1]

Home rule advocates felt that the Founding Fathers wanted congressional control only to avoid conflicts between local and federal interests, and that where no conflict existed District citizens could control their own government.

A 1953 Supreme Court decision lent support to self-government proponents. In *District of Columbia v. John R. Thompson Co.* (346 U.S. 100) which sustained the validity of anti-segregation ordinances adopted by the District's territorial government in 1872-73, Justice William O. Douglas said: "It would seem then that...there is no con-

stitutional barrier to the delegation by Congress to the District of Columbia of full legislative power, subject of course to constitutional limitations to which all lawmaking is subservient and subject also to the power of Congress at any time to revise, alter or revoke the authority granted."

Limited self-government was granted the District as soon as the federal government moved from Philadelphia to Washington in 1800 and it endured for nearly 70 years. Then, after a brief experiment with a territorial form of government, Congress took back into its own hands virtually all governing authority for the growing city.

A century later, in 1973, Congress again gave local residents limited control over their own affairs. By mid-1976, the experiment in home rule had been in effect for little more than a year and relations between the locally elected government and its congressional overseers had not always been smooth. But although Congress did not appear ready to grant full home rule to District residents, it did not seem anxious to reassume complete control of the city.

A parallel goal of many District residents has been voting representation in Congress. The Constitution does not speak directly to that matter and the intent of the Founding Fathers is unclear. Article I, Section 2 reads: "The House of Representatives shall be composed of Members chosen every second Year by the People of the several States...." Article I, Section 3 reads: "The Senate of the United States shall be composed of two Senators from each State...."

To answer this, advocates of D.C. congressional representation cited another section of *The Federalist* No. 43: "[T]he inhabitants [of the state areas to be ceded to the federal government] will find sufficient inducements of interest to become willing parties to the cession; as they have had their voice in the election of the government which is to exercise authority over them...."[2]

Opponents, however, claim this passage refers only to the time before cession.

Although Congress has occasionally become involved in more mundane District matters, the overriding concern and controversy have centered on these two related issues.

Creation of District of Columbia

Before there was a District of Columbia, and before the Constitution was adopted, the seat of government of the

Seats of Government

Prior to the selection of Washington, D.C., as the permanent seat of the federal government, Congress met in eight cities in four states. Following are the seats of government under the Continental Congress, the Articles of Confederation and the Constitution:

Continental Congress

Philadelphia	Sept. 5, 1774-Dec. 12, 1776
Baltimore	Dec. 20, 1776-March 4, 1777
Philadelphia	March 5, 1777-Sept. 18, 1777
Lancaster, Pa.	Sept. 27, 1777
York, Pa.	Sept. 30, 1777-June 27, 1778
Philadelphia	July 2, 1778-March 1, 1781

Articles of Confederation

Philadelphia	March 2, 1781-June 21, 1783
Princeton	June 30, 1783-Nov. 4, 1783
Annapolis	Nov. 26, 1783-June 3, 1784
Trenton	Nov. 1, 1784-Dec. 24, 1784
New York	Jan. 11, 1785-March 2, 1789

Constitution

New York	March 4, 1789-Aug. 12, 1790
Philadelphia	Dec. 6, 1790-May 14, 1800
Washington, D.C.	Nov. 17, 1800-

Source: *Biographical Directory of the American Congress, 1774-1971,* S. Doc. 92-8, 92nd Cong., 1st sess. (U.S. Government Printing Office, 1971).

United States was located wherever the Continental Congress met.[3] There were eight such places: Philadelphia, Lancaster and York in Pennsylvania; Trenton and Princeton in New Jersey; New York City; and Baltimore and Annapolis in Maryland. The Continental Congress made a number of abortive attempts to agree on a permanent site for the capital, including a decision on Oct. 7, 1783, to establish a federal town on the Delaware River and a decision 10 days later to set aside Georgetown, on the Potomac River, as a second federal town. *(Seats of government, above)*

Decision on the Site

In the light of the constitutional provision on the seat of government, the general assemblies of Maryland and Virginia on Dec. 19, 1791,[4] and Dec. 3, 1789, adopted resolutions offering up to 10 miles square of any portion of their respective states for use in laying out the federal city. But opposition to a site in the Maryland-Virginia area developed in the New England and Middle Atlantic states, where a more northerly site was preferred.

On Sept. 22, 1789, the House passed a bill naming a site on the Susquehanna River in Pennsylvania as the permanent capital. The Senate on Sept. 24 amended the bill to make Germantown, Pa., the permanent location. The conflicting bills were lost in the rush as the First Session of the First Congress headed for adjournment on Sept. 29. In the ensuing months, southern advocates of a site on the Potomac River rallied their forces.

Meanwhile, another North-South dispute was brewing, and it provided an ingredient for compromise on location of the seat of government. Northerners favored assumption by the federal government of debts which the states had incurred as a result of their participation in the Revolutionary War. These debts in the late 1780s were largely in the form of bonds which northern financiers had bought up at low prices. Since Virginia had already paid its debts of this kind, many Virginians, along with other southerners, objected to assumption of the state debts by the national government. But in mid-May 1790, Secretary of State Thomas Jefferson, Secretary of the Treasury Alexander Hamilton (who favored the "assumption" proposal), and two members of Congress from Virginia met around Jefferson's supper table in New York and agreed that, in return for Hamilton's aligning of northern support for a southern capital, the Virginians would vote for assumption.

An Act of Congress of July 16, 1790, provided that the seat of government should be located in Philadelphia from 1790 to 1800 and thereafter in "a district...on the river Potomac." And by an Act of Aug. 4, 1790, the federal government assumed the states' Revolutionary War debts.

Definition of the Boundaries

The July 16th act accepted the offers of land from Maryland and Virginia for a federal district and bounded it as follows: "...a district of territory, not exceeding ten miles square, to be located as hereafter directed on the river Potomac," at some place between the mouths of the Eastern Branch (now called the Anacostia River) and Conococheague Creek (which empties into the upper Potomac some 70 miles north near Williamsport, Md.). Three commissioners, appointed by President Washington and serving under his direction, were to survey the area and lay out the district's boundaries within those limits.

The exact boundaries preferred by Washington and the commissioners did not accord with the specifications. The 1790 law required that the district be located wholly to the west of the mouth of Maryland's Eastern Branch. But the area selected lay in part to the east of that stream and extended south along the Potomac to a point opposite Alexandria, Virginia. The area included the latter settlement and a slice of Virginia stretching northward from Alexandria along the west side of the Potomac to a point opposite Georgetown, a settlement that was also included in the district.

By an Act of March 3, 1791, Congress obligingly redefined the area to accord with the preferences of the President and the commissioners. Washington on March 30, 1791, issued a proclamation specifying the boundaries of the federal district. The boundaries formed a square, 10 miles on each side, comprising the portion on the Maryland side of the Potomac which is the present District of Columbia and a portion on the Virginia side that completed the square. *(Map, next page)*

Deal With the Landowners

It was understood by all parties that what Maryland and Virginia were ceding was governmental jurisdiction only. Ownership of land and buildings in the ceded area was to remain in the hands of deedholders. Land for governmental purposes in the new district was actually acquired through an arrangement which Washington, Jefferson and Madison negotiated with landowners in the general area before the decision on an exact site for the federal capital had been made. Washington himself conducted the principal talks with the landowners in a Georgetown tavern in the early part of 1791. On March 30 of that year, he obtained the owners' agreement to a plan under which they might expect to profit handsomely by ceding their land even though the government would not be required to levy taxes to pay for it. The plan provided:

1. Each landowner would cede one-half of his land to the federal government.

2. The government would keep that portion of the ceded land needed for public buildings, streets and parks, and would sell the remainder.

3. The landowners who had ceded one-half of their holdings would benefit in two ways: First, they would receive $66.67 an acre from the government for those portions of the ceded land which the government decided to keep for public buildings, streets and parks; secondly, the value of the one-half of their holdings which they did not sell to the government was expected to rise because of its proximity to the seat of government.

4. The government would benefit in that the money needed to pay for the acreage selected for buildings, streets and parks would have entered its coffers through the sale to private persons of those portions of the ceded land which it did not need. The Treasury stood to benefit also from contributions of $120,000 and $72,000 pledged by Virginia and Maryland, respectively, toward construction of public buildings in the new capital.

Naming the City

President Washington in March 1791 appointed Pierre Charles L'Enfant to prepare a plan of the new capital city and to participate in execution of the plan. Washington referred to the place as "the federal territory" as well as "the seat of government." The commissioners whom he had appointed to oversee development of the city called it, in a letter of Sept. 9, 1791, to Major L'Enfant, "the city of Washington" and named the whole district "the Territory of Columbia." Congress formally named the city and the district almost by indirection. An act of Congress approved May 6, 1796, was entitled "An Act Authorizing a Loan for the City of Washington, in the District of Columbia, and for other purposes therein mentioned." The text of the act merely referred to "the said city" and did not mention either the city or the district by name.[5]

L'Enfant's design for the capital city, completed in 1791, was greatly admired as combining features of the arrangement of avenues at Versailles with innovations to meet the special needs of an American capital city. However, in moving to carry out the plan, L'Enfant displayed an overbearing temperament. He repeatedly defied the authority of the commissioners and of the President himself. At one point, without waiting for approval, he had a large private dwelling, still under construction, torn down because it would block a proposed street. And he insisted on proceeding with development of the new city at a pace which would have forced the government into borrowing on a scale it was not prepared to undertake. On Feb. 27, 1792, President Washington asked for his resignation.

After 1800, L'Enfant haunted the halls of Congress, seeking compensation for his plan for the federal city. He claimed $95,500, but was authorized payments totaling less than $3,000. The bulk of that amount was paid, under a court order, to one of L'Enfant's creditors. L'Enfant died in

poverty in 1825. His plan was revived in 1901 and used as a basis for further development of the capital city.

Government's Move to Washington

The Act of July 16, 1790, which established a federal district on the Potomac, stipulated that during the 10 years in which the seat of government would be at Philadelphia a three-man commission should arrange for suitable buildings to accommodate Congress, the President and public offices, and that on the first Monday in December 1800 the government would be transferred to Washington.

Early in 1800 it became clear that the buildings erected in Washington for the government would be ready long before December. Accordingly Congress April 24, 1800, authorized the President to move to the new city after Congress adjourned. The act provided: "That the President of the United States shall be, and hereby is authorized and empowered, to direct the various offices belonging to the several executive departments of the United States, to be removed to the city of Washington, at any time that he shall judge proper, after the adjournment of the present session of Congress...."

The First Session of the Sixth Congress adjourned on May 14, 1800. Later that month, sloops carrying government records from Philadelphia sailed up the Potomac to the new city. President John Adams supervised the opening of government offices in June, and Abigail Adams, according to contemporary records, hung her washing in the East Room of the unfinished White House. The Second Session of the Sixth Congress, the first session of Congress to be held in Washington, convened Nov. 17, 1800, but for lack of a quorum did not actually sit until Nov. 21.

Congress was not in session during the summer of 1814, when British troops invaded Washington and burned the Capitol and other buildings. A special session of Congress convened on Sept. 19 of that year. On Sept. 26, 1814, Rep. Jonathan Fisk (D N.Y.) offered a resolution proposing a committee to study moving the seat of government to a more secure location. The resolution was adopted after a short debate, 72-51.

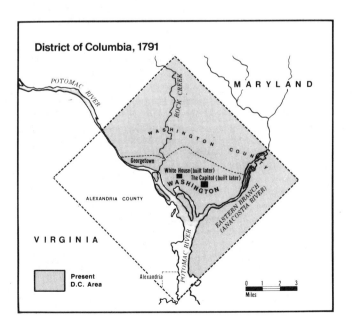

The study committee's Oct. 3 report said that it was "inexpedient to remove the seat of government at this time from the city of Washington." However, Fisk proposed an amendment to substitute the word "expedient" for "inexpedient," and the amendment carried, 69-68, with Speaker Langdon Cheves (D S.C.) casting the tie-breaking vote in favor of moving the government. House debate on the report continued until Oct. 6 when by a 72-71 vote it adopted the amended report and appointed a committee to prepare a bill for transferring the government. The committee bill, brought in Oct. 13, provided for moving the government to another location during the war with Britain.

No alternate sites were mentioned in the bill, but among the possible choices were Philadelphia, New York and Lancaster, Pa. It was widely assumed that such a temporary removal would develop into a permanent absence, and residents of the District of Columbia urged defeat of the measure. Finally on Oct. 15 the debate ended. The House defeated the bill on a 74-83 vote.

Thereafter, continuation of the seat of government in Washington was not seriously questioned, except that after the nation had been extended to the Pacific, a feeble voice was occasionally heard in favor of a more centrally located capital.

Return of Alexandria to Virginia

Congress, by an Act of Feb. 27, 1801, created two counties in the District of Columbia: Washington County on the Maryland side of the Potomac and Alexandria County on the Virginia side. Although the general provisions of the act, especially those concerning courts of law, were set forth for both counties, the two already incorporated communities of the new District—Georgetown and Alexandria—were exempted from the operation of most of these provisions.

In 1840, toward the end of Martin Van Buren's presidency, Washington in particular and the District of Columbia in general became a battleground between Washington's Whig mayor, William W. Seaton, and the Democrats, who were dominant in Congress. Because Seaton had been elected under a system which limited the franchise to property holders, the Democrats in Congress initiated a move to extend the franchise in the District of Columbia to all male adults. In addition, Congress virtually legislated D.C. banks out of existence by forbidding them, in an Act of July 3, 1840, to receive deposits, issue checks, or make loans. Renewal of the banks' charters was not effected until Aug. 25, 1841, after the Whigs had gained a majority in Congress.

When the banks of the District were deprived of their privileges, the city of Georgetown and the rural parts of Washington County, as well as the County of Alexandria, sought retrocession to Maryland and Virginia, respectively. The Maryland legislature was not willing to assume the financial burden of reintegrating Georgetown and the nearby countryside into the state. But much later, on Feb. 3, 1846, the Virginia legislature indicated its willingness to take back all of Alexandria County.

By an Act of July 9, 1846, Congress agreed to retrocede to Virginia the portion of the District of Columbia which lay in that state, if and when the residents of Alexandria County registered their approval. After a referendum resulted in a vote of 763 for retrocession and 222 against, President James K. Polk on Sept. 7, 1846, proclaimed Alexandria County retroceded to Virginia. Since then, the District of Columbia has consisted of about 70 square miles on the Maryland side of the Potomac.

Consolidation of District of Columbia

The three political entities remaining in the District of Columbia after the retrocession of the Virginia section were the city of Washington, Washington County, and the city of Georgetown. The first step toward erasing the inner boundaries of the District was taken in 1861, when Congress, by an act approved Aug. 6, established the Metropolitan Police District of the District of Columbia. The act assigned responsibility for law enforcement throughout the District to a board consisting of five commissioners appointed by the President, "three...from the city of Washington, one from Georgetown and one from the county of Washington at large," plus "the mayors of the cities of Washington and Georgetown, ex officio."

Ten years later, Congress established a territorial government for the District. The Act of Feb. 21, 1871, stipulated that the entire District would be considered as a single entity for municipal purposes. It also repealed the charters of the cities of Washington and Georgetown. The two cities, however, retained their names and the law provided that two members of the D.C. legislative assembly should come from Georgetown and two from the rural areas of the county.

The final consolidation came under the Act of Feb. 11, 1895. Georgetown was merged into the city of Washington and that city was made coterminous with the District of Columbia.

Changing Forms of Government

The Act of Feb. 27, 1801, relating to the government of the District of Columbia provided that the laws of Maryland and Virginia should continue to apply respectively in the portions of the District taken from those states. This situation continued in Alexandria city and county until the retrocession of 1846, and in Georgetown and Washington city and county until 1871. Georgetown, which had been governed before 1801 by a popularly elected council and board of aldermen under an appointed mayor, continued to be so governed thereafter; no change was made until 1830, when Congress authorized Georgetown's citizens to elect their mayor. Washington County, formerly governed by a so-called levy court whose members were appointed by the governor of Maryland, was governed after February 1801 by a levy court whose members were appointed by the President of the United States.

Mayor-Council Government, 1802-71

An Act of Congress approved May 3, 1802, set up a government for the city of Washington consisting of a mayor appointed by the President and a 12-member, two-chamber council elected by the people. Two changes were made in the early years of the century in the direction of fuller self-government. First, an Act of May 4, 1812, authorized the popularly elected council to elect the mayor. Then, by an Act of May 15, 1820, Congress authorized the city's residents themselves to elect the mayor.

Slavery was abolished in the District of Columbia on April 16, 1862. In 1867, three years before ratification of the Fifteenth Amendment to the Constitution (which prohibited voting discrimination on the basis of race), Congress conferred the franchise "without any distinction on account of color or race" on male citizens over 21 years of age who had resided in the District of Columbia for one year. President Andrew Johnson vetoed the franchise bill, but his veto was overridden by the Senate Jan. 7, 1867, and by the House the next day.

Those two events made the city an attractive haven for blacks and by 1870 they comprised about one-third of the District's population. Their numbers increased from 14,216 in 1860 to 43,404 in 1870.[6]

Blacks quickly became influential in city politics. When the first city election under the new suffrage law was held in June 1867, many whites refrained from voting. Blacks voted solidly for the party that had given them freedom and the Republicans controlled both chambers of the council. In 1868, however, whites went back to the polls. Nevertheless, with black support, the Republican candidate for mayor, Sayles J. Bowen, won a narrow victory. The council, however, was split between the parties.

Bowen launched a series of projects that promptly put the District into financial trouble. Whites blamed Bowen for the city's debt, Congress refused to bail him out and in the 1870 elections, even the black electorate deserted him. When Bowen's successor fared no better at solving the city's fiscal ills, Congress looked to another form of government for the District.

Territorial Government, 1871-74

Early in the 1870s, Alexander Shepherd, a Washington native who had risen from the job of plumber's helper to be the city's leading entrepreneur, suggested a modified territorial form of government for the District of Columbia. Acting on this suggestion, Congress enacted a law Feb. 21, 1871, providing for a governor appointed by the President; an elected nonvoting delegate in the House of Representatives; a territorial assembly consisting of an 11-member council appointed by the President and a 22-member house of delegates elected by the people; and a five-member board of public works appointed by the President.

Shepherd was made executive officer of the District of Columbia's board of public works. Under his direction, the city was modernized. Water mains and sewers were laid, streets paved, and parks developed. However, the bill for this work totaled some $20-million, nearly three times the estimate. Shepherd may have been extravagant, but he apparently sought no personal profit. Three congressional investigations into Shepherd's activities found no profit taking by him. As Martha Derthick wrote in *City Politics in Washington, D.C.,* Shepherd made the city bankrupt but he also made it habitable.[7]

The situation was aggravated in September 1873 when President Ulysses S. Grant named Shepherd to the post of governor of the District of Columbia. Aggrieved taxpayers presented a memorial to Congress which led to the appointment in February 1874 of a joint congressional committee to investigate District affairs. The committee, headed by Sen. William B. Allison (R Iowa), asserted in its report in June 1874 that the existing government, ridden by graft and financial mismanagement, was a failure.

The committee recommended that, for a temporary period, the governorship be replaced by an appointed three-member commission; that the assembly, the board of public works, and the post of D.C. delegate in the House of Representatives be abolished; and that Congress perform legislative functions for the District. Thus, representative government in the District would be brought to an end, but supposedly only for the time being. The investigating committee recommended that Congress appoint a new committee to propose a permanent form of government for the District.

Key Dates in D.C. History

July 16, 1790—Legislation establishing the District of Columbia as the permanent seat of the government is enacted.

Nov. 17, 1800—The Second Session of the Sixth Congress, the first session to be held in Washington, is convened, but does not actually sit until Nov. 21.

May 3, 1802—Congress establishes a local government structure for the District, consisting of a mayor appointed by the President and a city council whose lower chamber is popularly elected.

May 4, 1812—Congress authorizes the city council to elect the mayor.

May 15, 1820—Congress authorizes District residents to elect the mayor.

July 9, 1846—Legislation ceding Alexandria County back to Virginia is enacted.

Jan. 8, 1867—Congress gives the right to vote to all males, regardless of race, who are over 21 and have lived in the District for one year. (The Fifteenth Amendment to the Constitution granting that right nationwide was not ratified until March 30, 1870.)

Feb. 21, 1871—Congress revokes home rule; establishes a modified territorial government including one nonvoting delegate to the House of Representatives.

June 20, 1874—Congress revokes territorial government in the District, abolishes the nonvoting delegate office and establishes a three-member commission to govern the District.

Feb. 11, 1895—Legislation effecting the final consolidation of the County of Washington and the cities of Washington and Georgetown into a single governmental unit—the District of Columbia—is enacted.

Aug. 12, 1955—Legislation allowing District residents to elect delegates to the national presidential nominating conventions is enacted.

March 29, 1961—Twenty-third Amendment to the Constitution granting District residents the right to vote for President is ratified.

Aug. 11, 1967—The District government is reorganized to replace the three commissioners with a commissioner, an assistant commissioner and a nine-member city council, all appointed by the President.

April 22, 1968—Legislation allowing District residents to elect school board members is enacted.

Sept. 22, 1970—Legislation authorizing the District of Columbia to elect a nonvoting delegate to the House of Representatives is enacted.

Dec. 24, 1973—Legislation granting District residents limited home rule for the first time since 1871 is enacted.

Jan. 2, 1975—An elected mayor and city council took office Jan. 2, 1975.

March 23, 1976—House rejects proposed constitutional amendment giving the District voting representation in Congress.

Commission Government, 1874-1967

By an act of Congress approved June 20, 1874, the investigating committee's basic recommendations were put into effect. A furor developed when President Grant nominated Shepherd as one of the three new commissioners. The vote in the Senate June 23, 1874, was 6 in favor of confirmation and 32 opposed. A substitute nominee, William Dennison, one-time governor of Ohio, was approved. Shepherd, his fortune gone and his name besmirched, moved with his family to Mexico in 1876.

The joint congressional committee appointed to propose a permanent government for the District of Columbia recommended in 1875 that the commission form of government be continued, but with provision for popular election of three of the eight members of the school board. Action on this proposal in the next three years was prevented by disagreement over the franchise for District residents. Those favoring the franchise were embarrassed by pilfering of government property by popularly elected black members of the D.C. house of delegates when it went out of existence in 1874.

The commission form of government, without any voting rights for District residents, was made permanent from July 1, 1878, by an act of June 11 of that year, which came to be known as the Organic Act of the District of Columbia. Basic to the decision to prolong the commission form of government were two factors: the desire of the business community to assure the District of a sound financial future and hostility to black suffrage. The second factor was of importance not so much among members of Congress as among white residents of the District, many of whom preferred to do without the franchise rather than share it with the black residents.

The new law provided that two of the three commissioners must have resided in the District for at least three years before their appointment. The third commissioner—in charge of public works—was to be a member of the U.S. Army Corps of Engineers. The three commissioners decided which of them served as president.

Congress kept tight control over the manner in which Washington developed. In the late 1890s, construction of a 14-story apartment hotel nine blocks north of the White House (the Cairo, still standing in 1976) caused dismay in Congress, whose members wanted no private buildings in the capital to overshadow government structures. An Act of March 1, 1899, limited new residential buildings to five stories or 60 feet in height; buildings of any kind on a residential street to 90 feet; and buildings on a business street to 130 feet. Church spires could go higher with the approval of the District commissioners. As a rule of thumb, no buildings taller than 12 or 13 stories were allowed. The height limitations on residential buildings were subsequently modified, but the overall top limit of 130 feet was never relaxed.

Commissioner-Council Government 1967-74

The commission form of government prevailed in the District of Columbia for more than 90 years. In the latter part of that period, sentiment in favor of self-government for the national capital gathered substantial support. Although such sentiment reached a high point in the 1960s, moves in Congress to grant home rule to the District were obstructed, mainly by the House District Committee. Accordingly, strategists turned their attention to other ways of effecting changes in the District's government.

President Lyndon B. Johnson's advisers on District affairs persuaded him to make changes in the city's government through his power to submit to Congress government reorganization plans. Such plans take effect unless disapproved by either house within 60 days. On June 1, 1967, Johnson sent to Congress a plan to replace the three-member commission with a single commissioner, an assistant commissioner and a nine-member city council, all to be appointed by the President and confirmed by the Senate. The new commissioner would have the right to veto the council's action, but the council would be empowered to override his veto by a three-fourths vote.

The plan was referred to the Senate and House Committees on Government Operations. But the House District of Columbia Committee took the most active role. One of its subcommittees held hearings on the D.C. government in June, July and early August. The full District Committee on Aug. 7 reported to the House a substitute proposal to continue the three-member Board of Commissioners with a number of changes in the D.C. government, including a provision for popular election of the school board.

However, on Aug. 3 the Government Operations Committee had reported a resolution disapproving the President's plan, with the committee's recommendation that the resolution be rejected. The House followed the committee's recommendation Aug. 9 when it voted down the disapproval resolution, 160-244. Since no disapproval resolution was introduced in the Senate, the reorganization plan went into effect Aug. 11.

President Johnson nominated Walter E. Washington, a black, as commissioner and included five blacks on the council. At that time about 65 per cent of Washington's residents were blacks. The Senate confirmed all of the President's nominees.

Election of Board of Education

District residents received a second concession in 1968. Congress, responding to continued pressures for more self-government for the District and taking account of controversies over Washington's educational programs, authorized direct election of an 11-member D.C. Board of Education. Previously, under an Act of June 20, 1906, the board had been chosen by the judges of the U.S. District Court for the District of Columbia. The new law, signed April 22, 1968, provided that eight of the members of the board should be elected from wards and three at large; that the first election should be held on Nov. 5, 1968, and later elections in November of odd-numbered years; and that the members should serve in staggered four-year terms.

Limited Home Rule Restored

Proposals to restore to Washingtonians the right to elect local officials made little legislative headway or political impact until the 1940s, when evidence of a turn-around in public sentiment became apparent. The Democratic Party platform endorsed home rule as early as 1940; the Republican Party first called for it in 1948.

A bill to grant self-government to the District reached the House floor in 1948 but southern members killed the bill through delaying tactics. And for the next 24 years, southerners on the House District Committee were able to block passage of any home rule legislation.

Between 1949 and 1959 the Senate passed five successive bills providing for home rule, but they all died in the House District Committee. In 1960, supporters of home rule tried to obtain the necessary 219 names on a petition to force a bill out of the House District Committee but they received only 204 signatures.

From 1961 through 1964, the Senate made no serious attempt to pass a home rule bill. On July 22, 1965, the Senate passed a home rule bill, and on Sept. 3 a discharge petition in the House gained the required number of signatures. The House District Committee reported a bill which differed from the Senate's, and it was passed on Sept. 29, 1965. But the House District Committee effectively killed it by voting May 11, 1966, not to send the bill to conference for reconciliation of the Senate and House measures.

Congress was occupied in 1967 with President Johnson's reorganization plan for the D.C. government, and in 1968 with the legislation for election of the D.C. Board of Education. Action on home rule remained in abeyance. President Nixon revived the hopes of home rule advocates the following year. In his message to Congress on District affairs, April 28, 1969, he urged enactment of home rule legislation, saying: "At issue is whether the city will be enabled to take hold of its future: whether its institutions will be reformed so that its government can truly represent its citizens and act upon their needs."[8]

In 1970, the House District Committee relaxed its opposition somewhat, approving a bill allowing three members of the nine-member council to be elected. But the full House did not approve the measure.

In 1971, the Senate passed a home rule measure that expanded the size of the council and provided for the election of the council and the mayor. However, in 1972, largely because of delaying tactics by House District Committee Chairman John L. McMillan (D S.C.) and several Republican opponents, the committee failed repeatedly to obtain a quorum to consider any of the self-government proposals before it, including the Senate bill.

Arguments For and Against Home Rule

Arguments in favor of home rule changed little over the years. Proponents contended that the drafters of the Constitution intended the District to have home rule and pointed out that Washington did govern itself for three-quarters of a century. They also argued that Congress should not have to concern itself with the local housekeeping problems of the District, that local problems would be better solved by the local citizenry who had a stake in the outcome and that the nation's capital should be a showcase of democracy for the United States and the rest of the world.

Traditional arguments advanced by opponents of home rule included the following: Home rule led to bankruptcy in the 1870s; Congress would distribute less money for District needs if it did not control D.C. affairs; an elected D.C. government might subordinate the interests of the federal government to the desires of local citizens; and home rule probably would end the enviable record that Washington had of clean municipal government.

Underlying the arguments against home rule was the issue of race. According to the journalist Stewart Alsop, many white Washingtonians with southern attitudes were afraid that blacks would win control of a local government.[9] That attitude was reinforced by many of the southern members of the House District Committee.[10]

Washington is the largest of American cities with a black majority. The proportion of blacks in the city's population was about 25 per cent in Jefferson's time. A substantial influx of blacks during and after the Civil War lifted the proportion to one-third and the black population remained at about that level until the 1940s when it again started to grow rapidly. According to the 1970 Census, 71 per cent of the District's population was black.

The Turning Point

The 1972 congressional elections erased a major barrier to adoption of home rule legislation by the House. Committee Chairman McMillan was defeated in his district's Democratic primary runoff election. In addition, five other southern Democrats on the committee who generally supported McMillan either lost their bids for re-election or retired.

When the committee convened in 1973, its chairman was Charles C. Diggs Jr. (D Mich.), a black. Only four southern Democrats served on the committee; three of them were freshmen. Diggs reorganized the committee structure, adding a new Government Operations Subcommittee. Chaired by Brock Adams (D Wash.), that panel reported a draft home rule bill to the full committee in late June despite a boycott of the subcommittee's work sessions by its three Republican members.

The full committee followed suit, ordering the home rule bill reported July 31 by a 20-4 vote. "In a country such as ours where the tenets of democracy have reached full flower, it is an anomaly that the people of our nation's capital have virtually no voice in their own government," the committee wrote in its report issued Sept. 11.[11]

As reported, the House bill established an elected mayor and 13-member city council that would have control over how the city spent its revenues, including an annual payment made to the city by the federal government to compensate for revenue lost on nontaxable federal property. The bill also contained several recommendations made by a study commission authorized in 1969. Headed by Rep. Ancher Nelsen (R Minn.), the ranking minority member on the House District Committee, the study commission, after exhaustive research, suggested in early 1973 several steps to make the existing District government more efficient and recommended that the duties performed for the District by several federal and quasi-federal agencies be turned over to the local government.

That version proved too liberal for several non-committee members whose opposition probably would have killed the bill on the floor. Consequently, Diggs agreed to a compromise that was weaker than the original committee version but not as limiting as three substitute bills, one of which most likely would have been adopted had Diggs refused to compromise.

When the compromise version came to the floor Oct. 9, it won crucial support from William H. Natcher (D Ky.), the powerful chairman of the House Appropriations District of Columbia Subcommittee. Natcher's endorsement, it was widely believed, influenced the votes of several other members who otherwise were unlikely to support the bill.[12]

The Diggs compromise retained congressional line-item control over the city's budget, authorized the President to take control over the local police force in an emergency and prohibited the city council from making any changes in the criminal code. Another weakening amendment, adopted on the House floor, continued the President's authority to appoint local judges. But home rule supporters fended off other debilitating amendments and the compromise version was approved Oct. 10 on a 343-74 vote.

Meanwhile, the Senate July 10 had passed a stronger version, along the lines of the original House committee bill, by a 69-17 vote. Aware that its version was unlikely to be approved by the House, Senate conferees agreed to most of the major provisions of the House compromise. The House agreed to the conference report on the bill Dec. 17 on a 272-74 vote and the Senate cleared the bill Dec. 19, 77-13.[13]

Provisions

President Nixon signed the bill into law Dec. 24. As enacted, the bill provided for an elected mayor and 13-member city council. The elections would be partisan and the term of office was four years. The home rule law allowed the mayor to veto an act of the city council. The council could override a veto by a two-thirds vote but the President then could sustain the mayor's veto.

Congress would continue to make annual appropriations for the District as well as set the amount of the annual federal payment.

The President would continue to appoint judges to the local courts although his nominations would come from a list put together largely by local officials. The President was also given emergency control of the police department.

The act further limited city council activities by prohibiting it from imposing any taxes on United States property, from amending or repealing any act of Congress affecting the District, from reforming the city's criminal code until two years after the council was elected, and from raising the height limitation on buildings.

To ensure its continued control over the District, Congress reserved the right to legislate for the District at any time and established a procedure to veto any action taken by the city council.

Finally, Congress established a "federal enclave" consisting of most of the government buildings and grounds. The enclave was to be administered by a presidentially appointed director and the city would be prohibited from taking any action that might affect the area. Although neither President Nixon nor President Ford had appointed a director, in 1975 legislation was introduced in the House to abolish the enclave. The proposal was killed when the House adopted a substitute measure to retain the enclave. As of mid-1976, the Senate had taken no action on the legislation.

Participation in National Politics

At the same time that the District was embroiled in the home rule debate, it was also the focus of a drive to give its residents a voice in national politics.

Residents of the national capital area which Maryland and Virginia ceded to the federal government voted in 1800, in both national and local elections. Thereafter, they continued to vote in local elections until 1874. In national politics, they were deprived not only of an elected representative in Congress (except for a few years in the early 1870s), but also of participation in the nomination and election of the President and Vice President of the United States. Exclusion of D.C. residents from presidential politics continued for more than a century and a half.

After World War II, leaders of both major political parties sent up trial balloons on the possibility of permitting residents of the District of Columbia to participate in presidential elections. The reaction was predominantly favorable. Congress took the first step toward implementing the proposal in 1954 and 1955.

Convention Delegates

The Senate on July 10, 1954, and the House of Representatives on Aug. 9 of that year, passed a bill authorizing residents of the District to elect committeemen to represent them in the councils of the national political parties and delegates to the national nominating conven-

tions. President Dwight D. Eisenhower vetoed the bill Aug. 20 because it included a provision to which he was strongly opposed. The provision would have allowed employees of the federal government in the District of Columbia to engage in partisan political activities, contrary to the Hatch Act of 1939.

In 1955, both houses of Congress passed a sanitized version of the bill, excluding the controversial provision. President Eisenhower signed the bill Aug. 12, 1955. Under its provisions, the District of Columbia for the first time since 1874 set up and operated official election machinery. The act authorized the election by qualified voters in the District of Columbia of members and alternate members of the national committees of the political parties; delegates and alternates to the national nominating conventions; and "such members and officials of local committees of political parties as may be designated by the duly authorized local committees of such parties for election at large in the District of Columbia."

Right to Vote for President

The Constitution provides in Article II, Section 1, for election of the President and Vice President of the United States by electors chosen in each state. To enable the residents of the District of Columbia to participate in choosing the electors, an amendment to the Constitution was required. A resolution proposing such an amendment was first introduced in Congress in 1890. In the next 70 years, more than 65 amendments on the subject were proposed.[14] They failed to elicit substantial support until after the admission of Alaska and Hawaii to the Union in 1959.

The Senate on Feb. 2, 1960, adopted a resolution proposing an amendment to the Constitution which would grant to the District of Columbia the right to participate in the election of President and Vice President and, in addition, the right to elect a nonvoting delegate in the House of Representatives. In the House, the resolution, amended by removal of any reference to a delegate in Congress, was adopted on June 14. Two days later, the Senate accepted the House change. Under the proposed amendment, D.C. voters would elect "a number of electors of President and Vice President equal to the whole number of senators and representatives in Congress to which the District would be entitled if it were a state, but in no event more than the least populous state."

Opposition developed on two fronts. Only Tennessee among the southern and border states, where legislatures were disinclined to enfranchise Washington's black majority, ratified the amendment; Arkansas went on record against it, the only state in the nation to do so; and others took no action. Opposition in traditionally Republican states reflected fear that the District would regularly vote for Democratic nominees. Success of efforts by D.C. Republican leaders to allay this fear was indicated by the fact that it was a Republican-controlled legislature, that of Kansas, which on March 29, 1961, gave the needed 38th ratification of the Twenty-third Amendment. Ratification was completed in 286 days, a shorter ratification period than that of any other amendment up to that time except the Twelfth, which modified the voting procedures for election of the President and Vice President. (*Time Taken to Ratify Amendments, box p. 229*)

Congress implemented the new amendment by an act of Oct. 4, 1961. President John F. Kennedy had proposed a 90-day residence requirement and 18 years as the minimum age for D.C. voters. But Sen. Russell B. Long (D La.) fought vigorously for a 21-year minimum, and the act as passed conformed to his position and also established a one-year residence requirement. District of Columbia voters gave their three electoral votes in each of the presidential elections of 1964, 1968 and 1972 to the Democratic nominee.

Representation in Congress

D.C. residents still had no voting representation in Congress. The act of Congress approved Feb. 21, 1871, which established a territorial form of government for the national capital, gave local residents the right to elect a nonvoting delegate to the House of Representatives, who was to serve as a member of the Committee on the District of Columbia. Norton P. Chipman, a brigadier general in the Union Army who had settled in Washington after the Civil War, was elected to the post on the Republican ticket on April 21, 1871, and re-elected on Oct. 14, 1873. The Act of June 20, 1874, which replaced the territorial government of the District of Columbia by a commission form of government included a clause stating that repeal of the earlier legislation "shall not affect the term of office of the present Delegate in Congress." Chipman served as a delegate from the convening of the first regular session of the 42nd Congress on Dec. 4, 1871, to final adjournment of the 43rd Congress on March 4, 1875.

Bills providing for re-establishment of nonvoting representation for the District of Columbia were introduced repeatedly after the demise of the territorial government in 1874, but they made little progress until the 1950s. The Senate passed such bills in 1951, 1953, 1955, 1958 and 1959. Each time, however, the bill was killed in the House Committee on the District of Columbia.

In 1960, House supporters of a bill on the question gained 204 of the 219 signatures needed on a petition to take the bill from the District Committee's hands and bring it to the floor for a vote. Their near-success was hailed as a moral victory, but it led to no legislation. When the Senate passed a similar bill in 1965, the House passed, instead, a bill to set up a complex procedure for determining by referendum whether the people of the District really wanted the suffrage and, if so, what kind of suffrage they wanted. Differences between the two bills were not reconciled.

President Nixon on April 28, 1969, endorsed a constitutional amendment giving the District voting representation in Congress and advocating a nonvoting delegate to the House until the states ratified such an amendment. Legislation providing for a nonvoting delegate from the District to the House and for a study commission of the city's government was passed by the House Aug. 10, 1970, and by the Senate Sept. 9. President Nixon signed it into law on Sept. 22.

Democrat Walter E. Fauntroy, a black Baptist minister, was elected the District's nonvoting delegate on March 23, 1971, and was re-elected in 1972 and 1974. Fauntroy was appointed to the House District of Columbia Committee.

Moves for Voting Representation

Article I of the Constitution provides that the House of Representatives shall be composed of "Members chosen...by the People of the several States" and that the Senate shall be composed of "two Senators from each State." Supreme Court decisions handed down beginning in

1805 made it clear that the District of Columbia, for constitutional purposes, was not a state and that a constitutional amendment would be required to authorize voting representation of the District in Congress.

Resolutions proposing such a constitutional amendment were periodically introduced over the years but little further action occurred. In 1960, the Senate adopted a representation resolution but the House did not act on it. In 1967, at President Johnson's urging, both the House and Senate Judiciary Committees, which have jurisdiction over constitutional amendments, held hearings on the representation issue. Only the House committee reported a resolution supporting a constitutional amendment and it died when the Rules Committee took no further action.

In response to President Nixon's 1969 request for a constitutional amendment, the Senate Judiciary Subcommittee on Constitutional Amendments held hearings in 1970 but decided on July 28 to take no action on the issue.

The House Judiciary Committee again reported a constitutional amendment in 1972 and again the resolution died when the Rules Committee took no action.

Undaunted by its past defeats, the House Judiciary Committee Dec. 11, 1975, reported a resolution, sponsored by Fauntroy, proposing a constitutional amendment that would allow District residents to elect two voting senators and as many representatives in the House as it would be entitled to if it were a state. Based on the 1976 population of 723,000, the District would probably be allotted two House members. Unlike previous years, the Rules Committee took up the resolution and agreed by voice vote Feb. 18, 1976, to send it to the House floor.

During extensive floor debate March 16 and March 23, 1976, proponents of the resolution claimed that to continue

D.C. Appropriations

Fiscal Year	Millions of Dollars
1960	199.8
1961	199.5*
1962	209.6
1963	224.6
1964	240.9
1965	265.1
1966	285.1
1967	318.1
1968	371.3
1969	435.5
1970	529.0
1971	591.3
1972	641.5
1973	718.1
1974	777.8
1975	845.6
1976 (est.)	939.2

* Excludes appropriations for capital outlays beginning with fiscal 1961.

Source: *The Federal Payment, FY 1977* (District of Columbia Government, 1976).

to deny District residents a voice in Congress was to continue the tyranny of taxation without representation. They pointed out that District residents paid federal taxes, lived under federal law and served in the armed forces—clear indications that they were not trying to avoid the obligations of citizenship.

But opponents argued that the state must remain the basic unit of the federal system. If the District was given the right to elect representatives to Congress, they said, that right would have to be extended at least to such territories as Guam and the Virgin Islands. The District should seek statehood if it desired congressional representation, some opponents contended. Granting the city representation without statehood would give it all of a state's benefits with none of the responsibilities, they said.

The debate was salted with criticisms of the District and its management under the limited home rule granted in 1973. When it became apparent that the committee proposal would not receive the two-thirds majority vote needed to approve a constitutional amendment, Fauntroy and his backers agreed to support a weaker substitute amendment that would give the District one voting representative in the House immediately and authorize Congress to determine later if the District should be granted senators and an additional House member. That substitute was adopted, but the resolution was defeated, 229-181—45 votes short of the two-thirds needed for passage.

Powers of Congress Over D.C.

Between 1874, when Congress assumed dominance over District affairs, and 1975, when the city regained a modicum of self-government, four committees had filled the roles of mayor and city council: the House and Senate Committees on Appropriations and the House and Senate Committees on the District of Columbia.

Occasionally other committees have had jurisdiction over special aspects of District matters. For instance, the Government Operations Committees in both chambers have dealt with government reorganization plans while the Judiciary Committees have considered constitutional amendments that would expand the District's representation in Congress. The Committees on Labor and on the Post Office and Civil Service have also dealt with matters strictly affecting the District.

But it was the Appropriations and District Committees, particularly those on the House side, that controlled the city. The former determined how the city would spend its revenues, derived from local taxes, government grants and the federal payment, while the latter handled matters ranging in importance from whether slavery should be abolished in the District to fixing the local license fee for dog tags.

Despite the limited home rule granted the city in the mid-1970s, congressional control over the city has not diminished. Congress still tells the city how to spend its money and it can, when it chooses, pass legislation affecting the District or veto actions the city government has taken. But home rule has lessened considerably the day-to-day control once exercised by Congress.

District Committees

Among the oldest of standing committees in both chambers, the House District of Columbia Committee was

---

Annual Federal Payment to D.C.

Fiscal year	Authorized (millions of dollars)	Actual (millions of dollars)	Per cent of total revenues
1960	32	25.0	12.5%
1961	32	25.0	12.5*
1962	32	30.0	14.3
1963	32	30.0	13.6
1964	50	37.5	15.6
1965	50	37.5	14.1
1966	50	44.3	15.5
1967	60	58.0	18.2
1968	70	70.0	18.9
1969	90	89.4	20.5
1970	105	116.2**	22.0
1971	126	131.0***	22.2
1972	179	173.7	27.1
1973	190	181.5	25.3
1974	190	187.5	24.1
1975	230	226.2	26.7
1976 (est.)	254	254.0	27.0

*Percentage based on total appropriations that excludes capital outlays beginning with fiscal 1961.

** Includes $5-million authorized under PL 91-106 for law enforcement activities and $8-million authorized under PL 91-297 for retroactive pay increase for District personnel.

*** Includes $5-million authorized under PL 91-358 to carry out the D.C. Court Reform and Criminal Procedures Act of 1970.

Source: *The Federal Payment, FY 1977,* (District of Columbia Government, 1976).

---

set up in 1808 and the corresponding Senate committee was established in 1816.

For the quarter century prior to enactment of the 1973 home rule legislation, the House committee was dominated by southerners who were willing to serve on the committee while most northerners were not. Led by McMillan, the committee blocked all home rule legislation until the 1970s.

Daniel M. Berman, a professor of government at American University, wrote in his book *In Congress Assembled* (1964): "...there are certain committees on which practically no one wants to serve, notably those that deal with the District of Columbia.... The only Congressmen who generally want to serve on...(these committees) are those from nearby Maryland districts, and southern Democrats (whose motive is to block 'home rule' for the residents of the District, a majority of whom are Negroes)."[15]

"The role that veteran southerners play there satisfies the interests of their constituents as few other committee assignments could do," expanded Martha Derthick in her book, *City Politics in Washington, D.C.*[16]

But since the 1972 elections when McMillan and most of his southern compatriots on the committee either retired or were defeated, the character of the House D.C. Committee has changed radically. McMillan was succeeded by Diggs, only the third black man to hold a committee chairmanship. Under his guidance, the committee's first action was to push through the House the limited home rule charter. Since the popularly elected government took office in 1975, the committee often has taken a more permissive attitude toward the D.C. government than has its Senate counterpart.

Considered more liberal than the House committee throughout the McMillan rein, the Senate District Committee, under Thomas F. Eagleton (D Mo.), has taken a close look at the actions of the new government and has not hesitated to express its disapproval of some local decisions. An audit of city finances, ordered by Eagleton in November 1975, found substantial fiscal mismanagement but implied some of the fault lay with Congress as well as with city officials.

Committees on Appropriations

The budget of the District of Columbia government goes through basically the same steps as the budgets of federal departments and agencies. Briefly, units of the District government prepare estimates of the year's receipts and proposed expenditures which are reviewed and amended by the mayor and his budget office. The mayor then submits his budget proposals to the city council which may make further changes. The budget is next submitted to the President who may make further changes before sending it to Congress.

The District of Columbia Subcommittees of both Appropriations Committees then conduct hearings, and report through the full committees, appropriation bills which are often amended further during floor debate.

The key figure in the appropriations process has been William H. Natcher (D Ky.), who has served as chairman of the House Appropriations District of Columbia Subcommittee since November 1961. With Natcher leading it, the subcommittee has not only controlled appropriations but also imposed various requirements on the District government.

Natcher, for instance, singlehandedly held up funds for the city's share of construction costs of a metropolitan area subway system until direct intervention by the White House in 1971 persuaded the House to override his opposition.[17]

Federal Payment to the District

Congress since 1878 has made an annual contribution to the District of Columbia from the federal Treasury. The amount of the contribution is recommended by the Appropriations Committees and is considered part of the revenue available to the city for various municipal purposes.

The rationale for the contribution is based on several factors. In the first place, the federal government owns 43.3 per cent of the land area of the District as well as many government buildings and pays no real estate taxes on its holdings. In addition, other tax-exempt property owners, such as the D.C. government, foreign embassies and the headquarters of patriotic organizations, own 12.2 per cent of the land area. Further, values of taxable real property are kept down by the congressional ban on skyscrapers.

The amount of the federal contribution to the District was set initially by an Act of June 11, 1878, at one-half of the expenses of the D.C. government. The proportion was cut to 40 per cent by an Act of June 5, 1920. Four years later, Congress abandoned a fixed percentage and started appropriating a specific amount each year. *(Box, p. 296)*

President Johnson in 1965 proposed a permanent annual federal payment to the city equal to the real estate, personal property and business income taxes which the federal government would pay if it were a taxable entity. Failure by the House and Senate to come to agreement on home rule legislation which incorporated the Johnson proposal scuttled that plan.

In 1969, President Nixon recommended that the federal payment be equal to 30 per cent of the local tax and other general fund revenues. The Senate approved that proposal in 1970 but it died in the House.

During the 1973 debate on the limited home rule measure, the Senate passed a provision setting the federal payment at 40 per cent of the local tax effort. The House authorized open-ended appropriations through fiscal 1980 for the payment. The final version authorized specific amounts for the payment, increasing it to $300-million in fiscal 1978 and thereafter until changed by Congress.

Full Home Rule?

Despite congressional complaints of mismanagement and poor administration by the new city government, some District residents look to Congress to ultimately grant the capital city total local control over local matters. Full home rule could be accomplished by granting the existing government the authority to perform those local functions that Congress retained for itself, such as establishment of the city budget. Others have suggested that the District be granted statehood. In addition to giving city residents full self-government, statehood would ensure the city of voting representation in Congress without the need for passage of a constitutional amendment.

But numerous objections have been raised to the idea of statehood. The constitutionality of such a move has been questioned. There are also the questions of whether the city has a broad enough tax base to support itself as a state and whether the federal payment would be continued if the District were to become the 51st state.

But the chief question is what relationship would be drawn between the city and the federal government. Whatever form of government the city might be given, it is almost certain that Congress would insist on maintaining control over federal property and buildings within the city and a police force to protect such a federal enclave. Congress is unlikely to place itself in the position of the Congress of Confederation in 1783, which was forced to decamp to Princeton when Pennsylvania refused to provide protection against soldiers who marched on Philadelphia to press demands for long overdue pay.

Footnotes

1. *The Federalist Papers*, with an Introduction by Clinton Rossiter (Mentor, 1961), No. 43, p. 272.

2. *Ibid.*

3. For general historical background on the creation of the District of Columbia and changes in the city's form of government, see Wilhelmus B. Bryan, *A History of the National Capital*, 2 Vols.

(Macmillan, 1914-16); Martha Derthick, *City Politics in Washington, D.C.* (Harvard University Press, 1962); Constance McLaughlin Green, *Washington, Village and Capital, 1800-1878* (Princeton University Press, 1962); Green, *Washington, Capital City 1879-1950* (Princeton University Press, 1963); Laurence F. Schmeckebier, *The District of Columbia; Its Government and Administration* (Johns Hopkins Press, 1928); and William Tindall, *Standard History of the City of Washington From a Study of the Original Sources* (H. W. Crew & Co., 1914).

4. A Maryland resolution providing only for the appropriation of land to the federal government was approved Dec. 23, 1788; the 1791 resolution included an appropriation of funds to defray cost of public buildings. See Bryan, *A History of the National Capital*, p. 114, and Tindall, *Standard History of the City of Washington*, p. 31.

5. Schmeckebier, *The District of Columbia*, p. 35-36.

6. Derthick, *City Politics in Washington, D.C.*, p. 38.

7. *Ibid.*, p. 39.

8. U.S. President, *Public Papers of the Presidents of the United States, Richard Nixon, 1969* (U.S. Government Printing Office, 1971), p. 326.

9. Stewart Alsop, *The Center, People and Power in Political Washington* (Harper and Row, 1968), p. 28.

10. Derthick, *City Politics in Washington, D.C.*, pp. 176-78.

11. U.S. Congress, House, Committee on the District of Columbia, *District of Columbia Self-Government and Governmental Reorganization Act*, H Rept. 93-482, 93rd Cong., 1st sess., 1973, p. 50.

12. *The Washington Post*, Oct. 11, 1973.

13. For more background, see Congressional Quarterly, *1973 Almanac*, pp. 734-41.

14. Derthick, *City Politics in Washington, D.C.*, p. 73.

15. Daniel M. Berman, *In Congress Assembled, The Legislative Process in the National Government*, (Macmillan, 1964), p. 149.

16. Derthick, *City Politics in Washington, D.C.*, p. 54.

17. Congressional Quarterly, *Congress and the Nation, 1969-1972, Vol. III*, pp. 464-66.

Selected Bibliography

Books

Alsop, Stewart, *The Center, People and Power in Political Washington*, New York: Harper and Row, 1968.

Berman, Daniel M., *In Congress Assembled; The Legislative Process in the National Government*, New York: Macmillan, 1964.

Bryan, Wilhelmus B., *A History of the National Capital*, New York: Macmillan, 1914-16. 2 vols.

Derthick, Martha, *City Politics in Washington, D.C.*, Cambridge: Harvard University Press, 1962. (Prepared for Joint Center for Urban Studies, Massachusetts Institute of Technology and Harvard University.)

The Federalist Papers. Introduction by Clinton Rossiter. New York: Mentor, 1961.

Green, Constance McLaughlin, *The Secret City; A History of Race Relations in the Nation's Capital*, Princeton, N.J.: Princeton University Press, 1967.

———. *Washington, Capital City 1879-1950*, Princeton, N.J.: Princeton University Press, 1963.

———. *Washington, Village and Capital, 1800-1878*, Princeton, N.J.: Princeton University Press, 1962.

Hanson, Royce, *Governing the District of Columbia: An Introduction*, Washington: Washington Center for Metropolitan Studies, 1971.

Porter, J. A., *City of Washington: Its Origin and Administration*, New York: Johnson Reprint Corp., 1973.

Ross, Bernard H., *The Delegate and the District Building: The Potential for Conflict of Cooperation*, Washington: Washington Center for Metropolitan Studies, 1971.

Schmeckebier, Laurence F., *The District of Columbia; Its Government and Administration*, Baltimore: Johns Hopkins Press, 1928.

Tindall, William, *Standard History of the City of Washington From a Study of the Original Sources*, Knoxville, Tenn.: H. W. Crew & Co., 1914.

Young, James, *The Washington Community, 1800-1828*, New York: Columbia University Press, 1966.

Articles

Barth, Alan, "Exiles in the Capital," *Reporter*, February 4, 1960, pp. 26-29.

Breckinridge, John B., "The District of Columbia Home Rule Act," *Judicature*, March 1974, pp. 360-363.

Fenning, F. A., "Federal Management of the Federal City," *National Municipal Review*, January 1931, pp. 16-18.

Gelman, Norman I., "Self Government for the City of Washington," *Editorial Research Reports*, July 10, 1959, pp. 515-532.

Raven-Hasen, Peter, "Congressional Representation for the District of Columbia: A Constitutional Analysis," *Harvard Journal on Legislation*, February 1975, pp. 167-192.

"Washington, D.C.: An Unofficial View of the Seat of Government," *Fortune*, December 1934, pp. 54-64.

Wood, J. B., "Washington: Stepchild of the Nation," *Nation's Business*, August 1946, pp. 41-43.

Government Publications

Caemmerer, Hans P. *Washington, the National Capital*. U.S. Government Printing Office, 1932.

District of Columbia. *District of Columbia Code, Annotated*. U.S. Government Printing Office.

———. *The Federal Payment, FY 1977* (1976).

Padover, Saul K. (ed.). *Thomas Jefferson and the National Capital, Containing Notes and Correspondence Exchanged between Jefferson, Washington, L'Enfant and Others, 1783-1818*. U.S. Government Printing Office, 1946.

U.S. Congress. Joint Committee on Washington Metropolitan Problems. *The Governing of Metropolitan Washington*. 85th Cong., 2d sess., 1958.

U.S. Congress. House. Committee on the District of Columbia. *District of Columbia Self-Government and Governmental Reorganization Act*. H. Rept. 93-482 to accompany H.R. 9682. 93rd Cong., 1st sess., 1973.

———. *Report of the Commission on the Organization of the Government of the District of Columbia*. H. Doc. 317. 92nd Cong., 2d sess., 1972.

———. Committee on the Judiciary. *Providing Representation of the District of Columbia in Congress*. H. Rept. 94-714 to accompany H. J. Res 280. 94th Cong., 1st sess., 1975.

U.S. Congress. Senate. Committee on the District of Columbia. *Legislative History of District of Columbia Self-Government and Governmental Reorganization Act S 1435 (PL 93-198)*. 93rd Cong., 2d sess., 1974.

Private Bills

Private bills are lawmakers' admission of fallibility, for private bills generally are used to address some particular problem which public laws either created or overlooked.

The history of private bills dates at least from Roman times when they were called *constitutionis privilegia*, privileges accorded to specified individuals. They are a part of the history of Parliament, which the Founding Fathers drew upon in establishing the American legislative system. They have been a part of the activity of Congress since the beginning. In the 93rd Congress (1973-74), 1,097 private bills were considered by the House Judiciary Committee, and of them, 123 were enacted. *(Box, p. 303)*

Private bills have been challenged on constitutional grounds. It has been asserted that private bills are unconstitutional because they violate the equal protection clause, the separation of powers, or are in fact bills of attainder. Nevertheless, courts have rejected these challenges and have approved as constitutional a variety of provisions first enacted as private bills.

Private bills have been used for a number of purposes over the years by Congress. At present, they are used principally in claims and immigration cases. Congressional consideration of a private bill is similar to consideration of a public law: it must be passed by both chambers in identical form and be signed by the President.

Private bills have constituted a large proportion of laws enacted by Congress over the years, and Congress frequently has felt that considering the inherently narrow scope of private bills they have consumed a disproportionately large share of Congress' attention and time. Congress is also aware of the recurring opportunities for abuse which private bills present. In an effort to deal with both of these problems, Congress occasionally has tried to reduce the need for numerous private bills by broadening the discretionary authority of federal administrative agencies to deal with exceptional situations. Congress also created, and from time to time has broadened the jurisdiction of the U.S. Court of Claims in an attempt to reduce the need for numerous private bills.

In spite of Congress' efforts, the number of private bills remains high, and abuses still occur. In 1976, Rep. Henry Helstoski (D N.J.) was indicted on charges involving the introduction of private bills to postpone the deportation of aliens living illegally in the United States. *(p. 303)*

Constitutional Questions

Lawmakers in the United States sometimes have viewed their consideration of private bills as based on the right of individuals, under the First Amendment to the Constitution, to petition Congress for redress of grievances. "But the right to petition," according to an unsigned note in the June 1966 *Harvard Law Review*, "cannot confer upon Congress the power to enact bills dealing with any subject regarding which they are petitioned; otherwise, passage of any bill, no matter how local the subject matter or how far beyond stated constitutional limitations on Congress, might be justified by a mere petition."[1] The note added: "Enactment of private bills no doubt makes meaningful the right to petition, but the constitutional basis for passing such bills must be found elsewhere...."[2]

Relevant provisions elsewhere in the Constitution include Article I, Section 8, Clause 1, which authorizes Congress to pay the nation's debts; Article I, Section 8, Clause 4, which authorizes Congress "To establish an uniform Rule of Naturalization, and uniform Laws on the subject of Bankruptcies throughout the United States"; and Article I, Section 9, Clause 8, which requires the consent of Congress for acceptance of a gift or title from a foreign state by a government employee. As regards the word "uniform" in the clause on naturalization, the note in the *Harvard Law Review* commented, "While there is a constitutional requirement that such laws be 'uniform,' this appears to mean uniform among the states, not among the applicants."[3]

Among the serious constitutional questions which have been raised about private laws, three have been paramount: equal protection, separation of powers, and the ban on bills of attainder.

Equal Protection

In the words of the *Harvard Law Review* note, "unanswered problems related to the notion of 'equal protection' are raised when an individual denied a bill is in all relevant respects in the same position as one for whom a bill has been passed."[4] The Supreme Court ruled on this question in the case of *Paramino Lumber Co. v. Marshall* (309 U.S. 379) which concerned the constitutionality of a private law of April 10, 1936, for the relief of a claimant un-

Private and Public Laws

Congress	Private Laws	Public Laws	Total	Ratio of Private to Total (%)
1st 1789-91	10	108	118	8.6
20th 1827-29	101	134	235	43.0
40th 1867-69	415	354	769	53.9
59th 1905-07	6,249	775	7,024	89.0
60th 1907-09	234	411	645	36.4
80th 1947-48	457	906	1,363	33.5
87th 1961-62	684	885	1,569	43.6
88th 1963-64	360	666	1,026	35.1
89th 1965-66	473	810	1,283	36.9
90th 1967-68	362	640	1,002	36.1
91st 1969-71	247	696	943	26.2
92nd 1971-73	161	607	768	20.9
93rd 1973-74	123	650	773	15.9

Source: *Statutes at Large.*

der the Longshoremen's and Harbor Workers' Compensation Act of March 4, 1927. The private law allowed reconsideration, to raise the award, of an order for compensation under the 1927 act, although the statute of limitations had expired and the compensation would be paid by a private party.

Justice Stanley Reed on March 11, 1940, delivered the opinion of the court upholding the law: "It is urged by appellant...that the equal protection clause of the Fourteenth Amendment should be read into the due process clause of the Fifth Amendment. If so read, it is argued, this private act violates the rule of equal protection. This conclusion, however, we find untenable. Private acts, as such, are not forbidden by the Constitution."

Private legislation involves another type of equal protection issue. The question arose in 1950 whether the mere introduction of a private bill to cancel deportation proceedings entitled the beneficiary to a stay of deportation (postponement of deportation until final action on the private bill) in every case on the equal-protection ground that a stay is granted in most cases. The Second Circuit Court of Appeals in that case ruled in favor of a stay for the beneficiary of the bill because the Department of Justice had not provided special reasons for not granting it in that case. *(see p. 305)*

Separation of Powers

The Supreme Court has held that a private bill does not violate the constitutional separation of powers by permitting a congressional usurpation of judicial power.

The Supreme Court in 1940 took up this question in the *Paramino* case. The appellant in that case contended, with reference to the private law of April 10, 1936, mentioned above: "The Act is an attempted usurpation by Congress of judicial functions. It is judicial in nature and authorizes a readjudication between individuals of private property rights arising out of past transactions. Legislative grant of a new trial, rehearing or further determination in a cause which has proceeded to final adjudication under existing statutes is an attempted exercise of judicial power.... Congress possesses no judicial power."

The court's opinion, after rejecting the equal-protection argument, added: "Nor can we say that this legislation is an excursion of the Congress into the judicial function." The reason given by the court was that in this case the private law affected an administrative order rather than a judicial decision.

Bills of Attainder

A private bill which benefits one individual to the possible detriment of another may plausibly be held to be a bill of attainder and, as such, barred by Article I, Section 9, Clause 3, of the Constitution. Many U.S. private bills concern not only claims against the government but also relations between private persons. The question whether a private bill could successfully be attacked as a bill of attainder has not as such arisen in the courts, but a Supreme Court decision of June 7, 1965, came close to this subject-matter area. *(United States v. Brown, 381 U.S. 437).*

In the context of the cited clause of the Constitution, the author of the *Harvard Law Review* note discussed the constitutionality of private laws which abrogate the statute of limitations in claims cases arising between individuals. He wrote that in the light of recent decisions, especially the 1965 case of *United States v. Brown,* such a law, if passed now, "might be taken by the courts to be a bill of attainder against the individual suffering detriment under it."[5] The Supreme Court's opinion declared that the Labor-Management Reporting and Disclosure Act of Sept. 14, 1959, which barred Communists from all except custodial tasks as employees of labor unions, "plainly constitutes a bill of attainder" (381 U.S. 449).

Private Bills in History

Because of the nature of the matters they deal with, private bills seldom are the stuff of history. But occasionally, they have involved widely publicized situations, most recently in connection with attempts to deport alleged Mafia figures in the early 1950s and alleged abuses surrounding private immigration bills in the 1960s and 1970s.

In the 19th and early 20th centuries, noteworthy instances of private bills involved the French spoliation cases, efforts to correct an error in the estate of George Washington and efforts to compensate Queen Liliuokalani for the U.S. takeover of the Hawaiian Islands.

French Spoliation Claims

American citizens and companies unsuccessfully sought passage of private bills to pay their claims in the French spoliation cases. These cases arose mainly from the fact that the United States remained neutral in the wars between France and Great Britain in the late 18th and early 19th centuries. When American goods were shipped commercially to Great Britain during those wars, the French Navy in many cases seized both the goods and the vessels in which the goods were carried. By treaties of Sept. 30, 1800, and July 4, 1831, the United States government released the French government from responsibility for paying for the goods or vessels, in exchange for certain intergovernmental payments and concessions on other matters.

Congress in 1885, after many appeals from heirs of the owners of the goods and vessels, authorized the Court of Claims to consider the spoliation claims. Estimates of the total damages incurred by American merchants and shipping companies ranged from $20 million to $40 million. The

(Continued on p. 302)

Fine Line Separates Public and Private Bills

The two houses of the U.S. Congress during the 19th century developed criteria for differentiating between public and private bills. The identifying characteristics of the two categories of legislation were sorted out more fully by the House of Representatives, in its Rules of Procedure and by on-the-spot rulings of the Speaker, than by the Senate.

House, Senate and Statutory Definitions

Asher C. Hinds, in his *Precedents of the House of Representatives* (1907), quoted the following description of private bills from the House Manual in use at that time: "It has been the practice in [the British] Parliament, and also in Congress, to consider as private such [bills] as are 'for the interest of individuals, public companies or corporations, a parish, city, or county, or other locality.' "[1]

Hinds noted that, in the classification of bills as public or private, some varieties of bills previously had been counted in one category but were classed in the other category at the time of his writing. For example, bills granting American registration to foreign-built vessels, labeled public in earlier periods, had come to be classed as private, while bills incorporating companies, authorizing construction of bridges, or allowing rights of way through Indian reservations had often been classed as private but were "now generally treated as public."[2]

In an attempt to summarize the precedents, Hinds proposed the following definition: "A private bill is a bill for the relief of one or several specified persons, corporations, institutions, etc., and is distinguished from a public bill, which relates to public matters and deals with individuals only by classes."[3] He added the following admonition from the House Manual: "The line of distinction between public and private bills is so difficult to be defined in many cases that it must rest on the opinion of the Speaker and the details of the bill."[4]

The U.S. Senate, in a series of rulings by the presiding officer, touched the fringes of the question of what distinguishes a public from a private bill. The question as it arose in the Senate concerned the definition not of a private bill as such but of a private-claim amendment to a general appropriation bill. Such an amendment, however, possesses all the features of a private bill with the exception that it is part of a public bill and not a separate piece of legislation.

Senate Rule XVI reads: "No amendment, the object of which is to provide for a private claim, shall be received to any general appropriation bill, unless it be to carry out the provision of an existing law or a treaty stipulation, which shall be cited on the face of the amendment." The earliest case requiring an interpretation of that rule concerned a claim put forward by an attorney for an Indian tribe. The attorney sought payment out of Indian funds, not out of the federal Treasury, for legal services rendered.

On March 23, 1904, during debate on an Indian affairs appropriation bill, Sen. William P. Frye (R Maine), president pro tempore of the Senate, ruled that an amendment providing for payment of the attorney's claim was not a private-claim amendment and therefore was in order. He said that to be barred under Rule XVI a claim must be one which "would take money from the United States Treasury."[5] A similar ruling was made on Feb. 25, 1913.

A proposed amendment to a deficiency appropriation bill for 1935 raised a comparable question. On July 24, 1935, when the bill was under consideration, Sen. William G. McAdoo (D Calif.) offered an amendment which provided for payment of almost $6.5-million to the State of California for expenditures made in aiding the United States during the Civil War. The question arose whether the amendment concerned a private claim of the kind banned by Rule XVI. Sen. McAdoo observed that "...[O]n two occasions it [the Senate] held that this type of claims of States for reimbursement for expenditures made during the Civil War were private claims, and on two other occasions it ruled by a majority vote that they were public claims."[6] He contended that they were public claims, and Sen. Key Pittman (D Nev.), president pro tempore, ruled in his favor.[7] This ruling, taken with those of 1904 and 1913, amounted to a liberal interpretation of Rule XVI in that it kept to a narrow span the category of private claims banned by the rule.

The only federal statutory definition of private laws appeared in an Act of Jan. 12, 1895, as amended Jan. 20, 1905. The 1895 act stated: "The term private bill shall be construed to mean all bills for the relief of private parties, bills granting pensions, and bills removing political disabilities." This definition was embedded in a provision establishing the number of copies of bills of various kinds to be printed and the distribution of those copies in the Senate and the House. In the 1905 act, which likewise concerned the printing and distribution of bills in Congress, the definition was changed to read: "The term 'private bill' shall be construed to mean all bills for the relief of private parties, bills granting pensions, bills removing political disabilities, and bills for the survey of rivers and harbors."

Digest of Public General Bills

In 1936 the Library of Congress began publishing a *Digest of Public General Bills* for the 74th Congress, second session. The *Digest* is published five times a year. The *Digest* includes all public bills considered by Congress. All bills not included in the *Digest* may be considered private bills.

All public and private *laws* are published by the U.S. Government Printing Office in *Statutes at Large*. Since 1937, a volume of *Statutes at Large* has been published for each session of Congress. In this series, public laws and private laws are grouped separately. *(Box on publication of private laws, p. 302)*

---

1. Asher C. Hinds, *Hinds' Precedents of the House of Representatives of the United States*, 5 vols. (Washington: Government Printing Office, 1907), Vol. 4, p. 247.
2. *Ibid.*, p. 248.
3. *Ibid.*, p. 247.
4. *Ibid.*

5. U.S. Congress, Senate, 58th Cong., 2nd sess., 23 March 1904, *Congressional Record.* Vol. 38, p. 3548.
6. U.S., Congress, Senate, 74th Cong., 1st sess., 24 July 1935, *Congressional Record.* Vol. 79, p. 11761.
7. *Ibid.*, pp. 11762-11763.

(Continued from p. 300)

Court of Claims, from 1886 to 1916, made awards aggregating a little over $7-million. Congress, in 1891, 1899, 1902 and 1905, appropriated sums totaling approximately $3.9-million for payment of the awards. Claims amounting to more than $3-million, although approved by the Court of Claims, remained unpaid. After 1905, Congress was reluctant to pay the remaining sums to heirs so many generations removed from the events that had given rise to the claims.

Special Problems, 1890s and After

Private bills for the payment of claims included, toward the end of the 19th century, many cases having dubious foundations. Thomas B. Reed (R Maine), who was Speaker of the House in 1889-91 and 1895-99, showed relentless opposition to most private-claims bills from the time he first came to Congress in 1877. A bill to pay the College of William and Mary for property destroyed by northern forces in the Civil War was under discussion in the House on April 12, 1878. Reed, referring to the eloquence of proponents of the bill, said: "You may bring together Bunker Hill and Yorktown, Massachusetts and Virginia, and tie them together with all the flowers of rhetoric that ever bloomed since the Garden of Eden, but you cannot change the plain,

---

Publication of Private Laws

In the eight-volume compilation of the *Statutes at Large* covering the first 28 Congresses (1789-1845), Vol. 6 contains the private laws enacted by those Congresses.

In the volumes of the *Statutes at Large* covering the 29th-74th Congresses (1845-1936), there is a separately numbered volume for each Congress, but a volume in this series may consist physically of more than one book. For example, Vol. 49, covering the 74th Congress (1935-36), contains in Part 1 the public laws of that Congress and in Part 2 the private laws along with concurrent resolutions and other papers. Even when the private laws appeared in the same book with the public laws, the private laws were grouped separately.

For many years until 1936, the federal government published not only a volume of the *Statutes at Large* for each Congress, but also a paper-bound edition of the laws of each session of Congress, known as the Session Laws. When the Session Laws were published in two parts, the private laws appeared in Part 2.

Since 1937, a volume of the *Statutes at Large* has been published for each session of Congress rather than each Congress. In this series, as previously, the private laws are printed in a separate part if their inclusion in the same book with public laws would make the book unwieldy; and when they are printed in the same book, they are grouped separately.

Each public or private law is published as a separate sheet or pamphlet, depending on its length, as soon as it is enacted. These publications are known as slip laws. They are listed in the *Monthly Catalog, United States Government Publications,* issued by the Superintendent of Documents, Government Printing Office. Private slip laws may be obtained, so long as the supply lasts, from the Document Room of the Senate or the Document Room of the House of Representatives.

---

historic fact that no nation on earth ever was so imbecile and idiotic as to establish a principle [reimbursing those who have engaged in hostilities against the government, for damage done by the government in resisting them] that would more nearly bankrupt its treasury after victory than after defeat."[6]

Reed eventually took a somewhat more moderate position. The number of private laws enacted actually rose while he was Speaker during the last half-decade of the century, increasing from 514 in the 54th Congress (1895-97) to 885 in the 55th Congress (1897-99). A still further rise, to 1,499, occurred in the 56th Congress (1899-1901).[7] Reed had resigned from his House seat in September 1899.

Two private-claims bills in the 60th Congress (1907-09) attracted wide attention. One was a House bill "To reimburse the estate of General George Washington for certain lands of his in the state of Ohio, lost by conflicting grants made under the authority of the United States." The claim in this case arose from the fact that, through oversight on the part of public land officials, various individuals were permitted to settle on and obtain title to a 3,000-acre tract of which Washington was clearly the owner. When Washington was notified a year before he died that his title to the land might be in danger, he made inquiries and was officially assured that his title would prevail. Nevertheless, those who had located on his land were given rights there and exercised them.

Descendants of Washington, residing in Virginia, other southern states and California, arranged for introduction of a House bill (and a similar bill in the Senate) on the ground that Washington's estate had been deprived of the tract by negligence on the part of public land officers. Col. Robert E. Lee Jr. of Lexington, Va., son of the Confederate general, was administrator of the estate. The House Committee on Claims, of which Charles A. Lindbergh (R Minn.), father of the aviator, was a member, held a hearing on the bill, Jan. 14, 1909. Washington's heirs would have received $305,000 under the bill. However, the committee did not report the bill, and it never reached the floor of either house.

The other famous private-claim bill of the 60th Congress provided for payment of $250,000 to Her Majesty Liliuokalani, former Queen of the Hawaiian Islands. The claim was based on the fact that John L. Stevens, American minister at Honolulu, had collaborated with the American-born revolutionaries who overthrew the Queen in January 1893. Stevens, without authorization from Washington, offered the revolutionaries the support of the American cruiser *Boston,* then in Honolulu harbor. Marines were landed, marched to the palace grounds, and prevented the Queen's forces from resisting the rebels.

Secretary of State Walter Q. Gresham on Oct. 18, 1893, recommended to President Cleveland the restoration of the legitimate government in Honolulu. Cleveland, in his first annual message to Congress on Dec. 4, 1893, summarized the report of his special representative to Hawaii, James H. Blount, "showing beyond all question that the constitutional government of Hawaii had been subverted with the active aid of our representative to that government and through the intimidation caused by the presence of an armed naval force of the United States, which was landed for that purpose at the instance of our minister."[8] Cleveland took steps to promote the restoration of the Queen's government, but the steps were unavailing.

The Legislature of the Territory of Hawaii on Feb. 23 and 25, 1907, nine years after the annexation of Hawaii to the United States, adopted a concurrent resolution supporting action in Congress which would result in "the payment to Queen Liliuokalani of an ample sum in settlement of all existing claims on her behalf." The bill for the relief of the Queen died in the Committee on Claims.

Recent Abuses

1969 Immigration Bills. A newspaper investigation in 1969 which produced accusations of impropriety in the introduction of hundreds of private immigration bills to help Chinese seamen stay in the United States resulted in a Senate probe and a change in procedures.

The stories were published in August 1969 by Knight Newspapers, which after several weeks of investigation reported evidence that New York lawyers and Washington lobbyists had been getting $500 to $2,500 for each Chinese immigration bill involved.

The Senate Select Committee on Standards and Conduct had begun a preliminary investigation into allegations that some senators or their aides received gifts and campaign contributions for introducing bills to help Chinese ship-jumpers escape deportation. Chairman John C. Stennis (D Miss.) asked the committee staff to make a study of all private relief bills introduced in recent years to determine whether there had been any abuse in handling them. Such bills usually delay deportation while awaiting congressional action.

The Senate majority and minority leaders took action to halt the practice of staff aides' introducing private bills in the Senate. In a letter to Senate Secretary Francis R. Valeo, Mansfield and Scott instructed that "bills and resolutions should no longer be received at the desk by the Parliamentarian for reference to the appropriate standing committees unless they were signed by and delivered at the desk in person by the senator introducing them."[9]

Among those who figured in the upsurge of such bills since 1967 were Sens. Gaylord Nelson (D Wis.), Daniel K. Inouye (D Hawaii), Harrison A. Williams (D N.J.), and former Sen. Daniel Brewster (D Md.). Although these senators said they had had little or no connection with the Chinese nationals, bills introduced by them constituted almost half the 700 Chinese immigration bills brought before Congress in the period 1967-69.

The immigration issue had become increasingly important since 1967, when U.S. immigration officials and federal courts began a crackdown on aliens who stayed in the country illegally.

By law, the U.S. Immigration and Naturalization Service must deport alien seamen who extend their stays beyond normal shore leave time. However, if private legislation is pending in Congress, immigration authorities generally allow the bills to be resolved in Congress before taking action against such aliens.

Introduction of private immigration bills was not uncommon, but the increase in such bills for Chinese after 1967 had been dramatic. During the preceding two years of the 89th Congress—in 1965 and 1966—there were bills for fewer than 25 such individuals. Beginning in 1967, 700 such bills had been filed by several dozen senators.

1976 Helstoski Indictment. Rep. Henry Helstoski (D N.J.) was indicted by a federal grand jury, June 2, 1976, on charges that he solicited and accepted bribes in return for introducing bills to delay deportation of Chilean and Argentinian aliens who were living in the United States illegally.

The indictment alleged Helstoski received "at least" $8,735 for his sponsorship of the immigration bills. It alleged

Subjects of Private Bills in the House, 1961-74*

(Introduced in House or passed by Senate and referred to House)

Congress	Claims	Immigration and Naturalization	Patents
87th 1961-62	849	3,020	9
88th 1963-64	723	3,003	3
89th 1965-66	847	4,481	2
90th 1967-68	779	6,278	2
91st 1969-71	715	4,854	0
92nd 1971-72	609	2,142	0
93rd 1973-74	479	606	12

*The House Judiciary Committee publishes separate totals of the private bills pending before the House. The Senate Judiciary Committee does not publish totals.

Source: House Judiciary Committee, *Legislative Calendars.*

he received $5,500 on behalf of five Chilean aliens, $1,500 on behalf of two Argentinians, and at least $1,735 from two New Jersey lawyers specializing in immigration matters.

Categories of Private Bills

From time to time, various kinds of cases which Congress had previously handled through enactment of private laws have been made ineligible for such treatment. Cases in those areas are now handled by one or another agency in the executive branch or by the courts, thereby reducing the volume of minor bills before Congress. However, each of the main categories of private bills remaining within the purview of Congress is extensive.

Of the kinds of private congressional legislation which remain alive, two are paramount: claims cases and immigration cases. Bills for the relief of individuals in those two fields have been introduced in large numbers in every session of Congress for many years. Examples of other types of private bills now occur infrequently. Before 1950, private bills dealing with matters other than claims or immigration were more fully represented. Among these were land claims, military justice and pensions.

Private Claims Cases

The Constitution provides in Article I, Section 8, Clause 1, that "The Congress shall have Power...to pay the Debts...of the United States." This provision has been construed broadly to include not only legal but also moral obligations. The Supreme Court stated in *U.S. v. Realty Company* (1895) with reference to the cited clause: "The term 'debts' includes those debts or claims which rest upon a merely equitable or honorary obligation, and which would not be recoverable in a court of law if existing against an individual. The nation, broadly speaking, owes a 'debt' to an individual when his claim grows out of general principles of right and justice" (163 U.S. 427).

Bills introduced in Congress for payment of private claims against the government are of three kinds—refund cases, waiver cases and tort claims.

Refund Cases. One kind aims to wipe out the obligation of individuals to refund to the government payments made to them through error. Typically, in these cases, the money was received in good faith and repayment would cause hardship. The category consists, in large part, of cases in which work was done for the government in the mistaken belief that it had been authorized.

Also included in the refund category are bills to forgive obligations resulting from the fact that an individual was hired as a government employee, or given a government contract, when he was receiving a government pension or was not a citizen. Although the individual and the responsible government office both acted in good faith, the wages or other payments made were illegal and therefore subject to refund. Still another example consists of cases in which a government employee was mistakenly given a promotion, in innocent contravention of the rules.

Waiver Cases. Some private-claims bills provide for waiver of the statute of limitations on the government's obligation to make a payment to an individual, company, or organization. This kind of bill is considered particularly in order when the claimant, to his own detriment, relied on advice to the effect that the statute of limitations was inapplicable.

Tort Claims. The remaining category of private-claims bills concerns tort claims not covered by the Federal Tort Claims Act of Aug. 2, 1946. That act, while laying down procedures for the settlement of certain tort claims against the government, exempted from its provisions claims arising from activities of the Tennessee Valley Authority, the Panama Canal Co., and certain federal banks; combat activities in time of war; fiscal operations of the U.S. Treasury or regulation of the monetary system; "assault, battery, false imprisonment, false arrest, malicious prosecution, abuse of process, libel, slander, misrepresentation, deceit, or interference with contract rights"; events in a foreign country; establishment of a quarantine by the United States; detention of goods by a customs officer; loss of mail; and certain other situations.

These tort claims, exempted from the act of 1946 and therefore still eligible for relief by private legislation, may have their origin in injuries caused by government agents (as in a collision with a government truck) but not covered by compensation provisions of any applicable laws, or in situations where money was honestly promised by a government agent but never paid.

Private Immigration and Naturalization Bills, 1957-74

Congress	Bills Introduced	Laws Enacted
85th 1957-58	4,364	927
86th 1959-60	3,069	488
87th 1961-62	3,592	544
88th 1963-64	3,647	196
89th 1965-66	5,285	279
90th 1967-68	7,293	218
91st 1969-71	6,266	113
92nd 1971-72	2,866	62
93rd 1973-74	1,085	63

Source: *Annual Report,* Immigration and Naturalization Service, 1975, p. 139.

The number of private-claims bills introduced in the past two decades has averaged about 2,000 in each Congress. Many such bills in the past prohibited transfer of any part of the settlement amount to an attorney or agent for services rendered in connection with the claim. In recent years, private-claims bills generally have limited the amount that may be transferred to an attorney or agent to 10 per cent of the settlement amount.

Immigration and Naturalization Bills

Private laws for the relief of aliens are necessitated by the fact that public laws on admission of aliens to the United States, their residence in the United States, and change of nationality do not cover all hardship cases. Some private laws in this area permit aliens residing abroad to come to the United States although technically they are not eligible. Others permit aliens residing in the United States to remain in the country although technically they are not eligible. Still others permit aliens to become citizens although technically they are not eligible.

The number of private bills on immigration and naturalization rose significantly after enactment of strict provisions on both subjects in the Immigration and Nationality Act of June 27, 1952. Such bills, totaling on the average a few hundred in each Congress in the 1940s, reached a crest in the 83rd Congress (1953-54) of 4,797, of which 755 were enacted. The number introduced remained at a comparable level for several years and then increased to 5,285 in the 89th Congress (1965-66) and to 7,293 in the 90th Congress (1967-68). The number dropped off steadily after that; in the 93rd Congress (1973-74) 1,085 private immigration bills were introduced.[10] *(Box, this page)*

Private Immigration Bills. Federal statutes on immigration exclude from admission to the United States for permanent residence individuals who have not received a visa in accordance with the statutory provisions on preference in allocation of visas. The laws also exclude individuals having specified mental, physical, or moral defects. They provide for deportation or other penalties if an individual succeeds in entering the United States in violation of these bans. The immigration laws, although providing for exceptions in stated hardship situations, are otherwise stringent and are stringently enforced. In accordance with the clear intent of Congress, the Department of Justice exercises sparingly its authority to grant exceptions.

On the other hand, members of Congress, when faced with hardship cases, have little hesitation in introducing bills aimed at relaxing application of the law in those cases. A foreigner who wishes to move to the United States but is excluded under the moral-defects provision may have close relatives in the country who can effectively explain to a representative or senator that the moral defect does not warrant ineligibility to immigrate to the United States. An American couple desiring to bring in and adopt a Korean or Vietnamese child may be technically ineligible to do so. Often, however, a member of Congress may agree to seek passage of a bill authorizing an exception in their favor.

Many private immigration bills provide for exceptions in the case of a single individual; some affect more than one person. In 1949, the Immigration and Naturalization Service in the Department of Justice analyzed, from this standpoint, more than 3,500 private immigration bills introduced in the preceding 10 years. The analysis showed that the bills applied to an average of 1.6 persons. Private immigration bills in the 90th Congress (1967-68) applied to an average of 1.3 persons.[11]

Private Bills to Avert Deportation

An immigrant who has entered the country illegally and wishes to avoid deportation or other penalties may appeal to a representative's or senator's humanitarian feelings and hope for introduction and enactment of a private bill according him status as a legal immigrant. He may plead that he is needed as a breadwinner by members of his family, already legal residents of the United States. There may be medical reasons why he needs to stay in the country. The illegal immigrant may be a widow or widower of an American citizen. Or there may be danger of political persecution in the event of deportation to the country of origin. About 80 per cent of all private bills on immigration or naturalization involve threatened deportation of illegal immigrants.

If an alien is about to be deported, and a private bill is introduced in Congress to allow him to stay in the country, the Immigration and Naturalization Service is placed in a quandary. If it deports the individual and Congress later exempts him, the service will have prevented the congressional action from achieving its purpose; but if the service refrains from deporting the individual, it may be showing more leniency than Congress itself will show in the ultimate decision on the bill.

In an effort to deal with this situation, the Immigration and Naturalization Service and the Judiciary Committees of the House and Senate developed a series of agreements over the years. The end effect of the agreements was that deportation was suspended when a private bill had been introduced. Deportation proceedings were continued up to and including entry of a final administrative order; but final action to enforce departure was held up while Congress considered the bill.[12]

Court Cases on Deportation

Two important court cases have involved the question of whether the alien has a legal right to a stay of deportation on the basis of the introduction of a private bill for his relief. Attorneys for the aliens argued that a departure from the general practice of granting a stay would be arbitrary.

The first case was that of Ellen Knauff, a German who arrived in New York in 1948 and claimed admission under the War Brides Act of Dec. 28, 1945. When the Attorney General decided to exclude Mrs. Knauff and deport her on the basis of confidential adverse information, Sen. William Langer (R N.D.) on Feb. 2, 1950, and Rep. Francis E. Walter (D Pa.) on March 8, 1950, introduced private bills to cancel the deportation proceedings. Rep. Walter's bill passed the House, with amendments, on May 2.

Mrs. Knauff's attorneys sought a stay of deportation while the bills were pending. The Department of Justice declined to hold up deportation for this reason, whereupon the attorneys filed suit. The U.S. Court of Appeals, Second Circuit, on March 28, 1950, decided in Mrs. Knauff's favor. *(Knauff v. McGrath,* 181 F. 2d 839) The Supreme Court on March 5, 1951, declined to review the decision of the Court of Appeals.

Some weeks later, the Department of Justice revived the deportation order, on grounds it considered valid, and was about to put Mrs. Knauff on a plane when on May 17 Supreme Court Justice Robert H. Jackson granted a stay. The Board of Immigration Appeals later recommended that Mrs. Knauff be allowed to reside in the United States, and Attorney General J. Howard McGrath on Nov. 2, 1951, approved the recommendation.

The second court case involving the right to a stay of deportation while a private bill was pending concerned Mr. and Mrs. Konstantinos Roumeliotis, Greek visitors who had overstayed their visas and were about to be deported. On Feb. 6, 1962, Sen. Everett M. Dirksen (R Ill.) introduced a private bill on their behalf, but the Department of Justice indicated that it nevertheless would go ahead with the deportation. The would-be immigrants' lawyers filed suit.

The U.S. Court of Appeals, Seventh Circuit, in denying a stay of deportation, noted that the Senate Judiciary Committee had decided on March 7, 1962, not to take action on the bill for the relief of Mr. and Mrs. Roumeliotis, on the ground that, in the words of the committee's record of the decision, "Similar bills HR 1342 and HR 1343 (for the relief of Mr. and Mrs. Roumeliotis, respectively) were acted on adversely by the House Judiciary Committee on July 25, 1961."[13] Review was denied by the Supreme Court on Dec. 3, 1962.

Mafia Figures

Considerable public attention was focused, from about 1948 to the mid-1950s, on the deportation of individuals considered to be members of the Mafia. Charles (Lucky) Luciano was perhaps the most prominent gangster deported in the period. For some members or supposed members of the Mafia who were facing deportation, private relief bills were introduced in Congress.

At least one bill in this general category became a law. Sen. Herbert H. Lehman (D N.Y.) introduced a private bill in 1954 to cancel deportation proceedings against Martin A. Madden, brother of a notorious gangster of the Prohibition era. Lehman told a newspaper reporter, April 20, 1954, that as far as he knew, the beneficiary of the bill had committed no significant crime since serving time for burglary some 35 years earlier. The Immigration and Naturalization Service contended that Madden had violated a provision of the immigration law in 1953 by claiming American citizenship when he returned from a weekend trip to Cuba. Sen. Lehman reintroduced his private bill in 1955. It passed both houses, and President Eisenhower signed it on August 12, 1955.

Private bills introduced on behalf of individuals connected or supposedly connected with the Mafia fell off after a flurry of cases in the early 1950s. The total number of exemptions from deportation was small in comparison with the number of successful deportation efforts.

Nationality Bills

Senators and representatives from time to time introduce private bills on behalf of persons who wish to gain or retain status as American citizens notwithstanding provisions of law which normally would prevent them from doing so. To receive citizenship without waiting the required length of time would enable an alien, in some cases, to work at a job for which only citizens are eligible. If candidates for the job are scarce, and the alien is well qualified, a private bill for relief of the alien may gain quick approval. In other cases, a person who is already an American citizen may be in danger of losing that status. For example, a naturalized American citizen who is a servant of an American ambassador, and therefore resides abroad for extended periods, may be unable to fulfill requirements of the law relating to residence in the United States by naturalized citizens. Congress is likely to view with favor a private bill in such a case.

On grounds of compassion or sentiment, the 90th Congress during its Second Session (1968) enacted seven private laws bestowing American citizenship on individuals who had not strictly fulfilled the residence or physical-presence requirements of the naturalization laws, but who nevertheless were deemed worthy of the privileges of citizenship. Three of these laws conferred citizenship posthumously on men who had joined the U.S. Army in 1965 or 1966 and died while on active duty in Vietnam in 1967: John R. Aneli, native of Italy; John P. Collopy, native of Ireland; and Ivan C. King, native of Germany.

Private Bills in Other Areas

Matters other than claims, immigration, and naturalization call from time to time for private legislation. For one thing, the Constitution provides in Article I, Section 9, Clause 8, that "no Person holding any Office of Profit or Trust under...(the United States), shall, without the Consent of Congress, accept of any present, Emolument, Office, or Title, of any kind whatever, from any King, Prince, or foreign State." Congress grants consent in such cases by private laws.

An additional category of private legislation has developed because Congress, in a number of cases, wanted to reward an inventor or other benefactor. For example, Private Law 86-10, approved May 13, 1959, authorized the payment of $15,000 to Mrs. Paul M. Tedder of Gainesville, Fla., in recognition of the fact that her husband, a research engineer, had, in the words of the law, "conceived many ideas and inventions...which have resulted in savings to the United States of many millions of dollars and for which he received no compensation other than his salary from the University of Florida."

Procedures in Enactment

The general course of a private bill, from introduction to presidential approval, is much the same as that of a public bill. But there are some important differences, and they begin to appear at the very outset.

A private bill generally is initiated at the instance of the individual, company, group or locality that stands to benefit from its enactment. By contrast, public laws usually originate in the executive branch of the government or in Congress itself. The intended beneficiary of a private bill may get in touch with his representative or one of his senators directly, presenting the facts and considerations which he believes will justify introduction of the bill, or he may use the services of a lawyer, lobbyist or other intermediary.

Requests of Congress for legislative relief may come from two sources other than the interested party or a senator or representative acting in his behalf. By an Act of April 10, 1928, the Comptroller General of the United States was authorized to direct the attention of Congress to cases in which, through error or otherwise, citizens, business concerns, or institutions merited relief not authorized by existing law.

Congress by various acts has authorized the Attorney General to suspend the deportation of certain classes of deportable aliens and to report to Congress on each case in which he has exercised this authority. Congress may then confirm or end the suspension by measures which are not private laws in the full sense, since they do not require approval by the President, but which are comparable in

many respects to private laws. In some cases, either chamber may end the suspension and order the alien deported by adopting a resolution to that effect; if neither House nor Senate does so in a specified period, the deportation proceedings are canceled. In other cases, affirmative approval by Congress is required: both houses must adopt a concurrent resolution confirming the suspension; if they do not do so "prior to the close of the session of Congress next following the session at which...[the] case is reported,"[14] the Attorney General is required to deport the alien.

The Department of State initiates private bills authorizing retired personnel of the government to accept gifts or decorations from foreign governments. This source of private bills, unlike the two just mentioned, is based on tradition and the general statutory duties of the department rather than on specific legislation.

Committee Action

Virtually all private bills introduced in the Senate are referred to the Senate Committee on the Judiciary, and private bills introduced in the House are almost always referred to the House Committee on the Judiciary. Bills are referred to appropriate subcommittees, or to individual members if no appropriate subcommittee exists, and are taken up for consideration only upon a specific request for action from a sponsor. Reports are requested from the appropriate executive agencies. Subcommittee hearings are held in many cases. The subcommittee's decisions are presented to the full committee, which usually concurs. Committee approval of a bill places it on the Private Calendar in the House, and on the Calendar of Business in the Senate.

Floor Action

In the House, Rule XXIV provides for calling the Private Calendar on the first and third Tuesday of each month. On the third Tuesday, preference is to be given to omnibus bills, which include bills or resolutions previously objected to on a call of the Private Calendar. In the Senate, where private bills are listed in chronological order on the Calendar, they may be taken up on any day after the conclusion of the Morning Hour. *(Omnibus bills, box p. 307)*

Both chambers use a system of objectors to monitor consideration of private bills. The duty of House objectors, who are appointed by the Speaker, is to screen private bills reported by the Judiciary Committee, before the bills are called up on the Calendar. If one of them objects during floor consideration, the bill is passed over for later consideration. If two or more object, the bill is recommitted. Often, this kills the bill.

In the Senate, the function which the House assigns to the objectors is carried out by the Democratic and Republican Policy Committees. They screen private bills reported by the Committee on the Judiciary to ensure that objection will be voiced to bills that conflict with policy objectives.

Referral to Court of Claims

The Bowman Act of March 3, 1883, authorized referral of a claim from Congress to the U.S. Court of Claims. It provided that either house of Congress, or any committee of either house, might refer a claim involving determination of facts to the Court of Claims for investigation.

Referral of additional categories of cases to the court was authorized by the Tucker Act of March 3, 1887. The additional categories included claims "legal or equitable, or for a grant, gift, or bounty to any person." The Tucker Act empowered the court to render judgment in certain cases, Congress reserving the power to appropriate funds for carrying out the judgments. The cases to be so decided were those involving claims based on the Constitution or any law of Congress, except for pensions; a regulation of an executive department; a contract with the government; or non-tort injury by an agent of the government.

Senate Rule XV, Paragraph 2, provides: "Whenever a private bill is under consideration, it shall be in order to move, as a substitute for it, a resolution of the Senate referring the case to the Court of Claims, under the provisions of the act approved March 3, 1883." The House, while it does not have a corresponding rule, was authorized by the same law to make such a referral. The latest re-enactment of this authority appears in the Act of Oct. 15, 1966, which provides: "Any bill, except a bill for a pension, may be referred by either House of Congress to the chief commissioner of the Court of Claims for a report."

As stated by Supreme Court Justice Tom Clark, in a concurring opinion on June 25, 1962, "Congress still makes legislative references to the court [Court of Claims], averaging some 10 a year." *(Glidden Co. v. Zdanok,* 370 U.S. 530) In the 1970s, about 12 private bills a year were referred to the court according to the clerk of the court.

Private Amendment to Public Bill

The question of whether it would be in order to amend a general appropriation bill by attaching to it a provision for payment of a particular private claim has arisen in the Senate on a number of occasions. Sen. George F. Edmunds (R Vt.), president pro tempore, decided on May 13, 1884, that an amendment of this kind was subject to a point of order unless it served "to carry out the provisions of an existing law or a treaty stipulation, which shall be cited on the face of the amendment" (quoted from a Senate rule then in effect). This decision was confirmed in 1885, 1925, and 1933, and was included, as still in force, in the officially published 1964 digest of Senate procedure compiled by Charles L. Watkins and Floyd M. Riddick.[15]

On July 2, 1884, less than two months after Edmunds' ruling, an exception was allowed. The Treasury Department, administering a law which entitled various government employees to extra compensation, had ruled that the law was inapplicable to a particular group, but the Supreme Court decided later that that group was covered by the law. An amendment to a general appropriation bill, authorizing payment to these employees, was ruled in order.

Presidential Approval or Veto

The first private bill vetoed by a President was a bill to incorporate the Protestant Episcopal Church in Alexandria, Va. President Madison's veto of the bill on Feb. 21, 1811, was his first veto of any bill and the third veto in U.S. history. When Madison returned the bill to the House of Representatives, discussion arose as to whether the Constitution required immediate consideration of the returned bill. It was agreed that the bill should be passed over to the next day. Actually, the bill was taken up two days later, and the veto was sustained.

The question whether a vetoed private bill must be reconsidered immediately under the Constitution arose in another form almost a half-century later. President

Omnibus Private Bills

A private bill passed over by the House of Representatives because an official objector or anyone else has expressed opposition to it is reconsidered by the House Committee on the Judiciary. The committee, if it still favors the bill, may include the bill's provisions in a conglomerate piece of legislation called an omnibus bill. House Rule XXIV, Clause 6, governs, among other things, the consideration of omnibus bills. In its present form, adopted May 27, 1935, the clause reads, in part:

"On the third Tuesday of each month after the disposal of such business on the Speaker's table as requires reference only, the Speaker may direct the Clerk to call the bills and resolutions on the Private Calendar, preference to be given to omnibus bills containing bills or resolutions which have previously been objected to on a call of the Private Calendar....

"Omnibus bills shall be read for amendment by paragraph, and no amendment shall be in order except to strike out or to reduce amounts of money stated or to provide limitations. Any item or matter stricken from such an omnibus bill shall not thereafter during the same session of Congress be included in any omnibus bill.

"Upon passage of any such omnibus bill, said bill shall be resolved into the several bills and resolutions of which it is composed, and such original bills and resolutions, with any amendments adopted by the House, shall be engrossed, where necessary, and proceedings thereon had as if said bills and resolutions had been passed in the House severally."

Senate procedure is similar in respect to revival of deferred bills in omnibus bills and floor consideration of omnibus bills. In either house, one objection to a particular bill within an omnibus bill is enough to strike that particular bill.

Buchanan on April 17, 1860, vetoed a bill for the relief of individuals who claimed payment for services rendered in transporting mail. The House, on receiving the veto message, considered referring it to a committee. This proposal was rejected, but no further action on the message was taken until June 7, 1860, when the veto was sustained.

Veto messages for private bills are handled in the same manner as messages for public bills. There may be an immediate vote to override or sustain the veto, the vote may be postponed to a fixed date, or the message may be referred to a committee. Referral to a committee in effect kills the bill in most cases.

Two-thirds of all vetoed bills since 1789 have been private bills. A considerable proportion of the private bills vetoed would have waived the statute of limitations, particularly in tax cases. Another sizable category of vetoed private bills has consisted of bills to reverse unfavorable judicial decisions. Presidents generally have felt, in these cases, that the individuals already had had their day in court. *(Presidential vetoes, p. 628)*

Of private bills referred by Congress to the Court of Claims for examination, reported favorably by the court, and then passed by Congress, only a few have been vetoed. One case arose when federal officials who had filed a tax lien against a hotel refused to let the tenants pay their rent but failed to collect the rent themselves. The principal stockholder in the corporation that owned the hotel was a horse-race bookmaker. President Kennedy on Oct. 18, 1962, vetoed a bill for the relief of the corporation. He noted in his veto message that the primary beneficiary would be the bookmaker whose fraudulent evasion of taxes had caused the case. Congress later passed the bill again. It was vetoed this time by President Johnson on Aug. 11, 1964; and that ended the efforts of the hotel to obtain compensation.

Only once since the Cleveland administration has Congress overridden a Presidential veto of a private bill. A Tennessee tobacco factory was destroyed by fire in 1945. Internal Revenue stamps worth more than $8,000, for which the factory owners had paid the government in full, reportedly went up in flames. Congress early in 1949 passed a private bill to reimburse the factory owners for the value of the stamps, but President Truman on April 21, 1949, vetoed the bill because evidence was lacking that the stamps had been destroyed. The veto was overridden by the House on May 18 (318 yeas, 49 nays) and by the Senate on Sept. 15 (45 yeas, 6 nays).

Efforts to Reduce Workload

A significant proportion of the laws enacted by Congress consists of private laws. The ratio of private laws to public laws reached an all-time peak of almost 8 to 1 in the 59th Congress (December 1905-March 1907), which enacted 6,249 private laws and 775 public laws. The total number of private laws enacted since 1789 constitutes between one-third and one-half of all laws enacted in the same period. The ratio dropped from 54.9 per cent in the 79th Congress (1945-46) to 33.5 per cent in the 80th Congress (1947-48) after the Legislative Reorganization Act of Aug. 2, 1946, banned the introduction of various categories of private bills. In the 93rd Congress (1973-74) the ratio had dropped to 15.9 per cent.

Congress has taken steps, over the years, to avoid excessive allocation of the time of members and committees to the consideration of bills which directly affect only one person or a small number of persons. These steps have included, in the first place, a series of public laws delegating to executive agencies the authority to act on cases previously handled by Congress. In the second place, Congress has set up streamlined procedures for investigating the merits of cases which still can be settled only by means of private legislation.

In 1896, Congress enacted a public law which eliminated the need for Congress to pass a private bill to authorize every donation of an obsolete Civil War cannon to a town, civic association, or other group. The law, approved May 22, 1896, provided "That the Secretary of War and the Secretary of the Navy are each hereby authorized, in their discretion, to loan or give to soldiers' monument associations, posts of the Grand Army of the Republic, and municipal corporations, condemned ordnance, guns, and cannon balls which may not be needed in the service of either of said Departments." More comprehensive public laws to make unnecessary the passage of private laws followed over an extended period in the field of private claims.

Public Laws for Settling Private Claims

By an act of Feb. 24, 1855, Congress established the Court of Claims and gave it authority to investigate contrac-

tual and other legal claims against the government and report on them to Congress. An opinion by Supreme Court Justice John M. Harlan, handed down June 25, 1962. *(Glidden Company v. Zdanok,* 370 U.S. 530), provided a brief history lesson: "The Court of Claims was created...primarily to relieve the pressure on Congress caused by the volume of private bills.... By the end of 1861, however, it was apparent that the limited powers conferred on the court were insufficient to relieve Congress from the laborious necessity of examining the merits of private bills."

President Lincoln, in his first annual message to Congress, Dec. 3, 1861, requested that the Court of Claims be given authority to make final decisions:

"It is as much the duty of Government to render prompt justice against itself in favor of its citizens as it is to administer the same between private individuals. The investigation and adjudication of claims in their nature belong to the Judicial department. Besides, it is apparent that the attention of Congress will be more than usually engaged for some time to come with great national questions. It was intended by the organization of the Court of Claims mainly to remove this branch of business from the halls of Congress; but while the court has proved to be an effective and valuable means of investigation, it in great degree fails to effect the object of its creation for want of power to make its judgments final. Fully aware of the delicacy, not to say danger, of the subject, I commend to your careful consideration whether this power of making judgments final may not properly be given to the court, reserving the right of appeal on questions of law to the Supreme Court, with such other provisions as experience may have shown to be necessary."[16] Congress expanded the powers of the Court of Claims by the Bowman Act of 1883 and the Tucker Act of 1887, but not to the extent recommended by Lincoln.

A complication affecting referral of cases to the Court of Claims arose in the 1960s. The situation was summarized in a report submitted to the Senate by the Judiciary Committee on Sept. 22, 1966:

"In 1962,...in the case of *Glidden Co. v. Zdanok,* 370 U.S. 530, the Supreme Court held that the Court of Claims was a court of the United States within the meaning of Article III of the Constitution. It is well settled that an Article III court may only decide cases and controversies, and may not render merely advisory opinions that other branches of the Government are free to disregard.... Since the *Glidden* decision, the Court of Claims has regretfully declined to accept any further Congressional reference cases."[17]

The impasse was resolved by the Act of Oct. 15, 1966, which authorized trial commissioners of the Court of Claims, rather than the court as such, to consider and report on congressional reference cases.

Over the years, Congress has authorized executive departments and agencies in general, or particular departments and agencies, to settle small claims such as previously had required the introduction of private bills. Types of claims thus sloughed off by Congress were supplementary to those that the Court of Claims had been empowered to consider.

Changes Under Legislative Reorganization Act

Congressional committees considering legislative reforms in 1946 found it possible to eliminate three categories of private bills: those to settle certain tort claims, those to authorize construction of bridges, and those to correct military records. The Legislative Reorganization Act of

Aug. 2, 1946, prescribed other means of handling such matters.

Tort Claims. The act of 1946 provided, in Title IV, Sec. 403, for settlement by executive departments and agencies of "any claim against the United States for money only...on account of damage to or loss of property or on account of personal injury or death, where the total amount of the claim does not exceed $1,000, caused by the negligent or wrongful act or omission of any employee of the Government, while acting within the scope of his office or employment." Similar claims exceeding $1,000 were authorized to be settled in U.S. district courts. Title IV was called the Federal Tort Claims Act. Twenty years later, by an act of July 18, 1966, Congress eliminated the $1,000 maximum on tort claims to be settled by departments and agencies but added the provision "That any award, compromise, or settlement in excess of $25,000 shall be effected only with the prior written approval of the Attorney General or his designee."

Bridges and Military Records. Title V of the act of 1946 was called the General Bridge Act. In Sec. 502, it provided: "The consent of Congress is hereby granted for the construction, maintenance, and operation of bridges and approaches thereto over the navigable waters of the United States, in accordance with the provisions of this title." Among the provisions specified were approval by the chief of engineers and the Secretary of War (now the Secretary of the Army) of the location of such bridges and the plans for them, limitation of privately owned toll bridges, and special requirements for bridges connecting American with foreign territory.

The act provided in Title II, Sec. 207: "The Secretary of War, the Secretary of the Navy, and the Secretary of the Treasury with respect to the Coast Guard, respectively, under procedures set up by them, and acting through boards of civilian officers or employees of their respective departments, are authorized to correct any military or naval record where in their judgment such action is necessary to correct an error or to remove an injustice."

Immigration Appeals

Following enactment of the Immigration and Nationality Act of 1952, requests for relief from immigration restrictions increased markedly. During the fiscal year ended June 30, 1953, the number of private immigration bills introduced was 48 per cent greater than in the preceding fiscal year, but, because of restrictive attitudes in Congress, the number of such bills passed declined by 53 per cent. Nevertheless, in the fiscal year ended June 30, 1954, almost 43 per cent of all private laws enacted had to do with immigration. In the 93rd Congress (1973-74), private immigration bills accounted for 51 per cent of the private laws enacted.

President Eisenhower on Jan. 31, 1957, asked Congress to broaden the authority of the Attorney General to exempt deserving individuals from provisions of the immigration laws. The President proposed transferring authority from Congress to the Attorney General to grant relief to three classes of persons not likely to become public charges or to be undesirable citizens: "I recommend that the Attorney General be granted authority, subject to such safeguards as Congress may prescribe, to grant relief from exclusion and expulsion to aliens having close relatives in this country, to veterans, and to functionaries of religious organizations. Generally these are the classes of cases which have been favorably regarded by Congress because of the hardship involved."[18]

Congress adopted amendments to the immigration laws granting additional authority to the Attorney General, but the classes of persons whom the Attorney General was empowered to exempt differed from those recommended by the President. The act of Sept. 11, 1957, authorized admission, without regard to quotas, of a few categories of relatives previously not eligible for nonquota visas, such as stepchildren. It authorized the Attorney General to let down the bars also for a few additional groups, such as aliens who, though legally admitted, had failed to fulfill the requirements for permanent residence.

Further amendments of this kind were adopted in 1958. The act of Aug. 8, 1958, authorized the Attorney General to legalize the stay in the United States of persons who had entered the country improperly before June 28, 1940, had resided in the United States continuously since such entry, and were "of good moral character." The act of Aug. 21, 1958, added to the groups whose status the Attorney General could regularize aliens admitted as nonimmigrants who could have been admitted as immigrants.

Footnotes

1. "Private Bills in Congress," *Harvard Law Review* vol. 79 (June 1966) p. 1685.
2. *Ibid.,* p. 1685.
3. *Ibid.*
4. *Ibid.,* p. 1686.
5. *Ibid.,* pp. 1684-85.
6. *Congressional Record,* April 12, 1878, p. 2488.
7. *Statutes at Large,* vol. 29, pp. xix-xxviii; vol. 30, pp. xxi-xxxv; vol. 31, pp. xix-xliv.
8. Grover Cleveland, "First Annual Message," in *The State of the Union Messages of the Presidents 1790-1966,* vol. II, ed.
9. *Congressional Record,* Oct. 20, 1969, p. 30528.
10. *Annual Report,* Immigration and Naturalization Service, 1975, p. 139.
11. *Annual Report,* Immigration and Naturalization Service, 1968, p. 127.
12. Immigration and Naturalization Service, exchange of letters of Commissioner Raymond F. Farrell and Peter W. Rodino Jr. (D

N.J.), chairman, House Judiciary Committee, dated Feb. 7, 1973 and Feb. 26, 1973.
13. Cited in *Roumeliotis v. Immigration and Naturalization Service,* 304 F. 2nd 453.
14. 18 United States Code 1254.
15. Charles Watkins and Floyd M. Riddick, *Senate Procedure,* (U.S. Government Printing Office, 1964), p. 106.
16. Abraham Lincoln, "First Annual Message to Congress," in *The State of the Union Messages of the Presidents 1790-1966,* vol. II, ed. Fred L. Israel (New York: Chelsea House, Robert Hector Publishers, 1966), p. 1060.
17. U.S. Congress, Senate, *Congressional Reference Cases, U.S. Court of Claims,* S. Rept. 1643, 89th Cong., 2nd sess., Sept. 22, 1966, p. 3.
18. Public Papers of the Presidents, Dwight D. Eisenhower, (U.S. Government Printing Office, 1957), p. 115.

Selected Bibliography

Books

Bailey, Stephen K. and Samuel, Howard D., *Congress at Work.* New York: Holt, 1952.

Berman, Daniel M., *In Congress Assembled.* New York: Macmillan, 1964.

Digested Summary and Alphabetical List of Private Claims Which Have Been Presented to the House of Representatives from the First to the Thirty-First Congress. Baltimore: Genealogical Publishing Co., 1970.

Gordon, Charles and Rosenfield, Harry N., *Immigration Law and Procedure,* Banks, 1966 (revised edition).

Griffith, Ernest S., *Congress: Its Contemporary Role.* New York: New York University Press, 1961.

Luce, Robert, *Legislative Problems.* Boston: Houghton-Mifflin, 1935.

Schmeckebier, Laurence F. and Eastin, Roy B., *Government Publications and Their Use.* Washington: Brookings Institution, 1936 (revised edition, 1969).

Story, Joseph, *Commentaries on the Constitution of the United States.* New York: Da Capo Press, 1969. 3 vols.

Willoughby, William F., *Principles of Legislative Organization and Administration.* Washington: Brookings Institution, 1934.

Articles

Berdahl, Clarence A., "The President's Veto of Private Bills," *Political Science Quarterly,* December 1937, pp. 505-531.

Boeckel, Richard M., "The Veto Power of the President," *Editorial Research Reports,* Dec. 16, 1932, pp. 405-423.

Galloway, George B., "Reform of Private Bill Procedure" (memorandum, May 2, 1949); *Congressional Record,* Vol. 95 (81st Congress, 1st Session, 1949), Appendix, p. A 2901-A 2904.

Gellhorn, Walter and Lauer, Louis, "Congressional Settlement of Tort Claims Against the United States," *Columbia Law Review,* January 1955, pp. 1-36.

Large, Arlen J., "Drama in the Capitol: Private Bills Assist Lovers and a Cowman." *Wall Street Journal,* April 14, 1967, pp. 1, 14.

Luce, Robert, "Petty Business in Congress," *American Political Science Review,* October 1932, p. 815-827.

Orth, Samuel P., "Special Legislation," *Atlantic Monthly,* January 1906, pp. 69-76.

"Private Bills and the Immigration Law," *Harvard Law Review,* April 1956, pp. 1083-1096.

"Private Bills in Congress," *Harvard Law Review,* June 1966; pp. 1684-1706.

Steinberg, Alfred, "When to Use Your Right of Petition," *Nation's Business,* August 1951, pp. 56-59.

Government Publications

Bennett, Marion T., *Private Claims Acts and Congressional References.* Government Printing Office, 1968. (Printed for House Judiciary Committee; reprint from *U.S. Air Force JAG Law Review,* November-December 1967.)

Hinds, Asher C., *Hinds' Precedents of the House of Representatives.* Government Printing Office, 1907.

Statutes at Large. vol. 29 (December 1895-March 1897); vol. 30 (March 1897-March 1899); vol. 31 (December 1899-March 1901).

U.S. Congress, House. Committee on the Judiciary, Subcommittee on Immigration, Citizenship and International Law, *Rules of Procedure: Private Legislation.* Washington: Government Printing Office, 1975.

U.S. Congress, Senate. *Congressional Reference Cases, U.S. Court of Claims,* S. Rept. 1643, 89th Cong., 2nd sess., Sept. 22, 1966.

U.S. Congress, Senate. *List of Private Claims Brought Before the Senate of the United States from the Commencement of the Fourteenth to the Close of the Forty-sixth Congress.* Government Printing Office, 1881. 2 vols.

U.S. Congress, Senate. *List of Private Claims Brought Before the Senate of the United States from the Commencement of the Forty-seventh to the Close of the Fifty-first Congress.* Government Printing Office, 1895. 3 vols.

U.S. Congress, Senate, Committee on Claims. *Alphabetical List of Private Claims Which Were Brought Before the Senate of the United States...from December 4, 1899, to March 4, 1903.* Government Printing Office, 1903.

U.S. Congress, Senate, Committee on Claims. *Alphabetical List of Private Claims Which Were Brought Before the Senate of the United States...from November 9, 1903, to March 4, 1905.* Government Printing Office, 1905.

U.S. Congress, Senate Library, *Presidential Vetoes: Record of Bills Vetoed and Action Taken Thereon by the Senate and House of Representatives, First Congress through the Ninetieth Congress, 1789-1968.* Washington: Government Printing Office, 1969.

U.S. Immigration and Naturalization Service, *Annual Reports,* Government Printing Office, 1968, 1975.

CONGRESSIONAL PROCEDURES

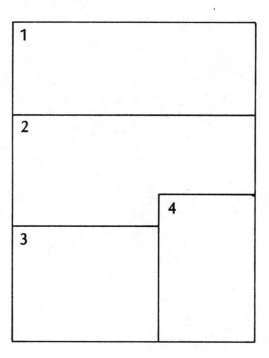

1. Senate Finance Committee marking up the tax-cut bill, March 14, 1975.

2. House Agriculture Committee meeting on the emergency farm bill, March 4, 1975.

3. Speaker Joseph G. Cannon (R Ill.) on the floor of the House. (Library of Congress photo no. LC-F82-5457.)

4. Contest for election of House Speaker, a two-month battle which resulted in the election of Nathaniel Banks (American Party Mass.) in February 1856 on the 133rd vote. (Library of Congress photo no. LC-USZ62-3546.)

Leadership in House and Senate

Few institutions of Congress exert as much influence on the legislative process as do the party leaderships of the House and the Senate. In each chamber, the two parties have established leadership mechanisms that define the party's legislative policies and apply pressure to achieve them. Without these mechanisms, the two chambers might be paralyzed by factional bickering and the pace of legislative activity in all probability would slow to a crawl.

In the House, the leadership structure consists of the Speaker, who is both the chamber's presiding officer and the majority party's overall leader; a majority and minority floor leader; assistant floor leaders (called whips) who have numerous assistants, and a variety of supporting organizations such as special committees to assist with party strategy, legislative scheduling and the assignment of party members to the standing committees of the House.

In the Senate, there is no party official comparable to the Speaker. The Vice President is the constitutional president of the Senate and, in his absence, the president pro tempore presides, but neither office ever has been endowed with political power comparable to that of the Speaker. The remainder of the Senate leadership apparatus, however, is similar in function and power to that of the House. Today, these leadership structures are so influential that few bills sponsored by individual members have any chance of passage without the endorsement of at least one party's leadership group.

Of all the leadership positions in Congress, the only one that has functioned continuously since 1789 is the Speaker—a post established by the Constitution. Although the post of president pro tempore of the Senate also was established by the Constitution, it was not filled on a continuing basis until 1890. Prior to that time, the Senate elected a president pro tempore only on occasions when the Vice President was absent, and in some sessions it let the office stand vacant. All the other leadership posts in both chambers were set up by party caucuses or conferences.

Speaker of the House

For the first two decades of Congress, the Speaker was largely a figurehead, but by the eve of the War of 1812, he had become the dominating leader in Congress. The power of the Speaker ebbed and flowed until the early 1900s, when the significance of the office reached its peak. By 1910, however, arbitrary use of power by a series of autocratic Speakers had culminated in drastic reform of the rules. The Speaker was stripped of most of his power, including authority to sit on the House Rules Committee (which Speakers had both sat on and chaired since 1858), authority to appoint committee members and absolute authority over recognition of members.

Those changes have stood. All subsequent Speakers who have achieved influence in the House have done so through personal prestige and persuasion. Today, the Speaker's primary powers are presiding over the House; deciding points of order; referring bills and resolutions to the appropriate House committees; and appointing members of select committees and conference committees and chairmen of the Committee of the Whole, the parliamentary format in which most House floor action is transacted. (Democrats have their party leader—who is the Speaker when they are the majority—name the Democratic members of the Rules Committee.) The Speaker may participate in debate and may vote, like any other member, although most recent Speakers have voted only to break a tie.

Most 20th-century Speakers have sought to apply their authority within parliamentary limits and yet to aid their own party whenever possible. As Floyd M. Riddick noted in his book *The U.S. Congress: Organization and Procedure,* "Tradition and unwritten law require that the Speaker apply the rules of the House consistently, yet in the twilight zone a large area exists where he may exercise great discrimination and where he has many opportunities to apply the rules to his party's advantage."[1] One notable example of such discrimination occurred in 1941, when a ruling by House Speaker Sam Rayburn (D Texas) won him credit for having made possible the passage of a bill extending the

---

Reference

See Appendix pp. 173-A and 184-A for list of all Speakers of the House, presidents pro tempore of the Senate and majority and minority leaders and whips of both chambers.

---

military draft. After the measure passed by the narrow margin of 203 to 202, Rayburn employed a series of parliamentary maneuvers to prevent the bill's reconsideration despite a considerable outcry from Republicans that he was using his power arbitrarily. Historians have observed that the entire preparedness program for World War II might have been disrupted if the bill had not been passed when it was.

Although the Constitution does not specify that the Speaker must be a member of the House, no non-member has ever been elected to the post. Since the 19th century, only relatively senior members have been named Speaker. (Prior to 1896, the average period of House service by members becoming Speaker was seven years; from 1896 to 1971, it was more than 22 years.) It also has become an unwritten tradition to elevate the party's floor leader to Speaker once an opening occurs, or in the case of the minority party, when it comes into the majority. Since the Civil War, neither party has ousted a sitting Speaker as long as the party remained in the majority, and only two former Speakers (J. Warren Keifer, R Ohio 1881-83 and Joseph W. Martin Jr., R Mass. 1947-49, 1953-55) have been removed from leadership positions when the party was in the minority. As Randall B. Ripley observed in his book *Party Leaders in the House of Representatives,* "In general, the Speaker retains leadership status in his party as long as he remains in the House."[2]

Leaders of the Senate

Because of the Senate's smaller size, leadership structures in that chamber developed more slowly than they did in the House. Some individual senators created their own followings at times, but it was not until the 1890s that an effective party structure appeared. From 1890 until 1911, a Republican clique led by Sens. William B. Allison (Iowa) and Nelson W. Aldrich (R.I.) was able to dominate the Senate even though neither senator was formally designated as party floor leader.

Toward the latter part of the Allison-Aldrich era, both parties formally organized their leadership in the Senate, vesting power in appointed party leaders (but not in the president pro tem, whose function has been limited for the most part to presiding in the Vice President's absence). Since the Allison-Aldrich period, there have been only four powerful leadership organizations in the Senate—those of Majority Leaders John W. Kern (D Ind.) during the Wilson administration, Joseph T. Robinson (D Ark.) in the New Deal era of the 1930s, Lyndon B. Johnson (D Texas) in the 1950s, and Minority Leader Everett McKinley Dirksen (R Ill.) in the 1960s. Subsequent Senate floor leaders Mike Mansfield (D Mont.), the majority leader since 1961, and Hugh Scott (R Pa.), minority leader since late 1969, were more reluctant than Johnson and Dirksen to use the full power of their offices and thus achieved less striking results. Mansfield and Scott were to retire at the end of the 94th Congress.

Tools of Leadership

Party leaders in both houses have relied on a variety of resources to achieve their objectives. Whenever possible, both parties take advantage of the chamber's rules, particularly by filibustering in the Senate. Leaders rely upon a variety of tangible rewards to influence the course of legislation, including selective use of committee assignments, allocation of public works projects, award of campaign funds from the Congressional and Senatorial Campaign Committees, help in obtaining outside campaign contributions and promises to campaign for a member's re-election.

A less tangible but equally important tool has been the leadership's expression of approval and personal friendliness toward the party faithful and coolness toward party defectors. As Randall Ripley noted in his study of the House, "The party leaders are in good position to influence the attitude of the House toward a member early in his career by telling other members what they think of him. There are also visible ways, such as the Speaker's selection of members to preside over the House or over the Committee of the Whole, by which party leaders indicate the younger members whom they regard highly."[3]

Most party leaders have been eager to dispense favors to members both of their own and of the opposition party so as to create a stack of IOUs to call upon in the event of close votes on important measures. In recent years, most leaders have relied on tact and persuasion instead of threats or harsh criticism to win members' support.

Following is a discussion of the evolution of the speakership and the recent development of other leadership posts. Also discussed are contested elections for leadership positions and the relations of leaders with Presidents.

History of the Speakership

The intentions of the framers of the Constitution with respect to the speakership were not set forth either in the Constitution itself or in the records of the Constitutional Convention. As adopted, the Constitution's only reference to the office came in Article I, Section 2, Clause 5, which stated that "The House of Representatives shall chuse their Speaker and other Officers...." There is no evidence that the provision was put to debate.

Two respected authorities on the speakership, Mary P. Follett and Hubert Bruce Fuller, have suggested that the failure of the Founding Fathers to elaborate on the Speaker's office indicated that the role they envisioned for the post was one similar to the speakership of the colonial legislatures—a post with which the framers were intimately familiar. In most cases, the colonial speakers were active politicians who not only presided over the legislatures but also used their positions to further their own or their faction's legislative aims. This concept of the office differed sharply from that of the speakership of the House of Commons; the British speaker is a strictly non-partisan presiding officer.

Follett, whose 1896 book, *The Speaker of the House of Representatives,* is widely regarded as an authoritative study of the office, contended that a proposal put before the Constitutional Convention for a Council of State—consisting of the Speaker, the President, the president of the Senate, the Chief Justice of the United States and the heads of federal departments—further indicated that the Founding Fathers intended the Speaker's office to be a political post. The proposal for a Council of State was seriously considered but was rejected by the Convention.

Follett asserted: "Surely, those who advocated this important board could not have thought of the Speaker as a non-political moderator, as a mere parliamentary officer whom it was necessary to dissociate from politics. What

(Continued on p. 318)

Order of Presidential Succession

The order in which congressional leaders and Cabinet officers succeed to the presidency in the event of a vacancy in that office and in the office of Vice President has been acted upon by Congress three times since 1789. Each time—in 1792, 1886 and 1947—the central question has been whether the President should be succeeded by an official appointed by him or by a member of Congress elected by the people. Congress took the latter course in 1792, switched to appointive officials in 1886, and then to elective followed by appointive officials in 1947. Although the Twenty-fifth Amendment, ratified in 1967, provided for appointment by the President of a new Vice President in the event of a vacancy in that office, it did not change the order of subsequent succession.

The original succession law, passed in 1792, provided that the president pro tempore of the Senate and the Speaker of the House, in that order, would assume the presidency in the event that both the President and Vice President died or were disabled. In 1886, Congress removed the two congressional leaders from the line of succession and added in their place all of the members of the President's Cabinet, in the order in which their departments had been established. In 1947, the Speaker of the House and the president pro tem of the Senate were put back on the list in that order and placed ahead of the Cabinet members.

Authority for the action of Congress was contained in Article II, Section 1, of the Constitution, which states: "In case of the Removal of the President from Office, or of his Death, Resignation or Inability to Discharge the Powers and Duties of the said Office, the Same shall devolve on the Vice President, and the Congress may by Law provide for the Case of Removal, Death, Resignation or Inability, both of the President and Vice President, declaring what Officer shall then act as President, and such Officer shall act accordingly, until the Disability be removed, or a President shall be elected." The Twenty-fifth Amendment provided a method of transferring power from a disabled President to the Vice President.

1886 Law. The 1886 revision of the line of succession was made in recognition of the possibility that both the President and the Vice President might die between the expiration of Congress on March 3 of odd-numbered years and the first session of the new Congress, not regularly held until the first Monday of the following December. If there had been no special session in that interim, there might be no Senate president pro tem, and there definitely would be no Speaker, because the Speaker's term expires with the Congress that elected him.

Therefore, unless there happened to be a holdover president pro tem, because the Vice President had been absent from the Senate at the end of the preceding session, there would be no one in the line of succession to assume the presidency of the United States in event of the cited emergency.

Sen. George F. Hoar (R Mass.), who proposed the 1886 revision, argued, moreover, that if either the president pro tem or the Speaker were available, he would have to combine the responsibility of the presidency with that of the pro tem's or the Speaker's office, whichever the case might be. Hoar asserted also that it was unlikely that anyone would be tempted to assassinate the President and the Vice President if the presidency would then desolve upon the President's chief political advisers, his Cabinet officers. The bill passed easily and was signed into law by President Cleveland.

1947 Revision. On June 19, 1945, President Truman sent Congress a message in which he asked for a re-examination of the order of presidential succession. At that time, the office of Vice President was vacant. Criticizing the 1886 law, Truman asserted: "It now lies within my power to nominate the person (Secretary of State or other Cabinet officers) who would be my immediate successor.... I do not believe that in a democracy this power should rest with the Chief Executive."[4] Accordingly, he asked for legislation which would put an elective official in line for the presidency and suggested for first place, after the Vice President, the Speaker of the House as being more in touch with the people than the president pro tem of the Senate. By that time, the Twentieth Amendment, ratified in 1933, had eliminated the gap between the expiration of one Congress and the beginning of its successor, both the life of the old ending and the life of the new starting at noon on Jan. 3 of odd-numbered years.

The administration bill embodying President Truman's proposal was passed by the House in 1945 but was not acted upon by the Senate. In his 1946 State of the Union Message, the President renewed his request for the bill's enactment, but the Senate still took no action. In 1947, the measure finally passed when the Republican-dominated Senate of the 80th Congress looked with favor on the possibility that one of their own rank—the Speaker of the House or president pro tem of the Senate—might succeed to the presidency. By a strict party-line vote in the Senate and by an overwhelming margin in the House, the President's 1945 proposal finally was enacted.

The Presidential Succession Act of 1947 provided the following new line of succession after the Vice President: the Speaker of the House; the president pro tempore of the Senate; the Secretaries of State, Treasury and War (changed to Secretary of Defense by the National Security Act of 1947); the Attorney General; the Postmaster General; and the Secretaries of Navy (removed from Cabinet rank and thus from the line of succession by the 1947 National Security Act), Interior, Agriculture, Commerce, and Labor. The order of Cabinet succession was the same as under the 1886 law except for addition of the Secretaries of Commerce and of Labor, whose departments had not been established when that law was enacted. The Secretaries of Health, Education and Welfare, of Housing and Urban Development, and of Transportation joined the line of succession later under new legislation providing for automatic addition of the heads of new departments as the departments are created. The position of Postmaster General was removed from the President's Cabinet by 1970 legislation setting up an independent Postal Service.

they intended must be inferred from that with which they were familiar: they knew a speaker in the colonial assemblies who was at the same time a political leader; they knew a presiding officer of (the Continental) Congress who was both a political leader and the official head of the state with important administrative functions; they knew a president of the Constitutional Convention who to his power as chairman added all the influence to be expected of one acknowledged as the foremost man of the nation. Few of their number had ever been in England, and there is no reason for believing, as has been frequently asserted, that they provided for a speaker similar to the presiding officer of the House of Commons."[5]

The term "speaker" first appeared in Commons in 1377, when Sir Thomas Hungerford assumed the post. Until the late 17th century, the speaker was directly responsible to the Crown. The term was derived from the fact that it was the duty of the presiding officer to interpret the will of Commons to the Crown.

First House Speakers

The House of Representatives spelled out the duties of the Speaker on April 7, 1789, when a select committee of 11 members reported a suggested code of standing rules and orders of procedure. The code, discussed and adopted the same day by the full House, assigned the following duties to the Speaker: presiding at House sessions, preserving decorum and order, putting questions to the House, deciding points of order, announcing the results of division and teller votes, appointing committees of not more than three members and voting in cases where his vote would be decisive (a practice known as the Speaker's "casting" vote). At first, the Speaker was elected by secret ballot, but since 1839 his selection has been made on a roll-call vote.

Because political parties had not yet been formed, Frederick A. C. Muhlenberg (Pa.), the first Speaker (1789 to 1791), was nonpartisan. In the 2nd Congress, however, clearly defined party divisions began to appear, and Muhlenberg's successor, Jonathan Trumbull (Conn.), displayed definite leanings toward President Washington's legislative program. Partisanship had become pronounced by 1799, when the Federalists elected Theodore Sedgwick (Mass.) to the Speaker's post. According to Follett's book, "Sedgwick made many enemies by decided and even partisan acts. He was Speaker during the debates on the repeal of the Alien and Sedition Acts, and gave his influence and cast votes in favor of the Bankrupt Act and the Sedition Acts (two important Federalist measures)."[6] In addition, Sedgwick denied a request by two reporters from the *National Intelligencer,* a leading anti-Federalist newspaper, to cover House proceedings. Sedgwick later made that decision final by exercising his casting vote on the matter when the reporters applied directly to the House.

Speakership of Henry Clay

One of the most important periods in the evolution of the speakership was from 1811 to 1825, during which Henry Clay, a Democratic Republican and later Whig, held the post for six terms. Clay, a popular Kentuckian who had resigned a seat in the Senate in order to run for the House, was one of only two members ever elected Speaker during a first term in the House. (The other was William Pennington (Whig N.J.) in 1859.) Clay owed his election to the Speaker's post in 1811 to a faction of young Democratic Republicans known as the War Hawks, who had swept 70

House seats in the election of 1810 by promising western expansion and war with England over its interference with American shipping. On these and other issues, Clay sought to assert the supremacy of Congress over the other branches of government, and of the speakership over affairs of the House.

In one of his first acts as Speaker, Clay stacked key House committees with proponents of his war policy. To the Foreign Affairs Committee he named three War Hawks: Peter B. Porter (DR N.Y.), who was named chairman; John C. Calhoun (DR S.C.) and Felix Grundy (DR Tenn.). In other important appointments, Clay named David R. Williams (DR N.Y.) chairman of the Committee on Military Affairs and Langdon Cheves (DR S.C.) chairman of the Naval Affairs Committee. The newly organized House immediately set out to push the government into war with England. On Nov. 29, 1811, less than four weeks after Congress had convened, the Foreign Affairs Committee issued a report recommending war.

Although President Madison sought a peaceful settlement with England, continuous pressure from Clay finally resulted in a declaration of war. On March 15, 1812, Clay presented to the administration a program calling for a 30-day embargo on British goods, followed by a declaration of war and the acceptance of 10,000 volunteers into the Army on short-term enlistments. Clay noted that while the declaration of war lay within the constitutional powers of Congress, he expected the administration to take the responsibility of recommending it. After considerable deliberation, Madison agreed to the embargo, and on June 1 sent Congress a war message. As George Rothwell Brown noted in his book *The Leadership of Congress,* "Clay had lifted the Speakership of the House to a point of new power and responsibility, the Speaker to a place in the state where, backed by the party organization behind him, he could present to the President a program determining national policy and involving a declaration of war.... Mr. Clay brought to bear upon Mr. Madison...the influence of his great office in an appeal to arms, against the pacifist sentiment of the President and most of the Cabinet."[7]

Clay, a gifted orator, was the first House Speaker to use debate extensively as a tool to achieve his party's legislative aims. In a series of heated discussions with Josiah Quincy, a powerful Federalist from Massachusetts who thought the war would endanger New England's trade interests, Clay mobilized national support for war by casting the issue in terms of patriotism. Hubert Bruce Fuller noted in his book, *The Speakers of the House:* "No subject was so well suited to Clay's native talents [as debate]; he touched the keys of inspiration and the nation echoed one strain; the boundless resources of the country, the glamor of successful war, the magic of enlarged domain, the prestige of victory. This stamped Clay, not the traditional moderator of the House, but rather party leader who could control the House.... In the stirring times of his first term in the Chair, with all the bitterness of party feeling, there was scarcely a day when he did not give voice to his sentiments."[8]

Clay reinforced his control of the House by taking advantage of such rules as that governing recognition of members desiring to speak. A notable example was afforded in debate on the declaration of war, when John Randolph, a Virginia Democrat who had long intimidated weaker House members with his rhetoric, sought to take the floor to oppose the war policy. Clay ruled that Randolph could not speak unless he submitted a motion to the House. When the motion was submitted, Clay ruled that Randolph still could not speak until the House considered the motion. The House refused to consider it, and Randolph was denied the floor. Clay frequently resorted to similar strategy on important issues. In his six terms as Speaker, none of his rulings from the Chair was overturned, though many were sustained only by strict party-line votes.

Unlike his predecessors, Clay remained a vigorous spokesman for his congressional district despite his position as Speaker. He was the first Speaker, and one of the few in history, to vote in instances when his vote could make no difference in the result. Clay's voting practices and his participation in debate set the precedent that Speakers forfeited none of their normal privileges as members.

Notwithstanding setbacks in the war, Clay's personal popularity was not diminished. He kept his influence over the House and later attained equal or even greater influence when he returned to the Senate. Just as he had forced the war policy of the House upon President Madison in 1812, Clay imposed other foreign and domestic policies upon President Monroe after the war. Among the measures he pushed through over Monroe's opposition were various internal improvements, a protective tariff, recognition of South American governments and the Missouri Compromise. In her study of the speakership, Mary P. Follett concluded that Clay was "the most powerful man in the nation from 1811 to 1825."[9] According to Follett, his legacy to the House included three important elements: the increase of the Speaker's parliamentary power, the broadening of the Speaker's personal influence and establishment of the Speaker's prestige as a legislative leader.

Clay's Successors Up to Civil War

With few exceptions, the members who succeeded Clay as Speaker in the pre-Civil War era attempted to follow Clay's model of the speakership. Among the most vigorous political partisans of that period were two Democrats, Andrew Stevenson (Va.), who held the post from 1827 to 1834, and James K. Polk (Tenn.), who served from 1835 to 1839. Both were strong advocates of the programs put forth by the Democratic Presidents who served during their tenures in the speakership. In 1832, Stevenson cast the deciding vote against a motion that a committee to investigate the Bank of the United States (an institution strongly opposed by President Jackson) be chosen by ballot of the House; defeat of the motion meant that Stevenson was free to appoint the committee himself. Polk, who was to become President in 1845, drew considerable criticism from John Quincy Adams (Whig Mass.), a former President, who accused him of appointing House committees "in favor of the administration" and of being "partial."

The main attempt at nonpartisanship in this period was made in 1839-41, when Robert M. T. Hunger (D Va.) was in the Speaker's chair. Hunter, elected as a compromise candidate after Whigs and Democrats had deadlocked over their own candidates, was considered fair but indecisive as a presiding officer. John Quincy Adams described him as a "good-hearted, weak-headed, young man."[10] In his closing speech, Hunter said, "It is something if I can hope I have made it easier for those who succeed me to act on some better principle than that of giving the whole power of the House to one of the parties without regard to the rights and feelings of others. Clothe this station with the authority of justice and how much may it not do to elevate the views of parties from themselves to their country. But arm it with the mere power of numbers and administer it with an ex-

clusive eye to the interests of a party and it may become the engine of as much fraud and oppression as can be practiced in a country as free as ours."[11]

Post-Civil War Speakers

The political character of the speakership became even more pronounced during and after the Civil War. Schuyler Colfax (R Ind.), who served in the post from 1863 to 1869, frequently left the chair to participate in House debates on party issues. One House member said of Colfax that "he sometimes announces the passage of a bill as if it were the triumph of his own work, not as if he were merely reading the record of the House." In April 1864, when a member advocated recognition of the Confederate states, Colfax took the floor to recommend the member's expulsion. "I recognize," Colfax said, "that there is a double duty incumbent upon me: first to the House of Representatives, to administer the duties of the Chair and the rules of the House faithfully and impartially to the best of my ability and judgment. But I feel that I owe still another duty to the people of the ninth Congressional district of Indiana, who sent me here as their Representative to speak and act and vote in their stead. It is in conforming with this latter duty to those who cannot speak here for themselves, and who, I believe, would endorse the sentiment of this resolution, that I have felt my duty to rise in my place as a Member of Congress from the state of Indiana and offer this resolution."[12]

The speakership of Colfax's successor, James G. Blaine (R Maine), was even more political in nature. Not since the time of Clay had a Speaker attempted so consciously to frame the committees of the House in a manner favorable to his party's program. As George Rothwell Brown noted: "Blaine created the committees as he desired them to be, bearing in mind the party necessity, naming as chairmen tried and trusted men of his own selection, men of proved ability and loyalty, who owed their allegiance to him as the head of the party in the House. Through these lieutenants, occupying every strategic place in the organization, the Speaker controlled the House and made it instantly responsive to the will of the party of which, at this period, he was one of the great leaders, if, indeed, not the greatest leader."[13] The result of this structuring of committees was a flood of legislation favorable to business (particularly railroad) interests.

Carlisle, Reed, Crisp

Dimensions of the Speaker's office were further broadened in the late 19th century under two Democrats, John G. Carlisle (Ky.) and Charles F. Crisp (Ga.), and one Republican, Thomas B. Reed (Maine), often called "Czar" Reed.

Carlisle, who held the post from 1883 to 1889, established the concept, which endured for more than two decades, that it was the duty of the Speaker not to follow the dictates of his party, but to impose his own will on the House. Carlisle achieved that objective primarily through the power of recognition, which he used arbitrarily to further his legislative ends. Follett observed that Carlisle "considered it the Speaker's duty to be the leader of Congress, to have a definite legislative policy, and to take every means in his power to secure the accomplishment of that policy. He himself shirked neither the duty nor the responsibility; again and again he opposed the will of a large majority of the House by refusing recognition to members who wished to take up important business; his committees also, while fair and able, represented Carlisle's views more closely than anyone's else. By every other means which his office afforded, he sought, entirely regardless of his position as chairman, to impose his will on the House and to be the real source of the legislation of the United States."[14]

Carlisle's successor, Reed, who served from 1889-91 and again from 1895-99, expanded the powers of his office more than has any other Speaker in history except Clay. In essence, Reed's rulings from the Chair, later formally incorporated into the House rules, established the absolute right of the majority to legislate regardless of attempted obstruction by a minority.

At the outset of the 51st Congress, when Reed assumed office, filibustering by the minority had grown to such lengths that it had become difficult for the majority to transact business. The minority was able to paralyze the House by introducing a series of dilatory motions, such as motions to recess or adjourn, and then demanding time-consuming roll-call votes on the motions. (As provided by the Constitution, one-fifth of a House quorum could demand a roll-call vote.) Another method of obstruction was a system of "constructive absences" under which members of the minority would fail to vote on certain questions even though they were present in the House chamber. Under established procedures, only those voting were counted for purposes of establishing the presence of a quorum, which was necessary for the transaction of business; thus a minority could stall House action by simply refusing to answer to their names on roll-call votes. Reed's rulings, attacked as arbitrary by the Democratic minority, put an end to these procedures.

On Jan. 21, 1890, Reed took his first major step against obstruction by refusing to consider a member's demand for a teller vote on a motion to adjourn. Later that month, he announced his intention to disregard all motions and appeals, however parliamentary in character, if intended simply to delay House business. On Jan. 30, 1890, Reed made a second ruling to curb obstruction. When the yeas and nays were demanded on consideration of a contested election case, the vote came to 161 yeas, 2 nays, and 165 not voting. After the result was announced, Democrats immediately claimed that the vote was invalid because a quorum had not voted. Reed then startled the House by ruling that 130 Democrats present but not voting would be counted for the purpose of establishing a quorum. The motion thus carried by a majority of those voting. An appeal from the decision was tabled by a majority of those voting (again with a quorum present but not voting).

On the following day, the Speaker declined to reconsider the ruling. Follett recalled that Reed was "denounced as a tyrant, despot, czar;...never before had the House of Representatives witnessed such a scene—its presiding officer condemned, and subjected to the most violent abuse on account of a parliamentary decision. But Mr. Reed by his calmness under personal accusations, and by the firmness with which he stood his ground against both importunity and attack, guided the House through its stormy crisis and the establishment of a more sound and salutary principle of parliamentary law."[15]

On Feb. 14, 1890, the House formally adopted new rules incorporating Reed's recent rulings and other new procedures. The new code, reported by the Rules Committee chaired by Reed, provided that (1) all members must vote unless they had a pecuniary interest in the question at issue; (2) motions to take a recess and to fix a date of adjournment would not be entertained when a question was

---

McCormack Aide Conviction

In recent years, only one major scandal has directly involved the office of a top congressional leadership official. This was the conviction in 1970 of Martin Sweig, a longtime aide to House Speaker John W. McCormack (D Mass.), on a perjury charge arising from Sweig's alleged misuse of the Speaker's office.

Some political figures and members of the press sought in the mid-1960s to link another scandal—alleged influence-peddling by Robert G. Baker secretary to the Senate majority in the late 1950s and early 1960s—to the office of then Senate Majority Leader Lyndon B. Johnson (D Texas). But no evidence of Johnson's involvement was established.

Sweig, who had been suspended by McCormack pending the final outcome of the case, was found guilty by a jury in the U.S. District Court in New York, July 9, 1970, on one count of perjury. He was acquitted on five other perjury counts and on a charge of conspiring with Nathan M. Voloshen, a New York lawyer, to misuse the office of Speaker McCormack. On Sept. 3, Sweig, 48, was sentenced to 30 months in prison and fined $2,000. He appealed the conviction and was released on a recognizance bond of $50,000.

After exhausting the appeals process, Sweig began serving his prison sentence July 22, 1971. He was later tried and convicted on a new charge of misusing the Speaker's office to influence government decisions. He was sentenced to three years in prison, with the sentence to run concurrently with the 30-month sentence he was already serving. Sweig was granted parole and released from the Lewisburg, Pa., federal penitentiary on July 17, 1972.

Voloshen pleaded guilty on June 17, 1970, to charges of conspiring to use the Speaker's office to influence matters before federal government agencies and to three counts of lying to a grand jury about the charges. He was fined $10,000 and given a suspended one-year prison sentence because of failing health on Nov. 24, 1970. Voloshen died Aug. 23, 1971.

---

under debate; (3) 100 members would constitute a quorum in the Committee of the Whole; and (4) no dilatory motion should be entertained by the Speaker. In its report to the House, the Rules Committee majority stated: "The abuse has grown to such proportions that the parliamentary law which governs American assemblies has found it necessary to keep pace with the evil, and to enable the majority by the intervention of the presiding officer to meet by extraordinary means the extraordinary abuse of power on the part sometimes of a very few members."[16]

The "Reed Rules" were adopted by the House after bitter debate; their most controversial provision—the counting of present but nonvoting members to make a quorum—was upheld by the U.S. Supreme Court in an 1891 test case.

Crisp, who succeeded Reed as Speaker in the Democratic-controlled House of 1891-95, contributed to the evolution of the speakership by strengthening the Rules Committee as an element of the Speaker's power. Although the Reed Rules as such were dropped in the 52nd Congress

(1891-93), essentially the same powers were lodged in the Rules Committee. Speakers had sat on and chaired the Rules Committee since 1858 and had derived much of their power from that arrangement.

The rules of the 53rd Congress (1893-95) permitted the Rules Committee to retire from the House at any time and report a motion to put an immediate stop to filibustering. Hubert Bruce Fuller has noted that the expanded role of the Rules Committee was "a radical departure from the long-established rules and principles of parliamentary law and practice." He added: "The tyranny of Reed seemed beneficence when Crisp ruled that not even "the question of consideration could be raised against a report from the Committee on Rules.' This committee, dominated of course by the Speaker, became the dictator of the House and the members were forbidden even to question its wisdom or decision...."[17]

Era of Cannonism

The peak of the Speaker's power came during the incumbency of Joseph G. Cannon (R Ill.), a staunch conservative who instituted few parliamentary changes in the House but fully exploited those made by Carlisle, Reed and Crisp. Like Reed, Cannon also was known as "Czar." Under his reign, from 1903 to 1911, recognition of members was made entirely arbitrary. It was reported that when members rose without first consulting Cannon, the Speaker would say "For what purpose does the gentleman rise?"[18] If the explanation was unsatisfactory, Cannon would invariably deny the member the floor. Fuller reported that on days set aside for enactment by unanimous consent of purely local bills of a minor character, Cannon moved arbitrarily to reward his friends and punish his enemies. "Often on the success of these bills would depend the re-election of many men to Congress. Each member was compelled first to consult the Speaker and secure his consent to recognition. The Speaker on these days had before him a list of the members to be recognized and this order was scrupulously followed. Thus the Speaker's power was neither to be ignored nor defied. His smile and assent made and unmade members, accordingly as he bestowed or withheld those powerful benefices."[19]

Under Cannon, the House Rules Committee became an even more powerful instrument of the speakership than it had been under Crisp. Before any House committee could report to the House, the committee was required to obtain clearance from the Rules panel, and clearance was usually granted only for measures which Cannon desired passed. Terms of the Rules Committee's clearance for consideration of bills desired by Cannon usually included sharp limits on debate and foreclosure of floor amendments. The latter practice made it possible for Cannon and his associates to attach legislative "riders" in committee which might have been voted down on the floor if brought to a separate vote. Rather than kill the entire bill, the House usually accepted such riders, which most frequently were attached to appropriation bills that were virtually assured of passage.

Unlike Speaker Reed, who had ruled the House alone, Cannon established a network of trusted lieutenants. Key committee assignments went to a group of Republicans who had become associated with Cannon in evening poker games: Sereno E. Payne (N.Y.), John Dalzell (Pa.), James R. Mann (Ill.) and Nicholas Longworth (Ohio). The Speaker and his leadership group reportedly decided much of the business of the House during the after-hours poker games.

Cannon finally was shorn of much of his power in 1910 after insurgent Republicans joined with Democrats to force a liberalization of the rules. Among other changes, the new rules prohibited the Speaker from naming or serving on the Rules Committee, denied the Speaker the right to appoint standing committees, and reduced the power of recognition by instituting procedures (Calendar Wednesday and the Calendar for Unanimous Consent) under which bills could be considered without the sponsor having to get recognition by the Speaker. All standing committees, including the Rules Committee, were to be appointed by the full House, meaning in effect the Democratic and Republican Committees on Committees, whose recommendations usually are approved by the party caucuses and the House.

Rule by Caucus or Steering Committee

Democratic Caucus. The first Speaker to preside under the liberalized rules was James Beauchamp (Champ) Clark (D Mo.), who served from 1911 to 1919. During this period, real power was in the hands of Oscar W. Underwood (D Ala.), who was made House majority leader and chairman of the Ways and Means Committee (and thus chairman of the newly established Democratic Committee on Committees made up of the Democrats on Ways and Means). Democrats in 1909 had adopted caucus rules which bound all party members to support any party position adopted by two-thirds of the caucus, unless a member considered the position unconstitutional or had made "contrary pledges to his constituents prior to his election or received contrary instructions by resolutions or platform from his nominating authority."[20] Democrats later adopted a resolution pledging their support to all bills presented to the House by the Ways and Means Committee. These procedures produced considerable party unity and gave Democrats tight control of the House throughout the first term of President Woodrow Wilson, when a large body of reform legislation was enacted.

Republican Steering Committee. Clark's successor, Speaker Frederick H. Gillett (R Mass.), who served from 1919 to 1925, attempted to diminish the partisan character of the speakership and restore its judicial character. With Gillett declining to assert political leadership, power in the House shifted to Majority Leader Franklin W. Mondell (R Wyo.) and a five-member Republican Steering Committee. From 1919 to 1925, the committee met almost daily to discuss party positions and to map strategy with committee chairmen and other Republican leaders. Randall B. Ripley observed in his book *Party Leaders in the House of Representatives:* "For the most part...the Steering Committee carried out the wishes of the Republican leaders in the House, even when these were not in accord with the Republican Administration. For example, a bill in the 68th Congress to increase civil service pensions was held up for an entire Congress and thus killed by an unfavorable Steering Committee decision despite support for it from a unanimous House Civil Service Committee, the Senate and the administration."[21]

Leadership under this system was so diffuse that House Republicans accomplished little during the period. Republicans found it difficult to achieve party unity even on such a traditionally partisan issue as the tariff. According to Ripley, the Steering Committee was plagued with "occasional lapses in communications between the various leaders" and its "communications with the White House were even more uncertain." "The Members," he said, "including some committee chairmen, used the loose leadership structure to pursue legislative ends other than those officially sanctioned."[22]

Longworth, Rayburn, McCormack, Albert

Longworth. The shortcomings of leadership by the Steering Committee prompted the next House Speaker, Nicholas Longworth (R Ohio), to again centralize power in the Speaker's office. Upon assuming the post in 1925, Longworth set forth his conception of the Speaker as party leader: "I believe it to be the duty of the Speaker, standing squarely on the platform of his party, to assist in so far as he properly can the enactment of legislation in accordance with the declared principles and policies of his party and by the same token to resist the enactment of legislation in violation thereof."[23]

Like Cannon, Longworth established a small group of trusted associates to help him run the House. This group, called the "Big Four," consisted of Longworth; John Q. Tilson (R Conn.), the majority leader; Bertrand H. Snell (R N.Y.), chairman of the Rules Committee, and James Begg (R Ohio), a longtime personal friend of Longworth's. Longworth, who served as Speaker until the Democrats took control of the House in 1931, was able to achieve through personal persuasion what Cannon had done by arbitrary interpretation of the House rules.

Rayburn. The prestige of the speakership increased considerably in the 1940s and 1950s during the tenure of Sam Rayburn (D Texas), another master of the art of persuasion. Faced after World War II with a party badly split over civil rights and other domestic issues, Rayburn found that he could minimize disunity by making party decisions himself and bargaining with individuals rather than with the party as a whole. During a large share of Rayburn's 18 years as Speaker (1940-47; 1949-53; 1955-61), many of his party's domestic programs were emasculated by a "conservative coalition" of Republicans and southern Democrats; still, Rayburn was able to push through considerable legislation in the field of foreign affairs as well as several important domestic bills, including two far-reaching civil rights acts (1957 and 1960). In Ripley's opinion, the Speaker's record, in view of the split in his own party, was "enough to earn for Rayburn a reputation as an incomparable legislative wizard when faced with unfavorable odds."[24]

McCormack. The mode of leadership adopted by Rayburn's successor, John W. McCormack (D Mass.), was more like that of the Republican leadership of the 1919-25 era than of any other recent period. He was Speaker from 1962 to 1971. Lacking the persuasive ability of a Rayburn or Longworth, McCormack placed considerable reliance on Majority Leader Carl Albert (D Okla.) and Majority Whip Hale Boggs (D La.). Ripley has noted: "Each element of the collegial leadership has its own importance, but the lack of cohesion that had troubled the Republicans in the early 1920s was not present in this arrangement. The functions were split between the various leaders, but there were numerous integrating meetings of the three principal leaders with committee chairmen and legislative liaison officials. The unity of the Democrats was still far from perfect and some major bills were lost, especially in 1962 and 1963. But the Democrats cohered well enough in 1964, 1965 and 1966 to pass many presidential proposals."[25]

Albert. While personally popular, Speaker Carl Albert (D Okla.) was considered by his colleagues to be a weak leader when compared to the influential Sam Rayburn. However, Albert's leadership was not usually compared un-

---

Pay of Congressional Leaders

Six of the top leaders of Congress—the Speaker of the House, the president pro tempore of the Senate and the majority and minority leaders of both chambers—receive additional pay for their leadership duties.

Speaker. Highest paid of all is the House Speaker: $65,625 as of May 1976. The amount was increased from $62,500 a year in 1975 under a law passed that July that granted members of Congress and top government officials an automatic annual cost-of-living pay increase. In addition to his salary, the Speaker is allowed $10,000 for official expenses (with no accounting required except for income tax purposes). He also receives annual appropriations for staff and other operating costs of running the Speaker's office (as distinguished from his own congressional office). In fiscal 1976, the appropriation for the Speaker's office including his $10,000 personal expense allowance was $333,000.

Following is a tabulation of the changes in the Speaker's salary, with the dates on which the authorizing legislation was enacted:

Salary	Date Signed into Law
$12 per day in session	Sept. 22, 1789
$3,000 per annum	March 19, 1816
$16 per day in session	Jan. 22, 1818
$6,000 per annum	Aug. 16, 1856
$8,000 per annum	Jan. 20, 1874
$12,000 per annum	Feb. 26, 1907
$15,000 per annum	March 4, 1925
$20,000 per annum	Aug. 2, 1946
$30,000 per annum	Jan. 19, 1949
$35,000 per annum	March 2, 1955
$43,000 per annum	Aug. 14, 1964
$62,500 per annum	Sept. 15, 1969
$65,625 per annum	Aug. 9, 1975

President Pro Tempore. Under the 1975 salary legislation (PL 94-82), the salary of the president pro tem of the Senate was raised from $49,500 to $51,975 (and to $65,625 when there is no Vice President and the president pro tem becomes the sole presiding officer). The Senate pro tem receives no allowance for staff and other operating costs.

Party Floor Leaders. The pay of the majority and minority leaders of both houses was increased from $49,500 to $51,975 under the 1975 law. The floor leaders receive appropriations for staff and other operating expenses. In fiscal 1976, the appropriation for the office of the House majority leader was $240,965 and that for the House minority leader was $183,650. Their Senate counterparts received a total appropriation of $239,000 in fiscal 1976 for staff and operating expenses. The majority and minority leaders in both chambers received $3,000 for their own official expenses. Appropriations for staff and operating expenses of House whips came to $198,860 each for the majority and minority. The offices of Senate whips received a total of $185,440.

favorably with that of his immediate predecessor, McCormack. Albert, who became Speaker in 1971, announced June 5, 1976, that he would retire from the House at the end of his term in the 94th Congress.

Albert's leadership style was described by a colleague as being "accommodating, on good terms with everyone."

Prior to the opening of the 94th Congress, the Democratic Caucus enacted reforms giving the Speaker additional powers. Albert was given the power to nominate Democratic members of the House Rules Committee, which decides what legislation will go to the House floor and under what terms it can be debated. The Democratic Steering and Policy Committee, which Albert chaired, was given the authority to make Democratic committee assignments.

Albert drew special criticism from many of the younger and more active party members in the House, most of whom also were moderate to liberal in their political views. In the 94th Congress, he received sharp criticism from a number of the 75 freshman Democrats who had been elected in 1974. The freshmen, as well as a number of their more senior colleagues, were especially distressed when House Democrats, with a 2-1 majority over Republicans, were unable to override many of President Ford's vetoes of Democratic-backed legislation.

Several freshman Democrats talked openly about removing Albert after the House in mid-1975 upheld a Ford veto of a strip-mining control bill, a proposal on which the Democrats had placed considerable importance and which was rejected, on the override attempt, by only three votes. Albert met with some dissatisfied freshmen in June and discussed the need for more effective work by party whips, better communication between leaders and freshmen and improved publicity for Democratic-backed legislation.

No effort was made to oust Albert from his position, and public criticism subsided as the 94th Congress continued into 1976.

Although hampered by the fact that he was not a forceful leader, Albert also faced important obstacles that were beyond his control. One was a White House occupied by a Republican President, Richard Nixon, intent on expanding his own power and acting with minimal consultation with and concern for Congress. In addition, the Nixon administration was committed to conservative political and economic programs opposed by the bulk of the liberal and moderate Democrats in Congress; in this situation, congressional Democrats were faced first with halting Nixon efforts to revamp or terminate existing Democratic programs and only secondly with enacting new programs. The long congressional-executive stalemate that grew from this divided view of government gave rise to frustration in Democratic congressional ranks that found expression in criticism of House (and to a lesser extent, Senate) leadership.

In addition, the House during Albert's speakership was a far different institution than in the days of Sam Rayburn. By Albert's time, the House had seen a huge infusion of new Democratic blood as younger members replaced older ones who retired or died. This turnover in membership came at the same time, and in many ways made possible, an important transformation in the formal rules and the party folkways of the House. Rules were changed to diminish the once nearly absolute power of the most senior members. The seniority system was cracked by subjecting committee chairmen to secret-ballot election by the Democratic Caucus. The powers exercised by committees, and many of the subcommittee chairmanships, had to be shared with junior and even some first and second-term members.

The fundamental result of these changes was to spread power in the House more evenly through the Democratic Party ranks, but the offshoot of that was to make the party more difficult to manage. There were far fewer members who were willing to follow Rayburn's famous exhortation: "to get along, go along." Consequently, the House during Albert's term had many power centers and dozens of members who were less amenable to party discipline than in the past.

Vice President and President Pro Tem

The Constitution's only references to leadership posts in the Senate are contained in two passages of Article I, Section 3. One passage provides that the Vice President "shall be President of the Senate, but shall have no vote, unless they be equally divided" (Clause 4). The other passage provides that the "Senate shall choose...a President pro tempore, in the absence of the Vice President, or when he shall exercise the office of President of the United States" (Clause 5).

With few exceptions, the Senate has been reluctant to place substantial political power in these offices. It has entrusted power instead to the majority and minority leaders. Thus the powers of the Vice President and of the president pro tempore consist of little more than presiding over the Senate, and neither post has equalled the significance of the speakership. Even the authority to preside is less significant in the upper chamber than it is in the House, because the Senate's rules, such as almost unlimited debate, are less strict.

Historical studies attempting to explain the Senate's attitude toward these top offices have stressed disinclination of senators to delegate power to a non-member (the Vice President) or to a member (the president pro tempore) who may preside only at times of the Vice President's absence. If the Vice President and president pro tempore are of different political parties—as has often been the case—the Vice President is able to neutralize the pro tem's authority at any point by merely taking the chair. Accordingly, the Senate has vested the real leadership in its party floor leaders, who in turn attempt to persuade the presiding officers (depending upon their party affiliation) to use their parliamentary powers where possible in support of party goals.

Evolution of Pro Tempore Post

The first president pro tempore, John Langdon of New Hampshire, was elected on April 6, 1789, before the first Vice President, John Adams, had appeared in the Senate. On April 21, 1789, Adams took his seat as presiding officer, and Langdon's service in that capacity ended. Until 1890, the Senate continued to act on the theory that a president pro tem could be elected only in the Vice President's absence and that his term expired when the Vice President returned. By 1890, when the president pro tem was first chosen to serve until "the Senate otherwise ordered," the Senate had elected presidents pro tem on 163 occasions. In the 42nd Congress alone (1871-73), 10 such elections (all of the same man) were held.

Problems that had arisen under this procedure came under scrutiny in 1876, when the Senate directed its Committee on Privileges and Elections to make a thorough study of the matter. After considerable debate on the committee's report, the Senate adopted the report's recommendations: (1) that the term of a president pro tem elected at one session be considered to extend into the next session in the continuing absence of the Vice President; (2) that the death of the Vice President did not automatically vacate the office of president pro tem; and (3) that the Senate had the right to replace a president pro tem at any time it pleased.

Fourteen years later, in 1890, the Senate gave the president pro tem tenure of a sort by adopting a resolution stating that "...It is competent for the Senate to elect a president pro tempore, who shall hold the office during the pleasure of the Senate and until another is elected, and shall execute the duties thereof during all future absences of the Vice President until the Senate otherwise order."[26] That resolution was still in effect in the 1970s. Under its terms, the president pro tem holds the office as long as he serves in the Senate, unless the Senate elects another in his place. Thus no new election is necessary at the start of each new Congress, as it is for the Speaker of the House, unless the Senate wishes to elect a different member to the office.

Almost inevitably, the Senate has elected members of the majority party as president pro tem, usually on straight party-line votes. In recent years, a sitting pro tem has failed of re-election only when his party has lost its majority. Since 1945, it has become customary to elect as pro tem only the most senior member of the majority party. Of six pro tems since 1945, only one has held less than senior rank in his party—Sen. Arthur H. Vandenberg (R Mich.), who was second-ranking Republican when elected in 1947. Before 1945, however, there were some notable exceptions to this rule. For example, Sen. George H. Moses (R N.H.) ranked only 15th in party seniority when elected in 1925, and Willard Saulsbury (D Del.) was still in his first term when elected in 1916.

Powers of President Pro Tempore

Powers of the pro tem as presiding officer have differed little from those of the Vice President. Among the powers of both officers (applicable to the pro tem, of course, only when he is in the chair) are recognition of members for debate and introduction of bills, amendments and motions; the authority to decide points of order (subject to appeal to the full Senate); appointment of senators to conference committees, though it is traditional that the presiding officer appoint the members suggested by the floor manager of the bill in question, subject to normal party ratios; enforcement of decorum; power to administer oaths and affirmations; and appointment of the members of select committees.

The main difference in the powers of the two offices is that the pro tem, but not the Vice President, may appoint a substitute to replace him in the chair. Also, the pro tem, as a member of the Senate, may vote on all matters, while the Vice President may vote only in the case of a tie. At various times in the 19th century, the pro tem was authorized to appoint members of standing committees. According to Walter Kravitz and Walter Oleszek, authors of *The President Pro Tempore of the U.S. Senate,* the pro tem exercised that authority in the years 1823-26, 1828-33, 1838, 1841, 1843 and 1863.

In recent years, the only president pro tem who exerted considerable political influence was Arthur H. Vandenberg (R Mich.), who held the post during the 80th Congress (1947-49). Floyd M. Riddick (later named Senate parliamentarian) said in 1949, in his book *The United States Congress: Organization and Procedure,* that Vandenberg, who was both president pro tem and chairman of the Foreign Relations Committee, "took quite an important part in the legislative program and no doubt exerted as much influence in what was done and not done as the Speaker of the House." Riddick added: "He was firm in his rulings, of which all but one or two stood as the decision of the Senate, even though several appeals were taken; he participated in discussions of the pending legislation from the chair perhaps to an unprecedented extent during any Congress of recent years...."[27]

A more recent pro tem, the late Sen. Richard B. Russell (D Ga.), wielded power potentially equal to that of Vandenberg through his posts as chairman of the Senate Appropriations Committee and of its Defense Appropriations Subcommittee. Russell, however, was hospitalized during much of his term as pro tem (1969-71).

Other Leadership Posts

Since the late 19th century, both political parties have developed highly centralized party organizations to formulate and carry out party programs in the House and the Senate. In each chamber, the parties have officially designated a majority and minority leader (party floor leaders), party whips (assistant floor leaders) and various advisory bodies such as committees to develop party policy, assign members to standing committees, and formulate party strategy for the scheduling of legislation. In the House, this party apparatus has normally been directed by the Speaker, in the Senate by the majority and minority leaders.

In both chambers, leadership organizations have become so important to a party's success that major bills are rarely brought to the floor without extensive study of their prospects as well as exertion of considerable pressure from the party organizations on both sides. These leadership structures are particularly important in the House, because of its greater size and consequent unwieldiness. In his study of the House, *Forge of Democracy,* Neil MacNeil called the chamber's leadership organizations its "priesthood." "The Speaker," MacNeil asserted, "...has never run the House of Representatives without help. The House has been from the beginning such a sprawling, discordant mass of men that the Speaker has had to depend on lieutenants to guide and oversee its multiple operations in its committees and on the floor, and to ensure the orderly flow of responsible legislation. Indeed, over the years, a hierarchy of leaders has been constructed in the House to support the Speaker, and opposing this hierarchy has been another, created by the minority party and led by the 'shadow' Speaker, the leader of the opposition party. With the hierarchy also has been built a vast array of political and party organizations to assist the Speaker and his lieutenants in the complicated task of making the House a viable, responsible legislative body."[28]

House

Majority Leader

The first House member to be officially designated majority leader was Sereno E. Payne (R N.Y.), who assumed the post in 1899. Prior to that time, the chairman of the Ways and Means Committee was normally looked upon as party floor leader, primarily because his committee handled tariff and tax measures, which were usually the most important to come up in the House. Occasionally, the Speaker designated a trusted lieutenant other than the Ways and

Means Committee chairman as the party's leader. In the interest of party harmony, he sometimes named to that post his leading rival within the party.

Until 1911, majority leaders were designated by the Speaker; after the revolt against Speaker Cannon in 1910, however, rank-and-file House members took it upon themselves to exercise this authority, usually through the party caucus or conference—groups made up of the full membership of the party in the House.

In 1911 the House Democratic Caucus elected Oscar W. Underwood (D Ala.) majority leader; when the Republicans returned to power in 1919, their Committee on Committees chose Franklin W. Mondell (R Wyo.). The Democratic Caucus has continued to select the party's floor leader. Since 1923, Republicans have vested the power of selection in their party conference (a body identical except in name to the Democratic Caucus).

The height of power for the majority leader came during President Wilson's first term, when Underwood dominated the House through the party caucus and his chairmanship of the Ways and Means Committee. George B. Galloway pointed out in his *History of the House of Representatives:* "As floor leader, Underwood was supreme, the Speaker a figurehead. The main cogs in the machine were the caucus, the floor leadership, the Rules Committee, the standing committees, and special rules. Oscar Underwood became the real leader in the House. He dominated the party caucus, influenced the rules, and as chairman of Ways and Means chose the committees. Champ Clark was given the shadow, Underwood the substance of power."[29] After 1925, the speakership regained much of its former power and prestige, and since then the majority leader has been the chief lieutenant of the Speaker.

Duties of the majority and minority leaders are not spelled out in the standing rules of the House, nor is official provision made for the offices (except through appropriations specifically made for their offices). In practice, the majority leader's job has been to formulate the party's legislative program in cooperation with the Speaker and other party leaders, steer the program through the House, ensure that committee chairmen report bills deemed of importance to the party, and fix the legislative schedule of the House by securing unanimous consent agreements from the membership. In this latter duty, the majority leader has a significant parliamentary advantage in that if a member objects to his proposal to consider a given bill, the majority leader can usually achieve the same result by putting the matter to a simple majority vote on the floor.

Minority Leader

The position of minority leader first became identifiable in 1883. Since that time, the post has always been assumed by the candidate nominated by the minority party for the speakership. As in the case of the majority leader, the selection of the minority leader is made by the Democratic Caucus or Republican Conference, depending upon which party is in the minority. For the most part, the minority leader's principal duty has been to organize the forces of his own party to counter the legislative program of the majority. Rarely has the minority offered its own legislative program. The only major legislative successes for the minority in the 20th century were in the 75th Congress (1937-39) and in the 87th Congress (1961-62), when a number of liberal proposals put forth by the Democratic majority were rejected. In both cases, however, large-scale defections of conservative Democrats were largely responsible for the outcome.

Everyday duties for the minority leader correspond to those of his majority counterpart, except that the minority leader has no authority over scheduling; if he objects to majority proposals for scheduling, he can always be defeated by a party-line vote on the floor. The minority leader is spokesman for his party and its field general on the floor. It is his duty to consult ranking minority members of House committees and see that they follow adopted party positions. If his party occupies the White House, he will probably be the President's spokesman in the House.

Randall B. Ripley observed in *Party Leaders in the House of Representatives:* "One of the minority leader's greatest problems is the generally demoralizing condition of minority party status. Minority members—especially those in a long-standing minority—are less likely to be informed about what the House is doing. They are on the losing side much of the time both in committee and on the floor. They have little patronage inside the Capitol. Their smaller committee staffs make it difficult to prepare legislative positions, and they usually are unable to obtain such assistance from the executive branch. Yet they want to be informed, to win, and to have patronage, committee staffs and executive branch cooperation. When they cannot gain these objectives, one target of their frustrations is the minority leader."[30]

Ripley found that minority leaders were much more likely than majority leaders to retire voluntarily or to be ousted from their positions. Ripley's study, conducted in 1967, showed that of 13 minority leaders until that time, five had stepped down voluntarily, while only two of 12 majority leaders had done so. No majority leader had been ousted by his party, while three minority leaders had been thrown out. Six majority leaders had succeeded to the speakership, while only three minority leaders had become Speaker. After Ripley's study was made, another majority leader Carl Albert (D Okla.), became Speaker. Albert was elected to the post in 1971 following the retirement from Congress of Speaker John W. McCormack (D Mass.).

Whips

From the outset, parties have relied on their more influential members to ensure party regularity on important issues before the House. During most of the 19th century, however, such members were employed in that capacity only on the occasion of a particular floor fight. It was not until 1899 that one of the parties officially designated a member as a party whip. Randall Ripley found that the term "derives from the British fox-hunting term 'whipper-in' used to describe the man responsible for keeping the hounds from leaving the pack."[31] It was first applied to the British Parliament around 1770.

Whips help their floor leader keep track of the whereabouts of party members, assist in exerting pressure on members to vote the party line, induce members to turn out for votes, compile lists on how members are likely to vote, and arrange "pairs" between opposing members. A whip serves as the party's acting floor leader in the absence of the regular leader. In recent years, the Democratic whip organization has consisted of a chief whip, appointed by the Democratic floor leader, and 15 to 18 assistant whips selected on a regional basis by state delegations. The Republican organization has consisted of a chief whip, a deputy whip, four regional whips and 15 area whips. From

1919 to 1965, the Republican whip was selected by the party's Committee on Committees. Since 1965, the selection has been made by the party conference. Traditionally, the chief Republican whip has selected his own assistants.

In recent years, whip organizations of the two parties have sometimes pooled their information in order to attain an accurate overall picture of the mood of the House respecting important bills. Neil MacNeil said in *Forge of Democracy:* "On some whip counts, or 'nose counts' as they have been called,...each [whip] has told the other how his party members would divide on a given bill. Between them, they have sometimes been able to forecast a House vote almost to the man as much as a week in advance. Armed with such intelligence, the majority and minority leaders have mapped out their strategy on floor action. If the whip's nose count has shown that the House would vote down a bill as it stood, the leaders have agreed to alter the bill with an amendment or two to woo at least some of the bill's opponents into favoring it."[32]

Because of the liberal-conservative split that has troubled the Democratic Party since the 1930s, House Democratic whips have had more difficulty than their Republican counterparts in controlling their members. A study by Randall Ripley of seven key roll-call votes in 1962 showed that while the average support score for all assistant Democratic whips was 84 per cent, scores for those whips from the following southern states were considerably lower: Tennessee, Kentucky and Arkansas, 71 per cent; Alabama and Florida, 67 per cent; Virginia and North Carolina, 43 per cent; and Texas, 29 per cent. Ripley noted, however, that one assistant whip who supported the administration only rarely in 1962 did "an excellent job" of reporting accurately on the voting inclinations of members in his zone, while his successor in 1963 achieved a high support score but did an inadequate job of reporting. "Voting loyalty," Ripley concluded, "is far less important than accuracy and thoroughness."[33]

Party Caucus

Use of party caucuses—meetings of the party's full House membership—for organizational purposes dates back to the beginning of Congress. In the Jeffersonian period, Democratic Republicans, in conjunction with the administration, used the caucus to formulate party legislative strategy. From 1800 to 1824, party caucuses in the House chose the party's nominees for the presidency and the vice presidency. After the 1820s, caucus activity diminished and caucuses met rarely over the next 60 years except to nominate the party candidate for the speakership at the beginning of each Congress.

Revival of the caucus as a forum for discussing legislative strategy came in the 1890s, when Speaker Reed used caucuses to a limited extent for discussing policy questions. For the most part, however, the caucus under Reed functioned only to give the party's stamp of approval to decisions Reed already had made. In the early 1900s, Speaker Cannon called caucus meetings occasionally but manipulated them in much the same manner as had Reed. It was not until Cannon's overthrow that the caucus was restored to its earlier legislative significance.

Democrats. The Democrats for many years had a caucus rule providing that by a two-thirds vote it could bind its members on a floor vote. It was adopted in 1909 and used effectively throughout President Wilson's first term. It was employed during Franklin Roosevelt's first term also, but fell into disuse after that. In recent times, the rule was used infrequently and then only on procedural or party issues, such as voting for the Speaker. It was used most recently in 1971 when Democrats were bound on a vote repealing a House rule that gave Republicans one-third of all committee staff. The binding rule was repealed by the caucus in 1975.

Caucus Activity. The Democratic Caucus has had a checkered history. Following an active period during the Wilson administration, it was little used for much of the next half-century. Its actions during this time were confined largely to nominating a candidate for Speaker, selecting floor leaders and approving committee assignments.

Beginning in the late 1960s, younger House Democrats with relatively little seniority began a campaign to revitalize the caucus as a means of countering the arbitrary authority exercised by committee chairmen and other very senior members. The campaign began in the 91st Congress, when regular monthly meetings were established, and gained momentum in subsequent Congresses. The result was a basic transformation of power in the party and the House. The most important change was to alter the seniority system by making committee chairmen subject to secret-ballot election by the caucus. This was achieved in steps and took its final form—automatic secret-ballot votes on all committee chairmen—in 1975. Also in that year, the caucus rejected three chairmen, an action that effectively ended the absolute operation of the seniority system. The defeat of the three individuals meant that all chairmen in the future would be accountable to their colleagues and thus could never again be the absolute powers unto themselves that they had been when the seniority system guaranteed them the reins of power. *(Seniority system, p. 397)*

The caucus also forced other changes that helped transform the House in the early 1970s into a more open and accountable institution. It helped enact a House rule requiring that committee bill-drafting sessions be open to the public (Republicans played an important part in this reform, also). It set up a Steering and Policy Committee under the leadership's control to develop party and legislative priorities. It limited a member to one subcommittee chairmanship, and guaranteed each Democrat a major committee assignment. It transferred the committee assignment power to the Steering and Policy Committee (from the Democrats on the Ways and Means Committee), thus putting that vital function directly under the leadership's control.

In addition, the caucus created a "bill of rights" for subcommittees that gave these units considerable independence from the full committee's chairman. In the past subcommittees were virtual creatures of the full committee chairman. *(For additional details on caucus and other reforms, see box, p. 368)*

Most of the rejuvenated caucus' work centered on procedural reforms for the House, but attention also was given to substantive legislative issues. For example, in 1972 the caucus forced an end-the-Vietnam-War resolution to the House floor and in 1975 it opposed more military aid to Indochina. In 1975, it ordered proposals to end the oil depletion allowance be brought to the House floor for a vote. (The allowance was repealed.)

These forays into substantive legislation plunged the caucus into new controversy, partly because it was seen as usurping the powers of committees and undermining the committee system and partly—in the eyes of conservative Democrats—because the caucus' positions generally were in favor of liberal-backed proposals. These conservatives, joined by many Republicans, charged that the caucus was trying to seize control of the House; Republicans began to talk about a return to "King Caucus," a pejorative term that came from the earlier period when the caucus dominated House activities.

By the end of the 94th Congress, the controversy had subsided as fewer legislative issues were brought before the caucus. This was a conscious decision of Democratic leaders who conceded that the earlier caucus actions offended many Democrats and threatened to harm the effectiveness of the caucus on key issues and on procedural matters at the beginning of each new Congress.

Republicans. Republicans, who never adopted a binding caucus rule, nonetheless used the caucus (renamed "conference" in 1911) effectively in the 1940s and 1950s to achieve a consensus among party members on important legislative proposals.

The conference was normally dominated by the party leadership, who resorted to it much as Reed and Cannon had done to achieve party support for their own predetermined courses of action.

The conference has rarely served as a deliberative body in the true sense; an exception was its occasional use in the period 1965-69 to develop policy positions for the consideration of party floor leaders. With the Democrats swollen majorities and the increasing power of the Democratic Caucus during the 1970s, House Republicans increasingly began to use the conference to get their objections to Democratic Caucus actions on the record.

Committee on Committees

After the House revolt against Speaker Cannon in 1910, power to appoint members of standing committees was taken from the Speaker and vested in the membership of the full House. In 1911, the Democratic Caucus delegated the authority to choose the party's committee members to a special Committee on Committees, which was composed of the Democrats on the Ways and Means Committee. The assignment task remained there until the reorganization moves of the 1970s.

In December 1974, just prior to the beginning of the 94th Congress, the caucus transferred the assignment power to the Steering and Policy Committee. The unit is composed of party leaders and their nominees and regionally elected members *(see below)*. The transfer of this function was part of the effort by junior and freshman Democrats to wrest some power away from committee chairmen. The choices of either group were subject to ratification by the caucus, but that usually was perfunctory.

In 1917, the Republican Conference established a Committee on Committees which in recent times has been composed of a representative from each state with a GOP member. It is chaired by the House GOP leader. Its decisions are subject to approval by the Republican Conference.

Speakers often have exercised much influence on committee assignments, even when not formally involved in the panel making the choices. In the late 1920s, for example, Speaker Longworth had four uncooperative members of the Rules Committee replaced with his own choices.

In the 1940s and 1950s, Speaker Sam Rayburn intervened frequently to influence the makeup of the Ways and Means Committee, which he insisted be stacked with member favorable to reciprocal trade agreements and opposed to reduction of the oil and gas depletion allowance.

Steering, Policy Committees

During the present century, both parties have established groups called "steering committees" to assist the leadership with legislative scheduling and the formulation of party strategy.

The Republican Steering Committee, appointed in 1919, dominated the House until 1925 when power again shifted to the Speaker. Although the new Speaker, Nicholas Longworth, largely ignored the Steering Committee, it continued in existence until 1949, when it was renamed the Policy Committee and expanded from eight to 22 members. Subsequently, the size of the committee was increased to 35. The Policy Committee was considered the chief advisory board for the minority leader from 1959 to 1965, but it was then replaced in that role by the party conference.

Democrats established a Steering Committee in 1933, abandoned it in 1956 and reconstituted it in 1962. In the decade after 1962, its membership was set at about 24 including the leadership; its duties and role in the party structure were vague.

In 1973, however, the Democratic Caucus voted to create a new Democratic Steering and Policy Committee to give coherence and direction to the party's legislative strategy. The 24-member unit was composed of the Speaker, the Democratic floor leader, the caucus chairman, 12 regionally elected members and nine members appointed by the Speaker. The committee's power was further increased in December 1974 when the authority to make Democratic committee assignments was transferred to it from the Ways and Means Committee.

Senate

Floor Leaders

Emergence of readily recognizable floor leaders in the Senate did not occur until the period 1911-13. Designation of these positions was the culmination of an increasing party influence in the chamber which began around 1890. Prior to that time, leadership in the Senate, when identifiable at all, was usually vested in powerful individuals or small factions of senators. As late as 1885, Woodrow Wilson wrote in his graduate thesis, *Congressional Government:* "The public now and again picks out here and there a senator who seems to act and to speak with true instinct of statemanship and who unmistakably merits the confidence of colleagues and of people. But such a man, however eminent, is never more than *a* senator. No one is *the* senator. No one may speak for his party as well as for himself; no one exercises the special trust of acknowledged leadership. The Senate is merely a body of individual critics...."[34]

Until 1846, party organization in the Senate was virtually nonexistent. Committee members were selected by ballot of the full Senate without any formal recommendation by parties, or they were appointed by the Vice President or the president pro tempore. In 1846, parties began nominating the membership of standing committees for routine ratification by the full Senate. Further steps toward party control were slow to develop until well after the Civil War. According to David J. Rothman in his book *Politics and Power,* party pressures on senators were still negligible as late as the 1870s: "No one had the authority to keep his colleagues in line, and positions of influence were distributed without regard for personal loyalties. Democratic and Republican organizations rarely attempted to schedule legislation or enforce unity in voting. In brief, senators were free to go about their business more or less as they pleased."[35]

Republicans. In the 1870s, Republicans sought to strengthen party control by appointing a caucus chairman, who was assumed to be the party's floor leader. The power of the chairman, Henry Anthony (R R.I.), was overshadowed, however, by the influence of a small faction of senators led by Roscoe Conkling (R N.Y.) which sought to develop and pursue its own policies regardless of the overall party interest. The influence of the Conkling faction, which was never great enough to control the Senate, eventually dissipated as the result of a series of unsuccessful feuds with Republican Presidents over patronage matters in New York State. But it was not until the 1890s and the emergence of another Republican faction led by Sens. William B. Allison (Iowa) and Nelson W. Aldrich (R.I.) that a consistently effective leadership organization was established.

Allison derived his power from the chairmanship of the Appropriations Committee. Aldrich achieved his through force of personality; he held no formal position in the Senate until he became chairman of the Finance Committee in 1899. By pooling their influence, the two Republican leaders were able to dictate committee assignments, caucus positions, decisions of standing committees and scheduling decisions. Like Speaker Cannon, who dominated the House for much of the same period, Allison and Aldrich were largely successful in imposing their own conservative political views upon the entire Senate. According to Rothman, the Allison-Aldrich clique "instituted once and for all, the prerogatives of power" in the Senate. "Would-be successors or Senate rivals would now be forced to capture and effectively utilize the party posts. Allison understood clearly that 'both in the committees and in the offices, we should use the machinery for our own benefit and not let other men have it.' His heirs had no choice but to follow his dictum."[36]

In the opinion of Rothman and other authorities, Allison and Aldrich used the tactic of after-hours poker games to cement the loyalties of key senators. About six or eight Republican senators usually attended the sessions, which were held at the home of Sen. James McMillan (R Mich.) and came to be known as the "School of Philosophy Club."[37] Eventually, two principal lieutenants emerged from the group: John C. Spooner (R Wis.) and Orville H. Platt (R Conn.). Defeats for the Allison-Aldrich group were rare until President Theodore Roosevelt was able to push through a part of his progressive legislative program in the early 1900s. The group retained much of its power after Allison's death in 1908, but it disintegrated soon after Aldrich retired in 1911.

Democrats. The evolution of a centralized Democratic organization in the Senate dates back to 1889, when Sen. Arthur P. Gorman (D Md.) was named chairman of the party's caucus. Like the Allison-Aldrich group, Gorman solidified his control by appointing his political allies to positions of influence. (Gorman further merged the real power with formal party positions by assuming all of the party's top leadership posts himself, including floor leader, chairman of the Steering Committee and chairman of the Committee on Committees.) Unlike the Allison-Aldrich appointments, however, Gorman's appointments were permanent and the responsibilities of his party lieutenants were clearly defined. In this sense, Gorman is credited with contributing more to modern party organization in the Senate than did Allison and Aldrich, even though the Republican clique attained far greater political influence at the time. (During Gorman's 10 years as caucus chairman, 1889-99, Democrats were in the minority for all except two years.) Leadership in the party was dispersed after Gorman left the Senate.

In 1911, Democrats broke new ground by formally designating a floor leader (Thomas S. Martin of Virginia). It was not until 1913 and the appointment of John W. Kern (D Ind.) to the post, however, that Democrats were able to create an organization as strong as the Allison-Aldrich group had been. Kern, who worked closely with President Wilson, mobilized solid Democratic support behind the President's tariff reform, currency reform and antitrust reform programs. As Randall B. Ripley observed in his book *Power in the Senate*, Kern's "leadership was unobtrusive and effective. He wielded his powers of influencing committee assignments, scheduling and chairing the caucus to unite Democrats behind the New Freedom legislative program."[38]

New Deal Era. Students of government have characterized the Senate floor leaders of both parties who served from 1919-1933 as largely ineffective, with the exception of Republican Majority Leader Henry Cabot Lodge (Mass.) on the issue of ratification of the Treaty of Versailles, which embodied the Covenant of the League of Nations. Lodge managed to bring about the treaty's defeat twice, in 1919 and on a second vote in 1920, despite enormous pressure from President Wilson. The next strong leader appeared in the New Deal era, when Majority Leader Joseph T. Robinson (D Ark.) pushed President Roosevelt's far-reaching legislative program through the chamber. Robinson achieved solid party support even though he sometimes disagreed personally with specific New Deal measures. It was almost 20 years before other strong floor leaders appeared.

Johnson, Dirksen. The only two Senate leaders widely acclaimed as effective in the period since Robinson have been Lyndon B. Johnson (D Texas), who served as minority leader from 1953 to 1955 and as majority leader from 1955 to 1960, and Everett McKinley Dirksen (R Ill.), minority leader from 1959 until his death in 1969.

Johnson, whose entire tenure as majority leader was spent while President Eisenhower was in the White House, became a master of compromise and thus was able to obtain legislation satisfactory both to the Democratic majority in Congress and to the Republican President. Johnson was a highly persuasive leader. He used a variety of techniques to win cooperation, including influence on committee assignments, logrolling and personal favors.

Dirksen, whose party was in the minority throughout his tenure, was able to put a Republican imprint on many Democratically inspired bills by maintaining tight party unity. Using methods similar to Johnson's, Dirksen translated party unity into amendments and other concessions although his party was seldom able to defeat important bills.

Mansfield, Scott. Mike Mansfield (D Mont.) and Hugh Scott (R Pa.), who replaced Johnson and Dirksen as Senate majority and minority leaders, were well liked by their colleagues but less effective than their predecessors. While generally successful in their leadership roles, they were not arm-twisting, high-pressure, flamboyant men. They chose to lead by gentle persuasion and compromise and often let their whips line up members for specific votes and take care of the practical politics. Both men sometimes were charged with not being sufficiently partisan. Mansfield encountered the charge because of his willingness to compromise with Republican Presidents Nixon and Ford. Scott was criticized because his moderate-liberal philosophy sometimes led him to oppose conservative positions taken by Nixon and Ford. Both Mansfield and Scott were to retire at the end of the 94th Congress.

Whip Organizations

The first whips appeared in the Senate shortly after the positions of majority and minority leader were formally established. Democrats named their first whip in 1913, Republicans theirs in 1915. Although duties of the Senate whips have been essentially the same as those of their House counterparts, the Senate whip organizations have rarely achieved as much success.

Senate whips at times have openly defied stands taken by their party leaders. Such clashes have resulted largely from the fact that the Democratic and Republican Conferences elect their floor leaders and whips and have sometimes been forced into regional logrolling to get agreement on their choices. Occasionally the breach between a party leader and a whip has become public knowledge.

The most serious breach of this sort was between Majority Leader Mike Mansfield (D Mont.) and Whip Russell B. Long (D La.) in the years 1965-69. Long and Mansfield clashed openly in 1966 over a proposal by Long for federal subsidies in presidential election campaigns. Long exacerbated the dispute in 1967 by publishing a newsletter for constitutents in which he listed his disagreements with President Johnson (which also were disagreements with Mansfield). Mansfield sought to circumvent Long's influence by appointing four assistant whips. In 1969, Long was defeated by Sen. Edward M. Kennedy (D Mass.), a Mansfield supporter, in his bid for re-election to the whip's post.

The occasional differences between party leaders and whips, coupled with the fact that the Senate is smaller and thus easier to control than the House, have left many Senate leaders reluctant to share power with their whips. As Ripley observed in his 1969 book *Power in the Senate,* the assistance of the whips has been "peripheral, not central, to the impact of the floor leaders."[39] He added that only a few whips had "developed into major influences in the party, usually through their performance of the persuasion function."

A recent exception to this generalization has been Sen. Robert C. Byrd (D W.Va.) who in 1971 defeated Kennedy for the position of majority whip. At the time, Byrd was secretary of the Democratic Conference. He had used that position shrewdly for the four years he had held it to build a broad base of support among colleagues. This was done largely through hard work on his part. A key part of this work was exacting attention to detail and willingness to assist Democratic colleagues in many diverse ways that indebted them to him.

Central to Byrd's effort was his willingness to spend many hours on the Senate floor looking after the details of the legislative program, a job often exercised by the whip or majority leader but which frequently fell to him. (A principal reason this occurred was Majority Leader Mansfield's willingness to delegate the task and Kennedy's apparent unwillingness to involve himself in the often mundane work of managing the Senate's legislative activities.)

Senators are extremely busy persons, usually serving on several committees and subcommittees and often in demand for personal appearances outside the Senate and for interviews by lobbyists, reporters and others. Byrd capitalized on this situation by seeing that the interests of senators were taken care of on the floor—for example, that

bills of concern to a senator came up at the right time, that amendments on which a senator wanted to vote were called to the senator's attention, that accommodations and compromises were arranged.

Caucuses

Early development of party caucuses in the Senate was concurrent with that in the House. In 1846, caucuses increased in importance when they acquired power over committee assignments. During the Civil War and the Reconstruction era, Republicans used the caucus frequently to discuss and adopt party positions on legislation.

In the 1890s both the Republican organization of Allison and Aldrich and the Democratic organization of Gorman used the caucus extensively, with Republicans achieving more control than Democrats. As Rothman observed in *Politics and Power:* "The Republican caucus was not binding, and yet its decisions commanded obedience, for party leadership was capable of enforcing discipline. Senators could no longer act with impunity unless they were willing to forego favorable committee posts and control of the chamber proceedings."[40]

In 1903, Senate Democrats officially adopted a binding caucus rule, but there is no evidence that they ever put it to use. In 1933, Democrats readopted the rule, but again did not use it. Since that time, neither party has seriously considered using a binding caucus. In recent years, both parties have employed the caucus (now called "conference" by both) to collect and distribute information to members. The Republican Conference, which meets more frequently than the Democratic Conference, has served also as a forum of persuasion for the leadership; the Democratic Conference has been used only rarely for that purpose.

Committee on Committees

The tradition of committees on committees in the Senate goes back to the Civil War era, when Republicans utilized a special panel appointed by the party caucus to make both Republican and Democratic committee assignments. After the war, Republicans took control of the committee away from the caucus as a whole and vested it in the caucus chairman. Democrats set up a similar committee in 1879, appointed and chaired by the caucus chairman. The Democratic committee on committees in the Senate now is known as the Steering Committee.

As in the House, decisions of the committee on committees of both parties are subject to approval of the party conferences and the full chamber, but approval has been perfunctory.

Steering, Policy Committees

What was in effect the first committee on order of business in the Senate was established in 1874, when the Republican caucus appointed a special committee to prepare a legislative schedule. That committee was replaced in the mid-1880s by a formal Steering Committee, appointed by the caucus chairman. Democrats established a Steering Committee in 1879, but discontinued it in periods when Republicans controlled the Senate and thus the legislative schedule. In 1947, both Democrats and Republicans created new Policy Committees which were assigned the scheduling duties of the old Steering Committees. (As previously noted, the Democratic Steering Committee, while retaining its name, was reconstituted as a committee on committees.) In years in which the

Republicans have been in the minority, the Policy Committee has studied legislation and recommended policy positions to the conference and the minority leader. The Democratic Policy Committee has not assumed an actual policy role.

Leadership Contests

Of the top leadership positions in Congress, only the office of House Speaker is filled by a formal vote on the floor. Other posts, not recognized in the House rules, are filled by action of a party caucus or conference. The latter bodies also make nominations for the speakership. In most elections for Speaker, the House has merely ratified the choice of the majority party; in some instances, the majority party has been splintered by factions, however, and spirited election battles have developed on the House floor.

Pre-Civil War Era

In the years before the Civil War, regional disputes, mostly over slavery, gave rise to at least 10 heated battles for the speakership. The first was in 1809, when none of the Democratic Republican candidates could achieve a majority on the first ballot; the election finally went to Joseph B. Varnum (Mass.) after the southern candidate, Nathaniel Macon (N.C.), withdrew for reasons of health. Other minor antebellum battles occurred in 1820, when an anti-slavery candidate, John W. Taylor (D N.Y.), won on the 22nd ballot; in 1821, when Philip P. Barbour (D Va.) won on the 12th; in 1825, when Taylor recaptured the post on the second ballot; in 1834, when John Bell (Whig Tenn.) won on the 10th vote; in 1847, when Robert C. Winthrop (Whig Mass.) won on the third; and in 1861, when Galusha A. Grow (R Pa.) won on the second. Major contests for the speakership in which the House became deadlocked for a matter of weeks or months took place in 1839, 1849, 1855 and 1859.

1839 New Jersey Controversy

The first of the prolonged battles over the speakership began on Dec. 2, 1839, when election of the Speaker hinged on the outcome of five contested House seats in New Jersey. Excluding the five New Jersey members, the party lineup in the House would have been 119 Democrats and 118 Whigs. Democrats sought to organize the House (and elect the new Speaker) before the New Jersey cases were decided; Whigs, in hope of winning control of the House, wanted to await the outcome of the New Jersey contests.

Chaos reigned for several days while the clerk of the House, according to custom, refused to put any question to the House until a quorum was present. After four days of disorder, John Quincy Adams (Whig Mass.), the most powerful member of the House, took the floor and demanded that the body proceed with the roll call, including those members from New Jersey who held election certificates signed by the governor of the state. The House voted overwhelmingly that Adams should take the Chair; finally, on Dec. 14, the House consented to vote for Speaker, with both New Jersey delegations excluded from participating. Although the decision was what the Democrats had been seeking, the party's leaders were unable to hold a sufficient number of members in line to win on the ensuing votes. Finally, on Dec. 16, Robert M. T. Hunter (D Va.), who had declared himself an independent, was elected Speaker on the 11th ballot. As Adams concluded in his

Memoirs, Hunter "finally united all the Whig votes, and all the malcontents of the Administration."[41]

1849 Free-Soil Dispute

The next major contest for the speakership developed in 1849, when neither the Whigs nor the Democrats could achieve a majority because Free-Soil factions of both parties decided to act independently. The resulting deadlock lasted for three weeks and 63 ballots.

The main issue underlying the deadlock was the makeup of the House Committee on the District of Columbia and on Territories, which Free-Soilers contended should be organized in favor of the opponents of expansion of slavery. Free-Soilers thus opposed the election of both of the leading candidates for the office, Robert C. Winthrop (Whig Mass.), who they felt had been lukewarm on the slavery issue as Speaker from 1847 to 1849, and Howell Cobb (D Ga.), a strong proponent of slavery. Each faction put up its own candidate (at one time there were 11), preventing either Cobb or Winthrop from achieving a majority. At various points in the controversy, compromise solutions were considered and rejected, including proposals that the Speaker be divested of his power to appoint committees (thus leaving that authority to the full House), that the Speaker be chosen by lottery and that members receive no salary or mileage until a Speaker was elected.

Finally, after the 59th vote, a motion was carried that the Speaker be elected by a plurality, provided that it be a majority of a quorum. On the 60th vote, Cobb led, on the 61st, Winthrop, and on the 62nd, the vote was tied. On the 63rd ballot, the issue was finally decided when Cobb won a plurality of two votes with a quorum voting. The House then confirmed his election by adopting a resolution "That Howell Cobb, a representative from the state of Georgia, be declared duly elected Speaker of the House of Representatives for the Thirty-First Congress."[42]

Commenting on the significance of Cobb's election, Mary P. Follett concluded in *Speaker of the House:* "Southern suspense was now relieved. If the Whigs had elected their candidate in 1849 the Civil War might have been delayed, for the committees of this Congress effected the Compromise of 1850. It is probable that Mr. Winthrop's prestige would have carried him into the Senate and eventually have affected the makeup of the Republican party. The choice of a very pronounced pro-slavery and southern man at this crisis undoubtedly aggravated the struggles of the following decade."[43]

1855 Kansas Controversy

Six years after the Cobb-Winthrop contest, another multi-faction battle based on the slavery issue led to a deadlock in the election of a Speaker. Like the 1849 battle, the 1855 dispute focused on the question of composition of House committees either for or against slavery. The immediate concern of both sides was the effect those committees might have on the question of admission of Kansas as a free or a slave state. The dispute, which began in December 1855, lasted through 133 ballots taken over a period of almost two months.

Although anti-slavery forces held a majority of House seats, their ranks were so split by factions (mostly the new Republican Party and various Free-Soil groups), that they could not unite behind a single candidate. At the outset of the election battle, on Dec. 3, 1855, 21 candidates were nominated. After 129 ballots, the House decided that, following three more roll calls, the candidate receiving the greatest number of votes would be elected. On Feb. 2, 1856, on the 133rd ballot, Nathaniel P. Banks (American Mass.) was elected with 103 votes out of 214 cast.

As in 1849, the election was subsequently confirmed by a resolution adopted by majority vote. Author Follett pointed out: "...Mr. Banks was elected above all because it was expected that he would constitute the committees in favor of the Free-Soilers. He justified the expectation by putting a majority of anti-slavery men on the Kansas Investigation Committee, which act practically delayed the settlement of the Kansas episode until after 1857, and this gave time for the anti-slavery forces to organize."[44]

1859 Pennington Election

The last of the great pre-war battles over the speakership occurred in 1859. The House took 44 ballots over a period of nearly two months to decide the question. On the first day of the session, Dec. 5, the tone for the battle was set when slavery advocates proposed a resolution that any candidate who endorsed the sentiments of *The Impending Crisis of the South: How to Meet It,* a book hostile to slavery, was not fit to be Speaker of the House. The next day, a second resolution was proposed, stating that "it is the duty of every good citizen of this Union to resist all attempts at renewing in Congress or out of it the slavery agitation, under whatever shape and color the attempt may be made. And that no member shall be elected Speaker of this House whose political opinions are not known to conform to the foregoing sentiment."[45]

Both resolutions were directed at John Sherman (R Ohio), who had endorsed the book opposing slavery. As Follett wrote, "The ball thus set rolling, the discussion of slavery began, bitter and passionate on one side, eager and vehement on the other. The state of the country was reflected in the struggle for Speaker. The House was the scene of a confusion and uproar which the clerk could not control.... Bitter personal invectives nearly led to personal encounters... It seemed as though the Civil War was to begin in the House of Representatives."[46]

Sherman led in the early voting, falling only six votes short of a majority on the third ballot. By the end of January, however, Republicans saw that Sherman could not be elected and shifted their support to William Pennington (Whig N.J.), a new and unknown member. On Feb. 1, Pennington was elected with 117 votes, the minimum required to win. According to Follett's book, Pennington as Speaker was regarded as an "impartial" presiding officer although "notably ignorant of the practice of the House."[47] Pennington was the only Speaker other than Henry Clay ever elected to the speakership during his first term in the House.

Progressive Insurgency of 1923

The only deadlock over the speakership since the Civil War was in 1923, when 20 Progressive Republicans held the balance of power in the House. (Officially, there were 225 Republicans including Progressives, 205 Democrats, 1 Independent, 1 Farmer-Laborite and 1 Socialist.) The Progressives put up their own candidate, Henry A. Cooper (R Wis.), as a protest against the rules. After eight inconclusive votes, Nicholas Longworth (R Ohio), the GOP floor leader, made an agreement with the Progressives to liberalize the rules. The next day the Progressives threw their support behind the Republican candidate, Frederick

H. Gillett (R Mass.), Speaker since 1919, who was re-elected.

From 1923 to 1975, there were no other floor battles for the speakership. Over that period, one party always held a clear majority and was able to elect its man on the first ballot.

Other Leadership Disputes

In recent years, there have been several major contests within parties for leadership posts. Among the more important of the contests:

● In 1951, Senate Democrats elected Ernest W. McFarland (Ariz.), a moderate, over Joseph C. O'Mahoney (Wyo.), a strong advocate of President Truman's Fair Deal program, for the majority leadership. McFarland's election set a pattern for the success of Democratic moderates or conservatives in contests with liberals.

In 1965, Russell B. Long (La.), a moderate conservative, defeated the more liberal John O. Pastore (R.I.) and Mike Monroney (Okla.) in a race for party whip. In 1967, conservative Robert C. Byrd (W.Va.) won the post of secretary of the conference against liberal Joseph S. Clark (Pa.). The only liberal victory in these Democratic contests came in 1969, when Edward M. Kennedy (Mass.) defeated Long in his bid for re-election as whip. In 1971, however, Kennedy was defeated in his bid for re-election as majority whip by Byrd. The outcome resumed the pattern among Senate Democrats of electing conservatives or moderates over liberals to leadership positions. Byrd had campaigned for the position in a quiet and cautious manner while talking to every Democratic senator to determine his strength. He had also spent a lot of time on the Senate floor and been very attentive to his colleague's needs while Kennedy had not.

● In 1969, Sen. Hugh Scott (R Pa.), a moderate, defeated conservative Sen. Roman Hruska (R Neb.) for Senate Republican whip. Following the death of Senate Minority Leader Everett McKinley Dirksen (Ill.) later in the year, Scott defeated Hruska and Howard H. Baker Jr. (Tenn.) for Dirksen's old post. Robert P. Griffin (Mich.), another moderate Republican, then defeated Baker for party whip. These developments ran counter to the GOP's postwar practice of electing mostly conservative floor leaders in contests with moderates or liberals. In four previous contested elections for top Republican leadership posts over the 1947-68 period, conservatives had won three. In 1971, Scott again defeated Baker for the minority leadership; Griffin was unopposed for whip.

● After a bitter 1959 battle, House Republicans replaced their longtime floor leader, Joseph W. Martin Jr. (Mass.), with a younger and more vigorous leader, Charles A. Halleck (Ind.). Halleck's unyielding conservatism and strong-arm leadership tactics annoyed many House Republicans, particularly moderates, and in 1965 the conference replaced him with Gerald R. Ford (Mich.), a younger and more moderately conservative leader.

● In 1971, Hale Boggs (D La.) defeated four other candidates for the post of House majority leader when Carl Albert became Speaker.

Through the 94th Congress, the selection of House majority and minority leaders was peaceful. Thomas P. O'Neill (D Mass.) was elected House majority leader for the 93rd and 94th Congresses without opposition. He had been the majority whip under Boggs, who perished in an airplane accident in late 1972. John J. Rhodes (R Ariz.) was unanimously elected minority leader in December of 1973 upon Ford's accession to the vice presidency. Rhodes was re-elected without opposition at the start of the 94th Congress.

Leadership vs. White House

For the most part, congressional leaders have sought to cooperate with a President of their own political party and to defeat or amend programs put forth by a President belonging to the opposite party. Over the years, however, there have been several important instances in which congressional leaders have resisted the program of a same-party President or have developed their own legislative program and imposed it on the White House. Cases in which a party's congressional leadership has cooperated in a substantial way with an opposing party's President are less frequent and have been limited mainly to national defense and foreign policy issues. One notable exception occurred at the beginning of the New Deal era when House Minority Leader Bertrand H. Snell (R N.Y.) threw his support behind President Roosevelt's emergency banking bill with the statement: "The House is burning down, and the President of the United States says this is the way to put out the fire."[48]

Strong Presidents

Many of the conflicts between the White House and Congresses controlled by the same party have come at times of strong presidential leadership. Lincoln, Wilson and the two Roosevelts all had difficulties with their party's congressional leaders, although all four Presidents were largely successful in executing their programs.

The first important conflict of this kind arose during the Civil War, when Republican extremists dominated Congress and sought to interfere with Lincoln's prosecution of the war and with his plans for postwar reconstruction. The so-called Radical Republicans, like the Whigs before them, strongly espoused the theory of congressional domination of the government. In application of that theory, Congress in 1861 created a Joint Committee on the Conduct of the War, which went so far as to intervene in military operations. In 1864, Congress sought to undermine President Lincoln's liberal reconstruction program by passing the Wade-Davis bill to transfer responsibility for reconstruction from the President to Congress. Lincoln pocket-vetoed the bill and, so far as possible, ignored the congressional extremists. He managed to hold the upper hand by resort to executive orders, but Congress, after Lincoln's assassination, achieved the supremacy it was seeking and retained it for more than 30 years.

The next strong President to experience difficulty with his own party's leadership in Congress was Theodore Roosevelt (R), who clashed sharply with Sen. Nelson W. Aldrich (R R.I.), the unofficial but acknowledged leader of Senate Republicans. Roosevelt was able to work successfully for the most part with the powerful House leader, Speaker Joseph G. Cannon (R Ill.), by compromising on various parts of his program. Although Speaker Cannon had agreed to support the President's bill to regulate railroad rates in exchange for Roosevelt's agreement to drop tariff reform, Aldrich refused to go along. After relying mostly on Democrats to report the rate bill from the Senate committee, Roosevelt won agreement from William B. Allison (R Iowa), another leading Republican in the Senate, to take a moderate position on judicial review of government-administered rates. This maneuver split the opposition and

led to passage of the bill by an overwhelming vote. However, Aldrich continued to oppose other administration measures and occasionally won important concessions from the President.

Although relations between President Wilson and the Democratic congressional leadership were generally good, party leaders sometimes deserted the President on foreign policy matters. On the eve of the opening of the Panama Canal in 1914, both Speaker Champ Clark (Mo.) and House Majority Leader Oscar W. Underwood (Ala.) opposed Wilson's request to repeal a provision of existing law that would have exempted American coastwise vessels from payment of canal tolls. The exemption, which Great Britain insisted would be in violation of an Anglo-American treaty, was nevertheless eliminated.

In 1917, when Wilson asked Congress to declare war on Germany, he was opposed by Rep. Claude Kitchin (N.C.), then the House majority leader. Later, he was opposed by Speaker Clark on his program for military conscription. Near the end of Wilson's second term, relations between Clark and the White House were almost severed.

President Franklin D. Roosevelt, whose overall relations with Congress were as good or better than Wilson's, also experienced some difficulty with his party's congressional leaders in the latter part of his administration. During his third (wartime) term, party leaders sometimes deserted the President on domestic measures; in 1944, Senate Majority Leader Alben W. Barkley (Ky.) resigned that post when Roosevelt vetoed a revenue bill. Barkley, however, was promptly reelected by the party caucus, and the bill was passed over the President's veto. The most active Presidents since Roosevelt—Truman, Kennedy and Johnson, all Democrats—generally commanded the support of the party's congressional apparatus.

Weak Presidents

To a somewhat lesser extent, congressional leaders have clashed with less active Presidents of their own party, mostly in cases of congressional initiative on legislation. The first and most prominent of these cases was that in which Henry Clay forced President Madison into the War of 1812 and President Monroe into a series of unwanted post-war measures, including tariff revision.

Following the Civil War, the Radical Republicans in Congress were able to push through their reconstruction policy over President Andrew Johnson's veto and almost managed to convict Johnson in impeachment proceedings. In 1871, Charles Sumner (R Mass.), chairman of the Senate Foreign Relations Committee, was deposed by the Republican caucus for opposing President Grant's foreign policy and refusing to consult with the President. The next major conflict of this sort came in 1898, also over foreign policy. Speaker Thomas B. Reed (R Maine), a strong isolationist, sought but failed to block three important parts of President McKinley's foreign policy program—war with Spain, the annexation of Hawaii and acquisition of the Philippine Islands. Reed's failure to stop these moves, which led to his retirement from Congress, was largely due to their popularity with the public, not to successful application of pressure by McKinley.

The only other instances of such intra-party conflicts occurred during the administrations of Presidents Harding and Coolidge, who were generally regarded as among the weakest of all Presidents of the United States. The Washington Naval Conference of 1921-22 was thrust on

Harding by Sen. William E. Borah (R Idaho). Congressional investigations of the Harding administration produced examples of widespread corruption and led to prosecution of a number of administration officials. In the Coolidge ad-

ministration, the Republican Congress passed a veterans' adjusted compensation (bonus) bill over the President's veto and drastically amended various administration bills.

Footnotes

1. Floyd M. Riddick, *The United States Congress: Organization and Procedure* (Washington: National Capitol Publishers, 1949), p. 67.
2. Randall B. Ripley, *Party Leaders in the House of Representatives* (Washington: The Brookings Institution, 1967), p. 13.
3. *Ibid.*, p. 7.
4. Harry S Truman, *Public Papers of the Presidents of the United States*, April 12 to Dec. 31, 1945 (Washington: U.S. Government Printing Office, 1961), p. 129.
5. Mary P. Follett, *The Speaker of the House of Representatives* (New York: Burt Franklin Reprints, 1974), pp. 25-26. (Reprint of 1896 ed.).
6. *Ibid.*, p. 67.
7. George Rothwell Brown, *The Leadership of Congress* (New York: Arno Press, 1974), pp. 37-38. (Reprint of 1922 ed.)
8. Hubert Bruce Fuller, *The Speakers of the House* (Boston: Little, Brown, 1909), pp. 40-41.
9. Follett, *The Speaker of the House of Representatives*, p. 79.
10. *Ibid.*, p. 89.
11. *Ibid.*, pp. 89-90.
12. *Ibid.*, pp. 99-100.
13. Brown, *The Leadership of Congress*, p. 74.
14. Follett, *The Speaker of the House of Representatives*, p. 115.
15. *Ibid.*, p. 193.
16. *Congressional Record*, 51st Congress, 1st Session, Feb. 7, 1890, p. 1150.
17. Fuller, *The Speakers of the House*, p. 244.
18. *Ibid.*, p. 256.
19. *Ibid.*, p. 257.
20. George B. Galloway, *History of the House of Representatives* (New York: Crowell, 1961) p. 139.
21. Ripley, *Party Leaders in the House of Representatives*, p. 101.
22. *Ibid.*
23. Galloway, *History of the House of Representatives*, p. 144.
24. Ripley, *Party Leaders in the House of Representatives*, p. 93.
25. *Ibid.*, p. 102.
26. George H. Haynes, *The Senate of the United States: Its History and Practice*, Vol. I (Boston: Houghton Mifflin, 1938), p. 251.
27. Riddick, *The United States Congress: Organization and Procedure*, p. 66.
28. Neil MacNeil, *Forge of Democracy: The House of Representatives* (New York: David McKay Company, 1963), p. 87.
29. Galloway, *History of the House of Representatives*, p. 108.
30. Ripley, *Party Leaders in the House of Representatives*, pp. 29 and 32.
31. *Ibid.*, p. 33.
32. MacNeil, *Forge of Democracy*, p. 100.
33. Ripley, *Party Leaders in the House of Representatives*, p. 41.
34. Woodrow Wilson, *Congressional Government* (Cleveland: Meridian, 1956), pp. 146-47. (Reprint of 1885 ed.)
35. David J. Rothman, *Politics and Power: The United States Senate 1869-1901* (Cambridge, Mass.: Harvard University Press, 1966), p. 4.
36. *Ibid.*, p. 44.
37. *Ibid.*, p. 45.
38. Randall B. Ripley, *Power in the Senate* (New York: St. Martin's Press, 1969), p. 31.
39. *Ibid.*, p. 35.
40. Rothman, *Politics and Power*, p. 60.
41. Galloway, *History of the House of Representatives*, p. 43.
42. Follett, *The Speaker of the House of Representatives*, pp. 55-56.
43. *Ibid.*, p. 56.
44. *Ibid.*, p. 59.
45. *Ibid.*, p. 61.
46. *Ibid.*, pp. 61-62.
47. *Ibid.*, p. 95.
48. Galloway, *History of the House of Representatives*, p. 260.

Selected Bibliography

Books

Alexander, De Alva Stanwood. *History and Procedure of the House of Representatives*. Boston: Houghton Mifflin, 1916.
Bolling, Richard W. *House Out of Order*. New York: Dutton, 1965.
_____. *Power in the House: A History of the Leadership of the House of Representatives*. New York: Dutton, 1968.
Brown, George Rothwell. *The Leadership of Congress*. New York: Arno Press, 1974.
Chiu, Chang-Wei. *The Speaker of the House of Representatives Since 1896*. New York: Columbia University Press, 1928.
Clark, Joseph S. *The Senate Establishment*. New York: Hill and Wang, 1963.
Follett, Mary P. *The Speaker of the House of Representatives*. Longmans, Green and Co., 1896; reprinted, New York: Burt Franklin Reprints, 1974.
Fuller, Hubert Bruce. *The Speakers of the House*. Boston: Little, Brown, 1909.
Galloway, George B. *History of the House of Representatives*. New York: Crowell, 1961.
Hasbrouck, Paul DeWitt. *Party Government in the House of Representatives*. New York: Macmillan, 1927.
Haynes, George H. *The Senate of the United States: Its History and Practice*. 2 vols. Boston: Houghton Mifflin, 1938.
Jones, Charles O. *The Minority Party in Congress*. Boston: Little, Brown, 1970.
MacNeil, Neil. *Forge of Democracy: The House of Representatives*. New York: David MacKay Company, 1963.
Peabody, Robert L. *Leadership in Congress: Stability, Succession and Change*. Boston: Little, Brown, 1976.
_____. "Political Parties: House Republican Leadership. In *American Political Institutions and Public Policy*, pp. 202-12. Edited by Allan B. Sindler. Boston: Little, Brown, 1969.

_____ and Polsby, Nelson W., eds. "Two Strategies of Influence: Choosing a Majority Leader, 1962." *In New Perspective on the House of Representatives,* pp. 237-70. Chicago: Rand McNally, 1972.

Riddick, Floyd M. *The United States Congress: Organization and Procedures.* Manassas, Va: National Capitol Publishers, 1949.

Ripley, Randall B. *Majority Party Leadership in Congress.* Boston: Little, Brown, 1969.

—————. *Party Leaders in the House of Representatives.* Washington: Brookings Institution, 1967.

_____. *Power in the Senate.* New York: St. Martins Press, 1969.

Rothman, David J. *Politics and Power: The United States Senate, 1869-1901.* Cambridge, Mass.: Harvard University Press, 1966.

Smith, William H. *Speakers of the House of Representatives of the United States.* Baltimore: S. J. Gaeng, 1928; reprint ed., New York: AMS Press, 1971.

Stewart, John. "The Strategies of Leadership: Johnson and Mansfield." In *Congressional Behavior,* pp. 61-92. Edited by Nelson W. Polsby. New York: Random House, 1971.

Wilson, Woodrow, *Congressional Government: A Study in American Politics.* Boston: Houghton Mifflin, 1885; reprint ed., Cleveland: Meridian, 1956.

Articles

Froman, Lewis A. Jr. and Ripley, Randall B. "Conditions for Party Leadership: The Case of the House Democrats." *American Political Science Review,* vol. 59, 1965, pp. 52-63.

Goodman, Paul. "Social Status of Party Leadership: The House of Representatives 1779-1804." *William and Mary Quarterly,* vol. 25, 1958, pp. 465-74.

Hinckley, Barbara. "Congressional Leadership Selection and Support: A Comparative Analysis." *Journal of Politics,* May 1970, pp. 268-87.

Hitchner, Dell G. "The Speaker of the House of Representatives." *Parliamentary Affairs,* Spring 1960, pp. 185-97.

Huit, Ralph K. "Democratic Party Leadership in the Senate." *American Political Science Review,* vol. 55, 1961, pp. 334-35.

Patterson, Samuel C. "Legislative Leadership and Political Ideology." *Public Opinion Quarterly,* vol. 27, 1963, pp. 399-410.

Peabody, Robert L. "Party Leadership Change in the United States House of Representatives." *American Political Science Review,* vol. 61, 1976, pp. 673-75.

Ripley, Randall B. "The Party Whip Organizations in the United States House of Representatives." *American Political Science Review,* vol. 58, 1964, pp. 561-76.

Sullivan, William E. "Criteria for Selecting Party Leadership in Congress." *American Political Quarterly,* January 1975, pp. 25-44.

Government Publications

U.S. Congress. House. *The History and Operation of the House Majority Whip Organization. H. Doc. 94-162, 94th Cong., 1st sess.* Washington: Government Printing Office, 1975.

U.S. Congress. Senate. *Majority and Minority Leaders of the Senate: History and Development of the Offices of the Floor Leaders,* by Floyd M. Riddick. S. Doc. 94-66, 94th Cong., 1st sess. Washington: Government Printing Office, 1975.

The Legislative Process

Article I of the Constitution vests "all legislative powers herein granted" to a Congress consisting of two chambers, a Senate and a House of Representatives, and provides that proposed legislation must be passed by both chambers and submitted to the President for his approval before it can become law. The Founding Fathers, it has been said, did not expect the lawmaking function to be unduly burdensome, because they thought Congress would confine itself chiefly to external affairs and leave domestic affairs to state and local governments. Alexander Hamilton even surmised that Congress would have little to do once the central government was established

The First Congress, from 1789 to 1791, consisted of 26 senators and 65 representatives, serving a population of about four million in 13 states along the Atlantic coast. Concerns of the Congress were limited in scope and volume, and a few simple rules were sufficient to guide its deliberations. Only a few hundred bills were introduced in the First Congress; 108 were enacted into public law. Most dealt with the establishment of the new government and its relations with the states, or with matters of defense or foreign relations.

Period of Congressional Supremacy

At first, Congress apparently expected to conduct most of its significant deliberations on the chamber floor. In early years the full chambers considered any question brought before them and indicated the line of action to be followed before appointing select committees to work out proper legislation. But as time passed the volume and complexity of legislative business increased, and the recurrent nature of many questions led gradually to the establishment of standing committees. For a time these continuing groups functioned as advisers whose reports were carefully considered on the floor, but by 1885 they had become such a powerful force in determining the shape of legislation that Woodrow Wilson could write: "It is now, though a wide departure from the form of things, no great departure from the fact to describe ours as a government by the standing committees of Congress."[1]

A succession of weak Presidents in the years following the Civil War had made possible the congressional supremacy Wilson deplored, but Congress would not long be able to retain its commanding role. World War I marked the beginning of a dramatic expansion of federal authority into almost every area of human activity, and strong Presidents were quick to reassert eroded executive prerogatives. Congress, operating under antiquated procedures more in keeping with a simpler era, gradually relinquished its policy-making role, and legislative initiative shifted from the Capitol to the White House.

Presidential Leadership

The President's control over policy was strengthened by the Budget and Accounting Act of 1921, which enabled him to draw up a unified national budget—a detailed business and financial plan for the government which reconciled proposed spending and estimated revenues. Prior to 1921, no system existed, either in Congress or the executive branch, for unified consideration or control of fiscal policy.

From time to time Congress still tries to seize for itself the policy-making functions now exercised by the executive branch, but these ventures into congressional government have only limited success. Congress may be able to block presidential programs, but it does not speak with a unified voice and it has no means of developing a comprehensive program of its own.

Today the President's budget, submitted to Congress shortly after it assembles each January, offers the framework of the President's program for the nation in the coming year. Together with the State of the Union address and various special messages, it forms the basis of legislative action to meet the needs of more than 200 million Americans.

In 1974, Congress took a potentially momentous.step toward more responsible action on federal economic policy by enacting legislation (HR 7130—PL 93-344) revising the procedures it uses to handle the federal budget.

The measure, which was to be tested in 1975 and fully implemented in 1976, established a framework for timely and comprehensive congressional action on appropriations, revenue and debt proposals in the President's annual budget message to Congress. *(Fiscal Powers, p. 111)*

Gathered to exercise its legislative responsibilities is a Congress of 100 senators and 435 representatives elected from 50 states extending from Maine to Hawaii and from Florida to Alaska. Membership in Congress is no longer a part-time job: Congress meets in almost year-round

Terms and Sessions of Congress

The two-year period for which a House of Representatives is elected constitutes a Congress. Under the Twentieth Amendment to the Constitution, adopted in 1933, this period begins at noon Jan. 3 of each odd-numbered year and ends at noon Jan. 3 of the next odd-numbered year. Congresses are numbered consecutively, and the Congress that met in January 1975 was the 94th in a series that began in 1789.

Under the Constitution, Congress is required to "assemble" at least once each year, and the Twentieth Amendment provides that these annual meetings shall begin at noon on Jan. 3 unless Congress "shall by law appoint a different day." Each Congress, therefore, has two regular sessions, the first beginning in January of the odd-numbered year and the second beginning in January of the even-numbered year. In addition, the President may "on extraordinary occasions" convene one or both houses in special session.

In practice, the annual sessions may run as long as 12 months. The Legislative Reorganization Act of 1970 stipulates that "unless otherwise provided by the Congress," the Senate and House "shall adjourn *sine die* not later than July 31 of each year" or, in the case of a nonelection year, take a 30-day recess in August. The provision is not applicable if "a state of war exists pursuant to a declaration of war by the Congress." *Sine die* adjournment ends a session of Congress. Within a session, Congress may adjourn to a day certain, although neither house can adjourn for more than three days without the consent of the other.

In 1973, reviving a procedure that had not been used in 25 years, Congress twice gave its leaders authority to call it back into session during adjournment.

A resolution to adjourn *sine die* was approved Dec. 22 only after the House accepted a Senate amendment permitting the leadership to reconvene Congress if national needs required. A resolution providing for adjournment from Aug. 3 to Sept. 5 also permitted the leaders to call Congress back into session.

Congress used a similar procedure four times during the 1940s, according to former Senate parliamentarian Floyd M. Riddick. On June 19, 1949, Congress adjourned for six months under a similar resolution. President Truman reconvened the 80th Congress July 26, 1948.

---

sessions, and its concerns are encyclopedic. The 93rd Congress (1973-75) was in session for 688 days, during which 26,219 bills were introduced and 649 were enacted into public law.

Institutional Structure of Congress

As its membership has grown and the volume and complexity of its business have multiplied, the institutional characteristics of Congress also have changed. Congress today is a very different institution from that contemplated by its creators.

Perhaps the most noteworthy characteristic of the modern Congress is its diffusion of power. The Senate and House both are marked by a disintegrated internal structure coupled with a lack of strong party control. Leadership is divided between the committee chairmen and the party leaders; there is no unity of command.

The institutional structure is decentralized through the committee system. The standing committees of Congress— 22 in the Senate, 18 in the House in 1975, each with a specialized jurisdiction—are the cornerstone of the legislative process. The committee system provides a convenient division of labor for the awesome congressional workload and makes it possible for members, through long experience, to develop expertise in complex fields of legislation. It also creates an independent power base for chairmen and senior minority members.

The committees hold virtually life-or-death power over legislation. They may approve, alter, kill or ignore any measure referred to them, and by and large the committees' decisions will not be overruled by the parent chamber. When a bill reaches the floor, the committee guides it to passage; when it goes to conference, committee members are chosen to meet with their counterparts from the other chamber to hammer out its final language. At every stage the committee plays a determining role.

Seniority System vs. Party Leadership

Until the 1970s, party cohesion was difficult to achieve in both houses because committee chairmen held power through the seniority system—that is, by tenure in office rather than election—and were therefore not subject to direct control by the elected party leaders. Changes in the committee assignment process and chairman selection procedures between 1970 and 1975 led to some strengthening of the congressional party apparatus. Nonetheless, the party leadership structure in Congress is itself so fragmented (among the House Speaker, floor leaders and the like) that real party government is impossible to achieve. This fragmentation is one of the fruits of the "revolution of 1910," which decentralized the party leadership that previously had been exercised by the Speaker of the House.

Party leadership is difficult in Congress because, in practice, there are no parties to be led. Members of Congress are responsible to a local electorate, independent of the national party and frequently at variance with it. Thus party unity is difficult to achieve, and attempts to bind party membership on voting are rarely made. Voting blocs in Congress represent shifting coalitions of divergent interests that frequently cross party lines. The "conservative coalition" of Republicans and southern Democrats voting against northern Democrats, for example, has been a potent legislative force for many years.

Characteristics of Senate and House

Each chamber of Congress also has its own special characteristics. The Senate, with only 100 members, can afford to be more relaxed in its procedures than the 435-member House of Representatives. Furthermore, each senator is an ambassador from a "sovereign" state and as such is accorded more deference, even indulgence, than a representative from a smaller district within a state.

In consequence, the House is more hierarchically organized and power is less evenly distributed than in the Senate, where even a freshman member occupies a position of some stature. A representative must expect to serve a

The Congressional Day

Ordinarily the Senate and House meet at noon daily, although sometimes an earlier meeting is scheduled. (This occurs more frequently in the Senate than the House.) In each chamber the session opens with a prayer, followed by "reading" and approval of the *Journal*. (Actual reading usually is dispensed with but occasionally is demanded for dilatory purposes. Under the Legislative Reorganization Act of 1970, the House *Journals* cannot be read unless the Speaker or a majority of those present so orders.)

What happens next depends on whether the chamber recessed or adjourned at the conclusion of its last previous sitting. If it adjourned, a new "legislative day" (the period from adjournment to adjournment) now begins, and the rules set forth certain matters to be taken up and disposed of at the beginning of the session. If it recessed, the same legislative day continues, and the chamber may move on to its unfinished business without further preliminaries. The distinction is less significant in the House, which normally adjourns from day to day, than in the Senate, where a legislative day frequently extends over several calendar days.

Senate. The Senate sets aside the first two hours of a legislative day as a "morning hour" for the consideration of routine business. This business includes such matters as messages from the President, communications from department heads, messages from the House, presentations of petitions and memorials, reports of standing and select committees and the introduction of bills and resolutions. Senators are limited to brief statements, usually three minutes.

During the first hour of the morning hour, no motion to proceed to the consideration of any bill on the calendar is in order except by unanimous consent. During the second hour, motions may be made but must be decided without debate. At the conclusion of morning business or after the hour of 1 o'clock, any senator may move to take up a bill out of its regular order on the calendar; if the bill is not disposed of by the time the morning hour ends, it is displaced by the unfinished business, if any.

Although not required under the rules, a morning hour frequently is arranged by unanimous consent following a recess.

At 2 o'clock, or earlier if the morning business has been completed, the Senate moves on to unfinished business or to the business planned by the majority leader for the day. Unlike the more orderly House, the Senate frequently interrupts consideration of a bill to take care of other business. The Senate may take up a bill, lay it aside temporarily to consider another, return to consideration of the first, then pause for speeches unrelated to the subject technically under consideration, etc. Generally its pace is leisurely, and it may take days or weeks to dispose of one piece of legislation.

House. The House tends to operate on a Monday-to-Thursday schedule, with Mondays reserved primarily for noncontroversial legislation considered under special procedures.

Although the House rules provide for a morning hour, that procedure is rarely employed. Following approval of the *Journal*, the Speaker recognizes members for one-minute speeches and submission of material to be inserted in the *Congressional Record*. Bills are introduced, reports filed and messages, petitions and memorials received. This constitutes the morning business of the House, after which the chamber turns to legislative business, sitting either as the House or in Committee of the Whole.

The House is able to dispose of most bills in one or two days. Once it takes up a bill, it generally sticks with it until action is completed, and the stringent House rules preclude undue delay.

Typically, the House sets aside a time at the close of the day's session—following the disposal of legislative business—for "special orders." At this time, members who have requested time in advance are permitted to make speeches on various subjects for inclusion in the *Congressional Record*. Few other members stay in the chamber to listen. Indeed, many of the speeches are not even delivered; only the texts of the remarks are inserted in the *Congressional Record*. The special-orders time is followed by adjournment.

Bells. Daily life on Capitol Hill is punctuated by the ringing of bells, intended to alert members not in their seats to what is going on in Senate or House. Systems of electric bells or buzzers are installed in the Capitol and the Senate and House office buildings (and even in some nearby restaurants) to summon members when their presence is required for votes or other purposes. Conveniently located wall lights show how many bells have rung. Different systems are used in each chamber.

In the Senate, one bell means a roll-call vote; two, a quorum call; three, a call of absentees (live quorum); four, adjournment or recess; five, not currently used; six, morning business concluded.

In the House, one bell means a teller vote; two, a recorded teller or a roll-call vote; three, a quorum call; four, adjournment; and five, a recess.

---

long apprenticeship before he can rise to prominence in the House (although this traditional rule has become somewhat less true in recent years). Similarly, the House operates under a more rigid system of rules designed to expedite its business. Because debate is limited and the amending process frequently curtailed, the House is able to dispose of legislation with great speed.

By comparison, the Senate is a leisurely and informal institution. It usually operates in a spirit of comity where the prerogatives of all members are respected. Much of its business is handled by unanimous consent, rather than by elaborate procedures spelled out in the rules. One of its most cherished traditions is the privilege of extensive debate; its amending powers are broad. Given these conditions, it is not surprising that the Senate may spend days considering a measure that the House dispatched in one sitting.

The key steps in formulating and enacting legislation are described in the following pages. The legislative process is complex and varied. Accomplished lawmakers know how to select the methods best suited to advance their legislative goals. For, as George B. Galloway observed, "In the end, the statutes that emerge from the travail of the legislative process reflect the influence of many forces. For better or for worse, they are affected by the way in which Congress is organized and by its rules of procedures."[2]

Origin and Sponsorship of Legislation

Legislative proposals may originate in a number of different ways. A member of Congress, of course, may himself develop the idea for a piece of legislation; assistance in drafting legislative language is available from the Office of Legislative Counsel in the Senate and House. Pressure groups—business, labor, farm, civil rights organizations and the like—are another fertile source of legislation; many such organizations not only provide detailed technical knowledge in specialized fields but also employ experts in the art of drafting bills. Constituents, either as individuals or groups, also may propose legislation; frequently a member of Congress will introduce such a bill "by request" whether or not he supports its purposes.

Today the bulk of legislation considered by Congress originates in the executive branch (although key members of Congress may participate in the formulation of administration programs). Each year the President outlines his legislative program in his State of the Union and budget messages and in special messages. Executive departments and agencies then transmit to Congress drafts of proposed legislation to carry out the President's program. These bills usually are introduced by the chairman of the committee or subcommittee having jurisdiction over the subject involved—or by the ranking minority member if the chairman is not of the President's party.

Sometimes committees consider proposals that have not been formally introduced in bill form. The committee then formulates its own bill, which is introduced by the chairman. This is the usual practice with appropriation and revenue bills.

No matter how a legislative proposal originates, it can be introduced only by a member of Congress. In the House a member (including the Resident Commissioner of Puerto Rico and the nonvoting delegates of the District of Columbia, Guam and the Virgin Islands) may introduce any one of several types of bills and resolutions by handing the measure to the clerk of the House or by placing it in a box called the hopper; he need not seek recognition for the purpose. A senator first gains recognition of the presiding officer to announce the introduction of a bill. If objection is offered by any senator, introduction of the bill is postponed until the following day. If there is no objection, the bill is read twice by title and referred to the appropriate committee. A House bill is considered read for the first time when it is referred to committee.

As the next step, in the House and the Senate, the bill is numbered (in order of introduction), referred to committee, labeled with the sponsor's name and sent to the Government Printing Office so that copies can be made for subsequent study and action.

There is no limit to the number of bills a member may introduce. Senate bills may be jointly sponsored and carry several senators' names; since 1967, the House also has per-

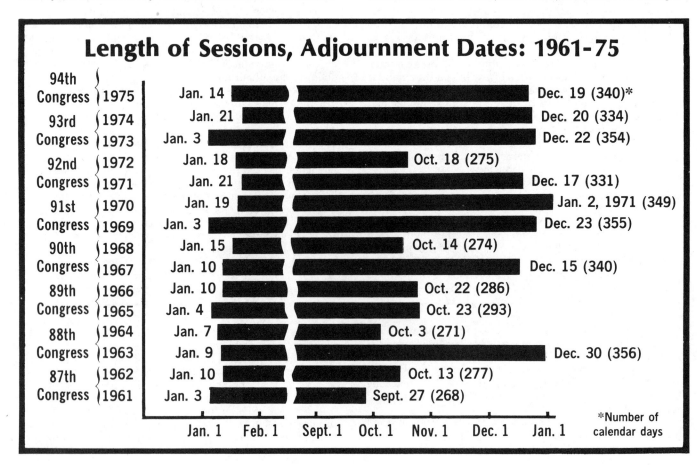

Length of Sessions, Adjournment Dates: 1961-75

94th Congress	1975	Jan. 14 — Dec. 19 (340)*
93rd Congress	1974	Jan. 21 — Dec. 20 (334)
	1973	Jan. 3 — Dec. 22 (354)
92nd Congress	1972	Jan. 18 — Oct. 18 (275)
	1971	Jan. 21 — Dec. 17 (331)
91st Congress	1970	Jan. 19 — Jan. 2, 1971 (349)
	1969	Jan. 3 — Dec. 23 (355)
90th Congress	1968	Jan. 15 — Oct. 14 (274)
	1967	Jan. 10 — Dec. 15 (340)
89th Congress	1966	Jan. 10 — Oct. 22 (286)
	1965	Jan. 4 — Oct. 23 (293)
88th Congress	1964	Jan. 7 — Oct. 3 (271)
	1963	Jan. 9 — Dec. 30 (356)
87th Congress	1962	Jan. 10 — Oct. 13 (277)
	1961	Jan. 3 — Sept. 27 (268)

Jan. 1   Feb. 1   Sept. 1   Oct. 1   Nov. 1   Dec. 1   Jan. 1

*Number of calendar days

mitted multiple sponsorship of bills, with a limit of 25 cosponsors on any one bill. The Constitution stipulates that "all bills for raising revenue shall originate in the House of Representatives," and this stipulation has generally been interpreted to include appropriation bills. All other bills may originate in either chamber; major legislation usually is introduced in both houses in the form of companion bills.

Although thousands of pieces of legislation are introduced in every Congress, most never receive any consideration. In the 93rd Congress (1973-74), 26,219 bills were introduced in the Senate and House; of these, only 2,786 were reported by committees. Bills not disposed of die with the Congress in which they were introduced and must be reintroduced in the following Congress to be eligible for consideration.

Types of Congressional Measures

Measures considered and acted upon by the House and the Senate include not only bills but also a variety of resolutions. The nomenclature and designations follow:

Bills are prefixed with "HR" when introduced in the House and with "S" when introduced in the Senate, followed by a number assigned in the order of introduction from the beginning of each Congress. Bills are used as the form for most legislation, whether general or special, public or private. When passed by both chambers in identical form and signed by the President (or repassed over his veto), they become public or private laws.

Joint Resolutions are designated H J Res or S J Res. A joint resolution requires the approval of both houses and the signature of the President, just as a bill does, and has the force of law if approved. There is no real difference between a bill and a joint resolution. The latter is generally used in dealing with limited matters, such as a single appropriation for a specific purpose. Joint resolutions are used also to propose amendments to the Constitution. These must be approved by two-thirds of both houses; they do not require the President's signature but become a part of the Constitution when ratified by three-fourths of the states.

Concurrent Resolutions are designated H Con Res or S Con Res. They are used for matters affecting the operations of both houses, such as fixing the time of adjournment of a Congress or expressing the "sense" of the two chambers on some question. They must be passed by both houses but do not require the signature of the President and do not have the force of law.

Resolutions are designated H Res or S Res. A simple resolution deals with matters entirely within the prerogatives of one house or the other. It requires neither passage by the other chamber nor approval by the President and does not have the force of law. Most resolutions deal with the rules of one house. They also are used to express the opinion of a single house on a current issue. Special orders or rules governing the time and manner of debate, as laid down by the House Rules Committee, are also designated H Res.

Committee Referral

Nearly all bills are referred to committees. A bill is referred to the appropriate committee by the House parliamentarian on the Speaker's order or by the Senate president, subject to the will of the chamber. In the Senate, the sponsor of a bill may indicate his preference for referral, but this is not binding.

Longest Sessions of Congress

Congress	Session	Convened	Adjourned	No. of days
76th	3rd	Jan. 3, 1940 -	Jan. 3, 1941	366
77th	1st	Jan. 3, 1941 -	Jan. 2, 1942	365
81st	2nd	Jan. 3, 1950 -	Jan. 2, 1951	365[1]
80th	2nd	Jan. 6, 1948 -	Dec. 31, 1948	361[2]
88th	1st	Jan. 9, 1963 -	Dec. 30, 1963	356
91st	1st	Jan. 3, 1969 -	Dec. 23, 1969	355[3]
65th	2nd	Dec. 3, 1917 -	Nov. 21, 1918	354
93rd	1st	Jan. 3, 1973 -	Dec. 22, 1973	354
79th	1st	Jan. 3, 1945 -	Dec. 21, 1945	353[4]
80th	1st	Jan. 3, 1947 -	Dec. 19, 1947	351[5]
78th	1st	Jan. 6, 1943 -	Dec. 21, 1943	350[6]
91st	2nd	Jan. 19, 1970 -	Jan. 2, 1971	349[7]
77th	2nd	Jan. 5, 1942 -	Dec. 16, 1942	346
40th	2nd	Dec. 2, 1867 -	Nov. 10, 1868	345[8]
78th	2nd	Jan. 10, 1944 -	Dec. 19, 1944	345[9]
90th	1st	Jan. 10, 1967 -	Dec. 15, 1967	340
94th	1st	Jan. 14, 1975 -	Dec. 19, 1975	340
93rd	2nd	Jan. 21, 1974 -	Dec. 20, 1974	334
83rd	2nd	Jan. 6, 1954 -	Dec. 2, 1954	331[10]
92nd	1st	Jan. 21, 1971 -	Dec. 17, 1971	331
63rd	2nd	Dec. 1, 1913 -	Oct. 24, 1914	328
50th	1st	Dec. 5, 1887 -	Oct. 20, 1888	321
51st	1st	Dec. 2, 1889 -	Oct. 1, 1890	304
31st	1st	Dec. 3, 1849 -	Sept. 30, 1850	302
89th	1st	Jan. 4, 1965 -	Oct. 23, 1965	293
67th	2nd	Dec. 5, 1921 -	Sept. 22, 1922	292
82nd	1st	Jan. 3, 1951 -	Oct. 20, 1951	291

1. Congress recessed from Sept. 23 to Nov. 27.
2. Congress recessed from June 20 to July 26 and Aug. 7 to Dec. 31.
3. Congress recessed from Aug. 15 to Sept. 3.
4. The House was in recess from July 21 to Sept. 5 and the Senate from Aug. 1 to Sept. 5.
5. Congress recessed from July 27 to Nov. 17.
6. Congress recessed from July 8 to Sept. 14.
7. The House was in recess from Aug. 14 to Sept. 9, and both chambers recessed from Oct. 14 to Nov. 16.
8. No business was transacted after July 27. Congress took three recesses between July 27 and Nov. 10.
9. Congress recessed from April 1-12, June 23 to Aug. 1 and Sept. 21 to Nov. 14.
10. The House adjourned sine die on Aug. 20. The Senate was in recess from Aug. 20 to Nov. 8 and from Nov. 18 to Nov. 29, and adjourned sine die on Dec. 2.

Generally, custom and rule govern the referral of legislation to committees; the jurisdiction of the standing committees is spelled out in House Rule 10 and Senate Rule 25. Sometimes, however, the presiding officer has a measure of discretion—for example, in the case of new programs or bills involving overlapping jurisdictions—and bills may be drafted to take advantage of this situation. In 1963 a controversial civil rights bill was referred to the Senate Commerce Committee instead of the southern-dominated Judiciary Committee because its subject matter, public accommodations, fell within the commerce clause of the Constitution. Occasionally when problems of overlapping jurisdiction arise, bills may be referred to more than one committee.

Committee Action

The standing committees of Congress, operating as little legislatures, determine the fate of most legislative proposals. Committee members and staff frequently have a high degree of expertise in the subjects under their jurisdiction, and it is at the committee stage that a bill comes under the sharpest congressional scrutiny.

A committee has several options with respect to a piece of legislation: it may consider and report it favorably, with or without amendments; rewrite it entirely; reject it or report it unfavorably; or simply refuse to consider it. Failure of a committee to act on a bill usually is equivalent to killing it; the measure can be withdrawn from the group's purview only by a discharge petition signed by a majority of the House membership on House bills, or by adoption of a special resolution in the Senate. Discharge attempts rarely succeed.

When a bill reaches a committee, it is placed on the group's calendar. (Most standing committees periodically publish cumulative calendars of business, detailing all action on measures referred to them.) Then the normal course of action for major bills is as follows:

Agency Views. The committee first requests comment from interested agencies of the government. The agencies give their views on the effect of the proposed legislation and how it would accord with the President's program.

Subcommittee Assignment. A bill may be considered by the full committee in the first instance, but more often the committee chairman assigns it to a subcommittee for study and hearings. Especially in the House, where chairmen tend to exercise tight control over their committees, this power of assignment may be used to promote or impede the suggested legislation. (The chairman's powers of referral were somewhat qualified in 1973.)

Hearings. The subcommittee usually schedules hearings on the bill and invites testimony from interested public and private witnesses. Other witnesses may testify at their own request. Most witnesses offer prepared statements, following which they may be questioned by subcommittee members. The hearings may be brief and perfunctory or they may go on for weeks. Because the demands on a member's time are so great, frequently only a few subcommittee members with a special interest in the subject will participate in the hearings.

Most hearings are held in open session, but some are held in closed (executive) session, or a combination of open and closed hearings may be used. Until 1971, all hearings of the House Appropriations Committee were in closed session. Hearings on national security matters frequently are closed.

In 1973, both houses adopted new rules to encourage open committee meetings. The House rule on committee secrecy that was adopted in March of 1973 required all committee meetings to be open unless a majority of members voted—by roll call, in open session with a quorum present—to close a meeting. The only exception was for meetings on internal committee business, such as budget and personnel matters.

Under the new rule, members could vote to close hearings only if public disclosure of the testimony would violate House rules or "endanger the national security."

The Senate rule, also adopted in March of 1973, was weaker. After defeating a proposal similar to the House resolution, the Senate adopted a resolution allowing committees to make their own rules governing mark-up session. Three committees chose that year to hold open mark-ups unless the members voted to close a meeting.[3] In November 1975, the Senate adopted "sunshine" rules for its committees that were similar to those in the House.

Hearings on legislation may serve a variety of purposes: to seek information on the subject under consideration; to test public opinion; to build support for the bill; or even to delay action on it. Sometimes hearings serve primarily as a safety valve for the release of group tensions.

Mark-up Session. After the hearings have ended, the subcommittee meets to "mark up" the bill—that is, to decide on legislative language for recommendation to the full committee. The subcommittee may approve the bill unaltered, amend it, rewrite it—or block it altogether. It then reports its recommendations to the full committee. In 1974, House panels opened most of their mark-ups while Senate committees continued to hold the majority of their mark-ups behind closed doors.

Full Committee Action. When the full committee receives the bill, it may repeat the subcommittee procedures, all or in part, or it may—as in the case of the Appropriations Committees—simply ratify the action of the subcommittee. When a committee votes on its recommendation to the House or Senate, it is said to "order the bill reported." Occasionally a committee may order a bill reported unfavorably; most of the time a report, submitted by the chairman of the committee to the House or Senate, calls for favorable action on the legislation, since the committee can effectively kill legislation by simply failing to take any action.

Frequently the committee proposes amendments to the bill. If they are substantial and the legislation is complicated, the committee may order introduction of a "clean bill" embodying the proposed amendments. The original bill is then put aside and the "clean bill," with a new number, is reported to the floor. If the amendments are not extensive, the original bill is "reported with amendments." The chamber must approve, alter or reject the committee amendments before the bill itself can be put to a vote.

Report. When a committee sends a bill to the chamber floor, it justifies its actions in a written statement, called a report, which accompanies the bill. The report describes the purposes and scope of the bill, explains the committee amendments, notes proposed changes in existing law and usually includes the texts of communications from department and agency heads whose views on the legislation have been solicited. Often committee members opposing a measure submit a dissenting minority report.

Reports are numbered, by Congress and chamber, in the order in which they are filed (S Rept 94-1, H Rept 94-1, etc.) and immediately printed. The reported bill also is printed, with committee amendments indicated by showing insertions in italics and deletions in stricken-through type. The report number also is shown on the bill, and the bill and report both carry the calendar number.

House and Senate Calendars

After a bill is reported back to the house where it originated, it is placed on a calendar. Although bills are placed on the calendar in chronological order, they are not necessarily called up for floor action in that order.

House. There are five legislative calendars in the House, issued in one cumulative calendar titled *Calendars of the United States House of Representatives and History of Legislation.* This calendar, which is printed daily when Congress is in session, lists all bills on each of the five legislative calendars. It also gives a capsule legislative history of all measures reported by Senate and House committees, together with other valuable reference material. Each Monday's edition carries a subject index.

The five legislative calendars are:

The Union Calendar to which are referred "bills raising revenue, general appropriations bills and bills of a public character directly or indirectly appropriating money or property." Technically it is the Calendar of the Committee of the Whole House on the State of the Union, so called because bills listed on it are first considered in the Committee of the Whole House on the State of the Union and reported back to the House for its final approval.

The House Calendar to which are referred "all bills of a public character not raising revenue nor directly or indirectly appropriating money or property." These measures are usually not considered in the Committee of the Whole but are taken up directly by the House.

The Consent Calendar to which are referred bills of a noncontroversial nature which already are on either the Union or House Calendars. The Consent Calendar is called on the first and third Mondays of each month; bills are passed without objection and without debate.

The Private Calendar to which are referred bills for relief in the nature of claims against the United States or private immigration bills. The Private Calendar can be called on the first and third Tuesdays of each month. Most private bills are passed without debate, but if two or more members object to a bill, it is recommitted to the committee reporting it.

The Discharge Calendar to which are referred motions to discharge committees from further consideration of a bill when the necessary signatures are signed to a discharge petition.

Discharge motions may be taken up on the second and fourth Mondays in each month. Those days are also set aside for consideration of business presented by the District Committee.

Consent Calendar and discharge procedures are described in detail later in this subchapter; private bill procedure is discussed in Chapter III.

Senate. The Senate has only two calendars, the *Executive Calendar,* on which treaties and nominations are listed, and the *Calendar of Business* (General Orders), to which all legislation is assigned.

A bill is brought before the Senate in one of two ways, either on call of the calendar (when bills must be considered in the order in which they were placed on the calendar) or by special action to take up a bill out of order.

The call of the calendar is used for noncontroversial legislation (similar to bills on the Consent Calendar in the House). This procedure is described below.

Scheduling of Floor Action

House. Although a variety of methods exist for bringing up legislation on the House floor, for most major bills the route to floor action lies through the House Rules Committee. This committee is empowered to report "rules" governing the floor consideration of legislation. *(A history of the committee appears on pp. 385-87)*

Usually the chairman of the committee that favorably reported the bill, supported by the bill's sponsor and other committee members, appears before the Rules Committee to request a special rule. The request, considered by the Rules Committee in the same fashion that other committees consider legislative measures, is in the form of a simple resolution providing for consideration of the bill. The resolu-

---

Obstruction in the House

Although stringent House curbs on debate preclude a filibuster in the Senate fashion, members sometimes make use of parliamentary stalling tactics with similar effect.

A dramatic example of dilatory tactics that became the equivalent of a Senate filibuster was given in 1968. The stalling maneuvers delayed adjournment a few days and at one point kept the House in continuous session for 32 hours and 17 minutes, the longest sitting in 93 years. Three bills were involved—a legislative reorganization bill, a campaign spending reform measure and a bill to permit television debates among the three major presidential candidates. All failed of enactment.

The principal delaying effort came Oct. 8 and 9 when Republicans—saying they sought action on the reform bills—forced the House to stay in its third longest session in history before it passed the TV debate bill. When Senate Republicans—also using delaying maneuvers—succeeded in having the measure killed, a group of House Democratic liberals then used stalling tactics to hold up adjournment from Oct. 10 to Oct. 14 in an unsuccessful effort to force the Senate to act on the TV bill.

On Oct. 8 the Republican group combined full reading of the *Journal*, 33 quorum calls, three roll-call votes and other tactics to delay proceedings for 20 hours before the House considered the TV debate bill. Democrats asserted that Republican presidential candidate Richard M. Nixon did not want to debate his Democratic opponent, Vice President Hubert H. Humphrey, while the Republicans responded that they were concerned with the two reform measures.

During the entire 32-hour, 17-minute Oct. 8-9 session, 45 roll calls were taken (37 quorum calls and eight record votes). The doors of the House were closed during quorum calls for the first time since 1950 and later were locked for the first time since 1917.

According to the Congressional Research Service of the Library of Congress, the Oct. 8-9 session was surpassed in length only twice: by a 46-hour, 25-minute session in 1875 on a civil rights bill, and by a 35½-hour session in 1854 on the Kansas-Nebraska bill to repeal the Missouri Compromise of 1820-21 (compromise on admission to the Union of slave and free states).

---

tion sets the time limit on general debate and governs the amending process. It may forbid all amendments or all amendments except, in some cases, those proposed by the legislative committee that handled the bill. In this instance it is known as a "closed rule," as opposed to an "open rule," which permits amendments from the floor. The resolution also may waive points of order against provisions of the bill or against specified amendments intended to be proposed to the bill. This waiver permits the House to violate its own rules by barring any objection to such violation; a typical example might involve legislative provisions in a general appropriations bill, not permitted under the House rules.

When the Rules Committee reports a rule, ordinarily action cannot occur for at least one day. The rule then is called up, debated and adopted by majority vote. (Very few

Closed Rule Changes

House Democrats in January 1973 modified the closed rule which had been used by the Ways and Means Committee to protect its bills from change on the House floor. The party caucus adopted a proposal that allowed 50 or more Democrats to bring amendments to Ways and Means bills to the caucus for debate. If the caucus voted to approve them, the Rules Committee was instructed to write a rule permitting the amendments to be offered on the floor.

One month later, however, on Feb. 27, the 410 members of the House who were not on the Ways and Means Committee passed up an opportunity to offer amendments to a tax bill reported by the committee. It was the first such bill given an "open rule"—allowing floor amendments—in almost 41 years.

In a departure from a tradition followed since the late 1920s, the House Rules Committee granted an open rule allowing floor amendments to a bill (HR 3577) extending the interest equalization tax for 15 months. During the brief Feb. 27 debate on HR 3577, however, no amendments were proposed.

Before Feb. 27, the last tax bill considered on the House floor with amendments allowed was the Revenue Act of 1932, passed by the House on April 1, 1932. That measure was considered without a formal rule, and a floor amendment was adopted deleting a controversial committee provision imposing a manufacturers' sales tax.

During the 92nd Congress, the House Rules Committee granted 13 closed or modified closed rules and 191 open rules, according to an informal tally by Bill Crosby, committee minority counsel.

The 1973 closed-rule reform was first used early in 1974, when the Democratic Caucus voted to allow floor consideration of amendments that would reduce oil industry tax preferences. However, Ways and Means Chairman Wilbur D. Mills (D Ark.) evaded the requirement by threatening to bring the bill to the floor without any rule at all. He never brought the bill out of committee at all.

Use of the closed-rule reform was more successful in 1975, when combined with the new requirement that all Ways and Means revenue bills must receive a rule prior to floor action. On Feb. 26, 1975, the Rules Committee adopted a rule permitting floor votes on seven amendments to a $21-billion tax cut bill (HR 2166). The committee's action came one day after the Democratic Caucus voted overwhelmingly (153-98) to couple repeal of the 22 per cent oil depletion allowance with the tax cut, despite opposition of the party leadership. Ways and Means Committee Chairman Al Ullman (D Ore.) pleaded for defeat of all amendments, but the House voted 248-163 to attach the oil depletion allowance phase-out (the other amendments were defeated).

rule must be adopted by a two-thirds vote rather than the customary simple majority. When the committee approves a rule, its report must be filed within three legislative days. If not immediately considered, the resolution goes on the calendar; if the member making the report does not call it up within seven legislative days, any member of the committee may do so. The resolution cannot be called up on the day it is reported except by two-thirds vote, although this does not apply during the last three days of the session.

The committee does not always grant rules when it is asked to do so, and frequently it has been subject to criticism on this ground. Sometimes the committee arbitrarily blocks or delays legislation—as happened with civil rights bills in the early 1960s, when the committee was under the chairmanship of Rep. Howard W. Smith (D Va.). At other times the committee may require substantive changes in a bill as the price for granting a rule for floor action. For the most part the committee works closely with the majority leadership, and it is probably fair to say that most bills it blocks either are opposed by the leaders or by a majority of the House.

If the Rules Committee refuses to grant a rule for a bill, it may be brought up under suspension of the rules or through the use of discharge or Calendar Wednesday procedures. These procedures, seldom successful, are described below. Another method of getting around the committee was the 21-day rule, adopted in 1965 but abandoned in 1967. (Under that rule, the Speaker could recognize a committee member to call up for House consideration any bill reported by the committee that had been before the Rules Committee for 21 days.) Enlargement of the committee from 12 to 15 members in 1961 and a change in 1974 that allowed the House Democratic leader to appoint all Democratic members of the committee (subject to caucus approval) helped to strengthen leadership control over the group's action.

Bills from certain committees have privileged status and may be considered by the House without a rule from the Rules Committee. Until 1975, revenue bills originating in the Ways and Means Committee did not require a rule, but the committee had usually sought one anyway in order to get a closed rule that precluded floor amendments. *(Box this page)*

General appropriations bills are privileged, as are matters required to be reported by the Committee on the Budget in accordance with the Congressional Budget Act of 1974 and certain matters under the jurisdictions of the House Administration and Standards of Official Conduct Committees.

Conference reports, presidential veto messages and certain amendments to Senate bills are also privileged; the member in charge may call them up at practically any time, although usually only after consulting with the majority and minority floor leaders.

Generally, a bill cannot be considered on the floor until the third day after a committee report has been filed, although this requirement can be waived by a two-thirds majority vote in the House. House rules also require that no bill may be considered unless copies of the legislation have been available to members for at least two hours. (The Rules Committee and the House by majority vote can suspend this two-hour requirement to allow immediate consideration of legislation, even before copies have been printed. This is most likely to occur in the hectic final days of a session.)

rules are rejected.) This clears the way for action on the bill itself.

There are certain limitations on the Rules Committee's power. It is not allowed to report a rule that denies the minority the right to make a motion to recommit a bill. If it reports a rule to dispense with Calendar Wednesday, such a

Senate. Unlike the House, the Senate has no elaborate rules or procedures for bringing bills to the floor, and it has no counterpart of the House Rules Committee.

Theoretically, under the rules, any senator at almost any time may offer a motion to call up a bill; a simple majority is required for adoption. During the morning hour (before 2 p.m. at the beginning of a legislative day) such a motion is undebatable; at other times, however, it is subject to debate—or even filibuster, which can only be stopped by invoking cloture, a process that requires a majority vote of three-fifths of all senators—60 votes. Occasionally controversial bills meet defeat at this stage.

In practice, floor action is scheduled by the majority leader with the help of the majority Policy Committee and after consultation with the minority leader. Effort is made to accommodate the wishes of individual senators, and important bills are seldom kept from the floor. The most common way to call up bills is by unanimous consent.

House Floor Procedures

Floor action on a major House bill ordinarily begins when the Speaker recognizes the member of the Rules Committee who has been designated to call up the rule for the bill's consideration. The rule may be debated for up to one hour, with half the time allotted to opponents of the bill. A typical open rule may provide:

"Resolved, That upon the adoption of this resolution it shall be in order to move that the House resolve itself into the Committee of the Whole House on the State of the Union for the consideration of the bill (H.R.—), entitled, etc. After general debate, which shall be confined to the bill and continue not to exceed —— hours, to be equally divided and controlled by the chairman and the ranking minority member of the committee on ——, the bill shall be read for amendment under the five-minute rule. At the conclusion of the consideration of the bill for amendment, the committee [of the whole] shall rise and report the bill to the House with such amendments as may have been adopted and the previous question shall be considered as ordered on the bill and amendment thereto to final passage without intervening motion except one motion to recommit with or without instructions."

After the rule has been adopted, by simple majority, the House resolves itself into the Committee of the Whole House on the State of the Union (working title: Committee of the Whole) for preliminary consideration of the bill.

Action in Committee of the Whole

Although only bills on the Union Calendar must be considered in Committee of the Whole, other bills may be so considered on motion. In practice, most important bills are considered in Committee of the Whole. (If a bill is considered in the House proper, the amount of time for debate is determined either by special rule or is allocated with an hour for each member if the bill is under consideration without a rule.)

The Committee of the Whole procedure goes back to a period in English history when the speaker of the House of Commons was regarded as a friendly agent of the King; the committee of the whole was devised so that during periods of strained King-Commons relations members could elect a chairman of their own and proceed to discuss matters, par-

ticularly matters pertaining to the King's household expenses, without the normal restrictions of a House of Commons session.

As used in the House of Representatives, Committee of the Whole procedure differs in several ways from procedure of the House proper. The Speaker does not preside but appoints a chairman to take his place. A quorum consists of 100 members, rather than a majority of the House (218 if there are no vacancies). No roll-call votes are taken in the Committee of the Whole; action is by voice, division (standing) or teller vote, and members' votes are not individually recorded except in the case of record teller votes, authorized under the Legislative Reorganization Act of 1970. *(For explanation of voting methods, see box, p. 346)*

The committee debates and amends bills, subject to approval by the full House, but it cannot pass them. It cannot itself recommit a bill, although it may report to the House with a recommendation that the bill be recommitted or that the enacting clause be stricken (a means of killing the measure); these recommendations must be voted on by the full House.

Role of Floor Manager

Floor action is guided by the legislative committee that reported the bill; its members occupy seats at the tables on either side of the center aisle. Ordinarily the committee chairman (or someone designated by him) acts as floor manager for the proponents of the bill, while the ranking minority member leads the opposition. *Cannon's Procedure* describes the floor manger's role:

"A chairman directed to report a bill to the House ceases to function individually so far as that measure is concerned and becomes the representative of the committee in charge of the bill. Although he may have opposed the bill or parts of it in committee, he either steps aside and permits the next ranking member of the committee to take charge of the bill on the floor or subordinates his personal views and devotes every effort to securing its consideration and passage in the form in which reported to the House. He is precluded from accepting modifications and is under the obligation of interposing points of order against vulnerable

---

Electronic Voting

The House began taking votes electronically at the start of the 93rd Congress. The first recorded vote using the new system was taken Jan. 31, 1973.

The rules of the House require the use of an electronic voting system for quorum calls and all recorded votes unless the Speaker invokes a call of the roll.

Under the rules, members have 15 minutes to answer quorum calls and recorded votes (roll calls and recorded teller votes). Members are able to vote at any of 48 consoles in the House chamber by inserting a plastic card and pressing a button to indicate a yea or nay vote. Boards installed on the walls of the chamber show instantly how each member voted as well as a running breakdown of votes cast. Voting ceases when the Speaker locks the vote total into the machine.

The leadership tables on the majority and minority sides of the House floor are equipped with consoles to allow the leadership to see how members voted.

amendments although personally he may approve of them. If for exceptional reasons he deems it necessary to offer an amendment or digress from the instructions under which the bill was reported, he should yield his seat to the next ranking member and explain unequivocally that the action is taken in his individual capacity and not as a member of the committee. So binding are the obligations of a chairman in the handling of a bill reported by his committee that charges to the effect that he is not sincerely cooperating to secure its passage give rise to a question of privilege."[4]

The rule under which the bill is considered provides for a certain number of hours of general debate to be divided equally between the chairman and ranking minority member of the committee that reported the bill. The chairman controls time for supporters of the bill, the ranking minority member for opponents. Usually each opens and closes debate for his side and yields remaining time first to other committee members, then to other representatives who wish to speak. No amendments may be offered during general debate.

At the conclusion of general debate under an open rule, the bill is read for amendment under the five-minute rule. This constitutes the second reading of the bill. The measure may be read section by section (or line by line, title by title, etc.), with amendments in order to each section as it is read, or it may be considered as read and open to amendment at any point. Debate on an amendment is limited to five minutes for supporters and five minutes for opponents, but additional time may be obtained by offering pro forma amendments to "strike out the last word." In contrast to Senate practice, amendments must be germane, not only to the bill but also to the section to which they are offered. *(Box, p. 350)*

Committee amendments are always taken up first but may be changed, as may all amendments, up to the second degree; an amendment to an amendment to an amendment is not in order. Although amendments in the third degree are not permitted, up to four amendments in the first and second degree may be pending at the same time: an amendment to the bill, an amendment to the amendment, a substitute for the original amendment and an amendment to the substitute. They are voted on in the following order, as diagrammed in *Cannon's Procedure.*[5]

TEXT

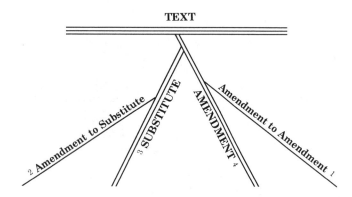

If the substitute is agreed to, the fourth vote is on the amendment as amended by the substitute.

More than one vote may be taken on a given amendment. The Committee of the Whole may first take a voice vote, then move on to standing or teller votes before finally deciding a question. (Amendments accepted in Committee of the Whole also are subject to roll-call votes after the bill is reported to the full House.)

The mark of an accomplished floor manager is his ability to get his bill through the House intact, and in voting on amendments representatives are under considerable pressure to support the actions of the committee that reported the bill. Expressing the traditional view of the House hierarchy, Cannon gives the following advice to members:

"Generally speaking, and in the absence of convictions to the contrary, members are justified in voting with the committee. Committees are not infallible but they have had long familiarity with the subject under discussion, and have made an intimate study of the particular bill before the House and after mature deliberation have made formal recommendations and, other considerations being equal, are entitled to support on the floor. *Members should be particularly wary of proponents of amendments disapproved by the committee who station members or employees at the doors to accost members arriving in response to the bells and who have not heard the debate.* It is a questionable practice and should serve to put members on their guard until they have ascertained the committee's point of view."[6]

The Legislative Reorganization Act of 1970 provides for 10 minutes of debate on any amendment offered on the floor—even if debate has been closed on the section to which the amendment is proposed—so long as the amendment has been printed in the *Congressional Record* at least one day before consideration. Previously, an amendment received no explanation at all during consideration of a bill when a majority of the Committee of the Whole agreed to cut off debate on a section before there had been any debate on the amendment.

Action by the Full House

When the Committee of the Whole has completed action on a bill, it "rises," the Speaker returns to the chair, and the erstwhile chairman of the Committee of the Whole reports the action of the committee and its recommendations. Only amendments *adopted* in Committee of the Whole are reported to the House.

If the previous question has been ordered, the full House votes immediately on amendments reported by the committee. At this point members may demand a roll call on any amendment adopted in the Committee of the Whole. There is no way to obtain another vote on an amendment rejected in the Committee of the Whole unless it can be incorporated in a recommittal motion with instructions.

(The previous question motion is a device to cut off debate and force a vote on the subject under consideration. Unless it is ordered, the bill and amendments would be subject to further debate and amendment. The previous question is not used in the Senate.)

Once the amendments have been disposed of, the question is on engrossment and third reading (by title only) of the bill. A member opposed to the bill may offer a motion to recommit the measure to the committee that reported it. There are two kinds of recommittal motions: a simple motion to recommit, which defeats the bill if it is adopted; or a motion to recommit with instructions (to report the bill back with amendments, after study, by a certain date, etc.). The motion to recommit with instructions, on which 10 minutes of debate is allowed under the 1970 act, is frequently used by the minority to present an alternative program. Although recommittal votes seldom succeed, they often

(Continued on p. 347)

HOW A BILL BECOMES LAW

This graphic shows the most typical way in which proposed legislation is enacted into law. There are more complicated, as well as simpler, routes, and most bills fall by the wayside and never become law. The process is illustrated with two hypothetical bills, House bill No. 1 (HR 1) and Senate bill No. 2 (S 2).

Each bill must be passed by both houses of Congress in identical form before it can become law. The path of HR 1 is traced by a solid line, that of S 2 by a broken line. However, in practice most legislation begins as similar proposals in both houses.

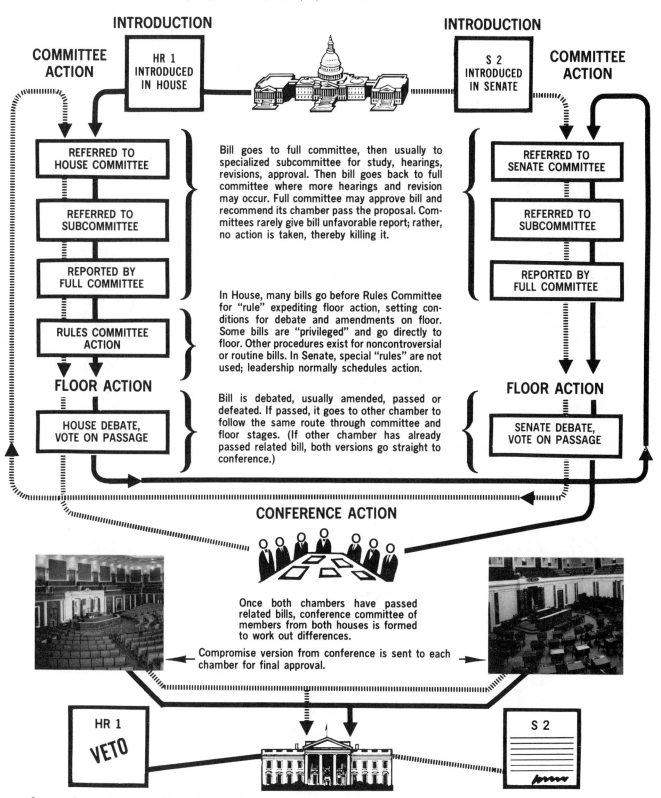

INTRODUCTION

COMMITTEE ACTION

HR 1 INTRODUCED IN HOUSE

REFERRED TO HOUSE COMMITTEE

REFERRED TO SUBCOMMITTEE

REPORTED BY FULL COMMITTEE

RULES COMMITTEE ACTION

FLOOR ACTION

HOUSE DEBATE, VOTE ON PASSAGE

INTRODUCTION

COMMITTEE ACTION

S 2 INTRODUCED IN SENATE

REFERRED TO SENATE COMMITTEE

REFERRED TO SUBCOMMITTEE

REPORTED BY FULL COMMITTEE

FLOOR ACTION

SENATE DEBATE, VOTE ON PASSAGE

Bill goes to full committee, then usually to specialized subcommittee for study, hearings, revisions, approval. Then bill goes back to full committee where more hearings and revision may occur. Full committee may approve bill and recommend its chamber pass the proposal. Committees rarely give bill unfavorable report; rather, no action is taken, thereby killing it.

In House, many bills go before Rules Committee for "rule" expediting floor action, setting conditions for debate and amendments on floor. Some bills are "privileged" and go directly to floor. Other procedures exist for noncontroversial or routine bills. In Senate, special "rules" are not used; leadership normally schedules action.

Bill is debated, usually amended, passed or defeated. If passed, it goes to other chamber to follow the same route through committee and floor stages. (If other chamber has already passed related bill, both versions go straight to conference.)

CONFERENCE ACTION

Once both chambers have passed related bills, conference committee of members from both houses is formed to work out differences.

Compromise version from conference is sent to each chamber for final approval.

HR 1 VETO

S 2

Compromise version approved by both houses is sent to President who can either sign it into law or veto it and return it to Congress. Congress may override veto by a two-thirds majority vote in both houses; bill then becomes law without President's signature.

345

Methods of Voting in House and Senate

House

The House has four different methods of voting, one or more of which may be used in deciding a single question. Occasionally the House takes several votes on the same proposition, using first simple and then more complex voting methods, before a final decision is reached. The four methods of voting:

Voice Vote. This is the usual method of voting when a proposition is first put to the House, although other methods also are in order. The presiding officer calls for the "ayes" and "noes" in turn, members answer in chorus, and the chair decides the result.

Division (Standing) Vote. If the result of a voice vote is in doubt or a further test is desired, a division may be demanded. In this case, members in favor of a proposal stand and are counted by the presiding officer; then members opposed stand and are counted. Only vote totals are announced; there is no record of how individual members voted.

Teller Vote. A teller vote may be ordered upon demand of one-fifth of a quorum (20 in the Committee of the Whole and 44 in the House). Traditionally, the chair appointed two tellers from opposite sides and directed the members to pass between them up the center aisle to be counted. The ayes would pass through first, then the nays. (This method has been superseded by electronic voting. *See box, p. 343*)

Prior to 1971, only vote totals were announced, but a House floor amendment to the Legislative Reorganization Act of 1970 opened the way to recorded teller votes. Under the 1970 act, it is possible to record the votes of individual members on a teller vote taken during consideration of a bill in the Committee of the Whole at the request of one-fifth of a quorum (20), or, in the case of the full House, at the request of 44 members. Members are permitted at least 15 minutes from the beginning of the vote to reach the floor and be counted.

When the change first went into effect, members were required to write their names on red or green cards they handed to tellers. Since January 1973, an electronic voting system has been used. It is within the Speaker's discretion, however, to require members to write their names on red or green cards handed to tellers in lieu of using the electronic voting system.

Roll-Call Vote. Yeas and nays are ordered by one-fifth of those present (as opposed to one-fifth of a quorum for tellers). They are not taken in the Committee of the Whole.

Prior to the installation of the electronic voting system, roll calls were a time-consuming process in the 435-member House, with each yea-and-nay vote taking about a half hour. After the first call of the roll, the clerk went through the list again repeating the names of those who failed to respond before. Following the second call, members standing in the "well" of the House could be recorded. The Speaker still has the discretion to require an alphabetical call of the role rather than using electronic voting.

During roll calls, members are required to vote yea or nay. Members who do not wish to vote may answer "present." The Speaker's name is called only at his own request: he is required to vote only if his vote would be deciding, but sometimes Speakers have voted on other occasions. (The Speaker also votes, if he chooses, on recorded teller votes in the Committee of the Whole.)

The Constitution requires yea-and-nay votes on the question of overriding a veto. Under the House rules, the yeas and nays are required automatically whenever a member objects to a nonrecord vote taken when a quorum was not present, if the question is one that requires a quorum. This is known as an automatic roll call.

Senate

Like the House, the Senate uses voice, division (standing) and roll-call votes. It does not employ the teller vote. Vote totals are seldom made public on division votes; usually only the result is announced.

The Senate does not follow the House practice of voting on a single proposition by several different methods; once the result of a vote has been announced in the Senate, the demand for a different kind of vote is not in order. But the same result sometimes occurs when the Senate votes to re-consider an earlier vote. Normally, this is a routine action taken on all votes, but on a closely contested issue it gives the Senate an opportunity to change its mind.

Roll calls are easier to obtain in the Senate than in the House. As in the House, they are available upon demand of one-fifth of those present, but in practice a senator is seldom denied a roll-call vote on an issue if he insists on one. Roll calls usually are planned and announced in advance. Yeas and nays are required on a vote to override a veto. The Vice President votes only in case of a tie.

Pairs. Pairs are "gentlemen's agreements" used by members of the House and Senate to cancel out the effect of absences on roll-call votes. A member who expects to be absent for a roll call pairs off with another member, both of them agreeing not to vote. Pairs are not counted in vote totals, although the names of lawmakers pairing on a given vote and their stands, if known, are printed in the *Congressional Record*. If the roll call is one that requires a two-thirds majority, a pair requires two members favoring the action to one opposed to it.

A *live pair* covers one or several specific issues. A member who would vote "yea" pairs with a member who would vote "nay." Thus both announce their stands. Live pairs may determine the outcome of a vote if a member who is present withholds his vote because he has a pair with one who is absent.

A *general pair*, widely used in the House, is a more arbitrary method of matching absent members while not involving announcement of their stands. No agreement is involved and the pair does not tie up votes. A representative expecting to be absent may notify the House clerk that he wishes to make a general pair. His name is then paired with that of another member desiring a general pair, and the list is printed in the *Congressional Record*. He may or may not be paired with a member taking the opposite position.

(Continued from p. 344)
provide a better test of members' views than a vote on passage.

If the recommittal vote fails, the next question is on final passage. That vote may be followed by a pro forma motion to reconsider, and this motion itself may be followed by a move to lay the motion on the table. Usually those voting for the bill's passage vote for the tabling motion, thus safeguarding the final passage action. With that, the bill has been formally passed by the chamber. While a motion to reconsider is pending, the bill cannot be sent to the Senate.

At this point, the bill officially becomes an "act," although it continues generally to be referred to as a bill. An engrossed copy of the bill as passed by the House, certified by the clerk of the House, is printed on blue paper and transmitted to the Senate for its action.

Alternative House Procedures

The procedures described above indicate the usual route of a major bill through the House, but certain alternative methods, described below, are available.

Consent Calendar

Members of the House may place on this calendar any bill on the House or Union Calendar which is considered to be noncontroversial. Bills on the Consent Calendar are normally called on the first and third Mondays of each month. On these days, immediately after the reading of the Journal, the Speaker directs the clerk to call the bills that have been for three legislative days on the Consent Calendar in the order of appearance on that calendar.

When a bill is called in this manner the first time, consideration may be blocked by the objection of any member. If objection is made the first time, the bill is carried over on the calendar to the next day when the Consent Calendar is called. The second time, if there are three objections, the bill is stricken from the Consent Calendar. If there are less than three objections, the bill is passed by unanimous consent without debate. Ordinarily the only amendments considered are those sponsored by the committee that reported the bill.

To avoid passage without debate of controversial measures or bills sufficiently important or complex to require full debate there are six official objectors—three from each party—who police the bills on the Consent Calendar and act for absent members.

A bill on the Consent Calendar may be postponed in another way. A member may ask that the measure be passed over "without prejudice." In that case, no objection is recorded against the bill and its status on the Consent Calendar remains unchanged.

A bill stricken from the Consent Calendar remains on the Union or House Calendar.

Suspension of the Rules

This is often a time-saving procedure for passing bills in the House. The wording of the motion, which may be made by any member recognized by the Speaker (arrangement for recognition must be made in advance) is: "I move to suspend the rules and pass the bill...." Before being considered by the House, the motion must be seconded by a majority of the members present, by teller vote, if demanded. Debate is limited to 40 minutes. The motion may not be amended and if amendments to the bill are proposed they must be included in the motion when it is made. The rules may be suspended only by affirmative vote of two-thirds of the members voting, with a quorum present. If a two-thirds favorable vote is not obtained, the bill may be considered later under regular procedures.

Suspension of the rules is in order on the first and third Mondays of each month and (since 1973) on the Tuesdays immediately following those days, as well as during the last six days of a session.

Discharge Petition

The discharge petition is a little-used device designed to permit a majority of representatives to bring to the House floor legislation blocked by a legislative committee or by the Rules Committee.

The modern discharge rule was first adopted in 1910.[7] The present form of the rule, adopted in 1935, enables a majority of the House to bring to the House floor after a complicated series of parliamentary steps: (1) any public bill that has been before a standing committee of the House for 30 days; or (2) any committee-approved bill that has been before the House Rules Committee for seven legislative days without receiving a special rule for floor debate. In addition, the discharge rule may be used to dislodge from the Rules Committee a special rule for debate on a bill that has been before a standing committee for 30 days—a combination of the first two procedures.

This is how the procedure works: If a bill has been before a legislative committee for 30 days (or the Rules Committee for seven days), any member may file a discharge motion, popularly called a discharge "petition." When 218 members, a majority of the House, have signed the petition, it is placed on the Discharge Calendar where it must remain for seven legislative days before it can be called up. This seven-day "grace period" makes it possible for the committee, if it chooses, to act on the bill before the discharge petition is considered. On the second and fourth Mondays of each month, except during the last six days of a session, any member who has signed the petition may be recognized to move that the committee be discharged. Debate on the motion is limited to 20 minutes, equally divided between proponents and opponents, and if the motion carries, consideration of the bill becomes a matter of high privilege. The House may consider the measure immediately or place it on one of the calendars.

Although the discharge method is seldom used successfully, the threat of such a move may be used to spur committee action. *(For actual use of the discharge petition since 1910, see box next page)*

Once during the first session of the 92nd Congress, a bill was brought to the floor by means of a discharge petition. This was on the constitutional amendment to allow prayer in public schools, and it received the 218 signatures necessary to dislodge it from the House Judiciary Committee, which had refused to act. The amendment was the target of a lobbying campaign by religious leaders and laymen on both sides of the issue, with most major church groups opposing it but a majority of the American people reported by polls to be in favor. The amendment came to the House floor Nov. 13, 1971, and failed as the 240 votes in its favor fell 28 short of the two-thirds majority necessary for a constitutional amendment.

Calendar Wednesday

This is a method for bringing to the House floor a bill that has been blocked by the Rules Committee. Under the procedure, each Wednesday committees may be called in the order in which they appear in Rule 10 of the House Manual (that is, alphabetically), for the purpose of bringing up any of their bills from the House or Union Calendars, except bills that are privileged. General debate is limited to two hours. Bills called up from the Union Calendar are considered in Committee of the Whole and amendments are taken up under the five-minute rule. Since the Calendar Wednesday procedure requires action to be completed in the same legislative day, it is vulnerable to dilatory action by opponents of the bill in question.

Calendar Wednesday is not observed during the last two weeks of a session and may be dispensed with at other times by a two-thirds vote. In practice, it usually is dispensed with by unanimous consent.

Many built-in hindrances make the procedure cumbersome:

● Since the committees must be called in alphabetical order, those at the end of the list may have to wait 15 to 20 weeks before they are reached.

● Many delaying tactics are available to opponents of any bill called up because the procedure requires that it be disposed of in one day.

● If a committee has had one opportunity to call up a bill, it cannot have another bill considered until all other committees have been called.

● Only the chairman is authorized to call up a bill reported by the committee.

Between 1950 and 1974, the Calendar Wednesday procedure was used successfully only twice: on Feb. 15, 1950, on the Fair Employment Practices Act, and on May 4, 1960, on the Area Redevelopment Act.

Other Methods

Special legislative days are set aside twice each month for the consideration of private bills and District of Columbia business. *(Private Bills chapter, p. 299; Control of the Seat of Government, p. 287)*

The so-called "21-day rule," a device under which legislative committees could bring to the floor bills that had been blocked by the Rules Committee, was in force in the House in the 81st (1949-51) and 89th (1965-67) Congresses. The 1965 rule permitted the chairman or any other member of a committee that had favorably reported a bill to bring a rule (authorizing House action on the bill) directly to the floor for adoption by majority vote. This was permitted on the second or fourth Monday of the month, if the Rules Committee had not granted clearance to the bill within 21 calendar days after a resolution to call up the bill had been filed by the legislative committee. Discretion remained with the Speaker to recognize the member from the committee, so that it was highly unlikely, if not impossible, for a bill to come up successfully under this procedure without leadership approval. (The 1949 rule *required* the Speaker to recognize the member who was calling up a 21-day resolution.) The 21-day rule was employed successfully only eight times in the 89th Congress.

Senate Floor Procedures

Although the Senate has an elaborate framework of parliamentary machinery to guide its deliberations, in practice its procedures are far more flexible than those of the House. Almost anything can be done by unanimous consent, or the rules can be suspended by a two-thirds vote.

Discharge Petition

The discharge petition is a little-used device designed to enable a majority of representatives to bring to the House floor legislation blocked by a legislative committee or the Rules Committee.

The following table shows the extent to which the discharge petition was used between its adoption in 1910 and the close of the 93rd Congress in 1975. Although 25 bills were pried loose from committee by the discharge method and 20 of them ultimately passed the House, only two were finally enacted: the Fair Labor Standards Act of 1938 and the 1960 federal pay raise bill.

Congress	Petitions Filed	Bills Discharged	Discharged Bills That Passed House
61 (1909-11)	223	figures not	
62-67 (1911-23)	241	available	
68 (1923-25)	4	1	0
69 (1925-27)	4	0	0
70 (1927-29)	2	0	0
71 (1929-31)	5	0	0
72 (1931-33)	12	1	1
73 (1933-35)	31	1	1
74 (1935-37)	33	2	0
75 (1937-39)	43	3	2
76 (1939-41)	37	2	2
77 (1941-43)	15	1	1
78 (1943-45)	21	3	3
79 (1945-47)	35	1	1
80 (1947-49)	20	1	1
81 (1949-51)	34	3	3
82 (1951-53)	14	0	0
83 (1953-55)	10	1	1
84 (1955-57)	6	0	0
85 (1957-59)	7	1	1
86 (1959-61)	5	1	1
87 (1961-63)	6	0	0
88 (1963-65)	5	0	0
89 (1965-67)	6	1	1
90 (1967-69)	4	0	0
91 (1969-71)	12	1	1
92 (1971-73)	15	1	0
93 (1973-75)	10	0	0
TOTAL	860	25	20

Bills may be brought to the Senate floor on call of the calendar (a process described below) or they may be called up through adoption, by majority vote, of a motion to consider a particular measure. A motion to consider a bill is not debatable if it is made during the morning hour (before 2 p.m.); after that hour it is subject to debate which can only be limited by invoking cloture. In practice, most major bills are taken up by unanimous consent in accord with the schedule worked out by the majority leader.

Unlike the House, the Senate does not consider bills in Committee of the Whole, and it does not set aside a period for general debate before the amending process begins.

Once he is recognized by the presiding officer, a senator may speak virtually as long as he likes and on any subject he chooses unless he violates the rules of the Senate. He may yield temporarily for the consideration of other business, or he may yield to another senator for a question, but he may not parcel out time to other members as is the practice in the House. Under the rules, no senator is permitted to speak more than twice on the same subject in the same legislative day; however, since each amendment is considered a different subject, this is not an effective limit on debate. Under a rule adopted in 1964, debate is required to be germane for three hours following the morning hour, but this stricture usually is ignored.

The previous question as a device for bringing debate to a close is not used in the Senate. The only bar to unlimited debate is the cloture rule (Rule 22), which requires the assent of three-fifths of the entire Senate membership to cut off debate. This rule is discussed in detail below.

In practice, unanimous consent agreements are widely used to expedite business and schedule votes. In a typical situation the procedure is as follows: After debate on a bill (or amendment, motion, etc.) has gone on for some time, the majority leader will consult with the minority leader and other interested senators in an effort to work out an agreement on control of remaining debate and the time of voting. Because a single objection will block a unanimous consent request, care is taken to protect the rights of all senators and to assure that those who wish to speak will have an opportunity to do so. The majority leader then rises on the floor and, following a quorum call to alert absent senators, asks for unanimous consent to end debate and vote at a particular time.

Amendment Process in Senate

When a bill is taken up, it is immediately open to virtually unlimited amendment. Committee amendments are taken up first and, like other amendments, may be amended to the second degree. Frequently the Senate by unanimous consent agrees to the committee amendments en bloc and provides that the bill as amended be considered as an original text for the purpose of further amendment. Substitute amendments are in order, in which case both the original amendment and the substitute would be open to amendment at the same time. The text of one bill may be offered as a substitute for another.

Except in the case of general appropriations bills, amendments need not be germane. An amendment may be modified or withdrawn before some action has been taken on it; once adopted, an amendment is not subject to further amendment unless a motion to reconsider the previous action is adopted by majority vote. Occasionally a bill's floor manager will agree to inclusion of an amendment, saying he will "take it to conference"; it is likely to die there. Pro forma amendments, used in the House to gain additional speaking time, are not offered in the Senate since debate is unlimited anyway.

Voting in the Senate is by voice, division (standing) or roll-call vote. There is no teller vote, and unlike the House, the Senate uses only one method of voting on a single question. Roll calls, required on demand of one-fifth of those present, are easily obtained and, until 1971, the Senate took many more such votes than the House did. *(For description of voting methods, see box p. 346.)*

When action on amendments is completed, the bill is ready for engrossment and third reading (usually by title only, although if demanded, it must be read in full) followed by the vote on passage. A motion to reconsider may be offered by any senator on the winning side, or one who did not vote, within two days of that vote. If the bill passed without a record vote, any senator may make the motion. In practice, a pro forma motion to reconsider usually is offered and in turn tabled, in order to nail down the final action.

Motions to recommit are seldom used in the Senate, partly because the amending process is so much more flexible than it is in the House.

Alternative Senate Procedures

Because the normal Senate procedures are so flexible, there is less need than in the House for alternative methods of bringing bills to the floor. In the Senate reported bills usually can be taken up without difficulty, and legislative obstruction is more likely to occur on the floor, in the form of a filibuster.

Reported bills may be taken up on call of the calendar, which is used for noncontroversial legislation similar to bills on the Consent Calendar in the House. Although the calendar may be called following the conclusion of morning business on any day and is privileged on Mondays, it usually is called only once or twice a month. When the calendar is called, bills that are not objected to are taken up in order and each senator is limited to five minutes' debate on each bill. If objection is raised, the bill may either be passed over or, upon motion, considered. If the majority votes to proceed to consider the bill, the five-minute rule no longer applies.

Under the discharge rule, any senator during the morning hour may submit a motion to discharge a committee from further consideration of proposed legislation. The motion must lie over for one legislative day; it then may be brought up and a simple majority vote is sufficient to discharge the committee. This procedure is seldom used.

A more common method of forcing action on a legislative proposal is by offering it as a floor amendment to a pending bill. Because—except in the case of general appropriations bills—there is no Senate rule requiring amendments to be germane to the bill to which they are offered, this is a simple way of bringing a bill to the floor.

An outstanding example occurred in 1960 when the Senate leadership made good on a promise to act on civil rights legislation, although none had been reported by the Judiciary Committee. It did so by calling up a minor House-passed bill and inviting senators to offer civil rights amendments to it. In 1965, Sen. Everett McKinley Dirksen (R Ill.) brought to the floor a minor baseball bill and then succeeded in substituting for its text the text of a proposed constitutional amendment, blocked by the Judiciary Committee, which dealt with state legislative apportionment.

The prohibition on riders to appropriations bills may be suspended by two-thirds vote on a motion to permit consideration of such an amendment upon one day's notice in writing.

Tax legislation is frequently subject to nongermane riders for a special reason: the Constitution requires that revenue measures originate in the House, which means in the Ways and Means Committee; the Senate is restricted to amending House-passed tax bills. The Senate does not often load a bill with unrelated amendments, but when it does the event can be spectacular. An example was the 1966 Foreign Investors Tax Act, which became known as the "Christmas Tree Bill" because of the multitude of unrelated

Nongermane Amendments: Old Senate-House Feud

The House Oct. 13, 1972, passed by a resolution amending its rules governing consideration of committee reports, House-Senate conference reports and nongermane amendments added by the Senate. Under the new rules which took effect at the beginning of the 93rd Congress:

● Conference reports and provisions reported in disagreement by House-Senate conferees had to be printed in the *Congressional Record* when reported and could not be considered by the House until at least the third day thereafter. (Under the former rule, conference reports could not be considered until the fourth day. There was no provision dealing with voting on provisions reported by conferees in disagreement; therefore they could be considered immediately by the House. There was no requirement for printing conference reports in the *Congressional Record,* although in practice such reports were published in the Record on or before the report was considered by the House.)

● A bill could not be considered on the House floor until the third day a committee report on the bill had been available to members. (Previously, a bill could not be considered until the fourth day.)

● During House consideration of conference reports, any Senate amendment accepted by House conferees, which if introduced in the House would be ruled nongermane under House rules, was subject to 40 minutes debate and a majority vote on acceptance of the amendment. If a nongermane amendment was rejected, the entire conference report would be rejected and the bill, without the rejected amendment, would be returned to the Senate for further action.

Background. The primary impetus for the resolution was the issue of nongermane amendments added by the Senate—a long-standing irritant between the two chambers.

The House had strict rules forbidding consideration of amendments not germane to the bill before the House. The Senate, however, for years had attached nongermane amendments to House-passed bills. House members complained that the practice prevented them from considering these amendments because they were not considered in a House committee and, incorporated in conference reports, could not be voted on separately.

During the 92nd Congress, the House operated under the new rule dealing with nongermane amendments to conference reports. The 1970 change was intended to rectify a problem which the previous House rule forbidding the House from considering nongermane amendments apart from the rest of a conference report had presented. But as written into the 1970 reorganization act, the new rule failed to achieve the desired result, partly because the 1970 act did not spell out the parliamentary procedure to follow in taking a separate recorded vote on nongermane portions of conference

reports and partly because the new rule appeared to conflict with other House rules that were not repealed, requiring an up-or-down vote on the entire bill with no chance to amend it.

Therefore, when a conference committee did agree to nongermane amendments, it was necessary in the House to obtain a special rule from the Rules Committee waiving points of order against nongermane amendments before bringing the conference report to the floor. On two major bills in the 92nd Congress—the fiscal 1972 military procurement authorization and the rural development bill—the germaneness issue was central.

On Nov. 10, 1971, the House agreed to a rule waiving points of order against a military procurement conference report and allowing separate votes on three sections of the conference report. The House actually voted on only one—allowing the importation of Rhodesian chrome—which it approved.

On July 27, 1972, the House took up consideration of a Rules Committee resolution (H Res 1057) on the conference report of the rural development bill. The bill included eight provisions which Rules Committee members thought were nongermane. The resolution waived points of order against the nongermane amendments and did not provide an opportunity to vote on the eight provisions separately.

H. Allen Smith (R Calif. 1957-73), ranking Republican on the Rules Committee, was ready to offer an amendment to H Res 1057 to provide for separate votes if the House defeated the previous question on the rule ordering an immediate vote on the conference report. However, the House voted 214-162 to order the previous question and then approved H Res 1057 by a voice vote. Subsequently, the House agreed to the conference report.

Under the 1972 procedure for nongermane amendments, House members could make points of order against a conference report after it was read but before debate began on it. If any portion of the conference report was ruled nongermane, that portion was immediately subject to 40 minutes of debate and a separate vote on it. This could be repeated until all points of order were offered. If no points of order were sustained or if the House accepted all nongermane amendments, the House would then consider and accept or reject the conference report as a whole.

If any or all of the nongermane amendments were rejected by the House, the House would then consider a motion to accept the Senate version with an amendment—the amendment consisting of all provisions of the conference report not rejected by the House. If the House agreed to this motion, according to House Rules Committee members, the Senate could then agree to the House version, without the nongermane amendments, or request a second conference on the bill.

amendments added in committee and on the floor—among them an amendment to establish a Presidential Election Campaign Fund, which was itself killed by a nongermane rider to another tax bill the following year.

Senate riders sometimes are the result of logrolling, sometimes are accepted out of courtesy to the sponsoring senator who has a strong interest in the proposal, and sometimes are approved simply because they are popular but with the knowledge that they will be quietly dropped in conference later.

In the case of a House-passed bill, another method of bypassing committees is available: Senate rules provide that a House-passed bill may be placed directly on the Senate calendar without being referred to committee. This method was used to keep the civil rights bills of 1957 and 1964 out of the hostile Senate Judiciary Committee.

Senate Cloture Rule

A unique characteristic of the Senate, compared to the House, is the right of extended—almost unlimited—debate on the floor. Occasionally, this right becomes a device to prevent action on legislative proposals. Continuing debate designed to prevent Senate action is known as a filibuster.

The Senate for many years has had in its rules a method by which to end a filibuster, but until the late 1960s it was rarely used successfully and even after that time it remained a difficult instrument to employ. That method is known as the cloture rule and it refers specifically to Senate Rule 22.

The rule has provided during most of the period that it has been in existence since 1917 that a filibuster may be stopped by a two-thirds majority; usually this has meant two-thirds of the senators present and voting but at certain times it has meant two-thirds of the full Senate. When this test has been met, cloture has been invoked and a filibuster ended. *(Cloture attempts, box next page)*

The cloture rule was revised in 1975 to make the limitation on debate easier to obtain. As revised, Rule 22 requires a three-fifths majority of the entire Senate membership (60 votes if there are no vacancies), rather than the previous requirement of two-thirds of those senators present and voting.

A cloture vote is taken two days after a cloture motion has been filed by 16 senators. Following adoption of a cloture motion, debate is limited to one hour for each senator on the bill itself and on all motions and amendments affecting it. No new amendments may be offered except by unanimous consent; only those amendments formally before the Senate when cloture was invoked may be considered. Amendments that are not germane to the pending business and amendments and motions clearly designed to delay action are out of order. The three-fifths requirement applies to ordinary Senate business; in the case of efforts to change the standing rules of the Senate, a two-thirds vote of senators present and voting still is required.

Rule Adopted in 1917. The original Rule 22 was adopted by the Senate in 1917 following a furor over the "talking to death" of President Woodrow Wilson's proposal, before American entry into World War I, to arm American merchant ships against the German submarine menace.

In its 1917 form, Rule 22 required two-thirds of the senators present and voting to invoke cloture. Over the years, however, a series of rulings and precedents made the rule virtually inoperative by holding that it could not be applied to debate on procedural questions, although it could be used on attempts to change Senate rules.

In 1949, when the Truman administration was seeking enactment of a civil rights measure, the rule was changed to require two-thirds of the entire Senate membership to invoke cloture, but it allowed cloture to operate on any pending business or motions, with the exception of debate on motions to change the Senate rules themselves.

In 1959, the rule was changed again, largely at the instigation of then Majority Leader Lyndon B. Johnson (D Texas). Under the 1959 rule, once again cloture could be imposed by two-thirds of those present and voting, and it could be applied to motions to change the Senate rules. At the same time, language was added to Senate Rule 32 stating that: "The rules of the Senate shall continue from one Congress to the next unless they are changed as provided in these rules."

The language added to Rule 32 was aimed at a key question with which the Senate had wrestled for years: Was the Senate, since one-third of its membership was elected every two years, a continuing body that should operate under rules carried over from Congress to Congress, or should it adopt new rules by general parliamentary procedure—majority vote—at the beginning of each Congress? (The House, all of whose members are elected every two years, adopts its rules at the beginning of each Congress.) If the Senate was a continuing body, rules changes could be talked to death unless two-thirds of the membership supported the proposed changes and would support cloture. If not, a filibuster could be stopped by majority vote at the beginning of a new Congress and substantive proposals for changes in the rules could be voted on. The language added to Rule 32 buttressed the position of those who maintained that the Senate was a continuing body, but liberal opponents of the filibuster never conceded the point. For sixteen years they tried without success to make it easier to cut off filibusters. Attempts were made at the opening of every Congress since the 86th—with the exception of the 93rd in 1973—but every effort was thwarted by the filibuster itself.

Senate liberals renewed their efforts early in 1975 with a proposal to require only a three-fifths majority of senators present and voting to invoke cloture. A compromise between advocates and opponents of a rules change was reached later to require a three-fifths majority of the entire Senate membership. The change was expected to produce more successful cloture efforts on the first vote rather than on the third or fourth vote. This would expedite Senate action on the proposal at issue as well as on other legislation that was being delayed by the filibuster.

Between 1917 and adjournment of the first session of the 94th Congress in 1975, only 34 of 123 cloture votes taken were successful. *(Table, next page. Background on the filibuster and 1975 reform, p. 100)*

Action in Second Chamber

After a bill has been passed by one house, an engrossed copy is transmitted to the other house.

When the Senate receives a House-passed bill, usually it refers the measure to the appropriate committee which frequently already is considering a similar measure. However, on rare occasions the House-passed bill is referred directly to the Senate calendar. A bill first passed by the Senate and transmitted to the House must go to committee unless a similar House bill has already been reported from committee and placed on the calendar.

Under normal procedure, then, a bill passed by one chamber and transmitted to the other is referred to the appropriate committee, from which it must follow the same route to passage as a bill originating in that chamber. Amendments may be offered at both the committee and floor action stages, and the bill as it emerges from the sec-

(Continued on p. 353)

List of Cloture Votes Since Adoption of Rule 22

Between 1917, when Senate Rule 22 was adopted, and Dec. 15, 1975, 123 cloture votes were taken of which 34 (in **dark type**) were successful. Cloture efforts through March 7, 1975, required a two-thirds majority for success. (Figures in the right-hand column through that date are hypothetical: the vote majorities that would have been needed to invoke cloture had Rule 22 required only a three-fifths majority of senators present and voting, as reform advocates wanted. Italic lines show votes that would have succeeded under that standard.) In 1975, Rule 22 was changed so that three-fifths of the full Senate, or 60 votes, was required for cloture after March 7.

Issue	Date	Vote	Yeas Needed 2/3 Majority	Yeas Needed 3/5 Majority
Versailles Treaty	Nov. 15, 1919	78-16	63	57
Emergency tariff	Feb. 2, 1921	36-35	48	43
Tariff bill	July 7, 1922	45-35	54	48
World Court	Jan. 25, 1926	68-26	63	57
Migratory birds	June 1, 1926	46-33	53	47
Branch banking	Feb.15, 1927	65-18	56	50
Disabled officers	Feb. 26, 1927	51-36	58	52
Colorado River	Feb. 26, 1927	32-59	61	55
D.C. buildings	Feb. 28, 1927	52-31	56	50
Prohibition Bureau	Feb. 28, 1927	55-27	55	49
Banking Act	Jan. 19, 1933	58-30	59	53
Anti-lynching	Jan. 27, 1938	37-51	59	53
Anti-lynching	Feb. 16, 1938	42-46	59	53
Anti-poll tax	Nov. 23, 1942	37-41	52	47
Anti-poll tax	May 15, 1944	36-44	54	48
Fair Employment Practices Commission	Feb. 9, 1946	48-36	56	50
British loan	May 7, 1946	41-41	55	49
Labor disputes	May 25, 1946	3-77	54	48
Anti-poll tax	July 31, 1946	39-33	48	43
FEPC	May 19, 1950	52-32	64*	58*
FEPC	July 12, 1950	55-33	64*	58*
Atomic Energy Act	July 26, 1954	44-42	64*	58*
Civil Rights Act	March 10, 1960	42-53	64	57
Amend Rule 22	Sept. 19, 1961	37-43	54	48
Literacy tests	May 9, 1962	43-53	64	58
Literacy tests	May 14, 1962	42-52	63	57
Comsat Act	Aug. 14, 1962	63-27	60	54
Amend Rule 22	Feb. 7, 1963	54-42	64	58
Civil Rights Act	June 10, 1964	71-29	67	60
Legislative reapportionment	Sept. 10, 1964	30-63	62	56
Voting Rights Act	May 25, 1965	70-30	67	60
Right-to-work repeal	Oct. 11, 1965	45-47	62	55
Right-to-work repeal	Feb. 8, 1966	51-48	66	59
Right-to-work repeal	Feb. 10, 1966	50-49	66	59
Civil Rights Act	Sept. 14, 1966	54-42	64	58
Civil Rights Act	Sept. 19, 1966	52-41	62	56
D.C. Home Rule	Oct. 10, 1966	41-37	52	47
Amend Rule 22	Jan. 24, 1967	53-46	66	59
Open Housing	Feb. 20, 1968	55-37	62	55
Open Housing	Feb. 26, 1968	56-36	62	55
Open Housing	March 1, 1968	59-35	63	57
Open Housing	March 4, 1968	65-32	65	58
Fortas Nomination	Oct. 1, 1968	45-43	59	53
Amend Rule 22	Jan. 16, 1969	51-47	66	59
Amend Rule 22	Jan. 28, 1969	50-42	62	55
Electoral College	Sept. 17, 1970	54-36	60	54
Electoral College	Sept. 29, 1970	53-34	58	53
Supersonic transport	Dec. 19, 1970	43-48	61	55
Supersonic transport	Dec. 22, 1970	42-44	58	52
Amend Rule 22	Feb. 18, 1971	48-37	57	51
Amend Rule 22	Feb. 23, 1971	50-36	58	52
Amend Rule 22	March 2, 1971	48-36	56	50
Amend Rule 22	March 9, 1971	55-39	63	57
Military Draft	June 23, 1971	65-27	62	55
Lockheed Loan	July 26, 1971	42-47	60	54
Lockheed Loan	July 28, 1971	59-39	66	59
Lockheed Loan	July 30, 1971	53-37	60	54
Military Draft	Sept. 21, 1971	61-30	61	55
Rehnquist nomination	Dec. 10, 1971	52-42	63	57
Equal Job Opportunity	Feb. 1, 1972	48-37	57	51
Equal Job Opportunity	Feb. 3, 1972	53-35	59	53
Equal Job Opportunity	Feb. 22, 1972	71-23	63	57
U.S.-Soviet Arms Pact	Sept. 14, 1972	76-15	61	55
Consumer Agency	Sept. 29, 1972	47-29	51	46
Consumer Agency	Oct. 3,1972	55-32	58	53
Consumer Agency	Oct. 5, 1972	52-30	55	49
School Busing	Oct. 10, 1972	45-37	55	49
School Busing	Oct. 11, 1972	49-39	59	53
School Busing	Oct. 12, 1972	49-38	58	53
Voter Registration	April 30, 1973	56-31	58	53
Voter Registration	May 3, 1973	60-34	63	57
Voter Registration	May 9, 1973	67-32	66	59
Public Campaign Financing	Dec. 2, 1973	47-33	54	48
Public Campaign Financing	Dec. 3, 1973	49-39	59	53
Rhodesian Chrome Ore	Dec. 11, 1973	59-35	63	57
Rhodesian Chrome Ore	Dec. 13, 1973	62-33	64	57
Legal Services Program	Dec. 13, 1973	60-36	64	58
Legal Services Program	Dec. 14, 1973	56-29	57	51
Rhodesian Chrome Ore	Dec. 18, 1973	63-26	60	54
Legal Services Program	Jan. 30, 1974	68-29	65	58
Genocide Treaty	Feb. 5, 1974	55-36	61	55
Genocide Treaty	Feb. 6, 1974	55-38	62	56
Government Pay Raise	March 6, 1974	67-31	66	59
Public Campaign Financing	April 4, 1974	60-36	64	58
Public Campaign Financing	April 9, 1974	64-30	63	57
Public Debt Ceiling	June 19, 1974	50-43	62	56
Public Debt Ceiling	June 19, 1974	45-48	62	56
Public Debt Ceiling	June 26, 1974	48-50	66	59
Consumer Agency	July 30, 1974	56-42	66	59
Consumer Agency	Aug. 1, 1974	59-39	66	59
Consumer Agency	Aug. 20, 1974	59-35	63	57
Consumer Agency	Sept. 19, 1974	64-34	66	59
Export-Import Bank	Dec. 3, 1974	51-39	60	54
Export-Import Bank	Dec. 4, 1974	48-44	62	55
Trade Reform	Dec. 13, 1974	71-19	60	54
Fiscal 1975 Supplemental Funds	Dec. 14, 1974	56-27	56	50
Export-Import Bank	Dec. 14, 1974	49-35	56	50
Export-Import Bank	Dec. 16, 1974	54-34	59	53
Social Services Programs	Dec. 17, 1974	70-23	62	56
Tax Law Changes	Dec. 17, 1974	67-25	62	55
Rail Reorganization Act	Feb. 26, 1975	86-8	63	57
Amend Rule 22	March 5, 1975	73-21	63	57
Amend Rule 22	March 7, 1975	73-21	63	57
Tax Reduction	March 20, 1975	59-38		60
Tax Reduction	March 21, 1975	83-13		60
Agency for Consumer Advocacy	May 13, 1975	71-27		60
Senate Staffing	June 11, 1975	77-19	64**	60
New Hampshire Senate Seat	June 24, 1975	57-39		60
New Hampshire Senate Seat	June 25, 1975	56-41		60
New Hampshire Senate Seat	June 26, 1975	54-40		60
New Hampshire Senate Seat	July 8, 1975	57-38		60
New Hampshire Senate Seat	July 9, 1975	57-38		60
New Hampshire Senate Seat	July 10, 1975	54-38		60
Voting Rights Act	July 21, 1975	72-19		60
Voting Rights Act	July 23, 1975	76-20		60
Oil Price Decontrol	July 30, 1975	54-38		60
Labor-HEW Appropriations	Sept. 23, 1975	46-48		60
Labor-HEW Appropriations	Sept. 24, 1975	64-33		60
Common-Site Picketing	Nov. 11, 1975	66-30		60
Common-Site Picketing	Nov. 14, 1975	58-31		60
Common-Site Picketing	Nov. 18, 1975	62-37		60
Rail Reorganization	Dec. 4, 1975	61-27		60
New York City Aid	Dec. 5, 1975	70-27		60

* Between 1949 and 1959, the cloture rule required a two-thirds majority of the Senate membership, rather than two-thirds of senators who voted.

** In 1975, Rule 22 was changed to require a three-fifths majority of the Senate membership for cloture except for changes in Senate rules, in which a two-thirds majority of senators voting still would be required.

Symbols of Authority: Mace and Gavel

Mace in the House. The most treasured possession of the House of Representatives is the mace, a traditional symbol of legislative authority. The concept, which the House borrowed from the British House of Commons, had its origin in republican Rome, where the fasces—an axe bound in a bundle of rods—symbolized the power of the magistrates.

The mace was adopted by the House in its first session in 1789 as a symbol of office for the sergeant at arms, who is charged with preserving order on the House floor. The first mace was destroyed when the British burned the Capitol in 1814, and for the next 27 years a mace of painted wood was used. The present mace, in use since 1841, is a replica of the original mace of 1789. It consists of a bundle of 13 ebony rods bound in silver, terminating in a silver globe topped by a silver eagle with outstretched wings—46 inches high in all. It was made by William Adams, a New York silversmith, for the sum of $400.

The sergeant at arms, custodian of the mace, is charged with its use when necessary to preserve order. There have been a number of occasions in the history of the House when the sergeant at arms, on order of the Speaker, has lifted the mace from its pedestal and "presented" it before an unruly member. On each such occasion order is said to have been promptly restored. At other times the sergeant at arms, bearing the mace, has

passed up and down the aisles to quell boisterous behavior in the chamber.

The mace also serves a second purpose. When the House is in regular session, it rests on a tall green marble pedestal at the right of the Speaker's desk, but when the House is sitting in the Committee of the Whole it is moved to a low white marble pedestal nearby. Thus, upon entering the chamber a representative can tell at a glance whether the House is meeting in regular session or in the Committee of the Whole.

Gavel in the Senate. The Senate has no mace, but it cherishes to an almost equal degree another symbol—a small silver-capped ivory gavel without a handle which, according to tradition, was used by Vice President Adams in calling the first Senate to order in 1789. Evidence exists that it was in use at least as early as 1831, and it remained in use until 1954 when it began to disintegrate beyond repair.

A replica of the old gavel, a gift of the government of India, was presented to the Senate on Nov. 17, 1954. Since that time a case containing both the old and the new gavels is carried into the Senate chamber and placed on the Vice President's desk just before the opening of each Senate session. The new gavel is removed from the case for use by the presiding officer; the old gavel is not used but remains on the desk in its case, a symbol of the continuity of the Senate.

(Continued from p. 351)

ond house may differ significantly from the version passed by the first. Frequently, one chamber may approve a version of a bill that is greatly at variance with the version already passed by the other house, and then substitute its text for the language of the other, retaining only the latter's bill designation.

If a bill is passed in identical form by both House and Senate, no further legislative action is required. But if the versions passed by the two chambers are not identical, all differences must be reconciled before the measure can be sent to the President.

If the second house has made changes in the bill, it may simply return it to the chamber of origin, which then has the option of accepting the other chamber's amendments, accepting with further amendments or disagreeing and requesting a conference. Or the second house itself may request a conference at the time it returns the bill to the chamber of origin. Only the chamber in possession of the "papers"—engrossed bill, engrossed amendments and messages of transmittal—can request a conference.

If the amendments are of a minor or noncontroversial nature, they usually are agreed to without a conference. Major amendments sometimes are accepted to avoid further floor action that might end in scuttling the bill.

Under the Legislative Reorganization Act of 1970 a separate House vote may be taken, upon the request of any member, on any nongermane amendment added by the Senate to a House-passed bill. *(Box, p. 350)*

Conference Committee Action

Sen. Bennett Champ Clark of Missouri once introduced a resolution providing that "all bills and resolutions shall be

read twice and, without debate, referred to conference." He was joking, of course, but his proposal highlights the crucial role of the conference committee in hammering out the final form of legislation.

Not all legislation goes to conference. On minor bills, the second house often will make only minimal changes in the first chamber's version. The first house then will agree to those amendments, clearing the measure for the President's signature. But virtually no legislation of any consequence or controversy escapes the conference system. Approximately one-third of all the bills enacted into public law in the 93rd Congress, including all regular appropriations bills, were product of conference committees.[8]

Calling a Conference

Either chamber can request a conference once both have adopted differing versions of the same legislation. Generally, the chamber that approved the legislation first will disagree to the amendments made by the second body and request that a conference be convened. Sometimes, however, the second body will ask for a conference immediately after it has approved the legislation, assuming that the other chamber will not accept its changes.

A conference cannot take place until both chambers formally agree that it be held. The Senate usually requests or agrees to a conference by unanimous consent. In the House this action generally is taken either by unanimous consent or by majority adoption of a rule from the Rules Committee providing for a conference on a particular bill. Prior to 1965, the House could bypass the Rules Committee only by unanimous consent or by suspension of the rules, for which a two-thirds majority is required. Since 1965, it has been possible to send a bill to conference by simple majority vote, without recourse to the Rules Committee, if the committee with jurisdiction over the bill approves. This method is seldom employed.

Selection and Seniority

The selection of conferees (known as "managers") has often caused more controversy and criticism than the actions they have taken.

The two chambers have different rules for selecting conferees, but in practice both follow similar procedures. Senate rules allow the chamber to elect conferees, but the body has rarely done so. The common practice is for the presiding officer to appoint conferees on the recommendation of the chairman of the committee having jurisdiction over the legislation.

House rules grant the Speaker the right to appoint conferees, but he usually does so only after consultation with the appropriate committee chairman.

Each chamber's delegation to a conference can range in size from three to more than 20 members, depending on the length or complexity of the legislation involved. There may be five senators and three representatives on the conference committee, or the reverse (although the Senate usually sends larger groups than the House). But whatever the size, a majority in each delegation must be from the majority party in the chamber. Each delegation votes as a unit on issues in dispute, with the majority position in the delegation determining how the whole delegation will vote.

Seniority ordinarily governs the selection of conferees. On a major bill, the chairman of the committee that handled the legislation usually selects himself, the ranking minority member and other senior members of the committee to staff the conference delegation. Where a subcommittee has exercised major responsibility for a bill, its senior members may be chosen. Only rarely will a conferee be appointed who is not on the appropriate committee.

Few legislative committees have hard and fast rules guiding the chairman on his choice of conferees, although most chairmen consult with the ranking minority member in choosing conferees from the minority party. The lack of guidance frequently led to complaints that a chairman had stacked the conference in favor of his own personal position rather than the will of the full chamber.

Members have also complained that reliance on the seniority system and the conservative bent of senior members combine to thwart the will of the full body. That argument was used in 1975 against F. Edward Hebert (D La.) in the successful fight to depose him as chairman of the House Armed Services Committee. A staunch advocate of a strong military establishment, Hebert generally took only the most senior members of his committee to conference; like him, they favored more spending for military programs. Rarely, if ever, did Hebert choose a junior member as a conferee.

Hebert's opponents pointed particularly to his actions in 1973 during consideration of the military procurement bill. Les Aspin (D Wis.), a second-termer and member of Hebert's committee, offered a floor amendment, adopted on a 242-163 vote, that slashed $950-million from the amount the committee had recommended. The Senate subsequently approved a higher funding level.

When the bill went to conference, Hebert designated himself, the next four senior Democrats and the four senior Republicans from the committee as conferees, overlooking

---

Opening the Doors

Conference committees, which traditionally carried on their vital legislative work in secret, began to open their doors more frequently to the press and public in the mid-1970s. Until 1974, conferees almost always met privately to hammer out the concessions and compromises that blended differing House and Senate legislation into a single bill.

Beginning in the early 1970s, however, Congress came under increasing pressure to open most of its proceedings to the public. In 1974, 12 conferences voluntarily opened their sessions. A rules change to require open conferences was adopted by the House in January 1975. The new rule required open sessions unless a majority of either chamber's conferees voted in public to close a meeting. Senate Democrats and Republicans in caucus accepted the change, and the full Senate approved the change the following November.

Proponents of the change said the open conferences held in 1974, including one on a controversial strip mine regulation bill, disproved the claim that public scrutiny would disrupt the conference process.

Some members, aides and lobbyists felt that the openness might lead some conferees to make long speeches explaining their actions and others to hold out stubbornly on issues of particular interest to constituents.

Open conferences were an issue as far back as the first session of Congress in 1789. The first conference, on import and tonnage legislation, was held in open session. Nonconferees wandered in and out of the meeting room and the Senate finally had to adjourn for the day because its members, distracted by the conference action, were paying little attention to regular business. The next open conference was not recorded until 1911.

While its advocates have argued that the open conference would make conferees accountable to their chambers and the public, opponents have questioned how openly conference decisions would be made.

"Sunshine laws kid the public," said Richard Bolling (D Mo.) in 1975. "They imply a total openness and there never will be." Bolling, a chief advocate of institutional reform in the House, said openness was healthy but cautioned that some compromises and accommodations would have to be made in secret if the legislation was to succeed.

The movement toward open conference may produce one practical problem: where to hold them. Traditionally, conferences have been held in small rooms in the Capitol itself, usually as close as possible to a point midway between the two chambers. But those rooms would not be large enough for a crowd of observers and reporters.

Conferees on the 1974 strip mining bill saw a preview of the problem. "Members had to carve their way through a wall of human flesh," recalled Rep. John F. Seiberling (D Ohio).

Aspin altogether. The House conferees quickly abandoned the Aspin amendment, and the conference approved a higher funding level than even the Senate had approved.

Hebert reported to the House that Senate conferees had been adamant on the higher authorization, but they denied the allegation.[9]

Even more controversial than seniority is the question of whether the conferees, however they are appointed, are likely to uphold their chamber's position on key points in the conference. Precedent in both the House and Senate indicates that conferees are expected to support the legislative position of the chamber they represent. The Legislative Reorganization Act of 1946 stipulated that conferees must have demonstrated support for the bill which passed their chamber, but this provision was not enforced.

In an effort to ensure that its conferees would uphold its position, the House in 1974 modified its rules on their selection. The new rules say that in making appointments to conferences, "the Speaker shall appoint no less than a majority of members who generally supported the House position as determined by the Speaker."

Either chamber may try to enforce its will by instructing its conferees on how to vote when they go to conference, but the conferees are not obligated to follow the instructions. Since the instructions are little more than guidelines, they are rarely used. In 1974 the House on three separate occasions instructed conferees on the elementary and secondary education amendments bill (PL 93-380) to insist on the House language limiting busing. The House conferees nevertheless agreed to a modification of the much weaker Senate version.

Authority of Conferees

The authority of the conferees theoretically is limited to matters in disagreement between the two chambers; they are not authorized to delete matter agreed to by both the Senate and the House nor to bring in entirely new provisions. When the disagreement involves numbers, conferees are limited to the range between the figure proposed by one house and the figure proposed by the other.

In practice, however, the conferees have wide latitude except where the matters in disagreement are very specific. When one house has struck out everything after the enacting clause and inserted a substitute for the bill approved by the other house, the entire subject is technically in disagreement and the conferees may report an entirely new bill if they choose to do so. In such a case, the Legislative Reorganization Act of 1946 stipulates that they may not include in their report "matter not committed to them by either house," but they may include "matter which is a germane modification of subjects in disagreement." The Legislative Reorganization Act of 1970 reinforced this provision by amending House rules to provide that any language concerning "a specific additional topic, question, issue or proposition" that neither chamber sent to conference "shall not constitute a germane modification of the matter in disagreement." It also forbade House conferees to modify any topic beyond the scope of the differing versions of the bill sent to conference.

Conference Bargaining

Some of the hardest bargaining in the entire legislative process takes place in the conference committee, and frequently the conference takes days or even weeks. Conferences on involved appropriations bills sometimes are particularly drawn out.

Roll-Call Vote Records

The 93rd Congress took 2,216 roll-call votes (excluding quorum calls), by far the highest number for an entire Congress in at least two decades. (However, the 94th Congress—1975-76—was only 12 votes behind that total in August 1976, and was certain to set a new record by the time it adjourned.) The high for a single year was in 1975 when 1,214 roll calls were taken. Both chambers set individual highs that year.

Year	House	Senate	Total
1975	612	602	1,214
1974	537	544	1,081
1973	541	594	1,135
1972	329	532	861
1971	320	423	743
1970	266	422	688
1969	177	245	422
1968	233	281	514
1967	245	315	560
1966	193	235	428
1965	201	258	459
1964	113	305	418
1963	119	229	348
1962	124	224	348
1961	116	204	320
1960	93	207	300
1959	87	215	302
1958	93	200	293
1957	100	107	207
1956	73	130	203
1955	76	87	163
1954	76	171	247
1953	71	89	160
1952	72	129	201
1951	109	202	311
1950	154	229	383
1949	121	227	348
1948	79	189	268
1947	84	138	222

As a conference proceeds, conferees reconcile their differences, but generally they grant concessions only insofar as they remain sure that the chamber they represent will accept the compromises. Unwanted amendments that were hard to oppose publicly on the floor may be quietly weeded out. The threat of a Senate filibuster on the conference report may influence the conferees' deliberations. Time also may be a factor, especially at the end of a Congress when delay may cause a bill to die in conference.

If the conferees find they are unable to reach agreement, they may return to their respective chambers for instructions. (Conferees may be, but seldom are, instructed at the time of their appointment.) Or they may simply report their failure to reach agreement to the parent chamber and allow it to act as it wishes.

Under the rules, House conferees may be instructed or discharged and replaced if they fail to make a report within 20 calendar days of their appointment (or within 36 hours of their appointment during the last six days of a session). This rule was adopted in 1931 but has rarely been invoked.

The Conference Report

When the conferees have reached agreement, they prepare a conference report explaining their actions. One or more amendments may be "reported in disagreement"; these amendments are acted upon separately following floor action on the conference report.

The 1970 Reorganization Act prohibited House conferees from agreeing to a nongermane Senate amendment unless authorized to do so by a vote of the House. The House had often been forced to vote on the bill as a whole, having to defeat the bill or accept the nongermane amendment. The new rule applied the same rules to nongermane Senate amendments as were already applied to legislative amendments to appropriation bills. In practice, conferees reported such amendments in disagreement and moved for a House vote to agree to them. *(1972 changes, box, p. 350)*

The conference report must be signed in duplicate by a majority of conferees from each chamber and submitted in document form to each house for its approval. Minority reports are not permitted. Traditionally the report was printed only in the House, together with an explanation by the House conferees, but under the 1970 act an explanatory statement must be prepared jointly by the House and Senate conferees and the conference report must be printed in the Senate as well as the House.

In both chambers consideration of conference reports is highly privileged and can interrupt most other business. The house that agreed to the conference acts first on the report, followed by the house that requested it. Approval of the report constitutes approval of the compromise bill.

Under the 1970 act, conference reports are supposed to be available for three days before the House may consider them. (In 1972, this was changed to allow floor consideration on the third day.) The act stipulated also that debate on a conference report was to be equally divided between the majority and minority in each chamber.

The House, though it does so infrequently, may send a completed conference report to its Rules Committee before the report reaches the floor. This has happened when the conferees inserted into a bill new material that might make the conference report subject to a point of order. The Rules Committee then may grant a rule waiving points of order against the report.

All or Nothing

Once conferees report the final bill, it must be approved or rejected in its entirety by both bodies. Exceptions are made only for nongermane Senate amendments which may be deleted in the House, and for certain other amendments which are reported in technical disagreement because they do not conform with House rules.

Unlike the Senate, the House has strict rules forbidding consideration of amendments not germane to the bill under consideration. The Senate for years attached nongermane amendments to House-passed bills, and they were frequently retained in conference. Until 1970, such amendments could not be voted on separately in the House, and many House members complained that the practice prevented them from considering the amendments at all.

In 1970 the House adopted a rule that allowed separate votes to be taken on nongermane Senate amendments. But the rule failed to achieve the desired result, partly because it did not spell out the procedure under which the separate votes could be taken, and partly because the new rule appeared to conflict with other House rules requiring an up-or-down vote on the entire conference report with no chance to amend it.[10]

In 1972, the House again amended its rules to allow members to make points of order against a conference report after it is read but before debate begins. If any portion of the conference report is ruled nongermane, that portion is immediately subject to 40 minutes of debate and a separate vote. If no points of order are sustained or if the House accepts all nongermane amendments, the House then considers and accepts or rejects the conference report as a whole.

If any of the nongermane amendments are rejected, the conference report is considered rejected. Then, the House can consider a motion to accept the Senate version with an amendment—the amendment consisting of all provisions of the conference report not rejected by the House. If the House agrees to this motion, the Senate can agree to the House version, without the nongermane amendments, or request a second conference on the bill.

This rule was employed at the end of the 1974 session. The House had approved a bill calling for a White House symposium on libraries; the Senate added two nongermane amendments, one to clarify a recently enacted law on the privacy of student records and one to exempt certain organizations from compliance with federal sex discrimination regulations. The provisions were retained in the conference and when the bill reached the House floor Dec. 19, William A. Steiger (R Wis.) raised a point of order against the provision dealing with sex discrimination. The point of order was sustained, but the House on a 37-102 standing vote rejected the motion to delete the nongermane provision. Thus the bill was accepted as it had been reported from the conference.

Conference Disputes

The conference machinery does not always work smoothly. In 1962 a feud between the Senate and House Appropriations Committees blocked conference action on major appropriation bills for months, and in 1970 several conference disputes marred the closing days of the 91st Congress.

The most frequently voiced complaint about the conference system is the charge—raised from time to time in both Senate and House—that conferees are not in sympathy with the position taken by their own chamber and do not sufficiently defend it against the opposition of the other chamber's conferees. This question figured in a 1970 dispute over continued provision of funds for development of the supersonic transport (SST) plane. The House had included $290-million for the plane in the fiscal 1971 Transportation Department appropriation bill; the Senate had provided no funds at all, but four of the seven Senate conferees had voted for full funding. The conferees, after only three hours of deliberation, agreed on $210-million. "If we stayed there until the cows came home, the answer would have been the same," said Senate conferee John O. Pastore (D R.I.). "The fact is that the House was adamant, but the Senate did try." The House promptly adopted the conference report, but in the Senate opponents of the SST launched a filibuster that delayed adjournment of the 91st Congress until an agreement on temporary funding was reached. Early in the 92nd Congress, both chambers voted to kill the SST program.[11]

A similar battle raged in the House in 1972, when a coalition of House Republicans and southern Democrats objected so strenuously to proposed conferees on a bill raising

Congress Resists Plans for Televising Sessions

In January of 1947, television crews entered the House chamber to record the opening session of the 80th Congress. Except for special and ceremonial occasions, they have not been in either the House or Senate chambers since.

Almost 30 years later, a concerted effort was made to open House sessions to television coverage. But the effort failed when the House leadership opposed it.

The reasons for that opposition appeared to be grounded in the apprehension that many members have toward televising their activities. The leadership's opposition reflected this fear of many rank-and-file members.

The defeat for proponents of TV coverage came in March 1976 when the House Rules Committee killed a resolution that would have permitted live broadcast coverage.

In the Senate, proposals to permit TV into the chamber were being held back by the leadership for similar reasons. At one point, the Senate seemed ready to permit TV but enthusiasm cooled abruptly after the chamber in 1975 endured many weeks of convoluted debate and voting on a dispute over the true winner of the 1974 election in New Hampshire. The dispute, which the Senate never resolved and had to send back to the New Hampshire voters for a new election, embarrassed many senators and made them leary of televising such activities directly into voters' homes. *(Wyman-Durkin election dispute p. 690)*

Following are the major arguments for and against television sessions of Congress:

Public Access

By denying itself access to television, said Sen. Hubert H. Humphrey (D Minn.), Congress is doubly damned. "On the one hand, we cast a blurred and confusing image for the man-in-the street; on the other, we are regularly made victim to end-runs and upstaging by the President."

A Harris poll in 1974 showed that Congress had received a public approval rating of less than 20 per cent—the lowest accorded any institution studied in the survey, including the presidency. Supporters of broadcast coverage have said the remedy is to open direct lines of communication to the public. "Congress is obviously not coming through loud and clear," complained Sen. Lee Metcalf (D Mont.).

Metcalf and other members saw the proposals as an opportunity to redress a growing imbalance of power between the executive and legislative branches. Former Sen. J. William Fulbright, an Arkansas Democrat, argued that the President's instant access to television has changed the Constitution without an amendment. "Communications is power," Fulbright has said, "and exclusive access to it is a dangerous unchecked power."

Showboats

"Participation of the public in the formulation and execution of public policy is essential in a democratic system," said Sen. Jesse A. Helms (R N.C.), "but not at every stage of the process."

Noting that the Founding Fathers met in secrecy to draw up the Constitution, Helms argued that the people were never intended to participate directly in congressional proceedings. The glare of television would not only complicate the proceedings, he said, but distort them by focusing on the final stage. "Indeed," argued Helms, "the proposal ignores the complexities of the legislative process, which requires decision-making and compromise in legislative committees." Helms was a former broadcaster himself.

Even Rep. Jack Brooks (D Texas), author of a House resolution to broadcast floor debate, questioned whether it would spark much viewer interest. "Gavel-to-gavel coverage of the proceedings," he has said, "would be similar to continuous coverage of hospital operating rooms for the purpose of improving the image and understanding of the medical professions."

---

the hourly minimum wage that they blocked the bill from going to conference.

Generally regarded as more liberal than the rest of the House, the Education and Labor Committee had reported the minimum wage bill in 1971. When the bill came to the floor in May 1972, after a long delay in the Rules Committee, the House approved a more conservative substitute bill offered by John N. Erlenborn (R Ill.). Erlenborn's bill made the increase more gradual, deleted a proposed extension of coverage to additional workers, and added a controversial provision that would allow employers to hire youths under 18 at a subminimum wage.

Subsequently, the Senate passed a bill even more generous than the original House committee proposals.

When Education and Labor Chairman Carl D. Perkins (D Ky.) asked unanimous consent to send the bill to conference with the Senate, Erlenborn asked him for the names of members he had recommended to be conferees. Perkins said they would be 10 members from the General Labor Subcommittee which had originally considered the bill—six Democrats and four Republicans. Ten of the 11 Democratic

members of the subcommittee had voted against the Erlenborn substitute.

Erlenborn objected to the unanimous consent request, thereby blocking it. He said it was unfair to send to the conference a delegation whose majority opposed the final House bill.

Certain that a second unanimous consent request would be objected to, Perkins offered a motion that the House disagree with the Senate version and request a conference to resolve the differences. Only a simple majority was needed to pass the motion. But Erlenborn again objected: "If we refuse to send the bill to conference at this time, then we may receive assurances in the future that when the bill does go to conference a majority of the managers on the part of the House will fight for the position the House has taken."

Perkins' motion was defeated, 190-198. Later the House killed the bill by voting 188-196 against a second Perkins motion to request a conference with the Senate. "All too often," Erlenborn said, summing up his opposition to the motion, "the House speaks its will by amending legislation...or adopting substitute bills and sending the legislation to the other body. All too often the other body passes a bill very similar to that rejected by the House. And almost without exception the conference committee members appointed by the House accede more to the provisions of the other body than they try to protect the provisions which the House had adopted."[12]

Final Steps

After a bill has been passed by both the House and the Senate, all of the original papers are sent to the enrolling clerk of the chamber in which the bill originated. He then prepares an enrolled bill which is printed on parchment paper. When this bill has been certified as correct by the secretary of the Senate or the clerk of the House, depending on which chamber originated the bill, it is signed first (no matter whether it originated in Senate or House) by the Speaker of the House and then by the president of the Senate. It is next sent to the White House to await presidential action.

The President has 10 days (Sundays excepted) from the time he receives the bill to act upon it. If he approves the measure, he signs it, dates it and usually writes the word "Approved" on the document. Under the Constitution, however, only his signature is required.

If the President does not want the bill to become law, he may veto it by returning it to the chamber in which it originated without his signature and with a message stating his objections. If no action on the message is taken there, the bill dies.

However, an attempt may be made to override the President's veto and enact the bill, "the objections of the President to the contrary notwithstanding." Such action requires a two-thirds vote of those present, who must number a quorum and vote by roll call. Debate may precede this vote, with motions permitted to lay the message on the table, to postpone action on it or to refer it to committee. If the vote to override the veto succeeds in the first house, the measure is sent to the second house for its action. If the veto is overridden by a two-thirds vote in both houses, the bill becomes law without the President's signature. But if either house fails to register a two-thirds vote for the bill, the veto stands, and the bill is dead. Senate or House action on a veto can be taken at any time during either session of the Congress in which the veto is received.

A bill may become law without the President's signature, not only by the overriding of a veto, but also if the President fails to sign it within 10 days (Sundays excepted) from the time he receives it, provided Congress is in session. Under this provision, the President may occasionally permit the enactment of legislation that he does not care to veto but does not wish to approve affirmatively. But if Congress adjourns before the 10 days expire, a bill not signed by the President does not become law. It has been what is called pocket-vetoed. *(Pocket Veto Controversy, box, p. 630)*

Under the Constitution, Congress does not have an opportunity to override a pocket veto. The question of whether a President could pocket veto legislation during a congressional recess became an issue when President Nixon's use of such a veto during a six-day recess in 1970 was challenged in court by Sen. Edward M. Kennedy (D Mass.). The pocket-vetoed measure, a medical training bill, had passed both houses by nearly unanimous votes, indicating that a regular veto would have been overridden. The U.S. Court of Appeals for the District of Columbia Aug. 14, 1974, upheld Kennedy's challenge and declared that Nixon had improperly used his pocket veto power.

When bills are passed and signed, or passed over a veto, they are given numbers in numerical order as they become law. There are two series of numbers, one for public and one for private laws, starting at the number "1" for each two-year term of Congress. They are then identified by law number and by Congress—i.e., Private Law 21, 94th Congress; Public Law 250, 94th Congress (or PL 94-250).

Footnotes

1. Woodrow Wilson, *Congressional Government* (Meridian edition, 1956), p. 55.
2. George B. Galloway, *Congress at the Crossroads* (Thomas Y. Crowell Co., 1946), p. 203.
3. See Congressional Quarterly, *1973 Almanac*, p. 1074.
4. Clarence Cannon, *Cannon's Procedures in the House of Representatives* (Government Printing Office, 1963), p. 220.
5. *Ibid.,* p. 6.
6. *Ibid.,* p. 221.
7. See W. Holmes Brown, *Constitution, Jefferson's Manual and Rules of the House of Representatives,* 94th Congress (Government Printing Office, 1975), p. 611.
8. For a discussion of conference committees, see Congressional Quarterly, *Weekly Report,* Feb. 8, 1975, p. 290 ff.
9. Congressional Quarterly, *1973 Almanac,* p. 902.
10. Congressional Quarterly, *Congress and the Nation,* Vol. III, p. 382.
11. Congressional Quarterly, *Congress and the Nation,* Vol. III, pp. 158, 167.
12. Congressional Quarterly, *1972 Almanac,* p. 361.

Selected Bibliography

Books

Bailey, Stephen K. *Congress Makes A Law.* New York: Columbia University Press, 1950.

Binkley, Wilfrid E. *President and Congress.* New York: Vintage, 1962.

Clapp, Charles L. *The Congressman: His Work as He Sees It.* Washington: The Brookings Institution, 1963.

Froman, Lewis A. Jr. *The Congressional Process.* Boston: Little, Brown, 1967.

Galloway, George B. *History of the United States House of Representatives.* New York: Thomas Y. Crowell, 1961.

——. *The Legislative Process in Congress.* New York: Thomas Y. Crowell, 1953.

Goodwin, George. *The Little Legislatures: Committees of Congress.* Amherst: University of Massachusetts Press, 1970.

Gross, Bertram M. *The Legislative Struggle.* New York: McGraw-Hill, 1953.

House Republican Task Force on Congressional Reform and Minority Staffing. *We Propose: A Modern Congress.* New York: McGraw-Hill, 1966.

Luce, Robert. *Legislative Procedure.* Boston: Houghton Mifflin, 1922; reprint ed., New York: Da Capo Press, 1972.

McConachie, Lauros. *Congressional Committees: A Study of the Origins and Development of Our National and*

Local Legislative Methods. New York: Thomas Y. Crowell, 1898.

Morrow, William L. *Congressional Committees.* New York: Scribner, 1969.

Pressman, Jeffery L. *House vs. Senate: Conflict in the Appropriations Process.* New Haven: Yale University Press, 1966.

Riddick, Floyd M. *The U.S. Congress: Organization and Procedure.* Manassas, Va.: National Capitol Publishers, 1949.

Rieselbach, Leroy N., ed. *The Congressional System: Notes and Readings.* Belmont, Calif.: Wadsworth, 1970.

Steiner, Gilbert. *The Congressional Conference Committee.* Urbana: University of Illinois Press, 1951.

Volger, David. *The Third House: Conference Committees in the United States Congress.* Evanston, Ill.: Northwestern University Press, 1971.

Wilson, Woodrow. *Congressional Government: A Study in American Politics.* Boston: Houghton Mifflin, 1885; reprint ed., Cleveland: Meridian, 1965.

Articles

Bolling, Richard. "Committees in the House." *Annals of the American Academy of Political and Social Science,* January 1974, pp. 1-14.

Brock, William E. "Committees in the Senate." *Annals of the American Academy of Political and Social Science,* January 1974, pp. 15-26.

Kravitz, Walter. "Evolution of the Senate's Committee System." *Annals of the American Academy of Political and Social Science,* January 1974, pp. 27-38.

Oleszek, Walter J. "House Senate Relationships: Comity and Conflict." *Annals of the American Academy of Political and Social Science,* January 1974, pp. 75-86.

Government Documents

Brown, W. Holmes. *Constitution, Jefferson's Manual and Rules of the House of Representatives.* 94th Cong., 1st sess. Washington: Government Printing Office, 1975.

Cannon, Clarence. *Cannon's Procedure in the House of Representatives.* Washington: Government Printing Office, 1963.

U.S. Congress. Joint Committee on Congressional Operations. *Rules Adopted by the Committees of Congress.* Committee print. 94th Cong., 1st sess., 1975.

U.S. Congress. Senate. Committee on Rules and Administration. *Senate Cloture Rule.* Compiled by the Congressional Research Service and the Office of the Legislative Counsel. Committee print, 94th Cong., 1st sess., 1975.

U.S. Congress. Senate. Committee on Rules and Administration. *Standing Rules of the United States Senate and Provisions of the Legislative Reorganization Acts of 1946 and 1970 Relating to Operation of the Senate.* 94th Cong., 1st sess., 1975.

U.S. Library of Congress. Congressional Research Service. *Committee Structure and Procedures of the House of Representatives.* Dec. 13, 1973.

Watkins, Charles L. and Riddick, Floyd M. *Senate Procedure, Precedents and Practices.* Washington: Government Printing Office, 1958.

Zinn, Charles J. *How Our Laws Are Made.* Washington: Government Printing Office, 1974.

The Parliamentarians of House and Senate

Two of the most influential—and publicly unnoticed—Capitol Hill officials are the parliamentarians of the House and the Senate. Their roles extend far beyond that of mere arbiters of parliamentary practice.

Consulted by White House legislation-drafters, relied upon heavily by congressional leaders, and sought out for advice by experienced members of both parties, the parliamentarians' influence is greatest in the guarded, private, behind-the-scenes procedural mechanics that transform an idea into a piece of enacted legislation.

The parliamentarians, serving unbroken terms in Congress after Congress, become masters of the legal and technical skills which are the backbone of successful legislating. They are at home in the specialized congressional world of bills, resolutions, amendments, rules, precedents and parliamentary maneuvering. And they are acknowledged experts in routing a bill to the right committee, preparing it for floor debate and protecting it from opposition attacks.

Long-Term Nature of the Job

Parliamentarians are appointed by the leadership of the House and Senate, but because of their highly skilled, technical functions, the parliamentarians traditionally remain in office regardless of changes in political control of the two chambers.

The acquired experience of the parliamentarians admits them to the innermost political councils. Former House Parliamentarian Lewis Deschler, for example, was a member of Speaker Sam Rayburn's "Board of Education." This was a group of House friends of the Speaker which would meet about sundown over drinks for political policy and strategy talks.[1] Deschler drew key roles in preparing the

---

Knowing the Rules

The penalty for speaking out without knowing just what is involved can be more than acute embarrassment, as a bit of inspired congressional doggerel suggests:

> "The Clerk's reading a bill
> when an eager young pill
> bounces up and moves to amend,
> which all comes to naught,
> he didn't move when he ought,
> and all that he did was offend."

Source: Donald G. Tacheron and Morris K. Udall, *The Job of the Congressman,* 1966, p. 193.

Bolling on Deschler

In his 1966 book, *House Out of Order*, Rep. Richard Bolling (D Mo.) had this to say about then-parliamentarian Lewis Deschler:

"The title (of parliamentarian) conjures up a vision of a dried, parchment-paper-like blinkered figure narrowly looking at the House through the prism of its general rules.

"Deschler is none of these things. He is a large-sized man with large-sized influence growing out of his encyclopedic knowledge. He cultivates anonymity. He never speaks to the press for quotation. There is little written about him....

"Many members sit in the House for years without being able to tell just why something happened or did not happen on the floor on certain occasions. They should ask Deschler. He would probably know, but he might not tell.

"And Lew Deschler does know the rules. He knows the practical application of them better than any group of members ever have and probably ever will. Deschler...has made himself the second most influential person in the House, during his service of more than three decades. Only the Speaker, at whose right hand he sits when the House is in session, has more influence. The word is 'influential,' rather than 'powerful,' because members who hold the power are influenced in their exercise of it by Deschler. The influence to a point, of course, is derivative. He has the Speaker's confidence. He knows the Speaker's mind. He can act on this.

"When consulted, Deschler can tell the inquiring member just what can be done under the rules. Then, as always, deferential, he may suggest how a desired purpose can be attained within the rules. Perhaps the timing is discussed, and lurking in the background is perhaps an implication that the purpose of the member may not really be a very good idea....

"Deschler, the anonymous parliamentarian, is the catalyst that makes the House function, rent as it is by partisanship, faction, personal jealousies, logrolling, rivalries, and hearty dislikes. Each member in a position of leadership consults him about parliamentary procedure. So, too, does the perceptive member of whatever rank who wants to have an amendment adopted. Deschler is available. His 'open door' policy brings a flow of inquiring members. Thus he knows more of what has happened, is happening, and will happen than any oligarch and, on occasions, more than the Speaker. He becomes the Speaker's 'man,' his adviser, his confidant, his sometime companion after hours, a major source of information and, if asked, advice."

Source: Richard Bolling, *House Out of Order* (E. P. Dutton & Co., 1966), pp. 110-12.

1957 civil rights bill for House action. He checked the draft bill to make sure the wording would permit consideration by a sympathetic committee. He checked committee changes in the measure to make sure the House germaneness rule still would bar unwanted floor amendments, and he cleared the rule for the bill, readying it for floor action. Because civil rights advocates and opponents both had sought parliamentary advice from Deschler, he could warn the Speaker of an upcoming floor fight and could predict the mood of the House.

Evolution of the Office

Despite the importance of the parliamentarians, the origin of the office is uncertain. In the 19th century, presiding officers of the House and Senate either made their own parliamentary rulings or turned for advice to senior members, or to senior clerks around the desk. Gradually it became a practice to rely on one of the clerks for advice on parliamentary matters. Finally, as sessions became longer, and legislation (and congressional rules and precedents) became more complex, a separate position was created with sole responsibility for parliamentary matters. The House established the post of parliamentarian in 1927; the Senate in 1937.

The position of parliamentarian is an ambiguous one, with few clearly defined responsibilities. In fact, the parliamentarians are available to perform virtually any task assigned by the leadership.

The parliamentarians of the House and Senate, together with their assistants, do share some common functions. They advise the presiding officers on the always changing parliamentary situation and on parliamentary procedures. To do so a parliamentarian is present at all floor sessions, sitting directly in front of the presiding officer in the Senate, and just to his right in the House. The parliamentarians are responsible for referring bills, resolutions and other communications to committees with proper jurisdiction. The parliamentarians also prepare and maintain compilations of the precedents of each chamber.

The House parliamentarian is appointed by the Speaker; the Senate parliamentarian is appointed by the secretary of the Senate.

Influence of Parliamentarians

For a number of reasons, the House parliamentarian has emerged as a more influential figure than the parliamentarian of the Senate.

In part, the disparity is a matter of differing personalities of the men who have held the posts. House Parliamentarian Deschler, whose long tenure left an immense mark on the office, was an aggressive man, prepared to assume new functions and new responsibilities. His Senate counterparts, Charles L. Watkins and Floyd M. Riddick, have been considered more self-effacing and less prone to seek additional duties. (*List of parliamentarians, box p. 361*)

More importantly, the disparity reflects basic differences in the power and composition of the House and Senate. In the Senate, power is diffused; there is no single overriding political post. Thus the parliamentarian, who serves the presiding officer, may find himself working with the Vice President (constitutional president of the Senate), the president pro tem or a senator picked as the acting president pro tem. Furthermore, the Vice President and the Senate majority may be of different political parties. As a result, the parliamentarian of the Senate lacks a firm base of political power from which to operate.

Quite a different situation exists in the House. The House parliamentarian is first, last and always the Speaker's man. And the Speaker is an important political power, regardless of varying personal operating styles. With the Speaker's political weight behind him, the House parliamentarian can afford to play off one committee chairman against another, or to upset a senior House member. The House parliamentarian never can thwart the Speaker, but in areas of indifference to the Speaker, such as routine bills or minor committees, the parliamentarian can exercise some discretionary authority as the Speaker's representative.

The comparatively smaller size of the Senate, its greater stability and its less restrictive rules also contribute to the disparity. The value of an expert in procedural technicalities is measurably enhanced when his constituency is a 435-member body that includes a sizable contingent of freshman and junior members, and the group is governed by numerous, complex and restrictive rules and precedents.

As one representative put it in 1966: "...you are going to run into occasions when you have a bill of your own that's coming up and you want to explore whether or not it would be possible to bring it up under suspension of the rules or some other procedure.... Then you might want to dig in the rule book for that, but for the commonly accepted procedures the best way to learn is by watching and then when you see something you don't understand, ask an older member or ask (the parliamentarian)....

"He is available on the phone most of the day, and he is available on the floor of the House when the House is in session.... Rather than end up making what may appear to others to be a foolish point of order, it might perhaps be best to talk to [the parliamentarian] ahead of time and find out or get some notion. He won't make a ruling for you, but he will certainly give you a few notions of just what you are getting into."[2]

Parliamentarians and Legislation

The influence wielded by parliamentarians on the shape of legislation and the course of floor action is subtle but important. Does the White House or the leadership want a certain committee to consider a new bill? The parliamentarians can suggest how to word the measure so it will fall under that committee's jurisdiction. Is a Senate filibuster blocking action on a measure favored by the leadership? The Senate parliamentarian can guide the leadership in attempts to end the filibuster by invoking the cloture process. Do potential House floor amendments threaten to unravel carefully worded compromises on a controversial bill? The House parliamentarian can protect the agreements through skilled application of the House germaneness rule—supported by judiciously selected precedents.

The public rarely sees one of the parliamentarians at work as adviser and tactician. These roles are carried out in private sessions, sometimes involving only the parliamentarian and a single member. Both sides are understandably reluctant to break this confidential relationship.

One example, drawn from the House side, shows parliamentarian Deschler openly at work as adviser and tactician. In a 1969 dispute over seating Rep. Adam Clayton Powell (D N.Y.), the House leadership favored admitting Powell to the 91st Congress without any sanctions. Others sought to penalize the flamboyant Harlem member, who had been excluded by the House from the 90th Congress for misusing public funds.

When Judiciary Committee Chairman Emanuel Celler (D N.Y.) offered a leadership resolution for the swearing-in

---

Congressional Parliamentarians

Listed below are persons who have performed the functions of parliamentarian in the House and Senate. The House did not formally establish the post until 1927, the Senate not until 1937.

House

Charles R. Crisp	1891-95
Asher C. Hinds	1895-1911
Joel Bennett Clark	1911-15
Clarence Cannon	1915-21
Lehr Fess	1921-28
Lewis Deschler	1928-74
William H. Brown	1974-

Senate

Edward J. Hickey	(?)-1923
Charles L. Watkins	1923-65
Floyd M. Riddick	1965-74
Murray Zweben	1975-

The House parliamentarian presides over a staff of three assistants and a clerk and (in fiscal 1976) an annual budget of $220,000. His salary in 1975 was $42,192. The staff is housed in the Speaker's room, off the House chamber. The parliamentarian's own office is around the corner, also off the chamber and several steps closer to the floor than even the office of the Speaker.

Two assistants and a secretary comprise the Senate parliamentarian's staff. The parliamentarian, whose salary in 1975 was $39,000, and his staff share a first floor Capitol office, a flight below the Senate chamber and the offices of the leadership.

---

of Powell, Speaker John W. McCormack (D Mass.) blocked a move by Powell opponents to add a $30,000 fine and a forfeit of seniority. In doing so, McCormack upheld a point of order by Celler against the opposition amendment for failing to meet the House rule of germaneness. Yet the Powell debate was taking place before the House had adopted its rules for the new Congress. McCormack quickly demonstrated that he had prepared himself for the obvious question of how he could invoke a House rule before it had been adopted. "The Chair anticipated that the question of germaneness would be raised and has had the precedents of the House thoroughly researched," the Speaker said. Then he sustained Celler's point of order. Citing a precedent based on a 1913 decision of Speaker Champ Clark (D Mo.), McCormack explained: "While the House is governed by general parliamentary usage prior to the adoption of rules, the Speakers have been inclined to give weight to the precedents of the House in the interpretation of that usage."[3] Thus the leadership, through the help of Deschler's research and advice, won its point. However, Powell's opponents won the battle when the House in a subsequent resolution agreed to seat Powell but to fine him $25,000 and to strip him of his seniority. *(Powell controversy, p. 687)*

Codification of Precedents

Although the parliamentarians of both chambers shun publicity and attempt to avoid controversies, they are not always successful.

Former House parliamentarian Deschler became involved in a political controversy over codifying recent House precedents. The precedents were last codified in 1936. Precedents established since then were scattered through the pages of House debate in the *Congressional Record.* (There is no current codification of Senate precedents either, but the more informal atmosphere of the Senate renders precedents less important.)

Pressure to compile a new House codification and to keep it up to date built up among younger representatives. They frequently found themselves at odds with the House leadership, particularly under Speaker McCormack, but often were caught off guard when forced to match precedents with Deschler. Deschler maintained a private file of post-1936 precedents, clipped from the *Record* and pasted in notebooks kept in his office.

Starting in 1965, Congress provided money annually in the legislative branch appropriations bill specifically for codification. Deschler hired his daughter, Mrs. Joan Deschler Eddy, as a $13,399-a-year research assistant to help with the task. The 1970 Legislative Reorganization Act directed the Speaker to complete a compilation of precedents by Jan. 1, 1977, and to prepare an updated version every two years thereafter. For fiscal 1976, $235,000 was authorized for this purpose. The job was nearly completed at the time of Deschler's death on July 12, 1976.

Footnotes

1. Neil MacNeil, *Forge of Democracy* (David MacKay Co., 1963), pp. 82-83.

2. Donald G. Tacheron and Morris K. Udall, *The Job of the Congressman* (The Bobbs-Merrill Co., Inc., 1966), p. 193; see also, pp. 231-33.

3. *Congressional Record*, Jan. 3, 1969, p. 25.

Selected Bibliography

Bolling, Richard. *House Out of Order.* New York: E. P. Dutton & Co., 1966.

Cannon, Clarence, ed. *Cannon's Precedents of the House of Representatives.* Washington, D.C.: Government Printing Office, 1936.

Hinds, Asher C., ed. *Hinds' Precedents of the House of Representatives.* Washington, D.C.: Government Printing Office, 1907.

Kennedy, Lawrence, comp. *Biographical Directory of the American Congress, 1774-1971.* Washington, D.C.: Government Printing Office, 1971.

MacNeil, Neil. *Forge of Democracy.* New York: David MacKay Co., 1963.

Tacheron, Donald G. and Udall, Morris K. *The Job of the Congressman.* Indianapolis: The Bobbs-Merrill Co. Inc., 1966.

Legislative Reorganization Act of 1970

Some major changes in legislative procedures were approved by Congress in 1970 with passage of the Legislative Reorganization Act (PL 91-510). The reforms were intended to improve the operations of Congress, particularly to open up many hitherto hidden procedures governing the way Congress conducted its committee meetings and disposed of legislation on the floor.

The bill was also designed to provide Congress with better tools for evaluating the federal budget along with improved research and information resources and services.

Under the new law, most provisions of which took effect with the convening of the 92nd Congress in January 1971, much of the secrecy surrounding the actions of members and their positions on various issues, particularly in the House, was peeled off. All roll-call votes taken in committee—where the vast majority of legislation is formulated—were to be made public. For the first time, House members' positions on floor amendments were to be individually recorded and printed in the *Congressional Record* in the same manner as senators' on roll-call votes (previously members had voted in virtual anonymity by non-recorded teller votes, and often a large percentage did not vote at all). The televising of House committee hearings was authorized.

Genesis of the Act

The 1970 act grew out of a study by the Joint Committee on the Organization of Congress in 1965-1966. The Senate in 1967 passed a bill embodying most of the Joint Committee's recommendations, but that measure met stubborn opposition in the House and never reached the floor.

Persistent pressure finally forced the House to pass a reform bill of its own in 1970; floor amendments substantially strengthened the modest reforms recommended by the House Rules Committee which reported the bill. Prospects for enactment of reform legislation in the 91st Congress seemed so poor that the Senate had decided not to consider any such measure unless the House acted first, but when the House-passed bill reached the upper chamber the Senate quickly added provisions relating to its own operations and the measure was enacted into law.

Neither the 1946 nor the 1970 act was really a comprehensive reform measure. Questions directly involving the distribution of power within Congress were largely excluded from both acts, and neither touched upon such sensitive and controversial subjects as the seniority system, the power of the House Rules Committee or limitation of debate in the Senate. *(For details of the 1946 act, see pp. 52-53; for provisions of 1970 act, see appendix)*

Structure of the 1970 Act

The 1970 reform act contained six parts, the last five of which—fiscal controls (Title II), sources of information (Title III), Congress as an institution (Title IV), the House Office of Legislative Counsel (Title V) and effective dates (Title VI)—applied primarily to matters outside the internal operations of each chamber.

All of Title I and some of Title II dealt with the rules of the House and the Senate which govern committee and floor procedures. The Constitution gives each chamber the right to make its own rules.

Title I and the relevant parts of Title II thus followed a two-part style in the legislation to achieve similar reforms in the rules of both houses without one house seeming to infringe upon the other's prerogatives. Each provision affecting the rules of both chambers had two sections: one amending the rules of the House directly; the other, in language identical or similar to that of the 1967 reform bill approved by the Senate, amending the Legislative Reorganization Act of 1946 to amend the rules of the Senate indirectly.

Principal Reforms

Despite its limitations, the 1970 act—like its predecessor—contained a number of provisions that promised to have a significant impact on the future actions of Congress. The most dramatic procedural reform was a provision that made it possible for House members to be individually recorded on teller votes. Previously, many crucial questions had been decided by non-recorded teller votes while the House was sitting in the committee of the whole; members had voted in virtual anonymity, and often many of them did not vote at all.

In its second experience with the recorded teller-vote procedure, the House on March 18, 1971, voted to cut off funds for further development of the supersonic transport (SST) aircraft. In 1970, the House had voted $290-million for the plane, but the only record votes relating to the SST controversy were on procedural questions. Thus the recorded teller vote in 1971 marked the first occasion on which representatives were directly recorded on the issue, and the House, reversing its earlier stand, voted 217-204 to delete the funds. "I think the teller vote made the difference," said Rep. Sidney R. Yates (D Ill.), one of the leaders of the SST opponents.

The 1970 act opened to the public eye more of the operations of Congress and the positions of its members by:
● Encouraging more open committee meetings and hearings.
● Requiring that all committee roll-call votes be made public.
● Allowing broadcasting and television coverage of committee hearings.
● Providing that House teller votes be recorded upon request, ending the secrecy surrounding members' positions on important amendments.

The measure was expected to expedite House proceedings by:
● Allowing all House committees to sit without special leave while the House was in session so long as it was not reading a bill for amendment under the five-minute rule.
● Dispensing with the reading of the *Journal* unless the Speaker or a majority of the members present so ordered.
● Allowing the call of the roll for a quorum to be suspended as soon as a quorum was obtained.

The law would safeguard the rights of the ideological or political minority by:
● Writing into the rules a specific time period for additional views to be added to a committee report.
● Allowing minority members of a committee to select two of the committee's six permanent professional staff. (This provision was changed subsequently. *For details on change, see p. 394*)
● Stating that minority members could call witnesses of their choosing during at least one day of hearings on a measure or topic.

Reforms Disregarded

The 92nd Congress, within two months after it convened in January 1971, had disregarded or suspended at least four key provisions of the Legislative Reorganization Act of 1970:
● The House agreed to disregard a provision of the 1970 act that required one-third of each committee's investigative funds to be used to hire minority staff members.
● The Senate, in approving a resolution to create a Joint Committee on Environment, included language exempting appointments to the committee from a provision of the 1970 act that limited senators to one joint committee assignment.
● The House by unanimous consent waived a provision of the act barring the House from considering a conference report until it had been printed and made available to members for three days. The waiver, requested by Ways and Means Committee Chairman Wilbur D. Mills (D Ark.) in connection with a bill to raise the debt ceiling and increase Social Security benefits, also precluded any member from requesting a separate House vote on the nongermane Social Security amendment, which the Senate had added to the bill. The procedure for a separate vote on nongermane Senate riders was established by the 1970 act.
● Committees varied in their compliance with a provision specifying that the results of all record votes taken by committees to report bills to the floor must be printed in the committee reports, and that the positions of individual members on such votes must be made available to the public. Some committees complied in full with these provisions. However, the House Agriculture Committee, in reporting one bill, did not include the vote in its report, although it made it available upon request. And the Ways and Means Committee, in its report on the debt limit bill, included in its report the 20-3 vote by which its action was taken but did not make the names available, stating that no record vote was taken.

● Requiring that debate on a conference report be evenly divided between the majority and minority sides.

Provisions which might slow congressional proceedings but which would give members a better opportunity to base their votes on knowledge of a particular measure would:
● Require the committee report on a bill (and committee hearings on an appropriations bill) to be available for at least three days before the House or Senate voted on the bill.
● Allow 10 minutes debate on any amendment offered on the floor of the House which had been printed in the *Congressional Record* at least one day prior to consideration.
● Require a conference report to be available for three days before the House voted on its adoption.

The act also provided for a modernized data processing system for federal fiscal and budgetary information, closer scrutiny by Congress of the current and projected costs of all federal programs, increased staff assistance for congressional committees, and a continuing study of the operations of Congress by a joint committee.

Effect of 1970 Reforms

The precedents for faithful implementation of congressional reform were not strong if the results of the postwar reorganization act of 1946 were any guide. Many provisions of that law were easily circumvented; others were merely ignored.

To cope with the multiplication of standing committees, the 1946 act cut the number in half—to 15 in the Senate and 19 in the House. At the beginning of the 91st Congress, there were 16 Senate and 21 House committees. But subcommittees proliferated. At the beginning of the 91st Congress there were 122 subcommittees in the Senate and 145 in the House.

The 1946 act required all committees to fix a regular meeting day. But in 1969 a survey by Congressional Quarterly found that although most committees had set such a day, few observed it.

The 1946 act directed Congress each year to prepare a legislative budget fixing a ceiling on the amounts which could be appropriated for each function. This was unsuccessful and was dropped in 1949. (However, a new congressional budget law was passed in 1974. *Details, p. 129)*

The test of the effectiveness of the 1970 reform measure would be the extent to which the new committee procedures were implemented—particularly in the House. With more members, more committees and more rules, the House of Representatives traditionally resisted rules reform more strenuously than the Senate.

And the key to implementation of the new procedures was the attitude of the House's senior members, who ruled its committees, and the amount of effort its junior members were willing to exert to demand that the rules be observed.

Barber B. Conable Jr. (R N.Y.), who led the bipartisan effort to enact PL 91-510, said of the new law that it provided the basis for major improvements in committee procedures but that it all depended on the congressional will to enforce it. He added that the demand for observance of procedural safeguards was directly related to the degree of frustration that junior members of a committee felt—the extent to which they perceived themselves disenfranchised by the chairmen.

Thomas M. Rees (D Calif.), long an advocate of congressional reform, pointed out that even before the 1970 act the rules of the House contained many provisions designed explicitly to protect the rights of the ideological or political or chronological minority, but that these rules were rarely if ever invoked because of the repercussions which would follow such imprudent action.

Recorded Teller Votes

Despite an inauspicious start—Congressional Quarterly reported in 1971 that within two months of the date the new law went into effect Congress had disregarded or suspended at least four of its key provisions—the act's new procedure for voting on the House floor brought about some dramatic changes. *(Box, p. 363)*

In the first full year of operation, 108 recorded teller votes were taken, most of them on amendments to bills which under the previous system would have been decided by a small number of anonymous members.

The 1970 act for the first time allowed recorded votes on amendments to bills when the House assembled as a committee of the whole. One-fifth of the committee (20 members) could demand "tellers with clerks." Members would still file up the aisle, but would hand the tellers colored pieces of paper bearing their names and positions.

A survey by Congressional Quarterly, based on the 108 recorded teller votes, found that voting participation increased by more than 90 per cent compared to voting on amendments the previous year. The study showed that only 23 of the 108 recorded teller votes were decided by a margin of 150 votes or more.

Pressures were exerted to modify the recorded teller vote procedure by some disgruntled members who claimed that the procedure was being abused by small numbers of representatives seeking votes on minor issues. Although some members backed a move to modify the rule—perhaps by increasing the number of people who would have to request a recorded teller vote—support for the 1970 reform voiced by Speaker Carl Albert (D Okla.) early in 1972 effectively squelched the attack.

On Feb. 23, 1972, the Democratic Caucus voted to change the recorded teller vote to permit such votes to last 15 minutes rather than the existing 12 minutes. In addition, it voted to change the rules to allow quorum calls to be taken by a 15-minute teller vote procedure rather than by calling the roll.

Both changes were adopted by the House by voice vote. No attempt was made during the caucus session to modify the procedure for having recorded teller votes.

Richard P. Conlon, staff director of the Democratic Study Group, comprised of liberal and moderate House Democrats, said in 1972 that the recorded teller vote was "working beyond any expectations" of its original backers. He said that the House leaders "underestimated its potency" before the SST vote, but the popularity of that vote made it "untouchable."

As important as whether liberals or conservatives, Republicans or Democrats, benefited most from the recorded teller vote was the increase in House voting participation which resulted from the reform. Rep. Conable observed that it ensured majority participation in the amending process. Before its adoption, 100 members could usually amend a bill any way they sought—"a serious gap in the legislative process," Conable said.

The Evolution of Committees

Probably the most outstanding characteristic of the United States Congress is the dominant role committees play in its proceedings. Committees are the gears and springs of the clock—the mechanism that propels this branch of government.

Their power reflects this role. So extensive is their influence in the legislative process that scholars over the years have called them "little legislatures"[1] and their chairmen, "petty barons."[2] The descriptions often have been apt: congressional committees have initial jurisdiction over legislation and the chairmen wield substantial influence over committee operations.

A committee may approve, alter (even totally revamp), kill or ignore proposals referred to it. It is difficult—almost impossible—to circumvent a committee that is determined not to act; a bill that has been approved by a committee may be amended when it reaches the House or Senate floor, but extensive changes are difficult and seldom occur. The work of a committee essentially becomes the work of Congress.

In the past, this vast power often was exercised arbitrarily by committees and their chairmen. Until the 1970s, when important reforms were made, committees and their chairmen usually were powers unto themselves. Strong party leadership in Congress might influence committee actions, but most committees had sufficient independence to do as they wished.

This independence began to be eroded in the 1970s, particularly in the House, as an increasing number of new members were elected to Congress. In the first half of the decade, Congress approved numerous and fundamental changes in its procedures that ended the nearly absolute authority enjoyed by senior members, and particularly by committee chairmen, and redistributed power among junior and even freshmen members. The iron hand of the seniority system was removed, making senior members who had risen to power by longevity subject to challenges and discipline for arbitrary use of that power.

Chairmen had to be elected by their colleagues, and were made subject to committee rules that restricted their past freedom to act as they saw fit. Subcommittees proliferated and took on institutional characteristics with their own spheres of influence, which produced a diffusion of power. *(Description of major changes, box p. 368; further discussion of subcommittees p. 382).*

The result of these changes was that congressional committees remained at the center of the legislative process but had become subject to many new pressures that made them in fact, as well as in theory, responsible to their parent bodies—the House and Senate—that created them.

Historical Background

Committees have become a major organizational factor in Congress by evolution, not by constitutional design. The committee concept was borrowed from the British Parliament and transmitted to the New World by way of the colonial legislatures, most notably those of Pennsylvania and Virginia. But the committee system as it developed in Congress has been colored by the peculiar characteristics of American life.

In the earliest days, when the nation's population was small and the duties of the central government were carefully circumscribed, Congress had little need for the division of labor which the committee system provides. A people who viewed with grave suspicion the need to delegate authority to elected representatives were served by a Congress that only grudgingly delegated its own powers to committees. Originally, legislative proposals were considered initially on the Senate or House floor, and then a special or select committee was "raised" to work out details. Once the committee reported, it was dissolved. Approximately 350 such committees were created during the Third Congress alone.[3]

In the House, initial consideration occurred in committee of the whole, followed by reference to a select committee. (The committee of the whole is not a committee as the word is usually understood, but rather the entire House operating under special rules. During the early years, when it was used to oversee the select committees, debate was unlimited.)

Gradually the select committees evolved into permanent standing committees, and legislation came to be referred directly to committees without prior consideration by the parent body. This procedure gave the committees initial power over legislation, each in its specialized area, subject to subsequent review by the full chamber.

The House led the way in the creation of standing committees. The Committee on Elections, created in 1789, was followed by Claims in 1794 and by Interstate and Foreign

Dates of Creation of Standing Committees

Only committees in existence in 1975 are listed. Where committees have been consolidated, the date cited is that of the component committee that was established first. Names in parentheses are of present committees where they differ from the original name.

HOUSE	SENATE
1789 Enrolled Bills (House Administration)	1789 Enrolled Bills (Rules & Administration)
1795 Commerce and Manufacturers (Interstate & Foreign Commerce)	
1795 Ways & Means	
1805 Public Lands (Interior & Insular Affairs)	
1808 Post Office and Post Roads (Post Office & Civil Service)	
1808 District of Columbia	
1813 Judiciary	
1813 Pensions and Revolutionary Claims (Veterans' Affairs)	
1816 Expenditures in Executive Departments (Government Operations)	1816 Commerce and Manufacturers (Commerce)
	1816 District of Columbia
	1816 Finance
	1816 Foreign Relations
	1816 Judiciary
	1816 Military Affairs (Armed Services)
	1816 Naval Affairs (Armed Services)
	1816 Post Office and Post Roads (Post Office & Civil Service)
	1816 Public Lands & Survey (Interior & Insular Affairs)
1820 Agriculture	
1822 Foreign Affairs (International Relations)	
1822 Military Affairs (Armed Services)	
1822 Naval Affairs (Armed Services)	
	1825 Agriculture (Agriculture & Forestry)
1837 Public Buildings and Grounds (Public Works and Transportation)	1837 Public Buildings and Grounds (Public Works)
	1842 Expenditures in Executive Departments (Government Operations)
1865 Appropriations	
1865 Banking & Currency (Banking, Currency & Housing)	
1867 Education & Labor	1867 Appropriations
	1869 Education & Labor (Labor & Public Welfare)
1880 Rules	
1887 Merchant Marine & Fisheries	
	1913 Banking & Currency (Banking, Housing & Urban Affairs)
1942 Select Small Business (Small Business)	
1958 Science & Astronautics (Science & Technology)	1958 Aeronautical & Space Sciences
1967 Standards of Official Conduct	
	1970 Veterans' Affairs
1975 Budget	1975 Budget

Source: George Goodwin Jr., *The Little Legislatures* (University of Massachusetts Press, 1970), and *Congressional Directories.*

Commerce and Revision of the Laws in 1795. The number had risen to 10 by 1810, and a further substantial expansion occurred under President James Monroe (1817-25). Between the War of 1812 and the Civil War the standing committee became the standard vehicle for consideration of the business of the House but was not fully exploited as a source of independent power.[4]

The Senate in its first quarter-century established only four standing committees, and all were, on the whole, more administrative than legislative. Most of the committee work fell to select committees, usually of three members, appointed as the occasion demanded. These occasions were so frequent that by the session of 1815-16 between 90 and 100 select committees were appointed. Frequently, however, related subjects would be referred to a committee that had already been set up, and the same men were often named to committees dealing with similar subjects. In 1816, the Senate, finding inconvenient the appointment of so many committees at each session, added 11 standing committees to the existing four. By 1863 the number had grown to 19.[5]

Methods of Appointing Committees

Different methods of making committee appointments developed in the two chambers. The first rule established by the House with respect to committee appointments in 1789 reserved to the House the choice of membership on all committees of more than three members. That rule gave way, in 1790, to a rule delegating this power to the Speaker, with the reservation that the House might direct otherwise in special cases. Finally, however, the Speaker was given the right to appoint members and chairmen of all of the standing committees, a power he retained until 1911. The principle that the committees were to be bipartisan but weighted in favor of the majority and its policies was established early.[6]

Certain principles governed the choices of the Speaker in making committee appointments. The wishes of the minority leadership usually were respected. Generally, seniority, length of service on the committee and factors such as geographical distribution and party regularity were considered. But the Speaker was not bound to respect this formula, and there were cases where none of the principles outweighed the Speaker's wishes. Despite complaints and attempts to change the rule, the system remained in force until 1911, when the House again reserved the right to elect members to all standing committees.

Senate committees were chosen by ballot, with pluralities decisive, until 1823. In that year a proposal that the chairmen of the five most important committees be chosen by ballot and then granted power to choose the membership of their own and other committees was rejected. The Senate instead adopted an amendment to the rules giving the "presiding officer" authority to name committees, unless otherwise ordered by the Senate. Since Vice President Daniel D. Tompkins scarcely ever entered the chamber, the choice of committees was left to the president pro tempore, who had been chosen by and was responsible to the Senate. But when the next Vice President, John C. Calhoun, used the appointing power with obvious bias, the Senate quickly and with little dissent returned to the system of electing committees.[7]

This time the chairmen were to be picked by majority vote, and other committee members were to be chosen on one ballot with their rank determined by the size of their pluralities. A major difficulty of this arrangement was that it failed to assure the majority party of succession to the chairmanship in the event of a vacancy, or to assure it of a majority on the committees.

The Senate in 1828 changed the rules to provide for appointment to committees by the president pro tempore, but in 1833 it reverted to choice by ballot. Choice by ballot has remained in the Senate rules down to the present, but for a time the Senate experimented with a variety of methods. It then became customary to suspend the rule by unanimous consent and designate an officer (the Vice President, the president pro tempore or the "presiding officer") to name the committees.

The method of selecting committee members that was still in use in the 1970s was developed in 1846. At that time a motion to entrust the Vice President with the task was defeated, and the Senate proceeded under the regular rules to name committees by ballot. But after six chairmen had been selected, a debate ensued on the method of choosing the remaining members of the committees. At first, several committees were filled by approving lists—arranged in order of succession to the chairmanship—submitted by the majority leader. After a number of committees had been filled in this manner, the ballot rule was suspended and the Senate approved a list for all remaining vacancies that had been agreed upon by both the majority and minority.[8] Since 1846, the choice of committees has usually amounted to routine acceptance by the Senate of lists agreed upon by representatives of the caucus or conference of the two major parties.

Proliferation of Standing Committees

The standing committee system, firmly established in the first half of the 19th century, continued to expand in the second half. During this period the standing committees developed into powerful and autonomous institutions, increasingly independent of chamber and party control, and the committee chairmen assumed ever greater powers over legislative action. So great was their influence that Woodrow Wilson in 1885 could write: "I know not how better to describe our form of government in a single phrase than by calling it a government by the chairmen of the standing committees of Congress."[9]

The committee chairmen became even more powerful figures following the House "revolution" of 1909-10, which curtailed the powers of the Speaker and split up the House leadership. Seniority, already a leading criterion in the Speaker's choice of committee chairmen, was firmly established from that time on until the reforms of the 1970s.

The number of standing committees has varied from one period to another. It reached a peak in 1913, when there were 61 standing committees in the House and 74 in the Senate. Not all were of equal importance. Some—such as Appropriations, Ways and Means, Finance and Rules—exercised great influence, but many others were created and continued chiefly as a means of providing members of Congress with offices and clerical staff. Until 1921 the Senate declined to abolish its Committee on Revolutionary Claims because its room belonged by custom to the minority caucus.[10]

Consolidation of Committees

Efforts to consolidate the committee system were undertaken in 1909, when six minor committees were dropped; but, as Galloway noted, "The reorganizations of 1910 and 1911 (were) the most spectacular and best known of any associated with Congress."[11] In 1911, when the Democrats obtained a majority, they abolished six superfluous committees as well as the Speaker's power to appoint committee members and chairmen. The new rule provided for election of standing committees by the House.

Ten years later, in 1921, another major reorganization took place, with the passage of the Budget and Accounting Act. At that time, the House restored to its Appropriations Committee exclusive jurisdiction over appropriations. Prior to the creation of Appropriations Committees in the House (1865) and the Senate (1867), one committee in each

(Continued on p. 370)

Power Flows Away from Senior Members . . .

Congress in the first half of the 1970s approved numerous and fundamental changes in its procedures that ended the nearly absolute authority enjoyed by senior members and redistributed power among junior and even freshmen members.

The impact of the revisions was on the way Congress conducts its business. The changes made the two chambers—and the House in particular—more pluralistic by spreading power among many members. The changes did not divest senior members of control, but they made them subject to influence by junior members—a situation that was almost unheard of in the past. And the changes also made Congress a more open institution by exposing most committee work sessions to the public and the press.

Following is a summary of the most important revisions approved during this period:

House

A number of the changes involved the Democratic Party in the House and were accomplished through the party's caucus. These revisions in effect influenced how the House was run because Democrats were in the majority. In addition, changes were made in the House's rules that applied to all members.

Committee Chairmen. Democrats in 1975 decided to make all nominees for committee chairmanships subject to automatic, secret-ballot election by the caucus. This change began modestly in 1971 with a requirement that 10 or more caucus members could demand a separate vote on any chairman nominee. It was known as the kamikaze rule because the challengers had to stand up publicly in the caucus to demand the vote. In 1973, Democrats decided that any chairman would be subject to a secret ballot vote if 20 per cent of the caucus demanded it—a liberalization of the 1971 requirement that in effect guaranteed a vote on all chairmen. In 1975, the secret-ballot election requirement was made automatic and was extended to the powerful chairmen of Appropriations subcommittees.

In 1975, Democrats further refined their method of selecting chairmen by allowing competitive nominations for the posts to be made on the caucus floor if the original selection, made by the Democratic Steering and Policy Committee, was voted down. Existing rules provided for a vote on the next Steering Committee choice.

In 1971, the Democrats had decided that no member could be chairman of more than one legislative subcommittee. That broke the hold of senior Democrats on key subcommittees. When adopted, it gave 16 Democrats elected since 1958 their first subcommittee chairmanships. This was expanded in 1975 to prevent a chairman of a legislative committee from chairing any other committees including special, select or joint ones.

Steering Committee. Democrats in 1973 created a Steering and Policy Committee to assist the leadership in developing party and legislative priorities.

Committee Assignments. Democrats in 1973 adopted a party rule guaranteeing each Democrat a major committee assignment. In December 1974, at an organizing session for the next Congress, the caucus gave the power to assign Democrats to House committees to the party's Steering and Policy Committee, composed of party leaders and their nominees and regionally elected members. The action took the appointive power away from Ways and Means Committee Democrats, who had held it since 1911.

In an effort to assure that all Democrats had a chance at good subcommittee slots, the caucus in December 1974 specified that beginning in 1975 no member could become a member of a second subcommittee on any full committee until every member of the full committee had chosen one subcommittee position. A grandfather clause allowed existing subcommittee members to protect two slots. The change was aimed at the Appropriations subcommittees where senior Democrats dominated the important units handling defense, agriculture, health, education and welfare funding.

Committee Rules. Committees are required to have written rules. This rule, adopted in the 1970 Legislative Reorganization Act, opened the way to checking the arbitrary use of power by committee chairmen.

Subcommittees. Subcommittee members were protected by a "bill of rights" adopted by the Democratic caucus in 1973. The new rules established a Democratic caucus on each committee and forced committee chairmen to start sharing authority with other Democratic members. Each committee caucus was granted the authority to select subcommittee chairmen, establish subcommittee jurisdictions, set party ratios on subcommittees to reflect the ratio in the full House, provide adequate subcommittee budgets and guarantee all members a major subcommittee slot where vacancies make that possible. In 1974, the caucus gave the committee members the power to determine the number of subcommittees their committee would have.

Under the "bill of rights," committee chairmen no longer could kill legislation by quietly pocketing it. They were required to refer bills to subcommittees within two weeks.

All committees with more than 20 members must establish at least four subcommittees. This requirement was made in 1974 and modified slightly in 1975. It was aimed at the Ways and Means Committee, which had not had subcommittees since 1961, but it also institutionalized subcommittees for the first time.

Subcommittee Staffing. In 1975, House rules were changed to allow subcommittee chairmen and ranking minority members to hire one staff person each to work directly with them on their subcommittees. The new staffing power strengthened subcommittees.

Proxy Voting. The House restricted the use of proxy voting in committee. The practice was banned in 1974, but partially restored by Democrats in 1975 by allowing committees to decide if proxies could be used. If they were, they could be used only on a specific amendment or on procedural matters and they had to be in writing and given to a specific person. The proxy vote also had to be

. . . As Congress Changes Many Procedures

dated and could not be used to make a quorum. General proxies, often given between Democrats for use as the recipient saw fit, no longer were possible. Republicans had long complained that Democrats abused proxy votes by using them to control committee activity even though few Democrats were present.

Open Meetings. The House in 1973 required that all committee and subcommittee bill-drafting sessions and other business meetings be open to the public unless a majority of the committee in open session voted to close the doors to the public. Hearings had been open, but markup sessions to draft legislation usually were closed. The change allowed interested citizens and—more importantly—reporters to watch bill-drafting work to see how committee members were performing and how they were voting on amendments and other changes in legislation.

The House in 1975 went a step further and voted to require that conference committee sessions be open to the public. The Senate went along later in the year.

Closed Rule. Democrats in 1973 modified the closed rule which had been used almost exclusively by the Ways and Means Committee to protect its bills from change on the House floor. Under the revision, 50 or more Democrats could bring a proposed amendment to the caucus. If a majority of the caucus approved the recommendation of the 50, the Democratic members of the Rules Committee would be instructed to write a rule allowing that specific amendment to reach the House floor for a vote when the bill to which it pertained came up.

Rules Committee Members. The Democrats in 1974 took a step to strengthen the party's leadership by allowing the Speaker to nominate all Democratic members of the Rules Committee, subject to caucus ratification.

Organization. In 1974, the House decided that beginning that year it would return between Dec. 1 and 20 in election years to organize the next Congress in advance. The purpose was to speed action on substantive matters at the beginning of new Congresses.

Teller Votes. The House took an important step to make members' actions more visible by requiring that teller votes on the floor be recorded. In the past, these votes were tabulated only in total; no record was made of each member's position even though the procedure was used to decide some of the most controversial issues that came before the House. The change was adopted in the 1970 Legislative Reorganization Act and put the House on a par with the Senate, where all important floor votes can be—and usually are—recorded.

Minority Rights. The 1970 Legislative Reorganization Act extended certain safeguards to minority members of Congress. For example, the minority was assured the right to call witnesses, House minority party conferees on a bill were given control over one-half of the debate time when the conference report came to the floor and minority members of a committee were given a specific length of time to get their views in a committee report.

Proceedings. The 1970 Legislative Reorganization Act made many changes in Senate and House procedures designed to expedite congressional activity and make more information available to members. For example, House committees were allowed to sit during a House session, House quorum calls were shortened, committee reports in both chambers had to be available at least three days before the bill was taken up on the floor and a minimum 10 minutes' debate was provided for any amendment on the House floor if the proposal had been printed previously in the *Congressional Record* so that members had an opportunity to study it.

Senate

There were fewer changes approved by the Senate during this period, but the Senate was a more open body and power was more evenly distributed than in the House. This was because Senate debate was unrestricted and floor amendments could be offered under most circumstances, and because the relatively small size of the Senate allowed most members to have good committee seats and at least one committee or subcommittee chairmanship and often more than one. Nevertheless, a number of fundamental changes were made.

Filibuster. Rule 22, which prescribed the way to terminate filibusters, was modified in 1975 after years of battle. The existing rule required two-thirds of senators present and voting to invoke cloture and bring a proposal to a vote. The 1975 change set the number of votes required at two-thirds of the full Senate, or 60 if there were no vacancies. Advocates believed the change would ease the task of ending filibusters.

Open Meetings. The Senate in 1975 voted to require each standing, select or special committee or subcommittee to open all its meetings, including bill-drafting sessions, to the public and press. Sessions could be closed by a majority vote of the members taken in open session, but only for one of about half a dozen reasons written into the new rule. In this regard, the open-meetings requirement was more strict than the similar House rule which set no standards for voting to close a meeting.

The Senate in 1975 also agreed—like the House—to open conference committee sessions.

Committee Chairmen. Senate Democrats in 1975 decided in their caucus to select committee chairmen by secret ballot whenever one-fifth of the caucus requests it. The procedure to carry out the change provides that a list of chairmen nominees by the Democratic Steering Committee will be distributed to all Democrats. The Democrats will check off the names of the nominees they wish to subject to a secret ballot and will submit the list without signing it. If at least 20 per cent of the caucus members want a secret vote on a nominee, it will be held automatically two days later.

Staff Assistance. Junior senators in 1975 obtained committee staff assistance to aid them on legislative matters. The change allowed them to hire up to three staffers who would work on a senator's committees. In the past, committee staffs were tightly controlled by senior senators.

Closed Committee Meetings

Congressional committees have opened their doors to the public and press in increasing numbers since 1973, when the House adopted new rules aimed at keeping closed sessions to a minimum. Before that time at least 30 per cent of all committee meetings had been closed. Senate open-meeting rules adopted in 1975 further increased public access to committee proceedings.

The figures used in the following chart were compiled from the lists of committee meetings published in the Daily Digest section of the *Congressional Record.* Subcommittee meetings were included in the totals along with full committee sessions. Open meetings followed by closed meetings were counted twice, once in each category. Joint meetings of separate committees or subcommittees were counted as one meeting for each.

The tabulations exclude meetings held when Congress was not in regular session; meetings held outside of Washington, D.C.; informal meetings without official status, and meetings of the House Rules Committee to consider sending legislation to the floor.

The Legislative Reorganization Act of 1946 required information on congressional committee meetings to be published daily in the *Record,* but the listings have not always reflected exactly the number of meetings held or whether they were closed to the public.

Year	Total Meetings	Number Closed	Per Cent Closed
1953	2,640*	892	35%*
1954	3,002*	1,243	41*
1955	2,940*	1,055	36*
1956	3,120*	1,130	36*
1957	2,517*	854	34*
1958	3,472*	1,167	34*
1959	3,152*	940	30*
1960	2,424*	840	35*
1961	3,159*	1,109	35*
1962	2,929*	991	34*
1963	3,868*	1,463	38*
1964	2,393*	763	32*
1965	3,903	1,537	39
1966	3,869	1,626	42
1967	4,412	1,716	39
1968	3,080	1,328	43
1969	4,029	1,470	36
1970	4,506	1,865	41
1971	4,816	1,731	36
1972	4,073	1,648	40
1973	5,520	887	16
1974	4,731	707	15
1975	6,325	449	7
Total*	84,880	27,411	32%

Meetings of the House Appropriations Committee, all reported closed until 1971, were not included in the study until 1965.

(Continued from p. 367)

chamber had handled both revenue and spending legislation. In 1885, the House dispersed the powers of its Appropriations Committee among nine committees.[12] The Senate followed the House example, and by 1914 eight of the 14 appropriations bills were not referred to the Appropriations Committee. Although this method allowed committees most familiar with a subject to consider pertinent appropriations, it resulted in a division of responsibility that permitted no unified consideration or control of financial policy as a whole. Accordingly, the House in 1920 restored exclusive spending powers to its Appropriations Committee; the Senate took similar action in 1922.

Another reorganization designed to streamline Congress was a reduction in 1921 in the number of Senate committees from 74 to 34. In many respects this "reform" was simply the formal abandonment of long defunct bodies like the Committee on Revolutionary Claims.[13] The House in 1927 reduced the number of its committees by merging 11 expenditures committees into a single Committee on Expenditures in the Executive Departments.

A major overhaul of the committee structure was effected by the Legislative Reorganization Act of 1946. By dropping minor committees and merging those with related functions, the act achieved a reduction from 33 to 15 committees in the Senate and from 48 to 19 in the House. The act also carefully defined the jurisdictions of each committee and attempted to set gound rules for their operations.[14]

Until 1974, the committee structure created by the Legislative Reorganization Act of 1946 underwent only minor changes, but its influence was weakened by the proliferation of subcommittees within the standing committee system, as well as by the creation of numerous select, special and joint committees. By the 1970s there were 268 congressional subcommittees. *(See further discussion of subcommittees p. 382)*

In addition to the standing committees—21 in the House and 16 in the Senate—there were seven major joint committees and a growing number of select committees which had been set up to examine specific problems.

The Legislative Reorganization Act of 1970 changed some committee procedures but made only minor revisions in the committee structure itself. It created a new Senate Committee on Veterans' Affairs and changed the name of the Senate Banking and Currency Committee to Banking, Housing and Urban Affairs, thus providing a more accurate reflection of the committee's jurisdiction. The defunct Joint Committee on Immigration and Nationality Policy was abolished, and a new Joint Committee on Congressional Operations was established. *(1970 Act, see Appendix)*

The House in 1974 made an abortive effort to restructure its committee system. Major changes were blocked by entrenched interests both in and out of Congress that benefited from the existing committee system.

Between the late 1960s and 1975, however, many important procedural changes were made that had a drastic impact on the way committees operated. These are discussed below and in the section on the chairman. *(p. 376)*

Senate Inaction

Unlike the House, the Senate by 1975 had considered no major committee reorganization plan in the 30 years since passage of the 1946 Legislative Reorganization Act.

Hearings on reorganization were held by the Government Operations Committee in 1951 and the Joint Committee on Congressional Operations in 1966. No major changes resulted from the hearings.

The Senate committee system was affected by two important changes in the 1970s:

● A 1975 Senate rules change requiring most committee meetings, including bill-drafting sessions, to be open to the public.

● A decision by both parties—the Republicans in 1971 and 1973 and the Democrats in 1975—to subject their top-ranking committee member to a secret-ballot vote of approval in the party caucuses.

Moreover, by 1975 many senators were pressing for a complete review of the committee system. It appeared that a majority of the Senate favored such a review, but the proposal continued to be blocked by senior senators who feared that some of their power and prerogatives would be eroded if the system underwent substantial revision.

Open Meetings

Both the Senate and the House in the 1970s adopted a fundamental change in the rules governing the operation of their committees: they required committees to open up their bill-drafting sessions to the public.

With some exceptions, these sessions were closed to the public and press, thereby preventing citizens from knowing how their elected officials voted on important issues in committee.

The cloak of secrecy began to be pulled away in 1970 with the requirement that roll-call votes taken in closed sessions be made public. This change led in the House in 1973 and in the Senate in 1975 to a requirement, written into the rules, that meetings be open unless a committee specifically voted in public session to close a meeting. A presumption in favor of open meetings was established. In addition, both chambers in 1975 applied the same rule to the powerful conference committees that resolve Senate-House differences on bills.

Partial House Reforms

An effort at consolidation and reorganization of the House's committee structure was made in 1973 and 1974, with limited success. The House defeated an ambitious plan of reform that was proposed by a special study committee.[15]

The changes eventually adopted were known as the Hansen plan after Rep. Julia Butler Hansen (D Wash.) who headed a special unit of the Democratic Caucus known as the Committee on Organization, Study and Review.

The Hansen plan made some jurisdictional shifts—such as giving the Public Works Committee control over most transportation matters—but mainly it retained the existing committee structure dating from 1946.

The Hansen plan also included a number of procedural changes such as directing the House to organize itself in December of election years for the next Congress. The plan also gave the Speaker wider latitude in referring bills to committees and required committees to have at least four subcommittees.

The Hansen plan was a substitute for the more far-reaching proposal, drafted by a select committee headed by Rep. Richard Bolling (D Mo.) composed of five Democrats and five Republicans with a $1.5-million budget. The Bolling committee was created in January 1973 and put forth its

Conference Committees

The conference committee is an ad hoc joint committee appointed to reconcile the differences between Senate and House versions of proposed legislation. A conference becomes necessary when the two chambers do not pass a bill in identical form and neither is willing to yield to the other. Then a conference committee, consisting of senators and representatives, is appointed to determine the final shape of the legislation. Only rarely does the Senate or House reject the work of a conference committee.

Traditionally, conference committees are composed of the senior members of the committees or subcommittees that handled the bill. They are appointed by the Speaker of the House and the presiding officer of the Senate upon the recommendation of the floor manager of the bill, usually the committee or subcommittee chairman. There need not be an equal number of conferees (or "managers" as they are styled) from each house, because a majority vote determines the position of each group. Therefore a majority of both the Senate and House delegations must agree before a provision emerges from conference as part of the bill.

Both parties are represented on a conference committee, with the majority party having a larger number, and a majority of conferees from each house must sign the conference report.

Until 1975, most conference committees met in secret. In November of that year, both chambers amended their rules to require open meetings. However, a majority of either chamber's conferees could vote in open session and on the record to close the meeting for that day.

In the past, conference committees met on the Senate side of the Capitol, with the most senior senator presiding, but this is no longer always the case.

Conferees have broad powers over the measure before them. Theoretically, they are not permitted to write new legislation in reconciling the Senate and House versions of bills, but this prohibition is sometimes bypassed. Many bills have become acceptable only after new language was provided by the conferees.

Once the conferees have reached agreement, they prepare a conference report for submission to their parent chambers. Conference reports cannot be amended on the floor; they must be accepted or rejected in their entirety, and they are very seldom rejected. When the report is approved by the Senate and the House, the conference committee dissolves.

The conference device, used by Congress since 1789, had developed into its modern pattern by the middle of the 19th century. *(For current conference procedures, see p. 353)*

plan the following December. It was much broader than the Hansen plan that was later devised.

For example, the Bolling plan set up new committees on Energy and Environment, Public Works and Transportation and Commerce and Health. The purpose was to consolidate related subjects in specific committees; a frequent criticism of the existing system was the dispersal of subject jurisdiction among many panels. The plan also took substantial power away from the Administration and Ways and Means Committees.

The Bolling plan drew a flood of protest from members and lobbyists whose interests would be affected. The House Democratic Caucus, reflecting this opposition, shunted the plan to Hansen's committee where it was watered down. Both plans finally were brought to the floor in the fall of 1974, where the Bolling proposal was decisively defeated and the Hansen substitute approved.

Changes Approved. The Hansen plan made the following changes in House rules, procedures and jurisdictions, effective at the beginning of the 94th Congress in 1975:

Procedural

● Increased each committee's permanent staff from six to 18 professionals and 12 clerks and granted the minority control of one-third (10) of the employees. However, this staffing provision was revised in 1975. The statutory staff was increased to 42 with the majority getting 26 and the minority 16. In effect, each side received six additional staff members to be used on subcommittees. (The 1975 changes dropped another provision of the Hansen plan that gave the minority control of one-third of a committee's fund for investigatory staff.)

● Banned proxy voting in committee. In 1975, proxy voting was partially restored, but under tight controls. Proxies could be used only on a specific amendment or on procedural matters and they had to be in writing and given to a specific person. Proxies also had to be dated and could not be used to make a quorum. General proxies (undesignated proxies given for the recipient to use as he saw fit) were outlawed.

● Required that committees with more than 15 members (increased to 20 members in 1975) establish at least four subcommittees.

● Required the House to return between Dec. 1 and 20 in election years to organize the next Congress in advance, effective in 1974.

● Authorized the Speaker to refer bills to more than one committee at a time or to several committees in sequence. He also could split up bills and send the parts to different committees.

● Required all committee reports to include a statement of the bill's impact on inflation, and required all reports on appropriations bills to include statements on changes in law made in the accompanying bill.

● Required a 100-word summary of the contents of each House bill introduced to be filed for public inspection.

● Gave all standing committees across-the-board subpoena authority without the necessity for individually approved House resolutions, and required that all subpoenas be authorized by a majority of a committee.

● Directed the Speaker to complete compilation of House precedents by Jan. 1, 1977, and to update them every two years after that.

● Established a Commission on Information and Facilities, controlled by the House members of the Joint Committee on Congressional Operations.

● Established a Legislative Classification Office to develop a system linking federal programs and expenditures to the authorizing statutes, and showing the committee jurisdiction for each authorization.

● Allowed resident commissioners and delegates to sit on conference committees and required that a majority of

House conferees support the House position on the bill in question.

Jurisdictional

The resolution also made a number of jurisdictional changes, including:

● Giving the Interstate and Foreign Commerce Committee jurisdiction over biomedical research (from Science and Astronautics), nursing home construction (from Banking) and health care programs except those financed through payroll taxes (from Ways and Means).

● Consolidating most transportation matters in the Public Works Committee, renamed Public Works and Transportation. The panel, which already had jurisdiction over highways, gained urban mass transit from Banking and Currency, and civil aviation and surface transit from Interstate and Foreign Commerce. Commerce kept railroads.

● Giving Banking and Currency, renamed Banking, Currency and Housing, jurisdiction over renegotiation (from Ways and Means) and international financial organizations (from Foreign Affairs).

● Giving Science and Astronautics, renamed Science and Technology, jurisdiction over civil aviation research and development (from Commerce), environmental research and development (from several committees) and all energy research and development except nuclear (from several committees).

● Giving the Foreign Affairs Committee (later renamed the International Relations Committee) authority over some international trade matters (from Banking and Currency), the Food for Peace Program (PL 480) except domestic production (from Agriculture), international commodity agreements and export controls (from Banking and Ways and Means).

● Transferring revenue sharing from Ways and Means to Government Operations.

● Moving legal services from Education and Labor to Judiciary.

● Setting up a new Select Committee on Aging.

● Making the Select Committee on Small Business a legislative committee with the jurisdiction of the Banking and Currency Committee's Small Business Subcommittee.

Additional Changes

Additional blows were delivered to the established committee system in the House in 1974 and 1975, partly as a result of the 1974 election of 75 mostly liberal Democratic freshmen who gave their party a 291-144 majority.

Meeting in December 1974 to organize for the 94th Congress, Democrats made these important changes:

● Stripped the Democratic members of the Ways and Means Committee of their power to make Democratic committee assignments and transferred that responsibility to the Steering and Policy Committee, a unit of the party leadership.

● Increased the Ways and Means Committee from 25 to 37 members (to allow packing the committee with liberals who would support party-backed proposals on tax reform, health insurance and other issues—a plan which had not accomplished its purposes by mid-way in the 94th Congress).

● Established a Democrat to Republican ratio of 2-1 plus one Democrat on all committees except ethics.

• Allowed the Speaker to nominate Rules Committee members, subject to caucus approval.

• Allowed members of committees, rather than just the chairmen, to determine the number and jurisdiction of subcommittees.

The Committee Structure

There are three principal kinds of committees: standing committees, permanent units with broad powers over legislation; select or special committees, usually temporary and chiefly investigative in nature; and joint committees, also usually investigative, with a membership drawn from both houses of Congress. Conference committees, a special variety of joint committee, serve only on an ad hoc basis to **resolve differences in Senate and House versions of legislation.** *(Box, p. 371)*

In addition, there are numerous subcommittees, which are functional subdivisions of the full committees. All of these groups are composed of members of the majority and minority parties, with the majority party having a numerical advantage.

At the start of the 94th Congress in 1975, there were 358 committees (standing, special and select) and subcommittees:

• 24 Senate committees with 139 subcommittees.
• 28 House committees with 146 subcommittees.
• 7 joint committees with 14 subcommittees.

The Senate had 18 standing (permanent) committees and the House 22, only three more in each chamber than there were in 1947, when the Legislative Reorganization Act of 1946 took effect, drastically reducing the number of committees in existence then.

But these standing committees had 268 subcommittees (126 Senate and 142 House), compared to 148 in 1947 (59 Senate and 89 House)—a growth rate of just over four new subcommittees every year since 1947. In 1975 there were five more subcommittees than there were at the end of 1974—four in the House, one in the Senate.

Standing Committees

The standing committees are the keystone of the legislative process because they have the power to review legislative proposals and report bills to the floor. Under the Legislative Reorganization Act of 1946, Senate and House committees are organized along similar but not precisely parallel lines.

One of the purposes of the 1946 act was to eliminate confusing and overlapping jurisdictions by grouping related subjects. The legislative committees (as distinct from the money committees) were in general regrouped to follow the major organizational divisions of the federal government. Responsibility for overseeing the executive branch was divided roughly as follows: Appropriations Committees were to review requests for spending authority, the Expenditures Committees (now Government Operations) were to oversee administration of appropriations and the quality of administration in general, and the legislative committees were to oversee administration of policy in their respective fields.

The size of the standing committees is fixed by the rules of their parent chamber; in the 94th Congress, House committees ranged in size from 12 (Standards of Official Conduct) to 55 (Appropriations), Senate committees from seven (District of Columbia) to 26 (Appropriations).

Traditionally, party ratios on the committees corresponded roughly with the party ratio in the full chamber.

Select and Special Committees

Select or special committees are established from time to time in the Senate or House to study special problems. Their size is fixed by the resolutions that create them. Ordinarily they are not permitted to report bills. Such committees may go on from Congress to Congress, as have the Senate and House Small Business Committees (the House Small Business Committee became a standing committee in 1974 and its Senate counterpart became a standing committee in 1976), but most have only a brief lifespan.

One exception to the usual prohibition on select committees' reporting legislation is the Senate Select Committee on Intelligence, established in May 1976. Recommended by a special intelligence investigating panel set up by the Senate in 1975, the new select committee was given exclusive legislation and budget authorization authority over the Central Intelligence Agency (CIA), but it shared jurisdiction over the intelligence components of the Federal Bureau of Investigation (FBI) and Defense Department with the Judiciary and Armed Services Committees respectively. Because the panel's subject-matter—intelligence—was narrower than that of most standing committees, it was decided that it be designated a "select" rather than a "standing" committee. *(Details on the CIA probe and new committee, see CIA Investigation, pp. 168-71)*

Joint Committees

Joint committees are created by statutes or resolutions which also fix their size. Of the seven joint committees in existence in 1975, only one—the Joint Committee on Atomic Energy—had the authority to report bills. Others, such as the Joint Economic Committee, examine public problems or review the execution of programs, but they must depend on standing committees to frame legislative proposals. The Joint Committee on Internal Revenue Taxation, made up of senior members of the House Ways and Means and Senate Finance Committees, may make policy recommendations to those committees but serves chiefly to provide a professional staff on tax issues. A few joint committees never meet.

Function of Subcommittees

Subcommittees provide the ultimate division of labor within the committee system. Although they enable members of Congress to develop technical expertise in specialized fields, they are often criticized on grounds that they fragment responsibility and increase the difficulty of overall policy review.[16]

Quite junior members of a full committee may be given subcommittee chairmanships which permit them to play more significant roles in the legislative process than they would otherwise be able to do. Sen. Birch Bayh (D Ind.) became chairman of the Senate Judiciary Subcommittee on Constitutional Amendments shortly after he took office in 1963; from that post he directed Senate action on the presidential disability amendment two years later.

Subcommittees vary in importance from committee to committee. Some, notably the Appropriations subcommittees in both chambers, have well-defined jurisdictions and function with great autonomy; most of their actions are routinely endorsed by their parent committees. Their im-

Congressional Oversight: . . .

Over the years, Congress has created a vast array of agencies and programs, but often it pays only scant attention to how the agencies are operating or the programs working.

Some examples:

● As of 1975, it had been almost 30 years since Congress took a thorough look at the Social Security Administration, a huge bureaucracy that distributes more than $80-billion a year in benefits to retired and disabled workers.

● Congress took its last close look at the Internal Revenue Code, the nation's basic tax law, in 1952.

● Until 1975, the Central Intelligence Agency and the Federal Bureau of Investigation were almost immune to close congressional scrutiny.

● After creating the Highway Trust Fund in the mid-1950s to pay for the interstate highway system, Congress never took the time to examine how the spending of $4-billion a year from the fund affected the nation's rail system.

The list could go on.

By 1975, however, Congress began to show signs that it intended to pay closer attention to head off problems afflicting those agencies and programs. The Social Security system was facing serious financial problems. The Internal Revenue Code was being attacked as loophole-ridden. The FBI and CIA were accused of **abuses in domestic and foreign intelligence. And the**

bankrupt Northeast railroads, undermined in part by truck competition aided by highway subsidies, required federal assistance to keep them running.

Members of Congress conceded that some of those problems might have been averted by preventive reviews, including hearings and studies to determine what went wrong. Congress calls this process "oversight."

Background. Congress periodically has demonstrated its concern for better oversight since 1946 when it first officially recognized its responsibility for such activity in the Legislative Reorganization Act (PL 79-601). Its problem since then has been to put its intent into practice. Propelled by its struggle to regain power from the executive branch, Congress moved in 1974 to improve its conduct of oversight when it passed the Congressional Budget and Impoundment Act (PL 93-344) and the House Committee Reform Amendments (H Res 988).

Specifically, H Res 988 required committees with more than 15 members either to set up an oversight subcommittee or to require their legislative committees to carry out oversight functions. In January 1975, the minimum committee size needed to trigger the oversight option was raised to 20 under the new House rules.

Legislative subcommittees carrying out oversight can do it only within their limited jurisdictions. On the other hand, most subcommittees set up specifically to

---

portance was one reason that House Democrats in late 1974 voted to make all Appropriations subcommittee chairmen subject to confirmation by secret-ballot in the party caucus.

Other committees carefully review and on occasion reverse the action of their subcommittees. A few committees leave little opportunity for subcommittee initiative. As George Goodwin has noted in his book, *The Little Legislatures,* "A conservative chairman usually will not want to see much development of subcommittees, especially if he heads one of the important control committees of Congress.... For a conservative chairman, perhaps the next best thing to having no subcommittees is to have numbered subcommittees without specified jurisdiction and to assign bills to them according to their responsiveness to his desires."[17]

Finally, a few committees—notably the powerful House Ways and Means and Senate Finance Committees—resisted the creation of subcommittees, although there were logical subdivisions into which their work could be divided. Subcommittees were established for the Senate Finance Committee in 1970 and for House Ways and Means in 1974, in the latter case partly from dissatisfaction with the power and performance of the full committee chairman Wilbur Mills (D Ark.). The House Rules and House and Senate Budget Committees were among those that had no subcommittees in the 94th Congress. *(Further discussion of subcommittees, p. 382)*

Committee Assignments

The current method of appointing committees—through chamber approval of a list of names sub-

mitted by party leaders—was adopted by the Senate in 1846 and by the House in 1911. This procedure takes place at the beginning of each new Congress. In practice it rarely involves more than assignment of new members to committees and filling of vacancies caused by death, retirement or voluntary transfer to another committee.[18]

Until the 1970s, committee assignments generally were made on the basis of seniority, with seats on the most powerful committees going to the more experienced members. Opponents of the seniority system have scored some successes, however, in broadening control over committee assignments. *(Seniority changes, p. 397)*

In the Senate, the Democratic committee roster is drawn up by the Democratic Steering Committee, headed by the party leader, who also names the other Steering Committee members. In 1971, the roster was made subject to caucus approval. The Republican committee roster is drawn up by the Republican Committee on Committees, which is appointed by the chairman of the Republican Conference, but the caucus does not vote on committee nominations. On the floor, the leaders of the two parties offer resolutions, which usually are adopted virtually automatically by the full chamber, making the committee appointments suggested by the party groups and in the process formalizing party ratios agreed upon by the leaders.

In the House, the Democratic committee roster is drawn up by the party's Steering and Policy Committee, whose nominations are subject to caucus approval. (Until 1975, Democratic committee assignments were made by the Democratic Committee on Committees, which was composed of the Democratic members of the Ways and Means Committee.) An exception is the membership of the Rules

. . . Renewed Interest in a Neglected Duty

conduct oversight can carry out their work within most of the full committee's jurisdiction, a much broader area.

The resolution required the House Government Operations Committee to report to the House within 60 days after Congress convened on the oversight plans of all the standing committees and on any recommendations for coordinating the activities.

It also gave seven committees—Budget, Armed Services, Education and Labor, Foreign Affairs, Interior and Insular Affairs, Science and Technology, and Small Business—special oversight responsibilities that permitted them to cross jurisdictional lines in any investigations.

Of the 22 standing House committees, eight had oversight subcommittees in the 94th Congress, an increase of four over the 93rd. Three of the new oversight panels were established on committees that acquired more vigorous, reform-minded chairmen in January 1975:—Agriculture, Banking and Currency, and Ways and Means.

Committees that already had oversight panels in the 93rd Congress were Government Operations, Interstate and Foreign Commerce, Foreign Affairs, and Public Works.

The Small Business Committee, whch became a legislative committee in the 94th Congress, had five oversight subcommittees and one legislative subcommittee. The seven subcommittees of the House Government Operations Committee were oversight-oriented although they also handled legislation.

Senate. By 1975, the Senate had not displayed the introspective bent that the House had. Moves to establish a Senate committee on committees that would closely scrutinize the committees' operations and propose reforms continued to be blocked.

The Senate and House shared some of the same problems in coping with oversight chores. But the Senate has some of its own, too. Because it is smaller, the Senate's problems of time, interest and priority are more acute. And the predilections of conservative committee chairmen often mitigate against vigorous oversight activity.

The average senator in 1975 served on 16 committes and subcommittees. Only one of the 16 standing committees that handled legislation—the Banking, Housing and Urban Affairs Committee—had established an oversight subcommittee. The Senate Government Operations Committee had combined legislative-oversight responsibilities.

The small size of the Senate and the large number of subcommittees hinders senators from giving full attention to oversight. Thus, the oversight responsibility in many cases is left to subcommittee staff members, who generally reflect the chairman's attitudes. As in the House, oversight has brought few publicity pay-offs and has often been neglected.

Committee; in 1975, the Speaker was given the power to nominate all Democratic members of that panel, subject to ratification by the caucus.

Republican committee nominations in the House are determined by the party's Committee on Committees, made up of one representative from each state having at least one Republican in its House delegation. The nominations are then submitted to the House Republican Policy Committee for approval. The Republican Conference does not vote on all committee nominations, but, under a 1971 innovation, it does vote on the ranking Republican member of each committee. As in the Senate, the committee rosters prepared by the two parties are incorporated in resolutions which must be adopted by the full chamber.

Factors in Choice of Members

Various factors govern selection of committee members, including seniority of service in the chamber, party loyalty, regional distribution, personal preference and the favor of the leadership.[19] Some committees typically have a special-interest cast: the Agriculture Committees are manned largely by members from farm states, the Interior Committees by members from public land states. Others—notably the "prestige" committees such as Appropriations, Ways and Means and Rules—have members from many states which provide these panels with a broader, more national outlook.

Traditionally, new members of Congress have had to serve an apprenticeship on minor committees before being appointed to major committees. However, since 1953 the Senate Democratic leadership has followed the so-called "Johnson rule" under which freshman senators are given at least one major committee assignment each. Senate Republicans have followed a similar practice since 1965. Although the Legislative Reorganization Act of 1946 attempted to limit the number of committees upon which an individual member could serve, this effort was not entirely successful.

The Legislative Reorganization Act of 1970 limited future assignment of senators to two major committees and one minor select or joint committee. It stipulated also that no senator could serve on more than one of the following: Armed Services, Appropriations, Finance or Foreign Relations. These restrictions did not affect existing committee assignments. In the larger House, few members serve on more than two committees. (In January 1971, House Democrats voted that henceforth no Democratic representative could serve on more than two committees with legislative jurisdiction.)

In the 94th Congress, the high ratio of Democratic freshmen to their senior party colleagues—the 75 freshman Democratic representatives comprised 26 per cent of the 289 Democratic members of the House—caused some interesting lineups on committees. According to initial committee assignments, 14 of 25 Democrats on the Science and Technology Committee were freshmen, as were 13 of 27 on Agriculture, 13 of 29 on Banking, Currency and Housing and 12 of 29 on Interstate and Foreign Commerce. However, the three most powerful House committees—Appropriations, Rules and Ways and Means—had only seven freshmen among their 73 Democratic members. Rules had no freshmen, nor did House Administration and Standards of Official Conduct.

Once on a congenial committee, a member of Congress usually remains there, gradually working his way up by longevity to the position of chairman or ranking minority member. He may have an opportunity to transfer from one committee to another, where he will have to start again at the bottom of the ladder. Or, if he is a very junior member, he may be bumped from his committee as a result of party realignments following an election. On rare occasions committee members have been stripped of their seniority or even denied their committee seats as a punishment for party disloyalty. Two southern representative—John Bell Williams (D Miss.) and Albert W. Watson (D S.C.)—lost their Democratic seniority in 1965 after they had supported the Republican presidential candidate the preceding year. It was the first such action since 1911. In the Senate, Wayne Morse (Ore.) lost his seat on two Senate committees in 1953 after he bolted the Republican Party and became an independent.[20]

Powers of Committee Chairmen

Initially little more than moderators of committee deliberations, the committee chairmen rapidly developed into powerful figures with broad influence over legislation. George B. Galloway in 1953 offered the following description of the role of committee chairmen at the time: "Just as the standing committees control legislative action, so the chairmen are masters of their committees. Selected on the basis of seniority, locally elected and locally responsible, these 'lord-proprietors' hold key positions in the power structure of Congress. They arrange the agenda of the committees, appoint the subcommittees, and refer bills to them. They decide what pending measures shall be considered and when, call committee meetings, and decide whether or not to hold hearings and when. They approve lists of scheduled witnesses, select their staffs and authorize staff studies, and preside at committee hearings. They handle reported bills on the floor and participate as principal managers in conference committees. They are in a position to expedite measures they favor and to retard or pigeonhole those they dislike. Strong chairmen can often induce in executive sessions the kind of committee action that they desire. In the House of Representatives, where debate is limited, the chairman in charge of a bill allots time to whomever he pleases during debate on the floor; he also has the right to open and close the debate on bills reported by his committee; and he may move the previous question whenever he thinks best. In short, committee chairmen exercise crucial powers over the legislative process."[21] However, this description of the chairman was no longer entirely accurate—particularly in the House—after reforms made between the late 1960s and the mid-1970s. *(Details in Post of Chairman section, this page)*

"Many factors work to give a chairman power," noted Goodwin in 1970, among them "the experience that generally comes from seniority, the demands for leadership that come from both within and outside a committee, control over the parliamentary process by virtue of being a focal point, and the availability of rewards and punishments. Yet a chairman is dependent at a minimum, on the toleration of his fellow committee members."[22]

Of course, the powers of a chairman vary from committee to committee and from chairman to chairman. And in nearly every recent Congress examples can be found of committee rebellions. Thus the House Education and Labor Committee in 1966 adopted a set of rules to limit the power of its chairman, Adam Clayton Powell (D N.Y.), who had angered members by delaying committee action on some bills and by refusing to call up for floor action others that the committee actually had reported. The rules left the initiative for action with Powell in most cases but eliminated his power to block action desired by a majority. A few months later Powell was deprived of his chairmanship, but the rules remained in force.[23]

Similarly, a revolt in the House Banking and Currency Committee led, in 1967, to a series of rules changes that stripped Chairman Wright Patman (D Texas) of much of his authority, including control over subcommittee appointments and staff hire. Patman had acquired the reputation of running the committee in high-handed fashion.

The House Rules Committee, following the 1966 election defeat of Chairman Howard W. Smith (D Va.), adopted a set of rules governing committee procedures for the first time in its history. The new regulations took from the chairman the right to set meeting dates, required the consent of a majority to table a bill and set limits on proxy voting. It was widely reported that these rules resulted from pressure by the Democratic leadership rather than pressure from within the committee. *(See pp. 385-387)*

In 1973 and 1974, the House Ways and Means Committee underwent major changes, culminating in the resignation of Wilbur Mills (D Ark.), the panel's chairman for 17 years (1958-75). Members both inside and outside the committee began to chafe at Mills' dominance of the panel, as exemplified by House rejection in 1973 of a major Ways and Means compromise engineered by Mills involving cost-of-living increases in Social Security payments. Mills' personal and health problems, which made headlines in the fall of 1974, added more fuel to growing dissatisfaction with his performance. As a result, the Democratic Caucus in late 1974 adopted a series of reforms designed to weaken the power of the Ways and Means Committee and its chairman. Henceforth, committee bills could be open for floor amendment under certain conditions. (Previously, most Ways and Means bills had been granted a "closed rule" which prohibited floor amendments.) The panel was required to establish subcommittees (six were established in the 94th Congress) and its Democratic members were stripped of their committee assignment powers for the party. The committee's size was increased to 37 from 25 members.

The Post of Chairman

The committee chairman is a central figure in the legislative process. Until the 1970s, the chairman was *the* central figure—his power equalled only by a few party leaders of great influence such as long-time House Speaker Sam Rayburn (D Texas 1913-61) or Senate Majority Leader Lyndon Johnson (D Texas 1937-61).

Although this influence was waning in the 1970s under the pressure of many events, the chairman remained a crucial figure. Congress functions primarily through its committees and the person who heads one has considerable influence over the advancement (or the defeat) of legislation.

At one time, the authority of a committee chairman was almost absolute. This power resulted from the rigid operation of the seniority system under which a person rose to a chairmanship simply through longevity in Congress. The unwritten seniority rule conferred a committee chairmanship on the member of the majority party with the longest continuous service on the committee. As long as his

TV Cameras in Committee: A Senate Tradition

Most House and Senate committees allow television and radio to cover hearings that are open to the public.

The Senate has a long tradition allowing broadcast coverage of committee hearings. Senate rules leave to individual committees the decision whether or not to admit radio and television. That decision usually is made by committee chairmen or, if there is an objection by a member, by a majority of the committee. In practice, most committees encourage coverage and require only advance notification from the news crew in order to provide suitable accommodations.

The only Senate committees that traditionally have not allowed broadcast coverage have been Armed Services and Judiciary. The Armed Services panel cited the small size of its meeting room as one reason for the policy. Nevertheless, the committee occasionally arranged for meetings in larger rooms to permit television broadcast of particularly newsworthy events.

The Judiciary Committee has not allowed cameras or tape recorders in the room when the full panel was in session. Sen. James O. Eastland (D Miss.), who became committee chairman in 1956 and continued in that position at the end of the 94th Congress in 1976, was said to believe that the function of his committee was similar to that of a court. The presence of cameras and other electronic equipment, an aide said, would destroy decorum as well as distract witnesses and committee members. Individual subcommittees have been allowed to set their own policies, however, and some have permitted broadcast coverage.

The House has traditionally been less hospitable to broadcasters than the Senate. After permitting a historic first telecast of floor proceedings in 1947, the leadership of the House closed the chamber to television and prescribed the same policy for House committees. It was not until passage of the 1970 Legislative Reorganization Act (PL 91-510) that broadcast coverage of committee hearings was legally sanctioned by the House.

While the Senate leaves broadcast decisions to its committees, the House has adopted a stringent set of standards for use by committees that do admit cameras. Among them are requirements that broadcast coverage not "distort the objects and purposes of the hearings...cast discredit or dishonor on the House, the committee, or any member or bring the House, the committee or any member into disrepute." When those provisions were adopted by the Interior and Insular Affairs Committee in 1975, some questions were raised in the written press about setting limitations on "journalistic integrity." Broadcasters were aware of the rules but said they have not interfered with their coverage of committees.

Television and radio seldom are allowed in the hearings of three House committees: Armed Services, Rules and Ways and Means. The Armed Services Committee flatly prohibits broadcast coverage, a staff member said, simply because "the committee doesn't want it."

The Rules Committee has admitted television cameras at least once, for hearings in the spring of 1973 on budget control and impoundment, but normally they are not allowed.

The Rules Committee considered but rejected proposals in 1974 to allow broadcast of its Rockefeller vice-presidential confirmation debate and its consideration of the articles of impeachment approved by the Judiciary Committee, if they had come to Rules.

The Ways and Means Committee early in 1975 considered opening hearings for telecasting, but under conditions that broadcasters found unacceptable.

In general, House committees seemed in the 1970s to be moving toward more open acceptance of broadcasting. In 1974, in order to permit television coverage of the Judiciary Committee sessions on impeachment, the House amended its rules to allow broadcasting of mark-up meetings as well as hearings. Previously, rules had barred television and radio from mark-up sessions and other meetings, and few if any committee meetings had ever been broadcast.

The Appropriations Committee, which in the past had permitted telecasting only of its formal budget hearings at the beginning of each year, opened its doors early in 1975 for coverage of testimony on Central Intelligence Agency activities by Defense Secretary James R. Schlesinger and CIA Director William E. Colby.

---

party retained control of Congress, he normally kept this position; if control passed to the other party, he changed places with the ranking member of the other party.

Only rarely was the rule not followed. Occasionally a member who held a top-ranking position on more than one committee would waive his seniority to the person next in line. This was more likely in the Senate where the small number of senators, relative to the number of representatives in the House, allowed some members to serve on several important committees.

Sometimes a chairman relinquished his post because of age or health and on very rare occasions a chairman was stripped of his position. For the most part, however, the seniority rule reigned supreme until the 1970s.

Then, changing circumstances caught up with it. The principal change was the election to Congress of dozens of new members—persons who had less patience with the traditional rule, credited to House Speaker Rayburn, which admonished newcomers "to get along, go along." The new members didn't want to wait 10 to 20 years to gain enough seniority to have some influence in the Senate or House. Moreover, they chafed under the often heavy handed rule of arbitrary chairmen. Thus, in the late 1960s and early 1970s began the revolt that was to undermine the seniority system and lead to numerous other changes that redefined the role and power of committee chairmen.

The single most important change that undermined the seniority system was the secret-ballot election of committee chairmen and ranking minority members by the parties in each chamber. The change came in steps, starting in 1971 with the House Republicans leading the way. Democrats at first resisted the idea, but by 1975 had come around. In that year, three House chairmen were dumped in elections. *(Details in seniority chapter, p. 397)*

The secret-ballot requirement made chairmen and ranking minority members accountable to their colleagues for their conduct; the defeat of the three chairmen in 1975 made clear that the accountability power could be used. But the election rule was only one of a number of changes that restricted the power of chairmen.

Committees were required under the 1970 Legislative Reorganization Act to have written rules. House Democrats in 1973 adopted a "bill of rights" to protect subcommittee members. They established a caucus of the Democratic members on a committee and gave them the power to select subcommittee chairmen, establish subcommittee jurisdictions, set party ratios on subcommittees to reflect the ratio in the full House, establish subcommittee budgets and guarantee all members a major subcommittee slot where vacancies made that possible. Under the "bill of rights," committee chairmen had to refer bills to subcommittees within two weeks, thus ending the chairman's ability to kill legislation by quietly pocketing it. In 1974, the House Democratic Caucus gave committee members the power to determine the number of subcommittees their committee would have. However, all committees with more than 20 members had to have at least four subcommittees under the House rules.

In another change, use of proxy voting in committee was curtailed in 1974 and 1975 in the House. A proxy vote, if allowed by a committee at all, could be used only on a specific amendment and had to be in writing and given to a specific person. General proxies, which a holder can use as he sees fit, were banned, Previously, chairmen could enhance control of their committees, particularly when controversial issues were before them, by collecting numerous general proxies from other members.

Staffing prerogatives were extended to members other than the chairman. In the House in 1975, subcommittee chairmen and ranking minority members were allowed to hire one staff person each to work on their subcommittees. In the Senate in 1975, junior members were allowed to hire up to three staffers who would work on a senator's committee. In both chambers, this change made committee members less subservient to the chairman by giving them professional staff help on legislative issues.

Both chambers also took steps to limit the influence of chairmen, and other senior members by restricting the number of chairmanships or committee slots that a person could fill. In the Senate, no senator could hold the chairmanship of more than one full committee and one subcommittee of a major committee (there were 13 committees designated as major, covering the most important and controversial areas of legislation).

In a related restriction, the Senate specified that senators may be members of only two major committees and one minor, select or joint committee. It also prohibited any senator from serving on more than one of the following committees: Armed Services, Appropriations, Finance or Foreign Relations. These restrictions, although not specifically directed at chairmen, prevented senior senators from rising to high-ranking positions on a variety of important committees or on more than one of the four so-called super committees.

However, the Senate rules applied only to future assignments and did not affect any senator holding a position when the restriction took effect under the Legislative Reorganization Act of 1970.

In the House, Democrats in 1971 decided that no member could be chairman of more than one legislative sub-committee. That broke the hold of senior Democrats on key subcommittees; it gave 16 Democrats elected since 1958 their first subcommittee chairmanships. This restriction was expanded in 1975 to prevent a chairman of a legislative committee from chairing any other committees including special, select or joint. Another 1975 rules change—not specifically aimed at chairmen—specified that no member could become a member of a second subcommittee on any full committee until every member of the full committee had chosen one subcommittee position. A grandfather clause allowed existing members to protect two subcommittee slots. The rule was aimed at the Appropriations Committee where senior Democrats dominated the most important subcommittees.

Joint Committees. Chairmanships of joint committees offer a special situation. Although historically their chairmen tended to be drawn from the Senate, in recent years the chairmanships of the major joint committees have rotated from one chamber to another at the beginning of each new Congress. When a senator serves as chairman, the vice chairman usually is a representative, and vice versa.

Rules and Procedures

Although Congress has no comprehensive code of committee procedure, general guidelines are provided by the Senate and House rules, which incorporate reforms enacted in the Legislative Reorganization Acts of 1946 and 1970.

One of the basic goals of the 1946 act was to regularize committee procedures in regard to regular meeting days, the keeping of committee records, reporting of approved measures, the presence of a majority of committee members as a condition of committee action and the conduct of hearings. However, the 1946 rules were not uniformly observed by all committees, and continuing dissatisfaction with committee operations led, in the 1970 Reorganization Act, to further efforts to reform committee procedures—particularly to make them more democratic and more open to public scrutiny.

Senate and House committees are required to establish and publish rules of committee procedure. Since the 1970 act, these rules have stipulated that each chamber's standing panels must fix regular meeting days. The rules also have authorized the chairman to call additional meetings, and have outlined a procedure under which a meeting may be called by the committee majority if the chairman fails to do so.

In addition, committees were required by the 1970 reorganization act to keep complete records of their actions and to make public certain roll-call votes. In the House, the rule requires information about each roll call be made available at the committee offices for inspection; it is to include a description of each amendment, motion, order or "other proposition" and the name of each member voting for or against the issue, as well as those present but not voting. The rule also requires that the division on any motion to report a bill be put into the committee's report on the measure; but the names of members or their positions on the action do not have to be included.

In the Senate, the disclosure rule is less specific. It requires that a committee's report on a bill include the results of roll-call votes on "any measure or any amendment thereto" unless the results had been announced previously by the committee. However, the Senate rule requires that the announcement of the roll call vote include the position taken by each member of the committee who was present for the vote.

The rules stipulate that it is the chairman's "duty" to see to it that legislation approved by his committee is reported, and they outline steps by which a committee majority may force a bill to be reported if the chairman fails to do so. The rules prohibit a committee from reporting any measure unless a majority of its members are actually present, and they place certain limits on proxy voting. Members are allowed time to file supplemental and minority views for inclusion in the committee report. Committees are required to announce hearings at least one week in advance, to hold them in open session and to require witnesses to file written statements in advance. The rules allow minority party members to call witnesses during at least one day of hearings on a subject.

Power Relationships

The standing committees of Congress, wrote Stephen K. Bailey in 1966, "exist to speed the work load; to facilitate meaningful deliberations on important measures and issues; to develop a degree of expertise among committee members and committee staff; and to serve as a convenient graveyard for inept proposals. They constitute the great baronies of congressional power. Many of them look outward in jealous competition with the President, with their opposite committee in the other house, and with the whole house of which they are a part. When internally unified and buttressed in parliamentary privilege by special rules, as in the case of the House Appropriations Committee, they can almost at will dominate the business of the parent chamber."[24]

Basis of Committee Power

Although committees also perform important investigative and oversight functions, the basis of committee power is control over legislation. *(Investigations, p. 141; Oversight, p. 374)*

Most of the legislative decisions of Congress actually are made in committee. Modern law-making requires understanding of many complex subjects, and the committee system provides a means by which members can attain a high degree of specialization in different areas. A committee that has subjected a bill to expert scrutiny expects its decisions to be upheld on the floor. Committees, says *Cannon's Procedure*, "are not infallible but they have had long familiarity with the subject under discussion, and have made an intimate study of the particular bill before the House and after mature deliberation have made formal recommendations and, other considerations being equal, are entitled to support on the floor."[25]

This attitude is more prevalent in the House than in the Senate, but in both chambers members usually are reluctant to challenge the committee, not only because they lack expert knowledge of the subject involved, but also because they would resent such a challenge if it were offered to a bill reported by one of their own committees. Thus committee power is sustained both by the practice of specialization and by the spirit of reciprocity that figures so prominently in the operations of Congress.

Conflicts Between Committees

Jurisdictional conflicts between rival committees have been a feature of congressional history since the inception of

Proxy Voting

Proxy voting, widely used in congressional committees, is a practice that permits one committee member to authorize another committee member to cast his votes for him in his absence. Proxy voting is not permitted on the Senate or House floor.

Until 1975, proxies could be general—covering all matters before a committee for a specific time or for an indefinite period, or special—limited to a particular bill and amendments.

Proponents of congressional reform long have argued for an outright ban on proxy voting in committee. Not only does it encourage absenteeism and irresponsibility, they contend, but it also contributes to the domination of committees by their chairmen, since the chairmen are in an ideal position to wrest proxies from committee members in return for the favors they can bestow.

Prior to 1970, the use of proxies was regulated either by custom or by the rules of individual committees, and different committees permitted them in different circumstances. In some committees they were never used. The Legislative Reorganization Act of 1970 prohibited proxy voting in House committees except when the committee's rules allowed, when the proxy was limited to a specific matter, and when it was in writing, designating the person to whom it was given. For Senate committees, the act provided that no proxy vote was to be cast on a motion to report a bill if the committee rules barred the use of a proxy on such a motion; if proxies were not barred on a motion to report a bill, they could nevertheless be voted only upon the affirmative request of an absent member.

House Limits. In October 1974, during floor debate on committee reform proposals, the House voted 196-166 to ban proxy voting entirely. But the ban didn't last long, primarily because Democrats benefit from use of proxies. Republicans, who had been in the minority in the House for most of the years since 1933, had long complained that Democrats use proxies to retain control of legislative action in committees when party colleagues are absent.

To retain the advantage of proxies, the Democratic caucus at the beginning of the 94th Congress in 1975 partially lifted the ban. The revision, which the majority Democrats wrote into the House rules, first allowed committees to decide whether to permit proxy voting. If proxies are allowed, they may be used only for a specific amendment or on procedural matters (general proxies were outlawed), and they must be in writing and given to a specific person. The proxy vote also must be dated and cannot be used to make a quorum.

the standing committee system.[26] The Legislative Reorganization Act of 1946 attempted to eliminate the problem by defining each committee's jurisdiction in detail. That this effort was not entirely successful was illustrated the very next year when a fight broke out in the Senate over referral of the armed forces unification bill. In the House the measure had been handled by the Committee on Executive Expenditures, which theoretically had jurisdiction over all proposals for government reorganization. But in the Senate the Expenditures Committee's claim to the bill was challenged successfully by the Armed Services Committee on a floor vote.

Such tangles have continued to arise because the complexities of modern legislative problems make it impossible to define jurisdictional boundaries precisely. Sometimes committees attempt to use jurisdictional ambiguities to expand their own powers. On other occasions the ambiguities serve as a pretext for efforts to place controversial bills in friendly (or perhaps hostile) committee hands.

The relationships between the Appropriations Committees and legislative committees frequently provide striking illustrations of inter-committee rivalries. Legislative committees handle bills authorizing funds, but only the Appropriations Committees are permitted to report actual appropriations, and the legislative committees observe this restriction. The Appropriations Committees, in turn, are barred by the rules from including legislative provisions in their appropriations bills, but they habitually do so and, despite grumbling from the legislative committees, are seldom overruled on the floor. In the Senate, some senior members of legislative committees participate in Appropriations Committee deliberations on bills in their fields of interest, thus reducing one area of conflict.

Committees are often in competition with their counterparts in the other chamber. Again, the Appropriations Committees offer a vivid example: in 1962, the decorum of Congress shattered when the two committees, each headed by an octogenarian chairman, brought their long-smoldering differences into public view. At issue were questions of whether the Senate had a right to initiate its own appropriation bills, whether it could add funds to House-passed bills, who would chair conferences between the two chambers and where the conferences would be held. The dispute blocked appropriations conferences for three months and virtually bankrupted several government agencies. Although the deadlock finally was broken, the two committees never reached full agreement on their respective roles in the appropriations process.

Committees compete for power not only with each other and with their parent chambers—on occasion they are willing to challenge the President himself. In 1967, the House Ways and Means Committee refused to act on President Johnson's proposal for a 10 per cent income tax surcharge until the President came up with an effective plan for reducing government expenditures. The President said committee Chairman Mills would live to "rue the day" he decided to block the proposal, but in fact Mills won his point.

The President finally got his tax increase in 1968, but Congress exacted as its price mandatory reductions in spending, appropriations and federal employment levels which Johnson said "would really bring chaos to the government." Although Mills had maintained throughout that a tax increase without expenditure controls would not be effective in curbing inflationary pressures, some observers attributed a part of his recalcitrance to pique. "I think Mills got upset because we didn't show him more attention," a high administration official said.[27]

Guarding of Committee Status Quo

Proposals to create new committees or to realign the jurisdictions of existing ones illustrate the determination of the committees to preserve their existing powers. For years after the House had created a separate Veterans' Affairs Committee, the Senate Finance Committee refused to relinquish jurisdiction over veterans' legislation; a Senate Committee on Veterans' Affairs was finally created under the Legislative Reorganization Act of 1970. Similarly, a proposal to split the House Education and Labor Committee into two separate committees was one of the stumbling blocks to House action on legislative reorganization in the 90th Congress; the plan was abandoned during consideration of the 1970 Reorganization Act. Reformers long have urged Congress to make greater use of joint committees to expedite business, but Congress declines to do so since such a practice would threaten the existing power structure.

It is very difficult to abolish a committee, once established, even though it no longer serves any purpose. Congress in 1952 created a Joint Committee on Immigration and Nationality Policy; the committee never met and never performed any function, yet it was not abolished until 1970.

Another well-known example of committee longevity is the House Un-American Activities Committee, established in 1945 (in 1969, its name was changed to the Internal Security Committee). Despite persistent efforts to abolish the panel and transfer its functions to the Judiciary Committee, the committee flourished until January 1975, when the House Democratic Caucus voted to recommend a series of changes in the House rules that included abolishing the committee. The recommendations were adopted by the House and the committee died at the beginning of the 94th Congress. *(For a review of the committee's history, see box, p. 166)*

The desire to maintain existing committee jurisdiction figured prominently in the debate over establishment of a new Senate Select Committee on Intelligence in May 1976. The committee was given exclusive legislative and budget authorization authority over the Central Intelligence Agency (CIA), but jurisdiction over the intelligence components of the Federal Bureau of Investigation (FBI) and the Defense Department was shared with the Judiciary and Armed Services Committees respectively. Some members of those two committees had objected strenuously to the transfer of intelligence jurisdiction from their panels' purviews to the new committee.

The compromise, as finally worked out, provided that in the case of shared jurisdiction, legislation approved by one panel would have to be referred to the other and then reported to the Senate floor within 30 days. The legislation creating the new committee (S Res 400) also required that two members of the new panel be chosen from each of four committees that had had jurisdiction over intelligence operations: Appropriations, Armed Services, Judiciary and Foreign Relations. The remaining seven members of the 15-member committee were to be selected at large. *(See p. 171)*

Footnotes

1. See George Goodwin Jr., *The Little Legislatures* (University of Massachusetts Press, 1970).

2. Woodrow Wilson, *Congressional Government* (Meridian edition, 1956), p. 59.

3. George B. Galloway, *Congress at the Crossroads* (Thomas Y. Crowell Co., 1946), p. 88.

4. On the evolution of the committee system, see Galloway, *Congress at the Crossroads,* pp. 127-31, and Goodwin, *The Little Legislatures,* p. 10

5. Galloway, *Congress,* pp. 139-44; Goodwin, *The Little Legislatures,* pp. 11-12.

6. Galloway, *Congress,* pp. 127, 137.

7. George H. Haynes, *The Senate of the United States* (Houghton Mifflin, 1938), pp. 273 ff.

8. *Ibid.,* p. 277.

9. Wilson, *Congressional Government,* p. 82.

10. Haynes, *The Senate,* p. 282.

11. Galloway, *Congress,* p. 135.

12. *Ibid.,* pp. 129-30.

13. Haynes, *The Senate,* p. 284.

14. For a concise discussion of the 1946 act, see Goodwin, *The Little Legislatures,* pp. 18-22.

15. For background on 1974 House reforms, see Congressional Quarterly, *1974 Almanac,* pp. 634-41.

16. On the role of subcommittees, see Goodwin, *The Little Legislatures,* pp. 50-59.

17. *Ibid.,* p. 59.

18. Background and discussion of assignment process, see Goodwin, *The Little Legislatures,* pp. 69-100.

19. On selection of members, cf. Randall B. Ripley, *Congress: Process and Policy* (W. W. Norton & Co., Inc., 1975), pp. 96 ff.

20. Goodwin, *The Little Legislatures,* pp. 94-96.

21. George B. Galloway, *The Legislative Process* in Congress (Thomas Y. Crowell Co., 1953), p. 289.

22. Goodwin, *The Little Legislatures,* p. 136; cf. also Ripley, *Congress,* pp. 108-11.

22. Ripley, *Congress,* p. 110.

24. Stephen K. Bailey, *The New Congress* (St. Martin's Press, 1966), p. 55.

25. Clarence Cannon, *Cannon's Procedure in the House of Representatives* (Government Printing Office, 1963), p. 221.

26. On jurisdictional conflicts, see William L. Morrow, *Congressional Committees* (Charles Scribner's Sons, 1969), p. 20.

27. Congressional Quarterly, *Congress and the Nation,* Vol. I, pp. 157-58, 167.

Selected Bibliography

Books

Bailey, Stephen K. *The New Congress.* New York: St. Martin's Press, 1966.

Cooper, Joseph. *The Origins of The Standing Committees and The Development of the Modern House.* Rice University Studies, vol. 56, no. 3. Houston: William Marsh Rice University, 1970.

Galloway, George B. *History of the United States House of Representatives.* New York: Crowell, 1961.

—. *The Legislative Process.* New York: Crowell, 1953.

Goodwin, George. *The Little Legislatures: Committees of Congress.* Amherst: University of Massachusetts Press, 1970.

Gross, Bertram M. *The Legislative Struggle.* New York: McGraw-Hill, 1953.

Haynes, George H. *The Senate of the United States.* 2 vols. Boston: Houghton Mifflin, 1938.

McConachie, Lauros. *Congressional Committees.* New York: Crowell, 1898.

McGown, Ada C. *The Congressional Conference Committee.* New York: Columbia University Press, 1927.

Manley, John F. *The Politics of Finance: The House Committee on Ways and Means.* Boston: Little, Brown, 1970.

Morrow, William L. *Congressional Committees.* New York: Scribner, 1969.

Ripley, Randall B. *Power in the Senate.* New York: St. Martin's Press, 1969.

Robinson, James A. *The House Rules Committee.* Indianapolis: Bobbs-Merrill, 1963.

Steiner, Gilbert. *The Congressional Conference Committee.* Urbana: University of Illinois Press, 1951.

Volger, David. *The Third House: Conference Committees in the United States Congress.* Evanston, Ill.: Northwestern University Press, 1971.

Articles

Asher, Herbert B. "Committees and the Norm of Specialization." *Annals of the American Academy of Political and Social Science,* January 1974, pp. 63-74.

Bolling, Richard. "Committees in the House." *Annals of the American Academy of Political and Social Science,* January 1974, pp. 1-14.

Brenner, Philip. "Committee Conflict in the Congressional Arena." *Annals of the American Academy of Political and Social Science,* January 1974, pp. 87-101.

Brock, William E. "Committees in the Senate." *Annals of the American Academy of Political and Social Science,* January 1974, pp. 15-26.

Davidson, Roger H. "Representation and Congressional Committees." *Annals of the American Academy of Political and Social Science,* January 1974, pp. 48-52.

Eckhardt, Bob. "The Presumption of Committee Openness Under House Rules." *Harvard Journal on Legislation,* February 1974, pp. 279-302.

Entin, Kenneth. "Information Exchange in Congress: The Case of House Armed Services Committee." *Western Political Quarterly,* September 1973, pp. 427-39.

Masters, Nicholas A. "Committee Assignments in the House of Representatives." *American Political Science Review,* vol. 55, 1961, pp. 345-57.

Ornstein, Norman J. "Causes and Consequences of Congressional Change: Subcommittee Reforms in the House of Representatives, 1970-1973." Papers delivered at the 1973 annual meeting of the *American Political Science Association,* 1973.

———. Towards Restructuring the Congressional Committee System. *Annals of the American Academy of Political and Social Science,* January 1974, pp. 133-46.

Peabody, Robert L. "Committees from the Leadership Perspective: Party Leadership in the House." *Annals of the American Academy of Political and Social Science,* January 1974, pp. 133-46.

Rohde, David W. "Committee Reform in the House of Representatives and the Subcommittee Bill of Rights." *Annals of the American Academy of Political and Social Science,* January 1974, pp. 39-47.

Wolanin, Thomas R. "Committee Seniority and the Choice of House Subcommittee Chairmen." *Journal of Politics,* August 1974, pp. 687-702.

Government Publications

U.S. Congress. House. Committee on Government Operations. *Oversight Plans of the Committee of the U.S. House of Representatives.* H. Rept. 94-61, 94th Cong., 1st sess., 1975.

U.S. Congress. House. Select Committee on Committees. *Hearings on Committee Organization in the House,* 3 vols. 93rd Cong., 1st sess., 1973. Reissued as H. Doc. 94-187, 94th Cong., 1st sess., 1975.

_____. *Committee Organization in the House: Index to Hearings and Panel Discussions,* 3 vols. Committee Print, 93rd Cong., 2nd sess., 1974.

_____. *Hearings on H. Res. 988, Committee Reform Amendments of 1974,* 2 parts. 93rd Cong., 2nd sess., 1974.

_____. *Committee Reform Amendments of 1974,* 2 parts. H. Rept. 93-916 to accompany H. Res. 988, 93rd Cong., 2nd sess., 1974.

_____. *Working Papers on House Committee Organization and Operation: Congressional Committees and the Two Party System,* by Charles O. Jones. Committee Print, 93rd Cong., 1st sess. Washington: Government Printing Office, 1973.

_____. *Working Papers on House Committee Organization and Operation: Congressional Oversight Methods and Reform Proposals,* by Walter Oleszek. Committee Print, 93rd Cong., 1st sess. Washington: Government Printing Office, 1973.

_____. *Working Papers on House Committee Organization and Operation: House Leadership, Party Caucuses and the Committee Structure,* by Robert L. Peabody. Committee Print, 93rd Cong., 1st sess. Washington: Government Printing Office, 1973.

_____. *Working Papers on House Committee Organization and Operation: Party Leaders and Standing Committees in the House of Representatives,* by Randall B. Ripley. Committee Print, 93rd Cong., 1st sess. Washington: Government Printing Office, 1973.

U.S. Library of Congress. Congressional Research Service. *Committee Structure and Procedures of the House of Representatives.* Dec. 13, 1973.

The Changing Role of Subcommittees

In January 1975, the House Democratic Caucus took the unprecedented step of deposing three senior committee chairmen as it organized for the 94th Congress. To many congressional observers, that action symbolized the end of "committee government" in the House as the once powerful barons, who had dominated the lower chamber in the 1950s and 1960s, were humbled publicly by the younger, more activist Democratic members.

But the ouster of F. Edward Hebert (D La.), Wright Patman (D Texas) and W. R. Poage (D Texas), the three southern elders who chaired the Armed Services, Banking, Currency and Housing and Agriculture Committees, overshadowed another significant power shift in the House—the rise in importance of the subcommittee.

The move to strengthen the autonomy of House subcommittees began in 1971 and culminated in decisions taken by the Democrats in the winter of 1974-75 forcing the Ways and Means Committee to establish subcommittees and authorizing subcommittee chairmen and ranking minority members to hire their own staffs.

As a result, subcommittees have taken over from their parent committees much of the legislative workload. In 1975, they drafted major legislation in important areas such as energy and the environment, and their chairmen managed bills on the House floor. On some committees, such as Interior, subcommittees operated autonomously with large staffs of their own.

Because of these changes, some House members and congressional observers began to talk about "subcommittee government" much as they had spoken of "committee government" in the 1960s.

Despite general support by Democrats for strengthening subcommittees, some members questioned whether the shift had gone too far. Few talked about undoing the procedural changes that enhanced the power of subcommittees or wanted to return to the days of the committee barons. But the increased importance of subcommittees raised these questions:

● Has the House become too fragmented?

● Are subcommittees operating too autonomously?

● Has the House leadership exerted strong enough leadership to effectively coordinate the efforts of the committees in drafting legislation and scheduling controversial measures for floor action?

Past Subcommittee Role

Subcommittee power became a new phenomenon in the House. Until the early 1970s, subcommittees in most instances did not play a dominant role in the legislative process. Major exceptions were the Appropriations subcommittees and the Banking Committee's housing subcommittee. The former were organized to parallel the executive departments and agencies. The staggering size and complexity of the federal budget required (and allowed) each subcommittee to develop an expertise and an autonomy respected and rarely challenged by other subcommittees or the full committee. The housing subcommittee had a long tradition of independent operation. It had control of its own budget and was able to hire and retain a widely respected staff.

The Legislative Reorganization Act of 1946 (PL 79-601) reduced the number of standing House committees from 48 to 19. But as that reduction took place at the top, an explosion occurred at the bottom as the 19 standing committees spawned 106 subcommittees in the 80th Congress.

The creation of a larger network of subcommittees did not mean that power gravitated there. Until the early 1970s, most House committees were run by chairmen who were able to keep much of the authority for themselves and a few senior members while giving little to junior members or subcommittees.

Those chairmen could dominate committees because they had the backing of Speaker Sam Rayburn (D Texas 1913-61) and Speaker John W. McCormack (D Mass. 1928-71) and the support, or at least the acquiescence, of their panels' members. They could pack subcommittees with members who would do their bidding, decide how active subcommittees would be, when they would meet, what legislation they would consider and how much staff, if any, they could have.

The day of the dominant committee chairman began to wane with the revival of the House Democratic Caucus in 1969 and the retirement of McCormack as Speaker in 1970. With McCormack's exit, these chairmen lost a powerful ally at the top of the House power structure.

The caucus revival meant that moderate and liberal Democrats elected to the House in the late 1950s and in the 1960s, who were frustrated by the old committee system that tended to freeze them out of power, at last had a vehicle to change the rules. They began to undercut the power of committee chairmen and strengthen that of the subcommittees where their potential power lay.

The drive for subcommittee reform had a sharp generational edge. Middle-ranking Democrats who came into the House together between the late 1950s and mid-1960s were allied against the senior membership.

Between 1958 and 1970, 293 new Democrats entered the House. Between 1970 and 1974, another 150 Democrats were elected. Many of those representatives, who tended to be moderate or liberal, provided the incentive for reform.

By the 94th Congress, Democratic members who had been elected since 1958 held 108 of the 146 subcommittee chairmanships on House standing and select committees.

Many of those members would have received subcommittee chairmanships even if the reforms had not been adopted, because they had accrued enough seniority. What the reforms did, however, was to give them real power when they finally took over a subcommittee.

Between 1971 and 1975, the old committee structure underwent many changes. During those four years, the House Democratic Caucus contributed to the ascendancy of the subcommittee by approving a series of innovations that guaranteed junior and middle-ranking Democrats greater power on subcommittees. The thrust of the changes was twofold: the authority of committee chairmen was curbed, and that of subcommittee leaders was strengthened. By the end of 1975, subcommittees were acting more independently and subcommittee chairmen were playing a more active role on the House floor.

Committee Chairman

The principal losers in the House power struggle of the late 1960s and early 1970s were the committee chairmen. By the time the 94th Congress organized, they had given up much of their control to the chairmen of subcommittees and to junior committee members. They still could delay bills coming before the full committee, or take a more active role in amending them, if they wanted to.

Their powers were pared in several ways through changes in House rules and positions adopted by the **Democratic Caucus.**

1. No House member could be chairman of more than one legislative subcommittee. That, in effect, made it possible to break the hold of senior conservative Democrats on key subcommittees and opened up opportunities for middle-level and junior Democrats on them. Adopted at the beginning of the 92nd Congress, that rule was responsible for giving 16 Democrats elected since 1958 their first subcommittee chairmanships in 1971 on such key committees as Judiciary, Foreign Affairs and Banking, Currency and Housing.

2. Subcommittee members were protected by a "bill of rights" adopted by the caucus in 1973. The new rules es-

tablished a Democratic caucus on each committee and forced committee chairmen to start sharing authority with the panel's other Democratic members. It did that by giving the committee caucus the authority to select subcommittee chairmen, establish subcommittee jurisdictions, set party ratios on subcommittees that reflect the party ratios in the full House, provide adequate budgets for subcommittees and guarantee all members a major subcommittee assignment where vacancies make that possible.

Committee chairmen no longer could kill legislation **quietly by pocketing it. They must refer bills to subcommittees** within two weeks. Establishing fixed subcommittee jurisdictions also prevented committee chairmen from referring bills to subcommittees that they knew would do their bidding.

3. All committees with more than 20 members were required to establish at least four subcommittees. This was directed at Ways and Means, which had operated without subcommittees during most of the 16-year chairmanship of Rep. Wilbur D. Mills (D Ark.). It also established an important precedent in the House because it institutionalized subcommittees for the first time.

4. Another change was in subcommittee staffing. Subcommittee chairmen and ranking minority subcommittee members were authorized to hire one staff person each to work directly for them on their subcommittees.

5. Committees were required to have written rules. This opened the way to checking the arbitrary power of committee chairmen and institutionalizing the subcommittees.

6. In an effort to spread participation even further, the **Democratic Caucus in December 1974 restricted senior** Democrats to membership on two of a committee's subcommittees. This was aimed mainly at the House Appropriations Committee, where senior conservative Democrats dominated important subcommittees handling defense, agriculture, and labor, health, education and welfare appropriations.

7. As of the beginning of the 94th Congress, chairmen of all the Appropriations subcommittees had to be approved by the House Democratic Caucus.

Impact on Committees

These reforms affected committees differently. They had little effect on some, such as Agriculture, which had a tradition of largely autonomous subcommittees and good relations between the committee chairman and the members.

The impact was much greater on those committees that until the mid-1970s had a tradition of strong central direction. In those cases—Ways and Means, Interstate and Foreign Commerce and Interior were prime examples—the committees tended to become fragmented, with the chairman exercising much weaker control over the full committee and the subcommittees becoming much more aggressive.

Workload

The strengthening of subcommittees in the 1970s created more work for House members. Subcommittees began holding more hearings and preparing more reports. For example, the three International Relations Committee subcommittees taken over by middle-level Democrats in 1971—Foreign Economic Policy, Europe, and the Near

(Continued on p. 385)

Proliferation of Subcommittees

The proliferation of congressional subcommittees since World War II has been deplored by students of Congress who believe it has led to unmanageable dispersion of power and accountability. In the 94th Congress, standing committees had 268 subcommittees, compared to 148 in 1947. In addition, subcommittees attached to special and select committees brought the overall total of such units to 299.

Subcommittees have proliferated partly because the 1946 Legislative Reorganization Act limited the number of standing committees to 34, a total that by 1975 had grown by only six.

Some experts on Congress, however, believe that this explanation—although correct—only begs the question. More important is whether many of these new subcommittees have been created to accomplish legislative work, and whether some of them even meet.

Although subcommittees do have a legislative purpose, more than a few have been created over the years primarily to give the status of a chairmanship to a senator or representative. In addition, subcommittees have been used as sources of employment for staff members whose principal—and sometimes, sole—purpose is to serve the political needs of the chairman.

The Hays Affair

In a spectacular, but rare, revelation about subcommittee staffers, a young woman—Elizabeth Ray—in 1976 said she had been put on the payroll of a House Administration subcommittee to serve as the mistress of the full committee's chairman, Wayne Hays (D Ohio). She said she did no work and did not possess typing, filing or other office skills. Hays admitted having a "relationship" with Ray but denied that she did no work.

The Ray allegation led to examination of some of the subcommittees on the House Administration panel. The subcommittee which had been paying Ray's $14,000 a year salary was the Oversight unit headed by Rep. Mendel J. Davis (D S.C.). The subcommittee rarely met and held only one meeting in the nearly seven months Ray was on its payroll. A number of congressional sources said the subcommittee was created by Hays in the summer of 1975 to reward Davis who backed Hays in 1974 when Hays faced a challenge to his chairmanship.

The Ray story led to further reports that some Administration subcommittees met rarely or, in one case, not at all by the time of Ray's May 1976 revelations. That one was the Paper Conservation Subcommittee. Other relatively inactive Administration subcommittees in 1975 were: Library and Memorials, which met twice; Parking which met once and Restaurant which met once.

Slots for Staffers

The misuse of subcommittees, and particularly subcommittee staff slots funded through full committee budgets, has never been thoroughly examined by Congress—at least partly because the practice benefits many members.

The situation with Ray—at least insofar as she did no congressional work—was thought to be quite rare. But it was not unusual for staffers on committee or subcom-mittee payrolls to do personal and political work—including constituent work—for the chairman of the subcommittee to which they were attached.

The *Washington Post* in a series of articles Feb. 16-24, 1975, examined Senate payroll data and reported that this practice was used by a number of senators.

Subcommittees That Don't Meet

Another bit of evidence that some subcommittees are less than beehives of activity was given to the Senate in 1976. A Library of Congress survey of Senate committee work found that almost half of the chamber's 138 subcommittees held four or fewer meetings in 1975, and that 28 of them did not meet at all. Included under the definition of subcommittees for the study were special subcommittees, ad hoc subcommittees, panels, task forces of the Budget Committee and regular standing subcommittees.

Ironically, the survey resulted not from a concern by senators that some subcommittees might not be needed, but rather as part of an effort by a few junior members of the chamber to obtain subcommittee chairmanships.

Freshman Sen. Dale Bumpers (D Ark.), who requested the study, had been joined earlier by six other first-term senators in co-sponsoring a Senate rules change to limit a senator to chairing either two subcommittees or one subcommittee and one major committee. In publicizing the study, Bumpers said "there is a high correlation between subcommittees which meet seldom and subcommittees which are chaired by senators who have two or more subcommittees under their leadership or who are chairmen of standing committees."

The 28 Senate subcommittees that did not meet in 1975 were:

- Armed Services: Preparedness Investigating.
- Banking, Housing and Urban Affairs: Oversight.
- Commerce: Special, to Study Textile Industry; Special, to Study Transportation on Great Lakes and St. Lawrence Seaway; Special, on Freight Car Shortage.
- Finance: Health; Foundations; Private Pension Plans; Social Security Financing; Supplemental Security Income.
- Foreign Relations: Far Eastern Affairs.
- Interior and Insular Affairs: Special, on Legislative Oversight; Ad Hoc, on Integrated Oil Operations.
- Judiciary: FBI Oversight; Federal Charters, Holidays and Celebrations; Immigration and Naturalization; Revision and Codification (disbanded Feb. 28, 1975).
- Labor and Public Welfare: Special, on Human Resources.
- Post Office and Civil Service: Civil Service Policies and Practices; Postal Operations.
- Public Works: Disaster Relief; Panel on Materials Policy.
- Rules and Administration: Privileges and Elections; Printing; Library; Smithsonian Institution; Restaurant; Computer Services.

Sources: The Library of Congress Study is reprinted in *The Congressional Record*, March 30, 1976, p. S 4565-69. See also Congressional Quarterly, 1975 *Weekly Report*, pp. 837-38.

(Continued from p. 383)
East—held 61 more days of hearings in the 92nd Congress than they did in the 91st Congress. The Commerce Committee's Investigations Subcommittee, chaired by John E. Moss (D Calif.), held 25 days of hearings through the first 10 months of 1975. Under its previous chairman, it held only 18 days of hearings in the entire 93rd Congress. The subcommittee issued seven reports in 1974 compared to one in 1973.

With the broadening of committee opportunities, junior members had to cope with a heavier workload as they participated more in subcommittee deliberations and floor debate.

Contrasted with this picture of the newfound activism of many subcommittees was a 1976 study conducted by the Library of Congress that reported 28 Senate subcommittees never met in 1975 and 67 (49 per cent) held four or fewer meetings that year.

Voting Cues

Subcommittee chairmen also gained more influence on the House floor. On routine legislation, there was a growing tendency for them rather than the committee chairmen to give the cues to members on how to vote. On major legislation, subcommittee chairmen were dealing almost as equals with the chairmen of other committees.

The House Rules Committee

The House Rules Committee has long stood as a strategic gateway between the legislative committees and the floor of the House for a small but important part of the chamber's legislative business. The power of the committee lies in its role of setting the agenda and allotting time for debate on those important and usually controversial bills that are not disposed of by the more routine procedures of the House. Thus the committee often has been able to prevent or delay bills it opposes from reaching the House floor.

The only ways of bypassing the Rules Committee are the discharge petition, which requires 218 signatures to free a bill from a committee; Calendar Wednesday, a day on which committee chairmen or members they designate may, in turn, call up bills reported by their committees that have not been granted a rule; and suspension of the rules, which requires a two-thirds majority vote. These methods, seldom used successfully, are beyond the direct control of the leadership. *(For a description of these procedures, see The Legislative Process, p. 335)*

There have been frequent controversies over what functions the Rules Committee should perform in its strategic position: whether it should serve merely as a clearinghouse for legislative business, as the agent of the majority leadership, or as a super-legislator editing the work of the legislative committees. A basic question has been whether the fate of important and highly controversial legislation should be decided by a small handful of men or by the majority of the entire House.

Defenders of the Rules Committee system of routing legislation argue that it promotes parliamentary efficiency in the 435-member House, and that the committee performs a unique service in blocking expensive or ill-advised bills that most House members would not dare to oppose openly on the floor.

Background

The Committee on Rules was established by the First Congress in 1789. Originally it was a select committee, authorized at the beginning of each new Congress, with jurisdiction over House rules. However, because the rules of one Congress were usually readopted by the next, this function was not of great importance and for many years the committee never made a report.[1]

In 1858, the Speaker was made a member of the committee, and from that time on the group gradually increased its power in the House. Rules became a standing committee as part of the general rules revision of 1880. In 1883 it began the practice of reporting special orders for the consideration of particular legislation, subject to a majority vote of the House. Previously the House could take up bills out of the regular order only by unanimous consent or by suspension of the rules, which required a two-thirds majority. Other powers acquired by the committee over the years included the right to sit while the House was in session, to have its reports immediately considered and even to report new business that had not been reported by a legislative committee. The latter power is exercised very infrequently. The committee used it in 1964 to grant rules for two measures, both dealing with apportionment of state legislatures, that the Judiciary Committee had refused to report. One of the measures went on to House passage; the other, a proposed constitutional amendment that required a two-thirds vote for approval, was never brought up on the floor.

Before 1910, the Rules Committee functioned as an arm of the leadership in deciding what legislation could come to the floor. But in the Progressive revolt of 1909-10 against Speaker "Uncle Joe" Cannon, the committee was made independent of the leadership. Establishment of the Discharge Calendar, Consent Calendar and Calendar Wednesday procedures in 1909 was followed in 1910 by adoption of a resolution, promoted by a coalition of Democrats and insurgent Republicans, to enlarge the Rules Committee and exclude the Speaker from membership on it. (This ban was repealed by the Legislative Reorganization Act of 1946, but no subsequent Speakers have sat on the Committee.)

By the late 1930s the committee had come to be dominated, not by the leadership, but by a coalition of conservative Democrats and Republicans which continued in control of the committee for most of the next quarter-century and which was successful in blocking a number of liberal measures.

Opposition to the obstructive tactics of the Rules Committee led, at the beginning of the 81st Congress in 1949, to the adoption of the "21-day rule," a device for bypassing the committee in bringing legislation to the floor. The rule provided that the chairman of a legislative committee which had favorably reported a bill and had requested a resolution from the Rules Committee for House consideration, might bring the resolution directly to the floor for adoption if the committee had failed to grant a rule within 21 calendar days of the request. The rule required the Speaker to recognize the member calling up the 21-day resolution.

Two years later, after the Democrats had lost 29 seats in the mid-term elections, the House repealed the 21-day rule. Although it had been used only eight times during the 1949-51 period, the threat of its use was credited with prying other bills out of the Rules Committee. Once it was repealed, the group was again free to block legislation without effective restraint.

Revolt

At the beginning of the 86th Congress in 1959, a group of House Democratic liberals sought Speaker Sam Rayburn's (D Texas) support for a change in House rules that would break the conservative grip on the committee. Following a conference with the Speaker, the group issued a statement saying that Rayburn had assured them that bills reported from legislative committees would reach the House floor and therefore they would not press for a rules change that year. However, the record of the 86th Congress showed that Rayburn often could not deliver on his promise. After the Rules Committee had blocked or delayed several measures that were destined to become key elements in the program of the new Kennedy administration, the Democratic leadership decided that the roadblock could not be allowed to stand.

Accordingly, at the beginning of the 87th Congress in 1961, the House by a narrow margin adopted a resolution to enlarge the committee's membership from 12 to 15 for the 87th Congress. This gave Rayburn and the Kennedy administration a delicate but favorable 8-7 majority on most issues that came before the committee. The plan was chosen by Rayburn over several others proposed, including a "purge" of an anti-administration committee Democrat, as the least "painful." By raising the number of Democratic members to 10 from 8 (Republicans to 5 from 4), it permitted the appointment to the committee of two pro-administration Democrats. This enlargement of the committee was made permanent in 1963.

Nevertheless, dissatisfaction with the Rules Committee continued, and following the Democratic sweep in the 1964 elections, the 21-day rule was revived. The new version of the rule, adopted by the House at the opening of the 89th Congress in 1965, did not require the Speaker to recognize a member calling up a 21-day resolution as the 1949 rule had done. Under the 1965 rule the Speaker retained discretion to recognize the member, so that it was highly unlikely, if not impossible, for a bill to come up successfully through this procedure without leadership approval. The new rule, which also was employed successfully only eight times, was abandoned in 1967, following the Republican resurgence in the mid-term elections.

The House retained another rule, adopted in 1965, that curbed the committee's power to block conferences on legislation. Prior to 1965, most bills were sent to conference either by unanimous consent or by House adoption of a resolution reported by the Rules Committee. The 1965 change made it possible to send a bill to conference by majority vote of the House.

Despite repeal of the 21-day rule in 1967, the committee continued to pursue a moderate course. Several factors contributed to the committee's less conservative posture. First, it had lost its chairman, Howard W. Smith (D Va.), as a result of his defeat in a 1966 primary election. Smith,

chairman since 1955, was a skilled parliamentarian and the acknowledged leader of the House conservative coalition—a voting alliance of Republicans and southern Democrats against northern Democrats. He was replaced as chairman by William M. Colmer (D Miss.), also a conservative southerner, but Colmer was unable to exert the high degree of control over legislation that had characterized Smith's 12-year tenure as chairman.

Two liberal members had been added to the committee, thus creating a more secure liberal majority, and a set of rules had been introduced to govern committee procedure. The rules took from the chairman the right to set meeting dates, a power Smith frequently had used to postpone or thwart action on bills backed by liberals or the administration. They also required the consent of a majority to table a bill and set limits on proxy voting.

The committee's latent powers of obstruction were partially obscured as long as it forbore to flaunt them, but in the closing days of the 91st Congress in 1970 the committee reverted to its old ways by refusing to clear two major bills for House floor action. The bills—one to establish an independent consumer agency and the other to strengthen the Equal Employment Opportunity Commission—had been passed by the Senate and enjoyed broad support in the House. Acting in the absence of Richard Bolling (D Mo.), a liberal who usually voted with the majority, the committee by 7-7 tie votes refused to grant rules for the measures. This reminder of the committee's power over legislation gave rise to new demands for reform, but when the 92nd Congress convened a few weeks later, a coalition of Republicans and southern Democrats succeeded in killing a proposal to reinstitute a variation of the 21-day rule.

Madden's Chairmanship

Liberal Democrats predicted that a new era was at hand in 1973, when Colmer's retirement gave Ray J. Madden (Ind.) the chairmanship and permitted the leadership to fill Colmer's own seat with a loyal, national Democrat.[2]

Three Democrats joined Rules in 1973: Gillis W. Long (La.), Morgan F. Murphy (Ill.) and Clem Rogers McSpadden (Okla.). In a departure from past procedure, the Speaker and the majority leader sat on the panel that made the assignments. Only Long actively sought the job on hhs own. Murphy was boosted for it by allies in his Illinois delegation, while McSpadden was Speaker Carl Albert's (Okla.) hand-picked choice.

All three were chosen for the loyalty they were expected to show toward the leadership's program. "All McSpadden has to do is go along when Albert calls him up on something," one Democrat explained after the choices were announced. "We didn't put him on there to exercise his judgment on substantive questions of legislation." (McSpadden retired from the House to run, unsuccessfully, for governor in 1974.)

In 1973, the Rules Committee did the job the leadership expected it to do. It reported a great deal of liberal legislation to the floor without regard to its chances of passage. The House itself, more conservative than the Rules Committee for the first time in years, began looking critically at the bills it scheduled for floor action and at the rules under which they were to be debated.

Before 1973, the vast majority of the rules were approved with little opposition by the House; opponents of the legislation usually saved their fire for the bill itself. But in 1973, goaded into action by the new composition of the Rules Committee, conservative Republicans and Democrats began to attack the rules.

Between 1929 and 1972 the Rules Committee was beaten 50 times. In 1973 alone it was beaten 13 times, on issues as important as wage and price controls and as parochial as emergency assistance to eucalyptus farmers.

The most awkward defeat came on economic controls. In April the Banking and Currency Committee came out with a bill which would have rolled back prices to January 1973 levels. The Rules Committee was skeptical of the bill, but still granted a rule with a less drastic one-month rollback. When the new version reached the floor, the product of what seemed like endless wrangling between Rules, the Democratic leadership and the Banking and Currency Committee, the House refused to accept it. It then extended the expiring controls with authority for the President to control wages and prices in whatever way he saw fit.

Of the committee's 1973 record, B.F. Sisk (D Calif.) said: "It caused some of us to step back and think a bit, and to discuss with the leadership whether there was sufficient support to carry some of the programs they might have desired."

Others took the position that the Rules Committee should not feel responsible. "It's not a reflection on the rule," said Long. "It's a reflection on the basic legislation."

Criticism in 1974

Having just about shed its old obstructionist image in 1973 by sending a flood of liberal legislation to the floor, the Rules Committee came under renewed criticism in 1974, after rejecting two major bills in little more than a week in February and March.

On Feb. 26, the committee voted not to let the full House consider a bill establishing national guidelines for land use. Eight days later, it blocked a House-Senate conference report on an urban mass transit subsidy bill that had already been passed by both houses. Just two weeks before that, the committee had bucked the House Democratic leadership by sending emergency energy legislation to the floor under guidelines that would have placed in jeopardy a provision rolling back the price of crude oil. Under prodding from Speaker Albert, the House revised the committee's rule on the floor.

Case Studies. A look at the way the Rules Committee handled two of the bills before it in 1974 revealed quite a bit about the committee and the way it worked. But it offered little evidence that the committee had declared its independence from the House leadership.

The committee supplied a textbook demonstration of its powers of delay when it twice refused to permit floor action on a bill to set up plans for voluntary conversion to the metric system in the United States. On Oct. 25, 1973, and again on Feb. 26, 1974, the committee declined to grant the bill a rule. On March 6, it met again and finally approved a rule by a vote of 10-3, with Sisk voting present.

Within the committee, Dave Martin (R Neb.) led the opposition and was in part responsible for the delay. He felt conversion to a metric system would be awkward and expensive for small businessmen in the western Nebraska district he represented. But Madden also played a key role. He was sensitive to objections by the AFL-CIO that the bill would provide inadequate protection for workers who lost

their jobs when plants changed over to the metric system. As chairman, Madden had the procedural weapons to delay the bill's progress. "Ray just didn't want to take it up," said Sisk. "He kept stalling it off, and stalling it off."

On emergency energy legislation, the Rules Committee found itself in a doubly awkward position. It broke with the leadership in the way it sent a conference report to the floor, then found itself overruled by the House the next day.

The conference report on the bill (S 2589) reached the Rules Committee Feb. 20. S 2589 contained a new provision, drafted by the conference committee, rolling back crude oil prices, and it was the price rollback that became the central issue.

The Democratic leadership, along with Commerce Committee Chairman Harley O. Staggers (D W.Va.), wanted the conference report sent to the floor under a rule barring points of order against it. That way, no House member would have an opportunity to vote separately on language added in conference that was not germane to the original House or Senate versions.

But a coalition of Republicans and oil-state Democrats was adamant against such a rule because it wanted a separate vote in which the price rollback could be removed. And it was this coalition that prevailed in the Rules Committee. All five Republicans, and four southern Democrats voted in favor of a rule permitting a separate vote.

The next day, on the House floor, John B. Anderson (R Ill.) explained the Rules Committee's action. He said it was a reminder to conferees that they were agents of the House, "not a supercommittee which may impose new positions on both houses."

But the House voted 144-259 against a motion to adopt the rule as offered by the committee. The House then passed the bill by a 258-151 vote, the President vetoed it, and the veto was upheld in the Senate.

Commenting on the independence of the Rules Committee, Anderson said, "Basically it has to be an arm of the leadership. But it can only be an arm of the leadership when there's strong leadership. When there isn't, the committee is likely to...ride off in all directions."

In an attempt to strengthen the Democratic leadership's control over the Rules Committee, the party caucus voted in December 1974 to give the Speaker the power to nominate all Democratic members of the panel, subject to caucus approval. Using this power, Albert nominated liberals John Joseph Moakley (Mass.) and Andrew Young (Ga) to fill two vacant positions.

"By the mid-1970s," concluded Ripley, "the Democrats on the Rules Committee had become reliable supporters of the leaders. It seems unlikely that party leaders would sanction committee appointments that might jeopardize future control of the committee by the majority party."[3]

---

1. For background and history of the Rules Committee, cf. George Goodwin Jr., *The Little Legislatures* (University of Massachusetts Press, 1970), pp. 182 ff; James A. Robinson, *The House Rules Committee* (Indianapolis, Bobbs-Merrill Co., 1963); and Legislative Reference Service, "A Short History of the Development of the House Committee on Rules," *Congressional Record,* 86th Congress, 2nd sess., 1960, pp. 7098-99.

2. The discussion of the committee in 1973 and 1974 is based on an article appearing in the March 30, 1974, Congressional Quarterly *Weekly Report,* pp. 804-10.

3. Randall B. Ripley, *Congress: Process and Policy* (W.W. Norton & Co., Inc., 1975), p. 113.

Development of Committee Staffs

Staff members of committees in Congress have been credited with doing much of the legislative work undertaken during each congressional session.

Commenting in 1943, Rep. Charles M. La Follette (R Ind.) pointed to the need for professional committee staffs on Capitol Hill. "It is rather asinine for the Congress to appropriate millions of dollars, yes, even billions of dollars, for the staffing of the executive branch of the government with lawyers, statisticians, engineers, and economists, and fail to have the courage to set up a similar body for themselves and to appropriate ample funds for obtaining the best impartial body of experts in America upon any and all legislative subjects," he said.[1]

Three years later, Congress took La Follette's concern to heart, passing the 1946 Legislative Reorganization Act, which allowed committees to hire their own staffs to assist them. The professional and clerical employees of committees increased in both size and quality after passage of the act. Total number of committee staffers rose from fewer than 400 in 1946 to nearly 4,000 in 1975.

Such growth caused some members of Congress to complain about a "government of staffs." "We are having legislation by staff rather than by elected officials," said Sen. Carl T. Curtis (R Neb.) in 1959. "Far be it from me to challenge the qualifications of any of the staff members. So far as I know, all of them are brilliant and well educated, but they are not elected by anyone. They do not represent the people. They are not answerable to the people. The public does not know who they are."[2]

Other members of Congress, however, have contended that additional staff employees were needed by committees. They cited the following reasons:

● Paucity in staffing has led to shifting of the initiative in policymaking to the executive branch.

● Understaffing of standing committees has forced a proliferation of special investigating committees and subcommittees, each with their own staffs.

● Some committee staffs are so small they cannot do effective research.

Lack of Staffs in Early Days

Senators and representatives were reluctant during the early years of Congress to admit that they required staff assistance for committees, or for that matter in their own personal offices. William L. Morrow wrote in his book *Congressional Committees,* "Legislators were considered more erudite than most citizens and they believed any suggestion for staff assistance might be interpreted as a lack of confidence in their ability to master their jobs."[3] Thus, most chairmen kept the records of their own committees in the early part of the 19th century, although some committees occasionally hired clerks during heavy legislative periods.

Various motions to employ permanent clerks were rejected by Congress until about 1840 when, after pleas by chairmen, some clerical assistance was allowed in emergencies on a per diem or hourly basis. Funds for the part-time assistants were made available through special appropriations.[4]

Only four clerks were employed by House committees in 1853. In 1856, the House Ways and Means and the Senate Finance Committees became the first committees to obtain regular appropriations for full-time clerks. Other committees followed, but their staffing generally was limited to persons hired for housekeeping duties—clerks, stenographers and receptionists. Committee activities and drafting of bills usually were handled by members or their personal aides. After the middle of the 19th century, however, several of the more important committees began to appoint full-time clerks. By 1893, 41 House committees employed clerks on an annual basis and a large number of clerks and messengers for the duration of a session of Congress.

Increased Hiring at Turn of Century

It was not until about 1900, according to George B. Galloway, that appropriations acts began to carry items specifying funds for the standing committees in both houses.[5] The first comprehensive legislative pay bill authorizing appropriations for all legislative employees, including committee clerks, was enacted in 1924. That act appropriated $270,100 for 141 Senate committee clerks and $200,490 for 120 House committee employees.

Committee staffs and personal office staffs of members have been separated by an ill-defined line, both in practice and by statute, although the 1946 Legislative Reorganization Act states that the professional staff members of committees "shall not engage in any work other than committee business, and no other duties may be assigned to them." Staff aides on relatively inactive committees often have been used to supplement members' office forces. Under the express provisions of the Legislative Pay Act of 1929, when a senator assumed the chairmanship of a committee, the three senior clerks on his office staff became *ex officio* clerk and assistant clerks of that committee. Further, the act stipulated that the clerical employees of a Senate committee also would serve as secretarial workers for the chairman of the committee.[6] The differentiation between senators' personal and committee staffs was further weakened by passage in 1975 of S Res 60, allowing senators to hire their own additional staff to help them with their committee duties.

Changes Under 1946 and 1970 Acts

One of the major changes brought about by the Legislative Reorganization Act of 1946 was the creation of professional committee staffs. Prior to passage of the act, the Joint Committee on the Organization of Congress reported in 1946 a "shocking lack" of skilled staff and proposed, in order to lessen congressional dependence on executive departments and on interest groups, the appointment of qualified committee personnel "without regard to political affiliation" and with qualifications determined by a director of congressional personnel. The proposed personnel director was dropped, but the other committee recommendations were adopted.[7]

1946 Reorganization. Committee staffing underwent substantial change after passage of the Legislative Reorganization Act of 1946. The number of standing committees in the Senate was reduced from 33 to 15 and in the

---

Committee Investigators

Every committee of Congress is to some degree an investigative unit. Each professional staff member is usually part investigator in discharging his duty of keeping the members on the committee well informed. But some committee staff personnel are hired specifically for investigative work.

Many committees, whether they have regular staff investigators or not, occasionally use the research services of other agencies. The General Accounting Office (GAO) and the Federal Bureau of Investigation (FBI) are two of the agencies used by committees seeking additional investigative help.

Investigative budgets account for only a part of each committee's expenditures. Permanent staff positions are budgeted under separate legislation. For fiscal 1976, the House authorized a $21.2-million investigative budget for 21 committees. The corresponding fiscal 1976 budget request for investigations by Senate committees was $23-million, compared to $16.6-million for the previous year. The increase in committee investigating staffs was due partly to the creation of new oversight subcommittees and expansion of the number of subcommittees. *(See also Congressional Oversight, p. 374 and Congressional Investigations, p. 141)*

House from 48 to 19, and the jurisdiction of each committee was more strictly defined. Early in the 1947 session, the Republican-controlled Congress added four new select and special committees to the roster of standing committees set up by the reorganization act. In subsequent years, a number of other special and select committees were created, but the standing committee structure remained essentially unchanged.

Committees were allowed by the 1946 act to hire four professional staff members and up to six clerical workers each, "without regard to political affiliations and solely on the basis of fitness to perform the duties of the office." The Appropriations Committees, however, were allowed to determine the number of their employees by a majority vote of the committee. Thus, the total number of staff employees allowed under the 1946 act was 340, plus the additional numbers needed by the Appropriations Committees.

The size of committee staffs has fluctuated above that level during much of the time since the law was passed. Additional staff members have been acquired through the adoption of resolutions in each house authorizing an increase in personnel. Some members have believed that use of special resolutions has given better control over the size of staffs than would have resulted from amending the 1946 act.

The establishment of more than 125 special and select subcommittees in subsequent years also increased staff hiring. Most subcommittees were authorized for a specific time period, to investigate a legislative or national problem, and were then to pass out of existence. But many of these subcommittees have continued to receive increasing appropriations, and consequently have become more firmly established, with larger staffs.

The 1946 act vested the hiring and firing function in the committee majority, although the general pattern was to delegate the power to the chairman, who often consulted with the ranking minority member. Usually, chairmen were able to obtain the funds they wanted from the House Administration and Senate Rules Committees and enjoyed flexibility in spending the funds.

1970 Reorganization. Passage of the Legislative Reorganization Act of 1970 (PL 91-510) brought significant changes in committee staffing procedures. As enacted, the law:

● Increased to six from four the number of permanent professional staff members for each standing committee. Two members of the professional staff, in addition to one of the six permanent clerical staff members, might be selected by a majority of the committee's minority party members. This provision did not apply to the House and Senate Appropriations Committees or to the House Committee on Standards of Official Conduct.

● Authorized standing committees—with the approval of the Senate Rules and Administration or House Administration Committee—to hire temporary consultants.

● Authorized standing committees—with the approval of the Senate Rules and Administration or House Administration Committee—to provide staff members with specialized training.

● Authorized salaries of Senate committee staff personnel comparable to those of House committee staff personnel.

● Redesignated the Legislative Reference Service in the Library of Congress as the Congressional Research Service, redefined its duties to assist congressional committees by providing research and analytical services, records, documents and other information and data, including memoranda on proposed legislation, and expanded its staff resources.

● Required that no less than one-third of a House committee's funds be used for minority staff. (The House, however, voted in 1971 to disregard this provision. It was revived in 1974 but killed again in 1975. *See below, p. 392*)

Expansion of Committee Staffs

The growth in size of committee staffs has been given a hard look by many economy-minded senators and representatives in recent years.

In December 1947, one year after the 1946 Reorganization Act went into effect, House committees employed 254 persons, according to a 1963 statistical study of House committee staffing prepared by the Legislative Reference Service. By December 1969, according to the *Congressional Record* of Jan. 28, 1970, a total of 917 House committee and subcommittee staff members were employed.

Senate committee employees in 1946 numbered approximately 150. But in March 1970, the total for all Senate committee and subcommittee aides stood at 728, according to figures compiled by the Senate Committee on Rules and Administration.

In a report issued June 5, 1975, the Senate Rules and Administration Committee projected 1,262 committee staff members in 1975, plus an additional 1,073 for the new committee staff personnel for individual senators authorized earlier in the year.[8] A report of the House Appropriations Committee on fiscal 1976 legislative branch funds noted that total authorized personnel for standing committees would rise from 380 in 1974 to 608 in 1975, excluding the Committees on Appropriations and the Budget, which had no ceilings on the number of employees that could be hired.[9] (The 1975 *Congressional Staff Directory* listed 38 and 62 employees, respectively, for those committees.) The committee also noted that special and select committee staffs had increased from 485 in 1971 to 706 in 1974 and were expected to be "considerably larger" in 1975.

Because senators generally serve on three times as many committees as House members, they often must lean more heavily on committee staffs for information and assistance. One consequence has been that House staffs have been smaller than their Senate counterparts. For example, the Senate Judiciary Committee had 177 employees in 1975 while the House Education and Labor Committee, which had the largest staff of any legislative committee in the House, had an average monthly staff of about 100 employees that year, according to the panel's personnel office.[10] (The number of employees on Senate and House committee staffs fluctuates monthly, with employment of summer interns, temporary investigators, etc.)

Recruitment and Tenure. Most committee aides and clerks have been appointed by the chairman or the ranking minority member, as a perquisite of office, subject only to nominal approval of the full committee. Their tenure generally was subject to the political and mortal hazards of the members who hired the employees. Turnover on committee staffs was great but some staffers made working for committees a career.

Even the most partisan members of Congress generally agree that competence has become a basic criterion for appointment to the professional staff. Practically all major staff members have college degrees; many are lawyers or have other advanced study experience.

A survey of 217 biographies of committee employees listed in the 1968 edition of the *Congressional Staff Directory* showed that nearly half of the group had law degrees and a significant number had had teaching or journalistic experience. Sixty-two had had previous congressional jobs before joining the committee that employed them during the 90th Congress, while 82 had had previous experience in the executive branch.[11]

The value of professional committee staffs as a source of information and assistance was described by one senior member of the House in 1966. "I would like to emphasize...the importance of the committee staff, the professional staff, many of whom, such as on Ways and Means, have been with us for years," he said. "A good bit of the staffs on most of the committees are not on a partisan basis. They are professional people, there to serve all members of the committee, and you frequently find in dealing with another committee, as well as your own committee, that the best source of information will be from the staff members, as well as the assistance that they can give you in following a piece of legislation that you are interested in before another committee or even following it before your own committee."[12]

Committee Organization. The majority of congressional committees tend to have dual staffs, one professional and one clerical. These are generally headed by a "staff director" and a "chief clerk," respectively.[13]

Although the distinction between professional and clerical staff is blurred on many committees, the duties of each can be roughly separated. The clerical staff is responsible for keeping the committee calendar up to date, for processing committee publications, for referring bills to the appropriate departments for comment, for preparing the bill dockets, for maintaining the files, for stenographic work, and for opening and sorting mail.

Professional staffers are primarily responsible for policy matters handled by the committee. They fill the need for legal, public relations, statistical, accounting, investigative and other technical services.

Salaries. Amounts appropriated for salaries of committee staff members increased dramatically during the period from 1945 to 1970. Some top executive staffers now earn almost as much as members themselves. In 1945, each House employee was listed under "clerk hire" with annual base pay of $2,500. But during the next 25 years, there were 17 federal pay raises.

The 1970 reorganization act converted the "base pay" system of the House into a monthly salary system and raised the compensation of committee employees. By 1975, the highest paid professional and clerical members of committee staffs were receiving an annual salary of nearly $40,000.

For fiscal 1976, the House appropriated $20,766,000 for committee expenses and staff salaries, an increase of $8,792,385 over the fiscal 1975 appropriation. The Senate appropriated $8,934,592 for its committees in fiscal 1976, an increase of $440,072 over the previous year. An additional $3.5-million was authorized for new staff positions for individual committee members. Congress authorized an appropriation of $4,307,495 for operation of joint committees in fiscal 1976.

However, the total cost of running committees is much greater—although almost impossible to determine because of the way Congress keeps its books.

But one large addition is clear: funds for committee investigators. The appropriations noted above are for regular

Senators' Use of Committee Staffs for Personal Work

A series of articles by Stephen Isaacs appearing in *The Washington Post* Feb. 16-24, 1975, described how numerous senators diverted committee staff personnel to non-committee work. The study was based on statistics, gathered by the paper's data processing staff, fed to an IBM computer.

The survey showed that about one-third of all senators were using committee staffers for business not connected with their committee assignments. About the same number of senators were using committees to attract favorable publicity by conducting field hearings in their home states; 85.5 per cent of all field hearings held in the 93rd Congress (1971-73) were held in the home states of members of the committees holding the hearings. In addition, the study found that more than 10 per cent of Senate committee employees "work not in committee offices, but in the suites of their Senate members" and were usually engaged in work for the senators rather than committee business.

As an example, the Post Feb. 19 cited the Judiciary Subcommittee on Refugees and Escapees, chaired by Sen. Edward M. Kennedy (D Mass.). The panel was authorized to spend $182,000 in 1974, but no bills were referred to it in the 93rd Congress and the panel held only two days of hearings in 1974. Eleven people were on the payroll, but only four worked in the subcommittee's office. On the diversion of staff, Kennedy said, "It does happen. There are people that are on payrolls that are working on other responsibilities." Appearing before the Senate Committee on Rules and Administration Feb. 28, Kennedy said he did not question whether one senator should have more staff assistants than another, but added that "I do resent quite deeply, as just an individual member of the Senate, not being afforded the kind of staff opportunity to meet responsibilities as a member of the Senate.

"We are competing with a major executive office that has extraordinary kinds of resources in every possible area, and we are constantly being challenged to represent our interests and represent them in an important way," he said.

Among the explanations for diverting committee staff to personal business were the enormous growth of constituent business (requiring letters, casework, etc.), the lack of office space in committee offices, and the fact that senators had obligations on other committees that required staff help.

In the Senate, any chairman has the prerogative as to what he will do with the committee staff, but there has been increasing pressure to distribute staff among committee members. According to the Post (Feb. 18), Sen. Henry M. Jackson (D Wash.) controlled a Senate staff budget totaling $1,901,970 a year. During the period Jan. 1-June 30, 1974, Jackson's Interior Committee employed 38 people, 31 of whom were under Jackson's control. Six others were controlled by the six Republican members of the committee. Jackson also was chairman of the Permanent Investigations Subcommittee of the Government Operations Committee; in that position, he controlled 32 of the subcommittee's 42 employees, with Republicans controlling the rest. Commenting on the situation, Sen. Lee Metcalf (D Mont.), who had one staff member on the Interior Committee, said: "I think staff should be a professional staff that we use as a staff...and the lowest ranking person in seniority on the committee should have access to all of the staff for legislative work just the same as everybody else." But Jackson said, "I think the problem is that if each individual member has the staffing...you get away from the idea of a professional staff, acting for the whole committee."

Funds for committee staffs are authorized by the Senate Committee on Rules and Administration, chaired by Sen. Howard W. Cannon (D Nev.). Of his role, Cannon said, "I can't be a policeman. I can't ask a United States senator to stand before me and swear an oath as to what he's going to do with that money."

In introducing his resolution providing for committee staff for individual senators (the measure was passed in modified form), Sen. Mike Gravel (D Alaska) said: "We all know that hundreds of people come to work in the Senate every day who are on committee payrolls who do no committee work. They perform services for members not related to committee activities.... The only (way to get staff) is to curry the favor of one's committee chairman in the hopes of gaining additional staff.... Machinations take place, well hidden from public view, under layers of seniority, senatorial courtesy, private back-scratching and negotiations. I submit that this is a rather silly process in which grown men are involved. But we all do it...."

Part of the committee staff problem may be attributed to the cross-jurisdictions of committees, with staffs of several panels handling the same issues. In March 1975, Sens. Adlai E. Stevenson III (D Ill.) and Bill Brock (R Tenn.), along with 50 other senators, introduced a resolution to establish a select committee to study the Senate committee system with a view to restructuring it so as to create more and better staffs and more effective and relevant committees. (A similar proposal in the 93rd Congress foundered when it ran up against opposition from senior Senate members.)

Sources: Articles by Stephen Isaacs in Feb. 16, 17, 18, 19, 20, 22, 23, 24, 1975. *The Washington Post:* Congressional Quarterly, Weekly Report, March 8, 1975, p. 496.

committee expenses; investigative funds are provided separately. In 1975, the Senate authorized an investigative budget of $19.4-million for 22 standing committees, and the House authorized $21.2-million for 21 committees. *(Details on committee investigative work, Investigations chapter p. 141)*

The true cost of running committees, including staff expenses, undoubtedly is much larger. For example, *The Washington Post* in early 1975 reported on research it had conducted into Senate committee costs. In a Feb. 16 article it placed total Senate committee expenses in the 93rd Congress at $54-million. According to the Post, the total cost is higher than the sum formally appropriated for committees at the beginning of each session. By law, the Senate has to publish a listing of all its payments, but the outlays are listed chronologically which makes it extremely difficult to determine how much a committee is spending. The Post did much of its work by feeding the published Senate data into a computer.

Both the House and the Senate are required by law to publish every six months a report on salaries, allowances and expenses paid to members, their personal and committee staffs. They are published in book form and called "Report of the Secretary of the Senate" and "Report of the Clerk of the House." The House in the past has not been as open as the Senate in detailing its monthly reports of staff salaries; however, the House Administration Committee adopted a new reporting requirement in June 1976. *(See p. 465)* House committee travel vouchers are not available for public scrutiny.

Description of Work

Committee aides, working within the jurisdiction of the committee and in close association with members, generate and shape much of the legislation considered by Congress. A classic example of committee staff work has been given by Stephen K. Bailey in his book, *Congress Makes a Law,* which describes the passage of the Full Employment Act of 1946 and shows how staff gathered basic economic data, prepared the case for the bill and arranged committee hearings.[14]

As George Goodwin has noted, "The amount of staff influence will vary with congressional and staff concepts of the proper role for committee staff, as well as with the amount of time committee members can give to overseeing staff work."[15]

Following are the major functions performed by committee staffs:[16]

● **Organizing Hearings.** Staffers set up hearings on legislation and current issues. They select witnesses, prepare questions, inform the press, brief committee members, and occasionally substitute for members or chairmen who cannot attend hearings. In many instances a member will prepare a list of questions for aides to ask witnesses if he cannot be present.

● **Investigations.** Much original research is conducted by staff members on issues which come before a committee. This usually involves looking into existing legislation, court decisions and current practices. Aides often travel to areas under consideration by the committee, and sometimes hold regional hearings to get opinions from citizens interested in certain legislation.

● **Bill and Amendment Drafting.** Although staff members occasionally may actually write bills and amendments, they usually serve as liaison between the Office of the Legislative Counsel, committee members, government agencies and special interest groups during the drafting of measures.

● **Preparing Reports.** Committee reports to accompany bills are almost entirely staff products. Often the reports are the only reference concerning the legislative matter being considered. Staff aides consult with the chairman or the majority to decide what should be emphasized in the report, including minority views. Then the staff writes the report, usually conforming to a standard format. Reports usually include three basic ingredients—the main body, which explains the bill and gives background and interpretation; the section-by-section analysis of the provisions of the bill, and a written comparison of the bill with existing law.

● **Preparation for Floor Action.** Staff aides assist in marking up bills by explaining technical provisions, outlining policy questions, analyzing proposed changes, following committee decisions and incorporating the decisions in successive revisions of the bill. The top committee aides often will accompany a bill's sponsor in the House or Senate to assist him during the floor action.

● **Conference Committee Work.** Staffs of correspondending committees in each house work together on preparation of conference reports and in resolving differences in a bill passed by both the House and the Senate.

● **Lobby Liaison.** Staff aides communicate frequently with lobbyists on legislative proposals before the committee. Some members regard this activity as the most consequential of all staff work. Rep. Bob Eckhardt (D Texas) said in September 1969: "The key point of contact is usually between a highly specialized lobbyist and the specialized staff people of a standing committee. Intimate friendships spring up there—it's the rivet point. Friendships that outlast terms. They probably have a greater influence on legislation, especially if it's technical."

As Kenneth Kofmehl noted in a 1962 study of professional committee staffs, "Most of the relations between committee aides and the staffs of organized interest groups in their fields centered around the exchange of various kinds of information. Often they were on each other's mailing lists.... The prevailing flow of information was from the interest groups to the committee staffs.... Generally, committee staffs turned to organized interest groups for data not available elsewhere. But fairly often, committee staff members secured information from them as a check on that supplied by the executive branch. In this regard, a number of committee aides observed that their efficiency was considerably increased through the operations of interest group representatives.[17]

A 1963 study of Washington lobbyists found that, when asked about the best contacts on Capitol Hill, 25 per cent of a sample of lobbyists named committee staff members. This was the single largest category—followed by 24 per cent naming staffs of executive agencies and 23 per cent naming members of Congress.[18]

Minority Staffing

A continuing controversy about committee staffing is the question of hiring employees affiliated with the minority party. Because the chairman's prerogative has usually prevailed in placing staff members on his committee, most employees have tended to be from the majority party.

The 1946 Legislative Reorganization Act did not contain any provision for apportioning the professional staff of a committee between the chairman and ranking minority member. The act simply stated that "said staff members shall be assigned to the chairman and ranking minority member of such committee as the committee may deem advisable." Until 1970, committees interpreted this provision in various ways; moreover, the quota of minority employees for a given committee sometimes fluctuated from Congress to Congress, "depending on the generosity of the chairman."[19]

Writing in 1961, columnist Roscoe Drummond deplored the lack of minority staffing for House committees, stating, "If the Republican members of Congress are ever to be in a position to clarify, expound and defend their stand on the major issues...and to advance constructive alternatives of their own, they must get a steady flow of adequate, reliable, competent research and information from an adequate,

---

Cloak of Anonymity

Philip W. Kelliher, counsel for the House Armed Services Committee, used poetry to describe the role of staff members in 1962:

"Silent he sits
Amid the applause,
Words,
His words still echoing in his ears.
Warmed only by an inward smile
The pro, the cynosure of no one,
Basks in the infra red light
Of anonymity."

Source: George Goodwin, Jr., *The Little Legislatures* (University of Massachusetts Press, 1970).

---

reliable and competent professional staff. This staff must be in the service of the minority, selected by the minority, and working for it."[20]

Other observers and members of both houses have argued that the balance of committee personnel between the two parties should more nearly approximate the division of party strength in the House or Senate, or in the individual committee. Non-partisan staffing also has been advocated, but some critics feel that a non-partisan staff would be nothing more than a funnel for the views of the departments whose operations most nearly coincide with the fields of interest of the respective committees.

Noted Ripley in 1975, "For policy-related committee staff positions chairmen usually hire individuals from their own party who share their general policy orientation. Ranking minority members appoint members who share their party and political orientation.... Even though hiring is on a partisan basis, retention of professional staff members may be non-partisan.... Nor is there a necessary conflict between a partisan staff and a professional staff. Individuals whose hiring and tasks are imbued with partisanship may simultaneously be first-rate professionals. In general, congressional staffs have become increasingly professional although they may well have remained at about the same level of partisanship."[21]

House Changes. Access to staff for minority members of House committees was facilitated by the 1970 Legislative Reorganization Act, which provided for at least three full-time staff aides for the minority on most congressional committees. In January 1971, however, the House voted to delete a section of the act providing that one-third of committee investigative funds be used for minority staff members. The Democratic Caucus by a vote had bound all House Democrats to vote for the deletion, an action which angered Republicans and revealed as clearly as any action in recent times the importance which attaches to the issue of congressional staffing.

The minority staffing issue surfaced again in late 1974, as representatives debated the House committee reorganization plan.

Under that plan, Republicans would be given 10 of 30 staff members assigned to committees by statute and one-third of the investigative staff for subcommittees allotted by the House Administration Committee. But when the Democratic Caucus met in January 1975, Jack Brooks (D Texas) introduced a resolution to nullify the one-third minority staffing guarantee for subcommittees. The caucus

finally agreed to a compromise under which the statutory staff for committees was increased to 42, with the majority party getting 26 and the minority 16. In effect, each side received six additional staff members to be used for subcommittees. The guarantee of one-third minority investigatory staff was removed.

The minority staffing compromise produced one of the most significant changes of the many revisions made in House rules over the period 1970-75. The compromise allowed subcommittee chairmen and ranking minority members to hire one staff person to work on their subcommittees. This new authority was seen as crucial to strengthening the subcommittees and giving minority members a meaningful opportunity to influence legislation. In general, dispersing power among committee members and reducing the authority of House committee chairmen also meant a dispersal of control over committee staffs and budget in 1975. *(See section on subcommittees, p. 382)*

Senate Staff Increases. The Senate dealt with the committee staff issue in a different way in 1975, when junior senators obtained committee staff assistance to aid them on legislative issues.[22] In the past, committee staff members had been controlled by chairmen and other senior committee members. Few junior members had regular and dependable access to staff personnel.

The junior members launched their campaign to get extra staff help when the 94th Congress convened in January 1975. They were finally victorious in June, when the Senate adopted a resolution (S Res 60) that gave senators new authority to hire staff persons responsible directly to them to assist on committee legislative work. The resolution allowed a senator to hire up to three staffers at a maximum annual salary of a total of $101,925 for a senator.

The number of staffers a given senator would get would depend on which committees he served and how many. The resolution was written in a way intended to prevent a senator who currently had staff on a committee from getting more staff for that committee. Thus, the resolution directly benefitted junior senators who had been excluded from staff help because of their low status on committees, and prevented senior senators from getting more staff help. The plan cut directly into the traditional power base that senior members enjoyed through their control of committee staff—and it was opposed by many of them for just that reason.

Specifically, the resolution allowed senators serving on certain major committees to hire one staff aide for each of two of the committees. These units were: Aeronautical and Space Sciences; Agriculture; Appropriations; Armed Services; Banking; Budget; Commerce; Finance; Foreign Relations; Government Operations; Interior; Judiciary; Labor and Public Welfare; and Public Works.

In addition, senators who had certain other committee assignments were allowed to hire one staff member. This category applied to senators serving on the following committees: District of Columbia; Post Office and Civil Service; Rules and Administration; and Veterans Affairs. It also applied to senators serving on more than two of the major standing committees named in the previous paragraph and to senators serving on select, special or joint committees.

The resolution specified that any staff person hired under its provision would have all the privileges of a regular professional committee staff member. The resolution was adopted June 12 by a 63-35 vote after cloture was invoked, 77-19, June 11 on a filibuster against the proposal. Subsequently, an appropriation of $3.5-million for fiscal 1976 was authorized to pay for the increased staff. It was estimated that implementation of the resolution would add 1,073 committee-related employees to the 1,262 regular committee staff members projected for the Senate in 1975, and would increase the cost of Senate staffing by almost $41 million a year.

During the lengthy debate on the measure, Sen. Mike Gravel (D Alaska), who introduced the original resolution, argued, "When we go up to the floor to vote, half, or more than half, the time we do not know what we are voting on until we ask the gentleman in the back of the room, or somebody at the front of the room and they tell us how to vote. They will give a thumbnail sketch, on the substance of the issue—on something that had maybe 20 hours debate—in half a minute.

"That is the informational process we have here. We are like blind men running to the Senate, like sheep with no knowledge of what is going on except when we get to the chamber itself."

Herman E. Talmadge (D Ga.), who opposed the additional staff proposal, countered by saying the Senate committees needed staffs "who know what they are doing, and if we have every senator who serves on a committee appointing a member of the professional staff who is not acceptable to the committee, we will have things so fouled up it will be like the Army going to sea."

Size and Professionalism

Although the quality of committee staffs remains high in most cases, recommendations for employment of more professional staff workers have come from diverse quarters. Private research groups and members themselves have pointed to increased committee workloads, emphasized the importance of having specialists for each of the major jurisdictions of a technical committee, and complained that, in the face of the more generous staffing of executive agencies, the Congress is frustrated in its efforts to perform properly its surveillance function.

A report entitled "Making Congress More Effective," issued in September 1970 by the Committee for Economic Development, called for expert capabilities in committee staffs. The report said in part:

"We recommend that Congress strengthen its staff resources by recruitment of highly qualified specialists—physical scientists, engineers, environmentalists, physicians, economists and other social scientists, nutritionists, mathematicians, management experts, and others as occasion may require.

"Some of these resources should be pooled—as in the Legislative Reference Service and the General Accounting Office—where every committee would have access to the best technical and analytical service. Minority staffing is essential, and could also be pooled in party policy or research committees. Serious attention should be given to professional training and development of all these staffs. Special attention to data collection problems is urgently needed."[23]

Perhaps a more realistic view was offered by George H.E. Smith of the Senate Republican Policy Committee in a "Memo on Staff Organization" in 1946: "In certain committees dealing with statistics and similar factual data, it will be possible in time to build a professional staff capable of serving both political parties alike. The nature of the subject matter itself minimizes partisan leanings.... Nonpartisan staff operations will not be so easily achieved in other

Office of the Legislative Counsel

The Office of the Legislative Counsel was created in 1919 under the Revenue Act of 1918. Originally called the Legislative Drafting Service, the office was established to provide professional assistance to members in the drafting of legislation. Each chamber has its own chief counsel, appointed in one case by the Speaker of the House and in the other by the president pro tempore of the Senate. Each counsel has a legal staff of between 11 and 20 persons.

Members who want to introduce a bill on a specific subject rely on the lawyers in the Office of the Legislative Counsel to put the proposal into legislative language. The lawyers analyze and research the precedents, compare the bill with existing laws, and sometimes suggest alternatives. Title V of the Legislative Reorganization Act of 1970 reconstituted the House office, upgrading its responsibilities and making its services more readily available to individual House members.

Although the Office of the Legislative Counsel continues to perform important service in the drafting of bills, there is a growing tendency on the part of executive branch agencies and even of some outside pressure groups to have their own experts draft the bills introduced on their behalf by members of Congress.

For fiscal 1976, the Senate and House authorized an appropriation of $1,749,110 for the office.

Sources: For background, cf. George B. Galloway, *Congress at the Crossroads* (Thomas Y. Crowell Co., 1946), p. 93; and Kenneth Kofmehl, *Professional Staffs of Congress* (Purdue Research Foundation, 1962), pp. 183-203, 229.

committees where political differences generate sharp controversies. This is likely to be the case with the greater number of committees."[24]

"Thoughtful members and staff members alike express concern about the development of independent influence on the part of staffers," noted Ripley in 1975. "Staff members are, of course not elected but speak in the name of individuals who are.... Perhaps the most serious threat is that professional staff members in Congress may join with civil servants in the executive branch and representatives of interest groups to dominate policy in a variety of specialized areas. None of these individuals directly represents any segment of the electorate.... (A) growing bureaucratization of Congress may reduce its representative character."[25]

The optimum size of congressional committee staffs poses another problem. "There is considerable sentiment for continuing to expand the staffs of Congress as a major way of seeking to offset the superior numbers and superior informational base of the executive branch," wrote Ripley. "There has also been some opposition simply to continuing the expansion of numbers.... First, large staffs have the potential of becoming uncontrollable bureaucracies. Second, as staffs get larger there is probably a greater likelihood that staffers will simply perform chores for individual members that have little or no relation to the legitimate business of the committee—that is, every committee member will want his 'man' on the committee. Third, it is impossible for the size of congressional staffs ever to match the size of the executive bureaucracy with which they interact."[26]

Footnotes

1. Quoted in George B. Galloway, *Congress at the Crossroads* (Thomas Y. Crowell Co., 1946), p. 180.
2. Quoted in George Goodwin Jr., *The Little Legislatures* (University of Massachusetts Press, 1970), pp. 147-8.
3. William L. Morrow, *Congressional Committees* (Charles Scribner's Sons, 1969), p. 52.
4. For background, see Galloway, *Congress*, p. 91.
5. *Ibid.*, p. 91.
6. Kenneth Kofmehl, *Professional Staffs of Congress* (Purdue Research Foundation, 1962), p. 4.
7. Joint Committee on the Organization of Congress, *Organization of Congress* (S Rept 1011, pursuant to H Con Res 18, 79th Congress, 2nd sess., 1946), pp. 9-11; cited in Goodwin, *op. cit.*, p. 143.
8. S Rept 94-185, 94th Congress, 1st sess.
9. H Rept 94-208, 94th Congress, 1st sess., p. 9.
10. Data on committee size from *The Washington Post*, Feb. 24, 1975, "House Unit Expenses Hidden," p. 1.
11. Goodwin, *The Little Legislatures*, p. 146.

12. Donald G. Tacheron and Morris K. Udall, *The Job of a Congressman* (Bobbs-Merrill Co., Inc., 1966), pp. 170-71.
13. On staff organization, see Kofmehl, *Professional Staffs*, pp. 37-51.
14. Stephen K. Bailey, *Congress Makes a Law* (Columbia University Press, 1950).
15. Goodwin, *The Little Legislatures*, p. 147.
16. For a description of staff work, see Kofmehl, *Professional Staffs*, pp. 110-26; and Randall B. Ripley, *Congress: Process and Policy* (W.W. Norton & Co., Inc., 1975), pp. 159 ff.
17. Kofmehl, *Professional Staffs*, p. 162.
18. Lester W. Milbrath, *The Washington Lobbyists* (Rand McNally, 1963), p. 266; quoted in Ripley, *op. cit.*, p. 161.
19. Kofmehl, *Professional Staffs*, p. 55.
20. Quoted in Kofmehl, p. 212
21. Ripley, *Congress*, p. 162.
22. The following discussion on Senate changes is taken from Congressional Quarterly, 1975 *Weekly Report*, pp. 1235-6, 1294.
23. Committee for Economic Development, "Making Congress More Effective" (CED, N.Y., September 1970), p. 51.
24. Quoted in Goodwin, *The Little Legislatures*, p. 151.
25. Ripley, *Congress*, p. 164.
26. *Ibid.*, pp. 163-4.

Selected Bibliography

Books

Committee for Economic Development, "Making Congress More Effective." CED, New York, September, 1970.

Galloway, George B., *Congress at the Crossroads.* Thomas Y. Crowell Co., 1946.

Goodwin, George, Jr. *The Little Legislatures.* University of Massachusetts Press, 1970.

Gross, Bertram, *The Legislative Struggle.* McGraw-Hill Inc., 1953.

Kofmehl, Kenneth, *Professional Staffs of Congress.* Purdue Research Foundation, 1962.

McInnis, Mary, ed., *We Propose: A Modern Congress.* McGraw-Hill Inc., 1966.

Morrow, William L., *Congressional Committees.* Charles Scribner's Sons, 1969.

Ripley, Randall B., *Congress: Process and Policy.* W.W. Norton & Co., Inc., 1975.

Tacheron, Donald G., and Udall, Morris K., *The Job of the Congressman.* Bobbs-Merrill Co., Inc., 1966.

Articles

Isaacs, Stephen, articles in *The Washington Post*, Feb. 16-24, 1975.

Government Publications

U.S. Congress. House. Select Committee on Committees. *Working Papers on House Committee Organization and Operation: Committee Staffing;* by James A. Robinson. Committee Print, 93rd Cong., 1st sess. Washington: Government Printing Office, 1973.

———. *Working Papers on House Committee Organization and Operation: Improving Some Skills of Committee Staff*, by Walter Kravitz. Committee Print, 93rd Cong., 1st sess. Washington: Government Printing Office, 1973.

———. *Working Papers on House Committee Organization and Operation: Proposals for Meeting Congressional Staff Needs*, by John S. Saloma III. Committee Print, 93rd Cong., 1st sess. Washington: Government Printing Office, 1973.

———. *Working Papers on House Committee Organization and Operation: Staffing House Committees*, by Samuel C. Patterson. Committee Print, 93rd Cong., 1st sess. Washington: Government Printing Office, 1973.

———. *Working Papers on House Committee Organization and Operation: Three Major Aspects of House Committee Staffing*, by Kenneth Kofmehl. Committee Print, 93rd Cong., 1st sess. Washington: Government Printing Office, 1973.

U.S. Congress. Joint Committee on the Organization of the Congress. *Organization of Congress, Interim Report.* H. Rept. 89-426, 89th Cong., 1st sess., 1965.

———. *Organization of Congress, Second Interim Report.* H. Rept. 89-1218, 89th Cong., 2nd sess., 1966.

U.S. Library of Congress. Legislative Reference Service. *Statistical Study of the Staffing of Committees of the House of Representatives.* November 1963.

———. *Senate Committee Staffing.* S. Doc. 88-16, 88th Cong., 1st sess., 1963.

The Seniority System

Seniority—status based on length of service, to which are attached certain rights and privileges—pervades nearly all social institutions. But in no other political group has its sway been stronger than in the United States Congress. As Barbara Hinckley points out in her study, *The Seniority System in Congress*, "The seniority system is unique to the United States Congress. No other national legislative assemblies, no state legislatures use seniority as the sole criterion for choosing leaders."[1]

Until the 1970s there had been few concerted or successful attacks on a system that tended to reward members' electoral longevity with favorable committee assignments and powerful committee chairmanships. Beginning around 1970, however, liberal—often, the younger—members of both houses, aided by outside pressure groups, started to chip away at the system. By 1975 their efforts had taken their toll in the defeat of three of the most senior House committee chairmen. To John Gardner, chairman of the self-styled citizens' lobby Common Cause, the ouster of the three chairmen was "the final healthy act of demolition that brings the seniority system crashing down."[2]

The epitaph may have been premature. Other observers noted that most senior members held onto their positions of rank despite the restlessness of many freshmen and more liberal members of the 94th Congress who tried to make substantial inroads into the seniority system. Moreover, there remained considerable debate over whether the system should be abolished at all. Some observers seemed to agree with a comment made by Rep. Champ Clark (D Mo.), Speaker of the House from 1911-19. Speaking to the "Baby Congressmen" on "The Making of a Representative," Clark remarked: "A man has to learn to be a representative, just as he must learn to be a blacksmith, a carpenter, a farmer, an engineer, a lawyer, or a doctor." And, "as a rule," he continued, "the big places [on the committees] go to old and experienced members" of the House.[3]

"The seniority system is the least objectionable of all systems for elevation of men to chairmanships," contended Rep. Emanual Celler (D N.Y. 1923-73), dean of the House of Representatives in the 92nd Congress. "We have tried in the history of Congress all manner and kind of selection, and they have all been discarded because they were not flawless, they were objectionable."[4]

The power of chairmen—and senior committee members—is discussed more fully elsewhere *(p. 365)*, but sometimes, noted Rep. Richard Bolling (D Mo.), it "can heighten a member's self-esteem to the point of insolence." As an example, Bolling cites a remark by one committee chairman in the 1920s, who told his colleagues: "You can go to hell; it makes no difference what a majority of you decide; if it meets with my disapproval it shall not be done; I am the committee; in me reposes absolute obstructive power."[5]

Tradition, Not Rule

It is perhaps ironic that the seniority system itself, as it developed in the House, was a reform of the early 1900s when representatives revolted against the arbitrary leadership of the Speaker who often doled out chairmanships according to whim or favor. Seniority at least guaranteed that chairmanships and top minority positions went to those members who had been around the longest.

As it took hold, the seniority system assumed a role of major importance in Congress. It affected the assignment of office space, members' access to congressional patronage, the deference shown members on the floor—even invitations to dinner. But seniority was most apparent (and important) in the committee system: it played a significant role in determining assignments to committees and subcommittees as well as in selection of their chairmen.

Despite frequent references to a "seniority rule" and a "seniority system," observance of seniority in Congress has never been dictated by law or formal ruling. It developed as a tradition: the formal rules simply state that the House or Senate shall determine committee memberships and chairmen. Nonetheless, there have been very few violations of the system since it became firmly entrenched. *(Violations of seniority tradition, p. 402)*

Seniority on Capitol Hill is based on the length of service in Congress, referred to as congressional seniority; or on the length of consecutive service on a committee, called committee seniority. As it developed in both houses, the system dictated that the member with the most years of service, regardless of other qualifications (or limitations), generally would be given first choice of better office space, assignment to an important committee or election to a committee chairmanship.

Seniority inherently has been an ally of older members and of the congressional establishment. As such, younger members (and some older ones) periodically have brought it under attack. The application of seniority in doling out perquisites has seldom been questioned. Most of the debate has centered on the role of seniority in the committee system. *(For a fuller discussion of perquisites, see p. 457)*

Committee Seniority

Committee assignments are affected by factors other than strict seniority, such as party loyalty, regional distribution and the favor of the leadership. However, a member high on the seniority ladder is more apt to receive the assignment he seeks than one further down. Sometimes the failure to follow seniority in assignments creates resentment. Sen. Joseph S. Clark (D Pa.) staged a three-day protest in 1963 against the Senate Democratic committee-assignment process. Clark asserted that liberals who had sought changes in Senate procedures had not received committee assignments they were entitled to by seniority.

Once on a committee, a member is not dropped except in unusual circumstances. The most junior members of a committee may be bumped from it if elections change party ratios. Members have been purged from committees (or lost seniority in some cases) when they switched party allegiance or bolted the party during a presidential election. *(Seating and discipline of members, p. 681)*

The fact that committee seniority is not transferable affects members who wish to move from one committee to another. As one representative commented, "Now this presents a problem if, after you have been here a couple of terms, you decide you want to switch from one committee to another. If you switch from one committee to another you go on at the bottom of the new committee and start the seniority process all over again.... Some time in the future you may find the problem of transferring is that although you like another committee a little bit better, you will lose the seniority you have built up in the meantime on the committee to which you were first assigned."[6]

As a member rises in rank on a committee, his chances of being heard, of asking witnesses questions, and of handling major legislation increase. So too do his chances of heading a subcommittee, although the senior member of a subcommittee is not always selected to be chairman. (Until 1973 all subcommittee chairmen were appointed by the committee chairmen.) When a member of the majority party becomes senior on the committee, he is entitled to be chairman. The honor has seldom been declined in the House, where most members are restricted to one major committee assignment apiece. But it more frequently is declined in the Senate, where a senator may be senior on two or more committees but is generally restricted to one major committee chairmanship.

Traditionally, senior committee members have been picked to serve on the conference committees that iron out differences between House and Senate versions of a bill.

Congressional Seniority

The term "seniority rule" generally refers to length of service on a committee, not in Congress. However, a member's length of service as ranked on a scale with the entire party membership of his house has a significant bearing on his committee seniority.

At the beginning of each congressional session, members of each house are given a seniority ranking vis-a-vis their party colleagues. Senate rank generally is determined according to the official date of the beginning of a member's service, which is Jan. 3, except in the case of a new member sworn in after Congress is in session. For those elected or appointed to fill unexpired terms, the date of appointment, certification or swearing-in determines the senator's rank. When members are sworn in on the same date, custom decrees that those with prior political experience take precedence. Counted as political experience, in order of importance, are senatorial, House and gubernatorial service.

In the House, rank generally is determined according to the official date of the beginning of a member's service, which is Jan. 3 except in cases when a member has been elected to fill a vacancy. In such cases, the date of election determines the rank. When members enter the House on the same date, those with prior House service take precedence, starting with those with the longest consecutive service. Experience as a senator or governor is disregarded.

History of the Seniority System

The history of the seniority system in Congress has become inextricably tied to development of the committee system and to party control of assignments. Parties have relied on seniority as a widely recognized—and neutral—arbiter for settling intra-party quarrels over lucrative positions. On occasion, parties have threatened their recalcitrant members with loss of seniority. In a few cases, the threat has been carried out.

Hinckley has pointed to factors other than party dominance that had a bearing on the gradual entrenchment of the committee seniority system. The growing complexity of legislation led to pressures for specialization and "professionalization"; at the same time, House and Senate careers were growing longer.[7] According to Bolling, in 1868, only 98 out of 243 House members, or 40 per cent, had served in previous Congresses. But by January 1904, the House had only 71 first-term members (out of a total of 386). "Perhaps in the early 1800s the electorate felt that emoluments and status of office should be passed around, and more candidates competed," he commented. "Then, too, members found traveling to, and living conditions in Washington uncongenial. But the increasing complexity of the legislative process and the growth of urban political machines helped to change the trend.... The longer a member remains in the House, the greater his seniority. The defeat, retirement, or death of fellow committee members helps him up the ladder to the apex of power."[8]

Development in the Senate

The emergence of the seniority system in the Senate closely paralleled the development of the standing committee system. Until 1816 the Senate had no standing committees; late that year, however, eleven were authorized. Until 1823, members of these committees were selected by ballot by the entire membership. In the following decade, various methods of selection were used. "During much of the period before 1833, seniority for initial assignments and for rank on committees was so unimportant that chairmenships were rotated," noted Ripley in his book, *Power in the Senate.*[9]

The relative unimportance of seniority in these early years was due in large part to the weakness of the party system. Party lines were not clearly drawn, and there was

Impact of the Seniority System

Although it plays an important role, seniority is only one of many factors influencing selection of committee chairmen. Party ratios in Congress, initial committee assignments and subsequent transfers, the number of committee slots open due to death, resignation or shifts in assignment—all can play a role in elevation of a member to a committee chairmanship.

In his book *Congress: Process and Policy,* Ripley concludes that "in general, the impact of the seniority system is limited. The distribution of chairmanships is regionally biased, but these biases are not necessarily attributable to the operation of the seniority rule itself. Many may be due to initial decisions made about assignments to the committee. Only in the case of southern overrepresentation in the Democratic Party in the House and Senate is an obvious tie between the seniority system and regional overrepresentation present."[1]

Ripley's assessment concurs with that of Hinckley. She, too, concluded in a 1971 study that "the effect of the seniority system on the kind of committee chairmen selected by Congress is at most a limited one. Democratic committee chairmen or ranking minority members, taken as a group, reflect with fair accuracy the composition of the Democratic members in Congress, and the Republican leaders even more accurately reflect their party's membership. Thus southerners have filled more than 50 per cent of the Democratic committee chairs in the past two decades, and southerners have usually comprised more than 50 per cent of the Democratic membership of the House and Senate.

"The effect of the seniority system is limited because its requirement of continuous service in House or Senate can be met by a majority of congressmen. The majority of House and Senate seats are safe for the incumbents. Indeed, there are more congressmen qualified by long congressional service for committee chairs than there are chairs to be filled; hence factors other than congressional seniority...can and do influence the selection of chairmen."[2]

In her study of the seniority system, Hinckley found that Democratic members from rural districts were overrepresented by committee chairmen but that this was not true of Republicans. Nor were small states (by population) overrepresented in the Senate.

As to policy stands, the study showed Democratic committee chairmen to have some conservative bias, and some bias against support for their party or President, while Republican committee leaders followed almost exactly the same voting pattern as the rest of their party colleagues.[3]

Hinckley has concluded that the seniority system serves a useful purpose. "Congress differs from many other organizations in that it does not control the selection of its own members," she points out. "Members of Congress are elected by the voters. The seniority rule...provides a key organizational link between the party system and Congress and between the members of Congress and its leaders. Under the system, leaders are chosen from among the senior members, those who know well the organization's rules and customs. And they are chosen in a way that reinforces the main areas of strength, the established interests in the majority party in Congress. The process reflects fairly accurately the composition of the party in Congress as it has been formed over time.... It thus reinforces traditional areas of party strength. It helps the political parties to organize the Congress in a way that ensures that established *party* interests and established *congressional* interests will not conflict, and in a way that strengthens them both."[4]

"Finally, and crucially important in a Congress which is characterized by plural, decentralized leadership and multiple interests, and in which the political process requires the forming and reforming of coalitions, the seniority system offers stability in the distribution of influence. It offers *predictability* concerning who has power in what area. Such predictability would seem a necessary prerequisite for carrying on political business. Thus the seniority system offers something valuable to leaders—both party and committee leaders—and members alike, as well as to interested parties outside Congress."[5]

1. Ripley, Randall B., *Congress: Process and Policy* (W. W. Norton and Co. Inc. 1975), p. 98.
2. Hinckley, Barbara, *The Seniority System in Congress* (Indiana University Press, 1971), pp. 108-9.
3. *Ibid.,* p. 110.
4. *Ibid.,* p. 111.
5. *Ibid.,* pp. 112-13.

little political control over committee assignments. By 1846, however, party control had become so firm that committee assignment lists supplied by the parties were approved routinely. And with party domination of assignments also appeared the principle of seniority. Seniority was applied both to committee assignments and to advancement within a committee.

Strains within the parties developed over the slavery issue, however, and from 1849 to 1857 committee assignments were made by the president pro tempore, although they were still subject to party influence. During that period, according to Ripley, southern Democrats who dominated committee chairmanships "supported the hardening of seniority to protect their position so that they could defend slavery."[10]

During the Civil War and Reconstruction period between 1861 and 1875, when Democrats had virtually disappeared from Congress, Republican senators disregarded seniority in committee assignments. But seniority rapidly came to dominate committee advancement as the character of the post-Civil War Senate changed—as Democrats regained seats and as members, accumulating year after year of uninterrupted service, began to consider the Senate a career.

Figures supplied by Ripley show a dramatic increase in the length of Senate service between 1875 and 1893. Prior to

1875, the average senator in most Congresses had served about four years. In most of the post-1893 Congresses, the average length of Senate service had about doubled.[11] With increased professionalization, the seniority system hardened, until by the middle of the 20th century it was firmly entrenched in the Senate.

Ripley also attributes the hardening of the seniority system in the Senate to the fact that after 1875 Republicans had a sizable Democratic contingent to contend with. Before that time, "the ruling Republican clique could afford to alienate some of the Republican senators and, because of the party's complete domination in numbers, still count on legislative success." But with the election of Democrats, Republican leaders found they had to rely on the support of all their party colleagues. And one way to gain this support was to agree to an "automatic and impartial rule for committee advancement. The leaders of the party thus helped institute this limit on their own power."[12]

Another explanation given by Ripley for the early emergence of seniority in the Senate was that the Senate lacked a powerful central leader—a counterpart to the House Speaker, who controlled representatives' committee assignments and committee chairmanships. "Thus, seniority emerged (in the Senate) as the only practical way of solving the problem of status on the committees, although it did not solve the problem of initial assignment."[13]

The Senate seniority system was considerably strengthened by passage of the Legislative Reorganization Act in 1946 (which required reshuffling committee assignments) and the elections of that year which returned a substantial number of southern Democrats to the Senate but reduced the overall Democratic majority. Gradually, the southern Democrats—due partly to their steady electoral success—solidified their hold over committee chairmanships and ranking committee positions. By the mid-1960s, however, the institutional sway of southern Democrats had begun to decline. As Ripley describes it, "a new situation had emerged in which a number of moderately senior and very junior Democrats, virtually all liberals, had begun to develop significant impact on important legislative matters. They began to make impressive records of their own in their subcommittees. At the same time, several of the senior conservative oligarchs were removed by defeat, death or retirement."[14]

Institutional power in the Republican Party was more widely dispersed than in the Democratic Party in the early post-World War II period, although midwestern conservative Republicans tended to be overrepresented vis-à-vis their relative numbers on important committee positions.

Before 1965, Republican committee assignments were made by the party committee on committees solely on the basis of seniority, although some bargaining over exceptions did occur. In 1965, the Republican Conference formally ruled that except for members already sitting, no Republican could be a member of more than one of the four most important committees: Foreign Relations, Appropriations, Finance and Armed Services. The change opened up some seats on these committees to more junior Republicans.

Prior to 1971, Democratic committee assignments were determined by the Senate Democratic Steering Committee, chaired by the floor leader and generally composed of quite senior members. (In 1971, the committee's roster of nominations was made subject to caucus approval.) The Steering Committee was guided but not bound by seniority, with the majority leader having a significant voice in the

committee selection process. In making assignments, factors other than seniority—such as personal preference, region and party loyalty—were also frequently taken into account by both parties.

Development in the House

In the House, seniority at first played a secondary role. Committee members were elected from the floor for only one Congress before the House gave the task to the Speaker. It was he who made all committee assignments, minority as well as majority, and selected chairmen; and although a member's seniority was a useful guide, the Speaker could violate seniority for personal or political reasons.

A 1969 study of seniority in the House showed that from 1880 to 1910, Speakers had appointed 750 chairmen, and that in doing so they had followed seniority in 429 cases and disregarded it in 321 cases.[15] *(Details, box p. 402)*

Through the years the House Speaker amassed vast power, until 1910-11, when insurgents revolted against Speaker Joseph G. Cannon. Cannon, a conservative, used his powers of committee appointment to frustrate the legislative aims of his opponents. He switched members among committees to create working majorities, bypassed senior committee members to find chairmen that agreed with him, and occasionally appointed a friend to be chairman of a committee on which he had not even served. *(History of the House, p. 35; History of the Speakership, p. 316)*

In 1910 and early 1911, an alliance of Democrats and progressive Republicans took this power away from Cannon, giving the formal power of committee appointment to party committees on committees. The choices made by the committees on committees, though subject to ratification by the party caucuses and approval by the full House, were almost always final.[16]

Following the revolt of 1910, the seniority rule became increasingly important, although it still was frequently ignored. A 1969 study by Polsby, et al., showed that from 1910 to the end of World War II, seniority was followed in 676 of 901 appointments of committee chairmen and violated 225 times. Between World War II and the 1970s, the power of seniority in the House, dating traditionally from the 1910 revolt, became virtually absolute.

Until 1974, Democratic committee assignments in the House were made by the Democratic committee on committees, which was composed of the Democratic members of the Ways and Means Committee. The assignments were usually approved routinely by the party caucus.

The Republican committee on committees, made up of one representative from each state having at least one Republican in its House delegation, drew up a list of assignments, subject to approval by the House Republican Policy Committee.

Attempts to Modify Seniority

On a number of occasions members of both houses have tried to modify the seniority system. Most of the tampering has been aimed at the congressional committees. Until 1974, however, few attempts were successful.

Senate

Two early attempts at modification were made in the Senate. In 1882, Wilkinson Call (D Fla.) proposed to prohibit a member from occupying a seat on more than one major committee. In 1919, George W. Norris (R Neb.) proposed to limit a member to seats on no more than two major committees. Neither move was successful.

In 1953, Lyndon B. Johnson (D Texas), acting as minority leader, succeeded where others had failed. Johnson proposed, in what was to become known as the "Johnson Rule," that all Democratic senators have a seat on one major committee before any Democrat is assigned to a second major committee. The proposal was a stunning blow to seniority, but it had the backing of the powerful Richard B. Russell (D Ga.) and was approved by the Democratic Steering Committee, which made Democratic committee assignments in the Senate.

On Jan. 12, 1953, Johnson assigned two freshman senators to key committees. Sen. Mike Mansfield (D Mont.), who had been a member of the House Foreign Affairs Committee, was assigned to the Senate Foreign Relations Committee. Sen. Stuart Symington (D Mo.), who had been the first Secretary of the Air Force in 1947, was assigned to the Armed Services Committee.

Within four years' time Johnson had assigned four other Democrats who came to the Senate in 1953 to key committees: Price Daniel (Texas) to Judiciary and Interstate and Foreign Commerce; Albert Gore (Tenn.) to Finance and the Joint Committee on Atomic Energy; Henry M. Jackson (Wash.) to Armed Services and Atomic Energy; John F. Kennedy (Mass.) to Foreign Relations.

Later, Senate Republicans adopted a similar practice, informally in 1959 and formally through the Republican Conference in 1965.

In 1971, under renewed pressure to modify the seniority system, Senate Democrats and Republicans agreed to further changes. Democratic Majority Leader Mike Mansfield announced Feb. 10 that a meeting of the party caucus would be held at the request of any senator, and that any senator would be free to challenge any nomination of a committee chairman, and that the practice of submitting Steering Committee nominations of committee chairmen and members would be continued as a regular procedure. Republicans adopted a proposal that a senator could be the ranking minority member of only one standing committee of the Senate.

Democrats and Republicans alike established committees to study the seniority system. The three-member Democratic committee was composed of Senators Fred R. Harris (Okla.), Hubert H. Humphrey (Minn.), and Herman E. Talmadge (Ga.). The five-member Republican committee included Senators Wallace F. Bennett (Utah), J. Caleb Boggs (Del.), Clifford P. Hansen (Wyo.), Robert W. Packwood (Ore.) and Robert Taft Jr. (Ohio).

On March 16, 1971, the Senate rejected a major challenge to the seniority system, when it tabled, 48-26, a resolution that would have permitted the selection of committee chairmen on some basis other than seniority. The resolution, sponsored by Harris and Charles McC. Mathias Jr. (R Md.), provided that in making committee assignments "neither [party] conference shall be bound by any tradition, custom or principle of seniority."

House

A major challenge to the seniority system in the House was made during floor action on the Legislative Reorganization Act of 1970. On July 28, 1970, the House debated two amendments to modify the system. Both were rejected.

Alternatives to Seniority

Numerous alternatives to the seniority system have been suggested over the years. The major alternatives printed below were compiled in 1970 by the Democratic Study Group, an organization of House liberals.

Although Democrats and Republicans in both chambers had by 1975 substantially modified the seniority system's operation, none of the proposals listed below were adopted in exactly the form suggested.

● Use the seniority system to nominate chairmen, subject to majority approval by the party caucus.

● Have the caucus elect committee chairmen from among the three most senior members of each committee.

● Authorize the Speaker to nominate chairmen, subject to approval by a majority of the caucus.

● Authorize the majority members of each committee to nominate the chairman, subject to caucus approval.

● Authorize the members of each committee—both majority and minority—to select the chairmen, subject to approval of the House as a whole.

● Establish a new special committee to nominate chairmen, subject to majority approval by the caucus.

● Set an age limit, and require chairmen to give up their chairmanships when they reach that age.

● Set a limit on the number of years a member can serve as chairman and require that, after serving as chairman, the member leave the committee and begin service on another committee.

● Rotate the chairmanship among the top three committee members every two years.

Source: Democratic Study Group, "The Seniority System in the U.S. House of Representatives," reprinted in the *Congressional Record*, Feb. 26, 1970, p. E 5170-72.

The primary amendment, offered by Henry S. Reuss (D Wis.), provided that seniority need not be the sole consideration in the selection of committee chairmen. It was defeated by a teller vote, 73-160.

The House also rejected, by a teller vote of 28-196, an amendment proposed by Fred Schwengel (R Iowa) as a substitute for the Reuss amendment. The substitute provided that the chairman of each committee should be chosen, by the majority members of the committee, from among the committee's three most senior majority members.

Opponents of the Reuss and Schwengel amendments argued that "campaigns" for chairmanships would provide the opportunity for pressure groups to "wheel and deal" in support of their candidates for chairmen of certain committees. They also said that only through the seniority system could minority group members—such as William L. Dawson (D Ill.), chairman of the House Government Operations Committee at the time—become committee chairmen.

Limited 1971 House Changes. Also during 1970, special committees appointed by both parties prepared recommendations for changes in the seniority system when the House reorganized for the 92nd Congress in January 1971.[17]

House Democrats voted Jan. 20, 1971, to adopt modest changes in the seniority system of selecting committee chairmen. The changes were recommended by the Committee on Organization, Study and Review headed by Rep. Julia Butler Hansen (D Wash.).

The principal changes agreed upon were:

● The Democratic committee on committees would recommend to the caucus nominees for the chairmanship and membership of each committee, and such recommendations need not necessarily follow seniority.

● The committee on committees would make recommendations to the caucus, one committee at a time; upon the

---

Exceptions to the Seniority Tradition

As a 1969 study* of House seniority demonstrated, violations do occur and exceptions are made. Party leaders can tamper with the seniority system, probably not as frequently as its critics would like, but certainly more often than some of its beneficiaries would prefer. Lyndon Johnson, as one example, violated seniority among Senate Democrats, distributing political favors as he built a base of power for his climb to domination of the Senate in the 1950s.

Stripping a member of his seniority as a punishment for political heresy also has been resorted to, but not frequently. In the Senate of 1866, for example, three Republican committee chairmen were dropped to the bottom of their committees for failing to vote with the radical Republicans on overriding a presidential veto of a civil rights bill.

A selection of examples of major departures from seniority follows.

Senate

In 1859 the Democratic Caucus removed Stephen A. Douglas (D Ill.) from the chairmanship of the Committee on Territories because he refused to go along with President Buchanan and the southern wing of the party on the question of slavery in the territories.

In 1871 Charles Sumner (R Mass.) was removed from the chairmanship of (and membership on) the Foreign Relations Committee because of disagreement with President Grant over Grant's project for annexation of the Dominican Republic.

In 1913 Benjamin R. Tillman (D S.C.) was denied the chairmanship of the Appropriations Committee, at least in part because of his age and impaired health.

In 1924 Albert R. Cummins (R Iowa) lost his chairmanship of the Interstate Commerce Committee because he was also president pro tempore. The next-ranking Republican, Robert M. La Follette (R Wis.), was then passed over because of his unpopularity with the regulars of his own party, and the chairmanship was finally given to the ranking Democrat, Ellison D. Smith (D S.C.).

In 1952 Wayne L. Morse (R Ore.) was dropped from the Armed Services and Labor and Public Welfare Committees when he left the Republican Party. Morse served in the Senate as an independent from 1952 to 1955 and as a Democrat from 1955 to 1969.

In 1965 Strom Thurmond (R S.C.) was placed third on the Republican side of the Armed Services Committee after he bolted the Democratic Party to support the 1964 presidential candidacy of Barry Goldwater. As a Democrat, Thurmond had ranked seventh during the 88th Congress of 1963-65. Thurmond also had requested a seat on the Commerce Committee equivalent in rank to the one he had held on that committee as a Democrat. But he was assigned to the Banking and Currency Committee. Thurmond's full seniority, dating from his entry into the Senate as a Democrat in 1955, though honored by the Republicans since he switched parties, was not formally recognized by the Senate Republican Conference until 1971.

House

In 1965 the Democratic Caucus censured and stripped of their seniority rights Reps. John Bell Williams (Miss.) and Albert W. Watson (S.C.). Both were to continue to be recognized as Democrats. Williams and Watson had openly supported Goldwater as Republican nominee for the presidency in 1964. The caucus action put Williams, second-ranking Democrat on the Interstate and Foreign Commerce Committee and fifth-ranking Democrat on the District of Columbia Committee, at the bottom of both committees. Watson, a low-ranking member of the Post Office and Civil Service Committee, stood to lose little seniority. Watson resigned his seat and successfully sought re-election in 1965 as a Republican.

In 1967 Adam Clayton Powell (D N.Y.) was investigated by a select committee which found that he had misused congressional funds, acted contemptuously toward the courts of New York in a libel suit and kept his wife on his congressional payroll although she did not work either in his district or in the District of Columbia, as required by law. The House on March 1, 1967, excluded Powell from the 90th Congress. The House Democratic Caucus already had removed Powell from the chairmanship of the Education and Labor Committee. In 1969 Powell was seated in the 91st Congress but was fined $25,000 and made the lowest-ranking Democrat on the same committee that he had headed. *(See Seating and Disciplining of Members, p. 681)*

In 1969 the Democratic Caucus stripped Rep. John R. Rarick (D La.) of his seniority on the Agriculture Committee for having supported third-party candidate George C. Wallace in the 1968 presidential campaign. Rarick was the lowest-ranking Democrat on the committee in the 90th Congress but would have moved ahead in the 91st Congress.

* **Source:** Polsby, Nelson W., et al., "The Growth of the Seniority System in the U.S. House of Representatives," *American Political Science Review*, September 1969; and Congressional Quarterly, 1971 *Weekly Report*, p. 134.

demand of 10 or more caucus members, nominations could be debated and voted on.

● If a nomination was rejected, the committee on committees would submit another nomination. (The Democratic committee on committees then consisted of the Democratic members of the House Ways and Means Committee.)

The Democrats also agreed that no member could be chairman of more than one legislative subcommittee. This would open up subcommittee chairmanships to younger members.

The issue of seniority was first raised in the Democratic Caucus Jan. 19 when Rep. John Conyers Jr. (Mich.) challenged the seniority rights of the all-Democratic Mississippi House delegation. Conyers pointed out that the five Mississippians had refused to run on the racially integrated Democratic ticket recognized by the national party, but had run instead on an all-white ticket. Conyers argued that if the Mississippians refused to adhere to the principles of the national Democratic Party, they should be stripped of their seniority and denied the right to hold committee chairmanships as Democrats. The challenge was rejected by a standing vote of 55-111.

House Republicans on Jan. 20 agreed to allow all their members to vote on nominations for ranking minority members of each House committee.

The Republican Conference adopted without change the recommendations of a task force on seniority headed by Rep. Barber B. Conable Jr. of New York. The major change proposed in the report would allow the ranking Republican on each committee to be selected by vote, not merely by seniority. If Republicans gained control of the House the system would apply to selection of committee chairmen.

The report set up a procedure for selection of ranking members. The Republican committee on committees would nominate a member to be top Republican on each committee, not necessarily on the basis of seniority. The Republican Conference would vote separately by secret ballot on each nomination. If the nomination were rejected, the committee on committees would submit another nomination. The committee is comprised of one representative from each state that has Republican members.

Action of Democrats. When House Democrats met in caucus Feb. 3, committee assignments for the 92nd Congress proposed by the committee on committees encountered more opposition than usual. Rep. Herman Badillo, a freshman member representing a poor Puerto Rican district in New York City, won a fight to have his assignment to the Agriculture Committee changed to the Committee on Education and Labor. But Rep. Donald M. Fraser (Minn.), outgoing chairman of the liberal Democratic Study Group, lost his bid to win a seat on the Ways and Means Committee. Liberals lost also, by a vote of 96-126, their fight in caucus to unseat Rep. John L. McMillan (S.C.) as chairman of the District of Columbia Committee, which he had headed for 22 years. McMillan was accused of being unresponsive to the needs of the capital city.

The Democratic liberals carried the fight against McMillan to the floor of the House on Feb. 4 but lost there by a roll-call vote of 32-258. Many of the Democratic liberals who had voted in caucus to unseat McMillan changed their votes on the floor. Rep. Hale Boggs (D La.), the new majority floor leader, warned that "if a minority on the Democratic side and a majority on the minority side get together, they could take over control of the entire committee system in the House."

Lobbying on Chairmen

Prior to 1975, political pressure groups were discreet about lobbying on internal congressional matters. But when the House in 1975 chose its committee chairmen for the 94th Congress, the lobbying was public.

Most prominent was Common Cause, the liberal, self-styled citizens' reform lobby, which had worked hard to alter House procedures for several years. Two days before the first vote on chairmen, Common Cause released a study charging that F. Edward Hebert (D La.) of Armed Services flagrantly violated standards of fairness and compliance with House and caucus rules. It said that Wayne L. Hays (D Ohio) of House Administration and W. R. Poage (D Texas) of Agriculture, while not as bad as Hebert, showed patterns of serious abuses.

Common Cause lobbyists were prominent outside the caucus room during the crucial week, and Hebert blamed his defeat on the organization. He called the group "insidious," and its lobbying effort "reprehensible."

Common Cause also was critical of Wright Patman (D Texas), the Banking, Currency and Housing Committee chairman. It said his leadership showed significant shortcomings. But on the Patman fight, there was public lobbying in the other direction. Consumer spokesman Ralph Nader asked the Democrats to support Patman, arguing that the Texan had pressed his fight against big banks and monopolies before it was fashionable to do so. The Consumer Federation of America said that Patman "should be honored for his constant efforts over a period of 46 years in Congress to protect consumers' pocketbooks."

When it came to the Hays chairmanship, nearly all the public lobbying was on the negative side. The National Committee for an Effective Congress, which provided financial and consulting help for many of the freshman Democrats in their campaigns, lobbied actively among them against Hays and for his opponent, Frank Thompson Jr. (D N.J.). But none of the groups was able to prevent Hays' eventual decisive victory over Thompson in the caucus.

Source: Congressional Quarterly, 1975 *Weekly Report*, p. 212.

Democrats who changed their votes recognized that submission of this party conflict to decision by the whole House might open the way for future conservative coalitions to unseat liberal chairmen or even block the majority party's choice of a Speaker. Thus the real issue was protection of the right of the two parties to make their own committee assignments. And while McMillan retained his chairmanship, the fight against him seemed to have had some effect when, a week later, the committee by an 8-to-7 vote adopted new rules designed to correct procedural abuses of which the chairman had been accused. But McMillan soon reasserted his powers when, ignoring seniority, he bypassed his critics on the committee and appointed his own supporters as chairmen of the newly reorganized subcommittees. (McMillan was defeated for re-election in 1972.)

1973 Changes in Seniority System

In the last days of the 92nd Congress in 1972, seniority was under fire as much as ever. Witnesses at an ad hoc Senate committee hearing on congressional reform in mid-December gave it a high place on the list of reforms they wanted to make.[18]

The system survived new challenges in the early days of the 93rd Congress.[19] Although Senate Republicans and House Democrats approved changes in the selection process, all the committee chairmanships and ranking minority positions were won by the members who would have held them through seniority.

Senate Republicans. Senate Republicans attracted the most attention in January 1973 as they debated and in large part adopted a plan to limit the seniority system by having members of each standing committee elect the top-ranking Republican on that committee, subject to approval by a vote of all Senate Republicans.

The Republicans narrowly defeated a bolder plan, offered by Robert W. Packwood (Ore.) and Robert Taft Jr. (Ohio), which would have set up an elected seven-member committee on committees to make all committee assignments, including the selection of top-ranking Republicans. The conference also refused, by a 20-16 vote, to block all changes by sending them back to a committee for further study.

The plan that finally emerged was a compromise, put forward by Howard H. Baker Jr. (Tenn.) in consultation with Jacob K. Javits (N.Y.). Ultimately approved by a 31-5 margin, Baker's plan preserved the notion of electing the top-ranking Republicans but dropped the idea of a special committee on committees. It made no change in the existing system of selecting all committee members below the top on a strict seniority basis.

As approved by the GOP Conference, Baker's compromise specifically asked that committees not use seniority as the exclusive criterion in choosing top-ranking members. It also provided that the member selected as top-ranking Republican by each committee must have his nomination approved by the full conference. Competing nominations were not allowed in the conference. But if the committee choice was not accepted, the conference could recommit the nomination with instructions to name someone else. All these votes would be a matter of public record.

When Senate Republicans made their committee assignments Jan. 11, all the ranking positions were won under election by the men who would have held them through seniority.

House Democrats. Like the Senate Republicans, House Democrats in January 1973 placed a procedural obstacle in the path of seniority, then stepped around it and awarded all committee chairmanships to the same members who would have received them if the system had gone untouched.

For the first time in recent years, Democratic committee chairmen had to win their jobs by majority vote of the full party caucus. This occurred when the caucus decided that a secret-ballot vote would be taken on any committee chairman when 20 per cent of the caucus demanded it. It was expected that votes would be taken on all candidates because 20 per cent of all Democrats could normally be expected to demand a tally.

This is what did occur, but all the chairmen survived and seven ranking Democrats eligible for elevation by the retirement or defeat of their predecessors also were

approved. The margins varied—from only two negative votes against Melvin Price (Ill.) of Standards of Official Conduct to 29 against Richard H. Ichord (Mo.) of Internal Security. But none of the contests was close. Chet Holifield (Calif.) of Government Operations, the only chairman to face organized opposition, survived by a vote of 172-46. Nevertheless, reformers in the House hailed the procedural change as an important step toward a more open and accountable Congress. They were particularly pleased that Speaker Carl Albert (Okla.) and Majority Leader Thomas P. O'Neill Jr. (Mass.) fought to prevent the changes from being watered down.

House Republicans. House Republicans, also meeting in January, elected their top-ranking committee members in accordance with the procedure established in 1971. But as on the Democratic side, all senior committee members aspiring to the top-ranking positions received them.

The most formidable challenge was made against Frank Horton (N.Y.), in line to become top-ranking Republican on the Government Operations Committee. John N. Erlenborn (Ill.), just below Horton in seniority on the committee, challenged him on the grounds that his own conservative views were more in line with the thinking of most House Republicans than those of the liberal Horton. But in a victory for seniority, the caucus upheld Horton by a 100-36 vote.

1974-75: Reform and Revolt

Committee seniority in the House was considerably weakened in late 1974 and early 1975, when Democratic members of the 94th Congress voted to institute far-reaching reforms of the committee system.

The first of many changes in the House committee structure occurred a month before the 1974 elections when the House, on Oct. 8, adopted the Committee Reform Amendments of 1974. Although this reorganization did not reduce the number of committees, it did consolidate some jurisdictions that had been spread among several committees and also required an increase in the number of subcommittees. (*Committee reorganization, pp. 371-72*)

Two further blows were delivered to the established committee and seniority systems in the House, first by the 1974 election, which ushered in 75 mostly liberal Democratic freshmen and gave the Democrats a 291-144 majority. The second blow was dealt by the House Democratic Caucus, including the 75 freshmen-elect, meeting Dec. 2-5, 1974, for the purpose of organizing the 94th Congress.

1974 Democratic Caucus Actions

Meeting under authority of the 1974 Committee Reform Amendments that permitted House party leaders to organize for a new Congress before it officially convened, the Democratic Caucus selected as its chairman a liberal activist, Phillip Burton (Calif.). Several hours after his election, Democrats strengthened their hitherto armless Steering and Policy Committee by giving it the committee assignment powers that had rested with Ways and Means since 1911.

In addition, Democrats made a secret-ballot vote on all chairman nominations automatic in the caucus. Under the 1973 rule, 20 per cent of the caucus had to demand a vote before one was taken.

However, the switch in the committee assignment power was the more significant change adopted. It came about when the caucus voted 146-122 to adopt a motion by Donald M. Fraser (D Minn.) to give the power to the 24-member Steering Committee, which was chaired by the Speaker, Albert, and the majority leader, O'Neill, as well as Burton and 12 regionally elected members and nine Albert appointees.

According to Fraser, "The whole exercise in shifting the committee on committees from Ways and Means to the Steering Committee was to enhance the Steering Committee's status. Now it amounts to something."[20]

A major reason for the change, however, lay in Democratic dissatisfaction with Wilbur Mills (D Ark.), then powerful chairman of the Ways and Means Committee. Mills' personal and health problems prompted his congressional party colleagues to institute a series of measures designed to weaken his influence as Ways and Means chairman. (Subsequently, Mills announced he would not seek to continue as committee chairman. Mills later decided not to seek re-election and retired from Congress at the end of 1976.) In the past, many representatives had felt that they had to curry favor with Mills and support him on legislative issues in order to get choice committee assignments.

The following day—Dec. 3—House Democrats decided by voice vote to enlarge the Ways and Means Committee by almost 50 per cent, a move to permit revamping the conservative cast of the House's major tax-writing committee. Under the change, the panel was expanded to include 25 Democrats and 12 Republicans. Of the 25 Democrats, 13 were incumbent committee members and the remaining 12 were required to be new to the panel. For the 12 new

---

Deposing Chairmen: Precedents

There was little precedent when the House Democratic Caucus in January 1975 removed three committee chairmen—F. Edward Hebert (La.), chairman of the Armed Services Committee; W. R. Poage (Texas), chairman of the Agriculture Committee and Wright Patman, chairman of the Banking, Currency and Housing Committee. The House and the Senate both have been reluctant to tamper with the prerogatives of seniority by removing chairmen from their positions.

Prior to the 1975 action, the most recent instance of removal of a chairman took place in January 1967, when the Democratic Caucus removed Adam Clayton Powell (N.Y.) from the chairmanship of the Education and Labor Committee.

Before the Powell case, the most recent precedent in the House deposing committee chairmen came in 1925 when the 69th Congress opened. In that case, the reason was party disloyalty. John M. Nelson and Florian Lampert, both Wisconsin Republicans, were stripped of seniority rights along with the nine other members of the Wisconsin delegation, for campaigning as LaFollette Progressives in the 1924 elections. Nelson was chairman of the Committee on Elections and Lampert the Patents Committee. All of the mavericks were stripped of their seniority and dropped to the bottom of the list or moved to less important committees.

A much earlier precedent—one not connected with party politics—was in 1807, when John Randolph of Virginia lost chairmanship of the Ways and Means Committee for what the records say was eccentric and arbitrary behavior. What he had done was not described, but several years later he brought hunting dogs into the chamber. Speaker Henry Clay evicted him.

---

members, nominations were permitted from the caucus floor in addition to those made by the Democratic Steering and Policy Committee. "This will avoid an undue cluster of power" in the Steering Committee, Burton said.

The composition of the Ways and Means Committee was further altered when the caucus voted to require the panel to establish subcommittees.

Also adopted was a plan whereby senior members on each committee could chose two of their current subcommittee positions for the 94th Congress. Once they had done so, the more junior members would have first crack at the remaining subcommittee slots. (However, senior members of the Ways and Means Committee were allowed first choice for only one subcommittee, not two as was the case for other committees. No senior member of Ways and Means could make a second choice until the junior members had each made one.)

Further inroads into the committee seniority system were made when the caucus voted 147 to 116 to make all subcommittee chairmen on the Appropriations Committee subject to confirmation by the caucus. (At the same time, the caucus rejected a plan to make subcommittee chairmen on all committees, not just Appropriations, subject to caucus confirmation.) Appropriations is a highly decentralized committee, with most of the important decisions made in subcommittee, and it was argued that the subcommittee chairmen on Appropriations were as powerful as most chairmen of full committees.

The House Democrats also voted to give members of each committee the power to determine the number and jurisdiction of its subcommittees. In the past, committee chairmen frequently had exercised this power on their own, without consulting their junior colleagues.

The caucus also voted 106 to 65 to allow the Speaker to nominate all Democratic members of the Rules Committee, subject to ratification by the caucus.

Finally, the caucus slightly refined its method of selecting committee chairmen by approving a proposal that would allow competitive nominations for committee chairmen on the caucus floor if the original selection of the Steering Committee were voted down. Existing rules had provided for a caucus vote on the next recommendation.

One minor restriction on the activities of committee chairmen was adopted when the caucus approved a resolution preventing chairmen of legislative committees from chairing any other committees, including special, select or joint ones.

But two drastic suggestions for curbing the power of chairmanships were rejected when Democrats decided not to apply an age limit of 70 to all chairmen and not to limit them to serving more than three consecutive terms.

1975 House Revolt

As a result of these changes, and the continuing attack on the seniority system, strengthened by the large number of Democratic freshmen, three committee chairmen were ousted by the caucus in January 1975 and a fourth had to engage in a hotly contested caucus election in order to retain his post.[21] While this was going on, the Republican Conference routinely approved committee assignments made by the House Republican committee on committees.

On Jan. 16, the Democratic Caucus voted to unseat F. Edward Hebert (La.) as chairman of the Armed Services Committee and W. R. Poage (Texas) as chairman of the Agriculture Committee. The day before, the Democratic Steering and Policy Committee had voted to depose Wright Patman (Texas) as chairman of the Banking, Currency and Housing Committee and Wayne L. Hays (Ohio) as chairman of the House Administration Committee. In their place, the committee recommended Henry S. Reuss (Wis.) to head the Banking Committee and Frank Thompson Jr. (N.J.) to take over the Administration Committee.

The caucus, however, rejected the Reuss and Thompson nominations at the same time that it turned

down Hebert and Poage. Meeting Jan. 17, the Steering Committee then unanimously nominated Patman for Banking, Currency and Housing, Thomas S. Foley (Wash.) for Agriculture, Melvin Price (D Ill.) for Armed Services and Hays for Administration.

But on Jan. 22, the caucus reversed its previous position, voting to replace Patman with Reuss as chairman of the Banking, Currency and Housing Committee. Foley and Price were approved by the caucus without any opposition. Thompson, however, failed in his second bid to unseat Hays, who retained his chairmanship by a 161 to 111 caucus vote. *(Box on lobbying, p. 403)*

Subcommittee Challenges. Two House committee chairmen lost key subcommittee positions Jan. 28 as the challenge to seniority reached below the party caucus level. The Banking, Currency and Housing Committee voted to replace Leonor K. Sullivan (D Mo.) as chairman of the Consumer Affairs Subcommittee and elected Frank Annunzio (D Ill.) in her stead. Sullivan was chairman of the Merchant Marine and Fisheries Committee. Harley O. Staggers (D W.Va.) retained his chairmanship of the Interstate and Foreign Commerce Committee but lost the chairmanship of its Subcommittee on Oversight and Investigations to John E. Moss (D Calif.). The Commerce Committee also became the first in the House to decide to elect its subcommittee chairmen by secret ballot among committee Democrats.

Senate Action

There were no dramatic revolts against sitting chairmen, but Senate Democrats for the first time created a system that would make chairmen accountable to their colleagues.

Democrats in 1971 had allowed any senator to call a meeting of the caucus to challenge a person nominated by the party's Steering Committee to be a chairman. But, like a similar earlier rule for House Democrats, this approach exposed a challenging senator to retribution by a chairman if the challenge failed.

In 1975, Democrats decided to select chairmen by secret ballot whenever one-fifth of the caucus requested it. The procedure to carry out the change provided that a list of chairmen nominees by the Democratic Steering Committee would be distributed to all Democrats. The Democrats would check off the names of the nominees they wished to subject to a secret ballot and would submit the list without signing it. If at least 20 per cent of the caucus members wanted a secret vote on a nominee, it would be held automatically two days later.

Footnotes

1. Barbara Hinckley, *The Seniority System in Congress* (Indiana Univ. Press, 1971), p. 5.

2. Quoted in the *Christian Science Monitor*, Jan. 20, 1975.

3. Quoted in George B. Galloway, *Congress at the Crossroads* (Thomas Y. Crowell Co., 1946), p. 187.

4. Interview with Congressional Quarterly in September 1972; quoted in CQ *Weekly Report*, Jan. 6, 1973, p. 22.

5. Richard Bolling, *House Out of Order* (E. P. Dutton and Co., Inc., 1965), p. 39.

6. Quoted in Donald G. Tacheron and Morris K. Udall, *The Job of Congressman* (Bobbs-Merrill Co., Inc., 1966), p. 163-164.

7. Hinckley, *The Seniority System*, p. 6.

8. Bolling, *House Out of Order*, p. 38.

9. Randall B. Ripley, *Power in the Senate* (St. Martin's Press, 1969), p. 22. This book contains a thorough discussion of the development of seniority in the Senate.

10. *Ibid.*, p. 23.

11. *Ibid.*, p. 43.

12. *Ibid.*, p. 47.

13. Ripley, *Power in the Senate*, p. 50.

14. *Ibid.*, p. 69.

15. Nelson W. Polsby, Miriam Gallaher and Barry Rundquist, "The Growth of the Seniority System in the U.S. House of Representatives," *American Political Science Review*, September 1969.

16. For a fuller discussion, Galloway, *History of the House of Representatives* (Thomas Y. Crowell Company, 1961), pp. 53-55.

17. For this section, see Congressional Quarterly, *Congress and the Nation*, Vol. III, pp. 353-354.

18. Congressional Quarterly, 1972 *Weekly Report*, p. 3128.

19. For this section, see Congressional Quarterly, *1973 Almanac*, pp. 43 ff.

20. See Congressional Quarterly, 1974 *Weekly Report*, p. 3250, for 1974 caucus action.

21. See Congressional Quarterly, 1975 *Weekly Report*, pp. 111, 210, for articles on 1975 actions.

Selected Bibliography

Books

Bolling, Richard, *House Out of Order*, E. P. Dutton and Co. Inc., 1965.

Congressional Quarterly, *1973 Almanac*, Washington, 1974; *Congress and the Nation*, Vol. III, Washington, 1973.

Evans, Rowland, and Novak, Robert, *Lyndon B. Johnson, The Exercise of Power*, New American Library, 1966.

Galloway, George B., *Congress at the Crossroads*. Thomas Y. Crowell Co., 1946.

Galloway, *History of the House of Representatives*. Thomas Y. Crowell Co., 1961.

Haynes, George H., *The Senate of the United States*. Houghton-Mifflin Co., 1938.

Hinckley, Barbara, *The Seniority System in Congress*. Indiana University Press, 1971.

Morrow, William L., *Congressional Committees*. Charles Scribner's Sons, 1969.

Ripley, Randall B., *Power in the Senate*. St. Martin's Press, 1969.

Ripley, *Congress: Process and Policy*. W. W. Norton and Co. Inc., 1975.

Tacheron, Donald G., and Udall, Morris K., *The Job of a Congressman*. Bobbs-Merrill Co. Inc., 1966.

Articles

Celler, Emanuel, "The Seniority Rule in Congress," *Western Political Quarterly*, March 1961.

Democratic Study Group, "The Seniority System in the U.S. House of Representatives," reproduced in the *Congressional Record*, Feb. 26, 1970, pp. E 5170-72.

Goodwin, George Jr., "The Seniority System in Congress," *American Political Science Review*, June 1959.

Huitt, Ralph K., "The Morse Committee Assignment Controversy," *American Political Science Review*, June 1957.

Malbin, Michael J., "House Democrats Oust Senior Members from Power," *National Journal Reports*, January 25, 1975, pp. 129-134.

Polsby, Nelson W., Gallaher, Miriam, and Rundquist, Barry, "The Growth of the Seniority System in the U.S. House of Representatives," *American Political Science Review*, September 1969.

Sullivan, G. R., "Ain't an Old House, No More, No More: Challenging Seniority Rule," *America*, April 26, 1975, pp. 314-16.

Wolanin, Thomas R., "Committee Seniority and the Choice of House Subcommittee Chairmen," *Journal of Politics*, August 1974, pp. 687-702.

HOUSING AND SUPPORT OF CONGRESS

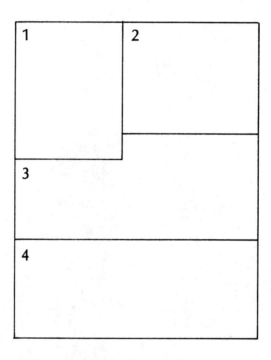

1. Great hall of the main building of the Library of Congress. (Library of Congress photo.)

2. Main building of the Library of Congress. (Library of Congress photo.)

3. East front of the U.S. Capitol Building. Earliest known photographic image of the Capitol; daguerreotype attributed to John Plumbe Jr., ca. 1846. (Library of Congress photo no. LC-USZ62-46801.)

4. View of the Capitol when first occupied by Congress, 1880. Collection of the Architect of the Capitol. (Library of Congress photo no. LC-USA7-11568.)

Capitol and Office Buildings

To some Americans, the United States Capitol is the magnificent symbol of a proud nation. It stands for a great and vital democracy. Only a few years younger than the Constitution, the Capitol has witnessed nearly 200 years of the nation's history and often has been at the center of that history. It has seen the United States grow from a weak strand of former colonies on the Atlantic seaboard into a continent-sized nation whose influence circles the globe.

To other Americans, the Capitol, while heroically scaled and elaborately decorated, is in essence a functional public building. It is a meeting place and a forum for national politicians, where legislation can be proposed, debated, amended and enacted or rejected. Designed for the business of government, the Capitol has been built, remodeled, burned, rebuilt, expanded and expanded again. It has changed as the nation has changed, and it may continue to change as time exacts new demands.

Varied Nature of the Capitol

The fact is that the Capitol is both symbol and building. The profile of the Capitol dome is as typically American as the Eiffel Tower is typically French, or the pyramids are typically Egyptian. It is a shrine for perhaps 2.5 million tourists each year.[1] Yet the building is the hub of activity for a few thousand congressional employees, and within its walls the Senate, House, Library of Congress and Supreme Court have shifted from room to room in a continuing search for adequate quarters.

Designed originally to be a home for the Senate and the House of Representatives, the Capitol has been pressed into service by others almost from the start. The Library of Congress did not leave until 1897; the Supreme Court stayed until 1935. Presidential inaugurations have taken place inside Capitol chambers and outside the East Front. The bodies of national leaders have lain in state in the Rotunda. A vast collection of art, some of it priceless and some of it worthless, crowds the floors, walls, ceilings, corridors and rooms of the Capitol.

Home of House and Senate

As the home of the House and the Senate, the Capitol has been the place where Congress works. Within the Capitol, Congress has developed and exercised its powers, enjoyed its perquisites and felt the varied pressures Americans have devised to influence Congress. From the Capitol, members of succeeding congresses have gone forth to meet the electorate, some returning to pursue careers of fame and power, others vanishing anonymously into the countryside.

Controversy has dogged the Capitol from its beginning. Designers failed to produce acceptable plans. Builders quarreled with architects. And in the end, members of Congress grumbled about the results. The Capitol has been expanded, and a jumble of huge office buildings has been erected to serve it. Recently, plans to extend the West Front have aroused strong protests. There even have been suggestions that Congress abandon the Capitol for a more modern, wholly utilitarian home elsewhere.[2]

Phases of Construction

In general terms, the Capitol has undergone four major periods of construction. The first period, which included the original design work and early construction, stretched from 1792 to about 1811. The second period, from 1815 to 1829, involved repair of damage caused by the British in 1814 and completion of the originally planned building, which had been halted by the War of 1812. The third period, covering from 1851 to 1892, included erection of the present wings used by the House and Senate, and landscaping of the grounds. The fourth period, not yet concluded, began in 1949 with extensive repairs to the roofs of the House and Senate wings. Extension of the East Front was completed in 1962. Proposals to extend or to restore the West Front still are under debate.

Early Construction, 1792-1811

After the Constitution was adopted and ratified, Congress met first in New York and then in Philadelphia. *(Box, New York and Philadelphia Capitols, p. 412)* The Act of July 16, 1790, which shifted the seat of government to "a district or territory...on the river Potomac," made it clear that a new city would have to be laid out, sites selected for

New York and Philadelphia

Under the Constitution, but before the seat of government was moved to Washington, D.C. in 1800, Congress met temporarily in public buildings in New York and Philadelphia.

Federal Hall in New York. The first session of the First Congress opened March 4, 1789, in Federal Hall at Broad and Wall Streets, New York City. The building, on the site of the old city hall, had been used previously by the Continental Congress. Private citizens raised $32,500 for Pierre Charles L'Enfant to redesign the structure.

The House chamber was on the first floor and the Senate chamber on the second floor. The actual cost of the renovations was almost $65,000, with half the total paid from tax revenues and half from lottery receipts.

The House and the Senate met in Federal Hall until the end of the second session of the First Congress on Aug. 12, 1790.

Congress Hall in Philadelphia. Congress met for a decade in Congress Hall at Sixth and Chestnut Streets, Philadelphia. The building, next to the famous Independence Hall, originally was the county courthouse. The House chamber was on the first floor, the Senate chamber on the second floor.

Congress Hall was used by the House and the Senate from the opening of the third session of the First Congress on Dec. 6, 1790, to the closing of the first session of the Sixth Congress on May 14, 1800.

Source: Architect of the Capitol, Art and Reference Division; National Park Service.

the government buildings, and the buildings themselves designed and erected.

Selection of Capitol Site

The task of selecting a site for the Capitol fell to Pierre Charles L'Enfant, who had been appointed by President Washington in March 1791 to prepare a plan for the new city. L'Enfant at times referred to the proposed building as "Congressional House," but the name "Capitol" appears to have been chosen by consensus. The President and others associated with its planning used "Capitol" from the beginning.[3] (*Selection of Washington, D.C., as National Capital, p. 287*)

Washington had instructed L'Enfant to locate the city on the Maryland side of the Potomac. L'Enfant made several tours of the area, studied maps of European cities and developed his plan. In a letter to Washington on June 22, 1791, he outlined a plan for the city which called for a rectangular grid of streets that would be intersected by broad avenues radiating from the "principal places." The Capitol would be one of the "principal places," and L'Enfant recommended putting it "on the west end of Jenkins Heights, which stand as a pedestal waiting for a monument...."

The President accepted L'Enfant's recommendations and on Dec. 13, 1791, forwarded them to Congress for its in-

formation. Although L'Enfant was dismissed in February 1792, his plans were used in preparing maps of the city. His recommendation of a site for the Capitol was retained on the maps. The area has been known ever since as Capitol Hill.

The area had been occupied earlier by a subtribe of the Algonquin Indians, known as the Powhatans, whose council house had been located at the foot of the hill. The original Capitol grounds were a part of Cerne Abbey Manor, owned by Daniel Carroll of Duddington. The land was purchased by the government for 25 pounds an acre, the equivalent at the time of $66.66.[4]

Design Competition

The three commissioners, appointed by Washington to oversee development of the city and the public buildings, originally had expected L'Enfant to provide designs for the buildings as well as the city. But by early 1792, it had become clear that the commissioners could not rely on L'Enfant for the building designs, and they decided to conduct a public design competition.

Throughout the month of March the commissioners advertised for designs. They set July 15, 1792, as a deadline for the competition and offered a prize of $500 and a city lot for the winning design.

The specifications laid down by the commissioners called for a brick building to include a conference room and a room for the representatives, each capable of accommodating 300 persons; a room for the Senate, containing 1,200 square feet; 12 rooms of 600 square feet each for committees and clerks' offices; and appropriate lobbies and anterooms.[5] They recommended that the central part of the building be designed so that, while it appeared to be complete, additions could be made later if desired.

Proposed Plans. The results of the competition were disappointing. Only 14 to 16 plans were received, according to different sources. Plans submitted by 10 individuals still exist: Andrew Mayfield Carshore, James Diamond, Samuel Dobie, Abram Faw, Stephen H. Hallet, Philip Hart, Robert G. Lanphier, Samuel McIntire, Jacob Small and Charles Wintersmith. One other extant plan is unattributed. Drawings supposedly submitted by five other individuals no longer exist: John Collins, Samuel Blodget Jr., Leonard Harbagh, Judge George Turner and Collen Williamson.[6]

There were few trained architects in the United States at the time. Some of the designs pictured oddly proportioned structures or proposed impossible details. A design by James Diamond, for example, included a monstrously oversized weathercock atop the building.

From among the designs that had been received, the commissioners favored Hallet's. Washington favored Turner's. Blodget's also attracted attention. Each of the three men was asked to revise his drawings and to submit them again. This second competition was not entirely successful either, but the commissioners agreed to ask Hallet to prepare more detailed plans, incorporating some suggested alterations.

Accepted Design. In the meantime, Dr. William Thornton, a physician and inventor, had written the commissioners in October 1792 from the island of Tortola, West Indies, asking whether he could submit a design even though the July 15 deadline had passed. The commissioners on Dec. 4, 1792, told Thornton to go ahead. They suggested that he send his proposal directly to Secretary of State

Thomas Jefferson for study by Washington. Hallet's revisions were to be ready for the President in January 1793.

After studying both plans, Washington said that he favored Thornton's. "Grandeur, simplicity and convenience appear to be so well combined in this plan of Dr. Thornton's," he wrote. Jefferson commented that "the beauty of the exterior; the propriety with which the apartments are distributed, and the economy in the mass of the whole structure recommended this plan."[7]

The commissioners agreed with Washington. On April 5, 1793, they wrote Thornton that "the President has given formal approbation of your plan."[8] Jefferson, himself an accomplished architect, said Thornton's design "captivated the eyes and judgment of all."[9]

The winning design called for a stately, three-story building, surmounted by a low dome. For the design, Thornton received the $500 award and a lot on North Capitol Street, about two blocks from the building site.[10]

Thornton was an amateur architect and his design was merely an elevation sketch. The commissioners hired Hallet, who was a professional French architect, to prepare working drawings. A clash was inevitable. As modifications of Thornton's design (some of them required for structural and practical reasons) crept into Hallet's drawings, Thornton raised a series of noisy objections. To settle the dispute, Washington called a meeting of Thornton, Hallet, James Hoban (winner of the design competition for the White House), and two builders. The group agreed to some of the modifications proposed by Hallet. In a letter to Washington concerning the changes Thomas Jefferson said that Hallet had "preserved the most valuable ideas of the original and rendered them acceptable of execution, so that it is considered Dr. Thornton's plan rendered into practical form."[11] Historians still are uncertain abut which man had greater influence over the Capitol's ultimate design.

Building of the Capitol

The Capitol was laid out on a north-south axis, so that descriptions mention north and south wings (ends) and east and west fronts (sides).

The first cornerstone was laid Sept. 18, 1793, by George Washington amid colorful Masonic rites. Although contemporary accounts put the cornerstone at the southeast corner of the north wing, it was not found during the 1958-62 extension of the East Front.

Hallet was placed in charge of the construction, under the supervision of Hoban. As work progressed, Hallet persisted in altering the design without approval of either the President or the commissioners. Hallet was tolerated for a year but finally was discharged on Nov. 15, 1794. Two months earlier, on Sept. 12, 1794, Washington had named Thornton to a vacancy on the three-man board of commissioners, putting Thornton for the first time in a place of direct authority over the construction.

Nearly a year passed before a successor to Hallet was appointed. In the interval, Hoban superintended construction of both the White House and the Capitol. Then on Oct. 15, 1795, the commissioners appointed as the new construction superintendent George Hadfield, a prize-winning student at the Royal Academy in London. At first, Hadfield quarreled with the commissioners over following the agreed plans, but the quarreling ended abruptly when the commissioners indicated they would instantly accept Hadfield's threatened resignation.

Although Thornton's basic design for the Capitol was executed by three other men—Hallet, Hoban and Had-

Architect of the Capitol

The present position of architect of the Capitol has existed since 1876, when Congress transferred to the architect the functions performed previously by the commissioner for public buildings and grounds. However, beginning with William Thornton in 1793, nine presidential appointees have had the architect's responsibility for construction and maintenance of the Capitol.

In the early years an architect was appointed only when the Capitol was under construction. The titles varied and some duties were shared with other officials. The position has been continuous since 1851.

The architect of the Capitol need not be a professional architect, for the position today is largely an administrative one. The architect is charged with the structural and mechanical care of the following buildings: the Capitol and its grounds, the Senate and House office buildings, the Library of Congress buildings and grounds, the U.S. Supreme Court building and grounds, the Senate garage, the Robert A. Taft Memorial and the Capitol Power Plant, which heats and cools some buildings in addition to the Capitol complex.

The architect also is charged with the operation of the U.S. Botanic Garden and the Senate restaurants. He serves as a member of the Capitol Police Board, the Capitol Guide Board, the Commission for Extension of the United States Capitol, the board of directors of the Pennsylvania Avenue Development Corporation, the District of Columbia Zoning Board, and is coordinator for civilian defense for Capitol Hill. In performing these tasks the architect is under the direction of the Speaker of the House, the Senate Committee on Rules and Administration, the House Office Building Commission and the Joint Committee on the Library.

The architect's main offices are in the Capitol. He has a permanent staff of about 70 to assist him in administrative work. However, in 1975 he was responsible for a total of 1,781 employees, most of whom served in the operation and maintenance of the House and Senate office buildings. On Oct. 1, 1975, the architect's annual salary was increased to $39,900.

Following is a list of the nine men appointed by the President as architect of the Capitol, though under other titles in the early years:

1793-1794	William Thornton
1803-1811 } 1815-1817 }	Benjamin Henry Latrobe
1818-1829	Charles Bulfinch
1851-1865	Thomas Ustick Walter
1865-1902	Edward Clark
1902-1923	Elliott Woods
1923-1954	David Lynn
1954-1970	J. George Stewart
1971-	George M. White

Source: Architect of the Capitol, Art and Reference Division, releases of June 28, 1974, and November 1974; *U.S. Government Manual,* 1974-75, pp. 40-42.

field—only Thornton was appointed by the President to the position that has come to be called "architect of the Capitol." The other three were hired by the board of commissioners. Congress abolished the board in 1802, when its responsibilities were taken over by a superintendent of public buildings. *(Box, Architect of the Capitol, p. 415)*

Despite the controversies, construction continued. It took slave labor to build the home of a free government. The Capitol work force was composed in large part of black slaves hired out by their masters in the District of Columbia and nearby Maryland and Virginia, as was then a common custom. By March 1796, the foundations had been laid, and the north wing was rising above the ground. The roof of the north wing had been boarded, shingled and painted by the fall of 1798. When Congress arrived from Philadelphia in the autumn of 1800, the foundations of the south wing had risen a few feet above the ground. The two wings were not connected by a permanent structure for more than 20 years.

The first public function held at the Capitol was a reception given by the citizens of Washington for President John Adams on June 5, 1800.

Arrival of Congress

The Act of July 16, 1790, designating a Potomac site as the permanent seat of government, had set the first Monday in December 1800 as the deadline for moving to the new capital. When it became clear that the government buildings would be ready before December, Congress by an Act of April 24, 1800, authorized the President to make an earlier transfer. By an Act of May 13, 1800, Congress fixed Nov. 17, 1800, as the date of its own Washington opening in the Capitol.

Congress was late for its debut. It convened Nov. 17 but for lack of a quorum did not actually sit until Nov. 21. Then on Nov. 22, representatives and senators attending the second session of the 6th Congress filled the Senate chamber to hear President Adams deliver a message of welcome. It was not until 1913 that another President, Woodrow Wilson, made a speech to Congress in the Capitol.

The citizens of Washington had planned a parade and a formal reception for Congress on Nov. 22. But plans collapsed in a dispute over selection of a master of ceremonies, and because of a surprise three-inch snowfall. Thus the welcome for Congress consisted of a congratulatory letter from local residents and a newly written, and long since forgotten, song.

Both the House and the Senate were quartered in the north wing, because it was the only part of the Capitol that had been completed. The wing was three stories high and was faced with sandstone on three sides. The fourth (south) side, to be connected later to the center section and south wing, was enclosed temporarily with brick.

The north wing, and the entire Capitol until the 1850s, was built primarily of sandstone from the Aquia Creek Quarry in Virginia. The quarry, on an island in the Potomac about 40 miles south of Washington, supplied the stone for all public buildings in the new capital from 1791 to 1837. The soft, light gray "freestone" could be quarried easily and shipped economically to Washington. But it did not wear well and was not used extensively after other quarries came into production. Much of the original sandstone in the Capitol has been replaced or covered over by subsequent construction.[12]

Inside the north wing, both the House and Senate chambers were two stories high. The House chamber was on the west side of the second floor. The Senate chamber was on the east side of the first floor, a floor below the space it later was to occupy and still later to turn over to the Supreme Court. On the walls of the Senate chamber hung portraits of Louis XVI and Marie Antoinette, the first art in the Capitol. The portraits had been presented by the King to the Continental Congress in 1784. Both paintings are thought to have been burned by the British in 1814. *(Box, the Capitol Art Collection, p. 418)*

Bursting out of its admittedly temporary quarters in the north wing, the House ordered construction of other temporary quarters on the foundations of its own south wing. The result was a one-story, elliptical brick building. Because of its shape and the stifling summer temperatures inside, the structure quickly was nicknamed "the oven." The House met there from the beginning of the 7th Congress on Dec. 7, 1801, until the end of the first session of the 8th Congress on March 27, 1804, when it abandoned the site so that construction of the south wing could continue. The House met again in its north wing chamber from Nov. 5, 1804, to March 3, 1807.

Continuation of Work Under Latrobe

In the meantime, Jefferson had become President. On March 6, 1803, he appointed Benjamin Henry Latrobe, an English architect, as surveyor of public buildings and placed him in charge of finishing the Capitol.

After demolition of "the oven," work was resumed on the south wing. The completed north wing determined the exterior design of the south wing, and the completed foundations of the south wing set the form of the interior. But like Hallet and Hadfield before him, Latrobe, as a professional architect, found flaws in Thornton's design. Thornton answered on Jan. 1, 1805, with an open letter to members of the House. The bitter pamphlet war that ensued rocked Congress and threatened further construction appropriations. Jefferson supported Latrobe, while cautioning him to "deviate as little as possible from the plan approved by General Washington."[13] Latrobe survived the criticism and remained in charge of the work.

The roof of the south wing was completed during the winter of 1806-07, and by March 1807 construction of the wing was virtually completed. The House moved from the north wing into what was considered its permanent home (later Statuary Hall) for the opening of the 10th Congress on Oct. 26, 1807. Problems arose almost at once. Latrobe had succeeded in changing Thornton's design for an elliptical House chamber into two semicircles joined by parallel lines, and the acoustics were horrible. Hanging curtains between the stone columns helped somewhat, but faulty acoustics plagued the House throughout its occupancy of the chamber.

Upon completion of the south wing, Latrobe turned to repairing some of the mediocre construction in the north wing. He replaced with stone some of the wood, plaster and brick interiors. He raised the floor of the two-story Senate chamber, dividing the area into two one-story chambers. He designed cornstalk motifs on columns in 1809 for the vestibule outside the first floor chamber. Latrobe hired Italian sculptors to execute his plans for the Capitol's interior.

During the remodeling, occupants of the north wing were shunted about. Following adjournment of the first session of the 10th Congress on April 25, 1808, the Senate moved into a first floor room on the west side of the north wing. The Supreme Court moved into the old House chamber on the west side of the second floor, sharing the space with the Library of Congress. The Court had moved to Washington for the opening of its February 1801 term and had been sitting in a small room adjoining the south side of the Senate chamber. After the Court adjourned in 1809, the Senate moved upstairs to share the old House quarters with the Library.

By the winter of 1809-10, new quarters were ready for both the Senate and the Court. On Jan. 1, 1810, the Senate moved into its remodeled chamber on the second floor of the east side. The Court opened its 1810 term in the first floor chamber beneath the Senate. Both chambers were used later for other purposes, but for the Bicentennial they were restored to their appearance of the 1850s.

The threat of an approaching war with Britain began to cut into construction appropriations for the Capitol. Work slowed, then halted. The two sections, the north wing and the south wing, stood apart, separated by the unfinished center section. In 1811, before work was completely suspended, a temporary wooden covered walk was built to connect the two wings.

Cost. Estimates of the cost of erecting the two wings are at best tentative. Part of the cost was defrayed by the original contributions of $72,000 from Maryland and $120,-000 from Virginia for construction of public buildings at Washington. The first congressional appropriation for the Capitol, in 1803, provided $50,000, although Congress had appropriated $9,000 in 1800 for furnishings. After studying Treasury records, Glenn Brown, author of a two-volume history of the Capitol published in 1900, put the cost of the north and south wings at $788,077.98.[14]

Reconstruction, 1815-1829

Most of the fighting during the War of 1812 took place far from Washington. But in response to American raids into Canada and in hopes of demoralizing the government, Vice Adm. Sir Alexander Cochrane authorized a series of Atlantic seaboard operations. Carrying out one of those operations, a British force under the command of Maj. Gen. Robert Ross and Rear Adm. Sir George Cockburn moved up the Patuxent River in Maryland in August 1814. The troops were put ashore near Benedict, Md., and marched overland through Upper Marlboro and Bladensburg toward Washington. American troops offered ineffective resistance.

The capital city was nearly deserted. Many residents had fled before the approaching troops. Most members of Congress, after a routine adjournment April 18, had long since left for their homes. President Madison and most of the Cabinet had gone to Bladensburg with the American troops.[15]

The British entered Washington around dusk on Aug. 24, 1814. That night a detachment of troops headed by Ross and Cockburn set the Capitol afire. The building was burned, according to tradition, after Cockburn had mounted the Speaker's chair in the House chamber and asked, "Shall this harbor of Yankee democracy be burned?" The soldiers shouted "Aye," tradition adds.[16] Leaving the Capitol in flames, the troops moved through the city and burned the White House and the Treasury building. Later on the night of Aug. 24-25, a violent rainstorm drowned the flames, preventing complete destruction of the buildings. The British again roamed through the city on Aug. 25. Before withdrawing that night, they also burned buildings used by the State and War Departments and a government arsenal.

As the President and other government officials returned to Washington Aug. 27, the slow work of reconstruction began.

Task of Rebuilding

On Aug. 8, 1814, President Madison had called a special session of Congress for Sept. 19. The Capitol had been damaged too heavily to meet there, and on Sept. 17 the President announced that Congress would convene in Blodget's Hotel, which had been taken over previously by the Post Office and the Patent Office. The huge structure, on E street between 7th and 8th Streets, Northwest, was the only government building not burned by the British. It had been built by Samuel Blodget Jr., one of the competitors for the original Capitol design, and it once was offered as a lottery prize but never served as a hotel. The building was demolished later in the 19th century.

The special session in Blodget's lasted from Sept. 19, 1814, to March 3, 1815. On Oct. 15, the House by a 74-83 vote defeated a bill to transfer the seat of government elsewhere. The vote was part of an intermittent effort from 1800 until after the Civil War to move the capital out of Washington.

Latrobe Recalled. An Act of Feb. 15, 1815, authorized the President to accept a $500,000 loan from Washington banks to pay for rebuilding the Capitol. On March 14, Labrobe was recalled to oversee the work. According to his reports, damage to the north wing was more extensive than that to the south wing. The wooden covered walk between them had been completely destroyed.

In repairing the interiors, Latrobe again redesigned the House chamber, making it semicircular but failing to improve its acoustics. He designed the central section west of the Rotunda, and the tobacco capitals of the small rotunda on the second floor. For the East Front, Latrobe designed the main portico and exterior steps. The new steps were to lead from the ground level to the second floor, which had become, and remains, the principal floor of the Capitol. *(Floor plan, p. 424)*

Work on reconstruction was well under way when Latrobe became entangled in a dispute with Samuel Lane, who had been named in 1816 to the newly created post of commissioner of public buildings and grounds. Latrobe resigned Nov. 20, 1817.

Brick Capitol. Meanwhile, Congress had moved from Blodget's Hotel into new quarters. A group of Washington landowners, worried that Congress might move to another city, had raised $25,000 to build a temporary "capitol" at First and A Streets, Northeast. The cornerstone was laid July 4, 1815, and both the House and Senate met in the new building at the opening of the 14th Congress on Dec. 4, 1815. The Senate chamber was on the ground floor and the House met on the floor above. Known as the Brick Capitol, the three-story brick building was rented to Congress for $1,650 per year.

James Monroe's first inaugural took place in front of the Brick Capitol on March 4, 1817. *(Box, Inaugural Sites, p. 425)* Congress met in the building for two terms. Later it was used as a rooming house, a military prison during the Civil War, and finally as headquarters of the National Woman's Party. The site now is occupied by the Supreme Court building. *(Continued on p. 420)*

The Capitol Art Collection Includes...

Although the Capitol was designed to provide a home for Congress, it has acquired a vast collection of works of art and other objects. Some of the art is excellent, and any museum would be proud to display it. Some is of doubtful value. An 1871 newspaper article called it the world's "most wretched collection," and suggested that a protest leap from the Rotunda would be "justifiable suicide."*

The earliest works in the Capitol were portraits of Marie Antoinette and Louis XVI by Madame Vigee Le Brun. Hung in the old Senate chamber, they are thought to have been destroyed by the British in 1814. An early statue, "Liberty and the Eagle" by Giuseppe Franzoni, is known to have been destroyed in the 1814 fire.

By 1975, according to the architect of the Capitol, the collection consisted of 677 pieces. But a precise count is impossible because so much of the art is part of the building's decoration. The collection includes paintings and portraits, frescoes and murals, statues, busts, relief portraits, sculptured reliefs, stained glass windows and skylights, woodcarving, lunettes, plaques and mantels. The Capitol also has historically important objects such as the silver-and-ebony mace of the House, the Senate desk of Daniel Webster and the couch on which John Quincy Adams died.

Responsibility for the art collection, as for most things in the Capitol, is shared. The architect has supervision over works of art in the Rotunda and public corridors, but he is guided by the Joint Committee on the Library. On the House side the architect's responsibility is shared with the Speaker and, in some instances, with interested committee chairmen. The Senate Commission on Art and Antiquities supervises the collection on the Senate side.

Some of the more notable works of art in the Capitol are described below:

Portraits and Paintings. The collection includes portraits of George Washington by Gilbert Stuart, Charles Willson Peale and Rembrandt Peale. Thomas Sully's paintings of Jefferson and Jackson also are in the Capitol. Francis B. Carpenter's huge painting of Lincoln reading the Emancipation Proclamation to his Cabinet was painted at the White House, where Lincoln himself authenticated details. The walls of the Rotunda are hung with eight large oil paintings, including four scenes from the Revolution by John Trumbull, who served briefly as an aide to General Washington. Another is Robert W. Weir's famous scene, "Puritans on Their Way to America."

The Capitol contains many murals, including several by Brumidi (below). Emanuel Leutze's dramatic account of the westward migration, painted in 1862, is at the west staircase of the House wing. Since 1970 Allyn Cox has been at work on murals in the House corridors depicting scenes from the nation's past.

Statues and Busts. When the House moved into new quarters in 1857 its old chamber was left unused. Congress in 1864 designated it the National Statuary Hall and invited "all the states to provide and furnish statues, in marble or bronze, not exceeding two in number for each state, of deceased persons who have been citizens thereof and illustrious for their historic renown or distinguished civil or military service...."

The states made their selections, and Rhode Island sent the first statue in 1870, a marble sculpture of Revolutionary hero Nathanael Greene. The room soon began to fill with images of statesmen, educators, suffragettes, generals, scientists, Indians, pioneers and other heroes. In 1975 the collection numbered 91 men and women. The Capitol also has nine statues other than those contributed by states. Their quality varies greatly, but together they form one of the finest and most representative collections of American sculpture, especially the 19th century works.

By 1933 the combined weight of the statues threatened to collapse the floor. Congress limited Statuary Hall to a single statue per state and authorized the placement of others throughout the Capitol. Many were moved to the Hall of Columns below the present House chamber. Statuary Hall remains one of the most popular rooms in the Capitol, and visitors search the corridors for such favorites as the bronze statute of Oklahoma's Will Rogers.

The Capitol has about 80 busts, including the heads of five Presidents, 10 Chief Justices and two Indian chiefs. An enormous marble head of Lincoln by Gutzon Borglum is in the Rotunda. There are 35 busts of Vice Presidents, 20 of them displayed in niches around the Senate gallery. The House gallery is surrounded by large relief medallions of 23 great lawgivers, from Hammurabi to Jefferson.

Works by Brumidi

Perhaps no other artist had as great an impact on the Capitol as Constantino Brumidi, an Italian immigrant hired in 1855 to decorate the interior. He continued for 25 years and his works can be seen throughout the building.

Brumidi's first work was the decoration of a House committee room (H-144) used at the time by the Agriculture Committee. The artist worked in fresco, applying paint to the surface of the plaster in its initial wet state. His murals in this room, "Calling of Cincinnatus from the Plow" and "Calling of Putnam from the Plow to the Revolution," were the first frescoes in the Capitol. There were to be many more, and Brumidi was to execute most of them.

Brumidi's masterpiece in the Rotunda, the symbolic "Apotheosis of Washington," decorates the canopy of the dome. Working in fresco, Brumidi took 11 months to cover 4,664 square feet of concave surface, often lying on his back nearly 180 feet above the stone floor. He completed the work in 1866.

The 300-foot frieze encircling the Rotunda, which Brumidi began in 1877 when he was 72, illustrates events in American history since the landing of Columbus. From the floor 58 feet below, the frieze appears to be a

...the Priceless and the Curious

sculptured relief, but it was painted in fresco on a flat surface. When the frieze was about one-third completed in 1879, Brumidi fell from the scaffold. He managed to catch a rope and was rescued, but the shock of the accident led to his death a few months later.

Filippo Costaggini, Brumidi's assistant, continued the work from 1880 to 1888, executing the designs Brumidi had prepared to circle the Rotunda. But either because of poor judgment or by his own planning, a 31-foot gap remained undecorated. A congressional resolution in 1950 provided for completion of the frieze, and Allyn Cox painted three final scenes in 1953. The frieze ends with the birth of aviation in 1903.

Brumidi's interior decoration elsewhere in the Capitol is spectacular. Working in fresco and with oils, he filled every inch of certain walls and vaulted ceilings with colorful designs, scrollwork, painted frames, portraits, landscapes, historical scenes, and pictures of plants and animals. His decoration can be seen in the "Brumidi Corridor" and the "Patent Corridor" on the ground floor of the Senate wing, and in the Senate Reception Room (S-213) and the President's Room (S-216), surely among the most elaborate rooms in America.

House Wing Corridors. The East corridor of the House wing, which Brumidi did not have time to decorate, finally was painted between early 1973 and mid-1974 by Allyn Cox, with the assistance of Cliff Young and John Charles Roach. Using oils, the artists filled the varied spaces with ornaments in harmony with the rest of the Capitol's interiors, and painted the vaults with scenes depicting the history of the Capitol. The last bay of the corridor, where an elevator had been installed, was disguised by a simulated vault.

Bronze Doors

Four pairs of cast bronze doors were executed for the major entrances to the Capitol, but only three of the four have been installed.

The best known doors are located at the eastern entrance to the Rotunda. Designed and modeled in high relief by Randolph Rogers in 1858, the doors are decorated with scenes from the life of Christopher Columbus. Total weight of the double doors and transom is 10 tons. In November 1863, the doors were installed between the old House chamber and the south wing, but they were moved to the Rotunda entrance in 1871.

The two pairs of doors at the eastern entrances of the House and Senate wings were designed in 1855-57 by sculptor Thomas Crawford, who also modeled the Statue of Freedom on top of the dome. The panels of the doors depict great events in American history. The Senate doors were installed in 1868 and the House doors in 1905.

The fourth pair of doors, modeled by Louis Amateis and completed in 1910, were designed for the central western entrance of the Capitol. But they could not be installed because enabling legislation for improvement of the West Front had not been enacted. They were exhibited first at the Corcoran Gallery of Art and then (1914-1967) at the Smithsonian Institution. The doors now are displayed on the first floor of the Capitol near the crypt. Panels in the doors depict symbolic accomplishments, and statuettes and medallions honor famous people.

Other Objects. Two of the most unusual objects in the Capitol collection are the Centennial Safe and the memorial to the pioneers of women's suffrage.

The Centennial Safe was a gift to the government from Mrs. Charles F. Deihm of New York, publisher of the weekly newspaper, *Our Second Century.* More than five feet tall, the safe was displayed at the 1876 Centennial Exposition in Philadelphia and later was moved to Statuary Hall. It was closed and locked with a key on February 22, 1879, and was opened July 1, 1976. The safe was displayed in the Capitol through the Bicentennial. It contained photographs of distinguished citizens, two volumes of autographs, a silver inkstand and other mementoes.

The suffragist memorial in the crypt below the Rotunda was presented in 1921. Sculptured by Adelaide Johnson, the monument consists of busts of Elizabeth Cady Stanton, Susan B. Anthony and Lucretia Mott emerging from an eight-ton block of Carrara marble. Its unusual appearance has given the memorial its nickname, "Ladies in a Bathtub."

Capitol Decoration. The Capitol is filled with outstanding examples of crafts. The building's decoration includes beautiful brasswork, marble staircases, carved wood and etched glass, intricate masonry, bronze railings, crystal chandeliers and antique furniture.

In the late 1850s the corridors of the House and Senate wings and several Capitol rooms were laid with glazed ceramic tile manufactured in England by Minton, Hollins and Company. The colorful tile patterns are a distinctive interior feature of the Capitol. The Minton tile was removed from most of the House wing in 1924 because it was badly worn and could not be matched. It was replaced by marble tile.

The basic appearance of the Capitol's interior was set by Benjamin H. Latrobe in his 11 years as architect before and after the 1814 fire. Latrobe's unique designs include the tobacco leaf and cornstalk motifs on columns in the small Senate Rotunda and at the entrance of the old Supreme Court chamber. His work was much admired by Thomas Jefferson.

Magna Carta Display. To commemorate the American Bicentennial, the British sent an original signed copy of the Magna Carta for display in the Rotunda. The "great charter" of English liberties, signed by King John at Runnymede on June 15, 1215, was scheduled for exhibition for a year beginning in May 1976. A facsimile was to remain permanently in the Capitol.

Lonnelle Aikman, We, the People: The Story of the United States Capitol, *U.S. Capitol Historical Society, 1974, p. 78.*

Source: Architect of the Capitol, U.S. Capitol Historical Society; Senate Commission on Art and Antiquities; Joint Committee on Printing.

(Continued from p. 417)

Appointment of Bulfinch. To succeed Latrobe, President Monroe on Jan. 8, 1818, appointed Charles Bulfinch of Boston, the first American-born architect to hold the position.

Bulfinch completed the reconstruction of the north and south wings, enabling Congress to resume meeting in the Capitol at the beginning of the 16th Congress on Dec. 6, 1819. The Supreme Court had returned for the February 1819 term.

The principal contribution of Bulfinch was to supervise work on the central section, for which the cornerstone was laid Aug. 24, 1818. With some modifications, Bulfinch completed the designs of Thornton and Latrobe for the center and the East and West fronts. There was some discussion of substituting a grand staircase and salon in place of an open rotunda, but Bulfinch decided in favor of the original plan.

In October 1824 the unfinished rotunda was used for a public reception for the Marquis de Lafayette. Then in his late sixties, the last surviving major general of the American Revolution was greeted as a hero. The same year John Trumbull's four paintings of scenes from the Revolution, commissioned in 1817, were hung in the Rotunda.

The original Capitol dome, much lower than the present dome and made of wood sheathed in copper, was completed in 1827. The pediment over the East Portico, "Genius of America" by Luigi Persico, was completed in 1828. The following year, initial construction of the Capitol was at last completed. The office Bulfinch had held since 1818 was abolished June 25, 1829.

The Capitol as completed in 1829 was 351 feet, 7½ inches long at ground level and 282 feet, 10½ inches wide. It took 37 years of construction and repair for the Capitol to achieve its original design, which it was to retain for only 22 years.

Cost. Treasury records indicate that the cost of repairing the damage wrought by the British was $687,126. Erection of the central section cost $957,647.36. The architect of the Capitol lists the cost of the original building, including repairs and grading of the Capitol grounds, as $2,432,851.34 up to the year 1827.[17]

Washington's Tomb

In the Capitol basement, two stories below the Rotunda, is an area that was intended to serve as a tomb for George and Martha Washington.

Within a few days after Washington's death on Dec. 14, 1799, Congress adopted a joint resolution providing that the first President was to be honored by placing his body in a special tomb in a section of the Capitol yet to be built. Meanwhile, Washington was buried at Mount Vernon in accordance with the terms of his will. In a letter of Dec. 31, 1799, Martha Washington gave permission to have his body moved to the Capitol.

Interior construction of the Rotunda was completed by 1824, but nearly five years more were needed to finish the entire central section. A circular opening about 10 feet in diameter was left in the center of the Rotunda floor, to permit visitors to look down upon a statue of Washington which was to have been placed in the crypt on the first floor. The tomb itself was to be one floor below the statue.

In 1828 the opening in the Rotunda floor was closed, because dampness from the lower levels was damaging the John Trumbull paintings hung in the Rotunda four years earlier. In 1830 a House committee recommended that both Washington and his wife be reinterred in the basement tomb.

As the 1832 centennial of Washington's birth approached, Congress asked John A. Washington, grandnephew of the first President, and George Washington Parke Custis, grandson of Mrs. Washington, for permission to move the bodies to the Capitol. Custis consented but John Washington refused. In 1832 the General Assembly of Virginia also adopted a resolution objecting to reinterment. The bodies have remained at Mount Vernon.

The area for the tomb is used to store the Lincoln catafalque, which serves as a bier when bodies of prominent citizens lie in state in the Rotunda.

Source: Architect of the Capitol, Art and Reference Division, release of June 1972.

Expansion, 1851-1892

Neither the House chamber nor the Senate chamber proved to be very comfortable. In addition to the acoustical problems in the House, both chambers were difficult to heat adequately in winter and difficult to ventilate.

As the mid-point of the 19th century approached, a new problem arose. The two chambers were becoming overcrowded by additional members representing newly admitted states. It was clear that the Capitol would have to be expanded.

Search for Designs. In response to a congressional request in 1843, the War Department prepared plans for an addition to the south wing to provide an enlarged chamber for the House. No further action was taken, however.

In May 1850 another set of requested drawings was rejected, although the Capitol by then was crowded with 62 senators and 232 representatives. The new drawings had been prepared by Robert Mills, the architect of public buildings, at the request of the Senate Public Buildings Committee. Mills had proposed adding two wings and enlarging the dome. Mills is more widely known as the architect of the Washington Monument, the Treasury Building and the Patent Office.

Then in September 1850 Congress adopted a resolution for a design competition under the supervision of the House and Senate Committees on Public Buildings. Plans were to be submitted by Dec. 1, 1850, and the winning design would receive a $500 award. As advertised in newspapers, "...these plans and estimates shall provide for the extension of the Capitol, either by additional wings, to be placed on the north and south of the present building, or by the erection of a separate and distinct building" to the east of the existing Capitol.[18]

A variety of plans was submitted. Some merely extended the old building further to the north and the south. Others proposed adding wings to the east and the west. At least one plan called for a duplicate building to the east. Four of the plans were selected, and Mills was asked to prepare a composite, incorporating certain features of each.

Appointment of Walter. In the meantime, a modified Senate amendment had been added to a routine appropriations bill authorizing President Fillmore to select a suitable plan and to appoint an architect. The appropriations measure, approved Sept. 30, 1850, also provided an initial $100,000 for the expansion. The legislation thwarted Mills' effort to develop a composite plan, although the Capitol extension inevitably included adaptations and compromises.

On June 10, 1851, Fillmore approved the general outline of a plan submitted by Thomas Ustick Walter, a Philadelphia architect who had designed Girard College, considered to be an outstanding example of the Greek Revival style in America. Walter was sworn in as architect of the Capitol extension on June 11. His accepted design provided for the erection at either end of the old building of the two wings which have been used for the House and Senate ever since they were built. The House is in the south wing, the Senate in the north.

Building of House and Senate Wings

The President laid the cornerstone for the extension on July 4, 1851, in the northeast corner of the House wing. The ceremonies included an oration by Daniel Webster. Work began immediately, but it was soon halted. Congress blocked further appropriations in the winter of 1851, when a controversy arose over charges of fraud and poor construction. The charges apparently were initiated by unsuccessful contractors and by the commissioner of public buildings and grounds. President Fillmore had made the Interior Department responsible for the extensions, leaving the commissioner in charge only of the central section. Investigating committees found the charges groundless, and appropriations were resumed in April 1852.

After renewed congressional sniping at Walter in 1853, President Pierce on March 23 transferred responsibility for the construction from the Interior Department to the War Department. War Secretary Jefferson Davis, who as a senator had led the drive for expansion, named Capt. M. C. Meigs of the Corps of Engineers to superintend the construction, and Meigs began a review of Walter's plans.

Meigs' review left Walter's basic design intact, but altered the location of the Senate and House chambers within their respective wings. Walter had put the Senate chamber on the east side of the north wing and arranged it so that the senators would sit facing east. The House, in the Walter plan, was to be on the east side of the south wing, arranged so that the representatives would face south. At Meigs' suggestion, Walter redesigned the location of the chambers to place them in the center of their respective wings, with the Senate facing north and the House south.

By the fall of 1854, the walls of the House and Senate wings were up to the ceiling level, but the chambers were not covered over until 1856. The present House chamber was occupied Dec. 16, 1857. As had been the case in the past, representatives were provided with individual desks and chairs. The desks were replaced by semi-circular benches in 1859, but the benches were removed and the desks reinstalled in 1860. Not until 1913 were the desks replaced by semicircular rows of seats.

Adequate acoustics remained a problem for the House even when it moved into its new chamber in 1857. Finally, in 1939, a system of microphones and loudspeakers was installed. After years of obstinate opposition, the Senate also had a public address system installed in 1970.

A delay in receiving certain ironwork held up completion of the north wing in the 1850s, so that the Senate was unable to meet in its chamber until Jan. 4, 1859. The

---

Capitol Building Facts

Site. On the western end of a plateau known previously as Jenkins Heights, 88 feet above the Potomac River. Located at the intersection of The Mall and North, East and South Capitol Streets.

Grounds. Total of 155 acres, including the Capitol, several congressional office buildings, the Library of Congress, the Supreme Court, and surrounding grounds, sidewalks and roads. Additional acres nearby.

Dimensions. Over-all length 751 feet, 4 inches. Greatest width, including approaches, 350 feet. Height 287 feet, 5½ inches from the East Front base to the top of the Statue of Freedom. Covers about four acres.

Capacity. Floor area of 16½ acres on five levels. Contains approximately 540 rooms devoted to offices, committee rooms, restaurants, storage and other purposes. There are 658 windows and 850 doorways.

Statue of Freedom. Female figure cast in bronze from plaster original by Thomas Crawford. Height 19 feet, 6 inches. Weight 14,985 pounds.

Dome. Width at base 135 feet, 5 inches. Made of cast iron. Weight 4,454.6 tons, or nearly 9 million pounds. Receives light through 108 windows.

Rotunda. Interior of the dome is 96 feet in diameter. Height 180 feet, 3 inches.

House Chamber. Length 139 feet. Width 93 feet. Greatest height 42 feet, 6 inches.

Senate Chamber. Length 113 feet, 3 inches. Width 80 feet, 3 inches. Greatest height 42 feet, 6 inches.

Source: Architect of the Capitol.

Senate's old desks were moved to the new chamber; new desks were added from time to time as the number of senators increased.

The exterior marble for the two wings came from quarries in Massachusetts, and marble for the columns was quarried in Maryland. One hundred columns, each cut from a single block of marble, were dressed by stonemasons on the Capitol grounds. Granite was used for the foundations. Until this phase of construction, the Capitol was made of Aquia Creek sandstone, with some granite foundations.

Construction of the New Dome

Although the original plans for extending the Capitol had made no provision for replacing the Bulfinch dome, it soon became apparent that the greatly enlarged building dwarfed the old dome. By an Act of April 4, 1855, Congress authorized replacement, and Walter drew up plans.

The tiered dome Walter designed is the distinguishing feature of the Capitol. It is a considerable accomplishment of art and engineering. Walter evidently was influenced by the domes of St. Paul's Cathedral in London and St. Peter's in Rome.[19] The entire dome, including the 36 columns in its lower section, is made of cast iron painted to match the Capitol's stonework. It consists of inner and outer shells girded and bolted together, and was assembled with the help of an internal crane which Meigs built from the floor of the Rotunda. The dome is more than 135 feet wide at its base and the Rotunda inside is 96 feet in diameter.

Work on the dome began in 1856 and was completed in 1865. Construction continued during the Civil War because President Lincoln wanted the expanding Capitol to be "a sign we intend the Union shall go on."[20]

On Dec. 2, 1863, the last section of the Statue of Freedom atop the dome was bolted into place, crowning the Capitol. Originally designed by sculptor Thomas Crawford as "Armed Liberty," wearing a soft cap of freed Roman slaves, the female statue was modified at the request of War Secretary Jefferson Davis.[21]

After installation of the dome's statue, work continued elsewhere on the Capitol. The pediment over the east portico of the Senate wing, "The Progress of Civilization" by Crawford, was erected in 1863. The north and west porticoes of the Senate wing were not completed until several years later. The porticoes of the House wing were completed by 1867, but the pediment over the east portico, "The Apotheosis of Democracy" by Paul Wayland Bartlett, was not installed until 1916.

Walter resigned as architect on May 26, 1865, as a result of a conflict over enlarging the quarters of the Library of Congress, then near the West Front of the Capitol. An accidental fire in 1851 had destroyed much of the Library.

Capitol During the Civil War

Congress, or what was left of it following secession, had adjourned March 3, 1861, the day before Lincoln's inauguration. When the President on April 15 issued a call for 75,000 volunteers, the Capitol was still vacant; and when the requested troops began arriving in Washington, they were quartered in the building.

The Sixth Massachusetts Regiment was camped in the Senate chamber. The House chamber contained the Seventh New York. The Eighth Massachusetts was quartered in the Rotunda. In all, some 14 units were bivouacked in the Capitol at one time or another, a total of 3,000 troops.

The soldiers called the Capitol the "Big Tent." Mock sessions of Congress were a favorite pastime. Basement vaults were turned into storehouses for firewood, flour, beef

and pork. Heating furnaces were used for cooking food. Committee rooms were lined with firebrick and converted into giant bread ovens.[22]

The Capitol itself became a heavily guarded defensive position. It was one of three centers, along with the City Hall hill and the White House, around which Col. Charles P. Stone of the District of Columbia Volunteers had planned his defense of Washington. The doors and windows were blocked with boards, stones and casks of cement. Heavy planking protected paintings and statues. Heavy iron plates, delivered for work on the dome, were erected as breastworks on the porticoes. Fifty armed men had been hidden beneath the platform erected for Lincoln's inauguration at the East Front.

In his request for volunteers following the Confederate attack on Ft. Sumter, Lincoln also had called a special session of Congress for July 4. As the date for the special session approached, the troops were cleared out, and the Capitol was given a thorough scouring.

In 1862, after the adjournment of Congress on July 17, the Capitol again was temporarily requisitioned, as a hospital for the wounded from the Second Bull Run and Antietam battles. Up to 1,500 cots were set up in the corridors, the Rotunda and the House and Senate chambers. The patients were transferred to other hospitals before the return of Congress on Dec. 1, and the Capitol once again was cleaned and refurbished.

Landscaping of Capitol Grounds

As major work on the Capitol expansion drew to a close in the late 1860s, the task of landscaping the Capitol grounds remained. The most prominent landscape architect of the time was Frederick Law Olmsted, the designer of New York's Central Park. By an Act of June 23, 1874, Olmsted was commissioned to landscape the grounds of the Capitol. The results of his work still surround the building.

Initial work on the grounds was carried out from 1874 to 1882. In 1881, additional funds were sought for the grand marble stairway and terraces on the west side of the Capitol, also designed by Olmsted. Congress approved the request, and work began in 1884. Space beneath the terraces was designed for use as committee rooms. Because the landscaping was virtually completed, Olmsted resigned in 1885, and the final work, finished in 1892, was supervised by Architect of the Capitol Edward Clark.

Cost. According to Treasury records, the Capitol expansion cost $8,075,299.04 for the new wings and $1,047,291.89 for the new dome. Landscaping the Capitol grounds cost $3,626,579.83.[23]

Recent Capitol Alterations

For 75 years following completion of the dome in 1865, little important architectural work was done on the Capitol. The roofs of the old north and south wings, over the original Senate chamber and Statuary Hall, were reconstructed and fireproofed in 1902. Then in 1940, Congress authorized remodeling of the House and Senate chambers and replacement of their cast iron and glass ceilings with new ceilings of stainless steel and plaster.

Remodeling. In 1940, temporary supports were installed under the old, weakened ceilings of the House and the Senate. Further work was delayed by World War II. The remodeling itself, under appropriations totaling $5,102,000, took place from July 1949 to January 1951. Plans for

---

Capitol Fires and Explosions

Several fires and explosions, some accidental and some not, have damaged the Capitol throughout its history. The most serious incidents are listed:

Aug. 24, 1814. A detachment of British troops led by Maj. Gen. Robert Ross and Rear Adm. Sir George Cockburn set fire to the Capitol, heavily damaging the interior.

Dec. 24, 1851. An accidental fire burned the West Front quarters of the Library of Congress, destroying 35,000 of the Library's 55,000 books.

Nov. 6, 1898. A gas explosion and fire heavily damaged the Supreme Court Chamber, the room used previously by the Senate.

July 2, 1915. The Senate Reception Room was damaged by the explosion of a homemade bomb, placed there by Erich Muenter (first identified as Frank Holt), a former instructor of German at Harvard who was upset by private sales of American munitions to the allies in World War I.

March 1, 1971. A bomb explosion at 1:32 a.m. damaged a small area on the ground floor of the Senate wing. *(Details, box p. 426)*

Source: Architect of the Capitol.

remodeling incorporated designs from sources of Federal architecture used by Thornton and Latrobe in the Supreme Court and Statuary Hall sections of the Capitol, and from other buildings of the period.

During the renovation, the Senate and House vacated their chambers on three occasions to allow the work to progress. The Senate held its sessions in the old Senate chamber, or Supreme Court room. The House met in the caucus room of the Longworth House Office Building.

When the temporary ceiling supports were being installed, the two bodies met in their substitute quarters from Nov. 22, 1940, to Jan. 3, 1941. When the first stage of construction work was being performed, the two bodies met away from their chambers from July 1, 1949, to Jan. 3, 1950. When construction on the final stage was under way, the Senate met in its old chamber from Aug. 11, 1950, to Jan. 3, 1951, and the House met in the Longworth Building from Sept. 1, 1950, to Jan. 1, 1951.[24]

Extension of East Front

The most controversial recent alteration of the Capitol was the 1958-62 extension of the East Front. Although such an extension had been proposed before, and had been discussed for years, its authorization by Congress in 1956 led to a heated dispute.

When Architect Thomas Ustick Walter designed the wings for the House and Senate and the new dome, he had suggested extending the east central section of the Capitol to make it symmetrical with the west central section and avoid any appearance of inadequate support for the larger dome. Walter wrote in his 1863 report to Congress: "The eastern portion of the old building will certainly be taken down at no very distant day, and the front be extended eastward."[25] But the day was more distant than Walter expected.

In 1903, the House passed a bill for extension of the East Front, but the bill died in the Senate. Congress in 1904 established a joint commission to study the question. The commission asked the firm of Carrere and Hastings, which had just designed the first House and Senate office buildings, to prepare plans for a proposed eastern extension. The architects submitted two proposals. One, labeled scheme A, provided for an extension of 12 feet, 10 inches. The other, called scheme B, provided for a 32½-foot extension. Once again, no further action was taken.

In 1935 and in 1937, the Senate passed bills providing for an extension. Both measures died in the House.

Finally in 1955, in the fiscal 1956 Legislative Appropriations Act, Congress authorized the extension of the East Front and provided an initial appropriation of $5-million. The extension was to follow the Carrere and Hastings proposal for a 32½-foot extension (scheme B). The work was to be directed by a Commission for Extension of the United States Capitol, then comprised of the President of the Senate, the Speaker of the House, the minority leader of each chamber and the architect of the Capitol.

There was little discussion about the project at first. Contributing to its acceptance were the deteriorating condition of the sandstone facing and the need of Congress for additional space. House Speaker Sam Rayburn (D Texas) was one of the strongest advocates of extension.

As public awareness of the impending project grew, however, strong opposition developed among architectural and historical groups. Opponents of the extension said the East Front should be repaired and preserved as it was. They

---

Final Tributes in the Rotunda

There is no law, regulation or written rule to determine whose body may lie in state in the Rotunda of the Capitol. Use of the Rotunda is controlled generally by concurrent resolution of the House and Senate, but it has been used without full concurrence during recesses or between sessions of Congress.

Twenty-four American citizens have lain in state in the Rotunda. They have included nine Presidents, six military men and the city planner who chose the site for the Capitol. The simple bier of cloth-covered boards constructed for Abraham Lincoln's coffin has been used for all tributes since 1865. The Lincoln catafalque was used also for services in the Senate Chamber for Chief Justice Salmon P. Chase in 1873 and in the House Chamber for Rep. Samuel Hooper in 1875.

Following is a list of persons who have been honored in the Rotunda and the dates on which their bodies lay in state:

Henry Clay	July 1, 1852
Abraham Lincoln	April 19-21, 1865
Thaddeus Stevens	Aug. 13-14, 1868
Charles Sumner	March 13, 1874
Henry Wilson	Nov. 25-26, 1875
James A. Garfield	Sept. 21-23, 1881
John A. Logan	Dec. 30-31, 1886
William McKinley	Sept. 17, 1901
Pierre Charles L'Enfant (reinterment)	April 28, 1909
George Dewey	Jan. 20, 1917
Unknown Soldier of World War I	Nov. 9-11, 1921
Warren G. Harding	Aug. 8, 1923
William Howard Taft	March 11, 1930
John Joseph Pershing	July 18-19, 1948
Robert A. Taft	Aug. 2-3, 1953
Unknown Soldiers of World War II and the Korean War* (2)	May 28-30, 1958
John F. Kennedy	Nov. 24-25, 1963
Douglas MacArthur	April 8-9, 1964
Herbert Hoover	Oct. 23-25, 1964
Dwight D. Eisenhower	March 30-31, 1969
Everett McKinley Dirksen	Sept. 9-10, 1969
J. Edgar Hoover	May 3-4, 1972
Lyndon Baines Johnson	Jan. 24-25, 1973

A duplicate catafalque was constructed, and each coffin rested for a time on the Lincoln catafalque.

Source: Architect of the Capitol, Art and Reference Division, releases of January 1973 and November 1974.

---

forced a one-day hearings before the Senate Public Works Subcommittee on Public Buildings and Grounds. The hearing was held on Feb. 17, 1958. On Feb. 21, the commission ordered the project to go ahead.

Work began in 1958. On July 4, 1959, President Eisenhower laid the cornerstone. Under the approved plans, a new East Front in marble was constructed 32½ feet east of the old front. The east walls of the connections between the central section of the Capitol and the Senate and House wings also were extended to the east and reproduced in

(Continued on p. 425)

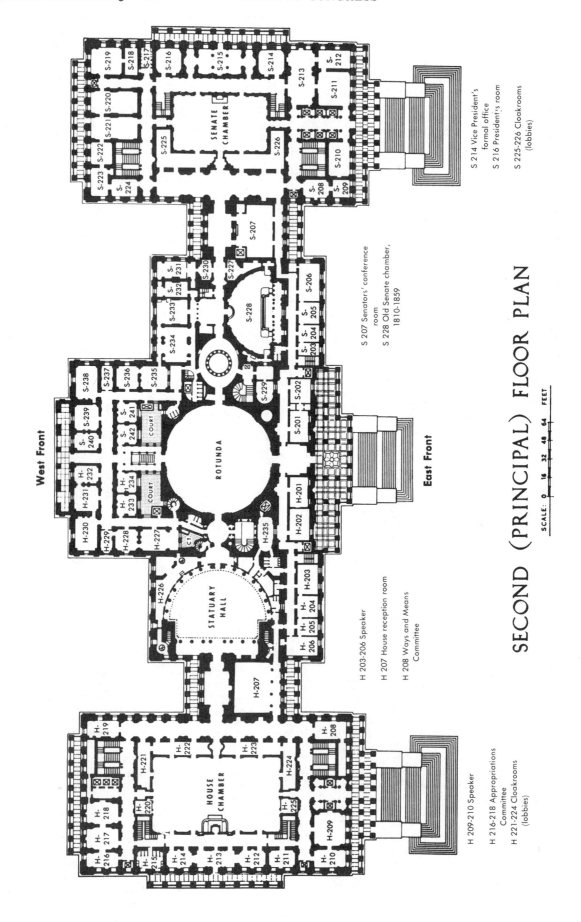

SECOND (PRINCIPAL) FLOOR PLAN

West Front

East Front

SCALE: 0 16 32 48 64 FEET

ROTUNDA

SENATE CHAMBER

HOUSE CHAMBER

STATUARY HALL

S 214 Vice President's formal office
S 216 President's room
S 225-226 Cloakrooms (lobbies)

S 207 Senators' conference room
S 228 Old Senate chamber, 1810-1859

H 203-206 Speaker
H 207 House reception room
H 208 Ways and Means Committee

H 209-210 Speaker
H 216-218 Appropriations Committee
H 221-224 Cloakrooms (lobbies)

(Continued from p. 423)

marble. The old sandstone walls were retained as a part of the interior wall construction. The original stonework and carvings were copied exactly in marble. The old sandstone columns were removed and stored at the Capitol Power Plant. Crumbling statuary from the East Front finally was transferred to the Smithsonian Institution in 1975.

The work was completed in 1962, although it was far enough along for President Kennedy's inauguration at the East Front in January 1961. During construction J. George Stewart was architect of the Capitol

Inaugural Sites

A President may take the oath of office anywhere, in public or private. Beginning in 1829 with Andrew Jackson, 34 inaugural ceremonies have been held outdoors near the East Front Portico of the Capitol. Nine other inaugurations have taken place inside the Capitol. Seven Presidents have taken the oath privately when they assumed the office in an emergency. Three Presidents—Hayes, Wilson and Eisenhower—took the oath in private on the day required by the Constitution, then repeated it in public ceremonies a day or two later.

Following is a list of public inaugural sites other than the East Front Portico:

Federal Hall, Broad and Wall Streets, New York City:

1789—George Washington

Congress Hall, Sixth and Chestnut Streets, Philadelphia:

1793—George Washington
1797—John Adams

Senate Chamber of the Capitol:

1801—Thomas Jefferson
1805—Thomas Jefferson
1909—William Howard Taft

House Chamber of the Capitol:

1809—James Madison
1813—James Madison
1821—James Monroe
1825—John Quincy Adams
1833—Andrew Jackson
1850—Millard Fillmore

"Brick Capitol," First and A Streets, N.E., Washington, D.C.:

1817—James Monroe

South Portico of the White House:

1945—Franklin D. Roosevelt

East Room of the White House:

1974—Gerald R. Ford

Source: Architect of the Capitol, Art and Reference Division.

Additions. The East Front extension added 100,000 square feet of space to the Capitol's five floors. It provided 102 new rooms, including 54 offices for individuals and committees, reception rooms, dining rooms and kitchens, document rooms, entrance foyers, additional elevators, and a private corridor for members between the Senate and House wings.

The construction project included more than an extension of the East Front. The Capitol's cast iron dome was sandblasted and repainted; a subway terminal was built under the Senate wing steps and the steps were rebuilt; the exterior marble of the Senate and House wings was cleaned for the first time since 1872; the entire building was "birdproofed"; all new rooms were furnished; and lighting throughout the Capitol was improved.

Cost. The total cost of the extension and all additional construction and repairs came to $24-million.[26] Extending the East Front alone cost $11,383,000.[27]

West Front Controversy

Although the authority of the fiscal 1956 Legislative Appropriations Act was used initially to extend the East Front, its broad language authorized the "extension, reconstruction, and replacement of the central portion of the United States Capitol." As work on the East Front drew to a close in 1962, the Commission for Extension of the U.S. Capitol turned its attention to the West Front.

The question of whether to restore, replace or extend the West Front is perhaps the most controversial construction issue in the Capitol's long history. After years of congressional debate, it still has not been settled.

Structural Weakness. At the heart of the controversy is a serious problem which must be solved in some way. There is a structural weakness in the west wall of the Capitol's central section. The last exposed portion of the original Capitol, the wall is constructed of Aquia Creek sandstone on the exterior, brick and stone on the interior, and is filled with loose rubble. The wall bears much of the lateral load of the huge building and for some time has been moving slightly, perhaps as much as one-fourth inch each year.[28] The sandstone, long known to be an inferior building material, has deteriorated since Bulfinch completed the original Capitol 150 years ago.

In a review of the wall's condition in 1973 the architect of the Capitol wrote: "Not only do many cracks exist from the footings through to the roof, but many of the lintels are cracked and sagging, the portico is unstable without supporting bracing, carved stones have broken and fallen, and the face of the stone itself is substantially deteriorated both in spite of and because of the many layers of paint (as much as one-fourth inch thick in places) with which all of the stone has been covered since 1829."[29]

First Studies. In 1964, Congress appropriated $125,000 for engineering studies of the West Front, and the commission hired a Brookline, Mass., engineering concern, Thompson and Lichtner Co. Inc. The studies were completed and submitted to the commission early in 1965. The firm recommended "an extended building...as the least hazardous and as causing the least interference with the occupancy of the present structure." Restoration of the existing West Front was specifically not recommended.[30] After a public hearing on the studies June 24, 1965, the commission agreed to ask Congress for money for preliminary plans, cost estimates and a model. Congress appropriated $300,000 for the project in October.

(Continued on p. 427)

1971 Capitol Bombing: Tighter Security

A bomb explosion in the Capitol in 1971, which caused extensive damage but no injuries, resulted in an improved security system for Capitol Hill.

Site of the explosion was an unmarked rest room on the ground floor of the original Senate wing, the oldest part of the Capitol. The blast demolished the rest room and caused extensive damage to six other rooms, including the Senate barbershop, a hearing room of the Senate Appropriations Committee and hideaway offices used by several senators. By 1976 the case still had not been solved.

Telephone Warning

The explosion occurred at 1:32 a.m. on March 1—33 minutes after a telephone caller warned the Capitol switchboard: "This building will blow up in 30 minutes. You will get many calls like this, but this one is real. Evacuate the building. This is in protest against the Nixon involvement in Laos."

Immediately after the warning call, a search of the Capitol was conducted by the 15 members of the Capitol Police then on duty. Their search took them to the general area of the rest room, but they did not check the room itself, they said, because it had been inspected only a few minutes before the call was received.

Subsequently, an Army munitions expert told a Senate subcommittee "it is our belief" that the explosive had been concealed behind a false wall in the rest room. He speculated that the blast could have been caused by 15 to 20 pounds of dynamite connected to a "delayed timing device" and smuggled into the Capitol "in an ordinary briefcase." It was noted that the building had been open to tourists until 4:30 p.m. on the day preceding the bombing, a Sunday, and that while entrances to the Capitol were routinely guarded, no check of visitors or inspection of parcels was customary.

Responsibility for the blast was promptly claimed by a group calling itself the Weather Underground. In identical letters to *The New York Times* and the Associated Press, the group wrote: "We have attacked the Capitol because it is, along with the White House and the Pentagon, the worldwide symbol of the government which is now attacking Indochina."

Tighter Security Proposed

In the wake of the bombing, there was widespread agreement on the need for additional security measures on Capitol Hill. The Capitol was briefly closed to visitors on the morning following the bombing but was reopened at midday. Thereafter the Capitol Police were instructed to check all briefcases and large packages brought into the Capitol itself and the Senate and House office buildings by employees as well as tourists. The bombing site remained closed pending repairs. Senate Sergeant at Arms Robert G. Dunphy said that during the tourist season as many as 25,000 people pass through the Rotunda daily and that thorough inspection of all visitors would be extremely difficult.

Following the bombing, a number of improvements were made in the Capitol's security system.

● Inspection of packages and briefcases at all entrances to the Capitol and congressional office buildings has continued since the day of the bombing. At 10 entrances the guards are aided by X-ray machines, installed at a total cost of $300,000. Guards at other stations inspect packages by hand.

● An electronic surveillance system using closed circuit television and automatic alarms was installed at strategic points throughout the Capitol complex. The system has more than 100 TV cameras, which are monitored by the Capitol Police. It was fully installed in May 1975 at a cost of $4-million.

● The tunnels from the Capitol Power Plant to all buildings in the Capitol complex were wired with an alarm system.

● The Capitol Police force was increased from 622 officers in 1971 to a total force of 1,113 in 1975. Political patronage was reduced substantially. In addition, 50 officers and detective sergeants from the District of Columbia Metropolitan Police Department are detailed to the Capitol during daily meetings of the House and Senate.

● A hazardous device unit was established by the Capitol Police to respond to bomb threats, search Capitol areas and examine suspicious packages. A group of dogs, owned by the Capitol Police, was trained especially to detect explosives.

● Potential hiding places for explosives in the Capitol were patched up or sealed off in a series of minor construction projects. For example, false walls of the sort where the 1971 bomb was hidden can no longer be opened. The public now is directed away from the remote sections of the Capitol where bombs might be left.

The bombing also gave new life to a study authorized in 1970 to modernize the House and Senate galleries, including the possible installation of bulletproof glass. Such a measure was first suggested in 1954, following the shooting of five representatives by Puerto Rican nationalists. *(Box, "Violence in the Capitol," p. 428)* The study concluded in 1973 that the glass was not advisable. But in January 1976, electronic metal detectors were installed at seven entrances to the House gallery. The walk-through sensors, similar to those used at airports, were purchased for about $40,000.

Extent of Damage

The damage from the blast consisted of cracked and battered walls, weakened floors and arches, blown-out doors and windows, and damaged trim, chandeliers and artwork. It cost approximately $200,000 to repair the damage.

Source: Capitol Police Chief James M. Powell; Architect of the Capitol, Art and Reference Division.

(Continued from p. 425)

Extension Plan. Private engineers and architects developed three plans for extension. In a surprise announcement on June 17, 1966, the commission approved an elaborate plan to extend the entire West Front. Designed to add as much as 270,000 square feet of floor space—nearly three times the capacity of the East Front extension—the plan called for extending the central section 44 feet, the two original wings 88 feet, and the corridors connecting the present Senate and House wings 56 feet. The original estimated cost was $35-million, but by 1973 it had escalated to $60-million.

The proposed use of all that space has varied in subsequent discussions of the plan, which never has been made final. A commission report issued in 1967 and published in the March 28, 1972, *Congressional Record* said the extension would add 285 rooms.[31] From time to time, advocates and opponents of the West Front extension have said it would include 115 offices, two auditoriums, two cafeterias, four dining rooms, committee rooms, a tourist center, an all-weather bus terminal, underground truck docks, a document room, press room, lounges, cloakrooms, reception rooms, and a vague number of private hideaways for members of Congress. The extension would cover nearly an acre of the grounds and terraces west of the present building.

A storm of congressional protest erupted when details of the proposed extension were made public. The objections were based on economic, historical and architectural grounds. Strenuous opposition developed in the Senate where 30 members, led by A. S. Mike Monroney (D Okla.) and William Proxmire (D Wis.), sponsored bills to block the project. A small but vocal House protest was organized by Samuel S. Stratton (D N.Y.). Architect of the Capitol J. George Stewart, a former representative from Delaware, was criticized almost daily in both the House and Senate for his strong advocacy of the extension plan.

Congressional Debate. Stewart did not follow up his announced intention to seek appropriations for the extension in 1966, apparently because of the hostile reaction in Congress. The debate continued in 1967.

Opposing the extension and favoring in its place a restoration of the west wall, the American Institute of Architects (AIA) said in a special April 1967 report: "The West Front of the Capitol can be restored and its structural weaknesses corrected." While restoration would be costly and "would entail some inconvenience," the AIA said, it was "unlikely that the cost of the restoration would approach the total cost of extension." The AIA, stressing the historical importance of the existing West Front, also called for a "permanent policy prohibiting any further major alteration to the Capitol."[32]

Discussing the AIA-backed restoration plan, Stewart's office told the House Legislative Branch Appropriations Subcommittee in early 1967: "What a shame it would be to butcher this old building in the manner they propose. Their program, if it can be called that, ...is an open invitation to endless expense, ...continued admittedly poor structural conditions, ...a scabby appearance...and stifling any further space growth for congressional operations in the Capitol."[33]

Debate over the West Front extension marked time in 1968, although Congress appropriated $135,000 to brace portions of the west wall and to caulk and paint the old sandstone. In 1965 the most obviously weak portions of the West Front had been shored with heavy timbers.

In 1969 Congress appropriated $2,275,000 for final extension plans, but earmarked $250,000 to be spent first for an independent study of restoration. The commission was authorized to proceed with extension unless the restoration study met five conditions, including a $15-million limit on the cost of restoration.

An Act of Sept. 29, 1969, increased the membership of the commission from five to seven. The majority leaders of the Senate and House joined the two minority leaders, the Speaker of the House, the Vice President and the architect of the Capitol.

New Architect. Stewart died in office May 24, 1970. President Nixon on Jan. 27, 1971, appointed George M. White as the ninth architect of the Capitol. A former vice president and board member of the AIA, White became the Capitol's first professional architect since Walter resigned in 1865. White was also an engineer and a lawyer.

Restoration Study. The New York architectural and engineering firm of Praeger-Kavanaugh-Waterbury completed its restoration study in January 1971. It concluded that a safe and attractive restoration of the west wall could be accomplished for slightly less than $15-million. It estimated the work could be done "in about three years, with no single wall section being scaffolded for more than one year."[34]

The commission did not pass judgment on the restoration study until March 8, 1972, when it decided that the five conditions specified in the 1969 act could not be met. It directed White to prepare final plans for extension. White, following a year-long review of all West Front proposals, had concluded before the commission met that the west wall needed repair and strengthening, that restoration would cost more than $15-million, and that Congress would have to weigh its need for office space against the desire for preservation.[35]

Senate Opposition. The Senate on March 28, 1972, amended the fiscal 1973 appropriations bill (PL 92-342) to deny funds for final plans or any construction of the West Front extension "until specifically approved and appropriated therefor by the Congress." There followed a three-month deadlock in conference until the House, by a roll-call vote (197-181) on June 28, accepted the Senate amendment.

The commission met Feb. 28, 1973, and again recommended extending the West Front according to the preliminary plan. White was directed to request $58-million ($60-million less $2-million appropriated in 1969) for fiscal 1974.

The House approved the request by voice vote April 18, after failing by six votes on the previous day to delete all funds for extension. The Senate, still opposed to extension, instead approved $18-million for restoration of the West Front and an additional $15-million to build underground offices. This led to another conference deadlock, which was resolved Oct. 11 by deleting all language relating to West Front construction.[36]

White, "after two years of intensive study and concern, and evaluation of the many ramifications," issued a statement in June 1973 strongly in favor of extending the West Front.[37] He doubted the feasibility of restoration, which he believed would cost at least $30-million, without alleviating the need for space.

White argued that Thomas U. Walter "had made numerous studies for the Congress, showing both the original East Front and the original West Front extended and modified to bring the central portion into harmony with the large dome and the Senate and House wings of his design."[38] When that point had been raised in previous con-

Violence in the Capitol

Violence has flared in the Capitol from time to time, particularly during the 19th century. Strong personal feelings have led to brawls among members in both chambers. In 1835, Vice President Martin Van Buren regularly wore a brace of pistols while presiding over the Senate. The House became known in frontier days as the "Bear Garden" because of its many quarrels. A picture in the files of the Library of Congress shows a wild melee on the House floor during a debate in 1858 on the Kansas statehood bill. Members of Congress and other officials have been attacked in the Capitol by private citizens as well.

Following is a selected list of major incidents:

Attempt on Jackson. On Jan. 30, 1835, a man later identified as Richard Lawrence fired two pistols at Andrew Jackson as the President stood in the Rotunda. Both pistols misfired. Jackson had come to the Capitol to attend funeral services in the House Chamber for Rep. Warren R. Davis (State Rights Democrat, S.C.). Lawrence, who was captured immediately, was found to be insane.

Foote-Benton Quarrel. On April 17, 1850, during the controversy surrounding the Compromise of 1850, Sen. Henry S. Foote (Unionist Miss.), a supporter of the Compromise, drew a pistol on Sen. Thomas Hart Benton (D Mo.), who opposed the Compromise. The incident occurred when Benton rushed to threaten Foote after Foote had directed bitter personal abuse at him. Other senators intervened before Foote could fire.

Beating of Sumner. On May 22, 1856, Rep. Preston S. Brooks (State Rights Democrat S.C.) used a heavy cane in an attack on Sen. Charles Sumner (R Mass.) in the Senate chamber. The attack came during discussion of the Kansas-Nebraska bill, and it followed a May 20 speech in which Sumner had personally denounced Brooks' uncle, Sen. A. P. Butler (State Rights Democrat S.C.). Sumner was beaten unconscious and was not able to resume his Senate duties for more than three years. Brooks, censured, resigned his seat but was re-elected.

Shooting of Taulbee. On Feb. 28, 1890, Charles E. Kincaid, a correspondent for the Louisville *Times,* shot former Rep. William P. Taulbee (D Ky.) on the stairs leading from the eastern corridor of the House to the basement. The shooting apparently resulted from *Times* stories of a scandal involving Taulbee. Taulbee died of the wounds on March 11, 1890.

Gunman in the House. On Dec. 13, 1932, a young man entered the House gallery, drew a loaded revolver and began waving it wildly, demanding time to address the House. As bedlam broke loose on the House floor, Rep. Melvin J. Maas (R Minn.) approached the gunman, a department store clerk named Marlin R. M. Kemmerer, and talked him into dropping the gun. Police arrested Kemmerer without a shot being fired.

Bricker Shooting. On July 12, 1947, Sen. John W. Bricker (R Ohio) was shot at twice as he entered the Senate subway. Both shots missed. The gunman was William L. Kaiser, a former Capitol policeman who had lost money when an Ohio building and loan firm was liquidated 15 years earlier.

Puerto Rican Attack. Five representatives were shot March 1, 1954, on the floor of the House. Their assailants, three pistol-wielding Puerto Rican extremists of the Nationalist party, fired about 30 shots from a visitors' gallery into a crowd of about 200 representatives. Wounded were Reps. Alvin M. Bentley (R Mich.), Ben F. Jensen (R Iowa), Clifford Davis (D Tenn.), George H. Fallon (D Md.) and Kenneth A. Roberts (D Ala.). The three assailants, and a fourth member of the group captured later, received prison sentences.

Source: Architect of the Capitol, Art and Reference Division; U.S. Capitol Historical Society.

gressional debate, Sen. Ernest F. Hollings (D S.C.), a strong opponent of extension, had scoffed. If the commission-approved extension were constructed, Hollings said, the Capitol dome would "look like the beanie on a freshman's head."[39]

Question Deferred. The controversy continued in 1974. The House included no funds for either extension or restoration in the fiscal 1975 appropriations bill, partly because of Senate opposition and partly because members did not wish to have the Capitol under construction during the Bicentennial. But a Senate amendment added $20.9-million for restoration and a master plan for the Capitol grounds. The bill was reported in disagreement by the conference committee, and the House rejected the Senate amendment Aug. 1, 1974, by a 192-203 vote.[40]

Hollings said, "The question of extension has been put to rest and the House of Representatives is coming toward restoration." But Rep. Bob Casey (D Texas), floor manager of the bill in the House, saw things differently: "So let us postpone action and then have our fight after the Bicentennial, and settle it once and for all if we possibly can."[41]

In the fiscal 1976 legislative appropriations bill, neither the House nor the Senate included any funds for West Front construction. They even denied White's request for $1.4-million to replace walkways and steps approaching the West Front from the foot of Capitol Hill. The bill, which cleared Congress July 22, 1975, did include $350,000 for a master plan to develop and enlarge the Capitol grounds. But the Senate Appropriations Committee got assurances from White that it was "his intention not to include in the development of the master plan any changes to the West Front of the Capitol, including either full or partial extension thereof."[42]

The desire of Congress not to disrupt Bicentennial observances with Capitol construction was not the only reason the West Front controversy cooled off in 1975. A National Visitors' Center under construction at Union Station, only a few blocks north of the Capitol, was expected to provide many of the tourist services originally planned for the extension. Moreover, the House had acquired over 500,-000 square feet in two nearby buildings and was considering erecting a new office building.

Capitol Historical Society

Since 1962 the Capitol has had a sort of fan club, the United States Capitol Historical Society. By its own description the society is "privately financed, patriotically motivated and charged with a profound sense of mission." It is a nonprofit educational organization that helps professional scholars, amateur historians and the public to gain a better understanding of the Capitol and its history.

The society has about 5,000 members who contribute from $5 to $1,000 to support its research and projects, which are coordinated with the architect of the Capitol. The society also operates an information center and souvenir stand on the ground floor of the Capitol, where mementoes on sale include paperweights and book ends made from sandstone fragments of the original East Front.

Special publications head the society's activities, including Lonnelle Aikman's popular book, *We the People: The Story of the United States Capitol.* Published with the assistance of the National Geographic Society, the full-color book has sold more than three million copies in several editions and languages. Other society publications include a guide to Washington, a Capitol coloring book, illustrated calendars, quarterly newsletters and occasional scholarly studies of the art and architecture of the Capitol.

Special projects of the society include a documentary film, "Washington: City Out of Wilderness," and a sound and light production planned for the East Front. With contributions from the Daughters of the American Revolution and others, the society is supporting new paintings and murals by Allyn Cox in the House wing of the Capitol. It intends to continue the project "until every corridor of the Capitol is illuminated by scenes from our past."

The founder and president of the society is Fred Schwengel, former Republican representative from Iowa. Several members of Congress serve as trustees. The society's office is at 200 Maryland Avenue N.E., Washington, D.C. 20515.

Source: U.S. Capitol Historical Society.

Still, the West Front controversey could only be considered dormant, not dead. The problem of the weakened west wall remained to be solved. The proponents of restoration, extension or other modification of the Capitol were prepared to take up their causes as soon as the nation began its third century.

Remodeling Projects

Construction projects of such scope as extending the West Front are extraordinary. More modest remodeling of the Capitol goes on continually. The building requires a great deal of special maintenance, including restoration of works of art and replacement of some hard-used furnishings. The Speaker's Lobby, a 100-foot corridor just outside the House chamber, was remodeled in 1972 for the first time since 1901.

Four recent remodeling projects were designed especially to prepare the Capitol for the Bicentennial and the unusually large number of tourists expected in 1976 and the following years. The Bicentennial projects were supervised by the architect of the Capitol and the Senate Commission on Art and Antiquities.

Rotunda. Early in 1975 the Rotunda was refurbished for the first time in more than 70 years. The stone walls were cleaned with a special mixture and water pressure, and tiny cracks were sealed. The exposed metal of the dome was painted to match a color drawing prepared by Walter in the 1860s. The eight oil paintings were restored, special lighting was installed, and 16 upholstered benches designed for the House chamber in 1859 were placed around the Rotunda.

Statuary Hall. In 1975 and 1976 Statuary Hall was partially restored to resemble its appearance in the 1820s, when it served as the House chamber. Some statues were moved to other parts of the Capitol. The ceiling was repainted; new scarlet draperies were hung; and two fireplaces were opened and restored. But the old House furnishings were not replaced. An electric replica of the chamber's original crystal chandelier was to be installed in 1976.

Old Supreme Court Chamber. On May 22, 1975, the public got its first look at the restored Supreme Court chamber on the first floor of the original Senate wing. The chamber, which the Court used for 50 years from Latrobe's remodeling until Walter's expansion, was fully restored to its appearance of about 1850. For 20 years it had been a storeroom. Cost of the restoration was nearly $480,000.[43]

Old Senate Chamber. Restoration of the old Senate chamber, on the second floor north of the Rotunda, was completed in 1976. The original lights, draperies and furniture used by the Senate in the 1850s were restored, and carpeting and other period furnishings were reproduced. The Senate met there from 1810 to 1859, when it was remodeled and used by the Supreme Court for 75 years. Cost of the restoration was estimated to be about $1-million.[44]

House and Senate Office Buildings

The construction of separate office buildings for senators and representatives is a relatively recent occurrence in the history of Congress. The first congressional office building, for members of the House, was not ready for use until 1908. Until then, a member's office consisted of his desk in the House or Senate chamber, or his rented room in a Washington boarding house. His files were carried in his head or the pockets of his jacket. The Capitol was the neatly self-contained home of the legislative branch.

The record of change from the traditional situation to the contemporary housing of Congress parallels the growth of Congress itself.

For years after the organization of the legislative branch under the Constitution, serving as a member of Congress was at most a part-time occupation. Sessions were short. Standing committees were few. And Washington was both inaccessible and inhospitable, protecting members from visits by constituents.

At the Capitol, if a member was not actually on the floor he had virtually no sanctuary, except his boarding house. The lobbies just off the chambers provided some relaxation. But the lobbies were open to the public, and favor-seekers took advantage of the chance to buttonhole legislators; hence the term "lobbying."

(Continued on p. 431)

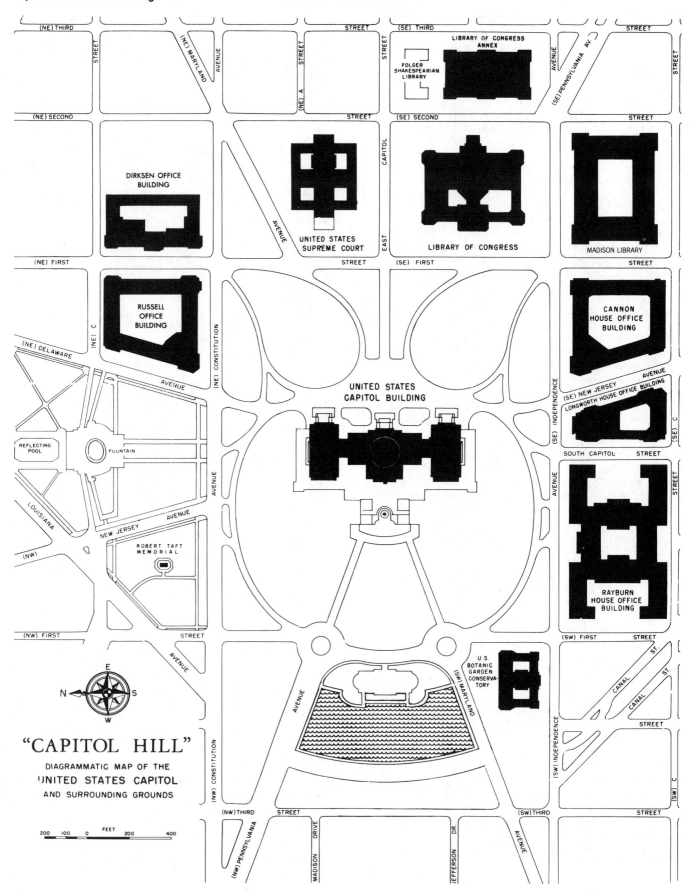

(NE) THIRD STREET

STREET

(NE) MARYLAND AVENUE

STREET

STREET

(SE) THIRD STREET

LIBRARY OF CONGRESS ANNEX

FOLGER SHAKESPEARIAN LIBRARY

(SE) PENNSYLVANIA AV.

STREET

(NE) SECOND STREET

STREET

(SE) SECOND STREET

STREET

DIRKSEN OFFICE BUILDING

(NE) A STREET

UNITED STATES SUPREME COURT

CAPITOL

LIBRARY OF CONGRESS

MADISON LIBRARY

(NE) FIRST STREET

EAST STREET

(SE) FIRST STREET

STREET

RUSSELL OFFICE BUILDING

(NE) C

(NE) CONSTITUTION AVENUE

CANNON HOUSE OFFICE BUILDING

(NE) DELAWARE AVENUE

(SE) NEW JERSEY AVENUE

(SE) INDEPENDENCE AVENUE

LONGWORTH HOUSE OFFICE BUILDING

UNITED STATES CAPITOL BUILDING

(SE) C

REFLECTING POOL

FOUNTAIN

SOUTH CAPITOL STREET

LOUISIANA AVENUE

NEW JERSEY AVENUE

(NW)

ROBERT TAFT MEMORIAL

RAYBURN HOUSE OFFICE BUILDING

(NW) FIRST STREET

AVENUE

(SW) FIRST STREET

CANAL ST.

STREET

E
N — S
W

U.S. BOTANIC GARDEN CONSERVATORY

(SW) MARYLAND

CANAL ST.

STREET

"CAPITOL HILL"

DIAGRAMMATIC MAP OF THE
UNITED STATES CAPITOL
AND SURROUNDING GROUNDS

(SW) INDEPENDENCE AVENUE

(SW) C

(NW) CONSTITUTION

200 100   0   200   400
              FEET

(NW) THIRD STREET

MADISON DRIVE

(NW) PENNSYLVANIA

JEFFERSON DR.

(SW) THIRD STREET

AVENUE

Growth of Pressure for Office Space

The first pressure for additional office space came from the congressional committees. The groups quickly overflowed the rooms allocated to them in the unfinished Capitol. At times, several Senate committees would meet in separate areas of the Senate chamber. When Bulfinch was at work on the Capitol's center section, he erected a temporary building for committees on the site of the present House wing. The long wooden building stood for only a few years until the original Capitol was completed.[45] The expansion of the Capitol by Walter in the 1850s provided more committee rooms, and much of the space beneath the terraces built in the 1880s was designated for committees.

The proliferation of committees devoured new space almost as fast as it was provided. Not all of the proliferation, however, was dictated by the press of legislative business. A committee office in the Capitol frequently doubled as a personal office for the committee chairman. The committee clerks doubled as a personal staff. This dual role of committees was widely acknowledged and occasionally criticized.

Criticized or not, the committees and their perquisites proved attractive. As a result, some committees survived long after their business was completed. The Senate Committee on Revolutionary (War) Claims, for example, existed until 1921.

As the committees outgrew the space provided even in the expanded Capitol, additional space was rented in nearby privately owned buildings. By 1891, the Maltby Building, at B Street and New Jersey Avenue, Northwest, had become known as the Senate Annex. It had been converted into 81 offices.

By the end of the 19th century, Congress had grown too large for the Capitol, and the use of converted buildings was judged inconvenient, if not hazardous because of the danger of fire. The Maltby Building had been condemned as an unsafe structure before the Senate finally left it. As the nation grew, the increased membership of the Senate and House produced a demand for additional rooms to accommodate members. The House authorized its first office building in 1903, the Senate in 1904.

Construction of Office Buildings

Once the first buildings set the precedent, pressure for additional buildings was impossible to resist. The pressure rose as the staffs of members increased, and as committees (and their expanded staffs) moved out of the Capitol and into the office buildings. The House currently has three office buildings of its own, two annexes, and is considering erecting its fourth building. The Senate has two office buildings, two temporary annexes and is planning to extend one of the main buildings. Assignment of space in the congressional buildings is based on seniority of members.

For years the House buildings were unnamed, known prosaically as the House Office Building, or, when a second one was built, as the Old House Office Building and the New House Office Building. When a third building was under construction in 1962, the House decided to name all three. It named each building for the House Speaker in office during a major part of the construction. Thus on Jan. 10, 1962, the old building was named for Joseph G. Cannon (R Ill.), the new one for Nicholas Longworth (R Ohio), and the third building for Sam Rayburn (D Texas).

The buildings on the Senate side for many years were called simply the Old and New Senate Office Buildings. On

---

Oct. 11, 1972, they were named for two former leaders of the Senate, the old building for Richard Brevard Russell (D Ga.) and the new one for Everett McKinley Dirksen (R Ill.).

All the office buildings are within a short walk of the Capitol *(map p. 430)*. They are connected by tunnels, and electric subway cars run from three of the buildings to the Capitol.

Most committees of Congress have space in the office buildings, although a handful of House and Senate and joint House-Senate committees have retained rooms in the Capitol. Miscellaneous organizations of members, such as the Democratic Study Group, the House Republican Conference and the Congressional Rural Caucus, all have space in the office buildings. The buildings also house a number of non-congressional organizations, including branch offices of the U.S. Employment Service and the Civil Service Commission, and liaison offices of all the armed forces.

In the meantime, senior members anxious to escape visiting constituents and lobbyists in the office buildings have been assigned unmarked hideaways in the Capitol. The development of these Capitol offices has brought the housing of Congress nearly full circle, reverting to an era that preceded construction of the first office building.

The Different Buildings

Cannon House Office Building. The first of the congressional offices, the Cannon Building was authorized by

Congress in 1903. President Theodore Roosevelt participated in cornerstone ceremonies April 14, 1906. Designed by Carrere and Hastings, the building was occupied Jan. 10, 1908.[46]

As designed, it was large enough for the existing House membership. But Congress in 1911 authorized an increase in the size of the House to 435 members (the present limit), and an additional story was erected on the building in 1913-14. Overall, the building contains about 500 rooms. The total cost of the building, including site, construction, furnishings, equipment and a tunnel to the Capitol, was $4,860,155.

As part of the later Rayburn House Office Building project, the Cannon Building was remodeled in the 1960s under a $5.2-million appropriation.

Russell Office Building. The first office building for the Senate was authorized in 1904. Adapted by Carerre and Hastings from their plans for the Cannon Building, the Russell Building was occupied March 5, 1909. However, the First Street side of the building, along with other alterations, was not completed until 1933. It has 315,000 square feet of floor space, excluding parking. The cost of the completed building was $8,390,892.

Longworth House Office Building. Authorized in 1929, the second building for the House was completed and ready for occupancy April 20, 1933. The eight floors occupied by representatives contain 251 two-room suites and 16 committee rooms. The total cost of the Longworth Building was $7,805,705.

Dirksen Office Building. Congress authorized the Senate's second building in 1948, and the site was soon purchased and cleared. But the Korean War delayed groundbreaking ceremonies until 1955. The building was ready for occupancy Oct. 15, 1958. It has 419,000 square feet of usable floor space. The total appropriated for the Dirksen Building was $24,196,000.

Rayburn House Office Building

The Rayburn Building was conceived in controversy and completed in conflict. Its legislative history began in 1955 when the Dirksen Building was under construction, and Speaker Sam Rayburn reminded the House of its own space needs.

At Rayburn's personal request, $25,000 for a study of the need for a third House office building was inserted in a supplemental appropriations bill in committee. When the bill reached the House floor, March 18, 1955, Rayburn left the chair and moved to strike the $25,000 item from the bill. In its place he offered an amendment authorizing the House Office Building Commission to spend $2-million and "such additional sums as may be necessary" for acquisition of a site and immediate construction of an additional House office building. Clarence Cannon (D Mo.), chairman of the Appropriations Committee, promptly accepted the amendment "in view of the emergency involved and the urgent need of the facility for which the appropriation is proposed."

Under House rules, appropriation bills are supposed to be limited to providing money for projects authorized by previous legislation. No new building had been authorized by Congress. Rep. Clare E. Hoffman (R Mich.) tried to make a point of order that Rayburn's amendment was legislation in an appropriation bill, a point which, if accepted, would have automatically killed the amendment. But Rep. Clark Thompson (D Texas), a trusted lieutenant to whom Rayburn had yielded the chair, ruled that

Hoffman had been too late in making the point of order. When Hoffman protested that he had spoken even before the clerk finished reading the amendment, Thompson declared: "That was not the proper time."

During the brief debate that followed, Hoffman received support only from Rep. H. R. Gross (R Iowa). Gross questioned the emergency that compelled construction of a new building, and expressed fears about the eventual cost. Rayburn replied that the matter would be handled by the three-member House Office Building Commission. Rayburn, then age 73, was chairman of this group, and the other members were Rep. Carl Vinson (D Ga.), 72, and Rep. James C. Auchincloss (R N.J.), 70. "I do not think this commission is going to run wild on anything," Rayburn assured the House. His amendment was accepted by voice vote.[47]

By the time the supplemental appropriations bill emerged from conference, it provided $5-million for a new House office building. Congress gave its final approval April 20, 1955, and the Rayburn Building project was underway.

While the act fixed no total cost, the three commission members were given authority to set the limit. The House itself still controlled the appropriations, and it could have stopped the project, especially during the early years, simply by cutting off the funds. Funds were appropriated on 11 occasions from 1955 to 1964. Only in 1957, after $14.9-million had been obligated for the acquisition of land and preliminary work, was the project challenged on the House floor. Rep. Gross objected to a $7.5-million appropriation to carry on the work for the next fiscal year, but his motion to recommit the bill was rejected on a roll-call vote, 206 to 176.

Construction. The company chosen to design the building was the Philadelphia architectural firm of Harbeson, Hough, Livingston & Larson. Architect John Harbeson was a friend of Capitol Architect J. George Stewart. He was a friend also of fellow Philadelphian Matthew H. McCloskey, treasurer and chief fund raiser for the Democratic Party.

McCloskey's construction firm, McCloskey & Co., was the Rayburn Building's principal contractor, by virtue of submitting the low bid of $6.66-million for excavation and construction of the foundation. Subsequently, the firm also won the contract for construction of the building's superstructure, with a low bid of $50.8-million. Stewart's office supervised all construction work.

The commission, headed by Rayburn until his death in November 1961, played an active role in designing the building. Writing in *Fortune* magazine, Harold B. Meyers said, "From the start the architects had limited scope for exercising discretion in the design.... Every decision of any moment—including the controversial layout of the suites and such accoutrements as the commodious safe in each one—had to be referred to the strongminded, busy members of the commission, with Stewart as intermediary."[48] From the time that specifications for the superstructure were drawn until bids were submitted, at least seven costly modifications were made in the plans.

Cost. The actual cost of the Rayburn Building was confused not only by design changes and faulty estimates, but because other Capitol Hill construction and renovation was going on at the same time. Appropriations totaling $135,279,000 included the Rayburn Building and its site, remodeling of the Cannon and Longworth Buildings, and construction of three underground garages and House subways. According to the architect of the Capitol's office, final cost of the Rayburn Building itself was $87.7-million, including land acquisition and furnishings.

Same Architects for Many Recent Hill Projects

The recent history of construction on Capitol Hill revealed that a small group of architects was involved in all major projects begun while J. George Stewart was architect of the Capitol (1954-70). During Stewart's administration, more than $250-million was spent or authorized for government construction around the Capitol.

Under the direction of Stewart, who was not an architect but had experience as a construction engineer, the East Front of the Capitol was extended, the Rayburn House Office Building was erected, older congressional buildings were remodeled, parking garages and subways were built, the Library of Congress James Madison Memorial Building was begun, and preliminary plans were approved for extending the West Front of the Capitol.

Without exception, the names of a tiny and sometimes rotating constellation of architects were attached to all these projects. This prompted charges that an architectural monopoly held sway on Capitol Hill. Stewart's office responded that contracts were awarded on the basis of open, competitive bidding, and that relatively few firms bid on the monumental construction that characterizes Capitol Hill.

House Speaker Sam Rayburn, chairman of the three-man House Office Building Commission, started the ball rolling in 1955 when the Philadelphia firm of Harbeson, Hough, Livingston & Larson was chosen to design what was to become the Rayburn Building. Architect John Harbeson was a friend of Stewart.

A little later, three other firms—Roscoe Dewitt and Fred L. Hardison of Dallas, well known to Rayburn; Alfred Easton Poor and Albert Homer Swanke of New York City; and Jesse M. Shelton and Alan G. Stanford of Atlanta, well known to Rep. Carl Vinson (D Ga.), a member of Rayburn's commission—were brought in for future work on related remodeling projects. Eventually, Dewitt and Hardison got the Cannon House Office Building remodeling job, Poor and Swanke the Longworth House Office Building project, and Shelton and Stanford the garage construction under and behind the Rayburn Building as well as the House-Capitol subway.

Meanwhile, Congress in 1955 established the Commission for Extension of the U.S. Capitol, composed at the time of the Speaker, the Vice President, the minority leaders of both the House and Senate, and Stewart. Because no remodeling work had been authorized yet on either the Cannon or Longworth Buildings, Stewart hired Dewitt and Hardison, Poor and Swanke, and Shelton and Stanford—who joined forces as Dewitt, Poor & Shelton—to draw up plans for extending the Capitol. An advisory panel was established consisting of Harbeson (whose firm would design the Rayburn Building), and Henry R. Shepley of Boston and Arthur Brown Jr. of San Francisco.

In 1957 Dewitt, Poor & Shelton, who were also to do the design work for remodeling the old Senate and Supreme Court chambers in the Capitol, presented the commission with plans for extending both the East and West Fronts. After bitter controversy, most of which developed in the Senate, Rayburn in 1958 pushed through the East Front extension project, which was completed in 1962 for a total cost of $24-million.

Subsequently, Dewitt, Poor & Shelton were picked to design the $90-million Library of Congress James Madison Memorial Building, first authorized in 1965. Stewart cited the "highly satisfactory" East Front project as the basis for selection.

In 1966 the extension commission, then headed by Speaker John W. McCormack (D Mass.), surprised Congress by approving a preliminary plan to extend the West Front for an estimated cost of $35-million. Again the architects were Dewitt, Poor & Shelton, who contended, with the support of the commission, that they were hired in 1956 for all work that might be done on the Capitol.

Stewart died in office in 1970 and was succeeded by George M. White in 1971. Under White, the tight group of Capitol Hill architects appeared to crack. The Washington firm of John Carl Warnecke & Associates was hired to design the Dirksen Office Building Extension, expected to cost $85-million. The original Dirksen Building, planned before Stewart became architect of the Capitol, was designed by Eggers & Higgins of New York City.

Source: Architect of the Capitol; Congressional Quarterly, *Weekly Report,* July 7, 1967, p. 1170.

Rayburn Building Profile. Completed and occupied in the early spring of 1965, the Rayburn Building is larger than the Capitol itself. When approached from the west along Independence Avenue, it appears to dominate Capitol Hill. It is 720 feet long and 450 feet wide (covering about two blocks) and has 50 acres of floor space on nine stories. It is served by 25 passenger elevators and 23 escalators.

Primary accommodations include 169 three-room suites for representatives, nine hearing rooms for standing committees and 16 subcommittee rooms. A typical suite is about 54 feet long and 32 feet wide. It consists of a large reception area and three rooms—one for the member, one for the administrative assistant and one for general office work. Eight of the hearing rooms are two stories high, 56 feet

long and 46 feet wide, and with a large rostrum which seats 41 representatives. Committee and subcommittee rooms have anterooms and adjoining staff offices. An underground garage was built for 1,600 cars and takes up 42 per cent of the building's gross floor space. Health facilities include a fully equipped gymnasium, a 20-by-60 foot swimming pool (with a ceiling too low for a diving board), and compartments identified as "slumber rooms."

Visitors to the Rayburn Building are struck by its opulence and inefficiency. It appears to contain immense amounts of unusable space, and features 13-foot, 9-inch ceilings in most areas and four long, dead-end corridors on the upper floors. Critics have noted that only 15 per cent of the gross floor space is used for representatives' offices—the

U.S. Botanic Garden

At the foot of Capitol Hill stands the glass-roofed conservatory of the United States Botanic Garden. The purpose of the Botanic Garden is to collect, cultivate and grow various plants for public display and for study by students, scientists and garden clubs. It produces annual plants and flowers, shrubs and certain trees for the Capitol grounds. The garden also provides cut flowers and potted plants for congressional offices and public ceremonies.

The United States Botanic Garden was founded in 1820 under the auspices of the Columbia Institute for the Promotion of Arts and Sciences. It was operated by the institute until 1837, when the organization became inactive and the garden was abandoned.

In 1842 the government had to accommodate the botanical collections brought to Washington from the South Seas by the U.S. Exploring Expedition of 1838-42, led by Capt. Charles Wilkes. The collections were housed temporarily in the Patent Office but soon were moved to a greenhouse behind the building. The Joint Committee on the Library named the commissioner of patents to oversee the collections.

In 1850 the Botanic Garden was moved to the west end of the Capitol grounds. It was relocated to its present site in 1933 when the conservatory was completed. The garden did not come under the specific direction of the Joint Committee on the Library until 1856. At present, the committee exercises its supervision through the architect of the Capitol, who has served since 1934 as acting director of the Botanic Garden.

The conservatory, between Independence and Maryland Avenues at First Street, Southwest, is open to the public daily. Its large rooms simulate a variety of climates for plant growth. Directly across Independence Avenue the garden maintains a park, which has at its center the 30-foot Bartholdi Fountain built for the Philadelphia Exposition of 1876. It was designed by Frederic Auguste Bartholdi, better known as the designer of the Statue of Liberty.

The garden also operates the Poplar Point Nursery in southeast Washington. The 24-acre arboretum, which includes many greenhouses, is also open to the public daily. In all, the Botanic Garden grows over 10,-000 species and varieties of plants, including palms, cycads, ferns, cacti, orchids and rare tropical and subtropical plants.

Source: Architect of the Capitol, U.S. Botanic Garden.

original reason for the building. The office of the architect of the Capitol responded to such charges with a detailed classification of space in the Rayburn Building: If the space used for the garage floors, plus space taken up with automatic ramps, was subtracted from the gross square footage in the building, a total of 1,189,200 square feet remained. This total was to be used as follows: congressional offices and files, 34 per cent; committee staff rooms, full committee hearing rooms, subcommittee hearing rooms, 13 per cent; cafeteria, first aid, health facilities, library, pressroom, television room, public telephone rooms, telegraph rooms, recording studio, mailroom, liaison offices, 9 per cent; stairs, escalators, elevators, entrance lobbies, halls, corridors, 21 per cent; mechanical and electrical rooms, janitorial and maintenance space, 18 per cent; undeveloped office or committee space, 5 per cent.

Architectural Criticism. Aside from the cost and extravagance, most of the criticism leveled at the Rayburn Building dealt with its architectural style. Built of marble and granite, it is known technically as "simplified classic." But critics derided it as "Mussolini Modern" and "Texas Penitentiary." One critic said it could be defended only militarily.

Ada Louise Huxtable wrote in *The New York Times:* "Architecturally, the Rayburn Building is a national disaster. Its defects range from profligate mishandling of 50 acres of space to elephantine esthetic banality at record costs.... It is quite possible that this is the worst building for the most money in the history of the construction art. It stuns by sheer mass and boring bulk.... The Rayburn Building's ultimate claim to fame may well be that it is the biggest star-spangled architectural blunder of our time."[49]

Stewart's office issued a long statement in reply to the architectural criticism. It read, in part: "Esthetics are often matters of opinion. What one person thinks is beautiful, another finds repulsive, and both could be sincere. In architecture, some prefer the classic treatment which has stood the test of time. Presidents Washington and Jefferson did, and our capital city is the more beautiful today because of their early leadership in this respect. We are not opposed to so-called modern architecture, but the House Office Building Commision wisely determined that it had no place adjoining the U.S. Capitol."[50]

In his *Fortune* article, Harold B. Meyers commented: "What is most outrageous about the Rayburn Building is not its appearance (which is actually well suited to its location); not its cost (which can be defended); nor the fact that Matthew McCloskey, who came into such sharp view in the Bobby Baker investigation, held the major construction contracts (his company won them through competitive bidding). The worst thing about the Rayburn Building is the very thing it symbolizes best: the power system that created it.... The Rayburn House Office Building is in every way a fitting monument to congressional power and a great Speaker's genius for using it."[51]

Continuing Controversy. Controversy continued to plague the Rayburn project, even after completion of the building itself. A number of claims for associated projects were submitted by contractors. Among them were claims totaling more than $5-million from Baltimore Contractors Inc., builder of underground parking garages behind the Rayburn Building. Some of its claims were settled. The rest were challenged and subjected to legal actions.

Plans for Expansion

As each congressional office building was completed it quickly overflowed with staff members, committees, auxiliary offices and equipment. By 1975 both the Senate and the House had taken steps toward further expansion of their offices.

Dirksen Building Extension. The Senate broke ground at the beginning of 1976 for an extension of the Dirksen Office Building. It was designated the Philip A. Hart Office Building after the Democratic senator from Michigan who was retiring at the end of the 94th Congress. The original building fills half of the block bounded by First, Second and C Streets and Constitution Avenue, Northeast. Congress in 1969 appropriated $1.25-million to purchase the remainder of the block, except for the historic 1799 Belmont House, which is to remain intact as headquarters of the National Women's Party. The site eventually cost $2-million.

An extension, to double the size of the Dirksen Building and provide offices for 50 senators, was authorized Oct. 31, 1972. Three separate appropriations totaling $85,147,000 were provided for the entire project. Although final plans were not approved until late 1975, the extension was scheduled to be completed by early 1979. It was to have 546,000 square feet of usable office space, including 50 rooms with 18-foot ceilings for senators' offices, a huge gymnasium suitable for tennis and other sports, and a two-story public hearing room with built-in television lights and glass booths for network broadcasters.

In the meantime, Senate staff and the Capitol Police moved into two former hotels, the Plaza and the Capitol Hill, in the block immediately north of the Dirksen Building. The Senate had begun purchasing the block in 1973 as the site for a parking garage. Plans called for demolishing the two annexes and constructing the garage after the Dirksen Building Extension was completed.

On Dec. 10, 1975, the Senate approved an amendment to the fiscal 1976 supplemental appropriations bill of $2,550,000 for possible leasing of a building at 400 North Capitol Street for Senate offices. But an audit and further Senate approval were required before any lease could be signed.[52]

Russell Building Renovation. In October 1975 the architect of the Capitol announced tentative plans to modernize the Russell Office Building after the Dirksen Extension was in use. The renovation plan called for expanding the Russell Building's four-room suites for senators and their staffs into seven-room suites.

House Office Expansion. The Rayburn Building was hardly 10 years old before the House was taking steps to have a fourth office building. Late in the first session of the 94th Congress it was not clear whether the House would erect its own building, commandeer new buildings designed for other government use, or make do with remodeled buildings acquired from others.

On Jan. 29, 1975, the House Office Building Commission—composed by then of Speaker Carl Albert (D Okla.), Majority Leader Thomas P. O'Neill Jr. (D Mass.) and Minority Leader John J. Rhodes (R Ariz.)—directed White to request $22.5-million in fiscal 1976 for land acquisition and preliminary planning for a new House office building. The commission envisioned a structure approximately as large as the Rayburn Building.

In May 12, 1975, hearings before the Public Buildings and Grounds Subcommittee, White maintained that the 1955 law authorizing the Rayburn Building—the floor amendment which Speaker Sam Rayburn himself pushed through—also authorized additional lands and buildings. But that interpretation was challenged by some representatives, civic organizations and residents of the neighborhood south of the Rayburn parking garage, where the new office building would be located.

The House Appropriations Committee deferred action on White's request in May, saying, "Many unanswered questions were raised during the committee's consideration of this proposal, particularly as to site and space requirements." Instead, the committee approved $350,000 "for the preparation of studies and the development of a long-range master plan for future development" of the area around the Capitol.[53] The Senate Appropriations Committee also approved the master plan, saying it was "cognizant of the criticism that Congress has not always been a good neighbor to the residents of Capitol Hill."[54] The plan was to be prepared by private consultants outside the Capitol establishment.

Ever since the Library of Congress James Madison Memorial Building was authorized in 1965, the House has toyed with the idea of taking over at least part of it for its own offices. A 1971 vote failed to defer funds for the new library in order to consider other uses for the building. In 1974 approximately 220 representatives signed a petition to designate part of the building for use by the House, but no vote was taken. In October 1975 the House leadership officially asked the Senate to permit the House to take over the entire Madison Building. Senate leaders were reluctant.

Then on Nov. 18, 1975, the House Office Building Commission met and decided to force a vote on the issue. They quickly introduced legislation to convert the building, already three-fourths completed, for exclusive use of the House. The Madison Building was designed specifically for the Library of Congress, with low ceilings, few windows, special interior layout and other facilities for storing information.[55]

The legislation was withdrawn Dec. 12, when the commission acknowledged it did not have sufficient support for its plan, even in the House. Instead, Albert and the others said they would seek an appropriation of $30-million to complete the building as a library. They also began negotiations to permit the House to use from 6 to 7 per cent of the building as offices for its research-related employees.[56] *(Details, The Library of Congress and the Congressional Research Service, p. 439)*

Meanwhile, the House Commission on Information and Facilities, composed of nine representatives, had suggested in the summer of 1975 that the House take over a new office building at Independence Avenue and Third Street, Southwest, being built by the General Services Administration for the Department of Health, Education and Welfare. Such a move would cause a legislative and bureaucratic wrangle of some size. The commission, headed by Rep. Jack Brooks (D Texas), was expected to issue a comprehensive report in 1976 on the office space needs of the House.

Without fanfare, the House had moved into 500,000 square feet of usable office space in two annexes by 1975. The first annex, the old Congressional Hotel south of the Cannon Building, was purchased in 1958 but not converted to House offices until the early 1970s. It has 84,300 square feet of usable office space. The second annex, an old federal building used for FBI files until mid-1975, has 432,840 square feet of office space at Third and D Streets, Southwest. In February 1975, Congress appropriated $17,175,000 to convert the old building for use by the House. Some members of the House were considering swapping the converted building for the new HEW building.

Any expansion of the House offices would have to wait until completion of studies by the House Office Building Commission, the Commission on Information and Facilities, and—most important—consultants for the Capitol Hill master plan. What was clear in 1976 was that the House was determined to acquire new office space, somewhere, and as soon as possible.

Footnotes

1. The Capitol Guides, who conducted free tours of the Capitol for 1,156,887 visitors in 1974, estimate that they accommodate only

40 to 45 per cent of the total number of tourists who enter the Capitol.

2. *The Capitol: A Pictorial History,* 6th edition (Joint Committee on Printing, Government Printing Office, 1973), p. 58.

3. Conclusion of historians for the Architect of the Capitol and the U.S. Capitol Historical Society. From interviews, July 1975.

4. Office of the Architect of the Capitol, Art and Reference Division, release of June 1972.

5. Glenn Brown, *History of the United States Capitol* (Government Printing Office, 1900), vol. 1, p. 5.

6. List of competitors was compiled in 1975 by the American Institute of Architects Foundation for a Bicentennial exhibition of the original Capitol designs.

7. Brown, *History of the United States Capitol,* vol. I, p. 8.

8. *Ibid.*

9. Lonnelle Aikman, *We the People: The Story of the United States Capitol,* 9th edition (U.S. Capitol Historical Society, 1974), p. 19.

10. Dr. Thornton was awarded lot 15 in square 634. The land is now part of the Capitol grounds. Information provided by the Office of the Architect of the Capitol, Art and Reference Division.

11. Brown, *History of the United States Capitol,* vol. 1, p. 12.

12. "Capitol Sandstone," *The Capitol Dome,* vol. 9, no. 3 (1974). (Newsletter of the U.S. Capitol Historical Society.)

13. Benjamin H. Latrobe, "A Private Letter to Individual Members of Congress on the Subject of the Public Buildings of the United States," Nov. 28, 1806, quoted in Brown, *History of the United States Capitol,* vol. 1, p. 40.

14. Brown, *History of the United States Capitol,* Vol. 1, pp. 32, 101.

15. Richard B. Morris, editor, *Encyclopedia of American History* (Harper & Brothers, 1953), p. 151.

16. Aikman, *We, the People,* p. 31.

17. Office of the Architect of the Capitol, Art and Reference Division, release of June 1972.

18. Brown, *History of the United States Capitol,* vol. 2, p. 116.

19. *The Capitol: A Pictorial History,* p. 9.

20. Aikman, *We, the People,* p. 49.

21. *Ibid.,* pp. 4, 54.

22. *Ibid.,* pp. 46-47.

23. Brown, *History of the United States Capitol,* vol. 2, pp. 211, 221.

24. Office of the Architect of the Capitol, Art and Reference Division, release of June 1972.

25. *The Capitol: A Pictorial History,* p. 10.

26. Architect of the Capitol, Art and Reference Division, release of June 1972.

27. *The Capitol: A Pictorial History,* p. 10.

28. J. George Stewart, Architect of the Capitol, "Extension of the Capitol: Authority - Commission" release of Dec. 12, 1969.

29. George M. White, Architect of the Capitol, "West Front of the Capitol" release of June 1973.

30. Letter from Miles N. Clair, president, Thompson and Lichtner Co. Inc., to J. George Stewart, Architect of the Capitol,

31. summarizing a "Report on the Structural Condition of the West Central Portion of the United States Capitol," reprinted in the *Congressional Record,* 92nd Cong., 2nd sess., March 28, 1972, pp. 10584-85.

31. *Congressional Record,* 92nd Cong., 2nd sess., March 28, 1972, p. 10577.

32. American Institute of Architects, "Report on Conditions of the West Front of the Capitol," reprinted in the *Congressional Record,* 90th Cong., 1st sess., April 20, 1967, pp. 10231-34.

33. Congressional Quarterly, *1967 Almanac,* p. 1033.

34. "West Front of Capitol Summary Report—1956 to 1973," Office of the Architect of the Capitol, June 1973, p. 24.

35. George M. White, Architect of the Capitol, "Memorandum to the Members of the Commission for Extension of the United States Capitol," March 6, 1972, pp. 9-10.

36. Congressional Quarterly, *1973 Almanac,* pp. 145, 147.

37. George M. White, Architect of the Capitol, "West Front of the Capitol," release of June 1973.

38. *Ibid.,* p. 3.

39. Congressional Quarterly, *Congress and the Nation, 1969-1972,* Vol. III, p. 379.

40. Congressional Quarterly, *1974 Almanac,* pp. 74-77.

41. *Ibid.,* p. 77.

42. U.S. Congress, Senate, Committee on Appropriations, *Legislative Branch Appropriations, 1976,* report to accompany HR 6950, S Rept 94-262, 94th Cong., 1st sess., p. 29.

43. Figure for cost of restoration from Commission on Arts and Antiquities of the U.S. Senate.

44. *Ibid.*

45. Florian H. Thayn, Office of the Architect of the Capitol, Art and Reference Division, interview, July 23, 1975.

46. Information about the office buildings of Congress was taken from the *1976 Congressional Directory,* 94th Congress, 2nd sess. (Government Printing Office), pp. 461-63.

47. *Congressional Record,* 84th Cong., 1st sess., March 18, 1955, p. 3204.

48. Harold B. Meyers, "A Monument to Power," *Fortune,* March 1965, p. 174.

49. *The New York Times,* March 30, 1965.

50. *Congressional Record,* 89th Cong., 1st ses., March 11, 1965, p. 4814.

51. Meyers, *Fortune,* p. 122.

52. Congressional Quarterly, *Weekly Report,* Dec. 13, 1975, pp. 2757-58.

53. U.S. Congress, House, Committee on Appropriations, *Legislative Branch Appropriation Bill, 1976,* report to accompany HR 6950, H Rept 94-208, 94th Cong., 1st sess., pp. 21-22.

54. U.S. Congress, Senate, Committee on Appropriations, *Legislative Branch Appropriations, 1976,* report to accompany HR 6950, S Rept. 94-262, 94th Cong., 1st sess., p. 29.

55. Congressional Quarterly, *Weekly Report,* Nov. 29, 1975, pp. 2579-81.

56. Congressional Quarterly, *Weekly Report,* Dec. 13, 1975, p. 2757.

Selected Bibliography

Books

Aikman, Lonnelle, *We, the People: The Story of the United States Capitol.* 9th ed. Washington, U.S. Capitol Historical Society, 1974.

Brown, Glenn. *History of the U.S. Capitol.* Washington: Government Printing Office, 1903; reprint ed., New York: Da Capo Press, 1970.

Bryan, Wilhelmus B. *A History of the National Capital.* 2 vols. New York: Macmillan, 1914-1916.

Feeley, Stephen V. *Story of the Capitol.* Buffalo: H. Stewart, 1957.

Frary, Ihna T. *They Built the Capitol.* Plainview, N.Y.: Books for Libraries, 1940.

Hazelton, George C. Jr. *The National Capitol.* New York: J. F. Taylor and Co., 1902.

Leech, Margaret. *Reveille in Washington.* New York: Grosset and Dunlap, 1941.

Government Publications

Architect of the Capitol, *Report,* Washington: Government Printing Office, 19-

Compilation of Works of Art and Other Objects in the U.S. Capitol. Washington: Government Printing Office, 1970.

Documentary History of the Construction and Development of the U.S. Capitol Building and Grounds. Washington: Government Printing Office, 1904.

Providing for the Installation of Security Apparatus for the Protection of the Capitol Complex. H. Rept. 92-925 to accompany H. Con. Res. 550, 92nd Cong., 2nd sess., 1972.

U.S. Congress. House. Committee on Education and Labor. Special Subcommittee on Labor. *Capitol Architecture and Planning. Hearings on H.R. 16100,* 89th Cong., 2nd sess., 1966.

U.S. Congress. House. Committee on Public Works, *Safety of Capitol Buildings and Grounds.* H. Rept. 90-745 to accompany H.R. 13178, 90th Cong., 1st sess., 1967.

————. *Safety of Capitol Building and Grounds, Hearings on H.R. 13178.* 90th Cong., 1st sess., 1967.

U.S.Congress. Joint Committee on Congressional Operations, "Right to Demonstrate on the Capitol Grounds," pp. 459-480, *Court Proceedings and Actions of Vital Interest to the Congress.* Committee Print, 92nd Cong., 2nd sess., 1972.

U.S. Congress. Joint Committee on Printing, *The Capitol: A Pictorial History.* Washington: Government Printing Office, 1973.

U.S. Congress. Senate. *Our Capitol: Factual Information Pertaining to our Capitol and Places of Historic Interest in the National Capitol.* S. Doc. 105, 89th Cong., 2nd sess., 1966.

U.S. Congress. Senate. Committee on Public Works. *Comprehensive Plan for the Development of the Capitol Grounds,* S. Rept. 236 to Accompany S. J. Res. 74, 90th Cong., 1st sess., 1967.

U.S. Congress. Senate. Committee on Public Works. *Security of the Capitol Grounds Relating to the Bombing of the U.S. Capitol, Hearing before the Subcommittee on Public Buildings and Grounds.* Committee Serial 92-H7, 92nd Cong., 1st sess., 1971.

————. *Security of the Capitol Building, Hearings on S. 2310.* 90th Cong., 1st sess., 1967.

Articles

Meyers, Harold B. "A Monument to Power." *Fortune,* March 1965, pp. 122-125, 174, 176, 178.

"U.S. Capitol: Scene of Violence Since 1814 Fire." Congressional *Quarterly Weekly Report* March 5, 1971, pp. 503-505.

The Library of Congress and the Congressional Research Service

Information is indispensable to a legislator. Although it cannot take the place of intelligence, judgment or concern, information is essential as a guide to the practical solution of problems of public policy. And it is valuable only if it is accurate.

An officer of the Library of Congress, Charles A. Goodrum, wrote in 1974: "Like every other legislative body in the world, the American Congress frets over its ability to secure the information it needs to govern wisely. Its members know the distress of all legislators over the increasing number of decisions to be made, each concerning matters of the utmost complexity and usually involving highly technical, intricately related, courses of action.... Here, where an increasing amount of legislation is generated by the executive branch..., the Congress is asked to approve or reject, pass or modify, increase or limit, thousands of the most complicated pieces of legislation without the equivalent of the bureaucracy available to the President."[1]

Senators and representatives rely on a variety of sources for the information they seek. They read, listen to visitors, travel to problem areas for direct observation, and conduct hearings. They also use the facilities of one of the world's great repositories of information, the Library of Congress. Of the two functions of the Library of Congress—to assist Congress and to serve as a national library—the first is probably less well known, but it has a more immediate impact on public affairs.

The Library's dual role causes considerable strain throughout the organization. As a national library it maintains its huge collections and provides central services to other libraries throughout the United States. But the fact remains that Congress established the Library for its own use and that the Library gives first priority to serving Congress.

Service to Congress

Senators and representatives cannot keep in their own heads or their own offices all the information required to make decisions on agricultural programs, consumer needs, international trade, environmental protection, labor and employment, weapons systems, mass transportation, energy policy and so on. They must turn to published sources for facts, and interpretations of facts, that will help them to make sound judgments. In choosing published sources the members must go beyond the special pleadings of people with axes to grind. The Library of Congress stands ready to furnish them with unbiased information.

The Library, on request, supplies members of the two houses and congressional committees with published material relevant to problems that concern them, finds the answers to specific questions, makes up reading lists, compiles and analyzes pertinent literature, and distills the pros and cons of policy issues. In many cases, it makes available the services of an expert from its staff, who confers with a senator or representative or provides advice on conducting public hearings. The Library sometimes will write a speech for a member, but it tries hard to remain nonpartisan in politics and impartial on public questions.

The Joint Committee on the Library oversees the Library's services to Congress. The committee traces its origin to the Act of April 24, 1800, which provided for the purchase of books for the use of Congress at the new seat of government on the Potomac River, "pursuant to such directions as shall be given...by a joint committee of both houses of Congress to be appointed for that purpose." The committee consists of five senators and five representatives. When a senator is chairman, a representative is vice chairman, and the positions are reversed with each new Congress. The committee oversees every administrative unit of the Library but pays special attention to the Congressional Research Service, which has Congress as its sole client.

A 1975 Library pamphlet stated the relationship clearly: "The primary role of the Library of Congress is to perform research work for members and committees of Congress."[2] A recent congressional publication put the matter bluntly: "The Congress of the United States commands the Library of Congress."[3]

Service as a National Library

The 10th librarian of Congress, Luther H. Evans, cited statistics in a 1945 radio broadcast which were soon outdated, but he made a point which is still valid. Referring to the Library's second function, he said: "The Library of Congress is the national library of the United States. This is so in the sense that the Library's work touches the life of every American citizen whether he is aware of it or not. He may never have sat in one of its 20 reading rooms to read one

SCORPIO Aids Congress

A computer data service developed by the Library's Information Systems Office instantly provides a wide variety of information to congressional offices that have the necessary receiving equipment. Installed in 1974, the system is called SCORPIO, for Subject-Content-Oriented Retriever for Processing Information On-line. By March 1976 the system was being used by approximately 90 senators, 75 representatives, and a large number of committees.

The offices of members and committees can receive five kinds of information from SCORPIO:

● A legislative history file, which gives background information on bills before Congress.

● A major-issue file containing objective briefs on 180 important issues and policy questions.

● A bibliography of magazine articles on specific subjects.

● A file listing more than 10,000 organizations willing to provide information on topics in science, technology and social science.

● A file of 90,000 references in science, technology, library science and bibliography.

Congressional staff members trained to use SCORPIO telephone the Library service, identify their office by a code number, name the subject they are interested in, and then either browse through the subject file that appears on the computer terminal screen or ask specific questions. Answers are provided quickly so that questions from constituents, for example, may be answered by mail the same day they arrive in Washington.

The SCORPIO service is provided free by the Library of Congress, but members must rent the terminals and other equipment for their offices in order to use the system. The Senate in 1975 installed complete sets—consisting of the computer terminal, a telephone hook-up, and a print-out device—in the offices of 83 senators who requested them. The rent for each complete set was $262 a month in 1975, which was paid from Senate funds.

In the House, members had to rent their equipment individually, and not all chose complete three-piece sets. Print-out devices, for example, rented for about $100 a month in 1975 and were considered luxuries by some members. Each representative was allowed to spend as much as $1,000 a month from staff salary funds to pay for computer services.

Members of Congress and committees that have computer terminals in their offices of course may use many other services in addition to the Library's SCORPIO. By late 1975 congressional offices could plug into about 80 commercial systems that sold computer services at hourly rates.

Sources: Library of Congress, Information Systems Office; Committee on House Administration, Computer Subcommittee; *The Washington Post,* Sept. 21, 1975.

---

of its six million books, or studied American history in its 10 million manuscripts, or pored over its million and a half maps,...but through the legislation which is enacted by Congress, through the infinite variety of ways in which his life is affected by multitudinous government agencies, through the research carried on by universities, industrial organizations, and private scholars, he cannot escape its effects."[4]

Whether the Library of Congress is the greatest library on earth is a matter of opinion. It is probably the world's largest, but the ways of measuring quantity of library holdings are not yet standardized, especially as to manuscript, music and other nonbook possessions. In measuring greatness it also is hard to compare objectively such Library treasures as Thomas Jefferson's rough draft of the Declaration of Independence or James Madison's personal notes from the Constitutional Convention with, for example, the British Museum's two signed copies of the Magna Carta.

All things considered, the Library's collections are unparalleled. By the middle of 1975, it had more than 70.5 million items of astonishing variety. Although it does not acquire every book printed, or even every book published in the United States, the Library grew rapidly in the mid-20th century and became terribly overcrowded. The Library of Congress James Madison Memorial Building, scheduled for completion late in the 1970s, promised to give the Library a modern facility equal to its great collections.

History of the Library

Late in 1784, when the Continental Congress was preparing to move from Trenton to New York City, the New York Society offered to make its library of about 5,000 books available to the legislators. Congress began using the library in January 1785. The First Congress under the Constitution, which convened in New York in 1789, also used the society's library until the seat of the federal government was moved to Philadelphia in 1790. From 1790 to 1800, Congress had access to the collection of the Library Company of Philadelphia, the oldest library in America, established in 1731 and superintended for a time by Benjamin Franklin. It had about 7,700 volumes in the 1790s.

The Act of April 24, 1800, on the transfer of government offices to Washington appropriated $5,000 for purchasing "such books as may be necessary for the use of Congress" and "fitting up a suitable apartment for containing them." From a list prepared by the Joint Committee on the Library, London booksellers supplied 152 works in 740 volumes.[5] The books were placed in a room in the original north wing of the Capitol, under the supervision of the secretary of the Senate and the clerk of the House. Supervision of the library by a single person was intended by an Act of Jan. 26, 1802, which authorized the President to appoint a librarian of Congress. But President Thomas Jefferson thought the post was not a full-time job and appointed John Beckley, clerk of the House, to serve also as librarian of Congress. Beckley did so until his death in April 1807. *(Box, Librarian of Congress, next page)*

Replacement of Books Burned by British

In November 1807, Jefferson appointed Patrick Magruder to succeed Beckley both as clerk of the House and as librarian. Members of Congress were critical of Magruder in 1814 for what they deemed his lack of diligence in trying

Librarian of Congress

Congress on Jan. 26, 1802, established the position of librarian of Congress, who "shall be appointed by the President, and with the advice and consent of the Senate. He shall make rules and regulations for the government of the Library." President Jefferson, who made the first two appointments, directed the clerk of the House to manage the small Library in addition to his other duties. President Madison appointed the first full-time librarian in 1815, and the position has taken on greater responsibility as the Library has grown. By 1975 the librarian directed a staff of nearly 4,700 employees, and he earned a salary of $39,900.

Following is a list of the 12 librarians of Congress and their terms of service:

John Beckley, 1802-1807
Patrick Magruder, 1807-1814
George Watterston, 1815-1829
John S. Meehan, 1829-1861
John G. Stephenson, 1861-1864
Ainsworth R. Spofford, 1865-1897
John R. Young, 1897-1899
Herbert Putnam, 1899-1939
Archibald MacLeish, 1939-1944
Luther H. Evans, 1945-1953
L. Quincy Mumford, 1954-1974
Daniel J. Boorstin, 1975-

Source: Library of Congress, Information Office.

First Full-Time Librarian of Congress

The acquisition of Jefferson's library, according to author Lucy Salamanca, "proved to be the life-stream that restored energy and enterprise to the expiring...Library of Congress."[11] Whereas the Library's previous collection of books had been narrowly utilitarian, Jefferson's library took all knowledge for its province. Recognizing the new importance in store for the Library, Madison on Jan. 21, 1815, had appointed the first full-time librarian of Congress. The man he chose, George Watterston, was a lawyer, novelist, playwright and newspaper editor. Watterston, through his wit and zeal, made the Library of Congress the cultural center of life in Washington. In December 1818, the Library was moved from Blodget's Hotel to the Capitol, where it remained, though moved from time to time within the building, until 1897.

Meehan's 32 Years as Librarian

President Andrew Jackson's wholesale displacement of non-Democrats holding federal jobs reached Watterston, a Whig, less than three months after inauguration day. On May 28, 1829, the President dismissed Watterston and appointed as his successor John S. Meehan, publisher of a Washington newspaper, the *United States Telegraph,* which had supported Jackson in the election campaign. Meehan became the first of three librarians of Congress to stay in the post for more than three decades. He survived changes of administrations over a period of 32 years.

During Meehan's incumbency, the Library's collection of books in the field of law was notably expanded. A count in 1832 showed that the Library then owned 2,011 law books, of which 639 had been bought from Jefferson. Members of the two houses felt the need for a still larger law library. An Act of July 14, 1832, "to increase and improve the law department of the Library of Congress," provided for the establishment of a separate branch of the Library for law books, with a separate location in the Capitol. The act appropriated a lump sum of $5,000, and authorized subsequent annual appropriations of $1,000 for five years, for the purchase of additional books in the field of law, in accordance with recommendations to be made by the Chief Justice. After the expiration of the five-year expansion program, money for law books was included in the regular appropriations for the Library of Congress.

Prior to 1846, copyright applicants were required by law to deposit copies of their publications with the Secretary of State and the clerk of the nearest U.S. district court. By an Act of Aug. 10, 1846, Congress provided that one copy of every copyrighted work should be sent to the Library of Congress. This law, however, contained no teeth and was largely ignored by publishers. It was repealed by an Act of Feb. 5, 1859, which transferred jurisdiction over copyrights from the Department of State to the Department of the Interior. Disappointment in the Library of Congress over the failure of the 1846 act to increase its collections significantly had been compounded by an accidental fire in the Capitol on Dec. 24, 1851, which destroyed 35,000 of the Library's 55,000 books.

President Abraham Lincoln, apparently suspecting that Meehan was a southern sympathizer, removed him from office on May 24, 1861, and appointed in his place John G. Stephenson, a legislative aide to Sen. Henry S. Lane (R Ind.). But Stephenson left the work of the Library to his assistants and entered the Union forces, receiving a citation for bravery in the Gettysburg campaign of 1863. He

to save the Library when British troops entered Washington. On the night of Aug. 24, the invaders burned or pillaged most books that remained in the Capitol, including all of the Library's original purchase.[6] A newspaper published in Nottingham, England, not long afterward condemned the burning as "an act without example in modern wars."[7] Magruder, insisting that he had done all that was reasonably within his power, resigned as clerk of the House and automatically gave up his position as librarian of Congress.

During the fall and winter of 1814-15, while Congress was meeting temporarily in Blodget's Hotel several blocks northwest of the damaged Capitol, Jefferson, then in retirement at Monticello, offered to sell his 6,487-volume library to the government to make up for the loss sustained in the book-burning. Jefferson wrote of his collection, "I have been 50 years making it, & have spared no pains, opportunity or expence, to make it what it is."[8] But anti-Jeffersonian members of Congress opposed the offer because Jefferson's library included books by Voltaire and other unorthodox thinkers. After considerable debate, the House authorized the purchase by an 81-71 vote. A total of $23,950 was appropriated, pricing each book on the basis of its format.[9] President Madison signed the bill on Jan. 30, 1815, and the books were transported to Washington by horse cart.

Jefferson's library became the nucleus of the Library of Congress as it exists today, even though most of his books have been lost. Its 6,487 volumes contained 4,931 works in 44 categories. Jefferson's classification system, which followed Sir Francis Bacon's table of science, was the basis for the Library's entire catalog until 1897, when the present Library of Congress classification was developed.[10]

resigned in December 1864 to engage in private business. The meager reputation of the Library in that period is indicated by the fact that an article on American libraries published in *Harper's Monthly* in 1864 made no mention of the Library of Congress.[12]

Term of Spofford as Librarian

Lincoln in January 1865 appointed as the new librarian of Congress Ainsworth R. Spofford, a bookseller, publisher, editor and writer who had served as assistant librarian under Stephenson. Congress soon passed a copyright law, the Act of March 3, 1865, which was strong enough in its deposit requirements to build up in the Library a comprehensive collection representative of every trend in American literature and every facet of American thought. By an Act of July 8, 1870, the government's copyright work was transferred from the Department of the Interior to the Library of Congress, where it has remained.

Under Spofford's direction, the Library of Congress made a number of sizable additions to its holdings, including the transfer of a large collection of materials from the Smithsonian Institution in 1866-67 and the purchase in 1867 for $100,000 of the Peter Force collection of early American newspapers and other Americana. The Library acquired important publications of foreign governments under a system for the international exchange of official documents authorized by a joint resolution of Congress approved March 2, 1867. The number of books and pamphlets which the Library owned grew from about 100,-000 when Spofford took charge to more than one million in 1897.

When Spofford had completed 32 years as librarian, in 1897, advancing age led him to resign. President William McKinley on July 1, 1897, appointed John R. Young as librarian, and Spofford became Young's assistant. Young had been a foreign correspondent in Europe for the *New York Herald* and had served as minister to China from 1882 to 1885. He supervised the transfer of the Library from the Capitol to its own building during the period from August to November 1897. Young achieved distinction as the first librarian of Congress to hire women as librarians. He died on Jan. 17, 1899, after only one and one-half years in office.

Herbert Putnam's Long Tenure at Library

After Young's death, McKinley offered the post of librarian of Congress to Herbert Putnam, 38-year-old member of the Putnam publishing family, lawyer and librarian of the Boston Public Library. Putnam declined the offer initially but then reconsidered and was appointed on March 13, 1899.

Putnam during his long service as librarian was responsible for innovations, improvements, and enlargements in every area of the Library's work. He organized the Aeronautics, Music, and Orientalia Divisions, as well as other units. On the basis of a special appropriation, he established the Legislative Reference Service (now the Congressional Research Service).

He arranged for "chairs" and consultantships in the Library for specialists in political science, military history, Roman law, poetry, the fine arts, and other fields. He instituted the administration by the Library of funds donated by individuals for expansion of the Library's services.

Noteworthy among the special materials acquired during Putnam's service as librarian were the G. V. Yudin library of 80,000 books on Russia and Siberia, a Japanese library of 45,000 volumes, the J. B. Thacher collection of 840 European incunabula (books printed before 1501), the library of Harry Houdini on magic and occultism, and one of the three extant perfect copies of the Gutenberg Bible. Putnam initiated or supervised projects for the sale of printed catalog cards to other libraries, photocopying of European manuscripts pertaining to American history, distribution of braille books to the blind, and interlibrary loans of books. Another innovation was the *National Union Catalog* of books owned by large American libraries, which helps a researcher to locate a book he needs but cannot find in the city where he lives. The Library received, during Putnam's stewardship, a gift of almost $100,000 from Mrs. Elizabeth Sprague Coolidge of Boston which made possible the construction in the Library of an auditorium for chamber music performances and other uses.

In 1938, when Putnam reached the age of 77, Congress passed an Act, signed June 20, which provided "That upon separation from service, by resignation or otherwise,...Herbert Putnam, the present Librarian of Congress, who has served in that office for 39 years, shall become Librarian Emeritus." Putnam had written to President Franklin D. Roosevelt, June 15, of his satisfaction that the choice of his successor "rests with a President who can fully appreciate the requirements of the position under the recent evolution of the institution." He rounded out 40 years of service in April 1939, as the Library was expanding into its second building.

MacLeish: The Regime of the Poet

The ninth librarian of Congress, poet Archibald MacLeish, gave the Library a new dimension in his brief tenure. Roosevelt on May 3, 1939, wrote to his friend and mentor, Supreme Court Justice Felix Frankfurter: "I have had a bad time picking a librarian to succeed Putnam. What would you think of Archie MacLeish? He is not a professional librarian nor is he a special student of incunabula or ancient manuscripts. Nevertheless, he has lots of qualifications that said specialists have not." Frankfurter favored the choice of MacLeish. His reply of May 11 said in part: "The librarians that have left the most enduring marks have not been technical librarians.... What is wanted in the directing head of a great library is imaginative energy and vision. He should be a man who knows books, loves books, and makes books."[13]

The announcement of MacLeish's nomination, June 7, 1939, set off a torrent of opposition. David C. Mearns, chief of the Manuscript Division, wrote of the affair in the May 1965 issue of the *Atlantic:* "The professional library associations, with degrees of intensity varying from petulance to passion, protested with prideful, proprietary indignation. He was not even a recognized amateur; he had no standing in the guild; whatever his gifts for other callings might be, he was starkly disqualified for a position to which only their own anointed might aspire."[14] The governing body of the American Library Association (ALA) asked on June 13, 1939, that the Senate reject MacLeish's nomination.

The Senate rejected the ALA's advice and confirmed MacLeish on June 29 by a vote of 64 to 8. MacLeish took office early in October 1939, and Putnam became librarian emeritus. The period in the administration of the Library of Congress which followed was called by historian Paul Angle the regime of the poet.[15] Mearns wrote, some 26 years later, "Happily, they [the professionals] were soon conciliated...and when they found their voice again they found that it was his."[16] The librarian told an audience at the Carnegie Institute in Pittsburgh, two weeks after taking office, that his reason for accepting the librarianship was his desire to fight with intellectual weapons the growing threat of fascism.

MacLeish set out to strengthen the Library of Congress in three directions. (1) He associated some of the best minds with the Library and with the government by appointing, for example, Allen Tate to the Library's chair of poetry, Thomas Mann as consultant on German literature, and Saint-John Perse as consultant on French poetry. His leadership in these and related measures gave him in some respects the status of a minister of culture. (2) He was active personally, and used the Library as a springboard, in the war for the minds of men that was a part of World War II; concurrently with his librarianship, he served as head of the Office of Facts and Figures and as assistant director of war information. (3) He strengthened the Library's internal organization. Shortly before resigning in 1944 to become assistant secretary of state, he wrote in his annual report: "To succeed Mr. Putnam was a good deal like inheriting an enormous house...from a wise, well-loved, strong-minded, charming and particular uncle who knew where everything was and how everything worked and what everyone could do but had left no indications in his will."[17] Though best known as a poet, MacLeish was an able administrator. He brought order into the fiscal, personnel and management aspects of the Library's operations.

Changes under Evans and Mumford

Evans' Administration. MacLeish's successor was Luther H. Evans, whose career had included service as a teacher of political science at Stanford, Princeton, New York University and Dartmouth; head of the Library's Legislative Reference Service; and chief assistant librarian. President Harry S Truman nominated Evans for the top Library job June 18, 1945, and he was confirmed without opposition June 30. The choice of Evans was applauded by the world of scholarship as well as by the library profession. He had served as acting librarian during long periods when MacLeish was otherwise occupied.

Evans presided over the opening to the public at midnight July 26, 1947, of the collection of papers of Abraham Lincoln which had been deposited in the Library in 1919 by Robert Todd Lincoln, the President's son. The opening date, as stipulated by Robert Lincoln, was exactly 21 years after his own death. Evans also saw to the transfer from the Library of Congress to the National Archives, in 1952, of two documents—the signed originals of the Declaration of Independence and the Constitution of the United States—which had been brought to the Library in 1921 from the Department of State. The Declaration and the Constitution were placed in display vaults on permanent exhibit at the National Archives, along with other historic papers from the nation's earliest years. Evans and others preferred to keep the two documents in the Library, but the Joint Committee on the Library decided otherwise.

Evans represented the United States at the founding conference of the United Nations Educational, Scientific and Cultural Organization in November 1945, and at general conferences of the organization from 1947 to 1952. In 1953, UNESCO selected him as its director general, and he resigned as librarian of Congress on July 5. Verner W. Clapp, chief assistant librarian, served as acting librarian

from then until Sept. 1, 1954, when L. Quincy Mumford took office.

Mumford's Administration. Mumford had been director of the Cleveland Public Library. President Eisenhower nominated him as librarian on April 22, 1954, and the Senate confirmed him on July 29. Mumford was the first graduate of a professional library school to serve as librarian of Congress. In the course of his service in the post, he appointed outspoken nonconformists as consultants to the Library. These appointments served to balance an episode which occurred a little more than a year after he became librarian. Mumford then found himself in the middle of a battle between political liberals and those, like Sen. Joseph R. McCarthy (R Wis.), who saw liberals as unpatriotic.

The Library invited Dr. Albert Sprague Coolidge, son of one of the Library's principal benefactors, Mrs. Elizabeth Sprague Coolidge, to serve on the advisory committee of the Coolidge Foundation, which played a part in administering the Coolidge gifts to the Library. But when Coolidge's association with ultra-liberal causes came to public attention and aroused criticism, the invitation was withdrawn. The weekly *Library of Congress Information Bulletin* explained on Feb. 6, 1956: "The Librarian felt that Dr. Coolidge's past associations and activities, entirely aside from the 'loyalty' or 'security' issue, would impair that objectivity in the fulfillment of his duties that one has a right to expect of a public employee, even in an advisory capacity on cultural matters."[18]

Former Librarian MacLeish, in an address at Carleton College in Northfield, Minn., on Sept. 22, 1956, commented acidly on the Library's statement of the preceding February. MacLeish said, "What is clearly implied was that a man is not suitable for work in a library who has taken sides on public issues." But taking sides on issues of freedom to read and freedom to speak one's mind, MacLeish said, was exactly what a librarian should do. "No librarian," he said, "who believes in the freedom guaranteed by the Constitution, and who detests authoritarianism, can avoid taking positions on controversial issues."[19]

In 1940 Mumford had come to the Library at MacLeish's request to reorganize the technical divisions and to head the new Processing Department. He left in 1941. When he returned as librarian, Mumford guided the Library of Congress into the age of automation. The program began in 1963 with basic work looking toward mechanical preparation of bibliographies. Later, what is called the Card Automated Reproduction and Distribution System was installed. It is based on a network of electronic hookups dubbed MARC because of its concept of Machine-Readable Cataloging. The format of MARC was worked out in prolonged consultations between the Library of Congress and the American Library Association. Other activities which the Library began to automate during the Mumford regime include identification, storage and retrieval of single-sheet maps; compilation and publication by the Congressional Research Service of the *Digest of Public General Bills and Resolutions;* and data maintenance and reporting of the Reader Services Department's National Referral Center for Science and Technology. A program developed by the Library's Information Systems Office was used by the Senate Select Committee on Presidential Campaign Activities in the 1974 Watergate hearings, providing the first major applications of computers in evidentiary proceedings.[20]

The drive for automation came none too soon to accommodate the Library's growth. Collections which numbered over 33 million when Mumford took office in 1954 had more than doubled when he retired 20 years later. Computers also aided the Library's National Program for Acquisitions and Cataloging, begun in 1966, to make bibliographic information acquired on a worldwide basis quickly accessible to citizens and scholars.

Mumford retired Dec. 31, 1974, having stayed a year beyond his intended retirement at the request of the President. During most of 1975 Deputy Librarian John G. Lorenz served as acting librarian.

Appointment of Boorstin

President Ford's June 20, 1975, nomination of historian Daniel J. Boorstin to become the twelfth librarian of Congress set off the biggest wrangle over the position since the nomination of MacLeish in 1939. The public debate began six weeks before the formal nomination, when stories were leaked from the White House that Ford intended to choose Boorstin.

There was no challenge to Boorstin's scholarship. He had earned academic honors at Harvard, Oxford and Yale and had passed bar examinations in England and the United States. He was on the faculty of the University of Chicago for 25 years and was a visiting lecturer at four universities abroad. His writing of history included over a dozen books and several major awards, and he edited the 27-volume series, *The Chicago History of American Civilization.* In 1969 Boorstin was appointed director of the Smithsonian Institution's National Museum of History and Technology, and in 1973 he became the museum's senior historian and an adviser to Smithsonian Secretary S. Dillon Ripley.

Boorstin's political reputation was controversial. At Harvard in 1938-39 he had belonged to a Communist Party cell. Then on Feb. 23, 1953, he described that experience to the House Committee on Un-American Activities and listed the names of fellow party members at Harvard, which earned him the lifelong enmity of many liberals. He was a friend of Vice President Spiro T. Agnew, who had been forced out of office by scandal in 1973, and was reported to have written some of Agnew's more demagogic speeches.

Most of the opposition to Boorstin's nomination to be librarian of Congress came from two sources. Professional librarians, led by the American Library Association, argued that Boorstin's career, however distinguished, did not include the technical expertise or administrative experience required to supervise the Library. Boorstin also was opposed by minority interests. Some employees of the Library claimed that Boorstin's writings and his previous actions in the government indicated that he would not emphasize hiring minority employees.

The Senate Committee on Rules and Administration, which conducted the confirmation hearings, was most concerned with Boorstin's plans to continue his career as historian. He had continued writing, editing and consulting while at the Smithsonian, and he had a contract with Random House Inc. to write a 200,000-word history of the world by 1982. Boorstin told the committee: "[I]f I am confirmed as Librarian of Congress I will be a full-time Librarian...by full time, I mean 40 hours a week, plus as many more hours, any time of the day or night, or on weekends, as would be necessary to serve the Library."[21] The committee "accepted his repeated assurances that he would not let the administration of the Library suffer as a result of his writings and that he would consider the Library his primary obligation."[22]

Types of Library Holdings

The 70.5 million items in the Library of Congress collections include a vast array of material. The variety of the Library's collections is listed below:

Artifacts, instruments and mementos

Books in the ordinary sense

Books and magazines in braille

Books and magazines recorded for the blind

Drawings, etchings, prints and other graphic representations and designs

Incunabula

Manuscripts in scrolls, sheets, notebooks and codex form

Maps

Microfilms and microfiches

Motion pictures, silent and sound

Music in written and printed notations

Music on phonograph records and cylinders

Music on tapes and wires

Newspapers, loose and in bound volumes

Pamphlets

Periodicals and magazines

Photocopies and photostats

Photographic negatives, prints and slides

Posters and broadsides

Processed materials—usually typewritten material reproduced by near-print processes

Speeches, recitations, narratives, poetry and dramatic performances on film, phonograph records or tape

Technical reports

Source: Library of Congress, Information Office.

One more charge against Boorstin had to be settled. While he was director of the National Museum of History and Technology, Boorstin had completed work on his Pulitzer Prize-winning book, *The Americans—The Democratic Experience,* with the assistance of some federally paid research and secretarial employees. The committee learned from Ripley that when Boorstin took the museum job he was assured that he and any assistants would be paid only from the Smithsonian's privately endowed funds. During the work, some federal funds also had been used. The committee concluded that "Dr. Boorstin was not aware of this practice of using government employees for his private use...."[23] Boorstin told the senators, "I would certainly not use my position as Librarian of Congress, nor any government employees, or any employees of the Library of Congress to help me with my private writings."[24]

After all the controversy, the committee confirmed Boorstin Sept. 16 by an 8-0 vote. The full Senate confirmed him without debate and by a voice vote on Sept. 26, a few days before Boorstin's 61st birthday. He was sworn in as the twelfth librarian of Congress Nov. 12, 1975.

The Library in Operation

Whether it is serving Congress specifically or the public in general, the Library does its job by acquiring, organizing, storing and dispensing human knowledge. The information it is responsible for is not confined to the written word, but includes many other devices for recording and communicating ideas. In performing its services the Library requires a large staff, complex organization, huge physical plant, and special equipment and techniques.

Scope of the Library's Holdings

At the end of fiscal 1975, the Library of Congress had a total of 70,537,778 items.[25] The collections included approximately 17.5 million volumes and pamphlets, 31.7 million manuscript pieces, 3.5 million maps, 3.5 million volumes and pieces of music, and 8.5 million photographic negatives, prints and slides. The grand total was even higher a year earlier, before the Library transferred custody of nearly 4.6 million braille volumes and "talking books" for the blind and physically handicapped to the 53 regional libraries where they had been deposited for many years. *(Box, Types of Library of Congress Holdings, p. 444)*

The Library's holdings include the nation's largest collection of incunabula—many donated by Lessing J. Rosenwald and housed in Jenkintown, Pa.

The Library has the world's most extensive collection of aeronautical literature. It has more than a thousand miniature books, none more than four inches high. The manuscript collection includes the papers of 23 Presidents. In the graphic arts, two highly valued collections are the Joseph Pennell Collection of Whistleriana and an almost complete set of Civil War photographs by Matthew Brady.

Including music and other performances, the Library had 467,654 recordings at the end of fiscal 1975. The Archive of Recorded Poetry and Literature seeks recordings by every living English-speaking poet of note, and often commissions and records readings.

The Library's materials are in 468 languages. Its Russian collection is the largest outside the Soviet Union, and its Chinese and Japanese collections are the largest outside the Orient. The Library acquires books from some countries by standing orders with publishers and dealers for every important book published.

The eighth librarian of Congress, Herbert Putnam, wrote in one of his 40 annual reports: "The progress of the Library which is more significant cannot be expressed in figures. It consists in the gradual perfection of its equipment and of its service, in a development of its collections appropriate to its purpose as a library of research, and in a wider appreciation and acceptance of its functions as a national library, with a duty to the entire country."[26]

Administrative Organization

At the top of the Library's organizational structure is the Office of the Librarian, consisting of the librarian of Congress, deputy librarian and three assistant librarians. Publicity about the Library is the responsibility of three offices attached to the Office of the Librarian: Publications, Exhibits and Information. Seven departments do the major work of the Library, four having primarily reference duties and three primarily technical and housekeeping duties. Supplementing the seven departments are a corps of consultants and the Library of Congress Trust Fund Board. *(Box, Library Trust Fund Board, p. 447)*

Reference Units. The units of the Library responsible for reference work are the Research Department, the Reader Services Department, the Congressional Research Service and the Law Library.

Research has eight divisions concerned with geographic areas, music, books and nonbook material. Reader Services

(Continued on p. 447)

Treasures in the Library

The Library of Congress has a number of exceedingly rare and valuable possessions among its 70.5 million books, manuscripts, recordings, photographs and other items. Some have been displayed in the Library, but most are in fragile condition and must be preserved and stored with great care. Some of the Library's major treasures are described below:

Gutenberg Bible—One of three known perfect copies printed on vellum. It was the first large book printed on moveable type, completed by 1456. Other Bibles in the Library include the manuscript Giant Bible of Mainz (1452) and the Necksei-Lipozc Bible in two illuminated volumes from 14th century Hungary.

Bay Psalm Book—One of only 11 copies extant of John Eliot's translation of the Psalms. Published in Cambridge, Mass., in 1640, the book is the first example of printing in North America that has survived.

Stradivari Instruments—A set of five stringed instruments made by Antonio Stradivari (1644?-1737). The Julliard String Quartet plays them regularly in concert series at the Library.

Declaration of Independence—Thomas Jefferson's rough draft of the Declaration in his handwriting, with changes written in by Benjamin Franklin and John Adams. The Library also has two copies of the first published edition of the Declaration, printed on the night of July 4, 1776, by John Dunlop of Philadelphia.

Madison's Notes—James Madison's personal notes of debates during the 1787 Constitutional Convention in Philadelphia.

Bill of Rights—One of the original engrossed and certified copies. The Library also has George Mason's 1776 draft of the Virginia Bill of Rights.

Gettysburg Address—Lincoln's first and second drafts of his Gettysburg Address, written on ruled paper. The Lincoln collection includes his manuscript for the Second Inaugural Address.

Civil War Photographs—A nearly complete set of Matthew Brady's photographs of the Civil War. Others in the Library's collection include pictures taken during the Great Depression by Walker Evans and others.

Folk Music—The Library's Archive of Folk Song has 26,000 cylinders, discs and tapes of traditional American (including Indian) and foreign folk music, most of it preserved nowhere else. These are noncommercial archival recordings made in the field by folklorists.

Presidential Papers—The personal papers of 23 Presidents, from Washington through Coolidge. The two million documents include Washington's 1775 commission as commander-in-chief, Monroe's journal of negotiations for the Louisiana Purchase, and Wilson's penciled draft announcing the 1918 Armistice.

Music Manuscripts—Examples from virtually all 20th century composers and many earlier masters, including Bach, Beethoven, Haydn, Mozart, Schubert and the largest collection anywhere of Johannes Brahms' manuscripts. The Library also has a copy of the first printed book of music, *Odhecaton*, published by Petrucci in Venice in 1504.

Source: Library of Congress staff interviews.

Organization of the Library of Congress

(Units arranged alphabetically)

OFFICE OF THE LIBRARIAN
Librarian of Congress
Deputy Librarian of Congress
Assistant Librarians of Congress

American Revolution Bicentennial Office
Chief Internal Auditor
Exhibits Office
Federal Library Committee
General Counsel

Information Office
Office of the Permanent Committee
   for the Oliver Wendell Holmes
   Devise
Publications Office

ADMINISTRATIVE DEPARTMENT
Office of the Director
  Building Planning Office
  Information Systems Office
  Photoduplication Service

Assistant Director for Management Services
  Buildings Management Office
  Central Services Division
  Financial Management Office
  Procurement and Supply Division

Assistant Director for Personnel
  Employee Relations Office
  Personnel Operations Office
  Personnel Security Office
  Placement and Classification Office
  Training Office

Assistant Director for Preservation
  Binding Office
  Collections Maintenance Office
  Preservation Microfilming Office
  Preservation Research and Testing Office
  Restoration Office

CONGRESSIONAL RESEARCH SERVICE
Office of the Director
  American Law Division
  Congressional Reference Division
  Economics Division
  Education and Public Welfare Division
  Environmental Policy Division
  Foreign Affairs Division
  Government and General Research Division
  Library Services Division
  Science Policy Research Division
  Senior Specialists Division

COPYRIGHT OFFICE
Office of the Register
  Cataloging Division
  Examining Division
  Reference Division
  Service Division

LAW LIBRARY
Office of the Law Librarian
  American-British Law Division
  European Law Division
  Far Eastern Law Division

Hispanic Law Division
Near Eastern and African Law Division

PROCESSING DEPARTMENT
Office of the Director
  MARC Development Office
  National Serials Data Program
  National Union Catalog Publication Project
  Technical Processes Research Office

Office of the Assistant Director for Acquisitions and
  Overseas Operations
  Exchange and Gift Division
  Order Division
  Overseas Operations Division
  Selection Office

Office of the Assistant Director for Cataloging
  Cataloging Instruction Office
  Decimal Classification Division
  Descriptive Cataloging Division
  MARC Editorial Division
  Shared Cataloging Division
  Subject Cataloging Division

Office of the Assistant Director for Processing Services
  Cataloging and Distributive Services
  Catalog Management Division
  Catalog Publication Division
  Serial Record Division

READER SERVICES DEPARTMENT
Office of the Director
  Blind and Physically Handicapped Division
  Federal Research Division
  General Reference and Bibliography Division
  Loan Division
  Science and Technology Division,
    National Referral Center
  Serial Division
  Stack and Reader Division

RESEARCH DEPARTMENT
Office of the Director
  Geography and Map Division
  Latin America, Portuguese and Spanish Division
  Manuscript Division
  Music Division
  Orientalia Division
  Prints and Photographs Division
  Rare Book Division
  Slavic and Central European Division

Source: *Annual Report of the Librarian of Congress* (Government Printing Office, 1975 pp. xiv-xv; Library of Congress, Information Office.

(Continued from p. 445)

includes the Library stacks, loans, serials, general reference and bibliography, federal research, science and technology, and services for the blind and physically handicapped. Research and Reader Services formed one Reference Department until 1976, when Boorstin divided them into two units.

The Law Library was established as a separate branch in 1832. Its five divisions specialize in geographic and cultural areas. They concentrate on treaties, court cases, constitutions, statutes, decrees and regulations.

The fourth Library unit with reference duties, the Congressional Research Service (CRS) is described later in this chapter. *(p. 450)*

Excluding the CRS, reference units of the Library in fiscal 1974 performed 1,145,000 direct reference services—456,000 in person, 189,000 through correspondence, and 500,000 by telephone. In addition, they circulated 2,088,000 volumes for use within the Library and another 210,600 for outside use, and prepared 223 bibliographies.[27]

Technical and Housekeeping Units. The Library's technical work of facilitating the use of books is centered in the Processing Department. It contains 18 divisions, or units comparable to divisions. The first steps in this work are the selection, ordering, and exchange of books and the receipt of gifts. Subsequent steps include the classification of books by subjects, description of books for the catalog, and production and sale of the Library of Congress catalog—as cards, computer tapes, or volumes.

The Administrative Department is divided into three sections, each headed by an assistant director, for management services, personnel, and preservation of materials. The Information Systems Office and two other units are supervised by the director of the Administrative Department.

The preservation section tries to save older books printed on paper which is brittle and disintegrating. Some are microfilmed, while others are salvaged by pasting thin protective sheets over damaged pages. A survey made in 1970 indicated that about 25 per cent of the Library's brittle books were unavailable elsewhere in the United States and were in urgent need of preservation. Perhaps six million books in the Library are decaying. Acting Librarian John G. Lorenz said in 1975 that preserving the rotting books on microfilm would cost $200-million, while the Library spends only about $1-million a year for microfilming.[28]

The Copyright Office, which became a part of the Library in 1870, also is engaged in technical work. Its four divisions—for cataloging, examining, reference and service—are supervised by the register of copyrights. U.S. copyright law, intended to protect the creators of original works from exploitation, is based on an Act of March 4, 1909, which was scarcely amended for more than 65 years. Efforts to revise the copyright law began in the 1950s, but by the fall of 1976 Congress still had not amended the act sufficiently to accommodate technological changes such as photocopying, broadcasting of sound recordings and cable television.

Consultants and Trust Fund Board. In addition to the three reference and three administrative or technical departments are the Library's consultants, including a full-time consultant in poetry in English and part-time honorary consultants on 19 subjects. The consultants assist in the development of the collections, furnish expert advice in specialized fields of knowledge, and serve as liaison between the Library and persons conducting intensive research. Consultants in recent years have included Stanley Kunitz, Margaret Mead, C. Vann Woodward, Wallace Stegner,

---

Library Trust Fund Board

An Act of March 3, 1925, created the Library of Congress Trust Fund Board and authorized it to receive and administer gifts and bequests to the Library, apart from money donated or bequeathed for immediate disbursement. The board consists of the Secretary of the Treasury (chairman), the chairman of the Joint Committee on the Library, the librarian of Congress (secretary), and two persons appointed by the President for terms of five years each. The board may invest its assets in stocks or bonds and may lend money to the U.S. government and collect interest. Gifts to the Library of Congress, and earnings of the Trust Fund Board, are tax-exempt.

Assets of trust funds administered by the board in fiscal 1974 included (1) more than $5.2-million on permanent loan to the U.S. Treasury at 4 per cent annual interest, and (2) entitlement to one-half of the income from investments valued at slightly more than $1-million. The largest gifts administered by the board are: more than $1.5-million from the Gertrude Clarke Whittall Foundation for maintenance of the Stradivari instruments which Mrs. Whittall donated to the Library, and for presentation of programs in which the instruments are played; nearly $1-million from the Whittall Poetry and Literature Fund for the presentation of poetry and literary programs; more than $800,-000 from the Elizabeth Sprague Coolidge Foundation to further musical research, composition, performance and appreciation.

Source: *Annual Report of the Librarian of Congress* (Government Printing Office, 1974), pp. vi, 99-100, 122-25.

John Updike and Edgar Breitenbach. Honorary consultants serve for three years. The librarian relies on the Library of Congress Trust Fund Board for the administration of endowment funds established for the Library. *(Library Trust Fund Board, above)*

Buildings of Library of Congress

The Library of Congress was housed in the Capitol during most of the 19th century. William W. Bishop, librarian of the University of Michigan, writing of the expansion of the Library under Ainsworth R. Spofford in the three decades following the Civil War, remarked: "Dr. Spofford waxed old, and the Frankenstein he had created overwhelmed the Capitol."[29] Congress, by an Act of April 15, 1886, authorized the construction of a separate building for the Library of Congress. In 1888, Gen. Thomas L. Casey, Chief of Engineers of the U.S. Army, was appointed to supervise the construction. It was designed by John L. Smithmeyer and Paul J. Pelz, but architect Edward Pearce Casey was in charge of the building from 1892, including the interior design.

Main Building. The Library of Congress building was completed in 1897 at a cost of $6,360,000.[30] It is near the Capitol, filling the block bounded by East Capitol Street, Independence Avenue, and First and Second Streets, Southeast. The Library's old quarters in the Capitol were

Symbolism in Main Reading Room

The main reading room of the Library of Congress is one of Washington's showplaces. At the center of the Library's original 1897 building, the circular room (actually a modified octagon) is covered by a dome 100 feet in diameter and 160 feet high.

The room's circumference is divided into eight sections by massive pillars of red-brown marble, which are connected by three tiers of alcoves and balconies. The sections are surmounted by arches and semicircular windows of stained glass decorated with the seals of the 45 states and three territories which composed the Union in the 1890s.

The pillars are topped by statues symbolizing different features of civilized life, and under the arches are statues of historic figures from each field of knowledge. Thus, Science is flanked by Isaac Newton and Joseph Henry, Law by Solon and Chancellor James Kent, Poetry by Homer and Shakespeare, Philosophy by Plato and Bacon, Art by Michelangelo and Beethoven, History by Herodotus and Gibbon, Commerce by Columbus and Robert Fulton, and Religion by Moses and St. Paul.

Above the arches is the dome of the Library. Its lowest section contains 320 blue squares bordered in gold and ivory and containing gold rosettes. Above the squares is a painted collar-like area symbolizing the evolution of civilization, with winged figures corresponding to the following countries or periods and their contributions:

Egypt, written records	Italy, fine arts
Judea, religion	Germany, art of printing
Greece, philosophy	Spain, discovery
Rome, administration	England, literature
Islam, physics	France, emancipation
Middle Ages, modern languages	America, science

At the top of the dome, above the collar, is a painting on a blue field of a female figure representing human understanding. The murals in the dome are by Edwin Blashfield. The floor of the main reading room contains the central reference desk and concentric circles of tables for 250 readers and a portion of the Library's 25,200-tray card-catalog files. The room and its alcoves and balconies contain about 30,000 reference books.

The entire room may be viewed from the visitors' gallery on the westernmost balcony. The gallery was enclosed in glass in 1975 to reduce noise. Other temporary staff offices at the balcony level are to be removed when the Madison Building is occupied.

Source: *The Library of Congress* (pamphlet, Government Printing Office 1975); Library of Congress Information Office.

The inspiration for the gray granite building was the Paris Opera, built in the 1860s. It is in the ornate style of the Italian Renaissance, decorated more richly inside than out, with stairs, walls and floors of multi-colored marble from Tennessee, Italy, France and Algeria. It is considered a landmark of public building decoration in the United States. The spectacular Great Hall features staircases of sculpture by Philip Martiny, and the corridors contain murals by John W. Alexander and paintings and a marble mosaic by Elihu Vedder. A clock over the entrance to the main reading room is decorated with sculptured figures representing Father Time and the seasons. *(Symbolism in Main Reading Room, box this page)*

The main reading room was closed from May 4, 1964, to Aug. 16, 1965, to install new heating and air-conditioning systems and new lighting, to improve the book-carrying machinery, and to build temporary offices in the mezzanine of the great hall and the balconies of the main reading room. The partitions were to be removed by 1980.

Library Annex. The main building, after three decades of use, was filling its available space faster than had been anticipated. Congress on June 13, 1930, authorized construction of an annex immediately east of the main building. Completed April 5, 1939, at a cost of $9-million, the library annex is of white marble, five stories high with three additional stories below ground and a tunnel to the main building. Occupying 13 acres of land, the two buildings gave the Library 35 acres of floor space and 320 miles of bookshelves.

Madison Building. About 25 years after the annex was occupied, the need for additional space again became evident. An Act of Oct. 19, 1965, authorized $75-million for a building which would serve the double purpose of providing a second annex to the Library of Congress and memorializing President James Madison. Although Washington, D.C., is cluttered with statues of famous and obscure people, on the eve of the nation's Bicentennial there was no monument honoring the father of the Constitution.

Officially named the Library of Congress James Madison Memorial Building, the structure was to have six stories above ground and three below, with a tunnel to the main Library building. Congress had been stung by architectural criticism of the Rayburn House Office Building, so the law said that plans for the Madison Building were to be drawn up "after consultation with the American Institute of Architects." But Architect of the Capitol J. George Stewart commissioned the firm of Dewitt, Poor & Shelton without the knowledge of the AIA consultants. *(Discussion of the Rayburn Building and Stewart's construction projects, pp. 432-33)*

Congress put off appropriating the money needed to erect the Madison Building, largely because of the tightness of the budget. At a hearing before the House Subcommittee on Public Buildings and Grounds, Oct. 29, 1969, Rep. Kenneth J. Gray (D Ill.), the subcommittee chairman, reported that architects had made a new estimate of $90-million as the cost of the building. An act of March 16, 1970, increased the authorized expenditure to $90-million and thereby released $2.8-million for final plans which had been appropriated for fiscal 1970 on condition that the authorized total be increased. Money was appropriated in fiscal 1971 for excavation and other preliminary construction work.

There was no ground-breaking ceremony and the building's cornerstone was not laid until March 8, 1974. Because of strikes and other delays, the building was not expected to be completed until 1978, with a chance that it

closed in July 1897 and the new building was opened Nov. 1. One million books and pamphlets were transferred in the intervening period. A system of underground conveyor belts was used to move books and reference material between the Library and the Capitol. *(Map, Capitol Hill, p. 430)*

might not be fully occupied until 1980. Because of inflation the final cost was expected to be more than $120-million. Meanwhile, Library employees were afraid the House of Representatives would take over at least part of the new building for its own staff offices. (*House expansion plans, p. 435*)

Need for Library Space. While waiting for the Madison Building the Library suffered from serious overcrowding. By the mid-1950s all bookshelves were filled, even though temporary additions brought the total to 336 miles.[31] Mumford noted that during his 20 years as librarian the collections increased by over 100 per cent while Library space increased by only 42 per cent. By the end of fiscal 1974 the Library occupied 12 buildings in Washington, Virginia, Maryland and Ohio.[32] There was hardly room anywhere for materials or Library employees, who numbered nearly 4,700 late in 1975.

An article in *Parade* magazine in 1975 described some of the problems caused by lack of space: "Each year the Library is inundated with 16 million pieces of printed matter. The staff must sift through this paper avalanche, selecting the 3 or 4 million items judged worthy of admission to its shelves. Each book has to be catalogued, then stack attendants must try to squeeze them into the already overloaded shelves. There hasn't been enough room and the books get piled knee-deep on the floor. People seeking to use the Library may sit hour upon hour in the reading room, often vainly waiting.... Stack attendants freely admit that as many as 30 per cent of book requests cannot be filled."[33]

Library's Nationwide Services

The White House, executive departments, and other government agencies in Washington have their own libraries. Some of these collections are comprehensive, such as those of the National Agricultural Library and the National Library of Medicine, but many are narrowly limited in scope. All parts of the executive branch depend on the Library of Congress for published information not available in their own buildings. The Library regards the executive branch as, next to Congress, its primary client for quick provision of information and for loans of books needed for official business.

Services to Other Libraries. Libraries throughout the United States look to the Library of Congress for many kinds of services, of which five are perhaps the most important: (1) Cataloging of new books and sale of catalog cards and MARC tapes; (2) maintenance of the *National Union Catalog*, which shows the holdings of approximately 700 large libraries in the United States; (3) conducting research in library technology; (4) administering a worldwide cooperative acquisitions program; and (5) lending books.

In marketing the first of these services, the Library's Cataloging and Distribution Service Division (formerly Card Division) each year sells millions of individual catalog cards, plus magnetic tapes which each contain about 1,000 catalog entries and can be fed into a computer for printouts. Sales of individual cards reached a high of 78.8 million in 1968. the year before the MARC tapes were first offered. The division sold 44.9 million cards in fiscal 1975, as automation of libraries increased.[34]

The portion of the *National Union Catalog* that contains pre-1956 imprints—about 16 million cards—is being printed in bound volumes by a commercial firm for sale to libraries that can afford them. The series eventually will fill 600 volumes, 404 of which had been distributed by October 1975. The current *National Union Catalog*—covering books and other materials published since 1956—has been published by the Library itself in monthly volumes and quarterly cumulations. Five-year series are then printed by a commercial firm.

Supplementing the union catalog of books is a monthly Library publication, *New Serial Titles*. It includes the titles of newly established periodicals and other serials, changes in titles, changes in frequency of issue, and titles of periodicals and serials which have been discontinued; it also shows the major libraries that receive the new serials.

Additional Library of Congress publications for other libraries are the *National Union Catalog of Manuscript Collections*, the *Library of Congress Catalog—Books; Subjects*, and numerous technical reports. The Cataloging and Distribution Service Division in fiscal 1975 realized total gross sales of $7,309,646.25 from distributing all catalog-related materials.[35]

Loans of books and materials are important Library services. In fiscal 1975 the Library loaned 218,519 books and other items, of which 53 per cent went to other libraries—38 per cent to government libraries in and near Washington, and 15 per cent to libraries outside the Washington area. The rest were borrowed by members of Congress and their staffs (34 per cent) and other authorized borrowers (13 per cent).[36] Other libraries may borrow books and materials for scholarly research if the Library of Congress has the only copies. The Library will make a photocopy if the item requested is too rare or too fragile to lend.

Services to the Public. Any person over high school age may use the facilities of the main reading room, the Thomas Jefferson reading room in the library annex, or 14 other rooms of specialized materials such as music, maps and current periodicals. Admission is free, but materials may not be removed from the Library. Books requested by readers are delivered to them in the reading rooms, and readers may use the reference books available on the open shelves without filling in a request slip. Reference librarians are on duty to assist readers.

A million and a half tourists and elementary and secondary school students visit the Library each year.[37] Visitors may view the exhibits in the corridors of the Library, walk through the great hall, and observe the main reading room from the visitors' gallery. Guides conduct free 45-minute tours of the Library at hourly intervals.

Both the main building and the Library annex are filled with changing exhibits prepared by the Library staff. In fiscal 1974 there were 13 major displays ranging from the 270-item "An American Sampler: A Look at Life in the 1800s" to a collection of treasure maps. The White House News Photographers Association annual displays have been popular for over 30 years. Also in fiscal 1974, the Library lent 540 items from its collections to other institutions for exhibition, prepared eight traveling exhibits shown at 29 locations, and provided materials for display by other government agencies.[38]

The Library regularly presents, in the Elizabeth Sprague Coolidge Auditorium, concerts, readings, and dramatic performances open to the public. The admission charge for some of these performances is 25 cents. The Gertrude Clarke Whittall Foundation sponsors concerts featuring the Stradivari instruments, played for many years by the Budapest String Quartet and now by the Julliard String Quartet. Other concerts at the Library in recent years have included the Deller Consort, the French String Trio, the Tokyo String Quartet and the Beaux Arts Trio of New York. Readings, lectures and literary conferences have featured Ralph Ellison, John Barth, Allen Ginsberg, Allen Tate and many others. In all, there were 52 public performances at the Library in fiscal 1974.[39]

Hundreds of publications and recordings produced by the Library are available to the public. Approximately 400 publications, based mainly on the Library's collections, cover an enormous range of subjects. They include scholarly studies, guides to collections, bibliographies, lectures, checklists and directories, and papers presented at such meetings as the Library of Congress Symposium on the American Revolution. The Library also publishes facsimiles of historic documents, manuscripts and posters, and a variety of greeting cards and gift items. In addition, the Library sells over 100 long-playing record albums produced from its vast collection of folk music and other recordings. A Bicentennial series of 15 albums of traditional American music was produced for sale late in 1976.

Library publications, albums and other items may be purchased at the Library or ordered by mail from the Library or the Government Printing Office. (Free catalogs are available from: Publications Distribution Unit, Central Services Division, Library of Congress, Washington, D.C. 20540.) The free monthly *Calendar of Events in the Library of Congress* describes exhibits, concerts and other public events at the Library.

The Library of Congress provides special services to citizens who are blind, partially sighted or otherwise physically unable to read conventional printed materials. The Library and 53 cooperating regional libraries throughout the nation have books in raised characters (braille) and books in large type, "talking books" on discs and tapes, and other recorded aids for the physically handicapped. Record and tape players are provided free. The Library itself has 52,000 special items, and the other libraries have more than 4.6 million in their custody. In fiscal 1974, 421,870 handicapped readers borrowed 11.2 million special books from the libraries.[40]

Copyright Protection. Although the registration of copyrights differs markedly from furnishing books and presenting performances, it, too, is a public service of the Library of Congress. The Copyright Office, with more than 400 employees, records the ownership of literary and other intellectual property in order to secure to the owners any financial benefits derived from the use of the property. Works subject to copyrighting and copyright renewal include books, pamphlets and leaflets, periodicals, unpublished lectures and radio and television scripts, dramatic and musical compositions, maps, works of art and reproductions of a work of art, scientific and technical

drawings, diagrams and models, photographs, prints, labels used for articles of merchandise (but not trademarks), motion pictures and sound recordings. In fiscal 1975 total copyright registrations, including renewals, reached 401,274—an increase of 7.6 per cent over the previous year. Copyright fees for fiscal 1975 totaled $2,447,295.14.[41] *(Box, Copyright Registrations, this page)*

Congressional Research Service

A 1975 article about the Library of Congress in *National Geographic* noted, "Congressmen call the Library for virtually everything: analysis of issues, legal research, translations, assistance with statements and drafts of speeches, the drawing up of charts, and help with constituent mail."[42] For most of these services, representatives and senators go directly to their own research branch within the Library, the Congressional Research Service (CRS).

The predecessor of today's CRS attained separate status early in the 20th century, when the Library became so involved with its collections and general research that Congress wanted renewed staff emphasis on legislation. It is now a major part of the Library organization, and many members of Congress no doubt regard the CRS as the most important part because it helps them directly to do their job. By 1975 the service had 475 full-time specialists, plus a large support staff, answering about 2,000 queries from Congress each day.[43]

Over half of all the questions put to the CRS are answered the same day they are received. Thanks to a massive filing system and a high degree of automation, many short, factual answers are provided within minutes. CRS research is objective and strictly nonpartisan. Congressional inquiries are kept confidential. A survey in May 1974 found that 91 per cent of congressional users rated the quality of CRS response as good or superior.[44]

The role of the CRS is restricted. The assistant director of the CRS, Charles A. Goodrum, wrote in 1974: "The Congressional Research Service is not an investigative agency. It has no powers of subpoena, and indeed must and should limit its sources of research to information already available in the public domain. Investigation must be limited to the committees of the legislature. The Service does not and should not recommend courses of action. It endeavors to identify such choices, and to the best of its ability attempts to state the apparent strengths and weaknesses of the alternatives—but it must be the legislator who makes the decision."[45]

Founding and Expansion of the Service

An Act of June 30, 1906, appropriated funds to enable the Library of Congress to prepare law indexes, digests and compilations for the use of Congress during the fiscal year 1907. Similar appropriations were made for the fiscal years 1908, 1909 and 1910. Hearings were held in 1912-13 on a bill to establish a permanent reference service for analyzing proposed legislation, but Congress failed to pass it.

An amendment to the legislative appropriations bill for fiscal 1915 provided as follows: "Legislative reference. To enable the Librarian of Congress to employ competent persons to prepare such indexes, digests and compilations of law as may be required for Congress and other official use pursuant to the Act approved June thirtieth, nineteen hundred and six, $25,000." The bill was signed July 16, 1914, and the librarian shortly thereafter established the

---

Copyright Registrations

1870	5,600	1930	172,792
1880	20,686	1940	176,997
1890	42,794	1950	210,564
1900	94,798	1960	243,926
1910	109,074	1970	316,466
1920	126,562	1975	401,274

Note: 1870-90, calendar year; 1900-75, fiscal year.

Source: *Annual Report of the Librarian of Congress* (Government Printing Office 1969), p. 96; Copyright Office records.

Legislative Reference Service by administrative order. Corresponding legislation for fiscal 1916, signed March 4, 1915, used the following language proposed by Sen. Robert M. La Follette (R Wis.): "To enable the Librarian of Congress to employ competent persons to gather, classify, and make available, in translations, indexes, digests, compilations, and bulletins, and otherwise, data for or bearing upon legislation, and to render such data serviceable to Congress and committees and members thereof." That language, with little change, was repeated annually in the appropriations acts until 1946.

Meanwhile, Congress had given the Legislative Reference Service two specific jobs, of which one was discontinued, and the other has remained on the agenda. Beginning in 1926, the LRS—at the request of Congress—compiled and published a biennial index of state legislation. The last of 12 volumes in the series covered laws enacted in 1947-48. Beginning in 1935, Congress directed LRS to prepare and publish a digest of public bills introduced in Congress. The Legislative Reorganization Act of August 2, 1946, made this task a regular part of the LRS program.

The 1946 law enlarged the LRS and shifted the predominant staff from librarians to subject specialists. It added pro-and-con studies, comparative analyses, and subject-oriented reports to the service's continued information support.

CRS Established. The Legislative Reorganization Act of 1970 transformed the LRS into the Congressional Research Service and gave it greater responsibilities. The law required the CRS to maintain continuous liaison with all congressional committees. This has meant evaluating legislative proposals and alternatives, estimating results of proposed legislation, identifying all expiring programs at the beginning of each Congress, and citing policy areas which the committees might consider.

The 1970 law also directed the CRS to prepare "purpose and effect" reports on all bills scheduled for hearings. It authorized the CRS director to prepare the budget for the service independently, for inclusion in the Library's annual budget. The act directed the librarian of Congress to "encourage and assist the service in performing its work, and to grant it complete research independence and the maximum administrative independence."

The CRS was allowed five years (by the end of fiscal 1976) to complete the act's provisions. The service expanded rapidly. Budgeted staff positions increased by 70 per cent from the beginning of fiscal 1972 to the end of fiscal 1974, to a total of 618 positions.[46] The fiscal 1976 request was for 860 positions, but Congress allowed only 778. The total CRS budget for the year was $16.6-million. Growth and change were evident in all divisions of the service.

Organization of CRS

There are 10 divisions within the CRS, all under the Office of the Director. One division collects data for use by the rest of the service, another handles general questions, seven divisions do subject-oriented research, and one assigns senior specialists to work in all fields. Generally, each division has a chief, assistant chief, administrative secretary, six to 10 typists, and a large number of researchers with varied experience.

Following is an outline of the CRS divisions and what they do:[47]

Library Services Division—Professional librarians and clerical assistants maintain a filing system on 3,000 sub-

CRS Senior Specialists

The Legislative Reorganization Act of 1970 authorized the Congressional Research Service to employ senior specialists in specified subject areas and "such other broad fields as the (CRS) Director may consider appropriate." The positions are filled with nationally recognized experts who, as a rule, have published widely and have had extensive careers outside CRS—in government, private business or academic centers. They prepare high-level analyses and evaluations, and their salaries are in the "supergrade" category of the Civil Service.

At the beginning of 1975 the Senior Specialists Division of the CRS had positions for the following 25 subject areas:

Agriculture
American Government
American Government and Public Administration
American Public Law
Business Economics
Conservation
Engineering and Public Works
Environmental Policy
Federal Budget
Housing
International Economics
International Relations
Labor
National Defense
National Security
Price Economics
Russian Affairs
Science and Technology
Social Security
Social Welfare
Soviet Economics
Space and Transportation Technology
Taxation and Fiscal Policy
Transportation and Communication
Urban Afairs

Source: *Services to Congress* (Library of Congress, Congressional Research Service (January 1975), pp. 15-16.

jects, available for instant use by researchers. Files are kept on past CRS research, nine daily newspapers, 2,000 magazines and thousands of reports and documents by government and private organizations.

Congressional Reference Division—More than 50 reference librarians handle about 135,000 factual requests from Congress each year. Ninety per cent of the questions are answered within 24 hours.

American Law Division—Staff members answer inquiries concerning constitutional, statutory and case law, and prepare continuing publications.

Economics Division—Researchers cover money and banking, international trade, industrial organization, labor, communications, housing, urban development, transportation and commerce.

Education and Public Welfare Division—Fields of research include Social Security, public health, crime, immigration and education.

Environmental Policy Division—It deals with the role of government in water resources, agriculture, mining, forestry, petroleum, power, and air and water pollution.

Foreign Affairs Division—Staff members are organized according to State Department "desks," with a separate section for military affairs.

Government and General Research Division—Separate sections deal with (1) Congress and political institutions; (2) the executive branch, federal budget and national planning; and (3) civil rights and minorities, history and territories, and general public affairs.

Science Policy Research Division—Scientists on the staff evaluate federal programs on science topics and research, and government support of scientific development and professional education.

Senior Specialists Division—Specialists with national reputations in 25 subject areas are scattered throughout the CRS to work on specific assignments. *(Box, CRS Senior Specialists, p. 451)*

CRS divisions responded to a total of 202,334 congressional inquiries in fiscal 1974. Assistant Director Goodrum wrote that an inquiry "may be as simple as a question on the population of California, or as complex as a study of the possible ways to provide medical care to the aged. The one required a few seconds by a researcher, the other occupied three analysts for a period of six months."[48]

Inquiries may be placed by telephone, by letter or in person. About a dozen full-time inquiry recorders pass phoned requests along to the CRS coordinator of research, who forwards them to the appropriate division. For complex requests, the CRS urges members and their staffs to write a letter to the director or schedule an interview with a CRS analyst.

However they are received, congressional inquiries get immediate attention. A 1975 newspaper article on the CRS said, "From the depths of research material, the minds of men and the memory banks of computers, an answer is almost always forthcoming within the specified deadline."[49] The article added that inquiries from the 94th Congress were so frequent that in 1975 they reached a volume the CRS had not expected until 1978.

Services Performed by CRS

Publications issued by the CRS include four from the American Law Division: the *Digest of Public General Bills and Resolutions,* issued every two weeks, gives synopses of all bills introduced in the current session of Congress; *Major Legislation of Congress,* a monthly publication, describes the 200 most important bills as selected by CRS specialists and tells where they are in Congress; the *Legislative Status Checklist,* published weekly, keeps track of action on major bills; and the *Annotated Constitution of the United States,* published every 10 years, analyzes and interprets Supreme Court rulings.[50]

The CRS also publishes "issue briefs" on topics that have a general legislative interest. Such briefs on 150-200 topics are in stock at all times, and the CRS may print as many as 5,000 copies of a popular brief. "Green Sheets," or background reports prepared throughout the CRS, may number several thousand each year. Each month members of Congress receive a list of all the "Green Sheets" currently available so that they may place orders. Finally, the CRS will provide bibliographies on just about any topic, citing government documents, items from professional journals, other current public affairs articles, and selected monographs.

The CRS maintains three automated data bases which members may receive by computer terminals in the Library, and House and Senate office buildings. The data bases include the biweekly *Bill Digest,* the "issue briefs" and all bibliographies.

In fiscal 1974, the CRS identified nearly 500 major projects which consumed over a third of its research time. Three-fourths of the major projects undertaken were for 125 congressional committees and subcommittees. Of the 320 projects completed during the year, about 20 per cent resulted in committee prints or documents and 13 per cent contributed to congressional hearings.[51]

A telephone "hotline" from the floors of the House and Senate taps CRS researchers for up-to-the-minute information required in congressional debate. In fiscal 1974, the CRS handled more than 13,000 "hotline" requests, a 13 per cent increase over the previous year.[52]

The Government and General Research Division will translate members' official correspondence. In fiscal 1974 the division provided 1,681 translations, into or from 22 different languages.[53]

If given sufficient advance notice, the CRS will prepare drafts of statements and speeches for members of Congress. But the Service clearly prefers to supply background information which a member's staff can adapt for public pronouncements.

The CRS also provides graphics services to members to help them present statistics or other information in congressional documents, hearings or public meetings.

In a 1975 pamphlet listing its services to Congress, the CRS said, "Although we cannot undertake research for your constituents—please, no term papers or master's theses!—we do try to help with that portion of your constituent mail which can be answered with readily available material."[54] CRS does not answer such mail directly but sends appropriate materials to the members. The Service provided 18,300 such kits in fiscal 1974.[55]

Members of Congress, their families, and specific members of their staffs are among the privileged few who may borrow books from the Library of Congress. Books are delivered directly to congressional offices. There is also a special reading room in the Library's main building for the

---

Conflict of Functions

Sometimes the Library of Congress is tugged in two directions by its twin functions—to serve as a national library and to serve Congress. On a day in 1949, the following dialogue reportedly took place in the Library's main reading room:

Irate reader. "I've been asking for that book for six weeks now, and they keep telling me, 'It's in use—it's in use.' Wha'dya mean it's in use?"

Joseph Rubin, reference librarian. "It's being used by a member of Congress."

Irate reader. "A Congressman! Why is a Congressman using it? I thought Congress had its own library!"

Rubin. "You may believe it. They do. And you're in it."

Source: *Library Journal,* Feb. 1, 1965, p. 572.

use of members, their families and staffs, with reference librarians on duty at all times.

Despite its large staff, its automated systems and all the resources of the Library, the CRS occasionally has to hire professional consultants from the private sector to bolster its research capability. Contract authority provided by the Reorganization Act of 1970 was used for the first time in fiscal 1973, when 17 contracts were effected. There were 25 in fiscal 1974, under an appropriation of $251,000.[56]

The effort to provide all these services makes the CRS one of the busiest parts of the entire Library of Congress. A 1975 magazine article commented: "Contrasted with the scholarly hush of the main reading rooms, the Research Service offices resemble the city room of a major metropolitan newspaper. Phones ring constantly, computers whir, ticker-tape machines clatter as the requests are dealt with."[57]

Strengths and Shortcomings

The dual role of the Library of Congress—to assist Congress directly and to serve as a national library—has both advantages and disadvantages. Goodrum said in 1975: "On the one hand you have a congressional library furiously trying to live in the present—Congress needs to know right now and we're their brokers of information. On the other hand you have a national library furiously trying to gather and catalog material for the scholars of the future. Yet nothing could be more reasonable than combining the two to make the resources of the present and the future as rich as possible."[58]

That is the optimistic view, coming from one of the Library's officers. Non-congressional users of the Library complain that overworked staff members frequently are not helpful, that they have to wait for hours to see a book they need, and that some materials cannot be located or are otherwise unavailable. But many readers have found that the unexcelled scope of the Library's collections and the dedication and knowledge of many on its staff counterbalance the annoyance caused by delays or mistakes. Both scholars and staff at times are disturbed by throngs of visitors walking through the Library's halls and reading rooms. And the tourists complain that they do not get to see much of the Library.

The Library is most sensitive to criticism from Congress. Members occasionally do complain about inefficient staff or incomplete research. But for the most part, Congress has shown its appreciation by generous support for the Library. For fiscal 1976, Congress appropriated $116.2-million for Library operations—only $3.8-million less than the budget request.

At the same time, Congress was critical of some of the Library's work. The House Appropriations Committee urged "that a management survey be conducted to determine if the Congressional Research Service is focusing on the needs of the Congress or if it is going off into independent fields of endeavor not necessarily required to perform its basic functions."[59] The Senate Appropriations Committee complained of "insufficient coordination among the activities of the Congressional Research Service, General Accounting Office and the Office of Technology Assessment."[60]

Others on Capitol Hill offer praise. In 1975 *The Washington Post* quoted an aide to Sen. Jacob K. Javits (R N.Y.): "The CRS does an indispensable job. When we were going to Cuba, for instance, we called and said we needed the complete layout on Cuba for the past 15 years. Their

only question was what our deadline was. When all the information was sent over to us, it even included our probable itinerary."[61]

For their part, Library employees are on guard against abuses of Library services by members and their staffs. Apocryphal stories about writing a dissertation for some senator's nephew recur but are not taken seriously. Researchers usually can spot requests that are not related to something Congress is doing, and they may turn some work aside. Employees are protected because the Library's personnel program is not directed by Congress. There is no political patronage.

The most serious problem for the Library of Congress is lack of space. It is also the most fundamental problem. Without sufficient space and facilities six million books are decaying, millions of items piled on the floors cannot be easily found and used, many old manuscripts and films cannot be preserved, and some rare collections cannot even be exhibited. Most important, without sufficient workspace the growing staff simply cannot make the Library function efficiently.

The Library's need for space has been urgent for some time. The space problems could be solved for many years to come if the Library of Congress is permitted to fill the new Madison Building. Library materials and staff would be consolidated from temporary locations all over the Washington area into a huge building designed specifically for their needs. That had been the plan since the building was authorized in 1965.

Late in 1975, with the shell of the building virtually completed and contracts about to be awarded for interior construction, the House of Representatives made an official effort to take over the Madison Building as the fourth House office building. Speaker Carl Albert (D Okla.) and other House leaders wrote to Senate leaders Oct. 8, asking them to go along with the scheme, which would have given the Library space in two old government buildings several blocks away from the Capitol.

The Washington Post reported that Senate leaders were cool to the exchange plan. Sen. Ernest F. Hollings (D S.C.), chairman of the Appropriations subcommittee with jurisdiction over congressional buildings, said: "I'm very reluctant to go along with that. Extra costs have gone into making it [the Madison Building] a library—why, it cost $4-million for book stacks. It would be wasteful. We would have wasted millions and it will be 10 years before we get another library."[62]

Albert and others on the House Office Building Commission quickly discovered that opposition to the Madison Building takeover was not confined to the Senate. News of the plan was followed immediately by protests from educators and scholars, letters to newspapers, angry editorials, and calls and letters to members of Congress. Special legislation to enact the commission's plan was met with charges that conversion could cost up to $55-million and could delay completion of the building by another 15 months.[63]

The legislation was withdrawn Dec. 12, when the commission acknowledged it did not have sufficient support for its plan, even in the House. The leadership instead sought appropriations to complete the building as a library.[64] They began negotiations to permit certain research-related employees of the House to use from 6 to 7 per cent of the Madison Building, but even that compromise was blocked by representatives who insisted that the building be used exclusively by the Library.[65]

On March 3, 1976, Congress cleared a measure appropriating $33-million in fiscal 1976 supplemental funds for completion of the library.[66] Congress had authorized the additional funding, to a total of $123-million, in legislation cleared Feb. 18 (PL 94-219). The law made no reference to House use of the Madison Building.[67]

Footnotes

1. Charles A. Goodrum, *The Congressional Research Service of the United States Congress* (Library of Congress, Oct. 1, 1974), p. 1.
2. *The Library of Congress* (pamphlet, Government Printing Office, 1975).
3. U.S. Congress, Joint Committee on Printing, *The Capitol: A Pictorial History*, 6th ed. (Government Printing Office, 1973), p. 65.
4. Luther Evans, "The Job of the Librarian of Congress," a July 21, 1945, radio broadcast, quoted in the *Annual Report of the Librarian of Congress* (Government Printing Office, 1946), p. 19.
5. *The Rare Book Division: A Guide to Its Collections and Services*, revised ed. (Library of Congress, 1965), p. 3.
6. *Ibid.*
7. William Dawson Johnston, *History of the Library of Congress, Vol. 1, 1800-1864.* (Government Printing Office, 1904), p. 68.
8. *The Rare Book Division*, p. 3.
9. *Ibid.*
10. *Ibid.*, p. 4.
11. Lucy Salamanca, *Fortress of Freedom: The Story of the Library of Congress*, (J. B. Lippincott, 1942), p. 107.
12. David C. Mearns, *The Story Up to Now: The Library of Congress, 1800-1946*, (Library of Congress, 1947), p. 87.
13. David C. Mearns, "The Brush of a Comet," *The Atlantic*, May 1965, p. 90.
14. *Ibid.*, p. 92.
15. Paul M. Angle, *The Library of Congress: An Account, Historical and Descriptive*, (Kingsport Press, 1958).
16. Mearns, "The Brush of a Comet," p. 92.
17. Archibald MacLeish, "The Reorganization of the Library of Congress," quoted in the *Annual Report of the Librarian of Congress* (Government Printing Office, 1946), p. 108.
18. *Library of Congress Information Bulletin*, Feb. 6, 1956.
19. Archibald MacLeish, "A Tower Which Will Not Yield," *American Library Association Bulletin*, Vol. 50, No. 10, November 1956, p. 653.
20. *Annual Report of the Librarian of Congress*, (Government Printing Office, 1974), p. 5.
21. U.S. Congress, Senate, Committee on Rules and Administration, *Hearings on the Nomination of Daniel J. Boorstin of the District of Columbia to be Librarian of Congress*, 94th Cong., 1st sess., 1975, p. 26.
22. U.S. Congress, Senate, Committee on Rules and Administration, *Nomination of Daniel J. Boorstin of the District of Columbia to be Librarian of Congress*, Exec. Rept. 94-6, 94th Cong., 1st sess., 1975, p. 3.
23. *Ibid.*, p. 4.
24. Senate, *Hearings on the Nomination of Daniel J. Boorstin*, p. 332.
25. Library of Congress, Information Office, Fiscal 1975 statistics released in September 1975.
26. Quoted in *Annual Report of the Librarian of Congress*, (Government Printing Office, 1973), p. 18.
27. *Annual Report of the Librarian of Congress*, (Government Printing Office, 1974), p. 2.
28. James Ridgeway and Alexander Cockburn, "The World's Largest Library and Its Large Problems," *Parade*, July 6, 1975, p. 14.
29. W. W. Bishop and Andrew Keogh, eds., *Essays Offered to Herbert Putnam by His Colleagues and Friends on His Thirtieth Anniversary as Librarian of Congress, 5 April 1929*, (Yale University Press, 1929).
30. *The Library of Congress* (pamphlet, Government Printing Office, 1975).
31. Fred Kline, "Library of Congress: The Nation's Bookcase," *National Geographic*, November 1975, p. 674.
32. *Annual Report of the Library of Congress*, (Government Printing Office, 1974), p. 4.
33. Ridgeway and Cockburn, *Parade*, p. 14.
34. Figures supplied by the Library of Congress, Processing Department, Cataloging and Distribution Services Division, October 1975.
35. *Ibid.*
36. Figures supplied by Library of Congress, Reference Department, Loan Division.
37. Kline, *National Geographic*, p. 674.
38. *Annual Report of the Librarian of Congress*, (Government Printing Office, 1974), pp. 10-11.
39. *Ibid.*, pp. 143-45.
40. *Ibid.*, p. 3.
41. Library of Congress, Copyright Office, staff interviews, October 1975.
42. Kline, *National Geographic*, p. 681.
43. *Ibid.*, p. 675.
44. *Annual Report of the Librarian of Congress*, (Government Printing Office, 1974), p. 43.
45. Goodrum, *The Congressional Research Service*, p. 15.
46. *Annual Report of the Librarian of Congress* (Government Printing Office, 1974), p. 42.
47. Descriptions and figures from Goodrum, *The Congressional Research Service*, pp. 3-9.
48. *Ibid.*, p. 2.
49. *The Washington Post*, Oct. 29, 1975.
50. Unless otherwise identified, the information in this section comes from *Services to Congress* (pamphlet, Library of Congress, Congressional Research Service, January 1975).
51. *Annual Report of the Librarian of Congress* (Government Printing Office, 1974), p. 32.
52. *Ibid.*, p. 40.
53. Goodrum, *The Congressional Research Service*, p. 5.
54. *Services to Congress*, p. 8.
55. *Annual Report of the Librarian of Congress* (Government Printing Office, 1974), p. 40.
56. *Ibid.*, p. 32.
57. Ridgeway and Cockburn, *Parade*, p. 14.
58. Kline, *National Geographic*, p. 681.
59. U.S. Congress, House, Committee on Appropriations, *Legislative Branch Appropriation Bill, 1976*, H Rept 94-208 to Accompany HR 6950, 94th Cong., 1st sess., 1975, p. 26.
60. U.S. Congress, Senate, Committee on Appropriations, *Legislative Branch Appropriations, 1976*, S Rept 94-262 to Accompany HR 6950, 94th Cong., 1st sess., 1975, p. 35.
61. *The Washington Post*, Oct. 29, 1975.
62. *The Washington Post*, Oct. 24, 1975.
63. *The Washington Post*, Dec. 6, 1975.
64. Congressional Quarterly, *Weekly Report*, Dec. 13, 1975, p. 2757.
65. Congressional Quarterly, *Weekly Report*, Feb. 28, 1976, p. 478.
66. Congressional Quarterly, *Weekly Report*, March 6, 1976, p. 524.
67. Congressional Quarterly, *Weekly Report*, Feb. 28, 1976, p. 478.

Selected Bibliography

Books

Adams, James Truslow. *The Epic of America.* Boston: Atlantic Monthly Press, 1931.

Angle, Paul M. *The Library of Congress: An Account, Historical and Descriptive.* Kingsport, Tenn.: Kingsport Press, 1958.

Bishop, W. W. and Keogh, Andrew, eds. *Essays Offered to Herbert Putnam by His Colleagues and Friends on His Thirtieth Anniversary as Librarian of Congress, 5 April 1929.* New Haven: Yale University Press, 1929.

Goodrum, Charles A. *The Library of Congress.* New York: Praeger, 1975.

McBride, Margareta. *Reference Service for Congress Before 1915.* Philadelphia: Drexel Institute of Technology, School of Library Science, 1955.

MacCloskey, Monro. *Our National Attic: the Library of Congress, the Smithsonian Institution, the National Archives.* New York: Richard Rosen Press, 1968.

Salamanca, Lucy. *Fortress of Freedom: the Story of the Library of Congress.* Philadelphia: J. B. Lippincott, 1942.

Articles

Bishop, W. W. "Thirty Years of the Library of Congress, 1899-1929." *Library Journal,* May 1, 1929, pp. 379-382.

Kline, Fred. "The Library of Congress: The Nation's Bookcase." *National Geographic,* November 1975, pp. 670-87.

Lewis, Hunter. "Capitol Hill Ugliness Club." *The Atlantic* February 1967.

Library Journal. 1965 (articles on the Library of Congress in 13 issues).

MacLeish, Archibald. "The Reorganization of the Library of Congress." *Library Quarterly,* Oct. 1944, pp. 277-315.

Mearns, David C. "The Brush of a Comet." *The Atlantic,* May 1965, pp. 91-92.

Orne, Jerrold. "The Library of Congress Prepares for Emergencies." *ALA Bulletin,* June 1941, pp. 341-348.

Plumb, M. M. "Library of Congress Services to Social Science." *Social Science,* July 1949, pp. 168-173.

Putnam, Herbert. "The National Library: Recent Developments." *Library Journal,* June 15, 1928, pp. 531-538.

Ridgeway, James and Cockburn, Alexander. "The World's Largest Library and Its Large Problems." *Parade,* July 6, 1975, p. 14.

Government Publications

Evans, Luther H., *The Job of the Librarian of Congress.* Washington: Library of Congress, 1945.

——. *The National Library in the Life of the Nation.* Washington: Library of Congress, 1946.

Goodrum, Charles A. *The Congressional Research Service of the United States Congress.* Washington: Library of Congress, 1974.

Hastings, C.H. *Library of Congress and Its Work: Report Prepared for the Commission of the United States of America to the Brazil Centennial Exposition.* Washington: Library of Congress, 1922.

Johnston, William Dawson. *History of the Library of Congress; Volume I, 1800-1864.* Washington: Government Printing Office, 1904. (Only volume published)

Mearns, David C. *The Story Up to Now: The Library of Congress 1800-1946.* Washington: Library of Congress, 1947.

Roberts, M. A., *The Library of Congress in Relation to Research.* Washington: Library of Congress, 1939.

U.S. Congress. Joint Committee on Printing. *The Capitol: A Pictorial History.* 6th ed. Washington: Government Printing Office, 1973.

U.S. Congress. Joint Committee on the Organization of Congress. 16 parts. *Organization of Congress; Hearing Pursuant to S. Con. Res. 2,* 89th Cong., 1st sess., 1965.

U.S. Congress. Senate. *Nomination of Daniel J. Boorstin of the District of Columbia to be Librarian of Congress,* Exec. Rept. 94-6, 94th Cong., 1st sess., 1975.

U.S. Congress. Senate. Committee on Rules and Administration. *Hearings on the Nomination of Daniel J. Boorstin of the District of Columbia to be Librarian of Congress,* 94th Cong., 1st sess., 1975.

U.S. Library of Congress. *Annual Report of the Librarian of Congress.* 1866- .

——. *The Library of Congress* (pamphlet), 1975.

——. *Library of Congress Information Bulletin.*

——. *The Rare Book Division: A Guide to Its Collections and Services.* Revised ed., 1965.

——. Congressional Research Service. *Services to Congress.* 1975.

Pay, Perquisites and Patronage

For years, Congress and its members have been favorite targets of national humor. The origins of this humorous image are obscure but, fair or not, it has persisted. Perhaps the best illustration of the technique comes in Mark Twain's classic commentary: "Suppose you were an idiot. And suppose you were a member of Congress. But I repeat myself."

While the evidence is uncertain, suspicion has it that not all of the humor is lost on the members. Rep. Jim Wright (D Texas) in his book *You and Your Congressman* quoted another member as saying: "I came here to make laws, and what do I do? I send baby books to young mothers, listen to every maladjusted kid who wants out of the service, write sweet replies to pompous idiots who think a public servant is a public footstool, and give tours of the Capitol to visitors who are just as worn out as I am."[1]

In any event, it is clear that one of the fringe benefits or perquisites of serving in Congress is the opportunity to tickle the nation's funny bone. Other perquisites abound. Some are important; others are merely convenient. Some cost the taxpayers a lot of money; others simply inflate the members' self-importance. All perquisites were intended, at least when they began, to ease the burden of what can be a grinding, tedious and frustrating job.

Both the pay and perquisites of members of Congress have increased enormously since World War II. A 1975 study of the salary, staff allowances, benefits and special privileges of members of the House estimated that a representative's job was worth nearly $500,000 a year.[2]

Countering the increases in pay and perquisites, there has been a decrease in congressional patronage—the power of senators and representatives to select appointees for government jobs, and thus to bolster their political strength. Most patronage positions today are restricted to Capitol Hill itself.

A Member's Jobs

The late Rep. Clem Miller (D Calif.) once described for constituents an account of a typical day in his Washington office:

"I arise at 6:45, eat breakfast, and spend 10 minutes with the *Washington Post....* Leave for the office at 7:55 a.m.... (Alternatively, I may breakfast at 8:00 a.m. with a veterans group, Boy Scouts, or some other group.)

...Generally at 9:00 comes the first office appointment: A trade association to discuss an industrial problem or a lobbyist to explain his position on a bill.... At 10:00 there may well be a hearing of the committee to which I am assigned, or of the subcommittee.... Frequently it seems almost impossible to arrive on time for these hearings, what with the press of office work.... The House meets at 12:00 noon.... If there is a debate on a bill, I will generally be there. Fitting lunch into this schedule often becomes difficult.... Usually I eat at my office, and relax with a newspaper from the state capital or my district. Then during afternoon hours, I am busy cramming committee meetings between duties on the floor or in the office.... About 5:00 p.m. I return to the office to work over the mail, sign letters and see people. Getting away from the office is more and more difficult. In the beginning I left at 5:45 p.m. Now I am leaving at 6:15 or 6:30 p.m."[3]

The major functions of a member of Congress are legislative and representational. Some observers also add a third: they believe that a member should "educate" the public on the major national problems and issues.

While the legislative duties of members are their most prominent ones, members are not solely lawmakers. Not only is it their function to act as the representatives of their constituents in the national government; it is unlikely that they will be re-elected if they neglect to do so. Since most members consider their own re-election as paramount, scrupulous attention usually is paid to constituent mail and the problems it brings. Some senators and representatives even make such public relations gestures as congratulating newlyweds and parents of newborn babies.

A widespread complaint is that much of this "case work," as it is known, is trivial, but few members feel that they can afford to ignore constituents, even nonvoting ones who write for help with school assignments. As a result, most of the staff and office facilities of members are given over to processing mail and running errands for the constituents. Some congressional staffs pass along constituent requests for information to the Congressional Research Service of the Library of Congress, which consequently has less time to spend on its primary duties. The member himself at times feels compelled to answer certain letters, introduce and follow private bills, talk to visitors, and even lead high school classes on tours of the Capitol.

Occasionally, a maverick member will shatter the traditional image of the infinitely patient and courteous public servant. It happens rarely, but when it does occur, the event makes news headlines. Such a maverick was Sen. Stephen M. Young (D Ohio). A liberal, Young was subjected to frequent attacks from conservatives. His acid-tongued replies were widely publicized. One Young reply began, "Dear Sir: You are a liar."[4]

The chances of getting a personal reply to a letter depend partly on the population of the state in which the writer lives. A Wyoming resident may receive a personal answer. A New Yorker is more likely to draw a standardized response drafted by a junior staff member, signed by a machine and only scanned by the member.

In recent years, a number of machines have been used to speed replies to letters. Among them are the Robotype machine and the Autopen. These machines can insert a signature and a heading on form letters while making it appear to the constituent that he has received an individual letter with a personal signature.

The Robotype machine looks like a typewriter. It is capable of reproducing identical copies of form letters without the standardized look of a mimeographed letter. Once it is set up to reproduce the body of a letter, a secretary types only the individual heading for each letter. The Autopen is a console machine with a large wheel. On the wheel is placed a metal plate with an impression of the member's signature. As the prepared letters revolve around the wheel, the metal plate stamps an imprint of the signature in the proper place on the paper.

Together, these machines make it possible for a congressional staff to answer letters after scanning them for a few seconds to see what they are about.

A Member's Workload

Political reporter David S. Broder wrote in 1962: "The main reason...that Congress does not legislate better is simply that most congressmen can no longer afford to regard legislation as the most important part of their jobs. Indeed, many of them find it very difficult to sandwich legislative work into the busy schedule of what they describe—correctly—as their more important functions. These relate to their second role, as mediators between their districts and the central government."[5]

These activities necessarily reduce the resources which members can bring to bear on legislation. Yet the technical complexities of legislation increase constantly as the code of laws, the economy and the federal government grow larger and as science, commerce, defense and foreign policy become increasingly interconnected. The problem is perhaps more acute in the Senate than the House, because senators serve on two and often three major committees, while most representatives are limited to one or two committees.

Caught by the conflicting demands of constituents and legislative duties, few members have time to perform the "educational" function except sporadically. The constant pressure of elections, however, forces many members to inform their constituents of their positions on national issues through newsletters, press releases and speeches. This activity, and efforts to promote a particular bill or approach to a national or local problem, of course add that much more to the member's workload.

The average active member of Congress—allowing for considerable variation from one office to another—frequent-

---

'What Ails Congress'

The growth of congressional staff and the increase in congressional expenses have been so rapid since the mid-1950s that some members of Congress have expressed their dismay.

Rep. William L. Armstrong (R Colo.), a member of the House Appropriations Committee, voted against the fiscal 1976 legislative branch appropriations bill and explained why in "Additional Views" at the end of the committee report. His statement was accompanied by tables that showed the growth of congressional employees from 5,585 in 1955 to 17,728 in 1974, and the increase in legislative branch appropriations from $70.7-million in fiscal 1955 to an estimated $802.4-million in fiscal 1976 (actual appropriation $827.5-million). Rep. Armstrong's statement follows:

"Within the last two decades congressional staffing has tripled and the overall cost of operating Congress itself has increased ten fold.

"If this increase had been accompanied by a corresponding improvement in the ability of Congress to cope with the nation's problems, I would not object. But it appears to me that the opposite is the case: Congress seems gradually less and less able to come to grips with basic issues.

"What ails Congress, it seems to me, is a lack of stomach for hard decisions, a failure of nerve and judgment rather than lack of staff and facilities, needed though these may be. Merely increasing funding for congressional operations will not overcome the basic problems which have stymied action on curbing inflation, recession, the energy crisis and other issues of utmost importance.

"I commend the committee for substantially reducing the amount of several appropriations requested by various congressional agencies. But, even so, the bill includes large increases for which no real justification has been considered or even submitted. In large part this bill simply funds the estimates of other committees without any attempt to seriously evaluate the propriety or need of such spending. While it is natural for members of the committee to defer to our colleagues in this way, by extending this courtesy we effectively eliminate any meaningful review on a large portion of the legislative appropriation which now totals approximately $700 million....

"I believe the spending of Congress on itself could and should be substantially reduced without adversely affecting the legislative process. By doing so the House would save taxpayer funds at a time when such savings are particularly necessary. More important, however, Congress would thereby set an example of prudence and restraint instead of continuing an example of self-indulgence.

"Since portions of this appropriation which are most in need of reduction merely reflect recent decisions of the full House itself, I do not intend to offer amendments which would have little or no chance of adoption. Under the circumstances, however, I am constrained to vote against the bill."

Source: U.S. Congress, House, Committee on Appropriations, *Legislative Branch Appropriation Bill, 1976,* H. Rept. 94-208 to Accompany HR 6950, 94th Cong., 1st sess., 1975.

ly puts in a 10- to 12-hour day at the office and in the Capitol before going home to dinner and two or three hours of reading related to work. During a typical day the member would probably spend time talking to lobbyists and to visiting constituents, possibly show a high school class around the Capitol, read and answer some of the large amount of daily mail, telephone the home district or state, answer questions from reporters, discuss legislation and politics with other members, attend party or regional meetings, possibly work on a speech or a newsletter to constituents, read the *Congressional Record*, newspapers, magazines and committee hearings or reports. In addition, the member would attend committee meetings in the morning and sometimes the afternoon, attend floor sessions to speak and listen to debate, vote, and wait to vote. He or she would also spend time overseeing staff work. If the member is the chairman of an active committee or subcommittee, or occupies a leadership post (for example, as a member of the whip organization), he or she would have additional time-consuming duties and additional staff aides. In the evenings, members often have combined political and social obligations. *(Washington's Party Circuit, this page)*

A Member's Perquisites

Aside from the congressional salary, a member's single greatest perquisite is a personal staff. Staff aides multiply the member's arms, legs, eyes and ears, providing the best hope of meeting the demands on the member's time. Properly used, a personal staff can function as the member's strongest ally. Misused, a personal staff becomes little more than a reservoir of wasted talents. And abused, a personal staff can turn traitor; for like the gentleman and his valet, no member is a hero to his staff.

Among the other formal, statutory perquisites are the franking privilege, immunity from certain legal actions, free office space in federal buildings, and allowances for travel, telephone and telegraph services, stationery, office expenses and equipment, plus thousands of free publications. Other benefits members receive include free storage of files and records, inexpensive use of television and radio studios, certain patronage appointments, modern recreational facilities, and discounts from Capitol Hill shops and services.

In addition, there is a vast, ill-defined collection of informal perquisites based on the deference customarily shown a VIP. Such deference appears typically in delaying the departure of a plane to accommodate the tardy arrival of a member of Congress. Other informal perquisites include free parking, assured press coverage under many circumstances, and special treatment by government agencies.

Are congressional perquisites abused? Objectively, it is difficult to tell. Probably the best answer is that members abuse their privileges about as much as such privileges would be abused by the public in general. Large-scale abuses, while rare, are uncovered periodically, touching off widely publicized scandals. Abuses that seem to recur are the employment of members' relatives as staff aides and the misuse of allowances or other funds.

Pay of Members of Congress

In Article I, Section 6, the Constitution provides: "The Senators and Representatives shall receive a Compensation for their Services, to be ascertained by Law, and paid out of the Treasury of the United States."

Washington's Party Circuit

Official entertaining is widespread in Washington. For the unwary member of Congress, what began as mere social courtesy can balloon out of control and become a social nightmare. One of the more candid descriptions of Washington's social life—as seen from Capitol Hill—was offered in a newsletter to constituents by Sen. Stephen M. Young (D Ohio). It was written in 1963.

People inquire what about social life in Washington. "Terrific" would be the answer, were a senator to attend all functions to which he is invited. Frankly, unless a senator throws in the sponge and accepts only one-fourth of the invitations, he will be out socially five or six evenings weekly. This would be a hardship in many respects. For example, inability to see "Gunsmoke," "Wells Fargo," "The Dakotas," "Wagon Train," to say nothing of wasting time needed to study pending legislation, read committee reports, etc.

More than one hundred nations have embassies in Washington. Each holds two large receptions a year plus dinners and cocktail parties to which most senators are invited. Then there are 17 State dinners. Among other dinners, make a mental note that there are 262 national associations such as the American Legion, American Farm Bureau Federation, American Trucking Associations Inc., Veterans of Foreign Wars, American Medical Association, National Association of Home Builders, U.S. Chamber of Commerce and National Association of Manufacturers. These are registered pressure groups, so-called. They filed reports admitting expenditures in excess of $5,000,000 during 1962. Many of these national associations usually invite all members of the Congress to at least one dinner a year. In addition, various state associations and citizens' organizations give dinners, cocktail parties, and receptions. They wine and dine Congressmen who attend and individual members and speakers may discuss legislative proposals they are promoting. At least 40 senators give dinners or luncheons for their colleagues and usually senators give dinners for their own state congressional delegations or a representative throws an affair to which he invites the senators from his state. In addition, a comparatively new horror has been devised—that is breakfasts to which senators are invited. The time stated is generally 8:30 a.m. The place, usually a downtown hotel, more than a mile distant from the Capitol. If a senator attends, he is fortunate to leave by 10 o'clock. Furthermore, quite frequently groups from the senator's own state visiting in Washington desire him to lunch or dine with them. These are invitations a senator appreciates receiving and likes to accept; and in turn, a senator does not keep his own pocketbook padlocked. He "wines and dines" constituents and "throws parties" to repay obligations, and also because this is an American custom we like. Regarding "pressure groups" and various professional and business associations, many Congressmen say "too busy" and are happy to pay for their own meals, and eat at home a couple evenings a week.

The constitutional language settled one sensitive contemporary issue—whether a member's salary should be drawn from state or national funds—but it left settlement of a far more delicate question up to Congress itself—deciding what the salary should be. The inevitable result was development of the salary issue into a political hot potato.

In attempts to minimize the political impact of periodic salary increases, Congress fell into the practice of wrapping up a pay increase for itself in a general pay increase for other federal workers, including at times the judiciary and the President. On a few occasions, even that tactic failed to blunt critical reaction on the part of the public.

Public reaction against congressional pay increases was strong at times, leading to wholesale election defeats for members who approved increases that their constituents considered unwarranted. Two controversial salary increases were repealed by succeeding Congresses. Frequently, a few members would refuse higher pay and return the amount of the increase to the Treasury or donate it to a public charity. Technically, every member must accept full pay. However, after receiving the salary they may return any portion to the Treasury.

Despite all the turmoil, congressional pay has risen steadily over the years. From $6 a day in 1789, it had climbed to $44,600 a year by 1975. Although the salary of members has remained unchanged for long periods of time, only rarely has it ever been reduced. Since 1946, members have been eligible to participate in a retirement system. *(Box, Retirement Benefits, p. 475)*

Early Pay Legislation

During the Constitutional Convention, a principal question surrounding compensation for members of Congress was the source of the funds. Members of the Confederation Congress had been paid by the states; those of the British Parliament were not paid at all. It was felt, however, that members of Congress should be paid, and paid by the national government.

Another question raised at the Convention was whether senators and representatives should receive equal pay. Charles Pinckney of South Carolina twice moved "that no salary should be allowed" members of the Senate. "As this branch was meant to represent the wealth of the country," Pinckney asserted, "it ought to be composed of persons of wealth; and if no allowance was to be made, the wealthy alone would undertake the service." Pinckney's motion was seconded by Benjamin Franklin but was twice rejected, six states to five states.[6]

History of Congressional Pay

Year	Salary	Year	Salary
1789-1795	$6 per diem	1907-1925	$7,500 per year
1795-1796	$6 per diem (House)	1925-1932	$10,000 per year
	$7 per diem (Senate)	1932-1933	$9,000 per year
1796-1815	$6 per diem	1933-1935	$8,500 per year
1815-1817	$1,500 per year	1935-1947	$10,000 per year
1817-1855	$8 per diem	1947-1955	$12,500 per year
1855-1865	$3,000 per year	1955-1965	$22,500 per year
1865-1871	$5,000 per year	1965-1969	$30,000 per year
1871-1873	$7,500 per year	1969-1975	$42,500 per year
1873-1907	$5,000 per year	1975-	$44,600 per year

Per Diem Compensation. One of the first—and most controversial—measures enacted by the new Congress in 1789 was a bill fixing the compensation of members. As originally considered by the House, both representatives and senators were to be paid $6 a day. The proposal for equal pay reopened the debate over whether senators, by reason of greater responsibilities and presumably higher qualifications, should receive a pay differential. At the heart of the debate was an amendment by Rep. Theodore Sedgwick (Federalist Mass.) to lower House pay to $5 per day, thus creating a $1-per-day differential in favor of the Senate. The amendment was defeated by a voice vote. On Aug. 10, 1789, the House by a 30-16 roll call passed a bill providing for payment of $6 a day to members of both chambers.

In the Senate, the bill was amended to provide that senators be paid at the $6 rate until March 4, 1795, when their pay would be increased to $8 and the pay of representatives would remain at $6. The amended bill passed the Senate on Aug. 28, 1789.

Following a House-Senate conference, the House on Sept. 11, by a 29-25 roll call, voted to fix the pay of senators at $7 a day after March 4, 1795, and by a 28-26 roll call set March 4, 1796, as the expiration date of the legislation. The Senate agreed to the House amendments on Sept. 12, and the bill was signed into law on Sept. 22, 1789, seven days before the end of the first session of Congress.

As enacted, the measure provided the first perquisite—a travel allowance for senators and representatives of $6 per 20 miles. It also provided a $6-a-day differential for the House Speaker (making his pay $12 a day), and compensation for a number of lesser House and Senate officials.

When a new pay law was enacted in 1796, only a glancing reference was made to a differential for the Senate. Both the House and the Senate passed a bill equalizing the pay at $6 a day.

Short-Lived Salary Law. In 1816, Congress voted itself a pay increase and a shift from per diem compensation to an annual salary. The Act of March 19, 1816, raised congressional pay to $1,500 a year and made the raise retroactive to Dec. 4, 1815, when the first session of the 14th Congress convened. The pay raise had passed both houses easily, but it was roundly condemned by the people. A number of members who had voted for the bill were defeated in the 1816 elections; nine members resigned over the issue. One of the election victims was Rep. Daniel Webster. He was defeated and was not elected to Congress again until 1822.

Return to Per Diem. The short session of the 14th Congress in 1817 repealed the $1,500 salary act, effective with the end of the Congress on March 3, 1817. An Act of Jan. 22, 1818, restored per diem compensation and set the rate at $8, retroactive to March 3, 1817.

Members' Salaries from 1850s to 1930s

Almost four decades later, a successful conversion to annual congressional salaries was finally achieved. An Act of Aug. 16, 1856, replaced the $8-a-day rate by a $3,000 annual salary, retroactive to the start of the 34th Congress on Dec. 3, 1855. Another retroactive pay increase—to $5,000—was approved July 28, 1866, effective Dec. 4, 1865, when the 39th Congress had convened for its first session.

"Salary Grab." In the closing days of the 42nd Congress in 1873, still another retroactive pay raise was enacted, increasing the salary to $7,500. The higher salary was made retroactive to the beginning of the 42nd Congress, in effect providing for members a $5,000 windfall ($2,500 per year for the two preceding years). Despite precedents for making the increase retroactive, the size of the increase and the windfall effect boomeranged. Congressional critics, already primed by the Credit Mobilier scandal, attacked the pay increase as a "salary grab" and a "backpay steal." Some members returned their back pay to the Treasury; others donated it to colleges or charities.

When the 43rd Congress opened in December 1873, scores of bills were introduced to repeal the increase. By an Act of Jan. 20, 1874, congressional pay reverted to the previous $5,000, and it stayed at that level until a $7,500 salary was at length sanctioned by an Act of Feb. 26, 1907. A raise to $10,000 was provided by an Act of March 4, 1925.

Government austerity was the byword as the Great Depression of the 1930s deepened. Salaries of federal employees were reduced, and members of Congress likewise had to take a pay cut. The Economy Act of June 30, 1932, provided for a 10 per cent cutback in members' salaries, dropping them from $10,000 to $9,000. The cutback was increased to 15 per cent, meaning a further drop to $8,500, by the Economy Act of March 20, 1933. Gradually the cutbacks were rescinded, and by the end of 1935, congressional salaries had been restored to the $10,000 level.

Postwar Salaries and Expense Allowances

Congress included in the Legislative Reorganization Act of 1946 a provision increasing congressional salaries from $10,000 to $12,500 and retaining an existing $2,500 non-taxable expense allowance for all members. The increases took effect at the beginning of the 80th Congress in 1947. The Joint Committee on the Organization of Congress had recommended a $15,000 annual salary and elimination of the expense allowance, but the bill was amended in the House, and the House provision was retained in the final version of the measure. The act also provided $20,000 salaries for the Vice President and Speaker of the House.

Provision for the $2,500 expense allowance had been made in 1945. The House Appropriations Committee included in the legislative branch appropriation bill for fiscal 1946 an appropriation to cover a $2,500 annual expense allowance for representatives. Although the bill did not so stipulate, the committee said the allowance probably would be tax-exempt. When the bill reached the House floor opponents called the allowance an opening wedge for inflation and a pay increase by subterfuge. But a resolution to waive all points of order, and thus thwart efforts to eliminate the expense allowance section, was adopted, 229-124. Other attempts to eliminate or change the proposal also failed, and the bill was passed by voice vote May 10, 1945.

The Senate Appropriations Committee reported the bill with a $2,500 expense allowance for senators as well. The committee amendment was defeated on the floor, 9-43, and two compromise amendments also failed. An amendment to strike out the House expense allowance was narrowly defeated, 22-28. The Senate thus passed the bill with the allowance for representatives, but not for senators.

The question came up again during Senate consideration of the first deficiency appropriation bill for fiscal 1946. The Senate Appropriations Committee offered an amendment to extend the expense allowance to senators, but the Senate rejected the plan, 24-47. Senators finally received the $2,500 expense allowance in 1946, in the fiscal 1947 Legislative Branch Appropriation Act.

Tax-Free Provision Ended. In the Revenue Act of 1951, Congress eliminated the tax-free provision on congressional expense allowances, effective Jan. 3, 1953. Also made subject to taxation were the expense allowances of the President, Vice President and Speaker of the House. The provision was offered as a Senate amendment by Sen. John J. Williams (R Del.) and agreed to on a 77-11 roll call.

Congress in 1953 created a Commission on Judicial and Congressional Salaries to study the salary question and report to Congress by Jan. 15, 1954. As passed by the Senate, the bill would have empowered the commission to raise salaries. However, the measure was amended in the House to require congressional approval for any pay increase. The commission's report recommended a $10,000 salary boost, but Congress took no action.

In 1955, Congress enacted legislation raising congressional and judicial salaries. The bill increased the salary for members of Congress to $22,500 (from $12,500 plus a $2,-500 expense allowance). It also provided $35,000 for the Speaker and Vice President (up from $30,000), and retained the existing $10,000 taxable expense allowance in both cases. The increases became effective March 1, 1955.

The chief difference between the House and Senate bills was the $2,500 congressional expense allowance, which the House would have retained. Both the Senate version and the final version deleted this item. The House passed the bill Feb. 16, 283-118, and the Senate passed it Feb. 23, 62-24. The Senate rejected the first conference report Feb. 25, because it contained a compromise expense allowance provision. After that had been deleted, the second conference report was approved by the Senate Feb. 28 and by the House March 1.

Congress again raised its own salaries, and those of other federal personnel, in 1964. Members' salaries were raised by $7,500, to $30,000. Salaries of the Speaker of the House and the Vice President were raised to $43,000. The bill was enacted after the House had first killed another bill raising congressional salaries by $10,000. The first bill was rejected by the House March 12 on a 184-222 roll-call vote. Election-year worries were believed important in the defeat of the first bill. The second measure was strongly backed by President Johnson and voted upon after most of the 1964 primary elections had been held. It was passed by the House June 11 on a 243-157 roll call and by the Senate July 2 on a 58-21 roll call.

Special Salary Commission

In 1967, Congress modified a bill increasing postal rates and the salaries of federal employees by adding an amendment creating a nine-member Commission on Executive, Legislative, and Judicial Salaries to review the salaries of members of Congress, federal judges and top officers of the executive branch every four years and to recommend changes it felt desirable.

The congressionally established commission was to include three members appointed by the President, two by the President of the Senate, two by the Speaker of the House, and two by the Chief Justice of the United States. Beginning in fiscal 1969, the commission was to submit its recommendations to the President, who was to recommend in his budget the exact rates of pay "he deems advisable" for federal executives, judges and members of Congress. His recommendations could be either higher or lower than those of the commission, or he could propose that salaries not be altered. The recommendations would take effect within 30

Docking of Pay

It is often suggested that the way to curb absenteeism in Congress is to dock a member's pay for each day he fails to appear on the floor. The Constitution makes no provision for this, saying only that "each House shall be the Judge of the Elections, returns and Qualifications of its own Members, and a Majority of each shall constitute a Quorum to do Business; but a smaller Number may adjourn from day to day, and may be authorized to compel the Attendance of absent Members, in such Manner, and under such Penalties as each House may provide." (Article 1, Section 5)

The first session of the First Congress in 1789 provided for an automatic docking of pay. Salaries were $6 a day for each day of attendance.

A law enacted in 1856 provided that "The Secretary of the Senate and the Sergeant at Arms of the House, respectively, shall deduct from the monthly payments of each member or delegate the amount of his salary for each day that he has been absent from the Senate or House,...unless such member or delegate assigns as the reason for such absence the sickness of himself or of some member of his family."

Since then a few rare attempts to compel attendance have cited this law. During the 53rd Congress (1894), after a ruling by the chairman of the Committee of the Whole that the 1856 law was still in force, portions of House members' salaries were withheld.

The 1894 incident was recalled in 1914 when the House adopted a resolution revoking all leaves of absence granted to members and directing the sergeant at arms to deduct members' pay for each day they were absent. The 1914 resolution was enforced stringently for a brief time.

No docking of pay of absentees occurred for many years. The House Parliamentarian's office said there was no way of knowing when a member was away.

The 1856 law was repealed by the fiscal 1976 legislative branch appropriations bill. The Senate Appropriations Committee maintained that the law "has no contemporary meaning," and urged its repeal. In testimony before the committee, the secretary of the Senate, Francis R. Valeo, said: "The fact is that a senator has to be, and is, on duty at all times, 24 hours a day, whether in his home state, in committee, or in the chamber.... A senator's absence from Washington and the Senate floor at no time separates him from the continuing responsibilities of his office any more than when the President is away from Washington, or the Supreme Court justices are away from the court on recess. The obligations of their office remain with them at all times."*

---

* Congressional Quarterly, *Weekly Report*, July 12, 1975, p. 1474.

---

on June 3, 1968. Named to head the commission was Frederick R. Kappel, former chairman of the American Telephone & Telegraph Co. The commission, reporting in December 1968, recommended salary levels of $67,500 for the Chief Justice, $65,000 for associate justices, $60,000 for Cabinet members, $50,000 to $40,000 for Level II-V in the executive branch, and of $50,000 for members of Congress. With the exception of Cabinet members, all salary recommendations were scaled down by Johnson in his budget request. The congressional salary level was set at $42,500, an increase of $12,500 over members' previous salary, the same rate as for Level II of the executive schedule.

The new salary scales became effective March 1, 1969. Although numerous bills were introduced in 1969 to rescind the congressional pay increase and to abolish the salary commission, none was enacted.

Congressional salaries were not increased again for six and a half years, although there were some controversial attempts at raises. Because President Nixon did not appoint the second commission until December 1972, the quadrennial pay increase recommendations were delayed a year. The commission reported to Nixon on June 30, 1973, recommending a 25 per cent increase in 1974. Nixon modified the proposal to provide for 7.5 per cent increases in 1974, 1975 and 1976 for members of Congress and most officials, but with single 7.5 per cent increase in 1975 for Cabinet officers and Supreme Court justices. Under existing law, Nixon could not submit his pay recommendations until his budget message of January 1974.

Some members of Congress were impatient. The Senate on July 9, 1973, without debate and by voice vote, passed a bill which would have empowered the commission to recommend pay raises every two years and would have made a congressional increase possible by October 1973. But the House on July 30 rejected a rule (156-237) to bring the bill to the floor. Supporters of the measure said a biennial review would keep up with the rising cost of living and would avoid embarrassingly large increases after years of inaction. Opponents cried subterfuge, and noted that the commission's recommendations would come every year when there was no congressional election. Rep. David W. Dennis (R Ind.) said, "This bill is here on the cynical and insulting assumption that the American people are so stupid they won't realize what is going on."[7]

The increases recommended by Nixon were to have taken effect March 9, 1974. But members were uneasy about receiving a raise, from $42,500 to $45,700, in an election year. The Senate Post Office and Civil Service Committee on Feb. 28 reported a resolution to disapprove the congressional raise only. On March 6, the Senate voted 67-31 to invoke cloture and cut off debate on the measure, and then voted 71-26 to disapprove all pay increases. The action ended all pay-raise efforts for 1974. The House Post Office and Civil Service Committee on March 4 had reported a resolution disapproving all increases.[8]

Automatic Salary Increases

With surprising speed and ease, Congress in 1975 approved annual cost-of-living increases for its members and other top officials, tied to raises for all federal employees. The new plan was worked out secretly over several months by congressional leaders in consultation with the Ford administration. It was cleared by Congress only five days after most members had first heard of it.

days unless Congress either disapproved all or part of them or enacted a separate pay bill. Thus creation of the commission was an attempt to relieve members of Congress of the politically uncomfortable task of raising their own salaries.

President Johnson announced appointment of the Commission on Executive, Legislative and Judicial Salaries

The idea of Congress giving itself an automatic pay increase every year, based on the Consumer Price Index, arose from staff discussions in the Senate and House Post Office and Civil Service Committees after the Senate had killed the 1974 pay raise. The amount of the increase was to be left to the President when he made his regular cost-of-living recommendations for other federal employees. Sen. Gale W. McGee (D Wyo.), chairman of the Senate committee, began a series of discussions of the proposal in February 1975.

Congressional leaders met at the White House March 10 with President Ford and Chief Justice Warren E. Burger. The administration was alarmed because more than 20 per cent of the government's top officials were either retiring early or taking private-sector jobs because of the executive pay freeze. Burger was concerned because federal judges with lifetime tenure were returning to private life at the highest rate in more than 30 years. Between March 1969, the date of the previous pay raise, and May 1975 the Consumer Price Index had risen by 47.5 per cent. Although congressional salaries had not increased during that time, members had protected themselves from inflation by steadily increasing their allowances and other perquisites.

The automatic cost-of-living raise was added as a rider to a bill establishing a job safety program for postal workers. The Senate committee reported the bill on a Friday, July 25. The Senate began debating it July 28, defeated several amendments and then passed it July 29 by a 58-29 vote.

The bill cleared the House on July 30 by a one-vote margin, 214-213, after a short but furious debate. One representative called the debate "vicious, one of the ugliest, most disgusting things I've ever seen.... Members who rarely say a thing during floor debate were shouting and screaming at each other, saying, 'Don't be a hero, you want this raise as much as we do.' It was ugly."[9]

Under the legislation, the Executive Salary Cost-of-Living Adjustment Act (title II of PL 94-82), salaries for the executive schedule (and for related positions in the legislative and judicial branches) were to be adjusted each year, beginning in October 1975, by the average percentage adjustment of the general government pay schedule.

President Ford set the 1975 pay increase at 5 per cent, although his advisers had suggested at least 8 per cent. The House Oct. 1 voted 278-123 to uphold the 5 per cent increase, and the raise took effect that day. The salary of members of Congress thus increased from $42,500 to $44,600. Salaries for the Speaker and other congressional leaders also increased accordingly.

Opposition to the automatic cost-of-living raise was expected to continue both in and out of Congress. During the House debate Rep. E. G. Shuster (R Pa.) called the plan a "sly backdoor technique." He said, "The American people would be better off if Congress got a pay decrease when the cost-of-living went up and a pay increase when the cost-of-living went down."[10] (A year later, in September 1976, Congress—facing an election in less than two months—voted to deny members the automatic increase scheduled for 1976.)

The system of annual salary increases did not do away with the quadrennial Commission on Executive, Legislative and Judicial Salaries but was intended to help close the pay gap caused by inflation. A new commission was to be appointed in 1977. Meanwhile, the President's Panel on Federal Compensation on Dec. 1, 1975, gave Ford a broad set of recommendations for reorganizing the federal pay structures. Congressional salaries were not included, but some of the recommendations could affect Congress.

The panel recommended higher levels for the executive schedule, and also urged that the existing linkage between Level II of the executive schedule and congressional salaries should not be permitted to continue to distort or improperly depress executive salaries. Thus executive salaries could be set at levels independent of congressional salaries. The possible importance of this change was pointed out by the panel. It asserted that the failure of efforts to increase salaries in the Executive Schedule in 1973 at the time of the last quadrennial review was a consequence of the tacit equivalence between salary for Level II of the executive schedule and the salary for members of Congress.[11] Both salaries in 1973 were $42,500, and in 1976 were $44,600.

Personal Staffs of Members

For a century after the organization of Congress, no provision was made in either chamber for personal staff for a member, unless he was chairman of a committee.

The Senate was first to provide for staff aides. In 1885, a senator was authorized to employ a clerk when Congress was in session. The rate was set at $6 per day. In 1893, the House first authorized a clerk for its members and provided $100 monthly for the clerk's salary.

Over the years the number of aides and the size of their salaries increased steadily. Staff responsibilities expanded as well, to include clerical and bureaucratic support skills, technical and professional legislative skills and political skills. Employees usually have to perform in all three areas.

In addition to their personal staffs, senior members are assisted on legislative matters by staffs of the committees and subcommittees they head. The chairman of a standing committee actually has two staffs. It is not unusual for an aide to do both committee work and personal casework for a member, no matter which payroll he or she is on. Personal staffs and committee staffs combined gave the Senate approximately 6,000 employees in 1975.[12] The House at that time had about 11,000 employees on 700 separate payrolls.[13]

This section deals only with the personal staffs of members. Committee staffs are discussed elsewhere in the book. *(Details, Development of Committee Staffs, p. 389)*

House Staff Allowance

In 1975 the House increased the personal staff allowance of each representative to $227,270 a year to employ up to 18 aides in the Washington and home district offices. A cost-of-living increase on Oct. 1, 1975, boosted the total to $238,584, but at the time only one-third of the representatives were spending the full allowance and only one-third had hired the maximum of 18 aides. The unused monthly allowance does not accumulate; however up to $1,-000 each month may be used to cover charges for computer and related services.

The staff increases have benefitted mainly the junior representatives who do not have the additional help of committee staffs. Richard P. Conlon, staff director of the Democratic Study Group, an organization of moderate and liberal House Democrats, said in 1975, "New members have found they receive more complaints from constituents." He cited the case of freshman Rep. James L. Oberstar (D Minn.), whose constituent service workload was four times higher than that of former Rep. John A. Blatnik (D Minn.), whom Oberstar replaced.[14]

In 1976, the House Administration Committee instituted a series of reforms governing staff allowances (among other things) in the aftermath of the sex-payroll scandal that forced Rep. Wayne L. Hays (D Ohio) to resign as committee chairman. *(See Sexual Scandal, below.)*

The committee's reforms:

● Required House members and chairmen of committees and subcommittees to certify monthly the salaries and duties of their staff and to disclose any kinships between staff employees and any House member. This change was to become effective 30 days after the committee approved the certification forms.

● Required quarterly reports of how House funds are spent. The reports would be indexed according to employees and employing offices, showing titles and salaries. The first report under the new format was expected to cover the third quarter of 1976, ending Sept. 30.

● Gave the committee the power to adjust the clerk-hire allowance to reflect federal government cost-of-living raises.

Senate Staff Allowance. The personal staff allowance of senators depends upon the population of their states. In 1975 the annual allowance ranged from $413,082 for states with fewer than two million residents to $844,608 for states with more than 21 million. Senators may hire as many aides as they wish within the allowance, but only one may earn the maximum annual salary of $39,909. Senate staff allowances are cumulative within a calendar year, so that unused monthly allowances may be carried over.[15]

In June 1975, junior senators succeeded in amending the Standing Rules of the Senate to allow all senators to appoint up to three additional staff members for a total of $101,925 a year to help them with their committee assignments. In four days of debate the first-term senators and their allies also won the right to hire and control their own committee staff members, thus making an inroad on the seniority system. Employees in the new category are paid out of the contingency fund of the Senate. The resolution eventually was approved by voice vote on June 12.[16]

Problems of Nepotism

Nepotism has been a recurring issue in congressional annals. Some members have used their staff allowances to pay relatives and in effect supplement the member's personal salary.

On May 20, 1932, the House adopted a resolution by Rep. Lindsay C. Warren (D N.C.) which provided that: "The Clerk of the House of Representatives is hereby authorized and directed to keep open for public inspection the payroll records of the disbursing officer of the House." The resolution was adopted without debate. Few members on the floor understood its import. On the next day, however, stories based upon examinations of the disbursing officer's records were published in all newspapers. They disclosed that 97 members of the House devoted their clerk-hire allowance, in whole or in part, to payment of persons having the same names as their own. Presumably these persons were relatives. The names were published, and "nepotism in Congress" became a subject of wide public discussion.

Senate payroll information was not opened for public inspection until 1959. On June 26, 1959, the Senate by voice vote adopted a resolution requiring the Secretary of the Senate to make public the name, title, salary and employer of all Senate employees. The resolution was the outgrowth of critical newspaper stories on the withholding of payroll information, coupled with disclosures of congressional nepotism.

Touching off the new round of disclosures was a Jan. 5, 1959, news story by Scripps-Howard staff writer Vance Trimble, containing a lengthy list of relatives he said were employed by members in their offices in 1958. Trimble had obtained the names by checking out similar names on available House-Senate records. He filed a court suit to gain access to Senate payroll records.

On Feb. 23, 1959, the Associated Press published a list of 65 representatives who had persons with "the same or similar family name" on their January payrolls. Three members who were on the AP list denied that their payroll namesakes were in any way related to them.

Nepotism also was a problem for Rep. Adam Clayton Powell Jr. (D N.Y.). From the time of their marriage in December 1960 Powell employed his Puerto Rican wife—Yvette Marjorie Flores—as a paid member of his congressional office staff. Mrs. Powell remained in Puerto Rico after the birth of a son in 1962, but she continued to draw a $20,578 annual salary as a clerk whose job was to answer mail to Spanish-speaking constituents. The House in 1964 adopted a resolution aimed specifically at that situation; it forbade members from hiring employees who did not work either in the member's home district or in Washington, D.C. That provision was readopted as a part of the legislative branch appropriation in 1965. Mrs. Powell, however, remained in Puerto Rico. Following a select committee investigation of additional charges against Powell, he was excluded from the 90th Congress on March 1, 1967. The U.S. Supreme Court later ruled that the House action was unconstitutional, and Powell returned to Congress in 1969. *(Details, 'Ethics in Congress,' p. 703)*

In 1967, Congress included in the postal rate-federal pay increase bill a provision to curb nepotism in federal employment. The provision prohibited public officials, including members of Congress, from appointing or influencing the appointment of relatives in the agency in which the official served. The ban covered all officials, including the President, but did not cover relatives already employed. And it did not prevent an official in one agency or chamber of Congress from seeking to obtain employment for a relative in another agency or chamber.

The "Congressional Handbook," prepared for all members and updated continually by the Joint Committee on Congressional Operations, lists 25 classifications of relatives whose employment by representatives and senators "is not permitted by law under the staff allowances."[17]

Political Misuse

In recent years the political misuse of congressional staff has become a more common charge than nepotism. The issue comes to the surface every election year, when some members are accused of using employees on the congressional payroll to help get themselves re-elected.

A series of articles in *The Washington Post* Feb. 16-24, 1975, charged that more than 100 Senate committee staff members had been transferred to non-committee duties in senators' offices and that others were being used in political campaigns.

Sexual Scandal

Traditionally, little has been said about members' sexual relations with their staffs. As a result, rumors of abuses have circulated from time to time, but rarely if ever have been substantiated.

1976 House Changes in Members' Benefits

The House of Representatives and its Committee on Administration adopted a number of reforms in 1976 in the aftermath of a sex-payroll scandal that forced Rep. Wayne L. Hayes (D Ohio) to resign June 18 as chairman of the committee. Elizabeth Ray, a committee secretary, said May 23 that Hays kept her on the payroll to provide him sexual favors. Hays denied the assertion, but the widespread publicity of the assertion, and resulting adverse public and political reaction, led to Hays' resignation of the chairmanship. He resigned from Congress on Sept. 1, 1976.

Committee Actions

The House Administration Committee, meeting under its new chairman, Rep. Frank Thompson Jr. (D N.J.), adopted a series of reform proposals on June 28, 1976. No House action was required. They included:

● Reduced the current 20-cents-a-mile allowance for automobile travel for House members to 15 cents, the amount set by the General Services Administration for federal employees, effective July 1.

● Required House members and chairmen of committees and subcommittees to certify monthly the salaries and duties of their staffs and to disclose any kinships between staff employees and any House member. This change would become effective 30 days after the Administration Committee approved the certification forms, which it did on Sept. 1.

● Required quarterly reports of how House funds are spent. The reports would be indexed according to employees and employing offices, showing the titles and salaries.

● Required that disbursements be made only on the presentation of vouchers, effective Sept. 1.

The following were to go into effect in the 95th Congress:

● Eliminated the separate postage stamp allowance, currently $1,140 a year, and ended the so-called "cash-out" practice that permitted members to convert unused stationery and travel allowances into cash for their personal use.

● Gave the committee the power to adjust the clerk-hire allowance, currently $238,584 a year, to reflect federal government cost-of-living raises.

● Revised the telephone and telegraph allowance to permit each member to have two WATS (wide area telephone service) lines to reduce costs for long-distance phone calls. If a member opted for the WATS lines, he would give up half of his annual telecommunications allowance.

● Revised the system of allowances used by members to run their offices by permitting members for the first time to transfer money from one fund to another. The new system was to take effect in the 95th Congress.

House Actions

On July 1 the House adopted two resolutions which were also designed as reform measures. Both were attacked sharply by Republicans, but survived recommittal votes, and eventually were adopted by large majorities. One resolution (H Res 1368) established a 15-person study commission on House accounting and personnel procedures and members' benefits. The other resolution (H Res 1372) stripped the House Administration Committee in most instances of its unilateral authority to alter representatives' benefits.

H Res 1368. The resolution authorizing the study commission was adopted by a 380-30 roll-call vote after a Republican motion to recommit was rejected by a 143-269 vote that followed party lines.

The resolution created a Commission on Administrative Review, which was to be composed of eight representatives (five Democrats, three Republicans) appointed by the Speaker, and seven members of the public chosen for their backgrounds and experience, also appointed by the Speaker. The commission was to conduct a study and prepare recommendations covering the following areas: staff personnel, administration, accounting and purchasing procedures, office equipment and communications facilities, recordkeeping, emoluments, and allowances. The Commission was to report to the House by Dec. 31, 1977.

H Res 1372. The resolution dealing with the House Administration Committee was adopted by a 311-92 roll call after a Republican recommittal motion was rejected by a 165-236 vote.

The resolution would require House approval—instead of unilateral committee action—of most changes in representatives' benefits and allowances. Cases in which the committee could continue to act alone were ones in which there was a change in the price of materials, services or office space; a technological change or other improvement in equipment; or a cost-of-living increase.

The tradition was broken dramatically in 1976 when Elizabeth Ray, a House Administration Committee secretary, told *The Washington Post* May 23 that Chairman Wayne L. Hays (D Ohio) maintained her on the committee staff to provide him with sexual favors. Hays admitted he had had a "personal relationship" with Ray but denied he had retained her as his mistress. Ray told the Post she had been a committee staff member since April 1974 despite the fact that "I can't type, I can't file, I can't even answer the phone."

The case attracted wide attention, and pressure from the House Democratic leadership led Hays to resign as committee chairman on June 18. The House on July 1 adopted two resolutions establishing a 15-member Commission on Administrative Review to study House accounting and personnel procedures and members' perquisites, and stripping the House Administration Committee of its unilateral power to alter representatives' benefits and allowances. Earlier the committee had approved a series of orders that revamped House perquisites and instituted controls over payroll and personnel procedures. Newspapers reported a number of other cases of possible sexual misuse of female workers by male members. Hays later decided not to stand for re-election in 1976 and resigned his seat Sept. 1.

House Allowances, 1971-1975

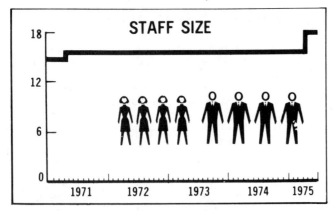

STAFF SIZE

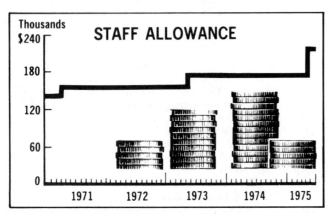

STAFF ALLOWANCE

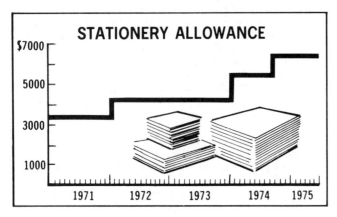

STATIONERY ALLOWANCE

Special Allowances

The travel allowance provided in the Act of Sept. 22, 1789, fixing the compensation of members of Congress was the first of what has become a handful of special allowances that members have created for themselves through the years. Senators and representatives still receive a travel allowance. Other special allowances cover office expenses, stationery, postage, telephone and telegraph service and publications. *(Information on special allowances is taken from the House and Senate versions of the "Congressional Handbook," see p. 484)*

The various allowances have been a persistent source of trouble for members. The stationery and other allowances are susceptible to abuse. At the same time, some members

find that the amounts provided by the allowances fail to keep up with rising costs. One answer to the money problem has been for members to apply campaign contributions to certain incidental expenses.

In general, allowances are more specific and more restrictive for representatives than for senators. While representatives have often had to limit spending within each account, senators may consolidate their allowances for stationery, postage, telephone and telegraph, travel, and state office expenses "with no limitation on the amount which can be spent in any one category."[18] Many House allowances must be spent a month at a time, whereas Senate allowances usually are cumulative within a calendar year. Most allowances in the House are the same for all members, but in the Senate they vary with the population of the states.

Each legislative body largely determines its own allowances and perquisites. Occasionally members on one side of the Capitol may decide that their colleagues on the other side are trying to boost their benefits too much. On Feb. 18, 1975, the House recommitted a bill which, perhaps inadvertently, would have amended Senate rules to allow senators and their aides to collect $35 per diem in expenses while traveling to, from and within their home states. Rep. Les Aspin (D Wis.) sent letters to all representatives, saying, "The new freebie will allow senators while they are out campaigning to rake off an extra $35 daily bonus."[19] Then on June 1 the representatives increased their own per diem to $50 for official business trips.

That incident was unusual. In contrast, the House Administration Committee on May 20, 1975, added a newsletter allowance and increased the allowances for staff, travel and telephone service without even asking members whether the perquisites were needed. A resolution approved in 1971 (but reversed in 1976) gave the committee the power to set allowances without a vote of the full House.[20]

Following a sex-payroll scandal that forced Rep. Wayne L. Hays to resign as chairman of the House Administration Committee, the committee in 1976 instituted a number of reform measures dealing with (among other things) the special allowances of representatives. In addition to making a series of specific changes, the committee reforms permitted House members for the first time to transfer funds from one allowance category to another. The new transfer system was to take effect in the 95th Congress.

Travel Allowance

The travel allowance of 1789—$6 for each 20 miles—has been altered to reflect increased mobility of the nation.

House. Representatives are allowed 26 free round trips each year to and from their home district. Their staffs are allowed six free trips a year. Six extra staff trips are permitted if they are deducted from a member's quota of 26. As recently as March 1971 each House office was allowed only 12 round trips a year.

Representatives may choose to withdraw their travel allowance in cash, up to a maximum of $2,250 a year. Until 1977, any remainder not used for travel could have gone toward members' personal expenses, if they paid income taxes on it.

As part of its reform package, the House Administration Committee in 1976 reduced the 20-cents-a-mile allowance for automobile travel for House members to 15 cents, the amount set by the General Services Administration for federal employees. The new rate became effective July 1, 1976.

The committee also ended the "cash-out" practice of allowing members to withdraw the unused balance of their travel allowance. This change was to become effective with the beginning of the 95th Congress.

Senate. The travel allowance for Senate offices is based on the cost of 40 round trips a year for states with fewer than 10 million people and 44 round trips for states with more than 10 million. The states' distance from Washington is figured in the computation. The Senate travel allowance makes no distinction between trips by senators or their staffs and it sets no limit on the number of trips to be taken each year.

Per Diem Travel. Members are reimbursed for travel on official business that is in addition to visits to their home districts or states. Representatives can receive $50 per diem for such travel within the United States. Senators and their staffs normally receive $35 per diem, but may be reimbursed for a maximum of $50 a day.

Stationery Allowance

House. Each representative is allowed $6,500 a year to purchase stationery and office supplies. Until 1977, members could convert the allowance into cash to pay for other publications or gifts for constituents, or for personal expenses provided they paid income taxes on it.

In 1976, the House Administration Committee eliminated the "cash-out" option as part of its reform package. This change was to become effective at the start of the 95th Congress.

In addition to the annual $6,500 allowance, each representative is allowed 40,000 brown "Public Document" envelopes a month without charge; the envelopes may be used anytime in a calendar year.

Senate. The stationery allowance for a senator's office ranges from $3,600 to $5,000 a year, depending on the state's population. It is part of the consolidated allowance of senators which may be used for a variety of official expenses. In addition to the cash allowance, each senator receives allotments of white envelopes and letterheads, blank sheets and brown "Public Document" envelopes, all based on the state's population.

Postage Allowance

The franking privilege of members of Congress applies only to regular surface mail. Special allowances are required for airmail and special delivery stamps.

House. Until 1977, each representative's office received a postage allowance for use on official mail that was ineligible for franking. In the 94th Congress, which began in 1975, the annual allowance was $1,140. Unused allowance balances could not accumulate.

In 1976, the House Administration Committee eliminated the postage allowance, effective with the start of the 95th Congress, as part of its reform efforts.

Senate. Senators whose states are east of the Mississippi River receive an annual postage allowance of $1,390; those whose states are wholly or partially west of the Mississippi receive $1,740 a year. It is part of the senators' consolidated allowance.

Telephone and Telegraph Allowance

House. Each year a represesnative is allowed 125,000 message units—for long-distance phone calls, telegrams and cablegrams—with the units freely transferable between the member's home district office and Washington office.

Unused units from one session may be carried over to a subsequent session of the same Congress. One long-distance telephone minute equals four units, one telegram word equals two units, and so on.

Senate. The Senate Rules and Administration Committee fixes telephone and telegraph allowances. Each senator may make 3,000 long-distance calls a year, totaling not more than 15,000 minutes. A senator from a state of more than 10 million persons is allowed an additional 1,500 calls a year (not more than 7,500 minutes). In addition, a senator is given a flat $2,200 a year for calls that exceed the per-call allowance. The committee uses a complicated formula to determine the telegraph allowance, based on state populations and Western Union rates from Washington. Both formulas go into a senator's total consolidated allowance.

FTS, WATS for Senate and House. Beyond these basic telephone and telegraph allowances, many members have access either to a nationwide, leased-line Federal Telecommunications System (FTS) or to wide-area telephone service (WATS) provided by telephone companies. The House Administration Committee in 1976 revised representatives' telephone and telegraph allowances to permit each member to have two WATS lines to reduce costs for long distance calls. If a representative chose to use WATS lines, half the annual telecommunications allowance would have to be given up. The change was part of the committee's reform package.

Newsletter Allowance

House. Since 1975 each representative has been allowed $5,000 a year for production and printing of newsletters, questionnaires and similar correspondence eligible to be mailed under the frank. The allowance about covers the cost of two newsletters a year. When the House Administration Committee first authorized the allowance, the chairman, Rep. Wayne L. Hays (D Ohio), said it would "assist members with district communication" and free them "from the necessity of private fund-raising." But Rep. Bill Frenzel (R Minn.), one of the committee members opposed to the new allowance, called it a "re-election campaign gimmick" that only increased the power of incumbents at the taxpayers' expense.[21]

Senate. Some services for printing and bulk mailing of newsletters, questionnaires, excerpts from the *Congressional Record* and other items are provided without charge by the Senate's Service Department. Senators receive a monthly printing allowance, based on state population, but they sometimes use part of the stationery allowance, trade-offs from other accounts, or private resources to cover newsletter expenses.

Office Allowances

House. The Washington office of a representative is provided free of charge. In 1975 a lobby group, Americans for Democratic Action, figured the average size of a member's office and the average rent for office space in Washington, D.C., and estimated that the free office saves each representative about $10,480 a year.[22] Office furnishings and decorations, housekeeping and maintenance all are free. Each member receives $5,500 a year to purchase electrical and mechanical office equipment, and $750 a month to lease equipment. The allowances are not cumulative.

In their home districts representatives are allowed up to three offices. Space in federal buildings is free. If private space must be rented, members are allowed $200 a month ($2,400 a year) for each office, or up to $500 a month in unusual circumstances. Each home office is allowed $5,000 for furnishings and equipment, and $1,500 for carpeting and draperies. An annual expense allowance of $2,000 is shared by all home offices.

Senate. The Washington office and furnishings for senators are provided free, as are housekeeping and maintenance services. Senators do not have allowances to buy or lease office equipment because it is provided by the sergeant at arms of the Senate.

A senator's home state office space is allocated according to the state's population. Within the allowed square footage there is no limit to the number of officers. Offices are provided free in federal buildings or leased from private owners at the GSA regional rate. Senators receive an aggregate furniture and equipment allowance of $20,500 for 4,800 square feet of office space, increased by $500 for each additional 200 square feet. All furnishings are provided through the General Services Administration. The expense allowance for home offices is part of the senators' consolidated allowance. Each senator also is allowed to rent one mobile office for use throughout the state.

Publications Allowance

In addition to their special allowances for office operations, communications and travel, members of Congress receive a number of free publications. Some are used directly in the member's work—a complete set of the U.S. Code and supplements, four subscriptions to the *Federal Register,* and office copies of the *Congressional Record* and the *Congressional Directory.* Others are offered as gifts to constituents. Besides three personal copies, representatives are allotted 68 subscriptions to the *Congressional Record* and senators are allotted 100. Members and their staffs receive engraved copies of the annual *Congressional Directory.* Representatives may distribute 33 copies and senators 58 copies.

Members also receive allotments of special publications to send off to constituents. One of the most popular is the Yearbook of the Department of Agriculture. Each representative was allotted 400 copies in 1975, worth $2,280.[23] Unused Yearbooks and certain other publications may be turned in to the Government Printing Office for exchange or credit toward other books and pamphlets. Among the gifts members may choose to distribute are wall calendars and pamphlets on American history, the legislative process and historic documents.

Americans for Democratic Action calculated in 1975 that each representative was allowed $10,659 worth of free publications.[24] But is is impossible to make an accurate estimate because members also receive, and use, hundreds of bills, annual reports from federal agencies, budget documents, manuals, published hearings and committee reports. Senators are given an unabridged dictionary and stand as part of their office furnishings.

Abuses of Allowances

With so much money involved in the special allowances, some members inevitably have taken advantage of them. Some abuses have been blatant and illegal. Others resulted from genuine confusion over what was proper or improper.

One classic example of abuse of the allowance for office expenses came to light in 1959. A Scripps-Howard dispatch on March 4, 1959, disclosed that Rep. Randall S. Harmon (D Ind.) was collecting $100 a month for use of the front porch of his home in Indiana as a district office. The incident was widely publicized and led to further news stories on the use that members make of their district offices. Randall was defeated in the 1960 elections.

Before travel allowances were made so generous, it was common for members to draw from other accounts to pay for their trips back home. On the other hand, members could pocket their travel allowance and pay for transportation with other funds. The postage allowance is frequently used because members find ways to trade in their sheets of stamps for cash.

Another abuse of travel funds was reported in 1976 by *The Wall Street Journal.* On April 30 it reported that a number of members filed reimbursement vouchers for 1975 automobile travel to their districts when they actually had traveled at lower cost by airline. Others had received reimbursement for trips on dates when the *Congressional Record* showed they had been in Washington voting on legislation. On June 18 *The Washington Post* reported the Justice Department had asked the House for financial records of nine members who allegedly overcharged the government for travel expenditures. The Post listed the names of the members as Reps. Ray J. Madden (D Ind.), Margaret M. Heckler (R Mass.), Tim Lee Carter (R Ky.), Walter Flowers (D Ala.), Otto E. Passman (D La.), Bill D. Burlison (D Mo.), George E. Shipley (D Ill.), Robert E. Jones (D Ala.), and Gene Taylor (R Mo.).

The stationery allowance is easily abused because its use is not specified and because representatives until 1977 were allowed to add the entire $6,500 a year to their annual salary. If they use it as personal income they must cover stationery expenses in some other way. In practice, most members deplete their stationery allowances on routine business and never withdraw the cash for personal use.

In both the House and Senate, stationery allowances routinely are used to purchase ashtrays, cuff links, pen and pencil sets and other souvenirs for constituents—especially at the end of the year. It is no secret that the funds cover a lot of official Christmas shopping.

In the House, stationery funds not spent during a given term are carried over in a member's account. The remainder served as a retirement bonus for some members. Early in the 94th Congress, 77 retired or defeated members withdrew a total of $198,306 from their accounts. The largest withdrawal was $23,611 by H. R. Gross (R Iowa), for years the House's leading opponent of federal spending, who said it was "one of the smallest withdrawals made over a 26-year period."[25] In 1976, the House Administration Committee eliminated the "cash-out" option. This change was to become effective at the start of the 95th Congress.

Increases in Allowances

Congress increased the special allowances so much in the early 1970s that the amounts themselves were criticized as improper. Americans for Democratic Action concluded in August 1975 that the total pay and perquisites of representatives, including special allowances, had risen by over $112,000 since the end of 1973—an increase of 30 per cent in about a year and a half.[26] The cost-of-living pay increases that took effect Oct. 1, 1975, added another $13,500 to that total.

The Washington Star reported Nov. 12, 1975: "Since 1970, consumer prices have risen by 39 per cent. In Congress, meanwhile, the legislators have raised allowances for staff salaries by 71 per cent, 116 per cent for stationery supplies, 63 per cent for special postage, and 275 per cent for the rental of district office space."[27]

Not all the critics of higher allowances were outside of Congress. Rep. Marjorie S. Holt (R Md.) chose not to increase her personal staff in 1975 when the maximum was raised from 16 to 18. "Increase the staff and you've got to increase the amount of paper you buy," Rep. Holt said. "Then you've got to buy more furniture for them. That means you need more rooms. And when you build more rooms you've got to hire more policemen to protect them."[28]

'Slush Funds' of Members

Despite all the allowances, many members still find their incomes insufficient to meet certain expenses associated with their duties. Thus they have established special accounts of private funds. The polite name for them is "office accounts" or even "constituent service accounts," but they are most frequently referred to simply as "slush funds."

Slush funds may be leftover campaign contributions, any donations from individuals or organizations, or part of members' personal wealth. They are used for many purposes: newsletter expenses, family or staff travel, lunches for constituents, public meetings, parking fees, opinion polls, flowers for funerals, mailings of Christmas cards, office coffee, and just about any job-related expense not covered by the allowances.

Slush funds essentially are not regulated. Some members report all sources and uses of slush funds; others avoid any mention of them.

A representative who requested anonymity told *Parade* magazine in 1975: "Office funds—or newsletter funds, office accounts, research and information funds—whatever they're called—are the last refuge for members of Congress who want to take unlimited amounts of money from any source, spend it on whatever they please and report it nowhere."[29]

The *Parade* article said at least half of the representatives were believed to have slush funds, although "a survey shows that most of the funds are relatively small—about $5,000 a year, most of it collected in small contributions from constituents."[30]

A Senate rule requires senators to file reports on the receipt and disposition of all contributions over $50, whether campaign gifts or not. Many senators handle slush funds through their campaign committees, and some keep more than one office account so that the amount does not appear embarrassingly large. Even so, a senator's slush fund may total tens of thousands of dollars a year.

The Federal Election Commission issued a regulation July 30, 1975, to apply the contribution and spending limits of the campaign finance law (PL 93-443) to the slush funds of members throughout their terms in Congress. When that was strongly opposed by Senate leaders, the commission Sept. 30 issued a compromise regulation that treated office accounts as campaign funds only for the last two years of a senator's term and the second year of a representative's term.

A Senate amendment to accept the revised regulation was defeated Oct. 8 by a 47-48 vote. Under the campaign finance law, the House and Senate have 30 legislative days to veto proposed commission regulations. Any regulation that is disapproved by one house is dead. Thus the commission was given the task of devising a new regulation governing slush funds, but without much guidance as to what Congress would accept.

Members' Honoraria

For many years members of Congress, especially senators, have supplemented their income by delivering speeches, making public appearances and broadcasts, and publishing articles for fees and royalties. Until 1975 there were no restrictions on such earnings, and it was not unusual for prominent or popular members to earn more from honoraria than from salary.

The era of no restrictions ended Jan. 1, 1975, when the campaign finance law took effect. It limited honoraria for members and other federal officials to $1,000 for any single appearance or article and a total of $15,000 a year.[31] *(See next page for 1976 change in limitations.)*

Senate. Senators, with larger constituencies and far more national publicity, always have received more than representatives in honoraria. In 1973, senators collected a record high of nearly $1.1-million. In 1974, the last year before the new law took effect, 77 senators reported honoraria totaling $939,619. Only 22 senators exceeded the $15,000 level, but they earned 69 per cent of the total. In 1975, with the new law in effect, 81 senators reported earning $637,893. The leading earner was Sen. Herman E. Talmadge (D Ga.), who reported $14,980.

The pattern of honoraria earnings followed a trend established over the years in which committee chairmen and members of committees with jurisdiction over economic issues reported the highest earnings.

In 1975 for the eighth straight year, colleges and universities spent more on Senate honoraria—$136,172 among 50 senators—than any other group. Jewish groups paid $33,500 to 19 senators; medical, dental and pharmaceutical associations paid $30,612 to 26 senators; labor groups paid $22,380 to 19 senators.

Senators were not required to report how they used their honoraria, but a few did so. Some used the funds to cover office expenses and other official activities, but most of the honoraria reported were donated by the senators to charitable institutions.

House. Reporting requirements were different in the House, where members must list activities for which honoraria were received but need not reveal the amount. In 1975, 231 representatives reported honoraria for speeches, writings and media appearances.

Of the total, 56 also reported their earnings, which came to $253,470. The leading earner was Rep. Shirley Chisholm (D N.Y.), who reported $15,000.

The leading provider of House honoraria in 1975 was the Grocery Manufacturers of America, which was listed on the reports of 20 representatives. The Brookings Institution appeared on the reports of 17 members. Other major contributors were the American Bankers Association and the American Podiatry Association.

Seven representatives reported honoraria from 20 or more sources.

(Reporting requirements of other outside earnings by members of Congress are discussed in Ethics in Congress, p. 703)

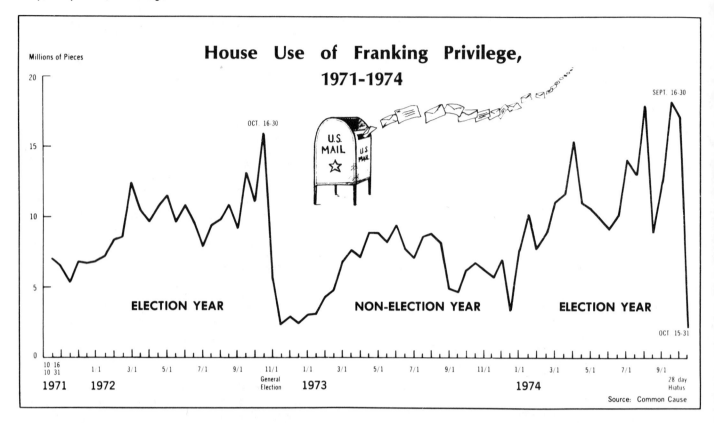

House Use of Franking Privilege, 1971-1974

Millions of Pieces

OCT. 16-30

SEPT. 16-30

ELECTION YEAR   NON-ELECTION YEAR   ELECTION YEAR

OCT. 15-31

10 16 / 10 31   1/1   3/1   5/1   7/1   9/1   11/1   1/1   3/1   5/1   7/1   9/1   11/1   1/1   3/1   5/1   7/1   9/1

1971   1972   General Election   1973   1974   28 day Hiatus

Source: Common Cause

1975 Rule Modified. The 1975 restrictions on honoraria were in effect for less than a year and a half. They were loosened considerably in May 1976 when Congress approved the Federal Election Campaign Act Amendments of 1976 (PL 94-283). The issue of honoraria was the last to be settled by conferees before the legislation could be passed. The House-approved bill had not changed the existing limits; the Senate bill had eliminated all restrictions on honoraria.

In the conference committee, Sen. Mark O. Hatfield (R Ore.) led the fight for increasing honoraria limits. Hatfield had been the Senate's third-highest recipient of honoraria in 1974, taking in $45,677 for 47 speeches before the $15,000 annual ceiling had gone into effect. He was opposed by Rep. Wayne L. Hays (D Ohio), who suggested only a slight increase to permit senators and representatives to receive $2,000 per individual event and a total of $20,000 annually.[32]

The 1976 law finally raised the limit on honoraria for members of Congress and federal employees to $2,000 for each event and a total of $25,000 a year. However, the $25,000 limit was a net amount; booking agents' fees, travel expenditures, subsistence, and expenses for an aide or a spouse to accompany the speaker could be deducted from the total honoraria in reaching a net amount. The law did not change existing reporting requirements.

Franking Privilege

One of the most valuable of members' perquisites is the frank, the privilege of mailing letters and packages under their signatures without being charged for postage. For fiscal 1976, Congress appropriated $46.1-million for its members and officials to send an estimated 322 million pieces of postage-free mail during the year.

The franking privilege is actually older than Congress itself. The first Continental Congress accorded its members mailing privileges, and one of the first acts of Congress under the Constitution was to continue the practice. Except for a brief time—the franking privilege was suspended for a few months in 1873—the privilege remained virtually unchanged. In 1973 Congress updated franking laws for the first time since the 19th century and established machinery for self-policing of franking practices.

Franking consists of a member's autograph or its facsimile on the envelope or package where stamps normally appear. Members submit three to five copies of their signature to the House Office Supply Service or the Senate Printing Clerk, and the most legible copy is selected for reproduction. Originally, franking was allowed on mail received by members as well as on mail sent.

Title 39 of the U.S. Code, which contains the rules of the franking privilege, limits it to correspondence "in which the Member deals with the addressee as a citizen of the United States or constituent." Members of Congress are not authorized to use the frank for letters in which they are acting as a personal friend, a candidate or a member of a political party.

The U.S. Postal Service keeps records of all franked mail as it passes through the post office in Washington. Every three months it sends Congress a bill for the cost of mail sent by members. The Postal Service computes the amount by weighing a random sample of the sacks of mail it receives each day from Congress. The rate of reimbursement is based on average weight, and was set at 14.3 cents per piece for fiscal 1976.

Neither the Postal Service nor its predecessor, the Post Office Department, has inspected franked mail to determine whether any members were abusing the privilege by sending personal or political correspondence postage-free.

Until 1968 the Post Office would issue rulings on specific abuses if private citizens made official complaints, and would ask the offending members to reimburse the Post Office. But the rulings were not binding, so some members refused to pay. On Dec. 27, 1968, the Post Office Department ruled that it no longer would attempt to collect from individual members who allegedly had abused the frank. The Postal Service has continued this policy.

No person allowed franking privileges may lend the privilege to any person, organization or committee, except House and Senate committees. Violators can be fined. Surviving spouses of members may use the frank for six months after a member's death.

Franked Mail Controversies

Special uses of the frank occasionally lead to controversy. In the early 1960s Congress had a fight each year over whether mail addressed to "occupant" could be sent under the frank. A compromise was finally adopted which permitted representatives to send some "occupant" mail but forbade senators from doing so.

The 1968 Post Office decision not to collect for franking abuses was followed by lawsuits taking some members to court. A 1970 decision awarded Democratic challenger John V. Tunney an injunction preventing incumbent Sen. George Murphy (R Calif.) from using the frank to send out campaign material. But a 1968 judgment had denied an injunction against similar use of the frank during a campaign by Rep. Jacob Gilbert (D N.Y.). In 1972 alone, 12 cases of alleged violations were brought before the courts.

In one franking case, a court decision was not necessary. In Georgia, the disclosure that Rep. Fletcher Thompson (R 1967-1973) was sending mail all over the state via the frank was considered a major reason he lost a race for a Senate seat. Thompson had sent a mass mailing at a cost to the taxpayers of more than $200,000, and Sam Nunn, his opponent, made it a campaign issue and was elected.

Conflicting court decisions, and a reluctance of many judges to rule on questions of congressional propriety, resulted in general confusion about proper use of the frank. The many disputes during the 1972 campaign convinced some members of Congress that new legislation was necessary. In addition, the House Post Office and Civil Service Committee in a 1973 report (H Rept 93-88) noted a marked increase in the amount of mail sent from Congress since the Post Office stopped policing use of the frank—from 178 million pieces in 1968 to an estimated 288 million pieces in 1973.[33]

1973 Franking Law

On Dec. 17, 1973, Congress approved HR 3180 (PL 93-191), which placed specific guidelines on the types of mail members could send free under the frank, set up mechanisms to rule on individual cases, and restricted the sending of mass mailings by members during the four weeks preceding congressional elections. The bill's sponsor, Rep. Morris K. Udall (D Ariz.) succeeded in establishing definitions of the franking privilege that were acceptable to most members and that represented little change from established practices. Udall said the issue was whether Congress would define the privilege or whether "the judges are going to write the law for us."[34]

The 1973 law provided the following:

● Authorized use of the frank "to expedite and assist the conduct of official business, activities and duties."

● Permitted use of the frank for mailings of any of the following: communications between members and the executive branch, newsletters and press releases dealing with legislative activity, public opinion polls, nonpartisan information on elections or voter registration, and biographies or pictures if sent in response to a specific request.

● Prohibited use of the frank for mailings that included purely personal communications, holiday greetings, information about the family of members, or political solicitations.

● Provided that material from the *Congressional Record* could be franked only if it would qualify as frankable on its own.

● Established a House Commission on Congressional Mailing Standards to make rulings on disputes arising in House election campaigns under the law.

● Assigned to the Senate Select Committee on Standards and Conduct the responsibility to make rulings on disputes arising in Senate election campaigns under the law.

● Prohibited mailings of more than 500 pieces of identical mail for the 28-day period immediately before an election by members who were candidates for re-election except for responses to inquiries, communications to government personnel, and news releases to the media.

The reforms did not anticipate every kind of abuse. Late in 1975 Congress voted to close a loophole in the 1973 law that had allowed former Rep. Frank M. Clark (D Pa.) to send out a franked newsletter mailing to his former constituents two months after his term had expired. The new legislation permitted former members to use the frank for 90 days after leaving Congress, but only for mailings to help close down their offices.

Increasing Use and Cost

Both the use and the cost of congressional franking increased enormously in the early 1970s. In 1970, members of Congress and others authorized to use the frank sent 190 million pieces of mail that cost a total of $11,224,000. For fiscal 1976 the volume and cost had jumped to 322 million pieces and $46,101,000. The 1976 appropriation was $7.3-million more than that for 1975. The Senate Appropriations Committee found in June 1975 "that the funds for fiscal year 1975 have been exhausted and that the reimbursements to the U.S. Postal Service are out of cycle by approximately $19-million."[35]

Some of the increase in cost was due to rising postal rates. The fiscal 1976 appropriation, for example, accounted for the first-class mail increase from 10 cents to 13 cents per ounce that began after Christmas 1975. On the other hand, Congress in 1974 renegotiated the status of certain types of its mail to reduce franking charges. At that time the *Congressional Record* was made eligible for less expensive second-class distribution instead of first-class mail.

The increase in volume was more significant in total franking costs. There is no franking allowance, so individual members may send as much postage-free mail as they wish. To no one's surprise, most members send out a lot more mail during campaign periods. Incumbent members realize that franking is one of their most valuable perquisites. *(Box, House Use of Franking Privileges, 1971-1974, p. 470)*

Travel Abroad—Junketing

Special allowances are available to members of Congress traveling abroad on government business. As

(Continued on p. 473)

Congressional Use of the Frank

Matter that may be franked	Persons authorized to use frank
Official business, which shall include all matters which directly or indirectly pertain to the legislative process or to any congressional representative function generally, or to the functioning, working or operating of the Congress and the performance of official duties in connection therewith. Mail matter which is frankable specifically includes but is not limited to: (1) the usual and customary newsletter, press release or questionnaire; (2) condolences and congratulations; (3) nonpartisan voter registration or election information or assistance; (4) mail matter which constitutes or includes a biography or autobiobiography of any member or member-elect, or of their spouse or other members of their family (or a picture, sketch, or other likeness of any member or member-elect), and which is mailed as a part of a federal publication or in response to a specific request therefor, and is not included for publicity purposes; (5) mail matter between members, from a member to any congressional district office (or between district offices), or from a member to a state or local legislator; (6) mail matter to any person and to any level of government regarding programs, decisions and other related matters of public concern, including any matter relating to actions of a past or current Congress; (7) mail matter including general mass mailings, which consist of federal laws, regulations, other federal publications, publications purchased with federal funds or containing items of general information.	The Vice President, members and members-elect, the secretary and sergeant-at-arms of the Senate, an elected officer of the House (other than a member), the legislative counsels of the House or the Senate. Members of Congress includes senators, representatives, delegates, resident commissioners. Term of use expires 90 days after the individual leaves office.
Public documents printed by the order of Congress.	The Vice President, members, the secretary and sergeant-at-arms of the Senate, an elected officer of the House (other than a member). (Members of Congress includes senators, representatives, delegates, resident commissioners.) Term of use expires on the first day of April following the expiration of their term of office.
The *Congressional Record,* a reprint, or any part of it.	Members of Congress (senators, representatives, delegates, resident commissioners).
Seeds and agricultural reports	Members of Congress (senators, representatives, delegates, resident commissioners). Term of use expires the 30th day of June following the expiration of their term of office.
Nonpolitical correspondence relating to the death of a member.	The surviving spouse of a member. Term of use expires 180 days after the member's death.
Mailgrams	The Vice President, members and members-elect, the secretary and sergeant-at-arms of the Senate, an elected officer of the House (other than a member), the legislative counsels of the House or the Senate. Members of Congress includes senators, representatives, delegates, resident commissioners.

Source: The Commission on Congressional Mailing Standards.

defined by William L. Safire's *The New Language of Politics,* "An overseas tour by a congressman or candidate is described by him as a *fact-finding trip,* and as a *junket* by his opponents, who usually add 'at the taxpayer's expense.' "[36]

A Congressional Quarterly survey published July 17, 1976, showed that 308 members of Congress had taken at least 544 trips abroad at government expense during 1975. The trips by members and their staff and committee aides cost at least $1,349,412.50. The travelers included 55 senators and 253 representatives, or 57.1 per cent of the members in 1975.[37]

Members generally undertake foreign travel on congressional (usually committee) business or by executive request or appointment. Members traveling abroad on committee business or as delegates to meetings of certain parliamentary groups are required by law to make public annually the government funds used. No public reports are required on other foreign trips.

Defense and Criticism of Members' Trips

As long as members of Congress have been taking trips abroad at government expense, there have been arguments between those who say that such travel is valuable and those who say it is a waste of time and money.

Defenders of foreign travel point out that it enables members to develop insight and to gain first-hand information needed for intelligent legislating and appropriating of funds. They say that such trips help members to overcome prejudice and provincialism and to spread goodwill, as well as giving them the chance to center their attention on foreign affairs and U.S. programs abroad.

Those who oppose overseas travel argue that trips at government expense are mainly a waste of the taxpayer's money. They say that visiting members expect to spend only a minimal amount of time on official business abroad, that they make unreasonable demands on U.S. personnel in the countries they visit, and that they sometimes damage American prestige through tactlessness or give foreign officials the impression that their comments reflect administration policy.

Critics also assert that the true cost of travel can be easily obscured, since expenses are not completely itemized or audited. Sometimes no cost of transportation is reported when flights are furnished by the State Department or the Department of Defense. Commercial airline fares and some other expenses are not always listed if they are defrayed out of Senate and House expense allowances.

Efforts To Control Travel Costs

Congress first initiated some control over members' foreign travel with the passage of the Mutual Security Act of 1954 (PL 83-665), which allowed congressional committees to use counterpart funds in their travels overseas. Members were required to make a full report to an appropriate oversight committee (House Administration, and Senate Rules and Administration), indicating the total amount of currency used and the purposes for which it was spent.

Public reporting in the *Record* was first required by amendments passed in the Mutual Security Act of 1958 (PL 85-477). The reports for 1958 were published in 1959. Members had to make itemized statements to their committee chairmen, showing the amount and dollar equivalent of counterpart funds they spent, plus the purposes for which the money was used, including lodging, meals, transporta-

---

Controversial Travel

Foreign travel at public expense traditionally has been a sensitive topic for some members of Congress. In past years, the press has reported on a number of such trips, or junkets, as they sometimes are called.

Probably the most notorious junketeer in Congress in recent years was the late Rep. Adam Clayton Powell Jr. (D N.Y.).

In one of his more celebrated trips in 1962, Powell traveled through Europe for six weeks accompanied by two assistants—Corinne Huff, a receptionist in his office, and Tamara J. Wall, an associate labor counsel for the House Education and Labor Committee, of which Powell was chairman.

According to one report, Powell's itinerary included London, Rome, Paris, Vienna, Spain and Greece. He requested State Department assistance to obtain tickets to the Vienna film festival, reservations at various European night clubs and a six-day cruise on the Aegean Sea.

Powell justified the trip on grounds that he and his two companions needed to study equal employment opportunities for women in Common Market countries.

'Lame-Duck Junkets'

In an example of "lame-duck" junketing, Sen. Edward V. Long (D Mo.) and Rep. Barrett O'Hara (D Ill.) both managed lengthy trips abroad after Congress had adjourned in 1968.

Both men had been defeated in primaries earlier in the year and were not returning for the new Congress. Long and his personal secretary traveled through 19 countries in six weeks. His administrative assistant explained that the trip was made for the Senate Banking and Currency Committee "to study export insurance and the Export-Import Bank." Officials of the bank subsequently said they never had been notified or consulted about the trip. O'Hara made a month-long journey to Africa accompanied by several staff members.

Hays' Headwaiter

In 1963, press reports revealed that Wayne L. Hays (D Ohio) had invited the headwaiter in the House dining room to accompany him to Paris for a NATO parliamentarians' conference. Hays reportedly had designated the waiter, Ernest Petinaud, to serve as a liaison man. One article reported that Hays was "unapologetic, calling Petinaud a fine American and an envoy of goodwill."

Source: CQ Weekly Report, May 18, 1974, p. 1292

---

tion and other reasons. Each committee was required to report this information to the proper oversight committee within the first 60 days of each session. The 1958 bill changed the Senate committee to Appropriations. Within 10 days of receipt, the two committees had to publish the reports in the *Record.*

In 1961, Congress required mandatory publication in the *Record* of individual itemized expenditures (Legislative

Branch Appropriations Act (PL 86-628)). It also stipulated that appropriated dollar funds be reported along with counterpart funds (Mutual Security Act of 1960 (PL 86-472)).

In 1963, the House took further steps to curb junketing, allowing only five House committees to use committee and counterpart funds for foreign travel. Ten other committees were restricted to travel within the United States, but could ask the Rules Committee for permission to travel abroad. Such requests would receive "respectful consideration," the Rules Committee chairman said.

In 1967, the Committee on House Administration banned the use of credit cards for transportation and accommodations and required uniform accounting and reporting from all House committees on a monthly basis.

In 1967, Rep. H. R. Gross (R Iowa) revealed that on 12 occasions during a single trip in 1966, five members collected their per diem twice by traveling to two countries in the same day. The House Committee on Standards of Official Conduct issued an ethics report March 14, 1968, calling for "clearer guidelines" regulating use and reporting of expenditures. One response of the House was to amend several committee travel authorizations to specifically limit collection of per diem rates to one period of time, regardless of the number of countries visited.

Then in October 1973, Congress passed a State Department authorization bill that contained a provision eliminating the requirement for disclosure in the *Congressional Record*. The change was engineered by Rep. Wayne L. Hays (D Ohio), chairman of the Foreign Affairs subcommittee where the bill originated. Hays also was chairman of the Committee on House Administration and a champion of generous perquisites for members.

Hays claimed he changed the old law to trim down the *Record*. "We decided we weren't going to spend eight or nine thousand dollars to let you guys (reporters) do your stories on congressional travel," he said. He told Congressional Quarterly that "there was no desire on anyone's part to cover up anything."

For a long time, Hays said, he has been "trying to cut the size of the *Record* down" and that "this was just another useless bit of using up space in the *Record*."[38]

Nevertheless, the effect of the change was to substantially reverse two decades of reform efforts aimed at preventing abuses of foreign travel and providing full public disclosure. Under the revised law, the detailed breakdown by committee and members was no longer published in the *Record*, and committees were no longer required to make public a separate accounting of tax dollars spent on travel for members and staff. There was no way to check the dates of arrival and departures in various countries, making it impossible to tell how long senators and representatives stayed abroad.

In the same amendment deleting the reporting requirements, Congress voted itself a 50 per cent increase in per diem allowance for foreign travel—from $50 to $75 each day.

Newspapers throughout the country printed stories about the congressional move and editorialized heavily against it. As a result, an amendment to the fiscal 1975 legislative branch appropriations bill (HR 14012—PL 93-371) reinstated language from the old law requiring that consolidated, detailed reports on foreign travel be made each year. But instead of being published in the *Record*, the amendment specified that the reports be made available to the public by the clerk of the House and the secretary of the

Senate. The law was signed by the President Aug. 13, 1974. It made no provision for the reports of such groups as the U.S. delegations to the Interparliamentary Union and the North Atlantic Assembly.

Still more changes were made in 1975 through amendments to the fiscal 1976 legislative branch appropriations bill (PL 94-59). It required all committee reports and all parliamentary delegation reports to be filed in only two places—the secretary of the Senate and the House Administration Committee. Rep. Hays thus gained control of the House foreign travel reports through his chairmanship of the committee.

The 1975 changes did not affect the requirement that all consolidated reports be filed within 60 days of the beginning of each session of Congress, but they did specify that the reports be open to public inspection. The changes became effective when the 1975 reports were filed in March 1976.

In 1976, the House adopted an amendment to the fiscal 1977 State Department authorization bill (HR 13179) requiring that annual foreign travel expense reports once again be printed in the *Record*. The House action was one of a number of reform developments following a sex-payroll scandal in which Hays, under pressure, resigned as chairman of the House Administration Committee. On May 23, 1976, Elizabeth Ray, a committee secretary, said Hays had kept her on the committee payroll to provide him with sexual favors. Hays resigned from Congress Sept. 1.

Sources of Travel Funds

Even before the reporting law was weakened in 1973, the information contained in the *Congressional Record* usually was the minimum required by law. It told where a member went, how long he stayed and how much he collected in government per diem payments. The listings rarely told why lawmakers went outside the United States. And they did not indicate the sources of the money used by members of Congress when they left the country on official business.

Some of the funds and facilities used for activities abroad by members include:

Appropriated Funds. Money is appropriated by Congress to pay the expenses, travel included, of its committees for routine and special investigations. Some committees also have confidential funds, which chairmen may spend without specific accounting.

Counterpart Funds. Members traveling abroad are allowed to use American-owned counterpart funds (foreign currencies held by U.S. embassies and credited to the United States in return for aid, and which may be used only in the country of origin). This surplus foreign currency generally is now disbursed on a $75-per-diem basis by embassies.

Representational Funds. American embassies and consulates abroad are allocated sums for official entertaining. Some of these funds are used for hospitality purposes for visiting members of Congress.

Contingency Funds. Emergency money is provided embassies to help stranded or financially strained American travelers. These funds usually are reimbursed when the traveler returns home.

Agency Funds. Many members of Congress travel as guests of government agencies, which have money appropriated for trips to their overseas posts. The Departments of State and Defense are the agencies most called upon to arrange travel.

Military Transportation. Members often travel without charge on ships of the Military Sea Transportation Service and planes of the Military Airlift Command.

Areas Visited by Members

Because of changes in the reporting law that began in 1973, the statistics for members' travel abroad in 1975 are incomplete. U.S. territories and possessions are not recorded as foreign travel. These include the U.S. Virgin Islands, Puerto Rico and Guam.

Areas visited by members in 1975, for both government and non-government trips, are shown below:[39]

	Senate	House	Total*
Western Europe (including Turkey)	60	291	351
Asia	22	105	127
People's Republic of China	7	18	25
South America	3	24	27
Middle East	19	81	100
Australia and New Zealand	0	3	3
Caribbean	7	15	22
Cuba	2	3	5
Africa	7	41	48
Russia and Eastern Europe	17	37	54
Canada	12	18	30
Mexico	10	16	26
India, Pakistan, Bangladesh and Sri Lanka	3	14	17
Antarctica	0	1	1

* Because most members visited more than one area on each trip, the number of areas visited is greater than the number of trips reported.

Additional Benefits

In addition to their pay, staff, allowances and other perquisites, members of Congress benefit from many other services, courtesies and special favors that go along with the job. It is impossible to compile a complete list of these other benefits or to compute their precise value. Selected additional benefits are described below:

Life Insurance. Regardless of age or health, members received $45,000 in term life insurance coverage under a group plan. The government matches one-third of the premium. An additional policy for $10,000 also is available, with the extra premium determined by the age of the member.

Health Insurance. Members are eligible for a generous health insurance plan. The government pays up to 40 per cent of the premium.

Health Care. A staff of doctors and nurses stands by in the Capitol to give members free medical care while at work. Services include physical examinations, laboratory work, electrocardiograms, ambulance service and supplies of prescription medicine. First aid stations in most House and Senate office buildings offer help for members and their staffs.

Taxes. Because members live in two places—their home towns and Washington, D.C.—federal tax law allows them to deduct up to $3,000 a year for living expenses in Washington. In October 1975 the House Ways and Means Committee attempted to raise the deduction to $44 a day while Congress is in session. If the rule had been in effect in

Retirement Benefits

Congress included in the Legislative Reorganization Act of 1946 a provision, recommended by the Joint Committee on the Organization of Congress, initiating a retirement system for senators and representatives. The Act brought members of Congress under the Civil Service Retirement Act, permitting them, at their option, to contribute 6 per cent of their salaries to a retirement fund. Retirement annuities were to be calculated at 2½ per cent of average salary multiplied by years of service, but could not exceed 80 per cent of a member's final congressional salary. A member became eligible for benefits upon retirement from Congress if the member was at least 62 years old and had served a minimum of five years (except in cases of disability).

In 1954, Congress liberalized the pension law and also adjusted retirement benefits for legislative employees. The basic rate of contribution remained 6 per cent of salary, but the bill included the congressional expense allowance in the salary computation. It also provided for reduced retirement benefits at age 60 and made other minor changes in the program. In 1956 the contribution rose to 7½ per cent. Further changes were enacted in 1960, although the basic retirement benefits were left unchanged.

In 1969, Congress again liberalized the pension law for both members and legislative employees. Retirement benefits were increased by specifying that the annuity computation formula would use an employee's average annual earnings during the highest consecutive three-year period, rather than during a five-year period, as had been required. The method of computing annuities for congressional employees was liberalized by eliminating a 15-year limitation on number of years of service for which the annuity would be computed at 2½ per cent of average pay. Other benefit changes also were made. In addition, the contribution of members of Congress was increased from 7½ per cent to 8 per cent, and the contribution of congressional employees from 6½ per cent to 7½ per cent, beginning in January 1970. The government matches participants' contributions to the plan.

Since 1969 the pension plan has included a "kicker," providing that each time pensions are raised for increases in the cost of living, an extra 1 per cent is added to compensate for the time lag between cost increases and the date of pension adjustment. Former Rep. Hastings R. Keith (R Mass.) told a House Post Office and Civil Service subcommittee Nov. 14, 1975, that in the two and one-half years since he had retired from Congress his monthly pension had increased from $1,560 to $2,095, or nine percentage points higher than the increase in living costs over the same period. Keith estimated he would receive an extra $76,000 from the "kicker" if he collected his pension through 1990. He said the increase was "becoming scandalous," and he urged Congress to save billions of dollars by ending the provision throughout the federal retirement system. Keith served 14 years in Congress, plus six years of other federal service.*

* U.S., Congress, House, Committee on Post Office and Civil Service, Civil Service Retirement System, Hearings before the Retirement and Employee Benefits Subcommittee, Serial No. 94-56, 94th Cong., 1st sess., Nov. 14, 1975, pp. 88-89.

Members' Recording Studios

Nearly all the perquisites of members of Congress give incumbents certain campaign advantages over their challengers. For example, a member's staff, the franking privilege, and special allowances for travel, office expenses, stationery, newsletters, telephone and telegraph services—all at public expense—may improve the member's chances of being re-elected. In addition, incumbents have inherent news-making powers which their opponents lack.

One of the greatest advantages—and perhaps a decisive one as electronic campaigning grows in importance—is the availability of radio and television recording facilities. The House Recording Studio, located in the Rayburn House Office Building, and the Senate Recording Studio, located in a tunnel between the Capitol and the Russell Office Building, are available to all members.

In theory the recording studios are designed to help members communicate with their constituents. Tapes recorded at the studios can be mailed to local stations for use in regular news or public affairs programing. In fact, much of the work performed at the studios is frankly campaign material.

Studio productions are subsidized with public funds. Tapes and films are produced at cost, and the film or tape is available at congressional stationery rooms. Members are billed individually each month. They may not pay in cash. Representatives may use their stationery allowance to purchase audio and video tapes.

Both recording studios are extensive. Color films for television are processed in-house within 24 hours. Teleprompter machines are available. Telephone "beeper" reports can be sent simultaneously to several broadcast stations. Members must design their programs and write the scripts, but the studios suggest a variety of formats and provide such services as TV sets and makeup. Members are urged to make appointments for filming and taping on a regular basis.

It is impossible to estimate the recording studios' value to members, but they are a bargain by any measure. Opponents of incumbent representatives and senators are charged full rates by commercial recording studios; they must pay for most of their broadcast time; and they are seldom seen and heard over the airwaves except during brief campaign periods.

Source: *Congressional Handbook: U.S. House of Representatives; Congressional Handbook: United States Senate.*

1974, a senator could have deducted as much as $7,392, and a representative could have deducted up to $6,996. The committee later dropped the idea and voted instead to instruct the Internal Revenue Service (IRS) to determine the amount to be deducted by applying "rules of reasonableness."[40]

The IRS maintains an office on Capitol Hill to help members prepare their income tax returns. Congressional staff also receive help when droves of IRS employees visit the Capitol each year at tax time.

Library. The Library of Congress provides members with free manpower and facilities to produce research, speechwriting and responses to constituents' questions. About 800 employees in the Library's Congressional Research Service work exclusively for members. *(Details, Library of Congress and Congressional Research Service, p. 450.)*

Books. The Library of Congress gives away to members and their staffs excess books that pile up every month and are not suitable for the Library's collections. Some members send the books to libraries and schools in their district or state. Many volumes wind up in the homes of congressional staff.

Legal Counsel. The Office of Legislative Counsel, with offices on both sides of Capitol Hill, assists members in drafting bills, resolutions and amendments. Its staff provides confidential help on legislative matters only and does no personal legal work for members. *(Box, Office of Legislative Counsel, p. 395)*

Recreation. Members of Congress have their own free health club, with a modern gymnasium in the Rayburn House Office Building and another in the Russell Office Building. Facilities include swimming pool, paddleball court and sauna.

Food. Government-subsidized food and facilities are available to members, staff and visitors. The Capitol and office buildings contain seven public restaurants and cafeterias, three members-only dining rooms, and six carryout services. In addition, members may reserve several private dining rooms or arrange banquets and parties in caucus rooms with low-cost catering from the House and Senate restaurants.

Loans. In the House only, members may receive personal loans through the Sergeant-at-Arms Office in amounts equal to the salary due them for the remainder of the current Congress. In theory, at the beginning of a term a representative could borrow double his annual salary of $44,600 if the full amount was repaid within two years. In fact, most loans are of much smaller amount and for shorter duration. Any loan must be repaid by the end of each term. Interest rates are set by commercial banks, for whom the sergeant at arms serves as the agent. Representatives may obtain the loans for virtually any purpose. The Senate has no comparable procedure for making loans to its members.[41]

Merchandise. Stationery stores located in the Capitol office buildings sell many gift items as well as normal office supplies, all at cost or slightly above. Members and their staffs can buy such things as wallets, briefcases, pocket calculators, typewriters, and drinking glasses and ashtrays with the seal of either the House or the Senate. Christmas cards also are available at bargain prices.

Parking. Each representative gets a free Capitol Hill garage space for personal use, plus four additional spaces and one outside parking permit for staff use. Each senator gets two garage spaces and several outside permits for staff. By 1976 parking spaces in prime business areas in Washington were rented for as high as $70 a month.

Grooming. Seven government-run barber shops in the office buildings give free or inexpensive haircuts to members and staff. Congress also has two in-house beauty shops that are much less expensive than private salons in Washington.

Photographs. The Senate spends at least $149,000 in public funds for what amounts to individual photographic service for senators. Democrats and Republicans maintain separate staffs and darkrooms in the basement of the Capitol. The photographers, who may earn more than $30,-

000 a year for taking hand-shaking shots of senators and constituents, are listed on public payrolls as "clerks" and "assistant clerks."[42]

Representatives have photography services in the Rayburn Building, but their photographers are paid from party campaign funds. In both the House and Senate, cameras, film and supplies are purchased with party campaign funds.

Office Decorations. The U.S. Botanic Garden will supply members' offices with three small potted plants every month and one large plant every three months. Members may request cut flowers as well. *(U.S. Botanic Garden, pp. 434, 477)*

Members may decorate their offices also with free wall maps, scenic photographs, reproductions of paintings and charts—all of which are framed and installed at no cost to members.

Other Benefits. Among the services and perquisites available to members are the following:

● Free storage space and storage trunks are provided for members' files and official records.

● Congressional license tags provided for each member permit unrestricted parking while on official business anywhere in Washington.

● American flags flown over the Capitol and certified by the Architect may be purchased at cost and presented as gifts.

● Members and staff may have packages wrapped free of charge for mailing, a service used heavily during the Christmas season. For years the man who does this for Senate offices has been called "Jack the Wrapper."

● Each year members give away thousands of wall calendars published by the Government Printing Office or the U.S. Capitol Historical Society. The Senate ordered 62,700 calendars for 1975, at a cost to the public of $30,465.[43]

● Members are allowed to accept free transportation on non-commercial carriers—primarily company planes—under certain circumstances. *(Details, Ethics in Congress, p. 703)*

Political Patronage in Congress

While the pay of members and their staffs has increased sharply and the perquisites of members have grown enormously, political patronage in Congress has decreased through the years. Patronage is supposed to be one of the advantages of holding political office, but many members of Congress always have regarded it as a nuisance.

As defined by William L. Safire's *The New Language of Politics*, political patronage means "governmental appointments made so as to increase political strength."[44] Senators and representatives once pulled the political strings on thousands of federal jobs. On Capitol Hill and back home, a powerful member could place scores of persons in such jobs as local postmaster, health inspector, tax collector, welfare commissioner and even custodian of public morals. The congressional patronage empire thus provided members with a healthy payoff list for political supporters.

Today on Capitol Hill, the only jobs remaining under patronage are those that generally require no special skills or technical knowledge. Elevator operators, doorkeepers, mail carriers and clerks comprise the bulk of the posts still available to patronage dispensers. All in all, a member now finds the available patronage jobs of little help in

strengthening his political position or rewarding his campaign supporters.

Andrew Jackson was the first President to give open support to political patronage. But when he spoke out in favor of patronage, the number of public jobs requiring technical skills was not large. The few misfits who slipped in through patronage appointments seemed to do little damage to the general efficiency of the government.

As the business of government grew more complex, and as it expanded, the inadequacies of the patronage system became glaringly apparent. The Pendleton Civil Service Act of 1883 made the first assault on the patronage system. Thereafter, successive statutes and executive orders virtually removed patronage rights on the state level from members of Congress. Ninety-five per cent of the persons now employed by federal agencies are hired under the merit system or Civil Service. *(Box, Origins of Civil Service, p. 478)*

Members of Congress do have a voice in presidential appointments when the President is a member of their party. The Nixon administration filled about 6,500 jobs when it took office in 1969, and many of the appointments were made after consultation with members. Jobs filled by the administration included Cabinet and subcabinet positions, White House staff posts and jobs in federal regulatory agencies, as well as some lesser positions exempt from Civil Service.

Congressional influence in these appointments is limited by the discretion of the President. Many of the appointments require Senate confirmation, but none requires prior consultation. A member's role in White House patronage affairs generally depends on his personal relationship with the President.

Patronage Machinery

There are more than a thousand acknowledged patronage jobs on Capitol Hill itself. The 435 representatives and 100 senators are responsible for filling these posts. Patronage privileges are meted out to members of Congress under a puzzling combination of written rules and contradictory traditions. The exceptions to the written procedures are so numerous and diverse that they have all but usurped the rules.

House. Of the two chambers of Congress, the House has the more clearly defined methods for distributing patronage jobs among its members. The five-member Patronage Committee of the majority party is ostensibly in control of all patronage jobs on the House side.

The committee assigns a small quota of the jobs to the minority party at the beginning of each session. These are jobs like those of clerk or page in the minority cloakroom. The remaining patronage jobs are divided among the state delegations, and the senior majority member of each delegation is responsible for distributing them among the other representatives from the state.

The Patronage Committee was first established by a caucus of Democratic representatives in 1911. Three members of the Ways and Means Committee were chosen by the caucus to distribute patronage positions to members. Committee chairmen were excluded from the general distribution of patronage because they already had the power to make appointments to committee staff positions.

When the Republicans won a majority in the House in 1918 they set up their own Patronage Committee, with rules that generally followed the Democrats' example.

Origins of Civil Service

American political patronage reached its peak in the post-Civil-War era, when senators spent much of their time keeping track of patronage in their states and were allowed to dictate major appointments.

In 1881, for example, both of New York's senators resigned after President James A. Garfield refused to nominate their choice for the lucrative position of Collector of the Port of New York.

Both senators expected the New York legislature to express its support by re-electing them. But before the legislature could meet, Garfield was assassinated by a disappointed patronage seeker.

Public revulsion over the assassination and the excesses of patronage led two years later to passage of the Pendleton Act, the first major attempt at civil service reform in America.

The Pendleton Act set up a three-man bipartisan board, the Civil Service Commission, and empowered it to certify applicants for federal employment after competitive examinations.

The original Act covered only about 10 per cent of federal employees, but its key provision gave the President power to expand the civil service classifications by executive order. A series of such orders and additional legislation in the following years removed from politics nearly all nonpolicy-level jobs in the government.

Following Garfield's assassination, Civil Service received unexpected support from the new President, Chester Alan Arthur.

In 1884, the Pendleton Act produced one more disappointed office seeker—its sponsor, Sen. George H. Pendleton (D Ohio). Pendleton was defeated for re-election by Henry Payne, an outspoken advocate of the patronage system.

In outlining the machinery for handling patronage assignments, the parties did not mention how the Speaker of the House might use his influence in the distribution of patronage. They failed also to say how behind-the-scenes bargaining for a crucial vote might involve paying off a reluctant member with a patronage job or two. Maneuvering of this kind is part of the system of exceptions by which patronage is distributed.

When Rep. Carl Albert (D Okla.) was elected Speaker in 1971 the membership of the Democrats' Patronage Committee was increased from three to five.

Patronage distribution has become highly informal, according to Rep. B. F. Sisk (D Calif.), a member of the Patronage Committee in the 1970s. He said the committee has no list of patronage jobs on Capitol Hill and does not know how many exist at any one time. For members who are not committee chairmen, seniority is a leading factor in obtaining patronage jobs. But this is not a formal rule, Sisk said, and no seniority quota exists. State delegations are still assigned quotas, however, and some of them have worked out their own systems of distribution. Majority members of the New York delegation, for example, pool their patronage jobs in order to obtain what they feel is an equitable distribution.[45]

Senate. There is a three-member committee for distributing patronage jobs among senators. The majority leader is in charge of the process. The minority party is granted about 20 per cent of the patronage posts in the minority cloakroom and a like proportion of such jobs as pages and telephone operators for the minority side of the Senate. The other jobs are distributed by seniority and as the majority leader may choose.

The minority party is not satisfied with its 20 per cent. Kenneth Davis, an aide to Senate Minority Leader Hugh Scott (R Pa.), complained about Democratic control of Capitol patronage in 1975. "We don't have 38 per cent of the patronage jobs around here," Davis said, "which we should have if they were divided equitably."[46]

What Are Patronage Jobs?

Many of the patronage jobs on Capitol Hill are filled by college students needing financial assistance. They work a shift as an elevator operator or chamber doorman and then go to classes. The turnover rate is high, but in most cases it does not greatly affect the efficiency of the operation.

An exception is the Capitol Police force, where the jobs require special skills and where patronage was sharply reduced in the early 1970s. As recently as 1971, patronage appointees constituted 25 per cent of the total force. By 1975 there were no patronage police jobs on the Senate side (486 positions) and only 109 out of 627 positions on the House side. Patronage appointees are required to meet the same standards and to undergo the same training as other members of the Capitol Police.[47]

There are almost no official figures on patronage, and members seldom admit which jobs they control. Some of the patronage positions are described below.[48]

House. The Office of the Doorkeeper oversees the largest number of patronage jobs in the House. Nearly all of the 301 positions authorized in 1975 were filled by patronage. The doorkeeper supervises officers of the press galleries, doormen for the visitors gallery and the House floor, custodians, barbers, pages, and employees of the House Document Room and the "folding room," which distributes newsletters, speeches and other materials for representatives.

The clerk of the House also had 301 employees in 1975, but relatively few were hired through patronage. The sergeant at arms of the House has partial responsibility for the Capitol Police, but the immediate office staff numbered only 16 in 1975 and none was a patronage employee. The House post office had 94 full-time employees in 1975, nearly all of them hired on a patronage basis.

Other patronage jobs in the House, less clearly defined, include several in the offices of the majority and minority leaders, the parliamentarian, the minority sergeant at arms, and the whips of both political parties.

Senate. The sergeant at arms of the Senate, who has partial responsibility for the Capitol Police, also supervises a large number of patronage employees. Among them are Senate pages, doormen, custodians, officers of the Senate press galleries and employees of the Senate post office.

The secretary of the Senate, an administrative official, had a staff of 175 in 1975, some of whom were patronage employees. There is a scattering of Senate patronage jobs in the offices of the majority and minority secretaries, the majority and minority leaders, and the party whips.

Architect's Office. Although the architect of the Capitol has an immediate staff of about 70 to assist him in his administrative tasks, he was responsible for a total of 1,781 employees in 1975. Most served in support of the House and Senate office buildings. Among the patronage employees supervised by the architect were 155 elevator operators, who each earned $7,715 a year.

Other Positions. While patronage is generally restricted to non-skilled jobs, there is a group of Capitol Hill officials (technically not of patronage status) whose jobs depend on the influence of sponsors or the swing of party control. The House doorkeeper, the House and Senate sergeants at arms, the secretary of the Senate and the clerk of the House work for all members of their respective houses, but are elected by the members by strict party-line votes.

Party leadership generally plays an important part in the election of these non-patronage officials. The postmaster of the House and Senate are elected by the members of each chamber, but under the sponsorship of some senior member.

An example of the influence of House leaders in patronage appointments occurred in 1969 when the job of chief printer became vacant following the death of Truman Ward, who had held the post for 48 years. The print shop had developed into a profitable operation, printing speeches, newsletters and other material needed by House members. The chief printer receives a salary and is allowed to keep all the profits he can make.

Print shop employees and many members believed the job would go to shop foreman Robert Cutter, a veteran printer who had served as Ward's assistant since 1954 and directed the operating during Ward's illness. But the selection was up to House Majority Leader (later Speaker) Carl Albert (D Okla.), and Albert bypassed Cutter in favor of David R. Ramage, a resident of Wewoka, Okla., in Albert's home district. Ramage was not a professional printer but a loyal Democrat who had served 15 years as a clerk in the House stationery room.

Committee Staffs. The selection of committee staffs is supposed to be based on a candidate's administrative credentials and expertise on the subject matter. To a degree this is the case, but most committee staff jobs are filled by appointees of the majority party. Members hire the employees they want. *(Details, Development of Committee Staffs, p. 388.)*

Personal Staffs. The personal staff of a senator or representative naturally includes persons chosen for partisan reasons. A member is hardly likely to hire a supporter of the opposition party. Members may hire and fire their personal staff at will—such employees are not protected by Civil Service—and in many congressional offices the staff turnover rate is quite high.

Debate Over Patronage

The use of patronage to fill positions requiring special skills or knowledge has been on the decline since 1883, when the Pendleton Civil Service Act removed 10 per cent of federal employees from the system of partisan appointments. Since that time the inequities, inefficiencies and justifications of patronage employment have been debated almost annually in Congress. The congressional patronage empire has so dwindled that some senior members count themselves fortunate if they can appoint a Capitol policeman, a few elevator operators and a mailman in the Senate or House post office.

Members of Congress lost one source of patronage in 1969 when the Nixon administration decided to remove 63,-000 postmaster and rural carrier appointments from politics

Congressional Employees

Federal civilian employment in Congress, Oct. 1955-1975.

Year	Senate	House	Total
1955	1,962	3,623	5,585
1956	2,342	3,965	6,307
1957	2,378	4,005	6,383
1958	2,516	4,082	6,598
1959	2,700	4,217	6,917
1960	2,643	4,148	6,791
1961	2,713	4,774	7,487
1962	2,889	4,968	7,857
1963	2,982	4,952	7,934
1964	3,071	5,020	8,091
1965	3,219	5,672	8,891
1966	3,294	6,190	9,484
1967	3,587	6,365	9,952
1968	3,632	6,446	10,078
1969	3,847	6,874	10,721
1970	4,140	7,134	11,274
1971	4,624	8,169	12,793
1972	4,626	8,976	13,602
1973	5,078	9,531	14,609
1974	5,284	12,444	17,728
1975	6,143	11,264	17,407

Sources: Civil Service Commission; U.S. Congress, House, Committee on Appropriations, *Legislative Branch Appropriation Bill, 1976,* H. Rept. 94-208 to Accompany HR 6950, 94th Cong., 1st sess., 1975.

and to use special boards to select candidates for the positions.

Previously, the jobs were filled by the Postmaster General upon the recommendation of the representative from the district in which the vacancy was located, provided the representative belonged to the same party as the President. If the representative belong to the opposition party, the choice went to either of the state's senators, if they belonged to the President's party. If the state had no members of the President's party, the state's national committeeman from the President's party was entitled to chose a candidate.

Nixon's Postmaster General, Winton M. Blount, approved no patronage appointments to postal jobs after he took office early in 1969. Legislation placing the appointments under a merit system was soon introduced. The Postal Reorganization Act of 1970, (PL 91-375), which established the U.S. Postal Service, put an end to post office patronage and relieved members of both power and problems.

In the fiscal 1976 legislative branch appropriations bill, approved July 22, 1975, Congress ordered a study to see if up to 50 per cent of the elevator operator jobs could be abolished. Sen. Dewey F. Bartlett (R Okla.) pointed out that many Capitol Hill elevators were automatic and did not need operators. He said that if half the jobs could be abolished patronage salaries could be cut by $540,000.[49]

For years a leading spokesman for patronage reform in the House was Rep. Joel T. Broyhill (R Va.), who was besieged by office-seekers from his suburban Washington district. In addition to the inconvenience of having his office used as an employment agency, Broyhill complained that patronage jobs on Capitol Hill were unfair to those who held them. He called the patronage market "cruel, costly and ugly" and said that all 31 of the patronage employees he had sponsored in 1954 were dismissed the next year when control of the House passed from the Republicans to the Democrats.[50]

Congressional defenders of patronage argue that most jobs remaining under the system require no special ability or training; and because the pay is rather low, they do not attract persons with families to support. They point out also that job turnover is so high that most patronage employees tend to leave within a short time regardless of what happens to their party in congressional elections.

Opponents of patronage point out that it disregards not only merit but also financial need. Critics note that many members of Congress fill patronage slots with the children of influential people from their districts. Some do seek out and sponsor disadvantaged scholarship students in the District of Columbia, but there seems to be little evidence that this is a widespread practice.

Appointments to Service Academies

One remnant of the patronage system has not only survived over the years but has continued to expand. Congressional appointees to the three major service academies account for more than three-fourths of their combined enrollment.

Until 1902, the privilege of appointing candidates for admission to the service academies was enjoyed only by representatives, the idea being to apportion academy enrollment on a national population basis. Each congressional district was to supply one appointee every four years, thus giving each class maximum geographic variance and allowing equal numbers of appointments from variously populated areas.

Eventually, senators and representatives alike were authorized to have as many as five appointees enrolled in each academy at one time. In December 1975 this added up to about 9,950 appointments in an enrollment total of 12,662, or nearly 79 per cent.[51]

In appointing young men and women for cadetships at the academies—U.S. Military Academy, West Point, N.Y.; U.S. Naval Academy, Annapolis, Md.; and U.S. Air Force Academy, Colorado Springs, Colo.—members of Congress have wide leeway in making their choices. Most senators and many representatives do not personally handle the screening of candidates. The job of selecting nominees usually falls to an administrative assistant in the senator's state office or the representative's home district.

Selection Methods. It was in 1964 that Congress set the quota of five cadet appointees in each academy at any one time. Either of two methods of selecting appointees may be used, the choice being left to the member.

● The general listing method allows for only minimal congressional influence in the selection. A list of as many as 10 candidates is submitted to each of the respective academies. Scholastic and physical tests are given the candidates and the one making the best combined performance wins the appointment.

● The principal-alternate method allows the member far greater discretion over the appointment. Again, a list of as many as 10 candidates is submitted to the academy, but each candidate is ranked in order of the member's preference. If the first-preference candidate meets the academic and physical entrance requirements, then that candidate wins the appointment regardless of how well the other candidates perform. If the first-preference candidate does not fulfill the entrance requirements, then the first-alternate is considered and so on down the list until a qualified candidate is found.

The principal-alternate method may be used by a member when he feels that a particular young person has outstanding potentialities in some area that is not weighted heavily in the entrance requirements, such as creative talents or outstanding athletic ability. Of course, the method can be used also to ensure the appointment of a member's relative, if qualified, or the relative of a friend.

Requirements. Before candidates can be considered for appointment, they must submit to scholastic, physical and medical testing. No candidate may be older than 21. He or she must be of "good moral character" and must never have been married. Candidates must also be United States citizens, unless they are entering one of the academies on a special program for foreigners. Persons already in military service who wish to attend one of the academies may take the annual competitive examination. If they score well they will be appointed.

Other Academies. A member of Congress also may nominate as many as 10 persons for appointment to the Merchant Marine Academy, New London, Conn. The candidates must take a nationally competitive examination to win appointment. No nominee on any member's list is guaranteed appointment. The highest-scoring candidates are appointed to the freshman class, regardless of who nominated them. No congressional appointments are made to the U.S. Coast Guard Academy, New London, Conn. Interested applicants contact the academy and take national examinations.

Evolution of Academy Appointments

West Point. The system of congressional appointments to the three major service academies had an obscure beginning in 1802 when Congress established what is today the U.S. Military Academy at West Point, N.Y. Congress envisioned the academy as an institution that would serve a dual purpose—teach cadets to be both officers and engineers.

Out of the initial class of 10, three had come from civilian backgrounds, the others from the Army. The three civilians were recommended by representatives and appointed by the Secretary of War. The course of study was unstructured, lasting for as long as a cadet cared to stay. Discipline was virtually nonexistent; compensation consisted of $16 a month and two daily rations.

Congress took an active interest in the academy when the United States declared war in 1812. Bold plans were drafted that year to create a standing Army of 145,000 men. But Congress had ignored requests from West Point for additional funds, and by 1812 the academy had graduated only 71 cadets.

After 1812, enrollment was expanded to 250, and representatives were told they should appoint only men between the ages of 14 and 20 who had excelled in their preparatory schooling. Officials in Washington, however, had no intention of limiting appointments to these specifications. Thus the academy had cadets ranging in age from 12 to 25. A Pennsylvania boy who had only one arm was appointed, and a married cadet kept his wife in a boarding house just outside the post and visited her every night.

As the prestige of West Point grew, increasing numbers of young men vied for appointments. By 1820 the President made all appointments to the academy with recommendations from members of Congress and the Secretary of War. Consideration for appointment was based on a boy's poverty and the service that his family had rendered the nation.

Naval Academy. In 1839 after years of demanding an academy to match the Army's facility at West Point, the Navy started an eight-month school in Philadelphia. Under pressure from the Secretary of the Navy, Congress in 1845 established a permanent facility at an old Army post called Fort Severn in Annapolis, Md. Money was appropriated the following year and a formalized curriculum was drafted. For the next seven years, all midshipmen at Annapolis were selected by the Secretary of the Navy from the ranks of enlisted men. Not until 1852 did Congress include the Naval Academy in the patronage appointment system. Every member of the House was allowed one appointed cadet in each academy at one time.

In 1862, after the Naval Academy had been moved temporarily to Newport, R.I., when Annapolis was threatened by the Confederacy, a representative's quota was raised to two appointments to both the Military and Naval Academies. After the Civil War, however, quotas were again cut to one per representative.

World War I. The demand for qualified officers in both the Navy and Army continued to grow during the years preceding World War I. In 1900 representatives were given two appointive positions and, for the first time, senators and territorial delegates also were granted appointment privileges—a quota of two per member at each academy. Quotas were increased to three in 1917 and to five, two years later. By 1919 the enrollment at the two academies was being filled also by appointments from the District of Columbia (5), from the ranks of enlisted men (100) and by presidential selections (25).

World War II. After the First World War, appointments were cut back to three a member (1923) and the other appointive categories also were reduced. By 1928, however, congressional quotas were again hiked to four. Presidential appointments were increased to 40 and for the first time (officially), the Vice President was given two places to fill.

During the 1930s, the number of congressional appointments to the military academies rose and fell in proportion to the size of military appropriations bills. But after the United States became involved in World War II, appointments were raised to five a member. After the war, the number was again cut to four.

Air Force Academy. When the Air Force Academy was established in 1954, it received a period of grace from the traditional patronage appointment system. During the Academy's first four years in Colorado Springs, candidates were selected for appointment under a strict geographic quota system. Each state was alloted a percentage of appointments in proportion to its population. Members of Congress were to draw up lists of aspiring candidates who were then tested on a statewide basis. The most highly qualified candidates from each state were admitted. By 1958, however, the Air Force Academy was using an appointment system similar to those in use at West Point and Annapolis except that more of the air cadets were con-

gressional appointees. By 1975, 85 per cent of the cadets were appointed by members.[52]

Changes in 1964. Congress approved legislation in 1964 providing for a doubling of the enrollment at West Point and the Air Force Academy by 1971 (Annapolis already had a substantially larger enrollment than the other two schools). The bill called for an eventual increase of the maximum capacity of each of the two academies from 2,529 cadets to 4,417. To provide for the increase, members of Congress were again given a five-cadet quota. Another section of the bill provided for appointment of the best qualified 150 of the "alternates" who failed of appointment under the principal-alternate system.

Women Cadets. The military procurement authorization bill for fiscal 1976, approved by Congress in June 1975, included an amendment to allow women to enter the three service academies. The legislation did not change any procedure for appointment, nor did it set quotas for women cadets. The academies began accepting women in 1976.

Patronage Reform. In 1969 Sen. Thomas J. Dodd (D Conn.) sponsored legislation to remove all academy appointments from the patronage system. It provided that any person desiring an appointment would be allowed to take a national examination, but that only the most qualified from the entire field would be appointed. The bill died in the Senate Armed Services Committee.

Academy appointments are the last sizeable part of the congressional patronage system, and members appear reluctant to let it slip away from them.

Legislative Budget

The legislative branch, like any government department or agency, operates on a budget, and the expenditures proposed in the budget have to be authorized and appropriated by Congress. However, there are some distinctive differences.

The legislative branch appropriations bill is prepared by Congress and is not subject to revision by the Office of Management and Budget. Nor is there a central point at which the legislative budget is screened on Capitol Hill. The clerk of the House and the secretary of the Senate are responsible for preparing appropriations requests for offices within their respective jurisdictions. In practice, they do little more than pass along requests submitted to them by others.

Legislative budget requests are reviewed by the Legislative Appropriations Subcommittee of each house. Traditionally, much of the legislative budget has gone unchallenged in both the Senate and House. But this acceptance became less prevalent in the late 1960s and the 1970s as many expenditures were subjected to closer scrutiny. Even once routine expenditures, such as for mail allowances or staff assistance, generated controversy as voters grew more disenchanted with government spending. Large congressional projects, such as construction of new office buildings, always generated considerable controversy and opposition in Congress.

The power of the Appropriations Committees to control the legislative budget, although considerable, has been less than absolute because large sums, such as salaries, are almost uncontrollable and because some items, such as office allowances, are authorized by other committees and by the full Congress and must be paid when the obligations are made by individual members.

(Continued on p. 483)

Legislative Branch Appropriations, Fiscal 1955-1976

Fiscal Year[1]	Senate	House of Representatives	Joint Items	Architect of The Capitol	Botanic Garden	Library of Congress	Government Printing Office	General Accounting Office[2]	Total[3]
1955	$14,665,223	$27,424,770	$1,542,225	$6,115,800	$223,100	$9,399,636	$11,325,000	($31,981,000)	$70,695,754
1956	16,315,720	31,123,305	2,542,120	21,163,890	246,000	9,767,937	11,650,000	(31,981,000)	92,808,972
1957	21,226,615	35,499,240	2,598,395	34,998,200	253,600	10,637,608	12,190,400	34,000,000	117,404,058
1958	22,271,890	37,827,705	2,638,065	17,009,000	275,500	11,647,500	13,175,000	36,050,000	104,844,660
1959	23,473,180	39,337,765	2,468,936	30,638,225	972,500	12,411,591	13,995,190	37,000,000	123,297,387
1960	26,406,345	42,398,065	2,929,430	27,412,900	327,500	14,302,790	15,020,350	41,800,000	128,797,380
1961	26,643,940	42,492,485	3,508,785	25,493,700	352,300	15,230,000	15,749,200	41,150,000	129,470,410
1962	28,421,840	47,856,835	4,090,090	19,256,600	489,000	17,193,700	18,124,000	43,000,000	135,432,065
1963	29,601,160	48,150,725	4,255,355	18,252,500	452,000	19,431,930	26,333,600	43,900,000	146,477,270
1964	30,675,350	50,131,550	6,271,369	33,279,500	454,500	20,488,800	26,992,000	45,700,000	168,293,069
1965	31,397,625	53,777,945	6,319,415	22,010,800	500,000	23,333,100[4]	26,062,000	46,900,000	210,300,885
1966	36,379,790	66,414,730	8,856,977	25,640,100	467,000	25,905,700	26,329,000	46,900,000	189,993,297
1967	39,655,180	77,676,145	9,716,988	14,281,000	504,600	29,974,100	42,655,900	48,500,000	214,463,913
1968	44,125,205	80,368,670	11,311,660	15,308,600	584,500	37,141,400	34,059,000	52,800,000	275,699,035
1969	47,082,247	85,039,420	12,711,299	15,614,700	565,000	40,638,000	39,000,000	57,500,000	298,678,396
1970	54,837,660	104,813,635	13,233,322	24,036,100	599,800	43,856,300	39,950,000	63,000,000	344,733,817
1971	60,929,464	110,526,455	14,558,775	36,568,126	672,800	50,396,600	65,382,000	74,020,000	413,104,220
1972	76,034,419	136,768,970	38,428,390	96,553,200	763,350	68,462,250	56,329,900	89,208,000	562,548,479
1973	82,046,675	145,266,770	26,151,320	102,574,500	811,300	79,104,450	88,874,100	98,065,000	622,894,115
1974	97,453,593	162,511,395	36,315,230	52,374,300	884,700	86,820,450	112,871,000	109,450,000	658,680,668
1975	111,135,870	185,546,445	45,789,324	68,288,500	1,018,000	98,990,000	129,065,000	124,989,000	764,822,139
1976	118,837,000	206,407,000	54,796,000	40,755,000	1,205,000	116,231,000	145,266,000	135,930,000	827,547,000[5]

Source: Senate Appropriations Committee.

1. 1972-75 includes supplementals.
2. Until fiscal 1968, the General Accounting Office was not regularly funded in the Legislative Branch Appropriations Act. GAO figures in parentheses are for years when appropriations were provided in other bills.
3. Beginning in fiscal 1969, the total includes funds (not included in individual for Senate, House, etc.) appropriated to liquidate contract authority. Contract authority allows agencies to enter into contracts ahead of appropriations, but requires appropriations in following years to pay off (liquidate) the contracts.
4. Includes $149,000 as a supplemental appropriation for fiscal 1964.
5. Includes $6,485,000 for the Office of Technology Assessment.

(Continued from p. 481)

A second barrier to tighter budget control in the legislative branch is the traditional rule of comity, by which each chamber is considered sovereign over its own affairs. Only rarely will one chamber interfere with a spending proposal for the other chamber.

A recent case in which the rule of comity was broken occurred in 1968 when the House of Representatives rejected a Senate-passed bill authorizing acquisition of land for future expansion of the Dirksen Office Building.

The accompanying box shows funds appropriated for the legislative branch over a period of 22 years. The appropriations provide funds not only for Congress itself but also for the major congressional supporting agencies, such as the Library of Congress, the General Accounting Office and others. These are the agencies most commonly funded in the legislative branch appropriations acts. Figures in the table represent regular appropriations; sums provided in supplemental appropriations have not been included except as indicated in footnotes. *(Table, p. 482)*

Footnotes

1. James C. Wright, *You and Your Congressman* (Coward-McCann, 1965), p. 17.
2. *ADA Special Report: Advantages of an Incumbent Seeking Re-Election* (Americans for Democratic Action, Aug. 25, 1975).
3. Clem Miller, *Member of the House: Letters of a Congressman,* ed. John W. Baker (Charles Scribner's Sons, 1962), p. 66.
4. *The New York Times,* Oct. 25, 1969.
5. David S. Broder, "Portrait of a Typical Congressman," *The New York Times Magazine,* Oct. 7, 1962, p. 31.
6. James Madison, *Notes of Debates in the Federal Convention of 1787,* with an Introduction by Adrienne Koch (Ohio University Press, 1966), p. 198.
7. Congressional Quarterly, *1973 Almanac,* p. 780.
8. Congressional Quarterly, *1974 Almanac,* pp. 663-65.
9. Congressional Quarterly, *Weekly Report,* Aug. 9, 1975, p. 1803.
10. Congressional Quarterly, *Weekly Report,* Aug. 2, 1975, p. 1684.
11. *Staff Report of the President's Panel on Federal Compensation* (Government Printing Office, 1976), p. 60.
12. From interview with staff of Senate Disbursing Office, Nov. 17, 1975.
13. From interview with staff of the Committee on House Administration, Nov. 13, 1975.
14. Congressional Quarterly, *Weekly Report,* June 21, 1975, p. 1292.
15. *Congressional Record,* 94th Cong., 1st sess., Oct. 30, 1975, p. S 18983.
16. Congressional Quarterly, *Weekly Report,* June 14, 1975, pp. 1235-36; June 21, 1975, p. 1294.
17. U.S., Congress, Joint Committee on Congressional Operations, *Congressional Handbook-U.S. House of Representatives,* 93rd Cong., 2nd sess., November 1974, p. 23; *Congressional Handbook-U.S. Senate,* 94th Cong., 1st sess., July 1975, p. 22.
18. *Congressional Handbook-U.S. Senate,* p. 3.
19. Congressional Quarterly, *Weekly Report,* Feb. 22, 1975, p. 411.
20. Congressional Quarterly, *Weekly Report,* June 21, 1975, pp. 1291-93.
21. *Ibid.,* p. 1291.
22. *ADA Special Report,* p. 2.
23. *Ibid.,* p. 3.
24. *Ibid.*
25. *The Washington Star,* Sept. 22, 1975.
26. Americans for Democratic Action, press release of Aug. 25, 1975.
27. William Taaffe, "The Costs of Keeping Congress Exceed Other Inflation," *The Washington Star,* Nov. 12, 1975.

28. *Ibid.*
29. Robert Walters, "How Some Congressmen Tap Extra Funds," *Parade,* Aug. 24, 1975.
30. *Ibid.*
31. Honoraria figures used in this section were taken from Congressional Quarterly, *Weekly Report,* July 31, 1976. pp. 2050-2060.
32. Congressional Quarterly, *Weekly Report,* April 24, 1976, p. 997.
33. Congressional Quarterly, *1973 Almanac,* p. 723.
34. *Ibid.,* p. 724.
35. U.S., Congress, Senate, Committee on Appropriations, *Legislative Branch Appropriations, 1976,* S. Rept. 94-262 to Accompany H.R. 6950, 94th Cong., 1st sess., 1975, p. 25.
36. William L. Safire, *The New Language of Politics: A Dictionary of Catchwords, Slogans and Political Usage,* rev. ed. (Collier Books, 1972), p. 196.
37. Congressional Quarterly, *Weekly Report,* July 17, 1976, pp. 1883-1902.
38. Congressional Quarterly, *Weekly Report,* May 18, 1974, p. 1289.
39. Congressional Quarterly, *Weekly Report,* Aug. 23, 1975, p. 1837.
40. Edward Stephens, "Bill Holds Tax Break for Congress," *The Washington Star,* Nov. 23, 1975.
41. From interviews with staff of the Committee on House Administration, House Sergeant at Arms and Senate Disbursing Office, March 17, 1976.
42. Congressional Quarterly, *Weekly Report,* March 9, 1974, p. 638.
43. Congressional Quarterly, *Weekly Report,* July 12, 1975, p. 1475.
44. Safire, *New Language,* p. 483.
45. Congressional Quarterly, *Weekly Report,* April 10, 1970, p. 966.
46. Congressional Quarterly, *Weekly Report,* Dec. 13, 1975, p. 2719.
47. Interview with Capitol Police Chief James M. Powell, Sept. 29, 1975.
48. Employment figures for 1975 are taken from fiscal 1976 budget hearings before the House and Senate Legislative Branch Appropriations Subcommittees.
49. *The Washington Star,* July 10, 1975.
50. Congressional Quarterly, *Weekly Report,* April 10, 1970, p. 969.
51. Enrollment figures for December 1975 were provided by the Washington offices for the three academies. West Point had 4,113 cadets with about 75 per cent congressional appointees; Annapolis had 4,302 with 76 per cent; and Colorado Springs had 4,247 with 85 per cent.
52. *Ibid.*

Selected Bibliography

Books

Ambrose, Stephen. *Duty, Honor, Country: A History of West Point.* Baltimore: Johns Hopkins Press, 1966.

Beise, J. Arthur. *The Brass Factories.* Washington: Public Affairs Press, 1969.

MacCloskey, Monro. *How to Qualify for the Service Academies.* New York: Richards Rosen Press Inc., 1964.

Madison, James. *Notes of Debates in the Federal Convention of 1787.* Introduction by Adrienne Koch. Athens, Ohio: Ohio University Press, 1966.

Miller, Clem. *Member of the House: Letters of a Congressman.* Edited by John W. Baker. New York: Charles Scribner's Sons, 1962.

Ripley, Randall B. *Congress: Process and Policy.* New York: W. W. Norton & Co. Inc., 1975.

Safire, William L. *The New Language of Politics: A Dictionary of Catchwords, Slogans and Political Usage.* rev. ed. New York: Collier Books, 1972.

Tacheron, Donald G., and Udall, Morris K. *The Job of the Congressman.* Indianapolis: Bobbs-Merrill, 1966.

Wright, James C. *You and Your Congressman.* New York: Coward-McCann, 1965.

Articles

ADA Special Report: Advantages of an Incumbent Seeking Re-election. Washington: Americans for Democratic Action, Aug. 25, 1975.

Boeckel, Richard M. "Wages and Hours of Members of Congress." *Editorial Research Reports,* Oct. 13, 1937, pp. 297-320.

Broder, David S. "Portrait of a Typical Congressman." *The New York Times Magazine,* Oct. 7, 1962, pp. 31, 97-99.

"Congressional Perquisites and Fair Elections: The Case of the Franking Privilege." *Yale Law Journal,* April 1974, pp. 1055-99.

Stephens, Edward. "Bill Holds Tax Break for Congress." *The Washington Star,* Nov. 23, 1975.

Taaffe, William. "The Costs of Keeping Congress Exceed Other Inflation." *The Washington Star,* Nov. 12, 1975.

Walters, Robert. "How Some Congressmen Tap Extra Funds." *Parade,* Aug. 24, 1975.

Government Publications

U.S. Congress. House. *Report of the Clerk of the House of Representatives.* Washington: Government Printing Office, 19—.

U.S. Congress. House. Committee on Post Office and Civil Service. Special Ad Hoc Subcommittee, *Use of the Congressional Frank, Hearings on H.R. 3180.* Committee Serial 93-1, 93rd Cong., 1st sess., 1973.

U.S. Congress. Joint Committee on Congressional Operations. *Congressional Handbook-U.S. House of Representatives.* 93rd Cong., 2nd sess., November 1974.

——. *Congressional Handbook-U.S. Senate.* 94th Cong., 1st sess., July 1975.

——. *Court Proceedings and Actions of Vital Interest to the Congress: The Franking Privilege of Members of Congress. Special Report, Pursuant to Section 402(a)(2) of the Legislative Reorganization Act of 1970.* 92nd Cong., 2nd sess., 1972.

U.S. Congress. Senate. *Report of the Secretary of the Senate.* Washington: Government Printing Office, 19—.

U.S. Congress. Senate. Committee on Appropriations. *Legislative Branch Appropriations, 1976.* S. Rept. 94-262 to Accompany H.R. 6950, 94th Cong., 1st sess., 1975.

U.S. Congress. Senate. Committee on Armed Services. *Report Relating to the Nomination and Selection of Candidates for Appointment to the Military, Naval and Air Force Academies.* 88th Cong., 2nd sess., Feb. 6, 1964.

U.S. Congress. Senate. Committee on Post Office and Civil Service. *Congressional Franking Reform: A Compilation of Legislative History.* Committee Print, 93rd Cong., 2nd sess., 1974.

U.S. Congress. Senate. Committee on Rules and Administration. Ad Hoc Subcommittee to Consider the Reimbursement of Actual Travel Expense of Senators. *Travel Expenses of Members of the Senate; Hearings on S.3231.* 92nd Cong., 2nd sess., 1972.

Supporting Organizations

In addition to their staffs, committees, facilities, privileges and the Library of Congress, senators and representatives are backed by a number of other supporting organizations and activities that help keep Capitol Hill running. These include the General Accounting Office, the Office of Technology Assessment, the Capitol Police, congressional pages and student interns, and Congress' own attempt at a diary, the *Congressional Record*.

The support forces, along with other institutions of Congress, often do not operate smoothly. Members have begun to re-examine their own institutions in an effort to improve them.

General Accounting Office

The General Accounting Office (GAO) is an arm of the legislative branch that was created to oversee the expenditures of the executive branch. Since it was established in 1921, the duties of the GAO have been expanded from routine audits of the accounts of executive branch departments to probing analyses of program management and planning, and often to controversial investigations of how government agencies are spending the taxpayers' money.

The GAO has been called the watchdog of Congress by those who support its actions and the "one-eyed watchdog" by critics who feel it is too responsive to political pressures. The agency has increasingly found itself in the center of controversy between Congress and the executive branch. GAO investigative audits have triggered hundreds of well-publicized news stories about everything from multimillion-dollar cost overruns for a weapons system to the remodeling of a Cabinet member's office.

The scope of the GAO has expanded since 1921, but its focus remains on helping Congress. Comptroller General Elmer B. Staats, the fifth head of the GAO, wrote in his annual report for fiscal 1974: "We view all of our work as being of assistance to the Congress in one way or another in carrying out its legislative and oversight functions. We, therefore, make every effort to direct our staff resources to work that produces information on federal programs and agency operations that will be useful to the Congress and in areas which, in our judgment, will fulfill the greatest apparent need and benefit to the government."[1]

GAO Activities. When Congress needs information about a program that will require additional funds, the GAO is contacted to conduct an investigation. When the Appropriations Committees of the Senate and House are working on the annual appropriations bills, GAO staff members act as consultants. The audits and management-analysis reports done by the GAO may be used as reference material. If an area of government activity is of particular interest to a committee or member, the GAO may be asked to make a special investigation.

The activities of the GAO are wide-ranging. Late in 1972, the GAO confirmed the existence of a secret "slush fund" at the Committee to Re-elect the President, a disclosure which spurred the Watergate investigations. In fiscal 1970, at the request of Congress, the GAO sent investigating teams to Vietnam to study refugee-camp management by the United States and the South Vietnamese, performance under U.S. construction contracts, and black-market pilfering of American goods from military warehouses. GAO accountants in 1974 revealed controversial details of a U.S.-Soviet wheat deal. And in 1974 the GAO reviewed the federal revenue-sharing program.

In addition to the routine auditing of all major department budgets, the GAO has monitored federal election campaigns and their funding and has reviewed Medicare and Medicaid programs. The GAO evaluates health maintenance organizations, studies water pollution control, provides advice to Congress on pending legislation, and examines military procurement contracts, foreign aid and domestic social programs. For years, the GAO divided its activities into military and civilian categories, and devoted about half of its staff time to defense matters.

Congress keeps giving the GAO new responsibilities. The GAO listed 24 public laws enacted in fiscal 1974 that were related to it.[2] The list did not include GAO appropriations, which totaled $109,450,000 in fiscal 1974. The GAO budget rose to $135,930,000 for fiscal 1976. *(Legislative Branch Appropriations, p. 480)*

Organization. The GAO is headed by the comptroller general of the United States, a presidential appointee with a single 15-year term, who is assisted by the deputy comptroller. *(Box, Comptrollers General, p. 486)* The office is organized by function, with most of its divisions supervised by assistant comptrollers general.

Comptrollers General

To isolate the General Accounting Office from political influence, the Budget and Accounting Act of 1921 provided that the comptroller general and the assistant comptroller general would be appointed for 15-year terms and could serve no more than one term. The appointments would be made by the President, subject to Senate confirmation, and the appointees could be removed from office only by joint resolution of Congress for a specific cause or through impeachment proceedings. In 1971 the title of assistant comptroller general was changed to deputy comptroller general.

Comptrollers General

John R. McCarl	July 1, 1921—June 30, 1936
Fred H. Brown	April 11, 1939—June 19, 1940
Lindsay C. Warren	Nov. 1, 1940—April 30, 1954
Joseph V. Campbell	Dec. 14, 1954—July 31, 1965
Elmer B. Staats	March 8, 1966—

Assistant Comptrollers General

Lurtin R. Ginn	July 1, 1921—Nov. 11, 1930
Richard N. Elliott	March 9, 1931—April 30, 1943
Frank L. Yates	May 1, 1943—June 29, 1953
Frank H. Weitzel	Oct. 12, 1953—Jan. 17, 1969*

Deputy Comptroller General

Robert F. Keller	Oct. 3, 1969—

* Weitzel served as acting comptroller general in the period between the resignation of Campbell and the appointment of Staats—time not counted as a part of his 15-year term as assistant comptroller general.

Source: *Annual Report of the Comptroller General of the United States, 1974.*

The GAO had a total of 5,188 employees on June 30, 1974. About 69 per cent were members of the professional staff. Thirty per cent of the professionals were not accountants but were trained in other disciplines.[3] More than 2,000 employees were assigned to GAO field operations. The next largest division, with over 600 employees, was concerned with routine checks and audits relating to the billions of dollars expended by the government each year for commercial transportation.[4]

At the request of Congress, 98 GAO staff members were assigned to the staffs of 29 congressional committees and subcommittees for at least part of fiscal 1974. In all, about 27 per cent of the GAO professional staff's time during the year was spent directly assisting Congress.[5]

Work Volume. The accomplishments of the GAO in fiscal 1974 included the following:[6]

● Performed 1,700 audits of federal programs and activities in the United States and 58 other countries.

● Issued 1,079 reports, including 553 to Congress and 322 to executive agencies, plus 204 reports by the GAO's Office of Federal Elections.

● Completed 221 audits of political committees and worked on 197 others.

● Audited transportation charges for four million freight shipments and 2.1 million passenger movements, for which the government paid $1.5-billion.

● Collected $9.5-million in transportation overpayments (out of $11.3-million stated against carriers), and settled for $2.1-million almost 10,000 claims by carriers.

● Testified 61 times before congressional committees.

● Prepared 533 reports on pending legislation for congressional committees—325 for the Senate and 208 for the House.

● Settled 8,727 claims against the United States for $142.4-million, and settled 26,580 claims made by the United States resulting in the collection of $4.9-million.

● Disposed of 4,716 legal matters, including more than 1,000 procurement bid protests.

In addition, according to the GAO's annual report, the adoption of numerous GAO recommendations by Congress and the executive agencies saved an estimated $562-million in federal expenditures during fiscal 1974. *(Box, p. 487)*

Background of GAO

The authority and influence now enjoyed by the General Accounting Office have been gradually attained. The GAO and the Office of Management and Budget (OMB), known originally as the Bureau of the Budget, both date back to the Budget and Accounting Act of 1921. The OMB, an arm of the executive branch, was given the responsibility of planning how and where federal funds should be spent. It was the function of the GAO, as an agency of the legislative branch, to provide Congress with an independent review of executive expenditures.

The Budget and Accounting Act transferred to the GAO the powers formerly vested in the comptroller of the Treasury and six Treasury auditors. The general audit function, the settlement of claims and the power to review methods of disbursing funds, which were shifted by the 1921 Act from the executive to the legislative branch, gave Congress new means to guard against lax or improper spending of government funds.

The comptroller general was empowered to investigate "all matters relating to the receipt, disbursement and application of public funds...making recommendations looking to greater economy or efficiency in public expenditures." "All claims and demands" for and against the government also were to be settled and adjusted by the GAO. As routine procedure, the GAO was required to review the adequacy of accounting systems in all departments.

Early Development of GAO

Although the GAO was established primarily to audit the books of government agencies, some members of Congress pointed out during House debate on the bill in 1921 that the agency would have other important functions, especially reporting on program efficiency. What the legislation purported to do was to give the House and Senate a tool by which each chamber could better control the spending of federal funds once they had been appropriated. With the GAO working as an independent auditing agency responsible to Congress, the audit became an instrument for preventing waste and extravagance as well as fraud.

Despite expression of high hopes by many members, the value of the GAO's work was limited in the early years. Auditing was restricted almost entirely to Washington. Departments and agencies sent the original copies of their financial documents to the GAO, and checking was carried out by a centralized desk audit. Major emphasis was placed on detecting illegal expenditures and errors in arithmetic. Only limited numbers of audits in the field were made before World War II.

Congress was generally enthusiastic about the work that the GAO did accomplish, but members made few requests for investigations. When requests were made, the GAO at times tended to be overzealous. (Critics of the agency still maintain that it spends too much time and money on investigating projects that have relatively small budgets while virtually ignoring huge expenditures in more "politically sensitive" areas.) During an investigation of the Tennessee Valley Authority in 1939, TVA Comptroller E. L. Kohler was highly critical of the GAO. He told the House-Senate investigating committee:

"It has long been recognized that the Comptroller General regards himself not as an accountant but as a glorified watchdog, and that he has surrounded himself with a narrow-visioned legal staff that recognizes no superior except a decision of the Supreme Court directly in point. In my opinion, he has more than once been sadly out of line with the spirit of the Budget and Accounting Act of 1921....

"A review of his report (1934) and frequent contact this year with the (GAO) field staff, convinced me quickly and decisively that the field staff had made no real audit originally and had made none since; the staff has consisted of persons styled as 'investigators' who have had little accounting training or experience; and the 1934 report was in no sense an audit report, but rather a disorderly miscellany of fact and fancy that could succeed only in misleading the reader, regardless of his skill in auditing, accounting or sleuthing."[7]

Grants of Additional Authority

During the middle and late 1940s, the GAO staff swelled to almost 15,000 persons. Wartime expenditures created masses of vouchers and routine claims that needed to be processed by the GAO. A need arose also for clarification of GAO authority. Disagreement between the General Accounting Office and such government corporations as the TVA were in part responsible for the passage of the Government Corporation Control Act of 1945. Its primary purpose was to bring government corporations under the effective control of Congress, thus plugging another loophole in congressional supervision of government spending.

Provisions of the 1945 act required the GAO to conduct its audits at the location of a government corporation's place of business. The extent of the audit was left to the discretion of the comptroller general, who in 1957-61, for example, ordered a complete study of TVA's methods, procedures, programs and management approaches as well as a straight audit. (A government corporation is funded at least in part by government money but is managed as if it were a private enterprise.) In 1974 Congress began to require audits of government corporations every three years rather than annually.

Legislative Reorganization Act of 1946. In 1946 the GAO was accorded new powers intended to facilitate its efforts to bring about greater government efficiency. Recognizing the financial expertise of the GAO, Congress in the Legislative Reorganization Act of 1946, gave the GAO the authority to "make an expenditure analysis of each agency in the executive branch of the government (including corporations), which, in the opinion of the Comptroller General, will enable Congress to determine where public funds have been economically and efficiently administered."

Anti-Kickback Act. Another major piece of legislation in 1946 was the Anti-Kickback Act (later amended by Public Law 86-695, approved Sept. 2, 1960). The act empowered the GAO to "inspect the plants and to audit the books and records of any prime contractor or subcontractor engaged in the performance of a negotiated contract with the government."

Property Audits. When the General Services Administration was established in 1949 to manage the government's property holdings, the duties of the GAO were again expanded. The agency was empowered to "audit all types of property accounts," which "as far as practicable shall be conducted at the places where the property or records of the executive agencies are kept and shall include, but not necessarily be limited to, an evaluation of the effectiveness of internal controls and audits."

Accounting and Auditing Act. A major piece of legislation concerning the GAO was the Accounting and Auditing Act of 1950. The act clarified in specific terms the existing audit authority of the GAO. Where the 1921 act had been vague, the 1950 measure fully outlined the authority granted to, and the restrictions placed on, the agency.

GAO Savings

A primary goal of the General Accounting Office is to eliminate wasteful practices throughout the federal government and thereby to improve program efficiency and save tax dollars. The GAO estimated that adoption of some of its recommendations saved $562-million in fiscal 1974 alone. The amount was more than five times the GAO's appropriations for the same year.

However, Comptroller General Elmer B. Staats cautioned: "It isn't really possible to determine the full effect of GAO activities.... For the most part, actions taken on our recommendations cannot be measured in dollar savings.... Even more important, in some ways, are the recommendations we make that may not result in dollar savings but do lead to increased effectiveness of government programs."

As an example, Staats cited a GAO study recommending removal of obstacles which were creating serious highway hazards throughout the states. The GAO estimated that the expenditure of $375-million for the improvements, appropriated in 1973, should save 1,450 lives and prevent 22,000 injuries a year.

In its fiscal 1974 report to Congress, the GAO described the "nondollar accomplishments" of 35 federal programs or procedures—all previously recommended by the GAO—which had "improved day-to-day operations at federal, state and local levels" or had had "a direct favorable effect on the well-being of individual citizens." The accomplishments included protection of consumers from defective pesticides, improved home ownership opportunities, coordination of natural gas reserve data and the return of unclaimed savings bonds to veterans and other individuals.

Source: *Annual Report of the Comptroller General of the United States, 1974.*

By 1950, the GAO was legally in a position to develop its "comprehensive" audit approach. This meant that it could go beyond questions of the legality and propriety of expenditures into other aspects of management. It could reach into nearly every phase of government spending with an eye to efficiency.

Cost-Benefit Studies. The Legislative Reorganization Act of 1970 expanded GAO authority by specifically empowering the comptroller general to make cost-benefit studies of government programs and activities, upon his own initiative or at the request of either chamber or any committee of Congress. The act also directed the comptroller general to assist committees in conducting cost-benefit studies themselves and in analyzing any such studies furnished by a federal agency. In addition, the comptroller general was directed to cooperate with the Secretary of the Treasury and the director of the Office of Management and Budget in developing a standardized information and data-processing system for budgetary and fiscal data.

Campaign Financing. For a brief time in the early 1970s, the GAO had some responsibility for political campaign financing and reporting. The Presidential Election Campaign Fund Act of 1971 (PL 92-178), which allowed individuals to designate one dollar of their annual income tax to support presidential campaigns, required the GAO to audit candidates' expenses and to certify the federal payments to which candidates were entitled. The Federal Election Campaign Act of 1971 (PL 92-225) required the GAO to supervise the disclosure of campaign funds, contributions and expenditures of presidential and vice presidential candidates, and to set regulations for the use of communications media in all federal elections.

The Federal Elections Campaign Act Amendments of 1974 (PL 93-443) transferred these functions, and gave additional responsibilities, to the new Federal Election Commision (FEC). *(Details, Campaign Financing, p. 544)*

Transportation Audits. Congress late in 1974 transferred from the GAO to the General Services Administration (GSA) the initial auditing of federal transportation bills and the recovery of overcharges. The change required the transfer of about 400 GAO employees to the GSA, with the first transfers taking place after July 1, 1975.

Budget Responsibilities. The Congressional Budget and Impoundment Control Act of 1974 (PL 93-344) specified numerous additional ways by which the GAO was to assist Congress in developing the annual federal budget. The act required the GAO to help congressional committees in evaluating government programs, and to provide information, services, facilities and personnel to the Congressional Budget Office (CBO). *(Details on CBO, p. 131)*

Main Functions of GAO

The General Accounting Office has five broad areas of responsibility—to initiate independently audits and reviews of agencies and programs, to establish accounting standards, provide legal opinions, settle claims for and against the government, and make studies at the request of Congress. Of GAO's 5,188 employees (as of June 30, 1974), 3,564 were classified as professionals—accountants and auditors, administrators, economists, attorneys, actuaries and specialists in several categories. An additional 335 GAO employees were classified as technical staff.[8]

Audit and Review

The basic function of the GAO is to audit agency and program spending and to review management effectiveness. The Budget and Accounting Act of 1921 stated that "the independent audit will...serve to inform Congress at all times as to the actual conditions surrounding the expenditure of public funds in every department of the government."

The GAO's audit approach is to review the organization, management and controls of each agency system; identify weaknesses; report on conditions found; and recommend improvements. Accordingly, the comptroller general orders selective reviews of management activities, financial transactions and accounts of 11 executive departments, about 60 independent agencies and commissions, and selected special programs.

Although the auditing and review functions of the GAO are expected to aid the respective departments, Congress also is indirectly benefited by every agency and project audit conducted. The findings of an audit may help Congress in exercising legislative oversight when considering requests by the executive branch. The audits may also provide congressional committees with information necessary to back up requests for further investigations of spending and management. At the same time, it has been asserted that Congress does not use the potentially valuable reports effectively.

The comptroller general often bases his choice of a selective audit on the interest of Congress in the subject or on whether consideration of proposed legislation will be aided by having authoritative information at the disposal of members. The GAO does not have to wait for its orders. *The New York Times* reported in 1975 that one-third of the investigations the GAO undertakes are initiated by the Office itself, not at the request of Congress.[9]

The authority to audit and review extends to most federal activities. However, there are forbidden areas. The agency has no authority to make analytical audits or reviews in six general areas—the Federal Reserve System, the Office of the Comptroller of the Currency, the operation of the Exchange Stabilization Fund in the Treasury Department, the Federal Land Bank System, presidential expenditures and most intelligence activities (FBI, CIA and military intelligence). However, in June 1976, the FBI agreed after seven months of discussions to allow the GAO to study its files and review its effectiveness in both crime-fighting and intelligence-gathering programs. A particular area in which the GAO's activity is limited is federal grants-in-aid to states for such projects as highway construction. Unless a special clause is included in the appropriations bill, the GAO has no authority to audit the handling of federal funds of this type by the states.

When making an audit, the GAO has the right to demand access to any documents, books, papers or records of any department or office not restricted. It has the same authority when auditing the accounts of private concerns that have been awarded negotiated contracts of $100,000 or more. Although the comptroller general has authority to demand these things, he does not have the general power to serve a subpoena to obtain records. Subpoenas must be obtained from congressional committees, which have subpoena power, or from the courts at the request of the Justice Department.

The GAO has asked repeatedly for legislation to empower it to sue in court for the furnishing of information or records considered necessary to its investigations. Other proposed bills would enable the comptroller general to sue in federal courts when his determinations differ from those of the Attorney General. But by and large the GAO has been given only limited legal powers in specific pieces of legislation.

Accounting Standards

The General Accounting Office not only conducts audits but also establishes accounting standards and management guidelines for all government departments and programs. The GAO prescribes the standards, helps the executive agencies to develop efficient accounting systems, and approves the systems when they are deemed adequate.

One criticism of this phase of the GAO's work is that there are no allowances for follow-up. The GAO can make all the recommendations it cares to, but it cannot require them to be put into effect. Once the GAO studies an agency or program and recommends changes, it can do no more. If Congress does not press for the suggested changes, the agency in question can go right on with inefficient management and improper accounting methods which may result in great expense to the taxpayer.

Legal Opinions

Attorneys working for GAO submitted 4,716 legal advisory opinions during fiscal 1974.[10] The bulk of legal work involves interpretations of the law as regards the extent of departmental or agency authority in the expenditure of public funds. Before undertaking new programs or executing contracts, department heads and disbursing officers may request advice from the GAO's legal staff. *(Box, Philadelphia Plan, this page)*

Settlement of Claims

As stated in the statues (31 U.S. Code 71), "All claims and demands whatever by the government or against it...shall be settled and adjusted in the General Accounting Office." The initial responsibility for collection of debts owed the government rests with the individual agency involved, but claims involving doubtful legal questions or claims that the agency has been unable to collect are referred to the GAO.

Congressional Studies

One of the ways in which the GAO gives Congress direct assistance is by making special investigative reports either at the request of Congress as a whole or at the request of committees or individual members. Of the 553 GAO reports completed for Congress in fiscal 1974, 145 were for the whole Congress, 167 for committees, and 241 for individual senators and representatives.[11] Many of the 98 GAO staff members who worked for Congress in fiscal 1974 are permanently assigned to various committees. Many additional GAO employees work on reports issued by special request of Congress.

The GAO increasingly has taken on the job of analyzing legislative proposals under consideration by committees of Congress. GAO staff members provide assistance in drafting bills, give technical advice and provide information based on ongoing work or previous GAO studies. According to estimates in the comptroller general's annual reports, the amount of GAO staff assistance devoted directly to Congress increased from 20 per cent in 1970 to 27 per cent in 1974. Many GAO studies are conducted in anticipation of congressional audits.

Philadelphia Plan

Comptroller General Elmer B. Staats used the power of his office in 1969 to challenge the Department of Labor, the Department of Justice and the President. The challenge involved a plan, first agreed to in Philadelphia, under which contractors on federally assisted construction projects were pledged to make every effort to hire a certain quota of minority-group workers.

The Philadelphia Plan was announced by the Labor Department in June 1969 and went into effect in September. Before the effective date, Comptroller General Staats ruled that the plan, though aimed to promote employment of blacks, would constitute discrimination in violation of the Civil Rights Act of 1964. Accordingly, Staats said he would sign pay releases to the contractors whether or not they met Labor Department hiring goals. Attorney General John N. Mitchell, on the other hand, denied that the Philadelphia Plan violated the law.

A controversy erupted on the floor of the Senate in December 1969 after the Appropriations Committee had added to a fiscal 1970 supplemental appropriations bill an amendment forbidding use of any federal funds through contracts or agreements which the comptroller general "holds to be in contravention of any federal statute." The Senate nevertheless accepted the amendment, whose effect would have been to nullify the Philadelphia Plan and give the comptroller general unprecedented power to interpret the law.

After President Nixon threatened to veto the bill, the House refused to accept the Senate amendment. The Senate later agreed to the deletion and the Philadelphia Plan continued in effect despite the objections of the comptroller general.

By March 1971, the Labor Department's Office of Federal Contract Compliance in Philadelphia had reported more than 50 instances in which building contractors were found in violation of the plan. The first cutoff of funds for a contractor not complying with the regulations was announced March 27, 1971.

Source: *Congress and the Nation, 1969-1972,* Vol. III (1973), pp. 497-98.

Criticism of GAO

A study of the GAO in 1970 by the Citizens Advocate Center, a public-interest law firm based in Washington, raised two basic questions about the GAO's increasing emphasis on serving as an information agency for Congress on popular issues: (1) Does the priority given to congressional requests diminish the GAO's ability to initiate and plan independent systematic audits and reviews of federal programs? (2) Does a close interdependence of the Office and Congress mean that the GAO must be responsive to the political power structure of Congress?

The study concluded that both questions might have to be answered in the affirmative. By anticipating congressional demands, the study said, the GAO was relinquishing its responsibility for planning independent audits of programs that might hold little interest for Congress but that were recipients of large amounts of federal money.[12]

Some critics of the GAO feel that Congress is to blame for the agency's weak points. They say that the GAO is only as strong as the Congress it serves. In some cases the GAO has been unable to do complete audits on certain projects because of bureaucratic power plays between branches of the government; and, critics add, because the comptroller general does not want to offend members of Congress who control or at least influence appropriations necessary to expand the agency.

Rep. William A. Steiger (R Wis.) said in 1975 that most members of the House make poor use of the GAO. "It's not used properly because there is no comprehensive, rational approach to how it should be used," Steiger said. "By and large, a congressman will tell GAO, 'Here's a problem, look at it and report back.' There's no understanding of the types of questions that should be asked or how programs should be evaluated."[13]

On the other hand, some members are accused—by their colleagues, not by GAO—of using the office all too skillfully. One is Sen. William Proxmire (D Wis.), who frequently calls for GAO audits and reports in his continual investigation of cost overruns and inefficiency in the Defense Department.

Proxmire's frequent requests were defended, in a 1975 interview, by Roland Sawyer, the GAO's chief information officer. "Theoretically, the GAO will take on any legitimate non-political issue," Sawyer said. "Proxmire has learned how to use the GAO and he does."[14]

Other critics of GAO complain that the office spends so much time pursuing a problem that by the time it issues a report the problem has either been surpassed by others or has grown so large that a whole new investigation is necessary. In one case, GAO investigators went to court to obtain contract information from Hewlett-Packard, a Defense Department contractor. The GAO won, but it took five years and three months of litigation. By that time "the trail was pretty cold," one GAO investigator said.[15]

Because it lacks subpoena power or other authority to enforce its findings, the GAO at times is thwarted by private organizations or government agencies not willing to provide necessary information. And sometimes even Congress is not very helpful.

During the last six months of 1970, for example, the GAO attempted to audit and review one of the Pentagon's weapons programs—Lockheed Aircraft Corporation's C-5A cargo plane. The Joint Economic Committee had requested a review of Lockheed's financial outlook because the company was requesting an additional $558-million to finish the project. The committee wanted to know if Lockheed was in danger of going bankrupt even if that sum were paid to the company. Both Lockheed and the Department of Defense at first refused to give the GAO any information. But after receiving a series of letters defining the agency's statutory rights, the Pentagon made a minor concession. The GAO was given permission to look at a Defense Department cash-flow analysis of Lockheed, but the auditors were not allowed to remove the books from the Pentagon, to copy down any figures or to tell anyone what the figures were they had audited. All the Defense Department would allow the auditors to do was to make a judgment on the solvency of Lockheed.

Pentagon officials said the prohibitions were necessary because of the "sensitivity" of the disputed program—the political sensitivity, not that of defense. Neither the GAO nor the Joint Economic Committee could enforce GAO's statutory authority to fully audit the defense contractor's cash-flow statement. Neither the committee nor the GAO had the authority to subpoena Lockheed's books which were in the hands of the Pentagon. The watchdog of Congress was immobilized in the Lockheed dispute because the company insisted that the government had no right to scrutinize its commercial programs (and, therefore, no broad-based analysis of the company's stability could be conducted).

The GAO has had less difficulty exercising its statutory authority on domestic programs concerning departments other than Defense. It has a record of relentless probing into matters such as job training, education, pollution and numerous others. Critics—including officials of the federal agencies investigated—call many of the unfavorable GAO analyses of domestic programs unfair. They say the agency gets good publicity uncovering minor corruption in the management of comparatively small projects, while making only cursory attempts to root out discrepancies in defense programs.

Office of Technology Assessment

In 1972 Congress approved legislation (PL 92-484) amending the National Science Foundation Act of 1950 to give Congress an additional supporting organization. It established the Office of Technology Assessment (OTA) to aid Congress in evaluating scientific and technical proposals for legislation. The office began operations in January 1974.

By law the OTA serves congressional committees, not individual members. Its large staff and even larger corps of consultants conduct studies to assess both the beneficial and adverse consequences of technologies, together with analyses of alternate policies. The office cannot operate laboratories, pilot projects or test facilities.

Organization. The OTA is governed by the bipartisan Technology Assessment Board, consisting of six senators, six representatives and the OTA director, who is appointed by the board for a six-year term. It is guided also by an advisory council whose members are the comptroller general (General Accounting Office), the director of the Congressional Research Service (Library of Congress), and 10 public members appointed by the board. The OTA also maintains liaison with the National Science Foundation and the Congressional Budget Office.

The OTA is organized along the lines of nine broad policy areas: energy, exploratory assessments, food, health, materials, oceans, research and development policy, transportation and world trade.

The initial growth of the OTA was very rapid. For fiscal 1974, which covered the establishment of the office and its first six months of operation, Congress appropriated $2-million. That was doubled in fiscal 1975, and the fiscal 1976 appropriation for the OTA jumped again to nearly $6.5-million.

Staff. In January 1976, OTA had a full-time staff of about 110 working in several offices scattered over Capitol Hill. The staff included 80 permanent employees (51 professional and 29 clerical), 10 full-time consultants, 8-10 employees on loan from executive agencies and 11 OTA Fellows who were supported by either private or public scientific organizations. In addition, the office had an active list of 220 consultants who could be called upon to do specialized work for one day or weeks at a time.[16] The director of OTA was Emilio Q. Daddario.

Accomplishments. The Senate Appropriations Committee reported in June 1975 that the OTA had received more than 60 requests from committees identifying approximately 130 specific issues to be assessed. The committee praised "the great strides OTA has made in becoming the focal point for supplying the Congress with competent and unbiased information on the application of technology...." But the committee complained of "a tendency to write OTA assessments into legislation," pointing out that requests were supposed to come from congressional committees and that there was no need for "so-called 'mandated' assessments in legislation."[17]

A tally of requests, prepared by the OTA in January 1976, revealed that 44 per cent had come from Senate committees, 39 per cent from House committees, 7 per cent from joint committees and 10 per cent of the requests had been made for committees through members of the Technology Assessment Board.[18]

The early OTA reports dealt with energy problems, drugs, automobile safety, agriculture and food supply, and transportation. In general, the OTA received stronger support from the Senate than from the House. In April 1974, the House rejected an amendment offered by Rep. H. R. Gross (R Iowa) to cut the Appropriations Committee recommendation for the OTA from $3.5-million to $2-million (the Senate approved $4-million) in fiscal 1975. Gross complained that the function of OTA overlapped with existing committees of Congress.[19]

Other Organizations

One of the most important supporting organizations of Congress is the Congressional Research Service (CRS), a part of the Library of Congress. By 1976, the CRS had about 800 employees who worked exclusively for members, responding to approximately 2,000 requests a day. *(Details, Congressional Research Service, p. 450)*

A more recent but very important supporting organization is the Congressional Budget Office, established under the Congressional Budget and Impoundment Control Act of 1974 (PL 93-344). The office was designed to help Congress coordinate all federal spending and taxing, and thus gain more control over the annual budget process. *(Details, p. 131)*

Of course, the committees themselves provide the most assistance to Congress. Members are supported not only by the committees and their large staffs, but also by organizations that branch out from the committees. For example, House Information Systems, created by the House Administration Committee to take charge of the growing computer-related operations of Congress, had a staff of 160 by 1976.

For its day-to-day operations, Congress is supported by the offices and staffs of the architect of the Capitol *(p. 415)*, the House and Senate sergeants at arms, the clerk of the House, the secretary of the Senate, the House doorkeeper and others. *(p. 478)*

U.S. Capitol Police

The U.S. Capitol Police is the private security force of Congress. The members of the force are responsible for security inside the Capitol, in the Senate and House office buildings and on the grounds surrounding the Capitol. Because the members of this force are stationed at one of the most popular tourist attractions in the United States, they must be to some extent tour guides and public relations officers as well as police officers.

By mid-1975 there were 1,113 men and women on the Capitol Police force, with 627 assigned to the House and its offices and 486 assigned to the Senate. Only 109 positions—all on the House side—were filled through political patronage. In addition, 50 officers and detective sergeants from the District of Columbia Metropolitan Police Department were detailed to the Capitol during daily meetings of Congress.[20]

Development of Police Force

From 1800 (when Congress first met in Washington) to 1857, watchmen were hired to guard the inside of the Capitol, and patrol of the Capitol grounds was left to the District of Columbia police. Congress appropriated $200 on March 3, 1857, to pay the watchmen, and for the first time these security men were referred to as the Capitol Police. Five years later, annual appropriations for the Capitol Police totaled $10,225. By 1876, a 31-man force had been organized with one captain, three lieutenants, 22 privates and six watchmen at a cost of $33,700 a year. Salaries ranged from $900 for watchmen to $1,600 for the captain.

The responsibility of selecting men for the force was split evenly between the sergeants at arms of the Senate and House. Actually, all the two sergeants at arms did was to accept appointments made by members of Congress. As outlined in an Act of April 29, 1876: "An appointment as a member of the Capitol Police is held subject to the will of the appointing power, which may remove at its pleasure, and both the appointment and the removal may be made informally."

Uniforms. By 1902, the Capitol Police were required to buy uniforms tailored to the specifications of the two sergeants at arms. Each man had to pay for his own uniform. A $20 allowance was made for a pistol and gun belt. Although Congress required members of the force to buy a standard uniform, there was no regulation about wearing it. To correct that situation, Congress passed a law two years later (March 18, 1904) stating: "The officers, privates and watchmen of the Capitol shall, when on duty, wear the regulation uniform."

Aid of Metropolitan Police. The District of Columbia Metropolitan Police Department was initially responsible for patrolling the grounds of nearly all government buildings in Washington. But, as the federal departments multiplied and expanded, separate security divisions for such areas as the White House, the State Department and the Capitol were organized.

The Capitol Police still rely on the Metropolitan Police for assistance in emergencies and for personnel. The professional assistance of officers and detectives cost an estimated $1.4-million in salaries for fiscal 1976, which was reimbursed by Congress to the Metropolitan Police Department.

Capitol Police and Patronage

Until 1967 all members of the Capitol Police were patronage appointees (except for the special officers on loan from the Metropolitan Police). Their continued service as policemen depended on remaining in the good graces of their sponsors and on the sponsor's tenure in office. When a senior member of Congress was defeated or retired, the member's patronage appointees generally left the Capitol also.

In 1966 the Capitol Police had about 250 men. Although some of them were able to hold their jobs after they lost sponsorship, the annual turnover rate was 82 per cent among the privates. The effectiveness of the training program for new men was limited because of the high turnover rate. A college student who was appointed was often put on the beat with an unloaded gun until he could be enrolled in the FBI training school. (Not until 1968 did the Capitol Police have facilities for its own training school.)

Professionalism. The first break with the patronage recruitment tradition came in 1967. The House needed more policemen to handle security for the Rayburn House Office Building, which had opened two years before. Instead of expanding the force through patronage appointments, the House adopted a resolution adding 78 men to the force "without regard to political affiliation and solely on the basis of fitness to perform the duties...." The result was an increasingly professional police force, which delighted Capitol Police Chief James M. Powell. For years he had explained to the House and Senate Appropriations Committees that Capitol security could be improved by hiring more career police officers and fewer student appointees. In 1971, Powell told a Senate subcommittee, "Over the long run, Congress should consider doing away with the patronage system of hiring Capitol Police."[21]

Much of the growth of professionalism was informal. Some men who had come onto the force through patronage decided to make police work their career. As their sponsors left Congress, Powell would ask the House or Senate Patronage Committee to allow the men to remain rather than give other members the right to appoint replacements. The committees generally cooperated with the chief's requests.

Patronage on the Capitol Police force dropped from nearly 100 per cent in 1966 to 41 per cent by 1970 and to 25 per cent late in 1971. By September 1975 it was less than 10 per cent.

Growth of the Force. The patronage percentage dropped so rapidly because the total Capitol Police force increased at the same time that patronage appointments decreased. In only nine years—from 1966 to 1975—the force grew from about 250 officers to more than 1,100. The total salary expense for fiscal 1976 was estimated to be $14.2-million.

When rising crime in the late 1960s pushed the District of Columbia up among the 10 metropolitan centers with the highest crime rates, members of Congress began to expand the Capitol Police. Mass demonstrations in Washington opposing the Vietnam War also emphasized the need for a larger and more professional force. A bomb explosion in the Capitol on March 1, 1971, resulted in greater police protection throughout the Capitol Hill complex. *(Box, 1971 Capitol Bombing: Tighter Security, p. 426)*

The increase in staff was accompanied by increases in police equipment. By 1975 the Capitol Police had scout cars, cruisers, motor scooters, buses, package x-ray machines, a closed-circuit TV system and a dozen police dogs trained to detect explosives.

Control of Capitol Police

The Capitol Police are under the direction and control of the sergeant at arms of the Senate and the sergeant at arms of the House. The force is technically divided into two parts—one for the House, one for the Senate. When one side

of Congress needs additional security forces, officers are added to the appropriate part of the force.

The Act of April 29, 1876, stated: "The Captain and lieutenants shall be selected jointly by the Sergeant at Arms of the Senate and the Sergeant at Arms of the House...." Today the chief is responsible for recommending promotions, which are then reviewed by the sergeants at arms. The Capitol Police are on the payroll of the sergeant at arms in each chamber.

Police Board. The sergeants at arms and the architect of the Capitol are the three members of the Capitol Police Board. The board has a general supervisory function. It reviews recommendations for suspension of an officer, considers requests for more men and submits reports to congressional committees.

The architect of the Capitol is generally responsible for maintenance of the Capitol and the surrounding grounds and buildings. Since Capitol Police duties include protection of the "Capitol grounds and terraces from use as playgrounds..." and protection of the buildings from defacement or destruction, the architect sits on the board to make sure that the interests of his office are respected by the Capitol Police.

Final authority over the Capitol Police rests, of course, with Congress, but its direct control over individual Capitol police officers is decreasing as the number of patronage appointments declines. Congress is increasingly shifting its responsibility for overseeing the force to the Police Board and the sergeants at arms.

Requirements and Selection. Patronage appointees and candidates for professional positions on the force must meet the same physical standards. All applicants must be between 21 and 45 years old. There is no written examination or civil service test. A routine security check is made of all applicants. Late in 1974 the Capitol Police began to accept female candidates. By the beginning of 1976 there were about 40 women on the force. Men and women are assigned to the same duties.[22]

Training. All members of the Capitol Police—patronage and professional, men and women—must complete the same 12-week training course. The first week, at the Capitol, provides a general introduction to police work. Candidates then undergo eight weeks of training at the Federal Consolidated Law Enforcement Training Center in Glenco, Georgia, where many other federal police officers are trained. The final three weeks, back in Washington, concentrate on the special duties of the Capitol Police.

Some officers receive additional training. One member from each graduating class is sent to a special 12-week course in security training at the FBI Academy. A special operations unit of the Capitol Police trains selected officers for riot control and other unusual duties. The Capitol Police Training School in the basement of the Rayburn Building has classrooms and a seven-lane firing range.

In fiscal 1974 the Capitol Police made 24 arrests for felonies, 43 for misdemeanors and 234 for traffic violations.[23]

Capitol Pages

Serving as messengers and floor assistants to the 535 members of Congress is a force of young patronage appointees called "pages." They range in age from 14 to 18 years and usually serve from six months to a year, although some stay as long as three years. In the 94th Congress there were 61 pages in the House and 30 in the Senate.

Congressional Interns

Over many years members of Congress have been assisted by temporary employees known generally as congressional interns. The origins of the practice are obscure, but probably it began with members hiring students of American government or the sons and daughters of constituents to work in their offices during the summer. The diverse and informal method of employment expanded greatly during the 1960s. Even estimates of their numbers are difficult to reach, but it seemed likely by the mid-1970s that about 1,500 interns were working in Congress each year.

Congressional interns vary widely in their experience and their office responsibilities. Younger students may work at clerical tasks, help answer mail or conduct visitors around the Capitol. Those with more experience may be assigned to constituent casework, drafting speeches and reports or helping committee staff. Some students receive college credit for working in Congress and others coordinate their jobs with independent research projects.

Many interns are not students at all. They are teachers, journalists, lawyers and young people who already have launched political careers of their own. Usually they are supported by private foundations, professional associations, schools or corporations during their congressional assignments, which may last up to a year. These older, more experienced interns take on greater responsibility and may serve with a member's top staff. Many are hired by the senator or representative after their internship is completed.

The way in which interns are paid varies as well. Those under private internships are paid by their sponsors. The Congressional Fellows program of the American Political Science Association, for example, each year brings a few dozen experienced journalists, teachers, and government officials to Congress. Employees of federal agencies may be assigned to Congress for a time and then returned to the executive branch.

In the Senate, interns may be paid from the annual staff allowance or other funds available to the office. The House has a more precise system. The Lyndon Baines Johnson congressional internship program was established in 1973 to employ students and teachers of government and social studies. Under the program, each representative is allocated $1,000 a year to hire one intern for two months or two interns for one month each. The interns must work in the member's Washington office.[1]

The House first established an internship program in 1965, with an annual allowance of $750 for each member's office. But the program was ended abruptly in 1967 because many representatives objected to some interns' protests against the war in Vietnam. The program was not reinstated until 1971. In the interim many representatives employed interns from the staff allowance.[2]

---

1. *Details, Congressional Quarterly,* 1973 Almanac, *p. 783.*
2. *Details, Congressional Quarterly,* Congress and the Nation, 1965-1968, *Vol. II, p. 918.*

Five days a week the pages attend a special school on the third floor of the Library of Congress. Classes for the ninth through twelfth grades are held from 6:10 to 10:30 a.m., then the pages go to their jobs at the Capitol. Until early evening—or much later if there is a night session—the pages answer phones, run errands, deliver messages or distribute information. If they have time or energy at the end of the day, they may practice with the Capitol Page School basketball team, work for the school newspaper or yearbook, debate school issues in student council or simply do their homework.

Although the demands on a page's time are uncommonly strict, hundreds of young men and women vie for these positions each year. The opportunity to observe Congress is unsurpassed, and the pay is remarkably high for anyone so young. In 1975 bench pages earned $7,215 a year, telephone pages earned $8,298 and three page overseers each earned $9,561.[24]

History of the Pages

Working as a page has not always been so lucrative, and the side benefit of going to school while toiling on the Hill is a relatively new development in the long history of this patronage job. Congress has always used messengers, but the earliest record of boys filling these positions was in 1827. Three youngsters were then employed as "runners" in the House of Representatives, serving as errand boys for the 227 House members and four delegates.

Runners. Many of the boys who served as runners were orphans or children of poor families. Their plight came to the attention of a senator or representative and the boys were given jobs running errands. There was apparently no law authorizing the use of young boys for these patronage jobs, yet hundreds were appointed over the years as a matter of practice. Members often paid the boys a bonus if they performed their duties well, but this practice was discontinued in 1843 after a special review of financial allocations in the House.

The first Senate "runner" was a nine-year-old boy named Grafton Hanson. He was appointed under the august sponsorship of Senators Daniel Webster and Henry Clay. Hanson served his sponsors for 10 years and later became postmaster of the Senate.

The name "pages" appeared first in the *Congressional Globe,* predecessor of the *Congressional Record,* of the 26th Congress, 1839-41. At about that time, a page was paid $1.50 a day and his activities were restricted to the immediate vicinity of the Capitol.

Riding and Telegraph Pages. Older persons were hired as "riding pages" to carry messages by horseback around Washington and as "telegraph pages" to deliver telegrams that came in through the Capitol telegraph office. There are still riding pages, but they have switched from horses to cars, and they deliver press releases and letters to federal offices and foreign embassies. The sole job of some pages is to answer telephones.

Dress Code. A code of dress was established for pages during the era when knickers were in vogue for young boys. The Supreme Court, which had a small corps of pages until 1975, was the last body to revise the dress code. Until 1963 the court pages had to report for duty in knickers, long black stockings and double-breasted jackets. More remarkable, until late in 1950, court pages could be no taller than five feet, four inches—the height of the backs of the justices' chairs.

Currently, all Capitol pages wear dark blue suits, black ties, black shoes and socks, and long-sleeved white shirts. Pages do not have to wear their jackets at all times. The dress code is the same for boys and girls.

Girl Pages. Until 1971 all pages were boys. The Senate passed a resolution on May 13, 1971, permitting the appointment of girl pages in the Senate, and the first two were sworn in the following day.[25] The House appointed its first girl pages in June 1973. Midway through the 94th Congress, 25 pages were girls.

House Pages

Pages for the House of Representatives are under the direction of the doorkeeper of the House. Each morning after classes they report for work to either the Democratic or Republican cloakroom. Their tasks are assigned by long-time patronage employees who report directly to the doorkeeper. One supervisor serves each party in the House.

A page with less than a year's experience is generally assigned to the floor of the House. Before a session begins, he or she distributes pertinent documents to each House seat in preparation for the day's business. When the session is called to order, the page retires to a bench in the rear of the chamber to await a representative's call. A button next to a member's seat triggers a light on a board in the rear of the chamber when a page is wanted. A page with more experience may be assigned to answer phones in one of the cloakrooms, to work in the document room or to run errands from the doorkeeper's office.

Selection. As is the case with other patronage appointments in the House, a five-member committee of the majority party is responsible for rationing page appointments. The Patronage Committee informs a member, who is usually high on the seniority list, that the member is eligible to appoint a page for the coming session. If the member has a candidate, the appointment is made.

Requirements. Pages for the House must be 16 or 17 years old when they begin serving, and no page turning 18 during a session may serve beyond the end of that session. Since 1970 the minimum appointment period has been two months and, because of the age restrictions, no page can serve much longer than two years. The length of a page's appointment also depends on the sponsor's tenure in office. If the sponsor loses an election, the page goes out of office also. House pages must maintain a grade average of C while attending the Capitol Page School, but dismissal for poor academic work is at the discretion of the page's sponsor and parents.

Senate Pages

The 30 pages of the Senate are under the direction of the sergeant at arms. He assigns pages to the majority and minority cloakrooms and to the Senate floor, where they are supervised by the secretaries of each party. Pages assigned to the Senate floor sit on the rostrum at the front of the chamber and are called to run errands by the snapping of a senator's fingers. The duties of the Senate page are virtually the same as those of pages in the House—messages are carried, documents gathered and distributed, telephones answered.

Selection. Senate pages are appointed by high-seniority members of each party. The distribution of appointments is generally controlled by the majority leader.

Requirements. Senate page must be at least 14 years old and not more than 16. Pages who turn 17 during a ses-

sion may hold their jobs only until the session adjourns. They must maintain "adequate" grades at the Capitol Page School, but the definition of "adequate" is left up to the page's sponsor and parents. The appointee must be willing to serve for at least two months.

Capitol Page School

Not until the Legislative Reorganization Act of 1946 became law were pages provided with any kind of uniform schooling. They had to rely on private tutors if they wanted to continue their education while working on Capitol Hill. After Congress established the Capitol Page School, three years passed before semi-permanent quarters were acquired. From 1946 to 1949, pages were bused to the YMCA for classes. In 1949 space was cleared on the third floor of the Library of Congress, classrooms were set up, and the school was officially opened.

During the 94th Congress the school had a principal who doubled as counselor, an administrative assistant, six teachers, and a part-time basketball coach. When Congress decided to establish a special school for pages, it allocated extra funds to the District of Columbia school system for administration of the Capitol Page School.

Curriculum. The school's curriculum differs somewhat from that of most public schools. The students attend five 45-minute classes every morning, with a 30-minute break in the middle of the schedule for a hot breakfast. Because of the short hours, classes are restricted almost entirely to academic subjects. Chemistry is excluded from the curriculum because the Library of Congress forbids laboratory work in the school's attic classrooms that might damage the books and archives on the floors below.

Courses at the Capitol Page School are geared toward college preparation because nearly all pages go on to college. Some eventually return to the Capitol as members of Congress. Two representatives in the 94th Congress were former pages: Robert E. Bauman (R Md.) and John D. Dingell (D Mich.). Many former members also had been pages.

New School. In the Legislative Reorganization Act of 1970 (PL 91-510), Congress authorized construction of a residential page school to be named for Speaker John W. McCormack (D Mass.). The architect of the Capitol selected a site, at Second and D Streets, S.E., and Congress purchased the land for $1.4-million.[26] Funds for construction of the classrooms and dormitories still had not been appropriated by mid-1976.

Criticism of the System

Congress has debated for years over how pages are appointed, how old they should be, who supervises them once they arrive in Washington and how much it costs to educate them. A day of hearings by the Select House Committee on the Welfare and Education of Congressional Pages, on Dec. 17, 1964, brought to light many of the questions that had been stalling action for years. One of the broadest questions under debate concerned the possibility of drastically altering the existing page system. Opponents of the school-dormitory asserted that a more economical system could be found. They favored raising the age limit of pages, thus allowing only high school graduates to take the jobs. The expense of running the Capitol Page School would thus be eliminated, and the worry over proper supervision of minors would no longer be a problem.

Supervision. The most consistent problem through the years has been the lack of supervision of the pages when they are not attending classes or working in the Capitol. Although some pages are as young as 14, they are required to find their own housing and to buy or prepare their own meals. Some sponsoring members are very conscientious about looking after their pages, but others appoint them and leave them on their own. No member or employee of Congress is responsible for supervising off-duty pages.

The Washington Star, in a report published Oct. 17, 1975, said of the pages: "Loosed unsupervised on the city, some of the teenagers...drink their way through the bars on Capitol Hill and party late into the night, some forgoing regular meals. Others see and experience the most distasteful aspects of life in the big city." The article cited one 17-year-old girl page who "was found this summer to be living in an apartment...in the heart of the city's red light district. The apartment was nice, but her parents didn't know the area."[27]

Of course, the pages are not without guardians. Principal John C. Hoffman of the Capitol Page School said in 1976 that about one-fourth of the pages are from the Washington area and live with their parents.[28] Some are placed in nearby residences by senators and representatives who appoint them. House Doorkeeper James T. Molloy maintains a list of approved housing for pages and works with area groups to set up after-hours activities for the pages. Local churches and civic clubs, notably the Capitol Hill Jaycees, have taken an interest in both the housing and supervision of the pages.[29]

Housing. The chief argument in favor of a residential page school is that it would provide both a safe home and a more modern school for the teenagers. It would also have recreation facilities. Resident counselors would live in the building and could help pages with any problems.

Age Restrictions. Some members have recommended repeatedly that the minimum age for pages be raised, because an older group would not require supervision and would not need either classrooms or dormitories. The Supreme Court did essentially that in 1975 when it decided that instead of pages it would use older employees already on its payroll. The Court had employed only four pages, under the direction of the marshal of the Court.

In 1973 the Senate approved a bill to change the age requirements for all pages to 18-21 years. The House took no action on the bill; and in the end, the Senate did not even set higher age limits for its own pages.[30]

Discrimination. Because individual members have full discretion in selecting pages under the patronage system, the most qualified youngsters have not always been appointed. Outright discrimination has been charged in some instances.

Congress did not have any black pages until 100 years after the Civil War. Sen. Jacob K. Javits (R N.Y.) appointed the first black page in 1965. Javits broke another long-standing tradition in December 1970, when he appointed the first girl page. She was not allowed to join the ranks of the pages until the following May.

Congressional Record

After each daily session of Congress, the Government Printing Office (GPO) publishes the *Congressional Record*—the official report of congressional proceedings. About 50,000 copies of the *Record,* averaging more than 200

Prior Publications

1789-1790—*The Congressional Register.* An early attempt to publish a record of congressional debates. Taken down in shorthand by Thomas Lloyd of New York. Four volumes.

1790-1825—Debate in House reported in haphazard way by some of better newspapers. Senate debates scarcely reported at all.

1834—Publication of first volume of *Annals of Congress.* Produced by Gales and Seaton. Brought together material from newspapers, magazines and other sources on congressional proceedings from 1st through 12th Congresses (March 3, 1789, to May 27, 1824). Forty-two volumes.

1824-1837—*Register of Debate.* Produced by Gales and Seaton; directly reported congressional proceedings.

1833-1873—*The Congressional Globe.* Published by Blair and Rives; F. and J. Rives; F. and J. Rives and George A. Bailey. Covered 23rd through 42nd Congresses (Dec. 2, 1833, to March 3, 1873). Forty-six volumes.

1873 to Present—*Congressional Record.* Produced by the Government Printing Office. Dec. 1, 1873, to present.

---

pages a copy, are printed and delivered the following morning. The *Record* is produced in less than 13 hours and involves the efforts of about 2,500 of the 8,500 GPO employees.

Background. Before 1825, debates in the House were not reported except in a haphazard way by some newspapers. Senate debates were seldom reported at all. Not until 1855 were reporters of congressional proceedings and debates paid at public expense, and only in 1863 were annual appropriations established in both chambers to cover reporting of proceedings.

The proceedings were not printed systematically before 1865, when the *Congressional Globe*—the forerunner of the *Record*—took on a form and style that later became standard. When the government contract for publication of the *Globe* expired in 1873, Congress passed an appropriations act which provided that with the 43rd Congress later that year the *Congressional Record* would be produced by the GPO. *(Box, Prior Publications, this page)*

Present Practice. Proceedings in both the Senate and the House are taken down by separate staffs of reporters, eight in the Senate and seven in the House. The shorthand notes of the debates are recorded later and typed by a transcriber. The typed copy is then proofread by the reporters, given an appropriate heading and sent to the members for their own editing and correction.

Reporting in the House is done on a half-hour schedule, requiring that each reporter spend five minutes of each half hour on the floor and the remaining time dictating, transcribing and correcting his notes. The Senate operates under the same procedures, but on an hourly basis. Each Senate reporter spends 10 minutes of each hour on the floor.

Corrected transcripts of debates must be returned to the GPO by 9 p.m. the same day if they are to be included in the following day's *Record.*

Contents of the *Record*

The *Congressional Record* chronologically reports daily what is said on the floor of both houses of Congress. Biweekly and hard-bound versions also are produced to provide a corrected and permanent record. The proceedings of the House and Senate alternately appear first in each daily printing of the *Record* when schedules permit.

The *Record* contains four separate sections:

● Proceedings of the House.
● Proceedings of the Senate.
● Extensions of Remarks.
● Daily Digest—a summary of the proceedings in both houses, including a calendar of committee meetings for the following day.

At the beginning of each month a resume of congressional activity is printed in the *Record,* providing statistical data for the preceding month on the following:

● Days Congress was in session.
● Number of pages of proceedings printed in the *Record.*
● Number of pages for extensions of remarks.
● Bills enacted into law.
● Measures reported by committees.
● Reports, quorum calls, votes and bills vetoed by the President.

Cost of the *Record*

The cost of printing each page of the *Congressional Record* more than doubled in the first half of the 1970s. The per-page cost was estimated to be $287 in fiscal 1976, and the complete *Record* was expected to increase by 5,000 pages to a total of 51,000 for the year.

Printed copies of hearings, congressional debates, bills and resolutions would undergo an estimated volume increase of 43 per cent over fiscal 1975, according to the public printer. Labor rates were cited for 52 per cent of the increase in cost of publication. Only 5 per cent of the increase was due to the higher cost of materials.

The following 10-year table covers the cost of all *Record* publications, including indexes, digests and the bound volumes provided for members of Congress. The per-page cost for each fiscal year has been rounded to the nearest dollar.

Fiscal Year	Cost per Page
1967	$110
1968	113
1969	116
1970	128
1971	140
1972	171
1973	228
1974	230
1975	260
1976	(estimate) 287

Source: Government Printing Office, Information Office; Congressional Quarterly, *Weekly Report,* May 24, 1975, p. 1119; *Weekly Report,* July 12, 1975, p. 1478.

The summary also provides information on the status of executive nominations.

Proceedings. Although the *Record* purports to print an exact account of the proceedings on the floor of both chambers, members of the Senate and the House edit and revise their remarks before they are published.

A member may request "unanimous consent to extend my remarks at this point in the *Record*" at any time the member is able to gain recognition on the floor. When the request is granted, a member may include a statement, newspaper article or speech, and it will appear in the body of the *Record* just as if it had been actually spoken on the floor during debate.

Extensions of Remarks. Following the record—actual or apparent—of floor debate in both chambers, senators and representatives are given additional space to extend their remarks. They may add such extraneous material as speeches given outside Congress, selected editorials, magazine articles or letters. Senators may add such material to the body of the *Record;* representatives must place it in the Extensions of Remarks section.

Daily Digest. The Legislative Reorganization Act of 1946 directed the Joint Committee on Printing, which controls the publication of the *Congressional Record,* to incorporate into the *Record* a list of congressional committee meetings and hearings, their places and subject matter. This section of the *Record,* titled the Daily Digest, summarizes the following material:

● Highlights of the day's congressional activities.
● Senate action.
● Senate committee meetings.
● House action.
● House committee meetings.
● Joint committee meetings.
● Time and date of next Senate and House meetings.

The Daily Digest lists also the committee meetings scheduled the day the *Record* is distributed.

Friday issues of the *Record* contain a section outlining the congressional program for the coming week, including schedules of major floor action and of House and Senate committee meetings.

Index. Published about twice a month, the index is the key to using the *Congressional Record.* It is a guide to the contents and a means of tracing floor action on legislation. The index consists of two parts: an index to the proceedings, which includes material both in the body and in the Extensions of Remarks section, and an index to the history of bills and resolutions.

Costs and Production Schedule

Costs. On June 12, 1970, the subscription price of the *Record* was raised for the first time in 87 years. Since 1883, the *Record* had cost $1.50 a month by mail. The new price was $3.75 a month, which has remained unchanged since then. It hardly covers mailing costs. Price increases mean nothing to about 90 per cent of the *Record's* 50,000 subscribers, because they receive their copies free.

The cost of printing the *Record* was estimated to be $287 a page for fiscal 1976. Printing volume for the year was expected to increase, from 46,000 to 51,000 pages.[31] *(Box, Cost of the Record, this page)*

Schedule. The texts of the Senate and House floor debates, matter for the Extensions and Daily Digest sections are assembled by the GPO each night before printing. The size of the *Record* never can be accurately determined beforehand, since it depends on the length of floor proceedings. The only known fact is that the *Record* must be printed and delivered by 8 a.m., regardless of its size or how late Congress remained in session.

GPO officials say that to their knowledge the *Record* never has missed its morning delivery deadline. Occasionally, late proceedings are held for printing in the next day's *Record*.

Production begins at 6:30 p.m., when "preparers" check incoming copy, note sections to be printed in specific type sizes and ascertain that the material to be printed is in proper sequential order. The copy is set by nearly 400 composing and casting machines, proofed, corrected and readied for stereotyping by 2 a.m. The double-deck, 64-page rotary magazine presses that print the *Record* are supposed to be in operation by 2:15 a.m., running at 18,000 impressions an hour. These presses print about 50,000 copies of the *Record* each night, using nearly 22 tons of paper. *(Box, Government Printing Office, this page)*

Approximately 35,000 copies are delivered each morning to congressional offices. About 100 copies are hand-delivered to the homes of members requesting such service in the Washington area; more than 200 are delivered to area libraries, offices and universities; from 6,000 to 7,000 are mailed or otherwise delivered to individual subscribers, and about 6,000 go to federal agencies.

Each senator is allotted 100 copies of the *Record* to distribute free to staff and constituents; each representative is allotted 68 copies. In addition to the daily *Record*, each member receives one subscription to what is called the "Greenbound Record," which is a semi-monthly bound compilation of the dailies. The permanent bound volume of the *Record*, printed on book paper, is published some months after a session ends. Each member is allotted one complete set.

Criticism of the *Record*

Untrue Account. The most persistent criticism of the *Congressional Record*, by some members of Congress as well as by the public, is that the published document is not a true account of what goes on in Congress. It records not only what is said in Congress, but what members want believed they would have said if they had been debating. There is no way to tell one from the other.

For example, on Oct. 18, 1972, according to the *Record*, Rep. Hale Boggs (D La.) addressed the House. "In the next few minutes," he was quoted as saying, "I would like to note for members the great amount of significant legislation enacted during the session." At the end of his speech, according to the *Record*, Boggs wished every member a Merry Christmas and a Happy New Year.[32] All of this was bizarre fiction. Hale Boggs was presumed dead on Oct. 18, the victim of a plane crash in the Alaska mountains two days earlier. As is routine, he had left behind a written speech to be printed at the close of the year's session. Anyone reading the *Record* would have assumed that Boggs was standing on the House floor.

Only rarely does a member try to expose the deception. One who did was Rep. Ken Hechler (D W.Va.), in a mischievously candid "speech" during a debate in 1971 on a bill to aid coal miners.

"Having received unanimous consent to extend my remarks in the record," Hechler said, "I would like to indicate that I am not really speaking these words.... I do not want to kid anyone into thinking that I am now on my feet

---

Government Printing Office

The Government Printing Office (GPO) was established by Congress in 1861 to print for "the Senate and House of Representatives, the executive and judicial departments, and the Court of Claims." Buildings, equipment and machinery were acquired from Cornelius Wendell, a private printer, for $135,000. The original plant stood on the site now occupied by the newest of the GPO's buildings. It was staffed by a work force of 350.

By its own reckoning, the GPO is now one of the largest and best-equipped complete printing plants in the world. It had a budget of $145.3-million for fiscal 1976 and employed about 8,500 persons, 90 per cent of them in Washington.

Not only does the Government Printing Office manufacture and buy printing; it also runs a sizable distribution and sales operation. The Public Documents Division, established in 1895 as an organic part of the GPO, performs this function. There are five GPO bookstores in Washington, and 18 others spread throughout the country. In fiscal 1975 the GPO sold 81 million publications for a total of $34-million. A much larger number of GPO publications were distributed free to Congress, government agencies at all levels, private organizations and the general public.

Source: Government Printing Office, Public Information Office.

---

delivering a stirring oration. As a matter of fact, I am back in my office typing this out on my own hot little typewriter, far from the madding crowd and somewhat removed from the House chamber. Such is the pretense of the House that it would have been easy to just quietly include these remarks in the record, issue a brave press release, and convince thousands of cheering constituents that I was in there fighting every step of the way, influencing the course of history in the heat of debate."[33]

Questionable as Hechler makes the practice sound, virtually everyone on Capitol Hill agrees that members should have some way to express their views in a debate without having to speak. In the House, for example, there are 435 members. If each spoke for one minute on any bill, more than seven hours would be consumed in debate—assuming that with unparalled restraint no one spoke more than once.

Some *Record* critics believe change is needed simply because the *Congressional Record* ought to be an honest document. Others have a more specific reason; they worry that the existing goulash of speeches and insertions is making it difficult for executive agencies to determine what Congress actually intended to do in passing a law.

"It allows you to have a legislative history that is warped, because it is not accurate," said Rep. William A. Steiger (R Wis.). Steiger believes that sooner or later, a federal agency is going to make a serious error by relying on the remarks of a member who was not even present during the debate.[34]

Steiger and other members have urged for years that the *Record* separate floor proceedings from inserted material. They have proposed use of a different type face for remarks not delivered in person. Steiger offered this as an amendment to the 1970 Legislative Reorganization Act, but it was defeated on a voice vote.

When legislation is debated in the House, a representative can even decide which position to argue after a vote is taken. Since 1974, members have been required to sign their written insertions and present them within 15 minutes of the close of the day's business. But the rule enables a member to bring two opposing speeches into the chamber, remain silent until the vote is nearly completed, be recorded for the winning side, and then insert into the published debate a speech explaining the recorded position.

Some corrections and additions are indeed necessary. Remarks made in heated debates may be judged offensive and edited out of the *Record* by a reporter or the member who made them. Grammar is often improved and the transcripts are often polished.

In the 1950s, members frequently inserted into the transcripts of their own remarks such words as "laughter" and "applause." Such additions have become infrequent. If they appear, the reporter has included them.

Extensions of Remarks. One step further from the reality of the House floor is the "Extensions of Remarks" section at the back of the *Congressional Record,* which on a busy day can run to 80 pages or more. "Extensions of Remarks" is a misnomer; nothing is extended because no remarks are made. The section is a collection of newspaper articles, outside speeches and other contributions, some related to legislative business, some to constituent matters, and some to hardly anything of general interest.

Occasionally, an economy-minded member of Congress is willing to say in public that the bulk of the material inserted in the extensions section is not worth what it costs. "Just take a look at the *Congressional Record* almost any day," complained Rep. Marjorie S. Holt (R Md.) in 1974. "It is bloated with tributes, memorials, and messages on every conceivable subject except the subjects under consideration by Congress on that day.... We often spend $15,-000 to $20,000 a day on such effluvia. We could save millions every year if we could eliminate it."[35]

Additions to the proceedings or the extensions section do cost money. Sen. Robert M. La Follette (R Wis.) on May 5, 1914, inserted a 365-page speech on railroad rates. The cost of printing this extension, according to the Joint Committee on Printing, was $13,760.85. In 1935 a speech opposing the National Recovery Administration by Sen. Huey P. Long (D La.) took up 85 pages of the *Record* and cost $4,493. One of the longest *Record* insertions was by Rep. Royal C. Johnson (R S.D.), who listed 504 pages of names of World War I slackers. No figures on the cost of this extension are available.

On May 24, 1972, the Joint Committee on Printing began to require members who planned inserting lengthy material to first obtain an estimate of the cost from the public printer. Members were then required, when seeking unanimous consent to extend their remarks, to state the probable cost of the material but not its content.[36]

Extensions have been known to cause trouble as well as expense. In the summer of 1974, false statements attributed to three representatives were placed in the *Record,* apparently as pranks. One, under the name of Rep. Earl F. Landgrebe (R Ind.), appeared a week after President Nixon resigned in disgrace. It proposed that President Ford nominate Nixon to be his Vice President, and then resign the presidency to allow Nixon to accede to the office under the Twenty-fifth Amendment.

Landgrebe was not amused by the prank, and neither was the House leadership. The Joint Committee immediately tightened the rules for submitting an insertion for the *Congressional Record* and required the signatures of members on all written statements.[37]

Efforts Toward Reform

More supporting organizations, like more staff members, do not necessarily make Congress more efficient. Representatives and senators have worried at times that they may be getting more motion than action from their back-up forces.

The House Appropriations Committee, in its report on the fiscal 1976 budget, offered this comment on the Office of Technology Assessment: "The committee is concerned over the rapid growth of this new office and possible duplication of effort and activities with other agencies of the government.... The House Commission on Information and Facilities is charged with the function of conducting a thorough and complete study of 'House resources for information, including the Congressional Research Service, the General Accounting Office, and the Office of Technology Assessment, and the organizational framework that makes them effective or ineffective.' The committee is anticipating that the report of the commission will be of great assistance in determining the future needs of these agencies."[38]

The House Commission on Information and Facilities was established Oct. 8, 1974 (H Res 998) with a mandate to complete its study and offer recommendations by late 1976. Headed by Rep. Jack Brooks (D Texas), the commission had nine members, five of them from the Joint Committee on Congressional Operations. It was composed of two task forces—Facilities and Space Utilization, headed by Rep. Elizabeth Holtzman (D N.Y.), and Information Resources, headed by Rep. Don Fuqua (D Fla.).

The Senate on July 29, 1975 (S Res 227), created the Commission on the Operation of the Senate. Nicknamed the Culver Commission after its chief sponsor, Sen. John C. Culver (D Iowa), the panel was composed of nine private citizens selected by the Senate leadership. It was not entirely independent of the Senate, since its chairman was former Sen. Harold E. Hughes (D Iowa) and it had two ex-officio members from the Senate's professional staff.

The Culver Commission was charged with recommending changes in the operating procedures and business practices of the Senate by September 1976. It was expected to concentrate on management problems but apparently had the authority to delve into all aspects of the Senate except Senate rules and committee jurisdictions. Among the topics to be studied were information technology, perquisites and allowances, office space and conflict-of-interest codes.[39]

Neither commission has the authority to implement its recommendations. The recommendations, no matter how thorough or sound or fool-proof, will have no effect whatever unless the House and Senate adopt them. Congress, like the White House, has a long record of appointing study commissions to do difficult jobs and of then ignoring them.

Perhaps in recognition of this political trait, a bipartisan group of former members of Congress, executive branch officials and prominent citizens announced Dec. 7, 1975, the formation of the Institute for Congress. Intended to give the House and Senate an independent policy research arm, the institute had a 15-member board of directors headed by former Rep. Martha W. Griffiths (D Mich.) and William D. Ruckelshaus, former administrator of the Environmental Protection Agency and former deputy attorney general. House and Senate leaders were ex-officio members of the board.[40]

The institute planned to develop a staff of 80 professionals and to seek both private funds and congressional research contracts. Griffiths and Ruckelshaus, in a statement describing the institute, suggested that it be a three-to-five-year experiment. The institute's advantage over the congressional bureaucracy with 535 bosses, they wrote, was that it "could protect its professionals against unmanageable loads and target them most effectively on a carefully selected set of issues of concern to Congress."[41]

Footnotes

1. *Annual Report of the Comptroller General of the United States, 1974* (Government Printing Office), p. 1.
2. *Ibid.,* pp. 282-86.
3. *Ibid.,* p. 9.
4. *Ibid.,* p. 181.
5. *Ibid.,* pp. 2-3.
6. Statistics in this section were taken from the *Annual Report, 1974.*
7. Quoted in Richard E. Brown, *The GAO: Untapped Source of Congressional Power* (The University of Tennessee Press, 1970), p. 20.
8. *Annual Report, 1974,* p. 180.
9. Jon Margolis, "The GAO Is Congress's Unpopular Watchdog," *The New York Times,* May 18, 1975.
10. *Annual Report, 1974,* p. 16.
11. *Ibid.,* p. 1.
12. Eliot Stanley, *The General Accounting Office: One-Eyed Watchdog?* (Citizens Advocate Center, 1970).
13. Congressional Quarterly, *Weekly Report,* March 22, 1975, p. 597.
14. Robert Signer, "GAO Frequent Target of Criticism," *The Forum,* Nov. 20, 1975.
15. *Ibid.*
16. Thomas P. McGurn, administrative officer, Office of Technology Assessment, interview, Jan. 9, 1976.
17. U.S. Congress, Senate, Committee on Appropriations, *Legislative Branch Appropriations, 1976,* S Rept 94-262 to Accompany HR 6950, 94th Cong., 1st sess., 1975, pp. 26-27.
18. McGurn interview.
19. Congressional Quarterly, *1974 Almanac,* pp. 75-76.
20. James M. Powell, chief, Capitol Police, interview, Sept. 29, 1975. See also U.S. Congress, House, Committee on Appropriations, Subcommittee on Legislative Branch Appropriations, *Hearings, Legislative Branch Appropriations for 1976,* 94th Cong., 1st sess., 1975, pt. 1, pp. 798-99; and U.S. Congress, House, Committee on Appropriations, *Legislative Branch Appropriation Bill, 1976,* H Rept 94-208 to Accompany HR 6950, 94th Cong., 1st sess., 1975, pp. 17-18.
21. Congressional Quarterly, *1971 Almanac,* p. 770.
22. Capt. George B. Carver, Capitol Police, interview, Jan. 9, 1976.
23. House, *Hearings, Legislative Branch Appropriations for 1976,* p. 799.
24. *Ibid.,* p. 834.
25. Congressional Quarterly, *Congress and the Nation, 1969-1972,* Vol. III, p. 375.
26. Lance Gay, "By Day, Pages Learn of Government, But at Night...," *The Washington Star,* Oct. 17, 1975.
27. *Ibid.*
28. John C. Hoffman, principal, Capitol Page School, interview, Jan. 12, 1976.
29. Gay, *The Washington Star,* Oct. 17, 1975.
30. Congressional Quarterly, *1973 Almanac,* p. 790.
31. Congressional Quarterly, *Weekly Report,* May 24, 1975, p. 1119.
32. Congressional Quarterly, *Weekly Report,* March 15, 1975, p. 527.
33. *Ibid.,* p. 529.
34. *Ibid.,* p. 528.
35. *Ibid.,* p. 529.
36. *Congress and the Nation,* Vol. III, pp. 378 and 380.
37. Congressional Quarterly, *Weekly Report,* Aug. 31, 1974, pp. 2382-83.
38. House, *Legislative Branch Appropriation Bill, 1976,* p. 19.
39. Congressional Quarterly, *Weekly Report,* Dec. 13, 1975, pp. 2715-21.
40. *Ibid.,* p. 2722.
41. Martha Griffiths and William Ruckelshaus, "Why Congress Needs Even More Help," *The Washington Star,* Oct. 12, 1975.

Selected Bibliography

Books

Brown, Richard E. *The GAO: Untapped Source of Congressional Power.* Knoxville: University of Tennessee Press, 1970.

Donham, Philip and Fahey, Robert J. *Congress Needs Help.* New York: Random House, 1966.

Madison, Frank. *A View from the Floor: The Journal of a U.S. Senate Pageboy.* Englewood Cliffs, N.J.: Prentice-Hall, 1967.

Mansfield, Harvey C. *The Comptroller General: A Study in the Law and Practice of Financial Administration.* New Haven: Yale University Press, 1939.

McInnis, Mary, ed. *We Propose: A Modern Congress.* New York: McGraw-Hill, 1966.

Stanley, Eliot. *The General Accounting Office: One-Eyed Watchdog?* Citizens Advocate Center, 1970.

Articles

Congressional Quarterly. "Congressional Record: A Daily Publishing Triumph on Congress' Doorstep." *Weekly Report,* Nov. 28, 1969, pp. 2408-09.

Congressional Quarterly. "The Record: Stirring Speeches in Absentia." *Weekly Report,* March 15, 1975, pp. 527-29.

Congressional Quarterly. "Technology Assessment: A New Tool for Congress." *Weekly Report,* April 7, 1973, pp. 772-75.

"Congressional Record." *New Republic,* Dec. 7, 1975, pp. 7-8.

Knoll, Edwin. "The Half-Hearted GAO: The Congress Gets What It Wants." *Progressive,* May 1971, pp. 19-23.

Mantel, Howard N. "The Congressional Record: Fact or Fiction of the Legislative Process." *Western Political Quarterly,* December 1959, pp. 981-95.

Morgan, Thomas D. "The General Accounting Office: One Hope for Congress to Regain Parity of Power with the President." *North Carolina Law Review,* October 1973, pp. 1279-1368.

Pearce, John M. "Senate Seeks to Expand GAO's Watchdog Capabilities." *National Journal Reports,* Feb. 6, 1971, pp. 273-79.

Rubin, Harold H. "The Role of the GAO in the Seventies and What GAO is Doing to Prepare for It." *GAO Report,* Winter 1971, pp. 45-52.

Staats, Elmer B. "The GAO: Government Watchdog, Analyst, Critic." *GAO Report,* Fall 1972, pp. 1-10.

Government Publications

U.S. Congress. House. Committee on Appropriations. *Legislative Branch Appropriation Bill, 1976.* H. Rept. 94-208 to Accompany HR 6950, 94th Cong., 1st sess., 1975.

U.S. Congress. House. Committee on Appropriations. Subcommittee on Legislative Branch Appropriations. *Hearings, Legislative Branch Appropriations for 1976.* 94th Cong., 1st sess., 1975.

U.S. Congress. House. Committee on Government Operations. *The General Accounting Office: A Study of Its Organization and Administration with Recommendations for Increasing Effectiveness.* Washington: Government Printing Office, 1956.

U.S. Congress. Joint Committee on Congressional Operations. *Availability of Information to Congress.* 93rd Cong., 1st sess., 1973.

U.S. Congress. Joint Committee on Congressional Operations. *Congressional Research Support and Information Services: A Compendium of Materials.* Committee Print, 93rd Cong., 2nd sess., 1974.

U.S. Congress. Joint Committee on Congressional Operations. *Hearings on Fiscal and Budgetary Information for the Congress.* 92nd Cong., 2nd sess., 1974.

U.S. Congress. Senate. Committee on Appropriations. *Legislative Branch Appropriations, 1976.* S. Rept. 94-262 to Accompany HR 6950, 94th Cong., 1st sess., 1975.

U.S. Congress. Senate. Committee on Rules and Administration. Subcommittee on Computer Services. *Office of Technology Assessment for Congress, Hearings, March 2, 1972.* 92nd Cong., 2nd sess., 1972.

U.S. General Accounting Office. *Annual Report of the Comptroller General of the United States, 1974.* Washington: Government Printing Office, 1975.

U.S. General Accounting Office. *The U.S. General Accounting Office: Purpose, Functions, Services.* Washington: 1973.

CONGRESS AND THE ELECTORATE

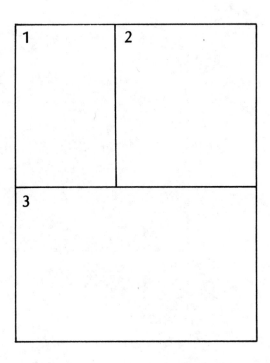

1. Voter in Lancaster, Pa., Nov. 2, 1948. (USIA photo, National Archives photo no. 49-1757, 1st accession.)

2. Gen. Walter Faulkner, congressional candidate, campaigning in June 1938 in Crossville, Tenn. (Farm Security Administration photo by Dorothea Lange, Library of Congress photo no. LC-USF34-18220-E.)

3. Herbert E. Harris II (D Va.), on right, campaigning for a House seat with the aid of former Virginia Lt. Gov. Henry Howell (D), Oct. 19, 1974.

The Voting Population

Few elements of American government have changed so markedly over the years as has the electorate. From the early days of the nation, when the voting privilege was limited to the upper economic classes, one voting barrier after another has fallen to pressures for wider suffrage. First nonproperty-holding males, then women, then black Americans and finally young people pushed for the franchise. By 1976, almost every restriction on voting had been removed and virtually every adult citizen had won the right to vote.

Actions to expand the electorate have taken place at both the state and federal levels. (Voting qualifications have varied widely in the states because of a provision of the federal Constitution (Article I, Section 2) permitting the states to set their own voting standards.) Early in the nation's history, the states dropped their property qualifications for voting but some retained literacy tests as late as 1970.

Constitutional Amendments on Voting

On the federal level, the Constitution has been amended five times to circumvent state qualifications denying the franchise to certain categories of persons. The Fourteenth Amendment, ratified in 1868, directed Congress to reduce the number of representatives from any state that disfranchised any adult male citizen for any reason other than commission of a crime, but no such reduction was ever made. The Fifteenth Amendment in 1870 prohibited denial of the right to vote "on account of race, color or previous condition of servitude," while the Nineteenth Amendment in 1920 prohibited denial of that right "on account of sex." The Twenty-fourth Amendment in 1964 outlawed denial of the right to vote in any federal election "by reason of failure to pay any poll tax or other tax." Finally, in 1971, the Twenty-sixth Amendment lowered the voting age to 18 in all the states.

Congress in the 1950s and 1960s enacted a series of statutes to enforce the Fifteenth Amendment's guaranty against racial discrimination in voting. A law passed in 1970 nullified state residence requirements of longer than 30 days for voting in presidential elections, suspended literacy tests for a five-year period and lowered the minimum voting age from 21 years (the level in most states) to 18 years. A Supreme Court ruling upheld the voting-age change with

respect to federal elections but invalidated it with respect to state and local elections. In the same decision *(Oregon v. Mitchell,* 400 U.S. 112, 1970) the court upheld the provision on residence requirements and sustained the suspension of literacy tests with respect to both state and local elections. The Twenty-sixth Amendment was ratified six months after the court's decision.

The right to vote in presidential elections was extended to citizens of the District of Columbia by the Twenty-third Amendment, ratified in 1961. District residents had been disfranchised for national elections except for a brief period in the 1870s, when they elected a nonvoting delegate to the House of Representatives. In 1970, Congress took another step toward full suffrage for District residents by again authorizing the election of a nonvoting delegate to the House, beginning in 1971.

Increases in Persons Voting

Statistics show that each major liberalization of election laws has resulted in a sharp increase in the number of persons voting. From 1824 to 1856, a period in which states gradually relaxed their property and taxpaying qualifications for voting, voter participation in presidential elections increased from 3.8 per cent to 16.7 per cent of the total population. From 1912, when women intensified their campaign for the ballot, until 1920, when the Constitution was amended to prohibit voter discrimination against women, participation increased from 15.8 to 25.1 per cent. Largely because of growing political awareness by women and passage of new civil rights laws enfranchising blacks, participation increased to 38.1 per cent of the population by 1960 but fell off slightly thereafter.[1] Total voter turnout rose to 77,719,000 in 1972.[2] The total in 1972 was 4.5 million more than the 1968 vote, reflecting the addition of voters as young as 18. *(Voter participation, p. 519)*

Despite a steady increase in the numbers of persons voting, voter turnout has actually decreased in terms of percentages of *eligible voters* voting. For the purpose of voting studies, eligible voters normally are defined as all adult civilians of voting age (whether registered or not) except persons housed in penal and other institutions. Voter participation reached a modern peak of 62.8 per cent in the 1960 presidential election. But it declined steadily over the next decade to 61.8 per cent in 1964, 60.9 per cent in 1968 and only 55.4 per cent in 1972. Voting in the off-year congressional elections, always lower than the presidential years, also declined during this period.[3]

Political scientists have attributed the percentage decline in voter participation to several factors: long periods of political stability; the predictable outcome of many races; the lack of appeal of some candidates; and the fact that many eligible voters do not bother to register to vote.

Differences in Voter Participation

Studies by the Bureau of the Census have shown a marked difference in participation among various classes of voters. In general, the studies have found higher participation rates among men, whites, persons 45 to 54 years of age, non-southerners, persons with higher family incomes, and white-collar employees and professionals. Private studies have shown repeatedly that higher turnout rates generally favor Democrats while lower ones favor Republicans. Far more voters are registered as Democrats.

As the voting population has grown, political parties have become increasingly important in the electoral process. As the power of the individual's vote became more and more diluted, voters found parties a convenient mechanism for defining political issues and mobilizing the strength to push a particular policy through to enactment and execution. After the rise and fall of numerous different political parties during the first half of the 19th century, most voting strength became and remained polarized in two major parties—the Republican and the Democratic.

What follows is a history of voting qualifications in the United States, together with details of actions by the state and federal governments to expand suffrage. The role of political parties in the process is examined, and studies on voter participation levels among various groups are provided.

Property Qualifications

During the first few decades after establishment of the new national government, all 13 of the original states limited the franchise to property holders and taxpayers. Seven of the states required ownership of land or a life estate as opposed to a leased estate as a qualification for voting, while the other six permitted persons to substitute either evidence of ownership of certain amounts of personal property or payment of taxes as a prerequisite to exercise of the franchise.

The framers of the Constitution were apparently content to have the states limit the right to vote to adult males who had a real stake in good government; this meant, in most cases, persons in the upper economic levels. Not wishing to discriminate against any particular type of property owner (uniform federal voting standards inevitably would have conflicted with some of the state standards), the convention adopted without dissent the recommendation of its Committee of Detail providing that qualifications for the electors of the House of Representatives "shall be the same...as those of the electors in the several states of the most numerous branch of their own legislatures."[4]

Under this provision fewer than one-half of the adult white men in the United States were eligible to vote at the outset in federal elections. Because no state made women eligible (although none was forbidden to do so), only one white adult in four qualified to go to the polls. Slaves, both black and Indian, were ineligible, and they comprised almost one-fifth of the American population as enumerated in the census of 1790. Also ineligible were white indentured servants, whose status was little better than that of slaves.

Actually, these early state practices represented a liberalization of restrictions on voting that had prevailed at one time in the colonial period. Roman Catholics had been disfranchised in almost every colony, Jews in most colonies, Quakers and Baptists in some. In Rhode Island, Jews remained legally ineligible to vote until 1842.

For upwards of half a century before the Civil War there was a steady broadening of the electorate. The new western settlements supplied a sharp and continuing stimulus to the principle of universal manhood suffrage, and Jacksonian democracy encouraged its acceptance. Gradually, the seven states making property ownership a condition for voting substituted a taxpaying requirement: Delaware in 1792; Maryland in 1810; Connecticut in 1818; Massachusetts in 1821; New York in 1821; Rhode Island in 1842, and Virginia in 1850. By the mid-19th century, most states had removed even the taxpaying qualifications although some jurisdictions persisted in this practice into the 20th century.

The Black Vote

In no period of American history were all black people excluded from the polls. At the time of the Constitutional Convention free blacks had the right of suffrage in all the original states except Georgia, South Carolina and Virginia. Their right to vote stemmed from the fact that the first blacks in America had been regarded not as slaves but as indentured servants who could expect freedom after a term of years. By 1800, however, the greater part of black people was held in slavery; and, as the institution of slavery for life was more firmly established, disfranchisement became widespread. At the outbreak of the Civil War black Americans were disfranchised, solely on the basis of their race, in all except six of the 33 states.

President Lincoln's Emancipation Proclamation of 1863 was the prelude to enfranchisement of former slaves after the Civil War. Lincoln himself preferred to move cautiously in expanding the black electorate, however, so as to ease the impact of change on the southern states. In 1864, he wrote a letter for the private consideration of the interim governor of Louisiana in which he broached the matter of allowing some blacks to vote, especially the "very intelligent" and those who had fought on the Union side. Lincoln was not disposed to force the southern states to accept all blacks as qualified voters.[5]

Black Voting in South after Civil War

Soon after Lincoln's assassination, several southern states enacted so-called "Black Codes" barring the newly liberated slaves from voting or holding office. Radical Republicans in Congress responded by passing the Reconstruction Act of 1867, which established provisional military governments in the southern states. Return of control to state officials was made dependent upon ratification of the Fourteenth Amendment. The second section of the amendment provided for reducing the representation in Congress of any state denying the franchise to any male citizen over 21 years of age, in the proportion which the number of the disfranchised bore to the whole adult male population of the state.

The Reconstruction Act conditioned readmission to the Union on extension of the franchise to all adult males "of whatever race, color or previous condition." On Feb. 26, 1869, Congress submitted to the states the Fifteenth Amendment, the first section of which provided: "The right of citizens of the United States to vote shall not be denied or abridged by the United States or by any state on account of race, color or previous condition of servitude." Ratification was completed in less than one year.

The Radical Republican majority in Congress feared that unless blacks were allowed to vote, Democrats and ex-rebels would quickly regain control of the national government. In the presidential election of 1868, in fact, Gen. Ulysses S. Grant defeated his Democratic opponent, Horatio Seymour, by a margin of less than 305,000 votes, with the new black vote probably deciding the election in favor of Grant.

The newly enfranchised blacks obtained many important posts in the governments formed under the Reconstruction Act of 1867. Louisiana, Mississippi and South Carolina had black lieutenant governors. Between 1870 and 1900, 22 blacks were sent to Congress from southern states. Hiram R. Revels and Blanche Kelso Bruce represented Mississippi in the Senate. Bruce served a full six-year term (1875-1881) and was a presiding officer of the Republican National Convention of 1880.[6]

During the decade of the 1870s there was mounting opposition in the South to the participation of former slaves in the electorate. Gunnar Myrdal noted in his landmark study of blacks in America, *An American Dilemma,* that: "The Fourteenth and Fifteenth Amendments were...looked upon as the supreme foolishness of the North and, worse still, as an expression of ill-will of the Yankees toward the defeated South. The Negro franchise became the symbol of the humiliation of the South."[7]

Loss of Vote After Reconstruction

Congress passed various enforcement acts to protect black rights in the South, but the North clearly was growing weary of the crusade for betterment of the condition of blacks. When the first federal troops were withdrawn in April 1877, the remaining Radical Reconstruction governments in the South quickly disintegrated. Some blacks continued to vote; but by 1900, according to historian Paul Lewinson in his book *Race, Class and Party,* "all factions united in a white man's party once more, to put the Negro finally beyond the pale of political activity."[8]

Mississippi led the way in prohibiting black political activity. A new state constitution drawn up in 1890 required prospective voters to pay a poll tax of $2 and to demonstrate their ability to read any section of the state constitution or to interpret it when read to them. In Mississippi and the other southern states which adopted voter literacy tests, care was taken not to disfranchise illiterate whites. Five states exempted white voters from literacy and some other requirements by "grandfather clauses"—regulations allowing prospective voters, if not otherwise qualified, to register if they were descended from persons who had voted, or served in the state's military forces, before 1867. Other provisions allowed illiterates to register if they owned a certain amount of property or could show themselves to be of good moral character.

Perhaps the most effective weapon for disfranchising southern blacks was the "white primary" in which blacks were excluded from participation in affairs of the Democratic Party. Southerners defended the white primary on the ground that the Democratic Party was a private

organization and hence not subject to the limitations of the Fourteenth and Fifteenth Amendments. Because victory in a southern Democratic primary was for many years equivalent to election, the small numbers of registered blacks were as effectively stripped of political rights as the vast unregistered majority.

Voter Intimidation. Legal devices to curtail black political activity were buttressed by physical and economic intimidation. Gunnar Myrdal, writing of conditions in the South in the early 1940s, noted that "Physical coercion is not so often practiced against the Negro, but the mere fact that it can be used with impunity and that it is devastating in its consequences creates a psychic coercion that exists nearly everywhere in the South. A Negro can seldom claim the protection of the police and the courts if a white man knocks him down, or if a mob burns his house or inflicts bodily injury on him or on members of his family. If he defends himself against a minor violence, he may expect a major violence. If he once 'gets in wrong' he may expect the loss of his job or other economic injury, and constant insult or loss of whatever legal rights he may have had. In such circumstances it is no wonder that the great majority of Negroes in the South make no attempt to vote and—if they make attempts which are rebuffed—seldom demand their full rights under the federal Constitution."[9]

Any black who summoned up the courage to try to register encountered various forms of delay and harassment. The scornful question "What do you want here, nigger?" often sufficed to send a black away from the registration office. If the applicant persisted, the registrar was likely to ignore him, tell him that there were no more registration forms, or direct him to another place of registration which, if it existed, was usually closed. Southern registrars also displayed a tendency to lose registration forms filled out by blacks who wanted to vote.

According to the U.S. Civil Rights Commission, by 1910 every former Confederate state had either disfranchised blacks or deprived them of their political effectiveness. More subtle practices limited black political participation in the northern states. With the exception of Chicago, white-controlled city machines excluded black people from any significant role in politics for the first half of the 20th century. During that time, Congress did virtually nothing to encourage black voting and the courts generally did not take an activist role in enforcing the Fifteenth Amendment and other black suffrage laws.[10]

Supreme Court Decisions. After years of litigation, two of the devices used to curtail black voting were struck down by the U.S. Supreme Court in the first half of the 20th century. The "grandfather clause," exempting prospective voters from literacy and certain other qualifications if they or their ancestors had been eligible to vote before Reconstruction, was declared unconstitutional in 1915 *(Guinn v. United States,* 238 U.S. 347). The all-white primary was finally outlawed in 1944 *(Smith v. Allwright,* 319 U.S. 738). The Supreme Court refused, in the white primary case, to accept the contention that a political party was the counterpart of a private club with the right to restrict its membership as it chose and to limit voting for candidates, as for club officers, to members only. In ruling that primaries were essential parts of the electoral process, the court voided the device that had been the most widely used to keep blacks from gaining effective political influence. The Supreme Court in 1966 outlawed the poll tax as a condition for voting in state and local elections *(Harper v.*

Virginia State Board of Elections, 383 U.S. 663). (The Twenty-fourth Amendment, ratified in 1964, had banned payment of poll taxes for participation in federal elections.) Justice William O. Douglas wrote the majority opinion in *Harper,* declaring that "Voter qualifications have no relation to wealth nor to paying or not paying this or any other tax. Wealth, like race, creed or color, is not germane to one's ability to participate intelligently in the electoral process."

Civil Rights Legislation

Despite the Supreme Court decisions, actual or threatened intimidation, coupled with discriminatory application of literacy tests, kept black political activity at a minimum. It was not until Congress and the White House intervened in behalf of blacks in the 1950s and 1960s that the tide began to turn.

Acts of 1957, 1960, 1964. The Civil Rights Act of 1957 added to the meager legal weapons previously possessed by the Attorney General the authority to institute civil actions to enjoin any public official or private person from interfering with a citizen's right to vote in any election—federal, state or local. Other provisions of the statute gave the federal district courts jurisdiction over such cases; authorized contempt proceedings whenever court orders were disobeyed; provided for appointment of an additional Assistant Attorney General, thus raising the status of the Civil Rights Section of the Justice Department to that of a full division.

The 1957 act, however, failed to take account of the ingenuity of southern registrars in sidestepping or ignoring the law. Accordingly, the Civil Rights Act of 1960 made states themselves liable to suits for enforcement of voting rights in cases where registrars had resigned and no successors had been appointed. Registration and voting records were declared public records, and it was required that they be preserved for 22 months after any general or special election. Such records thus became available to the U.S. Attorney General prior to institution of any legal proceedings. Instead of providing for appointment of federal registrars, as the U.S. Civil Rights Commission had recommended, the 1960 act set up complicated machinery by which federal voting "referees" might be appointed in cases where state registrars were found to have disqualified applicants on discriminatory grounds.

Title I of the Civil Rights Act of 1964 further strengthened the 1957 statute by prohibiting unequal application of voter registration requirements. Moreover, it enjoined registrars from rejecting registration forms on account of immaterial errors or omissions and required that all literacy tests be administered in writing. Most important of all, the 1964 act made a sixth-grade education (if in English) a presumption of literacy.

Voting Rights Act of 1965. The most sweeping piece of federal voting legislation in a century was yet to come. On March 17, 1965, 10 days after black demonstrators were attacked by Alabama law enforcement officers at Selma, President Johnson sent to Congress a bill aimed at eliminating the remaining obstacles to black voting in the South. The Voting Rights Act of 1965 suspended all literacy tests and similar devices in states where less than 50 per cent of the population of voting age had been registered or had voted in the 1964 presidential election. The act provided also for appointment of federal examiners with authority to register voters in areas covered by the legislation. The bill's formula applied to all of Alabama, Alaska, Georgia, Louisiana, Mississippi, South Carolina and Virginia, 40 counties in North Carolina and one county in Arizona.

The 1965 act was extended for five years in 1970, and was amended to suspend literacy tests nationwide and to bring more areas under the coverage of its provisions. The basic law was extended again in the summer of 1975, this time for seven years. It continued Justice Department oversight of elections in certain areas, extended the law's protections to "language minorities" (including American Indians), required bilingual elections in some instances, and abolished all literacy tests permanently.

Rise in Black Registration and Voting

Passage of the Voting Rights Act heralded a significant increase in the numbers of blacks registered, voting and running for office in the southern states. The Civil Rights Commission reported in 1968 that registration of blacks had climbed to more than 50 per cent of the voting-age population in every southern state. (Before the act, black registration had exceeded 50 per cent only in Florida, Tennessee and Texas.) The report cited black registration gains in the southern states as follows: Mississippi, from 6.7 per cent to 59.8 per cent of voting-age population; Alabama, from 19.3 to 51.6; Georgia, from 27.4 to 52.6; Louisiana, from 31.6 to 58.9; and South Carolina, from 37.3 to 51.2.[11]

In the first 10 years of the Voting Rights Act an estimated 2 million blacks were added to the voting rolls in the South, bringing total registration to about 3.5 million.[12] Despite that, voter participation among blacks and other minorities remained relatively low. The commission reported that surveys conducted after the 1972 general election showed that nationwide minority turnout was significantly less than white turnout: white, 64.5 per cent; black, 52.1; Puerto Rican, 44.6; Mexican-American, 37.4 per cent. No figure was available for American Indian voting.[13]

As the number of black voters increased, so did the number of blacks in elective office. The Joint Center for Political Studies, a nonprofit organization affiliated with Howard University in Washington, D.C., reported that the number of black elected officials in the seven southern states covered by the Voting Rights Act increased from fewer than 100 in 1964 to 963 in April 1974. The total included one member of the House of Representatives, 36 state legislators, 427 county and 500 municipal officials.[14]

Poll Taxes and Voting

Payment of poll taxes as a requirement for voting in the United States appeared in two different eras. The levies were introduced in some states during the early days of the republic as a substitute for property qualifications for voting. The intent of the early levies was to enlarge the electorate. These taxes were gradually eliminated, and by the time of the Civil War, few states still imposed them.

During the second era of the poll tax, which began in the early 1890s, the levy, though imposed in some other states, was used in the South as one of a number of devices to restrict suffrage. Poll taxes tied to the right to vote were adopted in 11 southern states—Florida (1889), Mississippi and Tennessee (1890), Arkansas (1892), South Carolina (1895), Louisiana (1898), North Carolina (1900), Alabama (1901), Virginia and Texas (1902) and Georgia (1908).[15]

The ostensible purpose of the levies was to "cleanse" elections of mass abuse, but the records of constitutional

The Growing Franchise in the United States, 1930-1974

YEAR	ESTIMATED POPULATION OF VOTING AGE	VOTE CAST FOR PRESIDENTIAL ELECTORS		VOTE CAST FOR U.S. REPRESENTATIVES	
		Number	Per Cent	Number	Per Cent
1930	73,623,000	—	—	24,777,000	33.7
1932	75,768,000	39,732,000	52.4	37,657,000	49.7
1934	77,997,000	—	—	32,256,000	41.4
1936	80,174,000	45,643,000	56.9	42,886,000	53.5
1938	82,354,000	—	—	36,236,000	44.0
1940	84,728,000	49,900,000	58.9	46,951,000	55.4
1942	86,465,000	—	—	28,074,000	32.5
1944	85,654,000	47,977,000	56.0	45,103,000	52.7
1946	92,659,000	—	—	34,398,000	37.1
1948	95,573,000	48,794,000	51.1	45,933,000	48.1
1950	98,134,000	—	—	40,342,000	41.1
1952	99,929,000	61,551,000	61.6	57,571,000	57.6
1954	102,075,000	—	—	42,580,000	41.7
1956	104,515,000	62,027,000	59.3	58,426,000	55.9
1958	106,447,000	—	—	45,818,000	43.0
1960	109,674,000	68,838,000	62.8	64,133,000	58.5
1962	112,958,000	—	—	51,261,000	46.3
1964	114,085,000	70,645,000	61.8	65,886,000	58.1
1966	116,638,000	—	—	52,900,000	45.4
1968	120,285,000	73,212,000	60.9	66,109,000	55.2
1970	124,498,000	—	—	54,173,000	43.5
1972	140,068,000	77,719,000	55.4	71,188,000	50.9
1974	144,928,000	—	—	52,397,000	36.2

Source: Bureau of the Census, *Statistical Abstracts of the United States, 1975*, p. 450.

conventions held in five southern states during the period contained statements praising the poll tax as a measure to bar blacks as well as poor whites from the franchise. Many historians have asserted that the main intent of these measures was to limit the popular base of the agrarian revolution inspired by the Populist Party.

State Action To Eliminate Tax

In the years following the Populist era, seven southern states dropped their poll taxes voluntarily. North Carolina, which repealed its tax with the granting of women's suffrage in 1920, was the first. Other states repealing the tax, all during periods of keen interest in political races, were: Louisiana (1934), Florida (1937), Georgia (1945), South Carolina (1951), Tennessee (1953) and Arkansas (1964).[16] In each of the first six states to drop the tax, voter participation increased sharply in the election following repeal, decreased in subsequent elections, and then rose again.

Constitutional amendments to repeal poll taxes were rejected by Virginia voters in 1949 and Texas voters in both 1949 and 1963. Alabama voters in 1953 amended the state constitution to restrict collection of accumulated unpaid back poll taxes from a maximum of 24 years with a maximum payment of $36 to two years with a ceiling of $3. In May 1965, the Alabama Senate voted overwhelmingly to

approve a state constitutional amendment repealing the tax; action on a similar amendment in the Alabama House was deferred. The Texas legislature in May 1965 approved a referendum to abolish state and local poll taxes for the following year's election. In the meantime, federal courts outlawed the tax as a voting qualification in a series of legal rulings.

Supreme Court Ban on Poll Tax

On March 24, 1966, the U.S. Supreme Court by a 6-3 vote held that the $1.50 poll tax imposed by Virginia on citizens desiring to vote in state and local elections violated the Equal Protection clause of the Constitution. (The Fourteenth Amendment stated: "...nor shall any State...deny to any person within its jurisdiction the equal protection of the law.") The Court's decision in *Harper v. Virginia State Board of Elections* and *Butts v. Harrison* (383 U.S. 663), decided as one case, struck down Virginia's poll tax and by extension that of Mississippi. Vermont, by legislation enacted on Feb. 23, 1966, eliminated its poll tax, while three-judge federal district courts declared unconstitutional the poll taxes in Texas (*U.S. v. Texas*, Feb. 9, 1966) and in Alabama (*U.S. v. Alabama*, March 3, 1966). The rulings completed a series of federal actions to eliminate the payment of a poll tax as a prerequisite for voting. The Twenty-fourth Amendment, approved by Congress in 1962 and ratified by the states in 1964, had banned the tax only in federal elections.

For more than two decades, there had been controversy in Congress over the proper approach to banning the poll tax. Some opponents of the levy favored an outright ban by congressional statute while others favored court action. The issue came to a head in 1965 when the Senate narrowly rejected (45-49 roll-call vote) an amendment to the Voting Rights Act which would have imposed a flat ban on the tax in all elections. Instead, Congress approved a provision declaring that payment of the poll tax abridged the right to vote and directing the U.S. Attorney General to institute "forthwith" court suits challenging the validity of the tax. The successful cases in Alabama and Texas were filed under that authority. The Virginia case was filed by a private citizen, Mrs. Annie E. Harper.

Women's Suffrage

The drive for women's suffrage, which began in the late 1830s, was closely related in the beginning to the movement for abolition of slavery. Women, because of their extensive legal disadvantages under the common law, often compared their lot to that of slaves and thus directed the bulk of their political activity against proposals for extension of slavery. Women were disfranchised at every level of government. Only in New Jersey did they have a theoretical right to vote, but the right had been included inadvertently in the state constitutions of 1776 and 1797. The state legislature repealed the provision at the outset of the 19th century when some women actually attempted to vote.

Gradual Gains for Women's Suffrage

Early victories for the women's suffrage movement came mostly in connection with school elections. Kentucky in 1838 gave the vote to widows and unmarried women with property subject to taxation for school purposes. Kansas in 1861 gave women the vote on all school questions, and Michigan, Utah, Minnesota, Colorado, New Hampshire and Massachusetts followed by 1880.

The Woman's Rights Convention at Seneca Falls, N.Y., in July 1848, is generally cited as the beginning of the women's suffrage movement in the United States. But the Declaration of Principles which Elizabeth Cady Stanton read at that meeting and which thereafter became a sacred text for the movement, was a much broader and more revolutionary document than a simple claim for the franchise.

Direct-action tactics were first applied by suffragists shortly after the Civil War, when Susan B. Anthony urged women to go to the polls and claim the right to vote under terms of the newly adopted Fourteenth Amendment. In the national elections of 1872, Anthony voted in her home city of Rochester, N.Y., and was tried and convicted of the crime of "voting without having a lawful right to vote." For almost a quarter of a century, Anthony and her followers pressed Congress for a constitutional amendment granting women's suffrage. On Jan. 25, 1887, almost 12 years after the suffragists had formally proposed such an amendment to Congress, it finally came up for consideration in the Senate but was rejected by a 16-34 roll-call vote. The suffrage forces then focused the bulk of their effort on the states, where they enjoyed considerable success in the West.

Wyoming (then a territory) extended full suffrage to women in 1869 (a right retained when Wyoming became a state in 1890). Three other western states extended the franchise to women before the turn of the century—Colorado in 1893, and Utah and Idaho in 1896.

After 1896, advocates of suffrage for women encountered stronger opposition, and it was not until the height of the Progressive movement in 1910 that other states, mostly in the West, gave women full voting rights. Equal suffrage was granted by Washington in 1910, California in 1911, Arizona, Kansas and Oregon in 1912, and Montana and Nevada in 1914. New York followed suit in 1917.

Grounds for Opposition

Opponents argued that women were the "weaker sex," that their temperament was unsuited to make the kinds of decisions necessary in casting a ballot, and that suffrage might alter the relationship between the sexes.

In the two decades preceding women's enfranchisement, extravagant claims were made by extremists on both sides. Radical feminists often insisted that women voters would be able to cleanse American politics of its corruption and usher in some ill-defined, utopian golden age. Anti-franchise forces were no less impractical in their claims. During World War I, Henry A. Wise Wood, president of the Aero Club of America, told the House Committee on Woman Suffrage that giving women the vote would mean "the dilution with the qualities of the cow, of the qualities of the bull upon which all the herd's safety must depend." And the January 1917 issue of *Remonstrance*, an anti-suffrage journal, cautioned that women's suffrage would lead to the nationalization of women, free love and communism."[17]

Fight for Constitutional Amendment

About the time of the outbreak of World War I in Europe, the advocates of militant tactics, commonly called suffragettes rather than suffragists, took the lead in the national campaign. In the congressional elections of 1914, in the nine (later in the year, 11) states permitting women to vote, they set out to defeat all Democratic candidates on the ground that the Democrats, as the majority party, were responsible for the failure of Congress to submit to the states a constitutional amendment granting women suffrage. Suffrage advocates opposed all Democratic candidates regardless of their stand on the suffrage question. In the election, only 20 of the 43 Democratic candidates in the suffrage states were elected. The outcome of the election failed, however, to move President Wilson, who preferred state rather than federal action on women's suffrage.

Wilson's opposition to a constitutional amendment prompted a series of stormy demonstrations by the suffragettes around the White House and other sites in Washington after the United States had entered the war. The demonstrators insisted that it was unconscionable for this country to be denying its own female citizens a right to participate in government at the same time it was fighting a war on the premise of "making the world safe for democracy." At the direction of the administration, thousands of the women demonstrators were arrested and brought to trial. Some were beaten by hostile crowds—often made up of soldiers and sailors who viewed the demonstrations as unpatriotic. At their trials, many of the women stood mute or made speeches advocating suffrage and attacking President Wilson for his refusal to endorse the constitutional amendment. Sentencing of the women to jail caused a severe housing problem for District of Columbia penal authorities and created considerable public sympathy for the suffragettes. Public support for their position was heightened by claims of the prisoners that they had been treated inhumanely and had been subjected to unsanitary conditions in prison. To protest such conditions, many of the prisoners went on a hunger strike, and the authorities resorted to forced feeding—an action which gave rise to even greater public furor.

On Jan. 9, 1918, Wilson finally came out for the proposed suffrage amendment. The House of Representatives approved it the next day by a 274-136 roll-call vote, one vote more than the necessary two-thirds majority, but that majority was not attained when the Senate voted in October 1918 or on a second try in February 1919. However, when the new Congress (elected in November 1918) met for the first time (in special session) on May 19, 1919, it took little more than two weeks to gain the required majorities in both House (304-89 on May 21) and Senate (56-25 on June 3).

On Aug. 18, 1920, Tennessee became the 36th and last state needed to ratify the amendment, and on Aug. 26 the final proclamation giving women the right to vote was signed by Secretary of State Bainbridge Colby. The new Nineteenth Amendment provided simply that "the right of citizens of the United States to vote shall not be denied or abridged by the United States or any state on account of sex."

Results of the Nineteenth Amendment

In the 1920 presidential election—the first in which women were allowed to vote—only about 30 per cent of the eligible women were believed to have cast their ballots. Analyses of the 1924 election indicated that scarcely one-third of all eligible women voted while more than two-thirds of the eligible men had done so. The women's electoral performance came as a bitter blow to the suffragists.

In more recent national elections, however, surveys by the Census Bureau have found that voting participation by women is only slightly below that of men. There has not been much evidence either that women and men differ significantly in their preferences for political parties or candidates.

Voting in District of Columbia

The right of residents of the District of Columbia to vote in federal elections was withdrawn in December 1800—shortly after the move of Congress from Philadelphia to Washington—when the Supreme Court ruled that the constitutional provision granting Congress exclusive jurisdiction over "such district...as may...become the seat of the Government of the United States" had taken effect.

Except for a brief period in the 1870s, when the District of Columbia had a territorial form of government and its citizens elected a nonvoting delegate to Congress, they took no part in any federal election until 1964, after the Twenty-third Amendment had authorized District voters to participate in presidential elections. For the first time since 1875, District residents in 1971 elected a nonvoting delegate to the House of Representatives.

For almost a century, the District itself was governed in effect by the District Committees of Congress, with day-to-day administration carried out by commissioners and, from

1967 through 1974, a city council appointed by the President. In December 1973, Congress approved legislation providing for partial self-government for the District, with a locally elected mayor and 13-member city council. The new government began to operate in January 1975. *(Background on District of Columbia government, p. 293)*

Twenty-third Amendment

In 1960, the Senate adopted a resolution to amend the Constitution to allow District residents the right to vote in presidential and vice presidential elections and to elect a delegate to the House of Representatives. Under this proposal, separate legislation would have determined whether or not the District delegate would have a vote. The House approved only the provision for participation in presidential elections, and the amendment in that form was ratified by the requisite number of states early in 1961. *(Details, p. 294)*

In 1964, District residents finally were allowed to vote for President and Vice President. The city's three electoral votes went to Lyndon B. Johnson; in 1968, they were cast for Hubert H. Humphrey. George S. McGovern received 78.1 per cent of the District's votes in 1972; the only other jurisdiction the Democratic candidate carried that year was Massachusetts, with 54.2 per cent.[18]

Nonvoting Delegate

In 1970, Congress enacted legislation enabling the District to elect its first representative to the House in nearly a century. The bill (PL 91-405), signed into law Sept. 22, 1970, authorized the District, beginning in 1971, to elect a delegate who would have all the privileges of other House members except that of voting on the House floor. Democrat Walter E. Fauntroy, a black Baptist minister, easily defeated his major opponent on March 23, 1971. Fauntroy was re-elected to the 93rd and 94th Congresses, and was assigned to the House District of Columbia Committee.

It would take a constitutional amendment to give the District of Columbia voting representation in Congress. The legislative changes which brought partial self-government to the District did not stop the home rule movement in the District, and many residents advocated full statehood. They argued that despite its small area (less than 70 square miles), Washington, D.C., had a larger population in 1970 than 10 of the 50 states—each of which had two senators and one or two representatives in the Capitol.

Changes in Voter Qualifications

Special qualifications for voting that have been dropped or modified over the years have included voter literacy, the minimum age for voting, and the period of residence required in a state to qualify as a voter.

Suspension of Literacy Tests

Although blacks and recent immigrants were the main target of voter literacy tests, such tests were used also to limit the electorate to persons thought to possess the qualities necessary for responsible citizenship. At one time or another, 21 states imposed literacy requirements as a condition for voting. The first to do so were Connecticut and Massachusetts (in 1855 and 1857, respectively), which imposed the tests in order to disqualify a flood of European immigrants. Primarily as a means of limiting the black electorate, eight southern states imposed the test between 1890 and 1910: Mississippi (1890), South Carolina (1895), Louisiana (1898), North Carolina (1900), Alabama (1901), Virginia (1902), Georgia (1908) and Oklahoma (1910). Other states adopting literacy requirements have been Wyoming (1889), Maine (1892), California (1894), Washington (1896), Delaware (1897), New Hampshire (1902), Arizona (1912), New York (1921), Oregon (1924), Alaska (1959) and Hawaii (1959).[19]

Requirements under the tests varied widely from state to state. Nineteen of the states applying the tests required the ability to read and 14 of the states the ability to write. Of the 19 states that imposed reading tests, all except four (New York, Washington, Alaska and Hawaii) required reading of some legal document or passage from the state or federal constitution. Four states expressly required reading with understanding—New York, Washington, Louisiana and Alabama.

As applied in the southern states, the tests, together with other voting requirements, virtually disfranchised blacks. Outside the South, the New York test was by far the most stringent although there were seldom any complaints that it was applied in a discriminatory way.

Despite pressures by civil libertarians, Congress declined for years to take action to void literacy requirements. Federal action modifying the application of the tests, it was feared, would interfere with the states' constitutional rights to impose their own voting requirements. In the 1950s and 1960s, however, reports of extreme examples of voter discrimination in the South prompted Congress to enact remedial legislation. Basing their actions on authority of the Fourteenth and Fifteenth Amendments, which guarantee due process of law and prohibit voter discrimination on the basis of race, creed or color, Congress passed three civil rights acts dealing in part with voter discrimination (1957, 1960 and 1964). In 1965 it passed a sweeping Voting Rights Act which suspended literacy tests in seven southern states and in a part of another state.

In 1970, the new voting act suspended all literacy tests, whether discriminatory or not, for a five-year period (through Aug. 6, 1975). The Supreme Court in *Oregon v. Mitchell* (400 U.S. 112) upheld the constitutionality of that provision. Suspension of the tests was expected to extend the franchise to about two million previously disfranchised persons in 12 states where the tests still applied—Alaska, Arizona, California, Connecticut, Delaware, Maine, Massachusetts, New Hampshire, New York, North Carolina (only with respect to counties not covered under provisions of the 1965 Voting Rights Act), Washington and Wyoming. When the act was amended again in 1975, literacy tests were abolished permanently in all jurisdictions.

Lowering of Voting Age

In the years before World War II, no state allowed persons to vote before the age of 21. In 1943, during World War II, Georgia lowered the voting age to 18 after suffrage advocates had attracted considerable public support with the slogan, "Fight at 18, vote at 18." In 1946, South Carolina Democrats authorized 18-year-olds to vote in party primaries, but later they withdrew that privilege. In 1955, Kentucky voters amended the state constitution to permit 18-year-olds to vote. The new states of Alaska and Hawaii, upon entering the Union in 1959, adopted minimum voting ages of 19 and 20 years, respectively.

In 1954, President Eisenhower proposed a constitutional amendment granting 18-year-olds the right to vote, but the proposal was rejected by the Senate. Eventually, in 1970, Congress in the Voting Rights Act of 1970 lowered the voting age to 18 for all federal, state and local elections, effective Jan. 1, 1971. The provision was sustained by the Supreme Court (*Oregon v. Mitchell,* 400 U.S. 112) with regard to federal elections but ruled unconstitutional with regard to state and local elections. The Twenty-sixth Amendment, ratified June 30, 1971, settled the issue: "The right of citizens of the United States, who are 18 years of age or older, to vote shall not be denied or abridged by the United States or any state on account of age. Congress shall have power to enforce this article by appropriate legislation."

Residence Requirements

Every state at some time has imposed a minimum period of residence in the state (and some of them a shorter period of residence in a county or voting district) as a qualification for voting. The rationale for this practice has been that individuals cannot vote intelligently, at least on state and local affairs, until they have lived in an area for a given period of time. In some southern states, unusually long periods of residence were required on the theory that they would help disqualify black voters.

Most of the states have required one year's residence for voting, but five (Alabama, Louisiana, Mississippi, Rhode Island and South Carolina) have required two years at one time or another. At one time Alabama required two years in the state, one year in the county and three months in the voting district.

In 1970, 33 states imposed residence requirements of one year, 15 required six months, and two (New York and Pennsylvania), three months. As a condition for voting in 1970, every state except New Hampshire required residents to have lived in the same county and/or voting district, as well as the state, for a stipulated period of time. The most stringent of these requirements were in Maryland and Texas, where voters had to have resided one year in the state, six months in the county and six months in the voting district.[20]

The federal voting-rights legislation of 1970 provided that any person could vote in a presidential election in the place where he had lived for at least 30 days immediately prior to the election. This provision of the law, upheld by the Supreme Court, extended the franchise to about five million people who might otherwise have been disqualified from voting in the 1972 presidential election.

Soon thereafter the court decided (*Dunn v. Blumstein,* 405 U.S. 330) that a state cannot constitutionally restrict the franchise to persons who have lived in the state at least one year and in the county at least three months. The 6-1 opinion, rendered March 21, 1972, caused all the states to change their residence requirements. By 1974, 18 states and the District of Columbia had no minimum requirement, and no state required more than 60 days of residence.[21]

Voters Living Abroad

At the beginning of 1976 President Ford signed legislation (PL 94-203) establishing uniform voting procedures for American citizens who live overseas. It gave Americans abroad the right to vote by absentee ballot in federal elections in the state in which they had their last voting address. The law imposed fines and prison sentences for voting fraud.

The law was expected to end voting discrimination against more than 750,000 Americans of voting age who live abroad. The Senate Rules Committee reported in May 1975 that it had examined studies showing that "nearly all of these private citizens outside of the United States in one way or another are strongly discouraged, or are even barred by the rules of the states of their last domicile, from participation in presidential and congressional elections."[22]

The absentee voting law, together with the amended Voting Rights Act, the constitutional amendments, and Supreme Court decisions, had the effect of extending suffrage to almost every American citizen of voting age. In general, the only remaining restrictions prevented voting by the insane, convicted felons, and otherwise eligible voters unable to meet the remaining residence requirements for voting.

Postcard Voter Registration

Congress began hearings in 1971 to establish a nationwide system of voter registration by mail. In theory, the system would increase voter participation by making registration easy. Census Bureau surveys show that 87 per cent of those who succeed in registering also vote.[23]

In 1976, the House Aug. 9 passed a bill which would establish a nationwide registration system enabling individuals to register in federal elections by mail. But the bill was weakened by an amendment deleting a provision requiring the Postal Service to mail voter registration postcards to every household in the country. Instead, the amendment provided that such forms be made available in post offices and other public buildings.

The outlook for the bill in the 94th Congress was dim; Senate leaders said in September it was dead.

Political Parties and the Electorate

Throughout the nation's history, political parties have played a dominant part in organizing the electorate and thus in shaping the character of the government. From the outset of the Republic, citizens turned to political parties to define issues, to support or oppose candidates on the basis of those issues, and then to carry out the agreed-upon policies when the party was in power.

One student of government, E. E. Schattschneider, described the process in his book, *Party Government:* "People submit to this assumption of power because they cannot help themselves. The immobility and inertia of large masses are to politics what the law of gravity is to physics. This characteristic compels people to submit to a greater channelization of the expresssion of their will, and is due to numbers, not to want of intelligence. An electorate of six million Aristotles would be equally restricted. In other words, parties take from the people powers that are merely theoretical. Nature, having first made numbers what they are, limits the effective power of the people, and the parties merely take advantage of the fact.... As interlocutors of the people, the parties frame the question and elicit the answers.... The greater the numbers involved in the scheme, the more necessary become the organization and management of politics by the parties."[24]

For nearly a century and a half the United States has had an established two party system. Yet such a system was never envisioned by the Founding Fathers, who viewed the existence of political parties with suspicion.

The Constitution did not provide either authority for or prohibitions against political parties. Historians have pointed out that most of the Founders had only a dim understanding of the function of political parties and thus were ambivalent, if not hostile, toward parties when they laid down the framework of the new government. Nevertheless, the delegates to the Constitutional Convention and their successors in Congress ensured a role for parties in the government when they gave protection to civil rights and the right to organize. The Founders set up what they regarded as safeguards against excesses of party activity by providing an elaborate governmental system of checks and balances. The prevailing attitude of the Convention on this matter was summed up by James Madison, who wrote in *The Federalist* (No. 10) that the "great object" of the new government was "to secure the public good and private rights against the danger of such a faction [party], and at the same time to preserve the spirit and the form of popular government."[25]

Emergence of Parties

The first two great American political parties, the Federalists and the Democratic-Republicans, developed as a result of public sentiment for and against adoption of the Constitution. The Federalist Party—a loose association of merchants, shippers, financiers and other business interests—favored the strong central government provided by the Constitution, while the Democratic-Republicans (at first called Anti-Federalists) were intent upon preservation of state sovereignty. Underlying the controversy was the desire of the interests represented by the Federalists to create a government with power to guarantee the value of the currency (and thus protect the position of creditors) and the desire of the agrarians and frontiersmen who made up the Anti-Federalist Party to maintain easy credit conditions and to protect the power of state legislatures to fend off encroachments by a remote federal government.

During the first 12 years of the Republic, Federalists controlled the government. From 1801 until 1829, Democratic-Republicans held the White House and dominated Congress. Although the Federalists continued to put up candidates until 1816, they were never again a serious threat to the "Republicans," as members of Jefferson's party usually called themselves. (Historians use the "Democratic-Republican" designation to avoid confusion with the modern, unrelated Republican Party, founded in 1854.[26])

Unlike the Federalist Party, which was never more than a loose alliance of particular interests, the Jeffersonians achieved a high degree of organization. The Federalists, in fact, never considered themselves a political party but rather a gentlemanly coalition of interests representing respectable society. What party management there was, they kept clandestine.

Groundwork for the Democratic-Republican organization was laid as early as 1792, when Jefferson and Madison traveled to New York State and struck a political alliance between the Virginia planters and New York's professional politicians. By the early 1800s, the party was so tightly unified that Jefferson was able to dominate its congressional wing through use of the binding legislative caucus. After the election of 1816, the Democratic-Republican gains were so substantial that even the semblance of a two-party system disappeared.

Party Affiliation of Voters

For four decades, representatives of the Gallup Poll have asked voting-age Americans this question: "In politics, as of today, do you consider yourself a Republican, Democrat, or Independent?" Results of the poll are shown below. Although Democrats have maintained a strong lead over Republicans in recent years, both major parties have lost voters to the Independent category, which increased by 50 per cent between 1964 and 1975. Persons polled who do not classify themselves in one of the three categories—ranging from two to three per cent—have been excluded from each set of figures.

	Repub-lican	Demo-crat	Indepen-dent
Sept.-Nov. 1975	22%	45%	33%
June-Aug. 1975	21	44	35
March-May 1975	22	44	34
Nov. 1974-March 1975	22	46	32
July-Oct. 1974	23	47	30
March-June 1974	23	44	33
Sept. 1973-Jan. 1974	24	42	34
May-Aug. 1973	24	43	33
March-May 1973	26	43	31
Nov. 1972-Feb. 1973	27	42	31
June-Oct. 1972	28	43	29
June-Sept. 1971	25	44	31
Jan.-March 1971	26	45	29

(Twenty-sixth Amendment ratified—18-year old vote)

	Repub-lican	Demo-crat	Indepen-dent
Sept.-Oct. 1970	29	45	26
July-Aug. 1969	29	44	27
May-June 1969	28	42	30
Jan.-June 1968	27	46	27
Aug.-Oct. 1967	27	42	31
Jan.-Feb. 1967	27	46	27
Nov.-Dec. 1966	27	48	25
March-May 1965	27	50	23
Jan.-Feb. 1964	25	53	22
1960	30	47	23
1954	34	46	20
1953	37	44	19
1952	34	41	25
1951	32	40	28
1950	33	45	22
1949	32	48	20
1946	40	39	21
1944	39	41	20
1942	38	46	16
1940	38	42	20
1937	34	50	16

Source: *The Gallup Opinion Index*, Report No. 125, November-December 1975, p. 83.

History of Parties

Controversy soon developed within the Democratic-Republican Party over Henry Clay's proposed "American System," a program of extensive internal improvements and a planned economy based on the protective tariff. When John Quincy Adams, the former Federalist turned Democratic-Republican, became President in 1825, he incorporated much of the program as his own, in particular a higher tariff.

The American System infuriated agrarian interests, who blamed Clay and the ruling classes for a severe economic depression that hit the nation in the 1820s. The growing schism in the party became complete in 1828, when Andrew Jackson, who had lost out to Adams when the election of 1824 was thrown into the House of Representatives, won the presidency as the champion of the rural and urban masses. Clay and his followers adopted the party designation of "National Republicans," while the Jacksonians soon took the name of "Democrats."

The Jacksonian power base consisted of small grain farmers in the South and West, cotton planters of the lesser plantations in the South, southern tobacco growers, almost the entire voting population of the Piedmont region and anti-aristocratic urban voters in the Northeast. The modern Democratic Party, with a much different constituency, traces its lineage directly to Jackson's day and then beyond to Jefferson's Democratic-Republican Party.

Jackson's program evoked strong opposition from the National Republicans—a coalition of eastern manufacturers, large southern plantation owners and westerners who sought greater outlays for internal improvements than the Democrats were willing to provide. By 1834, the party had become a collecting point for all the elements in the country who were disenchanted with the "mob rule" of the Jacksonians. In that year the National Republicans changed their names to "Whigs"—an English political term signifying antagonism to excessive use of executive prerogative. The party remained in existence until 1856 and won two presidential elections, in 1840 and 1848, when it ran two popular military figures, William Henry Harrison and Zachary Taylor. Every President elected since Taylor has been either a Democrat or a Republican.

Intense opposition in the northern states to the Kansas-Nebraska Act of 1854, which allowed the new territories to decide the slavery issue for themselves and subsequently to enter the Union as free or slave states, led to the formation of a new political party opposed to the extension of slavery. Called the Republican Party, it was composed originally of some Whigs and Democrats and members of the "Free Soil" factions of both parties. The Republicans held their first national convention in Philadelphia in 1856. Their presidential nominee, John Charles Fremont, won a third of the popular vote, and the Republican Party grew rapidly over the next four years.

Republicans broadened their constituency by promising a homestead law for the territories and a protective tariff in addition to the party's main objective of blocking the extension of slavery. These programs attracted numerous small farmers from the Democratic Party as well as a number of businessmen from the Whig Party. After 1856, the Whig Party became defunct; party members opposed to slavery became Republicans and the slaveholders became Democrats. In 1860, the Republicans won the national election when Democrats split into two factions, and Abraham Lincoln became the first Republican President.

During the Civil War and the Reconstruction period, Republicans (called the National Union Party during and just after the war) moved increasingly toward the old Federalist policy of championing the nation's business interests. Tariffs were raised to the highest level ever. Except following Democratic victories in the presidential elections of 1884 and 1892 (by Cleveland) and 1912 and 1916 (by Wilson), Republicans occupied the White House until 1933 and, during much of that period, controlled Congress. *(Political party affiliations in Congress and the White House, 1789-1975, appendix, p. 182-a)*

The Great Depression that followed the stock-market crash of 1929 inevitably brought about a sharp reversal of political fortunes. Democrats gained control of the House of Representatives in the mid-term elections of 1930, and Franklin D. Roosevelt won a sweeping victory in the presidential election two years later. Roosevelt, whose coalition included the South, small farmers and businessmen, minority groups and intellectuals all over the country, was re-elected in 1936 and went on to break all precedents by winning election for not only a third but also a fourth term. Throughout his long presidency, Roosevelt enjoyed Democratic majorities in both the House and Senate.

A turn by the electorate toward conservatism, coupled with the overwhelming popularity of Gen. Dwight D. Eisenhower, the Republican presidential candidate in 1952 and 1956, resulted in Republican control of the White House during most of the 1950s. Recurrent economic recessions under Eisenhower and rising concern over the problems of minority groups, helped the old Roosevelt coalition to produce victories for the Democrats in the presidential elections of 1960 and 1964.

The Republicans regained the presidency in 1968, when the Democrats were badly split over the Vietnam War issue and when third-party candidate George C. Wallace won 13.5 per cent of the popular vote. President Richard M. Nixon, who was re-elected by a huge majority in 1972, tried to form a new party alignment by courting the once solidly Democratic South with conservative domestic programs. But the results were mixed, and the Republican Party was badly damaged when the Watergate scandals forced Nixon to resign in 1974.

Despite the four terms won by Eisenhower and Nixon, the Republican Party was continually outmatched by the Democrats in Congress. The Democratic Party had control of both the House and the Senate in every Congress from 1933 to 1976, with the exception of the 80th in 1947-48 and the 83rd in 1953-54. Also since Roosevelt's time the Democrats have outnumbered the Republicans in voter registration throughout the nation.

Nomination of Party Candidates

In pre-Jacksonian times, the legislative caucus was the primary means of nominating party candidates for both state and national offices. From 1800 to 1824, congressional Republicans even used the caucus to select the party's nominee for the presidency. In 1824, Jackson's followers, realizing their candidate had no chance of winning the endorsement of the party caucus, set out to discredit "King Caucus" and substitute party conventions as a more democratic means of nomination. By 1832, they had largely succeeded. National conventions were called for the purpose of selecting presidential candidates, and most states also had shifted to conventions for nominating candidates for state races.

In the early 1900s, pressures emanated from the Progressive Movement to abolish the convention and replace it with an even more democratic selection process—the direct primary. Proponents of the primary contended that powerful organizations had seized control of the nominating conventions and had frequently ignored the preferences of the party rank and file. Under leadership of Robert M. La Follette, a leading Progressive, Wisconsin in 1903 enacted the first mandatory primary law. By 1917, the direct primary had been adopted for most nominations in almost every state. Use of the convention persisted only for the selection of presidential candidates and candidates for a few state offices, and for Republican Party nominations in the Democratic South.

Use of the direct primary considerably broadened the range of positions that a given political party might take. Political scientist V. O. Key Jr. has noted: "Rival factions and leaders now could fight out their differences in a campaign directed to the electorate—or a substantial segment of it—rather than be bound by the decisions of an assembly of delegates. Aspirants for nomination could likewise appeal directly to voters—or to those who voted in the primary—rather than be limited largely to the cultivation of the professionals who controlled the convention and constituted the operating core of the party. By the same token, new elements of power were introduced into the nominating process. Prominent among them were newspaper publishers and others in control of channels to reach the public."[27]

Southern Primaries. Primaries have been particularly important in districts (many of them in the South) in which one party is dominant and victory in that party's primary is usually equivalent to election. The U.S. Supreme Court recognized the importance of the party primary when it observed in its opinion in *United States v. Classic* (313 U.S. 299, 1941) that the primary in many areas determined the choice of the person elected and thus was an integral part of the electoral process.[28]

Because of the overwhelming dominance of the Democratic Party in the South during the first half of the 20th century, Democratic Party primaries became in effect the region's significant elections. The 11 states comprising the South—all members of the Civil War Confederacy—are Alabama, Arkansas, Florida, Georgia, Louisiana, Mississippi, North Carolina, South Carolina, Tennessee, Texas and Virginia.

Even in 1975, Republicans were a distinct minority in the South. On the national level, they were outnumbered 16 to 6 in Senate seats and 81 to 27 in House seats. Thus, the Democratic primaries continued in the South to be the deciding election more than in any other region.

Closely connected with the history of southern Democratic primaries is the question of race. In many southern states, blacks were long barred from participation in the Democratic primary, either on a statewide basis or in various counties. In order to exclude blacks, the Democratic Party was designated as a private association or club which could freely exclude blacks from participation and thereby prevent them from voting in the Democratic primaries. The practice was defended as constitutional since the Fifteenth Amendment, ratified in 1870, only prohibited *states*, not private associations, from denying the right to vote to persons on account of race or color. However, in 1944, the Supreme Court, in the case of *Smith v. Allwright* (319 U.S. 738) declared the white primary unconstitutional, holding that the primary was an integral part of the election machinery for choosing state and federal officials.

Election to the Senate

Constitutional Provisions

Article I, Section 3.

The Senate of the United States shall be composed of two Senators from each State, chosen by the Legislature thereof, for six Years; and each Senator shall have one Vote.

Immediately after they shall be assembled in Consequence of the first Election, they shall be divided as equally as may be into three Classes. The Seats of the Senators of the first Class shall be vacated at the Expiration of the second Year, of the second Class at the Expiration of the fourth Year, and of the third Class at the Expiration of the sixth Year, so that one third may be chosen every second Year; and if Vacancies happen by Resignation, or otherwise, during the Recess of the Legislature of any State, the Executive thereof may make temporary Appointments until the next Meeting of the Legislature, which shall then fill such Vacancies.

No Person shall be a Senator who shall not have attained to the Age of thirty Years, and been nine Years a Citizen of the United States, and who shall not, when elected, be an Inhabitant of that State for which he shall be chosen....

Article I, Section 4.

The Times, Places and Manner of holding Elections for Senators and Representatives, shall be prescribed in each State by the Legislature thereof; but the Congress may at any time by Law make or alter such Regulations, except as to the Places of chusing Senators....

Article I, Section 5.

Each House shall be the Judge of the Elections, Returns and Qualifications of its own Members, and a Majority of each shall constitute a Quorum to do Business; but a smaller Number may adjourn from day to day, and may be authorized to compel the Attendance of absent Members in such Manner, and under such Penalties as each House may provide....

Seventeenth Amendment.

The Senate of the United States shall be composed of two Senators from each State, elected by the people thereof for six years; and each Senator shall have one vote. The electors in each State shall have the qualifications requisite for electors of the most numerous branch of the State legislatures.

When vacancies happen in the representation of any State in the Senate, the executive authority of such State shall issue writs of election to fill such vacancies: *Provided*, That the legislature of any State may empower the executive thereof to make temporary appointments until the people fill the vacancies by election as the legislature may direct.

This amendment shall not be so construed as to affect the election or term of any Senator chosen before it becomes valid as part of the Constitution.

Senate Elections

The creation of the United States Senate was a result of the so-called "great compromise" at the Constitutional Convention in 1787. The small states wanted equal representation in Congress, fearing domination by the large states under a population formula. The larger states, however, naturally wished for a legislature based on population, where their strength would prevail.[29]

In compromising this dispute, delegates simply split the basis of representation between the two houses—population for the House of Representatives, equal representation by state for the Senate. By the terms of the compromise, each state was entitled to two senators. In a sense, they were conceived to be ambassadors from the states, representing the sovereign interests of the states to the federal government. *(Details p. 17)*

Early Election Procedure

To elect these "ambassadors," the Founding Fathers chose state bodies—the state legislatures—instead of the people themselves. The argument was that legislatures would be able to give more sober and reflective thought than the people at large to the kind of persons needed to represent the states' interests to the federal government. Moreover, the delegates felt, the state legislatures, and thus the states, would take a greater supportive interest in the fledgling national government if they were involved in its operations this way. Also, the state legislatures had chosen the members of the Continental Congress (the Congress under the Articles of Confederation), as well as the members of the Constitutional Convention itself, so the procedure was not an unfamiliar one.

So deeply entrenched was the ambassadorial aspect of a senator's duty that state legislatures sometimes took it upon themselves to instruct senators on how to vote. This sometimes raised severe problems of conscience among senators and resulted in several resignations.

Another problem for the Founders was the length of the senatorial term. The framers of the Constitution tried to balance two principles: the belief that relatively frequent elections were necessary in order to promote good behavior; and the need for steadiness and continuity in government. Delegates proposed terms of three, four, five, six, seven and nine years. They finally settled on six-year staggered terms, with one third of the senators coming up for election every two years.

At first, states made their own arrangements regarding how their state legislatures would elect the senators. Many states required an election made by the two houses of the legislature, sitting separately. That is, each house separately had to vote for the same candidate in order for him to be elected. Other states, however, provided for election by a joint ballot of the two houses sitting together.

Congressionally Enacted Procedure

The Constitution specifically authorized Congress to regulate senatorial elections if it so chose. Article I, Section 4, Paragraph 1 states, "The times, places and manner of holding elections for Senators and Representatives shall be prescribed in each state by the legislature thereof; but the Congress may at any time by law make or alter such regulations, except as to the places of chusing Senators."

In 1866, Congress decided to exercise its authority. Procedures in some states, particularly those requiring concurrent majorities in both houses of the state legislatures for election to the Senate, had resulted in numerous delays and vacancies.

The new federal law set up the following procedure: The first ballot for senator was to be taken by the two houses of each state legislature voting separately. If no candidate received a majority of the vote in both houses—that is, if a deadlock resulted—then the two houses were to meet and vote jointly until a majority choice emerged.

The new uniform system did not have the desired effect. The requirement for a majority vote continued the frequency of deadlock. In addition, critics charged that the party caucuses in the state legislatures, as well as individual members, were subject to intense and unethical lobbying practices by supporters of various senatorial candidates. The relatively small size of the electing body and the high stakes involved—a seat in the Senate—often tempted the use of questionable methods in conducting the elections.

Because of the frequency of allegations of illegal methods used in securing election, the Senate found itself involved in election disputes. The Constitution makes Congress the judge of its own members. Article I, Section 5, Paragraph 1, states, "Each House shall be the judge of the elections, returns, and qualifications of its own members...." *(Election disputes p. 689)*

Critics had still another grievance against the legislative method of choosing senators. They contended that elections to the state legislatures were often overshadowed by senatorial contests. Thus when voters went to the polls to choose their state legislators, they would sometimes be urged to disregard state and local issues and vote for a legislator who promised to support a certain candidate for the U.S. Senate. This, the critics said, led to a neglect of state government and issues. Moreover, drawn-out Senate contests tended to hold up the consideration of state business.

The main criticism of legislative elections was that they distorted, or even blocked, the will of the people. Throughout the 19th century, the movement toward popular election had taken away from legislatures the right to elect governors and presidential electors in states that had such provisions. Now attention focused on the Senate.

Five times around the turn of the century, the House passed constitutional amendments for popular Senate elections—in the 52nd Congress on Jan. 16, 1893; in the 53rd Congress on July 21, 1894; in the 55th Congress on May 11, 1898; in the 56th Congress on April 13, 1900, and in the 57th Congress on Feb. 13, 1902. But each time the Senate refused to act.

Frustrated in their desire for direct popular elections to the Senate, reformers began implementing various formulas for pre-selecting Senate candidates, attempting to reduce the legislative balloting to something approaching a mere formality.

In some cases, party conventions endorsed nominees for the Senate, allowing the voters at least to know who the members of the legislature were likely to support. Southern states adopted the party primary to choose Senate nominees early in the century. However, legislators never could be legally bound to support anyone, because the Constitution gave them the unfettered power of electing whomever they chose to the U.S. Senate.

Seventeenth Amendment Adopted

Despite these palliatives, pressures continued to mount for a switch to straight popular elections. Frustrated at the failure of the Senate to act, proponents of change began to push for a special convention to propose amendments, as provided by the Constitution. Meanwhile, progressives of both parties made strong gains in the midterm elections of 1910. Some successful Senate candidates had made pledges to work for adoption of a constitutional amendment providing for popular election. In this atmosphere, the Senate debated and finally passed the amendment on June 12, 1911, by a vote of 64-24. The House concurred in the Senate version on May 13, 1912, by a vote of 238-39. Ratification of the Seventeenth Amendment was completed by the requisite number of states on April 8, 1913.

There was no wholesale changeover in membership when the amendment became effective. In fact, every one of the 23 senators elected by state legislatures for their previous terms, and running for re-election to full terms in November 1914, was successful. Seven had retired or died, and two had been defeated for renomination.

The changeover in method of electing senators ended the frequent legislative stalemates in choosing members of the Senate. Otherwise, many things remained the same. There were still election disputes, including charges of corruption, as well as miscounting of votes.

House Elections

The House of Representatives was designed by the Founding Fathers to be the branch government closest to the people.[30]

Its members, unlike the Senate or the presidency—elected by state legislatures and presidential electors—were to be chosen directly by the people. They would have two-year terms, so the people would have a chance to monitor and pass on their activities at brief intervals. And the House would be a numerous branch, with members having relatively small constituencies.

The lower houses of the state legislatures served as a model for the U.S. House. All the states had at least one house of their legislatures elected by popular vote. The Constitution left the qualification of voters to the states, with one exception: the qualifications could be no more restrictive than for the most numerous branch of each of the states' own legislatures.

Many delegates to the Constitutional Convention preferred annual elections for the House, believing that the body should reflect as closely as possible the wishes of the people. James Madison, however, argued for a three-year term, in order to allow the representatives to gain knowledge and experience of national affairs, as well as the affairs of their own localities. The result was a compromise on a two-year term.

The size of the original House was written into Article I, Section 2 of the Constitution, along with directions to apportion the House according to population after the first census in 1790. Until the first census and apportionment, the 13 states were to have the following numbers of representatives: New Hampshire 3; Massachusetts, 8; Rhode Island, 1; Connecticut, 5; New York, 6; New Jersey, 4; Pennsylvania, 8; Delaware, 1; Maryland, 6; Virginia, 10; North Carolina, 5; South Carolina, 5; Georgia, 3. This apportionment of seats—65 in all—thus mandated by the Constitution remained in effect during the First and Second Congresses (1789-93).

By act of Congress (April 14, 1792), an apportionment measure provided for a ratio of one member for every 33,000

Election to the House of Representatives

(Constitutional Provisions)

Article I, Section 2.

The House of Representatives shall be composed of Members chosen every second Year by the People of the several States, and the Electors in each State shall have the Qualifications requisite for Electors of the most numerous Branch of the State Legislature.

No Person shall be a Representative who shall not have attained to the Age of twenty five Years, and been seven Years a Citizen of the United States, and who shall not, when elected, be an Inhabitant of that State in which he shall be chosen.

Representatives and direct Taxes shall be apportioned among the several States which may be included within this Union, according to their respective Numbers, which shall be determined by adding to the whole Number of free Persons, including those bound to Service for a Term of Years, and excluding Indians not taxed, three fifths of all other Persons. The actual Enumeration shall be made within three Years after the first Meeting of the Congress of the United States, and within every subsequent Term of ten Years, in such Manner as they shall by Law direct. The Number of Representatives shall not exceed one for every thirty Thousand, but each State shall have at Least one Representative; and until such enumeration shall be made, the State of New Hampshire shall be entitled to chuse three, Massachusetts eight, Rhode-Island and Providence Plantations one, Connecticut five, New-York six, New Jersey four, Pennsylvania eight, Delaware one, Maryland six, Virginia ten, North Carolina five, South Carolina five, and Georgia three.

When vacancies happen in the Representation from any State, the Executive Authority thereof shall issue Writs of Election to fill such Vacancies....

Article I, Section 4.

The Times, Places and Manner of holding Elections for Senators and Representatives, shall be prescribed in each State by the Legislature thereof; but the Congress may at any time by Law make or alter such Regulations, except as to the Places of chusing Senators....

Article I, Section 5.

Each House shall be the Judge of the Elections, Returns and Qualifications of its own Members, and a Majority of each shall constitute a Quorum to do Business; but a smaller Number may adjourn from day to day, and may be authorized to compel the Attendance of absent Members in such Manner, and under such Penalties as each House may provide....

Fourteenth Amendment, Section 2.

Representatives shall be apportioned among the several States according to their respective numbers, counting the whole number of persons in each State, excluding Indians not taxed. But when the right to vote at any election for the choice of electors for President and Vice President of the United States, Representatives in Congress, the Executive and Judicial officers of a State, or the members of the Legislature thereof, is denied to any of the male inhabitants of such State, being twenty-one years of age, and citizens of the United States, or in any way abridged, except for participation in rebellion, or other crime, the basis of representation therein shall be reduced in the proportion which the number of such male citizens shall bear to the whole number of male citizens twenty-one years of age in such State.

Twentieth Amendment, Section 1.

The terms of the President and Vice President shall end at noon on the 20th day of January, and the terms of Senators and Representatives at noon on the 3d day of January, of the years in which such terms would have ended if this article had not been ratified; and the terms of their successors shall then begin.

Section 2.

The Congress shall assemble at least once in every year, and such meeting shall begin at noon on the 3d day of January, unless they shall by law appoint a different day.

---

inhabitants and fixed the exact number of representatives to which each state was entitled. The total membership of the House was to be 105. In dividing the population of the various states by 33,000, all remainders were to be disregarded. This was known as the method of rejected fractions and was devised by Thomas Jefferson. Congress enacted a new apportionment measure, including the mathematical formula to be used, every ten years (except 1920) until a permanent law became effective in 1929. *(Details on reapportionment and redistricting, p. 559)*

Changing Election Practices

The New England states had a requirement for majority victory in congressional elections. Five New England states had such a provision at one time or another, but all phased them out by the end of the 19th century. The requirement provided that in order to win a seat in the U.S. House, a candidate had to achieve a majority of the popular vote. If no candidate gained such a majority, new elections were held until one contender managed to do so.

Another anomaly of early House elections was the multi-member district. Several states had districts which elected more than one representative. But the practice ended in 1842 when Congress enacted a law that "no one district may elect more than one Representative." The provision was a part of the reapportionment legislation following the census of 1840.

Another practice that has faded out over the years was general elections in odd-numbered years for the House. Prior to ratification of the Twentieth Amendment in 1933, regular sessions of Congress began in December of odd-numbered years. There was, therefore, an 11-month period in the odd-numbered year to elect members before the beginning of the congressional session.

The practice continued until late in the century. In 1875, four states still chose their representatives in regular odd-year elections: California, Connecticut, Mississippi and New Hampshire. But by 1881, all members of the House were being chosen in even-numbered years (except for special elections to fill vacancies). One of the major problems encountered by states choosing their representatives in odd-numbered years was the possibility of a special session of the new Congress being called before the states' elections were held. Depending on the date of the election, a state could be unrepresented in the House.

Practices in the South

Many of the anomalies in election of U.S. representatives occurred in the South. That region's experience with slavery, Civil War, Reconstruction, and racial antagonisms created special problems for the regular electoral process.

Article I, Section 2 of the Constitution contained a formula for counting slaves for apportionment purposes: every five slaves would be counted as three persons. Thus, the total population of a state to be used in determining its congressional representation would be the free population plus three-fifths of the slave population.

After the Civil War and the emancipation of the slaves, blacks were fully counted for the purposes of apportionment. The Fourteenth Amendment, ratified in 1868, required that apportionment be based on "the whole number of persons in each State...." On this basis, several southern states tried to claim immediate additional representation on their readmission to the Union. But the House declined to seat the additional representatives, and declared that states would have to await the regular reapportionment following the 1870 census for any changes in their representation.

Part of the Fourteenth Amendment affected—or was intended to affect—southern representation in the House. The second paragraph of the amendment provided for reducing the representation in the House of any state denying the franchise to any male citizen over 21 years of age, in the proportion which the number of the disfranchised bore to the whole adult male population of the state.

Designed as a club to use in forcing the South to accept black voting participation, the provision was incorporated in the reapportionment legislation of 1872. But the provision was never put into effect because of the difficulty of determining the exact number of persons whose right to vote was being abridged, and also because of the decline of northern enthusiasm for forcing reconstruction policies on the South.

As an alternative to invoking the difficult Fourteenth Amendment provision, Congress often considered election challenges filed against members from the South. When Republicans were in control of the House, several Democrats from the former Confederate states found themselves unseated, often on charges that black voting rights were abused in their districts. During the 47th Congress (1881-83) five Democrats from former Confederate states were unseated; in the 51st Congress (1889-91) there were six and in the 54th Congress (1895-97) there were seven Confederate states' Democrats who lost their seats by action of the House.

Procedures for Filling Vacancies

When vacancies occur in the House, the usual procedure is for the governor of the state concerned to call a special

---

Non-Voters, 1974

Voter turnout for the 1974 congressional elections was the lowest in a dozen years. Only about four in 10 eligible voters exercised their franchise. A Gallup Poll of non-voters shortly after the elections asked them to give their reasons for not voting. The results follow. Responses total more than 100 per cent due to multiple answers.

Didn't bother to register or prevented
from registering by residency
requirements 42%
Not interested in politics/
discouraged by political process/
just didn't vote 24
Didn't like the candidates 13
Sick or disabled 8
Could not leave job or working
two shifts 7
Away from home/traveling 6
Other reasons 4
Don't know 5

Source: *The Gallup Opinion Index,* Report No 118, April 1975, p. 24.

---

election. These may be held at any time throughout the year, and there are usually several in each Congress. During the 93rd Congress (1973-75), for example, there were 10 special House elections held to replace members who had died or resigned.

In the days of the lame duck sessions of Congress, elections for the remainder of a term were quite often held simultaneously with the general election, because the session following the election was an important, working meeting which lasted until March 4. However, since the passage of the Twentieth Amendment and the ending of most lame duck sessions, elections for the remaining two months of a term have become less usual.

Voter Participation

A precise breakdown to show which identifiable groups of voters (blacks, women, etc.) have higher turnout rates than others has never been possible. It would require the preparation of an elaborate questionnaire, to be passed out to every eligible voter, asking whether she or he had participated in the election under study.

In every election year since 1964, the Bureau of the Census has attempted to determine the relative turnout of various categories of voters (civilian noninstitutional population) on the basis of a random sample of the electorate. Again, the survey is not precise because it is based on what people say about whether they voted. Estimates made from the survey run above the actual ballot count, because people frequently report that they or members of their families voted when in fact they did not.

The Census Bureau reported that its survey following the 1972 presidential election confirmed "the results of earlier surveys in this series, as well as independent research efforts" about who participates in elections: "Thus, higher levels of registration and voting were associated with persons who were male, white, those in the middle age group (35-64), those persons with at least a high school diploma, those in families with incomes greater than $10,000, and those in white collar occupations. Conversely, females, Negroes, persons of Spanish ethnic origin, the youngest (18-34) and oldest age groups (65 or older), those who did not complete elementary school education, those in families with incomes less than $5,000, and those in unskilled occupations, such as laborers and private household workers, were less likely to be registered and to vote."[31] These characteristics remained "generally consistent" in the 1974 congressional election.[32]

Percentages of Voters in Various Groups

For a decade, total voter participation had declined steadily. In 1972, 63.0 per cent of Americans of voting age reported that they did vote in the presidential election. That compared with 67.8 per cent in 1968. Other surveys by the Census Bureau have found lower participation in the off-year congressional elections: 44.7 per cent in 1974, 54.6 per cent in 1970 and 55.4 per cent in 1966.[33]

Sex. In 1972, as in other years, voter participation for men was slightly above that for women—64.1 per cent to 62.0 per cent.[34] The same was true in the 1974 congressional elections, with a participation rate of 46.2 per cent for men and 43.4 per cent for women.[35]

Age. Up to age 65, voter participation in 1972 and 1974 increased as voters grew older. The breakdown by age groups follows:

Age in Years	Per Cent Voted 1972[36]	Per Cent Voted 1974[37]
18-20	48.2	20.8
21-24	50.7	26.4
25-29	57.8	33.8
30-34	61.9	40.7
35-44	66.3	49.1
45-54	70.9	55.9
55-64	70.7	58.3
65-74	68.1	55.8
75+	55.6	43.7

Race. The total voter participation of 63 per cent in 1972 included 64.5 per cent of white voters, 52.1 per cent of black voters and 37.5 per cent of voters of Spanish origin.[38] The total voter participation of 44.7 per cent in 1974 included 46.3 per cent of white voters, 33.8 per cent of black voters and 22.9 per cent of voters of Spanish origin.[39]

Education. Voter participation in 1972 and 1974 increased with the level of education. The breakdown by years of schooling completed follows:[40]

Years of School Completed	Per Cent Voted 1972	Per Cent Voted 1974
Elementary		
0-4 years	33.0	21.8
8 years	55.2	41.5
High School		
4 years	65.4	44.7
College		
4 years	82.3	58.3
5+years	85.6	65.7

Footnotes

1. Figures provided by U.S. Bureau of the Census.
2. U.S. Bureau of the Census, *Statistical Abstracts of the United States, 1975* (Government Printing Office, 1975), p. 450.
3. *Ibid.*
4. Max Farrand, ed., *The Records of the Federal Convention of 1787,* 4 vols. (Yale University Press, 1966), vol. 2, p. 178.
5. Thomas F. Gossett, *Race: The History of an Idea in America* (Southern Methodist University Press, 1963), p. 255.
6. William B. Dickinson Jr., "Negro Voting," *Editorial Research Reports, 1964,* vol. 2, p. 754.
7. Gunnar Myrdal, *An American Dilemma: The Negro Problem and Modern Democracy* (Harper & Row, 1944), p. 445.
8. Paul Lewinson, *Race, Class and Party: A History of Negro Suffrage and White Politics in the South* (Oxford University Press, 1932), p. 194.
9. Myrdal, *An American Dilemma,* p. 485.
10. Mary Costello, "Minority Voting Rights," *Editorial Research Reports, 1975,* vol. 1, pp. 150-51.
11. U.S. Commission on Civil Rights, *Political Participation* (May 1968), p. 223.
12. Costello, "Minority Voting Rights," p. 143.
13. U.S. Commission on Civil Rights, *The Voting Rights Act: Ten Years Later* (January 1975), p. 60.
14. Compiled from *National Roster of Black Elected Officials,* vol. 4 (Joint Center for Political Studies, April 1974).
15. Frederic D. Ogden, *The Poll Tax in the South* (University of Alabama Press, 1958), pp. 2-4.
16. *Ibid.,* pp. 178-200.
17. Mary Costello, "Women Voters," *Editorial Research Reports, 1972,* vol. 2, p. 776.
18. Congressional Quarterly, *Guide to U.S. Elections* (1975), p. 299.
19. Robert Luce, *Legislative Principles* (Houghton Mifflin Co., 1930; reprint ed., Da Capo Press, 1971), pp. 323-24.
20. *The Book of the States, 1970-71,* vol. 18 (The Council of State Governments, 1970), p. 40.
21. *The Book of the States, 1974-75,* vol. 20 (The Council of State Governments, 1974), p. 38.
22. U.S. Congress, Senate, Committee on Rules and Administration, *Overseas Citizens Voting Rights Act of 1975,* S Rept 94-121 to accompany S 95, 94th Cong., 1st sess., 1975, p. 2.
23. Costello, "Minority Voting Rights," p. 158.
24. E. E. Schattschneider, *Party Government* (Holt, Rinehart and Winston Inc., 1942), p. 52.
25. *The Federalist Papers,* with an Introduction by Clinton Rossiter (Mentor, 1961), No. 10, p. 80.
26. Arthur M. Schlesinger Jr., ed., *History of U.S. Political Parties,* vol. 1 (Bowker, 1973), p. 240; Roy F. Nichols, *The Invention of the American Political Parties* (Macmillan, 1967), p. 176.
27. V. O. Key Jr., *Politics, Parties and Pressure Groups,* 5th ed. (Thomas Y. Crowell Co., 1964), p. 378.
28. This section was drawn from Congressional Quarterly, *Guide to U.S. Elections,* pp. 889-93. For southern Senate primary popular vote returns, 1920-1974, see *Guide to U.S. Elections,* pp. 909-18.
29. This section was drawn from Congressional Quarterly, *Guide to U.S. Elections,* pp. 447-53. For Senate popular vote returns, 1913-1975, see *Guide to U.S. Elections,* pp. 484-510.
30. This section was drawn from Congressional Quarterly, *Guide to U.S. Elections,* pp. 519-22. For House popular vote returns, 1824-1975, see *Guide to U.S. Elections,* pp. 545-881.
31. U.S. Bureau of the Census, *Current Population Reports,* Series P-20, No. 253, "Voting and Registration in the Election of November 1972" (Government Printing Office, 1973), p. 1.
32. U.S. Bureau of the Census, *Current Population Reports,* Series P-20, No. 293, "Voting and Registration in the Election of November 1974" (Government Printing Office, 1976), p. 1.
33. U.S. Bureau of the Census, *Current Population Reports,* Series P-20, No. 275, "Voter Participation in November 1974 (Advance report)" (Government Printing Office, 1975), p. 2.
34. Computed from U.S. Bureau of the Census, *Current Population Reports,* Series P-20, No. 253, p. 17.

35. U.S. Bureau of the Census, *Current Population Reports,* Series P-20, No. 293, p. 11.

36. Computed from U.S. Bureau of the Census, *Current Population Reports,* Series P-20, No. 253, p. 17.

37. U.S. Bureau of the Census, *Current Population Reports,* Series P-20, No. 293, p. 11.

38. Computed from U.S. Bureau of the Census, *Current Population Reports,* Series P-20, No. 253, pp. 17-18.

39. U.S. Bureau of the Census, *Current Population Reports,* Series P-20, No. 293, pp. 11-12.

40. U.S. Bureau of the Census,. *Current Population Reports,* Series P-20, No. 293, p. 5.

Selected Bibliography

Books

Binkley, Wilfred E. *American Political Parties: Their Natural History.* 4th ed. New York: Alfred A. Knopf, Inc., 1962.

Bone, Hugh A. *American Politics and the Party System.* New York: McGraw-Hill, 1955.

Bone, Hugh A. and Austin Ranney. *Politics and Voters.* New York: McGraw-Hill, 1963.

Campbell, Angus. *The Voter Decides.* New York: Harper & Row, 1954.

Claude, Richard. *The Supreme Court and the Electoral Process.* Baltimore: Johns Hopkins Press, 1970.

Cummings, Milton C. *Congressmen and the Electorate: Elections for the U.S. House and the President, 1920-1964.* New York: Free Press, 1966.

Farrand, Max, ed. *The Records of the Federal Convention of 1787.* 4 vols. New Haven: Yale University Press, 1966.

The Federalist Papers. With an Introduction by Clinton Rossiter. New York: Mentor, 1961.

Gossett, Thomas F. *Race: The History of an Idea in America.* Dallas: Southern Methodist University Press, 1963.

Guide to U.S. Elections. Washington: Congressional Quarterly, 1975.

Haynes, George H. *The Election of Senators.* New York: Henry Holt and Co., 1906.

Heard, Alexander and Donald S. Strong. *Southern Primaries and Elections, 1920-1949.* University of Alabama Press, 1950; reprint ed., Plainview, New York: Books for Libraries Press, 1970.

Jennings, M. Kent. *The Electoral Process.* Englewood Cliffs, N.J.: Prentice-Hall, 1966.

Jones, Charles O. *Every Second Year.* Washington: Brookings Institution, 1967.

Key, V.O. *Politics, Parties and Pressure Groups.* 5th ed. New York: Thomas Y. Crowell Co., 1964.

—. *Southern Politics in State and Nation.* New York: Vintage Books, 1949.

Lane, Robert E. *Political Life.* New York: Free Press, 1959.

Leuthold, David A. *Electioneering in a Democracy.* New York: John Wiley & Sons, 1968.

Lewinson, Paul. *Race, Class and Party: A History of Negro Suffrage and White Politics in the South.* New York: Oxford University Press, 1932.

McGovney, Dudley O. *The American Suffrage Medley.* Chicago: University of Chicago Press, 1949.

McPhee, William N. and Glaser, William A. *Public Opinion and Congressional Elections.* New York: Free Press, 1962.

Mayhew, David R. *Congress: The Electoral Connection.* New Haven: Yale University Press, 1974.

Myrdal, Gunnar. *An American Dilemma: The Negro Problem and Modern Democracy.* New York: Harper & Row, 1944.

Ogden, Frederic D. *The Poll Tax in the South.* University, Ala.: University of Alabama Press, 1958.

Schattschneider, E.E. *Party Government.* New York: Holt, Rinehart and Winston, Inc., 1942.

Articles

Costello, Mary. "Minority Voting Rights." *Editorial Research Reports,* 1975 Vol. I, pp. 141-60.

—. "Women Voters." *Editorial Reesearch Reports,* 1972 Vol. II, pp. 764-84.

Davidson, Roger H., "Choosing Congressmen," *Current History,* August 1974, pp. 60-63.

Dickinson, William B. Jr. "Negro Voting." *Editorial Research Reports,* 1964 Vol. II, pp. 741-60.

The Gallup Opinion Index. Princeton: American Institute of Public Opinion, monthly publication.

Gilliland, Joseph F. "Racial Gerrymandering in the Deep South," *Alabama Law Review,* Spring 1970, pp. 319-48.

McIntyre, William R. "Right to Vote." *Editorial Research Reports,* 1958 Vol. I, pp. 201-19.

Meyers, B. F. "Single Vote in Congressional Elections." *North American Review,* June 1890, pp. 782-85.

Paper, Lewis J. "Legislative History of Title III of the Voting Rights Act of 1970." *Harvard Journal of Legislation,* November 1970, pp. 123-57.

Sullivan, John L. "Electoral Choice and Popular Control of Policy: The Case of the 1966 House Elections." *American Political Science Review,* December 1972, pp. 1256-68.

Worsnop, Richard L. "Changing Southern Politics." *Editorial Research Reports,* 1966 Vol. I, pp. 41-59.

—. "Protection of Voting Rights." *Editorial Research Reports,* 1962 Vol. I, pp. 277-95.

Government Publications

Riddick, Floyd M. *The Term of A Senator, When Does It Begin and End?, Constitution, Laws and Precedents Pertaining to the Term of A Senator.* Prepared under the direction of Emery L. Frazier, Secretary of the Senate. Washington: Government Printing Office, 1966.

U.S. Bureau of the Census. *Current Population Reports.* "Voter Participation in the National Election: November 1964." Oct. 25, 1965.

—. *Current Population Reports.* "Voting and Registration in the Election of November 1966." Aug. 8, 1968.

—. *Current Population Reports.* "Voting and Registration in the Election of November 1968." Dec. 2, 1969.

—. *Historical Statistics of the United States; Continuation to 1962 and Revisions.* Washington: Government Printing Office, 1965.

—. *Statistical Abstract of the United States.* Washington: Government Printing Office, 1975.

U.S. Commission on Civil Rights. *Political Participation.* May 1968.

—. "The Voting Rights Act: Ten Years Later." January 1975.

U.S. Congress. Senate. Committee on Rules and Administration. *Overseas Citizens Voting Rights Act of April 1975.* S. Rept. 94-121 to Accompany S. 95, 94th Cong., 1st sess., 1975.

—. *Senate Election, Expulsion and Censure Cases from 1793 to 1972.* Compiled by Richard D. Hupman for the Subcommittee on Privileges and Elections. S. Doc. 92-7, 92nd Cong., 1st sess., 1972.

—. *Senate Manual.* Prepared by John P. Coder and Jack L. Sapp. S. Doc 94-1, 94th Cong., 1st sess., 1975.

Facts on
Members of Congress

The American electorate makes its decision on a new Congress in November of even-numbered years. Early the following January the elected representatives and senators gather at the Capitol to begin their first session. Always there are many new members along with the veterans of varying seniority, especially in the House. But there is a certain uniformity as well, for the general composition of Congress changes but gradually. The names of persons elected to Congress change more rapidly than the characteristics of members.

A popular textbook of the 1960s, *American Democracy,* presented a description of the "average" member of Congress: "He is a little over fifty, has served in Congress for a number of years, and has had previous political experience before coming to Congress, such as membership in his state legislature. He has a college degree, is a lawyer by profession, a war veteran, and, before coming to Congress, was a well-known and popular member of the community. He has been reasonably successful in business or the practice of law, although not so successful that he is sacrificing a huge income in giving up his private occupation for a public job. Congress is clearly not an accurate cross section of the American people but neither is it a community of intellectuals and technicians."[1]

Any composite description of members of Congress might well note that by a great majority they are male, Caucasian and Christian—especially Protestant. In 1976 there were only 19 women in Congress—all in the House—just 17 blacks, and a scattering of members of Hispanic, Asian or Middle Eastern heritage. And since 1955 the Democrats have been in the majority.

Apart from these predominant characteristics, chances are good that a new senator served earlier in the House, but almost none that a new House member has served in the Senate. Only two former Presidents have served in Congress after their terms in the White House—John Quincy Adams and Andrew Johnson. *(Box, Members Who Became President, p. 524)*

Although the legal profession has long been dominant in the occupational background of members, most other vocations, including banking, business, journalism, farming and education, also have been well represented. The leading occupational groups that have been underrepresented are the clergy and workingmen. Almost no blue-collar workers have served in recent decades, although a few members were manual laborers before they began their professional careers.

Only a handful of Protestant ministers have served in Congress, and no Catholic priest had been a full-fledged member until Rep. Robert F. Drinan (D Mass.), a Jesuit, took his House seat in 1971. (Father Gabriel Richard was the nonvoting delegate of the Territory of Michigan from 1821 to 1823.) The 94th Congress contained five clergymen, including the nonvoting delegate from the District of Columbia. Scientists and physicians also have been underrepresented in Congress.

From the early days of the republic until the present, the American public often has criticized the qualifications of members of Congress. Through the years the House has received more such criticism than the Senate, perhaps because senators were not elected by popular vote until 1914.

An early but still familiar critique of Congress was written in the 1830s by Alexis de Tocqueville, the French aristocrat and scholar. After he had observed both chambers in session, Tocqueville wrote the following in *Democracy in America:*

"On entering the House of Representatives at Washington, one is struck by the vulgar demeanor of that great assembly. Often there is not a distinguished man in the whole number. Its members are almost all obscure individuals, whose names bring no associations to mind. They are mostly village lawyers, men in trade, or even persons belonging to the lower classes of society. In a country in which education is very general, it is said that the representatives of the people do not always know how to write correctly.

"At a few yards' distance is the door of the Senate, which contains within a small space a large proportion of the celebrated men of America. Scarcely an individual is to be seen in it who has not had an active and illustrious career: the Senate is composed of eloquent advocates, distinguished generals, wise magistrates, and statesmen of note, whose arguments would do honor to the most remarkable parliamentary debates of Europe."[2]

The public's characterization of members of Congress may have changed since Tocqueville's day, at least to the extent of blurring the distinctions between the House and Senate. But citizens' complaints and criticisms have continued. A Gallup Poll early in 1975 found that that only 32

Members Who Became President

When Gerald R. Ford became President in 1974, he brought to 23 the number of Presidents who had previous service in the House of Representatives or the Senate, or both. Following is a list of these Presidents and the chambers in which they served. Three other Presidents—George Washington, John Adams and Thomas Jefferson—had served in the Continental Congress, as had two of those listed, James Madison and James Monroe. James A. Garfield was elected to the Senate in January 1880, for a term beginning March 4, 1881, but declined to accept in December 1880 because he had been elected President. John Quincy Adams served in the House for 17 years after he had been President, and Andrew Johnson returned to the Senate five months before he died.

House Only	Senate Only
James Madison	James Monroe
James K. Polk	John Quincy Adams
Millard Fillmore	Martin Van Buren
Abraham Lincoln	Benjamin Harrison
Rutherford B. Hayes	Warren G. Harding
James A. Garfield	Harry S Truman
William McKinley	
Gerald R. Ford	

Both Chambers

Andrew Jackson	Andrew Johnson
William Henry Harrison	John F. Kennedy
John Tyler	Lyndon B. Johnson
Franklin Pierce	Richard M. Nixon
James Buchanan	

Source: *Biographical Directory of the American Congress, 1774-1971* (Government Printing Office, 1971).

per cent of Americans approved of the way Congress was doing its job, and 50 per cent disapproved.[3]

Characteristics of Members

Age. The average age of members of Congress went up substantially between the Civil War period and the 1950s, but it remained fairly constant from then to the mid-1970s. In the 41st Congress (1869-71), the average age of members was 44.6 years; by the 85th Congress (1957-58), the average had increased by more than nine years, to 53.8. Over the next 18 years, the average fluctuated only slightly. But when the 94th Congress met in January 1975 the average dropped to 50.9 years. The difference was made in the House, where 92 freshmen members reduced the average age of representatives to 49.8 years, the first time since World War II that the average in either chamber had fallen below 50 years.[4]

Proponents of congressional reform often contend that the average age of both senators and representatives means that persons under 40 are underrepresented while those over 40 are vastly overrepresented, and they claim that the age differential tends to make Congress more conservative than the country as a whole. When the 94th Congress convened, 87 representatives and five senators were 40 or under, an increase of 50 per cent from the previous Congress.[5] The

youngest member of the House was Thomas J. Downey (D N.Y.), who turned 26 shortly after Congress convened. The youngest senator was Joseph Biden (D Del.), who was 32 at the opening of the 94th Congress.

Occupation. From the early days of the republic, the legal profession has been the dominant occupational background of members of Congress—a development that has given that profession substantial overrepresentation. From a level of 37 per cent of the House members in the First Congress, the proportion of members with a legal background rose to 70 per cent in 1840, then declined slightly in subsequent years and remained at a level of 55 to 60 per cent from 1950 to the mid-1970s. More than 53 per cent of members of the 94th Congress listed law among their occupations.

The next most common profession of members is business or banking. Other occupations that have been prominently represented in recent Congresses are education, agriculture and journalism. Oddly, although all members are professional politicians, many still do not list public service or politics among their occupations. *(Box, Occupations of Members, 94th Congress, p. 525)*

Critics of Congress argue that the predominance of lawyers and businessmen is another factor, along with age, tending to give Congress a conservative bias. An earlier edition of the *American Democracy* textbook cited previously said: "Since a lawyer's business is, after all, with the law and government, it is not strange that so many lawyers should go into politics or ultimately become congressmen. However, the lawyer's approach to the business of *making* laws is but one of many and is, more often than not, a conservative one because of the strong influence of precedent and tradition in the practice of law. Charles A. Beard once observed that American politics has long been under bondage to lawyers. Whether this bondage has served the country as well as it has served members of the legal profession is a debatable point. Although the average law school undoubtedly gives the lawyer excellent technical preparation in the field of law, it is all too frequently true that the social and economic approaches to the problems of modern society have been ignored or but lightly treated. Moreover, the practicing lawyer has often been closely associated with business interests."[6]

Religion. Among religious groups, Protestants have comprised nearly three-fourths of the membership of both houses in recent years, although Roman Catholic members have become more numerous than members belonging to

Average Ages of Members

	93rd Congress (As of Jan. 3, 1973)	94th Congress (As of Jan. 3, 1975)
Both Chambers	52.1	50.9
Democrats	53.0	51.2
Republicans	51.0	50.3
House	51.3	49.8
Democrats	52.5	50.4
Republicans	49.8	48.6
Senate	55.5	55.5
Democrats	55.1	55.0
Republicans	56.1	56.2

Occupations of Members

A Congressional Quarterly survey of members of the 94th Congress (elected in November 1974) asked them to list their occupations. Nearly all members listed more than one occupation, and some listed four or five.

As is usual, more than half (53 per cent) of the 435 representatives and 100 senators were lawyers. All but 95 members listed public service or politics as their occupation, and 162 had been engaged in business or banking. There were 380 veterans of the armed forces in the 94th Congress.

Occupation	HOUSE D	R	Total	SENATE D	R	Total	Congress Total
Agriculture	13	18	31	5	5	10	41
Business or Banking	84	56	140	12	10	22	162
Educator	51	13	64	6	2	8	72
Engineering	1	2	3	2	0	2	5
Journalism	19	5	24	4	1	5	29
Labor leader	3	0	3	0	0	0	3
Law	158	63	221	45	22	67	288
Law enforcement	2	0	2	0	0	0	2
Medicine	3	2	5	1	0	1	6
Public service/Politics	235	111	346	59	35	94	440
Clergyman	4	1	5	0	0	0	5
Scientist	2	0	2	0	0	0	2
Veteran	198	109	307	45	28	73	380

any single Protestant denomination. Catholics took the lead from Methodists in 1965 and retained it through 1975.

In the 94th Congress the number of Catholics increased to 124 from 114 in the previous Congress. More than half of the Protestant members were affiliated with four denominations: Methodists led with 81, followed by Presbyterians with 67, Episcopalians with 66 and Baptists with 55. The number of Jewish members increased from 14 to 23.[7]

Veterans. Another dominant characteristic of the membership of Congress is former service in the armed forces. In 1975 there were 380 veterans in the House and Senate—more than 70 per cent of the combined membership. The high percentage of veterans has prompted critics of waste in military spending to charge that members' military loyalty makes Congress eager to fund new weapons systems, generous pensions and other military programs that the critics consider to be unnecessary. Every Congress includes many veterans who retain their military status as reserve officers.

Women in Congress

Women, who were not allowed to vote until 1920, always have been underrepresented in Congress. Starting with Rep. Jeannette Rankin (R Mont), elected in 1916, a total of 95 women had been elected or appointed to Congress by the end of 1975. The total included 84 in the House only, 10 in the Senate only, and one—Margaret Chase Smith (R Maine)—in both chambers. (Box, *Women Members of Congress, next page*)

Even the total of 95 is misleading. Two women were never sworn in because Congress was not in session between their election and the expiration of their terms. Another sat in the Senate for just one day. Several were appointed or elected to fill unexpired terms, and served in Congress for less than a year. Only three women have been elected to full Senate terms.

By the end of 1975, 40 per cent of the women members had entered Congress after their husbands. Thirty-eight were married to members who served before them; 36 of these (four senators and 32 representatives) were appointed or elected to fill the unexpired terms of their late husbands. Rep. Charlotte T. Reid (R Ill.) and Rep. Marilyn Lloyd (D Tenn.) became their parties' nominees when their husbands

died between the primary and general elections. One woman, Rep. Emily Taft Douglas (R Ill.), was elected to Congress before her husband, Sen. Paul H. Douglas (D Ill.).

Following the election of Rep. Rankin in 1916, the number of women in Congress increased only slightly until 1928, when nine were elected to the House for the 71st Congress. Women's membership reached a peak of 19 (two senators, 17 representatives) in the 87th Congress (1961-62) and did not match that until 1975, when 19 women served in the House.

The first woman named to the Senate served there only one day. On Oct. 2, 1922, Rebecca L. Felton (Independent Democrat Ga.) was appointed to fill the vacancy created by

(Continued on p. 527)

Number of Women Members, 1947-1975

Listed below by Congress are the number of women members of the Senate and House of Representatives since the 80th Congress. The figures include women appointed to office as well as those chosen by voters in general elections and special elections.

Congress	Senate	House
94th, 1st sess.	0	19
93rd	0	16
92nd	2	13
91st	1	10
90th	1	11
89th	2	10
88th	2	11
87th	2	17
86th	1	16
85th	1	15
84th	1	16
83rd	3	12
82nd	1	10
81st	1	9
80th	1	7

Women Members of Congress

By the end of 1975 a total of 95 women had been elected or appointed to Congress. Eighty-three served in the House only, 10 in the Senate only, and one—Margaret Chase Smith (R Maine)—in both chambers. Following is a list of the women members, their parties and states, and the years in which they served.

In addition to these 94 members, Mary Elizabeth Farrington (R), was a nonvoting delegate from Hawaii from 1954 to 1957. Hawaii did not become a state until 1959.

Senate

Rebecca L. Felton (Ind. D Ga.)*	1922
Hattie W. Caraway (D Ark.)	1931-45
Rose McConnell Long (D La.)	1936-37
Dixie Bibb Graves (D Ala.)	1937-38
Gladys Pyle (R S.D.)†	1938-39
Vera C. Bushfield (R S.D.)	1948
Margaret Chase Smith (R Maine)	1949-73
Hazel H. Abel (R Neb.)	1954
Eva K. Bowring (R Neb.)	1954
Maurine B. Neuberger (D Ore.)	1960-67
Elaine S. Edwards (D La.)	1972

House

Jeannette Rankin (R Mont.)	1917-19, 1941-43
Alice M. Robertson (R Okla.)	1921-23
Winnifred S. M. Huck (R Ill.)	1922-23
Mae E. Nolan (R Calif.)	1923-25
Florence P. Kahn (R Calif.)	1925-37
Mary T. Norton (D N.J.)	1925-51
Edith N. Rogers (R Mass.)	1925-60
Katherine G. Langley (R Ky.)	1927-31
Ruth H. McCormick (R Ill.)	1929-31
Pearl P. Oldfield (D Ark.)	1929-31
Ruth B. Owen (D Fla.)	1929-33
Ruth S. B. Pratt (R N.Y.)	1929-33
Effiegene Wingo (D Akr.)	1930-33
Willa M. B. Eslick (D Tenn.)	1932-33
Marian W. Clarke (R N.Y.)	1933-35
Virginia E. Jenckes (D Ind.)	1933-39
Kathryn O'Loughlin McCarthy (D Kan.)	1933-35
Isabella S. Greenway (D Ariz.)	1934-37
Caroline L. G. O'Day (D N.Y.)	1935-43
Nan W. Honeyman (D Ore.)	1937-39
Elizabeth H. Gasque (D S.C.)†	1938-39
Clara G. McMillan (D S.C.)	1939-41
Jessie Sumner (R Ill.)	1939-47
Frances P. Bolton (R Ohio)	1940-69
Florence R. Gibbs (D Ga.)	1940-41
Margaret Chase Smith (R Maine)	1940-49
Katherine E. Byron (D Md.)	1941-43

Veronica G. Boland (D Pa.)	1942-43
Clare Boothe Luce (R Conn.)	1943-47
Winifred C. Stanley (R N.Y.)	1943-45
Willa L. Fulmer (D S.C.)	1944-45
Emily T. Douglas (D Ill.)	1945-47
Helen G. Douglas (D Calif.)	1945-51
Chase G. Woodhouse (D Conn.)	1945-47, 1949-51
Helen D. Mankin (D Ga.)	1946-47
Eliza J. Pratt (D N.C.)	1946-47
Georgia L. Lusk (D N.M.)	1947-49
Katherine P.C. St. George (R N.Y.)	1947-65
Reva Z. B. Bosone (D Utah)	1949-53
Cecil M. Harden (R Ind.)	1949-59
Edna F. Kelly (D N.Y.)	1949-69
Vera D. Buchanan (D Pa.)	1951-55
Marguerite S. Church (R Ill.)	1951-63
Maude E. Kee (D W.Va.)	1951-65
Ruth Thompson (R Mich.)	1951-57
Gracie B. Pfost (D Idaho)	1953-63
Leonor K. Sullivan (D Mo.)	1953—
Iris F. Blitch (D Ga.)	1955-63
Edith Green (D Ore.)	1955-74
Martha W. Griffiths (D Mich.)	1955-74
Coya G. Knutson (D Minn.)	1955-59
Kathryn E. Granahan (D Pa.)	1956-63
Florence P. Dwyer (R N.J.)	1957-73
Catherine D. May (R Wash.)	1959-71
Edna O. Simpson (R Ill.)	1959-61
Jessica McC. Weis (R N.Y.)	1959-63
Julia B. Hansen (D Wash.)	1960-74
Catherine D. Norrell (D Ark.)	1961-63
Louise G. Reece (R Tenn.)	1961-63
Corinne B. Riley (D S.C.)	1962-63
Charlotte T. Reid (R Ill.)	1963-71
Irene B. Baker (R Tenn.)	1964-65
Patsy T. Mink (D Hawaii)	1965—
Lera M. Thomas (D Texas)	1966-67
Margaret M. Heckler (R Mass.)	1967—
Shirley Chisholm (D N.Y.)	1969—
Bella S. Abzug (D N.Y.)	1971—
Ella T. Grasso (D Conn.)	1971-75
Louise Day Hicks (D Mass.)	1971-73
Elizabeth B. Andrews (D Ala.)	1972-73
Yvonne B. Burke (D Calif.)	1973—
Marjorie S. Holt (R Md.)	1973—
Elizabeth Holtzman (D N.Y.)	1973—
Barbara C. Jordan (D Texas)	1973—
Patricia Schroeder (D Colo.)	1973—
Corinne C. Boggs (D La.)	1973—
Cardiss R. Collins (D Ill.)	1973—
Millicent Fenwick (R N.J.)	1975—
Martha E. Keys (D Kan.)	1975—
Marilyn Lloyd (D Tenn.)	1975—
Helen S. Meyner (D N.J.)	1975—
Virginia Smith (R Neb.)	1975—
Gladys N. Spellman (D Md.)	1975—
Shirley N. Pettis (R Calif.)	1975—

*Felton was sworn in Nov. 21, 1922, to fill the vacancy created by the death of Thomas E. Watson (D 1921-22); the next day she gave up her seat to Walter F. George (D 1922-57), the elected candidate for the vacancy.

†Never sworn in because Congress was not in session between election and expiration of term.

Sources: Biographical Directory of the American Congress, 1774-1971 (Government Printing Office, 1971); Hope Chamberlin, A Minority of Members: Women in the U.S. Congress (Praeger Publishers, 1973), pp. 356-63.

(Continued from p. 525)

the death of Sen. Thomas E. Watson (D Ga.); Sen. Felton was not sworn in until Nov. 21, however, and on the next day she turned the seat over the Walter F. George (D), who had been elected to fill the vacancy. In 1931, Hattie W. Caraway (D Ark.) became the second woman in the Senate's history when she was named to fill the vacancy created by the death of her husband, Thaddeus H. Caraway (D). In 1932 and 1938, she was elected to full six-year terms. Through the election of 1974, only two other woman—Maurine B. Neuberger (D Ore.) and Margaret Chase Smith—had been elected to full Senate terms.

Although many women elected to Congress on the basis of "widow's mandate" have served only the remainder of the husband's term, others have stayed to build strong political reputations for themselves. Both Sen. Smith and Rep. Frances P. Bolton (R Ohio)—who hold the records for the longest service by women in their respective chambers—were elected to the House in 1940 to fill the unexpired terms of their late husbands. Smith served in the House until 1948, when she won the first of four terms in the Senate. Bolton served in the House until she was defeated in 1968 when redistricting led to a contest with another incumbent, Charles A. Vanik (D).

As women have become more active in politics at all levels, the congressional tradition of "widow's mandate" has weakened. Only four of the 19 women in the first session of the 94th Congress—half the historical percentage—held the seats of their late husbands, and all had been elected to the positions. More women now plan for congressional careers. For example, Rep. Elizabeth Holtzman (D N.Y.) stunned Congress and her party with a 1972 primary challenge and victory over Rep. Emanuel Celler, a 50-year veteran and chairman of the House Judiciary Committee.

In her book about women who had served in Congress from 1917 through 1972, Hope Chamberlin wrote:

"Most members of this numerically select group were reared in modest economic circumstances; almost all attended college; only a few never married. The majority have been white, Anglo-Saxon, and Protestant. Beyond hard work and the gift of intuition, however, they have had little else in common. The laws of chance, if nothing else, argue against parallels. Their geographical heritage embraces 38 of the 50 states; their precongressional careers, if any, span a broad spectrum: teaching, stenography, journalism, social work, broadcasting, the theater, law—even cowpunching."[8]

Blacks in Congress

By the end of 1975 a total of 44 black Americans had served in Congress—three in the Senate and 41 in the House. Exactly half had served in the 19th century after the Civil War. All but five of the 22 blacks elected in the 20th century were serving in the 94th Congress. *(Box, Black Members of Congress, next page)*

The first black elected to Congress was John W. Menard (R La.), who won election in 1868 to an unexpired term in the 40th Congress. Menard's election was disputed, however, and the House denied him his seat. Thus the distinction of being the first black to serve in Congress went to Hiram Revels (R Miss.), who served in the Senate from Feb. 25, 1870, to March 3, 1871. The first black to serve in the House was Joseph H. Rainey (R S.C.), from 1870 to 1879.

In 1874, a second black, Blanche K. Bruce (R Miss.) was elected to the Senate; Bruce was the first member of his race to serve a full term in the Senate and the last elected to that chamber until Edward W. Brooke (R Mass.) won in 1966.

The last black elected to Congress in the 19th century was George Henry White (R N.C.), who won election in 1896 and 1898, but did not seek renomination in 1900.

For three decades there were no blacks in Congress. In 1928, Rep. Oscar DePriest (R Ill.) became the first black member elected in the 20th century. Only three more blacks were elected during the next 25 years. But beginning with the election of Rep. Charles C. Diggs (D Mich.) in 1954, black membership increased steadily. Three new black representatives were elected in the next decade. Sen. Brooke won his first term in 1966. Three more blacks were elected to the House in 1968, five more in 1970, three more in 1972, one in a special election in 1973, and one more in the 1974 general elections.

While black membership increased, two older black representatives—William L. Dawson (D Ill.) and Adam Clayton Powell Jr. (D N.Y.)—achieved enough seniority to be named chairmen of two important House committees. Dawson served as chairman of the Government Operations Committee from 1949 until his death in 1970; Powell was chairman of the Education and Labor Committee from 1961 until the House stripped him of the post in 1967 because of alleged misuse of committee funds.

In 1968, Rep. Shirley Chisholm (D N.Y.) became the first black woman to be elected to Congress. She was joined in the House by Yvonne Brathwaite Burke (D Calif.). and Barbara C. Jordan (D Texas), elected in 1972. In a special election the following year, Cardiss Collins (D Ill.) won the House seat previously held by her late husband, George W. Collins, and became the fourth black woman in Congress.

Rep. Jordan and Rep. Andrew Young (D Ga.), both elected in 1972, were the first blacks in the 20th century to represent southern constituencies. After the 1974 election they were joined by Rep. Harold E. Ford (D Tenn.).

All 22 black members of Congress in the 19th century were Republicans, reflecting the political alignment of the

---

Number of Black Members, 1947-1975

Listed below by Congress are the numbers of black members of the Senate and House of Representatives since the 80th Congress. The figures do not include the nonvoting delegate from the District of Columbia.

Congress	Senate	House
94th, 1st sess.	1	16
93rd	1	15
92nd	1	12
91st	1	9
90th	1	5
89th		6
88th		5
87th		4
86th		4
85th		4
84th		3
83rd		2
82nd		2
81st		2
80th		2

Black Members of Congress

By the end of 1975 a total of 44 black Americans had served in Congress—three in the Senate and 41 in the House. Following is a list of the black members, their parties and states, and the years of service.

In addition to these 44, John W. Menard (R La.) won a disputed election in 1868 but was not permitted to take his seat in·Congress. Walter E. Fauntroy (D D.C.), began serving as nonvoting delegate in 1971.

Senate

Hiram R. Revels (R Miss.)	1870-71
Blanche K. Bruce (R Miss.)	1875-81
Edward W. Brooke (R Mass.)	1967—

House

Joseph H. Rainey (R S.C.)	1870-79
Jefferson F. Long (R Ga.)	1870-71
Robert B. Elliott (R S.C.)	1871-74
Robert C. DeLarge (R S.C.)	1871-73
Benjamin S. Turner (R Ala.)	1871-73
Josiah T. Walls (R Fla.)	1871-76
Richard H. Cain (R S.C.)	1873-75; 1877-79
John R. Lynch (R Miss.)	1873-77; 1882-83
James T. Rapier (R Ala.)	1873-75
Alonzo J. Ransier (R S.C.)	1873-75
Jeremiah Haralson (R Ala.)	1875-77
John A. Hyman (R N.C.)	1875-77
Charles E. Nash (R La.)	1875-77
Robert Smalls (R S.C.)	1875-79; 1882-83; 1884-87
James E. O'Hara (R N.C.)	1883-87
Henry P. Cheatham (R N.C.)	1889-93
John M. Langston (R Va.)	1890-91
Thomas E. Miller (R S.C.)	1890-91
George W. Murray (R S.C.)	1893-95; 1896-97
George H. White (R N.C.)	1897-1901
Oscar De Priest (R Ill.)	1929-35
Arthur W. Mitchell (D Ill.)	1935-43
William L. Dawson (D Ill.)	1943-70
Adam C. Powell Jr. (D N.Y.)	1945-67; 1969-71
Charles C. Diggs Jr. (D Mich.)	1955—
Robert N.C. Nix (D Pa.)	1958—
Augustus F. Hawkins (D Calif.)	1963—
John Conyers Jr. (D Mich.)	1965—
Louis Stokes (D Ohio)	1969—
William L. Clay (D Mo.)	1969—
Shirley Chisholm (D N.Y.)	1969—
George W. Collins (D Ill.)	1970-72
Ronald V. Dellums (D Calif.)	1971—
Ralph H. Metcalfe (D Ill.)	1971—
Parren J. Mitchell (D Md.)	1971—
Charles B. Rangel (D N.Y.)	1971—
Yvonne B. Burke (D Calif.)	1973—
Cardiss Collins (D Ill.)	1973—
Barbara C. Jordan (D Texas)	1973—
Andrew Young (D Ga.)	1973—
Harold E. Ford (D Tenn.)	1975—

Sources: Maurine Christopher, *America's Black Congressmen* (Thomas Y. Crowell Co., 1971), pp. 267-69; *Biographical Directory of the American Congress, 1774-1971* (Government Printing Office, 1971).

Civil War. But in the 20th century, through 1975, only two black members were Republicans and 20 were Democrats.

In 1971 a loose alliance of black representatives formally organized the Congressional Black Caucus, calling themselves congressmen-at-large who represented all black citizens. They pointed out that 172 congressional districts in 1971 had at least a 25 per cent black population.[9] From 1971 through mid-1976, every black person elected to the House had joined the caucus. Another caucus member was Walter E. Fauntroy (D), nonvoting delegate from the District of Columbia, first elected in 1971.

Turnover in Membership

After experiencing high turnover rates in the 19th and early 20th centuries, the membership of both the House and the Senate became more stable from one Congress to another. But in the 1970s the rate of turnover began to increase.

Throughout the 19th century, turnover in the House was greater than in the Senate, primarily because of the exigencies of campaign travel every two years and the tendency of state legislatures to continue re-electing the same men to the Senate.

In 1869, for example, only 98 of 243 House members had served in previous Congresses. For several years after the direct election of senators was instituted by the Seventeenth Amendment in 1913, Senate turnover increased, particularly in the larger states.

In the middle of the 20th century congressional turnover held steady at a relatively low rate. In the quarter century after World War II, each Congress had an average of about 78 new members—65 in the House and 12.7 in the Senate.[10] The 92nd Congress opened in 1971 with 67 new members; the 93rd had 82 freshmen—69 in the House and 13 in the Senate.

The 1974 elections brought a big increase. The 94th Congress convened early in 1975 with 103 new members—92 representatives and 11 senators. There had been a comparable turnover when the 86th Congress began in 1959 with 95 new members.

Several factors contributed to the increasing turnover. The elections of 1972 and 1974 were affected by redistricting that followed the 1970 Census; many House veterans had retired rather than face strong new opposition. Those two elections also were the first in which 18-year-olds were allowed to vote for members of Congress. In 1974, probably the chief reason for change was the Watergate scandal, which put an end to the Nixon administration and badly damaged the Republican Party. The Democrats gained 43 seats from the Republicans in the House, and 75 of the 92 freshmen representatives in the 94th Congress were Democrats.

In the 94th Congress, members elected for the first time in either 1972 or 1974 made up more than one-third of the total membership of the House. Procedural reforms pushed through early in 1975, which weakened the power of committee chairmen and decreased the advantages of seniority, were expected to encourage other House veterans to retire within a few years—thus permitting further turnover in membership. *(Details, p. 397)*

Shifts Between Chambers

From the early days of Congress there has been shifting of membership from one chamber to another. The House and the Senate are equal under the law, and representatives tend to bristle when anyone refers to their chamber as the "lower house." But that does not stop them from running for the Senate whenever they see an opening. From 1789 to 1975, a total of 512 former House members had served in the Senate, while only 57 former senators had become representatives.

In recent years few former senators have gone to the House, and those who did usually had been defeated in their efforts to be re-elected to the Senate. From 1962 to 1974, 62 House members tried for a place in the Senate; however not one person left the Senate to run for the House.

In explaining why they have left the House to try for the Senate, former representatives have cited the Senate's greater prestige and publicity, the more stable six-year term, large staffs and more generous perquisites, their increased effectiveness as legislators in a chamber of 100 members instead of 435, the Senate's greater role in foreign affairs, and the challenge of moving into a new job with a larger constituency.

Shifting of members from one chamber to the other began in the 1790s, when 19 former representatives became senators, and three former senators moved to the House. The number of House members who became senators increased over the next several decades, reaching 55 in the years from 1800 to 1820 and 39 in the 1840s alone. The trend continued. Between 1964 and 1974, 17 former House members assumed Senate seats. By contrast, the greatest number of former senators to become House members in any one decade was nine in the years between 1810 and 1820. From 1900 through 1976, only 11 former senators became members of the House. The only former senator in the House at the convening of the 94th Congress was Rep. Claude Pepper (D Fla.), who had served continuously as a representative since 1963. Pepper had been a senator from 1936 through 1951.

Perhaps the most notable shift from the Senate to the House was that of Henry Clay (Democratic-Republican Ky.), who gave up his Senate seat in 1811 to assume a House seat. In his first term in the House, Clay was elected Speaker—an office he used successfully to help push the country into the War of 1812. After five terms in the House, he returned to the Senate in 1823. Another prominent House member who had once been a senator was John Quincy Adams (Whig Mass.), who also was one of only two former Presidents to serve in Congress after his term in the White House. Adams, who was known as "Old Man Eloquent,"

Record of Congressional Service

As of 1976, the record for the longest service in Congress—56 years—was held by Carl Hayden (D Ariz.), who retired from the Senate in 1968 at the age of 91. Hayden gave up his job as a county sheriff to become Arizona's first representative in 1912. He was sworn in Feb. 19, 1912, five days after Arizona became a state, and served in the House for 15 years. In 1927, he moved to the Senate where he served seven six-year terms. When Hayden retired, he was president pro tempore of the Senate and chairman of the Senate Appropriations Committee. Runner-up to Hayden was Rep. Emanuel Celler (D N.Y.), who served in the House for 25 consecutive terms (1923-1973). Celler was defeated in a Democratic primary in 1972.

---

was one of the most influential members of the Whig opposition in the House to President Jackson in the 1830s.

Those representatives who aspire to become senators usually are taking a risk. Of the 62 representatives who ran for the Senate from 1962 to 1974, only 20 succeeded. Six out of 16 won in 1970, four out of 10 in 1972, and just one out of six in 1974. The risks are higher if the House members are older and have considerable seniority.

Footnotes

1. Robert K. Carr, Marver H. Bernstein, Walter F. Murphy, *American Democracy,* 5th ed. (Holt, Rinehart and Winston, 1968), p. 231.
2. Alexis de Tocqueville, *Democracy in America,* vol. 1 (Vintage Books, (1971), pp. 211-12.
3. *The Gallup Opinion Index,* Report No. 118 (American Institute of Public Opinion, April 1975), pp. 16-17.
4. Congressional Quarterly, *1974 Almanac, p. 852.*
5. *Ibid.*
6. Robert K. Carr, Marver H. Bernstein, Donald H. Morrison, Joseph E. McLean, *American Democracy in Theory and Practice: National, State, and Local Government,* 3rd ed. (Rinehart & Company Inc., 1959), p. 300.
7. Congressional Quarterly, *1975 Almanac,* p. 44.
8. Hope Chamberlin, *A Minority of Members: Women in the U.S. Congress* (Praeger Publishers, 1973), pp. 3-4.
9. Congressional Quarterly, *Congress and the Nation, 1969-1972,* vol. III, p. 505.
10. Congressional Quarterly, *Weekly Report,* Jan. 6, 1973, p. 13.

Selected Bibliography

Books

Chamberlin, Hope. *A Minority of Members: Women in the U.S. Congress.* New York: Praeger Publishers, 1973.

Christopher, Maurine. *Black Americans in Congress.* New York: Crowell, 1971.

Engelbarts, Rudolf. *Women in the United States Congress, 1917-1972: Their Accomplishments with Biographies.* Littleton, Colo.: Libraries Unlimited, 1974.

Ewing, Cortez. *Congressional Elections, 1896-1944: The Sectional Basis of Political Democracy in the House of Representatives.* Norman: University of Oklahoma Press, 1947.

Fishel, Jeff. *Party and Opposition: Congressional Challengers in American Politics.* New York: McKay, 1973.

Fribourg, Marjorie. *The U.S. Congress: Men Who Steered Its Course.* Philadelphia: M. Smith, 1972.

Huckshorn, Robert J. and Spencer, Robert C. *Politics of Defeat: Campaigning for Congress.* Amherst: University of Massachusetts Press.

Moos, Malcolm C. *Politics, Presidents and Coattails.* New York: Greenwood Press, 1969.

Rieselbach, Leroy N. *Congressional Politics.* New York: McGraw-Hill, 1973.

Scammon, Richard M., ed. *American Votes: A Handbook of Contemporary American Election Statistics.* Washington; Congressional Quarterly, 1956.

Smith, Samuel D. *The Negro in Congress, 1870-1901.* Chapel Hill: University of North Carolina Press, 1940.

de Tocqueville, Alexis. *Democracy in America.* 2 vols. New York: Vintage Books, 1971.

Articles

Bullock, Charles S. "Recruitment of Women for U.S. Congress: A Research Note," *Western Political Quarterly,* September 1972, pp. 416-423.

Colon, Frank T. "The Elected Woman," *Social Studies,* November 1967, pp. 256-261.

"The New Congress: Its Members and Its Moods." *Congressional Quarterly Weekly Report,* Jan. 6, 1973, pp. 13-14.

"Characteristics of Members of the 94th Congress." *Congressional Quarterly Weekly Report,* Jan. 18, 1975, p. 120.

Gore, William J. and Peabody, Robert L. "The Function of the Political Campaign: A Case Study," *Western Political Quarterly,* March 1958, pp. 55-70.

McCamey, Denis. "Four Critical Senate Races Highlights 1970 Politics in the South." *National Journal Reports,* Oct. 10, 1970, pp. 2217-2227.

Meyer, Mary. "Black Congressmen and How They Grew: One Hundred Years in Congress." *Black Politician,* April 1970, pp. 3-11.

"Nationwide Black Gains for Elected Office."

Congressional Quarterly Weekly Report. Dec. 11, 1970, pp. 2951-2952.

Paulin, Charles O. "The First Elections Under the Constitution." *Iowa Journal of History and Politics,* January 1904, p. 28.

Walker, David B. "The Age Factor in the 1958 Congressional Elections." *Midwest Journal of Political Science,* February 1960, pp. 1-26.

Government Publications

U.S. Congress. Clerk of the House of Representatives. *Statistics of the Presidential and Congressional Election.* Washington: Government Printing Office, 19—.

U.S. Congress. Senate. *Biographical Directory of the American Congress 1774-1971.* Compiled by Lawrence Kennedy for the Joint Committee on Printing. S. Doc. 92-8, 92nd Cong., 1st sess., 1971.

U.S. Library of Congress. Congressional Research Service. *Election Law Guidebook: Summary of Federal and State Laws Regulating the Nomination and Election of U.S. Senators,* 1952—.

U.S. Library of Congress. Legislative Reference Service. *Members of Congress Who Have Served in Both Houses.* By William R. Tansill, 1965.

——. *Women in the Congress of the United States.* By Morrigene Van Helden, 1968.

Campaign Financing

The cost of running for the offices of senator, representative or President rose to dizzying heights in the decades after World War II and spawned a variety of ploys to fill the treasuries of candidates.

With the cost for some offices going into the millions and for most offices into at least the tens of thousands of dollars, candidates increasingly turned for help to wealthy individuals and business, labor and other organizations with well-filled coffers.

Money became the dominant influence on the election process, and the influence on public affairs of generous givers grew accordingly. But the public saw very little of this. Campaign financing was a sub rosa activity.

The result—the inevitable result, in the opinion of some critics of the campaign financing system—was the Watergate scandal of the Nixon administration. Watergate became the code word in the 1970s for governmental corruption. And although there were many aspects to the scandal, money in politics was at its roots. John Gardner, chairman of the self-styled citizens' lobby Common Cause, gave this analysis: "Watergate is not primarily a story of political espionage, or even of White House intrigue. It is a particularly malodorous chapter in the annals of campaign financing. The money paid to the Watergate conspirators before the break-in—and the money passed to them later—was money from campaign gifts."[1]

Indeed, the "smoking gun" evidence that precipitated Richard Nixon's resignation in 1974 was the disclosure that for almost two years he had concealed his knowledge that the June 1972 break-in of Democratic national headquarters had been financed by private contributions to Nixon's re-election campaign.

Included in the unprecedented catalog of misdeeds were specific violations of campaign spending laws, violations of other criminal laws facilitated by the availability of virtually unlimited campaign contributions, and still other instances where campaign funds were used in a manner that strongly suggested influence peddling or—at the very least—gave the appearance of gross improprieties in the conduct of public life.

Congress Responds

Watergate focused public attention on campaign spending at all levels of government. The public concern forced Congress to enact legislation in 1974 and in 1976 to reform the way that federal elections were financed. (Many state governments did the same for their elections.)

But Congress had begun to move even before Watergate. In the early 1970s, it had approved the concept of paying for an election with public tax money. This was done in 1971 through a check-off provision on federal income tax returns that allowed a taxpayer to put aside a dollar of his tax payment to help pay the costs of a presidential campaign.

Also in 1971, Congress in another law required disclosure of campaign contributions to candidates for federal office and placed limits on the amount of money candidates could spend. The law was greatly expanded and strengthened in 1974, and again in 1976 after the Supreme Court had struck down certain parts of the two earlier statutes.

Taken together, the 1971-76 laws provided public financing through federal tax dollars of presidential campaigns and nominating conventions (although not of congressional election campaigns), placed limits on private campaign contributions to federal candidates, required essentially complete disclosure of contribution sources and expenditure purposes and set up an independent commission to oversee and enforce the law. In a period of less than five years, Congress rewrote the manual of financing federal elections.

Issues Raised by Big Expenditures

Americans became concerned over the orgy of political spending mainly because it struck at the heart of the general assumption that every able and honest citizen of a democracy should have a chance to seek public office whether the person is rich, poor or somewhere in between. It follows that an aspirant for public service should not have to become obligated during a campaign to contributors who will expect him to vote for or against specified measures if elected. There is, however, no simple way to control campaign financing. Regulations to cope effectively with the problem of runaway costs must meet several requirements. The regulations must:

● Be enforceable; that is, they must not have the effect of unreasonably restricting use of the means of publicity necessary for a meaningful election contest. (If the rules are unrealistic, they will encourage evasion.)

• Have as equal an effect as possible on the candidates who are already in office and well known and the candidates not previously in the public eye.

• Be tightly drafted, to guard against loopholes.

• Avoid curtailment of freedom of expression.

The laws of the 1970s attempted to meet these requirements. But by doing so they ran certain risks. Restrictions imposed on campaign financing, if too severe, may trespass on the constitutional rights of individuals, as the Supreme Court found in 1976. Tight restrictions may interfere also with the fulfillment of the democratic process. That is, it does take money to win elections, and citizens should be encouraged to contribute and participate.

High Costs of Campaigns

Until quite recently when specific accounting was required by law, there were few topics in American politics about which less was known than the cost of election campaigns. But one fact is certain: modern political campaigns for Congress and the presidency are terribly expensive. The most detailed and reliable figures supplied into the mid-1970s showed that costs were rising with every presidential campaign.

The Citizens' Research Foundation (CRF) of Princeton, N.J., founded in 1958, was regarded for years as the most comprehensive source of itemized campaign contributions and expenditures. According to CRF estimates, in 1952 the total cost of campaigns for all elective offices in the United States was $140-million. These costs rose to an estimated $155-million in 1956, $175-million in 1960, $200-million in 1964, $300-million in 1968, and $425-million in 1972. After economic and political adjustments were made, the actual increase in campaign costs over the 20-year period was estimated at 45 per cent.[2]

The amount of spending per vote cast increased enormously during that time, from an average of $2.27 in 1952 to $5.66 in 1972. Spending per eligible voter, many of whom did not vote in primaries or general elections, jumped from $1.40 to $3.04 in the 20-year period.[3]

Increased use of the broadcast media, particularly television, has accented the growing problem of campaign costs. Television and radio, a major source of news for Americans, are ideally suited to large constituencies. Television emerged after 1952 as the dominant form of communications in presidential and some congressional campaigns. The spurt in broadcast time spending testified to the increase in use of television and radio. Total charges for political broadcasts in general elections at all levels of government increased from $9.8-million in 1956 to $59.6-million in 1972.[4]

A large share of the total spending for all campaigns is devoted to the presidential nominations and elections. But the costs of congressional campaigns have increased as well. In 1970, the reported total primary and general election costs of all campaigns for the House and Senate was an estimated $71.6-million. In 1972, the outlays for House and Senate campaigns came to $77.2-million; that too was an estimate, and the totals for the year may have been several million dollars higher.[5]

The high costs of individual campaigns for Congress have been striking. Wisconsin Gov. Gaylord Nelson (D) spent less than $200,000 in 1964 to win a seat in the Senate; six years later he spent more than $450,000 to retain it, even

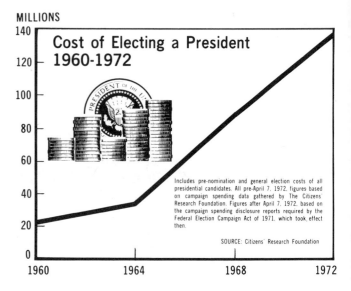

though he did not face strong opposition. In the 1970 California race for the Senate, Democrat John Tunney spent $1,338,200 to defeat Republican incumbent George Murphy, who spent $1,946,400. Campaigns for seats in the House also can be expensive. In 1972, Democratic House candidates in Connecticut averaged expenditures of $74,400; Republican candidates averaged $86,800.[6]

Campaign Expenditures

To be sure, the costs of campaigns have soared since the mid-20th century. But the price tags on elections were a public concern before then. Will Rogers noted in his syndicated newspaper column of June 28, 1931: "Politics has got so expensive that it takes a lot of money to even get beat with."

There are many reasons why the costs of campaigning keep going up. One is the general economic inflation that makes everything else more expensive. Another is the increasing number of citizens who are eligible to vote and who must be reached by the candidates. The widespread use of television in political contests has added greatly to the costs. Public opinion polling, never a cheap venture, has become common even in local campaigns. Mail costs have gone up; in 1976 every first-class letter to voters cost 13 cents to mail, in addition to the costs of preparation, printing and return postage. Transportation has grown steadily more expensive. Finally, all the costs associated with political organization have increased—office space, accommodations for volunteer workers, canvassing, communications and the hiring of specialists to direct campaigns in the field.

Political Consultants

A well-heeled non-incumbent candidate in a typical campaign for an important political office may enlist the services of a professional political consultant, a computer firm, a pollster, an advertising agency, a film-maker, a speechwriter, a television and radio time-buyer, a direct mail organization and possibly an accounting firm.

The cost of such services for a tight House race easily could run to more than $100,000 per candidate in the early 1970s—exclusive of television time expenses.

The political consultant may visit his candidate's state or district only occasionally, preferring instead to closet himself with poll results, computer breakdowns of voting patterns and demographic profiles. He prefers to plan a campaign as early before the primary as possible. He generally prefers newcomers for whom he can build an image. He is expensive. Some consultants command $500 a day for their full-time personal services.

A well-versed campaign consultant must be qualified to work in public opinion surveys, electronic data processing, fund-raising, budgeting, media, research, public relations and press services, advertising and volunteer recruitment. Some participate in policy decisions as well.

No organization has the talent or resources to take on all these jobs at once, but some offer prospective clients a "package" of related services. This practice assures that one firm will be responsible for victory or defeat. Some experienced politicians, however, still prefer to draw on a variety of experienced individuals and firms for their campaigns. Other firms act only as consultants for work contracted out to other individuals or agencies.

For a large enough fee, professional experts in this field will manage every step in a campaign from the candidate's announcement of availability to the post-election victory party. They will conduct opinion polls to determine what issues most concern the voters and even what kind of clothes it would be advantageous for the candidate to wear. They will accept responsibility for fund-raising, recruitment of volunteers, research, computerization of voting and demographic patterns of the electorate, preparation of brochures and documentaries, speechwriting, advertising, holding of rallies, trips through neighborhoods, and every other activity needed for an effective campaign.

Professional campaign management has become one of the most expensive elements in American politics, and questions have been raised as to the effectiveness of political consultant firms. Since only one candidate wins, all the others can conclude that they have sent their consultation money down the drain.

Polls

William R. Hamilton and Staff is a division of a Washington public opinion and marketing research firm, Independent Research Associates Inc., one of dozens of such firms that play an increasingly important part in campaigns. "In the past," says a Hamilton booklet, "candidates have gone through entire campaigns without polls; in today's politics, however, the chances are about five to one that the opposition is making his campaign decisions based on knowledge of how the voters feel about the candidates and issues."

Hamilton, whose firm did more than 125 studies for political, governmental and commercial clients from 1963 to 1971, recommends a basic, in-depth poll prior to any major campaign activity. Trained resident interviewers in randomly selected urban blocks or rural areas of a particular constituency interview five to eight probable voters in each area. The interviewer spends about 45 minutes to an hour with each voter.

When campaign funds are "extremely scarce," Hamilton recommends a telephone poll in place of an in-the-home poll. He also offers "telephone panel-backs," or follow-up polls, and scout studies—quick spot studies—of a particular group of voters.

The cost of Hamilton's statewide personal interview poll of 300 to 800 probable voters ranged from $5,000 to

---

Reasons for Higher Costs

Bills for campaigning for public office were higher than ever in the late 1960s and early 1970s chiefly because of the following developments:

- Enlargement of the electorate (the number of persons to be reached in campaigning) by the coming to voting age of the postwar bumper baby crop and by expansion of opportunities for voting by blacks.
- Revitalization of the Republican Party in the South, making it necessary for southern Republicans—and Democrats—to campaign more vigorously.
- Decline in straight-ticket voting; that is, the rise of independent voting, which resulted largely from virtual disappearance of old-style party machines in the precincts. Split-ticket voting requires each candidate for each office to intensify his efforts to get elected.
- Growing use of radio and television to reach prospective voters.
- Increase in numbers of young volunteer workers, whose services, though nominally free, are costly to administer, involving maintenance of headquarters, transportation of canvassers, arrangement of "socials" to sustain enthusiasm, and other expense items.
- Use of computers to categorize voters for specialized appeals.
- Growing reliance on costly public opinion surveys geared to campaigners' needs.
- Use of other new and costly campaign techniques, including "packaged" campaigns managed by political consultants.
- Inflation.

Source: Adapted from David Adamany, "Money for Politics," *National Civic Review,* April 1970, pp. 192-93.

$10,000. Telephone polls usually accounted for about 50 to 60 per cent of the costs of a personal interview poll, or $2,500 to $5,000. Telephone follow-ups ranged from $750 to $2,500.[7]

Broadcasting

The Federal Communications Commission reported that candidates for all offices—President, Senate, House, governor and local positions—spent $59.6-million for television and radio broadcasts in 1972. In 1970, when there was no presidential election, the total was only $400,000 less.

The 1970 total was almost double that for 1966, the previous non-presidential year. The totals include commissions paid to salesmen and others responsible for the broadcast advertisements.

Clearly, candidates increasingly are relying on radio and television to gain recognition for themselves and to explain their programs to the voters. But there are campaigns where television is not much of a factor, either because of the location of media markets or the area's political makeup. For example, only a rare congressional candidate from Manhattan could afford substantial television time at New York City rates. Candidates from New Jersey have the same problem, because that state has no television stations of its own and depends on New York facilities.

In rural areas candidates still find it more effective to get out and meet the voters in person. Citizens of sparsely settled states who know their senator by his first name are less likely to pay attention to half-hour television specials in which the candidate describes his record. Spot announcements and reminders are supplemented by billboards, posters, cards and—most of all—handshakes and personal greetings.

Print Advertising

Broadcasts cannot handle all political advertising. Some information from candidates has to be read because it is too complicated to be flashed over the airwaves. Politicians long ago learned the importance of getting their printed name before the voters exactly as it will appear on the ballot. Despite radio and TV, political consultants still emphasize print advertising.

Agencies determine the execution of posters, billboards, brochures, newspaper and magazine ads and handouts. Although some politicians discredit the effectiveness of newspaper ads, the medium consumed 10 to 15 per cent of the total budget of a modern statewide campaign in 1970.

Billboards are bought by market, rather than by state, and by what are called "showings," according to Jack Bowen of a Washington advertising agency, Bailey, Deardourff and Bowen. A showing is a projection of the percentage of people in an area who will see a billboard message at least once a week. Billboards are bought in advance, by the month. In the New York metropolitan area in 1971, Bowen said, a billboard for one month at a 100 showing would total 232 different boards costing $34,160. At a 75 showing, or 174 boards, the cost would be $25,620.

In the Billings, Mont., area, a 100 showing, or 14 boards, would cost $1,050; a 75 showing, or 11 boards, $825. In Atlanta, Ga., a 100 showing, or 80 boards, would cost $8,630; a 75 showing, or 60 boards, $6,480.

Persons buying billboards for a presidential campaign, Bowen said, usually buy within a selected list of 50 to 100 top markets.[8]

Besides the agency fee, campaigns must pay for the advertising itself. Ad agencies also handle such campaign paraphernalia as buttons, bumper stickers, balloons, posters and placards, hats, brochures, printed speeches and position papers, costume jewelry and even paper dresses. For national or statewide elections, campaign committees often produce favorable books about their candidates.

Staff and Office Expenses

Although headquarters and staff generally account for less than 20 to 30 per cent of most campaign budgets, a long-time aide to a western senator refused to estimate a probable cost for his boss' next campaign. "It depends on who you find," he said, "a retiree who will work for just about expenses or someone you hire away from a full-time job. Staff costs are among the imponderables."[9]

As long as the campaign continues, dollars flow from campaign headquarters not only for broadcasts and professional expertise, but also for a myriad of campaign services of other kinds. Some expenditures are made directly for equipment, supplies and services. Others take the form of contributions by a national committee to a local committee, or vice versa, to help the recipient committee pay its bills. Some costs are peculiar to the process of running for office; others, such as the Social Security tax on payrolls, are common to any business enterprise.

At campaign headquarters, costs continue through election day for items such as rent, supplies, utilities and salaries of some employees. There are expenses for transporting voters to the polls if not enough persons volunteer for such duty. And poll-watchers may have to be paid.

The administration of a campaign's volunteer work force is costly. Indirect expenses include recruitment drives, maintenance of headquarters, transportation of canvassers, social events to sustain enthusiasm and other items.

Speechwriting and Reseach

Speechwriters and researchers are usually included on the campaign staff, but occasionally freelance writers are hired. Commercial research firms and clipping services are often contracted to provide extensive background information and continuous updating on candidate publicity.

Professional gag men have been retained by parties or candidates at least as far back as the Herbert Hoover-Al Smith campaign, but these have been partisan volunteers whose activities were kept as secret as possible. Today the candidate's joke writers have been openly credited with making or breaking several campaigns.

Transportation

Reported campaign travel costs may be considerably inflated since as much as half the total is reimbursed by the organizations of reporters traveling with candidates. The reimbursement is for flying on a plane provided by the campaign or in the candidate's plane, and occasionally for ground transportation such as press buses. Substantial portions of travel costs can be recouped when the candidate and his staff fly with enough reporters.

Transportation accommodations vary widely among candidates—from flying private jets to riding tourist-class on commercial airlines. All travel costs have increased, however, and in large states or national campaigns they can use up a lot of the candidates' budgets.

Free Goods and Services

Some candidates receive goods and services without charge from their supporters. For instance, a friend may lend his private plane to a candidate or may lend a building rent-free for an office. Incumbents have certain financial advantages, too, such as computerized mail files of correspondence during their tenures.

Furthermore, when campaign totals are given, they represent committed costs, not actual expenditures. Some of the debts from the Kennedy, McCarthy and Humphrey campaigns of 1968 were settled for less than their full amount, for example.

Pre-Nomination Expenses

The most comprehensive estimates of campaign spending generally date only from the primaries, but it has been argued that campaigns and their attendant expenses begin several years before the nomination contests. For example, Richard M. Nixon's extensive travel in 1966 on behalf of Republican congressional candidates made him a major presidential contender after the Republicans' impressive election results that year. The 30,000-mile tour, including the salary and expenses of one assistant, cost $90,000. The money was raised independently of the campaigns.[10]

Mr. Nixon's first campaign planning session for his 1968 presidential race was held in early January 1967. He spent about $10-million during the next 19 months before he became the Republican Party's nominee.

Pre-nomination and post-nomination campaign organizations are often almost identical. The number of workers increases as election day nears. So do expenses. But the campaign managers, press secretaries, policy advisers, pollsters, advance men, schedulers and speechwriters, researchers and political intelligence staff have been hired months earlier.

Primary elections, especially presidential preference primaries, can be enormously expensive. Since the stakes are so high, campaign offices in primary states often open months before an election. And nominating conventions present candidates with still more campaign costs.

Effectiveness of Spending

The extent to which an election can be won by outspending the opposition is debated during and after almost every political contest. But big campaign spenders say they can point to better-than-random correlation between financial outlay and victory. Other political consultants analyze the situation this way:

● The majority of voters have made up their minds about the candidate they will vote for by the start of the campaign. Unswayed by bids for their favor during the campaign, they will vote for their pre-chosen candidate.

● About 10 to 15 per cent of the electorate, the voters who are "independent and susceptible" when the campaign begins, often hold the balance of power.

● The candidate with the most money cannot be sure of winning to his side enough of the undecided voters to give him a victory, but the candidate with less money may be unable to present his case adequately to the crucial group of undecided voters.

Campaign Fund-Raising

Obviously, before candidates can spend money on their campaigns they have to raise the funds. Where the money comes from is no less important than where it goes after it is turned over to the politicians. Campaign fund-raising traditionally was among the better kept secrets of American electoral politics. But again, the excesses of the Watergate scandals in the early 1970s brought about considerable reform. The most significant change was the beginning of public funding of part of the campaign process.

The changes in federal campaign finance laws are discussed in detail later in the chapter. This section describes the general methods and sources of campaign fund-raising.

The reform measures of the 1970-75 period, which originally imposed strict limits on campaign contributions and expenditures and provided for the public financing of presidential campaigns, were supposed to curtail drastically the role of money in campaigns. Candidates were expected to devote less effort to wooing contributors. Overall campaign spending was expected to be reduced. Challengers and incumbents were supposed to be placed on a more equal footing than in previous campaigns, because big money at last had been de-emphasized and the spending and fund-raising advantages of incumbents had been curbed.

But campaign financing law was altered in the winter and spring of 1976, first by a Supreme Court decision and then by new legislation. The over-all effect was to void recent restrictions on campaign contributions. However, the post-Watergate political climate and the economic down-

turn of the previous three years made 1975 and early 1976 a difficult period in which to raise money. Even before the temporary $1,000 limit on donations was lifted, many previously generous donors made only small contributions.

The cumulative effect of these difficulties was to push candidates to seek new givers to make up for the loss of large contributors and the slowness of fund-raising. Several campaigns in the past were able to expand greatly their contributor base and to tap large numbers of people who had never given before. Barry Goldwater did that on the Republican right in his 1964 presidential campaign. So did George McGovern on the Democratic left in his 1972 campaign. And Alabama Gov. George C. Wallace found many new small contributors to finance his 1968, 1972 and 1976 presidential campaigns.

Direct Mail

Direct mail is the only way that large numbers of small contributors can be reached. But increases in postage rates and paper prices pushed the cost of a direct-mail fund-raising letter to more than 20 cents, far too high a price if a mailing has a low response. Many candidates and political fund-raising organizations found in 1975 and 1976 that direct mail was not bringing in as much money as in previous years. The exceptions, according to reports for 1975, were Wallace and Republican presidential contender Ronald Reagan, whose conservative constituencies yielded them good direct-mail returns. Historically, the political extremes have found direct mail a much better source of money than have moderates.[11]

Millions of letters soliciting funds are sent out by computers in an election year. With the increasing need for large sums of money and the use of computer techniques by direct mail professionals, mass mail solicitation has become the most important means of fund-raising in a number of major political campaigns.

According to direct mail specialist Richard Viguerie, "direct mail comes close to being a science. We know the importance of the color of envelopes, length of letters, personalized variables in letters, because we've tested all of these variables. The results are analyzed...and the success of each variation is measured.

"It's exciting what can be done," Viguerie said, "but you seldom find a client who is interested in using all of this information in a sophisticated manner." Most users of direct mail are interested in geographic and financial breakdowns—for example, all of the contributors in a given state who have contributed $10 or more to a conservative cause.[12]

Direct mail works against the traditional premise that in order to finance large campaigns a candidate has to rely on big business, labor and large contributors. A small contribution goes to a candidate or committee with a personal commitment by the donor. It comes from people who expect nothing in return.

Direct mail experts estimate conservatively that there are more than 500 million names on computers. An official of the Direct Mail Advertising Association has said that "people's names get on lists because people exist.... Only hermits could avoid getting on lists but then they'll probably get on somebody's list of hermits."[13]

The collection of personal data by direct mail list brokers has raised questions similar to those concerning credit data banks. Lists include information on what publications an individual reads, what charities he contributes to, what candidates he is supporting financially and his stands on political issues. And the lists are available for sale by the list brokers.

Buying and selling political mailing lists has become a successful business. Periodicals and book clubs sell lists to all comers. Viguerie sells lists of anything from "active Americans" to "retired military" to conservative Republicans. The United Nations International Childrens Emergency Fund (UNICEF) has sold its lists to the Democratic National Committee and the 1970 Campaign Fund. The Internal Revenue Service sells aggregate income statistics about taxpayers broken down by zip code. This is valuable to identify high-income communities for fund-raising.

Interest Groups

Special-interest groups spent an estimated $13-million on campaign contributions and related political activities in the first eight months of 1974, according to a study of reports filed with federal officials.[14]

A total of 526 groups representing business, labor, agriculture, doctors, educators and other interests reported expenditures of $15.3-million by Aug. 31. About $2-million of this was simply transfers of cash between national groups and their state committees, however. In addition, the same political committees reported another $12.9-million in cash on hand ready for use before the November elections.

The reports, required by the Federal Election Campaign Act of 1971, provided the first timely, comprehensive picture available during an election year of total campaign spending. With seven weeks to go in the 1974 campaigns, spending by special-interest committees already was running about $2-million ahead of the previous record for an entire non-presidential year. Similar groups reporting spending $11-million on the 1970 election campaigns, according to records then available.

Part of the increase could be attributed to the tougher reporting requirements of the 1971 law, which replaced the Federal Corrupt Practices Act of 1925, often described as more loophole than law. But a larger flow of campaign dollars from some older groups and a proliferation of new committees also added to the record outpouring of funds.

The biggest spenders by category as of Aug. 31 were labor, $6.3-million; medical and health professionals, $3.9-million, and business, $2.2-million. These were gross figures, not adjusted for transfers. Actual labor spending, for instance, was closer to $5-million.

Teachers, contributing through new political action committees, joined the top spenders for the first time, disbursing $682,833 and reporting another $740,999 in cash available for the final weeks of the congressional campaigns.

The largest amounts are usually spent on campaigns in the final weeks before an election. By combining expenditures through Aug. 31 with cash on hand, it was possible to calculate the total funds available as of that date to various groups for political spending in 1974.

Business Executives

Executives of the largest defense-related contractors gave eight times more money in 1972 to the campaigns of President Nixon and other Republican candidates than to their Democratic counterparts.

Officers and directors of these companies gave $2,555,-740 to Republicans and $319,983 to Democrats, according to data compiled by the Citizens' Research Foundation of Princeton, N.J.[15]

The amounts, as well as the margin by which Republicans were favored, were up sharply from 1968. A similar Citizens' Research survey for that presidential election year showed Republicans favored 6 to 1 in donations. They received $1,235,402, compared with $180,550 for Democrats.

Both surveys covered campaign gifts reported by officials of the companies ranking among the top 25 contractors to the Defense Department (DOD), Atomic Energy Commission (AEC) and National Aeronautics and Space Administration (NASA).

The three agencies were the federal government's largest buyers of military and other hardware. DOD spent more than $20-billion a year on weapons systems and equipment. The AEC (later broken into two agencies) supplied nuclear warheads for bombs and missiles. And NASA rocketry helped the development of intercontinental ballistic missiles.

The old Federal Corrupt Practices Act of 1925 required no reporting of campaign gifts made before the nominating primary or convention. This loophole ceased as of April 7, 1972. The change did not affect the long-standing prohibition on campaign contributions by corporations. Executives of corporations may make campaign contributions as individuals.

Because of overlapping on the DOD, AEC and NASA lists, the survey covered 52 separate companies rather than a total of 75. Forty-six of the 52 companies had officials who gave to political campaigns. Not all the officers and directors of these 46 companies made campaign contributions. But the 483 who did gave an average of $5,953, compared with an average of $4,202 in 1968.

The compilation showed that 54 individuals contributed $10,000 or more. In 1968, only 43 corporate executives had given $5,500 or more.

All 25 companies on the DOD list had officers or directors who contributed to 1972 campaigns.

Sixteen of the companies on the AEC list also had officials who gave, including the four companies that were duplicated on the DOD or NASA lists.

All companies except one on the NASA list had officials who contributed. The exception was Computing Software Inc. All but six of the top 25 NASA contractors also were among the largest DOD and AEC contractors.

There was no direct correlation between the amount of business a company got from the defense agencies and the size of campaign contributions from the company's officials.

Fund-Raising Dinners

A fund-raising dinner is an effective tool for extracting a hefty check from a well-to-do voter. Where formerly a prospective donor was invited to a dinner and there subjected to give-'em-hell partisan appeals for a contribution or pledge, his gift now is assured in advance by the sale of expensive tickets of admission. President Eisenhower on Jan. 20, 1956, spoke by closed-circuit TV to 53 banquets held simultaneously in 37 states. Ticket sales netted between $4-million and $5-million for the Republican Party.

In the 1960s, techniques for holding political dinners were developed further. President Kennedy's Inaugural Eve Gala in Washington, D.C., grossed $1,250,000. In the administrations of Presidents Kennedy and Lyndon B. Johnson, those who paid $1,000 a plate at major political dinners were known as members of the President's Club. The most profitable form of fund-raising is the $1,000-a-plate political dinner. Overhead on a $1,000-a-plate dinner is approximately 5 per cent to 10 per cent while it can run as high as 50 per cent on a $10-a-plate dinner.

Campaign committees peddle tickets costing from $25 up for other politically oriented meals—breakfast, brunch and lunch. In addition, there are teas, cocktail parties, bean feeds and snack parties. Favorite invitees are Washington lobbyists and representatives of trade associations, as well as friendly corporation executives and labor union officials.

Other Methods

Another way in which candidates and parties raise money is to sell ads in special publications. The Democrats in 1964, for example, published a program booklet called "Toward an Age of Greatness." Large corporations bought advertising space in the booklet at rates approaching those charged by nationally circulated magazines. The Republicans quickly decided to fill their coffers in the same way. Prior to 1966, some corporations not only placed ads in such publications—for up to $15,000 a page—but also deducted the cost as business expenses in their federal tax returns. An act of March 15, 1966, put an end to these deductions, but both parties continue to sell ads.

In seeking campaign contributions from individuals, political committees often resort to the psychologically effective device of seeing to it that prospective donors are solicited by persons whom they will want to please. A prospective donor's best customer, for example, may be sent to ask him for a contribution. The desire of the donor to stand well with the solicitor may transcend, as a motive for giving, any tangible favors hoped for from the victory of a political candidate or his party.

Appointment of millionaire members of the party to office has long been another standard technique for inducing political contributions. Cabinet posts and other high offices in the executive branch, as well as membership on blue-ribbon commissions, are sometimes awarded in recognition of contributions already made or to encourage future contributions.

Wealthy Candidates

One of the best ways for a party to hold down its expenses is to nominate a candidate whose personal wealth is sufficient to absorb many campaign costs. A legislative attempt to limit how much of their own money candidates could spend on their campaigns was ended by a Supreme Court decision of Jan. 30, 1976, which held that such a restriction was unconstitutional. The ruling was thought to open the way for more wealthy candidates for federal office. However, candidates who use their own wealth in campaigning often suffer at the polls from opponents' attacks that they are attempting to buy the election.

Bad Political Debts

Questions have been raised in recent years as to the legality of a long-standing corporation practice which is tantamount to contributing funds to a candidate or a political committee. The practice involves post-election settlement, by a corporation, of campaign debts, especially those incurred by the loser, at less than 100 cents on the dollar. "Winners pay their debts; losers negotiate theirs," according to an election adage. Hotel bills, debts to airlines for candidates' and newsmen's fares, car rental fees, and telephone bills sometimes are paid off by a loser at 25 to 50 cents on the dollar.

Ambassadors and Money

Ambassadors and persons seeking ambassadorships often have made large contributions to presidential campaigns. After his 1972 re-election, President Nixon appointed 13 more non-career ambassadors, eight of whom had donated a minimum of $25,000 each and $706,000 in aggregate to his campaign. This led to charges that the Nixon administration was brokering ambassadorships.

According to the Senate Watergate Committee report, over $1.8-million in presidential campaign contributions was attributable, in whole or in part, to persons holding ambassadorial appointments from Nixon. The report said further that about 30 per cent of all foreign envoy posts were held in July 1974 by non-career appointees. The largest concentration was in Western Europe, where there was also a high concentration of persons contributing $100,000 or more.

While White House officials maintained they told persons seeking ambassadorships that no *quid pro quo* could follow contributions, the Senate Watergate Committee report concluded that "at the very least, a number of persons saw the making of a contribution as a means of obtaining the recognition needed to be actively considered."

A list of nine U.S. ambassadors to Western Europe and their contributions to Nixon's 1972 re-election campaign follows:

Country	Ambassador	Contribution
Great Britain	Walter H. Annenberg	$ 250,000
Switzerland	Shelby Davis	100,000
Luxembourg	Ruth L. Farkas	300,000
Belgium	Leonard K. Firestone	112,600
Netherlands	Kingdon Gould	100,900
Austria	John F. Humes	100,000
France	John N. Irwin II	50,500
France	Arthur K. Watson	300,000
Ireland	John D. Moore	10,442
Total		**$1,324,442**

Source: Congressional Quarterly, *Dollar Politics* (1974), vol. 2, p. 15.

Power of Incumbents

Incumbent members of Congress, Democrats and Republicans alike, have a powerful advantage over their challengers when it comes to raising money for re-election. But when neither major-party candidate is an incumbent, the ability to raise funds evens out.

These were two of the findings of a study on campaign spending conducted by Common Cause, the self-styled citizens' lobby. The results, based on analysis of reports filed by congressional candidates and their campaign committees, were announced on Sept. 13, 1973.

Further data collected by Common Cause on the 1972 House and Senate Campaigns was released on Nov. 30, 1973. At that time Fred Wertheimer, Common Cause legislative director, commented, "In Congress today we have neither a Democratic nor a Republican Party. Rather we have an incumbency party which operates a monopoly."[16]

The 106 candidates who ran for the Senate in the November 1972 elections raised about $27.3-million and spent about $26.4-million, according to Common Cause. Winners of the 33 elections outspent their major-party opponents by about two to one. And incumbents outspent challengers by about the same ratio. The study found that:

- In 19 of 25 races, incumbents outspent challengers.
- In 28 of 33 races, winners outspent losers.
- In all eight races in which there was no incumbent, winners outspent losers.

Similar patterns prevailed in the contests for House seats. The 318 incumbents who had majority-party challengers out-collected and out-spent their opponents by wide margins, but not so wide as in the Senate.

Races without incumbents not only featured a more equal distribution of spending, but a lot more spending in general. Democrats in these House districts spent an average of $90,074, Republicans a nearly identical $90,030. In 52 House districts, incumbents had no major-party challengers in 1972.

Common Cause reported finding a connection between plurality and cost—the closer a race was, the more expensive it was likely to be. House candidates who won with more than 60 per cent of the vote spent an average of less than $55,000. Elections won with less than 55 per cent cost more than $100,000, on the average, not only for the winner but for the loser as well.

Costs of Fund-Raising

No matter how it is done, campaign fund-raising is an expensive proposition. As much as two-thirds of every dollar raised is spent by some political committees for soliciting the funds. In July and August, 1971, Congressional Quarterly examined records in the House Clerk's office and interviewed officials of several political committees to determine the costs of raising money for various types of groups.[17]

The study found that fund-raising costs ranged from as low as 13 per cent for one direct mail effort to 58-65 per cent for comprehensive fund-raising programs. Probably the highest fund-raising costs were reported in 1968 by the United Republicans of America. Candidates supported by the committee received less than 10 per cent of the $473,453 it raised.

Finding the Funds

The 1976 campaign was especially difficult for fund-raising, as candidates and their managers puzzled over new campaign financing laws. Candidates had to spend more time raising money. The problem was especially acute in the presidential campaign, where the largest amounts had to be raised.

"We've done everything," a staff man for one liberal Democratic candidate told Congressional Quarterly. "We've held tennis parties, dinners, cocktail parties, breakfasts, receptions and concerts. We've even passed the hat at dances."[18]

Contributors also were making fund-raising more time consuming in the 1976 elections. They apparently wanted to see who was receiving their money and to take the candidates' measure before making donations.

Douglas L. Bailey, a political consultant in Washington, D.C., said, "The members of a candidate's finance committee have far more difficulty raising dough than the candidate. There's no automatic giving to establishment fund-raisers."[19]

Bailey saw nothing wrong with contributors wanting to personally size up the candidate they are helping to finance. But he and other campaign consultants worried that campaigns might suffer from the time it takes. "Candidates who have to spend most of their time raising money spend proportionately less time reaching voters," said Joseph Napolitan, a campaign consultant from Springfield, Mass. "If I had my choice, I'd like to see candidates spend their time meeting voters, not contributors."[20]

Campaigns and Broadcasting

Regulation of campaign expenditures entails, among other things, decisions on who may compete for purchase of television time and under what conditions such competition may occur. The basic legislation on the subject, Section 315 (a) of the Communications Act of 1934, apparently raised more questions than it answered. Section 315 (a) provided: "If any licensee shall permit any person who is a legally qualified candidate for any public office to use a broadcasting station, he shall afford equal opportunities to all other such candidates for that office in the use of such broadcasting station."

In 1959, Lar Daly, write-in candidate for Mayor of Chicago, made a demand on Chicago television stations which, if complied with, would have provided him with exposure on television without any expenditure on his part. He said that under the Act of 1934 he was entitled to receive as much time on Chicago news broadcasts as was given to Democratic and Republican candidates. He based his demand on a 20-second news shot of Mayor Richard J. Daley, Democratic candidate for re-election, greeting a foreign dignitary, and a one-minute news report on Daley's opening of the March of Dimes campaign. On Feb. 19, 1959, the Federal Communications Commission, in a surprise decision, ruled by a vote of four to three that Daly's demand was justified.

The commission's application of the equal-time provision to news broadcasts aroused a wave of protests. President Eisenhower on March 19, 1959, called the ruling "ridiculous." Congress, by an act of Sept. 14, 1959, nullified the commission's ruling by inserting, at the end of Section 315 (a), the words: "Appearance by a legally qualified candidate on any (1) bona fide newscast, (2) bona fide news interview, (3) bona fide news documentary (if the appearance of the candidate is incidental to the presentation of the subject or subjects covered by the news documentary), or (4) on-the-spot coverage of bona fide news events (including but not limited to political conventions and activities incidental thereto), shall not be deemed to be use of a broadcasting station within the meaning of this subsection."

Equal-Time Provision in the 1960s

The equal-time provision of the Act of 1934 was suspended in part by an act of Aug. 24, 1960, to make possible a series of television debates between the 1960 presidential candidates of the two major parties, John F. Kennedy (D) and Richard M. Nixon (R). Congress also considered but did not enact a proposal to suspend Section 315 (a) for the period of the 1962 congressional campaign.

The Senate and the House in 1964 passed different bills to make possible a television debate between the two major presidential contenders of that year, President Johnson and Sen. Barry Goldwater (R Ariz.). Although a conference committee reconciled the two bills, the measure was allowed to die, because President Johnson did not want to appear with Sen. Goldwater on a basis which implied equality of status for the incumbent and the challenger. Similarly, in 1968 and 1972 there were no debates between Richard M. Nixon and challengers Hubert H. Humphrey and George McGovern. However, in 1976 plans were well along in September for a resumption of campaign debates *(see next column).*

Legislation

In 1970 Congress passed a bill which would have limited spending on political broadcasts by candidates for election to Congress, the presidency and state governorships. The bill also would have made possible televised debates between the major parties' candidates for President by repealing the equal time requirements of the 1934 act. President Nixon vetoed the bill.

The Federal Election Campaign Act of 1971 (PL 92-225) set limits on the amounts candidates could spend for

---

Equal Time, Fairness

The "equal time" provision of the Communications Act of 1934—Section 315(a)—and the "fairness doctrine" of the Federal Communications Commission, although related to the federal regulation of broadcasting, differed significantly in their intent and effect.

The equal time provision required almost mathematical equality in television and radio broadcast treatment of legally qualified candidates for public office. The fairness doctrine, promulgated by the FCC after extensive hearings in 1949, required only fair or balanced treatment of community issues. Congress in 1959 added the fairness standard to Section 315(a) of the Communications Act by providing that broadcast licensees "must operate in the public interest and afford reasonable opportunity for the discussion of conflicting views on controversial issues of public interest."

The key distinction was between individuals, in equal time questions of law, and community issues, in fairness doctrine questions of policy. In no case under existing law or policy was there provision for equal time or fair broadcast treatment of political or social groups, organizations or institutions. That is, no group, organization, institution or individual—except legally qualified political candidates for public office—was guaranteed a right of access to the broadcast media.

Under the fairness doctrine, each licensee was compelled to seek responsible contrasting opinions on public issues once the broadcaster had provided time for raising an issue.

But the licensee was left with full discretion to determine what issues he would raise or permit to be raised on the air, who would be the "responsible spokesman" for opposing views, and at what length and in what context or format those issues would be raised and opposing views aired.

The FCC in 1964 said: "In passing on any complaint (under the fairness doctrine), the commission's role is not to substitute its judgment for that of the licensee as to any...programming decisions, but rather to determine whether the licensee can be said to have acted reasonably and in good faith."

---

broadcasting and other forms of advertising, and restricted the rates to be charged by broadcasters during campaigns. The law retained the 1934 equal time requirements.

In 1973 the Senate approved campaign reform legislation (S 372) which would have repealed the equal time provision, but the House did not act on the bill. The broadcasting industry contended that because Section 315 required broadcasters to make equal time available to all candidates, it discouraged them from making time available to major party candidates.[21]

The limits on broadcast advertising were tested in the 1972 elections and appeared not to have been unreasonable. The Federal Communications Commission reported that presidential candidates spent a total of $14.3-million on radio, television and cable TV advertising in 1972, compared with $28.5-million in the previous presidential election. Senatorial candidates spent $6.4-million in 1972, compared with $16-million in 1970 and $10.4-million in 1968. Broadcast spending in House races increased, however, from $6.1-million in 1970, when the FCC first computed it, to $7.4-million in 1972.[22]

In the Federal Election Campaign Amendments of 1974 (PL 93-443), Congress repealed the media spending limitations of the 1971 law. The Senate-approved bill again would have repealed the equal time provision of the 1934 Federal Communications Act, but House conferees eliminated that from the final legislation.

FCC Reversal, 1976 Debates

The Federal Communications Commission itself revised the equal time provision in a Sept. 25, 1975, decision. By a 5-2 vote, the commission ruled that broadcast news conferences and political debates sponsored by a third party would not be subject to Section 315 requirements. The change exempted from Section 315 press conferences held not only by the President, but by governors, mayors "and any candidates whose press conferences may be considered newsworthy and subject to on-the-spot coverage."[23]

As a result of this change, plans were well along in September 1976 for televised debates between President Ford and Democratic challenger Jimmy Carter. The series of three or four debates were to be sponsored by the League of Women Voters.

The FCC's majority opinion stated: "The undue stifling of broadcast coverage of news events involving candidates for public office has been unfortunate, and we believe that this remedy will go a long way toward ameliorating the paucity of coverage accorded these events during the past 15 years." But a dissenter who called the new ruling a "tragic mistake," Commissioner Benjamin L. Hooks, wrote that "by exempting two popular forms of political weaponry, the press conference and the debate, the delicate balance of egalitarian precepts underlying political 'equal time' has suffered a severe and, perhaps, mortal blow."[24]

The FCC ruling was appealed by a public-interest law firm in Washington called the Media Access Project and by the Democratic National Committee. Their joint appeal was heard late in 1975 by the U.S. Circuit Court of Appeals in the District of Columbia, but by Aug. 30, 1976, no decision had been given.

Robert Smith, a lawyer for the Democratic National Committee, argued that the 1975 ruling gave President Ford a "natural edge" over his opponents. "The decision means that he could hold three press conferences a week before election day and the network coverage will show him there against the White House background with the flags and all the other trappings," Smith said. He added that networks would be less likely to carry the press conferences of Ford's opponents.[25]

Campaign Finance Legislation

Legislation on campaign spending in the United States has had three aims: (1) to limit and regulate donations made to candidates and their campaign committees; (2) to limit and regulate disbursements made by candidates and their committees, and (3) to inform voters of the amounts and sources of the donations and the amounts, purposes and payees of the disbursements. Disclosure was intended to reveal which candidates, if any, were unduly indebted to interest groups, in time to forewarn the voters. But more than a century of legislative attempts to regulate campaign financing resulted in much controversy and minimal control.

Money has been a major issue in American politics since colonial times. In his race for the House of Burgesses in Virginia in 1757, George Washington was accused of campaign irregularities. He was charged with dispensing during his campaign 28 gallons of rum, 50 gallons of rum punch, 34 gallons of wine, 46 gallons of beer and two gallons of cider royal. "Even in those days," noted George Thayer, a historian of American campaign financing, "this was considered a large campaign expenditure, because there were only 391 voters in his district, for an average outlay of more than a quart and a half per person."[26]

Campaign spending was a central issue in the 1832 presidential race, in which President Andrew Jackson and Henry Clay, his Whig opponent, fought over the fate of the United States Bank. During the campaign, the U.S.-chartered but semi-autonomous bank spent heavily to support Clay. The strategy backfired, however. Jackson met the challenge with a strong veto message against legislation renewing the bank's charter, in which he described the bank as a "money monster," and he used it as an effective issue to defeat Clay.

Money played an important role in the victory of Republican William McKinley over populist Democrat William Jennings Bryan in the 1896 presidential election. McKinley's campaign was managed by Marcus A. Hanna, the wealthy Ohio financier and industrialist who turned the art of political fund raising into a system.

The first provision of federal law on campaign financing was incorporated in an act of March 2, 1867, making naval appropriations for the fiscal year 1868. The final section of the act read: "And be it further enacted, That no officer or employee of the government shall require or request any workingman in any navy yard to contribute or pay any money for political purposes, nor shall any workingman be removed or discharged for political opinion; and any officer or employee of the government who shall offend against the provisions of this section shall be dismissed from the service of the United States."

Reports circulated in the following year that at least 75 per cent of the money raised by the Republican Congressional Committee came from federal officeholders. Continuing agitation on this and other aspects of the spoils system in federal employment led to adoption of the Civil Service Reform Act of Jan. 16, 1883, which authorized establishment of Civil Service rules. One of the rules stated "That no person in the public service is for that reason under any obligation to contribute to any political fund...and that he will not be removed or otherwise prejudiced for refusing to do so." The law made it a crime for any federal employee to solicit campaign funds from another federal employee.

Federal Corrupt Practices Laws

Muckrakers in the early part of the 20th century exposed the influence on government that was exerted by big business through unrestrained spending on behalf of favored candidates. After the 1904 election, a move for federal legislation took shape in the National Publicity Law Association headed by former Rep. Perry Belmont (D N.Y.). President Theodore Roosevelt, in his annual message to Congress on Dec. 5, 1905, proposed that: "All contributions by corporations to any political committee or for any political purpose should be forbidden by law." Roosevelt repeated the proposal in his message of Dec. 3, 1906, suggesting that it be the first item of congressional business.[27]

Tillman Act

In response to the President's urging, Congress on Jan. 26, 1907, passed the Tillman Act, which made it unlawful for a corporation or a national bank to make "a money contribution in connection with any election" of candidates for federal office. Additional regulation of campaign financing was provided in 1910. The new law required every political committee "which shall in the two or more states influence the result or attempt to influence the result of an election at which Representatives in Congress are to be elected" to file with the Clerk of the House of Representatives, within 30 days after the election, the name and address of each contributor of $100 or more, the name and address of each recipient of $10 or more from the committee, and the total amounts that the committee received and disbursed. Individuals who engaged in similar activities outside the framework of committees were also required to submit such reports.

Legislation was passed in 1911 extending the filing requirements to committees influencing senatorial elections and to require filing of financial reports by candidates for the office of either senator or representative. In addition, it required statements to be filed both before and after an election. The most important innovation of the 1911 act was the limitation of the amount that a candidate might spend toward nomination and election: a candidate for the Senate, no more than $10,000 or, if less, the maximum amount permitted in his state; for the House, no more than $5,000 or, if less, the maximum amount permitted in his state.

Corrupt Practices Act

The basic campaign financing law in effect through 1971 was the Federal Corrupt Practices Act, approved Feb. 28, 1925. It limited its restrictions to campaigns for election, in view of the unsettled state at that time of the question whether Congress had power to regulate primary elections. Unless a state law prescribed a smaller amount, the act set the limit of campaign expenditures at (1) $10,000 for a would-be senator and $2,500 for a would-be member of the House; or (2) an amount equal to three cents for each vote cast in the last preceding election for the office sought, but not more than $25,000 for the Senate and $5,000 for the House.

The 1925 act incorporated the existing prohibition of campaign contributions by corporations or national banks, the ban on solicitation of political contributions from federal employees by candidates or other federal employees and the requirement that reports be filed on campaign finances. It prohibited giving or offering money to anyone in exchange for his vote. In amending the provisions of the act of 1907 on contributions, the new law substituted for the word "money" the expression "a gift, subscription, loan, advance, or deposit of money, or anything of value."

The Senate in 1927 barred Senator-elect William S. Vare (R Pa.) from taking his seat after reports indicated that his campaign had cost $785,000. In the same year, the Senate refused to seat Sen.-elect Frank L. Smith (R Ill.). More than 80 per cent of Smith's campaign fund had come from three men who had a direct interest in a decision of the Illinois Commerce Commission, of which Smith continued to be a member throughout the campaign. One of the three donors was Samuel Insull, owner of a controlling interest in a network of utility companies.

In 1934, a case reached the Supreme Court which required the court to rule on, among other things, the constitutionality of the requirement in the 1925 act that lists and amounts of campaign contributions and expenditures be filed publicly. The case, *Burroughs and Cannon v. United States*, involved primarily the applicability of the act to the election of presidential electors. Justice George Sutherland on Jan. 8, 1934, delivered the opinion of the court. Applicability of the act to presidential campaigns was upheld. The decision included the following statement on disclosure: "Congress reached the conclusion that public disclosure of political contributions, together with the names of contributors and other details, would tend to prevent the corrupt use of money to affect elections. The verity of this conclusion reasonably cannot be denied" (290 U.S. 548).

'Clean Politics' and Other Laws

Between the early efforts to regulate spending and the broad reforms of the 1970s, some legislation related to campaign financing had less direct effects than the corrupt practices laws.

Hatch Act

An act of Aug. 2, 1939, commonly called the Hatch Act but also known as the Clean Politics Act, affected campaign financing in only a secondary way. It barred federal employees from active participation in national politics and prohibited collection of political contributions from persons receiving relief funds provided by the federal government. But an amendment to the Hatch Act, approved July 19, 1940, made three significant additions to legislation on campaign financing. It forbade individuals or business concerns doing work for the federal government under contract to contribute to any political committee or candidate. It asserted the right of Congress to regulate primary elections for the nomination of candidates for federal office and made it unlawful for anyone to contribute more than $5,000 "during any calendar year, or in connection with any campaign for nomination or election, to or on behalf of any candidate for an elective federal office." However, the act specifically exempted from this limitation "contributions made to or by a state or local committee." The 1940 amendment also placed a ceiling of $3-million in a calendar year on expenditures by a political committee operating in two or more

states. Legislation in 1943 temporarily, and the Taft-Hartley Act of 1947 permanently, forbade labor unions to contribute to political campaigns from their general funds.

Congress on March 31, 1976, approved legislation to amend the Hatch Act. It would have allowed federal employees to run for federal office and to participate in partisan election campaigns for the first time since enactment of the original Hatch Act. The bill would have permitted workers, except while on federal grounds, to solicit and make political contributions. But President Ford vetoed the bill April 12, saying it would "deny the lessons of history" by "endangering the entire concept of employee independence and freedom from coercion which has been largely successful in preventing undue political influence in government programs or personnel management."[28] The veto was sustained.

Financing of Primary Campaigns

Application of federal laws on campaign financing to primary elections made a complete circuit on the wheel of judicial and legislative fortune. The act of 1911 limiting campaign expenditures in congressional elections covered primaries as well as general elections. However, the Supreme Court in 1921 in *Newberry v. United States* (256 U.S. 232) struck down the application of the law to primaries, on the ground that the power the Constitution gave Congress to regulate the "manner of holding election" did not extend to party primaries and conventions. The Federal Corrupt Practices Act of 1925 exempted primaries from its operation.

The Hatch Act amendments of 1940, as noted, made primaries again subject to federal restrictions on campaign contributions despite the Newberry decision. This new legislation was upheld in 1941, when the Supreme Court handed down its decision in *United States v. Classic et al.* (313 U.S. 299), which reversed the Newberry decision. The *Classic* decision was confirmed by the Supreme Court in 1944 in *Smith v. Allwright* (321 U.S. 649). When the Taft-Hartley Act was adopted in 1947, its prohibition of political contributions by corporations, national banks and labor organizations was phrased so as to cover primaries as well as general elections.

Tax Checkoff

Proponents of governmental subsidization of election campaigns appeared to have won a major victory in 1966. An act approved Nov. 13 of that year authorized any individual paying federal income tax to direct that $1 of the tax due in any year be paid into a Presidential Election Campaign Fund. The fund, to be set up in the U.S. Treasury, was to disburse its receipts, on a proportional basis, among political parties whose presidential candidates had received 5 million or more votes in the preceding presidential election.

However, an act of June 13 of the following year provided that "Funds which become available under the Presidential Election Campaign Fund Act of 1966 shall be appropriated and disbursed only after the adoption by law of guidelines governing their distribution." But Congress failed to adopt any guidelines, so the 1966 act was in effect voided in 1967.

State Laws on Campaign Financing

New York State in 1883 enacted a law prohibiting solicitation of campaign contributions from state employees

State Campaign Financing Laws

State legislatures, feeling the reverberations of the Watergate scandals, responded with a flurry of measures to reform campaign financing laws. Many states, in fact, responded faster than Congress.

The wave of reform began during the 1972 elections, when Washington and Colorado passed "open government" initiatives. In 1973 and 1974, as many as 40 state legislatures enacted 67 measures concerned with limiting campaign contributions and expenditures, and monitoring ethical standards of politicians.

Early in 1976 the reform movement in the states stood as follows:

Campaign Finance Disclosure. Forty-nine of the 50 states had statutes requiring public disclosure of campaign financing. Only North Dakota had no such law. Seven other states did not require disclosure until after the elections had taken place.

Public Financing. Eleven states had some form of tax checkoff or tax add-on (added liability) to help finance elections with public funds. In addition, New Jersey, which had no state income tax at the time, provided matching funds for gubernatorial general elections starting in 1977. Oregon citizens were scheduled to vote on public financing in 1976.

Contribution Limits. Twenty-two states set limits on the amounts of money that individuals could contribute to political campaigns.

Personal Finances. Thirty-eight states required some public officials to disclose their personal finances. In 28 of those 38 states, such laws were either enacted or strengthened in the three years before 1976.

Lobbying Disclosure. All 50 states at least required lobbyists to register. Between November 1972 and 1976, 24 states and the District of Columbia enacted new or stronger lobbying laws.

Open Meetings. From November 1972 to 1976, 27 states adopted or strengthened laws requiring open meetings of public agencies.

Source: Common Cause, March 1976.

and in 1890 required candidates to file sworn financial statements. California in 1893 limited the total amount of money that could be spent on behalf of a candidate and established a list of legitimate campaign expenses. By 1905, some type of regulation of campaign finances was in effect in 14 states. However, Justice Felix Frankfurter, delivering the opinion of the Supreme Court, March 11, 1957, in *United States v. U.A.W.* (352 U.S. 571), said: "These state publicity laws either became dead letters or were found to be futile."

Florida in 1951 adopted a law on campaign financing which often is cited as a model. It requires each candidate to appoint a campaign treasurer and to designate a single bank as the campaign depository. Contributions to the campaign must be deposited within 24 hours of receipt, with deposit slips showing the names and addresses of donors and the amounts contributed by each. Candidates are required to publish periodic reports of campaign expenditures during the campaign, every week in the case of candidates for the U.S. Senate and the governorship and every month in the case of candidates for all other offices.

By 1971, eight states regulated campaign financing by imposing limits on spending by candidates and political committees and by requiring candidates and committees to report receipts and expenditures. Twelve states made some, but not all, of the foregoing requirements. Twenty-one other states had less comprehensive regulations. Nine states—Alaska, Delaware, Georgia, Illinois, Louisiana, Maine, Nevada, Pennsylvania, Rhode Island—had no regulations. Prosecutions for violation of state laws on campaign financing have been rare.

Enforcement and Loopholes

In the six decades from 1907 to 1968, the Tillman Act, the Corrupt Practices Act and other federal laws on campaign financing were rarely enforced. All the campaign regulatory legislation passed through 1925 was largely ignored. Alexander Heard wrote in *The Costs of Democracy* in 1960 that the prohibition in the Federal Corrupt Practices Act of direct purchases of goods or advertising for the benefit of a candidate was "manifestly violated right and left;" that the prohibition of campaign contributions by federal contractors "goes ignored;" and that the prohibition of loans to candidates by banks was "disregarded."[29]

Then, in the late 1960s, Washington's attitude toward enforcement of the Federal Corrupt Practices Act seemed to change. The Nixon administration successfully pressed charges in 1969 against corporations (mostly in California) that had contributed campaign money in 1968.

Another form of violation, failure to report or false reporting under the Corrupt Practices Act, had also been ignored despite the fact that newsmen repeatedly uncovered instances of failure to file reports or the filing of incomplete reports. Attorney General Herbert Brownell in 1954 had stated as the position of the Department of Justice that the initiative in such cases rested with the secretary of the Senate and the clerk of the House, and that policy was continued.

Secretaries of the Senate and clerks of the House for many years winked at violations of the legal requirement that candidates and supporting committees periodically file with them detailed statements of contributions received and disbursements made. The situation changed in 1967 when former Rep. W. Pat Jennings (D Va., 1955-67) was elected clerk of the House. He began sending lists of violations to the Department of Justice for prosecution, but then the department refused to act.

Federal Loopholes

Enforcement efforts could hardly succeed because the federal laws were so flawed. It became common knowledge long ago that the limitations supposedly imposed by campaign financing legislation did not limit, that the prohibitions did not prohibit and that the restrictions did not restrict.

Some loopholes were available to donors. The Corrupt Practices Act required reporting the name and address of every donor of $100 or more to a campaign; a donor could give less than $100 to each of numerous committees supporting his candidate, and the gifts would not be recorded. Members of the same family could legally contribute up to $5,000 each; a wealthy donor could privately subsidize gifts by his relatives to one candidate. Corporations could skirt the prohibition against political contributions by giving bonuses or salary increases to executives in the expectation that they would make corresponding contributions to candidates favored by the corporations. Labor unions could contribute to a candidate or political committee funds collected from members apart from dues. They could also use such funds for nonpartisan registration and voting drives even if the drives were confined to precincts loaded with voters who favored pro-union candidates or to areas where registration was poor for the party they favored.

Other loopholes were available to candidates. The 1925 law referred to candidates' "knowledge or consent" of campaign gifts and expenditures. Thus many candidates, by insisting that all financing be handled by independent committees, could report that they personally received and spent not one cent on their campaigns. In addition, the law applied only to political committees operating in two or more states, and not to those operating in one state only that were not subdivisions of a national committee.

Limits on the expenditures that a political committee could make were evaded by establishing more than one committee and apportioning receipts and expenditures among them so that no one committee exceeded the limit. Since the law limited annual spending by a political committee to $3-million, the major parties formed committees under various names, each of which was free to spend up to $3-million.

Loopholes in State Laws

A law on campaign finances adopted in Massachusetts in 1962 was hailed as uncommonly tough. It limited the number of committees supporting a candidate to three. The law also required that each committee have a bank account, that the bank report money deposited in the account or paid out from it, and that names and addresses of donors of more than $25, and the addresses of persons whose bills were paid, be made public. Despite the supposed stringency of the law, when Edward M. Kennedy in 1964 reported expenditures of $100,292.45 for his successful bid for the Democratic nomination for the U.S. Senate, newspapers estimated that his staff, billboard, television and other expenses amounted to 10 times that sum.

Some state laws exempt from the ceilings and reporting requirements money spent directly on publicity, such as the costs of television and radio spots, advertisements in newspapers and handbills and booklets. Exemptions apply in other states to renting of halls for meetings, hiring of publicity agents and conveyance of voters to and from the polls. Some states require reports from candidates but not committees, or reports on receipts but not expenditures. Places where reports are to be filed, such as the headquarters of the candidate's party, or the place "where the candidate resides," often constitute obstruction rather than promotion of disclosure.

Reform in the 1970s

Government officials, political scientists, public interest organizations and others made dozens of proposals aimed at plugging loopholes in campaign statutes, curtailing inflation of campaign costs, and reducing the threats to democratic ideals that arise from the financial demands of campaigning. Many proposals came from practicing politicians, in and out of Congress. But for decades no action was taken.

Perennial discussions about reforming campaign financing began coming to a head as the 1970s approached. Both sessions of the 91st Congress (1969-70) showed signs of movement. However, only one bill, which concerned allocation of broadcasting time, was passed by both the House and Senate. It was vetoed.

The need for new legislation on campaign financing was acknowledged on all sides when the 92nd Congress convened in 1971. Within five years, Congress passed four major laws which changed the ways in which political campaigns for national office are financed and conducted. Stunned by the campaign abuses that came to light during the Watergate scandals, state governments and the courts also moved to alter the methods of campaign financing.

Tax Checkoff Campaign Fund

After a bitter partisan debate dominated by the approaching 1972 presidential election campaign, Congress on Dec. 8, 1971, approved legislation to establish a federal fund from public tax revenues to finance presidential election campaigns. The measure was initially adopted by the Senate as a non-germane amendment to the Revenue Act of 1971 (PL 92-178) reducing business and individual taxes to stimulate the economy.

A similar plan was cleared by Congress in 1966 but was rendered inoperative in 1967. *(See p. 541)*

As approved by Congress, however, the campaign funding plan was to become effective in time for the 1976 election. House-Senate conferees, faced with a threat by President Nixon to veto the bill, delayed the effective date of the campaign financing provision until after 1972.

At the insistence of House conferees, the conference committee set up to iron out differences between House and Senate versions of the bill also revised the Senate amendment by requiring Congress annually to appropriate to the campaign fund the money designated by federal taxpayers as contributions to presidential campaigns. Citizens first had an opportunity to contribute to the fund on their 1972 federal income tax returns, filed in 1973.

Despite his continued opposition to the campaign funding provision, the President signed the bill Dec. 10. Nixon reportedly planned to leave further challenges to the plan to congressional action or the courts.

Had the plan gone into effect before the 1972 election, about $20.4-million of federal funds would have been made available to each of the major party candidates. About $6.3-million would have been available for Democratic Gov. George C. Wallace (Ala.) running for President as a third-party candidate.

The plan gave each taxpayer the option starting in 1973 of designating $1 of his annual federal income tax payment for use by the presidential candidate of the eligible political party of his choice or for a general campaign fund to be divided among eligible presidential candidates.

Democrats, whose party was $9-million in debt following the 1968 presidential election, said the voluntary tax checkoff was needed to free presidential candidates from obligation to wealthy contributors to their election campaigns.

Republicans, whose party treasury was well stocked, charged that the plan was a device to rescue the Democratic Party from financial difficulty and assure a Wallace candidacy in 1972 that would lessen President Nixon's re-election chances.

Provisions. Officially called the Presidential Election Campaign Fund Act, the 1971 law (PL 92-178) included the following major campaign financing provisions:

● Allowed a tax credit of $12.50 ($25 for a married couple) or, alternatively, a deduction against income of $50 ($100 for a married couple) for political contributions to candidates for local, state or federal office.

● Allowed taxpayers to designate on their federal income tax returns $1 of their tax payment as a contribution to the presidential and vice presidential candidates of the political party of their choice, beginning with the 1972 taxable year.

● As an alternative, allowed taxpayers to contribute to a general fund for all eligible presidential and vice presidential candidates by authorizing $1 of their annual income tax payment to be placed in such a fund.

● Authorized to be distributed to the candidates of each major party (one which obtained 25 per cent of the votes cast in the previous presidential election) an amount equal to 15 cents multiplied by the number of U.S. residents age 18 and over.

● Established a formula for allocating public campaign funds to candidates of minor parties whose candidates received 5 per cent or more but less than 25 per cent of the previous presidential election vote.

● Authorized payments after the election to reimburse the campaign expenses of a new party whose candidate received enough votes to be eligible or of an existing minor party whose candidate increased its vote to the qualifying level.

● Prohibited major party candidates who chose public financing of their election campaign from accepting private campaign contributions unless their shares of funds contributed through the income tax check-off procedure fell short of the amounts to which they were entitled.

● Prohibited a major party candidate who chose public financing and all campaign committees authorized by the candidate from spending more than the mount to which the candidate was entitled under the contributions formula.

● Provided penalties of $5,000 or one year in prison, or both, for candidates or campaign committees which spent more on a campaign than the amounts they received from the campaign fund or which accepted private contributions when sufficient public funds were available.

● Provided penalties of $10,000 or five years in prison, or both, for candidates or campaign committees which used public campaign funds for unauthorized expenses, gave or accepted kickbacks or illegal payments involving public campaign funds or knowingly furnished false information to the Comptroller General.

Campaign Fund Status. At first, relatively few taxpayers bothered to designate their $1 payments for the presidential campaign fund. But participation increased as more people became aware of the fund, as the checkoff feature was displayed more prominently on income tax forms, and as the 1976 presidential campaign drew closer. The Internal Revenue Service reported that payments were authorized on 23.9 per cent of the 1974 tax forms, higher than any previous year. But 25.9 per cent of the 1975 forms tabulated through July 1976 designated payments to the fund.

Although participation was not as high as proponents of public-supported elections may have hoped, the fund grew steadily. The fund received $4-million for the 1972 tax year, $26.2-million for 1973, $31.8-million for 1974, and $33.4-million for 1975 (tabulated through July 1976)—for a total of $95.4-million. The Federal Election Commission reported

in September 1976 that it had disbursed $24.1-million in matching funds to 15 presidential candidates and $3.9-million combined for the Democratic and Republican national conventions. The two nominees, President Ford and Jimmy Carter, were slated to receive $21.8-million each for the 1976 general election campaign.

1971-1976 Election Law Changes

The income tax checkoff and public financing of presidential campaigns was the beginning of extensive election law reforms that were to be passed over the following five years.

Laws passed in 1971 (PL 92-225), 1974 (PL 93-443) and 1976 (PL 94-283) placed limits on contributions, imposed some expenditure limits, required public disclosure of campaign financing details and set up a federal commission to enforce the law.

Provisions. The major provisions of the three laws dealing with candidates and committees, reporting, contributions, expenditures, publication and broadcast notices, the Federal Election Commission and compliance and penalties are compared in tabular form beginning on page 553. *(For contribution limits, see box p. 549.)*

Immediately following are highlights of action on the three laws and summaries of important sections of each law.

1971 Federal Election Law

The first major reform following the tax checkoff law went into effect early in 1972 with enactment of the Federal Election Campaign Act of 1971 (PL 92-225). The law placed a ceiling on expenditures by candidates for President, Vice President, the Senate or the House, and required full disclosure of campaign contributions and expenditures. The law went into effect April 7, 1972, 60 days after it was signed by the President.

The heart of the new law was the spending ceiling of 10 cents per eligible voter for all forms of media advertising—radio and television time, newspapers, magazines, billboards and automatic telephone equipment.

Attempts at reform began early in the 92nd Congress when numerous bills to reform election campaigning were introduced in the House and the Senate. President Nixon was committed to a major overhaul of campaign practices. In October 1970, he had vetoed a bill to limit broadcast spending by candidates for President, Congress and governor. The bill set ceilings on general election campaign broadcast spending by candidates at seven cents per vote cast in the previous election. It also repealed the equal time provision of the 1934 Communications Act for presidential and vice presidential candidates.

In vetoing the bill, Nixon said it would have discriminated against broadcasters, would have given an unfair advantage to incumbents and would not have provided much needed overall campaign reform.[30]

Pressure for Reform. The 1968 and 1970 federal election campaigns saw a skyrocketing of political campaign spending by both major parties. There also was a profusion of affluent candidates which made political spending a major campaign issue in itself. By 1971, after Nixon's veto of the first reform bill, members came under considerable pressure to pass a bill that would be applicable to the 1972 presidential and congressional elections. Even as the proposals were being introduced, potential candidates from both major parties were collecting and spending sizable amounts to finance campaign organizations in preparation for the elections.

Proponents of reform, cognizant of the partisan considerations that could have threatened any revision of campaign laws, worked to avoid writing a law that would favor any political party or candidate. Republicans, aware of the relatively healthy financial condition of their party in 1971, were eager to protect their coffers; Democrats did not want to jeopardize their large contributions from organized labor.

The reform thrust was also pushed by various groups outside Congress, including the National Committee for an Effective Congress, the chief pressure group, the self-styled citizens' lobby Common Cause, labor unions and some media organizations.

Key Provisions. The Federal Election Campaign Act of 1971 (PL 92-225) was the first major election reform law to be passed since the Federal Corrupt Practices Act of 1925. Major provisions included the following:

● Limited the amount that could be spent by federal candidates for advertising time in communications media to 10 cents per eligible voter, or $50,000, whichever was greater. Included in the definition of "communications media" were radio and television broadcasting stations, newspapers, magazines, billboards and automatic telephone equipment. Of the total amount permitted to be spent in a campaign, up to 60 per cent could be used for broadcast advertising time.

● Defined "election" to mean any general, special, primary or runoff election, nominating convention or caucus, delegate selection primary, presidential preference primary or constitutional convention.

● Prohibited promises of employment or other political rewards or benefits by any candidate in exchange for political support, and prohibited contracts between candidates and any federal department or agency.

● Placed a ceiling on contributions by any candidate or his immediate family to his own campaign of $50,000 for President or Vice President, $35,000 for senator, and $25,000 for representative.

● Required all political committees that anticipated receipts in excess of $1,000 during the calendar year to file a statement of organization with the appropriate federal supervisory officer, which was to include the names of all principal officers, the scope of the committee, the names of all candidates the committee supported and other information as required by law.

● Stipulated that the appropriate federal supervisory officer to oversee election campaign practices, reporting and disclosure was the clerk of the House for House candidates, the secretary of the Senate for Senate candidates and the comptroller general of the General Accounting Office (GAO) for presidential candidates.

● Required each political committee to report any individual expenditure of more than $100 and any expenditures of more than $100 in the aggregate during the calendar year.

● Required disclosure of all contributions to any committee or candidate in excess of $100, including a detailed report with the name and address of the contributor and the date the contribution was made.

● Required candidates and committees to file reports of contributions and expenditures on the 10th day of March, June and September of every year, on the 15th and fifth days preceding the date on which an election was held and on the 31st day of January. Any contribution of $5,000 or more was to be reported within 48 hours after its receipt.

● Required reporting of the names, addresses and occupations of any lender and endorser of any loan in excess of $100 as well as the date and amount of such loans.

● Required reporting of the total proceeds from the sales of tickets to all fund-raising events, mass collections made at such events and sales of political campaign materials.

● Required any person who made any contribution in excess of $100, other than through a political committee or directly to the candidate, to report such contribution to the appropriate supervisory officer.

● Prohibited any contribution to a candidate or committee by one person in the name of another person.

Loopholes in the Act of 1971

The 1972 presidential and congressional elections highlighted some major failures of the new spending law. A loophole that existed previously that was not satisfactorily corrected was the "pass-through" political contribution. This occurs when a donor gives a sum of money to another person, committee or organization who in turn hands over the money, according to the wishes of the original donor, to a candidate for public office.

Although the pass-through tactic was prohibited under PL 92-225 in 1971, a loophole was created which allowed an organization such as a social club, which was not established primarily to influence the outcome of an election, to use some of its dues for such purposes. If the organization contributed to a particular candidate an amount exceeding $1,000, it would have to report the total amount, but the names of the contributors would be shielded from public view. There was no requirement in the law to force such an organization to disclose the names of its members who had paid the dues which eventually became the political donation.

Another loophole was the loose definition of the word "candidate" in Title I of the law establishing media spending limitations for candidates. The language was construed in such a way as to permit persons to accept contributions and to spend money to aid their own prospects for public office and still not come under the law's spending ceiling for political advertising of 10 cents per eligible voter. The definition, moreover, was narrower than that contained in Titles II and III of the same law or that used by the Federal Communications Commission in dealing with requests for political broadcast time. Thus the Title I definition permitted unlimited spending during a time when a person might be a candidate in every way but name. Presidential candidates, for example, in recent years had made a habit of running unannounced for long periods before making an official announcement of candidacy, sometimes almost up to the eve of the first presidential primary.

A continuing tax loophole that was not plugged was the exemption from federal gift taxes of political contributions under $3,000. It was evident from the 1972 campaigns that many persons had contributed substantially more than this amount to a single candidate—while avoiding the gift tax —by making more than one donation under $3,000 to numerous political committees working on behalf of the same candidate.

A big loophole that showed up during 1972 was in the use of loans to candidates. While the law provided that all debts had to be reported until they were terminated, it was silent on the means by which such loans were to be paid off. Thus a supporter of a particular candidate could forgive a debt to him or require only a token payment on the loan, and the report that was later made public would indicate only that the debt had been terminated. The source of the loan would not have to be named.

A related loophole involved the provision limiting the amount that a candidate or his immediate family could contribute to his own campaign. The restriction did not apply to relatives of the family, and there was no regulation against a member of a family giving the maximum contribution allowed and, in addition, making a loan to the candidate.

A serious flaw according to many observers was the failure of Congress to approve an independent election campaign commission to monitor and enforce the law, particularly Title I setting spending limits. Under the arrangement finally agreed to in PL 92-225, the clerk of the House was responsible for overseeing House elections, the secretary of the Senate for Senate elections and the comptroller general of the GAO for presidential elections.

One of the defects of this procedure was the way in which the Justice Department was given responsibility for prosecuting any violations brought to its attention by the House or Senate overseers or by the comptroller general. While Justice was required to act in any civil case, the language of the law allowed the department complete discretion in deciding whether or not to prosecute in criminal cases.

It was reported that during the 1972 campaigns the department had only one full-time attorney supervising enforcement of the act.

Enforcement was further impeded by another provision in the law requiring periodic reporting of contributions and expenditures. According to many members of Congress, the frequency required for the filing of these reports during election campaigns by all political committees of candidates—required for both primary and general elections—created monumental bookkeeping chores for the candidates. Correspondingly, the mammoth number of reports filed with the House clerk, the Senate secretary and the comptroller general made closer scrutiny practically impossible.

Under the law, only contributions "in excess of $100" had to be reported and thus made public. Some members felt this language went counter to the intent of the act to open up the election process because it shielded from public view substantial sums donated in amounts of $100 and less.

Efforts to Amend 1971 Act

The Senate in 1972 refused to consider a bill passed earlier by the House to modify a provision of the Federal Election Campaign Act of 1971 prohibiting corporations and labor unions having federal government contracts from making direct political contributions to candidates for federal office. The House-passed bill would have allowed these corporations and unions to engage in the same kinds of political activity as those not having government contracts.

The Senate in 1973, motivated in part by the Watergate scandals, twice voted to tighten federal laws on financing of political campaigns. Portions of the legislation were opposed by House members responsible for initiating such legislation, and House action went no further than the hearings stage.

However, the failure of campaign reform legislation in 1973 did not mean that it was dead in the second session. Soon after Congress reconvened following its Christmas recess, the Senate Rules and Administration Committee began work on a comprehensive public financing bill. Many

---

T. R. and the 1974 Law

The 1974 campaign financing law works against the stability of minor parties by allowing a presidential candidate who qualifies for public financing in one election to take the money with him if he switches parties in the next election.

If the new law had been in effect in 1912, for example, Theodore Roosevelt, the Progressive Party candidate that year, would have become eligible for full public financing in 1916, because he polled 27 per cent of the vote with his "Bull Moose" campaign. Winning more than 25 per cent would have given him major-party status.

In the same election, the Republican Party, under whose banner Roosevelt had served as President from 1901 until 1909, collected only 23 per cent of the vote and thus would have been a minor party in 1916 and would have had only partial public financing.

But if Roosevelt had rejoined the Republicans and been their candidate in 1916, they would have taken the full public funding away from the Progressives.

---

reforms which the Senate had passed previously were incorporated in the new legislation.

1974 Campaign Act Amendments

Almost two and a half years after it passed the Federal Election Campaign Act of 1971 that was a factor in breaking open the Watergate scandal, Congress, reacting to presidential campaign abuses, enacted another landmark campaign reform bill that substantially overhauled the existing system of financing election campaigns. Technically the 1974 law (PL 93-443) was a set of amendments to the 1971 legislation, but in fact it was the most comprehensive of the three campaign reform laws passed in the early 1970s.

The new measure, which President Ford signed into law Oct. 15, established the first spending limits ever for candidates in presidential primary and general elections and in primary campaigns for the House and Senate. It set new expenditure ceilings for general election campaigns for Congress to replace the limits established by the 1925 Federal Corrupt Practices Act that were never effectively enforced and were repealed in the 1971 law. Further changes were made in 1976. *(See table p. 549)*

The 1974 law also introduced the first use of public money to pay for political campaign costs by providing for optional public financing in presidential general election campaigns and establishing federal matching grants to cover up to 45 per cent of the cost of presidential primary campaigns. The final bill did not contain Senate-passed provisions for partial public financing of congressional campaigns.

Major Provisions. The major sections of PL 93-443 established contribution and expenditure limits and created a Federal Election Commission to enforce the law. The expenditure, contribution and other provisions were affected by a 1976 Supreme Court decision and subsequently revised by Congress. These and other major provisions are compared in tabular form beginning on page 553. Immediately below are details of the law's public financing and disclosure provisions.

Public Financing. PL 93-443 made the following provisions for public financing:

• Presidential general elections—voluntary public financing. Major party candidates would automatically qualify for full funding before the campaign. Minor party and independent candidates would be eligible to receive a proportion of full funding based on past or current votes received. If a candidate opted for full public funding, no private contributions would be permitted.

• Presidential nominating conventions—optional public funding. Major parties would automatically qualify. Minor parties would be eligible for lesser amounts based on their proportion of votes received in a past or current election.

• Presidential primaries—matching public funds of up to $5-million per candidate after meeting fund-raising requirement of $100,000 raised in amounts of at least $5,000 in each of 20 states or more. Only the first $250 of individual private contributions would be matched. The matching funds were to be divided among the candidates as quickly as possible. In allocating the money, the order in which the candidates qualified would be taken into account. Only private gifts raised after Jan. 1, 1975, would qualify for matching for the 1976 election. No federal payments would be made before January 1976.

• All federal money for public funding of campaigns would come from the Presidential Election Campaign Fund. Money received from the federal income tax dollar checkoff would be automatically appropriated to the fund.

Disclosure. PL 93-443 made the following stipulations for disclosure and reporting dates:

• Required each candidate to establish one central campaign committee through which all contributions and expenditures on behalf of a candidate must be reported. Required designation of specific bank depositories of campaign funds.

• Required full reports of contributions and expenditures to be filed with the Federal Election Commission 10 days before and 30 days after every election, and within 10 days of the close of each quarter unless the committee received or expended less than $1,000 in that quarter. A year-end report was due in non-election years.

• Required that contributions of $1,000 or more received within the last 15 days before an election be reported to the commission within 48 hours.

• Prohibited contributions in the name of another.

• Treated loans as contributions. Required a cosigner or guarantor for each $1,000 of outstanding obligation.

• Required every person who spent or contributed over $100 other than to or through a candidate or political committee to report.

• Permitted government contractors, unions and corporations to maintain separate, segregated political funds. (Formerly all contributions by government contractors were prohibited.)

Enforcement, Penalties. The 1974 law set up a Federal Election Commission to enforce the law and spelled out detailed and stringent penalties. However, the Supreme Court in 1976 *(see following section)* declared the method of appointing commissioners unconstitutional. Congress then rewrote the commission appointment procedures and in the process made many other changes in the law. Major changes, including those involving enforcement and penalties, are summarized in the text beginning on page 548.

1976 Supreme Court Decision

As soon as the Campaign Act Amendments of 1974 took effect, the law was challenged in court. Several plaintiffs filed suit against PL 93-443 on Jan. 2, 1975.

The plaintiffs included Sen. James L. Buckley (Cons-R N.Y.), former Sen. Eugene J. McCarthy (D Minn. 1959-71), the New York Civil Liberties Union and *Human Events*, a conservative publication.

Their basic arguments were that the law's new limits on campaign contributions and expenditures curbed the freedom of contributors and candidates to express themselves in the political marketplace and that the public financing provisions discriminated against minor parties and lesser-known candidates in favor of the major parties and better-known candidates.

The U.S. Court of Appeals for the District of Columbia on Aug. 14, 1975, upheld all of the law's major provisions, thus setting the stage for Supreme Court action.

The Supreme Court handed down its ruling *(Buckley v. Valeo)* on Jan. 30, 1976, in an unsigned 137-page opinion. In five separate, signed opinions, several justices concurred with and dissented from separate issues in the case.

In its decision, the court upheld the provisions of PL 93-443 that:

• Set limits on how much individuals and political committees may contribute to candidates.

• Provided for the public financing of presidential primary and general election campaigns.

• Required the disclosure of campaign contributions of more than $100 and campaign expenditures of more than $10.

But the court overturned other features of the law, ruling that the campaign spending limits were unconstitutional violations of the First Amendment guarantee of free expression. For presidential candidates who accepted federal matching funds, however, the ceiling on expenditures remained intact. The court also struck down the method for selecting members of the Federal Election Commission, the agency established to oversee and enforce the 1974 law.

"A restriction on the amount of money a person or group can spend on political communication during a campaign necessarily reduces the quantity of expression," the court stated, "by restricting the number of issues discussed, the depth of their exploration and the size of the audience reached. This is because virtually every means of communicating ideas in today's mass society requires the expenditure of money." Only Justice Byron R. White dissented on this point; he would have upheld the limitations.

Although the court acknowledged that both contribution limits and spending limits had First Amendment implications, it distinguished between the two by saying that the act's "expenditure ceilings impose significantly more severe restrictions on protected freedom of political expression and association than do its limitations on financial contributions."

The court removed all the limits imposed on political spending and, by so doing, weakened the effect of the contribution ceilings. The law had placed spending limits on House, Senate and presidential campaigns and on party nominating conventions. To plug a loophole in the contribution limits, it also placed a $1,000 annual limit on how much an individual could spend independently on behalf of a candidate.

The independent expenditure ceiling, the opinion said, was a clear violation of the First Amendment. "While the...ceiling thus fails to serve any substantial government interest in stemming the reality or appearance of corruption in the electoral process, it heavily burdens core First Amendment expression," the court wrote. "...Advocacy of the election or defeat of candidates for federal office is no less entitled to protection under the First Amendment than the discussion of political policy generally or advocacy of the passage or defeat of legislation."

The court struck down the limits on how much of their own money candidates could spend on their campaigns. The law had set a $25,000 limit on House candidates, $35,000 on Senate candidates and $50,000 on presidential candidates. "The candidate, no less than any other person, has a First Amendment right to engage in the discussion of public issues and vigorously and tirelessly to advocate his own election and the election of other candidates," the opinion said.

The ruling made it possible for a wealthy candidate to finance his own campaign and thus to avoid the limits on how much others could give him. That aspect did not concern the court, which wrote that "the use of personal funds reduces the candidate's dependence on outside contributions and thereby counteracts the coercive pressures and attendant risks of abuse to which the act's contribution limitations are directed."

Associate Justice Byron R. White dissented on expenditure limits. Rejecting the argument that money is speech, he wrote that there are "many expensive campaign activities that are not themselves communicative or remotely related to speech." Furthermore, he wrote, the expenditure and contribution limits are integral to the spending limit, "lessening the chance that the contribution ceiling will be violated."

Associate Justice Thurgood Marshall rejected the court's reasoning in striking down the limit on how much candidates may spend on their own campaigns. "It would appear to follow," he said, "that the candidate with a substantial personal fortune at his disposal is off to a significant 'head start.'" Moreover, he added, keeping the limitations on contributions but not on spending "put[s] a premium on a candidate's personal wealth."

Federal Election Commission. The court held unanimously that the Federal Election Commission was unconstitutional. The court said the method of appointment of commissioners violated the Constitution's separation-of-powers and appointments clauses because some members were named by congressional officials but exercised executive powers.

The justices refused to accept the argument that the commission, because it oversaw congressional as well as presidential elections, could have congressionally appointed members. "We see no reason to believe that the authority of Congress over federal election practices is of such a wholly different nature from the other grants of authority to Congress that it may be employed in such a manner as to offend well established constitutional restrictions stemming from the separation of powers," the court wrote.

According to the decision, the commission may exercise only those powers Congress is allowed to delegate to congressional committees—investigating and information-gathering. Only if the commission's members were appointed by the President, as required under the Constitution's appointments clause, could the commission carry out the administrative and enforcement responsibilities the law originally gave it, the court ruled.

That last action put Congress on the spot, because the justices stayed their ruling for 30 days—until Feb. 29—to give the House and Senate time to "reconstitute the commission by law or adopt other valid enforcement mechanisms." As things developed, Congress took much longer than 30 days to act, and instead of merely reconstituting the commission it passed a whole new campaign financing law.

Supporters and opponents of the 1974 law hailed the court's ruling, with each side claiming victory. John Gardner, chairman of Common Cause, called the decision a triumph "for all those who have worked so hard to clean up politics in this country. The fat cats won't be able to buy elections or politicians any more." Sen. Buckley said the court "struck a major blow for the forces of freedom" by allowing unchecked political spending. But Buckley added that the court had left standing "a clearly unworkable set of ground rules" that Congress would have to revise.

Campaign Act Amendments of 1976

The court decision forced Congress to return to campaign finance legislation for the fourth time in five years. The 1976 election campaign was already underway, but the court said that the Federal Election Commission could not continue to disburse public funds to presidential candidates as long as some commission members were congressional appointees.

Congress did not begin its work until late February. The court extended the original Feb. 29 deadline until March 22, but the extra three weeks still did not give Congress the time members wanted to revise the law. One result was that for two months after March 22 the presidential candidates did not receive the federal matching funds they had expected.

President Ford had wanted only a simple reconstitution of the commission, but Congress insisted on going much further and writing an extensive new campaign finance law. The new law, arrived at after much maneuvering and arguing between Democrats and Republicans, closed old loopholes in existing law and opened new ones, depending on the point of view of the observer.

In its basic provision, the law (PL 94-283), signed by the President May 11, reconstituted the Federal Election Commission as a six-member panel appointed by the President and confirmed by the Senate.

Commission members could not engage in outside business activities. The commission was given exclusive

---

Unchanged Provisions

The Federal Election Campaign Act amendments of 1976 (PL 94-283) did not change the following provisions of the 1974 campaign finance legislation:

● The public financing provisions for presidential campaigns.

● Spending limits for the prenomination and general election campaigns of presidential candidates accepting public funds.

● The prohibition against political contributions by foreign nationals, earmarked contributions and cash contributions of more than $100.

● The dates by which campaign finance reports have to be filed with the election commission.

● The 30-legislative-day time period for Congress to disapprove election commission regulations.

Limits on Campaign Contributions

This table shows the limits on campaign contributions for federal elections. The figures are those in effect following the 1976 amendments to the 1971 and 1974 financing laws.

Contribution from:	To candidate or his/her authorized committee	**To national party committees[5] (per calendar year)[6]	**To any other committee (per calendar year)[6]	Total contributions (per calendar year)[7]
Individual	$1,000 per election[3]	$20,000	$5,000	$25,000
Multicandidate committee[1]	$5,000 per election	$15,000	$5,000	No limit
Party committee	$1,000 or $5,000[4] per election	No limit	$5,000	No limit
Republican or Democratic senatorial campaign committee,[2] or the national party committee, or a combination of both**	$17,500 to Senate candidate per calendar year[6] in which candidate seeks election	Not applicable	Not applicable	Not applicable
Any other committee	$1,000 per election	$20,000	$5,000	No limit

1. A multicandidate committee is any committee with more than 50 contributors which has been registered for at least six months and, with the exception of state party committees, has made contributions to five or more federal candidates.

2. Republican and Democratic senatorial campaign committees are subject to all other limits applicable to a multicandidate committee.

3. Each of the following elections is considered a separate election: primary election, general election, run-off election, special election, and party caucus or convention which, instead of a primary, has authority to select the nominee.

4. Limit depends on whether or not party committee is a multicandidate committee.

** See footnote 6.

5. For purposes of this limit, national party committees include a party's national committee, the Republican and Democratic Senate and House campaign committees and any other committee established by the party's national committee, provided they are not authorized by any candidate.

6. In 1976 only, and solely in the case of contribution limits established in the 1976 amendments (those indicated by double asterisk), the calendar year extends from May 11 (date of enactment of the act) through Dec. 31, 1976.

7. Calendar year extends from Jan. 1 through Dec. 31, 1976. Individual contributions made or earmarked before or after 1976 to influence the 1976 election of a specific candidate are counted as if made during 1976.

Source: Federal Election Commission.

---

authority to prosecute civil violations of the campaign finance law and was vested with jurisdiction over violations formerly covered only in the criminal code, thus strengthening its power to enforce the law.

A major controversy that delayed enactment was the insistence of organized labor that corporate fund-raising activity through political action committees be curtailed. Labor won some but not all of its goal. The final law permitted company committees to seek contributions only from stockholders, executives and administrative personnel and their families. It restricted union political action committees to soliciting contributions from union members and their families. However, twice a year, union and corporate political action committees were permitted to seek campaign contributions by mail only from all employees. Contributions would have to remain anonymous and would be received by an independent third party that would keep records but pass the money to the committees.

The final bill also included provisions restricting the commission's use of advisory opinions and giving Congress the power to veto discrete sections of commission regulations. President Ford objected particularly to the latter provision. He said the provision "not only circumvents the original intent of campaign reform but, in my opinion, violates the Constitution." He directed the Justice Department to challenge the constitutionality of the provision in court.

The final bill also contained another provision prompted by the Supreme Court decision. In addition to finding the make-up of the election commission unconstitutional, the court had thrown out the 1974 law's limitations on independent political expenditures as a clear violation of the First Amendment. Members of Congress feared that the ruling would open a major new loophole. As a result, they included a provision in the new bill requiring that political committees and individuals making independent political expenditures of more than $100 to advocate the defeat or election of a candidate swear that the expenditures were not made in collusion with the candidate.

Other Major Provisions. The 1976 legislation also revised contribution limits (see table above) and contained these other important provisions:

• Required an affirmative vote of four members for the commission to issue regulations and advisory opinions and initiate civil actions and investigations.

• Required labor unions, corporations and membership organizations to report expenditures of over $2,000 per election for communications to their stockholders or members advocating the election or defeat of a clearly identified candidate. The costs of communications to members or stockholders on issues would not have to be reported.

• Required that candidates and political committees keep records of contributions of $50 or more. The 1974 law required records of contributions of $10 or more.

● Required that independent expenditures of $1,000 or more made within 15 days of an election be reported within 24 hours.

● Limited the commission to issuing advisory opinions only for specific fact situations. Advisory opinions could not be used to spell out commission policy. Advisory opinions were not to be considered as precedents unless an activity was "indistinguishable in all its material aspects" from an activity already covered by an advisory opinion.

● Permitted the commission to initiate investigations only after it received a properly verified complaint or had reason to believe, based on information it obtained in the normal course of its duties, that a violation had occurred or was about to occur. The commission was barred from relying on anonymous complaints to institute investigations.

● Required the commission to rely initially on conciliation to deal with alleged campaign law violations before going to court.

● Restricted the proliferation of membership organization, corporate and union political action committees. All political action committees established by a company or an international union would be treated as a single committee for contribution purposes. The contributions of political action committees of a company or union would be limited to no more than $5,000 overall to the same candidate in any election.

● Raised the limit on honoraria members of Congress and federal employees may receive to $2,000 per individual event and a total of $25,000 a year from $1,000 per individual event and a total of $15,000 a year. The $25,000 limit was a net amount; booking agents' fees, travel expenditures, subsistence and expenses for an aide or a spouse to accompany the speaker could be deducted.

● Provided for a one-year jail sentence and a fine of up to $25,000 or three times the amount of the contribution or expenditure involved in the violation, whichever was greater, if an individual was convicted of knowingly committing a campaign law violation that involved more than $1,000.

● Provided for civil penalties of fines of $5,000 or an amount equal to the contribution or expenditure involved in the violation, whichever was greater. For violations knowingly committed, the fine would be $10,000 or an amount equal to twice the amount involved in the violation, whichever was greater. The fines could be imposed by the courts or by the commission in conciliation agreements. The 1974 law included penalties for civil violations of a $1,000 fine and/or a one-year prison sentence.

● Limited spending by presidential candidates to no more than $50,000 of their own, or their family's money, on their campaigns, if they accepted public financing.

● Cut off federal campaign subsidies to a presidential candidate who won less than 10 per cent of the vote in two consecutive presidential primaries in which he ran.

Commission Reconstituted. The President appointed six members of the new commission in May soon after signing the legislation. The commission was formally reconstituted May 21 and tax funds began to flow to candidates for the presidency soon after.

Footnotes

1. Congressional Quarterly, *Dollar Politics* (1974), vol. 2, p. iv.
2. Congressional Quarterly, *Dollar Politics* (1971), vol. 1, p. 1.
3. David W. Adamany and George E. Agree, *Political Money: A Strategy for Campaign Financing in America* (Johns Hopkins University Press, 1975), p. 19.
4. *Dollar Politics*, vol. 1, p. 1 and *Dollar Politics*, vol. 2, p. 60.
5. Adamany and Agree, *Political Money*, pp. 19-20.
6. *Ibid.*, pp. 20-21.
7. *Dollar Politics*, vol. 1, p. 12.
8. *Ibid.*, p. 13.
9. *Ibid.*
10. *Ibid.*, p. 11.
11. Congressional Quarterly, *Weekly Report*, March 13, 1976, p. 554.
12. *Dollar Politics*, vol. 1, p. 5.
13. *Ibid.*
14. *Dollar Politics*, vol. 2, p. 55.
15. *Ibid.*, pp. 83-84.
16. *Ibid.*, pp. 73-75.
17. *Dollar Politics*, vol. 1, pp. 4-5.

18. Congressional Quarterly, *Weekly Report*, March 13, 1976, p. 555.
19. *Ibid.*
20. *Ibid.*
21. Congressional Quarterly, *1973 Almanac*, p. 750.
22. *Dollar Politics*, vol. 2, pp. 61-62.
23. Congressional Quarterly, *Weekly Report*, Oct. 4, 1975, p. 2131.
24. *Ibid.*
25. *Ibid.*, p. 2132.
26. George Thayer, *Who Shakes the Money Tree?* (Simon and Schuster, 1973), p. 25.
27. Yorick Blumenfeld and Bruce Freed, "Campaign Spending in Europe and America," *Editorial Research Reports*, Oct. 11, 1974, p. 776.
28. Congressional Quarterly, *Weekly Report*, April 17, 1976, p. 902.
29. Cited in Blumenfeld and Freed, "Campaign Spending," *Editorial Research Reports*, p. 777.
30. Congressional Quarterly, *Congress and the Nation, 1969-1972*, vol. 3, p. 397.

Selected Bibliography

Books

Adamany, David W. and Agree, George E. *Political Money: A Strategy for Campaign Financing in America.* Baltimore: Johns Hopkins University Press, 1975.

The American Bar Association. Special Committee on Election Reform. *Symposium on Campaign Financing Regulation.* Tiburon, Calif.: April 25-27, 1975.

Alexander, Herbert E. *Financing the 1960 Election.* Princeton: Citizens' Research Foundation, 1962.

_____. *Financing the 1964 Election.* Princeton: Citizens' Research Foundation, 1968.

_____. *Financing the 1968 Election.* Lexington, Mass.: D.C. Heath, 1971.

_____. *Financing the 1972 Election.* Lexington, Mass.: D.C. Heath, 1976.

_____. *Financing Politics.* Washington: Congressional Quarterly Press, 1976.

_____. *Political Financing.* Minneapolis: Burgess Publishing Co., 1972.

_____. *Money, Politics and Public Reporting.* Princeton: Citizens' Research Foundation, 1960.

_____. *Money in Politics.* Washington: Public Affairs Press, 1972.

_____. *Regulation of Political Finance.* Published jointly by Institute of Governmental Studies, Berkeley and Citizens' Research Foundation, Princeton, 1966.

_____, ed. *Studies in Money in Politics.* 2 vols. Princeton: Citizens' Research Foundation, 1965-1970.

Boyd, James. *Above the Law.* New York: New American Library, 1968.

Committee for Economic Development. Research and Policy Committee. *Financing a Better Election System.* New York, 1968.

Congressional Quarterly. *Dollar Politics.* Vol. I (1971), Vol. II (1974). Washington.

Domhoff, G. William. *Fat Cats and Democrats: The Role of the Big Rich in the Party of the Common Man.* Englewood Cliffs, N.J.: Prentice-Hall, 1972.

Dunn, Delmer D. *Financing Presidential Campaigns.* Washington: The Brookings Institution, 1972.

Felknor, Bruce L. *Dirty Politics.* New York: Norton, 1966.

Heard, Alexander. *The Costs of Democracy.* Chapel Hill: University of North Carolina Press, 1960.

McCarthy, Max. *Elections for Sale.* Boston: Houghton Mifflin, 1972.

Nichols, David. *Financing Elections: The Politics of an American Ruling Class.* New York: New Viewpoints, 1974.

1972 Congressional Finances. 10 vols. Prepared by the Campaign Finance Monitoring Project, Common Cause. Washington: 1974.

1972 Federal Campaign Finances: Interest Groups and Political Parties. 2 vols. Prepared by Campaign Monitoring Project, Common Cause. Washington, 1974.

1974 Congressional Campaign Finances. 5 vols. Prepared by Campaign Monitoring Project, Common Cause. Washington, 1976.

Overacker, Louise. *Money in Elections.* New York: Macmillan, 1932.

Peabody, Robert L. *To Enact a Law: Congress and Campaign Financing.* New York: Praeger, 1972.

Shannon, Jasper B. *Money and Politics.* New York: Random House, 1959.

Stinnett, Ronald F. *Democrats, Dinners, & Dollars.* Introduction by Hubert H. Humphrey. Ames: Iowa State University Press, 1967.

Thayer, George. *Who Shakes the Money Tree?* New York: Simon and Schuster, 1973.

Twentieth Century Fund. Commission on Campaign Costs in the Electronic Era. *Voters' Time; Report.* New York, 1969.

_____. Task Force on Financing Congressional Campaigns. *Electing Congress; The Financial Dilemma; Report* (and) *Background Paper* by David L. Rosenbloom. New York, 1970.

Articles

Adamany, David. "Election Campaign Financing: the 1974 Reforms." *Political Science Quarterly,* Summer, 1975, pp. 201-20.

_____. "Sources of Money: An Overview." *Annals of the American Academy of Political and Social Science,* May 1976, pp. 17-32.

Alexander, Herbert E., "Financing American Politics." *Political Quarterly,* October/December 1974, pp. 439-48.

_____, ed. "Political Finance: Reform and Reality; Symposium." *Annals of the American Academy of Political and Social Science,* May 1976, pp. 1-149.

_____, et al. "The High Costs of TV Campaigns." *Television Quarterly,* Winter 1966, pp. 47-65.

Berry, Jeffrey M. "Congress and Public Policy: A Study of the Federal Election Campaign Act of 1971." *Harvard Journal on Legislation,* February 1973, p. 331.

Biden, Joseph R. Jr. "Public Financing of Elections: Legislative Proposals and Constitutional Questions." *Northwestern University Law Review,* March/April 1974, pp. 1-70.

Boeckel, Richard. "Excessive Expenditures in Election Campaigns." *Editorial Research Reports,* 1926, vol. 2. pp. 636-58.

"Campaign Spending in the 1968 Elections." Congressional Quarterly, *Weekly Report,* Dec. 5, 1969, Part 1, pp. 2433-61.

Dawson, P. A. and Zinser, J. E. "Political Finance and Participation in Congressional Elections." *Annals of the American Academy of Political and Social Science,* May 1976, pp. 59-73.

Dean, E. Joseph. "Undisclosed Earmarking: Violation of the Federal Election Campaign Act of 1971." *Harvard Journal on Legislation,* February 1973, p. 175.

"The Federal Election Campaign Act of 1971: Reform of the Political Process?" *Georgetown Law Review,* May 1972, p. 1309.

Heard, Alexander. "Political Financing." *International Encyclopedia of the Social Sciences* (Macmillan, 1968, 17 vols.), Vol. 12, pp. 235-44.

Lambert, Jeremiah D. "Corporate Political Spending and Campaign Finance." *New York University Law Review,* December 1965, pp. 1033-78.

Lobel, Martin. "Federal Control of Campaign Contributions." *Minnesota Law Review,* 1966-67, pp. 1-62.

"Loophole Legislation—State Campaign Finance Laws." *University of Pennsylvania Law Review,* April 1967, pp. 983-1006.

Macdonald, George P. "Union Political Involvement and Reform of Campaign Financing Regulation." *Prospectus; A Journal of Law Reform,* April 1969, pp. 347-70.

Rauh, Joseph L. Jr. "Legality of Union Political Expenditures." *Southern California Law Review,* Winter 1961, pp. 152-64.

Sterling, Carleton W. "Control of Campaign Spending: The Reformers Paradox." *American Bar Association Journal,* October 1973, p. 1148.

Walters, Robert. "Campaign Spending from Loopholes." *National Journal Reports,* Jan. 11, 1975, p. 67.

Government Documents

U.S. Congress. House. Committee on House Administration. *Election Reform Act of 1966;* Hearings on H.R. 15317 and related Bills. 89th Cong., 2nd sess., 1966.

———. *Federal Election Campaign Act of 1971.* H. Rept. 92-752, conference report on S. 382. 92nd Cong., 1st sess., 1971.

U.S. Congress. House. Committee on Standards of Official Conduct. *Report Under the Authority of H. Res. 1031.* H. Rept. 91-1803. 91st Cong., 2nd sess., 1970.

———. *Campaign Finances; Hearings on H. Res. 1031, Regulation of Lobbying and Management of Campaign Money.* 92nd Cong., 1st sess., 1971.

U.S. Congress. House. Special Committee to Investigate Campaign Expenditures. *Reports.* H. Rept. 88-1946, 88th Cong., 2nd sess., 1964; H. Rept. 89-2348, 89th Cong., 2nd sess., 1966; H. Rept. 91-2, 91st Cong., 1st sess., 1968; Committee Print, 92nd Cong., 1st sess.,

1970; H. Rept. 93-1 and 93-286, 93rd Cong., 1st sess., 1973.

U.S. Congress. Senate. Committee on Finance. *Political Campaign Financing Proposals; Hearings on Various Proposals for Financing Political Campaigns.* 90th Cong., 1st sess., 1967.

———. *Report on Honest Elections Act of 1967.* S. Rept. 90-714. 90th Cong., 1st sess., 1967.

U.S. Congress. Senate. Committee on Rules and Administration. *Election Law Guidebook 1976.* S. Doc. 94-216. 94th Cong., 2nd sess., 1976.

———. *Federal Election Campaign Act of 1973, Report.* S. Rept. 93-310 to accompany S. 372. 93rd Cong., 1st sess., 1973.

———. *Hearings Before the Subcommittee on Privileges and Elections on Proposed Amendments to and Improvements in the Federal Election Laws.* 3 parts. 87th Cong., 1st sess., 1961.

———. *Hearings on 1956 Presidential and Senatorial Campaign Contributions and Practices.* 84th Cong., 2nd sess., 1956.

U.S. Congress. Senate. Select Committee on Presidential Campaign Activities. *Final Report.* S. Rept. 93-981, 93rd Cong., 2nd sess., 1974.

U.S. Congress. Senate. Office of the Secretary. *Report on Audits, Field Investigations, Complaints and Referrals in Connection with the Election of the U.S. Senate.* Washington: Government Printing Office, 19—.

U.S. Federal Election Commission. *Federal Election Campaign Laws.* Washington: Government Printing Office, 1976.

U.S. Library of Congress. American Law Division. *Analysis of Federal and State Campaign Finance Law: Summaries,* 1976.

Major Campaign Finance Law Provisions

Source: Federal Election Commission.

The material below gives major provisions of the campaign finance laws passed in 1971, 1974 and 1976. The material is presented in a form to show the major changes made by each law. The material does not include provisions on public financing of presidential elections or nominating conventions *(see text pp. 544, 547)*; in addition, the summary below does not include many detailed provisions relating to the fundamental disclosure, reporting, contribution and enforcement sections of the law that are summarized.

Column 2 (1971/1974 provisions) highlights the law in effect prior to the 1976 amendments. Column 3 (1976 amendments) highlights the changes made by the 1976 law.

SUBJECT	1971/1974 PROVISIONS	1976 AMENDMENTS
1) CANDIDATES AND COMMITTEES		
(A) ORGANIZATION **Principal Campaign Committee Support**	Could not support any other candidate.	Now may provide "occasional, isolated, or incidental" support of another candidate.
(B) REGISTRATION		(No change)
(C) RECORD-KEEPING **Records of contributions**	Had to be kept for contributions over $10.	Now only requires record-keeping of contributions over $50. Note: No change, however, in requirement that donors who contribute over $100 in the aggregate be identified in the reports where committee has knowledge of such aggregated contributions.
Campaign depositories	Candidate had to have "a" checking account for deposit of any contributions.	Now may also maintain "such other accounts" as desired (including checking accounts, savings accounts, or certificates of deposit).
(D) REPORTING **Filing with Principal Campaign Committee**	Every committee supporting a candidate had to file its report with that candidate's Principal Campaign Committee.	New law clarifies that only committees authorized by a candidate to raise contributions or make expenditures must file with the Principal Campaign Committee.
Treasurer's "best efforts"	(No provision)	Committee treasurers and candidates who show they have used "best efforts" to obtain and submit all required information shall be deemed in compliance with the law.
Waiver of quarterly report filing	Quarterly reports waived for any quarter in which $1,000 is not received or spent. (Except for end-of-year report due in January regardless of amount).	In addition, in non-election year, candidates and committees authorized by candidates do not have to file reports in quarters when combined contributions and expenditures do not exceed $5,000 (except for end-of-year report due in January regardless of amount).
Internal communications	(No provision)	Adds new requirement that membership organizations (including labor organizations or corporations) must report their expenditures for all communications primarily devoted to express advocacy of the election or defeat of a clearly identified candidate, when the total actual cost of such communications relating to all candidates in an election exceeds $2,000.
(2) CONTRIBUTIONS		
(A) CONTRIBUTION LIMITS **(i) FROM AN INDIVIDUAL** **To a candidate or that candidate's authorized committee(s)**	$1,000 per election.	Same.
To national political party committees	No limit (except $25,000 limit on total contributions per year).	$20,000 per year.
To any other political committee	No limit (except $25,000 limit on total contributions per year).	$5,000 per year.
Total aggregate contributions per year.	$25,000 per year.	Same.

SUBJECT	1971/1974 PROVISIONS	1976 AMENDMENTS
(ii) FROM A POLITICAL COMMITTEE QUALIFYING AS A "MULTI-CANDIDATE COMMITTEE"* (See definition p. 557)		
To a candidate or that candidate's authorized committee(s)	$5,000 per election.	Same.
To national political party committees	No limit.	$15,000 per year.
To any other political committee	No limit.	$5,000 per year.
Total aggregate contributions per year	No limit.	Same.
(iii) FROM ANY OTHER POLITICAL COMMITTEE OR ORGANIZATION		
To a candidate or that candidate's authorized committee(s)	$1,000 per election.	Same.
To national political party committees	No limit.	$20,000 per year.
To any other political committee	No limit.	$5,000 per year.
Total aggregate contributions per year	No limit.	Same.

(iv) SPECIAL EXCEPTIONS ADDED TO THE 1976 AMENDMENTS

Senate Elections: The Republican or Democratic Senatorial Campaign Committee, or the National Committee of a political party, or any combination of such committees may contribute not more than $17,500 in an election year to a Senate candidate.

Party Committee Limits: No limits on "transfers" between political committees of the same political party.

Subsidiary Committee Limits: For purposes of applying contribution limits, all political committees (including corporate or union separate segregated funds) established, financed, maintained or controlled by the same organization (such as subsidiaries, divisions, local units, etc.) are treated as a single political committee for purposes of contribution limits.

NOTE: There is an exception to this "single political committee" rule for political parties. Contributions by a single national political party committee and by a single state political party committee are not treated as one committee for purposes of applying the contribution limits.

(B) CONTRIBUTION DEFINITIONS

SUBJECT	1971/1974 PROVISIONS	1976 AMENDMENTS
"Contract"	Defined as "a contract, promise, or agreement, express or implied."	Now only defined as a "written" contract. Also the words "express or implied" were deleted.
Legal or accounting services	(No provision)	Not counted as "contribution" so long as lawyer/accountant is paid by his or her regular employer and does not engage in general campaign activities. But amounts paid or incurred must be reported.
$500 exemption	Costs to an individual, up to $500, of sale of food or beverage by a vendor at cost.	$500 exemption for vendor applies to a person (including committees, corporations, groups, etc.), not just an individual.

(3) EXPENDITURES
(A) EXPENDITURE LIMITS

SUBJECT	1971/1974 PROVISIONS	1976 AMENDMENTS
Candidate personal spending limits from own funds	Presidential, $50,000; Senate, $35,000; House, $25,000.	No limits except for presidential candidates accepting public funds, which remain the same.
Campaign spending limits	Presidential: primary, $10-million; general, $20-million. Senate: primary, greater of 8¢ per voter or $100,000; general, greater of 12¢ per voter or $150,000. House: $70,000 each election. Annual cost-of-living increase in spending limits. Exemption of fund-raising costs up to 20% of the spending limits.	No limits except for presidential candidates accepting public funds, which remain the same.

SUBJECT	1971/1974 PROVISIONS	1976 AMENDMENTS
(B) EXPENDITURE DEFINITIONS		
Legal or accounting services	(No provision)	Not counted as "expenditure" so long as lawyer/accountant is paid by his or her regular employer and does not engage in general campaign activities. But amounts paid or incurred must be reported.
(4) INDEPENDENT EXPENDITURES		
Definition	An expenditure "relative to a clearly identified candidate...advocating the election or defeat of a clearly identified candidate."	Changed to refer to expenditures "expressly" advocating a candidate. To be "independent" an expenditure also cannot involve any "cooperation," "consultation," or be in "concert" with or "be at the request or suggestion of" any candidate or candidate's agent. An expenditure made with any such involvement with a candidate is a "contribution" subject to contribution limits.
Independent spending limit	$1,000 per candidate per election.	No limit.
Reports: (i) Filed by individuals	Reports of independent expenditures over $100 on dates political committees file, but reports need not be cumulative.	Basically same reporting requirements, except the language "need not be cumulative" is stricken. Additional language added that must file the same information required of contributors over $100, and the same information required of political committees. Must also report name(s) of candidate(s) independently supported or opposed, and state "under penalty of perjury" whether there was any cooperation, etc., with any candidate. Must report any "independent expenditure" of $1,000 or more within 24 hours if made within 15 days of an election.
(ii) Filed by political committees	No special requirement. Same reports required of any political committee.	Basically same, except must also report name(s) of candidate(s) independently supported or opposed, and state "under penalty of perjury" whether there was any cooperation, etc., with any candidate. Must report any "independent expenditure" of $1,000 or more within 24 hours if made within 15 days of an election.
(5) PUBLICATION/BROADCAST NOTICES		
(A) Unauthorized literature or advertisements	Must contain statement that unauthorized by candidate, and that candidate not responsible.	These two sections (A) and (B) are replaced by a single new section covering communications "expressly advocating the election or defeat of a clearly identified candidate" through use of media, direct mail, or any advertisements. In such cases, the communication must either: (1) if authorized, state the name of the candidate or candidate's agent who authorized the communication, or (2) if unauthorized, state that the communication is unauthorized, identify who "made or financed" it, and list the name(s) of any affiliated or connected organization.
(B) Pamphlets or advertisements	Must state who is responsible, and list names of officers for any organization.	
(C) Fund-raising solicitation	There is no change in the requirement that any fund-raising solicitation (whether authorized or unauthorized) contain a statement that reports are filed with, and available for purchase from, the FEC.	
(6) MISCELLANEOUS PROVISIONS		
Definition of "election"	Included any political party caucus or convention "held" to nominate a candidate.	**Changed to include those which have "authority to"** nominate a candidate.
FEC indexes	————	FEC required to compile 2 new indexes: (1) Independent expenditures made on behalf of each candidate; (2) All political committees supporting more than one candidate, including the dates they qualify for the "multicandidate committee" contribution levels.

SUBJECT	1971/1974 PROVISIONS	1976 AMENDMENTS
Honorariums	Federal officeholders or officers limited to $15,000 per year, and $1,000 per "appearance, speech, or article." Exemption for recipient's actual travel and subsistence.	Limits increased to $25,000 per year and $2,000 per honorarium. Travel and subsistence exemption extended to spouse or one aide. Additional exemption added for agent or booking fees. Honorariums exempt from definition of "contribution" to a candidate.
Issue-oriented organization report	Reports required by an organization making any reference to a candidate, including voting record lists, issue-oriented comments, etc.	Deleted.

(7) FEDERAL ELECTION COMMISSION

SUBJECT	1971/1974 PROVISIONS	1976 AMENDMENTS
Appointment	6 Commissioners, 2 each appointed by President, Senate and House. Staggered terms every year. 6-year terms.	6 Commissioners, all appointed by the President. Confirmed by the Senate with 6-year terms staggered every 2 years (so terms expire in non-election years).
Authority to prescribe regulations	Only for Title 2 disclosure provisions. No authority to prescribe regulations for Title 18 limitations provisions.	Since all the provisions of the FECA formerly codified in Title 18 are now included in Title 2, FEC now has authority to prescribe regulations for all provisions of the act.
Advisory opinions Who may request	Any federal officeholder, any federal candidate, or any political committee.	Also, the national committee of any political party.
Scope	Must relate to specific transaction or activity of requestor.	Basically same, but language now reads that advisory opinions must relate to the "application" of a general rule of law in the act or regulations to a specific factual situation.
Immunity	Person receiving advisory opinion and acting in good faith reliance on it "presumed to be in compliance" with the law. Limited to person asking and receiving advisory opinion.	Basically same, but language now reads that such person "shall not...be subject to any sanction" of the law. Extended to any person involved in same transaction, or in another transaction "indistinguishable in all its material aspects."

(8) COMPLIANCE PROCEDURES

SUBJECT	1971/1974 PROVISIONS	1976 AMENDMENTS
Authority	FEC had "primary" civil jurisdiction authority.	Now has "exclusive" primary civil jurisdiction authority.
Form of complaints	(No provision)	Now must be in writing, signed and sworn, notarized, and subject to false reporting laws. FEC may not act solely on basis of an anonymous complaint.
FEC investigation	Any complaint filed.	Only if FEC "has reason to believe" violation has been committed.
Rights of person complained against	Right to request hearing concerning any complaint.	Hearings eliminated, but when FEC investigates (see above), right to demonstrate that no action should be taken.
Voluntary compliance	FEC to utilize "informal means of conference, conciliation or persuasion" to settle cases.	Basically same, except minimum of 30 days (or half the number of days before an election) to use informal methods. Cases to be settled by adoption of "conciliation agreement." Civil penalties can be included in conciliation agreement involving "knowing and willful violations."
Civil actions	FEC authority to seek civil action in court, or ask Justice Department to seek civil relief.	Now sole FEC authority.
Referral of cases to Justice Department	If apparent violation of a Title 18 provision (see (9), below), or if FEC unable to correct a violation of Title 2 provision (see (9)).	Now only if FEC determines there is probable cause of a knowing and willful violation, and if the violation involves contributions or expenditures aggregating $1,000 or more.
Confidentiality	FEC barred from making any information public about any investigation without consent of subject of investigation.	Same. However, new provision requires FEC after investigation to make public any conciliation agreement, any attempt at conciliation, and any determination that no violation has occurred.

SUBJECT	1971/1974 PROVISIONS	1976 AMENDMENTS
FEC inaction	(No provision)	Right to appeal to U.S. district court for FEC failure to act on complaint within 90 days or for FEC dismissal of a complaint.
Court enforcement	No specific language, except referral to Justice Department.	FEC has authority to seek court enforcement of a conciliation agreement, or of a court order.
(9) PENALTIES STRUCTURE **Title 2 reporting and disclosure provisions**	A fine up to $1,000; or 1 year prison; or both.	For any violation, a fine up to the greater of $5,000 or the amount of any contribution or expenditure involved; (or in the case of a knowing and willful violation, a fine up to the greater of $10,000 or twice the amount of any contribution or expenditure involved).

Limitations sections codified in the 1971/1974 Provisions in Title 18, and re-codified in the 1976 Amendments in Title 2	A fine up to $25,000; 1 or 5 years prison (depending on the section); or both.	Same as above for any violation, except:
		For knowing and willful violations of contribution and expenditure provisions aggregating $1,000 or more, a fine up to the greater of $25,000 or 300% of any amount involved; or 1 year prison; or both.
		Exceptions:
		(i) these additional penalties apply to violations over $250 for:
		  corporate/union provisions
		  $100 cash contribution limit
		  prohibition of contributions in the name of another.
		(ii) these additional penalties apply to violations of any amount for misrepresentation of campaign authority.

---

*Definition of "Multicandidate Committee"—A political committee meeting all of the following three conditions: (1) has been registered under the act for six months; (2) has received contributions from more than 50 persons; (3) has made contributions to five or more federal candidates. A state political party committee need only meet (1) and (2). Note: There is no change in these conditions from the 1971/1974 provisions, but the special term "multicandidate committee" was added in the 1976 amendments.

Reapportionment and Redistricting

When the 55 delegates to the Constitutional Convention emerged from their remarkable nation-creating endeavor in September 1787, their work was seen to contain many unique features. Among them was a national legislative body (the House of Representatives) whose membership was to be elected by the people and apportioned on the basis of population. But, as with almost everything in the Constitution, only a few basic rules and regulations were laid down. How to interpret and implement the instructions contained in the document was left to the future. Practical reactions to concrete problems would shape the institutions and create the customs by which the new nation would develop and prosper.

Within this framework, many questions soon arose concerning the lower house of Congress. How large was it to be? What mathematical formula was to be used in calculating the distribution of seats to the various states? Were the Representatives to be elected at large or by districts? If by districts, what standards should be used in fixing their boundaries? The Congress and the courts have been wrestling with these questions for almost 200 years.

Nor were such problems considered to be minor or routine. George Washington's only speech at the Constitutional Convention concerned the question of the ratio of population per Representative in the House. Moreover, his first veto as President—and therefore the first Presidential veto in American history—was of the Reapportionment Bill of 1792. Other such prominent figures in American history as Alexander Hamilton, Thomas Jefferson and Daniel Webster played leading roles in reapportionment and redistricting debates.

Until the mid-twentieth century, such questions generally remained in the hands of the legislators. But with growing concentration of the population in urban areas, variations in population among Congressional districts became more pronounced—and more noticeable. Moves in Congress to redress the grievance of heavily populated but under-represented areas proved unsuccessful. So intent were rural legislators on preventing power from slipping out of their hands that they managed to block reapportionment of the House following the Census of 1920. That census showed urban residents in the majority for the first time in American history.

Before long, the focus shifted to the Supreme Court, where litigants tried to get the Court to order the states to revise Congressional district boundaries in line with population shifts. After initial failure, a breakthrough occurred in 1964 in the case of *Wesberry v. Sanders.* The Court declared that the Constitution required that "as nearly as practicable, one man's vote in a Congressional election is to be wroth as much as another's."[1]

Background and Early History

Modern legislative bodies are descended from the councils of feudal lords and gentry which medieval kings summoned for the purpose of raising revenues and armies. These councils did not represent a king's subjects in any modern sense; they represented certain groups of subjects, such as the nobility, the clergy, the landed gentry and town merchants. Thus representation was by interest groups and had no relation to equal representation for equal numbers of people. In England, the king's council became Parliament, with the higher nobility and clergy making up the House of Lords and representatives of the gentry and merchants making up the House of Commons.

Beginning as little more than administrative and advisory arms of the throne, royal councils in time developed into lawmaking bodies and acquired powers which eventually eclipsed those of the monarchs they served. The power struggle in England was climaxed during the Cromwellian period when the Crown gave way, temporarily, to the Commonwealth. By 1800, Parliament was clearly the superior branch of Government.

During the 18th and early 19th centuries, as the power of Parliament grew, Englishmen became increasingly concerned about the "representativeness" of their system of apportionment. Newly developing industrial cities had no more representation in the House of Commons than small, almost deserted country towns. Small constituencies were bought and sold. Men from these empty "rotten boroughs" were often sent to Parliament representing a single "patron" landowner or clique of wealthy men. It was not until the Reform Act of 1832 that Parliament curbed such excesses and turned toward a representative system based on population.

The growth of the powers of Parliament as well as the development of Englishmen's ideas of representation during the 17th and 18th centuries had a profound effect on the colonists in America. Representative assemblies were unifying forces behind the breakaway of the colonies from England and the establishment of the newly independent country.

Colonists in America, generally modeling their legislatures after England's, used both population and land units as bases for apportionment. Patterns of early representation varied. "Nowhere did representation bear any uniform relation to the number of electors. Here and there the factor of size had been crudely recognized," Robert Luce pointed out in his book *Legislative Principles.*[2]

In the New England states, the town was usually the basis for representation. In the Middle Atlantic states, the county was frequently used. Some southern states used the county with extra representation for specified cities. In many areas, towns and counties were fairly equal in population. Thus territorial representation afforded roughly equal representation for equal numbers of people. Delaware's three counties, for example, were of almost equal population and had the same representation in the state legislature. But in Virginia the disparity was enormous (from 951 people in one county to 22,015 in another), and Thomas Jefferson criticized the state's constitution on the ground that "among those who share the representation, the shares are unequal"[3]

The Continental Congress, with representation from every colony, proclaimed in the Declaration of Independence in 1776 that Governments derive "their just powers from the consent of the governed" and that "the right of representation in the legislature" is an "inestimable right" of the people. The Constitutional Convention of 1787 included representatives from all the states. However, in neither of these bodies were the state delegations or voting powers proportional to population.

Intentions of Founding Fathers

Andrew Hacker, in his book *Congressional Districting,* said that to ascertain what the framers of the Constitution had in mind when they drew up the section concerning the House of Representatives, it was necessary to study closely (1) the Constitution itself, (2) the recorded discussions and debates at the Constitutional Convention, (3) *The Federalist Papers* (essays written by Alexander Hamilton, John Jay and James Madison in defense of the Constitution) and (4) the deliberations of the state ratifying conventions.

Provisions of Constitution. The Constitution states only that each state is to be allotted a certain number of representatives. It does not state specifically that Congressional districts must be equal or nearly equal in population. Nor does it even require specifically that a state create districts at all. However, it seems clear that the first clause of Article I, Section 2, providing that House Members should be chosen "by the people of the several states," indicated that the House of Representatives, in contrast to the Senate, was to represent people rather than states. "It follows," Hacker wrote, "that if the states are to have equal representation in the upper chamber, then individuals are to be equally represented in the lower body."

The third clause of Article I, Section 2, provided that Congressional apportionment among the states must be according to population. But, Hacker argued, "there is little point in giving the states Congressmen 'according to their respective numbers' if the states do not redistribute the members of their delegations on the same principle. For Representatives are not the property of the states, as are the Senators, but rather belong to the people who happen to reside within the boundaries of those states. Thus, each citizen has a claim to be regarded as a political unit equal in value to his neighbors." In this and similar ways, Constitutional scholars have argued the case for single-member Congressional districts deduced from the wording of the Constitution itself.[4]

Constitutional Convention. As for the debates in the Constitutional Convention, the issue of unequal representation arose only once. The occasion was Madi-

son's defense of Article I, Section 4, of the proposed Constitution giving Congress the power to override state regulations on "the times...and manner" of holding elections for United States Senators and Representatives. Madison's argument related to the fact that many state legislatures of the time were badly malapportioned: "The inequality of the representation in the legislatures of particular states would produce a like inequality in their representation in the national legislature, as it was presumable that the counties having the power in the former case would secure it to themselves in the latter."[5]

The implication was twofold: that states would create Congressional districts and that unequal districting was bad and should be prevented.

Constitutional Provisions on Apportionment and Districting

Article I, Section 2: The House of Representatives shall be composed of Members chosen every second Year by the People of the several States, and the Electors in each State shall have the Qualifications requisite for Electors of the most numerous Branch of the State Legislature....

Representatives and direct Taxes shall be apportioned among the several States which may be included within this Union, according to their respective Numbers, which shall be determined by adding to the whole Number of free Persons, including those bound to Service for a Term of Years, and excluding Indians not taxed, three fifths of all other Persons. The actual Enumeration shall be made within three Years after the first Meeting of the Congress of the United States, and within every subsequent Term of ten Years, in such Manner as they shall by Law direct. The Number of Representatives shall not exceed one for every thirty thousand, but each State shall have at least one Representative....

Article I, Section 4: The Times, Places and Manner of holding Elections for Senators and Representatives, shall be prescribed in each State by the Legislature thereof; but the Congress may at any time by Law make or alter such Regulations, except as to the Place of Chusing Senators....

Article (Amendment) XIV, Section 2: Representatives shall be apportioned among the several States according to their respective numbers, counting the whole number of persons in each State, excluding Indians not taxed. But when the right to vote at any election for the choice of electors for President and Vice President of the United States, Representatives in Congress, the Executive and Judicial officers of a State, or the members of the Legislature thereof, is denied to any of the male inhabitants of such State, being twenty-one years of age, and citizens of the United States, or in any way abridged, except for participation in rebellion, or other crime, the basis of representation therein shall be reduced in the proportion which the number of such male citizens shall bear to the whole number of male citizens twenty-one years of age in such State.

Federalist Papers. Madison made this interpretation even more clear in his contributions to *The Federalist Papers.* Arguing in favor of the relatively small size of the projected House of Representatives, he wrote in Paper No. 56: "Divide the largest state into ten or twelve districts and it will be found that there will be no peculiar local interests in either which will not be within the knowledge of the Representative of the district."

In the same paper, Madison said: "The Representatives of each State will not only bring with them a considerable knowledge of its laws, and a local knowledge of their respective districts, but will probably in all cases have been members, and may even at the very time be members, of the state legislature, where all the local information and interests of the state are assembled, and from whence they may easily be conveyed by a very few hands into the legislature of the United States." And finally, in the next *Federalist* paper (No. 57), Madison made the statement that "...each Representative of the United States will be elected by five or six thousand citizens." In making these arguments, Madison seems to have assumed that all or most Representatives would be elected by districts rather than at large.[6]

State Conventions. In the state ratifying conventions, the grant to Congress by Article I, Section 4, of ultimate jurisdiction over the "times, places and manner of holding elections" (except the places of choosing Senators) held the attention of many delegates. There were differences over the merits of this section, but no justification of unequal districts was prominently used to attack the grant of power. Further evidence that individual districts were the intention of the Founding Fathers was given in the New York ratifying convention, when Alexander Hamilton said: "The natural and proper mode of holding elections will be to divide the state into districts in proportion to the number to be elected. This state will consequently be divided at first into six."[7]

From his study of the sources relating to the question of Congressional districting, Hacker concluded: "There is, then, a good deal of evidence that those who framed and ratified the Constitution intended that the House of Representatives have as its constituency a public in which the votes of all citizens were of equal weight. In the final analysis, the aristocratic pronouncements of Hamilton, Gerry and Morris cannot be regarded as having been written into the document's provisions dealing with the lower chamber of the national legislature. The House of Representatives was designed to be a popular chamber, giving the same electoral power to all who had the vote. And the concern of Madison, King and Pinckney that districts be equal in size was an institutional step in the direction of securing this democratic principle."[8]

The Early Years: 1789-1842

Article I, Section 2, Clause 3 of the Constitution laid down the basic rules for apportionment and reapportionment of seats in the House of Representatives: "Representatives...shall be apportioned among the several states which may be included within this Union, according to their respective numbers, which shall be determined by adding to the whole number of free persons, including those bound to service for a term of years, and excluding

Indians not taxed, three-fifths of all other persons. The actual enumeration shall be made within three years after the first meeting of the Congress of the United States, and within every subsequent term of ten years, in such manner as they shall by law direct. The number of Representatives shall not exceed one for every thirty thousand, but each state shall have at least one Representative...."

Until the first census had been taken, the 13 states were to have the following numbers of Representatives: New Hampshire, three; Massachusetts, eight; Rhode Island and Providence Plantations, one; Connecticut, five; New York, six; New Jersey, four; Pennsylvania, eight; Delaware, one; Maryland, six; Virginia, ten; North Carolina, five; South Carolina, five; and Georgia, three. The apportionment of seats—65 in all—thus mandated by the Constitution remained in effect during the First and Second Congresses (1789-93).

Apparently realizing that apportionment of the House of Representatives was likely to become a major bone of contention, the First Congress submitted to the states a proposed constitutional amendment containing a formula to be used in future reapportionments. The amendment, which was not ratified, provided that following the taking of a decennial census there would be one Representative for every 30,000 persons until the House membership reached 100, "after which the proportion shall be so regulated by Congress that there shall be not less than 100 Representatives, nor less than one Representative for every 40,000 persons, until the number of Representatives shall amount to 200, after which the proportion shall be so regulated by Congress, that there shall not be less than 200 Representatives, nor more than one Representative for every 50,000 persons."[9]

First Apportionment by Congress

The failure to ratify this amendment made it necessary for Congress to enact apportionment legislation after the first census had been taken in 1790. The first apportionment bill was sent to the President on March 23, 1792. Washington, at the urging of Secretary of State Thomas Jefferson, sent the bill back to Congress without his signature—the first Presidential veto.

The bill had incorporated the constitutional minimum of 30,000 as the size of each district. But the population of each state was not a simple multiple of 30,000. Significant fractions were left over when the number of people in each state was divided by 30,000. Thus, for example, Vermont was found to be entitled to 2.851 Representatives, New Jersey to 5.98 and Virginia to 21.018. Therefore, a formula had to be found that would deal in the fairest possible manner with unavoidable variations from exact equality.

Accordingly, Congress proposed in the first apportionment bill to distribute the Members on a fixed ratio of one Representative per 30,000 inhabitants, and give an additional Member to each state with a fraction exceeding one-half. Washington's veto was based on the belief that eight states would receive more than one Representative per 30,000 people under this formula.

A motion to override the veto was unsuccessful. A new bill meeting the President's objections was introduced April 9, 1792, and approved April 14. The Act provided for a ratio of one Member for every 33,000 inhabitants and fixed the exact number of Representatives to which each state was entitled. The total membership of the House was to be 105. In dividing the population of the various states by 33,000, all remainders were to be disregarded. This was known as the Method of Rejected Fractions; it was devised by Thomas Jefferson.

Reapportionment by Jefferson's Method

Jefferson's method of reapportionment resulted in great inequalities among states. A Vermont district would contain 42,766 inhabitants, a New Jersey district 35,911 and a Virginia district only 33,187. Emphasis was placed on what was considered the ideal size of a Congressional district rather than on what the size of the House ought to be. This method was in use until 1840.

The reapportionment act based on the Census of 1800 continued the ratio of 33,000, which provided a House of 141 Members. Debate on the third apportionment bill began in the House on Nov. 22, 1811, and the bill was sent to the President on December 21. The ratio was fixed at 35,000, yielding a House of 181 Members. Following the Census of 1820, Congress approved an apportionment bill providing a ratio of 40,000 inhabitants per district. The sum of the quotas for the various states produced a House of 213 Members.

The Act of May 22, 1832, fixed the ratio at 47,700, resulting in a House of 240 Members. Dissatisfaction with the method in use continued, and Daniel Webster launched a vigorous attack against it. He urged adoption of a method that would assign an additional Representative to each state with a large fraction. His philosophical approach to the reapportionment process was made in a report he submitted to Congress in 1832: "The Constitution, therefore, must be understood not as enjoining an absolute relative equality—because that would be demanding an impossibility—but as requiring of Congress to make the apportionment of Representatives among the several states according to their respective numbers, *as near as may be.* That which cannot be done perfectly must be done in a manner as near perfection as can be... In such a case approximation becomes a rule."[10]

Following the Census of 1840, Congress adopted a reapportionment method similar to that advocated by Webster. The method fixed a ratio of one Representative for every 70,680 persons. This figure was reached by deciding on a fixed size of the House in advance (223), dividing that figure into the total national "Representative population" and using the result (70,680) as the fixed ratio. The population of each state was then divided by this ratio to find the number of its Representatives and was assigned an additional Representative for each fraction over one-half.

Redistricting Problems

Another new feature of the legislation following the Census of 1840 was a redistricting provision that became law on June 25, 1842. Under that provision, Representatives were to be "elected by districts composed of contiguous territory equal in number to the Representatives to which said state may be entitled, no one district electing more than one Representative." This provision climaxed a 50-year struggle to enact some sort of districting legislation. Despite substantial evidence of the intent of Congress, many states had not divided themselves into Congressional districts.

In the first few elections to the House, New Hampshire, Pennsylvania, New Jersey and Georgia elected their Representatives at large, as did Rhode Island and Delaware—the two states with only a single Representative. Districts were used in Massachusetts, New York, Maryland, Virginia and South Carolina. In Connecticut, a preliminary election was held to nominate three times as many persons as the number of Representatives to be chosen at large in the subsequent election. In 1840, 22 of the 31 states elected their Representatives by districts. New Hampshire, New Jersey, Georgia, Alabama, Mississippi and Missouri, with a combined representation of 33 out of a total of 232, elected their Representatives at large; three states, Arkansas, Delaware and Florida, had only one Representative each.

Constant efforts had been made during the early 1800s to lay down national rules, by means of a constitutional amendment, for Congressional districting. The first resolution proposing a mandatory division of each state into districts was introduced in Congress in 1800. In 1802 the Legislatures of Vermont and North Carolina adopted resolutions in support of such action. From 1816 to 1826, 22 state resolutions were adopted proposing the election of Representatives by districts.

In Congress, Sen. Mahlon Dickerson (D N.J.) proposed an amendment regularly almost every year from 1817 to 1826. The resolution embodying the Dickerson amendment was adopted by the Senate three times, in 1819, 1820 and 1822, but each time it failed to reach a vote in the House.

Acceptance by most states of the principle of local representation put an end to Congressional efforts in behalf of a constitutional amendment and led to the enactment of the 1842 law requiring contiguous single-member Congressional districts.

When President Tyler signed the bill, he appended to it a memorandum voicing doubt as to the constitutionality of the districting provisions. The memorandum precipitated a minor constitutional crisis. The House, urged on by Rep. John Quincy Adams (Whig Mass.), appointed a select committee to consider the action of the President. Chaired by the aging ex-President, the committee drew up a resolution protesting the President's action as "unwarranted by the Constitution and laws of the United States, injurious to the public interest, and of evil example for the future; and this House do hereby solemnly protest against the said act of the President and against its ever being repeated or adduced as a precedent hereafter." The House took no action on the resolution; several attempts to call it up under suspension of the rules failed to receive the necessary two-thirds vote.[11]

The action of the Congress in enacting districting legislation along with apportionment legislation did stand as a precedent, however. For the next 80 years, some sort of districting requirements were included in successive reapportionment laws.

Another phenomenon encountered—or perhaps only named—in this era was the gerrymander. Gerrymandering was the practice of drawing district lines so as to maximize the advantage of a political party or interest group. The name originated from a salamander-shaped Congressional district created by the Massachusetts Legislature in 1812 when Elbridge Gerry was Governor.

The Gerrymander

The practice of "gerrymandering"—the excessive manipulation of the shape of a legislative district to benefit a certain incumbent or party—is probably as old as the Republic, but the name originated in 1812.

In that year, the Massachusetts Legislature carved out of Essex County a district which historian John Fiske said had a "dragonlike contour." When the painter Gilbert Stuart saw the misshapen district, he penciled in a head. wings and claws and exclaimed: "That will do for a salamander!"—to which editor Benjamin Russell replied: "Better say a Gerrymander"—after Elbridge Gerry, then Governor of Massachusetts.

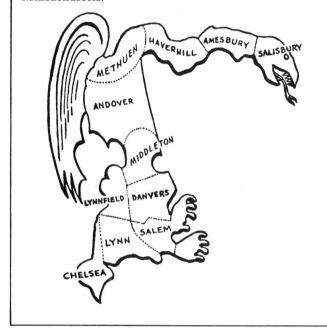

The Middle Years: 1850-1920

The modified reapportionment formula adopted by Congress in 1842 was found more satisfactory than the previous method, but another change was made following the Census of 1850. The new system was proposed by Rep. Samuel F. Vinton (Whig Ohio) and became known as the Vinton method.

Vinton Apportionment Formula

Under this formula, Congress first fixed the size of the House and then distributed the seats. The new method of distribution involved the same procedure as the 1842 system. The total Representative population of the country was divided by the desired number of Representatives and the resulting number became the ratio of population to each Representative. The population of each state was divided by this ratio and each state received the number of Representatives equal to the whole number in the quotient for that state. Then, to reach the required size

of the House, additional Representatives were assigned based on the remaining fractions, beginning with the state having the largest fraction. This procedure differed from the 1842 method only in the last step, which assigned one Representative to every state having a fraction larger than ½. The Vinton method was used from 1850 through 1900.

Advantages and Difficulties

Proponents of the Vinton method pointed out that it had the distinct advantage of making it possible to fix the size of the House in advance and to take into account at least the largest fractions. The concern of the House, grown in size from 65 in 1789 to 240 in 1833, turned from the ideal size of a Congressional district to the ideal size of the House itself. The 1842 legislation resulted in an actual reduction in the size of the House, to 233 Members.

Under the 1842 reapportionment formula, the exact size of the House could not be fixed in advance. If every state with a fraction over ½ were given an additional Representative, the House might wind up with a few more or a few less than the desired number. However, under the Vinton method, only states with the largest fractions were given additional House Members and only up to the desired total size of the House.

Despite the apparent advantages of the Vinton method, certain difficulties began to reveal themselves as the formula was applied. Zechariah Chafee Jr. of the Harvard Law School summarized these difficulties in an article in the *Harvard Law Review* in 1929. The method, he pointed out, suffered from a fatal defect called the "Alabama paradox." Under the paradox, an increase in the total size of the House might be accompanied by an actual loss of a seat by some state, even though there had been no corresponding change in population. This phenomenon first appeared in tables prepared for Congress in 1881, which gave Alabama eight Members in a House of 299 but only seven Members in a House of 300. It could even happen that the state which lost a seat was the one state which had expanded in population, while all the others had fewer people.

Chafee concluded from his study of the Vinton method: "Thus, it is unsatisfactory to fix the ratio of population per Representative before seats are distributed. Either the size of the House comes out haphazard, or, if this be determined in advance the absurdities of the 'Alabama paradox' vitiate the apportionment. Under present conditions, it is essential to determine the size of the House in advance; the problem thereafter is to distribute the required number of seats among the several states as nearly as possible in proportion to their respective populations so that no state is treated unfairly in comparison with any other state."[12]

Reapportionments by Vinton Method

Six reapportionments were carried out under the Vinton method. The 1850 Census Act contained three provisions not included in any previous law. First, it provided not only for reapportionment after the Census of 1850 but also for reapportionment after all subsequent censuses; secondly, it purported to fix the size of the House permanently at 233 Members; and thirdly, it provided in advance for an automatic apportionment by the Secretary of the Interior under the method prescribed in the Act.

Following the Census of 1860, according to the provisions of the Act passed a decade before, an automatic reapportionment was to be carried out by the Interior Department. However, because the size of the House was to remain at the 1850 level, some states faced loss of representation and others would gain less than they expected. To avert these eventualities, an Act was approved March 4, 1862, increasing the size of the House to 241 and giving an extra Representative to eight states— Illinois, Iowa, Kentucky, Minnesota, Ohio, Pennsylvania, Rhode Island and Vermont.

Apportionment legislation following the Census of 1870 contained several new provisions. The Act of Feb. 2, 1872, fixed the size of the House at 283, with the proviso that the number should be increased if new states were admitted. A supplemental Act of May 30, 1872, assigned one additional Representative each to Alabama, Florida, Indiana, Louisiana, New Hampshire, New York, Pennsylvania, Tennessee and Vermont.

Another section of the 1872 Act provided that no state should thereafter be admitted "without having the necessary population to entitle it to at least one Representative fixed by this bill." That provision was found to be unenforceable because no Congress can bind a succeeding Congress.

The Reconstruction era being at its height in the South, the reapportionment legislation of 1872 reflected the desire of Congress to enforce Section 2 of the new 14th Amendment. That section attempted to protect the right of Negroes to vote by providing for reduction of the House representation of a state which interfered with exercise of that right. The number of Representatives of such a state was to be reduced in proportion to the number of inhabitants of voting age whose right to go to the polls was denied or abridged. The reapportionment bill repeated the language of the section, but it was never put into effect because of the difficulty of determining the exact number of persons whose right to vote was being abridged.

The reapportionment Act of Feb. 25, 1882, provided for a House of 325 Members, with additional Members for any new states admitted to the Union. No new apportionment provisions were added. The acts of Feb. 7, 1891, and Jan. 16, 1901, were routine pieces of legislation as far as apportionment was concerned. The 1891 measure provided for a House of 356 Members, and the 1901 statute increased the number to 386.

Maximum Membership of House

On Aug. 8, 1911, the membership of the House was fixed at 433. Provision was made in the reapportionment Act of that date for the addition of one Representative each from Arizona and New Mexico, which were expected to become states in the near future. Thus, the size of the House reached 435, where it has remained up to the present with the exception of the brief period 1959-63, when the admission of Alaska and Hawaii raised the total temporarily to 437.

Limiting the size of the House amounted to recognition that the body would soon expand to unmanageable proportions if the practice of adding new seats every 10 years, to match population gains without depriving any

state of its existing representation, were continued. The limitation to a fixed number made the task of reapportionment all the more difficult when the population not only increased but became much more mobile. Population shifts brought Congress up hard against the politically painful necessity of taking seats away from slow-growing states to give the fast-growing states adequate representation.

A new mathematical calculation was adopted for the reapportionment following the Census of 1910. Devised by Prof. W. F. Willcox of Cornell University, the new system established a priority list which assigned seats progressively beginning with the first seat above the constitutional minimum of at least one seat per state. When there were 48 states, this method was used to assign the 49th Member, the 50th Member, and so on, until the desired size of the House was reached. The method was called Major Fractions and was used after the Censuses of 1910, 1930 and 1940. *(There was no reapportionment in 1920. See below.)*

Districting Legislation, 1850-1910

The districting provisions of the 1842 Act were not repeated in the legislation that followed the Census of 1850. But in 1862 an Act separate from the reapportionment Act revived the provisions of the Act of 1842 requiring districts to be composed of contiguous territory.

The 1872 reapportionment Act again repeated the districting provisions and went even further by adding that districts should contain "as nearly as practicable an equal number of inhabitants." Similar provisions were included in the Acts of 1881 and 1891. In the Act of Jan. 16, 1901, the words "compact territory" were added, and the clause then read "contiguous and compact territory and containing as nearly as practicable an equal number of inhabitants." This requirement appeared also in the legislation of Aug. 8, 1911.

Attempts to Enforce Redistricting. Several attempts, none of them successful, were made to enforce redistricting provisions. Despite the districting requirements of the Act of June 25, 1842, New Hampshire, Georgia, Mississippi and Missouri elected their Representatives at large that autumn. When the House elected at that time convened for its first session on Dec. 4, 1843, objection was made to seating the Representatives of the four states. The matter was referred to the Committee on Elections. The majority report of the Committee, made by its chairman, Rep. Stephen A. Douglas (D Ill.), asserted that the Act of 1842 was not binding upon the states and that the Representatives in question were entitled to their seats. A minority report by Rep. Garrett Davis (Whig Ky.) contended that the Members had not been elected according to the Constitution and the laws and were not entitled to their seats.

The matter was debated in the House from Feb. 6 to 14, 1844. With the Democratic party holding a majority of more than 60, and with 18 of the 21 challenged Members being Democrats, the House decided to seat the Members. An amendment to the majority report in the form of a substitute deleted all reference to the apportionment law. However, by 1848, all four states had come around to electing their Representatives by districts.

Methods of Apportioning House Seats

Fixed Ratio With Rejected Fractions, 1790-1830

The Method of Fixed Ratio With Rejected Fractions was devised by Thomas Jefferson at the time of the first reapportionment following the Census of 1790. Under this method, a predetermined ratio of inhibitants per Representative (say 33,000) was divided into the population of each state. The result was the quota for the state. A Representative was assigned for every whole number in the quota and the fractions were disregarded. Thus a state with a quota of 3.9 got three Representatives.

This method was subject to the population paradox. With a fixed ratio of representation, an increase in the total population might result in a decrease in the size of the House. An example was constructed by Edward V. Huntington in *Methods of Apportionment in Congress:* A fixed ratio of 250,000 persons per district would result in a House of 435 members if the population totaled 102,750,113 but in a House of only 391 members if the population rose to 102,958,798.

Fixed Ratio With Major Fractions, 1840

The Method of Fixed Ratio With Major Fractions was used only once—after the Census of 1840. It was based on an idea formulated by Daniel Webster. As under the Method of Fixed Ratio With Rejected Fractions, a predetermined ratio of persons per district was selected and divided into the population of each state. But in this case, the fractions were not discarded.

For every fraction over one-half, an additional Representative was assigned. Thus, a state with a quota of 3.51 got four Representatives but a state with a quota of 3.49 got only three. This method also was subject to the population paradox.

Vinton Method, 1850-1900

The Vinton method was based on a fixed ratio and a fixed size of the House. The total population of the country was divided by the number of House members to determine the ratio, or number of persons per district. This ratio was then divided into the population of each state, resulting in the quota for each state. Each state received a Representative for each whole number in its quota (with every state getting at least one Representative, fulfilling the Constitutional requirement). The remaining Representatives were then assigned in order to the states having the highest fractions, until the predetermined size of the House was reached.

The Vinton method was subject to the Alabama paradox, in which a state might lose a Representative even though the size of the House was increased.

Major Fractions, 1910-1940

The Method of Major Fractions, in use after the Censuses of 1910, 1930 and 1940, was based on the same principles as the previous method but some new, complex mathematical formulas were added to make the distribution fairer. Furthermore, a priority list system of ranking states' claims to Representatives was introduced. *(See Method of Equal Proportions for explanation of the priority list system, p. 569)*

Sources: Laurence F. Schmeckebier, *Congressional Apportionment;* Edward V. Huntington, *Methods of Apportionment in Congress.*

The next challenge to a Member of the House based on Federal districting laws occurred in 1901. It was charged that the Kentucky redistricting law then in force was contrary to the redistricting provisions of the Federal reapportionment law of Jan. 16, 1901. The specific challenge was to Rep. George G. Gilbert (D) of the eighth Kentucky district. The committee assigned to investigate the matter turned aside the challenge, asserting that the Federal act was not binding on the states. The reasons given were practical and political:

"Your committee are therefore of opinion that a proper construction of the Constitution does not warrant the conclusion that by that instrument Congress is clothed with power to determine the boundaries of Congressional districts, or to revise the acts of a State Legislature in fixing such boundaries; and your committee is further of opinion that even if such power is to be implied from the language of the Constitution, it would be in the last degree unwise and intolerable that it should exercise it. To do so would be to put into the hands of Congress the ability to disfranchise, in effect, a large

body of the electors. It would give Congress the power to apply to all the States, in favor of one party, a general system of gerrymandering. It is true that the same method is to a large degree resorted to by the several states, but the division of political power is so general and diverse that notwithstanding the inherent vice of the system of gerrymandering, some kind of equality of distribution results."[13]

In 1908, the Virginia Legislature transferred Floyd County from the fifth to the sixth Congressional district. As a result, the population of the fifth district was reduced from 175,579 to 160,191 and that of the sixth district was increased from 181,571 to 196,959. The average for the state was 185,418.

When the newly elected Representative from the fifth district, Rep. Edward W. Saunders (D), was challenged by his opponent in the 1908 elections, the majority of the investigating committee upheld the challenge. They concluded that the Virginia law of 1908 was null and void as it did not conform with the Federal law of Jan. 16, 1901, or with the constitution of Virginia, and that the

Malapportionment and Gerrymandering

The prevalence of malapportionment and "gerrymandering" in the creation of U.S. Congressional districts was, to many observers, one of the chief evils in the American system prior to reforms brought about by a Feb. 17, 1964, U.S. Supreme Court decision declaring that "as nearly as is practicable, one man's vote in a Congressional election is to be worth as much as another's."

Malapportionment. Malapportionment involved creating districts of grossly unequal populations—either through actions of state legislatures in establishing new districts or, as was the more frequent practice, simply by failing to redistrict despite major population movements that resulted in population inequalities. At the time of the 1964 Supreme Court decision, for instance, Louisiana had not redistricted since 1912, nor had Colorado or Georgia since 1931, or South Carolina since 1932.

Examples of great disparity in Congressional district sizes in modern U.S. history: New York (1930) 776,425 in largest district and 90,671 in smallest district; Ohio (1946) 698,650 and 163,561; Illinois (1946) 914,053 and 112,116; Arkansas (1946) 423,152 and 177,476; Texas (1962) 951,527 and 216,371; Michigan (1962) 802,994 and 177,431; Maryland (1962) 711,045 and 243,570; South Dakota (1962) 497,669 and 182,845.

The decennial census and ensuing reapportionment of House seats eventually forced reapportionment in most states, although some resorted to the expedient of electing Members at large (like Texas, Hawaii, Ohio, Michigan and Maryland in 1962) rather than face the process of redrawing district lines.

Gerrymandering. Gerrymandering was the name given to excessive manipulation of the shape of legislative districts. The gerrymander was named after Elbridge Gerry, Governor of Massachusetts in 1812 when the Legislature created a peculiar salamander-shaped district to benefit the Democratic party to which Gerry belonged.

Like malapportionment, gerrymandering was practiced by both political parties. In 1961, for example, Republican redistricters in New York created one gerrymander-like creature stretching across the greater part of upstate New York, his head hanging over Albany in the east and his tail reaching for Rochester in the west. Such salamander, tadpole and fishlike creatures sprang to life on the maps of New York City's boroughs. In California, Democrats in control of the Legislature connected two pockets of strong Republican strength in Los Angeles by a thin strip of land to form an unwieldly district running for miles along the coastline. In North Carolina, Democratic redistricters formed an almost perfect gerrymander shape to throw the state's sole Republican Representative in with a strong Democratic opponent.

The basic intent of practically every gerrymander was political—to create a maximum number of districts which would elect the party candidates or types of candidates favored by the controlling group in the state legislature that did the redistricting. The effect was almost always to increase the political power of the already politically dominant group. Up to the 1950s, this was said to be the Republicans in the North and the Democrats in the South. Growing Democratic strength in many northern states tended to cancel out the Republican advantage in that part of the country, however, and signs of the reverse happening in the South could be detected in the 1950s.

---

district should be regarded as including the counties which were a part of it before enactment of the 1908 state legislation. In that case the contestant would have had a majority of the votes, so the committee recommended that he be seated. Thus, for the first time, it looked as though the districting legislation would be enforced, but the House did not take action on the committee's report and the contestant was not seated.

Reapportionment Struggle of 1920s

Conflict Over Urban Growth. The results of the 14th decennial census were announced Dec. 17, 1920, just after the short session of the 66th Congress convened. The Census of 1920 showed that, for the first time in history, a majority of Americans were urban residents. Disclosure of this fact came as a profound shock to the many persons who were used to emphasizing the nation's rural traditions and the virtues of life on farms and in small towns. Rural legislators immediately mounted an attack on the census results which postponed reapportionment legislation for almost a decade.

Thomas Jefferson once wrote: "Those who labor in the earth are the chosen people of God, if ever He had a chosen people, whose breasts He had made His peculiar deposit for substantial and genuine virtue....The mobs of great cities add just as much to the support of pure government as sores do to the strength of the human body....I think our governments will remain virtuous for many centuries as long as they are chiefly agricultural; and this shall be as long as there shall be vacant lands in any part of America. When they get piled up upon one another in large cities as in Europe, they will become corrupt as in Europe."[14]

As their power waned throughout the latter part of the 19th century and the early part of the 20th, farmers and their spokesmen clung to the Jeffersonian belief that they were somehow more pure and virtuous than the growing number of urban residents. When finally faced with the fact that they were in the minority, they put up a strong rearguard action to prevent the inevitable shift of Congressional districts to the cities.

In the first place, rural Representatives insisted that, since the census was taken as of Jan. 1, the farm population had been undercounted. Supporting this contention, they argued that many farm laborers were seasonally employed in the cities at that time of year. Furthermore, mid-winter road conditions probably had prevented enumerators from visiting many farms; and other farmers were said to have been counted incorrectly because they were absent on winter vacation trips. The change of the census date to Jan. 1 in 1920 had been made to conform

(Continued on p. 568)

Congressional Apportionment 1789-1970

YEAR OF CENSUS [x]

	Con-stitu-tion† (1789)	1790	1800	1810	1820	1830	1840	1850	1860	1870	1880	1890	1900	1910	1930#	1940	1950	1960	1970
Ala.				1*	3	5	7	7	6	8	8	9	9	10	9	9	9	8	7
Alaska																	1*	1	1
Ariz.														1*	1	2	2	'	4
Ark.						1*	1	2	3	4	5	6	7	7	7	7	6	4	4
Calif.							2*	2	3	4	6	7	8	11	20	23	30	38	43
Colo.										1*	1	2	3	4	4	4	4	4	5
Conn.	5	7	7	7	6	6	4	4	4	4	4	4	5	5	6	6	6	6	6
Del.	1	1	1	2	1	1	1	1	1	1	1	1	1	1	1	1	1	1	1
Fla.							1*	1	1	2	2	2	3	4	5	6	8	12	15
Ga.	3	2	4	6	7	9	8	8	7	9	10	11	11	12	10	10	10	10	10
Hawaii																	1*	2	2
Idaho											1*	1	1	2	2	2	2	2	2
Ill.				1*	1	3	7	9	14	19	20	22	25	27	27	26	25	24	24
Ind.				1*	3	7	10	11	11	13	13	13	13	13	12	11	11	11	11
Iowa							2*	2	6	9	11	11	11	11	9	8	8	7	6
Kan.									1	3	7	8	8	8	7	6	6	5	5
Ky.		2	6	10	12	13	10	10	9	10	11	11	11	11	9	9	8	7	7
La.				1*	3	3	4	4	5	6	6	6	7	8	8	8	8	8	8
Maine				7*	7	8	7	6	5	5	4	4	4	4	3	3	3	2	2
Md.	6	8	9	9	9	8	6	6	5	6	6	6	6	6	6	6	7	8	8
Mass.	8	14	17	13‡	13	12	10	11	10	11	12	13	14	16	15	14	14	12	12
Mich.							1*	3	4	6	9	11	12	12	13	17	17	18	19	19
Minn.								2*	2	3	5	7	9	10	9	9	9	8	8
Miss.				1*	1	2	4	5	5	6	7	7	8	8	7	7	6	5	5
Mo.				1	2	5	7	9	13	14	15	16	16	13	13	11	10	10
Mont.											1*	1	1	2	2	2	2	2	2
Neb.								1*	1	3	6	6	6	5	4	4	3	3
Nev.									1*	1	1	1	1	1	1	1	1	1	1
N.H.	3	4	5	6	6	5	4	3	3	3	2	2	2	2	2	2	2	2	2
N.J.	4	5	6	6	6	6	5	5	5	7	7	8	10	12	14	14	14	15	15
N.M.														1*	1	2	2	2	2
N.Y.	6	10	17	27	34	40	34	33	31	33	34	34	37	43	45	45	43	41	39
N.C.	5	10	12	13	13	13	9	8	7	8	9	9	10	10	11	12	12	11	11
N.D.											1*	1	2	3	2	2	2	2	1
Ohio			1*	6	14	19	21	21	19	20	21	21	21	22	24	23	23	24	23
Okla.													5*	8	9	8	6	6	6
Ore.								1*	1	1	1	2	2	3	3	4	4	4	4
Pa.	8	13	18	23	26	28	24	25	24	27	28	30	32	36	34	33	30	27	25
R.I.	1	2	2	2	2	2	2	2	2	2	2	2	2	3	2	2	2	2	2
S.C.	5	6	8	9	9	9	7	6	4	5	7	7	7	7	6	6	6	6	6
S.D.											2*	2	2	3	2	2	2	2	2
Tenn.		1	3	6	9	13	11	10	8	10	10	10	10	10	9	10	9	9	8
Texas							2*	2	4	6	11	13	16	18	21	21	22	23	24
Utah												1*	1	2	2	2	2	2	2
Vt.		2	4	6	5	5	4	3	3	3	2	2	2	2	1	1	1	1	1
Va.	10	19	22	23	22	21	15	13	11	9	10	10	10	10	9	9	10	10	10
Wash.											1*	2	3	5	6	6	7	7	7
W.Va.									3	4	4	4	5	6	6	6	6	5	4
Wis.							2*	3	6	8	9	10	11	11	10	10	10	10	9
Wyo.											1*	1	1	1	1	1	1	1	1
Total	65	106	142	186	213	242	232	237	243	293	332	357	391	435	435	435	437**	435	435

x Apportionment effective with Congressional election two years after census.
† Original apportionment made in Constitution pending first census.
# No apportionment was made in 1920.
* These figures are not based on any census, but indicate the provisional representation accorded newly admitted states by the Congress, pending the following census.

‡ Twenty Members were assigned to Massachusetts, but seven of these were credited to Maine when that area became a state.
**Normally 435 but temporarily increased two seats by Congress when Alaska and Hawaii became states.

Source: *Biographical Directory of the American Congress* and Bureau of the Census.

(Continued from p. 566)

with recommendations of the Agriculture Department, which had asserted that the census should be taken early in the year if an accurate statistical picture of farming conditions was desired.

Another point raised by rural legislators was that large numbers of unnaturalized aliens were congregated in northern cities, with the result that these cities gained at the expense of constituencies made up mostly of citizens of the United States. Rep. Homer Hoch (R Kan.) submitted a table showing that, in a House of 435 Representatives, exclusion from the census count of persons not naturalized would have altered the allocation of seats to 16 states. Southern and western farming states would have retained the number of seats allocated to them in 1911 or would have gained, while northern industrial states and California would have lost or at least would have gained fewer seats.

A constitutional amendment to exclude all aliens from the enumeration for purposes of reapportionment was proposed during the 70th Congress (1927-29) by Rep. Hoch, Sen. Arthur Capper (R Kan.) and others. During the Senate Commerce Committee's hearings on reapportionment, Sen. Frederic M. Sackett (R Ky.) and Sen. Lawrence D. Tyson (D Tenn.) said they too intended to propose amendments to the same effect. But nothing further came of the proposals.

Lack of Progress on Bills

The first bill to reapportion the House according to the Census of 1920 was drafted by the House Census Committee early in 1921. Proceeding on the theory that no state should have its representation reduced, the Committee proposed to increase the total number of Representatives from 435 to 483. But the House voted 267 to 76 to keep its membership at 435 and passed the bill so amended on Jan. 19, 1921. Under this bill, 11 states would have lost seats and eight would have gained. The Senate sent the bill to a committee, where it died when the 66th Congress expired March 4, 1921.

Early in the 67th Congress, the House Census Committee again reported a bill, this time fixing the total membership at 460, an increase of 25. Two states—Maine and Massachusetts—would have lost one Representative each and 16 states would have gained. On the floor of the House an attempt to fix the number at the existing 435 failed, and the House voted to send the bill back to committee, where it remained until that Congress came to an end on March 4, 1923.

During the 68th Congress (1923-25), the House Census Committee failed to report any reapportionment bill, and midway in the 69th Congress (1925-27) it again looked as if no reapportionment measure would come out of the Committee. Accordingly, on April 8, 1926, Rep. Henry E. Barbour (R Calif.) moved that the Committee be discharged from further consideration of a bill identical with that passed by the House in 1921 continuing membership at 435.

Chairman Bertrand H. Snell (R N.Y.) of the House Rules Committee, representing the Republican leadership of the House, raised a point of order against Barbour's motion. The Speaker of the House, Nicholas Longworth (R Ohio), pointed out that decisions of earlier Speakers tended to indicate that reapportionment had been considered a matter of "constitutional privilege,"

and that Rep. Barbour's motion must be held in order if these precedents were followed. But the Speaker said he doubted whether the precedents had been interpreted correctly. He therefore submitted to the House the question of whether the pending motion should be considered privileged. The House sustained the Rules Committee by a vote of 87 to 265.

Intervention by President Coolidge

President Coolidge, who previously had made no reference to reapportionment in his communications to Congress, announced in January 1927 that he favored passage of a new apportionment bill during the short session of the 69th Congress, which would end in less than two months. The House Census Committee refused to act. Its chairman, Rep. E. Hart Fenn (R Conn.) therefore moved in the House on March 2, 1927, to suspend the rules and pass a bill he had introduced authorizing the Secretary of Commerce to reapportion the House immediately after the 1930 census. The motion was voted down 183 to 197.

The Fenn bill was rewritten early in the 70th Congress (1927-29) to give Congress itself a chance to act before the proposed reapportionment by the Secretary of Commerce should go into effect. The bill was submitted to the House, which on May 18, 1928, voted 186 to 165 to recommit it to the Census Committee. After minor changes, the Fenn bill was again reported to the House and was passed on Jan. 11, 1929. No record vote was taken on passage of the bill, but a motion to return it to the Committee was rejected 134-227.

Four days later, the reapportionment bill was reported out of the Senate Committee on Commerce. Repeated efforts to bring it up for floor action ahead of other bills were made in vain. Its supporters gave up the fight on Feb. 27, 1929—five days before the end of the session, when it became evident that Senators from states which would lose representation were ready to carry on a filibuster that would have blocked not only reapportionment but all other measures then awaiting final passage.

Intervention by President Hoover

With the time for the next census rapidly approaching, President Hoover listed provision for the 1930 census and reapportionment as "matters of emergency legislation" that should be acted upon in the special session of the 71st Congress that was convened on April 15, 1929. In response to this urgent request, the Senate June 13 passed, 48 to 37, a combined census-reapportionment bill which had been approved by voice vote of the House two days earlier.

The 1929 law established a permanent system of reapportioning the 435 House seats following each census. It provided that immediately after the convening of the 71st Congress for its short session in December 1930, the President should transmit to Congress a statement showing the apportionment population of each state together with an apportionment of Representatives to each state based on the existing size of the House. Failing enactment of new apportionment legislation, that apportionment would go into effect without further action and would remain in effect for ensuing elections to the House of Repre-

(Continued on p. 570)

Method of Equal Proportions

The basic problem in reapportionment is to determine the most equitable distribution of the 435 House seats among the states. There is no way of assigning a fractional Representative to a state or of giving a Representative a fractional vote. Nor is there any way by which two states could share the same Representative. To surmount such difficulties and achieve the fairest possible distribution of seats, Congress in 1941 adopted the Method of Equal Proportions. By this method, the proportional differences in the number of persons per Representative for any pair of states are reduced to a minimum.

Under the Constitution, each state is entitled to at least one seat in the House of Representatives. Thus, the first 50 seats are fixed. The question then becomes how to divide the remaining 385—which states are entitled to a second, third, fourth, etc., seat? To make the computation according to the Method of Equal Proportions, the apportionment population of each state is multiplied by the decimal of the fraction $\frac{1}{\sqrt{n(n-1)}}$ where "n" is the number of seats for the state. The result of this multiplication is a number called a priority value.

For example, for 1970 the priority value for a second seat for California was determined by multiplying the apportionment population (residents plus residents overseas) of the state for that year, 20,098,863, by $\frac{1}{\sqrt{2(2-1)}}$ (or 0.707 10678). The result of this multiplication was 14,212,042. The same computation was then made for New York, which involved multiplying New York's apportionment population, 18,287,529, by the same factor, 0.707 10678. The result was 12,931,236. This operation was repeated for every state. The result for the least populous state, Alaska, was 215,008.

To determine the priority value for each state's claim to a third seat, the population of the state is multiplied by $\frac{1}{\sqrt{3(3-1)}}$, or 0.408 24829. The result for California was a priority value of 8,205,326. This process is repeated for every state for any desired number of seats. Thus, to determine the strength of California's claim to a 40th seat, the multiplier was $\frac{1}{\sqrt{40(40-1)}}$ or 0.025 31848. The resulting priority value for the state in 1970 was 508,873.

When the necessary priority values for all the states have been computed, they are arranged in order, largest first. California, with the largest priority value for a second seat in 1970, received that seat, which was number 51 for the entire House. New York came next in line for a second seat, which was number 52.

The first 10 and bottom 10 priority values and the states involved, calculated by the Census Bureau on the basis of the 1970 census, were as follows:

Size of House	State	Size of State Delegation	Priority Value
51	California	2	14,212,042
52	New York	2	12,931,236
53	Pennsylvania	2	8,403,479
54	California	3	8,205,326
55	Texas	2	7,989,449
56	Illinois	2	7,908,509
57	Ohio	2	7,587,397
58	New York	3	7,465,852
59	Michigan	2	6,319,552
60	California	4	5,802,042
426	Michigan	19	483,268
427	Texas	24	480,908
428	South Carolina	6	477,855
429	Ohio	23	477,016
430	South Dakota	2	476,058
431	Illinois	24	476,036
432	New York	39	475,041
433	Florida	15	473,088
434	California	43	472,947
435	Oklahoma	6	472,043

The test of fairness of the Method of Equal Proportions is whether the percentage difference in population per Representative is the smallest possible for any pair of states. Again using the Census Bureau calculations for 1970, states can be compared with each other to test the method.

With six seats for Oklahoma, the average number of persons per Representative was 430,914. The state of Connecticut also was allocated six seats. The average number of persons per seat in Connecticut was 508,449, 17.99 percent more than the average for Oklahoma. But if a seat were taken from Oklahoma and given to Connecticut, the difference in the number of persons per Representative would have been 18.65 per cent.

South Dakota received two seats, North Dakota only one. The difference was 85.2 percent in population of Congressional districts. However, if the situation had been reversed, North Dakota receiving two and South Dakota one seat, the difference would have been 115.72 per cent. In each of these comparisons, the test is met: the proportional difference between the numbers per Representative is smaller for the apportionment as computed than would be the case with alternative methods. A similar comparison could be carried out in relation to the number of Representatives per million of the population, and the results would be the same.

Source: Conrad Taeuber (Associate Director, Bureau of the Census), "Reapportionment," *U.S. Department of Commerce News,* Dec. 7, 1970, p. 1-6.

sentatives until another census had been taken and another reapportionment made.

Because two whole decades had passed between reapportionments, a greater shift than usual took place following the Census of 1930. California's House delegation was almost doubled, rising from 11 to 20. Michigan gained four seats, Texas three, and New Jersey, New York and Ohio two each. Twenty-one states lost a total of 27 seats: Missouri alone lost three and Georgia, Iowa, Kentucky and Pennsylvania each lost two.

The 1929 Act required the President to report the distribution of seats by two methods, major fractions and equal proportions. This was in the nature of a test to see which method yielded the fairer result. However, pending legislation to the contrary, the method of major fractions was to be used.

The two methods gave an identical distribution of seats based on 1930 census figures. However, in 1940 the two methods gave different results: under major fractions, Michigan would have gained a seat lost by Arkansas; under equal proportions, there would have been no change in either state. The automatic reapportionment provisions of the 1929 Act went into effect in January 1941. But the House Census Committee moved to reverse the result, favoring the certain Democratic seat in Arkansas over a possible Republican gain if the seat were shifted to Michigan. Congress went along, adopting Equal Proportions as the method to be used in reapportionment calculations after the 1950 and subsequent censuses, and making this action retroactive to January 1941 in order to save Arkansas its seat.

While politics doubtless played a part in timing of the action taken in 1941, the Method of Equal Proportions had come to be accepted as the best available. It had been worked out by Prof. Edward V. Huntington of Harvard in 1921. At the request of the Speaker of the House, all known methods of apportionment were considered in 1929 by the National Academy of Sciences Committee on Apportionment. The Committee expressed its preference for Equal Proportions.

This method involves complicated mathematical calculations. In brief, each of the states (now 50) is initially assigned the one seat to which every state is entitled by the Constitution. The population of each state then is multiplied by a series of multipliers. There are 59 of these multipliers, each one decreasing in size. The products of all the multiplications are arranged in order of size, beginning with the largest, to form what is known as the priority list. Seats numbered 51 through 435 are then distributed according to that list. *(For full explanation, see box, p. 569)*

Court Action on Apportionment

After the long and desultory battle over reapportionment in the 1920s, those who were unhappy over the inaction of Congress or the state legislatures began taking their cases to court. At first, they had no luck. But as the disparity in both Federal and state legislative districts grew, and the Supreme Court began to show a tendency to intervene, plaintiffs were more successful. Finally, in a series of decisions beginning with *Baker v. Carr* in 1962, the Court intervened massively in the redistricting process, ordering that Congressional districts as well as state and local legislative districts be drawn so that their populations would be as nearly equal as possible.

Supreme Court's 1932 Decisions

In 1932 the Supreme Court handed down several important decisions on Congressional redistricting. In each case, petitioners asserted that state legislatures had not complied with the 1911 Act's requirement that districts be separate, compact, contiguous and equally populated. The question was whether that requirement, neither specifically repealed nor reaffirmed in the 1929 Act, was still in effect.

In *Smiley v. Holm* the petitioner also attacked a Minnesota redistricting statute which the Legislature had not repassed over the Governor's veto because it contended that districting legislation was not subject to veto. The Supreme Court, ignoring the question of compliance with the 1911 Act and ruling solely on the issue of the gubernatorial veto, declared that the U.S. Constitution did not exempt districting statutes from a Governor's veto. Two other 1932 Congressional districting cases—*Koenig v. Flynn,* from the New York Court of Appeals, and *Carroll v. Becker,* from the Missouri Supreme Court, were decided by the Supreme Court on similar questions regarding gubernatorial vetoes.

The question of the 1911 Act's applicability was reached in *Wood v. Broom,* a 1932 case challenging the constitutionality of a new Mississippi redistricting law. Speaking for the Court, Chief Justice Charles Evans Hughes ruled that the 1911 Act had, in effect, expired with the approval of the 1929 apportionment Act and that the standards of the 1911 Act were therefore no longer applicable. The Court reversed the decision of a lower Federal court which had permanently enjoined elections under the new Mississippi redistricting act because it violated the standards of the 1911 Act. Later the same year the Court made a similar ruling in *Mahan v. Hume,* a Kentucky Congressional districting case.

Four Members of the Supreme Court—Justices Louis D. Brandeis, Harlan F. Stone, Owen J. Roberts and Benjamin N. Cardozo—while concurring in the majority opinion, said they would have dismissed the Wood suit for "want of equity." The "want-of-equity" phrase in this context suggested a policy of judicial self-limitation with respect to the entire question of judicial involvement in essentially "political" questions.

Court's Decision in 1946 Case

Not until 1946, in *Colegrove v. Green,* did the Court again rule in a significant case dealing with Congressional redistricting. The case was brought by Kenneth Colegrove, a political science professor at Northwestern University, who alleged that Illinois' Congressional districts—varying between 112,116 and 914,053 in population—were so unequal that they violated the 14th Amendment's guarantee of equal protection of the laws. A seven-man Supreme Court divided 4-3 in dismissing the suit.

Justice Felix Frankfurter gave the plurality opinion of the Court, speaking for himself and Justices Stanley F. Reed and Harold H. Burton. Frankfurter's opinion cited *Wood v. Broom* to indicate that Congress had deliberately removed the standard set by the 1911 Act. "We also agree," he said, "with the four Justices (Brandeis, Stone, Roberts and Cardozo) who were of the opinion that the bill in *Wood v. Broom* should be 'dismissed for want of equity.' " The issue, Frankfurter said, was "of a peculiarly political nature and therefore not meet for judicial interpretation....The short of it is that the Constitution has conferred upon Congress exclusive authority to secure fair representation by the states in the popular House and has left to that House determination whether states have fulfilled their responsibility. If Congress failed in exercising its powers, whereby standards of fairness are offended, the remedy lies ultimately with the people...To sustain this action would cut very deep into the very being of Congress. Courts ought not to enter this political thicket. The remedy for unfairness in districting is to secure state legislatures that will apportion properly, or to invoke the ample powers of Congress." Frankfurter said, in addition, that the Court could not affirmatively remap Congressional districts and that elections at large would be politically undesirable.

Justice Hugo L. Black, joined in a dissenting opinion by Justices William O. Douglas and Frank Murphy, expressed the belief that the District Court had jursidiction under a section of the U.S. Code giving district courts the right to redress deprivations of constitutional rights occurring through action of the states. Black's opinion also rested on a previous case in which the Court had indicated that Federal constitutional questions, unless "frivolous," fall under the jursidiction of the Federal courts. Black asserted that the appellants had standing to sue, that the population disparities did violate the **equal protection clause of the 14th Amendment** and that relief should be granted. Black specifically rejected the view that *Smiley v. Holm* had set a precedent of nonjusticiability. *Smiley v. Holm,* he said, merely decided that the 1911 Act was no longer applicable. Only a minority of the Court, he pointed out, had thought the case should be dismissed for "want of equity."

With the Court split 3-3 on whether the Judiciary had or should exercise jurisdiction, the deciding opinion in *Colegrove v. Green* was that of Justice Wiley B. Rutledge. On the question of justiciability, Rutledge agreed with Black, Douglas and Murphy that the issue could be considered by the Federal courts. "But for the ruling in *Smiley v. Holm,"* Rutledge said, he would have thought that the Constitution specifically reserved the regulation of Congressional elections to the states and Congress. Rutledge believed, however, that Smiley "rules squarely to the contrary." Thus a majority of the Court participating in the Colegrove case felt that Congressional redistricting cases were justiciable.

On the other hand, on the question of granting relief in this specific instance, Rutledge agreed with Frankfurter, Reed and Burton that the case should be dismissed. He pointed out that four of the nine justices in *Wood v. Broom* had felt that dismissal should be for want of equity. Rutledge saw a "want-of-equity" situation in *Colegrove v. Green* as well. "I think the gravity of the constitutional questions raised so great, together with the possibility of collision (with the political departments of the Government), that the admonition (against avoidable constitutional decision) is appropriate to be followed here," Rutledge said. Jurisdiction, he thought, should be exercised "only in the most compelling circumstances." He thought that "the shortness of time remaining (before the forthcoming election) makes it doubtful whether action could or would be taken in time to

secure for petitioners the effective relief they seek." Rutledge warned that Congressional elections at large would deprive citizens of representation by districts, "which the prevailing policy of Congress demands." In the case of at-large elections, he warned, "the cure sought may be worse than the disease." For all these reasons he concluded that the case was "one in which the Court may properly, and should, decline to exercise its jurisdiction."

Factors Leading to New Court Position

In the ensuing years, law professors, political scientists and other commentators expressed growing dislike for the Colegrove doctrine and growing impatience with the Supreme Court's position. Yet the membership of the Court was changing, and the new members were more inclined toward judicial action on redistricting. By 1962, only three members of the Colegrove Court remained: Justices Black and Douglas, dissenters in that case, and Justice Frankfurter, aging spokesman for restraint in the exercise of judicial power.

Already in the 1950s, the Court had decided two cases which laid some groundwork for its subsequent reapportionment decisions. The first was *Brown v. Board of Education* (1954), the historic school desegregation case, in which the Court decided that an individual citizen could assert a right to equal protection of the laws under the 14th Amendment, contrary to the "separate but equal" doctrine of public facilities for white and Negro citizens. Six years later, in *Gomillion v. Lightfoot* (1960), the Court held that the Alabama Legislature could not draw the city limits of Tuskegee so as to exclude the Negro community. Justice Frankfurter based his opinion on the 15th Amendment, but Justice Charles E. Whittaker said that the equal protection clause was the proper constitutional basis for the decision. One commentator later remarked that *Gomillion* amounted to a "dragon" in the "political thicket" of Colegrove.

With this groundwork already laid, during the years 1962-64 the Supreme Court rendered a series of four landmark decisions in the politically sensitive area of Congressional and state legislative apportionment and districting. The precedent-breaking decisions all had a common theme—that "as nearly as practicable, one man's vote... is to be worth as much as another's." By entering the "political thicket" of apportionment and redistricting, the Court extended its authority far beyond its previous scope and seemed certain to cause a revolution in the complexion of state government and the bases of Congressional power.

A major element causing the reversal of the Court's previous decision on reapportionment and redistricting was the population migration from country to city, which had been under way ever since the turn of the century. By 1960, there was not a single legislative body in a single state in which there was not at least a 2-1 population disparity between the most and the least heavily populated districts. For example, the disparity was 242 to 1 in the Connecticut House, 223 to 1 in the Nevada Senate, 141 to 1 in the Rhode Island Senate and 9 to 1 in the Georgia Senate. Studies of the effective vote of large and small counties in state legislatures between 1910 and 1960 showed that the effective vote of the large counties had slipped while their percentage of the national population had more than doubled. The most lightly populated counties, on the other hand, advanced from a position of slight over-representation to one of extreme over-representation, holding almost twice as many seats as they would be entitled to by population alone. Predictably, the rural-dominated state legislatures resisted every move toward reapportioning districts to reflect new population patterns.

By no means as gross, but still substantial, was population imbalance among Congressional districts. In Texas, the Census of 1960 showed the most heavily populated district had four times as many inhabitants as the most lightly populated. Arizona, Maryland and Ohio each had at least one district with three times as many inhabitants as the most lightly populated. In a majority of cases, it was rural areas which benefited from Congressional malapportionment. As a result of the postwar population movement out of central cities to the surrounding areas, the suburbs were the most under-represented.

Historic 1962 Decision

It was against this background that a group of Tennessee city dwellers successfully broke the long-standing precedent against Federal court involvement in legislative apportionment problems. For more than half a century, since 1901, the Tennessee Legislature had refused to reapportion itself, even though a decennial reapportionment based on population was specifically required by the state's constitution. In the meantime, Tennessee's population had grown and shifted dramatically to urban areas. By 1960, the House legislative districts ranged from 3,454 to 36,031 in population, while the Senate districts ranged from 39,727 to 108,094. Appeals by urban residents to the rural-controlled Tennessee Legislatures proved fruitless. A suit brought in the state courts to force reapportionment was rejected on the ground that the courts should stay out of legislative matters.

The urban interests then appealed to the Federal courts, stating that they had no redress: the Legislature had refused to act for more than half a century; the state courts had refused to intervene; Tennessee had no referendum or initiative laws. The city dwellers charged that there was "a debasement of their votes by virtue of the incorrect, obsolete and unconstitutional apportionment" to such an extent that they were being deprived of their right to "equal protection of the laws" under the 14th Amendment. (The 14th Amendment reads, in part: "No state shall...deny to any person within its jurisdiction the equal protection of the laws.")

The Supreme Court on March 26, 1962, handed down its historic decision in *Baker v. Carr*, ruling in favor of the Tennessee city dwellers by a 6-2 margin. In the majority opinion, Justice William J. Brennan Jr. emphasized that the Federal judiciary had the power to review the apportionment of state legislatures under the 14th Amendment's equal protection clause. "The mere fact that a suit seeks protection as a political right," Brennan wrote, "does not mean that it presents a political question" which the courts should avoid.

In a vigorous dissent, Justice Frankfurter said the majority decision constituted "a massive repudiation of the experience of our whole past" and was an assertion of "destructively novel judicial power." He contended that the lack of any clear basis for relief "catapults

the lower courts" into a "mathematical quagmire." Frankfurter insisted that "there is not under our Constitution a judicial remedy for every political mischief." Appeal for relief, he maintained, should not be made in the courts, but rather "to an informed civically militant electorate."

One Man, One Vote for Representatives

Shortly after the Baker decision was handed down, James P. Wesberry Jr., an Atlanta resident and a member of the Georgia Senate, filed suit in a Federal court in Atlanta claiming that gross disparity in the population of Georgia's Congressional districts violated 14th Amendment rights of equal protection of the laws. At the time, Georgia districts ranged in population from 272,154 in the rural 9th district in the northeastern part of the state to 823,860 in the 5th district in Atlanta and its suburbs. District lines had not been changed since 1931. The state's number of House seats remained the same in the interim, but Atlanta's district population— already high in 1931 compared with the others—had more than doubled in 30 years, making a 5th District vote worth about one-third that of a vote in the 9th.

On June 20, 1962, the three-judge Federal court divided 2-1 in dismissing Wesberry's suit. The majority reasoned that the precedent of *Colegrove* still controlled in Congressional district cases. The judges cautioned against Federal judicial interference with Congress and against "depriving others of the right to vote" it the suit should result in at-large elections. They suggested that the Georgia Legislature (under court order to reapportion itself) or the U.S. Congress might better provide relief. Wesberry then appealed to the Supreme Court, which heard arguments on the case in November 1963.

On Feb. 17, 1964, the Supreme Court ruled in the case of *Wesberry v. Sanders* that Congressional districts must be substantially equal in population. The Court, which upheld Wesberry's challenge by a 6-3 decision, based its ruling on the history and wording of Article I, Section 2, of the Constitution providing that Representatives shall be apportioned among the states according to their respective numbers and be chosen by the people of the several states. This language, the Court stated, meant that "as nearly as is practicable, one man's vote in a Congressional election is to be worth as much as another's."

The majority opinion, written by Justice Black and supported by Chief Justice Earl Warren and Justices Brennan, Douglas, Arthur J. Goldberg and Byron R. White, said that "While it may not be possible to draw Congressional districts with mathematical precision, that is no excuse for ignoring our Constitution's plain objective of making equal representation for equal numbers of people the fundamental goal for the House of Representatives."

Predictably, the decision referred to the findings of the Baker case to show that districting questions were justiciable and to the *Gray v. Sanders* case to establish the principle of "one man, one vote." (*Gray v. Sanders*, 1963, overturned Georgia's county unit system of voting in statewide and Congressional primary elections.) Unlike those two decisions, however, the Wesberry decision did not attempt to use the 14th Amendment as its justification.

In a strongly worded dissent, Justice John M. Harlan asserted that the Constitution did not establish population as the only criterion of Congressional districting and that the subject was left in the Constitution to the discretion of the states, subject only to the supervisory power of Congress.

Justice Potter Stewart said he found that the Constitution gave "no mandate to this Court or to any court to ordain that Congressional districts within each state must be equal in population," but he disagreed with Harlan in that he thought the matter was justiciable.

Justice Tom C. Clark also found the matter justiciable but rejected the idea that Article I, Section 2, required a "one man, one vote" standard in Congressional elections. Clark said the case should be returned to the lower court for a hearing on the merits based on the 14th Amendment's equal protection requirements set down in the Baker case.

The Wesberry opinion established no precise standards for districting beyond declaring that districts must be as nearly equal in population "as is practicable." In his dissent, Harlan suggested that a disparity of more than 100,000 between a state's largest and smallest districts would "presumably" violate the equality standard enunciated by the majority. On that basis, Harlan estimated, the districts of 37 states with 398 Representatives would be unconstitutional, "leaving a constitutional House of 37 Members now sitting."

Neither did the Court's decision make any reference to gerrymandering, since it discussed only the population, not the shape of districts. In a separate districting opinion handed down the same day as *Wesberry*, the Court dismissed a challenge to Congressional districts in New York City, which had been brought by voters who charged that Manhattan's 17th "silk-stocking" District had been gerrymandered to exclude Negroes and Puerto Rican citizens.

Decision on Variance in Size of Districts

The next step in the Court's districting rulings came on April 7, 1969. On that date, the Court in a 6-3 decision tightened the "one man, one vote" principle by declaring Missouri's redistricting statute unconstitutional (*Kirkpatrick v. Preisler*). Justice Brennan, speaking for the Court, said that states must strive to create Congressional districts of precisely equal population. Any variance in population, "no matter how small," must be justified by the state or shown to result in spite of a "good-faith effort," he said.

In *Wesberry v. Sanders*, Brennan pointed out, the Court had held that the Constitution required "as nearly as is practicable one man's vote in a Congressional election...be worth as much as another's." Defining the phrase "as nearly as is practicable," Brennan said there was no fixed population variance small enough to be considered negligible. The Wesberry standard directed states to create districts absolutely equal in population. In the Court's words: "Equal representation for equal numbers of people is a principle designed to prevent debasement of voting power and diminution of access to elected Representatives. Toleration of even small deviations detracts from these purposes."

Maximum Population Variations From State Averages
(At time of Wesberry v. Sanders, February 1964)

The following list shows for each state the maximum variation from the state's average population per congressional district. For example, in Alabama, one of the state's eight districts had in 1964 a population 21.4 per cent higher than the state's average population per district. No other district in Alabama varied from the average population by as high a percentage.

State*	Maximum Variation	Total Districts
Alabama	+ 21.4%	8
Arizona	− 54.3	3
Arkansas	+ 28.8	4
California	+ 42.4	38
Colorado	− 55.4	4
Connecticut	− 37.1	6
Florida	+ 60.3	12
Georgia	+108.9	10
Idaho	22.9 #	2
Illinois	− 33.6	24
Indiana	+ 64.6	11
Iowa	+ 12.3	7
Kansas	+ 23.9	5
Kentucky	+ 40.8	7
Louisiana	− 35.2	8
Maine	4.3 #	2
Maryland	+ 83.5	8
Massachusetts	− 12.3	12
Michigan	+ 84.8	19
Minnesota	− 13.2	8
Mississippi	+ 39.7	5
Missouri	+ 17.3	10
Montana	18.7 #	2
Nebraska	− 14.0	3
New Hampshire	9.3 #	2
New Jersey	+ 44.8	15
New York	+ 15.1	41
North Carolina	− 32.9	11
North Dakota	5.4 #	2
Ohio	+ 72.1	24
Oklahoma	+ 42.5	6
Oregon	− 40.0	4
Pennsylvania	+ 31.9	27
Rhode Island	7.0 #	2
South Carolina	+ 33.9	6
South Dakota	46.3 #	2
Tennessee	+ 58.2	9
Texas	+118.5	23
Utah	28.6 #	2
Virginia	+ 36.0	10
Washington	+ 25.2	7
West Virginia	− 18.6	5
Wisconsin	+ 3.4	10

*Alaska, Delaware, Hawaii, Nevada, New Mexico, Vermont and Wyoming seats were filled at large and therefore are not listed.

#State had only two districts; thus one district is the stated percentage above the average and the other district is the stated percentage below the average.

The only permissible variances in population, the Court ruled, were those unavoidable despite the effort to achieve absolute equality or those which could be legally justified. The variances in Missouri, which amounted to 3.1 per cent among Congressional districts on a statewide basis, could have been avoided, the Court said.

None of Missouri's arguments for the plan qualified as "legally acceptable" justifications. The Court rejected the argument that population variance was necessary to allow representation of distinct interest groups. It held acceptance of such variances in order to produce districts with specific interests as "antithetical" to the basic purpose of equal representation.

The Court also rejected the argument that political reality—legislative compromise or the integrity of existing political boundaries—justified population variance. It dismissed arguments that nonvoting military personnel and students inflated census figures for certain districts, that post-1960 population trends were reflected in the new districts and that geographical compactness dictated the new boundaries and some population inequality.

Dissenting Opinions. Justice White dissented from the Court's opinion, which he characterized as "an unduly rigid and unwarranted application of the Equal Protection Clause which will unnecessarily involve the courts in the abrasive task of drawing district lines." The Justice added that some "acceptably small" population variance could be established. He indicated that considerations of existing political boundaries and geographical compactness could justify to him some variation from "absolute equality" of population.

Justice Harlan, joined by Justice Stewart, objected that "whatever room remained under this Court's prior decisions for the free play of the political process in matters of reapportionment is now all but eliminated by today's Draconian judgments."

As a result of the Court decisions of the 1960s, nearly every state was forced to redraw its Congressional district lines—sometimes more than once. By the end of the decade, 39 of the 45 states with more than one Representative had made the necessary adjustments.

However, the effect of the "one person, one vote" standard on Congressional districts did not bring about immediate equality in districts in the years 1964-70. Most of the new districts were far from equal in population, since the only official population figures came from the 1960 Census. Massive population shifts during the decade rendered most post-*Wesberry* efforts to achieve equality useless.

But following redistricting in 1971-72, based on the 1970 Census, the result achieved was that House Members elected in November 1972 to the 93rd Congress represented districts which differed only slightly in population from the state average. In 385 of the 435 districts, the district's variance was less than 1 per cent from the state average district population.

By contrast, only nine of the districts in the 88th Congress (elected in 1962) deviated less than 1 per cent from the state average; 81 were between 1 and 5 per cent; 87 from 5 to 10 per cent; and in 236 districts, the deviation was 10 per cent or greater. Twenty-two House members were elected at large.

The Supreme Court made only one major ruling concerning Congressional districts following the 1971-72

redistricting. On June 18, 1973, the Court declared the Texas Congressional districts, as redrawn in 1971, unconstitutional because of excessive population variance among districts. The variance between the largest and smallest districts was 4.9872 per cent. The Court returned the case to a three-judge Federal panel, which adopted a new Congressional district plan, effective Oct. 17, 1973.

The case *(White v. Weiser)* began on Oct. 19, 1971, when Dan Weiser, a mathematician, and others, challenged the legislature's congressional redistricting plan as unconstitutional because of unnecessarily large population variances. The challengers submitted two alternate plans—Plan B, which generally followed the redistricting plan set up by the state legislature, and Plan C, which radically altered district lines.

A federal three-judge panel chose Plan C on Jan. 22, 1972, but the U.S. Supreme Court stayed the decision, pending its own consideration of the case. The 1972 elections were held under the legislature's Congressional district plan.

The Supreme Court's June 1973 decision agreed that a new plan reducing population variances was needed. But the three-judge panel erred, concluded the Court, in choosing Plan C to replace the legislature's plan. Plan B, to a greater extent than Plan C, adhered to the desires of the state legislature while attempting to achieve population equality among districts. Since redistricting is primarily a state and legislative function, the courts should interfere only to the extent necessary to achieve a satisfactory population variance, and not intrude on the overall nature of the plan, concluded the Court.

Congress and Redistricting

Several attempts were made during the period of court action to enact new legislation on redistricting. Only one of the efforts was successful—the passage of a measure to rule out at-large elections in states with more than one Representative.

On Jan. 9, 1951, President Truman, upon presentation of the official state population figures of the Census of 1950, asked for changes in the existing law which would tighten Federal control of state redistricting. Specifically, he asked for a ban on gerrymandering, an end to "at-large" seats in states having more than one Representative and a sharp reduction in the huge differences in size between Congressional districts in each state.

On behalf of the Administration, Chairman Emanuel Celler (D N.Y.) of the House Judiciary Committee introduced a bill to require compact and contiguous Congressional districts which would not vary by more than 15 per cent between districts within a state. The bill also would have eliminated at-large seats and made redistricting mandatory every 10 years in accordance with population changes. But the House Judiciary Committee took no action on the proposals.

Rep. Celler regularly introduced his bill throughout the 1950s and early 1960s, but it made no headway until the Supreme Court handed down the Wesberry decision in 1964. On June 24, 1964, a Celler bill was approved by a House Judiciary Subcommittee. But the full Committee did not act on the bill before adjournment.

On March 16, 1965, the House passed a new Celler bill. It established 15 per cent as the maximum percentage by which a Congressional district's population might deviate from the average size of the state's districts; prohibited at-large elections for any state with more than one House seat; required that districts be composed of "contiguous territory in as compact form as practicable," and forbade more than one redistricting of a state between decennial censuses. A major reason for House approval of Celler's bill appeared to be a desire to gain protection from Court imposition of even more rigid criteria. But the measure encountered difficulties in the Senate Judiciary Committee. After considerable wrangling over its provisions, the committee voted to report the bill without precise agreement on its wording. No actual report was ever filed by the Senate Judiciary Committee.

In 1967, a redistricting bill was passed by both the Senate and the House, but not in the same form. And the bill had a different purpose from that of previous bills dealing with the subject. Instead of trying to establish standards of fairness in drawing district lines, the chief purpose in 1967 was to prevent the courts, until after the House had been reapportioned on the basis of the Census of 1970, from ordering redistricting of House seats or from ordering any state to hold elections at large—a procedure that many incumbent Representatives feared.

A combination of liberal Democrats and Republicans in the Senate managed to defeat the conference report Nov. 8, 1967, by a vote of 22-55. Liberals favored court action which they believed would eliminate many conservative rural districts, while Republicans felt that redistricted areas, especially in the growing suburbs, would elect more Republicans than Democrats.

To avoid at-large elections, the Senate added a rider to a House-passed private bill. Under the rider, at-large elections of U.S. Representatives were banned in all states entitled to more than one Representative, with the exceptions of New Mexico and Hawaii. Those states had a tradition of electing their two Representatives at large. Both of them, however, soon passed districting laws—New Mexico for the 1968 elections and Hawaii for 1970.

Following the Census of 1960, an attempt had been made to increase the size of the House to avoid some of the losses of seats that would otherwise be suffered by several states. By a vote of 12-14, the House Judiciary Committee on Sept. 9, 1961, rejected a motion to recommend enlarging the House to 453 seats. And by a vote of 14-15, the same Committee rejected a bill reported by a subcommittee which would have increased the permanent size of the House to 438. In Committee voting, a majority of Democrats favored the House-increase bills while Republicans were almost unanimous in opposition. Republican National Chairman William E. Miller and other Republican leaders reportedly reached the conclusion that any increase in the size of the House was more likely to benefit Democrats than Republicans.

Footnotes

1. Andrew Hacker, *Congressional Districting, The Issue of Equal Representation*, rev. ed. (Brookings Institution, 1964), p. 126.
2. Robert Luce, *Legislative Principles* (Houghton Mifflin Co., 1930, reprinted by Da Capo Press, 1971), p. 342.
3. Thomas Jefferson, *The Portable Thomas Jefferson*, ed. Merrill D. Peterson, pt. 3: *Notes on the State of Virginia* (The Viking Press, 1975), p. 163.
4. Hacker, *Congressional Districting*, pp. 6-7.
5. Max Farrand, ed., *The Records of the Federal Convention of 1787*, rev. ed., vol. 2 (Yale University Press, 1911, 1966), p. 241.
6. *The Federalist Papers*, with an introduction by Clinton Rossiter (Mentor, 1961), pp. 347-48, 354.
7. Laurence F. Schmeckebier, *Congressional Apportionment* (Brookings Institution, 1941), p. 131.

8. Hacker, *Congressional Districting*, p. 14.
9. U.S. Congress, Library of Congress, Congressional Research Service, *The Constitution of the United States of America*, S. Doc. 92-82, 92nd Cong., 2nd sess. (U.S. Government Printing Office, 1973), p. 51.
10. U.S. Congress, *Report of Select Committee*, S. Doc. 119, 22nd Cong., 1st sess., 1832, p. 4, quoted in Schmeckebier, *Congressional Apportionment*, p. 113.
11. Quoted in Schmeckebier, *Congressional Apportionment*, p. 134.
12. Zechariah Chafee, "Congressional Reapportionment," *Harvard Law Review*, 1929, pp. 1015-47.
13. Quoted in Schmeckebier, *Congressional Apportionment*, p. 137.
14. Thomas Jefferson, *Notes on the State of Virginia*, p. 217.

Selected Bibliography

Books

Apportionment in the Nineteen Sixties: State Legislatures and Congressional Districts. New York: National Municipal League, 1967.

Baker, Gordon E. *The Reapportionment Revolution: Representation, Political Power and the Supreme Court.* New York: Random House, 1966.

Boyd, William J. D. *Changing Patterns of Apportionment.* New York: National Municipal League, 1965.

Cortner, Richard C. *The Apportionment Cases.* Knoxville, Tenn. University of Tennessee Press, 1970.

Dean, J. W. *History of the Gerrymander.* Boston: 1892.

De Grazia, Alfred. *Essay on Apportionment and Representative Government.* Washington: American Enterprise Institute for Public Policy Research, 1963.

Dixon, Robert G. Jr. *Democratic Representation: Reapportionment in Law and Politics.* New York: Oxford University Press, 1968.

Erikson, Ann M. *Congressional Redistricting.* Columbus: Legislative Service Commission, 1965.

Farrand, Max. *Records of the Federal Convention*, 4 vols. New Haven: Yale University Press, 1966.

The Federalist Papers. Introduction by Clinton Rossiter. New York: Mentor, 1961.

Hacker, Andrew. *Congressional Districting: The Issue of Equal Representation.* Washington: Brookings Institution, 1963.

Hamilton, Howard D. *Legislative Apportionment: Key to Power.* New York: Harper, 1964.

Hanson, Royce. *The Political Thicket: Reapportionment and Constitutional Democracy.* Englewood Cliffs: Prentice-Hall, 1966.

Hutchins, Robert M. *Reapportioning the States.* Santa Barbara: Center for the Study of Democratic Institutions, 196-.

Jewell, Malcolm E., ed. *The Politics of Reapportionment.* New York: Atherton Press, 1962.

Luce, Robert. *Legislative Principles.* Boston: Houghton Mifflin, 1930; reprint ed., New York: Da Capo Press, 1971.

McKay, Robert B. *Reapportionment: The Law and Politics of Equal Representation.* New York: Twentieth Century Fund, 1965.

Myres, Sandra L. *One Man, One Vote: Gerrymandering vs. Reapportionment.* Austin, Texas: Steck-Vaugh, 1970.

"One Man, One Vote." Report of Conference Sponsored by the Twentieth Century Fund. New York: 1962.

Reapportionment in the Seventies. Lexington: The Council of State Governments, 1973.

Schmeckebier, Laurence F. *Congressional Apportionment.* Washington: Brookings Institution, 1941.

Schubert, Glendon, ed. *Reapportionment.* New York: Scribner, 1965.

Articles

Baker, Gordon E. "Redistricting in the Seventies: The Political Thicket Deepens." *National Civic Review,* June, 1972, pp. 277-85.

"Congress in the Thicket: The Congressional Redistricting Bill of 1967." *George Washington Law Review,* Volume 36, 1967, pp. 224-34.

"Congressional Reapportionment: Equal Representation Requirement Requires a Good Faith Effort to Achieve Absolute Equality." *Villanova Law Review,* Fall, 1969, p. 223.

"Congressional Redistricting: One Man, One Vote Demands Near Mathematical Precision." *De Paul Law Review,* Autumn, 1969, pp. 152-71.

Dixon, Robert G. "Apportionment Standards and Judicial Power." *Notre Dame Lawyer,* June, 1963, pp. 367-400.

Dixon, Robert G. "Reapportionment in the Supreme Court and Congress: The Constitutional Struggle for Fair Representation." *Michigan Law Review,* December, 1964, pp. 209-242.

"Equal Representation and the Weighted Voter Alternative." *Yale Law Review,* Spring, 1970, pp. 311-21.

Gazell, James A. One Man, One Vote: Its Long Germination." *Western Political Quarterly,* September, 1970, pp. 445-62.

Irwin, William P. "Representation and Apportionment." *Parliamentary Affairs,* Summer, 1968, pp. 226-45.

Irwin, W. P. "Representation and Election: The Reapportionment Cases in Retrospect." *Michigan Law Review,* Volume 67, 1969, pp. 729-754.

Jones, Charles O. "Inter-Party Competition for Congressional Seats." *Western Political Quarterly,* September, 1964, pp. 461-76.

Katz, Ellis. "Apportionment and Majority Rule." *Publius,* 1971, pp. 141-161.

Lehne, Richard. "Shape of the Future: Suburbs Seen as Biggest Bloc in Congress for the First Time After 1970 Reapportionment." *National Civic Review,* September, 1969, pp. 351-5.

Leiserson, Avery. "National Party Organization and Congressional Districts." *Western Political Quarterly,* September, 1963, pp. 33-49.

Linton, Robert N. "Further Exploration in the Political Thicket: The Gerrymander and the Constitution." *Loyola Law Review,* October, 1973, pp. 1-47.

"Reapportionment." *Harvard Law Review,* Volume 79, 1966, pp. 1226-87.

Sullivan, John L. "Electoral Choice and Popular Control of Policy: The Case of the 1966 House Elections." *American Political Science Review,* December, 1972, pp. 1256-68.

Government Publications

Huntington, Edward V. *Methods of Apportionment in Congress.* Washington: Government Printing Office, 1940.

Taeuber, Conrad. "Reapportionment." *U.S. Department of Commerce News,* Dec. 7, 1970.

PRESSURES ON CONGRESS

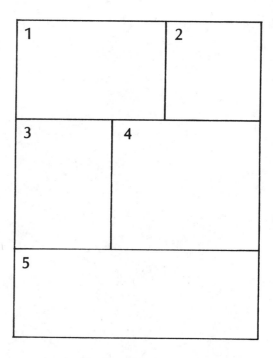

1. Press covering hearings on the Central Intelligence Agency held by the Senate Select Committee on Intelligence Activities, Sept. 16, 1975.

2. President Lyndon B. Johnson with Senate Minority Leader Everett M. Dirksen (R Ill.) and Senate Majority Leader Mike Mansfield (D Mont.) June 1965. (White House photo.)

3. Supreme Court Building. (Photo by Dan De Vay.)

4. Common Cause member lobbying passers-by on the steps of the Russell Senate Office Building. (Common Cause photo.)

5. Lobby of the House during the passage of the civil rights bill, 1866. Wood engraving in *Harper's Weekly.* (Library of Congress photo no. LC-USZ62-3545.)

Constituency Pressures

The relationship between a member of Congress and his constituents is the crux of self-government in the United States. The vitality of that relationship alone assures that government by laws enacted in Congress is also government by the people. How can the people be said to govern themselves unless they are effectively *represented* in their national legislature?

From the beginnings of the Republic, there ensued a philosophical conflict between those who favored a strong central government and those who feared it would be too distant geographically and too remote governmentally to be responsive to the will of the people.

Representative Government

In a pure, or direct, democracy, there are no constituents; each citizen represents himself. Execution and interpretation of the laws may be delegated, but the full body of citizens makes the laws. Early New England town meetings, using the Athenian city-state of Ancient Greece as a model, tried to approximate the ideal of pure democracy.[1]

Prior to the American Revolution the colonists were English subjects represented, in theory, in the English Parliament. It was precisely the fictitious character of this representation against which the colonists rebelled. Having experienced government by their own elected representatives in the colonial legislatures, their patience with remote rulers was limited. The frustrations imposed by a government in which they did not participate impressed upon Americans the importance of exercising continuous control over the government. They expected lawmakers to be dominated by their constituents because they were rebelling against a regime too independent of its subjects.

The colonists could derive representative government from the social-contract theories of Englishmen such as John Locke, which based legitimate authority on the consent of the governed. Not only consent, but active participation in government could be demanded on the basis of the colonists' experience of creating their own social order out of a state of nature. The absence of hereditary privileges and the prevalence of equal opportunities in a new land encouraged the conviction that representative government should be based on a broad, popular electorate. Thus the ex-

perience of the frontier, like the experience of rebellion against unrepresentative government, pushed the Americans toward the view that constituents should control their legislators.

Belief in a right of constituents to instruct their representatives was widespread late in the 18th century. Efforts to instruct members of Congress and state legislators were not uncommon, and several state constitutions explicitly recognized this right. Members of the Congress of the Confederation considered the instructions of their state legislatures as binding.[2]

Instruction of Representatives

In the first session of the First Congress, an amendment to the Bill of Rights was proposed which would have constitutionally guaranteed the right of the people "to instruct their representatives." Reps. Elbridge Gerry of Massachusetts and John D. Page of Virginia argued the case for instructions.

Much of the debate in the House centered on the question whether instructions would be binding upon the representatives. Thomas Hartley of Pennsylvania, holding that Congress itself was the best judge of proper legislation, anticipated that instructions would never be resorted to except for party purposes, that they would embarrass the best and wisest men, and make it impossible to accommodate various viewpoints. James Madison of Virginia did not believe the residents of any one constituency could speak for all the people.

An analysis of instructions by Roger Sherman of Connecticut implied they would turn representatives into messenger boys.

Thus, despite the inclusion of the principle of instructions in several state constitutions, the preponderance of opinion in the First Congress was that members should act as trustees for the whole nation, and not merely as agents for their constituencies. So the Constitution was not amended.[3]

Doctrine of Direct Representation

With the coming of the 19th Century, the triumph of Thomas Jefferson over the Federalists, the suffrage was widened and the electorate expanded. The idea of direct representation now came into vogue, an idea which "exalted the majority principle, brought social institutions as close to the individual as possible, challenged the division of labor between officers and public, and decried any failure of the representative to reflect immediately and faithfully the mathematical sum of his constituents' desires and characteristics."[4]

Andrew Jackson, elected President in 1828, inherited the party of Jefferson and set forth his own concept of representation in reacting to the pre-Civil War issue of nullification of the Constitution and secession from the Union. In addressing the South Carolina nullification movement, Jackson's proclamation spoke of the members of the House: "However, they may in practice, as it is their duty to do so, consult and prefer the interests of their particular constituents when they come in conflict with any other particular or local interest, yet is their first or highest duty, as representatives of the United States, to promote the general good."[5]

But the view for direct representation was summed up in 1836 when a young candidate for re-election to the Illinois Legislature, Abraham Lincoln, opened his campaign by saying, "If elected, I shall consider the whole people of Sangamon my constituents, as well those that oppose as those who support me. While acting as their representative I shall be governed by their will on all subjects upon which I have the means of knowing what their will is, and upon all others I shall do what my own judgment teaches me will best advance their interests."[6]

The great defender of states' rights and nullification, John C. Calhoun, created a theory of representation that denied majority rule and called for the separate representation of classes and interests, each of which would possess a veto over the others. In a discourse published posthumously in 1851, Calhoun called his principle the "concurrent majority," by which he meant that any law of general application must receive the assent of each interest before becoming valid. Otherwise, the legislation would be null and void in states that had rejected it.[7]

Thus in its earliest years the House itself took up and debated most of the limitations that might legitimately be placed on control of representatives by constituents even though the people were recognized as sovereign. The dangers of momentary popular passion or caprice; the priority of considered popular judgment expressed in the Constitution; the practical difficulties of establishing authentic constituent instructions, and of reconciling conflicting ones; the information often available to the representatives but not to constituents; the need to deliberate, and to combine different viewpoints; the sufficiency of the ballot for controlling legislators; and the priority of the national interest over local interests—all these arguments have been used down to the present to justify independence from constituency pressures.

Senators and State Legislatures

The Senate was deliberately separated from the voters. Its constituents were not the people, but the state governments whose legislators chose them. They came to the seat of government somewhat in the guise of ambassadors of semi-sovereign states. Their august name suggested the patrician traditions of the Roman Senate; and the analogous upper chamber in Great Britain, the House of Lords, was not elected at all. The functions of senators included those of an executive council—advice and consent in international affairs and approval of presidential ap-

pointments. At first, their debates were held in closed session, for they were not responsible to the general electorate.

In the Constitutional Convention, the small states gave vent to their fears of domination by the more populous states. After it was determined that the House of Representatives would be chosen by popular election, the small states made a stand for election of the second body of Congress, the Senate, by the state legislatures. The Great Compromise shaped the function of the Senate by securing equality of state representation in it.

Selection of senators by state legislatures posed no problem for the majority of delegates in 1787. During the American Revolution, the states entrusted their legislatures with paramount powers. The legislatures had elected delegates to the Continental Congress, to the Congress of the Confederation, and to the Constitutional Convention itself.

Selection of senators by the state legislators separated senators from direct influence by the people—furthered by giving senators six-year terms. Since the voters could not show their preferences for U.S. senators, the state legislators enjoyed great freedom in naming them and sometimes adopted the practice of instruction of senators they elected.

Insofar as the senator was considered an ambassador of his state, the practice of giving instructions seemed perfectly normal. The size and operation of the legislatures made the practice of instruction a simple matter. To strengthen the state's control over its senators, some urged that legislatures be empowered to recall them. Legislatures had enjoyed such power under the Articles of Confederation, and constitutional amendments to provide such recall were frequently introduced in the early years of the Republic.

Instruction of Senators

William Maclay was a senator from Pennsylvania in the First Congress who kept a journal. He reported a debate on instructions from state legislatures, which he advocated, on Feb. 24, 1791. The heated discussion was prompted by Virginia's senators, mentioning their instructions, who moved that the doors of the Senate chamber be opened to permit public attendance at the next session.

Oliver Ellsworth of Connecticut said that legislative instructions ought to be regarded as no more than a wish. Ralph Izard of South Carolina said legislatures had no right to instruct at all, any more than electors had a right to instruct the President of the United States. Maclay wrote that his Pennsylvania colleague, Robert Morris, said: "senators owed their existence to the Constitution; the Legislatures were only the machines to choose them.... We were senators of the United States, and had nothing to do with one state more than another."[8]

Maclay thought he might be considered imprudent for speaking up, but added he considered it his duty to the public to bear testimony against those who attacked the doctrine of instructions.

"Were we chosen with dictatorial powers, or were we sent as servants of the public, to do their business? The latter, clearly, in my opinion. The first question, then, which presented itself was, were my constituents here, what would they do? The answer, if known, was the rule of the representative," Maclay said.[9]

In practice, those members who received instructions from their constituents in the early years of Congress generally obeyed them. A conception of how the role of senator was conceived may be obtained from the tenor of a resolution adopted by the Virginia Legislature in 1812 when its two U.S. senators, William B. Giles and Richard Brent, refused to follow legislative instructions. The resolution asserted that the instruction of members had been a legal practice in the English House of Commons since early times, that it was "much more unquestionable in the United States, where the people are acknowledged to be the only legitimate source of all legislation," that the nature of representation required the right of instruction, and that the confidence and discretion with which a representative is endowed "is grounded on the supposition, that he is charged with the will, acquainted with the opinions, and devoted to the interests of his constituents."[10]

State legislatures, not surprisingly, were more inclined than the senators themselves to consider their wishes binding on their senators' actions. From the First Congress, some of them sent instructions to the men they had chosen for the Senate, a practice which reached a peak in the second quarter of the 19th century. Southern states in particular adopted the practice in the pre-Civil War decades. The distinction between responsibility of senators and representatives to legislatures was evident in the formula commonly used, of which one adopted by the Tennessee General Assembly in 1840 serves as an example: "That our Senators to Congress be *instructed* and our Representatives *requested* to vote against the chartering by Congress of a National Bank." (Italics added)[11]

The force of these instructions was illustrated in an ongoing battle over the National Bank, one of the major presidential-congressional conflicts in American history. An opponent of the bank, President Andrew Jackson precipitated a crisis when in 1833 he removed governmental funds from the National Bank and deposited them in 23 state banks.

When Jackson refused to justify his action to the Senate, Henry Clay of Kentucky introduced in the chamber a resolution, which was adopted, censuring Jackson. It stated that "the President, in the late executive proceedings in relation to the public revenue, has assumed upon himself authority and power not conferred by the Constitution and laws, but in derogation of both."[12]

Sen. John Tyler of Virginia, later to become the 10th President, had voted for the Jackson censure. In so doing, Tyler had followed the instructions of his state legislature.

A bitter fight developed over expunging the Jackson censure from the Senate Journal, which was done in 1837. Meanwhile, Jacksonians had won control of the Virginia Legislature, which, reversing itself, sent instructions to its senators telling them to support the expunging motion, and adding, "It is the duty of the representative to obey the instructions of his constituents or resign the trust with which they have clothed him."[16] Unwilling to follow the mandate of the legislature but recognizing its right of instruction, Tyler resigned from the Senate on Feb. 29, 1836.[13]

Senators' Position After Civil War

According to George H. Haynes in *The Senate of the United States,* more senators probably received instructions from their legislatures in the impeachment trial of President Andrew Johnson than have been instructed upon any other matter in American history. However, the triumph of the Union in the Civil War vitiated the force attached to legislative instructions in the heyday of the states' rights doctrine. Increasingly, senators felt as free as represen-

tatives to disregard them. An illustration of the change in attitude was provided by Sen. Lucius Q. C. Lamar (D Miss.), the first of the Confederate generals to gain prominence in Congress. On three major issues Lamar defied the Mississippi Legislature's instructions: to oppose the retirement of Gen. Grant with pay; to oppose the seating of Sen. Frank B. Kellogg of Louisiana; and to support the Bland Silver Bill.

The resentment in Mississippi was so strong that everyone agreed Lamar had committed political suicide. But after he toured the state explaining his actions, the legislature re-elected him by an overwhelming majority. His first speech after his return to Mississippi typified his rationale for disobeying instructions. He recounted how, when he had been on a ship preparing to run the Union blockade of Savannah Harbor, prominent Confederate officers on board concluded that they could safely proceed. But the captain of the ship sent a sailor to the topmast where, with his telescope, he counted 10 Yankee gunboats in the harbor. The officers conferred and concluded that the sailor must be mistaken because they knew where the Yankee fleet was then located. The captain nevertheless refused to proceed. Although he recognized that the officers knew more of naval affairs than an ordinary seaman, he realized that the topmast provided a much better view of the real situation. By the same token, Lamar said, he made no claim to be wiser than the Mississippi Legislature, but he believed that as a member of the U.S. Senate he was in a better position to judge what was in the interest of his constituents.[14]

Direct Election of Senators

In 1913 the 17th Amendment, requiring direct election of senators, entirely freed members of the upper house from the constraints of legislative instructions. They were thenceforth representatives of a different constituency—the people of their states. Indeed, in many states they could have claimed to represent the will of the people more effectively than legislatures elected from malapportioned districts. The shift to direct election did not imply, however, that the popular electorate would instruct senators as legislatures had done. Indeed, the foremost leader in the struggle for direct election, Sen. William E. Borah (R Idaho), protested when Sen. David A. Reed (R Pa.) announced some years later his intention of asking his state legislature to conduct a popular referendum on repeal of prohibition. "The fundamental principle upon which this government was originated," Borah said, "was that of representative government, not referendum or a pure democracy, but that the people select a representative, and that that representative is to represent their views if they are in harmony with his. If he has convictions against them, their remedy is to retire him...."[15]

20th Century Members

George B. Galloway, in his 1969 book, *History of the House of Representatives,* characterized the role of members of Congress in the 20th century as increasingly that of a broker for his constituency in its dealings with the federal government. He wrote: "many members have regarded themselves and have behaved as free agents, enjoying a large range of discretion, guided by their own best judgment, their convictions, and the dictates of conscience. Other members have acted as delegates of their districts, bound to follow instructions received from or pledges given to their constituents, even when they have conflicted with their own judgment or principles. In actual practice most representatives have combined both roles with changing circumstances, acting at times as free agents in making decisions on matters on which they were uninstructed, and at other times as delegates with a mandate to follow the wishes of the folks back home. At still other times they have acted as brokers seeking compromises between conflicting interests in a system of checks and balances."[16]

A 1959 *American Political Science Review* article identified three major role-types of senators and representatives: the "trustee" who is a free agent and follows his own convictions, principles, judgments or conscience; the "delegate" who consults and follows the wishes of his constituents; and the "politico" who expresses both orientations either simultaneously or serially. Under modern conditions, the authors concluded that Congress has become an agency for the coordination and integration of diverse social, economic and political interests, and that "the representative has become less and less a delegate and more and more a trustee as the business of government has become more and more intricate and technical."[17]

Congressional Views of Function

That shift toward the "trustee" position was endorsed by a House member of the 1950s, Coya Knutson (D-FL Minn.). She said, "Congressmen are elected on the basis of their party and personal principles. These principles govern our judgment and our actions. It would be impossible to let the various shadings of constituent opinion guide our actions. We would be stuck on dead center of every issue. It would be unrealistic to base actions on a numerical average of opinion-letters on various measures. These do not necessarily reflect cross-section opinion as there are many people who never write letters to representatives."[18]

One of the dilemmas that sometime faces every member is whether he should put aside his convictions in order to keep his seat in Congress. Many members have expressed reluctance to cloak their every decision in moral terms.

Rep. Robert Luce (R Mass.) expressed this view in 1926: "He (a representative) is to deal fairly by his constituents and by himself. Such a man deems it necessary to break with constituency or with party only on those very rare occasions when judgment must step aside and let conscience rule. The great mass of legislation is matter of expediency. Not once in a thousand times is it matter of what is usually thought of as right and wrong. Only when right and wrong are at stake may the legislator refuse to concede, to compromise, or to yield."[19]

In a 1959 survey, former Sen. William Benton (D Conn.) explored the attitudes of onetime colleagues. Rep. John M. Vorys (R Ohio) told Benton: "I am extremely cautious about calling political decisions moral issues. On the other hand, I think that congressmen and senators are expendable rather than indispensable, and no congressman or senator should cast a vote he knows is wrong in order to be re-elected. It makes no difference whether wrongness is on a moral, legal, economic or other issue."[20]

A reply made by Rep. John W. McCormack (D Mass.), then majority leader and later Speaker, stated: "I never place myself mentally in the position of compromising principle and conscience. But there are times when I might harmonize differences in order to make progress, or maintain

unity, and then start the journey from there. The extent of compromise or harmonization depends upon the circumstances of each case, the atmosphere, the strength of the opposition, as well as the support for a measure, and other factors. But sometimes there can be no compromise or harmonization, such as the Selective Service Act of 1941, three months before Pearl Harbor."[21]

Growing Independence of Members

Students of Congress believe that long-range trends have tended to increase the independence of members. There are a number of factors. It would seem that modern communications as well as voter sampling techniques would make it easier for members to determine what constituents want, but that advantage has been negated by such other developments as population growth.

An act of 1792 provided for a ratio of one House member for every 33,000 inhabitants and fixed total House membership at 105. During the 20th century, the total number was fixed at 435 House members. Any increase above that number is seen as making the body too unwieldy. The 1970 census made the count one representative for each 470,000 persons. The same census showed a senator from California represented 19,953,134 constituents, or five times the population of the whole United States in 1790.[22] Large, heterogeneous constituencies make it difficult to gauge constituent opinion on each issue because of the increased volume and complexity of legislation.

The variety of issues decided between elections make senators and representatives less dependent on public support on any particular one of them, unless it is judged of overriding importance by the voters. And the growing complexity of legislation widens the gap in information and expertise between the member and most of his constituents. But, on questions of first importance, members are subjected to greater pressures than ever by reason of the increased power of the President and the existence of highly organized national lobbies. Both the White House and the lobbies may try to influence them directly and, indirectly, through their constituents.

The relationship between a senator or representative and his community has been transformed by the slow growth of a national community. In an age of mass production, nationwide television and jet travel, it is difficult to imagine an earlier American society in which local and state loyalties were more real than the sense of national identity. Heightened awareness of foreign problems, coming particularly from the experience of two World Wars, the Cold War, Korea and Indochina, has deepened the American sense of belonging to one distinct nation. The urgent demands of foreign policy and national defense inevitably shifted the attention of members of Congress from local toward national and international concerns.

Because foreign and defense issues are the least familiar to constituents, their prominence has compelled Congress to exercise more independence of local opinion. Indeed, the complexity of these issues has tended to make members dependent to a considerable extent on specialists in the executive branch. From representatives making decisions on behalf of their constituents, they have become, rather, mediators between those constituents and the decision-makers. They have the dual responsibility of trying to make the State and Defense Departments understand the mood of the citizens, and the citizens understand the problems faced by those departments. The same mediating role assumes importance also in domestic affairs, as technology and urbanization render the government increasingly remote and incomprehensible to the common man.

Conflicting Pressures

Gradually the development of national party organizations and spirit, and the establishment of internal loyalties and leadership in House and Senate—with the leaders often acting as agents for national party positions—introduced pressures competing against those of constituents.

The pressures on members from the congressional leadership were once described by Speaker Sam Rayburn: "A congressman has two constituencies. He has his constituents at home, and his colleagues here in the House. To serve his constituents at home, he must also serve his colleagues here in the House.... To get along you have to go along. Anybody who tries will find a way to go along with his leaders 60 to 70 per cent of the time."[23]

Until the second decade of the 20th century, there tended to be long lulls between national crises when the primary of local interests tended to reassert itself as the focus of politics. But with World War I, the crises came to follow each other in rapid succession—the Great Depression, World War II, Cold War confrontation with the communist world (Berlin, Formosa, Korea, the Middle East, Cuba, Indochina), domestic race relations and the upheaval in cities and on campuses. As a consequence a member of Congress is forced to consider many matters in addition to the immediate concerns of the voters who send him to Washington.

But it is still the constituents , and not the President, or the party, or the congressional leadership, who grant and can take away the member's job. A senator or representative popular with his constituency can defy all three in a way unthinkable in a country such as England, where the leadership of the legislature, the executive and the party are one and the same.

Looking after his district, however, may make the representative dependent on the President and congressional leaders, who have power to influence the location of federal projects. In return for their channeling of federal funds into the district, the member may be expected to support their positions on national issues. The bargaining, which is often implicit rather than spoken, works both ways. The party leadership is anxious to win friends for key roll calls, and to help its supporters gain re-election, through distribution of federal projects.[24]

The leadership conserves support thus won by keeping demands to a minimum, or they may be non-existent if the leadership position clashes with a member's conscience or constituency, which sometimes are synonymous. In that case, a member is usually free to "vote his conscience or constituency." Said Speaker John W. McCormack (D Mass.), "I have never asked a member to vote against his conscience. If he mentions his conscience—that's all. I don't press him any further." His successor, Speaker Carl Albert (D Okla.), said, "If you whip them into line every time, by the time you reach the third vote you're through."[25]

The 'Pork Barrel'

The process of obtaining jobs for constituents largely depends on bringing federal projects and money into the constituency. Sums flowing into states and congressional districts from the U.S. Treasury in the latter 20th century have ballooned enormously. Injection of federal funds into the local economy often has more effect on a member's chances for re-election than his votes on controversial issues.

The member with a reputation for "bringing home the bacon" is very hard to beat. By securing the construction of a dam or preventing the closing of a military base in his constituency, a representative or senator contributes directly to the livelihood of both business and labor. The benefits to the voters are tangible and unambiguous in a way that most campaign issues are not. Those who gain from federal projects attributable to their representative or one of their senators may feel that contributions of effort and funds to his re-election are merely practical investments in their own well-being. Conversely, a constituency with an ailing economy and starving for federal projects may put heavy pressure on its member to get some or to retire him from Congress in favor of one who can.

The fight for a share of the federal project-pie is invariably lively and intense. In a 1960 book, former Speaker Joe Martin (R Mass.) quoted a predecessor, Speaker John Nance Garner (D Texas) as once saying: "Every time those damn Yankees get a hambone, I'm going to get a hog."[26]

On rare occasions, members unblushingly talk about the force of constituency pressure for a piece of the "pork-barrel" action. In the 1950s, Rep. Kenneth Gray (D Ill.) openly appealed to the House to approve funds for a project for his district on the grounds he could not be otherwise reelected. Rep. D. R. (Billy) Matthews (D Fla.) made the same sort of plea in 1960. In both cases, their House colleagues, amused by their candor and sympathetic to their plight, accepted the amendments they offered.[27]

Defense installations and contracts provide the largest share of federal expenditures. Rivers and harbors bills which periodically authorize Army Corps of Engineers water projects, and programs included in the annual omnibus public works appropriations bills, are most often cited as "pork barrel" legislation. But the types of federal largesse are unlimited, ranging from a peanut research laboratory to designation of the United States bicentennial city. Members of Congress are not averse to claiming credit for allocation of projects whose location was in fact decided within an executive department, and it was common practice for announcements of new projects to be made by the member representing the constituency. However, the fiscal 1971 defense procurement bill abolished that custom because it was felt that the practice prompted suspicion of improper congressional influence in the awarding of contracts. All military contracts were to be announced first by the Secretary of Defense.[28]

Pressuring of the Executive. Members of Congress, of course, have direct control over the location only of projects specified in legislation. The Defense Department is supposed to distribute its installations as national security requires, and other departments are required to award grants impartially according to criteria written into the authorizing legislation. But the opportunities for congressional pressure are considerable, and the President himself may intercede to help a senator or representative from his own party.

Candidates from the President's party sometimes imply that constituents have more to gain by electing them than members of the party that is not in the White House. Thus Sen. Edward M. Kennedy (D Mass.), brother of the President, campaigned in 1962 as "the man that can do more for Massachusetts." Some Republicans the next year voiced the suspicion that the location of a $50-million electronics research center in Boston was a favor from President Kennedy, and they sought unsuccessfully to block its construction. But the leading Republican representative from Massachusetts, former Speaker Joseph W. Martin Jr., called allegations of favoritism "a red herring...to defeat the New England proposal."[29]

Powerful figures on the Armed Services and Appropriations Committees may obtain for their states and districts an impressive array of military installations. The late House Armed Services Chairman L. Mendel Rivers (D S.C.), for example, had in his district the big Charleston shipyard, a naval weapons station, a Polaris submarine base, an Air Force base, the Parris Island Marine Corps recruit depot, a Marine Corps air base, an Army supply station and two naval hospitals. The Charleston Chamber of Commerce estimated in 1969 that the military installations alone accounted for more than $317 million in payrolls, and that 55 per cent of the area's payrolls came from defense industries attracted to the area.

Rank-and-file members may find, on the other hand, that there is little they can do to attract, or even keep, defense spending in their constituencies. When Defense Secretary Robert S. McNamara announced in 1964 plans to close 95 military installations in the United States and abroad, eliminating 63,401 military and civilian jobs at estimated annual savings of $477 million, many members were apprehensive about the economic consequences in their districts. They put through a bill requiring congressional review of base closings, but it was vetoed by President Johnson as a "fundamental encroachment" on powers of the executive branch. A watered-down version was then passed and signed into law.[30]

Public Works. Although congressional control of the purse strings does not usually extend to precise geographic distribution of federal funds, rivers and harbors authorizations and some public works bills explicitly designate the location of projects. While these projects constitute only a small portion of the total federal budget, their usefulness as aids to re-election makes them important counters in the internal politics of Capitol Hill. Chairmen of committees and subcommittees controlling authorizations and appropriations for such projects are in a position to exert pressure on colleagues eager to obtain similar favors for their own constituents. Votes on questions that have no intrinsic connection with public works may thus be determined by "pork-barrel" considerations.

One dispenser of "pork barrel" largess was Rep. Mike Kirwin (R Ohio) whose death ended a 33-year House career in 1970. As chairman of the House Appropriations Subcommittee on Public Works, he was a House force that no member dared anger. The Cleveland *Plain Dealer* once wrote, "Kirwin is almost a dictator when it comes to dispensing favors and funds for congressmen's pet projects."

Kirwin had his own pet projects, including a canal in his home district which would link Lake Erie and the Ohio River. The project was promoted by several Youngstown (Ohio) industrialists who wanted a federally-built waterway capable of carrying low-rate freight. Nearly no one else wanted the canal, including the New York State Power Authority, the mayors of Cleveland and Pittsburgh, and the governor of Pennsylvania who called it "utterly worthless." But when the issue came to the House floor, Rep. John Bell Williams (D Miss.), renowned for his flair, roared, "Yesterday, we voted $3.5 or $3.6 billion to throw away (on foreign aid). Let's build this ditch for Mike!" The House approved Kirwin's canal by a clamorous voice vote and preliminary planning was begun.[31]

Constituency Influence

The extent to which a member of Congress seeks to follow the wishes of his constituents is determined to a considerable extent by the issue at stake. Probably no member would actively oppose construction in his district of a dam or post office wanted by his constituents. Few, if any, would follow locally popular policies which they were convinced would seriously endanger the nation. Between these extremes lie a full spectrum of different blends of pressure from constituents and from conscience. It is in this grey area that members must make most of their decisions.

Frequently, of course, a senator or representative experiences no conflict between his own views and what he believes are the views of most of his constituents. In Roger H. Davidson's study, *The Role of the Congressman*, 53 percent of the 87 representatives surveyed in the 88th Congress agreed with the statement: "I seldom have to sound out my constituents because I think so much like them that I know how to react to almost any proposal." Members would be less than human if they did not sometimes rationalize their convictions to fit the demands of voters, or filter their perception of voter demands to fit their convictions. But agreement between the member and his constituents is more normal than disagreement, especially in homogeneous districts and states, because of the shared experiences of living, working, and usually growing up, in the same environment. Moreover, a member may readily "vote his constituency" against his own convictions if he knows that he could not change the final result by voting his convictions.[32]

Constituent opinion may set clear limits beyond which the representative or senator cannot trespass. Unless he was planning to retire, a representative from a farm district could not push policies designed to lower the price of foods grown by those who elect him. But on most questions the member has great leeway. The character of his constituency may have more effect on the kinds of questions he gives priority to than on how he votes on them. Thus a representative from a district with a large ethnic minority might become a champion of immigration reform, and a senator from a western state might concentrate his efforts on natural resources policies. The committees on which the senator or representative seeks membership also are often determined by the type of constituency he serves.

The Representative Role

The extent to which a legislator feels obliged to follow the opinion of his constituents depends in part on his own electoral vulnerability. In his House survey, Davidson divided the 87 respondents into three types according to their "style" of representation: "trustees," who see themselves as following their own knowledge or conscience; "delegates," who view themselves as following "instructions" (either actual or implied) from their constituents; and "politicos," who combine the two other viewpoints. Interviews showed 28 per cent trustees, 23 per cent delegates, 46 per cent politicos, and 3 per cent undetermined.[33] In safe districts the percentage of trustees rose to 35, while that of delegates fell to 11. Only 19 per cent of representatives holding marginal seats were in the trustee category, compared to 44 per cent classified as delegates.[34]

The tendency to emphasize local rather than national concerns increased with the competitiveness of the district. Only 19 per cent of representatives in the marginal group were predominantly concerned with national affairs, while 53 per cent focused on local matters. Among those with safe seats, 34 per cent emphasized national and 38 per cent local considerations.[35] (The remainder in each classification were equally divided on national and local interests, or their interests were primarily nongeographic.)

Davidson found that the relationship between safety of the seat and the ease of assuming trustee and national roles produced the following distinctions among categories of members: "Trustee and national roles are more common among Democrats, leaders, southerners, and high-seniority members. Delegate and local roles are more typical of Republicans, nonleaders, nonsoutherners, and freshmen."[36] Other factors appeared to exercise independent influence, but were less clearly identifiable.

To illustrate the limitation of a competitive constituency on a congressman's independence, Davidson recounted the lament of a California liberal Democrat who was disappointed by the state legislature's failure to redraw his district to enhance his electoral chances. "I would have been a statesman if they had cut off a few of those conservatives. Now I'll have to continue going this way, that way, back and forth. I'm a cracker-ass Congressman—and I could have been a statesman!"[37]

Power of Constituents

Uninformed Voters. The voters' lack of information about their senators and representatives makes some wonder how they can exercise any influence on those who represent them. A March 1970 Gallup Poll showed that only 53 per cent of American adults could name their representative in the House, but that was a 7 per cent increase over Gallup findings in August 1966. But since Americans go to the polls in modest numbers compared to the total voting strength, it may be that those who do know the names of their representatives are the ones who vote.

Potential Opposition. The local leaders are likely to include some who would like to see the representative replaced. Whether it's a candidate who wants to fill the seat himself, leaders of the opposition party, an opposing faction within his own party, a hostile newspaper publisher, or a powerful interest group which he has antagonized, they will be monitoring his past and current performance in Washington. Any move he makes that might be unpopular in his district or state is likely to be seized upon by his opponents and publicized as widely as possible. The fact that a member is little known may testify to the fact that his record in Congress had given opponents little opportunity to point with alarm at his defiance of his constituents.

In safer constituencies, the advantages enjoyed by an incumbent may discourage potential opponents from trying to unseat him. But even a "safe" member may provoke a challenge if his actions convince local leaders that they should, and can, persuade voters they have been forgotten or betrayed. In most election years, representatives see a few of their colleagues unpleasantly surprised at the polls, a harsh reminder of the precariousness of their occupation. It is reported in the press that a member is "back home mending fences," meaning that he is in his constituency to renew ties with voters.

Election Margin. Unless a member's behavior outrages opinion at home, his opponents have an uphill struggle to arouse opposition to him. An ill-informed electorate is not a tinder waiting for a spark. But a swing of only a small percentage of the voters may spell the difference between a new term and retirement from Congress. Thus the member's concern with constituent response to his actions is not rendered entirely unrealistic by the fact that most constituents are unaware of those actions. The minority which is informed is the minority which is more volatile, and its members may provide the losing margin.

A comfortable margin might encourage indifference to constituent opinion were it not for occasional reversals of normal political trends. A crisis or a combination of events may produce a sharp national swing in voter sentiment and a higher rate of mortality among incumbents of one of the parties. Thus many Democrats accustomed to easy reelection went down in 1946, and well-established Republicans were unseated in the Democratic sweep of 1958.[38] Regional or state conditions may also prompt departures from familiar voter habits. Thus GOP perennials were hurt in 1958 by the extra effort of organized labor in states where "right-to-work" laws were on the ballots.[39] To build up the kind of margin which will enable him to survive such unforeseen hostile trends, the member may be more cautious about alienating voters than his usual election margin would seem to require.

Constituent Communications

Whatever the senator's or representative's concept of his role, he needs information on the views of his constituents. He also seeks to keep them informed on national issues and his own activities in Congress. A variety of channels of communication between the member and his constituents are available.

Elections

Election returns are perhaps the most impressive indicators of constituent opinion. A member of Congress is highly conscious of the margins by which he and his predecessors have been elected. Because so many factors affect voting patterns—candidate personality, party affiliation, specific issues, etc.—the bare figures give only crude hints of local sentiment. Breakdown of these figures by neighborhood may indicate which interest groups supported or opposed a member, and inferences can be drawn to explain the causes of that support or opposition. Shifts in population and voter registration within a district may indicate shifts in the strength of opinion on some issues.

Ward-by-ward, precinct-by-precinct analysis of voting statistics assumes major significance when state legislatures redistrict House seats. A representative whose constituency is significantly altered through redistricting may assess the views of his new constituents through consideration of their past voting records as well as their ethnic, occupational, and other characteristics.

Elections for other offices, when held between congressional races, also serve as indicators of tends within the constituency. Senators, with six-year terms, are in the best position to observe trends in intervening elections.

Mail

Of all the sources of information about his constituents, their letters to him consume the largest share of the time of the Congressman and his staff. *(Box, p. 588)*

Volume of Congressional Mail

Precise figures on the volume of constituent mail to members of Congress are not available. However, during hearings on the fiscal 1977 legislative branch appropriations, House Postmaster Robert V. Rota testified that the House Post Office handled a record 39.6 million incoming pieces of mail during calendar year 1975, compared to 22.3 million similar pieces in 1970. In addition, during 1975 statistics provided by Rota showed his unit received and distributed 463,075 newspapers, 3.7 million parcels and 44,629 pieces of registered and certified mail.

Some of the comparative figures are deceptive because of changes in accounting procedures. For example, Rota's compilations showed that 6 million newspapers were received in 1965, nearly 15 times the units listed in 1975. The postmaster explained many of these items were received as bulk rate mailings in 1975 while in the past they were received and counted as individual mailings—if each of the 435 House members received one edition of a metropolitan newspaper each day, they were formerly counted as 435 units. In 1975 they were counted as one unit.

A spokesman in the Senate Sergeant at Arms office said that rough estimates showed that the Senate received 19 million first class letters and 1.5 million pieces of second and third class mail during 1975. The Senate Post Office received and distributed about 5,000 copies of the *Congressional Record* each day of publication. Estimates

were made by the Capitol Architect and Senate Post Office.

As in the case of incoming mail, no precise count of mail sent out by members is made. In fiscal 1969, franked mail volume was 190 million pieces, costing the taxpayers $11.2-million. The fiscal 1976 figures were 322 million pieces and $46.1-million in cost.

Franked mail sent out by senators and representatives is paid for under a joint appropriation approved by Congress each year. The appropriation is based upon figures supplied by the U.S. Postal Service which bills Congress each quarter for franked mailings. The Postal Service in 1976 arrived at its figures by picking a random week in each quarter and sampling the mail generated from the House and Senate.

Acting upon a House request, the Postal Service in October 1975 made future projections of franked mail, and estimated that by 1981 Congress would be sending out 353 million free pieces at a cost of $50.4-million.

Franked Mail Sent By Members of Congress

Year	Pieces (millions)	Fiscal Year	Pieces (millions)
1969	190	1973	311
1970	201	1974	315
1971	238	1975	304
1972	309	1976	322

Sources: Hearings for fiscal 1970-77 before the Subcommittee on Legislative Branch Appropriations of the House Committee on Appropriations.

The volume of correspondence rises and falls with public interest in legislative issues, and it can be suddenly expanded by a pressure group campaign. Mail dealing with the problems of individual constituents tends to remain rather constant. Variation in the volume of mail from one office to another will depend on both the characteristics of the state or district and the policies of the members. Senators from more populous states get more mail.

Generally, a responsiveness to letters tends to generate more correspondence. Although complaints about the volume of mail are commonplace, many members of Congress actively stimulate correspondence by such devices as mass mailings, soliciting opinions. Those who write are usually put on mailing lists for newsletters, polls, and other literature.[40]

Personal requests usually involve "casework" with agencies of the federal government. But they also cover a wide variety of other services. Requests for theater tickets and hotel or plane reservations are not uncommon, but the member may be asked to perform almost any service—to purchase an outsize pair of overalls or to match a constituent's pair of draperies.

Some letters express a constituent's frustrations and bewilderment with enigmatic directives from the federal bureaucracy. In a "Dear Congressman" letter, one tongue-in-cheek constituent wrote: "Some ninny working for the government has informed me that under the law, oats are not a feed grain. Would you please explain that to my mule, I sure can't."[41]

Means of Supplying Information

Constituent requests for information are numerous. A telephone call from a member's office to an appropriate executive agency or congressional committee may get the facts in a hurry for a constituent who has a query. Several departments make popular government publications available to members for mailing to constituents.

The member's office staff often clips wedding and birth announcements from local newspapers so the member can send publications along with a congratulatory message.[42]

The Congressional Research Service (CRS) of the Library of Congress deals with many requests for specific information from members of Congress. A CRS spokesman told Congressional Quarterly that in fiscal 1975 CRS answered 244,498 inquiries, of which 176,819 were for the members themselves and 67,679 were information requests from constituents forwarded to CRS by senators and representatives.

Appropriations for the CRS were set at $17,050,000 for fiscal 1976. House and Senate committees overseeing the Library of Congress urged that a management survey of the CRS be made to determine if it was "focusing on the needs of Congress...." Budget proposals called for as many as 157 new CRS positions to increase the total staff to 860 persons.[43]

Purpose of the CRS is to assist members in their constitutional and legislative functions, which it does through such services as drawing up briefs and digests on bills, and drafting members' speeches. CRS has specialists dealing with American law, education and public welfare, economics, foreign affairs, history and government, agriculture, national defense, labor, Russian affairs and other areas.

Much legislative mail is "inspired" by pressure groups. Sometimes it takes the form of printed or mimeographed postcards. Identical letters reveal that the writers have been supplied with the message and have given it little consideration. Other letters generated by pressure groups are usually easy to recognize by the recurrence of phrases and arguments, the timing, or even the stationery. Such mail is given less weight than spontaneous communications which reflect individual thought.[44] However, inspired mail may contain an implied threat: If an organization can prompt people to write, it may be able to deliver their votes, though the possibility is usually considered slight. Letters from personal or political friends have the greatest impact.

As an indicator of constituent opinion on business before Congress, the mail has grave limitations. Few Americans ever write their representatives and senators. The highly educated, prosperous, and politically active are overrepresented.[45] Constituents are more inclined to write to members with whom they agree than to those with whom they take issue.

In their study of pressures affecting tariff legislation, Bauer, Pool and Dexter found that persons most likely to write were "those who saw the act of writing as part of a recognized professional role, likely to contribute to specific and short-run objectives and contributing effectively to the special interest for which the writer spoke." Neither moral conviction, nor a sense of the question's importance, nor a desire for self-expression differentiated those who wrote to Congressmen from those who did not. "A man was more likely to write on a trivial point if it were part of his job and a practical thing to do than if he were burning with deep conviction about the nation's future welfare."[46]

What is true about mail on tariff legislation, does not apply to issues that inflame the public consciousness. Events such as invasion of Cambodia in April 1970 can produce a tidal wave of mail, but then again the concerned member of Congress has the problem of judging what part of the mail deluge is spontaneous and what part is inspired by pressure organizations geared up to make a massive response. For example, the national commander of the American Legion, J. Milton Patrick, acting in support of Nixon, wrote to Legionnaires asking them to write or telephone their members of Congress. Americans for Democratic Action announced it was mounting the widest possible campaign against the war in Indochina. ADA national director, Leon Shull, told his members: "It is of the highest importance to keep the pressure high on Congress.... Keep your letters, telegrams, statements and visits going to Congress."[47]

Extreme distortion of constituent opinion may be produced by the mail. President Roosevelt's proposal in 1939 to repeal a provision of the existing Neutrality Act requiring imposition of an embargo on arms shipments to nations at war provoked an unprecedented flood of mail (reaching 487,000 items in a single day). Robert A. Dahl's *Congress and Foreign Policy* noted that the ratio of opposition to repeal ran about five to one in mail sent to the House; the ratio in Senate mail was even higher. Yet a public opinion poll at the time indicated that the public supported repeal by 56 to 44 per cent. In this case Congress disregarded the mail, repealing the embargo by majorities of 68 per cent in the Senate and 59 per cent in the House. A year later, when a large sample of Senate mail showed 90 per cent opposition to Selective Service, a public opinion poll indicated 70 per cent support for the same measure. It passed the Senate with a 68 per cent majority.[48]

And yet members of Congress normally treat the mail with great respect. That attitude reflects in part the inadequacies of other sources of information. But the mail's distortion of constituent opinion often is an advantage to the senator or representative. The views which are overrepresented are likely to be those held by the more active, informed, influential and organized voters. They are also the constituents whose votes, and perhaps campaign funds or efforts, may depend on the member's stand on the question at issue. Many members periodically tabulate the opinion expressed in the mail on key issues, though "inspired" mail may be discounted or tabulated separately.

No senator or representative has time to read all his mail. Usually only complex matters and letters from friends or politically potent individuals are referred to him. Some members ask to see all significant case mail or all mail concerning legislation. However, when replies drafted by the staff are given to the member for his signature, often with the previous correspondence attached, he exercises control of his mail. Routine requests may be handled by a staff member authorized to use the member's signature.

On uncomplicated matters which may generate a flow of letters, members often devise a standardized "policy-line" answer to inquiries on those subjects. Special typewriters can produce identical copies of the text, outlining the member's position, that look like individual letters; the staffer himself types the name, address and salutation, then switches to automatic typing for the body of the reply. The letters are then individually signed by the member himself, by an assistant authorized to use his name, or by an autopen device. Few congressional offices employ mimeographed form letters to answer constituent mail.[49]

Thoughtful, concerned letters from constituents are likely to prompt careful replies. If the issue is complex, additional materials may be enclosed—a speech or article, a committee report, or a bulletin from an executive agency. Some members of Congress prepare "issue packets" on controversial subjects. One seasoned representative suggested to his freshman colleagues that when a particular group wants detailed information or is applying heavy pressure, they send transcripts of committee hearings, which may run to four volumes. The constituents can be told: "Please read this and then if you have any further questions I will be glad to answer them." Many House and Senate offices keep a record of all correspondents, with the subjects of their letters noted. Such a file may provide addresses for special mailings and serve other purposes.[50]

A special file is often reserved for "crackpots." Most members of Congress ignore chronic writers of crank mail on whom replies would be wasted. Occasionally a senator or representative may respond sharply to abusive mail. "Dear Friend," one replied to a constituent, "I want to call attention to the fact that some crackpot in your city is writing me and signing your name." But some members of Congress go out of their way to court sharp critics with extra attention, hoping perhaps that the antagonist's surprise will prompt him to report the unexpected courtesy to his acquaintances.[51]

Each senator and representative is granted allowances for stationery, stamps, and telephone and telegraph

Writing to Members of Congress

Citizens with complaints, suggestions and comments on how the government is being run can voice their views directly to the executive branch and to Congress by letters and telegrams.

Writing Tips

The following hints on how to write a member of Congress were suggested by congressional sources and the League of Women Voters.

● Write to your own senators or representative. Letters sent to other members will end up on the desk of members from your state.

● Write at the proper time, when a bill is being discussed in committee or on the floor.

● Use your own words and your own stationery. Avoid signing and sending a form or mimeographed letter.

● Don't be a pen pal. Don't try to instruct the representative or senator on every issue that comes up.

● Don't demand a commitment before all the facts are in. Bills rarely become law in the same form as introduced.

● Whenever possible, identify all bills by their number.

● If possible, include pertinent editorials from local papers.

● Be constructive. If a bill deals with a problem you admit exists but you believe the bill is the wrong approach, tell what you think the right approach is.

● If you have expert knowledge or wide experience in particular areas, share it with the member. But don't pretend to wield vast political influence.

● Write to the member when he does something you approve of. A note of appreciation will make him remember you more favorably the next time.

● Feel free to write when you have a question or problem dealing with procedures of government departments.

● Be brief, write legibly and be sure to use the proper form of address.

A 15-word telegram called a Public Opinion Message (P.O.M.) can be sent to the President, Vice President or a member of Congress from anywhere in the United States for $2. Name and address are not counted as part of the message unless there are additional signers.

Correct Form for Letters
President

The President
The White House
Washington, D.C. 20500

Dear Mr. President: _____

Very respectfully yours,

Vice President

The Vice President
The White House
Washington, D.C. 20500

Dear Mr. Vice President:

Sincerely yours,

Senator

Honorable _____
United States Senate
Washington, D.C. 20510

Dear Senator_____

Sincerely yours,

Representative

Honorable_____
House of Representatives
Washington, D.C. 20515

Dear Mr. _____

Sincerely yours,

Member of the Cabinet

Honorable _____
The Secretary of State
Washington, D.C. 20520

Dear Mr. Secretary:

Sincerely yours,

---

messages. All members of Congress enjoy franking privileges under which all surface mail related to official business is carried free of postage. "Official business" is defined broadly to include all matters related to a member's work in Congress. However, if personal comments or political appeals are included in the official correspondence, postage must be paid. Public documents printed by order of Congress, such as bills or committee hearings and report, can be mailed under franking privilege. Copies of speeches or of articles reprinted in the *Congressional Record* can be mailed at no charge regardless of the subject. It is not uncommon for members to have politically useful material inserted in the *Record* so that it can be reproduced and posted under frank.

Office Visitors

Constituents may come to Washington to contact their representatives or senators about legislation or to seek their assistance on individual matters. They may request help on business with a government agency, job hunting, a term paper, introductions to officials, or other matters. But the largest number of visitors from the home state or district are tourists who stop by the member's office. They may take advantage of the opportunity to make known their views or needs, but they are more likely to seek information and aid as tourists in the nation's capital. Often the visitors appear in groups—high school classes, delegates to conventions and tours organized by home district organizations.

The staff welcomes constituents, knowing the importance of the direct impression they will take back to the district or state. Information about Washington tourist attractions and the federal government are provided in a variety of booklets and brochures; the office staff may prepare calendars of events as well. Passes to House and Senate visitors' galleries are handed out, and special tours of the White House and some executive agencies may be arranged.

Though the staff can usually handle the needs of visitors, some are anxious to see the member himself. He may be reluctant to interrupt his other work, yet even more reluctant to turn down such a request. Unless he is hard-pressed for time, he is likely to speak with the caller or callers. He may arrange to be photographed with a group of constituents, providing them with copies to take home. Some legislators will even conduct groups on a tour of the Capitol or sponsor luncheons with them. Others attempt to keep time spent with visitors to a minimum.[52]

Visits to the Constituency

Earlier in the century, when sessions of Congress did not take up most of the year, hectic fence-mending trips to the home state or district were not urgent. Today, with members buried in work in Washington, these trips are much more difficult and much more necessary. The constituents have less opportunity to get acquainted with their senators or representatives at a time when, with the growth of legislation affecting their daily lives, they have greater need to know them. The members, meanwhile, have more voters to woo but less time to devote to that task.

Politicians know that the most effective electioneering is done between campaigns. The officeholder has no opponent at such times, and he carries the aura of his office more than the stigma of a "politician." The member of Congress who neglects to spend time in his constituency, despite—or indeed because of—his achievements as a legislator, is liable to find himself out of a job.

In 1976 House members were entitled to 26 free round trips to their district each year. Also allowed were six government-paid trips for each member's staff; six extra staff trips were permitted if they were deducted from a member's quota of 26. Representatives were allowed to draw a travel allowance of $2,250 a year in cash in lieu of trip quotas.

Each senator received a free trip to Washington and back home at the beginning and end of regular sessions. Beyond that, senators from states with fewer than 10 million people were reimbursed for 40 round trips to the state a year. Senators from states having populations of more than 10 million received 44 round trips to their state. They were reimbursed on a sliding scale based on mileage that ranged from 14 cents a mile for those senators whose states were within 375 miles of Washington to seven cents a mile for those senators from states more than 3,000 miles from the nation's capital. Members of a senator's staff received eight round trips annually to the senator's home staff; in the case of states with more than 10 million population, two additional staff trips were allowed. Members of Congress frequently exceed their travel allowances, and pay the added expense out of their own pockets or from other sources.[53]

District Offices

Nearly all senators and representatives have offices in their districts. The division of work between the district and Washington offices varies widely. Some members have a staffer handle substantial amounts of casework in the district, especially if regional offices of federal agencies are located there. Others prefer to deal with all casework in Washington and use the district office primarily for public relations work or keeping track of events in the district. Former Rep. George W. Grider (D Tenn.) set up "Dial-a-Congressman" hours on Monday afternoons when constitutents could visit his Memphis office to place a free telephone call to him in Washington. He observed that "The constituents, when they talk with me personally, know that through me they have a voice in what happens." Some members have no district office at all, while those within a striking distance of Washington may appear for regular weekend office hours.[54]

According to listings in the 1975 *Congressional Staff Directory,* the number of year-round offices maintained by senators in their states was: six offices, one senator; five offices, three senators; four offices, 11 senators; three offices, 22 senators; two offices, 27 senators; one office, 29 senators; and no offices, five senators. For the House, the number of year-round offices maintained by representatives in their districts was: five offices, one representative; four offices, 14 representatives; three offices, 83 representatives; two offices, 130 representatives; one office, 204 representatives; no offices, three representatives. Two representatives reported they opened a district office only when they were in the constituency.[55]

Members of Congress are allowed office space in federal buildings in their states or district, or, in lieu of available space, are given varying allowances to rent offices in private buildings.

Newsletters, Special Mailings

The flow of information from a senator or representative to his constituents is as important as that in the reverse direction. It is vital not only to the member's re-election but also to public understanding of the issues and processes of government. Some of the congressional dissemination of information takes one of the forms of communication already discussed—individual responses to mail and direct contacts in Washington or at home. Members also employ instruments of mass communication.

Newsletters. Newsletters have gained great favor. Some members have come to regard them as their most effective single activity among constituents. Newsletters are published weekly, fortnightly or monthly. Twelve of the offices mailed their newsletters to all postal patrons in the district, and 98 used special mailing lists.[56]

The format of the newsletter varies from mimeographed sheets stapled together to polished photo offset productions embellished with a picture of the member and one of the Capitol and a map of the district. The content ranges from resumes of various legislative activities to analysis of a single issue. The member's own activities are usually highlighted. Items of special interest to the district are more likely to be included, and some newsletters list visitors from the district to the Washington office. Some newsletters adopt a chatty tone; others are more formal.

One experienced member advised freshmen lawmakers on newsletters: "I do believe it helped me more in vote-getting than any single thing I did that I kept them advised. They don't ask for weighty information. They don't ask that you agree with them, I may say. What they do want is to know that you care enough about them to write home and that makes a big hit, that you are still aware of the fact that they sent you here.... Include in it some little homely news, at the bottom maybe a list of the visitors who came in. Keep a visitors' guest book. People are honored to be asked to sign it. Keep the guest book and then write in that newsletter that 'Mr. and Mrs. So-and-So came in this week to see me. They were on their way through to Florida...and I was happy to see them,' and mention all these people. They love to see their names in print even if your newsletter has a small circulation."[57]

On June 1, 1975, the House began to pay for the production and printing of two newsletters a year mailed by its 435 members and four non-voting delegates. Rep. James C. Cleveland (R N.H.) estimated that the cost of two newsletters per year ran about $6,000, and new rules permitted House members to convert their stationery allowance of $6,500 a year into cash to pay for newsletters.

Special Mailings. A mass mailing that does not take the form of a newsletter is often used to publicize a special issue or event. Such mailings may be specially prepared for the occasion or may consist of reproductions of a government report, a magazine article, or a speech from the *Congressional Record*. The material may be accompanied by a covering news release.

Mailing Lists. Mailing lists for newsletters and special mailings are built from a wide variety of sources. If the target is a particular town or county, the telephone directory may suffice. Cities usually have directories organized by address, permitting ward and precinct lists and concentration on specific ethnic or class neighborhoods. Voter registration lists, tax rolls, specialized directories, and membership lists of clubs, labor unions and voluntary associations can all be used to compile lists. Constituents who write to members are usually added to mailing lists. People identified as opinion molders—school principals, clergy, newsmen, presidents of local organizations, local officials, etc.—are particularly sought, and the local press is culled for names of newsmakers to be added to the lists. Some members list doctors' offices, beauty parlors, and barber shops.[58]

Questionnaires and Polls. Increasingly members mail questionnaires to their constituents.

Questionnaires are distributed by a variety of methods. They may be incorporated in a newsletter, published in newspapers, mailed separately to any of a wide variety of mailing lists, or even handed out at meetings. As a means of determining constituent opinion, congressional polls have been criticized by social scientists. Unsophisticated sampling methods with consequent distortion of findings have been found to characterize most polls. Members of Congress are seldom surprised by the results, but their frequent distribution to the press and insertion in the *Congressional Record* may create false impressions.

Use of professional polling organizations by individual members is rare, largely because of the expense. The national surveys of organizations such as the Gallup Poll do not help members of Congress much, because they are not broken down by state and district. Senators are less likely than representatives to distribute questionnaires because of their larger constituencies.

The unscientific character of the sampling does not interfere with the representative's principal purpose in distributing questionnaires. He considers the device especially useful for establishing a sense of connection between himself and his constituents. Some respondents take pains to elaborate on their answers, and it is not uncommon for them to note that "this is the first time anyone ever asked me for my views." Some make known

their doubts that the member will ever pay any attention to their answers, and most never bother to reply at all, but representatives believe questionnaires win friends in their districts.[59]

Press and Electronic Media

Members of Congress have to rely heavily on the press to inform their constituents, but they are not generally satisfied with the performance of the press in this regard. An individual representative's activities are largely lost in the flood of news competing for space in newspapers and on television. Senators, however, have less difficulty than representatives in attracting the attention of newspapers and networks.

Members and reporters often differ in their views of what is newsworthy. Members are apt to think that reporters neglect the substance of news in their eagerness for an "angle" that will attract attention. The complexities of public questions and of the legislative process sometimes appear to members to get less coverage than stories that tend to denigrate the public image of a member.

The extent to which members depend on the press may prompt some of their dissatisfaction with it. At the same time, their dependence makes them normally cordial to reporters, including those they dislike and fear. Reporters are well aware of the politician's quest for publicity, and understandably skeptical of the importance he attaches to keeping constituents aware of what he is doing.

Some members of Congress have former newsmen on their staffs to handle press relations. News releases are frequently dispatched to state and district media, often accompanied by the full text of a speech. Telephone calls may be made to direct the attention of the press to the member's activities. Releases are distributed to the House and Senate press galleries. Weekly newspapers in the constituencies, which have small staffs and tend to welcome stories connecting the community with a larger world, may print the releases verbatim.[60] Congressional staff members regularly scan local papers for figures of local prominence to be added to mailing lists, and for weddings, births, honors, elections and other events deserving congratulatory letters.

TV and Radio

Some members make weekly, bi-weekly, or monthly reports to their constituents on local TV and radio stations. Typically these reports consume from three to five minutes. Because licensed stations are required to devote a portion of their time to public service broadcasts, they are relatively receptive to such programs. A one-minute commentary on a major news event or item of particular local interest may also be supplied by the member to fit into newscasts. Interviews, typically lasting 5 to 15 minutes and often including a federal executive, provide a popular format for current issues of concern to constituents.[61]

Once a senator or representative is officially a candidate for re-election, he can no longer obtain free radio or television time. The high cost of TV then reduces most of his broadcasting to spot announcements at peak listening hours. Reports and interviews or panel shows tend during the campaign to give way to documentaries on the candidate's life and achievements. The House and Senate have studios where films and transcripts can be produced at cost to be dispatched to networks and stations.[62]

Services for Constituents

The volume of services which members of Congress perform for their constituents has grown enormously in recent years. Before 1900, when senators and representatives did not have offices of their own, Congress was not in session half of the time, and the population of constituencies was much smaller, requests for help on particular problems demanded little time or effort. With population growth, easier communication, and the spread of education, the volume of private requests expanded. But it is the expansion of the federal government into many areas directly affecting the private lives of individuals which has produced a revolution in the volume of services members perform for their constituents.

Variety of Casework

A member's dealings with administrative agencies of the federal government on behalf of his constituents is usually called "casework." The variety of casework is almost unlimited. Typical requests concern military service, social security benefits, veterans' affairs, immigration, passports, unemployment claims, and problems arising from federal aid programs such as housing. The character of requests also varies widely among constituencies. Thus agricultural districts generate casework related to acreage quotas and delayed crop subsidy checks. But even districts that are much alike sometimes show substantial variation in the type of problems brought to their representatives.

While some casework involves complaints, a good deal has to do with requests for assistance in approaching federal agencies. Government contracts, loans, grants, jobs and patents are among the benefits sought by constituents. They may ask only for referral to an appropriate agency, or, at the opposite extreme, they may ask their legislator to appear before an agency to argue the merits of a specific claim. Some requests are for introductions to federal officials, ranging from the Secretary of the Treasury to "the right man" in the Pentagon about the purchase of surplus goods.

A routine procedure has been worked out for one popular request. Schools and other organizations often ask for an American flag that has flown over the Capitol building. The representative may purchase a flag from the House stationery room. The page service then has it hoisted to the top of the Capitol, after which it is delivered to the representative with a letter from the Clerk's office certifying that it has been flown as requested by the specified individual or group.[63]

Casework Procedures

Most casework is handled by the staff. A telephone call to the appropriate agency is often sufficient, especially when the request is only for information. More complex matters, or those requiring a record of the transaction, are usually sent to the agency in writing. The constituent's letter, or a restatement of it by the senator or representative, may be used. A reply signed by the head of the agency is expected, and the member often forwards copies of it to the constituent.

To cope with the volume of constituents' problems, federal agencies and the three military services have liaison offices to assist members of Congress. The armed services, the Civil Service Commission and the Veterans Administration maintain offices in the House Office Buildings; other agencies send liaison personnel periodically to visit congressional offices. When cases involve agencies which have regional offices—Internal Revenue, Civil Service and the Veterans Administration, for example—Members may urge their constituents to pursue the matter first at that level.

"Service" and "watchdog" committees, such as the House and Senate Select Committees on Small Business or the Joint Committee on Defense Production, encourage members to channel constituents' affairs through them. Staffs of legislative committees also handle some matters having to do with constituents.

Often one or more members of a senator's or representative's staff specialize in casework; and an assistant skilled in handling constituents' affairs with federal agencies is valued highly. Legal education or experience in the executive branch are particularly helpful. In some offices, staff members specialize in problems relating to specific federal agencies; in others, all persons handle all types of requests, thus avoiding difficulties that would occur should a specialist be absent. Staff members have little opportunity to develop expertise in the wide variety of problems that prompt requests from constituents.

Most members of Congress deal personally with difficult cases, or those involving personal friends, important supporters, influential figures in the district, or large numbers of constituents. When the member does intervene personally, he increases the chances of a prompt and favorable response. While some members will pursue cases to the point of appearing as counsel for constituents, many are reluctant to spend the time or exert the influence required to press individual matters that far.

Effectiveness of Members' Efforts

A study by Walter Gellhorn in 1965 found unanimity among congressional staff members and administrators that "a congressional referral assures exceptionally quick attention and a courteous response." Most authorities agree also that the chances of favorable action for the constituent improve with the expression of interest by a senator or representative. Gellhorn's survey, on the other hand, discovered few who believed that administrative decisions were easily or frequently revised at the behest of a member of Congress. One representative told Gellhorn: "At least some agencies are becoming pretty sophisticated. They seem to realize that usually all I need or want is a demonstration that I have done everything possible on my constituent's behalf.... Some of the other agencies, though, seem to be dazzled by the fact that my office is involved, and then they get distracted from the real merit of the matter." Frequently, however, the official gets no clear indication of the extent of a member's interest in a case. Because matters before federal agencies often entail an element of discretion, the benefit of the doubt is likely to go to the member's client.[64]

Political Importance

The value of casework for re-election is a commonplace on Capitol Hill; many consider it more important in garnering votes than the stand the member takes on legislative matters. As long as he does not outrage the people of his district or state by consistently or blatantly ignoring their opinions on controversial issues, the representative or senator who carefully tends to constituents' requests is considered very hard to beat. The cultivation of election support based on services rendered tends to increase the independence of the member on legislative matters, and may even be justified on those grounds.

Members sometimes complain about increased constituency demands, but few downgrade its importance in keeping their congressional careers alive. One member stated, "I feel the errand boy function is contrary to the Founding Fathers' intent, but it's necessary for election. Glad-handing is degrading, but it's desired by constituents." Another said, "You have to represent your district in contacts with federal agencies. This is often criticized as 'errand running,' but letters from the district instruct you as to how a program is operating. I don't object to that."[65]

Why is the handling of problems of individual constituents considered to have such valuable political payoff? As already noted, cases may add up to several thousand a year, and over the years a representative or senator may build up a substantial personal following, the kind of following which has little incentive to abandon an incumbent for a challenger. In closely contested constituencies, such a following can itself make the difference between victory or defeat, especially because it cuts across party lines. In more homogeneous districts, where rival candidates are likely to agree on basic legislative matters, the member's effectiveness in serving the interests of constituents may be the principal election issue.[66]

The support gained is not limited to the individuals served. Their families and friends are likely to hear how helpful the representative or senator was. Of course, not everyone who has been helped votes for the candidate seeking re-election. But at least he has made himself known directly to individuals through matters of real concern to them. Anyone seeking to replace the incumbent has no such means of making individual voters notice him.

Controversy Over Casework

Congressional handling of casework has prompted serious criticism, which can be divided into two basic types. On the one hand, the volume of requests from constituents is said to interfere with the member's legislative responsibilities. On the other hand, congressional efforts to meet those requests are said to constitute an inefficient, or positively harmful, means of reviewing administrative decisions and procedures.

Critics of congressional intervention on behalf of constituents with federal agencies assert that members, by utilizing friendly contacts or by "going to the top," undermine the orderliness, efficiency, and even impartiality, within the executive branch. The level of ad hoc con-

gressional intervention diffuses responsibility within the executive, overburdens high-level officials, and contributes to needless duplication.[67] This evaluation argues, "Systematic government—a government whose organizational methods are discoverable and operable—is the best alternative to a government in which knowing the right people is the only reliable way of getting things done."[68]

Another argument asserts that constituent casework and service have no upper limits and that their continued growth threatens to subvert the professional and institutional staff that Congress has created for other purposes. Members have increased their casework by inviting more communications and requests from their constituents. Saloma said, "To keep pace with the workload, members have increased their own staff, borrowed professional committee staff, and turned to the institutional resources of the Library of Congress. Concern about this trend was evidenced in the Report of the Joint Committee of the Organization of the Congress which warned against the dissipation of the research resources of the Legislative (now Congressional) Reference Service."[69]

Others justify a vigorous congressional role in constituency service maintaining that the amount of time members actually spend on casework is greatly overstated, and note that Congress has the power to increase and control the use of its staff as it sees fit. They may admit that any form of congressional intervention reduces administrative efficiency, but hold that positive considerations clearly outweigh any negative effects.[70]

Members of Congress do feel they have a significant impact upon federal agency action. As Charles Clapp reported: "Through his handling of complaints the congressman feels that he learns about laws that need revision and agencies that would benefit from reorganization. The mail, then, helps the legislator carry out his legislative responsibilities as well as his representative function. In pointing up weaknesses in the executive branch, it contributes to the administrative process."[71]

Kenneth G. Olson went further in his analysis of the service function of government: "A major source of the total knowledge required by the federal government to govern effectively resides in the constant press of constituent requests upon members of Congress. That knowledge is essentially indivisible; it can be used for remedial legislation as well as for stimulating administrative changes within the bureaucracy. Knowledge of a constituent's problem can lead to a single, specific solution, or it can be the germ of a creative legislative idea ultimately affecting millions of persons as it is made the law of the land. Certainly, however, such knowledge is a necessary—if not a sufficient—condition of creative legislation."[72]

Footnotes

1. Frederic A. Ogg and P. Orman Ray, *Introduction to American Government* (Appleton-Century-Crofts Inc., 1948), p. 6.

2. *Ibid.*, pp. 1-13; Wilfred E. Binkley and Malcolm C. Moos, *A Grammar of American Politics: The National Government* (Alfred A. Knopf, 1958), pp. 19-24.

3. George B. Galloway, *History of the House of Representatives* (Thomas Y. Crowell, 1969), pp. 212-14.

4. Alfred deGrazia, *Public and Republic: Political Representation in America* (Alfred A. Knopf, 1951), p. 246.

5. *Ibid.*, p. 128.

6. Galloway, *History of the House*, p. 215.

7. *Ibid.*

8. Quoted in George H. Haynes, *The Senate of the United States*, 2 vols. (Houghton Mifflin Co., 1938), vol. 2, p. 1026.

9. *Ibid.*

10. Galloway, *History of the House*, p. 214.

11. Haynes, *The Senate of the United States*, vol. 2, p. 1027.

12. Richard B. Morris, ed., *Encyclopedia of American History* (Harper & Brothers, 1953) pp. 174-75.

13. Haynes, *The Senate of the United States*, vol. 2, p. 1028.

14. *Ibid.*, p. 1030.

15. *Ibid.*, p. 1031.

16. Galloway, *History of the House*, p. 217.

17. Heinz Eulau and others, "The Role of the Representative," *American Political Science Review*, September 1959, pp. 742-56.

18. Galloway, *History of the House,* p. 219.
19. *Ibid.*
20. William Benton, "The Big Dilemma: Conscience or Votes? *The New York Times Magazine,* April 26, 1959, p. 12.
21. *Ibid.,* p. 84.
22. Bureau of the Census, *Number of Inhabitants* (Government Printing Office, 1971).
23. Martin Tolchin and Susan Tolchin, *To the Victor...Political Patronage from the Clubhouse to the White House* (Random House, 1971), p. 187.
24. *Ibid.,* p. 188.
25. Neil MacNeil, *Forge of Democracy: The House of Representatives* (David McKay Co. Inc., 1963), pp. 93-94.
26. *Ibid.,* p. 143.
27. *Ibid.*
28. Congressional Quarterly, *1970 Almanac, p. 381.*
29. Congressional Quarterly, *1963 Almanac,* pp. 416-17.
30. Congressional Quarterly, *1965 Almanac,* p. 697.
31. Quoted in Drew Pearson and Jack Anderson, *The Case Against Congress: A Compelling Indictment of Corruption on Capitol Hill* (Simon and Schuster, 1968), pp. 284-88.
32. Roger H. Davidson, *The Role of the Congressman* (Pegasus, 1969), p. 199.
33. *Ibid.,* p. 117.
34. *Ibid.,* p. 128.
35. *Ibid.*
36. *Ibid.,* p. 140.
37. *Ibid.,* p. 141.
38. Congressional Quarterly, *Congress and the Nation, 1945-1964, vol. 1, p. 3.*
39. Ibid., p. 29.
40. Donald G. Tacheron and Morris K. Udall, *The Job of the Congressman: An Introduction to Service in the U.S. House of Representatives* (Bobbs-Merrill Co., 1966), pp. 71-72.
41. *Ibid.,* p. 64.
42. *Ibid.,* pp. 301-03.
43. Congressional Quarterly, *Inside Congress* (1976), p. 27.
44. Tacheron and Udall, *The Job of the Congressman,* p. 78.
45. Raymond A. Bauer, Ithiel de Sola Pool and Lexis Anthony Dexter, *American Business and Public Policy; The Politics of Foreign Trade* (Atherton Press, 1963), p. 201.

46. *Ibid.,* p. 202.
47. Congressional Quarterly, *Weekly Report,* May 29, 1970, p. 1461.
48. Robert Dahl, *Congress and Foreign Policy* (Harcourt Brace and Co., 1950), p. 34.
49. Tacheron and Udall, *The Job of the Congressman,* p. 79.
50. *Ibid.,* pp. 76-78.
51. *Ibid.,* pp. 74-75.
52. *Ibid.,* pp. 79-81.
53. Congressional Quarterly, *Inside Congress,* pp. 30-31.
54. Tacheron and Udall, *The Job of the Congressman,* pp. 93-97.
55. Charles B. Brownson, *1975 Congressional Staff Directory* (The Congressional Staff Directory, 1975), pp. 125-52, 247-321.
56. Tacheron and Udall, *The Job of the Congressman,* pp. 286-87.
57. *Ibid.,* pp. 111-13.
58. *Ibid.,* pp. 119-21.
59. *Ibid.,* pp. 113-14.
60. *Ibid.,* pp. 107-09.
61. *Ibid.,* pp. 109-11.
62. *Ibid.,* pp. 58-59.
63. Tacheron and Udall, *The Job of the Congressman,* p. 119.
64. Walter Gellhorn, *When Americans Complain: Governmental Grievance Procedures* (Harvard University Press, 1966), pp. 77-80.
65. Davidson, *The Role of the Congressman,* pp. 101-02.
66. John S. Saloma III, *Congress and the New Politics* (Little, Brown and Co., 1969), p. 183.
67. *Ibid.,* p. 180.
68. Gellhorn, *When Americans Complain,* p. 126.
69. Saloma, *Congress and the New Politics,* p. 180.
70. *Ibid.,* p. 181.
71. Charles L. Clapp, *The Congressman, His Work as He Sees It* (Brookings Institution, 1963), p. 79.
72. Kenneth G. Olson, "The Service Function of the United States Congress," in *Congress: The First Branch of Government, Twelve Studies of the Organization of Congress,* coordinated by Alfred deGrazia (American Enterprise Institute for Public Policy Research, 1966), pp. 373-74.

Selected Bibliography

Books

Anderson, John B. *Between Two Worlds: A Congressman's Choice.* Grand Rapids: Zondervan Publishing House, 1970.

Anderson, John B., ed. *Congress and Conscience.* Philadelphia: J. P. Lippincott, 1970.

Bauer, Raymond A., Pool, Ithiel de Sola; and Dexter, Lewis Anthony. *American Business and Public Policy: The Politics of Foreign Trade.* New York: Atherton Press, 1963.

Clapp, Charles L. *The Congressman, His Work as He Sees It.* Washington: Brookings Institution, 1963.

Dahl, Robert. *Congress and Foreign Policy.* New York: Harcourt Brace and Co., 1950.

Davidson, Roger H. *The Role of the Congressman.* New York: Pegasus, 1969.

DeGrazia, Alfred. *Public and Republic: Political Representation in America.* New York: Alfred A. Knopf, 1951.

Dexter, Lewis A. *The Sociology and Politics of Congress.* Chicago: Rand McNally, 1969.

Froman, Lewis A. Jr. *Congressmen and their Constituencies.* Chicago: Rand McNally and Co., 1963.

Gellhorn, Walter. *When Americans Complain: Governmental Grievance Procedures.* Cambridge: Harvard University Press, 1966.

Groennings, Sven and Hawley, Jonathan P., eds. *To Be A Congressman: The Promise and the Power.* Washington: Acropolis Press, 1973.

Haynes, George H. *The Senate of the United States: Its History and Practice.* Boston: Houghton Mifflin Co., 1938.

Hyneman, Charles S. and Carey, George W., eds. *A Second Federalist.* New York: Appleton-Century-Crofts, 1967.

Jackson, John E. *Constituencies and Leaders in Congress: Their Effects on Senate Voting Behavior.* Cambridge: Harvard University Press, 1974.

Key, V.O. Jr. *Public Opinion and American Democracy.* New York: Alfred A. Knopf, 1961.

MacRae, Duncan Jr. *Dimensions of Congressional Voting: A Statistical Study of the House of Representatives in the Eighty-First Congress.* Berkeley: University of California Press, 1958.

Matthews, Donald R. *U.S. Senators and Their World.* Chapel Hill: University of North Carolina Press, 1960.

Miller, Clem *Member of the House.* New York: Scribner's, 1962.

Olson, Kenneth G. "The Service Function of the United States Congress." In *Congress: The First Branch.* Edited by Alfred deGrazia. Washington: American Enterprise Institute for Public Policy Research, 1966.

Peabody, Robert L. and Polsby, Nelson W. *New Perspectives on the House of Representatives.* Chicago: Rand McNally, 1969.

Pennock, J. Roland, and Chapman, John W., *Representation.* New York: Atherton Press, 1968.

Polsby, Nelson W. *Congressional Behavior.* New York: Random House, 1971.

Saloma, John S. III *Congress and the New Politics.* Boston: Little, Brown and Co., 1969.

Shannon, W. Wayne *Party, Constituency, and Congressional Voting.* Baton Rouge: Louisiana State University Press, 1968.

Tacheron, Donald G. and Udall, Morris K., *The Job of the Congressman: An Introduction to Service in the House of Representatives.* Indianapolis: Bobbs-Merrill, 1966.

Truman, David B. (ed.) *Congress and America's Future.* Englewoods Cliffs, N.J.: Prentice-Hall, 1965.

Truman, David B. *The Governmental Process.* New York: Alfred A. Knopf, 1964.

Turner, Julius. *Party and Constituency: Pressures on Congress.* Baltimore: Johns Hopkins Press, 1951.

Wise, Sidney and Schier, Richard F. *Studies on Congress.* New York: Thomas Y. Crowell, 1969.

Wright, James. *You and Your Congressman.* New York: Coward McCann, 1965.

Young, James Sterling. *The Washington Community, 1800-1828.* New York: Columbia University, 1966.

Articles

Cnudde, Charles F. and McCrone, Donald J. "The Linkage Between Constituency Attitudes and Congressional Voting Behavior: A Causal Model." *American Political Science Review,* March 1966.

Davidson, Roger. "Public Prescriptions for the Job of the Congressman." *Midwest Journal of Political Science,* November 1970, pp. 648-666.

Froman, Lewis A., Jr. "Inter-Party Constituency Differences and Congressional Voting Behavior." *American Political Science Review,* March 1963.

Heighberger, Neil. "Representatives' Constituency and National Security." *Western Political Quarterly,* June 1973, pp. 224-235.

Ingram, Helen. "The Impact of Constituency on the Process of Legislating." *American Political Science Review,* March 1963, pp. 45-56.

Kravitz, Walter. "Casework by Members of Congress: A Survey of the Literature." The Library of Congress, Legislative Reference Service, May 4, 1965, revised and expanded Jan. 22, 1968.

Huntington, Samuel P. "A Revised Theory of American Party Politics." *American Political Science Review,* September 1950.

Marascuilo, Leonard A. and Amster, Harriet. "Survey of 1961-62 Congressional Polls." *Public Opinion Quarterly,* Fall 1964.

Miller, Warren E. and Stokes, Donald E. "Constituency Influence in Congress." *American Political Science Review,* Vol. 57 (1963), pp. 45-56.

Oleszek, Walter J., "Age and Political Careers," *Public Opinion Quarterly,* Spring 1969, pp. 100-103.

Rieselbach, Wayne, "Congressmen as 'Small Town' Boys: A Research Note," *Midwest Journal of Political Science,* May 1970, pp. 321-330.

The Press

Of all the pressures on Congress, none is such a two-way proposition as the relationship between members and the press.

While senators and representatives must contend with the peculiarities of the news-gathering business, such as deadlines and limited space or time to describe events, and with constant press scrutiny of their actions, they also must rely on news organizations to inform the public of their legislative accomplishments. At the same time, reporters must depend to some extent on "inside" information from members, a condition that makes many of them reluctant to displease their sources lest the pipeline of information be shut off.

But Congress basically is an open organization. Information flows freely on Capitol Hill and secrets rarely remain secret for long. It has always been true that an enterprising reporter can usually learn what is necessary to write newsworthy copy. But in the 1970s, rules and procedural changes opened to the public and press more activities of Congress than ever before. In the process, new pressures on members were created.

As a result of these changes, almost all committees meet in public session to do their work, including drafting bills. Even the very important conference committee meetings, where final decisions are made on bills, are open. Most floor votes of any significance now are recorded and reporters can observe how members vote in committee.

This new openness has created pressures on members that, although present before, were less intense. Members' actions are subject to closer scrutiny by the press and by constituents—as well as by political opponents.

In terms of numbers of journalists assigned to the congressional "beat," the Hill is covered more thoroughly than any other branch of the federal government. In 1976, the House and Senate press galleries had a membership of approximately 2,700 accredited reporters (including newspaper, periodical, radio and television reporters and photographers)—several times the size of the White House Correspondents Association.

At least a few reporters normally cover every floor session of both chambers and every committee proceeding of any importance except those closed to the public. Reporters often outnumber the members on hand for a committee hearing and sometimes even outnumber the legislators present on the House or Senate floor. As the late Rep. Clement W. Miller (D Calif. 1959-62) put it in his book *Member of the House:* "If the press did not report Congress, Congress could hardly function. If the sound of congressional voices carried no farther than the bare walls of the Chambers, Congress could disband."[1]

Most members of the House and Senate are skilled in public relations and realize that almost every Capitol Hill reporter must file one or more stories each day. That the legislators seek to benefit from this situation is indicated by the stacks of press releases and background statements that almost always inundate both the House and Senate press galleries. Rep. Richard Bolling (D Mo.) said in *House Out of Order:* "...almost any mimeographed statement placed in the gallery is seized upon for news copy. City-reared members, whose only view of a cow has been on a can of condensed milk, can get their names quoted in the press as experts in agriculture. A House member whose travels consist of a triangular course between West Wetdrip, Washington, and the Army-Navy game in Philadelphia can make the news with outrageous remarks about our foreign aid program simply by getting a press handout to the gallery early in the morning. A member who can't keep his family accounts in balance can be quoted on the President's economic message to the Congress provided he looks at an advance copy and sends a statement to the gallery first thing in the morning."[2]

Impact of Press on Government

In exercising their discretion about which news developments to report and how much emphasis to give them, reporters and editors exert considerable impact on the governmental process. James Reston, a vice president and columnist of *The New York Times,* observed in his book *The Artillery of the Press* that, through the news tickers on Capitol Hill and outside the President's office, "the reporters at the White House are constantly conveying the views of the President to the members of the federal legislature, and the reporters in the House and Senate press galleries are similarly serving as a link between what is happening on Capitol Hill and the President and his Cabinet members, who also have news tickers in their offices." Reston added: "The politicians at both ends of Pennsylvania Avenue are particularly sensitive to what the reporters select, what is going out on the air and into the

Freedom of Information and Newsmen's Privilege

Newspaper reporters and other journalists have argued for years that the public's right to know and access to government information are guaranteed by the First Amendment and are essential to the press' functioning as a watchdog over government.

Finding little sympathy in the courts for this interpretation of the First Amendment and faced with widespread executive branch secrecy in the era after World War II, the news media turned to Congress for support. The result was enactment in 1966 of the Federal Public Records Law, known as the Freedom of Information Act.

The law's purpose was to reduce executive branch secrecy by guaranteeing public access to information held by departments and agencies. (Congress was careful not to place itself under the law.) The law was of particular interest to journalists, but was available to anyone who sought government-held information. Consequently, the law was used by some members of Congress and by many lawyers and lobbyists for private interests.

Changes in Law

By the 1970s, however, it was apparent that the law was not operating as intended. A principal problem was the list of exemptions in the law for certain types of documents that allowed agencies to refuse requests for information. As demands for information grew, the tendency of officials to very broadly interpret the exemptions also grew. Other problems were bureaucratic delay, the high cost of bringing suit to force disclosure and excessive charges levied by the agencies to locate and provide requested information.

As a consequence, Congress in 1974 enacted, over the President's veto, the Freedom of Information Act amendments, designed to correct many of the original law's deficiencies. Chief among the 1974 changes were those allowing a federal judge to review a decision of the

government to classify certain material. Classified material had been exempt from the reach of the law. Another provision—particularly irritating to the bureaucracy—set deadlines for an agency or department to respond to a request for information under the law. *(For additional discussion of government secrecy, see p. 282)*

Newsmen's Shield Law

As of 1976, the news media had been less successful in its attempt to obtain shield legislation to protect confidentiality of sources. Hearings on the issue first began in 1971 in the Senate Judiciary Subcommittee on Constitutional Rights, chaired by Sam J. Ervin Jr. (D N.C.). House hearings in September 1972 followed a Supreme Court decision in June of that year (*Branzburg v. Hayes*, 408 U.S. 665) in which the court held that the government may compel newsmen to reveal sources of information during the course of grand jury investigations.

A qualified shield bill failed to reach the House floor in 1973 due to opposition from newsmen who felt that partial protection was worse than no legislation at all.

During the 1973 hearings on legislative proposals to delineate a newsman's right to withhold information from his government, the following questions were raised:

● Does Congress have authority to enact such a privilege?

● Should the privilege be absolute or qualified?

● Should it apply at federal and state levels, although 19 states had some form of newsman's shield law?

Some of the proposed bills were opposed by spokesmen for the news media on the grounds that the protection did not go far enough; others were opposed by the Justice Department as too broad. The result was an impasse: "This is the most difficult field I have ever tried to write a bill in," admitted Ervin on the final day of hearings before his committee.

Sources: Congressional Quarterly, *1974 Almanac*, pp. 648-54; *1973 Almanac*, pp. 383-88; and Robert O. Blanchard, ed., *Congress and the News Media* (Hastings House Publishers, 1974), pp. 439-57.

headlines, for this often produces strong reactions among the voters outside Washington. In the battle for the appropriation of money, for example, the dramatic news of military requirements tends to get a larger play than the less spectacular news about foreign aid, and this news emphasis on the military undoubtedly helps assure more votes for the armed services than for the foreign aid programs."[3]

Some students of government fear that constant headline-grabbing by legislators creates an imbalance in Washington news coverage at the expense of the other branches of government. Journalist Douglass Cater observed in *The Fourth Branch of Government:* "Collectively, reinforced by the publicity-making mechanisms of the congressional committees, it [the headline-grabbing] gives a congressional bias to the news which creates certain advantages for the legislative branch of government in its continuing power struggle with the executive. It contributes

at times to a constitutional imbalance that seems to be a recurrent disorder in American government.... When Congress is in session, Capitol Hill becomes a mecca for large numbers of the press. The syndicated columnist and the reporter for the provincial paper hurry along the long corridors to the committee sessions or crowd into the congested press conferences called by the legislative potentates. Day after day the bulk of the news that flows out of Washington is congressional-oriented."[4]

On the other hand, numerous members of Congress have complained that the executive branch dominates the news. During 1970 hearings on legislation that would guarantee to Congress public service time on the national television networks, Sen. J. William Fulbright (D Ark.) said: "...Congress is at a great disadvantage...in discussing most issues because the executive has a near monopoly on effective access to the public attention. The President can command a national television audience to hear his views on controversial matters at prime time, on short notice, at whatever length he chooses, and at no expense to the federal government or to his party. Other constitutional office-holders are compelled to reply on highly selective newspaper articles and television news spots, which at most will convey bits and snatches of their points of view, usually selected in such a way as to create an impression of cranky carping at an heroic and beleaguered President."5

Early Fight for Press Freedom

As first conceived, the American form of government provided no legal protection for a press bent on purusing the activities of government officials. The Constitution, as originally framed, omitted any guaranty of freedom of speech or of the press. This omission was criticized by Thomas Jefferson, who was in France at the time of the Constitutional Convention. In early 1787, Jefferson had written from Paris: "The people are the only censors of their governors; and even their errors will tend to keep these to the true principles of their institution. To punish these errors too severely would be to suppress the only safeguard of the public liberty. The way to prevent these irregular interpositions of the people is to give them full information of their affairs thru the channel of the public papers, & to contrive that those papers should penetrate the whole mass of the people. The basis of our government being the opinion of the people, the very first object should be to keep that right; and were it left to me to decide whether we should have a government without newspapers or newspapers without a government, I should not hesitate for a moment to prefer the latter."6

The main opposition to a guaranty of press freedom came from Alexander Hamilton, who wrote in *The Federalist* (No. 84): "What signifies a declaration that 'the liberty of the press shall be inviolably preserved'? What is the liberty of the press? Who can give it any definition which would not leave the utmost latitude for evasion? I hold it to be impracticable; and from this, I infer, that its security, whatever fine declarations may be inserted in any Constitution respecting it, must altogether depend on public opinion, and on the general spirit of the people and of the government."7 At the Constitutional Convention, Hamilton had been able to repel attempts by James Madison and George Mason to add to the Constitution a Bill of Rights including a guarantee of freedom of the press.

Advocates of constitutional protection of freedom of the press finally won the struggle in 1791, when Virginia became the necessary tenth state to ratify a new Bill of Rights consisting of 10 constitutional amendments. The first of the amendments provided that "Congress shall make no law respecting an establishment of religion, or prohibiting the free exercise thereof; or abridging the freedom of speech, or of the press; or the right of the people peaceably to assemble, and to petition the government for a redress of grievances."

The rivalry that had developed between Hamilton and Jefferson and their opposing concepts of government grew more intense during the first decade of the Republic. Both Hamilton, the leader of the Federalist party, and Jefferson, leader of the Democratic-Republican (later simply Democratic) Party, relied heavily on the press to advance their own views of government. The result was an era of partisan journalism in which both sides used party organs to at-tack the other. This vigorous press battle, fought mainly by the Federalist *Gazette of the United States* and the Republican *National Gazette* and later the *Aurora,* culminated in the several Alien and Sedition Acts of 1798. One of the main purposes of the acts passed by the Federalist Congress was to curb the Republican press and to deport some Republican journalists born abroad and not yet naturalized.

The Alien Act, which was never actually enforced and which expired by limitation in 1800, authorized the President to deport all such aliens "as he shall judge dangerous to the peace and safety of the United States, or shall have reasonable grounds to suspect are concerned in any treasonable or secret machinations against the government." The Alien Enemies Act, aimed at the French, did not go into force because current naval hostilities with France did not lead to a declaration of war. The Sedition Act, among other things, made it a crime, punishable by up to two years' imprisonment and $2,000 in fines, to speak, write or publish any "false, scandalous and malicious" writing against the government or its high officials with "intent to defame the said government...."8 Several newspapermen were fined under the act and a few were sent to prison. All were pardoned, however, when Jefferson became President on March 4, 1801, the day after the act expired by limitation. Congress eventually reimbursed the journalists for the fines they had paid.

First Press Coverage of Congress

Like the concept of freedom of the press, newspaper coverage of Congress was not envisioned by the Founders of the Republic. Following the example of the British Parliament, which had never admitted reporters to its proceedings (and continued to exclude them until 1834), the U.S. House and Senate both adopted rules in 1789 excluding reporters from their sessions. The rules were short-lived, however, as the House opened its proceedings to press coverage in 1790 and the Senate did the same in 1793.9 In 1841, the Senate excluded reporters of local Washington newspapers in order to benefit the national party organs then prevalent in the capital. Since that time, neither chamber has sought to exclude correspondents except from executive sessions. However, some individual reporters have been excluded for misconduct or other violation of the standing rules of the press galleries.

The next major step in the evolution of press coverage of Congress was taken in 1802, when Samuel Harrison Smith, editor of a Republican paper, the *National Intelligencer,* obtained permission from the House Speaker to make and publish stenographic reports of House debates. Such permission had been denied Smith the year before when the House was evenly divided between Federalists and Republicans. For years, the reports in the *Intelligencer* were the only printed records of congressional proceedings. The *Intelligencer* became the official organ of the Republican administration and remained so until the outset of the John Quincy Adams administration in 1825, when the *National Journal* became the official organ.

Under the Jackson administration, *The Globe* was the administration organ, and it remained so through the Van Buren administration. While all three of these papers were administration organs, they received lucrative government printing contracts. For a time, the owners of the *Intelligencer* did a thriving business in reporting the debates and proceedings of Congress in book form under the name of

Register of Debates. In 1832, the *Globe* entered this field with a similar publication called the *Congressional Globe.* In 1838, the *Register of Debates* ceased publication, leaving the field to the *Congressional Globe.*[10]

Checks on Votes of Members

In modern times, the *Congressional Record,* a nonpartisan publication of Congress, has provided a check for the press and public on the breakdown of roll-call votes. The *Record* has been unreliable, however, as a reference on congressional debates, because members are permitted to edit their remarks before the *Record* goes to the printer. In addition, the *Record* did not record the breakdown of teller and standing votes, under which much important business was conducted in the House. However, the Legislative Reorganization Act of 1970 required that a breakdown of teller votes be recorded. Previously, the only check on members during a non-record vote was provided by teams of reporters who watched the vote and published the breakdown. *(See p. 337 for additional discussion of the Record)*

In the years since World War II, a further check on members has been made by Congressional Quarterly, which publishes breakdowns of every roll-call vote taken in the House and Senate and provides an annual analysis of each member's voting record from the standpoint of party support and other considerations. In addition, CQ prints the highlights of congressional debates, detailed provisions of bills, analyses of legislative strategy and lobbying campaigns, reports on members' financial interests, reports on the number of committee proceedings held in closed session and provides various other analyses of congressional activities.

In addition, a number of pressure groups keep tabs on members' voting records and publish periodic ratings. *(See chapter on lobbies, p. 653)*

Growth of Press Corps at Capitol

Over the years, the number of correspondents covering Congress has increased markedly. In 1813-14, there were only four congressional correspondents, and in 1823 only 12. By 1868 the number had risen to 58; by 1900 to 171; and by 1930 to 251. By 1960 the size of the congressional press corps had jumped to 1,326 and by 1976 to about 2,700.

Facilities for accommodating the correspondents have been expanded accordingly. Galleries above the House and Senate chambers provide ample room for viewing congressional debates. Typewriters, telephones and teletype machines are available. Huge leather couches, coffee and candy machine also are provided.

Studios just off the House and Senate floor provide facilities for television and radio broadcasts and interviews. (TV and radio coverage of floor sessions was not allowed in either house as of 1976, although proposals to change this restriction were receiving serious consideration. However, exceptions are made in the case of such major events as the President's State of the Union Message and other presidential appearances and speeches by other prominent persons. The Senate long has consented to live television and radio coverage of committee proceedings, but the House banned such coverage from 1952 until late 1970, when the Legislative Reorganization Act carried a provision authorizing it at the discretion of a majority of each House committee. But few committees took advantage of the opportunity. *(Box, p. 357)*

Congress has made ample provisions to help members get their message through to the vast press apparatus on Capitol Hill. Most members (particularly senators) have a full-time press specialist, usually an experienced journalist, who is paid out of the member's staff allowance. These specialists crank out reams of press releases, directed at both the national and the local press.

An equally important public relations tool is provided by the House and Senate recording studios, which enable members to make low-cost TV and radio reports to their constituents. In these studios members can make a five-minute color film for a minimal cost. The tapes are sent to television and radio stations in the member's district or state, which are usually glad to put them on the air. The station not only gets free Washington coverage but applies the air time for the tapes against its obligation to devote a share of its programing to public service broadcasts. *(See chapter on pay and perquisites, p. 457)*

Congressional Use of the Press

The mere size of the Capitol Hill press corps puts such a premium on "exclusive" information that most reporters find themselves pressured to court news sources more assiduously than might be necessary on other beats. As Douglass Cater observed, "A great amount of news is dispensed to...[the reporter] as a favor and must be regarded as such."[11] Reporters who ruffle the feathers of too many congressional sources are likely to find themselves consistently "beaten" on stories by competing media.

Pressures to conform are a particularly serious problem for the small Washington bureau, which usually centers its coverage on a handful of congressional offices and relies on legislators to keep it informed of executive or regulatory agency action concerning its city or state. Pat Munroe, a veteran Washington newsman, observed in a 1966 study, *The Press in Washington:* "To cover Washington effectively for a paper interested in the local angle... [the reporter] is almost compelled to keep the lines to the congressional office open and friendly. If they are not, he can be effectively frozen out of major news stories, since the Hill is the nerve center for all the Washington news concerning his state. He runs this risk if he writes stories that are critical of the senator or congressman from his state. Yet there are always occasions when a good reporter feels compelled to write a story that reveals the legislator as something less than the great white knight. The reporter in this case must have the complete support of his editor. If the editor is not willing to risk getting scooped by the competition at some time in the future because the congressional source decides to retaliate, the reporter's hands are tied...."[12]

Just as reporters obtain much useful information from members of Congress, so the press frequently transmits substantive information that senators and representatives find useful in their work. Members read newspapers to discover what is occurring in Congress itself, because the number of committee meetings makes it virtually impossible to keep abreast of everything. In addition, members of Congress frequently rely on newspapers to keep up with events in their constituencies and to gauge constituency reactions.

In his discussion of Congress and the press, Delmer D. Dunn has noted: "Understanding congressional press relations requires differentiation not only between national and local media but also between their use by senators and representatives. While senatorial advantages are strongest with regard to the national media, they at times extend to the local or regional media as well. Senators are more interesting news targets than congressmen for several reasons. Many openly aspire to higher political office.... In addition, the Senate generally considers questions of broad public policy more openly than the House....

"Although representatives, by comparison to senators, rarely make the national media, there is some reversal with regard to the local or regional media. Representatives usually have deeper roots within their constituencies than do senators."[13]

Members of Congress seeking press coverage can acquire it in a variety of ways: through press releases, weekly news columns or radio or television programs, personal interviews with reporters, floor speeches, press conferences and briefings and investigations. Ironically, diligent attention to congressional work often does not help a member gain public attention and press coverage.

Senator Johnson and the Press

Leaders of both houses of Congress work especially hard to ensure that their own and their party's actions get favorable publicity. For instance, Sen. Lyndon B. Johnson (D Texas) benefited enormously in the mid-1950s from his close relationship with William S. White, a Texan who was covering the Senate for *The New York Times.* James Reston has noted that after White's resignation Johnson became disturbed when Reston, then the *Times'* Washington bureau chief, assigned first one reporter and then another to the job. "At this point," Reston said, "Mr. Johnson took me aside and asked what was going on. He had to know who was covering him, he said. He couldn't have one fellow one day and another the next. I tried to explain, but it was no use. He simply thought of the job in personal terms...."[14]

Not all members seek the favor of the press as vigorously as some do. A few members actually shun publicity because of fears of being misquoted or of having their views oversimplified or taken out of context. Among the members who have expressed such misgivings was the late Rep. Clem Miller, who complained in *Member of the House* that the press expected members to talk in cliches in order to simplify their reporting job and help them to meet deadlines. "We have become a nation of headline readers," Miller said. "It is not at all surprising that the working press has come to require the same of politicians in its day-to-day reporting. The result is distortion, the inevitable distortion that comes from oversimplification and compression.... What all this means in terms of Congress is that the congressman who tailors his speech and remarks to the strictures of modern reporting is going to get in the news; and he who doesn't is going to have difficult sledding. It means that many capable legislators operate fairly silently, while others who might be of inferior competence are heard from quite frequently."[15]

Publicity Through Investigations

By far the member's most effective method of achieving publicity is through congressional investigations, particularly investigations that lend themselves to sensational headlines. As Douglass Cater observed, the investigation "is geared to the production of headlines on a daily and even twice daily basis. It is able to create the news story which lingers week after week on the front pages to form an indelible impression on the public mind. No institution of the executive branch is capable of such sustained and well-manipulated publicity."[16]

The Problem of Leaks

While representatives and senators frequently attempt to use news leaks for their own advantage, Congress has long been plagued by improper or injudicious release of information received in confidence.

As early as 1812, Nathaniel Rounsavell, editor of the Alexandria, Virginia, *Herald,* was cited for contempt of Congress for refusing to answer questions about leaks from a secret House session. During the Civil War, the Radical Republicans on the Joint Committee on the Conduct of the War publicized information gathered in closed sessions when it suited their purposes.

"But never, it is safe to say, has Congress experienced such a frenetic outpouring of supposedly confidential information as emanated from the [Senate Watergate Committee]," wrote James Hamilton, who was on the panel's legal staff, in his book, *The Power to Probe.* "The leaks were the major stain on the committee's performance. They severely jeopardized its credibility and the integrity of its proceedings. At times they made committee members and staff—including those *not* leaking—appear as publicity-grabbing buffoons incapable of keeping their own counsel and conducting conscientious investigations into serious matters. Moreover, the leaks were illegal in that they violated the committee's own rules, and arguably some of them had criminal implications."

Hamilton's observation was seconded by Sen. Howard Baker, Jr. (R Tenn.), vice chairman of the committee, who commented "The [Senate] committee did not invent the leak, but we elevated it to its highest art form."

The leaks assumed what Hamilton termed "ludicrous proportions" as the committee staff began preparing the final report. Every draft section of the report was released to the press within moments after being sent to the committee members for review. Such leakage was "shamefully unfair to certain persons under investigation," he noted. Part of the blame, however, lay with the recipients of the leaks. "The coverage of the [Watergate] committee investigations was marked by strenuous competition among newsmen for confidential information," wrote Hamilton. "For a reporter to obtain a major leak was viewed in the press as a badge of honor." On the other hand, he also pointed out that Watergate—and many other major investigations— might not have been undertaken without the independent investigations and disclosures of the press.

Source: James Hamilton, *The Power to Probe. A Study of Congressional Investigations* (Random House, 1976), chapter IX. See also Robert O. Blanchard, ed., *Congress and the News Media* (Hastings House Publishers, 1974), pp. 458-87.

In the early 1950s, televised hearings of the Senate Special Committee to Investigate Organized Crime in Interstate Commerce and the probe by the Permanent Investigations Subcommittee of the Senate Government Operations Committee into alleged Communist infiltration of the government made national celebrities out of the committee chairmen, Senators Estes Kefauver (D Tenn.) and Joseph R. McCarthy (R Wis.), respectively. Kefauver was transformed almost instantly from a little-known senator to a leading competitor for his party's presidential nomination. McCarthy dominated the headlines for months and became one of the most powerful and most feared members of the Senate until the public tired of his attacks on government officials and his colleagues censured him for misconduct. *(See also Kefauver, McCarthy and Watergate investigations, pp. 165-68)*

According to Cater, "The most notable committee investigations are seldom in point of fact 'investigations.'" He said: "They are planned deliberately to move from a preconceived idea to a predetermined conclusion. The skill and resourcefulness of the chairman and a sizable staff are pitted against any effort to alter its destined course. Whatever investigating is done takes place well in advance of the public hearing. The hearing is the final act of the drama. Its intent, by the staging of an arresting spectacle, is to attract public attention, to alarm or to allay, to enlighten, or, yes, sometimes to obscure."[17]

That members consciously plan such spectacles was documented by a committee memorandum which fell into the hands of the press. This memo, written in 1943 by the counsel of a House committee investigating the Federal Communications Commission, advised committee members as follows:

"(1) Decide what you want the newspapers to hit hardest and then shape each hearing so that the main point becomes the vortex of the testimony. Once that vortex is reached, *adjourn.*

"(2) In handling press releases, first put a release date on them, reading something like this: 'For release at 10 a.m. EST July 6,' etc. If you do this, you can give releases out as much as 24 hours in advance, thus enabling reporters to study them and write better stories.

"(3) Limit the number of people authorized to speak for the committee, to give out press releases or to provide the press with information to the *fewest number possible.* It plugs leaks and helps preserve the concentration of purpose.

"(4) Do not permit distractions to occur, such as extraneous fusses with would-be witnesses, which might provide news that would bury the testimony which you want featured.

"(5) Do not space hearings more than 24 or 48 hours apart when on a controversial subject. This gives the opposition too much opportunity to make all kind of counter-charges and replies by issuing statements to the newspapers.

"(6) Don't ever be afraid to recess a hearing even for five minutes, so that you can keep the proceedings completely in control so far as creating news is concerned.

"(7) *And this is most important:* don't let the hearings or the evidence ever descend to the plane of a personal fight between the committee chairman and the head of the agency being investigated. The high plane of a duly-authorized committee of the House of Representatives *examining* the operations of an agency of the executive branch for constructive purposes should be maintained at all costs."[18]

Impact of Press on Congress

When the press chooses to exert its influence on Congress, the impact is often enormous. Throughout the nation's history, press coverage has mobilized public opin-

ion behind positions—both constructive and otherwise—that have influenced congressional action.

Recent examples of this impact have included news media coverage of the Vietnam War as well as the Senate Foreign Relations Committee hearings on the subject, and the press and TV coverage of the Senate Watergate Committee hearings and House Judiciary Committee impeachment proceedings. In these cases, the interdependent and reciprocal actions of the media and Congress served to intensify public concern about the subjects under investigation. Below are other examples of the impact that the press can have on congressional actions:

War With Spain. Newspaper reports by the so-called "yellow press" in New York in the late 1890s created a climate of hostility toward Spain that helped to precipitate the Spanish-American War. For months, the *New York World,* owned by Joseph Pulitzer, and the *New York Journal,* owned by William Randolph Hearst, sought to outdo each other with stories on Spanish atrocities in Cuba, then a possession of Spain. Hearst's *Journal* was generally the more aggressive of the two papers in sensationalizing the Cuban incidents, and Hearst candidly admitted that war would be good for his paper's circulation.

President William McKinley sought to keep the nation out of the war, but the wave of hysteria whipped up by the *World* and the *Journal* eventually proved too much for both Congress and McKinley. The final blow came on Feb. 15, 1898, when the U.S. battleship *Maine* was blown up in Havana harbor. The *Journal's* banner headline Feb. 17 read, "The warship *Maine* was Split in Two by an Enemy's Secret Infernal Machine."[19] Even before a naval court of inquiry could investigate the incident, the Hearst press was contending that the Spanish were responsible. (As it developed, the court of inquiry was unable to fix the blame.) On April 25, 1898, Congress declared war on Spain.

'Muckrakers.' In the early 1900s, a number of investigative articles by magazine reporters, who became known collectively as the "muckrakers," resulted in a large body of reform legislation, including the Seventeenth Amendment (providing for direct election of senators), the Pure Food and Drug Act and other measures.

Among the most notable of the muckraking reports was a series of articles by David Graham Phillips, appearing in *Cosmopolitan* magazine in 1906, entitled "The Treason of the Senate." In his first article, Phillips charged: "The treason of the Senate! Treason is a strong word, but not too strong, rather too weak, to characterize the situation in which the Senate is eager, resourceful, indefatigable agent of interests as hostile to the American people as any invading Army could be, and vastly more dangerous: interests that manipulate the prosperity produced by all, so that it heaps up riches for the few, interests whose growth and power can only mean the degradation of the people, of the educated into sycophants, of the masses toward serfdom.... The senators are not elected by the people; they are elected by the 'interests.'"[20] Phillips proceeded to link many of the leading members of the Senate to large corporations and political machines.

Louis Filler concluded in a book entitled *Crusaders for American Liberalism* that the impact of Phillips' articles had "broken down those adamant walls of the Senate." He then pointed out: "Freer discussion of senatorial personages and powers followed. A number of senators were unseated in the next elections, and others were dropped from the rolls in succeeding years until, by 1912, the composition of the chamber had changed completely.... An amendment to the

An Exchange of Telegrams

William Randolph Hearst's attitude toward prospects of war with Spain over Cuba was illuminated in 1897 by the following telegraphic exchange between the publisher of the *New York Journal* and Frederic Remington, his special correspondent in Havana:

HEARST, JOURNAL, NY:
      EVERYTHING IS QUIET. THERE IS NO TROUBLE HERE. THERE WILL BE NO WAR. WISH TO RETURN. REMINGTON.

REMINGTON, HAVANA:
      PLEASE REMAIN. YOU FURNISH THE PICTURES AND I'LL FURNISH THE WAR. W. R. HEARST.

Constitution was drafted and triumphantly adopted, and the power of direct election of senators was at last given to the people."[21]

Muckraking reports by Mark Sullivan in *Collier's* magazine had a similar effect on reform in the House. Throughout 1909 and 1910, Sullivan, in his weekly column, "Comment About Congress," campaigned for the defeat of Rep. Joseph G. Cannon (R Ill.) in his bid for re-election as Speaker in the 1911 session of Congress. Sullivan's columns showed systematically how Cannon had carried out the will of special interests and had thwarted democratic rule in the House through his exploitation of the House rules and domination of the Rules Committee. This situation, as Sullivan described it, pressured House members "to act on bills the way Cannon wished them acted upon; to report out for action those that Cannon wanted out, to keep in committee those that Cannon wanted repressed."[22] With public opinion running strongly against Cannon, Republican insurgents banded together with Democrats early in the 1910 session to strip Cannon of much of his power. Cannon lost his post as Speaker when Democrats won control of the House in the next session of Congress *(See pp. 43-45)*

League of Nations. Press coverage of President Wilson's drive for Senate ratification of the Treaty of Versailles, containing the Covenant of the League of Nations, was believed to have helped tip the scales against ratification in 1919. As journalist Ray Tucker described it in a magazine article in 1933, a small group of correspondents "conspired hourly with the 'irreconcilables,'...tipped off most of the congressmen to Wilsonian statements and maneuvers, and started senatorial counterattacks before the war President could unlimber his orators." Tucker continued: "They wrote philippics for the Borahs, Johnsons and Reeds, cooked up interviews, ...carried on independent research into the League's implications, dug up secret material. Their dispatches bristled with personal hostility to the League, and the carbon copies which they distributed to pro-Wilson writers affected even the latter's supposedly favorable articles. The Covenant was defeated by the Senate press gallery long before it was finally rejected by the Senate."[23] *(See also League of Nations p. 259)*

Teapot Dome. Investigative reports by the press in 1922 prompted congressional action that led to full exposure of the Teapot Dome oil scandal and prosecution of the government officials involved. Reporters from the *Denver Post* and *Albuquerque Morning Journal* traced receipts for racehorses and cattle received by Interior Secretary Albert B. Fall and found that they had been sent by oilman Harry F. Sinclair, whom Fall had permitted, without competitive bidding, to lease the Teapot Dome oil field in east central Wyoming, a reserve long set aside for the Navy. A subsequent investigation by Paul Y. Anderson of the *St. Louis Post-Dispatch* gave Senate investigators the information they needed to fully document the scandal. The Senate investigation led to criminal convictions of Fall and several other prominent officials of the Harding administration.[24] *(See also Teapot Dome p. 163)*

Dodd, Powell Incidents. In the late 1960s, press reports of alleged improprieties by Rep. Adam C. Powell (D N.Y.) and Sen. Thomas J. Dodd (D Conn.) led to Powell's exclusion from the House and Dodd's censure by the Senate. In the aftermath of the two incidents, the House and Senate both adopted tougher codes of ethics regarding the conduct of their members. *(See chapter on seating and disciplining of members, p. 681)*

Similar pressures for reform occurred in 1976, following news reports of alleged improprieties on the part of Rep. Wayne L. Hays (D Ohio) and several other members of Congress. *(See ethics chapter, p. 699)*

Several congressional observers have attributed Congress' increased sensitivity to the 1976 Capitol Hill scandals to the aggressive coverage of the allegations in the national press and the fact that the scandals became known in an election year.

Renegotiation Board. In 1968, a single newsman was widely credited with providing the impetus that steered a major bill through Congress. Over a period of several months, Sanford Watman, Washington correspondent of the *Cleveland Plain Dealer,* filed a series of stories revealing pressures by powerful business interests against renewing the life of the Rengotiation Board, the agency that handles recapture of excessive profits realized by private companies on contracts with government agencies. The *Plain Dealer* articles spurred four members of the Ohio delegation—Reps. Jackson E. Betts (R), Michael A. Feighan (D), William E. Minshall (R) and Charles A. Vanik (D) into supporting continuation of the board.

Two of the Ohio representatives—Betts and Vanik—were members of the House Ways and Means Committee, which had jurisdiction over the bill. In the committee, the Ohioans were joined in support of the measure by Reps. Martha W. Griffiths (D Mich.), a former government procurement officer, and James A. Burke (D Mass.), who also was under pressure from his hometown newspaper, *The Boston Globe.* Together, these four members pushed the bill through to enactment. Committee sources told Congressional Quarterly that the bill probably would have died in committee without the *Plain Dealer* articles.[25]

Members' Attacks on Newsmen

Despite the constitutional guarantee of freedom of the press, Congress sometimes has attempted to intimidate reporters and editors and to discredit their papers' editorial policies.

One of the most noteworthy of these cases occurred in 1915, when a Senate committee chaired by Sen. Thomas J. Walsh (D Mont.) probed the motives of the *New York Times* in publishing editorials opposing an administration

'The Selling of the Pentagon': Congress vs. TV

A major confrontation between Congress and the news media occurred in 1971, after CBS on Feb. 23 and March 23 broadcast on television a controversial and award-winning documentary, "The Selling of the Pentagon." The program, which attacked the public relations efforts of the Defense Department, led to a clash between television and Congress that was similar in many respects to the clash between the print media *(The New York Times)* and the executive branch over publication of the Pentagon Papers that year.

The documentary drew strong criticism from some members of Congress as well as Defense Department officials who charged that CBS during film editing had altered the words and meaning of statements made in interviews used in the telecast.

On April 7, the Interstate and Foreign Commerce Investigations Subcommittee, chaired by Rep. Harley O. Staggers (D W.Va.), who also was chairman of the full committee, subpoenaed all materials related to the documentary—film, recordings outtakes, transcripts, identification of staff and records of funds disbursed. Staggers insisted that the outtakes (film and sound recordings) were needed to determine what editing practices CBS had used. This was necessary, he said, so Congress could protect the public interest.

On April 20, CBS refused to comply with the subpoena. The network's president, Dr. Frank Stanton, contended that the subpoenaed materials were like a reporter's notes, protected by the First Amendment. The network, however, did furnish a transcript and copy of the televised film; later it supplied some other material related to the subpoena. On May 26, the subcommittee rescinded its original subpoena and issued an order for the outtakes and Stanton's appearance.

"The crucial issue," wrote Jerome Barron in an article on the subject, "was whether the outtakes, film shot for use in the program but not actually used, must be submitted to Congress.

"From the point of view of the House committee, the capacity of television to propagandize a nation was something that was within the scope of both legislative control and legislative inquiry.... In the view of CBS, the

editing processes of television were obviously protected by the First Amendment. Surely the government would not be permitted to subpoena a newspaper editor's notes. How therefore could a governmental inquiry into film editing on television be justified?"

Appearing before the subcommittee June 24, Stanton refused to provide the specified materials. The refusal brought a prompt statement from Staggers: "In my opinion, you are now in contempt." On July 1, the full committee voted 25-13 to cite CBS and Stanton for contempt of Congress.

But the House refused to do so; on July 13, it voted 226-181 to send the contempt resolution back to committee, in effect killing the measure.

During floor debate, Staggers said the entire issue was a "very simple one." He argued that since CBS had refused to supply the requested material, the network was in contempt of Congress. To his critics he said: "There has been an awful lot of talk about the First Amendment. I do not believe the First Amendment is involved in this question in any way whatsoever."

But House Judiciary Chairman Emanuel Celler (D N.Y.) disagreed. "The First Amendment," he said, "towers over these proceedings like a colossus."

"The collision here is between the privilege of the press to edit for journalistic purposes and the privilege of the Congress to investigate for legislative purposes," argued Richard H. Poff (R Va.) in opposing the resolution. "The collision is between the government and the governed.... Whenever two great constitutional privileges collide," he concluded, "one must yield.... I will prefer the governed. I will choose freedom."

Although most members usually support a committee's contempt recommendation, that congressional courtesy was disregarded as the House leadership, committee chairmen, liberal Democrats, freshmen representatives and some conservatives backed away from Staggers' request. As a result of the recommittal, concluded Barron, "a case that might have resulted in a great judicial decision which would have identified the First Amendment responsibilities and obligations of government and broadcasting...was aborted."

Sources: Jerome Barron, " 'The Selling of the Pentagon': Partisan Involvements and Antagonisms," in Robert O. Blanchard, ed., *Congress and the News Media* (Hastings House Publishers, 1974), pp. 406-10; excerpts from the House debate in Blanchard, pp. 410-38; Congressional Quarterly, *1971 Almanac,* pp. 801-803. See also chapter on Congressional Investigations, p. 141, for discussion of the contempt power.

bill to authorize purchase of foreign ships interned in American harbors at the start of World War I. Charles Ransom Miller, editor-in-chief of the *Times,* and Carr V. Van Anda, managing editor, were brought before the committee and queried on the *Times'* financial backing and its news and editorial policies. Both editors answered the committee's questions, but at the close of the hearing Miller said: "I can see no ethical, moral or legal right that you have to put many of the questions you put to me today. Inquisitorial proceedings of this kind would have a very marked tendency, if continued and adopted as a policy, to reduce the press of the United States to the level of the press

in some of the Central European empires, the press that has been known as the reptile press, that crawls on its belly every day to the foreign office or to the government officials and ministers to know what it may say or shall say—to receive its orders."[26]

The next major confrontation between a congressional committee and the press was in 1936. The House Committee on Military Affairs subpoenaed a *Washington Herald* reporter who had linked Rep. John J. McSwain (D S.C.), a member of the committee, to a group of war-surplus speculators. The reporter, Frank C. Waldrop, declined to answer the committee's questions on the ground that the panel was proceeding improperly "pursuant to a threat of its chairman and without legislative purpose."[27] J. R. Wiggins, then managing editor of *The Washington Post,* gave this account of the proceedings years later in an article in *Nieman Reports:*

"The committee, particularly its chairman, became enraged at this challenge. The chairman ordered the reporter to take the stand, administered the oath, and then asked, 'Your name is Frank C. Waldrop, is it not?'

"With a smile, the witness replied, 'Upon the advice of counsel, I decline to answer.'

"Then followed one of the most disgraceful exhibitions in the history of congressional inquisitions...; finally he [Waldrop] was told to stand down, but to hold himself subject to recall.

"The committee proceeded for several days with its inquiry. As witness after witness gave more and more damaging testimony, its chairman became more and more embarrassed.

"On April 15, a halt was called. At an executive session the committee voted unanimously to end its inquiry, not to print the record of its proceedings, and to make no report to the House.

"The following day Mr. Waldrop's counsel demanded and obtained a cancellation of his subpoena. Thus did a courageous reporter, in the face of threats, innuendo, and malicious insult, uphold the traditions of American journalism."[28]

An even more stormy episode occurred in 1953, when the McCarthy subcommittee questioned James A. Wechsler, editor of the *New York Post,* on his paper's editorial policy. According to an account by journalist Alan Barth in his book *Government by Investigation,* "...Wechsler was led by the subcommittee counsel, Roy Cohn, to acknowledge what was already well known and what he had never attempted to conceal—that he had joined the Young Communist League when he was 18 years old, in his junior year at Columbia University; he managed to say also what was equally well known, that he had left the Young Communist League and the whole of the Communist movement by the end of 1937, when he was 22, and had been militantly and articulately anti-Communist every since."[29]

Following this discussion, McCarthy launched a lengthy attack on Wechsler's editorial page, which the senator contended "...always leads the vanguard, with the *Daily Worker,* follows the same line, against anyone who is willing to expose Communists in government." At the close of the hearing, Wechsler retorted: "I regard this proceeding, as the first in a long line of attempts to intimidate editors who do not equate McCarthyism with patriotism."[30] The Wechsler incident produced much public animosity toward McCarthy and the committee. Thereafter, congressional committees were more wary about subpoenaing reporters.

Conflict and Cooperation

While relations between Congress and the press may at times be hostile, there is also considerable cooperation between them. In a series of interviews with congressional correspondents, Robert O. Blanchard found that in general they seemed to enjoy a cooperative relationship with members of Congress. Following are selected comments by reporters.

● "Newsmen and legislators generally have a cooperative attitude with each other concerning records, public affairs, the congressional business. The exceptions are when you get situations where legislators are in a minority position and in a position where they are holding legislative deliberations in less than the public light, in closed session.... Then there tends to be conflict. I think these are somewhat exceptional situations."

● "The essential role of the reporter to the public official is a hostile one. If he steps out of line, you're going to nail him. He knows it and you know it."

● "It depends on what you are doing. This gets right back down to a problem that starts at the lowest point in the newspaper business, covering the police beat. You have to be able to get along with the cops, and you have to be in a position to blow the whistle on the cops. Every newspaperman has gone through this, and you have to resolve it at every level. The question is how close do you get to your sources. If you get so close to them that you can't write anything ugly about them, then you might as well not know them."[31]

Concluding his discussion of Congress and the press, Dunn commented: "Regardless of occasional hostility and suspicion between them, the working relationship of newsman and legislator is fundamental to the democratic process; to be a congressman is to work with the press."[32]

"Communications media have a vast power to shape government—both its policies and its leaders," wrote Cater. "This is not an editorial page power. It is the power to select—out of the tens of thousands of words spoken in Washington each day and the tens of dozens of events—which words and events are projected for mankind to see. Equally powerful is the media's capacity to ignore; those words and events that fail to get projected might as well not have occurred."[33]

Footnotes

1. Clem Miller, *Member of the House: Letters of a Congressman* (Scribner's, 1962), p. 60.
2. Richard Bolling, *House Out of Order* (E. P. Dutton & Co., 1965), p. 147.
3. James Reston, *The Artillery of the Press* (Harper & Row, 1966), pp. 72-73.
4. Douglass Cater, *The Fourth Branch of Government* (Houghton-Mifflin Co., 1959), pp. 47-48.
5. Quoted in Robert O. Blanchard, ed., *Congress and the News Media* (Hastings House Publishers, 1974), p. 104.
6. Willard Grosvenor Bleyer, *Main Currents in the History of American Journalism* (Houghton-Mifflin Co., 1927), p. 103.
7. *The Federalist Papers,* with an Introduction by Clinton Rossiter (Mentor, 1961), No. 84, p. 514.

8. The Alien Act, section 1, *U.S. Statutes at Large,* vol. 1, pp. 570 ff; the Sedition Act, section 2, *U.S. Statutes at Large,* vol. 1, pp. 596-97.
9. Blanchard, *Congress and the News Media,* p. 7.
10. For background on early press coverage of Congress, see Blanchard, pp. 7-40; and F. B. Marbut, *News from the Capital. The Story of Washington Reporting* (Southern Illinois University Press, 1971), pp. 13-83.
11. Cater, *The Fourth Branch of Government,* p. 54.
12. Ray Eldon Hiebert, ed., *The Press in Washington* (Dodd Mead & Co., 1966), p. 15.
13. Delmer D. Dunn, "Symbiosis: Congress and the Press," in Sven Groennings and Jonathan P. Hawley, eds., *To Be a Congressman: The Promise and the Power* (Acropolis Books Ltd., 1973), p. 44.
14. Reston, *The Artillery of the Press,* p. 54.

15. Miller, *Member of the House,* p. 62.
16. Cater, *The Fourth Branch of Government,* p. 56.
17. *Ibid.,* p. 58.
18. *Ibid.,* pp. 58-59.
19. W. A. Swanberg, *Citizen Hearst* (Scribner's, 1961), p. 163.
20. Arthur and Lila Weinberg, *The Muckrakers* (Simon & Schuster, 1961), p. 69.
21. Louis Filler, *Crusaders for American Liberalism* (Harcourt Brace & Co., 1939), pp. 256-57.
22. Mark Sullivan, *The Education of an American* (Doubleday & Co., 1938), p. 248.
23. Ray Tucker, "Part-Time Statesmen," *Collier's,* Oct. 28, 1933, pp. 28-36.

24. William L. Rivers, *The Adversaries. Politics and the Press* (Beacon Press, 1970), p. 24.
25. Congressional Quarterly, *Congress and the Nation, 1965-68,* Vol. II, pp. 857-58.
26. Alan Barth, *Government by Investigation* (Viking Press, 1955), p. 185.
27. *Ibid.,* p. 186.
28. Quoted in *ibid.,* p. 186.
29. *Ibid.,* p. 187.
30. *Ibid.,* p. 189.
31. Blanchard, *Congress and the News Media,* pp. 201-204.
32. Dunn, "Symbiosis: Congress and the Press," p. 50.
33. Quoted in Max M. Kampelman, "Congress, the Media, and the President," in Harvey C. Mansfield Sr., ed., *Congress Against the President* (Praeger Publishers, 1975), p. 90.

Selected Bibliography

Books

Agee, Warren K. *The Press and the Public Interest.* Washington: Public Affairs Press, 1968.

Barth, Alan. *Government by Investigation.* New York: Viking Press, 1955.

Blanchard, Robert O., ed. *Congress and the News Media.* New York: Hastings House Publishers, 1974.

Bleyer, Willard Grosvenor. *Main Currents in the History of American Journalism.* Boston: Houghton Mifflin Co., 1927.

Bolling, Richard. *House Out of Order.* New York: E. P. Dutton & Co., 1965.

Cater, Douglass, *The Fourth Branch of Government.* Boston: Houghton Mifflin Co., 1959.

Chafee, Zechariah, Jr. *Government and Mass Communication.* Chicago: University of Chicago Press, 1947.

Clark, Joseph H. *Congress: The Sapless Branch.* New York: Harper & Row, 1964.

Cohen, Bernard C. *The Press and Foreign Policy.* Princeton: Princeton University Press, 1963.

Daniels, Jonathan. *They Will Be Heard.* New York: McGraw-Hill, 1965.

Dunn, Delmer D. "Symbiosis: Congress and the Press." In *To Be a Congressman: The Promise and the Power."* Edited by Sven Groennings and Jonathan P. Hawley. Washington: Acropolis Books Ltd., 1973.

Edwards, Verne E. Jr. *Journalism in a Free Society.* Dubuque, Iowa: William C. Brown Co., 1970.

Emery, Edwin. *The Press and America: An Interpretative History of the Mass Media.* Englewood Cliffs, N.J.: Prentice-Hall, 1972.

Essery, J. Frederick. *Covering Washington: Government Reflected to the Public in the Press, 1822-1926.* Boston: Houghton Mifflin, 1927.

Filler, Louis. *Crusaders for American Liberalism.* New York: Harcourt Brace and Co., 1939. .

Hamilton, James. *The Power To Probe.* New York: Random House, 1976.

Hiebert, Ray Eldon, ed. *The Press in Washington.* New York: Dodd Mead & Co., 1966.

Kampelman, Max M. "Congress, the Media, and the President." In *Congress Against the President.* Edited by Harvey C. Mansfield Sr. New York: Praeger, 1975.

Key, V. O. Jr. *Public Opinion and American Democracy.* New York: Alfred A. Knopf, 1961.

Krieghbaum, Hillier. *Pressures on the Press.* New York: Thomas Y. Crowell Co., 1972.

Krock, Arthur. *Memoirs: Sixty Years on the Firing Line.* New York: Funk & Wagnalls, 1968.

McGaffin, William and Knoll, Erwin. *Anything But the Truth: The Credibility Gap; How the News is Managed in Washington.* New York: Putnam, 1968.

Marbut, F. B. *News from the Capital. The Story of Washington Reporting.* Carbondale: Southern Illinois University Press, 1971.

Merrill, John C. *The Imperative of Freedom: A Philosophy of Journalistic Autonomy.* New York: Hastings House, 1974.

Miller, Clem. *Member of the House: Letters of a Congressman.* New York: Scribner's, 1962.

Mott, Frank Luther. *American Journalism: A History 1690-1960.* New York: Macmillan Co., 1962.

Nimmo, Dan D. *Newsgathering in Washington.* New York: Atherton Press, 1964.

Phillips, Cabell, ed. *Dateline: Washington.* New York: Doubleday & Co., 1949.

Reston, James. *The Artillery of the Press.* New York: Harper & Row, 1966.

Rivers, William L. *The Adversaries. Politics and the Press.* Boston: Beacon Press, 1970.

Ross, Ishbel. *Ladies of the Press.* New York: Harper & Bros., 1936.

Rosten, Leo C. *The Washington Correspondents.* New York: Harcourt, Brace & Co., 1937.

Rubin, Bernard. *Political Television.* Belmont, Calif.: Wadsworth Publishing Co., 1967.

Siebert, Fredrick Seaton. *The Rights and Privileges of the Press.* New York: D. Appleton Century Co., 1931.

Small, William J. *Political Power and the Press.* New York: W. W. Norton, 1972.

Sullivan, Mark. *The Education of an American.* New York: Doubleday & Co., 1938.

Swanberg, W. A. *Citizen Hearst.* New York: Scribner's, 1961.

Weinberg, Arthur and Lila. *The Muckrackers.* New York: Simon & Schuster, 1961.

Whale, John. *The Half-Shut Eye: Television and Politics in Britain and America.* New York: Macmillan & Co., 1969.

Will, George F., ed. *Press, Politics and Popular Government.* Washington: American Enterprise Institute for Public Policy Research, 1972.

Articles

Bagdikan, Ben H. "Congress and the Media: Partners in Propaganda; Why We Don't Know More About What Our Congressmen Are Doing." *Columbia Journalism Review,* January/February 1974, pp. 3-10.

Costello, Mary. "Newsmen's Rights." *Editorial Research Reports,* vol. 2, 1972, pp. 949-68.

Evans, Harold M. "Is the Press Too Powerful?" *Columbia Journalism Review,* January/February 1972, pp. 8-16.

"The First Amendment on Trial." *Columbia Journalism Review,* September/October 1971, pp. 7-50.

Gimlin, Hoyt. "Credibility Gaps and the Presidency." *Editorial Research Reports,* vol. 1, 1968, pp. 83-100.

———. "First Amendment and Mass Media." *Editorial Research Reports,* vol. 1, 1970, pp. 41-60.

Kraft, Joseph. "Politics of the Washington Press Corps." *Harper's,* June 1965, pp. 100-05.

Patch, Buel W. "Government and the Press." *Editorial Research Reports,* vol. 1, 1953, pp. 317-36.

Reston, J. B. "Press, the President and Foreign Policy." *Foreign Affairs,* July 1966, pp. 553-73.

Tucker, Ray. "Part-Time Statesmen." *Collier's,* Oct. 28, 1933, pp. 28-36.

Wiggins, J. R. "Background on Investigations of the Press." *Nieman Reports,* October 1953.

Witcover, Jules. "Washington: The News Explosion." *Columbia Journalism Review,* Spring 1969, pp. 23-27.

Worsnop, Richard L. "Secrecy in Government." *Editorial Research Reports,* vol. 2, 1971, pp. 629-50.

Internal Pressures

Internal pressures within Congress can exert as forceful an influence on a member's actions as the better known external pressures applied by constituents, lobbyists, the press and others. Internal pressures, however, are less visible because they operate between colleagues and at institutional, professional and social levels that are less likely to attract the public's attention.

The pressures include rewards and punishments, appeals to party loyalty, political trades, and the ever-present expectation that members ought to act within an unwritten but generally accepted code of conduct that allows a large organization of persons with equal claim to membership to get its work done.

The congressional leadership of a member's political party, the chairman of the committee on which he serves, members of his state's delegation and other party members all vie with and supplement outside pressures in an effort to win a member's support on an issue.

The significance of internal pressures was summed up succinctly years ago by a powerful House leader, Speaker Sam Rayburn (D Texas), who advised members that "to get along, you have to go along."[1] Rules and customs of both houses of Congress place powerful weapons in the hands of the power structure to help it work its will. Members who cooperate often are rewarded with a choice committee assignment or a coveted public works project, or by a display of personal approval from the leadership—an act that enhances the member's prestige among his colleagues and his effectiveness as a legislator.

By the same token, members who have not supported party leaders on important issues have been relegated to minor committees, denied the benefits of "pork barrel" appropriations and shunned by the leadership and even rank-and-file party colleagues. Their refusal to go along may make them so ineffective at serving their constituents' interests that their chances of re-election are endangered.

The price of acting independently of party leaders and committee chairmen was reduced in the 1970s by structural and procedural reforms that weakened the arbitrary power of senior party members, broadened the influence of subcommittees and made the committee assignment and chairmen selection processes more democratic. Nonetheless, members still had to contend with many formidable internal pressures when deciding how to cast their votes.

Sources of Party Pressures

Speaker

A principal source of pressure in the House is the Speaker, an official who is nominated by his party's caucus or conference and elected by the whole House, usually on a party-line vote. The Speaker's duties, which spring from the Constitution and from rules and traditions of the House, include presiding over House sessions, recognizing members to address the House, deciding points of order, referring bills and reports to the appropriate committees and House calendars, appointing the House conferees for House-Senate conferences on legislation, and appointing members of select committees. The Speaker normally wields considerable influence within his party's committee on committees, which assigns party members to standing committees. Although the Constitution does not stipulate that the Speaker must be a member of the House, no non-member has ever been elected to the post. The Speaker, like any other member, may vote and may lead debate on the floor. *(For detailed description of the speakership and other leadership posts, see Leadership chapter, p. 315)*

Over the years, some Speakers have been dominated by committee chairmen or other powerful House members, while others have run the chamber with their own iron will. According to Hubert Bruce Fuller's study of the speakership, *The Speakers of the House*, Henry Clay as Speaker in 1811 "organized the committees for war."[2] Speaker Thomas B. Reed (R Maine), who served in the 1890s, acted with such strength that he became known as "Czar" Reed. Reed transferred obstructionist members of both parties from committee to committee in order to achieve his desired policy objectives (at that time the Speaker had authority to appoint committees) and made far-reaching parliamentary rulings which broke the power of the minority to filibuster and ensured the right of the majority to transact business in the House.[3]

Champ Clark (D Mo.), Reed's House contemporary who himself became Speaker in 1910, recalled in his memoirs that "no company of soldiers in the regular army was ever more thoroughly drilled" than were the Republicans under Reed. "Time and again I have seen Mr. Reed bring every Republican up standing by waving his hands upward; and just as often, when they had risen inadvertently, I have seen him make them take their seats by waving his hands downwards."[4]

Reed's strong policies were continued in the early 1900s by Speaker Joseph G. Cannon (R Ill.), whose methods came to be known as "Cannonism." In *A Grammar of American Politics*, Wilfred E. Binkley and Malcolm C. Moos wrote that Cannon achieved a "dictatorship" in the House "through the Speaker's power of recognition and even more his power to appoint committees whereby he could make or break members virtually at will." In addition, "As chairman of the Committee on Rules, which he appointed and dominated, the Speaker could determine what measures the House would consider."[5]

Cannon's dictatorial methods and his sponsorship of conservative legislation despite a rising tide of progressive sentiment in the country led to his downfall in 1910 and 1911. First, a combination of Democrats and progressive Republicans succeeded in 1910 in barring the Speaker permanently from a seat on the Rules Committee—one of the major sources of Cannon's power. Then, a year later, Cannon was defeated for the speakership and the office of the Speaker was permanently deprived of the power to appoint standing committees;[6] that power was given to the full House (in effect, the committees on committees of the two parties). Although these specific powers were never restored to the Speaker, resourceful incumbents of that office in later years were able to restore much of the post's earlier influence through their own personal prestige as head of their party's House majority apparatus.

Floor Leaders

Both the majority and minority parties of the House and Senate appoint officials to shape and direct party strategy on the floor. These officials, known as the majority and minority leaders, devote their efforts to tying together the loose alliances which compose their parties in hopes of shaping them into voting majorities to pass or defeat bills. Majority floor leaders have considerable influence over the scheduling of debate and the selection of members to speak on bills. The majority leader in the House ranks just below the Speaker in importance. In the Senate, the majority leader is the most powerful officer, because neither the Vice President nor the President pro tempore holds substantive powers over the chamber's proceedings. In both houses, the floor leaders are in position to wield considerable pressure on members through their influence over the party apparatus.

Whips

Each party appoints a whip and a number of assistant whips to assist the floor leader in execution of the party's legislative program. The main job of the whip is to canvass party members on a pending issue and give the floor leader an accurate picture of the support or opposition he may expect for the measure. Whips also are responsible for making sure that party members are on hand to vote. At the direction of the floor leader, the whips also may apply pressure to ensure that party members follow the leadership line.

Party Caucus

Both major parties over the years have relied periodically on caucuses of party members (called "conferences" by Republicans in both houses and by Senate Democrats) to adopt party positions on legislation and, in the case of Democrats until 1975, to bind party members to support those positions. The concept of the caucus began in the Jefferson administration, continued under the speakership of Henry Clay, and was used sporadically in both chambers throughout the 19th century.

Between 1903 and 1916, the caucus or conference type of party government was revived and was used extensively by Democrats in both the House and the Senate. Senate Democrats in 1903 adopted a rule binding members to follow party positions.[7] House Democrats adopted a similar rule in 1909 and used it frequently until the end of the first Wilson administration.[8] A rule binding party members to support a presidentially proposed measure on a majority vote in caucus was adopted at the outset of the New Deal era by Democrats in both chambers.[9] Republicans in the 1940s and 1950s frequently used nonbinding conferences, but never adopted a binding caucus rule. (House Democrats in 1975 formally abandoned the binding rule which had been rarely used since the Wilson administration.)

Leadership Committees

Both parties maintain extra-legal party committees in each chamber to assist the party leadership and to enable more party members to participate in the leadership process. Steering committees recommend the order in which measures should be taken up and help with floor tactics, while policy committees research proposed legislation and recommend party positions. The two functions may be combined in a single committee.

The House Republican Policy Committee was quite active in the period from 1959 to 1965 when it frequently took positions on legislative business and thus became an important instrument of party leadership. The full GOP Conference began taking positions in 1965 and its influence was widely considered to be larger than the Policy Committee in the following years.[10] The House Democratic Steering and Policy Committee was rejuvenated in the mid-1970s and was showing signs of becoming an influential source of party leadership

Techniques of Applying Pressure

Most congressional leaders in recent years have preferred to use tact and persuasion rather than overt pressure to win support for party measures. Speaker Sam Rayburn once said: "My experience with the speakership has been that you can't lead people by driving them. Persuasion and reason are the only ways to lead them. In that way, the Speaker has influence and power in the House." On another occasion, Rayburn said that the Speaker must "feel" his way in the House, "receptive to...rolling waves of sentiment" among House members. "And if a man can't see and hear and feel, why then, of course, he's lost."[11]

Distribution of Favors

After the revolt of 1910, the House leaders turned to the tactic of passing around enough favors to members to have a significant number of IOUs to call on in the event of a close vote on an important bill. The master of this tactic was Speaker Rayburn, who had carefully cultivated his personal popularity with other members during his 25 terms in the House. In his book, *House Out of Order*, Rep. Richard Bolling (D Mo.), a Rayburn protege, wrote: "There was hardly a member, however strong a political opponent, for whom [Rayburn] had not done a favor—securing a more desirable committee assignment, obtaining a federal project to help in a difficult re-election campaign, an appointment to a board or commission for prestige purposes, or the assignment of extra space. Rayburn knew that the speakership had been shorn of much of its substantive power. Therefore, he built up, in place of it, a vast backlog of political IOUs with a compound interest."[12]

Some congressional leaders have enhanced their influence with rank-and-file members by withholding pressure in cases where the member's vote would be against his constituents' interests. Joseph W. Martin Jr. (R Mass.), a contemporary of Rayburn's who served two terms as Speaker and eight more as House minority leader, wrote in his memoirs: "Unless it was absolutely necessary, I never asked a man to side with me if his vote would hurt him in his district. Whenever I could spare a man this kind of embarrassment, I did so and saved him for another time when I might need him more urgently. In fact, I often counseled members against taking positions on legislation that could cost them the next election."[13] John McCormack (D Mass.), Rayburn's successor as Speaker of the House, had much the same philosophy.

Expressions of personal friendship toward fellow members also help congressional leaders stack up IOUs. One of the most obvious of these tactics is for the House Speaker to call a young member to the rostrum to preside over the House in the late afternoon hours while the members make speeches. If the Speaker permits a member to preside over the Committee of the Whole House while the House is actively debating major legislation, the member is likely to be even more appreciative. Another reward is the Speaker's selection of members to read to the House the traditional messages such as Washington's Farewell Address on Washington's Birthday. In his study of the House, *Forge of Democracy*, journalist Neil MacNeil wrote: "Such assignments, denoting the Speaker's approval of a member, have always been carefully watched by members of the House. The men receiving them have acquired immediately, in the inner life of the House, recognition by their fellows as friends of the Speaker with the added influence and prestige that such friendship has always meant. These assignments have denoted that the men receiving them have become members, if only minor members at times, of the Speaker's trusted inner circle. Men frequently called to the chair by the Speaker have even acquired the reputation of being likely successors to the Speaker."[14]

Committee Assignments

When a congressional leader resorts to overt pressure tactics, one of the most effective methods is the "carrot-and-stick" approach of promising prestigious committee assignments for members who cooperate and undesirable ones for those who don't.

One of the first and most severe applications of this tactic came in 1858, when Sen. Stephen A. Douglas (D Ill.) was removed from the chairmanship of the Committee on Territories for failure to follow the Democratic stand on the expansion of slavery.[15] Speaker Cannon removed 14 insurgent Republicans from choice committee assignments in 1909, and Speaker Nicholas Longworth (R Ohio) punished 13 progressive Republicans in the same way in 1925.[16] In 1965, the House Democratic Caucus stripped two Democrats—John Bell Williams (Miss.) and Albert W. Watson (S.C.)—of their committee seniority for supporting the Republican presidential candidate in the 1964 election. (Watson left the Democratic Party, resigned his seat and was re-elected as a Republican.) The loss of seniority cost

Williams the chairmanship of the House Interstate and Foreign Commerce Committee, which he would have been in line to receive in 1966 upon the retirement of Chairman Oren Harris (D Ark.).[17]

No other leader in the history of Congress was more proficient at this tactic than was Lyndon B. Johnson (D Texas), when he served as Senate Democratic floor leader from 1953 through 1960 (minority leader 1953-54, majority leader 1955-1960).

When Sen. John C. Stennis (D Miss.) supported Johnson's effort to censure Sen. Joseph R. McCarthy (R Wis.) for misconduct in his stormy probe of suspected Communists in government, Stennis was quickly rewarded with a seat on the prestigious Appropriations Committee.[18] Sen. J. Allen Frear Jr. (D Del.), a conservative who voted a moderate position at Johnson's behest on a number of important bills, was rapidly placed on the Finance Committee, while Sen. Paul H. Douglas (D Ill.), a strong liberal and Johnson foe, waited for nine years to be named to that panel.[19] Freshman senators who voted with Johnson in his successful effort in 1959 to resist liberalization of Senate Rule 22, governing application of cloture on filibusters, were rewarded with good committee assignments, while those voting for liberalization were given unattractive ones. For example, Sen. Thomas J. Dodd (D Conn.), who voted to uphold Rule 22, was rewarded with membership on the Appropriations, Judiciary and Aeronautics and Space Sciences Committees—three of the most prestigious in the Senate.[20] And Sen. Vance Hartke (D Ind.), who supported Johnson on Rule 22, was named to the powerful Finance and Commerce Committees. But Edmund S. Muskie (D Maine), who opposed Johnson on the vote, was relegated to two less desirable committees—Government Operations and Public Works.[21]

For years, Johnson and Rayburn teamed up to protect Texas oil interests through careful assignment of members to the tax-writing Senate Finance and House Ways and Means Committees. Drew Pearson and Jack Anderson asserted in *The Case Against Congress* that no one was admitted to the Ways and Means Committee who couldn't give Rayburn the answer he wanted to one question: "Do you favor the oil depletion allowance?"[22] When a Democratic vacancy occurred on the Finance Committee in 1955, Johnson assumed it himself rather than turn it over to Paul Douglas, a strong foe of percentage depletion.[23] Although Douglas was elected to the Senate in 1948, it was not until 1957 that he finally won a seat on the Finance Committee. *(For changes in the committee assignment process, see p. 374)*

Isolation of Rebels

The threat of unpopularity among their peers stands as a constant deterrent to members inclined to engage in unpopular activities. As political scientist Randall B. Ripley described it in *Party Leaders of the House of Representatives:* "For most members of the House, the life of an habitual maverick would be intolerable. Acting against the party involves a substantial amount of personal discomfort, which can even be expressed physically. The only Republican to vote against his party's recommittal motion on a major administration bill in 1963 answered the roll call while crouching behind the rail on the Democratic side of the House chamber. He explained, 'It's 190 degrees over there (pointing to the Republican side).' Another Republican, after voting with the Democrats on the Area Redevelopment Act amendments in 1963, said that he simply refused to go into the Republican cloakroom any more. He indicated that he could no longer talk to his Republican Party colleagues: 'Those old men don't ever want to do anything.' "[24]

Another House member, a Democrat, told Ripley: "When you vote against the leadership it gets sticky over there in the chamber. As a personal matter, you hate teller votes more than roll calls. The pressure on teller votes is meaner: the Speaker, majority leader and whip stand in the aisle where you have to walk by them. That's mean. There's lots of pressure from that stare. And diminished numbers on divisions and teller votes make each vote more important. This is the psychology of the group. You don't really get chewed out. They are polite to me. When the Speaker or Carl Albert [then House majority leader] say 'Can't you help us out?' this is worse than if they were nasty. It is tough to refuse."[25]

Distribution of Public Works

Another effective pressure method is the selective distribution of public works projects to members' states or districts. This can be a powerful lever in the hands of a congressional leader or committee chairman, because the political success or failure of members is based at least partly on how much "boodle" the member can win for his district.

During his eight-year term as Senate Democratic leader, Lyndon B. Johnson frequently employed this tactic in order to win key votes on important Senate bills. As majority leader in 1956, Johnson won the crucial vote of conservative Sen. George W. Malone (R Nev.) for a controversial Social Security bill by pushing to enactment of legislation providing government subsidies for tungsten production—a measure important to Malone's state. In effect, Malone's was the swing vote for the Social Security bill. It passed by the margin of 47-45 over the opposition of the Eisenhower administration and the American Medical Association.[26] A year later, when Johnson needed northern votes on a compromise version of the 1957 civil rights bill, he won support from Sens. Margaret Chase Smith (R Maine) and Frank Church (D Idaho) by securing appropriations for important reclamation projects in their states. Later in the year when the civil rights bill came up, both senators voted with Johnson.[27]

Another expert at the use of the pork-barrel tactic was Rep. Michael J. Kirwan (D Ohio), the longtime chairman of the House Appropriations Subcommittee on Public Works. When Kirwan experienced opposition in his House district for the first time in more than 20 years, a number of influential House members who had important public works projects pending for their districts took to the House floor to praise Kirwan for his work in the House.[28]

On an earlier occasion, Kirwan made a public show of his power after his committee's $10-million appropriation for an aquarium for Washington, D.C.—a pet project of Kirwan's—ran into unexpected difficulty in the Senate. Sen. Wayne Morse (D Ore.) attacked the aquarium project—which came to be known as Kirwan's "fish hotel"—as a "luxury the capital cannot afford while there is an acute shortage of classrooms here." Kirwan, then chairman of the Appropriations Subcommittee for the Interior Department, denounced Morse and dropped most Oregon projects from the Interior appropriations bill. "Morse was the cause of it," Kirwan said. "I'll hold up all of Oregon's water projects until Morse learns something about fish." It took President

Kennedy's personal intervention to get the Oregon projects restored.[29]

Rivaling Kirwan's expertise as a distributor of public works projects was Sen. Robert S. Kerr (D Okla.), one of the most powerful members of the Senate from the late 1950s until his death in 1963. According to an account in *Newsweek* by Kenneth G. Crawford, "The base of Kerr's power was never his major committees. Rather, it was his chairmanship of the Rivers and Harbors Subcommittee of the Public Works Committee, an obscure post that makes few national headlines, but much political hay. Kerr not only used it to consolidate his position in Oklahoma by festooning the state with public works but placed practically all senators under obligation to him by promoting their pet home projects. He never hesitated to collect on these obligations later, when the votes were needed."[30]

Distribution of Campaign Funds

Congressional leaders may also exert pressure on members through promises of financial aid in the member's re-election campaign. Both the Democratic and Republican parties have Senate and House Campaign Committees which parcel out funds to party members for help in their campaigns. The committees date from 1866 when Democratic members of both houses, who were opposing the attempt by Radical Republicans to impeach President Andrew Johnson, appointed their own committees to run the mid-term campaign.[31]

The committees do not participate in party primaries, only in the general elections. Their effectiveness as a pressure tool is limited, because party leaders will rarely threaten to cut off funds to a recalcitrant member if it might mean the election of a candidate of the opposition party. Thus while party leaders can offer the "carrot" of additional campaign money as an inducement to follow the party line, they can scarcely afford to employ the "stick" of cutting off funds altogether.

Careful decisions over how the money is allotted, however, may work to the party leaders' benefit. Just as Lyndon Johnson mastered the other facets of party leadership, he was able also to mold the Senate Campaign Committee into an effective pressure instrument. In their book *Lyndon B. Johnson: The Exercise of Power*, Rowland Evans and Robert Novak wrote:

"De facto control of the Campaign Committee's funds was one of Johnson's least obvious but most effective tools in building his network (of supporters). He controlled the distribution of committee funds through both its chairmen—first Earle Clements (D Ky.) and later George Smathers (D Fla.)—and through its secretary, Bobby Baker. More often than not, the requests for campaign funds were routinely made to Baker, and the money was physically distributed by him. Johnson further tightened his control when Clements was named the committee's executive director after his Senate defeat in 1956. Johnson got the most out of the committee's limited funds—at that time a mere four hundred thousand dollars—by shrewdly distributing them where they would do the most work. In the small mountain states like Idaho, a ten-thousand contribution could change the course of an election. But in New York or Pennsylvania, ten thousand dollars was the merest drop in the bucket. Johnson and Baker tried to reduce contributions to Democrats in the industrial northeast to the minimum. Because senators seldom bite the hand that feeds them, these westerners were naturally drawn into the

Johnson network, while the eastern liberals tended to remain outside."[32] *(For further discussion of congressional campaign financing, see p. 531)*

Meetings of State Delegations

State party delegations in the House can provide an effective forum for party pressures. Most state delegations hold informal meetings that are observed closely and sometimes attended by the party leadership. Votes may be swayed at these meetings, and at the very least, the party's whip organization will have a means of gauging the delegation's sentiment on pending issues.[33]

In large delegations whose members have similar constituencies, members with individual expertise in a given field often are able to sway part, if not all, of the state group. In a study of state delegations, Alan Fiellin found that 'A division of labor, corresponding to the committee structure of the House, develops in some groups and provides benefits for the individual." He added: "By virtue of his informal ties, the New York Democrat, for example, has ready access to committees of which he is not a member. Individual members may, and do, use group connections to check on the status and prospects of legislation in committees other than their own. In the absence of personal ties with members of most House committees, the task of quickly getting trustworthy information on the work of many committees would be most difficult. The New York Democrat may save many hours of legwork, reading and anxious deliberation by holding a brief conversation with a like-minded colleague who knows the material and has previously sifted through it."[34]

During a 1959 series of round table discussions conducted by the Brookings Institution, participating members of Congress expressed varying opinions on the usefulness of state delegations. Discussing the functioning of his own state delegation, one representative commented, "The state delegations are not very powerful. We used to meet together, though not too regularly, for informal discussions of issues with no attempt to bind members. There are few meetings of the delegation as a whole now, but we are a fairly close working group and by informal means we manage to cooperate closely."[35]

Power of Committee Chairmen

Strong pressures come from congressional committee chairmen, both on committee members and on the full chamber once the committee has acted. A special panel of the American Political Science Association reported in 1945 on the vast powers of the committees. The chairmen, it said, "arrange the schedules of work and the agenda of committee meetings.... They parcel out the personnel of subcommittees and determine the scope of their work. They or their subordinate chairmen of the subcommittees report to Congress on decisions for legislation and manage the floor debates in defense of such decisions. In these debates the committee chairman's word carries great weight because the subject is his peculiar province. In effect, the committee chairmen are able in large measure to dictate what proposals for legislation may be considered by Congress. The ordinary member proposes, but the chair disposes."[36] Although their arbitrary powers had been reduced by 1976, committee chairmen continued to hold considerable sway over the fate of legislation under their purview. *(See role of chairmen, Evolution of Committees, p. 365)*

Writing in 1963, Neil MacNeil observed: "The greatest power of a committee chairman in the House has been his ability to impede or hasten any given bill to House passage. The chairman largely has controlled the timing of legislation to be taken up for consideration—and timing alone can determine a bill's fate.... This power...has given them the means to intimidate ordinary members of the House and even to force the Speaker himself to cater to their whims or idiosyncracies. The chairmen have been able to help or hurt the individual representative's chances of re-election by endorsing or repudiating specific bills. They have been able also, more importantly, to influence and even determine the nature of American law; for they have held the decisive role in the vast screening process through which all legislation has had to pass in the House."[37]

Sometimes a philosophy or tradition springs up around a particular committee which serves as a type of psychological pressure on committee members. In a 1962 study of the House Appropriations Committee, Richard F. Fenno Jr. found a consensus among committee members that "all of their House-prescribed tasks can be fulfilled by superimposing upon them one single paramount task—to guard the federal Treasury." Committee members "state their goals in the essentially negative terms of guardianship—screening requests for money, checking against ill-advised expenditures, and protecting the taxpayer's dollar."[38]

The committee's official history states that the job of each member is "constantly and courageously to protect the federal Treasury against thousands of appeals and imperative demands for unnecessary, unwise and excessive expenditures."[39] Fenno found that procedures of the committee were so rigid that it was frowned upon if a member offered an amendment in the full committee unless he was a member of the pertinent subcommittee, and that it was frowned on even more if a committee member failed to support the committee bill on the House floor.[40] One subcommittee chairman told Fenno: "I tell them [the full committee] we should have a united front. If there are any objections or changes, we ought to hear it now and not wash our dirty linen out on the floor. If we don't have a bill that we can all agree on and support, we ought not to report it out. To do that is like throwing a piece of meat to a bunch of hungry animals."[41]

Another unwritten policy of the House Appropriations Committee which has exerted pressure on committee members has been the tradition against minority reports, both in subcommittee and full committee. Fenno noted that over the period from 1947 to 1957, only nine minority reports had been filed out of a possible 141.[42] Because of the immense prestige of the Appropriations Committee in the House, its unanimous reports have served as a powerful lever on the full House to adopt committee recommendations.

Logrolling as a Pressure Tool

Because of the diversity of interests in both House and Senate, members must often trade their votes to get their pet bills enacted. Such maneuvering, which is known as "logrolling," has been practiced in Congress since the early days of the Republic and in state legislatures before that. Two examples of the practice:

● In 1868, former Rep. Ransom Gillet (D N.Y. 1833-37) recalled that the way to enact a tariff bill was to provide protection for the local interests of enough representatives to ensure the bill's passage. "Interest and not principle," he said, "determines what shall be done. If votes from Louisiana and Texas are needed, sugar will come in for favor. If support is needed from Illinois, Wisconsin, Minnesota and Michigan, lead, copper and pine lumber are provided for. If the votes of Pennsylvania are wanted, coal and iron receive full attention.... The principle of protection under a tariff never expands beyond the objects necessary to carry a bill."[43]

● In 1964, liberal Democrats in the House voted for wheat and cotton subsidies in return for the support of rural conservatives for a new food stamp program. Both bills were passed April 8, the food stamp measure by a 229-189 roll-call vote and the wheat-cotton bill by a roll call of 211-203. The Johnson administration had arranged the trade after both bills appeared to be foundering in the House.[44]

In his book on the House leadership, Randall B. Ripley testified to the success of the trade: "Twelve Democrats," Ripley noted, "were absent for all three votes. Six more were absent for one or more of the three roll calls [two of them on the food stamp bill] but supported the administration when they voted. One hundred eighty Democrats supported the administration on all three roll calls and might best be labeled as 'reliable traders.' Twenty-six members were 'hard-line liberals,' voting with the administration twice on the food stamp bill and against the wheat-cotton bill. Twelve members were 'hard-line conservatives,' voting against the food stamp bill twice and for the wheat-cotton bill. Eight members were 'half-hearted traders,' voting with the administration on one food stamp roll call and against it on the other and for the wheat-cotton bill. Eight Democrats were against both programs on all three roll calls. The trade was 82 per cent successful in that only the hard-line liberals, hard-line conservatives and half-hearted traders explicitly violated the terms of the bargain. Even if only the reliable traders are counted, the trade was 71 per cent successful."[45]

Many students of government defend logrolling as a legitimate means of enabling the legislator to protect his constituency's interests. As Neil MacNeil put it, "In the inside struggle to set the House's stance on a question of public policy, rarely has the decision involved for the individual representative a moral choice between right and wrong.... Normally on legislation, there has always been an area of possible compromise, legitimate compromise, and this possibility has caused the bargaining implicit in the formulation of almost all legislation. The adoption of even an amendment of seemingly little or no consequence sometimes has provided the votes needed to pass an entire bill." Political scientist Nelson W. Polsby, another defender of logrolling, notes that cooperative effort of this sort in Congress "dilutes the power of the most entrenched, and enhances tremendously the powers of all senators, however low on the totem pole."[46]

Power of Voting Coalitions

In addition to logrolling, which entails a member's voting for proposals which may have little or no relation to his own interests in order to obtain support for his own objectives, coalitions of disparate groups of members often spring up in Congress to work for measures which may accrue to their common interests. The most important of these voting alliances has been the "conservative coalition" of Republicans and southern Democrats—a powerful influence in both the House and the Senate since 1937.[47]

Disillusioned with liberal economic policies, southern Democrats banded together with Republicans to defeat or

weaken some Roosevelt administration bills.[48] Under the direction of Rep. Howard W. Smith (D Va.), and House Minority Leader Charles A. Halleck (R Ind.), the coalition dominated the House in the 1950s and early 1960s, defeating many important bills submitted by the Kennedy administration. It was somewhat less powerful in the Senate, but still had an important impact on legislation. The coalition lost considerable House strength in the 1964 election when liberal Democrats won a landslide victory—a factor which subsequently resulted in passage of President Johnson's "Great Society" program of domestic social legislation. After recouping some of its losses in 1966 and 1968, the coalition again was able to stymie liberal proposals. Although still in existence in the late 1960s and the 1970s, the coalition was not as strong as in its heyday. Partly, this was due to the election of many new and younger members to Congress throughout the 1960s and into the 1970s. These newer members tended to be more interested in finding acceptable legislative compromises to deal with the issues pressing on Congress than in obstructing action of any sort, a characteristic of the old coalition's tactics.

The coalition did not function on every House and Senate roll-call vote but only on the major economic or social issues. Neil MacNeil has explained how the coalition took shape before a major vote in the House: "The Republican strategists conferred with the southern Democratic tacticians, and together they agreed on a joint plan of action. The secret of success was for [Joseph W.] Martin [Halleck's predecessor as minority leader] to permit the southern Democrats to carry the fight on the House floor. They would make the main speeches, they would make the motions, they would offer the substitutes and the amendments. The design was to encourage Democrats to join the opposition.... The technique once learned proved a major weapon in the conservative coalition's arsenal. Martin used it against Roosevelt measures and Truman measures and Charles Halleck used it against Kennedy bills. It was no accident that Phillip Landrum of Georgia, a conservative Democrat, offered the Eisenhower labor bill in 1959 or that James C. Davis of Georgia, even more conservative than Landrum, offered the Eisenhower airport-construction bill. Both had been chosen by Halleck and Smith as the southerners most likely to encourage other Democrats to join the conservative cause."[49]

By 1975, the top-heavy Democratic majorities in the House and Senate pushed the conservative coalition's success level down to its lowest point since the 89th Congress. The 89th was the last Congress in which the Democrats enjoyed a comparable 2-to-1 dominance over the Republicans.

The coalition (defined as a majority of Republicans and southern Democrats voting against the position taken by a majority of northern Democrats) formed on 28 per cent of the votes in each chamber during 1975. This represented a slight drop in the Senate from the 30 per cent level of the previous year, but a substantial increase over the 19 per cent of the time the coalition appeared in the House during 1974. Overall, the coalition appeared on 28 per cent of the votes in Congress, compared with a 1974 average of 24 per cent.

However, because there were fewer Republicans in each chamber in 1975, the coalition's victory percentage dropped sharply. The coalition won only 48 per cent of the 166 Senate votes on which it appeared, down from 54 per cent in 1974. This was its worst showing there since 1965, when it was successful only 39 per cent of the time.

In the House, the coalition performed slightly better, winning 52 per cent of the 170 votes on which it formed. But this was still 15 percentage points below the 67 per cent level of 1974, and the poorest showing since a 32 per cent victory level in 1966.[50]

Pressure by Informal Groups

Among the more inscrutable elements of internal pressure on Congress are the numerous informal groupings of senators and representatives. By definition, the groups operate outside the regular procedures of Congress, and their impact on regular congressional procedures is frequently hard to discern.

The groups are difficult to characterize. They tend to be short-lived insurgent coalitions. But some, such as the Democratic Study Group in the House, have survived for years; and one of the better known groups, called the Board of Education, served as a strategy council for legislative leaders in the House. The Board of Education was popular with Speakers from Nicholas Longworth to Sam Rayburn.

Many of the groups go unrecorded, organizing temporarily because of a shared interest in a certain bill or amendment, and disbanding once the bill or amendment has been adopted or defeated. Some of the groups, particularly in the Senate, consist of little more than a circle of lunch-table companions. Other groups have scores of members, regular assessments for dues, assigned space in a congressional office building, and paid staff aides.

Underlying all of the groups is the bond of personal friendship that plays such a large part in the functioning of Congress, and a shared desire to short-circuit the more cumbersome regular procedures of House and Senate.

Informal but somewhat "institutionalized" groupings thrive in Congress, particularly in the House, where the size of the chamber may give members a sense of isolation and anonymity, even within their own party. Among House Republicans, there were in 1976 the moderate-conservative discussion groups, SOS and Chowder and Marching Society (the groups meet jointly on Wednesdays) and Acorns; the moderate-liberal 36-member Wednesday Club and the conservative 60-member House Republican Study Committee. Democratic groups included the moderate-conservative 100-member United Democrats of Congress; the 75-member New Members Caucus; the moderate-conservative 75-member House Democratic Research Organization; and the powerful and liberal Democratic Study Group. (The size of the DSG was 226 in 1976.) Bipartisan groups included the 17-member House Congressional Black Caucus (in fact, all-Democratic in 1976); the 25-member New England Congressional Caucus; and the 50-member House Congressional Rural Caucus. The only bicameral and bipartisan informal group in 1976 was Members of Congress for Peace through Law, composed of 174 moderate-liberal House and Senate members.

In an assessment of these House groups, Sven Groennings, former staff director of the Wednesday Group, said: "The impact of informal groups upon the legislative system is largely subtle. Informal groups are mechanisms for the development of close rapport, confidence in one another's political judgment and mutual support. Some groups develop patterns of cue-giving and cue-taking, and it is normal that members help one another with problems. Collectively they serve as a quiet communications network, with some overlapping of membership. Selective in membership,

the Republican clubs tend to recruit those men who are particularly able or promising as well as compatible."[51]

Compared to the House, the Senate, whose members regard their entire body as a club, has not developed similar institutionalized groups. The structural conditions and size are such that there has been little demand for such groups. (In 1975-76, there was an informal moderate-liberal Senate Republican Wednesday club, but the group had no staff.)

Democratic Study Group

An organization of liberal Democrats in the House of Representatives, the Democratic Study Group was founded in 1959 to counter the roadblocks to liberal legislation erected by the conservative coalition of Republicans and southern Democrats.[52] The DSG played a supporting role for the New Frontier and Great Society legislation of Democratic administrations from 1961 to 1969. DSG members supplied crucial votes for passage of major education, civil rights and other social welfare legislation.

History

During the Eisenhower years (1953-61), Republicans and southern Democrats frustrated attempts of moderate and liberal Democrats to pass legislation. In the 85th Congress (1957-58), liberals tried to combat the conservative coalition in the House. Based on the 1956 national party platform, a legislative program was drafted by Democratic Reps. Eugene J. McCarthy of Minnesota, Lee Metcalf of Montana and Frank Thompson Jr. of New Jersey. The program, presented in 1957 with the support of 80 House Democrats, became known as the "Liberal Manifesto."

During the next two years, efforts to push the program were crippled by lack of organization, by lack of staff and by legislative machinery inadequate to sustain a coordinated operation, according to DSG literature.[53]

In the 1958 congressional elections, Democrats gained 15 seats in the Senate and 48 in the House, giving them a 2-to-1 majority in both chambers. Many of the newcomers belonged to the liberal wing of the party. With the gains, the liberals' hopes rose. But an unsuccessful attempt in 1959 to liberalize the House Rules Committee—controlled by Republicans and southern Democrats—tightened the conservative alliance. The session produced little action on measures advocated by the progressive Democrats—housing, civil rights, higher minimum wages, aid to education, medical care for the aged.

Because of the lack of legislative accomplishments, the group decided to put its operations on a more formal basis. A series of meetings was held in September 1959 to discuss the defeat of progressive legislation. Some 70 House Democrats attended the meetings. Metcalf, chairman of the first meeting, appointed a committee headed by Rep. B. F. Sisk (Calif.) to draw up the group's organizational structure. Metcalf was subsequently elected chairman of the group, and Thompson was named secretary.

The members named the organization the Democratic Study Group. They stressed the need to avoid words such as "liberal" or "action" because they feared the connotations the press might give these words. Metcalf sent a letter to northern, midwestern and western Democrats who were not members of the DSG, explaining: "Democrats in this Congress are being criticized, unfairly at times, for failure to carry out to a greater extent the legislative program spelled out in the Democratic platform. One reason for lack of success in some of our efforts has been a breakdown of communication among members who favor such a program. To remedy this lack of communication, and thus to achieve a better record next year than this, a number of us felt that we should have an organization before which we could discuss legislation, both as introduced and as reported, and be able to present the problems of our districts, states and regions to others."[54]

By January 1960, about 120 members from 34 states had been recruited into the DSG. In May 1960, the DSG hired a full-time staff member whose salary and expenses were paid by contributions from several members' clerk-hire allowance.

The DSG claimed in the months that followed that it had reversed the trend of defeat on legislative issues. The group took credit for beating the conservative coalition in 1960 on 12 of 19 key roll-call votes. According to the DSG, its first major victory came in March 1960, when opposition by its members delayed and finally killed a Treasury-backed bill raising long-term interest rates on Treasury bonds. The bill had been reported by the House Ways and Means Committee.[55]

When John F. Kennedy became President in 1961, the group had to change its focus—it began to mobilize support for the programs of a liberal administration rather than build opposition to a conservative one. The DSG researched and promoted efforts to write laws on civil rights, minimum wage, medicare and federal aid to education.

The mid-1960s brought new problems. In the 89th Congress, from 1965 to 1967, the Democratic majority in the House was so large that the Johnson administration could steer liberal bills through without an elaborate effort by the DSG. And the 90th Congress, from 1967 to 1969, saw the emergence of a split among House Democrats that divided the issue-oriented, generally peace-minded liberals from the bread-and-butter Democrats who had been their allies for more than a generation. In early 1969, the DSG had about 120 dues paying members, some 60 less than in the peak years of 1965 and 1966. It also had to face a hostile Democratic leadership. Many DSG activists supported an attempt to defeat Speaker John McCormack (D Mass. 1928-71) for re-election to his post in 1969.

But it was in these years that the first real moves toward reform were made. Under James G. O'Hara (Mich.), chairman from 1967 to 1969, the DSG persuaded House Democrats to hold regular party caucuses for the first time. Little was accomplished at most of these meetings, but they established the caucus as an available tool for liberal Democrats.

The DSG also mounted an active effort in the congressional campaigns in 1968, including a fund-raising operation, and fought successfully for some important liberal legislation. But the split between Democratic hawks and doves was beginning to affect its operation.

"When I was chairman," O'Hara recalled in 1973, "Johnson was President, and the DSG members were deeply divided about our role in Southeast Asia. I thought it was more important to keep the DSG together on those issues where we did agree than to break it up on issues where we differed. If we had a consensus then like we do now, we'd have been operating on foreign policy issues."[56]

That change came in the 91st Congress, under the chairmanship of Donald M. Fraser (Minn.), who was instrumental in directing the group toward anti-war and foreign policy issues. At the same time, the group was pushing House reform a little further. Caucuses became

more frequent; and in the summer of 1970, the DSG drafted an amendment to the Legislative Reorganization Act of that year which provided for the first recorded votes on major amendments. *(See Legislative Reorganization Act, p. 362)*

Other DSG proposals for reform, particularly of seniority, met with their first major success in January 1971, at the start of the 92nd Congress. The Democratic Caucus adopted a proposal forcing a vote on any committee chairman if 10 members of the caucus demanded it. This change fell short of what DSG leaders wanted at the time, but it opened the first crack in the seniority system. Another reform limited each member to chairmanship of one subcommittee. *(See Evolution of Committees and the Seniority System chapters, pp. 365, 397)*

The reform action that began with the 1970 changes reached a height in late 1974 and 1975. The DSG was a leading force in the successful effort to overturn the traditional power preserves. By the end of the first session of the 94th Congress in December 1975, the rigid seniority system was in shambles as the sole method by which members rose to power. The system still functioned as a useful device for ordering the hierarchy on committees, but it no longer was the dominant force it was in the past. Both chambers had created methods by which committee chairmen had to stand for election by their colleagues, and in the House three senior chairmen were deposed at the beginning of 1975.

Activities of the Study Group

Much of the DSG's mission is to provide information to members on key liberal issues. The group's main function is to help pass liberal legislation by alerting its members to important votes through a whip system. The DSG's importance lies mainly in its research activities and in giving its members an opportunity, through the exchange of information, to find a middle ground on which many of them can agree on certain issues.

The DSG staff issues weekly reports on bills about to come to the House floor, longer fact sheets and special reports on major legislative issues, and campaign ammunition for members to use against Republican opponents. The group also has had an elaborate whip call system to give members advance warning about caucuses and unexpected votes on the floor.

The weekly legislative reports summarize bills likely to come up in the week ahead, with an explanation of how the bill was handled in committee, a brief description of likely amendments, and arguments for and against both sides of controversial issues. The fact sheets and special reports do the same thing in more detail on selected topics. There were 20 fact sheets and 16 special reports in 1975.

For campaign purposes, the DSG has published a quarterly booklet listing each vote taken in the House during the previous quarter and explaining what was being decided. That way, a member who found one of his votes being questioned would have quick recall on how he cast his vote and why.

In election years, the service has been broadened to include source material for members and liberal Democratic challengers to use in speeches and in rebuttals to Republican campaign releases.

DSG activities are financed by members' dues ($100 per year) and donations, contributions from private citizens and an annual fund-raising banquet. Numerous members have contributed part of their office salary allowance to pay DSG staffers. The size of the staff, headed by Richard Conlon since 1968, fluctuates, but in 1976 stood at 22 employees, 10 of whom were professionals. Chairman of the group for the 1975-77 period was Bob Eckhardt (Texas).

Membership

The number of DSG members rose from about 80 in 1959 to a high of 180 during the 89th Congress (1965-66). But in the 1966 elections the Democrats suffered a net loss of 47 seats in the House, and in the 1968 election a net loss of five seats. As a result, DSG membership dropped sharply and by 1969 stood at only around 120. However, the upturn of Democratic fortunes in 1970 gave the party a net gain of nine House seats, and DSG membership moved up to an estimated 140 in 1971. By 1976, the membership list stood at 226.

There is an agreement among DSG members and supporters not to divulge the names on the lists, except those of the group's officers. The reason, according to staff director Conlon, is that publicizing the names might alienate some members, a few of whom are southerners who might be embarrassed in their conservative districts. For much the same reason—fear of alienating a small number of members on certain issues—the DSG does not officially issue public stands on specific bills. Conlon said the theory is that 90 per cent of the time, 90 per cent of the group can be counted on to support liberal measures anyway. In a 1963 letter to House members, DSG chairman John A. Blatnik (Minn.) pointed out: "No attempt is ever made to bind any member to any group action pertaining to his responsibilities. No 'membership' lists are kept and no press releases are issued in the name of the DSG endorsing specific legislation or publicizing any position."[57]

The House Wednesday Group

Like the DSG, the Republican Wednesday Group developed from a desire for constructive opposition. It was formed in 1963, at a time when Democrats controlled the White House and Republicans were the minority party in both chambers. The idea of establishing such a group was proposed on a Wednesday afternoon in the office of F. Bradford Morse (Mass.). Six other representatives were present and became co-founders: Robert Ellsworth (Kan.), John Lindsay (N.Y.), Charles McC. Mathias (Md.), Abner Sibal (Conn.), Robert Stafford (Vt.) and Stanley Tupper (Maine). According to Sven Groennings, who served two years as staff director of the group, "These men joined in an informal group because they shared similar experiences and perspectives. Most of them had developed a sense of comradeship by voting against the overwhelming majority of Republicans to expand the Rules Committee. All but Ellsworth had established voting records well to the left of most of their party, and all except Lindsay had been freshmen together, having entered Congress in 1961. These men were issue-oriented and wished to combat the frequent negativism of the Republican Party in its role of opposition.

"The first purpose, as in all other informal groups, was to broaden communications. In expanding the membership, the group's progressive ideological bias was clear and dominant but never narrowly rigid. There was no intention of becoming a faction, operating as a unified and bargaining bloc of all the party's liberals."[58]

Although the original seven had doubled their numbers in the year and a half prior to the 1964 elections, the group was badly divided and had not yet settled upon a long-term role. To remedy the situation, activists in the group proceeded to hire a researcher, Douglas Bailey, who was to play a major role in establishing the Wednesday Group as the first Republican legislative organization of its kind. As staff director, Bailey developed members' ideas into position papers, some of which were endorsed by as many as 40 members of Congress and were given much press coverage.[59]

Until mid-1972, when he left Congress to become Under-Secretary General of the United Nations, Morse "served as the principal innovator and enthusiastic energizer at every stage of the group's institutionalization and expansion," according to Groennings.[60]

The membership expanded steadily, reaching 20 in 1965, 26 by the end of 1967, and 36 by 1976. Growth had the advantage of broadening communications, the range of viewpoints presented, and the potential support for research. It also had the effect of weakening the group's activist impulse, as it became more difficult to approach consensus with larger numbers.

Membership, as in all other Republican groups, is by invitation (this is not the case with the DSG). The membership criteria vary; in the 1970s, there was emphasis on gaining representation from particular committees so as to gain breadth of information; from the freshman and sophomore classes in order to prevent ossification; and from various geographic areas in order to broaden the range of viewpoints. A principal guiding criterion remains an ideological bias toward the party's moderates and liberals.

Unlike the DSG, the group's members pay no dues. The group is financed through contributions.

Operations

In 1976, the group had a staff of four, three of whom were professionals. Its chairman was Charles A. Mosher (Ohio).

The group meets at 5 p.m. on Wednesday afternoons when Congress is in session. The members rotate as hosts, with the host serving as chairman. Meetings are relaxed and informal, with members reporting on whatever may be of interest from their committees.

The group has no equivalent of the DSG whip system for handling communications regarding action on the floor of the House; it does not conceive floor power as one of its basic purposes. Rather, its emphasis is on preparation of studies. Sponsorship of the finished study paper is open to all group members and selected Republican non-members who may be interested in the topic. The group tends to avoid issues that might be ideologically divisive. Major studies have included reports on air safety, the volunteer army, "Crisis in Urban Education" and "Organized Crime and the Urban Poor." In 1976, the group produced a major study on U.S.-Canadian relations.

In 1970 the staff began preparing a weekly "legislative summary" outlining the salient points in major bills.

Unlike the DSG, the Wednesday Group does not prepare campaign literature, nor does it engage in campaign fund-raising.

Black Caucus

The House Congressional Black Caucus, which emerged formally in 1971, was composed in 1976 of all 17 black members of the House (including D.C. non-voting delegate Walter E. Fauntroy) and was chaired by Charles B. Rangel (D N.Y.). As in the past, all members of the caucus were Democrats. Republican Sen. Edward W. Brooke (Mass.), the only black member of the Senate, was not a member of the caucus.

Origins

The group's origins can be traced to the late 1960s when Rep. Charles C. Diggs Jr. (D Mich.) formed the Democratic Select Committee. That committee, however, met only sporadically. In 1969, black members of Congress began coordinating their efforts; one of their first actions was public opposition to the nomination of Clement Haynsworth to be an associate justice of the Supreme Court.

In February 1970, the black members of the House sent a letter to President Nixon requesting a conference on issues of special interest to black and poor people in the United States. After an initial refusal, Nixon met 14 months later with the then-13 member caucus which presented him 61 recommendations for governmental action on domestic and foreign issues.

According to Marguerite Ross Barnett, in her study of the group, the meeting with Nixon "marked a turning point for the caucus. In a short time its members were caught in a transformation from a small, relatively powerless, and ignored group of junior representatives to a national cynosure.... During the first year (from mid-1971 to mid-1972) the [caucus] saw itself as 'congressmen at large for 20 million black people.' "[61]

Much of the caucus' visibility in its first year came from a series of hearings held around the country on issues of interest to blacks. The results of these hearings were to be incorporated in a "Black Agenda" which would be used inside Congress as the basis for caucus legislative action.

During this early stage, a staff nucleus was appointed and a method of financing the group was institutionalized through an annual $100-a-plate dinner. (The caucus netted $96,384 from the annual dinner in fiscal 1973 and $50,000 from the 1974 dinner.) An internal structure was established consisting of a chairman, executive committee and policy oriented subcommittees.

Emphasis on Legislation

The thrust of the group's activities changed in 1972, with the election of Louis Stokes (Ohio) as chairman. By mid-1972, members of the caucus had turned away from the turbulence of visible national collective leadership to concentrate on their effectiveness as legislators.

Between 1972 and the end of 1974, the caucus undertook two major unified efforts: extension of the Office of Economic Opportunity (OEO) programs under the Economic Opportunity Act of 1964 and countering President Nixon's impoundment (refusal to spend) of funds appropriated for social programs supported by the caucus.

All members of the caucus introduced or cosponsored legislation on impoundment and OEO. In addition, the caucus staff organized a nationwide lobbying effort on these issues. One result was to strengthen the group's base of support with other powerful national organizations.

At the beginning of the 94th Congress, caucus members worked out improved methods of exchanging information and discussing legislation to increase their unity on issues. The group devised a strategy to win more legislative victories for items on its agenda. In addition, the group decided to concentrate on one piece of legislation—the equal opportunity and full employment bill. Other important bills on the 1975 agenda included extension of the 1965 Voting

Rights Act, tax reform, passage of a universal voter registration law, and amendment and modification of the Revenue Sharing Act and the Higher Education Act.

Large Staff

Although the caucus was the smallest of the unofficial groups in the 94th Congress, its staff of seven (including four professionals) was the third largest. It was also, according to Barnett, "one of the most ambitious and highly organized groups."[62] The caucus staff published a newsletter, produced legislative alerts and larger research reports, held briefings and oversaw realization of the caucus strategy. The caucus as a group did not have formal ties with any other unofficial group in the House. However, in the 94th Congress, all four black congresswomen participated in the informal discussions of the women's "caucus." All members of the black caucus also belonged to the Democratic Study Group.

The caucus' "ability to demand and get better committee assignments has been one of the few clear achievements of black representatives organizing as a caucus," wrote Barnett.[63] Caucus members in 1975 were represented on the three most powerful House Committees: Appropriations, Ways and Means and Rules.

Peace Through Law Group

The precursor of the Members of Congress for Peace through Law was an informal lunch group formed in 1959 by Sen. Joseph S. Clark (D Pa.), Sen. Jacob K. Javits (R N.Y.), Rep. Robert W. Kastenmeier (D Wis.) and Rep. James G. Fulton (R Pa.). Until it was disbanded in 1963, the group met periodically to discuss foreign policy issues of mutual interest.[64]

The group was reconstituted in January 1967, when MCPL held its first steering committee meeting, attended by the five original members and eight other senators and representatives. They agreed that the organization should serve as an information clearinghouse to keep members abreast of legislation, undertake and promote research through contact with outside experts, arrange formal discussion meetings and provide a liaison with citizens' groups.

By the end of the year, MCPL had a membership roster of 46 senators and representatives; in 1976, its membership included 35 senators and 139 representatives.

Budget

The formal organization was launched with $10,000 provided by two contributors. The budget for 1967 was $25,000; by 1970, it had increased fourfold.

Operating expenses in 1976 were met through membership dues ($10 annually), with the bulk of MCPL revenue coming from individual private contributors. Like the DSG, the group has not made public a formal membership list, although it does make public a list of its officers and steering committee. Chairman of the group in 1976 was Sen. Dick Clark (D Iowa).

Generally, MCPL members comprise the more liberal segments of both houses; they are drawn to join it through a common interest in foreign policy issues. Many participants—particularly those in the House—are younger members of Congress who have been dissatisfied with the formal committee structure and party leadership. Although there is a broad consensus among the membership on issues such as arms control, closer scrutiny of military spending and strengthening the United Nations, MCPL has remained a heterogeneous and fluid grouping. It has rarely performed a whip function.

Operations

The organization's substantive work is carried on by standing and special committees that schedule luncheon meetings with outside experts to which the entire membership is invited. The group has sponsored periodic conferences (in 1970, it sponsored an all-day conference on a "feasible Timetable for Peace" in Indochina). In 1970, it issued a lengthy report on military spending which provided support for attempts to cut the defense budget that year. In 1976, the group focused on an effort to delay funding the controversial B-1 bomber.

The majority of letters, reports and petitions originating in MCPL committees are not identified as MCPL work as such but simply bear the names of members who subscribe to the statement. The relative anonymity may be helpful in recruiting new participants because members of Congress may join without subscribing to a stated set of positions or implicitly pledging to sponsor all MCPL-initiated work.

The group's staff of five (there are three professionals) publishes a newsletter twice a year.

Footnotes

1. Richard Bolling, *House Out of Order* (E.P. Dutton & Co., 1965), p. 48. A slightly different version of the quotation ("If you want to get along in the House, go along.") appears in Neil MacNeil, *Forge of Democracy* (David McKay Co., 1963), p. 75.
2. Hubert Bruce Fuller, *The Speakers of the House* (Little, Brown & Co., 1909), p. 40.
3. *Ibid.*, pp. 215-34.
4. Champ Clark, *My Quarter Century in American Politics*, 2 vols. (Harper & Bros., 1920), Vol. 1, p. 294.
5. Wilfred E. Binkley and Malcolm C. Moos, *A Grammar of American Politics*, 3rd ed. (Alfred A. Knopf, 1958), p. 439.
6. *Ibid.*
7. David J. Rothman, *Politics and Power: The United States Senate, 1869-1901* (Harvard University Press, 1966), p. 68.
8. George B. Galloway, *History of the House of Representatives* (Thomas Y. Crowell Co., 1961), p. 114; Hugh A. Bone, *American Politics and the Party System* 3rd ed. (McGraw-Hill, 1965), p. 590; Randall B. Ripley, *Party Leaders in the House of Representatives* (Brookings Institution, 1967), pp. 95-97.
9. George H. Haynes, *The Senate of the United States* (Houghton-Mifflin, 1938), p. 478.
10. Ripley, *Party Leaders*, p. 48.
11. MacNeil, *Forge of Democracy*, p. 75.
12. Bolling, *House Out of Order*, p. 68.
13. Joe Martin, *My First Fifty Years in Politics* (McGraw-Hill, 1960), p. 183.
14. MacNeil, *Forge of Democracy*, pp. 111-12.
15. Rothman, *Politics and Power*, p. 14.
16. MacNeil, *Forge of Democracy*, p. 111.
17. Bolling, *House Out of Order*, p. 232.
18. Rowland Evans and Robert Novak, *Lyndon B. Johnson: The Exercise of Power* (The New American Library, 1966), p. 102.
19. *Ibid.*, p. 96.
20. Jack Anderson and Drew Pearson, *The Case Against Congress* (Simon and Schuster, 1968), p. 53.
21. Evans and Novak, *Lyndon B. Johnson*, pp. 200-202.
22. Anderson and Pearson, *The Case Against Congress*, p. 140.
23. *Ibid.*, p. 141.
24. Ripley, *Party Leaders*, p. 159.
25. *Ibid.*, pp. 151-52.
26. Evans and Novak, *Lyndon B. Johnson*, pp. 157-59.
27. *Ibid.*, pp. 128-30, 137.
28. Anderson and Pearson, *The Case Against Congress*, pp. 284-86.
29. *Ibid.*, pp. 286-87.
30. Kenneth Crawford, "The Senate's Ways," *Newsweek*, Jan. 14, 1963, p. 27, cited by Nelson W. Polsby, *Congress and Presidency* (Prentice-Hall Inc., 1964), p. 38.
31. Bone, *American Politics*, pp. 127-28.
32. Evans and Novak, *Lyndon B. Johnson*, pp. 103-104.
33. Writing in 1973, former Wednesday Group staff director Sven Groennings questioned the use of state delegations: "Because state delegations may consist of one member or more than 20 with personal rivalries or differences of philosophy, these delegations have limited usefulness." Sven Groennings, "The Clubs in Congress: The House Wednesday Group," in Groennings and Jonathan P. Hawley, eds., *To Be a Congressman: The Promise and the Power* (Acropolis Books, Ltd., 1973), p. 76.
34. Alan Fiellin, "The Functions of Informal Groups in Legislative Institutions," *Journal of Politics*, February 1962, pp. 72-91.
35. Charles L. Clapp, *The Congressman: His Work as He Sees It* (Brookings Institution, 1963), p. 42.
36. "The Reorganization of Congress," *Report of the Committee of the American Political Science Association* (Public Affairs Press, 1945), p. 45.
37. MacNeil, *Forge of Democracy*, pp. 173-74.
38. Richard F. Fenno Jr., "The House of Representatives as a Political System: The Problem of Integration," *American Political Science Review*, June 1962, p. 311.
39. *Ibid.*, p. 311, quoting from "History of the Committee on Appropriations," H. Doc. 299, 77th Congress, 1st session, 1941-42, p. 11.
40. *Ibid.*, pp. 316-17.
41. *Ibid.*
42. *Ibid.*
43. MacNeil, *Forge of Democracy*, pp. 273-74.
44. Ripley, *Party Leaders*, pp. 132-35.
45. *Ibid.*, pp. 135-36.
46. Polsby, *Congress and Presidency*, p. 34.
47. MacNeil, *Forge of Democracy*, p. 281. See also annual conservative coalition voting studies by Congressional Quarterly in the annual *Almanacs*.
48. MacNeil, *Forge of Democracy*, p. 283.
49. *Ibid.*, pp. 283-84.
50. Congressional Quarterly, *1975 Almanac*, p. 972.
51. Groennings, "The Wednesday Group," p. 78.
52. For background on the group, see Congressional Quarterly, *Weekly Report*, Jan. 8, 1960, pp. 39-40; *Weekly Report*, June 2, 1973, pp. 1366-71; and Democratic Study Group brochure published in 1963.
53. DSG brochure, p. 2.
54. *Ibid.*, p. 7.
55. *Ibid.*, pp. 3-4.
56. Congressional Quarterly, *Weekly Report*, June 2, 1973, p. 1368.
57. DSG brochure, p. 7.
58. Groennings, "The Wednesday Group," p. 79.
59. *Ibid.*, p. 81.
60. *Ibid.*
61. Marguerite Ross Barnett, "The Congressional Black Caucus," in Harvey C. Mansfield Sr., ed., *Congress Against the President* (Praeger Publishers, 1975), p. 36.
62. *Ibid.*, p. 45.
63. *Ibid.*, p. 46.
64. The section on MCPL has been adapted from an article appearing in Congressional Quarterly, *Weekly Report*, July 31, 1970, pp. 1952-55.

Selected Bibliography

Books

Anderson, Jack and Pearson, Drew. *The Case Against Congress.* New York: Simon & Schuster, 1968.

Barnett, Marguerite Ross. "The Congressional Black Caucus." In *Congress Against the President.* Edited by Harvey C. Mansfield Sr. New York: Praeger, 1975.

Bibby, John F. and Davidson, Roger H. *On Capitol Hill.* Hinsdale, Ill.: Dryden, 1972.

Binkley, Wilfred E. and Moos, Malcolm C. *A Grammar of American Politics,* 3rd ed. New York: Alfred A. Knopf, 1958.

Bolling, Richard. *House Out of Order.* New York: E. P. Dutton & Co., 1965.

———. *Power in the House.* New York: E. P. Dutton & Co., 1968.

Bone, Hugh A. *American Politics and the Party System,* 3rd ed. New York: McGraw-Hill, 1965.

———. *Party Committees and National Politics.* Seattle: University of Washington Press, 1958.

Burns, James MacGregor. *Congress on Trial.* New York: Gordian Press, Inc., 1966.

Chi, Chang-wei. *The Speaker of the House of Representatives Since 1896.* New York: Columbia University Press, 1928.

Clapp, Charles L. *The Congressman: His Work As He Sees It.* Washington: Brookings Institution, 1963.

Clark, Champ. *My Quarter Century in American Politics.* 2 vols. New York: Harper & Bros., 1920.

Clark, Joseph S. *Congress: The Sapless Branch.* New York: Harper & Row, 1964.

Clausen, Aage R. *How Congressmen Decide.* New York: St. Martin's Press, 1973.

Evans, Rowland and Novak, Robert. *Lyndon B. Johnson: The Exercise of Power.* New York: The New American Library, 1966.

Fenno, Richard F. Jr. "The Internal Distribution of Influence: The House." In *The Congress and America's Future.* Edited by David B. Truman. Englewood Cliffs, N.J.: Prentice-Hall, 1973.

Ferber, Mark F. "The Formation of the Democratic Study Group." In *Congressional Behavior.* Edited by Nelson W. Polsby. New York: Random House, 1971.

Follett, Mary P. *The Speaker of the House of Representatives.* New York: Longmans, Green, 1896.

Fuller, Hubert Bruce. *The Speakers of the House.* Boston: Little, Brown & Co., 1909.

Galloway, George B. *History of the House of Representatives.* New York: Thomas Y. Crowell Co., 1961.

Groennings, Sven. "The Clubs in Congress: The House Wednesday Group." In *To Be a Congressman: The Promise and the Power.* Edited by Groennings and Jonathan P. Hawley. Washington: Acropolis Books Ltd., 1973.

Gross, Bertrand M. *The Legislative Struggle.* New York: McGraw-Hill, 1953.

Harbrouck, Paul DeWitt. *Party Government in the House of Representatives.* New York: Macmillan, 1927.

Haynes, George H. *The Senate of the United States.* Boston: Houghton Mifflin, 1938.

Jones, Charles O. *Party and Policy-Making: The House Republican Policy Committee.* New Brunswick, N.J.: Rutgers University Press, 1964.

Kingdon, John W. *Congressmen's Voting Decisions.* New York: Harper & Row, 1973.

MacNeil, Neil. *Forge of Democracy.* New York: David McKay Co., 1963.

Martin, Joe. *My First Fifty Years in Politics.* New York: McGraw-Hill, 1960.

Matthews, Donald R. *U.S. Senators and Their World.* Chapel Hill; University of North Crolina Press, 1960; reprint ed., New York: Norton, 1973.

Mayhew, David R. *Party Loyalty Among Congressmen.* Cambridge: Harvard University Press, 1966.

Polsby, Nelson W. *Congress and Presidency.* Englewood Cliffs, N.J.: Prentice-Hall, Inc., 1964.

Riddick, Floyd M. *The United States Congress: Organization and Procedure.* Manassas, Va.: National Capitol Publishers, Inc., 1949.

Ripley, Randall B. *Party Leaders in the House of Representatives.* Washington: Brookings Institution, 1967.

———. *Power in the Senate.* New York: St. Martin's, 1969.

Rothman, David J. *Politics and Power: The United States Senate, 1869-1901.* Cambridge: Harvard University Press, 1966.

Saloma, John S. *Congress and the New Politics.* Boston: Little, Brown, 1969.

Truman, David B. *The Governmental Process.* New York: Alfred A. Knopf, 1964.

Ulmer, S. Sidney, ed. *Political Decision Making.* Cincinnati: Van Nostrand Reinhold, 1970.

White, William S. *Citadel.* New York: Harper & Bros., 1955.

Articles

Clausen, Aage R. "State Party Influence on Congressional Party Decisions." *Midwest Journal of Political Science,* vol. 16, 1972, pp. 77-101.

Deckard, Barbara. "State Party Delegations in the U.S. House of Representatives—A Comparative Study of Group Cohesion." *Journal of Politics,* vol. 34, 1972, pp. 199-222.

Fenno, Richard F. Jr. "The House of Representatives as a Political System: The Problem of Integration." *American Political Science Review,* June 1962, pp. 310-24.

Fiellin, Alan. "The Functions of Informal Groups in Legislative Institutions." *Journal of Politics,* February 1962, pp. 72-91.

Polsby, Nelson W. "Institutionalization in the U.S. House of Representatives." *American Political Science Review,* vol. 62, 1968, pp. 144-68.

"The Reorganization of Congress." Report of the Committee on Congress of the American Political Science Association. Public Affairs Press, 1945.

Truman, David B. "The State Delegation and the Structure of Voting in the United States House of Representatives." *American Political Science Review,* vol. 50, 1956, pp. 1023-45.

The Executive Branch

The executive branch constitutes the most important source of pressure exerted on Congress.

In his great constitutional, official and political functions, the President is many men. He is the Commander in Chief of the Army, Navy and Air Force. He directs foreign relations. He executes the laws, and in doing so, he interprets them. Beyond these functions, he is, according to political scientist Bertram M. Gross, "the most important single legislative leader in the government. Except in wartime, Presidents are now judged more by the quality of the legislation they propose or succeed in getting enacted than by their records as executives."[1]

A great many of the President's legislative functions and activities are unmentioned in the Constitution although Gross indicated that those among the Founding Fathers who later became President had no trouble discovering them. The President is able to influence congressional action through the manipulation of patronage, the allocation of federal funds and projects that may be vital to the reelection of a member of Congress, and the handling of constituents' cases in which senators and representatives are interested.[2]

The President is also the leader of the Democratic or Republican Party, and thus is his party's chief election campaigner. As President and supreme political leader, he occupies a strategic position for promoting broad coalitions of social groups and interests. The President also has ready access to the news media for promoting administration policy.

Rivalry and Cooperation

There is an ongoing institutional struggle between the executive and legislative branches, embedded in the American system by the constitutional separation of powers. Some political scientists regard the rivalry as no more than a means by which members of Congress best develop public stature by demonstrating their ability to thwart the President's objectives. British political scientist Harold Laski subscribed to such a view when he wrote, "There can be no doubt that in its own eyes, Congress establishes its prestige when it either refuses to let the President have his own way, or compels him to compromise with it."[3]

The tendency to see President and Congress forever locked in combat with one adversary seeking to dominate the other falls short of the complete picture. In the post-World-War-II period, American foreign policy could have slipped into chaos without the collaboration of President Truman, a Democrat, and Sen. Arthur H. Vandenberg (Mich.), Republican president pro tempore of the Senate.

While the Republican 80th Congress was systematically chopping away at Truman's domestic program, the legislators did not oppose the President's foreign policy when he could persuade Vandenberg to go along. The senator reminded Truman that the Congress had constitutional responsibilities and often improved legislation. Against such Republican skeptics as Sen. Robert A. Taft (Ohio), Vandenberg argued successfully that bipartisanship, far from eliminating discussion, required that foreign policy be totally debated. Once debate was finished, bipartisanship became the means, as Vandenberg put it, of placing "national security ahead of partisan advantage."[4]

Legislative Leader

Although the President's legislative role has always been important, the growing complexity of running the government has put him at the center of the legislative process. Political scientist Lawrence H. Chamberlain has observed that "When so much of the life of the individual is influenced by federal legislation, the attitude of the President toward this legislation and his skill in gaining legislative approval of his proposals are matters of practical interest to millions of people...."[5]

The President's role as legislative leader derives, at least in part, from the Constitution. While the Constitution vests "all legislative powers" in Congress, it also directs the President to "give to the Congress information of the state of the union and recommend to their consideration such measures as he shall judge necessary and expedient."[6] Congress has broadened this function to direct the President to present to Congress each year, in addition to his State of the Union Message, two other general statements of presidential aims—an Economic Report including proposals directed to the maintenance of maximum employment, and a budget message outlining appropriations proposals. During a typical session, the President transmits to Congress scores of other legislative proposals, some on his own initiative and others in conformity with various statutes.[7]

Another legislative vehicle for presidential leadership in Congress is the constitutional power to veto acts it passes, or to threaten to veto them. Presidents often use veto messages as vehicles to suggest their alternative legislative proposals.

Evolution of Presidential Pressures

The hope of strict constructionists that the executive branch would remain aloof from Congress was dashed almost at the beginning of the American Republic. President Washington carefully avoided pressuring Congress in person after his first and only attempt failed. Washington sought to receive in person the advice of the Senate on an Indian treaty. Visiting the Senate, he anticipated prompt action on the treaty, but the senators declined to act quickly. After this experience, Washington stayed away from both chambers except to deliver annual messages.

Washington's chief assistants, Secretary of the Treasury Alexander Hamilton and Secretary of State Thomas Jefferson, did present the administration's views in person. In the House where the great debates of the day were conducted, Hamilton became so influential on fiscal matters that the chamber established its Ways and Means Committee as a buffer against his pressures. As President, Jefferson held effective control over Congress through influence over his Democratic-Republican Party's congressional leadership apparatus. On legislative matters, Jefferson discovered private means to modify and temper the House's action. When in 1808 he persuaded the House to reduce a proposed increase in the size of the Army, John Quincy Adams termed Jefferson's intervention an "extra-official hint."[8]

Other early Presidents varied considerably in their approach to the legislative branch. The years between Jefferson and Andrew Jackson were not marked by notable instances of executive attempts to pressure Congress. But Jackson, elected in 1828, clashed with Congress repeatedly when he sought to enlarge executive power and make the presidency responsive to the masses.

Jackson was the first to use the veto as a major weapon, thus departing from precedents set by his six presidential predecessors who used the veto sparingly, mainly to register objections on constitutional grounds. (John Adams and Thomas Jefferson did not veto a single bill.) But Jackson employed the veto to make war on the Bank of the United States which he hated and on numerous other bills he opposed.[9]

Neil MacNeil described most of the attempted encroachments upon the prerogatives of Senate and House by 19th century presidents as "sporadic and inconclusive."[10] Even a forceful President, Abraham Lincoln, found himself on the defensive with Congress, mostly over his conduct of the Civil War. But he was able to persevere, largely because of his skill in manipulating public opinion.

For several decades after Lincoln, Congress dominated the government. As late as 1893, one Washington correspondent, Theron Crawford, wrote: "No one has apparently less influence on congressional legislation than the President of the United States. His message is treated always as a perfunctory document and while it is regularly and respectfully referred to the proper committees for consideration, it is very rare that any suggestion made by the Executive has any practical result."[11]

Theodore Roosevelt and Wilson

The pendulum swung back toward the executive at the outset of the 20th century, when President Theodore Roosevelt asked Congress to approve a far-reaching legislative program. This reform package, which Roosevelt called the "Square Deal," was the first formalized presidential program ever submitted to Congress. (In the past, such programs normally had been submitted by the Speaker of the House, as in the case of Henry Clay's American Plan, a broad program of internal improvements and tariff protection.) Major bills passed at Roosevelt's request included some of the nation's basic conservation and railroad legislation.

When Woodrow Wilson assumed the presidency in 1913, he presented Congress with a broad legislative program and saw himself in the role of a prime minister in getting laws enacted. He was an admirer of the British parliamentary system in which the head of government, the prime minister, as Cabinet leader and member of the House of Commons guides legislation through the chamber.

During his first five years in office, Wilson showed considerable political skill in getting his domestic programs enacted. He used postmaster patronage as effectively as any predecessor in the interest of passing his legislation. Wilson, the 28th President, became the first chief executive since John Adams, the second President, to appear personally before Congress to deliver his annual messages. He appeared before joint sessions or only one chamber 19 other times to advocate specific domestic or foreign programs. *(Presidential appearances, box p. 623)*

Sen. Joseph S. Clark (D Pa.) wrote that Wilson "pleaded for party unity and it worked. When Wilson sought tariff revision, he used every tactic ever devised by a President, even to dropping in on legislative committee meetings. When the Underwood reform tariff bill received the vote of every Democratic senator, it seemed as though the scholar turned politician had found the elusive cure for executive-legislative ills. His legislative accomplishments were impressive. In addition to the tariff, the Federal Reserve Act, the Clayton Act, the Federal Trade Commission Act and child labor legislation were a few results of Wilson's executive leadership."[12]

But at the middle of his second term, after the Allied victory in World War I, Wilson was shattered by the election of a Republican Senate which refused to ratify U.S. participation in his cherished League of Nations. The defeat of the League of Nations marked a resumption of congressional supremacy that was to continue through the administrations of Warren G. Harding, Calvin Coolidge and Herbert Hoover.[13]

FDR's One Hundred Days

A President even more adept than Wilson at pushing his program through Congress was Franklin D. Roosevelt, whose first 100 days in the White House have no counterpart in U.S. history. Like Wilson, Roosevelt considered the presidency a position of leadership. "The Presidency is not merely an administrative office," he observed during the 1932 campaign. "That is the least of it.... It is preeminently a place of moral leadership...."[14]

Roosevelt scored his first major legislative victory within days after taking office, when he appeared before Congress to ask special powers to ward off the threat of a nationwide banking panic. "In the event that the Congress shall fail to take these courses," he said, "and in the event

(Continued on p. 624)

Presidential Appearances Before Congress

Only 12 of the 38 Presidents have appeared personally before Congress as a means of promoting their legislative programs. George Washington set a brief precedent in 1789 when he addressed the members on the occasion of his first Annual Message. John Adams stood before Congress six times, but successor Thomas Jefferson dropped the practice of personal appearances.

From 1797 until 1913—from Adams' last appearance to speak on relations with France until Woodrow Wilson's first appearnce on Capitol Hill to deliver his first Annual Message—a line of 25 Presidents entered neither House nor Senate chamber to address members.

Wilson's return to the custom of Washington and Adams was controversial. Some members mocked it as the President's "speech from the throne." But Wilson appeared 25 more times to establish a record. Runners-up are Harry S Truman, 17 appearances, and Franklin D. Roosevelt, 16 times. Between Wilson, the 28th President, and Gerald R. Ford, the 38th, all Presidents have addressed Congress except Herbert Hoover. Since Truman, Annual Messages have been called State of the Union Messages.

Following is a list of the direct appearances by Presidents before Congress through May 1976 (appearances are before joint sessions unless otherwise indicated):

President	Number of Appearances	Occasions
Washington	10	8 Annual Messages (1789-1796); 2 Inaugural Addresses (1789, 1793—second Inaugural before Senate only).
Adams	6	4 Annual Messages (1797-1800); Inaugural Address (1797); Relations With France Message (1797).
Wilson	26	6 Annual Messages (1913-1918). Also *1913:* Tariff Reform, Bank Reform, Relations with Mexico; *1914:* Antitrust Laws, Panama Canal Tolls, Relations with Mexico, New Tax Revenue. *1916:* Impending Rail Strike. *1917:* "Peace Without Victory" (Senate only), Breaking Relations with Germany, Arming of Merchant Ships, Request for War Declaration Against Germany. *1918:* Federal Takeover of Railroads, "14 Points" for Peace, Peace Outlook, Need for New Revenue, Request for Ratification of Women's Suffrage Amendment (Senate only), Announcing Armistice. *1919:* Request for Ratification of Versailles Treaty (Senate only), High Cost of Living.
Harding	7	2 Annual Messages (1921-22); Federal Problems Message (1921); 2 Merchant Marine Messages (1922); Coal and Railroad Message (1922); Debt Message (1923).
Coolidge	2	Annual Message (1923); George Washington's Birthday Message (1927).
Roosevelt	16	10 Annual Messages (1934-43); 100th Anniversary of Lafayette's Death (1934); 150th Anniversary of First Congress (1939);

President	Number of Appearances	Occasions
Roosevelt		Neutrality Address (1939); National Defense Message (1940); Declaration of War (1941); Yalta Conference Report (1945).
Truman	17	6 State of the Union Messages (1947-52); Prosecution of the War Message (1945); Submission of UN Charter (Senate only, 1945); Congressional Medal of Honor Ceremony (1945); Universal Military Training Message (1945); Railroad Strike Message (1946); Greek-Turkish Aid Policy (1947); Aid to Europe Message (1947); National Security and Conditions in Europe Message (1948); 50th Anniversary of the Liberation of Cuba (1948); Inflation, Housing and Civil Rights Message (1948); Steel Industry Dispute (1952).
Eisenhower	7	6 State of the Union Messages (1953-54; 1957-60); Message on Middle East (1957).
Kennedy	3	State of the Union Messages (1961-63).
Johnson	8	6 State of the Union Messages (1964-69); Assumption of Office (1963); Voting Rights (1965).
Nixon	7	4 State of the Union Messages (1970-72, 1974); Vietnam Policy (1969—separate addresses before House and Senate); Economic Policy Message (1971); Message on return from the Soviet Union (1972).
Ford*	5	2 State of the Union Messages (1975-76); Assumption of Office (1974); Inflation Message (1974); State of the World Message (1975).

*On Oct. 17, 1974, President Ford testified before the House Judiciary Subcommittee on Criminal Justice on his pardon of former President Nixon for alleged Watergate crimes.

Sources: Congressional Research Service, Library of Congress; *Congressional Record.*

(Continued from p. 622)

the national emergency is still critical, I shall not evade the clear course of duty that will then confront me. I shall ask Congress for the one remaining instrument to meet the crisis—broad executive power to wage a war against the emergency as great as the power that would be given me if we were in fact invaded by a foreign foe."[15] The requested powers were granted that day; they were even supported by House Republican Minority Leader, Bertrand Snell (N.Y.), who declared that "The house is burning down, and the President of the United States says this is the way to put out the fire."[16]

Congress went on, in the spring of 1933, to approve a flood of administration proposals, scarcely pausing to change as much as a comma. At the time, the President's program became known as the "Roosevelt Revolution," but the President said he preferred the term "New Deal." In the first 100 days alone, Congress approved the bank reorganization bill, authority to cut government operating expenses by 25 per cent, a farm relief bill, a massive public works program, relief grants to the states, establishment of a Civilian Conservation Corps, and other important measures. Although the going got much tougher in subsequent sessions of Congress, Roosevelt still won enactment of such landmark measures as the Trade Agreements Act, the Social Security Act, the Public Utilities Holding Company Act and other important legislation.

Postwar Leadership

Postwar Presidents came to exert a new kind of pressure on Congress in matters of national security—a pressure that sought to have Congress endorse presidential initiatives and decisions.

Historian Arthur Schlesinger summarized the postwar pre-eminence of the White House in this way: "The postwar Presidents, though Eisenhower and Kennedy markedly less than Truman, Johnson and Nixon, almost came to see the sharing of power with Congress in foreign policy as a derogation of the presidency. Congress, in increasing self-abasement, almost came to love its impotence. The image of the President acting by himself in foreign affairs, imposing his own sense of reality and necessity on a waiting government and people, became the new orthodoxy."[17]

Dwarfed by the presidential giant on issues of peace and war, Congress did fight, often successfully, to deny postwar Presidents much of what they wanted in the realm of domestic legislation. Harry S Truman, Dwight D. Eisenhower and John F. Kennedy all maintained the executive's initiative in proposing legislation, but none matched the legislative record of a Wilson or a Franklin Roosevelt.[18]

Johnson's Handling of Congress

No President ever came to office more schooled in the ways of Congress than did Lyndon Johnson. He had worked at the Capitol for 32 years, first as a congressional secretary, then as a House member, senator, Senate minority leader, Senate majority leader and Vice President. With Johnson applying the pressure, the 89th Congress in a single year, 1965, put on the books the broadest domestic legislative program since Roosevelt's first 100 days. Among its landmark enactments were federal aid to elementary and secondary education, a voting rights act, a comprehensive federal health care program for the aged, rent supplements for needy families and a major liberalization of the immigration laws.[19]

An important aspect of Johnson's legislative strategy was explained at a meeting of administration legislative liaison officers in January 1965. "I have watched the Congress from either the inside or the outside, man and boy, for more than 40 years," he said, "and I've never seen a Congress that didn't eventually take the measure of the President it was dealing with." Johnson therefore urged quick enactment of his entire "Great Society" program against the day when relations with Congress should turn sour.[20]

For the most part, the immense Democratic majorities that Johnson swept into office in the 1964 election were eager to do the President's bidding. He was always ready to put on the pressure, however, if a member stepped out of line.

Whatever the pressure method he employed, Johnson was amazingly successful. According to a Congressional Quarterly study, Congress in 1965 approved 68.9 per cent of the President's requests, the highest score since CQ began its tabulations in 1953. The figure was in marked contrast to President Kennedy's low of 27.2 per cent, recorded only two years earlier.[21]

But just as other strong Presidents had experienced, Congress eventually rebelled at the pressure treatment, and after 1966, the pace of legislation slowed. Divided over the President's Vietnam War policy and the inflation it had wrought on the economy, the nation elected 47 more Republicans to the House in 1966. Johnson proposed civil rights open-housing legislation in 1966 and 1967, but it was not enacted until 1968 when many American cities were torn by racial disorders and riots. The 90th Congress (1967-69), still Democratic but less liberal than the 89th, was often hostile to Johnson programs.

Nixon and Democratic Congresses

Richard M. Nixon, like Kennedy and Johnson, had served in both the House and Senate before entering the White House. But unlike the two Democratic Presidents, Republican Nixon was confronted by a Congress controlled by the opposition party. As a result, he was repeatedly at odds with Congress. Within the first 15 months of his presidency, the Senate refused to confirm his two southern nominees to the Supreme Court.

After the 1970 congressional elections which resulted in minor Senate gains for the Republicans and minor House gains for the Democrats, Nixon in January 1971 outlined to Congress "six great goals" of his administration: welfare reform, revenue sharing with the states and municipalities, health insurance reform, environmental initiatives, government reorganization and full employment. But by the end of 1972, and Nixon's first term, Congress had passed only one Nixon objective, revenue sharing. And in 1973, Congress, growing rebellious about executive dominance over international policies, dealt Nixon a severe setback on Nov. 7, when it voted to override his veto of the War Powers Act, the first time in the history of the nation that Congress had put limits on presidential powers to act in international emergencies.[22]

The abbreviated second Nixon administration was marked by the President's all-consuming fight to survive the Watergate scandal. Although Congress was initially criticized for acting slowly in the scandal, the House Judiciary Committee voted three articles of impeachment 10 days before Nixon resigned the presidency on Aug. 9, 1974.

Ford vs. Congress

When Gerald R. Ford assumed the presidency, he became the first to do so without being elected by the people to that office or to the vice presidency. He entered the White House after 25 years service in the House, the last nine as Republican minority leader.

Taking up the presidential burden in the wake of Watergate, Ford won a measure of cooperation from his former congressional colleagues. His first request, for a wage-price council to monitor inflation, cleared Congress in little more than a week. But his pardon of Nixon soon soured that early rapport, and while Ford did win some legislative victories, they came only after long struggles. His major initiative in 1974, a series of proposals for legislation to combat the soaring inflation, died a quiet death on Capitol Hill.

The first session of the 94th Congress ended in December 1975 on the same note of conflict that had typified its relations with the Ford administration throughout the year. Congress had begun the session resolutely opposed to the President's request for more military aid to the collapsing regime in South Vietnam. On the last day of the session, Dec. 19, the Senate voted down Ford's request for military aid for a pro-Western faction involved in a civil war in the African nation of Angola.

Throughout 1975, Ford and the Democratic-controlled Congress remained in a legislative stalemate. Ford vetoed 17 bills passed by Congress and only four bills were enacted over his veto.

Executive Liaison With Congress

Woodrow Wilson was the first President to devise the specific technique of lobbying Congress for measures he wanted by quietly using intimates to act as his liaison with members. Wilson made the lobbying operation as discreet as possible. His unofficial chief congressional liaison officer was Postmaster General Albert Burleson, a Texas Democrat who had quit the House to take the Cabinet position. With the disposal of post offices and postmasterships at his command, Burleson held considerable influence over representatives.

At Burleson's suggestion, Wilson enlisted another Texan, Rep. John Nance Garner, a member of the Ways and Means Committee and later Speaker and Vice President, to act as the President's confidential lobbyist inside the House. This relationship was hidden from the House Democratic hierarchy. Supposedly on his own business, Garner left Capitol Hill twice a week by streetcar, got off near the White House, entered the mansion through a side door, and was ushered into Wilson's private study where he reported to the President.[23]

Franklin D. Roosevelt used several White House aides, James Rowe, Thomas Corcoran and Benjamin Cohen, to exert pressure on members of Congress. However, their official duties ranged beyond congressional relations, including the role of drafting New Deal legislation, which made them natural choices for lobbying to get bills enacted. Postmaster General James A. Farley, who simultaneously was Democratic national chairman, used additional powers as Roosevelt's patronage dispenser, to influence decisions in the House. Like his predecessor, Harry S Truman used White House assistants Clark Clifford and Charles Murphy in part-time legislative liaison work.

Wrote Neil MacNeil, "Wilson, Roosevelt and Truman, in not publicly designating their liaison men to Congress, kept up a pretense of staying within the traditional strictures of the assumed independence of the President and the Congress. They felt the need for such intimate contact with the members of Congress, but they hesitated to offend the sensibilities of the House and Senate as institutions."[24]

Institutionalized Liaison

Beginning with Dwight D. Eisenhower, to bolster their direct-pressure efforts, Presidents have appointed full-time legislative liaison officers to their White House staff. In addition, all federal departments now have their own congressional liaison force. The practice began in 1945, when the War Department created the office of assistant secretary for congressional liaison, thus centralizing congressional relations which had been handled separately by the respective military services.

Eisenhower named Bryce N. Harlow, long an employee of the House Armed Services Committee, as his top special assistant for congressional affairs, a post he held under various titles for eight years. The position no longer was anonymous, nor did Harlow have other White House assignments, as did his predecessors.

According to MacNeil, Harlow "normally operated from his White House office, answering and making telephone calls, perhaps as many as 125 a day." MacNeil's account of Harlow's liaison methods continued: "Only rarely did he slip up to the House of Representatives and usually then only to have a private lunch with Charles Halleck of Indiana, one of the Republican leaders.... Harlow kept the Republican party's congressional leaders informed of forthcoming Eisenhower legislative proposals and kept in touch with the Democratic leaders. Frequently he escorted Speaker Sam Rayburn and Senate Majority Leader Lyndon Johnson into the White House late in the day for a highball and chat with the President.... Harlow tried to satisfy the requests of members and tried to persuade them to support the President's program. 'In this game,' he said, 'it's what you've done lately that counts.' "[25]

Kennedy-O'Brien Liaison Team

President Kennedy sought to beef up the liaison function, appointing his long-time associate Lawrence F. O'Brien as chief lobbyist and giving O'Brien full authority to speak for him on legislative matters. O'Brien, who was designated "Special Assistant for Congressional Affairs," was given coequal rank with other top White House aides and was assigned assistants for both House and Senate. MacNeil reported that "to even the most influential senators who telephoned Kennedy in the first weeks of his presidency, the President had a stock reply: 'Have you discussed this with Larry O'Brien?' "[26]

At the outset of the Kennedy administration, O'Brien organized a series of cocktail parties, all held in House committee rooms, in which he sought to meet House members on a purely social basis. Later, O'Brien invited House members in groups of 50 for coffee at the White House. For committee chairmen, he set up private discussions with the President. At a dinner with the Democratic Study Group, a bloc of about 100 House liberals, O'Brien promised that the President would support them for re-election if they backed his legislative program. "The White House certainly remembers who its friends are," he said, "and can be counted on to apply significant assistance in the campaign."[27]

Clearing their activities with O'Brien, Cabinet officials sought to cultivate key congressional leaders. Defense Secretary Robert S. McNamara courted House Armed Services Committee Chairman Carl Vinson (D Ga.), Vinson's Senate counterpart Richard B. Russell (also a Georgia Democrat) and other key members of the House and Senate military committees. Treasury Secretary Douglas Dillon kept in close touch with House Ways and Means Committee Chairman Wilbur D. Mills (D Ark.). Agriculture Secretary Orville L. Freeman consulted frequently with congressional leaders on the President's farm program. Other Cabinet officers and their liaison staffs made similar contacts.[28]

Kennedy and O'Brien made extensive use of the congressional liaison offices of the Cabinet departments and executive agencies. When an administration bill was introduced in Congress, the department involved was given the prime responsibility for getting the measure through the subcommittee and committee stages. When the bill neared House or Senate floor for debate and vote, O'Brien and his corps of White House lobbyists joined forces with the agency liaison teams. There were about 35 agency lobbyists working during the Kennedy-Johnson era although not all of them devoted full time to legislation.[29]

The Kennedy tactics were often successful in removing major legislative obstacles, but the obstacles appeared so frequently that the President's program foundered in Congress. Some members, primarily the older, more conservative ones, resented the pressure treatment. As Meg Greenfield reported: "The most widely shared and loudly voiced grievance that Congress has against administration practices concerns the unremitting attention it receives from those it describes simply and without affection as the 'young men.' They badger, to hear the members tell it. They hector. They even chase.... Legislators who still cherish the notion that they themselves will decide how to vote appear to have been at various times amused, confused and infuriated by the discombobulation of incoming messages.... 'Why are you calling me, son?' an august legislator asked an all but anonymous administration phoner not long ago.... To the White House counterclaim that pushing and prodding sometimes helps and never hurts, one congressman replies by citing the case of a young liaison man, the very sight of whom at the cloakroom door, he claims, is enough to cost the administration 25 votes. Under questioning, he lowered the figure to three, but this time he seemed serious."[30]

Liaison Under Johnson

The liaison system Kennedy nurtured paid dividends during the Johnson administration. Loyal Democrats had picked up a working margin of seats in the 1964 election, and with O'Brien still supervising the liaison job, almost all of the old Kennedy measures sailed through Congress. Even after Johnson appointed O'Brien to be Postmaster General, he continued as chief White House lobbyist, after Johnson himself.[31]

O'Brien abided by one self-imposed rule. He would not enter the public congressional galleries, either to listen to debate or watch the members vote. MacNeil added, "He could read the debate and count the vote in the *Congressional Record* the next day. To appear in the gallery, however, might smack of an impropriety; it might seem that he was asserting an undue pressure on the members of Congress. O'Brien's sensitivity here was a trace, a faint trace, of the old constitutional separatism between the executive and legislative branches of the government. There were scarcely any others left. The rest had been eroded by the imperious demands of modern America."[32]

Nixon and Ford

Although President Nixon sought to slow down the furious pace of legislation that had marked the Johnson years, he still relied on a large liaison staff to push key administration bills. As chief lobbyist, he named Bryce Harlow, who came back to the White House after eight years of lobbying for the Procter and Gamble Co. In Nixon's first two years, his lobby force lost critical battles over two Supreme Court nominations and over restrictions on the administration's Southeast Asia policy but won a notable victory on funds for deployment of a controversial antiballistic missile system.

Harlow served Nixon until April 1974, four months before Nixon's resignation. In addition to Harlow, during the Nixon years, much of the day-to-day congressional liaison was handled by William E. Timmons, who had served in both Senate and House members' offices.

When Timmons resigned as chief liaison officer Dec. 31, 1974, President Ford promoted Max L. Friedersdorf to the position. A former newspaper reporter, Friedersdorf had been an administrative assistant to a House member and a congressional relations officer with the Office of Economic Opportunity.

Appeals to Public Opinion

Other pressure methods available to the President include the manipulation of public opinion through television, radio and the press. Since the early days of the Republic, Presidents have gone over the head of Congress, often successfully, to work up support for their legislative programs.

The most effective practitioner of public relations among the early Presidents was Andrew Jackson, who used the partisan press to considerable advantage in his frequent battles with Congress. Jackson arranged release of official policies to sustain his favorite publications, a practice that his successors continued until Lincoln's time. James E. Pollard has written: "[Jackson] knew what he wanted, he meant to have his way, and he was fortunate in finding journalists devoted to him and capable of carrying out his desires. The result was the most effective employment of the press for partisan purposes in the long history of the Presidency."[33]

Lincoln, highly sensitive to public opinion, vastly broadened the presidency's channels for mobilizing grassroots support. With little regard for partisanship, Lincoln passed out stories to correspondents and editors and wrote numerous letters outlining his views, which eventually found their way into print. His many eloquent addresses received widespread publicity and also helped to galvanize public support for his policies. George Fort Milton has asserted that no President ever surpassed and few equaled Lincoln as "chief of public opinion." He always tried to inform the people of the controlling reasons for his policies and acts. "While he paid some heed to the sanctity of military secrets, he declined to worship at that shrine. He knew that the people had ears, whether the walls had them or not, and took advantage of every appropriate occasion to tell them his innermost thoughts."[34]

Presidents and the Press

Andrew Johnson was the first President to grant a formal interview to the press. Between October 1865 and May 1868, Johnson gave 12 exclusive interviews, most of them dealing with his troubles with Congress. The interviews were ineffective, however, in evoking support for his position.[35]

Presidential relations with the press took a major step forward in Theodore Roosevelt's administration. The President made himself readily available to newsmen and instituted the practice of systematic White House issuance of news releases.[36]

Roosevelt visualized the Presidency as a "bully pulpit" and used his flair for showmanship to mobilize popular support. When in December 1907 he dispatched the whole U.S. battleship fleet on a 14-month cruise around the world, the Navy lacked funds to pay the costs of such a long voyage. But the public was so impressed by this display of American naval power that Congress lost no time in approving the necessary appropriations.

Roosevelt is credited with having developed the "background" news conference, often called the "trial balloon," a technique later Presidents used extensively for testing public opinion prior to announcing a course of action.

Presidential newsmaking techniques also advanced under Woodrow Wilson, who instituted the regular and formal White House press conference and increased the frequency of presidential statements to the public. Until the war in Europe absorbed virtually all of his time, Wilson held press conferences on the average of twice a week.[37]

Of all his opinion-molding techniques, Wilson was most effective with the direct appeal to the public. Several weeks after his inauguration, he issued a statement attacking the "extraordinary exertions" being made by private lobby groups to alter his tariff legislation. "The newspapers are being filled with paid advertisements," he said, "calculated to mislead the judgment of public men, not only, but also the public opinion of the country itself." It was unfair, he added, that "the people at large should have no lobby and be voiceless in these matters, while great bodies of astute men seek to create an artificial public opinion and to overcome the interests of the public for their profit."[38] While usually successful, this technique failed Wilson in 1919. His whistle-stop tour of the country in September, undertaken to generate popular support for the League of Nations, did not arouse enough public backing to force Senate ratification of the Treaty of Versailles, which contained the Covenant of the League.[39]

'Fireside Chats'

Probably no President in history has used the news media to such advantage as did Franklin D. Roosevelt, particularly in the period of legislative fervor that was his first 100 days. Roosevelt showered attention on White House correspondents, holding 998 news conferences during his 147 months in office.[40] As a result, Pollard has written: "He was on an unprecedented footing with the working press. He knew its ways, he understood many of its problems and he more than held his own in his twice-weekly parry and thrust with the correspondents. In time, of course, some of the glamor wore off and occasionally he was quite out of patience. But on the whole, he made the relationship such an integral part of his working program that any comparison with any previous Administration is futile."[41]

In the nationwide radio hookup, Roosevelt found a powerful new opinion-making tool. At the conclusion of his first week in office, he allayed widespread apprehension with a radio message urging confidence in his banking reforms.

Similar radio messages followed, and they became known as "fireside chats." As Arthur Schlesinger Jr. has put it, these discussions were effective because they "conveyed Roosevelt's conception of himself as a man at ease in his own house talking frankly and intimately to neighbors as they sat in their living rooms."[42] Wilfred Binkley observed: "[Roosevelt] had only to glance toward a microphone or suggest that he might go on the air again and a whole congressional delegation would surrender. They had no relish for the flood of mail and telegrams they knew would swamp them after another fireside chat to the nation."[43]

Presidential Use of Television

The next innovation in White House public relations techniques occurred in the Eisenhower administration, when the President permitted increased use of the direct quotation and opened his news conferences to television filming, subject to White House editing. The first news conference televised, after previewing by White House press aides, occurred Jan. 19, 1955.

President Kennedy broke new ground by permitting live televising of his press conferences, which meant the public saw his actual response to questions without White House editing. But the Kennedy administration was bombarded with charges of "managed news" after Arthur Sylvester, assistant secretary of defense for public affairs, defended managed news as "part of the arsenal of weaponry that a President has." Sylvester also asserted that it was "the government's inherent right to lie, if necessary,"[44] in a major crisis. Professor James Pollard, in his books discussing press relations President-by-President, stated that Kennedy administration attempts to manage the news "had ample historical precedent since nearly every President, from Washington through Eisenhower, at one time or other and in one way or other, sought to manipulate the news and control it to a degree."[45]

President Johnson and the Press

The Johnson administration suffered from what the press and opposing politicians called a "credibility gap" to express their doubts about official truthfulness. Johnson's credibility troubles were rooted mainly in the Vietnam War.

Congress, as it became increasingly critical of Vietnam policy, was to exploit the credibility gap by criticizing the Johnson position, sometimes doing so through nationally televised hearings. Thus, the Senate Foreign Relations Committee in 1966 turned a televised hearing on a fiscal 1966 supplemental appropriations request for military operations in Vietnam into a full-scale debate on the essentials of U.S. policy. That was the intention of Chairman J. William Fulbright (D Ark.) who had become the chief congressional critic of the administration's involvement in the war.

Nixon, Watergate and the Media

Presidents have used television—either through the press conference format or in speeches to the American public—to state their positions in national crises. Thus, President Nixon used the medium on several occasions to defend his actions on Watergate.

(Continued on p. 629)

Vetoes and Vetoes Overridden, 1789-1976

From 1789 through June 30, 1976, Presidents had vetoed a grand total of 2,342 bills, with all except 58 of the vetoes occurring in the years since President Lincoln's administration. The pocket veto, authorized under Article I, Section 7 of the Constitution, was used 987 times. *(Box on pocket vetoes, p. 630)* Of the vetoed bills, only 86, or 3.7 per cent, became law through action by Congress overriding the President's veto. The Presidents who vetoed the most bills were Franklin D. Roosevelt (635 during his 12 years in the White House) and Grover Cleveland (584 during an eight-year period). The President who had the most vetoes overridden was Andrew Johnson (15 of the 29 bills vetoed).

Public and Private Bills

The following list shows the number of private and public bills vetoed by each President through Roosevelt, the type of veto used, and the number of vetoes overridden:

1789-1945

Public and Private Bills

President	All Bills Vetoed	Regular Vetoes	Pocket Vetoes	Vetoes Overriden
Washington	2	2	0	0
J. Adams	0	0	0	0
Jefferson	0	0	0	0
Madison	7	5	2	0
Monroe	1	1	0	0
J.Q. Adams	0	0	0	0
Jackson	12	5	7	0
Van Buren	1	0	1	0
W.H. Harrison	0	0	0	0
Tyler	10	6	4	1
Polk	3	2	1	0
Taylor	0	0	0	0
Fillmore	0	0	0	0
Pierce	9	9	0	5
Buchanan	7	4	3	0
Lincoln	6	2	4	0
A. Johnson	29	21	8	15
Grant	93	45	48	4
Hayes	13	12	1	1
Garfield	0	0	0	0
Arthur	12	4	8	1
Cleveland (1st term)	414	304	110	2
B. Harrison	44	19	25	1
Cleveland (2nd term)	170	42	128	5
McKinley	42	6	36	0
T. Roosevelt	82	42	40	1
Taft	39	30	9	1
Wilson	44	33	11	6
Harding	6	5	1	0
Coolidge	50	20	30	4
Hoover	37	21	16	3
F.D. Roosevelt	635	372	263	9

Up until 1969, Presidents usually vetoed more private bills than public bills. President Truman, for example, vetoed 83 public bills, and 167 private bills. Likewise, President Eisenhower vetoed 81 public bills and 100 private bills. But Presidents Nixon and Ford reversed the picture. President Nixon vetoed only three private bills during his years in office, and President Ford had vetoed only three private bills as of June 30, 1976.

Generally, a private bill names a particular individual or entity who is to receive relief from the federal government under the terms of the bill—payment of claims, a pension, citizenship, etc. This distinguished from a public bill which relates to public matters and deals with individuals only by classifications or categories. *(Private bills chapter, p. 299)*

Beginning with the Truman administration, Congressional Quarterly has divided presidential vetoes into public and private bills. The table below lists total bills and public bills vetoed since 1945. If listed in the bill status section of the *Digest of Public General Bills*, a bill was categorized as public; if not, it was classified as private.

In earlier periods, the distinction between public and private bills was hazy, with some bills now considered public designated as private and vice versa. The *Digest of Public General Bills* was first published by the Library of Congress for the 74th Congress, 2nd session (1936). (The *Digest* is published five times a year.) Consequently a reliable breakdown of vetoes into public and private bills for administrations prior to Truman's is not feasible. The following list shows the total number of bills (public and private) and for public bills the type of action taken and the number of vetoes overridden:

1945-1976

Public Bills

President	All Bills Vetoed	Total Vetoed	Regular Vetoes	Pocket Vetoes	Vetoes Overridden
Truman	250	83	54	29	11 [1]
Eisenhower	181	81	36	45	2
Kennedy	21	9	4	5	0
Johnson	30	13	6	7	0
Nixon	43 [2]	40	24	16 [2]	5
Ford	49 [3]	46	35	11	8

1. *Truman also had one private bill overridden, making a total of 12 Truman vetoes overridden.*

2. *Includes Nixon pocket veto of a bill during the 1970 congressional Christmas recess which was later ruled invalid by the District Court for the District of Columbia and the U.S. Court of Appeals for the District of Columbia.*

3. *Figures for Ford as of June 30, 1976.*

Sources: *Presidential Vetoes, Record of Bills Vetoed and Action Taken Thereon by the Senate and House of Representatives, First Congress Through the Ninetieth Congress, 1789-1968,* compiled by the Senate Library, under the direction of Richard D. Hupman, librarian (U.S. Government Printing Office, 1969); *Digest of Public General Bills,* Congressional Reference Service, Library of Congress, U.S. Government Printing Office.

(Continued from p. 627)

Addressing a national television audience on April 30, 1973, Nixon announced the resignations of aides H. R. Haldeman and John D. Ehrlichman, describing them as "two of the finest public servants it has been my privilege to know."[46] Nixon added that the two, who later were convicted of Watergate crimes, were leaving the White House in the interest of restoring confidence in the presidency.

Later in 1973 in an effort to stem the growing tide of public opinion against him, Nixon launched "Operation Candor," an attempt to downgrade Watergate as a matter of presidential, congressional and public concern. He made several speeches in the South where his support was strongest. Then, on Nov. 17, 1973, he stunned the nation at a nationally televised press conference at the annual Association Press Managing Editors meeting. Under fire about his personal finances and income tax payments, the President stated, "I made my mistakes, but in all my years in public life, I have never profited, never profited from public service. I have earned every cent.... Well, I am not a crook."[47]

"Operation Candor" had a transitory impact. In early December, the Gallup Poll showed a slight improvement for the President. Thereafter, Nixon's position in the polls plummeted until his resignation Aug. 9, 1974.

Ford and the Press

After President Ford assumed the office on Aug. 9, 1974, he promised an "open administration."[48] However, despite general gratitude from White House reporters for their accessibility to Ford and many key members of his administration, relations between the White House and the press grew increasingly testy during 1975.

The National Press Club, in a study released Dec. 29, 1975, praised Ford for his openness. The President had held 24 news conferences and more than 50 interviews since he took office 19 months before, compared with former President Nixon's 37 press conferences in 5½ years. But the Press Club report criticized White House Press Secretary Ron Nessen for being unprepared or less than candid at press briefings, especially regarding foreign policy.

For his part, Nessen lashed out at the press for making Ford appear inept and awkward by emphasizing through photographs and editorial cartoons a number of minor accidents, beginning with Ford's stumbling down the steps of Air Force One in Salzburg, Austria.

The Veto and Threat of Veto

From a purely defensive standpoint, the most powerful weapon in the President's arsenal is his authority to veto bills. Under terms of the Constitution, Congress must submit to the President every bill or joint resolution, which he must then approve or else send back to Congress. In the event he disapproves, Congress can override the veto only by a 2/3 vote of both houses. (Under a Supreme Court decision, a quorum must be present for the override to be effective.)

Because a President usually finds it relatively easy to marshal the support of at least one-third plus one member of the House or the Senate, the veto has been used with deadly effect.

From 1789 through June 1976, 2,342 bills have been vetoed. The direct veto has been used 1,355 times and the pocket veto 987 times. On 86 occasions a presidential veto has been overridden by Congress. *(Box on vetoes, p. 628; pocket vetoes, p. 630)*

The concept of *veto* (I forbid) originated in the Roman Empire as a means of protecting the plebeians from injustice at the hands of the patricians. Roman tribunes, representing the masses, were authorized to veto acts of the Senate, dominated by the patricians. English rulers were given absolute veto power, and in 1597, Queen Elizabeth I rejected more parliamentary bills than she accepted. The English veto, which is absolute and cannot be overridden, is still nominally in effect but has not been used since 1707.

Early American Presidents conceived of the veto as a device to be used rarely and then only against legislative encroachment on the prerogatives of another branch of government. Washington vetoed only two bills; Adams and Jefferson, none. Although Madison and Monroe vetoed seven bills between them, they cited constitutional grounds for doing so in all except one case. John Quincy Adams, like his father John Adams, did not veto a bill.[49]

Jackson's View of Veto

The concept of the veto underwent a marked change under Andrew Jackson, who vetoed 12 bills, mostly because he took issue with their content or purpose. His most noteworthy veto was that of a bill to recharter the Bank of the United States, which Jackson considered a creature of special interests. Binkley has described Jackson's message vetoing that bill "a landmark in the evolution of the presidency." Binkley said: "For the first time in American history, a veto message was used as an instrument of party warfare. Through it, the Democratic Party, as the Jacksonians were now denominated, dealt a telling blow to their opponents, the National Republicans. Though addressed to Congress, the veto message was an appeal to the nation. Not a single opportunity to discredit the old ruling class was missed."[50]

President John Tyler's veto of a tariff bill in 1843 brought on the first attempt by Congress to impeach a President. An impeachment resolution, introduced in the House by Whig Members, charged the President "with the high crime and misdemeanor of withholding his assent to laws indispensable to the just operation of the government."[51] When the impeachment move failed, Henry Clay proposed a constitutional amendment to enable Congress to override the President's veto by a simple majority instead of the required two-thirds vote. Noting that the President's right of veto gave him power equal to that of almost two-thirds of Congress, Clay declared that such power would ultimately make the President "ruler of the nation."[52]

Use of Veto After the Civil War

After the Civil War, the determination of Radical Republican Congresses to write their own reconstruction policy in defiance of the executive represented a new landmark in legislative-executive relations. When President Andrew Johnson vetoed a bill to protect the rights of freedmen, Congress passed the measure over his head—the first time in the nation's history that Congress had overridden the President's veto on a major issue. The civil rights bill was only the first of a number of measures to be passed over Johnson's veto. Among others was the Tenure of Office Act, which led indirectly to Johnson's impeachment. When Johnson refused to abide by the provisions of the act, which prohibited the President from removing appointed officials from office until their successors had been confirmed, the House initiated impeachment proceedings. Although

Pocket Veto Controversy and Court Rulings

Under the veto procedure outlined in the Constitution, the President must return a bill within 10 days of its receipt to the chamber where it originated. The bill automatically becomes a law if the President has not returned it within that time.

A second clause of Article I, Section 7, of the Constitution provides that a bill "shall not be a law" if "Congress by their adjournment prevent its return." The President then can "pocket veto" the bill, since he does not have an opportunity to return it to Congress together with his objections.

A controversy arose in the 1970s over what kind of a congressional adjournment "prevents" the return of a bill by the President. Court decisions in 1974 and 1976 specified that a President's power to use the pocket veto was restricted to final adjournments of Congresses. The 1974 decision stemmed from a case brought by Sen. Edward M. Kennedy (D Mass.) challenging former President Richard M. Nixon's use of the pocket veto in the 1st session of the 92nd Congress on a bill for which the 10-day period had expired during the 1971 Christmas recess. The President Dec. 14, 1971, received the Family Practice of Medicine Act (S 3418). The Family Practice of Medicine Act had been passed by a nearly unanimous vote of 64-1 in the Senate and 346-2 in the House.

Kennedy, Aug. 2, 1972, initiated a suit *(Kennedy v. Sampson)* in federal district court in the District of Columbia against two administration officials—Arthur F. Sampson, acting administrator of the General Services Administration, and Thomas M. Jones, White House records chief—asking the court to declare Nixon's veto of S 3418 invalid and to order the defendents to publish the bill as a law.

A final decision was issued in the case on Aug. 14, 1974, by the United States Court of Appeals for the District of Columbia. Citing a 1932 Supreme Court decision, *Edwards v. United States,* the court said the pocket veto served two main functions: 1) to give the President a suitable opportunity to consider the bills presented to him, and 2) to give Congress a suitable opportunity to consider the President's objections to bills and on such consideration to override his veto provided there were the necessary two-thirds majority vote. The court concluded that, although both chambers had adjourned, they had provided agents for each house to receive messages from the President and thus he had not

been prevented from returning the bills to Congress.

The court also pointed to the modern practice of short adjournments within a session in countering the decision of the Supreme Court in the "pocket veto case" of 1929. That case was based on President Calvin Collidge's veto of an Indian claims bill during a four-month congressional recess. Fearing that long congressional adjournments would keep the status of a bill in "suspended animation," the court, in the unanimous 1929 decision, held that the term adjournment applied to any congressional break preventing the return of a bill within the 10-day period. But in *Kennedy v. Sampson,* the court of appeals said the new shorter adjournments, coupled with modern methods of communication "generate no more public uncertainty [about the status of a bill] than does the return of a disapproved bill while Congress is in session."

The interpretation in *Kennedy v. Sampson* was greatly broadened by a second suit, again brought by Kennedy, against Jones on Jan. 29, 1974. Kennedy challenged Nixon's alleged pocket veto of a bill to amend the Federal-Aid Highway Act of 1973 (HR 10511). The bill had been presented to the President Dec. 22, 1973, the day the 93rd Congress adjourned its first session. Nixon issued a memorandum of diapproval Jan. 4, 1974, maintaining that he had pocket vetoed the bill. Two years later, on Jan. 19, 1976, the U.S. District Court for the District of Columbia used the principles established in *Kennedy v. Sampson* to deny the Justice Department's request for a dismissal of the case. The court said that during adjournments between sessions, as for those within a session, the chambers still appointed agents to receive messages so that the President would not be prevented from returning a bill.

The Department of Justice announced April 13, 1976, that it would not appeal the District Court's decision. In that statement, Attorney General Edward H. Levi said the Ford administration "will use the return veto rather than the pocket veto" when Congress adjourns and has "specifically authorized an officer or other agent to receive return vetoes during such periods."

The effect of the two cases brought by Kennedy was to make the two public bills become laws since the 10-day period had expired without the President returning the bills to Congress. S 3418 became PL 91-696, and HR 10511 became PL 93-650.

Johnson was impeached, he escaped conviction by a single vote when tried by the Senate.[53]

During the remainder of the 19th century, the veto was used mainly to prevent corruption through the passage of private bills. President Grover Cleveland's direct veto of 346 bills included 301 private pension bills which most previous Presidents had been signing perfunctorily. Cleveland's actions incurred the wrath of veterans' organizations even though his intention was to discourage fraudulent claims.[54] *(Private bills, p. 299)*

Use of the Veto After 1933

Cleveland established a record for total number of vetoes which stood until the presidency of Franklin D.

Roosevelt. Roosevelt vetoed 635 bills, including 372 direct vetoes and 263 pocket vetoes. *(Box, p. 628)* Nine Roosevelt vetoes were overridden from 1933 to 1945.

Professors Binkley and Moos pointed out in a 1958 book that there had been an increase in the number and ratio of vetoes to the total number of bills passed, attributable to the increase of legislation and its broadening scope as a consequence of the growing complexity of American society. The two educators noted that, while Cleveland's vetoes concentrated on private pensions, Roosevelt's vetoes swept the entire range of legislation. Until he vetoed a revenue bill during World War II, it had been assumed, since no President before him had ever vetoed that type measure, that precedent had exempted tax bills from the veto power.[55]

Presidents Truman and Eisenhower continued to make extensive use of the veto. When the coal and railroad strikes of 1946 prompted Congress to pass a measure restricting strikes, Truman vetoed the bill and Congress was not able to override. The votes for sustaining came largely from members who represented big city constituencies. Thus, Truman used the veto to safeguard metropolitan organized labor against the combined power of industry, business and agriculture as represented in Congress. Following the same considerations, Truman in 1947 vetoed the Taft-Hartley Labor Act, claiming that it was manifestly unfair to labor. However, in that year, Republicans were in control of Congress, the veto was overridden.

President Eisenhower used the veto and the veto threat to defeat or restrict social programs favored by the Democrats who controlled Congress six of his eight years in office. In 1959 alone, Eisenhower was able to galvanize the Republican minority and use a Republican-southern Democratic coalition to prevent passage of most liberal measures. Eisenhower defeated Democratic proposals for a wide program of aid for school construction and teachers' salaries, for a massive area redevelopment program, for increased minimum wage and medical care for the aged under Social Security. He vetoed two major housing bills and a rural electrification measure, and Congress was unable to override either.

The veto was seldom used or threatened by Presidents Kennedy and Johnson, two activist Democrats whose main concern was getting their own programs through Democratic Congresses. An exception was Johnson's veto in 1965 of a military construction authorization bill which required advance congressional review of presidential decisions to close military bases.

Presidents Nixon and Ford followed the Eisenhower pattern in using the veto and veto threat to prevent enactment of many Democratic programs.[56] Nixon's argument in vetoing measures was often that they were inflationary. For example, Congress passed $19.7-billion in appropriations an increase of $1.1-billion over presidential requests, for fiscal 1970 for the Departments of Labor and Health, Education and Welfare and the Office of Economic Opportunity. On the night of Jan. 20, 1970, Nixon vetoed the measure over nationwide television and radio. The House sustained his veto.

Other Democratic bills vetoed by Nixon included a $9.5-billion authorization for fiscal years 1971-74 for federal manpower training and public service employment programs, and a $6.3-billion authorization for fiscal 1972 for Office of Economic Opportunity antipoverty programs. Congress sustained the vetoes of the two authorization bills.

In 1973, Congress, seeking to reassert its powers over foreign policy, dealt Nixon a setback when it voted to override his veto of legislation limiting the executive's power to commit U.S. armed forces abroad without congressional approval. On Nov. 7, the War Powers Act was enacted after the House by four votes and the Senate by 13 overcame the two-thirds requirement needed for overriding.[57] Only on war powers did Congress prevail in 1973; nine other measures were killed by Nixon.

An ideological clash between President Ford and the heavily Democratic 94th Congress in 1975 resulted in the veto of 17 major bills, only four of which were overridden. Legislative stalemate encompassed many areas, but the focal points were national energy and economic policies. Of the 17 Ford vetoes, seven directly involved these two issues. Not one of the seven was overridden.

Pressure of Patronage, Preferment

Historically, the dispensation of patronage has been one of the President's most powerful means of exerting political pressure on Congress. Soon after the birth of the Republic, patronage became part of the fabric of the American political system despite George Washington's view that government jobs should be filled by "those who seem to have the greatest fitness for public office."

De Alva Stanwood Alexander, (R N.Y.) wrote in a 1916 book that the constitutional framers sought to protect members of Congress from the presidential appointive power. Thus, Article I, Section 6, Clause 2 of the Constitution stated: "No senator or representative shall, during the time for which he was elected, be appointed to any civil office under the authority of the United States, which shall have been created, or the emoluments whereof shall have been increased, during such time; and no person holding any office under the United States shall be a member of either House during his continuance in office."

Alexander commented, "In other words, a legislator was not to be induced to create an office, or to increase the emoluments of one, in the hope of an appointment; nor was the Executive able to appoint him while he continued in Congress. But in practice these constitutional limitations neither preserved the legislator's independence nor restrained executive influence. In fact, the President's possession of an ever-increasing patronage has enabled him at times to absorb the legislative branch of the Government."[58]

But the Constitution made no prohibition against the appointment to office of friends, relatives or political party and campaign supporters of either members of Congress or Presidents. In fact, the emergence of political parties in the first decade of the government under the Constitution created a demand for federal jobs by party loyalists.

The inauguration of Thomas Jefferson as the third President in 1801 marked the first time a switch in political parties was made at the White House. The new President found himself surrounded by Federalist Party appointees of predecessors Washington and John Adams. Jefferson replaced enough of the Federalists with Democratic-Republicans from his own party to assure, he said, a more even distribution of power between the two parties.[59]

Jefferson's election initiated, as a component of the power to dispense patronage, the "spoils system," which allowed victors to appoint persons to public office. But it was President Andrew Jackson, 20 years after Jefferson, who went on the develop and justify the spoils system. Martin Tolchin and Susan Tolchin wrote, "Jackson's contribution to patronage was that he was the first to articulate, legitimize, and translate the spoils system into the American experience...."[60]

Patronage and the spoils system engendered several power struggles. Jackson's administration had a House controlled by his own Democratic Party and a Senate in the hands of the opposition Whigs. The President and Congress spent much of their time dealing with patronage controversies.

Jackson was challenged from the Senate floor by John Tyler and John C. Calhoun. Calhoun led the battle against confirming some of the President's appointees, and the senator conducted a formal inquiry into the extent of federal patronage and the practicability of reducing it. The Tolchins wrote, "Calhoun's inquiry propounded the theory that patronage made government too big: If this practice continued, he warned, states' rights would be crushed under the force of an ever-expanding federal bureaucracy. His investigation revealed the shocking fact that the 60,294 employees of the federal government, together with their dependents and other pensioners, made up a payroll of more than 100,000 people dependent on the federal treasury."[61]

Lincoln and McKinley

President Lincoln once resorted to the spoils system when he needed votes for a key bill. According to De Alva Stanwood Alexander, Lincoln turned to patronage in 1864 to promote adoption of a constitutional amendment abolishing slavery. Not sure that enough states would vote to ratify the amendment, Lincoln sought to hasten the admission of a new state, Nevada. With the bill for that purpose bogged down in the House, the President learned that the votes of three representatives might be up for bargaining. When Assistant Secretary of War Charles A. Dana, whom the President authorized to negotiate with the legislators, asked Lincoln what they expected for their votes, he replied: "I don't know. It makes no difference. We must carry this vote.... Whatever promises you make, I will perform."[62] Dana made a deal with the three representatives, and Nevada was brought into the Union on Oct. 31, 1864. As Lincoln expected, it ratified the Thirteenth Amendment, which was submitted to the states Feb. 1, 1865, and was proclaimed in effect Dec. 18, 1865.

Alexander noted that President William McKinley appointed members of Congress to distinguished and lucrative positions on several presidential commissions, and thereby breached the constitutional prohibition against members during their term of office serving in another federal post. McKinley named members to commissions negotiating peace with Spain, settling the Bering Sea controversy, establishing the boundary between Alaska and Canada, arranging a treaty of commerce with Great Britain, and securing information upon which to base legislation for Hawaii. In the case of the Hawaiian commission, McKinley asked the Senate to confirm senators named to it. The Senate declined to confirm them.[63]

Wilson and Patronage

Perhaps the most successful dispenser of patronage ever to hold the presidency was Woodrow Wilson, who made patronage an important instrument of his party leadership. Although patronage jobs had been cut back severely under President Cleveland, as part of his civil service reform, Wilson used what patronage was left him with maximum effect. Alexander quoted from an article in the *New York Sun:* "This [Wilson's use of patronage] was never better illustrated than last Saturday, when at four o'clock, it became apparent that the senators from the cotton-growing states of the South had effected a coalition with the Republican side to kill the war-revenue bill or suspend it until legislation was put into the measure for the relief of the cotton planters. Immediately a strong arm was extended from the White House which promptly throttled the movement within thirty minutes after the fact of the revolt became known to Postmaster General Burleson, with the immense post-office patronage of the country at his disposal.... When the test came, four hours later, three of the eight revolters faltered and the scheme collapsed."[64]

FDR, Eisenhower, Kennedy and Johnson

The next Democrat in the White House, Franklin Roosevelt, also made effective use of his patronage power.

His patronage chief, Postmaster General James A. Farley, asked congressional patronage seekers such questions as "What was your pre-convention position on the Roosevelt candidacy?" and "How did you vote on the economy bill?" As Wilfred Binkley reported, if a member was asked to vote for a presidential measure against local pressures, the matter was put "on the frank basis of quid pro quo."[65]

The Eisenhower administration used patronage more as a stick than a carrot. The President's patronage dispenser, Postmaster General Arthur Summerfield, frequently set up shop in the office of House Minority Leader Charles A. Halleck (R Ind.) and berated Republican representatives who broke party ranks. Insurgents were warned that key jobs such as postmasterships might be cut back unless they got behind the President's program. The President himself sought to broaden the spoils, however, by removing some 134,000 classified jobs from the Civil Service.[66]

Under the Kennedy and Johnson administrations, patronage was assigned to John Bailey, chairman of the Democratic National Committee. Although clever use of patronage swayed votes on several key bills, Kennedy was not overly enamored of the tactic and preferred the direct pressure technique.

In recent years, many legislators and government officials have concluded that patronage is overrated as a presidential pressure tool. Rep. Paul J. Kilday (D Texas), said in 1961 that a representative normally had as many as 100 applicants for every patronage job. "You make 99 fellows mad at you and get one ingrate."[67]

Postal Reorganization

Congress in 1970 cut off its own influence in Post Office patronage when it passed a reform bill converting the 141-year-old, Cabinet-level Post Office Department into an independent government operation. Congress' main objective was to overcome the postal system's deep financial problems, but large postal deficits continued under the new system into the mid-1970s. However, the 1970 reform eliminated most congressional and other political influence in postal affairs, namely the appointment and promotion of postmasters and all postal employees.

Nixon and Ford

President Nixon began his first term with about 2,000 patronage jobs to distribute, and by the end of the year most of them were filled. Most of the appointees were white, male Republicans. The President came under fire at various times throughout the year for failing to appoint many members of minority groups, women or people whose party affiliation was not easily identifiable.

The *Baltimore Sun* estimated that 85 per cent of all patronage jobs had gone to Republicans, 5 per cent to blacks and the remainder to independents or people whose party affiliation was unknown. It noted that a higher number of southerners had received patronage appointments under President Nixon than ever before.

President Ford kept Nixon appointees temporarily in place after Nixon resigned Aug. 9, 1974. But in succeeding weeks and months, Ford put his own men in positions of power, beginning with the White House staff. By the end of 1975, Ford had replaced all but three of the 11 Cabinet members he had inherited from Nixon. The Nixon holdovers were Secretary of State Henry A. Kissinger, Secretary of the Treasury William E. Simon and Secretary of Agriculture Earl L. Butz.

Preferment

A weapon that is usually more effective than patronage is preferment, the selective use of the President's powers to assign federal contract awards and to choose the location of government installations. Political scientist Nelson W. Polsby has observed that use of this authority as a pressure tool makes it possible "to reward and punish congressional friends and foes quite vigorously." Going into particulars, he said: "Small Business Administration and Area Redevelopment Administration loans to certain areas may get more and more difficult to obtain, as applications fail to 'qualify.' Pilot programs and demonstration projects may be funneled here rather than there. Defense contracts and public works may be accelerated in some areas, retarded in others.... These administrative decisions have great potential impact because they affect the prosperity of areas where they are put into effect and they are often of acute concern to local political leaders. And so they can become weapons in the hands of a politically astute President."[68]

Distribution of federal contracts became increasingly important in the postwar years as federal budgets grew phenomenally. The greatest beneficiaries were members of the powerful House and Senate Armed Services Committees and Defense Appropriations Subcommittees, who received defense plants and installations in their districts in return for their support of military requests.

Regulation of Executive Pressures

Over the years, Congress has sought to restrict activities of federal agencies designed to influence legislative action or public opinion. The two major statutes governing these activities were enacted as far back as the Wilson administration, but they have not been vigorously enforced.

The chief measure restricting agency public relations activities was passed in 1913, following a groundswell of congressional criticism of administration plans to hire a "publicity expert" for the Office of Public Roads. The resulting legislation (5 U.S.C. 54) stipulated that "No money appropriated by this or any other act shall be used for the compensation of any publicity expert unless specifically appropriated for that purpose." Although Congress has made no subsequent provision for hiring such officials, federal agencies have countered by designating public relations officers as "Information Specialist," "Special Assistants," or "Public Affairs Officers."

Congress in 1919 enacted a law (18 U.S.C. 1913) prohibiting use of public funds "to pay for any personal service, advertisement, telegram, telephone, letter, printed or written matter, or other device, intended or designed to influence in any manner a member of Congress, to favor or oppose, by vote or otherwise, any legislation or appropriation by Congress." This law has been circumvented by broad interpretation of a clause permitting executive contacts concerning legislation when made through "the proper official

channels" at a member's request. Numerous other laws have sought to block executive agencies from engaging in publicity or propaganda campaigns.[69]

Executive lobbying came under congressional scrutiny in 1950 in a probe by the House Select Committee on Lobbying Activities. The committee's ranking minority member, Rep. Charles A. Halleck (R Ind.), proposed that the Federal Regulation of Lobbying Act, requiring lobbyists to register, be extended to officials of the executive branch. The proposal was resisted by committee Democrats, who defended Truman administration lobbying procedures.

At the 1950 hearings, a high General Accounting Office official testified on the difficulty of enforcing the 1919 law. Frank H. Weitzel, assistant to the Comptroller General, told the panel: "In many cases it is obviously hard, if not impossible, to recognize the unlawful use of federal funds for lobbying activities from documents submitted with the accounts to the General Accounting Office, except possibly from the context of telegrams included therein. For example, a trip of a government official to Washington might in fact have been intended and directed because of the official's capacity to enlist the aid of a certain member or members of Congress in legislation of interest to the department. The vouchers for the reimbursement of travel expenses covering such a trip will very seldom reveal the true purpose of the trip, which is usually described as being 'for official business.' Concrete evidence of irregular methods on the part of federal personnel involving either direct or indirect attempts to influence congressional action, is quite elusive. When personnel of the departments testify before congressional committees, the General Accounting Office is hardly in a position to say they are lobbying, when in fact their testimony may have been requested, as is usually the case. Also, much necessary liaison work goes on perfectly legitimately between congressional committees and executive agencies. Any member of Congress has a perfect right to request an official of the executive department to come up and advise him, or inform him, or discuss with him the effect of legislation that he may propose to introduce."[70]

Notwithstanding continuing complaints by members of Congress about administration "arm-twisting," no laws have been enacted to place new curbs on such activities. Nor has there been a serious court test of the 1913 and 1919 statutes. Consequently, these laws have fallen into disuse, and the bounds of administration lobbying activities appear to be limited only by the extent to which an administration thinks Congress will let it go.

On April 26, 1976, the Senate Government Operations Committee reported a bill to strengthen the public disclosure of lobbying activities in Washington, but lobbying the executive branch was not covered in the bill. Also in 1976, the Senate Judiciary Subcommittee on Administrative Practice and Procedure was working on a measure to require executive branch employees to log contacts from lobbyists and outside parties.[71]

Footnotes

1. Bertram M. Gross, *The Legislative Struggle: A Study in Social Combat* (New York: McGraw-Hill Book Co., Inc., 1953), p. 101.
2. *Ibid.*, p. 102.
3. Harold J. Laski, *The American Presidency: An Interpretation* (New York: Harper & Bros., 1940), p. 116.

4. Arthur M. Schlesinger, Jr., *The Imperial Presidency* (Boston: Houghton-Mifflin Co., 1973), p. 129.
5. Lawrence H. Chamberlain, "The President as Legislator," in *President and Congress: The Conflict of Powers*, ed. Joan Coyne MacLean (New York: H. W. Wilson Co., 1955), p. 56.
6. Gross, *The Legislative Struggle*, p. 101.
7. *Ibid.*, p. 102.
8. Neil MacNeil, *Forge of Democracy* (New York: David McKay Co., Inc., 1963), p. 236.

9. Edward S. Corwin and Louis W. Koenig, *The Presidency Today* (New York: New York University Press, 1956), p. 87.

10. MacNeil, *Forge of Democracy*, p. 237.

11. *Ibid.*

12. Joseph S. Clark, *Congress: The Sapless Branch* (New York: Harper & Row, Publishers, 1964), p. 97.

13. *Ibid.*, p. 98.

14. Corwin and Koenig, *The Presidency Today*, p. 63.

15. Wilfred E. Binkley, *President and Congress* (New York: Vintage Books, 1962), pp. 293-94.

16. *Ibid.*, p. 295.

17. Schlesinger, *The Imperial Presidency*, p. 206.

18. MacNeil, *Forge of Democracy*, pp. 88-89.

19. Rowland Evans and Robert Novak, *Lyndon B. Johnson: The Exercise of Power* (New York: The New American Library, 1966), pp. 492-93.

20. *Ibid.*, p. 490.

21. Congressional Quarterly, *Congress and the Nation,* Vol. II, p. 625.

22. Congressional Quarterly, *1973 Almanac,* p. 906.

23. MacNeil, *Forge of Democracy*, pp. 252-53.

24. *Ibid.*, pp. 253-54.

25. *Ibid.*, pp. 254-55.

26. *Ibid.*, p. 257.

27. *Ibid.*, p. 260.

28. *Ibid.*, p. 261.

29. John Deakin, *The Lobbyists* (Washington, D.C.: Public Affairs Press, 1966), pp. 45-46.

30. Meg Greenfield, "Why Are You Calling Me, Son?," *The Reporter,* Aug. 16, 1962, pp. 29-31.

31. Deakin, *The Lobbyists*, pp. 45-46.

32. MacNeil, *Forge of Democracy*, p. 268.

33. James E. Pollard, *The Presidents and the Press* (New York: Macmillan Co., 1947), p. 147.

34. George Fort Milton, *The Use of Presidential Power* (Boston: Little, Brown and Co., 1944), pp. 131-33.

35. Pollard, *The Presidents and the Press*, p. 413.

36. *Ibid.*, pp. 569-73.

37. *Ibid.*, p. 630.

38. *Ibid.*, p. 645.

39. *Ibid.*, p. 687.

40. James E. Pollard, *The Presidents and the Press: Truman to Johnson* (Washington, D.C.: Public Affairs Press, 1964), p. 27.

41. Pollard, *The Presidents and the Press*, p. 773.

42. Arthur M. Schlesinger, Jr., *The Coming of the New Deal* (Boston: Houghton-Mifflin Co., 1958), p. 559.

43. Binkley, *President and Congress*, p. 305.

44. Pollard, *Presidents and the Press: Truman to Johnson*, p. 100.

45. *Ibid.*, p. 101.

46. Congressional Quarterly, *Watergate: Chronology of a Crisis,* p. 24.

47. *Ibid.*, p. 432.

48. Congressional Quarterly, *Presidency 1974,* p. 76-A.

49. Wilfred E. Binkley and Malcolm C. Moos, *A Grammar of American Politics: The National Government* (New York: Alfred A. Knopf, 1958), pp. 328-29.

50. Binkley, *President and Congress*, p. 86.

51. *Ibid.*, p. 119.

52. *Ibid.*, p. 120.

53. *Ibid.*, pp. 172-77.

54. Binkley and Moos, *A Grammar of American Politics*, p. 330.

55. *Ibid.*

56. Congressional Quarterly, *Congress and the Nation,* Vol. III, pp. 101a-105a.

57. Congressional Quarterly, *1973 Almanac,* pp. 28, 905.

58. DeAlva Stanwood Alexander, *History and Procedure of the House of Representatives* (Boston: Houghton-Mifflin Co., 1916), pp. 378-79.

59. Martin Tolchin and Susan Tolchin, *To the Victor: Political Patronage From the Clubhouse to the White House* (New York: Random House, 1971), p. 323.

60. *Ibid.*

61. *Ibid.*, p. 325.

62. Alexander, *History and Procedure of the House of Representatives,* p. 379.

63. *Ibid.*, pp. 380-81.

64. *Ibid.*, pp. 381-82.

65. Binkley, *President and Congress*, p. 301.

66. MacNeil, *Forge of Democracy*, p. 255.

67. *Ibid.*, pp. 247-48.

68. Nelson W. Polsby, *Congress and the Presidency* (Englewood Cliffs, N.J.: Prentice-Hall Inc., 1964), pp. 106-07.

69. U.S., Congress, House, *Legislative Activities of Executive Agencies,* Hearings before the Select Committee on Lobbying Activities, 81st Cong., 2nd Sess., part 10, pp. 30-31.

70. *Ibid.*, p. 33.

71. Congressional Quarterly, *Weekly Report,* March 27, 1976, p. 715, and *Weekly Report,* May 1, 1976, p. 1047.

Selected Bibliography

Books

Acheson, Dean. *Present at the Creation.* New York: W. W. Norton & Co. Inc., 1969.

Alexander, DeAlva Stanwood. *History and Procedure of the House of Representatives.* Boston: Houghton-Mifflin Co., 1916.

Bailey, Stephen Kemp. *Congress Makes A Law.* New York: Columbia University Press, 1950.

Bell, Jack. *The Presidency: Office of Power.* Boston: Allyn and Bacon Inc., 1967.

Bentley, Arthur F. *The Process of Government.* Principia Press, 1949.

Binkley, Wilfred E. *Powers of the President.* New York: Doubleday and Co., 1937.

Binkley, Wilfred E. *President and Congress.* New York: Vintage Books, 1962.

Binkley, Wilfred E. and Malcolm C. Moos. *A Grammar of American Politics: The National Government.* New York: Alfred A. Knopf, 1958.

Cater, Douglass. *Power in Washington.* New York: Random House, 1964.

Chamberlain, Lawrence H. *President, Congress and Legislation.* New York: Columbia University Press, 1946.

Clark, Joseph S. *Congress: The Sapless Branch.* New York: Harper & Row, Publishers, 1964.

Congress and the Nation, 1965-1968. Vol. II. Washington: Congressional Quarterly, 1969.

Congress and the Nation, 1969-1972. Vol. III. Washington: Congressional Quarterly, 1973.

Corwin, Edward S. *The President: Office and Powers.* New York: New York University Press, 1948.

Corwin, Edward S. and Louise W. Koenig. *The Presidency Today.* New York: New York University Press, 1956.

Davis, James W. *The President and Congress: Toward a New Power Balance.* Woodbury, N.Y.: Barron's Educational Series, 1975.

Deakin, John. *The Lobbyists.* Washington: Public Affairs Press, 1966.

Egger, Rowland A. *The President and Congress.* New York: McGraw-Hill, 1963.

Evans, Rowland, Jr. and Novak, Robert. *Lyndon B. Johnson: The Exercise of Power.* New York: The New American Library, 1966.

Gross, Bertram M. *The Legislative Struggle: A Study in Social Combat.* New York: McGraw-Hill Co., 1953.

Herring, Edward P. *Presidential Leadership: The Political Relations of the Congress and Chief Executive.* Westport, Conn.: Greenwood Press, 1972.

Holtzman, Abraham. *Legislative Liaison: Executive Leadership in Congress.* Chicago: Rand McNally, 1970.

Key, V. O. *Politics, Parties and Pressure Groups.* 5th ed. New York: Thomas Y. Crowell Co., 1964

Laski, Harold J. *The American Presidency: An Interpretation.* New York: Harper & Bros., 1940.

MacLean, Joan Coyne, ed. *President and Congress: The Conflict of Powers.* New York: H. W. Wilson Co., 1955.

MacNeil, Neil. *Forge of Democracy.* New York: David McKay Co., 1963.

Mansfield, Harvey C., ed. *Congress Against the President.* New York Academy of Political Science, 1975.

Milton, George Fort. *The Use of Presidential Power.* Boston: Little, Brown and Co., 1944.

Mondale, Walter F. *The Accountability of Power: Toward a Responsible Presidency.* New York: David McKay, 1976.

Neustadt, Richard E. *Presidential Power.* New York: John Wiley and Sons Inc., 1960

Pollard, James E. *The Presidents and the Press.* New York: The Macmillan Co., 1947.

Pollard, James E. *The Presidents and the Press: Truman to Johnson.* Washington: Public Affairs Press, 1964.

Polsby, Nelson W. *Congress and the Presidency.* Englewood Cliffs, N.J.: Prentice-Hall Inc., 1964.

Presidency 1974. Washington: Congressional Quarterly, 1975.

Reston, James. *The Artillery of the Press.* New York: Harper and Row, 1966.

Schlesinger, Arthur M., Jr. *The Coming of the New Deal.* Boston: Houghton-Mifflin Co., 1959.

Schlesinger, Arthur M., Jr. *The Imperial Presidency.* Boston: Houghton-Mifflin Co., 1973.

Tolchin, Martin, and Tolchin, Susan. *To the Victor: Political Patronage From the Clubhouse to the White House.* New York: Random House, 1971.

Truman, David B. *The Governmental Process.* 10th ed. New York: Alfred A. Knopf, 1964.

Watergate: Chronology of a Crisis. Washington: Congressional Quarterly, 1975.

Wilson, Woodrow. *Congressional Government.* Cleveland: The World Publishing Co., 1956.

Articles

Binkley, Wilfred E. "The President and Congress." *Journal of Politics,* February 1949, p. 69.

Congressional Quarterly. *Weekly Report.* March 27, 1976, pp. 715-716, and May 1, 1976, pp. 1047-1049.

Cornwell, Elmer E. Jr. "Wilson Creel and the Presidency." *Public Opinion Quarterly,* Summer 1959, pp. 182-202.

Dorsen, Norman and Shattuck, John H. F. "Executive Privilege, the Congress and the Court." *Ohio State Law Journal,* Vol. 35, Number I, 1974, pp. 1-40.

Duscha, Julius. "The Undercover Fight Over the Wilderness." *Harper's,* April 1962, pp. 55-59.

Evans, Rowland Jr. "Louisiana's Passman: The Scourge of Foreign Aid." *Harper's,* January 1962, pp. 78-83.

Fisher, Louis "Presidential Spending Discretion and Congressional Controls." *Law and Contemporary Problems,* Winter 1972, pp. 135-172.

Greenfield, Meg. "Why Are You Calling Me, Son?" *The Reporter,* Aug. 16, 1962, pp. 29-31.

Herring, E. Pendleton. "The First Session of the 73rd Congress." *American Political Science Review,* Vol. 28, Number 1, p. 69.

Johannes, John R. "Where Does the Buck Stop? Congress, President and the Responsibility of Legislative Initiation." *Western Political Quarterly,* September 1972, pp. 396-415.

Miller, Nathan. "The Making of a Majority: The Senate and the ABM." *Washington Monthly,* October 1969, pp. 60-72.

Neustadt, Richard E. "President and Legislation: The Growth of Central Clearance." *American Political Science Review,* September 1954, pp. 641-671.

Neustadt, Richard E. "President and Legislation: Planning the President's Program." *American Political Science Review,* December 1955, pp. 980-1021.

Packman, Martin. "Government Jobs." *Editorial Research Reports,* May 18, 1955, pp. 357-375.

Parris, Judith H. "Congress in the American Presidential System." *Current History,* June 1974, pp. 259-263.

Patch, Buel W. "Political Reform and Federal Patronage." *Editorial Research Reports,* July 2, 1934, pp. 1-20.

Pipe, G. Russell. "Congressional Liaison: The Executive Branch Consolidates Its Relations With Congress." *Public Administration Review,* March 1966, pp. 14-24.

Reinstein, Robert J. and Silverglate, Harvey A., "Legislative Privilege and the Separation of Powers." *Harvard Law Review,* May 1973, pp. 1113-1182.

Shaffer, Helen. "Presidential Accountability." *Editorial Research Reports,* March 7, 1973, pp. 167-184.

Truman, David B. "The Presidency and Congressional Leadership: Some Notes on Our Changing Constitution." *American Philosophical Society Proeedings.* October 15, 1959, pp. 687-692.

Worsnop, Richard L. "Presidential Power." *Editorial Research Reports,* October 2, 1968, pp. 723-740.

Government Publications

U.S. Congress. House. Committee on the Judiciary. *The Pocket Veto Power, Hearings on HR 6225 to Implement Article I, Section 7 of the Constitution.* 92nd Cong., 1st sess., 1971.

U.S. Congress. House. Select Committee on Lobbying Activities. *General Interim Report.* 81st Cong., 2nd sess. Washington: Government Printing Office, 1950.

————. *Legislative Activities of Executive Agencies. Hearings before the Select Committee on Lobbying Activities,* 81st Cong., 2nd sess., 1950.

————. *Lobbying, Direct and Indirect. Hearings before the Select Committee on Lobbying Activities,* 81st Cong., 2nd sess., 1950.

————. *The Role of Lobbying in Representative Self-Government. Hearings before the Select Committee on Lobbying Activities,* 81st Cong., 2nd sess., 1950.

U.S. Congress. Senate. Committee on the Judiciary. *Congressional Oversight of Executive Agreements, Hearings April 24-May 19, 1972.* 92nd Cong., 2nd sess., 1972.

————. *Constitutionality of the President's "Pocket Veto."* 92nd Cong., 1st sess., 1971.

U.S. Congress, Senate Library. *Presidential Vetoes: Record of Bills Vetoed and Action Taken Thereon by the Senate and House of Representatives, First Congress through the Ninetieth Congress, 1789-1968.* Washington: Government Printing Office, 1969.

The Supreme Court

The Supreme Court exerts a strong restraining influence upon Congress through its power to declare that certain legislative acts are unconstitutional and, hence, invalid. Although the Constitution did not expressly authorize the court to strike down acts it deemed unconstitutional, the court assumed that important authority in 1803 through its own broad interpretation of its vested powers. Without this process, known as judicial review, there would be no assurance (not even the President's veto) against domination of the entire government by runaway congressional majorities.

Surprisingly, the incidence of court rulings overturning acts of Congress is not high; only about 100 acts or parts of acts have been declared unconstitutional in 187 years of the Republic. Of those invalidated, many were unimportant and others, such as the measures prohibiting the spread of slavery and those carrying out parts of Franklin D. Roosevelt's New Deal program, were replaced by legislation so revised as to pass muster with the Supreme Court. In early 1976, the court struck down the law creating a Federal Election Commission; Congress quickly passed a revised version of the law. Most constitutional scholars agree that the significance of judicial review lies primarily in the deterrent effect on Congress of a possible Supreme Court veto. *(List of acts declared unconstitutional, p. 238-A)*

With few exceptions, the court has interpreted the legislature's power to enact specific legislation as broadly as it has its own authority to sit in review of the statutes. The court's approach to its duties was defined in 1827, when Justice Bushrod Washington observed that "it is but a decent respect due to the wisdom, the integrity and the patriotism of the legislative body, by which any law is passed, to presume in favor of its validity until its violation of the Constitution is proved beyond all reasonable doubt."[1] Justices on almost every court since Justice Washington's day have reaffirmed that attitude.

Changes in Court's Philosophy

Because Supreme Court justices are appointed for life terms, changes in the court's philosophy come about with less regularity than in the other two branches of the federal government. For its first 150 years, the court served primarily as a bulwark against encroachment on property rights. This concept was maintained even in the 1930s, when the need was evident for precedent-shattering legislation to grapple with the country's economic crisis. In 1935 and 1936, the court struck down 11 New Deal statutes—the heart of the recovery program. But after President Roosevelt's overwhelming victory in the 1936 election and his threat to "pack" the court with additional justices who presumably would favor his program, the court relented and the remainder of the New Deal legislation was upheld. From that point on, the court's philosophy leaned more toward a flexible reading of the Constitution to permit achievement of national social goals than it did toward the traditional practice of giving priority to protection of property. This shift of doctrine was completed during the term of Chief Justice Earl Warren (1954-1969), when the court promulgated a series of sweeping decisions in support of individual rights.

But with Warren's retirement, the pendulum began to swing back. The membership of the court changed. By 1976 only four Warren court justices remained. The court's rulings in the 1970s interpreted individual rights more narrowly, making clear that they were rarely absolute.

Moreover, in 1976, the court struck down a piece of economic legislation enacted under the commerce clause that applied federal wages and hours legislation to state and local government employees. The action was reminiscent of the court's actions 40 years earlier overturning economic legislation applying to the private sector of the economy, and raised questions about whether the justices in future years would place additional limits on the power of Congress to control the actions of state and local governments.

Whatever the court's philosophy, it has always had its share of congressional critics quick to accuse it of usurping undue powers. The early Anti-Federalists (later known as Democratic-Republicans and finally as Democrats) thought the court nullified the Constitution by a series of rulings strengthening federal power at the expense of individuals and the states. New Deal Democrats thought the court was attempting to seize the preeminent role in government by voiding much of their legislative program. In the 1950s and 1960s, Republicans and southern Democrats were driven virtually to despair by the Warren court's decisions on school desegregation, criminal law, and voter representation.

In the 1970s, as the court became more conservative, criticism came again from liberal observers who worried that the court unduly favored the state at the expense of the individual.

Such criticism of the court has led to a number of proposals to curb the tribunal's powers. Among the proposals have been a requirement of more than a majority vote to render a statute unconstitutional, removal of justices upon concurrence of the President and both houses of Congress, and restriction of the court's appellate jurisdiction to exclude certain types of cases in which the court has made decisions not to the liking of some members of Congress. Although certain of these proposals have attracted wide support, none has ever been enacted into law. The only effective sanction available to Congress has been the Senate's refusal to confirm court nominees. The court's critics have been moderately successful in use of that sanction, blocking 26 of 139 court nominations submitted by successive Presidents. Eleven of the 26 nominations were rejected outright, and the others were withdrawn or allowed to lapse in the face of Senate opposition. *(See p. 642)*

Sources of Court's Power

Unlike the rebels who framed the Declaration of Independence, the men who met at Philadelphia in 1787 to shape the U.S. Constitution represented conservative financial interests. These interests had suffered heavily during the period of national confederation following the Revolution, when state legislatures, controlled mostly by agrarian interests, made repeated assaults on vested rights.

While the framers of the Constitution deprecated the excesses of the legislatures, they held a high respect for the courts, which gave judgments in favor of creditors and sent delinquent debtors to jail. As political scientist Charles A. Beard, a leading constitutional scholar, once put it, "The conservative intersts, made desperate by the imbecilities of the Confederation and harried by the state legislatures, roused themselves from their lethargy, drew together in a mighty effort to establish a government that would be strong enough to pay the national debt, regulate interstate and foreign commerce, provide for national defense, prevent fluctuations in the currency created by paper emissions, and control the propensities of legislative majorities to attack private rights."[2]

At the time the Framers met, judicial review had not yet been instituted in any country in the world. And despite considerable discussion of some means to check the excesses of Congress, the matter of a judicial veto never came up for a direct vote. The closest the Convention got to considering such a scheme was when it rejected the Virginia Plan of government. That plan contained a section establishing a Council of Revision, consisting of Supreme Court justices and the President, to consider the constitutionality of proposed acts prior to final congressional passage. As submitted to the state conventions for ratification, the Constitution was not clear on the final arbiter of constitutional disputes. Wilfred E. Binkley and Malcolm C. Moos have pointed out that there were matters the delegates "dared

not baldly assert in the Constitution without imperiling its ratification, but they doubtless hoped that implications would eventually be interpreted to supply the thing desired."[3] Judicial review appeared to be one of those things. Most other constitutional scholars have supported this view.

In *The Federalist*, a series of essays written to promote adoption of the Constitution, Alexander Hamilton made clear that the Framers expected the judiciary to rule on constitutional issues. In Number 78 of *The Federalist*, Hamilton wrote: "The complete independence of the courts of justice is peculiarly essential in a limited constitution. By a limited constitution, I understand one which contains certain specified exceptions to the legislative authority, such for instance, as that it shall pass no bills of attainder, no ex-post facto laws, and the like. Limitations of this kind can be preserved in practice no other way than through the courts of justice, whose duty it must be to declare all acts contrary to the manifest tenor of the Constitution void. Without this, all the reservations of particular rights or privileges would amount to nothing."[4]

In a 1912 study of the history of judicial review, Beard found that of the 25 members of the Convention who appeared to be most influential in shaping the Constitution, 17 (including Hamilton) were on record as favoring "the proposition that the judiciary would, in the normal course of things, pass upon the constitutionality of acts of Congress." Of the less prominent members, Beard said, eight went on record as understanding and approving the doctrine. Opponents of the concept have placed five members of the Convention against judicial review, but only one of these, Pierce Butler of South Carolina, was in the influential group. Beard observed that "The accepted canons of historical criticism warrant the assumption that, when a legal proposition is before a lawmaking body (the Constitutional Convention) and a considerable number of the supporters of that proposition definitely assert that it involves certain important and fundamental implications, and it is nevertheless approved by that body without any protests worthy of mention, these implications must be deemed part of that legal proposition when it becomes law...."[5] Binkley and Moos asserted: "Whether or not the Supreme Court 'usurped' the practice of judicial review is now purely an academic question. So completely has the practice been woven into the warp and woof of our constitutional fabric that the garment could now scarcely endure its elimination."[6]

Acts Declared Unconstitutional

No major constitutional clashes occurred during the Republic's first decade. Congress and the executive branch were firmly in the hands of the Federalist Party, which was united in its determination to stifle the political opposition—the states'-rights-minded Anti-Federalists. When Congress passed the far-reaching Sedition Act of 1798, which led to the imprisonment of several Anti-Federalist editors for criticizing the government, the court refused to strike down the acts despite Anti-Federalist assertions of its probable unconstitutionality.

Only once in that decade did the courts question an act of Congress, and that was on a minor matter. In the *Hayburn* case of 1792, two Supreme Court justices sitting on a circuit court (as they then had to do in addition to performing their Supreme Court duties) declined to implement

---

References

See Appendix for list of Acts of Congress declared unconstitutional by the Supreme Court *(p. 238-A)* and for excerpts from Chief Justice John Marshall's opinion in *Marbury v. Madison. (p. 237-A)*

---

an act requiring the circuit courts to pass upon certain claims of invalid pensioners, subject to later revision by the Secretary of War and Congress. Before the full Supreme Court could rule on the case, Congress revised the law involved.[7]

Case of *Marbury v. Madison*

The doctrine of judicial review was first enunciated by the Supreme Court in the famous case of *Marbury v. Madison* (5 U.S. (1 Cranch) 137) in 1803.

After Republican presidential candidate Thomas Jefferson had defeated Federalist John Adams in the latter's bid for re-election in 1800—but before the Republicans took office—Adams nominated a number of Federalists to judicial posts created by court-reform legislation passed by the lame-duck Federalist Congress. The nominations of 16 judges and some other officials were confirmed by the Senate and the commissions signed by Adams in the waning hours of his administration. When Adams' term expired at midnight on March 3, 1801, several of the commissions had not been delivered. Jefferson, who entered office at the stroke of midnight, ordered that these commissions be withheld.

One of the appointees whose commission had not been delivered was William Marbury, who had been named to the post of justice of the peace for the District of Columbia. Marbury sought to test Jefferson's executive power by filing suit in the Supreme Court requiring Jefferson's Secretary of State, James Madison, to deliver the commission. Marbury filed the suit under terms of the Judiciary Act of 1789, which empowered the court to issue writs of mandamus compelling federal officials to perform their duties.

The Chief Justice at the time of the case was John Marshall, a staunch Federalist who had been Secretary of State in the Adams administration and had been responsible in that capacity for delivering the commissions to Marbury and the other appointees. Notwithstanding his personal interest, Marshall refused to disqualify himself from participation in the court's action in the case. On the contrary, he delivered the opinion of the court.

Marshall first held that Marbury was entitled to his commission and that he should be granted the writ of mandamus if the court had proper jurisdiction. Although the Judiciary Act of 1789 purported to grant the Supreme Court the jurisdiction necessary in this case, Marshall asserted that that part of the Act was unconstitutional because Congress had no power to enlarge the court's original jurisdiction.

Article III of the Constitution gave the Supreme Court original jurisdiction over "cases affecting ambassadors, other public ministers and consuls, and those in which a state shall be party." In other cases the Supreme Court was given only appellate jurisdiction "both as to law and fact, with such exceptions and under such regulations as the Congress shall make."

Under the guise of handing his Jeffersonian foes a political victory, Marshall had laid the cornerstone of federal judicial power. Charles Warren, a leading constitutional authority, has commented: "Marshall naturally felt that in view of the recent attacks on judicial power, it was important to have the great principle firmly established, and undoubtedly he welcomed the opportunity of fixing the precedent in a case in which his action would necessitate a decision in favor of his political opponents.... In comprehensive and forceful terms, which for over 100

years have never been successfully controverted, he proceeded to lay down the great principles of the supremacy of the Constitution over statute law, and of the duty and power of the judiciary to act as the arbiter in case of any conflict between the two."[8]

Ironically, the doctrine of Supreme Court authority to strike down unconstitutional legislation, which Marshall established in the *Marbury* case, attracted little comment at the time. Republicans were critical instead of Marshall's comment that mandamus should have been granted if the court held proper jurisdiction. According to Charles Warren, Jefferson felt that Marshall and the other Federalists on the court had "intentionally gone out of their way to rule on points unnecessary for the decision, and he regarded it as a deliberate assumption of a right to interfere with his executive functions."[9] Jefferson remained indignant about that aspect of the decision until his death in 1826. As late as 1823, he wrote that "the practice of Judge Marshall in travelling out of his case to prescribe what the law would be in a moot case not before the Court" was "very irregular and very censurable" and amounted to an unwarranted lecture to the President from a political opponent on the bench.[10]

Dred Scott Decision

It was not until the eve of the Civil War that the Supreme Court again held an act of Congress unconstitutional. It did so in the case of *Scott v. Sanford* (60 U.S. 393) in 1857, probably the court's most controversial decision of all time and the one most criticized by students of the Constitution.

Dred Scott, a slave, had been taken by his former master from the slave state of Missouri into territory made free by the act of Congress known as the Missouri Compromise. After returning to Missouri, Scott sued to establish his freedom on the ground that his sojourn in free territory had made him a free man. The Missouri Supreme Court held that he had indeed gained his freedom through being on free soil, but that he had lost it when he returned to the slave state of Missouri.

Since Scott's present master (Sanford) was a citizen of New York, the case could now be considered by a federal court as a controversy between citizens of different states, provided that Scott was a citizen of Missouri. When the case reached the U.S. Supreme Court, a majority of the justices decided initially that the case should have been dismissed in lower federal court for lack of jurisdiction, because no Negro could be a citizen under terms of the Constitution. But the court did not stop there despite the finding of no jurisdiction. Chief Justice Roger Brooke Taney, who wrote what is considered the majority decision in the case (although nine separate opinions were filed by the justices), asserted that Scott was a slave because the Missouri Compromise—which had been repealed three years earlier by the Kansas-Nebraska Act—was unconstitutional. Congress, Taney declared, had no authority to limit the extension of slavery. (The decision was voided by the Thirteenth Amendment outlawing slavery.)

The *Dred Scott* decision aroused tremendous resentment in the North, especially among members of the newly organized Republican Party whose cardinal tenet was that Congress should abolish slavery in all of the territories. The *New York Tribune* asserted editorially that the decision was "entitled to just so much moral weight as would be the judgment of a majority of those congregated in any Washington barroom.... Until that remote period when different judges sitting in this same court shall reverse this wicked and false judgment, the Constitution of the United States is nothing better than the bulwark of inhumanity and repression."[11]

Greenback and Tax Cases

Greenback Cases. The *Dred Scott* decision was a prime example of what a later Supreme Court Chief Justice, Charles Evans Hughes, called the court's "self-inflicted wounds." As he noted, "It was many years before the Court, even under new judges, was able to retrieve its reputation."[12] Before it had been able to do so, another decision on a constitutional issue brought the court into further disrepute. In the case of *Hepburn v. Griswold* (75 U.S. (8 Wall.) 603), the court by a 4-3 decision in 1870 ruled unconstitutional the provision of a Civil War statute making United States notes, popularly known as "greenbacks," legal tender in payment of debts contracted before passage of the act.

On the day the opinion was rendered, President Grant, a proponent of the greenback clause, nominated William Strong and Joseph P. Bradley to fill two vacant seats on the court. Soon after their confirmation, the court ordered reargument of the case and reversed itself. In a 5-4 decision, with Bradley and Strong voting with the majority, the greenback statute was held constitutional. Even Chief Justice Salmon P. Chase joined critics in contending that the President had packed the court in order to win the reversal. The decision worked to the advantage of the railroads, whose long-term bonds were becoming due. The notes could now be paid in depreciated currency instead of gold, as would have been required under the first greenback decision.

In the opinion of Justice Hughes, "The reopening of the case was a serious mistake and the overruling in such a short time, and by one vote, of the previous decision, shook popular confidence in the Court." Hughes concluded: "The argument for reopening was strongly presented in view of the great importance of the question but the effect of such a sudden reversal of judgment might easily have been foreseen. Stability in judicial opinions is of no little importance in maintaining respect for the Court's work."[13]

Income Tax Case. The next controversial overturning of a congressional statute came in the income tax case of 1895, *Pollock v. Farmers' Loan and Trust Co.* (157 U.S. 429, 158 U.S. 601). Under assault in the case were the income tax provisions of the Tariff Act of 1894, which imposed a tax of 2 per cent on incomes of more than $4,000. The court at first held the statute constitutional by a 4-4 vote but later ruled it void by a vote of 5-4. The court's reasoning was that the levy was a "direct tax," and the Constitution required that direct taxes be apportioned among the states according to population. The decision was widely interpreted as a predisposition by the court to the doctrines of rugged individualism and Social Darwinism (survival of the fittest). This theme seemed to run through the concurring opinion of Justice Stephen J. Field, who said: "If the provisions of the Constitution can be set aside by an act of Congress, where is the course of usurpation to end? The present assault upon capital is but the beginning. It will be but the stepping stone to others, larger and more sweeping, till our political contests will become a war of the poor against the rich; a war constantly growing in intensity and bitterness." The decision was bitterly assailed by Democrats in Congress who contended that such protection of wealth was unconscionable in view of the severe depression then afflicting the country. The decision was nullified by the ratification in 1913 of the Sixteenth Amendment empowering Congress to levy taxes on income without apportionment among the states. *(See p. 226)*

Wave of Invalidations in Taft Court

Solicitude for property rights reached its high-water mark on the Supreme Court during the chief justiceship of William Howard Taft, who served from 1921 to 1930.

To ward off what it regarded as unwarranted governmental intrusion on property rights, the Taft court struck down an unusually large number of state and federal statutes. While the court had invalidated only two acts of Congress in the period from 1789 to 1865 (the *Marbury* and *Dred Scott* cases), it struck down 32 in the period from 1920 to 1936. Among the congressional statutes invalidated were curbs on the use of child labor *(Bailey v. Drexel Furniture Co.,* 259 U.S. 20) and a minimum wage for women and children in the District of Columbia *(Adkins v. Children's Hospital,* 261 U.S. 525). In the D.C. minimum wage case, decided in 1923, Justice George Sutherland wrote that the freedom of an individual to make his own labor arrangements was "the general rule and restraint the exception." Taft himself voted with the minority, but he wrote in dissent that "It is a disputable question in the field of political economy how far a statutory requirement of maximum hours or minimum wages may be a useful remedy" for the sweatshop system.

Fate of New Deal Legislation

The appointment in 1930 of Charles Evans Hughes to succeed Taft as Chief Justice seemed at the time to herald a new, less conservative era on the Supreme Court. In his six years on the court as an associate justice (1910-1916), Hughes had become known for his liberal attitude in the field of civil liberties. As it developed, however, the Hughes court became involved in an unprecedented clash with the legislative and executive branches over the New Deal's intrusion on property rights.

One after another, the depression-born statutes passed by Congress at President Roosevelt's urging were struck down by the Hughes court. During the 1935 and 1936 terms, laws invalidated by the court included such key New Deal measures as the Railroad Retirement Act, the National Industrial Recovery Act (NIRA), the Agricultural Adjustment Act (AAA), the Bituminous Coal Conservation (Guffey) Act, a part of the Home Owners' Loan Act, an act providing for readjustment of municipal indebtedness, and the Frazier-Lemke Act designed to delay foreclosures of farm mortgages.

The only major New Deal statute to survive Supreme Court scrutiny (the important Reciprocal Trade Agreements Act did not come up for judicial review) was the Tennessee Valley Authority Act, which created a public regional development authority. In the NIRA and certain other cases, the court ruled that Congress had made unconstitutional delegations of legislative power to the executive branch—unconstitutional because they set no standards to be followed in carrying out the acts or prescribed no findings of fact to be made before invoking the delegated powers. In most of the other cases, the court narrowly interpreted the authority of Congress to regulate commerce or ruled that Congress was encroaching upon powers reserved to the states. Fear rose that the court might strike down two 1935

New Deal enactments, the National Labor Relations (Wagner) Act and the Social Security Act, if given the opportunity.

President Roosevelt, stung by the Supreme Court's piecemeal destruction of his legislative program, resolved after the 1936 elections to do something about it. In a surprise message to Congress, Feb. 5, 1937, he asked for legislation that would authorize the President, when any federal judge who had been in service for 10 years did not retire within six months after becoming 70 years old, to appoint an additional judge to the court in question. Such a law would have made it possible for the President to add six justices to the Supreme Court and thus presumably ensure a majority sympathetic to the New Deal.

Although the court had come under heavy fire for its anti-New Deal decisions, the court-packing plan ran into strong opposition within and outside of Congress. Hughes presented an able defense of the court before the Senate Judiciary Committee, which, on June 14, 1937, submitted an adverse report on the administration bill. A measure finally approved in August provided only for procedural reforms in the lower courts.

Nonetheless, the President's campaign succeeded in bringing about a change of heart on the part of the Supreme Court. In *West Coast Hotel v. Parrish* (300 U.S. 379), decided soon after the court-packing plan was submitted to Congress, a minimum wage law, similar to one ruled unconstitutional a year before, was held to be valid. Revised versions of several of the other acts struck down by the Hughes court were passed by Congress and sustained by the court. On April 12, 1937, the court in *NLRB v. Jones and Laughlin Steel Corp.* (301 U.S. 1) upheld the constitutionality of the Wagner Act. In that decision, Chief Justice Hughes put forward a broad and encompassing definition of interstate commerce, contending that Congress had power to protect the lifelines of the national economy from private industrial warfare. Arguments that had proved effective in the NIRA and coal cases were unavailing. "These cases," Hughes asserted, "are not controlling here." Of the court's change of direction, it was said that "A switch in time saved nine."

Civil Rights Cases in Warren Court

The Supreme Court under Chief Justice Earl Warren (1954-1959) clashed repeatedly with Congress over a series of court rulings protecting individual rights. Although most of the controversy had to do with alleged court usurpation of states' rights, several of the court's decisions, including three important ones in the field of internal security, involved reversal of acts of Congress.

The first of the controversial rulings in the security field came in 1956, when the court curbed dismissal of government employees who were considered security risks. By a 6-3 decision in *Cole v. Young* (351 U.S. 536), the court ruled that the term "national security" in PL 81-733, the statute establishing the government's industrial security program, was not used "in an all-inclusive sense, but was intended to refer only to the protection of 'sensitive' activities. It followed that an employee could be dismissed 'in the interests of the national security' under the Act only if he occupied a 'sensitive' position."

Another controversial decision was handed down the following year in the case of *Yates v. United States* (354 U.S. 298). In that case the Warren court ruled that the Smith Act of 1940 did not outlaw advocacy of forcible overthrow of the government as an abstract doctrine but only as an in-

citement to action. The court ruled also that the term "organize," as used in the Smith Act's prohibition against organizing a group advocating forcible overthrow, referred only to the initial act of bringing the group into being and not to continued organizing activities such as the recruitment of members. For the American Communist Party, the court held, the act of organization had taken place in 1945, when the Communist Political Association was dissolved and the party brought into being. In 1962, Congress finally succeeded in enacting legislation to broaden the term "organize" to include continuing organizational activities.

A third major internal security case in which the Warren court struck down federal legislation was the 1964 case of *Aptheker v. Secretary of State* (378 U.S. 500) in which the court held unconstitutional a section of the Subversive Activities Control Act of 1950 depriving all U.S. Communist Party members of passport privileges. The court, in a 6-3 decision, ruled that the clause was in violation of the due process clause of the Fifth Amendment.

Other acts or parts of acts of Congress overturned by the Warren court included provisions of the Uniform Code of Military Justice; a law depriving of citizenship (1) citizens leaving the country or remaining abroad during wartime in order to escape military service, (2) citizens voting in foreign elections, and (3) naturalized citizens having extended residence in the country of their birth or prior citizenship; a law prohibiting Communists from serving as officers or employees of labor unions; a provision for compulsory registration of Communist Party members.

Elections, Women and Children

In the first half of the 1970s, the court under Chief Justice Warren E. Burger held a dozen acts of Congress unconstitutional. Most notable among these was the 1976 ruling striking down limits on campaign expenditures as a violation of the First Amendment. Those limits had been set by Congress in the Federal Election Campaign Amendments of 1974. In that same decision in the case of *Buckley v. Valeo,* the court struck down part of that law which violated the separation of powers by giving executive responsibility to a Federal Election Commission appointed in part by Congress.

The court in 1970 held that Congress exceeded its powers by enacting a law lowering to 18 the voting age for state and local elections *(Oregon v. Mitchell,* 400 U.S. 112). In this period, the justices also invalidated portions of the Social Security Act which unfairly denied or reduced benefits paid to illegitimate children. *(Richardson v. Davis, Richardson v. Griffin,* 409 U.S. 1069, 1972; *Jimenez v. Weinberger,* 417 U.S. 628, 1974) and which provided survivor's benefits to widows with children but not to widowers with children *(Weinberger v. Wiesenfeld,* 420 U.S. 636, 1975).

During this period, in one of its first rulings recognizing sex discrimination, the justices invalidated laws under which women in the military were required to prove the dependence of their spouses in order to receive dependents' benefits while men in the military were not required to prove such dependence in order for their wives to receive such benefits *(Frontiero v. Richardson,* 411 U.S. 677, 1973).

Congressional Investigations

Alleged abuse of congressional investigatory powers has produced a number of Supreme Court decisions through the

(Continued on p. 644)

Supreme Court Appointments, 1789-1975

Name	State	Date of Birth	Nomi-nated by	To Replace	Date of Ap-pointment	Date Confirmed	Other Action	Date Resigned	Date of Death	Years of Service
John Jay*	N.Y.	12/12/1745	Washington		9/24/1789	9/26/1789		6/29/1795	5/17/1829	6
John Rutledge	S.C.	1739	Washington		9/24/1789	9/26/1789		3/5/1791	7/23/1800	1
William Cushing	Mass.	3/1/1732	Washington		9/24/1789	9/26/1789			9/13/1810	21
Robert H. Harrison	Md.	1745	Washington		9/24/1789	9/26/1789	Jan. 1790(D)		4/20/1790	
James Wilson	Pa.	9/14/1742	Washington		9/24/1789	9/26/1789			8/28/1798	9
John Blair	Va.	1732	Washington		9/24/1789	9/26/1789		1/27/1796	8/31/1800	6
James Iredell	N.C.	10/5/1751	Washington	Harrison	2/9/1790	2/10/1790			10/2/1799	9
Thomas Johnson	Md.	11/4/1732	Washington	Rutledge	11/1/1791	11/7/1791		3/4/1793	10/25/1819	1
William Paterson	N.J.	12/24/1745	Washington	Johnson	2/27/1793		2/28/1793(W)**			
William Paterson	(See above)		Washington	Johnson	3/4/1793	3/4/1793			9/9/1806	13
John Rutledge*	(See above)		Washington	Jay	7/1/1795		12/15/1795(R)			
William Cushing*	(See above)		Washington	Jay	1/26/1796	1/27/1796	2/2/1796(D)			
Samuel Chase	Md.	4/17/1741	Washington	Blair	1/26/1796	1/27/1796			6/19/1811	15
Oliver Ellsworth*	Conn.	4/29/1745	Washington	Jay	3/3/1796	3/4/1796		9/30/1800	11/26/1807	4
Bushrod Washington	Va.	6/5/1762	Adams	Wilson	12/19/1798	12/20/1798			11/26/1829	31
Alfred Moore	N.C.	5/21/1755	Adams	Iredell	12/6/1799	12/10/1799		March, 1804	10/15/1810	4
John Jay*	(See above)		Adams	Ellsworth	12/18/1800	12/19/1800	1/2/1801(D)			
John Marshall*	Va.	9/24/1755	Adams	Ellsworth	1/20/1801	1/27/1801			7/6/1835	34
William Johnson	S.C.	12/27/1771	Jefferson	Moore	3/22/1804	3/24/1804			8/11/1834	30
Henry B. Livingston	N.Y.	11/26/1757	Jefferson	Paterson	12/13/1806	12/17/1806			3/18/1823	16
Thomas Todd	Ky.	1/23/1765	Jefferson	New Seat	2/28/1807	3/3/1807			2/7/1826	19
Levi Lincoln	Mass.	5/15/1749	Madison	Cushing	1/2/1811	1/3/1811	1/20/1811(D)		4/14/1820	
Alexander Wolcott	Conn.	9/15/1758	Madison	Cushing	2/4/1811		2/13/1811(R)		6/26/1828	
John Quincy Adams	Mass.	7/11/1767	Madison	Cushing	2/21/1811	2/22/1811	April, 1811(D)		2/23/1848	
Joseph Story	Mass.	9/18/1779	Madison	Cushing	11/15/1811	11/18/1811			9/10/1845	33
Gabriel Duval	Md.	12/6/1752	Madison	Chase	11/15/1811	11/18/1811		Jan., 1835	3/6/1844	23
Smith Thompson	N.Y.	1/17/1768	Monroe	Livingston	12/8/1823	12/19/1823			12/18/1843	20
Robert Trimble	Ky.	1777	J. Q. Adams	Todd	4/11/1826	5/9/1826			8/25/1828	2
John J. Crittenden	Ky.	9/10/1787	J. Q. Adams	Trimble	12/17/1828		2/12/1829(P)		7/26/1863	
John McLean	Ohio	3/11/1785	Jackson	Trimble	3/6/1829	3/7/1829			4/4/1861	32
Henry Baldwin	Pa.	1/14/1780	Jackson	Washington	1/4/1830	1/6/1830			4/21/1844	14
James M. Wayne	Ga.	1790	Jackson	Johnson	1/7/1835	1/9/1835			7/5/1867	32
Roger B. Taney	Md.	3/17/1777	Jackson	Duval	1/15/1835		3/3/1835(P)			
Roger B. Taney*	(See above)		Jackson	Marshall	12/28/1835	3/15/1836			10/12/1864	28
Philip P. Barbour	Va.	5/25/1783	Jackson	Duval	12/28/1835	3/15/1836			2/24/1841	5
William Smith	Ala.	1762	Jackson	New Seat	3/3/1837	3/8/1837	March, 1837(D)		6/10/1840	
John Catron	Tenn.	1786	Jackson	New Seat	3/3/1837	3/8/1837			5/30/1865	28
John McKinley	Ala.	5/1/1780	Van Buren	New Seat	9/18/1837	9/25/1837			7/19/1852	15
Peter V. Daniel	Va.	4/24/1784	Van Buren	Barbour	2/26/1841	3/2/1841			6/30/1860	19
John C. Spencer	N.Y.	1/8/1788	Tyler	Thompson	1/9/1844		1/31/1844(R)		5/18/1855	
Reuben H. Walworth	N.Y.	10/26/1788	Tyler	Thompson	3/13/1844		6/17/1844(W)		11/27/1867	
Edward King	Pa.	1/31/1794	Tyler	Baldwin	6/5/1844		6/15/1844(P)			
Edward King	(See above)		Tyler	Baldwin	12/4/1844		2/7/1845(W)		5/8/1873	
Samuel Nelson	N.Y.	11/10/1792	Tyler	Thompson	2/4/1845	2/14/1845		11/28/1872	12/13/1873	27
John M. Read	Pa.	2/21/1797	Tyler	Baldwin	2/7/1845	No action			11/29/1874	
George W. Woodward	Pa.	3/26/1809	Polk	Baldwin	12/23/1845		1/22/1846(R)		5/10/1875	
Levi Woodbury	N.H.	12/22/1789	Polk	Story	12/23/1845	1/3/1846			9/4/1851	5
Robert C. Grier	Pa.	3/5/1794	Polk	Baldwin	8/3/1846	8/4/1846		1/31/1870	9/26/1870	23
Benjamin R. Curtis	Mass.	11/4/1809	Fillmore	Woodbury	12/11/1851	12/29/1851		9/30/1857	9/15/1874	5
Edward A. Bradford	La.	9/27/1813	Fillmore	McKinley	8/16/1852	No action				
George E. Badger	N.C.	4/13/1795	Fillmore	McKinley	1/10/1853		2/11/1853(P)		5/11/1866	
William C. Micou	La.	1806	Fillmore	McKinley	2/24/1853	No action				
John A. Campbell	Ala.	6/24/1811	Pierce	McKinley	3/21/1853	3/25/1853		April, 1861	3/13/1889	8
Nathan Clifford	Maine	8/18/1803	Buchanan	Curtis	12/9/1857	1/12/1858			7/25/1881	23
Jeremiah S. Black	Pa.	1/10/1810	Buchanan	Daniel	2/5/1861		2/21/1861(R)		8/19/1883	
Noah H. Swayne	Ohio	12/7/1804	Lincoln	McLean	1/21/1862	1/24/1862		1/24/1881	6/8/1884	19
Samuel F. Miller	Iowa	4/5/1816	Lincoln	Daniel	7/16/1862	7/16/1862			10/13/1890	28
David Davis	Ill.	3/9/1815	Lincoln	Campbell	12/1/1862	12/8/1862		3/7/1877	6/26/1886	14
Stephen J. Field	Calif.	11/4/1816	Lincoln	New Seat	3/6/1863	3/10/1863		12/1/1897	4/9/1899	34
Salmon P. Chase*	Ohio	1/13/1808	Lincoln	Taney	12/6/1864	12/6/1864			5/7/1873	8
Henry Stanbery	Ohio	2/20/1803	Johnson	Catron	4/16/1866	No action			6/26/1881	
Ebenezer R. Hoar	Mass.	2/21/1816	Grant	New Seat	12/15/1869		2/3/1870(R)		1/31/1895	
Edwin M. Stanton	Pa.	12/19/1814	Grant	Grier	12/20/1869	12/20/1869			12/24/1869	
William Strong	Pa.	3/6/1808	Grant	Grier	2/7/1870	2/18/1870		12/14/1880	8/19/1895	10
Joseph P. Bradley	N.J.	3/14/1813	Grant	New Seat	2/7/1870	3/21/1870			1/22/1892	21
Ward Hunt	N.Y.	6/14/1810	Grant	Nelson	12/3/1872	12/11/1872		1/7/1882	3/24/1886	9
George H. Williams*	Ore.	3/23/1823	Grant	Chase	12/1/1873		1/8/1874(W)		4/4/1910	
Caleb Cushing*	Mass.	1/17/1800	Grant	Chase	1/9/1874		1/13/1874(W)		1/2/1879	

* *Chief Justice*   ** *Withdrawn for technical reasons*   ‡ *Motion to invoke cloture rejected*   D - Declined   W - Withdrawn   R - Rejected   P - Postponed

Other service on court listed separately in table.

Name	State	Date of Birth	Nomi-nated by	To Replace	Date of Ap-pointment	Date Confirmed	Other Action	Date Resigned	Date of Death	Years of Service
Morrison R. Waite*	Ohio	11/29/1816	Grant	Chase	1/19/1874	1/21/1874			3/23/1888	14
John M. Harlan	Ky.	6/1/1833	Hayes	Davis	10/17/1877	11/29/1877			10/14/1911	34
William B. Woods	Ga.	8/3/1824	Hayes	Strong	12/15/1880	12/21/1880			5/14/1887	6
Stanley Matthews	Ohio	7/21/1824	Hayes	Swayne	1/26/1881	No action				
Stanley Matthews		(See above)	Garfield	Swayne	3/14/1881	5/12/1881			3/22/1889	7
Horace Gray	Mass.	3/24/1828	Arthur	Clifford	12/19/1881	12/20/1881		7/9/1902	9/15/1902	20
Roscoe Conkling	N.Y.	10/30/1829	Arthur	Hunt	2/24/1882	3/2/1882	March, 1882(D)		4/18/1888	
Samuel Blatchford	N.Y.	3/9/1820	Arthur	Hunt	3/13/1882	3/27/1882			7/7/1893	11
Lucius Q. C. Lamar	Miss.	9/17/1825	Cleveland	Woods	12/6/1887	1/16/1888			1/23/1893	5
Melville W. Fuller*	Ill.	2/11/1833	Cleveland	Waite	4/30/1888	7/20/1888			7/4/1910	22
David J. Brewer	Kan.	1/20/1837	Harrison	Matthews	12/4/1889	12/18/1889			3/28/1910	20
Henry B. Brown	Mich.	3/21/1836	Harrison	Miller	12/23/1890	12/29/1890		5/28/1906	9/4/1913	15
George Shiras, Jr.	Pa.	1/26/1832	Harrison	Bradley	7/19/1892	7/26/1892		2/23/1903	8/21/1924	10
Howell E. Jackson	Tenn.	4/8/1832	Harrison	Lamar	2/2/1893	2/18/1893			8/8/1895	2
William B. Hornblower	N.Y.	5/13/1851	Cleveland	Blatchford	9/19/1893		1/15/1894(R)		6/16/1914	
Wheeler H. Peckham	N.Y.	1/1/1833	Cleveland	Blatchford	1/22/1894		2/16/1894(R)		9/27/1905	
Edward D. White	La.	11/3/1845	Cleveland	Blatchford	2/19/1894	2/19/1894			(See below)	17#
Rufus W. Peckham	N.Y.	11/8/1838	Cleveland	Jackson	12/3/1895	12/9/1895			10/24/1909	13
Joseph McKenna	Calif.	8/10/1843	McKinley	Field	12/16/1897	1/21/1898		1/5/1925	11/21/1926	26
Oliver W. Holmes	Mass.	3/8/1841	Roosevelt	Gray	12/2/1902	12/4/1902		1/12/1932	3/6/1935	29
William R. Day	Ohio	4/17/1849	Roosevelt	Shiras	2/19/1903	2/23/1903		11/13/1922	7/9/1923	19
William H. Moody	Mass.	12/23/1853	Roosevelt	Brown	12/3/1906	12/12/1906		11/20/1910	7/2/1917	3
Horace H. Lurton	Tenn.	2/26/1844	Taft	Peckham	12/13/1909	12/20/1909			7/12/1914	4
Edward D. White*		(On court, see above)	Taft	Fuller	12/12/1910	12/12/1910			5/19/1921	10#
Charles E. Hughes	N.Y.	4/11/1862	Taft	Brewer	4/25/1910	5/2/1910		6/10/1916	(See below)	6#
Willis Van Devanter	Wyo.	4/17/1859	Taft	Moody	12/12/1910	12/15/1910		6/2/1937	2/8/1951	26
Joseph R. Lamar	Ga.	10/14/1857	Taft	White	12/12/1910	12/15/1910			1/2/1916	5
Mahlon Pitney	N.J.	2/5/1858	Taft	Harlan	2/19/1912	3/13/1912		12/31/1922	12/9/1924	10
James C. McReynolds	Tenn.	2/3/1862	Wilson	Lurton	8/19/1914	8/29/1914		1/31/1941	8/24/1946	26
Louis D. Brandeis	Mass.	11/13/1856	Wilson	Lamar	1/28/1916	6/1/1916		2/13/1939	10/5/1941	22
John H. Clarke	Ohio	9/18/1857	Wilson	Hughes	7/14/1916	7/24/1916		9/18/1922	3/22/1945	6
William H. Taft*	Conn.	9/15/1857	Harding	White	6/30/1921	6/30/1921		2/3/1930	3/8/1930	8
George Sutherland	Utah	3/25/1862	Harding	Clarke	9/5/1922	9/5/1922		1/17/1938	7/18/1942	15
Pierce Butler	Minn.	3/17/1866	Harding	Day	11/23/1922	12/21/1922			11/16/1939	17
Edward T. Sanford	Tenn.	7/23/1865	Harding	Pitney	1/24/1923	1/29/1923			3/8/1930	7
Harlan F. Stone	N.Y.	10/11/1872	Coolidge	McKenna	1/5/1925	2/5/1925			(See below)	16#
Charles E. Hughes* (Former justice, see above)			Hoover	Taft	2/3/1930	2/13/1930		7/1/1941	8/27/1948	11#
John J. Parker	N.C.	11/20/1885	Hoover	Sanford	3/21/1930		5/7/1930(R)		3/17/1958	
Owen J. Roberts	Pa.	5/2/1875	Hoover	Sanford	5/9/1930	5/20/1930		7/31/1945	5/19/1955	15
Benjamin N. Cardozo	N.Y.	5/24/1870	Hoover	Holmes	2/15/1932	2/24/1932			7/9/1938	6
Hugo L. Black	Ala.	2/27/1886	Roosevelt	Van Devanter	8/12/1937	8/17/1937		9/17/1971	10/25/1971	34
Stanley F. Reed	Ky.	12/31/1884	Roosevelt	Sutherland	1/15/1938	1/25/1938		2/26/1957		19
Felix Frankfurter	Mass.	11/15/1882	Roosevelt	Cardozo	1/5/1939	1/17/1939		8/28/1962	2/22/1965	23
William O. Douglas	Conn.	10/16/1898	Roosevelt	Brandeis	3/20/1939	4/4/1939		8/28/1962		36
Frank Murphy	Mich.	4/13/1890	Roosevelt	Butler	1/4/1940	1/15/1940		11/12/1975	7/19/1949	9
Harlan F. Stone*		(On court, see above)	Roosevelt	Hughes	6/12/1941	6/27/1941			4/22/1964	5#
James F. Byrnes	S.C.	5/2/1879	Roosevelt	Stone	6/12/1941	6/12/1941		10/3/1942	4/9/1972	1
Robert H. Jackson	N.Y.	2/13/1892	Roosevelt	McReynolds	6/12/1941	7/7/1941			10/9/1954	13
Wiley B. Rutledge	Iowa	7/20/1894	Roosevelt	Byrnes	1/11/1943	2/8/1943			9/10/1949	6
Harold H. Burton	Ohio	6/22/1888	Truman	Roberts	9/19/1945	9/19/1945		10/13/1958	10/28/1964	13
Fred M. Vinson*	Ky.	1/22/1890	Truman	Stone	6/6/1946	6/20/1946			9/8/1953	7
Tom C. Clark	Texas	9/23/1899	Truman	Murphy	8/2/1949	8/19/1949		6/12/1967		18
Sherman Minton	Ind.	10/20/1890	Truman	Rutledge	9/15/1949	10/4/1949		10/15/1956	4/9/1965	7
Earl Warren*	Calif.	3/19/1891	Eisenhower	Vinson	9/30/1953	3/1/1954		6/23/1969	6/9/1974	15
John M. Harlan	N.Y.	5/20/1899	Eisenhower	Jackson	1/10/1955	3/16/1955		9/23/1971	12/29/1971	16
William J. Brennan Jr.	N.J.	4/25/1906	Eisenhower	Minton	10/16/1956	3/19/1957				
Charles E. Whittaker	Mo.	2/22/1901	Eisenhower	Reed	3/2/1957	3/19/1957		4/1/1962	11/26/73	5
Potter Stewart	Ohio	1/23/1915	Eisenhower	Burton	1/17/1959	5/5/1959				
Byron R. White	Colo.	6/8/1917	Kennedy	Whittaker	4/3/1962	4/11/1962				
Arthur J. Goldberg	Ill.	8/8/1908	Kennedy	Frankfurter	8/31/1962	9/25/1962		7/25/1965		3
Abe Fortas	Tenn.	6/19/1910	Johnson	Goldberg	7/28/1965	8/11/1965		5/14/1969		4
Thurgood Marshall	N.Y.	6/2/1908	Johnson	Clark	6/13/1967	8/30/1967				
Abe Fortas*		(On court, see above)	Johnson	Warren	6/26/1968		10/4/1968 (W)†			
Homer Thornberry	Texas	1/9/1909	Johnson	Fortas	6/26/1968		No action			
Warren E. Burger	Minn.	9/17/1907	Nixon	Warren	5/21/1969	6/9/1969				
Clement Haynsworth Jr.	S.C.	10/30/1912	Nixon	Fortas	8/18/1969		11/21/1969(R)			
G. Harrold Carswell	Fla.	12/22/1919	Nixon	Fortas	1/19/1970		4/8/1970(R)			
Harry A. Blackmun	Minn	11/12/1908	Nixon	Fortas	4/14/1970	5/12/1970				
Lewis F. Powell Jr.	Va.	9/19/1907	Nixon	Black	10/21/71	12/6/71				
William H. Rehnquist	Ariz.	10/1/24	Nixon	Harlan	10/21/71	12/10/71				
John Paul Stevens	Ill.	4/20/20	Ford	Douglas	11/28/75	12/17/75				

Sources: Leon Friedman and Fred L. Israel, eds., *The Justices of the United States Supreme Court, 1789-1969;* Congressional Quarterly, 1971 and 1975 Almanacs.

(Continued from p. 641)

years. After some inconclusive disputes over the power of Congress to penalize contempt, the Supreme Court in 1821 *(Anderson v. Dunn,* 19 U.S. 204) upheld the authority of a house of Congress to punish "contempts committed against themselves." Imprisonment could not extend beyond the adjournment of Congress. Considering the limitation of imprisonment to the legislative session inadequate, Congress in 1857 enacted a law making it a criminal offense to refuse information demanded by either house. This statute is the original version of the law generally used by Congress today to enforce observance of its investigative authority.

In 1881 *(Kilbourn v. Thompson,* 103 U.S. 168), the Supreme Court asserted the right of the courts to review the investigative activities of Congress. The decision was an extension of the principle of judicial review established by Chief Justice Marshall in the 1803 *Marbury* decision. The 1881 decision concerned a House investigation of a private real estate pool, with one of whose bankrupt members the federal government had deposited funds.

Congress delegated its investigative powers to the Interstate Commerce Commission, established in 1887, and subsequently to other regulatory agencies. The Supreme Court in 1894 *(Interstate Commerce Commission v. Brimson,* 154 U.S. 447) sustained the ICC's investigative authority, but in 1906 *(Harriman v. Interstate Commerce Commission,* 211 U.S. 407) held that the power was limited to obtaining information connected with possible violations of law.

A series of Supreme Court decisions delineated the balance between the powers of investigating committees and the rights of witnesses. The most important of these decisions was made in 1927 *(McGrain v. Daugherty,* 273 U.S. 135), when the court ruled that the Senate could require information from Mally S. Daugherty, brother of former Attorney General Harry M. Daugherty.

In 1929 *(Sinclair v. United States,* 279 U.S. 263) the Supreme Court held that a witness who refused to answer questions asked by a congressional committee could be punished if he were mistaken as to the ground on which he based his refusal, even if he acted in good faith on the advice of counsel. This precedent made any challenge of committee powers risky; a jail sentence might be in store for a witness seeking to test his rights in court. *(See p. 148)*

Following World War II, the Supreme Court was far more protective of the rights of witnesses. In the 1953 case of *United States v. Rumely* (344 U.S. 812), the Supreme Court upheld a Court of Appeals decision reversing the conviction, for contempt of Congress, of Edward A. Rumely. Rumely had refused to tell the House Select Committee on Lobbying Activities the names of individuals making bulk purchases of books distributed by the Committee for Constitutional Government, an arch-conservative organization. He had asserted to the committee that "under the Bill of Rights, that is beyond the power of your committee to investigate."

A majority of the court avoided the constitutional questions by narrowly construing the authority granted by the resolution establishing the committee. It held that the mandate to investigate "lobbying activities" was limited to "representations made directly to the Congress, its Members, or its committees," and excluded attempts to influence Congress indirectly through public dissemination of literature.

The court again placed strictures on the investigative powers of Congress in 1957, when it ruled in *Watkins v. United States* (354 U.S. 178) that John T. Watkins was not guilty of contempt of Congress for refusing to answer certain questions before the House Un-American Activities Committee. The court based its decision on a finding that the committee's legislative mandate was "loosely worded" and "excessively broad" and that the committee had failed to show that its questions were pertinent to the subject of the inquiry.

The court backtracked somewhat from this position in its decision in a 1959 case, *Barenblatt v. United States* (360 U.S. 109). By a 5-4 vote, it ruled that First Amendment rights may be limited where the public interest outweighs the private interest. While the court in that case criticized the "vagueness" of that section of House Rule XI defining the powers and duties of the Un-American Activities Committee (in the language of the resolution establishing the committee), it concluded that "we may not read it in isolation from its long history in the House."

Shifting gears again, the court in 1963, by another 5-4 decision, reversed the conviction of Edward Yellin for contempt of Congress on the ground that the Un-American Activities Committee violated its own rules by failing to consider his request for an executive session before he was questioned. *(See also chapter on investigative power of Congress)*

On a related issue, the court ruled several times during the early 1970s on the scope of the immunity which the Constitution grants to members of Congress for actions taken in their official capacity. The court held in 1972 that this immunity protected members and their aides as long as the conduct in question was part of their legislative function *(Gravel v. U.S.,* 408 U.S. 606), but that it did not protect a member from prosecution on charges that he had taken a bribe to vote a certain way on a legislative matter *(U.S. v. Brewster,* 408 U.S. 501). In a 1973 case *(Doe v. McMillan,* 412 U.S. 306) involving a challenge by persons who felt that their privacy had been invaded by their being named in a committee report, the court held that there were limits to this immunity, especially as it extended to persons outside Congress "who publish and distribute otherwise actionable materials beyond the reasonable requirements of the legislative function." *(Congressional immunity, p. 713)*

Court-Curbing Proposals

Intermittently throughout American history, congressional critics of judicial power have sought to impose restrictions on the Supreme Court. The methods have ranged from proposed curbs on the court's authority to the Senate's rejection of court nominees.

Early Proposals

The first move against the court was made in 1802, when the newly elected Congress dominated by Jeffersonian Republicans abolished the additional federal circuit courts set up the year before by the old Congress and staffed with 16 Federalist judges (the "midnight judges") appointed by President Adams on the eve of his departure from office. To delay a decision in the *Marbury* and controversial cases, Congress also enacted legislation postponing the Supreme Court's term for 14 months, until February 1803. In 1805, Rep. John Randolph, a Virginia Republican, proposed a constitutional amendment providing for removal of Supreme Court justices by the President upon the approval of both houses of Congress. However, Randolph's proposal attracted little support and was dropped.[14]

Alarmed by a series of Supreme Court decisions strengthening federal power at the expense of the states,

states' rights advocates in Congress introduced a variety of other court-curbing proposals. In 1807, Republicans proposed a constitutional amendment providing for a limited tenure of office for federal judges and for their removal by the President upon a two-thirds vote of each house.

In 1831, congressional Democrats (the old Jeffersonian Republican Party) launched a determined effort to repeal Section 25 of the Judiciary Act of 1789, which authorized writs of error to the Supreme Court to review state court judgments. (A writ of error is a process under which an appellate court may bring up a case from a lower court to examine the trial record as to questions of law but not of fact.) On Jan. 29, 1831, the House rejected this proposal by a 51-158 roll-call vote, with all but six of the minority votes coming from southern and western states.[15] Later that year, Democrats introduced another proposal directing the House Judiciary Committee to study the feasibility of amending the Constitution to limit the tenure of federal judges. That proposal was rejected by a 61-115 roll-call vote.[16]

Another series of attacks on the court was launched in the early 1900s by critics of the court's decisions protecting property rights. In 1923, Sen. William E. Borah (R Idaho) introduced a bill to require concurrence by seven of the nine justices to invalidate an act of Congress. The following year Sen. Robert M. La Follette (R Wis.) proposed a constitutional amendment providing that a statute once struck down by the Supreme Court could be declared constitutional and immune from further court consideration by a two-thirds majority of both houses of Congress. Neither the Borah nor the La Follette proposal received serious consideration.[17]

After Congress rejected the Roosevelt court-packing plan in 1937, the Supreme Court experienced a period of relatively placid relations with Congress until the Warren court launched on its course of judicial activism in the mid-1950s. The only proposed curb on the court that attracted much support from the mid-1930s to the early 1950s was a 1953 proposal to amend the Constitution to make retirement mandatory for all federal judges at age 75. The resolution proposing the amendment, suggested by the American Bar Association, was adopted by the Senate in 1954 but was shelved by the House.[18]

Attacks on the Warren Court

Congressional attacks on the Warren court began in 1954, the year of the court's famous school desegregation decision. On May 17, 1954, the court had declared in the case of *Brown v. Board of Education of Topeka, Kansas* (347 U.S. 483) that racial segregation in public schools was inherently discriminatory and therefore in contravention of the equal protection clause of the Fourteenth Amendment. The period of the next four years was a time of unusual anti-court activity in Congress, spurred at first by southern members. Some 19 senators and 74 representatives from the South signed a "Declaration of Constitutional Principles"—the so-called Southern Manifesto—on March 12, 1956, protesting the "decision of the Supreme Court in the school cases as a clear abuse of judicial power." The southerners were joined in time by colleagues from other sections who were dismayed by the court's decisions in such matters as federal-state relations, Communist activities, and contempt of Congress.

From 1955 through 1962, proposals were introduced in Congress to curb the Supreme Court's power to strike down state laws as pre-empted by federal laws. Under Article VI, Section 2, of the Constitution, making federal law the "supreme law of the land," the courts had invalidated state laws in cases where: (1) Congress had stated an intention to take over ("preempt") a given field of legislation; (2) there was a direct conflict between a federal law and a state law; or (3) congressional intention to preempt a field of legislation could be inferred, even though it had not been specified by Congress (the doctrine of "preemption by implication"). In 1958, a broad anti-preemption bill was passed overwhelmingly by the House and was defeated in the Senate by only one vote.[19]

Jenner-Butler Bill. The Jenner-Butler bill (for Republican Sens. William E. Jenner of Indiana and John Marshall Butler of Maryland), would have deprived the Supreme Court of authority to review several types of cases, including those concerning contempt of Congress, the federal loyalty-security program, state anti-subversive statutes, and admission to the practice of law in any state. After lengthy committee hearings and bitter floor debate, the Senate tabled the bill by a vote of 49 to 41 on Aug. 20, 1958.[20]

Attacks on the Supreme Court came not only from Congress but also from the judiciary itself. Three days after the Jenner-Butler bill was shelved by the Senate, the Conference of State Chief Justices approved a statement asserting that the court "too often has tended to adopt the rule of policy-maker without proper judicial restraint." The statement added: "We are not alone in our view that the Court, in many cases...has assumed what seems to us primarily legislative powers."

Dirksen Amendments. Congressional attacks on the court intensified in the early 1960s. The court in 1962 ruled unconstitutional the use of a 22-word prayer in New York state public schools. Justice Hugo L. Black, speaking for the court in the case of *Engel v. Vitale* (370 U.S. 421), said the prayer requirement violated the First Amendment's clause forbidding laws "respecting the establishment of religion." Soon afterward, Senate Republican Leader Everett McKinley Dirksen (Ill.) championed a proposed constitutional amendment to legalize voluntary student participation in prayers in public schools. Four years later, the proposal came to a vote in the Senate and fell nine votes short of receiving the necessary two-thirds majority. In 1971 a similar constitutional amendment came to a vote in the House and failed by 28 votes.[21]

Dirksen also was leader of congressional efforts to modify the Supreme Court's "one man, one vote" doctrine on legislative apportionment set out in a series of decisions during the early 1960s. The House passed a bill in 1964 to deny federal courts jurisdiction over apportionment of state legislatures, but it was blocked in the Senate. At this juncture, court foes proposed a constitutional amendment to permit states to apportion one house of their legislatures on some basis other than population. The proposal came to a vote in the Senate in 1965 and again in 1966—each time failing by seven votes to achieve a two-thirds majority. *(See p. 221)*

Court Pay Raises. Anti-court sentiment triumphed in Congress in 1964 when pay raises of $7,500 were voted for federal judges—except Supreme Court justices, whose salaries were raised by only $4,500. The following year, an attempt to restore the pay differential was beaten down. For the next five years, the salary of the Chief Justice remained at $40,000 and that of associate justices at $39,500. In 1969, the Chief Justice's salary was raised to $62,500 and the salaries of associate justices to $60,000. In 1975, Congress brought the Supreme Court and other federal judges under a federal pay law that made government workers eligible for annual cost-of-living salary increases.

Supreme Court and 1968 Crime Act

Later in the 1960s, anti-court sentiment found expression in the Omnibus Crime and Safe Streets Act of 1968, portions of which attempted to reverse three decisions of the Supreme Court—*Miranda, Mallory* and *Wade*. In *Mallory v. United States* (354 U.S. 449), the court in 1957 ruled that if there was unnecessary delay in bringing a suspect before a judge for arraignment, any confession he made during that period could not be admitted in court as evidence against him. Although the *Mallory* decision affected only federal police practices, it worried both federal and state law enforcement officers. They said it would hamper police investigations.

In *Miranda v. Arizona* (384 U.S. 436), the court in 1966 set rules for stationhouse questioning of suspects. Before the police could conduct an interrogation or obtain a confession, the court ruled, they must advise the suspect that anything he says may become evidence against him; that he has a right to remain silent, and that he is entitled to have a lawyer present during questioning. The following year, in the case of *United States v. Wade* (354 U.S. 449), the court held that a pre-trial lineup in which a defendant is exhibited to identifying witnesses constitutes a critical step in a criminal prosecution and that the defendant is entitled to assistance of counsel at the lineup.

Title II of the 1968 Act contained language governing admissibility of evidence and eyewitness testimony which many considered inconsistent with the three court decisions. "These Supreme Court decisions are based on constitutional principles," the magazine *Judicature* commented in its June-July 1968 issue. "If the law enforcement practices to which *Miranda, Mallory* and *Wade* objected were unconstitutional, it is hard to see how an act of Congress alone can make them constitutional."

Abortion and Busing

Abortion and busing were the issues which provoked the most determined efforts in Congress during the early 1970s to curb or undo Supreme Court actions through constitutional amendments.

Early in 1973, the court had limited the power of states to ban abortions, allowing such prohibitions only in the last months of pregnancy. In 1975 a Senate subcommittee rejected several amendments intended to reverse that ruling; in April 1976 the Senate refused, 47-40, to debate such an amendment.

In several rulings, the Supreme Court upheld the use of court-ordered busing to desegregate public school systems.

The proposed anti-busing constitutional amendments before Congress would have denied lower federal courts the power to issue such orders. By mid-1976, none had won approval in either chamber.

Rejection of Court Nominees

Congress exerts influence over the judiciary in another major way—through the Senate's prerogative to "advise and consent" in the President's selection of candidates for judicial offices, including not only Supreme Court justices but also other federal court judges.

Starting with George Washington, 15 Presidents have seen 26 of their nominees for the Supreme Court fail to win Senate confirmation—among a total of 139 appointments. In contrast, only eight Cabinet nominees have been rejected by the Senate. The last time a Cabinet nomination was rejected was in 1959, when Senate Democrats refused to approve President Eisenhower's selection of Lewis L. Strauss as Secretary of Commerce. *(See p. 180)*

Although Congress also has authority to remove federal judges by impeachment, only one such attempt with respect to a Supreme Court justice has moved past the preliminary stage, and that attempt failed. In 1804, the House impeached Justice Samuel Chase, a staunch Federalist who had rankled Republicans with his partisan political statements and his vigorous prosecution of the Sedition Act (which had finally been repealed in 1802. But Chase was not convicted by the Senate even though his opponents obtained a majority on three of the eight articles of impeachment. (A total of 23 senators—two-thirds of the Senate—was necessary for conviction. The greatest number of votes for conviction on any of the articles was 19.) After the trial, President Jefferson, a strong foe of the Federalist-dominated court, criticized impeachment as "a bungling way of removing judges" and "a farce which will not be tried again."[22] *(See p. 211)*

Senate rejection of court nominations was common in the 19th century, when political ideology often colored the confirmation process. But from 1900 to 1968, the Senate refused a seat on the Supreme Court to only one man, John J. Parker in 1930. Then, in a 19-month period from late 1968 to early 1970, the Senate refused to approve four Supreme Court nominees—Abe Fortas and Homer Thornberry, nominated by President Johnson, and Clement F. Haynsworth Jr. and G. Harrold Carswell, nominated by President Nixon. (Fortas, already an associate justice, had been nominated for Chief Justice. Thornberry was to take his place as an associate justice. Both nominations were withdrawn when Senate supporters of the nominees were unable to break a Republican-southern Democratic filibuster on the Fortas nomination.) *(For complete listing of justices, see table p. 642)*

Despite the low incidence of rejection for most of the 20th century, at least four other court nominations faced stiff opposition—those of Louis D. Brandeis in 1916, Harlan F. Stone in 1925, Charles Evans Hughes in 1930, and Hugo L. Black in 1937. To this list might be added Thurgood Marshall, the only black ever named to the court. The Senate Judiciary Committee, under the chairmanship of Sen. James O. Eastland (D Miss.), was able to induce President Johnson to hold back his intended nomination of Marshall for a year. When the nomination did come, in 1965, Marshall was confirmed, 54 to 16.

Action on the Brandeis nomination a half-century earlier was delayed for months by the same committee while it pondered the nominee's "radical views." When the nomination of Hughes as Chief Justice was made in 1930, the country was entering the Great Depression and the nominee's views were attacked as too conservative.

Despite the opposition to Hughes, voiced before his confirmation on Feb. 13, 1930, President Hoover thought Parker would be a non-controversial nominee. He was a federal judge and a Republican from North Carolina. Hoover later wrote in his memoirs that "No member of the Court at that time was from the southern states, and the regional distribution of justices had always been regarded as of some importance."[23] But Hoover misjudged the temper of

Supreme Court Nominations Not Confirmed by the Senate

From 1789 through 1975, 26 Supreme Court nominations have failed to receive Senate confirmation. Of these 11 have been rejected outright and the remainder withdrawn or allowed to lapse when Senate rejection appeared imminent. Following is the complete list of nominees failing to receive confirmation:

Nominee	President	Date of Nomination	Senate Action	Date of Senate Action
John Rutledge (for Chief Justice)	Washington	July 1, 1795	Rejected (10-14)	Dec. 15, 1795
Alexander Wolcott	Madison	Feb. 4, 1811	Rejected (9-24)	Feb. 13, 1811
John J. Crittenden	John Quincy Adams	Dec. 17, 1828	Postponed	Feb. 12, 1829
Roger Brooke Taney	Jackson	Jan. 15, 1835	Postponed	March 3, 1825 (later nominated for Chief Justice and confirmed)
John C. Spencer	Tyler	Jan. 9, 1844	Rejected (21-26)	Jan. 31, 1844
Reuben H. Walworth	Tyler	March 13, 1844	Withdrawn	
Edward King	Tyler	June 5, 1844	Postponed	June 15, 1844
Edward King	Tyler	Dec. 4, 1844	Withdrawn	
John M. Read	Tyler	Feb. 7, 1845	Not Acted Upon	
George W. Woodward	Polk	Dec. 23, 1845	Rejected (20-29)	Jan. 22, 1846
Edward A. Bradford	Fillmore	Aug. 16, 1852	Not Acted Upon	
George E. Badger	Fillmore	Jan. 10, 1853	Postponed	Feb. 11, 1853
William C. Micou	Fillmore	Feb. 24, 1853	Not Acted Upon	
Jeremiah S. Black	Buchanan	Feb. 5, 1861	Rejected (25-26)	Feb. 21, 1861
Henry Stanbery	Andrew Johnson	April 16, 1866	Not Acted Upon	
Ebenezer R. Hoar	Grant	Dec. 15, 1869	Rejected (24-33)	Feb. 3, 1870
George H. Williams (for Chief Justice)	Grant	Dec. 1, 1873	Withdrawn	
Caleb Cushing (for Chief Justice)	Grant	Jan. 9, 1874	Withdrawn	
Stanley Matthews	Hayes	Jan. 26, 1881	Not Acted Upon	(later renominated and confirmed)
William B. Hornblower	Cleveland	Sept. 19, 1893	Rejected (24-30)	Jan. 15, 1894
Wheeler H. Peckham	Cleveland	Jan. 22, 1894	Rejected (32-41)	Feb. 16, 1894
John J. Parker	Hoover	March 21, 1930	Rejected (39-41)	May 7, 1930
Abe Fortas (for Chief Justice)	Lyndon Johnson	June 26, 1968	Withdrawn	
Homer Thornberry	Lyndon Johnson	June 26, 1968	Not Acted Upon	
Clement F. Haynsworth Jr.	Nixon	Aug. 18, 1969	Rejected (45-55)	Nov. 21, 1969
G. Harrold Carswell	Nixon	Jan. 19, 1970	Rejected (45-51)	April 8, 1970

Source: Library of Congress, Congressional Research Service

the times. Social and economic issues were more important than was geography. A bipartisan group in Congress charged that Parker had made anti-Negro statements as a political candidate and an anti-Negro ruling from the bench. His nomination was rejected, 39 to 41, on May 7, 1930.

Hugo L. Black encountered difficulty getting confirmed because he had once been a member of the Ku Klux Klan in his native Alabama.

Stone, at the time of his nomination, was U.S. Attorney General and was in the midst of prosecuting Burton K. Wheeler, a recently elected Democratic senator from Montana. Wheeler was accused, but later acquitted of charges of participating in an oil-land fraud.

Wheeler's home state Democratic colleague, Sen. Thomas J. Walsh, used the committee hearings on Stone's nomination to criticize the Justice Department's handling of the Wheeler case.

The Senate's refusal to take up the Fortas and Thornberry nominations resulted largely from Fortas' affirmative votes in some of the most controversial decisions of the Warren court and from the desire of Senate Republicans to have a Republican President name the new Chief Justice. The GOP strategy paid off when Republican presidential candidate Richard M. Nixon won the 1968 election. But after Nixon's nominee for Chief Justice, Warren E. Burger, had been confirmed, Senate Democrats retaliated for the Fortas affair by successfully opposing confirmation of the President's next two court nominees—Haynsworth and Carswell. *(See p. 185)* Critics of the nominations based their opposition primarily on allegations that Haynsworth had failed to observe high standards of professional ethics while serving as an appellate judge, and that Carswell was not qualified for such a high judicial post. Republicans contended, however, that the avowedly conservative views of both men were responsible for their rejection.

GUIDE TO CONGRESS

The Federal Judicial System

Under the United States system of checks and balances, the Supreme Court stands at the pinnacle of the federal judicial structure as the final reviewing authority of congressional legislation and executive action. However, as is implicit in a checks-and-balance system of government, the high court, and also the lower federal judiciary, does not function with complete independence. On the one hand, the size, salaries and jurisdiction of the judicial branch are determined by the legislative branch. On the other hand, the membership of the judicial branch is selected by the executive branch.

Federal and State Courts

Two types of judicial systems, state and federal, provide forums for the resolution of disputes. The state judicial systems are composed of the state supreme court, or state court of appeals, intermediate appellate courts and trial courts with general jurisdiction over disputes where most cases of a serious nature begin. In addition, states usually have a group of lower courts, such as municipal, police and justice-of-the-peace courts, which are the lowest courts in the judicial hierarchy and have limited jurisdiction in both civil and criminal cases. The federal system forms a tri-level pyramid, comprised of district courts at the bottom, circuit courts of appeals in the middle, and the Supreme Court at the top.

Provision for a federal judiciary was made by Article III, Section 1, of the Constitution, which stated: "The judicial power of the United States shall be vested in one supreme court, and in such inferior courts as the Congress may from time to time ordain and establish." Thus, aside from the required "supreme court," the structure of the lower federal judicial system was left entirely to the discretion of Congress.

Congress and Federal Courts

The Judiciary Act of 1789 established the Supreme Court; 13 district courts, each with a single judge; and, above the district courts, three circuit courts, each presided over by one district and two Supreme Court judges. Thereafter, as the nation grew and the federal judiciary's workload increased, Congress established additional circuit and district courts. In 1975, there were 11 circuit courts of appeals, 88 district courts, and four territorial courts (Canal Zone, Guam, Puerto Rico and Virgin Islands).

The influence of Congress over the federal judiciary goes beyond the creation of courts. Although the power to appoint federal judges resides with the President, by and with the Senate's advice and consent, the power to create judgeships to which appointments could be made resides with Congress. It was in this area that politics historically plays its most important role. For example, in 1801, the Federalist Congress created additional circuit court judgeships to be filled by a Federalist President. However, in 1802, when the Jefferson Republicans came into power, the new posts were abolished.

As federal judges are appointed to serve during good behavior, the power of Congress to abolish judgeships is limited to providing in the creation of a judgeship that, when it becomes vacant, it cannot be filled. The history of the Supreme Court's size provides the best illustration of

the earlier habit of creating and abolishing judgeships. Originally, the Supreme Court was composed of six justices. Subsequently, however, its membership varied: five justices, 1801-07; seven justices, 1807-37; nine justices, 1837-63; 10 justices, 1863-66; seven justices, 1866-69; and nine justices since 1869.

Jurisdiction of Federal Courts

Article III, Section 2, of the Constitution vests in the Supreme Court original jurisdiction—the power to hear a case argued before other courts do—over only a few kinds of cases. The most important of these were suits between two states, which might concern such issues as water rights, offshore lands, etc. Article III, Section 2, also extended to the court "judicial power" over all cases arising under the Constitution, federal laws and treaties. This jurisdiction, however, was appellate (i.e., limited to review of decisions from lower courts) and was subject to "such exceptions and...regulations as Congress shall make." Most of the high court's present jurisdiction is defined by the Judiciary Act of 1925, largely drafted by the court itself under Chief Justice William Howard Taft.

The Judiciary Act of 1925 made the exercise of the court's appellate jurisdiction largely discretionary, giving the justices more leeway to refuse to review cases.

Except for certain limited types of cases in which the court was still "obligated" to take appeals, the court was allowed to decide whether the decisions from the lower courts presented questions or conflicts important enough or of such a constitutional nature as to warrant the court's consideration on review.

But only in this way is the court able to control the issues with which it deals. Its power is limited by the fact that it cannot reach out to bring issues before it, but must wait until they are properly presented in a case which has made its way through the lower courts.

In the relationship between federal and state judicial systems, federal courts have jurisdiction—usually where $10,000 or more is involved—over cases relating to federal rights or actions in which the parties are citizens of different states. The state courts, on the other hand, are concerned with cases generally involving citizens of that state and their own state laws.

There is some overlap of jurisdiction. The state courts are empowered to hear litigation concerning some federal rights, and federal constitutional rights often form the basis of decision in state court cases.

In the federal courts, where jurisdiction is based on a "diversity of citizenship" (i.e., the litigants are from different states), the court is obliged to find and apply the pertinent law of the state in which the court is sitting. In state court cases, similarly, in those few instances where a "federal question" might be resolved, the court is obliged to disregard its own precedents and apply appropriate federal law.

Judicial Appointments

The power to name members of the federal judiciary is perhaps the strongest patronage lever possessed by an incumbent President. As a result, federal judgeships, which are filled by the President with Senate confirmation,

Federal Judicial System

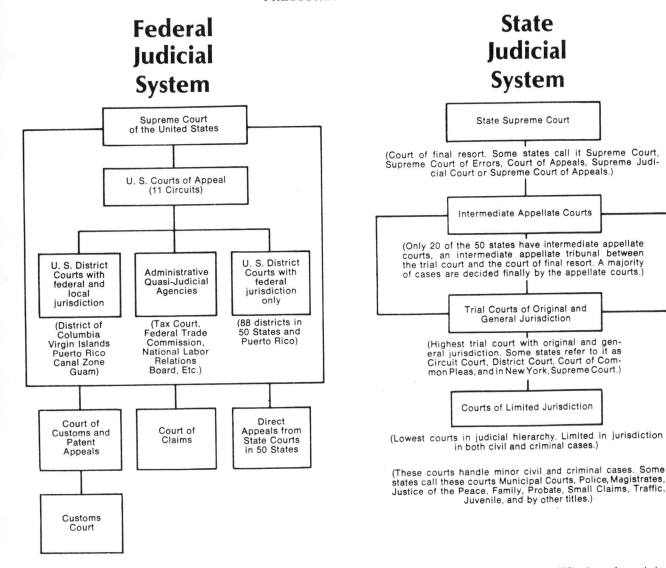

State Judicial System

```
┌─────────────────────────────┐
│      Supreme Court          │
│   of the United States      │
└─────────────────────────────┘

┌─────────────────────────────┐
│    U. S. Courts of Appeal   │
│        (11 Circuits)        │
└─────────────────────────────┘

┌──────────────┬──────────────┬──────────────┐
│ U. S. District│ Administrative│ U. S. District│
│ Courts with  │ Quasi-Judicial│ Courts with  │
│ federal and  │   Agencies   │   federal    │
│    local     │              │ jurisdiction │
│ jurisdiction │              │     only     │
└──────────────┴──────────────┴──────────────┘

(District of        (Tax Court,       (88 districts in
 Columbia           Federal Trade      50 States and
 Virgin Islands     Commission,        Puerto Rico)
 Puerto Rico        National Labor
 Canal Zone         Relations
 Guam)              Board, Etc.)

┌──────────────┬──────────────┬──────────────┐
│  Court of    │   Court of   │   Direct     │
│ Customs and  │    Claims    │ Appeals from │
│   Patent     │              │ State Courts │
│   Appeals    │              │ in 50 States │
└──────────────┴──────────────┴──────────────┘

┌──────────────┐
│  Customs     │
│   Court      │
└──────────────┘
```

```
┌─────────────────────────────┐
│     State Supreme Court     │
└─────────────────────────────┘

(Court of final resort. Some states call it Supreme Court,
Supreme Court of Errors, Court of Appeals, Supreme Judi-
cial Court or Supreme Court of Appeals.)

┌─────────────────────────────┐
│ Intermediate Appellate Courts│
└─────────────────────────────┘

(Only 20 of the 50 states have intermediate appellate
courts, an intermediate appellate tribunal between
the trial court and the court of final resort. A majority
of cases are decided finally by the appellate courts.)

┌─────────────────────────────┐
│  Trial Courts of Original and│
│     General Jurisdiction    │
└─────────────────────────────┘

(Highest trial court with original and gen-
eral jurisdiction. Some states refer to it as
Circuit Court, District Court, Court of Com-
mon Pleas, and in New York, Supreme Court.)

┌─────────────────────────────┐
│  Courts of Limited Jurisdiction│
└─────────────────────────────┘

(Lowest courts in judicial hierarchy. Limited in jurisdiction
in both civil and criminal cases.)

(These courts handle minor civil and criminal cases. Some
states call these courts Municipal Courts, Police, Magistrates,
Justice of the Peace, Family, Probate, Small Claims, Traffic,
Juvenile, and by other titles.)
```

traditionally go to those having the same political affiliation as the President. Throughout the nation's history, however, Presidents generally have indicated their intention to make judicial appointments nonpartisan. Nevertheless, since a judge is appointed for life, appointees to the federal bench, with few exceptions, have been of the same political party as the President appointing them.

Stages of Appointment Process

Two sections of the Constitution govern judicial appointments. Article II, Section 2, Clause 2, provides: The President "...shall nominate, and by and with the advice and consent of the Senate, shall appoint...judges of the Supreme Court, and all other officers of the United States...." Article II, Section 3, provides: The President "...shall commission all officers of the United States...."

From these two sections evolved three stages in the appointment process: (1) the nomination, (2) the appointment, and (3) the commission. The "nomination" is the independent act of the President, and is completely voluntary. In the selection, or nomination, of a prospective district or circuit court judge, however, the President usually takes into consideration a number of things—for example, political views and party affiliation, the opinions of congressional advisers who aided the President on other partisan matters, the recommendations of national, state and local political organizations and the qualification ratings given prospective nominees by national, state and local bar associations. In the selection of Supreme Court nominees, on the other hand, the President usually acts with more independence and gives more weight to political philosophy.

Usually when a judicial post becomes vacant or is created within a state, the senator or senators from the state who are of the President's party send to the office of the deputy attorney general a list of prospective nominees. The possible nominees then undergo scrutiny by the White House, the FBI and the American Bar Association's committee on the federal judiciary.

Once the nominee is selected, the nomination is sent to the Senate, where it is referred to the Judiciary Committee. Usually, after a perfunctory hearing, the committee recommends that the Senate confirm the nominee and the Senate does so by voice vote.

The "appointment" is also the sole act of the President, and is also a voluntary act, but can be performed only with the advice and consent of the Senate. In effect, the appointment is made automatically upon Senate confirmation.

Prior to confirmation, a senator can object to a nominee for patronage or other reasons—for example, when a nomination to a district circuit judgeship is made without consulting the senators of the district or circuit concerned. Then a senator can use the stock, but rare, objection that the nominee is "personally obnoxious" to him. In this case, other senators usually—but not always—join in blocking confirmation out of courtesy to their colleague.

The first person to lose a post to this "senatorial courtesy" was Benjamin Fishbourn, nominated naval officer of the port of Savannah, Ga., by President Washington in 1789. In 1976, the Senate Judiciary Committee demonstrated the strength of this custom by tabling—and thereby killing—President Ford's nomination of William B. Poff to a federal judgeship in Virginia. Poff's nomination was opposed by Sen. William Lloyd Scott (R Va.).

The "commission" is also the sole act of the President. It simply means that the appointee is given by the President the authority to carry out the duties of his office.

Types of Appointments

There are two types of judicial appointments. One is the regular appointment route outlined above. The other is the "recess" appointment prescribed by the Constitution's Article II, Section 2, Clause 3, which states: "The President shall have power to fill up all vacancies that may happen during the recess of the Senate, by granting commissions which shall expire at the end of their next session."

The recess appointment is an often criticized means of making appointments by temporarily bypassing Senate confirmation. Under this procedure, the President, when a judgeship becomes vacant and when Congress is not in session, can extend a "commission" for a judgeship, and the new judge can then take office without Senate confirmation. However, when Congress reconvenes, the President has to submit the name of his recess nominee for confirmation within 40 days. If he does not do so, the judge's pay is terminated. On the other hand, if the name is submitted in the required time and Congress fails to confirm or reject the nomination during the session, the appointment is good until Congress adjourns.

To prevent a President from leaving a vacancy which occurred in mid-session unfilled until Congress adjourns, so that he can make a recess appointment, law requires that the President nominate a person to fill a vacancy within 30 days. If the President fails to do this, he can still wait until Congress adjourns and then make the recess appointment, but the appointee would not be eligible to draw a salary.

Footnotes

1. *Ogden v. Saunders* (12 Wheat. 213), cited by Leon Friedman and Fred L. Israel, eds., in *The Justices of the United States Supreme Court, 1789-1969* (R.R. Bowker Co., 1969), vol. 1, p. 266.

2. Charles A. Beard, *The Supreme Court and the Constitution* (Macmillan, 1912), p. 76.

3. Wilfred E. Binkley and Malcolm C. Moos, *A Grammar of American Politics* (Alfred A. Knopf, 1958 ed.), p. 519.

4. *The Federalist Papers*, with an Introduction by Clinton Rossiter (Mentor, 1961), No. 78, p. 466.

5. Beard, *The Supreme Court*, pp. 63-64.

6. Binkley and Moos, *A Grammar of American Politics*, pp. 519-20.

7. Charles Warren, *The Supreme Court in United States History* (Little, Brown, 1922, 1926), vol. 1, pp. 69-83.

8. *Ibid.*, p. 243.

9. *Ibid.*, p. 244.

10. Letter of Jefferson to William Johnson, June 12, 1823, cited in Warren, *The Supreme Court*, vol. 1, p. 245.

11. *New York Tribune* editorials of March 1857, cited by Warren, *The Supreme Court*, vol. 1, pp. 305-06.

12. Charles Evans Hughes, *The Supreme Court of the United States* (Columbia University Press, 1928), p. 51.

13. *Ibid.*, pp. 52-53.

14. Warren, *The Supreme Court*, vol. 1, p. 295.

15. *Ibid.*, pp. 736-41.

16. *Ibid.*, p. 743.

17. Charles Warren, *Congress, The Constitution and the Supreme Court* (Little, Brown, 1925), pp. 138-42, 178-221.

18. Congressional Quarterly, *Congress and the Nation, 1945-1964*, vol. 1, p. 1442.

19. *Ibid.*

20. *Ibid.*

21. Congressional Quarterly, *Congress and the Nation, 1965-1968*, vol. 2, pp. 410-11; *Congress and the Nation, 1969-1972*, vol. 3, p. 486.

22. Letter of Jefferson to Spencer Roane, Sept. 6, 1819, cited in Warren, *The Supreme Court*, vol. 1, p. 295.

23. Herbert Hoover, *The Memoirs of Herbert Hoover*, vol. 2: *The Cabinet and the Presidency 1920-1933* (Macmillan Co., 1952), p. 268.

Selected Bibliography

Books

Beard, Charles A. *The Supreme Court and the Constitution.* New York: Macmillan, 1912.

Berger, Raoul. *Congress v. The Supreme Court.* Cambridge: Harvard University Press, 1969.

Berle, Adolf A. *The Three Faces of Power.* New York: Harcourt, Brace and World, 1967.

Bickel, Alexander M. *The Least Dangerous Branch.* Indianapolis: Bobbs-Merrill, 1962.

———. *Politics and the Warren Court.* New York: Harper and Row, 1965 ed.

Binkley, Wilfred E. and Moos, Malcolm C. *A Grammar of American Politics.* New York: Alfred A. Knopf, 1958 ed.

Boudin, Louis B. *Government by the Judiciary.* New York: Russell & Russell, 1968.

Breckenridge, Adam C. *Congress Against the Court.* Lincoln: University of Nebraska Press, 1970.

Corwin, Edward S. *Court Over Constitution.* Princeton: Princeton University Press, 1938.

———. *Doctrine of Judicial Review.* Princeton: Princeton University Press, 1914.

———. *The Twilight of the Supreme Court.* New Haven: Yale University Press, 1934.

Cushman, Robert Eugene. *Leading Constitutional Decisions.* New York: Appleton-Century-Crofts, 1955.

Davis, Horace. *A Judicial Veto.* Boston Houghton Mifflin, 1914; reprint ed., New York: Da Capo Press, 1971.

Ervin, Sam J. Jr. *Role of the Supreme Court: Policy Maker or Adjudicator.* Washington: American Enterprise Institute for Public Policy Research, 1970.

Forte, David F. *The Supreme Court in American Politics: Judicial Activism vs. Judicial Restraint.* Lexington, Mass.: D.C. Heath, 1972.

Friedman, Leon and Israel, Fred L., eds. *The Justices of the United States Supreme Court, 1789-1969.* 4 vols. New York: R.R. Bowker Co., 1969.

Harris, Richard. *Decision.* New York: E. P. Dutton & Co., Inc., 1971.

Hughes, Charles Evans. *The Supreme Court of the United States.* New York: Columbia University Press, 1928.

Krislov, Samuel. *Supreme Court in the Political Process.* New York: Macmillan, 1965.

Moore, Blaine F. *Supreme Court and Unconstitutional Legislation.* New York: Columbia University Press, 1913; reprint ed., New York: AMS Press, 1968.

Morgan, Donald G. *Congress and the Constitution.* Cambridge: Belknap Press of Harvard University Press, 1966.

Murphy, Walter F. *Congress and the Court.* Chicago: University of Chicago Press, 1962.

Post, C. Gordon. *Supreme Court and Political Questions.* Baltimore: Johns Hopkins University, 1936; reprint ed., New York: Da Capo Press, 1969.

Pritchett, C. Herman. *Congress vs. the Supreme Court, 1957-1960.* Minneapolis: University of Minnesota Press, 1961; reprint ed., New York: Da Capo Press, 1973.

Schlesinger, Arthur M. Jr. *The Politics of Upheaval.* Houghton Mifflin Co., 1960.

Schmidhauser, John R. *The Supreme Court and Congress: Conflict and Interaction 1945-1968.* New York: Free Press, 1972.

Warren, Charles. *Congress, The Constitution and the Supreme Court.* Boston: Little, Brown, 1925.

———. *The Supreme Court in United States History.* 2 vols. Boston: Little, Brown, 1922, 1926.

Articles

Berger, Raoul. "The President, Congress and the Courts." *Yale Law Journal,* May 1974, pp. 1111-55.

Chase, Harold W. "The Warren Court and Congress." *Minnesota Law Review,* March 1960, pp. 595-637.

Edgerton, Henry W. "The Incidence of Judicial Control Over Congress." *Cornell Law Quarterly,* vol. 22, no. 3, 1937, pp. 299-348.

Ervin, Sam J. Jr. "The Gravel and Brewster Cases: An Assault on Congressional Independence." *Virginia Law Review,* February 1973, pp. 175-95.

Frank, John P. "The Historic Role of the Supreme Court." *Kentucky Law Journal,* Fall 1959, pp. 26-47.

Gimlin, Hoyt. "Challenging of Supreme Court." *Editorial Research Reports,* 1968, vol. 2, pp. 741-60.

Hankin, C. A. "The Supreme Court and the New Deal." *Editorial Research Reports,* 1935, vol. 2, pp. 413-28.

Hankin, Gregory. "The New Deal in the Courts." *Editorial Research Reports,* 1934, vol. 2, pp. 347-62.

Hochman, Charles B. "The Supreme Court and the Constitutionality of Retroactive Legislation." *Harvard Law Review,* February 1960, pp. 692-727.

Shaffer, Helen B. "Separation of Powers." *Editorial Research Reports,* 1973, vol. 2, pp. 691-708.

Swindler, William F. "The Supreme Court, the President and Congress." *Comparative Law Quarterly,* October 1970, pp. 671-92.

Putney, Bryant. "The President, the Constitution and the Supreme Court." *Editorial Research Reports,* 1935, vol. 1, pp. 449-70.

Ulmer, S. Sidney. "Judicial Review as Political Behavior: A Temporary Check on Congress." *Administrative Science Quarterly,* March 1960, pp. 426-45.

Vetter, George M. "Who Is Supreme: People, Court or Legislature? Role of the Supreme Court in the History of Judicial Supremacy." *American Bar Association Journal,* October 1959, pp. 1051-55.

Worsnop, Richard L. "Supreme Court: Legal Storm Center." *Editorial Research Reports,* 1966, vol. 2, pp. 701-20.

Government Publications

U.S. Library of Congress, Congressional Research Service. *The Constitution of the United States: Analysis and Interpretation,* 1973.

Lobbying

Of all the pressures on Congress, none has received such widespread publicity and yet is so dimly understood as the role of Washington-based lobbyists and the groups they represent. The popular image of a rotund agent for special interests buying up members' votes is a vast over-simplification. The role of today's lobbyist is far more subtle, his or her techniques more refined.

Lobbyists and lobby groups have played an increasingly active part in the modern legislative process. The corps of Washington lobbyists has grown markedly since the 1930s, in line with the expansion of federal authority into new areas and with the huge increase in federal spending. The federal government has become a tremendous force in the life of the nation, and the number of fields in which changes in federal policy may spell success or failure for special interest groups has been greatly enlarged. Thus commercial and industrial interests, labor unions, ethnic and racial groups, professional organizations, citizen groups and representatives of foreign interests—all from time to time and some continuously—have sought by one method or another to exert pressure on Congress to attain their legislative goals.

The pressure usually has selfish aims—to assert rights or to win a special privilege or financial benefit for the group exerting it. But in other cases the objective may be disinterested—to achieve an ideological goal or to further a group's particular conception of the national interest.

Lobbying: Pros and Cons

It is widely recognized that pressure groups, whether operating through general campaigns designed to sway public opinion or through direct contacts with members of Congress, perform some important and indispensable functions. Such functions include helping to inform both Congress and the public about problems and issues, stimulating public debate, opening a path to Congress for the wronged and needy, and making known to Congress the practical aspects of proposed legislation—whom it would help, whom it would hurt, who is for it and who against it. The spin-off from this process is considerable technical information produced by research on legislative proposals.

Against benefits to the public that result from pressure activities, critics point to certain serious liabilities. The most important is that in pursuing their own objectives, the pressure groups are apt to lead Congress into decisions which benefit the pressure group but which do not necessarily serve other parts of the public. A group's power to influence legislation often is based less on its arguments than on the size of its membership, the amount of financial and manpower resources it can commit to a legislative pressure campaign and the astuteness of its representatives.

Origins of Lobbying

Representatives of special interests haunted the environs of the First Continental Congress, but the word "lobby" was not recorded until 1808 when it appeared in the annals of the 10th Congress. By 1829, the term "lobby-agents" was applied to favor-seekers at the state capitol in Albany, N.Y. By 1832, it had been shortened to "lobbyist" and was in wide use at the U.S. Capitol.[1]

Although the term had not yet been coined, the right to "lobby" was made implicit by the First Amendment to the Constitution, which provided that "Congress shall make no law...abridging the freedom of speech or of the press; or the right of the people peaceably to assemble and to petition the Government for redress of grievances." Among the Founding Fathers, only James Madison expressed concern over the dangers posed by pressure groups. In *The Federalist* (No. 10), Madison warned against the self-serving activities of the "factions." "Among the numerous advantages promised by a well-constructed union," he wrote, "none deserves to be more accurately developed than its tendency to break and control the violence of faction.... By a faction, I understand a number of citizens, whether amounting to a majority or minority of the whole, who are united and actuated by some common impulse of passion, or of interest, adverse to the rights of other citizens, or to the permanent and aggregate interests of the community." A strong federal government, Madison concluded, was the only effective counterbalance to the influence of such "factions."[2]

Regulation of Lobbying

In the 19th and early 20th centuries, abundant evidence accumulated that venal, selfish or misguided methods used by pressure groups could often result in legislation designed to enrich the pressure group at the expense of the public or to impose the group's own standards on the nation.

What Is a Lobbyist?

Five years before he became President of the United States, Sen. John F. Kennedy (D Mass.) described a lobbyist's functions in an article for the Sunday Magazine section of *The New York Times.* Kennedy said:

"...lobbyists are in many cases expert technicians and capable of explaining complex and difficult subjects in a clear, understandable fashion. They engage in personal discussions with members of Congress in which they can explain in detail the reason for positions they advocate.

"Lobbyists prepare briefs, memoranda, legislative analyses, and draft legislation for use by committees and members of Congress; they are necessarily masters of their subject and, in fact, they frequently can provide useful statistics and information not otherwise available....

"Concededly, each is biased; but such a procedure is not unlike the advocacy of lawyers in court which has proven so successful in resolving judicial controversies. Because our congressional representation is based on geographical boundaries, the lobbyists who speak for the various economic, commercial, and other functional interests of this country serve a very useful purpose and have assumed an important role in the legislative process."

Source: John F. Kennedy, "To Keep the Lobbyist Within Bounds," *New York Times Magazine,* Feb. 19, 1956, p. 42.

Following a series of congressional investigations, which began in 1913 with a probe of lobbying activities by the National Association of Manufacturers, proposals were repeatedly made for some kind of congressional regulation of pressure groups and lobbyists in the nation's capital. Bills requiring lobbyists to register and report on their activities were passed by one chamber or the other on several occasions, including 1928, 1935 and 1936, but were not enacted into law.

Laws were passed in 1935 and 1936 which required registration of utilities and shipping representatives who appeared before committees of Congress or specified federal agencies; and in 1938, Congress first enacted the Foreign Agents Registration Act, requiring persons in the United States acting for foreign governments or principals in any capacity to register with the Justice Department. It was not until 1946 that a general lobbyist registration law was put on the statute books.

As it turned out, the 1946 measure was full of loopholes, and it was further emasculated by a narrow Supreme Court interpretation. *(Details, pp. 656, 671, 673)*

The problem in gaining the approval of Congress and the courts for federal legislation regulating lobbying was how to curb dishonest pressure activities without interfering with constitutional rights of free speech and petition. Equally significant was congressional reluctance to delve into activity that might result in a lowered public image of Congress.

Pressure Methods

A Washington lobby group is out to get results. It pursues them wherever results are likely to be found in the governmental process. Many organizations, directed by professionals in the art of government, focus major efforts at key points where decisions are made and policy interpreted into action. They use the methods they deem appropriate for the circumstances within the limits of their resources, group policies and ethical outlook.

If a group loses a round in Congress, it may continue the fight in the agency charged with execution or in the courts. A year or two later, it may resume the struggle in Congress. This process can continue indefinitely.

Groups' goals are as numerous and varied as the organizations themselves. Many are primarily bent on protecting or promoting their specialized interests. Some assert public benefit purposes.

One group might work, for example, for the reduction of a tax burden, the passage of a subsidy program or the defense of existing advantages against proposals to eliminate them. A competing organization might actively work against some or all of the other group's main purposes. Even so, they might find themselves on the same side upon occasion.

On a long-range basis, both groups naturally might strive through the years to build up what they consider a sympathetic or at least neutral attitude in places of power where their particular interests are affected.

These and other factors can induce some organizations not only to attempt to influence the views of members of Congress on specific issues, but also to participate in the political activities which select the occupants of positions in which they are interested.

Background. Bribery of members of Congress was a well-documented occurrence in the 19th and early 20th centuries.

When Congress in the 1830s became embroiled in President Andrew Jackson's battle with the Bank of the United States, it was disclosed that Daniel Webster, then a senator from Massachusetts, enjoyed a retainer from the bank. On Dec. 21, 1833, Webster complained to bank president Nicholas Biddle: "My retainer has not been renewed or refreshed as usual. If it is wished that my relation to the Bank should be continued, it may be well to send me the usual retainers." Historian Arthur M. Schlesinger Jr. observed in *The Age of Jackson* that Henry Clay supported the bank "because it fitted in with his superb vision of America, but Webster was fighting for it in great part because it was a dependable source of private income."[3]

In the biggest scandal of the Grant administration, it was rumored that 12 members of Congress had received stock in the Crédit Mobilier, a joint stock company, in return for large congressional grants for construction of the transcontinental Union Pacific Railroad, which controlled the Crédit Mobilier. Following an investigation, two of the alleged participants were censured by the House.

Col. Martin M. Mulhall, a lobbyist for the National Association of Manufacturers, stated publicly in 1913 that he had bribed members of Congress for legislative favors, had paid the chief House page $50 a month for inside information from the cloakrooms, and had influenced House leaders to place members friendly to the NAM on House committees and subcommittees. In a subsequent congressional probe, six members were exonerated but one was censured and resigned.

After World War II, direct vote-buying by lobbyists was replaced by sophisticated techniques. Indirect, grass-roots pressures and political support became the predominant methods.

Campaign Support

While corporations have been barred since 1907, and labor unions since 1943, from making direct contributions to campaigns for federal office, it is widely acknowledged that contributors have found numerous ways to get around the restrictions. Although unions are prohibited from using dues money to assist political candidates in federal elections, it is legal for them to set up separate political arms, such as the AFL-CIO's Committee on Political Education (COPE), which collect voluntary contributions from union members and their families and use the funds for political expenditures calculated to benefit senators and representatives friendly to labor. It is also legal for unions to endorse political candidates.

Similarly, while corporations are prohibited from making direct campaign contributions, they can set up corporate political action committees to seek contributions from stockholders and executive and administrative personnel and their families. (Twice a year both union and corporate political action committees may seek anonymous contributions by mail from all employees, not just those they are initially restricted to.)

The same general resources for political support and opposition are available to members of citizens' groups and, indeed, to a wide range of organizations seeking to exert political pressure on members of Congress.

In approaching the typical member, a pressure group has no need to tell the member outright that future political support or opposition, and perhaps future political expenditures and the voluntary campaign efforts of its members, depend on how the member votes on a particular bill or whether, over a long period, the member acts favorably toward the group. The member understands this without being told. The member understands that, in the nature of the political process, positions taken on legislation help to determine which groups will provide support. The member understands that when the vital interests of some group are at stake in legislation, a vote for it would normally win the group's friendship and future support, and a vote against it would mean the group's enmity and future opposition.

Journalist James Deakin pointed out in *The Lobbyists* that when lobbyists themselves are asked to assess the main value of campaign contributions, "they frequently reply with one word: access." The campaign donation helps them to gain access to the legislator to present their case. "The reasoning is that the other fellow is contributing to the campaign of Congressman Doe and therefore is likely to get a cordial reception when he visits Doe's office, so we had better do the same. This, according to many lobbyists, is all that is gained from a campaign donation—a chance to present facts, figures and arguments to the lawmaker in the privacy of his office."[4]

In 1971, 1974 and 1976 Congress enacted legislation dealing with campaign financing, which included detailed provisions on political contributions by pressure groups. *(Details, Campaign Financing, p. 540)*

Grass-Roots Pressures

Except on obscure or highly specialized legislation, most lobby campaigns now are accompanied by massive propaganda or "educational" drives in which pressure groups seek to mobilize public opinion to support their aims. In most cases, citizens are urged to respond by contacting members of Congress in support of or opposition to a particular bill.

One of the most notable successes for this technique came in 1962, when the U.S. Savings and Loan League sought to defeat President Kennedy's proposal for withholding the taxes due on interest earned on savings deposits. Because the speedup in collections would have cut back the funds on deposit at the savings and loan institutions, it would have reduced the amount of S & L money available for housing loans.

After the plan had been approved by the House, the league launched a massive effort to generate pressures that would kill the proposal in the Senate. Some of the league's advertisements depicted the plan as a new tax on savings, not a mere speedup in the collection of existing levies on interest from the savings. "The result," James Deakin has said, "was an avalanche, a flood, a torrent of letters to members of the Senate. So many stacks of letters piled up that Senate staffs had to drop everything else to cope with the deluge. The Senate post office said there had been nothing to compare with it since Truman fired General MacArthur, or possibly the Army-McCarthy hearings."[5] The plan was summarily dropped by the Senate Finance Committee.

Another grass-roots effort acknowledged as highly successful came in the mid-1960s, when the National Rifle Association instigated an outpouring of mail against administration proposals for tighter gun controls. Even after the assassinations of President Kennedy, the Rev. Martin Luther King Jr. and Sen. Robert F. Kennedy (D N.Y.), the gun lobby was able to bottle up proposals for tough controls, and all that was passed was watered-down legislation not vigorously opposed by the NRA.

Anti-Saloon League Drive. Sometimes lobbying efforts originate at the grass roots and then attract national attention. A classic campaign of this type was the drive by the Anti-Saloon League and associated organizations to bar the sale of alcoholic beverages. After 15 years devoted to building up local support, particularly among Protestant denominations, the league met in Washington in 1911 to map strategy for its assault on Congress. To sway public opinion, the league launched an advertising campaign that blamed all the evils of society on the saloon.

Although the league's initial effort was not immediately productive, Congress deferred to this increasingly powerful lobby two years later by passing the Webb-Kenyon Act, which outlawed transportation of alcoholic beverages into states where their sale was illegal. Spurred by that victory, the league went on to push through nationwide prohibition.

Following substantial gains by "dry" candidates in the congressional election of 1916, Congress the next year submitted the Eighteenth Amendment, prohibiting the sale or consumption of alcoholic beverages, to the states for ratification. Ratification was completed early in 1919, and the amendment went into effect in January 1920 (it was repealed in 1933).

Disadvantages. Despite the frequent success of grassroots lobbying, such an approach has several inherent limitations which make its use questionable unless it is carefully and cleverly managed. If a member's mail on an issue appears artificially generated, the member may feel that the response is not representative of the member's constituency. Such pressure mail is easily recognized because the letters all arrive at about the same time, are mimeographed or printed, or are identically or similarly worded. Political scientist David B. Truman has observed that "Filling up the legislator's mailbag is essentially a crude device, a shotgun technique which may only wound

(Continued on p. 657)

Lobbying Act Federal Court Cases Since 1946

The Justice Department in mid-1976 told Congressional Quarterly it knew of only five federal court cases involving the Federal Regulation of Lobbying Act of 1946. Only four of the cases were prosecuted. Following are summaries of the cases:

NAM Test Suit. The National Association of Manufacturers on Jan. 28, 1948, brought a test suit challenging the validity of the lobbying law. On March 17, 1952, a federal court in Washington, D.C., ruled that the law was unconstitutional. It held that definitions in the law were too "indefinite and vague to constitute an ascertainable standard of guilt." Eight months later, on Oct. 13, 1952, the U.S. Supreme Court on a technicality reversed the lower court, leaving the 1946 law in full force but open to further challenge. *(J. Howard McGrath v. National Association of Manufacturers of the U.S.,* 344 U.S. 804).

Harriss Case. The government on June 16, 1948, obtained indictments of several individuals and an organization for alleged violations of the registration or reporting sections of the 1946 lobbying law. It was charged that, without registering or reporting, New York cotton broker Robert M. Harriss had made payments to Ralph W. Moore, a Washington commodity trader and secretary of the National Farm Committee, for the purpose of pressuring Congress on legislation, and that Moore had made similar payments to James E. McDonald, the agricultural commissioner of Texas, and Tom Linder, the agricultural commissioner of Georgia. A lower court ruling, Jan. 30, 1953, by Judge Alexander Holtzoff held the lobbying law unconstitutional on grounds that it was too vague and indefinite to meet the requirements of due process, that the registration and reporting requirements violated the First Amendment (freedom of speech, assembly, etc.) and that certain of the penalty provisions violated the constitutional right to petition Congress. Holtzoff's ruling was appealed by the government to the Supreme Court. On June 7, 1954, in a 5-3 decision, the Supreme Court reversed Holtzoff and upheld the constitutionality of the 1946 lobbying law, though construing it narrowly *(United States v. Harriss,* 347 U.S. 612). *(Text of decision, p. 244-A)*

In upholding the validity of the lobbying law, the Supreme Court sent the cases of the individual defendants back to the lower court to decide whether the individuals involved were guilty. None of the defendants was found guilty. The case against Harriss was dismissed on the ground that the lobbying law, as construed by the Supreme Court, applied only to those who solicited or received money for the purpose of lobbying, whereas Harriss was charged merely with paying money to Moore. The case against Linder was dismissed because he was exempt from the lobbying law under a specific provision exempting public officials. The charge against McDonald were dropped because of his death earlier in the case. The lower court dismissed the charges against Moore and acquitted the National Farm Committee, Nov. 2, 1955.

The importance of the *Harriss* case lay not in the decisions on the individual defendants but in the ruling that the 1946 lobbying law was constitutional.

Savings & Loan League. A federal grand jury in Washington, D.C., March 30, 1948, indicted the U.S. Savings and Loan League for failure to comply with the 1946 lobbying law. The case was dismissed April 19, 1949, by a federal district court. *(United States v. U.S. Savings and Loan League)*

Slaughter Case. On Nov. 23, 1948, ex-Rep. Roger C. Slaughter (D Mo.), a bitter political foe of President Truman, was indicted on charges he had lobbied for the North American Grain Association without registering under the lobbying act. Slaughter's defense was that he had merely acted as an attorney and had helped prepare testimony for witnesses. On April 17, 1950 Slaughter was acquitted, with the judge holding that the specific provision of the lobbying act which exempted persons who merely testified before a congressional committee applied, also, to those who helped such persons prepare testimony. *(United States v. Slaughter,* 89 F. Supp. 205).

Natural Gas Case. On Feb. 3, 1956, Sen. Francis Case (R S.D.) announced on the floor of the Senate that he would vote against the natural gas bill because an out-of-state lawyer who was interested in passage of the bill, and who had learned that Case was favorably inclined to the measure, had left a $2,500 campaign contribution for the senator. (Case had refused the contribution.) As a result of this incident, President Eisenhower on Feb. 17 vetoed the natural gas bill on the ground that agents of a natural gas producer had made an "arrogant" effort to influence legislation with a campaign contribution. John M. Neff of Lexington, Neb., the man who had offered the contribution to Sen. Case, was indicted, July 24, on charges of violating the Federal Regulation of Lobbying Act. Also indicted were Elmer Patman of Austin, Texas, and the Superior Oil Co. of California. Both Neff and Patman were attorneys for Superior Oil. In a Senate investigation and at court proceedings, Neff and Patman said the $2,500 offered to Case came from the personal funds of Superior Oil President Howard B. Keck. The money was given by Keck to Patman, who in turn gave it to Neff. Neff than offered it to Case. The accused denied any attempt at bribery and said the purpose of the offer was to aid senators they believed to be of the economic school of thought that would favor the natural gas bill, which would exempt producers from certain federal regulation.

On Dec. 14, 1956, both Neff and Patman pleaded guilty of violating the lobbying act by failing to register although engaged in lobbying the natural gas bill. They were fined $2,500 each and given one-year suspended sentences by Judge Joseph C. McGarraghy in Washington, D.C. Superior Oil was fined $5,000 on each of two counts of aiding and abetting Neff and Patman to violate the lobbying law. Bribery charges arising from the case were dropped. The convictions of Neff, Patman and Superior Oil were the first (and through the mid-1970s the only) convictions ever obtained under the 1946 lobbying law. There was never any suggestion that Sen. Case had sought the campaign contribution or had accepted it or had in any way acted improperly.

(Continued from p. 655)

where a rifle would kill." While Truman concedes that there may be times when a member will add up the pros and cons and vote with the majority, he cautions that "one fact is clear" in such instances: "The usual channels of access to him are empty or silent."[6]

Occasionally, this method may boomerang and leave the lobbyist worse off than when he started. A noteworthy example was the utility fight of 1935, when lobbyists for private utilities sought unsuccessfully to defeat President Roosevelt's proposed curbs on utility holding companies. A congressional investigation brought out the fact that thousands of phony telegrams to Congress had been financed by utility interests. A resulting wave of adverse publicity helped assure passage of Roosevelt's proposals.

Direct Lobbying

Much lobbying still is conducted on a face-to-face basis. In a study of pressures on the Senate, Donald R. Matthews, a political scientist, observed that the vast majority of such lobbying was directed at members "who are already convinced." He added: "The services a lobby can provide a friendly senator are substantial. Few senators could survive without them. First, they can perform much of the research and speech-writing chores of the senator's office. This service is especially attractive to the more publicity-oriented senators. Members of the party that does not control the White House also find this service especially valuable, since they cannot draw upon the research services of the departments as much as can the other members. But most senators find this service at first a convenience and soon a necessity."[7]

Once established, Matthews has said, "Senator-lobbyist friendships also tend to reinforce the senator's commitment to a particular group and line of policy.... Relatively few senators are actually changed by lobbyists from a hostile or neutral position to a friendly one. Perhaps a few on every major issue are converted and this handful of votes may carry the day. But quantitatively, the conversion effect is relatively small."[8]

Ensuring continued access to members of Congress requires considerable tact on the part of the lobbyist. Lobbyists must be particularly wary of overstaying their welcome and appearing overly aggressive. Rep. Emanuel Celler (D N.Y.) wrote: "The man who keeps his appointment, presents his problem or proposal and lets the congressman get on with his other work comes to be liked and respected. His message has an excellent chance of being effective. The man who feels that it somehow adds to his usefulness and prestige to be seen constantly in the company of one legislator or another, or who seeks to ingratiate himself with congressional staffs, gets under foot and becomes a nuisance. He does his principal and cause no good."[9]

Above all, the lobbyist must be certain that the information he gives the member is accurate and complete. Former White House aide Douglass Cater has said: "The smart lobbyist...knows he can be most effective by being helpful, by being timely, and, not least, by being accurate. According to the testimony of lobbyists themselves, the cardinal sin is to supply faulty information which puts a trusting policy-maker in an exposed position."[10]

Most contemporary lobbyists carefully avoid approaches that the member may interpret as threatening or as constituting excessive pressure. An adverse reaction by a member may lead to unfavorable publicity or even a damaging congressional investigation. Matthews has described the lobbyist as a "sitting duck—their public reputation is so low that public attack is bound to be damaging.... To invite public attack, or even worse a congressional investigation, is, from the lobbyist's point of view, clearly undesirable." Matthews adds: "It is the threat of and use of these countermeasures which help explain why so little lobbying is aimed at conversion. A lobbyist minimizes the risk of his job, the cause which he serves, and his ego by staying away from those senators clearly against him and his program. For, of all types of lobbying, attempts at conversion are most likely to boomerang."[11]

Information-Gathering Function. Some lobbyists may be of more use to their employers as a conduit of information than as a source of direct pressure on Congress. Merriman Smith, longtime White House correspondent for United Press International, wrote in 1962: "[The typical lobbyist] arises when he feels like it, usually midmorning, in a spacious, comfortable, but definitely unflashy home in the Northwest residential section of town. Over breakfast, he reads four or five major morning newspapers. If interested, he skims through the *Congressional Record* for the day before.... These are the golden hours of his day. He may earn his keep more from intelligent reading than from any other single activity. Years of experience have taught him to read between the lines and to search for indicative but seemingly small details....

"Once 'read' for the day, he may make it to town for luncheon with one or two key men in government at the Carlton or the Mayflower. Mostly, they talk about golf or fishing. Possibly in parting, he may ask casually, 'You fellows heard anything new on depreciation allowances?'... This man is more effective for his employer than a dozen more energetic fellows patrolling the halls of the Senate and House office buildings.... By being highly selective in his friendships, he manages to keep in touch with virtually any government move that might help or hinder his company.... Our man's effectiveness would be destroyed if he had to play the lobbyist's conventional role in attempting to push or halt specific bills before Congress."[12]

Strategic Contacts. In fights over a specific bill, most direct approaches by lobbyists are likely to center on a few strategic members instead of a large part of the membership of the House or Senate. In most lobby battles, approval of a measure by a congressional committee is tantamount to final passage. Except on highly controversial issues, committee decisions are almost always upheld by the full chamber. Lobby pressures may focus not only on key members of a committee but also on the committee's professional staff. Particularly on legislation involving highly technical matters, such staffs are extremely influential. Political scientist Lester W. Milbrath has noted that "failure to locate such key persons (members and staff) may result in the sending of many superfluous messages, and if the key persons cannot be persuaded, there is a high likelihood that the decision will go adversely."[13] Any inroads the lobbyist may have made outside the circle of strategic members are likely to be negated if these key members start pushing the other way.

Testimony at Hearings

Another useful technique for lobbyists is testimony at congressional hearings. The hearing provides the lobbyist with a propaganda forum that has few parallels in Washington. It also provides access to key members whom the lobbyist may not have been able to contact in any other

Famous Lobbyists Reflect . . .

Most Washington lobbyists are known only to their clients and contacts; the public never hears about them. A few over the years have run counter to the pattern. They either have achieved fame as lobbyists, or have carried into a lobbying career fame earned elsewhere. Below are brief profiles of selected lobbyists who have achieved some measure of fame. Their working styles tend to reflect the changing styles of lobbying.

Samuel Ward. Most colorful of all the early Washington lobbyists was Samuel Ward, brother of Julia Ward Howe, author of "The Battle Hymn of the Republic." Ward, known widely as "King of the Lobby," reigned in Washington for 15 years in the period following the Civil War. His clients included the railroads and other financial interests concerned with federal legislation.

In his study of the House of Representatives, journalist Neil MacNeil described Ward as "a short, stout man with the imperial white beard of a French count...a man of refined education, who sported diamond studs in his shirts and never appeared without a rose in his coat lapel.... He entertained nightly the political leaders of Washington at a table groaning with choice viands and fine wines. Himself a wit and gentleman of culture, Ward lavished on his guests a plentiful bounty with never so much as an indelicate suggestion of his ulterior motives; he never asked a man for a favor at his table. That came later." Ward is reported to have bragged repeatedly that "The way to a man's 'Aye' is through his stomach."

The size of Ward's fees was not a matter of record. On one occasion, however, he wrote his friend Henry Wadsworth Longfellow: "When I see you again, I will tell you how a client, eager to prevent the arrival at a committee of a certain member before it should adjourn, offered me $5,000 to accomplish his purpose, which I did by having his (the congressman's) boots mislaid while I smoked a cigar and condoled with him until they would be found at 11:45. I had the satisfaction of a good laugh, a good fee in my pocket, and of having prevented a conspiracy." By "conspiracy," Ward is reported to have meant legislation in which he saw no merit.

On other occasions, Ward reportedly received $50,-000 for influencing tariff legislation and $1-million for his work on a mail subsidy case. When a congressional committee asked him what he had done to earn his fee in the mail case, Ward denied that he had bribed anyone to influence the legislation. He supposed he had been retained, he said, because "I am called King of the Lobby, but I am not Treasurer of the Lobby, that is certain."

Edward Pendleton. A lobbyist of the immediate pre-Civil War era who achieved a reputation almost equal to Ward's was Edward Pendleton, who operated a popular gambling house on Pennsylvania Avenue. Pendleton's establishment, known as the "Palace of Fortune" and "Hall of the Bleeding Heart," was elaborately furnished and equipped with a wine cellar in which

Pendleton was said to have invested $10,000. Perley Poore, a contemporary of Pendleton's, wrote: "The people who nightly assemble to see and to take part in the entertainments of the house consisted of candidates for the presidency, senators and representatives, members of the Cabinet, editors and journalists and the master workmen of the third house, the lobby. Pendleton's in its palmiest days might have been called the vestibule of the lobby."

It was reported that the transfer of bribes to members of Congress in the form of winnings at cards was another of the methods followed at Pendleton's. But lending money to members who went broke at his tables was Pendleton's main stock in trade. Neil MacNeil has observed that "This was the source of his power as a lobbyist, and he proved successful many times in having bills passed for his clients." Perley Poore said of Pendleton that "A broker in parliamentary notes is an inevitable retainer of broker votes."

Thomas G. Corcoran. Among contemporary lobbyists, one of the best-known and most influential has been Thomas G. Corcoran, a powerful White House adviser in New Deal days who later became a highly paid lobbyist for Washington business interests.

During five years in the White House, Corcoran (dubbed "Tommy the Cork" by President Roosevelt) assisted in writing much of the major New Deal legislation, including the Securities and Exchange Act, the Public Utility Holding Company Act and the Fair Labor Standards Act. Corcoran also helped on Roosevelt's abortive plan to "pack" the Supreme Court with additional justices. He thus became one of the most controversial of the White House staff members, and when he sought the post of solicitor general in 1940, President Roosevelt declined to nominate him for fear the Senate would deny confirmation. Corcoran resigned his White House job and, almost overnight, reappeared as representative of the same business interests he had opposed as a New Deal crusader. Within a few months, he testified before a congressional committee that he had received $100,000 in legal fees and was turning away clients "by the hundreds."

Louis W. Koenig has described Corcoran as "an adventurer who...sought to introduce banana-growing on the island fortress of Taiwan and to establish across the length and breadth of Brazil a chain of restaurants under the auspices of the Union News Company." He added: "In reality, he belongs not to the twentieth century, but to another age. He is a medieval character who operated in the era of the New Deal with the fervor, bravado and finesse of a top-notch grand duke of an Italian principality.... 'The way to get ahead,' he would say, 'is to fish in troubled waters.' "

Journalist James Deakin has observed that when a 1960 House subcommittee investigating lobbyist contacts with members of the Federal Power Commission

way. On important legislation, lobbyists normally rehearse their statements before the hearing, seek to ensure a large turnout from their constituency on the hearing day, and may even hand friendly committee members leading questions for the group's witness to answer.

The degree of propaganda success for the hearing, however, is likely to depend on how well the committee's controlling factions are disposed to the group's position. In his book, *House Out of Order*, Rep. Richard Bolling (D Mo.) says that within congressional committees "proponents and

. . . Changing Styles of Lobbying

began probing the alleged activities of Corcoran, the panel "got out of its league." Deakin went on to say: "This was no plodding political hack caught cozying up to the industry, but a wily old pro who had forgotten more about the regulatory agencies and regulatory law than the subcommittee members ever knew.... Corcoran ran rings around the subcommittee in some of the stormiest and funniest hearings ever held on Capitol Hill."

Clark M. Clifford. Another highly paid representative for powerful business interests has been Clark M. Clifford, prominent Washington attorney and a former White House aide in the Truman administration, adviser to Presidents Kennedy and Johnson, and Secretary of Defense (1968-69) for the last 11 months of the Johnson administration. Clifford has long been a senior partner in the Washington law firm of Clifford, Warnke, Glass, McIlwain and Finney (formerly Clifford and Miller), which has held retainers from some of the nation's largest corporations, including Du Pont, General Electric, Standard Oil of California, Phillips Petroleum Co., Hughes Tool Co. and a number of mutual funds.

Clifford's firm declined for many years to register as a lobby group, contending that it did no actual lobbying. (Finally, in 1969, it did register for Hughes Tool, the Avco Corp. and several smaller clients.) Soon after setting up the firm, Clifford told reporters: "I have not and will not register as a lobbyist, for that is not the kind of work we do. We run a law office here, with a background of experience in the general practice of law, topped off by an intimate knowledge of how the government operates." Associates of Clifford's firm often said their role in the legislative process was to advise clients on positions to take on legislation and to suggest the tactics that they use in lobbying campaigns. The firm followed the legislation closely for the client, but if the situation called for active lobbying, it recommended someone else for that job.

It was widely rumored that Clifford's firm received a fee of $1-million from the DuPont Co. for its assistance in a stock divestiture case. The firm claimed that the size of the fee was exaggerated and said it had received only its regular retainer as DuPont's Washington counsel. The bulk of the fee, it said, went to the Washington law firm of Cleary, Gottlieb and Steen, which Clifford's firm recommended for the lobbying job.

Andrew J. Biemiller. The most prominent labor lobbyist in Washington has been Andrew J. Biemiller, a former U.S. representative from Wisconsin, who registered as a lobbyist for the AFL in 1953, became chief lobbyist for the AFL-CIO when the organizations merged in 1955, and was still in that position in 1976. James Deakin has called Biemiller "one of the best-known men on Capitol Hill" and points out that he has "one of the toughest jobs in Washington (because) he is caught in the occasional crossfire between the AFL and CIO and beset by the prickly personalities of some of labor's top

brass." Deakin quotes Biemiller as saying: "The only labor lobbyists over which I have control are those directly employed by the AFL-CIO. There are some 95 other labor lobbyists in Washington. With these, all I can use is suasion."

Despite Biemiller's widely acclaimed skills in mobilizing a united labor front, Congress during his tenure as labor's top lobbyist has passed relatively few of the major bills of direct interest to labor. However, Biemiller's overall effectiveness is not questioned. Many of the flood of labor-supported civil rights and welfare bills that have won approval during that period were at the top of the AFL-CIO's priorities list, right after the bills of exclusive interest to labor.

Charls E. Walker. Charls E. Walker, a 20-year veteran of Washington politics and banking interests, was deputy secretary of the Treasury during the first Nixon presidential term. In that post, Walker managed a wide range of legislative activities for the administration—tax measures, economic stabilization legislation, general revenue sharing. He also played a major role in Phase I, II and III wage and price control planning.

In leaving the Nixon administration early in 1973 to set up his own economic consulting firm (Charls E. Walker Associates Inc.), Walker followed the custom of other high-ranking officials who have put their government experience to work in private business.

Like them, he left with an intimate knowledge of government affairs and a reservoir of political connections throughout Washington and the world of finance. (Before serving as President Nixon's No. 2 man at the Treasury, Walker was executive vice president of the American Bankers Association (1961-69); during the second Eisenhower administration, he was special assistant to Treasury Secretary Robert B. Anderson.)

His experience—when something is needed "I know where to get it and who to call"—proved irresistible to many corporations. Walker himself recalled in a 1973 interview that when he told President Nixon of his plans at Camp David, Nixon observed: "You're going to be doing what you have been, but now making money at it."

Only six months after the Walker firm was incorporated, three of the four corporations (General Motors, Ford and General Electric) that headed *Fortune* magazine's ranking of the 500 largest manufacturers in the nation had hired Walker as a lobbyist. In all, 14 major corporations were Walker clients—12 of them ranked in the top 90 on *Fortune's* list in 1973. Besides the two auto giants and General Electric, Walker represented Gulf Oil, Procter and Gamble, Bethlehem Steel, Allied Chemical and Time Inc.

Sources: Neil MacNeil, *Forge of Democracy* (David McKay Co., 1963); James Deakin, *The Lobbyists* (Public Affairs Press, 1966); Louis W. Koenig, *The Invisible Presidency* (Rinehart and Co. Inc., 1960); *Congressional Quarterly*, Weekly Report, *Aug. 18, 1973, p. 2269.*

opponents of legislation jockey for position—each complementing the activities of their alter egos in lobbies outside." He points out: "Adverse witnesses can be kept to a minimum, for example, or they can be sandwiched among friendly witnesses in scheduled appearances so that their

testimony does not receive as much attention from the press as it deserves. Scant attention will be given, for example, to a knowledgeable opponent of the federal fallout shelter program if he is scheduled to testify on such legislation on the same day as are Dr. Edward Teller, an Assistant

Secretary of Defense and a three-star general. The opponent is neatly boxed in"[14]

Lobby Coalitions

Most major legislation is backed by alliances of interest groups on one side and opposed by alliances on the other. Such lobby coalitions, while having the advantage of bigger memberships and more financial resources for lobbying, are difficult to control because of the differences of viewpoint that are likely within the coalition. Despite these inner tensions, however, lobby coalitions have been instrumental in obtaining passage of much major legislation, such as Medicare, civil rights bills and housing legislation. Notable coalition efforts that failed have included a 1967 push for import restrictions, which ran into trouble when too many industries sought protective quotas, and a 1970 drive for cuts in military spending, which lost impact when liberal and conservative critics of Pentagon spending levels fell to quarreling over use of the prospective savings. Liberals sought to earmark the cuts for domestic programs, while the conservatives favored tax reductions.

In a broad sense, lobby coalitions have broken down into liberal and conservative camps, the former usually led by the labor unions and civil rights groups and the latter by business associations such as the Chamber of Commerce of the United States and the National Association of Manufacturers. Disparities within these groups usually lead to shifting of alliances among individual organizations as issues change and to formation of ad hoc coalitions to exert pressure on a particular issue.

Although there is considerable log-rolling, with organizations getting assistance on one issue by promising future support on another, the activity of many groups is limited mainly to matters of immediate concern to them. Thus, the American Medical Association, one of the most powerful pressure groups in the capital, is extremely active on questions of medical practice and health but normally shows little interest in such questions as agricultural policy, foreign trade or economic policy in general.

Defensive Lobby Alignments. While massive promotional campaigns by lobbyists have attracted wide public attention, a large share of lobby activity is defensive or preventive. Political scientist Lewis Dexter has observed that this is only natural because "it is much easier to get successful people—the kind who finance and initiate most lobbies—excited about having a favorable situation disturbed than to stir them up—at least in American society—about a contingent benefit."[15]

The bicameral structure of the legislative branch and the constitutional separation of powers also gives a considerable natural advantage to defensive lobbying efforts. David B. Truman has written that these structures "operate, as they were designed, to delay or obstruct action rather than to facilitate it." He adds: "Requirement of extensive majorities for particular kinds of measures and the absence of limits on the duration of debate have a like effect as do numerous technical details of the parliamentary rules. Finally, the diffuseness of leadership, and the power and independence of committees and their chairmen, not only provide a multiplicity of points of access...but also furnish abundant activities for obstruction and delay, opportunities that buttress the position of defensive groups."[16]

Sources of Pressure

Traditionally, pressure groups in the United States were comprised of similar economic or social interests.

Classic examples of such traditional groups were farmers, businessmen, workers, veterans. Their interests were few, and usually drew the united support of a large majority of members.

As the federal government broadened its activities, a new type of pressure group developed—the coalition of diverse economic and social interests brought together by concern for a certain issue. A coalition of this type could include, for example, both business and labor interests. An historic example of the broad coalition was the protectionist bloc, which was effective in raising protective U.S. tariffs. A more modern example is the education lobby. *(Details p. 664)*

Foreign nations increasingly are concerned with American policies. Their representatives comprise a special group of lobbyists.

Finally, there is a collection of groups with no single special interest to promote or protect. These self-styled citizens' or public interest lobbies are concerned with a vast array of issues, and usually have large numbers of individual members.

Selected examples are described briefly in the following section.

Veterans

In the period from World War I to World War II, the veterans' bloc, led by the American Legion, the Disabled American Veterans and the Veterans of Foreign Wars, exercised considerable influence over legislation within its purview. In legislation enacted in 1930, veterans' groups won extension of World War I veterans' disability compensation to veterans who had become disabled since the war, whether or not the disability was service-connected. In 1924, pressure from veterans' groups pushed Congress into overriding President Coolidge's veto of a bill calling for eventual payment of a World War I veterans' bonus. Similar pressure in 1934 caused Congress to override President Roosevelt's veto of a bill restoring certain veterans' benefits which had been curtailed for economy reasons a year earlier. And in 1936, veterans' groups again persuaded Congress to override Roosevelt and pass a bill requiring immediate payment of the World War I bonus.

After World War II, veterans' groups (still dominated by the American Legion, Disabled American Veterans and Veterans of Foreign Wars) did not exhibit the same legislative potency. One reason was that they did not have to. An extremely generous program of veterans' benefits enacted by Congress for World War II and Korean War veterans undermined present and future claims that veterans had been mistreated or forgotten, which had been a major argument after earlier wars.

Veterans' groups remained active on Capitol Hill, nevertheless. One example of their success was the continued growth and expansion of the Veterans Administration, the largest non-Cabinet agency in the federal government. Veterans groups lobbied actively each year for VA appropriations. Amid fluctuating congressional interest in national health insurance, veterans' groups worked carefully to retain their preferred free health care at VA hospitals and to assure VA hospitals of a continuing role under a national health insurance program.

Farmers

The farm lobby underwent a substantial change in character as the number of farmers declined, as family farms disappeared and as farming became big business. In

(Continued on p. 662)

Alliance Building: Major Strategy of Pressure Groups

Masses of unorganized individuals ordinarily exert little direct influence on the major activities of the federal government. As they organize in groups geared to specialized interests and goals, they build power bases from which their leaders and spokesmen can promote those interests.

Hence the formation of trade associations, labor and professional political action committees, self-styled citizens' groups and other organizations of many kinds that exert lobbying pressure.

As the nation has grown, and with it the crush of competing interests, individual interest groups even as large as the American Farm Bureau Federation, AFL-CIO or the Chamber of Commerce of the United States have found they sometimes lack sufficient impact to achieve their legislative purposes unassisted.

A major trend in the mid-20th century has been the pyramiding of pressure group on pressure group into combinations aimed at accumulating enough collective strength to compel power holders to heed them.

'Far From New'

While this movement toward coalitions has accelerated since World War II, it is far from new. For example, secretary-treasurer Roger Fleming of the American Farm Bureau Federation in 1971 noted the emergence of an opposition farm coalition and said: "But the greatest farm coalition ever assembled was when the American Farm Bureau Federation was founded in 1919." He explained its basis as follows:

"Farm Bureau offered a means whereby producers of every commodity in every area of the country could get together, regardless of their political affiliations, to reconcile their differences, and thereby develop honest-to-goodness farm unity." As for intergroup alliances on the legislative front, Fleming said: "We, in fact, have allies on practically every issue in which we are involved."

Education is another of the many fields in which interest groups have formed alliances to pressure national policy. John Lumley, former director of the National Education Association's office of legislation, told *Congressional Quarterly* in 1970 while discussing proposals to merge the NEA and the AFL-CIO's American Federation of Teachers: "Legislatively, we've worked together through the years with the AFL-CIO."

By 1950 the House Select Committee on Lobbying Activities said in a report: "The lone-wolf pressure group, wanting nothing more from other groups than to be left unmolested, is largely a thing of the past."

Prof. Stephen K. Bailey went so far as to tell the House committee his conclusion was "that lobbying can be understood only as the reflection of interests shared by shifting coalitions made up by members of Congress, outside pressures, and executive agencies." He added: "If this is a correct assumption, then it seems to me that your problem is the enormously complicated one of analyzing the interrelationships among private group interests, members of Congress and agency personnel."

In the pursuit of power, the ways of coalition are many. Their workings are sometimes open, easily traced and readily acknowledged by all. At other times, the cooperation is concealed, perhaps detectable mainly through after-the-fact disclosure that participants with seemingly variant interests arrive at the same legislative or executive result by divergent routes or that the same individuals show up in different places wearing different hats.

'More Apparent Than Real'

Some coalitions may be more apparent than real. Rather than indicating strength, they can at times suggest weakness among the separate entities and a lack of unity within the organizations. A frequent practice is the selection of certain top officers of various organizations to head a cluster of groups under a separate name.

Such a coalition may in fact be composed of a comparative handful of individuals and may operate under its own internal governing structure and bylaws which may or may not conform with those of the cooperating groups. Their responsible posts put coalition leaders in a position to draw upon the financial and educational resources, prestige and pressure mechanisms of individual groups to exert pressure on public officials.

In the case of organizations with millions of members, real internal unity would suggest the strong possibility of remedies at the polls and less necessity for combined pressure activities. This aspect sometimes prompts opponents in Congress to refer to coalitions of leaders as "generals without troops." This naturally draws stout rebuttals, and there are strong incentives for alliances from group leaders' viewpoint.

Two fairly lasting coalitions which have operated from time to time since the 1930s have been a coalition of northern liberals, civil rights and labor organizations opposed on some issues by a coalition of Republicans and southern conservatives. This has been demonstrated in pressure groups as in Congress. The clash between the two forces came into evidence in the battles over Senate confirmation of Supreme Court nominees Clement F. Haynsworth Jr. (1969) and G. Harrold Carswell (1970), both rejected.

'Mutual Interest'

Bayard Rustin, an anti-war activist since World War II and a leading strategist of the civil rights and anti-poverty movements, told the AFL-CIO convention that alliances of the kind formed during the 1969 battle over the nomination of Clement F. Haynsworth to the Supreme Court "are not made in the way in which one marries his wife. Alliances are not made out of affection. Alliances are made out of mutual interest, and although there will be difficult times for us, we must remember that this mutual interest does in fact exist and we must hold on to it.... Let us build upon that which unites us."

effect, what had been a "people's lobby" slowly became an interest group, subject to much the same public suspicion and criticism as other special interests.

Three major organizations claimed to represent the majority of American farmers—the American Farm Bureau Federation, the National Grange and the National Farmers Union. Occasionally the groups were able to work together. More frequently they were divided and fought against each other. In 1973 some 20 farm groups formed a loose, working coalition to coordinate their efforts against a Nixon administration farm bill. Standing aloof from the coalition was the conservative American Farm Bureau Federation.

The coalition was the first effort by farm organizations to ban together for a joint purpose. National Farmers Union officials, who together with the National Grange had sponsored the coalition, explained that a number of the groups had worked together in the past, in shifting alliances, on different pieces of farm legislation, but that no major concerted effort previously had developed on a farm bill.

Labor

Before World War II, labor union lobbying was a relatively negligible force in the nation's capital. There was a remarkable growth in union membership from 1935 to 1945. At the same time, many labor union officials "learned the ropes" in Washington when they came to the capital during the Second World War to serve on the War Labor Board's tripartite dispute settlement sections. These developments set the stage for the emergence of labor unions as an important pressure group in the nation's capital. The unions carried on both grass roots pressure campaigns designed to influence public opinion and active lobbying of Congress (and frequently of the President and other executive branch leaders). Their large membership, strength in urban centers, comparatively substantial financial resources, organizational know-how and, in many cases, the liberally oriented idealism of most of their spokesmen made them a formidable force in legislative pressure activities. An important aspect of their influence was that many unions, and notably the AFL-CIO, maintained research and publications staffs which contributed importantly to the development and popularization of many new policy proposals in the welfare and labor fields.

Also important, probably even more than research and propaganda activities, was the willingness of the unions to use political means to achieve their ends. Both the AFL and the CIO maintained political action arms (the AFL Labor's League for Political Education and the CIO Political Action Committee) which, when the two federations merged in 1955, were united to form the AFL-CIO Committee on Political Education (COPE).

If there is one trademark of AFL-CIO and union lobbyists, it is their physical presence at the Capitol. Members of Congress sympathetic to labor goals never need to guess what the AFL-CIO lobbyists want them to do. There are almost always one or more of them around to make sure members know.

Despite their usefulness as shorthand, terms such as "labor victory" and "labor defeat" imply a cohesiveness among unions that rarely exists. Even within the AFL-CIO, there are 109 unions ranging from teachers and government employees to craft-based building trades unions.

The affiliates vary almost as much in the intensity of their lobbying as they do in ideology. Sometimes individual unions not only refuse to help with the lobbying, but actual-

ly oppose an AFL-CIO position. The federation supported federal land use planning legislation, but the United Brotherhood of Carpenters fought it in 1974 and was instrumental in its defeat in the House.

Organized labor wins its share of arguments in Congress. Much of the civil rights and Great Society legislation of the 1960s was largely the product of its lobbying. But the irony that frustrates many union lobbyists is that labor has rarely won on the issues that affect it most directly.

The unions lost in 1948 when Congress overrode President Truman's veto of the Taft-Hartley Act. They lost in 1959, when they could not prevent passage of the restrictions in the Landrum-Griffin Labor-Management Reporting Act.

They lost in 1966, when the House failed to pass legislation repealing Section 14B of Taft-Hartley, which permits states to enact "right-to-work" laws sanctioning a non-union shop.

In 1975-76 labor thought for a time it had achieved a long-sought success in encouraging Congress to enact a common-site picketing bill. Congress enacted the bill, but it was vetoed by President Ford. The measure would have allowed a local union with a grievance against one contractor to picket all other contractors or subcontractors at the same construction site.

The reason labor fails to win on its own issues, members and lobbyists agree, is that it comes to be perceived as a special interest, rather than the public interest lobby it can portray itself as on behalf of social legislation.

For many legislators, fear of union retaliation when the legislator did not vote as the unions wished was lessened by the recognition that union leaders, on many non-"bread and butter" issues, tended to be far more liberal than their members and that union leaders did not always control the vote of members on election day. Moreover, there was a general feeling that the strength of labor unions as a pressure group was greatest in the 1940s and early 1950s and had begun to decline in the later 1950s and 1960s—in part because unions were no longer expanding their membership very rapidly, in part because the experience of the preceding 15-20 years demonstrated that unions alone simply were not strong enough to dominate congressional elections in a way which once was feared.

Business

Modern business groups no longer wield the power over members of Congress that business magnates wielded during the 70 years between the Civil War and the New Deal. The groups, nevertheless, continue to exert considerable influence on legislative decisions.

Journalist James Deakin illustrated some of the past and present techniques of business influence. He described the Senate in the late years of the 19th century as a home for business barons who had paid their way in Congress. Quoting William Allen White, Deakin continued: "One Senator represented the Union Pacific Railway system, another the New York Central, still another the insurance interests.... Coal and iron owned a coterie.... Cotton had half a dozen Senators. The collar of any great financial interest was worn with pride."[17]

Deakin also told about a luncheon in the 1960s in the private Pentagon dining room of Secretary of Defense Robert S. McNamara. At the head of the table was McNamara. Arrayed around him were four top defense aides and five men from the U.S. Chamber of Commerce,

Mass Pressure Demonstrations in Washington

Over the years, some pressure groups that lacked large financial resources have sought to make their pressure felt by staging demonstrations in the nation's capital. This method was particularly popular among civil rights and anti-war groups in the 1960s and early 1970s.

The first of these large demonstrations came in 1894, when an army of the unemployed was organized by Jacob S. Coxey to pressure Congress into authorizing a $500,000,000 highway improvement program and interest-free loans to state and local governments to finance public improvements. Coxey's army set out from Massillon, Ohio; others were soon organized in many parts of the West. The total number of men involved has been estimated at 6,000 to 11,000.

Only about 500 men reached Washington. The District of Columbia police department was greatly enlarged for their arrival and government buildings were heavily guarded. When Coxey and his men arrived May 1 and started to march into the Capitol grounds the police assaulted the men with clubs. Coxey and two other leaders reached the Senate steps but were arrested and subsequently convicted of trampling the shrubbery and unlawfully displaying banners.

Coxey's army established camps at various places in and around Washington. They subsisted on donated food and by begging. By mid-July they had been abandoned by most of their leaders. The demonstration ended when the Virginia militia drove the men out of a large encampment on the Virginia side of the Potomac and burned down their camp. The District of Columbia government then offered to provide transportation to the West, which most accepted.

The Bonus Expeditionary Force. The Bonus Expeditionary Force which marched on Washington in 1932 was much larger than Coxey's army. An estimated 15,-000 men participated.

The Bonus marchers, like Coxey's army, were the product of a depression era. The specific purpose of the Bonus Expeditionary Force was to pressure Congress into providing immediate payment to World War I veterans of bonus certificates that were scheduled to mature in 1945. Late in 1931 Rep. Wright Patman (D Texas) had introduced a bill to that end.

The Bonus marchers, led by Walter W. Waters, started arriving in Washington at the end of May 1932, three weeks after Patman's bill had been reported out unfavorably by the Ways and Means Committee. Some of the men found shelter in partly razed buildings along Pennsylvania Ave. The main camp of the Bonus marchers was on the Anacostia Flats and consisted of tents and shacks. Food, clothing and other supplies were donated by private individuals and charities.

The House passed the bonus bill June 15 by a 211-176 roll-call vote but it was rejected by the Senate June 17 on an 18-62 roll-call vote. A contemporary journalist described the Senate action as a "rebuke to what some senators regarded as practically physical intimidation by the bonus marchers."

The Bonus marchers remained in Washington hoping to pressure the Senate into reversing its vote. Congress adjourned on July 16 without reconsidering the bonus bill, but it authorized $100,000 in loans to veterans to enable them to return home. However, an estimated 11,000 people were still in camps a week after Congress had adjourned.

The Bonus Expeditionary Force was finally dispersed by federal troops on July 28. Troops were called to quell a riot which broke out when the police tried to evict marchers who were camping out in federally owned buildings. The federal troops were led by the Army Chief of Staff, General Douglas MacArthur. Major Dwight D. Eisenhower commanded a tank detachment. The marchers were driven towards Anacostia and the encampment there was burned that night. The following day President Hoover said of the marchers, "Government cannot be coerced by mob rule."

1963 March on Washington. On Aug. 28, 1963, about 200,000 persons descended on the capital for a "March on Washington for Jobs and Freedom." Goals of the massive demonstration included stronger civil rights laws and tougher enforcement of existing laws. A massive federal training program for the unemployed and a broadened minimum wage law also were demanded.

Lafayette Park Camp-in. A group of about 90 unemployed Mississippi blacks organized a camp-in in Lafayette Park, across from the White House, in April 1966. The campers were protesting delays in processing their application for poverty funds. Four tents were set up in Lafayette Park April 4-7. The demonstrators took turns living in them. They were given a permit by the Department of the Interior.

Poor People's Campaign. Some 3,000 persons, most of them black, camped near the Lincoln Memorial from April 29 through June 23, 1968, in a demonstration for jobs and welfare legislation. Termed the "Poor People's Campaign," the demonstration was dispersed when federal officials refused to renew the demonstrators' camping permit.

Anti-War Demonstrations. Crowds estimated in the tens of thousands turned out on numerous occasions from 1966 into 1971 to demonstrate for American withdrawal from the war in Vietnam. Pro-war groups also demonstrated, but turnouts were much smaller.

Sources: *Encyclopedia of American History,* edited by Richard B. Morris (Harper & Row, 1965); Congressional Quarterly, *Congress and the Nation,* Vols. I-III.

---

including Theron J. (Terry) Rice, then the chamber's manager of the national defense committee and later its chief lobbyist. During the cordial luncheon, the 10 men discussed various defense issues likely to come up in the next session of Congress, including the military assistance part of the foreign aid program, civil defense and fallout shelters, the Renegotiation Act, government patent policy on inventions resulting from government-financed research, conflict of interest legislation and the Defense Production Act.[18]

The two best known business groups have been the United States Chamber of Commerce and the National Association of Manufacturers (NAM) The two organizations have spoken for American business in the councils of government, usually with one voice, but not always. In 1976, the two groups announced agreement on plans to merge.

Chamber Lobbying Methods. Of the two groups, the chamber has been the more active in attempting to influence Congress. In a 1975 interview with Congressional Quarterly, R. Hilton (Dixie) Davis, general manager of the chamber's legislative action department, described some of the group's lobbying methods.

Davis' principal objective was to get chamber members to write their senators or representatives on any given issue, and he had four techniques for doing this:

● What he called the "lowest key" method was the use of the legislative action operation's weekly newsletter, "Congressional Action," which was distributed to all organizational members of the chamber, all local chamber congressional action committees and any business members requesting the service. Mailed as a newspaper under second-class postage, the newsletter was used to provide general information and to generate letters when there were no time pressures.

● Much more sophisticated were "action calls," a direct mail campaign to a selected audience "when issues start to reach the critical stage." An action call memorandum provided the information a letter-writer would need to send a detailed message to his lawmaker. However, Davis emphasized that the chamber avoided suggesting the wording of letters and never distributed form letters.

● The next step in intensity was the distribution of a memorandum from Davis, similar in format to the "action call" but briefer and printed on a different letterhead intended to make it look even more urgent. These memos were mailed to a very small group of members, primarily those whose lawmakers' votes were critical to the outcome of the issue at hand.

● When time was extremely short and the issue deemed sufficiently vital, Davis sent out mailgrams. He said he tried to keep them to a minimum because "the cost builds up."

One reason the chamber was able to be selective was the computerization of its membership lists, which were broken down by congressional districts and states. Davis and his aides needed only to determine which legislators held the swing votes and the computer would churn out address labels for chamber members in those districts.

Other lobbying activities undertaken by the national chamber included the preparation of a variety of publications and audio-visual aids. The national chamber encouraged local and state chambers to form their own congressional action committees, and supplied them with such materials as a monthly videotaped discussion of pending legislation.

Davis also tried to maintain a rapport with other business lobbyists in Washington. He hosted a breakfast meeting of corporate lobbyists at chamber headquarters twice each month when Congress is in session, and a similar meeting twice a month for trade association lobbyists. A member of Congress usually was invited to speak, and the status of legislation was discussed.

Foreign Trade

The high point of high-tariff sentiment in the United States was reached when the 1930 Smoot-Hawley Act imposed the highest tariff barriers in history. It was not long, however, before the Roosevelt administration began a move away from protectionism with passage of the Trade Agreements Act of 1934. Successive liberalizations of the

Trade Agreements Act followed. It became clear in the post-1945 period that protectionist forces, led by the American Tariff League (renamed Trade Relations Council of the United States in 1958), though still powerful were not able to regain the strength and influence they had held before 1934. Despite the efforts of this group and some others, the nation never went back to a position of rigorous protectionism and it maintained, on the whole, a favorable attitude toward the lowering of trade barriers.

The reasons for this development were partly ideological, partly practical. The cold war and the national interest in the development of a Western alliance and Western community of nations led to internationalist attitudes and the need for closer ties with Western Europe and other non-Communist areas—ends which would be served, many believed, by a low tariff policy. At the same time there was a development within the United States of economic interests which would benefit by liberal trade policies—corporations with large investments and subsidiaries overseas which sought access to the American market, and agricultural interests fearing exclusion from overseas markets if the United States pursued a protectionist policy. The upshot was that the business community in the postwar era was far less united than it had been on many occasions in the past in favor of protectionism.

Still, congressional consideration of a major foreign trade bill could produce intense lobbying by a variety of interests. Such lobbying occurred in 1970 over a bill imposing quotas on textile and footwear imports, and setting up machinery for imposing quotas on many other imports.

A new factor took on importance—the multinational corporation. The 1970 contest found some of the largest U.S.-based international business concerns, including a faction which contained three of the top five U.S. defense contractors and 10 of the top 25, throwing their substantial weight against tariffs, quotas and other trade barriers.

Major free trade and protectionist lobby coalition groups took active parts in the 1970 legislative action. The leading free trade groups were the Emergency Committee for American Trade and the Committee for a National Trade Policy. The leading protectionist groups were the Nation-Wide Committee on Import-Export Policy and the Trade Relations Council of the United States.

A major trade reform act in 1974 (PL 93-618) also was accompanied by heavy lobbying. The measure gave the President trade negotiating authority for five years. The bill had been actively supported by the Nixon and Ford administrations and by major multinational corporations and business groups interested in trade with the Soviet Union, working primarily through the Emergency Committee for American Trade. Also involved in lobbying on the bill's sections dealing with Soviet emigration and trade benefits were various Jewish groups, particularly the National Conference on Soviet Jewry, an umbrella organization. The major opponent of the bill was the AFL-CIO which had favored more protectionist legislation.

Education

The idea that the federal government should take some part in the support of education is an old one, dating from the post-Revolutionary years when certain land in every township in the Northwest Territory was set aside by Congress for support of public schools.

Not until 1862 did Congress act again to aid education, then establishing in each state land-grant colleges of agricultural and mechanical arts. In 1867, Congress approved a bill introduced by Rep. (later President) James A. Garfield, creating a non-Cabinet Department of Education. In 1917, Congress authorized federal aid to vocational education.

The federal government made its largest total financial contribution to education through the GI bill (Servicemen's Readjustment Act, 1944) and its successor laws.

In 1950, Congress authorized federal grants for schools in areas where federal activities were adding population while removing property from the tax rolls. But only after the Russians launched Sputnik did Congress pass the National Defense Education Act (NDEA) authorizing $1-billion in federal aid to education.

The decade of the 1960s, particularly the administration of former schoolteacher Lyndon B. Johnson, brought the greatest extension of federal aid to education through the Higher Education Facilities Act of 1963, the Elementary and Secondary Education Act of 1965 and the Higher Education Act of 1965.

As Congress enlarged the federal role in aiding education, many education groups set up Washington offices.

The American Federation of Teachers (AFT) moved from Chicago—where it had been chartered by Samuel Gompers in 1916—to Washington. The Association of American Universities (AAU) moved to Washington in 1962 at age 62. The National School Boards Association, founded in 1940, set up a Washington office in 1966.

By the 1970s, there were hundreds of such groups represented in Washington. Almost every type of institution and teacher was represented, as well as parents, libraries and educational administrators. School librarians and school secretaries each had their own group; as did college governing boards, college registrars and college business officers. In addition, dozens of the colleges and universities had their own Washington representatives.

The education community covers a wide spectrum of groups and specific interests from the 1.8-million-member National Education Association and the seven-million-member National Congress of Parents and Teachers to the 56-member Council of Chief State School Officers and the exclusive 48-member Association of American Universities.

No umbrella is large enough to cover all education interest groups although for a brief period in 1970 it seemed that the Emergency Committee for Full Funding might be able to.

The emergency committee—its creation and operations—cast into relief the difficulty of fusing these diverse groups into an effective cooperating community and the sensitivity of many of them to any suggestion that they were lobbies in the traditional meaning of the word.

Despite a basic common interest, many conflicts arose between groups, related to the various sectors of education which each represented. Black colleges and community colleges often did not benefit from the same programs as did large universities. The all-teacher membership of the AFT might not have seen things the same way as the teacher-administrator groups within NEA.

Because of these divisions, categorical aid programs—library services and school lunch—were enacted by Congress long before any type of general aid to schools. A proposal for general aid brought out all the contradictions in the educational community—church-state, public-private—while categorical grant programs won support from certain groups without incurring the opposition of others.

Ex-Members as Lobbyists

Among the most influential and active lobbyists in Washington have been former members of Congress, who, after leaving office, have been hired as lobbyists for private organizations.

In some cases, former members become permanently associated with a single organization whose views they share. On the other hand, some former members work for many different organizations as lobbyists, frequently changing or adding employers from year to year.

Because of their service in Congress, former members of the House or Senate enjoy several advantages in lobbying activities. They have an excellent knowledge of the legislative process and frequently a good "feel" for the operations of the House or Senate which tell them precisely when and what kind of pressure to exert on behalf of their clients. They often enjoy easy access to congressional staff members and members who are friends and former colleagues. This enables them to see and speak with key legislative personnel, perhaps the chairman of a committee or subcommittee, at the proper time. The ordinary lobbyist might spend weeks trying to obtain an appointment. Former members also frequently have an expert knowledge of the subject matter of legislation through having dealt with it while in Congress.

The privilege of being admitted to the floor and private lobbies of the House and Senate, which is granted in each chamber to former members of that chamber, is used relatively little by former members directly for lobbying purposes, although it is useful for maintaining contacts and old acquaintances. In the House, use of the floor by former members for lobbying purposes has been circumscribed by House Rule 32 and a chair ruling in 1945 by Speaker Sam Rayburn (D Texas). Under the "Rayburn rule," a former member is forbidden the privilege of the floor at any time the House is debating or voting on legislation in which he is interested, either personally or as an employee of some other person or group.

In the Senate, no similar formal rule exists. But as a matter of custom, it is considered improper for a former senator, or any other non-member granted the privilege of the floor, to use the privilege to lobby for legislation in which he is interested either personally or as a representative or lobbyist for another person or organization.

In 1971, external threats contributed to an unusual unity within the educational community. The financial crunch produced the cooperative effort of the emergency committee where the groups could hash out their differences and then arrive at a common strategy.

Its "package approach," developing one amendment increasing funding for a variety of education programs, was designed to overcome the fragmentation which had often beset the education community.

Early in 1971, most of the major higher education groups agreed upon one statement on institutional aid; later they agreed upon the best formula for allocating such aid. This unified pressure won an institutional aid proposal from the Nixon administration which had said early in 1971 that it would not submit such a bill during the year.

A number of other prominent and often-disagreeing groups united to oppose a program of education vouchers, which was seen as a serious threat to the public school system.

Yet the divisions remained, submerged only temporarily. One participant in the Government Relations Group, the congressional liaison representatives of the various associations, said that there often was more infighting than communication.

Foreign Interests

Since World War II, lobbying by foreign interests and by American groups with foreign members or interests has become an increasingly important factor in Washington's legislative and executive decision-making. Foreign-oriented lobbying is based on international politics, world trade and many American domestic issues, for any action by the U.S. government may have foreign or global implications.

Some examples of foreign interests which registered in 1975 included: American Hellenic Institute Public Affairs Committee Inc., interested in U.S.-Greece and U.S.-Cyprus trade and commerce; the Australian Meat Board, concerned with legislation affecting meat imports into the United States; Cuba Claims Commission, interested in procuring an additional five-year period in which to deduct Cuban losses allowed by the Internal Revenue Service; the Government of the Netherlands Antilles, interested in all bills relating to the business and diplomatic affairs of that country; and the Jamaica National Guild, USA, concerned with immigration bills.[19]

Arab and Israeli Interests. Recently a new type of foreign lobbying has developed. The 1973 Yom Kippur war in the Middle East resulted in new instability in the area, in growing doubts about Israel's security and in more aggressive control of oil production by the Arab states. In the aftermath of the war, Arab and Israeli interests in the United States, some of them long-standing groups, have taken on new roles.

On the one hand are various groups representing the interests of Israel: the American Israel Public Affairs Committee, the American Jewish Committee and B'nai B'rith's Anti-Defamation League. In the view both of people on Capitol Hill and of representatives of Jewish organizations, the Jewish lobby gains much of its power from citizen activism—both Jewish and non-Jewish—and widespread public backing for the longstanding U.S. policy of support for an independent Israel.

On the other hand are Arab interests in the United States, represented by a number of organizations. Two major groups are the National Association of Arab-Americans (NAAA) and the Arab Information Centers (AIC).

The NAAA presented position papers to the platform committees at the 1976 Democratic and Republican national conventions—a first for any Arab-American group. The organization was to support candidates for Congress in 1976 who pursued a sympathetic approach.

For years, according to Hatem I. Hussaini, assistant director of the Arab Information Center in Washington, the Arab Information Center has worked with this set of facts: "The Congress is in general pro-Israel. The Congress in general is not interested in the Arab point of view." The 1973-74 oil crisis changed these attitudes only a bit, he said. Now the AIC gets a few more queries from individual members of Congress regarding the Arab side of the Israeli conflict, on oil policy or other Middle East matters, Hussaini commented in a 1975 Congressional Quarterly interview.

Public Interest Groups

Public interest lobbies are a relatively new development in the long history of attempts to influence members of Congress. The League of Women Voters and Americans for Democratic Action are examples of public interest lobbies, and their activities helped to set the pattern for groups that were to follow. Two of the groups which followed have attracted wide public attention and have almost come to characterize public interest lobbies. The two groups are Common Cause, headed by John Gardner, and Public Citizen, developed by Ralph Nader.

While Common Cause and Public Citizen share the general goal of giving the average citizen more influence in political, economic and social matters, the two organizations have evolved their own areas of specialty.

Public Citizen groups pursue a broad agenda of substantive economic, consumer, environmental, legal and social policy issues while Common Cause has focused on issues of political structure and procedure.

Skillful use of publicity, shrewd legislative and political tactics and recognized expertise on previously undeveloped issues were key ingredients in the groups' success. They also profited from good timing.

Both groups can claim some notable successes. Common Cause, for example, is credited with a major role in the enactment of the 1974 campaign finance law (PL 93-443), with helping to develop public pressure for House and Senate reforms and with aiding pending "government in the sunshine" legislation.

Nader's groups have won lawsuits against corporations, professional organizations and the federal government. Nader lobbyists helped shape congressional energy and tax legislation, including repeal of the oil depletion allowance, and won approval for a fund to help consumers petition the Federal Trade Commission.

Both groups also have succeeded in involving the public in their work. Common Cause has approximtely 265,000 members. Public Citizen, though not a membership organization, is supported by an estimated 175,000 contributors annually. By way of comparison, Consumers Union has about 285,000 members, the League of Women Voters 160,000 and Americans for Democratic Action 65,000.

Common Cause and Public Citizen have adopted most of the normal pressure techniques used by interest groups with one major exception—neither group endorses candidates or makes campaign contributions. However, the groups do rate legislators' votes on selected issues.

Both Public Citizen and Common Cause have done organizational work at the grassroots level—but in different ways and with different objectives.

Common Cause has attempted to develop an indirect lobbying operation capable of producing letters and constituent contacts in response to important issues. Approximately 10 per cent of the organization's membership participates in the lobbying work, organized by congressional district and linked with Washington through an elaborate telephone "chain" and newsletter "action alerts."

The Nader operation's grassroots objective, in contrast, is to stimulate local action on local problems. One of Nader's main themes in his speeches is to urge his audience to become actively involved in public affairs.

Lobby Groups Rate Members

The number of organizations that rate members of Congress on their votes has increased steadily in recent years. More than 50 groups are now in the ratings business, compared with only a handful a few years ago.

Some of the newer raters are established organizations that have decided to adapt the ratings techniques successfully used for years by labor and political groups such as the Americans for Democratic Action, Americans for Constitutional Action and the AFL-CIO's COPE (Committee on Political Education).

Another reason for the increase is the proliferation of public interest groups, many of which issue congressional ratings. One of the most recent entrants to this field is Ralph Nader's Public Citizen organization, which in 1976 released its first consumer ratings of Congress.

Praise for and protests against group ratings of Congress are particularly intense during election years, when they provide handy weapons in the campaigns of members or their opponents.

The ratings provide a percentage or numerical label that can be used to characterize a member or a voting record, favorably or unfavorably, on an ideological scale or in a particular area of interest.

Voters may not believe a candidate's charge that a senator or representative is against consumers, particularly if the incumbent has some pro-consumer votes that can be pointed to in rebuttal. But the opponent's task is simplified if the incumbent appears on the Consumer Federation of America's list of "Consumer Zeroes," who have voted 100 per cent "wrong" from the organization's standpoint on its selection of key votes. On the other hand, an incumbent "Consumer Hero" can turn that label to an advantage.

Democrats running for re-election in heavily Republican districts fear a 100 per cent rating from the liberal Americans for Democratic Action (ADA). Republicans highly rated by the Americans for Constitutional Action (ACA) run a similar risk. They can be branded as conservatives, and risk losing Democratic votes.

Labels and numerical scores can be used by the opposition as a convenient "objective proof" of campaign charges and can force an incumbent onto the defensive.

Since members of Congress win re-election largely because they are incumbents and often face underfinanced and unpublicized opposition, unfavorable ratings from national interest groups can focus unwanted attention on a local campaign and pose a threat to these advantages.

Listed below are some of the major organizations that regularly compile congressional ratings:

Business. Chamber of Commerce of the United States, National Association of Businessmen, National Federation of Independent Businessmen.

Conservatives. American Conservative Union, Americans for Constitutional Action, Liberty Lobby.

Consumer Affairs. Consumer Federation of America, Public Citizen.

Defense/Foreign Policy. American Security Council, Coalition for a New Foreign and Military Policy, Friends Committee on National Legislation, SANE.

Education. American Federation of Teachers, Committee for Full Funding of Education Programs, National Education Association, National Student Lobby.

Environment. Environmental Action, League of Conservation Voters.

Labor. AFL-CIO Committee on Political Education; Amalgamated Clothing Workers of America; American Federation of Government Employees; American Federation of State, County and Municipal Employees; Building and Construction Trades Department, AFL-CIO; Communications Workers of America; International Association of Machinists; International Brotherhood of Teamsters; United Auto Workers; United Mine Workers.

Liberals. Americans for Democratic Action, *The New Republic,* Ripon Society.

Rural/Farm. American Farm Bureau Federation, National Farmers Organization, National Farmers Union.

Other. American Parents Committee, Common Cause, Council on National Priorities and Resources, League of Women Voters, National Council of Senior Citizens, National Taxpayers Union, Taxation With Representation, Women's Lobby.

Lobbying Investigations

Investigations of lobbying have stemmed from a wide range of motives and have sought to achieve nearly as broad a range of objectives. Lobbying investigations have been used to respond to intense public concern about lobbying, to gather information on the workings of existing regulatory legislation and to help prepare the way for, and to shape, proposed new regulatory legislation.

The first thorough investigation of lobbying was undertaken by the Senate in 1913 in reaction to President Wilson's charges of a massive grass roots lobbying effort by the tariff lobby opposing the administration's tariff program. Since 1913, committees in 24 Congresses have investigated particular allegations of lobbying abuses or lobbying activities in general

Following are summary accounts of selected major lobbying investigations.

Business Lobbying, 1913

Senate Investigation. In 1913, President Woodrow Wilson was enraged over alleged lobbying activity by the National Association of Manufacturers (NAM) and other protectionist groups on the Underwood tariff bill. On May 26, 1913, Wilson denounced the presence of an "insidious" lobby which sought to bring on a new tide of protectionism. "I think the public ought to know," he said, "that extraordinary exertions are being made by the lobby in Washington to gain recognition for certain alterations in the tariff bill.... Washington has seldom seen so numerous, so industrious, or so insidious a lobby.... There is every evidence that money without limit is being spent to sustain this lobby.... The government ought to be relieved from this intolerable burden and the constant interruption to the calm progress of debate."[20]

In the Senate hearings that followed, testimony disclosed that large amounts had been spent for entertainment and for other lobbying purposes both by the interests seeking high tariff duties and by those interested in low duties, such as the sugar refiners. Following the hearings, a bill for registration of lobbyists was introduced, but farm, labor and other special interests succeeded in warding off a vote on it.

House Investigation. Also in 1913, Col. Martin M. Mulhall, lobbyist for the NAM published a sensational account of his activities in a front-page article in the *New York World.* Among other disclosures, Mulhall said he had paid "between $1,500 and $2,000" to help Rep. James T. McDermott (D Ill.) for legislative favors.

A four-month inquiry by a select House panel chaired by Majority Leader Finis J. Garrett (D Tenn.) found that many of Mulhall's allegations were exaggerated. The panel established that Mulhall had set up his own office in the Capitol, had paid the chief House page $50 a month for inside information, had received advance information on pending legislation from McDermott and House Republican leader John Dwight (N.Y.), and had influenced the appointment of members to House committees and subcommittees. Six of seven House members implicated by Mulhall were exonerated, but the panel recommended that McDermott be "strongly censured." The House adopted the panel's recommendations. Although McDermott was not expelled from the House, he resigned the following year.[21]

Tax and Utilities Lobbying, 1927

Interest in lobbying activities was rekindled in the 1920s after the American Legion and other veterans' groups had succeeded in obtaining passage of a bonus bill over the veto of President Coolidge.

In 1927 an investigating committee under Sen. Thaddeus H. Caraway (D Ark.) conducted extensive public hearings on lobbying efforts. One of the immediate reasons for the 1927 investigation was the pressure being brought to bear on the Ways and Means Committee for repeal of the federal estate tax. More than 200 witnesses, including one governor and many state legislators, had been brought to Washington by the American Taxpayers League to appear before the committee. All travel expenses were paid and some of the witnesses received additional compensation. The second activity to which Congress objected at the time was the establishment of Washington headquarters by the Joint Committee of National Utility Associations to block a proposed Senate investigation of utility financing. The joint committee succeeded in having the investigation transferred to the Federal Trade Commission, but that agency took its assignment seriously and gave the utility situation a thorough going-over.

At the end of the investigation, a sweeping registration bill was recommended. The bill defined lobbying as "...any effort in influencing Congress upon any matter coming before it, whether it be by distributing literature, appearing before committees of Congress, or seeking to interview members of either the House or Senate." A lobbyist was defined as "...one who shall engage, for pay, to attempt to influence legislation, or to prevent legislation by the national Congress."[22] The bill passed the Senate by a unanimous vote but was pigeon-holed by a House committee.

Despite failure of the Caraway bill, the Senate Judiciary Committee's report on the measure contributed greatly to the public's knowledge of lobbying. The panel

asserted that about 90 per cent of the 300 to 400 lobbying associations listed in the Washington telephone directory were "fakes" whose aim was to bilk unwary clients. These organizations, according to the committee report, included groups that purported to represent scientific, agricultural, religious, temperance, and anti-prohibition interests. "In fact," the panel said, "every activity of the human mind has been capitalized by some grafter." The committee estimated that $99 of every $100 paid to these groups "go into the pockets of the promoters." Caraway himself disclosed that one of the lobbyists had collected $60,000 in one year from business interests by simply writing them every time a bill favorable to business was passed and claiming sole credit for its passage.[23]

Naval Armaments, 1929

The next congressional probe of lobbying came in 1929, when a Senate Naval Affairs Subcommittee looked into the activities of William B. Shearer, who represented shipping, electrical, metals, machinery and similar concerns interested in blocking limitation of naval armaments and in obtaining larger appropriations for Navy ships. The path to Shearer's exposure had been paved when he filed a suit in the New York courts to recover $257,655, which he said was owed to him by the New York Shipbuilding Co. Shearer claimed the money was due for lobbying services he had performed in Washington and at the Geneva naval limitation conference of 1927.

Testimony before the subcommittee showed that Shearer had been sent to Geneva by shipbuilding interests and had done everything he could to torpedo an agreement. Following the conference, at which no agreement was reached, Shearer had led industry lobbying efforts for bigger naval appropriations and for subsidies for the merchant marine. His other activities included preparing pro-Navy articles for the Hearst newspaper chain, writing articles for the 1938 Republican presidential campaign, in which he characterized peace advocates as traitors, and writing speeches for the American Legion and like-minded lobby groups.

Utility Lobbies, 1935

A decade of congressional concern over the influence exerted by private utilities led to a stormy probe of that industry's lobbying activities in 1935. Although Congress nine years earlier had instructed the Federal Trade Commission to investigate utility lobbying, a two-year probe by the FTC had been largely inconclusive.

After intensive lobbying by the utilities had threatened to emasculate an administration bill to regulate utility holding companies, President Roosevelt in a special message to Congress described the holding companies as "private empires within the nation" and denounced their lobbying techniques. Congressional supporters of the measure demanded an investigation to bring out the lengths to which the power interests' lobbying had gone.[24]

A special investigative panel was set up in the Senate under the chairmanship of Sen. Hugo L. Black (D Ala.), an administration stalwart who later was to become an associate justice of the Supreme Court. Following a sometimes raucous hearing, Black concluded that the utilities had spent about $4-million to defeat the utility bill and had engaged in massive propagandizing to convince the public that the bill was an iniquitous invasion of private rights and a sharp turn toward socialism. Among other findings, Black's panel stated that the utilities had financed thousands of phony telegrams to Congress, in which the names of the senders had been picked at random from telephone books.[25]

Amid a furor over the telegrams, Congress passed the Public Utilities Holding Company Act, which included provisions requiring reports to federal agencies on some utility lobbying activities. *(Details, p. 672)*

The Senate and House also passed lobbyist registration bills. A conference agreement was reached but the House rejected the agreement and final adjournment came before a new agreement could be reached. The defeat of the measure was attributed to the combined efforts of hundreds of lobbyists.

Munitions Lobby, 1935

Another investigation during 1935 involved the munitions lobby and the Senate Special Committee Investigating the Munitions Industry, under Sen. Gerald P. Nye (R N.D.). Committee disclosures of bribery and arms deals brought sharp responses in Latin America and Great Britain, where the incidents had occurred. *(Details, Congressional Investigations, p. 164)*

Further Studies, 1938 and 1945

The Temporary National Economic Committee, set up by Congress at President Roosevelt's request, under the chairmanship of Sen. Joseph O'Mahoney (D Wyo.), included lobbying among its subjects of study in 1938.

The Joint Committee on the Organization of Congress, established in 1945, studied lobbying activities along with other matters pertaining to Congress. On the basis of the committee's recommendations, Congress in 1946 passed the Legislative Reorganization Act, which included the first general lobby registration law. *(Details, p. 672)*

Omnibus Lobbying Probe, 1950

A House Select Committee on Lobbying Activities headed by Rep. Frank M. Buchanan (D Pa.) investigated the lobbying and related activities of a wide range of organizations in 1950. The committee's probe had been prompted largely by the assertion of President Truman that the 80th Congress was "the most thoroughly surrounded...with lobbies in the whole history of this great country of ours." Truman said: "There were more lobbyists in Washington, there was more money spent by lobbyists in Washington, than ever before in the history of the Congress of the United States. It's disgraceful...."[26] Most of the publicity centered on the efforts of the Committee for Constitutional Government to distribute low-cost or free "right-wing" books and pamphlets designed to influence the public.

In an effort to determine more accurately the amount of money spent by organizations to influence legislation, the House investigating committee requested detailed information from 200 corporations, labor unions and farm groups. Replies from 152 corporations gave a total of $32-million spent for this purpose from Jan. 1, 1947, through May 31, 1950. Over 100 of these corporations had not filed reports under the 1946 Federal Regulation of Lobbying Act. Reports of the 37 which had done so showed expenditures of $776,000, which was less than three per cent of the amount reported by respondents to the committee questionnaire. In releasing results of the questionnaire, Chairman Buchanan noted that the survey covered activities of only 152 of the country's 500,000 corporations. "I firmly believe," he said,

"that the business of influencing legislation is a billion-dollar industry."[27]

The House committee made recommendations for strengthening the 1946 lobbying law but no action was taken.

Omnibus Lobbying Probe, 1956

In 1956 a major lobbying inquiry was conducted by the Senate Special Committee to Investigate Political Activities, Lobbying and Campaign Contributions. The inquiry was initiated against a background of an alleged campaign contribution to Sen. Francis Case (R S.D.) in connection with voting on a natural gas bill. The panel was chaired by Sen. John L. McClellan (D Ark.).

Following a long investigation, McClellan on May 31, 1957, introduced a new lobbying registration bill designed to replace the 1946 act. The bill proposed to tighten the existing law by making the comptroller general responsible for enforcing it (there was no administrator under the 1946 act); by eliminating a loophole that required registration of only those lobbyists whose "principal purpose" was lobbying; by extending the coverage to anyone who spent $50,000 or more a year on grass-roots lobbying; and by eliminating an exemption which made the law inapplicable to persons who merely testified on proposed legislation.

The bill was vigorously opposed by the Chamber of Commerce of the United States and was criticized on certain points by the National Association of Manufacturers, the Association of American Railroads and the American Medical Association, although the latter endorsed the measure as a whole. The bill did not reach the floor and died with the close of the 85th Congress.

Retired Military Lobbyists, 1959

In 1959 the Special Investigations Subcommittee of the House Armed Services Committee held three months of hearings on the employment of former Army, Navy and Air Force officers by defense contractors, and the influence of the retired officers in obtaining government contracts for their new employers. The subcommittee found that more than 1,400 retired officers with the rank of major or higher—including 261 of general or flag rank—were employed by the top 100 defense contractors.

In its report in 1960, the subcommittee said that "The coincidence of contracts and personal contacts with firms represented by retired officers and retired civilian officials sometimes raises serious doubts as to the objectivity of these [contract] decisions."[28] Congress largely accepted subcommittee recommendations for tighter restrictions on sales to the government by former retired personnel.

Foreign Lobbyists, 1962

Lobbying in connection with the Sugar Act of 1962 led the Senate Foreign Relations Committee to vote, July 6, 1962, to launch an investigation of foreign lobbies and the extent to which they attempted to influence United States policies. At the request of Foreign Relations Committee Chairman J. William Fulbright (D Ark.) and Sen. Paul H. Douglas (D Ill.), the Senate Finance Committee, which had jurisdiction over the sugar bill, had queried sugar lobbyists on their arrangements with their employers, mostly foreign countries. A compendium of the answers, made public June 26, 1962, showed that some payments to the sugar lobbyists were made on the basis of the size of the sugar quotas granted by Congress.

Tax Deductions for Lobbying

Under a 1919 regulation by the Internal Revenue Service interpreting federal tax laws, money spent by businesses or individuals for lobbying purposes was not deductible from taxable income. The application of the regulation led to protests by businesses and several attempts to upset the regulation. Finally, in the omnibus tax bill of 1962 (HR 10650—PL 87-834), Congress authorized federal income tax deductions for sums of money spent for lobbying purposes. The authorization permitted a business to deduct the cost of lobbying for legislation—whether federal, state or local legislatures were involved—if the legislation was of direct interest to the taxpayer concerned. The company's interest had to be truly direct (e.g., tax or labor legislation affecting it) and not remote and speculative. Lobbying for a presidential disability amendment, for example, was considered remote and therefore not deductible. Deductions were made permissible for any otherwise legal type of direct contact with a legislative body designed to influence the public. Under the legislation, a business could also deduct any portion of the dues it paid to a trade organization or chamber of commerce allocable to lobbying, and an individual union member could deduct union dues allocable to lobbying purposes.

Hearings conducted some months later by the Foreign Relations Committee produced evidence that some lobbyists also lobbied their own clients. Fulbright disclosed, for example, that Michael B. Deane, a Washington public relations man who had been hired by the Dominican Sugar Commission to lobby for its interests before Congress, had apparently filed exaggerated, sometimes inaccurate reports to the commission regarding his effectiveness. Deane admitted that he had falsely reported to commission officials that he had been invited by the President to the White House and had talked with the Secretary of Agriculture. Deane said he occasionally gave himself "too much credit," but "one tends to do that a little bit when they have a client who is outside of Washington."[29] Similar testimony was elicited from other sugar lobbyists.

The Fulbright probe continued well into 1963, and at its conclusion, Fulbright introduced a bill to tighten registration requirements under the Foreign Agents Registration Act of 1938 for persons in the United States representing foreign interests. The bill passed the Senate in 1964 but died in the House. It was revived in the 89th Congress and enacted in 1966. *(Details, p. 672)*

Regulation of Lobbying

In 1876 the House first passed a resolution requiring lobbyists to register during the 44th Congress with the clerk of the House. Since the advent of the 62nd Congress in 1911, federal lobbying legislation has continued to be proposed in practically every Congress.[30] Yet by mid-1976 only one comprehensive lobbying regulation law and only a handful of more specialized measures, had been enacted. (In June 1976, legislation was passed by the Senate and was pending in the House. *See p. 674)*

The principal method of regulating lobbying has been disclosure rather than control. In four laws, lobbyists have been required to identify themselves, whom they represent and their legislative interests. In one law, lobbyists also have been required to report how much they and their employers spend on lobbying. But definitions have been unclear, and enforcement has been minimal. As a result, the few existing disclosure laws have produced only limited information, and its effects have been questionable.

One reason for the relative lack of restrictions on lobbies has been the difficulty of imposing meaningful restrictions without infringing on the constitutional rights of free speech, press, assembly and petition. Other reasons include a fear that restrictions would hamper legitimate lobbies without reaching more serious lobby abuses; the consolidated and highly effective opposition of lobbies; the desire of some members to keep open avenues to a possible lobbying career they may wish to pursue later.

The two major lobbying laws which Congress has succeeded in enacting have dealt with lobbyists in general who meet certain definitions of lobbying. The Foreign Agents Registration Act was first enacted in 1938 amid reports of Facist and Nazi propaganda circulating in the United States in the period before World War II. It has been amended frequently since then, and its history is as much a part of this country's struggle with internal security as it is a part of efforts to regulate lobbying.

The one existing omnibus lobbying law, the Federal Regulation of Lobbying Act, was enacted in 1946 as part of the Legislative Reorganization Act. The act's vague language and subsequent court interpretations have combined to reduce seriously the effectiveness of the law's spending and lobbying disclosure provisions.

The following sections review controls on spending by lobbyists and lobby registration requirements.

Spending Controls

Lobbying Expenditures

Although lobby spending by private individuals or groups is not restricted by federal law, a federal statute, first passed in 1919, attempted to restrict pressure on Congress by the federal executive branch. This statute (18 USC 1913) forbade federal employees and officials from using appropriated funds to lobby Congress on legislation. The provision was not designed to prevent normal federal employee communications and contacts with Congress in connection with legislative requests by executive branch agencies. Rather, it was designed to prevent flagrant spending to manipulate public opinion or to bombard members of Congress with letters and telegrams from the executive branch. In practice the law did not block high officials from publicly advocating legislation and pressuring Congress.

Judicial Restraints. A Supreme Court decision in 1961 somewhat limited the financial resources upon which railway labor unions could draw for their lobbying and similar activities.

The decision was handed down by a five-member majority in a Railway Labor Act case *(International Assn. of Machinists v. Street, 367 U.S. 740)*. The case involved several employees of the Southern Railway System. They contended their rights were being interfered with because, under a union shop contract sanctioned by a 1951 amendment to the Railway Labor Act, they were required to join a union and pay dues, part of which was used to promote legislation and public policies which they opposed.

The court majority held that the employees had a valid grievance. The court held that under the 1951 Railway Labor Act provision, the union could not use an employee's dues to support legislation and general public policies to which the employee objected. As a remedy, it suggested to the lower federal courts that they order the return to the complaining employees of that portion of their dues which had been used, not for collective bargaining activities, but for legislative and lobbying activities to which the employees objected.

Charitable Groups. Charitable organizations which engage in lobbying—and many of them do—face an uncertain test on limiting their lobbying expenditures. The problem arises out of the wording of a portion of section 501 (c)(3) of the Internal Revenue Code of 1954, under which the groups are granted tax-exempt status, and the way in which courts and the Internal Revenue Service have interpreted the wording.

As a condition of exemption, organizations are prohibited from engaging in "substantial" activities relating to lobbying. No statutory definition is provided for "substantial." One court has ruled that if less than 5 per cent of an exempt group's expenditures were for influencing legislation, the political activity was not substantial (*Murray Seasongood v. Commissioner*, 227 F. 2d 907 (6th Cir. 1955)). Other judges and the IRS have listed an exempt group's legislative activities and non-legislative activities in parallel columns, and have used human judgment to determine whether the lobbying activity was substantial.[31]

In recent years there have been a number of legislative proposals to provide a statutory base for judging the extent of an exempt group's lobbying efforts. While specific approaches have varied, most have sought to apply some percentage limitation on the dollar amount of total organizational spending which can be spent on legislative activity. None of the proposals, which are unusually sensitive politically, has been enacted, although Congress was considering such provisions in 1976.

Spending Reports. Under terms of the 1946 Federal Regulation of Lobbying Act, persons employed for the "principal purpose" of lobbying Congress were required to file financial reports with the clerk of the House and the secretary of the Senate. Because of loopholes in the act, however, the reports filed were scarcely an indication of the amounts spent on lobbying. *(1950 investigation, p. 669)*

One of the loopholes in the lobby law resulted from its vague language on who had to file, what information was to be included and who was to ensure enforcement. Some organizations, after filing reports for the first few years after 1946, stopped reporting on the ground that lobbying was not their "principal purpose." Others, such as the Chamber of Commerce of the United States and the National Association of Manufacturers, filed reports but did so under protest, contending that they were not covered under their interpretations of the act.

Many groups engaged primarily in grass-roots lobbying filed for a time but stopped after the Supreme Court ruled in *United States v. Harriss* (347 U.S. 612) in 1954 that grass-roots activities were not covered unless the organization, in effect, urged the public to contact Congress on legislation. Some groups that filed began subtracting the amounts they spent on their grass-roots work.

Another weakness was that the law left it up to each group or lobbyist to determine what portion of total expenditures were to be reported as spending for lobbying. As a result, some organizations whose budgets for their Washington, D.C., operation ran into the hundreds of thousands of dollars reported only very small amounts for spending on lobbying activities, contending that the remainder of their spending was for general public information purposes, research and other matters. Other organizations, interpreting the law quite differently, reported a much larger percentage of their total budgets as being for lobbying. The result was that some groups which year after year reported a large portion of their budgets gained reputations as "big lobby spenders" when, in fact, they simply were reporting more fully, at least under one view of the law, than other groups spending just as much.

Political Spending

The promise of electoral support or opposition has been probably the most effective device available to pressure groups in their attempts to influence Congress on legislation. Precisely for this reason, Congress attempted on several occasions to limit campaign contributions made by corporations, organizations and individuals in connection with federal elections. The limitations were intended to prevent those with great financial resources from using them to dominate the selection of members of Congress and thereby the legislative decisions of Congress.

Two major sets of federal laws long restricted campaign spending and contributions by pressure groups. The first, the Federal Corrupt Practices Act of 1925, strengthened a 1907 ban on campaign contributions by corporations in connection with federal elections. This prohibition was extended to labor unions temporarily by the 1943 wartime Smith-Connally (War Labor Disputes) Act and permanently by the 1947 Taft-Hartley Act. The Taft-Hartley Act also broadened the prohibition on both corporations and unions.

The second set of restrictions was contained in the second Hatch Act, passed in 1940, which (among other things) limited to $5,000 the amount an individual or group could contribute to any one candidate in a single calendar year in connection with any federal election campaign. *(Further details p. 541)*

Had either of these restrictions been truly effective, they might well have sealed off unions, businesses and other pressure groups from any major influence over federal elections. But loopholes in these laws, coupled with lack of clarity about the applicability and constitutionality of the ban on contributions by unions and corporations, left labor, business and other pressure groups numerous ways to continue effective political activity in federal elections.

Taft-Hartley Restrictions. The Taft-Hartley Act prohibition actually consisted of two parts: the ban on campaign contributions and the ban on direct expenditures. With regard to the prohibition on campaign contributions, there was no question that such contributions were barred in connection with federal elections and primaries if proposed to be made from corporate funds or from general union revenue derived from member dues. The ban applied whether the contribution was made directly to a candidate or to some group which used it on the candidate's behalf. But there was nothing in the law which stated that business executives or union members were barred from making voluntary contributions from their own personal funds to candidates for federal office.

Labor unions developed an additional technique which later was adopted by businesses. The unions set up separate political arms which were technically not labor unions and which received funds not from dues money but from voluntary contributions made by union members. These groups, the best known of which was the AFL-CIO's Committee on Political Education (COPE), were, in effect, simply voluntary political organizations and were not subject to the Taft-Hartley Act prohibition against political contributions by unions in federal elections. COPE and similar groups were free to make campaign contributions in connection with federal elections, primaries, conventions and caucuses. A major business political action committee was the Business-Industrial Political Action Committee (BIPAC), set up by the National Association of Manufacturers.

With regard to the second part of the Taft-Hartley prohibition, which barred direct expenditures by corporations and unions in connection with federal elections, "leakages" developed there too. The reason was, in part, that the ban on direct expenditures had to be construed narrowly lest it run afoul of the guarantees of freedom of speech contained in the First Amendment to the U.S. Constitution. In the years following the Taft-Hartley Act, a long list of expenditures in federal elections came to be accepted as permissible for corporations and unions.

Hatch Act Restrictions. The $5,000 limitation on campaign contributions in the Hatch Act did help to prevent massive spending in small areas by political and pressure organizations. But it was vitiated by several glaring loopholes. The $5,000 limitation did not prevent an individual, the individual's spouse, their children and other relatives from giving $5,000 each to the same candidate. Nor did it prevent a single wealthy individual from making contributions of $5,000 each to many different candidates and political committees. The limit was lowered to $1,000 by the Federal Election Campaign Act Amendments of 1974.

Campaign Finance Act Restrictions. In 1971, 1974 and 1976 Congress enacted campaign finance legislation which included provisions affecting political expenditures by pressure groups.

The Federal Election Campaign Act of 1971 (PL 92-225), which repealed the Federal Corrupt Practices Act of 1925, included a series of provisions which more strictly defined the roles unions and corporations could play in political campaigns. *(Details p. 544)*

The Federal Election Campaign Amendments of 1974 (PL 93-443) included provisions which set contribution limits for individuals and organizations. *(Details p. 546)*

The 1976 act (PL 94-283) tightened the contribution limits established in the 1974 campaign law for individuals and political committees and limited the ability of corporate and union political action committees to proliferate to circumvent the statute's contribution ceilings. The law also restricted the fund-raising ability of union and corporate political action committees. *(Details p. 548)*

Lobby Registration Laws

Utilities Holding Company Act

Section 12(i) of the Public Utilities Holding Company Act of 1935 required anyone employed or retained by a registered holding company or a subsidiary to file certain information with the Securities and Exchange Commission before attempting to influence Congress, the Federal Power Commission or the Securities and Exchange Commission on any legislative or administrative matter affecting any registered companies. Information required to be filed included a statement of the subject matter in which the individual was interested, the nature of the individual's employment and the nature of the individual's compensation.

Merchant Marine Act

Section 807 of the Merchant Marine Act of 1936 required any persons employed by or representing firms affected by various federal shipping laws to file certain information with the Secretary of Commerce before attempting to influence Congress, the Commerce Department and certain federal shipping agencies on shipping legislation or administrative decisions. The information included a statement of the subject matter in which the person was interested, the nature of the person's employment and the amount of the person's compensation.

Foreign Agents Registration Act

The Foreign Agents Registration Act of 1938, as amended, required registration with the Justice Department of anyone in the United States representing a foreign government or principal. Exceptions from the registration requirement were allowed for purely commercial groups and certain other categories. The act brought to public view many groups, individuals and associations that, while not necessarily engaged in lobbying Congress directly, carried on propaganda activities which might ultimately affect congressional legislation and national policy. The Foreign Agents Registration Act was amended frequently following its passage in 1938—for example, in 1939, 1942, 1946, 1950, 1956, 1961 and 1966—without changing its broad purposes. From 1950 on, the Justice Department followed the practice of reporting annually to Congress, in the form of a booklet listing registrants under the act and their receipts and the names of the foreign principals of registrants.

The 1966 amendments sought to clarify and strengthen the act by imposing stricter disclosure requirements for foreign lobbyists, by adding to the scope of activities for which individuals must register under the act, by requiring foreign agents to disclose their status as agents when contacting members of Congress and other government officials, and by prohibiting contingent fees for contracts (where the fee was based upon the success of political activities) and campaign contributions on behalf of foreign interests.

In 1976, the Justice Department, acting under the 1966 amendments, filed a civil suit in federal district court in Washington, D.C., against two trade organizations, the United States-Japan Trade Council Inc. and the Japan Trade Promotion Office, charging the groups with filing misleading statements with the department under the Foreign Agents Registration Act. The suit alleged that the council claimed it was a nonprofit trade association with U.S. members interested in promoting trade between the United States and Japan, when it actually was an organization using a trade association facade to conceal its foreign agent activities in representing Japanese governmental interests.

The 1976 action marked the first time a suit had been filed under the act alleging fraudulent reporting. There was speculation the suit could reflect a tougher enforcement policy toward the activities of foreign agents.

Federal Regulation of Lobbying Act

The Federal Regulation of Lobbying Act was actually passed as part of the Legislative Reorganization Act of 1946 (S 2177—PL 79-601). The lobbying provisions prompted little debate at the time. The Federal Regulation of Lobbying Act was never subsequently amended, and, as of mid-

1976, there had been only five federal court cases involving the act, of which four were prosecuted. *(Box, p. 656)*

The 1946 act did not in any way directly restrict the activities of lobbyists. It simply required any person who was hired by someone else for the principal purpose of lobbying Congress to register with the secretary of the Senate and clerk of the House and to file certain quarterly financial reports so that the lobbyist's activities would be known to Congress and the public. Organizations which solicited or received money for the principal purpose of lobbying Congress did not necessarily have to register, but they did have to file quarterly spending reports with the clerk detailing how much they spent to influence legislation. In 1954 the Supreme Court upheld the constitutionality of the 1946 lobbyist law (*United States v. Harriss*, 347 U.S. 612).

Loopholes. The court said that the law applied only to groups and individuals which collected or received money for the principal purpose of influencing legislation through direct contacts with members of Congress. This interpretation, based upon the court's reading of the legislative history, contained several major loopholes or vague areas permitting various organizations and individuals to avoid registering and/or reporting on spending under the 1946 law.

One loophole involved collection or receipt of money. Under the language of the law as interpreted by the court, groups or individuals that merely spent money out of their own funds to finance activities designed to influence legislation apparently were not covered by the law unless they also solicited, collected or received money for that purpose.

Another loophole involved the term "principal purpose." A number of organizations argued that since influencing Congress was not the principal purpose for which they collected or received money, they were not covered by the law regardless of what kind of activities they carried on. This argument was used by both the National Association of Manufacturers and the Chamber of Commerce of the United States as a basis for refusal to report any spending as an organization under the lobbyist law. The lobbyists for these groups personally reported their spending but they did so under protest.

The court held, in addition, that an organization or individual was not covered unless the method used to influence Congress contemplated some direct contact with members. The significance of this interpretation was that individuals or groups whose activities were confined to influencing the public on legislation or issues (so-called "grass-roots" lobbying) were not subject to the 1946 law.

The law left vague precisely what kind of contacts with Congress constituted lobbying subject to the law's reporting and registration requirements. The language of the law itself specifically exempted testimony before a congressional committee, and in 1950, in *United States v. Slaughter* (89 F. Supp. 205), a lower federal court held that this exemption applied also to those helping to prepare the testimony. Other direct contacts presumably were covered, but a gray area soon emerged, with some groups contending that their contacts with members of Congress were informational and could not be considered subject to the law.

Another weakness in the lobbying law was that it applied only to attempts to influence Congress, not administrative agencies or the executive branch where a considerable amount of legislation was generated which was later enacted by Congress, and where many decisions and regulations similar to legislation were put into effect under administrative rule-making and quasi-judicial powers.

Antitrust Action Against Lobbying

An attempt to use federal antitrust laws to restrain lobbying activities failed in 1961 when the U.S. Supreme Court held the antitrust laws inapplicable to campaigns for or against legislation. In the case of *Eastern Railroad v. Noerr* (365 U.S. 127) the Supreme Court held unanimously, Feb. 20, 1961, that attempts by any group to obtain legislation harmful to a competitor could not be considered a conspiracy in restraint of trade or any other violation of the federal antitrust laws. The court, speaking through Justice Hugo L. Black, said that because of the importance of the right to petition in the U.S. constitutional system, the federal antitrust laws could not be construed as outlawing action that was genuinely aimed at securing legislation—even if the legislation would injure a competitor and reduce competition, even if the legislative campaign had the effect of injuring the competitor's reputation and business or even if the publicity used in the legislative campaign was not wholly ethical.

The *Noerr* case arose in 1953 when 41 Pennsylvania truck operators and the Pennsylvania Motor Truck Association brought suit against 24 railroads associated in the Eastern Railroad Presidents' Conference. The truckers alleged that the railroads had engaged the Carl Byoir public relations firm to conduct a publicity campaign against truckers designed to foster adoption and retention of laws and law enforcement policies destructive of the trucking industry. The real motive, it was alleged, was to destroy the trucking industry as a competitor of the railroads in the long-haul freight business. It was alleged that the Byoir agency had, among other things, "planted" antitrucker editorials and articles in newspapers and magazines, helped to create supposedly spontaneous grass-roots citizens' organizations, which called for antitrucker legislation, conducted public opinion polls with questions loaded against the trucking industry and publicized the results as if they were unbiased findings. These tactics, it was asserted, resulted in a number of state actions injurious to the trucking industry, including Pennsylvania Gov. John S. Fine's (R) 1951 veto of a state "fair-truck" bill which would have permitted heavier loads on Pennsylvania highways. The truckers contended that this campaign violated the federal antitrust laws.

A lower court decision on Oct. 10, 1957, by federal Judge Thomas J. Clary upheld the truckers' position. Judge Clary conceded that legitimate lobbying activities and efforts to influence public opinion were not actionable under the antitrust laws, but he held that in this case the antitrust laws did apply because the objective of the railroad campaign was to destroy competition in the long-haul freight industry, the methods used to secure legislation were deceitful and the result had been to destroy the trucking industry's good will with the public. When the case reached the Supreme Court in 1961, however, it reversed the lower court, holding that the antitrust laws could not be construed as intended to permit injunctions or damage suits in a campaign involving a genuine attempt to obtain legislation, even when the campaign and the legislation sought would be injurious to a particular group.

Finally, reinforcing all the other weaknesses was the fact that the 1946 law did not designate anyone to investigate the truthfulness of lobbying registrations and reports and to seek enforcement. The clerk of the House and secretary of the Senate were to receive registrations and reports but were not directed or empowered to investigate reports or to compel anyone to register. Since violation of the law was made a crime, the Justice Department had power to prosecute violators but no mandate was given the department to investigate reports. In fact, the Justice Department eventually adopted a policy of investigating only when it received complaints and initiated only five prosecutions (some involving several individuals) from 1946 to mid-1976.

1970s Legislative Proposals

Congress renewed its interest in lobbying legislation in the 1970s. A proposed Legislative Activities Disclosure Act, drafted as a possible replacement for the Federal Regulation of Lobbying Act of 1946, was the subject of hearings in 1971 by the House Committee on Standards of Official Conduct. The bill stemmed from exploratory committee hearings in 1970 and was patterned after a bill with the same title recommended by the Special Committee to Investigate Political Activities, Lobbying, and Campaign Contributions in 1957. The 1971 proposal was broader, however.

The bill declared as its purpose "to provide for the disclosure to the Congress, to the President, and to the public, of the activities, and the origin, amounts and utilization of funds and other resources, of and by persons who seek to influence the legislative process." The proposal transferred administration to the comptroller general, avoided such words as "regulation" in favor of disclosure, and eliminated the controversial "principal purpose" test of the 1946 act.

It required registration of persons defined as falling within the measure's provisions and required detailed reports of receipts and expenditures every six months.

1976 Proposal

In 1976 there was action in both the Senate and the House on major lobbying legislation.

Senate Action. The Senate June 15 overrode the objections of an unusual coalition of lobby groups to pass, 82-9,

the Lobbying Disclosure Act of 1976 (S 2477). The bill would repeal the 30-year-old Federal Regulation of Lobbying Act and replace it with tighter regulation of organizations that seek to influence legislation before Congress directly and through "grass-roots" efforts.

Although there appeared to be unanimous agreement on the need for a new lobby law, as it came to the floor, the bill was opposed by virtually every major lobby group in Washington, with the exception of Common Cause. Among the groups critical of the measure were the AFL-CIO, Ralph Nader's Congress Watch, the National Association of Manufacturers, the Sierra Club, the American Civil Liberties Union, the Chamber of Commerce of the United States, the League of Women Voters and the U.S. Catholic Conference. Their reasons for opposition varied: some felt the disclosure requirements would unduly burden smaller organizations, some felt that the First Amendment freedoms of expression and association were abridged by the various disclosure requirements.

Groups meeting the bill's definition of lobbyists were required to register with the General Accounting Office and to provide information on the organization, its contributors, legislative interests, and on the persons lobbying on its behalf. Each quarter a lobbying group was to file a report on issues on which the organization had lobbied, and on gifts, loans or honoraria above a certain amount to a member or an employee of Congress. Also, in certain cases, it was to provide samples of its lobbying materials. The bill provided for both civil and criminal action against violators.

House Action. The House Judiciary Committee Aug. 25 ordered reported a bill (HR 15) regarded as less stringent than the measure passed by the Senate. Among the more important differences from the Senate bill were HR 15's exemption from coverage of small citizens' groups and voluntary associations; less voluminous record-keeping and reporting requirements and a less inclusive definition of a lobbyist than under the Senate bill.

HR 15 was under consideration by both the House Judiciary Committee and the Committee on Standards of Official Conduct (ethics committee). The ethics committee voted Sept. 2, 6-5, not to approve a speed-up plan that would have waived its jurisdiction over the bill. The plan had been proposed in order to enable the House to act on the measure prior to the scheduled Oct. 2 adjournment of the 94th Congress.

Footnotes

1. Douglass Cater, *Power in Washington* (Random House, 1964), p. 206.
2. *The Federalist Papers* (Mentor, 1961), No. 10, pp. 77-78.
3. Arthur M. Schlesinger Jr., *The Age of Jackson* (Little, Brown and Co., 1946), p. 84.
4. James Deakin, *The Lobbyists* (Public Affairs Press, 1966), p. 101.
5. *Ibid.*, pp. 197-99.
6. David B. Truman, *The Governmental Process* 10th ed. (Alfred A. Knopf, 1964), p. 389.
7. Donald R. Matthews, "Senators and Lobbyists," *Congressional Reform*, ed. Joseph Clark (Thomas Y. Crowell Co., 1965), pp. 182-83.
8. *Ibid.*, pp. 191-93.
9. Emanuel Celler, "Pressure Groups in Congress," *Annals of the American Academy of Political and Social Science*, September 1958, p. 241.
10. Cater, *Power in Washington*, p. 209.
11. Matthews, "Senators and Lobbyists," pp. 194-96.

12. Merriman Smith, *The Good New Days* (Bobbs-Merrill, 1962), pp. 198-200.
13. Lester W. Milbrath, *The Washington Lobbyists* (Rand McNally Co., 1963), pp. 216-17.
14. Richard Bolling, *House Out of Order* (E. P. Dutton Co., 1965), p. 141.
15. Lewis Anthony Dexter, *How Organizations Are Represented in Washington* (Bobbs-Merrill, 1969), p. 62.
16. Truman, *The Governmental Process*, p. 354.
17. Deakin, *The Lobbyists*, p. 107.
18. *Ibid.*, pp. 103-104.
19. Congressional Quarterly, *Weekly Report*, June 21, 1975, p. 1310.
20. Kenneth G. Crawford, *The Pressure Boys* (Julian Messner Inc., 1939), pp. 46-52.
21. Deakin, *The Lobbyists*, pp. 74-75.
22. George H. Haynes, *The Senate of the United States: Its History and Practice*, 2 vols. (Houghton Mifflin Co., 1938), vol. 1, pp. 499-500.
23. Karl Schriftgiesser, *The Lobbyists* (Little, Brown & Co., 1951), pp. 52-53, 155.

24. *Ibid.,* p. 68.

25. Crawford, *The Pressure Boys,* p. 56.

26. *Public Papers of the Presidents of the United States: Harry S Truman, 1948* (Government Printing Office, 1964), p. 916.

27. Frank M. Buchanan, press statement, Oct. 18, 1950.

28. U.S. Congress, House, Committee on Armed Services, *Report on Employment of Retired Commissioned Officers by Defense Department Contractors,* H Res 19, 86th Cong., 1st sess., 1960, p. 11.

29. U.S. Congress, Senate, Committee on Foreign Relations, *Activities of Nondiplomatic Representatives of Foreign Principals in the United States, Hearings,* 88th Cong., 1st sess., 1963, pt. 5, p. 553.

30. U.S. Congress, Senate, Committee on Government Operations, *Lobbying Disclosure Act of 1976,* S Rept 94-763 to accompany S 2477, 94th Cong., 2nd sess., 1976, pp. 3-4.

31. Stuart D. Halpert, *Participation in the Development of Legislative Policy: Some Guidelines for 501(c)(3) Tax-Exempt Organizations* (National Health Council Inc., 1975), p. 12.

Selected Bibliography

Books

Blaisdell, Donald C. *American Democracy Under Pressure.* New York: Ronald Press, 1957.

——. *Unofficial Government: Pressure Groups and Lobbies.* Philadelphia: American Academy of Political and Social Science, 1958.

Bolling, Richard. *House Out of Order.* New York: E.P. Dutton Co., 1965.

Cater, Douglass. *Power in Washington.* New York: Random House, 1964.

Chase, Stuart. *Democracy Under Pressure.* Westport, Conn.: Greenwood Press, 1945.

Clark, Joseph, ed. *Congressional Reform.* New York: Thomas Y. Crowell, 1965.

Crawford, Kenneth G. *The Pressure Boys.* New York: Julian Messner, Inc., 1939.

Deakin, James. *The Lobbyists.* Washington D.C.: Public Affairs Press, 1966.

Dexter, Lewis Anthony. *How Organizations Are Represented in Washington.* Indianapolis: Bobbs-Merrill, 1969.

Greenstone, J. David. *Labor in American Politics.* New York: Alfred A. Knopf, 1969.

Haider, Donald H. *When Governments Come to Washington: Governors, Mayors and Intergovernmental Lobbying.* New York: Free Press, 1974.

Hall, Donald R. *Cooperative Lobbying: The Power of Pressure.* Tucson: University of Arizona Press, 1969.

Harris, Joseph P. Congress and the Legislative Process. New York: McGraw-Hill, 1963.

Haynes, George H. *The Senate of the United States: Its History and Practice.* 2 vols. Boston: Houghton Mifflin, 1938.

Herring, E. Pendleton. *Group Representation before Congress.* Baltimore: Johns Hopkins Press, 1929.

Key, V. O. *Politics, Parties and Pressure Groups.* 5th ed. New York: Thomas Y. Crowell Co., 1964.

Koenig, Louis W. *The Invisible Presidency.* New York: Rinehart and Co., Inc., 1960.

Lane, Edgar. *Lobbying and the Law.* Berkeley: University of California Press, 1964.

Mahood, H.R. *Pressure Groups in American Politics.* New York: Charles Scribner's Sons, 1967.

Milbrath, Lester W. *The Washington Lobbyists.* Chicago: Rand McNally Co., 1963.

Murphy, Thomas P. *Pressures Upon Congress: Legislation by Lobby.* New York: Barron's Education Series, 1973.

Poore, Ben Perley. *Perley's Reminiscences of Sixty Years in The National Metropolis.* New York: W. A. Houghton, 1886.

Schlesinger, Arthur M. Jr. *The Age of Jackson.* Boston: Little, Brown and Co., 1946.

Scott, Andrew and Hunt, Margaret. *Congress and Lobbies: Image and Reality.* Chapel Hill: University of North Carolina Press, 1966.

Shriftgiesser, Karl. *The Lobbyists.* Boston: Little, Brown and Co., 1951.

Smith, Merriman. *The Good News Days.* Indianapolis: Bobbs-Merrill, 1962.

Truman, David B. *The Governmental Process.* 10th ed. New York: Alfred A. Knopf, 1964.

The Washington Lobby. Washington: Congressional Quarterly, 1971.

Articles

Boeckel, Richard. "Regulation of Congressional Lobbies." *Editorial Research Reports,* vol. 1, 1928, pp. 207-34.

Brewer, F. M. "Congressional Lobbying." *Editorial Research Reports,* vol. 1, 1946, pp. 314-33.

Celler, Emanuel. "Pressure Groups in Congress." *Annals of the American Academy of Political and Social Science,* September 1958.

Freeman, Dale C. "The Poor and the Political Process: Equal Access to Lobbying." *Harvard Journal on Legislation,* March 1969, pp. 369-92.

Halpert, Stuart D. *Participation in the Development of Legislative Policy: Some Guidelines for 501 (c)(3) Tax-Exempt Organizations.* Washington, D.C.: National Health Council, 1975.

Government Publications

U.S. Congress. Committee on Armed Services. *Report on Employment of Retired Commissioned Officers by Defense Department Contractors.* 86th Cong., 1st sess., 1960.

U.S. Congress. House. Committee on Standards of Official Conduct. *Regulation of Lobbying. Hearings, October 1-8, 1970, on House Resolution 1031.* 91st Cong., 2nd sess., 1970.

U.S. Congress. House Select Committee on Lobbying Activities. *General Interim Report.* 81st Cong., 2nd sess., 1950.

——. *Hearings on Lobbying. Direct and Indirect.* 81st Cong., 2nd sess., 1950.

——. *Hearings on the Role of Lobbying in Representative Self-Government.* 81st Cong., 2nd sess., 1950.

U.S. Congress. Senate. Committee on Foreign Relations. *Hearings on the Activities of Nondiplomatic Representatives of Foreign Principals in the United States.* 88th Cong., 1st sess., 1963.

U.S. Congress. Senate. Committee on Government Operations. *Lobbying Disclosure Act of 1976.* S Rept 94-763 to accompany S 2477. 94th Cong., 2nd sess., 1976.

QUALIFICATIONS AND CONDUCT OF MEMBERS

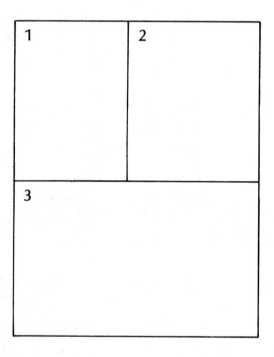

1. Assault on Sen. Charles Sumner (R Mass.) by Rep. Preston S. Brooks (State Rights Dem S.C.) in the Senate chamber, May 22, 1856. (Library of Congress photo no. LC-USZ62-3548.)

2. Congressional row in the House, midnight of Feb. 5, 1858, during debate on the Kansas statehood bill. (Library of Congress photo no. LC-USZ62-3547.)

3. Members of the House being sworn in, Jan. 3, 1953; Speaker Joseph W. Martin Jr. (R Mass.) presiding. (USIA photo, National Archives photo no. 53-365, 1st accession.)

Seating and Disciplining
of Members

In laying down the authority of Congress to seat, unseat and punish its members, the Constitutional Convention of 1787 drew inspiration from its favorite concept, that of checks and balances. The Constitution, while empowering Congress to pass judgment on the qualifications of members, put bounds on that power by listing certain mandatory qualifications. In carrying out the concept of a balance of power among the branches of the federal government, the judicial branch has been called on at various times to interpret the authority of Congress under the constitutional clauses on membership qualifications and on punishment of members' misconduct.

The power of Congress to determine whether a member-elect fulfills the requirements for service as a national legislator has come into conflict, over the years, with the right of voters in each state to decide who shall represent them. When Congress has ruled on disputed elections, the uncertain citizenship of a member-elect, or other questions of competence, senators or representatives from all over the country have decided whether a state may or may not be represented in Washington by a person certified by the state as the choice of its electorate.

Although Congress has acted often to determine the winner in contested elections, it has rejected the clear choice of the voters, for lack of the requisite qualifications, in fewer than 20 cases since 1789. Congress has shown like restraint in exercise of its constitutional right to punish or expel members for disorderly or improper conduct. Seven senators, 18 representatives and one territorial delegate have been formally censured by their colleagues for misconduct. Expulsions have numbered 15 in the Senate and three in the House.

Constitutional Provisions

The authority of Congress to judge the qualifications of members and to punish those who behave improperly rests on two clauses in Article I of the Constitution. The first is Clause 1 of Article I, Section 5, which reads in part: "Each House shall be the Judge of the Elections, Returns and Qualifications of its own members...." This clause would appear to give each house carte blanche in the validation of elections and the seating of members-elect. However, the election of members of Congress is regulated elsewhere in

Article I and in the Seventeenth Amendment. In addition, the Constitution specifically lists the qualifications required for membership in Congress.

The second clause on seating, unseating, and punishment of members is Clause 2 of Article I, Section 5, reading: "Each House may determine the Rules of its Proceedings, punish its Members for disorderly Behavior, and, with the Concurrence of two thirds, expel a Member." The original draft of this clause did not include the words "with the concurrence of two thirds." When the clause was considered in the Constitutional Convention, Aug. 10, 1787, James Madison of Virginia said that the right of expulsion was "too important to be exercised by a bare majority of a quorum, and in emergencies might be dangerously abused."[1] He therefore proposed requiring a two-thirds vote for expulsion.

Gouverneur Morris of Pennsylvania opposed Madison's proposal. He said: "This power may be safely trusted to a majority. To require more may produce abuses on the side of the minority. A few men from fractious motives may keep in a member who ought to be expelled."[2] But Edmund Randolph and George Mason of Virginia and Daniel Carroll of Maryland spoke in support of Madison's proposal, and it was adopted by a vote of 10 states in favor, one (Pennsylvania) divided and none opposed.

Judicial Interpretations

Litigation on the seating and disciplining of members of Congress reached the Supreme Court in the latter part of the 19th century in suits pivoting mainly on legalistic questions such as the power of Congress to subpoena witnesses when considering the qualifications of members. These suits afforded the court an opportunity to indicate bases upon which to judge the qualifications of members and to suggest the scope of punishment that may be imposed on members. In cases argued during the present century, the court has ruled more directly on the nature of the power of Congress to exclude members-elect and to punish or expel sitting members.

Application of the constitutional clause on judgment of the qualifications of members-elect has raised more questions of interpretation than has use of the authority to punish members. Perhaps the most serious of the issues involved in these cases has been whether exclusion of a member-elect deprives a state unwarrantedly, even for a short time, of its constitutionally guaranteed representation in Congress. The court ruled on this question in a case based on the 1926 contested election to the Senate of William S. Vare of Pennsylvania. It said that exclusion in such a case did not violate a state's rights. But the right of a state to send to Congress anyone it chooses, if he has the constitutionally listed qualifications and is legally elected, was upheld by the court in a 1969 case in which it reversed the exclusion of Adam Clayton Powell Jr. (D N.Y.) from the House of Representatives. *(Details, p. 687)*

Right to Compel Testimony, Imprison Members

The Supreme Court, in its 1880-81 term, handed down a decision which did not involve the seat or good standing of a member of either house of Congress but which specified a form of punishment which the House of Representatives might impose on a member guilty of misconduct. The case stemmed from an order by the House, March 14, 1876, for the arrest and detention of Hallett Kilbourn, a business broker in the District of Columbia, who had refused to produce papers needed in a House investigation of the bankruptcy of Jay Cooke and Co. Kilbourn brought suit, contending that punishment of an individual in his situation was not included in the powers allotted to Congress by the Constitution.

The year in which the House ordered Kilbourn's arrest was notable for financial scandals allegedly involving House members. Although the bankruptcy of the Cooke firm raised questions about the conduct of officers in an executive department rather than members of Congress, charges which arose in 1876 over trading in Union Pacific Railroad bonds and maneuverings of the Credit Mobilier affected several House members, including Speaker James G. Blaine (R Maine). The *Kilbourn* case therefore proceeded in an atmosphere of suspicion about the financial dealings of House members.

Justice Samuel F. Miller delivered the opinion of the Supreme Court in *Kilbourn v. Thompson* (103 U.S. 168). The court ruled that the House had exceeded its jurisdiction in investigating the Cooke bankruptcy and, thus, denied the right of the House to imprison Kilbourn for refusing to testify.

The court then went on to discuss the circumstances under which the House could use imprisonment and compel testimony. Speaking in the context of calls for punishment of members accused of unethical financial involvement in the businesses under investigation, it said:

● "The Constitution expressly empowers each House to punish its own members for disorderly behavior. We see no reason to doubt that this punishment may in a proper case be imprisonment."

● "Each House is by the Constitution made the judge of the election and qualifications of its members. In deciding on these it has an undoubted right to examine witnesses and inspect papers, subject to the usual rights of witnesses in such cases; and it may be that a witness would be subject to like punishment at the hands of the body engaged in trying a contested election, for refusing to testify, that he would if the case were pending before a court of judicature."

Although the *Kilbourn* case established the right of each house of Congress to compel testimony, that right was nevertheless challenged in a subsequent case which centered on legislation enacted prior to the *Kilbourn* case. That legislation, enacted in 1857 and amended in 1862, required witnesses to answer summonses and respond to questions on "any matter" before either chamber or any congressional committee.[3] Interpretation of the words "any matter" as used in the legislation came into play in an investigation of stock deals of senators charged with corruption in regard to tariff legislation.

Elverton R. Chapman, a New York stockbroker, was indicted Oct. 1, 1894, for violating the 1857 and 1862 statutes by refusing to answer questions about the accounts of the senators under question. Chapman's lawyers contended that the statutes were unconstitutional and that the Senate had no right to demand answers to questions about the accounts. The case reached the Supreme Court on appeal. Chief Justice Melville W. Fuller on April 19, 1897, delivered the opinion of the court, which reaffirmed the right of either chamber to compel testimony in matters which were within that chamber's jurisdiction. The opinion also defined the circumstances under which either chamber might expel a member. The court said:

"Nor will it do to hold that the Senate had no jurisdiction to pursue the particular inquiry because the preamble and resolutions did not specify that the proceedings were taken for the purpose of censure or expulsion, if certain facts were disclosed by the investigation. The matter was within the range of the constitutional powers of the Senate. The resolutions adequately indicated that the transactions referred to were deemed by the Senate reprehensible and deserving of condemnation and punishment. The right to expel extends to all cases where the offense is such as in the judgment of the Senate is inconsistent with the trust and duty of a member" (*In re Chapman,* 166 U.S. 661).

Question of Automatic Expulsion

The reference to expulsion in the court's opinion of 1897 was supplemented in an opinion handed down in 1906 interpreting an act of Congress approved June 11, 1864. The act provided that any senator or representative found guilty of illegally receiving compensation for services rendered in connection with a claim, contract or other proceeding before a government agency "shall...be rendered forever thereafter incapable of holding any office...under the government of the United States."[4] Sen. Joseph R. Burton (R Kan.) had been convicted on a charge of illegally receiving such compensation, and the question of his right to retain his seat in the Senate consequently arose. Burton's lawyers contended that the 1864 law violated the constitutional right of the Senate to decide on expulsion of its members.

Justice John M. Harlan, delivering the court's opinion on May 21, 1906, said: "The final judgment of conviction did not operate, *ipso facto,* to vacate the seat of the convicted senator nor compel the Senate to expel him or to regard him as expelled by force alone of the judgment" (*Burton v. United States,* 202 U.S. 344). On the following day, the Senate asked its Committee on Privileges and Elections to report what options remained and what further action, if any, should be taken in relation to Burton's seat. Burton resigned on June 4, 1906, before the committee had prepared a report.

Exclusion for Misconduct in Primary Election

Misconduct, not by sitting members of Congress, but by a member-elect was the problem in the next major case requiring the Supreme Court to rule on the power of Congress to judge its members' qualifications. This case grew out of the Federal Corrupt Practices Act of June 25, 1910, as amended Aug. 19, 1911. The two laws limited the amount of money that a candidate for Congress could spend on his campaign.

Truman H. Newberry and 16 others were found guilty of conspiring to violate the corrupt practices legislation in the Democratic senatorial primary election of Aug. 27, 1918, in Michigan. Newberry's opponent in the primary was Henry Ford. The conviction was appealed up to the Supreme Court. Here, the issue was whether Congress, despite its lack of express authority to regulate primary elections, might exercise some control over them through its right to pass judgment on its members' qualifications.

In *Newberry v. United States* (256 U.S. 232), the court took a restrictive view of that right. It decided, May 2, 1921, that Congress did not have power to control in any way a state's party primaries or conventions for designating candidates for the Senate or the House. A concurring opinion by Justice Mahlon Pitney, in which Justices Louis D. Brandeis and John H. Clarke joined, went beyond the inapplicability of the Corrupt Practices Act to primaries. On the right of Congress to exclude Newberry, Pitney said: "I am unable to see how, in right reason, it can be held that one of the houses of Congress, on the just exercise of its power, may exclude an elected member for securing by bribery his nomination at the primary, if the regulation by law of his conduct at the primary is beyond the constitutional power of Congress itself."

The concurring opinion made the additional point that neither house, in judging the qualifications of its members, is authorized to set up standards having the effect of legislation.

Twenty years after the *Newberry* decision, the Supreme Court reversed itself on the right of Congress to legislate on primary elections. Justice Harlan F. Stone on May 26, 1941, delivered the opinion of the court in *United States v. Classic.* He said that the power to regulate national elections, assigned by the Constitution to Congress, "includes the authority to regulate primary elections when, as in this case, they are a step in the exercise by the people of their choice of representatives in Congress" (313 U.S. 299).

Right to Subpoena Ballot Boxes

Investigative powers inherent in the right of each house of Congress to judge the qualifications of its members, although passed on by the Supreme Court in the *Kilbourn* and *Chapman* cases, came up again as an unsettled question following the senatorial election of Nov. 2, 1926, in Pennsylvania. William S. Vare, Republican, was declared the winner of the election over William B. Wilson, Democrat. But in view of reports of corruption in the election, the Senate established a committee consisting of James A. Reed (D Mo.) and others to investigate the Pennsylvania election campaign. Reed and his committee filed a suit aimed at compelling local officials to produce ballot boxes for inspection. The ballot boxes were produced, but the question of the committee's right to sue remained open.

The question reached the Supreme Court in *Reed et al. v. County Commissioners of Delaware County, Pa.* (277 U.S. 376). Lawyers for the committee contended that its right to sue was derived from "powers of inquiry auxiliary to the power to judge the elections, returns, and qualifications of the members of the Senate, or auxiliary to the power to legislate for the regulation of the times and manner of holding senatorial elections." The court's opinion, delivered May 28, 1928, by Justice Pierce Butler, reaffirmed the right of each house of Congress to "secure information upon which to decide concerning elections" but ruled that the

---

Constitutional Qualifications for Membership in Congress

- A senator must be at least 30 years old and have been a citizen of the United States not less than nine years (Article I, Section 3, Clause 3).
- A representative must be at least 25 years old and have been a citizen not less than seven years (Article I, Section 2, Clause 2).
- Every member of Congress must be, when elected, an inhabitant of the state that he is to represent (Article I, Section 2, Clause 2, and Section 3, Clause 3).
- No one may be a member of Congress who holds any other "Office under the United States" (Article I, Section 6, Clause 2).
- No person may be a senator or a representative who, having previously taken an oath as a member of Congress to support the Constitution, has engaged in rebellion against the United States or given aid or comfort to its enemies, unless Congress has removed such disability by a two-thirds vote of both houses (Fourteenth Amendment, Section 3).

---

wording of the resolution setting up the Reed committee did not give it the right to sue. The Senate on Dec. 6, 1929, denied Vare his seat. *(p. 690)*

Denial of State Representation

Not until 1929 was the Supreme Court required to rule on the question whether a house of Congress, in excluding a member-elect, deprives a state, though only temporarily, of its right to representation. Presented for decision was a case involving that question in only a secondary way, but the court took the occasion to state its view on the question. The case arose because Thomas W. Cunningham, member of a William S. Vare-for-Senator organization, refused to answer a Senate committee's questions on the organization's funds. On March 22, 1928, the Senate adopted a resolution ordering Cunningham to be taken into custody. He petitioned for a writ of habeas corpus, contending that the Senate had exceeded its powers.

The case was appealed to the Supreme Court as *Barry et al. v. United States ex rel. Cunningham* (279 U.S. 597). In an opinion delivered by Justice George Sutherland on May 27, 1929, the court ruled that the Senate had not exceeded its jurisdiction in investigating Vare's election and confirmed its right to examine witnesses during the investigation.

The court referred to the contention that the power which the Constitution conferred on the Senate was the power of judging the elections, returns and qualifications of its members and that, the Senate having refused to seat Vare, he was not a member. "When a candidate is elected to either house, he of course is elected a member of the body; and when that body determines, upon presentation of his credentials, without first giving him his seat, that the election is void, there would seem to be no real substance in the claim that the election of a 'member' has not been adjudged. To hold otherwise would be to interpret the word 'member' with a strictness in no way required by the obvious purpose of the constitutional provisions,...which, so far as the present case is concerned, was to vest the Senate with the authority to exclude persons asserting membership, who either had not been elected or, what amounts to the same thing, had been elected by resort to fraud, bribery, corruption, or other sinister methods having the effect of vitiating the election."

The court then made a pronouncement on the most important issue presented in the case, although the issue was not central to the situation affecting Cunningham: "Nor is there merit in the suggestion that the effect of the refusal of the Senate to seat Vare pending investigation was to deprive the state of its equal representation in the Senate. The equal representation clause is found in Article V, which authorizes and regulates amendments to the Constitution, 'provided,...that no state, without its consent, shall be deprived of its equal suffrage in the Senate.' This constitutes a limitation upon the power of amendment and has nothing to do with a situation such as the one here presented. The temporary deprivation of equal representation which results from the refusal of the Senate to seat a member pending inquiry as to his election or qualifications is the necessary consequence of the exercise of a constitutional power, and no more deprives the state of its 'equal suffrage' in the constitutional sense than would a vote of the Senate vacating the seat of a sitting member or a vote of expulsion."

The Vare case was significant for one other question answered by the Supreme Court: whether Congress, in judging election cases, was violating the principle of separation of powers by exercising a judicial function. The court said that the Constitution, by authorizing Congress to be the judge of its members' qualifications, conferred on each house "certain powers which are not legislative but judicial in character," including the power "to render a judgment which is beyond the authority of any other tribunal to review."

Additional Qualifications for Membership

The Supreme Court in 1969, while pointing to the right of either house to expel a member for any kind of misconduct, limited the grounds on which a member-elect might be excluded to those specifically listed in the Constitution. Adam Clayton Powell Jr. (D N.Y.), whose exclusion gave rise to the case, was elected to the House of Representatives in 1944 and every two years thereafter. When the 90th Congress in 1967 denied Powell the seat to which he had been re-elected in 1966, on the ground that he had misappropriated public funds, Powell and 13 voters in his district brought suit against the officers of the House. *(Details of Powell case, p. 687)*

The central legal issues in the Powell suit were:
● Could the House add to the Constitution's three qualifications for House membership? The three were that the member be at least 25 years old, have been a U.S. citizen for at least seven years and be, when elected, an inhabitant of the state from which he was elected.
● Could the courts properly examine the actions of the House in such cases, order the House not to add to the Constitution's qualifications, and enforce this order?

U.S. District Judge George L. Hart Jr. ruled April 7, 1967, that he had no jurisdiction in the case and dismissed the suit.

The U.S. Court of Appeals for the District of Columbia on Feb. 28, 1968, affirmed the action of the lower court in dismissing the suit. The Court of Appeals stated that the case involved a political question, which, if decided, would constitute a violation of the separation of powers and produce an embarrassing confrontation between Congress and the courts.

Powell appealed the case to the Supreme Court where it was entered on the docket as *Adam Clayton Powell Jr. et al., Petitioners, v. John W. McCormack et al.* (395 U.S. 486). While the case was pending, the 91st Congress seated Powell, who had been re-elected again in 1968, but the court felt that the issues that had been raised, including Powell's claim for back pay, required settlement. By a 7-1 decision on June 16, 1969, the Supreme Court reversed the lower court. Chief Justice Earl Warren, delivering the opinion of the court, ruled that the House had improperly excluded Powell, a duly elected representative who met the constitutional requirements of age, residence and citizenship.

"In judging the qualifications of its members Congress is limited to the standing qualifications prescribed in the Constitution. Respondents (McCormack et al.) concede that Powell met these.... Therefore, we hold that, since Adam Clayton Powell Jr. was duly elected...and was not ineligible to serve under any provision of the Constitution, the House was without power to exclude him from its membership," Warren wrote.

In response to the question whether the court had jurisdiction over the matter, the court pointed out that the suit had been brought against the Speaker of the House, the majority and minority leaders, the ranking members of the committee that investigated Powell, and three functionaries of the House who had withheld his pay and denied him such perquisites as an office and staff. The Supreme Court held that under the speech or debate clause of the Constitution, the five members of Congress were immune from prosecution but that the three employees were liable for action. The court ruling was limited to the case at hand. No ruling was made on the power of a house of Congress to exclude or expel a properly elected member.

A claim for back pay was remanded to the U.S. District Court for the District of Columbia for further proceedings but was dismissed by Judge George L. Hart Jr. May 14, 1971, when Powell failed to press the matter.

Seating of Members-Elect

The Constitution provides in Article VI that senators and representatives "shall be bound by Oath or Affirmation, to support this Constitution." Congress in implementing that provision, has enacted laws, adopted rules and made ad hoc decisions. These determinations not only prescribed the form of the oath and procedures for administering it, but also settled such questions as whether a member whose right to his seat is disputed should take an oath before the dispute is settled or only after it has been settled in his favor. The ad hoc decisions have gone sometimes one way and sometimes another.

The oath of office of members of Congress was worded as follows by an Act of June 1, 1789: "I, A B, do solemnly swear (or affirm) that I will support the Constitution of the United States."[5] In the light of Civil War experience, this language was expanded by an Act of July 11, 1868, to read: "I, A B, do solemnly swear (or affirm) that I will support and defend the Constitution of the United States against all enemies, foreign and domestic; that I will bear true faith and allegiance to the same; that I take this obligation freely, without any mental reservation or purpose of evasion; and that I will well and faithfully discharge the duties of the office on which I am about to enter. So help me God."[6]

Before the first meeting of each Congress, the secretary of the Senate and the clerk of the next preceding House of Representatives compile lists of members-elect on the basis of certifications signed by the state governors and secretaries of state. At the first meeting of each house in the new Congress, the presiding officer (the Speaker in the House and the Vice President in the Senate) administers the oath orally in the form of a question beginning "Do you solemnly swear (or affirm)...?" and the answer by each new member is "I do." New members chosen by the states between regular elections are similarly sworn in when they take their seats.

The number of new members who are sworn in together has varied. In the Senate, the oath was administered in some Congresses to groups of four and in later Congresses to all new members at once; since 1927, the oath again has been administered to groups of four. In the House, the oath was administered for many years by state delegations; since 1929, to all new members at once.

Challenge Procedure

The right of a member-elect to take the oath of office and be seated may be challenged by an already seated member or by a private individual or group. A member-elect whose title to his seat is questioned presents himself in the usual way for the purpose of taking an oath. The presiding officer then, either on his own authority or, more often, on the basis of a motion, may ask the individual to stand aside while the oath is administered to other members-elect. Sometimes, instead, a member-elect is permitted to take the oath of office without prejudice, and a resolution calling for investigation of his right to the seat is introduced later.

If a member-elect has stood aside while others were sworn in, he nevertheless may be accorded the privilege of the floor. The House in particular has accorded to election contestants the privilege of speaking in behalf of their right to be seated. House Rule 33, which lists those who may be "admitted to the Hall of the House," includes "contestants in election cases during the pendency of their cases in the House." The Senate rule on admission to the floor does not address those involved in election contests. Traditionally, however, contestants have been granted the right to be present during consideration of their cases.

The question whether a claimant to a seat in Congress is entitled to it is usually referred to a committee. Sometimes, a select committee is established for this purpose; at other times, the question is referred to the Senate or House Committee on Administration or another standing committee. Often, the committee assigned such a question conducts hearings. The committee, in reporting its findings, usually presents a draft resolution incorporating its recommendations.

Controversies Over Qualifications

Whether Congress, or either house of Congress, had power to set up qualifications for membership beyond those listed by the Constitution, or power to overlook the lack of one of the constitutional requirements, was a question answered sometimes in the affirmative and sometimes in the negative. Until the Supreme Court gave a negative answer in the *Powell* case, Congress had acted from time to time as if it was entitled to add qualifications as well as to wink at failure to fulfill a stated qualification.

Alexander Hamilton initiated discussion of the question. In No. 60 of *The Federalist*, he wrote: "The qualifications of the persons who may...be chosen are defined and fixed in the Constitution, and are unalterable by the legislature."[7]

However, later authorities, including a committee of the House appointed in 1900 to consider the seating of a Mormon who had been convicted for polygamy, contended that the Constitutional Convention intended to empower Congress to add to the listed qualification. The committee concluded that if the Constitutional Convention had meant to limit the qualifications to those listed in the Constitution, it would have phrased them in the affirmative. They maintained, for example, that the framers would have written: "Every member of the House of Representatives shall be of the age of 25 years at least," rather than deliberately setting on the supposedly more flexible negative phrasing: "No person shall be a Representative who shall not have attained to the age of twenty-five years."

The question of qualifications was widely discussed over an extended period of time and Congress faced a dilemma on the matter. If it adhered rigidly to the constitutional list of requirements, it would be obligated to seat individuals regarded as obnoxious. If it excluded such individuals, it would be open to the charge of exceeding its powers. The issue first came to a head at the start of the Civil War.

The two houses added a qualification for membership in 1862. An act approved July 2 of that year, known as the "Ironclad Oath Law" or the "Test Oath Law," required members of the House and Senate to swear, before taking the oath of office, that they had never voluntarily borne arms against the United States or aided, recognized, or supported a jurisdiction hostile to the United States. This law remained in effect until the Fourteenth Amendment was ratified in 1868. Westel W. Willoughby wrote in *The Constitutional Law of the United States* that during the period in which this act was in force, "Congress imposed, in effect, a disqualification for membership in either of its houses which was not imposed by the Constitution."

At the same time, Willoughby pointed out: "Though neither house may formally impose qualifications additional to those mentioned in the Constitution, or waive those that are mentioned, they may, in practice, do either of these things. That is to say, in case these constitutional provisions are disregarded or added to by either of the houses of Congress, there is no judicial means of overruling their action."[8] The Supreme Court found otherwise in the *Powell* case. (p. 687)

Cases Occurring in the Senate

Only three senators-elect have been denied seats for lack of the requisite qualifications:

(1) Albert Gallatin, born in Geneva, became a citizen of the United States in 1785. When elected to the Senate by the Pennsylvania Legislature in 1793, he had not been a citizen nine years as required by the Constitution. He contended, however, that every man who had taken part in the Revolution was a citizen according to the law of reason and nature. The Senate on Feb. 28, 1794, adopted the following resolution by a vote of 14 yeas to 12 nays: "Resolved, That the election of Albert Gallatin to be a Senator of the United States was void, he not having been a citizen of the United States the term of years required as a qualification to be a Senator of the United States."[9]

(2) James Shields, a native of Ireland, was elected a senator from Illinois in 1848. When he appeared, March 5, 1849, to take his seat, at a special session of the Senate, the question of whether he had been a citizen the required

Senate Cases Involving Qualifications for Membership

Congress	Session	Year	Member-elect	Grounds	Disposition
3rd	1st	1793	Albert Gallatin (D Pa.)	Citizenship	*Excluded*
11th	1st	1809	Stanley Griswold (D Ohio)	Residence	Admitted
28th	1st	1844	John M. Niles (D Conn.)	Sanity	Admitted
31st	Special Senate	1849	James Shields (D Ill.)	Citizenship	*Excluded*
37th	2nd	1861	Benjamin Stark (D Ore.)	Loyalty	Admitted
40th	1st	1867	Phillip F. Thomas (D Md.)	Loyalty	*Excluded*
41st	2nd	1870	Hiram R. Revels (R Miss.)	Citizenship	Admitted
41st	2nd	1870	Adelbert Ames (R Miss.)	Residence	Admitted
59th	2nd	1907	Reed Smoot (R Utah)	Mormonism	Admitted*
69th	2nd	1926	Arthur R. Gould (R Maine)	Character	Admitted
74th	1st	1935	Rush D. Holt (D W.Va.)	Age	Admitted
75th	1st	1937	George L. Berry (D Tenn.)	Character	Admitted
77th	2nd	1942	William Langer (R N.D.)	Character	Admitted*
80th	1st	1947	Theodore G. Bilbo (D Miss.)	Character	Died before Senate acted

*Senate decided that a two-thirds majority, as in expulsion cases, would be required for exclusion. The resolution proposing exclusion did not receive a two-thirds majority.

Source: U.S. Senate, Committee on Rules and Administration, Subcommittee on Privileges and Elections, *Senate Election, Expulsion and Censure Cases from 1793 to 1972,* compiled by Richard D. Hupman, S. Doc. 92-7, 92nd Cong. 1st sess., 1972.

number of years was raised. Shields had been naturalized Oct. 21, 1840, and would not be a citizen until Oct. 20, 1849. Although Shields was seated on March 6, the Senate on March 15 adopted a resolution declaring his election void on the ground of insufficient years of citizenship. Shields then was elected to fill the vacancy thus created and was allowed to serve from Oct. 27, 1849.

(3) Philip F. Thomas of Maryland had given $100 to his son when the son entered the military service of the Confederacy. When Thomas was elected a U.S. senator by the Maryland Legislature in 1866, he was charged with being disloyal for giving aid and comfort to the enemy. The Senate voted 27 to 20 to exclude Thomas.

Exclusion proceedings based on the age qualification for senators were avoided, in two cases, by different means. When Henry Clay (D-R Ky.) arrived in Washington to take his seat, he lacked five months of the required 30 years. The Senate tacitly ignored this fact, and he was sworn in, Nov. 19, 1806. Rush D. Holt (D W.Va.) also had not reached the age of 30 when the time came for him to enter the Senate in 1935. He delayed the presentation of his credentials until his 30th birthday and was then admitted. The Senate later rejected, 62-17, a proposal to declare Holt's election invalid on the ground of age.

Exclusion Cases Rejected. Several cases in which exclusion proceedings were begun and failed are noteworthy. John M. Niles, elected to the Senate by the Connecticut Legislature in 1842, was unable to take his seat, owing to severe illness, when the 28th Congress first convened in December 1843. Because Niles showed signs of mental strain when he first appeared with his credentials in April 1844, the Senate appointed a committee to consider his case. After interviewing him, it reported that it was "satisfied that Mr. Niles is at this time laboring under mental and physical debility, but is not of unsound mind in the technical sense of that phrase; the faculties of his mind are subject to the control of his will; and there is no sufficient reason why he be not qualified and permitted to take his seat as a member of the Senate."[10] The Senate on May 16, 1844, accepted the committee's conclusion, and Niles took his seat.

Hiram R. Revels (R Miss.), a former slave, was elected to the Senate in 1870. He was challenged on the ground that he had not become a citizen until 1868, when the Fourteenth Amendment was ratified. The Senate ruled that the amendment made Revels retroactively a citizen, and the oath was administered to him.

On Feb. 23, 1903, Reed Smoot (R Utah) presented his credentials as a senator-elect. A group of Utah citizens opposed his seating on the ground that as a Mormon he favored polygamy and opposed the separation of church and state. The Senate administered the oath to Smoot on a tentative basis on March 4, 1903. The senator's eligibility was then studied by the Committee on Privileges and Elections, which on June 11, 1906, reported a resolution which would have declared Smoot not entitled to his seat. Sen. Philander C. Knox (R Pa.) contended Feb. 14, 1907, that Smoot's case involved expulsion rather than exclusion and therefore required a two-thirds vote: "There is no question as to Sen. Smoot's possessing the qualifications prescribed by the Constitution, and therefore we cannot deprive him of his seat by a majority vote."[11]

Knox's amendment requiring a two-thirds vote was agreed to as a first step. But an amendment to expel Smoot failed on a 27-43 vote. Then the exclusion resolution, with Knox's amendment, also failed, 28-42.

When Arthur R. Gould (R Maine) was elected to the Senate in 1926, various colleagues made an issue of the fact that some 14 years earlier he had been accused of involvement in bribery. Vice President Charles G. Dawes ruled out of order a resolution which would have prevented Gould from being sworn in. Gould later voted for a resolution, which was adopted, directing the Committee on Privileges and Elections to look into his case. In the committee's hearings on the matter, Gould contended that the attempt to deny him his seat contravened the right of Maine's citizens to send to Washington a senator of their choice. The committee on March 4, 1927, reported that Gould's alleged part in the bribery case had not been proved. He was later reimbursed by the Senate for the expenses he had incurred in defending himself before the committee.

In 1941, the right of William Langer (R N.D.) to a seat in the Senate was challenged. Opponents cited alleged misconduct on Langer's part during his service as governor of North Dakota and in other posts in that state's government. When an investigating committee recommended that Langer be excluded, the Senate added a two-thirds requirement, as it had done in the case of Reed Smoot, and then on March 27, 1942, voted down the proposed resolution.

The most recent exclusion case involving a senator-elect arose in January 1947, when Theodore G. Bilbo (D Miss.) presented himself for swearing in. Bilbo had been accused of fraud, violence in preventing blacks from voting, and other offenses. He was asked to stand aside when other senators-elect took the oath. In August 1947, before the question of his right to his seat had been settled, Bilbo died.

Cases Occurring in the House

Ten members-elect have been excluded from the House of Representatives on the ground that they were not qualified to serve. John Bailey of Massachusetts was the first to be excluded. He was challenged on the ground that he was not a resident of the district that he purported to represent. The House, by a resolution of March 18, 1824, declared that Bailey was not entitled to his seat. He returned home, was elected to fill the vacancy created by his exclusion, and was seated Dec. 13, 1824.

In 1867, southern states elected to Congress four citizens whom the House found to be tainted with acts of disloyalty during the Civil War. They were John Y. Brown and John D. Young of Kentucky; W. D. Simpson of South Carolina; and John A. Wimpy of Georgia. The Kentuckians were Democrats; the two others, independents. All four were excluded.

South Carolina had another representative-elect excluded three years later. Benjamin F. Whittemore, a Republican, was censured by the House in 1870 for selling appointments to the U.S. Military Academy and resigned on Feb. 24 of that year. When Whittemore was re-elected to the same Congress, Rep. John A. Logan (D Ill.) discussed his case on the House floor: "It is said that the constituency has the right to elect such member as they deem proper. I say no. We cannot say that he shall be of a certain politics, or of a certain religion, or anything of that kind; but, Sir, we have the right to say that he shall not be a man of infamous character."[12] The House on June 21, 1870, excluded Whittemore by a vote of 130 to 76.

The House based two exclusions on polygamy. George Q. Cannon was elected in 1872 as a delegate from Utah Territory. In the first and second sessions of the 43rd Congress, the question of his eligibility was raised and was settled in his favor. Cannon served in the House until 1881 without being challenged, but in 1882 the issue arose again. The House, taking account both of Cannon's practice of polygamy and of doubts about the validity of his election, declared the seat vacant, in effect excluding Cannon.

In 1900, members of the House questioned the right of Brigham H. Roberts, elected as a representative from Utah, to take his seat. Roberts had been found guilty some years earlier of violating an 1882 law which prohibited polygamy. This was the case, mentioned earlier, in which an investigating committee argued that the Founding Fathers had not foreclosed the right of Congress to establish qualifications for membership other than those mentioned in the Constitution. The House refused to seat Roberts. There were 268 votes for exclusion, 50 against. *(p. 685)*

In the 20th century, only Victor L. Berger, Wisconsin Socialist, and Adam Clayton Powell Jr., New York Democrat, have been excluded from the House. Berger had been convicted in 1919 of violating the Espionage Act of June 15, 1917, by publishing anti-war statements. While an appeal was pending, he was elected to the 66th Congress. By resolution of the House, Nov. 10, 1919, Berger was declared "not entitled to take the oath of office as a representative."[13] He was re-elected during the same Congress and excluded again on Jan. 10, 1920. But after the Supreme Court had reversed Berger's conviction, he was elected to the House three more times, in 1922, 1924 and 1926, and was seated without question.

Cases in which House proceedings on exclusion ended in admission of the representative-elect evoked various memorable exchanges on the floor. An example is the case of John C. Conner (D Texas), who was accused of having whipped black soldiers under his command in 1868 and of having boasted in 1869 that he would escape conviction by a military court by bribing witnesses. Rep. James A. Garfield (R Ohio), speaking in the House on March 31, 1870, raised a constitutional question on this case: "Allow me to ask...if anything in the Constitution of the United States...forbids that a 'moral monster' shall be elected to Congress?"[14] Rep. Ebon C. Ingersoll (R Ill.) replied: "I believe the people may elect a moral monster to Congress if they see fit, but I believe that Congress has a right to exclude that moral monster from a seat if they see fit."[15] A resolution allowing Conner to take his seat was adopted the same day.

The Powell Case

One of the stormiest episodes in congressional history was the precedent-shattering case of Rep. Adam Clayton Powell Jr. It was Powell's exclusion from the House that resulted in the Supreme Court ruling that Congress could not add to the constitutional qualifications for membership in Congress. In 1937, Powell succeeded his father as pastor of the Abyssinian Baptist Church in Harlem, one of the largest congregations in the country. The new pastor was elected to the 79th Congress in 1944 with the nomination of both the Democratic and Republican Parties. He took his seat with the Democrats, was re-elected regularly by large majorities, served as chairman of the House Committee on Education and Labor from 1961 to 1967, and was considered by many observers the most powerful black in the United States. Throughout his legislative career, he retained his pastorate.

Court Suits

Powell's downfall was brought on in part by his flamboyant personality and his apparent disregard for the law. On the eve of Powell's 1952 re-election bid, he was informed by the Internal Revenue Service that he had underestimated his 1945 income tax by $2,749. A federal grand

House Cases Involving Qualifications for Membership

Congress	Session	Year	Member-elect	Grounds	Disposition
1st	1st	1789	William L. Smith (Fed S.C.)	Citizenship	Admitted
10th	1st	1807	Philip B. Key (Fed Md.)	Residence	Admitted
10th	1st	1807	William McCreery (— Md.)	Residence	Admitted
18th	1st	1823	Gabriel Richard (Ind Mich. Terr.)	Citizenship	Admitted
18th	1st	1823	John Bailey (Ind Mass.)	Residence	*Excluded*
18th	1st	1823	John Forsyth (D Ga.)	Residence	Admitted
27th	1st	1841	David Levy (R Fla. Terr.)	Citizenship	Admitted
36th	1st	1859	John Y. Brown (D Ky.)	Age	Admitted
40th	1st	1867	William H. Hooper (D Utah Terr.)	Mormonism	Admitted
40th	1st	1867	Lawrence S. Trimble (D Ky.)	Loyalty	Admitted
40th	1st	1867	John Y. Brown (D Ky.)	Loyalty	*Excluded*
40th	1st	1867	John D. Young (D Ky.)	Loyalty	*Excluded*
40th	1st	1867	Roderick R. Butler (R Tenn.)	Loyalty	Admitted
40th	1st	1867	John A. Wimpy (Ind Ga.)	Loyalty	*Excluded*
40th	1st	1867	W. D. Simpson (Ind S.C.)	Loyalty	*Excluded*
41st	1st	1869	John M. Rice (D Ky.)	Loyalty	Admitted
41st	2nd	1870	Lewis McKenzie (Unionist Va.)	Loyalty	Admitted
41st	2nd	1870	George W. Booker (Conservative Va.)	Loyalty	Admitted
41st	2nd	1870	Benjamin F. Whittemore (R S.C.)	Malfeasance	*Excluded*
41st	2nd	1870	John C. Conner (D Texas)	Misconduct	Admitted
43rd	1st	1873	George Q. Cannon (R Utah Terr.)	Mormonism	Admitted
43rd	2nd	1874	George Q. Cannon (R Utah Terr.)	Polygamy	Admitted
47th	1st	1881	John S. Barbour (D Va.)	Residence	Admitted
47th	1st	1882	George Q. Cannon (R Utah Terr.)	Polygamy	Seat vacated[1]
50th	1st	1887	James B. White (R Ind.)	Citizenship	Admitted
56th	1st	1899	Robert W. Wilcox (Ind Hawaii Terr.)	Bigamy, treason	Admitted
56th	1st	1900	Brigham H. Roberts (D Utah)	Polygamy	*Excluded*
59th	1st	1905	Anthony Michalek (R Ill.)	Citizenship	Admitted
66th	1st	1919	Victor L. Berger (Socialist Wis.)	Sedition	*Excluded*
66th	2nd	1920	Victor L. Berger (Socialist Wis.)	Sedition	*Excluded*
69th	1st	1926	John W. Langley (R Ky.)	Criminal misconduct	Resigned
70th	1st	1927	James M. Beck (R Pa.)	Residence	Admitted
71st	1st	1929	Ruth B. Owen (D Fla.)	Citizenship	Admitted
90th	1st	1967	Adam C. Powell Jr. (D N.Y.)	Misconduct	*Excluded*[2]

1. *Discussions of polygamy and an election contest led to a declaration that the seat was vacant.*
2. *Supreme Court June 16, 1969, ruled that the House had improperly excluded Powell.*

Sources: Hinds and Cannon, *Precedents of the House of Representatives of the United States,* 11 vols. (1935-41); Joint Committee on Congressional Operations, *House of Representatives Exclusion, Censure and Expulsion Cases from 1789 to 1973,* committee print, 93rd Cong., 1st sess., 1973.

jury indicted him in 1958 on a charge of tax evasion. In the ensuing trial, held in 1960, the jury was unable to reach a verdict. The case was dismissed the following year, but the IRS continued to dun Powell. In 1966, he paid $27,833.17 in back taxes and penalties.

The Harlem representative became involved in civil litigation after he had said, in a television interview in 1960, that Esther James, a widow in his district, was a "bag woman," or graft collector, for New York City policemen. James sued Powell for libel. He was ordered by the court to pay her an amount set originally at $211,739 and reduced, on appeal, to $46,500. That sum plus court costs was paid in 1965-67, in part by Powell directly and in part by a record company from royalties on Powell's record "Keep the Faith, Baby."

A second civil case against Powell was instituted by James in 1964 on the basis of an allegation that the representative had fraudulently transferred property to avoid paying the original libel judgment. In this case, a jury awarded James $350,000. That amount was reduced later to $155,785, including $100,000 in punitive damages. The New York Court of Appeals in 1967 eliminated the punitive damages. Powell, after further delays, ultimately paid the remainder. Meanwhile, he had been held in contempt of court on four occasions.

Committee Revolt

In 1966, Powell also ran into trouble from the members of his Education and Labor Committee. That committee had reported a bill authorizing President Johnson's anti-poverty program. Powell favored the legislation but, by long absences and for personal reasons, he delayed bringing it up for floor debate. Angered by the delay, Powell's Democratic colleagues on the committee moved to strip him of most of his basic powers as committee chairman. By a vote of 27 to 1, the committee Sept. 22, 1966, adopted new rules, one of which provided that if the chairman failed to bring a bill to the floor, one of the six subcommittee chairmen could do so.

The House Democratic Caucus on Jan. 9, 1967, removed Powell from the chairmanship of the Committee on Education and Labor for the duration of the 90th Congress. This was the first time since 1925 that a committee chairman had been deposed in either house of Congress. Powell, who attended the caucus, called the action "a lynching, northern style."[16] A day later, Powell was embroiled in a challenge to his seat in the House.

Exclusion Proceedings

In the 1950s and the early 1960s, Powell repeatedly went on costly pleasure trips at government expense. In addition, he incurred criticism for taking a staff member, Corinne A. Huff, on many trips to Bimini Island in the Bahamas. Out of government funds, he paid his wife $20,578 a year as a clerk while she lived in Puerto Rico. The Special Contracts Subcommittee of the House Committee on Administration on Jan. 3, 1967, recommended that Mrs. Powell be dropped from the payroll, as was done soon thereafter.

But Powell's apparent misuse of public funds and his continued legal problems in New York had generated much furor among the public and members of Congress, and on Jan. 10, 1967, the House took up the question of whether Powell should be seated.

A resolution submitted by Morris K. Udall (D Ariz.) proposed that Powell be sworn in, pending the result of a 60-day investigation of his conduct by a select committee. Udall contended that stripping Powell of his chairmanship was punishment enough, since his malfeasance was based on his misuse of that position. But the resolution was rejected on a 126-305 vote.

The House then adopted a resolution, offered by Minority Leader Gerald R. Ford (R Mich.), which denied Powell his seat pending an investigation. The vote was 363 to 65.

House Judiciary Committee Chairman Emanuel Celler (D N.Y.) was chairman of the select committee appointed to investigate Powell's qualifications for his seat. The committee conducted hearings beginning Feb. 8, 1967. Its report, submitted Feb. 23, included a recommendation, unprecedented in congressional history, that Powell be fined. The committee proposed that he be sworn in; that his seniority be based on the date of his swearing in; that he be censured for "gross misconduct" through misuse of funds of the Committee on Education and Labor, refusal to pay the judgment against him, and noncooperation with House investigating committees; and that he be fined $40,000, to be paid to the clerk of the House in the form of a monthly deduction of $1,000 from Powell's salary, in order to "offset any civil liability of Mr. Powell to the United States."[17]

The House on March 1, 1967, rejected the committee's proposals and adopted instead a resolution excluding Powell from the 90th Congress—the first exclusion since Victor L. Berger was barred in 1919 and 1920. On the select committee's proposals, the vote was 202 in favor, 222 against; on the exclusion resolution, 307 in favor, 116 against.

As in his ouster from his committee chairmanship, Powell ascribed his downfall to racism. That racial feeling played a part in the vote to exclude Powell seemed probable. Rep. Celler said on television and on the House floor that he saw "an element of racism in the vote."[18] Arlen

J. Large, a Washington correspondent, wrote in the *Wall Street Journal,* March 22, 1967: "Disclaimers of race as a factor in Mr. Powell's exclusion don't jibe with the nearly solid anti-Powell votes of southern congressmen, reflecting the bitterly worded letters from white voters back home."

Suit Filed

In his appearances before the select committee, Powell responded only to questions relating to the constitutional requirements for House membership—his age, citizenship and inhabitancy. These were the only questions that the House could properly inquire into, Powell and his lawyers claimed. Upon his exclusion by the House, Powell filed suit. The case eventually reached the Supreme Court, which on June 16, 1969, ruled that the House had improperly excluded Powell, a duly elected representative who met the constitutional requirements for membership. *(Details p. 684)*

Powell Seated

Meanwhile, New York State conducted a special election April 11, 1967, in Powell's Harlem district to fill the vacancy. Powell entered his name as a candidate but was unable to return to New York City to campaign without being arrested for contempt. Nevertheless, he was elected with 86 per cent of the vote. Powell, however, did not apply to the House to be seated but remained at his vacation retreat on Bimini, waiting the outcome of his lawsuit against the exclusion.

On April 5, 1968, Powell returned to his district where he was arrested and then released because the litigation in which he was involved was under appeal. In the general election of 1968, he again became a candidate for a seat in Congress and once more was victorious at the polls. The 91st Congress on Jan. 3, 1969, ended his two-year exile. Powell was sworn in and seated but subjected to loss of seniority and fined $25,000. In the voting on the resolution imposing these penalties, there were 254 yeas, 158 nays.

Although he had won the right to be seated, Powell rarely attended Congress, preferring instead his retreat in Bimini. In 1970 Charles B. Rangel successfully challenged Powell in the Democratic primary and went on to win the general election. Powell died in Miami, Fla., April 4, 1972.

Contested Elections

Decentralization of control over elections in the United States may have strengthened participatory democracy, but it has led frequently to controversy over election results. Losing candidates and their supporters believe in many cases that more voters were on their side than the official count showed. Floyd M. Riddick wrote in *The United States Congress; Organization and Procedure:* "Seldom if ever has a Congress organized without some losing candidate for a seat in either the Senate or House contesting the right of the member-elect to be senator or representative, as the case might be, as a result of the election in which the losing candidate participated."[19]

To avert partisanship in settling election disputes involving members of the House, an act of 1798 established procedures to be followed in handling contested cases; by its own terms the act expired in 1804. A law approved Feb. 19, 1851, renewed the effort to give the proceedings in contested elections of House members a judicial rather than partisan character, and amendments in 1873 and 1875 improved the procedure for taking testimony in such cases. But despite these efforts, fidelity to party determined the outcome in a large majority of the cases.

The Federal Contested Election Act of 1969 superseded the earlier legislation. The new law, which again applied only to House contests, prescribed procedures for instituting a challenge and presenting testimony, but it did not establish criteria to govern decisions. It was more restrictive than the 1798 and 1851 laws in providing that only candidates listed on the ballot or bona fide write-in candidates might contest election results. Previously, anyone having an interest in a congressional election could initiate proceedings by filing a petition.

Senators were chosen by state legislatures until the adoption in 1913 of the Seventeenth Amendment to the Constitution which provided for direct popular elections. Before then, contested senatorial elections often involved accusations of corruption in the legislatures. Neither before nor after 1913 did Congress enact any law on contested Senate elections comparable to the legislation on contested elections in the House.

It is generally agreed that since 1789, the number of contested elections in the House and Senate has run into the hundreds. An exact number is difficult to ascertain because students of the subject disagree on what constitutes a contested election. George B. Galloway of the Legislative Reference Service stated in 1953 that there had been 136 election contests in the Senate from 1789 to 1952. John T. Dempsey, in an unpublished 1956 University of Michigan doctoral dissertation, counted only 125 in the Senate from 1789 to 1955. [It appears that Galloway included, and Dempsey excluded, contested appointments made by state governors to fill seats vacated by death or otherwise.] In these same time periods, Galloway counted 541 House election contests while Dempsey put the number at 546.

Senate Cases

An illustrative 19th century election contest was that of Henry A. Du Pont (R Del.), who was excluded from the Senate because he had not been duly elected by the Delaware Legislature. Delaware law stated that 15 votes would be sufficient to elect a U.S. senator if the legislature consisted of 29 members; 16 votes, if it consisted of 30 members. Du Pont, in an election held in 1895, received 15 votes, but there was a question whether the legislature consisted of 29 or 30 members. Du Pont admitted that 30 votes had been cast, but he contended that one of the votes had been cast by a person who had no right to participate, because he had succeeded to the governorship through the death of the incumbent. The Senate on May 15, 1895, decided, by a vote of 31 to 30, that Du Pont was not entitled to the seat.

The more important 20th century cases have included those of Lorimer and Vare. William Lorimer (R Ill.) was elected a senator by the Illinois Legislature and took his seat in the Senate on June 18, 1909. In May 1910, he requested that the Committee on Privileges and Elections examine allegations made in the press that bribery and corruption had entered into his election. Following an investigation, the Senate on March 1, 1911, rejected a proposed resolution declaring that Lorimer had not been "duly and legally elected."[20] The vote was 40 for adoption of the resolution, 46 against.

The case, however, was reopened in the next Congress and the first decision reversed. A specially appointed committee took further testimony. While the committee majori-

ty favored dropping the charges, the minority proposed adoption of a resolution declaring Lorimer's election invalid on the ground of corruption. On June 13, 1912, the Senate adopted the resolution, 55-28.

Corruption was also the crux of the case of William S. Vare. During the primaries in Pennsylvania in 1926, newspapers charged that persons favoring Vare as the Republican nominee for senator were engaging in corrupt practices. Vare won the primary contest and the November election. The Senate meanwhile, on May 19, 1926, had appointed a committee to investigate Pennsylvania's senatorial primaries and the fall election. Following the election, Vare's Democratic rival, ex-Secretary of Labor William B. Wilson, charged that Vare had won through corruption. When Congress met, Vare was asked to stand aside while other senators-elect were sworn in.

Proceedings in Vare's case dragged on for two years, during which time Vare became seriously ill. The Senate received a series of reports on the case, including the report of a special committee, Feb. 22, 1929, asserting that Vare, owing to his excessive use of money to get nominated and elected, was not entitled to a seat in the Senate. Not until December 1929 did the Senate take final action on the matter. On Dec. 5, the Senate Committee on Privileges and Elections reported that Vare had received a plurality of the legal votes cast in the election. But the Senate on the following day voted 58-22 to deny Vare a seat. At the same time, it concluded by a vote of 66 to 15 that Wilson had not been elected. Subsequently, the governor of Pennsylvania appointed Joseph R. Grundy to the vacant Senate seat.

Wyman-Durkin Contest. The closest Senate election since popular voting for the Senate was instituted in 1913 occurred Nov. 5, 1974, in New Hampshire where Republican Louis C. Wyman led Democrat John A. Durkin by only two votes.

The election resulted in a prolonged dispute in the Senate covering seven months and 41 roll-call votes, and ending when the Senate reached a compromise and for the first time declared a vacancy due to its inability to decide an election contest.[21]

The dispute began when final unofficial returns gave Wyman a 355-vote margin over Durkin. A recount then found Durkin the winner by 10 votes. The state ballot commission examined the recount and found Wyman the winner by two votes.

Durkin filed a petition of contest with the Senate Dec. 27, 1974, challenging Wyman's right to the seat and defending the validity of his own recount victory. Wyman Jan. 5, 1975, filed a petition in the Senate urging that Durkin's petition be dismissed. He also asked that the seat be declared vacant which would open the way for a new election in New Hampshire. Wyman and his supporters feared that Durkin would win if the Senate, with its 61-38 Democratic majority, reviewed the ballot commission findings as the Democratic candidate requested.

The first skirmish occurred soon after the Senate convened. On Jan. 28, the Senate turned aside Republican attempts to temporarily seat Wyman and to declare the seat vacant and voted, 58-34, to send the dispute to the Senate Rules and Administration Committee. The Senate thus accepted the arguments of Senate Majority Leader Mike Mansfield (D Mont.) and Rules Chairman Howard W. Cannon (D Nev.), who cited the constitutional provision that each house of Congress should be the judge of its own elections and said the Rules Committee should at least try to determine who won before calling for a new election.

Democrats also said that the conflicting rulings of the New Hampshire authorities precluded seating either of the contestants, even though Wyman had the most recent certification. Republicans claimed that precedent dictated temporary seating of Wyman, without prejudice to Durkin's challenge. But the motion to temporarily seat Wyman failed on a 34-58 vote, while a motion to declare the seat vacant lost, 39-53.

The Rules Committee agreed to examine and recount the ballots in dispute. By April 25 nearly 1,000 ballots had been examined. But the committee failed to agree on 27 of the ballots, splitting on 4 to 4 tie votes. Tie votes also occurred on eight legal and procedural issues. The eight issues and 27 ballots were sent to the Senate floor to be resolved.

Floor consideration of the disputed election began June 12 with a second attempt by the Republicans to declare the seat vacant. The motion was defeated, 43-55, and a filibuster by Republicans and several southern Democrats supporting the Republican position began. An unprecedented six attempts were made to invoke cloture (shut off debate) but they all failed to obtain the required sixty votes. An attempt to settle one of the eight disputed issues in Wyman's favor July 15 was defeated on a 44-49 vote. After this loss, the Republicans charged that a Democratic "steamroller" was in operation and refused to allow a vote on any other issue.

The Senate began to spend less and less time each day on the New Hampshire dispute and returned to debate on substantive legislation. But neither side appeared ready to compromise. In the absence of any definitive Senate action, public pressure mounted for a vacancy to be declared and a new election held.

Finally, Durkin relented and asked for a new election. Durkin's change of mind came as a complete surprise to the Senate Democratic leadership, but there was a general feeling of relief that the impasse at last had been broken. The Senate June 30 voted 71-21 to declare the seat vacant as of Aug. 8.

Durkin won the special Sept. 16 election with 53.6 per cent of the vote and was sworn in Sept. 18, 1975.

Bellmon Challenged. A second case occurring during the 94th Congress proved the exception to the norm that a member of the minority party cannot win an election contest. Republican incumbent Henry Bellmon had been certified the victor of the November 1974 Oklahoma Senate election by 3,835 votes and was seated by the Senate in January 1975 pending the outcome of a challenge. The Democratic candidate, former Rep. Ed Edmondson, charged that the absence of a straight-ticket lever on voting machines in Tulsa County and confusing voter instructions cost him sufficient votes to have changed the outcome.

The Senate Rules and Administration Committee Dec. 15, 1975, declared that it could not decide which of the two candidates had won the election and sent the dispute to the floor. Under the committee resolution, the Senate could vote to dismiss the challenge, which would confirm Bellmon in office, or it could declare the seat vacant, as it ultimately did in the Wyman-Durkin contest.

After three days of debate, the Senate settled the issue by voting March 4, 1976, to seat Bellmon.[22]

House Cases

George F. Hoar (R Mass.), who served in both houses, wrote in his *Autobiography of Seventy Years* in 1903:

"Whenever there is a plausible reason for making a contest, the dominant party in the House almost always awards the seat to the man of its own side."[23] Thomas B. Reed (R Maine) went further than Hoar's "almost always." In an article on contested elections published in the *North American Review* in 1890, while he was Speaker of the House, Reed wrote: "Probably there is not an instance on record where the minority was increased by the decision of contested cases."[24] While preparing to write a history of the House of Representatives, De Alva Alexander found, in 1906, that up to that time only three persons not of the dominant party had obtained seats in that chamber through the settlement of some hundreds of election contests.

William F. Willoughby asserted in *Principles of Legislative Organization and Administration* in 1934 that "The whole history of the handling of election contests by the House has constituted one of the major scandals of our political system."[25] Willoughby noted that after enactment of the 1851 law on procedures for adjudicating elections, "for many years the House made little or no pretense of settling election contests on any basis of equity, political considerations in practically all cases determining the decision reached." In 1955, John T. Dempsey, a doctoral candidate at the University of Michigan, made a case-by-case examination of the 546 contested election cases he had counted in the House. He found that only on 47 occasions, less than 10 per cent of the total, did the controlling party award a contested seat to a member of the minority party.

Mississippi Dispute. Perhaps the most dramatic election dispute which the House has settled in recent years was that of the Mississippi Five in 1965. The governor of Mississippi certified the election to the House in 1964 of four Democrats and one Republican. The Democrats were Thomas G. Abernethy, William M. Colmer, Jamie L. Whitten and John B. Williams; the Republican was Prentiss Walker. Their right to be seated in the House was contested by a biracial group, the Mississippi Freedom Democratic Party (M.F.D.P.), formed originally to challenge the seating of all-white delegates from the state to the 1964 Democratic National Convention. This group, when unsuccessful in getting its candidates on the 1964 congressional election ballot, conducted a rump election in which Annie Devine, Virginia Gray and Fannie L. Hamer were the winners.[26]

The three women, when they sought entrance to the House floor, were barred. However, Speaker John W. McCormack (D Mass.) asked the regular Mississippi representatives-elect to stand aside while the other members of the House were sworn in. Rep. William F. Ryan (D N.Y.), sponsor of the challenge, contended that the regular congressional election in Mississippi was invalid because blacks had been systematically prevented from voting. A resolution to seat the regular Mississippi delegation was adopted on Jan. 4, 1965, by a voice vote.

The M.F.D.P. on May 16, 1965, filed a brief and petition, with 600 depositions, citing officially inspired harassment of black voters in Mississippi and the admission by state officials of participation in prevention of black voting. The House Committee on Administration on Sept. 15 reported, by a vote of 15 to 9, a proposed resolution rejecting the petition, partly because the contestants had not availed themselves of the proper legal steps and because alleged voting discrimination had been made moot by the Voting Rights Act of 1965. The full House approved the resolution Sept. 17 by a vote of 228 to 143.

Assault on Charles Sumner, 1856

Sen. Charles Sumner (R Mass.), in a speech on the Senate floor, May 20, 1856, denounced in scathing language supporters of the Kansas-Nebraska Act of 1854, which repealed the Missouri Compromise of 1820 and permitted the two new territories to decide whether slavery would be allowed there. Two days later, while Sumner was seated at his desk on the Senate floor after the day's session had ended, he heard his name called. Looking up, he saw a tall stranger, who berated him for his speech and then struck him on the head repeatedly with a heavy walking stick, which was broken by the blows. Sumner fell bleeding and unconscious to the floor. He was absent from the Senate, because of the injuries suffered in the assault, for three and a half years, until Dec. 5, 1859.

The attacker was Rep. Preston S. Brooks (State Rights Dem. S.C.), nephew of one of those whom Sumner had excoriated—Sen. A. P. Butler (State Rights Dem. S.C.). Expulsion proceedings against Brooks failed, on a strictly party vote. He resigned his House seat, July 15, 1856, but was elected to fill the vacancy caused by his resignation.

Rep. Laurence M. Keitt (D S.C.) was censured by the House on July 15, 1856, for having known of Brooks' intention to assault Sumner, for having taken no action to discourage or prevent the assault, and for having been "present on one or more occasions to witness the same." Keitt resigned, July 16, 1856, and was elected to fill the vacancy caused by his resignation. A resolution similar to the one censuring Keitt but directed against Rep. Henry A. Edmundson (D Va.) had failed of adoption, July 15, 1856.

Discipline

For offenses of sufficient gravity, each house of Congress punishes its members by expulsion or censure. Of the two, censure is milder, requiring a simple majority vote while expulsion requires a two-thirds majority vote. Censure also has the advantage of not depriving constituents of their elected senators or representatives. Grounds for disciplining members usually consist of a member's action during service in Congress. Both houses have distrusted their power to punish a member for offenses committed prior to an election and they also have been shy about punishing misdeeds committed during a previous Congress.

For minor transgressions of the rules, the presiding officer of either house may call a member to order, without a formal move to censure. For example, on Jan. 14, 1955, Sen. Russell B. Long (D La.), while presiding over the Senate, called Sen. Joseph R. McCarthy (R Wis.) to order when McCarthy questioned the motives of some senators who had voted with him for a resolution continuing an investigation of Communists in government. Long said: "The statement of the junior senator from Wisconsin was that other senators were insincere. In making that statement, the senator from Wisconsin spoke contrary to the rules of the Senate.... He must take his seat."[27] Later on the same day, Long again called McCarthy to order.

In recent years, Congress has turned to other methods when it wants to discipline members but yet wants to avoid the strong measure of censure or expulsion. These methods have included denial of the member's right to vote, fines, stripping of chairmanships and reprimand.

Expulsion

Fifteen senators have been expelled, one in 1797 and 14 during the Civil War. Expulsion proceedings in the Senate have been instituted 12 times since the Civil War, always without success. In the House, only three members have been expelled, all of them in 1861. Of the five expulsion cases in the House since the Civil War, all were changed to censure cases, and the accused members were censured. Conspiracy against a foreign country (the 1797 case in the Senate) and support of a rebellion (the Civil War cases of 14 senators and three representatives) have been the only grounds on which a senator or representative has been expelled. In a few cases, a senator or representative escaped expulsion by resigning.

Grounds for Expulsion

In the successful expulsion cases, the grounds were conspiracy or disloyalty. The unsuccessful cases were concerned with the killing of a representative in a duel, the assaulting of a senator or a representative, treasonable or offensive utterances, sedition, corruption and Mormonism.

Prior Offenses. The most important question raised about the validity of grounds for expulsion has been whether a member of either house may be expelled for offenses committed prior to his election. John Quincy Adams, while serving in the Senate, submitted a committee report which affirmed the right of the Senate to expel a member for pre-election conduct that came to light after he had taken his seat. The case was that of John Smith (D Ohio), who allegedly had been connected with Aaron Burr's conspiracy to separate several of the western states from the Union. Adams' committee, in its report of Dec. 31, 1807, said: "When a man whom his fellow citizens have honored with their confidence on the pledge of a spotless reputation has degraded himself by the commission of infamous crimes, which become suddenly and unexpectedly revealed to the world, defective, indeed, would be that institution which should be impotent to discard from its bosom the contagion of such a member."[28]

The expulsion case against Smith was lost by a single vote on April 9, 1808, when 19 yeas, not enough to make up the required two-thirds, were cast for expulsion, against 10 nays. Later Congresses which debated proposals to unseat members repeatedly took up the question whether acts committed prior to the member's election furnished legitimate grounds for expulsion.

Incompatible Office. The Constitution, in Article I, Section 6, provides: "...no Person holding any Office under the United States, shall be a Member of either House during his Continuance in Office." When a senator or representative has accepted appointment to another "Office under the United States," he has jeopardized but not always lost his privilege of remaining in Congress, depending on the type of office he accepted and the attitude of the house in which he was serving. If he lost his post in Congress by accepting another office, he is not considered to have been expelled; his seat is treated as having been vacated.

The first of two significant cases in which this provision resulted in a sitting member's loss of his seat was that of

Cases of Expulsion in the Senate

Congress	Session	Year	Member	Grounds	Disposition
5th	2nd	1797	William Blount (Ind Tenn.)	Anti-Spanish conspiracy	*Expelled*
10th	1st	1808	John Smith (D Ohio)	Disloyalty	Not expelled
35th	1st	1858	Henry M. Rice (D Minn.)	Corruption	Not expelled
37th	1st	1861	James M. Mason (D Va.)	Support of rebellion	*Expelled*
37th	1st	1861	Robert M. Hunter (D Va.)	Support of rebellion	*Expelled*
37th	1st	1861	Thomas L. Clingman (D N.C.)	Support of rebellion	*Expelled*
37th	1st	1861	Thomas Bragg (D N.C.)	Support of rebellion	*Expelled*
37th	1st	1861	James Chestnut Jr. (State Rights S.C.)	Support of rebellion	*Expelled*
37th	1st	1861	Alfred O. P. Nicholson (D Tenn.)	Support of rebellion	*Expelled*
37th	1st	1861	William K. Sebastian (D Ark.)	Support of rebellion	*Expelled*[1]
37th	1st	1861	Charles B. Mitchel (D Ark.)	Support of rebellion	*Expelled*
37th	1st	1861	John Hemphill (State Rights Dem. Texas)	Support of rebellion	*Expelled*
37th	1st	1861	Louis T. Wigfall[2] (D Texas)	Support of rebellion	Not expelled
37th	1st	1861	Louis T. Wigfall (D Texas)	Support of rebellion	*Expelled*
37th	1st	1861	John C. Breckinridge (D Ky.)	Support of rebellion	*Expelled*
37th	1st	1861	Lazarus W. Powell (D Ky.)	Support of rebellion	Not expelled
37th	2nd	1862	Trusten Polk (D Mo.)	Support of rebellion	*Expelled*
37th	2nd	1862	Jesse D. Bright (D Ind.)	Support of rebellion	*Expelled*
37th	2nd	1862	Waldo P. Johnson (D Mo.)	Support of rebellion	*Expelled*
37th	2nd	1862	James F. Simmons (Whig R.I.)	Corruption	Not expelled
42nd	3rd	1873	James W. Patterson (R N.H.)	Corruption	Not expelled
53rd	1st	1893	William N. Roach (D N.D.)	Embezzlement	Not expelled
58th	3rd	1905	John H. Mitchell (R Ore.)	Corruption	Not expelled
59th	2nd	1907	Reed Smoot (R Utah)	Mormonism	Not expelled
65th	3rd	1919	Robert M. La Follette (R Wis.)	Disloyalty	Not expelled
73rd	2nd	1934	John H. Overton (D La.)	Corruption	Not expelled
73rd	2nd	1934	Huey P. Long (D La.)	Corruption	Not expelled
77th	2nd	1942	William Langer (R N.D.)	Corruption	Not expelled

1. *The Senate reversed its decision on Sebastian's expulsion March 3, 1877. Sebastian had died in 1865 but his children were paid an amount equal to his Senate salary between the time of his expulsion and the date of his death.*

2. *The Senate took no action on an initial resolution expelling Wigfall because he represented a state that had seceded from the Union; three months later he was expelled for supporting the Confederacy.*

Source: U.S. Senate, Committee on Rules and Administration, Subcommittee on Privileges and Elections, *Senate Election, Expulsion and Censure Cases from 1793 to 1972,* compiled by Richard D. Hupman, S. Doc. 92-7, 92nd Cong., 1st sess., 1972.

Rep. John P. Van Ness (D N.Y.), who in the recess between the first and second sessions of the Seventh Congress was appointed a major in the District of Columbia militia. When the question of the compatibility of holding both that office and a seat in Congress was brought up, Van Ness argued that the pertinent provision of the Constitution was intended to apply only to civil offices, and he pointed out that his militia post carried no pay. On Jan. 11, 1803, however, the House, by a vote of 88 to 0, declared that Van Ness had forfeited his right to his House seat.

The second case was that of Rep. Samuel Hammond (Ind Ga.), who in October 1804 accepted an Army commission as colonel commandant for the District of Louisiana. On Feb. 2, 1805, the House declared the seat vacant.

In a similar situation which arose in 1846, the sitting representative involved, Edward D. Baker (Whig Ill.), resigned before the House had received a report on the matter from the Committee on Elections. Although the case was moot, the committee felt impelled to raise a hypothetical question. In its report of Feb. 21, 1847, the committee asked: "Now, suppose that every member of Congress were a colonel in the Army...and the President, who is by the Constitution the Commander in Chief of that Army, should come into the Halls of Congress and order each individual member to retire immediately...to his post in the Army, what would become of Congress?"[29]

War Service of Members. Cases arising in the Civil War and subsequent wars in which members of Congress served in the armed forces generally did not result in vacating of their seats. In the war with Spain, a House committee appointed to investigate the question reported on Feb. 21, 1899: "It cannot be contended that every position held by a member of Congress is an office within the meaning of the Constitution, even though the term office may usually be applied to many of these positions."[30] The committee cited as an example the position of official escort representative at the funeral of a public figure. To come under the constitutional prohibition, the committee said, a position "must not be merely transient, occasional, or incidental."[31]

The committee recommended adoption of a resolution declaring vacant the seats of four representatives who had

Cases of Expulsion in the House

Congress	Session	Year	Member	Grounds	Disposition
5th	2nd	1798	Matthew Lyon (Anti-Fed Vt.)	Assault on representative	Not expelled
5th	2nd	1798	Roger Griswold (Fed Conn.)	Assault on representative	Not expelled
5th	3rd	1799	Matthew Lyon (Anti-Fed Vt.)	Sedition	Not expelled
25th	2nd	1838	William J. Graves (Whig Ky.)	Killing of representative in duel	Not expelled
25th	3rd	1839	Alexander Duncan (Whig Ohio)	Offensive publication	Not expelled
34th	1st	1856	Preston S. Brooks (State Rights Dem. S.C.)	Assault on senator	Not expelled
34th	3rd	1857	Orsamus B. Matteson (Whig N.Y.)	Corruption	Not expelled
34th	3rd	1857	William A. Gilbert (— N.Y.)	Corruption	Not expelled
34th	3rd	1857	William W. Welch (American Conn.)	Corruption	Not expelled
34th	3rd	1857	Francis S. Edwards (— N.Y.)	Corruption	Not expelled
35th	1st	1858	Orsamus B. Matteson (Whig N.Y.)	Corruption	Not expelled*
37th	1st	1861	John B. Clark (D Mo.)	Support of rebellion	*Expelled*
37th	1st	1861	Henry C. Burnett (D Ky.)	Support of rebellion	*Expelled*
37th	1st	1861	John W. Reid (D Mo.)	Support of rebellion	*Expelled*
38th	1st	1864	Alexander Long (D Ohio)	Treasonable utterance	Not expelled*
38th	1st	1864	Benjamin G. Harris (D Md.)	Treasonable utterance	Not expelled*
39th	1st	1866	Lovell H. Rousseau (R Ky.)	Assault on representative	Not expelled*
41st	2nd	1870	Benjamin F. Whittemore (R S.C.)	Corruption	Not expelled*
41st	2nd	1870	Roderick R. Butler (R Tenn.)	Corruption	Not expelled*
42nd	3rd	1873	Oakes Ames (R Mass.)	Corruption	Not expelled*
42nd	3rd	1873	James Brooks (D N.Y.)	Corruption	Not expelled*
43rd	2nd	1875	John Y. Brown (D Ky.)	Insult to representative	Not expelled*
44th	1st	1875	William S. King (R Minn.)	Corruption	Not expelled
44th	1st	1875	John G. Schumaker (D N.Y.)	Corruption	Not expelled
48th	1st	1884	William P. Kellogg (R La.)	Corruption	Not expelled
67th	1st	1921	Thomas L. Blanton (D Texas)	Abuse of leave to print	Not expelled*

* Censured after expulsion move failed or was withdrawn.

Sources: Hinds and Cannon, *Precedents of the House of Representatives of the United States,* 11 vols. (1935-41); Joint Committee on Congressional Operations, *House of Representatives Exclusion, Censure and Expulsion Cases from 1789 to 1973,* committee print, 93rd Cong., 1st sess., 1973.

accepted commissions in the Army to serve in the war with Spain. "No mere patriotic sentiment," it said, "should be permitted to override the plain language of the fundamental written law."[32] On March 2, 1899, the House, by a vote of 77 yeas and 163 nays, declined to consider the proposed resolution.

Members of both houses have been appointed to serve as commissioners to negotiate peace and arbitrate disputes, as members of "blue ribbon" boards of inquiry, and so forth, without losing their seats in Congress. The House in 1919 authorized members who had been absent on military service to be paid their salaries minus the amount they were paid for military service. Judge Gerhard A. Gesell of the U.S. District Court for the District of Columbia ruled April 2, 1971, that the 117 members who held commissions in military reserve units were violating the incompatible-office clause of the Constitution. The decision was appealed all the way to the Supreme Court which ruled June 25, 1974, that the plaintiffs—present and former members of the reserves opposed to the Vietnam War—did not have legal standing to make the challenge. (*Schlesinger v. Reservists Committee to Stop the War,* 418 U.S. 208)

Civil War Cases

After the Senate's expulsion of William Blount (Ind Tenn.) in 1797 for conspiracy to incite members of two In-

dian tribes to attack Spanish Florida and Louisiana, the only successful expulsion cases were those resulting from the Civil War. *(Details on Blount case p. 211)* On Jan. 21, 1861, Jefferson Davis (D Miss.), like a number of other southern senators before and after that date, announced his support of secession and withdrew from the Senate. On March 14, 1861, ten days after Lincoln's inauguration, the Senate adopted a resolution ordering that inasmuch as the seats of these southerners had "become vacant,...the Secretary be directed to omit their names respectively from the roll."[33] Although Davis and the five other southern senators had left voluntarily, they had not formally resigned. Hence the Senate's action bore some resemblance to expulsion.

Senate Expulsions. On a single day, July 11, 1861, the Senate actually expelled 10 members, two each from Arkansas, North Carolina, Texas and Virginia, and one each from South Carolina and Tennessee, for failure to appear in their seats and for participation in secession. The vote was 32 in favor of expulsion, 10 against. Sen. John C. Breckinridge (D Ky.), who had been Vice President of the United States from 1857 to 1861, was expelled Dec. 4, 1861, by the following resolution: "Whereas John C. Breckinridge, a member of this body from the State of Kentucky, has joined the enemies of his country, and is now in arms against the Government he had sworn to support: Therefore, Resolved, That said John C. Breckinridge, the traitor, be, and he hereby is, expelled from the Senate."[34] On this resolution the vote was 37 to 0.

Of the 10 expulsions voted by the Senate on July 11, 1861, one was later annulled. In 1877, the Committee on Privileges and Elections reviewed the expulsion of Sen. William K. Sebastian (D Ark.), decided that the Senate had a right to reverse its earlier action, and recommended such reversal. The Senate on March 3, 1877, adopted the committee's recommendation, which was based on its findings that the charges made against Sebastian in 1861 were "occasioned by want of information, and by the overruling excitement of a period of great public danger."[35] Sebastian had remained loyal to the Union throughout the war.

In 1862, the Senate expelled three senators, all for disloyalty to the government—Missouri Democrats Trusten Polk and Waldo P. Johnson and Indiana Democrat Jesse D. Bright. Polk was accused of stating in a widely published letter his hopes that Missouri would secede from the Union. Johnson reportedly held similar feelings and furthermore did not appear to take his Senate seat. Bright was charged with treason for giving an arms salesman a letter of introduction to Confederate President Jefferson Davis.

House Expulsions. On July 13, 1861, the House expelled a member-elect, John B. Clark (D Mo.), who had not yet taken the oath. After a brief debate on Clark's entrance into the Confederate forces, and without referring the case to a committee, the House adopted the expulsion order by slightly more than a two-thirds vote, 94 to 45.

In December of the same year, the House adopted by two-thirds votes the only other expulsions in its history, affecting John W. Reid (D Mo.) and Henry C. Burnett (D Ky.). Reid was expelled for taking up arms against the country; Burnett was expelled for being in open rebellion against the federal government.

More Recent Expulsion Efforts

Sen. Robert M. La Follette (R Wis.) made a speech at St. Paul, Minn., Sept. 20, 1917, decrying American participation in the war in Europe. On the basis of that speech, Minnesota's Public Safety Commission petitioned the Senate to expel La Follette for sedition. The petition was referred to the Committee on Privileges and Elections, which held hearings during a 14-month period. On Dec. 2, 1918, three weeks after the World War I armistice, the committee recommended that the petition be dismissed. The Senate on Jan. 16, 1919, adopted the recommendation by a vote of 50 to 21.

In 1932-34, the two senators from Louisiana, Huey P. Long and John H. Overton, both Democrats, were accused of fraud and corruption in connection with their nomination and election. Resolutions of expulsion were introduced, and the Committee on Privileges and Elections conducted an investigation. Eventually it asked to be discharged from further consideration of the two cases. The Senate complied with this request on June 16, 1934, in effect burying the expulsion resolutions.

Charges of corruption against Sen.-elect William Langer (R N.D.) led to an effort to prevent his serving in the Senate. The effort took the form in part of a proposal to exclude Langer and in part of a proposal to expel him after he had taken the oath. On March 27, 1942, the Senate first rejected a resolution, 37-45, stating that the case did not fall within the constitutional provisions for expulsion. It then rejected, 30-52, a second resolution declaring that Langer was not entitled to his seat in the Senate.

Censure

In the entire history of the Congress, the Senate has censured seven of its members, the House 19. In the Senate, censure proceedings are carried out with a degree of moderation. The alleged offender, for example, is granted the privilege of speaking in his own behalf. The House often has denied that privilege to a representative accused of wrongdoing. In most cases in the House, a censured member is treated like a felon; the Speaker calls him to the bar and makes a solemn pronouncement of censure. For example, Speaker Frederick H. Gillett (R Mass.) on Oct. 27, 1921, directed the sergeant-at-arms to bring to the bar of the House Rep. Thomas L. Blanton (D Texas). The Speaker than made the following statement:

"Mr. Blanton, by a unanimous vote of the House—yeas, 293; nays, none—I have been directed to censure you because, when you had been allowed the courtesy of the House to print a speech which you did not deliver, you inserted in it foul and obscene matter, which you knew you could not have spoken on the floor; and that disgusting matter, which could not have been circulated through the mails in any other publication without violating the law, was transmitted as part of the proceedings of this House to thousands of homes and libraries throughout the country, to be read by men and women, and worst of all by children, whose prurient curiosity it would excite and corrupt. In accordance with the instructions of the House and as its representative, I pronounce upon you its censure."[36]

Censure by the Senate

Timothy Pickering (Fed Mass.) was the first member to be censured by the Senate. In December 1810, he had read aloud in the chamber secret documents relating to the 1803 convention with France for the cession of Louisiana. The Senate on Jan. 2, 1811, adopted the following resolution of censure: "Resolved, That Timothy Pickering, a Senator from the State of Massachusetts, having,...whilst the Senate was in session with open doors, read from his place certain documents confidentially communicated by the President of the United States to the Senate, the injunction of secrecy not having been removed, has, in so doing, committed a violation of the rules of this body."[37] Twenty senators voted for the resolution; seven, against it.

Benjamin Tappan (D Ohio) was similarly censured on May 10, 1844, when the Senate adopted a two-part resolution concerning his release to the press of confidential material relating to a treaty for the annexation of Texas. The first part, adopted 35 to 7, censured Tappan for releasing the documents in "flagrant violation" of the Senate rules. The second, adopted 39 to 3, accepted Tappan's apology and said that no further censure would "be inflicted on him."[38]

Threatened violence was involved in the next censure case in the Senate. On the Senate floor April 7, 1850, Thomas H. Benton (D Mo.) made menacing gestures and advanced toward Henry S. Foote (Unionist Miss.) while Foote was making a speech. Foote drew a pistol from his pocket and cocked it. Before any damage was done, other senators intervened and restored order. A committee appointed to consider the incident said in its report, July 30, that what the two men had done was deplorable. The committee recommended that Foote be censured, but the Senate took no action. This was the only Senate case in

Censure Proceedings in the Senate

Congress	Session	Year	Member	Grounds	Disposition
11th	3rd	1811	Timothy Pickering (Fed Mass.)	Breach of confidence	*Censured*
28th	1st	1844	Benjamin Tappan (D Ohio)	Breach of confidence	*Censured*
31st	1st	1850	Thomas H. Benton (D Mo.)	Disorderly conduct	Not censured
31st	1st	1850	Henry S. Foote (Unionist Miss.)	Disorderly conduct	Not censured
57th	1st	1902	John L. McLaurin (D S.C.)	Assault	*Censured*
57th	1st	1902	Benjamin R. Tillman (D S.C.)	Assault	*Censured*
71st	1st	1929	Hiram Bingham (R Conn.)	Bringing Senate into disrepute	*Censured*
83rd	2nd	1954	Joseph R. McCarthy (R Wis.)	Obstruction of legislative process, insult to senators, etc.	*Censured*
90th	1st	1967	Thomas J. Dodd (D Conn.)	Financial misconduct	*Censured*

Source: U.S. Senate, Committee on Rules and Administration, Subcommittee on Privileges and Elections, *Senate Election, Expulsion and Censure Cases from 1793 to 1972*, compiled by Richard D. Hupman, S. Doc. 92-7, 92nd Cong., 1st sess., 1972.

which an investigating committee's recommendation of censure was not adopted.

More than half a century later, on Feb. 22, 1902, while the Senate was debating Philippine affairs, Sen. Benjamin R. Tillman (D S.C.) made a statement questioning the integrity of Sen. John L. McLaurin (D S.C.). When McLaurin branded it as "a willful, malicious and deliberate lie,"[39] Tillman advanced toward McLaurin, and they engaged in a brief fistfight. After they had been separated, the Senate by a vote of 61 to 0 declared them to be "in contempt of the Senate" and by a voice vote referred the matter to the Committee on Privileges and Elections for a report on any further action that should be taken.

The committee on Feb. 27 reported a resolution declaring it to be the judgment of the Senate that the two men, "for disorderly behavior and flagrant violation of the rules of the Senate..., deserve the censure of the Senate, and they are hereby so censured, for their breach of the privileges and dignity of this body," and provided that after its adoption the previous declaration that the two men were in contempt of the Senate "shall be no longer in force and effect."[40] The Senate adopted the resolution by a vote of 54 to 12, with 22 senators (including the two participants in the affray) not voting.

The censure case of Sen. Hiram Bingham (R Conn.) occurred in 1929 when he placed on the Senate payroll, as a member of his staff, Charles L. Eyanson, a secretary to the president of the Connecticut Manufacturers' Association, to assist him in dealing with tariff legislation.

Sen. George W. Norris (R Neb.) introduced a resolution declaring that Bingham's action was "contrary to good morals and senatorial ethics."[41] During consideration of the resolution on Nov. 4, 1929, the Senate agreed to add language stating that Bingham's actions were "not the result of corrupt motives."[42] The resolution was then adopted by a vote of 54 to 22, with 18 senators (including Bingham) not voting.

McCarthy Case. The sixth member of the Senate to be censured was Joseph R. McCarthy (R Wis.). Proceedings on this case began in the 82nd Congress (1951-52) and were concluded in the 83rd (1953-54). Sen. William Benton (D

Conn.) in August 1951 offered a resolution calling on the Committee on Rules and Administration to investigate, among other things, McCarthy's participation in the defamation of Sen. Millard E. Tydings (D Md.) during the Maryland senatorial campaign, in order to determine whether expulsion proceedings should be instituted against McCarthy. On April 10, 1952, McCarthy submitted a resolution calling for investigation by the same committee of Benton's activities as Assistant Secretary of State, campaign contributions Benton had received, and other matters. Both proposals were referred to the Rules Committee's Privileges and Elections Subcommittee which, after conducting an investigation, submitted an inconclusive report on Jan. 2, 1953.

In the spring of 1954, the Senate Permanent Investigations Subcommittee conducted hearings on mutual accusations of misconduct by McCarthy and Army officials. *(Details p. 167)* During the hearings, McCarthy told Army Brig. Gen. Ralph W. Zwicker that he was "not fit to wear that uniform" and implied that Zwicker did not have "the brains of a five-year-old." In June, Sens. Ralph E. Flanders (R Vt.) and Herbert H. Lehman (D N.Y.) introduced resolutions to strip McCarthy of his chairmanship of the Senate Permanent Investigations Subcommittee. Both resolutions were referred to the Rules Committee.

The two resolutions became moot when 73-year-old Flanders on July 30 introduced a resolution censuring McCarthy. Among Flanders' reasons for pressing censure were McCarthy's refusal to testify before a Rules subcommittee in the 1952 Benton-McCarthy exchange of accusations, refusal to repudiate the "frivolous and irresponsible" conduct of Investigations Subcommittee Counsel Roy M. Cohn and consultant G. David Schine on their 1953 subversion-seeking trip to Europe, and "habitual contempt for people."[43] The Senate on Aug. 2 adopted, by a vote of 75 to 12, a proposal to refer Flanders' censure resolution to a select committee. Three days later, Vice President Richard M. Nixon appointed the select committee.

The Select Committee to Study Censure Charges held hearings from Aug. 31 to Sept. 13, 1954. McCarthy, in defending himself before the committee, contended that the

Senate Condemnation of Joseph R. McCarthy (R Wis.)

Resolution relating to the conduct of the Senator from Wisconsin, Mr. McCarthy. [S. Res. 301, 83rd Cong., 2nd sess., adopted Dec. 2, 1954.]

Section 1. Resolved, that the Senator from Wisconsin, Mr. McCarthy, failed to cooperate with the Subcommittee on Privileges and Elections of the Senate Committee on Rules and Administration in clearing up matters referred to that Subcommittee which concerned his conduct as a Senator and affected the honor of the Senate and, instead, repeatedly abused the Subcommittee and its Members who were trying to carry out assigned duties, thereby obstructing the constitutional processes of the Senate, and that this conduct of the Senator from Wisconsin, Mr. McCarthy, is contrary to Senatorial traditions and is hereby condemned.

Section 2. The Senator from Wisconsin (Mr. McCarthy), in writing to the chairman of the Select Committee to Study Censure Charges (Mr. Watkins) after the Select Committee had issued its report and before the report was presented to the Senate charging three members of the Select Committee with "deliberate deception" and "fraud" for failure to disqualify themselves;

In stating to the press on Nov. 4, 1954, that the special Senate session that was to begin Nov. 8, 1954, was a "lynch party";

In repeatedly describing this special Senate Session as a "lynch bee" in a nationwide television and radio show on Nov. 7, 1954;

In stating to the public press on Nov. 13, 1954, that the chairman of the Select Committee (Mr. Watkins) was guilty of "the most unusual, most cowardly thing I've ever heard of" and stating further: "I expected he would be afraid to answer the questions, but didn't think he'd be stupid enough to make a public statement"; and in characterizing the said Committee as the "unwilling handmaiden," "involuntary agent," and "attorneys-in-fact" of the Communist party and in charging that the said Committee in writing its report "imitated Communist methods—that it distorted, misrepresented, and omitted in its efforts to manufacture a plausible rationalization" in support of its recommendations to the Senate, which characterizations and charges were contained in a statement released to the press and inserted into the Congressional Record of Nov. 10, 1954, acted contrary to Senatorial ethics and tended to bring the Senate into dishonor and disrepute, to obstruct the constitutional processes of the Senate, and to impair its dignity.

And such conduct is hereby condemned.

Senate cannot punish a member for what he did in a previous Congress. The committee rejected that contention and on Sept. 27 submitted a 40,000-word report which included a unanimous recommendation that the Senate adopt a resolution censuring McCarthy. After a recess during the congressional election campaign, the Senate reconvened Nov. 8 to consider the censure proposal. Proceedings in the next few weeks led to modifications of that proposal and

substitution of the word "condemned" for "censured." *(Text of final resolution, this page)*

The Senate adopted the resolution of condemnation on Dec. 2 by a vote of 67 to 22. Republicans split evenly, 22 favoring and 22 opposing the resolution. All 44 Democrats, together with Sen. Wayne Morse (Ind Ore.), voted for the resolution. In January 1955, when control of Congress passed to the Democrats, McCarthy lost his committee and subcommittee chairmanships. His activities thereafter attracted less public attention, and he died May 2, 1957.

Dodd Case. House Speaker Sam Rayburn (D Texas) often said that the ethics of a member of Congress should be judged not by his peers but by the voters at re-election time. By the mid-1960s, it had become clear that neither Congress nor the public felt this was enough. In 1964, the Senate was jolted by adverse publicity over charges that Robert G. (Bobby) Baker had used his office as secretary to the Senate majority to promote his business interests. To allay public misgivings, the Senate on July 24 of that year established a Select Committee on Standards and Conduct with responsibility for investigating "allegations of improper conduct" by senators and Senate employees. In September, however, the Senate assigned jurisdiction over the Baker case to the Rules and Administration Committee. *(Baker case, p. 717)*

The new select committee's first inquiry, begun in 1966, concerned the Dodd case. On Jan. 24, 1966, and later dates, columnists Drew Pearson and Jack Anderson accused Sen. Thomas J. Dodd (D Conn.) of having (1) used for personal expenses funds contributed to him to help meet the costs of his campaign for re-election in 1964, (2) double-billed the government for travel expenses, and (3) improperly exchanged favors with Julius Klein, a public relations representative of West German interests. On the last charge, the columnists said that Dodd had gone to Germany for the purpose of interceding with Chancellor Konrad Adenauer on behalf of Klein's accounts, although the trip was supposedly made on Senate business.

Dodd on Feb. 23, 1966, requested the Select Committee on Standards and Conduct to investigate his relationship with Klein. The committee conducted hearings on all three of the Pearson-Anderson charges in June-July 1966 and March 1967. Dodd testified in his own defense.

● On the first charge, Dodd said he "truly believed" the proceeds from the testimonial dinners "to be donations to me from my friends."[44]

● The second charge, he said, stemmed from "sloppy bookkeeping" by Michael V. O'Hare, who had been an employee of Dodd. O'Hare and other former Dodd employees reportedly had taken documents from Dodd's files and made copies of them available to the committee. In the course of the hearings, Dodd called O'Hare a liar.[45]

● On charge three, Dodd denied that he had been a mere errand boy for Klein on the trip to Europe.

The committee on April 27, 1967, submitted its report on the Dodd case. It recommended that Dodd be censured for spending campaign contributions for personal purposes and for billing seven trips to both the Senate and private organizations. The committee dropped the third charge, saying that while Dodd's relations with Klein were indiscreet, there was not sufficient evidence of wrongdoing.

Voting on the committee's recommendations, June 23, 1967, the Senate censured Dodd on the first charge, by a vote of 92 to 5, but refused by a vote of 45 yeas to 51 nays to censure him on the second charge. The resolution as adopted recorded the judgment of the Senate that Dodd, "for having engaged in a course of conduct...from 1961 to 1965 of exer-

Censure Proceedings in the House

Congress	Session	Year	Member	Grounds	Disposition
5th	2nd	1798	Matthew Lyon (Anti-Fed Vt.)	Assault on representative	Not censured
5th	2nd	1798	Roger Griswold (Fed Conn.)	Assault on representative	Not censured
22nd	1st	1832	William Stanbery (D Ohio)	Insult to Speaker	*Censured*
24th	1st	1836	Sherrod Williams (Whig Ky.)	Insult to Speaker	Not censured
25th	2nd	1838	Henry A. Wise (Tyler Dem. Va.)	Service as second in duel	Not censured
25th	3rd	1839	Alexander Duncan (Whig Ohio)	Offensive publication	Not censured
27th	2nd	1842	John Q. Adams (Whig Mass.)	Treasonable petition	Not censured
27th	2nd	1842	Joshua R. Giddings (Whig Ohio)	Offensive paper	*Censured*
34th	2nd	1856	Henry A. Edmundson (D Va.) ⎫	Complicity in assault	Not censured
34th	2nd	1856	Laurence M. Keitt (D S.C.) ⎬	on senator	*Censured*
35th	1st	1858	Orsamus B. Matteson (Whig N.Y.)	Corruption	*Censured*
36th	1st	1860	George S. Houston (D Ala.)	Insult to representative	Not censured
38th	1st	1864	Alexander Long (D Ohio)	Treasonable utterance	*Censured*
38th	1st	1864	Benjamin G. Harris (D Md.)	Treasonable utterance	*Censured*
39th	1st	1866	John W. Chanler (D N.Y.)	Insult to House	*Censured*
39th	1st	1866	Lovell H. Rousseau (R Ky.)	Assault on representative	*Censured*
40th	1st	1867	John W. Hunter (Ind N.Y.)	Insult to representative	*Censured*
40th	2nd	1868	Fernando Wood (D N.Y.)	Offensive utterance	*Censured*
40th	3rd	1868	E. D. Holbrook[1] (D Idaho)	Offensive utterance	*Censured*
41st	2nd	1870	Benjamin F. Whittemore (R S.C.)	Corruption	*Censured*
41st	2nd	1870	Roderick R. Butler (R Tenn.)	Corruption	*Censured*
41st	2nd	1870	John T. Deweese (D N.C.)	Corruption	*Censured*
42nd	3rd	1873	Oakes Ames (R Mass.)	Corruption	*Censured*
42nd	3rd	1873	James Brooks (D N.Y.)	Corruption	*Censured*
43rd	2nd	1875	John Y. Brown (D Ky.)	Insult to representative	*Censured*[2]
44th	1st	1876	James G. Blaine (R Maine)	Corruption	Not censured
47th	1st	1882	William D. Kelley (R Pa.)	Offensive utterance	Not censured
47th	1st	1882	John D. White (R Ky.)	Offensive utterance	Not censured
47th	2nd	1883	John Van Voorhis (R N.Y.)	Offensive utterance	Not censured
51st	1st	1890	William D. Bynum (D Ind.)	Offensive utterance	*Censured*
67th	1st	1921	Thomas L. Blanton (D Texas)	Abuse of leave to print	*Censured*

1. Holbrook was a territorial delegate, not a representative.
2. The House later rescinded part of the censure resolution against Brown.

Sources: Hinds and Cannon, *Presidents of the House of Representatives of the United States,* 11 vols. (1935-41); Joint Committee on Congressional Operations, *House of Representatives Exclusion, Censure and Expulsion Cases from 1789 to 1973,* committee print, 93rd Cong., 1st sess., 1973.

cising the influence and favor of his office as a United States Senator...to obtain, and use for his personal benefit, funds from the public through political testimonials and a political campaign, deserves the censure of the Senate; and he is so censured for his conduct, which is contrary to accepted morals, derogates from the public trust expected of a Senator, and tends to bring the Senate into dishonor and disrepute."[46] The preponderance of affirmative votes was the largest in the history of censure proceedings in the Senate.

Dodd declined to seek the Democratic nomination for senator from Connecticut in 1970 but ran in the general election as an independent. He placed third, with 24 per cent of the votes, while the Democratic nominee lost to Republican Lowell P. Weicker Jr., 34 per cent to 42 per cent. Dodd had served four years in the House and 12 years in the Senate. He died May 24, 1971.

Censure by the House

The House in 1789 adopted a rule which, as amended in 1822 and 1880, is still in effect (Rule 14, Section 4). It reads:

"If any member, in speaking or otherwise, transgress the rules of the House, the Speaker shall, or any member may, call him to order; ...and if the case require it, he shall be liable to censure or such punishment as the House may deem proper."[47] The censure clause of this rule has been invoked 31 times, and censure has been voted 19 times, two-thirds of them in the 1860s and 1870s. Grounds for censure have included assault on a fellow member of the House, insult to the Speaker, treasonable utterance, corruption and other offenses. Only once in the 20th century has a representative been censured—Thomas L. Blanton (D Texas) in 1921 for abuse of the leave to print.

The first censure motion in the House was introduced following a physical attack in January 1798 by Rep. Matthew Lyon (Anti-Fed Vt.) on Rep. Roger Griswold (Fed Conn.), who had taunted Lyon on his allegedly poor military record. The censure motion failed. In the following month, Lyon and Griswold engaged in an affray with tongs and cane. Both fracases occurred on the House floor. Following the second incident, a motion was introduced to censure both members. The motion failed.

The first formal censure by the House was imposed in 1832 on William Stanbery (D Ohio) for saying, in objection to a ruling by the chair, "The eyes of the Speaker [Andrew Stevenson (D Va.)] are too frequently turned from the chair you occupy toward the White House."[48] There were 93 votes for censuring Stanbery; 44 were opposed. Censure for unacceptable language or offensive publication was imposed in seven other cases. For example, Rep. John W. Hunter (Ind N.Y.) was censured on Jan. 26, 1867, for saying, about a statement made by a colleague, "So far as I am concerned, it is a base lie."[49] The vote on censure was 77 to 23. One year later, on Jan. 15, 1868, the House by a vote of 114 to 39 censured Rep. Fernando Wood (D N.Y.) for describing a bill on the government of the southern states as "a monstrosity, a measure the most infamous of the many infamous acts of this infamous Congress."[50]

In 1842, censure was considered and rejected in the case of one of the most distinguished representatives in American history, John Quincy Adams, a former President of the United States. Adams had presented to the House, for 46 of his constituents, a petition asking Congress to dissolve the Union and allow the states to go their separate ways. A resolution proposing to censure him for this act was worded so strongly that Adams asserted his right, under the Sixth Amendment to the Constitution, to a trial by jury. He succeeded in putting his opponents on the defensive, and the resolution was not put to a vote.

Rep. Lovell H. Rousseau (R Ky.) during the evening of June 14, 1866, assaulted Rep. Josiah B. Grinnell (R Iowa) with a cane in the portico on the East Front of the Capitol. On the House floor, earlier in the month, Grinnell had imputed cowardice to Rousseau. A committee appointed to report on the case recommended that Rousseau be expelled. That recommendation was rejected, but the House voted on July 17, 1866, that he "be summoned to the bar of this House, and be there publicly reprimanded by the Speaker for his violation of its rights and privileges."[51] The order was carried out July 21, despite Rousseau's announcement that he had sent his resignation to the governor of Kentucky.

Corruption was the basis for censure or proposed censure in a number of cases. The House on Feb. 27, 1873, by a vote of 182 to 36, censured Reps. Oakes Ames (R Mass.) and James Brooks (D N.Y.) for their part in a financial scandal involving Crédit Mobilier stock given to members of Congress. Three years later, Speaker James G. Blaine (R Maine) was accused of involvement in that scandal as well as of receiving excessive payments from the Union Pacific Railroad Co. for bonds sold to the company. Two months before the convention at which Blaine hoped to be chosen the Republican candidate for President, he spoke in the House on the charges against him. By selective reading of a series of allegedly incriminating letters, Blaine managed to confuse the evidence sufficiently to rout the proponents of censure.

In one instance, the House rescinded part of a censure resolution. During debate on a bill in 1875, Rep. John Y. Brown (D Ky.) referred to Rep. Benjamin Butler (R Mass.) as "outlawed in his own home from respectable society; whose name is synonymous with falsehood; and who is the champion, and has been on all occasions, of fraud; who is the apologist of thieves; who is such a prodigy of vice and meanness that to describe him would sicken imagination and exhaust invective."[52]

Brown was censured Feb. 4, 1875, for that insult and for lying to the Speaker in order to continue his insulting

Censure for Dueling Withheld

The killing of one representative by another in a duel in 1838 went uncensured by the House. Rep. Jonathan Cilley (Jackson Dem. Maine) had made statements on the floor reflecting on the character of James W. Webb, prominent editor of a New York City newspaper which was a Whig organ. When Webb sent Cilley a note by the hand of Rep. William J. Graves (Whig Ky.), demanding an explanation of the statements, Cilley refused to receive the note. Further correspondence led to a challenge by Graves and agreement by Cilley to a duel with rifles.

The duel took place on Feb. 24, 1838, on the Marlboro Pike in Maryland, close to the District of Columbia. Graves and Cilley each fired twice, with no result. In the third volley, Cilley was shot fatally in the abdomen. Four days later, the House appointed a committee to investigate the affair. A majority of the committee recommended on April 21 that Graves be expelled from the House and that the seconds in the duel, Rep. Henry A. Wise (Tyler D Va.) and George W. Jones (a member of the Tennessee House of Representatives who served in the national House of Representatives, 1843-59), be censured. One of the minority group on the committee, Rep. Franklin H. Elmore (State Rights Dem S.C.), observed that dueling by members had been frequent and generally had gone unnoticed by the House. A motion to lay the committee's report on the table and to print the testimony was agreed to May 10, and an attempt on July 4 to take up the report was unsuccessful. Graves was not expelled and Wise and Jones were not censured.

speech. But a year later, on May 2, 1876, the House agreed to rescind that portion of the censure resolution condemning Brown for lying to the Speaker. The charge of insulting another member remained, however.[53]

Recent Cases

As of mid-1976, neither chamber had censured any of its members since the Dodd case in 1967. However, censure was discussed in two cases, one in the Senate, one in the House, both relating to the release of confidential information.

In 1971, Sen. Mike Gravel (D Alaska), frustrated in his attempts to read from the Pentagon Papers on the Senate floor, called a one-man, late-evening subcommittee hearing on June 29, 1971, and began reading from a censored version of the papers which detailed the nation's early involvement in the Vietnam War. He then passed these portions to reporters.

Minority Leader Hugh Scott (R Pa.) said at the time that Gravel might have violated a Senate rule that prohibited the divulging of confidential communications from the President or an executive department, or other secret or confidential information. Scott added that Senate Republicans were considering asking the Senate to censure Gravel. However, Majority Leader Mike Mansfield (D Mont.) said Gravel had not broken any Senate rule, and the Senate did not reprimand him. *(Details of Gravel case, p. 715)*

The second case occurred in 1975 when the House Committee on Standards of Official Conduct formally investigated a complaint that Michael J. Harrington (D Mass.) had violated House rules in 1974 by making public classified information. Harrington was charged with disclosing secret Armed Services Investigations Subcommittee testimony by CIA Director William E. Colby on alleged U.S. efforts to prevent the 1970 election of Salvador Allende as president of Chile.

Rep. Robin L. Beard Jr. (R Tenn.), who filed the complaint, had told the Associated Press June 18, 1975, that he hoped the complaint would result in a censure resolution. But the committee, also known as the ethics committee, dismissed the charges Nov. 6, 1975, on a 7 to 3 vote, after learning that the hearing at which Colby testified was not legally an executive session and thus not a hearing covered by the House rules. *(Details, p. 710)*

Other Forms of Discipline

Faced in recent years with cases of impropriety that it has not wanted to punish by expulsion or censure, the House has imposed less stringent forms of discipline. One method has been directed toward members who have been convicted in court of criminal actions carrying certain penalties.

Suspension

In 1972, the House began a move to formalize an unwritten rule that a member indicted for or convicted of a crime should refrain from voting on the House floor or in committee. Prior to 1972, the last time a member voluntarily refrained from voting was in 1929 when, under indictment in the District of Columbia, Frederick N. Zihlman (R Md.) did not vote on the floor and temporarily turned over his chairmanship of the House Committee on the District of Columbia to the committee's ranking member.

The move to formalize that unwritten rule was prompted by the case of John Dowdy (D Texas) who was convicted Dec. 31, 1971, of charges arising from acceptance of a bribe, conspiracy and perjury. While Dowdy appealed his conviction, the ethics committee reported a resolution May 3, 1972, stating that any House member convicted of a crime for which he could receive a sentence of two or more years in prison should not participate in committee business or House votes. The maximum sentence for the crimes Dowdy was convicted of was 40 years in prison and a $40,000 fine.

Because the Rules Committee failed to act, the resolution was not enacted. But Dowdy, in a June 21, 1972, letter to Speaker Carl Albert (D Okla.) promised he would refrain from voting.[54] He retired from the House at the end of 1972. *(Details, p. 717)*

Not until April 16, 1975, did the House enact a resolution similar to the one proposed in 1972. Under the 1975 rule, the voluntary prohibition against voting would apply during an appeal of the conviction but would end on reversal or when the member was re-elected subsequent to conviction, even if the verdict was upheld on appeal.

The first member affected by the 1975 rule was Andrew J. Hinshaw (R Calif.) who was convicted Jan. 26, 1976, and sentenced to one to 14 years in prison for accepting gifts of stereo equipment and a $1,000 campaign contribution from the Tandy Corporation during his term as assessor for Orange County, Calif. Hinshaw appealed. *(Details, p. 718)*

[In the wake of Hinshaw's conviction, Rep. Charles E. Wiggins (R Calif.) June 30, 1976, introduced a resolution (H Res 1392) to expell Hinshaw from the House. The House ethics committee Sept. 1, 1976, reported the resolution adversely by a 10-2 vote. Wiggins said he would call it up for a floor vote before the House adjourned. Hinshaw lost the June 8 Republican primary election.]

Loss of Chairmanships

Another method of punishment has been to strip a member of his committee chairmanship; such action was one of several disciplinary actions taken against Adam Clayton Powell Jr. (D N.Y.). *(p. 687)* In a recent case, Rep. Wayne L. Hays (D Ohio) in mid-1976 gave up the chairmanship of both the Democratic Congressional Campaign Committee and the House Administration Committee after it was alleged that he had kept a mistress on the latter committee's payroll. Hays was pressured to resign the posts by the House Democratic leadership and it was evident that the Democratic Caucus would have forced him to do so if he had not stepped aside voluntarily. Hays resigned from Congress Sept. 1, 1976. *(Details on investigation of Hays case, p. 711)*

Sikes Reprimand

The House July 29, 1976, voted 381-3, to reprimand Robert L. F. Sikes (D Fla.) for failure to disclose certain financial holdings. It was the first time that the House had formally punished a member since 1969 when it fined Adam Clayton Powell and stripped him of his seniority. *(Details of Sikes case, p. 710)*

John J. Flynt Jr. (D Ga.), chairman of the Standards of Official Coneduct Committee (Ethics Committee), which recommended the reprimand, said he saw no real difference between a reprimand and a censure, but that committee members decided to use the word reprimand. In the case of a vote to reprimand, no further action is taken against a member. Under censure, the member has to stand in the well and be publicly admonished by the Speaker.

Harrington Rebuke

Although the ethics committee decided Harrington could not be punished for releasing portions of the confidential Pentagon Papers, the House Armed Services Committee sought to rebuke him by refusing him further access to its files. On June 16, 1975, the committee voted 16-13 to deny Harrington access to the files pending an official response from the ethics committee setting forth criteria on future access to committee files by House members.

In conflict were two House rules and a rule of the Armed Services Committee. One House rule stated that any member of Congress could inspect any committee's files but a second House rule said that no evidence or testimony taken in executive session could be released without consent of the committee. The Armed Services Committee had regulations prohibiting anyone except its members from examining classified material; Harrington was not a committee member at the time of the incident.

Although the ethics committee informally told the Armed Services Committee that the matter involved a change in House rules and was therefore under the jurisdiction of the Rules Committee, rather than the Ethics Committee, the ethics committee had not formally responded to the Armed Services Committee resolution in mid-July 1976 and Harrington technically still was denied access to the latter committee's files.

Footnotes

1. Asher C. Hinds and Clarence Cannon, *Hinds' and Cannon's Precedents of the House of Representatives of the United States* (Government Printing Office, 1935-41), vol. 1, p. 525.
2. *Ibid.*
3. *Ibid.*, vol. 2, p. 1075.
4. *Ibid.*, vol. 2, p. 847.
5. *Ibid*, vol. 1, p. 84.
6. *Ibid.*
7. *The Federalist Papers*, with an Introduction by Clinton Rossiter (Mentor, 1961), No. 60, p. 371.
8. Westel W. Willoughby, *The Constitutional Law of the United States* (Baker, Voorhis, 1929), vol. 1, p. 608.
9. U.S. Congress, Senate, Committee on Rules and Administration, *Senate Election, Expulsion and Censure Cases*, S. Doc. 92-7, 92nd Cong., 1st sess., 1971, p. 1.
10. *Ibid.*, p. 12.
11. Hinds, *Precedents*, vol. 1, p. 588.
12. William F. Willoughby, *Principles of Legislative Organization and Administration* (Brookings Institution, 1934), p. 270.
13. Hinds, *Precedents*, vol. 6, p. 58.
14. *Ibid.*, vol. 1, p. 489.
15. *Ibid.*
16. Robert S. Getz, *Congressional Ethics; The Conflict of Interest Issue* (Van Nostrand, 1966), p. 110.
17. Kent M. Weeks, *Adam Clayton Powell and the Supreme Court* (Dunellen, 1971), p. 79.
18. *Ibid.*, p. 134.
19. Floyd M. Riddick, *The United States Congress; Organization and Procedure* (National Capitol Publishers, 1949), p. 12.
20. George H. Haynes, *The Senate of the United States* (Houghton-Mifflin Co., 1938), p. 131.
21. For more background, see Congressional Quarterly, *1975 Almanac*, p. 699.
22. For additional background, see Congressional Quarterly, *Weekly Report*, March 6, 1976, p. 508.
23. George F. Hoar, *Autobiography of Seventy Years* (Scribner's, 1903), vol. 1, p. 268.
24. Quoted in DeAlva Stanwood Alexander, *History and Procedure of the House of Representatives* (Lenox Hill, 1916), p. 323.
25. William Willoughby, *Principles*, p. 277.
26. For more background, see Congressional Quarterly, *1965 Almanac*, p. 609.
27. *Congressional Record*, 84th Cong., 1st sess., Jan. 14, 1955, p. 373.
28. Hinds, *Precedents*, vol. 2, p. 817.
29. *Ibid.*, vol. 1, p. 595.
30. *Ibid.*, p. 604.
31. *Ibid.*, p. 605.
32. *Ibid.*, p. 613.
33. *Senate Election, Expulsion and Censure Cases*, p. 29.
34. *Ibid.*, p. 31-32.
35. John T. Dempsey, *Control by Congress Over the Seating and Disciplining of Members* (Ph.D. dissertation, University of Michigan, 1956), p. 294.
36. Hinds, *Precedents*, vol. 6, p. 404-405.
37. *Senate Election, Expulsion and Censure Cases*, p. 6.
38. *Ibid.*, p. 14.
39. *Ibid.*, p. 96.
40. *Ibid.*, p. 97.
41. *Ibid.*, p. 128.
42. *Ibid.*
43. *Congressional Record*, 83rd Cong., 2nd sess., July 30, 1954, p. 12730.
44. U.S. Congress, Senate, Committee on Standards and Conduct, *Investigation of Senator Thomas J. Dodd, Hearings before the Select Committee on Standards and Conduct*, 89th Cong., 2nd sess., 1966, p. 846.
45. *Ibid.*, p. 847.
46. *Senate Election, Expulsion and Censure Cases*, p. 157.
47. Hinds, *Precedents*, vol. 5, p. 103.
48. *Ibid.*, vol. 2, p. 799.
49. *Ibid.*, p. 801.
50. *Ibid.*, p. 798.
51. *Ibid.*, p. 1134.
52. *Ibid.*, p. 802.
53. *Ibid.*, vol. 4, p. 26.
54. Dowdy actually voted three times by proxy in the House District of Columbia Committee June 22 after he had said he would not vote in committee or on the floor. Dowdy explained the votes by saying that he had given his proxy to the committee for use at a meeting scheduled on June 21 which was postponed until June 22 without his knowledge. Dowdy's pledge to refrain from voting was made the evening of June 21. For details, see Congressional Quarterly, *1972 Almanac*, p. 796.

Selected Bibliography

Books

Alexander, De Alva Stanwood, *History and Procedure of the House of Representatives*. New York: Lenox Hill, 1916.

Beck, James M. *The Vanishing Rights of the States*. New York: George H. Doran Co., 1926.

Berman, Daniel M. *In Congress Assembled; the Legislative Process in the National Government*. New York: Macmillan, 1964.

Dempsey, John T. *Control by Congress Over the Seating and Disciplining of Members*, Ph.D. dissertation. University of Michigan, 1956. (Microfilm copy in Library of Congress.)

Galloway, George B. *The Legislative Process in Congress*. New York: Thomas Y. Crowell, 1953.

Getz, Robert S. *Congressional Ethics; The Conflict of Interest Issue*. New York: Van Nostrand, 1966.

Haynes, George H. *The Senate of the United States*. 2 vols. Boston: Houghton-Mifflin Co., 1938.

Hoar, George F. *Autobiography of Seventy Years*. 2 vols. New York: Scribner's, 1903.

Jacobs, Andrew Jr. *The Powell Affair: Freedom Minus One*. Indianapolis: Bobbs Merrill, 1973.

Remick, Henry C. *The Powers of Congress in Respect to Membership and Elections*. 2 vols. Privately printed, 1929.

Riddick, Floyd M. *The United States Congress; Organization and Procedure*. Manassas, Va.: National Capitol Publishers, 1949.

Weeks, Kent M. *Adam Clayton Powell and the Supreme Court*. New York: Dunellen, 1971.

Willoughby, Westel W. *The Constitutional Law of the United States*. 2nd ed., 3 vols. New York: Baker, Voorhis, 1929.

Willoughby, William F. *Principles of Legislative Organization and Administration*. Washington: Brookings Institution, 1934.

Wilson, H. Hubert. *Congress; Corruption and Compromise*. New York: Rinehart, 1951.

Articles

Curtis, Thomas B. "Power of the House of Representatives to Judge the Qualifications of Its Members." *Texas Law Review*, July 1967, p. 1199.

Eckhardt, Robert C. "Adam Clayton Powell Case." *Texas Law Review*, July 1967, p. 1205.

Fleishman, Neill. "Power of Congress to Exclude Persons Duly Elected." *North Carolina Law Review*, April 1970, pp. 655-66.

"The Power of a House of Congress to Judge the Qualifications of Its Members." *Harvard Law Review*, January 1968, p. 673-84.

Wheildon, L.B. "Challenged Elections to the Senate." *Editorial Research Reports*, 1946, vol. 2, p. 799-817.

Government Publications

Deschler, Lewis. *Procedure in the U.S. House of Representatives.* Washington: Government Printing Office, 1975.

Hinds, Asher C. and Cannon, Clarence. *Hinds' and Cannon's Precedents of the House of Representatives of the United States.* 11 vols. Washington: Government Printing Office, 1935-41.

Hupman, Richard D. *Senate Election, Expulsion and Censure Cases from 1789 to 1972.* S. Doc. 92-7, 92nd Cong., 1st sess., 1972.

Riddick, Floyd. *Senate Procedure, Precedents and Practices.* Washington: Government Printing Office, 1975.

Rowell, Chester H. *A Historical and Legal Digest of All the Contested Election Cases in the House of Representatives from the First to the Fifty-sixth Congress, 1789-1901.* H. Doc. 510, 56th Cong., 2d sess., 1901.

Wickersham, Price. *The Right of the Senate to Determine the Qualifications of Its Members.* S. Doc. 4, 70th Cong., 1st sess., 1927.

U.S. Congress. House. Committee on House Administration. *Analysis of HR 14195, a Bill to Revise the Law Governing Contests of Elections of Members of the House of Representatives and for Other Purposes.* 91st Cong., 1st sess., 1970.

U.S. Congress. House. Select Committee Pursuant to H Res 1. *Report in re Adam Clayton Powell.* H. Rept 90-27. 90th Cong., 1st sess., 1967.

U.S. Congress. Joint Committee on Congressional Operations. *House of Representatives Exclusion, Censure and Expulsion Cases from 1789 to 1973.* Committee print, 93rd Cong., 1st sess., 1973.

U.S. Congress. Senate. Select Committee on Standards and Conduct. *Hearings on Senator Thomas J. Dodd.* 89th Cong., 2nd sess., and 90th Cong., 1st sess., 1966-67.

—. *Investigation of Senator Thomas J. Dodd.* 90th Cong., 1st sess., 1967.

—. *Report on the Investigation of Senator Thomas J. Dodd of Connecticut.* S. Rept. 90-193 to accompany S. Res. 112, 90th Cong., 1st sess., 1967.

—. *Standards of Conduct for Members of the Senate and Officers and Employees of the Senate.* S. Rept. 90-1015, 90th Cong., 2nd sess., 1968.

U.S. Congress. Senate. Select Committee to Study Censure Charges, Pursuant to S. Res. 301. *Hearings on a Resolution to Censure the Senator from Wisconsin, Mr. McCarthy.* 2 pts. 82nd Cong., 2nd sess., 1954.

Ethics and Criminal Prosecutions

Under the Constitution, each house of Congress has the power to punish members for misconduct. Article I, Section 5 states: "Each House may determine the Rules of its Proceedings, punish its Members for disorderly Behavior, and with the concurrence of two thirds, expel a Member."

It is a power Congress historically has been reluctant to use. Only seven senators, 18 representatives and one territorial delegate have been formally censured by their colleagues for misconduct. Fifteen senators and three representatives have been expelled. The instances of other disciplinary actions have been equally as rare. *(Details, p. 681)*

This reluctance has stemmed from a variety of reasons. There is a belief among some that, except in cases where a member's actions are illegal and punishable by the courts, the electorate must be the ultimate judge of his behavior rather than his colleagues. Loyalty among members, especially of the same party, and toward Congress as an institution is another factor. The difficulty of agreeing on what constitutes a conflict of interest and misuse of power has also clouded the question.

It is this grey area that Congress entered into in the 1960s when a series of scandals led to the formation of ethics committees to oversee the conduct of members of Congress. From their founding until 1976, the ethics panels have frequently been derided by critics as "do-nothing" committees.

The Senate committee launched its first investigation in 1966 when it probed charges against Thomas J. Dodd (D Conn.) which led to his censure. The panel conducted few publicly known investigations in the next decade. In mid-1976, however, it was reported to be investigating one senator and an aide to another senator.

Eight years after its establishment as a permanent committee, the House Committee on Standards of Official Conduct (House ethics committee) undertook its first investigation of a member. And within weeks after it launched an investigation of Robert L. F. Sikes (D Fla.) in May 1976—which resulted in the House reprimanding Sikes—it began a probe of Wayne L. Hays (D Ohio). *(Highlights of committee activities, p. 707)*

Congressional Immunity

The power of each house of Congress to judge the elections and qualifications of its own members and the power to punish members for disorderly behavior are essential to the functioning of Congress as a co-equal branch of the government, free from harassment and domination by the other branches. They are reinforced by the speech or debate clause of the Constitution (Article I, Section 6), which has been broadly interpreted by the courts as granting members of Congress immunity from prosecution for nearly all actions related to their legislative functions. *(Congressional Immunity p. 713)*

Senate Ethics Committee

The Senate Rules and Administration Committee, which conducted the investigations of the misconduct of Secretary to the Senate Majority Bobby Baker, asked the Senate in 1964 to give it jurisdiction to probe infractions of Senate rules. On the floor of the Senate, however, the request was turned down and the Senate voted instead to establish a six-member bipartisan committee to investigate allegations of improper conduct by senators and Senate employees. One reason for setting up the special committee was to avoid partisan bickering between the minority of Republicans on the Rules and Administration Committee and the Democratic majority. The Republicans had charged the Democrats with "whitewashing" Bobby Baker. *(Baker case, p. 717)*

In establishing the Select Committee on Standards and Conduct (Senate ethics committee) the Senate authorized it not only to receive complaints of unethical conduct but also to recommend disciplinary action if needed and to draw up a code of ethical conduct.

The six members of the select committee were not appointed until one year later, in July 1965. John C. Stennis (D Miss.) became the first chairman.

Following are highlights of Senate ethics committee activities:

Dodd Case

As its first business, the ethics committee undertook the investigation of Sen. Thomas J. Dodd (D Conn.). On Feb. 23, 1966, Dodd had invited the panel to probe charges, being aired in the press, that he had used campaign funds for personal expenses, billed both Congress and private organizations for the same travel expenses on speaking trips, and that he had used his position to do favors for a public relations representative of West German interests.

After conducting hearings the ethics committee recommended April 27, 1967, that the senator be censured. On June 23, the Senate on a 92-5 roll-call vote censured Dodd. *(Further details, p. 697)*

Long-Teamsters Probe

In 1967, the ethics committee made its second in vestigation into the activities of a member when it scrutinized charges made by *Life* magazine that Sen. Edward V. Long (D Mo.) had used his position to aid imprisoned Teamster Union President James R. Hoffa and had accepted fees for his efforts from one of Hoffa's lawyers. On Oct. 25, Chairman Stennis announced that the ethics committee had voted unanimously to exonerate Long of the *Life* charges.[1] When *Life* raised further, more specific charges, Stennis said the panel would consider the new charges.[2] Long was defeated in the 1968 primary.

Government's Code of Ethics

Congress in 1958 approved the following Code of Ethics (H Con Res 175, 85th Congress, second session) for all government employees, including members of Congress.*

Any person in Government service should:

1. Put loyalty to the highest moral principles and to country above loyalty to persons, party, or Government department.

2. Uphold the Constitution, laws, and legal regulations of the United States and of all governments therein and never be a party to their evasion.

3. Give a full day's labor for a full day's pay; giving to the performance of his duties his earnest effort and best thought.

4. Seek to find and employ more efficient and economical ways of getting tasks accomplished.

5. Never discriminate unfairly by the dispensing of special favors or privileges to anyone, whether for remuneration or not; and never accept, for himself or his family, favors or benefits under circumstances which might be construed by reasonable persons as influencing the performance of his governmental duties.

6. Make no private promises of any kind binding upon the duties of office, since a Government employee has no private word which can be binding on public duty.

7. Engage in no business with the Government, either directly or indirectly, which is inconsistent with the conscientious performance of his governmental duties.

8. Never use any information coming to him confidentially in the performance of governmental duties as a means for making private profit.

9. Expose corruption wherever discovered.

10. Uphold these principles, ever conscious that public office is a public trust.

*The report of the House Committee on Standards of Official Conduct *In the Matter of a Complaint Against Rep. Robert L. F. Sikes* (H Rept. 94-1364, July 23, 1976) stated the following: "Although the Code of Ethics for Government Service was adopted as a concurrent resolution, and, as such, may have expired with the adjournment of the 85th Congress, the standards of ethical conduct expressed therein represent continuing traditional standards of ethical conduct to be observed by Members of the House at all times, which were supplemented in 1968 by a specific Code of Official Conduct."

Chinese Immigration Bills

A third investigation was triggered by a series of news articles in late 1969 which implied that bribes were paid to Senate employees in the offices of 13 senators for introducing hundreds of private immigration bills to help Chinese seamen stay in the United States. After holding hearings, the committee reported May 28, 1970, that although there was no evidence of senatorial misconduct, there were indications of "apparent violations of law by some of the lawyers and lobbyists who sought the introduction of some of the bills."[3] *(Further details, p. 303)*

Luxury Car Leases

Reports in August 1970 that Ford Motor Company had leased insured Lincoln Continental sedans to at least 19 members, all but two of whom were committee chairmen or ranking minority members, at lower than average prices led to a unanimous committee recommendation that the leases be quickly terminated. Ford then cancelled them.[4]

Conflict of Interest Question

A fifth case did not involve a formal investigation but exemplified the more common committee procedure of what chief counsel Benjamin R. Fern described as "nipping in the bud." On Feb. 2, 1970, Sen. George L. Murphy (R Calif.) requested an opinion from Stennis on the propriety of receiving $20,000 a year as a private corporate retainer from Technicolor Inc. Stennis March 11 stated that he and Fern decided the arrangement was "not a conflict of interest.... This was so clear that it did not seem necessary to refer the question to the full committee." The committee, he continued, "by no means requires senators to bring matters to it for resolution, but at the express request of several senators, we have rendered opinions on matters relating to standards of conduct."[5]

Campaign Contributions Probe

In mid-1976 the ethics panel was investigating campaign contributions from Gulf Oil Corp. lobbyist Claude C. Wild Jr. Senate Minority Leader Hugh Scott (R Pa.) was reported by *The Washington Post* to have told the committee that he passed $45,000 he received from Wild along to other senators for their campaigns. The committee was also reported to be investigating Henry Giugni, administrative assistant to Sen. Daniel K. Inouye (D Hawaii), on charges that he accepted in early 1973 a $5,000 illegal contribution from Wild. The investigation was said to be concentrated on Giugni's failure to report it to the Inouye campaign treasurer and on his relationship with Wild at a time when the Senate Watergate Committee was investigating Wild's contributions to the Nixon campaign. Inouye was a member of the Watergate Committee.[6]

Senate Code of Conduct

On March 22, 1968, the Senate adopted four new rules intended to guide the ethical conduct of senators and Senate employees. In an opening statement in support of the four-point committee resolution, Chairman Stennis said that the resolution would "add rules [but]...not replace that great body of unwritten but generally accepted standards that will, of course, continue in effect."[7] Stennis pointed out that the resolution contained no provisions for punishing a violator. Censure of senators and dismissal of employees, he said would continue to be the remedies.

Regulations Governing Conduct of Members of Congress

Concern for the ethical conduct of members of Congress is reflected in the Constitution, federal statutes and Senate and House rules. Some key provisions affecting members' conduct follow:

Constitutional Provisions

"Each House may determine the Rules of its Proceedings, punish its Members for disorderly Behaviour, and, with the Concurrence of two thirds, expel a Member." (Article I, Section 5, Clause 2)

"...They shall in all Cases, except Treason, Felony and Breach of the Peace, be privileged from Arrest during their Attendance at the Session of their respective Houses, and in going to and returning from the same; and for any Speech or Debate in either House, they shall not be questioned in any other Place." (Article I, Section 6, Clause 1)

"No Senator or Representative shall, during the Time for which he was elected, be appointed to any civil Office under the Authority of the United States, which shall have been created, or the Emoluments whereof shall have been increased during such time; and no Person holding any Office under the United States, shall be a Member of either House during his Continuance in Office." (Article I, Section 6, Clause 2)

"No Title of Nobility shall be granted by the United States; And no Person holding any Office of Profit or Trust under them, shall, without the Consent of the Congress, accept of any present, Emolument, Office, or Title, of any kind whatever, from any King, Prince, or foreign State." (Article I, Section 9, Clause 8)

"The Senators and Representatives before mentioned...shall be bound by Oath or Affirmation, to support this Constitution...." (Article VI, Clause 3)

Criminal Statutes

A series of laws in Title 18 of the U.S. Code make it a federal crime for members of Congress to engage in certain actions. Prohibited acts, excluding those relating to campaign spending, include:

Soliciting or receiving a bribe for the performance of any official act, for the violation of an official duty or for participating in or permitting any fraud against the United States. The penalty is a $20,000 fine or three times the monetary equivalent of the thing of value, whichever is greater, or imprisonment for not more than 15 years, or both, plus possible disqualification from holding office. (18 USC 201c)

Soliciting or receiving anything of value for himself or because of any official act performed or to be performed by him. The penalty is a $10,000 fine or imprisonment for not more than two years, or both. (18 USC 201g)

Soliciting or receiving any compensation for services in relation to any proceeding, contract, claim, controversy, etc., in which the United States is a party or has a direct and substantial interest, before any department, agency, court martial, officer or civil or military commission. The penalty is a $10,000 fine and imprisonment for not more than two years, or both, plus disqualification from holding office. (18 USC 203a)

Practicing in the Court of Claims. The penalty is a $10,000 fine and imprisonment for not more than two years, or both, plus disqualification from holding office. (18 USC 204)

Receiving, as a political contribution or otherwise, anything of value for promising use of or using influence to obtain for any person an appointive office or place under the United States. The penalty is a $1,000 fine, or imprisonment for not more than one year, or both. (18 USC 211)

Entering into or benefiting from contracts with the United States or any agency thereof. The penalty is a $3,000 fine and voidance of the contract. (18 USC 431) Numerous exemptions are listed in 18 USC 433 and elsewhere.

Chamber Rules

Prior to the adoption of ethics codes in 1968, the chief ethical curbs on members' activities related to voting. *(Provisions of codes, this page and p. 711)*

In 1801, when he was Vice President and presiding over the Senate, Thomas Jefferson wrote in *Jefferson's Manual:*

"Where the private interests of a Member are concerned in a bill or question he is to withdraw. And where such an interest has appeared, his voice has been disallowed.... In a case so contrary, not only to the laws of decency, but to the fundamental principle of the social compact, which denies to any man to be a judge in his own cause, it is for the honor of the House that this rule of immemorial observance should be strictly adhered to."

Jefferson's rule gave rise to Rule 8 of the House, which requires each member present to vote "unless he has a direct personal or pecuniary interest in the event of such question." In most cases this decision has been left to the member. Under an 1874 ruling, a representative may vote for his private interests if the measure is not for his exclusive benefit, but for that of a group.

Under Rule 12 senators may be excused from voting, provided they give their reasons for abstaining, and senators have been excused in the past because of such a direct interest in the outcome.

The code provided for only limited public disclosure of the personal finances of senators, Senate candidates and those Senate employees making more than $15,000 a year. On a 40-44 vote, the Senate had rejected an amendment which would have required detailed public disclosure of members' and employees' assets, liabilities and business relationships. *(Financial disclosure, next page)*

Provisions of Senate Code

The resolution containing the new rules declared that a senator should use the power entrusted to him by the people "only for their benefit and never for the benefit of himself or of a few."

Outside Employment (Rule 41). Stipulated that no officer or employee of the Senate might engage in any other employment or paid activity unless it was not inconsistent with his duties in the Senate. Directed employees to report their outside employment to specified supervisors, including senators, who were to take such action as they considered necessary to avoid a conflict of interest by the employee.

Contributions (Rule 42). Directed that a senator and a declared candidate for the Senate might accept a contribution from a fund-raising event for his benefit only if he had given express approval before funds were raised and if he received a full accounting of the sources and amounts of each contribution. Official events of his party were exempted from these restrictions.

Permitted a senator or candidate to accept contributions from an individual or an organization provided that a complete accounting of the sources and amounts were made by the recipient.

Specified that a senator or candidate might use such contributions for the expenses of his nomination and election and for the following purposes: travel expenses to and from the senator's home state; printing and other expenses of sending speeches, newsletters and reports to his constituents; expenses of radio, television and other media reports to constituents; telephone, postage and stationery expenses not covered by Senate allowances; and subscriptions to home-state newspapers.

Required disclosure of gifts, from a single non-family source, of $50 or more under the provisions of Rule 44. *(See below.)*

Political Fund Raising (Rule 43). Prohibited employees of the Senate from receiving, soliciting or distributing funds collected in connection with a campaign for the Senate or any other federal office. Exempted from the rule senators' assistants who were designated to engage in such activity and who earned more than $10,000 a year. Required that the senator file the names of such designated aides with the secretary of the Senate, as public information.

Financial Disclosure (Rule 44). Required each senator, declared candidate and Senate employee earning more than $15,000 a year to file with the U.S. comptroller general, by May 15 each year, a sealed envelope containing the following reports:

• A copy of his U.S. income tax returns and declarations, including joint statements.

• The amount and source of each fee of $1,000 or more received from a client.

• The name and address of each corporation, business or professional enterprise in which he was an officer, director, manager, partner or employee, and the amount of compensation received.

• The identity of real or personal property worth $10,000 or more that he owned.

• The identity of each trust or fiduciary relation in which he held a beneficial interest worth $10,000 or more and the identity, if known, of any interest the trust held in real or personal property over $10,000.

• The identity of each liability of $5,000 or more owed by him or his spouse jointly.

• The source and value of all gifts worth $50 or more received from a single source.

Specified that the information filed with the comptroller general would be kept confidential for seven years and then returned to the filer or his legal representative. If the filer died or left the Senate, his reports would be returned within a year.

Provided that the Select Committee on Standards and Conduct might, by a majority vote, examine the contents of a confidential filing and make the file available for investigation to the committee staff. Required that due notice be given to an individual under investigation and an opportunity provided for him to be heard by the committee in closed session.

Required each senator, candidate and employee earning more than $15,000 a year to file with the secretary of the Senate by May 15 each year the following information, which was to be kept for three years and made available for public inspection:

• The accounting required under Rule 42 of all contributions received in the previous year (amounts under $50 might be totaled and not itemized).

• The amount, value and source of any honorarium of $300 or more.

House Ethics Committee

Largely in reaction to the Adam Clayton Powell Jr. (D N.Y.) case, the House in 1966 took its first step toward achieving an enforceable code of ethics. The effort was minimal, for the select committee empowered to draft a code was in existence only two months before the 89th Congress expired. It could only recommend that the next Congress create a permanent committee that would not only draft a code of ethical practices but would also, like the Senate ethics committee, investigate allegations of improper conduct and recommend disciplinary action. *(Details of Powell case, p. 687)*

Still moving slowly, the House the next year, early in the 90th Congress, created a 12-member, bipartisan standing Committee on Standards of Official Conduct. Rep. Melvin Price (D Ill.) became its first chairman. The committee was given no investigative authority. Its sole function was to recommend a code of conduct and the powers it might need to enforce the code. *(Code, p. 711)*

Committee Powers Increased

When the House adopted the code in 1968, it also made the Committee on Standards of Official Conduct a permanent committee with investigative and enforcement powers.

The committee was given several specific powers, including the following:

• It may consider measures related to the House Code of Official Conduct or financial disclosure requirements which have been referred to it.

• It may recommend to the House such legislative or administrative actions as it deems appropriate for establishing or enforcing standards of conduct.

• It may investigate, subject to limitations, any alleged violation of the code of official conduct or of any law, rule, regulation, or other standard of conduct applicable to members, officers or employees in the performance of their duties.

• It may report, with the approval of the House, to appropriate federal or state authorities, any substantial evidence of a violation of any law by a member, officer or employee of the House applicable to the discharge of his duties and responsibilities.

• It may consider a request of a member, officer or employee for an advisory opinion respecting the general propriety of any current or proposed conduct by him.

Certain limitations had been imposed on the committee by the resolution creating it. These included:

Disclosure Requirements for House and Senate

(as of mid-1976)

The House and Senate in 1968 adopted the first financial disclosure rules in the history of Congress. The regulations were different for each house, but in both cases members were required to make only limited public disclosures.

Senate

The Senate passed a resolution (S Res 266) March 22, 1968, setting down four new rules on conduct of members. Under the new rules, senators and senatorial candidates were required to make public the amount and source of each honorarium of $300 or more received during the preceding year. They also were asked to list the sources, amounts and disposition of the political contributions they received, as well as the source and amount of any gift in excess of $50 from persons other than relatives. *(Code, p. 705)*

The first Senate reports were filed in 1969, and members were allowed to account for only the second half of 1968. The reports are due each year by May 15.

In practice, the political contribution and gift disclosure requirements have yielded little information, because members must list only income received by themselves directly. Most senators have indicated that all such funds are received by their campaign committees. And although candidates and defeated incumbents have been officially required to file disclosure forms, few have done so.

Besides the public disclosures, senators were required to file with the comptroller general specific information on their income, assets and debts—including U.S. income tax returns.

House

The more detailed accounting required by House members was spelled out in H Res 1099, passed April 3, 1968. The resolution established a Code of Official Conduct for members and employees, as well as the disclosure rule. *(Code, p. 711)*

The new rules required representatives to disclose the following information by April 30 of each year:

● Interests worth more than $5,000 or income of $1,000 or more from any companies doing substantial business with the federal government or subject to federal regulatory agencies.

● Sources of any income for services (other than congressional salaries) exceeding $5,000 annually.

● Any capital gain from a single source exceeding $5,000.

In 1970, the House adopted a resolution (H Res 796) broadening the public disclosure requirements to include two new items—the source of each honorarium of $300 or more earned in one year, and the names of creditors to whom $10,000 or more was owed for 90 days or longer without the pledge of specific security. These new requirements were first added to reports for 1971.

Honoraria

Congress first limited how much its members could earn from honoraria in the 1974 campaign finance law (PL 93-443). For 1975, senators and representatives could receive no more than $15,000 annually for giving speeches and writing articles and were limited to $1,000 per item.

Under pressure from the Senate, that ceiling was raised in the 1976 amendments to the campaign law (PL 94-283) to allow members of Congress to receive $2,000 per individual event and an aggregate amount of $25,000 a year. The $25,000 limit was a net figure since members were allowed to deduct certain expenses such as booking agents' fees and travel expenditures.

Office Accounts

The 1974 campaign law also required senators and representatives to disclose contributions to and expenditures from office accounts, popularly known as "slush funds," that traditionally were used for official activities not covered by office allowances. However, the Federal Election Commission, which is responsible for enforcing the campaign law, had not implemented regulations spelling out what items were to be disclosed. The Senate rejected the initial office account regulation in late 1975 and the commission had not officially issued a new rule as of mid-1976. Until regulations were approved, members did not have to disclose their office accounts.

● No resolution, report, recommendation or advisory opinion may be made, and no investigation of conduct undertaken, unless approved by the vote of not less than 7 of the 12 members. (This assures that no action can be taken unless at least one member of the majority or minority is willing to join with those of the opposite political party.)

● Except when the committee undertakes an investigation on its own initiative it may act only upon receipt of a complaint, in writing and under oath, made by a member. If the complaint is submitted by an individual, not a member of the House, and as many as three members of the House have refused, in writing, to transmit the complaint, the committee may act on it.

● No member of the committee may participate in any committee proceeding relating to his own official conduct.

Following are highlights of House ethics committee activities:

Probe of Voting Irregularities

The House Committee on Standards of Official Conduct in 1968 investigated a controversy over "ghost" voting in the House which arose following newspaper reports of alleged irregularities in some House roll-call voting procedures. On June 19, 1969, the committee reported that "honest errors" accounted for the discrepancies in 1968 when members who were out of Washington were recorded as having voted. The committee blamed the errors on overwork and exhaustion on the part of the tally clerk, who later was dropped from the House payroll.[8]

(Continued on p. 709)

Members of Congress and the Practice of Law

Until World War II, to be a member of Congress was to hold a part-time job. Consequently, certain occupations which demand almost full-time attention—running a business or teaching school, for example—sent few representatives to Congress while others, notably the law, sent many. For years more than half of all members of Congress have been lawyers, while few have been active businessmen (though many have been retired businessmen). *(Occupations box, p. 525)*

Legal Practice and Past Scandals

Lawyers have never been forbidden to practice law while holding congressional office, but the combination of the two professions has led to numerous scandals.

Sen. Daniel Webster's retainer from the Bank of the United States is familiar to many. What is not so well known is that Webster's professional relationship with the bank was no secret; he represented the bank in 41 cases before the Supreme Court. It was not an unusual arrangement for the time; neither was it universally condoned. John Quincy Adams, for example, as a member of Congress declined to practice before federal courts.

It was not until the 1850s that members were forbidden to represent claimants against the U.S. government. This restriction grew out of a scandal surrounding Senator, and later Secretary of the Treasury, Thomas Corwin of Ohio. Corwin successfully recovered half a million dollars (an enormous sum for those days) in a mining case; scandal erupted when it was revealed that both the claimant and silver mine were frauds.

Legal practice played a supporting role in the great railroad robbery known as the Crédit Mobilier scandal of the Grant administration. In that case, as brought out in a congressional hearing, promoters of the Union Pacific Railroad used stock in Crédit Mobilier, a joint stock company they controlled, to bribe members of Congress to keep up federal subsidies to the railroad. *(See p. 162)*

The bribe-giver was a member of Congress, Rep. Oakes Ames of Massachusetts, and among those investigated were the Vice President Schuyler Colfax, and the Speaker of the House James G. Blaine. In the end, Ames, a Republican, and James Brooks, a Democrat from York, were censured but not expelled by the House, and censure was recommended but not carried out against Sen. James W. Patterson of New Hampshire. No unfavorable evidence was produced against Speaker Blaine, but Vice President Colfax's political career was ruined. *(Censure, p. 699)*

The early 1900s again brought congressional ethics to a low spot in public opinion. Heavily promoted by publisher William Randolph Hearst, a series of articles by David Graham Phillips called *Treason of the Senate* alleged corrupt behavior by 21 senators. The series played a major role in promoting direct election of senators.

Only one of the 21 senators replied publicly to Phillips' charges. He was Sen. Joseph W. Bailey of Texas, who had received more than $225,000 in legal fees for several months' services to a Texas oilman. Bailey vehemently defended his practice of law while serving in the Senate: "...I despise those public men who think they must remain poor in order to be considered honest. I am not one of them. If my constituents want a man who is willing to go to the poorhouse in his old age in order to stay in the Senate during his middle age, they will have to find another Senator. I intend to make every dollar that I can honestly make without neglecting or interfering with my public duty...."[1]

Bar Association Actions

The legal profession moved to discourage congressional law practice in the late 1960s. The move came after a series of scandals which involved, sometimes indirectly, congressional law practices. Among those were the cases of Rep. Thomas F. Johnson (D Md.), Senate Majority Secretary Bobby Baker, Sen. Edward Long (D Mo.), Sen. Thomas J. Dodd (D Conn.) and Rep. Cornelius Gallagher (D N.J.).[2]

The American Bar Association revised its canons in 1969. Its new Code of Professional Responsibility provided that the name of a public official should not be used in the name of a law firm or in the firm's professional notices "during any significant period in which he is not actively and regularly practicing law as a member of the firm."[3]

Most state bar associations adopted the code, as well as a number of state supreme courts, thus clearing the way for formal grievance proceedings if violated.

In an extensive study of congressional ethics, conducted in 1967-69, a special committee of the Association of the Bar of the City of New York made several recommendations on congressmen and the legal profession. The committee recommended that members of Congress voluntarily refrain from any form of law practice, except for first-termers who foresaw little prospect for re-election. The committee also recommended that Congress enact legislation to forbid "double door" law partnerships (under which the law partner of a member of Congress engages in federal agency practice prohibited by law to the member) and to forbid members from appearing for compensation in the courts.[4]

Income from Law Practices

In financial disclosure reports for the year 1975, 53 representatives reported at least $1,000 in income from a law practice. Nineteen of those were freshmen in the 94th Congress. Eight members of the House noted on their disclosure forms that they had withdrawn from practice.[5] (As of mid-1976, only information on the outside business activities of House members was made public.)

1. James C. Kirby, *Congress and the Public Trust: Report of the Association of the Bar of the City of New York Special Committee on Congressional Ethics* (Atheneum, 1970), pp. 81-82.

2. For details on the involvement of law practices in these cases, see *Congress and the Public Trust*, pp. 83-85.

3. *Ibid.*, p. 103.

4. *Ibid.*, pp. 234-35.

5. Congressional Quarterly, *Weekly Report*, July 31, 1976, p. 2053.

(Continued from p. 707)

The committee urged the installation of a modernized system of voting in the House. In 1972 the House changed its rules to allow the use of an electronic voting system for quorum calls and roll-call votes. The first recorded vote using the new system was taken Jan. 31, 1973.

Gallagher Charges

Life magazine on Aug. 9, 1968, raised charges of wrongdoing against Rep. Cornelius E. Gallagher (D N.J.), calling him a "tool and collaborator" of a reputed Mafia figure in New Jersey. The Committee on Standards of Official Conduct, after looking into the *Life* allegations, chose not to release any information on its inquiry and no action against Gallagher was taken by the committee. Chairman Price said in 1968 that "there was no proof of any violation of the code [of ethics] which the committee had adopted."[9]

On April 7, 1972, Gallagher was indicted for income tax evasion, perjury and conspiracy to hide kickbacks. He pleaded guilty to tax evasion. *(p. 718)*

Voting Ban

For the first time since its formation in 1967, the House ethics committee April 26, 1972, initiated action which would have had the effect of punishing a member. By a vote of 10-2, the committee approved a resolution stating that any representative convicted of a crime for which he might receive a sentence of two years or more in prison should refrain from participating in committee business or House votes.

The committee's report said that "the preservation of public confidence in the legislative process" demanded that guidelines be established for House members who were convicted of "serious" crimes.[10] The only member to whom the resolution was applicable at that time was John Dowdy (D Texas). *(Dowdy case, p. 717)*

The voting ban resolution never was voted on by the House in 1972 because the Rules Committee refused to recommend further action. But, on April 16, 1975, the House amended its rules to include a voluntary voting ban. *(Details, p. 700)*

Advisory Opinions on Travel

The House ethics committee on two occasions has counseled representatives on the acceptance of free trips, which long have raised ethical questions. On June 27, 1974, the committee advised members and employees of the House not to accept trips to foreign countries at the expense of foreign governments unless specifically approved by Congress.

The committee May 14, 1975, issued an advisory opinion to members recommending that they not accept free rides on noncommercial carriers—primarily company planes—when traveling to or from political campaign engagements "and the host carrier is one who would be prohibited by law from making a campaign contribution." In such cases, the committee said, the non-paid transportation would amount to a political contribution, "and should not be accepted."

Even if the trip were not for purposes of campaigning, said the opinion, representatives should not request special rides for their own convenience on a noncommercial carrier, as this could be interpreted "as an abuse of one's public position."

The committee said acceptance of free transportation would not be improper in the following situations:

Ban on Nepotism

In a move that surprised most members of Congress and reporters, the House voted in 1967 to prohibit nepotism by federal officials, including senators and representatives. The proposal was offered by Rep. Neal Smith (D Iowa) as a floor amendment to the postal rate and federal pay bill of 1967 and was adopted by a 49-33 standing vote. The Senate accepted the Smith proviso, with language extending it to less immediate relatives (sons-in-law, for example), and the ban was written into permanent law.

In explaining his amendment, Smith said it was aimed in particular at postmasters in small post offices who were inclined to hire their wives as post office clerks.

But nepotism by members of Congress—the hiring of wives, children, brothers and other close relatives for work on a member's own staff—was a frequent source of critical press comment. Columnists over the years had charged certain members with padding their official staffs or district offices with relatives who did no work for their government paycheck. *(See p. 464)*

The nepotism ban prohibited officers or employees of the federal or District of Columbia governments from appointing, or recommending for appointment or promotion, a relative to serve in the same agency or department as the official.

● If the purpose of the trip were personal or to carry out his job as a representative, and "if the host carrier's purpose in scheduling the transportation is solely for the general benefit of the host and the transportation is furnished on a space-available basis with no additional costs incurred in providing accommodations."

● If the purpose of the trip were to enable the member, as part of his official duties, to be present at an event for the general benefit of the audience—not the member.

● If the trip were in connection with the representatives' receipt of an honorarium. "Under such circumstances, the transportation may be accepted in lieu of monetary reimbursement for travel to which the passenger would otherwise be entitled."

● As a guest on scheduled airlines' inaugural flights, as long as the other conditions in the advisory opinion were met.

Complaint Against Harrington

The House ethics committee Nov. 6, 1975, dismissed a complaint brought by Robin L. Beard Jr. (R Tenn.) against Michael J. Harrington (D Mass.).

By a 7-3 vote, the committee set aside Beard's charges that Harrington had violated House rules by revealing secret information about the Central Intelligence Agency's political activities in Chile. The classified testimony had been presented to the Armed Services Investigations Subcommittee by CIA Director William E. Colby on April 22, 1974. The committee's vote came after John J. Flynt Jr. (D Ga.), who became chairman in 1975, told other members of the panel that the occasion on which Colby testified was not a legal executive session.

Flynt said no public notice of the meeting was issued, a quorum was not present, no vote was taken to meet in executive session as required by House rules and only one member of the panel was present when Colby testified.

On June 16 the House Armed Services Committee, reacting to Harrington's disclosure, had voted 16-13 to deny him future access to its files pending a ruling by the ethics panel on criteria for future access to committee files by House members. *(Details, p. 700)*

Lobby Legislation

The House ethics committee shares jurisdiction with the Judiciary Committee over lobby registration legislation in the House. The ethics panel began a study of lobbying activities in 1970, and reported a bill to the House in December 1971. The bill died at the end of that Congress. *(Lobby legislation, p. 674)*

Intelligence Leak Probe

The House Feb. 19, 1976, ordered the Committee on Standards of Official Conduct to investigate the unauthorized release of the House Select Intelligence Committee's final report on U.S. intelligence operations. The House on Jan. 29 had voted to bar the report's release on grounds that it contained classified information. On Feb. 11, a New York weekly newspaper, *The Village Voice*, published extensive excerpts from the document, and CBS News correspondent Daniel Schorr later admitted that he had transmitted the report to the newspaper.

On March 3, the House approved a resolution giving the ethics committee far-reaching power to subpoena "such witnesses...and documents as it deems necessary." Under House rules, the committee's subpoena power extends only to members, officers and employees of the House.

Following extensive interviews by the committee's investigative staff, the committee began public hearings in July 1976.

Sikes Investigation

The House July 29, 1976, voted to reprimand Rep. Robert L. F. Sikes (D Fla.) when it accepted, by a vote of 381-3, the House ethics committee finding that Sikes was guilty of financial misconduct. It was the first time the House had punished one of its members since the Powell case in 1969 and was the result of the first known investigation of a House member by the ethics committee. *(Powell case, p. 687)*

Sikes, chairman of the House Military Construction Appropriations Subcommittee, had been charged with conflicts of interest and failure to disclose certain financial holdings. *(See below.)* The complaint against Sikes had been filed by Common Cause, the self-styled citizens' lobby, and transmitted to the ethics committee by 44 House members. The formal backing for a complaint against a House member by other members was unprecedented in the history of the committee.

The ethics committee April 28 initiated an inquiry into the conflict-of-interest allegations. On May 12, by a 9-0 vote, the panel authorized a "factual investigation" into the charges. Chairman Flynt told reporters that "so far as I know" it was the first investigation of a House member by the panel. By elevating the probe from the status of an inquiry to an investigation, the panel gave itself the authority to subpoena financial records and question witnesses under oath.

Committee Findings. The committee July 21 voted 10-2 to approve a report (H Rept 94-1364) on Sikes' dealings

---

Senate Honoraria

Senate financial disclosure reports for 1975 showed information on both honoraria received by members and groups providing honoraria to members. Similar information was not available from House reports.

Top Earners

The following chart compares the 1974 and 1975 earnings of the 1974 top 10 recipients of honoraria. In 1974 there was no limit on the amount of honoraria a senator could receive. In 1975, the limit was $15,000.

	1974	1975
Howard H. Baker Jr. (R Tenn.)	$49,650	$ 8,500
William Proxmire (D Wis.)	46,279	13,000
Mark O. Hatfield (R Ore.)	45,677	14,964
Hubert H. Humphrey (D Minn.)	40,750	14,900
Henry M. Jackson (D Wash.)	34,350	7,700
Herman E. Talmadge (D Ga.)	32,165	14,980*
Daniel K. Inouye (D Hawaii)	29,550	14,389
Edmund S. Muskie (D Maine)	28,800	13,800
Edward W. Brooke (R Mass.)	28,700	9,000
Harrison A. Williams Jr. (D N.J.)	28,617	12,550

Highest earnings reported in 1975.

Top Spenders

The following chart shows the amounts of honoraria provided by the 10 groups which were reported as spending the most for such payments to senators in 1975.

American Mining Congress	$9,000
United Jewish Appeal	8,500
Grocery Manufacturers of America	7,000
American Podiatry Association	6,000
American Bakers Association	6,000
Heritage Foundation	5,500
Chicago Council on Foreign Relations	5,300
American Bankers Association	5,250
Brotherhood of Railway, Airline and Steamship Clerks, Freight Handlers, Express and Station Employees (AFL-CIO)	5,000
National Town Meeting	4,000

---

which recommended the House adopt H Res 1421 reprimanding Sikes.[11]

The report cited three instances where it said Sikes' actions "have violated standards of conduct applicable to all members of Congress." They were:

● Failure to report ownership of stock in Fairchild Industries, Inc., in annual disclosure statements from 1968 through 1973, and in the First Navy Bank at the Pensacola Naval Air Station, Pensacola, Fla., in his 1973 disclosure statement, as required by House Rule 44. (Sikes first disclosed stock ownership in both companies in his 1974 financial disclosure statement.) Although Sikes' failure to report these holdings did not appear to be "an effort to conceal" them from Congress or the public, the report declared: "The committee believes that the failure to report...is deserving of a reprimand."

• Sikes' investment in stock of the First Navy Bank which he was active in establishing violated Section 5 of the Code of Ethics for Government Service and was cause for a reprimand. *(Government code, p. 704)* "If an opinion had been requested of this committee in advance about the propriety of the investment, it would have been disapproved," according to the report.

• The sponsorship of legislation in 1961 that removed restrictions on Florida land parcels without disclosing that Sikes had an interest in the same land. The committee did not recommend any punishment for this action because, it said, it took place so long ago and "at least to some extent" the circumstances "appear to have been known to Representative Sikes' constituency which has continually re-elected him to Congress." The committee also noted that Sikes had sold some of the land after the bill he had sponsored passed the House, but before it passed the Senate. Although recommending no punishment, the committee said Sikes' involvement with the legislation "created an obvious and significant conflict of interest."

In the first two instances, the committee specified that adoption of the report would constitute a reprimand.

On another charge, the committee concluded that Sikes did not violate House rules when he voted for a fiscal year 1975 defense appropriations bill (HR 16243—PL 93-437) that contained a $73-million appropriation for an aircraft contract with Fairchild Industries. The committee determined that Sikes' ownership of 1,000 shares out of the more than 4.5 million shares outstanding in Fairchild was not "sufficient to disqualify him from voting on the bill."

Hays Scandal

Less than a month after undertaking the Sikes investigation, the ethics committee began a probe of a sex-and-public payroll scandal involving Wayne L. Hays (D Ohio), the powerful chairman of the House Administration Committee and the Democratic National Congressional Committee. In a story which broke in *The Washington Post* May 23, 1976, Elixabeth Ray accused Hays of giving her a $14,000-a-year job on the House Administration Committee in exchange for sexual favors.

Hays at first denied the Ray charge but then admitted to the House May 25 that he had had a "personal relationship" with Ray. However, he denied that he had hired her to be his mistress.[12]

On May 25, Hays asked the ethics committee to investigate the matter. The same day 28 House members, in a letter to ethics Chairman Flynt, asked the committee to take up the Hays case. On June 2, the committee voted 11-0 to begin an immediate investigation into the charges.

The Justice Department and FBI had entered the case soon after Ray made her charges, and by May 26, a federal grand jury in Washington, D.C., began hearing testimony relating to her allegations.

Pressure built up quickly in the House to oust Hays from his leadership positions. He relinquished June 3 his chairmanship of the Democratic Congressional Campaign Committee. Hays won renomination to his House seat in a close Democratic primary in Ohio's 18th District June 8. Then, bowing to pressure from the House Democratic leadership, Hays resigned the chairmanship of the House Administration Committee June 18 and Aug. 13 announced he would not run for re-election to Congress in 1976. On Sept. 1 Hays resigned from Congress. The ethics panel then voted, 12-0, to end its investigation of Hays.

John Young Accused

Meanwhile, a second House member was accused of keeping a woman on his staff in return for sexual favors. Colleen Gardner, a secretary, told *The New York Times* June 11, 1976, that Rep. John Young (D Texas) increased her salary to $26,000 a year after she submitted to his sexual advances. Young denied the allegation and asked the ethics committee to look into it. The Aug. 19 Times reported that the Justice Department ended its inquiry into the matter because it had been unable to substantiate the charge.

Travel Expense Vouchers

The ethics committee June 9, 1976, began an investigation into charges contained in *Wall Street Journal* articles alleging improprieties in travel expense vouchers submitted by members of Congress. *(Details, p. 468)*

House Code of Conduct

The House adopted its Official Code of Conduct April 3, 1968. The new ethics rules covered representatives, the resident commissioner from Puerto Rico and top employees of the chamber. In 1972, the definition of "members" was broadened to include the delegates from the District of Columbia, Guam and the Virgin Islands.

The House required its members to make more information public in their financial disclosure statements than did the Senate, but even the House provisions left many loopholes. The intent of the disclosure requirements, according to the House committee's report, was "to acquaint the voters with the areas in which it is possible for a conflict of interest to occur." This good intention, however, was just about nullified by strict rules the committee later laid down for members of the press or public who wanted to copy information from the non-confidential reports.

Provisions of House Code

Code of Official Conduct (Rule 43). Stipulates that a member, officer or employee of the House shall:

1. "...Conduct himself at all times in a manner which shall reflect creditably on the House of Representatives."

2. "...Adhere to the spirit and the letter of the rules of the House and to the rules of duly constituted committees thereof."

3. "...Receive no compensation nor shall he permit any compensation to accrue to his beneficial interest from any source, the receipt of which would occur by virtue of influence improperly exerted from his position in the Congress."

4. "...Accept no gift of substantial value, directly or indirectly, from any person, organization or corporation having a direct interest in legislation before the Congress."

5. "...Accept no honorarium for a speech, writing for publication, or other similar activity, from any person, organization or corporation in excess of the usual and customary value for such services."

6. "...Keep his campaign funds separate from his personal funds. Unless specifically provided by law, he shall convert no campaign funds to personal use in excess of reimbursement for legitimate and verifiable prior campaign expenditures and he shall expend no funds from his campaign account not attributable to bona fide campaign purposes." [The words "Unless specifically provided by law" added in 1975.]

7. "...Treat as campaign contributions all proceeds from testimonial dinners or other fund-raising events if the sponsors of such affairs do not give clear notice in advance to the donors or participants that the proceeds are intended for other purposes."

8. "...Retain no one from his clerk-hire allowance who does not perform duties commensurate with the compensation he receives."

9. "...Not discharge or refuse to hire any individual, or otherwise discriminate against any individual with respect to compensation, terms, conditions, or privileges of employment, because of such individual's race, color, religion, sex, or national origin." [Clause added in 1975.]

10. "A member of the House who has been convicted by a court of record for the commission of a crime for which a sentence of two or more years' imprisonment may be imposed should refrain from participation in the business of each committee of which he is a member and should refrain from voting on any question at a meeting of the House, or of the Committee of the Whole House, unless or until judicial or executive proceedings result in reinstatement of the presumption of his innocence or until he is reelected to the House after the date of such conviction." [Clause added in 1975.]

Financial Disclosure (Rule 44). Requires members and officers of the House, their principal assistants and professional staff members of committees to file with the Committee on Standards by April 30 each year a report naming the sources of certain financial interests—which are to be available to the public—and a sealed report on the amounts of income from each source. The sealed report may be opened by the committee only if it determines that it is essential to an investigation.

The public listing of financial interest is to include:

● The name of any business in which the filer has a financial interest of over $5,000 or from which he derives income of $1,000 or more, but only if it does substantial business with the federal government or is under federal regulation.

● The name and type of practice of any professional organization from which the filer receives income of $1,000 or more, but only if the filer or his spouse is an officer, director, partner or adviser.

● The source of income exceeding $5,000 from a service rendered (except to the government) or a capital gain (except sale of the filer's home) and of reimbursement for expenditures exceeding $1,000.

These reports are to be available for public inspection under regulations to be set by the committee, which may require full identification of the person making the examination and the reason for it and is to notify the member involved.

The confidential reports are to give the fair market value of the business holdings reported and the amount of income from each source reported publicly.

Persons without financial interests that must be reported are required to file statements to this effect.

Additional Disclosure Requirements. In 1969 *The Wall Street Journal* ran articles about the heavy indebtedness of Rep. Seymour Halpern (R N.Y.), third-ranking Republican on the House Banking Committee. The information showed, according to the *Journal*, that: "First National City Bank of New York extended Mr. Halpern a $40,000 usecured personal loan 'at our best lending rate' when he was already in debt to 13 other banks for more than $75,000; while that loan was outstanding, First National City's lobbyists were pressing Congress to enact a mild ver-

sion of the bill bringing one-bank holding companies under federal regulation."[13]

In 1970, the House added a new financial disclosure rule: It called for public reporting of any loan of $10,000 or more outstanding for 90 days or longer without a pledge of specific collateral. The amount of the indebtedness need not be made public, only the source. The House added also a requirement, matching the existing Senate requirement, for the disclosure of the sources of honoraria of $300 or more. Again, only the sources need be made public; the amounts received would be reported in the sealed file.

Financial Disclosure Reports

In mid-1976 Congress made another move toward tightening its financial disclosure rules that for the previous eight years had provided little information to the public on the financial holdings and outside income of its members. *(Summary of Financial Disclosure Requirements box p. 707)*

The Senate July 21, 1976, passed the Watergate reform bill that set out stringent financial disclosure requirements for members of Congress, candidates for federal office, judges and top level federal government officials. That represented the fourth time in four years that tough disclosure rules had been approved by the Senate. Those provisions, included in the Senate-passed versions of the 1971, 1974 and 1976 campaign finance laws, had been dropped at the insistence of the House conferees. *(Campaign finance legislation, p. 540)*

However, in mid-1976, some observers thought the House reprimand of Rep. Robert L.F. Sikes (D Fla.), in part for violating House disclosure rules, might weaken House resistance. Critics of the disclosure rules said that the Sikes case pointed up how inadequate the rules were at doing the job they were ostensibly intended to do.

CQ Study of Reports

Since 1969 Congressional Quarterly has examined and analyzed the House and Senate reports filed under the disclosure regulations.

Financial disclosure reports for 1975 filed by senators and representatives provided very limited information on their outside income, stock and property holdings.

A CQ study of the reports showed the following:

● The $15,000 ceiling on honoraria each member of Congress could receive in 1975—imposed in the 1974 campaign finance law (PL 93-443)—eliminated a source of substantial outside income for many senators. The campaign law also limited gratuities for speeches or articles to $1,000 per item. The total amount of honoraria senators received in 1975 fell by one-third to some $638,000 from almost $940,000 in 1974.

Senators' honoraria payments were expected to rise in 1976 following a relaxation of the limits included in the 1976 campaign finance law amendments (PL 94-283). Under the new law, members of Congress could receive $2,000 per individual event and $25,000 a year. However, the $25,000 limit was a net amount since booking agents' fees, travel expenditures, subsistence and expenses for an aide or spouse to accompany the speaker could be deducted. *(Box, Senate Honoraria, p. 710)*

● Special interest groups and other organizations spent considerably less on honoraria payments to senators in 1975 than in 1974. The biggest drop was recorded in honoraria paid by academic institutions, down to $136,172 in 1975 from $242,267 in 1974.

• In the House, 231 representatives listed honoraria payments in 1975, a 20 per cent jump over 1974. Fewer representatives, however, reported receiving income from outside law practices than in previous years. *(See p. 708)*

Reports filed by representatives and senators could not be compared because the two chambers required their members to disclose different items. Senators had to reveal only honoraria payments of $300 or more as well as political contributions and gifts of over $50.

Representatives, on the other hand, were required to disclose the sources but not the amounts of their honoraria. Representatives had to list companies in which they had substantial holdings and which did business with the government or were regulated by government agencies; they also had to list capital gains of more than $5,000 and sources of outside income exceeding $5,000 a year.

Congressional Immunity from Prosecution

The concept of congressional immunity from certain legal actions was a well-established principle in England when it was added to the American Constitution. Article I, Section 6 provides that senators and representatives "shall in all cases, except Treason, Felony and Breach of the Peace, be privileged from Arrest during their Attendance at the Session of their respective Houses, and in going to and returning from the same; and for any Speech or Debate in either House, they shall not be questioned in any other Place."

The privilege from arrest clause has become practically obsolete, as various court decisions have excluded more and more acts and proceedings from the protection of the clause. As presently interpreted, the clause applies only to arrests in civil suits, such as nonpayment of debts or breach of contract; and most state constitutions or statutes prohibit arrest generally in such actions. Civil arrests were more common at the time the Constitution was adopted.

Long v. Ansell (293 U.S. 76) in 1934 and *U.S. v. Cooper* (4 Dall. 341) in 1800 declared that the clause did not apply to service of process in civil or criminal cases; nor does it apply to arrest in any criminal case. Furthermore, *Williamson v. United States* (207 U.S. 425, 446) in 1908 interpreted the phrase "treason, felony, or breach of the peace" as excluding all criminal offenses from the privilege's coverage.

The speech or debate clause has been cited more frequently by members seeking immunity from actions against them. Various court decisions have broadly interpreted the phrase "speech or debate" to include virtually everything a member does in carrying out his legislative responsibilities.

'Speech or Debate' Broadly Construed

The first Supreme Court interpretation of the speech or debate clause occurred in 1880 in *Kilbourn v. Thompson* (103 U.S. 168). The case is also widely cited for its ruling on the limits of congressional investigations. It involved a contempt of Congress citation against Hallet Kilbourn, manager of a real estate pool, for refusing to answer questions before the House Select Committee on the Real Estate Pool and Jay Cooke Indebtedness. The House ordered Kilbourn jailed for contempt. He won release on a writ of habeus corpus and sued the Speaker, members of the investigating committee and Sergeant at Arms John G. Thompson for false arrest. The Supreme Court sustained Kilbourn's claim, on the grounds that it was not a legitimate investigation. *(Details, p. 150)*

The court decided the case on the basis of Congress' investigating powers. But the defendants, in the course of their arguments, raised the speech or debate clause as a defense, and the court also commented on this issue in its opinion. The court said the protection of the clause was not limited to words spoken in debate, but also was applicable to written reports, to resolutions offered, to the act of voting, and to all things generally done in a session of the House by one of its members in relation to the business before it.

Legislative Acts Protected

The Supreme Court on Feb. 24, 1966, held in a 7-0 decision that in prosecuting a former member of Congress the executive branch may not constitutionally inquire into the member's motives for making a speech on the floor, even though the speech was made for a bribe and was part of an unlawful conspiracy.

The holdings in *United States v. Johnson* (383 U.S. 169) left members immune from prosecution for their words and legislative deeds on the floor of Congress, with one exception reserved by the court—prosecution under a "narrowly drawn" law enacted by Congress itself "to regulate the conduct of its Members." Members of Congress already were immune from libel suits for speeches made on the floor.

Johnson was the first case of its kind. The court was unable to find among the English or American cases any direct precedent. The court did discuss cases holding that legislators were protected from private suits for their legislative words and deeds; and it cited approvingly a Supreme Court decision, the force of which appeared to extend the *Johnson* doctrine to state legislators.

Background. The *Johnson* case arose out of the conviction of former Rep. Thomas F. Johnson (D Md.) on June 13, 1963, by a federal jury in Baltimore. The government charged that Johnson, former Rep. Frank W. Boykin (D Ala.) and two officers of a Maryland savings and loan company then under indictment, J. Kenneth Edlin and William L. Robinson, entered into a conspiracy whereby Johnson and Boykin would approach the Justice Department to urge a "review" of the indictment and Johnson would make a speech on the floor of the House defending savings and loan institutions. Johnson made the speech June 30, 1960, and it was reprinted by the indicted company and distributed to the public. Johnson and Boykin allegedly received money in the form of "campaign contributions." Johnson's share was more than $20,000.

Court Rulings. Johnson was convicted on seven counts of violating the federal conflict of interest law (18 U.S.C. 281) and on one count of conspiring to defraud the United States (18 U.S.C. 371); the others were convicted of the same charges. President Johnson Dec. 17, 1965, granted Boykin a full pardon.

The 4th Circuit Court of Appeals Sept. 16, 1964, set aside Johnson's conspiracy conviction on grounds that it was unconstitutional under provisions of Article I, Section 6: "...for any Speech or Debate in either House, they [senators and representatives] shall not be questioned in any other Place." The court ordered a new trial on the other counts on grounds that evidence taken about Johnson's speech on the conspiracy count "infected" the entire case.

The Supreme Court affirmed the lower court's ruling, thus foreclosing further prosecution on the conspiracy count but permitting retrial on the other counts. In the majority opinion, Justice John Marshall Harlan said the purpose of the speech or debate clause was "prophylactic," that it was adopted by the Constitutional Convention (without discussion or opposition) because of the English experience with efforts of the Crown to intimidate and punish Parliament. The clause was intended to protect the independence and integrity of Congress, the justice said, and to reinforce the separation of powers by preventing an "unfriendly" executive and a "hostile" judiciary appointed by the executive from reaching into congressional activity for evidence of criminality.

The government's theory, rejected by Justice Harlan, was that Johnson's criminal act—acceptance of a bribe and entering into a conspiracy—predated his floor speech. Justice Harlan said the indictment particularized the speech as part of the conspiracy charged, and evidence about the speech was taken at trial.

On Jan. 26, 1968, Johnson was convicted for a second time on the conflict-of-interest charges by the U.S. District Court in Baltimore. He was sentenced to six months in prison.

Immunity Protection Narrowed

On June 29, 1972, the Supreme Court in effect narrowed the category of protected actions under the immunity clause. The court's ruling was issued in a case involving former Sen. Daniel B. Brewster (D Md.) who had been indicted, along with others, on charges of violating federal bribery laws.

Background. A federal grand jury Dec. 1, 1969, indicted Brewster, Spiegel Inc., a Chicago mail-order firm, and Cyrus T. Anderson, a lobbyist for the firm, on charges of violating federal bribery laws. The indictment announced by Attorney General John N. Mitchell, charged that Brewster received $24,500 from Spiegel Inc. and Anderson to influence his "action, vote and decision" on postal rate legislation.

The grand jury said the payments were made in five installments between Jan. 10, 1966 and Jan. 31, 1968. Brewster was a member of the Senate Post Office and Civil Service Committee during a 1967 debate on postal rate increases for regular third-class mail. Spiegel was a major user of such rates. Brewster had been defeated for re-election in 1968.

Court Rulings. Ten months after Brewster's indictment, a U.S. district court judge dismissed it on the grounds that the senator was immune from prosecution because of Article I, Section 6, Clause 1 of the Constitution—that the immunity granted members of Congress by the Constitution shielded him from prosecution for bribery related to performance of a legislative act.

The government took an appeal directly to the Supreme Court, which issued a decision June 29, 1972, narrowing the category of protected actions under the immunity clause. A six-man court majority ruled: "Taking a bribe is, obviously, no part of the legislative process or function." *(United States v. Brewster,* 408 U.S. 501)

Immunity in Washington

Members of Congress apparently were no longer to be immune from arrest in Washington, D.C., for crimes such as drunk driving and soliciting prostitutes, according to a 1976 Justice Department ruling.

Reports occasionally would appear in the press of such incidents in Washington involving a member. Invariably, once police confirmed that the suspect was a member of Congress, action against the member would be dropped.

The Justice Department ruling, which had been requested by Washington Police Chief Maurice J. Cullinane, stemmed from a case involving Rep. Joe D. Waggonner Jr. (D La.). Waggonner had been arrested after he allegedly solicited a District of Columbia policewoman posing as a prostitute. He was released when police identified him as a member of Congress.

Cullinane announced the Justice Department ruling on July 23, 1976. Based on the ruling, he said, members "and all other elected and appointed federal, state, and local officials are subject to arrest for the commission of criminal offenses to the same extent and in the same manner as all other citizens." An exception would be continued, he said, for most parking violations on private automobiles bearing congressional license plates.

Cullinane said the non-arrest policy, which had been in effect for more than 100 years, had been based on "a misinterpretation of the meaning" of the Privilege from Arrest Clause in Article I, Section 6 of the Constitution.

At least since *Williamson v. United States* (207 U.S. 425, 446) in 1908, this language was held to have been inserted in the Constitution to prevent political harassment through civil arrest. The more sweeping policy against arrest was thought to have been aimed at not offending the legislators, who controlled the D.C. police department budget.

Chief Justice Warren E. Burger, writing the opinion, continued: "The illegal conduct is taking or agreeing to take money for a promise to act in a certain way. There is no need for the government to show that [Brewster] fulfilled the alleged illegal bargain...for it is taking the bribe, not performance of the illicit compact, that is a criminal act." Importantly, the court upheld the validity of the indictment since it would not be necessary for the government to inquire into legislative acts or their motivations in order to prove a violation of the bribery statute. Brewster was ordered to stand trial, which began Oct. 30, 1972, and resulted in his conviction by a federal jury in Washington, D.C., on Nov. 17, 1972.

In its verdict, the jury found Brewster guilty of a lesser bribery charge, that of accepting an unlawful gratuity. Following the verdict, Spiegel Inc. pleaded guilty. Brewster was sentenced to two-to-six years in prison and fined $30,000. In August 1974 a federal appeals court reversed the conviction on grounds the jury had not been given proper instructions. A new trial was scheduled for August 1975. But on June 25, 1975, Brewster pleaded no contest to a felony charge of accepting an illegal gratuity while he was a senator.

Protected Acts Specified

On June 29, 1972, the Supreme Court took the unusual step of specifying in some detail certain acts of a legislator which were protected by the immunity clause. The case involved Sen. Mike Gravel (D Alaska) and his actions in releasing portions of the then-classified Pentagon Papers history of U.S. involvement in the Vietnam War.

Background. During the controversy over publication of the Pentagon Papers in 1971 by *The New York Times, The Washington Post* and several other newspapers, Sen. Gravel on June 29, 1971, convened a special meeting of the Public Works Subcommittee on Public Buildings, of which he was chairman. With the press and the public in attendance, Gravel read classified documents from the Pentagon Papers into the subcommittee record. Subsequently, the senator arranged for the verbatim publication of the subcommittee record by Beacon Press, the non-profit publishing arm of the Unitarian-Universalist Association.

In August 1971 a federal grand jury in Boston, investigating the release of the Pentagon Papers, ordered an aide to Gravel, Dr. Leonard S. Rodberg, to appear before it. Rodberg had been hired the night Gravel called the session of his subcommittee to read excerpts from the secret documents. Rodberg subsequently helped Gravel edit and make arrangements for publication of the papers. The grand jury also subpoenaed several persons associated with Beacon Press who were involved in publication of the papers.

Rodberg moved to quash the subpoena on the grounds he was protected from questioning by congressional immunity, contending such immunity extended to staff members. Gravel filed a motion to intervene on Rodberg's behalf, claiming Rodberg was acting under the senator's orders, which were immune from judicial inquiry.

The Justice Department, in a brief filed in the case Sept. 8, 1971, said no immunity existed for either Rodberg or Gravel. While not saying so directly, the department's action left open the possibility it might subpoena Gravel himself to testify.

A lower court ruled in October 1971 that the grand jury could not question any witness about Gravel's conduct at the special meeting or about his preparation for the meeting. The grand jury was also prohibited from questioning Rodberg about his own actions taken at Gravel's direction relating to the meeting.

Court Rulings. In January 1972 the Court of Appeals held that Gravel could be questioned about the subsequent publication of the subcommittee record by Beacon Press but not about the subcommittee meeting itself. The same immunities extended to Gravel were also to be applied to Rodberg, the court ruled. But third parties, the court ruled, could be questioned about any of their own actions regarding the publication and the ad hoc committee session.

In a 5-4 decision on June 29, 1972, the Supreme Court specifically enumerated the activities of Gravel and Rodberg which were protected by the immunity clause *(Gravel v. United States,* 408 U.S. 606).

The court said no witness could be questioned concerning: 1) the conduct of Gravel or his aides at the meeting of the Subcommittee on Public Buildings and Grounds of the Senate Public Works Committee on June 29, 1971; 2) the motives and purposes behind the conduct of Gravel or his aides at the June 29 meeting; 3) communications between Gravel and his aides during the terms of their employment and related to the June 29 meeting or any other legislative act of the senator; 4) any act, in itself not criminal, per-

formed by the senator or by his aides in the course of their employment in preparation for the subcommittee meeting, except as it proved relevant to investigating possible third-party crime.

The ruling held that Sen. Gravel's constitutional immunity did not shield him or his aides from grand jury questioning regarding their activities not directly related to their legislative responsibilities. "While the Speech or Debate Clause recognizes speech, voting and other legislative acts as exempt from liability that might attach," the court stated, "it does not privilege either senator or aide to violate an otherwise valid criminal law in preparing for or implementing legislative acts."

The court concluded that the immunity of Gravel's aide was identical to that of his employer and defined the latter's as immunity from "prosecutions that directly impinge upon or threaten the legislative process."

The court majority concurred with the lower court ruling that the negotiations leading to the unofficial publication of the committee record were outside the protection of the speech or debate clause; further, however, it also held that Gravel as well as Rodberg were vulnerable to grand jury questioning and possible liability regarding their roles in the Pentagon Papers publication.

As of mid-1976, no further action had taken place in the case.

Legislative Protection Restated

The Supreme Court on Oct. 9, 1973, upheld an appellate court ruling which had reversed five of eight conspiracy, bribery and perjury convictions against former Rep. John Dowdy (D Texas) on grounds they had violated the immunity clause. The Fourth Circuit Court of Appeals in Richmond had said evidence used in the trial was an unconstitutional examination of the defendant's acts as a member of Congress.

Background. A federal grand jury in Baltimore, Md., March 31, 1970, indicted Dowdy on charges of conspiracy, perjury and the use of interstate facilities to promote bribery. The indictment alleged Dowdy had accepted a $25,000 bribe at the Atlanta, Ga., airport on Sept. 22, 1965, to intervene in a federal and District of Columbia investigation of the Monarch Construction Company of Silver Spring, Md.

Dowdy's trial was set for Sept. 14, 1970, but the opening of the case was delayed after Dowdy entered a Texas hospital Sept. 8 for treatment of a recurring back condition. Lawyers for Dowdy attempted Sept. 1 to persuade the Fourth Circuit Court of Appeals to set aside the trial on grounds of congressional immunity. The lawyers argued that federal prosecutors were attempting to question privileged legislative acts. The court turned down the petition.

Court Rulings. Dowdy was convicted on Dec. 30, 1971, in U.S. District Court in Baltimore of crossing a state line to receive a bribe, conspiracy to obstruct justice, conspiracy to violate conflict of interest statutes, and five counts of perjury. He was sentenced to 18 months in prison and fined $25,000.

On March 13, 1973, the Fourth Circuit Court of Appeals reversed five of the eight convictions and reduced Dowdy's sentence to six months in prison and a $3,000 fine. Convictions on three counts of perjury were sustained. *(Dowdy v. United States,* 479 F.2d 213)

The court of appeals found that the first trial had violated the Speech or Debate clause of the Constitution, which provides that members of Congress cannot be questioned in any other forum for any speech or debate in which they participated in Congress.

The court held that the evidence used in the first trial "was an examination of the defendant's actions as a congressman, who was chairman of a subcommittee investigating a complaint, in gathering information in preparation for a possible subcommittee investigatory hearing."

These actions were privileged under the speech or debate clause of the Constitution. Thus a conviction based on such evidence violated the privilege and was unconstitutional.

Although the alleged criminal act—bribery—was the same in both the Dowdy and Brewster cases, the major difference, which resulted in one case being upheld and one case being reversed, was the source of the evidence. In Brewster's case there was sufficient evidence available outside of Brewster's legislative activities to permit the case to go forward. In Dowdy's case so much of the evidence was based on Dowdy's legislative activities that the court reversed five of the eight convictions.

On Oct. 9, 1973, the Supreme Court upheld the ruling of the lower court (*Dowdy v. United States,* 414 U.S. 866). After losing a bid to stay out of prison for health reasons, Dowdy began his term Jan. 28, 1974.

Criminal Actions Against Members Since 1941

Following is a list of members of Congress since 1941 who have been indicted or otherwise charged in criminal courts, and the disposition of their cases. The information was compiled from Congressional Quarterly publications, *The New York Times* and *Facts on File;* Congressional Quarterly does not claim that the list is definitive.

Senate

Daniel B. Brewster (D Md. House 1959-63; Senate 1963-69)—Dec. 1, 1969, indicted for accepting bribe from a mail-order house to influence his vote on postal rate legislation; Oct. 9, 1970, charges dismissed by U.S. District Court; June 29, 1972, U.S. Supreme Court ruling ordered Brewster to stand trial; Nov. 17, 1972, convicted of accepting an unlawful gratuity, a lesser charge than bribery; Feb. 2, 1973, sentenced to two-to-six years in prison and fined $30,000; Aug. 2, 1974, U.S. Court of Appeals, D.C. Circuit, ordered a new trial on the unlawful gratuity charge; June 25, 1975, pleaded no contest and was fined $10,000.

Edward J. Gurney (R Fla. House 1963-69; Senate 1969-75)—April 26, 1974, indicted by a Florida grand jury on a misdemeanor charge of violating a state campaign finance law; May 17, 1974, indictment dismissed; July 10, 1974, indicted by federal grand jury with six other defendants for conspiracy, perjury and soliciting bribes in form of campaign contributions from Florida builders with business pending before Department of Housing and Urban Development; Aug. 6, 1975, acquitted on soliciting bribes charge, but jury failed to reach a verdict on conspiracy to create a political slush fund and perjury charges; Sept. 1, 1976, Justice Department announced that it planned retrial on the perjury charge.

House

James M. Curley (D Mass. 1911-Feb. 4, 1914; 1943-47)—Sept. 16, 1943, indicted by federal grand jury, with five others, on charge of using mails to defraud by accepting retainers on false claims of ability to obtain war contracts; Nov. 1, 1943, indictment voided by U.S. District Court, Washington, D.C., on grounds grand jury was illegally summoned; Jan. 3, 1944, indicted on same charge; Jan. 18, 1946, convicted; Feb. 18, 1946, sentenced to six-to-18 months in prison and fined $1,000; Jan. 13, 1947, U.S. Court of Appeals, D.C. Circuit, upholds conviction; June 2, 1947, U.S. Supreme Court upholds conviction; June 26, 1947, begins serving sentence; Nov. 26, 1947, President Truman commutes remainder of sentence.

Andrew J. May (D Ky. 1931-47)—Jan. 23, 1947, indicted with three other men for conspiracy to defraud U.S. government and for accepting money to influence the War Department and other agencies to give contracts to a wartime munitions combine (May was one of its directors); July 3, 1947, convicted of conspiracy and bribery; Nov. 14, 1949, Supreme Court refused to review conviction; Dec. 5, 1949, entered prison and Sept. 18, 1950, paroled after serving nine months of an eight-to-24 month sentence; Dec. 24, 1950, pardoned by President Truman.

J. Parnell Thomas (R N.J. 1937-50)—Nov. 8, 1948, indicted for conspiracy to defraud the government through padding his congressional payroll and taking kickbacks from his staff; Nov. 30, 1949, pleaded no contest and Dec. 9, 1949, sentenced to six-to-18 months in prison and fined $10,000; Sept. 10, 1950, paroled after serving eight and a half months in prison.

Theodore Leonard Irving (D Mo. 1949-53)—June 8, 1951, indicted for violation of Corrupt Practices Act and the Taft-Hartley Act for misusing funds of the labor union he headed for his 1948 House campaign; Dec. 28, 1951, acquitted.

Walter E. Brehm (R Ohio 1943-53)—Dec. 20, 1950, indicted for accepting campaign contributions from two of his congressional office employees; April 30, 1951, convicted on charges involving one employee; June 11, 1951, sentenced to five-to-15 months in prison (sentence suspended) and fined $5,000.

John L. McMillan (D S.C. 1939-73)—Jan. 14, 1953, indicted for violating law barring members of Congress from contracting with the government (he leased oil and gas lands in Utah from Department of Interior); May 16, 1953, acquitted.

Ernest K. Bramblett (R Calif. 1947-55)—June 17, 1953, indicted for making false statements in connection with payroll padding and kickbacks from congressional employees; Feb. 9, 1954, convicted; April 14, 1954, sentence stayed pending Supreme Court review; April 4, 1955, Supreme Court upheld conviction; June 15, 1955, sentenced to four-to-12 months in prison (sentence suspended) and fined $5,000.

Thomas J. Lane (D Mass. Dec. 30, 1941-63)—March 5, 1956, indicted for federal income tax evasion in 1949-51; April 30, 1956, pleaded guilty and sentenced to four months in prison and fined $10,000.

William J. Green Jr. (D Pa. 1945-47; 1949-Dec. 21, 1963)—Dec. 14, 1956, indicted, with six others, for con-

Congressional Aides Misuse Power

Misuses of power and conflicts of interest have not been limited to members of Congress. Occasionally congressional aides have used their positions and their employers' prestige for personal gain. Following are two of the most famous cases in recent years.

Bobby Baker

Bobby Baker began his Capitol Hill career as a teenage page in the Senate. Ambitious and aggressive, Baker rose to the position of secretary to the Senate majority, making himself right-hand man to his mentor, Majority Leader Lyndon B. Johnson (D Texas), in the late 1950s. When he quit his post under fire, Baker on paper was worth $2-million, most of it gained, the subsequent court records showed, from combining law practice with influence peddling. The notoriety caused by the Baker case is credited with moving the Senate to create an ethics committee.

Baker resigned from his $19,600 Senate job in 1963 after a civil suit was brought against him, charging that he used his influence to obtain contracts for a vending machine concern in which he had a financial interest. Senate investigations conducted over the next two years concluded that Baker was guilty of "gross improprieties." The investigating committee recommended that the Senate require full financial disclosures by senators and top employees of the Senate.

Baker meanwhile was brought to trial on charges of income tax evasion, theft and conspiracy to defraud the government. He was found guilty in January 1967; after appeals had been exhausted, he began his prison term four years later. The major charge on which he was found guilty was that he had collected more than $99,000 from a group of California savings and loan executives, ostensibly as campaign contributions, but that in reality he had kept about 80,000 of the total for himself.

At the trial two of the California executives testified that in 1962 they gave Baker about $66,000 for campaign contributions to seven senators and one House member, Ways and Means Committee Chairman Wilbur D. Mills (D Ark.). Mills and one of the senators, Foreign Relations Committee Chairman J. W. Fulbright (D Ark.), testified that they had received none of the funds. Defense counsel stipulated that none of the other six senators had received any of the funds. One of the savings and loan executives testified that Baker told him the California savings and loan associations could improve their standing in Congress with a "very impressive" contribution to certain senators and House members and could "win friends" in Congress at a time when a bill was pending to increase taxes on the associations.

Baker testified he turned the money over to Sen. Robert S. Kerr (D Okla.), a power on the Senate Finance Committee, for his re-election campaign. Kerr was dead by the time Baker told his story.

Sweig and the Speaker's Office

A congressional scandal which attracted nationwide attention when it was revealed in 1969 involved influence-peddling in the office of Speaker John W. McCormack (D Mass.). In the end, one of his top aides, Dr. Martin Sweig, was convicted July 9, 1970, of perjury, and Jan. 28, 1972, of misusing the Speaker's office to influence government decisions.

Sweig, who had worked for McCormack 24 years and was drawing an annual salary of $36,000 in 1969, was implicated with Nathan M. Voloshen, New York City lawyer-lobbyist and longtime McCormack friend. On June 17, 1970, Voloshen pleaded guilty to charges of conspiring to use the Speaker's office to influence matters before federal government agencies and to three counts of lying to a federal grand jury about the charges.

---

spiracy to defraud the government by accepting money and bond business for his insurance firm from contractors in return for influencing decisions on the construction from 1951-54 of a $33-million Army Signal Corps depot in Tobyhanna, Pa.; Feb. 27, 1959, acquitted.

Thomas F. Johnson (D Md. 1959-63)—Oct. 16, 1962, indicted with Frank W. Boykin (D Ala.) and two other defendants, for conflict of interest and conspiracy to defraud the government by trying to influence Justice Department action on indictments in a Maryland savings and loan association scandal; Johnson was accused of receiving more than $20,000 for his part in the conspiracy, which included a House speech defending savings and loan institutions; June 13, 1963, convicted; Sept. 16, 1964, Fourth Circuit Court of Appeals set aside conviction on grounds that the House speech was protected by the speech or debate clause of the Constitution, and ordered new trial for Johnson on conflict of interest charges; Feb. 24, 1966, Supreme Court upheld ruling; Jan. 26, 1968, convicted of conflict of interest; Jan. 30, 1968, sentenced to six months in prison.

Frank W. Boykin (D Ala. 1935-63)—Oct. 16, 1962, indicted with Rep. Thomas F. Johnson (D Md.) on charges of conflict of interest and conspiracy to defraud the government *(see Johnson above)*; June 13, 1963, convicted; Oct. 7, 1963, Boykin placed on probation for six months and fined $40,000; Dec. 17, 1965, pardoned by President Johnson.

Adam Clayton Powell Jr. (D N.Y. 1945-67; 1969-71)—May 8, 1958, indicted for federal income tax evasion; April 5 and 7, 1960, federal judge dismissed two of three counts and trial on third count declared mistrial April 22, 1960, because of hung jury; May 23, 1960, judge refused to dismiss indictment; April 13, 1961, case dismissed at request of U.S. attorney. *(Powell's involvement in a libel suit in New York resulting in four contempt of court citations, p. 688)*

John V. Dowdy (D Texas Sept. 23, 1952-73)—March 31, 1970, indicted for bribery, conspiracy and perjury in connection with receipt of payment from a Maryland home improvements firm accused of defrauding its customers; Dec. 30, 1971, convicted; Feb. 23, 1972, sentenced to 18 months in prison and fined $25,000; March 13, 1973, Fourth Circuit Court of Appeals reversed conspiracy and bribery convictions on constitutional grounds, but left standing perjury conviction; Oct. 9, 1973, Supreme Court upheld ruling; Jan. 28, 1974, entered prison to serve a six-month term. *(p. 715)*

Martin B. McKneally (R N.Y. 1969-71)—Dec. 16, 1970, indicted for failure to file federal income tax returns for 1964-67; Oct. 18, 1971, pleaded guilty to charge that he filed no income tax in 1965 and government dropped other charges; Dec. 20, 1971, sentenced to one year in prison (sentence suspended), placed on one-year probation, and fined $5,000.

Cornelius Gallagher (D N.J. 1959-73)—April 7, 1972, indicted for federal income tax evasion in 1966-67, perjury and conspiracy to hide kickbacks for aiding two co-conspirators to evade taxes in 1966-68; Dec. 21, 1972, pleaded guilty to tax evasion charge involving his own income; June 15, 1973, sentenced to two years in prison and fined $10,000; Nov. 22, 1974, released from jail eight months before end of two-year sentence. *(Gallagher case, p. 709)*

Frank J. Brasco (D N.Y. 1967-75)—Oct. 23, 1973, indicted for conspiracy to receive bribes from a reputed Mafia figure who sought truck leasing contracts from the Post Office and loans to buy trucks; July 19, 1974, convicted; Oct. 22, 1974, sentenced to five years in prison (all but three months suspended) and fined $10,000; June 26, 1975, began three-month sentence; Oct. 6, 1975, Supreme Court upheld conviction.

Angelo D. Roncallo (R N.Y. 1973-75)—Feb. 21, 1974, indicted for extortion of political contribution from an incinerator contractor at the time Roncallo was comptroller of Nassau County, Long Island; May 17, 1974, acquitted.

Bertram L. Podell (D N.Y. Feb. 20, 1968-75)—July 12, 1973, indicted for conspiracy, bribery, perjury and conflict of interest for receipt of payment to appear before federal agencies to help Florida Atlantic Airlines to obtain approval of a Bahaman route; Oct. 1, 1974, Podell ended nine-day trial by pleading guilty to the conspiracy and conflict of interest charges; Jan. 9, 1975, sentenced to six months in prison and fined $5,000; Nov. 3, 1975, Supreme Court refused to review the case.

J. Irving Whalley (R Pa. Nov. 8, 1960-73)—July 5, 1973, indicted for mail fraud for using mail to deposit salary kickbacks he required from congressional staff and obstruction of justice for threatening an employee to prevent her from giving information to the Federal Bureau of Investigation; July 31, 1973, pleaded guilty; Oct. 15, 1973, sentenced to three years in prison (sentence suspended) and fined $11,000.

George V. Hansen (R Idaho 1965-69; 1975-)—Feb. 19, 1975, pleaded guilty to two misdemeanor counts of campaign spending violations in 1974 (failure to file a campaign finance report and filing an erroneous report); April 18, 1975, sentenced to one year in prison (ten months suspended and one-year probation); April 25, 1975, sentence reduced to a $2,000 fine.

Andrew J. Hinshaw (R Calif. 1973-)—May 6, 1975, indicted twice—first, for soliciting a bribe involving a 1972 campaign contribution, for two counts of bribery involving Tandy Corporation and for embezzlement and for misappropriation of public funds during time he served as assessor of Orange County, Calif., and second, for conspiracy, grand theft and embezzlement in connection with the use of employees for his 1972 House campaign; Oct. 10, 1975, judge dismissed from the first indictment embezzlement and misappropriation of public funds charges, but sustained bribery charges; Jan. 26, 1976, convicted of bribery charges and acquitted of charge of soliciting a bribe; Feb. 24, 1976, sentenced to a one-to-14-year sentence, announced he would appeal; trial on second indictment scheduled to begin in the fall of 1976.

James R. Jones (D Okla. 1973-)—Jan. 29, 1976, pleaded guilty to a misdemeanor charge that he failed to report a cash campaign contribution from the Gulf Oil Corp. in 1972; March 16, 1976, fined $200.

Wendell Wyatt (R Ore. Nov. 3, 1964-75)—June 11, 1975, pleaded guilty to misdemeanor charge of violating federal campaign spending laws by failing to report expenditures from a secret cash fund he controlled while heading the Nixon re-election campaign in Oregon in 1972; July 18, 1975, fined $750.

Henry J. Helstoski (D N.J. 1965-)—June 2, 1976, indicted for bribery, conspiracy, obstructing justice and perjury for his role in scheme to solicit and accept payment for the introduction of private immigration bills. *(See p. 303)*

Allan T. Howe (D Utah 1975-)—June 12, 1976, arrested in Salt Lake City on charge of soliciting two policewomen posing as prostitutes; July 23, 1976, convicted of soliciting sex acts for pay and sentenced to 30 days in prison and fined $150 (sentence suspended on payment of the fine); sentence stayed, pending appeal to state district court; Aug. 24, 1976, convicted and sentenced to 30 days in prison (suspended sentence) and assessed court costs.

Footnotes

1. U.S. Congress, Senate, Select Committee on Standards and Conduct, *Report on the Matter of Senator Edward V. Long of Missouri*, reprinted in *Congressional Record*, 90th Cong., 1st sess., Oct. 25, 1967, pp. 30096-98.

2. *Congressional Record*, 90th Cong., 1st sess., Nov. 7, 1967, p. 31530.

3. U.S. Congress, Senate, Select Committee on Standards and Conduct, *Investigation of the Introduction of Private Immigration Bills for Chinese Crewmen, 90th and 91st Congresses*, S. Rept. 91-911, 91st Cong., 2nd sess., May 28, 1970, p. 2.

4. *Congressional Record*, 91st Cong., 2nd sess., Aug. 24, 1970, p. 29880.

5. *The New York Times*, March 13, 1970.

6. *The Washington Post*, Aug. 10, 1976, and Aug. 31, 1976.

7. *Congressional Record*, 90th Cong., 2nd sess., March 18, 1968, p. 6833.

8. *Congressional Record*, 91st Cong., 1st sess., June 19, 1969, p. 16629.

9. Congressional Quarterly, *1968 Almanac*, p. 816.

10. U.S. Congress, House, Committee on Standards of Official Conduct, *Sense of the House of Representatives with Respect to Actions by Members Convicted of Certain Crimes*, H. Rept. 92-1039, 92nd Cong., 2nd sess., May 3, 1972.

11. U.S. Congress, House, Committee on Standards of Official Conduct, *In the Matter of A Complaint Against Representative Robert L. F. Sikes*, H. Rept. 94-1364 to accompany H. Res. 1421, 94th Cong., 2nd sess., July 23, 1976.

12. *Congressional Record*, 94th Cong., 2nd sess., May 25, 1976, p. H4895.

13. *The Wall Street Journal*, July 29, 1969.

Selected Bibliography

Books

Beard, Edmund and Horn, Stephen. *Congressional Ethics: The View from the House.* Washington D.C.: The Brookings Institution, 1975.

Bolling, Richard. *House Out of Order.* New York: E. P. Dutton Co., 1965.

Boyd, James. *Above the Law.* New York: New American Library, 1968.

Clark, Joseph S. *Congress: The Sapless Branch.* New York: Harper and Row, 1964.

Deakin, James. *The Lobbyists.* Washington, D.C.: Public Affairs Press, 1966.

Douglas, Paul H. *Ethics in Government.* Cambridge: Harvard University Press, 1952.

Getz, Robert S. *Congressional Ethics: The Conflict of Interest Issue.* Princeton: Van Nostrand, 1966.

Graham, George A. *Morality in American Politics.* New York: Random House, 1952.

Green, Mark J., Fallows, James M. and Zwick, David R. *Who Runs Congress?—The President, Big Business, or You.* New York: Grossman Publishers, 1972.

Kirby, James C. *Congress and the Public Trust: Report of the Association of the Bar of the City of New York Special Committee on Congressional Ethics.* New York: Atheneum, 1970.

Rienow, Robert and Rienow, Leona Train. *Of Snuff, Sin and the Senate.* Chicago: Follett Publishing Co., 1965.

Rogow, Arnold A. and Lasswell, Harold D. *Power, Corruption and Rectitude.* Englewood Cliffs: Prentice-Hall, 1963.

Weaver, Warren Jr. *Both Your Houses: The Truth About Congress.* New York: Praeger, 1972.

White, William S. *Citadel.* New York: Harper and Brothers, 1957.

Wilson, H. H. *Congress: Corruption and Compromise.* New York: Rinehart and Company, 1951.

Articles

Bernstein, Marver H. "Ethics in Government: The Problems in Perspective." *National Civic Review,* July 1972, pp. 341-47.

Clark, Joseph S. "Some Ethical Problems of Congress." *Annals of the American Academy of Political and Social Science,* January 1966, pp. 12-22.

"Bribed Congressman's Immunity from Prosecution." *Yale Law Journal,* December 1965, p. 335.

"Conflicts of Interest: A Symposium." *Federal Bar Journal,* Summer 1964.

"Conflict of Interest Acts." *Harvard Journal on Legislation,* January 1964, p. 68.

Hamer, John. "Ethics in Government." *Editorial Research Reports,* 1973, vol. 1, pp. 375-96.

Lee, Linda K. "Conflict of Interest: One Aspect of Congress' Problems." *George Washington Law Review,* vol. 32, 1963-1964, pp. 954-82.

"The Scope of Immunity for Legislators and Their Employees." *Yale Law Journal,* December 1967, pp. 366-89.

Government Publications

U.S. Congress. House. Committee on Rules. *Creating a Permanent Select Committee on Standards and Conduct.* House Report 89-1929. 89th Cong., 2nd sess., 1966.

U.S. Congress. House. Committee on Standards of Official Conduct. *Standards of Official Conduct, Hearings February 19, 1970 on House Resolution 796, Proposed Amendments to Financial Disclosure Rule.* 91st Cong., 2nd sess., 1970.

———. *Amendment of Financial Disclosure Rules.* House Report 91-938. 91st Cong., 2nd sess., 1973.

U.S. Congress. Joint Committee on Congressional Operations. *Constitutional Immunity of Members of Congress, Hearings March 21-July 19, 1973, on the Legislative Role of Congress in Gathering and Disclosing Information.* 93rd Cong., 1st sess., 1973.

———. *House of Representatives Exclusion, Censure and Expulsion Cases from 1789 to 1973.* Committee Print. 93rd Cong., 1st sess., 1973.

U.S. Congress. Senate. Committee on Labor and Public Welfare. *Hearings on the Establishment of a Commission on Ethics in Government, to Study Senate Concurrent Resolution 21.* 82nd Cong., 1st sess., 1951.

———. *Ethical Standards in Government.* Committee Print. 82nd Cong., 1st sess., 1951.

U.S. Congress. Senate. Committee on Rules and Administration. *Senate Election, Expulsion and Censure Cases from 1793 to 1972,* by Richard D. Hupman. Senate Document 92-7. 92nd Cong., 1st sess. Washington, D.C.: Government Printing Office, 1972.

U.S. Congress. Senate. Select Committee on Standards and Conduct. *Standards of Conduct for Members of the Senate and Officers and Employees of the Senate.* Senate Report 90-1015. 90th Cong., 2nd sess., 1968.

U.S. Library of Congress, American Law Division. *Provisions in the United States Code Prohibiting Conflicts of Interests by Members of Congress and by U.S. Government Officials and Employees.* By Elizabeth Yadlosky and Richard C. Ehlke. Library of Congress, 1973.

———. *Provisions in the United States Constitution, Federal Statutes and Rules of the House and Senate Governing the Conduct and Activities of Members of Congress.* By Robert L. Tienken. Library of Congress, 1972.

U.S. Library of Congress. Congressional Research Service. *The Constitutional Privileges from Arrest and of Speech or Debate of Members of Congress, U.S. Constitution Article I, Section 6: Historical Aspects and Legal Precedents.* Library of Congress, 1971.

APPENDIX

BIOGRAPHICAL INDEX

The names in this index include, alphabetically, all senators, representatives, resident commissioners and territorial delegates who served in Congress from March 4, 1789, through June 30, 1976—the 1st through 94th Congresses. The material is organized as follows: name, relationship to other members and Presidents, party, state (of service), date of birth, date of death (if applicable), congressional service, service as President, Vice President, member of the Cabinet or Supreme Court, governor, delegate to the Continental Congress, Speaker of the House, president pro tempore of the Senate and chairman of the Democratic or Republican National Committee. If member changed parties during his congressional service, party designation is that which applied at the end of such service and breakdown is included with congressional service. Party designation is multiple only if member was elected by two or more parties at the same time. Where service date is left open, member was still serving in 1976.

Dates of service are inclusive, starting in year of service and ending when service ends. From 1789 to 1933 terms of service were from March 4 to March 3; since 1934, service has been from January 3 to January 3. Exact date is shown (where available) if member began or ended his service in mid-term.

The major source for this list was the *Biographical Directory of the American Congress 1774-1971* compiled under the direction of the Joint Committee on Printing. Additional data were obtained from the files of the Joint Committee on Printing, the *Congressional Directory,* Congressional Quarterly's *Guide to U.S. Elections* and *Weekly Report, The New York Times* and *The Washington Post.*

A list of party and other abbreviations used follows.

Abbreviation	Party
AAD	Adams Anti Democrat
ABD	Anti Broderick Democrat
AD	Anti Democrat
Ad.D	Adams Democrat
AF	Anti Federalist
AJD	Anti Jackson Democrat
AL	American Laborite
Alliance D	Alliance Democrat
AM	Anti Monopolist
AMas.	Anti Mason
AMas. D	Anti Mason Democrat
AMD	Anti Monopoly Democat
AND	Anti Nebraska Democrat
AP	American Party
AR	Adams Republican
ASW	Anti Slavery Whig
ATD	Anti Tammany Democrat
AW	American Whig
C	Conservative
Cal.D	Calhoun Democrat
Cal.N	Calhoun Nullifier
CassD	Cass Democrat
CD	Clay Democrat
Clinton D	Clinton Democrat
Coal.	Coalitionist
Con.D	Conservative Democrat
Const. U	Constitutional Unionist
CR	Conservative Republican
CU	Conservative Unionist
CW	Clay Whig
D	Democrat
DD	Douglas Democrat
DFL	Democrat Farmer Labor
DR	Democratic Republican
E	Emancipationist
F	Federalist
FA	Farmers Alliance
FL	Farmer Laborite
FS	Free Soiler
FSD	Free Soil Democrat
FSil.	Free Silver
FSil.R	Free Silver Republican
FSW	Free Soil Whig

Abbreviation	Party
Fus.	Fusionist
Fus.D	Fusionist Democrat
G	Greenbacker
GD	Greenback Democrat
G Lab. Ref.	Greenback Labor Reformer
HCW	Henry Clay Whig
HTW	High Tariff Whig
I	Independent
ID	Independent Democrat
IR	Independent Republican
IRad.	Independent Radical
IRef.	Independent Reformer
ISil.R	Independent Silver Republican
IW	Independent Whig
JD	Jackson Democrat
Jeff.D	Jefferson Democrat
JFSt.	Jackson Free Statesman
KN	Know Nothing
L	Liberal
Lab.	Laborite
LD	Liberal Democrat
L&O	Law & Order
L&OW	Law & Order Whig
LR	Liberal Republican
LW	Liberation Whig
N	Nullifier
NAD	Native American Democrat
Nat.	Nationalist
Nat.A	National American
Nat.G	National Greenbacker
ND	Nullifier Democrat
New Prog.	New Progressive
Nonpart.R	Nonpartisan Republican
NR	National Republican
P	Populist
PD	Popular Democrat
PP	People's Party
PR	Progressive Republican
Pro.	Progressive

Abbreviation	Party
Prohib.	Prohibitionist
Protect.	Protectionist
Protect.TD	Protective Tariff Democrat
PSD	Popular Sovereignty Democrat
R	Republican
Rad.	Radical
Read.	Readjuster
RG	Republican Greenbacker
R Pro.	Republican Progressive
RR	Radical Republican
Sil.D	Silver Democrat
Sil.R	Silver Republican
Soc.	Socialist
SR	State Rights Party
SRD	State Rights Democrat
SRFT	State Rights Free Trader
SRW	State Rights Whig
SRWD	State Rights War Democrat
T	Temperance Party
TD	Tariff Democrat
Tyler D	Tyler Democrat
U	Unionist
UA	Ultra Abolitionist
UC	Union Conservative
UD	Union Democrat
UL	Union Laborite
UR	Union Republican
UU	Unconditional Unionist
UW	Union Whig
UWar	Union War Party
VBD	Van Buren Democrat
W	Whig
WD	War Democrat

Other Abbreviations

PI	Philippine Islands
PR	Puerto Rico
Rep.	Representative
Res.Comm.	Resident Commissioner
Terr.Del.	Territorial Delegate

A

AANDAHL, Fred George (R N.D.) April 9, 1897-April 7, 1966; House 1951-53; Gov. 1945-50.

ABBITT, Watkins Moorman (D Va.) May 21, 1908-___; House Feb. 17, 1948-73.

ABBOTT, Amos (W Mass.) Sept. 10, 1786-Nov. 2, 1868; House 1843-49.

ABBOTT, Jo (Joseph) (D Texas) Jan. 15, 1840-Feb. 11, 1908; House 1887-97.

ABBOTT, Joel (D Ga.) March 17, 1776-Nov. 19, 1826; House 1817-25.

ABBOTT, Joseph Carter (R N.C.) July 15, 1825-Oct. 8, 1881; Senate July 14, 1868-71.

ABBOTT, Josiah Gardner (D Mass.) Nov. 1, 1814-June 2, 1891; House July 28, 1876-77.

ABBOTT, Nehemiah (R Maine) March 29, 1804-July 26, 1877; House 1857-59.

ABDNOR, James (R S.D.) Feb. 13, 1923-___; House 1973-___.

ABEL, Hazel Hempell (R Neb.) July 10, 1888-July 30, 1966; Senate Nov. 8, 1954-Dec. 31, 1954.

ABELE, Homer E. (R Ohio) Nov. 21, 1916-___; House 1963-65.

ABERCROMBIE, James (UW Ala.) 1795-July 2, 1861; House 1851-55.

ABERCROMBIE, John William (D Ala.) May 17, 1866-July 2, 1940; House 1913-17.

ABERNETHY, Charles Laban (D N.C.) March 18, 1872-Feb. 23, 1955; House Nov. 7, 1922-35.

ABERNETHY, Thomas Gerstle (D Miss.) May 16, 1903-___; House 1943-73.

ABOUREZK, James G. (D S.D.) Feb. 24, 1931-___; House 1971-73; Senate 1973-___.

ABZUG, Bella S. (D N.Y.) July 24, 1920-___; House 1971-___.

ACHESON, Ernest Francis (R Pa.) Sept. 19, 1855-May 16, 1917; House 1895-1909.

ACKER, Ephraim Leister (D Pa.) Jan. 11, 1827-May 12, 1903; House 1871-73.

ACKERMAN, Ernest Robinson (R N.J.) June 17, 1863-Oct. 18, 1931; House 1919-Oct. 18, 1931.

ACKLEN, Joseph Hayes (D La.) May 20, 1850-Sept. 28, 1938; House Feb. 20, 1878-81.

ADAIR, Edwin Ross (R Ind.) Dec. 14, 1907-___; House 1951-71.

ADAIR, Jackson Leroy (D Ill.) Feb. 23, 1887-Jan. 19, 1956; House 1933-37.

ADAIR, John (D Ky.) Jan. 9, 1757-May 19, 1840; House 1831-33; Senate Nov. 8, 1805-Nov. 18, 1806; Gov. 1820-24.

ADAIR, John Alfred McDowell (D Ind.) Dec. 22, 1864-Oct. 5, 1938; House 1907-17.

ADAMS, Alva Blanchard (D Colo.) Oct. 29, 1875-Dec. 1, 1941; Senate May 17, 1923-Nov. 30, 1924, 1933-Dec. 1, 1941.

ADAMS, Benjamin (F Mass.) Dec. 16, 1764-March 28, 1837; House Dec. 2, 1816-21.

ADAMS, Brockman (Brock) (D Wash.) Jan. 13, 1927-___; House 1965-___.

ADAMS, Charles Francis (son of John Quincy Adams and grandson of President John Adams) (R Mass.) Aug. 18, 1807-Nov. 21, 1886; House 1859-May 1, 1861.

ADAMS, Charles Henry (R N.Y.) April 10, 1824-Dec. 15, 1902; House 1875-77.

ADAMS, George Everett (R Ill.) June 18, 1840-Oct. 5, 1917; House 1883-91.

ADAMS, George Madison (nephew of Green Adams) (D Ky.) Dec. 20, 1837-April 6, 1920; House 1867-75.

ADAMS, Green (uncle of George Madison Adams) (AP Ky.) Aug. 20, 1812-Jan. 18, 1884; House 1847-49, 1859-61 (1847-49 Whig, 1859-61 American Party).

ADAMS, Henry Cullen (R Wis.) Nov. 28, 1850-July 9, 1906; House 1903-July 9, 1906.

ADAMS, John (JD N.Y.) Aug. 26, 1778-Sept. 25, 1854; House March 4-Dec. 26, 1815, 1833-35 (1815 Democrat, 1833-35 Jackson Democrat).

ADAMS, John Joseph (D N.Y.) Sept. 16, 1848-Feb. 16, 1919; House 1883-87.

ADAMS, John Quincy (son of President John Adams and father of Charles Francis Adams) (W Mass.) July 11, 1767-Feb. 23, 1848; Senate 1803-June 8, 1808 (F); House 1831-Feb. 23, 1848 (W); Secy. of State 1817-25; President 1825-29.

ADAMS, Parmenio (—N.Y.) Sept. 9, 1776-Feb. 19, 1832; House Jan. 7, 1824-27.

ADAMS, Robert Jr. (R Pa.) Feb. 26, 1849-June 1, 1906; House Dec. 19, 1893-June 1, 1906.

ADAMS, Robert Huntington (JD Miss.) 1792-July 2, 1830; Senate Jan. 6, 1830-July 2, 1830.

ADAMS, Sherman (R N.H.) Jan. 8, 1899-___; House 1945-47; Governor 1949-53.

ADAMS, Silas (R Ky.) Feb. 9, 1839-May 5, 1896; House 1893-95.

ADAMS, Stephen (UD Miss.) Oct. 17, 1807-May 11, 1857; House 1845-47 (D); Senate March 17, 1852-1857 (UD).

ADAMS, Wilbur Louis (D Del.) Oct. 23, 1884-Dec. 4, 1937; House 1933-35.

ADAMSON, William Charles (D Ga.) Aug. 13, 1854-Jan. 3, 1929; House 1897-Dec. 18, 1917.

ADDABBO, Joseph P. (D N.Y.) March 17, 1925-___; House 1961-___.

ADDAMS, William (D Pa.) April 11, 1777-May 30, 1858; House 1825-29.

ADDONIZIO, Hugh Joseph (D N.J.) Jan. 31, 1914-___; House 1949-June 30, 1962.

ADGATE, Asa (D N.Y.) Nov. 17, 1767-Feb. 15, 1832; House June 7, 1815-17.

ADKINS, Charles (R Ill.) Feb. 7, 1863-March 31, 1941; House 1925-33.

ADRAIN, Garnett Bowditch (D N.J.) Dec. 15, 1815-Aug. 17, 1878; House 1857-61.

AHL, John Alexander (D Pa.) Aug. 16, 1813-April 25, 1882; House 1857-59.

AIKEN, David Wyatt (father of Wyatt Aiken and cousin of William Aiken) (D S.C.) March 17, 1828-April 6, 1887; House 1877-87.

AIKEN, George David (R Vt.) Aug. 20, 1892-___; Senate Jan. 10, 1941-75; Gov. 1937-41.

AIKEN, William (cousin of David Wyatt Aiken) (D S.C.) Aug. 4, 1806-Sept. 7, 1887; House 1851-57; Gov. 1844-46.

AIKEN, Wyatt (son of David Wyatt Aiken) (D S.C.) Dec. 14, 1863-Feb. 6, 1923; House 1903-17.

AINEY, William David Blakeslee (R Pa.) April 8, 1864-Sept. 4, 1932; House Nov. 7, 1911-15.

AINSLIE, George (D Idaho) Oct. 30, 1838-May 19, 1913; House (Terr. Del.) 1879-83.

AINSWORTH, Lucien Lester (AM Iowa) June 21, 1831-April 19, 1902; House 1875-77.

AITKEN, David Demerest (R Mich.) Sept. 5, 1853-May 26, 1930; House 1893-97.

AKERS, Thomas Peter (AP Mo.) Oct. 4, 1828-April 3, 1877; House Aug. 18, 1856-1857.

AKIN, Theron (PR N.Y.) May 23, 1855-March 26, 1933; House 1911-13.

ALBAUGH, Walter Hugh (R Ohio) Jan. 2, 1890-Jan. 21, 1942; House Nov. 8, 1938-39.

ALBERT, Carl Bert (D Okla.) May 10, 1908-___; House 1947-___; Speaker 1971-___.

ALBERT, William Julian (R Md.) Aug. 4, 1816-March 29, 1879; House 1873-75.

ALBERTSON, Nathaniel (D Ind.) June 10, 1800-Dec. 16, 1863; House 1849-51.

ALBRIGHT, Charles (R Pa.) Dec. 13, 1830-Sept. 28, 1880; House 1873-75.

ALBRIGHT, Charles Jefferson (R Ohio) May 9, 1816-Oct. 21, 1883; House 1855-57.

ALCORN, James Lusk (R Miss.) Nov. 4, 1816-Dec. 19, 1894; Senate Dec. 1, 1871-77; Gov. 1870-71.

ALDERSON, John Duffy (D W.Va.) Nov. 29, 1854-Dec. 5, 1910; House 1889-95.

ALDRICH, Cyrus (R Minn.) June 18, 1808-Oct. 5, 1871; House 1859-63.

ALDRICH, James Franklin (son of William Aldrich) (R Ill.) April 6, 1853-March 8, 1933; House 1893-97.

ALDRICH, Nelson Wilmarth (father of Richard Steere Aldrich and cousin of William Aldrich) (R R.I.) Nov. 6, 1841-April 16, 1915; House 1879-Oct. 4, 1881; Senate Oct. 5, 1881-1911.

ALDRICH, Richard Steere (son of Nelson Wilmarth Aldrich) (R R.I.) Feb. 29, 1884-Dec. 25, 1941; House 1923-33.

ALDRICH, Truman Heminway (brother of William Farrington Aldrich (R Ala.) Oct. 17, 1848-April 28, 1932; House June 9, 1896-97.

ALDRICH, William (father of James Franklin Aldrich and cousin of Nelson Wilmarth Aldrich) (R Ill.) Jan. 19, 1820-Dec. 3, 1885; House 1877-83.

ALDRICH, William Farrington (brother of Truman Heminway Aldrich) (R Ala.) March 11, 1853-Oct. 30, 1925; House March 13, 1896-97, Feb. 9, 1898-99 and March 8, 1900-01.

ALESHIRE, Arthur William (D Ohio) Feb. 15, 1900-March 11, 1940; House 1937-39.

ALEXANDER, Adam Rankin (F Tenn.) ?-?; House 1823-27.

ALEXANDER, Armstead Milton (D Mo.) May 26, 1834-Nov. 7, 1892; House 1883-85.

ALEXANDER, De Alva Stanwood (R N.Y.) July 17, 1846-Jan. 30, 1925; House 1897-1911.

ALEXANDER, Evan Shelby (cousin of Nathaniel Alexander) (— N.C.) about 1767-Oct. 28, 1809; House Feb. 24, 1806-09.

ALEXANDER, Henry Porteous (W N.Y.) Sept. 13, 1801-Feb. 22, 1867; House 1849-51.

ALEXANDER, Hugh Quincy (D N.C.) Aug. 7, 1911-___; House 1953-63.

ALEXANDER, James Jr. (D Ohio) Oct. 17, 1789-Sept. 5, 1846; House 1837-39.

ALEXANDER, John (D Ohio) April 16, 1777-June 28, 1848; House 1813-17.

ALEXANDER, John Grant (R Minn.) July 16, 1893-Dec. 8, 1971; House 1939-41.

ALEXANDER, Joshua Willis (D Mo.) Jan. 22, 1852-Feb. 27, 1936; House 1907-Dec. 15, 1919; Secy. of Commerce 1919-21.

ALEXANDER, Mark (SRD Va.) Feb. 7, 1792-Oct. 7, 1883; House 1819-33.

ALEXANDER, Nathaniel (cousin of Evan Shelby Alexander) (— N.C.) March 5, 1756-March 7, 1808; House 1803-Nov. 1805; Gov. 1805-07.

ALEXANDER, Sydenham Benoni (D N.C.) Dec. 8, 1840-June 14, 1921; House 1891-95.

ALEXANDER, William Vollie Jr. (D Ark.) Jan. 16, 1934-___; House 1969-___.

ALFORD, Julius Caesar (W Ga.) May 10, 1799-Jan. 1, 1863; House Jan. 2-March 3, 1837, 1839-Oct. 1, 1841 (1837 States Rights Whig; 1839-41 Harrison Whig).

ALFORD, Thomas Dale (D Ark.) Jan. 28, 1916-___; House 1959-63.

ALGER, Bruce Reynolds (R Texas) June 12, 1918-___; House 1955-65.

ALGER, Russell Alexander (R Mich.) Feb. 27, 1836-Jan. 24, 1907; Senate Sept. 27, 1902-Jan. 24, 1907; Gov. 1885-87; Secy. of War 1897-99.

ALLAN, Chilton (CD Ky.) April 6, 1786-Sept. 3, 1858; House 1831-37.

ALLEE, James Frank (R Del.) Dec. 2, 1857-Oct. 12, 1938; Senate March 3, 1903-07.

ALLEN, Alfred Gaither (D Ohio) July 23, 1867-Dec. 9, 1932; House 1911-17.

ALLEN, Amos Lawrence (R Maine) March 17, 1837-Feb. 20, 1911; House Nov. 6, 1899-Feb. 20, 1911.

ALLEN, Asa Leonard (D La.) Jan. 5, 1891-Jan. 5, 1969; House 1937-53.

ALLEN, Charles (FS Mass.) Aug. 9, 1797-Aug. 6, 1869; House 1849-53.

ALLEN, Charles Herbert (R Mass.) April 15, 1848-April 20, 1934; House 1885-89.

ALLEN, Clarence Emir (R Utah) Sept. 8, 1852-July 9, 1932; House Jan. 4, 1896-97.

ALLEN, Clifford Robertson (D Tenn.) Jan. 6, 1912-___; House Nov. 25, 1975-___.

ALLEN, Edward Payson (R Mich.) Oct. 28, 1839-Nov. 25, 1909; House 1887-91.

ALLEN, Elisha Hunt (son of Samuel Clesson Allen) (W Maine) Jan. 28, 1804-Jan. 1, 1883; House 1841-43.

ALLEN, Heman (W Vt.) June 14, 1777-Dec. 11, 1844; House 1831-39.

ALLEN, Heman (D Vt.) Feb. 23, 1779-April 7, 1852; House 1817-April 20, 1818.

ALLEN, Henry Crosby (R N.J.) May 13, 1872-March 7, 1942; House 1905-07.

ALLEN, Henry Dixon (D Ky.) June 24, 1854-March 9, 1924; House 1899-1903.

ALLEN, Henry Justin (R Kan.) Sept. 11, 1868-Jan. 17, 1950; Senate April 1, 1929-Nov. 30, 1930; Gov. 1919-23.

ALLEN, James Browning (D Ala.) Dec. 28, 1912-___; Senate 1969-___.

ALLEN, James Cameron (D Ill.) Jan. 29, 1822-Jan. 30, 1912; House 1853-July 18, 1856, Nov. 4, 1856-57 and 1863-65.

ALLEN, John (father of John William Allen) (F Conn.) June 12, 1763-July 31, 1812; House 1797-99.

ALLEN, John Beard (R Wash.) May 18, 1845-Jan. 28, 1903; House (Terr. Del.) March 4-Nov. 11, 1889; Senate Nov. 20, 1889-93.

ALLEN, John Clayton (R Ill.) Feb. 14, 1860-Jan. 12, 1939; House 1925-33.

ALLEN, John James (brother of Robert Allen) (W Va.) Sept. 25, 1797-Sept. 18, 1871; House 1833-35.

ALLEN, John Joseph Jr. (R Calif.) Nov. 27, 1899-___; House 1947-59.

ALLEN, John Mills (D Miss.) July 8, 1846-Oct. 30, 1917; House 1885-1901.

ALLEN, John William (son of John Allen) Aug. 1802-Oct. 5, 1887; House 1837-41.

ALLEN, Joseph (F Mass.) Sept. 2, 1749-Sept. 2, 1827; House Oct. 8, 1810-11.

ALLEN, Judson (D N.Y.) April 3, 1797-Aug. 6, 1880; House 1839-41.

ALLEN, Leo Elwood (R Ill.) Oct. 5, 1898-Jan. 19, 1973; House 1933-61.

ALLEN, Nathaniel (father-in-law of Robert Lawson Rose) (— N.Y.) 1780-Dec. 22, 1832; House 1819-21.

ALLEN, Philip (TD R.I.) Sept. 1, 1785-Dec. 16, 1865; Senate July 20, 1853-59; Gov. 1851-53.

ALLEN, Robert (D Tenn.) June 19, 1778-Aug. 19, 1844; House 1819-27.

ALLEN, Robert (brother of John James Allen) (D Va.) July 30, 1794-Dec. 30, 1859; House 1827-33.

ALLEN, Robert Edward Lee (D W.Va.) Nov. 28, 1865-Jan. 28, 1951; House 1923-25.

ALLEN, Robert Gray (D Pa.) Aug. 24, 1902-Aug. 9, 1963; House 1937-41.

ALLEN, Samuel Clesson (father of Elisha Hunt Allen (— Mass.) Jan. 5, 1772-Feb. 8, 1842; House 1817-29.

ALLEN, Thomas (D Mo.) Aug. 29, 1813-April 8, 1882; House 1881-April 8, 1882.

ALLEN, William (D Ohio) Dec. 27, 1803- July 11, 1879; House 1833-35; Senate 1837-49; Gov. 1874-76.

ALLEN, William (D Ohio) Aug. 13, 1827-July 6, 1881; House 1859-63.

ALLEN, William Franklin (D Del.) Jan. 19, 1883-June 14, 1946; House 1937-39.

ALLEN, William Joshua (son of Willis Allen) (D Ill.) June 9, 1829-Jan. 26, 1901; House June 2, 1862-65.

ALLEN, William Vincent (P Neb.) Jan. 28, 1847-Jan. 12, 1924; Senate 1893-99, Dec. 13, 1899-March 28, 1901.

ALLEN, Willis (father of William Joshua Allen) (D Ill.) Dec. 15, 1806-April 15, 1859; House 1851-55.

ALLEY, John Bassett (R Mass.) Jan. 7, 1817-Jan. 19, 1896; House 1859-67.

ALLGOOD, Miles Clayton (D Ala.) Feb. 22, 1878-___; House 1923-35.

ALLISON, James Jr. (father of John Allison) (W Pa.) Oct. 4, 1772-June 17, 1854; House 1823-25.

ALLISON, John (son of James Allison Jr.) (W Pa.) Aug. 5, 1812-March 23, 1878; House 1851-53, 1855-57.

ALLISON, Robert (W Pa.) March 10, 1777-Dec. 2, 1840; House 1831-33.

ALLISON, William Boyd (R Iowa) March 2, 1829-Aug. 4, 1908; House 1863-71; Senate 1873-Aug. 4, 1908.

ALLOTT, Gordon Llewellyn (R Colo.) Jan. 2, 1907-__; Senate 1955-73.

ALMON, Edward Berton (D Ala.) April 18, 1860-June 22, 1933; House 1915-June 22, 1933.

ALMOND, James Lindsay Jr. (D Va.) June 15, 1898-—; House Jan. 22, 1946-April 17, 1948; Gov. 1958-62.

ALSTON, Lemuel James (— S.C.) 1760-1836; House 1807-11.

ALSTON, William Jeffreys (W Ala.) Dec. 31, 1800-June 10, 1876; House 1849-51.

ALSTON, Willis (nephew of Nathaniel Macon) (WD N.C.) 1769-April 10, 1837; House 1799-1815, 1825-31.

ALVORD, James Church (W Mass.) April 14, 1808-Sept. 27, 1839; House 1839-Sept. 27, 1839.

AMBLER, Jacob A. (R Ohio) Feb. 18, 1829-Sept. 22, 1906; House 1869-73.

AMBRO, Jerome Anthony Jr. (D N.Y.) June 27, 1928-__; House 1975-__.

AMERMAN, Lemuel (D Pa.) Oct. 29, 1846-Oct. 7, 1897; House 1891-93.

AMES, Adelbert (father of Butler Ames) (R Miss.) Oct. 31, 1835-April 12, 1933; Senate Feb. 23, 1870-Jan. 10, 1874; Gov. 1868-69; 1874-76.

AMES, Butler (son of Adelbert Ames and grandson of Benjamin Franklin Butler) (R Mass.) Aug. 22, 1871-Nov. 6, 1954; House 1903-13.

AMES, Fisher (F Mass.) April 9, 1758-July 4, 1808; House 1789-97.

AMES, Oakes (R Mass.) Jan. 10, 1804-May 8, 1873; House 1863-73.

AMLIE, Thomas Ryum (Pro. Wis.) April 17, 1897-Aug. 22, 1973; House Oct. 13, 1931-33, 1935-39 (1931-33 Republican Progressive, 1935-39 Progressive).

ANCONA, Sydenham Elnathan (D Pa.) Nov. 20, 1824-June 20, 1913; House 1861-67.

ANDERSEN. Herman Carl (R Minn.) Jan. 27, 1897-__; House 1939-63.

ANDERSON, Albert Raney (IR Iowa) Nov. 8, 1837-Nov. 17, 1898; House 1887-89.

ANDERSON, Alexander Outlaw (son of Joseph Anderson) (D Tenn.) Nov. 10, 1794-May 23, 1869; Senate Feb. 26, 1840-41.

ANDERSON, Carl Carey (D Ohio) Dec. 2, 1877-Oct. 1, 1912; House 1909-Oct. 1, 1912.

ANDERSON, Chapman Levy (D Miss.) March 15, 1845-April 27, 1924; House 1887-91.

ANDERSON, Charles Arthur (D Mo.) Sept. 26, 1899-__; House 1937-41.

ANDERSON, Charles Marley (D Ohio) Jan. 5, 1845-Dec. 28, 1908; House 1885-87.

ANDERSON, Clinton Presba (D N.M.) Oct. 23, 1895-Nov. 11, 1975; House 1941-June 30, 1945; Senate 1949-1973; Secy. of Agriculture 1945-48.

ANDERSON, George Alburtus (D Ill.) March 11, 1853-Jan. 31, 1896; House 1887-89.

ANDERSON, George Washington (RR Mo.) May 22, 1832-Feb. 26, 1902; House 1865-69.

ANDERSON, Glenn M. (D Calif.) Feb. 21, 1913-__; House 1969-__.

ANDERSON, Hugh Johnston (D Maine) May 10, 1801-May 31, 1881; House 1837-41; Gov. 1844-47.

ANDERSON, Isaac (Jeff.D Pa.) Nov. 23, 1760-Oct. 27, 1838; House 1803-07.

ANDERSON, James Patton (D Wash.) Feb. 16, 1822-Sept. 20, 1872; House (Terr. Del.) 1855-57.

ANDERSON, John (Jeff.D Maine) July 30, 1792-Aug. 21, 1853; House 1825-33.

ANDERSON, John Alexander (R Kan.) June 26, 1834-May 18, 1892; House 1879-91, (1879-87 Republican, 1887-89 Independent, 1889-91 Republican).

ANDERSON, John B. (R Ill.) Feb. 15, 1922-__; House 1961-__.

ANDERSON, John Zuinglius (R Calif.) March 22, 1904-__; House 1939-53.

ANDERSON, Joseph (father of Alexander Outlaw Anderson) (— Tenn.) Nov. 5, 1757-April 17, 1837; Senate Sept. 26, 1797-1815; Pres. pro tempore 1804-05.

ANDERSON, Joseph Halstead (D N.Y.) Aug. 25, 1800-June 23, 1870; House 1843-47.

ANDERSON, Josiah McNair (W Tenn.) Nov. 29, 1807-Nov. 8, 1861; House 1849-51.

ANDERSON, LeRoy Hagen (D Mont.) Feb. 2, 1906-__; House 1957-61.

ANDERSON, Lucian (U Ky.) June 23, 1824-Oct. 18, 1898; House 1863-65.

ANDERSON, Richard Clough Jr. (— Ky.) Aug. 4, 1788-July 24, 1826; House 1817-21.

ANDERSON, Samuel (— Pa.) 1773-Jan. 17, 1850; House 1827-29.

ANDERSON, Simeon H. (father of William Clayton Anderson) (W Ky.) March 2, 1802-Aug. 11, 1840; House 1839-Aug. 11, 1840.

ANDERSON, Sydney (R Minn.) Sept. 18, 1881-Oct. 8, 1948; House 1911-25.

ANDERSON, Thomas Lilbourne (ID Mo.) Dec. 8, 1808-March 6, 1885; House 1857-61 (1857-59 American Party; 1859-61 Independent Democrat).

ANDERSON, William (Jeff.D Pa.) 1762-Dec. 16, 1829; House 1809-15, 1817-19.

ANDERSON, William Black (ID Ill.) April 2, 1830-Aug. 28, 1901; House 1875-77.

ANDERSON, William Clayton (son of Simeon H. Anderson and nephew of Albert Gallatin Talbott) (AP Ky.) Dec. 26, 1826-Dec. 23, 1861; House 1859-61.

ANDERSON, William Coleman (R Tenn.) July 10, 1853-Sept. 8, 1902; House 1895-97.

ANDERSON, William Robert (D Tenn.) June 17, 1921-__; House 1965-1973.

ANDRESEN, August Herman (R Minn.) Oct. 11, 1890-Jan. 14, 1958; House 1925-33 and 1935-Jan. 14, 1958.

ANDREW, Abram Piatt Jr. (R Mass.) Feb. 12, 1873-June 3, 1936; House Sept. 27, 1921-June 3, 1936.

ANDREW, John Forrester (D Mass.) Nov. 26, 1850-May 30, 1895; House 1889-93.

ANDREWS, Arthur Glenn (R Ala.) Jan. 15, 1909-__; House 1965-67.

ANDREWS, Charles (D Maine) Feb. 11, 1814-April 30, 1852; House 1851-April 30, 1852.

ANDREWS, Charles Oscar (D Fla.) March 7, 1877-Sept. 18, 1946; Senate Nov. 4, 1936-Sept. 18, 1946.

ANDREWS, Elizabeth Bullock (widow of George William Andrews) (D Ala.) Feb. 12, 1911-__; House April 4, 1972-73.

ANDREWS, George Rex (W N.Y.) Sept. 21, 1808-Dec. 5, 1873; House 1849-51.

ANDREWS, George William (D Ala.) Dec. 12, 1906-Dec. 25, 1971; House March 14, 1944-Dec. 25, 1971.

ANDREWS, Ike Franklin (D N.C.) Sept. 2, 1925-—; House 1973-—.

ANDREWS, John Tuttle (D N.Y.) May 29, 1803-June 11, 1894; House 1837-39.

ANDREWS, Landaff Watson (W Ky.) Feb. 12, 1803-Dec. 23, 1887; House 1839-43.

ANDREWS, Mark (R N.D.) May 19, 1926-__; House Oct. 22, 1963-__.

ANDREWS, Samuel George (R N.Y.) Oct. 16, 1796-June 11, 1863; House 1857-59.

ANDREWS, Sherlock James (W Ohio) Nov. 17, 1801-Feb. 11, 1880; House 1841-43.

ANDREWS, Walter Gresham (R N.Y.) July 16, 1889-March 5, 1949; House 1931-49.

ANDREWS, William Ezekiel (R Neb.) Dec. 17, 1854-Jan. 19, 1942; House 1895-97, 1919-23.

ANDREWS, William Henry (R N.M.) Jan. 14, 1846-Jan. 16, 1919; House (Terr. Del.) 1905-Jan. 7, 1912.

ANDREWS, William Noble (R Md.) Nov. 13, 1876-Dec. 27, 1937; House 1919-21.

ANDRUS, John Emory (R N.Y.) Feb. 16, 1841-Dec. 26, 1934; House 1905-13.

ANFUSO, Victor L'Episcopo (D N.Y.) March 10, 1905-Dec. 28, 1966; House 1951-53, 1955-63.

ANGEL, William G. (JD N.Y.) July 17, 1790-Aug. 13, 1858; House 1825-27, 1829-33 (1825-27 John Quincy Adams Democrat, 1829-33 Jackson Democrat).

ANGELL, Homer Daniel (R Ore.) Jan. 12, 1875-March 31, 1968; House 1939-55.

ANKENY, Levi (R Wash.) Aug. 1, 1844-March 29, 1921; Senate 1903-09.

ANNUNZIO, Frank (D Ill.) Jan. 12, 1915-__; House 1965-__.

ANSBERRY, Timothy Thomas (D Ohio) Dec. 24, 1871-July 5, 1943; House 1907-Jan. 9, 1915.

ANSORGE, Martin Charles (R N.Y.) Jan. 1, 1882-Feb. 4, 1967; House 1921-23.

ANTHONY, Daniel Read Jr. (R Kan.) Aug. 22, 1870-Aug. 4, 1931; House May 23, 1907-29.

ANTHONY, Henry Bowen (R R.I.) April 1, 1815-Sept. 2, 1884; Senate 1859-Sept. 2, 1884; Gov. 1850-51; President pro tempore 1869-73.

ANTHONY, Joseph Biles (D Pa.) June 19, 1795-Jan. 10, 1851; House 1833-37.

ANTONY, Edwin Le Roy (D Texas) Jan. 5, 1852-Jan. 16, 1913; House June 14, 1892-93.

APLIN, Henry Harrison (R Mich.) April 15, 1841-July 23, 1910; House Oct. 20, 1901-03.

APPLEBY, Stewart Hoffman (son of Theodore Frank Appleby) (R N.J.) May 17, 1890-Jan. 12, 1964; House Nov. 3, 1925-27.

APPLEBY, Theodore Frank (father of Stewart Hoffman Appleby) (R N.J.) Oct. 10, 1864-Dec. 15, 1924; House 1921-23.

APPLETON, John (D Maine) Feb. 11, 1815-Aug. 22, 1864; House 1851-53.

APPLETON, Nathan (cousin of William Appleton) (HTW Mass.) Oct. 6, 1779-July 14, 1861; House 1831-33, June 9-Sept. 28, 1842.

APPLETON, William (cousin of Nathan Appleton) (W Mass.) Nov. 16, 1786-Feb. 15, 1862; House 1851-55, March 4-Sept. 27, 1861.

APSLEY, Lewis Dewart (R Mass.) Sept. 29, 1852-April 11, 1925; House 1893-97.

ARCHER, John (father of Stevenson Archer) (D Md.) May 5, 1741-Sept. 28, 1810; House 1801-07.

ARCHER, Stevenson (son of John Archer) (D Md.) Oct. 11, 1786-June 26, 1848; House Oct. 26, 1811-17, 1819-21.

ARCHER, Stevenson (son of Stevenson Archer and grandson of John Archer) (D Md.) Feb. 28, 1827-Aug. 2, 1898; House 1867-75.

ARCHER, William Reynolds Jr. (R Texas) March 22, 1928-; House 1971-__.

ARCHER, William Segar (nephew of Joseph Eggleston) (W Va.) March 5, 1789-March 28, 1855; House Jan. 3, 1820-35; Senate 1841-47.

ARENDS, Leslie Cornelius (R Ill.) Sept. 27, 1895-__; House 1935-Dec. 31, 1974.

ARENS, Henry (F-L Minn.) Nov. 21, 1873-Oct. 6, 1963; House 1933-35.

ARENTZ, Samuel Shaw (Ulysses) (R Nev.) Jan. 8, 1879-June 17, 1934; House 1921-23, 1925-33.

ARMFIELD, Robert Franklin (D N.C.) July 9, 1829-Nov. 9, 1898; House 1879-83.

ARMSTRONG, David Hartley (D Mo.) Oct. 21, 1812-March 18, 1893; Senate Sept. 20, 1877-Jan. 26, 1879.

ARMSTRONG, James (brother of John Armstrong) (F Pa.) Aug. 29, 1748-May 6, 1828; House 1793-95.

ARMSTRONG, John (brother of James Armstrong) (— N.Y.) Nov. 25, 1755-April 1, 1843; Senate Nov. 6, 1800-Feb. 5, 1802; Nov. 10, 1803-June 30, 1804; Secy. of War 1813-14.

ARMSTRONG, Moses Kimball (D Dakota) Sept. 19, 1832-Jan. 11, 1906; House (Terr. Del.) 1871-75.

ARMSTRONG, Orland Kay (R Mo.) Oct. 2, 1893-__; House 1951-53.

ARMSTRONG, William (D Va.) Dec. 23, 1782-May 10, 1865; House 1825-33.

ARMSTRONG, William Hepburn (R Pa.) Sept. 7, 1824-May 14, 1919; House 1869-71.

ARMSTRONG, William Lester (R Colo.) March 16, 1937-—; House 1973-—.

ARNELL, Samuel Mayes (R Tenn.) May 3, 1833-July 20, 1903; House July 24, 1866-71.

ARNOLD, Benedict (brother-in-law of Matthias J. Bovee) (— N.Y.) Oct. 5, 1780-March 3, 1849; House 1829-31.

ARNOLD, Isaac Newton (R Ill.) Nov. 30, 1815-April 24, 1884; House 1861-65.

ARNOLD, Laurence Fletcher (D Ill.) June 8, 1891-Dec. 6, 1966; House 1937-43.

ARNOLD, Lemuel Hastings (great-great-uncle of Theodore Francis Green) (LW R.I.) Jan. 29, 1792-June 27, 1852; House 1845-47; Gov. 1831-32.

ARNOLD, Marshall (D Mo.) Oct. 21, 1845-June 12, 1913; House 1891-95.

ARNOLD, Samuel (D Conn.) June 1, 1806-May 5, 1869; House 1857-59.

ARNOLD, Samuel Greene (grand uncle of Theodore Francis Green) (R R.I.) April 12, 1821-Feb. 14, 1880; Senate Dec. 1, 1862-63.

ARNOLD, Samuel Washington (R Mo.) Sept. 21, 1879-Dec. 18, 1961; House 1943-49.

ARNOLD, Thomas Dickens (W Tenn.) May 3, 1798-May 26, 1870; House 1831-33, 1841-43.

ARNOLD, Warren Otis (R R.I.) June 3, 1839-April 1, 1910; House 1887-91, 1895-97.

ARNOLD, William Carlile (R Pa.) July 15, 1851-March 20, 1906; House 1895-99.

ARNOLD, William Wright (D Ill.) Oct. 14, 1877-Nov. 23, 1957; House 1923-Sept. 16, 1935.

ARNOT, John Jr. (D N.Y.) March 11, 1831-Nov. 20, 1886; House 1883-Nov. 20, 1886.

ARRINGTON, Archibald Hunter (uncle of Archibald Hunter Arrington Williams) (D N.C.) Nov. 13, 1809-July 20, 1872; House 1841-45.

ARTHUR, William Evans (D Ky.) March 3, 1825-May 18, 1897; House 1871-75.

ASH, Michael Woolston (— Pa.) March 5, 1789-Dec. 14, 1858; House 1835-37.

ASHBROOK, John Milan (son of William Albert Ashbrook) (R Ohio) Sept. 21, 1928-__; House 1961-__.

ASHBROOK, William Albert (father of John Milan Ashbrook) (D Ohio) July 1, 1867-Jan. 1, 1940; House 1907-21, 1935-Jan. 1, 1940.

ASHE, John Baptista (uncle of John Baptista Ashe of Tennessee, Thomas Samuel Ashe and William Shepperd Ashe) (F N.C.) 1748-Nov. 27, 1802; House 1789-93; Cont. Cong. 1787.

ASHE, John Baptista (brother of William Shepperd Ashe, nephew of John Baptista Ashe of N.C. and cousin of Thomas Samuel Ashe) (W Tenn.) 1810-Dec. 29, 1857; House 1843-45.

ASHE, Thomas Samuel (nephew of John Baptista Ashe of N.C. and cousin of John Baptista Ashe of Tenn. and of William Shepperd Ashe) (D N.C.) July 21, 1812-Feb. 4, 1887; House 1873-77 (1873-75 Conservative, 1875-77 Democrat).

ASHE, William Shepperd (brother of John Baptista Ashe of Tenn. and nephew of John Baptista Ashe of N.C. and cousin of Thomas Samuel Ashe) (D N.C.) Aug. 12, 1813-Sept. 14, 1862; House 1849-55.

ASHLEY, Chester (D Ark.) June 1, 1790-April 29, 1848; Senate Nov. 8, 1844-April 29, 1848.

ASHLEY, Delos Rodeyn (R Nev.) Feb. 19, 1828-July 18, 1873; House 1865-69.

ASHLEY, Henry (— N.Y.) Feb. 19, 1778-Jan. 14, 1829; House 1825-27.

ASHLEY, James Mitchell (great grandfather of Thomas William Ludlow Ashley) (R Ohio) Nov. 14, 1824-Sept. 16, 1896; House 1859-69; Gov. Terr. of Montana 1869-70.

ASHLEY, Thomas William Ludlow (great-grandson of James Mitchell Ashley) (D Ohio) Jan. 11, 1923-__; House 1955-__.

ASHLEY, William Henry (W Mo.) 1778-March 26, 1838; House Oct. 31, 1831-37.

ASHMORE, John Durant (D S.C.) Aug. 18, 1819-Dec. 5, 1871; House 1859-Dec. 21, 1860.

ASHMORE, Robert Thomas (D S.C.) Feb. 22, 1904-—; House June 2, 1953-69.

ASHMUN, Eli Porter (father of George Ashmun) (— Mass.) June 24, 1770-May 10, 1819; Senate June 12, 1816-May 10, 1818.

ASHMUN, George (son of Eli Porter Ashmun) (W Mass.) Dec. 25, 1804-July 16, 1870; House 1845-51.

ASHURST, Henry Fountain (D Ariz.) Sept. 13, 1874-May 31, 1962; Senate March 27, 1912-41.

ASPER, Joel Funk (RR Mo.) April 20, 1822-Oct. 1, 1872; House 1869-71.

ASPIN, Les (D Wis.) July 21, 1938-__; House 1971-—.

ASPINALL, Wayne Norviel (D Colo.) April 3, 1896-__; House 1949-1973.

ASWELL, James Benjamin (D La.) Dec. 23, 1869-March 16, 1931; House 1913-March 16, 1931.

ATCHISON, David Rice (W Mo.) Aug. 11, 1807-Jan. 26, 1886; Senate Oct. 14, 1843-55; President pro tempore 1846-54.

ATHERTON, Charles Gordon (son of Charles Humphrey Atherton) (D N.H.) July 4, 1804-Nov. 15, 1853; House 1837-43; Senate 1843-49, 1853-Nov. 15, 1853.

ATHERTON, Charles Humphrey (father of Charles Gordon Atherton) (F N.H.) Aug. 14, 1773-Jan. 8, 1853; House 1815-17.

ATHERTON, Gibson (D Ohio) Jan. 19, 1831-Nov. 10, 1887; House 1879-83.

ATKESON, William Oscar (R Mo.) Aug. 24, 1854-Oct. 16, 1931; House 1921-23.

ATKINS, John DeWitt Clinton (D Tenn.) June 4, 1825-June 2, 1908; House 1857-59, 1873-83.

ATKINSON, Archibald (D Va.) Sept. 15, 1792-Jan. 7, 1872; House 1843-49.

ATKINSON, George Wesley (R W.Va.) June 29, 1845-April 4, 1925; House Feb. 26, 1890-91; Gov. 1897-1901.

ATKINSON, Louis Evans (R Pa.) April 16, 1841-Feb. 5, 1910; House 1883-93.

ATKINSON, Richard Merrill (D Tenn.) Feb. 6, 1894-April 29, 1947; House 1937-39.

ATWATER, John Wilbur (P N.C.) Dec. 27, 1840-July 4, 1910; House 1899-1901.

ATWOOD, David (R Wis.) Dec. 15, 1815-Dec. 11, 1889; House Feb. 23, 1870-71.

ATWOOD, Harrison Henry (R Mass.) Aug. 26, 1863-Oct. 22, 1954; House 1895-97.

AUCHINCLOSS, James Coats (R N.J.) Jan. 19, 1885-__; House 1943-65.

AuCOIN, Les (D Ore.) Oct. 21, 1942-__; House 1975-__.

AUF DER HEIDE, Oscar Louis (D N.J.) Dec. 8, 1874-March 29, 1945; House 1925-35.

AUSTIN, Albert Elmer (stepfather of Clare Boothe Luce) (R Conn.) Nov. 15, 1877-Jan. 26, 1942; House 1939-41.

AUSTIN, Archibald (D Va.) Aug. 11, 1772-Oct. 16, 1837; House 1817-19.

AUSTIN, Richard Wilson (R Tenn.) Aug. 26, 1857-April 20, 1919; House 1909-19.

AUSTIN, Warren Robinson (R Vt.) Nov. 12, 1877-Dec. 25, 1962; Senate April 1, 1931-Aug. 2, 1946.

AVERETT, Thomas Hamlet (D Va.) July 10, 1800-June 30, 1855; House 1849-53.

AVERILL, John Thomas (R Minn.) March 1, 1825-Oct. 3, 1889; House 1871-75.

AVERY, Daniel (D N.Y.) Sept. 18, 1766-Jan. 30, 1842; House 1811-15, Sept. 30, 1816-17.

AVERY, John (R Mich.) Feb. 29, 1824-Jan. 21, 1914; House 1893-97.

AVERY, William Henry (R Kan.) Aug. 11, 1911-__; House 1955-65; Gov. 1965-67.

AVERY, William Tecumsah (D Tenn.) Nov. 11, 1819-May 22, 1880; House 1857-61.

AVIS, Samuel Brashear (R W.Va.) Feb. 19, 1872-June 8, 1924; House 1913-15.

AXTELL, Samuel Beach (D Calif.) Oct. 14, 1819-Aug. 6, 1891; House 1867-71; Gov. Utah Territory (R) 1874-75; Gov. Territory of N. Mexico (R) 1875.

AYCRIGG, John Bancker (W N.J.) July 9, 1798-Nov. 8, 1856; House 1837-39, 1841-43.

AYER, Richard Small (R Va.) Oct. 9, 1829-Dec. 14, 1896; House Jan. 31, 1870-71.

AYERS, Roy Elmer (D Mont.) Nov. 9, 1882-May 23, 1955; House 1933-37; Gov. 1937-41.

AYRES, Steven Beckwith (ID N.Y.) Oct. 27, 1861-June 1, 1929; House 1911-13.

AYRES, William Augustus (D Kan.) April 19, 1867-Feb. 17, 1952; House 1915-21, 1923-Aug. 22, 1934.

AYRES, William Hanes (R Ohio) Feb. 5, 1916-__; House 1951-71.

B

BABBITT, Clinton (D Wis.) Nov. 16, 1831-March 11, 1907; House 1891-93.

BABBITT, Elijah (R Pa.) July 29, 1795-Jan. 9, 1887; House 1859-63 (1859-61 Unionist, 1861-63 Republican).

BABCOCK, Alfred (W N.Y.) April 15, 1805-May 16, 1871; House 1841-43.

BABCOCK, Joseph Weeks (grandson of Joseph Weeks) (R Wis.) March 6, 1850-April 27, 1909; House 1893-1907.

BABCOCK, Leander (D N.Y.) March 1, 1811-Aug. 18, 1864; House 1851-53.

BABCOCK, William (— N.Y.) 1785-Oct. 20, 1838; House 1831-33.

BABKA, John Joseph (D Ohio) March 16, 1884-March 22, 1937; House 1919-21.

BACHARACH, Isaac (R N.J.) Jan. 5, 1870-Sept. 5, 1956; House 1915-37.

BACHMAN, Nathan Lynn (D Tenn.) Aug. 2, 1878-April 23, 1937; Senate Feb. 28, 1933-April 23, 1937.

BACHMAN, Reuben Knecht (D Pa.) Aug. 6, 1834-Sept. 19, 1911; House 1879-81.

BACHMANN, Carl George (R W.Va.) May 14, 1890-__; House 1925-33.

BACON, Augustus Octavius (cousin of William S. Howard) (D Ga.) Oct. 20, 1839-Feb. 14, 1914; Senate 1895-Feb. 14, 1914.

BACON, Ezekiel (son of John Bacon and father of William Johnson Bacon) (D Mass.) Sept. 1, 1776-Oct. 18, 1870; House Sept. 16, 1807-13.

BACON, Henry (D N.Y.) March 14, 1846-March 25, 1915; House Dec. 6, 1886-89, 1891-93.

BACON, John (father of Ezekiel Bacon and grandfather of William Johnson Bacon) (— Mass.) April 5, 1738-Oct. 25, 1820; House 1801-03.

BACON, Mark Reeves (R Mich.) Feb. 29, 1852-Aug. 20, 1941; House March 4-Dec. 13, 1917.

BACON, Robert Low (R N.Y.) July 23, 1884-Sept. 12, 1938; House 1923-Sept. 12, 1938.

BACON, William Johnson (son of Ezekiel Bacon and grandson of John Bacon) (R N.Y.) Feb. 18, 1803-July 3, 1889; House 1877-79.

BADGER, De Witt Clinton (D Ohio) Aug. 7, 1858-May 20, 1926; House 1903-05.

BADGER, George Edmund (W N.C.) April 17, 1795-May 11, 1866; Senate Nov. 25, 1846-55; Secy. of the Navy March 5-Sept. 11, 1841.

BADGER, Luther (— N.Y.) April 10, 1785-1869; House 1825-27.

BADILLO, Herman (D N.Y.) Aug. 21, 1929-__; House 1971-__.

BAER, George Jr. (F Md.) 1763-April 3, 1834; House 1797-1801, 1815-17.

BAER, John Miller (R N.D.) March 29, 1886-Feb. 18, 1970; House July 10, 1917-21 (1917-19 Nonpartisan League, 1919-21 Republican).

BAFALIS, Louis Arthur (R Fla.) Sept. 28, 1929-__; House 1973-__.

BAGBY, Arthur Pendleton (D Ala.) 1794-Sept. 21, 1858; Senate Nov. 24, 1841-June 16, 1848; Gov. 1837-41.

BAGBY, John Courts (D Ill.) Jan. 24, 1819-April 4, 1896; House 1875-77.

BAGLEY, George Augustus (R N.Y.) July 22, 1826-May 12, 1915, House 1875-79.

BAGLEY, John Holroyd Jr. (D N.Y.) Nov. 26, 1832-Oct. 23, 1902; House 1875-77; 1883-85.

BAILEY, Alexander Hamilton (R N.Y.) Aug. 14, 1817-April 20, 1874; House Nov. 30, 1867-71.

BAILEY, Cleveland Monroe (D W.Va.) July 15, 1886-July 13, 1965; House 1945-47, 1949-63.

BAILEY, David Jackson (SRD Ga.) March 11, 1812-June 14, 1897; House 1851-55.

BAILEY, Goldsmith Fox (R Mass.) July 17, 1823-May 8, 1862; House 1861-May 8, 1862.

BAILEY, James Edmund (D Tenn.) Aug. 15, 1822-Dec. 29, 1885; Senate Jan. 19, 1877-81.

BAILEY, Jeremiah (W Maine) May 1, 1773-July 6, 1853; House 1835-37.

BAILEY, John (— Mass.) 1786-June 26, 1835; House Dec. 13, 1824-31.

BAILEY, John Mosher (R N.Y.) Aug. 24, 1838-Feb. 21, 1916; House Nov. 5, 1878-81.

BAILEY, Joseph (D Pa.) March 18, 1810-Aug. 26, 1885; House 1861-65.

BAILEY, Joseph Weldon (father of Joseph Weldon Bailey Jr.) (D Texas) Oct. 6, 1862-April 13, 1929; House 1891-1901; Senate 1901-Jan. 3, 1913.

BAILEY, Joseph Weldon Jr. (son of Joseph Weldon Bailey) (D Texas) Dec. 15, 1892-July 17, 1943; House 1933-35.

BAILEY, Josiah William (D N.C.) Sept. 14, 1873-Dec. 15, 1946; Senate 1931-Dec. 15, 1946.

BAILEY, Ralph Emerson (R Mo.) July 14, 1878-April 8, 1948; House 1925-27.

BAILEY, Theodorus (D N.Y.) Oct. 12, 1758-Sept. 6, 1828; House 1793-97; 1799-1801; Oct. 6, 1801-03; Senate 1803-Jan. 16, 1804.

BAILEY, Warren Worth (D Pa.) Jan. 8, 1855-Nov. 9, 1928; House 1913-17.

BAILEY, Willis Joshua (R Kan.) Oct. 12, 1854-May 19, 1932; House 1899-1901; Gov. 1903-05.

BAIRD, David (father of David Baird Jr.) (R N.J.) April 7, 1839-Feb. 25, 1927; Senate Feb. 23, 1918-19.

BAIRD, David Jr. (son of David Baird) (R N.J.) Oct. 10, 1881-Feb. 28, 1955; Senate Nov. 30, 1929-Dec. 1, 1930.

BAIRD, Joseph Edward (R Ohio) Nov. 12, 1865-June 14, 1942; House 1929-31.

BAIRD, Samuel Thomas (D La.) May 5, 1861-April 22, 1899; House 1897-April 22, 1899.

BAKER, Caleb (— N.Y.) 1762-June 26, 1849; House 1819-21.

BAKER, Charles Simeon (R N.Y.) Feb. 18, 1839-April 21, 1902; House 1885-91.

BAKER, David Jewett (D Ill.) Sept. 7, 1792-Aug. 6, 1869; Senate Nov. 12-Dec. 11, 1830.

BAKER, Edward Dickinson (R Ill., Ore.) Feb. 24, 1811-Oct. 21, 1861; House 1845-Jan. 15, 1847 (W Ill.), 1849-51 (W Ill.); Senate Oct. 2, 1860-Oct. 21, 1861 (R Ore.).

BAKER, Ezra (— N.J.) ? - ?; House 1815-17.

BAKER, Henry Moore (R N.H.) Jan. 11, 1841-May 30, 1912; House 1893-97.

BAKER, Howard Henry (husband of Irene B. Baker, father of Howard Henry Baker Jr.) (R Tenn.) Jan. 12, 1902-Jan. 7, 1964; House 1951-Jan. 7, 1964.

BAKER, Howard Henry Jr. (son of Howard Henry Baker and Irene B. Baker, son-in-law of Everett McKinley Dirksen) (R Tenn.) Nov. 15, 1925-__; Senate 1967-__.

BAKER, Irene B. (widow of Howard Henry Baker and mother of Howard Henry Baker Jr.) (R Tenn.) Nov. 17, 1901-__; House March 10, 1964-65.

BAKER, Jacob Thompson (D N.J.) April 13, 1847-Dec. 7, 1919; House 1913-15.

BAKER, Jehu (Fus. Ill.) Nov. 4, 1822-March 1, 1903; House 1865-69, 1887-89, 1897-99 (1865-69 and 1887-89 Republican, 1897-99 Fusionist)

BAKER John (F Va.) ? - Aug. 18, 1823; House 1811-13.

BAKER, John Harris (R Ind.) Feb. 28, 1832-Oct. 21, 1915; House 1875-81.

BAKER, LaMar (R Tenn.) Dec. 19, 1915-__; House 1971-1975.

BAKER, Lucien (R Kan.) June 8, 1846-June 21, 1907; Senate 1895-1901.

BAKER, Osmyn (W Mass.) May 18, 1800-Feb. 9, 1875; House Jan. 14, 1840-45.

BAKER, Robert (D N.Y.) April 1862-June 15, 1943; House 1903-05.

BAKER, Stephen (R N.Y.) Aug. 12, 1819-June 9, 1875; House 1861-63.

BAKER, William (PP Kan.) April 29, 1831-Feb. 11, 1910; House 1891-97.

BAKER, William Benjamin (R Md.) July 22, 1840-May 17, 1911; House 1895-1901.

BAKER, William Henry (R N.Y.) Jan. 17, 1827-Nov. 25, 1911; House 1875-79.

BAKEWELL, Charles Montague (R Conn.) April 24, 1867-Sept. 19, 1957; House 1933-35.

BAKEWELL, Claude Ignatius (R Mo.) Aug. 9, 1912-__; House 1947-49, March 9, 1951-53.

BALDRIGE, Howard Malcolm (R Neb.) June 23, 1894-__; House 1931-33.

BALDUS, Alvin James (D Wis.) April 27, 1926-__; House 1975-__.

BALDWIN, Abraham (F Ga.) Nov. 2, 1754-March 4, 1807; House 1789-99; Senate 1799-March 4, 1807; Cont. Cong. 1785, 1787-89; Pres. pro tempore 1801-02.

BALDWIN, Augustus Carpenter (UD Mich.) Dec. 24, 1817-Jan. 21, 1903; House 1863-65.

BALDWIN, Harry Streett (D Md.) Aug. 21, 1894-Oct. 19, 1952; House 1943-47.

BALDWIN, Henry (F Pa.) Jan. 14, 1780-April 21, 1844; House 1817-May 8, 1822; Assoc. Justice U.S. Supreme Court Jan. 6, 1830-April 21, 1844.

BALDWIN, Henry Alexander (R Hawaii) Jan. 12, 1871-Oct. 8, 1946; House (Terr. Del.) March 25, 1922-23.

BALDWIN, Henry Porter (R Mich.) Feb. 22, 1814-Dec. 31, 1892; Senate Nov. 17, 1879-81; Gov. 1869-73.

BALDWIN, John (— Conn.) April 5, 1772-March 27, 1850; House 1825-29.

BALDWIN, John Denison (R Mass.) Sept. 28, 1809-July 8, 1883; House 1863-69.

BALDWIN, John Finley Jr. (R Calif.) June 28, 1915-March 9, 1966; House 1955-March 9, 1966.

BALDWIN, Joseph Clark (R N.Y.) Jan. 11, 1897-Oct. 27, 1957; House March 11, 1941-47.

BALDWIN, Melvin Riley (D Minn.) April 12, 1838-April 15, 1901; House 1893-95.

BALDWIN, Raymond Earl (R Conn.) Aug. 31, 1893-__; Senate Dec. 27, 1946-Dec. 16, 1949; Gov. 1939-41, 1943-46.

BALDWIN, Roger Sherman (son of Simeon Baldwin) (W Conn.) Jan. 4, 1793-Feb. 19, 1863; Senate Nov. 11, 1847-51; Gov. 1844-46.

BALDWIN, Simeon (father of Roger Sherman Baldwin) (F Conn.) Dec. 14, 1761-May 26, 1851; House 1803-05.

BALL, Edward (W Ohio) Nov. 6, 1811-Nov. 22, 1872; House 1853-57.

BALL, Joseph Hurst (R Minn.) Nov. 3, 1905-__; Senate Oct. 14, 1940-Nov. 17, 1942, 1943-49.

BALL, Lewis Heisler (R Del.) Sept. 21, 1861-Oct. 18, 1932; House 1901-03; Senate March 3, 1903-05, 1919-25.

BALL, Thomas Henry (D Texas) Jan. 14, 1859-May 7, 1944; House 1897-Nov. 16, 1903.

BALL, Thomas Raymond (R Conn.) Feb. 12, 1896-June 16, 1943; House 1939-41.

BALL, William Lee (D Va.) Jan. 2, 1781-Feb. 28, 1824; House 1817-Feb. 28, 1824.

BALLENTINE, John Goff (D Tenn.) May 20, 1825-Nov. 23, 1915; House 1883-87.

BALLOU, Latimer Whipple (R R.I.) March 1, 1812-May 9, 1900; House 1875-81.

BALTZ, William Nicolas (D Ill.) Feb. 5, 1860-Aug. 22, 1943; House 1913-15.

BANDSTRA, Bert (D Iowa) Jan. 25, 1922-__; House 1965-67.

BANKHEAD, John Hollis (Father of John Hollis Bankhead 2d and William Brockman Bankhead and grandfather of Walter Will Bankhead) (D Ala.) Sept. 13, 1842-March 1, 1920; House 1887-1907; Senate June 18, 1907-March 1, 1920.

BANKHEAD, John Hollis 2d (son of John Hollis Bankhead, brother of William Brockman Bankhead and father of Walter Will Bankhead) (D Ala.) July 8, 1872-June 12, 1946; Senate 1931-June 12, 1946.

BANKHEAD, Walter Will (son of John Hollis Bankhead 2d, grandson of John Hollis Bankhead and nephew of William Brockman Bankhead) (D Ala.) July 21, 1897-—; House Jan. 3-Feb. 1, 1941.

BANKHEAD, William Brockman (son of John Hollis Bankhead, brother of John Hollis Bankhead 2d and uncle of Walter Will Bankhead) (D Ala.) April 12, 1874-Sept. 15, 1940; House 1917-Sept. 15, 1940; Speaker June 4, 1936-Sept. 15, 1940.

BANKS, John (W Pa.) Oct. 17, 1793-April 3, 1864; House 1831-36.

BANKS, Linn (D Va.) Jan. 23, 1784-Jan. 13, 1842; House April 28, 1838-Dec. 6, 1841.

BANKS, Nathaniel Prentice (R Mass.) Jan. 30, 1816-Sept. 1, 1894; House 1853-Dec. 24, 1857, Dec. 4, 1865-1873, 1875-79, 1889-91; (1853-55 Coalition Democrat, 1855-57 American Party, March 4-Dec. 24, 1857 Republican, Dec. 4, 1865-67 Union Republican, 1867-73 Republican, 1875-79 Liberal Republican, 1889-91 Republican); Speaker 1855-57; Gov. 1858-61.

BANNING, Henry Blackstone (D Ohio) Nov. 10, 1836-Dec. 10, 1881; House 1873-79.

BANNON, Henry Towne (R Ohio) June 5, 1867-Sept. 6, 1950; House 1905-09.

BANTA, Parke Monroe (R Mo.) Nov. 21, 1891-May 12, 1970; House 1947-49.

BARBER, Hiram Jr. (R Ill.) March 24, 1835-Aug. 5, 1924; House 1879-81.

BARBER, Isaac Ambrose (R Md.) Jan. 26, 1852-March 1, 1909; House 1897-99.

BARBER, Joel Allen (R Wis.) Jan. 17, 1809-June 17, 1881; House 1871-75.

BARBER, Laird Howard (D Pa.) Oct. 25, 1848-Feb. 16, 1928; House 1899-1901.

BARBER, Levi (— Ohio) Oct. 16, 1777-April 23, 1833; House 1817-19, 1821-23.

BARBER, Noyes (uncle of Edwin Barbour Morgan and Christopher Morgan) (D Conn.) April 28, 1781-Jan. 3, 1844; House 1821-35.

BARBOUR, Henry Ellsworth (R Calif.) March 8, 1877-March 21, 1945; House 1919-33.

BARBOUR, James (brother of Philip Pendleton Barbour and cousin of John Strode Barbour) (AD/SR Va.) June 10, 1775-June 7, 1842; Senate Jan. 2, 1815-March 7, 1825; President pro tempore 1819; Gov. 1812-14; Secy. of War 1825-28.

BARBOUR, John Strode (father of John Strode Barbour, cousin of James Barbour and Philip Pendleton Barbour) (SRD Va.) Aug. 8, 1790-Jan. 12, 1855; House 1823-33.

BARBOUR, John Strode (son of John Strode Barbour) (D Va.) Dec. 29, 1820-May 14, 1892; House 1881-87; Senate 1889-May 14, 1892.

BARBOUR, Lucien (FS/T/KN Ind.) March 4, 1811-July 19, 1880; House 1855-57.

BARBOUR, Philip Pendleton (brother of James Barbour and cousin of John Strode Barbour) (D Va.) May 25, 1783-Feb. 25, 1841; House Sept. 19, 1814-25, 1827-Oct. 15, 1830; Speaker 1821-23; Assoc. Justice U.S. Supreme Court 1836-41.

BARBOUR, William Warren (R N.J.) July 31, 1888-Nov. 22, 1943; Senate Dec. 1, 1931-37, Nov. 9, 1938-Nov. 22, 1943.

BARCHFELD, Andrew Jackson (R Pa.) May 18, 1863-Jan. 28, 1922; House 1905-17.

BARCLAY, Charles Frederick (R Pa.) May 9, 1844-March 9, 1914; House 1907-11.

BARCLAY, David (D Pa.) 1823-Sept. 10, 1889; House 1855-57.

BARD, David (— Pa.) 1744-March 12, 1815; House 1795-99, 1803-March 12, 1815.

BARD, Thomas Robert (R Calif.) Dec. 8, 1841-March 5, 1915; Senate Feb. 7, 1900-05.

BARDEN, Graham Arthur (D N.C.) Sept. 25, 1896-Jan. 29, 1967; House 1935-61.

BARHAM, John All (R Calif.) July 17, 1843-Jan. 22, 1926; House 1895-1901.

BARING, Walter Stephan (D Nev.) Sept. 9, 1911-July 13, 1975; House 1949-53, 1957-73.

BARKER, Abraham Andrews (UR Pa.) March 30, 1816-March 18, 1898; House 1865-67.

BARKER, David Jr. (— N.H.) Jan. 8, 1797-April 1, 1834; House 1827-29.

BARKER, Joseph (D Mass.) Oct. 19, 1751-July 5, 1815; House 1805-09.

BARKLEY, Alben William (D Ky.) Nov. 24, 1877-April 30, 1956; House 1913-27; Senate 1927-Jan. 19, 1949, 1955-April 30, 1956; Vice President 1949-53.

BARKSDALE, Ethelbert (brother of William Barksdale) (D Miss.) Jan. 4, 1824-Feb. 17, 1893; House 1883-87.

BARKSDALE, William (brother of Ethelbert Barksdale) (SRD Miss.) Aug. 21, 1821-July 2, 1863; House 1853-Jan. 12, 1861.

BARLOW, Bradley (NR Vt.) May 12, 1814-Nov. 6, 1889; House 1879-81.

BARLOW, Charles Averill (P/D Calif.) March 17, 1858-Oct. 3, 1927; House 1897-99.

BARLOW, Stephen (D Pa.) June 13, 1779-Aug. 24, 1845; House 1827-29.

BARNARD, Daniel Dewey (W N.Y.) July 16, 1797-April 24, 1861; House 1827-29, 1839-45.

BARNARD, Isaac Dutton (F Pa.) July 18, 1791-Feb. 28, 1834; Senate 1827-Dec. 6, 1831.

BARNARD, William Oscar (R Ind.) Oct. 25, 1852-April 8, 1939; House 1909-11.

BARNES, Demas (D N.Y.) April 4, 1827-May 1, 1888; House 1867-69.

BARNES, George Thomas (D Ga.) Aug. 14, 1833-Oct. 24, 1901; House 1885-91.

BARNES, James Martin (D Ill.) Jan. 9, 1899-June 8, 1958; House 1939-43.

BARNES, Lyman Eddy (D Wis.) June 30, 1855-Jan. 16, 1904; House 1893-95.

BARNETT, William (SRD Ga.) March 4, 1761-April 1832; House Oct. 5, 1812-15.

BARNEY, John (F Md.) Jan. 18, 1785-Jan. 26, 1857; House 1825-29.

BARNEY, Samuel Stebbins (R Wis.) Jan. 31, 1846-Dec. 31, 1919; House 1895-1903.

BARNHART, Henry A. (D Ind.) Sept. 11, 1858-March 26, 1934; House Nov. 3, 1908-19.

BARNITZ, Charles Augustus (W Pa.) Sept. 11, 1780-Jan. 8, 1850; House 1833-35.

BARNUM, William Henry (D Conn.) Sept. 17, 1818-April 30, 1889; House 1867-May 18, 1876; Senate May 18, 1876-79; Chrmn. Dem. Nat. Comm. 1877-89.

BARNWELL, Robert (father of Robert Woodward Barnwell) (F S.C.) Dec. 21, 1761-Oct. 24, 1814; House 1791-93; Cont. Cong. 1788-89.

BARNWELL, Robert Woodward (son of Robert Barnwell) (D S.C.) Aug. 10, 1801-Nov. 24, 1882; House 1829-33; Senate June 4-Dec. 8, 1850.

BARR, Joseph Walker (D Ind.) Jan. 17, 1918-—; House 1959-61; Secy. of the Treasury 1968-69.

BARR, Samuel Fleming (R Pa.) June 15, 1829-May 29, 1919; House 1881-85.

BARR, Thomas Jefferson (D N.Y.) 1812-March 27, 1881; House Jan. 17, 1859-61.

BARRERE, Granville (nephew of Nelson Barrere) (R Ill.) July 11, 1829-Jan. 13, 1889; House 1873-75.

BARRERE, Nelson (uncle of Granville Barrere) (W Ohio) April 1, 1808-Aug. 20, 1883; House 1851-53.

BARRET, John Richard (D Mo.) Aug. 21, 1825-Nov. 2, 1903; House 1859-June 8, 1860, Dec. 3, 1860-61.

BARRETT, Frank A. (R Wyo.) Nov. 10, 1892-May 30, 1962; House 1943-Dec. 31, 1950; Senate 1953-59; Gov. 1951-53.

BARRETT, William A. (D Pa.) Aug. 14, 1896-April 12, 1976; House 1945-47, 1949-April 12, 1976.

BARRETT, William Emerson (R Mass.) Dec. 29, 1858-Feb. 12, 1906; House 1895-99.

BARRINGER, Daniel Laurens (uncle of Daniel Moreau Barringer) (D N.C.) Oct. 1, 1788-Oct. 16, 1852; House Dec. 4, 1826-35.

BARRINGER, Daniel Moreau (nephew of **Daniel Laurens Barringer**) (W N.C.) July 30, 1806-Sept. 1, 1873; House 1843-49.

BARROW, Alexander (W La.) March 27, 1801-Dec. 19, 1846; Senate 1841-Dec. 19, 1846.

BARROW, Middleton Pope (grandson of Wilson Lumpkin) (D Ga.) Aug. 1, 1839-Dec. 23, 1903; Senate Nov. 15, 1882-83.

BARROW, Washington (W Tenn.) Oct. 5, 1807-Oct. 19, 1866; House 1847-49.

BARROWS, Samuel June (R Mass.) May 26, 1845-April 21, 1909; House 1897-99.

BARRY, Alexander Grant (R Ore.) Aug. 23, 1892-Dec. 28, 1952; Senate Nov. 9, 1938-39.

BARRY, Frederick George (D Miss.) Jan. 12, 1845-May 7, 1909; House 1885-89.

BARRY, Henry W. (R Miss.) April 1840-June 7, 1875; House Feb. 23, 1870-75.

BARRY, Robert Raymond (R N.Y.) May 15, 1915-__; House 1959-65.

BARRY, William Bernard (D N.Y.) July 21, 1902-Oct. 20, 1946; House Nov. 5, 1935-Oct. 20, 1946.

BARRY, William Taylor (D Ky.) Feb. 15, 1784-Aug. 30, 1835; House Aug. 8, 1810-11; Senate Dec. 16, 1814-May 1, 1816; Postmaster General 1829-35.

BARRY, William Taylor Sullivan (D Miss.) Dec. 10, 1821-Jan. 29, 1868; House 1853-55.

BARSTOW, Gamaliel Henry (NR N.Y.) July 20, 1784-March 30, 1865; House 1831-33.

BARSTOW, Gideon (D Mass.) Sept. 7, 1783-March 26, 1852; House 1821-23.

BARTHOLDT, Richard (R Mo.) Nov. 2, 1855-March 19, 1932; House 1893-1915.

BARTINE, Horace Franklin (R Nev.) March 21, 1848-Aug. 27, 1918; House 1889-93.

BARTLETT, Bailey (F Mass.) Jan. 29, 1750-Sept. 9, 1830; House Nov. 27, 1797-1801.

BARTLETT, Charles Lafayette (D Ga.) Jan. 31, 1853-April 21, 1938; House 1895-1915.

BARTLETT, Dewey Follett (R Okla.) March 28, 1919-__; Senate 1973-__; Gov. 1967-1971.

BARTLETT, Edward Lewis (Bob) (D Alaska) April 20, 1904-Dec. 11, 1968; House (Terr. Del.) 1945-59; Senate 1959-Dec. 11, 1968.

BARTLETT, Franklin (D N.Y.) Sept. 10, 1847-April 23, 1909; House 1893-97.

BARTLETT, George Arthur (D Nev.) Nov. 30, 1869-June 1, 1951; House 1907-11.

BARTLETT, Ichabod (AD N.H.) July 24, 1786-Oct. 19, 1853; House 1823-29.

BARTLETT, Josiah Jr. (— N.H.) Aug. 29, 1768-April 16, 1838; House 1811-13.

BARTLETT, Thomas Jr. (D Vt.) June 18, 1808-Sept. 12, 1876; House 1851-53.

BARTLEY, Mordecai (— Ohio) Dec. 16, 1783-Oct. 10, 1870; House 1823-31; Gov. 1844-46.

BARTON, Bruce (R N.Y.) Aug. 5, 1886-July 5, 1967; House Nov. 2, 1937-41.

BARTON, David (— Mo.) Dec. 14, 1783-Sept. 28, 1837; Senate Aug. 10, 1821-31.

BARTON, Richard Walker (W Va.) 1800-March 15, 1859; House 1841-43.

BARTON, Samuel (JD N.Y.) July 27, 1785-Jan. 29, 1858; House 1835-37.

BARTON, Silas Reynolds (R Neb.) May 21, 1872-Nov. 7, 1916; House 1913-15.

BARTON, William Edward (cousin of Courtney Walker Hamlin) (D Mo.) April 11, 1868-July 29, 1955; House 1931-33.

BARWIG, Charles (D Wis.) March 19, 1837-Feb. 15, 1912; House 1889-95.

BASHFORD, Coles (I Ariz.) Jan. 24, 1816-April 25, 1878; House (Terr. Del.) 1867-69; Gov. of Wisconsin (Republican) 1855-58.

BASS, Lyman Kidder (R N.Y.) Nov. 13, 1836-May 11, 1889; House 1873-77.

BASS, Perkins (R N.H.) Oct. 6, 1912-__; House 1955-63.

BASS, Ross (D Tenn.) March 17, 1918-__; House 1955-Nov. 3, 1964; Senate Nov. 4, 1964-67.

BASSETT, Burwell (D Va.) March 18, 1764-Feb. 26, 1841; House 1805-13, 1815-19, 1821-29.

BASSETT, Edward Murray (D N.Y.) Feb. 7, 1863-Oct. 27, 1948; House 1903-05.

BASSETT, Richard (grandfather of Richard Henry Bayard and James Asheton Bayard Jr.) (— Del.) April 2, 1745-Aug. 15, 1815; Senate 1789-93; Gov. 1799-1801.

BATE, William Brimage (D Tenn.) Oct. 7, 1826-March 9, 1905; Senate 1887-March 9, 1905; Gov. 1883-87.

BATEMAN, Ephraim (D N.J.) July 9, 1780-Jan. 28, 1829; House 1815-23; Senate Nov. 10, 1826-Jan. 12, 1829.

BATES, Arthur Laban (nephew of John Milton Thayer) (R Pa.) June 6, 1859-Aug. 26, 1934; House 1901-13.

BATES, Edward (brother of James Woodson Bates) (A A-D Mo.) Sept. 4, 1793-March 25, 1869; House 1827-29; Atty. Gen. of the U.S. 1861-64.

BATES, George Joseph (father of William Henry Bates) (R Mass.) Feb. 25, 1891-Nov. 1, 1949; House 1937-Nov. 1, 1949.

BATES, Isaac Chapman (W Mass.) Jan. 23, 1779-March 16, 1845; House 1827-35 (Anti-Jackson); Senate Jan. 13, 1841-March 16, 1845 (Whig).

BATES, James (D Maine) Sept. 24, 1789-Feb. 25, 1882; House 1831-33.

BATES, James Woodson (brother of Edward Bates) (— Ark.) Aug. 25, 1788-Dec. 16, 1846; House (Terr. Del.) Dec. 21, 1819-23.

BATES, Joseph Bengal (D Ky.) Oct. 29, 1893-Sept. 10, 1965; House June 4, 1938-53.

BATES, Martin Waltham (D Del.) Feb. 24, 1787-Jan. 1, 1869; Senate Jan. 14, 1857-59.

BATES, William Henry (son of George Joseph Bates) (R Mass.) April 26, 1917-June 22, 1969; House Feb. 14, 1950-June 22, 1969.

BATHRICK, Elsworth Raymond (D Ohio) Jan. 6, 1863-Dec. 23, 1917; House 1911-15, March 4-Dec. 23, 1917.

BATTIN, James F. (R Mont.) Feb. 13, 1925-—; House 1961-Feb. 27, 1969.

BATTLE, Laurie Calvin (D Ala.) May 10, 1912-__; House 1947-55.

BAUCUS, Max Sieben (D Mont.) Dec. 11, 1941-__; House 1975-__.

BAUMAN, Robert Edmund (R Md.) April 4, 1937-—; House Aug. 21, 1973-—.

BAUMHART, Albert David Jr. (R Ohio) June 15, 1908-__; House 1941-Sept. 2, 1942, 1955-61.

BAXTER, Portus (R Vt.) Dec. 4, 1806-March 4, 1868; House 1861-67.

BAY, William Van Ness (D Mo.) Nov. 23, 1818-Feb. 10, 1894; House 1849-51.

BAYARD, James Asheton Sr. (father of Richard Henry Bayard and James Asheton Bayard Jr., grandfather of Thomas Francis Bayard Sr., and great-grandfather of **Thomas Francis Bayard Jr.**) (F Del.) July 28, 1767-Aug. 6, 1815; House 1797-1803; Senate Nov. 13, 1804-13.

BAYARD, James Asheton Jr. (son of James Asheton Bayard Sr., grandson of Richard Bassett, father of Thomas Francis Bayard Sr. and grandfather of Thomas Francis Bayard Jr.) (D Del.) Nov. 15, 1799-June 13, 1880; Senate 1851-Jan. 29, 1864, April 5, 1867-69.

BAYARD, Richard Henry (son of James Asheton Bayard Sr., and grandson of Richard Bassett) (W Del.) Sept. 23, 1796-March 4, 1868; Senate June 17, 1836-Sept. 19, 1839, Jan. 12, 1841-45.

BAYARD, Thomas Francis Sr. (son of James Asheton Bayard Jr. and father of Thomas Francis Bayard Jr.) (D Del.) Oct. 29, 1828-Sept. 28, 1898; Senate 1869-March 6, 1885; President pro tempore 1881; Secretary of State 1885-89.

BAYARD, Thomas Francis Jr. (son of Thomas Francis Bayard Sr.) (D Del.) June 4, 1868-July 12, 1942; Senate Nov. 8, 1922-29.

BAYH, Birch Evan (D Ind.) Jan. 22, 1928-__; Senate 1963-__.

BAYLIES, Francis (brother of William Baylies) (— Mass.) Oct. 16, 1784-Oct. 28, 1852; House 1821-27.

BAYLIES, William (brother of Francis Baylies) (WD Mass.) Sept. 15, 1776-Sept. 27, 1865; House March 4-June 28, 1809, 1813-17, 1833-35.

BAYLOR, Robert Emmett Bledsoe (nephew of Jesse Bledsoe) (D Ala.) May 10, 1793-Jan. 6, 1874; House 1829-31.

BAYLY, Thomas (D Md.) Sept. 13, 1775-1829; House 1817-23.

BAYLY, Thomas Henry (son of Thomas Monteagle Bayly) (SRD Va.) Dec. 11, 1810-June 23, 1856; House May 6, 1844-June 23, 1856.

BAYLY, Thomas Monteagle (father of Thomas Henry Bayly) (D Va.) March 26, 1775-Jan. 7, 1834; House 1813-15.

BAYNE, Thomas McKee (R Pa.) June 14, 1836-June 16, 1894; House 1877-91.

BEACH, Clifton Bailey (R Ohio) Sept. 16, 1845-Nov. 15, 1902; House 1895-99.

BEACH, Lewis (D N.Y.) March 30, 1835-Aug. 10, 1886; House 1881-Aug. 10, 1886.

BEAKES, Samuel Willard (D Mich.) Jan. 11, 1861-Feb. 9, 1927; House 1913-March 3, 1917, Dec.13, 1917-19.

BEALE, Charles Lewis (R N.Y.) March 5, 1824-Jan. 29, 1900; House 1859-61.

BEALE, James Madison Hite (D Va.) Feb. 7, 1786-Aug. 2, 1866; House 1833-37, 1849-53.

BEALE, Joseph Grant (R Pa.) March 26, 1839-May 21, 1915; House 1907-09.

BEALE, Richard Lee Tuberville (D Va.) May 22, 1819-April 21, 1893; House 1847-49, Jan. 23, 1879-81.

BEALES, Cyrus William (R Pa.) Dec. 16, 1877-Nov. 14, 1927; House 1915-17.

BEALL, James Andrew (Jack) (D Texas) Oct. 25, 1866-Feb. 12, 1929; House 1903-15.

BEALL, James Glenn (father of John Beall Jr. (R Md.) June 5, 1894-Jan. 14, 1971; House 1943-53; Senate 1953-65.

BEALL, John Glenn Jr. (son of James Glenn Beall) (R Md.) June 19, 1927-__; House 1969-71; Senate 1971-__.

BEALL, Reasin (W Ohio) Dec. 3, 1769-Feb. 20, 1843; House April 20, 1813-June 7, 1814.

BEAM, Harry Peter (D Ill.) Nov. 23, 1892__; House 1931-Dec. 6, 1942.

BEAMAN, Fernando Cortez (R Mich.) June 28, 1814-Sept. 27, 1882; House 1861-71.

BEAMER, John Valentine (R Ind.) Nov. 17, 1896-Sept. 8, 1964; House 1951-59.

BEAN, Benning Moulton (D N.H.) Jan. 9, 1782-Feb. 6, 1866; House 1833-37.

BEAN, Curtis Coe (R Ariz.) Jan. 4, 1828-Feb. 1, 1904; House (Terr. Del.) 1885-87.

BEARD, Edward Peter (D R.I.) Jan. 20, 1940-__; House 1975-__.

BEARD, Robin Leo Jr. (R Tenn.) Aug. 21, 1939-__; House 1973-__.

BEARDSLEY, Samuel (D N.Y.) Feb. 6, 1790-May 6, 1860; House 1831-March 29, 1836, 1843-Feb. 29, 1844.

BEATTY, John (— N.J.) Dec. 10, 1749-May 30, 1826; House 1793-95; Cont. Cong. Jan. 13-June 3, 1784, Nov. 11, 1784-Nov. 7, 1785.

BEATTY, John (R Ohio) Dec. 16, 1828-Dec. 21, 1914; House Feb. 5, 1868-73.

BEATTY, William (VBD Pa.) 1787-April 12, 1851; House 1837-41.

BEATY, Martin (W Ky.) ? - ?; House 1833-35.

BEAUMONT, Andrew (D Pa.) Jan. 24, 1790-Sept. 30, 1853; House 1833-37.

BECK, Erasmus Williams (D Ga.) Oct. 21, 1833-July 22, 1898; House Dec. 2, 1872-73.

BECK, James Burnie (D Ky.) Feb. 13, 1822-May 3, 1890; House 1867-75; Senate 1877-May 3, 1890.

BECK, James Montgomery (R Pa.) July 9, 1861-April 12, 1936; House Nov. 8, 1927-Sept. 30, 1934.

BECK, Joseph David (R Wis.) March 14, 1866-Nov. 8, 1936; House 1921-29.

BECKER, Frank John (R N.Y.) Aug. 27, 1899-__; House 1953-65.

BECKHAM, John Crepps Wickliffe (grandson of Charles Anderson Wickliffe and cousin of Robert Charles Wickliffe) (D Ky.) Aug. 5, 1869-Jan. 9, 1940; Senate 1915-21; Gov. Feb. 3, 1900-07.

BECKNER, William Morgan (D Ky.) June 19, 1841-March 14, 1910; House Dec. 3, 1894-95.

BECKWITH, Charles Dyer (R N.J.) Oct. 22, 1838-March 27, 1921; House 1889-91.

BECKWORTH, Lindley Gary (D Texas) June 30, 1913-__; House 1939-53, 1957-67.

BEDE, James Adam (R Minn.) Jan. 13, 1856-April 11, 1942; House 1903-09.

BEDELL, Berkley Warren (D Iowa) March 5, 1921-__; House 1975-__.

BEDINGER, George Michael (uncle of Henry Bedinger) (— Ky.) Dec. 10, 1756-Dec. 7, 1843; House 1803-07.

BEDINGER, Henry (nephew of George Michael Bedinger) (D Va.) Feb. 3, 1812-Nov. 26, 1858; House 1845-49.

BEE, Carlos (D Texas) July 8, 1867-April 20, 1932; House 1919-21.

BEEBE, George Monroe (D N.Y.) Oct. 28, 1836-March 1, 1927; House 1875-79.

BEECHER, Philemon (F Ohio) 1775-Nov. 30, 1839; House 1817-21, 1823-29.

BEEDY, Carroll Lynwood (R Maine) Aug. 3, 1880-Aug. 30, 1947; House 1921-35.

BEEKMAN, Thomas (— N.Y.) ? - ?; House 1829-31.

BEEMAN, Joseph Henry (D Miss.) Nov. 17, 1833-July 31, 1909; House 1891-93.

BEERMANN, Ralph F. (R Neb.) Aug. 13, 1912-__; House 1961-65.

BEERS, Cyrus (D N.Y.) June 21, 1786-June 5, 1850; House Dec. 3, 1838-39.

BEERS, Edward McMath (R Pa.) May 27, 1877-April 21, 1932; House 1923-April 21, 1932.

BEESON, Henry White (D Pa.) Sept. 14, 1791-Oct. 28, 1863; House May 31, 1841-43.

BEGG, James Thomas (R Ohio) Feb. 16, 1877-March 26, 1963; House 1919-29.

BEGICH, Nicholas J. (D Alaska) April 6, 1932-?; House 1971-1972. (Disappeared in a plane Oct. 16, 1972; congressional seat declared vacant Dec. 29, 1972.)

BEGOLE, Josiah Williams (R Mich.) Jan. 20, 1815-June 5, 1896; House 1873-75; Gov. 1883-85.

BEIDLER, Jacob Atlee (R Ohio) Nov. 2, 1852-Sept. 13, 1912; House 1901-07.

BEIRNE, Andrew (VBD Va.) 1771-March 16, 1845; House 1837-41.

BEITER, Alfred Florian (D N.Y.) July 7, 1894-March 11, 1974; House 1933-39, 1941-43.

BELCHER, Hiram (W Maine) Feb. 23, 1790-May 6, 1857; House 1847-49.

BELCHER, Nathan (D Conn.) June 23, 1813-June 2, 1891; House 1853-55.

BELCHER, Page Henry (R Okla.) April 21, 1899-__; House 1951-73.

BELDEN, George Ogilvie (D N.Y.) March 28, 1797-Oct. 9, 1833; House 1827-29.

BELDEN, James Jerome (R N.Y.) Sept. 30, 1825-Jan. 1, 1904; House Nov. 8, 1887-95, 1897-99.

BELFORD, James Burns (cousin of Joseph McCrum Belford) (R Colo.) Sept. 28, 1837-Jan. 10, 1910; House Oct. 3, 1876-Dec. 13, 1877, 1879-85.

BELFORD, Joseph McCrum (cousin of James Burns Belford) (R N.Y.) Aug. 5, 1852-May 3, 1917; House 1897-99.

BELKNAP, Charles Eugene (R Mich.) Oct. 17, 1846-Jan. 16, 1929; House 1889-91, Nov. 3, 1891-93.

BELKNAP, Hugh Reid (R Ill.) Sept. 1, 1860-Nov. 12, 1901; House Dec. 27, 1895-99.

BELL, Alphonzo (R Calif.) Sept. 19, 1914-__; House 1961-__.

BELL, Charles Henry (nephew of Samuel Bell and cousin of James Bell) (R N.H.) Nov. 18, 1823-Nov. 11, 1893; Senate March 13-June 18, 1879; Gov. 1881-83.

BELL, Charles Jasper (D Mo.) Jan. 16, 1885-__; House 1935-49.

BELL, Charles Keith (nephew of Reese Bowen Brabson) (D Texas) April 18, 1853-April 21, 1913; House 1893-97.

BELL, Charles Webster (PR Calif.) June 11, 1857-April 19, 1927; House 1913-15.

BELL, Hiram (W Ohio) April 22, 1808-Dec. 21, 1855; House 1851-53.

BELL, Hiram Parks (D Ga.) Jan. 19, 1827-Aug. 17, 1907; House 1873-75, March 13, 1877-79.

BELL, James (son of Samuel Bell, uncle of Samuel Newell Bell and cousin of Charles Henry Bell) (W N.H.) Nov. 13, 1804-May 26, 1857; Senate July 30, 1855-May 26, 1857.

BELL, James Martin (D Ohio) Oct. 16, 1796-April 4, 1849; House 1833-35.

BELL, John (W Ohio) June 19, 1796-May 4, 1869; House Jan. 7-March 3, 1851.

BELL, John (W Tenn.) Feb. 15, 1797-Sept. 10, 1869; House 1827-41 (1827-29 Democrat, 1829-41 Whig); Senate Nov. 22, 1847-59; Speaker 1834-35; Secretary of War March 5-Sept. 12, 1841.

BELL, John Calhoun (D Colo.) Dec. 11, 1851-Aug. 12, 1933; House 1893-1903.

BELL, John Junior (D Texas) May 15, 1910-Jan. 24, 1963; House 1955-57.

BELL, Joshua Fry (W Ky.) Nov. 26, 1811-Aug. 17, 1870; House 1845-47.

BELL, Peter Hansbrough (D Texas) March 11, 1810-March 8, 1898; House 1853-57; Gov. 1849-53.

BELL, Samuel (father of James Bell, grandfather of Samuel Newell Bell and uncle of Charles Henry Bell) (— N.H.) Feb. 9, 1770-Dec. 23, 1850; Senate 1823-35; Gov. 1819-23.

BELL, Samuel Newell (grandson of Samuel Bell and nephew of James Bell) (D N.H.) March 25, 1829-Feb. 8, 1889; House 1871-73, 1875-77.

BELL, Theodore Arlington (D Calif.) July 25, 1872-Sept. 4, 1922; House 1903-05.

BELL, Thomas Montgomery (D Ga.) March 17, 1861-March 18, 1941; House 1905-31.

BELLAMY, John Dillard (D N.C.) March 24, 1854-Sept. 25, 1942; House 1899-1903.

BELLINGER, Joseph (— S.C.) 1773-Jan. 10, 1830; House 1817-19.

BELLMON, Henry (R Okla.) Sept. 3, 1921-__; Senate 1969-__; Gov. 1963-67.

BELMONT, Oliver Hazard Perry (brother of Perry Belmont) (D N.Y.) Nov. 12, 1858-June 10, 1908; House 1901-03.

BELMONT, Perry (brother of Oliver Hazard Perry Belmont) (D N.Y.) Dec. 28, 1851-May 25, 1947; House 1881-Dec. 1, 1888.

BELSER, James Edwin (D Ala.) Dec. 22, 1805-Jan. 16, 1859; House 1843-45.

BELTZHOOVER, Frank Eckels (D Pa.) Nov. 6, 1841-June 2, 1923; House 1879-83, 1891-95.

BENDER, George Harrison (R Ohio) Sept. 29, 1896-June 18, 1961; House 1939-49, 1951-Dec. 15, 1954; Senate Dec. 16, 1954-57.

BENEDICT, Charles Brewster (D N.Y.) Feb. 7, 1828-Oct. 3, 1901; House 1877-79.

BENEDICT, Henry Stanley (R Calif.) Feb. 20, 1878-July 10, 1930; House Nov. 7, 1916-17.

BENET, Christie (D S.C.-) Dec. 26, 1879-March 30, 1951; Senate July 6-Nov. 5, 1918.

BENITEZ, Jaime (PD P.R.) Oct. 29, 1908__; House (Res Comm.) 1973-__.

BENHAM, John Samuel (R Ind.) Oct. 24, 1863-Dec. 11, 1935; House 1919-23.

BENJAMIN, John Forbes (RR Mo.) Jan. 23, 1817-March 8, 1877; House 1865-71.

BENJAMIN, Judah Philip (D La.) Aug. 6, 1811-May 8, 1884; Senate 1853-Feb. 4, 1861 (1853-59 Whig; 1859-Feb. 4, 1861 Democrat).

BENNER, George Jacob (D Pa.) April 13, 1859-Dec. 30, 1930; House 1897-99.

BENNET, Augustus Witschief (son of William Stiles Bennet) (R N.Y.) Oct. 7, 1897-__; House 1945-47.

BENNET, Benjamin (— N.J.) Oct. 31, 1764-Oct. 8, 1840; House 1815-19.

BENNET, Hiram Pitt (CR Colo.) Sept. 2, 1826-Nov. 11, 1914; House (Terr. Del.) Aug. 19, 1861-65.

BENNET, William Stiles (father of Augustus Witschief Bennet) (R N.Y.) Nov. 9, 1870-Dec. 1, 1962; House 1905-11, Nov. 2, 1915-17.

BENNETT, Charles Edward (D Fla.) Dec. 2, 1910-__; House 1949-__.

BENNETT, Charles Goodwin (R N.Y.) Dec. 11, 1863-May 25, 1914; House 1895-99.

BENNETT, David Smith (R N.Y.) May 3, 1811-Nov. 6, 1894; House 1869-71.

BENNETT, Granville Gaylord (R Dakota) Oct. 9, 1833-June 28, 1910; House (Terr. Del.) 1879-81.

BENNETT, Hendley Stone (D Miss.) April 7, 1807-Dec. 15, 1891; House 1855-57.

BENNETT, Henry (R N.Y.) Sept. 29, 1808-May 10, 1868; House 1849-59 (1849-51 Whig; 1851-59 Republican).

BENNETT, John Bonifas (R Mich.) Jan. 10, 1904-Aug. 9, 1964; House 1943-45, 1947-Aug. 9, 1964.

BENNETT, Joseph Bentley (R Ky.) April 21, 1859-Nov. 7, 1923; House 1905-11.

BENNETT, Marion Tinsley (son of Philip A. Bennett) (R Mo.) June 6, 1914-—; House Jan. 12, 1943-49.

BENNETT, Philip Allen (father of Marion T. Bennett) (R Mo.) March 5, 1881-Dec. 7, 1942; House 1941-Dec. 7, 1942.

BENNETT, Risden Tyler (D N.C.) June 18, 1840-July 21, 1913; House 1883-87.

BENNETT, Thomas Warren (I Idaho) Feb. 16, 1831-Feb. 2, 1893; House (Terr. Del.) 1875-June 23, 1876; Gov. 1871-75.

BENNETT, Wallace Foster (R Utah) Nov. 13, 1898-__; Senate 1951-Dec. 20, 1974.

BENNY, Allan (D N.J.) July 12, 1867-Nov. 6, 1942; House 1903-05.

BENSON, Alfred Washburn (R Kan.) July 15, 1843-Jan. 1, 1916; Senate June 11, 1906-Jan. 23, 1907.

BENSON, Carville Dickinson (D Md.) Aug. 24, 1872-Feb. 8, 1929; House Nov. 5, 1918-21.

BENSON, Egbert (— N.Y.) June 21, 1746-Aug. 24, 1833; House 1789-93, March 4-Aug. 2, 1813; Cont. Cong. 1784-88.

BENSON, Elmer Austin (F-L Minn.) Sept. 22, 1895-__; Senate Dec. 27, 1935-Nov. 3, 1936; Gov. 1937-39.

BENSON, Samuel Page (R Maine) Nov. 28, 1804-Aug. 12, 1876; House 1853-57 (1853-55 Whig; 1855-57 Republican).

BENTLEY, Alvin Morell (R Mich.) Aug. 30, 1918-April 10, 1969; House 1953-61.

BENTLEY, Henry Wilbur (D N.Y.) Sept. 30, 1838-Jan. 27, 1907; House 1891-93.

BENTON, Charles Swan (D N.Y.) July 12, 1810-May 4, 1882; House 1843-47.

BENTON, Jacob (R N.H.) Aug. 19, 1814-Sept. 29, 1892; House 1867-71.

BENTON, Lemuel (great-grandfather of George William Dargan) (D S.C.) 1754-May 18, 1818; House 1793-99.

BENTON, Maecenas Eason (D Mo.) Jan. 29, 1848-April 27, 1924; House 1897-1905.

BENTON, Thomas Hart (D Mo.) March 14, 1782-April 10, 1858; Senate Aug. 10, 1821-51; House 1853-55 (Missouri Compromise Democrat).

BENTON, William (D Conn.) April 1, 1900-March 18, 1973; Senate Dec. 17, 1949-53.

BENTSEN, Lloyd Millard Jr. (D Texas) Feb. 11, 1921-__; House Dec. 4, 1948-55; Senate 1971-__.

BERGEN, Christopher Augustus (R N.J.) Aug. 2, 1841-Feb. 18, 1905; House 1889-93.

BERGEN, John Teunis (second cousin of Teunis Garret Bergen) (D N.Y.) 1786-March 9, 1855; House 1831-33.

BERGEN, Teunis Garret (second cousin of John Teunis Bergen) (D N.Y.) Oct. 6, 1806-April 24, 1881; House 1865-67.

BERGER, Victor Luitpold (Soc. Wis.) Feb. 28, 1860-Aug. 7, 1929; House 1911-13, 1923-29.

BERGLAND, Bob (D Minn.) July 31, 1928-—; House 1971-__.

BERLIN, William Markle (D Pa.) March 29, 1880-Oct. 14, 1962; House 1933-37.

BERNARD, John Toussaint (F-L Minn.) March 6, 1893-__; House 1937-39.

BERNHISEL, John Milton (W Utah) July 23, 1799-Sept. 28, 1881; House (Terr. Del.) 1851-59, 1861-63.

BERRIEN, John Macpherson (W Ga.) Aug. 23, 1781-Jan. 1, 1856; Senate 1825-March 9, 1829, 1841-May 1845, Nov. 14, 1845-47, Nov. 13, 1847-May 28, 1852 (1825-29 Democrat, 1841-52 Whig); Attorney General 1829-31.

BERRY, Albert Seaton (D Ky.) May 13, 1836-Jan. 6, 1908; House 1893-1901.

BERRY, Campbell Polson (cousin of James Henderson Berry) (D Calif.) Nov. 7, 1834-Jan. 8, 1901; House 1879-83.

BERRY, Ellis Yarnal (R S.D.) Oct. 6, 1902-—; House 1951-71.

BERRY, George Leonard (D Tenn.) Sept. 12, 1882-Dec. 4, 1948; Senate May 6, 1937-Nov. 8, 1938.

BERRY, James Henderson (cousin of Campbell Polson Berry) (D Ark.) May 15, 1841-Jan. 30, 1913; Senate March 20, 1885-1907; Gov. 1883-85.

BERRY, John (D Ohio) April 26, 1833-May 18, 1879; House 1873-75.

BESHLIN, Earl Hanley (D/Prohib. Pa.) April 28, 1870-July 12, 1971; House Nov. 8, 1917-19.

BETHUNE, Lauchlin (JD N.C.) April 15, 1785-Oct. 10, 1874; House 1831-33.

BETHUNE, Marion (R Ga.) April 8, 1816-Feb. 20, 1895; House Dec. 22, 1870-71.

BETTON, Silas (— N.H.) Aug. 26, 1768-Jan. 22, 1822; House 1803-07.

BETTS, Jackson Edward (R Ohio) May 26, 1904-—; House 1951-73.

BETTS, Samuel Rossiter (D N.Y.) June 8, 1787-Nov. 2, 1868; House 1815-17.

BETTS, Thaddeus (W Conn.) Feb. 4, 1789-April 7, 1840; Senate 1839-April 7, 1840.

BEVERIDGE, Albert Jeremiah (R Ind.) Oct. 6, 1862-April 27, 1927; Senate 1899-1911.

BEVERIDGE, John Lourie (R Ill.) July 6, 1824-May 3, 1910; House Nov. 7, 1871-Jan. 4, 1873; Gov. 1873-77.

BEVILL, Tom (D Ala.) March 27, 1921-—; House 1967-—.

BIAGGI, Mario (D N.Y.) Oct. 26, 1917-—; House 1969-—.

BIBB, George Motier (— Ky.) Oct. 30, 1776-April 14, 1859; Senate 1811-Aug. 23, 1814, 1829-35; Secy. of the Treasury 1844-45.

BIBB, William Wyatt (D Ga.) Oct. 1, 1780-July 9, 1820; House Jan. 26, 1807-Nov. 6, 1813; Senate Nov. 6, 1813-Nov. 9, 1816; Gov. of Ala. 1817-20.

BIBIGHAUS, Thomas Marshal (W Pa.) March 17, 1817-June 18, 1853; House 1851-53.

BIBLE, Alan Harvey (D Nev.) Nov. 20, 1909-—; Senate Dec. 2, 1954-Dec. 17, 1974.

BICKNELL, Bennet (D N.Y.) Nov. 14, 1781-Sept. 15, 1841; House 1837-39.

BICKNELL, George Augustus (D Ind.) Feb. 6, 1815-April 11, 1891; House 1877-81.

BIDDLE, Charles John (nephew of Richard Biddle) (D Pa.) April 30, 1819-Sept. 28, 1873; House July 2, 1861-63.

BIDDLE, John (W Mich.) March 2, 1792-Aug. 25, 1859; House (Terr. Del.) 1829-Feb. 21, 1831.

BIDDLE, Joseph Franklin (R Pa.) Sept. 14, 1871-Dec. 3, 1936; House Nov, 8, 1932-33.

BIDDLE, Richard (uncle of Charles John Biddle) (W Pa.) March 25, 1796-July 6, 1847; House 1837-40.

BIDEN, Joseph Robinette Jr. (D Del.) Nov. 20, 1942-—; Senate 1973-—.

BIDLACK, Benjamin Alden (D Pa.) Sept. 8, 1804-Feb. 6, 1849; House 1841-45.

BIDWELL, Barnabas (— Mass.) Aug. 23, 1763-July 27, 1833; House 1805-July 13, 1807.

BIDWELL, John (U Calif.) Aug. 5, 1819-April 4, 1900; House 1865-67.

BIEMILLER, Andrew John (D Wis.) July 23, 1906-—; House 1945-47, 1949-51.

BIERMANN, Frederick Elliott (D Iowa) March 20, 1884-July 1, 1968; House 1933-39.

BIERY, James Soloman (R Pa.) March 2, 1839-Dec. 3, 1904; House 1873-75.

BIESTER, Edward G. Jr. (R Pa.) Jan. 5, 1931-—; House 1967-—.

BIGBY, John Summerfield (R Ga.) Feb. 13, 1832-March 28, 1898; House 1871-73.

BIGELOW, Abijah (F Mass.) Dec. 5, 1775-April 5, 1860; House Oct. 8, 1810-March 3, 1815.

BIGELOW, Herbert Seely (D Ohio) Jan. 4, 1870-Nov. 11, 1951; House 1937-39.

BIGELOW, Lewis (— Mass.) Aug. 18, 1785-Oct. 2, 1838; House 1821-23.

BIGGS, Asa (D N.C.) Feb. 4, 1811-March 6, 1878; House 1845-47; Senate 1855-May 5, 1858.

BIGGS, Benjamin Thomas (D Del.) Oct. 1, 1821-Dec. 25, 1893; House 1869-73; Gov. 1887-91.

BIGGS, Marion (D Calif.) May 2, 1823-Aug. 2, 1910; House 1887-91.

BIGLER, William (D Pa.) Jan. 1, 1814-Aug. 9, 1880; Senate Jan. 14, 1856-61; Gov. 1852-55.

BILBO, Theodore Gilmore (D Miss.) Oct. 13, 1877-Aug. 21, 1947; Senate 1935-Aug. 21, 1947; Gov. 1916-20, 1928-32.

BILLINGHURST, Charles (R Wis.) July 27, 1818-Aug. 18, 1865; House 1855-59.

BILLMEYER, Alexander (D Pa.) Jan. 7, 1841-May 24, 1924; House Nov. 4, 1902-03.

BINDERUP, Charles Gustav (D Neb.) March 5, 1873-Aug. 19, 1950; House 1935-39.

BINES, Thomas (D N.J.) ? - April 9, 1826; House Nov. 2, 1814-15.

BINGHAM, Henry Harrison (R Pa.) Dec. 4, 1841-March 22, 1912; House 1879-March 22, 1912.

BINGHAM, Hiram (father of Jonathan B. Bingham) (R Conn.) Nov. 19, 1875-June 6, 1956; Senate Dec. 17, 1924-33; Gov. 1925.

BINGHAM, John Armor (R Ohio) Jan. 21, 1815-March 19, 1900; House 1855-63, 1865-73.

BINGHAM, Jonathan B. (son of Hiram Bingham) (D N.Y.) April 24, 1914-—; House 1965-—.

BINGHAM, Kinsley Scott (R Mich.) Dec. 16, 1808-Oct. 5, 1861; House (Dem.) 1847-51; Senate 1859-Oct. 5, 1861; Gov. 1854-58.

BINGHAM, William (F Pa.) March 8, 1752-Feb. 7, 1804; Senate 1795-1801; President pro tempore 1797; Cont. Cong. 1787-88.

BINNEY, Horace (W Pa.) Jan. 4, 1780-Aug. 12, 1875; House 1833-35.

BIRCH, William Fred (R N.J.) Aug. 30, 1870-Jan. 25, 1946; House Nov. 5, 1918-19.

BIRD, John (D N.Y.) Nov. 22, 1768-Feb. 2, 1806; House 1799-July 25, 1801.

BIRD, John Taylor (D N.J.) Aug. 16, 1829-May 6, 1911; House 1869-73.

BIRD, Richard Ely (R Kan.) Nov. 4, 1878-Jan. 10, 1955; House 1921-23.

BIRDSALL, Ausburn (D N.Y.) ? - July 10, 1903; House 1847-49.

BIRDSALL, Benjamin Pixley (R Iowa) Oct. 26, 1858-May 26, 1917; House 1903-09.

BIRDSALL, James (D N.Y.) 1783-July 20, 1856; House 1815-17.

BIRDSALL, Samuel (D N.Y.) May 14, 1791-Feb. 8, 1872; House 1837-39.

BIRDSEYE, Victory (W N.Y.) Dec. 25, 1782-Sept. 16, 1853; House 1815-17, 1841-43.

BISBEE, Horatio Jr. (R Fla.) May 1, 1839-March 27, 1916; House 1877-Feb. 20, 1879, Jan. 22-March 3, 1881, June 1, 1882-85.

BISHOP, Cecil William (Runt) (R Ill.) June 29, 1890-Sept. 21, 1971; House 1941-55.

BISHOP, James (W N.J.) May 11, 1816-May 10, 1895; House 1855-57.

BISHOP, Phanuel (— Mass.) Sept. 3, 1739-Jan. 6, 1812; House 1799-1807.

BISHOP, Roswell Peter (R Mich.) Jan. 6, 1843-March 4, 1920; House 1895-1907.

BISHOP, William Darius (D Conn.) Sept. 14, 1827-Feb. 4, 1904; House 1857-59.

BISSELL, William Harrison (D Ill.) April 25, 1811-March 18, 1860; House 1849-55; Gov. 1857-60.

BIXLER, Harris Jacob (R Pa.) Sept. 16, 1870-March 29, 1941; House 1921-27.

BLACK, Edward Junius (father of George Robison Black) (D Ga.) Oct. 30, 1806-Sept. 1, 1846; House 1839-41, Jan. 3, 1842-45 (1839-41 States Rights Whig, 1842-45 Democrat).

BLACK, Eugene (D Texas) July 2, 1879-May 22, 1975; House 1915-29.

BLACK, Frank Swett (R N.Y.) March 8, 1853-March 22, 1913; House 1895-Jan. 7, 1897; Gov. 1897-99.

BLACK, George Robison (son of Edward Junius Black) (D Ga.) March 24, 1835-Nov. 3, 1886; House 1881-83.

BLACK, Henry (W Pa.) Feb. 25, 1783-Nov. 28, 1841; House June 28-Nov. 28, 1841.

BLACK, Hugo Lafayette (D Ala.) Feb. 27, 1886-Sept. 25, 1971. Senate 1927-Aug. 19, 1937; Assoc. Justice U.S. Supreme Court 1937-Sept. 17, 1971.

BLACK, James (D Pa.) March 6, 1793-June 21, 1872; House Dec. 5, 1836-37, 1843-47.

BLACK, James Augustus (Cal.D S.C.) 1793-April 3, 1848; House 1843-April 3, 1848.

BLACK, James Conquest Cross (D Ga.) May 9, 1842-Oct. 1, 1928; House 1893-March 4, 1895, Oct. 2, 1895-97.

BLACK, John (— Miss.) ? - Aug. 29, 1854; Senate Nov. 12, 1832-March 3, 1833, Nov. 22, 1833-Jan. 22, 1838.

BLACK, John Charles (D Ill.) Jan. 27, 1839-Aug. 17, 1915; House 1893-Jan. 12, 1895.

BLACK, Loring Milton Jr. (D N.Y.) May 17, 1866-May 21, 1956; House 1923-35.

BLACKBURN, Benjamin Bentley (R Ga.) Feb. 14, 1927-__; House 1967-75.

BLACKBURN, Edmond Spencer (R N.C.) Sept. 22, 1868-March 10, 1912; House 1901-03, 1905-07.

BLACKBURN, Joseph Clay Stiles (D Ky.) Oct. 1, 1838-Sept. 12, 1918; House 1875-85; Senate 1885-97, 1901-07.

BLACKBURN, Robert E. Lee (R Ky.) April 9, 1870-Sept. 20, 1935; House 1929-31.

BLACKBURN, William Jasper (R La.) July 24, 1820-Nov. 10, 1899; House July 18, 1868-69.

BLACKLEDGE, William (father of William Salter Blackledge) (D N.C.) ? - Oct. 19, 1828; House 1803-09, 1811-13.

BLACKLEDGE, William Salter (son of William Blackledge) (D N.C.) 1793-March 21, 1857; House Feb. 7, 1821-23.

BLACKMAR, Esbon (W N.Y.) June 19, 1805-Nov. 19, 1857; House Dec. 4, 1848-49.

BLACKMON, Fred Leonard (D Ala.) Sept. 15, 1873-Feb. 8, 1921; House 1911-Feb. 8, 1921.

BLACKNEY, William Wallace (R Mich.) Aug. 28, 1876-March 14, 1963; House 1935-37, 1939-53.

BLACKWELL, Julius W. (VBD Tenn.) ?-?; House 1839-41, 1843-45.

BLAINE, James Gillespie (R Maine) Jan. 31, 1830-Jan. 27, 1893; House 1863-July 10, 1876; Speaker 1869-75; Senate July 10, 1876-March 5, 1881; Secy. of State March 5-Dec. 12, 1881, March 7, 1889-June 4, 1892.

BLAINE, John James (R Wis.) May 4, 1875-April 18, 1934; Senate 1927-33; Gov. 1921-27.

BLAIR, Austin (R Mich.) Feb. 8, 1818-Aug. 6, 1894; House 1867-73; Gov. 1861-65.

BLAIR, Bernard (W N.Y.) May 24, 1801-May 7, 1880; House 1841-43.

BLAIR, Francis Preston Jr. (D Mo.) Feb. 19, 1821-July 8, 1875; House 1857-59 (Free-Soiler) June 8-25, 1860, 1861-July 1862, 1863-June 10, 1864; Senate Jan. 20, 1871-73 (Democrat).

BLAIR, Henry William (R N.H.) Dec. 6, 1834-March 14, 1920; House 1875-79, 1893-95; Senate June 20, 1879-March 3, 1885, March 5, 1885-91.

BLAIR, Jacob Beeson (U Va. and W.Va.) April 11, 1821-Feb. 12, 1901; House Dec. 2, 1861-63 (Va.), Dec. 7, 1863-65 (W.Va.).

BLAIR, James (D S.C.) 1790-April 1, 1834; House 1821-May 8, 1822, 1829-April 1, 1834 (1821-22 Democrat, 1829-31 Union Democrat, 1831-34 Democrat).

BLAIR, James Gorrall (LR Mo.) Jan. 1, 1825-March 1, 1904; House 1871-73.

BLAIR, John (D Tenn.) Sept. 13, 1790-July 9, 1863; House 1823-35.

BLAIR, Samuel Steel (R Pa.) Dec. 5, 1821-Dec. 8, 1890; House 1859-63.

BLAISDELL, Daniel (F N.H.) Jan. 22, 1762-Jan. 10, 1833; House 1809-11.

BLAKE, Harrison Gray Otis (R Ohio) March 17, 1818-April 16, 1876; House Oct. 11, 1859-63.

BLAKE, John Jr. (— N.Y.) Dec. 5, 1762-Jan. 13, 1826; House 1805-09.

BLAKE, John Lauris (R N.J.) March 25, 1831-Oct. 10, 1899; House 1879-81.

BLAKE, Thomas Holdsworth (AR Ind.) June 14, 1792-Nov. 28, 1849; House 1827-29.

BLAKENEY, Albert Alexander (R Md.) Sept. 28, 1850-Oct. 15, 1924; House 1901-03, 1921-23.

BLAKLEY, William Arvis (D Texas) Nov. 17, 1898-Jan. 5, 1976; Senate Jan. 15-April 28, 1957, Jan. 3-June 14, 1961.

BLANCHARD, George Washington (R Wis.) Jan. 26, 1884-Oct. 2, 1964; House 1933-35.

BLANCHARD, James Johnston (D Mich.) Aug. 8, 1942-__; House 1975-__.

BLANCHARD, John (W Pa.) Sept. 30, 1787-March 9, 1849; House 1845-49.

BLANCHARD, Newton Crain (D La.) Jan. 29, 1849-June 22, 1922; House 1881-March 12, 1894; Senate March 12, 1894-97; Gov. 1904-08.

BLAND, Oscar Edward (R Ind.) Nov. 21, 1877-Aug. 3, 1951; House 1917-23.

BLAND, Richard Parks (D Mo.) Aug. 19, 1835-June 15, 1899; House 1873-95, 1897-June 15, 1899.

BLAND, Schuyler Otis (D Va.) May 4, 1872-Feb. 16, 1950; House July 2, 1918-Feb. 16, 1950.

BLAND, Theodorick (— Va.) March 21, 1742-June 1, 1790; House 1789-June 1, 1790; Cont. Cong. 1780-83.

BLAND, William Thomas (grandson of John George Jackson and cousin of James Monroe Jackson) (D Mo.) Jan. 21, 1861-Jan. 15, 1928; House 1919-21.

BLANTON, Leonard Ray (D Tenn.) April 10, 1930-—; House 1967-73; Gov. 1975-—.

BLANTON, Thomas Lindsay (D Texas) Oct. 25, 1872-Aug. 11, 1957; House 1917-29, May 20, 1930-37.

BLATNIK, John Anton (D Minn.) Aug. 17, 1911-__; House 1947-Dec. 31, 1974.

BLEAKLEY, Orrin Dubbs (R Pa.) May 15, 1854-Dec. 3, 1927; House March 4-April 3, 1917.

BLEASE, Coleman Livingston (D S.C.) Oct. 8, 1868-Jan. 19, 1942; Senate 1925-31; Gov. 1911-15.

BLEDSOE, Jesse (uncle of Robert Emmett Bledsoe Baylor) (— Ky.) April 6, 1776-June 25, 1836; Senate 1813-Dec. 24, 1814.

BLEECKER, Harmanus (F N.Y.) Oct. 9, 1779-July 19, 1849; House 1811-13.

BLISS, Aaron Thomas (R Mich.) May 22, 1837-Sept. 16, 1906; House 1889-91; Gov. 1901-05.

BLISS, Archibald Meserole (D N.Y.) Jan. 25, 1838-March 19, 1923; House 1875-83, 1885-89.

BLISS, George (D Ohio) Jan. 1, 1813-Oct. 24, 1868; House 1853-55, 1863-65.

BLISS, Philemon (R Ohio) July 28, 1813-Aug. 25, 1889; House 1855-59.

BLITCH, Iris Faircloth (D Ga.) April 25, 1912-__; House 1955-63.

BLODGETT, Rufus (D N.J.) Oct. 9, 1834-Oct. 3, 1910; Senate 1887-93.

BLOODWORTH, Timothy (— N.C.) 1736-Aug. 24, 1814; House April 6, 1790-91; Senate 1795-1801; Cont. Cong. 1786-Aug. 13, 1787.

BLOOM, Isaac (— N.Y.) 1716-April 26, 1803; House March 4-April 26, 1803.

BLOOM, Sol (D N.Y.) March 9, 1870-March 7, 1949; House 1923-March 7, 1949.

BLOOMFIELD, Joseph (D N.J.) Oct. 5, 1753-Oct. 3, 1823; House 1817-21; Gov. 1801-12.

BLOUIN, Michael Thomas (D Iowa) Nov. 7, 1945 -__; House 1975 -__.

BLOUNT, James Henderson (D Ga.) Sept. 12, 1837-March 8, 1903; House 1873-93.

BLOUNT, Thomas (brother of William Blount and uncle of William Grainger Blount) (D N.C.) May 10, 1759-Feb. 7, 1812; House 1793-99, 1805-09, 1811-Feb. 7, 1812.

BLOUNT, William (father of William Grainger Blount and brother of Thomas Blount) (— Tenn.) March 26, 1749-March 21, 1800; Senate Aug. 2, 1796-July 8, 1797; Cont. Cong. (N.C.) 1782-83, 1786-87.

BLOUNT, William Grainger (son of William Blount and nephew of Thomas Blount) (D Tenn.) 1784-May 21, 1827; House Dec. 8, 1815-19.

BLOW, Henry Taylor (R Mo.) July 15, 1817-Sept. 11, 1875; House 1863-67.

BLUE, Richard Whiting (R Kan.) Sept. 8, 1841-Jan. 28, 1907; House 1895-97.

BOARDMAN, Elijah (father of William Whiting Boardman) (D Conn.) March 7, 1760-Aug. 18, 1823; Senate 1821-Aug. 18, 1823.

BOARDMAN, William Whiting (son of Elijah Boardman) (W Conn.) Oct. 10, 1794-Aug: 27, 1871; House Dec. 7, 1840-43.

BOARMAN, Alexander (Aleck) (L La.) Dec. 10, 1839-Aug. 30, 1916; House Dec. 3, 1872-73.

BOATNER, Charles Jahleal (D La.) Jan. 23, 1849-March 21, 1903; House 1889-95, June 10, 1896-97.

BOCKEE, Abraham (JD N.Y.) Feb. 3, 1784-June 1, 1865; House 1829-31, 1833-37.

BOCOCK, Thomas Stanhope (D Va.) May 18, 1815-Aug. 5, 1891; House 1847-61.

BODEN, Andrew (— Pa.) ? - Dec. 20, 1835; House 1817-21.

BODINE, Robert Nall (D Mo.) Dec. 17, 1837-March 16, 1914; House 1897-99.

BODLE, Charles (— N.Y.) 1787-Oct. 31, 1835; House 1833-35.

BOEHNE, John William (father of John William Boehne Jr.) (D Ind.) Oct. 28, 1856-Dec. 27, 1946; House 1909-13.

BOEHNE, John William Jr. (son of John William Boehne) (D Ind.) March 2, 1895-July 5, 1973; House 1931-43.

BOEN, Haldor Erickson (PP Minn.) Jan. 2, 1851-July 23, 1912; House 1893-95.

BOGGS, Corinne Claiborne (widow of Thomas Hale Boggs Sr.) (D La.) March 13, 1916 -__; House March 20, 1973 -__.

BOGGS, James Caleb (R Del.) May 15, 1909-__; House 1947-53; Senate 1961-73; Gov. 1953-60.

BOGGS, Thomas Hale Sr. (husband of Corinne Claiborne Boggs) (D La.) Feb. 15, 1914-?; House 1941-43, 1947-1973. (Disappeared in a plane Oct. 16, 1972; congressional seat declared vacant Jan. 3, 1973.)

BOGY, Lewis Vital (D Mo.) April 9, 1813-Sept. 20, 1877; Senate 1873-Sept. 20, 1877.

BOHN, Frank Probasco (R Mich.) July 14, 1866-June 1, 1944; House 1927-33.

BOIES, William Dayton (R Iowa) Jan. 3, 1857-May 31, 1932; House 1919-29.

BOILEAU, Gerald John (Pro. Wis.) Jan. 15, 1900-__; House 1931-39 (1931-35 Republican, 1935-39 Progressive).

BOKEE, David Alexander (W N.Y.) Oct. 6, 1805-March 15, 1860; House 1849-51.

BOLAND, Edward Patrick (D Mass.) Oct. 1, 1911-__; House 1953-__.

BOLAND, Patrick Joseph (husband of Veronica G. Boland) (D Pa.) Jan. 6, 1880-May 18, 1942; House 1931-May 18, 1942.

BOLAND, Veronica Grace (widow of Patrick J. Boland) (D Pa.) March 18, 1899-__; House Nov. 19, 1942-43.

BOLES, Thomas (R Ark.) July 16, 1837-March 13, 1905; House June 22, 1868-71, Feb. 9, 1872-73.

BOLLES, Stephen (R Wis.) June 25, 1866-July 8, 1941; House 1939-July 8, 1941.

BOLLING, Richard Walker (D Mo.) May 17, 1916-__; House 1949-__.

BOLTON, Chester Castle (husband of Frances P. Bolton and father of Oliver P. Bolton) (R Ohio) Sept. 5, 1882-Oct. 29, 1939; House 1929-37, Jan. 3,-Oct. 29, 1939.

BOLTON, Frances Payne (widow of Chester C. Bolton, grand-daughter of Henry B. Payne and mother of Oliver P. Bolton) (R Ohio) March 29, 1885-—; House Feb. 27, 1940-69.

BOLTON, Oliver Payne (son of Chester Castle Bolton and Frances Payne Bolton and great-grandson of Henry B. Payne) (R Ohio) Feb. 22, 1917-Dec. 13, 1972; House 1953-57, 1963-65.

BOLTON, William P. (D Md.) July 2, 1885-Nov. 22, 1964; House 1949-51.

BOND, Charles Grosvenor (nephew of Charles Henry Grosvenor) (R N.Y.) May 29, 1877-Jan. 8, 1974; House 1921-23.

BOND, Shadrack (D Ill.) Nov. 24, 1773-April 12, 1832; House (Terr. Del.) Dec. 3, 1812-Aug. 2, 1813; Gov. 1818-22.

BOND, William Key (W Ohio) Oct. 2, 1792-Feb. 17, 1864; House 1835-41.

BONE, Homer Truett (D Wash.) Jan. 25, 1883-March 11, 1970; Senate 1933-Nov. 13, 1944.

BONHAM, Milledge Luke (SRD S.C.) Dec. 25, 1813-Aug. 27, 1890; House 1857-Dec. 21, 1860; Gov. 1862-64.

BONIN, Edward John (R Pa.) Dec. 23, 1904-—; House 1953-55.

BONKER, Don Leroy (D Wash.) March 7, 1937-—; House 1975-—.

BONNER, Herbert Covington (D N.C.) May 16, 1891-Nov. 7, 1965; House Nov. 5, 1940-Nov. 7, 1965.

BONYNGE, Robert William (R Colo.) Sept. 8, 1863-Sept. 22, 1939; House Feb. 16, 1904-09.

BOODY, Azariah (W N.Y.) April 21, 1815-Nov. 18, 1885; House March 4-October 1853.

BOODY, David Augustus (D N.Y.) Aug. 13, 1837-Jan. 20, 1930; House March 4-Oct. 13, 1891.

BOOHER, Charles Ferris (D Mo.) Jan. 31, 1848-Jan. 21, 1921; House Feb. 19-March 3, 1889, 1907-Jan. 21, 1921.

BOOKER, George William (C Va.) Dec. 5, 1821-June 4, 1883; House Jan. 26, 1870-71.

BOON, Ratliff (JD Ind.) Jan. 18, 1781-Nov. 20, 1844; House 1825-27, 1829-39; Gov. Sept. 12-Dec. 5, 1822.

BOONE, Andrew Rechmond (D Ky.) April 4, 1831-Jan. 26, 1886; House 1875-79.

BOOTH, Newton (AM Calif.) Dec. 25, 1825-July 14, 1892; Senate 1875-81; Gov. 1871-75.

BOOTH, Walter (FS Conn.) Dec. 8, 1791-April 30, 1870; House 1849-51.

BOOTHMAN, Melvin Morella (R Ohio) Oct. 16, 1846-March 5, 1904; House 1887-91.

BOOZE, William Samuel (R Md.) Jan. 9, 1862-Dec. 6, 1933; House 1897-99.

BORAH, William Edgar (R Idaho) June 29, 1865-Jan. 19, 1940; Senate 1907-Jan. 19, 1940.

BORCHERS, Charles Martin (D Ill.) Nov. 18, 1869-Dec. 2, 1946; House 1913-15.

BORDEN, Nathaniel Briggs (W Mass.) April 15, 1801-April 10, 1865; House 1835-39, 1841-43 (1835-39 Van Buren Democrat, 1841-43 Whig).

BOREING, Vincent (R Ky.) Nov. 24, 1839-Sept. 16, 1903; House 1899-Sept. 16, 1903.

BOREMAN, Arthur Inghram (R W.Va.) July 24, 1823-April 19, 1896; Senate 1869-75; Gov. 1863-69.

BOREN, Lyle H. (D Okla.) May 11, 1909-__; House 1937-47.

BORLAND, Charles Jr. (— N.Y.) June 29, 1786-Feb. 23, 1852; House Nov. 8, 1821-23.

BORLAND, Solon (D Ark.) Sept. 21, 1808-Jan. 1, 1864; Senate March 30, 1848-April 3, 1853.

BORLAND, William Patterson (D Mo.) Oct. 14, 1867-Feb. 20, 1919; House 1909-Feb. 20, 1919.

BORST, Peter I. (JD N.Y.) April 24, 1797-Nov. 14, 1848; House 1829-31.

BOSCH, Albert Henry (R N.Y.) Oct. 30, 1908-__; House 1953-Dec. 31, 1960.

BOSONE, Reva Zilpha Beck (D Utah ? -__; House 1949-53.

BOSS, John Linscom Jr. (— R.I.) Sept. 7, 1780-Aug. 1, 1819; House 1815-19.

BOSSIER, Pierre Evariste John Baptiste (Cal. D La.) March 22, 1797-April 24, 1844; House 1843-April 24, 1844.

BOTELER, Alexander Robinson (AP Va.) May 16, 1815-May 8, 1892; House 1859-61.

BOTKIN, Jeremiah Dunham (Fus. Kan.) April 24, 1849-Dec. 29, 1921; House 1897-99.

BOTTS, John Minor (HCW Va.) Sept. 16, 1802-Jan. 8, 1869; House 1839-43, 1847-49.

BOTTUM, Joseph H. (R S.D.) Aug. 7, 1903-__; Senate July 11, 1962-63.

BOUCK, Gabriel (nephew of Joseph Bouck) (D Wis.) Dec. 16, 1828-Feb. 21, 1904; House 1877-81.

BOUCK, Joseph (uncle of Gabriel Bouck) (D N.Y.) July 22, 1788-March 30, 1858; House 1831-33.

BOUDE, Thomas (F Pa.) May 17, 1752-Oct. 24, 1822; House 1801-03.

BOUDINOT, Elias (— N.J.) May 2, 1740-Oct. 24, 1821; House 1789-95; Cont. Cong. 1777-78, 1781-83.

BOULDIN, James Wood (brother of Thomas Tyler Bouldin) (JD Va.) 1792-March 30, 1854; House March 15, 1834-39.

BOULDIN, Thomas Tyler (brother of James Wood Bouldin) (D Va.) 1781-Feb. 11, 1834; House 1829-33, Aug. 26, 1833-Feb. 11, 1834.

BOULIGNY, Charles Joseph Dominique (uncle of John Edward Bouligny) (— La.) Aug. 22, 1773-March 6, 1833; Senate Nov. 19, 1824-29.

BOULIGNY, John Edward (nephew of Charles Joseph Dominique Bouligny) (AP La.) Feb. 5, 1824-Feb. 20, 1864; House 1859-61.

BOUND, Franklin (R Pa.) April 9, 1829-Aug. 8, 1910; House 1885-89.

BOURN, Benjamin (F R.I.) Sept. 9, 1755-Sept. 17, 1808; House Aug. 31, 1790-96.

BOURNE, Jonathan Jr. (R Ore.) Feb. 23, 1855-Sept. 1, 1940; Senate 1907-13.

BOURNE, Shearjashub (— Mass.) June 14, 1746-March 11, 1806; House 1791-95.

BOUTELL, Henry Sherman (R Ill.) March 14, 1856-March 11, 1926; House Nov. 23, 1897-1911.

BOUTELLE, Charles Addison (R Maine) Feb. 9, 1839-May 21, 1901; House 1883-1901.

BOUTWELL, George Sewel (R Mass.) Jan. 28, 1818-Feb. 27, 1905; House 1863-March 12, 1869; Senate March 17, 1873-77; Gov. 1851-53; Secy. of the Treasury March 12, 1869-March 17, 1873.

BOVEE, Matthias Jacob (JD N.Y.) July 24, 1793-Sept. 12, 1872; House 1835-37.

BOW, Frank Townsend (R Ohio) Feb. 20, 1901-Nov. 13, 1972; House 1951-Nov. 13, 1972.

BOWDEN, George Edwin (nephew of Lemuel Jackson Bowden) (R Va.) July 6, 1852-Jan. 22, 1908; House 1887-91.

BOWDEN, Lemuel Jackson (uncle of George Edwin Bowden) (R Va.) Jan. 16, 1815-Jan. 2, 1864; Senate 1863-Jan. 2, 1864.

BOWDLE, Stanley Eyre (D Ohio) Sept. 4, 1868-April 6, 1919; House 1913-15.

BOWDON, Franklin Welsh (uncle of Sydney Johnston Bowie) (D Ala.) Feb. 17, 1817-June 8, 1857; House Dec. 7, 1846-51.

BOWEN, Christopher Columbus (R S.C.) Jan. 5, 1832-June 23, 1880; House July 20, 1868-71.

BOWEN, David Reece (D Miss.) Oct. 21, 1932-—; House 1973-—.

BOWEN, Henry (son of Rees Tate Bowen, nephew of John Warfield Johnston and cousin of William Bowen Campbell) (R Va.) Dec. 26, 1841-April 29, 1915; House 1883-85; 1887-89 (1883-85 Readjuster, 1887-89 Republican).

BOWEN, John Henry (D Tenn.) Sept. 1780-Sept. 25, 1822; House 1813-15.

BOWEN, Rees Tate (father of Henry Bowen) (C Va.) Jan. 10, 1809-Aug. 29, 1879; House 1873-75.

BOWEN, Thomas Mead (R Colo.) Oct. 26, 1835-Dec. 30, 1906; Senate 1883-89; Gov. (Idaho Terr.) 1871.

BOWER, Gustavus Miller (D Va.) Dec. 12, 1790-Nov. 17, 1864; House 1843-45.

BOWER, William Horton (D N.C.) June 6, 1850-May 11, 1910; House 1893-95.

BOWERS, Eaton Jackson (D Miss.) June 17, 1865-Oct. 26, 1939; House 1903-11.

BOWERS, George Meade (R W.Va.) Sept. 13, 1863-Dec. 7, 1925; House May 9, 1916-23.

BOWERS, John Myer (— N.Y.) Sept. 25, 1772-Feb. 24, 1846; House May 26-Dec. 20, 1813.

BOWERS, William Wallace (R Calif.) Oct. 20, 1834-May 2, 1917; House 1891-97.

BOWERSOCK, Justin De Witt (R Kan.) Sept. 19, 1842-Oct. 27, 1922; House 1899-1907.

BOWIE, Richard Johns (W Md.) June 23, 1807-March 12, 1888; House 1849-53.

BOWIE, Sydney Johnston (nephew of Franklin Welsh Bowdon) (D Ala.) July 26, 1865-May 7, 1928; House 1901-07.

BOWIE, Thomas Fielder (grandnephew of Walter Bowie and brother-in-law of Reverdy Johnson) (D Md.) April 7, 1808-Oct. 30, 1869; House 1855-59.

BOWIE, Walter (granduncle of Thomas Fielder Bowie) (D Md.) 1748-Nov. 9, 1810; House March 24, 1802-05.

BOWLER, James Bernard (D Ill.) Feb. 5, 1875-July 18, 1957; House July 7, 1953-July 18, 1957.

BOWLES, Chester Bliss (D Conn.) April 5, 1901-__; House 1959-61; Gov. 1949-51.

BOWLES, Henry Leland (R Mass.) Jan. 6, 1866-May 17, 1932; House Sept. 29, 1925-29.

BOWLIN, James Butler (D Mo.) Jan. 16, 1804-July 19, 1874; House 1843-51.

BOWLING, William Bismarck (D Ala.) Sept. 24, 1870-Dec. 27, 1946; House Dec. 14, 1920-Aug. 16, 1928.

BOWMAN, Charles Calvin (R Pa.) Nov. 14, 1852-July 3, 1941; House 1911-Dec. 12, 1912.

BOWMAN, Frank Llewellyn (R W.Va.) Jan. 21, 1879-Sept. 15, 1936; House 1925-33.

BOWMAN, Selwyn Zadock (R Mass.) May 11, 1840-Sept. 30, 1928; House 1879-83.

BOWMAN, Thomas (D Iowa) May 25, 1848-Dec. 1, 1917; House 1891-93.

BOWNE, Obadiah (W N.Y.) May 19, 1822-April 27, 1874; House 1851-53.

BOWNE, Samuel Smith (VBD N.Y.) April 11, 1800-July 9, 1865; House 1841-43.

BOWRING, Eva Kelly (R Neb.) Jan. 9, 1892-__; Senate April 16-Nov. 7, 1954.

BOX, John Calvin (D Texas) March 28, 1871-May 17, 1941; House 1919-31.

BOYCE, William Henry (D Del.) Nov. 28, 1855-Feb. 6, 1942; House 1923-25.

BOYCE, William Waters (SRD S.C.) Oct. 24, 1818-Feb. 3, 1890; House 1853-Dec. 21, 1860.

BOYD, Adam (D N.J.) March 21, 1746-Aug. 15, 1835; House 1803-05, March 8, 1808-13.

BOYD, Alexander (W N.Y.) Sept. 14, 1764-April 8, 1857; House 1813-15.

BOYD, John Frank (R Neb.) Aug. 8, 1853-May 28, 1945; House 1907-09.

BOYD, John Huggins (W N.Y.) July 31, 1799-July 2, 1868; House 1851-53.

BOYD, Linn (D Ky.) Nov. 22, 1800-Dec. 17, 1859; House 1835-37, 1839-55; Speaker 1851-55.

BOYD, Sempronius Hamilton (R Mo.) May 28, 1828-June 22, 1894; House 1863-65, 1869-71 (1863-65 Emancipationist, 1869-71 Republican).

BOYD, Thomas Alexander (R Ill.) June 25, 1830-May 28, 1897; House 1877-81.

BOYDEN, Nathaniel (R N.C.) Aug. 16, 1796-Nov. 20, 1873; House 1847-49, July 13, 1868-69 (1847-49 Whig, 1868-69 Republican).

BOYER, Benjamin Markley (D Pa.) Jan. 22, 1823-Aug. 16, 1887; House 1865-69.

BOYER, Lewis Leonard (D Ill.) May 19, 1886-March 12, 1944; House 1937-39.

BOYKIN, Frank William (D Ala.) Feb. 21, 1885-March 12, 1969; House July 30, 1935-63.

BOYLAN, John Joseph (D N.Y.) Sept. 20, 1878-Oct. 5, 1938; House March 4, 1923-Oct. 5, 1938.

BOYLE, Charles Augustus (D Ill.) Aug. 13, 1907-Nov. 4, 1959; House 1955-Nov. 4, 1959.

BOYLE, Charles Edmund (D Pa.) Feb. 4, 1836-Dec. 15, 1888; House 1883-87.

BOYLE, John (D Ky.) Oct. 28, 1774-Feb. 28, 1834; House 1803-09.

BRABSON, Reese Bowen (uncle of Charles Keith Bell) (D Tenn.) Sept. 16, 1817-Aug. 16, 1863; House 1859-61.

BRACE, Johathan (F Conn.) Nov. 12, 1754-Aug. 26, 1837; House Dec. 3, 1798-1800.

BRACKENRIDGE, Henry Marie (W Pa.) May 11, 1786-Jan. 18, 1871; House Oct. 13, 1840-41.

BRADBURY, George (F Mass.) Oct. 10, 1770-Nov. 7, 1823; House 1813-17.

BRADBURY, James Ware (D Maine) June 10, 1802-Jan. 7, 1901; Senate 1847-53.

BRADBURY, Theophilus (F Mass.) Nov. 13, 1739-Sept. 6, 1803; House 1795-July 24, 1797.

BRADEMAS, John (D Ind.) March 2, 1927-___; House 1959-___.

BRADFORD, Allen Alexander (R Colo.) July 23, 1815-March 12, 1888; House (Terr. Del.) 1865-67, 1869-71.

BRADFORD, Taul (D Ala.) Jan. 20, 1835-Oct. 28, 1883; House 1875-77.

BRADFORD, William (— R.I.) Nov. 4, 1729-July 6, 1808; Senate 1793-Oct. 1797; President pro tempore 1797.

BRADLEY, Edward (D Mich.) April 1808-Aug. 5, 1847; House March 4-Aug. 5, 1847.

BRADLEY, Frederick Van Ness (R Mich.) April 12, 1898-May 24, 1947; House 1939-May 24, 1947.

BRADLEY, Michael Joseph (D Pa.) May 24, 1897-___; House 1937-47.

BRADLEY, Nathan Ball (R Mich.) May 28, 1831-Nov. 8, 1906; House 1873-77.

BRADLEY, Stephen Row (father of William Czar Bradley) (D Vt.) Feb. 20, 1754-Dec. 9, 1830; Senate Oct. 17, 1791-95, Oct. 15, 1801-13; President pro tempore 1802-03, 1808.

BRADLEY, Thomas Joseph (D N.Y.) Jan. 2, 1870-April 1, 1901; House 1897-1901.

BRADLEY, Thomas Wilson (R N.Y.) April 6, 1844-May 30, 1920; House 1903-13.

BRADLEY, William Czar (son of Stephen Row Bradley) (D Vt.) March 23, 1782-March 3, 1867; House 1813-15, 1823-27 (1813-15 War Democrat, 1823-27 Democrat).

BRADLEY, William O'Connell (R Ky.) March 18, 1847-May 23, 1914; Senate 1909-May 23, 1914; Gov. 1895-99.

BRADLEY, Willis Winter (R Calif.) June 28, 1884-Aug. 27, 1954; House 1947-49.

BRADSHAW, Samuel Carey (W Pa.) June 10, 1809-June 9, 1872; House 1855-57.

BRADY, James Dennis (R Va.) April 3, 1843-Nov. 30, 1900; House 1885-87.

BRADY, James Henry (R Idaho) June 12, 1862-Jan. 13, 1918; Senate Feb. 6, 1913-Jan. 13, 1918; Gov. 1909-11.

BRADY, Jasper Ewing (W Pa.) March 4, 1797-Jan. 26, 1871; House 1847-49.

BRAGG, Edward Stuyvesant (D Wis.) Feb. 20, 1827-June 20, 1912; House 1877-83, 1885-87.

BRAGG, John (SRD Ala.) Jan. 14, 1806-Aug. 10, 1878; House 1851-53.

BRAGG, Thomas (D N.C.) Nov. 10, 1810-Jan. 21, 1872; Senate 1859-March 6, 1861; Gov. 1855-59.

BRAINERD, Lawrence (FS Vt.) March 16, 1794-May 9, 1870; Senate Oct. 14, 1854-55.

BRAINERD, Samuel Myron (R Pa.) Nov. 13, 1842-Nov. 21, 1898; House 1883-85.

BRAMBLETT, Ernest King (R Calif.) April 25, 1901-___; House 1947-55.

BRANCH, John (uncle of Lawrence O'Bryan Branch) (D N.C.) Nov. 4, 1782-Jan. 3, 1863; Senate 1823-March 9, 1829; House May 12, 1831-33; Gov. (N.C.) 1817-20; Gov. (Fla.) 1844-45; Secy. of the Navy 1829-31.

BRANCH, Lawrence O'Bryan (father of William Augustus Blount Branch and nephew of John Branch) (D N.C.) Nov. 28, 1820-Sept. 17, 1862; House 1855-61.

BRANCH, William Augustus Blount (son of Lawrence O'Bryan Branch) (D N.C.) Feb. 26, 1847-Nov. 18, 1910; House 1891-95.

BRAND, Charles (R Ohio) Nov. 1, 1871-May 23, 1966; House 1923-33.

BRAND, Charles Hillyer (D Ga.) April 20, 1861-May 17, 1933; House 1917-May 17, 1933.

BRANDEGEE, Augustus (father of Frank Bosworth Brandegee) (R Conn.) July 15, 1828-Nov. 10, 1904; House 1863-67.

BRANDEGEE, Frank Bosworth (son of Augustus Brandegee) (R Conn.) July 8, 1864-Oct. 14, 1924; House Nov. 5, 1902-May 10, 1905; Senate May 10, 1905-Oct. 14, 1924.

BRANTLEY, William Gordon (D Ga.) Sept. 18, 1860-Sept. 11, 1934; House 1897-1913.

BRASCO, Frank J. (D N.Y.) Oct. 15, 1932-___; House 1967-75.

BRATTON, John (D S.C.) March 7, 1831-Jan. 12, 1898; House Dec. 8, 1884-85.

BRATTON, Robert Franklin (D Md.) May 13, 1845-May 10, 1894; House 1893-May 10, 1894.

BRATTON, Sam Gilbert (D N.M.) Aug. 19, 1888-Sept. 22, 1963; Senate 1925-June 24, 1933.

BRAWLEY, William Huggins (cousin of John James Hemphill and great-uncle of Robert Witherspoon Hemphill) (D S.C.) May 13, 1841-Nov. 15, 1916; House 1891-Feb. 12, 1894.

BRAXTON, Elliott Muse (D Va.) Oct. 8, 1823-Oct. 2, 1891; House 1871-73.

BRAY, William Gilmer (R Ind.) June 17, 1903-___; House 1951-75.

BRAYTON, William Daniel (R R.I.) Nov. 6, 1815-June 30, 1887; House 1857-61.

BREAUX, John Berlinger (D La.) March 1, 1944-__; House Sept. 30, 1972-__.

BREAZEALE, Phanor (D La.) Dec. 29, 1858-April 29, 1934; House 1899-1905.

BRECK, Daniel (brother of Samuel Breck) (W Ky.) Feb. 12, 1788-Feb. 4, 1871; House 1849-51.

BRECK, Samuel (brother of Daniel Breck) (F Pa.) July 17, 1771-Aug. 31, 1862; House 1823-25.

BRECKINRIDGE, Clifton Rodes (son of John Cabell Breckinridge and great-grandson of John Breckinridge) (D Ark.) Nov. 22, 1846-Dec. 3, 1932; House 1883-Sept. 5, 1890, Nov. 4, 1890-Aug. 14, 1894.

BRECKINRIDGE, James (brother of John Breckinridge) (F Va.) March 7, 1763-May 13, 1833; House 1809-17.

BRECKINRIDGE, James Douglas (— Ky.) ? - May 6, 1849; House Nov. 21, 1821-23.

BRECKINRIDGE, John (brother of James Breckinridge, grandfather of John Cabell Breckinridge and William Campbell Preston Breckinridge and great-grandfather of Clifton Rodes Breckinridge) (D Ky.) Dec. 2, 1760-Dec. 14, 1806; Senate 1801-Aug. 7, 1805; Atty. Gen. of the U.S. 1805-06.

BRECKINRIDGE, John Bayne (D Ky.) Nov. 29, 1913-__; House 1973-__.

BRECKINRIDGE, John Cabell (grandson of John Breckinridge, father of Clifton Rodes Breckinridge and cousin of Henry Donnel Foster) (D Ky.) Jan. 21, 1821-May 17, 1875; House 1851-55; Senate March 4-Dec. 4, 1861; Vice Pres. 1857-61.

BRECKINRIDGE, William Campbell Preston (grandson of John Breckinridge and uncle of Levin Irving Handy) (D Ky.) Aug. 28, 1837-Nov. 18, 1904; House 1885-95.

BREEDING, James Floyd (D Kan.) Sept. 28, 1901-__; House 1957-63.

BREEN, Edward G. (D Ohio) June 10, 1908-__; House 1949-Oct. 1, 1951.

BREESE, Sidney (D Ill.) July 15, 1800-June 28, 1878; Senate 1843-49.

BREHM, Walter Ellsworth (R Ohio) May 25, 1892-__; House 1943-53.

BREITUNG, Edward (R Mich.) Nov. 10, 1831-March 3, 1887; House 1883-85.

BREMNER, Robert Gunn (D N.J.) Dec. 17, 1874-Feb. 5, 1914; House 1913-Feb. 5, 1914.

BRENGLE, Francis (W Md) Nov. 26, 1807-Dec. 10, 1846; House 1843-45.

BRENNAN, Martin Adlai (D Ill.) Sept. 21, 1879-July 4, 1941; House 1933-37.

BRENNAN, Vincent Morrison (R Mich.) April 22, 1890-Feb. 4, 1959; House 1921-23.

BRENNER, John Lewis (D Ohio) Feb. 2, 1832-Nov. 1, 1906; House 1897-1901.

BRENT, Richard (uncle of William Leigh Brent and nephew of Daniel Carroll) (— Va.) 1757-Dec. 30, 1814; House 1795-99, 1801-03; Senate 1809-Dec. 30, 1814.

BRENT, William Leigh (nephew of Richard Brent) (— La.) Feb. 20, 1784-July 7, 1848; House 1823-29.

BRENTANO, Lorenzo (R Ill.) Nov. 4, 1813-Sept. 18, 1891; House 1877-79.

BRENTON, Samuel (R Ind.) Nov. 22, 1810-March 29, 1857; House 1851-53, 1855-March 29, 1857 (1851-53 Whig, 1855-57 Republican).

BRENTS, Thomas Hurley (R Wash.) Dec. 24, 1840-Oct. 23, 1916; House (Terr. Del.) 1879-85.

BRETZ, John Lewis (D Ind.) Sept. 21, 1852-Dec. 25, 1920; House 1891-95.

BREVARD, Joseph (W S.C.) July 19, 1766-Oct. 11, 1821; House 1819-21.

BREWER, Francis Beattie (R N.Y.) Oct. 8, 1820-July 29, 1892; House 1883-85.

BREWER, John Hart (R N.J.) March 29, 1844-Dec. 21, 1900; House 1881-85.

BREWER, Mark Spencer (R Mich.) Oct. 22, 1837-March 18, 1901; House 1877-81, 1887-91.

BREWER, Willis (D Ala.) March 15, 1844-Oct. 30, 1912; House 1897-1901.

BREWSTER, Daniel Baugh (D Md.) Nov. 23, 1923-__; House 1959-63; Senate 1963-69.

BREWSTER, David P. (D N.Y.) June 15, 1801-Feb. 20, 1876; House 1839-43.

BREWSTER, Henry Colvin (R N.Y.) Sept. 7, 1845-Jan. 29, 1928; House 1895-99.

BREWSTER, Ralph Owen (R Maine) Feb. 22, 1888-Dec. 25, 1961; House 1935-41; Senate 1941-Dec. 31, 1952; Gov. 1925-29.

BRICE, Calvin Stewart (D Ohio) Sept. 17, 1845-Dec. 15, 1898; Senate 1891-97; Chrmn., De. Natl. Comm. 1889-1892.

BRICK, Abraham Lincoln (R Ind.) May 27, 1860-April 7, 1908; House 1899-April 7, 1908.

BRICKER, John William (R Ohio) Sept. 6, 1893-__; Senate 1947-59; Gov. 1939-45.

BRICKNER, George H. (D Wis.) Jan. 21, 1834-Aug. 12, 1904; House 1889-95.

BRIDGES, George Washington (U Tenn.) Oct. 9, 1825-March 16, 1873; House Feb. 25-March 3, 1863.

BRIDGES, Henry Styles (R N.H.) Sept. 9, 1898-Nov. 26, 1961; Senate 1937-Nov. 26, 1961; Gov. 1935-37.

BRIDGES, Samuel Augustus (D Pa.) Jan. 27, 1802-Jan. 14, 1884; House March 6, 1848-49, 1853-55, 1877-79.

BRIGGS, Clay Stone (D Texas) Jan. 8, 1876-April 29, 1933; House 1919-April 29, 1933.

BRIGGS, Frank Obadiah (son of James Frankland Briggs) (R N.J.) Aug. 12, 1851-May 8, 1913; Senate 1907-13.

BRIGGS, Frank Parks (D Mo.) Feb. 25, 1894-__; Senate Jan. 18, 1945-47.

BRIGGS, George (AP N.Y.) May 6, 1805-June 1, 1869; House 1849-53, 1859-61 (1849-53 Whig, 1859-61 American Party).

BRIGGS, George Nixon (W Mass.) April 12, 1796-Sept. 11, 1861; House 1831-43; Gov. 1844-51.

BRIGGS, James Frankland (father of Frank Obadiah Briggs) (R N.H.) Oct. 23, 1827-Jan. 21, 1905; House 1877-83.

BRIGHAM, Elbert Sidney (R Vt.) Oct. 19, 1877-July 5, 1962; House 1925-31.

BRIGHAM, Elijah (F Mass.) July 7, 1751-Feb. 22, 1816; House 1811-Feb. 22, 1816.

BRIGHAM, Lewis Alexander (R N.J.) Jan. 2, 1831-Feb. 19, 1885; House 1879-81.

BRIGHT, Jesse David (D Ind.) Dec. 18, 1812-May 20, 1875; Senate 1845-Feb. 5, 1862; President pro tempore 1854, 1856, 1860.

BRIGHT, John Morgan (D Tenn.) Jan. 20, 1817-Oct. 3, 1911; House 1871-81.

BRINKERHOFF, Henry Roelif (cousin of Jacob Brinkerhoff) (D Ohio) Sept. 23, 1787-April 30, 1844; House 1843-April 30, 1844.

BRINKERHOFF, Jacob (cousin of Henry Roelif Brinkerhoff) (D Ohio) Aug. 31, 1810-July 19, 1880; House 1843-47.

BRINKLEY, Jack Thomas (D Ga.) Dec. 22, 1930-__; House 1967-__.

BRINSON, Samuel Mitchell (D N.C.) March 20, 1870-April 13, 1922; House 1919-April 13, 1922.

BRISBIN, John (W Pa.) July 13, 1818-Feb. 3, 1880; House Jan. 13-March 3, 1851.

BRISTOW, Francis Marion (W Ky.) Aug. 11, 1804-June 10, 1864; House Dec. 4, 1854-55, 1859-61.

BRISTOW, Henry (R N.Y.) June 5, 1840-Oct. 11, 1906; House 1901-03.

BRISTOW, Joseph Little (R Kan.) July 22, 1861-July 14, 1944; Senate 1909-15.

BRITT, James Jefferson (R N.C.) March 4, 1861-Dec. 26, 1939; House 1915-17, March 1-3, 1919.

BRITTEN, Frederick Albert (R Ill.) Nov. 18, 1871-May 4, 1946; House 1913-35.

BROADHEAD, James Overton (D Mo.) May 29, 1819-Aug. 7, 1898; House 1883-85.

BROCK, Lawrence (D Neb.) Aug. 16, 1906-Aug. 28, 1968; House 1959-61.

BROCK, William Emerson (grandfather of William Emerson Brock III) (D Tenn.) March 14, 1872-Aug. 5, 1950; Senate Sept. 2, 1929-31.

BROCK, William Emerson III (grandson of William Emerson Brock) (R Tenn.) Nov. 23, 1930-___; House 1963-71; Senate 1971-___.

BROCKENBROUGH, William Henry (D Fla.) Feb. 23, 1812-Jan. 28, 1850; House Jan. 24, 1846-47.

BROCKSON, Franklin (D Del.) Aug. 6, 1865-March 16, 1942; House 1913-15.

BROCKWAY, John Hall (W Conn.) Jan. 31, 1801-July 29, 1870; House 1839-43.

BRODBECK, Andrew R. (D Pa.) April 11, 1860-Feb. 27, 1937; House 1913-15, 1917-19.

BRODERICK, Case (cousin of David Colbreth Broderick and Andrew Kennedy) (R Kan.) Sept. 23, 1839-April 1, 1920; House 1891-99.

BRODERICK, David Colbreth (cousin of Andrew Kennedy and Case Broderick) (D Calif.) Feb. 4, 1820-Sept. 16, 1859; Senate 1857-Sept. 16, 1859.

BRODHEAD, John (D N.H.) Oct. 5, 1770-April 7, 1838; House 1829-33.

BRODHEAD, John Curtis (D N.Y.) Oct. 27, 1780-Jan. 2, 1859; House 1831-33, 1837-39.

BRODHEAD, Joseph Davis (son of Richard Brodhead) (D Pa.) Jan. 12, 1859-April 23, 1920; House 1907-09.

BRODHEAD, Richard (father of Joseph Brodhead) (D Pa.) Jan. 5, 1811-Sept. 16, 1863; House 1843-49; Senate 1851-57.

BRODHEAD, William McNulty (D Mich.) Sept. 12, 1941-___; House 1975-___.

BROGDEN, Curtis Hooks (R N.C.) Nov. 6, 1816-Jan. 5, 1901; House 1877-79; Gov. 1874-77.

BROMBERG, Frederick George (LR/D Ala.) June 19, 1837-Sept. 4, 1930; House 1873-75.

BROMWELL, Henry Pelham Holmes (R Ill.) Aug. 26, 1823-Jan. 7, 1903; House 1865-69.

BROMWELL, Jacob Henry (R Ohio) May 11, 1848-June 4, 1924; House Dec. 3, 1894-1903.

BROMWELL, James E. (R Iowa) March 26, 1920-___; House 1961-65.

BRONSON, David (W Maine) Feb. 8, 1800-Nov. 20, 1863; House May 31, 1841-43.

BRONSON, Isaac Hopkins (D N.Y.) Oct. 16, 1802-Aug. 13, 1855; House 1837-39.

BROOCKS, Moses Lycurgus (D Texas) Nov. 1, 1864-May 27, 1908; House 1905-07.

BROOKE, Edward W. (R Mass.) Oct. 26, 1919-___; Senate 1967-___.

BROOKE, Walker (W Miss.) Dec. 25, 1813-Feb. 18, 1869; Senate Feb. 18, 1852-53.

BROOKHART, Smith Wildman (PR Iowa) Feb. 2, 1869-Nov. 15, 1944; Senate Nov. 7, 1922-April 12, 1926, 1927-33.

BROOKS, Charles Wayland (R Ill.) March 8, 1897-Jan. 14, 1957; Senate Nov. 22, 1940-49.

BROOKS, David (— N.Y.) 1756-Aug. 30, 1838; House 1797-99.

BROOKS, Edward Schroeder (R Pa.) June 14, 1867-July 12, 1957; House 1919-23.

BROOKS, Edwin Bruce (cousin of Edmund Howard Hinshaw) (R Ill.) Sept. 20, 1868-Sept. 18, 1933; House 1919-23.

BROOKS, Franklin Eli (R Colo.) Nov. 19, 1860-Feb. 7, 1916; House 1903-07.

BROOKS, George Merrick (R Mass.) July 26, 1824-Sept. 22, 1893; House Nov. 2, 1869-May 13, 1872.

BROOKS, Jack Bascom (D Texas) Dec. 18, 1922-___; House 1953-___.

BROOKS, James (D N.Y.) Nov. 10, 1810-April 30, 1873; House 1849-53, 1863-April 7, 1866; 1867-April 30, 1873 (1849-53 Whig, 1863-66 and 1867-73 Democrat).

BROOKS, Joshua Twing (D Pa.) Feb. 27, 1884-Feb. 7, 1956; House 1933-37.

BROOKS, Micah (— N.Y.) May 14, 1775-July 7, 1857; House 1815-17.

BROOKS, Overton (nephew of John Holmes Overton) (D La.) Dec. 21, 1897-Sept. 16, 1961; House 1937-Sept. 16, 1961.

BROOKS, Preston Smith (SRD S.C.) Aug. 5, 1819-Jan. 27, 1857; House 1853-July 15, 1856, Aug. 1, 1856-Jan. 27, 1857.

BROOKSHIRE, Elijah Voorhees (D Ind.) Aug. 15, 1856-April 14, 1936; House 1889-95.

BROOM, Jacob (son of James Madison Broom) (AW Pa.) July 25, 1808-Nov. 28, 1864; House 1855-57.

BROOM, James Madison (father of Jacob Broom) (F Del.) 1776-Jan. 15, 1850; House 1805-07.

BROOMALL, John Martin (R Pa.) Jan. 19, 1816-June 3, 1894; House 1863-69.

BROOMFIELD, William S. (R Mich.) April 28, 1922-___; House 1957-___.

BROPHY, John Charles (R Wis.) Oct. 8, 1901-___; House 1947-49.

BROSIUS, Marriott (R Pa.) March 7, 1843-March 16, 1901; House 1889-March 16, 1901.

BROTZMAN, Donald Glenn (R Colo.) June 28, 1922-___; House 1963-65, 1967-75.

BROUGHTON, Joseph Melville (D N.C.) Nov. 17, 1888-March 6, 1949; Senate Dec. 31, 1948-March 6, 1949; Gov. 1941-45.

BROUSSARD, Edwin Sidney (brother of Robert Foligny Broussard (D La.) Dec. 4, 1874-Nov. 19, 1934; Senate 1921-33.

BROUSSARD, Robert Foligny (brother of Edwin Sidney Broussard) (D La.) Aug. 17, 1864-April 12, 1918; House 1897-1915; Senate 1915-April 12, 1918.

BROWER, John Morehead (R N.C.) July 19, 1845-Aug. 5, 1913; House 1887-91.

BROWN, Aaron Venable (D Tenn.) Aug. 15, 1795-March 8, 1859; House 1839-45; Gov. 1845-47; Postmaster General 1857-59.

BROWN, Albert Gallatin (D Miss.) May 31, 1813-June 12, 1880; House 1839-41, 1847-53; Senate Jan. 7, 1854-Jan. 12, 1861; Gov. 1844-48.

BROWN, Anson (W N.Y.) 1800-June 14, 1840; House 1839-June 14, 1840.

BROWN, Arthur (R Utah) March 8, 1843-Dec. 12, 1906; Senate Jan. 22, 1896-97.

BROWN, Bedford (D N.C.) June 6, 1795-Dec. 6, 1870; Senate Dec. 9, 1829-Nov. 16, 1840.

BROWN, Benjamin (nephew of John Brown) (— Mass.) Sept. 23, 1756-Sept. 17, 1831; House 1815-17.

BROWN, Benjamin Gratz (grandson of John Brown of Virginia and Kentucky) (D Mo.) May 28, 1826-Dec. 13, 1885; Senate Nov. 13, 1863-67; Gov. 1871-73.

BROWN, Charles (D Pa.) Sept. 23, 1797-Sept. 4, 1883; House 1841-43, 1847-49.

BROWN, Charles Elwood (R Ohio) July 4, 1834-May 22, 1904; House 1885-89.

BROWN, Charles Harrison (D Mo.) Oct. 22, 1920-___; House 1957-61.

BROWN, Clarence J. (father of Clarence J. Brown Jr.) (R Ohio) July 14, 1893-Aug. 23, 1965; House 1939-Aug. 23, 1965.

BROWN, Clarence J. Jr. (son of Clarence J. Brown) June 18, 1927-___; House Nov. 2, 1965-___.

BROWN, Elias (W Md.) May 9, 1793-July 7, 1857; House 1829-31.

BROWN, Ernest S. (R Nev.) Sept. 25, 1903-July 23, 1965; Senate Oct. 1-Dec. 1, 1954.

BROWN, Ethan Allen (D Ohio) July 4, 1776-Feb. 24, 1852; Senate Jan. 3, 1822-25; Gov. 1818-22.

BROWN, Foster Vincent (father of Joseph Edgar Brown) (R Tenn.) Dec. 24, 1852-March 26, 1937; House 1895-97.

BROWN, Fred Herbert (D N.H.) April 12, 1879-Feb. 3, 1955; Senate 1933-39; Gov. 1923-25.

BROWN, Garry E. (R Mich.) Aug. 12, 1923-__; House 1967-__.

BROWN, George E. Jr. (D Calif.) March 6, 1920-—; House 1963-71, 1973-—.

BROWN, George Houston (W N.J.) Feb. 12, 1810-Aug. 1, 1865; House 1851-53.

BROWN, James (brother of John Brown of Virginia and Kentucky) (— La.) Sept. 11, 1776-April 7, 1835; Senate Feb. 5, 1813-17, 1819-Dec. 10, 1823.

BROWN, James Sproat (D Wis.) Feb. 1, 1824-April 15, 1878; House 1863-65.

BROWN, James W. (R Pa.) July 14, 1844-Oct. 23, 1909; House 1903-05.

BROWN, Jason Brevoort (D Ind.) Feb. 26, 1839-March 10, 1898; House 1889-95.

BROWN, Jeremiah (W Pa.) April 14, 1785-March 2, 1858; House 1841-45.

BROWN, John (uncle of Benjamin Brown and grandfather of John Brown Francis) (F R.I.) Jan. 27, 1736-Sept. 20, 1803; House 1799-1801.

BROWN, John (D Md.) ? -Dec. 13, 1815; House 1809-10.

BROWN, John (brother of James Brown and grandfather of Benjamin Gratz Brown) (— Va./Ky.) Sept. 12, 1757-Aug. 29, 1837; House 1789-June 1, 1792 (Ky. district of Va.); Senate June 18, 1792-1805 (Ky.); President pro tempore 1803-04; Cont. Cong. (Ky. district of Va.) 1787-88.

BROWN, John (— Pa.) Aug. 12, 1772-Oct. 12, 1845; House 1821-25.

BROWN, John Brewer (D Md.) May 13, 1836-May 16, 1898; House Nov. 8, 1892-93.

BROWN, John Robert (IR Va.) Jan. 14, 1842-Aug. 4, 1927; House 1887-89.

BROWN, John W. (D N.Y.) Oct. 11, 1796-Sept. 6, 1875; House 1833-37.

BROWN, John Young (nephew of Bryan Rust Young and William Singleton Young) (D Ky.) June 28, 1835-Jan. 11, 1904; House 1859-61, 1873-77; Gov. 1891-95.

BROWN, John Young (D Ky.) Feb. 1, 1900__; House 1933-35.

BROWN, Joseph Edgar (son of Foster Vincent Brown) (R Tenn.) Feb. 11, 1880-June 13, 1939; House 1921-23.

BROWN, Joseph Emerson (D Ga.) April 15, 1821-Nov. 30, 1894; Senate May 26, 1880-91; Gov. 1857-65.

BROWN, Lathrop (D N.Y.) Feb. 26, 1883-Nov. 28, 1959; House 1913-15.

BROWN, Milton (W Tenn.) Feb. 28, 1804-May 15, 1883; House 1841-47.

BROWN, Norris (R Neb.) May 2, 1863-Jan. 5, 1960; Senate 1907-13.

BROWN, Paul (D Ga.) March 31, 1880-Sept. 24, 1961; House July 5, 1933-61.

BROWN, Prentiss Marsh (D Mich.) June 18, 1889-Dec. 19, 1973; House 1933-Nov. 18, 1936; Senate Nov. 19, 1936-43.

BROWN, Robert (D Pa.) Dec. 25, 1744-Feb. 26, 1823; House Dec. 4, 1798-1815.

BROWN, Seth W. (R Ohio) Jan. 4, 1841-Feb. 24, 1923; House 1897-1901.

BROWN, Titus (— N.H.) Feb. 11, 1786-Jan. 29, 1849; House 1825-29.

BROWN, Webster Everett (R Wis.) July 16, 1851-Dec. 14, 1929; House 1901-07.

BROWN, William (— Ky.) April 19, 1779-Oct. 6, 1833; House 1819-21.

BROWN, William Gay (U Va./W.Va.) Sept. 25, 1800-April 19, 1884; House 1845-49, 1861-63, Dec. 7, 1863-65 (1845-49 Democrat, Va.; 1861-63 Unionist, Va.; 1863-65 Unionist, W.Va.).

BROWN, William Gay Jr. (son of William Gay Brown) (D W.Va.) April 7, 1856-March 9, 1916; House 1911-March 9, 1916.

BROWN, William John (D Ind.) Aug. 15, 1805-March 18, 1857; House 1843-45, 1849-51.

BROWN, William Ripley (R Kan.) July 16, 1840-March 3, 1916; House 1875-77.

BROWN, William Wallace (R Pa.) April 22, 1836-Nov. 4, 1926; House 1883-87.

BROWNE, Charles (D N.J.) Sept. 28, 1875-Aug. 17, 1947; House 1923-25.

BROWNE, Edward Everts (R Wis.) Feb. 16, 1868-Nov. 23, 1945; House 1913-31.

BROWNE, George Huntington (D R.I.) Jan. 6, 1811-Sept. 26, 1885; House 1861-63.

BROWNE, Thomas Henry Bayly (R Va.) Feb. 8, 1844-Aug. 27, 1892; House 1887-91.

BROWNE, Thomas McLelland (R Ind.) April 19, 1829-July 17, 1891; House 1877-91.

BROWNING, Gordon (D Tenn.) Nov. 22, 1889-May 23, 1976; House 1923-35; Gov. 1937-39, 1949-53.

BROWNING, Orville Hickman (R Ill.) Feb. 10, 1806-Aug. 10, 1881; Senate June 26, 1861-Jan. 12, 1863; Secy. of the Interior 1866-69; Atty. Gen. ad interim 1868.

BROWNING, William John (R N.J.) April 11, 1850-March 24, 1920; House Nov. 7, 1911-March 24, 1920.

BROWNLOW, Walter Preston (nephew of William Gannaway Brownlow) (R Tenn.) March 27, 1851-July 8, 1910; House 1897-July 8, 1910.

BROWNLOW, William Gannaway (uncle of Walter Preston Brownlow) (R Tenn.) Aug. 29, 1805-April 29, 1877; Senate 1869-75; Gov. April 5, 1865-Oct., 1867.

BROWNSON, Charles Bruce (R Ind.) Feb. 5, 1914-__; House 1951-59.

BROYHILL, James T. (R N.C.) Aug. 19, 1927-__; House 1963-__.

BROYHILL, Joel Thomas (R Va.) Nov. 4, 1919__; House 1953-Dec. 31, 1974.

BRUCE, Blanche Kelso (R Miss.) March 1, 1841-March 17, 1898; Senate 1875-81.

BRUCE, Donald Cogley (R Ind.) April 27, 1921-Aug. 31, 1969; House 1961-65.

BRUCE, Phineas (— Mass.) June 7, 1762-Oct. 4, 1809; elected to House 1803, but did not serve.

BRUCE, William Cabell (D Md.) March 12, 1860-May 9, 1946; Senate 1923-29.

BRUCKER, Ferdinand (D Mich.) Jan. 8, 1858-March 3, 1904; House 1897-99.

BRUCKNER, Henry (D N.Y.) June 17, 1871-April 14, 1942; House 1913-Dec. 31, 1917.

BRUMBAUGH, Clement Laird (D Ohio) Feb. 28, 1863-Sept. 28, 1921; House 1913-21.

BRUMBAUGH, David Emmert (R Pa.) Oct. 8, 1894-—; House Nov. 2, 1943-47.

BRUMM, Charles Napoleon (father of George Franklin Brumm) (RG Pa.) June 9, 1838-Jan. 11, 1917; House 1881-89, 1895-99, Nov. 6, 1906-Jan. 4, 1909.

BRUMM, George Franklin (son of Charles Napoleon Brumm) (R Pa.) Jan. 24, 1880-May 29, 1934; House 1923-27, 1929-May 29, 1934.

BRUNDIDGE, Stephen Jr. (D Ark.) Jan. 1, 1857-Jan. 14, 1938; House 1897-1909.

BRUNNER, David B. (D Pa.) March 7, 1835-Nov. 29, 1903; House 1889-93.

BRUNNER, William Frank (D N.Y.) Sept. 15, 1887-April 23, 1965; House 1929-Sept. 27, 1935.

BRUNSDALE, Clarence Norman (R N.D.) July 9, 1891-__; Senate Nov. 19, 1959-Aug. 7, 1960; Gov. 1951-57.

BRUSH, Henry (— Ohio) June 1778-Jan. 19, 1855; House 1819-21.

BRUYN, Andrew DeWitt (D N.Y.) Nov. 18, 1790-July 27, 1838; House 1837-July 27, 1838.

BRYAN, Guy Morrison (D Texas) Jan. 12, 1821-June 4, 1901; House 1857-59.

BRYAN, Henry H. (— Tenn.) ? -May 7, 1835; House 1819-21, re-elected 1820, but did not serve.

BRYAN, James Wesley (PR Wash.) March 11, 1874-Aug. 26, 1956; House 1913-15.

BRYAN, John Heritage (W N.C.) Nov. 4, 1798-May 19, 1870; House 1825-29.

BRYAN, Joseph (D Ga.) Aug. 18, 1773-Sept. 12, 1812; House 1803-06.

BRYAN, Joseph Hunter (— N.C.) ? - ?; House 1815-19.

BRYAN, Nathan (— N.C.) 1748-June 4, 1798; House 1795-June 4, 1798.

BRYAN, Nathan Philemon (brother of William James Bryan) (D Fla.) April 23, 1872-Aug. 8, 1935; Senate 1911-17.

BRYAN, William James (brother of Nathan Philemon Bryan) (D Fla.) Oct. 10, 1876-March 22, 1908; Senate Dec. 26, 1907-March 22, 1908.

BRYAN, William Jennings (father of Ruth Bryan Owen) (D Neb.) March 19, 1860-July 26, 1925; House 1891-95; Secy. of State 1913-15.

BRYCE, Lloyd Stephens (D N.Y.) Sept. 20, 1850-April 2, 1917; House 1887-89.

BRYSON, Joseph Raleigh (D S.C.) January 18, 1893-March 10, 1953; House 1939-March 10, 1953.

BUCHANAN, Andrew (D Pa.) April 8, 1780-Dec. 2, 1848; House 1835-39.

BUCHANAN, Frank (D Ill.) June 14, 1862-April 18, 1930; House 1911-17.

BUCHANAN, Frank (husband of Vera Daerr Buchanan) (D Pa.) Dec. 1, 1902-April 27, 1951; House May 21, 1946-April 27, 1951.

BUCHANAN, Hugh (D Ga.) Sept. 15, 1823-June 11, 1890; House 1881-85.

BUCHANAN, James (D Pa.) April 23, 1791-June 1, 1868; House 1821-31; Senate Dec. 6, 1834-March 5, 1845; Secy. of State 1845-49; President 1857-61.

BUCHANAN, James (R N.J.) June 17, 1839-Oct. 30, 1900; House 1885-93.

BUCHANAN, James Paul (cousin of Edward William Pou) (D Texas) April 30, 1867-Feb. 22, 1937; House April 5, 1913-Feb. 22, 1937.

BUCHANAN, John Alexander (D Va.) Oct. 7, 1843-Sept. 2, 1921; House 1889-93.

BUCHANAN, John Hall Jr. (R Ala.) March 19, 1928-___; House 1965-___.

BUCHANAN, Vera Daerr (wife of Frank Buchanan) (D Pa.) July 20, 1902-Nov. 26, 1955; House July 24, 1951-Nov. 26, 1955.

BUCHER, John Conrad (— Pa.) Dec. 28, 1792-Oct. 15, 1851; House 1831-33.

BUCK, Alfred Eliab (R Ala.) Feb. 7, 1832-Dec. 4, 1902; House 1869-71.

BUCK, Charles Francis (D La.) Nov. 5, 1841-Jan. 19, 1918; House 1895-97.

BUCK, Clayton Douglas (great-grandnephew of John M. Clayton) (R Del.) March 21, 1890-Jan. 27, 1965; Senate 1943-49; Gov. 1929-37.

BUCK, Daniel (father of Daniel Azro Ashley Buck) (F Vt.) Nov. 9, 1753-Aug. 16, 1816; House 1795-97.

BUCK, Daniel Azro Ashley (son of Daniel Buck) (D Vt.) April 19, 1789-Dec. 24, 1841; House 1823-25, 1827-29.

BUCK, Ellsworth Brewer (R N.Y.) July 3, 1892-Aug. 14, 1970; House June 6, 1944-49.

BUCK, Frank Henry (D Calif.) Sept. 23, 1887-Sept. 17, 1942; House 1933-Sept. 17, 1942.

BUCK, John Ransom (R Conn.) Dec. 6, 1835-Feb. 6, 1917; House 1881-83, 1885-87.

BUCKALEW, Charles Rollin (D Pa.) Dec. 28, 1821-May 19, 1899; Senate 1863-69; House 1887-91.

BUCKBEE, John Theodore (R Ill.) Aug. 1, 1871-April 23, 1936; House 1927-April 23, 1936.

BUCKINGHAM, William Alfred (R Conn.) May 28, 1804-Feb. 5, 1875; Senate 1869-Feb. 5, 1875; Gov. 1858-66.

BUCKLAND, Ralph Pomeroy (R Ohio) Jan. 20, 1812-May 27, 1892; House 1865-69.

BUCKLER, Richard Thompson (F-L Minn.) Oct. 27, 1865-Jan. 23, 1950; House 1935-43.

BUCKLEY, Charles Anthony (D N.Y.) June 23, 1890-Jan. 22, 1967; House 1935-65.

BUCKLEY, Charles Waldron (R Ala.) Feb. 18, 1835-Dec. 4, 1906; House July 21, 1868-73.

BUCKLEY, James Lane (C/R N.Y.) March 9, 1923-—; Senate 1971-—.

BUCKLEY, James Richard (D Ill.) Nov. 18, 1870-June 22, 1945; House 1923-25.

BUCKLEY, James Vincent (D Ill.) May 15, 1894-July 30, 1954; House 1949-51.

BUCKMAN, Clarence Bennett (R Minn.) April 1, 1851-March 1, 1917; House 1903-07.

BUCKNER, Alexander (— Mo.) 1785-June 6, 1833; Senate 1831-June 6, 1833.

BUCKNER, Aylette (son of Richard Aylett Buckner) (W Ky.) July 21, 1806-July 3, 1869; House 1847-49.

BUCKNER, Aylett Hawes (nephew of Aylett Hawes and cousin of Richard Hawes and Albert Gallatin Hawes) (D Mo.) Dec. 14, 1816-Feb. 5, 1894; House 1873-85.

BUCKNER, Richard Aylett (father of Aylett Buckner) (A-D Ky.) July 16, 1763-Dec. 8, 1847; House 1823-29.

BUDD, James Herbert (D Calif.) May 18, 1851-July 30, 1908; House 1883-85; Gov. 1895-99.

BUDGE, Hamer Harold (R Idaho) Nov. 21, 1910-___; House 1951-61.

BUEL, Alexander Woodruff (D Mich.) Dec. 13, 1813-April 19, 1868; House 1849-51.

BUELL, Alexander Hamilton (D N.Y.) July 14, 1801-Jan. 29, 1853; House 1851-Jan. 29, 1853.

BUFFETT, Howard Homan (R Neb.) Aug. 13, 1903-April 30, 1964; House 1943-49, 1951-53.

BUFFIN(G)TON, James (R Mass.) March 16, 1817-March 7, 1875; House 1855-63, 1869-March 7, 1875.

BUFFINGTON, Joseph (W Pa.) Nov. 17, 1803-Feb. 3, 1872; House 1843-47.

BUFFUM, Joseph Jr. (D N.H.) Sept. 23, 1784-Feb. 24, 1874; House 1819-21.

BUGG, Robert Malone (W Tenn.) Jan. 20, 1805-Feb. 18, 1887; House 1853-55.

BULKELEY, Morgan Gardner (cousin of Edwin Dennison Morgan) (R Conn.) Dec. 26, 1837-Nov. 6, 1922; Senate 1905-11; Gov. 1889-93.

BULKLEY, Robert Johns (D Ohio) Oct. 8, 1880-July 21, 1965; House 1911-15; Senate Dec. 1, 1930-39.

BULL, John (W Mo.) 1803-Feb. 1863; House 1833-35.

BULL, Melville (R R.I.) Sept. 29, 1854-July 5, 1909; House 1895-1903.

BULLARD, Henry Adams (W La.) Sept. 9, 1788-April 17, 1851; House 1831-Jan. 4, 1834, Dec. 5, 1850-51.

BULLOCH, William Bellinger (D Ga.) 1777-May 6, 1852; Senate April 8-Nov. 6, 1813.

BULLOCK, Robert (D Fla.) Dec. 8, 1828-July 27, 1905; House 1889-93.

BULLOCK, Stephen (F Mass.) Oct. 10, 1735-Feb. 2, 1816; House 1797-99.

BULLOCK, Wingfield (— Ky.) ?-Oct. 13, 1821; House 1821-Oct. 13, 1821.

BULOW, William John (D S.D.) Jan. 13, 1869-Feb. 26, 1960; Senate 1931-43; Gov. 1927-31.

BULWINKLE, Alfred Lee (D N.C.) April 21, 1883-Aug. 31, 1950; House 1921-29, 1931-Aug. 31, 1950.

BUMPERS, Dale (D Ark.) Aug. 12, 1925-___; Senate 1975-___; Gov. 1971-75.

BUNCH, Samuel (W Tenn.) Dec. 4, 1786-Sept. 5, 1849; House 1833-37.

BUNDY, Hezekiah Sanford (R Ohio) Aug. 15, 1817-Dec. 12, 1895; House 1865-67, 1873-75, Dec. 4, 1893-95.

BUNDY, Solomon (R N.Y.) May 22, 1823-Jan. 13, 1889; House 1877-79.

BUNKER, Berkeley Lloyd (D Nev.) Aug. 12, 1906-___; Senate Nov. 27, 1940-Dec. 6, 1942; House 1945-47.

BUNN, Benjamin Hickman (D N.C.) Oct. 19, 1844-Aug. 25, 1907; House 1889-95.

BUNNELL, Frank Charles (R Pa.) March 19, 1842-Sept. 11, 1911; House Dec. 24, 1872-73, 1885-89.

BUNNER, Rudolph (AD N.Y.) Aug. 17, 1779-July 16, 1837; House 1827-29.

BUNTING, Thomas Lathrop (D N.Y.) April 24, 1844-Dec. 27, 1898; House 1891-93.

BURCH, John Chilton (D Calif.) Feb. 1, 1826-Aug. 31, 1885; House 1859-61.

BURCH, Thomas Granville (D Va.) July 3, 1869-March 20, 1951; House 1931-May 31, 1946; Senate May 31-Nov. 5, 1946.

BURCHARD, Horatio Chapin (R Ill.) Sept. 22, 1825-May 14, 1908; House Dec. 6, 1869-79.

BURCHARD, Samuel Dickinson (D Wis.) July 17, 1836-Sept. 1, 1901; House 1875-77.

BURCHILL, Thomas Francis (D N.Y.) Aug. 3, 1882-March 28, 1960; House 1943-45.

BURD, George (__ Pa.) 1793-Jan. 13, 1844; House 1831-35.

BURDETT, Samuel Swinfin (R Mo.) Feb. 21, 1836-Sept. 24, 1914; House 1869-73.

BURDICK, Clark (R R.I.) Jan. 13, 1868-Aug. 27, 1948; House 1919-33.

BURDICK, Quentin Northrop (son of Usher L. Burdick and brother-in-law of Robert W. Levering) (D N.D.) June 19, 1908-__; House 1959-Aug. 8, 1960; Senate Aug. 8, 1960-__.

BURDICK, Theodore Weld (R Iowa) Oct. 7, 1836-July 16, 1898; House 1877-79.

BURDICK, Usher Lloyd (father of Quentin N. Burdick and father-in-law of Robert W. Levering) (R N.D.) Feb. 21, 1879-Aug. 19, 1960; House 1935-45, 1949-59.

BURGENER, Clair Walter (R Calif.) Dec. 5, 1921-__; House 1973-__.

BURGES, Dempsey (— N.C.) 1751-Jan. 13, 1800; House 1795-99.

BURGES, Tristam (great-great-uncle of Theodore Francis Green) (__R.I.) Feb. 26, 1770-Oct. 13, 1853; House 1825-35.

BURGESS, George Farmer (D Texas) Sept. 21, 1861-Dec. 31, 1919; House 1901-17.

BURGIN, William Olin (D N.C.) July 28, 1877-April 11, 1946; House 1939-April 11, 1946.

BURK, Henry (R Pa.) Sept. 26, 1850-Dec. 5, 1903; House 1901-Dec. 5, 1903.

BURKE, Aedanus (— S.C.) June 16, 1743-March 30, 1802; House 1789-91.

BURKE, Charles Henry (R S.D.) April 1, 1861-April 7, 1944; House 1899-1907, 1909-15.

BURKE, Edmund (D N.H.) Jan. 23, 1809-Jan. 25, 1882; House 1839-45.

BURKE, Edward Raymond (D Neb.) Nov. 28, 1880-Nov. 4, 1968; House 1933-35; Senate 1935-41.

BURKE, Frank Welsh (D Ky.) June 1, 1920-__; House 1959-63.

BURKE, J. Herbert (R Fla.) Jan. 14, 1913-__; House 1967-__.

BURKE, James Anthony (D Mass.) March 30, 1910-__; House 1959-__.

BURKE, James Francis (R Pa.) Oct. 21, 1867-Aug. 8, 1932; House 1905-15.

BURKE, John Harley (D Calif.) June 2, 1894-May 14, 1951; House 1933-35.

BURKE, Michael Edmund (D Wis.) Oct. 15, 1863-Dec. 12, 1918; House 1911-17.

BURKE, Raymond Hugh (R Ohio) Nov. 4, 1881-Aug. 18, 1954; House 1947-49.

BURKE, Robert Emmet (D Texas) Aug. 1, 1847-June 5, 1901; House 1897-June 5, 1901.

BURKE, Thomas A. (D Ohio) Oct. 30, 1898-Dec. 5, 1971; Senate Nov. 10, 1953-Dec. 2, 1954.

BURKE, Thomas Henry (D Ohio) May 6, 1904-Sept. 12, 1959; House 1949-51.

BURKE, William Joseph (R Pa.) Sept. 25, 1862-Nov. 7, 1925; House 1919-23.

BURKE, Yvonne Brathwaite (D Calif.) Oct. 5, 1932-__; House 1973-__.

BURKETT, Elmer Jacob (R Neb.) Dec. 1, 1867-May 23, 1935; House 1899-March 4, 1905; Senate 1905-11.

BURKHALTER, Everett Glenn (D Calif.) Jan. 19, 1897-May 24, 1975; House 1963-65.

BURLEIGH, Edwin Chick (R Maine) Nov. 27, 1843-June 16, 1916; House June 21, 1897-1911; Senate 1913-June 16, 1916; Gov. 1889-93.

BURLEIGH, Henry Gordon (R N.Y.) June 2, 1832-Aug. 10, 1900; House 1883-87.

BURLEIGH, John Holmes (son of William Burleigh) (R Maine) Oct. 9, 1822-Dec. 5, 1877; House 1873-77.

BURLEIGH, Walter Atwood (R Dakota) Oct. 25, 1820-March 7, 1896; House (Terr. Del.) 1865-69.

BURLEIGH, William (father of John Holmes Burleigh) (AD Maine) Oct. 24, 1785-July 2, 1827; House 1823-July 2, 1827.

BURLESON, Albert Sidney (D Texas) June 7, 1863-Nov. 24, 1937; House 1899-March 6, 1913; Postmaster General 1913-21.

BURLESON, Omar Truman (D Texas) March 19, 1906-__; House 1947-__.

BURLINGAME, Anson (R Mass.) Nov. 14, 1820-Feb. 23, 1870; House 1855-61 (1855-59 American Party, 1859-61 Republican).

BURLISON, Bill Dean (D Mo.) March 15, 1933-__; House 1969-__.

BURNELL, Barker (W Mass.) Jan. 30, 1798-June 15, 1843; House 1841-June 15, 1843.

BURNES, Daniel Dee (D Mo.) Jan. 4, 1851-Nov. 2, 1899; House 1893-95.

BURNES, James Nelson (D Mo.) Aug. 22, 1827-Jan. 23, 1889; House 1883-Jan. 23, 1889.

BURNET, Jacob (F N.J.) Feb. 22, 1770-May 10, 1853; Senate Dec. 10, 1828-31.

BURNETT, Edward (D Mass.) March 16, 1849-Nov. 5, 1925; House 1887-89.

BURNETT, Henry Cornelius (D Ky.) Oct. 5, 1825-Oct. 1, 1866; House 1855-Dec. 3, 1861.

BURNETT, John Lawson (D Ala.) Jan. 20, 1854-May 13, 1919; House 1899-May 13, 1919.

BURNEY, William Evans (D Colo.) Sept. 11, 1893-Jan. 29, 1969; House Nov. 5, 1940-41.

BURNHAM, Alfred Avery (R Conn.) March 8, 1819-April 11, 1879; House 1859-63.

BURNHAM, George (R Calif.) Dec. 28, 1868-June 28, 1939; House 1933-37.

BURNHAM, Henry Eben (R N.H.) Nov. 8, 1844-Feb. 8, 1917; Senate 1901-13.

BURNS, John Anthony (D Hawaii) March 30, 1909-Aug. 5, 1975; House (Terr.Del.) 1957-Aug. 21, 1959; Gov. 1962-74.

BURNS, Joseph (D Ohio) March 11, 1800-May 12, 1875; House 1857-59.

BURNS, Robert (D N.H.) Dec. 12, 1792-June 26, 1866; House 1833-37.

BURNSIDE, Ambrose Everett (R R.I.) May 23, 1824-Sept. 13, 1881; Senate 1875-Sept. 13, 1881; Gov. 1866-69.

BURNSIDE, Maurice Gwinn (D W.Va.) Aug. 23, 1902-__; House 1949-53, 1955-57.

BURNSIDE, Thomas (— Pa.) July 28, 1782-March 25, 1851; House Oct. 10, 1815-April 1816.

BURR, Aaron (cousin of Theodore Dwight) (D N.Y.) Feb. 6, 1756-Sept. 14, 1836; Senate 1791-97; Vice President 1801-05.

BURR, Albert George (D Ill.) Nov. 8, 1829-June 10, 1882; House 1867-71.

BURRELL, Orlando (R Ill.) July 26, 1826-June 7, 1922; House 1895-97.

BURRILL, James Jr. (great-grandfather of Theodore Francis Green) (— R.I.) April 25, 1772-Dec. 25, 1820; Senate 1817-Dec. 25, 1820.

BURROUGHS, Sherman Everett (R N.H.) Feb. 6, 1870-Jan. 27, 1923; House June 7, 1917-Jan. 27, 1923.

BURROUGHS, Silas Mainville (R N.Y.) July 16, 1810-June 3, 1860; House 1857-June 3, 1860.

BURROWS, Daniel (uncle of Lorenzo Burrows) (D Conn.) Oct. 26, 1766-Jan. 23, 1858; House 1821-23.

BURROWS, Joseph Henry (G Mo.) May 15, 1840-April 28, 1914; House 1881-83.

BURROWS, Julius Caesar (R Mich.) Jan. 9, 1837-Nov. 16, 1915; House 1873-75, 1879-83, 1885-Jan. 23, 1895; Senate Jan. 24, 1895-1911.

BURROWS, Lorenzo (nephew of Daniel Burrows) (W N.Y.) March 15, 1805-March 6, 1885; House 1849-53.

BURSUM, Holm Olaf (R N.M.) Feb. 10, 1867-Aug. 7, 1953; Senate March 11, 1921-25.

BURT, Armistead (D S.C.) Nov. 13, 1802-Oct. 30, 1883; House 1843-53.

BURTNESS, Olger Burton (R N.D.) March 14, 1884-Jan. 20, 1960; House 1921-33.

BURTON, Charles Germman (R Mo.) April 4, 1846-Feb. 25, 1926; House 1895-97.

BURTON, Clarence Godber (D Va.) Dec. 14, 1886-__; House Nov. 2, 1948-53.

BURTON, Harold Hitz (R Ohio) June 22, 1888-Oct. 28, 1964; Senate 1941-Sept. 30, 1945; Assoc. Justice of the Supreme Court 1945-58.

BURTON, Hiram Rodney (R Del.) Nov. 13, 1841-June 17, 1927; House 1905-09.

BURTON, Hutchins Gordon (A-D N.C.) 1782-April 21, 1836; House Dec. 6, 1819-March 23, 1824; Gov. 1824-27.

BURTON, John Lowell (brother of Phillip Burton) (D Calif.) Dec. 15, 1932-—; House June 25, 1974-—.

BURTON, Joseph Ralph (R Kan.) Nov. 16, 1850-Feb. 27, 1923; Senate 1901-June 4, 1906.

BURTON, Laurence Junior (R Utah) Oct. 30, 1926-—; House 1963-71.

BURTON, Phillip (brother of John Lowell Burton) (D Calif.) June 1, 1926-—; House Feb. 18, 1964-—.

BURTON, Theodore Elijah (R Ohio) Dec. 20, 1851-Oct. 28, 1929; House 1889-91, 1895-1909, 1921-Dec. 15, 1928; Senate 1909-15, Dec. 15, 1928-Oct. 28, 1929.

BURWELL, William Armisted (D Va.) March 15, 1780-Feb. 16, 1821; House Dec. 1, 1806-Feb. 16, 1821.

BUSBEY, Fred Ernst (R Ill.) Feb. 8, 1895-Feb. 11, 1966; House 1943-45, 1947-49, 1951-55.

BUSBY, George Henry (D Ohio) June 10, 1794-Aug. 22, 1869; House 1851-53.

BUSBY, Thomas Jefferson (D Miss.) July 26, 1884-Oct. 18, 1964; House 1923-35.

BUSEY, Samuel Thompson (D Ill.) Nov. 16, 1835-Aug. 12, 1909; House 1891-93.

BUSH, Alvin Ray (R Pa.) June 4, 1893-Nov. 5, 1959; House 1951-Nov. 5, 1959.

BUSH, George Herbert Walker (son of Prescott S. Bush) (R Texas) June 12, 1924-—; House 1967-71; Chrmn. Republican Nat. Comm. 1973-74.

BUSH, Prescott Sheldon (father of George Herbert Walker Bush) (R Conn.) May 15, 1895-Oct. 8, 1972; Senate Nov. 4, 1952-63.

BUSHFIELD, Harlan John (husband of Vera C. Bushfield) (R S.D.) Aug. 6, 1882-Sept. 27, 1948; Senate 1943-Sept. 27, 1948; Gov. 1939-43.

BUSHFIELD, Vera Cahalan (widow of Harlan J. Bushfield) (R S.D.) Aug. 9, 1889-—; Senate Oct. 6-Dec. 26, 1948.

BUSHNELL, Allen Ralph (D Wis.) July 18, 1833-March 29, 1909; House 1891-93.

BUSHONG, Robert Grey (grandson of Anthony Ellmaker Roberts) (R Pa.) June 10, 1883-April 6, 1951; House 1927-29.

BUTLER, Andrew Pickens (son of William Butler) (SRD S.C.) Nov. 19, 1796-May 25, 1857; Senate Dec. 4, 1846-May 25, 1857.

BUTLER, Benjamin Franklin (grandfather of Butler Ames) (R Mass.) Nov. 5, 1818-Jan. 11, 1893; House 1867-75, 1877-79; Gov. 1883-84 (Greenback & Democrat).

BUTLER, Chester Pierce (W Pa.) March 21, 1798-Oct. 5, 1850; House 1847-Oct. 5, 1850.

BUTLER, Ezra (D Vt.) Sept. 24, 1763-July 12, 1838; House 1813-15; Gov. 1826-28.

BUTLER, Hugh Alfred (R Neb.) Feb. 28, 1878-July 1, 1954; Senate 1941-July 1, 1954.

BUTLER, James Joseph (D Mo.) Aug. 29, 1862-May 31, 1917; House 1901-June 28, 1902, Nov. 4, 1902-Feb. 26, 1903, 1903-05.

BUTLER, John Cornelius (R N.Y.) July 2, 1887-Aug. 13, 1953; House April 22, 1941-49, 1951-53.

BUTLER, John Marshall (R Md.) July 21, 1897-—; Senate 1951-63.

BUTLER, Josiah (D N.Y.) Dec. 4, 1779-Oct. 27, 1854; House 1817-23.

BUTLER, Manley Caldwell (R Va.) June 2, 1925-—; House Nov. 7, 1972-—.

BUTLER, Marion (P N.C.) May 20, 1863-June 3, 1938; Senate 1895-1901.

BUTLER, Matthew Calbraith (son of William Butler) (D S.C.) March 8, 1836-April 14, 1909; Senate 1877-95.

BUTLER, Mounce Gore (D Tenn.) May 11, 1849-Feb. 13, 1917; House 1905-07.

BUTLER, Pierce (D S.C.) July 11, 1744-Feb. 15, 1822; Senate 1789-Oct. 25, 1796, Nov. 4, 1802-Nov. 21, 1804; Cont. Cong. 1787-88.

BUTLER, Robert Reyburn (grandson of Roderick Random Butler) (R Ore.) Sept. 24, 1881-Jan. 7, 1933; House Nov. 6, 1928-Jan. 7, 1933.

BUTLER, Roderick Random (grandfather of Robert Reyburn Butler) (R Tenn.) April 9, 1827-Aug. 18, 1902; House 1867-75, 1887-89.

BUTLER, Sampson Hale (D S.C.) Jan. 3, 1803-March 16, 1848; House 1839-Sept. 27, 1842.

BUTLER, Thomas (— La.) April 14, 1785-Aug. 7, 1847; House Nov. 16, 1818-21.

BUTLER, Thomas Belden (W Conn.) Aug. 22, 1806-June 8, 1873; House 1849-51.

BUTLER, Thomas Stalker (R Pa.) Nov. 4, 1855-May 26, 1928; House 1897-May 26, 1928.

BUTLER, Walter Halben (D Iowa) Feb. 13, 1852-April 24, 1931; House 1891-93.

BUTLER, William (father of Andrew Pickens Butler) (A-F S.C.) Dec. 17, 1759-Sept. 15, 1821; House 1801-13.

BUTLER, William (son of William Butler, brother of Andrew Pickens Butler and father of Matthew Calbraith Butler) (W S.C.) Feb. 1, 1790-Sept. 25, 1850; House 1841-43.

BUTLER, William Morgan (R Mass.) Jan. 29, 1861-March 29, 1937; Senate Nov. 13, 1924-Dec. 6, 1926; Chrmn. Republican Nat. Comm. 1924-28.

BUTLER, William Orlando (D Ky.) April 19, 1791-Aug. 6, 1880; House 1839-43.

BUTMAN, Samuel (— Maine) 1788-Oct. 9, 1864; House 1827-31.

BUTTERFIELD, Martin (R N.Y.) Dec. 8, 1790-Aug. 6, 1866; House 1859-61.

BUTTERWORTH, Benjamin (R Ohio) Oct. 22, 1837-Jan. 16, 1898; House 1879-83, 1885-91.

BUTTON, Daniel Evan (R N.Y.) Nov. 1, 1917-—; House 1967-71.

BUTTZ, Charles Wilson (R S.C.) Nov. 16, 1837-July 20, 1913; House Nov. 7, 1876-77.

BYNUM, Jesse Atherton (D N.C.) May 23, 1797-Sept. 23, 1868; House 1833-41.

BYNUM, William Dallas (D Ind.) June 26, 1846-Oct. 21, 1927; House 1885-95.

BYRD, Adam Monroe (D Miss.) July 6, 1859-June 21, 1912; House 1903-11.

BYRD, Harry Flood (father of Harry Flood Byrd Jr., nephew of Henry De La Warr Flood and Joel West Flood) (D Va.) June 10, 1887-Oct. 20, 1966; Senate 1933-Nov. 10, 1965; Gov. 1926-30.

BYRD, Harry Flood Jr. (son of Harry Flood Byrd) (D Va.) Dec. 20, 1914-—; Senate Nov. 12, 1965-— (1965-71 Democrat, 1971-Independent).

BYRD, Robert Carlyle (D W.Va.) Jan. 15, 1918-—; House 1953-59; Senate 1959-—.

BYRNE, Emmet Francis (R Ill.) Dec. 6, 1896-Sept. 25, 1974; House 1957-59.

BYRNE, James Aloysius (D Pa.) June 22, 1906-—; House 1953-73.

BYRNE, William Thomas (D N.Y.) March 6, 1876-Jan. 27, 1952; House 1937-Jan. 27, 1952.

BYRNES, James Francis (D S.C.) May 2, 1879-April 9, 1972; House 1911-25; Senate 1931-July 8, 1941; Assoc. Justice U.S. Supreme Court July 8, 1941-Oct. 3, 1942; Secy. of State 1945-47; Gov. 1951-55.

BYRNES, John William (R Wis.) June 12, 1913-—; House 1945-73.

BYRNS, Joseph Wellington (father of Joseph Wellington Byrns Jr.) (D Tenn.) July 20, 1869-June 4, 1936; House 1909-June 4, 1936; Speaker 1935-June 4, 1936.

BYRNS, Joseph Wellington Jr. (son of Joseph Wellington Byrns) (D Tenn.) Aug. 15, 1903-—; House 1939-41.

BYRNS, Samuel (D Mo.) March 4, 1848-July 9, 1914; House 1891-93.

BYRON, Goodloe Edgar (son of Katharine E. Byron and William D. Byron and great-grandson of Louis E. McComas) (D Md.) June 22, 1929-—; House 1971-—.

BYRON, Katharine Edgar (widow of William D. Byron, mother of Goodloe E. Byron and granddaughter of Louis E. McComas) (D Md.) Oct. 25, 1903-—; House May 27, 1941-43.

BYRON, William Devereux (husband of Katharine E. Byron and father of Goodloe E. Byron) (D Md.) May 15, 1895-Feb. 27, 1941; House 1939-Feb. 27, 1941.

C

CABANISS, Thomas Banks (cousin of Thomas Chipman McRae) (D Ga.) Aug. 31, 1835-Aug. 14, 1915; House 1893-95.

CABELL, Earle (D Texas) Oct. 27, 1906-Sept. 24, 1975; House 1965-73.

CABELL, Edward Carrington (W Fla.) Feb. 5, 1816-Feb. 28, 1896; House Oct. 6, 1845-Jan. 24, 1846, 1847-53.

CABELL, George Craighead (D Va.) Jan. 25, 1836-June 23, 1906; House 1875-87.

CABELL, Samuel Jordan (D Va.) Dec. 15, 1756-Aug. 4, 1818; House 1795-1803.

CABLE, Benjamin Taylor (D Ill.) Aug. 11, 1853-Dec. 13, 1923; House 1891-93.

CABLE, John Levi (great-grandson of Joseph Cable) (R Ohio) April 15, 1884-Sept. 15, 1971; House 1921-25, 1929-33.

CABLE, Joseph (great-grandfather of John Levi Cable) (D Ohio) April 17, 1801-May 1, 1880; House 1849-53.

CABOT, George (great-grandfather of Henry Cabot Lodge) (F Mass.) Dec. 16, 1751-April 18, 1823; Senate 1791-June 9, 1796.

CADMUS, Cornelius Andrew (D N.J.) Oct. 7, 1844-Jan. 20, 1902; House 1891-95.

CADWALADER, John (D Pa.) April 1, 1805-Jan. 26, 1879; House 1855-57.

CADWALADER, Lambert (— N.J.) 1742-Sept. 13, 1823; House 1789-91, 1793-95; Cont. Cong. 1784-87.

CADY, Claude Ernest (D Mich.) May 28, 1878-Nov. 30, 1953; House 1933-35.

CADY, Daniel (uncle of John Watts Cady) (F N.Y.) April 29, 1773-Oct. 31, 1859; House 1815-17.

CADY, John Watts (nephew of Daniel Cady) (W N.Y.) June 28, 1790-Jan. 5, 1854; House 1823-25.

CAFFERY, Donelson (grandfather of Patrick Thomson Caffery) (D La.) Sept. 10, 1835-Dec. 30, 1906; Senate Dec. 31, 1892-1901.

CAFFERY, Patrick Thomson (grandson of Donelson Caffery) (D La.) July 6, 1932-___; House 1969-73.

CAGE, Harry (— Miss.) ? -1859; House 1833-35.

CAHILL, William Thomas (R N.J.) June 25, 1912-___; House 1959-Jan. 19, 1970; Gov. 1970-74.

CAHOON, William (AMas Vt.) Jan. 12, 1774-May 30, 1833; House 1829-33.

CAIN, Harry Pulliam (R Wash.) Jan. 10, 1906-___; Senate Dec. 26, 1946-53.

CAIN, Richard Harvey (R S.C.) April 12, 1825-Jan. 18, 1887; House 1873-75, 1877-79.

CAINE, John Thomas (D Utah) Jan. 8, 1829-Sept. 20, 1911; House (Terr. Del.) Nov. 7, 1882-93 (1882-89 Democrat, 1889-93 People's Party).

CAKE, Henry Lutz (R Pa.) Oct. 6, 1827-Aug. 26, 1899; House 1867-71.

CALDER, William Musgrave (R N.Y.) March 3, 1869-March 3, 1945; House 1905-15; Senate 1917-23.

CALDERHEAD, William Alexander (R Kan.) Sept. 26, 1844-Dec. 18, 1928; House 1895-97, 1899-1911.

CALDWELL, Alexander (R Kan.) March 1, 1830-May 19, 1917; Senate 1871-March 24, 1873.

CALDWELL, Andrew Jackson (D Tenn.) July 22, 1837-Nov. 22, 1906; House 1883-87.

CALDWELL, Ben Franklin (D Ill.) Aug. 2, 1848-Dec. 29, 1924; House 1899-1905, 1907-09.

CALDWELL, Charles Pope (D N.Y.) June 18, 1875-July 31, 1940; House 1915-21.

CALDWELL, George Alfred (D Kan.) Oct. 18, 1814-Sept. 17, 1866; Houe 1843-45, 1849-51.

CALDWELL, Greene Washington (D N.C.) April 13, 1806-July 10, 1864; House 1841-43.

CALDWELL, James (D Ohio) Nov. 30, 1770-May 1838; House 1813-17.

CALDWELL, John Alexander (R Ohio) April 21, 1852-May 24, 1927; House 1889-May 4, 1894.

CALDWELL, John Henry (D Ala.) April 4, 1826-Sept. 4, 1902; House 1873-77.

CALDWELL, John William (D Ky.) Jan. 15, 1837-July 4, 1903; House 1877-83.

CALDWELL, Joseph Pearson (W N.C.) March 5, 1808-June 30, 1853; House 1849-53.

CALDWELL, Millard Fillmore (D Fla.) Feb. 6, 1897-___; House 1933-41; Gov. 1945-49.

CALDWELL, Patrick Calhoun (SRD S.C.) March 10, 1801-Nov. 22, 1855; House 1841-43.

CALDWELL, Robert Porter (D Tenn.) Dec. 16, 1821-March 12, 1885; House 1871-73.

CALDWELL, William Parker (D Tenn.) Nov. 8, 1832-June 7, 1903; House 1875-79.

CALE, Thomas (I Alaska) Sept. 17, 1848-Feb. 3, 1941; House (Terr. Del.) 1907-09.

CALHOON, John (W Ky.) 1797-?; House 1835-39.

CALHOUN, John Caldwell (cousin of John Ewing Colhoun and Joseph Calhoun) (WD S.C.) March 18, 1782-March 31, 1850; House 1811-Nov. 3, 1817; Senate Dec. 29, 1832-March 3, 1843, Nov. 26, 1845-March 31, 1850; Vice President 1825-Dec. 28, 1832; Secy. of War 1817-25; Secy. of State 1844-45.

CALHOUN, Joseph (cousin of John Caldwell Calhoun and John Ewing Colhoun) (D S.C.) Oct. 22, 1750-April 14, 1817; House June 2, 1807-11.

CALHOUN, William Barron (W Mass.) Dec. 29, 1796-Nov. 8, 1865; House 1835-43.

CALKIN, Hervey Chittenden (D N.Y.) March 23, 1828-April 20, 1913; House 1869-71.

CALKINS, William Henry (R Ind.) Feb. 18, 1842-Jan. 29, 1894; House 1877-Oct. 20, 1884.

CALL, Jacob (— Ind.) ? -April 20, 1826; House Dec. 23, 1824-25.

CALL, Richard Keith (uncle of Wilkinson Call) (D Fla.) Oct. 24, 1792-Sept. 14, 1862; House (Terr. Del.) 1823-25; Terr. Gov. 1835-40, 1841-44.

CALL, Wilkinson (nephew of Richard Keith Call and cousin of James David Walker) (D Fla.) Jan. 9, 1834-Aug. 24, 1910; Senate 1879-97.

CALLAHAN, James Yancy (FSil Okla.) Dec. 19, 1852-May 3, 1935; House (Terr. Del.) 1897-99.

CALLAN, Clair Armstrong (D Neb.) March 20, 1920-___; House 1965-67.

CALLAWAY, Howard Hollis (Bo) (R Ga.) April 2, 1927-___; House 1965-67.

CALLAWAY, Oscar (D Texas) Oct. 2, 1872-Jan. 31, 1947; House 1911-17.

CALLIS, John Benton (R Ala.) Jan. 3, 1828-Sept. 24, 1898; House July 21, 1868-69.

CALVERT, Charles Benedict (UW Md.) Aug. 24, 1808-May 12, 1864; House 1861-63.

CALVIN, Samuel (W Pa.) July 30, 1811-March 12, 1890; House 1849-51.

CAMBRELENG, Churchill Caldom (D N.Y.) Oct. 24, 1786-April 30, 1862; House 1821-39.

CAMDEN, Johnson Newlon (D W.Va.) March 6, 1828-April 25, 1908; Senate 1881-87, Jan. 25, 1893-95.

CAMDEN, Johnson Newlon Jr. (son of Johnson Newlon Camden) (D Ky.) Jan. 5, 1865-Aug. 16, 1942; Senate June 16, 1914-15.

CAMERON, Angus (R Wis.) July 4, 1826-March 30, 1897; Senate 1875-81, March 14, 1881-85.

CAMERON, James Donald (son of Simon Cameron) (R Pa.) May 14, 1833-Aug. 30, 1918; Senate March 20, 1877-97; Secy. of War 1876-77; Chrmn. Rep. Nat. Comm. 1879-80.

CAMERON, Ralph Henry (R Ariz.) Oct. 21, 1863-Feb. 12, 1953; House (Terr. Del.) 1909-Feb. 18, 1912; Senate 1921-27.

CAMERON, Ronald Brooks (D Calif.) Aug. 16, 1927-___; House 1963-67.

CAMERON, Simon (father of James Donald Cameron) (R Pa.) March 8, 1799-June 26, 1889; Senate March 13, 1845-49, 1857-March 4, 1861, 1867-March 12, 1877 (1845-49 Democrat, 1857-61 and 1867-77 Republican); Secy. of War 1861-62.

CAMINETTI, Anthony (D Calif.) July 30, 1854-Nov. 17, 1923; House 1891-95.

CAMP, Albert Sidney (D Ga.) July 26, 1892-July 24, 1954; House Aug. 1, 1939-July 24, 1954.

CAMP, John Henry (R N.Y.) April 4, 1840-Oct. 12, 1892; House 1877-83.

CAMP, John Newbold Happy (R Okla.) May 11, 1908-___; House 1969-75.

CAMPBELL, Albert James (D Mont.) Dec. 12, 1857-Aug. 9, 1907; House 1899-1901.

CAMPBELL, Alexander (— Ohio) 1779-Nov. 5, 1857; Senate Dec. 11, 1809-13.

CAMPBELL, Alexander (I Ill.) Oct. 4, 1814-Aug. 8, 1898; House 1875-77.

CAMPBELL, Brookins (D Tenn.) 1808-Dec. 25, 1853; House March 4-Dec. 25, 1853.

CAMPBELL, Courtney Warren (D Fla.) April 29, 1895-Dec. 22, 1971; House 1953-55.

CAMPBELL, Ed Hoyt (R Iowa) March 6, 1882-April 26, 1969; House 1929-33.

CAMPBELL, Felix (D N.Y.) Feb. 28, 1829-Nov. 8, 1902; House 1883-91.

CAMPBELL, George Washington (D Tenn.) Feb. 9, 1769-Feb. 17, 1848; House 1803-09; Senate Oct. 8, 1811-Feb. 11, 1814, Oct. 10, 1815-April 20, 1818; Secy. of the Treasury Feb. 9-Oct. 6, 1814.

CAMPBELL, Guy Edgar (R Pa.) Oct. 9, 1871-Feb. 17, 1940; House 1917-33 (1917-23 Democrat, 1923-33 Republican).

CAMPBELL, Howard Edmond (R Pa.) Jan. 4, 1890-___; House 1945-47.

CAMPBELL, Jacob Miller (R Pa.) Nov. 20, 1821-Sept. 27, 1888; House 1877-79, 1881-87.

CAMPBELL, James Edwin (nephew of Lewis Davis Campbell) (D Ohio) July 7, 1843-Dec. 18, 1924; House June 20, 1884-89; Gov. 1890-92.

CAMPBELL, James Hepburn (W Pa.) Feb. 8, 1820-April 12, 1895; House 1855-57, 1859-63.

CAMPBELL, James Romulus (D Ill.) May 4, 1853-Aug. 12, 1924; House 1897-99.

CAMPBELL, John (F Md.) Sept. 11, 1765-June 23, 1828; House 1801-11.

CAMPBELL, John (brother of Robert Blair Campbell) (SRD S.C.) ? -May 19, 1845; House 1829-31 (SRW), 1837-45 (SRD).

CAMPBELL, John Goulder (D Ariz.) June 25, 1827-Dec. 22, 1903; House (Terr. Del.) 1879-81.

CAMPBELL, John Hull (W Pa.) Oct. 10, 1800-Jan. 19, 1868; House 1845-47.

CAMPBELL, John Pierce Jr. (AP Ky.) Dec. 8, 1820-Oct. 29, 1888; House 1855-57.

CAMPBELL, John Wilson (D Ohio) Feb. 23, 1782-Sept. 24, 1833; House 1817-27.

CAMPBELL, Lewis Davis (uncle of James Edwin Campbell) (D Ohio) Aug. 9, 1811-Nov. 26, 1882; House 1849-May 25, 1858, 1871-73 (1849-1858 Whig, 1871-73 Democrat).

CAMPBELL, Philip Pitt (R Kan.) April 25, 1862-May 26, 1941; House 1903-23.

CAMPBELL, Robert Blair (brother of John Campbell of South Carolina) (W S.C.) ? -July 12, 1862; House 1823-25, Feb. 27, 1834-37 (1823-25 no party designation, 1834-35 Nullifier, 1835-37 Whig).

CAMPBELL, Samuel (— N.Y.) July 11, 1773-June 2, 1853; House 1821-23.

CAMPBELL, Thomas Jefferson (W Tenn.) 1786-April 13, 1850; House 1841-43.

CAMPBELL, Thompson (D Ill.) 1811-Dec. 6, 1868; House 1851-53.

CAMPBELL, Timothy John (D N.Y.) Jan. 8, 1840-April 7, 1904; House Nov. 3, 1885-89, 1891-95.

CAMPBELL, William Bowen (cousin of Henry Bowen) (D Tenn.) Feb. 1, 1807-Aug. 19, 1867; House 1837-43, July 24, 1866-67 (1837-43 Whig, 1866-67 Democrat); Gov. 1851-53.

CAMPBELL, William W. (AP N.Y.) June 10, 1806-Sept. 7, 1881; House 1845-47.

CAMPBELL, William Wildman (R Ohio) April 2, 1853-Aug. 13, 1927; House 1905-07.

CANBY, Richard Sprigg (W Ohio) Sept. 30, 1808-July 27, 1895; House 1847-49.

CANDLER, Allen Daniel (cousin of Ezekiel Samuel Candler Jr. and Milton Anthony Candler) (D Ga.) Nov. 4, 1834-Oct. 26, 1910; House 1883-91; Gov. 1898-1902.

CANDLER, Ezekiel Samuel Jr. (nephew of Milton A. Candler and cousin of Allen Daniel Candler) (D Miss.) Jan. 18, 1862-Dec. 18, 1944; House 1901-21.

CANDLER, John Wilson (R Mass.) Feb. 10, 1828-March 16, 1903; House 1881-83, 1889-91.

CANDLER, Milton Anthony (uncle of Ezekiel Samuel Candler Jr. and cousin of Allen Daniel Candler) (D Ga.) Jan. 11, 1837-Aug. 8, 1909; House 1875-79.

CANFIELD, Gordon (R N.J.) April 15, 1898-June 20, 1972; House 1941-61.

CANFIELD, Harry Clifford (D Ind.) Nov. 22, 1875-Feb. 9, 1945; House 1923-33.

CANNON, Arthur Patrick (D Fla.) May 22, 1904-Jan. 23, 1966; House 1939-47.

CANNON, Clarence Andrew (D Mo.) April 11, 1879-May 12, 1964; House 1923-May 12, 1964.

CANNON, Frank Jenne (son of George Quayle Cannon) (R Utah) Jan. 25, 1859-July 25, 1933; House (Terr. Del.) 1895-Jan. 4, 1896; Senate Jan. 22, 1896-99.

CANNON, George Quayle (father of Frank Jenne Cannon) (R Utah) Jan. 11, 1827-April 12, 1901; House (Terr. Del.) 1873-81.

CANNON, Howard Walter (D Nev.) Jan. 26, 1912-___; Senate 1959-___.

CANNON, Joseph Gurney (R Ill.) May 7, 1836-Nov. 12, 1926; House 1873-91, 1893-1913, 1915-23; Speaker 1903-11.

CANNON, Marion (PP/D Calif.) Oct. 30, 1834-Aug. 27, 1920; House 1893-95.

CANNON, Newton (D Tenn.) May 22, 1781-Sept. 16, 1841; House Sept. 16, 1814-17, 1819-23; Gov. 1835-39.

CANNON, Raymond Joseph (D Wis.) Aug. 26, 1894-Nov. 25, 1951; House 1933-39.

CANTOR, Jacob Aaron (D N.Y.) Dec. 6, 1854-July 2, 1921; House Nov. 4, 1913-15.

CANTRILL, James Campbell (D Ky.) July 9, 1870-Sept. 2, 1923; House 1909-Sept. 2, 1923.

CAPEHART, Homer Earl (R Ind.) June 6, 1897-___; Senate 1945-63.

CAPEHART, James (D W.Va.) March 7, 1847-April 28, 1921; House 1891-95.

CAPERTON, Allen Taylor (son of Hugh Caperton) (D W.Va.) Nov. 21, 1810-July 26, 1876; Senate 1875-July 26, 1876.

CAPERTON, Hugh (father of Allen Taylor Caperton) (F Va.) April 17, 1781-Feb. 9, 1847; House 1813-15.

CAPOZZOLI, Louis Joseph (D N.Y.) March 6, 1901-___; House 1941-45.

CAPPER, Arthur (R Kan.) July 14, 1865-Dec. 19, 1951; Senate 1919-49; Gov. 1915-19.

CAPRON, Adin Ballou (R R.I.) Jan. 9, 1841-March 17, 1911; House 1897-1911.

CAPSTICK, John Henry (R N.J.) Sept. 2, 1856-March 17, 1918; House 1915-March 17, 1918.

CARAWAY, Hattie Wyatt (wife of Thaddeus Horatius Caraway) (D Ark.) Feb. 1, 1878-Dec. 21, 1950; Senate Nov. 13, 1931-45.

CARAWAY, Thaddeus Horatius (husband of Hattie Wyatt Caraway) (D Ark.) Oct. 17, 1871-Nov. 6, 1931; House 1913-21; Senate 1921-Nov. 6, 1931.

CARDEN, Cap Robert (D Ky.) Dec. 17, 1866-June 13, 1935; House 1931-June 13, 1935.

CAREW, John Francis (nephew of Thomas Francis Magner) (D N.Y.) April 16, 1873-April 10, 1951; House 1913-Dec. 18, 1929.

CAREY, Hugh Leo (D N.Y.) April 11, 1919-___; House 1961-Dec. 31, 1974; Gov. 1975-___.

CAREY, John (R Ohio) April 5, 1792-March 17, 1875; House 1859-61.

CAREY, Joseph Maull (father of Robert Davis Carey) (R Wyo.) Jan. 19, 1845-Feb. 5, 1924; House (Terr. Del.) 1885-July 10, 1890; Senate Nov. 15, 1890-95; Gov. 1911-15.

CAREY, Robert Davis (son of Joseph Maull Carey) (R Wyo.) Aug. 12, 1878-Jan. 17, 1937; Senate Dec. 1, 1930-37; Gov. 1919-23.

CARLETON, Ezra Child (D Mich.) Sept. 6, 1838-July 24, 1911; House 1883-87.

CARLETON, Peter (D N.H.) Sept. 19, 1755-April 29, 1828; House 1807-09.

CARLEY, Patrick J. (D N.Y.) Feb. 2, 1866-Feb. 25, 1936; House 1927-35.

CARLILE, John Snyder (U Va.) Dec. 16, 1817-Oct. 24, 1878; House 1855-57 and March 4-July 9, 1861 (AP); Senate July 9, 1861-65 (U).

CARLIN, Charles Creighton (D Va.) April 8, 1866-Oct. 14, 1938; House Nov. 5, 1907-19.

CARLISLE, John Griffin (D Ky.) Sept. 5, 1835-July 31, 1910; House 1877-May 26, 1890; Senate May 26, 1890-Feb. 4, 1893; Speaker 1883-89; Secy. of the Treasury 1893-97.

CARLSON, Clifford Dale (R Ill.) Dec. 30, 1915-___; House April 4, 1972-73.

CARLSON, Frank (R Kan.) Jan. 23, 1893-___; House 1935-47; Senate Nov. 29, 1950-69; Gov. 1947-50.

CARLTON, Henry Hull (D Ga.) May 14, 1835-Oct. 26, 1905; House 1887-91.

CARLYLE, Frank Ertel (D N.C.) April 7, 1897-Oct. 2, 1960; House 1949-57.

CARMACK, Edward Ward (D Tenn.) Nov. 5, 1858-Nov. 9, 1908; House 1897-1901; Senate 1901-07.

CARMICHAEL, Archibald Hill (D Ala.) June 17, 1864-July 15, 1947; House Nov. 14, 1933-37.

CARMICHAEL, Richard Bennett (JD Md.) Dec. 25, 1807-Oct. 21, 1884; House 1833-35.

CARNAHAN, Albert Sidney Johnson (D Mo.) Jan. 9, 1897-March 24, 1968; House 1945-47, 1949-61.

CARNES, Thomas Petters (— Ga.) 1762-May 5, 1822; House 1793-95.

CARNEY, Charles Joseph (D Ohio) April 17, 1913-___; House Nov. 3, 1970-___.

CARPENTER, Cyrus Clay (R Iowa) Nov. 24, 1829-May 29, 1898; House 1879-83; Gov. 1872-76.

CARPENTER, Davis (W N.Y.) Dec. 25, 1799-Oct. 22, 1878; House Nov. 8, 1853-55.

CARPENTER, Edmund Nelson (R Pa.) June 27, 1865-Nov. 4, 1952; House 1925-27.

CARPENTER, Levi D. (D N.Y.) Aug. 21, 1802-Oct. 27, 1856; House Nov. 5, 1844-45.

CARPENTER, Lewis Cass (R S.C.) Feb. 20, 1836-March 6, 1908; House Nov. 3, 1874-75.

CARPENTER, Matthew Hale (R Wis.) Dec. 22, 1824-Feb. 24, 1881; Senate 1869-75, 1879-Feb. 24, 1881; President pro tempore 1873-75.

CARPENTER, Terry McGovern (D Neb.) March 28, 1900-___; House 1933-35.

CARPENTER, William Randolph (D Kan.) April 24, 1894-July 26, 1956; House 1933-37.

CARR, Francis (father of James Carr) (D Mass.) Dec. 6, 1751-Oct. 6, 1821; House April 6, 1812-13.

CARR, James (son of Francis Carr) (— Mass.) Sept. 9, 1777-Aug. 24, 1818; House 1815-17.

CARR, John (D Ind.) April 9, 1793-Jan. 20, 1845; House 1831-37, 1839-41.

CARR, Milton Robert (D Mich.) March 27, 1943-___; House 1975-___.

CARR, Nathan Tracy (D Ind.) Dec. 25, 1833-May 28, 1885; House Dec. 5, 1876-77.

CARR, Wooda Nicholas (D Pa.) Feb. 6, 1871-June 28, 1953; House 1913-15.

CARRIER, Chester Otto (R Ky.) May 5, 1897-___; House Nov. 30, 1943-45.

CARRIGG, Joseph Leonard (R Pa.) Feb. 23, 1901-___; House Nov. 6, 1951-59.

CARROLL, Charles (cousin of Daniel Carroll) (F Md.) Sept. 19, 1737-Nov. 14, 1832; Senate 1789-Nov. 30, 1792; Cont. Cong. 1776-78.

CARROLL, Charles Hobart (CW N.Y.) May 4, 1794-June 8, 1865; House 1843-47.

CARROLL, Daniel (uncle of Richard Brent, cousin of Charles Carroll) (F Md.) July 22, 1730-May 7, 1796; House 1789-91; Cont. Cong. 1780-84.

CARROLL, James (D Md.) Dec. 2, 1791-Jan. 16, 1873; House 1839-41.

CARROLL, John Albert (D Colo.) July 30, 1901-___; House 1947-51; Senate 1957-63.

CARROLL, John Michael (D N.Y.) April 27, 1823-May 8, 1901; House 1871-73.

CARSON, Henderson Haverfield (R Ohio) Oct. 25, 1893-Oct. 5, 1971; House 1943-45, 1947-49.

CARSON, Samuel Price (D N.C.) Jan. 22, 1798-Nov. 2, 1838; House 1825-33.

CARSS, William Leighton (FL Minn.) Feb. 15, 1865-May 31, 1931; House 1919-21, 1925-29 (1919-21 Independent, 1925-29 Farmer Laborite).

CARTER, Albert Edward (R Calif.) July 5, 1881-Aug. 8, 1964; House 1925-45.

CARTER, Charles David (D Okla.) Aug. 16, 1868-April 9, 1929; House Nov. 16, 1907-27.

CARTER, John (— S.C.) Sept. 10, 1792-June 20, 1850; House Dec. 11, 1822-29.

CARTER, Luther Cullen (UR N.Y.) Feb. 25, 1805-Jan. 3, 1875; House 1859-61.

CARTER, Steven V. (D Iowa) Oct. 8, 1915-Nov. 4, 1959; House Jan. 3-Nov. 4, 1959.

CARTER, Thomas Henry (R Mont.) Oct. 30, 1854-Sept. 17, 1911; House (Terr. Del.) March 4,-Nov. 7, 1889, (Representative) Nov. 8, 1889-91; Senate 1895-1901, 1905-11; Chrmn. Rep. Nat. Comm. 1892-96.

CARTER, Tim Lee (R Ky.) Sept. 2, 1910-___; House 1965-___.

CARTER, Timothy Jarvis (D Maine) Aug. 18, 1800-March 14, 1838; House Sept. 4, 1837-March 14, 1838.

CARTER, Vincent Michael (R Wyo.) Nov. 6, 1891-Dec. 30, 1972; House 1929-35.

CARTER, William Blount (W Tenn.) Oct. 22, 1792-April 17, 1848; House 1835-41.

CARTER, William Henry (R Mass.) June 15, 1864-April 23, 1955; House 1915-19.

CARTTER, David Kellogg (D Ohio) June 22, 1812-April 16, 1887; House 1849-53.

CARTWRIGHT, Wilburn (D Okla.) Jan. 12, 1892-___; House 1927-43.

CARUTH, Asher Graham (D Ky.) Feb. 7, 1844-Nov. 25, 1907; House 1887-95.

CARUTHERS, Robert Looney (W Tenn.) July 31, 1800-Oct. 2, 1882; House 1841-43.

CARUTHERS, Samuel (D Mo.) Oct. 13, 1820-July 20, 1860; House 1853-59 (1853-57 Whig, 1857-59 Democrat).

CARVILLE, Edward Peter (D Nev.) May 14, 1885-June 27, 1956; Senate July 25, 1945-47; Gov. 1939-45.

CARY, George (— Ga.) Aug. 7, 1789-Sept. 10, 1843; House 1823-27.

CARY, George Booth (D Va.) 1811-March 5, 1850; House 1841-43.

CARY, Glover H. (D Ky.) May 1, 1885-Dec. 5, 1936; House 1931-Dec. 5, 1936.

CARY, Jeremiah Eaton (D N.Y.) April 30, 1803-June 1888; House 1843-45.

CARY, Samuel Fenton (R Ohio) Feb. 18, 1814-Sept. 29, 1900; House Nov. 21, 1867-69.

CARY, Shepard (D Maine) July 3, 1805-Aug. 9, 1866; House May 10, 1844-45.

CARY, William Joseph (R Wis.) March 22, 1865-Jan. 2, 1934; House 1907-19.

CASE, Charles (D Ind.) Dec. 21, 1817-June 30, 1883; House Dec. 7, 1857-61.

CASE, Clifford Philip (R N.J.) April 16, 1904-___; House 1945-Aug. 16, 1953; Senate 1955-___.

CASE, Francis Higbee (R S.D.) Dec. 9, 1896-June 22, 1962; House 1937-51; Senate 1951-June 22, 1962.

CASE, Walter (— N.Y.) 1776-Oct. 7, 1859; House 1819-21.

CASEY, John Joseph (D Pa.) May 26, 1875-May 5, 1929; House 1913-17, 1919-21, 1923-25, 1927-May 5, 1929.

CASEY, Joseph (W Pa.) Dec. 17, 1814-Feb. 10, 1879; House 1849-51.

CASEY, Joseph Edward (D Mass.) Dec. 27, 1898-___; House 1935-43.

CASEY, Levi (— S.C.) about 1752-Feb. 3, 1807; House 1803-Feb. 3, 1807.

CASEY, Lyman Rufus (R N.D.) May 6, 1837-Jan. 26, 1914; Senate Nov. 25, 1889-93.

CASEY, Robert Randolph (Bob) (D Texas) July 17, 1915-___; House 1959-Jan. 22, 1976.

CASEY, Samuel Lewis (R Ky.) Feb. 12, 1821-Aug. 25, 1902; House March 10, 1862-63.

CASEY, Zadoc (JD Ill.) March 7, 1796-Sept. 4, 1862; House 1833-43.

CASKIE, John Samuels (D Va.) Nov. 8, 1821-Dec. 16, 1869; House 1851-59.

CASON, Thomas Jefferson (R Ind.) Sept. 13, 1828-July 10, 1901; House 1873-77.

CASS, Lewis (D Mich.) Oct. 9, 1782-June 17, 1866; Senate 1845-May 29, 1848, 1849-57; Gov. (Mich. Terr.) 1813-31; Secy. of War 1831-36; Secy. of State 1857-60.

CASSEDY, George (D N.J.) Sept. 16, 1783-Dec. 31, 1842; House 1821-27.

CASSEL, Henry Burd (R Pa.) Oct. 19, 1855-April 28, 1926; House Nov. 5, 1901-09.

CASSERLY, Eugene (D Calif.) Nov. 13, 1820-June 14, 1883; Senate 1869-Nov. 19, 1873.

CASSIDY, George Williams (D Nev.) April 25, 1836-June 24, 1892; House 1881-85.

CASSIDY, James Henry (R Ohio) Oct. 28, 1869-Aug. 23, 1926; House April 20, 1909-11.

CASSINGHAM, John Wilson (D Ohio) June 22, 1840-March 14, 1930; House 1901-05.

CASTELLOW, Bryant Thomas (D Ga.) July 29, 1876-July 23, 1962; House Nov. 8, 1932-37.

CASTLE, Curtis Harvey (P/D Calif.) Oct. 4, 1848-July 12, 1928; House 1897-99.

CASTLE, James Nathan (D Minn.) May 23, 1836-Jan. 2, 1903; House 1891-93.

CASTOR, George Albert (R Pa) Aug. 6, 1855-Feb. 19, 1906; House Feb. 16, 1904-Feb. 19, 1906.

CASWELL, Lucien Bonaparte (R Wis.) Nov. 27, 1827-April 26, 1919; House 1875-83, 1885-91.

CATCHINGS, Thomas Clendinen (D Miss.) Jan. 11, 1847-Dec. 24, 1927; House 1885-1901.

CATE, George Washington (IRef. Wis.) Sept. 17, 1825-March 7, 1905; House 1875-77.

CATE, William Henderson (D Ark.) Nov. 11, 1839-Aug. 23, 1899; House 1889-March 5, 1890, 1891-93.

CATHCART, Charles William (D Ind.) July 24, 1809-Aug. 22, 1888; House 1845-49; Senate Dec. 6, 1852-53.

CATLIN, George Smith (D Conn.) Aug. 24, 1808-Dec. 26, 1851; House 1843-45.

CATLIN, Theron Ephron (R Mo.) May 16, 1878-March 19, 1960; House 1911-Aug. 12, 1912.

CATRON, Thomas Benton (R N.M.) Oct. 6, 1840-May 15, 1921; House (Terr. Del.) 1895-97; Senate March 27, 1912-17.

CATTELL, Alexander Gilmore (R N.J.) Feb. 12, 1816-April 8, 1894; Senate Sept. 19, 1866-71.

CAULFIELD, Bernard Gregory (D Ill.) Oct. 18, 1828-Dec. 19, 1887; House Feb. 1, 1875-77.

CAULFIELD, Henry Stewart (R Mo.) Dec. 9, 1873-May 11, 1966; House 1907-09; Gov. 1929-33.

CAUSEY, John Williams (D Del.) Sept. 19, 1841-Oct. 1, 1908; House 1891-95.

CAUSIN, John M. S. (W Md.) 1811-Jan. 30, 1861; House 1843-45.

CAVALCANTE, Anthony (D Pa.) Feb. 6, 1897-Oct. 29, 1966; House 1949-51.

CAVANAUGH, James Michael (D Minn./Mont.) July 4, 1823-Oct. 30, 1879; House May 11, 1858-59 (Minn.), 1867-71 (Terr. Del.-Mont.).

CAVICCHIA, Peter Angelo (R N.J.) May 22, 1879-Sept. 11, 1967; House 1931-37.

CEDERBERG, Elford Alfred (R Mich.) March 6, 1918-___; House 1953-___.

CELLER, Emanuel (D N.Y.) May 6, 1888-___; House 1923-73.

CESSNA, John (R Pa.) June 29, 1821-Dec. 13, 1893; House 1869-71, 1873-75.

CHACE, Jonathan (R R.I.) July 22, 1829-June 30, 1917; House 1881-Jan. 26, 1885; Senate Jan. 20, 1885-April 9, 1889.

CHADWICK, E. Wallace (R Pa.) Jan. 17, 1884-Aug. 18, 1969; House 1947-49.

CHAFFEE, Calvin Clifford (AP Mass.) Aug. 28, 1811-Aug. 8, 1896; House 1855-59.

CHAFFEE, Jerome Bunty (R Colo.) April 17, 1825-March 9, 1886; House (Terr. Del.) 1871-75; Senate Nov. 15, 1876-79.

CHALMERS, James Ronald (son of Joseph Williams Chalmers) (I Miss.) Jan. 12, 1831-April 9, 1898; House 1877-April 29, 1882, June 25, 1884-85 (1877-82 Democrat, 1884-85 Independent).

CHALMERS, Joseph Williams (father of James Ronald Chalmers) (D Miss.) Dec. 20, 1806-June 16, 1853; Senate Nov. 3, 1845-47.

CHALMERS, William Wallace (R Ohio) Nov. 1, 1861-Oct. 1, 1944; House 1921-23; 1925-31.

CHAMBERLAIN, Charles Ernest (R Mich.) July 22, 1917-___; House 1957-Dec. 31, 1974.

CHAMBERLAIN, Ebenezer Mattoon (D Ind.) Aug. 20, 1805-March 14, 1861; House 1853-55.

CHAMBERLAIN, George Earle (D Ore.) Jan. 1, 1854-July 9, 1928; Senate 1909-21; Gov. 1903-09.

CHAMBERLAIN, Jacob Payson (R N.Y.) Aug. 1, 1802-Oct. 5, 1878; House 1861-63.

CHAMBERLAIN, John Curtis (F N.H.) June 5, 1772-Dec. 8, 1834; House 1809-11.

CHAMBERLAIN, William (F Vt.) April 27, 1755-Sept. 27, 1828; House 1803-05, 1809-11.

CHAMBERS, David (— Ohio) Nov. 25, 1780-Aug. 8, 1864; House Oct. 9, 1821-23.

CHAMBERS, Ezekiel Forman (W Md.) Feb. 28, 1788-Jan. 30, 1867; Senate Jan. 24, 1826-Dec. 20, 1834.

CHAMBERS, George (W Pa.) Feb. 24, 1786-March 25, 1866; House 1833-37.

CHAMBERS, Henry H. (D Ala.) Oct. 1, 1790-Feb. 24, 1826; Senate 1825-Feb. 24, 1826.

CHAMBERS, John (W Ky.) Oct. 6, 1780-Sept. 21, 1852; House Dec. 1, 1828-29, 1835-39; Gov. of Territory of Iowa 1841-45.

CHAMPION, Edwin Van Meter (D Ill.) Sept. 18, 1890-___; House 1937-39.

CHAMPION, Epaphroditis (F Conn.) April 6, 1756-Dec. 22, 1834; House 1807-17.

CHAMPLIN, Christopher Grant (— R.I.) April 12, 1768-March 18, 1840; House 1797-1801; Senate June 26, 1809-Oct. 2, 1811.

CHANDLER, Albert Benjamin (D Ky.) July 14, 1898-——; Senate Oct. 10, 1939-Nov. 1, 1945; Gov. 1935-39, 1955-59.

CHANDLER, John (brother of Thomas Chandler and uncle of Zachariah Chandler) (D Mass./Maine) Feb. 1, 1762-Sept. 25, 1841; House (Mass.) 1805-09; Senate (Maine) June 14, 1820-29.

CHANDLER, Joseph Ripley (W Pa.) Aug. 22, 1792-July 10, 1880; House 1849-55.

CHANDLER, Thomas (brother of John Chandler and uncle of Zachariah Chandler) (D N.H.) Aug. 10, 1772-Jan. 28, 1866; House 1829-33.

CHANDLER, Thomas Alberter (R Okla.) July 26, 1871-June 22, 1953; House 1917-19, 1921-23.

CHANDLER, Walter (Clift) (D Tenn.) Oct. 5, 1887-Oct. 1, 1967; House 1935-Jan. 2, 1940.

CHANDLER, Walter Marion (R N.Y.) Dec. 8, 1867-March 16, 1935; House 1912-19, 1921-23 (1912-19 Progressive, 1921-23 Republican).

CHANDLER, William Eaton (R N.H.) Dec. 28, 1835-Nov. 20, 1917; Senate June 14, 1887-March 3, 1889, June 18, 1889-1901; Secy. of the Navy 1882-85.

CHANDLER, Zachariah (nephew of John Chandler and Thomas Chandler and grandfather of Frederick Hale) (R Mich.) Dec. 10, 1813-Nov. 1, 1879; Senate 1857-75, Feb. 22, 1879-Nov. 1, 1879; Secy. of the Interior 1875-77; Chmn. Rep. Natl. Comm. 1876-79.

CHANEY, John (JD Ohio) Jan. 12, 1790-April 10, 1881; House 1833-39.

CHANEY, John Crawford (R Ind.) Feb. 1, 1853-April 26, 1940; House 1905-09.

CHANLER, John Winthrop (father of William Astor Chanler) (D N.Y.) Sept. 14, 1826-Oct. 19, 1877; House 1863-69.

CHANLER, William Astor (son of John Winthrop Chanler) (D N.Y.) June 11, 1867-March 4, 1934; House 1899-1901.

CHAPIN, Alfred Clark (D N.Y.) March 8, 1848-Oct. 2, 1936; House Nov. 3, 1891-Nov. 16, 1892.

CHAPIN, Chester Williams (D Mass.) Dec. 16, 1798-June 10, 1883; House 1875-77.

CHAPIN, Graham Hurd (D N.Y.) Feb. 10, 1799-Sept. 8, 1843; House 1835-37.

CHAPMAN, Andrew Grant (son of John Grant Chapman) (D Md.) Jan. 17, 1839-Sept. 25, 1892; House 1881-83.

CHAPMAN, Augustus Alexandria (VBD Va.) March 9, 1803-June 7, 1876; House 1843-47.

CHAPMAN, Bird Beers (D Neb.) Aug. 24, 1821-Sept. 21, 1871; House (Terr. Del.) 1855-57.

CHAPMAN, Charles (W Conn.) June 21, 1799-Aug. 7, 1869; House 1851-53.

CHAPMAN, Henry (D Pa.) Feb. 4, 1804-April 11, 1891; House 1857-59.

CHAPMAN, John (F Pa.) Oct. 18, 1740-Jan. 27, 1800; House 1797-99.

CHAPMAN, John Grant (father of Andrew Grant Chapman) (W Md.) July 5, 1798-Dec. 10, 1856; House 1845-49.

CHAPMAN, Pleasant Thomas (R Ill.) Oct. 8, 1854-Jan. 31, 1931; House 1905-11.

CHAPMAN, Reuben (D Ala.) July 15, 1799-May 16, 1882; House 1835-47; Gov. 1847-49.

CHAPMAN, Virgil Munday (D Ky.) March 15, 1895-March 8, 1951; House 1925-29, 1931-49; Senate 1949-March 8, 1951.

CHAPMAN, William Williams (D Iowa) Aug. 11, 1808-Oct. 18, 1892; House (Terr. Del.) Sept. 10, 1838-Oct. 27, 1840.

CHAPPELL, Absalom Harris (cousin of Lucius Quintus Cincinnatus Lamar) (SRW Ga.) Dec. 18, 1801-Dec. 11, 1878; House Oct. 2, 1843-45.

CHAPPELL, John Joel (SRWD S.C.) Jan. 19, 1782-May 23, 1871; House 1813-17.

CHAPPELL, William Venroe Jr. (D Fla.) Feb. 3, 1922-___; House 1969-___.

CHARLES, William Barclay (R N.Y.) April 3, 1861-Nov. 25, 1950; House 1915-17.

CHARLTON, Robert Milledge (— Ga.) Jan. 19, 1807-Jan. 18, 1854; Senate May 31, 1852-53.

CHASE, Dudley (uncle of Salmon Portland Chase and Dudley Chase Denison) (JD Vt.) Dec. 30, 1771-Feb. 23, 1846; Senate 1813-Nov. 3, 1817, 1825-31.

CHASE, George William (W N.Y.) ? -April 17, 1867; House 1853-55.

CHASE, Jackson Burton (R Neb.) Aug. 19, 1890-May 5, 1974; House 1955-57.

CHASE, James Mitchell (R Pa.) Dec. 19, 1891-Jan. 1, 1945; Houes 1927-33.

CHASE, Lucien Bonaparte (D Tenn.) Dec. 5, 1817-Dec. 4, 1864; House 1845-49.

CHASE, Ray P. (R Minn.) March 12, 1880-Sept. 18, 1948; House 1933-35.

CHASE, Salmon Portland (nephew of Dudley Chase and cousin of Dudley Chase Denison) (R Ohio) Jan. 13, 1808-May 7, 1873; Senate 1849-55 (F-S/D), March 4-6, 1861 (R); Governor 1856-60; Secy. of the Treasury 1861-64; Chief Justice of the Supreme Court 1864-73.

CHASE, Samuel (Ad.D N.Y.) ? -Aug. 3, 1838; House 1827-29.

CHASTAIN, Elijah Webb (UD Ga.) Sept. 25, 1813-April 9, 1874; House 1851-55.

CHATHAM, Richard Thurmond (D N.C.) Aug. 16, 1896-Feb. 5, 1957; House 1949-57.

CHAVES, Jose Francisco (R N.M.) June 27, 1833-Nov. 26, 1904; House (Terr. Del.) 1865-67, Feb. 20, 1869-71.

CHAVEZ, Dennis (D N.M.) April 8, 1888-Nov. 18, 1962; House 1931-35; Senate May 11, 1935-Nov. 18, 1962.

CHEADLE, Joseph Bonaparte (R Ind.) Aug. 14, 1842-May 28, 1904; House 1887-91.

CHEATHAM, Henry Plummer (R N.C.) Dec. 27, 1857-Nov. 29, 1935; House 1889-93.

CHEATHAM, Richard (W Tenn.) Feb. 20, 1799-Sept. 9, 1845; House 1837-39.

CHELF, Frank Leslie (D Ky.) Sept. 22, 1907-__; House 1945-67.

CHENEY, Person Colby (R N.H.) Feb. 25, 1828-June 19, 1901; Senate Nov. 24, 1886-June 14, 1887; Gov. 1875-77.

CHENOWETH, John Edgar (R Colo.) Aug. 17, 1897-__; House 1941-49, 1951-65.

CHESNEY, Chester Anton (D Ill.) March 9, 1916-__; House 1949-51.

CHESNUT, James Jr. (SRD S.C.) Jan. 18, 1815-Feb. 1, 1885; Senate Dec. 3, 1858-Nov. 10, 1860.

CHETWOOD, William (JD N.J.) June 17, 1771-Dec. 17, 1857;House Dec. 5, 1836-37.

CHEVES, Langdon (D S.C.) Sept. 17, 1776-June 26, 1857; House Dec. 31, 1810-15; Speaker 1814-15.

CHICKERING, Charles Addison (R N.Y.) Nov. 26, 1843-Feb. 13, 1900; House 1893-Feb. 13, 1900.

CHILCOTT, George Miles (R Colo.) Jan. 2, 1828-March 6, 1891; House (Terr. Del.) 1867-69; Senate April 17, 1882-Jan. 27, 1883.

CHILD, Thomas Jr. (D N.Y.) March 22, 1818-March 9, 1869; House 1855-57.

CHILDS, Robert Andrew (R Ill.) March 22, 1845-Dec. 19, 1915; House 1893-95.

CHILDS, Tomothy (W N.Y.) 1785-Nov. 8, 1847; House 1829-31, 1835-39, 1841-43.

CHILES, Lawton Mainor Jr. (D Fla.) April 3, 1930-__; Senate 1971-__.

CHILTON, Horace (grandson of Thomas Chilton) (D Texas) Dec. 29, 1853-June 12, 1932; Senate June 10, 1891-March 22, 1892, 1895-1901.

CHILTON, Samuel (W Va.) Sept. 7, 1804-Jan. 14, 1867; House 1843-45.

CHILTON, Thomas (grandfather of Horace Chilton) (W Ky.) July 30, 1798-Aug. 15, 1854; House Dec. 22, 1827-31, 1833-35.

CHILTON, William Edwin (D W.Va.) March 17, 1858-Nov. 7, 1939; Senate 1911-17.

CHINDBLOM, Carl Richard (R Ill.) Dec. 21, 1870-Sept. 12, 1956; House 1919-33.

CHINN, Joseph William (D Va.) Nov. 16, 1798-Dec. 5, 1840; House 1831-35.

CHINN, Thomas Withers (cousin of Robert Enoch Withers) (W La.) Nov. 22, 1791-May 22, 1852; House 1839-41.

CHIPERFIELD, Burnett Mitchell (father of Robert Bruce Chiperfield) (R Ill.) June 14, 1870-June 24, 1940; House 1915-17, 1929-33.

CHIPERFIELD, Robert Bruce (son of Burnett Mitchell Chiperfield) (R Ill.) Nov. 20, 1899-April 9, 1971; House 1939-63.

CHIPMAN, Daniel (brother of Nathaniel Chipman) (F Vt.) Oct. 22, 1765-April 23, 1850; House 1815-May 5, 1816.

CHIPMAN, John Logan (grandson of Nathaniel Chipman) (D Mich.) June 5, 1830-Aug. 17, 1893; House 1887-Aug. 17, 1893.

CHIPMAN, John Smith (D Mich.) Aug. 10, 1800-July 27, 1869; House 1845-47.

CHIPMAN, Nathaniel (brother of Daniel Chipman and grandfather of John Logan Chipman) (— Vt.) Nov. 15, 1752-Jan. 15, 1843; Senate Oct. 17, 1797-1803.

CHIPMAN, Norton Parker (R D.C.) March 7, 1836-Feb. 1, 1924; House (Delegate) April 21, 1871-75.

CHISHOLM, Shirley Anita (D N.Y.) Nov. 30, 1924-__; House 1969-__.

CHITTENDEN, Martin (— Vt.) March 12, 1763-Sept. 5, 1840; House 1803-13; Gov. 1813-15.

CHITTENDEN, Simeon Baldwin (R N.Y.) March 29, 1814-April 14, 1889; House Nov. 3, 1874-81.

CHITTENDEN, Thomas Cotton (W N.Y.) Aug. 30, 1788-Aug. 22, 1866; House 1839-43.

CHOATE, Rufus (W Mass.) Oct. 1, 1799-July 13, 1859; House 1831-June 30, 1834; Senate Feb. 23, 1841-45.

CHRISMAN, James Stone (D Ky.) Sept. 14, 1818-July 29, 1881; House 1853-55.

CHRISTGAU, Victor (R Minn.) Sept. 20, 1894-__; House 1929-33.

CHRISTIANCY, Isaac Peckham (R Mich.) March 12, 1812-Sept. 8, 1890; Senate 1875-Feb. 10, 1879.

CHRISTIANSON, Theodore (R Minn.) Sept. 12, 1883-Dec. 9, 1948; House 1933-37.

CHRISTIE, Gabriel (— Md.) 1755-April 1, 1808; House 1793-97, 1799-1801.

CHRISTOPHER, George Henry (D Mo.) Dec. 9, 1888-Jan. 23, 1959; House 1949-51, 1955-Jan. 23, 1959.

CHRISTOPHERSON, Charles Andrew (R S.D.) July 23, 1871-Nov. 2, 1951; House 1919-33.

CHUDOFF, Earl (D Pa.) Nov. 16, 1907-__; House 1949-Jan. 5, 1958.

CHURCH, Denver Samuel (D Calif.) Dec. 11, 1862-Feb. 21, 1952; House 1913-19, 1933-35.

CHURCH, Frank Forrester (D Idaho) July 25, 1924-__; Senate 1957-__.

CHURCH, Marguerite Stitt (widow of Ralph Edwin Church) (R Ill.) Sept. 13, 1892-__; House 1951-63.

CHURCH, Ralph Edwin (husband of Marguerite Stitt Church) (R Ill.) May 5, 1883-March 21, 1950; House 1935-41, 1943-March 21, 1950.

CHURCHILL, George Bosworth (R Mass.) Oct. 24, 1866-July 1, 1925; House March 4-July 1, 1925.

CHURCHILL, John Charles (R N.Y.) Jan. 17, 1821-June 4, 1905; House 1867-71.

CHURCHWELL, William Montgomery (D Tenn.) Feb. 20, 1826-Aug. 18, 1862; House 1851-55.

CILLEY, Bradbury (uncle of Jonathan Cilley and Joseph Cilley) (F N.H.) Feb. 1, 1760-Dec. 17, 1831; House 1813-17.

CILLEY, Jonathan (nephew of Bradbury Cilley and brother of Joseph Cilley) (JD Maine) July 2, 1802-Feb. 24, 1838; House 1837-Feb. 24, 1838.

CILLEY, Joseph (nephew of Bradbury Cilley and brother of Jonathan Cilley) (D N.H.) Jan. 4, 1791-Sept. 12, 1887; Senate June 13, 1846-47.

CITRON, William Michael (D Conn.) Aug. 29, 1896-June 8, 1976; House 1935-39.

CLAFLIN, William (R Mass.) March 6, 1818-Jan. 5, 1905; House 1877-81; Gov. 1869-71; Chmn. Rep. Natl. Comm. 1868-72.

CLAGETT, Clifton (— N.H.) Dec. 3, 1762-Jan. 25, 1829; House 1803-05, 1817-21.

CLAGETT, William Horace (uncle of Samuel Barrett Pettengill) (R Mont.) Sept. 21, 1838-Aug. 3, 1901; House (Terr. Del.) 1871-73.

CLAGUE, Frank (R Minn.) July 13, 1865-March 25, 1952; House 1921-33.

CLAIBORNE, James Robert (D Mo.) June 22, 1882-Feb. 16, 1944; House 1933-37.

CLAIBORNE, John (son of Thomas Claiborne) (—Va.) 1777-Oct. 9, 1808; House 1805-Oct. 9, 1808.

CLAIBORNE, John Francis Hamtramck (nephew of William Charles Cole Claiborne and Nathaniel Herbert Claiborne and great-grandfather of Herbert Claiborne Pell Jr.) (JD Miss.) April 24, 1809-May 17, 1884; House 1835-37, July 18, 1837-Feb. 5, 1838.

CLAIBORNE, Nathaniel Herbert (brother of William Charles Cole Claiborne and uncle of John Francis Hamtramck Claiborne) (R Va.) Nov. 14, 1777-Aug. 15, 1859; House 1825-37.

CLAIBORNE, Thomas (father of John Claiborne and Thomas Claiborne) (— Va.) Feb. 1, 1749-1812; House 1793-99, 1801-05.

CLAIBORNE, Thomas (son of Thomas Claiborne) (D Tenn.) May 17, 1780-Jan. 7, 1856; House 1817-19.

CLAIBORNE, William Charles Cole (brother of Nathaniel Herbert Claiborne and uncle of John Francis Hamtramck Claiborne) (Jeff. D Tenn.; D La.) 1775-Nov. 23, 1817; House 1797-1801 (Tenn.); Senate March 4-Nov. 23, 1817 (La.); Gov. of Terr. of Miss. 1801-03; Gov. of Terr. of Orleans 1804-12; Gov. of La. 1812-16.

CLANCY, Donald D. (R Ohio) July 24, 1921-__; House 1961-__.

CLANCY, John Michael (D N.Y.) May 7, 1837-July 25, 1903; House 1889-95.

CLANCY, John Richard (D N.Y.) March 8, 1859-April 21, 1932; House 1913-15.

CLANCY, Robert Henry (R Mich.) March 14, 1882-April 23, 1962; House 1923-25, 1927-33 (1923-25 Democrat, 1927-33 Republican).

CLAPP, Asa William Henry (D Maine) March 6, 1805-March 22, 1891; House 1847-49.

CLAPP, Moses Edwin (R Minn.) May 21, 1851-March 6, 1929; Senate Jan. 23, 1901-1917.

CLARDY, John Daniel (D Ky.) Aug. 30, 1828-Aug. 20, 1918; House 1895-99.

CLARDY, Kit Francis (R Mich.) June 17, 1892-Sept. 5, 1961; House 1953-55.

CLARDY, Martin Linn (D Mo.) April 26, 1844-July 5, 1914; House 1879-89.

CLARK, Abraham (— N.J.) Feb. 15, 1726-Sept. 15, 1794; House 1791-Sept. 15, 1794; Cont. Cong. 1776-78, 1779-83, 1787-89.

CLARK, Alvah Augustus (cousin of James Nelson Pidcock) (D N.J.) Sept. 13, 1840-Dec. 27, 1912; House 1877-81.

CLARK, Ambrose Williams (R N.Y.) Feb. 19, 1810-Oct. 13, 1887; House 1861-65.

CLARK, Amos Jr. (R N.J.) Nov. 8, 1828-Oct. 31, 1912; House 1873-75.

CLARK, Charles Benjamin (R Wis.) Aug. 24, 1844-Sept. 10, 1891; House 1887-91.

CLARK, Charles Nelson (R Mo.) Aug. 21, 1827-Oct. 4, 1902; House 1895-97.

CLARK, Christopher Henderson (brother of James Clark and uncle of John Bullock Clark) (Jeff. D Va.) 1767-Nov. 21, 1828; House Nov. 5, 1804-July 1, 1806.

CLARK, Clarence Don (R Wyo.) April 16, 1851-Nov. 18, 1930; House Dec. 1, 1890-1893; Senate Jan. 23, 1895-1917.

CLARK, Daniel (— Orleans) About 1766-Aug. 16, 1813; House (Terr. Del.) Dec. 1, 1806-09.

CLARK, Daniel (R N.H.) Oct. 24, 1809-Jan. 2, 1891; Senate June 27, 1857-July 27, 1866; President pro tempore 1864.

CLARK, David Worth (D Idaho) April 2, 1902-June 19, 1955; House 1935-39; Senate 1939-45.

CLARK, Ezra Jr. (AP/R Conn.) Sept. 12, 1813-Sept. 26, 1896; House 1855-59.

CLARK, Frank (D Fla.) March 28, 1860-April 14, 1936; House 1905-25.

CLARK, Frank Monroe (D Pa.) Dec. 24, 1915-__; House 1955-Dec. 31, 1974.

CLARK, Franklin (D Maine) Aug. 2, 1801-Aug. 24, 1874; House 1847-49.

CLARK, Henry Alden (R Pa.) Jan. 7, 1850-Feb. 15, 1944; House 1917-19.

CLARK, Henry Selby (D N.C.) Sept. 9, 1809-Jan. 8, 1869; House 1845-47.

CLARK, Horace Francis (D N.Y.) Nov. 29, 1815-June 19, 1873; House 1857-61.

CLARK, James (brother of Christopher Henderson Clark and uncle of John Bullock Clark) (CD Ky.) Jan. 16, 1770-Sept. 27, 1839; House 1813-16, Aug. 1, 1825-31; Gov. (Whig) 1836-39.

CLARK, James Beauchamp (Champ) (father of Joel Bennett Clark) (D Mo.) March 7, 1850-March 2, 1921; House 1893-95, 1897-March 2, 1921; Speaker 1911-19.

CLARK, James West (D N.C.) Oct. 15, 1779-Dec. 20, 1843; House 1815-17.

CLARK, Jerome Bayard (D N.C.) April 5, 1882-Aug. 26, 1959; House 1929-49.

CLARK, Joel Bennett (Champ) (son of James Beauchamp Clark) Jan. 8, 1890-July 13, 1954; Senate Feb. 4, 1933-45.

CLARK, John Bullock (nephew of Chrisopher Henderson Clark and James Clark) (D Mo.) April 17, 1802-Oct. 29, 1885; House Dec. 7, 1857-July 13, 1861.

CLARK, John Bullock Jr. (son of John Bullock Clark) (D Mo.) Jan. 14, 1831-Sept. 7, 1903; House 1873-83.

CLARK, John Chamberlain (W N.Y.) Jan. 14, 1793-Oct. 25, 1852; House 1827-29, 1837-43 (1827-29 and 1837-39 Democrat, 1839-43 Whig).

CLARK, Joseph Sill (D Pa.) Oct. 21, 1901-__; Senate 1957-69.

CLARK, Lincoln (D Iowa) Aug. 9, 1800-Sept. 16, 1886; House 1851-53.

CLARK, Linwood Leon (R Md.) March 21, 1876-Nov. 18, 1965; House 1929-31.

CLARK, Lot (W N.Y.) May 23, 1788-Dec. 18, 1862; House 1823-25.

CLARK, Richard Clarence (D Iowa) Sept. 14, 1929-__; Senate 1973-__.

CLARK, Robert (D N.Y.) June 12, 1777-Oct. 1, 1837; House 1819-21.

CLARK, Rush (R Iowa) Oct. 1, 1834-April 29, 1879; House 1877-April 29, 1879.

CLARK, Samuel (D N.Y./Mich.) Jan., 1800-Oct. 2, 1870; House 1833-35 (N.Y.), 1853-55 (Mich.).

CLARK, Samuel Mercer (R Iowa) Oct. 11, 1842-Aug. 11, 1900; House 1895-99.

CLARK, William (W Pa.) Feb. 18, 1774-March 28, 1851; House 1833-37.

CLARK, William Andrews (D Mont.) Jan. 8, 1839-March 2, 1925; Senate Dec. 4, 1899-May 15, 1900, 1901-07.

CLARK, William Thomas (R Texas) June 29, 1831-Oct. 12, 1905; House March 31, 1870-May 13, 1872.

CLARKE, Archibald Smith (brother of Staley Nichols Clarke) (— N.Y.) 1788-Dec. 4, 1821; House Dec. 2, 1816-17.

CLARKE, Bayard (AW N.Y.) March 17, 1815-June 20, 1884; House 1855-57.

CLARKE, Beverly Leonidas (D Ky.) Feb. 11, 1809-March 17, 1860; House 1847-49.

CLARKE, Charles Ezra (W N.Y.) April 8, 1790-Dec. 29, 1863; House 1849-51.

CLARKE, Frank Gay (R N.H.), Sept. 10, 1850-Jan. 9, 1901; House 1897-Jan. 9, 1901.

CLARKE, Freeman (R N.Y.) March 22, 1809-June 24, 1887; House 1863-65, 1871-75.

CLARKE, James Paul (D Ark.) Aug. 18, 1854-Oct. 1, 1916; Senate 1903-Oct. 1, 1916; President pro tempore 1913, 1915; Gov. 1895-97.

CLARKE, John Blades (D Ky.) April 14, 1833-May 23, 1911; House 1875-79.

CLARKE, John Davenport (husband of Marian Williams Clarke) (R N.Y.) Jan. 15, 1873-Nov. 5, 1933; House 1921-25, 1927-Nov. 5, 1933.

CLARKE, John Hopkins (W R.I.) April 1, 1789-Nov. 23, 1870; Senate 1847-53.

CLARKE, Marian Williams (wife of John Davenport Clarke) (R N.Y.) July 29, 1880-April 8, 1953; House Dec. 28, 1933-35.

CLARKE, Reader Wright (R Ohio) May 18, 1812-May 23, 1872; House 1865-69.

CLARKE, Richard Henry (D Ala.) Feb. 9, 1843-Sept. 26, 1906; House 1889-97.

CLARKE, Sidney (R Kan.) Oct. 16, 1831-June 18, 1909; House 1865-71.

CLARKE, Staley Nichols (brother of Archibald Smith Clarke) (W N.Y.) May 24, 1794-Oct. 14, 1860; House 1841-43.

CLASON, Charles Russell (R Mass.) Sept. 3, 1890-__; House 1937-49.

CLASSON, David Guy (R Wis.) Set. 27, 1870-Sept. 6, 1930; House 1917-23.

CLAUSEN, Don Holst (R Calif.) Apri. 27, 1923-__; House Jan. 22, 1963-__.

CLAWSON, Delwin (Del) Morgan (R Calif.) Jan. 11, 1914-__; House June 11, 1963-__.

CLAWSON, Isaiah Dunn (W N.J.) M⁻.ch 30, 1822-Oct. 9, 1879; House 1855-59.

CLAY, Alexander Stephens (D Ga.) Sept. 25, 1853-Nov. 13, 1910; Senate 1897-Nov. 13, 1910.

CLAY, Brutus Junius (U Ky.) July 1, 1808-Oct. 11, 1878; House 1863-65.

CLAY, Clement Claiborne Jr. (son of Clement Comer Clay) (D Ala.) Dec. 13, 1816-Jan. 3, 1882; Senate Nov. 29, 1853-Jan. 21, 1861.

CLAY, Clement Comer (father of Clement Claiborne Clay Jr.) (D Ala.) Dec. 17, 1789-Sept. 9, 1866; House 1829-35; Senate June 19, 1837-Nov. 15, 1841; Gov. 1835-37.

CLAY, Henry (father of James Brown Clay) (— Ky.) April 12, 1777-June 29, 1852; Senate Nov. 19, 1806-07, Jan. 4, 1810-11, Nov. 10, 1831-March 31, 1842, 1849-June 29, 1852; House 1811-Jan. 19, 1814, 1815-21, 1823-March 6, 1825; Speaker Nov. 4, 1811-Jan. 19, 1814, Dec. 4, 1815-Oct. 28, 1820, Dec. 1, 1823-25; Secy. of State March 7, 1825-29.

CLAY, James Brown (son of Henry Clay) (D Ky.) Nov. 9, 1817-Jan. 26, 1864; House 1857-59.

CLAY, James Franklin (D Ky.) Oct. 29, 1840-Aug. 17, 1921; House 1883-85.

CLAY, Joseph (— Pa.) July 24, 1769-Aug. 27, 1811; House 1803-08.

CLAY, Matthew (D Va.) March 25, 1754-May 27, 1815; House 1797-1813, March 4-May 27, 1815.

CLAY, William Lacey (D Mo.) April 30, 1931-__; House 1969-__.

CLAYPOOL, Harold Kile (son of Horatio Clifford Claypool and cousin of John Barney Peterson) (D Ohio) June 2, 1886-Aug. 2, 1958; House 1937-43.

CLAYPOOL, Horatio Clifford (father of Harold Kile Claypool and cousin of John Barney Peterson) (D Ohio) Feb. 9, 1859-Jan. 19, 1921; House 1911-15, 1917-19.

CLAYTON, Augustin Smith (SRD Ga.) Nov. 27, 1783-June 21, 1839; House Jan. 21, 1832-35.

CLAYTON, Bertram Tracy (brother of Henry De Lamar Clayton) (D N.Y.) Oct. 19, 1862-May 30, 1918; House 1899-1901.

CLAYTON, Charles (R Calif.) Oct. 5, 1825-Oct. 4, 1885; House 1873-75.

CLAYTON, Henry De Lamar (brother of Bertram Tracy Clayton) (D Ala.) Feb. 10, 1857-Dec. 21, 1929; House 1897-May 25, 1914.

CLAYTON, John Middleton (nephew of Joshua Clayton, cousin of Thomas Clayton and great-grand-uncle of C. Douglass Buck) (W Del.) July 24, 1796-Nov. 9, 1856; Senate 1829-Dec. 29, 1836, 1845-Feb. 23, 1849, 1853-Nov. 9, 1856 (1829-1836 National Republican, 1845-49 and 1853-56 Whig); Secy. of State March 7, 1849-July 22, 1850.

CLAYTON, Joshua (father of Thomas Clayton and uncle of John Middleton Clayton) (— Del.) July 20, 1744-Aug. 11, 1798; Senate Jan. 19, 1798-Aug. 11, 1798; Gov. 1789-96.

CLAYTON, Powell (R Ark.) Aug. 7, 1833-Aug. 25, 1914; Senate 1871-77; Gov. 1868.

CLAYTON, Thomas (son of Joshua Clayton and cousin of John Middleton Clayton) (W Del.) March 9, 1778-Aug. 21, 1854; House 1815-17 Federalist; Senate Jan. 8, 1824-27, Jan. 9, 1837-47 (1824-27 Federalist, 1837-47 Whig).

CLEARY, William Edward (D N.Y.) July 20, 1849-Dec. 20, 1932; House March 5, 1918-21, 1923-27.

CLEMENS, Jeremiah (D Ala.) Dec. 28, 1814-May 21, 1865; Senate Nov. 30, 1849-53.

CLEMENS, Sherrard (D Va.) April 28, 1820-June 30, 1881; House Dec. 6, 1852-53, 1857-61.

CLEMENTE, Louis Gary (D N.Y.) June 10, 1908-May 13, 1968; House 1949-53.

CLEMENTS, Andrew Jackson (U Tenn.) Dec. 23, 1832-Nov. 7, 1913; House 1861-63.

CLEMENTS, Earle C. (D Ky.) Oct. 22, 1896-__; House 1945-Jan. 6, 1948; Senate Nov. 27, 1950-57; Gov. Jan. 1948-Nov. 1950.

CLEMENTS, Isaac (R Ill.) March 31, 1837-May 31, 1909; House 1873-75.

CLEMENTS, Judson Claudius (D Ga.) Feb. 12, 1846-June 18, 1917; House 1881-91.

CLEMENTS, Newton Nash (— Ala.) Dec. 23, 1837-Feb. 20, 1900; House Dec. 8, 1880-81.

CLENDENIN, David (— Ohio) ? - ?; House Oct. 11, 1814-17.

CLEVELAND, Chauncey Fitch (D Conn.) Feb. 16, 1799-June 6, 1887; House 1849-53; Gov. 1842-44.

CLEVELAND, James Colgate (R N.H.) June 13, 1920-__; House 1963-__.

CLEVELAND, Jesse Franklin (UD Ga.) Oct. 25, 1804-June 22, 1841; House Oct. 5, 1835-39.

CLEVELAND, Orestes (D N.J.) March 2, 1829-March 30, 1896; House 1869-71.

CLEVENGER, Cliff (R Ohio) Aug. 20, 1885-Dec. 13, 1960; House 1939-59.

CLEVENGER, Raymond Francis (D Mich.) June 6, 1926-__; House 1965-67.

CLEVER, Charles P. (D N.M.) Feb. 23, 1830-July 8, 1874; House (Terr. Del.) Sept. 2, 1867-Feb. 20, 1869.

CLIFFORD, Nathan (D Maine) Aug. 18, 1803-July 25, 1881; House 1839-43; Atty. Gen. of U.S. 1846-1848; Assoc. Justice of Supreme Court 1858-1881.

CLIFT, Joseph Wales (R Ga.) Sept. 30, 1837-May 2, 1908; House July 25, 1868-69.

CLINCH, Duncan Lamont (W Ga.) April 6, 1787-Nov. 27, 1849; House Feb. 15, 1844-45.

CLINE, Cyrus (D Ind.) July 12, 1856-Oct. 5, 1923; House 1909-17.

CLINGMAN, Thomas Lanier (D N.C.) July 27, 1812-Nov. 3, 1897; House 1843-45, 1847-May 7, 1858 (1843-45 Whig, 1847-58 Democrat); Senate May 7, 1858-March 28, 1861.

CLINTON, De Witt (half brother of James Graham Clinton and cousin of George Clinton) (D N.Y.) March 2, 1769-Feb. 11, 1828; Senate Feb. 9, 1802-Nov. 4, 1803; Gov. 1817-21, 1825-28.

CLINTON, George (cousin of De Witt Clinton and James Graham Clinton) (D N.Y.) June 6, 1771-Sept. 16, 1809; House Feb. 14, 1805-09.

CLINTON, James Graham (half brother of De Witt Clinton and cousin of George Clinton) (D N.Y.) Jan. 2, 1804-May 28, 1849; House 1841-45.

CLIPPINGER, Roy (R Ill.) Jan. 13, 1886-Dec. 24, 1962; House Nov. 6, 1945-49.

CLOPTON, David (SRD Ala.) Sept. 19, 1820-Feb. 5, 1892; House 1859-Jan. 21, 1861.

CLOPTON, John (D Va.) Feb. 7, 1756-Sept. 11, 1816; House 1795-99; 1801-Sept. 11, 1816.

CLOUSE, Wynne F. (R Tenn.) Aug. 29, 1883-Feb. 19, 1944; House 1921-23.

CLOVER, Benjamin Hutchinson (FA Kan.) Dec. 22, 1837-Dec. 30, 1899; House 1891-93.

CLOWNEY, William Kennedy (SRD S.C.) March 21, 1797-March 12, 1851; House 1833-35, 1837-39 (1833-35 Nullifier, 1837-39 States Rights Democrat).

CLUETT, Ernest Harold (R N.Y.) July 13, 1874-Feb. 4, 1954; House 1937-43.

CLUNIE, Thomas Jefferson (D Calif.) March 25, 1852-June 30, 1903; House 1889-91.

CLYMER, George (F Pa.) March 16, 1739-Jan. 23, 1813; House 1789-91; Cont. Cong. 1776-78, 1780-83.

CLYMER, Hiester (nephew of William Hiester and cousin of Isaac Ellmaker Hiester) (D Pa.) Nov. 3, 1827-June 12, 1884; House 1873-81.

COAD, Merwin (D Iowa) Sept. 28, 1924-__; House 1957-63.

COADY, Charles Pearce (D Md.) Feb. 22, 1868-Feb. 16, 1934; House Nov. 4, 1913-21.

COBB, Amasa (R Wis.) Sept. 27, 1823-July 5, 1905; House 1863-71.

COBB, Clinton Levering (R N.C.) Aug. 25, 1842-April 30, 1879; House 1860-75.

COBB, David (F Mass.) Sept. 14, 1748-April 17, 1830; House 1793-95.

COBB, George Thomas (D N.J.) Oct. 13, 1813-Aug. 12, 1870; House 1861-63.

COBB, Howell (uncle of Howell Cobb) (— Ga.) Aug. 3, 1772-May 26, 1818; House 1807-12.

COBB, Howell (nephew of the preceding) (D Ga.) Sept. 7, 1815-Oct. 9, 1868; House 1843-51, 1855-57; Speaker 1849-51; Gov. 1851-53; Secy. of the Treasury 1857-60.

COBB, James Edward (— Ala.) Oct. 5, 1835-June 2, 1903; House 1887-April 21, 1896.

COBB, Seth Wallace (D Mo.) Dec. 5, 1838-May 22, 1909; House 1891-97.

COBB, Stephen Alonzo (R Kan.) June 17, 1833-Aug. 24, 1878; House 1873-75.

COBB, Thomas Reed (D Ind.) July 2, 1828-June 23, 1892; House 1877-87.

COBB, Thomas Willis (— Ga.) 1784-Feb. 1, 1830; House 1817-21, 1823-Dec. 6, 1824; Senate Dec. 6, 1824-28.

COBB, Williamson Robert Winfield (D Ala.) June 8, 1807-Nov. 1, 1864; House 1847-Jan. 30, 1861.

COBURN, Frank Potter (D Wis.) Dec. 6, 1858-Nov. 2, 1932; House 1891-93.

COBURN, John (R Ind.) Oct. 27, 1825-Jan. 28, 1908; House 1867-75.

COBURN, Stephen (R Maine) Nov. 11, 1817-July 4, 1882; House Jan. 2-March 3, 1861.

COCHRAN, Alexander Gilmore (D Pa.) March 20, 1846-May 1, 1928; House 1875-77.

COCHRAN, Charles Fremont (D Mo.) Sept. 27, 1846-Dec. 19, 1906; House 1897-1905.

COCHRAN, James (grandfather of James Cochrane Dobbin) (D N.C.) about 1767-April 7, 1813; House 1809-13.

COCHRAN, James (— N.Y.) Feb. 11, 1769-Nov. 7, 1848; House 1797-99.

COCHRAN, John Joseph (D Mo.) Aug. 11, 1880-March 6, 1947; House Nov. 2, 1926-47.

COCHRAN, Thomas Cunningham (R Pa.) Nov. 30, 1877-Dec. 10, 1957; House 1927-35.

COCHRAN, William Thad (R Miss.) Dec. 7, 1937-___; House 1973-___.

COCHRANE, Aaron Van Schaick (nephew of Isaac Whitbeck Van Schaick) (R N.Y.) March 14, 1858-Sept. 7, 1943; House 1897-1901.

COCHRANE, Clark Betton (R N.Y.) May 31, 1815-March 5, 1867; House 1857-61.

COCHRANE, John (SRD N.Y.) Aug. 27, 1813-Feb. 7, 1898; House 1857-61.

COCKE, John (son of William Cocke and uncle of William Michael Cocke) (— Tenn.) 1772-Feb. 16, 1854; House 1819-27.

COCKE, William (father of John Cocke and grandfather of William Michael Cocke (— Tenn.) 1747-Aug. 22, 1828; Senate Aug. 2, 1796-Mar. 3, 1797, April 22-Sept. 26, 1797, 1799-1805.

COCKE, William Michael (grandson of William Cocke and nephew of John Cocke) (D Tenn.) July 16, 1815-Feb. 6, 1896; House 1845-49.

COCKERILL, Joseph Randolph (D Ohio) Jan. 2, 1818-Oct. 23, 1875; House 1857-59.

COCKRAN, William Bourke (D N.Y.) Feb. 28, 1854-March 1, 1923; House 1887-89, Nov. 3, 1891-95, Feb. 23, 1904-09, 1921-March 1, 1923.

COCKRELL, Francis Marion (brother of Jeremiah Vardaman Cockrell) (D Mo.) Oct. 1, 1834-Dec. 13, 1915; Senate 1875-1905.

COCKRELL, Jeremiah Vardaman (brother of Francis Marion Cockrell) (D Texas) May 7, 1832-March 18, 1915; House 1893-97.

COCKS, William Willets (brother of Frederick Cocks Hicks) (R N.Y.) July 24, 1861-May 24, 1932; House 1905-11.

CODD, George Pierre (R Mich.) Dec. 7, 1869-Feb. 16, 1927; House 1921-23.

CODDING, James Hodge (R Pa.) July 8, 1849-Sept. 12, 1919; House Nov. 5, 1895-99.

COFFEE, Harry Buffington (D Neb.) March 16, 1890-Oct. 3, 1972; House 1935-43.

COFFEE, John (D Ga.) Dec. 3, 1782-Sept. 25, 1836; House 1833-Sept. 25, 1836.

COFFEE, John Main (D Wash.) Jan. 23, 1897-___; 1937-47.

COFFEEN, Henry Asa (D Wyo.) Feb. 14, 1841-Dec. 9, 1912; House 1893-95.

COFFEY, Robert Lewis Jr. (D Pa.) Oct. 21, 1918-April 20, 1949; House Jan. 3-April 20, 1949.

COFFIN, Charles Dustin (W Ohio) Sept. 9, 1805-Feb. 28, 1880; House Dec. 20, 1837-39.

COFFIN, Charles Edward (R Md.) July 18, 1841-May 24, 1912; House Nov. 6, 1894-97.

COFFIN, Frank Morey (D Maine) July 11, 1919-___; House 1957-61.

COFFIN, Howard Aldridge (R Mich.) June 11, 1877-Feb. 28, 1956; House 1947-49.

COFFIN, Peleg Jr. (— Mass.) Nov. 3, 1756-March 6, 1805; House 1793-95.

COFFIN, Thomas Chalkley (D Idaho) Oct. 25, 1887-June 8, 1934; House 1933-June 8, 1934.

COFFROTH, Alexander Hamilton (D Pa.) May 18, 1828-Sept. 2, 1906; House 1863-65, Feb. 19-July 18, 1866, 1879-81.

COGHLAN, John Maxwell (R Calif.) Dec. 8, 1835-March 26, 1879; House 1871-73.

COGSWELL, William (R Mass.) Aug. 23, 1838-May 22, 1895; House 1887-May 22, 1895.

COHELAN, Jeffery (D Calif.) June 24, 1914-___; House 1959-71.

COHEN, John Sanford (D Ga.) Feb. 26, 1870-May 13, 1935; Senate April 25, 1932-Jan. 11, 1933.

COHEN, William Sebastian (R Maine) Aug. 28, 1940-___; House 1973-___.

COHEN, William Wolfe (D N.Y.) Sept. 6, 1874-Oct. 12, 1940; House 1927-29.

COIT, Joshua (F Conn.) Oct. 7, 1758-Sept. 5, 1798; House 1793-Sept. 5, 1798.

COKE, Richard (nephew of Richard Coke Jr.) (D Texas) March 13, 1829-May 14, 1897; Senate 1877-95; Gov. Dec. 1873-Dec. 1, 1877.

COKE, Richard Jr. (uncle of Richard Coke) (JD Va.) Nov. 16, 1790-March 31, 1851; House 1829-33.

COLCOCK, William Ferguson (D S.C.) Nov. 5, 1804-June 13, 1889; House 1849-53.

COLDEN, Cadwallader David (D N.Y.) April 4, 1769-Feb. 7, 1834; House Dec. 12, 1821-23.

COLDEN, Charles J. (D Calif.) Aug. 24, 1870-April 15, 1938; House 1933-April 15, 1938.

COLE, Albert McDonald (R Kan.) Oct. 13, 1901-___; House 1945-53.

COLE, Cornelius (UR Calif.) Sept. 17, 1822-Nov. 3, 1924; House 1863-65; Senate 1867-73.

COLE, Cyrenus (R Iowa) Jan. 13, 1863-Nov. 14, 1939; House July 19, 1921-33.

COLE, George Edward (D Wash.) Dec. 23, 1826-Dec. 3, 1906; House (Terr. Del.) 1863-65; Terr. Gov. Nov. 1866-March 4, 1867.

COLE, Nathan (R Mo.) July 26, 1825-March 4, 1904; House 1877-79.

COLE, Orsamus (W Wis.) Aug. 23, 1819-May 5, 1903; House 1849-51.

COLE, Ralph Dayton (brother of Raymond Clinton Cole) (R Ohio) Nov. 30, 1873-Oct. 15, 1932; House 1905-11.

COLE, Raymond Clinton (brother of Ralph Dayton Cole) (R Ohio) Aug. 21, 1870-Feb. 8, 1957; House 1919-25.

COLE, William Clay (R Mo.) Aug. 29, 1897-Sept. 23, 1965; House 1943-49, 1953-55.

COLE, William Hinson (D Md.) Jan. 11, 1837-July 8, 1886; House 1885-July 8, 1886.

COLE, William Purington Jr. (D Md.) May 11, 1889-Sept. 22, 1957; House 1927-29, 1931-Oct. 26, 1942.

COLE, William Sterling (R N.Y.) April 18, 1904-___; House 1935-Dec. 1, 1957.

COLEMAN, Hamilton Dudley (R La.) May 12, 1845-March 16, 1926; House 1889-91.

COLEMAN, Nicholas Daniel (JD Ky.) April 22, 1800-May 11, 1874; House 1829-31.

COLEMAN, William Henry (R Pa.) Dec. 28, 1871-June 3, 1943; House 1915-17.

COLERICK, Walpole Gillespie (D Ind.) Aug. 1, 1845-Jan. 11, 1911; House 1879-83.

COLES, Isaac (father of Walter Coles) (— Va.) March 2, 1747-June 3, 1813; House 1789-91, 1793-97.

COLES, Walter (son of Isaac Coles) (D Va.) Dec. 8, 1790-Nov. 9, 1857; House 1835-45.

COLFAX, Schuyler (R Ind.) March 23, 1823-Jan. 13, 1885; House 1855-69; Speaker 1863-69; Vice Pres. 1869-73.

COLHOUN, John Ewing (cousin of John Caldwell Calhoun and Joseph Calhoun) (D S.C.) 1750-Oct. 26, 1802; Senate 1801-Oct. 26, 1802.

COLLAMER, Jacob (R Vt.) Jan. 8, 1792-Nov. 9, 1865; House 1843-49 (W); Senate 1855-Nov. 9, 1865; Postmaster General March 7, 1849-July 20, 1850.

COLLIER, Harold Reginald (R Ill.) Dec. 12, 1915-___; House 1957-75.

COLLIER, James William (D Miss.) Sept. 28, 1872-Sept. 28, 1933; House 1909-33.

COLLIER, John Allen (CD NY) Nov. 13, 1787-March 24, 1873; House 1831-33.

COLLIN, John Francis (D N.Y.) April 30, 1802-Sept. 16, 1889; House 1845-47.

COLLINS, Cardiss (widow of George Washington Collins) (D Ill.) Sept. 24, 1931-___; House June 5, 1973-___.

COLLINS, Ela (father of William Collins) (D N.Y.) Feb. 14, 1786-Nov. 23, 1848; House 1823-25.

COLLINS, Francis Dolan (D Pa.) March 5, 1841-Nov. 21, 1891; House 1875-79.

COLLINS, George Washington (D Ill.) March 5, 1925-Dec. 8, 1972; House Nov. 3, 1970-Dec. 8, 1972.

COLLINS, James M. (R Texas) April 29, 1916-__; House Aug. 24, 1968-__.

COLLINS, Patrick Andrew (D Mass.) March 12, 1844-Sept. 13, 1905; House 1883-89.

COLLINS, Ross Alexander (D Miss.) April 25, 1880-July 14, 1968; House 1921-35, 1937-43.

COLLINS, Samuel LaFort (R Calif.) Aug. 6, 1895-June 26, 1965; House 1933-37.

COLLINS, William (son of Ela Collins) (D N.Y.) Feb. 22, 1818-June 18, 1878; House 1847-49.

COLMER, William Meyers (D Miss.) Feb. 11, 1890-__; House 1933-73.

COLQUITT, Alfred Holt (son of Walter Terry Colquitt) (D Ga.) April 20, 1824-March 26, 1894; House 1853-55; Senate 1883-March 26, 1894; Gov. 1877-82.

COLQUITT, Walter Terry (father of Alfred Holt Colquitt) (VBD Ga.) Dec. 27, 1799-May 7, 1855; House 1839-July 21, 1840, Jan. 3, 1842-43 (1839-40 States Rights Whig, 1842-43 Van Buren Democrat); Senate 1843-Feb. 1848.

COLSON, David Grant (R Ky.) April 1, 1861-Sept. 27, 1904; House 1895-99.

COLSTON, Edward (F Va.) Dec. 25, 1786-April 23, 1852; House 1817-19.

COLT, LeBaron Bradford (R R.I.) June 25, 1846-Aug. 18, 1924; Senate 1913-Aug. 18, 1924.

COLTON, Don Byron (R Utah) Sept. 15, 1876-Aug. 1, 1952; House 1921-33.

COMBS, George Hamilton Jr. (D Mo.) May 2, 1899-__; House 1927-29.

COMBS, Jesse Martin (D Texas) July 7, 1889-Aug. 21, 1953; House 1945-53.

COMEGYS, Joseph Parsons (W Del.) Dec. 29, 1813-Feb. 1, 1893; Senate Nov. 19, 1856-Jan. 14, 1857.

COMER, Braxton Bragg (D Ala.) Nov. 7, 1848-Aug. 15, 1927; Senate March 5-Nov. 2, 1920; Gov. 1907-11.

COMINGO, Abram (D Mo.) Jan. 9, 1820-Nov. 10, 1889; House 1871-75.

COMINS, Linus Bacon (R Mass.) Nov. 29, 1817-Oct. 14, 1892; House 1855-59 (1855-57 American Party, 1857-59 Republican).

COMPTON, Barnes (great-grandson of Philip Key) (D Md.) Nov. 16, 1830-Dec. 4, 1898; House 1885-March 20, 1890, 1891-May 15, 1894.

COMPTON, C. H. Ranulf (R Conn.) Sept. 16, 1878-Jan. 26, 1974; House 1943-45.

COMSTOCK, Charles Carter (Fus. D Mich.) March 5, 1818-Feb. 20, 1900; House 1885-87.

COMSTOCK, Daniel Webster (R Ind.) Dec. 16, 1840-May 19, 1917; House March 4-May 19, 1917.

COMSTOCK, Oliver Cromwell (D N.Y.) March 1, 1780-Jan. 11, 1860; House 1813-19.

COMSTOCK, Solomon Gilman (R Minn.) May 9, 1842-June 3, 1933; House 1889-91.

CONABLE, Barber B. Jr. (R N.Y.) Nov. 2, 1922-__; House 1965-__.

CONARD, John (D Pa.) Nov. 1773-May 9, 1857; House 1813-15.

CONDICT, Lewis (A-F N.J.) March 3, 1772-May 26, 1862; House 1811-17, 1821-33.

CONDIT, John (father of Silas Condit) (D N.J.) July 8, 1755-May 4, 1834; House 1799-1803; Senate Sept. 1, 1803-March 3, 1809, March 21, 1809-17; House March 4-Nov. 4, 1819.

CONDIT, Silas (son of John Condit) (CD N.J.) Aug. 18, 1778-Nov. 29, 1861; House 1831-33.

CONDON, Francis Bernard (D R.I.) Nov. 11, 1891-Nov. 23, 1965; House Nov. 4, 1930-Jan. 10, 1935.

CONDON, Robert Likens (D Calif.) Nov. 10, 1912-__; House 1953-55.

CONGER, Edwin Hurd (R Iowa) March 7, 1843-May 18, 1907; House 1885-Oct. 3, 1890.

CONGER, Harmon Sweatland (W N.Y.) April 9, 1816-Oct. 22, 1882; House 1847-51.

CONGER, James Lockwood (F-S W Mich.) Feb. 18, 1805-April 10, 1876; House 1851-53.

CONGER, Omar Dwight (R Mich.) April 1, 1818-July 11, 1898; House 1869-81; Senate 1881-87.

CONKLING, Alfred (father of Frederick Augustus Conkling and Roscoe Conkling) (AJD N.Y.) Oct. 12, 1789-Feb. 5, 1874; House 1821-23.

CONKLING, Frederick Augustus (son of Alfred Conkling and brother of Roscoe Conkling) (R N.Y.) Aug. 22, 1816-Sept. 18, 1891; House 1861-63.

CONKLING, Roscoe (son of Alfred Conkling and brother of Frederick Augustus Conkling) (UR N.Y.) Oct. 3, 1829-April 18, 1888; House 1859-63, 1865-March 4, 1867 (R); Senate 1867-May 16, 1881 (UR).

CONLAN, John Bertrand (R Ariz.) Sept. 17, 1930-__; House 1973-__.

CONN, Charles Gerard (D Ind.) Jan. 29, 1844-Jan. 5, 1931; House 1893-95.

CONNALLY, Thomas Terry (Tom) (D Texas) Aug. 19, 1877-Oct. 28, 1963; House 1917-29; Senate 1929-53.

CONNELL, Charles Robert (son of William Connell) (R Pa.) Sept. 22, 1864-Sept. 26, 1922; House 1921-Sept. 26, 1922.

CONNELL, Richard Edward (D N.Y.) Nov. 6, 1857-Oct. 30, 1912; House 1911-Oct. 30, 1912.

CONNELL, William (father of Charles Robert Connell) (R Pa.) Sept. 10, 1827-March 21, 1909; House 1897-1903, Feb. 10, 1904-05.

CONNELL, William James (R Neb.) July 6, 1846-Aug. 16, 1924; House 1889-91.

CONNELLY, John Robert (D Kan.) Feb. 27, 1870-Sept. 9, 1940; House 1913-19.

CONNER, James Perry (R Iowa) Jan. 27, 1851-March 19, 1924; House Dec. 4, 1900-09.

CONNER, John Cogswell (D Texas) Oct. 14, 1842-Dec. 10, 1873; House March 31, 1870-73.

CONNER, Samuel Shepard (— Mass.) about 1783-Dec. 17, 1820; House 1815-17.

CONNERY, Lawrence Joseph (brother of William Patrick Connery Jr.) (D Mass.) Oct. 17, 1895-Oct. 19, 1941; House Sept. 28, 1937-Oct. 19, 1941.

CONNERY, William Patrick Jr. (brother of Lawrence Joseph Connery) (D Mass.) Aug. 24, 1888-June 15, 1937; House 1923-June 15, 1937.

CONNESS, John (UR Calif.) Sept. 22, 1821-Jan. 10, 1909; Senate 1863-69 (elected as a Douglass D).

CONNOLLY, Daniel Ward (D Pa.) April 24, 1847-Dec. 4, 1894; House 1883-85.

CONNOLLY, James Austin (R Ill.) March 8, 1843-Dec. 15, 1914; House 1895-99.

CONNOLLY, James Joseph (R Pa.) Sept. 24, 1881-Dec. 10, 1952; House 1921-35.

CONNOLLY, Maurice (D Iowa) March 13, 1877-May 28, 1921; House 1913-15.

CONNOR, Henry William (D N.C.) Aug. 5, 1793-Jan. 6, 1866; House 1821-41.

CONOVER, Simon Barclay (R Fla.) Sept. 23, 1840-April 19, 1908; Senate 1873-79.

CONOVER, William Sheldrick II (R Pa.) Aug. 27, 1928-__; House April 25, 1972-73.

CONRAD, Charles Mynn (W La.) Dec. 24, 1804-Feb. 11, 1878; Senate April 14, 1842-43; House 1849-August 17, 1850; Secy. of War Aug. 15, 1850-March 7, 1853.

CONRAD, Frederick (F Pa.) 1759-Aug. 3, 1827; House 1803-07.

CONRY, Joseph Aloysius (D Mass.) Sept. 12, 1868-June 22, 1943; House 1901-03.

CONRY, Michael Francis (D N.Y.) April 2, 1870-March 2, 1917; House 1909-March 2, 1917.

CONSTABLE, Albert (D Md.) June 3, 1805-Sept. 18, 1855; House 1845-47.

CONTE, Silvio Otto (R Mass.) Nov. 9, 1921-__; House 1959-__.

CONTEE, Benjamin (uncle of Alexander Contee Hanson and granduncle of Thomas Contee Worthington) (— Md.) 1755-Nov. 30, 1815; House 1789-91; Cont. Cong. 1787-88.

CONVERSE, George Leroy (D Ohio) June 4, 1827-March 30, 1897; House 1879-85.

CONWAY, Henry Wharton (cousin of Ambrose Hendley Sevier) (D Ark.) March 18, 1793-Nov. 9, 1827; House (Terr. Del.) 1823-Nov. 9, 1827.

CONWAY, Martin Franklin (R Kan.) Nov. 19, 1827-Feb. 15, 1882; House Jan. 29, 1861-63.

CONYERS, John Jr. (D Mich.) May 16, 1929-__; House 1965-__.

COOK, Burton Chauncey (R Ill.) May 11, 1819-Aug. 18, 1894; House 1865-Aug. 26, 1871.

COOK, Daniel Pope (— Ill.) 1794-Oct. 16, 1827; House 1819-27.

COOK, George Washington (R Colo.) Nov. 10, 1851-Dec. 18, 1916; House 1907-09.

COOK, Joel (R Pa.) March 20, 1842-Dec. 15, 1910; House Nov. 5, 1907-Dec. 15, 1910.

COOK, John Calhoun (ID Iowa) Dec. 26, 1846-June 7, 1920; House March 3, 1883 and Oct. 9, 1883-85.

COOK, John Parsons (W Iowa) Aug. 31, 1817-April 17, 1872; House 1853-55.

COOK, Marlow Webster (R Ky.) July 27, 1926-___; Senate Dec. 17, 1968-Dec. 27, 1974.

COOK, Orchard (— Mass.) March 24, 1763-Aug. 12, 1819; House 1805-11.

COOK, Philip (D Ga.) July 30, 1817-May 24, 1894; House 1873-83.

COOK, Robert Eugene (D Ohio) May 19, 1920-___; House 1959-63.

COOK, Samuel Andrew (R Wis.) Jan. 28, 1849-April 4, 1918; House 1895-97.

COOK, Samuel Ellis (D Ind.) Sept. 30, 1860-Feb. 22, 1946; House 1923-25.

COOK, Zadock (— Ga.) Feb. 18, 1769-Aug. 3, 1863; House Dec. 2, 1816-19.

COOKE, Bates (A-Mas. N.Y.) Dec. 23, 1787-May 31, 1841; House 1831-33.

COOKE, Edmund Francis (R N.Y.) April 13, 1885-May 13, 1967; House 1929-33.

COOKE, Edward Dean (R Ill.) Oct. 17, 1849-June 24, 1897; House 1895-June 24, 1897.

COOKE, Eleutheros (NR Ohio) Dec. 25, 1787-Dec. 27, 1864; House 1831-33.

COOKE, Thomas Burrage (D N.Y.) Nov. 21, 1778-Nov. 20, 1853; House 1811-13.

COOLEY, Harold Dunbar (D N.C.) July 26, 1897-Jan. 15, 1974; House July 7, 1934-67.

COOLIDGE, Frederick Spaulding (father of Marcus Allen Coolidge) (D Mass.) Dec. 7, 1841-June 8, 1906; House 1891-93.

COOLIDGE, Marcus Allen (son of Frederick Spaulding Coolidge) (D Mass.) Oct. 6, 1865-Jan. 23, 1947; Senate 1931-37.

COOMBS, Frank Leslie (R Calif.) Dec. 27, 1853-Oct. 5, 1934; House 1901-03.

COOMBS, William Jerome (D N.Y.) Dec. 24, 1833-Jan. 12, 1922; House 1891-95.

COON, Samuel Harrison (R Ore.) April 15, 1903-___; House 1953-57.

COONEY, James (D Mo.) July 28, 1848-Nov. 16, 1904; House 1897-1903.

COOPER, Allen Foster (R Pa.) June 16, 1862-April 20, 1917; House 1903-11.

COOPER, Charles Merian (D Fla.) Jan. 16, 1856-Nov. 14, 1923; House 1893-97.

COOPER, Edmund (brother of Henry Cooper) (C Tenn.) Sept. 11, 1821-July 21, 1911; House July 24, 1866-67.

COOPER, Edward (R W.Va.) Feb. 26, 1873-March 1, 1928; House 1915-19.

COOPER, George Byran (D Mich.) June 6, 1808-Aug. 29, 1866; House 1859-May 15, 1860.

COOPER, George William (D Ind.) May 21, 1851-Nov. 27, 1899; House 1889-95.

COOPER, Henry (brother of Edmund Cooper) (D Tenn.) Aug. 22, 1827-Feb. 4, 1884; Senate 1871-77.

COOPER, Henry Allen (R Wis.) Sept. 8, 1850-March 1, 1931; House 1893-1919, 1921-March 1, 1931.

COOPER, James (W Pa.) May 8, 1810-March 28, 1863; House 1839-43; Senate 1849-55.

COOPER, Jere (D Tenn.) July 20, 1893-Dec. 18, 1957; House 1929-Dec. 18, 1957.

COOPER, John Gordon (R Ohio) April 27, 1872-Jan. 7, 1955; House 1915-37.

COOPER, John Sherman (R Ky.) Aug. 23, 1901-___; Senate Nov. 6, 1946-49, Nov. 5, 1952-55, Nov. 7, 1956-73.

COOPER, Mark Anthony (cousin of Eugenius Aristides Nisbet) (D Ga.) April 20, 1800-March 17, 1885; House 1839-41, Jan. 3, 1842-June 26, 1843 (1839-41, 1842-March 3, 1843 States' Rights Whig; March 4-June 26, 1843 Democrat).

COOPER, Richard Matlack (— N.J.) Feb. 29, 1768-March 10, 1843; House 1829-33.

COOPER, Samuel Bronson (D Texas) May 30, 1850-Aug. 21, 1918; House 1893-1905, 1907-09.

COOPER, Thomas (F Del.) 1764-1829; House 1813-17.

COOPER, Thomas Buchecker (D Pa.) Dec. 29, 1823-April 4, 1862; House 1861-April 4, 1862.

COOPER, William (F N.Y.) Dec. 2, 1754-Dec. 22, 1809; House 1795-97, 1799-1801.

COOPER, William Craig (R Ohio) Dec. 18, 1832-Aug. 29, 1902; House 1885-91.

COOPER, William Raworth (D N.J.) Feb. 20, 1793-Sept. 22, 1856; House 1839-41.

COPELAND, Royal Samuel (D N.Y.), Nov. 7, 1868-June 17, 1938; Senate 1923-June 17, 1938.

COPLEY, Ira Clifton (nephew of Richard Henry Whiting) (R Pro. Ill.) Oct. 25, 1864-Nov. 1, 1947; House 1911-23.

CORBETT, Henry Winslow (UR Ore.) Feb. 18, 1827-March 31, 1903; Senate 1867-73.

CORBETT, Robert James (R Pa.) Aug. 25, 1905-April 25, 1971; House 1939-41, 1945-April 25, 1971.

CORDON, Guy (R Ore.) April 24, 1890-June 8, 1969; Senate March 4, 1944-55.

CÓRDOVA, Jorge Luis (New Prog. P.R.) April 20, 1907-___; House (Res. Comm.) 1969-73.

CORKER, Stephen Alfestus (D Ga.) May 7, 1830-Oct. 18, 1879; House Dec. 22, 1870-71.

CORLETT, William Wellington (R Wyo.) April 10, 1842-July 22, 1890; House (Terr. Del.) 1877-79.

CORLEY, Manuel Simeon (R S.C.) Feb. 10, 1823-Nov. 20, 1902; House July 25, 1868-69.

CORLISS, John Blaisdell (R Mich.) June 7, 1851-Dec. 24, 1929; House 1895-1903.

CORMAN, James C. (D Calif.) Oct. 20, 1920-___; House 1961-___.

CORNELL, Robert John (D Wis.) Dec. 16, 1919-___; House 1975-___.

CORNELL, Thomas (R N.Y.) Jan. 27, 1814-March 30, 1890; House 1867-69, 1881-83.

CORNING, Erastus (grandfather of Parker Corning) (D N.Y.) Dec. 14, 1794-April 9, 1872; House 1857-59, 1861-Oct. 5, 1863.

CORNING, Parker (grandson of Erastus Corning) (D N.Y.) Jan. 22, 1874-May 24, 1943; House 1923-37.

CORNISH, Johnston (D N.J.) June 13, 1858-June 26, 1920; House 1893-95.

CORWIN, Franklin (nephew of Moses Bledso Corwin and Thomas Corwin) (R Ill.) Jan. 12, 1818-June 15, 1879; House 1873-75.

CORWIN, Moses Bledso (brother of Thomas Corwin and uncle of Franklin Corwin) (W Ohio) Jan. 5, 1790-April 7, 1872; House 1849-51, 1853-55.

CORWIN, Thomas (brother of Moses Bledso Corwin and uncle of Franklin Corwin) (R Ohio) July 29, 1794-Dec. 18, 1865; House 1831-May 30, 1840, 1859-March 12, 1861 (1831-1840 Whig, 1859-61 Republican); Senate 1845-July 20, 1850 (W); Gov. 1840-42; Secy. of the Treasury 1850-53.

COSDEN, Jeremiah (— Md.) 1768-Dec. 5, 1824; House 1821-March 19, 1822.

COSGROVE, John (D Mo.) Sept. 12, 1839-Aug. 15, 1925; House 1883-85.

COSTELLO, John Martin (D Calif.) Jan. 15, 1903--Aug. 28, 1976; House 1935-45.

COSTELLO, Peter Edward (R Pa.) June 27, 1854-Oct. 23, 1935; House 1915-21.

COSTIGAN, Edward Prentiss (D Colo.) July 1, 1874-Jan. 17, 1939; Senate 1931-37.

COTHRAN, James Sproull (D S.C.) Aug. 8, 1830-Dec. 5, 1897; House 1887-91.

COTTER, William Ross (D Conn.) July 18, 1926-___; House 1971-___.

COTTMAN, Joseph Stewart (IW Md.) Aug. 16, 1803-Jan. 28, 1863; House 1851-53.

COTTON, Aylett Rains (R Iowa) Nov. 29, 1826-Oct. 30, 1912; House 1871-75.

COTTON, Norris (R N.H.) May 11, 1900-___; House 1947-Nov. 7, 1954; Senate Nov. 8, 1954-Dec. 31, 1974; Aug. 8-Sept. 18, 1975.

COTTRELL, James La Fayette (D Ala.) Aug. 25, 1808-Sept. 7, 1885; House Dec. 7, 1846-47.

COUDERT, Frederick René Jr. (R N.Y.) May 7, 1898-May 21, 1972; House 1947-59.

COUDREY, Harry Marcy (R Mo.) Feb. 28, 1867-July 5, 1930; House June 23, 1906-11.

COUGHLIN, Clarence Dennis (uncle of Robert Lawrence Coughlin) (R Pa.) July 27, 1883-Dec. 15, 1946; House 1921-23.

COUGHLIN, Robert Lawrence (nephew of Clarence Dennis Coughlin) (R Pa.) April 11, 1929-___; House 1969-___.

COULTER, Richard (D Pa.) March 1788-April 21, 1852; House 1827-31 (I), 1831-35 (D).

COURTNEY, William Wirt (D Tenn.) Sept. 7, 1889-April 6, 1961; House May 11, 1939-49.

COUSINS, Robert Gordon (R Iowa) Jan. 31, 1859-June 20, 1933; House 1893-1909.

COUZENS, James (R Mich.) Aug. 26, 1872-Oct. 22, 1936; Senate Nov. 29, 1922-Oct. 22, 1936.

COVERT, James Way (D N.Y.) Sept. 2, 1842-May 16, 1910; House 1877-81, 1889-95.

COVINGTON, George Washington (D Md.) Sept. 12, 1838-April 6, 1911; House 1881-85.

COVINGTON, James Harry (D Md.) May 3, 1870-Feb. 4, 1942; House 1909-Sept. 30, 1914.

COVINGTON, Leonard (D Md.) Oct. 30, 1768-Nov. 14, 1813; House 1805-07.

COVODE, John (R Pa.) March 18, 1808-Jan. 11, 1871; House 1855-63, 1867-69, Feb. 9, 1870-Jan. 11, 1871 (1855-57 Anti-Mason Whig; 1857-63, 1867-69, 1870-71 Republican).

COWAN, Edgar (R Pa.) Sept. 19, 1815-Aug. 29, 1885; Senate 1861-67.

COWAN, Jacob Pitzer (D Ohio) March 20, 1823-July 9, 1895; House 1875-77.

COWEN, Benjamin Sprague (W Ohio) Sept. 27, 1793-Sept. 27, 1860; House 1841-43.

COWEN, John Kissig (D Md.) Oct. 28, 1844-April 26, 1904; House 1895-97.

COWGER, William Owen (R Ky.) Jan. 1, 1922-Oct. 2, 1971; House 1967-71.

COWGILL, Calvin (R Ind.) Jan. 7, 1819-Feb. 10, 1903; House 1879-81.

COWHERD, William Strother (D Mo.) Sept. 1, 1860-June 20, 1915; House 1897-1905.

COWLES, Charles Holden (nephew of William Henry Harrison Cowles) (R N.C.) July 16, 1875-Oct. 2, 1957; House 1909-11.

COWLES, George Washington (R N.Y.) Dec. 6, 1823-Jan. 20, 1901; House 1869-71.

COWLES, Henry Booth (— N.Y.) March 18, 1798-May 17, 1873; House 1829-31.

COWLES, William Henry Harrison (uncle of Charles Holden Cowles) (D N.C.) April 22, 1840-Dec. 30, 1901; House 1885-93.

COX, Edward Eugene (D Ga.) April 3, 1880-Dec. 24, 1952; House 1925-Dec. 24, 1952.

COX, Isaac Newton (D N.Y.) Aug. 1, 1846-Sept. 28, 1916; House 1891-93.

COX, Jacob Dolson (R Ohio) Oct. 27, 1828-Aug. 4, 1900; House 1877-79; Gov. 1866-68; Secy. of the Interior 1869-70.

COX, James (D N.J.) June 14, 1753-Sept. 12, 1810; House 1809-Sept. 12, 1810.

COX, James Middleton (D Ohio) March 31, 1870-July 15, 1957; House 1909-Jan. 12, 1913; Gov. 1913-15, 1917-21.

COX, Leander Martin (AP Ky.) May 7, 1812-March 19, 1865; House 1853-55 (W), 1855-57 (AP).

COX, Nicholas Nichols (D Tenn.) Jan. 6, 1837-May 2, 1912; House 1891-1901.

COX, Samuel Sullivan (D Ohio/N.Y.) Sept. 30, 1824-Sept. 10, 1889; House (Ohio) 1857-65, (N.Y.) 1869-73, Nov. 4, 1873-May 20, 1885, Nov. 2, 1886-Sept. 10, 1889; Speaker pro tempore 1876.

COX, William Elijah (D Ind.) Sept. 6, 1861-March 11, 1942; House 1907-19.

COX, William Ruffin (D N.C.) March 11, 1831-Dec. 26, 1919; House 1881-87.

COXE, William Jr. (F N.J.) May 3, 1762-Feb. 25, 1831; House 1813-15.

COYLE, William Radford (R Pa.) July 10, 1878-Jan. 30, 1962; House 1925-27, 1929-33.

CRABB, George Whitfield (W Ala.) Feb. 22, 1804-Aug. 15, 1846; House Sept. 4, 1838-41.

CRABB, Jeremiah (D Md.) 1760-1800; House 1795-96.

CRADDOCK, John Durrett (R Ky.) Oct. 26, 1881-May 20, 1942; House 1929-31.

CRADLEBAUGH, John (— Nev.) Feb. 22, 1819-Feb. 22, 1872; House (Terr. Del.) Dec. 2, 1861-1863.

CRAFTS, Samuel Chandler (— Vt.) Oct. 6, 1768-Nov. 19, 1853; House 1817-25; Senate April 23, 1842-43; Gov. 1828-31.

CRAGIN, Aaron Harrison (AP N.H.) Feb. 3, 1821-May 10, 1898; House 1855-59 (1855-57 American Party, 1857-59 Republican); Senate 1865-77 (AP).

CRAGO, Thomas Spencer (R Pa.) Aug. 8, 1866-Sept. 12, 1925; House 1911-13, 1915-21, Sept. 20, 1921-23.

CRAIG, Alexander Kerr (D Pa.) Feb. 21, 1828-July 29, 1892; House Feb. 6, 1892-July 29, 1892.

CRAIG, George Henry (R Ala.) Dec. 25, 1845-Jan. 26, 1923; House Jan. 9-March 3, 1885.

CRAIG, Hector (JD N.Y.) 1775-Jan. 31, 1842; House 1823-25, 1829-July 12, 1830.

CRAIG, James (D Mo.) Feb. 28, 1818-Oct. 22, 1888; House 1857-61.

CRAIG, Robert (D Va.) 1792-Nov. 25, 1852; House 1829-33, 1835-41.

CRAIG, Samuel Alfred (R Pa.) Nov. 19, 1839-March 17, 1920; House 1889-91.

CRAIG, William Benjamin (D Ala.) Nov. 2, 1877-Nov. 27, 1925; House 1907-11.

CRAIGE, Francis Burton (D N.C.) March 13, 1811-Dec. 30, 1875; House 1853-61.

CRAIK, William (— Md.) Oct. 31, 1761-prior to 1814; House Dec. 5, 1796-1801.

CRAIL, Joe (R Calif.) Dec. 25, 1877-March 2, 1938; House 1927-33.

CRAIN, William Henry (D Texas) Nov. 25, 1848-Feb. 10, 1896; House 1885-Feb. 10, 1896.

CRALEY, Nathaniel Nieman Jr. (D Pa.) Nov. 17, 1927-___; House 1965-67.

CRAMER, John (D N.Y.) May 17, 1779-June 1, 1870; House 1833-37.

CRAMER, William Cato (R Fla.) Aug. 4, 1922-___; House 1955-71.

CRAMTON, Louis Convers (R Mich.) Dec. 2, 1875-June 23, 1966; House 1913-31.

CRANE, Joseph Halsey (W Ohio) Aug. 31, 1782-Nov. 13, 1851; House 1829-37.

CRANE, Philip M. (R Ill.) Nov. 3, 1930-___; House Nov. 25, 1969-___.

CRANE, Winthrop Murray (R Mass.) April 23, 1853-Oct. 2, 1920; Senate Oct. 12, 1904-13; Gov. 1900-03.

CRANFORD, John Walter (D Texas) 1862-March 3, 1899; House 1897-March 3, 1899.

CRANSTON, Alan (D Calif.) June 19, 1914-___; Senate 1969-___.

CRANSTON, Henry Young (brother of Robert Bennie Cranston) (W R.I.) Oct. 9, 1789-Feb. 12, 1864; House 1843-47.

CRANSTON, Robert Bennie (brother of Harry Young Cranston) (L&OW R.I.) Jan. 14, 1791-Jan. 27, 1873; House 1837-43 (W), 1847-49 (L&OW).

CRAPO, William Wallace (R Mass.) May 16, 1830-Feb. 28, 1926; House Nov. 2, 1875-83.

CRARY, Isaac Edwin (D Mich.) Oct. 2, 1804-May 8, 1854; House Jan. 26, 1837-41.

CRAVENS, James Addison (second cousin of James Harrison Cravens) (D Ind.) Nov. 4, 1818-June 20, 1893; House 1861-65.

CRAVENS, James Harrison (second cousin of James Addison Cravens) (W Ind.) Aug. 2, 1802-Dec. 4, 1876; House 1841-43.

CRAVENS, Jordan Edgar (cousin of William Ben Cravens) (D Ark.) Nov. 7, 1830-April 8, 1914; House 1877-83.

CRAVENS, William Ben (father of William Fadjo Cravens and cousin of Jordan Edgar Cravens) (D Ark.) Jan. 17, 1872-Jan. 13, 1939; House 1907-13, 1933-Jan. 13, 1939.

CRAVENS, William Fadjo (son of William Ben Cravens) (D Ark.) Feb. 15, 1889-___; House Sept. 12, 1939-49.

CRAWFORD, Coe Isaac (R S.D.) Jan. 14, 1858-April 25, 1944; Senate 1909-15; Gov. 1907-09.

CRAWFORD, Fred Lewis (R Mich.) May 5, 1888-April 13, 1957; House 1935-53.

CRAWFORD, George Washington (W Ga.) Dec. 22, 1798-July 22, 1872; House Jan. 7-March 3, 1843; Gov. 1843-47; Secy. of War 1849-50.

CRAWFORD, Joel (D Ga.) June 15, 1783-April 5, 1858; House 1817-21.

CRAWFORD, Martin Jenkins (D Ga.) March 17, 1820-July 23, 1883; House 1855-Jan. 23, 1861.

CRAWFORD, Thomas Hartley (JD Pa.) Nov. 14, 1786-Jan. 27, 1863; House 1829-33.

CRAWFORD, William (D Pa.) 1760-Oct. 23, 1823; House 1809-17.

CRAWFORD, William Harris (— Ga.) Feb. 24, 1772-Sept. 15, 1834; Senate Nov. 7, 1807-March 23, 1813; President pro tempore 1812; Secy. of War 1815-16; Secy. of the Treasury 1816-25.

CRAWFORD, William Thomas (D N.C.) June 1, 1856-Nov. 16, 1913; House 1891-95, 1899-May 10, 1900, 1907-09.

CREAGER, Charles Edward (R Okla.) April 28, 1873-Jan. 11, 1964; House 1909-11.

CREAL, Edward Wester (D Ky.) Nov. 20, 1883-Oct. 13, 1943; House Nov. 5, 1935-Oct. 13, 1943.

CREAMER, Thomas James (D N.Y.) May 26, 1843-Aug. 4, 1914; House 1873-75, 1901-03.

CREBS, John Montgomery (D Ill.) April 9, 1830-June 26, 1890; House 1869-73.

CREELY, John Vaudain (R Pa.) Nov. 14, 1839-Sept. 28, 1900; House 1871-73.

CREIGHTON, William Jr. (D Ohio) Oct. 29, 1778-Oct. 8, 1851; House May 4, 1813-17, 1827-28, 1829-33.

CRESWELL, John Andrew Jackson (R Md.) Nov. 18, 1828-Dec. 23, 1891; House 1863-65; Senate March 9, 1865-67; Postmaster General 1869-74.

CRETELLA, Albert William (R Conn.) April 22, 1897-__; House 1953-59.

CRIPPA, Edward David (R Wyo.) April 8, 1899-Oct. 20, 1960; Senate June 24-Nov. 28, 1954.

CRISFIELD, John Woodland (UR Md.) Nov. 8, 1806-Jan. 12, 1897; House 1847-49 (W), 1861-63 (UR).

CRISP, Charles Frederick (father of Charles Robert Crisp) (D Ga.) Jan. 29, 1845-Oct. 23, 1896; House 1883-Oct. 23, 1896; Speaker 1891-95.

CRISP, Charles Robert (son of Charles Frederick Crisp) (D Ga.) Oct. 19, 1870-Feb. 7, 1937; House Dec. 19, 1896-97, 1913-Oct. 7, 1932.

CRIST, Henry (— Ky.) Oct. 20, 1764-Aug. 11, 1844; House 1809-11.

CRITCHER, John (C Va.) March 11, 1820-Sept. 27, 1901; House 1871-73.

CRITTENDEN, John Jordan (uncle of Thomas Theodore Crittenden) (U Ky.) Sept. 10, 1787-July 26, 1863; Senate 1817-19, 1835-41, March 31, 1842-June 12, 1848, 1855-61, House 1861-63; Gov. 1848-50; Attorney General March 5-Sept. 13, 1841 and 1850-53.

CRITTENDEN, Thomas Theodore (nephew of John Jordan Crittenden) (D Mo.) Jan. 1, 1832-May 29, 1909; House 1873-75, 1877-79; Gov. 1881-85.

CROCHERON, Henry (brother of Jacob Crocheron) (D N.Y.) Dec. 26, 1772-Nov. 8, 1819; House 1815-17.

CROCHERON, Jacob (brother of Henry Crocheron) (JD N.Y.) Aug. 23, 1774-Dec. 27, 1849; House 1829-31.

CROCKER, Alva (R Mass.) Oct. 14, 1801-Dec. 26, 1874; House Jan. 2, 1872-Dec. 26, 1874.

CROCKER, Samuel Leonard (W Mass.) March 31, 1804-Feb. 10, 1883; House 1853-55.

CROCKETT, David (father of John Wesley Crockett) (W Tenn.) Aug. 17, 1786-March 6, 1836; House 1827-31, 1833-35 (1827-31 Democrat, 1833-35 Whig).

CROCKETT, John Wesley (W Tenn.) July 10, 1807-Nov. 24, 1852; House 1837-41.

CROFT, George William (father of Theodore Gaillard Croft) (D S.C.) Dec. 20, 1846-March 10, 1904; House 1903-March 10, 1904.

CROFT, Theodore Gaillard (son of George William Croft) (D S.C.) Nov. 26, 1874-March 23, 1920; House May 17, 1904-05.

CROLL, William Martin (D Pa.) April 9, 1866-Oct. 21, 1929; House 1923-25.

CROMER, George Washington (R Ind.) May 13, 1856-Nov. 8, 1936; House 1899-1907.

CRONIN, Paul William (R Mass.) March 14, 1938-__; House 1973-75.

CROOK, Thurman Charles (D Ind.) July 18, 1891-__; House 1949-51.

CROOKE, Philip Schuyler (R N.Y.) March 2, 1810-March 17, 1881; House 1873-75.

CROSBY, Charles Noel (D Pa.) Sept. 29, 1876-Jan. 26, 1951; House 1933-39.

CROSBY, John Crawford (D Mass.) June 15, 1859-Oct. 14, 1943; House 1891-93.

CROSS, Edward (D Ark.) Nov. 11, 1798-April 6, 1887; House 1839-45.

CROSS, Oliver Harian (D Texas) July 13, 1868-April 24, 1960; House 1929-37.

CROSSER, Robert (D Ohio) June 7, 1874-June 3, 1957; House 1913-19, 1923-55.

CROSSLAND, Edward (D Ky.) June 30, 1827-Sept. 11, 1881; House 1871-75.

CROUCH, Edward (D Pa.) Nov. 9, 1764-Feb. 2, 1827; House Oct. 12, 1813-15.

CROUNSE, Lorenzo (R Neb.) Jan. 27, 1834-May 13, 1909; House 1873-77; Gov. 1893-95.

CROUSE, George Washington (R Ohio) Nov. 23, 1832-Jan. 5, 1912; House 1887-89.

CROW, Charles Augustus (R Mo.) March 31, 1873-March 20, 1938; House 1909-11.

CROW, William Evans (father of William J. Crow) (R Pa.) March 10, 1870-Aug. 2, 1922; Senate Oct. 24, 1921-Aug. 2, 1922.

CROW, William Josiah (son of William Evans Crow) (R Pa.) Jan. 22, 1902-Oct. 13, 1974; House 1947-49.

CROWE, Eugene Burgess (D Ind.) Jan. 5, 1878-May 12, 1970; House 1931-41.

CROWELL, John (— Ala.) Sept. 18, 1780-June 25, 1846; House (Terr. Del.) Jan. 29, 1818-19; (Rep.) Dec. 14, 1819-21.

CROWELL, John (W Ohio) Sept. 15, 1801-March 8, 1883; House 1847-51.

CROWLEY, Joseph Burns (D Ohio) July 19, 1858-June 25, 1931; House 1899-1905.

CROWLEY, Miles (D Texas) Feb. 22, 1859-Sept. 22, 1921; House 1895-97.

CROWLEY, Richard (R N.Y.) Dec. 14, 1836-July 22, 1908; House 1879-83.

CROWNINSHIELD Benjamin Williams (brother of Jacob Crowninshield) (D Mass.) Dec. 27, 1772-Feb. 3, 1851; House 1823-31; Secy. of the Navy 1814-18.

CROWNINSHIELD, Jacob (brother of Benjamin Williams Crowninshield) (D Mass.) March 31, 1770-April 15, 1808; House 1803-April 15, 1808.

CROWTHER, Frank (R N.Y.) July 10, 1870-July 20, 1955; House 1919-43.

CROWTHER, George Calhoun (R Mo.) Jan. 26, 1849-March 18, 1914; House 1895-97.

CROXTON, Thomas (D Va.) March 8, 1822-July 3, 1903; House 1885-87.

CROZIER, John Hervey (W Tenn.) Feb. 10, 1812-Oct. 25, 1889; House 1845-49.

CROZIER, Robert (R Kan.) Oct. 13, 1827-Oct. 2, 1895; House Nov. 24, 1873-Feb. 12, 1874.

CRUDUP, Josiah (W N.C.) Jan. 13, 1791-May 20, 1872; House 1821-23.

CRUGER, Daniel (D N.Y.) Dec. 22, 1780-July 12, 1843; House 1817-19.

CRUMP, Edward Hull (D Tenn.) Oct. 2, 1874-Oct. 16, 1954; House 1931-35.

CRUMP, George William (JD Va.) Sept. 26, 1786-Oct. 1, 1848; House Jan. 21, 1826-27.

CRUMP, Rousseau Owen (R Mich.) May 20, 1843-May 1, 1901; House 1895-May 1, 1901.

CRUMPACKER, Edgar Dean (father of Maurice Edgar Crumpacker and cousin of Shepard J. Crumpacker Jr.) (R Ind.) May 27, 1851-May 19, 1920; House 1897-1913.

CRUMPACKER, Maurice Edgar (son of Edgar Dean Crumpacker and cousin of Shepard J. Crumpacker Jr.) (R Ore.) Dec. 19, 1886-July 24, 1927; House 1925-July 24, 1927.

CRUMPACKER, Shepard Jr. (cousin of Edgar Dean Crumpacker and Maurice Edgar Crumpacker) (R Ind.) Feb. 13, 1917-__; House 1951-57.

CRUTCHFIELD, William (R Tenn.) Nov. 16, 1824-Jan. 24, 1890; House 1873-75.

CULBERSON, Charles Allen (son of David Browning Culberson) (D Texas) June 10, 1855-March 19, 1925; Senate 1899-1923; Gov. 1895-99.

CULBERSON, David Browning (father of Charles Allen Culberson) (D Texas) Sept. 29, 1830-May 7, 1900; House 1875-97.

CULBERTSON, William Constantine (R Pa.) Nov. 25, 1825-May 24, 1906; House 1889-91.

CULBERTSON, William Wirt (R Ky.) Sept. 22, 1835-Oct. 31, 1911; House 1883-85.

CULBRETH, Thomas (D Md.) April 13, 1786-April 16, 1843; House 1817-21.

CULKIN, Francis Dugan (R N.Y.) Nov. 10, 1874-Aug. 4, 1943; House Nov. 6, 1928-Aug. 4, 1943.

CULLEN, Elisha Dickerson (AP Del.) April 23, 1799-Feb. 8, 1862; House 1855-57.

CULLEN, Thomas Henry (D N.Y.) March 29, 1868-March 1, 1944; House 1919-March 1, 1944.

CULLEN, William (R Ill.) March 4, 1826-Jan. 17, 1914; House 1881-85.

CULLOM, Alvan (brother of William Cullom and uncle of Shelby Moore Cullom) (W Tenn.) June 4, 1810-Dec. 6, 1896; House 1851-55.

CULLOM, Shelby Moore (nephew of Alvan Cullom and William Cullom) (R Ill.) Nov. 22, 1829-Jan. 28, 1914; House 1865-71; Senate 1883-1913; Gov. Jan. 8, 1877-Feb. 5, 1883.

CULLOM, William (brother of Alvan Cullom and uncle of Shelby Moore Cullom) (W Tenn.) June 4, 1810-Dec. 6, 1896; House 1851-55.

CULLOP, William Allen (D Ind.) March 28, 1853-Oct. 9, 1927; House 1909-17.

CULPEPPER, John (F N.C.) 1761-Jan. 1841; House 1807-Jan. 2, 1808, Feb. 23, 1808-09, 1813-17, 1819-21, 1823-25, 1827-29.

CULVER, Charles Vernon (R Pa.) Sept. 6, 1830-Jan. 10, 1909; House 1865-67.

CULVER, Erastus Dean (W N.Y.) March 15, 1803-Oct. 13, 1889; House 1845-47.

CULVER, John Chester (D Iowa) Aug. 8, 1932-__; House 1965-75; Senate 1975-__.

CUMBACK, William (R Ind.) March 24, 1829-July 31, 1905; House 1855-57.

CUMMING, Thomas William (D N.Y.) 1814 or 1815-Oct. 13, 1855; House 1853-55.

CUMMINGS, Amos Jay (D N.Y.) May 15, 1841-May 2, 1902; House 1887-89, Nov. 5, 1889-Nov. 21, 1894, Nov. 5, 1895-May 2, 1902.

CUMMINGS, Fred Nelson (D Colo.) Sept. 18, 1864-Nov. 10, 1952; House 1933-41.

CUMMINGS, Henry Johnson Brodhead (R Iowa) May 21, 1831-April 16, 1909; House 1877-79.

CUMMINGS, Herbert Wesley (D Pa.) July 13, 1873-March 4, 1956; House 1923-25.

CUMMINS, Albert Baird (R Iowa) Feb. 15, 1850-July 30, 1926; Senate Nov. 24, 1908-July 30, 1926; President pro tempore 1919-25; Gov. 1902-Nov. 24, 1908.

CUMMINS, John D. (D Ohio) 1791-Sept. 11, 1849; House 1845-49.

CUNNINGHAM, Francis Alanson (D Ohio) Nov. 9, 1804-Aug. 16, 1864; House 1845-47.

CUNNINGHAM, Glenn Clarence (R Neb.) Sept. 10, 1912-__; House 1957-71.

CUNNINGHAM, Paul Harvey (R Iowa) June 15, 1890-July 16, 1961; House 1941-59.

CURLEY, Edward Walter (D N.Y.) May 23, 1873-Jan. 6, 1940; House Nov. 5, 1935-Jan. 6, 1940.

CURLEY, James Michael (D Mass.) Nov. 20, 1874-Nov. 12, 1958; House 1911-Feb. 4, 1914, 1943-47, Gov. 1935-37.

CURLIN, William Prather Jr. (D Ky.) Nov. 30, 1933-__; House Dec. 4, 1971-73.

CURRIE, Gilbert Archibald (R Mich.) Sept. 19, 1882-June 5, 1960; House 1917-21.

CURRIER, Frank Dunklee (R N.H.) Oct. 30, 1853-Nov. 25, 1921; House 1901-13.

CURRY, Charles Forrest (father of Charles Forrest Curry Jr.) (R Calif.) March 14, 1858-Oct. 10, 1930; House 1913-Oct. 10, 1930.

CURRY, Charles Forrest Jr. (son of Charles Forrest Curry) (R Calif.) Aug. 13, 1893-__; House 1931-33.

CURRY, George (R N.M.) April 3, 1863-Nov. 27, 1947; House Jan. 8, 1912-13; Gov. (Terr. of N.M.) 1907-11.

CURRY, Jabez Lamar Monroe (SRD Ala.) June 5, 1825-Feb. 12, 1903; House 1857-Jan. 21, 1861.

CURTIN, Andrew Gregg (D Pa.) April 22, 1817-Oct. 7, 1894; House 1881-87; Gov. (R) 1861-67.

CURTIN, Willard Sevier (R Pa.) Nov. 18, 1905-__; House 1957-67.

CURTIS, Carl Thomas (R Neb.) March 15, 1905-__; House 1939-Dec. 31, 1954; Senate Jan. 1, 1955-__.

CURTIS, Carlton Brandaga (R Pa.) Dec. 17, 1811-March 17, 1883; House 1851-55 (D), 1873-75 (R).

CURTIS, Charles (R Kan.) Jan. 25, 1860-Feb. 8, 1936; House 1893-Jan. 28, 1907; Senate Jan. 29, 1907-13, 1915-29; President pro tempore 1911; Vice President 1929-33.

CURTIS, Edward (W N.Y.) Oct. 25, 1801-Aug. 2, 1856; House 1837-41.

CURTIS, George Martin (R Iowa) April 1, 1844-Feb. 9, 1921; House 1895-99.

CURTIS, Laurence (R Mass.) Sept. 3, 1893-__; House 1953-63.

CURTIS, Newton Martin (R N.Y.) May 21, 1835-Jan. 8, 1910; House Nov. 3, 1891-97.

CURTIS, Samuel Ryan (R Iowa) Feb. 3, 1805-Dec. 25, 1866; House 1857-Aug. 4, 1861.

CURTIS, Thomas Bradford (R Mo.) May 14, 1911-__; House 1951-69.

CUSACK, Thomas (D Ill.) Oct. 5, 1858-Nov. 19, 1926; House 1899-1901.

CUSHING, Caleb (W Mass.) Jan. 17, 1800-Jan. 2, 1879; House 1835-43; Attorney General 1853-57.

CUSHMAN, Francis Wellington (R Wash.) May 8, 1867-July 6, 1909; House 1899-July 6, 1909.

CUSHMAN, John Paine (— N.Y.) March 8, 1784-Sept. 16, 1848; House 1817-19.

CUSHMAN, Joshua (D Mass./Maine) April 11, 1761-Jan. 27, 1834; House 1819-21 (Mass.), 1821-25 (Maine).

CUSHMAN, Samuel (D N.H.) June 8, 1783-May 20, 1851; House 1835-39.

CUTCHEON, Byron M. (R Mich.) May 11, 1836-April 12, 1908; House 1883-91.

CUTHBERT, Alfred (brother of John Alfred Cuthbert) (D Ga.) Dec. 23, 1785-July 9, 1856; House Dec. 13, 1813-Nov. 9, 1816, 1821-27; Senate Jan. 12, 1835-43.

CUTHBERT, John Alfred (brother of Alfred Cuthbert) (D Ga.) June 3, 1788-Sept. 22, 1881; House 1819-21.

CUTLER, Augustus William (D N.J.) Oct. 22, 1827-Jan. 1, 1897; House 1875-79.

CUTLER, Manasseh (F Mass.) May 13, 1742-July 28, 1823; House 1801-05.

CUTLER, William Parker (R Ohio) July 12, 1812-April 11, 1889; House 1861-63.

CUTTING, Bronson Murray (R N.M.) June 23, 1888-May 6, 1935; Senate Dec. 29, 1927-Dec. 6, 1928, 1929-May 6, 1935.

CUTTING, Francis Brockholst (D N.Y.) Aug. 6, 1804-June 26, 1870; House 1853-55.

CUTTING, John Tyler (R Calif.) Sept. 7, 1844-Nov. 24, 1911; House 1891-93.

CUTTS, Charles (F N.H.) Jan. 31, 1769-Jan. 25, 1846; Senate June 21, 1810-March 3, 1813, April 2-June 10, 1813.

CUTTS, Marsena Edgar (R Iowa) May 22, 1833-Sept. 1, 1883; House 1881-Sept. 1, 1883.

CUTTS, Richard (D Mass.) June 28, 1771-April 7, 1845; House 1801-13.

D

DADDARIO, Emilio Quincy (D Conn.) Sept. 24, 1918-__; House 1959-71.

DAGGETT, David (F Conn.) Dec. 31, 1764-April 12, 1851; Senate May 13, 1813-19.

DAGGETT, Rollin Mallory (R Nev.) Feb. 22, 1831-Nov. 12, 1901; House 1879-81.

DAGUE, Paul Bartram (R Pa.) May 19, 1898-Dec. 2, 1974; House 1947-67.

DAHLE, Herman Bjorn (R Wis.) March 30, 1855-April 25, 1920; House 1899-1903.

DAILY, Samuel Gordon (R Neb.) 1823-Aug. 15, 1866; House (Terr. Del.) May 18, 1860-65.

DALE, Harry Howard (D N.Y.) Dec. 3, 1868-Nov. 17, 1935; House 1913-Jan. 6, 1919.

DALE, Porter Hinman (R Vt.) March 1, 1867-Oct. 6, 1933; House 1915-Aug. 11, 1923; Senate Nov. 7, 1923-Oct. 6, 1933.

DALE, Thomas Henry (R Pa.) June 12, 1846-Aug. 21, 1912; House 1905-07.

D'ALESANDRO, Thomas Jr. (D Md.) Aug. 1, 1903-__; House 1939-May 16, 1947.

DALLAS, George Mifflin (D Pa.) July 10, 1792-Dec. 31, 1864; Senate Dec. 13, 1831-33; Vice President 1845-49.

DALLINGER, Frederick William (R Mass.) Oct. 2, 1871-Sept. 5, 1955; House 1915-25, Nov. 2, 1926-Oct. 1, 1932.

DALTON, Tristram (— Mass.) May 28, 1738-May 30, 1817; Senate 1789-91.

DALY, John Burrwood (D Pa.) Feb. 13, 1872-March 12, 1939; House 1935-March 12, 1939.

DALY, William Davis (D N.J.) June 4, 1851-July 31, 1900; House 1899-July 31, 1900.

DALZELL, John (R Pa.) April 19, 1845-Oct. 2, 1927; House 1887-1913.

D'AMOURS, Norman Edward (D N.H.) Oct. 14, 1937-__; House 1975-__.

DAMRELL, William Shapleigh (R Mass.) Nov. 29, 1809-May 17, 1860; House 1855-57 (AP), 1857-59 (R).

DANA, Amasa (D N.Y.) Oct. 19, 1792-Dec. 24, 1867; House 1839-41, 1843-45.

DANA, Judah (D Maine) April 25, 1772-Dec. 27, 1845; Senate Dec. 7, 1836-37.

DANA, Samuel (D Mass.) June 26, 1767-Nov. 20, 1835; House Sept. 22, 1814-15.

DANA, Samuel Whittlesey (F Conn.) Feb. 13, 1760-July 21, 1830; House Jan. 3, 1797-May 10, 1810; Senate May 10, 1810-21.

DANAHER, John Anthony (R Conn.) Jan. 9, 1899-__; Senate 1939-45.

DANE, Joseph (F Maine) Oct. 25, 1778-May 1, 1858; House Nov. 6, 1820-23.

DANFORD, Lorenzo (R Ohio) Oct. 18, 1829-June 19, 1899; House 1873-79, 1895-June 19, 1899.

DANFORTH, Henry Gold (R N.Y.) June 14, 1854-April 8, 1918; House 1911-17.

DANIEL, Charles Ezra (D S.C.) Nov. 11, 1895-Sept. 13, 1964; Senate Sept. 6-Dec. 23, 1954.

DANIEL, Henry (JD Ky.) March 15, 1786-Oct. 5, 1873; House 1827-33.

DANIEL, John Reeves Jones (D N.C.) Jan. 13, 1802-June 22, 1868; House 1841-53.

DANIEL, John Warwick (D Va.) Sept. 5, 1842-June 29, 1910; House 1885-87; Senate 1887-June 29, 1910.

DANIEL, Price Marion (D Texas) Oct. 10, 1910-__; Senate 1953-Jan. 14, 1957; Gov. Jan. 15, 1957-Jan. 15, 1963.

DANIEL, Robert Williams Jr. (R Va.) March 17, 1936-__; House 1973-__.

DANIEL, W. C. (Dan) (D Va.) May 12, 1914-__; House 1969-__.

DANIELL, Warren Fisher (D N.H.) June 26, 1826-July 30, 1913; House 1891-93.

DANIELS, Charles (R N.Y.) March 24, 1825-Dec. 20, 1897; House 1893-97.

DANIELS, Dominick V. (D N.J.) Oct. 18, 1908-__; House 1959-__.

DANIELS, Milton John (R Calif.) April 18, 1838-Dec. 1, 1914; House 1903-05.

DANIELSON, George Elmore (D Calif.) Feb. 20, 1915-__; House 1971-__.

DANNER, Joel Buchanan (D Pa.) 1804-July 29, 1885; House Dec. 2, 1850-51.

DARBY, Ezra (D N.J.) June 7, 1768-Jan. 27, 1808; House 1805-Jan. 27, 1808.

DARBY, Harry (R Kan.) Jan. 23, 1895-__; Senate Dec. 2, 1949-Nov. 28, 1950.

DARBY, John Fletcher (W Mo.) Dec. 10, 1803-May 11, 1882; House 1851-53.

DARDEN, Colgate Whitehead, Jr. (D Va.) Feb. 11, 1897-__; House 1933-37, 1939-March 1, 1941; Gov. 1942-46.

DARGAN, Edmund Strother (D Ala.) April 15, 1805-Nov. 22, 1879; House 1845-47.

DARGAN, George William (great-grandson of Lemuel Benton) (D S.C.) May 11, 1841-June 29, 1898; House 1883-91.

DARLING, Mason Cook (D Wis.) May 18, 1801-March 12, 1866; House June 9, 1848-49.

DARLING, William Augustus (R N.Y.) Dec. 27, 1817-May 26, 1895; House 1865-67.

DARLINGTON, Edward (cousin of Isaac Darlington and William Darlington) (A-Mas. Pa.) Sept. 17, 1795-Nov. 21, 1884; House 1833-39 (1833-37 Whig, 1837-39 Anti-Mason).

DARLINGTON, Isaac (cousin of Edward Darlington and William Darlington) (F Pa.) Dec. 13, 1781-April 27, 1839; House 1817-19.

DARLINGTON, Smedley (second cousin of Edward Darlington, Isaac Darlington and William Darlington) (R Pa.) Dec. 24, 1827-June 24, 1899; House 1887-91.

DARLINGTON, William (cousin of Edward Darlington and Isaac Darlington) (D Pa.) April 28, 1782-April 23, 1863; House 1815-17; 1819-23.

DARRAGH, Archibald Bard (R Mich.) Dec. 23, 1840-Feb. 21, 1927; House 1901-09.

DARRAGH, Cornelius (W Pa.) 1809-Dec. 22, 1854; House March 26, 1844-47.

DARRALL, Chester Bidwell (R La.) June 24, 1842-Jan. 1, 1908; House 1869-Feb. 20, 1878, 1881-83.

DARROW, George Potter (R Pa.) Feb. 4, 1859-June 7, 1943; House 1915-37, 1939-41.

DAUGHERTY, James Alexander (D Mo.) Aug. 30, 1847-Jan. 26, 1920; House 1911-13.

DAUGHTON, Ralph Hunter (D Va.) Sept. 23, 1885-Dec. 22, 1958; House Nov. 7, 1944-47.

DAVEE, Thomas (D Maine) Dec. 9, 1797-Dec. 9, 1841; House 1837-41.

DAVENPORT, Franklin (— N.J.) Sept., 1755-July 27, 1832; Senate Dec. 5, 1798-99; House 1799-1801.

DAVENPORT, Frederick Morgan (R N.Y.) Aug. 27, 1866-Dec. 26, 1956; House 1925-33.

DAVENPORT, Harry James (D Pa.) Aug. 28, 1902-__; House 1949-51.

DAVENPORT, Ira (R N.Y.) June 28, 1841-Oct. 6, 1904; House 1885-89.

DAVENPORT, James (brother of John Davenport of Connecticut) (—Conn.) Oct. 12, 1758-Aug. 3, 1797; House Dec. 5, 1796-Aug. 3, 1797.

DAVENPORT, James Sanford (D Okla.) Sept. 21, 1864-Jan. 3, 1940; House Nov. 16, 1907-09, 1911-17.

DAVENPORT, John (brother of James Davenport) (F Conn.) Jan. 16, 1752-Nov. 28, 1830; House 1799-1817.

DAVENPORT, John (— Ohio) Jan. 9, 1788-July 18, 1855; House 1827-29.

DAVENPORT, Samuel Arza (R Pa.) Jan. 15, 1834-Aug. 1, 1911; House 1897-1901.

DAVENPORT, Stanley Woodward (D Pa.) July 21, 1861-Sept. 26, 1921; House 1899-1901.

DAVENPORT, Thomas (F Va.) ?-Nov. 18, 1838; House 1825-35.

DAVEY, Martin Luther (D Ohio) July 25, 1884-March 31, 1946; House Nov. 5, 1918-21, 1923-29; Gov. 1935-39.

DAVEY, Robert Charles (D La.) Oct. 22, 1853-Dec. 26, 1908; House 1893-95, 1897-Dec. 26, 1908.

DAVIDSON, Alexander Caldwell (D Ala.) Dec. 26, 1826-Nov. 6, 1897; House 1885-89.

DAVIDSON, Irwin Delmore (D/L N.Y.) Jan. 2, 1906-__; House 1955-Dec. 31, 1956.

DAVIDSON, James Henry (R Wis.) June 18, 1858-Aug. 6, 1918; House 1897-1913, 1917-Aug. 6, 1918.

DAVIDSON, Robert Hamilton McWhorta (D Fla.) Sept. 23, 1832-Jan. 18, 1908; House 1877-91.

DAVIDSON, Thomas Green (D La.) Aug. 3, 1805-Sept. 11, 1883; House 1855-61.

DAVIDSON, William (F N.C.) Sept. 12, 1778-Sept. 16, 1857; House Dec. 2, 1818-21.

DAVIES, Edward (W Pa.) Nov. 1779-May 18, 1853; House 1837-41.

DAVIES, John Clay (D N.Y.) May 1, 1920-__; House 1949-51.

DAVILA, Felix Cordova (U P.R.), Nov. 20, 1878-Dec. 3, 1938; House (Res Comm.) Aug. 7, 1917-April 11, 1932.

DAVIS, Alexander Mathews (— Va.) Jan. 17, 1833-Sept. 25, 1889; House 1873-March 5, 1874.

DAVIS, Amos (brother of Garrett Davis) (W Ky.) Aug. 15, 1794-June 11, 1835; House 1833-35.

DAVIS, Charles Russell (R Minn.) Sept. 17, 1849-July 29, 1930; House 1903-25.

DAVIS, Clifford (D Tenn.) Nov. 18, 1897-June 8, 1970; House Feb. 15, 1940-65.

DAVIS, Cushman Kellogg (R Minn.) June 16, 1838-Nov. 27, 1900; Senate 1887-Nov. 27, 1900; Gov. 1874-76.

DAVIS, David (cousin of Henry Winter Davis) (I/D Ill.) March 9, 1815-June 26, 1886; Senate 1877-83; President pro tempore 1881-83; Asso. Justice of Supreme Court 1862-77.

DAVIS, Ewin Lamar (D Tenn.) Feb. 5, 1876-Oct. 23, 1949; House 1919-33.

DAVIS, Garrett (brother of Amos Davis) (D Ky.) Sept. 10, 1801-Sept. 22, 1872; House 1839-47 (HCW); Senate Dec. 10, 1861-Sept. 22, 1872 (1861-67 Whig, 1867-72 Democrat).

DAVIS, George Royal (R Ill.) Jan. 3, 1840-Nov. 25, 1899; House 1879-85.

DAVIS, George Thomas (W Mass.) Jan. 12, 1810-June 17, 1877; House 1851-53.

DAVIS, Glenn Robert (R Wis.) Oct. 28, 1914-__; House April 22, 1947-57, 1965-Dec. 31, 1974.

DAVIS, Henry Gassaway (brother of Thomas Beall Davis and grandfather of Davis Elkins) (D W.Va.) Nov. 16, 1823-March 11, 1916; Senate 1871-83.

DAVIS, Henry Winter (cousin of David Davis) (UU Md.) Aug. 16, 1817-Dec. 30, 1865; House 1855-61, 1863-65 (1855-57 American Party, 1857-61 Republican, 1863-65 Unconditional Unionist).

DAVIS, Horace (R Calif.) March 16, 1831-July 12, 1916; House 1877-81.

DAVIS, Jacob Cunningham (D Ill.) Sept. 16, 1820-Dec. 25, 1883; House Nov. 4, 1856-57.

DAVIS, Jacob Erastus (D Ohio) Oct. 31, 1905-__; House 1941-43.

DAVIS, James Curran (D Ga.) May 17, 1895-__; House 1947-63.

DAVIS, James Harvey (Cyclone) (D Texas) Dec. 24, 1853-Jan. 31, 1940; House 1915-17.

DAVIS, James John (R Pa.) Oct. 27, 1873-Nov. 22, 1947; Senate Dec. 2, 1930-45; Secy of Labor 1921-30.

DAVIS, Jeff (D Ark.) May 6, 1862-Jan. 3, 1913; Senate 1907-Jan. 3, 1913; Gov. 1901-07.

DAVIS, Jefferson (D Miss.) June 3, 1808-Dec. 6, 1889; House 1845-June 1846; Senate Aug. 10, 1847-Sept. 23, 1851, 1857-Jan. 21, 1861; Secy. of War 1853-57.

DAVIS, John (W Mass.) Jan. 13, 1787-April 19, 1854; House 1825-Jan. 14, 1834 (NR); Senate 1835-Jan. 5, 1841, March 24, 1845-53; Gov. 1834-35, 1841-43.

DAVIS, John (D Pa.) Aug. 7, 1788-April 1, 1878; House 1839-41.

DAVIS, John (PP Kan.) Aug. 9, 1826-Aug. 1, 1901; House 1891-95.

DAVIS, John Givan (D Ind.) Oct. 10, 1810-Jan. 18, 1866; House 1851-55, 1857-61.

DAVIS, John James (father of John William Davis) (D W.Va.) May 5, 1835-March 19, 1916; House 1871-75.

DAVIS, John Wesley (D Ind.) April 16, 1799-Aug. 22, 1859; House 1835-37, 1839-41, 1843-47; Speaker 1845-47; Gov. of Oregon Terr. 1853-54.

DAVIS, John William (son of John James Davis) (D W.Va.) April 13, 1873-March 24, 1955; House 1911-Aug. 29, 1913.

DAVIS, John William (D Ga.) Sept. 12, 1916-__; House 1961-75.

DAVIS, Joseph Jonathan (D N.C.) April 13, 1828-Aug. 7, 1892; House 1875-81.

DAVIS, Lowndes Henry (D Mo.) Dec. 13, 1836-Feb. 4, 1920; House 1879-85.

DAVIS, Mendel Jackson (D S.C.) Oct. 23, 1942-__; House April 27, 1971-__.

DAVIS, Noah (R N.Y.) Sept. 10, 1818-March 20, 1902; House 1869-July 15, 1870.

DAVIS, Reuben (D Miss.) Jan. 18, 1813-Oct. 14, 1890; House 1857-Jan. 12, 1861.

DAVIS, Richard David (D N.Y.) 1799-June 17, 1871; House 1841-45.

DAVIS, Robert Lee (R Pa.) Oct. 29, 1893-__; House Nov. 8, 1932-33.

DAVIS, Robert Thompson (R Mass.) Aug. 28, 1823-Oct. 29, 1906; House 1883-89.

DAVIS, Robert Wyche (D Fla.) March 15, 1849-Sept. 15, 1929; House 1897-1905.

DAVIS, Roger (D Pa.) Oct. 2, 1762-Nov. 20, 1815; House 1811-15.

DAVIS, Samuel (F Mass.) 1774-April 20, 1831; House 1813-15.

DAVIS, Thomas (D R.I.) Dec. 18, 1806-July 26, 1895; House 1853-55.

DAVIS, Thomas Beall (brother of Henry Gassaway Davis) (D W.Va.) April 25, 1828-Nov. 26, 1911; House June 6, 1905-07.

DAVIS, Thomas Terry (— Ky.) ? - Nov. 15, 1807; House 1797-1803.

DAVIS, Thomas Treadwell (grandson of Thomas Tredwell) (U N.Y.) Aug. 22, 1810-May 2, 1872; House 1863-67.

DAVIS, Timothy (W Iowa) March 29, 1794-April 27, 1872; House 1857-59.

DAVIS, Timothy (R Mass.) April 12, 1821-Oct. 23, 1888; House 1855-59 (1855-57 American Party, 1857-59 Republican).

DAVIS, Warren Ransom (SRD S.C.) May 8, 1793-Jan. 29, 1835; House 1827-Jan. 29, 1835.

DAVIS, William Morris (R Pa.) Aug. 16, 1815-Aug. 5, 1891; House 1861-63.

DAVISON, George Mosby (R Ky.) March 23, 1855-Dec. 18, 1912; House 1897-99.

DAVY, John Madison (R N.Y.) June 29, 1835-April 21, 1909; House 1875-77.

DAWES, Beman Gates (son of Rufus Dawes) (R Ohio) Jan. 14, 1870-May 15, 1953; House 1905-09.

DAWES, Henry Laurens (R Mass.) Oct. 30, 1816-Feb. 5, 1903; House 1857-75; Senate 1875-93.

DAWES, Rufus (father of Vice President Charles Gates Dawes and Beman Gates Dawes) (R Ohio) July 4, 1838-Aug. 2, 1899; House 1881-83.

DAWSON, Albert Foster (R Iowa) Jan. 26, 1872-March 9, 1949; House 1905-11.

DAWSON, John (D Va.) 1762-March 31, 1814; House 1797-March 31, 1814; Cont. Cong. 1788-89.

DAWSON, John Bennett (D La.) March 17, 1798-June 26, 1845; House 1841-June 26, 1845.

DAWSON, John Littleton (D Pa.) Feb. 7, 1813-Sept. 18, 1870; House 1851-55, 1863-67.

DAWSON, William (D Mo.) March 17, 1848-Oct. 12, 1929; House 1885-87.

DAWSON, William Adams (R Utah) Nov. 5, 1903-__; House 1947-49; 1953-59.

DAWSON, William Crosby (SRW Ga.) Jan. 4, 1798-May 6, 1856; House Nov. 7, 1836-Nov. 13, 1841; Senate 1849-55.

DAWSON, William Levi (D Ill.) April 26, 1886-Nov. 9, 1970; House 1943-Nov. 9, 1970.

DAY, Rowland (D N.Y.) March 6, 1779-Dec. 23, 1853; House 1823-25, 1833-35.

DAY, Stephen Albion (R Ill.) July 13, 1882-Jan. 5, 1950; House 1941-45.

DAY, Timothy Crane (R Ohio) Jan. 8, 1819-April 15, 1869; House 1855-57.

DAYAN, Charles (D N.Y.) July 8, 1792-Dec. 25, 1877; House 1831-33.

DAYTON, Alston Gordon (R W.Va.) Oct. 18, 1857-July 30, 1920; House 1895-March 16, 1905.

DAYTON, Jonathan (F N.J.) Oct. 16, 1760-Oct. 9, 1824; House 1791-99; Speaker 1795-99; Senate 1799-1805; Cont. Cong. Nov. 6, 1787-89.

DAYTON, William Lewis (W N.J.) Feb. 17, 1807-Dec. 1, 1864; Senate July 2, 1842-51.

DEAL, Joseph Thomas (D Va.) Nov. 19, 1860-March 7, 1942; House 1921-29.

DEAN, Benjamin (D Mass.) Aug. 14, 1824-April 9, 1897; House March 28, 1878-79.

DEAN, Ezra (D Ohio) April 9, 1795-Jan. 25, 1872; House 1841-45.

DEAN, Gilbert (D N.Y.) Aug. 14, 1819-Oct. 12, 1870; House 1851-July 3, 1854.

DEAN, Josiah (D Mass.) March 6, 1748-Oct. 14, 1818; House 1807-09.

DEAN, Sidney (R Conn.) Nov. 16, 1818-Oct. 29, 1901; House 1855-59 (1855-57 American Party, 1857-59 Republican).

DEANE, Charles Bennett (D N.C.) Nov. 1, 1898-Nov. 24, 1969; House 1947-57.

DEAR, Cleveland (D La.) Aug. 22, 1888-Dec. 30, 1950; House 1933-37.

DEARBORN, Henry (father of Henry Alexander Scammell Dearborn) (D Mass.) Feb. 23, 1751-June 6, 1829; House 1793-97; Secy. of War 1801-09.

DEARBORN, Henry Alexander Scammell (son of Henry Dearborn) (— Mass.) March 3, 1783-July 29, 1851; House 1831-33.

DE ARMOND, David Albaugh (D Mo.) March 18, 1844-Nov. 23, 1909; House 1891-Nov. 23, 1909.

DEBERRY, Edmund (W N.C.) Aug. 14, 1787-Dec. 12, 1859; House 1829-31, 1833-45, 1849-51.

DEBOE, William Joseph (R Ky.) June 30, 1849-June 15, 1927; Senate 1897-1903.

DE BOLT, Rezin A. (D Mo.) Jan. 20, 1828-Oct. 30, 1891; House 1875-77.

DECKER, Perl D. (D Mo.) Sept. 10, 1875-Aug. 22, 1934; House 1913-19.

DEEMER, Elias (R Pa.) Jan. 3, 1838-March 29, 1918; House 1901-07.

DEEN, Braswell Drue (D Ga.) June 28, 1893- —; House 1933-39.

DEERING, Nathaniel Cobb (R Iowa) Sept. 2, 1827-Dec. 11, 1887; House 1877-83.

DE FOREST, Henry Schermerhorn (R N.Y.) Feb. 16, 1847-Feb. 13, 1917; House 1911-13.

DE FOREST, Robert Elliott (D Conn.) Feb. 20, 1845-Oct. 1, 1924; House 1891-95.

DEFREES, Joseph Hutton (R Ind.) May 13, 1812-Dec. 21, 1885; House 1865-67.

DEGENER, Edward (R Texas) Oct. 20, 1809-Sept. 11, 1890; House March 31, 1870-71.

DEGETAU, Federico (R P.R.) Dec. 5, 1862-Jan. 20, 1914; House (Res. Comm.) 1901-05.

DE GRAFF, John Isaac (D N.Y.) Oct. 2, 1783-July 26, 1848; House 1827-29; 1837-39.

DE GRAFFENREID, Reese Calhoun (D Texas) May 7, 1859-Aug. 29, 1902; House 1897-Aug. 29, 1902.

deGRAFFENRIED, Edward (D Ala.) June 30, 1899-Nov. 5, 1974; House 1949-53.

DE HAVEN, John Jefferson (R Calif.) March 12, 1849-Jan. 26, 1913; House 1889-Oct. 1, 1890.

DEITRICK, Frederick Simpson (D Mass.) April 9, 1875-May 24, 1948; House 1913-15.

DE JARNETTE, Daniel Coleman (D Va.) Oct. 18, 1822-Aug. 20, 1881; House 1859-61.

DE LACY, Emerson Hugh (D Wash.) May 9, 1910- —; House 1945-47.

de la GARZA II, Eligio (D Texas) Sept. 22, 1927- —; House 1965- —.

DE LA MATYR, Gilbert (Nat./D Ind.) July 8, 1825-May 17, 1892; House 1879-81.

DE LA MONTANYA, James (D N.Y.) March 20, 1798-April 29, 1849; House 1839-41.

DELANEY, James Joseph (D N.Y.) March 19, 1901- —; House 1945-47, 1949- —.

DELANEY, John Joseph (D N.Y.) Aug. 21, 1878-Nov. 18, 1948; House March 5, 1918-19, 1931-Nov. 18, 1948.

DELANO, Charles (R Mass.) June 24, 1820-Jan. 23, 1883; House 1859-63.

DELANO, Columbus (R Ohio) June 4, 1809-Oct. 23, 1896; House 1845-47, 1865-67, June 3, 1868-69 (1845-47 Whig, 1865-67 and 1868-69 Republican); Secy. of the Interior 1870-75.

DE LANO, Milton (R N.Y.) Aug. 11, 1844-Jan. 2, 1922; House 1887-91.

DELAPLAINE, Isaac Clason (Fus. N.Y.) Oct. 27, 1817-July 17, 1866; House 1861-63.

DE LARGE, Robert Carlos (R S.C.) March 15, 1842-Feb. 14, 1874; House 1871-Jan. 24, 1873.

DELGADO, Francisco Afan (Nat. P.I.) Jan. 25, 1886-Oct. 27, 1964; House (Res. Comm.) 1935-Feb. 14, 1936.

DELLAY, Vincent John (D N.J.) June 23, 1907- —; House 1957-59 (1957 Republican, 1958-59 Democrat).

DELLENBACK, John Richard (R Ore.) Nov. 6, 1918- —; House 1967-75.

DELLET, James (W Ala.) Feb. 18, 1788-Dec. 21, 1848; House 1839-41, 1843-45.

DELLUMS, Ronald V. (D Calif.) Nov. 24, 1935- —; House 1971- —.

DE LUGO, Ron (D V.I.) Aug. 2, 1930- —; House (Terr. Del.) 1973- —.

DEMING, Benjamin F. (W Vt.) 1790-July 11, 1834; House 1833-July 11, 1834.

DEMING, Henry Champion (R Conn.) May 23, 1815-Oct. 8, 1872; House 1863-67.

DE MOTT, John (D N.Y.) Oct. 7, 1790-July 31, 1870; House 1845-47.

DE MOTTE, Mark Lindsey (R Ind.) Dec. 28, 1832-Sept. 23, 1908; House 1881-83.

DEMPSEY, John Joseph (D N.M.) June 22, 1879-March 11, 1958; House 1935-41, 1951-March 11, 1958; Gov. 1943-47.

DEMPSEY, Stephen Wallace (R N.Y.) May 8, 1862-March 1, 1949; House 1915-31.

DE MUTH, Peter Joseph (D Pa.) Jan. 1, 1892- —; House 1937-39.

DENBY, Edwin (grandson of Graham Newell Fitch) (R Mich.) Feb. 18, 1870-Feb. 8, 1929; House 1905-11; Secy. of the Navy 1921-24.

DENEEN, Charles Samuel (R Ill.) May 4, 1863-Feb. 5, 1940; Senate Feb. 26, 1925-31; Gov. 1905-13.

DENHOLM, Frank E. (D S.D.) Nov. 29, 1923- —; House 1971-75.

DENISON, Charles (nephew of George Denison) (D Pa.) Jan. 23, 1818-June 27, 1867; House 1863-June 27, 1867.

DENISON, Dudley Chase (nephew of Dudley Chase and cousin of Salmon Portland Chase) (R Vt.) Sept. 13, 1819-Feb. 10, 1905; House 1875-79.

DENISON, Edward Everett (R Ill.) Aug. 28, 1873-June 17, 1953; House 1915-31.

DENISON, George (uncle of Charles Denison) (D Pa.) Feb. 22, 1790-Aug. 20, 1831; House 1819-23.

DE NIVERNAIS, Edward James (see: LIVERNASH, Edward James).

DENNEY, Robert Vernon (R Neb.) April 11, 1916- —; House 1967-71.

DENNING, William (— N.Y.) April 1740-Oct. 30, 1819; House 1809-10.

DENNIS, David Worth (R Ind.) June 7, 1912- —; House 1969-75.

DENNIS, George Robertson (D Md.) April 8, 1822-Aug. 13, 1882; Senate 1873-79.

DENNIS, John (father of John Dennis and uncle of Littleton Purnell Dennis) (F Md.) Dec. 17, 1771-Aug. 17, 1806; House 1797-1805.

DENNIS, John (son of John Dennis) (W Md.) 1807-Nov. 1, 1859; House 1837-41.

DENNIS, Littleton Purnell (nephew of John Dennis) (W Md.) July 21, 1786-April 14, 1834; House 1833-April 14, 1834.

DENNISON, David Short (R Ohio) July 29, 1918- —; House 1957-59.

DENNY, Arthur Armstrong (R Wash.) June 20, 1822-Jan. 9, 1899; House (Terr. Del.) 1865-67.

DENNY, Harmar (great-grandfather of Harmar Denny Denny Jr.) (W Pa.) May 13, 1794-Jan. 29, 1852; House Dec. 15, 1829-37 (1829-35 Anti Mason, 1835-37 Whig).

DENNY, Harmar Denny Jr. (great grandson of Harmar Denny) (R Pa.) July 2, 1886-Jan. 6, 1966; House 1951-53.

DENNY, James William (D Md.) Nov. 20, 1838-April 12, 1923; House 1899-1901, 1903-05.

DENNY, Walter McKennon (D Miss.) Oct. 28, 1853-Nov. 5, 1926; House 1895-97.

DENOYELLES, Peter (— N.Y.) 1766-May 6, 1829; House 1813-15.

DENSON, William Henry (D Ala.) March 4, 1846-Sept. 26, 1906; House 1893-95.

DENT, George (D Md.) 1756-Dec. 2, 1813; House 1793-1801.

DENT, John Herman (D Pa.) March 10, 1908-__; House Jan. 21, 1958-__.

DENT, Stanley Hubert Jr. (D Ala.) Aug. 16, 1869-Oct. 6, 1938; House 1909-21.

DENT, William Barton Wade (D Ga.) Sept. 8, 1806-Sept. 7, 1855; House 1853-55.

DENTON, George Kirkpatrick (father of Winfield Kirkpatrick Denton) (D Ind.) Nov. 17, 1864-Jan. 4, 1926; House 1917-19.

DENTON, Winfield Kirkpatrick (son of George Kirkpatrick Denton) (D Ind.) Oct. 28, 1896-Nov. 2, 1971; House 1949-53, 1955-Dec. 30, 1966.

DENVER, James William (father of Matthew Rombach Denver) (A-BD Calif.) Oct. 23, 1817-Aug. 9, 1892; House 1855-57; Gov. of Terr. of Kansas 1857-58.

DENVER, Matthew Rombach (son of James William Denver) (D Ohio) Dec. 21, 1870-May 13, 1954; House 1907-13.

DEPEW, Chauncey Mitchell (R N.Y.) April 23, 1834-April 5, 1928; Senate 1899-1911.

DE PRIEST, Oscar (R Ill.) March 9, 1871-May 12, 1951; House 1929-35.

DE ROUEN, Rene Louis (D La.) Jan. 7, 1874-March 27, 1942; House Aug. 23, 1927-41.

DEROUNIAN, Steven Boghos (R N.Y.) April 6, 1918-__; House 1953-65.

DERRICK, Butler Carson Jr. (D S.C.) Sept. 30, 1936-__; House 1975-__.

DERSHEM, Franklin Lewis (D Pa.) March 5, 1865-Feb. 14, 1950; House 1913-15.

DERWINSKI, Edward Joseph (R Ill.) Sept. 15, 1926-__; House 1959-__.

DE SAUSSURE, William Ford (D S.C.) Feb. 22, 1792-March 13, 1870; Senate May 10, 1852-53.

DESHA, Joseph (brother of Robert Desha) (D Ky.) Dec. 9, 1768-Oct. 11, 1842; House 1807-19; Gov. 1824-28.

DESHA, Robert (brother of Joseph Desha) (— Tenn.) Jan. 14, 1791-Feb. 6, 1849; House 1827-31.

DESTREHAN, John Noel (— La.) 1780-1824; Senate Sept. 3-Oct. 1, 1812.

DEUSTER, Peter Victor (D Wis.) Feb. 13, 1831-Dec. 31, 1904; House 1879-85.

DEVEREUX, James Patrick Sinnott (R Md.) Feb. 20, 1903-__; House 1951-59.

DE VEYRA, Jaime Carlos (Nat. P.I.) Nov. 4, 1873-March 7, 1963; House (Res. Comm.) 1917-23.

DEVINE, Samuel Leeper (R Ohio) Dec. 21, 1915-__; House 1959-__.

DEVITT, Edward James (R Minn.) May 5, 1911-__; House 1947-49.

DE VRIES, Marion (D Calif.) Aug. 15, 1865-Sept. 11, 1939; House 1897-Aug. 20, 1900.

DEWALT, Arthur Granville (D Pa.) Oct. 11, 1854-Oct. 26, 1931; House 1915-21.

DEWART, Lewis (father of William Lewis Dewart) (JD Pa.) Nov. 14, 1780-April 26, 1852; House 1831-33.

D'EWART, Wesley Abner (R Mont.) Oct. 1, 1889-Sept. 2, 1973; House June 5, 1945-55.

DEWART, William Lewis (son of Lewis Dewart) (D Pa.) June 21, 1821-April 19, 1888; House 1857-59.

DEWEESE, John Thomas (D N.C.) June 4, 1835-July 4, 1906; House July 6, 1868-Feb. 28, 1870.

DEWEY, Charles Schuveldt (R Ill.) Nov. 10, 1880-__; House 1941-45.

DEWEY, Daniel (W Mass.) Jan. 29, 1766-May 26, 1815; House 1813-Feb. 24, 1814.

DE WITT, Alexander (AP Mass.) April 2, 1798-Jan. 13, 1879; House 1853-57.

DE WITT, Charles Gerrit (JD N.Y.) Nov. 7, 1789-April 12, 1839; House 1829-31.

DE WITT, David Miller (D N.Y.) Nov. 25, 1837-June 23, 1912; House 1873-75.

DE WITT, Francis Byron (R Ohio) March 11, 1849-March 21, 1929; House 1895-97.

DE WITT, Jacob Hasbrouck (Clinton D N.Y.) Oct. 2, 1784-Jan. 30, 1867; House 1819-21.

DE WOLF, James (D R.I.) March 18, 1764-Dec. 21, 1837; Senate 1821-Oct. 31, 1825.

DEXTER, Samuel (F Mass.) May 14, 1761-May 3, 1816; House 1793-95; Senate 1799-May 30, 1800; Secy. of War May 13-Dec. 31, 1800; Secy. of the Treasury Jan. 1-May 6, 1801.

DEZENDORF, John Frederick (R Va.) Aug. 10, 1834-June 22, 1894; House 1881-83.

DIAL, Nathaniel Barksdale (D S.C.) April 24, 1862-Dec. 11, 1940; Senate 1919-25.

DIBBLE, Samuel (D S.C.) Sept. 16, 1837-Sept. 16, 1913; House June 9, 1881-May 31, 1882, 1883-91.

DIBRELL, George Gibbs (D Tenn.) April 12, 1822-May 9, 1888; House 1875-85.

DICK, Charles William Frederick (R Ohio) Nov. 3, 1858-March 13, 1945; House Nov. 8, 1898-March 23, 1904; Senate March 23, 1904-11.

DICK, John (father of Samuel Bernard Dick) (R Pa.) June 17, 1794-May 29, 1872; House 1853-59 (1853-55 Whig, 1855-59 Republican).

DICK, Samuel Bernard (son of John Dick) (R Pa.) Oct. 26, 1836-May 10, 1907; House 1879-81.

DICKENS, Samuel (— N.C.) ?-1840; House Dec. 2, 1816-17.

DICKERMAN, Charles Heber (D Pa.) Feb. 3, 1843-Dec. 17, 1915; House 1903-05.

DICKERSON, Mahlon (brother of Philemon Dickerson) (D N.J.) April 17, 1770-Oct. 5, 1853; Senate 1817-33; Gov. 1815-17; Secy. of the Navy 1834-38.

DICKERSON, Philemon (brother of Mahlon Dickerson) (JD N.J.) Jan. 11, 1788-Dec. 10, 1862; House 1833-Nov. 3, 1836 (D), 1839-41 (JD); Gov. 1836-37.

DICKERSON, William Worth (D Ky.) Nov. 29, 1851-Jan. 31, 1923; House June 21, 1890-93.

DICKEY, Henry Luther (D Ohio) Oct. 29, 1832-May 23, 1910; House 1877-81.

DICKEY, Jesse Column (W Pa.) Feb. 27, 1808-Feb. 19, 1890; House 1849-51.

DICKEY, John (father of Oliver James Dickey) (W Pa.) June 23, 1794-March 14, 1853; House 1843-45, 1847-49.

DICKEY, Oliver James (son of John Dickey) (R Pa.) April 6, 1823-April 21, 1876; House Dec. 7, 1868-73.

DICKINSON, Clement Cabell (D Mo.) Dec. 6, 1849-Jan. 14, 1938; House Feb. 1, 1910-21, 1923-29, 1931-35.

DICKINSON, Daniel Stevens (D N.Y.) Sept. 11, 1800-April 12, 1866; Senate Nov. 30, 1844-51.

DICKINSON, David W. (nephew of William Hardy Murfree) (W Tenn.) June 10, 1808-April 27, 1845; House 1833-35; 1843-45 (1833-35 Democrat, 1843-45 Whig).

DICKINSON, Edward (W Mass.) Jan. 1, 1803-June 16, 1874; House 1853-55.

DICKINSON, Edward Fenwick (D Ohio) Jan. 21, 1829-Aug. 25, 1891; House 1869-71.

DICKINSON, John Dean (W N.Y.) June 28, 1767-Jan. 28, 1841; House 1819-23, 1827-31 (1819-25 Federalist, 1827-31 Whig).

DICKINSON, Lester Jesse (cousin of Fred Dickinson Letts) (R Iowa) Oct. 29, 1873-June 4, 1968; House 1919-31; Senate 1931-37.

DICKINSON, Philemon (— N.J.) April 5, 1739-Feb. 4, 1809; Senate Nov. 23, 1790-93; Cont. Cong. (Del.) 1782-83.

DICKINSON, Rodolphus (D Ohio) Dec. 28, 1797-March 20, 1849; House 1847-March 20, 1849.

DICKINSON, William Louis (R Ala.) June 5, 1925-__; House 1965-__.

DICKSON, David (D Miss.) ?-July 31, 1836; House 1835-July 31, 1836.

DICKSON, Frank Stoddard (R Ill.) Oct. 6, 1876-Feb. 24, 1953; House 1905-07.

DICKSON, John (W N.Y.) June 1, 1783-Feb. 22, 1852; House 1831-35.

DICKSON, Joseph (F N.C.) April 1745-April 14, 1825; House 1799-1801.

DICKSON, Samuel (W N.Y.) March 29, 1807-May 3, 1858; House 1855-57.

DICKSON, William (— Tenn.) May 5, 1770-Feb. 1816; House 1801-07.

DICKSON, William Alexander (D Miss.) July 20, 1861-Feb. 25, 1940; House 1909-13.

DICKSTEIN, Samuel (D N.Y.) Feb. 5, 1885-April 22, 1954; House 1923-Dec. 30, 1945.

DIEKEMA, Gerrit John (R Mich.) March 27, 1859-Dec. 20, 1930; House March 17, 1908-11.

DIES, Martin (father of Martin Dies Jr.) (D Texas) March 13, 1870-July 13, 1922; House 1909-19.

DIES, Martin Jr. (son of Martin Dies) (D Texas) Nov. 5, 1900-Nov. 14, 1972; House 1931-45, 1953-59.

DIETERICH, William Henry (D Ill.) March 31, 1876-Oct. 12, 1940; House 1931-33; Senate 1933-39.

DIETRICH, Charles Elmer (D Pa.) July 30, 1889-May 20, 1942; House 1935-37.

DIETRICH, Charles Henry (R Neb.) Nov. 26, 1853-April 10, 1924; Senate March 28, 1901-05; Gov. Jan. 3-May 1, 1901.

DIETZ, William (D N.Y.) June 28, 1778-Aug. 24, 1848; House 1825-27.

DIFFENDERFER, Robert Edward (D Pa.) June 7, 1849-April 27, 1923; House 1911-15.

DIGGS, Charles Coles Jr. (D Mich.) Dec. 2, 1922-__; House 1955-__.

DILL, Clarence Cleveland (D Wash.) Sept. 21, 1884- —; House 1915-19; Senate 1923-35.

DILLINGHAM, Paul Jr. (father of William Paul Dillingham) (D Vt.) Aug. 10, 1799-July 26, 1891; House 1843-47; Gov. 1865-67.

DILLINGHAM, William Paul (son of Paul Dillingham, Jr.) (R Vt.) Dec. 12, 1843-July 12, 1923; Senate Oct. 18, 1900-July 12, 1923; Gov. 1888-90.

DILLON, Charles Hall (R S.D.) Dec. 18, 1853-Sept. 15, 1929; House 1913-19.

DILWEG, LaVern Ralph (D Wis.) Nov. 1, 1903-Jan. 2, 1968; House 1943-45.

DIMMICK, Milo Melankthon (brother of William Harrison Dimmick) (D Pa.) Oct. 30, 1811-Nov. 22, 1872; House 1849-53.

DIMMICK, William Harrison (brother of Milo Melankthon Dimmick) (D Pa.) Dec. 20, 1815-Aug. 2, 1861; House 1857-61.

DIMOCK, Davis Jr. (D Pa.) Sept. 17, 1801-Jan. 13, 1842; House 1841-Jan. 13, 1842.

DIMOND, Anthony Joseph (D Alaska) Nov. 30, 1881-May 28, 1953; House (Terr. Del.) 1933-45.

DINGELL, John David (father of John David Dingell Jr.) (D Mich.) Feb. 2, 1894-Sept. 19, 1955; House 1933-Sept. 19, 1955.

DINGELL, John David Jr. (son of John Dingell) (D Mich.) July 8, 1926-__; House Dec. 13, 1955-__.

DINGLEY, Nelson Jr. (R Maine) Feb. 15, 1832-Jan. 13, 1899; House Sept. 12, 1881-Jan. 13, 1899; Gov. 1874-76.

DINSMOOR, Samuel (WD N.H.) July 1, 1766-March 15, 1835; House 1811-13; Gov. 1831-34.

DINSMORE, Hugh Anderson (D Ark.) Dec. 24, 1850-May 2, 1930; House 1893-1905.

DIRKSEN, Everett McKinley (R Ill.) Jan. 4, 1896-Sept. 7, 1969; House 1933-49; Senate 1951-Sept. 7, 1969.

DISNEY, David Tiernan (D Ohio) Aug. 25, 1803-March 14, 1857; House 1849-55.

DISNEY, Wesley Ernest (D Okla.) Oct. 31, 1883-March 26, 1961; House 1931-45.

DITTER, John William (R Pa.) Sept. 5, 1888-Nov. 21, 1943; House 1933-Nov. 21, 1943.

DIVEN, Alexander Samuel (R N.Y.) Feb. 10, 1809-June 11, 1896; House 1861-63.

DIX, John Adams (son-in-law of John Jordan Morgan) (D N.Y.) July 24, 1798-April 21, 1879; Senate Jan. 27, 1845-49; Secy. of the Treasury Jan. 11-March 3, 1861; Gov. (R) 1873-75.

DIXON, Archibald (W Ky.) April 2, 1802-April 23, 1876; Senate Sept. 1, 1852-55.

DIXON, Henry Aldous (R Utah) June 29, 1890-Jan. 22, 1967; House 1955-61.

DIXON, James (R Conn.) Aug. 5, 1814-March 27, 1873; House 1845-49 (W); Senate 1857-69 (R)

DIXON, Joseph (R N.C.) April 9, 1828-March 3, 1883; House Dec. 5, 1870-71.

DIXON, Joseph Andrew (D Ohio) June 3, 1879-July 4, 1942; House 1937-39.

DIXON, Joseph Moore (R Mont.) July 31, 1867-May 22, 1934; House 1903-07; Senate 1907-13; Gov. 1921-25.

DIXON, Lincoln (D Ind.) Feb. 9, 1860-Sept. 16, 1932; House 1905-19.

DIXON, Nathan Fellows (father of the following) (W R.I.) Dec. 13, 1774-Jan. 29, 1842; Senate 1839-Jan. 29, 1842.

DIXON, Nathan Fellows (son of the preceding and father of the following) (R R.I.) May 1, 1812-April 11, 1881; House 1849-51, 1863-71 (1849-51 Whig, 1863-71 Republican).

DIXON, Nathan Fellows (son of the preceding) (R R.I.) Aug. 28, 1847-Nov. 8, 1897; House Feb. 12-March 3, 1885; Senate April 10, 1889-95.

DIXON, William Wirt (D Mont.) June 3, 1838-Nov. 13, 1910; House 1891-93.

DOAN, Robert Eachus (R Ohio) July 23, 1831-Feb. 24, 1919; House 1891-93.

DOAN, William (D Ohio) April 4, 1792-June 22, 1847; House 1839-43.

DOBBIN, James Cochrane (grandson of James Cochran of North Carolina) (D N.C.) Jan. 17, 1814-Aug. 4, 1857; House 1845-47; Secy. of the Navy 1853-57.

DOBBINS, Donald Claude (D Ill.) March 20, 1878-Feb. 14, 1943; House 1933-37.

DOBBINS, Samuel Atkinson (R N.J.) April 14, 1814-May 26, 1886; House 1873-77.

DOCKERY, Alexander Monroe (D Mo.) Feb. 11, 1845-Dec. 26, 1926; House 1883-99; Gov. 1901-05.

DOCKERY, Alfred (father of Oliver Hart Dockery) (W N.C.) Dec. 11, 1797-Dec. 7, 1875; House 1845-47, 1851-53.

DOCKERY, Oliver Hart (son of Alfred Dockery) (R N.C.) Aug. 12, 1830-March 21, 1906; House July 13, 1868-71.

DOCKWEILER, John Francis (D Calif.) Sept. 19, 1895-Jan. 31, 1943; House 1933-39.

DODD, Christopher John (son of Thomas Joseph Dodd) May 27, 1944-__; House 1975-__.

DODD, Edward (W N.Y.) Aug. 25, 1805-March 1, 1891; House 1855-59.

DODD, Thomas Joseph (father of Christopher John Dodd) (D Conn.) May 15, 1907-May 24, 1971; House 1953-57; Senate 1959-71.

DODDRIDGE, Philip (— Va.) May 17, 1773-Nov. 19, 1832; House 1829-Nov. 19, 1832.

DODDS, Francis Henry (R Mich.) June 9, 1858-Dec. 23, 1940; House 1909-13.

DODDS, Ozro John (D Ohio) March 22, 1840-April 18, 1882; House Oct. 8, 1872-73.

DODGE, Augustus Caesar (son of Henry Dodge) (D Iowa) Jan. 2, 1812-Nov. 20, 1883; House (Terr. Del.) Oct. 28, 1840-Dec. 28, 1846; Senate Dec. 7, 1848-Feb. 22, 1855.

DODGE, Grenville Mellen (R Iowa) April 12, 1831-Jan. 3, 1916; House 1867-69.

DODGE, Henry (father of Augustus Caesar Dodge) (D Wis.) Oct. 12, 1782-June 19, 1867; House (Terr. Del.) 1841-45; Senate June 8, 1848-57; Gov. (Terr.) 1836-41, 1845-48.

DODGE, William Earle (R N.Y.) Sept. 4, 1805-Feb. 9, 1883; House April 7, 1866-67.

DOE, Nicholas Bartlett (W N.Y.) June 16, 1786-Dec. 6, 1856; House Dec. 7, 1840-41.

DOIG, Andrew Wheeler (D N.Y.) July 24, 1799-July 11, 1875; House 1839-43.

DOLE, Robert J. (R Kan.) July 22, 1923-__; House 1961-69; Senate 1969-__; Chmn. Rep. Natl. Comte., 1971-73.

DOLLINGER, Isidore (D N.Y.) Nov. 13, 1903-__; House 1949-Dec. 31, 1959.

DOLLIVER, James Isaac (nephew of Jonathan Prentiss Dolliver) (R Iowa) Aug. 31, 1894-__; House 1945-57.

DOLLIVER, Jonathan Prentiss (uncle of James Isaac Dolliver) (R Iowa) Feb. 6, 1858-Oct. 15, 1910; House 1889-Aug. 22, 1900; Senate Aug. 22, 1900-Oct. 15, 1910.

DOLPH, Joseph Norton (uncle of Frederick William Mulkey) (R Ore.) Oct. 19, 1835-March 10, 1897; Senate 1883-95.

DOMENGEAUX, James (D La.) Jan. 6, 1907-__; House 1941-April 15, 1944; Nov. 7, 1944-49.

DOMENICI, Pete Vichi (R N.M.) May 7, 1932-__; Senate 1973-__.

DOMINICK, Frederick Haskell (D S.C.) Feb. 20, 1877-March 11, 1960; House 1917-33.

DOMINICK, Peter H. (R Colo.) July 7, 1915-__; House 1961-63; Senate 1963-75.

DONAHEY, Alvin Victor (D Ohio) July 7, 1873-April 8, 1946; Senate 1935-41; Gov. 1923-29.

DONDERO, George Anthony (R Mich.) Dec. 16, 1883-Jan. 29, 1968; House 1933-57.

DONLEY, Joseph Benton (R Pa.) Oct. 10, 1838-Jan. 23, 1917; House 1869-71.

DONNAN, William G. (R Iowa) June 30, 1834-Dec. 4, 1908; House 1871-75.

DONNELL, Forrest C. (R Mo.) Aug. 20, 1884-__; Senate 1945-51; Gov. 1941-45.

DONNELL, Richard Spaight (grandson of Richard Dobbs Spaight) (W N.C.) Sept. 20, 1820-June 3, 1867; House 1847-49.

DONNELLY, Ignatius (R Minn.) Nov. 3, 1831-Jan. 1, 1901; House 1863-69.

DONOHOE, Michael (D Pa.) Feb. 22, 1864-Jan. 17, 1958; House 1911-15.

DONOHUE, Harold Daniel (D Mass.) June 18, 1901-__; House 1947-Dec. 31, 1974.

DONOVAN, Dennis D. (D Ohio) Jan. 31, 1859-April 21, 1941; House 1891-95.

DONOVAN, James George (D/R/L N.Y.) Dec. 15, 1898-__; House 1951-57.

DONOVAN, Jeremiah (D Conn.) Oct. 18, 1857-April 22, 1935; House 1913-15.

DONOVAN, Jerome Francis (D N.Y.), Feb. 1, 1872-Nov. 2, 1949; House March 5, 1918-21.

DOOLEY, Edwin Benedict (R N.Y.) April 13, 1905-__; House 1957-63.

DOOLING, Peter Joseph (D N.Y.) Feb. 15, 1857-Oct. 18, 1931; House 1913-21.

DOOLITTLE, Dudley (D Kan.) June 21, 1881-Nov. 14, 1957; House 1913-19.

DOOLITTLE, James Rood (R Wis.) Jan. 3, 1815-July 23, 1897; Senate 1857-69.

DOOLITTLE, William Hall (R Wash.) Nov. 6, 1848-Feb. 26, 1914; House 1893-97.

DOREMUS, Frank Ellsworth (D Mich.) Aug. 31, 1865-Sept. 4, 1947; House 1911-21.

DORN, Francis Edwin (R N.Y.) April 18, 1911-__; House 1953-61.

DORN, William Jennings Bryan (D S.C.) April 14, 1916-__; House 1947-49; 1951-75.

DORR, Charles Philips (R W. Va.) Aug. 12, 1852-Oct. 8, 1914; House 1897-99.

DORSEY, Clement (— Md.) 1778-Aug. 6, 1848; House 1825-31.

DORSEY, Frank Joseph Gerard (D Pa.) April 26, 1891-July 13, 1949; House 1935-39.

DORSEY, George Washington Emery (R Neb.) Jan. 25, 1842-June 12, 1911; House 1885-91.

DORSEY, John Lloyd Jr. (D Ky.) Aug. 10, 1891-March 22, 1960; House Nov. 4, 1930-31.

DORSEY, Stephen Wallace (R Ark.) Feb. 28, 1842-March 20, 1916; Senate 1873-79.

DORSHEIMER, William (D N.Y.) Feb. 5, 1832-March 26, 1888; House 1883-85.

DOTY, James Duane (cousin of Morgan Lewis Martin) (FS Wis.) Nov. 5, 1799-June 13, 1865; House Jan. 14, 1839-41 as a territorial delegate, 1849-53 as a representative (1839-41 and 1849-51 Democrat, 1851-53 Free Soiler); Gov. (Terr. of Wis.) 1841-44, (Terr. of Utah) 1863-65.

DOUBLEDAY, Ulysses Freeman (JD N.Y.) Dec. 15, 1792-March 11, 1866; House 1831-33, 1835-37.

DOUGHERTY, Charles (D Fla.) Oct. 15, 1850-Oct. 11, 1915; House 1885-89.

DOUGHERTY, John (D Mo.) Feb. 25, 1857-Aug. 1, 1905; House 1899-1905.

DOUGHTON, Robert Lee (D N.C.) Nov. 7, 1863-Oct. 1, 1954; House 1911-53.

DOUGLAS, Albert (R Ohio) April 25, 1852-March 14, 1935; House 1907-11.

DOUGLAS, Beverly Browne (D Va.) Dec. 21, 1822-Dec. 22, 1878; House 1875-77 (C), 1877-Dec. 22, 1878 (D).

DOUGLAS, Emily Taft (wife of Senator Paul H. Douglas) (D Ill.) April 10, 1899-__; House 1945-47.

DOUGLAS, Fred James (R N.Y.) Sept. 14, 1869-Jan. 1, 1949; House 1937-45.

DOUGLAS, Helen Gahagan (D Calif.) Nov. 25, 1900-__; House 1945-51.

DOUGLAS, Lewis Williams (D Ariz.) July 2, 1894-March 7, 1974; House 1927-March 4, 1933.

DOUGLAS, Paul Howard (husband of Emily Taft Douglas) (D Ill.) March 26, 1892-__; Senate 1949-67.

DOUGLAS, Stephen Arnold (PSD Ill.) April 23, 1813-June 3, 1861; House 1843-47 (D); Senate 1847-June 3, 1861 (1847-53 Democrat, 1853-61 Popular Sovereignty Democrat).

DOUGLAS, William Harris (R N.Y.) Dec. 5, 1853-Jan. 27, 1944; House 1901-05.

DOUGLASS, John Joseph (D Mass.) Feb. 9, 1873-April 5, 1939; House 1925-35.

DOUTRICH, Isaac Hoffer (R Pa.) Dec. 19, 1871-May 28, 1941; House 1927-37.

DOVENER, Blackburn Barrett (R W.Va.) April 20, 1842-May 9, 1914; House 1895-1907.

DOW, John Goodchild (D N.Y. May 6, 1905-__; House 1965-69; 1971-73.

DOWD, Clement (D N.C.) Aug. 27, 1832-April 15, 1898; House 1881-85.

DOWDELL, James Ferguson (SRD Ala.) Nov. 26, 1818-Sept. 6, 1871; House 1853-59.

DOWDNEY, Abraham (D N.Y.) Oct. 31, 1841-Dec. 10, 1886; House 1885-Dec. 10, 1886.

DOWDY, John Vernard (D Texas) Feb. 11, 1912-__; House Sept. 23, 1952-73.

DOWELL, Cassius Clay (R Iowa) Feb. 29, 1864-Feb. 4, 1940; House 1915-35, 1937-Feb. 4, 1940.

DOWNEY, Sheridan (son of Stephen Wheeler Downey) (D Calif.) March 11, 1884-Oct. 25, 1961; Senate 1939-Nov. 30, 1950.

DOWNEY, Stephen Wheeler (father of Sheridan Downey) (R Wyo.) July 25, 1839-Aug. 3, 1902; House (Terr. Del.) 1879-81.

DOWNEY, Thomas Joseph (D N.Y.) Jan. 28, 1949-__; House 1975-__.

DOWNING, Charles (— Fla.) ?-1845; House (Terr. Del.) 1837-41.

DOWNING, Finis Ewing (D Ill.) Aug. 24, 1846-March 8, 1936; House 1895-June 5, 1896.

DOWNING, Thomas Nelms (D Va.) Feb. 1, 1919-__; House 1959-__.

DOWNS, Le Roy Donnelly (D Conn.) April 11, 1900-Jan. 18, 1970; House 1941-43.

DOWNS, Solomon Weathersbee (D La.) 1801-Aug. 14, 1854; Senate 1847-53.

DOWSE, Edward (D Mass.) Oct. 22, 1756-Sept. 3, 1828; House 1819-May 26, 1820.

DOX, Peter Myndert (grandson of John Nicholas) (D Ala.) Sept. 11, 1813-April 2, 1891; House 1869-73.

DOXEY, Charles Taylor (R Ind.) July 13, 1841-April 30, 1898; House Jan. 17-March 3, 1883.

DOXEY, Wall (D Miss.) Aug. 8, 1892-March 2, 1962; House 1929-Sept. 28, 1941; Senate Sept. 29, 1941-43.

DOYLE, Clyde Gilman (D Calif.) July 11, 1887-March 14, 1963; House 1945-47, 1949-March 14, 1963.

DOYLE, Thomas Aloysius (D Ill.) Jan. 9, 1886-Jan. 29, 1935; House Nov. 6, 1923-31.

DRAKE, Charles Daniel (R Mo.) April 11, 1811-April 1, 1892; Senate 1867-Dec. 19, 1870.

DRAKE, John Reuben (— N.Y.) Nov. 28, 1782-March 21, 1857; House 1817-19.

DRANE, Herbert Jackson (D Fla.) June 20, 1863-Aug. 11, 1947; House 1917-33.

DRAPER, Joseph (— Va.) Dec. 25, 1794-June 10, 1834; House Dec. 6, 1830-31, Dec. 6, 1832-33.

DRAPER, William Franklin (R Mass.) April 9, 1842-Jan. 28, 1910; House 1893-97.

DRAPER, William Henry (R N.Y.) June 24, 1841-Dec. 7, 1921; House 1901-13.

DRAYTON, William (UD S.C.) Dec. 30, 1776-May 24, 1846; House May 17, 1825-33.

DRESSER, Solomon Robert (R Pa.) Feb. 1, 1842-Jan. 21, 1911; House 1903-07.

DREW, Ira Walton (D Pa.) Aug. 31, 1878-—; House 1937-39.

DREW, Irving Webster (R N.H.) Jan. 8, 1845-April 10, 1922; Senate Sept. 2-Nov. 5, 1918.

DREWRY, Patrick Henry (D Va.) May 24, 1875-Dec. 21, 1947; House April 27, 1920-Dec. 21, 1947.

DRIGGS, Edmund Hope (D N.Y.) May 2, 1865-Sept. 27, 1946; House Dec. 6, 1897-1901.

DRIGGS, John Fletcher (R Mich.) March 8, 1813-Dec. 17, 1877; House 1863-69.

DRINAN, Robert F. (D Mass.) Nov. 15, 1920-—; House 1971-—.

DRISCOLL, Daniel Angelus (D N.Y.) March 6, 1875-June 5, 1955; House 1909-17.

DRISCOLL, Denis Joseph (D Pa.) March 27, 1871-Jan. 18, 1958; House 1935-37.

DRISCOLL, Michael Edward (R N.Y.) Feb. 9, 1851-Jan. 19, 1929; House 1899-1913.

DRIVER, William Joshua (D Ark.) March 2, 1873-Oct. 1, 1948; House 1921-39.

DROMGOOLE, George Coke (uncle of Alexander Dromgoole Sims) (D Va.) May 15, 1797-April 27, 1847; House 1835-41, 1843-April 27, 1847.

DRUKKER, Dow Henry (R N.J.) Feb. 7, 1872-Jan. 11, 1963; House April 7, 1914-19.

DRUM, Augustus (D Pa.) Nov. 26, 1815-Sept. 15, 1858; House 1853-55.

DRYDEN, John Fairfield (R N.J.) Aug. 7, 1839-Nov. 24, 1911; Senate Jan. 29, 1902-07.

DUBOIS, Fred Thomas (D Idaho) May 29, 1851-Feb. 14, 1930; House (Terr. Del.) 1887-July 3, 1890 (R); Senate 1891-97 (R), 1901-07 (Sil. R 1901, D 1901-07).

DU BOSE, Dudley McIver (D Ga.) Oct. 28, 1834-March 2, 1883; House 1871-73.

DUDLEY, Charles Edward (D N.Y.) May 23, 1780-Jan. 23, 1841; Senate Jan. 15, 1829-33.

DUDLEY, Edward Bishop (NR N.C.) Dec. 15, 1769-Oct. 30, 1855; House Nov. 10, 1829-31; Gov. 1837-41.

DUELL, Rodolphus Holland (R N.Y.) Dec. 20, 1824-Feb. 11, 1891; House 1859-63, 1871-75.

DUER, William (W N.Y.) May 25, 1805-Aug. 25, 1879; House 1847-51.

DUFF, James Henderson (R Pa.) Jan. 21, 1883-Dec. 20, 1969; Senate Jan. 16, 1951-57; Gov. 1947-51.

DUFFEY, Warren Joseph (D Ohio) Jan. 24, 1886-July 7, 1936; House 1933-July 7, 1936.

DUFFY, Francis Ryan (D Wis.) June 23, 1888-—; Senate 1933-39.

DUFFY, James Patrick Bernard (D N.Y.) Nov. 25, 1878-Jan. 8, 1969; House 1935-37.

DUGRO, Philip Henry (D N.Y.) Oct. 3, 1855-March 1, 1920; House 1881-83.

DUKE, Richard Thomas Walker (C Va.) June 6, 1822-July 2, 1898; House Nov. 8, 1870-73.

DULLES, John Foster (R N.Y.) Feb. 25, 1888-May 24, 1959; Senate July 7-Nov. 8, 1949; Secy. of State 1953-59.

DULSKI, Thaddeus J. (D N.Y.) Sept. 27, 1915-—; House 1959-75.

DUMONT, Ebenezer (U Ind.) Nov. 23, 1814-April 16, 1871; House 1863-67.

DUNBAR, James Whitson (R Ind.) Oct. 17, 1860-May 19, 1943; House 1919-23, 1929-31.

DUNBAR, William (D La.) 1805-March 18, 1861; House 1853-55.

DUNCAN, Alexander (W Ohio) 1788-March 23, 1853; House 1837-41, 1843-45.

DUNCAN, Daniel (W Ohio) July 22, 1806-May 18, 1849; House 1847-49.

DUNCAN, James (— Pa.) 1756-June 24, 1844; House 1821.

DUNCAN, James Henry (W Mass.) Dec. 5, 1793-Feb. 8, 1869; House 1849-53.

DUNCAN, John J. (R Tenn.) March 24, 1919-—; House 1965-—.

DUNCAN, Joseph (JD Ill.) Feb. 22, 1794-Jan. 15, 1844; House 1827-Sept. 21, 1834; Gov. 1834-38.

DUNCAN, Richard Meloan (D Mo.) Nov. 10, 1889-—; House 1933-43.

DUNCAN, Robert Blackford (D Ore.) Dec. 4, 1920-—; House 1963-67; 1975-—.

DUNCAN, William Addison (D Pa.) Feb. 2, 1836-Nov. 14, 1884; House 1883-Nov. 14, 1884.

DUNCAN, (William) Garnett (W Ky.) March 2, 1800-May 25, 1875; House 1847-49.

DUNGAN, James Irvine (D Ohio) May 29, 1844-Dec. 28, 1931; House 1891-93.

DUNHAM, Cyrus Livingston (D Ind.) Jan. 16, 1817-Nov. 21, 1877; House 1849-55.

DUNHAM, Ransom Williams (R Ill.) March 21, 1838-Aug. 19, 1896; House 1883-89.

DUNLAP, George Washington, (U Ky.) Feb. 22, 1813-June 6, 1880; House 1861-63.

DUNLAP, Robert Pinkney (D Maine) Aug. 17, 1794-Oct. 20, 1859; House 1843-47; Gov. 1834-38.

DUNLAP, William Claiborne (D Tenn.) Feb. 25, 1798-Nov. 16, 1872; House 1833-37.

DUNN, Aubert Culberson (D Miss.) Nov. 20, 1896-—; House 1935-37.

DUNN, George Grundy (R Ind.) Dec. 20, 1812-Sept. 4, 1857; House 1847-49 (W), 1855-57 (R).

DUNN, George Hedford (W Ind.) Nov. 15, 1794-Jan. 12, 1854; House 1837-39.

DUNN, John Thomas (D N.J.) June 4, 1838-Feb. 22, 1907; House 1893-95.

DUNN, Matthew Anthony (D Pa.) Aug. 15, 1886-Feb. 13, 1942; House 1933-41.

DUNN, Poindexter (D Ark.) Nov. 3, 1834-Oct. 12, 1914; House 1879-89.

DUNN, Thomas Byrne (R N.Y.) March 16, 1853-July 2, 1924; House 1913-23.

DUNN, William McKee (R Ind.) Dec. 12, 1814-July 24, 1887; House 1859-63.

DUNNELL, Mark Hill (R Minn.) July 2, 1823-Aug. 9, 1904; House 1871-83, 1889-91.

DUNPHY, Edward John (D N.Y.) May 12, 1856-July 29, 1926; House 1889-95.

DUNWELL, Charles Tappan (R N.Y.) Feb. 13, 1852-June 12, 1908; House 1903-June 12, 1908.

du PONT, Henry Algernon (cousin of Thomas Coleman du Pont) (R Del.) July 30, 1838-Dec. 31, 1926; Senate June 13, 1906-17.

du PONT, Pierre S. IV (R Del.) Jan. 22, 1935-—; House 1971-—.

du PONT, Thomas Coleman (cousin of Henry Algernon du Pont) (R Del.) Dec. 11, 1863-Nov. 11, 1930; Senate July 7, 1921-Nov. 7, 1922; 1925-Dec. 9, 1928.

DUPRÉ, Henry Garland (D La.) July 28, 1873-Feb. 21, 1924; House Nov. 8, 1910-Feb. 21, 1924.

DURAND, George Harman (D Mich.) Feb. 21, 1838-June 8, 1903; House 1875-77.

DURBOROW, Alan Cathcard Jr. (D Ill.) Nov. 10, 1857-March 10, 1908; House 1891-95.

DURELL, Daniel Meserve (— N.H.) July 20, 1769-April 29, 1841; House 1807-09.

DUREY, Cyrus (R N.Y.) May 16, 1864-Jan. 4, 1933; House 1907-11.

DURFEE, Job (D R.I.) Sept. 20, 1790-July 26, 1847; House 1821-25 (PP 1821-23, D 1823-25).

DURFEE, Nathaniel Briggs (R R.I.) Sept. 29, 1812-Nov. 9, 1872; House 1855-59 (AP 1855-57, R 1857-59).

DURGAN, George Richard (D Ind.) Jan. 20, 1872-Jan. 13, 1942; House 1933-35.

DURHAM, Carl Thomas (D N.C.) Aug. 28, 1892-April 29, 1974; House 1939-61.

DURHAM, Milton Jameson (D Ky.) May 16, 1824-Feb. 12, 1911; House 1873-79.

DURKEE, Charles (R Wis.) Dec. 10, 1805-Jan. 14, 1870; House 1849-53 (F-S); Senate 1855-61 (R); Gov. of Utah Terr. 1865-69.

DURKIN, John Anthony (D N.H.) March 29, 1936-—; Senate Sept. 18, 1975-—.

DURNO, Edwin R. (R Ore.) Jan. 26, 1899-—; House 1961-63.

DUVAL, Isaac Harding (R W.Va.) Sept. 1, 1824-July 10, 1902; House 1869-71.

DUVAL, William Pope (D Ky.) 1784-March 19, 1854; House 1813-15; Gov. of Terr. of Fla. 1822-34.

DUVALL, Gabriel (D Md.) Dec. 6, 1752-March 6, 1844; House Nov. 11, 1794-March 28, 1796; Asso. Justice, U.S. Supreme Court 1812-35.

DWIGHT, Henry Williams (— Mass.) Feb. 26, 1788-Feb. 21, 1845; House 1821-31.

DWIGHT, Jeremiah Wilbur (father of John Wilbur Dwight) (R N.Y.) April 17, 1819-Nov. 26, 1885; House 1877-83.

DWIGHT, John Wilbur (son of Jeremiah Wilbur Dwight) (R N.Y.) May 24, 1859-Jan. 19, 1928; House Nov. 2, 1902-13.

DWIGHT, Theodore (cousin of Aaron Burr) (F Conn.) Dec. 15, 1764-June 12, 1846; House Dec. 1, 1806-07.

DWIGHT, Thomas (F Mass.) Oct. 29, 1758-Jan. 2, 1819; House 1803-05.

DWINELL, Justin (— N.Y.) Oct. 28, 1785-Sept. 17, 1850; House 1823-25.

DWORSHAK, Henry Clarence (R Idaho) Aug. 29, 1894-July 23, 1962; House 1939-Nov. 5, 1946; Senate Nov. 6, 1946-49, Oct. 14, 1949-July 23, 1962.

DWYER, Florence Price (R N.J.) July 4, 1902-Feb. 29, 1976; House 1959-73.

DYAL, Kenneth Warren (D Calif.) July 9, 1910-—; House 1965-67.

DYER, David Patterson (uncle of Leonidas Carstarphen Dyer) (R Mo.) Feb. 12, 1838-April 29, 1924; House 1869-71.

DYER, Leonidas Carstarphen (nephew of David Patterson Dyer) (R Mo.) June 11, 1871-Dec. 15, 1957; House 1911-June 19, 1914, 1915-33.

E

EAGAN, John Joseph (D N.J.) Jan. 22, 1872-June 13, 1956; House 1913-21, 1923-25.

EAGER, Samuel Watkins (R N.Y.) April 8, 1789-Dec. 23, 1860; House Nov. 2, 1830-31.

EAGLE, Joe Henry (D Texas) Jan. 23, 1870-Jan. 10, 1963; House 1913-21, Jan. 28, 1933-37.

EAGLETON, Thomas F. (D Mo.) Sept. 4, 1929-—; Senate Dec. 28, 1968-—.

EAMES, Benjamin Tucker (R R.I.) June 4, 1818-Oct. 6, 1901; House 1871-79.

EARHART, Daniel Scofield (D Ohio) May 28, 1907-—; House Nov. 3, 1936-37.

EARLE, Elias (uncle of Samuel Earle and John Baylis Earle and great-grandfather of John Laurens Manning Irby and Joseph Haynsworth Earle) (D S.C.) June 19, 1762-May 19, 1823; House 1805-07, 1811-15, 1817-21.

EARLE, John Baylis (nephew of Elias Earle and cousin of Samuel Earle) (— S.C.) Oct. 23, 1766-Feb. 3, 1863; House 1803-05.

EARLE, Joseph Haynsworth (great-grandson of Elias Earle, cousin of John Laurens Manning Irby and nephew of William Lowndes Yancey) (D S.C.) April 30, 1847-May 20, 1897; Senate March 4-May 20, 1897.

EARLE, Samuel (nephew of Elias Earle and cousin of John Baylis Earle) (— S.C.) Nov. 28, 1760-Nov. 24, 1833; House 1795-97.

EARLL, Jonas Jr. (cousin of Nehemiah Hezekiah Earll) (D N.Y.) 1786-Oct. 28, 1846; House 1827-31.

EARLL, Nehemiah Hezekiah (cousin of Jonas Earll, Jr.) (D N.Y.) Oct. 5, 1787-Aug. 26, 1872; House 1839-41.

EARLY, Joseph Daniel (D Mass.) Jan. 31, 1933-—; House 1975-—.

EARLY, Peter (— Ga.) June 20, 1773-Aug. 15, 1817; House Jan. 10, 1803-07; Gov. 1813-15.

EARNSHAW, Manuel (I P.I.) Nov. 19, 1862-Feb. 13, 1936; House (Res. Comm.) 1913-17.

EARTHMAN, Harold Henderson (D Tenn.) April 13, 1900-—; House 1945-47.

EASTLAND, James Oliver (D Miss.) Nov. 28, 1940-—; Senate June 30-Sept. 18, 1941, 1943-—; President pro tempore July 29, 1972-—.

EASTMAN, Ben C. (D Wis.) Oct. 24, 1812-Feb. 2, 1856; House 1851-55.

EASTMAN, Ira Allen (nephew of Nehemiah Eastman) (D N.H.) Jan. 1, 1809-March 21, 1881; House 1839-43.

EASTMAN, Nehemiah (uncle of Ira Allen Eastman) (D N.H.) June 16, 1782-Jan. 11, 1856; House 1825-27.

EASTON, Rufus (D Mo.) May 4, 1774-July 5, 1834; House (Terr. Del.) Sept. 17, 1814-Aug. 5, 1816.

EATON, Charles Aubrey (uncle of William Robb Eaton) (R N.J.) March 29, 1868-Jan. 23, 1953; House 1925-53.

EATON, John Henry (D Tenn.) June 18, 1790-Nov. 17, 1856; Senate Sept. 5, 1818-21, Sept. 27, 1821-March 9, 1829; Secy. of War 1829-31; Gov. of Fla. Terr. 1834-36.

EATON, Lewis (— N.Y.) ? - ?; House 1823-25.

EATON, Thomas Marion (R Calif.) Aug. 3, 1896-Sept. 16, 1939; House Jan. 3-Sept. 16, 1939.

EATON, William Robb (nephew of Charles Aubrey Eaton) (R Colo.) Dec. 17, 1877-Dec. 16, 1942; House 1929-33.

EATON, William Wallace (D Conn.) Oct. 11, 1816-Sept. 21, 1898; Senate Feb. 5, 1875-1881; House 1883-85.

EBERHARTER, Herman Peter (D Pa.) April 29, 1892-Sept. 9, 1958; House 1937-Sept. 9, 1958.

ECHOLS, Leonard Sidney (R W.Va.) Oct. 30, 1871-May 9, 1946; House 1919-23.

ECKERT, Charles Richard (D Pa.) Jan. 20, 1868-Oct. 26, 1959; House 1935-39.

ECKERT, George Nicholas (W Pa.) July 4, 1802-June 28, 1865; House 1847-49.

ECKHARDT, Robert Christian (D Texas) July 16, 1913-—; House 1967-—.

ECKLEY, Ephraim Ralph (R Ohio) Dec. 9, 1811-March 27, 1908; House 1863-69.

ECTON, Zales Nelson (R Mont.) April 1, 1898-March 3, 1961; Senate 1947-53.

EDDY, Frank Marion (R Minn.) April 1, 1856-Jan. 13, 1929; House 1895-1903.

EDDY, Norman (D Ind.) Dec. 10, 1810-Jan. 28, 1872; House 1853-55.

EDDY, Samuel (D R.I.) March 31, 1769-Feb. 3, 1839; House 1819-25.

EDELSTEIN, Morris Michael (D N.Y.) Feb. 5, 1888-June 4, 1941; House Feb. 6, 1940-June 4, 1941.

EDEN, John Rice (D Ill.) Feb. 1, 1826-June 9, 1909; House 1863-65, 1873-79, 1885-87.

EDGAR, Robert William (D Pa.) May 29, 1943-__; House 1975-__.

EDGE, Walter Evans (R N.J.) Nov. 20, 1873-Oct. 29, 1956; Senate 1919-Nov. 21, 1929; Gov. 1917-19, 1944-47.

EDGERTON, Alfred Peck (brother of Joseph Ketchum Edgerton) (D Ohio) Jan. 11, 1813-May 14, 1897; House 1851-55.

EDGERTON, Alonzo Jay (R Minn.) June 7, 1827-Aug. 9, 1896; Senate March 12-Oct. 30, 1881.

EDGERTON, Joseph Ketchum (brother of Alfred Peck Edgerton) (D Ind.) Feb. 16, 1818-Aug. 25, 1893; House 1863-65.

EDGERTON, Sidney (R Ohio) Aug. 17, 1818-July 19, 1900; House 1859-63; Gov. of Montana Terr. 1865-66.

EDIE, John Rufus (W Pa.) Jan. 14, 1814-Aug. 27, 1888; House 1855-59.

EDMANDS, John Wiley (W Mass.) March 1, 1809-Jan. 31, 1877; House 1853-55.

EDMISTON, Andrew (D W.Va.) Nov. 13, 1892-Aug. 28, 1966; House Nov. 28, 1933-43.

EDMOND, William (F Conn.) Sept. 28, 1755-Aug. 1, 1838; House Nov. 13, 1797-1801.

EDMONDS, George Washington (R Pa.) Feb. 22, 1864-Sept. 28, 1939; House 1913-25, 1933-35.

EDMONDSON, Edmond Augustus (brother of James Howard Edmondson) (D Okla.) April 7, 1919-__; House 1953-1973.

EDMONDSON, James Howard (brother of Edmond Augustus Edmondson) (D Okla.) Sept. 27, 1925-Nov. 17, 1971; Senate Jan. 9, 1963-Nov. 3, 1964, Gov. 1959-63.

EDMUNDS, George Franklin (R Vt.) Feb. 1, 1828-Feb. 27, 1919; Senate April 3, 1866-Nov. 1, 1891, President pro tempore 1883-85.

EDMUNDS, Paul Carrington (D Va.) Nov. 1, 1836-March 12, 1899; House 1889-95.

EDMUNDSON, Henry Alonzo (D Va.) June 14, 1814-Dec. 16, 1890; House 1849-61.

EDSALL, Joseph E. (D N.J.) 1789-1865; House 1845-49.

EDWARDS, Benjamin (father of Ninian Edwards) (— Md.) Aug. 12, 1753-Nov. 13, 1829; House Jan. 2-March 3, 1795.

EDWARDS, Caldwell, (D-P Mont.) Jan. 8, 1841-July 23, 1922; House 1901-03.

EDWARDS, Charles Gordon (D Ga.) July 2, 1878-July 13, 1931; House 1907-17, 1925-July 13, 1931.

EDWARDS, Don (D Calif.) Jan. 6, 1915-__; House 1963-__.

EDWARDS, Don Calvin (R Ky.) July 13, 1861-Sept. 19, 1938; House 1905-11.

EDWARDS, Edward Irving (D N.J.) Dec. 1, 1863-Jan. 26, 1931; Senate 1923-29; Gov. 1920-23.

EDWARDS, Edwin Washington (husband of Elaine Schwartzenburg Edwards) (D La.) Aug. 7, 1927-__; House Oct. 2, 1965-May 9, 1972.

EDWARDS, Elaine Schwartzenburg (wife of Edwin Washington Edwards) (D La.) March 8, 1929-__; Senate Aug. 1, 1972-Nov. 13, 1972.

EDWARDS, Francis Smith (AP N.Y.) May 28, 1817-May 20, 1899; House 1855-Feb. 28, 1857.

EDWARDS, Henry Waggaman (D Conn.) Oct. 1779-July 22, 1847; House 1819-23; Senate Oct. 8, 1823-27; Gov. 1833, 1835-37.

EDWARDS, Jack (William Jackson) (R Ala.) Sept. 20, 1928-__; House 1965-__.

EDWARDS, John (— Ky.) 1748-1837; Senate June 18, 1792-95.

EDWARDS, John (D N.Y.) Aug. 6, 1781-Dec. 28, 1850; House 1837-39.

EDWARDS, John (granduncle of John Edwards Leonard) (W Pa.) 1786-June 26, 1843; House 1839-43.

EDWARDS, John (LR Ark.) Oct. 24, 1805-April 8, 1894; House 1871-Feb. 9, 1872.

EDWARDS, John Cummins (D Mo.) June 24, 1804-Oct. 14, 1888; House 1841-43; Gov. 1844-48.

EDWARDS, Ninian (son of Benjamin Edwards) (D Ill.) March 17, 1775-July 20, 1833; Senate Dec. 3, 1818-24; Terr. Gov. 1809-18; Gov. 1826-30.

EDWARDS, Samuel (F Pa.) March 12, 1785-Nov. 21, 1850; House 1819-27.

EDWARDS, Thomas McKey (R N.H.) Dec. 16, 1795-May 1, 1875; House 1859-63.

EDWARDS, Thomas Owen (W Ohio) March 29, 1810-Feb. 5, 1876; House 1847-49.

EDWARDS, Weldon Nathaniel (D N.C.) Jan. 25, 1788-Dec. 18, 1873; House Feb. 7, 1816-27.

EDWARDS, William Posey (R Ga.) Nov. 9, 1835-June 28, 1900; House July 25, 1868-69.

EFNER, Valentine (D N.Y.) May 5, 1776-Nov. 20, 1865; House 1835-37.

EGBERT, Albert Gallatin (D Pa.) April 13, 1828-March 28, 1896; House 1875-77.

EGBERT, Joseph (D N.Y.) April 10, 1807-July 7, 1888; House 1841-43.

EGE, George (— Pa.) March 9, 1748-Dec. 14, 1829; House Dec. 8, 1796-Oct. 1797.

EGGLESTON, Benjamin (R Ohio) Jan. 3, 1816-Feb. 9, 1888; House 1865-69.

EGGLESTON, Joseph (uncle of William Segar Archer) (D Va.) Nov. 24, 1754-Feb. 13, 1811; House Dec. 3, 1798-1801.

EICHER, Edward Clayton (D Iowa) Dec. 16, 1878-Nov. 29, 1944; House 1933-Dec. 2, 1938.

EICKHOFF, Anthony (D N.Y.) Sept. 11, 1827-Nov. 5, 1901; House 1877-79.

EILBERG, Joshua (D Pa.) Feb. 12, 1921-__; House 1967-__.

EINSTEIN, Edwin (R N.Y.) Nov. 18, 1842-Jan. 24, 1905; House 1879-81.

EKWALL, William Alexander (R Ore.) June 14, 1887-Oct. 16, 1956; House 1935-37.

ELA, Jacob Hart (R N.H.) July 18, 1820-Aug. 21, 1884; House 1867-71.

ELAM, Joseph Barton (D La.) June 12, 1821-July 4, 1885; House 1877-81.

ELDER, James Walter (D La.) Oct. 5, 1882-Dec. 16, 1941; House 1913-15.

ELDREDGE, Charles Augustus (D Wis.) Feb. 27, 1820-Oct. 26, 1896; House 1863-75.

ELDREDGE, Nathaniel Buel (D Mich.) March 28, 1813-Nov. 27, 1893; House 1883-87.

ELIOT, Samuel Atkins (great-grandfather of Thomas Hopkinson Eliot) (W Mass.) March 5, 1798-Jan. 29, 1862; House Aug. 22, 1850-51.

ELIOT, Thomas Dawes (R Mass.) March 20, 1808-June 14, 1870; House April 17, 1854-1855 (W), 1859-69 (R).

ELIOT, Thomas Hopkinson (great-grandson of Samuel Atkins Eliot) (D Mass.) June 14, 1907-__; House 1941-43.

ELIZALDE, Joaquin Miguel (— P.I.) Aug. 2, 1896-Feb. 9, 1965; House (Res. Comm.) Sept. 29, 1938-Aug. 9, 1944.

ELKINS, Davis (son of Stephen Benton Elkins and grandson of Henry Gassaway Davis) (R W.Va.) Jan. 24, 1876-Jan. 5, 1959; Senate Jan. 9-Jan. 31, 1911, 1919-25.

ELKINS, Stephen Benton (father of Davis Elkins) (R N.M./W.Va.) Sept. 26, 1841-Jan. 4, 1911; House (Terr. Del. N.M.) 1873-77; Senate (W.Va.) 1895-Jan. 4, 1911; Secy. of War 1891-93.

ELLENBOGEN, Henry (D Pa.) April 3, 1900-__; House 1933-Jan. 3, 1938.

ELLENDER, Allen Joseph (D La.) Sept. 24, 1890-July 27, 1972; Senate 1937-July 27, 1972. President pro tempore 1971-July 27, 1972.

ELLERBE, James Edwin (D S.C.) Jan. 12, 1867-Oct. 24, 1917; House 1905-13.

ELLERY, Christopher (D R.I.) Nov. 1, 1768-Dec. 2, 1840; Senate May 6, 1801-05.

ELLETT, Henry Thomas (D Miss.) March 8, 1812-Oct. 15, 1887; House Jan. 26-March 3, 1847.

ELLETT, Tazewell (D Va.) Jan. 1, 1856-May 19, 1914; House 1895-97.

ELLICOTT, Benjamin (D N.Y.) April 17, 1765-Dec. 10, 1827; House 1817-19.

ELLIOTT, Alfred James (D Calif.) June 1, 1895-Jan. 17, 1973; House May 4, 1937-49.

ELLIOTT, Carl Atwood (D Ala.) Dec. 20, 1913-__; House 1949-65.

ELLIOTT, Douglas Hemphill (R Pa.) June 3, 1921-June 19, 1960; House April 26-June 19, 1960.

ELLIOTT, James (F Vt.) Aug. 18, 1775-Nov. 10, 1839; House 1803-09.

ELLIOTT, James Thomas (R Ark.) April 22, 1823-July 28, 1875; House Jan. 13-March 3, 1869.

ELLIOTT, John (— Ga.) Oct. 24, 1773-Aug. 9, 1827; Senate 1819-25.

ELLIOTT, John Milton (D Ky.) May 20, 1820-March 26, 1879; House 1853-59.

ELLIOTT, Mortimer Fitzland (D Pa.) Sept. 24, 1839-Aug. 5, 1920; House 1883-85.

ELLIOTT, Richard Nash (R Ind.) April 25, 1873-March 21, 1948; House June 26, 1917-31.

ELLIOTT, Robert Brown (R S.C.) Aug. 11, 1842-Aug. 9, 1884; House 1871-Nov. 1, 1874.

ELLIOTT, William (D S.C.) Sept. 3, 1838-Dec. 7, 1907; House 1887-Sept. 23, 1890, 1891-93, 1895-June 4, 1896, 1897-1903.

ELLIS, Caleb (— N.H.) April 16, 1767-May 6, 1816; House 1805-07.

ELLIS, Chesselden (D N.Y.) 1808-May 10, 1854; House 1843-45.

ELLIS, Clyde Taylor (D Ark.) Dec. 21, 1908-__; House 1939-43.

ELLIS, Edgar Clarence (R Mo.) Oct. 2, 1854-March 15, 1947; House 1905-09, 1921-23, 1925-27, 1929-31.

ELLIS, Ezekiel John (D La.) Oct. 15, 1840-April 25, 1889; House 1875-85.

ELLIS, Hubert Summers (R W.Va.) July 6, 1887-Dec. 3, 1959; House 1943-49.

ELLIS, Powhatan (D Miss.) Jan. 17, 1790-March 18, 1863; Senate Sept. 28, 1825-Jan. 28, 1826, 1827-July 16, 1832.

ELLIS, William Cox (F Pa.) May 5, 1787-Dec. 13, 1871; House 1821 (elected 1820 but resigned before Congress assembled), 1823-25.

ELLIS, William Russell (R Ore.) April 23, 1850-Jan. 18, 1915; House 1893-99, 1907-11.

ELLIS, William Thomas (D Ky.) July 24, 1845-Jan. 8, 1925; House 1889-95.

ELLISON, Andrew (D Ohio) 1812-about 1860; House 1853-55.

ELLISON, Daniel (R Md.) Feb. 14, 1886-Aug. 20, 1960; House 1943-45.

ELLMAKER, Amos (— Pa.) Feb. 2, 1787-Nov. 28, 1851; House March 3-July 3, 1815 (elected but did not qualify, resigned before Congress assembled).

ELLSBERRY, William Wallace (D Ohio) Dec. 18, 1833-Sept. 7, 1894; House 1885-87.

ELLSWORTH, Charles Clinton (R Mich.) Jan. 29, 1824-June 25, 1899; House 1877-79.

ELLSWORTH, Franklin Fowler (R Minn.) July 10, 1879-Dec. 23, 1942; House 1915-21.

ELLSWORTH, Matthew Harris (R Ore.) Sept. 17, 1899-__; House 1943-57.

ELLSWORTH, Oliver (father of William Wolcott Ellsworth) (F Conn.) April 29, 1745-Nov. 26, 1807; Senate 1789-March 8, 1796; Cont. Cong. 1777-84; Chief Justice, U.S. Supreme Court 1796-99.

ELLSWORTH, Robert Fred (R Kan.) June 11, 1926-__; House 1961-67.

ELLSWORTH, Samuel Stewart (D N.Y.) Oct. 13, 1790-June 4, 1863; House 1845-47.

ELLSWORTH, William Wolcott (son of Oliver Ellsworth) (W Conn.) Nov. 10, 1791-Jan. 15, 1868; House 1829-July 8, 1834; Gov. 1838-42.

ELLWOOD, Reuben (R Ill.) Feb. 21, 1821-July 1, 1885; House 1883-July 1, 1885.

ELLZEY, Lawrence Russell (D Miss.) March 20, 1891-__; House March 15, 1932-35.

ELMENDORF, Lucas Conrad (D N.Y.) 1758-Aug. 17, 1843; House 1797-1803.

ELMER, Ebenezer (brother of Jonathan Elmer and father of Lucius Quintius Cincinnatus Elmer) (D N.J.) Aug. 23, 1752-Oct. 18, 1843; House 1801-07.

ELMER, Jonathan (brother of Ebenezer Elmer and uncle of Lucius Quintius Cincinnatus Elmer) (F N.J.) Nov. 29, 1745-Sept. 3, 1817; Senate 1789-91; Cont. Cong. 1776-78, 1781-84, 1787-88.

ELMER, Lucius Quintius Cincinnatus (son of Ebenezer Elmer and nephew of Jonathan Elmer) (D N.J.) Feb. 3, 1793-March 11, 1883; House 1843-45.

ELMER, William Price (R Mo.) March 2, 1871-May 11, 1956; House 1943-45.

ELMORE, Franklin Harper (SRD S.C.) Oct. 15, 1799-May 28, 1850; House Dec. 10, 1836-39; Senate April 11-May 28, 1850.

ELSAESSER, Edward Julius (R N.Y.) March 10, 1904-__; House 1945-49.

ELSTON, Charles Henry (R Ohio) Aug. 1, 1891-__; House 1939-53.

ELSTON, John Arthur (PR Calif.) Feb. 10, 1874-Dec. 15, 1921; House 1915-Dec. 15, 1921.

ELTSE, Ralph Roscoe (R Calif.) Sept. 13, 1885-__; House 1933-35.

ELVINS, Politte (R Mo.) March 16, 1878-Jan. 14, 1943; House 1909-11.

ELY, Alfred (R N.Y.) Feb. 15, 1815-May 18, 1892; House 1859-63.

ELY, Frederick David (R Mass.) Sept. 24, 1838-Aug. 6, 1921; House 1885-87.

ELY, John (D N.Y.) Oct. 8, 1774-Aug. 20, 1849; House 1839-41.

ELY, Smith Jr. (D N.Y.) April 17, 1825-July 1, 1911; House 1871-73, 1875-Dec. 11, 1876.

ELY, William (F Mass.) Aug. 14, 1765-Oct. 9, 1817; House 1805-15.

EMBREE, Elisha (W Ind.) Sept. 28, 1801-Feb. 28, 1863; House 1847-49.

EMERICH, Martin (D Ill.) April 27, 1846-Sept. 27, 1922; House 1903-05.

EMERSON, Henry Ivory (R Ohio) March 15, 1871-Oct. 28, 1953; House 1915-21.

EMERSON, Louis Woodard (R N.Y.) July 25, 1857-June 10, 1924; House 1899-1903.

EMERY, David Farnham (R Maine) Sept. 1, 1948-__; House 1975-__.

EMOTT, James (F N.Y.) March 9, 1771-April 7, 1850; House 1809-13.

EMRIE, Jonas Reece (R Ohio) April 25, 1812-June 5, 1869; House 1855-57.

ENGEL, Albert Joseph (R Mich.) Jan. 1, 1888-Dec. 2, 1959; House 1935-51.

ENGLAND, Edward Theodore (R W.Va.) Sept. 29, 1869-Sept. 9, 1934; House 1927-29.

ENGLE, Clair (D Calif.) Sept. 21, 1911-July 30, 1964; House Aug. 31, 1943-59; Senate 1959-July 30, 1964.

ENGLEBRIGHT, Harry Lane (son of William F. Englebright) (R Calif.) Jan. 2, 1884-May 13, 1943; House Aug. 31, 1926-May 13, 1943.

ENGLEBRIGHT, William Fellows (father of Harry Lane Englebright) (R Calif.) Nov. 23, 1855-Feb. 10, 1915; House Nov. 6, 1906-11.

ENGLISH, Glenn Lee Jr. (D Okla.) Nov. 30, 1940-__; House 1975-__.

ENGLISH, James Edward (D Conn.) March 13, 1812-March 2, 1890; House 1861-65; Senate Nov. 27, 1875-May 17, 1876; Gov. 1867-69, 1870-71.

ENGLISH, Thomas Dunn (D N.J.) June 29, 1819-April 1, 1902; House 1891-95.

ENGLISH, Warren Barkley (D Calif.) May 1, 1840-Jan. 9, 1913; House April 4, 1894-95.

ENGLISH, William Eastin (son of William Hayden English) (D Ind.) Nov. 3, 1850-April 29, 1926; House May 22, 1884-85.

ENGLISH, William Hayden (father of William Eastin English) (D Ind.) Aug. 27, 1822-Feb. 7, 1896; House 1853-61.

ENLOE, Benjamin Augustine (D Tenn.) Jan. 18, 1848-July 8, 1922; House 1887-95.

ENOCHS, William Henry (R Ohio) March 29, 1842-July 13, 1893; House 1891-July 13, 1893.

EPES, James Fletcher (cousin of Sydney Parham Epes) (D Va.) May 23, 1842-Aug. 24, 1910; House 1891-95.

EPES, Sydney Parham (cousin of James Fletcher Epes) (D Va.) Aug. 20, 1865-March 3, 1900; House 1897-March 23, 1898, 1899-March 3, 1900.

EPPES, John Wayles (D Va.) April 7, 1773-Sept. 13, 1823; House 1803-11, 1813-15; Senate 1817-Dec. 4, 1819.

ERDMAN, Constantine Jacob (grandson of Jacob Erdman) (D Pa.) Sept. 4, 1846-Jan. 15, 1911; House 1893-97.

ERDMAN, Jacob (grandfather of Constantine Jacob Erdman) (D Pa.) Feb. 22, 1801-July 20, 1867; House 1845-47.

ERICKSON, John Edward (D Mont.) March 14, 1863-May 25, 1946; Senate March 13, 1933-Nov. 6, 1934; Gov. 1925-33.

ERK, Edmund Frederick (R Pa.) April 17, 1872-Dec. 14, 1953; House Nov. 4, 1930-33.

ERLENBORN, John Neal (R Ill.) Feb. 8, 1927-__; House 1965-__.

ERMENTROUT, Daniel (D Pa.) Jan. 24, 1837-Sept. 17, 1899; House 1881-89, 1897-Sept. 17, 1899.

ERNST, Richard Pretlow (R Ky.) Feb. 28, 1858-April 13, 1934; Senate 1921-27.

ERRETT, Russell (R Pa.) Nov. 10, 1817-April 7, 1891; House 1877-83.

ERVIN, James (Protect. S.C.) Oct. 17, 1778-July 7, 1841; House 1817-21.

ERVIN, Joseph Wilson (brother of Samuel James Ervin Jr.) (D N.C.) March 3, 1901-Dec. 25, 1945; House Jan. 3-Dec. 25, 1945.

ERVIN, Samuel James Jr. (brother of Joseph Wilson Ervin) (D N.C.) Sept. 27, 1896-__; House Jan. 22, 1946-47; Senate June 5, 1954-Dec. 31, 1974.

ESCH, John Jacob (R Wis.) March 20, 1861-April 27, 1941; House 1899-1921.

ESCH, Marvin L. (R Mich.) Aug. 4, 1927-__; House 1967-__.

ESHLEMAN, Edwin D. (R Pa.) Dec. 4, 1920-__; House 1967-__.

ESLICK, Edward Everett (husband of Willa McCord Eslick) (D Tenn.) April 19, 1872-June 14, 1932; House 1925-June 14, 1932.

ESLICK, Willa McCord Blake (wife of Edward Everett Eslick) (D Tenn.) Sept. 8, 1878-Feb. 18, 1961; House Aug. 4, 1932-33.

ESSEN, Frederick (R Mo.) April 22, 1863-Aug. 18, 1946; House Nov. 5, 1918-19.

ESTABROOK, Experience (— Neb.) April 30, 1813-March 26, 1894; House (Terr. Del.) 1859-May 18, 1860.

ESTEP, Harry Allison (R Pa.) Feb. 1, 1884-Feb. 28, 1968; House 1927-33.

ESTERLY, Charles Joseph (R Pa.) Feb. 8, 1888-Sept. 3, 1940; House 1925-27, 1929-31.

ESTIL, Benjamin (— Va.) March 13, 1780-July 14, 1853; House 1825-27.

ESTOPINAL, Albert (D La.) Jan. 30, 1845-April 28, 1919; House Nov. 3, 1908-April 28, 1919.

ESTY, Constantine Canaris (R Mass.) Dec. 26, 1824-Dec. 27, 1912; House Dec. 2, 1872-73.

ETHERIDGE, Emerson (W Tenn.) Sept. 28, 1819-Oct. 21, 1902; House 1853-57, 1859-61.

EUSTIS, George Jr. (brother of James Biddle Eustis) (AP La.) Sept. 28, 1828-March 15, 1872; House 1855-59.

EUSTIS, James Biddle (brother of George Eustis, Jr.) (D La.) Aug. 27, 1834-Sept. 9, 1899; Senate Jan. 12, 1876-79, 1885-91.

EUSTIS, William (D Mass.) June 10, 1753-Feb. 6, 1825; House 1801-05, Aug. 21, 1820-23; Secy. of War 1809-13; Gov. 1823-25.

EVANS, Alexander (W Md.) Sept. 13, 1818-Dec. 5, 1888; House 1847-53.

EVANS, Alvin (R Pa.) Oct. 4, 1845-June 19, 1906; House 1901-05.

EVANS, Charles Robley (D Nev.) Aug. 9, 1866-Nov. 30, 1954; House 1919-21.

EVANS, David Ellicott (D N.Y.) March 19, 1788-May 17, 1850; House March 4-May 2, 1827.

EVANS, David Reid (D S.C.) Feb. 20, 1769-March 8, 1843; House 1813-15.

EVANS, David Walter (D Ind.) Aug. 17, 1946-__; House 1975-__.

EVANS, Frank Edward (D Colo.) Sept. 6, 1923-__; House 1965-__.

EVANS, George (W Maine) Jan. 12, 1797-April 6, 1867; House July 20, 1829-41; Senate 1841-47.

EVANS, Henry Clay (R Tenn.) June 18, 1843-Dec. 12, 1921; House 1889-91.

EVANS, Hiram Kinsman (R Iowa) March 17, 1863-July 9, 1941; House June 4, 1923-25.

EVANS, Isaac Newton (R Pa.) July 29, 1827-Dec. 3, 1901; House 1877-79, 1883-87.

EVANS, James La Fayette (R Ind.) March 27, 1825-May 28, 1903; House 1875-79.

EVANS, John Morgan (D Mont.) Jan. 7, 1863-March 12, 1946; House 1913-21, 1923-33.

EVANS, Joshua Jr. (D Pa.) Jan. 20, 1777-Oct. 2, 1846; House 1829-33.

EVANS, Josiah James (SRD S.C.) Nov. 27, 1786-May 6, 1858; Senate 1853-May 6, 1858.

EVANS, Lemuel Dale (AP Texas) Jan. 8, 1810-July 1, 1877; House 1855-57.

EVANS, Lynden (D Ill.) June 28, 1858-May 6, 1926; House 1911-13.

EVANS, Marcellus Hugh (D N.Y.) Sept. 22, 1884-Nov. 21, 1953; House 1935-41.

EVANS, Nathan (W Ohio) June 24, 1804-Sept. 27, 1879; House 1847-51.

EVANS, Robert Emory (R Neb.) July 15, 1856-July 8, 1925; House 1919-23.

EVANS, Thomas (— Va.) ? - ?; House 1797-1801.

EVANS, Walter (nephew of Burwell Clark Ritter) (R Ky.) Sept. 18, 1842-Dec. 30, 1923; House 1895-99.

EVANS, William Elmer (R Calif.) Dec. 14, 1877-Nov. 12, 1959; House 1927-35.

EVARTS, William Maxwell (grandson of Roger Sherman) (R N.Y.) Feb. 6, 1818-Feb. 28, 1901; Senate 1885-91; Atty. Gen. 1868-69; Secy. of State 1877-81.

EVERETT, Edward (father of William Everett) (NR Mass.) April 11, 1794-Jan. 15, 1865; House 1825-35; Senate 1853-June 1, 1854; Gov. 1836-40; Secy. of State 1852-53.

EVERETT, Horace (W Vt.) July 17, 1779-Jan. 30, 1851; House 1829-43.

EVERETT, Robert Ashton (D Tenn.) Feb. 24, 1915-Jan. 26, 1969; House Feb. 1, 1958-Jan. 26, 1969.

EVERETT, Robert William (D Ga.) March 3, 1839-Feb. 27, 1915; House 1891-93.

EVERETT, William (son of Edward Everett) (D Mass.) Oct. 10, 1839-Feb. 16, 1910; House April 25, 1893-95.

EVERHART, James Bowen (son of William Everhart) (R Pa.) July 26, 1821-Aug. 23, 1888; House 1883-87.

EVERHART, William (father of James Bowen Everhart) (W Pa.) May 17, 1785-Oct. 30, 1868; House 1853-55.

EVINS, John Hamilton (D S.C.) July 18, 1830-Oct. 20, 1884; House 1877-Oct. 20, 1884.

EVINS, Joseph Landon (Joe) (D Tenn.) Oct. 24, 1910-__; House 1947-__.

EWART, Hamilton Glover (R N.C.) Oct. 23, 1849-April 28, 1918; House 1889-91.

EWING, Andrew (brother of Edwin Hickman Ewing) (D Tenn.) June 17, 1813-June 16, 1864; House 1849-51.

EWING, Edwin Hickman (brother of Andrew Ewing) (W Tenn.) Dec. 2, 1809-April 24, 1902; House 1845-47.

EWING, John (W Ind.) May 19, 1789-April 6, 1858; House 1833-35, 1837-39.

EWING, John Hoge (W Pa.) Oct. 5, 1796-June 9, 1887; House 1845-47.

EWING, Presley Underwood (W Ky.) Sept. 1, 1822-Sept. 27, 1854; House 1851-Sept. 27, 1854.

EWING, Thomas (W Ohio) (father of the following) Dec. 28, 1789-Oct. 26, 1871; Senate 1831-37; July 20, 1850-51; Secy. of the Treasury 1841; Secy. of the Interior 1849-50.

WING, Thomas (son of the preceding) (D Ohio) Aug. 7, 1829-Jan. 21, 1896; House 1877-81.

WING, William Lee Davidson (JD Ill.) Aug. 31, 1795-March 25, 1846; Senate Dec. 30, 1835-37; Gov. Nov.-Dec. 1834.

F

FADDIS, Charles I. (D Pa.) June 13, 1890-April 1, 1972; House 1933-Dec. 4, 1942.

FAIR, James Graham (D Nev.) Dec. 3, 1831-Dec. 28, 1894; Senate 1881-87.

FAIRBANKS, Charles Warren (R Ind.) May 11, 1852-June 4, 1918; Senate 1897-1905; Vice President 1905-09.

FAIRCHILD, Benjamin Lewis (R N.Y.) Jan. 5, 1863-Oct. 25, 1946; House 1895-97, 1917-19, 1921-23, Nov. 6, 1923-27.

FAIRCHILD, George Winthrop (R N.Y.) May 6, 1854-Dec. 31, 1924; House 1907-19.

FAIRFIELD, John (D Maine) Jan. 30, 1797-Dec. 24, 1847; House 1835-Dec. 24, 1838; Senate 1843-Dec. 24, 1847; Gov. 1839-41, 1842-43.

FAIRFIELD, Louis William (R Ind.) Oct. 15, 1858-Feb. 20, 1930; House 1917-25.

FAISON, John Miller (D N.C.) April 17, 1862-April 21, 1915; House 1911-15.

FALCONER, Jacob Alexander (Pro Wash.) Jan. 26, 1869-July 1, 1928; House 1913-15.

FALL, Albert Bacon (R N.M.) Nov. 26, 1861-Nov. 30, 1944; Senate March 27, 1912-March 4, 1921; Secy. of the Interior 1921-23.

FALLON, George Hyde (D Md.) July 24, 1902-__; House 1945-71.

FANNIN, Paul Jones (R Ariz.) Jan. 29, 1907-__; Senate 1965-__; Gov. 1959-65.

FARAN, James John (D Ohio) Dec. 29, 1808-Dec. 12, 1892; House 1845-49.

FARBSTEIN, Leonard (D N.Y.) Oct. 12, 1902-__; House 1957-71.

FARIS, George Washington (R Ind.) June 9, 1854-April 17, 1914; House 1895-1901.

FARLEE, Isaac Gray (— N.J.) May 18, 1787-Jan. 12, 1855; House 1843-45.

FARLEY, Ephraim Wilder (W Maine) Aug. 29, 1817-April 3, 1880; House 1853-55.

FARLEY, James Indus (D Ind.) Feb. 24, 1871-June 16, 1948; House 1933-39.

FARLEY, James Thompson (D Calif.) Aug. 6, 1829-Jan. 22, 1886; Senate 1879-85.

FARLEY, Michael Francis (D N.Y.) March 1, 1863-Oct. 8, 1921; House 1915-17.

FARLIN, Dudley (D N.Y.) Sept. 2, 1777-Sept. 26, 1837; House 1835-37.

FARNSLEY, Charles Rowland Peaslee (D Ky.) March 28, 1907-__; House 1965-67.

FARNSWORTH, John Franklin (R Ill.) March 27, 1820-July 14, 1897; House 1857-61, 1863-73.

FARNUM, Billie Sunday (D Mich.) April 11, 1916-__; House 1965-67.

FARQUHAR, John Hanson (R Ind.) Dec. 20, 1818-Oct. 1, 1873; House 1865-67.

FARQUHAR, John McCreath (R N.Y.) April 17, 1832-April 24, 1918; House 1885-91.

FARR, Evarts Worcester (R N.H.) Oct. 10, 1840-Nov. 30, 1880; House 1879-Nov. 30, 1880.

FARR, John Richard (R Pa.) July 18, 1857-Dec. 11, 1933; House 1911-19, Feb. 25-March 3, 1921.

FARRELLY, John Wilson (son of Patrick Farrelly) (W Pa.) July 7, 1809-Dec. 20, 1860; House 1847-49.

FARRELLY, Patrick (father of John Wilson Farrelly) (D Pa.) 1770-Jan. 12, 1826; House 1821-Jan. 12, 1826.

FARRINGTON, James (D N.H.) Oct. 1, 1791-Oct. 29, 1859; House 1837-39.

FARRINGTON, Joseph Rider (husband of Mary Elizabeth Pruett Farrington) (R Hawaii) Oct. 15, 1897-June 19, 1954; House (Terr. Del.) 1943-June 19, 1954.

FARRINGTON, Mary Elizabeth Pruett (widow of Joseph Rider Farrington) (R Hawaii) May 30, 1898-__; House (Terr. Del.) July 31, 1954-57.

FARROW, Samuel (WD S.C.) 1759-Nov. 18, 1824; House 1813-15.

FARWELL, Charles Benjamin (R Ill.) July 1, 1823-Sept. 23, 1903; House 1871-May 6, 1876, 1881-83; Senate Jan. 19, 1887-91.

FARWELL, Nathan Allen (cousin of Owen Lovejoy) (R Maine) Feb. 24, 1812-Dec. 9, 1893; Senate Oct. 27, 1864-65.

FARWELL, Sewall Spaulding (R Iowa) April 26, 1834-Sept. 21, 1909; House 1881-83.

FARY, John George (D Ill.) April 11, 1911-__; House July 8, 1975-__.

FASCELL, Dante Bruno (D Fla.) March 9, 1917-__; House 1955-__.

FASSETT, Jacob Sloat (R N.Y.) Nov. 13, 1853-April 21, 1924; House 1905-11.

FAULKNER, Charles James (D Va./W.Va.) July 6, 1806-Nov. 1, 1884; House 1851-59 (Va.), 1875-77 (W.Va.).

FAULKNER, Charles James (son of the preceding) (D W.Va.) Sept. 21, 1847-Jan. 13, 1929; Senate 1887-99.

FAUNTROY, Walter Edward (D D.C.) Feb. 6, 1933-__; House (Delegate) March 23, 1971-__.

FAUST, Charles Lee (R Mo.) April 24. 1879-Dec. 17, 1928; House 1921-Dec. 17, 1928.

FAVROT, George Kent (D La.) Nov. 26, 1868-Dec. 26, 1934; House 1907-09, 1921-25.

FAY, Francis Ball (W Mass.) June 12, 1793-Oct. 6, 1876; House Dec. 13, 1852-53.

FAY, James Herbert (D N.Y.) April 29, 1899-Sept. 10, 1948; House 1939-41, 1943-45.

FAY, John (D N.Y.) Feb. 10, 1773-June 21, 1855; House 1819-21.

FEARING, Paul (F N.W. Terr.) Feb. 28, 1762-Aug. 21, 1822; House (Terr. Del.) 1801-03.

FEATHERSTON, Winfield Scott (D Miss.) Aug. 8, 1820-May 28, 1891; House 1847-51.

FEATHERSTONE, Lewis Porter (UL Ark.) July 28, 1851-March 14, 1922; House March 5, 1890-91.

FEAZEL, William Crosson (D La.) June 10, 1895-March 16, 1965; Senate May 18-Dec. 30, 1948.

FEELY, John Joseph (D Ill.) Aug. 1, 1875-Feb. 15, 1905; House 1901-03.

FEIGHAN, Michael Aloysius (D Ohio) Feb. 16, 1905-__; House 1943-71.

FELCH, Alpheus (D Mich.) Sept. 28, 1804-June 13, 1896; Senate 1847-53; Gov. 1846-47.

FELDER, John Myers (D S.C.) July 7, 1782-Sept. 1, 1851; House 1831-35.

FELLOWS, Frank (R Maine) Nov. 7, 1889-Aug. 27, 1951; House 1941-Aug. 27, 1951.

FELLOWS, John R. (D N.Y.) July 29, 1832-Dec. 7, 1896; House 1891-Dec. 31, 1893.

FELTON, Charles Norton (R Calif.) Jan. 1, 1828-Sept. 13, 1914; House 1885-89; Senate March 19, 1891-93.

FELTON, Rebecca Latimer (wife of William Harrell Felton) (D Ga.) June 10, 1835-Jan. 24, 1930; Senate Oct. 3-Nov. 22, 1922.

FELTON, William Harrell (husband of Rebecca Latimer Felton) (D Ga.) June 19, 1823-Sept. 24, 1909; House 1875-81.

FENERTY, Clare Gerald (R Pa.) July 25, 1895-July 1, 1952; House 1935-37.

FENN, Edward Hart (R Conn.) Sept. 12, 1856-Feb. 23, 1939; House 1921-31.

FENN, Stephen Southmyd (D Idaho) March 28, 1820-April 13, 1892; House (Terr. Del.) June 23, 1876-79.

FENNER, James (D R.I.) Jan. 22, 1771-April 17, 1846; Senate 1805-Sept. 1807; Gov. 1807-11, 1824-31, 1843-45.

FENTON, Ivor David (R Pa.) Aug. 3, 1889-__; House 1939-63.

FENTON, Lucien Jerome (R Ohio) May 7, 1844-June 28, 1922; House 1895-99.

FENTON, Reuben Eaton (R N.Y.) July 4, 1819-Aug. 25, 1885; House 1853-55, 1857-Dec. 20, 1864; Senate 1869-75; Gov. 1865-69.

FENWICK, Millicent Hammond (R N.J.) Feb. 25, 1910-__; House 1975-__.

FERDON, John William (R N.Y.) Dec. 13, 1826-Aug. 5, 1884; House 1879-81.

FERGUSON, Fenner (D Neb.) April 25, 1814-Oct. 11, 1859; House (Terr. Del.) 1857-59.

FERGUSON, Homer (R Mich.) Feb. 25, 1889-__; Senate 1943-55.

FERGUSON, Phillip Colgan (D Okla.) Aug. 15, 1903-__; House 1935-41.

FERGUSSON, Harvey Butler (D N.M.) Sept. 9, 1848-June 10, 1915; House (Terr. Del.) 1897-99; (Rep.) Jan. 8, 1912-15.

FERNALD, Bert Manfred (R Maine) April 3, 1858-Aug. 23, 1926; Senate Sept. 12, 1916-Aug. 23, 1926; Gov. 1909-11.

FERNANDEZ, Antonio Manuel (D N.M.) Jan. 17, 1902-Nov. 7, 1956; House 1943-Nov. 7, 1956.

FERNANDEZ, Joachim Octave (D La.) Aug. 14, 1896-__; House 1931-41.

FERNÓS-ISERN, Antonio (PD P.R.) May 10, 1895-Jan. 19, 1974; House (Res. Comm.) Sept. 11, 1946-65.

FERRELL, Thomas Merrill (D N.J.) June 20, 1844-Oct. 20, 1916; House 1883-85.

FERRIS, Charles Goadsby (JD N.Y.) about 1796-June 4, 1848; House Dec. 1, 1834-35, 1841-43.

FERRIS, Scott (D Okla.) Nov. 3, 1877-June 8, 1945; House Nov. 16, 1907-21.

FERRIS, Woodbridge Nathan (D Mich.) Jan. 6, 1853-March 23, 1928; Senate 1923-March 23, 1928; Gov. 1913-17.

FERRISS, Orange (R N.Y.) Nov. 26, 1814-April 11, 1894; House 1867-71.

FERRY, Orris Sanford (IR/D Conn.) Aug. 15, 1823-Nov. 21, 1875; House 1859-61 (R); Senate 1867-Nov. 21, 1875 (1867-74 R, 1874-75 IR/D).

FERRY, Thomas White (R Mich.) June 10, 1827-Oct. 13, 1896; House 1865-71; Senate 1871-83; President pro tempore 1875, 1877-79.

FESS, Simeon Davison (R Ohio) Dec. 11, 1861-Dec. 23, 1936; House 1913-23; Senate 1923-35; Chrmn. Rep. Nat. Comm. 1930-32.

FESSENDEN, Samuel Clement (brother of Thomas Amory Deblois Fessenden and William Pitt Fessenden) (R Maine) March 7, 1815-April 18, 1882; House 1861-63.

FESSENDEN, Thomas Amory Deblois (brother of Samuel Clement Fessenden and William Pitt Fessenden) (R Maine) Jan. 23, 1826-Sept. 28, 1868; House Dec. 1, 1862-63.

FESSENDEN, William Pitt (brother of Samuel Clement Fessenden and Thomas Amory Deblois Fessenden) (W Maine) Oct. 16, 1806-Sept. 9, 1869; House 1841-43; Senate Feb. 10, 1854-July 1, 1864, 1865-Sept. 9, 1869; Secy. of the Treasury 1864-65.

FEW, William (D Ga.) June 8, 1748-July 16, 1828; Senate 1789-93; Cont. Cong. 1780-88.

FICKLIN, Orlando Bell (D Ill.) Dec. 16, 1808-May 5, 1886; House 1843-49, 1851-53.

FIEDLER, William Henry Frederick (D N.J.) Aug. 25, 1847-Jan. 1, 1919; House 1883-85.

FIELD, David Dudley (D N.Y.) Feb. 13, 1805-April 13, 1894; House Jan. 11-March 3, 1877.

FIELD, Moses Whelock (R Mich.) Feb. 10, 1828-March 14, 1889; House 1873-75.

FIELD, Richard Stockton (R N.J.) Dec. 31, 1803-May 25, 1870; Senate Nov. 21, 1862-Jan. 14, 1863.

FIELD, Scott (D Texas) Jan. 26, 1847-Dec. 20, 1931; House 1903-07.

FIELD, Walbridge Abner (R Mass.) April 26, 1833-July 15, 1899; House 1877-March 28, 1878, 1879-81.

FIELDER, George Bragg (D N.J.) July 24, 1842-Aug. 14, 1906; House 1893-95.

FIELDS, William Craig (R N.Y.) Feb. 13, 1804-Oct. 27, 1882; House 1867-69.

FIELDS, William Jason (D Ky.) Dec. 29, 1874-Oct. 21, 1954; House 1911-Dec. 11, 1923; Gov. 1923-27.

FIESINGER, William Louis (D Ohio) Oct. 25, 1877-Sept. 11, 1953; House 1931-37.

FILLMORE, Millard (W N.Y.) Jan. 7, 1800-March 8, 1874; House 1833-35, 1837-43; Vice President 1849-July 9, 1850; President July 10, 1850-53.

FINCH, Isaac (D N.Y.) Oct. 13, 1783-June 23, 1845; House 1829-31.

FINCK, William Edward (D Ohio) Sept. 1, 1822-Jan. 25, 1901; House 1863-67, Dec. 7, 1874-75.

FINDLAY, James (brother of John Findlay and William Findlay) (JD Ohio) Oct. 12, 1770-Dec. 28, 1835; House 1825-33.

FINDLAY, John (brother of James Findlay and William Findlay) (D Pa.) March 31, 1766-Nov. 5, 1838; House Oct. 9, 1821-27.

FINDLAY, John Van Lear (D Md.) Dec. 21, 1839-April 19, 1907; House 1883-87.

FINDLAY, William (brother of James Findlay and John Findlay) (D Pa.) June 20, 1768-Nov. 12, 1846; Senate Dec. 10, 1821-27; Gov. 1817-20.

FINDLEY, Paul (R Ill.) June 23, 1921-__; House 1961-__.

FINDLEY, William (D Pa.) 1741 or 1742-April 4, 1821; House 1791-99, 1803-17.

FINE, John (D N.Y.) Aug. 26, 1794-Jan. 4, 1867; House 1839-41.

FINE, Sidney Asher (D N.Y.) Sept. 14, 1903-__; House 1951-Jan. 2, 1956.

FINERTY, John Frederick (ID Ill.) Sept. 10, 1846-June 10, 1908; House 1883-85.

FINKELNBURG, Gustavus Adolphus (LR Mo.) April 6, 1837-May 18, 1908; House 1869-71 (R), 1871-73 (LR).

FINLEY, Charles (son of Hugh Franklin Finley) (R Ky.) March 26, 1865-March 18, 1941; House Feb. 15, 1930-33.

FINLEY, David Edward (D S.C.) Feb. 28, 1861-Jan. 26, 1917; House 1899-Jan. 26, 1917.

FINLEY, Ebenezer Byron (nephew of Stephen Ross Harris) (D Ohio) July 31, 1833-Aug. 22, 1916; House 1877-81.

FINLEY, Hugh Franklin (father of Charles Finley) (R Ky.) Jan. 18, 1833-Oct. 16, 1909; House 1887-91.

FINLEY, Jesse Johnson (D Fla.) Nov. 18, 1812-Nov. 6, 1904; House April 19, 1876-77, Feb. 20-March 3, 1879, 1881-June 1, 1882.

FINNEGAN, Edward Rowan (D Ill.) June 5, 1905-Feb. 2, 1971; House 1961-Dec. 6, 1964.

FINNEY, Darwin Abel (R Pa.) Aug. 11, 1814-Aug. 25, 1868; House 1867-Aug. 25, 1868.

FINO, Paul Albert (R N.Y.) Dec. 15, 1913-__; House 1953-Dec. 31, 1968.

FISCHER, Israel Frederick (R N.Y.) Aug. 17, 1858-March 16, 1940; House 1895-99.

FISH, Hamilton (grandfather of Hamilton Fish Jr. and great-grandfather of Hamilton Fish Jr.) (W N.Y.) Aug. 3, 1808-Sept. 7, 1893; House 1843-45; Senate 1851-57; Gov. 1849-51; Secy. of State 1869-77.

FISH, Hamilton (son of the preceding, father of Hamilton Fish Jr. and grandfather of Hamilton Fish Jr.) (R N.Y.) April 17, 1849-Jan. 15, 1936; House 1909-11.

FISH, Hamilton Jr. (son of the preceding, grandson of Hamilton Fish and father of Hamilton Fish Jr.) (R N.Y.) Dec. 7, 1888-__; House Nov. 2, 1920-45.

FISH, Hamilton Jr. (son of the preceding, grandson of Hamilton Fish, great-grandson of Hamilton Fish) (R N.Y.) June 3, 1926-__; House 1969-__.

FISHBURNE, John Wood (cousin of Fontaine Maury Maverick) (D Va.) March 8, 1868-June 24, 1937; House 1931-33.

FISHER, Charles (D N.C.) Oct. 20, 1789-May 7, 1849; House Feb. 11, 1819-21, 1839-41.

FISHER, David (W Ohio) Dec. 3, 1794-May 7, 1886; House 1847-49.

FISHER, George (— N.Y.) March 17, 1788-March 26, 1861; House 1829-Feb. 5, 1830.

FISHER, George Purnell (UR Del.) Oct. 13, 1817-Feb. 10, 1899; House 1861-63.

FISHER, Horatio Gates (R Pa.) April 21, 1838-May 8, 1890; House 1879-83.

FISHER, Hubert Frederick (D Tenn.) Oct. 6, 1877-June 16, 1941; House 1917-31.

FISHER, John (R N.Y.) March 13, 1806-March 28, 1882; House 1869-71.

FISHER, Joseph Lyman (D Va.) Jan. 11, 1914-__; House 1975-__.

FISHER, Ovie Clark (D Texas) Nov. 22, 1903-__; House 1943-75.

FISHER, Spencer Oliver (D Mich.) Feb. 3, 1843-June 1, 1919; House 1885-89.

FISK, James (D Vt.) Oct. 4, 1763-Nov. 17, 1844; House 1805-09, 1811-15; Senate Nov. 4, 1817-Jan. 8, 1818.

FISK, Jonathan (D N.Y.) Sept. 26, 1778-July 13, 1832; House 1809-11, 1813-March 1815.

FITCH, Asa (F N.Y.) Nov. 10, 1765-Aug. 24, 1843; House 1811-13.

FITCH, Ashbel Parmelee (D N.Y.) Oct. 8, 1838-May 4, 1904; House 1887-89 (R), 1889-Dec. 26, 1893 (D).

FITCH, Graham Newell (grandfather of Edwin Denby) (D Ind.) Dec. 5, 1809-Nov. 29, 1892; House 1849-53; Senate Feb. 4, 1857-61.

FITCH, Thomas (R Nev.) Jan. 27, 1838-Nov. 12, 1923; House 1869-71.

FITE, Samuel McClary (D Tenn.) June 12, 1816-Oct. 23, 1875; House March 4-Oct. 23, 1875.

FITHIAN, Floyd James (D Ind.) Nov. 3, 1928-___; House 1975-___.

FITHIAN, George Washington (D Ill.) July 4, 1854-Jan. 21, 1921; House 1889-95.

FITZGERALD, Frank Thomas (D N.Y.) May 4, 1857-Nov. 25, 1907; House March 4-Nov. 4, 1889.

FITZGERALD, John Francis (grandfather of John F. Kennedy, Robert F. Kennedy and Edward M. Kennedy) (D Mass.) Feb. 11, 1863-Oct. 2, 1950; House 1895-1901, March 4-Oct. 23, 1919.

FITZGERALD, John Joseph (D N.Y.) March 10, 1872-May 13, 1952; House 1899-Dec. 31, 1917.

FITZGERALD, Roy Gerald (R Ohio) Aug. 25, 1875-Nov. 16, 1962; House 1921-31.

FITZGERALD, Thomas (D Mich.) April 10, 1796-March 25, 1855; Senate June 8, 1848-49.

FITZGERALD, William (JD Tenn.) Aug. 6, 1799-March 1864; House 1831-33.

FITZGERALD, William Joseph (D Conn.) March 2, 1887-May 6, 1947; House 1937-39, 1941-43.

FITZGERALD, William Thomas (R Ohio) Oct. 13, 1858-Jan. 12, 1939; House 1925-29.

FITZGIBBONS, John (D N.Y.) July 10, 1868-Aug. 4, 1941; House 1933-35.

FITZHENRY, Louis (D Ill.) June 13, 1870-Nov. 18, 1935; House 1913-15.

FITZPATRICK, Benjamin (SRD Ala.) June 30, 1802-Nov. 25, 1869; Senate Nov. 25, 1848-Nov. 30, 1849, Jan. 14, 1853-55, Nov. 26, 1855-Jan. 21, 1861; President pro tempore 1857-61; Gov. 1841-45.

FITZPATRICK, James Martin (D N.Y.) June 27, 1869-April 10, 1949; House 1927-45.

FITZPATRICK, Morgan Cassius (D Tenn.) Oct. 29, 1868-June 25, 1908; House 1903-05.

FITZPATRICK, Thomas Young (D Ky.) Sept. 20, 1850-Jan. 21, 1906; House 1897-1901.

FITZSIMONS, Thomas (F Pa.) 1741-Aug. 26, 1811; House 1789-95; Cont. Cong. 1782-83.

FJARE, Orvin Benonie (R Mont.) April 16, 1918-___; House 1955-57.

FLACK, William Henry (R N.Y.) March 22, 1861-Feb. 2, 1907; House 1903-Feb. 2, 1907.

FLAGLER, Thomas Thorn (W N.Y.) Oct. 12, 1811-Sept. 6, 1897; House 1853-57.

FLAHERTY, Lawrence James (R Calif.) July 4, 1878-June 13, 1926; House 1925-June 13, 1926.

FLAHERTY, Thomas Aloysius (D Mass.) Dec. 21, 1898-April 27, 1965; House Dec. 14, 1937-43.

FLANAGAN, De Witt Clinton (D N.J.) Dec. 28, 1870-Jan. 15, 1946; House June 18, 1902-03.

FLANAGAN, James Winright (R Texas) Sept. 5, 1805-Sept. 28, 1887; Senate March 30, 1870-75.

FLANDERS, Alvan (R Wash.) Aug. 2, 1825-March 14, 1884; House (Terr. Del.) 1867-69; Gov. of Terr. 1869-70.

FLANDERS, Benjamin Franklin (U La.) Jan. 26, 1816-March 13, 1896; House Dec. 3, 1862-63; Military Gov. 1867-68.

FLANDERS, Ralph Edward (R Vt.) Sept. 28, 1880-Feb. 19, 1970; Senate Nov. 1, 1946-59.

FLANNAGAN, John William Jr. (D Va.) Feb. 20, 1885-April 27, 1955; House 1931-49.

FLANNERY, John Harold (D Pa.) April 19, 1898-June 3, 1961; House 1937-42.

FLEEGER, George Washington (R Pa.) March 13, 1839-June 25, 1894; House 1885-87.

FLEETWOOD, Frederick Gleed (R Vt.) Sept. 27, 1868-Jan. 28, 1938; House 1923-25.

FLEGER, Anthony Alfred (D Ohio) Oct. 21, 1900-July 16, 1963; House 1937-39.

FLEMING, William Bennett (D Ga.) Oct. 29, 1803-Aug. 19, 1886; House Feb. 10-March 3, 1879.

FLEMING, William Henry (D Ga.) Oct. 18, 1856-June 9, 1944; House 1897-1903.

FLETCHER, Charles Kimball (R Calif.) Dec. 15, 1902-___; House 1947-49.

FLETCHER, Duncan Upshaw (D Fla.) Jan. 6, 1859-June 17, 1936; Senate 1909-June 17, 1936.

FLETCHER, Isaac (A-Mas. D Vt.) Nov. 22, 1784-Oct. 19, 1842; House 1837-41.

FLETCHER, Loren (R Minn.) April 10, 1833-April 15, 1919; House 1893-1903, 1905-07.

FLETCHER, Richard (W Mass.) Jan. 8, 1788-June 21, 1869; House 1837-39.

FLETCHER, Thomas (— Ky.) Oct. 21, 1779- ?; House Dec. 2, 1816-17.

FLETCHER, Thomas Brooks (D Ohio) Oct. 10, 1879-July 1, 1945; House 1925-29, 1933-39.

FLICK, James Patton (R Iowa) Aug. 28, 1845-Feb. 25, 1929; House 1889-93.

FLINT, Frank Putnam (R Calif.) July 15, 1862-Feb. 11, 1929; Senate 1905-11.

FLOOD, Daniel John (D Pa.) Nov. 26, 1903-___; House 1945-47, 1949-53, 1955-___.

FLOOD, Henry De La Warr (half brother of Joel West Flood and uncle of Harry Flood Byrd) (D Va.) Sept. 2, 1865-Dec. 8, 1921; House 1901-Dec. 8, 1921.

FLOOD, Joel West (half brother of Henry De La Warr Flood and uncle of Harry Flood Byrd) (D Va.) Aug. 2, 1894-April 27, 1964; House Nov. 8, 1932-33.

FLOOD, Thomas Schmeck (R N.Y.) April 12, 1844-Oct. 28, 1908; House 1887-91.

FLORENCE, Elias (W Ohio) Feb. 15, 1797-Nov. 21, 1880; House 1843-45.

FLORENCE, Thomas Birch (D Pa.) Jan. 26, 1812-July 3, 1875; House 1851-61.

FLORIO, James Joseph (D N.J.) Aug. 29, 1937-___; House 1975-___.

FLOURNOY, Thomas Stanhope (W Va.) Dec. 15, 1811-March 12, 1883; House 1847-49.

FLOWER, Roswell Pettibone (D N.Y.) Aug. 7, 1835-May 12, 1899; House Nov. 8, 1881-83, 1889-Sept. 16, 1891; Gov. 1892-95.

FLOWERS, Walter (D Ala.) April 12, 1933-___; House 1969-___.

FLOYD, Charles Albert (D N.Y.) 1791-Feb. 20, 1873; House 1841-43.

FLOYD, John (— Ga.) Oct. 3, 1769-June 24, 1839; House 1827-29.

FLOYD, John (D Va.) April 24, 1783-Aug. 17, 1837; House 1817-29; Gov. 1830-34.

FLOYD, John Charles (D Ark.) April 14, 1858-Nov. 4, 1930; House 1905-15.

FLOYD, John Gelston (D N.Y.) Feb. 5, 1806-Oct. 5, 1881; House 1839-43, 1851-53.

FLOYD, William (— N.Y.) Dec. 17, 1734-Aug. 4, 1821; House 1789-91; Cont. Cong. 1774-77, 1778-83.

FLYE, Edwin (R Maine) March 4, 1817-July 12, 1886; Dec. 4, 1876-77.

FLYNN, Dennis Thomas (R Okla.) Feb. 13, 1861-June 19, 1939; House (Terr. Del.) 1893-97, 1899-1903.

FLYNN, Gerald Thomas (D Wis.) Oct. 7, 1910-___; House 1959-61.

FLYNN, Joseph Vincent (D N.Y.) Sept. 2, 1883-Feb. 6, 1940; House 1915-19.

FLYNT, John James Jr. (D Ga.) Nov. 8, 1914-___; House Nov. 2, 1954-___.

FOCHT, Benjamin Kurtz (R Pa.) March 12, 1863-March 27, 1937; House 1907-13, 1915-23, 1933-March 27, 1937.

FOELKER, Otto Godfrey (R N.Y.) Dec. 29, 1875-Jan. 18, 1943; House Nov. 3, 1908-11.

FOERDERER, Robert Herman (R Pa.) May 16, 1860-July 26, 1903; House 1901-July 26, 1903.

FOGARTY, John Edward (D R.I.) March 23, 1913-Jan. 10, 1967; House 1941-Dec. 7, 1944; 1945-Jan. 10, 1967.

FOGG, George Gilman (R N.H.) May 26, 1813-Oct. 5, 1881; Senate Aug. 31, 1866-67.

FOLEY, James Bradford (D Ind.) Oct. 18, 1807-Dec. 5, 1886; House 1857-59.

FOLEY, John Robert (D Md.) Oct. 16, 1917-___; House 1959-61.

FOLEY, Thomas Stephen (D Wash.) March 6, 1929-___; House 1965-___.

FOLGER, Alonzo Dillard (brother of John Hamlin Folger) (D N.C.) July 9, 1888-April 30, 1941; House 1939-April 30, 1941.

FOLGER, John Hamlin (brother of Alonzo D. Folger) (D N.C.) Dec. 18, 1880-July 19, 1963; House June 14, 1941-49.

FOLGER, Walter Jr. (D Mass.) June 12, 1765-Sept. 8, 1849; House 1817-21.

FOLLETT, John Fassett (D Ohio) Feb. 18, 1831-April 15, 1902; House 1883-85.

FONG, Hiram Leong (R Hawaii) Oct. 1, 1907-___; Senate Aug. 21, 1959-___.

FOOT, Solomon (R Vt.) Nov. 19, 1802-March 28, 1866; House 1843-47 (W); Senate 1851-March 28, 1866 (1851-57 Whig, 1857-1866 Republican); President pro tempore 1861-64.

FOOTE, Charles Augustus (D N.Y.) April 15, 1785-Aug. 1, 1828; House 1823-25.

FOOTE, Ellsworth Bishop (R Conn.) Jan. 12, 1898-___; House 1947-49.

FOOTE, Henry Stuart (U Miss.) Feb. 28, 1804-May 19, 1880; Senate 1847-Jan. 8, 1852; Gov. 1852-54.

FOOTE, Samuel Augustus (W Conn.) Nov. 8, 1780-Sept. 15, 1846; House 1819-21, 1823-25, 1833-May 9, 1834; Senate 1827-33; Gov. 1834-35.

FOOTE, Wallace Turner Jr. (R N.Y.) April 7, 1864-Dec. 17, 1910; House 1895-99.

FORAKER, Joseph Benson (R Ohio) July 5, 1846-May 10, 1917; Senate 1897-1909; Gov. 1886-90.

FORAN, Martin Ambrose (D Ohio) Nov. 11, 1844-June 28, 1921; House 1883-89.

FORAND, Aime Joseph (D R.I.) May 23, 1895-Jan. 18, 1972; House 1937-39, 1941-61.

FORD, Aaron Lane (D Miss.) Dec. 21, 1903-___; House 1935-43.

FORD, George (D Ind.) Jan. 11, 1846-Aug. 30, 1917; House 1885-87.

FORD, Gerald R. Jr. (R Mich.) July 14, 1913-___; House 1949-Dec. 6, 1973; Vice Pres. Dec. 6, 1973-Aug. 9, 1974; Pres. Aug. 9, 1974-___.

FORD, Harold Eugene (D Tenn.) May 20, 1945-___; House 1975-___.

FORD, James (JD Pa.) May 4, 1783-Aug. 18, 1859; House 1829-33.

FORD, Leland Merritt (R Calif.) March 8, 1893-November 27, 1965; House 1939-43.

FORD, Melbourne Haddock (D Mich.) June 30, 1849-April 20, 1891; House 1887-89; March 4-April 20, 1891.

FORD, Nicholas (LR Mo.) June 21, 1833-June 18, 1897; House 1879-83.

FORD, Thomas Francis (D Calif.) Feb. 18, 1873-Dec. 26, 1958; House 1933-45.

FORD, Wendell Hampton (D Ky.) Sept. 8, 1924-___; Senate Dec. 28, 1974-___; Gov. 1971-74.

FORD, William D. (D N.Y.) 1779-Oct. 1, 1833; House 1819-21.

FORD, William David (D Mich.) Aug. 6, 1927-___; House 1965-___.

FORDNEY, Joseph Warren (R Mich.) Nov. 5, 1853-Jan. 8, 1932; House 1899-1923.

FOREMAN, Edgar Franklin (R Texas/N.M.) Dec. 22, 1933-___; House 1963-65 (Texas), 1969-71 (N.M.).

FORESTER, John B. (— Tenn.) ?-Aug. 31, 1845; House 1833-37.

FORKER, Samuel Carr (D N.J.) March 16, 1821-Feb. 10, 1900; House 1871-73.

FORMAN, William St. John (D Ill.) Jan. 20, 1847-June 10, 1908; House 1889-95.

FORNANCE, Joseph (D Pa.) Oct. 18, 1804-Nov. 24, 1852; House 1839-43.

FORNES, Charles Vincent (D N.Y.) Jan. 22, 1844-May 22, 1929; House 1907-13.

FORNEY, Daniel Munroe (son of Peter Forney) (— N.C.) May 1784-Oct. 15, 1847; House 1815-18.

FORNEY, Peter (father of Daniel Munroe Forney) (D N.C.) April 21, 1756-Feb. 1, 1834; House 1813-15.

FORNEY, William Henry (grandson of Peter Forney) (D Ala.) Nov. 9, 1823-Jan. 16, 1894; House 1875-93.

FORREST, Thomas (— Pa.) 1747-March 20, 1825; House 1819-21, Oct. 8, 1822-23.

FORREST, Uriah (F Md.) 1756-July 6, 1805; House 1793-Nov. 8, 1794; Cont. Cong. 1786-87.

FORRESTER, Elijah Lewis (D Ga.) Aug. 16, 1896-March 19, 1970; House 1951-65.

FORSYTH, John (D Ga.) Oct. 22, 1780-Oct. 21, 1841; House 1813-Nov. 23, 1818, 1823-Nov. 7, 1827; Senate Nov. 23, 1818-Feb. 17, 1819, Nov. 9, 1829-June 27, 1834; Secy. of State 1834-41; Gov. 1827-29.

FORSYTHE, Albert Palaska (R Ill.) May 24, 1830-Sept. 2, 1906; House 1879-81.

FORSYTHE, Edwin Bell (R N.J.) Jan. 17, 1916-___; House Nov. 3, 1970-___.

FORT, Franklin William (R N.J.) March 30, 1880-June 20, 1937; House 1925-31.

FORT, Greenbury Lafayette (R Ill.) Oct. 17, 1825-Jan. 13, 1883; House 1873-81.

FORT, Tomlinson (D Ga.) July 14, 1787-May 11, 1859; House 1827-29.

FORWARD, Chauncey (brother of Walter Forward) (D Pa.) Feb. 4, 1793-Oct. 19, 1839; House Dec. 4, 1826-31.

FORWARD, Walter (brother of Chauncey Forward) (D Pa.) Jan. 24, 1783-Nov. 24, 1852; House Oct. 8, 1822-25; Secy. of the Treasury 1841-43.

FOSDICK, Nicoll (W N.Y.) Nov. 9, 1785-May 7, 1868; House 1825-27.

FOSS, Eugene Noble (brother of George Edmund Foss) (D Mass.) Sept. 24, 1858-Sept. 13, 1939; House March 22, 1910-Jan. 4, 1911; Gov. 1911-14.

FOSS, Frank Herbert (R Mass.) Sept. 20, 1865-Feb. 15, 1947; House 1925-35.

FOSS, George Edmund (brother of Eugene Noble Foss) (R Ill.) July 2, 1863-March 15, 1936; House 1895-1913, 1915-19.

FOSTER, A. Lawrence (W N.Y.) ?-?; House 1841-43.

FOSTER, Abiel (— N.H.) Aug. 8, 1735-Feb. 6, 1806; House 1789-91, 1795-1803; Cont. Cong. 1783-85.

FOSTER, Addison Gardner (R Wash.) Jan. 28, 1837-Jan. 16, 1917; Senate 1899-1905.

FOSTER, Charles (R Ohio) April 12, 1828-Jan. 9, 1904; House 1871-79; Secy. of the Treasury 1891-93; Gov. 1880-84.

FOSTER, David Johnson (R Vt.) June 27, 1857-March 21, 1912; House 1901-March 21, 1912.

FOSTER, Dwight (brother of Theodore Foster) (F Mass.) Dec. 7, 1757-April 29, 1823; House 1793-June 6, 1800; Senate June 6, 1800-March 2, 1803.

FOSTER, Ephraim Hubbard (W Tenn.) Sept. 17, 1794-Sept. 14, 1854; Senate Sept. 17, 1838-1839; Oct. 17, 1843-45.

FOSTER, George Peter (D Ill.) April 3, 1858-Nov. 11, 1928; House 1899-1905.

FOSTER, Henry Allen (D N.Y.) May 7, 1800-May 11, 1889; House 1837-39; Senate Nov. 30, 1844-Jan. 27, 1845.

FOSTER, Henry Donnel (cousin of John Cabell Breckinridge) (D Pa.) Dec. 19, 1808-Oct. 16, 1880; House 1843-47, 1871-73.

FOSTER, Israel Moore (R Ohio) Jan. 12, 1873-June 10, 1950; House 1919-25.

FOSTER, John Hopkins (R Ind.) Jan. 31, 1862-Sept. 5, 1917; House May 16, 1905-09.

FOSTER, Lafayette Sabine (R Conn.) Nov. 22, 1806-Sept. 19, 1880; Senate 1855-67; President pro tempore 1865-67.

FOSTER, Martin David (D Ill.) Sept. 3, 1861-Oct. 20, 1919; House 1907-19.

FOSTER, Murphy James (D La.) Jan. 12, 1849-June 12, 1921; Senate 1901-13; Gov. 1892-1900.

FOSTER, Nathaniel Greene (D Ga.) Aug. 25, 1809-Oct. 19, 1869; House 1855-57 (elected as AP candidate).

FOSTER, Stephen Clark (R Maine) Dec. 24, 1799-Oct. 5, 1872; House 1857-61.

FOSTER, Theodore (brother of Dwight Foster) (L&O R.I.) April 29, 1752-Jan. 13, 1828; Senate June 7, 1790-1803.

FOSTER, Thomas Flournoy (D Ga.) Nov. 23, 1790-Sept. 14, 1848; House 1829-35, 1841-43.

FOSTER, Wilder De Ayr (R Mich.) Jan. 8, 1819-Sept. 20, 1873; House Dec. 4, 1871-Sept. 20, 1873.

FOUKE, Philip Bond (D Ill.) Jan. 23, 1818-Oct. 3, 1876; House 1859-63.

FOULKES, George Ernest (D Mich.) Dec. 25, 1878-Dec. 13, 1960; House 1933-35.

FOULKROD, William Walker (R Pa.) Nov. 22, 1846-Nov. 13, 1910; House 1907-Nov. 13, 1910.

FOUNTAIN, Lawrence H. (D N.C.) April 23, 1913-__; House 1953-__.

FOWLER, Charles Newell (R N.J.) Nov. 2, 1852-May 27, 1932; House 1895-1911.

FOWLER, Hiram Robert (D Ill.) Feb. 7, 1851-Jan. 5, 1926; House 1911-15.

FOWLER, John (— Ky.) 1755-Aug. 22, 1840; House 1797-1807.

FOWLER, John Edgar (P N.C.) Sept. 8, 1866-July 4, 1930; House 1897-99.

FOWLER, Joseph Smith (UR Tenn.) Aug. 31, 1820-April 1, 1902; Senate July 24, 1866-71.

FOWLER, Orin (F-SW Mass.) July 19, 1791-Sept. 3, 1852; House 1849-Sept. 3, 1852.

FOWLER, Samuel (JD N.J.) Oct. 30, 1779-Feb. 20, 1844; House 1833-37.

FOWLER, Samuel (grandson of the preceding) (D N.J.) March 22, 1851-March 17, 1919; House 1889-93.

FOX, Andrew Fuller (D Miss.) April 26, 1849-Aug. 29, 1926; House 1897-1903.

FOX, John (D N.Y.) June 30, 1835-Jan. 17, 1914; House 1867-71.

FRANCE, Joseph Irvin (R Md.) Oct. 11, 1873-Jan. 26, 1939; Senate 1917-23.

FRANCHOT, Richard (R N.Y.) June 2, 1816-Nov. 23, 1875; House 1861-63.

FRANCIS, George Blinn (R N.Y.) Aug. 12, 1883-May 20, 1967; House 1917-19.

FRANCIS, John Brown (grandson of John Brown of Rhode Island) (L&O R.I.) May 31, 1791-Aug. 9, 1864; Senate Jan. 25, 1844-45; Gov. 1833-38.

FRANCIS, William Bates (D Ohio) Oct. 25, 1860-Dec. 5, 1954; House 1911-15.

FRANK, Augustus (nephew of William Patterson of N.Y.) (R N.Y.) July 17, 1826-April 29, 1895; House 1859-65.

FRANK, Nathan (R/UL Mo.) Feb. 23, 1852-April 5, 1931; House 1889-91.

FRANKHAUSER, William Horace (R Mich.) March 5, 1863-May 9, 1921; House March 4-May 9, 1921.

FRANKLIN, Benjamin Joseph (D Mo.) March 1839-May 18, 1898; House 1875-79; Gov. (Ariz. Terr.) 1896-97.

FRANKLIN, Jesse (brother of Meshack Franklin) (D N.C.) March 24, 1760-Aug. 31, 1823; House 1795-97; Senate 1799-1805, 1807-13; President pro tempore 1804-05; Gov. 1820-21.

FRANKLIN, John Rankin (W Md.) May 6, 1820-Jan. 11, 1878; House 1853-55.

FRANKLIN, Meshack (brother of Jesse Franklin) (D N.C.) 1772-Dec. 18, 1839; House 1807-15.

FRASER, Donald MacKay (D Minn.) Feb. 20, 1924-__; House 1963-__.

FRAZIER, James Beriah (D Tenn.) Oct. 18, 1856-March 28, 1937; Senate March 21, 1905-11; Gov. 1903-05.

FRAZIER, James Beriah Jr. (son of the preceding) (D Tenn.) June 23, 1890-__; House 1949-63.

FRAZIER, Lynn Joseph (R N.D.) Dec. 21, 1874-Jan. 11, 1947; Senate 1923-41; Gov. 1917-21.

FREAR, James Archibald (R Wis.) Oct. 24, 1861-May 28, 1939; House 1913-35.

FREAR, Joseph Allen Jr. (D Del.) March 7, 1903-__; Senate 1949-61.

FREDERICK, Benjamin Todd (D Iowa) Oct. 5, 1834-Nov. 3, 1903; House March 3, 1885-87.

FREDERICKS, John Donnan (R Calif.) Sept. 10, 1869-Aug. 26, 1945; House May 1, 1923-27.

FREE, Arthur Monroe (R Calif.) Jan. 15, 1879-April 1, 1953; House 1921-33.

FREEDLEY, John (W Pa.) May 22, 1793-Dec. 8, 1851; House 1847-51.

FREEMAN, Chapman (R Pa.) Oct. 8, 1832-March 22, 1904; House 1875-79.

FREEMAN, James Crawford (R Ga.) April 1, 1820-Sept. 3, 1885; House 1873-75.

FREEMAN, John D. (U Miss.) ?-Jan. 17, 1886; House 1851-53.

FREEMAN, Jonathan (uncle of Nathaniel Freeman Jr.) (F N.H.) March 21, 1745-Aug. 20, 1808; House 1797-1801.

FREEMAN, Nathaniel Jr. (nephew of Jonathan Freeman) (— Mass.) May 1, 1766-Aug. 22, 1800; House 1795-99.

FREEMAN, Richard Patrick (R Conn.) April 24, 1869-July 8, 1944; House 1915-33.

FREER, Romeo Hoyt (R W.Va.) Nov. 9, 1846-May 9, 1913; House 1899-1901.

FRELINGHUYSEN, Frederick (father of Theodore Frelinghuysen and great-great-great-grandfather of Peter Hood Ballantine Frelinghuysen Jr.) (F N.J.) April 13, 1753-April 13, 1804; Senate 1793-Nov. 12, 1796; Cont. Cong. 1778-79, 1782-83.

FRELINGHUYSEN, Frederick Theodore (nephew and adopted son of Theodore Frelinghuysen, uncle of Joseph Sherman Frelinghuysen, and great-grandfather of Peter Hood Ballantine Frelinghuysen Jr.) (R N.J.) Aug. 4, 1817-May 20, 1885; Senate Nov. 12, 1866-69, 1871-77; Secy. of State 1881-85.

FRELINGHUYSEN, Joseph Sherman (nephew of Frederick Theodore Frelinghuysen and cousin of Peter Hood Ballentine Frelinghuysen Jr.) (R N.J.) March 12, 1869-Feb. 8, 1948; Senate 1917-23.

FRELINGHUYSEN, Peter Hood Ballantine Jr. (cousin of Joseph Sherman Frelinghuysen, great-grandson of Frederick T. Frelinghuysen, great-great-great-nephew of Theodore Frelinghuysen and great-great-great-grandson of Frederick Frelinghuysen) (R N.J.) Jan. 17, 1916-__; House 1953-75.

FRELINGHUYSEN, Theodore (son of Frederick Frelinghuysen and great-great-great-uncle of Peter Hood Ballantine Frelinghuysen Jr.) (Ad. D N.J.) March 28, 1787-April 12, 1862; Senate 1829-35.

FREMONT, John Charles (F-SD Calif.) Jan. 21, 1813-July 13, 1890; Senate Sept. 9, 1850-51; Gov. (Ariz. Terr.) 1878-81.

FRENCH, Burton Lee (R Idaho) Aug. 1, 1875-Sept. 12, 1954; House 1903-09, 1911-15, 1917-33.

FRENCH, Carlos (D Conn.) Aug. 6, 1835-April 14, 1903; House 1887-89.

FRENCH, Ezra Bartlett (R Maine) Sept. 23, 1810-April 24, 1880; House 1859-61.

FRENCH, John Robert (R N.C.) May 28, 1819-Oct. 2, 1890; House July 6, 1868-69.

FRENCH, Richard (D Ky.) June 20, 1792-May 1, 1854; House 1835-37, 1843-45, 1847-49.

FRENZEL, William E. (R Minn.) July 31, 1928-__; House 1971-__.

FREY, Louis Jr. (R Fla.) Jan. 11, 1934-__; House 1969-__.

FREY, Oliver Walter (D Pa.) Sept. 7, 1887-Aug. 26, 1939; House Nov. 7, 1933-39.

FRICK, Henry (W Pa.) March 17, 1795-March 1, 1844; House 1843-March 1, 1844.

FRIEDEL, Samuel Nathaniel (D Md.) April 18, 1898-__; House 1953-71.

FRIES, Frank William (D Ill.) May 1, 1893-__; House 1937-41.

FRIES, George (D Ohio) 1799-Nov. 13, 1866; House 1845-49.

FROEHLICH, Harold Vernon (R Wis.) May 12, 1932-__; House 1973-75.

FROMENTIN, Eligius (— La.) ?-Oct. 6, 1822; Senate 1813-19.

FROST, Joel (— N.Y.) ?-?; House 1823-25.

FROST, Richard Graham (D Mo.) Dec. 29, 1851-Feb. 1, 1900; House 1879-March 2, 1883.

FROST, Rufus Smith (R Mass.) July 18, 1826-March 6, 1894; House 1875-July 28, 1876.

FROTHINGHAM, Louis Adams (R Mass.) July 13, 1871-Aug. 23, 1928; House 1921-Aug. 23, 1928.

FRY, Jacob Jr. (D Pa.) June 10, 1802-Nov. 28, 1866; House 1835-39.

FRY, Joseph Jr. (D Pa.) Aug. 4, 1781-Aug. 15, 1860; House 1827-31.

FRYE, William Pierce (grandfather of Wallace Humphrey White Jr.) (R Maine) Sept. 2, 1830-Aug. 8, 1911; House 1871-March 17, 1881; Senate March 18, 1881-Aug. 8, 1911, President pro tempore 1896-1911.

FUGATE, Thomas Bacon (D Va.) April 10, 1899-___; House 1949-53.

FULBRIGHT, James Franklin (D Mo.) Jan. 24, 1877-April 5, 1948; House 1923-25, 1927-29, 1931-33.

FULBRIGHT, James William (D Ark.) April 9, 1905-___; House 1943-45; Senate 1945-Dec. 31, 1974.

FULKERSON, Abram (D Va.) May 13, 1834-Dec. 17, 1902; House 1881-83 (elected as a Readjuster).

FULKERSON, Frank Ballard (R Mo.) March 5, 1866-Aug. 30, 1936; House 1905-07.

FULLER, Alvan Tufts (R Mass.) Feb. 27, 1878-April 30, 1958; House 1917-Jan. 5, 1921; Gov. 1925-29.

FULLER, Benoni Stinson (D Ind.) Nov. 13, 1825-April 14, 1903; House 1875-79.

FULLER, Charles Eugene (R Ill.) March 31, 1849-June 25, 1926; House 1903-13, 1915-June 25, 1926.

FULLER, Claude Albert (D Ark.) Jan. 20, 1876-Jan. 8, 1968; House 1929-39.

FULLER, George (D Pa.) Nov. 7, 1802-Nov. 24, 1888; House Dec. 2, 1844-45.

FULLER, Hadwen Carlton (R N.Y.) Aug. 28, 1895-___; House Nov. 2, 1943-49.

FULLER, Henry Mills (W Pa.) Jan. 3, 1820-Dec. 26, 1860; House 1851-53, 1855-57.

FULLER, Philo Case (W N.Y.) Aug. 14, 1787-Aug. 16, 1855; House 1833-Sept. 2, 1836.

FULLER, Thomas James Duncan (D Maine) March 17, 1808-Feb. 13, 1876; House 1849-57.

FULLER, Timothy (D Mass.) July 11, 1778-Oct. 1, 1835; House 1817-25.

FULLER, William Elijah (R Iowa) March 30, 1846-April 23, 1918; House 1885-89.

FULLER, William Kendall (D N.Y.) Nov. 24, 1792-Nov. 11, 1883; House 1833-37.

FULLERTON, David (uncle of David Fullerton Robison) (— Pa.) Oct. 4, 1772-Feb. 1, 1843; House 1819-May 15, 1820.

FULMER, Hampton Pitts (husband of Willa L. Fulmer) (D S.C.) June 23, 1875-Oct. 19, 1944; House 1921-Oct. 19, 1944.

FULMER, Willa Lybrand, (widow of Hampton P. Fulmer) (D S.C.) Feb. 3, 1884-May 13, 1968; House Nov. 7, 1944-45.

FULTON, Andrew Steele (brother of John H. Fulton) (W Va.) Sept. 29, 1800-Nov. 22, 1884; House 1847-49.

FULTON, Charles William (brother of Elmer Lincoln Fulton) (R Ore.) Aug. 24, 1853-Jan. 27, 1918; Senate 1903-09.

FULTON, Elmer Lincoln (brother of Charles William Fulton) (D Okla.) April 22, 1865-Oct. 4, 1939; House Nov. 16, 1907-09.

FULTON, James Grove (R Pa.) March 1, 1903-Oct. 6, 1971; House Feb. 2, 1945-Oct. 6, 1971.

FULTON, John Hall (brother of Andrew Steele Fulton) (W Va.) ?-Jan. 28, 1836; House 1833-35.

FULTON, Richard Harmon (D Tenn.) Jan. 27, 1927-___; House 1963-Aug. 14, 1975.

FULTON, William Savin (D Ark.) June 2, 1795-Aug. 15, 1844; Senate Sept. 18, 1836-Aug. 15, 1844; Gov. (Terr.) 1835-36.

FUNK, Benjamin Franklin (father of Frank Hamilton Funk) (R Ill.) Oct. 17, 1838-Feb. 14, 1909; House 1893-95.

FUNK, Frank Hamilton (son of Benjamin Franklin Funk) (R Ill.) April 5, 1869-Nov. 24, 1940; House 1921-27.

FUNSTON, Edward Hogue (R Kan.) Sept. 16, 1836-Sept. 10, 1911; House March 21, 1884-Aug. 2, 1894.

FUQUA, Don (D Fla.) Aug. 20, 1933-___; House 1963-___.

FURCOLO, Foster (D Mass.) July 29, 1911-___; House 1949-Sept. 30, 1952; Gov. 1957-61.

FURLONG, Robert Grant (D Pa.) Jan. 4, 1886-March 19, 1973; House 1943-45.

FURLOW, Allen John (R Minn.) Nov. 9, 1890-Jan. 29, 1954; House 1925-29.

FYAN, Robert Washington (D Mo.) March 11, 1835-July 28, 1896; House 1883-85, 1891-95.

G

GABALDON, Isauro (Nat. P.I.) Dec. 8, 1875-Dec. 21, 1942; House (Res. Comm.) 1920-July 16, 1928.

GAGE, Joshua (D Mass.) Aug. 7, 1763-Jan. 24, 1831; House 1817-19.

GAHN, Harry Conrad (R Ohio) April 26, 1880-Nov. 2, 1962; House 1921-23.

GAILLARD, John (uncle of Theodore Gaillard Hunt) (D S.C.) Sept. 5, 1765-Feb. 26, 1826; Senate Dec. 6, 1804-Feb. 26, 1826; President pro tempore 1810, 1814-18, 1820-25.

GAINES, John Pollard (W Ky.) Sept. 22, 1795-Dec. 9, 1857; House 1847-49; Gov. (Ore. Terr.) 1850-53.

GAINES, John Wesley (D Tenn.) Aug. 24, 1860-July 4, 1926; House 1897-1909.

GAINES, Joseph Holt (R W.Va.) Sept. 3, 1864-April 12, 1951; House 1901-11.

GAINES, William Embre (R Va.) Aug. 30, 1844-May 4, 1912; House 1887-89.

GAITHER, Nathan (D Ky.) Sept. 15, 1788-Aug. 12, 1862; House 1829-33.

GALBRAITH, John (D Pa.) Aug. 2, 1794-June 15, 1860; House 1833-37, 1839-41.

GALE, George (father of Levin Gale) (— Md.) June 3, 1756-Jan. 2, 1815; House 1789-91.

GALE, Levin (son of George Gale) (— Md.) April 24, 1784-Dec. 18, 1834; House 1827-29.

GALE, Richard Pillsbury (R Minn.) Oct. 30, 1900-Dec. 4, 1973; House 1941-45.

GALIFIANAKIS, Nick (D N.C.) July 22, 1928-___; House 1967-73.

GALLAGHER, Cornelius Edward (D N.J.) March 2, 1921-___; House 1959-73.

GALLAGHER, James A. (R Pa.) Jan. 16, 1869-Dec. 8, 1957; House 1943-45, 1947-49.

GALLAGHER, Thomas (D Ill.) July 6, 1850-Feb. 24, 1930; House 1909-21.

GALLAGHER, William James (D Minn.) May 13, 1875-Aug. 13, 1946; House 1945-Aug. 13, 1946.

GALLATIN, Albert (D Pa.) Jan. 29, 1761-Aug. 12, 1849; Senate Dec. 2, 1793-Feb. 28, 1794; House 1795-1801; Secy. of the Treasury 1801-14.

GALLEGOS, Jose Manuel (D N.M.) Oct. 30, 1815-April 21, 1875; House (Terr. Del.) 1853-July 23, 1856, 1871-73.

GALLINGER, Jacob Harold (R N.H.) March 28, 1837-Aug. 17, 1918; House 1885-89; Senate 1891-Aug. 17, 1918.

GALLIVAN, James Ambrose (D Mass.) Oct. 22, 1866-April 3, 1928; House April 7, 1914-April 3, 1928.

GALLOWAY, Samuel (R Ohio) March 20, 1811-April 5, 1872; House 1855-57.

GALLUP, Albert (D N.Y.) Jan. 30, 1796-Nov. 5, 1851; House 1837-39.

GAMBLE, James (D Pa.) Jan. 28, 1809-Feb. 22, 1883; House 1851-55.

GAMBLE, John Rankin (brother of Robert Jackson Gamble and uncle of Ralph Abernethy Gamble) (R S.D.) Jan. 15, 1848-Aug. 14, 1891; House March 4-Aug. 14, 1891.

GAMBLE, Ralph Abernethy (son of Robert Jackson Gamble and nephew of John Rankin Gamble) (R N.Y.) May 6, 1885-March 4, 1959; House Nov. 2, 1937-57.

GAMBLE, Robert Jackson (brother of John Rankin Gamble and father of Ralph Abernethy Gamble) (R S.D.) Feb. 7, 1851-Sept. 22, 1924; House 1895-97, 1899-1901; Senate 1901-13.

GAMBLE, Roger Lawson (W Ga.) 1787-Dec. 20, 1847; House 1833-35 (D); 1841-43 (W).

GAMBRELL, David Henry (D Ga.) Dec. 20, 1929-__; Senate Feb. 1, 1971-Nov. 7, 1972.

GAMBRILL, Stephen Warfield (D Md.) Oct. 2, 1873-Dec. 19, 1938; House Nov. 4, 1924-Dec. 19, 1938.

GANDY, Harry Luther (D S.D.) Aug. 13, 1881-Aug. 15, 1957; House 1915-21.

GANLY, James Vincent (D N.Y.) Sept. 13, 1878-Sept. 7, 1923; House 1919-21; March 4-Sept. 7, 1923.

GANNETT, Barzillai (D Mass.) June 17, 1764-1832; House 1809-12.

GANSON, John (D N.Y.) Jan. 1, 1818-Sept. 28, 1874; House 1863-65.

GANTZ, Martin Kissinger (D Ohio) Jan. 28, 1862-Feb. 10, 1916; House 1891-93.

GARBER, Harvey Cable (D Ohio) July 6, 1866-March 23, 1938; House 1903-07.

GARBER, Jacob Aaron (R Va.) Jan. 25, 1879-Dec. 2, 1953; House 1929-31.

GARBER, Milton Cline (R Okla.) Nov. 30, 1867-Sept. 12, 1948; House 1923-33.

GARD, Warren (D Ohio) July 2, 1873-Nov. 1, 1929; House 1913-21.

GARDENIER, Barent (F N.Y.) ?-Jan. 10, 1822; House 1807-11.

GARDNER, Augustus Peabody (R Mass.) Nov. 5, 1865-Jan. 14, 1918; House Nov. 3, 1902-May 15, 1917.

GARDNER, Edward Joseph (D Ohio) Aug. 7, 1898-Dec. 7, 1950; House 1945-47.

GARDNER, Francis (— N.H.) Dec. 27, 1771-June 25, 1835; House 1807-09.

GARDNER, Frank (D Ind.) May 8, 1872-Feb. 1, 1937; House 1923-29.

GARDNER, Gideon (— Mass.) May 30, 1759-March 22, 1832; House 1809-11.

GARDNER, James Carson (R N.C.) April 8, 1933-__; House 1967-69.

GARDNER, John James (R N.J.) Oct. 17, 1845-Feb. 7, 1921; House 1893-1913.

GARDNER, Mills (R Ohio) Jan. 30, 1830-Feb. 20, 1910; House 1877-79.

GARDNER, Obadiah (D Maine) Sept. 13, 1850-July 24, 1938; Senate Sept. 23, 1911-13.

GARDNER, Washington (R Mich.) Feb. 16, 1845-March 31, 1928; House 1899-1911.

GARFIELD, James Abram (R Ohio) Nov. 19, 1831-Sept. 19, 1881; House 1863-Nov. 8, 1880; President March 4-Sept. 19, 1881.

GARFIELDE, Selucius (R Wash.) Dec. 8, 1822-April 13, 1881; House (Terr. Del.) 1869-73.

GARLAND, Augustus Hill (D Ark.) June 11, 1832-Jan. 26, 1899; Senate 1877-March 6, 1885; Gov. 1874-77; Attorney General 1885-89.

GARLAND, David Shepherd (D Va.) Sept. 27, 1769-Oct. 7, 1841; House Jan. 17, 1810-11.

GARLAND, James (D Va.) June 6, 1791-Aug. 8, 1885; House 1835-41.

GARLAND, Mahlon Morris (R Pa.) May 4, 1856-Nov. 19, 1920; House 1915-Nov. 19, 1920.

GARLAND, Peter Adams (R Maine) June 16, 1923-__; House 1961-63.

GARLAND, Rice (W La.) about 1795-1861; House April 28, 1834-July 21, 1840.

GARMATZ, Edward Alexander (D Md.) Feb. 7, 1903-__; House July 15, 1947-1973.

GARN, Edwin Jacob (R Utah) Oct. 12, 1932-__; Senate Dec. 21, 1974-__.

GARNER, Alfred Buckwalter (R Pa.) March 4, 1873-July 30, 1930; House 1909-11.

GARNER, John Nance (D Texas) Nov. 22, 1868-Nov. 7, 1967; House 1903-33; Speaker 1931-33; Vice President 1933-41.

GARNETT, James Mercer (brother of Robert Selden Garnett and grandfather of Muscoe Russell Hunter Garnett) (D Va.) June 8, 1770-April 23, 1843; House 1805-09.

GARNETT, Muscoe Russell Hunter (grandson of James Mercer Garnett) (D Va.) July 25, 1821-Feb. 14, 1864; House Dec. 1, 1856-61.

GARNETT, Robert Selden (brother of James Mercer Garnett and cousin of Charles Fenton Mercer) (D Va.) April 26, 1789-Aug. 15, 1840; House 1817-27.

GARNSEY, Daniel Greene (JD N.Y.) June 17, 1779-May 11, 1851; House 1825-29.

GARRETT, Abraham Ellison (D Tenn.) March 6, 1830-Feb. 14, 1907; House 1871-73.

GARRETT, Clyde Leonard (D Texas) Dec. 16, 1885-Dec. 18, 1959; House 1937-41.

GARRETT, Daniel Edward (D Texas) April 28, 1869-Dec. 13, 1932; House 1913-15; 1917-19; 1921-Dec. 13, 1932.

GARRETT, Finis James (D Tenn.) Aug. 26, 1875-May 25, 1956; House 1905-29.

GARRISON, Daniel (D N.J.) April 3, 1782-Feb. 13, 1851; House 1823-27.

GARRISON, George Tankard (D Va.) Jan. 14, 1835-Nov. 14, 1889; House 1881-83; March 20, 1884-85.

GARROW, Nathaniel (D N.Y.) April 25, 1780-March 3, 1841; House 1827-29.

GARTH, William Willis (D Ala.) Oct. 28, 1828-Feb. 25, 1912; House 1877-79.

GARTNER, Fred Christian (R Pa.) March 14, 1896-__; House 1939-41.

GARTRELL, Lucius Jeremiah (uncle of Choice Boswell Randell) (D Ga.) Jan. 7, 1821-April 7, 1891; House 1857-Jan. 23, 1861.

GARVIN, William Swan (D Pa.) July 25, 1806-Feb. 20, 1883; House 1845-47.

GARY, Frank Boyd (D S.C.) March 9, 1860-Dec. 7, 1922; Senate March 6, 1908-09.

GARY, Julian Vaughan (D Va.) Feb. 25, 1892-Sept. 6, 1973; House March 6, 1945-65.

GASQUE, Allard Henry (husband of Elizabeth (Bessie) Hawley Gasque) (D S.C.) March 8, 1873-June 17, 1938; House 1923-June 17, 1938.

GASQUE, Elizabeth Hawley (widow of Allard Henry Gasque—later Mrs. A. J. Van Exem) (D S.C.) ?-__; House Sept. 13, 1938-39.

GASSAWAY, Percy Lee (D Okla.) Aug. 30, 1885-May 15, 1937; House 1935-37.

GASTON, Athelston (D Pa.) April 24, 1838-Sept. 23, 1907; House 1899-1901.

GASTON, William (F N.C.) Sept. 19, 1778-Jan. 23, 1844; House 1813-17.

GATES, Seth Merrill (A-SW N.Y.) Oct. 10, 1800-Aug. 24, 1877; House 1839-43.

GATHINGS, Ezekiel Candler (D Ark.) Nov. 10, 1903-__; House 1939-69.

GATLIN, Alfred Moore (— N.C.) April 20, 1790-?; House 1823-25.

GAUSE, Lucien Coatsworth (D Ark.) Dec. 25, 1836-Nov. 5, 1880; House 1875-79.

GAVAGAN, Joseph Andrew (D N.Y.) Aug. 20, 1892-Oct. 18, 1968; House Nov. 5, 1929-Dec. 30, 1943.

GAVIN, Leon Harry (R Pa.) Feb. 25, 1893-Sept. 15, 1963; House 1943-Sept. 15, 1963.

GAY, Edward James (D La.) Feb. 3, 1816-May 30, 1889; House 1885-May 30, 1889.

GAY, Edward James (grandson of the preceding) (D La.) May 5, 1878-Dec. 1, 1952; Senate Nov. 6, 1918-21.

GAYDOS, Joseph M. (D Pa.) July 3, 1926-__; House Nov. 5, 1968-__.

GAYLE, John (W Ala.) Sept. 11, 1792-July 28, 1859; House 1847-49; Gov. 1831-35.

GAYLE, June Ward (D Ky.) Feb. 22, 1865-Aug. 5, 1942; House Jan. 15, 1900-01.

GAYLORD, James Madison (— Ohio) May 29, 1811-June 14, 1874; House 1851-53.

GAZLAY, James William (JFSt. Ohio) July 23, 1784-June 8, 1874; House 1823-25.

GEAR, John Henry (R Iowa) April 7, 1825-July 14, 1900; House 1887-91; 1893-95; Senate 1895-July 14, 1900; Gov. 1878-82.

GEARHART, Bertrand Wesley (R Calif.) May 31, 1890-Oct. 11, 1955; House 1935-49.

GEARIN, John McDermeid (D Ore.) Aug. 15, 1851-Nov. 12, 1930; Senate Dec. 13, 1905-Jan. 23, 1907.

GEARY, Thomas J. (D/AP Calif.) Jan. 18, 1854-July 6, 1929; House Dec. 9, 1890-95.

GEBHARD, John (— N.Y.) Feb. 22, 1782-Jan. 3, 1854; House 1821-23.

GEDDES, George Washington (D Ohio) July 16, 1824-Nov. 9, 1892; House 1879-87.

GEDDES, James (F N.Y.) July 22, 1763-Aug. 19, 1838; House 1813-15.

GEELAN, James Patrick (D Conn.) Aug. 11, 1901-__; House 1945-47.

GEHRMANN, Bernard John (Pro. Wis.) Feb. 13, 1880-July 12, 1958; House 1935-43.

GEISSENHAINER, Jacob Augustus (D N.J.) Aug. 28, 1839-July 20, 1917; House 1889-95.

GENSMAN, Lorraine Michael (R Okla.) Aug. 26, 1878-May 27, 1954; House 1921-23.

GENTRY, Brady Preston (D Texas) March 25, 1896-Nov. 9, 1966; House 1953-57.

GENTRY, Meredith Poindexter (W Tenn.) Sept. 15, 1809-Nov. 2, 1866; House 1839-43; 1845-53.

GEORGE, Henry Jr. (D N.Y.) Nov. 3, 1862-Nov. 14, 1916; House 1911-15.

GEORGE, James Zachariah (D Miss.) Oct. 20, 1826-Aug. 14, 1897; Senate 1881-Aug. 14, 1897.

GEORGE, Melvin Clark (R Ore.) May 13, 1849-Feb. 22, 1933; House 1881-85.

GEORGE, Myron Virgil (R Kan.) Jan. 6, 1900-April 11, 1972; House Nov. 7, 1950-59.

GEORGE, Newell A. (D Kan.) Sept. 24, 1904-__; House 1959-61.

GEORGE, Walter Franklin (D Ga.) Jan. 29, 1878-Aug. 4, 1957; Senate Nov. 22, 1922-57; President pro tempore 1955-57.

GERAN, Elmer Hendrickson (D N.J.) Oct. 24, 1875-Jan. 12, 1954; House 1923-25.

GERLACH, Charles Lewis (R Pa.) Sept. 14, 1895-May 5, 1947; House 1939-May 5, 1947.

GERMAN, Obadiah (D N.Y.) April 22, 1766-Sept. 24, 1842; Senate 1809-15.

GERNERD, Fred Benjamin (R Pa.) Nov. 22, 1879-Aug. 7, 1948; House 1921-23.

GERRY, Elbridge (great-grandfather of Peter Goelet Gerry) (D Mass.) July 17, 1744-Nov. 23, 1814; House 1789-93 (A-F); Cont. Cong. 1776-81 and 1782-85; (D) Gov. 1810-12; Vice President 1813-14 (D).

GERRY, Elbridge (grandson of the preceding) (D Maine) Dec. 6, 1813-April 10, 1886; House 1849-51.

GERRY, James (D Pa.) Aug. 14, 1796-July 19, 1873; House 1839-43.

GERRY, Peter Goelet (great-grandson of Elbridge Gerry) (D R.I.) Sept. 18, 1879-Oct. 31, 1957; House 1913-15; Senate 1917-29; 1935-47.

GEST, William Harrison (R Ill.) Jan. 7, 1838-Aug. 9, 1912; House 1887-91.

GETTYS, Thomas Smithwick (D S.C.) June 19, 1912-__; House Nov. 3, 1964-Dec. 31, 1974.

GETZ, James Lawrence (D Pa.) Sept. 14, 1821-Dec. 25, 1891; House 1867-73.

GEYER, Henry Sheffie (D Mo.) Dec. 9, 1790-March 5, 1859; Senate 1851-57.

GEYER, Lee Edward (D Calif.) Sept. 9, 1888-Oct. 11, 1941; 1939-Oct. 11, 1941.

GHOLSON, James Herbert (D Va.) 1798-July 2, 1848; House 1833-35.

GHOLSON, Samuel Jameson (D Miss.) May 19, 1808-Oct. 16, 1883; House Dec. 1, 1836-37; July 18, 1837-Feb. 5, 1838.

GHOLSON, Thomas Jr. (D Va.) ?-July 4, 1816; House Nov. 7, 1808-July 4, 1816.

GIAIMO, Robert Nicholas (D Conn.) Oct. 15, 1919-__; House 1959-__.

GIBBONS, Sam M. (D Fla.) Jan. 20, 1920-__; House 1963-__.

GIBBS, Florence Reville (widow of Willis Benjamin Gibbs) (D Ga.) April 4, 1890-Aug. 19, 1964; House Oct. 1, 1940-41.

GIBBS, Willis Benjamin (husband of Florence Reville Gibbs) (D Ga.) April 15, 1889-Aug. 7, 1940; House 1939-Aug. 7, 1940.

GIBSON, Charles Hopper (cousin of Henry Richard Gibson) (D Md.) Jan. 19, 1842-March 31, 1900; House 1885-91; Senate Nov. 19, 1891-97.

GIBSON, Ernest Willard (father of Ernest William Gibson) (R Vt.) Dec. 29, 1872-June 20, 1940; House Nov. 6, 1923-Oct. 19, 1933; Senate Nov. 21, 1933-June 20, 1940.

GIBSON, Ernest William (son of Ernest Willard Gibson) (R Vt.) March 6, 1901-Nov. 4, 1969; Senate June 24, 1940-41; Gov. 1947-50.

GIBSON, Eustace (D W.Va.) Oct. 4, 1842-Dec. 10, 1900; House 1883-87.

GIBSON, Henry Richard (cousin of Charles Hopper Gibson) (R Tenn.) Dec. 24, 1837-May 25, 1938; House 1895-1905.

GIBSON, James King (D Va.) Feb. 18, 1812-March 30, 1879; House Jan. 28, 1870-71.

GIBSON, John Strickland (D Ga.) Jan. 3, 1893-Oct. 19, 1960; House 1941-47.

GIBSON, Paris (D Mont.) July 1, 1830-Dec. 16, 1920; Senate March 7, 1901-05.

GIBSON, Randall Lee (D La.) Sept. 10, 1832-Dec. 15, 1892; House 1875-83; Senate 1883-Dec. 15, 1892.

GIDDINGS, De Witt Clinton (D Texas) July 18, 1827-Aug. 19, 1903; House May 13, 1872-75; 1877-79.

GIDDINGS, Joshua Reed (ASW Ohio) Oct. 6, 1795-May 27, 1864; House Dec. 3, 1838-March 22, 1842; Dec. 5, 1842-59.

GIDDINGS, Napoleon Bonaparte (D Neb.) Jan. 2, 1816-Aug. 3, 1897; House (Terr. Del.) Jan. 5-March 3, 1855.

GIFFORD, Charles Laceille (R Mass.) March 15, 1871-Aug. 23, 1947; House Nov. 7, 1922-Aug. 23, 1947.

GIFFORD, Oscar Sherman (R S.D.) Oct. 20, 1842-Jan. 16, 1913; House: Terr. Del. for Dakota 1885-89; Rep. Nov. 2, 1889-91.

GILBERT, Abijah (R Fla.) June 18, 1806-Nov. 23, 1881; Senate 1869-75.

GILBERT, Edward (D Calif.) about 1819-Aug. 2, 1852; House Sept. 11, 1850-51.

GILBERT, Ezekiel (— N.Y.) March 25, 1756-July 17, 1841; House 1793-97.

GILBERT, George Gilmore (father of Ralph Waldo Emerson Gilbert) (D Ky.) Dec. 24, 1849-Nov. 9, 1909; House 1899-1907.

GILBERT, Jacob H. (D N.Y.) June 17, 1920-__; House March 8, 1960-1971.

GILBERT, Newton Whiting (R Ind.) May 24, 1862-July 5, 1939; House 1905-Nov. 6, 1906.

GILBERT, Ralph Waldo Emerson (son of George Gilmore Gilbert) (D Ky.) Jan. 17, 1882-July 30, 1939; House 1921-29; 1931-33.

GILBERT, Sylvester (— Conn.) Oct. 20, 1755-Jan. 2, 1846; House Nov. 16, 1818-19.

GILBERT, William Augustus (W N.Y.) Jan. 25, 1815-May 25, 1875; House 1855-Feb. 27, 1857.

GILCHRIST, Fred Cramer (R Iowa) June 2, 1868-March 10, 1950; House 1931-45.

GILDEA, James Hilary (D Pa.) Oct. 21, 1890-__; House 1935-39.

GILES, William Branch (D Va.) Aug. 12, 1762-Dec. 4, 1830; House Dec. 7, 1790-Oct. 2, 1798, 1801-03 (1790-98 Anti Federalist, 1801-03 Democrat); Senate Aug. 11, 1804-15; Gov. 1827-30.

GILES, William Fell (D Md.) April 8, 1807-March 21, 1879; House 1845-47.

GILFILLAN, Calvin Willard (R Pa.) Feb. 20, 1832-Dec. 2, 1901; House 1869-71.

GILFILLAN, John Bachop (R Minn.) Feb. 11, 1835-Aug. 19, 1924; House 1885-87.

GILHAMS, Clarence Chauncey (R Ind.) April 11, 1860-June 5, 1912; House Nov. 6, 1906-09.

GILL, John Jr. (D Md.) June 9, 1850-Jan. 27, 1918; House 1905-11.

GILL, Joseph John (R Ohio) Sept. 21, 1846-May 22, 1920; House Dec. 4, 1899-Oct. 31, 1903.

GILL, Michael Joseph (D Mo.) Dec. 5, 1864-Nov. 1, 1918; House June 19, 1914-15.

GILL, Patrick Francis (D Mo.) Aug. 16, 1868-May 21, 1923; House 1909-11; Aug. 12, 1912-13.

GILL, Thomas P. (D Hawaii) April 21, 1922-__; House 1963-65.

GILLEN, Courtland Craig (D Ind.) July 3, 1880-Sept. 1, 1954; House 1931-33.

GILLESPIE, Dean Milton (R Colo.) May 3, 1884-Feb. 2, 1949; House March 7, 1944-47.

GILLESPIE, Eugene Pierce (D Pa.) Sept. 24, 1852-Dec. 16, 1899; House 1891-93.

GILLESPIE, James (— N.C.) ?-Jan. 11, 1805; House 1793-99; 1803-Jan. 11, 1805.

GILLESPIE, James Frank (D Ill.) April 18, 1869-Nov. 26, 1954; House 1933-35.

GILLESPIE, Oscar William (D Texas) June 20, 1858-Aug. 23, 1927; House 1903-11.

GILLET, Charles William (R N.Y.) Nov. 26, 1840-Dec. 31, 1908; House 1893-1905.

GILLET, Ransom Hooker (D N.Y.) Jan. 27, 1800-Oct. 24, 1876; House 1833-37.

GILLETT, Frederick Huntington (R Mass.) Oct. 16, 1851-July 31, 1935; House 1893-1925; Speaker 1919-25; Senate 1925-31.

GILLETT, James Norris (R Calif.) Sept. 20, 1860-April 20, 1937; House 1903-Nov. 4, 1906; Gov. 1907-11.

GILLETTE, Edward Hooker (son of Francis Gillette) (G Iowa) Oct. 1, 1840-Aug. 14, 1918; House 1879-81.

GILLETTE, Francis (father of Edward Hooker Gillette) (FSW Conn.) Dec. 14, 1807-Sept. 30, 1879; Senate May 24, 1854-55.

GILLETTE, Guy Mark (D Iowa) Feb. 3, 1879-March 3, 1973; House 1933-Nov. 3, 1936; Senate Nov. 4, 1936-45; 1949-55.

GILLETTE, Wilson Darwin (R Pa.) July 1, 1880-Aug. 7, 1951; House Nov. 4, 1941-Aug. 7, 1951.

GILLIE, George W. (R Ind.) Aug. 15, 1880-July 3, 1963; House 1939-49.

GILLIGAN, John J. (D Ohio) March 22, 1921-__; House 1965-67; Gov. 1971-75.

GILLIS, James Lisle (D Pa.) Oct. 2, 1792-July 8, 1881; House 1857-59.

GILLON, Alexander (— S.C.) 1741-Oct. 6, 1794; House 1793-Oct. 6, 1794.

GILMAN, Benjamin Arthur (R N.Y.) Dec. 6, 1922-__; House 1973-__.

GILMAN, Charles Jervis (grandnephew of Nicholas Gilman) (R Maine) Feb. 26, 1824-Feb. 5, 1901; House 1857-59.

GILMAN, Nicholas (granduncle of Charles Jervis Gilman) (D N.H.) Aug. 3, 1755-May 2, 1814; House 1789-97 (F); Senate 1805-May 2, 1814 (D); Cont. Cong. 1786-88.

GILMER, George Rockingham (D Ga.) April 11, 1790-Nov. 16, 1859; House 1821-23, Oct. 1, 1827-29; 1833-35; Gov. 1829-31, 1837-39.

GILMER, John Adams (AP N.C.) Nov. 4, 1805-May 14, 1868; House 1857-61.

GILMER, Thomas Walker (D Va.) April 6, 1802-Feb. 28, 1844; House 1841-43 (W); 1843-Feb. 16, 1844 (D); Gov. 1840-41; Secy. of the Navy Feb. 15-Feb. 28, 1844.

GILMER, William Franklin (Dixie) (D Okla.) June 7, 1901-June 9, 1954; House 1949-51.

GILMORE, Alfred (son of John Gilmore) (D Pa.) June 9, 1812-June 29, 1890; House 1849-53.

GILMORE, Edward (D Mass.) Jan. 4, 1867-April 10, 1924; House 1913-15.

GILMORE, John (father of Alfred Gilmore) (JD Pa.) Feb. 18, 1780-May 11, 1845; House 1829-33.

GILMORE, Samuel Louis (D La.) July 30, 1859-July 18, 1910; House March 30, 1909-July 18, 1910.

GINGERY, Don (D Pa.) Feb. 19, 1884-Oct. 15, 1961; House 1935-39.

GINN, Ronald Bryan (D Ga.) May 31, 1934-__; House 1973-__.

GIST, Joseph (D S.C.) Jan. 12, 1775-March 8, 1836; House 1821-27.

GITTINS, Robert Henry (D N.Y.) Dec. 14, 1869-Dec. 25, 1957; House 1913-15.

GLASCOCK, John Raglan (D Calif.) Aug. 25, 1845-Nov. 10, 1913; House 1883-85.

GLASCOCK, Thomas (UD Ga.) Oct. 21, 1790-May 19, 1841; House Oct. 5, 1835-39.

GLASGOW, Hugh (— Pa.) Sept. 8, 1769-Jan. 31, 1818; House 1813-17.

GLASS, Carter (D Va.) Jan. 4, 1858-May 28, 1946; House Nov. 4, 1902-Dec. 16, 1918; Senate Feb. 2, 1920-May 28, 1946; Secy. of the Treasury 1918-20.

GLASS, Presley Thornton (D Tenn.) Oct. 18, 1824-Oct. 9, 1902; House 1885-89.

GLATFELTER, Samuel Feiser (D Pa.) April 7, 1858-April 23, 1927; House 1923-25.

GLEN, Henry (— N.Y.) July 13, 1739-Jan. 6, 1814; House 1793-1801.

GLENN, John Herschel Jr. (D Ohio) July 18, 1921-__; Senate Dec. 24, 1974-__.

GLENN, Milton Willits (R N.J.) June 18, 1903-Dec. 14, 1967; House Nov. 5, 1957-65.

GLENN, Otis Ferguson (R Ill.) Aug. 27, 1879-March 11, 1959; Senate Dec. 3, 1928-33.

GLENN, Thomas Louis (P Idaho) Feb. 2, 1847-Nov. 18, 1918; House 1901-03.

GLONINGER, John (D Pa.) Sept. 19, 1758-Jan. 22, 1836; House March 4-Aug. 2, 1813.

GLOSSBRENNER, Adam John (D Pa.) Aug. 31, 1810-March 1, 1889; House 1865-69.

GLOVER, David Delano (D Ark.) Jan. 18, 1868-April 5, 1952; House 1929-35.

GLOVER, John Milton (nephew of John Montgomery Glover) (D Mo.) June 23, 1852-Oct. 20, 1929; House 1885-89.

GLOVER, John Montgomery (uncle of John Milton Glover) (D Mo.) Sept. 4, 1822-Nov. 15, 1891; House 1873-79.

GLYNN, James Peter (R Conn.) Nov. 12, 1867-March 6, 1930; House 1915-23; 1925-March 6, 1930.

GLYNN, Martin Henry (D N.Y.) Sept. 27, 1871-Dec. 14, 1924; House 1899-1901; Gov. 1913-15.

GODDARD, Calvin (F Conn.) July 17, 1768-May 2, 1842; House May 14, 1801-05.

GODSHALK, William (R Pa.) Oct. 25, 1817-Feb. 6, 1891; House 1879-83.

GODWIN, Hannibal Lafayette (D N.C.) Nov. 3, 1873-June 9, 1929; House 1907-21.

GOEBEL, Herman Philip (R Ohio) April 5, 1853-May 4, 1930; House 1903-11.

GOEKE, John Henry (D Ohio) Oct. 28, 1869-March 25, 1930; House 1911-15.

GOFF, Abe McGregor (R Idaho) Dec. 21, 1899-__; House 1947-49.

GOFF, Guy Despard (son of Nathan Goff and father of Mrs. Louise Goff Reece) (R W.Va.) Sept. 13, 1866-Jan. 7, 1933; Senate 1925-31.

GOFF, Nathan (father of Guy Despard Goff and grandfather of Mrs. Louise Goff Reece) (R W.Va.) Feb. 9, 1843-April 24, 1920; House 1883-89; Senate April 1, 1913-19; Secy. of the Navy Jan. 6-March 5, 1881.

GOGGIN, William Leftwich (W.Va.) May 31, 1807-Jan. 3, 1870; House 1839-43; April 25, 1844-45; 1847-49.

GOLD, Thomas Ruggles (F N.Y.) Nov. 4, 1764-Oct. 24, 1827; House 1809-13; 1815-17.

GOLDEN, James Stephen (R Ky.) Sept. 10, 1891-Sept. 6, 1971; House 1949-55.

GOLDER, Benjamin Martin (R Pa.) Dec. 23, 1891-Dec. 30, 1946; House 1925-33.

GOLDFOGLE, Henry Mayer (D N.Y.), May 23, 1856-June 1, 1929; House 1901-15; 1919-21.

GOLDSBOROUGH, Charles (great-grand-father of Thomas Alan Goldsborough and Winder Laird Henry) (F Md.) July 15, 1765-Dec. 13, 1834; House 1805-17; Gov. 1819.

GOLDSBOROUGH, Phillips Lee (R Md.) Aug. 6, 1865-Oct. 22, 1946; Senate 1929-35; Gov. 1912-16.

GOLDSBOROUGH, Robert Henry (great-grandfather of Winder Laird Henry) (W Md.) Jan. 4, 1779-Oct. 5, 1836; Senate May 21, 1813-19 (F); Jan. 13, 1835-Oct. 5, 1836 (W).

GOLDSBOROUGH, Thomas Alan (great-grandson of Charles Goldsborough) (D Md.) Sept. 16, 1877-June 16, 1951; House 1921-April 5, 1939.

GOLDTHWAITE, George Thomas (D Ala.) Dec. 10, 1809-March 18, 1879; Senate 1871-77.

GOLDWATER, Barry Morris (father of Barry Morris Goldwater Jr.) (R Ariz.) Jan. 1, 1909-—; Senate 1953-65, 1969-—.

GOLDWATER, Barry Morris Jr. (son of the preceding) (R Calif.) July 15, 1938-—; House April 29, 1969-—.

GOLDZIER, Julius (D Ill.) Jan. 20, 1854-Jan. 20, 1925; House 1893-95.

GOLLADAY, Edward Isaac (brother of Jacob Shall Golladay) (D Tenn.) Sept. 9 1830-July 11, 1897; House 1871-73.

GOLLADAY, Jacob Shall (brother of Edward Isaac Golladay) (D Ky.) Jan. 19, 1819-May 20, 1887; House Dec. 5, 1867-Feb. 28, 1870.

GONZALEZ, Henry B. (D Texas) May 3, 1916-—; House Nov. 4, 1961-—.

GOOCH, Daniel Linn (D Ky.) Oct. 28, 1853-April 12, 1913; House 1901-05.

GOOCH, Daniel Wheelwright (R Mass.) Jan. 8, 1820-Nov. 11, 1891; House Jan. 31, 1858-Sept. 1, 1865, 1873-75.

GOOD, James William (R Iowa) Sept. 24, 1866-Nov. 18, 1929; House 1909-June 15, 1921; Secy. of War March 5-Nov. 18, 1929.

GOODALL, Louis Bertrand (R Maine) Sept. 23, 1851-June 26, 1935; House 1917-21.

GOODE, John Jr. (D Va.) May 27, 1829-July 14, 1909; House 1875-81.

GOODE, Patrick Gaines (W Ohio) May 10, 1798-Oct. 17, 1862; House 1837-43.

GOODE, Samuel (— Va.) March 21, 1756-Nov. 14, 1822; House 1799-1801.

GOODE, William Osborne (D Va.) Sept. 16, 1798-July 3, 1859; House 1841-43, 1853-July 3, 1859.

GOODELL, Charles Ellsworth (R N.Y.) March 16, 1926-—; House May 26, 1959-Sept. 10, 1968; Senate Sept. 10, 1968-71.

GOODENOW, John Milton (JD Ohio) 1782-July 20, 1838; House 1829-April 9, 1830.

GOODENOW, Robert (brother of Rufus King Goodenow) (W Maine) April 19, 1800-May 15, 1874; House 1851-53.

GOODENOW, Rufus King (brother of Robert Goodenow) (W Maine) April 24, 1790-March 24, 1863; House 1849-51.

GOODHUE, Benjamin (— Mass.) Sept. 20, 1748-July 28, 1814; House 1789-June 1796; Senate June 11, 1796-Nov. 8, 1800.

GOODIN, John Randolph (D Kan.) Dec. 14, 1836-Dec. 18, 1885; House 1875-77.

GOODING, Frank Robert (R Idaho) Sept. 16, 1859-June 24, 1928; Senate Jan. 15, 1921-June 24, 1928; Gov. 1905-09.

GOODLING, George Atlee (father of William Franklin Goodling) (R Pa.) Sept. 26, 1896-—; House 1961-65, 1967-1975.

GOODLING, William Franklin (son of George Atlee Goodling) (R Pa.) Dec. 5, 1927-—; House 1975-—.

GOODNIGHT, Isaac Herschel (D Ky.) Jan. 31, 1849-July 24, 1901; House 1889-95.

GOODRICH, Chauncey (brother of Elizur Goodrich) (F Conn.) Oct. 20, 1759-Aug. 18, 1815; House 1795-1801; Senate Oct. 25, 1807-May 1813.

GOODRICH, Elizur (brother of Chauncey Goodrich) (F Conn.) March 24, 1761-Nov. 1, 1849; House 1799-1801.

GOODRICH, John Zacheus (W Mass.) Sept. 27, 1804-April 19, 1885; House 1851-55.

GOODRICH, Milo (R N.Y.) Jan. 3, 1814-April 15, 1881; House 1871-73.

GOODWIN, Angier Louis (R Mass.) Jan. 30, 1881-June 20, 1975; House 1943-55.

GOODWIN, Forrest (R Maine) June 14, 1862-May 28, 1913; House March 4-May 28, 1913.

GOODWIN, Godfrey Gummer (R Minn.) Jan. 11, 1873-Feb. 16, 1933; House 1925-Feb. 16, 1933.

GOODWIN, Henry Charles (R N.Y.) June 25, 1824-Nov. 12, 1860; House Nov. 7, 1854-55, 1857-59.

GOODWIN, John Noble (R Maine/Ariz.) Oct. 18, 1824-April 29, 1887; House (Rep. Maine) 1861-63 (Terr. Del. Ariz.) 1865-67; Gov. (Ariz. Terr.) 1863-65.

GOODWIN, Philip Arnold (R N.Y.) Jan. 20, 1882-June 6, 1937; House 1933-June 6, 1937.

GOODWIN, Robert Kingman (R Iowa) May 23, 1905-—; House March 5, 1940-41.

GOODWIN, William Shields (D Ark.) May 2, 1866-Aug. 9, 1937; House 1911-21.

GOODWYN, Albert Taylor (D Ala.) Dec. 17, 1842-July 2, 1931; House April 22, 1896-97.

GOODWYN, Peterson (D Va.) 1745-Feb. 21, 1818; House 1803-Feb. 21, 1818.

GOODYEAR, Charles (D N.Y.) April 26, 1804-April 9, 1876; House 1845-47, 1865-67.

GOODYKOONTZ, Wells (R W.Va.) June 3, 1872-March 2, 1944; House 1919-23.

GORDON, George Washington (D Tenn.) Oct. 5, 1836-Aug. 9, 1911; House 1907-Aug. 9, 1911.

GORDON, James (F N.Y.) Oct. 31, 1739-Jan. 17, 1810; House 1791-95.

GORDON, James (— Miss.) Dec. 6, 1833-Nov. 28, 1912; Senate Dec. 27, 1909-Feb. 22, 1910.

GORDON, John Brown (D Ga.) Feb. 6, 1832-Jan. 9, 1904; Senate 1873-May 26, 1880, 1891-97; Gov. 1886-90.

GORDON, Robert Bryarly (D Ohio) Aug. 6, 1855-Jan. 3, 1923; House 1899-1903.

GORDON, Samuel (D N.Y.) April 28, 1802-Oct. 28, 1873; House 1841-43, 1845-47.

GORDON, Thomas Sylvy (D Ill.) Dec. 17, 1893-Jan. 22, 1959; House 1943-59.

GORDON, William (— N.H.) April 12, 1763-May 8, 1802; House 1797-June 12, 1800.

GORDON, William (D Ohio) Dec. 15, 1862-Jan. 16, 1942; House 1913-19.

GORDON, William Fitzhugh (D Va.) Jan. 13, 1787-Aug. 28, 1858; House Jan. 25, 1830-35.

GORE, Albert Arnold (D Tenn.) Dec. 26, 1907-—; House 1939-Dec. 4, 1944, 1945-53; Senate 1953-71.

GORE, Christopher (— Mass.) Sept. 21, 1758-March 1, 1827; Senate May 5, 1813-May 30, 1816; Gov. 1809-10.

GORE, Thomas Pryor (D Okla.) Dec. 10, 1870-March 16, 1949; Senate Dec. 11, 1907-21, 1931-37.

GORHAM, Benjamin (— Mass.) Feb. 13, 1775-Sept. 27, 1855; House Nov. 6, 1820-23, July 23, 1827-31, 1833-35.

GORMAN, Arthur Pue (D Md.) March 11, 1839-June 4, 1906; Senate 1881-99, 1903-June 4, 1906.

GORMAN, George Edmund (D Ill.) April 13, 1873-Jan. 13, 1935; House 1913-15.

GORMAN, James Sedgwick (D Mich.) Dec. 28, 1850-May 27, 1923; House 1891-95.

GORMAN, John Jerome (R Ill.) June 2, 1883-Feb. 24, 1949; House 1921-23, 1925-27.

GORMAN, Willis Arnold (D Ind.) Jan. 12, 1816-May 20, 1876; House 1849-53; Terr. Gov. of Minn. 1853-57.

GORSKI, Chester Charles (D N.Y.) June 22, 1906-April 25, 1975; House 1949-51.

GORSKI, Martin (D Ill.) Oct. 30, 1886-Dec. 4, 1949; House 1943-Dec. 4, 1949.

GOSS, Edward Wheeler (R Conn.) April 27, 1893-—; House Nov. 4, 1930-35.

GOSS, James Hamilton (R S.C.) Aug. 9, 1820-Oct. 31, 1886; House July 18, 1868-69.

GOSSETT, Charles Clinton (D Idaho) Sept. 2, 1888-___; Senate Nov. 17, 1945-47; Gov. Jan.-Nov. 16, 1945.

GOSSETT, Ed Lee (D Texas) Jan. 27, 1902___; House 1939-July 31, 1951.

GOTT, Daniel (W N.Y.) July 10, 1794-July 6, 1864; House 1847-51.

GOULD, Arthur Robinson (R Maine) March 16, 1857-July 24, 1946; Senate Nov. 30, 1926-31.

GOULD, Herman Day (W N.Y.) Jan. 16, 1799-Jan. 26, 1852; House 1849-51.

GOULD, Norman Judd (grandson of Norman Buel Judd) (R N.Y.) March 15, 1877-Aug. 20, 1964; House Nov. 2, 1915-23.

GOULD, Samuel Wadsworth (D Maine) Jan. 1, 1852-Dec. 19, 1935; House 1911-13.

GOULDEN, Joseph Aloysius (D N.Y.) Aug. 1, 1844-May 3, 1915; House 1903-11; 1913-May 3, 1915.

GOURDIN, Theodore (D S.C.) March 20, 1764-Jan. 17, 1826; House 1813-15.

GOVAN, Andrew Robison (— S.C.) Jan. 13, 1794-June 27, 1841; House Dec. 4, 1822-27.

GOVE, Samuel Francis (R Ga.) March 9, 1822-Dec. 3, 1900; House June 25, 1868-69.

GRABOWSKI, Bernard F. (D Conn.) June 11, 1923-___; House 1963-67.

GRADISON, Willis David Jr. (R Ohio) Dec. 28, 1928-___; House 1975-___.

GRADY, Benjamin Franklin (D N.C.) Oct. 10, 1831-March 6, 1914; House 1891-95.

GRAFF, Joseph Verdi (R Ill.) July 1, 1854-Nov. 10, 1921; House 1895-1911.

GRAHAM, Frank Porter (D N.C.) Oct. 14, 1886-Feb. 16, 1972; Senate March 29, 1949-Nov. 26, 1950.

GRAHAM, George Scott (R Pa.) Sept. 13, 1850-July 4, 1931; House 1913-July 4, 1931.

GRAHAM, James (brother of William Alexander Graham) (W N.C.) Jan. 7, 1793-Sept. 25, 1851; House 1833-March 29, 1836; Dec. 5, 1836-1843; 1845-47.

GRAHAM, James Harper (R N.Y.) Sept. 18, 1812-June 23, 1881; House 1859-61.

GRAHAM, James McMahon (D Ill.) April 14, 1852-Oct. 23, 1945; House 1909-15.

GRAHAM, John Hugh (D N.Y.) April 1, 1835-July 11, 1895; House 1893-95.

GRAHAM, Louis Edward (R Pa.) Aug. 4, 1880-Nov. 9, 1965; House 1939-55.

GRAHAM, William (W Ind.) March 16, 1782-Aug. 17, 1858; House 1837-39.

GRAHAM, William Alexander (brother of James Graham) (W N.C.) Sept. 5, 1804-Aug. 11, 1875; Senate Nov. 25, 1840-43; Gov. 1845-49; Secy. of the Navy 1850-52.

GRAHAM, William Harrison (R Pa.) Aug. 3, 1844-March 2, 1923; House Nov. 29, 1898-1903; 1905-11.

GRAHAM, William Johnson (R Ill.) Feb. 7, 1872-Nov. 10, 1937; House 1917-June 7, 1924.

GRAMMER, Elijah Sherman (R Wash.) April 3, 1868-Nov. 19, 1936; Senate Nov. 22, 1932-33.

GRANAHAN, Kathryn Elizabeth (widow of William Thomas Granahan) (D Pa.) Dec. 7, 1906-___; House Nov. 6, 1956-63.

GRANAHAN, William Thomas (husband of Kathryn Elizabeth Granahan) (D Pa.) July 26, 1895-May 25, 1956; House 1945-47; 1949-May 25, 1956.

GRANATA, Peter Charles (R Ill.) Oct. 28, 1898-___; House 1931-April 5, 1932.

GRANFIELD, William Joseph (D Mass.) Dec. 18, 1889-May 28, 1959; House Feb. 11, 1930-37.

GRANGER, Amos Phelps (cousin of Francis Granger) (W N.Y.) June 3, 1789-Aug. 20, 1866; House 1855-59.

GRANGER, Bradley Francis (D Mich.) March 12, 1825-Nov. 4, 1882; House 1861-63.

GRANGER, Daniel Larned Davis (D R.I.) May 30, 1852-Feb. 14, 1909; House 1903-Feb. 14, 1909.

GRANGER, Francis (cousin of Amos Phelps Granger) (W N.Y.) Dec. 1, 1792-Aug. 31, 1868; House 1835-37; 1839-March 5, 1841; Nov. 27, 1841-1843; Postmaster General March 6-Sept. 18, 1841.

GRANGER, Miles Tobey (D Conn.) Aug. 12, 1817-Oct. 21, 1895; House 1887-89.

GRANGER, Walter Keil (D Utah) Oct. 11, 1888-___; House 1941-53.

GRANT, Abraham Phineas (D N.Y.) April 5, 1804-Dec. 11, 1871; House 1837-39.

GRANT, George McInvale (D Ala.) July 11, 1897-___; House June 14, 1938-65.

GRANT, John Gaston (R N.C.) Jan. 1, 1858-June 21, 1923; House 1909-11.

GRANT, Robert Allen (R Ind.) July 31, 1905-___; House 1939-49.

GRANTLAND, Seaton (U Ga.) June 8, 1782-Oct. 18, 1864; House 1835-39.

GRASSLEY, Charles Ernest (R Iowa) Sept. 17, 1933-___; House 1975-___.

GRASSO, Ella T. (D Conn.) May 10, 1919-___; House 1971-1975; Gov. 1975-___.

GRAVEL, Maurice Robert (D Alaska) May 13, 1930-___; Senate 1969-___.

GRAVELY, Joseph Jackson (R Mo.) Sept. 25, 1828-April 28, 1872; House 1867-69.

GRAVES, Alexander (D Mo.) Aug. 25, 1844-Dec. 23, 1916; House 1883-85.

GRAVES, Dixie Bibb (D Ala.) July 26, 1882-Jan. 21, 1965; Senate Aug. 19, 1937-Jan. 10, 1938.

GRAVES, William Jordan (W Ky.) 1805-Sept. 27, 1848; House 1835-41.

GRAY, Edward Winthrop (R N.J.) Aug. 18, 1870-June 10, 1942; House 1915-19.

GRAY, Edwin (— Va.) July 18, 1743-?; House 1799-1813.

GRAY, Finly Hutchinson (D Ind.) July 21, 1863-May 8, 1947; House 1911-17; 1933-39.

GRAY, George (D Del.) May 4, 1840-Aug. 7, 1925; Senate March 18, 1885-99.

GRAY, Hiram (D N.Y.) July 10, 1801-May 6, 1890; House 1837-39.

GRAY, John Cowper (— Va.) 1783-May 18, 1823; House Aug. 28, 1820-21.

GRAY, Joseph Anthony (D Pa.) Feb. 25, 1884-May 8, 1966; House 1935-39.

GRAY, Kenneth James (D Ill.) Nov. 14, 1924-___; House 1955-Dec. 31, 1974.

GRAY, Oscar Lee (D Ala.) July 2, 1865-Jan. 2, 1936; House 1915-19.

GRAYSON, William (father of William John Grayson and uncle of Alexander Dalrymple Orr) (— Va.) 1740-March 12, 1790; Senate 1789-March 12, 1790; Cont. Cong. 1784-87.

GRAYSON, William John (son of William Grayson and cousin of Alexander Dalrymple Orr) (W S.C.) Nov. 2, 1788-Oct. 4, 1863; House 1833-37.

GREELEY, Horace (W N.Y.) Feb. 3, 1811-Nov. 29, 1872; House Dec. 4, 1848-49.

GREEN, Byram (— N.Y.) April 15, 1786-Oct. 18, 1865; House 1843-45.

GREEN, Edith (D Ore.) Jan. 17, 1910-___; House 1955-Dec. 31, 1974.

GREEN, Frederick William (D Ohio) Feb. 18, 1816-June 18, 1879; House 1851-55.

GREEN, Henry Dickinson (D Pa.) May 3, 1857-Dec. 29, 1929; House Nov. 7, 1899-1903.

GREEN, Innis (D Pa.) Feb. 26, 1776-Aug. 4, 1839; House 1827-31.

GREEN, Isaiah Lewis (— Mass.) Dec. 28, 1761-Dec. 5, 1841; House 1805-09; 1811-13.

GREEN, James Stephen (D Mo.) Feb. 28, 1817-Jan. 19, 1870; House 1847-51; Senate Jan. 12, 1857-61.

GREEN, Robert Alexis (D Fla.) Feb. 10, 1892-Feb. 9, 1973; House 1925-Nov. 25, 1944.

GREEN, Robert Stockton (D N.J.) March 25, 1831-May 7, 1895; House 1885-Jan. 17, 1887; Gov. 1887-90.

GREEN, Theodore Francis (grandnephew of Samuel Greene Arnold, great-grandnephew of Tristam Burges, great-grandson of James Burrill Jr., great-great-nephew of Lemuel Hastings Arnold) (D R.I.) Oct. 2, 1867-May 19, 1966; Senate 1937-61; Gov. 1933-37.

GREEN, Wharton Jackson (grandson of Jesse Wharton and cousin of Matt Whitaker Ransom) (D N.C.) Feb. 28, 1831-Aug. 6, 1910; House 1883-87.

GREEN, William Joseph Jr. (father of William Joseph Green) (D Pa.) March 5, 1910-Dec. 21, 1963; House 1945-47; 1949-Dec. 21, 1963.

GREEN, William Joseph III (son the preceding) (D Pa.) June 24, 1938-___; House April 28, 1964-___.

GREEN, William Raymond (R Iowa) Nov. 7, 1856-June 11, 1947; House June 5, 1911-March 31, 1928.

GREEN, Willis (W Ky.) ? - ?; House 1839-45.

GREENE, Albert Collins (W R.I.) April 15, 1791-Jan. 8, 1863; Senate 1845-51.

GREENE, Frank Lester (R Vt.) Feb. 10, 1870-Dec. 17, 1930; House July 30, 1912-1923; Senate 1923-Dec. 17, 1930.

GREENE, George Woodward (D N.Y.) July 4, 1831-July 21, 1895; House 1869-Feb. 17, 1870.

GREENE, Ray (— R.I.) Feb. 2, 1765-Jan. 11, 1829; Senate Nov. 13, 1797-1801.

GREENE, Thomas Marston (— Miss.) Feb. 26, 1758-Feb. 7, 1813; House (Terr. Del.) Dec. 6, 1802-03.

GREENE, William Laury (P Neb.) Oct. 3, 1849-March 11, 1899; House 1897-March 11, 1899.

GREENE, William Stedman (R Mass.) April 28, 1841-Sept. 22, 1924; House May 31, 1898-Sept. 22, 1924.

GREENHALGE, Frederic Thomas (R Mass.) July 19, 1842-March 5, 1896; House 1889-91; Gov. 1894-96.

GREENLEAF, Halbert Stevens (D N.Y.) April 12, 1827-Aug. 25, 1906; House 1883-85; 1891-93.

GREENMAN, Edward Whitford (D N.Y.) Jan. 26, 1840-Aug. 3, 1908; House 1887-89.

GREENUP, Christopher (— Ky.) 1750-April 27, 1818; House Nov. 9, 1792-1797; Gov. 1804-08.

GREENWAY, Isabella Selmes (later Mrs. Harry Orland King) (D Ariz.) March 22, 1886-Dec. 18, 1953; House Oct. 3, 1933-37.

GREENWOOD, Alfred Burton (D Ark.) July 11, 1811-Oct. 4, 1889; House 1853-59.

GREENWOOD, Arthur Herbert (D Ind.) Jan. 31, 1880-April 26, 1963; House 1923-39.

GREENWOOD, Ernest (D N.Y.) Nov. 25, 1884-June 15, 1955; House 1951-53.

GREEVER, Paul Ranous (D Wyo.) Sept. 28, 1891-Feb. 16, 1943; House 1935-39.

GREGG, Alexander White (D Texas) Jan. 31, 1855-April 30, 1919; House 1903-19.

GREGG, Andrew (grandfather of James Xavier McLanahan) (— Pa.) June 10, 1755-May 20, 1835; House 1791-1807; Senate 1807-13; President pro tempore 1809.

GREGG, Curtis Hussey (D Pa.) Aug. 9, 1865-Jan. 18, 1933; House 1911-13.

GREGG, James Madison (D Ind.) June 26, 1806-June 16, 1869; House 1857-59.

GREGORY, Dudley Sanford (W N.J.) Feb. 5, 1800-Dec. 8, 1874; House 1847-49.

GREGORY, Noble Jones (brother of William Voris Gregory) (D Ky.) Aug. 30, 1897-Sept. 26, 1971; House 1937-59.

GREGORY, William Voris (brother of Noble Jones Gregory) (D Ky.) Oct. 21, 1877-Oct. 10, 1936; House 1927-Oct. 10, 1936.

GREIG, John (W N.Y.) Aug. 6, 1779-April 9, 1858; House May 21-Sept. 25, 1841.

GREIGG, Stanley Lloyd (D Iowa) May 7, 1931-___; House 1965-67.

GRENNELL, George Jr. (— Mass.) Dec. 25, 1786-Nov. 19, 1877; House 1829-39.

GRESHAM, Walter (D Texas) July 22, 1841-Nov. 6, 1920; House 1893-95.

GREY, Benjamin Edwards (grandson of Benjamin Edwards) (W Ky.) ? - ?; House 1851-55.

GRIDER, George William (D Tenn.) Oct. 1, 1912-___; House 1965-67.

GRIDER, Henry (W Ky.) July 16, 1796-Sept. 7, 1866; House 1843-47; 1861-Sept. 7, 1866.

GRIEST, William Walton (R Pa.) Sept. 22, 1858-Dec. 5, 1929; House 1909-Dec. 5, 1929.

GRIFFIN, Anthony Jerome (D N.Y.) April 1, 1866-Jan. 13, 1935; House March 5, 1918-Jan. 13, 1935.

GRIFFIN, Charles Hudson (great-great-grandson of Isaac Griffin) (D Miss.) May 9, 1926-___; House March 12, 1968-1973.

GRIFFIN, Daniel Joseph (D N.Y.) March 26, 1880-Dec. 11, 1926; House 1913-Dec. 31, 1917.

GRIFFIN, Isaac (great-grandfather of Eugene McLanahan Wilson and great-great-grandfather of Charles Hudson Griffin) (D Pa.) Feb. 27, 1756-Oct. 12, 1827; House Feb. 16, 1813-17.

GRIFFIN, John King (SRW S.C.) Aug. 13, 1789-Aug. 1, 1841; House 1831-41.

GRIFFIN, Levi Thomas (D Mich.) May 23, 1837-March 17, 1906; House Dec. 4, 1893-95.

GRIFFIN, Michael (R Wis.) Sept. 9, 1842-Dec. 29, 1899; House Nov. 5, 1894-99.

GRIFFIN, Robert Paul (R Mich.) Nov. 6, 1923-___; House 1957-May 10, 1966; Senate May 11, 1966-___.

GRIFFIN, Samuel (— Va.) ?-Nov. 3, 1810; House 1789-95.

GRIFFIN, Thomas (— Va.) 1773-Oct. 7, 1837; House 1803-05.

GRIFFITH, Francis Marion (D Ind.) Aug. 21, 1849-Feb. 8, 1927; House Dec. 6, 1897-1905.

GRIFFITH, John Keller (D La.) Oct. 16, 1882-Sept. 25, 1942; House 1937-41.

GRIFFITH, Samuel (D Pa.) Feb. 14, 1816-Oct. 1, 1893; House 1871-73.

GRIFFITHS, Martha Wright (D Mich.) Jan. 29, 1912-___; House 1955-Dec. 31, 1974.

GRIFFITHS, Percy Wilfred (R Ohio) March 30, 1893-___; House 1943-49.

GRIGGS, James Mathews (D Ga.) March 29, 1861-Jan. 5, 1910; House 1897-Jan. 5, 1910.

GRIGSBY, George Barnes (D Alaska) Dec. 2, 1874-May 9, 1962; House (Terr. Del.) June 3, 1920-March 1, 1921.

GRIMES, James Wilson (R Iowa) Oct. 20, 1816-Feb. 7, 1872; Senate 1859-Dec. 6, 1869; Gov. 1854-58.

GRIMES, Thomas Wingfield (D Ga.) Dec. 18, 1844-Oct. 28, 1905; House 1887-91.

GRINNELL, Joseph (brother of Moses Hicks Grinnell) (W Mass.) Nov. 17, 1788-Feb. 7, 1885; House Dec. 7, 1843-51.

GRINNELL, Josiah Bushnell (R Iowa) Dec. 22, 1821-March 31, 1891; House 1863-67.

GRINNELL, Moses Hicks (brother of Joseph Grinnell) (W N.Y.) March 3, 1803-Nov. 24, 1877; House 1839-41.

GRISWOLD, Dwight Palmer (R Neb.) Nov. 27, 1893-April 12, 1954; Senate Nov. 5, 1952-April 12, 1954; Gov. 1941-47.

GRISWOLD, Gaylord (F N.Y.) Dec. 18, 1767-March 1, 1809; House 1803-05.

GRISWOLD, Glenn Hasenfratz (D Ind.) Jan. 20, 1890-Dec. 5, 1940; House 1931-39.

GRISWOLD, Harry Wilbur (R Wis.) May 19, 1886-July 4, 1939; House Jan. 3-July 4, 1939.

GRISWOLD, John Ashley (D N.Y.) Nov. 18, 1822-Feb. 22, 1902; House 1869-71.

GRISWOLD, John Augustus (R N.Y.) Nov. 11, 1822-Oct. 31, 1872; House 1863-69 (1863-65 Democrat, 1865-69 Republican).

GRISWOLD, Matthew (grandson of Roger Griswold) (R Pa.) June 6, 1833-May 19, 1919; House 1891-93; 1895-97.

GRISWOLD, Roger (grandfather of Matthew Griswold) (F Conn.) May 21, 1762-Oct. 25, 1812; House 1795-1805; Gov. 1811-12.

GRISWOLD, Stanley (— Ohio) Nov. 14, 1763-Aug. 21, 1815; Senate May 18-Dec. 11, 1809.

GROESBECK, William Slocum (D Ohio) July 24, 1815-July 7, 1897; House 1857-59.

GRONNA, Asle Jorgenson (R N.D.) Dec. 10, 1858-May 4, 1922; House 1905-Feb. 2, 1911; Senate Feb. 2, 1911-21.

GROOME, James Black (D Md.) April 4, 1838-Oct. 5, 1893; Senate 1879-85; Gov. 1874-76.

GROSS, Chester Heilman (R Pa.) Oct. 13, 1888-Jan. 9, 1973; House 1939-41; 1943-49.

GROSS, Ezra Carter (D N.Y.) July 11, 1787-April 9, 1829; House 1819-21.

GROSS, Harold Royce (R Iowa) June 30, 1899-___; House 1949-1975.

GROSS, Samuel (D Pa.) Nov. 10, 1774-March 19, 1844; House 1819-23.

GROSVENOR, Charles Henry (uncle of Charles Grosvenor Bond) (R Ohio) Sept. 20, 1833-Oct. 30, 1917; House 1885-91; 1893-1907.

GROSVENOR, Thomas Peabody (F N.Y.) Dec. 20, 1778-April 24, 1817; House Jan. 29, 1813-17.

GROUT, Jonathan (D Mass.) July 23, 1737-Sept. 8, 1807; House 1789-91.

GROUT, William Wallace (R Vt.) May 24, 1836-Oct. 7, 1902; House 1881-83; 1885-1901.

GROVE, William Barry (F N.C.) Jan. 15, 1764-March 30, 1818; House 1791-1803.

GROVER, Asa Porter (D Ky.) Feb. 18, 1819-July 20, 1887; House 1867-69.

GROVER, James R. Jr. (R N.Y.) March 5, 1919-___; House 1963-1975.

GROVER, La Fayette (D Ore.) Nov. 29, 1823-May 10, 1911; House Feb. 15-March 3, 1859; Senate 1877-83; Gov. 1870-77.

GROVER, Martin (NAD N.Y.) Oct. 20, 1811-Aug. 23, 1875; House 1845-47.

GROW, Galusha Aaron (R Pa.) Aug. 31, 1823-March 31, 1907; House 1851-63; Feb. 26, 1894-1903 (1851-57 Free Soil Democrat, 1857-63 and 1894-1903 Republican); Speaker 1861-63.

GRUENING, Ernest (D Alaska) Feb. 6, 1887-June 26, 1974; Senate 1959-69; Gov. (Terr.) 1939-53.

GRUNDY, Felix (WD Tenn.) Sept. 11, 1777-Dec. 19, 1840; House 1811-14; Senate Oct. 19, 1829-July 4, 1838; Nov. 19, 1839-Dec. 19, 1840; Atty. Gen. 1838-39.

GRUNDY, Joseph Ridgway (R Pa.) Jan. 13, 1863-March 3, 1961; Senate Dec. 11, 1929-Dec. 1, 1930.

GUBSER, Charles Samuel (R Calif.) Feb. 1, 1916-___; House 1953-Dec. 31, 1974.

GUDE, Gilbert (R Md.) March 9, 1923___; House 1967-___.

GUDGER, James Madison Jr. (father of Katherine Gudger Langley) (D N.C.) Oct. 22, 1855-Feb. 29, 1920; House 1903-07; 1911-15.

GUENTHER, Richard William (R Wis.) Nov. 30, 1845-April 5, 1913; House 1881-89.

GUERNSEY, Frank Edward (R Maine) Oct. 15, 1866-Jan. 1, 1927; House Nov. 3, 1908-17.

GUEVARA, Pedro (Nat. P.I.) Feb. 23, 1879-Jan. 19, 1937; House (Res. Comm.) 1923-Feb. 14, 1936.

GUFFEY, Joseph F. (D Pa.) Dec. 29, 1870-March 6, 1959; Senate 1935-47.

GUGGENHEIM, Simon (R Colo.) Dec. 30, 1867-Nov. 2, 1941; Senate 1907-13.

GUILL, Ben Hugh (R Texas) Sept. 8, 1909-___; House May 6, 1950-51.

GUION, Walter (D La.) April 3, 1849-Feb. 7, 1927; Senate April 22-Nov. 5, 1918.

GUNCKEL, Lewis B. (R Ohio) Oct. 15, 1826-Oct. 3, 1903; House 1873-75.

GUNN, James (— Ga.) March 13, 1753-July 30, 1801; Senate 1789-1801; Cont. Cong. 1788-89.

GUNN, James (P Idaho) March 6, 1843-Nov. 5, 1911; House 1897-99.

GUNTER, Thomas Montague (D Ark.) Sept. 18, 1826-Jan. 12, 1904; House June 16, 1874-83.

GUNTER, William Dawson Jr. (D Fla.) July 16, 1934-___; House 1973-75.

GURLEY, Henry Hosford (W La.) May 20, 1788-March 16, 1833; House 1823-31.

GURLEY, John Addison (R Ohio) Dec. 9, 1813-Aug. 19, 1863; House 1859-63.

GURNEY, Chan (John Chandler) (R S.D.) May 21, 1896-___; Senate 1939-51.

GURNEY, Edward John (R Fla.) Jan. 12, 1914-___; House 1963-69; Senate 1969-Dec. 31, 1974.

GUSTINE, Amos (D Pa.) 1789-March 3, 1844; House May 4, 1841-43.

GUTHRIE, James (D Ky.) Dec. 5, 1792-March 13, 1869; Senate 1865-Feb. 7, 1868; Secy. of the Treasury 1853-57.

GUYER, Tennyson (R Ohio) Nov. 29, 1913-___; House 1973-___.

GUYER, Ulysses Samuel (R Kan.) Dec. 13, 1868-June 5, 1943; House Nov. 4, 1924-1925; 1927-June 5, 1943.

GUYON, James Jr. (F N.Y.) Dec. 24, 1778-March 9, 1846; House Jan. 14, 1820-21.

GWIN, William McKendree (D Miss/Calif.) Oct. 9, 1805-Sept. 3, 1885; House 1841-43 (Miss.); Senate Sept. 9, 1850-1855; Jan. 13, 1857-1861 (Calif.).

GWINN, Ralph Waldo (R N.Y.) March 29, 1884-Feb. 27, 1962; House 1945-59.

GWYNNE, John William (R Iowa) Oct. 20, 1889-___; House 1935-49.

H

HABERSHAM, Richard Wylly (SRD Ga.) Dec. 1786-Dec. 2, 1842; House 1839-Dec. 2, 1842.

HACKETT, Richard Nathaniel (D N.C.) Dec. 4, 1866-Nov. 22, 1923; House 1907-09.

HACKETT, Thomas C. (D Ga.) ?-Oct. 8, 1851; House 1849-51.

HACKLEY, Aaron Jr. (—N.Y.) May 6, 1783-Dec. 28, 1868; House 1819-21.

HACKNEY, Thomas (D Mo.) Dec. 11, 1861-Dec. 24, 1946; House 1907-09.

HADLEY, Lindley Hoag (R Wash.) June 19, 1861-Nov. 1, 1948; House 1915-33.

HADLEY, William Flavius Lester (R Ill.) June 15, 1847-April 25, 1901; House Dec. 2, 1895-97.

HAGAN, G. Elliott (D Ga.) May 24, 1916-___; House 1961-1973.

HAGANS, John Marshall (R W.Va.) Aug. 13, 1838-June 17, 1900; House 1873-75.

HAGEDORN, Thomas Michael (R Minn.) Nov. 27, 1943-—; House 1975-—.

HAGEN, Harlan Francis (D Calif.) Oct. 8, 1914-___; House 1953-67.

HAGEN, Harold Christian (R Minn.) Nov. 10, 1901-March 19, 1957; House 1943-55 (1943-45 Farmer Laborite, 1945-55 Republican).

HAGER, Alva Lysander (R Iowa) Oct. 29, 1850-Jan. 29, 1923; House 1893-99.

HAGER, John Sharpenstein (AMD Calif.) March 12, 1818-March 19, 1890; Senate Dec. 23, 1873-75.

HAGGOTT, Warren Armstrong (R Colo.) May 18, 1864-April 29, 1958; House 1907-09.

HAHN, John (D Pa.) Oct. 30, 1776-Feb. 26, 1823; House 1815-17.

HAHN, Michael (R La.) Nov. 24, 1830-March 15, 1886; House Dec. 3, 1862-1863; 1885-March 15, 1886 (1862-63 Unionist, 1885-86 Republican).

HAIGHT, Charles (D N.J.) Jan. 4, 1838-Aug. 1, 1891; House 1867-71.

HAIGHT, Edward (D N.Y.) March 26, 1817-Sept. 15, 1885; House 1861-63.

HAILE, William (— Miss.) 1797-March 7, 1837; House July 10, 1826-Sept. 12, 1828.

HAILEY, John (D Idaho) Aug. 29, 1835-April 10, 1921; House (Terr. Del.) 1873-75; 1885-87.

HAINER, Eugene Jerome (R Neb.) Aug. 16, 1851-March 17, 1929; House 1893-97.

HAINES, Charles Delemere (D N.Y.) June 9, 1856-April 11, 1929; House 1893-95.

HAINES, Harry Luther (D Pa.) Feb. 1, 1880-March 29, 1947; House 1931-39; 1941-43.

HALDEMAN, Richard Jacobs (D Pa.) May 19, 1831-Oct. 1, 1886; House 1869-73.

HALE, Artemas (W Mass.) Oct. 20, 1783-Aug. 3, 1882; House 1845-49.

HALE, Eugene (father of Frederick Hale) (R Maine) June 9, 1836-Oct. 28, 1918; House 1869-79; Senate 1881-1911.

HALE, Fletcher (R N.H.) Jan. 22, 1883-Oct. 22, 1931; House 1925-Oct. 22, 1931.

HALE, Frederick (son of Eugene Hale, grandson of Zachariah Chandler and cousin of Robert Hale) (R Maine) Oct. 7, 1874-Sept. 28, 1963; Senate 1917-41.

HALE, James Tracy (R Pa.) Oct.14, 1810-April 6, 1865; House 1859-65.

HALE, John Blackwell (D Mo.) Feb. 27, 1831-Feb. 1, 1905; House 1885-87.

HALE, John Parker (F-S N.H.) March 31, 1806-Nov. 19, 1873; House 1843-45 (D); Senate 1847-53; July 30, 1855-1865 (F-S).

HALE, Nathan Wesley (R Tenn.) Feb. 11, 1860-Sept. 16, 1941; House 1905-09.

HALE, Robert (cousin of Frederick Hale) (R Maine) Nov. 29, 1889-__; House 1943-59.

HALE, Robert Safford (R N.Y.) Sept. 24, 1822-Dec. 14, 1881; House Dec. 3, 1866-1867; 1873-75.

HALE, Salma (D N.H.) March 7, 1787-Nov. 19, 1866; House 1817-19.

HALE, William (F N.H.) Aug. 6, 1765-Nov. 8, 1848; House 1809-11; 1813-17.

HALEY, Elisha (D Conn.) Jan. 21, 1776-Jan. 22, 1860; House 1835-39.

HALEY, James Andrew (D Fla.) Jan. 4, 1899-__; House 1953-__.

HALL, Albert Richardson (R Ind.) Aug. 27, 1884-Nov. 29, 1969; House 1925-31.

HALL, Augustus (D Iowa) April 29, 1814-Feb. 1, 1861; House 1855-57.

HALL, Benton Jay (D Iowa) Jan. 13, 1835-Jan. 5, 1894; House 1885-87.

HALL, Bolling (WD Ga.) Dec. 25, 1767-Feb. 25, 1836; House 1811-17.

HALL, Chapin (R Pa.) July 12, 1816-Sept. 12, 1879; House 1859-61.

HALL, Darwin Scott (R Minn.) Jan. 23, 1844-Feb. 23, 1919; House 1889-91.

HALL, David McKee (D N.C.) May 16, 1918-Jan. 29, 1960; House 1959-Jan. 29, 1960.

HALL, Durward Gorham (R Mo.) Sept. 14, 1910-__; House 1961-73.

HALL, Edwin Arthur (R N.Y.) Feb. 11, 1909-__; House Nov. 7, 1939-53.

HALL, George (D N.Y.) May 12, 1770-March 20, 1840; House 1819-21.

HALL, Hiland (W Vt.) July 20, 1795-Dec. 18, 1885; House Jan. 1, 1833-43; Gov. (R) 1858-60.

HALL, Homer William (R Ill.) July 22, 1870-Sept. 22, 1954; House 1927-33.

HALL, James Knox Polk (D Pa.) Sept. 30, 1844-Jan. 5, 1915; House 1899-Nov. 29, 1902.

HALL, Joseph (D Maine) June 26, 1793-Dec. 31, 1859; House 1833-37.

HALL, Joshua Gilman (R N.H.) Nov. 5, 1828-Oct. 31, 1898; House 1879-83.

HALL, Lawrence Washington (D Ohio) 1819-Jan. 18, 1863; House 1857-59.

HALL, Leonard Wood (R N.Y.) Oct. 2, 1900-__; House 1939-Dec. 31, 1952; Chrmn. Rep. Nat. Comm. 1953-57.

HALL, Nathan Kelsey (W N.Y.) March 28, 1810-March 2, 1874; House 1847-49; Postmaster General 1850-52.

HALL, Norman (D Pa.) Nov. 17, 1829-Sept. 29, 1917; House 1887-89.

HALL, Obed (D N.H.) Dec. 23, 1757-April 1, 1828; House 1811-13.

HALL, Osee Matson (D Minn.) Sept. 10, 1847-Nov. 26, 1914; 1891-95.

HALL, Philo (R S.D.) Dec. 31, 1865-Oct. 7, 1938; House 1907-09.

HALL, Robert Bernard (R Mass.) Jan. 28, 1812-April 15, 1868; House 1855-57 (AP); 1857-59 (R).

HALL, Robert Samuel (D Miss.) March 10, 1879-June 10, 1941; House 1929-33.

HALL, Sam B. Jr. (D Texas) Jan. 11, 1924-__; House June 28, 1976-__.

HALL, Tim Lee (D Ill.) June 11, 1925-__; House 1975-__.

HALL, Thomas (R N.D.) June 6, 1869-Dec. 4, 1958; House Nov. 4, 1924-33.

HALL, Thomas H. (D N.C.) June 1773-June 30, 1853; House 1817-25; 1827-35.

HALL, Uriel Sebree (son of William Augustus Hall and nephew of Willard Preble Hall) (D Mo.) April 12, 1852-Dec. 30, 1932; House 1893-97.

HALL, Willard (D Del.) Dec. 24, 1780-May 10, 1875; House 1817-Jan. 22, 1821.

HALL, Willard Preble (brother of William Augustus Hall and uncle of Uriel Sebree Hall) (D Mo.) May 9, 1820-Nov. 2, 1882; House 1847-53; Gov. 1864-65.

HALL, William (D Tenn.) Feb. 11, 1775-Oct. 7, 1856; House 1831-33; Gov. 1829.

HALL, William Augustus (father of Uriel Sebree Hall and brother of Willard Preble Hall) (D Mo.) Oct. 15, 1815-Dec. 15, 1888; House Jan. 20, 1862-65.

HALL, Wilton Earle (D S.C.) March 11, 1901-__; Senate Nov. 20, 1944-45.

HALLECK, Charles Abraham (R Ind.) Aug. 22, 1900-__; House Jan. 29, 1935-69.

HALLOCK, John Jr. (D N.Y.) July 1783-Dec. 6, 1840; House 1825-29.

HALLOWAY, Ransom (W N.Y.) about 1793-April 6, 1851; House 1849-51.

HALLOWELL, Edwin (D Pa.) April 2, 1844-Sept. 13, 1916; House 1891-93.

HALPERN, Seymour (R N.Y.) Nov. 19, 1913-__; House 1959-73.

HALSELL, John Edward (D Ky.) Sept. 11, 1826-Dec. 26, 1899; House 1883-87.

HALSEY, George Armstrong (R N.J.) Dec. 7, 1827-April 1, 1894; House 1867-69; 1871-73.

HALSEY, Jehiel Howell (son of Silas Halsey) (JD N.Y.) Oct. 7, 1788-Dec. 5, 1867; House 1829-31.

HALSEY, Nicoll (son of Silas Halsey) (D N.Y.) March 8, 1782-March 3, 1865; House 1833-35.

HALSEY, Silas (father of Jehiel Howell Halsey and Nicoll Halsey) (D N.Y.) Oct. 6, 1743-Nov. 19, 1832; House 1805-07.

HALSEY, Thomas Jefferson (R Mo.) May 4, 1863-March 17, 1951; House 1929-31.

HALSTEAD, William (W N.J.) June 4, 1794-March 4, 1878; House 1837-39; 1841-43.

HALTERMAN, Frederick (R Pa.) Oct. 22, 1831-March 22, 1907; House 1895-97.

HALVORSON, Kittel (FA/Prohib. Minn.) Dec. 15, 1846-July 12, 1936; House 1891-93.

HAMBLETON, Samuel (D Md.) Jan. 8, 1812-Dec. 9, 1886; House 1869-73.

HAMER, Thomas Lyon (uncle of Thomas Ray Hamer) (D Ohio) July 1800-Dec. 2, 1846; House 1833-39.

HAMER, Thomas Ray (nephew of Thomas Lyon Hamer) (R Idaho) May 4, 1864-Dec. 22, 1950; House 1909-11.

HAMILL, James Alphonsus (D N.J.) March 30, 1877-Dec. 15, 1941; House 1907-21.

HAMILL, Patrick (D Md.) April 28, 1817-Jan. 15, 1895; House 1869-71.

HAMILTON, Andrew Holman (D Ind.) June 7, 1834-May 9, 1895; House 1875-79.

HAMILTON, Andrew Jackson (brother of Morgan Calvin Hamilton) (ID Texas) Jan. 28, 1815-April 11, 1875; House 1859-61; Military Gov. 1862-65; Provisional Gov. 1865-66.

HAMILTON, Charles Mann (R N.Y.) Jan. 23, 1874-Jan. 3, 1942; House 1913-19.

HAMILTON, Charles Memorial (R Fla.) Nov. 1, 1840-Oct. 22, 1875; House July 1, 1868-1871.

HAMILTON, Cornelius Springer (R Ohio) Jan. 2, 1821-Dec. 22, 1867; House March 4-Dec. 22, 1867.

HAMILTON, Daniel Webster (D Iowa) Dec. 20, 1861-Aug. 21, 1936; House 1907-09.

HAMILTON, Edward La Rue (R Mich.) Dec. 9, 1857-Nov. 2, 1923; House 1897-1921.

HAMILTON, Finley (D Ky.) June 19, 1886-Jan. 10, 1940; House 1933-35.

HAMILTON, James Jr. (SRFT S.C.) May 8, 1786-Nov. 15, 1857; House Dec. 13, 1822-29; Gov. 1830-32.

HAMILTON, John (D Pa.) Nov. 25, 1754-Aug. 22, 1837; House 1805-07.

HAMILTON, John M. (D W.Va.) March 16, 1855-Dec. 27, 1916; House 1911-13.

HAMILTON, John Taylor (D Iowa) Oct. 16, 1843-Jan. 25, 1925; House 1891-93.

HAMILTON, Lee Herbert (D Ind.) April 20, 1931-__; House 1965-__.

HAMILTON, Morgan Calvin (brother of Andrew Jackson Hamilton) (R Texas) Feb. 25, 1809-Nov. 21, 1893; Senate March 30, 1870-77.

HAMILTON, Norman Rond (D Va.) Nov. 13, 1877-March 26, 1964; House 1937-39.

HAMILTON, Robert (D N.J.) Dec. 9, 1809-March 14, 1878; House 1873-77.

HAMILTON, William Thomas (D Md.) Sept. 8, 1820-Oct. 26, 1888; House 1849-55; Senate 1869-75; Gov. 1880-84.

HAMLIN, Courtney Walker (cousin of William Edward Barton) (D Mo.) Oct. 27, 1858-Feb. 16, 1950; House 1903-05; 1907-19.

HAMLIN, Edward Stowe (W Ohio) July 6, 1808-Nov. 23, 1894; House Oct. 8, 1844-45.

HAMLIN, Hannibal (R Maine) Aug. 27, 1809-July 4, 1891; House 1843-47 (D); Senate June 8, 1848-Jan. 7, 1857, 1857-Jan. 17, 1861, 1869-81 (1848-57 Democrat, 1857-61 and 1869-81 Republican); Gov. Jan. 8-Feb. 20, 1857; Vice President 1861-65.

HAMLIN, Simon Moulton (D Maine) Aug. 10, 1866-July 27, 1939; House 1935-37.

HAMMER, William Cicero (D N.C.) March 24, 1865-Sept. 26, 1930; House 1921-Sept. 26, 1930.

HAMMERSCHMIDT, John Paul (R Ark.) May 4, 1922-__; House 1967-__.

HAMMETT, William H. (D Miss.) ? - ?; House 1843-45.

HAMMOND, Edward (D Md.) March 17, 1812-Oct. 19, 1882; House 1849-53.

HAMMOND, Jabez Delno (D N.Y.) Aug. 2, 1778-Aug. 18, 1855; House 1815-17.

HAMMOND, James Henry (SRD S.C.) Nov. 15, 1807-Nov. 13, 1864; House 1835-Feb. 26, 1836 (SRFT); Senate Dec. 7, 1857-Nov. 11, 1860 (SRD); Gov. 1842-44.

HAMMOND, John (R N.Y.) Aug. 17, 1827-May 28, 1889; House 1879-83.

HAMMOND, Nathaniel Job (D Ga.) Dec. 26, 1833-April 20, 1899; House 1879-87.

HAMMOND, Peter Francis (D Ohio) June 30, 1887-__; House Nov. 30, 1936-37.

HAMMOND, Robert Hanna (VBD Pa.) April 28, 1791-June 2, 1847; House 1837-41.

HAMMOND, Samuel (D Ga.) Sept. 21, 1757-Sept. 11, 1842; House 1803-Feb. 2, 1805; Gov. Upper Louisiana Terr. 1805-1824.

HAMMOND, Thomas (D Ind.) Feb. 27, 1843-Sept. 21, 1909; House 1893-95.

HAMMOND, Winfield Scott (D Minn.) Nov. 17, 1863-Dec. 30, 1915; House 1907-Jan. 6, 1915; Gov. Jan. 1915-Dec. 30, 1915.

HAMMONS, David (D Maine) May 12, 1808-Nov. 7, 1888; House 1847-49.

HAMMONS, Joseph (JD N.H.) March 3, 1787-March 29, 1836; House 1829-33.

HAMPTON, James Giles (W N.J.) June 13, 1814-Sept. 22, 1861; House 1845-49.

HAMPTON, Moses (W Pa.) Oct. 28, 1803-June 27, 1878; House 1847-51.

HAMPTON, Wade (D S.C.) 1752-Feb. 4, 1835; House 1795-97; 1803-05.

HAMPTON, Wade (grandson of the preceding) (D S.C.) March 28, 1818-April 11, 1902; Senate 1879-91; Gov. 1876-79.

HANBACK, Lewis (R Kan.) March 27, 1839-Sept. 7, 1897; House 1883-87.

HANBURY, Harry Alfred (R N.Y.) Jan. 1, 1863-Aug. 22, 1940; House 1901-03.

HANCHETT, Luther (R Wis.) Oct. 25, 1825-Nov. 24, 1862; House 1861-Nov. 24, 1862.

HANCOCK, Clarence Eugene (R N.Y.) Feb. 13, 1885-Jan. 3, 1948; House Nov. 8, 1927-47.

HANCOCK, Franklin Wills Jr. (D N.C.) Nov. 1, 1894-Jan. 23, 1969; House Nov. 4, 1930-39.

HANCOCK, George (D Va.) June 13, 1754-July 18, 1820; House 1793-97.

HANCOCK, John (D Texas) Oct. 24, 1824-July 19, 1893; House 1871-77; 1883-85.

HAND, Augustus Cincinnatus (D N.Y.) Sept. 4, 1803-March 8, 1878; House 1839-41.

HAND, Thomas Millet (R N.J.) July 7, 1902-Dec. 26, 1956; House 1945-Dec. 26, 1956.

HANDLEY, William Anderson (D Ala.) Dec. 15, 1834-June 23, 1909; House 1871-73.

HANDY, Levin Irving (nephew of William Campbell Preston Breckenridge) (D Del.) Dec. 24, 1861-Feb. 3, 1922; House 1897-99.

HANKS, James Millander (D Ark.) Feb. 12, 1833-May 24, 1909; House 1871-73.

HANLEY, James M. (D N.Y.) July 19, 1920-__; House 1965-__.

HANLY, James Franklin (R Ind.) April 4, 1863-Aug. 1, 1920; House 1895-97; Gov. 1905-09.

HANNA, John (R Ind.) Sept. 3, 1827-Oct. 24, 1882; House 1877-79.

HANNA, John Andre (grandfather of Archibald McAllister) (AF Pa.) 1762-July 23, 1805; House 1797-July 23, 1805.

HANNA, Louis Benjamin (R N.D.) Aug. 9, 1861-April 23, 1948; House 1909-Jan. 7, 1913; Gov. 1913-17.

HANNA, Marcus Alonzo (father of Ruth Hanna McCormick) (R Ohio) Sept. 24, 1837-Feb. 15, 1904; Senate March 5, 1897-Feb. 15, 1904; Chrmn. Rep. Natl. Comm. 1896-1904.

HANNA, Richard Thomas (D Calif.) June 9, 1914-__; House 1963-Dec. 31, 1974.

HANNA, Robert (W Ind.) April 6, 1786-Nov. 16, 1858; Senate Aug. 19, 1831-Jan. 3, 1832.

HANNAFORD, Mark Warren (D Calif.) Feb. 7, 1925-__; House 1975-__.

HANNEGAN, Edward Allen (D Ind.) June 25, 1807-Feb. 25, 1859; House 1833-37; Senate 1843-49.

HANRAHAN, Robert Paul (R Ill.) Feb. 25, 1934-__; House 1973-1975.

HANSBROUGH, Henry Clay (R N.D.) Jan. 30, 1848-Nov. 16, 1933; House Nov. 2, 1889-1891; Senate 1891-1909.

HANSEN, Clifford Peter (R Wyo.) Oct. 16, 1912-__; Senate 1967-__; Gov. 1963-67.

HANSEN, George Vernon (R Idaho) Sept. 14, 1930-__; House 1965-69, 1975-__.

HANSEN, John Robert (D Iowa) Aug. 24, 1901-Sept. 23, 1974; House 1965-67.

HANSEN, Julia Butler (D Wash.) June 14, 1907-__; House Nov. 8, 1960-Dec. 31, 1974.

HANSEN, Orval Howard (R Idaho) Aug. 3, 1926-__; House 1969-75.

HANSON, Alexander Contee (grandnephew of Benjamin Contee) (F Md.) Feb. 27, 1786-April 23, 1819; House 1813-16; Senate Dec. 20, 1816-April 23, 1819.

HARALSON, Hugh Anderson (D Ga.) Nov. 13, 1805-Sept. 25, 1854; House 1843-51.

HARALSON, Jeremiah (R Ala.) April 1, 1846-about 1916; House 1875-77.

HARD, Gideon (W N.Y.) April 29, 1797-April 27, 1885; House 1833-37.

HARDEMAN, Thomas Jr. (D Ga.) Jan. 12, 1825-March 6, 1891; House 1859-Jan. 23, 1861; 1883-85.

HARDEN, Cecil Murray (R Ind.) Nov. 21, 1894-__; House 1949-59.

HARDENBERGH, Augustus Albert (D N.J.) May 18, 1830-Oct. 5, 1889; House 1875-79; 1881-83.

HARDIN, Benjamin (cousin of Martin Davis Hardin) (W Ky.) Feb. 29, 1784-Sept. 24, 1852; House 1815-17; 1819-23; 1833-37.

HARDIN, John J. (son of Martin Davis Hardin) (W Ill.) Jan. 6, 1810-Feb. 23, 1847; House 1843-45.

HARDIN, Martin Davis (cousin of Benjamin Hardin and father of John J. Hardin) (D Ky.) June 21, 1780-Oct. 8, 1823; Senate Nov. 13, 1816-17.

HARDING, Aaron (UD Ky.) Feb. 20, 1805-Dec. 24, 1875; House 1861-67.

HARDING, Abner Clark (R Ill.) Feb. 10, 1807-July 19, 1874; House 1865-69.

HARDING, Benjamin Franklin (R Ore.) Jan. 4, 1823-June 16, 1899; Senate Sept. 12, 1862-65.

HARDING, John Eugene (R Ohio) June 27, 1877-July 26, 1959; House 1907-09.

HARDING, Ralph R. (D Idaho) Sept. 9, 1929-__; House 1961-65.

HARDING, Warren Gamaliel (R Ohio) Nov. 2, 1865-Aug. 2, 1923; Senate 1915-Jan. 13, 1921; President 1921-Aug. 2, 1923.

HARDWICK, Thomas William (D Ga.) Dec. 9, 1872-Jan. 31, 1944; House 1903-Nov. 2, 1914; Senate Nov. 4, 1914-19; Gov. 1921-23.

HARDY, Alexander Merrill (R Ind.) Dec. 16, 1847-Aug. 31, 1927; House 1895-97.

HARDY, Guy Urban (R Colo.) April 4, 1872-Jan. 26,1947; House 1919-33.

HARDY, John (D N.Y.) Sept. 19, 1835-Dec. 9, 1913; House Dec. 5, 1881-85.

HARDY, Porter Jr. (D Va.) June 1, 1903-__; House 1947-69.

HARDY, Rufus (D Texas) Dec. 16, 1855-March 13, 1943; House 1907-23.

HARE, Butler Black (father of James Butler Hare) (D S.C.) Nov. 25, 1875-Dec. 30, 1967; House 1925-33; 1939-47.

HARE, Darius Dodge (D Ohio) Jan. 9, 1843-Feb. 10, 1897; House 1891-95.

HARE, James Butler (son of Butler Black Hare) (D S.C.) Sept. 4, 1918-July 16, 1966; House 1949-51.

HARE, Silas (D Texas) Nov. 13, 1827-Nov. 26, 1907; House 1887-91.

HARGIS, Denver David (D Kan.) July 22, 1921-__; House 1959-61.

HARKIN, Thomas Richard (D Iowa) Nov. 19, 1939-__; House 1975-__.

HARLAN, Aaron (cousin of Andrew Jackson Harlan) (W Ohio) Sept. 8, 1802-Jan. 8, 1868; House 1853-59.

HARLAN, Andrew Jackson (cousin of Aaron Harlan) (D Ind.) March 29, 1815-May 19, 1907; House 1849-51; 1853-55.

HARLAN, Byron Berry (D Ohio) Oct. 22, 1886-Nov. 11, 1949; House 1931-39.

HARLAN, James (W Ky.) June 22, 1800-Feb. 18, 1863; House 1835-39.

HARLAN, James (R Iowa) Aug. 26, 1820-Oct. 5, 1899; Senate Dec. 31, 1855-Jan. 12, 1857, Jan. 29, 1857-May 15, 1865, 1867-73 (1855-57 Whig, 1857-65 and 1867-73 Republican); Secy. of the Interior May 15, 1865-July 27, 1866.

HARLESS, Richard Fielding (D Ariz.) Aug. 6, 1905-Nov. 24, 1970; House 1943-49.

HARMANSON, John Henry (D La.) Jan. 15, 1803-Oct.24, 1850; House 1845-Oct. 24, 1850.

HARMER, Alfred Crout (R Pa.) Aug. 8, 1825-March 6, 1900; House 1871-75; 1877-March 6, 1900.

HARMON, Randall S. (D Ind.) July 19, 1903-__; House 1959-61.

HARNESS, Forest Arthur (R Ind.) June 24, 1895-July 29, 1974; House 1939-49.

HARPER, Alexander (W Ohio) Feb.5, 1786-Dec. 1, 1860; House 1837-39; 1843-47; 1851-53.

HARPER, Francis Jacob (D Pa.) March 5, 1800-March 18, 1837; House March 4-18, 1837.

HARPER, James (W Pa.) March 28, 1780-March 31, 1873; House 1833-37 (1833-35 Clay Democrat, 1835-37 Whig).

HARPER, James Clarence (C N.C.) Dec. 6, 1819-Jan. 8, 1890; House 1871-73.

HARPER, John Adams (WD N.H.) Nov. 2, 1779-June 18, 1816; House 1811-13.

HARPER, Joseph Morrill (D N.H.) June 21, 1787-Jan. 15, 1865; House 1831-35.

HARPER, Robert Goodloe (F S.C./Md.) Jan. 1765-Jan. 14, 1825; House Feb.5, 1795-1801 (S.C.); Senate Jan. 29-Dec. 6, 1816 (Md.).

HARPER, William (SRD S.C.) Jan. 17, 1790-Oct. 10, 1847; Senate March 8-Nov. 29, 1826.

HARRELD, John William (R Okla.) Jan. 24, 1872-Dec. 26, 1950; House Nov. 8, 1919-21; Senate 1921-27.

HARRIES, William Henry (D Minn.) Jan. 15, 1843-July 23, 1921; House 1891-93.

HARRINGTON, Henry William (D Ind.) Sept. 12, 1825-March 20, 1882; House 1863-65.

HARRINGTON, Michael Joseph (D Mass.) Sept. 2, 1936-__; House Sept. 30, 1969-__.

HARRINGTON, Vincent Francis (D Iowa) May 16, 1903-Nov.29, 1943; House 1937-Sept. 5, 1942.

HARRIS, Benjamin Gwinn (D Md.) Dec. 13, 1805-April 4, 1895; House 1863-67.

HARRIS, Benjamin Winslow (father of Robert Orr Harris) (R Mass.) Nov. 10, 1823-Feb. 7, 1907; House 1873-83.

HARRIS, Charles Murray (D Ill.) April 10, 1821-Sept. 20, 1896; House 1863-65.

HARRIS, Christopher Columbus (D Ala.) Jan. 28, 1842-Dec. 28, 1935; House May 11, 1914-15.

HARRIS, Fred Roy (D Okla.) Nov. 13, 1930-__; Senate Nov. 4, 1964-Jan. 3, 1973; Chrmn Dem. Natl. Comm. 1969-70.

HARRIS, George Emrick (R Miss.) Jan. 6, 1827-March 19, 1911; House Feb. 23, 1870-73.

HARRIS, Henry Richard (D Ga.) Feb. 2, 1828-Oct. 15, 1909; House 1873-79; 1885-87.

HARRIS, Henry Schenck (D N.J.) Dec. 27, 1850-May 2, 1902; House 1881-83.

HARRIS, Herbert Eugene II (D Va.) April 14, 1926-__; House 1975-__.

HARRIS, Ira (grandfather of Henry Riggs Rathbone) (R N.Y.) May 31, 1802-Dec. 2, 1875; Senate 1861-67.

HARRIS, Isham Green (D Tenn.) Feb. 10, 1818-July 8, 1897; House 1849-53; Senate 1877-July 8, 1897; President pro tempore 1893-95; Gov. 1857-62.

HARRIS, James Morrison (AP Md.) Nov. 20, 1817-July 16, 1898; House 1855-61.

HARRIS, John (cousin of Robert Harris) (— N.Y.) Sept. 26, 1760-Nov., 1824; House 1807-09.

HARRIS, John Spafford (R La.) Dec. 18, 1825-Jan. 25, 1906; Senate July 9, 1868-71.

HARRIS, John Thomas (cousin of John Hill of Virginia) (D Va.) May 8, 1823-Oct. 14, 1899; House 1859-61; 1871-81.

HARRIS, Mark (— Maine) Jan. 27, 1779-March 2, 1843; House Dec. 2, 1822-23.

HARRIS, Oren (D Ark.) Dec. 20, 1903-__; House 1941-Feb. 2, 1966.

HARRIS, Robert (cousin of John Harris) (— Pa.) Sept. 5, 1768-Sept.3, 1851; House 1823-27.

HARRIS, Robert Orr (son of Benjamin Winslow Harris) (R Mass.) Nov. 8, 1854-June 13, 1926; House 1911-13.

HARRIS, Sampson Willis (D Ala.) Feb. 23, 1809-April 1, 1857; House 1847-57.

HARRIS, Stephen Ross (uncle of Ebenezer Byron Finley) (R Ohio) May 22, 1824-Jan. 15, 1905; House 1895-97.

HARRIS, Thomas K. (D Tenn.) ?-March 18, 1816; House 1813-15.

HARRIS, Thomas Langrell (D Ill.) Oct. 29, 1816-Nov. 24, 1858; House 1849-51; 1855-Nov. 24, 1858.

HARRIS, Wiley Pope (D Miss.) Nov. 9, 1818-Dec. 3, 1891; House 1853-55.

HARRIS, William Alexander (D Va.) Aug. 24, 1805-March 28, 1864; House 1841-43.

HARRIS, William Alexander (son of the preceding) (D Kan.) Oct. 29, 1841-Dec. 20, 1909; House 1893-95 (P); Senate 1897-1903 (D).

HARRIS, William Julius (great-grandson of Charles Hooks) (D Ga.) Feb. 3, 1868-April 18, 1932; Senate 1919-April 18, 1932.

HARRIS, Winder Russell (D Va.) Dec. 3, 1888-Feb. 24, 1973; House April 8, 1941-Sept.15, 1944.

HARRISON, Albert Galliton (VBD Mo.) June 26, 1800-Sept. 7, 1839; House 1835-39.

HARRISON, Benjamin (grandson of President William Henry Harrison; son of John Scott Harrison of Ohio; and grandfather of William Henry Harrison of Wyoming) (R Ind.) Aug. 20, 1833-March 13, 1901; Senate 1881-87; President 1889-93.

HARRISON, Burr Powell (son of Thomas Walter Harrison) (D Va.) July 2, 1904-Dec. 29, 1973; House Nov. 6, 1946-63.

HARRISON, Byron Patton (Pat) (D Miss.) Aug. 29, 1881-June 22, 1941; House 1911-19; Senate 1919-June 22, 1941; President pro tempore 1941.

HARRISON, Carter Bassett (brother of President William Henry Harrison) (— Va.) ?-April 18, 1808; House 1793-99.

HARRISON, Carter Henry (D Ill.) Feb. 15, 1825-Oct. 28, 1893; House 1875-79.

HARRISON, Francis Burton (D N.Y.) Dec. 18, 1873-Nov. 21, 1957; House 1903-05; 1907-Sept. 1, 1913.

HARRISON, George Paul (D Ala.) March 19, 1841-July 17, 1922; House Nov. 6, 1894-97.

HARRISON, Horace Harrison (R Tenn.) Aug. 7, 1829-Dec. 20, 1885; House 1873-75.

HARRISON, John Scott (son of President William Henry Harrison, and father of President Benjamin Harrison) (W Ohio) Oct. 4, 1804-May 25, 1878; House 1853-57.

HARRISON, Richard Almgill (UD Ohio) April 8, 1824-July 30, 1904; House July 4, 1861-63.

HARRISON, Robert Dinsmore (R Neb.) Jan. 26, 1897-—; House Dec. 4, 1951-59.

HARRISON, Samuel Smith (D Pa.) 1780-April 1853; House 1833-37.

HARRISON, Thomas Walter (father of Burr Powell Harrison) (D Va.) Aug. 5, 1856-May 9, 1935; House Nov. 7, 1916-Dec. 15, 1922; 1923-29.

HARRISON, William Henry (father of John Scott Harrison, brother of Carter Basset Harrison, grandfather of Benjamin Harrison and great-great-grandfather of William Henry Harrison of Wyoming) (W Ohio); Feb. 9, 1773-April 4, 1841; House (Terr. Del.) 1799-May 14, 1800; (Rep.) Oct. 8, 1816-19; Senate 1825-May 20, 1828; President March 4-April 4, 1841; Gov. (Indiana Terr.) 1801-13.

HARRISON, William Henry (great-great-grandson of President William Henry Harrison and grandson of President Benjamin Harrison and Alvin Saunders) (R Wyo.) Aug. 10, 1896-—; House 1951-55; 1961-65, 1967-69.

HARSHA, William Howard (R Ohio) Jan. 1, 1921-—; House 1961-—.

HART, Alphonso (R Ohio) July 4, 1830-Dec. 23, 1910; House 1883-85.

HART, Archibald Chapman (D N.J.) Feb. 27, 1873-July 24, 1935; House Nov. 5, 1912-March 3, 1913; July 22, 1913-17.

HART, Edward Joseph (D N.J.) March 25, 1893-April 20, 1961; House 1935-55.

HART, Elizur Kirke (D N.Y.) April 8, 1841-Feb. 18, 1893; House 1877-79.

HART, Emanuel Bernard (D N.Y.) Oct. 27, 1809-Aug. 29, 1897; House 1851-53.

HART, Gary Warren (D Colo.) Nov. 28, 1937-—; Senate 1975-—.

HART, Joseph Johnson (D Pa.) April 18, 1859-July 13, 1926; House 1895-97.

HART, Michael James (D Mich.) July 16, 1877-Feb. 14, 1951; House Nov. 3, 1931-35.

HART, Philip Aloysius (D Mich.) Dec. 10, 1912-—; Senate 1959-—.

HART, Roswell (R N.Y.) Aug. 4, 1824-April 20, 1883; House 1865-67.

HART, Thomas Charles (R Conn.) June 12, 1877-July 4, 1971; Senate Feb. 15, 1945-Nov. 5, 1946.

HARTER, Dow Watters (D Ohio) Jan. 2, 1885-Sept. 4, 1971; House 1933-43.

HARTER, John Francis (R N.Y.) Sept. 1, 1897-Dec. 20, 1947; House 1939-41.

HARTER, Michael Daniel (grandson of Robert Moore) (D Ohio) April 6, 1846-Feb. 22, 1896; House 1891-95.

HARTKE, Rupert Vance (D Ind.) May 31, 1919-—; Senate 1959-—.

HARTLEY, Fred Allan Jr. (R N.J.) Feb. 22, 1902-May 11, 1969; House 1929-49.

HARTLEY, Thomas (— Pa.) Sept. 7, 1748-Dec. 21, 1800; House 1789-Dec. 21, 1800.

HARTMAN, Charles Sampson (Sil R Mont) March 1, 1861-Aug. 3, 1929; House 1893-99 (1893-97 Republican, 1897-99 Silver Republican).

HARTMAN, Jesse Lee (R Pa.) June 18, 1853-Feb. 17, 1930; House 1911-13.

HARTRIDGE, Julian (D Ga.) Sept. 9, 1829-Jan. 8, 1879; House 1875-Jan. 8, 1879.

HARTZELL, William (D Ill.) Feb. 20, 1837-Aug. 14, 1903; House 1875-79.

HARVEY, David Archibald (R Okla.) March 20, 1845-May 24, 1916; House (Terr. Del.) Nov. 4, 1890-93.

HARVEY, James (R Mich.) July 4, 1922-—; House 1961-Jan. 31, 1974.

HARVEY, James Madison (R Kan.) Sept. 21, 1833-April 15, 1894; Senate Feb. 2, 1874-77; Gov. 1869-73.

HARVEY, Jonathan (brother of Matthew Harvey) (— N.H.) Feb. 25, 1780-Aug. 23, 1859; House 1825-31.

HARVEY, Matthew (brother of Jonathan Harvey) (D N.H.) June 21, 1781-April 7, 1866; House 1821-25; Gov. 1830-31.

HARVEY, Ralph (R Ind.) Aug. 9, 1901-—; House Nov. 4, 1947-59; 1961-Dec. 30, 1966.

HASBROUCK, Abraham Bruyn (cousin of Abraham Joseph Hasbrouck) (NR N.Y.) Nov. 29, 1791-Feb. 24, 1879; House 1825-27.

HASBROUCK, Abraham Joseph (cousin of Abraham Bruyn Hasbrouck) (Clinton D N.Y.) Oct. 16, 1773-Jan.m12, 1845; House 1813-15.

HASBROUCK, Josiah (— N.Y.) March 5, 1755-March 19, 1821; House April 28, 1803-05, 1817-19.

HASCALL, Augustus Porter (W N.Y.) June 24, 1800-June 27, 1872; House 1851-53.

HASKELL, Dudley Chase (grandfather of Otis Halbert Holmes) (R Kan.) March 23, 1842-Dec. 16, 1883; House 1877-Dec. 16, 1883.

HASKELL, Floyd Kirk (D Colo.) Feb. 7, 1916-—; Senate 1973-—.

HASKELL, Harry Garner Jr. (R Del.) May 27, 1921-—; House 1957-59.

HASKELL, Reuben Locke (R N.Y.) Oct. 5, 1878-—; House 1915-Dec. 31, 1919.

HASKELL, William T. (nephew of Charles Ready) (W Tenn.) July 21, 1818-March 12, 1859; House 1847-49.

HASKIN, John Bussing (D N.Y.) Aug. 27, 1821-Sept. 18, 1895; House 1857-61.

HASKINS, Kittredge (R Vt.) April 8, 1836-Aug. 7, 1916; House 1901-09.

HASTINGS, Daniel Oren (R Del.) March 5, 1874-May 9, 1966; Senate Dec. 10, 1928-37.

HASTINGS, George (D N.Y.) March 13, 1807-Aug. 29, 1866; House 1853-55.

HASTINGS, James Fred (R N.Y.) April 10, 1926-—; House 1969-Jan. 20, 1976.

HASTINGS, John (JD Ohio) 1778-Dec. 8, 1854; House 1839-43.

HASTINGS, Serranus Clinton (D Iowa) Nov. 14, 1813-Feb. 18, 1893; House Dec. 28, 1846-47.

HASTINGS, Seth (father of William Soden Hastings) (F Mass.) April 8, 1762-Nov. 19, 1831; House Aug. 24, 1801-07.

HASTINGS, William Soden (son of Seth Hastings) (D Mass.) June 3, 1798-June 17, 1842; House 1837-June 17, 1842.

HASTINGS, William Wirt (D Okla.) Dec. 31, 1866-April 8, 1938; House 1915-21; 1923-35.

HATCH, Carl Atwood (D N.M.) Nov. 27, 1889-Sept. 14, 1963; Senate Oct. 10, 1933-49.

HATCH, Herschel Harrison (R Mich.) Feb. 17, 1837-Nov. 30, 1920; House 1883-85.

HATCH, Israel Thompson (D N.Y.) June 30, 1808-Sept. 24, 1875; House 1857-59.

HATCH, Jethro Ayers (R Ind.) June 18, 1837-Aug. 3, 1912; House 1895-97.

HATCH, William Henry (D Mo.) Sept. 11, 1833-Dec. 23, 1896; House 1879-95.

HATCHER, Robert Anthony (D Mo.) Feb. 24, 1819-Dec. 4, 1886; House 1873-79.

HATFIELD, Henry Drury (R W.Va.) Sept. 15, 1875-Oct..23, 1962; Senate 1929-35; Gov. 1913-17.

HATFIELD, Mark Odom (R Ore.) July 12, 1922-__; Senate Jan. 10, 1967-__; Gov. 1959-67.

HATHAWAY, Samuel Gilbert (D N.Y.) July 18, 1780-May 2, 1867; House 1833-35.

HATHAWAY, William Dodd (D Maine) Feb. 21, 1924-__; House 1965-1973; Senate 1973-__.

HATHORN, Henry Harrison (R N.Y.) Nov. 28, 1813-Feb. 20, 1887; House 1873-77.

HATHORN, John (F N.Y.) Jan. 9, 1749-Feb. 19, 1825; House 1789-91; 1795-97; Cont. Cong. 1788.

HATTON, Robert Hopkins (AP Tenn.) Nov. 2, 1826-May 31, 1862; House 1859-61.

HAUGEN, Gilbert Nelson (R Iowa) April 21, 1859-July 18, 1933; House 1899-1933.

HAUGEN, Nils Pederson (R Wis.) March 9, 1849-April 23, 1931; House 1887-95.

HAUGHEY, Thomas (R Ala.) 1826-Aug. 1869; House July 21, 1868-69.

HAUN, Henry Peter (D Calif.) Jan. 18, 1815-June 6, 1860; Senate Nov. 3, 1859-March 4, 1860.

HAVEN, Nathaniel Appleton (F N.H.) July 19, 1762-March 13, 1831; House 1809-11.

HAVEN, Solomon George (W N.Y.) Nov. 27, 1810-Dec. 24, 1861; House 1851-57.

HAVENNER, Franck Roberts (D Calf.) Sept. 20, 1882-July 24, 1967; House 1937-41, 1945-53 (1937-39 Progressive, 1939-41 and 1945-53 Democrat).

HAVENS, Harrison Eugene (R Mo.) Dec. 15, 1837-Aug. 16, 1916; House 1871-75.

HAVENS, James Smith (D N.Y.) May 28, 1859-Feb. 27, 1927; House April 19, 1910-11.

HAVENS, Jonathan Nicoll (D N.Y.) June 18, 1757-Oct. 25, 1799; House 1795-Oct. 25, 1799.

HAWES, Albert Gallatin (brother of Richard Hawes, nephew of Aylett Hawes, grand-uncle of Harry Bartow Hawes, and cousin of Aylett Hawes Buckner) (JD Ky.) April 1, 1804-March 14, 1849; House 1831-37.

HAWES, Aylett (uncle of Richard Hawes, Albert Gallatin Hawes, and Aylett Hawes Buckner) (D Va.) April 21, 1768-Aug. 31, 1833; House 1811-17.

HAWES, Harry Bartow (grandnephew of Albert Gallatin Hawes) (D Mo.) Nov. 15, 1869-July 31, 1947; House 1921-Oct. 15, 1926; Senate Dec. 6, 1926-Feb. 3, 1933.

HAWES, Richard (brother of Albert Gallatin Hawes, nephew of Aylett Hawes and cousin of Aylett Hawes Buckner) (W Ky.) Feb. 6, 1797-May 25, 1877; House 1837-41.

HAWK, Robert Moffett Allison (R Ill.) April 23, 1839-June 29, 1882; House 1879-June 29, 1882.

HAWKES, Albert Wahl (R N.J.) Nov. 20, 1878-May 9, 1971; Senate 1943-49.

HAWKES, James (— N.Y.) Dec. 13, 1776-Oct. 2, 1865; House 1821-23.

HAWKINS, Augustus F. (D Calif.) Aug. 31, 1907-__; House 1963-__.

HAWKINS, Benjamin (uncle of Micajah Thomas Hawkins) (F N.C.) Aug. 15, 1754-June 6, 1816; Senate Nov. 27, 1789-1795; Cont. Cong. 1781-84, 1786-87.

HAWKINS, George Sydney (D Fla.) 1808-March 15, 1878; House 1857-Jan. 21, 1861.

HAWKINS, Isaac Roberts (R Tenn.) May 16, 1818-Aug. 12, 1880; House July 24, 1866-71.

HAWKINS, Joseph (Ad.D N.Y.) Nov. 14, 1781-April 20, 1832; House 1829-31.

HAWKINS, Joseph H. (F Ky.) ?-1823; House March 29, 1814-15.

HAWKINS, Micajah Thomas (nephew of Benjamin Hawkins and Nathaniel Macon) (D N.C.) May 20, 1790-Dec. 22, 1858; House Dec. 15, 1831-41.

HAWKS, Charles Jr. (R Wis.) July 7, 1899-Jan. 6, 1960; House 1939-41.

HAWLEY, John Baldwin (R Ill.) Feb. 9, 1831-May 24, 1895; House 1869-75.

HAWLEY, Joseph Roswell (R Conn.) Oct. 31, 1826-March 17, 1905; House Dec. 2, 1872-75, 1879-81; Senate 1881-1905; Gov. 1866-67.

HAWLEY, Robert Bradley (R Texas) Oct. 25, 1849-Nov.28, 1921; House 1897-1901.

HAWLEY, Willis Chatman (R Ore.) May 5, 1864-July 24, 1941; House 1907-33.

HAWS, John Henry Hobart (W N.Y.) 1809-Jan. 27, 1858; House 1851-53.

HAY, Andrew Kessler (W N.J.) Jan. 19, 1809-Feb. 7, 1881; House 1849-51.

HAY, James (D Va.) Jan. 9, 1856-June 12, 1931; House 1897-Oct. 1, 1916.

HAY, John Breese (R Ill.) Jan. 8, 1834-June 16, 1916; House 1869-73.

HAYDEN, Carl Trumbull (D Ariz.) Oct. 2, 1877-Jan. 25, 1972; House Feb. 19, 1912-27; Senate 1927-69; President pro tempore 1957-69.

HAYDEN, Edward Daniel (R Mass.) Dec. 27, 1833-Nov. 15, 1908; House 1885-89.

HAYDEN, Moses (— N.Y.) 1786-Feb. 13, 1830; House 1823-27.

HAYES, Everis Anson (R Calif.) March 10, 1855-June 3, 1942; House 1905-19.

HAYES, Philip Cornelius (R Ill.) Feb. 3, 1833-July 13, 1916; House 1877-81.

HAYES, Philip Harold (D Ind.) Sept. 1, 1940-__; House 1975-__.

HAYES, Rutherford Birchard (R Ohio) Oct. 4, 1822-Jan. 17, 1893; House 1865-July 20, 1867; President 1877-81; Gov. 1868-72, 1876-77.

HAYES, Walter Ingalls (D Iowa) Dec. 9, 1841-March 14, 1901; House 1887-95.

HAYMOND, Thomas Sherwood (W Va.) Jan. 15, 1794-April 5, 1869; House Nov. 8, 1849-51.

HAYMOND, William Summerville (D/L Ind.) Feb. 20, 1823-Dec. 24, 1885; House 1875-77.

HAYNE, Arthur Peronneau (brother of Robert Young Hayne) (D S.C.) March 12, 1790-Jan. 7, 1867; Senate May 11-Dec. 2, 1858.

HAYNE, Robert Young (brother of Arthur Peronneau Hayne) (TD S.C.) Nov. 10, 1791-Sept. 24, 1839; Senate 1823-Dec. 13, 1832; Gov. 1832-34.

HAYNES, Charles Eaton (U Ga.) April 15, 1784-Aug. 29, 1841; House 1825-31, 1835-39 (1825-31 Democrat, 1835-39 Unionist).

HAYNES, Martin Alonzo (R N.H.) July 30, 1842-Nov. 28, 1919; House 1883-87.

HAYNES, William Elisha (cousin of George William Palmer) (D Ohio) Oct. 19, 1829-Dec. 5, 1914; House 1889-93.

HAYS, Charles (R Ala.) Feb. 2, 1834-June 24, 1879; House 1869-77.

HAYS, Edward Dixon (R Mo.) April 28, 1872-July 25, 1941; House 1919-23.

HAYS, Edward Retilla (R Iowa) May 26, 1847-Feb. 28, 1896; House Nov. 4, 1890-91.

HAYS, Lawrence Brooks (D Ark.) Aug. 9, 1898-__; House 1943-59.

HAYS, Samuel (D Pa.) Sept. 10, 1783-July 1, 1868; House 1843-45.

HAYS, Samuel Lewis (D Va.) Oct. 20, 1794-March 17, 1871; House 1841-43.

HAYS, Wayne Levere (D Ohio) May 13, 1911-__; House 1949-Sept. 1, 1976.

HAYWARD, Monroe Leland (R Neb.) Dec. 22, 1840-Dec. 5, 1899; Senate March 8-Dec. 5, 1899.

HAYWARD, William Jr. (D Md.) 1787-Oct. 19, 1836; House 1823-25.

HAYWOOD, William Henry Jr. (D N.C.) Oct. 23, 1801-Oct. 7, 1852; Senate 1843-July 25, 1846.

HAYWORTH, Donald (D Mich.) Jan. 13, 1898-__; House 1955-57.

HAZARD, Nathaniel (D R.I.) 1776-Dec. 17, 1820; House 1819-Dec. 17, 1820.

HAZELTINE, Abner (W N.Y.) June 10, 1793-Dec. 20, 1879; House 1833-37.

HAZELTINE, Ira Sherwin (RG Mo.) July 13, 1821-Jan. 13, 1899; House 1881-83.

HAZELTON, George Cochrane (brother of Gerry Whiting Hazelton and nephew of Clark Betton Cochrane) (R Wis.) Jan. 3, 1832-Sept. 4, 1922; House 1877-83.

HAZELTON, Gerry Whiting (brother of George Cochrane Hazelton and nephew of Clark Betton Cochrane) (R Wis.) Feb. 24, 1829-Sept. 19, 1920; House 1871-75.

HAZELTON, John Wright (R N.J.) Dec. 10, 1814-Dec. 20, 1878; House 1871-75.

HAZLETT, James Miller (R Pa.) Oct. 14, 1864-Nov. 8, 1940; House March 4-Oct. 20, 1927.

HEALD, William Henry (R Del.) Aug. 27, 1864-June 3, 1939; House 1909-13.

HEALEY, Arthur Daniel (D Mass.) Dec. 29, 1889-Sept. 16, 1948; House 1933-Aug. 3, 1942.

HEALEY, James Christopher (D N.Y.) Dec. 24, 1909-__; House Feb. 7, 1956-65.

HEALY, Joseph (D N.H.) Aug. 21, 1776-Oct. 10, 1861; House 1825-29.

HEALY, Ned R. (D Calif.) Aug. 9, 1905-__; House 1945-47.

HEARD, John Thaddeus (D Mo.) Oct. 29, 1840-Jan. 27, 1927; House 1885-95.

HEARST, George (father of William Randolph Hearst) (D Calif.) Sept. 3, 1820-Feb. 28, 1891; Senate March 23-Aug. 4, 1886, 1887-Feb. 28, 1891.

HEARST, William Randolph (son of George Hearst) (D N.Y.) April 29, 1863-Aug. 14, 1951; House 1903-07.

HEATH, James P. (D Md.) Dec. 21, 1777-June 12, 1854; House 1833-35.

HEATH, John (R Va.) May 8, 1758-Oct. 13, 1810; House 1793-97.

HEATON, David (R N.C.) March 10, 1823-June 25, 1870; House July 15, 1868-June 25, 1870.

HEATON, Robert Douglas (R Pa.) July 1, 1873-June 11, 1933; House 1915-19.

HEATWOLE, Joel Prescott (R Minn.) Aug. 22, 1856-April 4, 1910; House 1895-1903.

HEBARD, William (W Vt.) Nov. 29, 1800-Oct. 20, 1875; House 1849-53.

HEBERT, Felix (R R.I.) Dec. 11, 1874-Dec. 14, 1969; Senate 1929-35.

HEBERT, Felix Edward (D La.) Oct. 12, 1901-__; House 1941-__.

HECHLER, Ken (D W.Va.) Sept. 20, 1914-__; House 1959-__.

HECKLER, Margaret M. (R Mass.) June 21, 1931-__; House 1967-__.

HEDGE, Thomas (R Iowa) June 24, 1844-Nov. 28, 1920; 1899-1907.

HEDRICK, Erland Harold (D W.Va.) Aug. 9, 1894-Sept. 20, 1954; House 1945-53.

HEFFERNAN, James Joseph (D N.Y.) Nov. 8, 1888-Jan. 27, 1967; House 1941-53.

HEFLIN, James Thomas (nephew of Robert Stell Heflin) (D Ala.) April 9, 1869-April 22, 1951; House May 10, 1904-Nov. 1, 1920; Senate Nov. 3, 1920-31.

HEFLIN, Robert Stell (uncle of James Thomas Heflin) (R Ala.) April 15, 1815-Jan. 24, 1901; House 1869-71.

HEFNER, Willie Gathrel (D N.C.) April 11, 1930-__; House 1975-__.

HEIDINGER, James Vandaveer (R Ill.) July 17, 1882-March 22, 1945; House 1941-March 22, 1945.

HEILMAN, William (great-grandfather of Charles Marion LaFollette) (R Ind.) Oct. 1, 1824-Sept.22, 1890; House 1879-83.

HEINER, Daniel Brodhead (R Pa.) Dec.30, 1854-Feb. 14, 1944; House 1893-97.

HEINKE, George Henry (R Neb.) July 22, 1882-Jan. 2, 1940; House 1939-Jan. 2, 1940.

HEINTZ, Victor (R Ohio) Nov. 20, 1876-Dec. 27, 1968; House 1917-19.

HEINZ, Henry John III (R Pa.) Oct. 23, 1938-__; House Nov. 2, 1971-__.

HEISKELL, John Netherland (D Ark.) Nov. 2, 1872-Dec. 28, 1972; Senate Jan. 6-Jan. 29, 1913.

HEITFELD, Henry (P Idaho) Jan. 12, 1859-Oct. 21, 1938; Senate 1897-1903.

HELGESEN, Henry Thomas (R N.D.) June 26, 1857-April 10, 1917; House 1911-April 10, 1917.

HELLER, Louis Benjamin (D N.Y.) Feb. 10, 1905-__; House Feb. 15, 1949-July 21, 1954.

HELM, Harvey (D Ky.) Dec. 2, 1865-March 3, 1919; House 1907-March 3, 1919.

HELMS, Jesse Alexander (R N.C.) Oct. 18, 1921-__; Senate 1973-__.

HELMICK, William (R Ohio) Sept. 6, 1817-March 31, 1888; House 1859-61.

HELMS, William (D N.J.) ?-1813; House 1801-11.

HELSTOSKI, Henry (D N.J.) March 21, 1925-__; House 1965-__.

HELVERING, Guy Tresillian (D Kan.) Jan. 10, 1878-July 4, 1946; House 1913-19.

HEMENWAY, James Alexander (R Ind.) March 8, 1860-Feb. 10, 1923; House 1895-1905; Senate 1905-09.

HEMPHILL, John (uncle of John James Hemphill and great-great-uncle of Robert Witherspoon Hemphill) (SRD Texas) Dec. 18, 1803-Jan. 7, 1862; Senate 1859-July 11, 1861.

HEMPHILL, John James (cousin of William Huggins Brawley, nephew of John Hemphill and great-uncle of Robert Witherspoon Hemphill) (D S.C.) Aug. 25, 1849-May 11, 1912; House 1883-93.

HEMPHILL, Joseph (JD Pa.) Jan. 7, 1770-May 29, 1842; House 1801-03, 1819-26, 1829-31 (1801-03 and 1819-26 Federalist 1829-31 Jackson Democrat).

HEMPHILL, Robert Witherspoon (great-great nephew of John Hemphill, great-nephew of John J. Hemphill and William Huggins Brawley, and great-great-grandson of Robert Witherspoon) (D S.C.) May 10, 1915-__; House 1957-May 1, 1964.

HEMPSTEAD, Edward (— Mo.) June 3, 1780-Aug. 10, 1817; House (Terr. Del.) Nov. 9, 1812-Sept. 17, 1814.

HENDEE, George Whitman (R Vt.) Nov. 30, 1832-Dec. 6, 1906; House 1873-79.

HENDERSON, Archibald (F N.C.) Aug. 7, 1768-Oct. 21, 1822; House 1799-1803.

HENDERSON, Bennett H. (— Tenn.) Sept. 5, 1784-?; House 1815-17.

HENDERSON, Charles Belknap (D Nev.) June 8, 1873-Nov. 8, 1954; Senate Jan. 12, 1918-21.

HENDERSON, David Bremner (R Iowa) March 14, 1840-Feb. 25, 1906; House 1883-1903; Speaker 1899-1903.

HENDERSON, David Newton (D N.C.) April 16, 1921-__; House 1961-__.

HENDERSON, James Henry Dickey (UR Ore.) July 23, 1810-Dec. 13, 1885; House 1865-67.

HENDERSON, James Pinckney (SRD Texas) March 31, 1808-June 4, 1858; Senate Nov. 9, 1857-June 4, 1858; Gov. 1846-47.

HENDERSON, John (W Miss.) 1795-Sept. 13, 1866; Senate 1839-45.

HENDERSON, John Brooks (D Mo.) Nov. 16, 1826-April 12, 1913; Senate Jan. 17, 1862-69.

HENDERSON, John Earl (R Ohio) Jan. 4, 1917-__; House 1955-61.

HENDERSON, John Steele (D N.C.) Jan. 6, 1846-Oct. 9, 1916; House 1885-95.

HENDERSON, Joseph (— Pa.) Aug. 2, 1791-Dec. 25, 1863; House 1833-37.

HENDERSON, Samuel (R Pa.) Nov. 27, 1764-Nov. 17, 1841; House Oct. 11, 1814-15.

HENDERSON, Thomas (— N.J.) Aug. 15, 1743-Dec. 15, 1824; House 1795-97.

HENDERSON, Thomas Jefferson (R Ill.) Nov. 29, 1824-Feb. 6, 1911; House 1875-95.

HENDRICK, John Kerr (D Ky.) Oct. 10, 1849-June 20, 1921; House 1895-97.

HENDRICKS, Joseph Edward (D Fla.) Sept. 24, 1903-__; House 1937-49.

HENDRICKS, Thomas Andrews (nephew of William Hendricks) (D Ind.) Sept. 7, 1819-Nov. 25, 1885; House 1851-55; Senate 1863-69; Gov. 1873-1877; Vice Pres. March 4-Nov. 25, 1885.

HENDRICKS, William (uncle of Thomas Andrews Hendricks) (D Ind.) Nov. 12, 1782-May 16, 1850; House Dec. 11, 1816-July 25, 1822; Senate 1825-37; Gov. 1822-25.

HENDRICKSON, Robert Clymer (R N.J.) Aug. 12, 1898-Dec. 7, 1964; Senate 1949-55.

HENDRIX, Joseph Clifford (D N.Y.) May 25, 1853-Nov. 9, 1904; House 1893-95.

HENKLE, Eli Jones (D Md.) Nov. 24, 1828-Nov. 1, 1893; House 1875-81.

HENLEY, Barclay (son of Thomas Jefferson Henley) (D Calif.) March 17, 1843-Feb. 15, 1914; House 1883-87.

HENLEY, Thomas Jefferson (father of Barclay Henley) (D Ind.) April 2, 1810-Jan. 2, 1865; House 1843-49.

HENN, Bernhart (D Iowa) 1817-Aug. 30, 1865; House 1851-55.

HENNEY, Charles William Francis (D Wis.) Feb. 2, 1884-Nov. 16, 1969; House 1933-35.

HENNINGS, Thomas Carey Jr. (D Mo.) June 25, 1903-Sept. 13, 1960; House 1935-Dec. 31, 1940; Senate 1951-Sept. 13, 1960.

HENRY, Charles Lewis (R Ind.) July 1, 1849-May 2, 1927; House 1895-99.

HENRY, Daniel Maynadier (D Md.) Feb. 19, 1823-Aug. 31, 1899; House 1877-81.

HENRY, Edward Stevens (R Conn.) Feb. 10, 1836-Oct. 10, 1921; House 1895-1913.

HENRY, John (D Md.) Nov. 1750-Dec. 16, 1798; Senate 1789-Dec. 10, 1797; Gov. 1797-98; Cont. Cong. 1778-81, 1784-87.

HENRY, John (W Ill.) Nov. 1, 1800-April 28, 1882; House Feb. 5-March 3, 1847.

HENRY, John Flournoy (— Ky.) Jan. 17, 1793-Nov. 12, 1873; House Dec. 11, 1826-27.

HENRY, Lewis (R N.Y.) June 8, 1885-July 23, 1941; House April 11, 1922-23.

HENRY, Patrick (D Miss.) Feb. 12, 1843-May 18, 1930; House 1897-1901.

HENRY, Patrick (nephew of the preceding) (D Miss.) Feb. 15, 1861-Dec. 28, 1933; House 1901-03.

HENRY, Robert Kirkland (R Wis.) Feb. 9, 1890-Nov. 20, 1946; House 1945-Nov. 20, 1946.

HENRY, Robert Lee (D Texas) May 12, 1864-July 9, 1931; House 1897-1917.

HENRY, Robert Pryor (CD Ky.) Nov. 24, 1788-Aug. 25, 1826; House 1823-Aug. 25, 1826.

HENRY, Thomas (W Pa.) 1779-July 20, 1849; House 1837-43.

HENRY, William (W Vt.) March 22, 1788-April 16, 1861; House 1847-51.

HENRY, Winder Laird (great-grandson of Charles Goldsborough and Robert Henry Goldsborough) (D Md.) Dec. 20, 1864-July 5, 1940; House Nov. 6, 1894-95.

HENSLEY, Walter Lewis (D Mo.) Sept. 3, 1871-July 18, 1946; House 1911-19.

HEPBURN, William Peters (great-grandson of Matthew Lyon) (R Iowa) Nov. 4, 1833-Feb. 7, 1916; House 1881-87; 1893-1909.

HERBERT, Hilary Abner (D Ala.) March 12, 1834-March 5, 1919; House 1877-93; Secy. of the Navy 1893-97.

HERBERT, John Carlyle (F Md.) Aug. 16, 1775-Sept. 1, 1846; House 1815-19.

HERBERT, Philemon Thomas (D Calif.) Nov. 1, 1825-July 23, 1864; House 1855-57

HEREFORD, Frank (D W.Va.) July 4, 1825-Dec. 21, 1891; House 1871-Jan. 31, 1877; Senate Jan. 31, 1877-81.

HERKIMER, John (D N.Y.) 1773-June 8, 1848; House 1817-19, 1823-25.

HERLONG, Albert Sydney Jr. (D Fla.) Feb. 14, 1909-—; House 1949-69.

HERMANN, Binger (R Ore.) Feb. 19, 1843-April 15, 1926; House 1885-97, June 1, 1903-07.

HERNANDEZ, Benigno Cardenas (R N.M.) Feb. 13, 1862-Oct. 18, 1954; House 1915-17, 1919-21.

HERNANDEZ, Joseph Marion (— Fla.) Aug. 4, 1793-June 8, 1857; House (Terr. Del.) Sept. 30, 1822-23.

HERNDON, Thomas Hord (D Ala.) July 1, 1828-March 28, 1883; House 1879-March 28, 1883.

HERNDON, William Smith (D Texas) Nov. 27, 1835-Oct. 11, 1903; House 1871-75.

HEROD, William (W Ind.) March 31, 1801-Oct. 20, 1871; House Jan. 25, 1837-39.

HERRICK, Anson (son of Ebenezer Herrick) (D N.Y.) Jan. 21, 1812-Feb. 6, 1868; House 1863-65.

HERRICK, Ebenezer (father of Anson Herrick) (— Maine) Oct. 21, 1785-May 7, 1839; House 1821-27.

HERRICK, Joshua (D Maine) March 18, 1793-Aug. 30, 1874; House 1843-45.

HERRICK, Manuel (R Okla.) Sept. 20, 1876-Feb. 29, 1952; House 1921-23.

HERRICK, Richard Platt (W N.Y.) March 23, 1791-June 20, 1846; House 1845-June 20, 1846.

HERRICK, Samuel (D Ohio) April 14, 1779-June 4, 1852; House 1817-21.

HERRING, Clyde LaVerne (D Iowa) May 3, 1879-Sept. 15, 1945; Senate Jan. 15, 1937-43; Gov. 1933-37.

HERSEY, Ira Greenlief (R Maine) March 31, 1858-May 6, 1943; House 1917-29.

HERSEY, Samuel Freeman (R Maine) April 12, 1812-Feb. 3, 1875; House 1873-Feb. 3, 1875.

HERSMAN, Hugh Steel (D Calif.) July 8, 1872-March 7, 1954; House 1919-21.

HERTER, Christian Archibald (R Mass.) March 28, 1895-Dec. 30, 1966; House 1943-53; Secy. of State 1959-61; Gov. 1953-57.

HESELTON, John Walter (R Mass.) March 17, 1900-Aug. 19, 1962; House 1945-59.

HESS, William Emil (R Ohio) Feb. 13, 1898-—; House 1929-37, 1939-49, 1951-61.

HEWITT, Abram Stevens (D N.Y.) July 31, 1822-Jan. 18, 1903; House 1875-79, 1881-Dec. 30, 1886, Chmn. Dem. Natl. Comm. 1876-77.

HEWITT, Goldsmith Whitehouse (D Ala.) Feb. 14, 1834-May 27, 1895; House 1875-79, 1881-85.

HEYBURN, Weldon Brinton (R Idaho) May 23, 1852-Oct. 17, 1912; Senate 1903-Oct. 17, 1912.

HIBBARD, Ellery Albee (cousin of Harry Hibbard) (D N.H.) July 31, 1826-July 24, 1903; House 1871-73.

HIBBARD, Harry (cousin of Ellery Albee Hibbard) (D N.H.) June 1, 1816-July 28, 1872; House 1849-55.

HIBSHMAN, Jacob (R Pa.) Jan. 31, 1772-May 19, 1852; House 1819-21.

HICKENLOOPER, Bourke Blakemore (R Iowa) July 21, 1896-Sept. 4, 1971; Senate 1945-69; Gov. 1943-45.

HICKEY, Andrew James (R Ind.) Aug. 27, 1872-Aug. 20, 1942; House 1919-31.

HICKEY, John Joseph (D Wyo.) Aug. 22, 1911-Sept. 22, 1970; Senate 1961-Nov. 6, 1962; Gov. 1959-61.

HICKMAN, John (R Pa.) Sept. 11, 1810-March 23, 1875; House 1855-63 (1855-59 Democrat, 1859-61 Douglas Democrat, 1861-63 Republican).

HICKS, Floyd Verne (D Wash.) May 29, 1915-__; House 1965-__.

HICKS, Frederick Cocks (original name, Frederick Hicks Cocks, brother of William Willets Cocks) (R N.Y.) March 6, 1872-Dec. 14, 1925; House 1915-23.

HICKS, Josiah Duane (R Pa.) Aug. 1, 1844-May 9, 1923; House 1893-99.

HICKS, Louise Day (D Mass.) Oct. 16, 1923-__; House 1971-1973.

HICKS, Thomas Holliday (R Md.) Sept. 2, 1798-Feb. 14, 1865; Senate Dec. 29, 1862-Feb. 14, 1865; Gov. 1858-62.

HIESTAND, Edgar Willard (R Calif.) Dec. 3, 1888-Aug. 19, 1970; House 1953-63.

HIESTAND, John Andrew (R Pa.) Oct. 2, 1824-Dec. 13, 1890; House 1885-89.

HIESTER, Daniel (brother of John Hiester, cousin of Joseph Hiester and uncle of William Hiester) (— Pa./Md.) June 25, 1747-March 7, 1804; House 1789-July 1, 1796 (Pa.), 1801-March 7, 1804 (Md.).

HIESTER, Daniel (son of John Hiester and nephew of the preceding) (— Pa.) 1774-March 8, 1834; House 1809-11.

HIESTER, Isaac Ellmaker (son of William Hiester and cousin of Hiester Clymer) (W Pa.) May 29, 1824-Feb. 6, 1871; House 1853-55.

HIESTER, John (brother of Daniel Hiester, cousin of Joseph Hiester, and uncle of William Hiester) (— Pa.) April 9, 1745-Oct. 15, 1821; House 1807-09.

HIESTER, Joseph (cousin of John Hiester and Daniel Hiester and grandfather of Henry Augustus Muhlenberg) (F Pa.) Nov. 18, 1752-June 10, 1832; House Dec. 1, 1797-1805, 1815-Dec. 1820; Gov. 1820-23.

HIESTER, William (father of Isaac Ellmaker Hiester, uncle of Hiester Clymer, and nephew of John Hiester and Daniel Hiester) (W Pa.) Oct. 10, 1790-Oct. 13, 1853; House 1831-37.

HIGBY, William (R Calif.) Aug. 18, 1813-Nov. 27, 1887; House 1863-69.

HIGGINS, Anthony (R Del.) Oct. 1, 1840-June 26, 1912; Senate 1889-95.

HIGGINS, Edwin Werter (R Conn.) July 2, 1874-Sept. 24, 1954; House Oct. 2, 1905-13.

HIGGINS, John Patrick (D Mass.) Feb. 19, 1893-Aug. 2, 1955; House 1935-Sept. 30, 1937.

HIGGINS, William Lincoln (R Conn.) March 8, 1867-Nov. 19, 1951; House 1933-37.

HIGHTOWER, Jack English (D Texas) Sept. 6, 1926-__; House 1975-__.

HILBORN, Samuel Greeley (R Calif.) Dec. 9, 1834-April 19, 1899; House Dec. 5, 1892-April 4, 1894, 1895-99.

HILDEBRANDT, Fred Herman (D S.D.) Aug. 2, 1874-Jan. 26, 1956; House 1933-39.

HILDEBRANT, Charles Quinn (R Ohio) Oct. 17, 1864-March 31, 1953; House 1901-05.

HILL, Benjamin Harvey (cousin of Hugh Lawson White Hill) (D Ga.) Sept. 14, 1823-Aug. 16, 1882; House May 5, 1875-77; Senate 1877-Aug. 16, 1882.

HILL, Charles Augustus (R Ill.) Aug. 23, 1833-May 29, 1902; House 1889-91.

HILL, Clement Sidney (ID Ky.) Feb. 13, 1813-Jan. 5, 1892; House 1853-55.

HILL, David Bennett (D N.Y.) Aug. 29, 1843-Oct. 20, 1910; Senate Jan. 7, 1892-97; Gov. 1885-92.

HILL, Ebenezer J. (R Conn.) Aug. 4, 1845-Sept. 27, 1917; House 1895-1913, 1915-Sept. 27, 1917.

HILL, Hugh Lawson White (cousin of Benjamin Harvey Hill) (D Tenn.) March 1, 1810-Jan. 18, 1892; House 1847-49.

HILL, Isaac (D N.H.) April 6, 1788-March 22, 1851; Senate 1831-May 30, 1836; Gov. 1836-39.

HILL, John (D N.C.) April 9, 1797-April 24, 1861; House 1839-41.

HILL, John (cousin of John Thomas Harris) (W Va.) July 18, 1800-April 19, 1880; House 1839-41.

HILL, John (R N.J.) June 10, 1821-July 24, 1884; House 1867-73, 1881-83.

HILL, John Boynton Philip Clayton (R Md.) May 2, 1879-May 23, 1941; House 1921-27.

HILL, Joseph Lister (D Ala.) Dec. 29, 1894-__; House Aug. 14, 1923-Jan. 11, 1938; Senate Jan. 11, 1938-69.

HILL, Joshua (UR Ga.) Jan. 10, 1812-March 6, 1891; House 1857-Jan. 23, 1861 (AP); Senate Feb. 1, 1871-73 (UR).

HILL, Knute (D Wash.) July 31, 1876-Dec. 3, 1963; House 1933-43.

HILL, Mark Langdon (— Mass./Maine) June 30, 1772-Nov. 26, 1842; House 1819-21 (Mass.), 1821-23 (Maine).

HILL, Nathaniel Peter (R Colo.) Feb. 18, 1832-May 22, 1900; Senate 1879-85.

HILL, Ralph (R Ind.) Oct. 12, 1827-Aug. 20, 1899; House 1865-67.

HILL, Robert Potter (D Ill./Okla.) April 18, 1874-Oct. 29, 1937; House 1913-15 (Ill.), Jan. 3,-Oct. 29, 1937 (Okla.)

HILL, Samuel Billingsley (D Wash.) April 2, 1875-March 16, 1958; House Sept. 25, 1923-June 25, 1936.

HILL, William David (D Ohio) Oct. 1, 1833-Dec. 26, 1906; House 1879-81, 1883-87.

HILL, William Henry (F N.C.) May 1, 1767-1809; House 1799-1803.

HILL, William Henry (R N.Y.) March 23, 1877-__; House 1919-21.

HILL, William Luther (D Fla.) Oct. 17, 1873-Jan. 5, 1951; Senate July 1-Nov. 3, 1936.

HILL, William Silas (R Colo.) Jan. 20, 1886-Aug. 28, 1972; House 1941-59.

HILL, Wilson Shedric (D Miss.) Jan. 19, 1863-Feb. 14, 1921; House 1903-09.

HILLELSON, Jeffrey Paul (R Mo.) March 9, 1919-__; House 1953-55.

HILLEN, Solomon Jr. (D Md.) July 10, 1810-June 26, 1873; House 1839-41.

HILLHOUSE, James (F Conn.) Oct. 21, 1754-Dec. 29, 1832; House 1791-96; Senate Dec. 6, 1796-June 10, 1810; President pro tempore 1801.

HILLIARD, Benjamin Clark (D Colo.) Jan. 9, 1868-Aug. 7, 1951; House 1915-19.

HILLIARD, Henry Washington (W Ala.) Aug. 4, 1808-Dec. 17, 1892; House 1845-51.

HILLINGS, Patrick Jerome (R Calif.) Feb. 19, 1923-__; House 1951-59.

HILLIS, Elwood Haynes (R Ind.) March 6, 1926-__; House 1971-__.

HILLYER, Junius (D Ga.) April 23, 1807-June 21, 1886; House 1851-55.

HIMES, Joseph Hendrix (R Ohio) Aug. 15, 1885-Sept. 9, 1960; House 1921-23.

HINDMAN, Thomas Carmichael (D Ark.) Jan. 28, 1828-Sept. 27, 1868; House 1859-61.

HINDMAN, William (— Md.) April 1, 1743-Jan. 19, 1822; House Jan. 30, 1793-1799; Senate Dec. 12, 1800-Nov. 19, 1801; Cont. Cong. 1784-88.

HINDS, Asher Crosby (R Maine) Feb. 6, 1863-May 1, 1919; House 1911-17.

HINDS, James (R Ark.) Dec. 5, 1833-Oct. 22, 1868; House June 22-Oct. 22, 1868.

HINDS, Thomas (D Miss.) Jan. 9, 1780-Aug. 23, 1840; House Oct. 21, 1828-31.

HINEBAUGH, William Henry (Pro. Ill.) Dec. 16, 1867-Sept. 22, 1943; House 1913-15.

HINES, Richard (D N.C.) ?-Nov. 20, 1851; House 1825-27.

HINES, William Henry (D Pa.) March 15, 1856-Jan. 17, 1914; House 1893-95.

HINRICHSEN, William Henry (D Ill.) May 27, 1850-Dec. 18, 1907; House 1897-99.

HINSHAW, Andrew Jackson (R Calif.) Aug. 4, 1923-__; House 1973-__.

HINSHAW, Edmund Howard (cousin of Edwin Bruce Brooks) (R Neb.) Dec. 8, 1860-June 15, 1932; House 1903-11.

HINSHAW, John Carl Williams (R Calif.) July 28, 1894-Aug. 5, 1956; House 1939-Aug. 5, 1956.

HIRES, George (R N.J.) Jan. 26, 1835-Feb. 16, 1911; House 1885-89.

HISCOCK, Frank (R N.Y.) Sept. 6, 1834-June 18, 1914; House 1877-87; Senate 1887-93.

HISE, Elijah (D Ky.) July 4, 1802-May 8, 1867; House Dec. 3, 1866-May 8, 1867.

HITCHCOCK, Gilbert Monell (son of Phineas Warren Hitchcock) (D Neb.) Sept. 18, 1859-Feb. 3, 1934; House 1903-05, 1907-11; Senate 1911-23.

HITCHCOCK, Herbert Emery (D S.D.) Aug. 22, 1867-Feb. 17, 1958; Senate Dec. 29, 1936-Nov. 8, 1938.

HITCHCOCK, Peter (— Ohio) Oct.19, 1781-March 4, 1854; House 1817-19.

HITCHCOCK, Phineas Warren (father of Gilbert Monell Hitchcock) (R Neb.) Nov. 30, 1831-July 10, 1881; House (Terr. Del.) 1865-March 1, 1867; Senate 1871-77.

HITT, Robert Roberts (R Ill.) Jan. 16, 1834-Sept. 19, 1906; House Nov. 7, 1882-Sept. 19, 1906.

HOAG, Truman Harrison (D Ohio) April 9, 1816-Feb. 5, 1870; House 1869-Feb.5, 1870.

HOAGLAND, Moses (D Ohio) June 19, 1812-April 16, 1865; House 1849-51.

HOAR, Ebenezer Rockwood (son of Samuel Hoar, brother of George Frisbie Hoar, and father of Sherman Hoar) (R Mass.) Feb. 21, 1816-Jan. 31, 1895; House 1873-75; Atty. Gen. 1869-70.

HOAR, George Frisbie (son of Samuel Hoar, brother of Ebenezer Rockwood Hoar, and father of Rockwood Hoar) (R Mass) Aug. 29, 1826-Sept. 30, 1904; House 1869-77; Senate 1877-Sept. 30, 1904.

HOAR, Rockwood (son of George Frisbie Hoar) (R Mass.) Aug. 24, 1855-Nov. 1, 1906; House 1905-Nov. 1, 1906.

HOAR, Samuel (father of Ebenezer Rockwood Hoar and George Frisbie Hoar), (W Mass.) May 18, 1778-Nov. 2, 1856; House 1835-37.

HOAR, Sherman (son of Ebenezer Rockwood Hoar) (D Mass.) July 30, 1860-Oct. 7, 1898; House 1891-93.

HOARD, Charles Brooks (R N.Y.) June 5, 1805-Nov. 20, 1886; House 1857-61.

HOBART, Aaron (D Mass.) June 26, 1787-Sept. 19, 1858; House Nov. 24, 1820-27.

HOBART, John Sloss (— N.Y.) May 6, 1738-Feb. 4, 1805; Senate Jan. 11-April 16, 1798.

HOBBIE, Selah Reeve (JD N.Y.) March 10, 1797-March 23, 1854; House 1827-29.

HOBBS, Samuel Francis (Sam) (D Ala.) Oct. 5, 1887-May 31, 1952; House 1935-51.

HOBLITZELL, Fetter Schrier (D Md.) Oct. 7, 1838-May 2, 1900; House 1881-85.

HOBLITZELL, John Dempsey Jr. (R W.Va.) Dec. 30, 1912-Jan. 6, 1962; Senate Jan. 25-Nov. 4, 1958.

HOBSON, Richmond Pearson (D Ala.) Aug. 17, 1870-March 16, 1937; House 1907-15.

HOCH, Daniel Knabb (D Pa.) Jan. 31, 1866-Oct. 11, 1960; House 1943-47.

HOCH, Homer (R Kan.) July 4, 1879-Jan. 30, 1949; House 1919-33.

HODGES, Asa (R Ark.) Jan. 22, 1822-June 6, 1900; House 1873-75.

HODGES, Charles Drury (D Ill.) Feb. 4, 1810-April 1, 1884; House Jan. 4-March 3, 1859.

HODGES, George Tisdale (R Vt.) July 4, 1789-Aug. 9, 1860; House Dec. 1, 1856-57.

HODGES, James Leonard (— Mass.) April 24, 1790-March 8, 1846; House 1827-33.

HOEPPEL, John Henry (D Calif.) Feb. 10, 1881-__; House 1933-37.

HOEVEN, Charles Bernard (R Iowa) March 30, 1895-__; House 1943-65.

HOEY, Clyde Roark (D N.C.) Dec. 11, 1877-May 12, 1954; House Dec. 16, 1919-21; Senate 1945-May 12, 1954; Gov. 1937-41.

HOFFECKER, John Henry (father of Walter Oakley Hoffecker) (R Del.) Sept. 12, 1827-June 16, 1900; House 1899-June 16, 1900.

HOFFECKER, Walter Oakley (son of John Henry Hoffecker) (R Del.) Sept. 20, 1854-Jan. 23, 1934; House Nov. 6, 1900-01.

HOFFMAN, Carl Henry (R Pa.) Aug. 12, 1896-__; House May 21, 1946-47.

HOFFMAN, Clare Eugene (R Mich.) Sept. 10, 1875-Nov. 3, 1967; House 1935-63.

HOFFMAN, Elmer Joseph (R Ill.) July 7, 1899-__; House 1959-65.

HOFFMAN, Harold Giles (R N.J.) Feb. 7, 1896-June 4, 1954; House 1927-31; Gov. 1935-38.

HOFFMAN, Henry William (AP Md.) Nov. 10, 1825-July 28, 1895; House 1855-57.

HOFFMAN, Josiah Ogden (W N.Y.) May 3, 1793-May 1, 1856; House 1837-41.

HOFFMAN, Michael (D N.Y.) Oct. 11, 1787-Sept. 27, 1848; House 1825-33.

HOFFMAN, Richard William (R Ill.) Dec. 23, 1893-July 6, 1975; House 1949-57.

HOGAN, Earl Lee (D Ind.) March 13, 1920-__; House 1959-61.

HOGAN, John (D Mo.) Jan. 2, 1805-Feb. 5, 1892; House 1865-67.

HOGAN, Lawrence Joseph (R Md.) Sept. 30, 1928-__; House 1969-75.

HOGAN, Michael Joseph (R N.Y.) April 22, 1871-May 7, 1940; House 1921-23.

HOGAN, William (JD N.Y.) July 17, 1792-Nov. 25, 1874; House 1831-33.

HOGE, John (brother of William Hoge) (D Pa.) Sept. 10, 1760-Aug. 4, 1824; House Nov. 2, 1804-05.

HOGE, John Blair (D W.Va.) Feb. 2, 1825-March 1, 1896; House 1881-83.

HOGE, Joseph Pendleton (D Ill.) Dec. 15, 1810-Aug. 14, 1891; House 1843-47.

HOGE, Solomon Lafayette (R S.C.) July 11, 1836-Feb. 23, 1909; House April 8, 1869-71, 1875-77.

HOGE, William (brother of John Hoge) (F Pa.) 1762-Sept. 25, 1814; House 1801-Oct. 15, 1804, 1807-09.

HOGEBOOM, James Lawrence (W N.Y.) Aug. 25, 1766-Dec. 23, 1839; House 1823-25.

HOGG, Charles Edgar (father of Robert Lynn Hogg) (D W.Va.) Dec. 21, 1852-June 14, 1935; House 1887-89.

HOGG, David (R Ind.) Aug. 21, 1886-Oct. 23, 1973; House 1925-33.

HOGG, Herschel Millard (R Colo.) Nov. 21, 1853-Aug. 27, 1934; House 1903-07.

HOGG, Robert Lynn (son of Charles Edgar Hogg) (R W.Va.) Dec. 30, 1893-July 21, 1973; House Nov. 4, 1930-33.

HOGG, Samuel (D Tenn.) April 18, 1783-May 28, 1842; House 1817-19.

HOIDALE, Einar (D Minn.) Aug. 17, 1870-Dec. 5, 1952; House 1933-35.

HOLADAY, William Perry (R Ill.) Dec. 14, 1882-Jan. 29, 1946; House 1923-33.

HOLBROCK, Greg John (D Ohio) June 21, 1906-__; House 1941-43.

HOLBROOK, Edward Dexter (D Idaho) May 6, 1836-June 18, 1870; House (Terr. Del.) 1865-69.

HOLCOMBE, George (D N.J.) March 1786-Jan. 14, 1828; House 1821-Jan. 14, 1828.

HOLIFIELD, Chester Earl (D Calif.) Dec. 3, 1903-__; House 1943-Dec. 31, 1974.

HOLLADAY, Alexander Richmond (D Va.) Sept. 18, 1811-Jan. 29, 1877; House 1849-53.

HOLLAND, Cornelius (D Maine) July 9, 1783-June 2, 1870; House Dec. 6, 1830-33.

HOLLAND, Edward Everett (D Va.) Feb. 26, 1861-Oct. 23, 1941; House 1911-21.

HOLLAND, Elmer Joseph (D Pa.) Jan. 8, 1894-Aug. 9, 1968; House May 19, 1942-43; Jan. 24, 1956-Aug. 9, 1968.

HOLLAND, James (A-F N.C.) 1754-May 19, 1823; House 1795-97; 1801-11.

HOLLAND, Kenneth Lamar (D S.C.) Nov. 24, 1934-__; House 1975-__.

HOLLAND, Spessard Lindsey (D Fla.) July 10, 1892-Nov. 6, 1971; Senate Sept. 25, 1946-71; Gov. 1941-45.

HOLLEMAN, Joel (VBD Va.) Oct. 1, 1799-Aug. 5, 1844; House 1839-40.

HOLLEY, John Milton (W N.Y.) Nov. 10, 1802-March 8, 1848; House 1847-March 8, 1848.

HOLLIDAY, Elias Selah (R Ind.) March 5, 1842-March 13, 1936; House 1901-09.

HOLLINGS, Ernest F. (D S.C.) Jan. 1, 1922-__; Senate Nov. 9, 1966-__; Gov. 1959-63.

HOLLINGSWORTH, David Adams (R Ohio) Nov. 21, 1844-Dec. 3, 1929; House 1909-11, 1915-19.

HOLLIS, Henry French (D N.H.) Aug. 30, 1869-July 7, 1949; Senate March 13, 1913-19.

HOLLISTER, John Baker (R Ohio) Nov. 7, 1890-__; House Nov. 3, 1931-37.

HOLLOWAY, David Pierson (PP Ind.) Dec. 7, 1809-Sept. 9, 1883; House 1855-57.

HOLMAN, Rufus Cecil (R Ore.) Oct. 14, 1877-Nov. 27, 1959; Senate 1939-45.

HOLMAN, William Steele (D Ind.) Sept. 6, 1822-April 22, 1897; House 1859-65, 1867-77, 1881-95, March 4-April 22, 1897.

HOLMES, Adoniram Judson (R Iowa) March 2, 1842-Jan. 21, 1902; House 1883-89.

HOLMES, Charles Horace (R N.Y.) Oct. 24, 1827-Oct. 2, 1874; House Dec. 6, 1870-71.

HOLMES, David (— Va./Miss.) March 10, 1769-Aug. 20, 1832; House 1797-1809 (Va.); Senate Aug. 30, 1820-Sept. 25, 1825 (Miss.); Gov. 1809-17 (Miss. Terr.), 1817-20 (Miss.).

HOLMES, Elias Bellows (W N.Y.) May 22, 1807-July 31, 1866; House 1845-49.

HOLMES, Gabriel (— N.C.) 1769-Sept. 26, 1829; House 1825-Sept. 26, 1829; Gov. 1821-24.

HOLMES, Isaac Edward (D S.C.) April 6, 1796-Feb. 24, 1867; House 1839-51.

HOLMES, John (D Mass./Maine) March 14, 1773-July 7, 1843; House 1817-March 15, 1820 (Mass.); Senate June 13, 1820-27, Jan. 15, 1829-33 (Maine).

HOLMES, Otis Halbert (Hal) (grandson of Dudley Chase Haskell) (R Wash.) Feb. 22, 1902-__; House 1943-59.

HOLMES, Pehr Gustaf (R Mass.) April 9, 1881-Dec.19, 1952; House 1931-47.

HOLMES, Sidney Tracy (R N.Y.) Aug. 14, 1815-Jan. 16, 1890; House 1865-67.

HOLMES, Uriel (F Conn.) Aug. 26, 1764-May 18, 1827; House 1817-18.

HOLSEY, Hopkins (UD Ga.) Aug. 25, 1779-March 31, 1859; House Oct, 5, 1835-39.

HOLT, Hines (W Ga.) April 27, 1805-Nov. 4, 1865; House Feb. 1-March 3, 1841.

HOLT, Joseph Franklin 3d (R Calif.) July 6, 1924-__; House 1953-61.

HOLT, Marjorie Sewell (R Md.) Sept. 17, 1920-__; House 1973-__.

HOLT, Orrin (D Conn.) March 13, 1792-June 20, 1855; House Dec. 5, 1836-39.

HOLT, Rush Dew (D W.Va.) June 19, 1905-Feb. 8, 1955; Senate June 21, 1935-41.

HOLTEN, Samuel (— Mass.) June 9, 1738-Jan. 2, 1816; House 1793-95; Cont. Cong. 1778-80, 1782-87.

HOLTON, Hart Benton (R Md.) Oct. 13, 1835-Jan. 4, 1907; House 1883-85.

HOLTZMAN, Elizabeth (D N.Y.) Aug. 11, 1941-__; House 1973-__.

HOLTZMAN, Lester (D N.Y.) June 1, 1913-__; House 1953-Dec. 31, 1961.

HONEYMAN, Nan Wood (D Ore.) July 15, 1881-Dec. 10, 1970; House 1937-39.

HOOD, George Ezekial (D N.C.) Jan. 25, 1875-March 8, 1960; House 1915-19.

HOOK, Enos (D Pa.) Dec. 3, 1804-July 15, 1841; House 1839-April 18, 1841.

HOOK, Frank Eugene (D Mich.) May 26, 1893-__; House 1935-43, 1945-47.

HOOKER, Charles Edward (D Miss.) 1825-Jan. 8, 1914; House 1875-83, 1887-95, 1901-03.

HOOKER, James Murray (D Va.) Oct. 29, 1873-Aug. 6, 1940; House Nov. 8, 1921-25.

HOOKER, Warren Brewster (R N.Y.) Nov. 24, 1856-March 5, 1920; House 1891-Nov. 10, 1898.

HOOKS, Charles (great-grandfather of William Julius Harris) (D N.C.) Feb. 20, 1768-Oct. 18, 1843; House Dec. 2, 1816-17, 1819-25.

HOOPER, Benjamin Stephen (Read. Va.) March 6, 1835-Jan. 17, 1898; House 1883-85.

HOOPER, Joseph Lawrence (R Mich.) Dec. 22, 1877-Feb. 22, 1934; House Aug. 18, 1925-Feb. 22, 1934.

HOOPER, Samuel (R Mass.) Feb. 3, 1808-Feb. 14, 1875; House Dec. 2, 1861-Feb. 14, 1875.

HOOPER, William Henry (D Utah) Dec. 25, 1813-Dec. 30, 1882; House (Terr. Del.) 1859-61; 1865-73.

HOPE, Clifford Ragsdale (R Kan.) June 9, 1893-May 16, 1970; House 1927-57.

HOPKINS, Albert Cole (R Pa.) Sept. 15, 1837-June 9, 1911; House 1891-95.

HOPKINS, Albert Jarvis (R Ill.) Aug. 15, 1846-Aug. 23, 1922; House Dec. 7, 1885-1903; Senate 1903-09.

HOPKINS, Benjamin Franklin (R Wis.) April 22, 1829-Jan. 1, 1870; House 1867-Jan. 1, 1870.

HOPKINS, David William (R Mo.) Oct. 31, 1897-Oct. 14, 1968; House Feb. 5, 1929-33.

HOPKINS, Francis Alexander (Frank) (D Ky.) May 27, 1853-June 5, 1918; House 1903-07.

HOPKINS, George Washington (D Va.) Feb. 22, 1804-March 1, 1861; House 1835-47, 1857-59.

HOPKINS, James Herron (D Pa.) Nov. 3, 1832-June 17, 1904; House 1875-77; 1883-85.

HOPKINS, Nathan Thomas (R Ky.) Oct. 27, 1852-Feb. 11, 1927; House Feb. 18-March 3, 1897.

HOPKINS, Samuel (D Ky.) April 9, 1753-Sept. 16, 1819; House 1813-15.

HOPKINS, Samuel Isaac (D Va.) Dec. 12, 1843-Jan. 15, 1914; House 1887-89.

HOPKINS, Samuel Miles (— N.Y.) May 9, 1772-March 9, 1837; House 1813-15.

HOPKINS, Stephen Tyng (R N.Y.) March 25, 1849-March 3, 1892; House 1887-89.

HOPKINSON, Joseph (F Pa.) Nov. 12, 1770-Jan.15, 1842; House 1815-19.

HOPWOOD, Robert Freeman (R Pa.) July 24, 1856-March 1, 1940; House 1915-17.

HORAN, Walter Franklin (R Wash.) Oct. 15, 1898-Dec. 19, 1966; House 1943-65.

HORN, Henry (JD Pa.) 1786-Jan. 12, 1862; House 1831-33.

HORNBECK, John Westbrook (W Pa.) Jan. 24, 1804-Jan. 16, 1848; House 1847-Jan. 16, 1848.

HORNOR, Lynn Sedwick (D W.Va.) Nov. 3, 1874-Sept. 23, 1933; House 1931-Sept. 23, 1933.

HORR, Ralph Ashley (R Wash.) Aug. 12, 1884-Jan. 26, 1960; House 1931-33.

HORR, Roswell Gilbert (R Mich.) Nov. 26, 1830-Dec.19, 1896; House 1879-85.

HORSEY, Outerbridge (F Del.) March 5, 1777-June 9, 1842; Senate Jan. 12, 1810-21.

HORSFORD, Jerediah (W N.Y.) March 8, 1791-Jan. 14, 1875; House 1851-53.

HORTON, Frank Jefferson (R N.Y.) Dec. 12, 1919-__; House 1963-__.

HORTON, Frank Ogilvie (R Wyo.) Oct. 18, 1882-Aug. 17, 1948; House 1939-41.

HORTON, Thomas Raymond (R N.Y.) April 1822-July 26, 1894; House 1855-57.

HORTON, Valentine Baxter (W Ohio) Jan. 29, 1802-Jan. 14, 1888; House 1855-59, 1861-63.

HOSKINS, George Gilbert (R N.Y.) Dec. 24, 1824-June 12, 1893; House 1873-77.

HOSMER, Craig (R Calif.) May 6, 1915-__; House 1953-Dec. 31, 1974.

HOSMER, Hezekiah Lord (— N.Y.) June 7, 1765-June 9, 1814; House 1797-99.

HOSTETLER, Abraham Jonathan (D Ind.) Nov. 22, 1818-Nov. 24, 1899; House 1879-81.

HOSTETTER, Jacob (D Pa.) May 9, 1754-June 29, 1831; House Nov. 16, 1818-21.

HOTCHKISS, Giles Waldo (R N.Y.) Oct. 25, 1815-July 5, 1878; House 1863-67, 1869-71.

HOTCHKISS, Julius (R Conn.) July 11, 1810-Dec. 23, 1878; House 1867-69.

HOUCK, Jacob Jr. (D N.Y.) Jan. 14, 1801-Oct. 2, 1857; House 1841-43.

HOUGH, David (— N.H.) March 13, 1753-April 18, 1831; House 1803-07.

HOUGH, William Jervis (D N.Y.) March 20, 1795-Oct. 4, 1869; House 1845-47.

HOUGHTON, Alanson Bigelow (R N.Y.) Oct. 10, 1863-Sept. 15, 1941; House 1919-Feb. 28, 1922.

HOUGHTON, Sherman Otis (R Calif.) April 10, 1828-Aug. 31, 1914; House 1871-75.

HOUK, George Washington (D Ohio) Sept. 25, 1825-Feb. 9, 1894; House 1891-Feb. 9, 1894.

HOUK, John Chiles (son of Leonidas Campbell Houk) (R Tenn.) Feb. 26, 1860-June 3, 1923; House Dec. 7, 1891-95.

HOUK, Leonidas Campbell (father of John Chiles Houk) (R Tenn.) June 8, 1836-May 25, 1891; House 1879-May 25, 1891.

HOUSE, John Ford (D Tenn.) Jan. 9, 1827-June 28, 1904; House 1875-83.

HOUSEMAN, Julius (D Mich.) Dec. 8, 1832-Feb. 8, 1891; House 1883-85.

HOUSTON, Andrew Jackson (son of Samuel Houston) (D Texas) June 21, 1854-June 26, 1941; Senate April 21-June 26, 1941.

HOUSTON, George Smith (D Ala.) Jan. 17, 1808-Dec. 31, 1879; House 1841-49, 1851-Jan. 21, 1861; Senate March 4-Dec. 31, 1879; Gov. 1874-78.

HOUSTON, Henry Aydelotte (D Del.) July 10, 1847-April 5, 1925; House 1903-05.

HOUSTON, John Mills (D Kan.) Sept. 15, 1890-April 29, 1975; House 1935-43.

HOUSTON, John Wallace (uncle of Robert Griffith Houston) (W Del.) May 4, 1814-April 26, 1896; House 1845-51.

HOUSTON, Robert Griffith (nephew of John Wallace Houston) (R Del.) Oct. 13, 1867-Jan. 29, 1946; House 1925-33.

HOUSTON, Samuel (father of Andrew Jackson Houston and cousin of David Hubbard) (D Tenn./Texas) March 2, 1793-July 26, 1863; House 1823-27 (Tenn.); Senate Feb. 21, 1846-59 (Texas), Gov. 1827-April 16, 1829 (Tenn.); 1859-61 (Texas).

HOUSTON, Victor Stewart Kaleoaloha (R Hawaii) July 22, 1876-July 31, 1959; House (Terr. Del.) 1927-33.

HOUSTON, William Cannon (D Tenn.) March 17, 1852-Aug. 30, 1931; House 1905-19.

HOVEY, Alvin Peterson (R Ind.) Sept. 6, 1821-Nov. 23, 1891; House 1887-Jan. 17, 1889; Gov. 1889-91.

HOWARD, Benjamin (— Ky.) 1760-Sept. 18, 1814; House 1807-April 10, 1810; Gov. (Louisiana Terr.) 1810-12.

HOWARD, Benjamin Chew (son of John Eager Howard) (D Md.) Nov. 5, 1791-March 6, 1872; House 1829-33, 1835-39.

HOWARD, Edgar (D Neb.) Sept. 16, 1858-July 19, 1951; House 1923-35.

HOWARD, Everette Burgess (D Okla.) Sept. 19, 1873-April 3, 1950; House 1919-21, 1923-25, 1927-29.

HOWARD, Guy Victor (R Minn.) Nov. 28, 1879-Aug. 20, 1954; Senate Nov. 4, 1936-37.

HOWARD, Jacob Merritt (R Mich.) July 10, 1805-April 2, 1871; House 1841-43 (W); Senate Jan. 17, 1862-71 (R).

HOWARD, James John (D N.J.) July 24, 1927-—; House 1965-—.

HOWARD, John Eager (father of Benjamin Chew Howard) (F Md.) June 4, 1752-Oct. 12, 1827; Senate Nov. 30, 1796-1803; Gov. 1789-91; Cont. Cong. 1784-88.

HOWARD, Jonas George (D Ind.) May 22, 1825-Oct. 5, 1911; House 1885-89.

HOWARD, Milford Wriarson (P Ala.) Dec. 18, 1862-Dec. 28, 1937; House 1895-99.

HOWARD, Tilghman Ashurst (D Ind.) Nov. 14, 1797-Aug. 16, 1844; House Aug. 5, 1839-July 1, 1840.

HOWARD, Volney Erskine (D Texas) Oct. 22, 1809-May 14, 1889; House 1849-53.

HOWARD, William (D Ohio) Dec. 31, 1817-June 1, 1891; House 1859-61.

HOWARD, William Alanson (R Mich.) April 8, 1813-April 10, 1880; House 1855-59, May 15, 1860-61; Gov. (Dakota Terr.) 1878-80.

HOWARD, William Marcellus (D Ga.) Dec. 6, 1857-July 5, 1932; House 1897-1911.

HOWARD, William Schley (cousin of Auggustus O. Bacon) (D Ga.) June 29, 1875-Aug. 1, 1953; House 1911-19.

HOWE, Albert Richards (R Miss.) Jan. 1, 1840-June 1, 1884; House 1873-75.

HOWE, Allan Turner (D Utah) Sept. 6, 1927-—; House 1975-—.

HOWE, James Robinson (R N.Y.) Jan. 27, 1839-Sept. 21, 1914; House 1895-99.

HOWE, John W. (FSW Pa.) 1801-Dec. 1, 1873; House 1849-53.

HOWE, Thomas Marshall (father-in-law of James W. Brown) (W Pa.) April 20, 1808-July 20, 1877; House 1851-55.

HOWE, Thomas Y. Jr. (D N.Y.) 1801-July 15, 1860; House 1851-53.

HOWE, Timothy Otis (UR Wis.) Feb. 24, 1816-March 25, 1883; Senate 1861-79; Postmaster General 1882-83.

HOWELL, Benjamin Franklin (R N.J.) Jan. 27, 1844-Feb. 1, 1933; House 1895-1911.

HOWELL, Charles Robert (D N.J.) April 23, 1904-July 5, 1973; House 1949-55.

HOWELL, Edward (D N.Y.) Oct. 16, 1792-Jan. 30, 1871; House 1833-35.

HOWELL, Elias (father of James Bruen Howell) (W Ohio) 1792-May 1844; House 1835-37.

HOWELL, George (R Pa.) June 28, 1859-Nov. 19, 1913; House 1903-Feb.10, 1904.

HOWELL, George Evan (R Ill.) Sept. 21, 1905-—; House 1941-Oct. 5, 1947.

HOWELL, James Bruen (son of Elias Howell) (R Iowa) July 4, 1816-June 17, 1880; Senate Jan. 18, 1870-71.

HOWELL, Jeremiah Brown (F R.I.) Aug. 28, 1771-Feb. 5, 1822; Senate 1811-17.

HOWELL, Joseph (R Utah) Feb. 17, 1857-July 18, 1918; House 1903-17.

HOWELL, Nathaniel Woodhull (— N.Y.) Jan. 1, 1770-Oct. 15, 1851; House 1813-15.

HOWELL, Robert Beecher (R Neb.) Jan. 21, 1864-March 11, 1933; Senate 1923-March 11, 1933.

HOWEY, Benjamin Franklin (nephew of Charles Creighton Stratton) (R N.J.) March 17, 1828-Feb. 6, 1895; House 1883-85.

HOWLAND, Benjamin (D R.I.) July 27, 1755-May 1, 1821; Senate Oct. 29, 1804-09.

HOWLAND, Leonard Paul (R Ohio) Dec. 5, 1865-Dec. 23, 1942; House 1907-13.

HOXWORTH, Stephen Arnold (D Ill.) May 1, 1860-Jan. 25, 1930; House 1913-15.

HRUSKA, Roman Lee (R Neb.) Aug. 16, 1904-—; House 1953-Nov. 8, 1954; Senate Nov. 8, 1954-—.

HUBARD, Edmund Wilcox (D Va.) Feb. 20, 1806-Dec. 9, 1878; House 1841-47.

HUBBARD, Asahel Wheeler (father of Elbert Hamilton Hubbard) (R Iowa) Jan. 19, 1819-Sept. 22, 1879; House 1863-69.

HUBBARD, Carroll Jr. (D Ky.) July 7, 1937-—; House 1975-—.

HUBBARD, Chester Dorman (father of William Pallister Hubbard) (R W.Va.) Nov. 25, 1814-Aug. 23, 1891; House 1865-69.

HUBBARD, David (cousin of Samuel Houston) (SRD Ala.) 1792-Jan. 20, 1874; House 1839-41, 1849-51.

HUBBARD, Demas Jr. (R N.Y.) Jan. 17, 1806-Sept. 2, 1873; House 1865-67.

HUBBARD, Elbert Hamilton (son of Asahel Wheeler Hubbard) (R Iowa) Aug. 19, 1849-June 4,1912; House 1905-June 4, 1912.

HUBBARD, Henry (D N.H.) May 3, 1784-June 5, 1857; House 1829-35; Senate 1835-41; Gov. 1842-44.

HUBBARD, Joel Douglas (R Mo.) Nov. 6, 1860-May 26, 1919; House 1895-97.

HUBBARD, John Henry (R Conn.) March 24, 1804-July 30, 1872; House 1863-67.

HUBBARD, Jonathan Hatch (F Vt.) May 7, 1768-Sept. 20, 1849; House 1809-11.

HUBBARD, Levi (D Mass.) Dec. 19, 1762-Feb. 18, 1836; House 1813-15.

HUBBARD, Richard Dudley (D Conn.) Sept. 7, 1818-Feb. 28, 1884; House 1867-69; Gov. 1877-79.

HUBBARD, Samuel Dickinson (W Conn.) Aug. 10, 1799-Oct. 8, 1855; House 1845-49; Postmaster General 1852-53.

HUBBARD, Thomas Hill (D N.Y.) Dec. 5, 1781-May 21, 1857; House 1817-19, 1821-23.

HUBBARD, William Pallister (son of Chester Dorman Hubbard) (R W.Va.) Dec. 24, 1843-Dec. 5, 1921; House 1907-11.

HUBBELL, Edwin Nelson (D N.Y.) Aug. 13, 1815-?; House 1865-67.

HUBBELL, James Randolph (R Ohio) July 13, 1824-Nov. 26, 1890; House 1865-67.

HUBBELL, Jay Abel (R Mich.) Sept. 15, 1829-Oct. 13, 1900; House 1873-83.

HUBBELL, William Spring (D N.Y.) Jan. 17, 1801-Nov. 16, 1873; House 1843-45.

HUBBS, Orlando (R N.C.) Feb. 18, 1840-Dec. 5, 1930; House 1881-83.

HUBER, Robert James (R Mich.) Aug. 29, 1922-__; House 1973-75.

HUBER, Walter B. (D Ohio) June 29, 1903-—; House 1945-51.

HUBLEY, Edward Burd (JD Pa.) 1792-Feb. 23, 1856; House 1835-39.

HUCK, Winnifred Sprague Mason (daughter of William Ernest Mason) (R Ill.) Sept. 14, 1882-Aug. 24, 1936; House Nov. 7, 1922-23.

HUDD, Thomas Richard (D Wis.) Oct. 2, 1835-June 22, 1896; House March 8, 1886-89.

HUDDLESTON, George (D Ala.) Nov. 11, 1869-Feb. 29, 1960; House 1915-37.

HUDDLESTON, George Jr. (son of the preceding) (D Ala.) March 19, 1920-Sept. 14, 1971; House 1955-65.

HUDDLESTON, Walter Darlington (D Ky.) April 15, 1926-__; Senate 1973-__.

HUDNUT, William Herbert III (R Ind.) Oct. 17, 1932-__; House 1973-75.

HUDSON, Charles (W Mass.) Nov. 14, 1795-May 4, 1881; House May 3, 1841-49.

HUDSON, Grant Martin (R Mich.) July 23, 1868-Oct. 26, 1955; House 1923-31.

HUDSON, Thomas Jefferson (P Kan.) Oct. 30, 1839-Jan. 4, 1923; House 1893-95.

HUDSPETH, Claude Benton (D Texas) May 12, 1877-March 19, 1941; House 1919-31.

HUFF, George Franklin (R Pa.) July 16, 1842-April 18, 1912; House 1891-93, 1895-97, 1903-11.

HUFFMAN, James Wylie (D Ohio) Sept. 13, 1894-—; Senate Oct. 8, 1945-Nov. 5, 1946.

HUFTY, Jacob (D N.J.) ?-May 20, 1814; House 1808-May 20, 1814.

HUGER, Benjamin (— S.C.) 1768-July 7, 1823; House 1799-1805, 1815-17.

HUGER, Daniel (father of Daniel Elliott Huger) (— S.C.) Feb. 20, 1742-July 6, 1799; House 1789-93; Cont. Cong. 1786-88.

HUGER, Daniel Elliott (son of the preceding) (SRD S.C.) June 28, 1779-Aug. 21, 1854; Senate 1843-45.

HUGHES, Charles (D N.Y.) Feb. 27, 1822-Aug. 10, 1887; House 1853-55.

HUGHES, Charles James Jr. (D Colo.) Feb. 16, 1853-Jan. 11, 1911; Senate 1909-Jan. 11, 1911.

HUGHES, Dudley Mays (D Ga.) Oct. 10, 1848-Jan. 20, 1927; House 1909-17.

HUGHES, George Wurtz (D Md.) Sept. 30, 1806-Sept. 3, 1870; House 1859-61.

HUGHES, Harold Everett (D Iowa) Feb. 10, 1922-—; Senate 1969-75; Gov. 1963-69.

HUGHES, James (D Ind.) Nov. 24, 1823-Oct. 24, 1873; House 1857-59.

HUGHES, James Anthony (R W.Va.) Feb. 27, 1861-March 2, 1930; House 1901-15, 1927-March 2, 1930.

HUGHES, James Frederic (D Wis.) Aug. 7, 1883-Aug. 9, 1940; House 1933-35.

HUGHES, James Hurd (D Del.) Jan. 14, 1867-Aug. 29, 1953; Senate 1937-43.

HUGHES, James Madison (D Mo.) April 7, 1809-Feb. 26, 1861; House 1843-45.

HUGHES, Thomas Hurst (W N.J.) Jan. 10, 1769-Nov. 10, 1839; House 1829-33.

HUGHES, William (D N.J.) April 3, 1872-Jan. 30, 1918; House 1903-05, 1907-Sept. 27, 1912; Senate 1913-Jan. 30, 1918.

HUGHES, William John (D N.J.) Oct. 17, 1932-__; House 1975-__.

HUGHSTON, Jonas Abbott (W N.Y.) 1808-Nov. 10, 1862; House 1855-57.

HUGUNIN, Daniel Jr. (— N.Y.) Feb. 6, 1790-June 21, 1850; House Dec. 15, 1825-27.

HUKRIEDE, Theodore Waldemar (R Mo.) Nov. 9, 1878-April 14, 1945; House 1921-23.

HULBERT, George Murray (D N.Y.) May 14, 1881-April 26, 1950; House 1915-Jan. 1, 1918.

HULBERT, John Whitefield (F Mass.) June 1, 1770-Oct. 19, 1831; House Sept. 26, 1814-17.

HULBURD, Calvin Tilden (R N.Y.) June 5, 1809-Oct. 25, 1897; House 1863-69.

HULICK, George Washington (R Ohio) June 29, 1833-Aug. 13, 1907; House 1893-97.

HULING, James Hall (R W.Va.) March 24, 1844-April 23, 1918; House 1895-97.

HULINGS, Willis James (R Pa.) July 1, 1850-Aug. 8, 1924; House 1913-15, 1919-21 (1913-15 Progressive, 1919-21 Republican).

HULL, Cordell (D Tenn.) Oct. 2, 1871-July 23, 1955; House 1907-21, 1923-31; Senate 1931-March 3, 1933; Secy. of State 1933-44; Chrmn. Dem. Natl. Comm. 1921-24.

HULL, Harry Edward (R Iowa) March 12, 1864-Jan. 16, 1938; House 1915-25.

HULL, John Albert Tiffin (R Iowa) May 1, 1841-Sept. 26, 1928; House 1891-1911.

HULL, Merlin (R Wis.) Dec. 18, 1870-May 17, 1953; House 1929-31, 1935-May 17, 1953 (1929-31 Republican, 1935-47 Progressive, 1947-53 Republican).

HULL, Morton Denison (R Ill.) Jan. 13, 1867-Aug. 20, 1937; House April 3, 1923-33.

HULL, Noble Andrew (D Fla.) March 11, 1827-Jan. 28, 1907; House 1879-Jan. 22, 1881.

HULL, William Edgar (R Ill.) Jan. 13, 1866-May 30, 1942; House 1923-33.

HULL, William Raleigh Jr. (D Mo.) April 17, 1906-—; House 1955-73.

HUMPHREY, Augustin Reed (R Neb.) Feb. 18, 1859-Dec. 10, 1937; House Nov. 7, 1922-23.

HUMPHREY, Charles (D N.Y.) Feb. 14, 1792-April 17, 1850; House 1825-27.

HUMPHREY, Herman Leon (R Wis.) March 14, 1830-June 10, 1902; House 1877-83.

HUMPHREY, Hubert Horatio Jr. (D Minn.) May 27, 1911-—; Senate 1949-Dec. 29, 1964, 1971-—; Vice President 1965-69.

HUMPHREY, James (R N.Y.) Oct. 9, 1811-June 16, 1866; House 1859-61, 1865-June 16, 1866.

HUMPHREY, James Morgan (D N.Y.) Sept. 21, 1819-Feb. 9, 1899; House 1865-69.

HUMPHREY, Reuben (— N.Y.) Sept. 2, 1757-Aug. 12, 1831; House 1807-09.

HUMPHREY, William Ewart (R Wash.) March 31, 1862-Feb. 14, 1934; House 1903-17.

HUMPHREYS, Andrew (D Ind.) March 30, 1821-June 14, 1904; House Dec. 5, 1876-77.

HUMPHREYS, Benjamin Grubb (father of William Yerger Humphreys) (D Miss.) Aug. 17, 1865-Oct. 16, 1923; House 1903-Oct. 16, 1923.

HUMPHREYS, Parry Wayne (D Tenn.) 1778-Feb. 12, 1839; House 1813-15.

HUMPHREYS, Robert (D Ky.) Aug. 20, 1893-__; Senate June 21-Nov. 6, 1956.

HUMPHREYS, William Yerger (son of Benjamin Grubb Humphreys) (D Miss.) Sept. 9, 1890-Feb. 26, 1933; House Nov. 27, 1923-25.

HUNGATE, William Leonard (D Mo.) Dec. 24, 1922-__; House Nov. 3, 1964-__.

HUNGERFORD, John Newton (R N.Y.) Dec. 31, 1825-April 2, 1883; House 1877-79.

HUNGERFORD, John Pratt (D Va.) Jan. 2, 1761-Dec. 21, 1833; House March 4-Nov. 29, 1811, 1813-17.

HUNGERFORD, Orville (D N.Y.) Oct. 29, 1790-April 6, 1851; House 1843-47.

HUNT, Carleton (nephew of Theodore Gaillard Hunt) (D La.) Jan. 1, 1836-Aug. 14, 1921; House 1883-85.

HUNT, Hiram Paine (W N.Y.) May 23, 1796-Aug. 14, 1865; House 1835-37, 1839-43.

HUNT, James Bennett (D Mich.) Aug. 13, 1799-Aug. 15, 1857; House 1843-47.

HUNT, John Edmund (R N.J.) Nov. 25, 1908-__; House 1967-75.

HUNT, John Thomas (D Mo.) Feb. 2, 1860-Nov. 30, 1916; House 1903-07.

HUNT, Jonathan (NR Vt.) Aug. 12, 1787-May 15, 1832; House 1827-May 15, 1832.

HUNT, Lester Callaway (D Wyo.) July 8, 1892-June 19, 1954; Senate 1949-June 19, 1954; Gov. 1943-49.

HUNT, Samuel (— N.H.) July 8, 1765-July 7, 1807; House Dec. 6, 1802-05.

HUNT, Theodore Gaillard (nephew of John Gaillard and uncle of Carleton Hunt) (W La.) Oct. 23, 1805-Nov. 15, 1893; House 1853-55.

HUNT, Washington (W N.Y.) Aug. 5, 1811-Feb. 2, 1867; House 1843-49; Gov. 1851-53.

HUNTER, Allan Oakley (R Calif.) June 15, 1916- —; House 1951-55.

HUNTER, Andrew Jackson (D Ill.) Dec. 17, 1831-Jan. 12, 1913; House 1893-95, 1897-99.

HUNTER, John (F S.C.) 1732-1802; House 1793-95; Senate Dec. 8, 1796-Nov. 26, 1798.

HUNTER, John Feeney (D Ohio) Oct. 19, 1896-Dec. 19, 1957; House 1937-43.

HUNTER, John Ward (— N.Y.) Oct. 15, 1807-April 16, 1900; House Dec. 4, 1866-67.

HUNTER, Morton Craig (R Ind.) Feb. 5, 1825-Oct. 25, 1896; House 1867-69, 1873-79.

HUNTER, Narsworthy (— Miss.) ?-March 11, 1802; House (Terr. Del.) 1801-March 11, 1802.

HUNTER, Richard Charles (D Neb.) Dec. 3, 1884-Jan. 23, 1941; Senate Nov. 7, 1934-35.

HUNTER, Robert Mercer Taliaferro (D Va.) April 21, 1809-July 18, 1887; House 1837-43, 1845-47; Senate 1847-March 28, 1861; Speaker 1839-41.

HUNTER, Whiteside Godfrey (R Ky.) Dec. 25, 1841-Nov. 2, 1917; House 1887-89, 1895-97,Nov. 10, 1903-05.

HUNTER, William (R Vt.) Jan. 3, 1754-Nov. 30, 1827; House 1817-19.

HUNTER, William (F R.I.) Nov. 26, 1774-Dec. 3,1849; Senate Oct. 28, 1811-21.

HUNTER, William Forrest (W Ohio) Dec. 10, 1808-March 30, 1874; House 1849-53.

HUNTER, William H. (D Ohio) ?-1842; House 1837-39.

HUNTINGTON, Abel (D N.Y.) Feb. 21, 1777-May 18, 1858; House 1833-37.

HUNTINGTON, Benjamin (— Conn.) April 19, 1736-Oct. 16, 1800; House 1789-91; Cont. Cong. 1780-84, 1787-88.

HUNTINGTON, Ebenezer (W Conn.) Dec. 26, 1754-June 17, 1834; House Oct. 11, 1810-11, 1817-19.

HUNTINGTON, Jabez Williams (W Conn.) Nov. 8, 1788-Nov. 1, 1847; House 1829-Aug. 16, 1834; Senate May 4, 1840-Nov. 1, 1847.

HUNTON, Eppa (D Va.) Sept. 24, 1822-Oct. 11, 1908; House 1873-81; Senate May 28, 1892-95.

HUNTSMAN, Adam (JD Tenn.) ?-?; House1835-37.

HUOT, Joseph Oliva (D N.H.) Aug. 11, 1917-—; House 1965-67.

HURD, Frank Hunt (D Ohio) Dec. 25, 1840-July 10, 1896; House 1875-77, 1879-81, 1883-85.

HURLBUT, Stephen Augustus (R Ill.) Nov. 29, 1815-March 27, 1882; House 1873-77.

HURLEY, Denis Michael (R N.Y.) March 14, 1843-Feb. 26, 1899; House 1895-Feb. 26, 1899.

HUSTED, James William (R N.Y.) March 16, 1870-Jan. 2, 1925; House 1915-23.

HUSTING, Paul Oscar (D Wis.) April 25, 1866-Oct. 21, 1917; Senate 1915-Oct. 21, 1917.

HUTCHESON, Joseph Chappell (D Texas) May 18, 1842-May 25, 1924; House 1893-97.

HUTCHINS, John (cousin of Wells Andrews Hutchins) (R Ohio) July 25, 1812-Nov. 20, 1891; House 1859-63.

HUTCHINS, Waldo (D N.Y.) Sept. 30, 1822-Feb. 8, 1891; House Nov. 4, 1879-85.

HUTCHINS, Wells Andrews (cousin of John Hutchins) (D Ohio) Oct. 8, 1818-Jan. 25, 1895; House 1863-65.

HUTCHINSON, Edward (R Mich.) Oct. 13, 1914-—; House 1963-—.

HUTCHINSON, Elijah Cubberley (R N.J.) Aug. 7, 1855-June 25, 1932; House 1915-23.

HUTTON, John Edward (D Mo.) March 28, 1828-Dec. 28, 1893; House 1885-89.

HUYLER, John (D N.J.) April 9, 1808-Jan. 9, 1870; House 1857-59.

HYDE, DeWitt Stephen (R Md.) March 21, 1909-—; House 1953-59.

HYDE, Henry John (R Ill.) April 18, 1924-—; House 1975-—.

HYDE, Ira Barnes (R Mo.) Jan. 18, 1838-Dec. 6, 1926; House 1873-75.

HYDE, Samuel Clarence (R Wash.) April 22, 1842-March 7, 1922; House 1895-97.

HYMAN, John Adams (R N.C.) July 23, 1840-Sept. 14, 1891; House 1875-77.

HYNEMAN, John M. (D Pa.) April 25, 1771-April 16, 1816; House 1811-Aug. 2, 1813.

HYNES, William Joseph (Reform R Ark.) March 31, 1843-April 2, 1915; House 1873-75.

I

ICHORD, Richard H. (D Mo.) June 27, 1926-—; House 1961-—.

IGLESIAS, Santiago (formerly Santiago Iglesias Pantin) (Coal. P.R.) Feb. 22, 1872-Dec. 5, 1939; House (Res. Comm.) 1933-Dec. 5, 1939.

IGOE, James Thomas (D Ill.) Oct. 23, 1883-—; House 1927-33.

IGOE, Michael Lambert (D Ill.) April 16, 1885-Aug. 21, 1967; House Jan. 3-June 2, 1935.

IGOE, William Leo (D Mo.) Oct. 19, 1879-April 20, 1953; House 1913-21.

IHRIE, Peter Jr. (JD Pa.) Feb. 3, 1796-March 29, 1871; House Oct. 13, 1829-33.

IKARD, Frank Neville (D Texas) Jan. 30, 1914-—; House Sept. 8, 1951-Dec. 15, 1961.

IKIRT, George Pierce (D Ohio) Nov. 3, 1852-Feb. 12, 1927; House 1893-95.

ILSLEY, Daniel (D Mass.) May 30, 1740-May 10, 1813; House 1807-09.

IMHOFF, Lawrence E. (D Ohio) Dec. 28, 1895-—; House 1933-39, 1941-43.

IMLAY, James Henderson (— N.J.) Nov. 26, 1764-March 6, 1823; House 1797-1801.

INGALLS, John James (R Kan.) Dec. 29, 1833-Aug. 16, 1900; Senate 1873-91; President pro tempore 1887-91.

INGE, Samuel Williams (nephew of William Marshall Inge) (D Ala.) Feb. 22, 1817-June 10, 1868; House 1847-51.

INGE, William Marshall (uncle of Samuel Williams Inge) (D Tenn.) 1802-46; House 1833-35.

INGERSOLL, Charles Jared (brother of Joseph Reed Ingersoll) (D Pa.) Oct. 3, 1782-May 14, 1862; House 1813-15, 1841-49.

INGERSOLL, Colin Macrae (son of Ralph Isaacs Ingersoll) (D Conn.) March 11, 1819-Sept. 13, 1903; House 1851-55.

INGERSOLL, Ebon Clark (R Ill.) Dec. 12, 1831-May 31, 1879; House May 20, 1864-71.

INGERSOLL, Joseph Reed (brother of Charles Jared Ingersoll) (W Pa.) June 14, 1786-Feb. 20, 1868; House 1835-37, Oct. 12, 1841-49.

INGERSOLL, Ralph Isaacs (father of Colin Macrae Ingersoll) (D Conn.) Feb. 8, 1789-Aug. 26, 1872; House 1825-33.

INGHAM, Samuel (D Conn.) Sept. 5, 1793-Nov. 10, 1881; House 1835-39.

INGHAM, Samuel Delucenna (Jeff. D Pa.) Sept. 16, 1779-June 5, 1860; House 1813-July 6, 1818, Oct. 8, 1822-29; Secy. of the Treasury 1829-31.

INOUYE, Daniel Ken (D Hawaii) Sept. 7, 1924-—; House Aug. 21, 1959-63; Senate 1963-—.

IRBY, John Laurens Manning (great-grandson of Elias Earle) (D S.C.) Sept. 10, 1854-Dec. 9, 1900; Senate 1891-97.

IREDELL, James (D N.C.) Nov. 2, 1788-April 13, 1853; Senate Dec. 15, 1828-31; Gov. 1827-28.

IRELAND, Clifford Cady (R Ill.) Feb. 14, 1878-May 24, 1930; House 1917-23.

IRION, Alfred Briggs (D La.) Feb. 18, 1833-May 21, 1903; House 1885-87.

IRVIN, Alexander (W Pa.) Jan. 18, 1800-March 20, 1874; House 1847-49.

IRVIN, James (W Pa.) Feb. 18, 1800-Nov. 28, 1862; House 1841-45.

IRVIN, William W. (D Ohio) 1778-March 28, 1842; House 1829-33.

IRVINE, William (— Pa.) Nov. 3, 1741-July 29, 1804; House 1793-95; Cont. Cong. 1786-88.

IRVINE, William (R N.Y.) Feb. 14, 1820-Nov. 12, 1882; House 1859-61.

IRVING, Theodore Leonard (D Mo.) March 24, 1898-March 8, 1962; House 1949-53.

IRVING, William (D N.Y.) Aug. 15, 1766-Nov. 9, 1821; House Jan. 22, 1814-19.

IRWIN, Donald J. (D Conn.) Sept. 7, 1926-__; House 1959-61, 1965-69.

IRWIN, Edward Michael (R Ill.) April 14, 1869-Jan. 30, 1933; House 1925-31.

IRWIN, Harvey Samuel (R Ky.) Dec. 10, 1844-Sept. 3, 1916; House 1901-03.

IRWIN, Jared (D Pa.) Jan. 19, 1768- ?; House 1813-17.

IRWIN, Thomas (D Pa.) Feb. 22, 1785-May 14, 1870; House 1829-31.

IRWIN, William Wallace (W Pa.) 1803-Sept. 15, 1856; House 1841-43.

ISACKS, Jacob C. (— Tenn.) ? - ?; House 1823-33.

ISACSON, Leo (AL N.Y.) April 20, 1910-__; House Feb. 17, 1948-49.

ITTNER, Anthony Friday (R Mo.) Oct. 8, 1837-Feb. 22, 1931; House 1877-79.

IVERSON, Alfred Sr. (D Ga.) Dec. 3, 1798-March 5, 1873; House 1847-49; Senate 1855-Jan. 28, 1861.

IVES, Irving McNeil (R N.Y.) Jan. 24, 1896-Feb. 24, 1962; Senate 1947-59.

IVES, Willard (D N.Y.) July 7, 1806-April 19, 1896; House 1851-53.

IZAC, Edouard Victor Michel (D Calif.) Dec. 18, 1891-__; House 1937-47.

IZARD, Ralph (— S.C.) Jan. 23, 1742-May 30, 1804; Senate 1789-95; President pro tempre 1794-95; Cont. Cong. 1782-83.

IZLAR, James Ferdinand (D S.C.) Nov. 25, 1832-May 26, 1912; House April 12, 1894-95.

J

JACK, Summers Melville (R Pa.) July 18, 1852-Sept. 16, 1945; House 1899-1903.

JACK, William (D Pa.) July 19, 1788-Feb. 28, 1852; House 1841-43.

JACKSON, Alfred Metcalf (D Kan.) July 14, 1860-June 11, 1924; House 1901-03.

JACKSON, Amos Henry (R Ohio) May 10, 1846-Aug. 30, 1924; House 1903-05.

JACKSON, Andrew (D Tenn.) March 15, 1767-June 8, 1845; House Dec. 5, 1796-97; Senate Sept. 26, 1797-April 1798, 1823-Oct. 14, 1825; Gov. of Florida Terr. March 10-July 18, 1821; President 1829-37.

JACKSON, David Sherwood (D N.Y.) 1813-Jan. 20, 1872; House 1847-April 19, 1848.

JACKSON, Donald L. (R Calif.) Jan. 23, 1910-__; House 1947-61.

JACKSON, Ebenezer Jr. (W Conn.) Jan. 31, 1796-Aug. 17, 1874; House Dec. 1, 1834-35.

JACKSON, Edward Brake (son of George Jackson and brother of John George Jackson) (D Va.) Jan. 25, 1793-Sept. 8, 1826; House Oct. 23, 1820-23.

JACKSON, Fred Schuyler (R Kan.) April 19, 1868-Nov. 21, 1931; House 1911-13.

JACKSON, George (father of John George Jackson and Edward Brake Jackson) (— Va.) Jan. 9, 1757-May 17, 1831; House 1795-97, 1799-1803.

JACKSON, Henry Martin (D Wash.) May 31, 1912-__; House 1941-53; Senate 1953-__; Chairman, Dem. Nat. Comm. 1960-61.

JACKSON, Howell Edmunds (D Tenn.) April 8, 1832-Aug. 8, 1895; Senate 1881-April 14, 1886; Assoc. Justice Supreme Court 1894-95.

JACKSON, Jabez Young (son of Senator James Jackson and uncle of Representative James Jackson) (UD Ga.) July 1790- ?; House Oct. 5, 1835-39.

JACKSON, James (father of Jabez Y. Jackson and grandfather of James Jackson) (— Ga.) Sept. 21, 1757-March 19, 1806; House 1789-91; Senate 1793-95, 1801-March 19, 1806; Gov. 1798-1801.

JACKSON, James (grandson of the preceding and nephew of Jabez Y. Jackson) (D Ga.) Oct. 18, 1819-Jan. 13, 1887; House 1857-Jan. 23, 1861.

JACKSON, James Monroe (cousin of William Thomas Bland) (D W.Va.) Dec. 3, 1825-Feb. 14, 1901; House 1889-Feb. 3, 1890.

JACKSON, James Streshley (U Ky.) Sept. 27, 1823-Oct. 8, 1862; House March 4-Dec. 13, 1861.

JACKSON, John George (son of George Jackson, brother of Edward Brake Jackson and grandfather of William Thomas Bland) (D Va.) Sept. 22, 1777-March 28, 1825; House 1803-Sept. 28, 1810, 1813-17.

JACKSON, Joseph Webber (D Ga.) Dec. 6, 1796-Sept. 29, 1854; House March 4, 1850-53.

JACKSON, Oscar Lawrence (R Pa.) Sept. 2, 1840-Feb. 16, 1920; House 1885-89.

JACKSON, Richard Jr. (F R.I.) July 3, 1764-April 18, 1838; House Nov. 11, 1808-15.

JACKSON, Samuel Dillon (D Ind.) May 28, 1895-March 8, 1951; Senate Jan. 28-Nov. 13, 1944.

JACKSON, Thomas Birdsall (D N.Y.) March 24, 1797-April 23, 1881; House 1837-41.

JACKSON, William (W Mass.) Sept. 2, 1783-Feb. 26, 1855; House 1833-37.

JACKSON, William Humphreys (father of William Purnell Jackson) (R Md.) Oct. 15, 1839-April 3, 1915; House 1901-05, 1907-09.

JACKSON, William Purnell (son of William Humphreys Jackson) (R Md.) Jan. 11, 1868-March 7, 1939; Senate Nov. 29, 1912-Jan. 28, 1914.

JACKSON, William Terry (W N.Y.) Dec. 29, 1794-Sept. 15, 1882; House 1849-51.

JACOBS, Andrew Sr. (father of Andrew Jacobs Jr.) (D Ind.) Feb. 22, 1906-__; House 1949-51.

JACOBS, Andrew Jr. (son of Andrew Jacobs Sr. and husband of Martha Elizabeth Keys) (D Ind.) Feb. 24, 1932-__; House 1965-73, 1975-__.

JACOBS, Ferris Jr. (R N.Y.) March 20, 1836-Aug. 30, 1886; House 1881-83.

JACOBS, Israel (— Pa.) June 9, 1726-about Dec. 10, 1796; House 1791-93.

JACOBS, Orange (R Wash.) May 2, 1827-May 21, 1914; House (Terr. Del.) 1875-79.

JACOBSEN, Bernhard Martin (father of William Sebastian Jacobsen) (D Iowa) March 26, 1862-June 30, 1936; House 1931-June 30, 1936.

JACOBSEN, William Sebastian (son of Bernhard Martin Jacobsen) (D Iowa) Jan. 15, 1887-April 10, 1955; House 1937-43.

JACOBSTEIN, Meyer (D N.Y.) Jan. 25, 1880-April 18, 1963; House 1923-29.

JACOWAY, Henderson Madison (D Ark.) Nov. 7, 1870-Aug. 4, 1947; House 1911-23.

JADWIN, Cornelius Comegys (R Pa.) March 27, 1835-Aug. 17, 1913; House 1881-83.

JAMES, Addison Davis (grandfather of John Albert Whitaker) (R Ky.) Feb. 27, 1850-June 10, 1947; House 1907-09.

JAMES, Amaziah Bailey (R N.Y.) July 1, 1812-July 6, 1883; House 1877-81.

JAMES, Benjamin Franklin (R Pa.) Aug. 1, 1885-Jan. 26, 1961; House 1949-59.

JAMES, Charles Tillinghast (Protect. TD R.I.) Sept. 15, 1805-Oct. 17, 1862; Senate 1851-57.

JAMES, Darwin Rush (R N.Y.) May 14, 1834-Nov. 19, 1908; House 1883-87.

JAMES, Francis (W Pa.) April 4, 1799-Jan. 4, 1886; House 1839-41.

JAMES, Hinton (D N.C.) April 24, 1884-Nov. 3, 1948; House Nov. 4, 1930-31.

JAMES, Ollie Murray (D Ky.) July 27, 1871-Aug. 28, 1918; House 1903-13; Senate 1913-Aug. 28, 1918.

JAMES, Rorer Abraham (D Va.) March 1, 1859-Aug. 6, 1921; House June 15, 1920-Aug. 6, 1921.

JAMES, William Francis (Frank) (R Mich.) May 23, 1873-Nov. 17, 1945; House 1915-35.

JAMESON, John (D Mo.) March 6, 1802-Jan. 24, 1857; House Dec. 12, 1839-41, 1843-45, 1847-49.

JAMIESON, William Darius (D Iowa) Nov. 9, 1873-Nov. 18, 1949; House 1909-11.

JANES, Henry Fisk (W/A-M Vt.) Oct. 10, 1792-June 6, 1879; House Dec. 2, 1834-37.

JARMAN, John (R Okla.) July 17, 1915-__; House 1951-__; 1951-75(D), 1975-__ (R).

JARMAN, Pete (D Ala.) Oct. 31, 1892-Feb. 17, 1955; House 1937-49.

JARNAGIN, Spencer (W Tenn.) 1792-June 25, 1853; Senate Oct. 17, 1843-47.

JARRETT, Benjamin (R Pa.) July 18, 1881-July 20, 1944; House 1937-43.

JARRETT, William Paul (D Hawaii) Aug. 22, 1877-Nov. 10, 1929; House (Terr. Del.) 1923-27.

JARVIS, Leonard (D Maine) Oct. 19, 1781-Oct. 18, 1854; House 1829-37.

JARVIS, Thomas Jordan (D N.C.) Jan. 18, 1836-June 17, 1915; Senate April 19, 1894-Jan. 23, 1895; Gov. 1879-85.

JAVITS, Jacob Koppel (R N.Y.) May 18, 1904-___; House 1947-Dec. 31, 1954; Senate Jan. 9, 1957-___.

JAYNE, William (— Dakota) Oct. 8, 1826-March 20, 1916; House (Terr. Del.) 1863-June 17, 1864; Gov. 1861-63.

JEFFERIS, Albert Webb (R Neb.) Dec. 7, 1868-Sept. 14, 1942; House 1919-23.

JEFFERS, Lamar (D Ala.) April 16, 1888-___; House June 7, 1921-35.

JEFFORDS, Elza (R Miss.) May 23, 1826-March 19, 1885; House 1883-85.

JEFFORDS, James Merrill (R Vt.) May 11, 1934-___; House 1975-___.

JEFFREY, Harry Palmer (R Ohio) Dec. 26, 1901-___; House 1943-45.

JEFFRIES, Walter Sooy (R N.J.) Oct. 16, 1893-Oct. 11, 1954; House 1939-41.

JENCKES, Thomas Allen (R R.I.) Nov. 2, 1818-Nov. 4, 1875; House 1863-71.

JENCKES, Virginia Ellis (D Ind.) Nov. 6, 1877-Jan. 9, 1975; House 1933-39.

JENIFER, Daniel (NR Md.) April 15, 1791-Dec. 18, 1855; House 1831-33, 1835-41.

JENISON, Edward Halsey (R Ill.) July 27, 1907-___; House 1947-53.

JENKINS, Albert Gallatin (D Va.) Nov. 10, 1830-May 21, 1864; House 1857-61.

JENKINS, John James (R Wis.) Aug. 24, 1843-June 8, 1911; House 1895-1909.

JENKINS, Lemuel (D N.Y.) Oct. 20, 1789-Aug. 18, 1862; House 1823-25.

JENKINS, Mitchell (R Pa.) Jan. 24, 1896-___; House 1947-49.

JENKINS, Robert (— Pa.) July 10, 1769-April 18, 1848; House 1807-11.

JENKINS, Thomas Albert (R Ohio) Oct. 28, 1880-Dec. 21, 1959; House 1925-59.

JENKINS, Timothy (D N.Y.) Jan. 29, 1799-Dec. 24, 1859; House 1845-49, 1851-53.

JENKS, Arthur Byron (R N.H.) Oct. 15, 1866-Dec. 14, 1947; House 1937-June 9, 1938, 1939-43.

JENKS, George Augustus (D Pa.) March 26, 1836-Feb. 10, 1908; House 1875-77.

JENKS, Michael Hutchinson (W Pa.) May 21, 1795-Oct. 16, 1867; House 1843-45.

JENNER, William Ezra (R Ind.) July 21, 1908-___; Senate Nov. 14, 1944-45, 1947-59.

JENNESS, Benning Wentworth (D N.H.) July 14, 1806-Nov. 16, 1879; Senate Dec. 1, 1845-June 13, 1846.

JENNINGS, David (— Ohio) 1787-1834; House 1825-May 25, 1826.

JENNINGS, John Jr. (R Tenn.) June 6, 1880-Feb. 27, 1956; House Dec. 30, 1939-51.

JENNINGS, Jonathan (D Ind.) 1784-July 26, 1834; House (Terr. Del.) Nov. 27, 1809-Dec. 11, 1816, (Rep.) Dec. 2, 1822-31; Gov. 1816-22.

JENNINGS, William Pat (D Va.) Aug. 20, 1919-___; House 1955-67.

JENRETTE, John Wilson Jr. (D S.C.) May 19, 1936-___; House 1975-___.

JENSEN, Benton Franklin (Ben) (R Iowa) Dec. 16, 1892-Feb. 5, 1970; House 1939-65.

JETT, Thomas Marion (D Ill.) May 1, 1862-Jan. 10, 1939; House 1897-1903.

JEWETT, Daniel Tarbox (R Mo.) Sept. 14, 1807-Oct. 7, 1906; Senate Dec. 19, 1870-Jan. 20, 1871.

JEWETT, Freeborn Garrettson (JD N.Y.) Aug. 4, 1791-Jan. 27, 1858; House 1831-33.

JEWETT, Hugh Judge (brother of Joshua Husband Jewett) (D Ohio) July 1, 1817-March 6, 1898; House 1873-June 23, 1874.

JEWETT, Joshua Husband (brother of Hugh Judge Jewett) (D Ky.) Sept. 30, 1815-July 14, 1861; House 1855-59.

JEWETT, Luther (F Vt.) Dec. 24, 1772-March 8, 1860; House 1815-17.

JOELSON, Charles S. (D N.J.) Jan. 27, 1916-___; House 1961-Sept. 4, 1969.

JOHANSEN, August Edgar (R Mich.) July 21, 1905-___; House 1955-65.

JOHNS, Joshua Leroy (R Wis.) Feb. 27, 1881-March 16, 1947; House 1939-43.

JOHNS, Kensey Jr. (F Del.) Dec. 10, 1791-March 28, 1857; House Oct. 2, 1827-31.

JOHNSON, Adna Romulus (R Ohio) Dec. 14, 1860-June 11, 1938; House 1909-11.

JOHNSON, Albert (R Wash.) March 5, 1869-Jan. 17, 1957; House 1913-33.

JOHNSON, Albert Walter (R Pa.) April 17, 1906-___; House Nov. 5, 1963-___.

JOHNSON, Andrew (R Tenn.) Dec. 29, 1808-July 31, 1875; House 1843-53 (D); Senate Oct. 8, 1857-62, March 4-July 31, 1875; Gov. 1853-57 (D); Vice Pres. March 4-April 15, 1865 (R); Pres. April 15, 1865-69 (R).

JOHNSON, Anton Joseph (R Ill.) Oct. 20, 1878-April 16, 1958; House 1939-49.

JOHNSON, Ben (D Ky.) May 20, 1858-June 4, 1950; House 1907-27.

JOHNSON, Byron Lindberg (D Colo.) Oct. 12, 1917-___; House 1959-61.

JOHNSON, Calvin Dean (R Ill.) Nov. 22, 1898-___; House 1943-45.

JOHNSON, Cave (D Tenn.) Jan. 11, 1793-Nov. 23, 1866; House 1829-37, 1839-45; Postmaster Gen. 1845-49.

JOHNSON, Charles (— N.Y.) ?-July 23, 1802; House 1801-July 23, 1802.

JOHNSON, Charles Fletcher (D Maine) Feb. 14, 1859-Feb. 15, 1930; Senate 1911-17.

JOHNSON, Dewey William (F-L Minn.) March 14, 1899-Sept. 18, 1941; House 1937-39.

JOHNSON, Edwin Carl (D Colo.) Jan. 1, 1884-May 30, 1970; Senate 1937-55; Gov. 1933-37, 1955-57.

JOHNSON, Edwin Stockton (D S.D.) Feb. 26, 1857-July 19, 1933; Senate 1915-21.

JOHNSON, Francis (Ad.D Ky.) June 19, 1776-May 16, 1842; House Nov. 13, 1820-27.

JOHNSON, Frederick Avery (— N.Y.) Jan. 2, 1833-July 17, 1893; House 1883-87.

JOHNSON, Fred Gustus (R Neb.) Oct. 16, 1876-April 30, 1951; House 1929-31.

JOHNSON, George William (D W.Va.) Nov. 10, 1869-Feb. 24, 1944; House 1923-25, 1933-43.

JOHNSON, Glen Dale (D Okla.) Sept. 11, 1911-___; House 1947-49.

JOHNSON, Grove Lawrence (father of Hiram Warren Johnson) (R Calif.) March 27, 1841-Feb. 1, 1926; House 1895-97.

JOHNSON, Harold Terry (D Calif.) Dec. 2, 1907-___; House 1959-___.

JOHNSON, Harvey Hull (D Ohio) Sept. 7, 1808-Feb. 4, 1896; House 1853-55.

JOHNSON, Henry (W La.) Sept. 14, 1783-Sept. 4, 1864; Senate Jan. 12, 1818-May 27, 1824, Feb. 12, 1844-49; House Sept. 25, 1834-39; Gov. 1824-28.

JOHNSON, Henry Underwood (R Ind.) Oct. 28, 1850-June 4, 1939; House 1891-99.

JOHNSON, Herschel Vespasian (D Ga.) Sept. 18, 1812-Aug. 16, 1880; Senate Feb. 4, 1848-49; Gov. 1853-57.

JOHNSON, Hiram Warren (son of Grove Lawrence Johnson) (R Calif.) Sept. 2, 1866-Aug. 6, 1945; Senate March 16, 1917-Aug. 6, 1945; Gov. 1911-17.

JOHNSON, Jacob (R Utah) Nov. 1, 1847-Aug. 15, 1925; House 1913-15.

JOHNSON, James (D Va.) ?-Dec. 7, 1825; House 1813-Feb. 1, 1820.

JOHNSON, James (brother of Richard Mentor Johnson and John Telemachus Johnson and uncle of Robert Ward Johnson) (D Ky.) Jan. 1, 1774-Aug. 14, 1826; House 1825-Aug. 14, 1826.

JOHNSON, James (U Ga.) Feb. 12, 1811-Nov. 20, 1891; House 1851-53; Provisional Gov. 1865.

JOHNSON, James Augustus (D Calif.) May 16, 1829-May 11, 1896; House 1867-71.

JOHNSON, James Hutchins (— N.H.) June 3, 1802-Sept. 2, 1887; House 1845-49.

JOHNSON, James Leeper (W Ky.) Oct. 30, 1818-Feb. 12, 1877; House 1849-51.

JOHNSON, James Paul (R Colo.) June 2, 1930-___; House 1973-___.

JOHNSON, Jed Joseph (father of Jed Johnson Jr.) (D Okla.) July 31, 1888-May 8, 1963; House 1927-47.

JOHNSON, Jed Jr. (son of the preceding) (D Okla.) Dec. 17, 1939-__; House 1965-67.

JOHNSON, Jeromus (D N.Y.) Nov. 2, 1775-Sept. 7, 1846; House 1825-29.

JOHNSON, John (I Ohio) 1805-Feb. 5, 1867; House 1851-53.

JOHNSON, John Telemachus (brother of James Johnson and Richard Mentor Johnson and uncle of Robert Ward Johnson) (JD Ky.) Oct. 5, 1788-Dec. 17, 1856; House 1821-25.

JOHNSON, Joseph (uncle of Waldo Porter Johnson) (D Va.) Dec. 19, 1785-Feb. 27, 1877; House 1823-27, Jan. 21-March 3, 1833, 1835-41, 1845-47; Gov. 1852-56.

JOHNSON, Joseph Travis (D S.C.) Feb. 28, 1858-May 8, 1919; House 1901-April 19, 1915.

JOHNSON, Justin Leroy (R Calif.) April 8, 1888-March 26, 1961; House 1943-57.

JOHNSON, Lester Roland (D Wis.) June 16, 1901-July 24, 1975; House Oct. 13, 1953-65.

JOHNSON, Luther Alexander (D Texas) Oct. 29, 1875-June 6, 1965; House 1923-July 17, 1946.

JOHNSON, Lyndon Baines (D Texas) Aug. 27, 1908-Jan. 22, 1973; House April 10, 1937-49; Senate 1949-61; Vice Pres. 1961-Nov. 22, 1963; President Nov. 22, 1963-69.

JOHNSON, Magnus (F-L Minn.) Sept. 19, 1871-Sept. 13, 1936; Senate July 16, 1923-25; House 1933-35.

JOHNSON, Martin Nelson (R N.D.) March 3, 1850-Oct. 21, 1909; House 1891-99, Senate March 4-Oct. 21, 1909.

JOHNSON, Noadiah (D N.Y.) 1795-April 4, 1839; House 1833-35.

JOHNSON, Noble Jacob (R Ind.) Aug. 23, 1887-March 17, 1968; House 1925-31, 1939-July 1, 1948.

JOHNSON, Paul Burney (D Miss.) March 23, 1880-Dec. 26, 1943; House 1919-23; Gov. 1940-43.

JOHNSON, Perley Brown (W Ohio) Sept. 8, 1798-Feb. 9, 1870; House 1843-45.

JOHNSON, Philip (R Pa.) Jan. 17, 1818-Jan. 29, 1867; House 1861-Jan. 29, 1867.

JOHNSON, Reverdy (brother-in-law of Thomas Fielder Bowie) (D Md.) May 21, 1796-Feb. 10, 1876; Senate 1845-March 7, 1849, 1863-July 10, 1868 (1845-49 Whig, 1863-68 Democrat); Attorney Gen. 1849-50.

JOHNSON, Richard Mentor (brother of James Johnson and John Telemachus Johnson and uncle of Robert Ward Johnson) (D Ky.) Oct. 17, 1781-Nov. 19, 1850; House 1807-19; 1829-37; Senate Dec. 10, 1819-29 (JD); Vice Pres. 1837-41.

JOHNSON, Robert Davis (D Mo.) Aug. 12, 1883-Oct. 23, 1961; House Sept. 29, 1931-33.

JOHNSON, Robert Ward (nephew of James Johnson, John Telemachus Johnson and Richard Mentor Johnson) (D Ark.) July 22, 1814-July 26, 1879; House 1847-53; Senate July 6, 1853-61.

JOHNSON, Royal Cleaves (R S.D.) Oct. 3, 1882-Aug. 2, 1939; House 1915-33.

JOHNSON, Thomas F. (D Md.) June 26, 1909-__; House 1959-63.

JOHNSON, Tom Loftin (D Ohio) July 18, 1854-April 10, 1911; House 1891-95.

JOHNSON, Waldo Porter (nephew of Joseph Johnson) (D Mo.) Sept. 16, 1817-Aug. 14, 1885; Senate March 17, 1861-Jan. 10, 1862.

JOHNSON, William Cost (W Md.) Jan. 14, 1806-April 14, 1860; House 1833-35, 1837-43.

JOHNSON, William Richard (R Ill.) May 15, 1875-Jan. 2, 1938; House 1925-33.

JOHNSON, William Samuel (— Conn.) Oct. 7, 1727-Nov. 14, 1819; Senate 1789-March 4, 1791; Cont. Cong. 1784-87.

JOHNSON, William Ward (R Calif.) March 9, 1892-June 8, 1963; House 1941-45.

JOHNSTON, Charles (W N.Y.) Feb. 14, 1793-Sept. 1, 1845; House 1839-41.

JOHNSTON, Charles Clement (brother of Joseph Eggleston Johnston and uncle of John Warfield Johnston) (SRD Va.) April 30, 1795-June 17, 1832; House 1831-June 17, 1832.

JOHNSTON, David Emmons (D W.Va.) April 10, 1845-July 7, 1917; House 1899-1901.

JOHNSTON, James Thomas (R Ind.) Jan. 19, 1839-July 19, 1904; House 1885-89.

JOHNSTON, John Bennett Jr. (D La.) June 10, 1932-__; Senate Nov. 14, 1972-__.

JOHNSTON, John Brown (D N.Y.) July 10, 1882-Jan. 11, 1960; House 1919-21.

JOHNSTON, John Warfield (uncle of Henry Bowen and nephew of Charles Clement Johnston and Joseph Eggleston Johnston) (C Va.) Sept. 9, 1818-Feb. 27,1889; Senate Jan. 26, 1870-March 3, 1871, March 15, 1871-83.

JOHNSTON, Joseph Eggleston (brother of Charles Clement Johnston and uncle of John Warfield Johnston) (D Va.) Feb. 3, 1807-March 21, 1891; House 1879-81.

JOHNSTON, Joseph Forney (D Ala.) March 23, 1843-Aug. 8, 1913; Senate Aug. 6, 1907-Aug. 8, 1913; Gov. 1896-1900.

JOHNSTON, Josiah Stoddard (D La.) Nov. 24, 1784-May 19, 1833; House 1821-23; Senate Jan. 15, 1824-May 19, 1833.

JOHNSTON, Olin DeWitt Talmadge (D S.C.) Nov. 18, 1896-April 18, 1965; Senate 1945-April 18, 1965; Gov. 1935-39; 1943-45.

JOHNSTON, Rienzi Melville (cousin of Benjamin Edward Russell) (D Texas) Sept. 9, 1849-Feb. 28, 1926; Senate Jan 4-Feb. 2, 1913.

JOHNSTON, Rowland Louis (R Mo.) April 23, 1872-Sept. 22, 1939; House 1929-31.

JOHNSTON, Samuel (F N.C.) Dec. 15, 1733-Aug. 18, 1816; Senate Nov. 27, 1789-93; Cont. Cong. 1780-82.

JOHNSTON, Thomas Dillard (D N.C.) April 1, 1840-June 22, 1902; House 1885-89.

JOHNSTON, William (D Ohio) 1819-May 1, 1866; House 1863-65.

JOHNSTONE, George (D S.C.) April 18, 1846-March 8, 1921; House 1891-93.

JOLLEY, John Lawlor (R S.D.) July 14, 1840-Dec. 14, 1926; House Dec. 7, 1891-93.

JONAS, Benjamin Franklin (D La.) July 19, 1834-Dec. 21, 1911; Senate 1879-85.

JONAS, Charles Andrew (father of Charles Raper Jonas) (R N.C.) Aug. 14, 1876-May 25, 1955; House 1929-31.

JONAS, Charles Raper (son of Charles Andrew Jonas) (R N.C.) Dec. 9, 1904-__; House 1953-73.

JONAS, Edgar Allan (R Ill.) Oct. 14, 1885-Nov. 14, 1965; House 1949-55.

JONES, Alexander Hamilton (R N.C.) July 21, 1822-Jan. 29, 1901; House July 6, 1868-71.

JONES, Andrieus Aristieus (D N.M.) May 16, 1862-Dec. 20, 1927; Senate 1917-Dec. 20, 1927.

JONES, Benjamin (D Ohio) April 13, 1787-April 24, 1861; House 1833-37.

JONES, Burr W. (D Wis.) March 9, 1846-Jan. 7, 1935; House 1883-85.

JONES, Charles William (D Fla.) Dec. 24, 1834-Oct. 11, 1897; Senate 1875-87.

JONES, Daniel Terryll (D N.Y.) Aug. 17, 1800-March 29, 1861; House 1851-55.

JONES, Ed (D Tenn.) April 20, 1912-__; House March 25, 1969-__.

JONES, Evan John (R Pa.) Oct. 23, 1872-Jan. 9, 1952; House 1919-23.

JONES, Francis (— Tenn.) ? - ?; House 1817-23.

JONES, Frank (D N.H.) Sept. 15, 1832-Oct. 2, 1902; House 1875-79.

JONES, George (— Ga.) Feb. 25, 1766-Nov. 13, 1838; Senate Aug. 27-Nov. 7, 1807.

JONES, George Wallace (— Mich./Wis./Iowa) April 12, 1804-July 22, 1896; House (Terr. Del.) 1835-April 1836 (Mich.), April 1836-Jan. 14, 1839 (Wis.); Senate Dec. 7, 1848-59 (Iowa).

JONES, George Washington (D Tenn.) March 15, 1806-Nov. 14, 1884; House 1843-59.

JONES, George Washington (G Texas) Sept. 5, 1828-July 11, 1903; House 1879-83.

JONES, Hamilton Chamberlain (D N.C.) Sept. 26, 1884-Aug. 10, 1957; House 1947-53.

JONES, Homer Raymond (R Wash.) Sept. 3, 1893-Nov. 26, 1970; House 1947-49.

JONES, Isaac Dashiell (W Md.) Nov. 1, 1806-July 5, 1893; House 1841-43.

JONES, James (R Ga.) ?-Jan. 11, 1801; House 1799-Jan. 11, 1801.

JONES, James (D Va.) Dec. 11, 1772-April 25, 1848; House 1819-23.

JONES, James Chamberlain (W Tenn.) April 20, 1809-Oct. 29, 1859; Senate 1851-57; Gov. 1841-45.

JONES, James Henry (D Texas) Sept. 13, 1830-March 22, 1904; House 1883-87.

JONES, James Kimbrough (D Ark.) Sept. 29, 1839-June 1, 1908; House 1881-Feb. 19, 1885; Senate March 4, 1885-1903; Dem. Natl. Comm. Chmn. 1896-1904.

JONES, James Robert (D Okla.) May 5, 1939-—; House 1973-__.

JONES, James Taylor (D Ala.) July 20, 1832-Feb. 15, 1895; House 1877-79, Dec. 3, 1883-89.

JONES, Jehu Glancy (D Pa.) Oct. 7, 1811-March 24, 1878; House 1851-53, Feb. 4, 1854-Oct. 30, 1858.

JONES, John James (D Ga.) Nov. 13, 1824-Oct. 19, 1898; House 1859-Jan. 23, 1861.

JONES, John Marvin (D Texas) Feb. 26, 1886-March 4, 1976; House 1917-Nov. 20, 1940.

JONES, John Percival (R Nev.) Jan. 27, 1829-Nov. 27, 1912; Senate 1873-1903.

JONES, John Sills (R Ohio) Feb. 12, 1836-April 11, 1903; House 1877-79.

JONES, John William (W Ga.) April 14, 1806-April 27, 1871; House 1847-49.

JONES, John Winston (D Va.) Nov. 22, 1791-Jan. 29, 1848; House 1835-45; Speaker 1843-45.

JONES, Morgan (D N.Y.) Feb. 26, 1830-July 13, 1894; House 1865-67.

JONES, Nathaniel (D N.Y.) Feb. 17, 1788-July 20, 1866; House 1837-41.

JONES, Owen (D Pa.) Dec. 29, 1819-Dec. 25, 1878; House 1857-59.

JONES, Paul Caruthers (D Mo.) March 12, 1901-__; House Nov. 2, 1948-69.

JONES, Phineas (R N.J.) April 18, 1819-April 19, 1884; House 1881-83.

JONES, Robert Emmett Jr. (D Ala.) June 12, 1912-__; House Jan. 28, 1947-__.

JONES, Robert Franklin (R Ohio) June 25, 1907-June 22, 1968; House 1939-Sept. 2, 1947.

JONES, Roland (D La.) Nov. 18, 1813-Feb. 5, 1869; House 1853-55.

JONES, Seaborn (D Ga.) Feb. 1, 1788-March 18, 1864; House 1833-35; 1845-47.

JONES, Thomas Laurens (D Ky.) Jan. 22, 1819-June 20, 1887; House 1867-71, 1875-77.

JONES, Walter (D Va.) Dec. 18, 1745-Dec. 31, 1815; House 1797-99, 1803-11.

JONES, Walter B. (D N.C.) Aug. 19, 1913-__; House Feb. 5, 1966-__.

JONES, Wesley Livsey (R Wash.) Oct. 9, 1863-Nov. 19, 1932; House 1899-1909; Senate 1909-Nov. 19, 1932.

JONES, William (D Pa.) 1760-Sept. 6, 1831; House 1801-03; Secy. of the Navy 1813-14.

JONES, William Atkinson (D Va.) March 21, 1849-April 17, 1918; House 1891-April 17, 1918.

JONES, William Carey (FSil. R Wash.) April 5, 1855-June 14, 1927; House 1897-99.

JONES, William Theopilus (R Wyo.) Feb. 20, 1842-Oct. 9, 1882; House (Terr. Del.) 1871-73.

JONES, Woodrow Wilson (D N.C.) Jan. 26, 1914-—; House Nov. 7, 1950-57.

JONKMAN, Bartel John (R Mich.) April 28, 1884-June 13, 1955; House Feb. 19, 1940-49.

JORDAN, Barbara Charline (D Texas) Feb. 21, 1936-__; House 1973-__.

JORDAN, Benjamin Everett (D N.C.) Sept. 8, 1896-March 15, 1974; Senate April 19, 1958-73.

JORDAN, Isaac M. (D Ohio) May 5, 1835-Dec. 3, 1890; House 1883-85.

JORDAN, Leonard Beck (R Idaho) May 15, 1899-—; Senate Aug. 6, 1962-73; Gov. 1951-55.

JORDEN, Edwin James (R Pa.) Aug. 30, 1863-Sept. 7, 1903; House Feb. 23-March 4, 1895.

JORGENSEN, Joseph (R Va.) Feb. 11, 1844-Jan. 21, 1888; House 1877-83.

JOSEPH, Antonio (D N.M.) Aug. 25, 1846-April 19, 1910; House (Terr. Del.) 1885-95.

JOST, Henry Lee (D Mo.) Dec. 6, 1873-July 13, 1950; House 1923-25.

JOY, Charles Frederick (R Mo.) Dec. 11, 1849-April 13, 1921; House 1893-April 3, 1894, 1895-1903.

JOYCE, Charles Herbert (R Vt.) Jan. 30, 1830-Nov. 22, 1916; House 1875-83.

JOYCE, James (R Ohio) July 2, 1870-March 25, 1931; House 1909-11.

JUDD, Norman Buel (grandfather of Norman Judd Gould) (R Ill.) Jan. 10, 1815-Nov. 10, 1878; House 1867-71.

JUDD, Walter Henry (R Minn.) Sept. 25, 1898-__; House 1943-63.

JUDSON, Andrew Thompson (D Conn.) Nov. 29, 1784-March 17, 1853; House 1835-July 4, 1836.

JULIAN, George Washington (R Ind.) May 5, 1817-July 7, 1899; House 1849-51, 1861-71 (1849-51 Free Soiler, 1861-71 Republican).

JUNKIN, Benjamin Franklin (R Pa.) Nov. 12, 1822-Oct. 9, 1908; House 1859-61.

JUUL, Niels (R Ill.) April 27, 1859-Dec. 4, 1929; House 1917-21.

K

KADING, Charles August (R Wis.) Jan. 14, 1874-June 19, 1956; House 1927-33.

KAHN, Florence Prag (wife of Julius Kahn) (R Calif.) Nov. 9, 1868-Nov. 16, 1948; House 1925-37.

KAHN, Julius (husband of Florence Prag Kahn) (R Calif.) Feb. 28, 1861-Dec. 18, 1924; House 1899-1903, 1905-Dec. 18, 1924.

KALANIANAOLE, Jonah Kuhio (R Hawaii) March 26, 1871-Jan. 7, 1922; House (Terr. Del.) 1903-Jan. 7, 1922.

KALBFLEISCH, Martin (D N.Y.) Feb. 8, 1804-Feb. 12, 1873; House 1863-65.

KANE, Elias Kent (D Ill.) June 7, 1794-Dec. 12, 1835; Senate 1825-Dec. 12, 1835.

KANE, Nicholas Thomas (D N.Y.) Sept. 12, 1846-Sept. 14, 1887; House March 4-Sept. 14, 1887.

KARCH, Charles Adam (D Ill.) March 17, 1875-Nov. 6, 1932; House 1931-Nov. 6, 1932.

KARST, Raymond Willard (D Mo.) Dec. 31, 1902-—; House 1949-51.

KARSTEN, Frank Melvin (D Mo.) Jan. 7, 1913-—; House 1947-69.

KARTH, Joseph Edward (D Minn.) Aug. 26, 1922-—; House 1959-__.

KASEM, George Albert (D Calif.) April 6, 1919-—; House 1959-61.

KASSON, John Adam (R Iowa) Jan. 11, 1822-May 19, 1910; House 1863-67, 1873-77, 1881-July 13, 1884.

KASTEN, Robert Walter Jr. (R Wis.) June 19, 1942-—; House 1975-__.

KASTENMEIER, Robert William (D Wis.) Jan. 24, 1924-__; House 1959-__.

KAUFMAN, David Spangler (D Texas) Dec. 18, 1813-Jan. 31, 1851; House March 30, 1846-Jan. 31, 1851.

KAVANAGH, Edward (D Maine) April 27, 1795-Jan. 20, 1844; House 1831-35; Gov. 1843-44.

KAVANAUGH, William Marmaduke (D Ark.) March 3, 1866-Feb. 21, 1915; Senate Jan. 30-March 3, 1913.

KAYNOR, William Kirk (R Mass.) Nov. 29, 1884-Dec. 20, 1929; House March 4-Dec. 20, 1929.

KAZEN, Abraham Jr. (D Texas) Jan. 17, 1919-—; House 1967-__.

KEAN, Hamilton Fish (father of Robert Winthrop Kean, brother of John Kean) (R N.J.) Feb. 27, 1862-Dec. 27, 1941; Senate 1929-35.

KEAN, John (brother of Hamilton Fish Kean and uncle of Robert Winthrop Kean) (R N.J.) Dec. 4, 1852-Nov. 4, 1914; House 1883-85, 1887-89; Senate 1899-1911.

KEAN, Robert Winthrop (son of Hamilton Fish Kean, nephew of John Kean) (R N.J.) Sept. 28, 1893-—; House 1939-59.

KEARNEY, Bernard William (R N.Y.) May 23, 1889-—; House 1943-59.

KEARNS, Carroll Dudley (R Pa.) May 7, 1900-June 11, 1976; House 1947-63.

KEARNS, Charles Cyrus (R Ohio) Feb. 11, 1869-Dec. 17, 1931; House 1915-31.

KEARNS, Thomas (R Utah) April 11, 1862-Oct. 18, 1918; Senate Jan. 23, 1901-05.

KEATING, Edward (D Colo.) July 9, 1875-March 18, 1965; House 1913-19.

KEATING, Kenneth Barnard (R N.Y.) May 18, 1900-May 5, 1975; House 1947-59; Senate 1959-65.

KEATING, William John (R Ohio) March 30, 1927-___; House 1971-Jan. 3, 1974.

KEE, James (son of John and Maude Elizabeth Kee) (D W.Va.) April 15, 1917-___; House 1965-1973.

KEE, John (husband of Maude Elizabeth Kee and father of James Kee) (D W.Va.) Aug. 22, 1874-May 8, 1951; House 1933-May 8, 1951.

KEE, Maude Elizabeth (widow of John Kee and mother of James Kee) (D W.Va.) ? - Feb. 16, 1975; House July 17, 1951-65.

KEEFE, Frank Bateman (R Wis.) Sept. 23, 1887-Feb. 5, 1952; House 1939-51.

KEENEY, Russell Watson (R Ill.) Dec. 29, 1897-Jan. 11, 1958; House 1957-Jan. 11, 1958.

KEESE, Richard (D N.Y.) Nov. 23, 1794-Feb. 7, 1883; House 1827-29.

KEFAUVER, Carey Estes (D Tenn.) July 26, 1903-Aug. 10, 1963; House Sept. 13, 1939-49; Senate 1949-Aug. 10, 1963.

KEHOE, James Nicholas (D Ky.) July 15, 1862-June 16, 1945; House 1901-05.

KEHOE, James Walter (D Fla.) April 25, 1870-Aug. 20, 1938; House 1917-19.

KEHR, Edward Charles (D Mo.) Nov. 5, 1837-April 20, 1918; House 1875-77.

KEIFER, Joseph Warren (R Ohio) Jan. 30, 1836-April 22, 1932; House 1877-85, 1905-11; Speaker 1881-83.

KEIGHTLEY, Edwin William (R Mich.) Aug. 7, 1843-May 4, 1926; House 1877-79.

KEIM, George May (uncle of William High Keim) (D Pa.) March 23, 1805-June 10, 1861; House March 17, 1838-43.

KEIM, William High (nephew of George May Keim) (D Pa.) June 13, 1813-May 18, 1862; House Dec. 7, 1858-59.

KEISTER, Abraham Lincoln (R Pa.) Sept. 10, 1852-May 26, 1917; House 1913-17.

KEITH, Hastings (R Mass.) Nov. 22, 1915-___; House 1959-73.

KEITT, Laurence Massillon (D S.C.) Oct. 4, 1824-June 4, 1864; House 1853-July 16, 1856; Aug. 6, 1856-Dec. 1860.

KELIHER, John Austin (D Mass.) Nov. 6, 1866-Sept. 20, 1938; House 1903-11.

KELLER, Kent Ellsworth (D Ill.) June 4, 1867-Sept. 3, 1954; House 1931-41.

KELLER, Oscar Edward (IR Minn.) July 30, 1878-Nov. 21, 1927; House July 1, 1919-27.

KELLEY, Augustine Bernard (D Pa.) July 9, 1883-Nov. 20, 1957; House 1941-Nov. 20, 1957.

KELLEY, Harrison (R Kan.) May 12, 1836-July 24, 1897; House Dec. 2, 1889-91.

KELLEY, John Edward (D/PP S.D.) March 27, 1853-Aug. 5, 1941; House 1897-99.

KELLEY, Patrick Henry (R Mich.) Oct. 7, 1867-Sept. 11, 1925; House 1913-23.

KELLEY, William Darrah (R Pa.) April 12, 1814-Jan. 9, 1890; House 1861-Jan. 9, 1890.

KELLOGG, Charles (— N.Y.) Oct. 3, 1773-May 11, 1842; House 1825-27.

KELLOGG, Francis William (R Mich./Ala.) May 30, 1810-Jan. 13, 1879; House 1859-65 (Mich.); July 22, 1868-69 (Ala.).

KELLOGG, Frank Billings (R Minn.) Dec. 22, 1856-Dec. 21, 1937; Senate 1917-23; Secy. of State 1925-29.

KELLOGG, Orlando (W N.Y.) June 18, 1809-Aug. 24, 1865; Houes 1847-49; 1863-Aug. 24, 1865.

KELLOGG, Stephen Wright (R Conn.) April 5, 1822-Jan. 27, 1904; House 1869-73.

KELLOGG, William (R Ill.) July 8, 1814-Dec. 20, 1872; House 1857-63.

KELLOGG, William Pitt (R La.) Dec. 8, 1831-Aug. 10, 1918; Senate July 9, 1868-Nov. 1, 1872, 1877-83; House 1883-85; Gov. 1873-77.

KELLY, Edna Flannery (D N.Y.) Aug. 20, 1906-___; House Nov. 8, 1949-69.

KELLY, Edward Austin (D Ill.) April 3, 1892-Aug. 30, 1969; House 1931-43, 1945-47.

KELLY, George Bradshaw (D N.Y.) Dec. 12, 1900-June 26, 1971; House 1937-39.

KELLY, James (— Pa.) July 17, 1760-Feb. 4, 1819; House 1805-09.

KELLY, James Kerr (D Ore.) Feb. 16, 1819-Sept. 15, 1903; Senate 1871-77.

KELLY, John (D N.Y.) April 21, 1821-June 1, 1886; House 1855-Dec. 25, 1858.

KELLY, Melville Clyde (R Pa.) Aug. 4, 1883-April 29, 1935; House 1913-15, 1917-35.

KELLY, Richard (R Fla.) July 31, 1924-___; House 1975-___.

KELLY, William (— Ala.) 1770-1832; Senate Dec. 12, 1822-25.

KELSEY, William Henry (R N.Y.) Oct. 2, 1812-April 20, 1879; House 1855-59, 1867-71 (1855-59 Whig, 1867-71 Republican).

KELSO, John Russell (IRad. Mo.) March 23, 1831-Jan. 26, 1891; House 1865-67.

KEM, James Preston (R Mo.) April 2, 1890-Feb. 24, 1965; Senate 1947-53.

KEM, Omar Madison (P Neb.) Nov. 13, 1855-Feb. 13, 1942; House 1891-97.

KEMBLE, Gouverneur (D N.Y.) Jan. 25, 1786-Sept. 16, 1875; House 1837-41.

KEMP, Bolivar Edwards (D La.) Dec. 28, 1871-June 19, 1933; House 1925-June 19, 1933.

KEMP, Jack French (R N.Y.) July 13, 1935-___; House 1971-___.

KEMPSHALL, Thomas (W N.Y.) about 1796-Jan. 14, 1865; House 1839-41.

KENAN, Thomas (D N.C.) Feb. 26, 1771-Oct. 22, 1843; House 1805-11.

KENDALL, Charles West (D Nev.) April 22, 1828-June 25, 1914; House 1871-75.

KENDALL, Elva Roscoe (R Ky.) Feb. 14, 1893-Jan. 29, 1968; House 1929-31.

KENDALL, John Wilkerson (father of Joseph Morgan Kendall) (D Ky.) June 26, 1834-March 7, 1892; House 1891-March 7, 1892.

KENDALL, Jonas (father of Joseph Gowing Kendall) (F Mass.) Oct. 27, 1757-Oct. 22, 1844; House 1819-21.

KENDALL, Joseph Gowing (son of Jonas Kendall) (— Mass.) Oct. 27, 1788-Oct. 2, 1847; House 1829-33.

KENDALL, Joseph Morgan (son of John Wilkerson Kendall) (D Ky.) May 12, 1863-Nov. 5, 1933; House April 21, 1892-93, 1895-Feb. 18, 1897.

KENDALL, Nathan Edward (R Iowa) March 17, 1868-Nov. 5, 1936; House 1909-13; Gov. 1921-25.

KENDALL, Samuel Austin (R Pa.) Nov. 1, 1859-Jan. 8, 1933; House 1919-Jan. 8, 1933.

KENDRICK, John Benjamin (D Wyo.) Sept. 6, 1857-Nov. 3, 1933; Senate 1917-Nov. 3, 1933; Gov. 1915-17.

KENNA, John Edward (D W.Va.) April 10, 1848-Jan. 11, 1893; House 1877-83; Senate 1883-Jan. 11, 1893.

KENNEDY, Ambrose (R R.I.) Dec. 1, 1875-March 10, 1967; House 1913-23.

KENNEDY, Ambrose Jerome (D Md.) Jan. 6, 1893-Aug. 29, 1950; House Nov. 8, 1932-41.

KENNEDY, Andrew (cousin of Case Broderick) (D Ind.) July 24, 1810-Dec. 31, 1847; House 1841-47.

KENNEDY, Anthony (brother of John Pendleton Kennedy) (U Md.) Dec. 21, 1810-July 31, 1892; Senate 1857-63.

KENNEDY, Charles Augustus (R Iowa) March 24, 1869-Jan. 10, 1951; House 1907-21.

KENNEDY, Edward Moore (brother of John Fitzgerald Kennedy and Robert Francis Kennedy and grandson of John Francis Fitzgerald) (D Mass.) Feb. 22, 1932-___; Senate Nov. 7, 1962-___.

KENNEDY, James (R Ohio) Sept. 3, 1853-Nov. 9, 1928; House 1903-11.

KENNEDY, John Fitzgerald (brother of Edward Moore Kennedy and Robert Francis Kennedy and grandson of John Francis Fitzgerald) (D Mass.) May 29, 1917-Nov. 22, 1963; House 1947-53; Senate 1953-Dec. 22, 1960; President 1961-Nov. 22, 1963.

KENNEDY, John Lauderdale (R Neb.) Oct. 27, 1854-Aug. 30, 1946; House 1905-07.

KENNEDY, John Pendleton (brother of Anthony Kennedy) (W Md.) Oct. 25, 1795-Aug. 18, 1870; House April 25, 1838-39, 1841-45; Secy. of the Navy 1852-53.

KENNEDY, Martin John (D N.Y.) Aug. 29, 1892-Oct. 27, 1955; House March 11, 1930-45.

KENNEDY, Michael Joseph (D N.Y.) Oct. 25, 1897-Nov. 1, 1949; House 1939-43.

KENNEDY, Robert Francis (brother of Edward Moore Kennedy and John Fitzgerald Kennedy and grandson of John Francis Fitzgerald) (D N.Y.) Nov. 20, 1925-June 6, 1968; Senate 1965-June 6, 1968; Atty. Gen. 1961-64.

KENNEDY, Robert Patterson (R Ohio) Jan. 23, 1840-May 6, 1918; House 1887-91.

KENNEDY, William (F N.C.) July 31, 1768-Oct. 11, 1834; House 1803-05, 1809-11, Jan. 30, 1813-15.

KENNEDY, William (D Conn.) Dec. 19, 1854-June 19, 1918; House 1913-15.

KENNETT, Luther Martin (AP Mo.) March 15, 1807-April 12, 1873; House 1855-57.

KENNEY, Edward Aloysius (D N.J.) Aug. 11, 1884-Jan. 27, 1938; House 1933-Jan. 27, 1938.

KENNEY, Richard Rolland (D Del.) Sept. 9, 1856-Aug. 14, 1931; Senate Jan. 19, 1897-1901.

KENNON, William Sr. (cousin of William Kennon Jr.) (D Ohio) May 14, 1793-Nov. 2, 1881; House 1829-33, 1835-37.

KENNON, William Jr. (cousin of William Kennon Sr.) (D Ohio) June 12, 1802-Oct. 19, 1867; House 1847-49.

KENT, Everett (D Pa.) Nov. 15, 1888-Oct. 13, 1963; House 1923-25, 1927-29.

KENT, Joseph (NR Md.) Jan. 14, 1779-Nov. 24, 1837; House 1811-15, 1819-Jan. 6, 1826 (1811-15 Federalist, 1819-26 Democrat); Senate 1833-Nov. 24, 1837 (NR); Gov. 1826-29.

KENT, Moss (F N.Y.) April 3, 1766-May 30, 1838; House 1813-17.

KENT, William (I Calif.) March 29, 1864-March 13, 1928; House 1911-17 (1911-13 Progressive Republican, 1913-17 Independent).

KENYON, William Scheuneman (R N.Y.) Dec. 13, 1820-Feb. 10, 1896; House 1859-61.

KENYON, William Squire (R Iowa) June 10, 1869-Sept. 9, 1933; Senate April 12, 1911-Feb. 24, 1922.

KEOGH, Eugene James (D N.Y.) Aug. 30, 1907-__; House 1937-67.

KERN, Frederick John (D Ill.) Sept. 6, 1864-Nov. 9, 1931; House 1901-03.

KERN, John Worth (D Ind.) Dec. 20, 1849-Aug. 17, 1917; Senate 1911-17.

KERNAN, Francis (D N.Y.) Jan. 14, 1816-Sept. 7, 1892; House 1863-65; Senate 1875-81.

KERR, Daniel (R Iowa) June 18, 1836-Oct. 8, 1916; House 1887-91.

KERR, James (D Pa.) Oct. 2, 1851-Oct. 31, 1908; House 1889-91.

KERR, John (father of John Kerr Jr., cousin of Bartlett Yancey, and grand-uncle of John Hosea Kerr) (D Va.) Aug. 4, 1782-Sept. 29, 1842; House 1813-15, Oct. 30, 1815-17.

KERR, John Jr. (son of John Kerr) (W N.C.) Feb. 10, 1811-Sept. 5, 1879; House 1853-55.

KERR, John Bozman (son of John Leeds Kerr) (W Md.) March 5, 1809-Jan. 27, 1878; House 1849-51.

KERR, John Hosea (grandnephew of John Kerr) (D N.C.) Dec. 31, 1873-June 21, 1958; House Nov. 6, 1923-53.

KERR, John Leeds (father of John Bozman Kerr) (W Md.) Jan. 15, 1780-Feb. 21, 1844; House 1825-29, 1831-33; Senate Jan. 5, 1841-43.

KERR, Joseph (D Ohio) 1765-Aug. 22, 1837; Senate Dec. 10, 1814-15.

KERR, Josiah Leeds (R Md.) Jan. 10, 1861-Sept. 27, 1920; House Nov. 6, 1900-01.

KERR, Michael Crawford (D Ind.) March 15, 1827-Aug. 19, 1876; House 1865-73, 1875-Aug. 19, 1876; Speaker 1875-76.

KERR, Robert Samuel (D Okla.) Sept. 11, 1896-Jan. 1, 1963; Senate 1949-Jan. 1, 1963; Gov. 1943-47.

KERR, Winfield Scott (R Ohio) June 23, 1852-Sept. 11, 1917; House 1895-1901.

KERRIGAN, James (D N.Y.) Dec. 25, 1828-Nov. 1, 1899; House 1861-63.

KERSHAW, John (D S.C.) Sept. 12, 1765-Aug. 4, 1829; House 1813-15.

KERSTEN, Charles Joseph (R Wis.) May 26, 1902-Oct. 31, 1972; House 1947-49; 1951-55.

KETCHAM, John Clark (R Mich.) Jan. 1, 1873-Dec. 4, 1941; House 1921-33.

KETCHAM, John Henry (R N.Y.) Dec. 21, 1832-Nov. 4, 1906; House 1865-73, 1877-93, 1897-Nov. 4, 1906.

KETCHUM, William Matthew (R Calif.) Sept. 2, 1921-__; House 1973-__.

KETCHUM, Winthrop Welles (R Pa.) June 29, 1820-Dec. 6, 1879; House 1875-July 19, 1876.

KETTNER, William (D Calif.) Nov. 20, 1864-Nov. 11, 1930; House 1913-21.

KEY, David McKendree (D Tenn.) Jan. 27, 1824-Feb. 3, 1900; Senate Aug. 18, 1875-Jan. 19, 1877; Postmaster Gen. 1877-80.

KEY, John Alexander (D Ohio) Dec. 30, 1871-March 4, 1954; House 1913-19.

KEY, Philip (cousin of Philip Barton Key and great-grandfather of Barnes Compton) (— Md.) 1750-Jan. 4, 1820; House 1791-93.

KEY, Philip Barton (cousin of Philip Key) (F Md.) April 12, 1757-July 28, 1815; House 1807-13.

KEYES, Elias (R Vt.) April 14, 1758-July 9, 1844; House 1821-23.

KEYES, Henry Wilder (R N.H.) May 23, 1863-June 19, 1938; Senate 1919-37; Gov. 1917-19.

KEYS, Martha Elizabeth (wife of Andrew Jacobs Jr.) (D Kan.) Aug. 10, 1930-__; House 1975-__.

KIDDER, David (W Maine) Dec. 8, 1787-Nov. 1, 1860; House 1823-27.

KIDDER, Jefferson Parish (R Dakota) June 4, 1815-Oct. 2, 1883; House (Terr. Del.) 1875-79.

KIDWELL, Zedekiah (D Va.) Jan. 4, 1814-April 27, 1872; House 1853-57.

KIEFER, Andrew Robert (R Minn.) May 25, 1832-May 1, 1904; House 1893-97.

KIEFNER, Charles Edward (R Mo.) Nov. 25, 1869-Dec. 13, 1942; House 1925-27, 1929-31.

KIESS, Edgar Raymond (R Pa.) Aug. 26, 1875-July 20, 1930; House 1913-July 20, 1930.

KILBOURNE, James (D Ohio) Oct. 19, 1770-April 9, 1850; House 1813-17.

KILBURN, Clarence Evans (R N.Y.) April 13, 1893-May 20, 1975; House Feb. 13, 1940-65.

KILDAY, Paul Joseph (D Texas) March 29, 1900-Oct. 12, 1968; House 1939-Sept. 24, 1961.

KILGORE, Constantine Buckley (D Texas) Feb. 20, 1835-Sept. 23, 1897; House 1887-95.

KILGORE, Daniel (D Ohio) 1793-Dec. 12, 1851; House Dec. 1, 1834-July 4, 1838.

KILGORE, David (R Ind.) April 3, 1804-Jan. 22, 1879; House 1857-61.

KILGORE, Harley Martin (D W.Va.) Jan. 11, 1893-Feb. 28, 1956; Senate 1941-Feb. 28, 1956.

KILGORE, Joe Madison (D Texas) Dec. 10, 1918-—; House 1955-65.

KILLE, Joseph (D N.J.) April 12, 1790-March 1, 1865; House 1839-41.

KILLINGER, John Weinland (R Pa.) Sept. 18, 1824-June 30, 1896; House 1859-63, 1871-75, 1877-81.

KIMBALL, Alanson Mellen (R Wis.) March 12, 1827-May 26, 1913; House 1875-77.

KIMBALL, Henry Mahlon (R Mich.) Aug. 27, 1878-Oct. 19, 1935; House Jan. 3-Oct. 19, 1935.

KIMBALL, William Preston (D Ky.) Nov. 4, 1857-Feb. 24, 1926; House 1907-09.

KIMMEL, William (D Md.) Aug. 15, 1812-Dec. 28, 1886; House 1877-81.

KINCAID, John (D Ky.) Feb. 15, 1791-Feb. 7, 1873; House 1829-31.

KINCHELOE, David Hayes (D Ky.) April 9, 1877-April 16, 1950; House 1915-Oct. 5, 1930.

KINDEL, George John (D Colo.) March 2, 1855-Feb. 28, 1930; House 1913-15.

KINDNESS, Thomas Norman (R Ohio) Aug. 26, 1929-__; House 1975-__.

KINDRED, John Joseph (D N.Y.) July 15, 1864-Oct. 23, 1937; House 1911-13, 1921-29.

KING, Adam (D Pa.) 1790-May 6, 1835; House 1827-33.

KING, Andrew (D Mo.) March 20, 1812-Nov. 18, 1895; House 1871-73.

KING, Austin Augustus (UD Mo.) Sept. 21, 1802-April 22, 1870; House 1863-65; Gov. 1848-53.

KING, Carleton James (R N.Y.) June 15, 1904-___; House 1961-Dec. 31, 1974.

KING, Cecil Rhodes (D Calif.) Jan. 13, 1898-March 17, 1974; House Aug. 25, 1942-69.

KING, Cyrus (half brother of Rufus King) (F Mass.) Sept. 6, 1772-April 25, 1817; House 1813-17.

KING, Daniel Putnam (W Mass.) Jan. 8, 1801-July 25, 1850; House 1843-July 25, 1850.

KING, David Sjodahl (son of William H. King) (D Utah) June 20, 1917-___; House 1959-63, 1965-67.

KING, Edward John (R Ill.) July 1, 1867-Feb. 17, 1929; House 1915-Feb. 17, 1929.

KING, George Gordon (W R.I.) June 9, 1807-July 17, 1870; House 1849-53.

KING, Henry (brother of Thomas Butler King and uncle of John Floyd King) (D Pa.) July 6, 1790-July 13, 1861; House 1831-35.

KING, James Gore (son of Rufus King and brother of John Alsop King) (W N.J.) May 8, 1791-Oct. 3, 1853; House 1849-51.

KING, John (D N.Y.) 1775-Sept. 1, 1836; House 1831-33.

KING, John Alsop (son of Rufus King and brother of James Gore King) (W N.Y.) Jan. 3, 1788-July 7, 1867; House 1849-51; Gov. 1857-59 (R).

KING, John Floyd (son of Thomas Butler King and nephew of Henry King) (D La.) April 20, 1842-May 8, 1915; House 1879-87.

KING, John Pendleton (D Ga.) April 3, 1799-March 19, 1888; Senate Nov. 21, 1833-Nov. 1, 1837.

KING, Karl Clarence (R Pa.) Jan. 26, 1897-April 16, 1974; House Nov. 6, 1951-57.

KING, Perkins (D N.Y.) Jan. 12, 1784-Nov. 29, 1875; House 1829-31.

KING, Preston (R N.Y.) Oct. 14, 1806-Nov. 12, 1865; House 1843-47, 1849-53 (D); Senate 1857-63 (R).

KING, Rufus (half brother of Cyrus King and father of John Alsop King and James Gore King) (F N.Y.) March 24, 1755-April 29, 1827; Senate July 16, 1789-May 23, 1796; 1813-25; Cont. Cong. (Mass.) 1784-87.

KING, Rufus H. (W N.Y.) Jan. 20, 1820-Sept. 13, 1890; House 1855-57.

KING, Samuel Wilder (R Hawaii) Dec. 17, 1886-March 24, 1959; House (Terr. Del.) 1935-43; Terr. Gov. 1953-57.

KING, Thomas Butler (brother of Henry King and father of John Floyd King) (W Ga.) Aug. 27, 1800-May 10, 1864; House 1839-43, 1845-50.

KING, William Henry (father of David S. King) (D Utah) June 3, 1863-Nov. 27, 1949; House 1897-99, April 2, 1900-01; Senate 1917-41.

KING, William Rufus deVane (D N.C./Ala.) April 7, 1786-April 18, 1853; House 1811-Nov. 4, 1816 (N.C.); Senate Dec. 14, 1819-April 15, 1844, July 1, 1848-Dec. 20, 1852 (Ala.); President pro tempore 1835-41, 1849-52; Vice President March 4-April 18, 1853.

KING, William Smith (R Minn.) Dec. 16, 1828-Feb. 24, 1900; House 1875-77.

KINGSBURY, William Wallace (D Minn.) June 4, 1828-April 17, 1892; House (Terr. Del.) 1857-May 11, 1858.

KINKAID, Moses Pierce (R Neb.) Jan. 24, 1856-July 6, 1922; House 1903-July 6, 1922.

KINKEAD, Eugene Francis (D N.J.) March 27, 1876-Sept. 6, 1960; House 1909-Feb. 4, 1915.

KINNARD, George L. (D Ind.) 1803-Nov. 26, 1836; House 1833-Nov. 26, 1836.

KINNEY, John Fitch (D Utah) April 2, 1816-Aug. 16, 1902; House (Terr. Del.) 1863-65.

KINSELLA, Thomas (D N.Y.) Dec. 31, 1832-Feb. 11, 1884; House 1871-73.

KINSEY, Charles (— N.J.) 1773-June 25, 1849; House 1817-19, Feb. 2, 1820-21.

KINSEY, William Medcalf (R Mo.) Oct. 28, 1846-June 20, 1931; House 1889-91.

KINSLEY, Martin (— Mass.) June 2, 1754-June 20, 1835; House 1819-21.

KINZER, John Roland (R Pa.) March 28, 1874-July 25, 1955; House Jan. 28, 1930-47.

KIPP, George Washington (D Pa.) March 28, 1847-July 24, 1911; House 1907-09, March 4-July 24, 1911.

KIRBY, William Fosgate (D Ark.) Nov. 16, 1867-July 26, 1934; Senate Nov. 8, 1916-21.

KIRK, Andrew Jackson (R Ky.) March 19, 1866-May 25, 1933; House Feb. 13, 1926-27.

KIRKLAND, Joseph (— N.Y.) Jan. 18, 1770-Jan. 26, 1844; House 1821-23.

KIRKPATRICK, Littleton (D N.J.) Oct. 19, 1797-Aug. 15, 1859; House 1843-45.

KIRKPATRICK, Sanford (D Iowa) Feb. 11, 1842-Feb. 13, 1932; House 1913-15.

KIRKPATRICK, Snyder Solomon (R Kan.) Feb. 21, 1848-April 5, 1909; House 1895-97.

KIRKPATRICK, William (D N.Y.) Nov. 7, 1769-Sept. 2, 1832; House 1807-09.

KIRKPATRICK, William Huntington (son of William Sebring Kirkpatrick) (R Pa.) Oct. 2, 1885-Nov. 28, 1970; House 1921-23.

KIRKPATRICK, William Sebring (father of William Huntington Kirkpatrick) (R Pa.) April 21, 1844-Nov. 3, 1932; House 1897-99.

KIRKWOOD, Samuel Jordan (R Iowa) Dec. 20, 1813-Sept. 1, 1894; Senate Jan. 13, 1866-67, 1877-March 7, 1881; Gov. 1860-64, 1876-77; Secy. of the Interior 1881-82.

KIRTLAND, Dorrance (— N.Y.) July 28, 1770-May 23, 1840; House 1817-19.

KIRWAN, Michael Joseph (D Ohio) Dec. 2, 1886-July 27, 1970; House 1937-July 27, 1970.

KISSEL, John (R N.Y.) July 31, 1864-Oct. 3, 1938; House 1921-23.

KITCHELL, Aaron (D N.J.) July 10, 1744-June 25, 1820; House 1791-93, Jan. 29, 1795-97, 1799-1801; Senate 1805-March 12, 1809.

KITCHEN, Bethuel Middleton (R W.Va.) March 21, 1812-Dec. 15, 1895; House 1867-69.

KITCHENS, Wade Hampton (D Ark.) Dec. 26, 1878-Aug. 22, 1966; House 1937-41.

KITCHIN, Alvin Paul (nephew of Claude Kitchin and William Walton Kitchin and grandson of William Hodges Kitchin) (D N.C.) Sept. 13, 1908-—; House 1957-63.

KITCHIN, Claude (son of William Hodges Kitchin, brother of William Walton Kitchin and uncle of A. Paul Kitchin) (D N.C.) March 24, 1869-May 31, 1923; House 1901-May 31, 1923.

KITCHIN, William Hodges (father of Claude Kitchin and William Walton Kitchin, and grandfather of A. Paul Kitchin) (D N.C.) Dec. 22, 1837-Feb. 2, 1901; House 1879-81.

KITCHIN, William Walton (son of William Hodges Kitchin, brother of Claude Kitchin, and uncle of A. Paul Kitchin) (D N.C.) Oct. 9, 1866-Nov. 9, 1924; House 1897-Jan. 11, 1909; Gov. 1909-13.

KITTERA, John Wilkes (father of Thomas Kittera) (F Pa.) Nov. 1752-June 6, 1801; House 1791-1801.

KITTERA, Thomas (son of John Wilkes Kittera) (F Pa.) March 21, 1789-June 16, 1839; House Oct. 10, 1826-27.

KITTREDGE, Alfred Beard (R S.D.) March 28, 1861-May 4, 1911; Senate July 11, 1901-09.

KITTREDGE, George Washington (AND N.H.) Jan. 31, 1805-March 6, 1881; House 1853-55.

KLEBERG, Richard Mifflin Sr. (nephew of Rudolph Kleberg and cousin of Robert Christian Eckhardt) (D Texas) Nov. 18, 1887-May 8, 1955; House Nov. 24, 1931-45.

KLEBERG, Rudolph (great uncle of Robert Christian Eckhardt and uncle of Richard Mifflin Kleberg Sr.) (D Texas) June 26, 1847-Dec. 28, 1924; House April 7, 1896-1903.

KLECZKA, John Casimir (R Wis.) May 6, 1885-April 21, 1959; House 1919-23.

KLEIN, Arthur George (D N.Y.) Aug. 8, 1904-Feb. 20, 1968; House July 29, 1941-45, Feb. 19, 1946-Dec. 31, 1956.

KLEINER, John Jay (D Ind.) Feb. 8, 1845-April 8, 1911; House 1883-87.

KLEPPE, Thomas S. (R N.D.) July 1, 1919-___; House 1967-71; Sec. of Interior, July 17, 1975-—.

KLEPPER, Frank B. (R Mo.) June 22, 1864-Aug. 4, 1933; House 1905-07.

KLINE, Ardolph Loges (R N.Y.) Feb. 21, 1858-Oct. 13, 1930; House 1921-23.

KLINE, Isaac Clinton (R Pa.) Aug. 18, 1858-Dec. 2, 1947; House 1921-23.

KLINE, Marcus Charles Lawrence (D Pa.) March 26, 1855-March 10, 1911; House 1903-07.

KLINGENSMITH, John Jr. (D Pa.) 1785- ?; House 1835-39.

KLOEB, Frank LeBlond (grandson of Francis C. LeBlond) (D Ohio) June 16, 1890-—; House 1933-Aug. 19, 1937.

KLOTZ, Robert (D Pa.) Oct. 27, 1819-May 1, 1895; House 1879-83.

KLUCZYNSKI, John Carl (D Ill.) Feb. 15, 1896-Jan. 26, 1975; House 1951-Jan. 26, 1975.

KLUTTZ, Theodore Franklin (D N.C.) Oct. 4, 1848-Nov. 18, 1918; House 1899-1905.

KNAPP, Anthony Lausett (brother of Robert McCarty Knapp) (D Ill.) June 14, 1828-May 24, 1881; House Dec. 12, 1861-65.

KNAPP, Charles (father of Charles Junius Knapp) (R N.Y.) Oct. 8, 1797-May 14, 1880; House 1869-71.

KNAPP, Charles Junius (son of Charles Knapp) (R N.Y.) June 30, 1845-June 1, 1916; House 1889-91.

KNAPP, Charles Luman (R N.Y.) July 4, 1847-Jan. 3, 1929; House Nov. 5, 1901-11.

KNAPP, Chauncey Langdon (R Mass.) Feb. 26, 1809-May 31, 1898; House 1855-59 (1855-57 American Party, 1857-59 Republican).

KNAPP, Robert McCarty (brother of Anthony Lausett Knapp) (D Ill.) April 21, 1831-June 24, 1889; House 1873-75, 1877-79.

KNICKERBOCKER, Herman (F N.Y.) July 27, 1779-Jan. 30, 1855; House 1809-11.

KNIFFIN, Frank Charles (D Ohio) April 26, 1894-April 30, 1968; House 1931-39.

KNIGHT, Charles Landon (R Ohio) June 18, 1867-Sept. 26, 1933; House 1921-23.

KNIGHT, Jonathan (W Pa.) Nov. 22, 1787-Nov. 22, 1858; House 1855-57.

KNIGHT, Nehemiah (father of Nehemiah Rice Knight) (A-F R.I.) March 23, 1746-June 13, 1808; House 1803-June 13, 1808.

KNIGHT, Nehemiah Rice (son of Nehemiah Knight) (D R.I.) Dec. 31, 1780-April 18, 1854; Senate Jan. 9, 1821-41 (1821-35 Anti-Federalist, 1835-41 Democrat); Gov. 1817-21 (A-F).

KNOPF, Philip (R Ill.) Nov. 18, 1847-Aug. 14, 1920; House 1903-09.

KNOTT, James Proctor (D Ky.) Aug. 29, 1830-June 18, 1911; House 1867-71, 1875-83; Gov. 1883-87.

KNOWLAND, Joseph Russell (father of William Fife Knowland) (R Calif.) Aug. 5, 1873-Feb. 1, 1966; House Nov. 8, 1904-15.

KNOWLAND, William Fife (son of Joseph Russell Knowland) (R Calif.) June 26, 1908-Feb. 23, 1974; Senate Aug. 26, 1945-59.

KNOWLES, Freeman Tulley (P S.D.) Oct. 10, 1846-June 1, 1910; House 1897-99.

KNOWLTON, Ebenezer (R Maine) Dec. 6, 1815-Sept. 10, 1874; House 1855-57.

KNOX, James (W Ill.) July 4, 1807-Oct. 8, 1876; House 1853-57.

KNOX, Philander Chase (R Pa.) May 6, 1853-Oct. 12, 1921; Senate June 10, 1904-March 4, 1909, 1917-Oct. 12, 1921; Atty. Gen. 1901-04; Secy. of State 1909-13.

KNOX, Samuel (R Mo.) March 21, 1815-March 7, 1905; House June 10, 1864-65.

KNOX, Victor Alfred (R Mich.) Jan. 13, 1899-__; House 1953-65.

KNOX, William Shadrach (R Mass.) Sept. 10, 1843-Sept. 21, 1914; House 1895-1903.

KNUTSON, Coya Gjesdal (D-FL Minn.) Aug. 22, 1912-__; House 1955-59.

KNUTSON, Harold (R Minn.) Oct. 20, 1880-Aug. 21, 1953; House 1917-49.

KOCH, Edward I. (D/L N.Y.) Dec. 12, 1924-__; House 1969-__.

KOCIALKOWSKI, Leo Paul (D Ill.) Aug. 16, 1882-Sept. 27, 1958; House 1933-43.

KONIG, George (D Md.) Jan. 26, 1865-May 31, 1913; House 1911-May 31, 1913.

KONOP, Thomas Frank (D Wis.) Aug. 17, 1879-Oct. 17, 1964; House 1911-17.

KOONTZ, William Henry (R Pa.) July 15, 1830-July 4, 1911; House July 18, 1866-69.

KOPP, Arthur William (R Wis.) Feb. 28, 1874-June 2, 1967; House 1909-13.

KOPP, William Frederick (R Iowa) June 20, 1869-Aug. 24, 1938; House 1921-33.

KOPPLEMANN, Herman Paul (D Conn.) May 1, 1880-Aug. 11, 1957; House 1933-39, 1941-43, 1945-47.

KORBLY, Charles Alexander (D Ind.) March 24, 1871-July 26, 1937; House 1909-15.

KORELL, Franklin Frederick (R Ore.) July 23, 1889-June 7, 1965; House Oct. 18, 1927-31.

KORNEGAY, Horace Robinson (D N.C.) March 12, 1924-__; House 1961-69.

KOWALSKI, Frank (D Conn.) Oct. 18, 1907-Oct. 11, 1974; House 1959-63.

KRAMER, Charles (D Calif.) April 18, 1879-Jan. 20, 1943; House 1933-43.

KRAUS, Milton (R Ind.) June 26, 1866-Nov. 18, 1942; House 1917-23.

KREBS, Jacob (D Pa.) March 13, 1782-Sept. 26, 1847; House Dec. 4, 1826-March 3, 1827.

KREBS, John Hans (D Calif.) Dec. 17, 1926-__; House 1975-__.

KREBS, Paul J. (D N.J.) May 26, 1912-__; House 1965-67.

KREIDER, Aaron Shenk (R Pa.) June 26, 1863-May 19, 1929; House 1913-23.

KREMER, George (— Pa.) Nov. 21, 1775-Sept. 11, 1854; House 1823-29.

KRIBBS, George Frederic (D Pa.) Nov. 8, 1846-Sept. 8, 1938; House 1891-95.

KRONMILLER, John (R Md.) Dec. 6, 1858-June 19, 1928; House 1909-11.

KRUEGER, Otto (R N.D.) Sept. 7, 1890-June 6, 1963; House 1953-59.

KRUEGER, Robert Charles (D Texas) Sept. 19, 1935-__; House 1975-__.

KRUSE, Edward H Jr. (D Ind.) Oct. 22, 1918-__; House 1949-51.

KUCHEL, Thomas Henry (R Calif.) Aug. 15, 1910-__; Senate Jan. 2, 1953-69.

KUHNS, Joseph Henry (W Pa.) Sept. 1800-Nov. 16, 1883; House 1851-53.

KULP, Monroe Henry (R Pa.) Oct. 23, 1858-Oct. 19, 1911; House 1895-99.

KUNKEL, Jacob Michael (D Md.) July 13, 1822-April 7, 1870; House 1857-61.

KUNKEL, John Christian (grandfather of John Crain Kunkel) (W Pa.) Sept. 18, 1816-Oct. 14, 1870; House 1855-59.

KUNKEL, John Crain (grandson of John Christian Kunkel, great-grandson of John Sergeant, and great-great-grandson of Jonathan Dickinson Sergeant and Robert Whitehill) (R Pa.) July 21, 1898-July 27, 1970; House 1939-51, May 16, 1961-Dec. 30, 1966.

KUNZ, Stanley Henry (D Ill.) Sept. 26, 1864-April 23, 1946; House 1921-31, April 5, 1932-33.

KUPFERMAN, Theodore R. (R N.Y.) May 12, 1920-__; House Feb. 8, 1966-69.

KURTZ, Jacob Banks (R Pa.) Oct. 31, 1867-Sept. 18, 1960; House 1923-35.

KURTZ, William Henry (D Pa.) Jan. 31, 1804-June 24, 1868; House 1851-55.

KUSTERMANN, Gustav (R Wis.) May 24, 1850-Dec. 25, 1919; House 1907-11.

KUYKENDALL, Andrew Jackson (R Ill.) March 3, 1815-May 11, 1891; House 1865-67.

KUYKENDALL, Dan H. (R Tenn.) July 9, 1924-__; House 1967-75.

KVALE, Ole Juulson (father of Paul John Kvale (FL Minn.) Feb. 6, 1869-Sept. 11, 1929; House 1923-Sept. 11, 1929 (1923-25 Independent Republican, 1925-29 Farmer Laborite).

KVALE, Ole Juulson (father of Paul John Kvale) (FL Minn.) March 27, 1896-June 14, 1960; House Oct. 16, 1929-39.

KYL, John Henry (R Iowa) May 9, 1919-__; House Dec. 15, 1959-65, 1967-73.

KYLE, James Henderson (I S.D.) Feb. 24, 1854-July 1, 1901; Senate 1891-July 1, 1901.

KYLE, John Curtis (D Miss.) July 17, 1851-July 6, 1913; House 1891-97.

KYLE, Thomas Barton (R Ohio) March 10, 1856-Aug. 13, 1915; House 1901-05.

KYROS, Peter N. (D Maine) July 11, 1925-__; House 1967-75.

L

LA BRANCHE, Alcee Louis (D La.) 1806-Aug. 17, 1861; House 1843-45.

LACEY, Edward Samuel (R Mich.) Nov. 26, 1835-Oct. 2, 1916; House 1881-85.

LACEY, John Fletcher (R Iowa) May 30, 1841-Sept. 29, 1913; House 1889-91, 1893-1907.

LACOCK, Abner (D Pa.) July 9, 1770-April 12, 1837; House 1811-13; Senate 1813-19.

LADD, Edwin Freemont (Nonpart. R N.D.) Dec. 13, 1859-June 22, 1925; Senate 1921-June 22, 1925.

LADD, George Washington (D/G Maine) Sept. 28, 1818-Jan. 30, 1892; House 1879-83.

LA DOW, George Augustus (D Ore.) March 18, 1826-May 1, 1875; House March 4-May 1, 1875.

LAFALCE, John Joseph (D N.Y.) Oct. 6, 1939-__; House 1975-__.

LAFEAN, Daniel Franklin (R Pa.) Feb. 7, 1861-April 18, 1922; House 1903-13, 1915-17.

LAFFERTY, Abraham Walter (PR Ore.) June 10, 1875-Jan. 15, 1964; House 1911-15.

LAFFOON, Polk (D Ky.) Oct. 24, 1844-Oct. 22, 1906; House 1885-89.

LAFLIN, Addison Henry (R N.Y.) Oct. 24, 1823-Sept. 24, 1878; House 1865-71.

LA FOLLETTE, Charles Marion (great-grandson of William Heilman) (R Ind.) Feb. 27, 1898-__; House 1943-47.

LA FOLLETTE, Robert Marion (R Wis.) June 14, 1855-June 18, 1925; House 1885-91; Senate Jan. 2, 1906-June 18, 1925; Gov. 1901-06.

LA FOLLETTE, Robert Marion Jr. (son of the preceding) (Prog. Wis.) Feb. 6, 1895-Feb. 24, 1953; Senate Sept. 30, 1925-35 (R/Prog.), 1935-47 (Prog.).

LA FOLLETTE, William Leroy (R Wash.) Nov. 30, 1860-Dec. 20, 1934; House 1911-19.

LAFORE, John Armand Jr. (R Pa.) May 25, 1905-__; House Nov. 5, 1957-61.

LAGAN, Matthew Diamond (D La.) June 20, 1829-April 8, 1901; House 1887-89, 1891-93.

LAGOMARSINO, Robert John (R Calif.) Sept. 4, 1926-__; House March 5, 1974-__.

LA GUARDIA, Fiorello Henry (R/Prog. N.Y.) Dec. 11, 1882-Sept. 20, 1947; House 1917-19, 1923-33 (1917-19 and 1923-25 Republican, 1925-27 Socialist, 1927-33 Republican/Progressive).

LAHM, Samuel (D Ohio) April 22, 1812-June 16, 1876; House 1847-49.

LAIDLAW, William Grant (R N.Y.) Jan. 1, 1840-Aug. 19, 1908; House 1887-91.

LAIRD, James (R Neb.) June 20, 1849-Aug. 17, 1889; House 1883-Aug. 17, 1889.

LAIRD, Melvin Robert (R Wis.) Sept. 1, 1922-__; House 1953-Jan. 21, 1969; Secy. of Defense 1969-73.

LAIRD, William Ramsey III (D W.Va.) June 2, 1916-Jan. 7, 1974; Senate March 13-Nov. 6, 1956.

LAKE, William Augustus (W Miss.) Jan. 6, 1808-Oct. 15, 1861; House 1855-57.

LAMAR, Henry Graybill (D Ga.) July 10, 1798-Sept. 10, 1861; House Dec. 7, 1829-33.

LAMAR, James Robert (D Mo.) March 28, 1866-Aug. 11, 1923; House 1903-05; 1907-09.

LAMAR, John Basil (D Ga.) Nov. 5, 1812-Sept. 15, 1862; House March 4-July 29, 1843.

LAMAR, Lucius Quintus Cincinnatus (uncle of William Bailey Lamar and cousin of Absalom Harris Chappell) (D Miss.) Sept. 17, 1825-Jan. 23, 1893; House 1857-December 1860, 1873-77; Senate 1877-March 6, 1885; Secy. of the Int. 1885-88, Assoc. Justice of the Supreme Court 1888-93.

LAMAR, William Bailey (nephew of Lucius Quintus Cincinnatus Lamar) (D Fla.) June 12, 1853-Sept. 26, 1928; House 1903-09.

LAMB, Alfred William (D Mo.) March 18, 1824-April 29, 1888; House 1853-55.

LAMB, John (D Va.) June 12, 1840-Nov. 21, 1924; House 1897-1913.

LAMB, John Edward (D Ind.) Dec. 26, 1852-Aug. 23, 1914; House 1883-85.

LAMBERT, John (D N.J.) Feb. 24, 1746-Feb. 4, 1823; House 1805-09; Senate 1809-15.

LAMBERTSON, William Purnell (R Kan.) March 23, 1880-Oct. 26, 1957; House 1929-45.

LAMBETH, John Walter (D N.C.) Jan. 10, 1896-Jan. 12, 1961; House 1931-39.

LAMISON, Charles Nelson (D Ohio) 1826-April 24, 1896; House 1871-75.

LAMNECK, Arthur Philip (D Ohio) March 12, 1880-April 23, 1944; House 1931-39.

LAMPERT, Florian (R Wis.) July 8, 1863-July 18, 1930; House Nov. 5, 1918-July 18, 1930.

LAMPORT, William Henry (R N.Y.) May 27, 1811-July 21, 1891; House 1871-75.

LANCASTER, Columbia (D Wash.) Aug. 26, 1803-Sept. 15, 1893; House (Terr. Del.) April 12, 1854-55.

LANDERS, Franklin (D Ind.) March 22, 1825-Sept. 10, 1901; House 1875-77.

LANDERS, George Marcellus (D Conn.) Feb. 22, 1813-March 27, 1895; House 1875-79.

LANDES, Silas Zephaniah (D Ill.) May 15, 1842-May 23, 1910; House 1885-89.

LANDGREBE, Earl F. (R Ind.) Jan. 21, 1916-__; House 1969-75.

LANDIS, Charles Beary (brother of Frederick Landis) (R Ind.) July 9, 1858-April 24, 1922; House 1897-1909.

LANDIS, Frederick (brother of Charles Beary Landis) (R Ind.) Aug. 18, 1872-Nov. 15, 1934; House 1903-07.

LANDIS, Gerald Wayne (R Ind.) Feb. 23, 1895-Sept. 6, 1971; House 1939-49.

LANDRUM, John Morgan (D La.) July 3, 1815-Oct. 18, 1861; House 1859-61.

LANDRUM, Phillip Mitchell (D Ga.) Sept. 10, 1909-__; House 1953-__.

LANDRY, Joseph Aristide (W La.) July 10, 1817-March 9, 1881; House 1851-53.

LANDY, James (D Pa.) Oct. 13, 1813-July 25, 1875; House 1857-59.

LANE, Amos (father of James Henry Lane) (D Ind.) March 1, 1778-Sept. 2, 1849; House 1833-37.

LANE, Edward (D Ill.) March 27, 1842-Oct. 30, 1912; House 1887-95.

LANE, Harry (grandson of Joseph Lane and nephew of LaFayette Lane) (D Ore.) Aug. 28, 1855-May 23, 1917; Senate 1913-May 23, 1917.

LANE, Henry Smith (R Ind.) Feb. 24, 1811-June 18, 1881; House Aug. 3, 1840-43 (W); Senate 1861-67 (R); Gov. Jan. 1861 (R).

LANE, James Henry (son of Amos Lane) (D Ind./R Kan.) June 22, 1814-July 11, 1866; House 1853-55 (D Ind.); Senate April 4, 1861-July 11, 1866 (R Kan.).

LANE, Joseph (father of LaFayette Lane and grandfather of Harry Lane) (D Ore.) Dec. 14, 1801-April 19, 1881; House (Terr. Del.) 1851-Feb. 14, 1859; Senate Feb. 14, 1859-61; Gov. (Terr.) 1849-50, May 16-19, 1853.

LANE, Joseph Reed (R Iowa) May 6, 1858-May 1, 1931; House 1899-1901.

LANE, LaFayette (son of Joseph Lane and uncle of Harry Lane) (D Ore.) Nov. 12, 1842-Nov. 23, 1896; House Oct. 25, 1875-77.

LANE, Thomas Joseph (D Mass.) July 6, 1898-__; House Dec. 30, 1941-63.

LANGDON, Chauncey (F Vt.) Nov. 8, 1763-July 23, 1830; House 1815-17.

LANGDON, John (D N.H.) June 25, 1741-Sept. 18, 1819; Senate 1789-1801; President pro tempore 1789, 1792-94; Cont. Cong. 1775-76, 1783; Gov. 1788, 1805-09, 1810-12.

LANGEN, Odin (R Minn.) Jan. 5, 1913-__; House 1959-71.

LANGER, William (R N.D.) Sept. 30, 1886-Nov. 8, 1959; Senate 1941-Nov. 8, 1959; Gov. 1933-34, 1937-39.

LANGHAM, Jonathan Nicholas (R Pa.) Aug. 4, 1861-May 21, 1945; House 1909-15.

LANGLEY, John Wesley (husband of Katherine Gudger Langley) (R Ky.) Jan. 14, 1868-Jan. 17, 1932; House 1907-Jan. 11, 1926.

LANGLEY, Katherine Gudger (wife of John Wesley Langley and daughter of James Madison Gudger Jr.) (R Ky.) Feb. 14, 1888-Aug. 15, 1948; House 1927-31.

LANGSTON, John Mercer (R Va.) Dec. 14, 1829-Nov. 15, 1897; House Sept. 23, 1890-91.

LANHAM, Fritz Garland (son of Samuel Willis Tucker Lanham) (D Texas) Jan. 3, 1880-July 31, 1965; House April 19, 1919-47.

LANHAM, Henderson Lovelace (D Ga.) Sept. 14, 1888-Nov. 10, 1957; House 1947-Nov. 10, 1957.

LANHAM, Samuel Willis Tucker (father of Fritz Garland Lanham) (D Texas) July 4, 1846-July 29, 1908; House 1883-93, 1897-Jan. 15, 1903; Gov. 1903-07.

LANING, Jay Ford (R Ohio) May 15, 1853-Sept. 1, 1941; House 1907-09.

LANKFORD, Menalcus (R Va.) March 14, 1883-Dec. 27, 1937; House 1929-33.

LANKFORD, Richard Estep (D Md.) July 22, 1914-___; House 1955-65.

LANKFORD, William Chester (D Ga.) Dec. 7, 1877-Dec. 10, 1964; House 1919-33.

LANMAN, James (D Conn.) June 14, 1767-Aug. 7, 1841; Senate 1819-25.

LANNING, William Mershon (R N.J.) Jan. 1, 1849-Feb. 16, 1912; House 1903-June 6, 1904.

LANSING, Frederick (R N.Y.) Feb. 16, 1838-Jan. 31, 1894; House 1889-91.

LANSING, Gerrit Yates (JD N.Y.) Aug. 4, 1783-Jan. 3, 1862; House 1831-37.

LANSING, William Esselstyne (R N.Y.) Dec. 29, 1821-July 29, 1883; House 1861-63, 1871-75.

LANTAFF, William Courtland (D Fla.) July 31, 1913-Jan. 28, 1970; House 1951-55.

LANZETTA, James Joseph (D N.Y.) Dec. 21, 1894-Oct. 27, 1956; House 1933-35, 1937-39.

LAPHAM, Elbridge Gerry (R N.Y.) Oct. 18, 1814-Jan. 8, 1890; House 1875-July 29, 1881; Senate Aug. 2, 1881-85.

LAPHAM, Oscar (D R.I.) June 29, 1837-March 29, 1926; House 1891-95.

LAPORTE, John (— Pa.) Nov. 4, 1798-Aug. 22, 1862; House 1833-37.

LARCADE, Henry Dominique Jr. (D La.) July 12, 1890-March 15, 1966; House 1943-53.

LARNED, Simon (— Mass.) Aug. 3, 1753-Nov. 16, 1817; House Nov. 5, 1804-05.

LARRABEE, Charles Hathaway (D Wis.) Nov. 9, 1820-Jan. 20, 1883; House 1859-61.

LARRABEE, William Henry (D Ind.) Feb. 21, 1870-Nov. 16, 1960; House 1931-43.

LARRAZOLO, Octaviano Ambrosio (R N.M.) Dec. 7, 1859-April 7, 1930; Senate Dec. 7, 1928-29; Gov. 1919-21.

LARRINAGA, Tulio (U P.R.) Jan. 15, 1847-April 28, 1917; House (Res. Comm.) 1905-11.

LARSEN, William Washington (D Ga.) Aug. 12, 1871-Jan. 5, 1938; House 1917-33.

LARSON, Oscar John (R Minn.) May 20, 1871-Aug. 1, 1957; House 1921-25.

LA SERE, Emile (D La.) 1802-Aug. 14, 1882; House Jan. 29, 1846-51.

LASH, Israel George (R N.C.) Aug. 18, 1810-April 1, 1878; House July 20, 1868-71.

LASSITER, Francis Rives (great-nephew of Francis Everod Rives) (D Va.) Feb. 18, 1866-Oct. 31, 1909; House April 19, 1900-03, 1907-Oct. 31, 1909.

LATHAM, George Robert (R W.Va.) March 9, 1832-Dec. 16, 1917; House 1865-67.

LATHAM, Henry Jepson (R N.Y.) Dec. 10, 1908-___; House 1945-Dec. 31, 1958.

LATHAM, Louis Charles (D N.C.) Sept. 11, 1840-Oct. 16, 1895; House 1881-83, 1887-89.

LATHAM, Milton Slocum (D Calif.) May 23, 1827-March 4, 1882; House 1853-55; Senate March 5, 1860-63; Gov. Jan. 9-Jan. 14, 1860.

LATHROP, Samuel (R Mass.) May 1, 1772-July 11, 1846; House 1819-27.

LATHROP, William (R Ill.) April 17, 1825-Nov. 19, 1907; House 1877-79.

LATIMER, Asbury Churchwell (D S.C.) July 31, 1851-Feb. 20, 1908; House 1893-1903; Senate 1903-Feb. 20, 1908.

LATIMER, Henry (— Del.) April 24, 1752-Dec. 19, 1819; House Feb. 14, 1794-Feb. 7, 1795; Senate Feb. 7, 1795-Feb. 28, 1801.

LATTA, Delbert Leroy (R Ohio) March 5, 1920-___; House 1959-___.

LATTA, James Polk (D Neb.) Oct. 31, 1844-Sept. 11, 1911; House 1909-Sept. 11, 1911.

LATTIMORE, William (— Miss.) Feb. 9, 1774-April 3, 1843; House (Terr. Del.) 1803-07, 1813-17.

LAURANCE, John (— N.Y.) 1750-Nov. 11, 1810; House 1789-93; Senate Nov. 9, 1796-Aug. 1800; President pro tempore 1798-99; Cont. Cong. 1785-87.

LAUSCHE, Frank John (D Ohio) Nov. 14, 1895-___; Senate 1957-69; Gov. 1945-47, 1949-57.

LAW, Charles Blakeslee (R N.Y.) Feb. 5, 1872-Sept. 15, 1929; House 1905-11.

LAW, John (son of Lyman Law and grandson of Amasa Learned) (D Ind.) Oct. 28, 1796-Oct. 7, 1873; House 1861-65.

LAW, Lyman (father of John Law) (F Conn.) Aug. 19, 1770-Feb. 3, 1842; House 1811-17.

LAWLER, Frank (D Ill.) June 25, 1842-Jan. 17, 1896; House 1885-91.

LAWLER, Joab (W Ala.) June 12, 1796-May 8, 1838; House 1835-May 8, 1838.

LAWRENCE, Abbott (W Mass.) Dec. 16, 1792-Aug. 18, 1855; House 1835-37, 1839-Sept. 18, 1840.

LAWRENCE, Cornelius Van Wyck (cousin of Effingham Lawrence) (JD N.Y.) Feb. 28, 1791-Feb. 20, 1861; House 1833-May 14, 1834.

LAWRENCE, Effingham (cousin of Cornelius Van Wyck Lawrence) (D La.) March 2, 1820-Dec. 9, 1878; House March 3, 1875.

LAWRENCE, George Pelton (R Mass.) May 19, 1859-Nov. 21, 1917; House Nov. 2, 1897-1913.

LAWRENCE, George Van Eman (son of Joseph Lawrence) (W Pa.) 1786-April 17, 1842; House 1865-69, 1883-85 (1865-69 Whig, 1883-85 Republican).

LAWRENCE, Henry Franklin (R Mo.) Jan. 31, 1868-Jan. 12, 1950; House 1921-23.

LAWRENCE, John Watson (D N.Y.) Aug. 1800-Dec. 20, 1888; House 1845-47.

LAWRENCE, Joseph (father of George Van Eman Lawrence) (W Pa.) 1786-April 17, 1842; House 1825-29, 1841-April 17, 1842.

LAWRENCE, Samuel (brother of William Thomas Lawrence) (— N.Y.) May 23, 1773-Oct. 20, 1837; House 1823-25.

LAWRENCE, Sidney (D N.Y.) Dec. 31, 1801-May 9, 1892; House 1847-49.

LAWRENCE, William (D Ohio) Sept. 2, 1814-Sept. 8, 1895; House 1857-59.

LAWRENCE, William (R Ohio) June 26, 1819-May 8, 1899; House 1865-71, 1873-77.

LAWRENCE, William Thomas (brother of Samuel Lawrence) (— N.Y.) May 7, 1788-Oct. 25, 1859; House 1847-49.

LAWS, Gilbert Lafayette (R Neb.) March 11, 1838-April 25, 1907; House Dec. 2, 1889-91.

LAWSON, John Daniel (R N.Y.) Feb. 18, 1816-Jan. 24, 1896; House 1873-75.

LAWSON, John William (D Va.) Sept. 13, 1837-Feb. 21, 1905; House 1891-93.

LAWSON, Thomas Graves (D Ga.) May 2, 1835-April 16, 1912; House 1891-97.

LAWYER, Thomas (—N.Y.) Oct. 14, 1785-May 21, 1868; House 1817-19.

LAXALT, Paul Dominque (R Neb.) Aug. 2, 1922-___; Senate Dec. 18, 1974-); Gov. 1967-7'.

LAY, Alfred Morrison (D Mo.) May 20, 1836-Dec. 8, 1879; House March 4-Dec. 8, 1879.

LAY, George Washington (W N.Y.) July 26, 1798-Oct. 21, 1860; House 1833-37.

LAYTON, Caleb Rodney (R Del.) Sept. 8, 1851-Nov. 11, 1930; House 1919-23.

LAYTON, Fernando Coello (D Ohio) April 11, 1847-June 22, 1926; House 1891-97.

LAZARO, Ladislas (D La.) June 5, 1872-March 30, 1927; House 1913-March 30, 1927.

LAZEAR, Jesse (D Pa.) Dec. 12, 1804-Sept. 2, 1877; House 1861-65.

LEA, Clarence Frederick (D Calif.) July 11, 1874-June 20, 1964; House 1917-49.

LEA, Luke (brother of Pryor Lea) (UD Tenn.) Jan. 21, 1783-June 17, 1851; House 1833-37.

LEA, Luke (great-grandson of the preceding) (D Tenn.) April 12, 1879-Nov. 18, 1945; Senate 1911-17.

LEA, Pryor (brother of Luke Lea) (JD Tenn.) Aug. 31, 1794-Sept. 14, 1879; House 1827-31.

LEACH, DeWitt Clinton (R Mich.) Nov. 23, 1822-Dec. 21, 1909; House 1857-61.

LEACH, James Madison (C N.C.) Jan. 17, 1815-June 1, 1891; House 1859-61, 1871-75 (1859-61 Whig, 1871-75 Conservative).

LEACH, Robert Milton (R Mass.) April 2, 1879-Feb. 18, 1952; House Nov. 4, 1924-25.

LEADBETTER, Daniel Parkhurst (JD Ohio) Sept. 10, 1797-Feb. 26, 1870; House 1837-41.

LEAHY, Edward Laurence (D R.I.) Feb. 9, 1886-July 22, 1953; Senate Aug. 24, 1949-Dec. 18, 1950.

LEAHY, Patrick Joseph (D Vt.) March 31, 1940-__; Senate 1975-__.

LEAKE, Eugene Walter (D N.J.) July 13, 1877-Aug. 23, 1959; House 1907-09.

LEAKE, Shelton Farrar (D Va.) Nov. 30, 1812-March 4, 1884; House 1845-47, 1859-61.

LEAKE, Walter (D Miss.) May 25, 1762-Nov. 17, 1825; Senate Dec. 10, 1817-May 15, 1820; Gov. 1822-25.

LEARNED, Amasa (grandfather of John Law) (—Conn.) Nov. 15, 1750-May 4, 1825; House 1791-95.

LEARY, Cornelius Lawrence Ludlow (U Md.) Oct. 22, 1813-March 21, 1893; House 1861-63.

LEATHERWOOD, Elmer O. (R Utah) Sept. 4, 1872-Dec. 24, 1929; House 1921-Dec. 24, 1929.

LEAVENWORTH, Elias Warner (R N.Y.) Dec. 20, 1803-Nov. 25, 1887; House 1875-77.

LEAVITT, Humphrey Howe (JD Ohio) June 18, 1796-March 15, 1873; House Dec. 6, 1830-July 10, 1834.

LEAVITT, Scott (R Mont.) June 16, 1879-Oct. 19, 1966; House 1923-33.

LEAVY, Charles Henry (D Wash.) Feb. 16, 1884-Sept. 25, 1952; House 1937-Aug. 1, 1942.

LE BLOND, Francis Celeste (grandfather of Frank LeBlond Kloeb) (D Ohio) Feb. 14, 1821-Nov. 9, 1902; House 1863-67.

LECOMPTE, Joseph (D Ky.) Dec. 15, 1797-April 25, 1851; House 1825-33.

LE COMPTE, Karl Miles (R Iowa) May 25, 1887-Sept. 30, 1972; House 1939-59.

LEE, Blair (D Md.) Aug. 9, 1857-Dec. 25, 1944; Senate Jan. 28, 1914-17.

LEE, Frank Hood (D Mo.) March 29, 1873-Nov. 20, 1952; House 1933-35.

LEE, Gideon (JD N.Y.) April 27, 1778-Aug. 21, 1841; House Nov. 4, 1835-37.

LEE, Gordon (D Ga.) May 29, 1859-Nov. 7, 1927; House 1905-27.

LEE, Henry (brother of Richard Bland Lee and grandfather of William Henry Fitzhugh Lee) (F Va.) Jan. 29, 1756-March 25, 1818; House 1799-1801; Cont. Cong. 1785-88; Gov. 1791-94.

LEE, John (D Md.) Jan. 30, 1788-May 17, 1871; House 1823-25.

LEE, Joshua (D N.Y.) 1783-Dec. 19, 1842; House 1835-37.

LEE, Joshua Bryan (D Okla.) Jan. 23, 1892-Aug. 10, 1967; House 1935-37; Senate 1937-43.

LEE, Moses Lindley (R N.Y.) May 29, 1805-May 19, 1876; House 1859-61.

LEE, Richard Bland (brother of Henry Lee) (—Va.) Jan. 20, 1761-March 12, 1827; House 1789-95.

LEE, Richard Henry (— Va.) Jan. 20, 1732-June 19, 1794; Senate 1789-Oct. 8, 1792; Cont. Cong. 1774-80, 1784-87.

LEE, Robert Emmett (D Pa.) Oct. 12, 1868-Nov. 19, 1916; House 1911-15.

LEE, Robert Quincy (D Texas) Jan. 12, 1869-April 18, 1930; House 1929-April 18, 1930.

LEE, Silas (F Mass.) July 3, 1760-March 1, 1814; House 1799-Aug. 20, 1801.

LEE, Thomas (D N.J.) Nov. 28, 1780-Nov. 2, 1856; House 1833-37.

LEE, Warren Isbell (R N.Y.) Feb. 5, 1876-Dec. 25, 1955; House 1921-23.

LEE, William Henry Fitzhugh (grandson of Henry Lee) (D Va.) May 31, 1837-Oct. 15, 1891; House 1887-Oct. 15, 1891.

LEECH, James Russell (R Pa.) Nov., 19, 1888-Feb. 5, 1952; House 1927-Jan. 29, 1932.

LEEDOM, John Peter (D Ohio) Dec. 20, 1847-March 18, 1895; House 1881-83.

LEET, Isaac (D Pa.) 1801-June 10, 1844; House 1839-41.

LE FEVER, Jacob (father of Frank Jacob LeFevre) (R N.Y.) April 20, 1830-Feb. 4, 1905; House 1893-97.

LE FEVER, Joseph (D Pa.) April 3, 1760-Oct. 17, 1826; House 1811-13.

LE FEVRE, Benjamin (D Ohio) Oct. 8, 1838-March 7, 1922; House 1879-87.

LE FEVRE, Frank Jacob (son of Jacob Le Fever) (R N.Y.) Nov. 30, 1874-April 29, 1941; House 1905-07.

LE FEVRE, Jay (R N.Y.) Sept. 6, 1893-April 26, 1970; House 1943-51.

LEFFERTS, John (D N.Y.) Dec. 17, 1785-Sept. 18, 1829; House 1813-15.

LEFFLER, Isaac (brother of Shepherd Leffler) (—Va.) Nov. 7, 1788-March 8, 1866; House 1827-29.

LEFFLER, Shepherd (brother of Isaac Leffler) (D Iowa) April 24, 1811-Sept. 7, 1879; House Dec. 28, 1846-51.

LEFTWICH, Jabez (— Va.) Sept. 22, 1765-June 22, 1855; House 1821-25.

LEFTWICH, John William (D Tenn.) Sept. 7, 1826-March 6, 1870; House July 24, 1866-67.

LEGARDA Y TUASON, Benito (— P.I.) Sept. 27, 1853-Aug. 27, 1915; House (Res. Comm.) Nov. 22, 1907-13.

LEGARE, George Swinton (D S.C.) Nov. 11, 1869-Jan. 31, 1913; House 1903-Jan. 31, 1913.

LEGARE, Hugh Swinton (UD S.C.) Jan. 2, 1797-June 20, 1843; House 1837-39; Atty. Gen. 1841-43; Secy. of State 1843.

LEGGETT, Robert L. (D Calif.) July 26, 1926-__; House 1963-__.

LEHLBACH, Frederick Reimold (nephew of Herman Lehlbach) (R N.J.) Jan. 31, 1876-Aug. 4, 1937; House 1915-37.

LEHLBACH, Herman (uncle of Frederick Reimold Lehlbach) (R N.J.) July 3, 1845-Jan. 11, 1904; House 1885-91.

LEHMAN, Herbert Henry (D N.Y.) March 28, 1878-Dec. 5, 1963; Senate Nov. 9, 1949-57; Gov. 1933-42.

LEHMAN, William (D Fla.) Oct. 4, 1913-__; House 1973-__.

LEHMAN, William Eckart (D Pa.) Aug. 21, 1821-July 19, 1895; House 1861-63.

LEHR, John Camillus (D Mich.) Nov. 18, 1878-Feb. 17, 1958; House 1933-35.

LEIB, Michael (D Pa.) Jan. 8, 1760-Dec. 22, 1822; House 1799-Feb. 14, 1806; Senate Jan. 9, 1809-Feb. 14, 1814.

LEIB, Owen D. (D Pa.) ? -June 17, 1848; House 1845-47.

LEIDY, Paul (D Pa.) Nov. 13, 1813-Sept. 11, 1877; House Dec. 7, 1857-59.

LEIGH, Benjamin Watkins (W Va.) June 18, 1781-Feb. 2, 1849; Senate Feb. 26, 1834-July 4, 1836.

LEIGHTY, Jacob D. (R Ind.) Nov. 15, 1839-Oct. 18, 1912; House 1895-97.

LEIPER, George Gray (D Pa.) Feb. 3, 1786-Nov. 18, 1868; House 1829-31.

LEISENRING, John (R Pa.) June 3, 1853-Jan. 19, 1901; House 1895-97.

LEITER, Benjamin Franklin (R Ohio) Oct. 13, 1813-June 17, 1866; House 1855-59.

LEMKE, William (R N.D.) Aug. 13, 1878-May 30, 1950; House 1933-41, 1943-May 30, 1950 (1933-41 Nonpartisan Republican, 1943-50 Republican).

LE MOYNE, John Valcoulon (D Ill.) Nov. 17, 1828-July 27, 1918; House May 6, 1876-77.

LENAHAN, John Thomas (D Pa.) Nov. 15, 1852-April 28, 1920; House 1907-09.

L'ENGLE, Claude (D Fla.) Oct. 19, 1868-Nov. 6, 1919; House 1913-15.

LENNON, Alton Asa (D N.C.) Aug. 17, 1906-__; Senate July 10, 1953-Nov. 28, 1954; House 1957-73.

LENROOT, Irvine Luther (R Wis.) Jan. 31, 1869-Jan. 26, 1949; House 1909-April 17, 1918; Senate April 18, 1918-27.

LENT, James (JD N.Y.) 1782-Feb. 22, 1833; House 1829-Feb. 22, 1833.

LENT, Norman Frederick (R N.Y.) March 23, 1931-__; House 1971-__.

LENTZ, John Jacob (D Ohio) Jan. 27, 1856-July 27, 1931; House 1897-1901.

LEONARD, Fred Churchill (R Pa.) Feb. 16, 1856-Dec. 5, 1921; House 1895-97.

LEONARD, George (— Mass.) July 4, 1729-July 26, 1819; House 1789-91, 1795-97.

LEONARD, John Edwards (grandnephew of John Edwards of Pa.) (R La.) Sept. 22, 1845-March 15, 1878; House 1877-March 15, 1878.

LEONARD, Moses Gage (D N.Y.) July 10, 1809-March 20, 1899; House 1843-45.

LEONARD, Stephen Banks (D N.Y.) April 15, 1793-May 8, 1876; House 1835-37, 1839-41.

LESHER, John Vandling (D Pa.) July 27, 1866-May 3, 1932; House 1913-21.

LESINSKI, John (D Mich.) Jan. 3, 1885-May 27, 1950; House 1933-May 27, 1950.

LESINSKI, John Jr. (son of the preceding) (D Mich.) Dec. 28, 1914-__; House 1951-65.

LESSLER, Montague (R N.Y.) Jan. 1, 1869-Feb. 17, 1938; House Jan. 7, 1902-03.

LESTER, Posey Green (D Va.) March 12, 1850-Feb. 9, 1929; House 1889-93.

LESTER, Rufus Ezekiel (D Ga.) Dec. 12, 1837-June 16, 1906; House 1889-June 16, 1906.

LETCHER, John (D Va.) March 29, 1813-Jan. 26, 1884; House 1851-59; Gov. 1860-64.

LETCHER, Robert Perkins (W Ky.) Feb. 10, 1788-Jan. 24, 1861; House 1823-33, Aug. 6, 1834-35 (1823-27 Clay Democrat, 1827-33 and 1834-35 Whig); Gov. 1840-44.

LETTS, Fred Dickinson (cousin of Lester Jesse Dickinson) (R Iowa) April 26, 1875-Jan. 19, 1965; House 1925-31.

LEVER, Asbury Francis (D S.C.) Jan. 5, 1875-April 28, 1940; House Nov. 5, 1901-Aug. 1, 1919.

LEVERING, Robert Woodrow (son-in-law of Usher L. Burdick and brother-in-law of Quentin N. Burdick) (D Ohio) Oct. 3, 1914-__; House 1959-61.

LEVIN, Lewis Charles (AP Pa.) Nov. 10, 1808-March 14, 1860; House 1845-51.

LEVITAS, Elliott Harris (D Ga.) Dec. 26, 1930-__; House 1975-__.

LEVY, David (R Fla.) (See YULEE, David Levy.)

LEVY, Jefferson Monroe (D N.Y.) April 16, 1852-March 6, 1924; House 1899-1901, 1911-15.

LEVY, William Mallory (D La.) Oct. 31, 1827-Aug. 14, 1882; House 1875-77.

LEWIS, Abner (W N.Y.) ? - ?; House 1845-47.

LEWIS, Barbour (R Tenn.) Jan. 5, 1818-July 15, 1893; House 1873-75.

LEWIS, Burwell Boykin (D Ala.) July 7, 1838-Oct. 11, 1885; House 1875-77, 1879-Oct. 1, 1880.

LEWIS, Charles Swearinger (D Va.) Feb. 26, 1821-Jan. 22, 1878; House Dec. 4, 1854-55.

LEWIS, Clarke (D Miss.) Nov. 8, 1840-March 13, 1896; House 1889-93.

LEWIS, David John (D Md.) May 1, 1869-Aug. 12, 1952; House 1911-17, 1931-39.

LEWIS, Dixon Hall (D Ala.) Aug. 10, 1802-Oct. 25, 1848; House 1829-April 22, 1844 (SRD); Senate April 22, 1844-Oct. 25, 1848 (D).

LEWIS, Earl Ramage (R Ohio) Feb. 22, 1887-Feb. 1, 1956; House 1939-41, 1943-49.

LEWIS, Edward Taylor (D La.) Oct. 26, 1834-April 26, 1927; House 1883-85.

LEWIS, Elijah Banks (D Ga.) March 27, 1854-Dec. 10, 1920; House 1897-1909.

LEWIS, Fred Ewing (R Pa.) Feb. 8, 1865-June 27, 1949; House 1913-15.

LEWIS, James Hamilton (D Wash./Ill.) May 18, 1863-April 9, 1939; House 1897-99 (Wash.); Senate March 26, 1913-19, 1931-April 9, 1939 (Ill.).

LEWIS, John Francis (R Va.) March 1, 1818-Sept. 2, 1895; Senate Jan. 26, 1870-75.

LEWIS, John Henry (R Ill.) July 21, 1830-Jan. 6, 1929; House 1881-83.

LEWIS, John William (R Ky.) Oct. 14, 1841-Dec. 20, 1913; House 1895-97.

LEWIS, Joseph Jr. (F Va.) 1772-March 30, 1834; House 1803-17.

LEWIS, Joseph Horace (D Ky.) Oct. 29, 1824-July 6, 1904; House May 10, 1870-73.

LEWIS, Lawrence (D Colo.) June 22, 1879-Dec. 9, 1943; House 1933-Dec. 9, 1943.

LEWIS, Robert Jacob (R Pa.) Dec. 30, 1864-July 24, 1933; House 1901-03.

LEWIS, Thomas (— Va.) ? - ?; House 1803-March 5, 1804.

LEWIS, William (R Ky.) Sept. 22, 1868-Aug. 8, 1959; House April 24, 1948-49.

LEWIS, William J. (D Va.) July 4, 1766-Nov. 1, 1828; House 1817-19.

LIBBEY, Harry (R Va.) Nov. 22, 1843-Sept. 30, 1913; House 1883-87.

LIBONATI, Roland Victor (D Ill.) Dec. 29, 1900-__; House Dec. 31, 1957-65.

LICHTENWALNER, Norton Lewis (D Pa.) June 1, 1889-May 3, 1960; House 1931-33.

LICHTENWALTER, Franklin Herbert (R Pa.) March 28, 1910-March 4, 1973; House Sept. 9, 1947-51.

LIEB, Charles (D Ind.) May 20, 1852-Sept. 1, 1928; House 1913-17.

LIEBEL, Michael Jr. (D Pa.) Dec. 12, 1870-Aug. 8, 1927; House 1915-17.

LIGON, Robert Fulwood (D Ala.) Dec. 16, 1823-Oct. 11, 1901; House 1877-79.

LIGON, Thomas Watkins (D Md.) May 10, 1810-Jan. 12, 1881; House 1845-49; Gov. 1854-58.

LILLEY, George Leavens (R Conn.) Aug. 3, 1859-April 21, 1909; House 1903-Jan. 5, 1909; Gov. 1909.

LILLEY, Mial Eben (R Pa.) May 30, 1850-Feb. 28, 1915; House 1905-07.

LILLY, Samuel (D N.J.) Oct. 28, 1815-April 3, 1880; House 1853-55.

LILLY, Thomas Jefferson (D W.Va.) June 3, 1878-April 2, 1956; House 1923-25.

LILLY, William (R Pa.) June 3, 1821-Dec. 1, 1893; House March 4-Dec. 1, 1893.

LINCOLN, Abraham (R Ill.) Feb. 12, 1809-April 15, 1865; House 1847-49 (W); Pres. 1861-April 15, 1865 (R).

LINCOLN, Enoch (son of Levi Lincoln and brother of Levi Lincoln) (— Mass./Maine) Dec. 28, 1788-Oct. 8, 1829; House Nov. 4, 1818-21 (Mass.), 1821-26 (Maine); Gov. of Maine 1827-Oct. 8, 1829.

LINCOLN, Levi (father of Enoch Lincoln and Levi Lincoln) (D Mass.) May 15, 1749-April 14, 1820; House Dec. 15, 1800-March 5, 1801; Atty. Gen. 1801-04; Gov. 1808-09.

LINCOLN, Levi (son of the preceding and brother of Enoch Lincoln) (W Mass.) Oct. 25, 1782-May 29, 1868; House Feb. 17, 1834-March 16, 1841; Gov. 1825-34.

LINCOLN, William Slosson (R N.Y.) Aug. 13, 1813-April 21, 1893; House 1867-69.

LIND, James Francis (D Pa.) Oct. 17, 1900-__; House 1949-53.

LIND, John (D Minn.) March 25, 1854-Sept. 18, 1930; House 1887-93, 1903-05 (1887-93 Republican, 1903-05 Democrat); Gov. 1899-1901 (D).

LINDBERGH, Charles Augustus (R Minn.) Jan. 20, 1859-May 24, 1924; House 1907-17.

LINDLEY, James Johnson (W Mo.) Jan. 1, 1822-April 18, 1891; House 1853-57.

LINDQUIST, Francis Oscar (R Mich.) Sept. 27, 1869-Sept. 25, 1924; House 1913-15.

LINDSAY, George Henry (father of George Washington Lindsay) (D N.Y.) Jan. 7, 1837-May 25, 1916; House 1901-13.

LINDSAY, George Washington (son of George Henry Lindsay) (D N.Y.) March 28, 1865-March 15, 1938; House 1923-35.

LINDSAY, John Vliet (R N.Y.) Nov. 24, 1921-__; House 1959-Dec. 31, 1965.

LINDSAY, William (D Ky.) Sept. 4, 1835-Oct. 15, 1909; Senate Feb. 15, 1893-1901.

LINDSEY, Stephen Decatur (R Maine) March 3, 1828-April 26, 1884; House 1877-83.

LINDSLEY, James Girard (R N.Y.) March 19, 1819-Dec. 4, 1898; House 1885-87.

LINDSLEY, William Dell (D Ohio) Dec. 25, 1812-March 11, 1890; House 1853-55.

LINEBERGER, Walter Franklin (R Calif.) July 20, 1883-Oct. 9, 1943; House 1921-27.

LINEHAN, Neil Joseph (D Ill.) Sept. 23, 1895-Aug. 23, 1967; House 1949-51.

LINK, Arthur A. (D N.D.) May 24, 1914-__; House 1971-73; Gov. 1973-__.

LINK, William Walter (D Ill.) Feb. 12, 1884-Sept. 23, 1950; House 1945-47.

LINN, Archibald Ladley (W N.Y.) Oct. 15, 1802-Oct. 10, 1857; House 1841-43.

LINN, James (D N.J.) 1749-Jan. 5, 1821; House 1799-1801.

LINN, John (— N.J.) Dec. 3, 1763-Jan. 5, 1821; House 1817-Jan. 5, 1821.

LINN, Lewis Fields (D Mo.) Nov. 5, 1796-Oct. 3, 1843; Senate Oct. 25, 1833-Oct. 3, 1843.

LINNEY, Romulus Zachariah (R N.C.) Dec. 26, 1841-April 15, 1910; House 1895-1901.

LINTHICUM, John Charles (D Md.) Nov. 26, 1867-Oct. 5, 1932; House 1911-Oct. 5, 1932.

LINTON, William Seelye (R Mich.) Feb. 4, 1856-Nov. 22, 1927; House 1893-97.

LIPPITT, Henry Frederick (R R.I.) Oct. 12, 1856-Dec. 28, 1933; Senate 1911-17.

LIPSCOMB, Glenard Paul (R Calif.) Aug. 19, 1915-Feb. 1, 1970; House Nov. 10, 1953-Feb. 1, 1970.

LISLE, Marcus Claiborne (D Ky.) Sept. 23, 1862-July 7, 1894; House 1893-July 7, 1894.

LITCHFIELD, Elisha (D N.Y.) July 12, 1785-Aug. 4, 1859; House 1821-25.

LITTAUER, Lucius Nathan (R N.Y.) Jan. 20, 1859-March 2, 1944; House 1897-1907.

LITTLE, Chauncey Bundy (D Kan.) Feb. 10, 1877-Sept. 29, 1952; House 1925-27.

LITTLE, Edward Campbell (R Kan.) Dec. 14, 1858-June 27, 1924; House 1917-June 27, 1924.

LITTLE, Edward Preble (D Mass.) Nov. 7, 1791-Feb. 6, 1875; House Dec. 13, 1852-53.

LITTLE, John (R Ohio) April 25, 1837-Oct. 18, 1900; House 1885-87.

LITTLE, John Sebastian (D Ark.) March 15, 1853-Oct. 29, 1916; House Dec. 3, 1894-Jan. 14, 1907; Gov. 1907.

LITTLE, Joseph James (D N.Y.) June 5, 1841-Feb. 11, 1913; House Nov. 3, 1891-93.

LITTLE, Peter (D Md.) Dec. 11, 1775-Feb. 5, 1830; House 1811-13, Sept. 2, 1816-29.

LITTLEFIELD, Charles Edgar (R Maine) June 21, 1851-May 2, 1915; House June 19, 1899-Sept. 30, 1908.

LITTLEFIELD, Nathaniel Swett (CassD Maine) Sept. 20, 1804-Aug. 15, 1882; House 1841-43, 1849-51 (1841-43 Democrat, 1849-51 Cass Democrat).

LITTLEJOHN, DeWitt Clinton (R N.Y.) Feb. 7, 1818-Oct. 27, 1892; House 1863-65.

LITTLEPAGE, Adam Brown (D W.Va.) April 14, 1859-June 29, 1921; House 1911-13, 1915-19.

LITTLETON, Martin Wiley (D N.Y.) Jan. 12, 1872-Dec. 19, 1934; House 1911-13.

LITTON, Jerry Lon (D Mo.) May 12, 1937-Aug. 3, 1976; House 1973-Aug. 3, 1976.

LIVELY, Robert Maclin (D Texas) Jan. 6, 1855-Jan. 15, 1929; House July 23, 1910-11.

LIVERMORE, Arthur (son of Samuel Livermore and brother of Edward St. Loe Livermore) (D N.H.) July 29, 1766-July 1, 1853; House 1817-21, 1823-25.

LIVERMORE, Edward St. Loe (son of Samuel Livermore and brother of Arthur Livermore) (F Mass.) April 5, 1762-Sept. 15, 1832; House 1807-11.

LIVERMORE, Samuel (father of Arthur Livermore and Edward St. Loe Livermore) (— N.H.) May 14, 1732-May 18, 1803; House 1789-93; Senate 1793-June 12, 1801; Cont. Cong. 1780-82 and 1785.

LIVERNASH, Edward James (subsequently Edward James de Nivernais) (UL/D Calif.) Feb. 14, 1866-June 1, 1938; House 1903-05.

LIVINGSTON, Edward (D N.Y./La.) May 26, 1764-May 23, 1836; House 1795-1801 (N.Y.), 1823-29 (La.); Senate 1829-May 24, 1831 (La.); Secy. of State 1831-33.

LIVINGSTON, Henry Walter (— N.Y.) 1768-Dec. 22, 1810; House 1803-07.

LIVINGSTON, Leonidas Felix (D Ga.) April 3, 1832-Feb. 11, 1912; House 1891-1911.

LIVINGSTON, Robert LeRoy (F N.Y.) ? - ?; House 1809-May 6, 1812.

LLOYD, Edward (D Md.) July 22, 1779-June 2, 1834; House Dec. 3, 1806-09; Senate 1819-Jan. 14, 1826; Gov. 1809-11.

LLOYD, James (D Md.) 1745-1820; Senate Dec. 11, 1797-Dec. 1, 1800.

LLOYD, James (F Mass.) Dec. 1769-April 5, 1831; Senate June 9, 1808-May 1, 1813, June 5, 1822-May 23, 1826.

LLOYD, James Frederick (D Calif.) Sept. 27, 1922-___; House 1975-___.

LLOYD, James Tilghman (D Mo.) Aug. 28, 1857-April 3, 1944; House June 1, 1897-1917.

LLOYD, Marilyn Laird (D Tenn.) Jan. 3, 1929-___; House 1975-___.

LLOYD, Sherman Parkinson (R Utah) Jan. 11, 1914-___; House 1963-65, 1967-73.

LLOYD, Wesley (D Wash.) July 24, 1883-Jan. 10, 1936; House 1933-Jan. 10, 1936.

LOAN, Benjamin Franklin (Rad. Mo.) Oct. 4, 1819-March 30, 1881; House 1863-69 (1863-67 Emancipationist, 1867-69 Radical).

LOBECK, Charles Otto (D Neb.) April 6, 1852-Jan. 30, 1920; House 1911-19.

LOCHER, Cyrus (D Ohio) March 8, 1878-Aug. 17, 1929; Senate April 5-Dec. 14, 1928.

LOCKE, Francis (nephew of Matthew Locke) (D N.C.) Oct. 31, 1776-Jan. 8, 1823; Senate 1814-Dec. 5, 1815.

LOCKE, John (— Mass.) Feb. 14, 1764-March 29, 1855; House 1823-29.

LOCKE, Matthew (uncle of Francis Locke and great-great-great-grandfather of Effiegene (Locke) Wingo) (D N.C.) 1730-Sept. 7, 1801; House 1793-99.

LOCKHART, James (D Ind.) Feb. 13, 1806-Sept. 7, 1857; House 1851-53, March 4-Sept. 7, 1857.

LOCKHART, James Alexander (D N.C.) June 2, 1850-Dec. 24, 1905; House 1895-June 5, 1896.

LOCKWOOD, Daniel Newton (D N.Y.) June 1, 1844-June 1, 1906; House 1877-79, 1891-95.

LODGE, Henry Cabot (great-grandson of George Cabot) (R Mass.) May 12, 1850-Nov. 9, 1924; House 1887-93; Senate 1893-Nov. 9, 1924.

LODGE, Henry Cabot Jr. (grandson of the preceding, brother of John Davis Lodge and nephew of Augustus P. Gardner) (R Mass.) July 5, 1902-___; Senate 1937-Feb. 3, 1944, 1947-53.

LODGE, John Davis (grandson of Henry Cabot Lodge, brother of Henry Cabot Lodge Jr., nephew of Augustus P. Gardner) (R Conn.) Oct. 20, 1903-___; House 1947-51; Gov. 1951-55.

LOFLAND, James Ruch (R Del.) Nov. 2, 1823-Feb. 10, 1894; House 1873-75.

LOFT, George William (D N.Y.) Feb. 6, 1865-Nov. 6, 1943; House Nov. 4, 1913-17.

LOFTIN, Scott Marion (D Fla.) Sept. 14, 1878-Sept. 22, 1953; Senate May 26-Nov. 3, 1936.

LOGAN, George (D Pa.) Sept. 9, 1753-April 9, 1821; Senate July 13, 1801-07.

LOGAN, Henry (D Pa.) April 14, 1784-Dec. 26, 1866; House 1835-39.

LOGAN, John Alexander (R Ill.) Feb. 9, 1826-Dec. 26, 1886; House 1859-April 2, 1862, 1867-71 (1859-62 Democrat, 1867-71 Republican); Senate (Republican) 1871-77, 1879-Dec. 26, 1886.

LOGAN, Marvel Mills (D Ky.) Jan. 7, 1875-Oct. 3, 1939; Senate 1931-Oct. 3, 1939.

LOGAN, William (D Ky.) Dec. 8, 1776-Aug. 8, 1822; Senate 1819-May 28, 1820.

LOGAN, William Turner (D S.C.) June 21, 1874-Sept. 15, 1941; House 1921-25.

LOGUE, James Washington (D Pa.) Feb. 22, 1863-Aug. 27, 1925; House 1913-15.

LONDON, Meyer (Soc. N.Y.) Dec. 29, 1871-June 6, 1926; House 1915-19, 1921-23.

LONERGAN, Augustine (D Conn.) May 20, 1874-Oct. 18, 1947; House 1913-15, 1917-21, 1931-33; Senate 1933-39.

LONG, Alexander (D Ohio) Dec. 24, 1816-Nov. 28, 1886; House 1863-65.

LONG, Chester Isaiah (R Kan.) Oct. 12, 1860-July 1, 1934; House 1895-97, 1899-March 4, 1903; Senate 1903-09.

LONG, Clarence Dickinson (D Md.) Dec. 11, 1908-___; House 1963-___.

LONG, Edward Henry Carroll (W Md.) Sept. 28, 1808-Oct. 16, 1865; House 1845-47.

LONG, Edward Vaughn (D Mo.) July 18, 1908-Nov. 6, 1972; Senate Sept. 23, 1960-Dec. 27, 1968.

LONG, George Shannon (brother of Huey Pierce Long, brother-in-law of Rose McConnell Long and uncle of Russell Billiu Long) (D La.) Sept. 11, 1883-March 22, 1958; House 1953-March 22, 1958.

LONG, Gillis William (cousin of Huey Pierce Long and of Rose McConnell Long, cousin of Russell Billiu Long and cousin of George Shannon Long) (D La.) May 4, 1923-___; House 1963-65, 1973-___.

LONG, Huey Pierce (husband of Rose McConnell Long, father of Russell B. Long and brother of George S. Long) (D La.) Aug. 30, 1893-Sept. 10, 1935; Senate Jan. 25, 1932-Sept. 10, 1935; Gov. 1928-32.

LONG, Jefferson Franklin (R Ga.) March 3, 1836-Feb. 5, 1900; House Dec. 22, 1870-71.

LONG, John (W N.C.) Feb. 26, 1785-Aug. 11, 1857; House 1821-29.

LONG, John Benjamin (D Texas) Sept. 8, 1843-April 27, 1924; House 1891-93.

LONG, John Davis (R Mass.) Oct. 27, 1838-Aug. 28, 1915; House 1883-89; Gov. 1880-83; Secy. of the Navy 1897-1902.

LONG, Lewis Marshall (D Ill.) June 22, 1883-Sept. 9, 1957; House 1937-39.

LONG, Oren Ethelbirt (D Hawaii) March 4, 1889-May 6, 1965; Senate Aug. 21, 1959-63; Gov. (Terr.) 1951-53.

LONG, Rose McConnell (widow of Huey Pierce Long, mother of Russell B. Long and sister-in-law of George S. Long) (D La.) April 8, 1892-May 27, 1970; Senate Jan. 31, 1936-37.

LONG, Russell Billiu (son of Huey Pierce Long and Rose McConnell Long and nephew of George S. Long) (D La.) Nov. 3, 1918-__; Senate Dec. 31, 1948-__.

LONG, Speedy O. (D La.) June 16, 1928-__; House 1965-73.

LONGFELLOW, Stephen (F Maine) June 23, 1775-Aug. 2, 1849; House 1823-25.

LONGNECKER, Henry Clay (R Pa.) April 17, 1820-Sept. 16, 1871; House 1859-61.

LONGWORTH, Nicholas (nephew of Bellamy Storer) (R Ohio) Nov. 5, 1869-April 9, 1931; House 1903-13, 1915-April 9, 1931; Speaker 1925-31.

LONGYEAR, John Wesley (R Mich.) Oct. 22, 1820-March 11, 1875; House 1863-67.

LOOFBOUROW, Frederick Charles (R Utah) Feb. 8, 1874-July 8, 1949; House Nov. 4, 1930-33.

LOOMIS, Andrew Williams (W Ohio) June 27, 1797-Aug. 24, 1873; House March 4-Oct. 20, 1837.

LOOMIS, Arphaxed (D N.Y.) April 9, 1798-Sept. 15, 1885; House 1837-39.

LOOMIS, Dwight (R Conn.) July 27, 1821-Sept. 17, 1903; House 1859-63.

LORD, Bert (R N.Y.) Dec. 4, 1869-May 24, 1939; House 1935-May 24, 1939.

LORD, Frederick William (W N.Y.) Dec. 11, 1800-May 24, 1860; House 1847-49.

LORD, Henry William (R Mich.) March 8, 1821-Jan. 25, 1891; House 1881-83.

LORD, Scott (D N.Y.) Dec. 11, 1820-Sept. 10, 1885; House 1875-77.

LORE, Charles Brown (D Del.) March 16, 1831-March 6, 1911; House 1883-87.

LORIMER, William (R Ill.) April 27, 1861-Sept. 13, 1934; House 1895-1901, 1903-June 17, 1909; Senate June 18, 1909-July 13, 1912.

LORING, George Bailey (R Mass.) Nov. 8, 1817-Sept. 13, 1891; House 1877-81.

LOSER, Joseph Carlton (D Tenn.) Oct. 1, 1892-__; House 1957-63.

LOTT, Chester Trent (R Miss.) Oct. 9, 1941-__; House 1973-__.

LOUD, Eugene Francis (R Calif.) March 12, 1847-Dec. 19, 1908; House 1891-1903.

LOUD, George Alvin (R Mich.) June 18, 1852-Nov. 13, 1925; House 1903-13, 1915-17.

LOUDENSLAGER, Henry Clay (R N.J.) May 22, 1852-Aug. 12, 1911; House 1893-Aug. 12, 1911.

LOUGHRIDGE, William (R Iowa) July 11, 1827-Sept. 26, 1889; House 1867-71, 1873-75.

LOUNSBERY, William (D N.Y.) Dec. 25, 1831-Nov. 8, 1905; House 1879-81.

LOUTTIT, James Alexander (R Calif.) Oct. 16, 1848-July 26, 1906; House 1885-87.

LOVE, Francis Johnson (R W.Va.) Jan. 23, 1901-__; House 1947-49.

LOVE, James (— Ky.) May 12, 1795-June 12, 1874; House 1833-35.

LOVE, John (D Va.) ?-Aug. 17, 1822; House 1807-11.

LOVE, Peter Early (D Ga.) July 7, 1818-Nov. 8, 1866; House 1859-Jan. 23, 1861.

LOVE, Rodney Marvin (D Ohio) July 18, 1908-__; House 1965-67.

LOVE, Thomas Cutting (W N.Y.) Nov. 30, 1789-Sept. 17, 1853; House 1835-37.

LOVE, William Carter (D N.C.) 1784-1835; House 1815-17.

LOVE, William Franklin (D Miss.) March 29, 1850-Oct. 16, 1898; House 1897-Oct. 16, 1898.

LOVEJOY, Owen (cousin of Nathan Allen Farwell) (R Ill.) Jan. 6, 1811-March 25, 1864; House 1857-March 25, 1864.

LOVERING, Henry Bacon (D Mass.) April 8, 1841-April 5, 1911; House 1883-87.

LOVERING, William Croad (R Mass.) Feb. 25, 1835-Feb. 4, 1910; House 1897-Feb. 4, 1910.

LOVETT, John (F N.Y.) Feb. 20, 1761-Aug. 12, 1818; House 1813-17.

LOVETTE, Oscar Byrd (R Tenn.) Dec. 20, 1871-July 6, 1934; House 1931-33.

LOVRE, Harold Orrin (R S.D.) Jan. 30, 1904-Jan. 17, 1972; House 1949-57.

LOW, Frederick Ferdinand (R Calif.) June 30, 1828-July 21, 1894; House June 3, 1862-63; Gov. 1863-67.

LOW, Philip Burrill (R N.Y.) May 6, 1836-Aug. 23, 1912; House 1895-99.

LOWDEN, Frank Orren (R Ill.) Jan. 26, 1861-March 20, 1943; House Nov. 6, 1906-11; Gov. 1917-21.

LOWE, David Perley (R Kan.) Aug. 22, 1823-April 10, 1882; House 1871-75.

LOWE, William Manning (GD Ala.) June 12, 1842-Oct. 12, 1882; House 1879-81, June 3, 1882-Oct. 12, 1882.

LOWELL, Joshua Adams (D Maine) March 20, 1801-March 13, 1874; House 1839-43.

LOWENSTEIN, Allard K. (D-L N.Y.) Jan. 16, 1929-__; House 1969-71.

LOWER, Christian (D Pa.) Jan. 7, 1740-Dec. 19, 1806; House 1805-Dec. 19, 1806.

LOWNDES, Lloyd Jr. (R Md.) Feb. 21, 1845-Jan. 8, 1905; House 1873-75; Gov. 1896-1900.

LOWNDES, Thomas (brother of William Lowndes) (F S.C.) Jan. 22, 1766-July 8, 1843; House 1801-05.

LOWNDES, William (brother of Thomas Lowndes) (D S.C.) Feb. 11, 1782-Oct. 27, 1822; House 1811-May 8, 1822.

LOWREY, Bill Green (D Miss.) May 25, 1862-Sept. 2, 1947; House 1921-29.

LOWRIE, Walter (D Pa.) Dec. 10, 1784-Dec. 14, 1868; Senate 1819-25.

LOWRY, Robert (D Ind.) April 2, 1824-Jan. 27, 1904; House 1883-87.

LOYALL, George (D Va.) May 29, 1789-Feb. 24, 1868; House March 9, 1830-31, 1833-37.

LOZIER, Ralph Fulton (D Mo.) Jan. 28, 1866-May 28, 1945; House 1923-35.

LUCAS, Edward (brother of William Lucas) (D Va.) Oct. 20, 1780-March 4, 1858; House 1833-37.

LUCAS, John Baptiste Charles (D Pa.) Aug. 14, 1758-Aug. 17, 1842; House 1803-05.

LUCAS, Scott Wike (D Ill.) Feb. 19, 1892-Feb. 22, 1968; House 1935-39; Senate 1939-51.

LUCAS, William (brother of Edward Lucas) (D Va.) Nov. 30, 1800-Aug. 29, 1877; House 1839-41, 1843-45.

LUCAS, William Vincent (R S.D.) July 3, 1835-Nov. 10, 1921; House 1893-95.

LUCAS, Wingate Hezekiah (D Texas) May 1, 1908-__; House 1947-55.

LUCE, Clare Boothe (stepdaughter of Albert E. Austin) (R Conn.) April 10, 1903-__; House 1943-47.

LUCE, Robert (R Mass.) Dec. 2, 1862-April 17, 1946; House 1919-35, 1937-41.

LUCKEY, Henry Carl (D Neb.) Nov. 22, 1868-Dec. 31, 1956; House 1935-39.

LUCKING, Alfred (D Mich.) Dec. 18, 1856-Dec. 1, 1929; House 1903-05.

LUDLOW, Louis Leon (D Ind.) June 24, 1873-Nov. 28, 1950; House 1929-49.

LUECKE, John Frederick (D Mich.) July 4, 1889-March 21, 1952; House 1937-39.

LUFKIN, Willfred Weymouth (R Mass.) March 10, 1879-March 28, 1934; House Nov. 6, 1917-June 30, 1921.

LUHRING, Oscar Raymond (R Ind.) Feb. 11, 1879-Aug. 20, 1944; House 1919-23.

LUJAN, Manuel Jr. (R N.M.) May 12, 1928-__; House 1969-__.

LUKEN, Thomas Andrew (D Ohio) July 9, 1925-___; House March 5, 1974-75.

LUKENS, Donald E. (Buz) (R Ohio) Feb. 11, 1931-___; House 1967-71.

LUMPKIN, Alva Moore (D S.C.) Nov. 13, 1886-Aug. 1, 1941; Senate July 22-Aug. 1, 1941.

LUMPKIN, John Henry (nephew of Wilson Lumpkin) (D Ga.) June 13, 1812-July 10, 1860; House 1843-49, 1855-57.

LUMPKIN, Wilson (uncle of John Henry Lumpkin and grandfather of Middleton Pope Barrow) (D Ga.) Jan. 14, 1783-Dec. 28, 1870; House 1815-17, 1827-31; Senate Nov. 22, 1837-41; Gov. 1831-35.

LUNA, Tranquillino (R N.M.) Feb. 25, 1849-Nov. 20, 1892; House (Terr. Del.) 1881-March 5, 1884.

LUNDEEN, Ernest (FL Minn.) Aug. 4, 1878-Aug. 31, 1940; House 1917-19, 1933-37 (1917-19 Republican, 1933-37 Farmer Laborite); Senate 1937-Aug. 31, 1940 (FL).

LUNDIN, Frederick (R Ill.) May 18, 1868-Aug. 20, 1947; House 1909-11.

LUNDINE, Stanley N. (D N.Y.) Feb. 4, 1939-___; House March 8, 1976-___.

LUNN, George Richard (D N.Y.) June 23, 1873-Nov. 27, 1948; House 1917-19.

LUSK, Georgia L. (D N.M.) May 12, 1893-Jan. 5, 1971; House 1947-49.

LUSK, Hall Stoner (D Ore.) Sept. 21, 1883-___; Senate March 16-Nov. 8, 1960.

LUTTRELL, John King (D Calif.) June 27, 1831-Oct. 4, 1893; House 1873-79.

LYBRAND, Archibald (R Ohio) May 23, 1840-Feb. 7, 1910; House 1897-1901.

LYLE, Aaron (D Pa.) Nov. 17, 1759-Sept. 24, 1825; House 1809-17.

LYLE, John Emmett Jr. (D Texas) Sept. 4, 1910-___; House 1945-55.

LYMAN, Joseph (R Iowa) Sept. 13, 1840-July 9, 1890; House 1885-89.

LYMAN, Joseph Stebbins (— N.Y.) Feb. 14, 1785-March 21, 1821; House 1819-21.

LYMAN, Samuel (— Mass.) Jan. 25, 1749-June 5, 1802; House 1795-Nov. 6, 1800.

LYMAN, Theodore (I Mass.) Aug. 23, 1833-Sept. 9, 1897; House 1883-85.

LYMAN, William (D Mass.) Dec. 7, 1755-Sept. 2, 1811; House 1793-97.

LYNCH, John (R Maine) Feb. 18, 1825-July 21, 1892; House 1865-73.

LYNCH, John (D Pa.) Nov. 1, 1843-Aug. 17, 1910; House 1887-89.

LYNCH, John Roy (R Miss.) Sept. 10, 1847-Nov. 2, 1939; House 1873-77, April 29, 1882-83.

LYNCH, Thomas (D Wis.) Nov. 21, 1844-May 4, 1898; House 1891-95.

LYNCH, Walter Aloysius (D N.Y.) July 7, 1894-Sept. 10, 1957; House Feb. 20, 1940-51.

LYNDE, William Pitt (D Wis.) Dec. 16, 1817-Dec. 18, 1885; House June 5, 1848-49, 1875-79.

LYON, Asa (F Vt.) Dec. 31, 1763-April 4, 1841; House 1815-17.

LYON, Caleb (I N.Y.) Dec. 7, 1822-Sept. 8, 1875; House 1853-55; Gov. (Idaho Terr.) 1864-66.

LYON, Chittenden (son of Matthew Lyon) (D Ky.) Feb. 22, 1787-Nov. 23, 1842; House 1827-35.

LYON, Francis Strother (W Ala.) Feb. 25, 1800-Dec. 31, 1882; House 1835-39.

LYON, Homer Le Grand (D N.C.) March 1, 1879-May 31, 1956; House 1921-29.

LYON, Lucius (D Mich.) Feb. 26, 1800-Sept. 24, 1851; House (Terr. Del.) 1833-35, (Rep.) 1843-45; Senate Jan. 26, 1837-39.

LYON, Matthew (father of Chittenden Lyon and great grandfather of William Peters Hepburn) (— Vt./Ky.) July 14, 1746-Aug. 1, 1822; House 1797-1801 (Vt.), 1803-11 (Ky.).

LYTLE, Robert Todd (nephew of John Rowan) (JD Ohio) May 19, 1804-Dec. 22, 1839; House 1833-March 10, 1834, Dec. 27, 1834-35.

M

MAAS, Melvin Joseph (R Minn.) May 14, 1898-April 13, 1964; House 1927-33, 1935-45.

MacCRATE, John (R N.Y.) March 29, 1885-___; House 1919-Dec. 30, 1920.

MacDONALD, John Lewis (D Minn.) Feb. 22, 1838-July 13, 1903; House 1887-89.

MACDONALD, Moses (D Maine) April 8, 1815-Oct. 18, 1869; House 1851-55.

MACDONALD, Torbert Hart (D Mass.) June 6, 1917-May 21, 1976; House 1955-May 21, 1976.

MacDONALD, William Josiah (Pro. Mich.) Nov. 17, 1873-March 29, 1946; House Aug. 26, 1913-15.

MacDOUGALL, Clinton Dugald (R N.Y.) June 14, 1839-May 24, 1914; House 1873-77.

MACE, Daniel (R Ind.) Sept. 5, 1811-July 26, 1867; House 1851-57 (1851-55 Democrat, 1855-57 Republican).

MacGREGOR, Clarence (R N.Y.) Sept. 16, 1872-Feb. 18, 1952; House 1919-Dec. 31, 1928.

MacGREGOR, Clark (R Minn.) July 12, 1922-___; House 1961-71.

MACHEN, Hervey Gilbert (D Md.) Oct. 14, 1916-___; House 1965-69.

MACHEN, Willis Benson (D Ky.) April 10, 1810-Sept. 29, 1893; Senate Sept. 27, 1872-73.

MACHIR, James (— Va.) ?-June 25, 1827; House 1797-99.

MACHROWICZ, Thaddeus Michael (D Mich.) Aug. 21, 1899-Feb. 17, 1970; House 1951-Sept. 18, 1961.

MACIEJEWSKI, Anton Frank (D Ill.) Jan. 3, 1893-Sept. 25, 1949; House 1939-Dec. 8, 1942.

MacINTYRE, Archibald Thompson (D Ga.) Oct. 27, 1822-Jan. 1, 1900; House 1871-73.

MACIORA, Lucien John (D Conn.) Aug. 17, 1902-___; House 1941-43.

MACK, Peter Francis Jr. (D Ill.) Nov. 1, 1916-___; House 1949-63.

MACK, Russell Vernon (R Wash.) June 13, 1891-March 28, 1960; House June 7, 1947-March 28, 1960.

MACKAY, James Armstrong (D Ga.) June 25, 1919-___; House 1965-67.

MACKEY, Edmund William McGregor (R S.C.) March 8, 1846-Jan. 27, 1884; House 1875-July 19, 1876, May 31, 1882-Jan. 27, 1884 (1875-76 Independent Republican, 1882-84 Republican).

MACKEY, Levi Augustus (D Pa.) Nov. 25, 1819-Feb. 8, 1889; House 1875-79.

MACKIE, John C. (D Mich.) June 1, 1920-___; House 1965-67.

MacKINNON, George Edward (R Minn.) April 22, 1906-___; House 1947-49.

MacLAFFERTY, James Henry (R Calif.) Feb. 27, 1871-June 9, 1937; House Nov. 7, 1922-25.

MACLAY, Samuel (brother of William Maclay and father of William Plunkett Maclay) (— Pa.) June 17, 1741-Oct. 5, 1811; House 1795-97; Senate 1803-Jan. 4, 1809.

MACLAY, William (brother of Samuel Maclay) (D Pa.) July 20, 1737-April 16, 1804; Senate 1789-91.

MACLAY, William (— Pa.) March 22, 1765-Jan. 4, 1825; House 1815-19.

MACLAY, William Brown (D N.Y.) March 20, 1812-Feb. 19, 1882; House 1843-49, 1857-61.

MACLAY, William Plunkett (son of Samuel Maclay) (D Pa.) Aug. 23, 1774-Sept. 2, 1842; House Oct. 8, 1816-21.

MACON, Nathaniel (uncle of Willis Alston and Micajah Thomas Hawkins and great-grandfather of Charles Henry Martin) (D N.C.) Dec. 17, 1757-June 29, 1837; House 1791-Dec. 13, 1815; Senate Dec. 13, 1815-Nov. 14, 1828; Speaker 1801-07; President pro tempore 1826-27.

MACON, Robert Bruce (D Ark.) July 6, 1859-Oct. 9, 1925; House 1903-13.

MACY, John B. (D Wis.) March 25, 1799-Sept. 24, 1856; House 1853-55.

MACY, William Kingsland (R N.Y.) Nov. 21, 1889-July 15, 1961; House 1947-51.

MADDEN, Martin Barnaby (R Ill.) March 20, 1855-April 27, 1928; House 1905-April 27, 1928.

MADDEN, Ray John (D Ind.) Feb. 25, 1892-___; House 1943-___.

MADDOX, John W. (D Ga.) June 3, 1848-Sept. 27, 1922; House 1893-1905.

MADIGAN, Edward Rell (R Ill.) Jan. 13, 1936-___; House 1973-___.

MADISON, Edmond Haggard (R Kan.) Dec. 18, 1865-Sept. 18, 1911; House 1907-Sept. 18, 1911.

MADISON, James (D Va.) March 16, 1751-June 28, 1836; House 1789-97; Cont. Cong. 1780-83, 1786-88; Secretary of State 1801-09; President 1809-17.

MAFFETT, James Thompson (R Pa.) Feb. 2, 1837-Dec. 19, 1912; House 1887-89.

MAGEE, Clare (D Mo.) March 31, 1899-Aug. 7, 1969; House 1949-53.

MAGEE, James McDevitt (R Pa.) April 5, 1877-April 16, 1949; House 1923-27.

MAGEE, John (D N.Y.) Sept. 3, 1794-April 5, 1868; House 1827-31.

MAGEE, John Alexander (D Pa.) Oct. 14, 1827-Nov. 18, 1903; House 1873-75.

MAGEE, Walter Warren (R N.Y.) May 23, 1861-May 25, 1927; House 1915-May 25, 1927.

MAGINNIS, Martin (D Mont.) Oct. 27, 1841-March 27, 1919; House (Terr. Del.) 1873-85.

MAGNER, Thomas Francis (uncle of John Francis Carew) (D N.Y.) March 8, 1860-Dec. 22, 1945; House 1889-95.

MAGNUSON, Donald Hammer (D Wash.) March 7, 1911-__; House 1953-63.

MAGNUSON, Warren Grant (D Wash.) April 12, 1905-__; House 1937-Dec. 13, 1944; Senate Dec. 14, 1944-__.

MAGOON, Henry Sterling (R Wis.) Jan. 31, 1832-March 3, 1889; House 1875-77.

MAGRADY, Frederick William (R Pa.) Nov. 24, 1863-Aug. 27, 1954; House 1925-33.

MAGRUDER, Allan Bowie (D La.) 1775-April 15, 1822; Senate Sept. 3, 1812-13.

MAGRUDER, Patrick (— Md.) 1768-Dec. 24, 1819; House 1805-07.

MAGUIRE, Gene Andrew (D N.J.) March 11, 1939-__; House 1975-__.

MAGUIRE, James George (D Calif.) Feb. 22, 1853-June 20, 1920; House 1893-99.

MAGUIRE, John Arthur (D Neb.) Nov. 29, 1870-July 1, 1939; House 1909-15.

MAHAN, Bryan Francis (D Conn.) May 1, 1856-Nov. 16, 1923; House 1913-15.

MAHANY, Rowland Blennerhassett (R N.Y.) Sept. 28, 1864-May 2, 1937; House 1895-99.

MAHER, James Paul (D N.Y.) Nov. 3, 1865-July 31, 1946; House 1911-21.

MAHON, Gabriel Heyward Jr. (D S.C.) Nov. 11, 1889-June 11, 1962; House Nov. 3, 1936-39.

MAHON, George Herman (D Texas) Sept. 22, 1900-__; House 1935-__.

MAHON, Thaddeus Maclay (R Pa.) May 21, 1840-May 31, 1916; House 1893-1907.

MAHONE, William (Read. Va.) Dec. 1, 1826-Oct. 8, 1895; Senate 1881-87.

MAHONEY, Peter Paul (D N.Y.) June 25, 1848-March 27, 1889; House 1885-89.

MAHONEY, William Frank (D Ill.) Feb. 22, 1856-Dec. 27, 1904; House 1901-Dec. 27, 1904.

MAILLIARD, William Somers (R Calif.) June 10, 1917-__; House 1953-March 5, 1974.

MAIN, Verner Wright (R Mich.) Dec. 16, 1885-July 6, 1965; House Dec. 17, 1935-37.

MAISH, Levi (D Pa.) Nov. 22, 1837-Feb. 26, 1899; House 1875-79, 1887-91.

MAJOR, James Earl (D Ill.) Jan. 5, 1887-Jan. 4, 1972; House 1923-25, 1927-29, 1931-Oct. 6, 1933.

MAJOR, Samuel Collier (D Mo.) July 2, 1869-July 28, 1931; House 1919-21, 1923-29, March 4-July 28, 1931.

MAJORS, Thomas Jefferson (R Neb.) June 25, 1841-July 11, 1932; House Nov. 5, 1878-79.

MALBONE, Francis (F R.I.) March 20, 1759-June 4, 1809; House 1793-97; Senate March 4-June 4, 1809.

MALBY, George Roland (R N.Y.) Sept. 16, 1857-July 5, 1912; House 1907-July 5, 1912.

MALLARY, Richard Walker (R Vt.) Feb. 21, 1929-—; House Jan. 7, 1972-75.

MALLARY, Rollin Carolas (— Vt.) May 27, 1784-April 16, 1831; House Jan. 13, 1820-April 16, 1831.

MALLORY, Francis (W Va.) Dec. 12, 1807-March 26, 1860; House 1837-39, Dec. 28, 1840-43.

MALLORY, Meredith (D N.Y.) ? - ?; House 1839-41.

MALLORY, Robert (UD Ky.) Nov. 15, 1815-Aug. 11, 1885; House 1859-65.

MALLORY, Rufus (UR Ore.) Jan. 10, 1831-April 30, 1914; House 1867-69.

MALLORY, Stephen Russell (father of the following) (D Fla.) 1812-Nov. 9, 1873; Senate 1851-Jan. 21, 1861.

MALLORY, Stephen Russell (son of the preceding) (D Fla.) Nov. 2, 1848-Dec. 23, 1907; House 1891-95; Senate May 15, 1897-Dec. 23, 1907.

MALONE, George Wilson (R Nev.) Aug. 7, 1890-May 19, 1961; Senate 1947-59.

MALONEY, Francis Thomas (D Conn.) March 31, 1894-Jan. 16, 1945; House 1933-35; Senate 1935-Jan. 16, 1945.

MALONEY, Franklin John (R Pa.) March 29, 1899-Sept. 15, 1958; House 1947-49.

MALONEY, Paul Herbert (D La.) Feb. 14, 1876-March 26, 1967; House 1931-Dec. 15, 1940, 1943-47.

MALONEY, Robert Sarsfield (R Mass.) Feb. 3, 1881-Nov. 8, 1934; House 1921-23.

MANAHAN, James (R Minn.) March 12, 1866-Jan. 8, 1932; House 1913-15.

MANASCO, Carter (D Ala.) Jan. 3, 1902-—; House June 24, 1941-49.

MANDERSON, Charles Frederick (R Neb.) Feb. 9, 1837-Sept. 28, 1911; Senate 1883-95; President pro tempore 1891-93.

MANGUM, Willie Person (W N.C.) May 10, 1792-Sept. 7, 1861; House 1823-March 18, 1826; Senate 1831-Nov. 26, 1836, Nov. 25, 1840-53; President pro tempore 1842-45.

MANKIN, Helen Douglas (D Ga.) Sept. 11, 1896-July 25, 1956; House Feb. 12, 1946-47.

MANLOVE, Joe Jonathan (R Mo.) Oct. 1, 1876-Jan. 31, 1956; House 1923-33.

MANN, Abijah Jr. (D N.Y.) Sept. 24, 1793-Sept. 6, 1868; House 1833-37.

MANN, Edward Coke (D S.C.) Nov. 21, 1880-Nov. 11, 1931; House Oct. 7, 1919-21.

MANN, Horace (FS Mass.) May 4, 1796-Aug. 2, 1859; House April 3, 1848-53 (1848-51 Whig, 1851-53 Free Soiler).

MANN, James (D La.) June 22, 1822-Aug. 26, 1868; House July 18-Aug. 26, 1868.

MANN, James Robert (R Ill.) Oct. 20, 1856-Nov. 30, 1922; House 1897-Nov. 30, 1922.

MANN, James Robert (D S.C.) April 27, 1920-—; House 1969-—.

MANN, Job (D Pa.) March 31, 1795-Oct. 8, 1873; House 1835-37, 1847-51.

MANN, Joel Keith (D Pa.) Aug. 1, 1780-Aug. 28, 1857; House 1831-35.

MANNING, John Jr. (D N.C.) July 30, 1830-Feb. 12, 1899; House Dec. 7, 1870-71.

MANNING, Richard Irvine (D S.C.) May 1, 1789-May 1, 1836; House Dec. 8, 1834-May 1, 1836; Gov. 1824-26.

MANNING, Vannoy Hartrog (D Miss.) July 26, 1839-Nov. 3, 1892; House 1877-83.

MANSFIELD, Joseph Jefferson (D Texas) Feb. 9, 1861-July 12, 1947; House 1917-July 12, 1947.

MANSFIELD, Michael Joseph (Mike) (D Mont.) March 16, 1903-—; House 1943-53; Senate 1953-—.

MANSON, Mahlon Dickerson (D Ind.) Feb. 20, 1820-Feb. 4, 1895; House 1871-73.

MANSUR, Charles Harley (D Mo.) March 6, 1835-April 16, 1895; House 1887-93.

MANTLE, Lee (R Mont.) Dec. 13, 1851-Nov. 18, 1934; Senate Jan. 16, 1895-99.

MANZANARES, Francisco Antonio (D N.M.) Jan. 25, 1843-Sept. 17, 1904; House (Terr. Del.) March 5, 1884-85.

MAPES, Carl Edgar (R Mich.) Dec. 26, 1874-Dec. 12, 1939; House 1913-Dec. 12, 1939.

MARABLE, John Hartwell (NR Tenn.) Nov. 18, 1786-April 11, 1844; House 1825-29.

MARAZITI, Joseph James (R N.J.) June 15, 1912-—; House 1973-75.

MARCANTONIO, Vito (AL N.Y.) Dec. 10, 1902-Aug. 9, 1954; House 1935-37, 1939-51 (1935-37 Republican, 1939-51 American Laborite).

MARCHAND, Albert Gallatin (son of David Marchand) (D Pa.) Feb. 27, 1811-Feb. 5, 1848; House 1839-43.

MARCHAND, David (father of Albert Gallatin Marchand) (— Pa.) Dec. 10, 1776-March 11, 1832; House 1817-21.

MARCY, Daniel (D N.H.) Nov. 7, 1809-Nov. 3, 1893; House 1863-65.

MARCY, William Learned (JD N.Y.) Dec. 12, 1786-July 4, 1857; Senate 1831-Jan. 1, 1833; Gov. 1833-39; Secy. of War 1845-49; Secy. of State 1853-57.

MARDIS, Samuel Wright (D Ala.) June 12, 1800-Nov. 14, 1836; House 1831-35.

MARION, Robert (— S.C.) ? — ?; House 1805-Dec. 4, 1810.

MARKELL, Henry (son of Jacob Markell) (D N.Y.) Feb. 7, 1792-Aug. 30, 1831; House 1825-29.

MARKELL, Jacob (father of Henry Markell) (F N.Y.) May 8, 1770-Nov. 26, 1852; House 1813-15.

MARKHAM, Henry Harrison (R Calif.) Nov. 16, 1840-Oct. 9, 1923; House 1885-87; Gov. 1891-95.

MARKLEY, Philip Swenk (D Pa.) July 2, 1789-Sept. 12, 1834; House 1823-27.

MARKS, William (D Pa.) Oct. 13, 1778-April 10, 1858; Senate 1825-31.

MARLAND, Ernest Whitworth (D Okla.) May 8, 1874-Oct. 4, 1941; House 1933-35; Gov. 1935-39.

MARQUETTE, Turner Mastin (R Neb.) July 19, 1831-Dec. 22, 1894; House March 2-3, 1867.

MARR, Alem (D Pa.) June 18, 1787-March 29, 1843; House 1829-31.

MARR, George Washington Lent (— Tenn.) May 25, 1779-Sept. 5, 1856; House 1817-19.

MARSALIS, John Henry (D Colo.) May 9, 1904-—; House 1949-51.

MARSH, Benjamin Franklin (R Ill.) 1839-June 2, 1905; House 1877-83, 1893-1901, 1903-June 2, 1905.

MARSH, Charles (father of George Perkins Marsh) (F Vt.) July 10, 1765-Jan. 11, 1849; House 1815-17.

MARSH, George Perkins (son of Charles Marsh) (W Vt.) March 15, 1801-July 24, 1882; House 1843-May 1849.

MARSH, John O. Jr. (D Va.) Aug. 7, 1926-—; House 1963-71.

MARSHALL, Alexander Keith (AP Ky.) Feb. 11, 1808-April 28, 1884; House 1855-57.

MARSHALL, Alfred (D Maine) about 1797-Oct. 2, 1868; House 1841-43.

MARSHALL, Edward Chauncey (D Calif.) June 29, 1821-July 9, 1893; House 1851-53.

MARSHALL, Fred (D Minn.) March 13, 1906-—; House 1949-63.

MARSHALL, George Alexander (D Ohio) Sept. 14, 1851-April 21, 1899; House 1897-99.

MARSHALL, Humphrey (grandfather of Humphrey Marshall, father of Thomas Alexander Marshall and cousin of John Marshall) (F Ky.) 1760-July 1, 1841; Senate 1795-1801.

MARSHALL, Humphrey (grandson of the preceding) (AP Ky.) Jan. 13, 1812-March 28, 1872; House 1849-Aug. 4, 1852, 1855-59 (1849-52 Whig, 1855-59 American Party).

MARSHALL, James William (D Va.) March 31, 1844-Nov. 27, 1911; House 1893-95.

MARSHALL, John (uncle of Thomas Francis Marshall and cousin of Humphrey Marshall) (— Va.) Sept. 24, 1755-July 6, 1835; House 1799-June 7, 1800; Secy. of State June 6, 1800-March 4, 1801; Chief Justice of the Supreme Court Feb. 4, 1801-July 6, 1835.

MARSHALL, Leroy Tate (R Ohio) Nov. 8, 1883-Nov. 22, 1950; House 1933-37.

MARSHALL, Lycurgus Luther (R Ohio) July 9, 1888-Jan. 12, 1958; House 1939-41.

MARSHALL, Samuel Scott (D Ill.) March 12, 1821-July 26, 1890; House 1855-59, 1865-75.

MARSHALL, Thomas Alexander (son of Humphrey Marshall) (W Ky.) Jan. 15, 1794-April 17, 1871; House 1831-35.

MARSHALL, Thomas Francis (nephew of John Marshall) (— Ky.) June 7, 1801-Sept. 22, 1864; House 1841-43.

MARSHALL, Thomas Frank (R N.D.) March 7, 1854-Aug. 20, 1921; House 1901-09.

MARSTON, Gilman (R N.H.) Aug. 20, 1811-July 3, 1890; House 1859-63, 1865-67; Senate March 4-June 18, 1889.

MARTIN, Alexander (— N.C.) 1740-Nov. 10, 1807; Senate 1793-99; Gov. 1782-84, 1789-92.

MARTIN, Augustus Newton (D Ind.) March 23, 1847-July 11, 1901; House 1889-95.

MARTIN, Barclay (uncle of Lewis Tillman) (D Tenn.) Dec. 17, 1802-Nov. 8, 1890; House 1845-47.

MARTIN, Benjamin Franklin (D W.Va.) Oct. 2, 1828-Jan. 20, 1895; House 1877-81.

MARTIN, Charles (D Ill.) May 20, 1856-Oct. 28, 1917; House March 4-Oct. 28, 1917.

MARTIN, Charles Drake (D Ohio) Aug. 5, 1829-Aug. 27, 1911; House 1859-61.

MARTIN, Charles Henry (great-grandson of Nathaniel Macon) (P N.C.) Aug. 28, 1848-April 19, 1931; House June 5, 1896-99.

MARTIN, Charles Henry (D Ore.) Oct. 1, 1863-Sept. 22, 1946; House 1931-35; Gov. 1935-39.

MARTIN, David Thomas (R Neb.) July 9, 1907-—; House 1961-Dec. 31, 1974.

MARTIN, Eben Wever (R S.D.) April 12, 1855-May 22, 1932; House 1901-07, Nov. 3, 1908-15.

MARTIN, Edward (R Pa.) Sept. 18, 1879-March 19, 1967; Senate 1947-59; Gov. 1943-47.

MARTIN, Edward Livingston (D Del.) March 29, 1837-Jan. 22, 1897; House 1879-83.

MARTIN, Elbert Sevier (brother of John Preston Martin) (AP Va.) about 1829-Sept. 3, 1876; House 1859-61.

MARTIN, Frederick Stanley (W N.Y.) April 25, 1794-June 28, 1865; House 1851-53.

MARTIN, George Brown (grandson of John Preston Martin) (D Ky.) Aug. 18, 1876-Nov. 12, 1945; Senate Sept. 7, 1918-19.

MARTIN, James D. (R Ala.) Sept. 1, 1918-—; House 1965-67.

MARTIN. James Grubbs (R N.C.) Dec. 11, 1935-—; House 1973-—.

MARTIN, John (D Kan.) Nov. 12, 1833-Sept. 3, 1913; Senate 1893-95.

MARTIN, John Andrew (D Colo.) April 10, 1868-Dec. 23, 1939; House 1909-13, 1933-Dec. 23, 1939.

MARTIN, John Cunningham (D Ill.) April 29, 1880-Jan. 27, 1952; House 1939-41.

MARTIN, John Mason (son of Joshua Lanier Martin) (D Ala.) Jan. 20, 1837-June 16, 1898; House 1885-87.

MARTIN, John Preston (brother of Elbert Sevier Martin and grandfather of George Brown Martin) (D Ky.) Oct. 11, 1811-Dec. 23, 1862; House 1845-47.

MARTIN, Joseph John (R N.C.) Nov. 21, 1833-Dec. 18, 1900; House 1879-Jan. 29, 1881.

MARTIN, Joseph William Jr. (R Mass.) Nov. 3, 1884-March 6, 1968; House 1925-67; Speaker 1947-49, 1953-55; Chrmn. Rep. Nat. Comm. 1940-42.

MARTIN, Joshua Lanier (father of John Mason Martin) (D Ala.) Dec. 5, 1799-Nov. 2, 1856; House 1835-39; Gov. 1845-47.

MARTIN, Lewis J. (D N.J.) Feb. 22, 1844-May 5, 1913; House March 4-May 5, 1913.

MARTIN, Morgan Lewis (cousin of James Duane Doty) (D Wis.) March 31, 1805-Dec. 10, 1887; House (Terr. Del.) 1845-47.

MARTIN, Patrick Minor (R Calif.) Nov. 25, 1924-July 18, 1968; House 1963-65.

MARTIN, Robert Nicols (D Md.) Jan. 14, 1798-July 20, 1870; House 1825-27.

MARTIN, Thomas Ellsworth (R Iowa) Jan. 18, 1893-June 27, 1971; House 1939-55; Senate 1955-61.

MARTIN, Thomas Staples (D Va.) July 29, 1847-Nov. 12, 1919; Senate 1895-Nov. 12, 1919.

MARTIN, Whitmell Pugh (D La.) Aug. 12, 1867-April 6, 1929; House 1915-April 6, 1929 (1915-19 Progressive, 1919-29 Democrat).

MARTIN, William Dickinson (D S.C.) Oct. 20, 1789-Nov. 17, 1833; House 1827-31.

MARTIN, William Harrison (D Texas) May 23, 1823-Feb. 3, 1898; House Nov. 4, 1887-91.

MARTINDALE, Henry Clinton (W N.Y.) May 6, 1780-April 22, 1860; House 1823-31, 1833-35.

MARTINE, James Edgar (D N.J.) Aug. 25, 1850-Feb. 26, 1925; Senate 1911-17.

MARVIN, Dudley (W N.Y.) May 9, 1786-June 25, 1856; House 1823-29, 1847-49 (1823-29 Adams Democrat, 1847-49 Whig).

MARVIN, Francis (R N.Y.) March 8, 1828-Aug. 14, 1905; House 1893-95.

MARVIN, James Madison (U N.Y.) Feb. 27, 1809-April 25, 1901; House 1863-69.

MARVIN, Richard Pratt (W N.Y.) Dec. 23, 1803-Jan. 11, 1892; House 1837-41.

MASON, Armistead Thomson (son of Stevens Thomson Mason) (D Va.) Aug. 4, 1787-Feb. 6, 1819; Senate Jan. 3, 1816-17.

MASON, Harry Howland (D Ill.) Dec. 16, 1873-March 10, 1946; House 1935-37.

MASON, James Brown (F R.I.) January 1775-Aug. 31, 1819; House 1815-19.

MASON, James Murray (JD Va.) Nov. 3, 1798-April 28, 1871; House 1837-39; Senate Jan. 21, 1847-March 28, 1861.

MASON, Jeremiah (F N.H.) April 27, 1768-Oct. 14, 1848; Senate June 10, 1813- June 16, 1817.

MASON, John Calvin (JD Ky.) Aug. 4, 1802-Aug. 1865; House 1849-53, 1857-59.

MASON, John Thomson (D Md.) May 9, 1815-March 28, 1873; House 1841-43.

MASON, John Young (D Va.) April 18, 1799-Oct. 3, 1859; House 1831-Jan. 11, 1837; Secy. of the Navy 1844-45 and 1846-49; Atty. Gen. 1845-46.

MASON, Jonathan (F Mass.) Aug. 30, 1752-Nov. 1, 1831; Senate Nov. 14, 1800-03; House 1817-May 15, 1820

MASON, Joseph (R N.Y.) March 30, 1828-May 31, 1914; House 1879-83.

MASON, Moses Jr. (D Maine) June 2, 1789-June 25, 1866; House 1833-37.

MASON, Noah Morgan (R Ill.) July 19, 1882-March 29, 1965; House 1937-63.

MASON, Samson (W Ohio) July 24, 1793-Feb. 1, 1869; House 1835-43.

MASON, Stevens Thomson (father of Armistead Thomson Mason) (D Va.) Dec. 29, 1760-May 10, 1803; Senate Nov. 18, 1794-May 10, 1803.

MASON, William (D N.Y.) Sept. 10, 1786-Jan. 13, 1860; House 1835-37.

MASON, William Ernest (father of Winnifred Sprague Mason Huck) (R Ill.) July 7, 1850-June 16, 1921; House 1887-91, 1917-June 16, 1921; Senate 1897-1903.

MASSEY, William Alexander (R Nev.) Oct. 7, 1856-March 5, 1914; Senate July 1, 1912-Jan. 29, 1913.

MASSEY, Zachary David (R Tenn.) Nov. 14, 1864-July 13, 1923; House Nov. 8, 1910-11.

MASSINGALE, Samuel Chapman (D Okla.) Aug. 2, 1870-Jan. 17, 1941; House 1935-Jan. 17, 1941.

MASTERS, Josiah (D N.Y.) Nov. 22, 1763-June 30, 1822; House 1805-09.

MATHEWS, Frank Asbury Jr. (R N.J.) Aug. 3, 1890-Feb. 5, 1964; House Nov. 6, 1945-49.

MATHEWS, George (— Ga.) Aug. 30, 1739-Aug. 30, 1812; House 1789-91; Gov. 1787, 1793-96.

MATHEWS, George Arthur (R Dakota) June 4, 1852-April 19, 1941; House (Terr. Del.) March 4-Nov. 2, 1889.

MATHEWS, James (D Ohio) June 4, 1805-March 30, 1887; House 1841-45.

MATHEWS, Vincent (F N.Y.) June 29, 1766-Aug. 23, 1846; House 1809-11.

MATHEWSON, Elisha (D R.I.) April 18, 1767-Oct. 14, 1853; Senate Oct. 26, 1807-11.

MATHIAS, Charles McC. Jr. (R Md.) July 24, 1922-—; House 1961-69; Senate 1969-—.

MATHIAS, Robert B. (R Calif.) Nov. 17, 1930-—; House 1967-1975.

MATHIOT, Joshua (W Ohio) April 4, 1800-July 30, 1849; House 1841-43.

MATHIS, Marvin Dawson (D Ga.) Nov. 30, 1940-—; House 1971-—.

MATLACK, James (— N.J.) Jan. 11, 1775-Jan. 16, 1840; House 1821-25.

MATSON, Aaron (— N.H.) 1770-July 18, 1855; House 1821-25.

MATSON, Courtland Cushing (D Ind.) April 25, 1841-Sept. 4, 1915; House 1881-89.

MATSUNAGA, Spark Masayuki (D Hawaii) Oct. 8, 1916-—; House 1963-—.

MATTESON, Orsamus Benajah (W N.Y.) Aug. 28, 1805-Dec. 22, 1889; House 1849-51, 1853-Feb. 27, 1857, March 4, 1857-59.

MATTHEWS, Charles (R Pa.) Oct. 15, 1856-Dec. 12, 1932; House 1911-13.

MATTHEWS, Donald Ray (Billy) (D Fla.) Oct. 3, 1907-—; House 1953-67.

MATTHEWS, Nelson Edwin (R Ohio) April 14, 1852-Oct. 13, 1917; House 1915-17.

MATTHEWS, Stanley (uncle of Henry Watterson) (R Ohio) July 21, 1824-March 22, 1889; Senate March 21, 1877-79; Assoc. Justice of Supreme Court 1881-89.

MATTHEWS, William (— Md.) April 26, 1755-?; House 1797-99.

MATTOCKS, John (W Vt.) March 4, 1777-Aug. 14, 1847; House 1821-23, 1825-27, 1841-43; Gov. 1843-44.

MATTOON, Ebenezer (F Mass.) Aug. 19, 1755-Sept. 11, 1843; House Feb. 2, 1801-03.

MAURICE, James (D N.Y.) Nov. 7, 1814-Aug. 4, 1884; House 1853-55.

MAURY, Abram Poindexter (cousin of Fontaine Maury Maverick) (W Tenn.) Dec. 26, 1801-July 22, 1848; House 1835-39.

MAVERICK, Fontaine Maury (cousin of Abram P. Maury, nephew of James L. Slayden, and

cousin of John W. Fishburne) (D Texas) Oct. 23, 1895-June 7, 1954; House 1935-39.

MAXEY, Samuel Bell (D Texas) March 30, 1825-Aug. 16, 1895; Senate 1875-87.

MAXWELL, Augustus Emmett (grandfather of Emmett Wilson) (D Fla.) Sept. 21, 1820-May 5, 1903; House 1853-57.

MAXWELL, George Clifford (father of John Patterson Bryan Maxwell) (— N.J.) May 31, 1771-March 16, 1816; House 1811-13.

MAXWELL, John Patterson Bryan (son of George Clifford Maxwell and uncle of George Maxwell Robeson) (W N.J.) Sept. 3, 1804-Nov. 14, 1845; House 1837-39, 1841-43.

MAXWELL, Lewis (N R Va.) April 17, 1790-Feb. 13, 1862; House 1827-33.

MAXWELL, Samuel (Fus. Neb.) May 20, 1825-Feb. 11, 1901; House 1897-99.

MAXWELL, Thomas (D N.Y.) Feb. 16, 1792-Nov. 4, 1864; House 1829-31.

MAY, Andrew Jackson (D Ky.) June 24, 1875-Sept. 6, 1959; House 1931-47.

MAY, Catherine Dean (Barnes) (R Wash.) May 18, 1914-—; House 1959-71.

MAY, Edwin Hyland Jr. (R Conn.) May 28, 1924-—; House 1957-59.

MAY, Henry (D Md.) Feb. 13, 1816-Sept. 25, 1866; House 1853-55, 1861-63.

MAY, Mitchell (D N.Y.) July 10, 1870-March 24, 1961; House 1899-1901.

MAY, William L. (D Ill.) about 1793-Sept. 29, 1849; House Dec. 1, 1834-39.

MAYALL, Samuel (D Maine) June 21, 1816-Sept. 17, 1892; House 1853-55.

MAYBANK, Burnet Rhett (D S.C.) March 7, 1899-Sept. 1, 1954; Senate Nov. 5, 1941-Sept. 1, 1954; Gov. 1939-41.

MAYBURY, William Cotter (D Mich.) Nov. 20, 1848-May 6, 1909; House 1883-87.

MAYFIELD, Earle Bradford (D Texas) April 12, 1881-June 23, 1964; Senate 1923-29.

MAYHAM, Stephen Lorenzo (D N.Y.) Oct. 8, 1826-March 3, 1908; House 1869-71, 1877-79.

MAYNARD, Harry Lee (D Va.) June 8, 1861-Oct. 23, 1922; House 1901-11.

MAYNARD, Horace (R Tenn.) Aug. 30, 1814-May 3, 1882; House 1857-63, July 24, 1866-75 (1857-63 American Party, 1866-75 Republican); Postmaster General 1880-81.

MAYNARD, John (W N.Y.) ? - March 24, 1850; House 1827-29, 1841-43.

MAYNE, Wiley (R Iowa) Jan. 19, 1917-—; House 1967-1975.

MAYO, Robert Murphy (Read. Va.) April 28, 1836-March 29, 1896; House 1883-March 20, 1884.

MAYRANT, William (— S.C.) ? - ?; House 1815-Oct. 21, 1816.

MAYS, Dannite Hill (D Fla.) April 28, 1852-May 9, 1930; House 1909-13.

MAYS, James Henry (D Utah) June 29, 1868-April 19, 1926; House 1915-21.

MAZZOLI, Romano Louis (D Ky.) Nov. 2, 1932- —; House 1971- —.

McADOO, William (D N.J.) Oct. 25, 1853-June 7, 1930; House 1883-91.

McADOO, William Gibbs (D Calif.) Oct. 31, 1863-Feb. 1, 1941; Senate 1933-Nov. 8, 1938; Secy. of the Treasury 1913-18.

McALEER, William (D Pa.) Jan. 6, 1838-April 19, 1912; House 1891-95, 1897-1901.

McALLISTER, Archibald (grandson of John Andre Hanna) (D Pa.) Oct. 12, 1813-July 18, 1883; House 1863-65.

McANDREWS. James (D Ill.) Oct. 22, 1862-Aug. 31, 1942; House 1901-05, 1913-21, 1935-41.

McARDLE, Joseph A. (D Pa.) June 29, 1903-Dec. 27, 1967; House 1939-Jan. 5, 1942.

McARTHUR. Clifton Nesmith (grandson of James Willis Nesmith) (R Ore.) June 10, 1879-Dec. 9, 1923; House 1915-23.

McARTHUR, Duncan (D Ohio) June 14, 1772-April 29, 1839; House March 4-April 5, 1813, 1823-25; Gov. 1830-32.

McBRIDE, George Wycliffe (brother of John Rogers McBride) (R Ore.) March 13, 1854-June 18, 1911; Senate 1895-1901.

McBRIDE, John Rogers (brother of George Wycliffe McBride) (R Ore.) Aug. 22, 1832-July 20, 1904; House 1863-65.

McBRYDE, Archibald (D N.C.) Sept. 28, 1766-Feb. 15, 1816; House 1809-13.

McCALL, John Ethridge (R Tenn.) Aug. 14, 1859-Aug. 8, 1920; House 1895-97.

McCALL, Samuel Walker (R Mass.) Feb. 28, 1851-Nov. 4, 1923; House 1893-1913; Gov. 1916-19.

McCANDLESS, Lincoln Loy (D Hawaii) Sept. 18, 1859-Oct. 5, 1940; House (Terr. Del.) 1933-35.

McCARRAN, Patrick Anthony (Pat) (D Nev.) Aug. 8, 1876-Sept. 28, 1954; Senate 1933-Sept. 28, 1954.

McCARTHY, Dennis (R N.Y.) March 19, 1814-Feb. 14, 1886; House 1867-71.

McCARTHY, Eugene Joseph (D Minn.) March 29, 1916- —; House 1949-59; Senate 1959-71.

McCARTHY, John Henry (D N.Y.) Nov. 16, 1850-Feb. 5, 1908; House 1889-Jan. 14, 1891.

McCARTHY, John Jay (R Neb.) July 19, 1857-March 30, 1943; House 1903-07.

McCARTHY, Joseph Raymond (R Wis.) Nov. 14, 1908-May 2, 1957; Senate 1947-May 2, 1957.

McCARTHY, Kathryn O'Loughlin (see O'Loughlin, Kathryn Ellen.)

McCARTHY, Richard Dean (D N.Y.) Sept. 24, 1927- —; House 1965-71.

McCARTY, Andrew Zimmerman (W N.Y.) July 14, 1808-April 23, 1879; House 1855-57.

McCARTY, Johnathan (W Ind.) Aug. 3, 1795-March 30, 1852; House 1831-37.

McCARTY, Richard (D N.Y.) Feb. 19, 1780-May 18, 1844; House 1821-23.

McCARTY, William Mason (W Va.) about 1789-Dec. 20, 1863; House Jan. 25, 1840-41; Terr. Gov. of Fla. 1827.

McCAUSLEN, William Cochran (D Ohio) 1796-March 13, 1863; House 1843-45.

McCLAMMY, Charles Washington (D N.C.) May 29, 1839-Feb. 26, 1896; House 1887-91.

McCLEAN. Moses (D Pa.) June 17, 1804-Sept. 30, 1870; House 1845-47.

McCLEARY, James Thompson (R Minn.) Feb. 5, 1853-Dec. 17, 1924; House 1893-1907.

McCLEERY, James (R La.) Dec. 2, 1837-Nov. 5, 1871; House March 4-Nov. 5, 1871.

McCLELLAN, Abraham (D Tenn.) Oct. 4, 1789-May 3, 1866; House 1837-43.

McCLELLAN, Charles A. O. (D Ind.) May 25, 1835-Jan. 31, 1898; House 1889-93.

McCLELLAN, George (D N.Y.) Oct. 10, 1856-Feb. 20, 1927; House 1913-15.

McCLELLAN, George Brinton (D N.Y.) Nov. 23, 1865-Nov. 30, 1940; House 1895-Dec. 21, 1903.

McCLELLAN, John Little (D Ark.) Feb. 25, 1896- —; House 1935-39; Senate 1943- —.

McCLELLAN, Robert (D N.Y.) Oct. 2, 1806-June 28, 1860; House 1837-39, 1841-43.

McCLELLAND, Robert (D Mich.) Aug. 1, 1807-Aug. 30, 1880; House 1843-49; Gov. 1851-53; Secy. of the Interior 1853-57.

McCLELLAND, William (D Pa.) March 2, 1842-Feb. 7, 1892; House 1871-73.

McCLENACHAN, Blair (— Pa.) ? - May 8, 1812; House 1797-99.

McCLERNAND, John Alexander (D Ill.) May 30, 1812-Sept. 20, 1900; House 1843-51, Nov. 8, 1859-Oct. 28, 1861.

McCLINTIC, James Vernon (D Okla.) Sept. 8, 1878-April 22, 1948; House 1915-35.

McCLINTOCK, Charles Blaine (R Ohio) May 25, 1886-Feb. 1, 1965; House 1929-33.

McCLORY, Robert (R Ill.) Jan. 31, 1908- —; House 1963- —.

McCLOSKEY, Augustus (D Texas) Sept. 23, 1878-July 21, 1950; House 1929-Feb. 10, 1930.

McCLOSKEY, Paul N. (Pete) Jr. (R Calif.) Sept. 29, 1927- —; House Dec. 12, 1967- —.

McCLURE, Addison S. (R Ohio) Oct. 10, 1839-April 17, 1903; House 1881-83, 1895-97.

McCLURE, Charles (D Pa.) 1804-Jan. 10, 1846; House 1837-39, Dec. 7, 1840-41.

McCLURE, James A. (R Idaho) Dec. 27, 1924-__; House 1967-1973; Senate 1973- —.

McCLURG, Joseph Washington (Rad. Mo.) Feb. 22, 1818-Dec. 2, 1900; House 1863-68 (1863-65 Emancipationist, 1865-68 Radical); Gov. 1869-71 (R).

McCOID, Moses Ayres (R Iowa) Nov. 5, 1840-May 19, 1904; House 1879-85.

McCOLLISTER, John Yetter (R Neb.) June 10, 1921- —; House 1971- —.

McCOMAS, Louis Emory (grandfather of Katharine E. Byron and great-grandfather of Goodloe E. Byron) (R Md.) Oct. 28, 1846-Nov. 10, 1907; House 1883-91; Senate 1899-1905.

McCOMAS, William (W Va.) 1795-June 3, 1865; House 1833-37.

McCONNELL, Felix Grundy (D Ala.) April 1, 1809-Sept. 10, 1846; House 1843-Sept. 10, 1846.

McCONNELL, Samuel Kerns Jr. (R Pa.) April 6, 1901- —; House Jan. 18, 1944-Sept. 1, 1957.

McCONNELL, William John (R Idaho) Sept. 18, 1839-March 30, 1925; Senate Dec. 18, 1890-91; Gov. 1893-97.

McCOOK, Anson George (R N.Y.) Oct. 10, 1835-Dec. 30, 1917; House 1877-83.

McCORD, Andrew (— N.Y.) about 1754-1808; House 1803-05.

McCORD, James Nance (D Tenn.) March 17, 1879-Sept. 2, 1968; House 1943-45; Gov. 1945-49.

McCORD, Myron Hawley (R Wis.) Nov. 26, 1840-April 27, 1908; House 1889-91; Gov. (Ariz. Terr.) 1897-98.

McCORKLE, Joseph Walker (D Calif.) June 24, 1819-March 18, 1884; House 1851-53.

McCORKLE, Paul Grier (D S.C.) Dec. 19, 1863-June 2, 1934; House Feb. 24-March 3, 1917.

McCORMACK, John William (D Mass.) Dec. 21, 1891- —; House Nov. 6, 1928-71; Speaker 1962-71.

McCORMACK, Mike (D Wash.) Dec. 14, 1921- —; House 1971- —.

McCORMICK, Henry Clay (R Pa.) June 30, 1844-May 26, 1902; House 1887-91.

McCORMICK, James Robinson (D Mo.) Aug. 1, 1824-May 19, 1897; House Dec. 17, 1867-73.

McCORMICK, John Watts (R Ohio) Dec. 20, 1831-June 25, 1917; House 1883-85.

McCORMICK, (Joseph) Medill (husband of Ruth Hanna McCormick) (R Ill.) May 16, 1877-Feb. 25, 1925; House 1917-19; Senate 1919-Feb. 25, 1925.

McCORMICK, Nelson B. (P Kan.) Nov. 20, 1847-April 10, 1914; House 1897-99.

McCORMICK, Richard Cunningham (U Ariz. & R N.Y.) May 23, 1832-June 2, 1901; House (Terr. Del. Ariz.) 1869-75, (Rep. N.Y.) 1895-97; Gov. (Ariz. Terr.) 1866.

McCORMICK, Ruth Hanna (daughter of Marcus Alonzo Hanna, wife of Joseph Medill McCormick and of Albert Gallatin Simms) (R Ill.) March 27, 1880-Dec. 31, 1944; House 1929-31.

McCORMICK, Washington Jay (R Mont.) Jan. 4, 1884-March 7, 1949; House 1921-23.

McCOWEN, Edward Oscar (R Ohio) June 29, 1877-Nov. 4, 1953; House 1943-49.

McCOY, Robert (— Pa.) ? - June 7, 1849; House Nov. 22, 1831-33.

McCOY, Walter Irving (D N.J.) Dec. 8, 1859-July 17, 1933; House 1911-Oct. 3, 1914.

McCOY, William (D Va.) ? - 1864; House 1811-33.

McCRACKEN, Robert McDowell (R Idaho) March 15, 1874-May 16, 1934; House 1915-17.

McCRARY, George Washington (R Iowa) Aug. 29, 1835-June 23, 1890; House 1869-77; Secy. of War 1877-79.

McCRATE, John Dennis (D Maine) Oct. 1, 1802-Sept. 11, 1879; House 1845-47.

McCREARY, George Deardorff (R Pa.) Sept. 28, 1846-July 26, 1915; House 1903-13.

McCREARY, James Bennett (D Ky.) July 8, 1838-Oct. 8, 1918; House 1885-97; Senate 1903-09; Gov. 1875-79, 1911-15.

McCREARY, John (— S.C.) 1761-Nov. 4, 1833; House 1819-21.

McCREDIE, William Wallace (R Wash.) April 27, 1862-May 10, 1935; House Nov. 2, 1909-11.

McCREERY, Thomas Clay (D Ky.) Dec. 12, 1816-July 10, 1890; Senate Feb. 19, 1868-71, 1873-79.

McCREERY, William (— Md.) 1750-March 8, 1814; House 1803-09.

McCREERY, William (D Pa.) May 17, 1786-Sept. 27, 1841; House 1829-31.

McCULLOCH, George (D Pa.) Feb. 22, 1792-April 6, 1861; House Nov. 20, 1839-41.

McCULLOCH, John (W Pa.) Nov. 15, 1806-May 15, 1879; House 1853-55.

McCULLOCH, Philip Doddridge Jr. (D Ark.) June 23, 1851-Nov. 26, 1928; House 1893-1903.

McCULLOCH, Roscoe Conkling (R Ohio) Nov. 27, 1880-March 17, 1958; House 1915-21; Senate Nov. 5, 1929-Nov. 30, 1930.

McCULLOCH, William Moore (R Ohio) Nov. 24, 1901-—; House Nov. 4, 1947-1973.

McCULLOGH, Welty (R Pa.) Oct. 10, 1847-Aug. 31, 1889; House 1887-89.

McCULLOUGH, Hiram (D Md.) Sept. 26, 1813-March 4, 1885; House 1865-69.

McCULLOUGH, Thomas Grubb (— Pa.) April 20, 1785-Sept. 10, 1848; House Oct. 17, 1820-21.

McCUMBER, Porter James (R N.D.) Feb. 3, 1858-May 18, 1933; Senate 1899-1923.

McDADE, Joseph Michael (R Pa.) Sept. 29, 1931-—; House 1963-—.

McDANIEL, William (D Mo.) ? - about 1854; House Dec. 7, 1846-47.

McDANNOLD, John James (D Ill.) Aug. 29, 1851-Feb. 3, 1904; House 1893-95.

McDEARMON, James Calvin (D Tenn.) June 13, 1844-July 19, 1902; House 1893-97.

McDERMOTT, Allan Langdon (D N.J.) March 30, 1854-Oct. 26, 1908; House Dec. 3, 1900-07.

McDERMOTT, James Thomas (D Ill.) Feb. 13, 1872-Feb. 7, 1938; House 1907-July 21, 1914, 1915-17.

McDILL, Alexander Stuart (R Wis.) March 18, 1822-Nov. 12, 1875; House 1873-75.

McDILL, James Wilson (R Iowa) March 4, 1834-Feb. 28, 1894; House 1873-77; Senate March 8, 1881-83.

McDONALD, Alexander (R Ark.) April 10, 1832-Dec. 13, 1903; Senate June 22, 1868-71.

McDONALD, Edward Francis (D N.J.) Sept. 21, 1844-Nov. 5, 1892; House 1891-Nov. 5, 1892.

McDONALD, Jack H. (R Mich.) June 28, 1932-—; House 1967-1973.

McDONALD, John (R Md.) May 24, 1837-Jan. 30, 1917; House 1897-99.

McDONALD, Joseph Ewing (D Ind.) Aug. 29, 1819-June 21, 1891; House 1849-51; Senate 1875-81.

McDONALD, Lawrence Patton (D Ga.) April 1, 1935-—; House 1975-—.

McDONOUGH, Gordon Leo (R Calif.) Jan. 2, 1895-June 25, 1968; House 1945-63.

McDOUGALL, James Alexander (D Calif.) Nov. 19, 1817-Sept. 3, 1867; House 1853-55; Senate 1861-67.

McDOWELL, Alexander (R Pa.) March 4, 1845-Sept. 30, 1913; House 1893-95.

McDOWELL, Harris Brown Jr. (D Del.) Feb. 10, 1906-—; House 1955-57, 1959-67.

McDOWELL, James (D Va.) Oct. 13, 1796-Aug. 24, 1851; House March 6, 1846-51; Gov. 1843-46.

McDOWELL, James Foster (D Ind.) Dec. 3, 1825-April 18, 1887; House 1863-65.

McDOWELL, John Anderson (D Ohio) Sept. 25, 1853-Oct. 2, 1927; House 1897-1901.

McDOWELL, John Ralph (R Pa.) Nov. 6, 1902-Dec. 11, 1957; House 1939-41, 1947-49.

McDOWELL, Joseph (father of Joseph Jefferson McDowell and cousin of Joseph (P G) McDowell) (— N.C.) Feb. 15, 1756-Feb. 5, 1801; House 1797-99.

McDOWELL, Joseph (P G) (cousin of Joseph McDowell) (— N.C.) Feb. 25, 1758-March 7, 1799; House 1793-95.

McDOWELL, Joseph Jefferson (son of Joseph McDowell) (D Ohio) Nov. 13, 1800-Jan. 17, 1877; House 1843-47.

McDUFFIE, George (D S.C.) Aug. 10, 1790-March 11, 1851; House 1821-34; Senate Dec. 23, 1842-Aug. 17, 1846; Gov. 1834-36.

McDUFFIE, John (D Ala.) Sept. 25, 1883-Nov. 1, 1950; House 1919-March 2, 1935.

McDUFFIE, John Van (R Ala.) May 16, 1841-Nov. 18, 1896; House June 4, 1890-91.

McENERY, Samuel Douglas (D La.) May 28, 1837-June 28, 1910; Senate 1897-June 28, 1910. Gov. 1881-88.

McETTRICK, Michael Joseph (D Mass.) June 22, 1848-Dec. 31, 1921; House 1893-95.

McEWAN, Thomas Jr. (R N.J.) Feb. 26, 1854-Sept. 11, 1926; House 1895-99.

McEWEN, Robert Cameron (R N.Y.) Jan. 5, 1920-—; House 1965-—.

McFADDEN, Louis Thomas (R Pa.) July 25, 1876-Oct. 1, 1936; House 1915-35.

McFADDEN, Obadiah Benton (D Wash.) Nov. 18, 1815-June 25, 1875; House (Terr. Del.) 1873-75.

McFALL, John Joseph (D Calif.) Feb. 20, 1918-—; House 1957-—.

McFARLAN, Duncan (— N.C.) ? - Sept. 7, 1816; House 1805-07.

McFARLAND, Ernest William (D Ariz.) Oct. 9, 1894-—; Senate 1941-53; Gov. 1955-59.

McFARLAND, William (D Tenn.) Sept. 15, 1821-April 12, 1900; House 1875-77.

McFARLANE, William Doddridge (D Texas) July 17, 1894-—; House 1933-39.

McGANN, Lawrence Edward (D Ill.) Feb. 2, 1852-July 22, 1928; House 1891-Dec. 2, 1895.

McGARVEY, Robert Neill (R Pa.) Aug. 14, 1888-June 28, 1952; House 1947-49.

McGAUGHEY, Edward Wilson (W Ind.) Jan. 16, 1817-Aug. 6, 1852; House 1845-47, 1849-51.

McGAVIN, Charles (R Ill.) Jan. 10, 1874-Dec. 17, 1940; House 1905-09.

McGEE, Gale William (D Wyo.) March 17, 1915-—; Senate 1959-—.

McGEHEE, Daniel Rayford (D Miss.) Sept. 10, 1883-Feb. 9, 1962; House 1935-47.

McGILL, George (D Kan.) Feb. 12, 1879-May 14, 1963; Senate Dec. 1, 1930-39.

McGILLICUDDY, Daniel John (D Maine) Aug. 27, 1859-July 30, 1936; House 1911-17.

McGINLEY, Donald Francis (D Neb.) June 30, 1920-—; House 1959-61.

McGLENNON, Cornelius Augustine (D N.J.) Dec. 10, 1878-June 13, 1931; House 1919-21.

McGLINCHEY, Herbert Joseph (D Pa.) Nov. 7, 1904-—; House 1945-47.

McGOVERN, George Stanley (D S.D.) July 19, 1922-—; House 1957-61; Senate 1963-—.

McGOWAN, Jonas Hartzell (R Mich.) April 2, 1837-July 5, 1909; House 1877-81.

McGRANERY, James Patrick (D Pa.) July 8, 1895-Dec. 23, 1962; House 1937-Nov. 17, 1943; Atty. Gen. 1952-53.

McGRATH, Christopher Columbus (D N.Y.) May 15, 1902-—; House 1949-53.

McGRATH, James Howard (D R.I.) Nov. 28, 1903-Sept. 2, 1966; Senate 1947-Aug. 23, 1949; Chrmn. Dem. Nat. Comm. 1947-49; Gov. 1941-45; Atty. Gen. 1949-52.

McGRATH, John Joseph (D Calif.) July 23, 1872-Aug. 25, 1951; House 1933-39.

McGRATH, Thomas C. Jr. (D N.J.) April 22, 1927-—; House 1965-67.

McGREGOR, J. Harry (R Ohio) Sept. 30, 1896-Oct. 7, 1958; House Feb. 27, 1940-Oct. 7, 1958.

McGREW, James Clark (R W.Va.) Sept. 14, 1813-Sept. 18, 1910; House 1869-73.

McGROARTY, John Steven (D Calif.) Aug. 20, 1862-Aug. 7, 1944; House 1935-39.

McGUGIN, Harold Clement (R Kan.) Nov. 22, 1893-March 7, 1946; House 1931-35.

McGUIRE, Bird Segle (cousin of William Neville) (R Okla.) Oct. 13, 1865-Nov. 9, 1930; House (Terr. Del.) 1903-07, (Rep.) Nov. 16, 1907-15.

McGUIRE, John Andrew (D Conn.) Feb. 28, 1906-May 28, 1976; House 1949-53.

McHATTON, Robert Lytle (JD Ky.) Nov. 17, 1788-May 20, 1835; House Dec. 7, 1826-29.

McHENRY, Henry Davis (son of John Hardin McHenry) (D Ky.) Feb. 27, 1826-Dec. 17, 1890; House 1871-73.

McHENRY, John Geiser (D Pa.) April 26, 1868-Dec. 27, 1912; House 1907-Dec. 27, 1912.

McHENRY, John Hardin (father of Henry Davis McHenry) (W Ky.) Oct. 13, 1797-Nov. 1, 1871; House 1845-47.

McHUGH, Matthew Francis (D N.Y.) Dec. 6, 1938-—; House 1975-—.

McILVAINE, Abraham Robinson (W Pa.) Aug. 14, 1804-Aug. 22, 1863; House 1843-49.

McILVAINE, Joseph (D N.J.) Oct. 2, 1769-Aug. 19, 1826; Senate Nov. 12, 1823-Aug. 19, 1826.

McINDOE, Walter Duncan (R Wis.) March 30, 1819-Aug. 22, 1872; House Jan. 26, 1863-67.

McINTIRE, Clifford Guy (R Maine) May 4, 1908-Oct. 1, 1974; House Oct. 22, 1951-65.

McINTIRE, Rufus (JD Maine) Dec. 19, 1784-April 28, 1866; House Sept. 10, 1827-35.

McINTIRE, William Watson (R Md.) June 30, 1850-March 30, 1912; House 1897-99.

McINTOSH, Robert John (R Mich.) Sept. 16, 1922-—; House 1957-59.

McINTYRE, John Joseph (D Wyo.) Dec. 17, 1904-Nov. 30, 1974; House 1941-43.

McINTYRE, Thomas James (D N.H.) Feb. 20, 1915-—; Senate Nov. 7, 1962-—.

McJUNKIN, Ebenezer (R Pa.) March 28, 1819-Nov. 10, 1907; House 1871-Jan. 1, 1875.

McKAIG, William McMahone (D Md.) July 29, 1845-June 6, 1907; House 1891-95.

McKAY, James Iver (D N.C.) 1793-Sept. 4, 1853; House 1831-49.

McKAY, Koln Gunn (D Utah) Feb. 23, 1925-—; House 1971-__.

McKEAN, James Bedell (nephew of Samuel McKean) (R N.Y.) Aug. 5, 1821-Jan. 5, 1879; House 1859-63.

McKEAN, Samuel (uncle of James Bedell McKean) (D Pa.) April 7, 1787-Dec. 14, 1841; House 1823-29; Senate 1833-39.

McKEE, George Colin (R Miss.) Oct. 2, 1837-Nov. 17, 1890; House 1869-75.

McKEE, John (— Ala.) 1771-Aug. 12, 1832; House 1823-29.

McKEE, Samuel (D Ky.) Oct. 13, 1774-Oct. 16, 1826; House 1809-17.

McKEE, Samuel (R Ky) Nov. 5, 1833-Dec. 11, 1898; House 1865-67, June 22, 1868-69.

McKEIGHAN, William Arthur (I Neb.) Jan. 19, 1842-Dec. 15, 1895; House 1891-95 (1891-93 Democrat, 1893-95 Independent).

McKELLAR, Kenneth Douglas (D Tenn.) Jan. 29, 1869-Oct. 25, 1957; House Nov. 9, 1911-17; Senate 1917-53; President pro tempore 1945-47, 1949-53.

McKENNA, Joseph (R Calif.) Aug. 10, 1843-Nov. 21, 1926; House 1885-92; Atty. Gen. 1897-98; Assoc. Justice of Supreme Court 1898-1925.

McKENNAN, Thomas McKean Thompson (W Pa.) March 31, 1794-July 9, 1852; House 1831-39, May 30, 1842-43; Secy. of the Interior Aug. 15-Sept. 12, 1850.

McKENNEY, William Robertson (D Va.) Dec. 2, 1851-Jan. 3, 1916; House 1895-May 2, 1896.

McKENTY, Jacob Kerlin (D Pa.) Jan. 19, 1827-Jan. 3, 1866; House Dec. 3, 1860-61.

McKENZIE, Charles Edgar (D La.) Oct. 3, 1896-June 7, 1956; House 1943-47.

McKENZIE, James Andrew (uncle of John McKenzie Moss) (D Ky.) Aug. 1, 1840-June 25, 1904; House 1877-83.

McKENZIE, John Charles (R Ill.) Feb. 18, 1860-Sept. 17, 1941; House 1911-25.

McKENZIE, Lewis (UC Va.) Oct. 7, 1810-June 28, 1895; House Feb. 16-March 3, 1863, Jan. 31, 1870-71 (1863 Unionist, 1870-71 Union Conservative).

McKEON, John (D N.Y.) March 29, 1808-Nov. 22, 1883; House 1835-37, 1841-43.

McKEOUGH, Raymond Stephen (D Ill.) April 29, 1888-—; House 1935-43.

McKEOWN, Thomas Deitz (D Okla.) June 4, 1878-Oct. 22, 1951; House 1917-21, 1923-35.

McKEVITT, James Douglas (Mike) (R Colo.) Oct. 26, 1928-__; House 1971-73.

McKIBBIN, Joseph Chambers (D Calif.) May 14, 1824-July 1, 1896; House 1857-59.

McKIM, Alexander (uncle of Isaac McKim) (D Md.) Jan. 10, 1748-Jan. 18, 1832; House 1809-15.

McKIM, Isaac (nephew of Alexander McKim) (D Md.) July 21, 1775-April 1, 1838; House Jan. 4, 1823-25, 1833-April 1, 1838.

McKINIRY, Richard Francis (D N.Y.) March 23, 1878-May 30, 1950; House 1919-21.

McKINLAY, Duncan E. (R Calif.) Oct. 6, 1862-Dec. 30, 1914; House 1905-11.

McKINLEY, John (JD Ala.) May 1, 1780-July 19, 1852; Senate Nov. 27, 1826-31, March 4-April 22, 1837; House 1833-35; Assoc. Justice of Supreme Court April 22, 1837-July 19, 1852.

McKINLEY, William (D Va.) ? - ?; House Dec. 21, 1810-11.

McKINLEY, William Jr. (R Ohio) Jan. 29, 1843-Sept. 14, 1901; House 1877-May 27, 1884, 1885-91; Gov. 1892-96; President 1897-1901.

McKINLEY, William Brown (R Ill.) Sept. 5, 1856-Dec. 7, 1926; House 1905-13; 1915-21; Senate 1921-Dec. 7, 1926.

McKINNEY, James (R Ill.) April 14, 1852-Sept. 29, 1934; House Nov. 7, 1905-13.

McKINNEY, John Franklin (D Ohio) April 12, 1827-June 13, 1903; House 1863-65, 1871-73.

McKINNEY, Luther Franklin (D N.H.) April 25, 1841-July 30, 1922; House 1887-89, 1891-93.

McKINNEY, Stewart Brett (R Conn.) Jan. 30, 1931-—; House 1971-—.

McKINNON, Clinton Dotson (D Calif.) Feb. 5, 1906-—; House 1949-53.

McKISSOCK, Thomas (W N.Y.) April 17, 1790-June 26, 1866; House 1849-51.

McKNEALLY, Martin B. (R N.Y.) Dec. 31, 1914-—; House 1969-71.

McKNIGHT, Robert (R Pa.) Jan. 20, 1820-Oct. 25, 1885; House 1859-63.

McLACHLAN, James (R Calif.) Aug. 1, 1852-Nov. 21, 1940; House 1895-97, 1901-11.

McLAIN, Frank Alexander (D Miss.) Jan. 29, 1852-Oct. 10, 1920; House Dec. 12, 1898-1909.

McLANAHAN, James Xavier (grandson of Andrew Gregg) (D Pa.) 1809-Dec. 16, 1861; House 1849-53.

McLANE, Louis (father of Robert Milligan McLane) (F Del.) May 28, 1786-Oct. 7, 1857; House 1817-27; Senate 1827-April 16, 1829; Secy. of the Treasury 1831-33; Secy. of State 1833-34.

McLANE, Patrick (D Pa.) March 14, 1875-Nov. 13, 1946; House 1919-Feb. 25, 1921.

McLANE, Robert Milligan (son of Louis McLane) (D Md.) June 23, 1815-April 16, 1898; House 1847-51, 1879-83; Gov. 1884-85.

McLAUGHLIN, Charles Francis (D Neb.) June 19, 1887-Feb. 5, 1976; House 1935-43.

McLAUGHLIN, James Campbell (R Mich.) Jan. 26, 1858-Nov. 29, 1932; House 1907-Nov. 29, 1932.

McLAUGHLIN, Joseph (R Pa.) June 9, 1867-Nov. 21, 1926; House 1917-19, 1921-23.

McLAUGHLIN, Melvin Orlando (R Neb.) Aug. 8, 1876-June 18, 1928; House 1919-27.

McLAURIN, Anselm Joseph (D Miss.) March 26, 1848-Dec. 22, 1909; Senate Feb. 7, 1894-95, 1901-Dec. 22, 1909; Gov. 1896-1900.

McLAURIN, John Lowndes (D S.C.) May 9, 1860-July 29, 1934; House Dec. 5, 1892-May 31, 1897; Senate June 1, 1897-1903.

McLEAN, Alney (—Ky.) June 10, 1779-Dec. 30, 1841; House 1815-17, 1819-21.

McLEAN, Donald Holman (R N.J.) March 18, 1884-Aug. 19, 1975; House 1933-45.

McLEAN, Finis Ewing (brother of John McLean and uncle of James David Walker) (W Ky.) Feb. 19, 1806-April 12, 1881; House 1849-51.

McLEAN, George Payne (R Conn.) Oct. 7, 1857-June 6, 1932; Senate 1911-29; Gov. 1901-03.

McLEAN, James Henry (R Mo.) Aug. 13, 1829-Aug. 12, 1886; House Dec. 15, 1882-83.

McLEAN, John (brother of William McLean) (WD Ohio) March 11, 1785-April 4, 1861; House 1813-16; Postmaster Gen. 1823-29; Assoc. Justice of Supreme Court 1829-61.

McLEAN, John (brother of Finis Ewing McLean and uncle of James David Walker) (D Ill.) Feb. 4, 1791-Oct. 14, 1830; House Dec. 3, 1818-19; Senate Nov. 23, 1824-25, 1829-Oct. 14, 1830.

McLEAN, Samuel (D Mont.) Aug. 7, 1826-July 16, 1877; House (Terr. Del.) Jan. 6, 1865-67.

McLEAN, William (brother of John McLean) (—Ohio) Aug. 10, 1794-Oct. 12, 1839; House 1823-29.

McLEAN, William Pinkney (D Texas) Aug. 9, 1836-March 13, 1925; House 1873-75.

McLEMORE, Atkins Jefferson (Jeff) (D Texas) March 13, 1857-March 4, 1929; House 1915-19.

McLENE, Jeremiah (D Ohio) 1767-March 19, 1837; House 1833-37.

McLEOD, Clarence John (R Mich.) July 3, 1895-May 15, 1959; House Nov. 2, 1920-21, 1923-37, 1939-41.

McLOSKEY, Robert Thaddeus (R Ill.) June 26, 1907-—; House 1963-65.

McMAHON, Gregory (R N.Y.) March 19, 1915-__; House 1947-49.

McMAHON, James O'Brien (D Conn.) Oct. 6, 1903-July 28, 1952; Senate 1945-July 28, 1952.

McMAHON, John A. (nephew of Clement Laird Vallandigham) (D Ohio) Feb. 19, 1833-March 8, 1923; House 1875-81.

McMANUS, William (— N.Y.) 1780-Jan. 18, 1835; House 1825-27.

McMASTER, William Henry (R S.D.) May 10, 1877-Sept. 14, 1968; Senate 1925-31; Gov. 1921-25.

McMILLAN, Alexander (—N.C.) ? - 1817; House 1817.

McMILLAN, Clara Gooding (widow of Thomas S. McMillan) (D S.C.) Aug. 17, 1894-—; House Nov. 7, 1939-41.

McMILLAN, James (R Mich.) May 12, 1838-Aug. 10, 1902; Senate 1889-Aug. 10, 1902.

McMILLAN, John Lanneau (D S.C.) ? - —; House 1939-73.

McMILLAN, Samuel (R N.Y.) Aug. 6, 1850-May 6, 1924; House 1907-09.

McMILLAN, Samuel James Renwick (R Minn.) Feb. 22, 1826-Oct. 3, 1897; Senate 1875-87.

McMILLAN, Thomas Sanders (husband of Clara Gooding McMillan) (D S.C.) Nov. 27, 1888-Sept. 29, 1939; House 1925-Sept. 29, 1939.

McMILLAN, William (— N.W. Terr.) March 2, 1764-May 1804; House (Terr. Del.) Nov. 24, 1800-01.

McMILLEN, Rolla Coral (R Ill.) Oct. 5, 1880-May 6, 1961; House June 13, 1944-51.

McMILLIN, Benton (D Tenn.) Sept. 11, 1845-Jan. 8, 1933; House 1879-Jan. 6, 1899; Gov. 1899-1903.

McMORRAN, Henry Gordon (R Mich.) June 11, 1844-July 19, 1929; House 1903-13.

McMULLEN, Chester Bartow (D Fla.) Dec. 6, 1902-Nov. 3, 1953; House 1951-53.

McMULLEN, Fayette (D Va.) May 18, 1805-Nov. 8, 1880; House 1849-57; Gov. of Wash. Terr. 1857-61.

McMURRAY, Howard Johnstone (D Wis.) March 3, 1901-Aug. 14, 1961; House 1943-45.

McNAGNY, William Forgy (D Ind.) April 19, 1850-Aug. 24, 1923; House 1893-95.

McNAIR, John (D Pa.) June 8, 1800-Aug. 12, 1861; House 1851-55.

McNAMARA, Patrick Vincent (D Mich.) Oct. 4, 1894-April 30, 1966; Senate 1955-April 30, 1966.

McNARY, Charles Linza (R Ore.) June 12, 1874-Feb. 25, 1944; Senate May 29, 1917-Nov. 5, 1918, Dec. 18, 1918-Feb. 25, 1944.

McNARY, William Sarsfield (D Mass.) March 29, 1863-June 26, 1930; House 1903-07.

McNEELY, Thompson Ware (D Ill.) Oct. 5, 1835-July 23, 1921; House 1869-73.

McNEILL, Archibald (— N.C.) ? - 1849; House 1821-23, 1825-27.

McNULTA, John (R Ill.) Nov. 9, 1837-Feb. 22, 1900; House 1873-75.

McNULTY, Frank Joseph (D N.J.) Aug. 10, 1872-May 26, 1926; House 1923-25.

McPHERSON, Edward (R Pa.) July 31, 1830-Dec. 14, 1895; House 1859-63.

McPHERSON, Isaac Vanbert (R Mo.) March 8, 1868-Oct. 31, 1931; House 1919-23.

McPHERSON, John Rhoderic (D N.J.) May 9, 1833-Oct. 8, 1897; Senate 1877-95.

McPHERSON, Smith (R Iowa) Feb. 14, 1848-Jan. 17, 1915; House 1899-June 6, 1900.

McQUEEN, John (D S.C.) Feb. 9, 1804-Aug. 30, 1867; House Feb. 12, 1849-Dec. 21, 1860.

McRAE, John Jones (SRD Miss.) Jan. 10, 1815-May 31, 1868; Senate Dec. 1, 1851-March 17, 1852 (D); House Dec. 7, 1858-Jan. 12, 1861 (SRD); Gov. 1854-58.

McRAE, Thomas Chipman (cousin of Thomas Banks Cabaniss) (D Ark.) Dec. 21, 1851-June 2, 1929; House Dec. 7, 1885-1903; Gov. 1921-25.

McREYNOLDS, Samuel Davis (D Tenn.) April 16, 1872-July 11, 1939; House 1923-July 11, 1939.

McROBERTS, Samuel (D Ill.) April 12, 1799-March 27, 1843; Senate 1841-March 27, 1843.

McRUER, Donald Campbell (R Calif.) March 10, 1826-Jan. 29, 1898; House 1865-67.

McSHANE, John Albert (D Neb.) Aug. 25, 1850-Nov. 10, 1923; House 1887-89.

McSHERRY, James (— Pa.) July 29, 1776-Feb. 3, 1849; House 1821-23.

McSPADDEN, Clem Rogers (D Okla.) Nov. 9, 1925-—; House 1973-75.

McSWAIN, John Jackson (D S.C.) May 1, 1875-Aug. 6, 1936; House 1921-Aug. 6, 1936.

McSWEEN, Harold Barnett (D La.) July 19, 1926-—; House 1959-63.

McSWEENEY, John (D Ohio) Dec. 19, 1890-Dec. 13, 1969; House 1923-29, 1937-39, 1949-51.

McVEAN, Charles (D N.Y.) 1802-Dec. 22, 1848; House 1833-35.

McVEY, Walter Lewis (R Kan.) Feb. 19, 1922-—; House 1961-63.

McVEY, William Estus (R Ill.) Dec. 13, 1885-Aug. 10, 1958; House 1951-Aug. 10, 1958.

McVICKER, Roy Harrison (D Colo.) Feb. 20, 1924-Sept. 15, 1973; House 1965-67.

McWILLIAMS, John Dacher (R Conn.) July 23, 1891-March 30, 1975; House 1943-45.

McWILLIE, William (D Miss.) Nov. 17, 1795-March 3, 1869; House 1849-51; Gov. 1858-60.

MEACHAM, James (W Vt.) Aug. 16, 1810-Aug. 23, 1856; House Dec. 3, 1849-Aug. 23, 1856.

MEAD, Cowles (— Ga.) Oct. 18, 1776-May 17, 1844; House March 4-Dec. 24, 1805.

MEAD, James Michael (D N.Y.) Dec. 27, 1885-March 15, 1964; House 1919-Dec. 2, 1938; Senate Dec. 3, 1938-47.

MEADE, Edwin Ruthven (D N.Y.) July 6, 1836-Nov. 28, 1889; House 1875-77.

MEADE, Hugh Allen (D Md.) April 4, 1907-July 8, 1949; House 1947-49.

MEADE, Richard Kidder (D Va.) July 29, 1803-April 20, 1862; House Aug. 5, 1847-53.

MEADE, Wendell Howes (R Ky.) Jan. 18, 1912-—; House 1947-49.

MEADER, George (R Mich.) Sept. 13, 1907-—; House 1951-65.

MEANS, Rice William (R Colo.) Nov. 16, 1877-Jan. 30, 1949; Senate Dec. 1, 1924-27.

MEBANE, Alexander (— N.C.) Nov. 26, 1744-July 5, 1795; House 1793-95.

MECHEM, Edwin Leard (R N.M.) July 2, 1912-—; Senate Nov. 30, 1962-Nov. 3, 1964; Gov. 1951-55, 1957-59, 1961-62.

MEDILL, William (D Ohio) 1802-Sept. 2, 1865; House 1839-43; Gov. 1853-56.

MEECH, Ezra (D Vt.) July 26, 1773-Sept. 23, 1856; House 1819-21, 1825-27.

MEEDS, Lloyd (D Wash.) Dec. 11, 1927-—; House 1965-—.

MEEKER, Jacob Edwin (R Mo.) Oct. 7, 1878-Oct. 16, 1918; House 1915-Oct. 16, 1918.

MEEKISON, David (D Ohio) Nov. 14, 1849-Feb. 12, 1915; House 1897-1901.

MEEKS, James Andrew (D Ill.) March 7, 1864-Nov. 10, 1946; House 1933-39.

MEIGS, Henry (D N.Y.) Oct. 28, 1782-May 20, 1861; House 1819-21.

MEIGS, Return Jonathan Jr. (D Ohio) Nov. 16, 1764-March 29, 1825; Senate Dec. 12, 1808-May 1, 1810; Gov. 1810-14; Postmaster Gen. 1814-23.

MEIKLEJOHN, George de Rue (R Neb.) Aug. 26, 1857-April 19, 1929; House 1893-97.

MELCHER, John (D Mont.) Sept. 6, 1924-—; House June 24, 1969-—.

MELLEN, Prentiss (— Mass.) Oct. 11, 1764-Dec. 31, 1840; Senate June 5, 1818-May 15, 1820.

MELLISH, David Batcheller (R N.Y.) Jan. 2, 1831-May 23, 1874; House 1873-May 23, 1874.

MENEFEE, Richard Hickman (W Ky.) Dec. 4, 1809-Feb. 21, 1841; House 1837-39.

MENGES, Franklin (R Pa.) Oct. 26, 1858-May 12, 1956; House 1925-31.

MENZIES, John William (U Ky.) April 12, 1819-Oct. 3, 1897; House 1861-63.

MERCER, Charles Fenton (cousin of Robert Selden Garnett) (D Va.) June 16, 1778-May 4, 1858; House 1817-Dec. 26, 1839.

MERCER, David Henry (R Neb.) July 9, 1857-Jan. 10, 1919; House 1893-1903.

MERCER, John Francis (D Md.) May 17, 1759-Aug. 30, 1821; House Feb. 5, 1792-April 13, 1794; Cont. Cong. (Va.) 1782-85; Gov. of Md. 1801-03.

MERCUR, Ulysses (R Pa.) Aug. 12, 1818-June 6, 1887; House 1865-Dec. 2, 1872.

MEREDITH, Elisha Edward (D Va.) Dec. 26, 1848-July 29, 1900; House Dec. 9, 1891-97.

MERIWETHER, David (father of James Meriwether) (D Ga.) April 10, 1755-Nov. 16, 1822; House Dec. 6, 1802-07.

MERIWETHER, David (D Ky.) Oct. 30, 1800-April 4, 1893; Senate July 6-Aug. 31, 1852; Gov. of N.M. Terr. 1853-55.

MERIWETHER, James (son of David Meriwether and uncle of James A. Meriwether) (— Ga.) 1789-1854; House 1825-27.

MERIWETHER, James A. (nephew of James Meriwether) (W Ga.) Sept. 20, 1806-April 18, 1852; House 1841-43.

MERRIAM. Clinton Levi (R N.Y.) March 25, 1824-Feb. 18, 1900; House 1871-75.

MERRICK, William Duhurst (father of William Matthew Merrick) (W Md.) Oct. 25, 1793-Feb. 5, 1857; Senate Jan. 4, 1838-45.

MERRICK, William Matthew (son of William Duhurst Merrick) (D Md.) Sept. 1, 1818-Feb. 4, 1889; House 1871-73.

MERRILL, D. Bailey (R Ind.) Nov. 22, 1912-—; House 1953-55.

MERRILL, Orsamus Cook (D Vt.) June 18, 1775-April 12, 1865; House 1817-Jan. 12, 1820.

MERRIMAN, Truman Adams (D N.Y.) Sept. 5, 1839-April 16, 1892; House 1885-89.

MERRIMON, Augustus Summerfield (D N.C.) Sept. 15, 1830-Nov. 14, 1892; Senate 1873-79.

MERRITT, Edwin Albert (R N.Y.) July 25, 1860-Dec. 4, 1914; House Nov. 5, 1912-Dec. 4, 1914.

MERRITT, Matthew Joseph (D N.Y.) April 2, 1895-Sept. 29, 1946; House 1935-45.

MERRITT, Samuel Augustus (D Idaho) Aug. 15, 1827-Sept. 8, 1910; House (Terr. Del.) 1871-73.

MERRITT, Schuyler (R Conn.) Dec. 16, 1853-April 1, 1953; House Nov. 6, 1917-31, 1933-37.

MERROW, Chester Earl (R N.H.) Nov. 15, 1906-Feb. 10, 1974; House 1943-63.

MERWIN, Orange (— Conn.) April 7, 1777-Sept. 4, 1853; House 1825-29.

MESICK, William Smith (R Mich.) Aug. 26, 1856-Dec. 1, 1942; House 1897-1901.

MESKILL, Thomas J. (R Conn.) Jan. 30, 1928-—; House 1967-71; Gov. 1971-75.

METCALF, Arunah (D N.Y.) Aug. 15, 1771-Aug. 15, 1848; House 1811-13.

METCALF, Jesse Houghton (R R.I.) Nov. 16, 1860-Oct. 9, 1942; Senate Nov. 5, 1924-37.

METCALF, Lee (D Mont.) Jan. 28, 1911-__; House 1953-61; Senate 1961-__.

METCALF, Victor Howard (R Calif.) Oct. 10, 1853-Feb. 20, 1936; House 1899-July 1, 1904; Secy. of Commerce and Labor 1904-06; Secy of the Navy 1906-08.

METCALFE, Henry Bleecker (D N.Y.) Jan. 20, 1805-Feb. 7, 1881; House 1875-77.

METCALFE, Lyne Shackelford (R Mo.) April 21, 1822-Jan. 31, 1906; House 1877-79.

METCALFE, Ralph Harold (D Ill.) May 29, 1910-—; House 1971-—.

METCALFE, Thomas (D Ky.) March 20, 1780-Aug. 18, 1855; House 1819-June 1, 1828; Senate June 23, 1848-49; Gov. 1828-32.

METZ, Herman August (D N.Y.) Oct. 19, 1867-May 17, 1934; House 1913-15.

METZENBAUM, Howard Morton (D Ohio) June 4, 1917-—; Senate Jan. 4, 1974-Dec. 23, 1974.

MEYER, Adolph (D La.) Oct. 19, 1842-March 8, 1908; House 1891-March 8, 1908.

MEYER, Herbert Alton (R Kan.) Aug. 30, 1886-Oct. 2, 1950; House 1947-Oct. 2, 1950.

MEYER, John Ambrose (D Md.) May 15, 1899-Oct. 2, 1969; House 1941-43.

MEYER, William Henry (D Vt.) Dec. 29, 1914-—; House 1959-61.

MEYERS, Benjamin Franklin (D Pa.) July 6, 1833-Aug. 11, 1918; House 1871-73.

MEYNER, Helen Stevenson (D N.J.) March 5, 1929-—; House 1975-—.

MEZVINSKY, Edward Maurice (D Iowa) Jan. 17, 1937-—; House 1973-—.

MICHAELSON, Magne Alfred (R Ill.) Sept. 7, 1878-Oct. 26, 1949; House 1921-31.

MICHALEK, Anthony (R Ill.) Jan. 16, 1878-Dec. 21, 1916; House 1905-07.

MICHEL, Robert Henry (R Ill.) March 2, 1923-—; House 1957-—.

MICHENER, Earl Cory (R Mich.) Nov. 30, 1876-July 4, 1957; House 1919-33, 1935-51.

MICKEY, J. Ross (D Ill.) Jan. 5, 1856-March 20, 1928; House 1901-03.

MIDDLESWARTH, Ner (W Pa.) Dec. 12, 1783-June 2, 1865; House 1853-55.

MIDDLETON, George (D N.J.) Oct. 14, 1800-Dec. 31, 1888; House 1863-65.

MIDDLETON, Henry (D S.C.) Sept. 28, 1770-June 14, 1846; House 1815-19; Gov. 1810-12.

MIERS, Robert Walter (D Ind.) Jan. 27, 1848- Feb. 20, 1930; House 1897-1905.

MIKVA, Abner J. (D Ill.) Jan. 21, 1926-—; House 1969-1973, 1975-—.

MILES, Frederick (R Conn.) Dec. 19, 1815-Nov. 20, 1896; House 1879-83, 1889-91.

MILES, John Esten (D N.M.) July 28, 1884-Oct. 7, 1971; House 1949-51; Gov. 1939-43.

MILES, Joshua Weldon (D Md.) Dec. 9, 1858-March 4, 1929; House 1895-97.

MILES, William Porcher (D S.C.) July 4, 1822-May 11, 1899; House 1857-Dec. 1860.

MILFORD, Dale (D Texas) Feb. 18, 1926-—; House 1973-—.

MILLARD, Charles Dunsmore (R N.Y.) Dec. 1, 1873-Dec. 11, 1944; House 1931-Sept. 29, 1937.

MILLARD, Joseph Hopkins (R Neb.) April 20, 1836-Jan. 13, 1922; Senate March 28, 1901-07.

MILLARD, Stephen Columbus (R N.Y.) Jan. 14, 1841-June 21, 1914; House 1883-87.

MILLEDGE, John (—Ga.) 1757-Feb. 9, 1818; House Nov. 22, 1792-93, 1795-99, 1801-May 1802; Senate June 19, 1806-Nov. 14, 1809; President pro tempore 1809; Gov. 1802-06.

MILLEN, John (D Ga.) 1804-Oct. 15, 1843; House March 4-Oct. 15, 1843.

MILLER, Arthur Lewis (R Neb.) May 24, 1892-March 16, 1967; House 1943-59.

MILLER, Bert Henry (D Idaho) Dec. 15, 1879-Oct. 8, 1949; Senate Jan. 3-Oct. 8, 1949.

MILLER, Clarence Benjamin (R Minn.) March 13, 1872-Jan. 10, 1922; House 1909-19.

MILLER, Clarence E. (R Ohio) Nov. 1, 1917-—; House 1967-—.

MILLER, Clement Woodnutt (nephew of Thomas W. Miller) (D Calif.) Oct. 28, 1916-Oct. 7, 1962; House 1959-Oct. 7, 1962.

MILLER, Daniel Fry (W Iowa) Oct. 4, 1814-Dec. 9, 1895; House Dec. 20, 1850-51.

MILLER, Daniel H. (JD Pa.) ? - 1846; House 1823-31.

MILLER, Edward Edwin (R Ill.) July 22, 1880-Aug. 1, 1946; House 1923-25.

MILLER, Edward Tylor (R Md.) Feb. 1, 1895-Jan. 20, 1968; House 1947-59.

MILLER, George (D Calif.) May 17, 1945-—; House 1975-—.

MILLER, George Funston (R Pa.) Sept. 5, 1809-Oct. 21, 1885; House 1865-69.

MILLER, George Paul (D Calif.) Jan. 15, 1891-—; House 1945-73.

MILLER, Homer Virgil Milton (D Ga.) April 29, 1814-May 31, 1896; Senate Feb. 24-March 3, 1871.

MILLER, Howard Shultz (D Kan.) Feb. 27, 1879-Jan. 2, 1970; House 1953-55.

MILLER, Jack Richard (R Iowa) June 6, 1916-—; Senate 1961-73.

MILLER, Jacob Welsh (W N.J.) Aug. 29, 1800-Sept. 30, 1862; Senate 1841-53.

MILLER, James Francis (D Texas) Aug. 1, 1830-July 3, 1902; House 1883-87.

MILLER, James Monroe (R Kan.) May 6, 1852-Jan. 20, 1926; House 1899-1911.

MILLER, Jesse (father of William Henry Miller) (D Pa.) 1800-Aug. 20, 1850; House 1833-Oct. 30, 1836.

MILLER, John (—N.Y.) Nov. 10, 1774-March 31, 1862; House 1825-27.

MILLER, John (VBD Mo.) Nov. 25, 1781-March 18, 1846; House 1837-43; Gov. 1826-32.

MILLER, John Elvis (D Ark.) May 15, 1888-—; House 1931-Nov. 14, 1937; Senate Nov. 15, 1937-March 31, 1941.

MILLER, John Franklin (R Calif.) (uncle of the following) Nov. 21, 1831-March 8, 1886; Senate 1881-March 8, 1886.

MILLER, John Franklin (nephew of the preceding) (R Wash.) June 9, 1862-May 28, 1936; House 1917-31.

MILLER, John Gaines (W Mo.) Nov. 29, 1812-May 11, 1856; House 1851-May 11, 1856.

MILLER, John Krepps (D Ohio) May 25, 1819-Aug. 11, 1863; House 1847-51.

MILLER, Joseph (D Ohio) Sept. 9, 1819-May 27, 1862; House 1857-59.

MILLER, Killian (W N.Y.) July 30, 1785-Jan. 9, 1859; House 1855-57.

MILLER, Louis Ebenezer (R Mo.) April 30, 1899-Nov. 1, 1952; House 1943-45.

MILLER, Lucas Miltiades (D Wis.) Sept. 15, 1824-Dec. 4, 1902; House 1891-93.

MILLER, Morris Smith (father of Rutger Bleecker Miller) (F N.Y.) July 31, 1779-Nov. 16, 1824; House 1813-15.

MILLER, Orrin Larrabee (R Kan.) Jan. 11, 1856-Sept. 11, 1926; House 1895-97.

MILLER, Pleasant Moorman (— Tenn.) ? - 1849; House 1809-11.

MILLER, Rutger Bleecker (son of Morris Smith Miller) (D N.Y.) July 28, 1805-Nov. 12, 1877; House Nov. 9, 1836-37.

MILLER, Samuel Franklin (R N.Y.) May 27, 1827-March 16, 1892; House 1863-65, 1875-77.

MILLER, Samuel Henry (R Pa.) April 19, 1840-Sept. 4, 1918; House 1881-85, 1915-17.

MILLER, Smith (D Ind.) May 30, 1804-March 21, 1872; House 1853-57.

MILLER, Stephen Decatur (N S.C.) May 8, 1787-March 8, 1838; House Jan. 2, 1817-19 (D); Senate 1831-March 2, 1833 (N); Gov. 1828-30.

MILLER, Thomas Byron (R Pa.) Aug. 11, 1896-—; House May 9, 1942-45.

MILLER, Thomas Ezekiel (R S.C.) June 17, 1849-April 8, 1938; House Sept. 24, 1890-91.

MILLER, Thomas Woodnutt (uncle of Clement W. Miller) (R Del.) June 26, 1886-May 5, 1973; House 1915-17.

MILLER, Ward MacLaughlin (R Ohio) Nov. 29, 1902-—; House Nov. 8, 1960-61.

MILLER, Warner (R N.Y.) Aug. 12, 1838-March 21, 1918; House 1879-July 26, 1881; Senate July 27, 1881-87.

MILLER, Warren (R W.Va.) April 2, 1847-Dec. 29, 1920; House 1895-99.

MILLER, William Edward (R N.Y.) March 22, 1914-—; House 1951-65; Chrmn. Rep. Nat. Comm. 1961-64.

MILLER, William Henry (son of Jesse Miller) (D Pa.) Feb. 28, 1829-Sept. 12, 1870; House 1863-65.

MILLER, William Jennings (R Conn.) March 12, 1899-Nov. 22, 1950; House 1939-41, 1943-45, 1947-49.

MILLER, William Starr (— N.Y.) Aug. 22, 1793-Nov. 9, 1854; House 1845-47.

MILLIGAN, Jacob Le Roy (D Mo.) March 9, 1889-March 9, 1951; House Feb. 14, 1920-21, 1923-35.

MILLIGAN, John Jones (W Del.) Dec. 10, 1795-April 20, 1875; House 1831-39.

MILLIKEN, Charles William (D Ky.) Aug. 15, 1827-Oct. 16, 1915; House 1873-77.

MILLIKEN, Seth Llewellyn (R Maine) Dec. 12, 1831-April 18, 1897; House 1883-April 18, 1897.

MILLIKEN, William H. Jr. (R Pa.) Aug. 19, 1897-July 4, 1969; House 1959-65.

MILLIKIN, Eugene Donald (R Colo.) Feb. 12, 1891-July 26, 1958; Senate Dec. 20, 1941-57.

MILLINGTON, Charles Stephen (R N.Y.) March 13, 1855-Oct. 25, 1913; House 1909-11.

MILLS, Daniel Webster (R Ill.) Feb. 25, 1838-Dec. 16, 1904; House 1897-99.

MILLS, Elijah Hunt (F Mass.) Dec. 1, 1776- May 5, 1829; House 1815-19; Senate June 12, 1820-27.

MILLS, Newt Virgus (D La.) Sept. 27, 1899-—; House 1937-43.

MILLS, Ogden Livingston (R N.Y.) Aug. 23, 1884-Oct. 11, 1937; House 1921-27; Secy. of the Treasury 1932-33.

MILLS, Roger Quarles (D Texas) March 30, 1832-Sept. 2, 1911; House 1873-March 28, 1892; Senate March 29, 1892-99.

MILLS, Wilbur Daigh (D Ark.) May 24, 1909-—; House 1939-__.

MILLS, William Oswald (R Md.) Aug. 12, 1924-May 24, 1973; House May 27, 1971-May 24, 1973.

MILLSON, John Singleton (D Va.) Oct. 1, 1808-March 1, 1874; House 1849-61.

MILLSPAUGH, Frank Crenshaw (R Mo.) Jan. 14, 1872-July 8, 1947; House 1921-Dec. 5, 1922.

MILLWARD, William (W Pa.) June 30, 1822-Nov. 28, 1871; House 1855-57, 1859-61.

MILNES, Alfred (R Mich.) May 28, 1844-Jan. 15, 1916; House Dec. 2, 1895-97.

MILNES, William Jr. (C Va.) Dec. 8, 1827-Aug. 14, 1889; House Jan. 27, 1870-71.

MILNOR, James (F Pa.) June 20, 1773-April 8, 1844; House 1811-13.

MILNOR, William (F Pa.) June 26, 1769-Dec. 13, 1848; House 1807-11, 1815-17, 1821-May 8, 1822.

MILTON, John Gerald (D N.J.) Jan. 21, 1881-__; Senate Jan. 18-Nov. 8, 1938.

MILTON, William Hall (D Fla.) March 2, 1864-Jan. 4, 1942; Senate March 27, 1908-09.

MINAHAN, Daniel Francis (D N.J.) Aug. 8, 1877-April 29, 1947; House 1919-21, 1923-25.

MINER, Ahiman Louis (W Vt.) Sept. 23, 1804-July 19, 1886; House 1851-53.

MINER, Charles (F Pa.) Feb. 1, 1780-Oct. 26, 1865; House 1825-29.

MINER, Henry Clay (D N.Y.) March 23, 1842-Feb. 22, 1900; House 1895-97.

MINER, Phineas (W Conn.) Nov. 27, 1777-Sept. 15, 1839; House Dec. 1, 1834-35.

MINETA, Norman Yoshio (D Calif.) Nov. 12, 1931--—; House 1975-—.

MINISH, Joseph George (D N.J.) Sept. 1, 1916-—; House 1963-—.

MINK, Patsy Takemoto (D Hawaii) Dec. 6, 1927-—; House 1965-—.

MINOR, Edward Sloman (R Wis.) Dec. 13, 1840-July 26, 1924; House 1895-1907.

MINSHALL, William Edwin Jr. (R Ohio) Oct. 24, 1911-—; House 1955-75.

MINTON, Sherman (D Ind.) Oct. 20, 1890-April 9, 1965; Senate 1935-41; Assoc. Justice of the Supreme Court 1949-56.

MITCHEL, Charles Burton (D Ark.) Sept. 19, 1815-Sept. 20, 1864; Senate March 4-July 11, 1861.

MITCHELL, Alexander (father of John Lendrum Mitchell) (D Wis.) Oct. 18, 1817-April 19, 1887; House 1871-75.

MITCHELL, Alexander Clark (R Kan.) Oct. 11, 1860-July 7, 1911; House March 4-July 7, 1911.

MITCHELL, Anderson (W N.C.) June 13, 1800-Dec. 24, 1876; House April 27, 1842-43.

MITCHELL, Arthur Wergs (D Ill.) Dec. 22, 1883-May 9, 1968; House 1935-43.

MITCHELL, Charles F. (W N.Y.) about 1808- ?; House 1837-41.

MITCHELL, Charles Le Moyne (D Conn.) Aug. 6, 1844-March 1, 1890; House 1883-87.

MITCHELL, Donald Jerome (R N.Y.) May 8, 1923-—; House 1973-—.

MITCHELL, Edward Archibald (R Ind.) Dec. 2, 1910-—; House 1947-49.

MITCHELL, George Edward (D Md.) March 3, 1781-June 28, 1832; House 1823-27, Dec. 7, 1829-June 28, 1832.

MITCHELL, Harlan Erwin (D Ga.) Aug. 17, 1924-—; House Jan. 8, 1958-61.

MITCHELL, Henry (JD N.Y.) 1784-Jan. 12, 1856; House 1833-35.

MITCHELL, Hugh Burnton (D Wash.) March 22, 1907-—; Senate Jan. 10, 1945-Dec. 25, 1946; House 1949-53.

MITCHELL, James Coffield (— Tenn.) March 1786-Aug. 7, 1843; House 1825-29.

MITCHELL, James S. (D Pa.) 1784-1844; House 1821-27.

MITCHELL, John (D Pa.) March 8, 1781-Aug. 3, 1849; House 1825-29.

MITCHELL, John Hipple (R Ore.) June 22, 1835-Dec. 8, 1905; Senate 1873-79, Nov. 18, 1885-97, 1901-Dec. 8, 1905.

MITCHELL, John Inscho (R Pa.) July 28, 1838-Aug. 20, 1907; House 1877-81; Senate 1881-87.

MITCHELL, John Joseph (D Mass.) May 9, 1873-Sept. 13, 1925; House Nov. 8, 1910-11, April 15, 1913-15.

MITCHELL, John Lendrum (son of Alexander Mitchell) (D Wis.) Oct. 19, 1842-June 29, 1904; House 1891-93; Senate 1893-99.

MITCHELL, John Murray (R N.Y.) March 18, 1858-May 31, 1905; House June 2, 1896-99.

MITCHELL, John Ridley (D Tenn.) Sept. 26, 1877-Feb. 26, 1962; House 1931-39.

MITCHELL, Nahum (F Mass.) Feb. 12, 1769-Aug. 1, 1853; House 1803-05.

MITCHELL, Parren James (D Md.) April 29, 1922-—; House 1971-—.

MITCHELL, Robert (D Ohio) 1778-Nov. 13, 1848; House 1833-35.

MITCHELL, Stephen Mix (F Conn.) Dec. 9, 1743-Sept. 30, 1835; Senate Dec. 2, 1793-95; Cont. Cong. 1783-88.

MITCHELL, Thomas Rothmaler (— S.C.) May 1783-Nov. 2, 1837; House 1821-23; 1825-29, 1831-33.

MITCHELL, William (R Ind.) Jan. 19, 1807-Sept. 11, 1865; House 1861-63.

MITCHILL, Samuel Latham (D N.Y.) Aug. 20, 1764-Sept. 7, 1831; House 1801-Nov. 22, 1804, Dec. 4, 1810-13; Senate Nov. 23, 1804-09.

MIZE, Chester L. (R Kan.) Dec. 25, 1917-—; House 1965-71.

MIZELL, Wilmer David (R N.C.) Aug. 13, 1930-—; House 1969-75.

MOAKLEY, John Joseph (ID Mass.) April 27, 1927-—; House 1973-—.

MOBLEY, William Carlton (D Ga.) Dec. 7, 1906-—; House March 2, 1932-33.

MOELLER, Walter Henry (D Ohio) March 15, 1910-—; House 1959-63, 1965-67.

MOFFATT, Seth Crittenden (R Mich.) Aug. 10, 1841-Dec. 22, 1887; House 1885-Dec. 22, 1887.

MOFFET, John (D Pa.) April 5, 1831-June 19, 1884; House March 4-April 9, 1869.

MOFFETT, Anthony Joseph (D Conn.) Aug. 18, 1944-—; House 1975-—.

MOFFITT, Hosea (F N.Y.) Nov. 17, 1757-Aug. 31, 1825; House 1813-17.

MOFFITT, John Henry (R N.Y.) Jan. 8, 1843-Aug. 14, 1926; House 1887-91.

MOLLOHAN, Robert Homer (D W.Va.) Sept. 18, 1909-—; House 1953-57, 1969-—.

MOLONY, Richard Sheppard (D Ill.) June 28, 1811-Dec. 14, 1891; House 1851-53.

MONAGAN, John Stephen (D Conn.) Dec. 23, 1911-—; House 1959-73.

MONAGHAN, Joseph Patrick (D Mont.) March 26, 1906-—; House 1933-37.

MONAHAN, James Gideon (R Wis.) Jan. 12, 1855-Dec. 5, 1923; House 1919-21.

MONAST, Louis (R R.I.) July 1, 1863-April 16, 1936; House 1927-29.

MONDALE, Walter F. (D Minn.) Jan. 5, 1928-—; Senate Dec. 30, 1964-—.

MONDELL, Franklin Wheeler (R Wyo.) Nov. 6, 1860-Aug. 6, 1939; House 1895-97, 1899-1923.

MONELL, Robert (— N.Y.) 1786-Nov. 29, 1860; House 1819-21, 1829-Feb. 21, 1831.

MONEY, Hernando De Soto (D Miss.) Aug. 26, 1839-Sept. 18, 1912; House 1875-85, 1893-97; Senate Oct. 8, 1897-1911.

MONKIEWICZ, Boleslaus Joseph (R Conn.) Aug. 8, 1898-July 2, 1971; House 1939-41, 1943-45.

MONROE, James (nephew of Joseph Jones and uncle of the following) (— Va.) April 28, 1758-July 4, 1831; Senate Nov. 9, 1790-May 27, 1794; Cont. Cong. 1783-86; Gov. 1799-1802, 1811; Secy. of State 1811-17; President 1817-25.

MONROE, James (nephew of the preceding) (W N.Y.) Sept. 10, 1799-Sept. 7, 1870; House 1839-41.

MONROE, James (R Ohio) July 18, 1821-July 6, 1898; House 1871-81.

MONRONEY, Almer Stillwell Mike (D Okla.) March 2, 1902-—; House 1939-51; Senate 1951-69.

MONTAGUE, Andrew Jackson (D Va.) Oct. 3, 1862-Jan. 24, 1937; House 1913-Jan. 24, 1937; Gov. 1902-06.

MONTET, Numa Francois (D La.) Sept. 17, 1892-—; House Aug. 6, 1929-37.

MONTGOMERY, Alexander Brooks (D Ky.) Dec. 11, 1837-Dec. 27, 1910; House 1887-95.

MONTGOMERY, Daniel Jr. (D Pa.) Oct. 30, 1765-Dec. 30, 1831; House 1807-09.

MONTGOMERY, Gillespie V. (D Miss.) Aug. 5, 1920-—; House 1967-—.

MONTGOMERY, John (D Md.) 1764-July 17, 1828; House 1807-April 29, 1811.

MONTGOMERY, John Gallagher (D Pa.) June 27, 1805-April 24, 1857; House March 4-April 24, 1857.

MONTGOMERY, Samuel James (R Okla.) Dec. 1, 1896-June 4, 1957; House 1925-27.

MONTGOMERY, Thomas (D Ky.) 1779-April 2, 1828; House 1813-15, Aug. 1, 1820-23.

MONTGOMERY, William (— Pa.) Aug. 3, 1736-May 1, 1816; House 1793-95; Cont. Cong. 1784-85.

MONTGOMERY, William (D N.C.) Dec. 29, 1789-Nov. 27, 1844; House 1835-41.

MONTGOMERY, William (D Pa.) April 11, 1818-April 28, 1870; House 1857-61.

MONTOYA, Joseph Manuel (D N.M.) Sept. 24, 1915-—; House April 9, 1957-Nov. 3, 1964; Senate Nov. 4, 1964-—.

MONTOYA, Nestor (R N.M.) April 14, 1862-Jan. 13, 1923; House 1921-Jan. 13, 1923.

MOODY, Arthur Edson Blair (D Mich.) Feb. 13, 1902-July 20, 1954; Senate April 23, 1951-Nov. 4, 1952.

MOODY, Gideon Curtis (R S.D.) Oct. 16, 1832-March 17, 1904; Senate Nov. 2, 1889-91.

MOODY, James Montraville (R N.C.) Feb. 12, 1858-Feb. 5, 1903; House 1901-Feb. 5, 1903.

MOODY, Malcolm Adelbert (R Ore.) Nov. 30, 1854-March 19, 1925; House 1899-1903.

MOODY, William Henry (R Mass.) Dec. 23, 1853-July 2, 1917; House Nov. 5, 1895-May 1, 1902; Secy. of the Navy 1902-04; Atty. Gen. 1904-06; Assoc. Justice of Supreme Court 1906-10.

MOON, John Austin (D Tenn.) April 22, 1855-June 26, 1921; House 1897-1921.

MOON, John Wesley (R Mich.) Jan. 18, 1836-April 5, 1898; House 1893-95.

MOON, Reuben Osborne (R Pa.) July 22, 1847-Oct. 25, 1919; House Nov. 2, 1903-13.

MOONEY, Charles Anthony (D Ohio) Jan. 5, 1879-May 29, 1931; House 1919-21, 1923-May 29, 1931.

MOONEY, William Crittenden (R Ohio) June 15, 1855-July 24, 1918; House 1915-17.

MOOR, Wyman Bradbury Seavy (D Maine) Nov. 11, 1811-March 10, 1869; Senate Jan. 5-June 7, 1848.

MOORE, Allen Francis (R Ill.) Sept. 30, 1869-Aug. 18, 1945; House 1921-25.

MOORE, Andrew (father of Samuel McDowell Moore) (— Va.) 1752-April 14, 1821; House 1789-97, March 5-Aug. 11, 1804; Senate Aug. 11, 1804-09.

MOORE, Arch Alfred Jr. (R W.Va.) April 16, 1923-—; House 1957-69; Gov. 1969-—.

MOORE, Arthur Harry (D N.J.) July 3, 1879-Nov. 18, 1952; Senate 1935-Jan. 17, 1938; Gov. 1926-29, 1932-35, 1938-41.

MOORE, Charles Ellis (R Ohio) Jan. 3, 1884-April 2, 1941; House 1919-33.

MOORE, Edward Hall (R Okla.) Nov. 19, 1871-Sept. 2, 1950; Senate 1943-49.

MOORE, Eliakim Hastings (R Ohio) June 19, 1812-April 4, 1900; House 1869-71.

MOORE, Ely (D N.Y.) July 4, 1798-Jan. 27, 1861; House 1835-39.

MOORE, Gabriel (— Ala.) 1785-June 9, 1845; House 1821-29; Senate 1831-37; Gov. 1829-31.

MOORE, Heman Allen (D Ohio) Aug. 27, 1809-April 3, 1844; House 1843-April 3, 1844.

MOORE, Henry Dunning (W Pa.) April 13, 1817-Aug. 11, 1887; House 1849-53.

MOORE, Horace Ladd (D Kan.) Feb. 25, 1837-May 1, 1914; House Aug. 2, 1894-95.

MOORE, Jesse Hale (R Ill.) April 22, 1817-July 11, 1883; House 1869-73.

MOORE, John (W La.) 1788-June 17, 1867; House Dec. 17, 1840-43, 1851-53.

MOORE, John Matthew (D Texas) Nov. 18, 1862-Feb. 3, 1940; House June 6, 1905-13.

MOORE, John William (D Ky.) June 9, 1877-Dec. 11, 1941; House Nov. 3, 1925-29, June 1, 1929-33.

MOORE, Joseph Hampton (R Pa.) March 8, 1864-May 2, 1950; House Nov. 6, 1906-Jan. 4, 1920.

MOORE, Laban Theodore (Nat. A. Ky.) Jan. 13, 1829-Nov. 9, 1892; House 1859-61.

MOORE, Littleton Wilde (D Texas) March 25, 1835-Oct. 29, 1911; House 1887-93.

MOORE, Nicholas Ruxton (D Md.) July 21, 1756-Oct. 7, 1816; House 1803-11, 1813-15.

MOORE, Orren Cheney (R N.H.) Aug. 10, 1839-May 12, 1893; House 1889-91.

MOORE, Oscar Fitzallen (R Ohio) Jan. 27, 1817-June 24, 1885; House 1855-57.

MOORE, Paul John (D N.J.) Aug. 5, 1868-Jan. 10, 1938; House 1927-29.

MOORE, Robert (grandfather of Michael Daniel Harter) (— Pa.) March 30, 1778-Jan. 14, 1831; House 1817-21.

MOORE, Robert Lee (D Ga.) Nov. 27, 1867-Jan. 14, 1940; House 1923-25.

MOORE, Robert Walton (D Va.) Feb. 6, 1859-Feb. 8, 1941; House May 27, 1919-31.

MOORE, Samuel (D Pa.) Feb. 8, 1774-Feb. 18, 1861; House Oct. 13, 1818-May 20, 1822.

MOORE, Samuel McDowell (son of Andrew Moore) (W Va.) Feb. 9, 1796-Sept. 17, 1875; House 1833-35.

MOORE, Sydenham (D Ala.) May 25, 1817-May 31, 1862; House 1857-Jan. 21, 1861.

MOORE, Thomas (— S.C.) 1759-July 11, 1822; House 1801-13, 1815-17.

MOORE, Thomas Love (— Va.) ? - 1862; House Nov. 13, 1820-23.

MOORE, Thomas Patrick (D Ky.) 1797-July 21, 1853; House 1823-29.

MOORE, William (R N.J.) Dec. 25, 1810-April 26, 1878; House 1867-71.

MOORE, William Henson (R La.) Oct. 4, 1939-—; House Jan. 7, 1975-—.

MOORE, William Robert (R Tenn.) March 28, 1830-June 12, 1909; House 1881-83.

MOORE, William Sutton (R Pa.) Nov. 18, 1822-Dec. 30, 1877; House 1873-75.

MOOREHEAD, Tom Van Horn (R Ohio) April 12, 1898-—; House 1961-63.

MOORES, Merrill (R Ind.) April 21, 1856-Oct. 21, 1929; House 1915-25.

MOORHEAD, Carlos John (R Calif.) May 6, 1922-—; House 1973-—.

MOORHEAD, James Kennedy (R Pa.) Sept. 7, 1806-March 6, 1884; House 1859-69.

MOORHEAD, William Singer (D Pa.) April 8, 1923-—; House 1959-—.

MOORMAN, Henry DeHaven (D Ky.) June 9, 1880-Feb. 3, 1939; House 1927-29.

MORAN, Edward Carleton Jr. (D Maine) Dec. 29, 1894-July 12, 1967; House 1933-37.

MORANO, Albert Paul (R Conn.) Jan. 18, 1908-—; House 1951-59.

MOREHEAD, Charles Slaughter (W Ky.) July 7, 1802-Dec. 21, 1868; House 1847-51; Gov. 1855-59 (AP).

MOREHEAD, James Turner (W Ky.) May 24, 1797-Dec. 28, 1854; Senate 1841-47; Gov. 1834-36.

MOREHEAD, James Turner (W N.C.) Jan. 11, 1799-May 5, 1875; House 1851-53.

MOREHEAD, John Henry (D Neb.) Dec. 3, 1861-May 31, 1942; House 1923-35; Gov. 1913-17.

MOREHEAD, John Motley (R N.C.) July 20, 1866-Dec. 13, 1923; House 1909-11.

MOREY, Frank (R La.) July 11, 1840-Sept. 22, 1889; House 1869-June 8, 1876.

MOREY, Henry Lee (R Ohio) April 8, 1841-Dec. 29, 1902; House 1881-June 20, 1884, 1889-91.

MORGAN, Charles Henry (R Mo.) July 5, 1842-Jan. 4, 1912; House 1875-79, 1883-85, 1893-95, 1909-11 (1875-95 Democrat, 1909-11 Republican).

MORGAN. Christopher (brother of Edwin Barbour Morgan and nephew of Noyes Barber) (W N.Y.) June 4, 1808-April 3, 1877; House 1839-43.

MORGAN, Daniel (F Va.) 1736-July 6, 1802; House 1797-99.

MORGAN, Dick Thompson (R Okla.) Dec. 6, 1853-July 4, 1920; House 1909-July 4, 1920.

MORGAN, Edwin Barbour (brother of Christopher Morgan and nephew of Noyes Barber) (R N.Y.) May 2, 1806-Oct. 13, 1881; House 1853-59.

MORGAN, Edwin Dennison (cousin of Morgan Gardner Bulkeley) (UR N.Y.) Feb. 8, 1811-Feb. 14, 1883; Senate 1863-69; Chrmn. Rep. Nat. Comm. 1856-64, 1872-76; Gov. 1859-63.

MORGAN, George Washington (D Ohio) Sept. 20, 1820-July 26, 1893; House 1867-June 3, 1868, 1869-73.

MORGAN, James (F N.J.) Dec. 29, 1756-Nov. 11, 1822; House 1811-13.

MORGAN, James Bright (D Miss.) March 14, 1833-June 18, 1892; House 1885-91.

MORGAN, John Jordan (father-in-law of John Adams Dix) (D N.Y.) 1770-July 29, 1849; House 1821-25, Dec. 1, 1834-35.

MORGAN, John Tyler (D Ala.) June 20, 1824-June 11, 1907; Senate 1877-June 11, 1907.

MORGAN, Lewis Lovering (D La.) March 2, 1876-June 10, 1950; House Nov. 5, 1912-17.

MORGAN, Robert Burren (D N.C.) Oct. 5, 1925-—; Senate 1975-—.

MORGAN, Stephen (R Ohio) Jan. 25, 1854-Feb. 9, 1928; House 1899-1905.

MORGAN, Thomas Ellsworth (D Pa.) Oct. 13, 1906-—; House 1945-—.

MORGAN, William Mitchell (R Ohio) Aug. 1, 1870-Sept. 17, 1935; House 1921-31.

MORGAN, William Stephen (D Va.) Sept. 7, 1801-Sept. 3, 1878; House 1835-39.

MORIN, John Mary (R Pa.) April 18, 1868-March 3, 1942; House 1913-29.

MORITZ, Theodore Leo (D Pa.) Feb. 10, 1892-—; House 1935-37.

MORPHIS, Joseph Lewis (R Miss.) April 17, 1831-July 29, 1913; House Feb. 23, 1870-73.

MORRELL, Daniel Johnson (R Pa.) Aug. 8, 1821-Aug. 20, 1885; House 1867-71.

MORRELL, Edward de Veaux (R Pa.) Aug. 7, 1863-Sept. 1, 1917; House Nov. 6, 1900-07.

MORRIL, David Lawrence (Ad.D N.H.) June 10, 1772-Jan. 28, 1849; Senate 1817-23; Gov. 1824-27.

MORRILL, Anson Peaslee (brother of Lot Myrick Morrill) (R Maine) June 10, 1803-July 4, 1887; **House 1861-63; Gov. 1855-56.**

MORRILL, Edmund Needham (R Kan.) Feb. 12, **1834-March 14, 1909; House 1883-91; Gov. 1895-97.**

MORRILL, Justin Smith (UR Vt.) April 14, 1810-Dec. 28, 1898; House 1855-67 (W); Senate 1867-Dec. 28, 1898.

MORRILL, Lot Myrick (brother of Anson Peaslee Morrill) (R Maine) May 3, 1813-Jan. 10, 1883; Senate Jan. 17, 1861-69; Oct. 30, 1869-July 7, **1876; Gov. 1858-61; Secy. of the Treasury 1876-77.**

MORRILL, Samuel Plummer (R Maine) Feb. 11, 1816-Aug. 4, 1892; House 1869-71.

MORRIS, Calvary (W Ohio) Jan. 15, 1798-Oct. 13, 1871; House 1837-43.

MORRIS, Daniel (R N.Y.) Jan. 4, 1812-April 22, 1889; House 1863-67.

MORRIS, Edward Joy (W Pa.) July 16, 1815-Dec. 31, 1881; House 1843-45; 1857-June 8, 1861.

MORRIS, Gouverneur (uncle of Lewis Robert Morris) (F N.Y.) Jan. 31, 1752-Nov. 6, 1816; Senate April 3, 1800-03; Cont. Cong. 1777-78.

MORRIS, Isaac Newton (son of Thomas Morris and brother of Jonathan David Morris) (D Ill.) Jan. 22, 1812-Oct. 29, 1879; House 1857-61.

MORRIS, James Remley (son of Joseph Morris) (D Ohio) Jan. 10, 1819-Dec. 24, 1899; House 1861-65.

MORRIS, Jonathan David (son of Thomas Morris and brother of Isaac Newton Morris) (D Ohio) Oct. 8, 1804-May 16, 1875; House 1847-51.

MORRIS, Joseph (father of James Remley Morris) (D Ohio) Oct. 16, 1795-Oct. 23, 1854; House 1843-47.

MORRIS, Joseph Watkins (D Ky.) Feb. 26, 1879-Dec. 21, 1937; House Nov. 30, 1923-25.

MORRIS, Lewis Robert (nephew of Gouverneur Morris) (F Vt.) Nov. 2, 1760-Dec. 29, 1825; House 1797-1803.

MORRIS, Mathias (W Pa.) Sept. 12, 1787-Nov. 9, 1839; House 1835-39.

MORRIS, Robert (father of Thomas Morris) (— Pa.) Jan. 20, 1734-May 8, 1806; Senate 1789-95; Cont. Cong. 1776-78.

MORRIS, Robert Page Walter (R Minn.) June 30, 1853-Dec. 16, 1924; House 1897-1903.

MORRIS, Samuel Wells (D Pa.) Sept. 1, 1786-May 25, 1847; House 1837-41.

MORRIS, Thomas (son of Robert Morris) (— N.Y.) Feb. 26, 1771-March 12, 1849; House 1801-03.

MORRIS, Thomas (father of Isaac Newton Morris and Jonathan David Morris) (D Ohio) Jan. 3, 1776-Dec. 7, 1844; Senate 1833-39.

MORRIS, Thomas Gayle (D N.M.) Aug. 20, 1919-—; House 1959-69.

MORRIS, Toby (D Okla.) Feb. 28, 1899-Sept. 1, 1973; House 1947-53, 1957-61.

MORRISON, Cameron A. (D N.C.) Oct. 5, 1869-Aug. 20, 1953; Senate Dec. 13, 1930-Dec. 4, 1932; House 1943-45; Gov. 1921-25.

MORRISON, George Washington (D N.H.) Oct. 16, 1809-Dec. 21, 1888; House Oct. 8, 1850-51, 1853-55.

MORRISON, James Hobson (D La.) Dec. 8, 1908-—; House 1943-67.

MORRISON, James Lowery Donaldson (D Ill.) April 12, 1816-Aug. 14, 1888; House Nov. 4, 1856-57.

MORRISON, John Alexander (D Pa.) Jan. 31, 1814-July 25, 1904; House 1851-53.

MORRISON, Martin Andrew (D Ind.) April 15, 1862-July 9, 1944; House 1909-17.

MORRISON, William Ralls (D Ill.) Sept. 14, 1825-Sept. 29, 1909; House 1863-65, 1873-87.

MORRISSEY, John (D N.Y.) Feb. 12, 1831-May 1, 1878; House 1867-71.

MORROW, Dwight Whitney (R N.J.) Jan. 11, 1873-Oct. 5, 1931; Senate Dec. 3, 1930-Oct. 5, 1931.

MORROW, Jeremiah (W Ohio) Oct. 6, 1771-**March 22, 1852; House Oct. 17, 1803-13,** Oct. 13, 1840-43 (1803-13 Democrat, 1840-43 Whig); Senate 1813-19 (D); Gov. 1822-26.

MORROW, John (— Va.) ? - ?; House 1805-09.

MORROW, John (D N.M.) April 19, 1865-Feb. 25, 1935; House 1923-29.

MORROW, William W. (R Calif.) July 15, 1843-July 24, 1929; House 1885-91.

MORSE, Elijah Adams (R Mass.) May 25, 1841-June 5, 1898; House 1889-97.

MORSE, Elmer Addison (R Wis.) May 11, 1870-Oct. 4, 1945; House 1907-13.

MORSE, F. Bradford (R Mass.) Aug. 7, 1921-—; House 1961-May 1, 1972.

MORSE, Freeman Harlow (R Maine) Feb. 19, 1807-Feb. 5, 1891; House 1843-45, 1857-61 (1843-45 Whig, 1857-61 Republican).

MORSE, Isaac Edward (D La.) May 22, 1809-Feb. 11, 1866; House Dec. 2, 1844-51.

MORSE, Leopold (D Mass.) Aug. 15, 1831-Dec. 15, 1892; House 1877-85, 1887-89.

MORSE, Oliver Andrew (R N.Y.) March 26, 1815-April 20, 1870; House 1857-59.

MORSE, Wayne Lyman (D Ore.) Oct. 20, 1900-July 22, 1974; Senate 1945-69 (1945-Oct. 24, 1952 Republican, Oct. 24, 1952-Feb. 17, 1955 Independent, Feb. 17, 1955-69 Democrat).

MORTON, Jackson (brother of Jeremiah Morton) (W Fla.) Aug. 10, 1794-Nov. 20, 1874; Senate 1849-55.

MORTON, Jeremiah (brother of Jackson Morton) (W Va.) Sept. 3, 1799-Nov. 28, 1878; House 1849-51.

MORTON, Levi Parson (R N.Y.) May 16, 1824-May 16, 1920; House 1879-March 21, 1881; Vice President 1889-93; Gov. 1895-97.

MORTON, Marcus (D Mass.) Dec. 19, 1784-Feb. 6, 1864; House 1817-21; Gov. 1840-41, 1843-44.

MORTON, Oliver Hazard Perry Throck (UR Ind.) Aug. 4, 1823-Nov. 1, 1877; Senate 1867-Nov. 1, 1877; Gov. 1861-67.

MORTON, Rogers Clark Ballard (brother of Thruston Ballard Morton) (R Md.) Sept. 19, 1914-__; House 1963-Jan. 29, 1971; Chrmn. Rep. Nat. Comm. 1969-71; Secy. of Interior 1971-75; Secy. of Commerce 1975-76.

MORTON, Thruston Ballard (brother of Rogers Clark Ballard Morton) (R Ky.) Aug. 19, 1907-__; House 1947-53; Senate 1957-Dec. 16, 1968; Chrmn. Rep. Nat. Comm. 1959-61.

MOSELEY, Jonathan Ogden (R Conn.) April 9, 1762-Sept. 9, 1838; House 1805-21.

MOSLEY, William Abbott (W N.Y.) Oct. 20, 1798-Nov. 19, 1873; House 1843-47.

MOSER, Guy Louis (D Pa.) Jan. 23, 1866-May 9, 1961; House 1937-43.

MOSES, Charles Leavell (D Ga.) May 2, 1856-Oct. 10, 1910; House 1891-97.

MOSES, George Higgins (R N.H.) Feb. 9, 1869-Dec. 20, 1944; Senate Nov. 6, 1918-33; President pro tempore 1925-33.

MOSES, John (D N.D.) June 12, 1885-March 3, 1945; Senate Jan. 3-March 3, 1945; Gov. 1939-45.

MOSGROVE, James (D/G Pa.) June 14, 1821-Nov. 27, 1900; House 1881-83.

MOSHER, Charles Adams (R Ohio) May 7, 1906-—; House 1961-—.

MOSIER, Harold Gerard (D Ohio) July 24, 1889-Aug. 7, 1971; House 1937-39.

MOSS, Frank Edward (D Utah) Sept. 23, 1911-—; Senate 1959-—.

MOSS, Hunter Holmes Jr. (R W.Va.) May 26, 1874-July 15, 1916; House 1913-July 15, 1916.

MOSS, John Emerson Jr. (D Calif.) April 13, 1913-—; House 1953-—.

MOSS, John McKenzie (nephew of James Andrew McKenzie) (R Ky.) Jan. 3, 1868-June 11, 1929; House March 25, 1902-03.

MOSS, Ralph Wilbur (D Ind.) April 21, 1862-April 26, 1919; House 1909-17.

MOTT, Gordon Newell (R Nev.) Oct. 21, 1812-April 27, 1887; House (Terr. Del.) 1863-Oct. 31, 1864.

MOTT, James (D N.J.) Jan. 18, 1739-Oct. 18, 1823; House 1801-05.

MOTT, James Wheaton (R Ore.) Nov. 12, 1883-Nov. 12, 1945; House 1933-Nov. 12, 1945.

MOTT, Luther Wright (R N.Y.) Nov. 30, 1874-July 10, 1923; House 1911-July 10, 1923.

MOTT, Richard (R Ohio) July 21, 1804-Jan. 22, 1888; House 1855-59.

MOTTL, Ronald Milton (D Ohio) Feb. 6, 1934-—; House 1975-—.

MOULDER, Morgan Moore (D Mo.) Aug. 31, 1904-—; House 1949-63.

MOULTON, Mace (D N.H.) May 2, 1796-May 5, 1867; House 1845-47.

MOULTON, Samuel Wheeler (D Ill.) Jan. 20, 1821-June 3, 1905; House 1865-67, 1881-85.

MOUSER, Grant Earl (father of the following) (R Ohio) Sept. 11, 1868-May 6, 1949; House 1905-09.

MOUSER, Grant Earl Jr. (son of the preceding) (R Ohio) Feb. 20, 1895-Dec. 21, 1943; House 1929-33.

MOUTON, Alexander (D La.) Nov. 19, 1804-Feb. 12, 1885; Senate Jan. 12, 1837-March 1, 1842; Gov. 1842-46.

MOUTON, Robert Louis (D La.) Oct. 20, 1892-Nov. 26, 1956; House 1937-41.

MOXLEY, William James (R Ill.) May 22, 1851-Aug. 4, 1938; House Nov. 23, 1909-11.

MOYNIHAN, Patrick Henry (R Ill.) Sept. 25, 1869-May 20, 1946; House 1933-35.

MOZLEY, Norman Adolphus (R Mo.) Dec. 11, 1865-May 9, 1922; House 1895-97.

MRUK, Joseph (R N.Y.) Nov. 6, 1903-—; House 1943-45.

MUDD, Sydney Emanuel (father of the following) (R Md.) Feb. 12, 1858-Oct. 21, 1911; House March 20, 1890-91, 1897-1911.

MUDD, Sydney Emanuel (son of the preceding) (R Md.) June 20, 1885-Oct. 11, 1924; House 1915-Oct. 11, 1924.

MUHLENBERG, Francis Swaine (son of John Peter Gabriel Muhlenberg and nephew of Frederick Augustus Conrad Muhlenberg) (NR Ohio) April 22, 1795-Dec. 17, 1831; House Dec. 19, 1828-29.

MUHLENBERG, Frederick Augustus (great-great-grandson of Frederick Augustus Conrad Muhlenberg, great-great-grand-nephew of John Peter Gabriel Muhlenberg) (R Pa.) Sept. 25, 1887-—; House 1947-49.

MUHLENBERG, Frederick Augustus Conrad (brother of John Peter Gabriel Muhlenberg, uncle of Francis Swaine Muhlenberg and of Henry Augustus Philip Muhlenberg and great great grandfather of Frederick Augustus Muhlenberg) (— Pa.) Jan. 1, 1750-June 5, 1801; House 1789-97; Speaker 1789-91, 1793-95; Cont. Cong. 1779-80.

MUHLENBERG, Henry Augustus (son of Henry Augustus Muhlenberg and grandson of Joseph Hiester) (D Pa.) July 21, 1823-Jan. 9, 1854; House 1853-Jan. 9, 1854.

MUHLENBERG, Henry Augustus Philip (father of Henry Augustus Muhlenberg and nephew of John Peter Gabriel Muhlenberg and of Frederick Augustus Conrad Muhlenberg) (JD Pa.) May 13, 1782-Aug. 11, 1844; House 1829-Feb. 9, 1838.

MUHLENBERG, John Peter Gabriel (father of Francis Swaine Muhlenberg, brother of Frederick Augustus Conrad Muhlenberg, and uncle of Henry Augustus Philip Muhlenberg and great-great-granduncle of Frederick Augustus Muhlenberg) (D Pa.) Oct. 1, 1746-Oct. 1, 1807; House 1789-91, 1793-95, 1799-1801; Senate March 4-June 30, 1801.

MULDOWNEY, Michael Joseph (R Pa.) Aug. 10, 1889-March 30, 1947; House 1933-35.

MULDROW, Henry Lowndes (D Miss.) Feb. 8, 1837-March 1, 1905; House 1877-85.

MULKEY, Frederick William (nephew of Joseph Norton Dolph) (R Ore.) Jan. 6, 1874-May 5, 1924; Senate Jan. 23-March 3, 1907, Nov. 6-Dec. 17, 1918.

MULKEY, William Oscar (D Ala.) July 27, 1871-June 30, 1943; House June 29, 1914-15.

MULLER, Nicholas (D N.Y.) Nov. 15, 1836-Dec. 12, 1917; House 1877-81, 1883-87, 1899-Dec. 1, 1902.

MULLIN, Joseph (R N.Y.) Aug. 6, 1811-May 17, 1882; House 1847-49.

MULLINS, James (R Tenn.) Sept. 15, 1807-June 26, 1873; House 1867-69.

MULTER, Abraham Jacob (D N.Y.) Dec. 24, 1900-—; House Nov. 4, 1947-Dec. 31, 1967.

MUMFORD, George (D N.C.) ? - Dec. 31, 1818; House 1817-Dec. 31, 1818.

MUMFORD, Gurdon Saltonstall (F N.Y.) Jan. 29, 1764-April 30, 1831; House 1805-11.

MUMMA, Walter Mann (R Pa.) Nov. 20, 1890-Feb. 25, 1961; House 1951-Feb. 25, 1961.

MUNDT, Karl Earl (R S.D.) June 3, 1900-Aug. 16, 1974; House 1939-Dec. 30, 1948; Senate Dec. 31, 1948-73.

MUNGEN, William (D Ohio) May 12, 1821-Sept. 9, 1887; House 1867-71.

MURCH, Thompson Henry (G Lab.Ref. Maine) March 29, 1838-Dec. 15, 1886; House 1879-83.

MURDOCK, John Robert (D Ariz.) April 20, 1885-Feb. 14, 1972; House 1937-53.

MURDOCK, Orrice Abram Jr. (Abe) (D Utah) July 18, 1893-—; House 1933-41; Senate 1941-47.

MURDOCK, Victor (R Kan.) March 18, 1871-July 8, 1945; House May 26, 1903-15; Chrmn. Progressive Party Nat. Comm. 1915-16.

MURFREE, William Hardy (uncle of David W. Dickinson) (D N.C.) Oct. 2, 1781-Jan. 19, 1827; House 1813-17.

MURPHEY, Charles (D Ga.) May 9, 1799-Jan. 16, 1861; House 1851-53.

MURPHY, Arthur Phillips (R Mo.) Dec. 10, 1870-Feb. 1, 1914; House 1905-07; 1909-11.

MURPHY, Benjamin Franklin (R Ohio) Dec. 24, 1867-March 6, 1938; House 1919-33.

MURPHY, Edward Jr. (D N.Y.) Dec. 15, 1836-Aug. 3, 1911; Senate 1893-99.

MURPHY, Everett Jerome (R Ill.) July 24, 1852-April 10, 1922; House 1895-97.

MURPHY, George Lloyd (R Calif.) July 4, 1902-—; Senate Jan. 1, 1965-Jan. 2, 1971.

MURPHY, Henry Cruse (D N.Y.) July 5, 1810-Dec. 1, 1882; House 1843-45, 1847-49.

MURPHY, James Joseph (D N.Y.) Nov. 3, 1898-Oct. 19, 1962; House 1949-53.

MURPHY, James William (D Wis.) April 17, 1858-July 11, 1927; House 1907-09.

MURPHY, Jeremiah Henry (D Iowa) Feb. 19, 1835-Dec. 11, 1893; House 1883-87.

MURPHY, John (D Ala.) 1786- Sept. 21, 1841; House 1833-35; Gov. 1825-29.

MURPHY, John Michael (D N.Y.) Aug. 3, 1926-—; House 1963-—.

MURPHY, John William (D Pa.) April 26, 1902-March 28, 1962; House 1943-July 17, 1946.

MURPHY, Maurice J. Jr. (R N.H.) Oct. 3, 1927-—; Senate Dec. 7, 1961-Nov. 6, 1962.

MURPHY, Morgan Francis (D Ill.) April 16, 1933-—; House 1971-—.

MURPHY, Nathan Oakes (R Ariz.) Oct. 14, 1849-Aug. 22, 1908; House (Terr. Del.) 1895-97; Gov. (Terr.) 1892-94, 1898-1902.

MURPHY, Richard Louis (D Iowa) Nov. 6, 1875-July 16, 1936; Senate 1933-July 16, 1936.

MURPHY, William Thomas (D Ill.) Aug. 7, 1899-—; House 1959-71.

MURRAY, Ambrose Spencer (brother of William Murray) (R N.Y.) Nov. 27, 1807-Nov. 8, 1885; House 1855-59.

MURRAY, George Washington (R S.C.) Sept. 22, 1853-April 21, 1926; House 1893-95, June 4, 1896-97.

MURRAY, James Cunningham (D Ill.) May 16, 1917-—; House 1955-57.

MURRAY, James Edward (D Mont.) May 3, 1876-March 23, 1961; Senate Nov. 7, 1934-61.

MURRAY, John (cousin of Thomas Murray, Jr.) (— Pa.) 1768-March 7, 1834; House Oct. 14, 1817-21.

MURRAY, John L. (D Ky.) Jan. 25, 1806-Jan. 31, 1842; House 1837-39.

MURRAY, Reid Fred (R Wis.) Oct. 16, 1887-April 29, 1952; House 1939-April 29, 1952.

MURRAY, Robert Maynard (D Ohio) Nov. 28, 1841-Aug. 2, 1913; House 1883-85.

MURRAY, Thomas Jr. (cousin of John Murray) (D Pa.) 1770-Aug. 26, 1823; House Oct. 9, 1821-23.

MURRAY, Thomas Jefferson (D Tenn.) Aug. 1, 1894-Nov. 28, 1971; House 1943-67.

MURRAY, William (brother of Ambrose Spencer Murray) (D N.Y.) Oct. 1, 1803-Aug. 25, 1875; House 1851-55.

MURRAY, William Francis (D Mass.) Sept. 7, 1881-Sept. 21, 1918; House 1911-Sept. 28, 1914.

MURRAY, William Henry (D Okla.) Nov. 21, 1869-Oct. 15, 1956; House 1913-17; Gov. 1931-35.

MURRAY, William Vans (F Md.) Feb. 9, 1760-Dec. 11, 1803; House 1791-97.

MURTHA, John Patrick Jr. (D Pa.) Jan. 17, 1932-—; House Feb. 5, 1974-—.

MUSKIE, Edmund Sixtus (D Maine) March 28, 1914-__; Senate 1959-__; Gov. 1955-59.

MUSSELWHITE, Harry Webster (D Mich.) May 23, 1868-Dec. 14, 1955; House 1933-35.

MUTCHLER, Howard (son of William Mutchler) (D Pa.) Feb. 12, 1859-Jan. 4, 1916; House Aug. 7, 1893-95, 1901-03.

MUTCHLER, William (father of Howard Mutcher) (D Pa.) Dec. 21, 1831-June 23, 1893; House 1875-77, 1881-85, 1889-June 23, 1893.

MYERS, Amos (R Pa.) April 23, 1824-Oct. 18, 1893; House 1863-65.

MYERS, Francis John (D Pa.) Dec. 18, 1901-July 5, 1956; House 1939-45; Senate 1945-51.

MYERS, Gary Arthur (R Pa.) Aug. 16, 1937-—; House 1975-—.

MYERS, Henry Lee (D Mont.) Oct. 9, 1862-Nov. 11, 1943; Senate 1911-23.

MYERS, John Thomas (R Ind.) Feb. 8, 1927-—; House 1967-—.

MYERS, Leonard (R Pa.) Nov. 13, 1827-Feb. 11, 1905; House 1863-69, April 9, 1869-75.

MYERS, William Ralph (D Ind.) June 12, 1836-April 18, 1907; House 1879-81.

N

NABERS, Benjamin Duke (U Miss.) Nov. 7, 1812-Sept. 6, 1878; House 1851-53.

NAPHEN, Henry Francis (D Mass.) Aug. 14, 1852-June 8, 1905; House 1899-1903.

NAREY, Harry Elsworth (R Iowa) May 15, 1885-Aug. 18, 1962; House Nov. 3, 1942-43.

NASH, Charles Edmund (R La.) May 23, 1844-June 21, 1913; House 1875-77.

NATCHER, William Huston (D Ky.) Sept. 11, 1909-__; House Aug. 1, 1953-__.

NAUDAIN, Arnold (NR Del.) Jan. 6, 1790-Jan. 4, 1872; Senate Jan. 13, 1830-June 16, 1836.

NAYLOR, Charles (W Pa.) Oct. 6, 1806-Dec. 24, 1872; House June 29, 1837-41.

NEAL, Henry Safford (R Ohio) Aug. 25, 1828-July 13, 1906; House 1877-83.

NEAL, John Randolph (D Tenn.) Nov. 26, 1836-March 26, 1889; House 1885-89.

NEAL, Lawrence Talbot (D Ohio) Sept. 22, 1844-Nov. 2, 1905; House 1873-77.

NEAL, Stephen Lybrook (D N.C.) Nov. 7, 1934-—; House 1975-—.

NEAL, William Elmer (R W.Va.) Oct. 14, 1875-Nov. 12, 1959; House 1953-55, 1957-59.

NEALE, Raphael (— Md.) ? - Oct. 19, 1833; House 1819-25.

NEDZI, Lucien Norbert (D Mich.) May 28, 1925-—; House Nov. 7, 1961-—.

NEECE, William Henry (D Ill.) Feb. 26, 1831-Jan. 3, 1909; House 1883-87.

NEEDHAM, James Carson (R Calif.) Sept. 17, 1864-July 11, 1942; House 1899-1913.

NEELEY, George Arthur (D Kan.) Aug. 1, 1879-Jan. 1, 1919; House Nov. 11, 1912-15.

NEELY, Matthew Mansfield (D W.Va.) Nov. 9, 1874-Jan. 18, 1958; House Oct. 14, 1913-21, 1945-47; Senate 1923-29, 1931-Jan. 12, 1941, 1949-Jan. 18, 1958; Gov. 1941-45.

NEGLEY, James Scott (R Pa.) Dec. 22, 1826-Aug. 7, 1901; House 1869-75, 1885-87.

NEILL, Robert (D Ark.) Nov. 12, 1838-Feb. 16, 1907; House 1893-97.

NELSEN, Ancher (R Minn.) Oct. 11, 1904-—; House 1959-1975.

NELSON, Adolphus Peter (R Wis.) March 28, 1872-Aug. 21, 1927; House Nov. 5, 1918-23.

NELSON, Arthur Emanuel (R Minn.) May 10, 1892-April 11, 1955; Senate Nov. 18, 1942-43.

NELSON, Charles Pembroke (son of John E. Nelson) (R Maine) July 2, 1907-June 8, 1962; House 1949-57.

NELSON, Gaylord (D Wis.) June 4, 1916-—; Senate 1963-—; Gov. 1959-63.

NELSON, Homer Augustus (D N.Y.) Aug. 31, 1829-April 25, 1891; House 1863-65.

NELSON, Hugh (D Va.) Sept. 30, 1768-March 18, 1836; House 1811-Jan. 14, 1823.

NELSON, Jeremiah (F Mass.) Sept. 14, 1769-Oct. 2, 1838; House 1805-07, 1815-25, 1831-33.

NELSON, John (son of Roger Nelson) (D Md.) June 1, 1794-Jan. 18, 1860; House 1821-23; Atty. Gen. 1843-45.

NELSON, John Edward (father of Charles Pembroke Nelson) (R Maine) July 12, 1874-April 11, 1955; House March 27, 1922-33.

NELSON, John Mandt (R Wis.) Oct. 10, 1870-Jan. 29, 1955; House Sept. 4, 1906-19, 1921-33.

NELSON, Knute (R Minn.) Feb. 2, 1843-April 28, 1923; House 1883-89; Senate 1895-April 28, 1923; Gov. 1893-95.

NELSON, Roger (father of John Nelson) (D Md.) 1759-June 7, 1815; House Nov. 6, 1804-May 14, 1810.

NELSON, Thomas Amos Rogers (U Tenn.) March 19, 1812-Aug. 24, 1873; House 1859-61.

NELSON, Thomas Maduit (D Va.) Sept. 27, 1782-Nov. 10, 1853; House Dec. 4, 1816-19.

NELSON, William (W N.Y.) June 29, 1784-Oct. 3, 1869; House 1847-51.

NELSON, William Lester (D Mo.) Aug. 4, 1875-Dec. 31, 1946; House 1919-21, 1925-33, 1935-43.

NES, Henry (I Pa.) May 20, 1799-Sept. 10, 1850; House 1843-45, 1847-Sept. 10, 1850.

NESBIT, Walter (D Ill.) May 1, 1878-Dec. 6, 1938; House 1933-35.

NESBITT, Wilson (D S.C.) ? - May 13, 1861; House 1817-19.

NESMITH, James Willis (cousin of Joseph Gardner Wilson and grandfather of Clifton Nesmith McArthur) (D Ore.) July 23, 1820-June 17, 1885; Senate 1861-67; House Dec. 1, 1873-75.

NEUBERGER, Maurine Brown (widow of Richard L. Neuberger) (D Ore.) Jan. 9, 1907-—; Senate Nov. 9, 1960-67.

NEUBERGER, Richard Lewis (husband of Maurine B. Neuberger) (D Ore.) Dec. 26, 1912-March 9, 1960; Senate 1955-March 9, 1960.

NEVILLE, Joseph (— Va.) 1730-March 4, 1819; House 1793-95.

NEVILLE, William (cousin of Bird Segle McGuire) (P Neb.) Dec. 29, 1843-April 5, 1909; House Dec. 4, 1899-1903.

NEVIN, Robert Murphy (R Ohio) May 5, 1850-Dec. 17, 1912; House 1901-07.

NEW, Anthony (D Va./Ky.) 1747-March 2, 1833; House 1793-1805 (Va.), 1811-13, 1817-19 and 1821-23 (Ky.).

NEW, Harry Stewart (R Ind.) Dec. 31, 1858-May 9, 1937; Senate 1917-23; Chrmn. Rep. Nat. Comm. 1907-08; Postmaster Gen. 1923-29.

NEW, Jeptha Dudley (D Ind.) Nov. 28, 1830-July 9, 1892; House 1875-77, 1879-81.

NEWBERRY, John Stoughton (father of Truman Handy Newberry) (R Mich.) Nov. 18, 1826-Jan. 2, 1887; House 1879-81.

NEWBERRY, Truman Handy (son of John Stoughton Newberry) (R Mich.) Nov. 5, 1864-Oct. 3, 1945; Senate 1919-Nov. 18, 1922; Secy. of the Navy 1908-09.

NEWBERRY, Walter Cass (D Ill.) Dec. 23, 1835-July 20, 1912; House 1891-93.

NEWBOLD, Thomas (D N.J.) Aug. 2, 1760-Dec. 18, 1823; House 1807-13.

NEWCOMB, Carman Adam (R Mo.) July 1, 1830-April 6, 1902; House 1867-69.

NEWELL, William Augustus (R N.J.) Sept. 5, 1817-Aug. 8, 1901; House 1845-51, 1865-67 (1845-51 Whig, 1865-67 Republican); Gov. (N.J.) 1857-60; Gov. (Wash. Terr.) 1880-84.

NEWHALL, Judson Lincoln (R Ky.) March 26, 1870-July 23, 1952; House 1929-31.

NEWHARD, Peter (D Pa.) July 26, 1783-Feb. 19, 1860; House 1839-43.

NEWLANDS, Francis Griffith (D Nev.) Aug. 28, 1848-Dec. 24, 1917; House 1893-1903; Senate 1903-Dec. 24, 1917.

NEWMAN, Alexander (D Va.) Oct. 5, 1804-Sept. 8, 1849; House March 4-Sept. 8, 1849.

NEWNAN, Daniel (SRD Ga.) about 1780-Jan. 16, 1851; House 1831-33.

NEWSHAM, Joseph Parkinson (R La.) May 24, 1837-Oct. 22, 1919; House July 18, 1868-69, May 23, 1870-71.

NEWSOME, John Parks (D Ala.) Feb. 13, 1893-Nov. 10, 1961; House 1943-45.

NEWTON, Cherubusco (D La.) May 15, 1848-May 26, 1910; House 1887-89.

NEWTON, Cleveland Alexander (R Mo.) Sept. 3, 1873-Sept. 17, 1945; House 1919-27.

NEWTON, Eben (W Ohio) Oct. 16, 1795-Nov. 6, 1885; House 1851-53.

NEWTON, Thomas Jr. (D Va.) Nov. 21, 1768-Aug. 5, 1847; House 1801-March 3, 1829, March 4, 1829-March 9, 1830, 1831-33.

NEWTON, Thomas Willoughby (W Ark.) Jan. 18, 1804-Sept. 22, 1853; House Feb. 6-March 3, 1847.

NEWTON, Walter Hughes (R Minn.) Oct. 10, 1880-Aug. 10, 1941; House 1919-June 30, 1929.

NEWTON, Willoughby (W Va.) Dec. 2, 1802-May 23, 1874; House 1843-45.

NIBLACK, Silas Leslie (cousin of William Ellis Niblack) (D Fla.) March 17, 1825-Feb. 13, 1883; House Jan. 29-March 3, 1873.

NIBLACK, William Ellis (cousin of Silas Leslie Niblack) (D Ind.) May 19, 1822-May 7, 1893; House Dec. 7, 1857-61, 1865-75.

NICHOLAS, John (brother of Wilson Cary Nicholas and uncle of Robert Carter Nicholas) (D Va.) about 1757-Dec. 31, 1819; House 1793-1801.

NICHOLAS, Robert Carter (nephew of John Nicholas and Wilson Cary Nicholas) (D La.) 1793-Dec. 24, 1857; Senate Jan. 13, 1836-41.

NICHOLAS, Wilson Cary (brother of John Nicholas and uncle of Robert Carter Nicholas) (D Va.) Jan. 31, 1761-Oct. 10, 1820; Senate Dec. 5, 1799-May 22, 1804; House 1807-Nov. 27, 1809; Gov. 1814-16.

NICHOLLS, John Calhoun (D Ga.) April 25, 1834-Dec. 25, 1893; House 1879-81, 1883-85.

NICHOLLS, Samuel Jones (D S.C.) May 7, 1885-Nov. 23, 1937; House Sept. 14, 1915-21.

NICHOLLS, Thomas David (ID Pa.) Sept. 16, 1870-Jan. 19, 1931; House 1907-11.

NICHOLS, Charles Archibald (R Mich.) Aug. 25, 1876-April 25, 1920; House 1915-April 25, 1920.

NICHOLS, John (I N.C.) Nov. 14, 1834-Sept. 22, 1917; House 1887-89.

NICHOLS, John Conover (Jack) (D Okla.) Aug. 31, 1896-Nov. 7, 1945; House 1935-July 3, 1943.

NICHOLS, Matthias H. (R Ohio) Oct. 3, 1824-Sept. 15, 1862; House 1853-59 (1853-55 Whig, 1855-59 Republican).

NICHOLS, William (D Ala.) Oct. 16, 1918-—; House 1967-—.

NICHOLSON, Alfred Osborn Pope (D Tenn.) Aug. 31, 1808-March 23, 1876; Senate Dec. 25, 1840-Feb. 7, 1842, 1859-61.

NICHOLSON, Donald William (R Mass.) Aug. 11, 1888-Feb. 16, 1968; House Nov. 18, 1947-59.

NICHOLSON, John (D N.Y.) 1765-Jan. 20, 1820; House 1809-11.

NICHOLSON, John Anthony (D Del.) Nov. 17, 1827-Nov. 4, 1906; House 1865-69.

NICHOLSON, Joseph Hopper (D Md.) May 15, 1770-March 4, 1817; House 1799-March 1, 1806.

NICHOLSON, Samuel Danford (R Colo.) Feb. 22, 1859-March 24, 1923; Senate 1921-March 24, 1923.

NICOLL, Henry (D N.Y.) Oct. 23, 1812-Nov. 28, 1879; House 1847-49.

NIEDRINGHAUS, Frederick Gottlieb (uncle of Henry Frederick Niedringhaus) (R Mo.) Oct. 21, 1837-Nov. 25, 1922; House 1889-91.

NIEDRINGHAUS, Henry Frederick (nephew of Frederick Gottlieb Niedringhaus) (R Mo.) Dec. 15, 1864-Aug. 3, 1941; House 1927-33.

NILES, Jason (R Miss.) Dec. 19, 1814-July 7, 1894; House 1873-75.

NILES, John Milton (D Conn.) Aug. 20, 1787-May 31, 1856; Senate Dec. 21, 1835-39, 1843-49; Postmaster Gen. 1840-41.

NILES, Nathaniel (— Vt.) April 3, 1741-Oct. 31, 1828; House Oct. 17, 1791-95.

NIMTZ, F. Jay (R Ind.) Dec. 1, 1915-—; House 1957-59.

NISBET, Eugenius Aristides (cousin of Mark Anthony Cooper) (W Ga.) Dec. 7, 1803-March 18, 1871; House 1839-Oct. 12, 1841.

NIVEN, Archibald Campbell (D N.Y.) Dec. 8, 1803-Feb. 21, 1882; House 1845-47.

NIX, Robert Nelson Cornelius Sr. (D Pa.) Aug. 9, 1905-—; House May 20, 1958-—.

NIXON, George Stuart (R Nev.) April 2, 1860-June 5, 1912; Senate 1905-June 5, 1912.

NIXON, John Thompson (R N.J.) Aug. 31, 1820-Sept. 28, 1889; House 1859-63.

NIXON, Richard Milhous (R Calif.) Jan. 9, 1913-__; House 1947-Nov. 30, 1950; Senate Dec. 1, 1950-Jan. 1, 1953; Vice Pres. 1953-61; Pres. 1969-Aug. 9, 1974.

NOBLE, David Addison (D Mich.) Nov. 9, 1802-Oct. 13, 1876; House 1853-55.

NOBLE, James (DR Ind.) Dec. 16, 1785-Feb. 26, 1831; Senate Dec. 11, 1816-Feb. 26, 1831.

NOBLE, Warren Perry (D Ohio) June 14, 1820-July 9, 1903; House 1861-65.

NOBLE, William Henry (D N.Y.) Sept. 22, 1788-Feb. 5, 1850; House 1837-39.

NODAR, Robert Joseph Jr. (R N.Y.) March 23, 1916-—; House 1947-49.

NOELL, John William (father of Thomas Estes Noell) (D Mo.) Feb. 22, 1816-March 14, 1863; House 1859-March 14, 1863.

NOELL, Thomas Estes (son of John William Noell) (Rad. Mo.) April 3, 1839-Oct. 3, 1867; House 1865-Oct. 3, 1867.

NOLAN, John Ignatius (husband of Mae Ella Nolan) (R Calif.) Jan. 14, 1874-Nov. 18, 1922; House 1913-Nov. 18, 1922.

NOLAN, Mae Ella (widow of John Ignatius Nolan) (R Calif.) Sept. 20, 1886-July 9, 1973; House Jan. 23, 1923-25.

NOLAN, Michael Nicholas (D N.Y.) May 4, 1833-May 31, 1905; House 1881-83.

NOLAN, Richard Michael (D Minn.) Dec. 17, 1943-—; House 1975-—.

NOLAN, William Ignatius (R Minn.) May 14, 1874-Aug. 3, 1943; House June 17, 1929-33.

NOLAND, James E. (D Ind.) April 22, 1920-—; House 1949-51.

NOONAN, Edward Thomas (D Ill.) Oct. 23, 1861-Dec. 19, 1923; House 1899-1901.

NOONAN, George Henry (R Texas) Aug. 20, 1828-Aug. 17, 1907; House 1895-97.

NORBECK, Peter (R S.D.) Aug. 27, 1870-Dec. 20, 1936; Senate 1921-Dec. 20, 1936; Gov. 1917-21.

NORBLAD, Albin Walter Jr. (R Ore.) Sept. 12, 1908-Sept. 20, 1964; House Jan. 11, 1946-Sept. 20, 1964.

NORCROSS, Amasa (R Mass.) Jan. 26, 1824-April 2, 1898; House 1877-83.

NORMAN, Fred Barthold (R Wash.) March 21, 1882-April 18, 1947; House 1943-45, Jan. 3-April 18, 1947.

NORRELL, Catherine Dorris (widow of William Frank Norrell) (D Ark.) March 30, 1901-—; House April 18, 1961-63.

NORRELL, William Frank (husband of Catherine D. Norrell) (D Akr.) Aug. 29, 1896-Feb. 15, 1961; House 1939-Feb. 15, 1961.

NORRIS, Benjamin White (R Ala.) Jan. 22, 1819-Jan. 26, 1873; House July 21, 1868-69.

NORRIS, George William (R Neb.) July 11, 1861-Sept. 2, 1944; House 1903-13; Senate 1913-43 (1913-37 Republican, 1937-43 Independent Republican).

NORRIS, Moses Jr. (D N.H.) Nov. 8, 1799-Jan. 11, 1855; House 1843-47; Senate 1849-Jan. 11, 1855.

NORTH, Solomon Taylor (R Pa.) May 24, 1853-Oct. 19, 1917; House 1915-17.

NORTH, William (F N.Y.) 1755-Jan. 3, 1836; Senate May 5-Aug. 17, 1798.

NORTHWAY, Stephen Asa (R Ohio) June 19, 1833-Sept. 8, 1898; House 1893-Sept. 8, 1898.

NORTON, Daniel Sheldon (UC Minn.) April 12, 1829-July 13, 1870; Senate 1865-July 13, 1870

NORTON, Ebenezer Foote (D N.Y.) Nov. 7, 1774-May 11, 1851; House 1829-31.

NORTON, Elijah Hise (D Mo.) Nov. 24, 1821-Aug. 5, 1914; House 1861-63.

NORTON, James (D S.C.) Oct. 8, 1843-Oct. 14, 1920; House Dec. 6, 1897-1901.

NORTON, James Albert (D Ohio) Nov. 11, 1843-July 24, 1912; House 1897-1903.

NORTON, Jesse Olds (R Ill.) Dec. 25, 1812-Aug. 3, 1875; House 1853-57, 1863-65.

NORTON, John Nathaniel (D Neb.) May 12, 1878-Oct. 5, 1960; House 1927-29, 1931-33.

NORTON, Mary Teresa (D N.J.) March 7, 1875-Aug. 2, 1959; House 1925-51.

NORTON, Miner Gibbs (R Ohio) May 11, 1857-Sept. 7, 1926; House 1921-23.

NORTON, Nelson Ira (R N.Y.) March 30, 1820-Oct. 28, 1887; House Dec. 6, 1875-77.

NORTON, Patrick Daniel (R N.D.) May 17, 1876-Oct. 14, 1953; House 1913-19.

NORTON, Richard Henry (D Mo.) Nov. 6, 1849-March 15, 1918; House 1889-93.

NORVELL, John (D Mich.) Dec. 21, 1789-April 24, 1850; Senate Jan. 26, 1837-41.

NORWOOD, Thomas Manson (D Ga.) April 26, 1830-June 19, 1913; Senate Nov. 14, 1871-77; House 1885-89.

NOTT, Abraham (F S.C.) Feb. 5, 1768-June 19, 1830; House 1799-1801.

NOURSE, Amos (— Maine) Dec. 17, 1794-April 7, 1877; Senate Jan. 16-March 3, 1857.

NOWAK, Henry James (D N.Y.) Feb. 21, 1935-—; House 1975-__.

NOYES, John (F Vt.) April 2, 1764-Oct. 26, 1841; House 1815-17.

NOYES, Joseph Cobham (W Maine) Sept. 22, 1798-July 28, 1868; House 1837-39.

NUCKOLLS, Stephen Friel (D Wyo.) Aug. 16, 1825-Feb. 14, 1879; House (Terr. Del.) Dec. 6, 1869-71.

NUCKOLLS, William Thompson (— S.C.) Feb. 23, 1801-Sept. 27, 1855; House 1827-33.

NUGEN, Robert Hunter (D Ohio) July 16, 1809-Feb. 28, 1872; House 1861-63.

NUGENT, John Frost (D Idaho) June 28, 1868-Sept. 18, 1931; Senate Jan. 22, 1918-Jan. 14, 1921.

NUNN, David Alexander (R Tenn.) July 26, 1833-Sept. 11, 1918; House 1867-69, 1873-75.

NUNN, Samuel Augustus (D Ga.) Sept. 8, 1938-—; Senate Nov. 8, 1972-—.

NUTE, Alonzo (R N.H.) Feb. 12, 1826-Dec. 24, 1892; House 1889-91.

NUTTING, Newton Wright (R N.Y.) Oct. 22, 1840-Oct. 15, 1889; House 1883-85, 1887-Oct. 15, 1889.

NYE, Frank Mellen (R Minn.) March 7, 1852-Nov. 29, 1935; House 1907-13.

NYE, Gerald Prentice (R N.D.) Dec. 19, 1892-July 17, 1971; Senate Nov. 14, 1925-45.

NYE, James Warren (R Nev.) June 10, 1815-Dec. 25, 1876; Senate Dec. 16, 1864-73; Gov. (Terr.) 1861-64.

NYGAARD, Hjalmar (R N.D.) March 24, 1906-July 18, 1963; House 1961-July 18, 1963.

O

OAKEY, Peter Davis (R Conn.) Feb. 25, 1861-Nov. 18, 1920; House 1915-17.

OAKLEY, Thomas Jackson (Clinton D. N.Y.) Nov. 10, 1783-May 11, 1857; House 1813-15, 1827-May 9, 1828 (1813-15 Federalist, 1827-28 Clinton Democrat).

OAKMAN, Charles Gibb (R Mich.) Sept. 4, 1903-Oct. 28, 1973; House 1953-55.

OATES, William Calvin (D Ala.) Nov. 30, 1835-Sept. 9, 1910; House 1881-Nov. 5, 1894; Gov. 1894-96.

OBERSTAR, James Louis (D Minn.) Sept. 10, 1934-—; House 1975-—.

OBEY, David Ross (D Wis.) Oct. 3, 1938-—; House April 1, 1969-__.

O'BRIEN, Charles Francis Xavier (D N.J.) March 7, 1879-Nov. 14, 1940; House 1921-25.

O'BRIEN, George Donoghue (D Mich.) Jan. 1, 1900-Oct. 25, 1957; House 1937-39, 1941-47, 1949-55.

O'BRIEN, George Miller (R Ill.) June 17, 1917-—; House 1973-—.

O'BRIEN, James (A-TD N.Y.) March 13, 1841-March 5, 1907; House 1879-81.

O'BRIEN, James Henry (D N.Y.) July 15, 1860-Sept. 2, 1924; House 1913-15.

O'BRIEN, Jeremiah (D Maine) Jan. 21, 1778-May 30, 1858; House 1823-29.

O'BRIEN, Joseph John (R N.Y.) Oct. 9, 1897-Jan. 23, 1953; House 1939-45.

O'BRIEN, Leo William (D N.Y.) Sept. 21, 1900-—; House April 1, 1952-67.

O'BRIEN, Thomas Joseph (D Ill.) April 30, 1878-April 14, 1964; House 1933-39, 1943-April 14, 1964.

O'BRIEN, William James (D Md.) May 28, 1836-Nov. 13, 1905; House 1873-77.

O'BRIEN, William Smith (D W.Va.) Jan. 8, 1862-Aug. 10, 1948; House 1927-29.

OCAMPO, Pablo (— P.I.) Jan. 25, 1853-Feb. 5, 1925; House (Res. Comm.) Nov. 22, 1907-Nov. 22, 1909.

OCHILTREE, Thomas Peck (I Texas) Oct. 26, 1837-Nov. 25, 1902; House 1883-85.

O'CONNELL, David Joseph (D N.Y.) Dec. 25, 1868-Dec. 29, 1930; House 1919-21, 1923-Dec. 29, 1930.

O'CONNELL, Jeremiah Edward (D R.I.) July 8, 1883-Sept. 18, 1964; House 1923-27, 1929-May 9, 1930.

O'CONNELL, Jerry Joseph (D Mont.) June 14, 1909-Jan. 16, 1956; House 1937-39.

O'CONNELL, John Matthew (D R.I.) Aug. 10, 1872-Dec. 6, 1941; House 1933-39.

O'CONNELL, Joseph Francis (D Mass.) Dec. 7, 1872-Dec. 10, 1942; House 1907-11.

O'CONNOR, Charles (R Okla.) Oct. 26, 1878-Nov. 15, 1940; House 1929-31.

O'CONNOR, James (D La.) April 4, 1870-Jan. 7, 1941; House June 5, 1919-31.

O'CONNOR, James Francis (D Mont.) May 7, 1878-Jan. 15, 1945; House 1937-Jan. 15, 1945.

O'CONNOR, John Joseph (D N.Y.) Nov. 23, 1885-Jan. 26, 1960; House Nov. 6, 1923-39.

O'CONNOR, Michael Patrick (D S.C.) Sept. 29, 1831-April 26, 1881; House 1879-April 26, 1881.

O'CONOR, Herbert Romulus (D Md.) Nov. 17, 1896-March 4, 1960; Senate 1947-53; Gov. 1939-47.

O'DANIEL, Wilbert Lee (D Texas) March 11, 1890-May 11, 1969; Senate Aug. 4, 1941-49; Gov. 1939-41.

O'DAY, Caroline Love Goodwin (D N.Y.) June 22, 1875-Jan. 4, 1943; House 1935-43.

ODDIE, Tasker Lowndes (R Nev.) Oct. 24, 1870-Feb. 17, 1950; Senate 1921-33; Gov. 1911-15.

ODELL, Benjamin Baker Jr. (R N.Y.) Jan. 14, 1854-May 9, 1926; House 1895-99; Gov. 1901-05.

ODELL, Moses Fowler (D N.Y.) Feb. 24, 1818-June 13, 1866; House 1861-65.

ODELL, Nathaniel (D N.Y.) Oct. 10, 1828-Oct. 30, 1904; House 1875-77.

O'DONNELL, James (R Mich.) March 25, 1840-March 17, 1915; House 1885-93.

O'FERRALL, Charles Triplett (D Va.) Oct. 21, 1840-Sept. 22, 1905; House May 5, 1884-Dec. 28, 1893; Gov. 1894-98.

OGDEN, Aaron (F N.J.) Dec. 3, 1756-April 19, 1839; Senate Feb. 28, 1801-03; Gov. 1812-13.

OGDEN, Charles Franklin (R Ky.) ? - April 10, 1933; House 1919-23.

OGDEN, David A. (F N.Y.) Jan. 10, 1770-June 9, 1829; House 1817-19.

OGDEN, Henry Warren (D La.) Oct. 21, 1842-July 23, 1905; House May 12, 1894-99.

OGLE, Alexander (father of Charles Ogle and grandfather of Andrew Jackson Ogle) (D Pa.) Aug. 10, 1766-Oct. 14, 1832; House 1817-19.

OGLE, Andrew Jackson (grandson of Alexander Ogle) (W Pa.) March 25, 1822-Oct. 14, 1852; House 1849-51.

OGLE, Charles (son of Alexander Ogle) (W Pa.) 1798-May 10, 1841; House 1837-May 10, 1841.

OGLESBY, Richard James (cousin of Woodson Ratcliffe Oglesby) (R Ill.) July 25, 1824-April 24, 1899; Senate 1873-79; Gov. 1865-69; Jan. 13-23, 1873; 1885-89.

OGLESBY, Woodson Ratcliffe (cousin of Richard James Oglesby) (D N.Y.) Feb. 9, 1867-April 30, 1955; House 1913-17.

O'GORMAN, James Aloysius (D N.Y.) May 5, 1860-May 17, 1943; Senate 1911-17.

O'GRADY, James Mary Early (R N.Y.) March 31, 1863-Nov. 3, 1928; House 1899-1901.

O'HAIR, Frank Trimble (D Ill.) March 12, 1870-Aug. 3, 1932; House 1913-15.

O'HARA, Barratt (D Ill.) April 28, 1882-Aug. 11, 1969; House 1949-51; 1953-69.

O'HARA, James Edward (R N.C.) Feb. 26, 1844-Sept. 15, 1905; House 1883-87.

O'HARA, James Grant (D Mich.) Nov. 8, 1925-—; House 1959-—.

O'HARA, Joseph Patrick (R Minn.) Jan. 23, 1895-March 4, 1975; House 1941-59.

OHLIGER, Lewis Phillip (D Ohio) Jan. 3, 1843-Jan. 9, 1923; House Dec. 5, 1892-93.

O'KONSKI, Alvin Edward (R Wis.) May 26, 1904-—; House 1943-73.

OLCOTT, Jacob Van Vechten (R N.Y.) May 17, 1856-June 1, 1940; House 1905-11.

OLCOTT, Simeon (F N.H.) Oct. 1, 1735-Feb. 22, 1815; Senate June 17, 1801-05.

OLDFIELD, Pearl Peden (widow of William Allan Oldfield) (D Ark.) Dec. 2, 1876-April 12, 1962; House Jan. 9, 1929-31.

OLDFIELD, William Allan (husband of Pearl Peden Oldfield) (D Ark.) Feb. 4, 1874-Nov. 19, 1928; House 1909-Nov. 19, 1928.

OLDS, Edson Baldwin (D Ohio) June 3, 1802-Jan. 24, 1869; House 1849-55.

O'LEARY, Denis (D N.Y.) Jan. 22, 1863-Sept. 27, 1943; House 1913-Dec. 31, 1914.

O'LEARY, James Aloysius (D N.Y.) April 23, 1889-March 16, 1944; House 1935-March 16, 1944.

OLIN, Abram Baldwin (son of Gideon Olin) (R N.Y.) Sept. 21, 1808-July 7, 1879; House 1857-63.

OLIN, Gideon (father of Abram Baldwin Olin and uncle of Henry Olin) (D Vt.) Nov. 2, 1743-Jan. 21, 1823; House 1803-07.

OLIN, Henry (nephew of Gideon Olin) (Jeff D Vt.) May 7, 1768-Aug. 16, 1837; House Dec. 13, 1824-25.

OLIVER, Andrew (D N.Y.) Jan. 16, 1815-March 6, 1889; House 1853-57.

OLIVER, Daniel Charles (D N.Y.) Oct. 6, 1865-March 26, 1924; House 1917-19.

OLIVER, Frank (D N.Y.) Oct. 2, 1883-Jan. 1, 1968; House 1923-June 18, 1934.

OLIVER, George Tener (R Pa.) Jan. 26, 1848-Jan. 22, 1919; Senate March 17, 1909-17.

OLIVER, James Churchill (D Maine) Aug. 6, 1895-—; House 1937-43 (R); 1959-61 (D).

OLIVER, Mordecai (W Mo.) Oct. 22, 1819-April 25, 1898; House 1853-57.

OLIVER Samuel Addison (R Iowa) July 21, 1833-July 7, 1912; House 1875-79.

OLIVER, William Bacon (cousin of Sydney Parham Epes) (D Ala.) May 23, 1867-May 27, 1948; House 1915-37.

OLIVER, William Morrison (D N.Y.) Oct. 15, 1792-July 21, 1863; House 1841-43.

OLMSTED, Marlin Edgar (R Pa.) May 21, 1847-July 19, 1913; House 1897-1913.

OLNEY, Richard (D Mass.) Jan. 5, 1871-Jan. 15, 1939; House 1915-21.

O'LOUGHLIN, Kathryn Ellen (after election was married to Daniel M. McCarthy and thereupon served under the name of Kathryn O'Loughlin McCarthy) (D Kan.) April 24, 1894-Jan. 16, 1952; House 1933-35.

OLPP, Archibald Ernest (R N.J.) May 12, 1882-July 26, 1949; House 1921-23.

OLSEN, Arnold (D Mont.) Dec. 17, 1916-—; House 1961-71.

OLSON, Alec G. (D Minn.) Sept. 11, 1930-—; House 1963-67.

O'MAHONEY, Joseph Christopher (D Wyo.) Nov. 5, 1884-Dec. 1, 1962; Senate Jan. 1, 1934-53; Nov. 29, 1954-61.

O'MALLEY, Matthew Vincent (D N.Y.) June 26, 1878-May 26, 1931; House March 4-May 26, 1931.

O'MALLEY, Thomas David Patrick (D Wis.) March 24, 1903-—; House 1933-39.

O'NEAL, Emmet (D Ky.) April 14, 1887-July 18, 1967; House 1935-47.

O'NEAL, Maston Emmett Jr. (D Ga.) July 19, 1907-—; House 1965-71.

O'NEALL, John Henry (D Ind.) Oct. 30, 1838-July 15, 1907; House 1887-91.

O'NEIL, Joseph Henry (D Mass.) March 23, 1853-Feb. 19, 1935; House 1889-95.

O'NEILL, Charles (R Pa.) March 21, 1821-Nov. 25, 1893; House 1863-71; 1873-Nov. 25, 1893.

O'NEILL, Edward Leo (D N.J.) July 10, 1903-Dec. 12, 1948; House 1937-39.

O'NEILL, Harry Patrick (D Pa.) Feb. 10, 1889-June 24, 1953; House 1949-53.

O'NEILL, John (D Ohio) Dec. 17, 1822-May 25, 1905; House 1863-65.

O'NEILL, John Joseph (D Mo.) June 25, 1846-Feb. 19, 1898; House 1883-89; 1891-93; April 3, 1894-95.

O'NEILL, Thomas Phillip Jr. (D Mass.) Dec. 9, 1912-—; House 1953-—.

O'REILLY, Daniel (ID N.Y.) June 3, 1838-Sept. 23, 1911; House 1879-81.

ORMSBY, Stephen (D Ky.) 1759-1844; House 1811-13; April 20, 1813-17.

ORR, Alexander Dalrymple (nephew of William Grayson and cousin of William John Grayson) (— Ky.) Nov. 6, 1761-June 21, 1835; House Nov. 8, 1792-97.

ORR, Benjamin (F Mass.) Dec. 1, 1772-Sept. 3, 1828; House 1817-19.

ORR, Jackson (R Iowa) Sept. 21, 1832-March 15, 1926; House 1871-75.

ORR, James Lawrence (D S.C.) May 12, 1822-May 5, 1873; House 1849-59; Speaker 1857-59; Gov. 1865-68 (R).

ORR, Robert Jr. (D Pa.) March 5, 1786-May 22, 1876; House Oct. 11, 1825-29.

ORTH, Godlove Stein (R Ind.) April 22, 1817-Dec. 16, 1882; House 1863-71, 1873-75; 1879-Dec. 16, 1882.

OSBORN, Thomas Ward (R Fla.) March 9, 1836-Dec. 18, 1898; Senate June 25, 1868-73.

OSBORNE, Edwin Sylvanus (R Pa.) Aug. 7, 1839-Jan. 1, 1900; House 1885-91.

OSBORNE, Henry Zenas (R Calif.) Oct. 4, 1848-Feb. 8, 1923; House 1917-Feb. 8, 1923.

OSBORNE, John Eugene (D Wyo.) June 19, 1858-April 24, 1943; House 1897-99; Gov. 1893-95.

OSBORNE, Thomas Burr (W Conn.) July 8, 1798-Sept. 2, 1869; House 1839-43.

OSGOOD, Gayton Pickman (D Mass.) July 4, 1797-June 26, 1861; House 1833-35.

O'SHAUNESSY, George Francis (D R.I.) May 1, 1868-Nov. 28, 1934; House 1911-19.

OSIAS, Camilo (Nat. P.I.) March 23, 1889-—; House (Res. Comm.) 1929-35.

OSMER, James H. (R Pa.) Jan. 23, 1832-Oct. 3, 1912; House 1879-81.

OSMERS, Frank Charles Jr. (R N.J.) Dec. 30, 1907-—; House 1939-43; Nov. 6, 1951-65.

OSTERTAG, Harold Charles (R N.Y.) June 22, 1896-—; House 1951-65.

O'SULLIVAN, Eugene Daniel (D Neb.) May 31, 1883-Feb. 7, 1968; House 1949-51.

O'SULLIVAN, Patrick Brett (D Conn.) Aug. 11, 1887-—; House 1923-25.

OTERO, Mariano Sabino (nephew of Miguel Antonio Otero) (R N.M.) Aug. 29, 1844-Feb. 1, 1904; House (Terr. Del.) 1879-81.

OTERO, Miguel Antonio (uncle of Mariano Sabino Otero) (D N.M.) June 21, 1829-May 30, 1882; House (Terr. Del.) July 23, 1856-61.

OTEY, Peter Johnston (D Va.) Dec. 22, 1840-May 4, 1902; House 1895-May 4, 1902.

OTIS, Harrison Gray (F Mass.) Oct. 8, 1765-Oct. 28, 1848; House 1797-1801; Senate 1817-May 30, 1822.

OTIS, John (W Maine) Aug. 3, 1801-Oct. 17, 1856; House 1849-51.

OTIS, John Grant (PP Kan.) Feb. 10, 1838-Feb. 22, 1916; House 1891-93.

OTIS, Norton Prentiss (R N.Y.) March 18, 1840-Feb. 20, 1905; House 1903-Feb. 20, 1905.

OTJEN, Theobald (R Wis.) Oct. 27, 1851-April 11, 1924; House 1895-1907.

O'TOOLE, Donald Lawrence (D N.Y.) Aug. 1, 1902-Sept. 12, 1964; House 1937-53.

OTTINGER, Richard Lawrence (D N.Y.) Jan. 27, 1929—; House 1965-71, 1975-—.

OURY, Granville Henderson (D Ariz.) March 12, 1825-Jan. 11, 1891; House (Terr. Del.) 1881-85.

OUTHWAITE, Joseph Hodson (D Ohio) Dec. 5, 1841-Dec. 9, 1907; House 1885-95.

OUTLAND, George Elmer (D Calif.) Oct. 8, 1906-—; House 1943-47.

OUTLAW, David (cousin of George Outlaw) (W N.C.) Sept. 14, 1806-Oct. 22, 1868; House 1847-53.

OUTLAW, George (cousin of David Outlaw) (JD N.C.) ? - Aug. 15, 1825; House Jan. 19-March 3, 1825.

OVERMAN, Lee Slater (D N.C.) Jan. 3, 1854-Dec. 12, 1930; Senate 1903-Dec. 12, 1930.

OVERMYER, Arthur Warren (D Ohio) May 31, 1879-March 8, 1952; House 1915-19.

OVERSTREET, James (— S.C.) Feb. 11, 1773-May 24, 1822; House 1819-May 24, 1822.

OVERSTREET, James Whetstone (D Ga.) Aug. 28, 1866-Dec. 4, 1938; House Oct. 3, 1906-07, 1917-23.

OVERSTREET, Jesse (R Ind.) Dec. 14, 1859-May 27, 1910; House 1895-1909.

OVERTON, Edward Jr. (R Pa.) Feb. 4, 1836-Sept. 18, 1903; House 1877-81.

OVERTON, John Holmes (uncle of Overton Brooks) (D La.) Sept. 17, 1875-May 14, 1948; House May 12, 1931-33; Senate 1933-May 14, 1948.

OVERTON, Walter Hampden (D La.) 1788-Dec. 24, 1845; House 1829-31.

OWEN, Allen Ferdinand (W Ga.) Oct. 9, 1816-April 7, 1865; House 1849-51.

OWEN, Emmett Marshall (D Ga.) Oct. 19, 1877-June 21, 1939; House 1933-June 21, 1939.

OWEN, George Washington (— Ala.) Oct. 20, 1796-Aug. 18, 1837; House 1823-29.

OWEN, James (D N.C.) Dec. 7, 1784-Sept. 4, 1865; House 1817-19.

OWEN, Robert Dale (D Ind.) Nov. 9, 1800-June 24, 1877; House 1843-47.

OWEN, Robert Latham (D Okla.) Feb. 3, 1856-July 19, 1947; Senate Dec. 11, 1907-25.

OWEN, Ruth Bryan (later Mrs. Borge Rohde; daughter of William Jennings Bryan) (D Fla.) Oct. 2, 1885-July 26, 1954; House 1929-33.

OWEN, William Dale (R Ind.) Sept. 6, 1846-1906; House 1885-91.

OWENS, Douglas Wayne (D Utah) May 2, 1937-—; House 1973-75.

OWENS, George Welshman (U Ga.) Aug. 29, 1786-March 2, 1856; House 1835-39.

OWENS, James W. (D Ohio) Oct. 24, 1837-March 30, 1900; House 1889-93.

OWENS, Thomas Leonard (R Ill.) Dec. 21, 1897-June 7, 1948; House 1947-June 7, 1948.

OWENS, William Claiborne (D Ky.) Oct. 17, 1849-Nov. 18, 1925; House 1895-97.

OWSLEY, Bryan Young (W Ky.) Aug. 19, 1798-Oct. 27, 1849; House 1841-43.

P

PACE, Stephen (D Ga.) March 9, 1891-April 5, 1970; House 1937-51.

PACHECO, Romualdo (R Calif.) Oct. 31, 1831-Jan. 23, 1899; House 1877-Feb. 7, 1878; 1879-83; Gov. 1875.

PACKARD, Jasper (R Ind.) Feb. 1, 1832-Dec. 13, 1899; House 1869-75.

PACKER, Asa (D Pa.) Dec. 29, 1805-May 17, 1879; House 1853-57.

PACKER, Horace Billings (R Pa.) Oct. 11, 1851-April 13, 1940; House 1897-1901.

PACKER, John Black (R Pa.) March 21, 1824-July 7, 1891; House 1869-77.

PACKWOOD, Robert William (R Ore.) Sept. 11, 1932-—; Senate 1969-—.

PADDOCK, Algernon Sidney (R Neb.) Nov. 9, 1830-Oct. 17, 1897; Senate 1875-81, 1887-93.

PADDOCK, George Arthur (R Ill.) March 24, 1885-Dec. 29, 1964; House 1941-43.

PADGETT, Lemuel Phillips (D Tenn.) Nov. 28, 1855-Aug. 2, 1922; House 1901-Aug. 2, 1922.

PAGAN, Bolivar (Coal. P.R.) May 16, 1897-Feb. 9, 1961; House (Res. Comm.) Dec. 26, 1939-45.

PAGE, Carroll Smalley (R Vt.) Jan. 10, 1843-Dec. 3, 1925; Senate Oct. 21, 1908-23; Gov. 1890-92.

PAGE, Charles Harrison (D R.I.) July 19, 1843-July 21, 1912; House Feb. 21-March 3, 1887, 1891-93, April 5, 1893-95.

PAGE, Henry (D Md.) June 28, 1841-Jan. 7, 1913; House 1891-Sept. 3, 1892.

PAGE, Horace Francis (R Calif.) Oct. 20, 1833-Aug. 23, 1890; House 1873-83.

PAGE, John (D Va.) April 17, 1744-Oct. 11, 1808; House 1789-97; Gov. 1802-05.

PAGE, John (D N.H.) May 21, 1787-Sept. 8, 1865; Senate June 8, 1836-37; Gov. 1839-42.

PAGE, Robert (F Va.) Feb. 4, 1765-Dec. 8, 1840; House 1799-1801.

PAGE, Robert Newton (D N.C.) Oct. 26, 1859-Oct. 3, 1933; House 1903-17.

PAGE, Sherman (JD N.Y.) May 9, 1779-Sept. 27, 1853; House 1833-37.

PAIGE, Calvin DeWitt (R Mass.) May 20, 1848-April 24, 1930; House Nov. 26, 1913-25.

PAIGE, David Raymond (D Ohio) April 8, 1844-June 30, 1901; House 1883-85.

PAINE, Elijah (F Vt.) Jan. 21, 1757-April 28, 1842; Senate 1795-Sept. 1, 1801.

PAINE, Halbert Eleazer (R Wis.) Feb. 4, 1826-April 14, 1905; House 1865-71.

PAINE, Robert Treat (AP N.C.) Feb. 18, 1812-Feb. 8, 1872; House 1855-57.

PAINE, William Wiseham (D Ga.) Oct. 10, 1817-Aug. 5, 1882; House Dec. 22, 1870-71.

PALEN, Rufus (W N.Y.) Feb. 25, 1807-April 26, 1844; House 1839-41.

PALFREY, John Gorham (W Mass.) May 2, 1796-April 26, 1881; House 1847-49.

PALMER, Alexander Mitchell (D Pa.) May 4, 1872-May 11, 1936; House 1909-15; Atty. Gen. 1919-21.

PALMER, Beriah (— N.Y.) 1740-May 20, 1812; House 1803-05.

PALMER, Cyrus Maffet (R Pa.) Feb. 12, 1887-Aug. 16, 1959; House 1927-29.

PALMER, Francis Wayland (Frank) (R Iowa) Oct. 11, 1827-Dec. 3, 1907; House 1869-73.

PALMER, George William (nephew of John Palmer and cousin of William Elisha Haynes) (R N.Y.) Jan. 13, 1818-March 2, 1916; House 1857-61.

PALMER, Henry Wilber (R Pa.) July 10, 1839-Feb. 15, 1913; House 1901-07, 1909-11.

PALMER, John (uncle of George William Palmer) (D N.Y.) Jan. 29, 1785-Dec. 8, 1840; House 1817-19, 1837-39.

PALMER, John McAuley (D Ill.) Sept. 13, 1817-Sept. 25, 1900; Senate 1891-97; Gov. (R) 1869-73.

PALMER, John William (R Mo.) Aug. 20, 1866-Nov. 3, 1958; House 1929-31.

PALMER, Thomas Witherell (R Mich.) Jan. 25, 1830-June 1, 1913; Senate 1883-89.

PALMER, William Adams (D Vt.) Sept. 12, 1781-Dec. 3, 1860; Senate Oct. 20, 1818-25; Gov. 1831-35.

PALMISANO, Vincent Luke (D Md.) Aug. 5, 1882-Jan. 12, 1953; House 1927-39.

PANTIN, Santiago Iglesias (see IGLESIAS, Santiago).

PAREDES, Quintin (Nat. P.I.) Sept. 9, 1884-—; House (Res. Comm.) Feb. 14, 1936-Sept. 29, 1938.

PARK, Frank (D Ga.) March 3, 1864-Nov. 20, 1925; House Nov. 5, 1913-25.

PARKE, Benjamin (D Ind.) Sept. 22, 1777-July 12, 1835; House (Terr. Del.) Dec. 12, 1805-March 1, 1808.

PARKER, Abraham X. (R N.Y.) Nov. 14, 1831-Aug. 9, 1909; House 1881-89.

PARKER, Amasa Junius (D N.Y.) June 2, 1807-May 13, 1890; House 1837-39.

PARKER, Andrew (D Pa.) May 21, 1805-Jan. 15, 1864; House 1851-53.

PARKER, Homer Cling (D Ga.) Sept. 25, 1885-June 22, 1946; House Sept. 10, 1931-35.

PARKER, Hosea Washington (D N.H.) May 30, 1833-Aug. 21, 1922; House 1871-75.

PARKER, Isaac (— Mass.) June 17, 1768-July 26, 1830; House 1797-99.

PARKER, Isaac Charles (R Mo.) Oct. 15, 1838-Nov. 17, 1896; House 1871-75.

PARKER, James (D Mass.) 1768-Nov. 9, 1837; House 1813-15, 1819-21.

PARKER, James (grandfather of Richard Wayne Parker) (D N.J.) March 3, 1776-April 1, 1868; House 1833-37.

PARKER, James Southworth (R N.Y.) June 3, 1867-Dec. 19, 1933; House 1913-Dec. 19, 1933.

PARKER, John Mason (W N.Y.) June 14, 1805-Dec. 16, 1873; House 1855-59.

PARKER, Josiah (— Va.) May 11, 1751-March 18, 1810; House 1789-1801.

PARKER, Nahum (— N.H.) March 4, 1760-Nov. 12, 1839; Senate 1807-June 1, 1810.

PARKER, Richard (D Va.) Dec. 22, 1810-Nov. 10, 1893; House 1849-51.

PARKER, Richard Elliott (D Va.) Dec. 27, 1783-Sept. 6, 1840; Senate Dec. 12, 1836-March 13, 1837.

PARKER, Richard Wayne (grandson of James Parker) (R N.J.) Aug. 6, 1848-Nov. 28, 1923; House 1895-1911, Dec. 1, 1914-19, 1921-23.

PARKER, Samuel Wilson (W Ind.) Sept. 9, 1805-Feb. 1, 1859; House 1851-55.

PARKER, Severn Eyre (— Va.) July 19, 1787-Oct. 21, 1836; House 1819-21.

PARKER, William Henry (— S.D.) May 5, 1847-June 26, 1908; House 1907-June 26, 1908.

PARKS, Gorham (D Maine) May 27, 1794-Nov. 23, 1877; House 1833-37.

PARKS, Tilman Bacon (D Ark.) May 14, 1872-Feb. 12, 1950; House 1921-37.

PARMENTER, William (D Mass.) March 30, 1789-Feb. 25, 1866; House 1837-45.

PARRAN, Thomas (R Md.) Feb. 12, 1860-March 29, 1955; House 1911-13.

PARRETT, William Fletcher (D Ind.) Aug. 10, 1825-June 30, 1895; House 1889-93.

PARRIS, Albion Keith (cousin of Virgil Delphini Parris) (D Mass./Maine) Jan. 19, 1788-Feb. 22, 1857; House (Mass.) 1815-Feb. 3, 1818; Senate (Maine) 1827-Aug. 26, 1828; Gov. (Maine) 1822-27.

PARRIS, Stanford E. (R Va.) Sept. 9, 1929-__; House 1973-75.

PARRIS, Virgil Delphini (cousin of Albion Keith Parris) (SRD Maine) Feb. 18, 1807-June 13, 1874; House May 29, 1838-41.

PARRISH, Isaac (D Ohio) March 1804-Aug. 9, 1860; House 1839-41; 1845-47.

PARRISH, Lucian Walton (D Texas) Jan. 10, 1878-March 27, 1922; House 1919-March 27, 1922.

PARROTT, John Fabyan (D N.H.) Aug. 8, 1767-July 9, 1836; House 1817-19; Senate 1819-25.

PARROTT, Marcus Junius (R Kan.) Oct. 27, 1828-Oct. 4, 1879; House (Terr. Del.) 1857-Jan. 29, 1861.

PARSONS, Claude VanCleve (D Ill.) Oct. 7, 1895-May 23, 1941; House Nov. 4, 1930-41.

PARSONS, Edward Young (D Ky.) Dec. 12, 1842-July 8, 1876; House 1875-July 8, 1876.

PARSONS, Herbert (R N.Y.) Oct. 28, 1869-Sept. 16, 1925; House 1905-11.

PARSONS, Richard Chappel (R Ohio) Oct. 10, 1826-Jan. 9, 1899; House 1873-75.

PARTRIDGE, Donald Barrows (R Maine) June 7, 1891-June 5, 1946; House 1931-33.

PARTRIDGE, Frank Charles (R Vt.) May 7, 1861-March 2, 1943; Senate Dec. 23, 1930-March 31, 1931.

PARTRIDGE, George (— Mass.) Feb. 8, 1740-July 7, 1828; House 1789-Aug. 14, 1790; Cont. Cong. 1779-82; 1783-85.

PARTRIDGE, Samuel (D N.Y.) Nov. 29, 1790-March 30, 1883; House 1841-43.

PASCHAL, Thomas Moore (D Texas) Dec. 15, 1845-Jan. 28, 1919; House 1893-95.

PASCO, Samuel (D Fla.) June 28, 1834-March 13, 1917; Senate May 19, 1887-April 19, 1899.

PASSMAN, Otto Ernest (D La.) June 27, 1900-__; House 1947-__.

PASTORE, John Orlando (D R.I.) March 17, 1907-__; Senate Dec. 19, 1950-__; Gov. 1945-50.

PATERSON, John (— N.Y.) 1744-July 19, 1808; House 1803-05.

PATERSON, William (F N.J.) Dec. 24, 1745-Sept. 9, 1806; Senate 1789-Nov. 13, 1790; Cont. Cong. 1780-81; 1787; Gov. 1790-92; Asso. Justice of Supreme Court 1793-1806.

PATMAN, Wright (D Texas) Aug. 6, 1893-March 7, 1976; House 1929-March 7, 1976.

PATRICK, Luther (D Ala.) Jan. 23, 1894-May 26, 1957; House 1937-43; 1945-47.

PATTEN, Edward James (D N.J.) Aug. 22, 1905-__; House 1963-__.

PATTEN, Harold Ambrose (D Ariz.) Oct. 6, 1907-Sept. 6, 1969; House 1949-55.

PATTEN, John (— Del.) April 26, 1746-Dec. 26, 1800; House 1793-Feb. 14, 1794; 1795-97; Cont. Cong.. 1785-86.

PATTEN, Thomas Gedney (D N.Y.) Sept. 12, 1861-Feb. 23, 1939; House 1911-17.

PATTERSON, David Trotter (D Tenn.) Feb. 28, 1818-Nov. 3, 1891; Senate July 24, 1866-69.

PATTERSON, Edward White (D Kan.) Oct. 4, 1895-March 6, 1940; House 1935-39.

PATTERSON, Ellis Ellwood (D Calif.) Nov. 28, 1897-__; House 1945-47.

PATTERSON, Francis Ford, Jr. (R N.J.) July 30, 1867-Nov. 30, 1935; House Nov. 2, 1920-27.

PATTERSON, George Robert (R Pa.) Nov. 9, 1863-March 21, 1906; House 1901-March 21, 1906.

PATTERSON, George Washington (brother of William Patterson) (R N.Y.) Nov. 11, 1799-Oct. 15, 1879; House 1877-79.

PATTERSON, Gilbert Brown (D N.C.) May 29, 1863-Jan. 26, 1922; House 1903-07.

PATTERSON, James O'Hanlon (D S.C.) June 25, 1857-Oct. 25, 1911; House 1905-11.

PATTERSON, James Thomas (R Conn.) Oct. 20, 1908-__; House 1947-59.

PATTERSON, James Willis (R N.H.) July 2, 1823-May 4, 1893; House 1863-67; Senate 1867-73.

PATTERSON, Jerry Mumford (D Calif.) Oct. 25, 1934-__; House 1975-__.

PATTERSON, John (half brother of Thomas Patterson) (D Ohio) Feb. 10, 1771-Feb. 7, 1848; House 1823-25.

PATTERSON, John James (R S.C.) Aug. 8, 1830-Sept. 28, 1912; Senate 1873-79.

PATTERSON, Josiah (father of Malcolm Rice Patterson) (D Tenn.) April 14, 1837-Feb. 10, 1904; House 1891-97.

PATTERSON, Lafayette Lee (D Ala.) Aug. 23, 1888-__; House Nov. 6, 1928-33.

PATTERSON, Malcolm Rice (son of Josiah Patterson) (D Tenn.) June 7, 1861-March 8, 1935; House 1901-Nov. 5, 1906; Gov. 1907-11.

PATTERSON, Roscoe Conkling (R Mo.) Sept. 15, 1876-Oct. 22, 1954; House 1921-23; Senate 1929-35.

PATTERSON, Thomas (half brother of John Patterson) (D Pa.) Oct. 1, 1764-Nov. 16, 1841; House 1817-25.

PATTERSON, Thomas J. (W N.Y.) about 1808- ?; House 1843-45.

PATTERSON, Thomas MacDonald (D Colo.) Nov. 4, 1839-July 23, 1916; House (Terr. Del.) 1875-Aug. 1, 1876; (Rep.) Dec. 13, 1877-79; Senate 1901-07.

PATTERSON, Walter (— N.Y.) ? - ?; House 1821-23.

PATTERSON, William (brother of George Washington Patterson and uncle of Augustus Frank) (W N.Y.) June 4, 1789-Aug. 14, 1838; House 1837-Aug. 14, 1838.

PATTERSON, William (D Ohio) 1790-Aug. 17, 1868; House 1833-37.

PATTISON, Edward Worthington (D N.Y.) April 29, 1932-—; House 1975-—.

PATTISON, John M. (D Ohio) June 13, 1847-June 18, 1906; House 1891-93; Gov. 1906.

PATTON, Charles Emory (son of John Patton and brother of John Patton Jr.) (— Pa.) July 5, 1859-Dec. 15, 1937; House 1911-15.

PATTON, David Henry (D Ind.) Nov. 26, 1837-Jan. 17, 1914; House 1891-93.

PATTON, John (father of Charles Emory Patton and John Patton Jr. and uncle of William Irvin Swoope) (R Pa.) Jan. 6, 1823-Dec. 23, 1897; House 1861-63; 1887-89.

PATTON, John Jr. (son of the preceding and brother of Charles Emory Patton) (R Mich.) Oct. 30, 1850-May 24, 1907; Senate May 5, 1894-Jan. 14, 1895.

PATTON, John Denniston (D Pa.) Nov. 28, 1829-Feb. 22, 1904; House 1883-85.

PATTON, John Mercer (D Va.) Aug. 10, 1797-Oct. 29, 1858; House Nov. 25, 1830-April 7, 1838.

PATTON, Nat (D Texas) Feb. 26, 1884-July 27, 1957; House 1935-45.

PAUL, John (Read. Va.) June 30, 1839-Nov. 1, 1901; House 1881-Sept. 5, 1883.

PAUL, John (son of the preceding) (R Va.) Dec. 9, 1883-Feb. 13, 1964; House Dec. 15, 1922-23.

PAUL, Ronald Ernest (R Texas) Aug. 20, 1935-—; House April 3, 1976-—.

PAULDING, William Jr. (D N.Y.) March 7, 1770-Feb. 11, 1854; House 1811-13.

PAWLING, Levi (D Pa.) July 25, 1773-Sept. 7, 1845; House 1817-19.

PAYNE, Frederick George (R Maine) July 24, 1904-—; Senate 1953-59; Gov. 1949-53.

PAYNE, Henry B. (grandfather of Frances P. Bolton) (D Ohio) Nov. 30, 1810-Sept. 9, 1896; House 1875-77; Senate 1885-91.

PAYNE, Sereno Elisha (R N.Y.) June 26, 1843-Dec. 10, 1914; House 1883-87; 1889-Dec. 10, 1914.

PAYNE, William Winter (D Ala.) Jan. 2, 1807-Sept. 2, 1874; House 1841-47.

PAYNTER, Lemuel (D Pa.) 1788-Aug. 1, 1863; House 1837-41.

PAYNTER, Thomas Hanson (D Ky.) Dec. 9, 1851-March 8, 1921; House 1889-Jan. 5, 1895; Senate 1907-13.

PAYSON, Lewis Edwin (R Ill.) Sept. 17, 1840-Oct. 4, 1909; House 1881-91.

PEACE, Roger Craft (D S.C.) May 19, 1899-Aug. 20, 1968; Senate Aug. 5-Nov. 4, 1941.

PEARCE, Charles Edward (R Mo.) May 29, 1842-Jan. 30, 1902; House 1897-1901.

PEARCE, Dutee Jerauld (D R.I.) April 3, 1789-May 9, 1849; House 1825-37.

PEARCE, James Alfred (D Md.) Dec. 8, 1804-Dec. 20, 1862; House 1835-39; 1841-43 (W); Senate 1843-Dec. 20, 1862 (1843-62 Whig, March-Dec. 1862 Democrat).

PEARCE, John Jamison (W Pa.) Feb. 28, 1826-May 26, 1912; House 1855-57.

PEARRE, George Alexander (R Md.) July 16, 1860-Sept. 19, 1923; House 1899-1911.

PEARSON, Albert Jackson (D Ohio) May 20, 1846-May 15, 1905; House 1891-95.

PEARSON, Herron Carney (D Tenn.) July 31, 1890-April 24, 1953; House 1935-43.

PEARSON, James Blackwood (R Kan.) May 7, 1920-—; Senate Jan. 31, 1962-—.

PEARSON, John James (W Pa.) Oct. 25, 1800-May 30, 1888; House Dec. 5, 1836-37.

PEARSON, Joseph (F N.C.) 1776-Oct. 27, 1834; House 1809-15.

PEARSON, Richmond (R N.C.) Jan. 26, 1852-Sept. 12, 1923; House 1895-99; May 10, 1900-01.

PEASE, Henry Roberts (R Miss.) Feb. 19, 1835-Jan. 2, 1907; Senate Feb. 3, 1874-75.

PEASLEE, Charles Hazen (D N.H.) Feb. 6, 1804-Sept. 18, 1866; House 1847-53.

PEAVEY, Hubert Haskell (R Wis.) Jan. 12, 1881-Nov. 21, 1937; House 1923-35.

PECK, Erasmus Darwin (R Ohio) Sept. 16, 1808-Dec. 25, 1876; House April 23, 1870-73.

PECK, George Washington (D Mich.) June 4, 1818-June 30, 1905; House 1855-57.

PECK, Jared Valentine (D N.Y.) Sept. 21, 1816-Dec. 25, 1891; House 1853-55.

PECK, Lucius Benedict (D Vt.) Nov. 17, 1802-Dec. 28, 1866; House 1847-51.

PECK, Luther Christopher (W N.Y.) Jan.1800-Feb. 5, 1876; House 1837-41.

PECKHAM, Rufus Wheeler (D N.Y.) Dec. 20, 1809-Nov. 22, 1873; House 1853-55.

PEDDIE, Thomas Baldwin (R N.J.) Feb. 11, 1808-Feb. 16, 1889; House 1877-79.

PEDEN, Preston Elmer (D Okla.) June 28, 1914-—; House 1947-49.

PEEK, Harmanus (— N.Y.) June 24, 1782-Sept. 27, 1838; House 1819-21.

PEEL, Samuel West (D Ark.) Sept. 13, 1831-Dec. 18, 1924; House 1883-93.

PEELLE, Stanton Judkins (R Ind.) Feb. 11, 1843-Sept. 4, 1928; House 1881-May 22, 1884.

PEERY, George Campbell (D Va.) Oct. 28, 1873-Oct. 14, 1952; House 1923-29; Gov. 1934-38.

PEFFER, William Alfred (P Kan.) Sept. 10, 1831-Oct. 7, 1912; Senate 1891-97.

PEGRAM, John (— Va.) Nov. 16, 1773-April 8, 1831; House April 21, 1818-19.

PEIRCE, Joseph (— N.H.) June 25, 1748-Sept.12, 1812; House 1801-02.

PEIRCE, Robert Bruce Fraser (R Ind.) Feb. 17, 1843-Dec. 5, 1898; House 1881-83.

PELHAM, Charles (R Ala.) March 12, 1835-Jan. 18, 1908; House 1873-75.

PELL, Claiborne de Borda (son of Herbert Claiborne Pell Jr.) (D R.I.) Nov. 22, 1918-__; Senate 1961-__.

PELL, Herbert Claiborne Jr. (great-grandson of John Francis Hamtramck Claiborne, great-great-grandnephew of William Charles Cole Claiborne and Nathaniel Herbert Claiborne and father of Claiborne de Borda Pell) (D N.Y.) Feb. 16, 1884-July 17, 1961; House 1919-21.

PELLY, Thomas Minor (R Wash.) Aug. 22, 1902-Nov. 21, 1973; House 1953-73.

PELTON, Guy Ray (W N.Y.) Aug. 3, 1824-July 24, 1890; House 1855-57.

PENCE, Lafayette (P/Sil.D Colo.) Dec. 23, 1857-Oct. 22, 1923; House 1893-95.

PENDLETON, Edmund Henry (W N.Y.) 1788-Feb. 25, 1862; House 1831-33.

PENDLETON, George Cassety (D Texas) April 23, 1845-Jan. 19, 1913; House 1893-97.

PENDLETON, George Hunt (son of Nathanael Greene Pendleton) (D Ohio) July 19, 1825-Nov. 24, 1889; House 1857-65; Senate 1879-85.

PENDLETON, James Monroe (R R.I.) Jan. 10, 1822-Feb. 16, 1889; House 1871-75.

PENDLETON, John Overton (D W.Va.) July 4, 1851-Dec. 24, 1916; House 1889-Feb. 26, 1890; 1891-95.

PENDLETON, John Strother (W Va.) March 1, 1802-Nov. 19, 1868; House 1845-49.

PENDLETON, Nathanael Greene (father of George Hunt Pendleton) (W Ohio) Aug. 25, 1793-June 16, 1861; House 1841-43.

PENINGTON, John Brown (D Del.) Dec. 20, 1825-June 1, 1902; House 1887-91.

PENN, Alexander Gordon (D La.) May 10, 1799-May 7, 1866; House Dec. 30, 1850-53.

PENNIMAN, Ebenezer Jenckes (W/F-S Mich.) Jan. 11, 1804-April 12, 1890; House 1851-53.

PENNINGTON, Alexander Cumming McWhorter (cousin of William Pennington) (W N.J.) July 2, 1810-Jan. 25, 1867; House 1853-57.

PENNINGTON, William (cousin of Alexander Cumming McWhorter Pennington) (W N.J.) May 4, 1796-Feb. 16, 1862; House 1859-61; Speaker 1859-61; Gov. 1837-43.

PENNYBACKER, Isaac Samuels (cousin of Green Berry Samuels) (D Va.) Sept. 3, 1805-Jan. 12, 1847; House 1837-39; Senate Dec. 3, 1845-Jan.12, 1847.

PENROSE, Boies (R Pa.) Nov. 1, 1860-Dec. 31, 1921; Senate 1897-Dec. 31, 1921.

PEPPER, Claude Denson (D Fla.) Sept. 8, 1900-—; Senate Nov. 4, 1936-51; House 1963-

PEPPER, George Wharton (R Pa.) March 16, 1867-May 24, 1961; Senate Jan. 9, 1922-27.

PEPPER, Irvin St. Clair (D Iowa) June 10, 1876-Dec. 22, 1913; House 1911-Dec. 22, 1913.

PERCE, Legrand Winfield (R Miss.) June 19, 1836-March 16, 1911; House Feb. 23, 1870-73.

PERCY, Charles Harting (R Ill.) Sept. 27, 1919-__; Senate 1967-__.

PERCY, Le Roy (D Miss.) Nov. 9, 1860-Dec. 24, 1929; Senate Feb. 23, 1910-13.

PEREA, Francisco (cousin of Pedro Perea) (R N.M.) Jan. 9, 1830-May 21, 1913; House (Terr. Del.) 1863-65.

PEREA, Pedro (cousin of Francisco Perea) (R N.M.) April 22, 1852-Jan. 11, 1906; House (Terr. Del.) 1899-1901.

PERHAM, Sidney (R Maine) March 27, 1819-April 10, 1907; House 1863-69; Gov. 1871-74.

PERKINS, Bishop (D N.Y.) Sept. 5, 1787-Nov. 20, 1866; House 1853-55.

PERKINS, Bishop Walden (R Kan.) Oct. 18, 1841-June 20, 1894; House 1883-91; Senate Jan. 1, 1892-93.

PERKINS, Carl Dewey (D Ky.) Oct. 15, 1912-__; House 1949-__.

PERKINS, Elias (F Conn.) April 5, 1767-Sept. 27, 1845; House 1801-03.

PERKINS, George Clement (R Calif.) Aug. 23, 1839-Feb. 26, 1923; Senate July 26, 1893-1915; Gov. 1880-83.

PERKINS, George Douglas (R Iowa) Feb. 29, 1840-Feb. 3, 1914; House 1891-99.

PERKINS, James Breck (R N.Y.) Nov. 4, 1847-March 11, 1910; House 1901-March 11, 1910.

PERKINS, Jared (W N.H.) Jan. 5, 1793-Oct. 15, 1854; House 1851-53.

PERKINS, John Jr. (D La.) July 1, 1819-Nov. 28, 1885; House 1853-55.

PERKINS, Randolph (R N.J.) Nov. 30, 1871-May 25, 1936; House 1921-May 25, 1936.

PERKY, Kirtland Irving (D Idaho) Feb. 8, 1867-Jan. 9, 1939; Senate Nov. 18, 1912-Feb. 5, 1913.

PERLMAN, Nathan David (R N.Y.) Aug. 2, 1887-June 29, 1952; House Nov. 2, 1920-27.

PERRILL, Augustus Leonard (D Ohio) Jan. 20, 1807-June 2, 1882; House 1845-47.

PERRY, Aaron Fyfe (R Ohio) Jan. 1, 1815-March 11, 1893; House 1871-72.

PERRY, Eli (D N.Y.) Dec. 25, 1799-May 17, 1881; House 1871-75.

PERRY, John Jasiel (R Maine) Aug. 2, 1811-May 2, 1897; House 1855-57; 1859-61.

PERRY, Nehemiah (Const.U N.J.) March 30, 1816-Nov. 1, 1881; House 1861-65.

PERRY, Thomas Johns (D Md.) Feb. 17, 1807-June 27, 1871; House 1845-47.

PERRY, William Hayne (D S.C.) June 9, 1839-July 7, 1902; House 1885-91.

PERSON, Seymour Howe (R Mich.) Feb. 2, 1879-April 7, 1957; House 1931-33.

PERSONS, Henry (D Ga.) Jan. 30, 1834-June 17, 1910; House 1879-81.

PESQUERA, Jose Lorenzo (Nonpart. P.R.) Aug. 10, 1882-July 25, 1950; House (Res. Comm.) April 15, 1932-33.

PETER, George (D Md.) Sept. 28, 1779-June 22, 1861; House Oct. 7, 1816-19; 1825-27.

PETERS, Andrew James (D Mass.) April 3, 1872-June 26, 1938; House 1907-Aug. 15, 1914.

PETERS, John Andrew (R Maine) Oct. 9, 1822-April 2, 1904; House 1867-73.

PETERS, John Andrew (nephew of the preceding) (R Maine) Aug. 13, 1864-Aug. 22, 1953; House Sept. 8, 1913-Jan. 2, 1922.

PETERS, Mason Summers (D/P Kan.) Sept. 3, 1844-Feb. 14, 1914; House 1897-99.

PETERS, Samuel Ritter (R Kan.) Aug. 16, 1842-April 21, 1910; House 1883-91.

PETERSEN, Andrew Nicholas (R N.Y.) March 10, 1870-Sept. 28, 1952; House 1921-23.

PETERSON, Hugh (D Ga.) Aug. 21, 1898-Oct. 3, 1961; House 1935-47.

PETERSON, James Hardin (D Fla.) Feb. 11, 1894-__; House 1933-51.

PETERSON, John Barney (cousin of Horatio Clifford Claypool and Harold Kile Claypool) (D Ind.) July 4, 1850-July 16, 1944; House 1913-15.

PETERSON, Morris Blaine (D Utah) March 26, 1906-__; House 1961-63.

PETRIE, George (R N.Y.) Sept. 8, 1793-May 8, 1879; House 1847-49.

PETRIKIN, David (D Pa.) Dec. 1, 1788-March 1, 1847; House 1837-41.

PETTENGILL, Samuel Barrett (nephew of William Horace Clagett) (D Ind.) Jan. 19, 1886-March 20, 1974; House 1931-39.

PETTIBONE, Augustus Herman (R Tenn.) Jan. 21, 1835-Nov. 26, 1918; House 1881-87.

PETTIGREW, Ebenezer (W N.C.) March 10, 1783-July 8, 1848; House 1835-37.

PETTIGREW, Richard Franklin (R S.D.) July 23, 1848-Oct. 5, 1926; House (Terr. Del.) 1881-83; Senate Nov. 2, 1889-1901.

PETTIS, Jerry Lyle (R Calif.) July 18, 1916-Feb. 14, 1975; House 1967-Feb. 14, 1975.

PETTIS, Shirley Neal (widow of Jerry Lyle Pettis) (R Calif.) July 12, 1924-__; House April 29, 1975-__.

PETTIS, Solomon Newton (R Pa.) Oct. 10, 1827-Sept. 18, 1900; House Dec. 7, 1868-69.

PETTIS, Spencer Darwin (D Mo.) 1802-Aug. 28, 1831; House 1829-Aug. 28, 1831.

PETTIT, John (D Ind.) June 24, 1807-Jan. 17, 1877; House 1843-49; Senate Jan. 11, 1853-55.

PETTIT, John Upfold (R Ind.) Sept. 11, 1820-March 21, 1881; House 1855-61.

PETTUS, Edmund Winston (D Ala.) July 6, 1821-July 27, 1907; Senate 1897-July 27, 1907.

PEYSER, Peter A. (R N.Y.) Sept. 7, 1921-__; House 1971-__.

PEYSER, Theodore Albert (D N.Y.) Feb. 18, 1873-Aug. 8, 1937; House 1933-Aug. 8, 1937.

PEYTON, Balie (brother of Joseph Hopkins Peyton) (W Tenn.) Nov. 26, 1803-Aug. 18, 1878; House 1833-37.

PEYTON, Joseph Hopkins (brother of Balie Peyton) (W Tenn.) May 20, 1808-Nov. 11, 1845; House 1843-Nov. 11, 1845.

PEYTON, Samuel Oldham (D Ky.) Jan. 8, 1804-Jan. 4, 1870; House 1847-49; 1857-61.

PFEIFER, Joseph Lawrence (D N.Y.) Feb. 6, 1892-April 19, 1974; House 1935-51.

PFEIFFER, William Louis (R N.Y.) May 29, 1907-__; House 1949-51.

PFOST, Gracie Bowers (D Idaho) March 12, 1906-Aug. 11, 1965; House 1953-63.

PHEIFFER, William Townsend (R N.Y.) July 15, 1898-__; House 1941-43.

PHELAN, James (D Tenn.) Dec. 7, 1856-Jan. 30, 1891; House 1887-Jan. 30, 1891.

PHELAN, James Duval (D Calif.) April 20, 1861-Aug. 7, 1930; Senate 1915-21.

PHELAN, Michael Francis (D Mass.) Oct. 22, 1875-Oct. 12, 1941; House 1913-21.

PHELPS, Charles Edward (UC Md.) May 1, 1833-Dec. 27, 1908; House 1865-69 (1865-67 Union War Party, 1867-69 Union Conservative).

PHELPS, Darwin (R Pa.) April 17, 1807-Dec. 14, 1879; House 1869-71.

PHELPS, Elisha (father of John Smith Phelps) (D Conn.) Nov. 16, 1779-April 6, 1847; House 1819-21; 1825-29.

PHELPS, James (son of Lancelot Phelps) (D Conn.) Jan. 12, 1822-Jan. 15, 1900; House 1875-83.

PHELPS, John Smith (son of Elisha Phelps) (D Mo.) Dec. 22, 1814-Nov. 20, 1886; House 1845-63; Gov. 1877-81.

PHELPS, Lancelot (father of James Phelps) (D Conn.) Nov. 9, 1784-Sept. 1, 1866; House 1835-39.

PHELPS, Oliver (D N.Y.) Oct. 21, 1749-Feb. 21, 1809; House 1803-05.

PHELPS, Samuel Shethar (W Vt.) May 13, 1793-March 25, 1855; Senate 1839-51; Jan. 17, 1853-March 16, 1854.

PHELPS, Timothy Guy (R Calif.) Dec. 20, 1824-June 11, 1899; House 1861-63.

PHELPS, William Wallace (D Minn.) June 1, 1826-Aug. 3, 1873; House May 11, 1858-59.

PHELPS, William Walter (R N.J.) Aug. 24, 1839-June 17, 1894; House 1873-75; 1883-89.

PHILBIN, Philip Joseph (D Mass.) May 29, 1898-June 14, 1972; House 1943-71.

PHILIPS, John Finis (D Mo.) Dec. 31, 1834-March 13, 1919; House 1875-77; Jan. 10, 1880-81.

PHILLIPS, Alfred Noroton (D Conn.) April 23, 1894-Jan.18, 1970; House 1937-39.

PHILLIPS, Dayton Edward (R Tenn.) March 29, 1910-__; House 1947-51.

PHILLIPS, Fremont Orestes (R Ohio) March 16, 1856-Feb. 21, 1936; House 1899-1901.

PHILLIPS, Henry Myer (D Pa.) June 30, 1811-Aug. 28, 1884; House 1857-59.

PHILLIPS, John (F Pa.) ? - ?; House 1821-23.

PHILLIPS, John (R Calif.) Sept. 11, 1887-__; House 1943-57.

PHILLIPS, Philip (D Ala.) Dec. 13, 1807-Jan. 14, 1884; House 1853-55.

PHILLIPS, Stephen Clarendon (W Mass.) Nov. 4, 1801-June 26, 1857; House Dec. 1, 1834-Sept. 28, 1838.

PHILLIPS, Thomas Wharton (father of Thomas Wharton Phillips Jr.) (R Pa.) Feb. 23, 1835-July 21, 1912; House 1893-97.

PHILLIPS, Thomas Wharton Jr. (son of the preceding) (R Pa.) Nov. 21, 1874-Jan. 2, 1956; House 1923-27.

PHILLIPS, William Addison (R Kan.) Jan. 14, 1824-Nov. 30, 1893; House 1873-79.

PHILSON, Robert (— Pa.) 1759-July 25, 1831; House 1819-21.

PHIPPS, Lawrence Cowle (R Colo.) Aug. 30, 1862-March 1, 1958; Senate 1919-31.

PHISTER, Elijah Conner (D Ky.) Oct. 8, 1822-May 16, 1887; House 1879-83.

PHOENIX, Jonas Phillips (W N.Y.) Jan. 14, 1788-May 4, 1859; House 1843-45; 1849-51.

PICKENS, Andrew (grandfather of Francis Wilkinson Pickens) (D S.C.) Sept. 13, 1739-Aug. 11, 1817; House 1793-95.

PICKENS, Francis Wilkinson (grandson of Andrew Pickens) (ND S.C.) April 7, 1805-Jan. 25, 1869; House Dec. 8, 1834-43; Gov. 1860-62.

PICKENS, Israel (D N.C./Ala.) Jan. 30, 1780-April 24, 1827; House (N.C.) 1811-17; Senate (Ala.) Feb. 17, 1826-Nov. 27, 1826; Gov. (Ala.) 1821-25.

PICKERING, Timothy (F Mass.) July 17, 1745-Jan. 29, 1829; Senate 1803-11; House 1813-17; Postmaster Gen. 1791-95; Secy. of War 1795; Secy. of State 1795-1800.

PICKETT, Charles Edgar (R Iowa) Jan. 14, 1866-July 20, 1930; House 1909-13.

PICKETT, Thomas Augustus (Tom) (D Texas) Aug. 14, 1906-__; House 1945-June 30, 1952.

PICKLE, J. J. (Jake) (D Texas) Oct. 11, 1913-__; House Dec. 21, 1963-__.

PICKLER, John Alfred (R S.D.) Jan. 24, 1844-June 13, 1910; House Nov. 2, 1889-97.

PICKMAN, Benjamin Jr. (— Mass.) Sept. 30, 1763-Aug. 16, 1843; House 1809-11.

PIDCOCK, James Nelson (cousin of Alvah Augustus Clark) (D N.J.) Feb. 8, 1836-Dec. 17, 1899; House 1885-89.

PIERCE, Charles Wilson (D Ala.) Oct. 7, 1823-Feb. 18, 1907; House July 21, 1868-69.

PIERCE, Franklin (D N.H.) Nov. 23, 1804-Oct. 8, 1869; House 1833-37; Senate 1837-Feb. 28, 1842; President 1853-57.

PIERCE, Gilbert Ashville (R N.D.) Jan. 11, 1839-Feb. 15, 1901; Senate Nov. 21, 1889-91; Gov. (Terr.) 1884-86.

PIERCE, Henry Lillie (R Mass.) Aug. 23, 1825-Dec. 17, 1896; House Dec. 1, 1873-77.

PIERCE, Ray Vaughn (R N.Y.) Aug. 6, 1840-Feb. 4, 1914; House 1879-Sept. 18, 1880.

PIERCE, Rice Alexander (D Tenn.) July 3, 1848-July 12, 1936; House 1883-85; 1889-93; 1897-1905.

PIERCE, Wallace Edgar (R N.Y.) Dec. 9, 1881-Jan. 3, 1940; House 1939-Jan. 3, 1940.

PIERCE, Walter Marcus (D Ore.) May 30, 1861-March 27, 1954; House 1933-43; Gov. 1923-27.

PIERSON, Isaac (W N.J.) Aug. 15, 1770-Sept. 22, 1833; House 1827-31.

PIERSON, Jeremiah Halsey (F N.Y.) Sept. 13, 1766-Dec. 12, 1855; House 1821-23.

PIERSON, Job (D N.Y.) Sept. 23, 1791-April 9, 1860; House 1831-35.

PIGOTT, James Protus (D Conn.) Sept. 11, 1852-July 1, 1919; House 1893-95.

PIKE, Austin Franklin (R N.H.) Oct. 16, 1819-Oct. 8, 1886; House 1873-75; Senate 1883-Oct. 8, 1886.

PIKE, Frederick Augustus (R Maine) Dec. 9, 1816-Dec. 2, 1886; House 1861-69.

PIKE, James (AP N.H.) Nov. 10, 1818-July 26, 1895; House 1855-59.

PIKE, Otis G. (D N.Y.) Aug. 31, 1921-__; House 1961-__.

PILCHER, John Leonard (D Ga.) Aug. 27, 1898-__; House Feb. 4, 1953-65.

PILE, William Anderson (R Mo.) Feb. 11, 1829-July 7, 1889; House 1867-69; Gov. (N.M.) 1869-70.

PILES, Samuel Henry (R Wash.) Dec. 28, 1858-March 11, 1940; Senate 1905-11.

PILLION, John Raymond (R N.Y.) Aug. 10, 1904-__; House 1953-65.

PILSBURY, Timothy (Cal.D Texas) April 12, 1789-Nov. 23, 1858; House March 30, 1846-49.

PINCKNEY, Charles (father of Henry Laurens Pinckney) (D S.C.) Oct. 26, 1757-Oct. 29, 1824; Senate Dec. 6, 1798-1801; House 1819-21; Cont. Cong. 1784-87; Gov. 1789-92; 1796-98; 1806-08.

PINCKNEY, Henry Laurens (son of Charles Pinckney) (D S.C.) Sept. 24, 1794-Feb. 3, 1863; House 1833-37.

PINCKNEY, John McPherson (D Texas) May 4, 1845-April 24, 1905; House Nov. 17, 1903-April 24, 1905.

PINCKNEY, Thomas (F S.C.) Oct. 23, 1750-Nov. 2, 1828; House Nov. 23, 1797-1801; Gov. 1787-89.

PINDALL, James (F Va.) about 1783-Nov. 22, 1825; House 1817-July 26, 1820.

PINDAR, John Sigsbee (D N.Y.) Nov. 18, 1835-June 30, 1907; House 1885-87; Nov. 4, 1890-91.

PINE, William Bliss (R Okla.) Dec. 30, 1877-Aug. 25, 1942; Senate 1925-31.

PINERO, Jesus T. (PD P.R.) April 16, 1897-Nov. 19, 1952; House (Res. Comm.) 1945-Sept. 2, 1946; Gov. 1946-48.

PINKNEY, William (— Md.) March 17, 1764-Feb. 25, 1822; House March 4-Nov. 1791; 1815-April 18, 1816; Senate Dec. 21, 1819-Feb. 25, 1822; Atty. Gen. 1811-14.

PIPER, William (— Pa.) Jan. 1, 1774-1852; House 1811-17.

PIPER, William Adam (D Calif.) May 21, 1826-Aug. 5, 1899; House 1875-77.

PIRCE, William Almy (R R.I.) Feb. 29, 1824-March 5, 1891; House 1885-Jan. 25, 1887.

PIRNIE, Alexander (R N.Y.) April 16, 1903-__; House 1959-73.

PITCHER, Nathaniel (D N.Y.) 1777-May 25, 1836; House 1819-23, 1831-33.

PITKIN, Timothy (F Conn.) Jan. 21, 1766-Dec. 18, 1847; House Sept. 16, 1805-19.

PITMAN, Charles Wesley (W Pa.) ?-June 8, 1871; House 1849-51.

PITNEY, Mahlon (R N.J.) Feb. 5, 1858-Dec. 9, 1924; House 1895-Jan. 10, 1899; Assoc. Justice of Supreme Court 1912-22.

PITTENGER, William Alvin (R Minn.) Dec. 29, 1885-Nov. 26, 1951; House 1929-33, 1935-37, 1939-47.

PITTMAN, Key (D Nev.) Sept. 19, 1872-Nov. 10, 1940; Senate Jan. 29, 1913-Nov. 10, 1940; President pro tempore March 9, 1933-Nov. 10, 1940.

PLAISTED, Harris Merrill (R Maine) Nov. 2, 1828-Jan. 31, 1898; House Sept. 13, 1875-77; Gov. 1881-83.

PLANT, David (NR Conn.) March 29, 1783-Oct. 18, 1851; House 1827-29.

PLANTS, Tobias Avery (R Ohio) March 17, 1811-June 19, 1887; House 1865-69.

PLATER, Thomas (— Md.) May 9, 1769-May 1, 1830; House 1801-05.

PLATT, Edmund (R N.Y.) Feb. 2, 1865-Aug. 7, 1939; House 1913-June 7, 1920.

PLATT, James Henry Jr. (R Va.) July 13, 1837-Aug. 13, 1894; House Jan. 26, 1870-75.

PLATT, Jonas (F N.Y.) June 30, 1769-Feb. 22, 1834; House 1799-1801.

PLATT, Orville Hitchcock (R Conn.) July 19, 1827-April 21, 1905; Senate 1879-April 21, 1905.

PLATT, Thomas Collier (R N.Y.) July 15, 1833-March 6, 1910; House 1873-77; Senate March 4-May 16, 1881; 1897-1909.

PLAUCHE, Vance Gabriel (D La.) Aug. 25, 1897-__; House 1941-43.

PLEASANTS, James (D Va.) Oct. 24, 1769-Nov. 9, 1836; House 1811-Dec. 14, 1819; Senate Dec. 14, 1819-Dec. 15, 1822; Gov. 1822-25.

PLOESER, Walter Christian (R Mo.) Jan. 7, 1907-__; House 1941-49.

PLOWMAN, Thomas Scales (D Ala.) June 8, 1843-July 26, 1919; House 1897-Feb. 9, 1898.

PLUMB, Preston B. (R Kan.) Oct. 12, 1837-Dec. 20, 1891; Senate 1877-Dec. 20, 1891.

PLUMB, Ralph (R Ill.) March 29, 1816-April 8, 1903; House 1885-89.

PLUMER, Arnold (D Pa.) June 6, 1801-April 28, 1869; House 1837-39, 1841-43.

PLUMER, George (D Pa.) Dec. 5, 1762-June 8, 1843; House 1821-27.

PLUMER, William (father of William Plumer Jr.) (F N.H.) June 25, 1759-Dec. 22, 1850; Senate June 17, 1802-07; Gov. (D) 1812-13, 1816-19.

PLUMER, William Jr. (son of William Plumer) (D N.H.) Feb. 9, 1789-Sept. 18, 1854; House 1819-25.

PLUMLEY, Charles Albert (son of Frank Plumley) (R Vt.) April 14, 1875-Oct. 31, 1964; House Jan. 16, 1934-51.

PLUMLEY, Frank (father of Charles Albert Plumley) (R Vt.) Dec. 17, 1844-April 30, 1924; House 1909-15.

PLUMMER, Franklin E. (— Miss.) ?-Sept. 24, 1847; House 1831-35.

POAGE, William Robert (D Texas) Dec. 28, 1899-__; House 1937-__.

PODELL, Bertram L. (D N.Y.) Dec. 27, 1925-__; House Feb. 20, 1968-75.

POEHLER, Henry (D Minn.) Aug. 22, 1833-July 18, 1912; House 1879-81.

POFF, Richard Harding (R Va.) Oct. 19, 1923-__; House 1953-Aug. 29, 1972.

POINDEXTER, George (— Miss.) 1779-Sept. 5, 1855; House (Terr. Del.) 1807-13; (Rep.) Dec. 10, 1817-19; Senate Oct. 15, 1830-35; Gov. 1820-22.

POINDEXTER, Miles (R Wash.) April 22, 1868-Sept. 21, 1946; House 1909-11; Senate 1911-23.

POINSETT, Joel Roberts (D S.C.) March 2, 1779-Dec. 12, 1851; House 1821-March 7, 1825; Secy. of War 1837-41.

POLANCO-ABREU, Santiago (PD P.R.) Oct. 30, 1920-__; House 1965-69.

POLAND, Luke Potter (R Vt.) Nov. 1, 1815-July 2, 1887; Senate Nov. 21, 1865-67; House 1867-75, 1883-85.

POLK, Albert Fawcett (D Del.) Oct. 11, 1869-Feb. 14, 1955; House 1917-19.

POLK, James Gould (D Ohio) Oct. 6, 1896-April 28, 1959; House 1931-41, 1949-April 28, 1959.

POLK, James Knox (brother of William Hawkins Polk) (D Tenn.) Nov. 2, 1795-June 15, 1849; House 1825-39; Speaker 1835-39; Gov. 1839-41; President 1845-49.

POLK, Rufus King (D Pa.) Aug. 23, 1866-March 5, 1902; House 1899-March 5, 1902.

POLK, Trusten (D Mo.) May 29, 1811-April 16, 1876; Senate 1857-Jan. 10, 1862; Gov. 1857.

POLK, William Hawkins (brother of James Knox Polk) (D Tenn.) May 24, 1815-Dec. 16, 1862; House 1851-53.

POLLARD, Ernest Mark (R Neb.) April 15, 1869-Sept. 24, 1939; House July 18, 1905-09.

POLLARD, Henry Moses (R Mo.) June 14, 1836-Feb. 24, 1904; House 1877-79.

POLLOCK, Howard W. (R Alaska) April 11, 1920-__; House 1967-71.

POLLOCK, James (W Pa.) Sept. 11, 1810-April 19, 1890; House April 5, 1844-49; Gov. 1855-58.

POLLOCK, William Pegues (D S.C.) Dec. 9, 1870-June 2, 1922; Senate Nov. 6, 1918-19.

POLSLEY, Daniel Haymond (R W.Va.) Nov. 28, 1803-Oct. 14, 1877; House 1867-69.

POMERENE, Atlee (D Ohio) Dec. 6, 1863-Nov. 12, 1937; Senate 1911-23.

POMEROY, Charles (R Iowa) Sept. 3, 1825-Feb. 11, 1891; House 1869-71.

POMEROY, Samuel Clarks (R Kan.) Jan. 3, 1816-Aug. 27, 1891; Senate April 4, 1861-73.

POMEROY, Theodore Medad (R N.Y.) Dec. 31, 1824-March 23, 1905; House 1861-69; Speaker March 3, 1869.

POND, Benjamin (D N.Y.) 1768-Oct. 6, 1814; House 1811-13.

POOL, Joe Richard (D Texas) Feb. 18, 1911-July 14, 1968; House 1963-July 14, 1968.

POOL, John (uncle of Walter Freshwater Pool) (W N.C.) June 16, 1826-Aug. 16, 1884; Senate July 4, 1868-73.

POOL, Walter Freshwater (nephew of John Pool) (R N.C.) Oct. 10, 1850-Aug. 25, 1883; House March 4-Aug. 25, 1883.

POOLE, Theodore Lewis (R N.Y.) April 10, 1840-Dec. 23, 1900; House 1895-97.

POPE, James Pinckney (D Idaho) March 31, 1884-Jan. 23, 1966; Senate 1933-39.

POPE, John (D Ky.) 1770-July 12, 1845; Senate 1807-13; House 1837-43; President pro tempore 1811; Terr. Gov. of Ark. 1829-35.

POPE, Nathaniel (— Ill.) Jan. 5, 1784-Jan. 22, 1850; House (Terr. Del.) Sept. 5, 1816-Sept. 5, 1818.

POPE, Patrick Hamilton (D Ky.) March 17, 1806-May 4, 1841; House 1833-35.

POPPLETON, Earley Franklin (D Ohio) Sept. 29, 1834-May 6, 1899; House 1875-77.

PORTER, Albert Gallatin (R Ind.) April 20, 1824-May 3, 1897; House 1859-63; Gov. 1881-85.

PORTER, Alexander (W La.) 1786-Jan. 13, 1844; Senate Dec. 19, 1833-Jan. 5, 1837.

PORTER, Augustus Seymour (nephew of Peter Buell Porter) (W Mich.) Jan. 18, 1798-Sept. 18, 1872; Senate Jan. 20, 1840-45.

PORTER, Charles Howell (R Va.) June 21, 1833-July 9, 1897; House Jan. 26, 1870-73.

PORTER, Charles Orlando (D Ore.) April 4, 1919-__; House 1957-61.

PORTER, Gilchrist (W Mo.) Nov. 1, 1817-Nov. 1, 1894; House 1851-53; 1855-57.

PORTER, Henry Kirke (— Pa.) Nov. 24, 1840-April 10, 1921; House 1903-05.

PORTER, James (D N.Y.) April 18, 1787-Feb. 7, 1839; House 1817-19.

PORTER, John (— Pa.) ? - ?; House Dec. 8, 1806-11.

PORTER, Peter Augustus (grandson of Peter Buell Porter) (IR/D N.Y.) Oct. 10, 1853-Dec. 15, 1925; House 1907-09.

PORTER, Peter Buell (grandfather of Peter Augustus Porter and uncle of Augustus Seymour Porter) (D N.Y.) Aug. 4, 1773-March 20, 1844; House 1809-13, 1815-Jan. 23, 1816; Secy. of War 1828-29.

PORTER, Stephen Geyer (R Pa.) May 18, 1869-June 27, 1930; House 1911-June 27, 1930.

PORTER, Timothy H. (— N.Y.) ?-about 1840; House 1825-27.

POSEY, Francis Blackburn (R Ind.) April 28, 1848-Oct. 31, 1915; House Jan. 29-March 3, 1889.

POSEY, Thomas (— La.) July 9, 1750-March 19, 1818; Senate Oct. 8, 1812-Feb. 4, 1813; Gov. of Ind. Terr. 1813-16.

POST, George Adams (D Pa.) Sept. 1, 1854-Oct. 31, 1925; House 1883-85.

POST, James Douglass (D Ohio) Nov. 25, 1863-April 1, 1921; House 1911-15.

OST, Jotham Jr. (F N.Y.) April 4, 1771-May 15, 1817; House 1813-15.

OST, Morton Everel (D Wyo.) Dec. 25, 1840-March 19, 1933; House (Terr. Del.) 1881-85.

OST, Philip Sidney (R Ill.) March 19, 1833-Jan. 6, 1895; House 1887-Jan. 6, 1895.

OSTON, Charles Debrille (R Ariz.) April 20, 1825-June 24, 1902; House (Terr. Del.) Dec. 5, 1864-65.

POTTER, Allen (I Mich.) Oct. 2, 1818-May 8, 1885; House 1875-77.

POTTER, Charles Edward (R Mich.) Oct. 30, 1916-___; House Aug. 26, 1947-Nov. 4, 1952; Senate Nov. 5, 1952-59.

POTTER, Clarkson Nott (D N.Y.) April 25, 1825-Jan. 23, 1882; House 1869-75; 1877-79.

POTTER, Elisha Reynolds (F R.I.) Nov. 5, 1764-Sept. 26, 1835; House Nov. 15, 1796-97; 1809-15.

POTTER, Elisha Reynolds (son of the preceding) (W R.I.) June 20, 1811-April 10, 1882; House 1843-45.

POTTER, Emery Davis (D Ohio) Oct. 7, 1804-Feb. 12, 1896; House 1843-45; 1849-51.

POTTER, John Fox (R Wis.) May 11, 1817-May 18, 1899; House 1857-63.

POTTER, Orlando Brunson (UD N.Y.) March 10, 1823-Jan. 2, 1894; House 1883-85.

POTTER, Robert (JD N.C.) about 1800-March 2, 1841; House 1829-Nov. 1831.

POTTER, Samuel John (— R.I.) June 29, 1753-Oct. 14, 1804; Senate 1803-Oct. 14, 1804.

POTTER, William Wilson (D Pa.) Dec. 18, 1792-Oct. 28, 1839; House 1837-Oct. 28, 1839.

POTTLE, Emory Bemsley (R N.Y.) July 4, 1815-April 18, 1891; House 1857-61.

POTTS, David Jr. (W Pa.) Nov. 27, 1794-June 1, 1863; House 1831-39.

POTTS, David Matthew (R N.Y.) March 12, 1906-___; House 1947-49.

POTTS, Richard (F Md.) July 19, 1753-Nov. 26, 1808; Senate Jan. 10, 1793-Oct. 24, 1796; Cont. Cong. 1781-82.

POU, Edward William (cousin of James Paul Buchanan) (D N.C.) Sept. 9, 1863-April 1, 1934; House 1901-April 1, 1934.

POULSON, Norris (R Calif.) July 23, 1895-___; House 1943-45; 1947-June 11, 1953.

POUND, Thaddeus Coleman (R Wis.) Dec. 6, 1833-Nov. 21, 1914; House 1877-83.

POWELL, Adam Clayton Jr. (D N.Y.) Nov. 29, 1908-April 4, 1972; House 1945-67, 1969-71.

POWELL, Alfred H. (— Va.) March 6, 1781-1831; House 1825-27.

POWELL, Cuthbert (son of Levin Powell) (W Va.) March 4, 1775-May 8, 1849; House 1841-43.

POWELL, Joseph (D Pa.) June 23, 1828-April 24, 1904; House 1875-77.

POWELL, Lazarus Whitehead (D Ky.) Oct. 6, 1812-July 3, 1867; Senate 1859-65; Gov. 1851-55.

POWELL, Levin (father of Cuthbert Powell) (F Va.) 1737-Aug. 23, 1810; House 1799-1801.

POWELL, Paulus (D Va.) 1809-June 10, 1874; House 1849-59.

POWELL, Samuel (— Tenn.) July 10, 1776-Aug. 2, 1841; House 1815-17.

POWELL, Walter E. (R Ohio) April 25, 1931-___; House 1971-75.

POWER, Thomas Charles (R Mont.) May 22, 1839-Feb. 16, 1923; Senate Jan. 2, 1890-95.

POWERS, Caleb (R Ky.) Feb. 1, 1869-July 25, 1932; House 1911-19.

POWERS, David Lane (R N.J.) July 29, 1896-March 28, 1968; House 1933-Aug. 30, 1945.

POWERS, Gershom (JD N.Y.) July 11, 1789-June 25, 1831; House 1829-31.

POWERS, Horace Henry (R Vt.) May 29, 1835-Dec. 8, 1913; House 1891-1901.

POWERS, Llewellyn (R Maine) Oct. 14, 1836-July 28, 1908; House 1877-79; April 8, 1901-July 28, 1908; Gov. 1897-1901.

POWERS, Samuel Leland (R Mass.) Oct. 26, 1848-Nov. 30, 1929; House 1901-05.

POYDRAS, Julien de Lallande (— Orleans) April 3, 1740-June 14, 1824; House (Terr. Del.) 1809-11.

PRACHT, Charles Frederick (R Pa.) Oct. 20, 1880-Dec. 22, 1950; House 1943-45.

PRALL, Anning Smith (D N.Y.) Sept. 17, 1870-July 23, 1937; House Nov. 6, 1923-35.

PRATT, Charles Clarence (R Pa.) April 23, 1854-Jan. 27, 1916; House 1909-11.

PRATT, Daniel Darwin (R Ind.) Oct. 26, 1813-June 17, 1877; Senate 1869-75.

PRATT, Eliza Jane (D N.C.) March 5, 1902-___; House May 25, 1946-47.

PRATT, Harcourt Joseph (R N.Y.) Oct. 23, 1866-May 21, 1934; House 1925-33.

PRATT, Harry Hayt (R N.Y.) Nov. 11, 1864-Nov. 13, 1932; House 1915-19.

PRATT, Henry Otis (R Iowa) Feb. 11, 1838-May 22, 1931; House 1873-77.

PRATT, James Timothy (D Conn.) Dec. 14, 1802-April 11, 1887; House 1853-55.

PRATT, Joseph Marmaduke (R Pa.) Sept. 4, 1891-July 19, 1946; House Jan. 18, 1944-45.

PRATT, Le Gage (D N.J.) Dec. 14, 1852-March 9, 1911; House 1907-09.

PRATT, Ruth Sears Baker (R N.Y.) Aug. 24, 1877-Aug. 23, 1965; House 1929-33.

PRATT, Thomas George (W Md.) Feb. 18, 1804-Nov. 9, 1869; Senate Jan. 12, 1850-57; Gov. 1845-48.

PRATT, Zadock (D N.Y.) Oct. 30, 1790-April 6, 1871; House 1837-39; 1843-45.

PRAY, Charles Nelson (R Mont.) April 6, 1868-Sept. 12, 1963; House 1907-13.

PRENTISS, John Holmes (brother of Samuel Prentiss) (D N.Y.) April 17, 1784-June 26, 1861; House 1837-41.

PRENTISS, Samuel (brother of John Holmes Prentiss) (W Vt.) March 31, 1782-Jan. 15, 1857; Senate 1831-April 11, 1842.

PRENTISS, Sergeant Smith (— Miss.) Sept. 30, 1808-July 1, 1850; House May 30, 1838-39.

PRESCOTT, Cyrus Dan (R N.Y.) Aug. 15, 1836-Oct.23, 1902; House 1879-83.

PRESSLER, Larry Lee (R S.D.) March 29, 1942-___; House 1975-___.

PRESTON, Francis (father of William Campbell Preston and uncle of William Ballard Preston and William Preston) (— Va.) Aug. 2, 1765-May 26, 1836; House 1793-97.

PRESTON, Jacob Alexander (W Md.) March 12, 1796-Aug. 2, 1868; House 1843-45.

PRESTON, Prince Hulon Jr. (D Ga.) July 5, 1908-Feb. 8,1961; House 1947-61.

PRESTON, William (nephew of Francis Preston) (W Ky.) Oct. 16, 1816-Sept. 21, 1887; House Dec. 6, 1852-55.

PRESTON, William Ballard (nephew of Francis Preston) (W Va.) Nov. 25, 1805-Nov. 16, 1862; House 1847-49; Secy. of the Navy 1849-50.

PRESTON, William Campbell (son of Francis Preston) (Cal.N S.C.) Dec. 27, 1794-May 22, 1860; House Nov. 26, 1833-Nov. 29, 1842.

PREYER, Lunsford Richardson (D N.C.) Jan. 11, 1919-___; House 1969-___.

PRICE, Andrew (D La.) April 2, 1854-Feb. 5, 1909; House Dec. 2, 1889-97.

PRICE, Charles Melvin (D Ill.) Jan. 1, 1905-___; House 1945-___.

PRICE, Emory Hilliard (D Fla.) Dec. 3, 1899-Feb. 11, 1976; House 1943-49.

PRICE, Hiram (R Iowa) Jan. 10, 1814-May 30, 1901; House 1863-69; 1877-81.

PRICE, Hugh Hiram (son of William Thompson Price) (R Wis.) Dec. 2, 1859-Dec. 25, 1904; House Jan. 18-March 3, 1887.

PRICE, Jesse Dashiell (D Md.) Aug. 15, 1863-May 14, 1939; House Nov. 3, 1914-19.

PRICE, Robert Dale (Bob) (R Texas) Sept. 7, 1927-___; House 1967-75.

PRICE, Rodman McCamley (D N.J.) May 5, 1816-June 7, 1894; House 1851-53; Gov. 1854-57.

PRICE, Samuel (— W.Va.) July 28, 1805-Feb. 25, 1884; Senate Aug. 26, 1876-Jan. 26, 1877.

PRICE, Sterling (D Mo.) Sept. 20, 1809-Sept. 29, 1867; House 1845-Aug. 12, 1846; Gov. 1853-57.

PRICE, Thomas Lawson (D Mo.) Jan. 19, 1809-July 15, 1870; House Jan. 21, 1862-63.

PRICE, William Pierce (D Ga.) Jan. 29, 1835-Nov. 4, 1908; House Dec. 22, 1870-73.

PRICE, William Thompson (father of Hugh Hiram Price) (R Wis.) June 17, 1824-Dec. 6, 1886; House 1883-Dec. 6, 1886.

PRIDEMORE, Auburn Lorenzo (D Va.) June 27, 1837-May 17, 1900; House 1877-79.

PRIEST, James Percy (D Tenn.) April 1, 1900-Oct. 12, 1956; House 1941-Oct. 12, 1956.

PRINCE, Charles Henry (R Ga.) May 9, 1837-April 3, 1912; House July 25, 1868-69.

PRINCE, George Washington (R Ill.) March 4, 1854-Sept. 26, 1939; House Dec. 2, 1895-1913.

PRINCE, Oliver Hillhouse (— Ga.) 1787-Oct. 9, 1837; Senate Nov. 7, 1828-29.

PRINCE, William (— Ind.) 1772-Sept. 8, 1824; House 1823-Sept. 8, 1824.

PRINDLE, Elizur H. (R N.Y.) May 6, 1829-Oct. 7, 1890; House 1871-73.

PRINGEY, Joseph Colburn (R Okla.) May 22, 1858-Feb. 11, 1935; House 1921-23.

PRINGLE, Benjamin (W N.Y.) Nov. 9, 1807-June 7, 1887; House 1853-57.

PRITCHARD, George Moore (son of Jeter Connelly Pritchard) (R N.C.) Jan. 4, 1886-April 24, 1955; House 1929-31.

PRITCHARD, Jeter Connelly (father of George Moore Pritchard) (R N.C.) July 12, 1857-April 10, 1921; Senate Jan. 23, 1895-1903.

PRITCHARD, Joel McFee (R Wash.) May 5, 1925-___; House 1973-___.

PROCTOR, Redfield (R Vt.) June 1, 1831-March 4, 1908; Senate Nov. 2, 1891-March 4, 1908; Gov. 1878-80; Secy. of War 1889-91.

PROFFIT, George H. (W Ind.) Sept. 7, 1807-Sept. 7, 1847; House 1839-43.

PROKOP, Stanley A. (D Pa.) ?-___; House 1959-61.

PROSSER, William Farrand (R Tenn.) March 16, 1834-Sept.23, 1911; House 1869-71.

PROUTY, Solomon Francis (R Iowa) Jan. 17, 1854-July 16, 1927; House 1911-15.

PROUTY, Winston Lewis (R Vt.) Sept. 1, 1906-Sept. 10, 1971; House 1951-59; Senate 1959-Sept. 10, 1971.

PROXMIRE, William (D Wis.) Nov. 11, 1915-___; Senate Aug. 28, 1957-___.

PRUYN, John Van Schaick Lansing (D N.Y.) June 22, 1811-Nov. 21, 1877; House Dec. 7, 1863-65; 1867-69.

PRYOR, David Hampton (D Ark.) Aug. 29, 1934-___; House Nov. 8, 1966-73; Gov. 1975-___.

PRYOR, Luke (D Ala.) July 5, 1820-Aug. 5, 1900; Senate Jan. 7-Nov. 23, 1880; House 1883-85.

PRYOR, Roger Atkinson (D Va.) July 19, 1828-March 14, 1919; House Dec. 7, 1859-61.

PUCINSKI, Roman Conrad (D Ill.) May 13, 1919-___; House 1959-73.

PUGH, George Ellis (D Ohio) Nov. 28, 1822-July 19, 1876; Senate 1855-61.

PUGH, James Lawrence (D Ala.) Dec. 12, 1820-March 9, 1907; House 1859-Jan. 21, 1861; Senate Nov. 24, 1880-97.

PUGH, John (D Pa.) June 2, 1761-July 13, 1842; House 1805-09.

PUGH, John Howard (R N.J.) June 23, 1827-April 30, 1905; House 1877-79.

PUGH, Samuel Johnson (R Ky.) Jan. 28, 1850-April 17, 1922; House 1895-1901.

PUGSLEY, Cornelius Amory (D N.Y.) July 17, 1850-Sept. 10, 1936; House 1901-03.

PUGSLEY, Jacob Joseph (R Ohio) Jan. 25, 1838-Feb. 5, 1920; House 1887-91.

PUJO, Arsène Paulin (D La.) Dec. 16, 1861-Dec. 31, 1939; House 1903-13.

PULITZER, Joseph (D N.Y.) April 10, 1847-Oct. 29, 1911; House 1885-April 10, 1886.

PURCELL, Graham Boynton Jr. (D Texas) May 5, 1919-___; House Jan. 27, 1962-73.

PURCELL, William Edward (D N.D.) Aug. 3, 1856-Nov. 23, 1928; Senate Feb. 1, 1910-Feb. 1, 1911.

PURDY, Smith Meade (D N.Y.) July 31, 1796-March 30, 1870; House 1843-45.

PURMAN, William James (R Fla.) April 11, 1840-Aug. 14, 1928; House 1873-Jan. 25, 1875, March 4, 1875-77.

PURNELL, Fred Sampson (R Ind.) Oct. 25, 1882-Oct. 21, 1939; House 1917-33.

PURTELL, William Arthur (R Conn.) May 6, 1897-___; Senate Aug. 29-Nov. 4, 1952, 1953-59.

PURVIANCE, Samuel Anderson (W Pa.) Jan. 10, 1809-Feb. 14, 1882; House 1855-59.

PURVIANCE, Samuel Dinsmore (F N.C.) Jan. 7, 1774-about 1806; House 1803-05.

PURYEAR, Richard Clauselle (W N.C.) Feb. 9, 1801-July 30, 1867; House 1853-57.

PUSEY, William Henry Mills (D Iowa) July 29, 1826-Nov. 15, 1900; House 1883-85.

PUTNAM, Harvey (W N.Y.) Jan. 5, 1793-Sept. 20, 1855; House Nov. 7, 1838-39, 1847-51.

PYLE, Gladys (R S.D.) Oct. 4, 1890-___; Senate Nov. 9, 1938-39.

Q

QUACKENBUSH, John Adam (R N.Y.) Oct. 15, 1828-May 11, 1908; House 1889-93.

QUARLES, James Minor (W Tenn.) Feb. 8, 1823-March 3, 1901; House 1859-61.

QUARLES, Joseph Very (R Wis.) Dec. 16, 1843-Oct. 7, 1911; Senate 1899-1905.

QUARLES, Julian Minor (D Va.) Sept. 25, 1848-Nov. 18, 1929; House 1899-1901.

QUARLES, Tunstall (D Ky.) about 1770-Jan. 7, 1855; House 1817-June 15, 1820.

QUAY, Matthew Stanley (R Pa.) Sept. 30, 1833-May 28, 1904; Senate 1887-99, Jan. 16, 1901-May 28, 1904; Chrmn. Rep. Nat. Comm. 1888-91.

QUAYLE, John Francis (D N.Y.) Dec. 1, 1868-Nov. 27, 1930; House 1923-Nov. 27, 1930.

QUEZON, Manuel Luis (Nat. P.I.) Aug. 19, 1878-Aug. 1, 1944; House (Res. Comm.) Nov. 23, 1909-Oct. 15, 1916; President of P.I. 1935-44.

QUIE, Albert Harold (R Minn.) Sept. 18, 1923-___; House Feb. 18, 1958-___.

QUIGG, Lemuel Ely (R N.Y.) Feb. 12, 1863-July 1, 1919; House Jan. 30, 1894-99.

QUIGLEY, James Michael (D Pa.) March 30, 1918-___; House 1955-57, 1959-61.

QUILLEN, James H. (Jimmy) (R Tenn.) Jan. 11, 1916-___; House 1963-___.

QUIN, Percy Edwards (D Miss.) Oct. 30, 1872-Feb. 4, 1932; House 1913-Feb. 4, 1932.

QUINCY, Josiah (F Mass.) Feb. 4, 1772-July 1, 1864; House 1805-13.

QUINN, James Leland (D Pa.) Sept. 8, 1875-Nov. 12, 1960; House 1935-39.

QUINN, John (D N.Y.) Aug. 9, 1839-Feb. 23, 1903; House 1889-91.

QUINN, Peter Anthony (D N.Y.) May 10, 1904-Dec. 23, 1974; House 1945-47.

QUINN, Terence John (D N.Y.) Oct. 16, 1836-June 18,1878; House 1877-June 18, 1878.

QUINN, Thomas Vincent (D N.Y.) March 16, 1903-___; House 1949-Dec. 30, 1951.

QUITMAN, John Anthony (D Miss.) Sept. 1, 1799-July 17, 1858; House 1855-July 17, 1858; Gov. 1850-51.

R

RABAUT, Louis Charles (D Mich.) Dec. 5, 1886-Nov. 12, 1961; House 1935-47, 1949-Nov. 12, 1961.

RABIN, Benjamin J. (D N.Y.) June 3,1896-Feb. 22, 1969; House 1945-Dec. 31, 1947.

RACE, John Abner (D Wis.) May 12, 1914-___; House 1965-67.

RADCLIFFE, Amos Henry (R N.J.) Jan. 16, 1870-Dec. 29, 1950; House 1919-23.

RADCLIFFE, George Lovick (D Md.) Aug. 22, 1877-July 29, 1974; Senate 1935-47.

RADFORD, William (D N.Y.) June 24, 1814-Jan. 18, 1870; House 1863-67.

RADWAN, Edmund Parick (R N.Y.) Sept. 22, 1911-Sept. 7, 1959; House 1951-59.

RAGON, Heartsill (D Ark.) March 20, 1885-Sept. 15, 1940; House 1923-June 16, 1933.

RAGSDALE, James Willard (D S.C.) Dec. 14, 1872-July 23, 1919; House 1913-July 23, 1919.

RAILSBACK, Thomas F. (R Ill.) Jan. 22, 1932-__; House 1967-__.

RAINES, John (R N.Y.) May 6, 1840-Dec. 16, 1909; House 1889-93.

RAINEY, Henry Thomas (D Ill.) Aug. 20, 1860-Aug. 19, 1934; House 1903-21, 1923-Aug. 19, 1934; Speaker 1933-34.

RAINEY, John William (D Ill.) Dec. 21, 1880-May 4, 1923; House April 2, 1918-May 4, 1923.

RAINEY, Joseph Hayne (R S.C.) June 21, 1832-Aug. 2, 1887; House Dec. 12, 1870-79.

RAINEY, Lilius Bratton (D Ala.) July 27, 1876-Sept. 27, 1959; House Sept. 30, 1919-23.

RAINS, Albert M. (D Ala.) March 11, 1902-__; House 1945-65.

RAKER, John Edward (D Calif.) Feb. 22, 1863-Jan. 22, 1926; House 1911-Jan. 22, 1926.

RALSTON, Samuel Moffett (D Ind.) Dec. 1, 1857-Oct. 14, 1925; Senate 1923-Oct. 14, 1925; Gov. 1913-17.

RAMEY, Frank Marion (R Ill.) Sept. 23, 1881-March 27, 1942; House 1929-31.

RAMEY, Homer Alonzo (R Ohio) March 2, 1891-April 13, 1960; House 1943-49.

RAMSAY, Robert Lincoln (D W.Va.) March 24, 1877-Nov. 14, 1956; House 1933-39, 1941-43, 1949-53.

RAMSEY, Alexander (W Pa./R Minn.) Sept. 8, 1815-April 22, 1903; House (W Pa.) 1843-47; Senate (R Minn.) 1863-75; Gov. (Terr. of Minn.) 1849-53, (State of Minn.) 1860-63; Secy. of War 1879-81.

RAMSEY, John Rathbone (R N.J.) April 25, 1862-April 10, 1933; House 1917-21.

RAMSEY, Robert (W Pa.) Feb. 15, 1780-Dec. 12, 1849; House 1833-35, 1841-43.

RAMSEY, William (D Pa.) Sept. 7, 1779-Sept. 29, 1831; House 1827-Sept. 29, 1831.

RAMSEY, William Sterrett (D Pa.) June 12, 1810-Oct. 17, 1840; House 1839-Oct. 17, 1840.

RAMSEYER, Christian William (R Iowa) March 13, 1875-Nov. 1, 1943; House 1915-33.

RAMSPECK, Robert C. Word (D Ga.) Sept. 5, 1890-Sept. 10, 1972; House Oct. 2, 1929-Dec. 31, 1945.

RANDALL, Alexander (W Md.) Jan. 3, 1803-Nov. 21, 1881; House 1841-43.

RANDALL, Benjamin (W Maine) Nov. 14, 1789-Oct. 11, 1859; House 1839-43.

RANDALL, Charles Hiram (Prohib./D/R/Pro. Calif.) July 23, 1865-Feb. 18, 1951; House 1915-21.

RANDALL, Charles Sturtevant (R Mass.) Feb. 20, 1824-Aug. 17, 1904; House 1889-95.

RANDALL, Clifford Ellsworth (R Wis.) Dec. 25, 1876-Oct. 16,1934; House 1919-21.

RANDALL, Samuel Jackson (D Pa.) Oct.10, 1828-April 13, 1890; House 1863-April 13, 1890; Speaker 1876-81.

RANDALL, William Harrison (R Ky.) July 15, 1812-Aug. 1, 1881; House 1863-67.

RANDALL, William Joseph (D Mo.) July 16, 1909-__; House March 3, 1959-__.

RANDELL, Choice Boswell (nephew of Lucius Jeremiah Gartrell) (D Texas) Jan. 1, 1857-Oct. 19, 1945; House 1901-13.

RANDOLPH, James Fitz (father of Theodore Fitz Randolph) (— N.J.) June 26, 1791-Jan. 25, 1872; House Dec. 1, 1827-33.

RANDOLPH, James Henry (R Tenn.) Oct. 18, 1825-Aug. 22, 1900; House 1877-79.

RANDOLPH, Jennings (D W.Va.) March 8, 1902-__; House 1933-47; Senate Nov. 5, 1958-__.

RANDOLPH, John (SRD Va.) June 2, 1773-May 24, 1833; House 1799-1813, 1815-17, 1819-Dec. 26, 1825, 1827-29, March 4-May 24, 1833; Senate Dec. 26, 1825-27.

RANDOLPH, Joseph Fitz (W N.J.) March 14, 1803-March 20, 1873; House 1837-43.

RANDOLPH, Theodore Fitz (son of James Fitz Randolph) (D N.J.) June 24, 1826-Nov. 7, 1883; Senate 1875-81; Gov. 1869-72.

RANDOLPH, Thomas Mann (D Va.) Oct. 1, 1768-June 20, 1828; House 1803-07; Gov. 1819-22.

RANEY, John Henry (R Mo.) Sept. 28, 1849-Jan. 23, 1928; House 1895-97.

RANGEL, Charles Bernard (D N.Y.) June 1, 1930-__; House 1971-__.

RANKIN, Christopher (D Miss.) 1788-March 14, 1826; House 1819-March 14, 1826.

RANKIN, Jeannette (R Mont.) June 11, 1880-May 18, 1973; House 1917-19, 1941-43.

RANKIN, John Elliott (D Miss.) March 29, 1882-Nov. 26, 1960; House 1921-53.

RANKIN, Joseph (D Wis.) Sept. 25, 1833-Jan. 24, 1886; House 1883-Jan. 24, 1886.

RANNEY, Ambrose Arnold (R Mass.) April 17, 1821-March 5, 1899; House 1881-87.

RANSDELL, Joseph Eugene (D La.) Oct. 7, 1858-July 27, 1954; House Aug. 29, 1899-1913; Senate 1913-31.

RANSIER, Alonzo Jacob (R S.C.) Jan. 3, 1834-Aug. 17, 1882; House 1873-75.

RANSLEY, Harry Clay (R Pa.) Feb. 5, 1863-Nov. 7, 1941; House Nov. 2, 1920-37.

RANSOM, Matt Whitaker (cousin of Wharton Jackson Green) (D N.C.) Oct. 8, 1826-Oct. 8, 1904; Senate Jan. 30, 1872-95.

RANTOUL, Robert Jr. (D Mass.) Aug. 13, 1805-Aug. 7, 1852; Senate Feb. 1-March 3, 1851; House March 4, 1851-Aug. 7, 1852.

RAPIER, James Thomas (R Ala.) Nov. 13, 1837-May 31, 1883; House 1873-75.

RARICK, John Richard (D La.) Jan. 29, 1924-—; House 1967-75.

RARIDEN, James (W Ind.) Feb. 14, 1795-Oct. 20, 1856; House 1837-41.

RATHBONE, Henry Riggs (grandson of Ira Harris) (R Ill.) Feb.12, 1870-July 15, 1928; House 1923-July 15, 1928.

RATHBUN, George Oscar (D N.Y.) 1803-Jan. 5, 1870; House 1843-47.

RAUCH, George Washington (D Ind.) Feb. 22, 1876-Nov. 4, 1940; House 1907-17.

RAUM, Green Berry (R Ill.) Dec. 3, 1829-Dec. 18, 1909; House 1867-69.

RAWLINS, Joseph Lafayette (D Utah) March 28, 1850-May 24, 1926; House (Terr. Del.) 1893-95; Senate 1897-1903.

RAWLS, Morgan (D Ga.) June 29, 1829-Oct. 18, 1906; House 1873-March 24, 1874.

RAWSON, Charles Augustus (R Iowa) May 29, 1867-Sept. 2, 1936; Senate Feb. 24-Dec. 1, 1922.

RAY, George Washington (R N.Y.) Feb. 3, 1844-Jan. 10, 1925; House 1883-85, 1891-Sept. 11, 1902.

RAY, John Henry (R N.Y.) Sept. 27, 1886-May 21, 1975; House 1953-63.

RAY, Joseph Warren (R Pa.) May 25, 1849-Sept. 15, 1928; House 1889-91.

RAY, Ossian (R N.H.) Dec. 13, 1835-Jan. 28, 1892; House Jan. 8, 1881-85.

RAY, William Henry (R Ill.) Dec. 14, 1812-Jan. 25, 1881; House 1873-75.

RAYBURN, Sam (D Texas) Jan. 6, 1882-Nov. 16, 1961; House 1913-Nov. 16, 1961; Speaker 1940-47, 1949-53, 1955-61.

RAYFIEL, Leo Frederick (D N.Y.) March 22, 1888-__; House 1945-Sept. 13, 1947.

RAYMOND, Henry Jarvis (R N.Y.) Jan. 24, 1820-June 18, 1869; House 1865-67; Chmn. Rep. Nat. Comm. 1864-66.

RAYMOND, John Baldwin (R Dakota) Dec. 5, 1844-Jan. 3, 1886; House (Terr. Del.) 1883-85.

RAYNER, Isidor (D Md.) April 11, 1850-Nov. 25, 1912; House 1887-89, 1891-95; Senate 1905-Nov. 25, 1912.

RAYNER, Kenneth (W N.C.) June 20, 1808-March 4, 1884; House 1839-45.

REA, David (D Mo.) Jan. 19, 1831-June 13, 1901; House 1875-79.

REA, John (D Pa.) Jan. 27, 1755-Feb. 26, 1829; House 1803-11, May 11, 1813-15.

READ, Almon Heath (D Pa.) June 12, 1790-June 3, 1844; House March 18, 1842-June 3, 1844.

READ, George (— Del.) Sept. 18, 1733-Sept. 21, 1798; Senate 1789-Sept. 18, 1793; Cont. Cong. 1774-77.

READ, Jacob (F S.C.) 1751-July 17, 1816; Senate 1795-1801; Cont. Cong. 1783-85.

READ, Nathan (F Mass.) July 2, 1759-Jan. 20, 1849; House Nov. 25, 1800-03.

READ, William Brown (D Ky.) Dec. 14, 1817-Aug. 5, 1880; House 1871-75.

READE, Edwin Godwin (AP N.C.) Nov. 13, 1812-Oct. 18, 1894; House 1855-57.

READING, John Roberts (D Pa.) Nov. 1, 1826-Feb. 14, 1886; House 1869-April 13, 1870.

READY, Charles (uncle of William T. Haskell) (W Tenn.) Dec. 22, 1802-June 4, 1878; House 1853-59.

REAGAN, John Henninger (D Texas) Oct. 8, 1818-March 6, 1905; House 1857-61, 1875-March 4, 1887; Senate March 4, 1887-June 10, 1891.

REAMES, Alfred Evan (D Ore.) Feb. 5, 1870-March 4, 1943; Senate Feb. 1-Nov. 8, 1938.

REAMS, Henry Frazier (I Ohio) Jan. 15, 1897-Sept. 15, 1971; House 1951-55.

REAVIS, Charles Frank (R Neb.) Sept. 5, 1870-May 26, 1932; House 1915-June 3, 1922.

REBER, John (R Pa.) Feb. 1, 1858-Sept. 26, 1931; House 1919-23.

REDDEN, Monroe Minor (D N.C.) Sept. 24, 1901-__; House 1947-53.

REDFIELD, William Cox (D N.Y.) June 18, 1858-June 13, 1932; House 1911-13; Secy. of Commerce 1913-19.

REDING, John Randall (D N.H.) Oct. 18, 1805-Oct. 8, 1892; House 1841-45.

REDLIN, Rolland W. (D N.D.) Feb. 29, 1920-__; House 1965-67.

REECE, Brazilla Carroll (husband of Louise G. Reece) (R Tenn.) Dec. 22, 1889-March 19, 1961; House 1921-31, 1933-47, 1951-March 19, 1961; Chrmn. Rep. Nat. Comm. 1946-48.

REECE, Louise Goff (widow of B. Carroll Reece, daughter of Guy Despard Goff and granddaughter of Nathan Goff) (R Tenn.) Nov. 6, 1898-May 14, 1970; House May 16, 1961-63.

REED, Charles Manning (W Pa.) April 3, 1803-Dec. 16, 1871; House 1843-45.

REED, Chauncey William (R Ill.) June 2, 1890-Feb. 9, 1956; House 1935-Feb. 9, 1956.

REED, Clyde Martin (R Kan.) Oct. 19, 1871-Nov. 8, 1949; Senate 1939-Nov. 8, 1949; Gov. 1929-31.

REED, Daniel Alden (R N.Y.) Sept. 15, 1875-Feb. 19, 1959; House 1919-Feb. 19, 1959.

REED, David Aiken (R Pa.) Dec. 21, 1880-Feb. 10, 1953; Senate Aug. 8, 1922-35.

REED, Edward Cambridge (D N.Y.) March 8, 1793-May 1, 1883; House 1831-33.

REED, Eugene Elliott (D N.H.) April 23, 1866-Dec. 15, 1940; House 1913-15.

REED, Isaac (W Maine) Aug. 22, 1809-Sept. 19, 1887; House June 25, 1852-53.

REED, James Alexander (D Mo.) Nov. 9, 1861-Sept. 8, 1944; Senate 1911-29.

REED, James Byron (D Ark.) Jan. 2, 1881-April 27, 1935; House Oct. 20, 1923-29.

REED, John (F Mass.) Nov. 11, 1751-Feb. 17, 1831; House 1795-1801.

REED, John (son of the preceding) (W Mass.) Sept. 2, 1781-Nov. 25, 1860; House 1813-17, 1821-41 (1813-17 Federalist, 1821-41 Whig).

REED, Joseph Rea (R Iowa) March 12, 1835-April 2, 1925; House 1889-91.

REED, Philip (— Md.) 1760-Nov. 2, 1829; Senate Nov. 25, 1806-13; House 1817-19, March 19, 1822-23.

REED, Robert Rentoul (W Pa.) March 12, 1807-Dec. 14, 1864; House 1849-51.

REED, Stuart Felix (R W.Va.) Jan. 8, 1866-July 4, 1935; House 1917-25.

REED, Thomas Brackett (R Maine) Oct. 18, 1839-Dec. 7, 1902; House 1877-Sept. 4, 1899; Speaker 1889-91, 1895-99.

REED, Thomas Buck (D Miss.) May 7, 1787-Nov. 26, 1829; Senate Jan. 28, 1826-27, March 4-Nov. 26, 1829.

REED, William (F Mass.) June 6, 1776-Feb. 18, 1837; House 1811-15.

REEDER, William Augustus (R Kan.) Aug. 28, 1849-Nov. 7, 1929; House 1899-1911.

REES, Edward Herbert (R Kan.) June 3, 1886-Oct. 25, 1969; House 1937-61.

REES, Rollin Raymond (R Kan.) Jan. 10, 1865-May 30, 1935; House 1911-13.

REES, Thomas M. (D Calif.) March 26, 1925-__; House Dec. 15, 1965-__.

REESE, David Addison (W Ga.) March 3, 1794-Dec.16, 1871; House 1853-55.

REESE, Seaborn (D Ga.) Nov. 28, 1846-March 1, 1907; House Dec. 4, 1882-87.

REEVES, Albert Lee Jr. (R Mo.) May 31, 1906-__; House 1947-49.

REEVES, Henry Augustus (D N.Y.) Dec. 7, 1832-March 4, 1916; House 1869-71.

REEVES, Walter (R Ill.) Sept. 25, 1848-April 9, 1909; House 1895-1903.

REGAN, Kenneth Mills (D Texas) March 6, 1893-Aug. 15, 1959; House Aug. 23, 1947-55.

REGULA, Ralph Strauss (R Ohio) Dec. 3, 1924-__; House 1973-__.

REID, Charles Chester (D Ark.) June 15, 1868-May 20, 1922; House 1901-11.

REID, Charlotte Thompson (R Ill.) Sept. 27, 1913-__; House 1963-Oct. 7, 1971.

REID, David Settle (nephew of Thomas Settle) (D N.C.) April 19, 1813-June 19, 1891; House 1843-47; Senate Dec. 6, 1854-59; Gov. 1851-54.

REID, Frank R. (R Ill.) April 18, 1879-Jan. 25, 1945; House 1923-35.

REID, James Wesley (D N.C.) June 11, 1849-Jan. 1, 1902; House Jan. 28, 1885-Dec. 31, 1886.

REID, John William (D Mo.) June 14, 1821-Nov. 22, 1881; House March 4-Aug. 3, 1861.

REID, Ogden Rogers (D N.Y.) June 24, 1925-__; House 1963-75 (1963-March 22, 1972 Republican, March 22, 1972-75 Democrat).

REID, Robert Raymond (D Ga.) Sept. 8, 1789-July 1, 1841; House Feb. 18, 1819-23; Gov. (Fla. Terr.) 1839-41.

REIFEL, Benjamin (R S.D.) Sept. 19, 1906-__; House 1961-71.

REILLY, James Bernard (D Pa.) Aug. 12, 1845-May 14, 1924; House 1875-79, 1889-95.

REILLY, John (D Pa.) Feb. 22, 1836-April 19, 1904; House 1875-77.

REILLY, Michael Kieran (D Wis.) July 15, 1869-Oct. 14, 1944; House 1913-17, Nov. 4, 1930-39.

REILLY, Thomas Lawrence (D Conn.) Sept. 20, 1859-July 6, 1924; House 1911-15.

REILLY, Wilson (D Pa.) Aug. 8, 1811-Aug. 26, 1885; House 1857-59.

REILY, Luther (D Pa.) Oct. 17, 1794-Feb. 20, 1854; House 1837-39.

REINECKE, Edwin (R Calif.) Jan. 7, 1924-__; House 1965-Jan. 21, 1969.

RELFE, James Hugh (D Mo.) Oct. 17, 1791-Sept. 14, 1863; House 1843-47.

REMANN, Frederick (R Ill.) May 10, 1847-July 14, 1895; House March 4-July 14, 1895.

RENCHER, Abraham (D N.C.) Aug. 12, 1798-July 6, 1883; House 1829-39, 1841-43; Gov. of N.M. 1857-61.

RESA, Alexander John (D Ill.) Aug. 4, 1887-July 4, 1964; House 1945-47.

RESNICK, Joseph Yale (D N.Y.) July 13, 1924-Oct. 6, 1969; House 1965-69.

REUSS, Henry Schoellkopf (D Wis.) Feb. 22, 1912-__; House 1955-__.

REVELS, Hiram Rhodes (R Miss.) Sept. 27, 1827-Jan. 16, 1901; Senate Feb. 23, 1870-71.

REVERCOMB, William Chapman (R W.Va.) July 20, 1895-__; Senate 1943-49, Nov. 7, 1956-59.

REYBURN, John Edgar (father of William Stuart Reyburn) (R Pa.) Feb. 7, 1845-Jan. 4, 1914; House Feb. 18, 1890-97, Nov. 6, 1906-March 31, 1907.

REYBURN, William Stuart (son of John Edgar Reyburn) (R Pa.) Dec. 17, 1882-July 25, 1946; House May 23, 1911-13.

REYNOLDS, Edwin Ruthvin (R N.Y.) Feb. 16, 1816-July 4, 1908; House Dec. 5, 1860-61.

REYNOLDS, Gideon (W N.Y.) Aug. 9, 1813-July 13, 1896; House 1847-51.

REYNOLDS, John (D Ill.) Feb. 26, 1789-May 8, 1865; House Dec. 1, 1834-37, 1839-43; Gov. 1830-34.

REYNOLDS, John Hazard (R N.Y.) June 21, 1819-Sept. 24, 1875; House 1859-61.

REYNOLDS, John Merriman (R Pa.) March 5, 1848-Sept. 14, 1933; House 1905-Jan. 17, 1911.

REYNOLDS, Joseph (D N.Y.) Sept. 14, 1785-Sept. 24, 1864; House 1835-37.

REYNOLDS, Robert Rice (D N.C.) June 18, 1884-Feb. 13, 1963; Senate Dec. 5, 1932-45.

REYNOLDS, Samuel Williams (R Neb.) Aug. 11, 1890-—; Senate July 3-Nov. 7, 1954.

RHEA, John (D Tenn.) 1753-May 27, 1832; House 1803-15, 1817-23.

RHEA, John Stockdale (D/P Ky.) March 9, 1855-July 29, 1924; House 1897-March 25, 1902, 1903-05.

RHEA, William Francis (D Va.) April 20, 1858-March 23, 1931; House 1899-1903.

RHETT, Robert Barnwell (formerly Robert Barnwell Smith) (D S.C.) Dec. 24, 1800-Sept. 14, 1876; House 1837-49; Senate Dec. 18, 1850-May 7, 1852.

RHINOCK, Joseph Lafayette (D Ky.) Jan. 4, 1863-Sept. 20, 1926; House 1905-11.

RHODES, George Milton (D Pa.) Feb. 24, 1898-—; House 1949-69.

RHODES, John Jacob (R Ariz.) Sept. 18, 1916-—; House 1953-—.

RHODES, Marion Edwards (R Mo.) Jan. 4, 1868-Dec. 25, 1928; House 1905-07, 1919-23.

RIBICOFF, Abraham Alexander (D Conn.) April 9, 1910-—; House 1949-53; Senate 1963-—; Gov. 1955-61; Secy. of HEW 1961-62.

RICAUD, James Barroll (AP Md.) Feb. 11, 1808-Jan. 24, 1866; House 1855-59.

RICE, Alexander Hamilton (R Mass.) Aug. 30, 1818-July 22, 1895; House 1859-67; Gov. 1876-79.

RICE, Americus Vespucius (D Ohio) Nov. 18, 1835-April 4, 1904; House 1875-79.

RICE, Benjamin Franklin (R Ark.) May 26, 1828-Jan. 19, 1905; Senate June 23, 1868-73.

RICE, Edmund (brother of Henry Mower Rice) (D Minn.) Feb. 14, 1819-July 11, 1889; House 1887-89.

RICE, Edward Young (D Ill.) Feb. 8, 1820-April 16, 1883; House 1871-73.

RICE, Henry Mower (brother of Edmund Rice) (D Minn.) Nov. 29, 1817-Jan. 15, 1894; House (Terr. Del.) 1853-57; Senate May 11, 1858-63.

RICE, John Birchard (R Ohio) June 23, 1832-Jan. 14, 1893; House 1881-83.

RICE, John Blake (R Ill.) May 28, 1809-Dec. 17, 1874; House 1873-Dec. 17, 1874.

RICE, John Hovey (R Maine) Feb. 5, 1816-March 14, 1911; House 1861-67.

RICE, John McConnell (D Ky.) Feb. 19, 1831-Sept. 18, 1895; House 1869-73.

RICE, Theron Moses (Natl. G Mo.) Sept. 21, 1829-Nov. 7, 1895; House 1881-83.

RICE, Thomas (— Mass.) March 30, 1768-Aug. 25, 1854; House 1815-19.

RICE, William Whitney (R Mass.) March 7, 1826-March 1, 1896; House 1877-87.

RICH, Carl West (R Ohio) Sept. 12, 1898-June 26, 1972; House 1963-65.

RICH, Charles (D Vt.) Sept. 13, 1771-Oct. 15, 1824; House 1813-15.

RICH, John Tyler (R Mich.) April 23, 1841-March 28, 1926; House April 5, 1881-83; Gov. 1893-97.

RICH, Robert Fleming (R Pa.) June 23, 1883-April 28, 1968; House Nov. 4, 1930-43, 1945-51.

RICHARD, Gabriel (— Mich.) Oct. 15, 1767-Sept. 13, 1832; House (Terr. Del.) 1823-25.

RICHARDS, Charles Lenmore (D Nev.) Oct. 3, 1877-Dec. 22, 1953; House 1923-25.

RICHARDS, Jacob (D Pa.) 1773-July 20, 1816; House 1803-09.

RICHARDS, James Alexander Dudley (D Ohio) March 22, 1845-Dec. 4, 1911; House 1893-95.

RICHARDS, James Prioleau (D S.C.) Aug. 31, 1894-—; House 1933-57.

RICHARDS, John (brother of Matthias Richards) (— Pa.) April 18, 1753-Nov. 13, 1822; House 1795-97.

RICHARDS, John (— N.Y.) April 13, 1765-April 18, 1850; House 1823-25.

RICHARDS, Mark (D Vt.) July 15, 1760-Aug. 10, 1844; House 1817-21.

RICHARDS, Matthias (brother of John Richards) (— Pa.) Feb. 26, 1758-Aug. 4, 1830; House 1807-11.

RICHARDSON, David Plunket (R N.Y.) May 28, 1833-June 21, 1904; House 1879-83.

RICHARDSON, George Frederick (D Mich.) July 1, 1850-March 1, 1923; House 1893-95.

RICHARDSON, Harry Alden (R Del.) Jan. 1, 1853-June 16, 1928; Senate 1907-13.

RICHARDSON, James Daniel (D Tenn.) March 10, 1843-July 24, 1914; House 1885-1905.

RICHARDSON, James Montgomery (D Ky.) July 1, 1858-Feb. 9, 1925; House 1905-07.

RICHARDSON, John Peter (SRD S.C.) April 14, 1801-Jan. 24, 1864; House Dec. 19, 1836-39; Gov. 1840-42.

RICHARDSON, John Smythe (D S.C.) Feb. 29, 1828-Feb. 24, 1894; House 1879-83.

RICHARDSON, Joseph (— Mass.) Feb. 1, 1778-Sept. 25, 1871; House 1827-31.

RICHARDSON, William (D Ala.) May 8, 1839-March 31, 1914; House Aug. 6, 1900-March 31, 1914.

RICHARDSON, William Alexander (D Ill.) Jan. 16, 1811-Dec. 27, 1875; House Dec. 6, 1847-Aug. 25, 1856, 1861-Jan. 29, 1863; Senate Jan. 30, 1863-65.

RICHARDSON, William Emanuel (D Pa.) Sept. 3, 1886-Nov. 3, 1948; House 1933-37.

RICHARDSON, William Merchant (F Mass.) Jan. 4, 1774-March 15, 1838; House Nov. 4, 1811-April 18, 1814.

RICHMOND, Frederick William (D N.Y.) Nov. 15, 1923-—; House 1975-—.

RICHMOND, Hiram Lawton (R Pa.) May 17, 1810-Feb. 19, 1885; House 1873-75.

RICHMOND, James Buchanan (D Va.) Feb. 27, 1842-April 30, 1910; House 1879-81.

RICHMOND, Jonathan (— N.Y.) July 31, 1774-July 28, 1853; House 1819-21.

RICKETTS, Edwin Darlington (R Ohio) Aug. 3, 1867-July 3, 1937; House 1915-17, 1919-23.

RIDDICK, Carl Wood (R Mont.) Feb. 25, 1872-July 9, 1960; House 1919-23.

RIDDLE, Albert Gallatin (R Ohio) May 28, 1816-May 16, 1902; House 1861-63.

RIDDLE, George Read (D Del.) 1817-March 29, 1867; House 1851-55; Senate Feb. 2, 1864-March 29, 1867.

RIDDLE, Haywood Yancey (D Tenn.) June 20, 1834-March 28, 1879; House Dec. 14, 1875-79.

RIDDLEBERGER, Harrison Holt (Read. Va.) Oct. 4, 1844-Jan. 24, 1890; Senate 1883-89.

RIDER, Ira Edgar (D N.Y.) Nov. 17, 1868-May 29, 1906; House 1903-05.

RIDGELY, Edwin Reed (PP/D Kan.) May 9, 1844-April 23, 1927; House 1897-1901.

RIDGELY, Henry Moore (F Del.) Aug. 6, 1779-Aug. 6, 1847; House 1811-15; Senate Jan. 12, 1827-29.

RIDGWAY, Joseph (W Ohio) May 6, 1783-Feb. 1, 1861; House 1837-43.

RIDGWAY, Robert (C Va.) April 21, 1823-Oct. 16, 1870; House Jan. 27-Oct. 16, 1870.

RIEGLE, Donald Wayne Jr. (D Mich.) Feb. 4, 1938-—; House 1967-— (1967-Feb. 27, 1973 Republican, Feb. 27, 1973-— Democrat).

RIEHLMAN, Roy Walter (R N.Y.) Aug. 26, 1899-—; House 1947-65.

RIFE, John Winebrenner (R Pa.) Aug. 14, 1846-April 17, 1908; House 1889-93.

RIGGS, James Milton (D Ill.) April 17, 1839-Nov. 18, 1933; House 1883-87.

RIGGS, Jetur Rose (D N.J.) June 20, 1809-Nov. 5, 1869; House 1859-61.

RIGGS, Lewis (D N.Y.) Jan. 16, 1789-Nov. 6, 1870; House 1841-43.

RIGNEY, Hugh McPheeters (D Ill.) July 31, 1873-Oct. 12, 1950; House 1937-39.

RIKER, Samuel (— N.Y.) April 8, 1743-May 19, 1823; House Nov. 5, 1804-05, 1807-09.

RILEY, Corinne Boyd (widow of John J. Riley) (D S.C.) July 4, 1893-—; House April 10, 1962-63.

RILEY, John Jacob (husband of Corinne Boyd Riley) (D S.C.) Feb. 1, 1895-Jan. 1, 1962; House 1945-49, 1951-Jan. 1, 1962.

RINAKER, John Irving (R Ill.) Nov. 1, 1830-Jan. 15, 1915; House June 5, 1896-97.

RINALDO, Matthew John (R N.J.) Sept. 1, 1931-—; House 1973-—.

RINGGOLD, Samuel (D Md.) Jan. 15, 1770-Oct. 18, 1829; House Oct. 15, 1810-15, 1817-21.

RIORDAN, Daniel Joseph (D N.Y.) July 7, 1870-April 28, 1923; House 1899-1901, Nov. 6, 1906-April 28, 1923.

RIPLEY, Eleazar Wheelock (brother of James Wheelock Ripley) (D La.) April 15, 1782-March 2, 1839; House 1835-March 2, 1839.

RIPLEY, James Wheelock (brother of Eleazar Wheelock Ripley) (D Maine) March 12, 1786-June 17, 1835; House Sept. 11, 1826-March 12, 1830.

RIPLEY, Thomas C. (— N.Y.) ? - ?; House Dec. 7, 1846-47.

RISENHOOVER, Theodore Marshall (D Okla.) Nov. 3, 1934-—; House 1975-—.

RISK, Charles Francis (R R.I.) Aug. 19, 1897-Dec. 26, 1943; House Aug. 6, 1935-37, 1939-41.

RISLEY, Elijah (W N.Y.) May 7, 1787-Jan. 9, 1870; House 1849-51.

RITCHEY, Thomas (D Ohio) Jan. 19, 1801-March 9, 1863; House 1847-49, 1853-55.

RITCHIE, Byron Foster (son of James Monroe Ritchie) (D Ohio) Jan. 29, 1853-Aug. 22, 1928; House 1893-95.

RITCHIE, David (R Pa.) Aug. 19, 1812-Jan. 24, 1867; House 1853-59.

RITCHIE, James Monroe (father of Byron Foster Ritchie) (R Ohio) July 28, 1829-Aug. 17, 1918; House 1881-83.

RITCHIE, John (D Md.) Aug. 12, 1831-Oct. 27, 1887; House 1871-73.

RITTER, Burwell Clark (uncle of Walter Evans) (C Ky.) Jan. 6, 1810-Oct. 1, 1880; House 1865-67.

RITTER, John (D Pa.) Feb. 6, 1779-Nov. 24, 1851; House 1843-47.

RIVERA, Luis Munoz (U P.R.) July 17, 1859-Nov. 15, 1916; House (Res. Comm.) 1911-Nov. 15, 1916.

RIVERS, Lucius Mendel (D S.C.) Sept. 28, 1905-Dec. 28, 1970; House 1941-Dec. 28, 1970.

RIVERS, Ralph Julian (D Alaska) May 23, 1903-Aug. 14, 1976; House 1959-67.

RIVERS, Thomas (AP Tenn.) Sept. 18, 1819-March 18, 1863; House 1855-57.

RIVES, Francis Everod (great uncle of Francis Rives Lassiter) (D Va.) Jan. 14, 1792-Dec. 26, 1861; House 1837-41.

RIVES, William Cabell (W Va.) May 4, 1792-April 25, 1868; House 1823-29 (D); Senate Dec. 10, 1832-Feb. 22, 1834, 1836-39, Jan. 18; 1841-45 (1832-34 and 1836-39 Democrat, 1841-45 Whig).

RIVES, Zeno John (R Ill.) Feb. 22, 1874-Sept. 2, 1939; House 1905-07.

RIXEY, John Franklin (D Va.) Aug. 1, 1854-Feb. 8, 1907; House 1897-Feb. 8, 1907.

RIZLEY, Ross (R Okla.) July 5, 1892-March 4, 1969; House 1941-49.

ROACH, Sidney Crain (R Mo.) July 25, 1876-June 29, 1934; House 1921-25.

ROACH, William Nathaniel (D N.D.) Sept. 25, 1840-Sept. 7, 1902; Senate 1893-99.

ROANE, John (father of John Jones Roane) (D Va.) Feb. 9, 1766-Nov. 15, 1838; House 1809-15, 1827-31, 1835-37.

ROANE, John Jones (son of John Roane) (D Va.) Oct. 31, 1794-Dec. 18, 1869; House 1831-33.

ROANE, William Henry (grandson of Patrick Henry) (D Va.) Sept. 17, 1787- May 11, 1845; House 1815-17; Senate March 14, 1837-41.

ROARK, Charles Wickliffe (R Ky.) Jan. 22, 1887-April 5, 1929; House March 4-April 5, 1929.

ROBB, Edward (D Mo.) March 19, 1857-March 13, 1934; House 1897-1905.

ROBBINS, Asher (W R.I.) Oct. 26, 1757-Feb. 25, 1845; Senate Oct. 31, 1825-39.

ROBBINS, Edward Everett (R Pa.) Sept. 27, 1860-Jan. 25, 1919; House 1897-99, 1917-Jan. 25, 1919.

ROBBINS, Gaston Ahi (D Ala.) Sept. 26, 1858-Feb. 22, 1902; House 1893-March 13, 1896, 1899-March 8, 1900.

ROBBINS, George Robbins (W N.J.) Sept. 24, 1808-Feb. 22, 1875; House 1855-59.

ROBBINS, John (D Pa.) 1808-April 27, 1880; House 1849-55, 1875-77.

ROBBINS, William McKendree (D N.C.) Oct. 26, 1828-May 5, 1905; House 1873-79.

ROBERTS, Anthony Ellmaker (grandfather of Robert Grey Bushong) (W Pa.) Oct. 29, 1803-Jan. 25, 1885; House 1855-59.

ROBERTS, Brigham Henry (D Utah) March 13, 1857-Sept. 27, 1933; House 1899-Jan. 25, 1900.

ROBERTS, Charles Boyle (D Md.) April 19, 1842-Sept. 10, 1899; House 1875-79.

ROBERTS, Edwin Ewing (R Nev.) Dec. 12, 1870-Dec. 11, 1933; House 1911-19.

ROBERTS, Ellis Henry (R N.Y.) Sept. 30, 1827-Jan. 8, 1918; House 1871-75.

ROBERTS, Ernest William (R Mass.) Nov. 22 1858-Feb. 27, 1924; House 1899-1917.

ROBERTS, Herbert Ray (D Texas) March 28 1913-—; House Jan. 30, 1962-—.

ROBERTS, Jonathan (DR Pa.) Aug. 16, 1771 July 24, 1854; House 1811-Feb. 24, 1814, Senate Feb. 24, 1814-21.

ROBERTS, Kenneth Allison (D Ala.) Nov. 1, 1912-—; House 1951-65.

ROBERTS, Robert Whyte (D Miss.) Nov. 28, 1784-Jan. 4, 1865; House 1843-47.

ROBERTS, William Randall (D N.Y.) Feb. 6, 1830-Aug. 9, 1897; House 1871-75.

ROBERTSON, Alice Mary (R Okla.) Jan. 2, 1854-July 1, 1931; House 1921-23.

ROBERTSON, A. Willis (D Va.) May 27, 1887-Nov. 1, 1971; House 1933-Nov. 5, 1946; Senate Nov. 6, 1946-67.

ROBERTSON, Charles Raymond (R N.D.) Sept. 5, 1889-Feb. 18, 1951; House 1941-43, 1945-49.

ROBERTSON, Edward Vivian (R Wyo.) May 27, 1881-April 15, 1963; Senate 1943-49.

ROBERTSON, Edward White (father of Samuel Matthews Robertson) (D La.) June 13, 1823-Aug. 2, 1887; House 1877-83, March 4-Aug. 2, 1887.

ROBERTSON, George (— Ky.) Nov. 18, 1790-May 16, 1874; House 1817-21.

ROBERTSON, John (brother of Thomas Bolling Robertson) (W Va.) April 13, 1787-July 5, 1873; House Dec. 8, 1834-39.

ROBERTSON, Samuel Matthews (son of Edward White Robertson) (D La.) Jan. 1, 1852-Dec. 24, 1911; House Dec. 5, 1887-1907.

ROBERTSON, Thomas Austin (D Ky.) Sept. 9, 1848-July 18, 1892; House 1883-87.

ROBERTSON, Thomas Bolling (brother of John Robertson) (D La.) Feb. 27, 1779-Oct. 5, 1828; House April 30, 1812-April 20, 1818; Gov. 1820-24.

ROBERTSON, Thomas James (R S.C.) Aug. 3, 1823-Oct. 13, 1897; Senate July 15, 1868-77.

ROBERTSON, William Henry (R N.Y.) Oct. 10, 1823-Dec. 7, 1898; House 1867-69.

ROBESON, Edward John Jr. (D Va.) Aug. 9, 1890-March 10, 1966; House May 2, 1950-59.

ROBESON, George Maxwell (nephew of George Clifford Maxwell) (R N.J.) March 16, 1829-Sept. 27, 1897; House 1879-83; Secy. of the Navy 1869-77.

ROBIE, Reuben (D N.Y.) July 15, 1799-Jan. 21, 1872; House 1851-53.

ROBINSON, Arthur Raymond (R Ind.) March 12, 1881-March 17, 1961; Senate Oct. 20, 1925-35.

ROBINSON, Christopher (AP R.I.) May 15, 1806-Oct. 3, 1889; House 1859-61.

ROBINSON, Edward (W Maine) Nov. 25, 1796-Feb. 19, 1857; House April 28, 1838-39.

ROBINSON, George Dexter (R Mass.) Jan. 20, 1834-Feb. 22, 1896; House 1877-Jan. 7, 1884; Gov. 1884-87.

ROBINSON, James Carroll (D Ill.) Aug. 19, 1823-Nov. 3, 1886; House 1859-65, 1871-75.

ROBINSON, James Kenneth (R Va.) May 14, 1916-—; House 1971-—.

ROBINSON, James McClellan (D Ind.) May 31, 1861-Jan. 16, 1942; House 1897-1905.

ROBINSON, James Sidney (R Ohio) Oct. 14, 1827-Jan. 14, 1892; House 1881-Jan. 12, 1885.

ROBINSON, James Wallace (R Ohio) Nov. 26, 1826-June 28, 1898; House 1873-75.

ROBINSON, James William (D Utah) Jan. 19, 1878-Dec. 2, 1964; House 1933-47.

ROBINSON, John Buchanan (R Pa.) May 23, 1846-Jan. 28, 1933; House 1891-97.

ROBINSON, John Larne (D Ind.) May 3, 1813-March 21, 1860; House 1847-53.

ROBINSON, John McCracken (D Ill.) April 10, 1794-April 25, 1843; Senate Dec. 11, 1830-41.

ROBINSON, John Seaton (D Neb.) May 4, 1856-May 25, 1903; House 1899-1903.

ROBINSON, Jonathan (brother of Moses Robinson) (— Vt.) Aug. 11, 1756-Nov. 3, 1819; Senate Oct. 10, 1807-15.

ROBINSON, Joseph Taylor (D Ark.) Aug. 26, 1872-July 14, 1937; House 1903-Jan. 14, 1913; Senate 1913-July 14, 1937; Gov. Jan. 16-March 8, 1913.

ROBINSON, Leonidas Dunlap (D N.C.) April 22, 1867-Nov. 7, 1941; House 1917-21.

ROBINSON, Milton Stapp (R Ind.) April 20, 1832-July 28, 1892; House 1875-79.

ROBINSON, Moses (brother of Jonathan Robinson) (D Vt.) March 20, 1741-May 26, 1813; Senate Oct. 17, 1791-Oct. 15, 1796; Gov. 1789-90.

ROBINSON, Orville (D N.Y.) Oct. 28, 1801-Dec. 1, 1882; House 1843-45.

ROBINSON, Thomas Jr. (D Del.) 1800-Oct. 28, 1843; House 1839-41.

ROBINSON, Thomas John Bright (R Iowa) Aug. 12, 1868-Jan. 27, 1958; House 1923-33.

ROBINSON, William Erigena (D N.Y.) May 6, 1814-Jan. 23, 1892; House 1867-69, 1881-85.

ROBISON, David Fullerton (nephew of David Fullerton) (W Pa.) May 28, 1816-June 24, 1859; House 1855-57.

ROBISON, Howard Winfield (R N.Y.) Oct. 30, 1915-—; House Jan. 14, 1958-75.

ROBSION, John Marshall (father of John Marshall Robsion Jr.) (R Ky.) Jan. 2,

1873-Feb. 17, 1948; House 1919-Jan. 10, 1930, 1935-Feb. 17, 1948; Senate Jan. 11-Nov. 30, 1930.

ROBSION, John Marshall Jr. (son of the preceding) (R Ky.) Aug. 28, 1904-—; House 1953-59.

ROCHESTER, William Beatty (D N.Y.) Jan. 29, 1789-June 14, 1838; House 1821-April 1823.

ROCKEFELLER, Lewis Kirby (R N.Y.) Nov. 25, 1875-Sept. 18, 1948; House Nov. 2, 1937-43.

ROCKHILL, William (D Ind.) Feb. 10, 1793-Jan. 15, 1865; House 1847-49.

ROCKWELL, Francis Williams (son of Julius Rockwell) (R Mass.) May 26, 1844-June 26, 1929; House Jan. 17, 1884-91.

ROCKWELL, Hosea Hunt (D N.Y.) May 31, 1840-Dec. 18, 1918; House 1891-93.

ROCKWELL, John Arnold (W Conn.) Aug. 27, 1803-Feb. 10, 1861; House 1845-49.

ROCKWELL, Julius (father of Francis Williams Rockwell) (W Mass.) April 26, 1805-May 19, 1888; House 1843-51; Senate June 3, 1854-Jan. 31, 1855.

ROCKWELL, Robert Fay (R Colo.) Feb. 11, 1886-Sept. 29, 1950; House Dec. 9, 1941-49.

RODDENBERY, Seaborn Anderson (D Ga.) Jan. 12, 1870-Sept. 25, 1913; House Feb. 16, 1910-Sept. 25, 1913.

RODENBERG, William August (R Ill.) Oct. 30, 1865-Sept. 10, 1937; House 1899-1901, 1903-13, 1915-23.

RODEY, Bernard Shandon (R N.M.) March 1, 1856-March 10, 1927; House (Terr. Del.) 1901-05.

RODGERS, Robert Lewis (R Pa.) June 2, 1875-May 9, 1960; House 1939-47.

RODINO, Peter Wallace Jr. (D N.J.) June 7, 1909-—; House 1949-—.

RODMAN, William (D Pa.) Oct. 7, 1757-July 27, 1824; House 1811-13.

RODNEY, Caesar Augustus (cousin of George Brydges Rodney) (D Del.) Jan. 4, 1772-June 10, 1824; House 1803-05, 1821-Jan. 24, 1822; Senate Jan. 24, 1822-Jan. 29, 1823; Atty. Gen. 1807-11.

RODNEY, Daniel (F Del.) Sept. 10, 1764-Sept. 2, 1846; House Oct. 1, 1822-23; Senate Nov. 8, 1826-Jan. 12, 1827; Gov. 1814-17.

RODNEY, George Brydges (cousin of Caesar Augustus Rodney) (W Del.) April 2, 1803-June 18, 1883; House 1841-45.

ROE, Dudley George (D Md.) March 23, 1881-Jan. 4, 1970; House 1945-47.

ROE, James A. (D N.Y.) July 9, 1896-April 22, 1967; House 1945-47.

ROE, Robert A. (D N.J.) Feb. 28, 1924-—; House Nov. 4, 1969-—.

ROGERS, Andrew Jackson (D N.J.) July 1, 1828-May 22, 1900; House 1863-67.

ROGERS, Anthony Astley Cooper (D Ark.) Feb. 14, 1821-July 27, 1899; House 1869-71.

ROGERS, Byron Giles (D Colo.) Aug. 1, 1900-—; House 1951-71.

ROGERS, Charles (W N.Y.) April 30, 1800-Jan. 13, 1874; House 1843-45.

ROGERS, Dwight Laing (father of Paul G. Rogers) (D Fla.) Aug. 17, 1886-Dec. 1, 1954; House 1945-Dec. 1, 1954.

ROGERS, Edith Nourse (wife of John Jacob Rogers) (R Mass.) 1881-Sept. 10, 1960; House June 30, 1925-Sept. 10, 1960.

ROGERS, Edward (D N.Y.) May 30, 1787-May 29, 1857; House 1839-41.

ROGERS, George Frederick (D N.Y.) March 19, 1887-Nov. 20, 1948; House 1945-47.

ROGERS, James (D S.C.) Oct. 24, 1795-Dec. 21, 1873; House 1835-37, 1839-43.

ROGERS, John (D N.Y.) May 9, 1813-May 11, 1879; House 1871-73.

ROGERS, John Henry (D Ark.) Oct. 9, 1845-April 16, 1911; House 1883-91.

ROGERS, John Jacob (husband of Edith Nourse Rogers) (R Mass.) Aug. 18, 1881-March 28, 1925; House 1913-March 28, 1925.

ROGERS, Paul Grant (son of Dwight L. Rogers) (D Fla.) June 4, 1921-—; House Jan. 11, 1955-—.

ROGERS, Sion Hart (D N.C.) Sept. 30, 1825-Aug. 14, 1874; House 1853-55, 1871-73 (1853-55 Whig, 1871-73 Democrat).

ROGERS, Thomas Jones (father of William Findlay Rogers) (D Pa.) 1781-Dec. 7, 1832; House March 3, 1818-April 20, 1824.

ROGERS, Walter Edward (D Texas) July 19, 1908-—; House 1951-67.

ROGERS, Will (D Okla.) Dec. 12, 1898-—; House 1933-43.

ROGERS, Will Jr. (D Calif.) Oct. 20, 1911-—; House 1943-May 23, 1944.

ROGERS, William Findlay (son of Thomas Jones Rogers) (D N.Y.) March 1, 1820-Dec. 16, 1899; House 1883-85.

ROGERS, William Nathaniel (D N.H.) Jan. 10, 1892-Sept. 25, 1945; House 1923-25, Jan. 5, 1932-37.

ROHRBOUGH, Edward Gay (R W.Va.) 1874-Dec. 12, 1956; House 1943-45, 1947-49.

ROLLINS, Edward Henry (R N.H.) Oct. 3, 1824-July 31, 1889; House 1861-67; Senate 1877-83.

ROLLINS, James Sidney (C Mo.) April 19, 1812-Jan. 9, 1888; House 1861-65.

ROLPH, Thomas (R Calif.) Jan. 17, 1885-May 10, 1956; House 1941-45.

ROMAN, James Dixon (W Md.) Aug. 11, 1809-Jan. 19, 1867; House 1847-49.

ROMEIS, Jacob (R Ohio) Dec. 1, 1835-March 8, 1904; House 1885-89.

ROMERO, Trinidad (R N.M.) June 15, 1835-Aug. 28, 1918; House (Terr. Del.) 1877-79.

ROMJUE, Milton Andrew (D Mo.) Dec. 5, 1874-Jan. 23, 1968; House 1917-21, 1923-43.

ROMULO, Carlos Pena (— P.I.) Jan. 14, 1901-—; House (Res. Comm.) Aug. 10, 1944-July 4, 1946.

RONAN, Daniel J. (D Ill.) July 13, 1914-Aug. 13, 1969; House 1965-Aug. 13, 1969.

RONCALIO, Teno (D Wyo.) March 23, 1916-—; House 1965-67, 1971-—.

RONCALLO, Angelo Dominick (R N.Y.) May 28, 1927-—; House 1973-75.

ROONEY, Fred B. (D Pa.) Nov. 6, 1925-—; House July 30, 1963-—.

ROONEY, John James (D N.Y.) Nov. 29, 1903-Oct. 26, 1975; House June 6, 1944-Dec. 31, 1974.

ROOSEVELT, Franklin Delano Jr. (son of President Franklin D. Roosevelt and brother of James Roosevelt) (D N.Y.) Aug. 17, 1914-—; House May 17, 1949-55 (1949-51 Liberal/Four Freedoms; 1951-55 Democrat).

ROOSEVELT, James (son of President Franklin D. Roosevelt and brother of Franklin Delano Roosevelt Jr.) (D Calif.) Dec. 23, 1907-—; House 1955-Sept. 30, 1965.

ROOSEVELT, James I. (uncle of Robert Barnwell Roosevelt) (D N.Y.) Dec. 14, 1795-April 5, 1875; House 1841-43.

ROOSEVELT, Robert Barnwell (nephew of James I. Roosevelt and uncle of President Theodore Roosevelt) (D N.Y.) Aug. 7, 1829-June 14, 1906; House 1871-73.

ROOT, Elihu (R N.Y.) Feb. 15, 1845-Feb. 7, 1937; Senate 1909-15; Secy. of War 1899-1904; Secy. of State 1905-09.

ROOT, Erastus (D N.Y.) March 16, 1773-Dec. 24, 1846; House 1803-05, 1809-11, Dec. 26, 1815-17, 1831-33.

ROOT, Joseph Mosley (W Ohio) Oct. 7, 1807-April 7, 1879; House 1845-51.

ROOTS, Logan Holt (R Ark.) March 26, 1841-May 30, 1893; House June 22, 1868-71.

ROSE, Charles Gradison III (D N.C.) Aug. 10, 1939-—; House 1973-—.

ROSE, John Marshall (R Pa.) May 18, 1856-April 22, 1923; House 1917-23.

ROSE, Robert Lawson (son of Robert Seldon Rose and son-in-law of Nathaniel Allen) (W N.Y.) Oct. 12, 1804-March 14, 1877; House 1847-51.

ROSE, Robert Selden (father of Robert Lawson Rose) (— N.Y.) Feb. 24, 1774-Nov. 24, 1835; House 1823-27, 1829-31.

ROSECRANS, William Starke (D Calif.) Sept. 6, 1819-March 11, 1898; House 1881-85.

ROSENBLOOM, Benjamin Louis (R W. Va.) June 3, 1880-March 22, 1965; House 1921-25.

ROSENTHAL, Benjamin S. (D/L N.Y.) June 8, 1923-—; House Feb. 20, 1962-—.

ROSIER, Joseph (D W.Va.) Jan. 24, 1870-Oct. 7, 1951; Senate Jan. 13, 1941-Nov. 17, 1942.

ROSS, Edmund Gibson (R Kan.) Dec. 7, 1826-May 8, 1907; Senate July 19, 1866-71; Gov. (N.M. Terr.) (D) 1885-89.

ROSS, Henry Howard (W N.Y.) May 9, 1790-Sept. 14, 1862; House 1825-27.

ROSS, James (F Pa.) July 12, 1762-Nov. 27, 1847; Senate April 24, 1794-1803.

ROSS, John (father of Thomas Ross) (— Pa.) Feb. 24, 1770-Jan. 31, 1834; House 1809-11, 1815-Feb. 24, 1818.

ROSS, Jonathan (R Vt.) April 30, 1826-Feb. 23, 1905; Senate Jan. 11, 1899-Oct. 18, 1900.

ROSS, Lewis Winans (D Ill.) Dec. 8, 1812-Oct. 20, 1895; House 1863-69.

ROSS, Miles (D N.J.) April 30, 1827-Feb. 22, 1903; House 1875-83.

ROSS, Robert Tripp (R N.Y.) June 4, 1903-—; House 1947-49, Feb. 19, 1952-53.

ROSS, Sobieski (R Pa.) May 16, 1828-Oct. 24, 1877; House 1873-77.

ROSS, Thomas (son of John Ross) (D Pa.) Dec. 1, 1806-July 7, 1865; House 1849-53.

ROSS, Thomas Randolph (D Ohio) Oct. 26, 1788-June 28, 1869; House 1819-25.

ROSSDALE, Albert Berger (R N.Y.) Oct. 23, 1878-April 17, 1968; House 1921-23.

ROSTENKOWSKI, Daniel David (Dan) (D Ill.) Jan. 2, 1928-—; House 1959-—.

ROTH, William V. Jr. (R Del.) July 22, 1921-—; House 1967-Dec. 31, 1970; Senate Jan. 1, 1971-—.

ROTHERMEL, John Hoover (D Pa.) March 7, 1856-Aug. 1922; House 1907-15.

ROTHWELL, Gideon Frank (D Mo.) April 24, 1836-Jan. 18, 1894; House 1879-81.

ROUDEBUSH, Richard Lowell (R Ind.) Jan. 18, 1918-—; House 1961-71.

ROUSE, Arthur Blythe (D Ky.) June 20, 1874-Jan. 25, 1956; House 1911-27.

ROUSH, John Edward (D Ind.) Sept. 12, 1920-—; House 1959-69, 1971-—.

ROUSSEAU, Lovell Harrison (R Ky.) Aug. 4, 1818-Jan. 7, 1869; House 1865-July 21, 1866, Dec. 3, 1866-67.

ROUSSELOT, John Harbin (R Calif.) Nov. 1, 1927-—; House 1961-63, June 30, 1970-—.

ROUTZOHN, Harry Nelson (R Ohio) Nov. 4, 1881-April 14, 1953; House 1939-41.

ROWAN, John (uncle of Robert Todd Lytle) (D Ky.) July 12, 1773-July 13, 1843; House 1807-09; Senate 1825-31.

ROWAN, Joseph (D N.Y.) Sept. 8, 1870-Aug. 3, 1930; House 1919-21.

ROWAN, William A. (D Ill.) Nov. 24, 1882-May 31, 1961; House 1943-47.

ROWBOTTOM, Harry Emerson (R Ind.) Nov. 3, 1884-March 22, 1934; House 1925-31.

ROWE, Edmund (Ed) (R Ohio) Dec. 21, 1892-—; House 1943-45.

ROWE, Frederick William (R N.Y.) March 19, 1863-June 20, 1946; House 1915-21.

ROWE, Peter (D N.Y.) March 10, 1807-April 17, 1876; House 1853-55.

ROWELL, Jonathan Harvey (R Ill.) Feb. 10, 1833-May 15, 1908; House 1883-91.

ROWLAND, Alfred (D N.C.) Feb. 9, 1844-Aug. 2, 1898; House 1887-91.

ROWLAND, Charles Hedding (R Pa.) Dec. 20, 1860-Nov. 24, 1921; House 1915-19.

ROY, Alphonse (D N.H.) Oct. 26, 1897-Oct. 5, 1967; House June 9, 1938-39.

ROY, William Robert (D Kan.) Feb. 23, 1926-—; House 1971-75.

ROYBAL, Edward R. (D Calif.) Feb. 10, 1916-—; House 1963-—.

ROYCE, Homer Elihu (R Vt.) June 14, 1819-April 24, 1891; House 1857-61.

ROYSE, Lemuel Willard (R Ind.) Jan. 19, 1847-Dec. 18, 1946; House 1895-99.

RUBEY, Thomas Lewis (D Mo.) Sept. 27, 1862-Nov. 2, 1928; House 1911-21, 1923-Nov. 2, 1928.

RUCKER, Atterson Walden (D Colo.) April 3, 1847-July 19, 1924; House 1909-13.

RUCKER, Tinsley White (D Ga.) March 24, 1848-Nov. 18, 1926; House Jan. 11-March 3, 1917.

RUCKER, William Waller (D Mo.) Feb. 1, 1855-May 30, 1936; House 1899-1923.

RUDD, Stephen Andrew (D N.Y.) Dec. 11, 1874-March 31, 1936; House 1931-March 31, 1936.

RUFFIN, James Edward (D Mo.) July 24, 1893-—; House 1933-35.

RUFFIN, Thomas (D N.C.) Sept. 9, 1820-Oct. 13, 1863; House 1853-61.

RUGGLES, Benjamin (D Ohio) Feb. 21, 1783-Sept. 2, 1857; Senate 1815-33.

RUGGLES, Charles Herman (— N.Y.) Feb. 10, 1789-June 16, 1865; House 1821-23.

RUGGLES, John (D Maine) Oct. 8, 1789-June 20, 1874; Senate Jan. 20, 1835-41.

RUGGLES, Nathaniel (F Mass.) Nov. 11, 1761-Dec. 19, 1819; House 1813-19.

RUMPLE, John Nicholas William (R Iowa) March 4, 1841-Jan. 31, 1903; House 1901-Jan. 31, 1903.

RUMSEY, David (W N.Y.) Dec. 25, 1810-March 12, 1883; House 1847-51.

RUMSEY, Edward (W Ky.) Nov. 5, 1796-April 6, 1868; House 1837-39.

RUMSFELD, Donald (R Ill.) July 9, 1932-__; House 1963-May 25, 1969; Secy. of Defense 1975-__.

RUNK, John (W N.J.) July 3, 1791-Sept. 22, 1872; House 1845-47.

RUNNELS, Harold Lowell (D N.M.) March 17, 1924-__; House 1971-__.

RUPLEY, Arthur Ringwalt (PR Pa.) Nov. 13, 1868-Nov. 11, 1920; House 1913-15.

RUPPE, Philip E. (R Mich.) Sept. 29, 1926-__; House 1967-__.

RUPPERT, Jacob Jr. (D N.Y.) Aug. 5, 1867-Jan. 13, 1939; House 1899-1907.

RUSK, Harry Welles (D Md.) Oct. 17, 1852-Jan. 28, 1926; House Nov. 2, 1886-97.

RUSK, Jeremiah McLain (R Wis.) June 17, 1830-Nov. 21, 1893; House 1871-77; Gov. 1882-89; Secy. of Agric. 1889-93.

RUSK, Thomas Jefferson (D Texas) Dec. 5, 1803-July 29, 1857; Senate Feb. 21, 1846-July 29, 1857; President pro tempore 1857.

RUSS, John (D Conn.) Oct. 29, 1767-June 22, 1833; House 1819-23.

RUSSELL, Benjamin Edward (cousin of Rienzi Melville Johnston) (D Ga.) Oct. 5, 1845-Dec. 4, 1909; House 1893-97.

RUSSELL, Charles Addison (R Conn.) March 2, 1852-Oct. 23, 1902; House 1887-Oct. 23, 1902.

RUSSELL, Charles Hinton (R Nev.) Dec. 27, 1903-__; House 1947-49; Gov. 1951-59.

RUSSELL, Daniel Lindsay (R N.C.) Aug. 7, 1845-May 14, 1908; House 1879-81; Gov. 1897-1901.

RUSSELL, David Abel (W N.Y.) 1780-Nov. 24, 1861; House 1835-41.

RUSSELL, Donald Stuart (D S.C.) Feb. 22, 1906-__; Senate April 22, 1965-1967; Gov. 1963-65.

RUSSELL, Gordon James (D Texas) Dec. 22, 1859-Sept. 14, 1919; House Nov. 4, 1902-June 14, 1910.

RUSSELL, James McPherson (father of Samuel Lyon Russell) (W Pa.) Nov. 10, 1786-Nov. 14, 1870; House Dec. 21, 1841-43.

RUSSELL, Jeremiah (D N.Y.) Jan. 26, 1786-Sept. 30, 1867; House 1843-45.

RUSSELL, John (— N.Y.) Sept. 7, 1772-Aug. 2, 1842; House 1805-09.

RUSSELL, John Edwards (D Mass.) Jan. 20, 1834-Oct. 28, 1903; House 1887-89.

RUSSELL, Jonathan (D Mass.) Feb. 27, 1771-Feb. 16, 1832; House 1821-23.

RUSSELL, Joseph (D N.Y.) ?-?; House 1845-57, 1851-53.

RUSSELL, Joseph James (D Mo.) Aug. 23, 1854-Oct. 22, 1922; House 1907-09, 1911-19.

RUSSELL, Joshua Edward (R Ohio) Aug. 9, 1867-June 21, 1953; House 1915-17.

RUSSELL, Leslie W. (— N.Y.) April 15, 1840-Feb. 3, 1903; House March 4-Sept. 11, 1891.

RUSSELL, Richard Brevard (D Ga.) Nov. 2, 1897-Jan. 21, 1971; Senate Jan. 12, 1933-Jan. 21, 1971; President pro tempore 1969-71; Gov. 1931-33.

RUSSELL, Richard Manning (D Mass.) March 3, 1891-__; House 1935-37.

RUSSELL, Sam Morris (D Texas) Aug. 9, 1889-Oct. 19, 1971; House 1941-47.

RUSSELL, Samuel Lyon (son of James McPherson Russell) (W Pa.) July 30, 1816-Sept. 27, 1891; House 1853-55.

RUSSELL, William (W Ohio) 1782-Sept. 28, 1845; House 1827-33, 1841-43 (1827-33 Jackson Democrat, 1841-43 Whig).

RUSSELL, William Augustus (R Mass.) April 22, 1831-Jan. 10, 1899; House 1879-85.

RUSSELL, William Fiero (D N.Y.) Jan. 14, 1812-April 29, 1896; House 1857-59.

RUSSO, Martin Anthony (D Ill.) Jan. 23, 1944-__; House 1975-__.

RUST, Albert (D Ark.) ?-April 3, 1870; House 1855-57; 1859-61.

RUTH, Earl B. (R N.C.) Feb. 7, 1916-__; House 1969-75.

RUTHERFORD, Albert Greig (R Pa.) Jan. 3, 1879-Aug. 10, 1941; House 1937-Aug. 10, 1941.

RUTHERFORD, J. T. (D Texas) May 30, 1921-__; House 1955-63.

RUTHERFORD, Robert (— Va.) Oct. 20, 1728-Oct. 1803; House 1793-97.

RUTHERFORD, Samuel (D Ga.) March 15, 1870-Feb. 4, 1932; House 1925-Feb. 4, 1932.

RUTHERFURD, John (F N.J.) Sept. 20, 1760-Feb. 23, 1840; Senate 1791-Dec. 5, 1799.

RUTLEDGE, John Jr. (F S.C.) 1766-Sept. 1, 1819; House 1797-1803.

RYALL, Daniel Bailey (D N.J.) Jan. 30, 1798-Dec. 17, 1864; House 1839-41.

RYAN, Elmer James (D Minn.) May 26, 1907-Feb. 1, 1958; House 1935-41.

RYAN, Harold M. (D Mich.) Feb. 6, 1911-__; House Feb. 13, 1962-65.

RYAN, James Wilfrid (D Pa.) Oct. 16, 1858-Feb. 26, 1907; House 1899-1901.

RYAN, Leo Joseph (D Calif.) May 5, 1925-__; House 1973-__.

RYAN, Thomas (R Kan.) Nov. 25, 1837-April 5, 1914; House 1877-April 4, 1889.

RYAN, Thomas Jefferson (R N.Y.) June 17, 1890-Nov. 10, 1968; House 1921-23.

RYAN, William (D N.Y.) March 8, 1840-Feb. 18, 1925; House 1893-95.

RYAN, William Fitts (D/L N.Y.) June 28, 1922-Sept. 17, 1972; House 1961-Sept. 17, 1972.

RYAN, William Henry (D N.Y.) May 10, 1860-Nov. 18, 1939; House 1899-1909.

RYON, John Walker (D Pa.) March 4, 1825-March 12, 1901; House 1879-81.

RYTER, John Francis (D Conn.) Feb. 4, 1914-__; House 1945-47.

S

SABATH, Adolph Joachim (D Ill.) April 4, 1866-Nov. 6, 1952; House 1907-Nov. 6, 1952.

SABIN, Alvah (W Vt.) Oct. 23, 1793-Jan. 22, 1885; House 1853-57.

SABIN, Dwight May (R Minn.) April 25, 1843-Dec. 22, 1902; Senate 1883-89; Chrmn. Rep. Nat. Comm. 1883-84.

SABINE, Lorenzo (W Mass.) Feb. 28, 1803-April 14, 1877; House Dec. 13, 1852-53.

SACKETT, Frederick Mosley (R Ky.) Dec. 17, 1868-May 18, 1941; Senate 1925-Jan. 9, 1930.

SACKETT, William Augustus (W N.Y.) Nov. 18, 1811-Sept. 6, 1895; House 1849-53.

SACKS, Leon (D Pa.) Oct. 7, 1902-__; House 1937-43.

SADLAK, Antoni Nicholas (R Conn.) June 13, 1908-Oct. 18, 1969; House 1947-59.

SADLER, Thomas William (D Ala.) April 17, 1831-Oct. 29, 1896; House 1885-87.

SADOWSKI, George Gregory (D Mich.) March 12, 1903-Oct. 9, 1961; House 1933-39, 1943-51.

SAGE, Ebenezer (D N.Y.) Aug. 16, 1755-Jan. 20, 1834; House 1809-15.

SAGE, Russell (W N.Y.) Aug. 4, 1816-July 22, 1906; House 1853-57.

SAILLY, Peter (D N.Y.) April 20, 1754-March 16, 1826; House 1805-07.

ST. GEORGE, Katharine Price Collier (R N.Y.) July 12, 1896-__; House 1947-65.

ST. GERMAIN, Fernand Joseph (D R.I.) Jan. 9, 1928-__; House 1961-__.

ST. JOHN, Charles (R N.Y.) Oct. 8, 1818-July 6, 1891; House 1871-75.

ST. JOHN, Daniel Bennett (W N.Y.) Oct. 8, 1808-Feb. 18, 1890; House 1847-49.

ST. JOHN, Henry (D Ohio) July 16, 1783-May 1869; House 1843-47.

ST. MARTIN, Louis (D La.) May 17, 1820-Feb. 9, 1893; House 1851-53; 1885-87.

ST. ONGE, William Leon (D Conn.) Oct. 9, 1914-May 1, 1970; House 1963-May 1, 1970.

SALINGER, Pierre Emil George (D Calif.) June 14, 1925-__; Senate Aug. 4-Dec. 31, 1964.

SALMON, Joshua S. (D N.J.) Feb. 2, 1846-May 6, 1902; House 1899-May 6, 1902.

SALMON, William Charles (D Tenn.) April 3, 1868-May 13, 1925; House 1923-25.

SALTONSTALL, Leverett (W Mass.) June 13, 1783-May 8, 1845; House Dec. 5, 1838-43.

SALTONSTALL, Leverett (great-grandson of the preceding) (R Mass.) Sept. 1, 1892-__; Senate Jan. 4, 1945-67; Gov. 1939-45.

SAMFORD, William James (D Ala.) Sept. 16, 1844-June 11, 1901; House 1879-81; Gov. 1900-01.

SAMMONS, Thomas (grandfather of John Henry Starin) (D N.Y.) Oct. 1, 1762-Nov. 20, 1838; House 1803-07, 1809-13.

SAMPLE, Samuel Caldwell (D Ind.) Aug. 15, 1796-Dec. 2, 1855; House 1843-45.

SAMPSON, Ezekiel Silas (R Iowa) Dec. 6, 1831-Oct. 7, 1892; House 1875-79.

SAMPSON, Zabdiel (D Mass.) Aug. 22, 1781-July 19, 1828; House 1817-July 26, 1820.

SAMUEL, Edmund William (R Pa.) Nov. 27, 1857-March 7, 1930; House 1905-07.

SAMUELS, Green Berry (cousin of Isaac Samuels Pennybacker) (D Va.) Feb. 1, 1806-Jan. 5, 1859; House 1839-41.

SANBORN, John Carfield (R Idaho) Sept. 28, 1885-May 16, 1968; House 1947-51.

SANDAGER, Harry (R R.I.) April 12, 1887-Dec. 24, 1955; House 1939-41.

SANDERS, Archie Dovell (R N.Y.) June 17, 1857-July 15, 1941; House 1917-33.

SANDERS, Everett (R Ind.) March 8, 1882-May 12, 1950; House 1917-25; Chrmn. Rep. Nat. Comm. 1932-34.

SANDERS, Jared Young (father of Jared Young Sanders Jr.) (D La.) Jan. 29, 1869-March 23, 1944; House 1917-21; Gov. 1908-12.

SANDERS, Jared Young Jr. (son of the preceding) (D La.) April 20, 1892-Nov. 29, 1960; House May 1, 1934-37, 1941-43.

SANDERS, Morgan Gurley (D Texas) July 14, 1878-Jan. 7, 1956; House 1921-39.

SANDERS, Newell (R Tenn.) July 12, 1850-Jan. 26, 1939; Senate April 11, 1912-Jan. 24, 1913.

SANDERS, Wilbur Fiske (R Mont.) May 2, 1834-July 7, 1905; Senate Jan. 1, 1890-93.

SANDFORD, James T. (— Tenn.) ? - ?; House 1823-25.

SANDFORD, Thomas (D Ky.) 1762-Dec. 10, 1808; House 1803-07.

SANDIDGE, John Milton (D La.) Jan. 7, 1817-March 30, 1890; House 1855-59.

SANDLIN, John Nicholas (D La.) Feb. 24, 1872-Dec. 25, 1957; House 1921-37.

SANDMAN, Charles William Jr. (R N.J.) Oct. 23, 1921-__; House 1967-75.

SANDS, Joshua (— N.Y.) Oct. 12, 1757-Sept. 13, 1835; House 1803-05, 1825-27.

SANFORD, John (father of Stephen Sanford) (D N.Y.) June 3, 1803-Oct. 4, 1857; House 1841-43.

SANFORD, John (son of Stephen Sanford and grandson of the preceding) (R N.Y.) Jan. 18, 1851-Sept. 26, 1939; House 1889-93.

SANFORD, John W. A. (UD Ga.) Aug. 28, 1798-Sept. 12, 1870; House March 4-July 25, 1835.

SANFORD, Jonah (great-grandfather of Rollin Brewster Sanford) (JD N.Y.) Nov. 30, 1790-Dec. 25, 1867; House Nov. 3, 1830-31.

SANFORD, Nathan (D N.Y.) Nov. 4, 1777-Oct. 17, 1838; Senate 1815-21, Jan. 14, 1826-31.

SANFORD, Rollin Brewster (great-grandson of Jonah Sanford) (R N.Y.) May 18, 1874-May 16, 1957; House 1915-21.

SANFORD, Stephen (son of John Sanford born in 1803 and father of John Sanford born in 1851) (R N.Y.) May 26, 1826-Feb. 13, 1913; House 1869-71.

SANTANGELO, Alfred Edward (D N.Y.) June 4, 1912-__; House 1957-63.

SANTINI, James David (D Nev.) Aug. 13, 1937-__; House 1975-__.

SAPP, William Fletcher (nephew of William R. Sapp) (R Iowa) Nov. 20, 1824-Nov. 22, 1890; House 1877-81.

SAPP, William Robinson (uncle of William F. Sapp) (W Ohio) March 4, 1804-Jan. 3, 1875; House 1853-57.

SARASIN, Ronald Arthur (R Conn.) Dec. 31, 1934-__; House 1973-__.

SARBACHER, George William Jr. (R Pa.) Sept. 30, 1919-March 4, 1973; House 1947-49.

SARBANES, Paul Spyros (D Md.) Feb. 3, 1933-__; House 1971-__.

SARGENT, Aaron Augustus (R Calif.) Sept. 28, 1827-Aug. 14, 1887; House 1861-63, 1869-73; Senate 1873-79.

SASSCER, Lansdale Ghiselin (D Md.) Sept. 30, 1893-Nov. 5, 1964; House Feb. 3, 1939-53.

SATTERFIELD, Dave Edward Jr. (father of David E. Satterfield III) (D Va.) Sept. 11, 1894-Dec. 27, 1946; House Nov. 2, 1937-Feb. 15, 1945.

SATTERFIELD, David Edward III (son of the preceding) (D Va.) Dec. 2, 1920; House 1965-__.

SAUERHERING, Edward (R Wis.) June 24, 1864-March 1, 1924; House 1895-99.

SAULSBURY, Eli (brother of Willard Saulsbury) (D Del.) Dec. 29, 1817-March 22, 1893; Senate 1871-89.

SAULSBURY, Willard (brother of Eli Saulsbury) (D Del.) June 2, 1820-April 6, 1892; Senate 1859-71.

SAULSBURY, Willard (son of the preceding) (D Del.) April 17, 1861-Feb. 20, 1927; Senate 1913-19; President pro tempore 1916-19.

SAUND, Daliph Singh (D Calif.) Sept. 20, 1899-April 22, 1973; House 1957-63.

SAUNDERS, Alvin (grandfather of William Henry Harrison of Wyoming) (R Neb.) July 12, 1817-Nov. 1, 1899; Senate March 5, 1877-83; Gov. (Neb. Terr.) 1861-67.

SAUNDERS, Edward Watts (D Va.) Oct. 20, 1860-Dec. 16, 1921; House Nov. 6, 1906-Feb. 29, 1920.

SAUNDERS, Romulus Mitchell (D N.C.) March 3, 1791-April 21, 1867; House 1821-27, 1841-45.

SAUTHOFF, Harry (Pro. Wis.) June 3, 1879-June 16, 1966; House 1935-39, 1941-45.

SAVAGE, Charles Raymon (D Wash.) April 12, 1906-Jan. 14, 1976; House 1945-47.

SAVAGE, John (D N.Y.) Feb. 22, 1779-Oct. 19, 1863; House 1815-19.

SAVAGE, John Houston (— Tenn.) Oct. 9, 1815-April 5, 1904; House 1849-53, 1855-59.

SAVAGE, John Simpson (D Ohio) Oct. 30, 1841-Nov. 24, 1884; House 1875-77.

SAWTELLE, Cullen (D Maine) Sept. 25, 1805-Nov. 10, 1887; House 1845-47, 1849-51.

SAWYER, Frederick Adolphus (R S.C.) Dec. 12, 1822-July 31, 1891; Senate July 16, 1868-73.

SAWYER, John Gilbert (R N.Y.) June 5, 1825-Sept. 5, 1898; House 1885-91.

SAWYER, Lemuel (D N.C.) 1777-Jan. 9, 1852; House 1807-13, 1817-23, 1825-29.

SAWYER, Lewis Ernest (D Ark.) June 24, 1867-May 5, 1923; House March 4-May 5, 1923.

SAWYER, Philetus (R Wis.) Sept. 22, 1816-March 29, 1900; House 1865-75; Senate 1881-93.

SAWYER, Samuel Locke (D Mo.) Nov. 27, 1813-March 29, 1890; House 1879-81.

SAWYER, Samuel Tredwell (D N.C.) 1800-Nov. 29, 1865; House 1837-39.

SAWYER, William (D Ohio) Aug. 5, 1803-Sept. 18, 1877; House 1845-49.

SAXBE, William B. (R Ohio) June 24, 1916-__; Senate 1969-Jan. 3, 1974; Attorney General 1974-75.

SAY, Benjamin (— Pa.) 1756-April 23, 1813; House Nov. 16, 1808-June 1809.

SAYERS, Joseph Draper (D Texas) Sept. 23, 1841-May 15, 1929; House 1885-Jan. 16, 1899; Gov. 1899-1903.

SAYLER, Henry Benton (cousin of Milton Sayler) (R Ind.) March 31, 1836-June 18, 1900; House 1873-75.

SAYLER, Milton (cousin of Henry Benton Sayler) (D Ohio) Nov. 4, 1831-Nov. 17, 1892; House 1873-79.

SAYLOR, John Phillips (R Pa.) July 23, 1908-Oct. 28, 1973; House Sept. 13, 1949-Oct. 28, 1973.

SCALES, Alfred Moore (D N.C.) Nov. 26, 1827-Feb. 9, 1892; House 1857-59, 1875-Dec. 30, 1884; Gov. 1885-89.

SCAMMAN, John Fairfield (D Maine) Oct. 24, 1786-May 22, 1858; House 1845-47.

SCANLON, Thomas Edward (D Pa.) Sept. 18, 1896-Aug. 9, 1955; House 1941-45.

SCARBOROUGH, Robert Bethea (D S.C.) Oct. 29, 1861-Nov. 23, 1927; House 1901-05.

SCHADEBERG, Henry C. (R Wis.) Oct. 12, 1913-—; House 1961-65, 1967-71.

SCHAEFER, Edwin Martin (D Ill.) May 14, 1887-Nov. 8, 1950; House 1933-43.

SCHAFER, John Charles (R Wis.) May 7, 1893-June 9, 1962; House 1923-33, 1939-41.

SCHALL, Thomas David (R Minn.) June 4, 1878-Dec. 22, 1935; House 1915-25; Senate 1925-Dec. 22, 1935.

SCHELL, Richard (D N.Y.) May 15, 1810-Nov. 10, 1879; House Dec. 7, 1874-75.

SCHENCK, Abraham Henry (uncle of Isaac Teller) (D N.Y.) Jan. 22, 1775-June 1, 1831; House 1815-17.

SCHENCK, Ferdinand Schureman (JD N.J.) Feb. 11, 1790-May 16, 1860; House 1833-37.

SCHENCK, Paul Fornshell (R Ohio) April 19, 1899-Nov. 30, 1968; House Nov. 6, 1951-65.

SCHENCK, Robert Cumming (R Ohio) Oct. 4, 1809-March 23, 1890; House 1843-51, 1863-Jan. 5, 1871 (1843-51 Whig, 1863-71 Republican).

SCHERER, Gordon Harry (R Ohio) Dec. 26, 1906-—; House 1953-63.

SCHERLE, William Joseph (R Iowa) March 14, 1923-—; House 1967-75.

SCHERMERHORN, Abraham Maus (W N.Y.) Dec. 11, 1791-Aug. 22, 1855; House 1849-53.

SCHERMERHORN, Simon Jacob (D N.Y.) Sept. 25, 1827-July 21, 1901; House 1893-95.

SCHEUER, James Haas (D N.Y.) Feb. 6, 1920-—; House 1965-73, 1975-—.

SCHIFFLER, Andrew Charles (R W.Va.) Aug. 10, 1889-March 27, 1970; House 1939-41, 1943-45.

SCHIRM, Charles Reginald (R Md.) Aug. 12, 1864-Nov. 2, 1918; House 1901-03.

SCHISLER, Darwin Gale (D Ill.) March 2, 1933-—; House 1965-67.

SCHLEICHER, Gustave (D Texas) Nov. 19, 1823-Jan. 10, 1879; House 1875-Jan. 10, 1879.

SCHLEY, William (D Ga.) Dec.15, 1786-Nov. 20, 1858; House 1833-July 1, 1835; Gov. 1835-37.

SCHMIDHAUSER, John Richard (D Iowa) Jan. 3, 1922-—; House 1965-67.

SCHMITZ, John George (R Calif.) Aug. 12, 1930-—; House June 30, 1970-73.

SCHNEEBELI, Gustav Adolphus (R Pa.) May 23, 1853-Feb. 6, 1923; House 1905-07.

SCHNEEBELI, Herman T. (R Pa.) July 7, 1907-—; House April 26, 1960-—.

SCHNEIDER, George John (Pro. Wis.) Oct. 30, 1877-March 12, 1939; House 1923-33, 1935-39 (1923-33 Republican, 1935-39 Progressive).

SCHOEPPEL, Andrew Frank (R Kan.) Nov. 23, 1894-Jan. 21, 1962; Senate 1949-Jan. 21, 1962; Gov. 1943-47.

SCHOOLCRAFT, John Lawrence (W N.Y.) 1804-July 7, 1860; House 1849-53.

SCHOONMAKER, Cornelius Corneliusen (grandfather of Marius Schoonmaker) (— N.Y.) June 1745-96; House 1791-93.

SCHOONMAKER, Marius (grandson of preceding) (W N.Y.) April 24, 1811-Jan. 5, 1894; House 1851-53.

SCHROEDER, Patricia Scott (D Colo.) July 30, 1940-—; House 1973-—.

SCHUETZ, Leonard William (D Ill.) Nov. 16, 1887-Feb. 13, 1944; House 1931-Feb. 13, 1944.

SCHULTE, William Theodore (D Ind.) Aug. 19, 1890-Dec. 7, 1966; House 1933-43.

SCHULZE, Richard Taylor (R Pa.) Aug. 7, 1929-—; House 1975-—.

SCHUMAKER, John Godfrey (D N.Y.) June 27, 1826-Nov. 23, 1905; House 1869-71, 1873-77.

SCHUNEMAN, Martin Gerretsen (D N.Y.) Feb. 10, 1764-Feb. 21, 1827; House 1805-07.

SCHUREMAN, James (F N.J.) Feb. 12, 1756-Jan. 22, 1824; House 1789-91, 1797-99, 1813-15; Senate 1799-Feb. 16, 1801; Cont. Cong. 1786-87.

SCHURZ, Carl (R Mo.) March 2, 1829-May 14, 1906; Senate 1869-75; Secy. of the Interior 1877-81.

SCHUYLER, Karl Cortlandt (R Colo.) April 3, 1877-July 31, 1933; Senate Dec. 7, 1932-33.

SCHUYLER, Philip Jeremiah (son of Philip John Schuyler) (—N.Y.) Jan. 21, 1768-Feb. 21, 1835; House 1817-19.

SCHUYLER, Philip John (father of Philip Jeremiah Schuyler) (F N.Y.) Nov. 20, 1733-Nov. 18, 1804; Senate 1789-91, 1797-Jan. 3, 1798; Cont. Cong. 1775-81.

SCHWABE, George Blaine (brother of Max Schwabe) (R Okla.) July 26, 1886-April 2, 1952; House 1945-49, 1951-April 2, 1952.

SCHWABE, Max (brother of George Blaine Schwabe) (R Mo.) Dec. 6, 1905-—; House 1943-49.

SCHWARTZ, Henry Herman (Harry) (D Wyo.) May 18, 1869-April 24, 1955; Senate 1937-43.

SCHWARTZ, John (D Pa.) Oct. 27, 1793-June 20, 1860; House 1859-June 20, 1860.

SCHWEIKER, Richard Schultz (R Pa.) June 1, 1926-—; House 1961-69; Senate 1969-—.

SCHWELLENBACH, Lewis Baxter (D Wash.) Sept. 20, 1894-June 10, 1948; Senate 1935-Dec. 16, 1940; Secy. of Labor 1945-48.

SCHWENGEL, Frederick Delbert (R Iowa) May 28, 1907-—; House 1955-65, 1967-73.

SCHWERT, Pius Louis (D N.Y.) Nov. 22, 1892-March 11, 1941; House 1939-March 11, 1941.

SCOBLICK, James Paul (R Pa.) May 10, 1909-—; House Nov. 5, 1946-49.

SCOFIELD, Glenni William (R Pa.) March 11, 1817-Aug. 30, 1891; House 1863-75.

SCOTT, Byron Nicholson (D Calif.) March 21, 1903-—; House 1935-39.

SCOTT, Charles Frederick (R Kan.) Sept. 7, 1860-Sept. 18, 1938; House 1901-11.

SCOTT, Charles Lewis (D Calif.) Jan. 23, 1827-April 30, 1899; House 1857-61.

SCOTT, David (— Pa.) ? - ?; House 1817.

SCOTT, Frank Douglas (R Mich.) Aug. 25, 1878-Feb. 12, 1951; House 1915-27.

SCOTT, George Cromwell (R Iowa) Aug. 8, 1864-Oct. 6, 1948; House Nov. 5, 1912-15, 1917-19.

SCOTT, Hardie (son of John Roger Kirkpatrick Scott) (R Pa.) June 7, 1907-—; House 1947-53.

SCOTT, Harvey David (R Ind.) Oct. 18, 1818-July 11, 1891; House 1855-57.

SCOTT, Hugh Doggett Jr. (R Pa.) Nov. 11, 1900-—; House 1941-45, 1947-59; Senate 1959-—; Chrmn. Rep. Nat. Comm. 1948-49.

SCOTT, John (— Mo.) May 18, 1785-Oct. 1, 1861; House (Terr. Del.) Aug. 6, 1816-Jan. 13, 1817, Aug. 5, 1817-March 3, 1821, (Rep.) Aug. 10, 1821-27.

SCOTT, John (— Pa.) Dec. 25, 1784-Sept. 22, 1850; House 1829-31.

SCOTT, John (son of the preceding) (R Pa.) July 24, 1824-Nov. 29, 1896; Senate 1869-75.

SCOTT, John Guier (D Mo.) Dec. 26, 1819-May 16, 1892; House Dec. 7, 1863-65.

SCOTT, John Roger Kirkpatrick (father of Hardie Scott) (R Pa.) July 6, 1873-Dec. 9, 1945; House 1915-Jan. 5, 1919.

SCOTT, Lon Allen (R Tenn.) Sept. 25, 1888-Feb. 11, 1931; House 1921-23.

SCOTT, Nathan Bay (R W.Va.) Dec. 18, 1842-Jan. 2, 1924; Senate 1899-1911.

SCOTT, Owen (D Ill.) July 6, 1848-Dec. 21, 1928; House 1891-93.

SCOTT, Ralph James (D N.C.) Oct. 15, 1905-—; House 1957-67.

SCOTT, Thomas (— Pa.) 1739-March 2, 1796; House 1789-91, 1793-95.

SCOTT, William Kerr (D N.C.) April 17, 1896-April 16, 1958; Senate Nov. 29, 1954-April 16, 1958; Gov. 1949-53.

SCOTT, William Lawrence (D Pa.) July 2, 1828-Sept. 19, 1891; House 1885-89.

SCOTT, William Lloyd (R Va.) July 1, 1915-—; House 1967-73; Senate 1973-—.

SCOVILLE, Jonathan (D N.Y.) July 14, 1830-March 4, 1891; House Nov. 12, 1880-83.

SCRANTON, George Whitfield (second cousin of Joseph Augustine Scranton) (R Pa.) May 11, 1811-March 24, 1861; House 1859-March 24, 1861.

SCRANTON, Joseph Augustine (second cousin of George Whitfield Scranton) (R Pa.) July 26, 1838-Oct. 12, 1908; House 1881-83, 1885-87, 1889-91, 1893-97.

SCRANTON, William Warren (R Pa.) July 19, 1917-—; House 1961-63; Gov. 1963-67.

SCRIVNER, Errett Power (R Kan.) March 20, 1898-—; House Sept. 14, 1943-59.

SCROGGY, Thomas Edmund (R Ohio) March 18, 1843-March 6, 1915; House 1905-07.

SCRUGHAM, James Graves (D Nev.) Jan. 19, 1880-June 23, 1945; House 1933-Dec. 7, 1942; Senate Dec. 7, 1942-June 23, 1945; Gov. 1923-27.

SCUDDER, Henry Joel (uncle of Townsend Scudder) (R N.Y.) Sept. 18, 1825-Feb. 10, 1886; House 1873-75.

SCUDDER, Hubert Baxter (R Calif.) Nov. 5, 1888-July 4, 1968; House 1949-59.

SCUDDER, Isaac Williamson (R N.J.) 1816-Sept. 10, 1881; House 1873-75.

SCUDDER, John Anderson (D N.J.) March 22, 1759-Nov. 6, 1836; House Oct. 31, 1810-11.

SCUDDER, Townsend (nephew of Henry Joel Scudder) (D N.Y.) July 26, 1865-Feb. 22, 1960; House 1899-1901, 1903-05.

SCUDDER, Tredwell (—N.Y.) Jan. 1, 1778-Oct. 31, 1834; House 1817-19.

SCUDDER, Zeno (W Mass.) Aug. 18, 1807-June 26, 1857; House 1851-March 4, 1854.

SCULL, Edward (R Pa.) Feb. 5, 1818-July 10, 1900; House 1887-93.

SCULLY, Thomas Joseph (D N.J.) Sept. 19, 1868-Dec. 14, 1921; House 1911-21.

SCURRY, Richardson (D Texas) Nov. 11, 1811-April 9, 1862; House 1851-53.

SEAMAN, Henry John (AP N.Y.) April 16, 1805-May 3, 1861; House 1845-47.

SEARING, John Alexander (D N.Y.) May 14, 1805-May 6, 1876; House 1857-59.

SEARS, William Joseph (D Fla.) Dec. 4, 1874-March 30, 1944; House 1915-29, 1933-37.

SEARS, Willis Gratz (R Neb.) Aug. 16, 1860-June 1, 1949; House 1923-31.

SEATON, Frederick Andrew (R Neb.) Dec. 11, 1909-Jan. 16, 1974; Senate Dec. 10, 1951-Nov. 4, 1952; Secy. of the Interior 1956-61.

SEAVER, Ebenezer (D Mass.) July 5, 1763-March 1, 1844; House 1803-13.

SEBASTIAN, William King (D Ark.) 1812-May 20, 1865; Senate May 12, 1848-July 11, 1861.

SEBELIUS, Keith G. (R Kan.) Sept. 10, 1916-—; House 1969-—.

SECCOMBE, James (R Ohio) Feb. 12, 1893-Aug. 23, 1970; House 1939-41.

SECREST, Robert Thompson (D Ohio) Jan. 22, 1904-—; House 1933-Aug. 3, 1942, 1949-Sept. 26, 1954, 1963-Jan. 3, 1967.

SEDDON, James Alexander (D Va.) July 13, 1815-Aug. 19, 1880; House 1845-47, 1849-51.

SEDGWICK, Charles Baldwin (R N.Y.) March 15, 1815-Feb. 3, 1883; House 1859-63.

SEDGWICK, Theodore (F Mass.) May 9, 1746-Jan. 24, 1813; House 1789-June 1796, 1799-1801; Senate June 11, 1796-99; Speaker 1799-1801; President pro tempore 1798; Cont. Cong. 1785-88.

SEELEY, John Edward (R N.Y.) Aug. 1, 1810-March 30, 1875; House 1871-73.

SEELY-BROWN, Horace Jr. (R Conn.) May 12, 1908-—; House 1947-49, 1951-59, 1961-63.

SEELYE, Julius Hawley (I Mass.) Sept. 14, 1824-May 12, 1895; House 1875-77.

SEERLEY, John Joseph (D Iowa) March 13, 1852-Feb. 23, 1931; House 1891-93.

SEGAR, Joseph Eggleston (U Va.) June 1, 1804-April 30, 1880; House March 15, 1862-63.

SEGER, George Nicholas (R N.J.) Jan. 4, 1866-Aug. 26, 1940; House 1923-Aug. 26, 1940.

SEIBERLING, Francis (R Ohio) Sept. 20, 1870-Feb. 1, 1945; House 1929-33.

SEIBERLING, John Frederick (D Ohio) Sept. 8, 1918-—; House 1971-—.

SELBY, Thomas Jefferson (D Ill.) Dec. 4, 1840-March 10, 1917; House 1901-03.

SELDEN, Armistead Inge Jr. (D Ala.) Feb. 20, 1921-—; House 1953-69.

SELDEN, Dudley (D N.Y.) ?-Nov. 7, 1855; House 1833-July 1, 1834.

SELDOMRIDGE, Harry Hunter (D Colo.) Oct. 1, 1864-Nov. 2, 1927; House 1913-15.

SELLS, Sam Riley (R Tenn.) Aug. 2, 1871-Nov. 2, 1935; House 1911-21.

SELVIG, Conrad George (R Minn.) Oct. 11, 1877-Aug. 2, 1953; House 1927-33.

SELYE, Lewis (I N.Y.) July 11, 1803-Jan. 27, 1883; House 1867-69.

SEMMES, Benedict Joseph (D Md.) Nov. 1, 1789-Feb. 10, 1863; House 1829-33.

SEMPLE, James (D Ill.) Jan. 5, 1798-Dec. 20, 1866; Senate Dec. 4, 1843-47.

SENER, James Beverley (R Va.) May 18, 1837-Nov. 18, 1903; House 1873-75.

SENEY, George Ebbert (D Ohio) May 29, 1832-June 11, 1905; House 1883-91.

SENEY, Joshua (— Md.) March 4, 1756-Oct. 20, 1798; House 1789-May 1, 1792; Cont. Cong. 1787-88.

SENNER, George Frederick Jr. (D Ariz.) Nov. 24, 1921-—; House 1963-67.

SENTER, William Tandy (W Tenn.) May 12, 1801-Aug. 28, 1848; House 1843-45.

SERGEANT, John (grandfather of John Sergeant Wise and Richard Alsop Wise, and great-grandfather of John Crain Kunkel) (F Pa.) Dec. 5, 1779-Nov. 23, 1852; House Oct. 10, 1815-23, 1827-29, 1837-Sept. 15, 1841.

SESSINGHAUS, Gustavus (R Mo.) Nov. 8, 1838-Nov. 16, 1887; House March 2-3, 1883.

SESSIONS, Walter Loomis (R N.Y.) Oct. 4, 1820-May 27, 1896; House 1871-75, 1885-87.

SETTLE, Evan Evans (D Ky.) Dec. 1, 1848-Nov. 16, 1899; House 1897-Nov. 16, 1899.

SETTLE, Thomas (uncle of David Settle Reid) (D N.C.) March 9, 1789-Aug. 5, 1857; House 1817-21.

SETTLE, Thomas (grandson of the preceding) (R N.C.) March 10, 1865-Jan. 20, 1919; House 1893-97.

SEVERANCE, Luther (W Maine) Oct. 26, 1797-Jan. 25, 1855; House 1843-47.

SEVIER, Ambrose Hundley (cousin of Henry Wharton Conway) (D Ark.) Nov. 10, 1801-Dec. 31, 1848; House (Terr. Del.) Feb. 13, 1828-June 15, 1836 (W); Senate Sept. 18, 1836-March 15, 1848 (D).

SEVIER, John (D N.C./Tenn.) Sept. 23, 1745-Sept. 24, 1815; House 1789-91 (N.C.) 1811-Sept. 24, 1815 (Tenn.); Gov. (Tenn.) 1796-1801, 1803-09.

SEWALL, Charles S. (—Md.) 1779-Nov. 3, 1848; House Oct. 1, 1832-33, Jan. 2-March 3, 1843.

SEWALL, Samuel (— Mass.) Dec. 11, 1757-June 8, 1814; House Dec. 7, 1796-Jan. 10, 1800.

SEWARD, James Lindsay (D Ga.) Oct. 30, 1813-Nov. 21, 1886; House 1853-59.

SEWARD, William Henry (R N.Y.) May 16, 1801-Oct. 16, 1872; Senate 1849-61 (1849-55 Whig, 1855-61 Republican); Secy of State 1861-69; Gov. 1839-43.

SEWELL, William Joyce (R N.J.) Dec. 6, 1835-Dec. 27, 1901; Senate 1881-87, 1895-Dec. 27, 1901.

SEXTON, Leonidas (R Ind.) May 19, 1827-July 4, 1880; House 1877-79.

SEYBERT, Adam (D Pa.) May 16, 1773-May 2, 1825; House Oct. 10, 1809-15, 1817-19.

SEYMOUR, David Lowrey (D N.Y.) Dec. 2, 1803-Oct. 11, 1867; House 1843-45, 1851-53.

SEYMOUR, Edward Woodruff (son of Origen Storrs Seymour) (D Conn.) Aug. 30, 1832-Oct. 16, 1892; House 1883-87.

SEYMOUR, Henry William (R Mich.) July 21, 1834-April 7, 1906; House Feb. 14, 1888-89.

SEYMOUR, Horatio (uncle of Origen Storrs Seymour) (CD Vt.) May 31, 1778-Nov. 21, 1857; Senate 1821-33.

SEYMOUR, Origen Storrs (father of Edward Woodruff Seymour and nephew of Horatio Seymour) (D Conn.) Feb. 9, 1804-Aug. 12, 1881; House 1851-55.

SEYMOUR, Thomas Hart (D Conn.) Sept. 29, 1807-Sept. 3, 1868; House 1843-45; Gov. 1850-53.

SEYMOUR, William (D N.Y.) about 1780-Dec. 28, 1848; House 1835-37.

SHACKELFORD, John Williams (D N.C.) Nov. 16, 1844-Jan. 18, 1883; House 1881-Jan. 18, 1883.

SHACKLEFORD, Dorsey William (D Mo.) Aug. 27, 1853-July 15, 1936; House Aug. 29, 1899-1919.

SHAFER, Jacob K. (D Idaho) Dec. 26, 1823-Nov. 22, 1876; House (Terr. Del.) 1869-71.

SHAFER, Paul Werntz (R Mich.) April 27, 1893-Aug. 17, 1954; House 1937-Aug. 17, 1954.

SHAFFER, Joseph Crockett (R Va.) Jan. 19, 1880-Oct. 19, 1958; House 1929-31.

SHAFROTH, John Franklin (D Colo.) June 9, 1854-Feb. 20, 1922; House 1895-Feb. 15, 1904 (1895-97 Republican, 1897-1903 Silver Republican/Democrat, 1903-04 Democrat); Senate 1913-19; Gov. 1909-13.

SHALLENBERGER, Ashton Cokayne (D Neb.) Dec. 23, 1862-Feb. 22, 1938; House 1901-03, 1915-19, 1923-29, 1931-35; Gov. 1909-11.

SHALLENBERGER, William Shadrack (R Pa.) Nov. 24, 1839-April 15, 1914; House 1877-83.

SHANKLIN, George Sea (D Ky.) Dec. 23, 1807-April 1, 1883; House 1865-67.

SHANKS, John Peter Cleaver (R Ind.) June 17, 1826-Jan. 23, 1901; House 1861-63, 1867-75.

SHANLEY, James Andrew (D Conn.) April 1, 1896-April 5, 1965; House 1935-43.

SHANNON, Joseph Bernard (D Mo.) March 17, 1867-March 28, 1943; House 1931-43.

SHANNON, Richard Cutts (R N.Y.) Feb. 12, 1839-Oct. 5, 1920; House 1895-99.

SHANNON, Thomas (brother of Wilson Shannon) (D Ohio) Nov. 15, 1786-March 16, 1843; House Dec. 4, 1826-27.

SHANNON, Thomas Bowles (R Calif.) Sept. 21, 1827-Feb. 21, 1897; House 1863-65.

SHANNON, Wilson (brother of Thomas Shannon) (D Ohio) Feb. 24, 1802-Aug. 31, 1877; House 1853-55; Gov. of Ohio 1838-40, 1842-44; Gov. Kansas Terr. 1855-56.

SHARON, William (R Neb.) Jan. 9, 1821-Nov. 13, 1885; Senate 1875-81.

SHARP, Edgar Allan (R N.Y.) June 3, 1876-Nov. 27, 1948; House 1945-47.

SHARP, Philip Riley (D Ind.) July 15, 1942-—; House 1975-—.

SHARP, Solomon P. (D Ky.) 1780-Nov. 7, 1825; House 1813-17.

SHARP, William Graves (D Ohio) March 14, 1859-Nov. 17, 1922; House 1909-July 23, 1914.

SHARPE, Peter (— N.Y.) ? - ?; House 1823-25.

SHARTEL, Cassius McLean (R Mo.) April 27, 1860-Sept. 27, 1943; House 1905-07.

SHATTUC, William Bunn (R Ohio) June 11, 1841-July 13, 1911; House 1897-1903.

SHAW, Aaron (D Ill.) Dec. 19, 1811-Jan. 7, 1887; House 1857-59, 1883-85.

SHAW, Albert Duane (R N.Y.) Dec. 21, 1841-Feb. 10, 1901; House Nov. 6, 1900-Feb. 10, 1901.

SHAW, Frank Thomas (D Md.) Oct. 7, 1841-Feb. 24, 1923; House 1885-89.

SHAW, George Bullen (R Wis.) March 12, 1854-Aug. 27, 1894; House 1893-Aug. 27, 1894.

SHAW, Guy Loren (R Ill.) May 16, 1881-May 19, 1950; House 1921-23.

SHAW. Henry (son of Samuel Shaw) (F Mass.) 1788-Oct. 17, 1857; House 1817-21.

SHAW, Henry Marchmore (D N.C.) Nov. 20, 1819-Nov. 1, 1864; House 1853-55, 1857-59.

SHAW, John Gilbert (D N.C.) Jan. 16, 1859-July 21, 1932; House 1895-97.

SHAW, Samuel (father of Henry Shaw) (D Vt.) Dec. 1768- Oct. 23, 1827; House Sept. 6, 1808-13.

SHAW, Tristram (— N.H.) May 23, 1786-March 14, 1843; House 1839-43.

SHEAFE, James (F N.H.) Nov. 16, 1755-Dec. 5, 1829; House 1799-1801; Senate 1801-June 14, 1802.

SHEAKLEY, James (D Pa.) April 24, 1829-Dec. 10, 1917; House 1875-77; Gov. of Alaska Terr. 1893-97.

SHEATS, Charles Christopher (R Ala.) April 10, 1839-May 27, 1904; House 1873-75.

SHEEHAN, Timothy Patrick (R Ill.) Feb. 21, 1909-—; House 1951-59.

SHEFFER, Daniel (D Pa.) May 24, 1783-Feb. 16, 1880; House 1837-39.

SHEFFEY, Daniel (F Va.) 1770-Dec. 3, 1830; House 1809-17.

SHEFFIELD, William Paine (R R.I.) Aug. 30, 1820-June 2, 1907; House 1861-63; Senate Nov. 19, 1884-Jan. 20, 1885.

SHEFFIELD, William Paine (son of the preceding) (R R.I.) June 1, 1857-Oct. 19, 1919; House 1909-11.

SHELDEN, Carlos Douglas (R Mich.) June 10, 1840-June 24, 1904; House 1897-1903.

SHELDON, Lionel Allen (R La.) Aug. 30, 1828-Jan. 17, 1917; House 1869-75; Gov. Terr. of N.M. 1881-85.

SHELDON, Porter (R N.Y.) Sept. 29, 1831-Aug. 15, 1908; House 1869-71.

SHELL, George Washington (D S.C.) Nov. 13, 1831-Dec. 15, 1899; House 1891-95.

SHELLABARGER, Samuel (R Ohio) Dec. 10, 1817-Aug. 7, 1896; House 1861-63, 1865-69, 1871-73.

SHELLEY, Charles Miller (D Ala.) Dec. 28, 1833-Jan. 20, 1907; House 1877-81, Nov. 7, 1882-Jan. 9, 1885.

SHELLEY, John Francis (D Calif.) Sept. 3, 1905-Sept. 1, 1974; House Nov. 8, 1949-Jan. 7, 1964.

SHELTON, Samuel Azariah (R Mo.) Sept. 3, 1858-Sept. 13, 1948; House 1921-23.

SHEPARD, Charles Biddle (D N.C.) Dec. 5, 1807-Oct. 31, 1843; House 1837-41.

SHEPARD, William (— Mass.) Dec. 1, 1737-Nov. 16, 1817; House 1797-1803.

SHEPARD, William Biddle (NR N.C.) May 14, 1799-June 20, 1852; House 1829-37.

SHEPLER, Matthias (D Ohio) Nov. 11, 1790-April 7, 1863; House 1837-39.

SHEPLEY, Ether (D Maine) Nov. 2, 1789-Jan. 15, 1877; Senate 1833-March 3, 1836.

SHEPPARD, Harry Richard (D Calif.) Jan. 10, 1885-April 28, 1969; House 1937-65.

SHEPPARD, John Levi (father of Morris Sheppard) (D Texas) April 13, 1852-Oct. 11, 1902; House 1899-Oct. 11, 1902.

SHEPPARD, Morris (son of John Levi Sheppard) (D Texas) May 28, 1875-April 9, 1941; House Nov. 15, 1902-Feb. 3, 1913; Senate Feb. 3, 1913-April 9, 1941.

SHEPPERD, Augustine Henry (W N.C.) Feb. 24, 1792-July 11, 1864; House 1827-39, 1841-43, 1847-51.

SHERBURNE, John Samuel (— N.H.) 1757-Aug. 2, 1830; House 1793-97.

SHEREDINE, Upton (D Md.) 1740-Jan. 14, 1800; House 1791-93.

SHERIDAN, George Augustus (L La.) Feb. 22, 1840-Oct. 7, 1896; House 1873-75.

SHERIDAN, John Edward (D Pa.) Sept. 15, 1902-—; House Nov. 7, 1939-47.

SHERLEY, Joseph Swagar (D Ky.) Nov. 28, 1871-Feb. 13, 1941; House 1903-19.

SHERMAN, James Schoolcraft (R N.Y.) Oct. 24, 1855-Oct. 30, 1912; House 1887-91, 1893-1909; Vice Pres. 1909-Oct. 30, 1912.

SHERMAN, John (R Ohio) May 10, 1823-Oct. 22, 1900; House 1855-March 21, 1861; Senate March 21, 1861-March 8, 1877, 1881-March 4, 1897; Secy. of the Treasury 1877-81; Secy. of State 1897-98.

SHERMAN, Judson W. (R N.Y.) 1808-Nov. 12, 1881; House 1857-59.

SHERMAN, Lawrence Yates (R Ill.) Nov. 8, 1858-Sept. 15, 1939; Senate March 26, 1913-21.

SHERMAN, Roger (— Conn.) April 19, 1721-July 23, 1793; House 1789-91; Senate June

13, 1791-July 23, 1793; Cont. Cong. 1774-81, 1783-84.

SHERMAN, Socrates Norton (R N.Y.) July 22, 1801-Feb. 1, 1873; House 1861-63.

SHERRILL, Eliakim (W N.Y.) Feb. 16, 1813-July 4, 1863; House 1847-49.

SHERROD, William Crawford (D Ala.) Aug. 17, 1835-March 24, 1919; House 1869-71.

SHERWIN, John Crocker (R Ill.) Feb. 8, 1838-Jan. 1, 1904; House 1879-83.

SHERWOOD, Henry (D Pa.) Oct. 9, 1813-Nov. 10, 1896; House 1871-73.

SHERWOOD, Isaac R. (D Ohio) Aug. 13, 1835-Oct. 15, 1925; House 1873-75, 1907-21, 1923-25 (1873-75 Republican, 1907-21 and 1923-25 Democrat).

SHERWOOD, Samuel (F N.Y.) April 24, 1779-Oct. 31, 1862; House 1813-15.

SHERWOOD, Samuel Burr (F Conn.) Nov. 26, 1767-April 27, 1833; House 1817-19.

SHIEL, George Knox (D Ore.) 1825-Dec. 12, 1893; House July 30, 1861-63.

SHIELDS, Benjamin Glover (W Ala.) 1808-?; House 1841-43.

SHIELDS, Ebenezer J. (W Tenn.) Dec. 22, 1778-April 21, 1846; House 1835-39.

SHIELDS, James (JD Ohio) April 13, 1762-Aug. 13, 1831; House 1829-31.

SHIELDS, James (nephew of the preceding) (D Ill./Minn./Mo.) May 10, 1810-June 1, 1879; Senate March 6-15, 1849, Oct. 27, 1849-55 (Ill.), May 11, 1858-59 (Minn.), Jan. 27-March 3, 1879 (Mo.).

SHIELDS, John Knight (D Tenn.) Aug. 15, 1858-Sept. 30, 1934; Senate 1913-25.

SHINN, William Norton (JD N.J.) Oct. 24, 1782-Aug. 18, 1871; House 1833-37.

SHIPHERD, Zebulon Rudd (F N.Y.) Nov. 15, 1768-Nov. 1, 1841; House 1813-15.

SHIPLEY, George Edward (D Ill.) April 21, 1927-__; House 1959-__.

SHIPSTEAD, Henrik (R Minn.) Jan. 8, 1881-June 26, 1960; Senate 1923-47 (1923-41 Farmer Laborite, 1941-47 Republican).

SHIRAS, George 3d (IR Pa.) Jan. 1, 1859-March 24, 1942; House 1903-05.

SHIVELY, Benjamin Franklin (D Ind.) March 20, 1857-March 14, 1916; House Dec. 1, 1884-85, 1887-93 (1884-85 National Anti Monopolist, 1887-93 Democrat); Senate 1909-March 14, 1916 (D).

SHOBER, Francis Edwin (father of Francis Emanuel Shober) (D N.C.) March 12, 1831-May 29, 1896; House 1869-73.

SHOBER, Francis Emanuel (son of Francis Edwin Shober) (D N.Y.) Oct. 24, 1860-Oct. 7, 1919; House 1903-05.

SHOEMAKER, Francis Henry (FL Minn.) April 25, 1889-July 24, 1958; House 1933-35.

SHOEMAKER, Lazarus Denison (R Pa.) Nov. 5, 1819-Sept. 9, 1893; House 1871-75.

SHONK, George Washington (R Pa.) April 26, 1850-Aug. 14, 1900; House 1891-93.

SHORT, Dewey Jackson (R Mo.) April 7, 1898-__; House 1929-31, 1935-57.

SHORT, Don Levingston (R N.D.) June 22, 1903-__; House 1959-65.

SHORTER, Eli Sims (D Ala.) March 15, 1823-April 29, 1879; House 1855-59.

SHORTRIDGE, Samuel Morgan (R Calif.) Aug. 3, 1861-Jan. 15, 1952; Senate 1921-33.

SHOTT, Hugh Ike (R W.Va.) Sept. 3, 1866-Oct. 12, 1953; House 1929-33; Senate Nov. 18, 1942-43.

SHOUP, George Laird (grandfather of Richard G. Shoup) (R Idaho) June 15, 1836-Dec. 21, 1904; Senate Dec. 18, 1890-1901; Gov. (Idaho Terr.) 1889-90; Gov. Oct. 1-Dec. 1890.

SHOUP, Richard Garner (grandson of George Laird Shoup) (R Mont.) Nov. 29, 1923-__; House 1971-75.

SHOUSE, Jouett (D Kan.) Dec. 10, 1879-June 2, 1968; House 1915-19.

SHOWALTER, Joseph Baltzell (R Pa.) Feb. 11, 1851-Dec. 3, 1932; House April 20, 1897-1903.

SHOWER, Jacob (I Md.) Feb. 22, 1803-May 25, 1879; House 1853-55.

SHREVE, Milton William (R Pa.) May 3, 1858-Dec. 23, 1939; House 1913-15, 1919-33.

SHRIVER, Garner E. (R Kan.) July 6, 1912-__; House 1961-__.

SHUFORD, Alonzo Craig (P N.C.) March 1, 1858-Feb. 8, 1933; House 1895-99.

SHUFORD, George Adams (D N.C.) Sept. 5, 1895-Dec. 8, 1962; House 1953-59.

SHULL, Joseph Horace (D Pa.) Aug. 17, 1848-Aug. 9, 1944; House 1903-05.

SHULTZ, Emanuel (R Ohio) July 25, 1819-Nov. 5, 1912; House 1881-83.

SHUSTER, E. G. (Bud) (R Pa.) Jan. 23, 1932-__; House 1973-__.

SIBAL, Abner Woodruff (R Conn.) April 11, 1921-__; House 1961-65.

SIBLEY, Henry Hastings (son of Solomon Sibley) (— Wis./Minn.) Feb. 20, 1811-Feb. 18, 1891; House (Terr. Del.) Oct. 30, 1848-49 (Wis.), July 7, 1849-53 (Minn.); Gov. of Minn. 1858-60.

SIBLEY, Jonas (D Mass.) March 7, 1762-Feb. 5, 1834; House 1823-25.

SIBLEY, Joseph Crocker (R Pa.) Feb. 18, 1850-May 19, 1926; House 1893-95, 1899-1907 (1893-95 Democrat/People's Party/Prohibitionist, 1899-1901 Democrat, 1901-07 Republican).

SIBLEY, Mark Hopkins (W N.Y.) 1796-Sept. 8, 1852; House 1837-39.

SIBLEY, Solomon (father of Henry Hastings Sibley) (— Mich.) Oct. 7, 1769-April 4, 1846; House (Terr. Del.) Nov. 20, 1820-23.

SICKLES, Carlton R. (D Md.) June 15, 1921-__; House 1963-67.

SICKLES, Daniel Edgar (D N.Y.) Oct. 10, 1825-May 3, 1914; House 1857-61, 1893-95.

SICKLES, Nicholas (D N.Y.) Sept. 11, 1801-May 13, 1845; House 1835-37.

SIEGEL, Isaac (R N.Y.) April 12, 1880-June 29, 1947; House 1915-23.

SIEMINSKI, Alfred Dennis (D N.J.) Aug. 23, 1911-__; House 1951-59.

SIKES, Robert Louis Fulton (D Fla.) June 3, 1906-__; House 1941-Oct. 19, 1944, 1945-__.

SILER, Eugene (R Ky.) June 26, 1900-__; House 1955-65.

SILL, Thomas Hale (NR Pa.) Oct. 11, 1783-Feb. 7, 1856; House March 14, 1826-27, 1829-31.

SILSBEE, Nathaniel (D Mass.) Jan. 14, 1773-July 14, 1850; House 1817-21; Senate May 31, 1826-35.

SILVESTER, Peter (grandfather of Peter Henry Silvester) (— N.Y.) 1734-Oct. 15, 1808; House 1789-93.

SILVESTER, Peter Henry (grandson of Peter Silvester) (W N.Y.) Feb. 17, 1807-Nov. 29, 1882; House 1847-51.

SIMKINS, Eldred (D S.C.) Aug. 30, 1779-Nov. 17, 1831; House Jan. 24, 1818-21.

SIMMONS, Furnifold McLendel (D N.C.) Jan. 20, 1854-April 30, 1940; House 1887-89; Senate 1901-31.

SIMMONS, George Abel (W N.Y.) Sept. 8, 1791-Oct. 27, 1857; House 1853-57.

SIMMONS, James Fowler (W R.I.) Sept. 10, 1795-July 10, 1864; Senate 1841-47, 1857-Aug. 15, 1862.

SIMMONS, James Samuel (nephew of Milton George Urner) (R N.Y.) Nov. 25, 1861-Nov. 28, 1935; House 1909-13.

SIMMONS, Robert Glenmore (R Neb.) Dec. 25, 1891-Dec. 27, 1969; House 1923-33.

SIMMS, Albert Gallatin (husband of Ruth Hanna McCormick) (R N.M.) Oct. 8, 1882-Dec. 29, 1964; House 1929-31.

SIMMS, William Emmett (D Ky.) Jan. 2, 1822-June 25, 1898; House 1859-61.

SIMON, Joseph (R Ore.) Feb. 7, 1851-Feb. 14, 1935; Senate Oct. 8, 1898-1903.

SIMON, Paul Martin (D Ill.) Nov. 29, 1928-__; House 1975-__.

SIMONDS, William Edgar (R Conn.) Nov. 24, 1842-March 14, 1903; House 1889-91.

SIMONS, Samuel (D Conn.) 1792-Jan. 13, 1847; House 1843-45.

SIMONTON, Charles Bryson (D Tenn.) Sept. 8, 1838-June 10, 1911; House 1879-83.

SIMONTON, William (W Pa.) Feb. 12, 1788-May 17, 1846; House 1839-43.

SIMPKINS, John (R Mass.) June 27, 1862-March 27, 1898; House 1895-March 27, 1898.

SIMPSON, Edna Oakes (widow of Sidney E. Simpson) (R Ill.) Oct. 28, 1891-___; House 1959-61.

SIMPSON, James Jr. (R Ill.) Jan. 7, 1905-Feb. 29, 1960; House 1933-35.

SIMPSON, Jeremiah (Jerry) (P Kan.) March 31, 1842-Oct. 23, 1905; House 1891-95, 1897-99.

SIMPSON, Kenneth Farrand (R N.Y.) May 4, 1895-Jan. 25, 1941; House Jan. 3-Jan. 25, 1941.

SIMPSON, Milward Lee (R Wyo.) Nov. 12, 1897-___; Senate Nov. 7, 1962-67; Gov. 1955-59.

SIMPSON, Richard Franklin (D S.C.) March 24, 1798-Oct. 28, 1882; House 1843-49.

SIMPSON, Richard Murray (R Pa.) Aug. 30, 1900-Jan. 7, 1960; House May 11, 1937-Jan. 7, 1960.

SIMPSON, Sidney Elmer (Sid) (husband of Edna Oakes Simpson) (R Ill.) Sept. 20, 1894-Oct. 26, 1958; House 1943-Oct. 26, 1958.

SIMS, Alexander Dromgoole (nephew of George Coke Dromgoole) (D S.C.) June 12, 1803-Nov. 22, 1848; House 1845-Nov. 22, 1848.

SIMS, Hugo Sheridan Jr. (D S.C.) Oct. 14, 1921-___; House 1949-51.

SIMS, Leonard Henly (D Mo.) Feb. 6, 1807-Feb. 28, 1886; House 1845-47.

SIMS, Thetus Willrette (D Tenn.) April 25, 1852-Dec. 17, 1939; House 1897-1921.

SINCLAIR, James Herbert (R N.D.) Oct. 9, 1871-Sept. 5, 1943; House 1919-35.

SINGISER, Theodore Frelinghuysen (R Idaho) March 15, 1845-Jan. 23, 1907; House (Terr. Del.) 1883-85.

SINGLETON, James Washington (D Ill.) Nov. 23, 1811-April 4, 1892; House 1879-83.

SINGLETON, Otho Robards (D Miss.) Oct. 14, 1814-Jan. 11, 1889; House 1853-55, 1857-Jan. 12, 1861, 1875-87.

SINGLETON, Thomas Day (N S.C.) ?-Nov. 25, 1833; House March 3-Nov. 25, 1833.

SINNICKSON, Clement Hall (grandnephew of Thomas Sinnickson) (R N.J.) Sept. 16, 1834-July 24, 1919; House 1875-79.

SINNICKSON, Thomas (granduncle of Clement Hall Sinnickson) (— N.J.) Dec. 21, 1744-May 15, 1817; House 1789-91, 1797-99.

SINNICKSON, Thomas (nephew of the preceding) (— N.J.) Dec. 13, 1786-Feb. 17, 1873; House Dec. 1, 1828-29.

SINNOTT, Nicholas John (R Ore.) Dec. 6, 1870-July 20, 1929; House 1913-May 31, 1928.

SIPE, William Allen (D Pa.) July 1, 1844-Sept. 10, 1935; House Dec. 5, 1892-95.

SIROVICH, William Irving (D N.Y.) March 18, 1882-Dec. 17, 1939; House 1927-Dec. 17, 1939.

SISK, Bernice Frederic (D Calif.) Dec. 14, 1910-___; House 1955-___.

SISSON, Frederick James (D N.Y.) March 31, 1879-Oct. 20, 1949; House 1933-37.

SISSON, Thomas Upton (D Miss.) Sept. 22, 1869-Sept. 26, 1923; House 1909-23.

SITES, Frank Crawford (D Pa.) Dec. 24, 1864-May 23, 1935; House 1923-25.

SITGREAVES, Charles (D N.J.) April 22, 1803-March 17, 1878; House 1865-69.

SITGREAVES, Samuel (F Pa.) March 16, 1764-April 4, 1827; House 1795-98.

SITTLER, Edward Lewis Jr. (R Pa.) April 21, 1908-___; House 1951-53.

SKELTON, Charles (D N.J.) April 19, 1806-May 20, 1879; House 1851-55.

SKILES, William Woodburn (R Ohio) Dec. 11, 1849-Jan. 9, 1904; House 1901-Jan. 9, 1904.

SKINNER, Charles Rufus (R N.Y.) Aug. 4, 1844-June 30, 1928; House Nov. 8, 1881-85.

SKINNER, Harry (brother of Thomas Gregory Skinner) (P N.C.) May 25, 1855-May 19, 1929; House 1895-99.

SKINNER, Richard (D Vt.) May 30, 1778-May 23, 1833; House 1813-15; Gov. 1820-23.

SKINNER, Thomas Gregory (brother of Harry Skinner) (D N.C.) Jan. 22, 1842-Dec. 22, 1907; House Nov. 20, 1883-87, 1889-91.

SKINNER, Thomas Joseph (D Mass.) May 24, 1752-Jan. 20, 1809; House Jan. 27, 1797-99, 1803-Aug. 10, 1804.

SKUBITZ, Joe (R Kan.) May 6, 1906-___; House 1963-___.

SLACK, John Mark Jr. (D W.Va.) March 18, 1915-___; House 1959-___.

SLADE, Charles (D Ill.) ?-July 26, 1834; House 1833-July 26, 1834.

SLADE, William (W Vt.) May 9, 1786-Jan. 18, 1859; House Nov. 1, 1831-43; Gov. 1844-46.

SLATER, James Harvey (D Ore.) Dec. 28, 1826-Jan. 28, 1899; House 1871-73; Senate 1879-85.

SLATTERY, James Michael (D Ill.) July 29, 1878-Aug. 28, 1948; Senate April 14, 1939-Nov. 21, 1940.

SLAUGHTER, Roger Caldwell (D Mo.) July 17, 1905-June 2, 1974; House 1943-47.

SLAYDEN, James (uncle of Maury Maverick) (D Texas) June 1, 1853-Feb. 24, 1924; House 1897-1919.

SLAYMAKER, Amos (— Pa.) March 11, 1755-June 12, 1837; House Oct. 11, 1814-15.

SLEMONS, William Ferguson (D Ark.) March 15, 1830-Dec. 10, 1918; House 1875-81.

SLEMP, Campbell (father of Campbell Bascom Slemp) (R Va.) Dec. 2, 1839-Oct. 13, 1907; House 1903-Oct. 13, 1907.

SLEMP, Campbell Bascom (son of Campbell Slemp) (R Va.) Sept. 4, 1870-Aug. 7, 1943; House Dec. 17, 1907-23.

SLIDELL, John (SRD La.) 1793-July 26, 1871; House 1843-Nov. 10, 1845; Senate Dec. 5, 1853-Feb. 4, 1861.

SLINGERLAND, John I. (R N.Y.) March 1, 1804-Oct. 26, 1861; House 1847-49.

SLOAN, Andrew (R Ga.) June 10, 1845-Sept. 22, 1883; House March 24, 1874-75.

SLOAN, Andrew Scott (brother of Ithamar Conkey Sloan) (R Wis.) June 12, 1820-April 8, 1895; House 1861-63.

SLOAN, Charles Henry (R Neb.) May 2, 1863-June 2, 1946; House 1911-19, 1929-31.

SLOAN, Ithamar Conkey (brother of Andrew Scott Sloan) (R Wis.) May 9, 1822-Dec. 24, 1898; House 1863-67.

SLOAN, James (— N.J.) ?-Nov. 1811; House 1803-09.

SLOANE, John (W Ohio) 1779-May 15, 1856; House 1819-29.

SLOANE, Jonathan (W Ohio) Nov. 1785-April 25, 1854; House 1833-37.

SLOCUM, Henry Warner (D N.Y.) Sept. 24, 1827-April 14, 1894; House 1869-73, 1883-85.

SLOCUMB, Jesse (F N.C.) 1780-Dec. 20, 1820; House 1817-Dec. 20, 1820.

SLOSS, Joseph Humphrey (Con.D Ala.) Oct. 12, 1826-Jan. 27, 1911; House 1871-75.

SMALL, Frank Jr. (R Md.) July 15, 1896-Oct. 24, 1973; House 1953-55.

SMALL, John Humphrey (D N.C.) Aug. 29, 1858-July 13, 1946; House 1899-1921.

SMALL, William Bradbury (R N.H.) May 17, 1817-April 7, 1878; House 1873-75.

SMALLS, Robert (R S.C.) April 5, 1839-Feb. 22, 1915; House 1875-79, July 19, 1882-83, March 18, 1884-87.

SMART, Ephraim Knight (D Maine) Sept. 3, 1813-Sept. 29, 1872; House 1847-49, 1851-53.

SMART, James Stevenson (R N.Y.) June 14, 1842-Sept. 17, 1903; House 1873-75.

SMATHERS, George Armistead (nephew of William H. Smathers) (D Fla.) Nov. 14, 1913-___; House 1947-51; Senate 1951-69.

SMATHERS, William Howell (uncle of George A. Smathers) (D N.J.) Jan. 7, 1891-Sept. 24, 1955; Senate April 15, 1937-43.

SMELT, Dennis (— Ga.) about 1750-?; House Sept. 1, 1806-11.

SMILIE, John (D Pa.) 1741-Dec. 30, 1812; House 1793-95, 1799-Dec. 30, 1812.

SMITH, Abraham Herr (R Pa.) March 7, 1815-Feb. 16, 1894; House 1873-85.

SMITH, Addison Taylor (R Idaho) Sept. 5, 1862-July 5, 1956; House 1913-33.

SMITH, Albert (D Maine) Jan. 3, 1793-May 29, 1867; House 1839-41.

SMITH, Albert (R N.Y.) June 22, 1805-Aug. 27, 1870; House 1843-47.

SMITH, Arthur (— Va.) Nov. 15, 1785-March 30, 1853; House 1821-25.

SMITH, Ballard (— Va.) ? - ?; House 1815-21.

SMITH, Benjamin A. II (D Mass.) March 26, 1916-___; Senate Dec. 27, 1960-Nov. 7, 1962.

SMITH, Bernard (— N.Y.) July 5, 1776-July 16, 1835; House 1819-21.

SMITH, Caleb Blood (W Ind.) April 16, 1808-Jan. 7, 1864; House 1843-49; Secy. of the Interior 1861-63.

SMITH, Charles Bennett (D N.Y.) Sept. 14, 1870-May 21, 1939; House 1911-19.

SMITH, Charles Brooks (R W.Va.) Feb. 24, 1844-Dec. 7, 1899; House Feb. 3, 1890-91.

SMITH, Clyde Harold (husband of Margaret Chase Smith) (R Maine) June 9, 1876-April 8, 1940; House 1937-April 8, 1940.

SMITH, Daniel (— Tenn.) Oct. 28, 1748-June 6, 1818; Senate Oct. 6, 1798-99, 1805-March 31, 1809.

SMITH, David Highbaugh (D Ky.) Dec. 19, 1854-Dec. 17, 1928; House 1897-1907.

SMITH, Delazon (D Ore.) Oct. 5, 1816-Nov. 19, 1860; Senate Feb. 14-March 3, 1859.

SMITH, Dietrich Conrad (R Ill.) April 4, 1840-April 18, 1914; House 1881-83.

SMITH, Edward Henry (D N.Y.) May 5, 1809-Aug. 7, 1885; House 1861-63.

SMITH, Ellison DuRant (D S.C.) Aug. 1, 1866-Nov. 17, 1944; Senate 1909-Nov. 17, 1944.

SMITH, Frances Ormand Jonathan (D Maine) Nov. 23, 1806-Oct. 14, 1876; House 1833-39.

SMITH, Francis Raphael (D Pa.) Sept. 25, 1911-___; House 1941-43.

SMITH, Frank Ellis (D Miss.) Feb. 21, 1918-___; House 1951-Nov. 14, 1962.

SMITH, Frank Leslie (R Ill.) Nov. 24, 1867-Aug. 30, 1950; House 1919-21; Senate (elected 1926 but never served).

SMITH, Frank Owens (D Md.) Aug. 27, 1859-Jan. 29, 1924; House 1913-15.

SMITH, Frederick Cleveland (R Ohio) July 29, 1884-July 16, 1956; House 1939-51.

SMITH, George (— Pa.) ? - ?; House 1809-13.

SMITH, George Joseph (R N.Y.) Nov. 7, 1859-Dec. 24, 1913; House 1903-05.

SMITH, George Luke (R La.) Dec. 11, 1837-July 9, 1884; House Nov. 24, 1873-75.

SMITH, George Ross (R Minn.) May 28, 1864-Nov. 7, 1952; House 1913-17.

SMITH, George Washington (R Ill.) Aug. 18, 1846-Nov. 30, 1907; House 1889-Nov. 30, 1907.

SMITH, Gerrit (UA N.Y.) March 6, 1797-Dec. 28, 1874; House 1853-Aug. 7, 1854.

SMITH, Gomer Griffith (D Okla.) July 11, 1896-May 26, 1953; House Dec. 10, 1937-39.

SMITH, Green Clay (son of John Speed Smith) (U Ky.) July 4, 1826-June 29, 1895; House 1863-July 13, 1866; Gov. (Montana Terr.) 1866-69.

SMITH, H. Allen (R Calif.) Oct. 8, 1909-___; House 1957-73.

SMITH, Henry (PP Wis.) July 22, 1838-Sept. 16, 1916; House 1887-89.

SMITH, Henry Cassorte (R Mich.) June 2, 1856-Dec. 7, 1911; House 1899-1903.

SMITH, Henry P. III (R N.Y.) Sept. 29, 1911-___; House 1965-75.

SMITH, Hezekiah Bradley (D/G N.J.) July 24, 1816-Nov. 3, 1887; House 1879-81.

SMITH, Hiram Ypsilanti (R Iowa) March 22, 1843-Nov. 4, 1894; House Dec. 2, 1884-85.

SMITH, Hoke (D Ga.) Sept. 2, 1855-Nov. 27, 1931; Senate Nov. 16, 1911-21; Secy. of the Interior 1893-96; Gov. 1907-09, 1911.

SMITH, Horace Boardman (R N.Y.) Aug. 18, 1826-Dec. 26, 1888; House 1871-75.

SMITH, Howard Alexander (uncle of Peter H. Dominick) (R N.J.) Jan. 30, 1880-Oct. 27, 1966; Senate Dec. 7, 1944-59.

SMITH, Howard Worth (D Va.) Feb. 2, 1883-___; House 1931-67.

SMITH, Isaac (F N.J.) 1740-Aug. 29, 1807; House 1795-97.

SMITH, Isaac (D Pa.) Jan. 4, 1761-April 4, 1834; House 1813-15.

SMITH, Israel (D Vt.) April 4, 1759-Dec. 2, 1810; House Oct. 17, 1791-1797, 1801-03; Senate 1803-Oct. 1, 1807; Gov. 1807-08.

SMITH, James Jr. (D N.J.) June 12, 1851-April 1, 1927; Senate 1893-99.

SMITH, James Strudwick (D N.C.) Oct. 15, 1790-Aug. 1859; House 1817-21.

SMITH, James Vernon (R Okla.) July 23, 1926-June 23, 1973; House 1967-69.

SMITH, Jedediah Kilburn (— N.H.) Nov. 7, 1770-Dec. 17, 1828; House 1807-09.

SMITH, Jeremiah (brother of Samuel Smith of N.H. and uncle of Robert Smith) (F N.H.) Nov. 29, 1759-Sept. 21, 1842; House 1791-July 26, 1797; Gov. 1809-10.

SMITH, John (D Ohio) 1735-June 10, 1816; Senate April 1, 1803-April 25, 1808.

SMITH, John (D Va.) May 7, 1750-March 5, 1836; House 1801-15.

SMITH, John (D N.Y.) Feb. 12, 1752-Aug. 12, 1816; House Feb. 6, 1800-Feb. 23, 1804; Senate Feb. 23, 1804-13.

SMITH, John (father of Worthington Curtis Smith) (D Vt.) Aug. 12, 1789-Nov. 26, 1858; House 1839-41.

SMITH, John Ambler (R Va.) Sept. 23, 1847-Jan. 6, 1892; House 1873-75.

SMITH, John Armstrong (R Ohio) Sept. 23, 1814-March 7, 1892; House 1869-73.

SMITH, John Cotton (F Conn.) Feb. 12, 1765-Dec. 7, 1845; House Nov. 17, 1800-Aug. 1806; Gov. 1812-17.

SMITH, John Hyatt (IR/D N.Y.) April 10, 1824-Dec. 7, 1886; House 1881-83.

SMITH, John Joseph (D Conn.) Jan. 25, 1904-___; House 1935-Nov. 4, 1941.

SMITH, John M. C. (R Mich.) Feb. 6, 1853-March 30, 1923; House 1911-21, June 28, 1921-March 30, 1923.

SMITH, John Quincy (R Ohio) Nov. 5, 1824-Dec. 30, 1901; House 1873-75.

SMITH, John Speed (father of Green Clay Smith) (D Ky.) July 1, 1792-June 6, 1854; House Aug. 6, 1821-23.

SMITH, John T. (D Pa.) ? - ?; House 1843-45.

SMITH, John Walter (D Md.) Feb. 5, 1845-April 19, 1925; House 1899-Jan. 12, 1900; Senate March 25, 1908-21; Gov. 1900-04.

SMITH, Joseph Luther (D W.Va.) May 22, 1880-Aug. 23, 1962; House 1929-45.

SMITH, Joseph Showalter (D Ore.) June 20, 1824-July 13, 1884; House 1869-71.

SMITH, Josiah (— Mass.) Feb. 26, 1738-April 4, 1803; House 1801-03.

SMITH, Lawrence Henry (R Wis.) Sept. 15, 1892-Jan. 22, 1958; House Aug. 29, 1941-Jan. 22, 1958.

SMITH, Madison Roswell (D Mo.) July 9, 1850-June 18, 1919; House 1907-09.

SMITH, Marcus Aurelius (D Ariz.) Jan. 24, 1851-April 7, 1924; House (Terr. Del.) 1887-95, 1897-99, 1901-03, 1905-09; Senate March 27, 1912-21.

SMITH, Margaret Chase (widow of Clyde Harold Smith) (R Maine) Dec. 14, 1897-___; House June 3, 1940-49; Senate 1949-73.

SMITH, Martin Fernand (D Wash.) May 28, 1891-Oct. 25, 1954; House 1933-43.

SMITH, Nathan (brother of Nathaniel Smith and uncle of Truman Smith) (W Conn.) Jan. 8, 1770-Dec. 6, 1835; Senate 1833-Dec. 6, 1835.

SMITH, Nathaniel (brother of Nathan Smith and uncle of Truman Smith) (F Conn.) Jan. 6, 1762-March 9, 1822; House 1795-99.

SMITH, Neal Edward (D Iowa) March 23, 1920-__; House 1959-__.

SMITH, O'Brien (— S.C.) about 1756-April 27, 1811; House 1805-07.

SMITH, Oliver Hampton (W Ind.) Oct. 23, 1794-March 19, 1859; House 1827-29 (JD), Senate 1837-43 (W).

SMITH, Perry (D Conn.) May 12, 1783-June 8, 1852; Senate 1837-43.

SMITH, Ralph Tyler (R Ill.) Oct. 6, 1915-Aug. 13, 1972; Senate Sept. 17, 1969-Nov. 3, 1970.

SMITH, Robert (nephew of Jeremiah Smith and Samuel Smith of N.H.) (D Ill.) June 12, 1802-Dec. 21, 1867; House 1843-49, 1857-59.

SMITH, Robert Barnwell (see RHETT, Robert Barnwell).

SMITH, Samuel (D Md.) July 27, 1752-April 22, 1839; House 1793-1803, Jan. 31, 1816-Dec. 17, 1822; Senate 1803-15, Dec. 17, 1822-33; President pro tempore 1805-08.

SMITH, Samuel (— Pa.) ?-?; House Nov. 7, 1805-11.

SMITH, Samuel (brother of Jeremiah Smith and uncle of Robert Smith) (F N.H.) Nov. 11, 1765-April 25, 1842; House 1813-15.

SMITH, Samuel A. (ID Pa.) 1795-May 15, 1861; House Oct. 13, 1829-33.

SMITH, Samuel Axley (D Tenn.) June 26, 1822-Nov. 25, 1863; House 1853-59.

SMITH, Samuel William (R Mich.) Aug. 23, 1852-June 19, 1931; House 1897-1915.

SMITH, Sylvester Clark (R Calif.) Aug. 26, 1858-Jan. 26, 1913; House 1905-Jan. 26, 1913.

SMITH, Thomas (F Pa.) ?-Jan. 29, 1846; House 1815-17.

SMITH, Thomas (D Ind.) May 1, 1799-April 12, 1876; House 1839-41, 1843-47.

SMITH, Thomas Alexander (D Md.) Sept. 3, 1850-May 1, 1932; House 1905-07.

SMITH, Thomas Francis (D N.Y.) July 24, 1865-April 11, 1923; House April 12, 1917-21.

SMITH, Thomas Vernor (D Ill.) April 26, 1890-May 24, 1964; House 1939-41.

SMITH, Truman (nephew of Nathan Smith and Nathaniel Smith) (W Conn.) Nov. 27, 1791-May 3, 1884; House 1839-43, 1845-49; Senate 1849-May 24, 1854.

SMITH, Virginia Dodd (R Neb.) June 30, 1911-__; House 1975-__.

SMITH, Walter Inglewood (R Iowa) July 10, 1862-Jan. 27, 1922; House Dec. 3, 1900-March 15, 1911.

SMITH, William (F Md.) April 12, 1728-March 27, 1814; House 1789-91; Cont. Cong. 1777-78.

SMITH, William (D S.C.) 1762-June 26, 1840; Senate Dec. 4, 1816-23, Nov. 29, 1826-31.

SMITH, William (— S.C.) Sept. 20, 1751-June 22, 1837; House 1797-99.

SMITH, William (— Va.) ?-?; House 1821-27.

SMITH, William (D Va.) Sept. 6, 1797-May 18, 1887; House 1841-43, 1853-61; Gov. 1846-49, 1864-65.

SMITH, William Alden (R Mich.) May 12, 1859-Oct. 11, 1932; House 1895-Feb. 9, 1907; Senate Feb. 9, 1907-19.

SMITH, William Alexander (R N.C.) Jan. 9, 1828-May 16, 1888; House 1873-75.

SMITH, William Ephraim (D Ga.) March 14, 1829-March 11, 1890; House 1875-81.

SMITH, William Jay (R Tenn.) Sept. 24, 1823-Nov. 29, 1913; House 1869-71.

SMITH, William Loughton (F S.C.) 1758-Dec. 19, 1812; House 1789-July 10, 1797.

SMITH, William Nathan Harrell (D N.C.) Sept. 24, 1812-Nov. 14, 1889; House 1859-61.

SMITH, William Orlando (R Pa.) June 13, 1859-May 12, 1932; House 1903-07.

SMITH, William Robert (D Texas) Aug. 18, 1863-Aug. 16, 1924; House 1903-17.

SMITH, William Russell (AP Ala.) March 27, 1815-Feb. 26, 1896; House 1851-57 (1851-55 Union Whig, 1855-57 American Party).

SMITH, William Stephens (F N.Y.) Nov. 8, 1755-June 10, 1816; House 1813-15.

SMITH, Willis (D N.C.) Dec. 19, 1887-June 26, 1953; Senate Nov. 27, 1950-June 26, 1953.

SMITH, Wint (R Kan.) Oct. 7, 1892-__; House 1947-61.

SMITH, Worthington Curtis (son of John Smith of Vt.) (R Vt.) April 23, 1823-Jan. 2, 1894; House 1867-73.

SMITHERS, Nathaniel Barratt (R Del.) Oct. 8, 1818-Jan. 16, 1896; House Dec. 7, 1863-65.

SMITHWICK, John Harris (D Fla.) July 17, 1872-Dec. 2, 1948; House 1919-27.

SMOOT, Reed (R Utah) Jan. 10, 1862-Feb. 9, 1941; Senate 1903-33.

SMYSER, Martin Luther (R Ohio) April 3, 1851-May 6, 1908; House 1889-91, 1905-07.

SMYTH, Alexander (— Va.) 1765-April 17, 1830; House 1817-25, 1827-April 17, 1830.

SMYTH, George Washington (D Texas) May 16, 1803-Feb. 21, 1866; House 1853-55.

SMYTH, William (R Iowa) Jan. 3, 1824-Sept. 30, 1870; House 1869-Sept. 30, 1870.

SNAPP, Henry (father of Howard Malcolm Snapp) (R Ill.) June 30, 1822-Nov. 26, 1895; House Dec. 4, 1871-73.

SNAPP, Howard Malcolm (son of Henry Snapp) (R Ill.) Sept. 27, 1855-Aug. 14, 1938; House 1903-11.

SNEED, William Henry (AP Tenn.) Aug. 27, 1812-Sept. 18, 1869; House 1855-57.

SNELL, Bertrand Hollis (R N.Y.) Dec. 9, 1870-Feb. 2, 1958; House Nov. 2, 1915-39.

SNIDER, Samuel Prather (R Minn.) Oct. 9, 1845-Sept. 24, 1928; House 1889-91.

SNODGRASS, Charles Edward (nephew of Henry Clay Snodgrass) (D Tenn.) Dec. 28, 1866-Aug. 3, 1936; House 1899-1903.

SNODGRASS, Henry Clay (uncle of Charles Edward Snodgrass) (D Tenn.) March 29, 1848-April 22, 1931; House 1891-95.

SNODGRASS, John Fryall (D Va.) March 2, 1804-June 5, 1854; House 1853-June 5, 1854.

SNOOK, John Stout (D Ohio) Dec. 18, 1862-Sept. 19, 1952; House 1901-05, 1917-19.

SNOVER, Horace Greeley (R Mich.) Sept. 21, 1847-July 21, 1924; House 1895-99.

SNOW, Donald Francis (R Maine) Sept. 6, 1877-Feb. 12, 1958; House 1929-33.

SNOW, Herman Wilber (D Ill.) July 3, 1836-Aug. 25, 1914; House 1891-93.

SNOW, William W. (D N.Y.) April 27, 1812-Sept. 3, 1886; House 1851-53.

SNYDER, Adam Wilson (VBD Ill.) Oct. 6, 1799-May 14, 1842; House 1837-39.

SNYDER, Charles Philip (D W.Va.) June 9, 1847-Aug. 21, 1915; House May 15, 1883-89.

SNYDER, Homer Peter (R N.Y.) Dec. 6, 1863-Dec. 30, 1937; House 1915-25.

SNYDER, John (— Pa.) Jan. 29, 1793-Aug. 15, 1850; House 1841-43.

SNYDER, John Buell (D Pa.) July 30, 1877-Feb. 24, 1946; House 1933-Feb. 24, 1946.

SNYDER, Marion Gene (R Ky.) Jan. 26, 1928-—; House 1963-65, 1967-—.

SNYDER, Melvin Claude (R W.Va.) Oct. 29, 1898-__; House 1947-49.

SNYDER, Oliver P. (R Ark.) Nov. 13, 1833-Nov. 22, 1882; House 1871-75.

SOLARZ, Stephen Joshua (D N.Y.) Sept. 12, 1940-__; House 1975-__.

SOLLERS, Augustus Rhodes (W Md.) May 1, 1814-Nov. 26, 1862; House 1841-43, 1853-55.

SOMERS, Andrew Lawrence (D N.Y.) March 21, 1895-April 6, 1949; House 1925-April 6, 1949.

SOMERS, Peter J. (D Wis.) April 12, 1850-Feb. 15, 1924; House Aug. 27, 1893-95.

SOMES, Daniel Eton (R Maine) May 20, 1815-Feb. 13, 1888; House 1859-61.

SORG, Paul John (D Ohio) Sept. 23, 1840-May 28, 1902; House May 21, 1894-97.

SOSNOWSKI, John Bartholomew (R Mich.) Dec. 8, 1883-July 16, 1968; House 1925-27.

SOULE, Nathan (— N.Y.) ? - ?; House 1831-33.

SOULE, Pierre (SRD La.) Aug. 28, 1801-March 26, 1870; Senate Jan. 21-March 3, 1847, 1849-April 11, 1853.

SOUTH, Charles Lacy (D Texas) July 22, 1892-Dec. 20, 1965; House 1935-43.

SOUTHALL, Robert Goode (D Va.) Dec. 26, 1852-May 25, 1924; House 1903-07.

SOUTHARD, Henry (father of Isaac Southard and Samuel Lewis Southard) (D N.J.) Oct. 7, 1747-May 22, 1842; House 1801-11, 1815-21.

SOUTHARD, Isaac (son of Henry Southard and brother of Samuel Lewis Southard) (CD N.J.) Aug. 30, 1783-Sept. 18, 1850; House 1831-33.

SOUTHARD, James Harding (R Ohio) Jan. 20, 1851-Feb. 20, 1919; House 1895-1907.

SOUTHARD, Milton Isaiah (D Ohio) Oct. 20, 1836-May 4, 1905; House 1873-79.

SOUTHARD, Samuel Lewis (son of Henry Southard and brother of Isaac Southard) (W N.J.) June 9, 1787-June 26, 1842; Senate Jan. 26, 1821-1823, 1833-June 26, 1842 (1821-23 Democrat, 1833-42 Whig); President pro tempore 1841-42; Secy. of the Navy 1823-29; Gov. 1832-33.

SOUTHGATE, William Wright (W Ky.) Nov. 27, 1800-Dec. 26, 1849; House 1837-39.

SOUTHWICK, George Newell (R N.Y.) March 7, 1863-Oct. 17, 1912; House 1895-99, 1901-11.

SOWDEN, William Henry (D Pa.) June 6, 1840-March 3, 1907; House 1885-89.

SPAIGHT, Richard Dobbs (grandfather of Richard Spaight Donnell and father of Richard Dobbs Spaight Jr.) (D N.C.) March 25, 1758-Sept. 6, 1802; House Dec. 10, 1798-1801; Cont. Cong. 1782-85; Gov. 1792-95.

SPAIGHT, Richard Dobbs Jr. (son of the preceding) (D N.C.) 1796-May 2, 1850; House 1823-25; Gov. 1835-36.

SPALDING, Burleigh Folsom (R N.D.) Dec. 3, 1853-March 17, 1934; House 1899-1901; 1903-05.

SPALDING, George (R Mich.) Nov. 12, 1836-Sept. 13, 1915; House 1895-99.

SPALDING, Rufus Paine (WD Ohio) May 3, 1798-Aug. 29, 1886; House 1863-69.

SPALDING, Thomas (— Ga.) March 26, 1774-Jan. 5, 1851; House Dec. 24, 1805-06.

SPANGLER, David (W Ohio) Dec. 2, 1796-Oct. 18, 1856; House 1833-37.

SPANGLER, Jacob (F Pa.) Nov. 28, 1767-June 17, 1843; House 1817-April 20, 1818.

SPARKMAN, John Jackson (D Ala.) Dec. 20, 1899-__; House 1937-Nov. 5, 1946; Senate Nov. 6, 1946-__.

SPARKMAN, Stephen Milancthon (D Fla.) July 29, 1849-Sept. 26, 1929; House 1895-1917.

SPARKS, Charles Isaac (R Kan.) Dec. 20, 1872-April 30, 1937; House 1929-33.

SPARKS, William Andrew Jackson (D Ill.) Nov. 19, 1828-May 7, 1904; House 1875-83.

SPAULDING, Elbridge Gerry (U N.Y.) Feb. 24, 1809-May 5, 1897; House 1849-51, 1859-63 (1849-51 Whig, 1859-63 Unionist).

SPAULDING, Oliver Lyman (R Mich.) Aug. 2, 1833-July 30, 1922; House 1881-83.

SPEAKS, John Charles (R Ohio) Feb. 11, 1859-Nov. 6, 1945; House 1921-31.

SPEARING, James Zacharie (D La.) April 23, 1864-Nov. 2, 1942; House April 22, 1924-31.

SPEED, Thomas (— Ky.) Oct. 25, 1768-Feb. 20, 1842; House 1817-19.

SPEER, Emory (I Ga.) Sept. 3, 1848-Dec. 13, 1918; House 1879-83 (1879-81 Democrat, 1881-83 (Independent).

SPEER, Peter Moore (R Pa.) Dec. 29, 1862-Aug. 3, 1933; House 1911-13.

SPEER, Robert Milton (D Pa.) Sept. 8, 1838-Jan. 17, 1890; House 1871-75.

SPEER, Thomas Jefferson (R Ga.) Aug. 31, 1837-Aug. 18, 1872; House 1871-Aug. 18, 1872.

SPEIGHT, Jesse (D N.C./Miss.) Sept. 22, 1795-May 1, 1847; House 1829-37 (N.C.); Senate 1845-May 1, 1847 (Miss.).

SPELLMAN, Gladys Noon (D Md.) March 1, 1918-__; House 1975-__.

SPENCE, Brent (D Ky.) Dec. 24, 1874-Sept. 18, 1967; House 1931-63.

SPENCE, Floyd Davidson (R S.C.) April 9, 1928-—; House 1971-—.

SPENCE, John Selby (uncle of Thomas Ara Spence) (D Md.) Feb. 29, 1788-Oct. 24, 1840; House 1823-25, 1831-33; Senate Dec. 31, 1836-Oct. 24, 1840.

SPENCE, Thomas Ara (nephew of John Selby Spence) (W Md.) Feb. 20, 1810-Nov. 10, 1877; House 1843-45.

SPENCER, Ambrose (father of John Canfield Spencer) (D N.Y.) Dec. 13, 1765-March 13, 1848; House 1829-31.

SPENCER, Elijah (D N.Y.) 1775-Dec. 15, 1852; House 1821-23.

SPENCER, George Eliphaz (R Ala.) Nov. 1, 1836-Feb. 19, 1893; Senate July 13, 1868-79.

SPENCER, George Lloyd (D Ark.) March 27, 1893-__; Senate April 1, 1941-43.

SPENCER, James Bradley (D N.Y.) April 26, 1781-March 26, 1848; House 1837-39.

SPENCER, James Grafton (D Miss.) Sept. 13, 1844-Feb. 22, 1926; House 1895-97.

SPENCER, John Canfield (son of Ambrose Spencer) (D N.Y.) Jan. 8, 1788-May 18, 1855; House 1817-19; Secy. of War 1841-43; Secy. of the Treasury 1843-44.

SPENCER, Richard (D Md.) Oct. 29, 1796-Sept. 3, 1868; House 1829-31.

SPENCER, Selden Palmer (R Mo.) Sept. 16, 1862-May 16, 1925; Senate Nov. 6, 1918-May 16, 1925.

SPENCER, William Brainerd (D La.) Feb. 5, 1835-Feb. 12, 1882; House June 8, 1876-Jan. 8, 1877.

SPERRY, Lewis (D Conn.) Jan. 23, 1848-June 22, 1922; House 1891-95.

SPERRY, Nehemiah Day (R Conn.) July 10, 1827-Nov. 13, 1911; House 1895-1911.

SPIGHT, Thomas (D Miss.) Oct. 25, 1841-Jan. 5, 1924; House July 5, 1898-1911.

SPINK, Cyrus (R Ohio) March 24, 1793-May 31, 1859; House March 4-May 31, 1859.

SPINK, Solomon Lewis (R Dakota) March 20, 1831-Sept. 22, 1881; House (Terr. Del.) 1869-71.

SPINNER, Francis Elias (D N.Y.) Jan. 21, 1802-Dec. 31, 1890; House 1855-61.

SPINOLA, Francis Barretto (D N.Y.) March 19, 1821-April 14, 1891; House 1887-April 14, 1891.

SPONG, William Belser Jr. (D Va.) Sept. 29, 1920-__; Senate Dec. 31, 1966-73.

SPOONER, Henry Joshua (R R.I.) Aug. 6, 1839-Feb. 9, 1918; House Dec. 5, 1881-91.

SPOONER, John Coit (R Wis.) Jan. 6, 1843-June 11, 1919; Senate 1885-91, 1897-April 30, 1907.

SPRAGUE, Charles Franklin (grandson of Peleg Sprague) (R Mass.) June 10, 1857-Jan. 30, 1902; House 1897-1901.

SPRAGUE, Peleg (— N.H.) Dec. 10, 1756-April 20, 1800; House Dec. 15, 1797-99.

SPRAGUE, Peleg (grandfather of Charles Franklin Sprague) (NR Maine) April 27, 1793-Oct. 13, 1880; House 1825-29; Senate 1829-Jan. 1, 1835.

SPRAGUE, William (W Mich.) Feb. 23, 1809-Sept. 19, 1868; House 1849-51.

SPRAGUE, William (uncle of the following) (W R.I.) Nov. 3, 1799-Oct. 19, 1856; House 1835-37; Senate Feb. 18, 1842-Jan. 17, 1844; Gov. 1838-39.

SPRAGUE, William (nephew of the preceding) (R R.I.) Sept. 12, 1830-Sept. 11, 1915; Senate 1863-75; Gov. 1860-63 (U).

SPRAGUE, William Peter (R Ohio) May 21, 1827-March 3, 1899; House 1871-75.

SPRIGG, James Cresap (brother of Michael Cresap Sprigg) (— Ky.) 1802-Oct. 3, 1852; House 1841-43.

SPRIGG, Michael Cresap (brother of James Cresap Sprigg) (D Md.) July 1, 1791-Dec. 18, 1845; House 1827-31.

SPRIGG, Richard Jr. (nephew of Thomas Sprigg) (— Md.) ? - ?; House May 5, 1796-99, 1801-Feb. 11, 1802.

SPRIGG, Thomas (uncle of Richard Sprigg Jr.) (— Md.) 1747-Dec. 13, 1809; House 1793-97.

SPRIGGS, John Thomas (D N.Y.) April 5, 1825-Dec. 23, 1888; House 1883-87.

SPRINGER, Raymond Smiley (R Ind.) April 26, 1882-Aug. 28, 1947; House 1939-Aug. 28, 1947.

SPRINGER, William Lee (R Ill.) April 12, 1909-__; House 1951-73.

SPRINGER, William McKendree (D Ill.) May 30, 1836-Dec. 4, 1903; House 1875-95.

SPROUL, Elliott Wilford (R Ill.) Dec. 28, 1856-June 22, 1935; House 1921-31.

SPROUL, William Henry (R Kan.) Oct. 14, 1867-Dec. 27, 1932; House 1923-31.

SPRUANCE, Presley (W Del.) Sept. 11, 1785-Feb. 13, 1863; Senate 1847-53.

SQUIRE, Watson Carvosso (R Wash.) May 18, 1838-June 7, 1926; Senate Nov. 20, 1889-97; Gov. (Terr.) 1884-87.

STACK, Edmund John (D Ill.) Jan. 31, 1874-April 12, 1957; House 1911-13.

STACK, Michael Joseph (D Pa.) Sept. 29, 1888-Dec. 14, 1960; House 1935-39.

STACKHOUSE, Eli Thomas (D S.C.) March 27, 1824-June 14, 1892; House 1891-June 14, 1892.

STAEBLER, Neil (D Mich.) July 11, 1905-__; House 1963-65.

STAFFORD, Robert Theodore (R Vt.) Aug. 8, 1913-__; House 1961-Sept. 16, 1971, Senate Sept. 16, 1971-__; Gov. 1959-61.

STAFFORD, William Henry (R Wis.) Oct. 12, 1869-April 22, 1957; House 1903-11, 1913-19, 1921-23, 1929-33.

STAGGERS, Harley Orrin (D W.Va.) Aug. 3, 1907-__; House 1949-__.

STAHLE, James Alonzo (R Pa.) Jan. 11, 1829-Dec. 21, 1912; House 1895-97.

STAHLNECKER, William Griggs (D N.Y.) June 20, 1849-March 26, 1902; House 1885-93.

STALBAUM, Lynn Ellsworth (D Wis.) May 15, 1920-__; House 1965-67.

STALKER, Gale Hamilton (R N.Y.) Nov. 7, 1889-__; House 1923-35.

STALLINGS, Jesse Francis (D Ala.) April 4, 1856-March 18, 1928; House 1893-1901.

STALLWORTH, James Adams (D Ala.) April 7, 1822-Aug. 31, 1861; House 1857-Jan. 21, 1861.

STANARD, Edwin Obed (R Mo.) Jan. 5, 1832-March 12, 1914; House 1873-75.

STANBERY, William (JD Ohio) Aug. 10, 1788-Jan. 23, 1873; House Oct. 9, 1827-33.

STANDIFER, James (W Tenn.) ?-Aug. 20, 1837; House 1823-25, 1829-Aug. 20, 1837.

STANDIFORD, Elisha David (D Ky.) Dec. 28, 1831-July 26, 1887; House 1873-75.

STANFIELD, Robert Nelson (R Ore.) July 9, 1877-April 13, 1945; Senate 1921-27.

STANFIL, William Abner (R Ky.) Jan. 16, 1892-__; Senate Nov. 19, 1945-Nov. 5, 1946.

STANFORD, Leland (R Calif.) March 9, 1824-June 21, 1893; Senate 1885-June 21, 1893; Gov. 1862-63.

STANFORD, Richard (grandfather of William Robert Webb) (D N.C.) March 2, 1767-April 9, 1816; House 1797-April 9, 1816.

STANLEY, Augustus Owsley (D Ky.) May 21, 1867-Aug. 13, 1958; House 1903-15; Senate May 19, 1919-25; Gov. 1915-19.

STANLEY, Thomas Bahnson (D Va.) July 16, 1890-July 10, 1970; House Nov. 5, 1946-Feb. 3, 1953; Gov. 1954-58.

STANLEY, Winifred Claire (R N.Y.) Aug. 14, 1909-__; House 1943-45.

STANLY, Edward (son of John Stanly) (W N.C.) July 13, 1810-July 12, 1872; House 1837-43, 1849-53.

STANLY, John (father of Edward Stanly) (— N.C.) April 9, 1774-Aug. 2, 1834; House 1801-03, 1809-11.

STANTON, Benjamin (W Ohio) June 4, 1809-June 2, 1872; House 1851-53, 1855-61.

STANTON, Frederick Perry (D Tenn.) Dec. 22, 1814-June 4, 1894; House 1845-55; Gov. of Kansas Terr. 1858-61.

STANTON, James Vincent (D Ohio) Feb. 27, 1932-__; House 1971-__.

STANTON, John William (R Ohio) Feb. 20, 1924-__; House 1965-__.

STANTON, Joseph Jr. (D R.I.) July 19, 1739-1807; Senate June 7, 1790-93; House 1801-07.

STANTON, Richard Henry (D Ky.) Sept. 9, 1812-March 20, 1891; House 1849-55.

STANTON, William Henry (D Pa.) July 28, 1843-March 28, 1900; House Nov. 7, 1876-77.

STARIN, John Henry (grandson of Thomas Sammons) (R N.Y.) Aug. 27, 1825-March 21, 1909; House 1877-81.

STARK, Benjamin (D Ore.) June 26, 1820-Oct. 10, 1898; Senate Oct. 29, 1861-Sept. 12, 1862.

STARK, Fortney Hillman (D Calif.) Nov. 11, 1931-__; House 1973-__.

STARK, William Ledyard (D Neb.) July 29, 1853-Nov. 11, 1922; House 1897-1903.

STARKEY, Frank Thomas (D Minn.) Feb. 18, 1892-May 14, 1968; House 1945-47.

STARKWEATHER, David Austin (D Ohio) Jan. 21, 1802-July 12, 1876; House 1839-41, 1845-47.

STARKWEATHER, George Anson (D N.Y.) May 19, 1794-Oct. 15, 1879; House 1847-49.

STARKWEATHER, Henry Howard (R Conn.) April 29, 1826-Jan. 28, 1876; House 1867-Jan. 28, 1876.

STARNES, Joe (D Ala.) March 31, 1895-Jan. 9, 1962; House 1935-45.

STARR, John Farson (R N.J.) March 25, 1818-Aug. 9, 1904; House 1863-67.

STAUFFER, Simon Walter (R Pa.) Aug. 13, 1888-Sept. 26, 1975; House 1953-55, 1957-59.

STEAGALL, Henry Bascom (D Ala.) May 19, 1873-Nov. 22, 1943; House 1915-Nov. 22, 1943.

STEARNS, Asahel (F Mass.) June 17, 1774-Feb. 5, 1839; House 1815-17.

STEARNS, Foster Waterman (R N.H.) July 29, 1881-June 4, 1956; House 1939-45.

STEARNS, Ozora Pierson (R Minn.) Jan. 15, 1831-June 2, 1896; Senate Jan. 23-March 3, 1871.

STEBBINS, Henry George (WD N.Y.) Sept. 15, 1811-Dec. 9, 1881; House 1863-Oct. 24, 1864.

STECK, Daniel Frederick (D Iowa) Dec. 16, 1881-Dec. 31, 1950; Senate April 12, 1926-31.

STEDMAN, Charles Manly (D N.C.) Jan. 29, 1841-Sept. 23, 1930; House 1911-Sept. 23, 1930.

STEDMAN, William (F Mass.) Jan. 21, 1765-Aug. 31, 1831; House 1803-July 16, 1810.

STEED, Thomas Jefferson (D Okla.) March 2, 1904-__; House 1949-__.

STEELE, George Washington (R Ind.) Dec. 13, 1839-July 12, 1922; House 1881-89, 1895-1903; Gov. Okla. Terr. 1890-91.

STEELE, Henry Joseph (D Pa.) May 10, 1860-March 19, 1933; House 1915-21.

STEELE, John (F N.C.) Nov. 1, 1764-Aug. 14, 1815; House 1789-93.

STEELE, John Benedict (D N.Y.) March 28, 1814-Sept. 24, 1866; House 1861-65.

STEELE, John Nevett (W Md.) Feb. 22, 1796-Aug. 13, 1853; House May 29, 1834-37.

STEELE, Leslie Jasper (D Ga.) Nov. 21, 1868-July 24, 1929; House 1927-July 24, 1929.

STEELE, Robert Hampton (R Conn.) Nov. 3, 1938-__; House Nov. 3, 1970-75.

STEELE, Thomas Jefferson (D Iowa) March 19, 1853-March 20, 1920; House 1915-17.

STEELE, Walter Leak (D N.C.) April 18, 1823-Oct. 16, 1891; House 1877-81.

STEELE, William Gaston (D N.J.) Dec. 17, 1820-April 22, 1892; House 1861-65.

STEELE, William Randolph (D Wyo.) July 24, 1842-Nov. 30, 1901; House (Terr. Del.) 1873-77.

STEELMAN, Alan Watson (R Texas) March 15, 1942-__; House 1973-__.

STEENERSON, Halvor (R Minn.) June 30, 1852-Nov. 22, 1926; House 1903-23.

STEENROD, Lewis (D Va.) May 27, 1810-Oct. 3, 1862; House 1839-45.

STEFAN, Karl (R Neb.) March 1, 1884-Oct. 2, 1951; House 1935-Oct. 2, 1951.

STEIGER, Sam (R Ariz.) March 10, 1929-__; House 1967-__.

STEIGER, William A. (R Wis.) May 15, 1938-__; House 1967-__.

STEIWER, Frederick (R Ore.) Oct. 13, 1883-Feb. 3, 1939; Senate 1927-Jan. 31, 1938.

STENGER, William Shearer (D Pa.) Feb. 13, 1840-March 29, 1918; House 1875-79.

STENGLE, Charles Irwin (D N.Y.) Dec. 5, 1869-Nov. 23, 1953; House 1923-25.

STENNIS, John Cornelius (D Miss.) Aug. 3, 1901-__; Senate Nov. 5, 1947-__.

STEPHENS, Abraham P. (D N.Y.) Feb. 18, 1796-Nov. 25, 1859; House 1851-53.

STEPHENS, Alexander Hamilton (great-great-uncle of Robert Grier Stephens Jr.) (D Ga.) Feb. 11, 1812-March 4, 1883; House Oct. 2, 1843-59, Dec. 1, 1873-Nov. 4, 1882; Gov. 1882-83.

STEPHENS, Ambrose Everett Burnside (R Ohio) June 3, 1862-Feb. 12, 1927; House 1919-Feb. 12, 1927.

STEPHENS, Dan Voorhees (D Neb.) Nov. 4, 1868-Jan. 13, 1939; House Nov. 7, 1911-19.

STEPHENS, Hubert Durrett (D Miss.) July 2, 1875-March 14, 1946; House 1911-21; Senate 1923-35.

STEPHENS, John Hall (D Texas) Nov. 22, 1847-Nov. 18, 1924; House 1897-1917.

STEPHENS, Philander (JD Pa.) 1788-July 8, 1842; House 1829-33.

STEPHENS, Robert Grier Jr. (great-great-nephew of Alexander Hamilton Stephens) (D Ga.) Aug. 14, 1913-__; House 1961-__.

STEPHENS, William Dennison (R Calif.) Dec. 26, 1859-April 25, 1944; House 1911-July 22, 1916; Gov. 1917-23.

STEPHENSON, Benjamin (D Ill.) ?-Oct. 10, 1822; House (Terr. Del.) Sept. 3, 1814-16.

STEPHENSON, Isaac (brother of Samuel Merritt Stephenson) (R Wis.) June 18, 1829-March 15, 1918; House 1883-89; Senate May 17, 1907-15.

STEPHENSON, James (F Va.) March 20, 1764-Aug. 7, 1833; House 1803-05, 1809-11, Oct. 28, 1822-25.

STEPHENSON, Samuel Merritt (brother of Isaac Stephenson) (R Mich.) Dec. 23, 1831-July 31, 1907; House 1889-97.

STERETT, Samuel (AF Md.) 1758-July 12, 1833; House 1791-93.

STERIGERE, John Benton (D Pa.) July 31, 1793-Oct. 13, 1852; House 1827-31.

STERLING, Ansel (brother of Micah Sterling) (— Conn.) Feb. 3, 1782-Nov. 6, 1853; House 1821-25.

STERLING, Bruce Foster (D Pa.) Sept. 28, 1870-April 26, 1945; House 1917-19.

STERLING, John Allen (brother of Thomas Sterling) (R Ill.) Feb. 1, 1857-Oct. 17, 1918; House 1903-13, 1915-Oct. 17, 1918.

STERLING, Micah (brother of Ansel Sterling) (F N.Y.) Nov. 5, 1784-April 11, 1844; House 1821-23.

STERLING, Thomas (brother of John Allen Sterling) (R S.D.) Feb. 21, 1851-Aug. 26, 1930; Senate 1913-25.

STETSON, Charles (D Maine) Nov. 2, 1801-March 27, 1863; House 1849-51.

STETSON, Lemuel (D N.Y.) March 13, 1804-May 17, 1868; House 1843-45.

STEVENS, Aaron Fletcher (R N.H.) Aug. 9, 1819-May 10, 1887; House 1867-71.

STEVENS, Bradford Newcomb (D Ill.) Jan. 3, 1813-Nov. 10, 1885; House 1871-73.

STEVENS, Charles Abbot (brother of Moses Tyler Stevens and cousin of Isaac Ingalls Stevens) (R Mass.) Aug. 9, 1816-April 7, 1892; House Jan. 27-March 3, 1875.

STEVENS, Frederick Clement (R Minn.) Jan. 1, 1861-July 1, 1923; House 1897-1915.

STEVENS, Hestor Lockhart (D Mich.) Oct. 1, 1803-May 7, 1864; House 1853-55.

STEVENS, Hiram Sanford (D Ariz.) March 20, 1832-March 22, 1893; House (Terr. Del.) 1875-79.

STEVENS, Isaac Ingalls (cousin of Charles Abbot Stevens and Moses Tyler Stevens) (D Wash.) March 25, 1818-Sept. 1, 1862; House (Terr. Del.) 1857-61; Gov. (Terr.) 1853-57.

STEVENS, James (D Conn.) July 4, 1768-April 4, 1835; House 1819-21.

STEVENS, Moses Tyler (brother of Charles Abbot Stevens and cousin of Isaac Ingalls Stevens) (D Mass.) Oct. 10, 1825-March 25, 1907; House 1891-95.

STEVENS, Raymond Bartlett (D N.H.) June 18, 1874-May 18, 1942; House 1913-15.

STEVENS, Robert Smith (D N.Y.) March 27, 1824-Feb. 23, 1893; House 1883-85.

STEVENS, Thaddeus (R Pa.) April 4, 1792-Aug. 11, 1868; House 1849-53, 1859-Aug. 11, 1868 (1849-53 Whig, 1859-68 Republican).

STEVENS, Theodore F. (Ted) (R Alaska) Nov. 18, 1923-__; Senate Dec. 24, 1968-__.

STEVENSON, Adlai Ewing (D Ill.) Oct. 23, 1835-June 14, 1914; House 1875-77, 1879-81; Vice Pres. 1893-97.

STEVENSON, Adlai Ewing III (grandson of the preceding) (D Ill.) Oct. 10, 1930-__; Senate Nov. 17, 1970-__.

STEVENSON, Andrew (father of John White Stevenson) (D Va.) Jan. 21, 1784-Jan. 25, 1857; House 1821-June 2, 1834; Speaker 1827-34.

STEVENSON, James S. (— Pa.) 1780-Oct. 16, 1831; House 1825-29.

STEVENSON, Job Evans (R Ohio) Feb. 10, 1832-July 24, 1922; House 1869-73.

STEVENSON, John White (son of Andrew Stevenson) (D Ky.) May 4, 1812-Aug. 10, 1886; House 1857-61; Senate 1871-77; Gov. 1867-71.

STEVENSON, William Francis (D S.C.) Nov. 23, 1861-Feb. 12, 1942; House 1917-33.

STEVENSON, William Henry (R Wis.) Sept. 23, 1891-__; House 1941-49.

STEWARD, Lewis (D Ill.) Nov. 21, 1824-Aug. 27, 1896; House 1891-93.

STEWART, Alexander (R Wis.) Sept. 12, 1829-May 24, 1912; House 1895-1901.

STEWART, Andrew (W Pa.) June 11, 1791-July 16, 1872; House 1821-29, 1831-35, 1843-49 (1821-29 and 1831-35 Democrat, 1843-49 Whig).

STEWART, Andrew (son of the preceding) (R Pa.) April 6, 1836-Nov. 9, 1903; House 1891-Feb. 26, 1892.

STEWART, Arthur Thomas (Tom) (D Tenn.) Jan. 11, 1892-Oct. 10, 1972; Senate Jan. 16, 1939-49.

STEWART, Charles (D Texas) May 30, 1836-Sept. 21, 1895; House 1883-93.

STEWART, David (W Md.) Sept. 13, 1800-Jan. 5, 1858; Senate Dec. 6, 1849-Jan. 12, 1850.

STEWART, David Wallace (R Iowa) Jan. 22, 1887-__; Senate Aug. 7, 1926-27.

STEWART, Jacob Henry (R Minn.) Jan. 15, 1829-Aug. 25, 1884; House 1877-79.

STEWART, James (— N.C.) Nov. 11, 1775-Dec. 29, 1821; House Jan. 5, 1818-19.

STEWART, James Augustus (D Md.) Nov. 24, 1808-April 3, 1879; House 1855-61.

STEWART, James Fleming (R N.J.) June 15, 1851-Jan. 21, 1904; House 1895-1903.

STEWART, John (D Pa.) ?-1820; House Jan. 15, 1801-05.

STEWART, John (D Conn.) Feb. 10, 1795-Sept. 16, 1860; House 1843-45.

STEWART, John David (D Ga.) Aug. 2, 1833-Jan. 28, 1894; House 1887-91.

STEWART, John George (R Del.) June 2, 1890-May 24, 1970; House 1935-37.

STEWART, John Knox (R N.Y.) Oct. 20, 1853-June 27, 1919; House 1899-1903.

STEWART, John Wolcott (R Vt.) Nov. 24, 1825-Oct. 29, 1915; House 1883-91; Senate March 24-Oct. 21, 1908; Gov. 1870-72.

STEWART, Paul (D Okla.) Feb. 27, 1892-Nov. 13, 1950; House 1943-47.

STEWART, Percy Hamilton (D N.J.) Jan. 10, 1867-June 30, 1951; House Dec. 1, 1931-33.

STEWART, Thomas Elliott (CR N.Y.) Sept. 22, 1824-Jan. 9, 1904; House 1867-69.

STEWART, William (R Pa.) Sept. 10, 1810-Oct. 17, 1876; House 1857-61.

STEWART, William Morris (R Nev.) Aug. 9, 1827-April 23, 1909; Senate Dec. 15, 1864-75, 1887-1905.

STIGLER, William Grady (D Okla.) July 7, 1891-Aug. 21, 1952; House March 28, 1944-Aug. 21, 1952.

STILES, John Dodson (D Pa.) Jan. 15, 1822-Oct. 29, 1896; House June 3, 1862-65, 1869-71.

STILES, William Henry (D Ga.) Jan. 1, 1808-Dec. 20, 1865; House 1843-45.

STILLWELL, Thomas Neel (R Ind.) Aug. 29, 1830-Jan. 14, 1874; House 1865-67.

STINESS, Walter Russell (R R.I.) March 13, 1854-March 17, 1924; House 1915-23.

STINSON, K. William (Bill) (R Wash.) April 20, 1930-___; House 1963-65.

STIVERS, Moses Dunning (R N.Y.) Dec. 30, 1828-Feb. 2, 1895; House 1889-91.

STOBBS, George Russell (R Mass.) Feb. 7, 1877-Dec. 23, 1966; House 1925-31.

STOCKBRIDGE, Francis Brown (R Mich.) April 9, 1826-April 30, 1894; Senate 1887-April 30, 1894.

STOCKBRIDGE, Henry Jr. (R Md.) Sept. 18, 1856-March 22, 1924; House 1889-91.

STOCKDALE, Thomas Ringland (D Miss.) March 28, 1828-Jan. 8, 1899; House 1887-95.

STOCKMAN, Lowell (R Ore.) April 12, 1901-Aug. 10, 1962; House 1943-53.

STOCKSLAGER, Strother Madison (D Ind.) May 7, 1842-June 1, 1930; House 1881-85.

STOCKTON, John Potter (son of Robert Field Stockton) Aug. 2, 1826-Jan. 22, 1900; Senate March 15, 1865-March 27, 1866, 1869-75.

STOCKTON, Richard (father of Robert Field Stockton) (F N.J.) April 17, 1764-March 7, 1828; Senate Nov. 12, 1796-99; House 1813-15.

STOCKTON, Robert Field (son of the preceding and father of John Potter Stockton) (D N.J.) Aug. 20, 1795-Oct. 7, 1866; Senate 1851-Jan. 10, 1853.

STODDARD, Ebenezer (— Conn.) May 6, 1785-Aug. 19, 1847; House 1821-25.

STODDERT, John Truman (JD Md.) Oct. 1, 1790-July 19, 1870; House 1833-35.

STOKELY, Samuel (W Ohio) Jan. 25, 1796-May 23, 1861; House 1841-43.

STOKES, Edward Lowber (R Pa.) Sept. 29, 1880-Nov. 8, 1964; House Nov. 3, 1931-35.

STOKES, James William (D S.C.) Dec. 12, 1853-July 6, 1901; House 1895-June 1, 1896; Nov. 3, 1896-July 6, 1901.

STOKES, Louis (D Ohio) Feb. 23, 1925-___; House 1969-___.

STOKES, Montfort (D N.C.) March 12, 1762-Nov. 4, 1842; Senate Dec. 4, 1816-23; Gov. 1830-32.

STOKES, William Brickly (R Tenn.) Sept. 9, 1814-March 14, 1897; House 1859-61, July 24, 1866-71 (1859-61 Whig, 1866-71 Republican).

STOLL, Philip Henry (D S.C.) Nov. 5, 1874-Oct. 29, 1958; House Oct. 7, 1919-23.

STONE, Alfred Parish (D Ohio) June 28, 1813-Aug. 2, 1865; House Oct. 8, 1844-45.

STONE, Charles Warren (R Pa.) June 29, 1843-Aug. 15, 1912; House Nov. 4, 1890-99.

STONE, Claudius Ulysses (D Ill.) May 11, 1879-Nov. 13, 1957; House 1911-17.

STONE, David (D N.C.) Feb. 17, 1770-Oct. 7, 1818; House 1799-1801; Senate 1801-Feb. 17, 1807, 1813-Dec. 24, 1814; Gov. 1808-10.

STONE, Eben Francis (R Mass.) Aug. 3, 1822-Jan. 22, 1895; House 1881-87.

STONE, Frederick (grandson of Michael Jenifer Stone) (D Md.) Feb. 7, 1820-Oct. 17, 1899; House 1867-71.

STONE, James W. (D Ky.) 1813-Oct. 13, 1854; House 1843-45, 1851-53.

STONE, John Wesley (R Mich.) July 18, 1838-March 24, 1922; House 1877-81.

STONE, Joseph Champlin (R Iowa) July 30, 1829-Dec. 3, 1902; House 1877-79.

STONE, Michael Jenifer (grandfather of Frederick Stone) (— Md.) 1747-1812; House 1789-91.

STONE, Richard Bernard (D Fla.) Sept. 22, 1928-___; Senate Jan. 1, 1975-___.

STONE, Ulysses Stevens (R Okla.) Dec. 17, 1878-Dec. 8, 1962; House 1929-31.

STONE, William (W Tenn.) Jan. 26, 1791-Feb. 18, 1853; House Sept. 14, 1837-39.

STONE, William Alexis (R Pa.) April 18, 1846-March 1, 1920; House 1891-Nov. 9, 1898; Gov. 1899-1903.

STONE, William Henry (D Mo.) Nov. 7, 1828-July 9, 1901; House 1873-77.

STONE, William Joel (D Mo.) May 7, 1848-April 14, 1918; House 1885-91; Senate 1903-April 14, 1918; Gov. 1893-97.

STONE, William Johnson (D Ky.) June 26, 1841-March 12, 1923; House 1885-95.

STORER, Bellamy (father of the following) (W Ohio) March 26, 1796-June 1, 1875; House 1835-37.

STORER, Bellamy (son of the preceding and uncle of Nicholas Longworth) (R Ohio) Aug. 28, 1847-Nov. 12, 1922; House 1891-95.

STORER, Clement (— N.H.) Sept. 20, 1760-Nov. 21, 1830; House 1807-09; Senate June 27, 1817-19.

STORKE, Thomas More (D Calif.) Nov. 23, 1876-Oct. 12, 1971; Senate Nov. 9, 1938-39.

STORM, Frederic (R N.Y.) July 2, 1844-June 9, 1935; House 1901-03.

STORM, John Brutzman (D Pa.) Sept. 19, 1838-Aug. 13, 1901; House 1871-75, 1883-87.

STORRS, Henry Randolph (brother of William Lucius Storrs) (F N.Y.) Sept. 3, 1787-July 29, 1837; House 1817-21, 1823-31.

STORRS, William Lucius (brother of Henry Randolph Storrs) (W Conn.) March 25, 1795-June 25, 1861; House 1829-33, 1839-June 1840.

STORY, Joseph (D Mass.) Sept. 18, 1779-Sept. 10, 1845; House May 23, 1808-09; Assoc. Just. of Supreme Court 1811-Sept. 10, 1845.

STOUGHTON, William Lewis (R Mich.) March 20, 1827-June 6, 1888; House 1869-73.

STOUT, Byron Gray (D Mich.) Jan. 12, 1829-June 19, 1896; House 1891-93.

STOUT, Lansing (D Ore.) March 27, 1828-March 4, 1871; House 1859-61.

STOUT, Tom (D Mont.) May 20, 1879-Dec. 26, 1965; House 1913-17.

STOVER, John Hubler (R Mo.) April 24, 1833-Oct. 27, 1889; House Dec. 7, 1868-69.

STOW, Silas (F N.Y.) Dec. 21, 1773-Jan. 19, 1827; House 1811-13.

STOWELL, William Henry Harrison (R Va.) July 26, 1840-April 27, 1922; House 1871-77.

STOWER, John G. (JD N.Y.) ?-?; House 1827-29.

STRADER, Peter Wilson (D Ohio) Nov. 6, 1818-Feb. 25, 1881; House 1869-71.

STRAIT, Horace Burton (R Minn.) Jan. 26, 1835-Feb. 25, 1894; House 1873-79, 1881-87.

STRAIT, Thomas Jefferson (Alliance D S.C.) Dec. 25, 1846-April 18, 1924; House 1893-99.

STRANAHAN, James Samuel Thomas (W N.Y.) April 25, 1808-Sept. 3, 1898; House 1855-57.

STRANGE, Robert (D N.C.) Sept. 20, 1796-Feb. 19, 1854; Senate Dec. 5, 1836-Nov. 16, 1840.

STRATTON, Charles Creighton (uncle of Benjamin Franklin Howey) (W N.J.) March 6, 1796-March 30, 1859; House 1837-39, 1841-43; Gov. 1845-48.

STRATTON, John (— Va.) Aug. 19, 1769-May 10, 1804; House 1801-03.

STRATTON, John Leake Newbold (R N.J.) Nov. 27, 1817-May 17, 1899; House 1859-63.

STRATTON, Nathan Taylor (D N.J.) March 17, 1813-March 9, 1887; House 1851-55.

STRATTON, Samuel Studdiford (D N.Y.) Sept. 27, 1916-___; House 1959-___.

STRATTON, William Grant (R Ill.) Feb. 26, 1914-___; House 1941-43, 1947-49; Gov. 1953-61.

STRAUB, Christian Markle (D Pa.) 1804-?; House 1853-55.

STRAUS, Isidor (D N.Y.) Feb. 6, 1845-April 15, 1912; House Jan. 30, 1894-95.

STRAWBRIDGE, James Dale (R Pa.) April 7, 1824-July 19, 1890; House 1873-75.

STREET, Randall S. (D N.Y.) 1780-Nov. 21, 1841; House 1819-21.

STRICKLAND, Randolph (R Mich.) Feb. 4, 1823-May 5, 1880; House 1869-71.

STRINGER, Lawrence Beaumont (D Ill.) Feb. 24, 1866-Dec. 5, 1942; House 1913-15.

STRINGFELLOW, Douglas (R Utah) Sept. 24, 1922-Oct. 19, 1966; House 1953-55.

STRODE, Jesse Burr (R Neb.) Feb. 18, 1845-Nov. 10, 1924; House 1895-99.

STROHM, John (W Pa.) Oct. 16, 1793-Sept. 12, 1884; House 1845-49.

STRONG, Caleb (F Mass.) Jan. 9, 1745-Nov. 7, 1819; Senate 1789-June 1, 1796; Gov. 1800-07, 1812-16.

STRONG, James (F N.Y.) 1783-Aug. 8, 1847; House 1819-21, 1823-31.

STRONG, James George (R Kan.) April 23, 1870-Jan. 11, 1938; House 1919-33.

STRONG, Julius Levi (R Conn.) Nov. 8, 1828-Sept. 7, 1872; House 1869-Sept. 7, 1872.

STRONG, Luther Martin (R Ohio) June 23, 1838-April 26, 1903; House 1893-97.

STRONG, Nathan Leroy (R Pa.) Nov. 12, 1859-Dec. 14, 1939; House 1917-35.

STRONG, Selah Brewster (D N.Y.) May 1, 1792-Nov. 29, 1872; House 1843-45.

STRONG, Solomon (F Mass.) March 2, 1780-Sept. 16, 1850; House 1815-19.

STRONG, Stephen (D N.Y.) Oct. 11, 1791-April 15, 1866; House 1845-47.

STRONG, Sterling Price (D Texas) Aug. 17, 1852-March 28, 1936; House 1933-35.

STRONG, Theron Rudd (cousin of William Strong of Pa.) (D N.Y.) Nov. 7, 1802-May 14, 1873; House 1839-41.

STRONG, William (D Vt.) 1763-Jan. 28, 1840; House 1811-15, 1819-21.

STRONG, William (cousin of Theron Rudd Strong) (D Pa.) May 6, 1808-Aug. 19, 1895; House 1847-51; Assoc. Justice of Supreme Court 1870-80.

STROTHER, George French (father of James French Strother) (D Va.) 1783-Nov. 28, 1840; House 1817-Feb. 10, 1820.

STROTHER, James French (son of George French Strother) (W Va.) Sept. 4, 1811-Sept. 20, 1860; House 1851-53.

STROTHER, James French (grandson of the preceding) (R W.Va.) June 29, 1868-April 10, 1930; House 1925-29.

STROUSE, Myer (D Pa.) Dec. 16, 1825-Feb. 11, 1878; House 1863-67.

STROWD, William Franklin (P N.C.) Dec. 7, 1832-Dec. 12, 1911; House 1895-99.

STRUBLE, Isaac S. (R Iowa) Nov. 3, 1843-Feb. 17, 1913; House 1883-91.

STRUDWICK, William Francis (F N.C.) ?-1812; House Nov. 28, 1796-97.

STUART, Alexander Hugh Holmes (cousin of Archibald Stuart) (W W.Va.) April 2, 1807-Feb. 13, 1891; House 1841-43; Secy. of the Interior 1850-53.

STUART, Andrew (D Ohio) Aug. 3, 1823-April 30, 1872; House 1853-55.

STUART, Archibald (cousin of Alexander Hugh Holmes Stuart) (W W.Va.) Dec. 2, 1795-Sept. 20, 1855; House 1837-39.

STUART, Charles Edward (D Mich.) Nov. 25, 1810-May 19, 1887; House Dec. 6, 1847-49, 1851-53; Senate 1853-59.

STUART, David (D Mich.) March 12, 1816-Sept. 12, 1868; House 1853-55.

STUART, John Todd (D Ill.) Nov. 10, 1807-Nov. 23, 1885; House 1839-43, 1863-65 (1839-43 Whig, 1863-65 Democrat).

STUART, Philip (F Md.) 1760-Aug. 14, 1830; House 1811-19.

STUBBLEFIELD, Frank Albert (D Ky.) April 5, 1907-___; House 1959-Dec. 31, 1974.

STUBBS, Henry Elbert (D Calif.) March 4, 1881-Feb. 28, 1937; House 1933-Feb. 28, 1937.

STUCKEY, Williamson Sylvester Jr. (D Ga.) May 25, 1935-___; House 1967-___.

STUDLEY, Elmer Ebenezer (R N.Y.) Sept. 24, 1869-Sept. 6, 1942; House 1933-35.

STUDDS, Gerry Eastman (D Mass.) May 12, 1937-___; House 1973-___.

STULL, Howard William (R Pa.) April 11, 1876-April 22, 1949; House April 26, 1932-33.

STUMP, Herman (D Md.) Aug. 8, 1837-Jan. 9, 1917; House 1889-93.

STURGEON, Daniel (D Pa.) Oct. 27, 1789-July 3, 1878; Senate Jan. 14, 1840-51.

STURGES, Jonathan (father of Lewis Burr Sturges) (— Conn.) Aug. 23, 1740-Oct. 4, 1819; House 1789-93; Cont. Cong. 1774-87.

STURGES, Lewis Burr (son of Jonathan Sturges) (F Conn.) March 15, 1763-March 30, 1844; House Sept. 16, 1805-17.

STURGISS, George Cookman (R W.Va.) Aug. 16, 1842-Feb. 26, 1925; House 1907-11.

STURTEVANT, John Cirby (R Pa.) Feb. 20, 1835-Dec. 20, 1912; House 1897-99.

SULLIVAN, Christopher Daniel (D N.Y.) July 14, 1870-Aug. 3, 1942; House 1917-41.

SULLIVAN, George (— N.H.) Aug. 29, 1771-April 14, 1838; House 1811-13.

SULLIVAN, John Andrew (D Mass.) May 10, 1868-May 31, 1927; House 1903-07.

SULLIVAN, John Berchmans (husband of Leonor Kretzer Sullivan) (D Mo.) Oct. 10, 1897-Jan. 29, 1951; House 1941-43, 1945-47, 1949-Jan. 19, 1951.

SULLIVAN, Leonor Kretzer (widow of John Berchmans Sullivan) (D Mo.) Aug. 21, 1903-___; House 1953-___.

SULLIVAN, Maurice Joseph (D Nev.) Dec. 7, 1884-Aug. 9, 1953; House 1943-45.

SULLIVAN, Patrick Joseph (R Wyo.) March 17, 1865-April 8, 1935; Senate Dec. 5, 1929-Nov. 20, 1930.

SULLIVAN, Patrick Joseph (R Pa.) Oct. 12, 1877-Dec. 31, 1946; House 1929-33.

SULLIVAN, Timothy Daniel (D N.Y.) July 23, 1862-Aug. 31, 1913; House 1903-July 27, 1906, March 4-Aug. 31, 1913.

SULLIVAN, William Van Amberg (D Miss.) Dec. 18, 1857-March 21, 1918; House 1897-May 31, 1898; Senate May 31, 1898-1901.

SULLOWAY, Cyrus Adams (R N.H.) June 8, 1839-March 11, 1917; House 1895-1913, 1915-March 11, 1917.

SULZER, Charles August (brother of William Sulzer) (D Alaska) Feb. 24, 1879-April 28, 1919; House (Terr. Del.) 1917-Jan. 7, 1919, March 4-April 28, 1919.

SULZER, William (brother of Charles August Sulzer) (D N.Y.) March 18, 1863-Nov. 6, 1941; House 1895-Dec. 31, 1912; Gov. 1913.

SUMMERS, George William (W Va.) March 4, 1804-Sept. 19, 1868; House 1841-45.

SUMMERS, John William (R Wash.) April 29, 1870-Sept. 25, 1937; House 1919-33.

SUMNER, Charles (R Mass.) Jan. 6, 1811-March 11, 1874; Senate April 24, 1851-March 11, 1874 (1851-57 Democrat/Free Soiler, 1857-74 Republican).

SUMNER, Charles Allen (D Calif.) Aug. 2, 1835-Jan. 31, 1903; House 1883-85.

SUMNER, Daniel Hadley (D Wis.) Sept. 15, 1837-May 29, 1903; House 1883-85.

SUMNER, Jessie (R Ill.) July 17, 1898-__; House 1939-47.

SUMNERS, Hatton William (D Texas) May 30, 1875-April 19, 1962; House 1913-47.

SUMTER, Thomas (grandfather of Thomas De Lage Sumter) (D S.C.) Aug. 14, 1734-June 1, 1832; House 1789-93, 1797-Dec. 15, 1801; Senate Dec. 15, 1801-Dec. 16, 1810.

SUMTER, Thomas De Lage (grandson of Thomas Sumter) (D S.C.) Nov. 14, 1809-July 2, 1874; House 1839-43.

SUNDSTROM, Frank Leander (R N.J.) Jan. 5, 1901-__; House 1943-49.

SUTHERLAND, Daniel Alexander (R Alaska) April 17, 1869-March 24, 1955; House (Terr. Del.) 1921-31.

SUTHERLAND, George (R Utah) March 25, 1862-July 18, 1942; House 1901-03; Senate 1905-17; Assoc. Justice of Supreme Court 1922-38.

SUTHERLAND, Howard (R W.Va.) Sept. 8, 1865-March 12, 1950; House 1913-17; Senate 1917-23.

SUTHERLAND, Jabez Gridley (D Mich.) Oct. 6, 1825-Nov. 20, 1902; House 1871-73.

SUTHERLAND, Joel Barlow (JD Pa.) Feb. 26, 1792-Nov. 15, 1861; House 1827-37.

SUTHERLAND, Josiah (D N.Y.) June 12, 1804-May 25, 1887; House 1851-53.

SUTHERLAND, Roderick Dhu (P Neb.) April 27, 1862-Oct. 18, 1915; House 1897-1901.

SUTPHIN, William Halstead (D N.J.) Aug. 30, 1887-Oct. 14, 1972; House 1931-43.

SUTTON, James Patrick (Pat) (D Tenn.) Oct. 31, 1915-__; House 1949-55.

SWAN, Samuel (— N.J.) 1771-Aug. 24, 1844; House 1821-31.

SWANK, Fletcher B. (D Okla.) April 24, 1875-March 16, 1950; House 1921-29, 1931-35.

SWANN, Edward (D N.Y.) March 10, 1862-Sept. 19, 1945; House Nov. 4, 1902-03.

SWANN, Thomas (D Md.) Feb. 3, 1809-July 24, 1883; House 1869-79; Gov. 1866-69 (U).

SWANSON, Charles Edward (R Iowa) Jan. 3, 1879-Aug. 22, 1970; House 1929-33.

SWANSON, Claude Augustus (D Va.) March 31, 1862-July 7, 1939; House 1893-Jan. 30, 1906; Senate Aug. 1, 1910-33; Gov. 1906-10; Secy. of the Navy 1933-39.

SWANWICK, John (D Pa.) 1740-Aug. 1, 1798; House 1795-Aug. 1, 1798.

SWART, Peter (— N.Y.) July 5, 1752-Nov. 3, 1829; House 1807-09.

SWARTZ, Joshua William (R Pa.) June 9, 1867-May 27, 1959; House 1925-27.

SWASEY, John Philip (R Maine) Sept. 4, 1839-May 27, 1928; House Nov. 3, 1908-11.

SWEARINGEN, Henry (D Ohio) about 1792-?; House Dec. 3, 1838-41.

SWEAT, Lorenzo De Medici (D Maine) May 26, 1818-July 26, 1898; House 1863-65.

SWEENEY, Martin Leonard (father of Robert E. Sweeney) (D Ohio) April 15, 1885-May 1, 1960; House Nov. 3, 1931-43.

SWEENEY, Robert E. (son of Martin L. Sweeney) (D Ohio) Nov. 4, 1924-__; House 1965-67.

SWEENEY, William Northcut (D Ky.) May 5, 1832-April 21, 1895; House 1869-71.

SWEENY, George (— Ohio) Feb. 22, 1796-Oct. 10, 1877; House 1839-43.

SWEET, Burton Erwin (R Iowa) Dec. 10, 1867-Jan. 3, 1957; House 1915-23.

SWEET, Edwin Forrest (D Mich.) Nov. 21, 1847-April 2, 1935; House 1911-13.

SWEET, John Hyde (R Neb.) Sept. 1, 1880-April 4, 1964; House April 9, 1940-41.

SWEET, Thaddeus C. (R N.Y.) Nov. 16, 1872-May 1, 1928; House Nov. 6, 1923-May 1, 1928.

SWEET, Willis (R Idaho) Jan. 1, 1856-July 9, 1925; House Oct. 1, 1890-95.

SWEETSER, Charles (D Ohio) Jan. 22, 1808-April 14, 1864; House 1849-53.

SWENEY, Joseph Henry (R Iowa) Oct. 2, 1845-Nov. 11, 1918; House 1889-91.

SWICK, Jesse Howard (R Pa.) Aug. 6, 1879-Nov. 17, 1952; House 1927-35.

SWIFT, Benjamin (F Vt.) April 3, 1781-Nov. 11, 1847; House 1827-31; Senate 1833-39.

SWIFT, George Robinson (D Ala.) Dec. 19, 1887-Sept. 10, 1972; Senate June 15-Nov. 5, 1946.

SWIFT, Oscar William (R N.Y.) April 11, 1869-June 30, 1940; House 1915-19.

SWIFT, Zephaniah (F Conn.) Feb. 27, 1759-Sept. 27, 1823; House 1793-97.

SWINBURNE, John (R N.Y.) May 30, 1820-March 28, 1889; House 1885-87.

SWINDALL, Charles (R Okla.) Feb. 13, 1876-June 19, 1939; House Nov. 2, 1920-21.

SWING, Philip David (R Calif.) Nov. 30, 1884-Aug. 8, 1963; House 1921-33.

SWITZER, Robert Mauck (R Ohio) March 6, 1863-Oct. 28, 1952; House 1911-19.

SWOOPE, Jacob (F Va.) ?-1832; House 1809-11.

SWOOPE, William Irvin (nephew of John Patton) (R Pa.) Oct. 3, 1862-Oct. 9, 1930; House 1923-27.

SWOPE, Guy Jacob (D Pa.) Dec. 26, 1892-July 25, 1969; House 1937-39; Gov. of Puerto Rico 1941.

SWOPE, John Augustus (D Pa.) Dec. 25, 1827-Dec. 6, 1910; House Dec. 23, 1884-March 3, 1885, Nov. 3, 1885-87.

SWOPE, King (R Ky.) Aug. 10, 1893-April 23, 1961; House Aug. 2, 1919-21.

SWOPE, Samuel Franklin (R Ky.) March 1, 1809-April 19, 1865; House 1855-57 (1855-56 American Party, 1856-57 Republican).

SYKES, George (D N.J.) Sept. 20, 1802-Feb. 25, 1880; House 1843-45, Nov. 4, 1845-47.

SYMES, George Gifford (R Colo.) April 28, 1840-Nov. 3, 1893; House 1885-89.

SYMINGTON, James Wadsworth (son of William Stuart Symington) (D Mo.) Sept. 28, 1927-__; House 1969-__.

SYMINGTON, William Stuart (father of James Wadsworth Symington) (D Mo.) June 26, 1901-__; Senate 1953-—.

SYMMS, Steven Douglas (R Idaho) April 23, 1938-__; House 1973-__.

SYPHER, Jacob Hale (R La.) June 22, 1837-May 9, 1905; House July 18, 1868-69, Nov. 7, 1870-75.

T

TABER, John (R N.Y.) May 5, 1880-Nov. 22, 1965; House 1923-63.

TABER, Stephen (son of Thomas Taber 2d) (D N.Y.) March 7, 1821-April 23, 1886; House 1865-69.

TABER, Thomas 2d (father of Stephen Taber) (D N.Y.) May 19, 1785-March 21, 1862; House Nov. 5, 1828-29.

TABOR, Horace Austin Warner (R Colo.) Nov. 26, 1830-April 10, 1899; Senate Jan. 27-March 3, 1883.

TACKETT, Boyd (D Ark.) May 9, 1911-__; House 1949-53.

TAFFE, John (R Neb.) Jan. 30, 1827-March 14, 1884; House 1867-73.

TAFT, Charles Phelps (brother of President William Howard Taft and uncle of Robert Alphonso Taft) (R Ohio) Dec. 21, 1843-Dec. 31, 1929; House 1895-97.

TAFT, Kingsley Arter (R Ohio) July 19, 1903-March 28, 1970; Senate Nov. 5, 1946-47.

TAFT, Robert Alphonso (son of President William Howard Taft, father of Robert Taft Jr., and nephew of Charles Phelps Taft) (R Ohio) Sept. 8, 1889-July 31, 1953; Senate 1939-July 31, 1953.

TAFT, Robert Jr. (son of the preceding) (R Ohio) Feb. 26, 1917-—; House 1963-65, 1967-71; Senate 1971-__.

TAGGART, Joseph (D Kan.) June 15, 1867-
Dec. 3, 1938; House Nov. 7, 1911-17.

TAGGART, Samuel (F Mass.) March 24,
1754-April 25, 1825; House 1803-17.

TAGGART, Thomas (D Ind.) Nov. 17, 1856-
March 6, 1929; Senate March 20-Nov. 7,
1916; Chrmn. Dem. Nat. Comm. 1904-08.

TAGUE, Peter Francis (D Mass.) June 4,
1871-Sept. 17, 1941; House 1915-19, Oct.
23, 1919-25.

TAIT, Charles (D Ga.) Feb. 1, 1768-Oct. 7,
1835; Senate Nov. 27, 1809-19.

TALBERT, William Jasper (D S.C.) Oct. 6,
1846-Feb. 5, 1931; House 1893-1903.

TALBOT, Isham (— Ky.) 1773-Sept. 25,
1837; Senate Jan. 3, 1815-19, Oct. 19,
1820-25.

TALBOT, Joseph Edward (R Conn.) March
18, 1901-April 30, 1966; House Jan. 20,
1942-47.

TALBOT, Silas (F N.Y.) Jan. 11, 1751-June
30, 1813; House 1793-95.

TALBOTT, Albert Gallatin (uncle of William
Clayton Anderson) (D Ky.) April 4, 1808-
Sept. 9, 1887; House 1855-59.

TALBOTT, Joshua Frederick Cockey (D Md.)
July 29, 1843-Oct. 5, 1918; House 1879-
85, 1893-95, 1903-Oct. 5, 1918.

TALCOTT, Burt L. (R Calif.) Feb. 22,
1920-__; House 1963-__.

TALCOTT, Charles Andrew (D N.Y.) June
10, 1857-Feb. 27, 1920; House 1911-15.

TALIAFERRO, Benjamin (— Ga.) 1750-
Sept. 3, 1821; House 1799-1802.

TALIAFERRO, James Piper (D Fla.) Sept.
30, 1847-Oct. 6, 1934; Senate April 20,
1899-1911.

TALIAFERRO, John (W Va.) 1768-Aug. 12,
1852; House 1801-03, Nov. 29, 1811-13,
March 24, 1824-31, 1835-43 (1801-03 and
1811-13 and 1824-31 Democrat, 1835-43
Whig).

TALLE, Henry Oscar (R Iowa) Jan. 12,
1892-March 14, 1969; House 1939-59.

TALLMADGE, Benjamin (father of Frederick
Augustus Tallmadge) (F Conn.) Feb. 25,
1754-March 7, 1835; House 1801-17.

TALLMADGE, Frederick Augustus (son of
Benjamin Tallmadge) (W N.Y.) Aug. 29,
1792-Sept. 17, 1869; House 1847-49.

TALLMADGE, James Jr. (D N.Y.) Jan.
20, 1778-Sept. 29, 1853; House June 6,
1817-19.

TALLMADGE, Nathaniel Pitcher (D N.Y.)
Feb. 8, 1795-Nov. 2, 1864; Senate 1833-
June 17, 1844; Gov. (Wis. Terr.) 1844-45.

TALLMAN, Peleg (D Mass.) July 24, 1764-
March 12, 1840; House 1811-13.

TALMADGE, Herman Eugene (D Ga.) Aug.
9, 1913-__; Senate 1957-__; Gov. 1947, 1948-
55.

TANNEHILL, Adamson (D Pa.) May 23,
1750-Dec. 23, 1820; House 1813-15.

TANNER, Adolphus Hitchcock (R N.Y.)
May 23, 1833-Jan. 14, 1882; House 1869-71.

TAPPAN, Benjamin (D Ohio) May 25, 1773-
April 12, 1857; Senate 1839-45.

TAPPAN, Mason Weare (R N.H.) Oct. 20,
1817-Oct. 25, 1886; House 1855-61.

TARBOX, John Kemble (D Mass.) May 6,
1838-May 28, 1887; House 1875-77.

TARR, Christian (— Pa.) May 25, 1765-Feb.
24, 1833; House 1817-21.

TARSNEY, John Charles (D Mo.) Nov. 7,
1845-Sept. 4, 1920; House 1889-Feb. 17,
1896.

TARSNEY, Timothy Edward (D Mich.) Feb.
4, 1849-June 8, 1909; House 1885-89.

TARVER, Malcolm Connor (D Ga.) Sept.
25, 1885-March 5, 1960; House 1927-47.

TATE, Farish Carter (D Ga.) Nov. 20, 1856-
Feb. 7, 1922; House 1893-1905.

TATE, Magnus (F Va.) 1760-March 30,
1823; House 1815-17.

TATGENHORST, Charles Jr. (R Ohio)
Aug. 19, 1883-Jan. 13, 1961; House Nov. 8,
1927-29.

TATOM, Absalom (R N.C.) 1742-Dec. 20,
1802; House 1795-June 1, 1796.

TATTNALL, Edward Fenwick (— Ga.) 1788-
Nov. 21, 1832; House 1821-27.

TATNALL, Josiah (— Ga.) 1764-June 6,
1803; Senate Feb. 20, 1796-99; Gov. 1801-
02.

TAUL, Micah (grandfather of Taul Bradford) (D Ky.) May 14, 1785-May 27, 1850;
House 1815-17.

TAULBEE, William Preston (D Ky.) Oct. 22,
1851-March 11, 1890; House 1885-89.

TAURIELLO, Anthony Francis (D N.Y.)
Aug. 14, 1899-__; House 1949-51.

TAVENNER, Clyde Howard (D Ill.) Feb. 4,
1882-Feb. 6, 1942; House 1913-17.

TAWNEY, James Albertus (R Minn.) Jan.
3, 1855-June 12, 1919; House 1893-1911.

TAYLER, Robert Walker (R Ohio) Nov. 26,
1852-Nov. 25, 1910; House 1895-1903.

TAYLOR, Abner (R Ill.) 1829-April 13,
1903; House 1889-93.

TAYLOR, Alexander Wilson (R Pa.) March
22, 1815-May 7, 1893; House 1873-75.

TAYLOR, Alfred Alexander (son of Nathaniel
Green Taylor and brother of Robert Love
Taylor) (R Tenn.) Aug. 6, 1848-Nov. 25,
1931; House 1889-95; Gov. 1921-23.

TAYLOR, Arthur Herbert (D Ind.) Feb. 29,
1852-Feb. 20, 1922; House 1893-95.

TAYLOR, Benjamin Irving (D N.Y.) Dec.
21, 1877-Sept. 5, 1946; House 1913-15.

TAYLOR, Caleb Newbold (R Pa.) July 27,
1813-Nov. 15, 1887; House 1867-69, April
13, 1870-71.

TAYLOR, Chester William (son of Samuel
Mitchell Taylor) (D Ark.) July 16, 1883-
July 17, 1931; House Oct. 31, 1921-23.

TAYLOR, Dean Park (R N.Y.) Jan. 1, 1902-__;
House 1943-61.

TAYLOR, Edward Livingston Jr. (R Ohio)
Aug. 10, 1869-March 10, 1938; House
1905-13.

TAYLOR, Edward Thomas (D Colo.) June
19, 1858-Sept. 3, 1941; House 1909-Sept.
3, 1941.

TAYLOR, Ezra Booth (R Ohio) July 9,
1823-Jan. 29, 1912; House Dec. 13, 1880-
93.

TAYLOR, Gene (R Mo.) Feb. 10, 1928-__;
House 1973-__.

TAYLOR, George (D N.Y.) Oct. 19, 1820-
Jan. 18, 1894; House 1857-59.

TAYLOR, George Washington (D Ala.) Jan.
16, 1849-Dec. 21, 1932; House 1897-1915.

TAYLOR, Glen Hearst (D Idaho) April 12,
1904-__; Senate 1945-51.

TAYLOR, Herbert Worthington (R N.J.)
Feb. 19, 1869-Oct. 15, 1931; House 1921-
23, 1925-27.

TAYLOR, Isaac Hamilton (R Ohio) April
18, 1840-Dec. 18, 1936; House 1885-87.

TAYLOR, James Alfred (D W.Va.) Sept.
25, 1878-June 9, 1956; House 1923-27.

TAYLOR, James Willis (R Tenn.) Aug. 28,
1880-Nov. 14, 1939; House 1919-Nov. 14,
1939.

TAYLOR, John (D Va.) May 17, 1754-Aug.
20, 1824; Senate Oct. 18, 1792-May 11,
1794, June 4-Dec. 7, 1803, Dec. 18,
1822-Aug. 20, 1824.

TAYLOR, John (D S.C.) May 4, 1770-April
16, 1832; House 1807-Dec. 30, 1810; Senate Dec. 31, 1810-Nov. 1816; Gov. 1826-28.

TAYLOR, John (— S.C.) ?-?; House 1815-17.

TAYLOR, John Clarence (D S.C.) March 2,
1890-__; House 1933-39.

TAYLOR, John James (D N.Y.) April 27,
1808-July 1, 1892; House 1853-55.

TAYLOR, John Lampkin (W Ohio) March 7,
1805-Sept. 6, 1870; House 1847-55.

TAYLOR, John May (D Tenn.) May 18,
1838-Feb. 17, 1911; House 1883-87.

TAYLOR, John W. (D N.Y.) March 26,
1784-Sept. 8, 1854; House 1813-33;
Speaker 1820-21, 1825-27.

TAYLOR, Jonathan (D Ohio) 1796-April
1848; House 1839-41.

TAYLOR, Joseph Danner (R Ohio) Nov.
7, 1830-Sept. 19, 1899; House Jan. 2,
1883-85, 1887-93.

TAYLOR, Miles (D La.) July 16, 1805-Sept. 23, 1873; House 1855-Feb. 5, 1861.

TAYLOR, Nathaniel Green (father of Alfred Alexander Taylor and Robert Love Taylor) (W Tenn.) Dec. 29, 1819-April 1, 1887; House March 30, 1854-55, July 24, 1866-67.

TAYLOR, Nelson (D N.Y.) June 8, 1821-Jan. 16, 1894; House 1865-67.

TAYLOR, Robert (— Va.) April 29, 1763-July 3, 1845; House 1825-27.

TAYLOR, Robert Love (D Tenn.) (son of Nathaniel Green Taylor and brother of Alfred Alexander Taylor) July 31, 1850-March 31, 1912; House 1879-81; Senate 1907-March 31, 1912; Gov. 1887-91, 1897-99.

TAYLOR, Roy Arthur (D N.C.) Jan. 31, 1910-__; House June 25, 1960-__.

TAYLOR, Samuel Mitchell (father of Chester William Taylor) (D Ark.) May 25, 1852-Sept. 13, 1921; House Jan. 15, 1913-Sept. 13, 1921.

TAYLOR, Vincent Albert (R Ohio) Dec. 6, 1845-Dec. 2, 1922; House 1891-93.

TAYLOR, Waller (D Ind.) before 1786-Aug. 26, 1826; Senate Dec. 11, 1816-25.

TAYLOR, William (D N.Y.) Oct. 12, 1791-Sept. 16, 1865; House 1833-39.

TAYLOR, William (D Va.) April 5, 1788-Jan. 17, 1846; House 1843-Jan. 17, 1846.

TAYLOR, William Penn (W Va.) ?-?; House 1833-35.

TAYLOR, Zachary (R Tenn.) May 9, 1849-Feb. 19, 1921; House 1885-87.

TAZEWELL, Henry (father of Littleton Waller Tazewell) (— Va.) Nov. 15, 1753-Jan. 24, 1799; Senate Dec. 29, 1794-Jan. 24, 1799; President pro tempore 1794-96.

TAZEWELL, Littleton Waller (son of Henry Tazewell) (D Va.) Dec. 17, 1774-May 6, 1860; House Nov. 26, 1800-01; Senate Dec. 7, 1824-July 16, 1832; President pro tempore 1832; Gov. 1834-36.

TEAGUE, Charles McKevett (R Calif.) Sept. 18, 1909-Jan. 1, 1974; House 1955-Jan. 1, 1974.

TEAGUE, Olin Earl (D Texas) April 6, 1910-__; House Aug. 24, 1946-__.

TEESE, Frederick Halstead (D N.J.) Oct. 21, 1823-Jan. 7, 1894; House 1875-77.

TEIGAN, Henry George (FL Minn.) Aug. 7, 1881-March 12, 1941; House 1937-39.

TELFAIR, Thomas (D Ga.) March 2, 1780-Feb. 18, 1818; House 1813-17.

TELLER, Henry Moore (D Colo.) May 23, 1830-Feb. 23, 1914; Senate Nov. 15, 1876-April 17, 1882, 1885-1909 (1876-82 and 1885-97 Republican, 1897-1903 Independent Silver Republican, 1903-09 Democrat); Secy. of the Interior 1882-85.

TELLER, Isaac (nephew of Abraham Henry Schenck) (D N.Y.) Feb. 7, 1799-April 30, 1868; House Nov. 7, 1854-55.

TELLER, Ludwig (D N.Y.) June 22, 1911-Oct. 4, 1965; House 1957-61.

TEMPLE, Henry Wilson (R Pa.) March 31, 1864-Jan. 11, 1955; House 1913-15, Nov. 2, 1915-33 (1913-15 Progressive Republican, 1915-33 Republican).

TEMPLE, William (D Del.) Feb. 28, 1814-May 28, 1863; House March 4-May 28, 1863.

TEMPLETON, Thomas Weir (R Pa.) Nov. 8, 1867-Sept. 5, 1935; House 1917-19.

TENER, John Kinley (R Pa.) July 25, 1863-May 19, 1946; House 1909-Jan. 16, 1911; Gov. 1911-15.

TENEROWICZ, Rudolph Gabriel (D Mich.) June 14, 1890-Aug. 31, 1963; House 1939-43.

TEN EYCK, Egbert (— N.Y.) April 18, 1779-April 11, 1844; House 1823-Dec. 15, 1825.

TEN EYCK, John Conover (R N.J.) March 12, 1814-Aug. 24, 1879; Senate 1859-65.

TEN EYCK, Peter Gansevoort (D N.Y.) Nov. 7, 1873-Sept. 2, 1944; House 1913-15, 1921-23.

TENNEY, Samuel (— N.H.) Nov. 27, 1748-Feb. 6, 1816; House Dec. 8, 1800-07.

TENZER, Herbert (D N.Y.) Nov. 1, 1905-__; House 1965-69.

TERRELL, George Butler (D Texas) Dec. 5, 1862-April 18, 1947, House 1933-35.

TERRELL, James C. (UD Ga.) Nov. 7, 1806-Dec. 1, 1835; House March 4-July 8, 1835.

TERRELL, Joseph Meriwether (D Ga.) June 6, 1861-Nov. 17, 1912; Senate Nov. 17, 1910-July 14, 1911; Gov. 1902-07.

TERRELL, William (D Ga.) 1778-July 4, 1855; House 1817-21.

TERRY, David Dickson (son of William Leake Terry) (D Ark.) Jan. 31, 1881-Oct. 7, 1963; House Dec. 19, 1933-43.

TERRY, John H. (R N.Y.) Nov. 14, 1924-__; House 1971-1973.

TERRY, Nathaniel (— Conn.) Jan. 30, 1768-June 14, 1844; House 1817-19.

TERRY, William (C Va.) Aug. 14, 1824-Sept. 5, 1888; House 1871-73, 1875-77.

TERRY, William Leake (father of David Dickson Terry) (D Ark.) Sept. 27, 1850-Nov. 4, 1917; House 1891-1901.

TEST, John (W Ind.) Nov. 12, 1771-Oct. 9, 1849; House 1823-27, 1829-31 (1823-27 Clay Democrat, 1829-31 Whig)

TEWES, Donald Edgar (R Wis.) Aug. 4, 1916-__; House 1957-59.

THACHER, George (F Mass.) April 12, 1754-April 6, 1824; House 1789-1801; Cont. Cong. 1787.

THACHER, Thomas Chandler (D Mass.) July 20, 1858-April 11, 1945; House 1913-15.

THATCHER, Maurice Hudson (R Ky.) Aug. 15, 1870-Jan. 6, 1973; House 1923-33.

THATCHER, Samuel (D Mass.) July 1, 1776-July 18, 1872; House Dec. 6, 1802-05.

THAYER, Andrew Jackson (D Ore.) Nov. 27, 1818-April 28, 1873; House March 4-July 30, 1861.

THAYER, Eli (father of John Alden Thayer) (R Mass.) June 11, 1819-April 15, 1899; House 1857-61.

THAYER, Harry Irving (R Mass.) Sept. 10, 1869-March 10, 1926; House 1925-March 10, 1926.

THAYER, John Alden (son of Eli Thayer) (D Mass.) Dec. 22, 1857-July 31, 1917; House 1911-13.

THAYER, John Milton (uncle of Arthur Laban Bates) (R Neb.) Jan. 24, 1820-March 19, 1906; Senate March 1, 1867-71; Gov. (Wyo. Terr.) 1875-79, (Neb.) 1887-91.

THAYER, John Randolph (D Mass.) March 9, 1845-Dec. 19, 1916; House 1899-1905.

THAYER, Martin Russell (R Pa.) Jan. 27, 1819-Oct. 14, 1906; House 1863-67.

THEAKER, Thomas Clarke (R Ohio) Feb. 1, 1812-July 16, 1883; House 1859-61.

THIBODEAUX, Bannon Goforth (— La.) Dec. 22, 1812-March 5, 1866; House 1845-49.

THILL, Lewis Dominic (R Wis.) Oct. 18, 1903-__; House 1939-43.

THISTLEWOOD, Napoleon Bonaparte (R Ill.) March 30, 1837-Sept. 15, 1915; House Feb. 15, 1908-13.

THOM, William Richard (D Ohio) July 7, 1885-Aug. 28, 1960; House 1933-39, 1941-43, 1945-47.

THOMAS, Albert (husband of Lera M. Thomas) (D Texas) April 12, 1898-Feb. 15, 1966; House 1937-Feb. 15, 1966.

THOMAS, Benjamin Franklin (CU Mass.) Feb. 12, 1813-Sept. 27, 1878; House June 11, 1861-63.

THOMAS, Charles Randolph (R N.C.) Feb. 7, 1827-Feb. 18, 1891; House 1871-75.

THOMAS, Charles Randolph (son of the preceding) (D N.C.) Aug. 21, 1861-March 8, 1931; House 1899-1911.

THOMAS, Charles Spalding (D Colo.) Dec. 6, 1849-June 24, 1934; Senate Jan. 15, 1913-21; Gov. 1899-1901.

THOMAS, Christopher Yancy (R Va.) March 24, 1818-Feb. 11, 1879; House March 5, 1874-75.

THOMAS, David (D N.Y.) June 11, 1762-Nov. 11, 1831; House 1801-May 1, 1808.

THOMAS, Elbert Duncan (D Utah) June 17, 1883-Feb. 11, 1953; Senate 1933-51.

THOMAS, Francis (UR Md.) Feb. 3, 1799-Jan. 22, 1876; House 1831-41, 1861-69 (1831-41 Democrat, 1861-69 Union Republican); Gov. 1842-45 (D).

THOMAS, George Morgan (R Ky.) Nov. 23, 1828-Jan. 7, 1914; House 1887-89.

THOMAS, Henry Franklin (R Mich.) Dec. 17, 1843-April 16, 1912; House 1893-97.

THOMAS, Isaac (D Tenn.) Nov. 4, 1784-Feb. 2, 1859; House 1815-17.

THOMAS, James Houston (D Tenn.) Sept. 22, 1808-Aug. 4, 1876; House 1847-51, 1859-61.

THOMAS, Jesse Burgess (W Ind./Ill.) 1777-May 4, 1853; House (Terr. Del.) Oct. 22, 1808-09 (Ind.); Senate Dec. 3, 1818-29 (Ill.).

THOMAS, John (R Idaho) Jan. 4, 1874-Nov. 10, 1945; Senate June 30, 1928-33, Jan. 27, 1940-Nov. 10, 1945.

THOMAS, John Chew (F Md.) Oct. 15, 1764-May 10, 1836; House 1799-1801.

THOMAS, John Lewis Jr. (R Md.) May 20, 1835-Oct. 15, 1893; House Dec. 4, 1865-67.

THOMAS, John Parnell (R N.J.) Jan. 16, 1895-Nov. 19, 1970; House 1937-Jan. 2, 1950.

THOMAS, John Robert (R Ill.) Oct. 11, 1846-Jan. 19, 1914; House 1879-89.

THOMAS, John William Elmer (D Okla.) Sept. 8, 1876-Sept. 19, 1965; House 1923-27; Senate 1927-51.

THOMAS, Lera M. (widow of Albert Thomas) (D Texas) Aug. 3, 1900-__; House March 30, 1966-67.

THOMAS, Lot (R Iowa) Oct. 17, 1843-March 17, 1905; House 1899-1905.

THOMAS, Ormsby Brunson (R Wis.) Aug. 21, 1832-Oct. 24, 1904; House 1885-91.

THOMAS, Philemon (D La.) Feb. 9, 1763-Nov. 18, 1847; House 1831-35.

THOMAS, Phillip Francis (D Md.) Sept. 12, 1810-Oct. 2, 1890; House 1839-41, 1875-77; Gov. 1848-51; Secy. of the Treasury 1860-61.

THOMAS, Richard (F Pa.) Dec. 30, 1744-Jan. 19, 1832; House 1795-1801.

THOMAS, Robert Young Jr. (D Ky.) July 13, 1855-Sept. 3, 1925; House 1909-Sept. 3, 1925.

THOMAS, William Aubrey (R Ohio) June 7, 1866-Sept. 8, 1951; House Nov. 8, 1904-11.

THOMAS, William David (R N.Y.) March 22, 1880-May 17, 1936; House Jan. 30, 1934-May 17, 1936.

THOMASON, Robert Ewing (D Texas) May 30, 1879-Nov. 8, 1973; House 1931-July 31, 1947.

THOMASSON, William Poindexter (W Ky.) Oct. 8, 1797-Dec. 29, 1882; House 1843-47.

THOMPSON, Albert Clifton (R Ohio) Jan. 23, 1842-Jan. 26, 1910; House 1885-91.

THOMPSON, Benjamin (W Mass.) Aug. 5, 1798-Sept. 24, 1852; House 1845-47, 1851-Sept. 24, 1852.

THOMPSON, Charles James (R Ohio) Jan. 24, 1862-March 27, 1932; House 1919-31.

THOMPSON, Charles Perkins (D Mass.) July 30, 1827-Jan. 19, 1894; House 1875-77.

THOMPSON, Charles Winston (D Ala.) Dec. 30, 1860-March 20, 1904; House 1901-March 20, 1904.

THOMPSON, Chester Charles (D Ill.) Sept. 19, 1893-Jan. 30, 1971; House 1933-39.

THOMPSON, Clark Wallace (D Texas) Aug. 6, 1896-__; House June 24, 1933-35, Aug. 23, 1947-Dec. 30, 1966.

THOMPSON, Fountain Land (D N.D.) Nov. 18, 1854-Feb. 4, 1942; Senate Nov. 10, 1909-Jan. 31, 1910.

THOMPSON, Frank Jr. (D N.J.) July 26, 1918-__; House 1955-__.

THOMPSON, George Western (D Va.) May 14, 1806-Feb. 24, 1888; House 1851-July 30, 1852.

THOMPSON, Hedge (— N.J.) Jan. 28, 1780-July 23, 1828; House 1827-July 23, 1828.

THOMPSON, Jacob (D Miss.) May 15, 1810-March 24, 1885; House 1839-51; Secy. of the Interior 1857-61.

THOMPSON, James (D Pa.) Oct. 1, 1806-Jan. 28, 1874; House 1845-51.

THOMPSON, Joel (F N.Y.) Oct. 3, 1760-Feb. 8, 1843; House 1813-15.

THOMPSON, John (D N.Y.) March 20, 1749-1823; House 1799-1801, 1807-11.

THOMPSON, John (R N.Y.) July 4, 1809-June 1, 1890; House 1857-59.

THOMPSON, John Burton (W Ky.) Dec. 14, 1810-Jan. 7, 1874; House Dec. 7, 1840-43, 1847-51; Senate 1853-59.

THOMPSON, John McCandless (brother of William George Thompson) (R Pa.) Jan. 4, 1829-Sept. 3, 1903; House Dec. 22, 1874-75, 1877-79.

THOMPSON, Joseph Bryan (D Okla.) April 29, 1871-Sept. 18, 1919; House 1913-Sept. 18, 1919.

THOMPSON, Philip (— Ky.) Aug. 20, 1789-Nov. 25, 1836; House 1823-25.

THOMPSON, Philip Burton Jr. (D Ky.) Oct. 15, 1845-Dec. 15, 1909; House 1879-85.

THOMPSON, Philip Rootes (D Va.) March 26, 1766-July 27, 1837; House 1801-07.

THOMPSON, Richard Wigginton (W Ind.) June 9, 1809-Feb. 9, 1900; House 1841-43, 1847-49; Secy. of the Navy 1877-80.

THOMPSON, Robert Augustine (father of Thomas Larkin Thompson) (D Va.) Feb. 14, 1805-Aug. 31, 1876; House 1847-49.

THOMPSON, Ruth (R Mich.) Sept. 15, 1887-April 5, 1970; House 1951-57.

THOMPSON, Standish Fletcher (R Ga.) Feb. 5, 1925-__; House 1967-1973.

THOMPSON, Theo Ashton (D La.) March 31, 1916-July 1, 1965; House 1953-July 1, 1965.

THOMPSON, Thomas Larkin (son of Robert Augustine Thompson) (D Calif.) May 31, 1838-Feb. 1, 1898; House 1887-89.

THOMPSON, Thomas Weston (— N.H.) March 15, 1766-Oct. 1, 1821; House 1805-07; Senate June 24, 1814-17.

THOMPSON, Waddy Jr. (W S.C.) Jan. 8, 1798-Nov. 23, 1868; House Sept. 10, 1835-41.

THOMPSON, Wiley (D Ga.) Sept. 23, 1781-Dec. 28, 1835; House 1821-33.

THOMPSON, William (D Iowa) Nov. 10, 1813-Oct. 6, 1897; House 1847-June 29, 1850.

THOMPSON, William George (brother of John McCandless Thompson) (R Iowa) Jan. 17, 1830-April 2, 1911; House Oct. 14, 1879-83.

THOMPSON, William Henry (D Neb.) Dec. 14, 1853-June 6, 1937; Senate May 24, 1933-Nov. 6, 1934.

THOMPSON, William Howard (D Kan.) Oct. 14, 1871-Feb. 9, 1928; Senate 1913-19.

THOMSON, Alexander (— Pa.) Jan. 12, 1788-Aug. 2, 1848; House Dec. 6, 1824-May 1, 1826.

THOMSON, Charles Marsh (PR Ill.) Feb. 13, 1877-Dec. 30, 1943; House 1913-15.

THOMSON, Edwin Keith (R Wyo.) Feb. 8, 1919-Dec. 9, 1960; House 1955-Dec. 9, 1960.

THOMSON, John (D Ohio) Nov. 20, 1780-Dec. 2, 1852; House 1825-27, 1829-37.

THOMSON, John Renshaw (D N.J.) Sept. 25, 1800-Sept. 12, 1862; Senate 1853-Sept. 12, 1862.

THOMSON, Mark (F N.J.) 1739-Dec. 14, 1803; House 1795-99.

THOMSON, Vernon Wallace (R Wis.) Nov. 5, 1905-__; House 1961-Dec. 31, 1974; Gov. 1957-59.

THONE, Charles (R Neb.) Jan. 4, 1924-__; House 1971-__.

THORINGTON, James (W Iowa) May 7, 1816-June 13, 1887; House 1855-57.

THORKELSON, Jacob (R Mont.) Sept. 24, 1876-Nov. 20, 1945; House 1939-41.

THORNBERRY, William Homer (D Texas) Jan. 9, 1909-__; House 1949-Dec. 20, 1963.

THORNBURGH, Jacob Montgomery (R Tenn.) July 3, 1837-Sept. 19, 1890; House 1873-79.

THORNTON, Anthony (D Ill.) Nov. 9, 1814-Sept. 10, 1904; House 1865-67.

THORNTON, John Randolph (D La.) Aug. 25, 1846-Dec. 28, 1917; Senate Dec. 7, 1910-15.

THORNTON, Raymond Hoyt Jr. (D Ark.) July 16, 1928-__; House 1973-__.

THORP, Robert Taylor (R Va.) March 12, 1850-Nov. 26, 1938; House May 2, 1896-97, March 23, 1898-99.

THORPE, Roy Henry (R Neb.) Dec. 13, 1874-Sept. 19, 1951; House Nov. 7, 1922-23.

THROCKMORTON, James Webb (D Texas) Feb. 1, 1825-April 21, 1894; House 1875-79, 1883-87; Gov. 1866-67.

THROOP, Enos Thompson (D N.Y.) Aug. 21, 1784-Nov. 1, 1874; House 1815-June 4, 1816; Gov. 1829-33.

THROPP, Joseph Earlston (R Pa.) Oct. 4, 1847-July 27, 1927; House 1899-1901.

THRUSTON, Bruckner (D Ky.) Feb. 8, 1764-Aug. 30, 1845; Senate 1805-Dec. 18, 1809.

THURMAN, Allen Granberry (D Ohio) Nov. 13, 1813-Dec. 12, 1895; House 1845-47; Senate 1869-81.

THURMAN, John Richardson (W N.Y.) Oct. 6, 1814-July 24, 1854; House 1849-51.

THURMOND, James Strom (R S.C.) Dec. 5, 1902-__; Senate Dec. 24, 1954-April 4, 1956, Nov. 7, 1956-__; (1954-1956 and 1956-Sept. 16, 1964 Democrat, Sept. 16, 1964-__ Republican); Gov. 1947-51.

THURSTON, Benjamin Babcock (D R.I.) June 29, 1804-May 17, 1886; House 1847-49, 1851-57.

THURSTON, John Mellen (R Neb.) Aug. 21, 1847-Aug. 9, 1916; Senate 1895-1901.

THURSTON, Lloyd (R Iowa) March 27, 1880-May 7, 1970; House 1925-39.

THURSTON, Samuel Royal (D Ore.) April 15, 1816-April 9, 1851; House (Terr. Del.) 1849-51.

THYE, Edward John (R Minn.) April 26, 1896-Aug. 28, 1969; Senate 1947-59; Gov. 1943-47.

TIBBATTS, John Wooleston (D Ky.) June 12, 1802-July 5, 1852; House 1843-47.

TIBBITS, George (F N.Y.) Jan. 14, 1763-July 19, 1849; House 1803-05.

TIBBOTT, Harve (R Pa.) May 27, 1885-Dec. 31, 1969; House 1939-49.

TICHENOR, Isaac (F Vt.) Feb. 8, 1754-Dec. 11, 1838; Senate Oct. 18, 1796-Oct. 17, 1797, 1815-21; Gov. 1797-1807, 1808-09.

TIERNAN, Robert Owens (D R.I.) Feb. 24, 1929-__; House March 28, 1967-1975.

TIERNEY, William Laurence (D Conn.) Aug. 6, 1876-April 13, 1958; House 1931-33.

TIFFIN, Edward (D Ohio) June 19, 1766-Aug. 9, 1829; Senate 1807-09; Gov. 1803-07.

TIFT, Nelson (D Ga.) July 23, 1810-Nov. 21, 1891; House July 25, 1868-69.

TILDEN, Daniel Rose (W Ohio) Nov. 5, 1804-March 4, 1890; House 1843-47.

TILLINGHAST, Joseph Leonard (cousin of Thomas Tillinghast) (W R.I.) 1791-Dec. 30, 1844; House 1837-43.

TILLINGHAST, Thomas (cousin of Joseph Leonard Tillinghast (—R.I.) Aug. 21, 1742-Aug. 26, 1821; House Nov. 13, 1797-99, 1801-03.

TILLMAN, Benjamin Ryan (brother of George Dionysius Tillman) (D S.C.) Aug. 11, 1847-July 3, 1918; Senate 1895-July 3, 1918; Gov. 1890-94.

TILLMAN, George Dionysius (brother of Benjamin Ryan Tillman) (D S.C.) Aug. 21, 1826-Feb. 2, 1902; House 1879-June 19, 1882, 1883-93.

TILLMAN, John Newton (D Ark.) Dec. 13, 1859-March 9, 1929; House 1915-29.

TILLMAN, Lewis (nephew of Barclay Martin) (R Tenn.) Aug. 18, 1816-May 3, 1886; House 1869-71.

TILLOTSON, Thomas (— N.Y.) 1750-May 5, 1832; House March 4-Aug. 10, 1801.

TILSON, John Quillin (R Conn.) April 5, 1866-Aug. 14, 1958; House 1909-13, 1915-Dec. 3, 1932.

TIMBERLAKE, Charles Bateman (R Colo.) Sept. 25, 1854-May 31, 1941; House 1915-33.

TINCHER, Jasper Napoleon (R Kan.) Nov. 2, 1878-Nov. 6, 1951; House 1919-27.

TINKHAM, George Holden (R Mass.) Oct. 29, 1870-Aug. 28, 1956; House 1915-43.

TIPTON, John (D Ind.) Aug. 14, 1786-April 5, 1839; Senate Jan. 3, 1832-39.

TIPTON, Thomas Foster (R Ill.) Aug. 29, 1833-Feb. 7, 1904; House 1877-79.

TIPTON, Thomas Weston (R Neb.) Aug. 5, 1817-Nov. 26, 1899; Senate March 1, 1867-75.

TIRRELL, Charles Quincy (R Mass.) Dec. 10, 1844-July 31, 1910; House 1901-July 31, 1910.

TITUS, Obadiah (D N.Y.) Jan. 20, 1789-Sept. 2, 1854; House 1837-39.

TOBEY, Charles William (R N.H.) July 22, 1880-July 24, 1953; House 1933-39; Senate 1939-July 24, 1953; Gov. 1929-31.

TOD, John (D Pa.) 1779-March 1830; House 1821-24.

TODD, Albert May (Fus. Mich.) June 3, 1850-Oct. 6, 1931; House 1897-99.

TODD, John Blair Smith (D Dakota) April 4, 1814-Jan. 5, 1872; House (Terr. Del.) Dec. 9, 1861-63, June 17, 1864-65.

TODD, Lemuel (R Pa.) July 29, 1817-May 12, 1891; House 1855-57, 1873-75.

TODD, Paul Harold Jr. (D Mich.) Sept. 22, 1921-__; House 1965-67.

TOLAN, John Harvey (D Calif.) Jan. 15, 1877-June 30, 1947; House 1937-47.

TOLAND, George Washington (W Pa.) Feb. 8, 1796-Jan. 30, 1869; House 1837-43.

TOLL, Herman (D Pa.) March 15, 1907-July 26, 1967; House 1959-67.

TOLLEFSON, Thor Carl (R Wash.) May 2, 1901-__; House 1947-65.

TOLLEY, Harold Sumner (R N.Y.) Jan. 16, 1894-May 20, 1956; House 1925-27.

TOMLINSON, Gideon (D Conn.) Dec. 31, 1780-Oct. 8, 1854; House 1819-27; Senate 1831-37; Gov. 1827-31.

TOMLINSON, Thomas Ash (W N.Y.) March 1802-June 18, 1872; House 1841-43.

TOMPKINS, Arthur Sidney (R N.Y.) Aug. 26, 1865-Jan. 20, 1938; House 1899-1903.

TOMPKINS, Caleb (— N.Y.) Dec. 22, 1759-Jan. 1, 1846; House 1817-21.

TOMPKINS, Christopher (— Ky.) March 24, 1780-Aug. 9, 1858; House 1831-35.

TOMPKINS, Cydnor Bailey (father of Emmett Tompkins) (R Ohio) Nov. 8, 1810-July 23, 1862; House 1857-61.

TOMPKINS, Emmett (son of Cydnor Bailey Tompkins) (R Ohio) Sept. 1, 1853-Dec. 18, 1917; House 1901-03.

TOMPKINS, Patrick Watson (W Miss.) 1804-May 8, 1853; House 1847-49.

TONGUE, Thomas H. (R Ore.) June 23, 1844-Jan. 11, 1903; House 1897-Jan. 11, 1903.

TONRY, Richard Joseph (D N.Y.) Sept. 30, 1893-Jan. 17, 1971; House 1935-37.

TOOLE, Joseph Kemp (D Mont.) May 12, 1851-March 11, 1929; House (Terr. Del.) 1885-89; Gov. 1889-93, 1901-08.

TOOMBS, Robert (SRD Ga.) July 2, 1810-Dec. 15, 1885; House 1845-53; Senate 1853-Feb. 4, 1861.

TORRENS, James H. (D N.Y.) Sept. 12, 1874-April 5, 1952; House Feb. 29, 1944-47.

TOUCEY, Isaac (D Conn.) Nov. 5, 1796-July 30, 1869; House 1835-39; Senate May 12, 1852-57; Gov. 1846-47; Atty. Gen. 1848-49; Secy. of the Navy 1857-61.

TOU VELLE, William Ellsworth (D Ohio) Nov. 23, 1862-Aug. 14, 1951; House 1907-11.

TOWE, Harry Lancaster (R N.J.) Nov. 3, 1898-__; House 1943-Sept. 7, 1951.

TOWELL, David Gilmer (R Nev.) June 9, 1937-__; House 1973-75.

TOWER, John Goodwin (R Texas) Sept. 29, 1925-__; Senate June 15, 1961-__.

TOWEY, Frank William Jr. (D N.J.) Nov. 5, 1895-__; House 1937-39.

TOWNE, Charles Arnette (D Minn./N.Y.) Nov. 21, 1858-Oct. 22, 1928; House 1895-97 (R Minn.), 1905-07 (D N.Y.); Senate Dec. 5, 1900-Jan. 28, 1901 (D Minn.).

TOWNER, Horace Mann (R Iowa) Oct. 23, 1855-Nov. 23, 1937; House 1911-April 1, 1923; Gov. of Puerto Rico 1923-29.

TOWNS, George Washington Bonaparte (D Ga.) May 4, 1801-July 15, 1854; House 1835-Sept. 1, 1836, 1837-39, Jan. 5, 1846-47 (1835-36 and 1837-39 Union Democrat, 1846-47 Democrat); Gov. 1847-51.

TOWNSEND, Amos (R Ohio) 1821-March 17, 1895; House 1877-83.

TOWNSEND, Charles Champlain (R Pa.) Nov. 24, 1841-July 10, 1910; House 1889-91.

TOWNSEND, Charles Elroy (R Mich.) Aug. 15, 1856-Aug. 3, 1924; House 1903-11; Senate 1911-23.

TOWNSEND, Dwight (D N.Y.) Sept. 26, 1826-Oct. 29, 1899; House Dec. 5, 1864-65, 1871-73.

TOWNSEND, Edward Waterman (D N.J.) Feb. 10, 1855-March 15, 1942; House 1911-15.

TOWNSEND, George (D N.Y.) 1769-Aug. 17, 1844; House 1815-19.

TOWNSEND, Hosea (R Colo.) June 16, 1840-March 4, 1909; House 1889-93.

TOWNSEND, John Gillis Jr. (R Del.) May 31, 1871-April 10, 1964; Senate 1929-41; Gov. 1917-21.

TOWNSEND, Martin Ingham (R N.Y.) Feb. 6, 1810-March 8, 1903; House 1875-79.

TOWNSEND, Washington (R Pa.) Jan. 20, 1813-March 18, 1894; House 1869-77.

TOWNSHEND, Norton Strange (D Ohio) Dec. 25, 1815-July 13, 1895; House 1851-53.

TOWNSHEND, Richard Wellington (D Ill.) April 30, 1840-March 9, 1889; House 1877-March 9, 1889.

TRACEWELL, Robert John (R Ind.) May 7, 1852-July 28, 1922; House 1895-97.

TRACEY, Charles (D N.Y.) May 27, 1847-March 24, 1905; House Nov. 8, 1887-95.

TRACEY, John Plank (R Mo.) Sept. 18, 1836-July 24, 1910; House 1895-97.

TRACY, Albert Haller (brother of Phineas Lyman Tracy) (D N.Y.) June 17, 1793-Sept. 19, 1859; House 1819-25.

TRACY, Andrew (W Vt.) Dec. 15, 1797-Oct. 28, 1868; House 1853-55.

TRACY, Henry Wells (IR Pa.) Sept. 24, 1807-April 11, 1886; House 1863-65.

TRACY, Phineas Lyman (brother of Albert Haller Tracy) (W N.Y.) Dec. 25, 1786-Dec. 22, 1876; House Nov. 5, 1827-33.

TRACY, Uri (D N.Y.) Feb. 8, 1764-July 21, 1838; House 1805-07, 1809-13.

TRACY, Uriah (F Conn.) Feb. 2, 1755-July 19, 1807; House 1793-Oct. 13, 1796; Senate Oct. 13, 1796-July 19, 1807; President pro tempore 1800.

TRAEGER, William Isham (R Calif.) Feb. 26, 1880-Jan. 20, 1935; House 1933-35.

TRAFTON, Mark (AP Mass.) Aug. 1, 1810-March 8, 1901; House 1855-57.

TRAIN, Charles Russell (R Mass.) Oct. 18, 1817-July 28, 1885; House 1859-63.

TRAMMELL, Park (D Fla.) April 9, 1876-May 8, 1936; Senate 1917-May 8, 1936; Gov. 1913-17.

TRANSUE, Andrew Jackson (D Mich.) Jan. 12, 1903-__; House 1937-39.

TRAXLER, Jerome Bob (D Mich.) July 21, 1931-__; House April 16, 1974-__.

TRAYNOR, Philip Andrew (D Del.) May 31, 1874-Dec. 5, 1962; House 1941-43, 1945-47.

TREADWAY, Allen Towner (R Mass.) Sept. 16, 1867-Feb. 16, 1947; House 1913-45.

TREADWAY, William Marshall (D Va.) Aug. 24, 1807-May 1, 1891; House 1845-47.

TREDWELL, Thomas (grandfather of Thomas Treadwell Davis) (— N.Y.) Feb. 6, 1743-Dec. 30, 1831; House May 1791-95.

TREEN, David Conner (R La.) July 16, 1928-__; House 1973-__.

TRELOAR, William Mitchellson (R Mo.) Sept. 21, 1850-July 3, 1935; House 1895-97.

TREMAIN, Lyman (R N.Y.) June 14, 1819-Nov. 30, 1878; House 1873-75.

TREZVANT, James (— Va.) ?-Sept. 2, 1841; House 1825-31.

TRIBBLE, Samuel Joelah (D Ga.) Nov. 15, 1869-Dec. 8, 1916; House 1911-Dec. 8, 1916.

TRIGG, Abram (brother of John Johns Trigg) (— Va.) 1750-?; House 1797-1809.

TRIGG, Connally Findlay (D Va.) Sept. 18, 1847-April 23, 1907; House 1885-87.

TRIGG, John Johns (brother of Abram Trigg) (— Va.) 1748-May 17, 1804; House 1797-May 17, 1804.

TRIMBLE, Carey Allen (R Ohio) Sept. 13, 1813-May 4, 1887; House 1859-63.

TRIMBLE, David (D Ky.) June 1782-Oct. 20, 1842; House 1817-27.

TRIMBLE, James William (D Ark.) Feb. 3, 1894-March 10, 1972; House 1945-67.

TRIMBLE, John (R Tenn.) Feb. 7, 1812-Feb. 23, 1884; House 1867-69.

TRIMBLE, Lawrence Strother (D Ky.) Aug. 26, 1825-Aug. 9, 1904; House 1865-71.

TRIMBLE, South (D Ky.) April 13, 1864-Nov. 23, 1946; House 1901-07.

TRIMBLE, William Allen (— Ohio) April 4, 1786-Dec. 13, 1821; Senate 1819-Dec. 13, 1821.

TRIPLETT, Philip (W Ky.) Dec. 24, 1799-March 30, 1852; House 1839-43.

TRIPPE, Robert Pleasant (W Ga.) Dec. 21, 1819-July 22, 1900; House 1855-59.

TROTTER, James Fisher (D Miss.) Nov. 5, 1802-March 9, 1866; Senate Jan. 22-July 10, 1838.

TROTTI, Samuel Wilds (— S.C.) July 18, 1810-June 24, 1856; House Dec. 17, 1842-43.

TROUP, George Michael (SRD Ga.) Sept. 8, 1780-April 26, 1856; House 1807-15 (D); Senate Nov. 13, 1816-Sept. 23, 1818, 1829-Nov. 8, 1833 (SRD); Gov. 1823-27.

TROUT, Michael Carver (D Pa.) Sept. 30, 1810-June 25, 1873; House 1853-55.

TROUTMAN, William Irvin (R Pa.) Jan. 13, 1905-__; House 1943-Jan. 2, 1945.

TROWBRIDGE, Rowland Ebenezer (R Mich.) June 18, 1821-April 20, 1881; House 1861-63, 1865-69.

TRUAX, Charles Vilas (D Ohio) Feb. 1, 1887-Aug. 9, 1935; House 1933-Aug. 9, 1935.

TRUMAN, Harry S (D Mo.) May 8, 1884-Dec. 26, 1972; Senate 1935-Jan. 17, 1945; Vice Pres. Jan. 20-April 12, 1945; Pres. April 12, 1945-53.

TRUMBO, Andrew (W Ky.) Sept. 15, 1797-Aug. 21, 1871; House 1845-47.

TRUMBULL, Jonathan (F Conn.) March 26, 1740-Aug. 7, 1809; House 1789-95; Senate 1795-June 10, 1796; Speaker 1791-93; Gov. 1797-1809.

TRUMBULL, Joseph (W Conn.) Dec. 7, 1782-Aug. 4, 1861; House Dec. 1, 1834-35, 1839-43; Gov. 1849-50.

TRUMBULL, Lyman (R Ill.) Oct. 12, 1813-June 25, 1896; Senate 1855-73.

TSONGAS, Paul Efthemios (D Mass.) Feb. 14, 1941-__; House 1975-__.

TUCK, Amos (I N.H.) Aug. 2, 1810-Dec. 11, 1879; House 1847-53.

TUCK, William Munford (D Va.) Sept. 28, 1896-__; House April 14, 1953-69; Gov. 1946-50.

TUCKER, Ebenezer (— N.J.) Nov. 15, 1758-Sept. 5, 1845; House 1825-29.

TUCKER, George (cousin of Henry St. George Tucker) (D Va.) Aug. 20, 1775-April 10, 1861; House 1819-25.

TUCKER, Henry St. George (father of John Randolph Tucker, cousin of George Tucker and nephew of Thomas Tudor Tucker) (— Va.) Dec. 29, 1780-Aug. 28, 1848; House 1815-19.

TUCKER, Henry St. George (son of John Randolph Tucker and grandson of the preceding) (D Va.) April 5, 1853-July 23, 1932; House 1889-97, March 21, 1922-July 23, 1932.

TUCKER, John Randolph (son of Henry St. George Tucker) (D Va.) Dec. 24, 1823-Feb. 13, 1897; House 1875-87.

TUCKER, Starling (— S.C.) 1770-Jan. 3, 1834; House 1817-31.

TUCKER, Thomas Tudor (uncle of Henry St. George Tucker) (F S.C.) June 25, 1745-May 2, 1828; House 1789-93; Cont. Cong. 1787-88.

TUCKER, Tilghman Mayfield (D Miss.) Feb. 5, 1802-April 3, 1859; House 1843-45; Gov. 1842-44.

TUFTS, John Quincy (R Iowa) July 12, 1840-Aug. 10, 1908; House 1875-77.

TULLY, Pleasant Britton (D Calif.) March 21, 1829-March 24, 1897; House 1883-85.

TUMULTY, Thomas James (D N.J.) March 2, 1913-__; House 1955-57.

TUNNELL, James Miller (D Del.) Aug. 2, 1879-Nov. 14, 1957; Senate 1941-47.

TUNNEY, John Varick (D Calif.) June 26, 1934-__; House 1965-Jan. 2, 1971; Senate Jan. 2, 1971-__.

TUPPER, Stanley Roger (R Maine) Jan. 25, 1921-—; House 1961-67.

TURLEY, Thomas Battle (D Tenn.) April 5, 1845-July 1, 1910; Senate July 20, 1897-1901.

TURNBULL, Robert (D Va.) Jan. 11, 1850-Jan. 22, 1920; House March 8, 1910-13.

TURNER, Benjamin Sterling (R Ala.) March 17, 1825-March 21, 1894; House 1871-73.

TURNER, Charles Jr. (WD Mass.) June 20, 1760-May 16, 1839; House June 28, 1809-13.

TURNER, Charles Henry (D N.Y.) May 26, 1861-Aug. 31, 1913; House Dec. 9, 1889-91.

TURNER, Clarence Wyly (D Tenn.) Oct. 22, 1866-March 23, 1939; House Nov. 7, 1922-23, 1933-March 23, 1939.

TURNER, Daniel (son of James Turner) (D N.C.) Sept. 21, 1796-July 21, 1860; House 1827-29.

TURNER, Erastus Johnson (R Kan.) Dec. 26, 1846-Feb. 10, 1933; House 1887-91.

TURNER, George (Fus. Wash.) Feb. 25, 1850-Jan. 26, 1932; Senate 1897-1903.

TURNER, Henry Gray (D Ga.) March 20, 1839-June 9, 1904; House 1881-97.

TURNER, James (father of Daniel Turner) (D N.C.) Dec. 20, 1766-Jan. 15, 1824; Senate 1805-Nov. 21, 1816; Gov. 1802-05.

TURNER, James (D Md.) Nov. 7, 1783-March 28, 1861; House 1833-37.

TURNER, Oscar (ID Ky.) Feb. 3, 1825-Jan. 22, 1896; House 1879-85.

TURNER, Oscar (son of the preceding) (D Ky.) Oct. 19, 1867-July 17, 1902; House 1899-1901.

TURNER, Smith Spangler (D Va.) Nov. 21, 1842-April 8, 1898; House Jan. 30, 1894-97.

TURNER, Thomas (D Ky.) Sept. 10, 1821-Sept. 11, 1900; House 1877-81.

TURNER, Thomas Johnston (D Ill.) April 5, 1815-April 4, 1874; House 1847-49.

TURNEY, Hopkins Lacy (D Tenn.) Oct. 3, 1797-Aug. 1, 1857; House 1837-43; Senate 1845-51.

TURNEY, Jacob (D Pa.) Feb. 18, 1825-Oct. 4, 1891; House 1875-79.

TURPIE, David (D Ind.) July 8, 1828-April 21, 1909; Senate Jan. 14-March 3, 1863, 1887-99.

TURPIN, Charles Murray (R Pa.) March 4, 1878-June 4, 1946; House June 4, 1929-37.

TURPIN, Louis Washington (D Ala.) Feb. 22, 1849-Feb. 3, 1903; House 1889-June 4, 1890, 1891-95.

TURRILL, Joel (JD N.Y.) Feb. 22, 1794-Dec. 28, 1859; House 1833-37.

TUTEN, James Russell (D Ga.) July 23, 1911-Aug. 16, 1968; House 1963-67.

TUTHILL, Joseph Hasbrouck (nephew of Selah Tuthill) (D N.Y.) Feb. 25, 1811-July 27, 1877; House 1871-73.

TUTHILL, Selah (uncle of Joseph Hasbrouck Tuthill) (— N.Y.) Oct. 26, 1771-Sept. 7, 1821; House March 4-Sept. 7, 1821.

TUTTLE, William Edgar Jr. (D N.J.) Dec. 10, 1870-Feb. 11, 1923; House 1911-15.

TWEED, William Marcy (D N.Y.) April 3, 1823-April 12, 1878; House 1853-55.

TWEEDY, John Hubbard (W Wis.) Nov. 9, 1814-Nov. 12, 1891; House (terr. Del.) 1847-May 29, 1848.

TWEEDY, Samuel (W Conn.) March 8, 1776-July 1, 1868; House 1833-35.

TWICHELL, Ginery (R Mass.) Aug. 26, 1811-July 23, 1883; House 1867-73.

TWYMAN, Robert Joseph (R Ill.) June 18, 1897-__; House 1947-49.

TYDINGS, Joseph Davies (son of Millard Evelyn Tydings) (D Md.) May 4, 1928-__; Senate 1965-71.

TYDINGS, Millard Evelyn (father of Joseph Davies Tydings) (D Md.) April 6,

1890-Feb. 9, 1961; House 1923-27; Senate 1927-51.

TYLER, Asher (W N.Y.) May 10, 1798-Aug. 1, 1875; House 1843-45.

TYLER, David Gardiner (son of John Tyler) (D Va.) July 12, 1846-Sept. 5, 1927; House 1893-97.

TYLER, James Manning (R Vt.) April 27, 1835-Oct. 13, 1926; House 1879-83.

TYLER, John (father of David Gardiner Tyler) (D-R Va.) March 29, 1790-Jan. 18, 1862; House Dec. 16, 1817-21; Senate 1827-Feb. 29, 1836; President pro tempore 1834-35; Gov. 1825-27; Vice Pres. March 4-April 4, 1841; Pres. April 6, 1841-45.

TYNDALL, William Thomas (R Mo.) Jan. 16, 1862-Nov. 26, 1928; House 1905-07.

TYNER, James Noble (R Ind.) Jan. 17, 1826-Dec. 5, 1904; House 1869-75; Postmaster General 1876-77.

TYSON, Jacob (— N.Y.) Oct. 8, 1773-July 16, 1848; House 1823-25.

TYSON, Joe Roberts (W Pa.) Feb. 8, 1803-June 27, 1858; House 1855-57.

TYSON, John Russell (D Ala.) Nov. 28, 1856-March 27, 1923; House 1921-March 27, 1923.

TYSON, Lawrence Davis (D Tenn.) July 4, 1861-Aug. 24, 1929; Senate 1925-Aug. 24, 1929.

U

UDALL, Morris King (brother of Stewart Lee Udall) (D Ariz.) June 15, 1922-__; House May 2, 1961-__.

UDALL, Stewart Lee (brother of Morris K. Udall) (D Ariz.) Jan. 31, 1920-__; House 1955-Jan. 18, 1961; Secy. of the Interior 1961-69.

UDREE, Daniel (D Pa.) Aug. 5, 1751-July 15, 1828; House Oct. 12, 1813-15, Dec. 26, 1820-21, Dec. 10, 1822-25.

ULLMAN, Albert Conrad (D Ore.) March 9, 1914-—; House 1957-—.

UMSTEAD, William Bradley (D N.C.) May 13, 1895-Nov. 7, 1954; House 1933-39; Senate Dec. 18, 1946-Dec. 30, 1948; Gov. 1953-54.

UNDERHILL, Charles Lee (R Mass.) July 20, 1867-Jan. 28, 1946; House 1921-33.

UNDERHILL, Edwin Stewart (D N.Y.) Oct. 7, 1861-Feb. 7, 1929; House 1911-15.

UNDERHILL, John Quincy (D N.Y.) Feb. 19, 1848-May 21, 1907; House 1899-1901.

UNDERHILL, Walter (W N.Y.) Sept. 12, 1795-Aug. 17, 1866; House 1849-51.

UNDERWOOD, John William Henderson (D Ga.) Nov. 20, 1816-July 18, 1888; House 1859-Jan. 23, 1861.

UNDERWOOD, Joseph Rogers (brother of Warner Lewis Underwood and grandfather of Oscar Wilder Underwood) (W Ky.) Oct. 24, 1791-Aug. 23, 1876; House 1835-43; Senate 1847-53.

UNDERWOOD, Mell Gilbert (D Ohio) Jan. 30, 1892-March 8, 1972; House 1923-April 10, 1936.

UNDERWOOD, Oscar Wilder (grandson of Joseph Rogers Underwood) (D Ala.) May 6, 1862-Jan. 25, 1929; House 1895-June 9, 1896, 1897-1915; Senate 1915-27.

UNDERWOOD, Thomas Rust (D Ky.) March 3, 1898-June 29, 1956; House 1949-March 17, 1951; Senate March 19, 1951-Nov. 4, 1952.

UNDERWOOD, Warner Lewis (brother of Joseph Rogers Underwood) (AP Ky.) Aug. 7, 1808-March 12, 1872; House 1855-59.

UPDEGRAFF, Jonathan Taylor (R Ohio) May 13, 1822-Nov. 30, 1882; House 1879-Nov. 30, 1882.

UPDEGRAFF, Thomas (R Iowa) April 3, 1834-Oct. 4, 1910; House 1879-83, 1893-99.

UPDIKE, Ralph Eugene (R Ind.) May 27, 1894-Sept. 16, 1953; House 1925-29.

UPHAM, Charles Wentworth (cousin of George Baxter Upham and Jabez Upham) (W Mass.) May 4, 1802-June 15, 1875; House 1853-55.

UPHAM, George Baxter (brother of Jabez Upham and cousin of Charles Wentworth Upham) (— N.H.) Dec. 27, 1768-Feb. 10, 1848; House 1801-03.

UPHAM, Jabez (brother of George Baxter Upham and cousin of Charles Wentworth Upham) (— Mass.) Aug. 23, 1764-Nov. 8, 1811; House 1807-10.

UPHAM, Nathaniel (D N.H.) June 9, 1774-July 10, 1829; House 1817-23.

UPHAM, William (W Vt.) Aug. 5, 1792-Jan. 14, 1853; Senate 1843-Jan. 14, 1853.

UPSHAW, William David (D Ga.) Oct. 15, 1866-Nov. 21, 1952; House 1919-27.

UPSON, Charles (R Mich.) March 19, 1821-Sept. 5, 1885; House 1863-69.

UPSON, Christopher Columbus (D Texas) Oct. 17, 1829-Feb. 8, 1902; House April 15, 1879-83.

UPSON, William Hanford (R Ohio) Jan. 11, 1823-April 13, 1910; House 1869-73.

UPTON, Charles Horace (R Va.) Aug. 23, 1812-June 17, 1877; House May 23, 1861-Feb. 27, 1862.

UPTON, Robert William (R N.H.) Feb. 3, 1884-April 28, 1972; Senate Aug. 14, 1953-Nov. 7, 1954.

URNER, Milton George (uncle of James Samuel Simmons) (R Md.) July 29, 1839-Feb. 9, 1926; House 1879-83.

UTT, James Boyd (R Calif.) March 11, 1899-March 1, 1970; House 1953-March 1, 1970.

UTTER, George Herbert (R R.I.) July 24, 1854-Nov. 3, 1912; House 1911-Nov. 3, 1912; Gov. 1905-07.

UTTERBACK, Hubert (cousin of John Gregg Utterback) (D Iowa) June 28, 1880-May 12, 1942; House 1935-37.

UTTERBACK, John Gregg (cousin of Hubert Utterback) (D Maine) July 12, 1872-July 11, 1955; House 1933-35.

V

VAIL, George (D N.J.) July 21, 1809-May 23, 1875; House 1853-57.

VAIL, Henry (D N.Y.) 1782-June 25, 1853; House 1837-39.

VAIL, Richard Bernard (R Ill.) Aug. 31, 1895-July 29, 1955; House 1947-49, 1951-53.

VAILE, William Newell (R Colo.) June 22, 1876-July 2, 1927; House 1919-July 2, 1927.

VALENTINE, Edward Kimble (R Neb.) June 1, 1843-April 11, 1916; House 1879-85.

VALK, William Weightman (AP N.Y.) Oct. 12, 1806-Sept. 20, 1879; House 1855-57.

VALLANDIGHAM, Clement Laird (uncle of John A. McMahon) (D Ohio) July 29, 1820-June 17, 1871; House May 25, 1858-63.

VAN AERNAM, Henry (R N.Y.) March 11, 1819-June 1, 1894; House 1865-69, 1879-83.

VAN ALEN, James Isaac (half brother of Martin Van Buren) (F N.Y.) 1776-Dec. 23, 1870; House 1807-09.

VAN ALEN, John Evert (— N.Y.) 1749-March 1807; House 1793-99.

VAN ALSTYNE, Thomas Jefferson (D N.Y.) July 25, 1827-Oct. 26, 1903; House 1883-85.

VAN AUKEN, Daniel Myers (D Pa.) Jan. 15, 1826-Nov. 7, 1908; House 1867-71.

VAN BUREN, John (D N.Y.) May 13, 1799-Jan. 16, 1855; House 1841-43.

VAN BUREN, Martin (half-brother of James Isaac Van Alen) (D N.Y.) Dec. 5, 1782-July 24, 1862; Senate 1821-Dec. 20, 1828; Gov. 1829; Secy. of State 1829-31; Vice Pres. 1833-37; Pres. 1837-41.

VANCE, John Luther (D Ohio) July 19, 1839-June 10, 1921; House 1875-77.

VANCE, Joseph (W Ohio) March 21, 1786-Aug. 24, 1852; House 1821-35, 1843-47 (1821-35 Democrat, 1843-47 Whig); Gov. 1836-38.

VANCE, Robert Brank (uncle of Zebulon Baird Vance) (D N.C.) 1793-1827; House 1823-25.

VANCE, Robert Brank (nephew of the preceding and brother of Zebulon Baird Vance) (D N.C.) April 24, 1828-Nov. 28, 1899; House 1873-85.

VANCE, Robert Johnstone (D Conn.) March 15, 1854-June 15, 1902; House 1887-89.

VANCE, Zebulon Baird (brother of Robe Brank Vance) (D N.C.) May 13, 183(April 14, 1894; House Dec. 7, 1858-6 Senate 1879-April 14, 1894; Gov. 186 65, 1877-79.

VAN CORTLANDT, Philip (brother of Pierre Va Cortlandt Jr.) (D N.Y.) Aug. 21, 1749-Nov. 1831; House 1793-1809.

VAN CORTLANDT, Pierre Jr. (brother of Philip Van Cortlandt (D N.Y.) Aug. 29, 1762-July 13, 1848; House 1811-13.

VAN DEERLIN, Lionel (D Calif.) July 25 1914-__; House 1963-__.

VANDENBERG, Arthur Hendrick (R Mich. March 22, 1884-April 18, 1951; Senat March 31, 1928-April 18, 1951; presiden pro tempore 1947-49.

VANDER JAGT, Guy Adrian (R Mich. Aug. 26, 1931-__; House Nov. 8, 1966-__.

VANDERPOEL, Aaron (D N.Y.) Feb. 5 1799-July 18, 1870; House 1833-37, 1839 41.

VANDER VEEN, Richard Franklin (D Mich. Nov. 26, 1922-__; House Feb. 18, 1974-__.

VANDERVEER, Abraham (D N.Y) 1781- July 21, 1839; House 1837-39.

VANDEVER, William (R Iowa/Calif.) March 31, 1817-July 23, 1893; House 1859-Sept. 24, 1861 (Iowa), 1887-91 (Calif.).

VANDIVER, Willard Duncan (D Mo.) March 30, 1854-May 30, 1932; House 1897-1905.

VAN DUZER, Clarence Dunn (D Nev.) May 4, 1866-Sept. 28, 1947; House 1903-07.

VAN DYKE, Carl Chester (D Minn.) Feb. 18, 1881-May 20, 1919; House 1915-May 20, 1919.

VAN DYKE, John (W N.J.) April 3, 1807-Dec. 24, 1878; House 1847-51.

VAN DYKE, Nicholas (F Del.) Dec. 20, 1769-May 21, 1826; House Oct. 6, 1807-11; Senate 1817-May 21, 1826.

VAN EATON, Henry Smith (D Miss.) Sept. 14, 1826-May 30, 1898; House 1883-87.

VAN GAASBECK, Peter (A-F N.Y.) Sept. 27, 1754-1797; House 1793-95.

VAN HORN, Burt (R N.Y.) Oct. 28, 1823-April 1, 1896; House 1861-63, 1865-69.

VAN HORN, George (D N.Y.) Feb. 5, 1850-May 3, 1904; House 1891-93.

VAN HORN, Robert Thompson (R Mo.) May 19, 1824-Jan. 3, 1916; House 1865-71, 1881-83, Feb. 27, 1896-97.

VAN HORNE, Archibald (— Md.) ?-1817; House 1807-11.

VAN HORNE, Espy (D Pa.) 1795-Aug. 25, 1829; House 1825-29.

VAN HORNE, Isaac (D Pa.) Jan. 13, 1754-Feb. 2, 1834; House 1801-05.

VAN HOUTEN, Isaac B. (D N.Y.) June 4, 1776-Aug. 16, 1850; House 1833-35.

VANIK, Charles Albert (D Ohio) April 7, 1913-___; House 1955-___.

VANMETER, John Inskeep (W Ohio) Feb. 1798-Aug. 3, 1875; House 1843-45.

VAN NESS, John Peter (D N.Y.) 1770-March 7, 1846; House Oct. 6, 1801-Jan. 17, 1803.

VAN NUYS, Frederick (D Ind.) April 16, 1874-Jan. 25, 1944; Senate 1933-Jan. 25, 1944.

VAN PELT, William Kaiser (R Wis.) March 10, 1905-___; House 1951-65.

VAN RENSSELAER, Henry Bell (son of Stephen Van Rensselaer) (W N.Y.) May 14, 1810-March 23, 1864; House 1841-43.

VAN RENSSELAER, Jeremiah (father of Solomon Van Vechten Van Rensselaer and cousin of Killian Killian Van Rensselaer) (— N.Y.) Aug. 27, 1738-Feb. 19, 1810; House 1789-91.

VAN RENSSELAER, Killian Killian (cousin of Jeremiah Van Rensselaer and uncle of Solomon Van Vechten Van Rensselaer) (D N.Y.) June 9, 1763-June 18, 1845; House 1801-11.

VAN RENSSELAER, Solomon Van Vechten (son of Jeremiah Van Rensselaer and nephew of Killian Killian Van Rensselaer) (F N.Y.) Aug. 6, 1774-April 23, 1852; House 1819-Jan. 14, 1822.

VAN RENSSELAER, Stephen (father of Henry Bell Van Rensselaer) (— N.Y.) Nov. 1, 1764-Jan. 26, 1839; House Feb. 27, 1822-29.

VAN SANT, Joshua (D Md.) Dec. 31, 1803-April 8, 1884; House 1853-55.

VAN SCHAICK, Isaac Whitbeck (uncle of Aaron Van Schaick Cochrane) (R Wis.) Dec. 7, 1817-Aug. 22, 1901; House 1885-87, 1889-91.

VAN SWEARINGEN, Thomas (— Va.) May 5, 1784-Aug. 19, 1822; House 1819-Aug. 19, 1822.

VAN TRUMP, Philadelph (D Ohio) Nov. 15, 1810-July 31, 1874; House 1867-73.

VAN VALKENBURGH, Robert Bruce (R N.Y.) Sept. 4, 1821-Aug. 1, 1888; House 1861-65.

VAN VOORHIS, Henry Clay (R Ohio) May 11, 1852-Dec. 12, 1927; House 1893-1905.

VAN VOORHIS, John (R N.Y.) Oct. 22, 1826-Oct. 20, 1905; House 1879-83, 1893-95.

VAN VORHES, Nelson Holmes (R Ohio) Jan. 23, 1822-Dec. 4, 1882; House 1875-79.

VAN WINKLE, Marshall (grandnephew of Peter G. Van Winkle) (R N.J.) Sept. 28, 1869-May 10, 1957; House 1905-07.

VAN WINKLE, Peter Godwin (granduncle of Marshall Van Winkle) (U W.Va.) Sept. 7, 1808-April 15, 1872; Senate Aug. 4, 1863-69.

VAN WYCK, Charles Henry (R N.Y./Neb.) May 10, 1824-Oct. 24, 1895; House 1859-63, 1867-69, Feb. 17, 1870-71 (N.Y.); Senate 1881-87 (Neb.).

VAN WYCK, William William (D N.Y.) Aug. 9, 1777-Aug. 27, 1840; House 1821-25.

VAN ZANDT, James Edward (R Pa.) Dec. 18, 1898-___; House 1939-Sept. 24, 1943, 1947-63.

VARDAMAN, James Kimble (D Miss.) July 26, 1861-June 25, 1930; Senate 1913-19; Gov. 1904-08.

VARE, William Scott (R Pa.) Dec. 24, 1867-Aug. 7, 1934; House April 24, 1912-Jan. 2, 1923, March 4, 1923-27, Senate (elected 1926 but never served).

VARNUM, John (F Mass.) June 25, 1778-July 23, 1836; House 1825-31.

VARNUM, Joseph Bradley (— Mass.) Jan. 29, 1750-Sept. 21, 1821; House 1795-June 29, 1811; Senate June 29, 1811-17; Speaker 1807-11; president pro tempore 1813-14.

VAUGHAN, Horace Worth (D Texas) Dec. 2, 1867-Nov. 10, 1922; House 1913-15.

VAUGHAN, William Wirt (D Tenn.) July 2, 1831-Aug. 19, 1878; House 1871-73.

VAUGHN, Albert Clinton Sr. (R Pa.) Oct. 9, 1894-Sept. 1, 1951; House Jan. 3-Sept. 1, 1951.

VAUX, Richard (D Pa.) Dec. 19, 1816-March 22, 1895; House May 20, 1890-91.

VEEDER, William Davis (D N.Y.) May 19, 1835-Dec. 2, 1910; House 1877-79.

VEHSLAGE, John Herman George (D N.Y.) Dec. 20, 1842-July 21, 1904; House 1897-99.

VELDE, Harold Himmel (R Ill.) April 1, 1910-___; House 1949-57.

VENABLE, Abraham Bedford (uncle of Abraham Watkins Venable) (— Va.) Nov. 20, 1758-Dec. 26, 1811; House 1791-99; Senate Dec. 7, 1803-June 7, 1804.

VENABLE, Abraham Watkins (nephew of Abraham Bedford Venable) (D N.C.) Oct. 17, 1799-Feb. 24, 1876; House 1847-53.

VENABLE, Edward Carrington (D Va.) Jan. 31, 1853-Dec. 8, 1908; House 1889-Sept. 23, 1890.

VENABLE, William Webb (D Miss.) Sept. 25, 1880-Aug. 2, 1948; House Jan. 4, 1916-21.

VERPLANCK, Daniel Crommelin (father of Gulian Crommelin Verplanck) (F N.Y.) March 19, 1762-March 29, 1834; House Oct. 17, 1803-09.

VERPLANCK, Gulian Crommelin (son of Daniel Crommelin Verplanck) (D N.Y.) Aug. 6, 1786-March 18, 1870; House 1825-33.

VERREE, John Paul (R Pa.) March 9, 1817-June 27, 1889; House 1859-63.

VEST, George Graham (D Mo.) Dec. 6, 1830-Aug. 9, 1904; Senate 1879-1903.

VESTAL, Albert Henry (R Ind.) Jan. 18, 1875-April 1, 1932; House 1917-April 1, 1932.

VEYSEY, Victor V. (R Calif.) April 14, 1915-___; House 1971-1975.

VIBBARD, Chauncey (D N.Y.) Nov. 11, 1811-June 5, 1891; House 1861-63.

VICKERS, George (D Md.) Nov. 19, 1801-Oct. 8, 1879; Senate March 7, 1868-73.

VIDAL, Michel (R La.) Oct. 1, 1824-?; House July 18, 1868-69.

VIELE, Egbert Ludoricus (D N.Y.) June 17, 1825-April 22, 1902; House 1885-87.

VIGORITO, Joseph Phillip (D Pa.) Nov. 10, 1918-___; House 1965-___.

VILAS, William Freeman (D Wis.) July 9, 1840-Aug. 28, 1908; Senate 1891-97; Postmaster General 1885-88; Secy. of the Interior 1888-89.

VINCENT, Beverly Mills (D Ky.) March 28, 1890-___; House 1937-45.

VINCENT, Bird J. (R Mich.) March 6, 1880-July 18, 1931; House 1923-July 18, 1931.

VINCENT, Earl W. (R Iowa) March 27, 1886-May 22, 1953; House June 4, 1928-29.

VINCENT, William Davis (P Kan.) Oct. 11, 1852-Feb. 28, 1922; House 1897-99.

VINING, John (— Del.) Dec. 23, 1758-Feb. 1802; House 1789-93; Senate 1793-Jan. 19, 1798; Cont. Cong. 1784-86.

VINSON, Carl (D Ga.) Nov. 18, 1883-___; House Nov. 3, 1914-65.

VINSON, Frederick Moore (Fred) (D Ky.) Jan. 22, 1890-Sept. 8, 1953; House Jan. 12, 1924-29, 1931-May 12, 1938; Secy. of the Treasury 1945-46; Chief Justice of Supreme Court 1946-53.

VINTON, Samuel Finley (W Ohio) Sept. 25, 1792-May 11, 1862; House 1823-37, 1843-51.

VIVIAN, Weston Edward (D Mich.) Oct. 25, 1924-___; House 1965-67.

VOIGT, Edward (R Wis.) Dec. 1, 1873-Aug. 26, 1934; House 1917-27.

VOLK, Lester David (R N.Y.) Sept. 17, 1884-April 30, 1962; House Nov. 2, 1920-23.

VOLLMER, Henry (D Iowa) July 28, 1867-Aug. 25, 1930; House Feb. 10, 1914-15.

VOLSTEAD, Andrew John (R Minn.) Oct. 31, 1860-Jan. 20, 1947; House 1903-23.

VOORHEES, Charles Stewart (son of Daniel Wolsey Voorhees) (D Wash.) June 4, 1853-Dec. 26, 1909; House (Terr. Del.) 1885-89.

VOORHEES, Daniel Wolsey (father of Charles Stewart Voorhees) (D Ind.) Sept. 26, 1827-April 9, 1897; House 1861-Feb. 23, 1866, 1869-73; Senate Nov. 6, 1877-97.

VOORHIS, Charles Henry (R N.J.) March 13, 1833-April 15, 1896; House 1879-81.

VOORHIS, Horace Jerry (D Calif.) April 6, 1901-__; House 1937-47.

VORYS, John Martin (R Ohio) June 16, 1896-Aug. 25, 1968; House 1939-59.

VOSE, Roger (F N.H.) Feb. 24, 1763-Oct. 26, 1841; House 1813-17.

VREELAND, Albert Lincoln (R N.J.) July 2, 1901-May 3, 1975; House 1939-43.

VREELAND, Edward Butterfield (R N.Y.) Dec. 7, 1856-May 8, 1936; House Nov. 7, 1899-1913.

VROOM, Peter Dumont (D N.J.) Dec. 12, 1791-Nov. 18, 1873; House 1839-41; Gov. 1829-32, 1833-36.

VURSELL, Charles Wesley (R Ill.) Feb. 8, 1881-Sept. 21, 1974; House 1943-59.

W

WACHTER, Frank Charles (R Md.) Sept. 16, 1861-July 1, 1910; House 1899-1907.

WADDELL, Alfred Moore (D N.C.) Sept. 16, 1834-March 17, 1912; House 1871-79.

WADDILL, Edmund Jr. (R Va.) May 22, 1855-April 9, 1931; House April 12, 1890-91.

WADDILL, James Richard (D Mo.) Nov. 22, 1842-June 14, 1917; House 1879-81.

WADE, Benjamin Franklin (brother of Edward Wade) (R Ohio) Oct. 27, 1800-March 2, 1878; Senate March 15, 1851-69 (1851-57 Whig, 1857-69 Republican); president pro tem 1867-69.

WADE, Edward (brother of Benjamin Franklin Wade) (R Ohio) Nov. 22, 1802-Aug. 13, 1866; House 1853-55 (FS), 1855-61 (R).

WADE, Martin Joseph (D Iowa) Oct. 20, 1861-April 16, 1931; House 1903-05.

WADE, William Henry (R Mo.) Nov. 3, 1835-Jan. 13, 1911; House 1885-91.

WADLEIGH, Bainbridge (R N.H.) Jan. 4, 1831-Jan. 24, 1891; Senate 1873-79.

WADSWORTH, James Wolcott (R N.Y.) Oct. 12, 1846-Dec. 24, 1926; House Nov. 8, 1881-85, 1891-1907.

WADSWORTH, James Wolcott Jr. (son of the preceding) (R N.Y.) Aug. 12, 1877-June 21, 1952; Senate 1915-27; House 1933-51.

WADSWORTH, Jeremiah (F Conn.) July 12, 1743-April 30, 1804; House 1789-95; Cont. Cong. 1787-88.

WADSWORTH, Peleg (— Mass.) May 6, 1748-Nov. 12, 1829; House 1793-1807.

WADSWORTH, William Henry (R Ky.) July 4, 1821-April 2, 1893; House 1861-65, 1885-87 (1861-65 Unionist, 1885-87 Republican).

WAGENER, David Douglas (D Pa.) Oct. 11, 1792-Oct. 1, 1860; House 1833-41.

WAGGAMAN, George Augustus (NR La.) 1790-March 22, 1843; Senate Nov. 15, 1831-35.

WAGGONNER, Joseph David Jr. (D La.) Sept. 7, 1918-—; House Dec. 19, 1961-—.

WAGNER, Earl Thomas (D Ohio) April 27, 1908-__; House 1949-51.

WAGNER, Peter Joseph (W N.Y.) Aug. 14, 1795-Sept. 13, 1884; House 1839-41.

WAGNER, Robert Ferdinand (D N.Y.) June 8, 1877-May 4, 1953; Senate 1927-June 28, 1949.

WAGONER, George Chester Robinson (R Mo.) Sept. 3, 1863-April 27, 1946; House Feb. 26-March 3, 1903.

WAINWRIGHT, Jonathan Mayhew (R N.Y.) Dec. 10, 1864-June 3, 1945; House 1923-31.

WAINWRIGHT, Stuyvesant II (R N.Y.) March 16, 1921-__; House 1953-61.

WAIT, John Turner (R Conn.) Aug. 27, 1811-April 21, 1899; House April 12, 1876-87.

WAKEFIELD, James Beach (R Minn.) March 21, 1825-Aug. 25, 1910; House 1883-87.

WAKEMAN, Abram (W N.Y.) May 31, 1824-June 29, 1889; House 1855-57.

WAKEMAN, Seth (R N.Y.) Jan. 15, 1811-Jan. 4, 1880; House 1871-73.

WALBRIDGE, David Safford (R Mich.) July 30, 1802-June 15, 1868; House 1855-59.

WALBRIDGE, Henry Sanford (cousin of Hiram Walbridge) (W N.Y.) April 8, 1801-Jan. 27, 1869; House 1851-53.

WALBRIDGE, Hiram (cousin of Henry Sanford Walbridge) (D N.Y.) Feb. 2, 1821-Dec. 6, 1870; House 1853-55.

WALCOTT, Frederic Collin (R Conn.) Feb. 19, 1869-April 27, 1949; Senate 1929-35.

WALDEN, Hiram (D N.Y.) Aug. 21, 1800-July 21, 1880; House 1849-51.

WALDEN, Madison Miner (R Iowa) Oct. 6, 1836-July 24, 1891; House 1871-73.

WALDIE, Jerome Russell (D Calif.) Feb. 15, 1925-—; House June 7, 1966-1975.

WALDO, George Ernest (R N.Y.) Jan. 11, 1851-June 16, 1942; House 1905-09.

WALDO, Loren Pinckney (D Conn.) Feb. 2, 1802-Sept. 8, 1881; House 1849-51.

WALDOW, William Frederick (R N.Y.) Aug. 26, 1882-April 16, 1930; House 1917-19.

WALDRON, Alfred Marpole (R Pa.) Sept. 21, 1865-June 28, 1952; House 1933-35.

WALDRON, Henry (R Mich.) Oct. 11, 1819-Sept. 13, 1880; House 1855-61, 1871-77.

WALES, George Edward (— Vt.) May 13, 1792-Jan. 8, 1860; House 1825-29.

WALES, John (— Del.) July 31, 1783-Dec. 3, 1863; Senate Feb. 3, 1849-51.

WALKER, Amasa (R Mass.) May 4, 1799-Oct. 29, 1875; House Dec. 1, 1862-63.

WALKER, Benjamin (D N.Y.) 1753-Jan. 13, 1818; House 1801-03.

WALKER, Charles Christopher Brainerd (D N.Y.) June 27, 1824-Jan. 26, 1888; House 1875-77.

WALKER, David (brother of George Walker and grandfather of James David Walker) (— Ky.) ?-March 1, 1820; House 1817-March 1, 1820.

WALKER, E. S. Johnny (D N.M.) June 18, 1911-__; House 1965-69.

WALKER, Felix (D N.C.) July 19, 1753-1828; House 1817-23.

WALKER, Francis (brother of John Walker) (— Va.) June 22, 1764-March 1806; House 1793-95.

WALKER, Freeman (D Ga.) Oct. 25, 1780-Sept. 23, 1827; Senate Nov. 6, 1819-Aug. 6, 1821.

WALKER, George (brother of David Walker) (— Ky.) 1763-1819; Senate Aug. 30-Dec. 16, 1814.

WALKER, Gilbert Carlton (D Va.) Aug. 1, 1833-May 11, 1885; House 1875-79 (1875-77 Conservative, 1877-79 Democrat); Gov. 1869-74.

WALKER, Isaac Pigeon (D Wis.) Nov. 2, 1815-March 29, 1872; Senate June 8, 1848-55.

WALKER, James Alexander (R Va.) Aug. 27, 1832-Oct. 21, 1901; House 1895-99.

WALKER, James David (grandson of David Walker, nephew of John McLean of Ill., and cousin of Wilkinson Call) (D Ark.) Dec. 13, 1830-Oct. 17, 1906; Senate 1879-85.

WALKER, James Peter (D Mo.) March 14, 1851-July 19, 1890; House 1887-July 19, 1890.

WALKER, John (brother of Francis Walker) (— Va.) Feb. 13, 1744-Dec. 2, 1809; Senate March 31-Nov. 9, 1790; Cont. Cong. 1780.

WALKER, John Randall (D Ga.) Feb. 23, 1874-?; House 1913-19.

WALKER, John Williams (father of Percy Walker) (D Ala.) Aug. 12, 1783-April 23, 1823; Senate Dec. 14, 1819-Dec. 12, 1822.

WALKER, Joseph Henry (R Mass.) Dec. 21, 1829-April 3, 1907; House 1889-99.

WALKER, Lewis Leavell (R Ky.) Feb. 15, 1873-June 30, 1944; House 1929-31.

WALKER, Percy (son of John Williams Walker) (AP Ala.) Dec. 1812-Dec. 31, 1880; House 1855-57.

WALKER, Prentiss Lafayette (R Miss.) Aug. 23, 1917-__; House 1965-67.

WALKER, Robert James (D Miss.) July 23, 1801-Nov. 11, 1869; Senate 1835-March 5, 1845; Secy. of the Treasury 1845-49; Gov. of Kan. Terr. 1857.

WALKER, Robert Jarvis Cochran (R Pa.) Oct. 20, 1838-Dec. 19, 1903; House 1881-83.

WALKER, Walter (D Colo.) April 3, 1883-Oct. 8, 1956; Senate Sept. 26-Dec. 6, 1932.

WALKER, William Adams (D N.Y.) June 5, 1805-Dec. 18, 1861; House 1853-55.

WALL, Garret Dorset (father of James Walter Wall) (D N.J.) March 10, 1783-Nov. 22, 1850; Senate 1835-41.

WALL, James Walter (son of Garret Dorset Wall) (D N.J.) May 26, 1820-June 9, 1872; Senate Jan. 14-March 3, 1863.

WALL, William (R N.Y.) March 20, 1800-April 20, 1872; House 1861-63.

WALLACE, Alexander Stuart (R S.C.) Dec. 30, 1810-June 27, 1893; House May 27, 1870-77.

WALLACE, Daniel (W S.C.) May 9, 1801-May 13, 1859; House June 12, 1848-53.

WALLACE, David (W Ind.) April 4, 1799-Sept. 4, 1859; House 1841-43; Gov. 1837-40.

WALLACE, James M. (— Pa.) 1750-Dec. 17, 1823; House Oct. 10, 1815-21.

WALLACE, John Winfield (R Pa.) Dec. 20, 1818-June 24, 1889; House 1861-63, 1875-77.

WALLACE, Jonathan Hasson (D Ohio) Oct. 31, 1824-Oct. 28, 1892; House May 27, 1884-85.

WALLACE, Nathaniel Dick (D La.) Oct. 27, 1845-July 16, 1894; House Dec. 9, 1886-87.

WALLACE, Robert Minor (D Ark.) Aug. 6, 1856-Nov. 9, 1942; House 1903-11.

WALLACE, Rodney (R Mass.) Dec. 21, 1823-Feb. 27, 1903; House 1889-91.

WALLACE, William Andrew (D Pa.) Nov. 28, 1827-May 22, 1896; Senate 1875-81.

WALLACE, William Copeland (R N.Y.) May 21, 1856-Sept. 4, 1901; House 1889-91.

WALLACE, William Henson (R Wash./Idaho) July 19, 1811-Feb. 7, 1879; House (Terr. Del.) 1861-63 (Wash.), Feb. 1, 1864-65 (Idaho) Gov. (Idaho Terr.) 1863.

WALLEY, Samuel Hurd (W Mass.) Aug. 31, 1805-Aug. 27, 1877; House 1853-55.

WALLGREN, Monrad Charles (D Wash.) April 17, 1891-Sept. 18, 1961; House 1933-Dec. 19, 1940; Senate Dec. 19, 1940-Jan. 9, 1945; Gov. 1945-49.

WALLHAUSER, George Marvin (R N.J.) Feb. 10, 1900-__; House 1959-65.

WALLIN, Samuel (R N.Y.) July 31, 1856-Dec. 1, 1917; House 1913-15.

WALLING, Ansel Tracy (D Ohio) Jan. 10, 1824-June 22, 1896; House 1875-77.

WALLS, Josiah Thomas (R Fla.) Dec. 30, 1842-May 5, 1905; House 1871-Jan. 29, 1873, March 4, 1873-April 19, 1876.

WALN, Robert (F Pa.) Feb. 22, 1765-Jan. 24, 1836; House Dec. 3, 1798-1801.

WALSH, Allan Bartholomew (D N.J.) Aug. 29, 1874-Aug. 5, 1953; House 1913-15.

WALSH, Arthur (D N.J.) Feb. 26, 1896-Dec. 13, 1947; Senate Nov. 26, 1943-Dec. 7, 1944.

WALSH, David Ignatius (D Mass.) Nov. 11, 1872-June 11, 1947; Senate 1919-25, Dec. 6, 1926-47; Gov. 1914-16.

WALSH, James Joseph (D N.Y.) May 22, 1858-May 8, 1909; House 1895-June 2, 1896.

WALSH, John Richard (D Ind.) May 22, 1913-__; House 1949-51.

WALSH, Joseph (R Mass.) Dec. 16, 1875-Jan. 13, 1946; House 1915-Aug. 2, 1922.

WALSH, Michael (D N.Y.) March 8, 1810-March 18, 1859; House 1853-55.

WALSH, Patrick (D Ga.) Jan. 1, 1840-March 19, 1899; Senate April 2, 1894-95.

WALSH, Thomas James (D Mont.) June 12, 1859-March 2, 1933; Senate 1913-March 2, 1933.

WALSH, Thomas Yates (W Md.) 1809-Jan. 20, 1865; House 1851-53.

WALSH, William (D Md.) May 11, 1828-May 17, 1892; House 1875-79.

WALSH, William Francis (R N.Y.) July 11, 1912-__; House 1973-__.

WALTER, Francis Eugene (D Pa.) May 26, 1894-May 31, 1963; House 1933-May 31, 1963.

WALTERS, Anderson Howell (R Pa.) May 18, 1862-Dec. 7, 1927; House 1913-15, 1919-23, 1925-27.

WALTERS, Herbert Sanford (D Tenn.) Nov. 17, 1891-Aug. 17, 1973; Senate Aug. 20, 1963-Nov. 3, 1964.

WALTHALL, Edward Cary (D Miss.) April 4, 1831-April 21, 1898; Senate March 9, 1885-Jan. 24, 1894; 1895-April 21, 1898.

WALTON, Charles Wesley (R Maine) Dec. 9, 1819-Jan. 24, 1900; House 1861-May 26, 1862.

WALTON, Eliakim Persons (R Vt.) Feb. 17, 1812-Dec. 19, 1890; House 1857-63.

WALTON, George (cousin of Matthew Walton) (— Ga.) 1750-Feb. 2, 1804; Senate Nov. 16, 1795-Feb. 20, 1796; Cont. Cong. 1776-78, 1780-81, 1787-88; Gov. 1779, 1789.

WALTON, Matthew (cousin of George Walton) (D Ky.) ?-Jan. 18, 1819; House 1803-07.

WALTON, William Bell (D N.M.) Jan. 23, 1871-April 14, 1939; House 1917-19.

WALWORTH, Reuben Hyde (D N.Y.) Oct. 26, 1788-Nov. 27, 1867; House 1821-23.

WAMPLER, Fred (D Ind.) Oct. 15, 1909-__; House 1959-61.

WAMPLER, William Creed (R Va.) April 21, 1926-__; House 1953-55, 1967-__.

WANGER, Irving Price (R Pa.) March 5, 1852-Jan. 14, 1940; House 1893-1911.

WARBURTON, Herbert Birchby (R Del.) Sept. 21, 1916-__; House 1953-55.

WARBURTON, Stanton (R Wash.) April 13, 1865-Dec. 24, 1926; House 1911-13.

WARD, Aaron (uncle of Elijah Ward) (D N.Y.) July 5, 1790-March 2, 1867; House 1825-29, 1831-37, 1841-43.

WARD, Andrew Harrison (D Ky.) Jan. 3, 1815-April 16, 1904; House Dec. 3, 1866-67.

WARD, Artemas (F Mass.) Nov. 26, 1727-Oct. 28, 1800; House 1791-95; Cont. Cong. 1780-82.

WARD, Artemas Jr. (son of the preceding) (F Mass.) Jan. 9, 1762-Oct. 7, 1847; House 1813-17.

WARD, Charles Bonnell (R N.Y.) April 27, 1879-May 27, 1946; House 1915-25.

WARD, David Jenkins (D Md.) Sept. 17, 1871-Feb. 18, 1961; House June 6, 1939-45.

WARD, Elijah (nephew of Aaron Ward) (D N.Y.) Sept. 16, 1816-Feb. 7, 1882; House 1857-59, 1861-65, 1875-77.

WARD, Hallett Sydney (D N.C.) Aug. 31, 1870-March 31, 1956; House 1921-25.

WARD, Hamilton (R N.Y.) July 3, 1829-Dec. 28, 1898; House 1865-71.

WARD, James Hugh (D Ill.) Nov. 30, 1853-Aug. 15, 1916; House 1885-87.

WARD, Jasper Delos (R Ill.) Feb. 1, 1829-Aug. 6, 1902; House 1873-75.

WARD, Jonathan (D N.Y.) Sept. 21, 1768-Sept. 28, 1842; House 1815-17.

WARD, Marcus Lawrence (R N.J.) Nov. 9, 1812-April 25, 1884; House 1873-75; Gov. 1866-69; Chrmn. Rep. Nat. Comm. 1866-68.

WARD, Matthias (D Texas) Oct. 13, 1805-Oct. 5, 1861; Senate Sept. 27, 1858-Dec. 5, 1859.

WARD, Thomas (D N.J.) about 1759-March 4, 1842; House 1813-17.

WARD, Thomas Bayless (D Ind.) April 27, 1835-Jan. 1, 1892; House 1883-87.

WARD, William (R Pa.) Jan. 1, 1837-Feb. 27, 1895; House 1877-83.

WARD, William Lukens (R N.Y.) Sept. 2, 1856-July 16, 1933; House 1897-99.

WARD, William Thomas (W Ky.) Aug. 9, 1808-Oct. 12, 1878; House 1851-53.

WARDWELL, Daniel (R N.Y.) May 28, 1791-March 27, 1878; House 1831-37.

WARE, John Haines III (R Pa.) Aug. 29, 1908-—; House Nov. 3, 1970-1975.

WARE, Nicholas (— Ga.) 1769-Sept. 7, 1824; Senate Nov. 10, 1821-Sept. 7, 1824.

WARE, Orie Solomon (D Ky.) May 11, 1882-Dec. 16, 1974; House 1927-29.

WARFIELD, Henry Ridgely (F Md.) Sept. 14, 1774-March 18, 1839; House 1819-25.

WARNER, Adoniram Judson (D Ohio) Jan. 13, 1834-Aug. 12, 1910; House 1879-81; 1883-87.

WARNER, Hiram (D Ga.) Oct. 29, 1802-June 30, 1881; House 1855-57.

WARNER, John De Witt (D N.Y.) Oct. 30, 1851-May 27, 1925; House 1891-95.

WARNER, Levi (brother of Samuel Larkin Warner) (D Conn.) Oct. 10, 1831-April 12, 1911; House Dec. 4, 1876-79.

WARNER, Richard (D Tenn.) Sept. 19, 1835-March 4, 1915; House 1881-85.

WARNER, Samuel Larkin (brother of Levi Warner) (R Conn.) June 14, 1828-Feb. 6, 1893; House 1865-67.

WARNER, Vespasian (R Ill.) April 23, 1842-March 31, 1925; House 1895-1905.

WARNER, Willard (R Ala.) Sept. 4, 1826-Nov. 23, 1906; Senate July 13, 1868-71.

WARNER, William (R Mo.) June 11, 1840-Oct. 4, 1916; House 1885-89; Senate March 18, 1905-11.

WARNOCK, William Robert (R Ohio) Aug. 29, 1838-July 30, 1918; House 1901-05.

WARREN, Cornelius (W N.Y.) March 15, 1790-July 28, 1849; House 1847-49.

WARREN, Edward Allen (D Ark.) May 2, 1818-July 2, 1875; House 1853-55, 1857-59.

WARREN, Francis Emroy (R Wyo.) June 20, 1844-Nov. 24, 1929; Senate Nov. 18, 1890-1893; 1895-Nov. 24, 1929; Gov. 1885-86, 1889-90 (Terr.); 1890.

WARREN, Joseph Mabbett (D N.Y.) Jan. 28, 1813-Sept. 9, 1896; House 1871-73.

WARREN, Lindsay Carter (D N.C.) Dec. 16, 1889-__; House 1925-Oct. 31, 1940.

WARREN, Lott (W Ga.) Oct. 30, 1797-June 17, 1861; House 1839-43.

WARREN, William Wirt (D Mass.) Feb. 27, 1834-May 2, 1880; House 1875-77.

WARWICK, John George (D Ohio) Dec. 23, 1830-Aug. 14, 1892; House 1891-Aug. 14, 1892.

WASHBURN, Cadwallader Colden (brother of Israel Washburn Jr., Elihu Benjamin Washburne, and William Drew Washburn) (R Wis.) April 22, 1818-May 15, 1882; House 1855-61, 1867-71; Gov. 1872-74.

WASHBURN, Charles Grenfill (R Mass.) Jan. 28, 1857-May 25, 1928; House Dec. 18, 1906-11.

WASHBURN, Henry Dana (R Ind.) March 28, 1832-Jan. 26, 1871; House Feb. 23, 1866-69.

WASHBURN, Israel Jr. (brother of Elihu Benjamin Washburne, Cadwallader Colden Washburn and William Drew Washburn) (R Maine) June 6, 1813-May 12, 1883; House 1851-Jan. 1, 1861 (1851-55 Whig, 1855-61 Republican); Gov. 1861-63.

WASHBURN, William Barrett (R Mass.) Jan. 31, 1820-Oct. 5, 1887; House 1863-Dec. 5, 1871; Senate April 17, 1874-75; Gov. 1872-74.

WASHBURN, William Drew (brother of Israel Washburn Jr., Elihu Benjamin Washburne and Cadwallader Colden Washburn) (R Minn.) Jan. 14, 1831-July 29, 1912; House 1879-85; Senate 1889-95.

WASHBURNE, Elihu Benjamin (brother of Israel Washburn Jr., Cadwallader Colden Washburn and William Drew Washburn) (W Ill.) Sept. 23, 1816-Oct. 22, 1887; House 1853-March 6, 1869; Secy. of State 1869.

WASHINGTON, George Corbin (grandnephew of President George Washington) (— Md.) Aug. 20, 1789-July 17, 1854; House 1827-33, 1835-37.

WASHINGTON, Joseph Edwin (D Tenn.) Nov. 10, 1851-Aug. 28, 1915; House 1887-97.

WASHINGTON, William Henry (W N.C.) Feb. 7, 1813-Aug. 12, 1860; House 1841-43.

WASIELEWSKI, Thaddeus Francis Boleslaw (D Wis.) Dec. 2, 1904-__; House 1941-47.

WASKEY, Frank Hinman (D Alaska) April 20, 1875-Jan. 18, 1964; House (Terr. Del.) Aug. 14, 1906-07.

WASON, Edward Hills (R N.H.) Sept. 2, 1865-Feb. 6, 1941; House 1915-33.

WATERMAN, Charles Winfield (R Colo.) Nov. 2, 1861-Aug. 27, 1932; Senate 1927-Aug. 27, 1932.

WATERS, Russell Judson (R Calif.) June 6, 1843-Sept. 25, 1911; House 1899-1901.

WATKINS, Albert Galiton (D Tenn.) May 5, 1818-Nov. 9, 1895; House 1849-53, 1855-59 (1849-53 Whig, 1855-59 Democrat).

WATKINS, Arthur Vivian (R Utah) Dec. 18, 1886-Sept. 1, 1973; Senate 1947-59.

WATKINS, Elton (D Ore.) July 6, 1881-June 24, 1956; House 1923-25.

WATKINS, George Robert (R Pa.) May 21, 1902-Aug. 7, 1970; House 1965-Aug. 7, 1970.

WATKINS, John Thomas (D La.) Jan. 1!, 1854-April 25, 1925; House 1905-21.

WATMOUGH, John Goddard (— Pa.) De- 6, 1793-Nov. 27, 1861; House 1831-35.

WATRES, Laurence Hawley (R Pa.) Jul 18, 1882-Feb. 6, 1964; House 1923-31.

WATSON, Albert William (R S.C.) Aug. 3(1922-—; House 1963-Feb. 1, 1965, June 1! 1965-1971 (1963-65 Democrat, 1965-71 Re publican).

WATSON, Clarence Wayland (D W.Va. May 8, 1864-May 24, 1940; Senate Fet 1, 1911-13.

WATSON, Cooper Kinderdine (F-S Ohic June 18, 1810-May 20, 1880; House 1855 57.

WATSON, David Kemper (R Ohio) Jun 18, 1849-Sept. 28, 1918; House 1895-97.

WATSON, Henry Winfield (R Pa.) June 24 1856-Aug. 27, 1933; House 1915-Aug. 27 1933.

WATSON, James (D N.Y.) April 6, 1750 May 15, 1806; Senate Aug. 17, 1798 March 19, 1800.

WATSON, James Eli (R Ind.) Nov. 2 1863-July 29, 1948; House 1895-97, 1899 1909; Senate Nov. 8, 1916-33.

WATSON, Lewis Findlay (R Pa.) April 14 1819-Aug. 25, 1890; House 1877-79, 1881 83, 1889-Aug. 25, 1890.

WATSON, Thomas Edward (D Ga.) Sept 5, 1856-Sept. 26, 1922; House 1891-93 (P); Senate 1921-Sept. 26, 1922 (D).

WATSON, Walter Allen (D Va.) Nov. 25 1867-Dec. 24, 1919; House 1913-Dec. 24 1919.

WATTERSON, Henry (son of Harvey Magee Watterson and nephew of Stanley Matthews) (D Ky.) Feb. 16, 1840-Dec. 22, 1921; House Aug. 12, 1876-77.

WATTS, John (— N.Y.) Aug. 27, 1749-Sept. 3, 1836; House 1793-95.

WATTS, John Clarence (D Ky.) July 9, 1902-Sept. 24, 1971; House April 14, 1951-Sept. 24, 1971.

WATTS, John Sebrie (R N.M.) Jan. 19, 1816-June 11, 1876; House (Terr. Del.) 1861-63.

WAUGH, Daniel Webster (R Ind.) March 7, 1842-March 14, 1921; House 1891-95.

WAXMAN, Henry Arnold (D Calif.) Sept. 12, 1939-__; House 1975-__.

WAYNE, Anthony (father of Isaac Wayne) (— Ga.) Jan. 1, 1745-Dec. 15, 1796; House 1791-March 21, 1792.

WAYNE, Isaac (son of Anthony Wayne) (F Pa.) 1772-Oct. 25, 1852; House 1823-25.

WAYNE, James Moore (JD Ga.) 1790-July 5, 1867; House 1829-Jan. 13, 1835; Assoc. Justice of Supreme Court 1835-67.

WEADOCK, Thomas Addis Emmet (D Mich.) Jan. 1, 1850-Nov. 18, 1938; House 1891-95.

WEAKLEY, Robert (— Tenn.) July 20, 1764-Feb. 4, 1845; House 1809-11.

WEARIN, Otha Donner (D Iowa) Jan. 10, 1903-__; House 1933-39.

WEATHERFORD, Zadoc Lorenzo (D Ala.) Feb. 4, 1888-__; House Nov. 5, 1940-41.

WEAVER, Archibald Jerard (grandfather of Phillip H. Weaver) (R Neb.) April 15, 1844-April 18, 1887; House 1883-87.

WEAVER, Claude (D Okla.) March 19, 1867-May 19, 1954; House 1913-15.

WEAVER, James Baird (D/G-Lab. Iowa) June 12, 1833-Feb. 6, 1912; House 1879-81, 1885-89 (1879-81 and 1885-87 Greenbacker, 1887-89 Democrat/Greenback Labor).

WEAVER, James Dorman (R Pa.) Sept. 27, 1920-__; House 1963-65.

WEAVER, James Howard (D Ore.) Aug. 8, 1927-__; House 1975-__.

WEAVER, Phillip Hart (grandson of Archibald Jerard Weaver) (R Neb.) April 9, 1919-__; House 1955-63.

WEAVER, Walter Lowrie (R Ohio) April 1, 1851-May 26, 1909; House 1897-1901.

WEAVER, Zebulon (D N.C.) May 12, 1872-Oct. 29, 1948; House 1917-March 1, 1919, March 4, 1919-29; 1931-47.

WEBB, Edwin Yates (D N.C.) May 23, 1872-Feb. 7, 1955; House 1903-Nov. 10, 1919.

WEBB, William Robert (grandson of Richard Stanford) (D Tenn.) Nov. 11, 1842-Dec. 19, 1926; Senate Jan. 24-March 3, 1913.

WEBBER, Amos Richard (R Ohio) Jan. 21, 1852-Feb. 25, 1948; House Nov. 8, 1904-07.

WEBBER, George Washington (R Mich.) Nov. 25, 1825-Jan. 15, 1900; House 1881-83.

WEBER, John Baptiste (R N.Y.) Sept. 21, 1842-Dec. 18, 1926; House 1885-89.

WEBSTER, Daniel (W N.H./Mass.) Jan. 18, 1782-Oct. 24, 1852; House 1813-17 (F N.H.); 1823-May 30, 1827 (F Mass.); Senate May 30, 1827-Feb. 22, 1841 (F Mass.) 1845-July 22, 1850 (W Mass.); Secy. of State 1841-43, 1850-52.

WEBSTER, Edwin Hanson (R Md.) March 31, 1829-April 24, 1893; House 1859-July 1865.

WEBSTER, John Stanley (R Wash.) Feb. 22, 1877-Dec. 24, 1962; House 1919-May 8, 1923.

WEBSTER, Taylor (JD Ohio) Oct. 1, 1800-April 27, 1876; House 1833-39.

WEDEMEYER, William Walter (R Mich.) March 22, 1873-Jan. 2, 1913; House 1911-Jan. 2, 1913.

WEEKS, Edgar (cousin of John Wingate Weeks) (R Mich.) Aug. 3, 1839-Dec. 17, 1904; House 1899-1903.

WEEKS, John Eliakim (R Vt.) June 14, 1853-Sept. 10, 1949; House 1931-33; Gov. 1927-31.

WEEKS, John Wingate (great uncle of John Wingate Weeks) (— N.H.) March 31, 1781-April 3, 1853; House 1829-33.

WEEKS, John Wingate (father of Sinclair Weeks and cousin of Edgar Weeks) (R Mass.) April 11, 1860-July 12, 1926; House 1905-March 4, 1913; Senate March 4, 1913-1919; Secy. of War 1921-25.

WEEKS, Joseph (grandfather of Joseph Weeks Babcock) (D N.H.) Feb. 13, 1773-Aug. 4, 1845; House 1835-39.

WEEKS, Sinclair (son of John Wingate Weeks) (R Mass.) June 15, 1893-Feb. 7, 1972; Senate Feb. 8-Dec. 19, 1944; Secy. of Commerce 1953-58.

WEEMS, Capell Lane (R Ohio) July 7, 1860-Jan. 5, 1913; House Nov. 3, 1903-09.

WEEMS, John Crompton (D Md.) 1778-Jan. 20, 1862; House Feb. 1, 1826-29.

WEFALD, Knud (FL Minn.) Nov. 3, 1869-Oct. 25, 1936; House 1923-27.

WEICHEL, Alvin F. (R Ohio) Sept. 11, 1891-Nov. 27, 1956; House 1943-55.

WEICKER, Lowell Palmer Jr. (R Conn.) May 16, 1931-—; House 1969-71; Senate 1971-—.

WEIDEMAN, Carl May (D Mich.) March 5, 1898-March 5, 1972; House 1933-35.

WEIGHTMAN, Richard Hanson (D N.M.) Dec. 28, 1816-Aug. 10, 1861; House (Terr. Del.) 1851-53.

WEIS, Jessica McCullough (R N.Y.) July 8, 1901-May 1, 1963; House 1959-63.

WEISS, Samuel Arthur (D Pa.) April 15, 1902-__; House 1941-Jan. 7, 1946.

WEISSE, Charles Herman (D Wis.) Oct. 24, 1866-Oct. 8, 1919; House 1903-11.

WELBORN, John (R Mo.) Nov. 20, 1857-Oct. 27, 1907; House 1905-07.

WELCH, Adonijah Strong (R Fla.) April 12, 1821-March 14, 1889; Senate June 25, 1868-69.

WELCH, Frank (R Neb.) Feb. 10, 1835-Sept. 4, 1878; House 1877-Sept. 4, 1878.

WELCH, John (W Ohio) Oct. 28, 1805-Aug. 5, 1891; House 1851-53.

WELCH, Philip James (D Mo.) April 4, 1895-April 26, 1963; House 1949-53.

WELCH, Richard Joseph (R Calif.) Feb. 13, 1869-Sept. 10, 1949, House Aug. 31, 1926-Sept. 10, 1949.

WELCH, William Wickham (AP Conn.) Dec. 10, 1818-July 30, 1892; House 1855-57.

WELKER, Herman (R Idaho) Dec. 11, 1906-Oct. 30, 1957; Senate 1951-57.

WELKER, Martin (R Ohio) April 25, 1819-March 15, 1902; House 1865-71.

WELLBORN, Marshall Johnson (D Ga.) May 29, 1808-Oct. 16, 1874; House 1849-51.

WELLBORN, Olin (D Texas) June 18, 1843-Dec. 6, 1921; House 1879-87.

WELLER, John B. (UD Ohio/Calif.) Feb. 22, 1812-Aug. 17, 1875; House 1839-45 (D Ohio); Senate Jan. 30, 1852-57 (UD Calif.); Gov. of Calif. 1858-60.

WELLER, Luman Hamlin (Nat. G/D Iowa) Aug. 24, 1833-March 2, 1914; House 1883-85.

WELLER, Ovington Eugene (R Md.) Jan. 23, 1862-Jan. 5, 1947; Senate 1921-27.

WELLER, Royal Hurlburt (D N.Y.) July 2, 1881-March 1, 1929; House 1923-March 1, 1929.

WELLING, Milton Holmes (D Utah) Jan. 25, 1876-May 28, 1947; House 1917-21.

WELLINGTON, George Louis (R Md.) Jan. 28, 1852-March 20, 1927; House 1895-97; Senate 1897-1903.

WELLS, Alfred (R N.Y.) May 27, 1814-July 18, 1867; House 1859-61.

WELLS, Daniel Jr. (D Wis.) July 16, 1808-March 18, 1902; House 1853-57.

WELLS, Erastus (D Mo.) Dec. 2, 1823-Oct. 2, 1893; House 1869-77; 1879-81.

WELLS, Guilford Wiley (R Miss.) Feb. 14, 1840-March 21, 1909; House 1875-77.

WELLS, John (W N.Y.) July 1, 1817-May 30, 1877; House 1851-53.

WELLS, John Sullivan (— N.H.) Oct. 18, 1803-Aug. 1, 1860; Senate Jan. 16-March 3, 1855.

WELLS, Owen Augustine (D Wis.) Feb. 4, 1844-Jan. 29, 1935; House 1893-95.

WELLS, William Hill (— Del.) Jan. 7, 1769-March 11, 1829; Senate Jan. 17, 1799-Nov. 6, 1804, May 28, 1813-17.

WELSH, George Austin (R Pa.) Aug. 9, 1878-Oct. 22, 1970; House 1923-May 31, 1932.

WELTNER, Charles Longstreet (D Ga.) Dec. 17, 1927-__; House 1963-67.

WELTY, Benjamin Franklin (D Ohio) Aug. 9, 1870-Oct. 23, 1962; House 1917-21.

WEMPLE, Edward (D N.Y.) Oct. 23, 1843-Dec. 18, 1920; House 1883-85.

WENDOVER, Peter Hercules (D N.Y.) Aug. 1, 1768-Sept. 24, 1834; House 1815-21.

WENE, Elmer H. (D N.J.) May 1, 1892-Jan. 25, 1957; House 1937-39, 1941-45.

WENTWORTH, John (R Ill.) March 5, 1815-Oct. 16, 1888; House 1843-51, 1853-55, 1865-67 (1843-51 and 1853-55 Democrat, 1865-67 Republican).

WENTWORTH, Tappan (W Mass.) Feb. 24, 1802-June 12, 1875; House 1853-55.

WERDEL, Thomas Harold (R Calif.) Sept. 13, 1905-Sept. 30, 1966; House 1949-53.

WERNER, Theodore B. (D S.D.) June 2, 1892-__; House 1933-37.

WERTZ, George M. (R Pa.) July 19, 1856-Nov. 19, 1928; House 1923-25.

WEST, Charles Franklin (D Ohio) Jan. 12, 1895-Dec. 27, 1955; House 1931-35.

WEST, George (R N.Y.) Feb. 17, 1823-Sept. 20, 1901; House 1881-83, 1885-89.

WEST, Joseph Rodman (R La.) Sept. 19, 1822-Oct. 31, 1898; Senate 1871-77.

WEST, Milton Horace (D Texas) June 30, 1888-Oct. 28, 1948; House April 22, 1933-Oct. 28, 1948.

WEST, William Stanley (D Ga.) Aug. 23, 1849-Dec. 22, 1914; Senate March 2-Nov. 3, 1914.

WESTBROOK, John (D Pa.) Jan. 9, 1789-Oct. 8, 1852; House 1841-43.

WESTBROOK, Theodoric Romeyn (D N.Y.) Nov. 20, 1821-Oct. 6, 1885; House 1853-55.

WESTCOTT, James Diament Jr. (D Fla.) May 10, 1802-Jan. 19, 1880; Senate July 1, 1845-49.

WESTERLO, Rensselaer (F N.Y.) April 29, 1776-April 18, 1851; House 1817-19.

WESTLAND, Aldred John (Jack) (R Wash.) Dec. 14, 1904-__; House 1953-65.

WETHERED, John (D Md.) May 8, 1809-Feb. 15, 1888; House 1843-45.

WETMORE, George Peabody (R R.I.) Aug. 2, 1846-Sept. 11, 1921; Senate 1895-1907, Jan. 22, 1908-1913; Gov. 1885-87.

WEVER, John Madison (R N.Y.) Feb. 24, 1847-Sept. 27, 1914; House 1891-95.

WEYMOUTH, George Warren (R Mass.) Aug. 25, 1850-Sept. 7, 1910; House 1897-1901.

WHALEN, Charles William Jr. (R Ohio) July 31, 1920-__; House 1967-__.

WHALEY, Kellian Van Rensalear (R Va./W.Va.) May 6, 1821-May 20, 1876; House 1861-63 (Va.); Dec. 7, 1863-67 (W.Va.).

WHALEY, Richard Smith (D S.C.) July 15, 1874-Nov. 8, 1951; House April 29, 1913-21.

WHALLEY, John Irving (R Pa.) Sept. 14, 1902-__; House Nov. 8, 1960-1973.

WHALLON, Reuben (JD N.Y.) Dec. 7, 1776-April 15, 1843; House 1833-35.

WHARTON, Charles Stuart (R Ill.) April 22, 1875-Sept. 4, 1939; House 1905-07.

WHARTON, James Ernest (R N.Y.) Oct. 4, 1899-__; House 1951-65.

WHARTON, Jesse (grandfather of Wharton Jackson Green) (— Tenn.) July 29, 1782-July 22, 1833; House 1807-09; Senate March 17, 1814-Oct. 10, 1815.

WHEAT, William Howard (R Ill.) Feb. 19, 1879-Jan. 16, 1944; House 1939-Jan. 16, 1944.

WHEATON, Horace (D N.Y.) Feb. 24, 1803-June 23, 1882; House 1843-47.

WHEATON, Laban (F Mass.) March 13, 1754-March 23, 1846; House 1809-17.

WHEELER, Burton Kendall (D Mont.) Feb. 27, 1882-Jan. 6, 1975; Senate 1923-47.

WHEELER, Charles Kennedy (D Ky.) April 18, 1863-June 15, 1933; House 1897-1903.

WHEELER, Ezra (D Wis.) Dec. 23, 1820-Sept. 19, 1871; House 1863-65.

WHEELER, Frank Willis (R Mich.) March 2, 1853-Aug. 9, 1921; House 1889-91.

WHEELER, Grattan Henry (— N.Y.) Aug. 25, 1783-March 11, 1852; House 1831-33.

WHEELER, Hamilton Kinkaid (R Ill.) Aug. 5, 1848-July 19, 1918; House 1893-95.

WHEELER, Harrison H. (D Mich.) March 22, 1839-July 28, 1896; House 1891-93.

WHEELER, John (D N.Y.) Feb. 11, 1823-April 1, 1906; House 1853-57.

WHEELER, Joseph (D Ala.) Sept. 10, 1836-Jan. 25, 1906; House 1881-June 3, 1882; Jan. 15-March 3, 1883; 1885-April 20, 1900.

WHEELER, Loren Edgar (R Ill.) Oct. 7, 1862-Jan. 8, 1932; House 1915-23, 1925-27.

WHEELER, Nelson Platt (R Pa.) Nov. 4, 1841-March 3, 1920; House 1907-11.

WHEELER, William Almon (R N.Y.) June 19, 1819-June 4, 1887; House 1861-63, 1869-77; Vice Pres. 1877-81.

WHEELER, William McDonald (D Ga.) July 11, 1915-__; House 1947-55.

WHELCHEL, Benjamin Frank (D Ga.) Dec. 16, 1895-May 11, 1954; House 1935-45.

WHERRY, Kenneth Spicer (R Neb.) Feb. 28, 1892-Nov. 29, 1951; Senate 1943-Nov. 29, 1951.

WHIPPLE, Thomas Jr. (— N.H.) 1787-Jan. 23, 1835; House 1821-29.

WHITACRE, John Jefferson (D Ohio) Dec. 28, 1860-Dec. 2, 1938; House 1911-15.

WHITAKER, John Albert (grandson of Addison Davis James) (D Ky.) Oct. 31, 1901-Dec. 15, 1951; House April 17, 1948-Dec. 15, 1951.

WHITCOMB, James (D Ind.) Dec. 1, 1795-Oct. 4, 1852; Senate 1849-Oct. 4, 1852; Gov. 1843-49.

WHITE, Addison (cousin of John White) (W Ky.) May 1, 1824-Feb. 4, 1909; House 1851-53.

WHITE, Albert Smith (R Ind.) Oct. 24, 1803-Sept. 24, 1864; House 1837-39, 1861-63 (1837-39 Whig, 1861-63 Republican; Senate 1839-45 (W).

WHITE, Alexander (F Va.) 1738-Sept. 19, 1804; House 1789-93.

WHITE, Alexander (R Ala.) Oct. 16, 1816-Dec. 13, 1893; House 1851-53, 1873-75 (1851-53 Union Whig, 1873-75 Republican).

WHITE, Alexander Colwell (R Pa.) Dec. 12, 1833-June 11, 1906; House 1885-87.

WHITE, Allison (D Pa.) Dec. 21, 1816-April 5, 1886; House 1857-59.

WHITE, Bartow (— N.Y.) Nov. 7, 1776-Dec. 12, 1862; House 1825-27.

WHITE, Benjamin (D Maine) May 13, 1790-June 7, 1860; House 1843-45.

WHITE, Campbell Patrick (JD N.Y.) Nov. 30, 1787-Feb. 12, 1859; House 1829-35.

WHITE, Cecil Fielding (D Calif.) Dec. 12, 1900-__; House 1949-51.

WHITE, Chilton Allen (D Ohio) Feb. 6, 1826-Dec. 7, 1900; House 1861-65.

WHITE, Compton Ignatius (father of Compton Ignatius White Jr.) (D Idaho) July 31, 1877-March 31, 1956; House 1933-47, 1949-51.

WHITE, Compton Ignatius Jr. (son of the preceding) (D Idaho) Dec. 19, 1920-__; House 1963-67.

WHITE, David (— Ky.) 1785-Oct. 19, 1834; House 1823-25.

WHITE, Dudley Allen (R Ohio) Jan. 3, 1901-Oct. 14, 1957; House 1937-41.

WHITE, Edward Douglass (son of James White and father of Edward Douglass White) (W La.) March 1795-April 18, 1847; House 1829-Nov. 15, 1834, 1839-43; Gov. 1834-38.

WHITE, Edward Douglass (son of the preceding) (D La.) Nov. 3, 1845-May 19, 1921; Senate 1891-March 12, 1894; Supreme Court Assoc. Justice 1894-1910; Chief Justice 1910-21.

WHITE, Francis (— Va.) ?- Nov. 1826; House 1813-15.

WHITE, Francis Shelley (Frank) (D Ala.) March 13, 1847-Aug. 1, 1922; Senate May 11, 1914-15.

WHITE, Frederick Edward (D Iowa) Jan. 19, 1844-Jan. 14, 1920; House 1891-93.

WHITE, George (D Ohio) Aug. 21, 1872-Dec. 15, 1953; House 1911-15, 1917-19; Chrmn. Dem. Nat. Comm. 1920-21; Gov. 1931-35.

WHITE, George Elon (R Ill.) March 7, 1848-May 17, 1935; House 1895-99.

WHITE, George Henry (R N.C.) Dec. 18, 1852-Dec. 28, 1918; House 1897-1901.

WHITE, Harry (R Pa.) Jan. 12, 1834-June 23, 1920; House 1877-81.

HITE, Hays Baxter (R Kan.) Sept. 21, 1855-Sept. 29, 1930; House 1919-29.

HITE, Hugh (R N.Y.) Dec. 25, 1798-Oct. 6, 1870; House 1845-51.

HITE, Hugh Lawson (— Tenn.) Oct. 30, 1773-April 10, 1840; Senate Oct. 28, 1825-Jan. 13, 1840; President pro tempore 1832-33.

WHITE, James (father of Edward Douglass White) (— Tenn.) June 16, 1749-Oct. 1809; House (Terr. Del.) Sept. 3, 1794-June 1, 1796; Cont. Cong. (N.C.) 1786-88.

WHITE, James Bain (R Ind.) June 26, 1835-Oct. 9, 1897; House 1887-89.

WHITE, James Bamford (D Ky.) June 6, 1842-March 25, 1931; House 1901-03.

WHITE, John (cousin of Addison White and uncle of John Daughterty White) (W Ky.) Feb. 14, 1802-Sept. 22, 1845; House 1835-45; Speaker 1841-43.

WHITE, John Daugherty (nephew of John White) (R Ky.) Jan. 16, 1849-Jan. 5, 1920; House 1875-77, 1881-85.

WHITE, Joseph Livingston (W Ind.) ?-Jan. 12, 1861; House 1841-43.

WHITE, Joseph M. (D Fla.) May 10, 1781-Oct. 19, 1839; House (Terr. Del.) 1825-37.

WHITE, Joseph Worthington (D Ohio) Oct. 2, 1822-Aug. 6, 1892; House 1863-65.

WHITE, Leonard (D Mass.) May 3, 1767-Oct. 10, 1849; House 1811-13.

WHITE, Michael Doherty (R Ind.) Sept. 8, 1827-Feb. 6, 1917; House 1877-79.

WHITE, Milo (R Minn.) Aug. 17, 1830-May 18, 1913; House 1883-87.

WHITE, Phineas (D Vt.) Oct. 30, 1770-July 6, 1847; House 1821-23.

WHITE, Richard Crawford (D Texas) April 29, 1923-__; House 1965-__.

WHITE, Samuel (F Del.) 1770-Nov. 4, 1809; Senate Feb. 28, 1801-Nov. 4, 1809.

WHITE, Sebastian Harrison (D Colo.) Dec. 24, 1864-Dec. 21, 1945; House Nov. 15, 1927-29.

WHITE, Stephen Mallory (D Calif.) Jan. 19, 1853-Feb. 21, 1901; Senate 1893-99.

WHITE, Stephen Van Culen (R N.Y.) Aug. 1, 1831-Jan. 18, 1913; House 1887-89.

WHITE, Wallace Humphrey Jr. (grandson of William Pierce Frye) (R Maine) Aug. 6, 1877-March 31, 1952; House 1917-31; Senate 1931-49.

WHITE, Wilbur McKee (R Ohio) Feb. 22, 1890-__; House 1931-33.

WHITE, William John (R Ohio) Oct. 7, 1850-Feb. 16, 1923; House 1893-95.

WHITEAKER, John (D Ore.) May 4, 1820-Oct. 2, 1902; House 1879-81; Gov. 1859-62.

WHITEHEAD, Joseph (D Va.) Oct. 31, 1867-July 8, 1938; House 1925-31.

WHITEHEAD, Thomas (C Va.) Dec. 27, 1825-July 1, 1901; House 1873-75.

WHITEHILL, James (son of John Whitehill and nephew of Robert Whitehill) (— Pa.) Jan. 31, 1762-Feb. 26, 1822; House 1813-Sept. 1, 1814.

WHITEHILL, John (father of James Whitehill and brother of Robert Whitehill) (— Pa.) Dec. 11, 1729-Sept. 16, 1815; House 1803-07.

WHITEHILL, Robert (brother of John Whitehill and uncle of James Whitehill) (— Pa.) July 21, 1738-April 8, 1813; House Nov. 7, 1805-April 8, 1813.

WHITEHOUSE, John Osborne (LD N.Y.) July 19, 1817-Aug. 24, 1881; House 1873-77.

WHITEHURST, George William (R Va.) March 12, 1925-__; House 1969-__.

WHITELAW, Robert Henry (D Mo.) Jan. 30, 1854-July 27, 1937; House Nov. 4, 1890-91.

WHITELEY, Richard Henry (R Ga.) Dec. 22, 1830-Sept. 26, 1890; House Dec. 22, 1870-75.

WHITELEY, William Gustavus (D Del.) Aug. 7, 1819-April 23, 1886; House 1857-61.

WHITENER, Basil Lee (D N.C.) May 14, 1915-__; House 1957-69.

WHITESIDE, Jenkin (— Tenn.) 1772-Sept. 25, 1822; Senate April 11, 1809-Oct. 8, 1811.

WHITESIDE, John (D Pa.) 1773-July 28, 1830; House 1815-19.

WHITFIELD, John Wilkins (D Kan.) March 11, 1818-Oct. 27, 1879; House (Terr. Del.) Dec. 20, 1854-Aug. 1, 1856; Dec. 9, 1856-57.

WHITING, Justin Rice (D/G Mich.) Feb. 18, 1847-Jan. 31, 1903; House 1887-95.

WHITING, Richard Henry (uncle of Ira Clifton Copley) (R Ill.) Jan. 17, 1826-May 24, 1888; House 1875-77.

WHITING, William (R Mass.) March 3, 1813-June 29, 1873; House March 4-June 29, 1873.

WHITING, William (R Mass.) May 24, 1841-Jan. 9, 1911; House 1883-89.

WHITLEY, James Lucius (R N.Y.) May 24, 1872-May 17, 1959; House 1929-35.

WHITMAN, Ezekiel (F Mass./Maine) March 9, 1776-Aug. 1, 1866; House 1809-11; 1817-21 (Mass.); 1821-June 1, 1822 (Maine).

WHITMAN, Lemuel (D Conn.) June 8, 1780-Nov. 13, 1841; House 1823-25.

WHITMORE, Elias (D N.Y.) March 2, 1772-Dec. 26, 1853; House 1825-27.

WHITMORE, George Washington (R Texas) Aug. 26, 1824-Oct. 14, 1876; House March 30, 1870-71.

WHITNEY, Thomas Richard (AP N.Y.) May 2, 1807-April 12, 1858; House 1855-57.

WHITTEMORE, Benjamin Franklin (R S.C.) May 18, 1824-Jan. 25, 1894; House July 18, 1868-Feb. 24, 1870.

WHITTEN, Jamie Lloyd (D Miss.) April 18, 1910-__; House Nov. 4, 1941-__.

WHITTHORNE, Washington Curran (D Tenn.) April 19, 1825-Sept. 21, 1891; House 1871-83, 1887-91; Senate April 16, 1886-87.

WHITTINGTON, William Madison (D Miss.) May 4, 1878-Aug. 20, 1962; House 1925-51.

WHITTLESEY, Elisha (uncle of William Augustus Whittlesey and cousin of Frederick Whittlesey and Thomas Tucker Whittlesey) (— Ohio) Oct. 19, 1783-Jan. 7, 1863; House 1823-July 9, 1838.

WHITTLESEY, Frederick (cousin of Elisha Whittlesey and Thomas Tucker Whittlesey) (W N.Y.) June 12, 1799-Sept. 19, 1851; House 1831-35.

WHITTLESEY, Thomas Tucker (cousin of Elisha Whittlesey and Frederick Whittlesey) (VBD Conn.) Dec. 8, 1798-Aug. 20, 1868; House April 29, 1836-39.

WHITTLESEY, William Augustus (nephew of Elisha Whittlesey) (D Ohio) July 14, 1796-Nov. 6, 1866; House 1849-51.

WHYTE, William Pinkney (D Md.) Aug. 9, 1824-March 17, 1908; Senate July 13, 1868-69, 1875-81, June 8, 1906-March 17, 1908; Gov. 1872-74.

WICK, William Watson (D Ind.) Feb. 23, 1796-May 19, 1868; House 1839-41; 1845-49.

WICKERSHAM, James (R Alaska) Aug. 24, 1857-Oct. 24, 1939; House (Terr. Del.) 1909-17, Jan. 7-March 3, 1919, March 1-3, 1921, 1931-33.

WICKERSHAM, Victor Eugene (D Okla.) Feb. 9, 1906-__; House April 1, 1941-47, 1949-57, 1961-65.

WICKES, Eliphalet (— N.Y.) April 1, 1769-June 7, 1850; House 1805-07.

WICKHAM, Charles Preston (R Ohio) Sept. 15, 1836-March 18, 1925; House 1887-91.

WICKLIFFE, Charles Anderson (grandfather of Robert Charles Wickliffe and John Crepps Wickliffe Beckham) (UW Ky.) June 8, 1788-Oct. 31, 1869; House 1823-33, 1861-63 (1823-33 Democrat, 1861-63 Union Whig); Gov. 1839-40; Postmaster Gen. 1841-45.

WICKLIFFE, Robert Charles (grandson of Charles Anderson Wickliffe and cousin of John Crepps Wickliffe Beckham) (D La.) May 1, 1874-June 11, 1912; House 1909-June 11, 1912.

WIDGERY, William (D Mass.) about 1753-July 31, 1822; House 1811-13.

WIDNALL, William Beck (R N.J.) March 17, 1906-__; House Feb. 6, 1950-Dec. 31, 1974.

WIER, Roy William (D Minn.) Feb. 25, 1888-June 27, 1963; House 1949-61.

WIGFALL, Louis Tresvant (D Texas) April 21, 1816-Feb. 18, 1874; Senate Dec. 5, 1859-March 23, 1861.

WIGGINS, Charles Edward (R Calif.) Dec. 3, 1927-—; House 1967-—.

WIGGINTON, Peter Dinwiddie (D Calif.) Sept. 6, 1839-July 7, 1890; House 1875-77, Feb. 7, 1878-79.

WIGGLESWORTH, Richard Bowditch (R Mass.) April 25, 1891-Oct. 22, 1960; House Nov. 6, 1928-Nov. 13, 1958.

WIKE, Scott (D Ill.) April 6, 1834-Jan. 15, 1901; House 1875-77, 1889-93.

WILBER, David (father of David Forrest Wilber) (R N.Y.) Oct. 5, 1820-April 1, 1890; House 1873-75; 1879-81; 1887-April 1, 1890.

WILBER, David Forrest (son of David Wilber) (R N.Y.) Dec. 7, 1859-Aug. 14, 1928; House 1895-99.

WILBOUR, Isaac (F R.I.) April 25, 1763-Oct. 4, 1837; House 1807-09.

WILCOX, James Mark (D Fla.) May 21, 1890-Feb. 3, 1956; House 1933-39.

WILCOX, Jeduthun (father of Leonard Wilcox) (F N.H.) Nov. 18, 1768-July 18, 1838; House 1813-17.

WILCOX, John A. (UW Miss.) April 18, 1819-Feb. 7, 1864; House 1851-53.

WILCOX, Leonard (son of Jeduthun Wilcox) (D N.H.) Jan. 29, 1799-June 18, 1850; Senate March 1, 1842-43.

WILCOX, Robert William (— Hawaii) Feb. 15, 1855-Oct. 23, 1903; House (Terr. Del.) Nov. 6, 1900-03.

WILDE, Richard Henry (D Ga.) Sept. 24, 1789-Sept. 10, 1847; House 1815-17; Feb. 7-March 3, 1825; Nov. 17, 1827-35.

WILDER, Abel Carter (R Kan.) March 18, 1828-Dec. 22, 1875; House 1863-65.

WILDER, William Henry (R Mass.) May 14, 1855-Sept. 11, 1913; House 1911-Sept. 11, 1913.

WILDMAN, Zalmon (D Conn.) Feb. 16, 1775-Dec. 10, 1835; House March 4-Dec. 10, 1835.

WILDRICK, Isaac (D N.J.) March 3, 1803-March 22, 1892; House 1849-53.

WILEY, Alexander (R Wis.) May 26, 1884-May 26, 1967; Senate 1939-63.

WILEY, Ariosto Appling (brother of Oliver Cicero Wiley) (D Ala.) Nov. 6, 1848-June 17, 1908; House 1901-June 17, 1908.

WILEY, James Sullivan (D Maine) Jan. 22, 1808-Dec. 21, 1891; House 1847-49.

WILEY, John McClure (D N.Y.) Aug. 11, 1846-Aug. 13, 1912; House 1889-91.

WILEY, Oliver Cicero (brother of Ariosto Appling Wiley) (D Ala.) Jan. 30, 1851-Oct. 18, 1917; House Nov. 3, 1908-09.

WILEY, William Halsted (R N.J.) July 10, 1842-May 2, 1925; House 1903-07, 1909-11.

WILFLEY, Xenophon Pierce (D Mo.) March 18, 1871-May 4, 1931; Senate April 30-Nov. 5, 1918.

WILKIN, James Whitney (father of Samuel Jones Wilkin) (D N.Y.) 1762-Feb. 23, 1845; House June 7, 1815-19.

WILKIN, Samuel Jones (son of James Whitney Wilkin) (D N.Y.) Dec. 17, 1793-March 11, 1866; House 1831-33.

WILKINS, Beriah (D Ohio) July 10, 1846-June 7, 1905; House 1883-89.

WILKINS, William (D Pa.) Dec. 20, 1779-June 23, 1865; Senate 1831-June 30, 1834 (D/AMas.); House 1843-Feb. 14, 1844; Secy. of War 1844-45.

WILKINSON, Morton Smith (R Minn.) Jan. 22, 1819-Feb. 4, 1894; Senate 1859-65; House 1869-71.

WILKINSON, Theodore Stark (D La.) Dec. 18, 1847-Feb. 1, 1921; House 1887-91.

WILLARD, Charles Wesley (R Vt.) June 18, 1827-June 8, 1880; House 1869-75.

WILLARD, George (R Mich.) March 20, 1824-March 26, 1901; House 1873-77.

WILLCOX, Washington Frederick (D Conn.) Aug. 22, 1834-March 8, 1909; House 1889-93.

WILLETT, William Forte Jr. (D N.Y.) Nov. 27, 1869-Feb. 12, 1938; House 1907-11.

WILLEY, Calvin (D Conn.) Sept. 15, 1776-Aug. 23, 1858; Senate May 4, 1825-31.

WILLEY, Earle Dukes (R Del.) July 21, 1889-March 17, 1950; House 1943-45.

WILLEY, Waitman Thomas (— Va./R W.Va.) Oct. 18, 1811-May 2, 1900; Senate July 9, 1861-63 (Va.); Aug. 4, 1863-71 (W.Va.).

WILLFORD, Albert Clinton (D Iowa) Sept. 21, 1877-March 10, 1937; House 1933-35.

WILLIAMS, Abram Pease (R Calif.) Feb. 3, 1832-Oct. 17, 1911; Senate Aug. 4, 1886-87.

WILLIAMS, Alpheus Starkey (D Mich.) Sept. 20, 1810-Dec. 20, 1878; House 1875-Dec. 20, 1878.

WILLIAMS, Andrew (R N.Y.) Aug. 27, 1828-Oct. 6, 1907; House 1875-79.

WILLIAMS, Archibald Hunter Arrington (nephew of Archibald Hunter Arrington) (D N.C.) Oct. 22, 1842-Sept. 5, 1895; House 1891-93.

WILLIAMS, Arthur Bruce (R Mich.) Jan. 27, 1872-May 1, 1925; House June 19, 1923-May 1, 1925.

WILLIAMS, Benjamin (— N.C.) Jan. 1, 1751-July 20, 1814; House 1793-95; Gov. 1799-1802, 1807-08.

WILLIAMS, Charles Grandison (R Wis) Oct. 18, 1829-March 30, 1892; House 187 83.

WILLIAMS, Christopher Harris (grandfath of John Sharp Williams) (W Tenn.) De 18, 1798-Nov. 27, 1857; House 1837-4 1849-53.

WILLIAMS, Clyde (D Mo.) Oct. 13, 187 Nov. 12, 1954; House 1927-29; 1931-43.

WILLIAMS, David Rogerson (D S.C March 8, 1776-Nov. 17, 1830; Hous 1805-09, 1811-13; Gov. 1814-16.

WILLIAMS, Elihu Stephen (R Ohio) Jan. 2 1835-Dec. 1, 1903; House 1887-91.

WILLIAMS, George Fred (D Mass.) July 1 1852-July 11, 1932; House 1891-93.

WILLIAMS, George Henry (UR Ore.) Marc 23, 1823-April 4, 1910; Senate 1865-71 Atty. Gen. 1872-75.

WILLIAMS, George Howard (R Mo.) Dec 1, 1871-Nov. 25, 1963; Senate May 25 1925-Dec. 5, 1926.

WILLIAMS, George Short (R Del.) Oct. 21 1877-Nov. 22, 1961; House 1939-41.

WILLIAMS, Guinn (D Texas) April 22 1871-Jan. 9, 1948; House May 13, 1922-33.

WILLIAMS, Harrison Arlington Jr. (D N.J. Dec. 10, 1919-—; House Nov. 3, 1953-57; Senate 1959-—.

WILLIAMS, Henry (D Mass.) Nov. 30, 1805-May 8, 1887; House 1839-41, 1843-45.

WILLIAMS, Hezekiah (D Maine) July 28, 1798-Oct. 23, 1856; House 1845-49.

WILLIAMS, Isaac Jr. (D N.Y.) April 5, 1777-Nov. 9, 1860; House Dec. 20, 1813-1815, 1817-19, 1823-25.

WILLIAMS, James (D Del.) Aug. 4, 1825-April 12, 1899; House 1875-79.

WILLIAMS, James Douglas (D Ind.) Jan. 16, 1808-Nov. 20, 1880; House 1875-Dec. 1, 1876; Gov. 1877-1880.

WILLIAMS, James Robert (D Ill.) Dec. 27, 1850-Nov. 8, 1923; House Dec. 2, 1889-95; 1899-1905.

WILLIAMS, James Wray (D Md.) Oct. 8, 1792-Dec. 2, 1842; House 1841-Dec. 2, 1842.

WILLIAMS, Jared (JD Va.) March 4, 1766-Jan. 2, 1831; House 1819-25.

WILLIAMS, Jared Warner (D N.H.) Dec. 22, 1796-Sept. 29, 1864; House 1837-41; Senate Nov. 29, 1853-July 15, 1854; Gov. 1847-49.

WILLIAMS, Jeremiah Norman (D Ala.) May 29, 1829-May 8, 1915; House 1875-79.

WILLIAMS, John (— N.Y.) Sept. 1752-July 22, 1806; House 1795-99.

WILLIAMS, John (brother of Lewis Williams and Robert Williams, father of Joseph Lanier Williams and cousin of Marmaduke Williams) (— Tenn.) Jan. 29, 1778-Aug. 10, 1837; Senate Oct. 10, 1815-23.

ILLIAMS, John (D N.Y.) Jan. 7, 1807-March 26, 1875; House 1855-57.

ILLIAMS, John Bell (D Miss.) Dec. 4, 1918-__; House 1947-Jan. 16, 1968; Gov. 1968-72.

ILLIAMS, John James (R Del.) May 17, 1904-__; Senate 1947-Dec. 31, 1970.

ILLIAMS, John McKeown Snow (R Mass.) Aug. 13, 1818-March 19, 1886; House 1873-75.

ILLIAMS, John Sharp (grandson of Christopher Harris Williams) (D Miss.) July 30, 1854-Sept. 27, 1932; House 1893-1909; Senate 1911-23.

ILLIAMS, John Stuart (D Ky.) July 10, 1818-July 17, 1898; Senate 1879-85.

ILLIAMS, Jonathan (— Pa.) May 20, 1750-May 16, 1815; House March 4-May 16, 1815.

ILLIAMS, Joseph Lanier (son of John Williams of Tenn.) (W Tenn.) Oct. 23, 1810-Dec. 14, 1865; House 1837-43.

ILLIAMS, Lawrence Gordon (R Pa.) Sept. 15, 1913-July 13, 1975; House 1967-75.

ILLIAMS, Lemuel (— Mass.) June 18, 1747-Nov. 8, 1828; House 1799-1805.

ILLIAMS, Lewis (brother of John Williams of Tenn. and Robert Williams and cousin of Marmaduke Williams) (— N.C.) Feb. 1, 1782-Feb. 23, 1842; House 1815-Feb. 23, 1842.

ILLIAMS, Marmaduke (cousin of John Williams of Tenn., Lewis Williams and Robert Williams) (D N.C.) April 6, 1774-Oct. 29, 1850; House 1803-09.

WILLIAMS, Morgan B. (R Pa.) Sept. 17, 1831-Oct. 13, 1903; House 1897-99.

WILLIAMS, Nathan (D N.Y.) Dec. 19, 1773-Sept. 25, 1835; House 1805-07.

WILLIAMS, Reuel (D Maine) June 2, 1783-July 25, 1862; Senate 1837-Feb. 15, 1843.

WILLIAMS, Richard (R Ore.) Nov. 15, 1836-June 19, 1914; House 1877-79.

WILLIAMS, Robert (brother of John Williams of Tenn. and Lewis Williams and cousin of Marmaduke Williams) (— N.C.) July 12, 1773-Jan. 25, 1836; House 1797-1803; Gov. of Miss. Terr. 1805-09.

WILLIAMS, Seward Henry (R Ohio) Nov. 7, 1870-Sept. 2, 1922; House 1915-17.

WILLIAMS, Sherrod (W Ky.) 1804-?; House 1835-41.

WILLIAMS, Thomas (R Pa.) Aug. 28, 1806-June 16, 1872; House 1863-69.

WILLIAMS, Thomas (D Ala.) Aug. 11, 1825-April 13, 1903; House 1879-85.

WILLIAMS, Thomas Hickman (D Miss.) Jan. 20, 1801-May 3, 1851; Senate Nov. 12, 1838-39.

WILLIAMS, Thomas Hill (D Miss.) 1780-1840; Senate Dec. 10, 1817-29.

WILLIAMS, Thomas Scott (— Conn.) June 26, 1777-Dec. 22, 1861; House 1817-19.

WILLIAMS, Thomas Sutler (R Ill.) Feb. 14, 1872-April 5, 1940; House 1915-Nov. 11, 1929.

WILLIAMS, Thomas Wheeler (W Conn.) Sept. 28, 1789-Dec. 31, 1874; House 1839-43.

WILLIAMS, William (D N.Y.) Sept. 6, 1815-Sept. 10, 1876; House 1871-73.

WILLIAMS, William (R Ind.) May 11, 1821-April 22, 1896; House 1867-75.

WILLIAMS, William Brewster (R Mich.) July 28, 1826-March 4, 1905; House Dec. 1, 1873-77.

WILLIAMS, William Elza (D Ill.) May 5, 1857-Sept. 13, 1921; House 1899-1901, 1913-17.

WILLIAMS, William Robert (R N.Y.) Aug. 11, 1884-May 9, 1972; House 1951-59.

WILLIAMSON, Ben Mitchell (D Ky.) Oct. 16, 1864-June 23, 1941; Senate Dec. 1, 1930-31.

WILLIAMSON, Hugh (F N.C.) Dec. 5, 1735-May 22, 1819; House 1789-93; Cont. Cong. 1782-85, 1787-88.

WILLIAMSON, John Newton (R Ore.) Nov. 8, 1855-Aug. 29, 1943; House 1903-07.

WILLIAMSON, William (R S.D.) Oct. 7, 1875-July 15, 1972; House 1921-33.

WILLIAMSON, William Durkee (D Maine) July 31, 1779-May 27, 1846; House 1821-23; Gov. 1821.

WILLIE, Asa Hoxie (D Texas) Oct. 11, 1829-March 16, 1899; House 1873-75.

WILLIS, Albert Shelby (D Ky.) Jan. 22, 1843-Jan. 6, 1897; House 1877-87.

WILLIS, Benjamin Albertson (D N.Y.) March 24, 1840-Oct. 14, 1886; House 1875-79.

WILLIS, Edwin Edward (D La.) Oct. 2, 1904-Oct. 24, 1972; House 1949-69.

WILLIS, Francis (— Ga.) Jan. 5, 1745-Jan. 25, 1829; House 1791-93.

WILLIS, Frank Bartlett (R Ohio) Dec. 28, 1871-March 30, 1928; House 1911-Jan. 9, 1915; Senate Jan. 14, 1921-March 30, 1928; Gov. 1915-17.

WILLIS, Jonathan Spencer (R Del.) April 5, 1830-Nov. 24, 1903; House 1895-97.

WILLIS, Raymond Eugene (R Ind.) Aug. 11, 1875-March 21, 1956; Senate 1941-47.

WILLITS, Edwin (R Mich.) April 24, 1830-Oct. 22, 1896; House 1877-83.

WILLOUGHBY, Westel Jr. (D N.Y.) Nov. 20, 1769-Oct. 3, 1844; House Dec. 13, 1815-17.

WILMOT, David (R Pa.) Jan. 20, 1814-March 16, 1868; House 1845-51 (D); Senate March 14, 1861-63 (R).

WILSHIRE, William Wallace (C Ark.) Sept. 8, 1830-Aug. 19, 1888; House 1873-June 16, 1874; 1875-77 (1873-74 Republican, 1875-77 Conservative).

WILSON, Alexander (— Va.) ?-?; House Dec. 4, 1804-09.

WILSON, Benjamin (D W.Va.) April 30, 1825-April 26, 1901; House 1875-83.

WILSON, Charles (D Texas) June 1, 1933-__; House 1973-__.

WILSON, Charles Herbert (D Calif.) Feb. 15, 1917-—; House 1963-—.

WILSON, Earl (R Ind.) April 18, 1906-__; House 1941-59; 1961-65.

WILSON, Edgar (Sil. R/D Idaho) Feb. 25, 1861-Jan. 3, 1915; House 1895-97, 1899-1901 (1895-97 Republican, 1899-1901 Silver Republican/Democrat).

WILSON, Edgar Campbell (son of Thomas Wilson of Va. and father of Eugene McLanahan Wilson) (W Va.) Oct. 18, 1800-April 24, 1860; House 1833-35.

WILSON, Emmett (grandson of Augustus Emmett Maxwell) (D Fla.) Sept. 17, 1882-May 29, 1918; House 1913-17.

WILSON, Ephraim King (father of Ephraim King Wilson) (D Md.) Sept. 15, 1771-Jan. 2, 1834; House 1827-31.

WILSON, Ephraim King (son of the preceding) (D Md.) Dec. 22, 1821-Feb. 24, 1891; House 1873-75; Senate 1885-Feb. 24, 1891.

WILSON, Eugene McLanahan (son of Edgar Campbell Wilson, grandson of Thomas Wilson of Va. and great-grandson of Isaac Griffin) (D Minn.) Dec. 25, 1833-April 10, 1890; House 1869-71.

WILSON, Francis Henry (R N.Y.) Feb. 11, 1844-Sept. 25, 1910; House 1895-Sept. 30, 1897.

WILSON, Frank Eugene (D N.Y.) Dec. 22, 1857-July 12, 1935; House 1899-1905, 1911-15.

WILSON, George Allison (R Iowa) April 1, 1884-Sept. 8, 1953; Senate Jan. 14, 1943-49; Gov. 1939-43.

WILSON, George Howard (D Okla.) Aug. 21, 1905-__; House 1949-51.

WILSON, George Washington (R Ohio) Feb. 22, 1840-Nov. 27, 1909; House 1893-97.

WILSON, Henry (D Pa.) 1778-Aug. 14, 1826; House 1823-Aug. 14, 1826.

WILSON, Henry (FS/AP/D Mass.) Feb. 16, 1812-Nov. 22, 1875; Senate Jan. 31, 1855-73; Vice Pres. (R) 1873-75.

WILSON, Isaac (— N.Y.) June 25, 1780-Oct. 25, 1848; House 1823-Jan. 7, 1824.

WILSON, James (father of James Wilson) (F N.H.) Aug. 16, 1766-Jan. 4, 1839; House 1809-11.

WILSON, James (son of the preceding) (W N.H.) March 18, 1797-May 29, 1881; House 1847-Sept. 9, 1850.

WILSON, James (D Pa.) April 28, 1779-July 19, 1868; House 1823-29.

WILSON, James (father of John Lockwood Wilson) (R Ind.) April 9, 1825-Aug. 8, 1867; House 1857-61.

WILSON, James (R Iowa) Aug. 16, 1835-Aug. 26, 1920; House 1873-77, 1883-85; Secy. of Agriculture 1897-1913.

WILSON, James Clifton (D Texas) June 21, 1874-Aug. 3, 1951; House 1917-19.

WILSON, James Falconer (R Iowa) Oct. 19, 1828-April 22, 1895; House Oct. 8, 1861-69; Senate 1883-95.

WILSON, James Jefferson (D N.J.) 1775-July 28, 1824; Senate 1815-Jan. 8, 1821.

WILSON, Jeremiah Morrow (R Ind.) Nov. 25, 1828-Sept. 24, 1901; House 1871-75.

WILSON, John (— S.C.) Aug. 11, 1773-Aug. 13, 1828; House 1821-27.

WILSON, John (F Mass.) Jan. 10, 1777-Aug. 9, 1848; House 1813-15, 1817-19.

WILSON, John Frank (D Ariz.) May 7, 1846-April 7, 1911; House (Terr. Del.) 1899-1901, 1903-05.

WILSON, John Haden (D Pa.) Aug. 20, 1867-Jan. 28, 1946; House 1919-21.

WILSON, John Henry (R Ky.) Jan. 30, 1846-Jan. 14, 1923; House 1889-93.

WILSON, John Lockwood (son of James Wilson of Ind.) (R Wash.) Aug. 7, 1850-Nov. 6, 1912; House Nov. 20, 1889-Feb. 18, 1895; Senate Feb. 19, 1895-99.

WILSON, John Thomas (R Ohio) April 16, 1811-Oct. 6, 1891; House 1867-73.

WILSON, Joseph Franklin (D Texas) March 18, 1901-Oct. 13, 1968; House 1947-55.

WILSON, Joseph Gardner (cousin of James Willis Nesmith) (R Ore.) Dec. 13, 1826-July 2, 1873; House March 4-July 2, 1873.

WILSON, Nathan (D N.Y.) Dec. 23, 1758-July 25, 1834; House June 3, 1808-09.

WILSON, Riley Joseph (D La.) Nov. 12, 1871-Feb. 23, 1946; House 1915-37.

WILSON, Robert (U Mo.) Nov. 1803-May 10, 1870; Senate Jan. 17, 1862-Nov. 13, 1863.

WILSON, Robert Carlton (Bob) (R Calif.) April 5, 1916-__; House 1953-__.

WILSON, Robert Patterson Clark (D Mo.) Aug. 8, 1834-Dec. 21, 1916; House Dec. 2, 1889-93.

WILSON, Stanyarne (D S.C.) Jan. 10, 1860-Feb. 14, 1928; House 1895-1901.

WILSON, Stephen Fowler (R Pa.) Sept. 4, 1821-March 30, 1897; House 1865-69.

WILSON, Thomas (father of Edgar Campbell Wilson and grandfather of Eugene McLanahan Wilson) (F Va.) Sept. 11, 1765-Jan. 24, 1826; House 1811-13.

WILSON, Thomas (D Pa.) 1772-Oct. 4, 1824; House May 4, 1813-17.

WILSON, Thomas (D Minn.) May 16, 1827-April 3, 1910; House 1887-89.

WILSON, Thomas Webber (D Miss.) Jan. 24, 1893-Jan. 31, 1948; House 1923-29.

WILSON, William (— Pa.) ?-?; House 1815-19.

WILSON, William (— Ohio) March 19, 1773-June 6, 1827; House 1823-June 6, 1827.

WILSON, William Bauchop (D Pa.) April 2, 1862-May 25, 1934; House 1907-13; Secy. of Labor 1913-21.

WILSON, William Edward (D Ind.) March 9, 1870-Sept. 29, 1948; House 1923-25.

WILSON, William Henry (R Pa.) Dec. 6, 1877-Aug. 11, 1937; House 1935-37.

WILSON, William Lyne (D W.Va.) May 3, 1843-Oct. 17, 1900; House 1883-95; Postmaster Gen. 1895-97.

WILSON, William Warfield (R Ill.) March 2, 1868-July 22, 1942; House 1903-13, 1915-21.

WINNANS, Edwin Baruch (D Mich.) May 16, 1826-July 4, 1894; House 1883-87; Gov. 1891-93.

WINANS, James January (R Ohio) June 7, 1818-April 28, 1879; House 1869-71.

WINANS, John (ID Wis.) Sept. 27, 1831-Jan. 17, 1907; House 1883-85.

WINCHESTER, Boyd (D Ky.) Sept. 23, 1836-May 18, 1923; House 1869-73.

WINDOM, William (R Minn.) May 10, 1827-Jan. 29, 1891; House 1859-69; Senate July 15, 1870-Jan. 22, 1871; March 4, 1871-March 7, 1881; Nov. 15, 1881-83; Secy. of the Treasury 1881, 1889-91.

WINFIELD, Charles Henry (D N.Y.) April 22, 1822-June 10, 1888; House 1863-67.

WING, Austin Eli (W Mich.) Feb. 3, 1792-Aug. 27, 1849; House (Terr. Del.) 1825-29, 1831-33.

WINGATE, Joseph Ferdinand (D Maine) June 29, 1786-?; House 1827-31.

WINGATE, Paine (F N.H.) May 14, 1739-March 7, 1838; Senate 1789-93; House 1793-95; Cont. Cong. 1787-88.

WINGO, Effiegene (Locke) (widow of Otis Theodore Wingo and great-great-great-granddaughter of Matthew Locke) (D Ark.) April 13, 1883-Sept. 19, 1962; House Nov. 4, 1930-33.

WINGO, Otis Theodore (husband of Effiegene Wingo) (D Ark.) June 18, 1877-Oct. 21, 1930; House 1913-Oct. 21, 1930.

WINN, Larry Jr. (R Kan.) Aug. 22, 1919-__; House 1967-__.

WINN, Richard (D S.C.) 1750-Dec. 1[?], 1818; House 1793-97, Jan. 24, 1803-13.

WINN, Thomas Elisha (Alliance D Ga[?]) May 21, 1839-June 5, 1925; House 1891-9[?].

WINSLOW, Samuel Ellsworth (R Mass[?]) April 11, 1862-July 11, 1940; House 191[3?]-25.

WINSLOW, Warren (D N.C.) Jan. 1[?], 1810-Aug. 16, 1862; House 1855-61.

WINSTEAD, William Arthur (D Miss.) Jan[?] 6, 1904-__; House 1943-65.

WINSTON, Joseph (D N.C.) June 17[?], 1746-April 21, 1815; House 1793-95, 1803[-]07.

WINTER, Charles Edwin (R Wyo.) Sept. 13[?], 1870-April 22, 1948; House 1923-29.

WINTER, Elisha I. (F N.Y.) July 15[?], 1781-June 30, 1849; House 1813-15.

WINTER, Thomas Daniel (R Kan.) July 7[?], 1896-Nov. 7, 1951; House 1939-47.

WINTHROP, Robert Charles (W Mass.[?]) May 12, 1809-Nov. 16, 1894; House Nov. 9, 1840-May 25, 1842, Nov. 29, 1842-July 30, 1850; Senate July 30, 1850-Feb. 1, 1851; Speaker, 1847-49.

WIRTH, Timothy Endicott (D Colo.) Sept. 22, 1939-__; House 1975-__.

WISE, George Douglas (cousin of John[?] Sergeant Wise and Richard Alsop Wise and nephew of Henry Alexander Wise) (D Va.) June 4, 1831-Feb. 4, 1898; House 1881-April 10, 1890, 1891-95.

WISE, Henry Alexander (father of John Sergeant Wise and Richard Alsop Wise and uncle of George Douglas Wise) (Tyler D Va.) Dec. 3, 1806-Sept. 12, 1876; House 1833-Feb. 12, 1844 (1833-37 Jackson Democrat, 1837-43 Whig, 1843-44 Tyler Democrat); Gov. 1856-60.

WISE, James Walter (D Ga.) March 3, 1868-Sept. 8, 1925; House 1915-25.

WISE, John Sergeant (son of Henry Alexander Wise, grandson of John Sergeant, brother of Richard Alsop Wise and cousin of George Douglas Wise) (Read. Va.) Dec. 27, 1846-May 12, 1913; House 1883-85.

WISE, Morgan Ringland (D Pa.) June 7, 1825-April 13, 1903; House 1879-83.

WISE, Richard Alsop (son of Henry Alexander Wise, grandson of John Sergeant, brother of John Sergeant Wise and cousin of George Douglas Wise) (R Va.) Sept. 2, 1843-Dec. 21, 1900; House April 26, 1898-99, March 12-Dec. 21, 1900.

WITCHER, John Seashoal (R W.Va.) July 15, 1839-July 8, 1906; House 1869-71.

WITHERELL, James (D Vt.) June 16, 1759-Jan. 9, 1838; House 1807-May 1, 1808.

WITHERS, Garrett Lee (D Ky.) June 21, 1884-April 30, 1953; Senate Jan. 20, 1949-Nov. 26, 1950; House Aug. 2, 1952-April 30, 1953.

WITHERS, Robert Enoch (cousin of Thomas Withers Chinn) (C Va.) Sept. 18, 1821-Sept. 21, 1907; Senate 1875-81.

WITHERSPOON, Robert (great-great-grandfather of Robert Witherspoon Hemphill) (D S.C.) Jan. 29, 1767-Oct. 11, 1837; House 1809-11.

WITHERSPOON, Samuel Andrew (D Miss.) May 4, 1855-Nov. 24, 1915; House 1911-Nov. 24, 1915.

WITHROW, Gardner Robert (R Wis.) Oct. 5, 1892-Sept. 23, 1964; House 1931-39, 1949-61 (1931-35 Republican, 1935-39 Progressive, 1949-61 Republican).

WITTE, William Henry (D Pa.) Oct. 4, 1817-Nov. 24, 1876; House 1853-55.

WOFFORD, Thomas Albert (D S.C.) Sept. 27, 1908-__; Senate April 5-Nov. 6, 1956.

WOLCOTT, Edward Oliver (R Colo.) March 26, 1848-March 1, 1905; Senate 1889-1901.

WOLCOTT, Jesse Paine (R Mich.) March 3, 1893-Jan. 28, 1969; House 1931-57.

WOLCOTT, Josiah Oliver (D Del.) Oct. 31, 1877-Nov. 11, 1938; Senate 1917-July 2, 1921.

WOLD, John Schiller (R Wyo.) Aug. 31, 1916-__; House 1969-71.

WOLF, George (D Pa.) Aug. 12, 1777-March 11, 1840; House Dec. 9, 1824-29; Gov. 1829-35.

WOLF, Harry Benjamin (D Md.) June 16, 1880-Feb. 17, 1944; House 1907-09.

WOLF, Leonard George (D Iowa) Oct. 29, 1925-March 28, 1970; House 1959-61.

WOLF, William Penn (R Iowa) Dec. 1, 1833-Sept. 19, 1896; House Dec. 6, 1870-71.

WOLFE, Simeon Kalfius (D Ind.) Feb. 14, 1824-Nov. 18, 1888; House 1873-75.

WOLFENDEN, James (R Pa.) July 25, 1889-April 8, 1949; House Nov. 6, 1928-47.

WOLFF, Joseph Scott (D Mo.) June 14, 1878-Feb. 27, 1958; House 1923-25.

WOLFF, Lester Lionel (D N.Y.) Jan. 4, 1919-__; House 1965-__.

WOLFORD, Frank Lane (D Ky.) Sept. 2, 1817-Aug. 2, 1895; House 1883-87.

WOLVERTON, Charles Anderson (R N.J.) Oct. 24, 1880-May 16, 1969; House 1927-59.

WOLVERTON, John Marshall (R W.Va.) Jan. 31, 1872-Aug. 19, 1944; House 1925-27, 1929-31.

WOLVERTON, Simon Peter (D Pa.) Jan. 28, 1837-Oct. 25, 1910; House 1891-95.

WON PAT, Antonio Borja (D Guam) Dec. 10, 1908-__; House 1973-__.

WOOD, Abiel (F Mass.) July 22, 1772-Oct. 26, 1834; House 1813-15.

WOOD, Alan Jr. (nephew of John Wood) (R Pa.) July 6, 1834-Oct. 31, 1902; House 1875-77.

WOOD, Amos Eastman (D Ohio) Jan. 2, 1810-Nov. 19, 1850; House Dec. 3, 1849-Nov. 19, 1850.

WOOD, Benjamin (brother of Fernando Wood) (D N.Y.) Oct. 13, 1820-Feb. 21, 1900; House 1861-65; 1881-83.

WOOD, Benson (R Ill.) March 31, 1839-Aug. 27, 1915; House 1895-97.

WOOD, Bradford Ripley (D N.Y.) Sept. 3, 1800-Sept. 26, 1889; House 1845-47.

WOOD, Ernest Edward (D Mo.) Aug. 24, 1875-Jan. 10, 1952; House 1905-June 23, 1906.

WOOD, Fernando (brother of Benjamin Wood) (D N.Y.) June 14, 1812-Feb. 13, 1881; House 1841-43, 1863-65, 1867-Feb. 13, 1881 (1841-43 Tammany Democrat, 1863-65 and 1867-1881 Democrat).

WOOD, Ira Wells (R N.J.) June 19, 1856-Oct. 5, 1931; House Nov. 8, 1904-13.

WOOD, John (uncle of Alan Wood Jr.) (R Pa.) Sept. 6, 1816-May 28, 1898; House 1859-61.

WOOD, John Jacob (JD N.Y.) Feb. 16, 1784-May 20, 1874; House 1827-29.

WOOD, John M. (R Maine) Nov. 17, 1813-Dec. 24, 1864; House 1855-59.

WOOD, John Stephens (D Ga.) Feb. 8, 1885-Sept. 12, 1968; House 1931-35, 1945-53.

WOOD, John Travers (R Idaho) Nov. 25, 1878-Nov. 2, 1954; House 1951-53.

WOOD, Reuben Terrell (D Mo.) Aug. 7, 1884-July 16, 1955; House 1933-41.

WOOD, Silas (D N.Y.) Sept. 14, 1769-March 2, 1847; House 1819-29.

WOOD, Thomas Jefferson (D Ind.) Sept. 30, 1844-Oct. 13, 1908; House 1883-85.

WOOD, Walter Abbott (R N.Y.) Oct. 23, 1815-Jan. 15, 1892; House 1879-83.

WOOD, William Robert (R Ind.) Jan. 5, 1861-March 7, 1933; House 1915-33.

WOODARD, Frederick Augustus (D N.C.) Feb. 12, 1854-May 8, 1915; House 1893-97.

WOODBRIDGE, Frederick Enoch (R Vt.) Aug. 29, 1818-April 25, 1888; House 1863-69.

WOODBRIDGE, William W. (W/D Mich.) Aug. 20, 1780-Oct. 20, 1861; House (Terr. Del.) 1819-Aug. 9, 1820; Senate 1841-47; Gov. 1840-41.

WOODBURN, William (R Nev.) April 14, 1838-Jan. 15, 1915; House 1875-77, 1885-89.

WOODBURY, Levi (D N.H.) Dec. 22, 1789-Sept. 4, 1851; Senate March 16, 1825-31, 1841-Nov. 20, 1845; Gov. 1823-24; Secy. of the Navy 1831-34; Secy. of the Treasury 1834-41; Assoc. Justice of Supreme Court 1845-51.

WOODCOCK, David (D N.Y.) 1785-Sept. 18, 1835; House 1821-23, 1827-29.

WOODFORD, Stewart Lyndon (R N.Y.) Sept. 3, 1835-Feb. 14, 1913; House 1873-July 1, 1874.

WOODHOUSE, Chase Going (D Conn.) ?-__; House 1945-47, 1949-51.

WOODMAN, Charles Walhart (R Ill.) March 11, 1844-March 18, 1898; House 1895-97.

WOODRUFF, George Catlin (D Conn.) Dec. 1, 1805-Nov. 21, 1885; House 1861-63.

WOODRUFF, John (AP Conn.) Feb. 12, 1826-May 20, 1868; House 1855-57; 1859-61.

WOODRUFF, Roy Orchard (R Mich.) March 14, 1876-Feb. 12, 1953; House 1913-15, 1921-53 (1913-15 Progressive Republican, 1921-53 Republican).

WOODRUFF, Thomas M. (D N.Y.) May 3, 1804-March 28, 1855; House 1845-47.

WOODRUM, Clifton Alexander (D Va.) April 27, 1887-Oct. 6, 1950; House 1923-Dec. 31, 1945.

WOODS, Frank Plowman (R Iowa) Dec. 11, 1868-April 25, 1944; House 1909-19.

WOODS, Henry (brother of John Woods) (— Pa.) 1764-1826; House 1799-1803.

WOODS, James Pleasant (D Va.) Feb. 4, 1868-July 7, 1948; House Feb. 25, 1919-23.

WOODS, John (brother of Henry Woods) (F Pa.) 1761-Dec. 16, 1816; House (elected 1814 but never served).

WOODS, John (W Ohio) Oct. 18, 1794-July 30, 1855; House 1825-29.

WOODS, Samuel Davis (R Calif.) Sept. 19, 1845-Dec. 24, 1915; House Dec. 3, 1900-03.

WOODS, William (D N.Y.) 1790-Aug. 7, 1837; House Nov. 3, 1823-25.

WOODSON, Samuel Hughes (— Ky.) Sept. 15, 1777-July 28, 1827; House 1821-23.

WOODSON, Samuel Hughes (son of the preceding) (AP Mo.) Oct. 24, 1815-June 23, 1881; House 1857-61.

WOODWARD, George Washington (D Pa.) March 26, 1809-May 10, 1875; House Nov. 21, 1867-71.

WOODWARD, Gilbert Motier (D Wis.) Dec. 25, 1835-March 13, 1913; House 1883-85.

WOODWARD, Joseph Addison (D S.C.) April 11, 1806-Aug. 3, 1885; House 1843-53.

WOODWARD, William (— S.C.) ? - ?; House 1815-17.

WOODWORTH, James Hutchinson (R Ill.) Dec. 4, 1804-March 26, 1869; House 1855-57.

WOODWORTH, Laurin Dewey (R Ohio) Sept. 10, 1837-March 13, 1897; House 1873-77.

WOODWORTH, William W. (D N.Y.) March 16, 1807-Feb. 13, 1873; House 1845-47.

WOODYARD, Harry Chapman (R W.Va.) Nov. 13, 1867-June 21, 1929; House 1903-11, Nov. 7, 1916-23, 1925-27.

WOOMER, Ephraim Milton (R Pa.) Jan. 14, 1844-Nov. 29, 1897; House 1893-97.

WOOTEN, Dudley Goodall (D Texas) June 19, 1860-Feb. 7, 1929; House July 13, 1901-03.

WORCESTER, Samuel Thomas (R Ohio) Aug. 30, 1804-Dec. 6, 1882; House July 4, 1861-63.

WORD, Thomas Jefferson (W Miss.) ? - ?; House May 30, 1838-39.

WORKS, John Downey (R Calif.) March 29, 1847-June 6, 1928; Senate 1911-17.

WORLEY, Francis Eugene (D Texas) Oct. 10, 1908-Dec. 17, 1974; House 1941-April 3, 1950.

WORMAN, Ludwig (F Pa.) 1761-Oct. 17, 1822; House 1821-Oct. 17, 1822.

WORTENDYKE, Jacob Reynier (D N.J.) Nov. 27, 1818-Nov. 7, 1868; House 1857-59.

WORTHINGTON, Henry Gaither (R Nev.) Feb. 9, 1828-July 29, 1909; House Oct. 31, 1864-65.

WORTHINGTON, John Tolley Hood (D Md.) Nov. 1, 1788-April 27, 1849; House 1831-33, 1837-41.

WORTHINGTON, Nicholas Ellsworth (D Ill.) March 30, 1836-March 4, 1916; House 1883-87.

WORTHINGTON, Thomas (D Ohio) July 16, 1773-June 20, 1827; Senate April 1, 1803-07, Dec. 15, 1810-Dec. 1, 1814; Gov. 1814-18.

WORTHINGTON, Thomas Contee (nephew of Benjamin Contee) (D Md.) Nov. 25, 1782-April 12, 1847; House 1825-27.

WREN, Thomas (R Nev.) Jan. 2, 1826-Feb. 5, 1904; House 1877-79.

WRIGHT, Ashley Bascom (R Mass.) May 25, 1841-Aug. 14, 1897; House 1893-Aug. 14, 1897.

WRIGHT, Augustus Romaldus (D Ga.) June 16, 1813-March 31, 1891; House 1857-59.

WRIGHT, Charles Frederick (brother of Myron Benjamin Wright) (R Pa.) May 3, 1856-Nov. 10, 1925; House 1899-1905.

WRIGHT, Daniel Boone (D Miss.) Feb. 17, 1812-Dec. 27, 1887; House 1853-57.

WRIGHT, Edwin Ruthvin Vincent (D N.J.) Jan. 2, 1812-Jan. 21, 1871; House 1865-67.

WRIGHT, George Grover (brother of Joseph Albert Wright) (R Iowa) March 24, 1820-Jan. 11, 1896; Senate 1871-77.

WRIGHT, George Washington (I Calif.) June 4, 1816-April 7, 1885; House Sept. 11, 1850-51.

WRIGHT, Hendrick Bradley (D Pa.) April 24, 1808-Sept. 2, 1881; House 1853-55, July 4, 1861-63, 1877-81.

WRIGHT, James Assion (D Pa.) Aug. 11, 1902-Nov. 7, 1963; House 1941-45.

WRIGHT, James Claude Jr. (D Texas) Dec. 22, 1922-__; House 1955-__.

WRIGHT, John Crafts (Ad.D Ohio) Aug. 17, 1783-Feb. 13, 1861; House 1823-29.

WRIGHT, John Vines (D Tenn.) June 28, 1828-June 11, 1908; House 1855-61.

WRIGHT, Joseph Albert (brother of George Grover Wright) (D Ind.) April 17, 1810-May 11, 1867; House 1843-45; Senate Feb. 24, 1862-Jan. 14, 1863; Gov. 1849-57.

WRIGHT, Myron Benjamin (brother of Charles Frederick Wright) (R Pa.) June 12, 1847-Nov. 13, 1894; House 1889-Nov. 13, 1894.

WRIGHT, Robert (D Md.) Nov. 20, 1752-Sept. 7, 1826; Senate Nov. 19, 1801-Nov. 12, 1806; House Nov. 29, 1810-17, 1821-23; Gov. 1806-09.

WRIGHT, Samuel Gardiner (W N.J.) Nov. 18, 1781-July 30, 1845; House March 4-July 30, 1845.

WRIGHT, Silas Jr. (D N.Y.) May 24, 1795-Aug. 27, 1847; House 1827-Feb. 16, 1829, Senate Jan. 4, 1833-Nov. 26, 1844; Gov. 1845-47.

WRIGHT, William (D N.J.) Nov. 13, 1790-Nov. 1, 1866; House 1843-47 (CW); Senate 1853-59, 1863-Nov. 1, 1866 (D).

WRIGHT, William Carter (D Ga.) Jan. 6, 1866-June 11, 1933; House Jan. 24, 1918-33.

WURTS, John (NR Pa.) Aug. 13, 1792-April 23, 1861; House 1825-27.

WURZBACH, Harry McLeary (uncle of Robert Christian Eckhardt) (R Texas) May 19, 1874-Nov. 6, 1931; House 1921-29, Feb. 10, 1930-Nov. 6, 1931.

WYANT, Adam Martin (R Pa.) Sept. 15, 1869-Jan. 5, 1935; House 1921-33.

WYATT, Wendell (R Ore.) June 15, 1917-__; House Nov. 3, 1964-1975.

WYDLER, John Waldemar (R N.Y.) June 9, 1924-__; House 1963-—.

WYLIE, Chalmers Pangburn (R Ohio) Nov. 23, 1920-__; House 1967-__.

WYMAN, Louis Crosby (R N.H.) March 16, 1917-__; House 1963-65, 1967-Dec. 31, 1974; Senate Dec. 31, 1974-Jan. 3, 1975.

WYNKOOP, Henry (— Pa.) March 2, 1737-March 25, 1816; House 1789-91; Cont. Cong. 1779-83.

WYNN, William Joseph (UL/D Calif.) June 12, 1860-Jan. 4, 1935; House 1903-05.

WYNNS, Thomas (F N.C.) 1764-June 3, 1825; House Dec. 7, 1802-07.

Y

YANCEY, Bartlett (cousin of John Kerr) (— N.C.) Feb. 19, 1785-Aug. 30, 1828; House 1813-17.

YANCEY, Joel (D Ky.) Oct. 21, 1773-Apr. 1838; House 1827-31.

YANCEY, William Lowndes (uncle of Joseph Haynsworth Earle) (D Ala.) Aug. 10, 1814-July 28, 1863; House Dec. 2, 1844-Sept. 1, 1846.

YANGCO, Teodoro Rafael (Nat. P.I.) Nov. 9, 1861-April 20, 1939; House (Res. Comm. 1917-20.

YAPLE, George Lewis (U Mich.) Feb. 20, 1851-Dec. 16, 1939; House 1883-85.

YARBOROUGH, Ralph Webster (D Texas) June 8, 1903-__; Senate April 29, 1957-71.

YARDLEY, Robert Morris (R Pa.) Oct. 9, 1850-Dec. 8, 1902; House 1887-91.

YATES, John Barentse (D N.Y.) Feb. 1, 1784-July 10, 1836; House 1815-17.

YATES, Richard (UR Ill.) Jan. 18, 1818-Nov. 27, 1873; House 1851-55 (W); Senate 1865-71 (UR); Gov. 1861-65.

YATES, Richard (son of the preceding) (R Ill.) Dec. 12, 1860-April 11, 1936; House 1919-33; Gov. 1901-05.

YATES, Sidney Richard (D Ill.) Aug. 27, 1909-__; House 1949-63, 1965-__.

YATRON, Gus (D Pa.) Oct. 16, 1927-__; House 1969-—.

YEAMAN, George Helm (U Ky.) Nov. 1, 1829-Feb. 23, 1908; House Dec. 1, 1862-65.

YEATES, Jesse Johnson (D N.C.) May 29, 1829-Sept. 5, 1892; House 1875-79; Jan. 29-March 3, 1881.

YELL, Archibald (VBD Ark.) 1797-Feb. 22, 1847; House Aug. 1, 1836-39; 1845-July 1, 1846; Gov. 1840-44.

YOAKUM, Charles Henderson (D Texas) July 10, 1849-Jan. 1, 1909; House 1895-97.

YOCUM, Seth Hartman (R Pa.) Aug. 2, 1834-April 19, 1895; House 1879-81.

YODER, Samuel S. (D Ohio) Aug. 16, 1841-May 11, 1921; House 1887-91.

YON, Thomas Alva (D Fla.) March 14, 1882-Feb. 16, 1971; House 1927-33.

YORK, Tyre (LD N.C.) May 4, 1836-Jan. 28, 1916; House 1883-85.

YORKE, Thomas Jones (W N.J.) March 25, 1801-April 4, 1882; House 1837-39, 1841-43.

YORTY, Samuel William (D Calif.) Oct. 1, 1909-__; House 1951-55.

YOST, Jacob (R Va.) April 1, 1853-Jan. 25, 1933; House 1887-89, 1897-99.

YOST, Jacob Senewell (D Pa.) July 29, 1801-March 7, 1872; House 1843-47.

YOUMANS, Henry Melville (D Mich.) May 15, 1832-July 8, 1920; House 1891-93.

YOUNG, Andrew Jackson (D Ga.) March 12, 1932-__; House 1973-__.

YOUNG, Augustus (W Vt.) March 20, 1784-June 17, 1857; House 1841-43.

YOUNG, Bryan Rust (brother of William Singleton Young and uncle of John Young Brown) (D Ky.) Jan. 14, 1800-May 14, 1882; House 1845-47.

YOUNG, Charles William (Bill) (R Fla.) Dec. 16, 1930-__; House 1971-__.

YOUNG, Clarence Clifton (R Nev.) Nov. 7, 1922-__; House 1953-57.

YOUNG, Donald Edwin (R Alaska) June 9, 1933-__; House March 6, 1973-__.

YOUNG, Ebenezer (F Conn.) Dec. 25, 1783-Aug. 18, 1851; House 1829-35.

YOUNG, Edward Lunn (R S.C.) Sept. 7, 1920-__; House 1973-75.

YOUNG, George Morley (R N.D.) Dec. 11, 1870-May 27, 1932; House 1913-Sept. 2, 1924.

YOUNG, Hiram Casey (D Tenn.) Dec. 14, 1828-Aug. 17, 1899; House 1875-81, 1883-85.

YOUNG, Horace Olin (R Mich.) Aug. 4, 1850-Aug. 5, 1917; House March 4, 1903-May 16, 1913.

YOUNG, Isaac Daniel (R Kan.) March 29, 1849-Dec. 10, 1927; House 1911-13.

YOUNG, James (D Texas) July 18, 1866-April 29, 1942; House 1911-21.

YOUNG, James Rankin (R Pa.) March 10, 1847-Dec. 18, 1924; House 1897-1903.

YOUNG, John (W N.Y.) June 12, 1802-April 23, 1852; House Nov. 9, 1836-37, 1841-43; Gov. 1847-49.

YOUNG, John Andrew (D Texas) Nov. 10, 1916-__; House 1957-__.

YOUNG, John Duncan (D Ky.) Sept. 22, 1823-Dec. 26, 1910; House 1873-75.

YOUNG, John Smith (D La.) Nov. 4, 1834-Oct. 11, 1916; House Nov. 5, 1878-79.

YOUNG, Lafayette (R Iowa) May 10, 1848-Nov. 15, 1926; Senate Nov. 12, 1910-April 11, 1911.

YOUNG, Milton Ruben (R N.D.) Dec. 6, 1897-__; Senate March 12, 1945-__.

YOUNG, Pierce Manning Butler (D Ga.) Nov. 15, 1836-July 6, 1896; House July 25, 1868-69, Dec. 22, 1870-75.

YOUNG, Richard (R N.Y.) Aug. 6, 1846-June 9, 1935; House 1909-11.

YOUNG, Richard Montgomery (D Ill.) Feb. 20, 1798-Nov. 28, 1861; Senate 1837-43.

YOUNG, Samuel Hollingsworth (R Ill.) Dec. 26, 1922-__; House 1973-75.

YOUNG, Stephen Marvin (D Ohio) May 4, 1889-__; House 1933-37, 1941-43, 1949-51; Senate 1959-71.

YOUNG, Thomas Lowry (R Ohio) Dec. 14, 1832-July 20, 1888; House 1879-83.

YOUNG, Timothy Roberts (D Ill.) Nov. 19, 1811-May 12, 1898; House 1849-51.

YOUNG, William Albin (D Va.) May 17, 1860-March 12, 1928; House 1897-April 26, 1898, 1899-March 12, 1900.

YOUNG, William Singleton (brother of Bryan Rust Young and uncle of John Young Brown) (D Ky.) April 10, 1790-Sept. 20, 1827; House 1825-Sept. 20, 1827.

YOUNGBLOOD, Harold Francis (R Mich.) Aug. 7, 1907-__; House 1947-49.

YOUNGDAHL, Oscar Ferdinand (R Minn.) Oct. 13, 1893-Feb. 3, 1946; House 1939-43.

YOUNGER, Jesse Arthur (R Calif.) April 11, 1893-June 20, 1967; House 1953-June 20, 1967.

YULEE, David Levy (formerly David Levy) (WD Fla.) June 12, 1810-Oct. 10, 1886; House (Terr. Del.) 1841-45; Senate July 1, 1845-51, 1855-Jan. 21, 1861.

Z

ZABLOCKI, Clement John (D Wis.) Nov. 18, 1912-__; House 1949-__.

ZEFERETTI, Leo C. (D N.Y.) July 15, 1927-__; House 1975-__.

ZELENKO, Herbert (D N.Y.) March 16, 1906-__; House 1955-63.

ZENOR, William Taylor (D Ind.) April 30, 1846-June 2, 1916; House 1897-1907.

ZIEGLER, Edward Danner (D Pa.) March 3, 1844-Dec. 21, 1931; House 1899-1901.

ZIHLMAN, Frederick Nicholas (R Md.) Oct. 2, 1879-April 22, 1935; House 1917-31.

ZIMMERMAN, Orville (D Mo.) Dec. 31, 1880-April 7, 1948; House 1935-April 7, 1948.

ZION, Roger Herschel (R Ind.) Sept. 17, 1921-__; House 1967-1975.

ZIONCHECK, Marion Anthony (D Wash.) Dec. 5, 1901-Aug. 7, 1936; House 1933-Aug. 7, 1936.

ZOLLICOFFER, Felix Kirk (SRW Tenn.) May 19, 1812-Jan. 19, 1862; House 1853-59.

ZWACH, John Matthew (R Minn.) Feb. 8, 1907-__; House 1967-1975.

Declaration of Independence

In Congress, July 4, 1776,

The Unanimous Declaration of the
Thirteen United States of America,

When in the Course of human events, it becomes necessary for one people to dissolve the political bands which have connected them with another, and to assume among the Powers of the earth, the separate and equal station to which the Laws of Nature and of Nature's God entitle them, a decent respect to the opinions of mankind requires that they should declare the causes which impel them to the separation.

We hold these truths to be self-evident, that all men are created equal, that they are endowed by their Creator with certain unalienable Rights, that among these are Life, Liberty and the pursuit of Happiness. That to secure these rights, Governments are instituted among Men, deriving their just powers from the consent of the governed. That whenever any form of Government becomes destructive of these ends, it is the Right of the People to alter or to abolish it, and to institute new Government, laying its foundation on such principles and organizing its powers in such form, as to them shall seem most likely to effect their Safety and Happiness. Prudence, indeed, will dictate that Government long established should not be changed for light and transient causes; and accordingly all experience hath shown, that mankind are more disposed to suffer, while evils are sufferable, than to right themselves by abolishing the forms to which they are accustomed. But when a long train of abuses and usurpations, pursuing invariably the same Object evinces a design to reduce them under absolute Despotism, it is their right, it is their duty, to throw off such Government, and to provide new Guards for their future security.—Such has been the patient sufferance of these Colonies; and such is now the necessity which constrains them to alter their former Systems of Government. The history of the present King of Great Britain is a history of repeated injuries and usurpations, all having in direct object the establishment of an absolute Tyranny over these States. To prove this, let Facts be submitted to a candid world.

He has refused his Assent to Laws, the most wholesome and necessary for the public good.

He has forbidden his Governors to pass Laws of immediate and pressing importance, unless suspended in their operation till his Assent should be obtained; and when so suspended, he has utterly neglected to attend to them.

He has refused to pass other Laws for the accommodation of large districts of people, unless those people would relinquish the right of Representation in the Legislature, a right inestimable to them and formidable to tyrants only.

He has called together legislative bodies at places unusual, uncomfortable, and distant from the depository of their Public Records, for the sole purpose of fatiguing them into compliance with his measures.

He has dissolved Representative Houses repeatedly, for opposing with manly firmness his invasions on the rights of the people.

He has refused for a long time, after such dissolutions, to cause others to be elected; whereby the Legislative Powers, incapable of Annihilation, have returned to the People at large for their exercise; the State remaining in the mean time exposed to all the dangers of invasion from without, and convulsions within.

He has endeavoured to prevent the population of these States; for that purpose obstructing the Laws of Naturalization of Foreigners; refusing to pass others to encourage their migration hither, and raising the conditions of new Appropriations of Lands.

He has obstructed the Administration of Justice, by refusing his Assent to Laws for establishing Judiciary Powers.

He has made Judges dependent on his Will alone, for the tenure of their offices, and the amount and payment of their salaries.

He has erected a multitude of New Offices, and sent hither swarms of Officers to harass our People, and eat out their substance.

He has kept among us, in times of peace, Standing Armies without the Consent of our legislature.

He has affected to render the Military independent of and superior to the Civil Power.

He has combined with others to subject us to a jurisdiction foreign to our constitution, and unacknowledged by our laws; giving his Assent to their acts of pretended legislation:

For quartering large bodies of armed troops among us:

For protecting them, by a mock Trial, from Punishment for any Murders which they should commit on the Inhabitants of these States:

For cutting off our Trade with all parts of the world:

For imposing taxes on us without our Consent:

For depriving us in many cases, of the benefits of Trial by Jury:

For transporting us beyond Seas to be tried for pretended offences:

For abolishing the free System of English Laws in a neighbouring Province, establishing therein an Arbitrary government, and enlarging its Boundaries so as to render it at once an example and fit instrument for introducing the same absolute rule into these Colonies:

For taking away our Charters, abolishing our most valuable Laws, and altering fundamentally the Forms of our Governments:

For suspending our own Legislature, and declaring themselves invested with Power to legislate for us in all cases whatsoever.

He has abdicated Government here, by declaring us out of his Protection and waging War against us.

He has plundered our seas, ravaged our Coasts, burnt our towns, and destroyed the lives of our people.

He is at this time transporting large armies of foreign mercenaries to compleat the works of death, desolation and tyranny, already begun with circumstances of Cruelty & perfidy scarcely paralleled in the most barbarous ages, and totally unworthy the Head of a civilized nation.

He has constrained our fellow Citizens taken Captive on the high Seas to bear Arms against their Country, to become the executioners of their friends and Brethren, or to fall themselves by their Hands.

He has excited domestic insurrections amongst us, and has endeavoured to bring on the inhabitants of our frontiers, the merciless Indian Savages, whose known rule of warfare, is an undistinguished destruction of all ages, sexes and conditions.

In every stage of these Oppressions We have Petitioned for Redress in the most humble terms: Our repeated Petitions have been answered only by repeated injury. A Prince, whose character is thus marked by every act which may define a Tyrant, is unfit to be the ruler of a free People.

Nor have We been wanting in attention to our Brittish brethren. We have warned them from time to time of attempts by their legislature to extend an unwarrantable jurisdiction over us. We have reminded them of the circumstances of our emigration and settlement here. We have appealed to their native justice and magnanimity, and we have conjured them by the ties of our common kindred to disavow these usurpations, which, would inevitably interrupt our connections and correspondence. They too have been deaf to the voice of justice and of consanguinity. We must, therefore, acquiesce in the necessity, which denounces our Separation, and hold them, as we hold the rest of mankind, Enemies in War, in Peace Friends.

We, therefore, the Representatives of the united States of America, in General Congress, Assembled, appealing to the Supreme Judge of the world for the rectitude of our intentions, do, in the Name, and by Authority of the good People of these Colonies, solemnly publish and declare, That these United Colonies are, and of Right ought to be Free and Independent States; that they are Absolved from all Allegiance to the British Crown, and that all political connection between them and the State of Great Britain, is and ought to be totally dissolved; and that as Free and Independent States, they have full Power to levy War, conclude Peace, contract Alliances, establish Commerce, and to do all other Acts and Things which Independent States may of right do. And for the support of this Declaration, with a firm reliance on the Protection of Divine Providence, we mutually pledge to each other our Lives, our Fortunes and our sacred Honor.

JOHN HANCOCK.

New Hampshire:
Josiah Bartlett,
William Whipple,
Matthew Thornton.

Massachusetts-Bay:
Samuel Adams,
John Adams,
Robert Treat Paine,
Elbridge Gerry.

Rhode Island:
Stephen Hopkins,
William Ellery.

Connecticut:
Roger Sherman,
Samuel Huntington,
William Williams,
Oliver Wolcott.

New York:
William Floyd,
Philip Livingston,
Francis Lewis,
Lewis Morris.

Pennsylvania:
Robert Morris,
Benjamin Rush,
Benjamin Franklin,
John Morton,
George Clymer,
James Smith,
George Taylor,
James Wilson,
George Ross.

Delaware:
Caesar Rodney,
George Read,
Thomas McKean.

Georgia:
Button Gwinnett,
Lyman Hall,
George Walton.

Maryland:
Samuel Chase,
William Paca,
Thomas Stone,
Charles Carroll of Carrollton.

Virginia:
George Wythe,
Richard Henry Lee,
Thomas Jefferson,
Benjamin Harrison,
Thomas Nelson Jr.,
Francis Lightfoot Lee,
Carter Braxton.

North Carolina:
William Hooper,
Joseph Hewes,
John Penn.

South Carolina:
Edward Rutledge,
Thomas Heyward Jr.,
Thomas Lynch Jr.,
Arthur Middleton.

New Jersey:
Richard Stockton,
John Witherspoon,
Francis Hopkinson,
John Hart,
Abraham Clark.

Articles of Confederation

Agreed to by Congress November 15, 1777; Ratified and in Force, March 1, 1781

To all to whom these Presents shall come, we the undersigned Delegates of the States affixed to our Names send greeting. Whereas the Delegates of the United States of America in Congress assembled did on the fifteenth day of November in the Year of our Lord One Thousand Seven Hundred and Seventy seven, and in the Second Year of the Independence of America agree to certain articles of Confederation and perpetual Union between the States of Newhampshire, Massachusetts-bay, Rhodeisland and Providence Plantations, Connecticut, New York, New Jersey, Pennsylvania, Delaware, Maryland, Virginia, North-Carolina, South-Carolina and Georgia in the Words ollowing, viz. "Articles of Confederation and perpetual Union between the states of Newhampshire, Massachusetts-bay, Rhodeisland and Providence Plantations, Connecticut, New-York, New-Jersey, Pennsylvania, Delaware, Maryland, Virginia, North-Carolina, South-Carolina and Georgia.

Art. I. The Stile of this confederacy shall be "The United States of America."

Art. II. Each state retains its sovereignty, freedom and independence, and every Power, Jurisdiction and right, which is not by this confederation expressly delegated to the United States, in Congress assembled.

Art. III. The said states hereby severally enter into a firm league of friendship with each other, for their common defence, the security of their Liberties, and their mutual and general welfare, binding themselves to assist each other, against all force offered to, or attacks made upon them, or any of them, on account of religion, sovereignty, trade, or any other pretence whatever.

Art. IV. The better to secure and perpetuate mutual friendship and intercourse among the people of the different states in this union, the free inhabitants of each of these states, paupers, vagabonds and fugitives from Justice excepted, shall be entitled to all privileges and immunities of free citizens in the several states; and the people of each state shall have free ingress and regress to and from any other state, and shall enjoy therein all the privileges of trade and commerce, subject to the same duties, impositions and restrictions as the inhabitants thereof respectively, provided that such restriction shall not extend so far as to prevent the removal of property imported into any state, to any other state of which the Owner is an inhabitant; provided also that no imposition, duties or restriction shall be laid by any state, on the property of the united states, or either of them.

If any Person guilty of, or charged with treason, felony, or other high misdemeanor in any state, shall flee from Justice, and be found in any of the united states, he shall upon demand of the Governor or executive power, of the state from which he fled, be delivered up and removed to the state having jurisdiction of his offence.

Full faith and credit shall be given in each of these states to the records, acts and judicial proceedings of the courts and magistrates of every other state.

Art. V. For the more convenient management of the general interests of the united states, delegates shall be annually appointed in such manner as the legislature of each state shall direct, to meet in Congress on the first Monday in November, in every year, with a power reserved to each state, to recal its delegates, or any of them, at any time within the year, and to send others in their stead, for the remainder of the Year.

No state shall be represented in Congress by less than two, nor by more than seven Members; and no person shall be capable of being a delegate for more than three years in any term of six years; nor shall any person, being a delegate, be capable of holding any office under the united states, for which he, or another for his benefit receives any salary, fees or emolument of any kind.

Each state shall maintain its own delegates in a meeting of the states, and while they act as members of the committee of the states.

In determining questions in the united states, in Congress assembled, each state shall have one vote.

Freedom of speech and debate in Congress shall not be impeached or questioned in any Court, or place out of Congress, and the members of congress shall be protected in their persons from arrests and imprisonments, during the time of their going to and from, and attendance on congress, except for treason, felony, or breach of the peace.

Art. VI. No state without the Consent of the united states in congress assembled, shall send any embassy to, or receive any embassy from, or enter into any conference, agreement, or alliance or treaty with any King, prince or state; nor shall any person holding any office of profit or trust under the united states, or any of them, accept of any present, emolument, office or title of any kind whatever from any king, prince or foreign state; nor shall the united states in congress assembled, or any of them, grant any title of nobility.

No two or more states shall enter into any treaty, confederation or alliance whatever between them, without the consent of the united states in congress assembled, specifying accurately the purposes for which the same is to be entered into, and how long it shall continue.

No state shall lay any imposts or duties, which may interfere with any stipulations in treaties, entered into by the united states in congress assembled, with any king, prince or state, in pursuance of any treaties already proposed by congress, to the courts of France and Spain.

No vessels of war shall be kept up in time of peace by any state, except such number only, as shall be deemed necessary by the united states in congress assembled, for the defence of such state, or its trade; nor shall any body of forces be kept up by any state, in time of peace, except such number only, as in the judgment of the united states, in congress assembled, shall be deemed requisite to garrison the forts necessary for the defence of such state; but every state shall always keep up a well regulated and disciplined militia, sufficiently armed and accoutred, and shall provide and constantly have ready for use, in public stores, a due number of field pieces and tents, and a proper quantity of arms, ammunition and camp equipage.

No state shall engage in any war without the consent of the united states in congress assembled, unless such state be actually invaded by enemies, or shall have received certain advice of a resolution being formed by some nation of Indians to invade such state, and the danger is so imminent as not to admit of a delay, till the united states in congress assembled can be consulted: nor shall any state grant commissions to any ships or vessels of war, nor letters of marque or reprisal, except it be after a declaration of war by the united states in congress assembled, and then only against the kingdom or state and the subjects thereof, against which war has been so declared, and under such regulations as shall be established by the united states in congress assembled, unless such state be infested by pirates, in which case vessels of war may be fitted out for that occasion, and kept so long as the danger shall continue, or until the united states in congress assembled shall determine otherwise.

Art. VII. When land-forces are raised by any state for the common defence, all officers of or under the rank of colonel, shall be appointed by the legislature of each state respectively by whom such forces shall be raised, or in such manner as such state shall direct, and all vacancies shall be filled up by the state which first made the appointment.

Art. VIII. All charges of war, and all other expences that shall be incurred for the common defence or general welfare, and allowed by the united states in congress assembled, shall be defrayed out of a common treasury, which whall be supplied by the several states, in proportion to the value of all land within each state, granted to or surveyed for any Person, as such land and the buildings and improvements thereon shall be estimated according to such mode as the united states in congress assembled, shall from time to time direct and appoint. The taxes for paying that proportion shall be laid and levied by the authority and direction of the legislatures of the several states within the time agreed upon by the united states in congress assembled.

Art. IX. The united states in congress assembled, shall have the sole and exclusive right and power of determining on peace and war, except in the cases mentioned in the sixth article—of sending and receiving ambassadors—entering into treaties and alliances, provided that no treaty of commerce shall be made whereby the legislative power of the respective states shall be restrained from imposing such imposts and duties on foreigners, as their own people are subjected to, or from prohibiting the exportation or importation of any species of goods or commodities whatsoever—of establishing rules for deciding in all cases, what captures on land or water shall be legal, and in what manner prizes taken by land or naval forces in the service of the united states shall be divided or appropriated—of granting letters of marque and reprisal in times of peace—appointing courts for the trial of piracies and felonies committed on the high seas and establishing courts for receiving and determining finally appeals in all cases of captures, provided that no member of congress shall be appointed a judge of any of the said courts.

The united states in congress assembled shall also be the last resort on appeal in all disputes and differences now subsisting or that hereafter may arise between two or more states concerning boundary, jurisdiction or any other cause whatever; which authority shall always be exercised in the manner following. Whenever the legislative or executive authority or lawful agent of any state in controversy with another shall present a petition to congress, stating the matter in question and praying for a hearing, notice thereof shall be given by order of congress to the legislative or executive authority of the other state in controversy, and a day assigned for the appearance of the parties by their lawful agents, who shall then be directed to appoint by joint consent, commissioners or judges to constitute a court for hearing and determining the matter in question: but if they cannot agree, congress shall name three persons out of each of the united states, and from the list of such persons each party shall alternately strike out one, the petitioners beginning, until the number shall be reduced to thirteen; and from that number not less than seven, nor more than nine names as congress shall direct, shall in the presence of congress be drawn out by lot, and the persons whose names shall be so drawn or any five of them, shall be commissioners or judges, to hear and finally determine the controversy, so always as a major part of the judges who shall hear the cause shall agree in the determination: and if either party shall neglect to attend at the day appointed, without shewing reasons, which congress shall judge sufficient, or being present shall refuse to strike, the congress shall proceed to nominate three persons out of each state, and the secretary of congress shall strike in behalf of such party absent or refusing; and the judgment and sentence of the court to be appointed, in the manner before prescribed, shall be final and conclusive; and if any of the parties shall refuse to submit to the authority of such court, or to appear to defend their claim or cause, the court shall nevertheless proceed to pronounce sentence, or judgment, which shall in like manner be final and decisive, the judgment or sentence and other proceedings being in either case transmitted to congress, and lodged among the acts of congress for the security of the parties concerned: provided that every commissioner, before he sits in judgment, shall take an oath to be administered by one of the judges of the supreme or superior court of the state where the cause shall be tried, "well and truly to hear and determine the matter in question, according to the best of his judgment, without favour, affection or hope of reward:" provided also that no state shall be deprived of territory for the benefit of the united states.

All controversies concerning the private right of soil claimed under different grants of two or more states, whose jurisdictions as they may respect such lands, and the states which passed such grants are adjusted, the said grants or either of them being at the same time claimed to have originated antecedent to such settlement of jurisdiction, shall on the petition of either party to the congress of the united states, be finally determined as near as may be in the same manner as is before prescribed for deciding disputes respecting territorial jurisdiction between different states.

The united states in congress assembled shall also have the sole and exclusive right and power of regulating the alloy and value of coin struck by their own authority, or by that of the respective states—fixing the standard of weights and measures throughout the united states—regulating the trade and managing all affairs with the Indians, not members of any of the states, provided that the legislative right of any state within its own limits be not infringed or violated—establishing and regulating post-offices from one state to another, throughout all the united states, and exacting such postage on the papers passing thro' the same as may be requisite to defray the expences of the said office—appointing all officers of the land forces, in the service of the united states, excepting regimental officers —appointing all the officers of the naval forces, and commissioning all officers whatever in the service of the united states—making rules for the government and regulation of the said land and naval forces, and directing their operations.

The united states in congress assembled shall have authority to appoint a committee, to sit in the recess of congress, to be denominated "A Committee of the States," and to consist of one delegate from each state; and to appoint such other committees and civil officers as may be necessary for managing the general affairs of the united states under their direction—to appoint one of their number to preside, provided that no person be allowed to serve in the office of president more than one year in any term of three years; to ascertain the necessary sums of Money to be raised for the service of the united states, and to appropriate and apply the same for defraying the public expences—to borrow money, or emit bills on the credit of the united states, transmitting every half year to the respective states an account of the sums of money so borrowed or emitted,—to build and equip a navy—to agree upon the number of land forces, and to make requisitions from each state for its quota, in proportion to the number of white inhabitants in such state; which requisition shall be binding, and thereupon the legislature of each state shall appoint the regimental officers, raise the men and cloath, arm and equip them in a soldier like manner, at the expence of the united states, and the officers and men so cloathed, armed and equipped shall march to the place appointed, and within the time agreed on by the united states in congress assembled: But if the united states in congress assembled shall, on consideration of circumstances judge proper that any state should not raise men, or should raise a smaller number than its quota, and that any other state should raise a greater number of men than the quota thereof, such extra number shall be raised, officered, cloathed, armed and equipped in the same manner as the quota of such state, unless the legislature of such state shall judge that such extra number cannot be safely spared out of the same, in which case they shall raise, officer, cloath, arm and equip as many of such extra number as they judge can be safely spared. And the officers and men so cloathed, armed and equipped, shall march to the place appointed, and within the time agreed on by the united states in congress assembled.

The united states in congress assembled shall never engage in a war, nor grant letters of marque and reprisal in time of peace, nor enter into any treaties or alliances, nor coin money, nor regulate the value thereof, nor ascertain the sums and expences necessary for the defence and welfare of the united states, or any of them, nor emit bills, nor borrow money on the credit of the united states, nor appropriate money, nor agree upon the number of vessels of war, to be built or purchased, or the number of land or sea forces to be raised, nor appoint a commander in chief of the army or navy, unless nine states assent to the same: nor shall a question on any other point, except for adjourning from day to day be determined, unless by the votes of a majority of the united states in congress assembled.

The congress of the united states shall have power to adjourn to any time within the year, and to any place within the united states, so that no period of adjournment be for a longer duration than the space of six Months, and shall publish the Journal of their proceedings monthly, except such parts thereof relating to treaties, alliances or military operations as in their judgment require secresy; and the yeas and nays of the delegates of each state on any question shall be entered on the Journal, when it is desired by any delegate; and the delegates of a state, or any of them, at his or their request shall be furnished with a transcript of the said Journal, except such parts as are above excepted, to lay before the legislatures of the several states.

Art. X. The committee of the states, or any nine of them, shall be authorised to execute, in the recess of congress, such of the powers of congress as the united states in congress assembled, by the consent of nine states, shall from time to time think expedient to vest them with; provided that no power be delegated to the said committee, for the exercise of which, by the articles of confederation, the voice of nine states in the congress of the united states assembled is requisite.

Art. XI. Canada acceding to this confederation, and joining in the measures of the united states, shall be admitted into, and entitled to all the advantages of this union: but no other colony shall be admitted into the same, unless such admission be agreed to by nine states.

Art. XII. All bills of credit emitted, monies borrowed and debts contracted by, or under the authority of congress, before the assembling of the united states, in pursuance of the present confederation, shall be deemed and considered as a charge against the united states, for payment and satisfaction whereof the said united states, and the public faith are hereby solemnly pledged.

Art. XIII. Every state shall abide by the determinations of the united states in congress assembled, on all questions which by this confederation are submitted to them. And the Articles of this confederation shall be inviolably observed by every state, and the union shall be perpetual; nor shall any alteration at any time hereafter be made in any of them; unless such alteration be agreed to in a congress of the united states, and be afterwards confirmed by the legislatures of every state.

And Whereas it hath pleased the Great Governor of the World to incline the hearts of the legislatures we respectively represent in congress, to approve of, and to authorize us to ratify the said articles of confederation and perpetual union. Know Ye that we the under-signed delegates, by virtue of the power and authority to us given for that purpose, do by these presents, in the name and in behalf of our respective constituents, fully and entirely ratify and confirm each and every of the said articles of confederation and perpetual union, and all and singular the matters and things therein contained: And we do further solemnly plight and engage the faith of our respective constituents, that they shall abide by the determinations of the united states in congress assembled, on all questions, which by the said confederation are submitted to them. And that the articles thereof shall be inviolably observed by the states we respectively represent, and that the union shall be perpetual. In Witness whereof we have hereunto set our hands in Congress. Done at Philadelphia in the state of Pennsylvania the ninth Day of July in the Year of our Lord one Thousand seven Hundred and Seventy-eight, and in the third year of the independence of America.

New Hampshire:	Josiah Bartlett, John Wentworth Jr.	**New York:**	James Duane, Francis Lewis, William Duer, Gouverneur Morris.
Massachusetts:	John Hancock, Samuel Adams, Elbridge Gerry, Francis Dana, James Lovell, Samuel Holten.	**New Jersey:**	John Witherspoon, Nathaniel Scudder.
		Pennsylvania:	Robert Morris, Daniel Roberdeau, Jonathan Bayard Smith, William Clingan, Joseph Reed.
Rhode Island:	William Ellery, Henry Marchant, John Collins.		
Connecticut:	Roger Sherman, Samuel Huntington, Oliver Wolcott, Titus Hosmer, Andrew Adams.	**Delaware:**	Thomas McKean, John Dickinson, Nicholas Van Dyke.
		Maryland:	John Hanson, Daniel Carroll.

Virginia:	Richard Henry Lee, John Banister, Thomas Adams, John Harvie, Francis Lightfoot Lee.
North Carolina:	John Penn, Cornelius Harnett, John Williams.
South Carolina:	Henry Laurens, William Henry Drayton, John Mathews, Richard Hutson, Thomas Heyward Jr.
Georgia:	John Walton, Edward Telfair, Edward Langworthy.

Constitution of the United States

We the People of the United States, in Order to form a more perfect Union, establish Justice, insure domestic Tranquility, provide for the common defence, promote the general Welfare, and secure the Blessings of Liberty to ourselves and our Posterity, do ordain and establish this Constitution for the United States of America.

Article I

Section 1. All legislative Powers herein granted shall be vested in a Congress of the United States, which shall consist of a Senate and House of Representatives.

Section 2. The House of Representatives shall be composed of Members chosen every second Year by the People of the several States, and the Electors in each State shall have the Qualifications requisite for Electors of the most numerous Branch of the State Legislature.

No Person shall be a Representative who shall not have attained to the age of twenty five Years, and been seven Years a Citizen of the United States, and who shall not, when elected, be an Inhabitant of that State in which he shall be chosen.

[Representatives and direct Taxes shall be apportioned among the several States which may be included within this Union, according to their respective Numbers, which shall be determined by adding to the whole Number of free Persons, including those bound to Service for a Term of Years, and excluding Indians not taxed, three fifths of all other Persons.]¹ The actual Enumeration shall be made within three Years after the first Meeting of the Congress of the United States, and within every subsequent Term of ten Years, in such Manner as they shall by Law direct. The Number of Representatives shall not exceed one for every thirty Thousand, but each State shall have at Least one Representative; and until such enumeration shall be made, the State of New Hampshire shall be entitled to chuse three, Massachusetts eight, Rhode-Island and Providence Plantations one, Connecticut five, New-York six, New Jersey four, Pennsylvania eight, Delaware one, Maryland six, Virginia ten, North Carolina five, South Carolina five, and Georgia three.

When vacancies happen in the Representation from any State, the Executive Authority thereof shall issue Writs of Election to fill such Vacancies.

The House of Representatives shall chuse their Speaker and other Officers; and shall have the sole Power of Impeachment.

Section 3. The Senate of the United States shall be composed of two Senators from each State, [chosen by the Legislature thereof,]² for six Years; and each Senator shall have one Vote.

Immediately after they shall be assembled in Consequence of the first Election, they shall be divided as equally as may be into three Classes. The Seats of the Senators of the first Class shall be vacated at the Expiration of the second Year, of the second Class at the Expiration of the fourth Year, and of the third Class at the Expiration of the sixth Year, so that one third may be chosen every second Year; [and if Vacancies happen by Resignation, or otherwise, during the Recess of the Legislature of any State, the Executive thereof may make temporary Appointments until the next Meeting of the Legislature, which shall then fill such Vacancies.]³

No Person shall be a Senator who shall not have attained to the Age of thirty Years, and been nine Years a Citizen of the United States, and who shall not, when elected, be an Inhabitant of that State for which he shall be chosen.

The Vice President of the United States shall be President of the Senate, but shall have no Vote, unless they be equally divided.

The Senate shall chuse their other Officers, and also a President pro tempore, in the Absence of the Vice President, or when he shall exercise the Office of President of the United States.

The Senate shall have the sole Power to try all Impeachments. When sitting for that Purpose, they shall be on Oath or Affirmation. When the President of the United States is tried the Chief Justice shall preside: And no Person shall be convicted without the Concurrence of two thirds of the Members present.

Judgment in Cases of Impeachment shall not extend further than to removal from Office, and disqualification to hold and enjoy any Office of honor, Trust or Profit under the United States: but the Party convicted shall nevertheless be liable and subject to Indictment, Trial, Judgment and Punishment, according to Law.

Section 4. The Times, Places and Manner of holding Elections for Senators and Representatives, shall be prescribed in each State by the Legislature thereof; but the Congress may at any time by Law make or alter such Regulations, except as to the Places of chusing Senators.

The Congress shall assemble at least once in every Year, and such Meeting shall [be on the first Monday in December],⁴ unless they shall by Law appoint a different Day.

Section 5. Each House shall be the Judge of the Elections, Returns and Qualifications of its own Members, and a Majority of each shall constitute a Quorum to do Business; but a smaller Number may adjourn from day to day, and may be authorized to compel the Attendance of absent Members, in such Manner, and under such Penalties as each House may provide.

Each House may determine the Rules of its Proceedings, punish its Members for disorderly Behaviour, and, with the Concurrence of two thirds, expel a Member.

Each House shall keep a Journal of its Proceedings, and from time to time publish the same, excepting such Parts as may in their Judgment require Secrecy; and the Yeas and Nays of the Members of either House on any question shall, at the Desire of one fifth of those Present, be entered on the Journal.

Neither House, during the Session of Congress, shall, without the Consent of the other, adjourn for more than three days, nor to any other Place than that in which the two Houses shall be sitting.

Section 6. The Senators and Representatives shall receive a Compensation for their Services, to be ascertained by Law, and paid out of the Treasury of the United States. They shall in all Cases, except Treason, Felony and Breach of the Peace, be privileged from Arrest during their Attendance at the Session of their respective Houses, and in going to and returning from the same; and for any Speech or Debate in either House, they shall not be questioned in any other Place.

No Senator or Representative shall, during the Time for which he was elected, be appointed to any civil Office under the Authority of the United States, which shall have been created, or the Emoluments whereof shall have been encreased during such time; and no Person holding any Office under the United States, shall be a Member of either House during his Continuance in Office.

Section 7. All Bills for raising Revenue shall originate in the House of Representatives; but the Senate may propose or concur with amendments as on other Bills.

Every Bill which shall have passed the House of Representatives and the Senate, shall, before it become a Law, be presented to the President of the United States; If he approve he shall sign it, but if not he shall return it, with his Objections to that House in which it shall have originated, who shall enter the Objections at large on their Journal, and proceed to reconsider it. If after such Reconsideration two thirds of that House shall agree to pass the Bill, it shall be sent, together with the Objections, to the other House, by which it shall likewise be reconsidered, and if approved by two thirds of that House, it shall become a Law. But in all such Cases the Votes of both Houses shall be determined by yeas and Nays, and the Names of the Persons voting for and against the Bill shall be entered on the Journal of each House respectively. If any Bill shall not be returned by the President within ten Days (Sunday excepted) after it shall have been presented to him, the Same shall be a Law, in like Manner as if he had signed it, unless the Congress by their Adjournment prevent its Return, in which Case it shall not be a Law.

Every Order, Resolution, or Vote to which the Concurrence of the Senate and House of Representatives may be necessary (except on a question of Adjournment) shall be presented to the President of the United States; and before the Same shall take Effect, shall be approved by him, or being disapproved by him, shall be repassed by two thirds of the Senate and House of Representatives, according to the Rules and Limitations prescribed in the Case of a Bill.

Section 8. The Congress shall have Power To lay and collect Taxes, Duties, Imposts and Excises, to pay the Debts and provide for the common Defence and general Welfare of the United States; but all Duties, Imposts and Excises shall be uniform throughout the United States;

To borrow Money on the credit of the United States;

To regulate Commerce with foreign Nations, and among the several States, and with the Indian Tribes;

To establish an uniform Rule of Naturalization, and uniform Laws on the subject of Bankruptcies throughout the United States;

To coin Money, regulate the Value thereof, and of foreign Coin, and fix the Standard of Weights and Measures;

To provide for the Punishment of counterfeiting the Securities and current Coin of the United States;

To establish Post Offices and post Roads;

To promote the Progress of Science and useful Arts, by securing for limited Times to Authors and Inventors the exclusive Right to their respective Writings and Discoveries;

To constitute Tribunals inferior to the supreme Court;

To define and punish Piracies and Felonies commited on the high Seas, and Offences against the Law of Nations;

To declare War, grant Letters of Marque and Reprisal, and make Rules concerning Captures on Land and Water;

To raise and support Armies, but no Appropriation of Money to that Use shall be for a longer Term than two Years;

To provide and maintain a Navy;

To make Rules for the Government and Regulation of the land and naval Forces;

To provide for calling forth the Militia to execute the Laws of the Union, suppress Insurrections and repel Invasions;

To provide for organizing, arming, and disciplining, the Militia, and for governing such Part of them as may be employed in the Service of the United States, reserving to the States respectively, the Appointment of the Officers, and the Authority of training the Militia according to the discipline prescribed by Congress;

To exercise exclusive Legislation in all Cases whatsoever, over such District (not exceeding ten Miles square) as may, by Cession of Particular States, and the Acceptance of Congress, become the Seat of the Government of the United States, and to exercise like Authority over all Places purchased by the Consent of the Legislature of the State in which the Same shall be, for the Erection of Forts, Magazines, Arsenals, dock-Yards, and other needful Buildings;—And

To make all Laws which shall be necessary and proper for carrying into Execution the foregoing Powers, and all other Powers vested by this Constitution in the Government of the United States, or in any Department or Officer thereof.

Section 9. The Migration or Importation of such Persons as any of the States now existing shall think proper to admit, shall not be prohibited by the Congress prior to the Year one thousand eight hundred and eight, but a Tax or duty may be imposed on such Importation, not exceeding ten dollars for each Person.

The Privilege of the Writ of Habeas Corpus shall not be suspended, unless when in Cases of Rebellion or Invasion the public Safety may require it.

No Bill of Attainder or ex post facto Law shall be passed.

No Capitation, or other direct, Tax shall be laid, unless in Proportion to the Census of Enumeration herein before directed to be taken.[5]

No Tax or Duty shall be laid on Articles exported from any State.

No Preference shall be given by any Regulation of Commerce or Revenue to the Ports of one State over those of another; nor shall Vessels bound to, or from, one State, be obliged to enter, clear or pay Duties in another.

No Money shall be drawn from the Treasury, but in Consequence of Appropriations made by Law; and a regular Statement and Account of the Receipts and Expenditures of all public Money shall be published from time to time.

No Title of Nobility shall be granted by the United States: And no Person holding any Office of Profit or Trust under them, shall, without the Consent of the Congress, accept of any present, Emolument, Office, or Title, of any kind whatever, from any King, Prince or foreign State.

Section 10. No State shall enter into any Treaty, Alliance, or Confederation; grant Letters of Marque and Reprisal; coin Money; emit Bills of Credit; make any Thing but gold and silver Coin a Tender in Payment of Debts; pass any Bill of Attainder, ex post facto Law, or Law impairing the Obligation of Contracts, or grant any Title of Nobility.

No State shall, without the Consent of the Congress, lay any Imposts or Duties on Imports or Exports, except what may be absolutely necessary for executing it's inspection Laws: and the net Produce of all Duties and Imposts, laid by any State on Imports or Exports, shall be for the Use of the Treasury of the United States; and all such Laws shall be subject to the Revision and Controul of the Congress.

No State shall, without the Consent of Congress, lay any Duty of Tonnage, keep Troops, or Ships of War in time of Peace, enter into any Agreement or Compact with another State, or with a foreign Power, or engage in War, unless actually invaded, or in such imminent Danger as will not admit of delay.

Article II

Section 1. The executive Power shall be vested in a President of the United States of America. He shall hold his Office during the Term of four Years, and, together with the Vice President, chosen for the same Term, be elected, as follows

Each State shall appoint, in such Manner as the Legislature thereof may direct, a Number of Electors, equal to the whole Number of Senators and Representatives to which the State may be entitled in the Congress: but no Senator or Representative, or Person holding an Office of Trust or Profit under the United States, shall be appointed an Elector.

[The Electors shall meet in their respective States, and vote by Ballot for two Persons, of whom one at least shall not be an Inhabitant of the same State with themselves. And they shall make a List of all the Persons voted for, and of the Number of Votes for each; which List they shall sign and certify, and transmit sealed to the Seat of the Government of the United States, directed to the President of the Senate. The President of the Senate shall, in the Presence of the Senate and House of Representatives, open all the Certificates, and the Votes shall then be counted. The Person having the greatest Number of Votes shall be the President, if such Number be a Majority of the whole Number of Electors appointed; and if there be more than one who have such Majority, and have an equal Number of Votes, then the House of Representatives shall immediately chuse by Ballot one of them for President; and if no Person have a Majority, then from the five highest on the list the said House shall in like Manner chuse the President. But in chusing the President, the Votes shall be taken by States, the Representation from each State having one Vote; a quorum for this Purpose shall consist of a Member or Members from two thirds of the States, and a Majority of all the States shall be necessary to a Choice. In every Case, after the Choice of the President, the Person having the greatest Number of Votes of the Electors shall be the Vice President. But if there should remain two or more who have equal Votes, the Senate shall chuse from them by Ballot the Vice President.][6]

The Congress may determine the Time of chusing the Electors, and the Day on which they shall give their Votes; which Day shall be the same throughout the United States.

No Person except a natural born Citizen, or a Citizen of the United States, at the time of the Adoption of this Constitution, shall be eligible to the Office of President; neither shall any Person be eligible to that Office who shall not have attained to the Age of thirty five Years, and been fourteen Years a Resident within the United States.

In Case of the Removal of the President from Office, or of his Death, Resignation, or Inability to discharge the Powers and Duties of the said Office,[7] the Same shall devolve on the Vice President, and the Congress may by Law provide for the Case of Removal, Death, Resignation or Inability, both of the President and Vice President, declaring what Officer shall then act as President, and such Officer shall act accordingly, until the Disability be removed, or a President shall be elected.

The President shall, at stated Times, receive for his Services, a Compensation, which shall neither be encreased nor dimished during the Period for which he shall have been elected, and he shall not receive within that Period any other Emolument from the United States, or any of them.

Before he enter on the Execution of his Office, he shall take the following Oath or Affirmation: —"I do solemnly swear (or affirm) that I will faithfully execute the Office of President of the United States, and will to the best of my Ability, preserve, protect and defend the Constitution of the United States."

Section 2. The President shall be Commander in Chief of the Army and Navy of the United States, and of the Militia of the several States, when called into the actual Service of the United States; he may require the Opinion, in writing, of the principal Officer in each of the executive Departments, upon any Subject relating to the Duties of their respective Offices, and he shall have Power to grant Reprieves and Pardons for Offenses against the United States, except in Cases of Impeachment.

He shall have Power, by and with the Advice and Consent of the Senate, to make Treaties, provided two thirds of the Senators present concur; and he shall nominate, and by and with the Advice and Consent of the Senate, shall appoint Ambassadors, other public Ministers and Consuls, Judges of the supreme Court, and all other Officers of the United States, whose Appointments are not herein otherwise provided for, and which shall be established by Law: but the Congress may by Law vest the Appointment of such inferior Officers, as they think proper, in the President alone, in the Courts of Law, or in the Heads of Departments.

The President shall have Power to fill up all Vacancies that may happen during the Recess of the Senate, by granting Commissions which shall expire at the End of their next Session.

Section 3. He shall from time to time give to the Congress Information of the State of the Union, and recommend to their Consideration such Measures as he shall judge necessary and expedient; he may, on extraordinary Occasions, convene both Houses, or either of them, and in Case of Disagreement between them, with Respect to the Time of Adjournment, he may adjourn them to such Time as he shall think proper; he shall receive Ambassadors and other public Ministers; he shall take Care that the Laws be faithfully executed, and shall Commission all the Officers of the United States.

Section 4. The President, Vice President and all Civil Officers of the United States, shall be removed from office on Impeachment for, and Conviction of, Treason, Bribery, or other high Crimes and Misdemeanors.

Article III

Section 1. The judicial Power of the United States, shall be vested in one supreme Court, and in such inferior Courts as the Congress may from time to time ordain and establish. The Judges, both of the supreme and inferior Courts, shall hold their Offices during good Behaviour, and shall, at stated Times, receive for their Services, a Compensation, which shall not be diminished during their Continuance in Office.

Section 2. The judicial Power shall extend to all Cases, in Law and Equity, arising under this Constitution, the Laws of the United States, and Treaties made, or which shall be made, under their Authority;—to all Cases affecting Ambassadors, other public Ministers and Consuls;—to all Cases of admiralty and maritime Jurisdiction;—to Controversies to which the United States shall be a Party;—to Controversies between two or more States;—between a State and Citizens of another State[8];—between Citizens of different States;—between Citizens of the same State claiming Lands under Grants of different States, and between a State, or the Citizens thereof, and foreign States, Citizens or Subjects.[8]

In all Cases affecting Ambassadors, other public Ministers and Consuls, and those in which a State shall be Party, the supreme Court shall have original Jurisdiction. In all the other Cases before mentioned, the supreme Court shall have appellate Jurisdiction, both as to Law and Fact, with such Exceptions, and under such Regulations as the Congress shall make.

The Trial of all Crimes, except in cases of Impeachment, shall be by Jury; and such Trial shall be held in the State where the said Crimes shall have been committed; but when not committed within any State, the Trial shall be at such Place or Places as the Congress may by Law have directed.

Section 3. Treason against the United States, shall consist only in levying War against them, or in adhering to their Enemies, giving them Aid and Comfort. No Person shall be convicted of Treason unless on the Testimony of two Witnesses to the same overt Act, or on Confession in open Court.

The Congress shall have Power to declare the Punishment of Treason, but no Attainder of Treason shall work Corruption of Blood, or Forfeiture except during the Life of the Person attainted.

Article IV

Section 1. Full Faith and Credit shall be given in each State to the public Acts, Records, and judicial Proceedings of every other State. And the Congress may by general Laws prescribe the Manner in which such Acts, Records and Proceedings shall be proved, and the Effect thereof.

Section 2. The Citizens of each State shall be entitled to all Privileges and Immunities of Citizens in the several States.

A Person charged in any State with Treason, Felony, or other Crime, who shall flee from Justice, and be found in another State, shall on Demand of the executive Authority of the State from which he fled, be delivered up, to be removed to the State having Jurisdiction of the Crime.

[No Person held to Service or Labour in one State, under the Laws thereof, escaping into another, shall, in Consequence of any Law or Regulation therein, be discharged from such Service or Labour, but shall be delivered up on Claim of the Party to whom such Service or Labour may be due.][9]

Section 3. New States may be admitted by the Congress into this Union; but no new State shall be formed or erected within the Jurisdiction of any other State; nor any State be formed by the Junction of two or more States, or Parts of States, without the Consent of the Legislatures of the States concerned as well as of the Congress.

The Congress shall have Power to dispose of and make all needful Rules and Regulations respecting the Territory or other Property belonging to the United States; and nothing in this Constitution shall be so construed as to Prejudice any Claims of the United States, or of any particular State.

Section 4. The United States shall guarantee to every State in this Union a Republican Form of Government, and shall protect each of them against Invasion; and on Application of the Legislature, or of the Executive (when the Legislature cannot be convened) against domestic Violence.

Article V

The Congress, whenever two thirds of both Houses shall deem it necessary, shall propose Amendments to this Constitution, or, on the Application of the Legislatures of two thirds of the several States, shall call a Convention for proposing Amendments, which, in either Case, shall be valid to all Intents and Purposes, as Part of this Constitution, when ratified by the Legislatures of three fourths of the several States, or by Conventions in three fourths thereof, as the one or the other Mode of Ratification may be proposed by the Congress; Provided [that no Amendment which may be made prior to the Year One thousand eight hundred and eight shall in any Manner affect the first and fourth Clauses in the Ninth Section of the first Article; and][10] that no State, without its Consent, shall be deprived of its equal Suffrage in the Senate.

Article VI

All Debts contracted and Engagements entered into, before the Adoption of this Constitution, shall be as valid against the United States under this Constitution, as under the Confederation.

This Constitution, and the Laws of the United States which shall be made in Pursuance thereof; and all Treaties made, or which shall be made, under the Authority of the United States, shall be the supreme Law of the Land; and the Judges in every State shall be bound thereby, any Thing in the Constitution or Laws of any State to the Contrary notwithstanding.

The Senators and Representatives before mentioned, and the Members of the several State Legislatures, and all executive and judicial Officers, both of the United States and of the several States, shall be bound by Oath or Affirmation, to support this Constitution; but no religious Test shall ever be required as a Qualification to any Office or public Trust under the United States.

Article VII

The Ratification of the Conventions of nine States, shall be sufficient for the Establishment of this Constitution between the States so ratifying the Same. Done in Convention by the Unanimous Consent of the States present the Seventeenth Day of September in the Year of our Lord one thousand seven hundred and Eighty seven and of the Independence of the United States of America the Twelfth In witness whereof We have hereunto subscribed our Names, George Washington, President and deputy from Virginia.

New Hampshire: John Langdon,
Nicholas Gilman.

Massachusetts: Nathaniel Gorham,
Rufus King.

Connecticut: William Samuel Johnson,
Roger Sherman.

New York: Alexander Hamilton.

New Jersey: William Livingston,
David Brearley,
William Paterson,
Jonathan Dayton.

Pennsylvania: Benjamin Franklin,
Thomas Mifflin,
Robert Morris,
George Clymer,
Thomas FitzSimons,
Jared Ingersoll,
James Wilson,
Gouverneur Morris.

Delaware: George Read,
Gunning Bedford Jr.,
John Dickinson,
Richard Bassett,
Jacob Broom.

Maryland: James McHenry,
Daniel of St. Thomas Jenifer,
Daniel Carroll.

Virginia: John Blair,
James Madison Jr.

North Carolina: William Blount,
Richard Dobbs Spaight,
Hugh Williamson.

South Carolina: John Rutledge,
Charles Cotesworth Pinckney,
Charles Pinckney,
Pierce Butler.

Georgia: William Few,
Abraham Baldwin.

[The language of the original Constitution, not including the Amendments, was adopted by a convention of the states on Sept. 17, 1787, and was subsequently ratified by the states on the following dates: Delaware, Dec. 7, 1787; Pennsylvania, Dec. 12, 1787; New Jersey, Dec. 18, 1787; Georgia, Jan. 2, 1788; Connecticut, Jan. 9, 1788; Massachusetts, Feb. 6, 1788; Maryland, April 28, 1788; South Carolina, May 23, 1788; New Hampshire, June 21, 1788.

Ratification was completed on June 21, 1788.

The Constitution subsequently was ratified by Virginia, June 25, 1788; New York, July 26, 1788; North Carolina, Nov. 21, 1789; Rhode Island, May 29, 1790; and Vermont, Jan. 10, 1791.]

Amendments

Amendment I

(First ten amendments ratified Dec. 15, 1791.)

Congress shall make no law respecting an establishment of religion, or prohibiting the free exercise thereof; or abridging the freedom of speech, or of the press; or the right of the people peaceably to assemble, and to petition the Government for a redress of grievances.

Amendment II

A well regulated Militia, being necessary to the security of a free State, the right of the people to keep and bear Arms, shall not be infringed.

Amendment III

No Soldier shall, in time of peace be quartered in any house, without the consent of the Owner, nor in time of war, but in a manner to be prescribed by law.

Amendment IV

The right of the people to be secure in their persons, houses, papers, and effects, against unreasonable searches and seizures, shall not be violated, and no Warrants shall issue, but upon probable cause, supported by Oath or affirmation, and particularly describing the place to be searched, and the persons or things to be seized.

Amendment V

No person shall be held to answer for a capital, or otherwise infamous crime, unless on a presentment or indictment of a Grand Jury, except in cases arising in the land or naval forces, or in the Militia, when in actual service in time of War or public danger; nor shall any person be subject for the same offence to be twice put in jeopardy of life or limb; nor shall be compelled in any criminal case to be a witness against himself, nor be deprived of life, liberty, or property, without due process of law; nor shall private property be taken for public use, without just compensation.

Amendment VI

In all criminal prosecutions, the accused shall enjoy the right to a speedy and public trial, by an impartial jury of the State and district wherein the crime shall have been committed, which district shall have been previously ascertained by law, and to be informed of the nature and cause of the accusation; to be confronted with the witnesses against him; to have compulsory process for obtaining witnesses in his favor, and to have the Assistance of Counsel for his defence.

Amendment VII

In Suits at common law, where the value in controversy shall exceed twenty dollars, the right of trial by jury shall be preserved, and no fact tried by a jury, shall be otherwise re-examined in any Court of the United States, than according to the rules of the common law.

Amendment VIII

Excessive bail shall not be required, nor excessive fines imposed, nor cruel and unusual punishments inflicted.

Amendment IX

The enumeration in the Constitution, of certain rights, shall not be construed to deny or disparage others retained by the people.

Amendment X

The powers not delegated to the United States by the Constitution, nor prohibited by it to the States, are reserved to the States respectively, or to the people.

Amendment XI *(Ratified Feb. 7, 1795)*

The Judicial power of the United States shall not be construed to extend to any suit in law or equity, commenced or prosecuted against one of the United States by Citizens of another State, or by Citizens or Subjects of any Foreign State.

Amendment XII *(Ratified June 15, 1804)*

The Electors shall meet in their respective states and vote by ballot for President and Vice-President, one of whom, at least, shall not be an inhabitant of the same state with themselves; they shall name in their ballots the person voted for as President, and in distinct ballots the person voted for as Vice-President, and they shall make distinct lists of all persons voted for as President, and of all persons voted for as Vice-President, and of the number of votes for each, which lists they shall sign and certify, and transmit sealed to the seat of the government of the United States, directed to the President of the Senate;—The President of the Senate shall, in the presence of the Senate and House of Representatives, open all the certificates and the votes shall then be counted;—The person having the greatest number of votes for President, shall be the President, if such number be a majority of the whole number of Electors appointed; and if no person have such majority, then from the persons having the highest numbers not exceeding three on the list of those voted for as President, the House of Representatives shall choose immediately, by ballot, the President. But in choosing the President, the votes shall be taken by states, the representation from each state having one vote; a quorum for this purpose shall consist of a member or members from two-thirds of the states, and a majority of all the states shall be necessary to a choice. [And if the House of Representatives shall not choose a President whenever the right of choice shall devolve upon them, before the fourth day of March next following, then the Vice-President shall act as President, as in the case of the death or other constitutional disability of the President—][11]The person having the greatest number of votes as Vice-President, shall be the Vice-President, if such number be a majority of the whole number of Electors appointed, and if no person have a majority, then from the two highest numbers on the list, the Senate shall choose the Vice-President; a quorum for the purpose shall consist of two-thirds of the whole number of Senators, and a majority of the whole number shall be necessary to a choice. But no person constitutionally ineligible to the office of President shall be eligible to that of Vice-President of the United States.

Amendment XIII *(Ratified Dec. 6, 1865)*

Section 1. Neither slavery nor involuntary servitude, except as a punishment for crime whereof the party shall have been duly convicted, shall exist within the United States, or any place subject to their jurisdiction.

Section 2. Congress shall have power to enforce this article by appropriate legislation.

Amendment XIV *(Ratified July 9, 1868)*

Section 1. All persons born or naturalized in the United States and subject to the jurisdiction thereof, are citizens of the United States and of the State wherein they reside. No State shall make or enforce any law which shall abridge the privileges or immunities of citizens of the United States; nor shall any State deprive any person of life, liberty, or property, without due process of law; nor deny to any person within its jurisdiction the equal protection of the laws.

Section 2. Representatives shall be apportioned among the several States according to their respective numbers, counting the whole number of persons in each State, excluding Indians not taxed. But when the right to vote at any election for the choice of electors for President and Vice President of the United States, Representatives in Congress, the Executive and Judicial officers of a State, or the members of the Legislature thereof, is denied to any of the male inhabitants of such State, being twenty-one years of age,[12] and citizens of the United States, or in any way abridged, except for participation in rebellion, or other crime, the basis of representation therein shall be reduced in the proportion which the number of such male citizens shall bear to the whole number of male citizens twenty-one years of age in such State.

Section 3. No person shall be a Senator or Representative in Congress, or elector of President and Vice President, or hold any office, civil or military, under the United States, or under any State, who, having previously taken an oath, as a member of Congress, or as an officer of the United States, or as a member of any State legislature, or as an executive or judicial officer of any State, to support the Constitution of the United States, shall have engaged in insurrection or rebellion against the same, or given aid or comfort to the enemies thereof. But Congress may by a vote of two-thirds of each House, remove such disability.

Section 4. The validity of the public debt of the United States, authorized by law, including debts incurred for payment of pensions and bounties for services in suppressing insurrection or rebellion, shall not be questioned. But neither the United States nor any State shall assume or pay any debt or obligation incurred in aid of insurrection or rebellion against the United States, or any claim for the loss or emancipation of any slave; but all such debts, obligations and claims shall be held illegal and void.

Section 5. The Congress shall have power to enforce, by appropriate legislation, the provisions of this article.

Amendment XV *(Ratified Feb. 3, 1870)*

Section 1. The right of citizens of the United States to vote shall not be denied or abridged by the United States or by any State on account of race, color, or previous condition of servitude.

Section 2. The Congress shall have power to enforce this article by appropriate legislation.

Amendment XVI *(Ratified Feb. 3, 1913)*

The Congress shall have power to lay and collect taxes on incomes, from whatever source derived, without apportionment among the several States, and without regard to any census or enumeration.

Amendment XVII *(Ratified Apr. 8, 1913)*

The Senate of the United States shall be composed of two Senators from each State, elected by the people thereof, for six years; and each Senator shall have one vote. The electors in each State shall have the qualifications requisite for electors of the most numerous branch of the State legislatures.

When vacancies happen in the representation of any State in the Senate, the executive authority of such State shall issue writs of election to fill such vacancies: *Provided,* That the legislature of any State may empower the executive thereof to make temporary appointments until the people fill the vacancies by election as the legislature may direct.

This amendment shall not be so construed as to affect the election or term of any Senator chosen before it becomes valid as part of the Constitution.

[Amendment XVIII *(Ratified Jan. 16, 1919)*

Section 1. After one year from the ratification of this article the manufacture, sale, or transportation of intoxicating liquors within, the importation thereof into, or the exportation thereof from the United States and all territory subject to the jurisdiction thereof for beverage purposes is hereby prohibited.

Section 2. The Congress and the several States shall have concurrent power to enforce this article by appropriate legislation.

Section 3. This article shall be inoperative unless it shall have been ratified as an amendment to the Constitution by the legislatures of the several States, as provided in the Constitution, within seven years from the date of the submission hereof to the States by the Congress.][13]

Amendment XIX *(Ratified Aug. 18, 1920)*

The right of citizens of the United States to vote shall not be denied or abridged by the United States or by any State on account of sex.

Congress shall have power to enforce this article by appropriate legislation.

Amendment XX *(Ratified Jan. 23, 1933)*

Section 1. The terms of the President and Vice President shall end at noon on the 20th day of January, and the terms of Senators and Representatives at noon on the 3d day of January, of the years in which such terms would have ended if this article had not been ratified; and the terms of their successors shall then begin.

Section 2. The Congress shall assemble at least once in every year, and such meeting shall begin at noon on the 3d day of January, unless they shall by law appoint a different day.

Section 3.[14] If, at the time fixed for the beginning of the term of the President, the President elect shall have died, the Vice President elect shall become President. If a President shall not have been chosen before the time fixed for the beginning of his term, or if the President elect shall have failed to qualify, then the Vice President elect shall act as President until a President shall have qualified; and the Congress may by law provide for the case wherein neither a President elect nor a Vice President elect shall have qualified, declaring who shall then act as President, or the manner in which one who is to act shall be selected, and

such person shall act accordingly until a President or Vice President shall have qualified.

Section 4. The Congress may by law provide for the case of the death of any of the persons from whom the House of Representatives may choose a President whenever the right of choice shall have devolved upon them, and for the case of the death of any of the persons from whom the Senate may choose a Vice President whenever the right of choice shall have devolved upon them.

Section 5. Sections 1 and 2 shall take effect on the 15th day of October following the ratification of this article.

Section 6. This article shall be inoperative unless it shall have been ratified as an amendment to the Constitution by the legislatures of three-fourths of the several States within seven years from the date of its submission.

Amendment XXI *(Ratified Dec. 5, 1933)*

Section 1. The eighteenth article of amendment to the Constitution of the United States is hereby repealed.

Section 2. The transportation or importation into any State, Territory or possession of the United States for delivery or use therein of intoxicating liquors, in violation of the laws thereof, is hereby prohibited.

Section 3. This article shall be inoperative unless it shall have been ratified as an amendment to the Constitution by conventions in the several States, as provided in the Constitution, within seven years from the date of the submission hereof to the States by the Congress.

Amendment XXII *(Ratified Feb. 27, 1951)*

Section 1. No person shall be elected to the office of the President more than twice, and no person who has held the office of President, or acted as President, for more than two years of a term to which some other person was elected President shall be elected to the office of the President more than once. But this Article shall not apply to any person holding the office of President when this Article was proposed by the Congress, and shall not prevent any person who may be holding the office of President, or acting as President, during the term within which this Article becomes operative from holding the office of President or acting as President during the remainder of such term.

Section 2. This Article shall be inoperative unless it shall have been ratified as an amendment to the Constitution by the legislatures of three-fourths of the several States within seven years from the date of its submission to the States by the Congress.

Amendment XXIII *(Ratified March 29, 1961)*

Section 1. The District constituting the seat of Government of the United States shall appoint in such manner as the Congress may direct:

A number of electors of President and Vice President equal to the whole number of Senators and Representatives in Congress to which the District would be entitled if it were a State, but in no event more than the least populous State; they shall be in addition to those appointed by the States, but they shall be considered, for the purposes of the election of President and Vice President, to be electors appointed by a State; and they shall meet in the District and perform such duties as provided by the twelfth article of amendment.

Section 2. The Congress shall have power to enforce this article by appropriate legislation.

Amendment XXIV *(Ratified Jan. 23, 1964)*

Section 1. The right of citizens of the United States to vote in any primary or other election for President or Vice President, for electors for President or Vice President, or for Senator or Representative in Congress, shall not be denied or abridged by the United States or any State by reason of failure to pay any poll tax or other tax.

Section 2. The Congress shall have power to enforce this article by appropriate legislation.

Amendment XXV *(Ratified Feb. 10, 1967)*

Section 1. In case of the removal of the President from office or of his death or resignation, the Vice President shall become President.

Section 2. Whenever there is a vacancy in the office of the Vice President, the President shall nominate a Vice President who shall take office upon confirmation by a majority vote of both Houses of Congress.

Section 3. Whenever the President transmits to the President pro tempore of the Senate and the Speaker of the House of Representatives his written declaration that he is unable to discharge the powers and duties of his office, and until he transmits to them a written declaration to the contrary, such powers and duties shall be discharged by the Vice President as Acting President.

Section 4. Whenever the Vice President and a majority of either the principal officers of the executive departments or of such other body as Congress may by law provide, transmit to the President pro tempore of the Senate and the Speaker of the House of Representatives their written declaration that the President is unable to discharge the

powers and duties of his office, the Vice President shall immediately assume the powers and duties of the office as Acting President.

Thereafter, when the President transmits to the President pro tempore of the Senate and the Speaker of the House of Representatives his written declaration that no inability exists, he shall resume the powers and duties of his office unless the Vice President and a majority of either the principal officers of the executive department or of such other body as Congress may by law provide, transmit within four days to the President pro tempore of the Senate and the Speaker of the House of Representatives their written declaration that the President is unable to discharge the powers and duties of his office. Thereupon Congress shall decide the issue, assembling within forty-eight hours for that purpose if not in session. If the Congress, within twenty-one days after receipt of the latter written declaration, or, if Congress is not in session, within twenty-one days after Congress is required to assemble, determines by two-thirds vote of both houses that the President is unable to discharge the powers and duties of his office, the Vice President shall continue to discharge the same as Acting President; otherwise, the President shall resume the powers and duties of his office.

Amendment XXVI *(Ratified July 1, 1971)*

Section 1. The right of citizens of the United States, who are eighteen years of age or older, to vote shall not be denied or abridged by the United States or by any State on account of age.

Section 2. The Congress shall have power to enforce this article by appropriate legislation.

Footnotes

1. The part in brackets was changed by section 2 of the Fourteenth Amendment.
2. The part in brackets was changed by section 1 of the Seventeenth Amendment.
3. The part in brackets was changed by the second paragraph of the Seventeenth Amendment.
4. The part in brackets was changed by section 2 of the Twentieth Amendment.
5. The Sixteenth Amendment gave Congress the power to tax incomes.
6. The material in brackets has been superseded by the Twelfth Amendment.
7. This provision has been affected by the Twenty-fifth Amendment.

8. These clauses were affected by the Eleventh Amendment.
9. This paragraph has been superseded by the Thirteenth Amendment.
10. Obsolete.
11. The part in brackets has been superseded by section 3 of the Twentieth Amendment.
12. See the Twenty-sixth Amendment.
13. This Amendment was repealed by section 1 of the Twenty-first Amendment.
14. See the Twenty-fifth Amendment.

Source: U.S. Congress, House, Committee on the Judiciary, *The Constitution of the United States of America, As Amended Through July 1971,* H. Doc. 93-215, 93rd Cong., 2nd sess., 1974.

Subsidiary Documents of the Pre-Constitutional Period

Albany Plan of Union
1754

It is proposed that humble application be made for an act of Parliament of Great Britain, by virtue of which one general government may be formed in America, including all the said colonies, within and under which government each colony may retain its present constitution, except in the particulars wherein a change may be directed by the said act, as hereafter follows.

1. That the said general government be administered by a President-General, to be appointed and supported by the crown; and a Grand Council, to be chosen by the representatives of the people of the several Colonies met in their respective assemblies.

2. That within ＿＿ months after the passing such act, the House of Representatives that happen to be sitting within that time, or that shall be especially for that purpose convened, may and shall choose members for the Grand Council, in the following proportion, that is to say,

Massachusetts Bay	7
New Hampshire	2
Connecticut	5
Rhode Island	2
New York	4
New Jersey	3
Pennsylvania	6
Maryland	4
Virginia	7
North Carolina	4
South Carolina	4
	48

3. ____who shall meet for the first time at the city of Philadelphia, being called by the President-General as soon as conveniently may be after his appointment.

4. That there shall be a new election of the members of the Grand Council every three years; and, on the death or resignation of any member, his place should be supplied by a new choice at the next sitting of the Assembly of the Colony he represented.

5. That after the first three years, when the proportion of money arising out of each Colony to the general treasury can be known, the number of members to be chosen for each Colony shall, from time to time, in all ensuing elections, be regulated by that proportion, yet so as that the number to be chosen by any one Province be not more than seven, nor less than two.

6. That the Grand Council shall meet once in every year, and oftener if occasion require, at such time and place as they shall adjourn to at the last preceding meeting, or as they shall be called to meet at by the President-General on any emergency; he having first obtained in writing the consent of seven of the members to such call, and sent duly and timely notice to the whole.

7. That the Grand Council have power to choose their speaker; and shall neither be dissolved, prorogued, nor continued sitting longer than six weeks at one time, without their own consent or the special command of the crown.

8. That the members of the Grand Council shall be allowed for their service ten shillings sterling per diem, during their session and journey to and from the place of meeting; twenty miles to be reckoned a day's journey.

9. That the assent of the President-General be requisite to all acts of the Grand Council, and that it be his office and duty to cause them to be carried into execution.

10. That the President-General, with the advice of the Grand Council, hold or direct all Indian treaties, in which the general interest of the Colonies may be concerned; and make peace or declare war with Indian nations.

11. That they make such laws as they judge necessary for regulating all Indian trade.

12. That they make all purchases from Indians, for the crown, of lands not now within the bounds of particular Colonies, or that shall not be within their bounds when some of them are reduced to more convenient dimensions.

13. That they make new settlements on such purchases, by granting lands in the King's name, reserving a quitrent to the crown for the use of the general treasury.

14. That they make laws for regulating and governing such new settlements, till the crown shall think fit to form them into particular governments.

15. That they raise and pay soldiers and build forts for the defence of any of the Colonies, and equip vessels of force to guard the coasts and protect the trade on the ocean, lakes, or great rivers; but they shall not impress men in any Colony, without the consent of the Legislature.

16. That for these purposes they have power to make laws, and lay and levy such general duties, imposts, or taxes, as to them shall appear most equal and just (considering the ability and other circumstances of the inhabitants in the several Colonies), and such as may be collected with the least inconvenience to the people; rather discouraging luxury, than loading industry with unnecessary burdens.

17. That they may appoint a General Treasurer and Particular Treasurer in each government when necessary; and, from time to time, may order the sums in the treasuries of each government into the general treasury; or draw on them for special payments, as they find most convenient.

18. Yet no money to issue but by joint orders of the President-General and Grand Council; except where sums have been appropriated to particular purposes, and the President-General is previously empowered by an act to draw such sums.

19. That the general accounts shall be yearly settled and reported to the several Assemblies.

20. That a quorum of the Grand Council, empowered to act with the President-General, do consist of twenty-five members; among whom there shall be one or more from a majority of the Colonies.

21. That the laws made by them for the purposes aforesaid shall not be repugnant, but, as near as may be, agreeable to the laws of England, and shall be transmitted to the King in Council for approbation, as soon as may be after their passing; and if not disapproved within three years after presentation, to remain in force.

22. That, in case of the death of the President-General, the Speaker of the Grand Council for the time being shall succeed, and be vested with the same powers and authorities, to continue till the King's pleasure be known.

23. That all military commission officers, whether for land or sea service, to act under this general constitution, shall be nominated by the President-General; but the approbation of the Grand Council is to be obtained, before they receive their commissions. And all civil officers are to be nominated by the Grand Council, and to receive the President-General's approbation before they officiate.

24. But, in case of vacancy by death or removal of any officer, civil or military, under this constitution, the Governor of the Province in which such vacancy happens may appoint, till the pleasure of the President-General and Grand Council can be known.

25. That the particular military as well as civil establishments in each Colony remain in their present state, the general constitution notwithstanding; and that on sudden emergencies any Colony may defend itself, and lay the accounts of expense thence arising before the President-General and General Council, who may allow and order payment of the same, as far as they judge such accounts just and reasonable.

Resolutions of the Stamp Act Congress October 19, 1765

THE members of this Congress, sincerely devoted with the warmest sentiments of affection and duty to His Majesty's person and Government, inviolably attached to the present happy establishment of the Protestant succession, and with minds deeply impressed by a sense of the present and impending misfortunes of the British colonies on this continent; having considered as maturely as time will permit the circumstances of the said colonies, esteem it our indispensable duty to make the following declarations of our humble opinion respecting the most essential rights and liberties of the colonists, and of the grievances under which they labour, by reason of several late Acts of Parliament.

I. That His Majesty's subjects in these colonies owe the same allegiance to the Crown of Great Britain that is owing from his subjects born within the realm, and all due subordination to that august body the Parliament of Great Britain.

II. That His Majesty's liege subjects in these colonies are intitled to all the inherent rights and liberties of his natural born subjects within the kingdom of Great Britain.

III. That it is inseparably essential to the freedom of a people, and the undoubted right of Englishmen, that no taxes be imposed on them but with their own consent, given personally or by their representatives.

IV. That the people of these colonies are not, and from their local circumstances cannot be, represented in the House of Commons in Great Britain.

V. That the only representatives of the people of these colonies are persons chosen therein by themselves, and that no taxes ever have been, or can be constitutionally imposed on them, but by their respective legislatures.

VI. That all supplies to the Crown being free gifts of the people, it is unreasonable and inconsistent with the principles and spirit of the British Constitution, for the people of Great Britain to grant to His Majesty the property of the colonists.

VII. That trial by jury is the inherent and invaluable right of every British subject in these colonies.

VIII. That the late Act of Parliament, entitled *An Act for granting and applying certain stamp duties, and other duties, in the British colonies and plantations in America, etc.*, by imposing taxes on the inhabitants of these colonies; and the said Act, and several other Acts, by extending the jurisdiction of the courts of Admiralty beyond its ancient limits, have a manifest tendency to subvert the rights and liberties of the colonists.

IX. That the duties imposed by several late Acts of Parliament, from the peculiar circumstances of these colonies, will be extremely burthensome and grievous; and from the scarcity of specie, the payment of them absolutely impracticable.

X. That as the profits of the trade of these colonies ultimately center in Great Britain, to pay for the manufactures which they are obliged to take from thence, they eventually contribute very largely to all supplies granted there to the Crown.

XI. That the restrictions imposed by several late Acts of Parliament on the trade of these colonies will render them unable to purchase the manufactures of Great Britain.

XII. That the increase, prosperity, and happiness of these colonies depend on the full and free enjoyments of their rights and liberties, and an intercourse with Great Britain mutually affectionate and advantageous.

XIII. That it is the right of the British subjects in these colonies to petition the King or either House of Parliament.

Lastly, That it is the indispensable duty of these colonies to the best of sovereigns, to the mother country, and to themselves, to endeavour by a loyal and dutiful address to His Majesty, and humble applications to both Houses of Parliament, to procure the repeal of the Act for granting and applying certain stamp duties, of all clauses of any other Acts of Parliament, whereby the jurisdiction of the Admiralty is extended as aforesaid, and of the other late Acts for the restriction of American commerce.

Declaration and Resolves of the First Continental Congress October 14, 1774

Whereas, since the close of the last war, the British parliament, claiming a power of right to bind the people of America by statute in all cases whatsoever, hath, in some acts expressly imposed taxes on them, and in others, under various pretences, but in fact for the purpose of raising a revenue, hath imposed rates and duties payable in these colonies, established a board of commissioners with unconstitutional powers, and extended the jurisdiction of courts of Admiralty not only for collecting the said duties, but for the trial of causes merely arising within the body of a county.

And whereas, in consequence of other statutes, judges who before held only estates at will in their offices, have been made dependent on the Crown alone for their salaries, and standing armies kept in times of peace. And it has lately been resolved in Parliament, that by force of a statute made in the thirty-fifth year of the reign of king Henry the Eighth, colonists may be transported to England, and tried there upon accusations for treasons and misprisions, or concealments of treasons committed in the colonies; and by a late statute, such trials have been directed in cases therein mentioned.

And whereas, in the last session of Parliament, three statutes were made...[the Boston Port Act, the Massachusetts Government Act, the Administration of Justice Act], and another statute was then made [the Quebec Act]... All which statutes are impolitic, unjust, and cruel, as well as unconstitutional, and most dangerous and destructive of American rights.

And whereas, Assemblies have been frequently dissolved, contrary to the rights of the people, when they attempted to deliberate on grievances; and their dutiful, humble, loyal, & reasonable petitions to the crown for redress, have been repeatedly treated with contempt, by His Majesty's ministers of state:

The good people of the several Colonies of New-hampshire, Massachusetts-bay, Rhode-island and

Providence plantations, Connecticut, New-York, New-Jersey, Pennsylvania, Newcastle Kent and Sussex on Delaware, Maryland, Virginia, North-Carolina, and South-Carolina, justly alarmed at these arbitrary proceedings of parliament and administration, have severally elected, constituted, and appointed deputies to meet, and sit in general Congress, in the city of Philadelphia, in order to obtain such establishment, as that their religion, laws, and liberties, may not be subverted:

Whereupon the deputies so appointed being now assembled, in a full and free representation of these Colonies, taking into their most serious consideration the best means of attaining the ends aforesaid, do in the first place, as Englishmen their ancestors in like cases have usually done, for asserting and vindicating their rights and liberties, declare,

That the inhabitants of the English Colonies in North America, by the immutable laws of nature, the principles of the English constitution, and the several charters or compacts, have the following Rights:

Resolved, N. C. D.

1. That they are entitled to life, liberty, and property, & they have never ceded to any sovereign power whatever, a right to dispose of either without their consent.

2. That our ancestors, who first settled these colonies, were at the time of their emigration from the mother country, entitled to all the rights, liberties, and immunities of free and natural-born subjects within the realm of England.

3. That by such emigration they by no means forfeited, surrendered, or lost any of those rights, but that they were, and their descendants now are entitled to the exercise and enjoyment of all such of them, as their local and other circumstances enable them to exercise and enjoy.

4. That the foundation of English liberty, and of all free government, is a right in the people to participate in their legislative council: and as the English colonists are not represented, and from their local and other circumstances, cannot properly be represented in the British parliament, they are entitled to a free and exclusive power of legislation in their several provincial legislatures, where their right of representation can alone be preserved, in all cases of taxation and internal polity, subject only to the negative of their sovereign, in such manner as has been heretofore used and accustomed. But, from the necessity of the case, and a regard to the mutual interest of both countries, we cheerfully consent to the operation of such acts of the British parliament, as are bona fide restrained to the regulation of our external commerce, for the purpose of securing the commercial advantages of the whole empire to the mother country, and the commercial benefits of its respective members excluding every idea of taxation, internal or external, for raising a revenue on the subjects in America without their consent.

5. That the respective colonies are entitled to the common law of England, and more especially to the great and inestimable privilege of being tried by their peers of the vicinage, according to the course of that law.

6. That they are entitled to the benefit of such of the English statutes, as existed at the time of their colonization; and which they have, by experience, respectively found to be applicable to their several local and other circumstances.

7. That these, his majesty's colonies, are likewise entitled to all the immunities and privileges granted and confirmed to them by royal charters, or secured by their several codes of provincial laws.

8. That they have a right peaceably to assemble, consider of their grievances, and petition the King; and that all prosecutions, prohibitory proclamations, and commitment for the same, are illegal.

9. That the keeping a Standing army in these colonies in times of peace, without the consent of the legislature of that colony in which such army is kept, is against law.

10. It is indispensably necessary to good government, and rendered essential by the English constitution, that the constituent branches of the legislature be independent of each other; that, therefore, the exercise of legislative power in several colonies, by a council appointed during pleasure by the crown, is unconstitutional, dangerous, and destructive to the freedom of American legislation.

All and each of which the aforesaid deputies, in behalf of themselves, and their constituents, do claim, demand, and insist on, as their indubitable rights and liberties; which cannot be legally taken from them, altered or abridged by any power whatever, without their own consent, by their representatives in their several provincial legislatures.

In the course of our inquiry, we find many infringements and violations of the foregoing rights, which, from an ardent desire that harmony and mutual intercourse of affection and interest may be restored, we pass over for the present, and proceed to state such acts and measures as have been adopted since the last war, which demonstrate a system formed to enslave America.

Resolved, That the following acts of Parliament are infringements and violations of the rights of the colonists; and that the repeal of them is essentially necessary, in order to restore harmony between Great Britain and the American colonies, ...viz.:

The several Acts of 4 Geo. 3, ch. 15 & ch. 34; 5 Geo. 3, ch. 25; 6 Geo. 3, ch. 52; 7 Geo. 3, ch. 41 & 46; 8 Geo. 3, ch. 22; which impose duties for the purpose of raising a revenue in America, extend the powers of the admiralty courts beyond their ancient limits, deprive the American subject of trial by jury, authorize the judges' certificate to indemnify the prosecutor from damages that he might otherwise be liable to, requiring oppressive security from a claimant of ships and goods seized before he shall be allowed to defend his property; and are subversive of American rights.

Also the 12 Geo. 3, ch. 24, entitled "An act for the better preserving his Majesty's dockyards, magazines, ships, ammunition, and stores," which declares a new offense in America, and deprives the American subject of a constitutional trial by jury of the vicinage, by authorizing the trial of any person charged with the committing any offense described in the said act, out of the realm, to be indicted and tried for the same in any shire or county within the realm.

Also the three acts passed in the last session of parliament, for stopping the port and blocking up the harbour of Boston, for altering the charter & government of the Massachusetts-bay, and that which is entitled "An Act for the better administration of Justice," &c.

Also the act passed the same session for establishing the Roman Catholick Religion in the province of Quebec, abolishing the equitable system of English laws, and erecting a tyranny there, to the great danger, from so great a dissimilarity of Religion, law, and government, of the neighbouring British colonies....

Also the act passed the same session for the better providing suitable quarters for officers and soldiers in his Majesty's service in North America.

Also, that the keeping a standing army in several of these colonies, in time of peace, without the consent of the legislature of that colony in which the army is kept, is against law.

To these grievous acts and measures Americans cannot submit, but in hopes that their fellow subjects in Great-Britain will, on a revision of them, restore us to that state in which both countries found happiness and prosperity, we have for the present only resolved to pursue the following peaceable measures: 1st. To enter into a non-importation, non-consumption, and non-exportation agreement or association. 2. To prepare an address to the people of Great-Britain, and a memorial to the inhabitants of British America, & 3. To prepare a loyal address to his Majesty, agreeable to resolutions already entered into.

Virginia or Randolph Plan
Presented to the Federal Convention
May 29, 1787

1. Resolved that the Articles of Confederation ought to be so corrected and enlarged as to accomplish the objects proposed by their institution; namely "common defence, security of liberty and general welfare."

2. Resolved therefore that the rights of suffrage in the National Legislature ought to be proportioned to the Quotas of contribution, or to the number of free inhabitants, as the one or the other rule may seem best in different cases.

3. Resolved that the National Legislature ought to consist of two branches.

4. Resolved that the members of the first branch of the National Legislature ought to be elected by the people of the several States every   for the terms of   ; to be of the age of   years at least, to receive liberal stipends by which they may be compensated for the devotion of their time to public service, to be ineligible to any office established by a particular State, or under the authority of the United States, except those peculiarly belonging to the functions of the first branch, during the term of service, and for the space of   after its expiration; to be incapable of reelection for the space of   after the expiration of their term of service, and to be subject to recall.

5. Resolved that the members of the second branch of the National Legislature ought to be elected by those of the first, out of a proper number of persons nominated by the individual Legislatures, to be of the age of   years at least; to hold their offices for a term sufficient to ensure their independency; to receive liberal stipends, by which they may be compensated for the devotion of their time to public service; and to be ineligible to any office established by a particular State, or under the authority of the United States, except those peculiarly belonging to the functions of the second branch, during the term of service, and for the space of   after the expiration thereof.

6. Resolved that each branch ought to possess the right of originating Acts; that the National Legislature ought to be impowered to enjoy the Legislative Rights vested in Congress by the Confederation and moreover to legislate in all cases to which the separate States are incompetent, or in which the harmony of the United States may be interrupted by the exercise of individual Legislation; to negative all laws passed by the several States, contravening in the opinion of the National Legislature the articles of Union; and to call forth the force of the Union against any member of the Union failing in its duty under the articles thereof.

7. Resolved that a National Executive be instituted; to be chosen by the National Legislature for the term of   years; to receive punctually, at stated times, a fixed compensation for the services rendered, in which no increase or diminution shall be made so as to affect the Magistracy, existing at the time of the increase or diminution, and to be ineligible a second time; and that besides a general authority to execute the National laws, it ought to enjoy the Executive rights vested in Congress by the Confederation.

8. Resolved that the Executive and a convenient number of the National Judiciary, ought to compose a Council or revision with authority to examine every act of the National Legislature before a Negative thereon shall be final; and that the dissent of the said Council shall amount to a rejection, unless the Act of the National Legislature be passed again, or that of a particular Legislature be again negatived by   of the members of each branch.

9. Resolved that a National Judiciary be established to consist of one or more supreme tribunals, and of inferior tribunals to be chosen by the National Legislature, to hold their offices during good behaviour; and to receive punctually at stated times fixed compensation for their services, in which no increase or diminution shall be made so as to affect the persons actually in office at the time of such increase or diminution. That the jurisdiction of the inferior tribunals shall be to hear and determine in the first instance, and of the supreme tribunal to hear and determine in the dernier resort, all piracies and felonies on the high seas, captures from an enemy; cases in which foreigners or citizens of other States applying to such jurisdictions may be interested, or which respect the collection of the National revenue; impeachments of any National officers, and questions which may involve the national peace and harmony.

10. Resolved that provision ought to be made for the admission of States lawfully arising within the limits of the United States, whether from a voluntary junction of Government and Territory or otherwise, with the consent of a number of voices in the National legislature less than the whole.

11. Resolved that a Republican Government and the territory of each State, except in the instance of a voluntary junction of Government and territory, ought to be guaranteed by the United States to each State.

12. Resolved that provision ought to be made for the continuance of Congress and their authorities and privileges, until a given day after the reform of the articles of Union shall be adopted, and for the completion of all their engagements.

13. Resolved that provision ought to be made for the amendment of the Articles of Union whensoever it shall seem necessary, and that the assent of the National Legislature ought not to be required thereto.

14. Resolved that the Legislative Executive and Judiciary powers within the several States ought to be bound by oath to support the articles of Union.

15. Resolved that the amendments which shall be offered to the Confederation, by the Convention ought at a proper time, or times, after the approbation of Congress to

be submitted to an assembly or assemblies of Representatives, recommended by the several Legislatures to be expressly chosen by the people, to consider and deci thereon.

The Paterson or New Jersey Plan Presented to the Federal Convention June 15, 1787

1. Resolved that the Articles of Confederation ought to be so revised, corrected, and enlarged as to render the federal Constitution adequate to the exigencies of Government, and the preservation of the Union.

2. Resolved that in addition to the powers vested in the United States in Congress, by the present existing articles of Confederation, they be authorized to pass acts for raising a revenue, by levying a duty or duties on all goods or merchandizes of foreign growth or manufacture, imported into any part of the United States, by Stamps on paper, vellum or parchment, and by a postage on all letters or packages passing through the general post-office, to be applied to such federal purposes as they shall deem proper and expedient; to make rules and regulations for the collection thereof; and the same from time to time, to alter and amend in such manner as they shall think proper: to pass Acts for the regulation of trade and commerce as well with foreign nations as with each other; provided that all punishments, fines, forfeitures and penalties to be incurred for contravening such acts rules and regulations shall be adjudged by the Common law Judiciaries of the State in which any offence contrary to the true intent and meaning of such Acts rules and regulations shall have been committed or perpetrated, with liberty of commencing in the first instance all suits and prosecutions for that purpose, in the superior common law Judiciary in such state, subject nevertheless, for the correction of errors, both in law and fact in rendering Judgement, to an appeal to the Judiciary of the United States.

3. Resolved that whenever requisitions shall be necessary, instead of the rule for making requisitions mentioned in the articles of Confederation, the United States in Congress be authorized to make such requisitions in proportion to the whole number of white and other free citizens and inhabitants of every age sex and condition including those bound to servitude for a term of years and three fifths of all other persons not comprehended in the foregoing description, except Indians not paying taxes; that if such requisitions be not complied with, in the time specified therein, to direct the collection thereof in the non-complying States and for that purpose to devise and pass acts directing and authorizing the same; provided that none of the powers hereby vested in the United States in Congress shall be exercised without the consent of at least   States, and in that proportion if the number of Confederated States should hereafter be increased or diminished.

4. Resolved that the United States in Congress be authorized to elect a federal Executive to consist of   persons, to continue in office for the term of   years, to receive punctually at stated times a fixed compensation for their services, in which no increase or diminution shall be made so as to affect the persons composing the Executive the time of such increase or diminution, to be paid out of the federal treasury; to be incapable of holding any other office or appointment during their time of service and for   years thereafter; to be ineligible a second time, and removeable by Congress on application by a majority of the Executives of the several States; that the Executive besides their general authority to execute the federal acts ought to appoint all federal officers not otherwise provided for, and to direct all military operations; provided that none of the persons composing the federal Executive shall on any occasion take command of any troops so as personally to conduct any enterprise as General or in other capacity.

5. Resolved that a federal Judiciary be established to consist of a supreme tribunal the Judges of which to be appointed by the Executive, and to hold their offices during good behaviour, to receive punctually at stated times a fixed compensation for their services in which no increase or diminution shall be made so as to affect persons actually in office at the time of such increase or diminution; that the Judiciary so established shall have authority to hear and determine in the first instance on all impeachments of federal officers, and by way of appeal in the dernier resort in all cases touching the rights of Ambassadors, in all cases of captures from an enemy, in all cases of piracies and felonies on the high Seas, in all cases in which foreigners may be interested, in the construction of any treaty or treaties, or which may arise on any of the Acts for regulation of trade, or the collection of the federal Revenue: that none of the Judiciary shall during the time they remain in office be capable of receiving or holding any other office or appointment during the time of service, or for thereafter.

6. Resolved that all Acts of the United States in Congress made by virtue and in pursuance of the powers hereby and by the articles of Confederation vested in them, and all Treaties made and ratified under the authority of the United States, shall be the supreme law of the respective States so far forth as those Acts or Treaties shall relate to the said States or their Citizens, and that the Judiciary of the several States shall be bound thereby in their decisions, any thing in the respective laws of the Individual States to the contrary notwithstanding; and that if any State, or any body of men in the State shall oppose or prevent carrying into execution such acts or treaties, the federal Executive shall be authorized to call forth the power of the Confederated States, or so much thereof as may be necessary to enforce and compel an obedience to such Acts or an observance of such Treaties.

7. Resolved that provision be made for the admission of new States into the Union.

8. Resolved the rule for naturalization ought to be the same in every State.

9. Resolved that a Citizen of one State committing an offence in another State of the Union, shall be deemed guilty of the same offence as if it had been committed by a Citizen of the State in which the offence was committed.

Sessions of the U.S. Congress, 1789-1976

Source: 1976 Official Congressional Directory

Congress	Session	Date of beginning[1]	Date of adjournment[2]	Length in days	President pro tempore of the Senate[3]	Speaker of the House of Representatives
1st	1	Mar. 4, 1789	Sept. 29, 1789	210	John Langdon of New Hampshire[4]	Frederick A. C. Muhlenberg of Pennsylvania
	2	Jan. 4, 1790	Aug. 12, 1790	221		
	3	Dec. 6, 1790	Mar. 3, 1791	88		
2nd	1	Oct. 24, 1791	May 8, 1792	197	Richard Henry Lee of Virginia	Jonathan Trumbull of Connecticut
	2	Nov. 5, 1792	Mar. 2, 1793	119	John Langdon of New Hampshire	
3rd	1	Dec. 2, 1793	June 9, 1794	190	Langdon	Frederick A. C. Muhlenberg of Pennsylvania
					Ralph Izard of South Carolina	
	2	Nov. 3, 1794	Mar. 3, 1795	121	Henry Tazewell of Virginia	
4th	1	Dec. 7, 1795	June 1, 1796	177	Tazewell	Jonathan Dayton of New Jersey
					Samuel Livermore of New Hampshire	
	2	Dec. 5, 1796	Mar. 3, 1797	89	William Bingham of Pennsylvania	
5th	1	May 15, 1797	July 10, 1797	57	William Bradford of Rhode Island	Dayton
	2	Nov. 13, 1797	July 16, 1798	246	Jacob Read of South Carolina	George Dent of Maryland[5]
					Theodore Sedgwick of Massachusetts	
	3	Dec. 3, 1798	Mar. 3, 1799	91	John Laurence of New York	
					James Ross of Pennsylvania	
6th	1	Dec. 2, 1799	May 14, 1800	164	Samuel Livermore of New Hampshire	Theodore Sedgwick of Massachusetts
					Uriah Tracy of Connecticut	
	2	Nov. 17, 1800	Mar. 3, 1801	107	John E. Howard of Maryland	
					James Hillhouse of Connecticut	
7th	1	Dec. 7, 1801	May 3, 1802	148	Abraham Baldwin of Georgia	Nathaniel Macon of North Carolina
	2	Dec. 6, 1802	Mar. 3, 1803	88	Stephen R. Bradley of Vermont	

Footnotes, p. 180-A

Congress	Session	Date of beginning[1]	Date of adjournment[2]	Length in days	President pro tempore of the Senate[3]	Speaker of the House of Representatives
8th	1	Oct. 17, 1803	Mar. 27, 1804	163	John Brown of Kentucky Jesse Franklin of North Carolina	Macon
	2	Nov. 5, 1804	Mar. 3, 1805	119	Joseph Anderson of Tennessee	
9th	1	Dec. 2, 1805	Apr. 21, 1806	141	Samuel Smith of Maryland	Macon
	2	Dec. 1, 1806	Mar. 3, 1807	93		
10th	1	Oct. 26, 1807	Apr. 25, 1808	182	Smith	Joseph B. Varnum of Massachusetts
	2	Nov. 7, 1808	Mar. 3, 1809	117	Stephen R. Bradley of Vermont John Milledge of Georgia	
11th	1	May 22, 1809	June 28, 1809	38	Andrew Gregg of Pennsylvania	Varnum
	2	Nov. 27, 1809	May 1, 1810	156	John Gaillard of South Carolina	
	3	Dec. 3, 1810	Mar. 3, 1811	91	John Pope of Kentucky	
12th	1	Nov. 4, 1811	July 6, 1812	245	William H. Crawford of Georgia	Henry Clay of Kentucky
	2	Nov. 2, 1812	Mar. 3, 1813	122	Crawford	
13th	1	May 24, 1813	Aug. 2, 1813	71		Clay
	2	Dec. 6, 1813	Apr. 18, 1814	134	Joseph B. Varnum of Massachusetts	
	3	Sept. 19, 1814	Mar. 3, 1815	166	John Gaillard of South Carolina	Langdon Cheves of South Carolina[6]
14th	1	Dec. 4, 1815	Apr. 30, 1816	148	Gaillard	Henry Clay of Kentucky
	2	Dec. 2, 1816	Mar. 3, 1817	92	Gaillard	
15th	1	Dec. 1, 1817	Apr. 20, 1818	141	Gaillard	Clay
	2	Nov. 16, 1818	Mar. 3, 1819	108	James Barbour of Virginia	
16th	1	Dec. 6, 1819	May 15, 1820	162	John Gaillard of South Carolina	Clay
	2	Nov. 13, 1820	Mar. 3, 1821	111	Gaillard	John W. Taylor of New York[7]
17th	1	Dec. 3, 1821	May 8, 1822	157	Gaillard	Philip P. Barbour of Virginia
	2	Dec. 2, 1822	Mar. 3, 1823	92	Gaillard	
18th	1	Dec. 1, 1823	May 27, 1824	178	Gaillard	Henry Clay of Kentucky
	2	Dec. 6, 1824	Mar. 3, 1825	88	Gaillard	
19th	1	Dec. 5, 1825	May 22, 1826	169	Nathaniel Macon of North Carolina	John W. Taylor of New York
	2	Dec. 4, 1826	Mar. 3, 1827	90	Macon	
20th	1	Dec. 3, 1827	May 26, 1828	175	Samuel Smith of Maryland	Andrew Stevenson of Virginia
	2	Dec. 1, 1828	Mar. 3, 1829	93	Smith	
21st	1	Dec. 7, 1829	May 31, 1830	176	Smith	Stevenson
	2	Dec. 6, 1830	Mar. 3, 1831	88	Littleton Waller Tazewell of Virginia	
22nd	1	Dec. 5, 1831	July 16, 1832	225	Tazewell	Stevenson
	2	Dec. 3, 1832	Mar. 2, 1833	91	Hugh Lawson White of Tennessee	
23rd	1	Dec. 2, 1833	June 30, 1834	211	George Poindexter of Mississippi	Stevenson
	2	Dec. 1, 1834	Mar. 3, 1835	93	John Tyler of Virginia	John Bell of Tennessee[8]

ongress	Session	Date of beginning[1]	Date of adjournment[2]	Length in days	President pro tempore of the Senate[3]	Speaker of the House of Representatives
24th	1	Dec. 7, 1835	July 4, 1836	211	William R. King of Alabama	James K. Polk of Tennessee
	2	Dec. 5, 1836	Mar. 3, 1837	89	King	
25th	1	Sept. 4, 1837	Oct. 16, 1837	43	King	Polk
	2	Dec. 4, 1837	July 9, 1838	218	King	
	3	Dec. 3, 1838	Mar. 3, 1839	91	King	
26th	1	Dec. 2, 1839	July 21, 1840	233	King	Robert M. T. Hunter of Virginia
	2	Dec. 7, 1840	Mar. 3, 1841	87		
27th	1	May 31, 1841	Sept. 13, 1841	106	Samuel L. Southard of New Jersey	John White of Kentucky
	2	Dec. 6, 1841	Aug. 31, 1842	269	Willie P. Mangum of North Carolina	
	3	Dec. 5, 1842	Mar. 3, 1843	89	Mangum	
28th	1	Dec. 4, 1843	June 17, 1844	196	Mangum	John W. Jones of Virginia
	2	Dec. 2, 1844	Mar. 3, 1845	92	Mangum	
29th	1	Dec. 1, 1845	Aug. 10, 1846	253	David R. Atchison of Missouri	John W. Davis of Indiana
	2	Dec. 7, 1846	Mar. 3, 1847	87	Atchison	
30th	1	Dec. 6, 1847	Aug. 14, 1848	254	Atchison	Robert C. Winthrop of Massachusetts
	2	Dec. 4, 1848	Mar. 3, 1849	90	Atchison	
31st	1	Dec. 3, 1849	Sept. 30, 1850	302	William R. King of Alabama	Howell Cobb of Georgia
	2	Dec. 2, 1850	Mar. 3, 1851	92	King	
32nd	1	Dec. 1, 1851	Aug. 31, 1852	275	King	Linn Boyd of Kentucky
	2	Dec. 6, 1852	Mar. 3, 1853	88	David R. Atchison of Missouri	
33rd	1	Dec. 5, 1853	Aug. 7, 1854	246	Atchison	Boyd
	2	Dec. 4, 1854	Mar. 3, 1855	90	Jesse D. Bright of Indiana Lewis Cass of Michigan	
34th	1	Dec. 3, 1855	Aug. 18, 1856	260	Jesse D. Bright of Indiana	Nathaniel P. Banks of Massachusetts
	2	Aug. 21, 1856	Aug. 30, 1856	10	Bright	
	3	Dec. 1, 1856	Mar. 3, 1857	93	James M. Mason of Virginia Thomas J. Rusk of Texas	
35th	1	Dec. 7, 1857	June 14, 1858	189	Benjamin Fitzpatrick of Alabama	James L. Orr of South Carolina
	2	Dec. 6, 1858	Mar. 3, 1859	88	Fitzpatrick	
36th	1	Dec. 5, 1859	June 25, 1860	202	Fitzpatrick Jesse D. Bright of Indiana	William Pennington of New Jersey
	2	Dec. 3, 1860	Mar. 3, 1861	93	Solomon Foot of Vermont	
37th	1	July 4, 1861	Aug. 6, 1861	34	Foot	Galusha A. Grow of Pennsylvania
	2	Dec. 2, 1861	July 17, 1862	228	Foot	
	3	Dec. 1, 1862	Mar. 3, 1863	93	Foot	
38th	1	Dec. 7, 1863	July 4, 1864	209	Foot Daniel Clark of New Hampshire	Schuyler Colfax of Indiana
	2	Dec. 5, 1864	Mar. 3, 1865	89	Clark	

Footnotes, p. 180-A

Congress	Session	Date of beginning[1]	Date of adjournment[2]	Length in days	President pro tempore of the Senate[3]	Speaker of the House of Representatives
39th	1	Dec. 4, 1865	July 28, 1866	237	Lafayette S. Foster of Connecticut	Colfax
	2	Dec. 3, 1866	Mar. 3, 1867	91	Benjamin F. Wade of Ohio	
40th	1	Mar. 4, 1867[9]	Dec. 2, 1867	274	Wade	Colfax
	2	Dec. 2, 1867[10]	Nov. 10, 1868	345	Wade	
	3	Dec. 7, 1868	Mar. 3, 1869	87	Wade	Theodore M. Pomeroy of New York[11]
41st	1	Mar. 4, 1869	Apr. 10, 1869	38	Henry B. Anthony of Rhode Island	James G. Blaine of Maine
	2	Dec. 6, 1869	July 15, 1870	222	Anthony	
	3	Dec. 5, 1870	Mar. 3, 1871	89	Anthony	
42nd	1	Mar. 4, 1871	Apr. 20, 1871	48	Anthony	Blaine
	2	Dec. 4, 1871	June 10, 1872	190	Anthony	
	3	Dec. 2, 1872	Mar. 3, 1873	92	Anthony	
43rd	1	Dec. 1, 1873	June 23, 1874	204	Matthew H. Carpenter of Wisconsin	Blaine
	2	Dec. 7, 1874	Mar. 3, 1875	87	Carpenter	
					Henry B. Anthony of Rhode Island	
44th	1	Dec. 6, 1875	Aug. 15, 1876	254	Thomas W. Ferry of Michigan	Michael C. Kerr of Indiana[12]
						Samuel S. Cox of New York, pro tempore[13]
						Milton Sayler of Ohio, pro tempore[14]
	2	Dec. 4, 1876	Mar. 3, 1877	90	Ferry	Samuel J. Randall of Pennsylvania
45th	1	Oct. 15, 1877	Dec. 3, 1877	50	Ferry	Randall
	2	Dec. 3, 1877	June 20, 1878	200	Ferry	
	3	Dec. 2, 1878	Mar. 3, 1879	92	Ferry	
46th	1	Mar. 18, 1879	July 1, 1879	106	Allen G. Thurman of Ohio	Randall
	2	Dec. 1, 1879	June 16, 1880	199	Thurman	
	3	Dec. 6, 1880	Mar. 3, 1881	88	Thurman	
47th	1	Dec. 5, 1881	Aug. 8, 1882	247	Thomas F. Bayard of Delaware	J. Warren Keifer of Ohio
					David Davis of Illinois	
	2	Dec. 4, 1882	Mar. 3, 1883	90	George F. Edmunds of Vermont	
48th	1	Dec. 3, 1883	July 7, 1884	218	Edmunds	John G. Carlisle of Kentucky
	2	Dec. 1, 1884	Mar. 3, 1885	93	Edmunds	
49th	1	Dec. 7, 1885	Aug. 5, 1886	242	John Sherman of Ohio	Carlisle
	2	Dec. 6, 1886	Mar. 3, 1887	88	John J. Ingalls of Kansas	
50th	1	Dec. 5, 1887	Oct. 20, 1888	321	Ingalls	Carlisle
	2	Dec. 3, 1888	Mar. 3, 1889	91	Ingalls	
51st	1	Dec. 2, 1889	Oct. 1, 1890	304	Ingalls	Thomas B. Reed of Maine
	2	Dec. 1, 1890	Mar. 3, 1891	93	Charles F. Manderson of Nebraska	
52nd	1	Dec. 7, 1891	Aug. 5, 1892	251	Manderson	Charles F. Crisp of Georgia
	2	Dec. 5, 1892	Mar. 3, 1893	89	Isham G. Harris of Tennessee	

Footnotes, p. 180-A

Congress	Session	Date of beginning[1]	Date of adjournment[2]	Length in days	President pro tempore of the Senate[3]	Speaker of the House of Representatives
53rd	1	Aug. 7, 1893	Nov. 3, 1893	89	Harris	Crisp
	2	Dec. 4, 1893	Aug. 28, 1894	268	Harris	
	3	Dec. 3, 1894	Mar. 3, 1895	97	Matt W. Ransom of North Carolina Isham G. Harris of Tennessee	
54th	1	Dec. 2, 1895	June 11, 1896	193	William P. Frye of Maine	Thomas B. Reed of Maine
	2	Dec. 7, 1896	Mar. 3, 1897	87	Frye	
55th	1	Mar. 15, 1897	July 24, 1897	131	Frye	Reed
	2	Dec. 6, 1897	July 8, 1898	215	Frye	
	3	Dec. 5, 1898	Mar. 3, 1899	89	Frye	
56th	1	Dec. 4, 1899	June 7, 1900	186	Frye	David B. Henderson of Iowa
	2	Dec. 3, 1900	Mar. 3, 1901	91	Frye	
57th	1	Dec. 2, 1901	July 1, 1902	212	Frye	Henderson
	2	Dec. 1, 1902	Mar. 3, 1903	93	Frye	
58th	1	Nov. 9, 1903	Dec. 7, 1903	29	Frye	Joseph G. Cannon of Illinois
	2	Dec. 7, 1903	Apr. 28, 1904	144	Frye	
	3	Dec. 5, 1904	Mar. 3, 1905	89	Frye	
59th	1	Dec. 4, 1905	June 30, 1906	209	Frye	Cannon
	2	Dec. 3, 1906	Mar. 3, 1907	91	Frye	
60th	1	Dec. 2, 1907	May 30, 1908	181	Frye	Cannon
	2	Dec. 7, 1908	Mar. 3, 1909	87	Frye	
61st	1	Mar. 15, 1909	Aug. 5, 1909	144	Frye	Cannon
	2	Dec. 6, 1909	June 25, 1910	202	Frye	
	3	Dec. 5, 1910	Mar. 3, 1911	89	Frye	
62nd	1	Apr. 4, 1911	Aug. 22, 1911	141	Frye[15]	Champ Clark of Missouri
	2	Dec. 4, 1911	Aug. 26, 1912	267	Augustus O. Bacon of Georgia[16]; Frank B. Brandegee of Connecticut[17]; Charles Curtis of Kansas[18]; Jacob H. Gallinger of New Hampshire[19]; Henry Cabot Lodge of Mass.[20]	
	3	Dec. 2, 1912	Mar. 3, 1913	92	Bacon[21]; Gallinger[22]	
63rd	1	Apr. 7, 1913	Dec. 1, 1913	239	James P. Clarke of Arkansas	Clark
	2	Dec. 1, 1913	Oct. 24, 1914	328	Clarke	
	3	Dec. 7, 1914	Mar. 3, 1915	87	Clarke	
64th	1	Dec. 6, 1915	Sept. 8, 1916	278	Clarke[23]	Clark
	2	Dec. 4, 1916	Mar. 3, 1917	90	Willard Saulsbury of Delaware	
65th	1	Apr. 2, 1917	Oct. 6, 1917	188	Saulsbury	Clark
	2	Dec. 3, 1917	Nov. 21, 1918	354	Saulsbury	
	3	Dec. 2, 1918	Mar. 3, 1919	92	Saulsbury	
66th	1	May 19, 1919	Nov. 19, 1919	185	Albert B. Cummins of Iowa	Frederick H. Gillett of Massachusetts
	2	Dec. 1, 1919	June 5, 1920	188	Cummins	
	3	Dec. 6, 1920	Mar. 3, 1921	88	Cummins	
67th	1	Apr. 11, 1921	Nov. 23, 1921	227	Cummins	Gillett
	2	Dec. 5, 1921	Sept. 22, 1922	292	Cummins	
	3	Nov. 20, 1922	Dec. 4, 1922	15	Cummins	
	4	Dec. 4, 1922	Mar. 3, 1923	90	Cummins	
68th	1	Dec. 3, 1923	June 7, 1924	188	Cummins	Gillett
	2	Dec. 1, 1924	Mar. 3, 1925	93	Cummins	

Footnotes, p. 180-A

Congress	Session	Date of beginning[1]	Date of adjournment[2]	Length in days	President pro tempore of the Senate[3]	Speaker of the House of Representatives
69th	1	Dec. 7, 1925	July 3, 1926	209	George H. Moses of New Hampshire	Nicholas Longworth of Ohio
	2	Dec. 6, 1926	Mar. 3, 1927	88	Moses	
70th	1	Dec. 5, 1927	May 29, 1928	177	Moses	Longworth
	2	Dec. 3, 1928	Mar. 3, 1929	91	Moses	
71st	1	Apr. 15, 1929	Nov. 22, 1929	222	Moses	Longworth
	2	Dec. 2, 1929	July 3, 1930	214	Moses	
	3	Dec. 1, 1930	Mar. 3, 1931	93	Moses	
72nd	1	Dec. 7, 1931	July 16, 1932	223	Moses	John N. Garner of Texas
	2	Dec. 5, 1932	Mar. 3, 1933	89	Moses	
73rd	1	Mar. 9, 1933	June 15, 1933	99	Key Pittman of Nevada	Henry T. Rainey of Illinois[24]
	2	Jan. 3, 1934	June 18, 1934	167	Pittman	
74th	1	Jan. 3, 1935	Aug. 26, 1935	236	Pittman	Joseph W. Byrns of Tennessee[25]
	2	Jan. 3, 1936	June 20, 1936	170	Pittman	William B. Bankhead of Alabama[26]
75th	1	Jan. 5, 1937	Aug. 21, 1937	229	Pittman	Bankhead
	2	Nov. 15, 1937	Dec. 21, 1937	37	Pittman	
	3	Jan. 3, 1938	June 16, 1938	165	Pittman	
76th	1	Jan. 3, 1939	Aug. 5, 1939	215	Pittman	Bankhead[27]
	2	Sept. 21, 1939	Nov. 3, 1939	44	Pittman	
	3	Jan. 3, 1940	Jan. 3, 1941	366	Pittman[28] William H. King of Utah[30]	Sam Rayburn of Texas[29]
77th	1	Jan. 3, 1941	Jan. 2, 1942	365	Pat Harrison of Mississippi[31]; Carter Glass of Virginia[32]	Rayburn
	2	Jan. 5, 1942	Dec. 16, 1942	346	Carter Glass of Virginia	
78th	1	Jan. 6, 1943[33]	Dec. 21, 1943	350	Glass	Rayburn
	2	Jan. 10, 1944[34]	Dec. 19, 1944	345	Glass	
79th	1	Jan. 3, 1945[35]	Dec. 21, 1945	353	Kenneth McKellar of Tennessee	Rayburn
	2	Jan. 14, 1946[36]	Aug. 2, 1946	201	McKellar	
80th	1	Jan. 3, 1947[37]	Dec. 19, 1947	351	Arthur H. Vandenberg of Michigan	Joseph W. Martin Jr. of Massachusetts
	2	Jan. 6, 1948[38]	Dec. 31, 1948	361	Vandenberg	
81st	1	Jan. 3, 1949	Oct. 19, 1949	290	Kenneth McKellar of Tennessee	Sam Rayburn of Texas
	2	Jan. 3, 1950[39]	Jan. 2, 1951	365	McKellar	
82nd	1	Jan. 3, 1951[40]	Oct. 20, 1951	291	McKellar	Rayburn
	2	Jan. 8, 1952[41]	July 7, 1952	182	McKellar	
83rd	1	Jan. 3, 1953[42]	Aug. 3, 1953	213	Styles Bridges of New Hampshire	Joseph W. Martin Jr. of Massachusetts
	2	Jan. 6, 1954[43]	Dec. 2, 1954	331	Bridges	
84th	1	Jan. 5, 1955[44]	Aug. 2, 1955	210	Walter F. George of Georgia	Sam Rayburn of Texas
	2	Jan. 3, 1956[45]	July 27, 1956	207	George	
85th	1	Jan. 3, 1957[46]	Aug. 30, 1957	239	Carl Hayden of Arizona	Rayburn
	2	Jan. 7, 1958[47]	Aug. 24, 1958	230	Hayden	
86th	1	Jan. 7, 1959[48]	Sept. 15, 1959	252	Hayden	Rayburn
	2	Jan. 6, 1960[49]	Sept. 1, 1960	240	Hayden	
87th	1	Jan. 3, 1961[50]	Sept. 27, 1961	268	Hayden	Rayburn[51]
	2	Jan. 10, 1962[52]	Oct. 13, 1962	277	Hayden	John W. McCormack of Massachusetts[53]

Footnotes, p. 180-A

Congress	Session	Date of beginning[1]	Date of adjournment[2]	Length in days	President pro tempore of the Senate[3]	Speaker of the House of Representatives
88th	1	Jan. 9, 1963[54]	Dec. 30, 1963	356	Hayden	McCormack
	2	Jan. 7, 1964[55]	Oct. 3, 1964	270	Hayden	
89th	1	Jan. 4, 1965	Oct. 23, 1965	293	Hayden	McCormack
	2	Jan. 10, 1966[56]	Oct. 22, 1966	286	Hayden	
90th	1	Jan. 10, 1967[57]	Dec. 15, 1967	340	Hayden	McCormack
	2	Jan. 15, 1968[58]	Oct. 14, 1968	274	Hayden	
91st	1	Jan. 3, 1969[59]	Dec. 23, 1969	355	Richard B. Russell of Georgia	McCormack
	2	Jan. 19, 1970[60]	Jan. 2, 1971	349	Russell	
92nd	1	Jan. 21, 1971[61]	Dec. 17, 1971	331	Russell[62]; Allen J. Ellender of Louisiana[63]	Carl Albert of Oklahoma
	2	Jan. 18, 1972[64]	Oct. 18, 1972	275	Ellender[65]; James O. Eastland of Mississippi[66]	
93rd	1	Jan. 3, 1973[67]	Dec. 22, 1973	354	Eastland	Albert
	2	Jan. 21, 1974[68]	Dec. 20, 1974	334	Eastland	
94th	1	Jan. 14, 1975[69]	Dec. 19, 1975	340	Eastland	Albert
	2	Jan. 19, 1976			Eastland	Albert

Footnotes, p. 180-A

1. The Constitution (art. I, sec. 4) provided that "The Congress shall assemble at least once in every year...on the first Monday in December, unless they shall by law appoint a different day." Pursuant to a resolution of the Continental Congress, the first session of the First Congress convened March 4, 1789. Up to and including May 20, 1820, 18 acts were passed providing for the meeting of Congress on other days in the year. After 1820 Congress met regularly on the first Monday in December until 1934, when the 20th Amendment to the Constitution became effective changing the meeting date to Jan. 3. [Until then, brief special sessions of the Senate only were held at the beginning of each presidential term to confirm Cabinet and other nominations—and occasionally at other times for other purposes. The Senate last met in special session from March 4 to March 6, 1933.]

The first and second sessions of the First Congress were held in New York City; subsequently, including the first session of the Sixth Congress, Philadelphia was the meeting place; since then, Congress has convened in Washington.

2. Until adoption of the 20th Amendment, the deadline for adjournment of Congress in odd-numbered years was March 3. However, the expiring Congress often extended the "legislative day" of March 3 up to noon of March 4, when the new Congress came officially into being. After ratification of the 20th Amendment, the deadline for adjournment of Congress in odd-numbered years was noon on Jan. 3.

3. Until within recent years the appointment or election of a President pro tempore was held by the Senate to be for the occasion only, so that more than one appears in several sessions and in others none was chosen. Since March 12, 1890, they have served until "the Senate otherwise ordered."

4. Elected to count the vote for President and Vice President, which was done April 6, 1789, a quorum of the Senate then appearing for the first time. John Adams, Vice President, appeared April 21, 1789, and took his seat as president of the Senate.

5. Elected Speaker pro tempore for April 20, 1798, and again for May 28, 1798.

6. Elected Speaker Jan. 19, 1814, to succeed Henry Clay, who resigned Jan. 19, 1814.

7. Elected Speaker Nov. 15, 1820, to succeed Henry Clay, who resigned Oct. 28, 1820.

8. Elected Speaker June 2, 1834, to succeed Andrew Stevenson of Virginia, who resigned.

9. There were recesses in this session from Saturday, Mar. 30, to Wednesday, July 1, and from Saturday, July 20, to Thursday, Nov. 21.

10. There were recesses in this session from Monday, July 27, to Monday, Sept. 21, to Friday, Oct. 16, and to Tuesday, Nov. 10. No business was transacted subsequent to July 27.

11. Elected Speaker Mar. 3, 1869, and served one day.

12. Died Aug. 19, 1876.

13. Appointed Speaker pro tempore Feb. 17, May 12, June 19.

14. Appointed Speaker pro tempore June 4.

15. Resigned as President pro tempore Apr. 27, 1911.

16. Elected to serve Jan. 11-17, Mar. 11-12, Apr. 8, May 10, May 30 to June 1 and 3, June 13 to July 5, Aug. 1-10, and Aug. 27 to Dec. 15, 1912.

17. Elected to serve May 25, 1912.

18. Elected to serve Dec. 4-12, 1911.

19. Elected to serve Feb. 12-14, Apr. 26-27, May 7, July 6-31, Aug. 12-26, 1912.

20. Elected to serve Mar. 25-26, 1912.

21. Elected to serve Aug. 27 to Dec. 15, 1912, Jan. 5-18, and Feb. 2-15, 1913.

22. Elected to serve Dec. 16, 1912, to Jan. 4, 1913, Jan. 19 to Feb. 1, and Feb. 16 to Mar. 3, 1913.

23. Died Oct. 1, 1916.

24. Died Aug. 19, 1934.

25. Died June 4, 1936.

26. Elected June 4, 1936.

27. Died Sept. 15, 1940.

28. Died Nov. 10, 1940.

29. Elected Sept. 16, 1940.

30. Elected Nov. 19, 1940.

31. Elected Jan. 6, 1941; died June 22, 1941.

32. Elected July 10, 1941.

33. There was a recess in this session from Thursday, July 8, Tuesday, Sept. 14.

34. There were recesses in this session from Saturday, Apr. 1, Wednesday, Apr. 12; from Friday, June 23, to Tuesday, Aug. 1; a from Thursday, Sept. 21, to Tuesday, Nov. 14.

35. The House was in recess in this session from Saturday, Ju 21, 1945, to Wednesday, Sept. 5, 1945, and the Senate fr Wednesday, Aug. 1, 1945, to Wednesday, Sept. 5, 1945.

36. The House was in recess in this session from Thursday, A 18, 1946, to Tuesday, Apr. 30, 1946.

37. There was a recess in this session from Sunday, July 27, 194 to Monday, Nov. 17, 1947.

38. There were recesses in this session from Sunday, June 2 1948, to Monday, July 26, 1948, and from Saturday, Aug. 7, 1948, Friday, Dec. 31, 1948.

39. The House was in recess in this session from Thursday, Ap 6, 1950, to Tuesday, Apr. 18, 1950, and both the Senate and t House were in recess from Saturday, Sept. 23, 1950, to Monda Nov. 27, 1950.

40. The House was in recess in this session from Thursday, Ma 22, 1951, to Monday, Apr. 2, 1951, and from Thursday, Aug. 2 1951, to Wednesday, Sept. 12, 1951.

41. The House was in recess in this session from Thursday, Ap 10, 1952, to Tuesday, Apr. 22, 1952.

42. The House was in recess in this session from Thursday, Ap 2, 1953, to Monday, Apr. 13, 1953.

43. The House was in recess in this session from Thursday, Ap 15, 1954, to Monday, Apr. 26, 1954, and adjourned sine die Aug. 2(1954. The Senate was in recess in this session from Friday, Aug. 2(1954, to Monday, Nov. 8, 1954; from Thursday, Nov. 18, 1954, t Monday, Nov. 29, 1954, and adjourned sine die December 2, 1954

44. There was a recess in this session from Monday, Apr. 4, 1955 to Wednesday, Apr. 13, 1955.

45. There was a recess in this session from Thursday, Mar. 29 1956, to Monday, Apr. 9, 1956.

46. There was a recess in this session from Thursday, Apr. 18 1957, to Monday, Apr. 29, 1957.

47. There was a recess in this session from Thursday, Apr. 3 1958, to Monday, Apr. 14, 1958.

48. There was a recess in this session from Thursday, Mar. 26, 1959, to Tuesday, Apr. 7, 1959.

49. The Senate was in recess in this session from Thursday, Apr. 14, 1960, to Monday, Apr. 18, 1960; from Friday, May 27, 1960, to Tuesday, May 31, 1960, and from Sunday, July 3, 1960, to Monday, Aug. 8, 1960. The House was in recess in this session from Thursday, Apr. 14, 1960, to Monday, Apr. 18, 1960; from Friday, May 27, 1960, to Tuesday, May 31, 1960, and from Sunday, July 3, 1960, to Monday, Aug. 15, 1960.

50. The House was in recess in this session from Thursday, Mar. 30, 1961, to Monday, Apr. 10, 1961.

51. Died November 16, 1961.

52. The House was in recess in this session from Thursday, Apr. 19, 1962, to Monday, Apr. 30, 1962.

53. Elected Jan. 10, 1962.

54. The House was in recess in this session from Thursday, Apr. 11, 1963, to Monday, Apr. 22, 1963.

55. The House was in recess in this session from Thursday, Mar. 26, 1964, to Monday, Apr. 6, 1964; from Thursday, July 2, 1964, to Monday, July 20, 1964; from Friday, Aug. 21, 1964, to Monday, Aug. 31, 1964. The Senate was in recess in this session from Friday, July 10, 1964, to Monday, July 20, 1964; from Friday, Aug. 21, 1964, to Monday, Aug. 31, 1964.

56. The House was in recess in this session from Thursday, Apr. 7, 1966, to Monday, Apr. 18, 1966; from Thursday, June 30, 1966, to Monday, July 11, 1966. The Senate was in recess in this session from Thursday, Apr. 7, 1966, to Wednesday, Apr. 13, 1966; from Thursday, June 30, 1966, to Monday, July 11, 1966.

57. There was a recess in this session from Thursday, Mar. 23, 1967, to Monday, Apr. 3, 1967; from Thursday, June 29, 1967, to Monday, July 10, 1967; from Thursday, Aug. 31, 1967, to Monday,

ot. 11, 1967; and from Wednesday, Nov. 22, 1967, to Monday, v. 27, 1967.

58. The House was in recess this session from Thursday, Apr. 11, 58, to Monday, Apr. 22, 1968; from Wednesday, May 29, 1968, to onday, June 3, 1968; from Wednesday, July 3, 1968, to Monday, ly 8, 1968; from Friday Aug. 2, 1968, to Wednesday, Sept. 4, 1968. ie Senate was in recess this session from Thursday, Apr. 11, 1968, Wednesday, Apr. 17, 1968; from Wednesday, May 29, 1968, to onday, June 3, 1968; from Wednesday, July 3, 1968, to Monday, ly 8, 1968; from Friday, Aug. 2, 1968, to Wednesday, Sept. 4, 58.

59. The House was in recess this session from Friday, Feb. 7, 69, to Monday, Feb. 17, 1969; from Thursday, Apr. 3, 1969, to onday, Apr. 14, 1969; from Wednesday, May 28, 1969, to Monday, June 2, 1969; from Wednesday, July 2, 1969, to Monday, July 1969; from Wednesday, Aug. 13, 1969, to Wednesday, Sept. 3, 69; from Thursday, Nov. 6, 1969, to Wednesday, Nov. 12, 1969; om Wednesday, Nov. 26, 1969 to Monday, Dec. 1, 1969. The nate was in recess this session from Friday, Feb. 7, 1969, to Mon- ay, Feb. 17, 1969; from Thursday, Apr. 3, 1969, to Monday Apr. 4, 1969; from Wednesday, July 2, 1969 to Monday, July 7, 1969; om Wednesday, Aug. 13, 1969, to Wednesday, Sept. 3, 1969; from ednesday, Nov. 26, 1969, to Monday, Dec. 1, 1969.

60. The House was in recess this session from Tuesday, Feb. 10, 70, to Monday, Feb. 16, 1970; from Thursday, Mar. 26, 1970, to uesday, Mar. 31, 1970; from Wednesday, May 27, 1970, to Mon- ay, June 1, 1970; from Wednesday, July 1, 1970, to Monday, July 1970; from Friday, Aug. 14, 1970, to Wednesday, Sept. 9, 1970; om Wednesday Oct. 14, 1970, to Monday, Nov. 16, 1970; from ednesday, Nov. 25, 1970, to Monday, Nov. 30, 1970; from uesday, Dec. 22, 1970, to Tuesday, Dec. 29, 1970. The Senate was recess this session from Tuesday, Feb. 10, 1970, to Monday, Feb. 6, 1970; from Thursday, Mar. 26, 1970, to Tuesday, Mar. 31, 1970; om Wednesday, Sept. 2, 1970, to Tuesday, Sept. 8, 1970; from ednesday, Oct. 14, 1970, to Monday, Nov. 16, 1970; from ednesday, Nov. 25, 1970, to Monday, Nov. 30, 1970; from uesday, Dec. 22, 1970, to Monday, Dec. 28, 1970.

61. The House was in recess this session from Wednesday, Feb. 0, 1971, to Wednesday, Feb. 17, 1971; from Wednesday, Apr. 7, 971, to Monday, Apr. 19, 1971; from Thursday, May 27, 1971, to uesday, June 1, 1971; from Thursday, July 1, 1971, to Tuesday, uly 6, 1971; from Friday Aug. 6, 1971, to Wednesday, Sept. 8, 1971; from Thursday, Oct. 7, 1971, to Tuesday, Oct. 12, 1971; from Thurs- day, Oct. 21, 1971, to Tuesday, Oct. 26, 1971; from Friday, Nov. 9, 1971, to Monday, Nov. 29, 1971. The Senate was in recess this ession from Thursday, Feb. 11, 1971, to Wednesday, Feb. 17, 1971; from Wednesday, Apr. 7, 1971, to Wednesday, Apr. 14, 1971; from Wednesday, May 26, 1971, to Tuesday, June 1, 1971; from Wednesday, June 30, 1971, to Tuesday, July 6, 1971; from Friday, Aug. 6, 1971, to Wednesday, Sept. 8, 1971; from Thursday, Oct. 21, 1971, to Tuesday, Oct. 26, 1971; from Wednesday, Nov. 24, 1971, to Monday, Nov. 29, 1971.

62. Died Jan. 21, 1971.

63. Elected Jan. 22, 1971.

64. The House was in recess this session from Wednesday, Feb. 9, 1972, to Wednesday, Feb. 16, 1972; from Wednesday, Mar. 29, 1972, to Monday, Apr. 10, 1972; from Wednesday, May 24, 1972, to **Tuesday, May 30, 1972; from Friday, June 30, 1972, to Monday,** July 17, 1972; from Friday, Aug. 18, 1972, to Tuesday, Sept. 5, 1972. The Senate was in recess this session from Wednesday, Feb. 9, 1972, to Monday, Feb. 14, 1972; from Thursday, Mar. 30, 1972, to Tuesday, Apr. 4, 1972; from Thursday, May 25, 1972, to Tuesday, May 30, 1972; from Friday, June 30, 1972, to Monday, July 17, 1972; from Friday, Aug. 18, 1972, to Tuesday, Sept. 5, 1972.

65. Died July 27, 1972.

66. Elected July 28, 1972.

67. The House was in recess this session from Thursday, Feb. 8, 1973, to Monday, Feb. 19, 1973; from Thursday, Apr. 19, 1973, to Monday, Apr. 30, 1973; from Thursday, May 24, 1973 to Tuesday, May 29, 1973; from Saturday, June 30, 1973, to Tuesday, July 10, 1973; from Friday, Aug. 3, 1973, to Wednesday, Sept. 5, 1973; from Thursday, Oct. 4, 1973, to Tuesday, Oct. 9, 1973; from Thursday, Oct. 18, 1973, to Tuesday, Oct. 23, 1973; from Thursday, Nov. 15, 1973 to Monday, Nov. 26, 1973. The Senate was in recess this ses- sion from Thursday, Feb. 8, 1973, to Thursday, Feb. 15, 1973; from Wednesday, Apr. 18, 1973, to Monday, Apr. 30, 1973; from Wednesday, May 23, 1973, to Tuesday, May 29, 1973; from Satur- day, June 30, 1973, to Monday, July 9, 1973; from Friday, Aug. 3, 1973 to Wednesday, Sept. 5, 1973; from Thursday, Oct. 18, 1973, to Tuesday, Oct. 23, 1973; from Wednesday, Nov. 21, 1973, to Mon- day, Nov. 26, 1973.

68. The House was in recess this session from Thursday, Feb. 7, 1974, to Wednesday, Feb. 13, 1974; from Thursday, Apr. 11, 1974, to Monday, Apr. 22, 1974; from Thursday, May 23, 1974, to Tuesday, May 28, 1974; from Thursday, Aug. 22, 1974, to Wednesday, Sept. 11, 1974; from Thursday Oct. 17, 1974, to Monday, Nov. 18, 1974; from Tuesday, Nov. 26, 1974, to Tuesday, Dec. 3, 1974. The Senate was in recess this session from Friday, Feb. 8, 1974, to Monday, Feb. 18, 1974; from Wednesday, Mar. 13, 1974, to Tuesday, Mar. 19, 1974; from Thursday, Apr. 11, 1974, to Monday, Apr. 22, 1974; from Wednesday, May 23, 1974, to Tuesday, May 28, 1974; from **Thursday, Aug. 22, 1974, to Wednesday, Sept. 4, 1974; from Thurs-** day, Oct. 17, 1974, to Monday, Nov. 18, 1974; from Tuesday Nov. 26, 1974, to Monday, Dec. 2, 1974.

69. The House was in recess this session from Wednesday, Mar. 26, 1975, to Monday, Apr. 7, 1975; from Thursday, May 22, 1975, to Monday, June 2, 1975; from Thursday, June 26, 1975, to Tuesday, July 8, 1975; from Friday, Aug. 1, 1975, to Wednesday, Sept. 3, 1975; from Thursday, Oct. 9, 1975, to Monday, Oct. 20, 1975; from Thursday, Oct. 23, 1975, to Tuesday, Oct. 28, 1975; from Thursday, Nov. 20, 1975, to Monday, Dec. 1, 1975. The Senate was in recess this session from Wednesday, Mar. 26, 1975, to Monday, Apr. 7, 1975; from Thursday, May 22, 1975, to Monday, June 2, 1975; from Friday, June 27, 1975, to Monday, July 7, 1975; from Friday, Aug. 1, 1975, to Wednesday, Sept. 3, 1975; from Thursday, Oct. 9, 1975, to Monday, Oct. 20, 1975; from Thursday, Oct. 23, 1975, to Tuesday, Oct. 28, 1975; from Thursday, Nov. 20, 1975, to Monday, Dec. 1, 1975.

Political Party Affiliations in Congress ..

(Letter symbols for political parties: Ad—Administration; AM—Anti-Masonic; C—Coalition; D—Democratic; DR—Democratic-Republican; F—Federalist; J—Jacksonian; NR—National Republican; Op—Opposition; R—Republican; U—Unionist; W—Whig. Figures are for the beginning of the first session of each Congress.)

Year	Congress	HOUSE Majority party	HOUSE Principal minority party	HOUSE Other (except vacancies)	SENATE Majority party	SENATE Principal minority party	SENATE Other (except vacancies)	President
1975-1977	94th	D-291	R-144	-	D-60	R-37	2	R (Ford)
1973-1975	93rd	D-239	R-192	1	D-56	R-42	2	R (Nixon-Ford)
1971-1973	92nd	D-254	R-180	-	D-54	R-44	2	R (Nixon)
1969-1971	91st	D-243	R-192	-	D-57	R-43	-	R (Nixon)
1967-1969	90th	D-247	R-187	-	D-64	R-36	-	D (L. Johnson)
1965-1967	89th	D-295	R-140	-	D-68	R-32	-	D (L. Johnson)
1963-1965	88th	D-258	R-177	-	D-67	R-33	-	D (L. Johnson) D (Kennedy)
1961-1963	87th	D-263	R-174	-	D-65	R-35	-	D (Kennedy)
1959-1961	86th	D-283	R-153	-	D-64	R-34	-	R (Eisenhower)
1957-1959	85th	D-233	R-200	-	D-49	R-47	-	R (Eisenhower)
1955-1957	84th	D-232	R-203	-	D-48	R-47	1	R (Eisenhower)
1953-1955	83rd	R-221	D-211	1	R-48	D-47	1	R (Eisenhower)
1951-1953	82nd	D-234	R-199	1	D-49	R-47	-	D (Truman)
1949-1951	81st	D-263	R-171	1	D-54	R-42	-	D (Truman)
1947-1949	80th	R-245	D-188	1	R-51	D-45	-	D (Truman)
1945-1947	79th	D-242	R-190	2	D-56	R-38	1	D (Truman)
1943-1945	78th	D-218	R-208	4	D-58	R-37	1	D (F. Roosevelt)
1941-1943	77th	D-268	R-162	5	D-66	R-28	2	D (F. Roosevelt)
1939-1941	76th	D-261	R-164	4	D-69	R-23	4	D (F. Roosevelt)
1937-1939	75th	D-331	R-89	13	D-76	R-16	4	D (F. Roosevelt)
1935-1937	74th	D-319	R-103	10	D-69	R-25	2	D (F. Roosevelt)
1933-1935	73rd	D-310	R-117	5	D-60	R-35	1	D (F. Roosevelt)
1931-1933	72nd	D-220	R-214	1	R-48	D-47	1	R (Hoover)
1929-1931	71st	R-267	D-167	1	R-56	D-39	1	R (Hoover)
1927-1929	70th	R-237	D-195	3	R-49	D-46	1	R (Coolidge)
1925-1927	69th	R-247	D-183	4	R-56	D-39	1	R (Coolidge)
1923-1925	68th	R-225	D-205	5	R-51	D-43	2	R (Coolidge)
1921-1923	67th	R-301	D-131	1	R-59	D-37	-	R (Harding)
1919-1921	66th	R-240	D-190	3	R-49	D-47	-	D (Wilson)
1917-1919	65th	D-216	R-210	6	D-53	R-42	-	D (Wilson)
1915-1917	64th	D-230	R-196	9	D-56	R-40	-	D (Wilson)
1913-1915	63rd	D-291	R-127	17	D-51	R-44	1	D (Wilson)
1911-1913	62nd	D-228	R-161	1	R-51	D-41	-	R (Taft)
1909-1911	61st	R-219	D-172	-	R-61	D-32	-	R (Taft)
1907-1909	60th	R-222	D-164	-	R-61	D-31	-	R (T. Roosevelt)
1905-1907	59th	R-250	D-136	-	R-57	D-33	-	R (T. Roosevelt)
1903-1905	58th	R-208	D-178	-	R-57	D-33	-	R (T. Roosevelt)
1901-1903	57th	R-197	D-151	9	R-55	D-31	4	R (T. Roosevelt) R (McKinley)
1899-1901	56th	R-185	D-163	9	R-53	D-26	8	R (McKinley)
1897-1899	55th	R-204	D-113	40	R-47	D-34	7	R (McKinley)
1895-1897	54th	R-244	D-105	7	R-43	D-39	6	D (Cleveland)
1893-1895	53rd	D-218	R-127	11	D-44	R-38	3	D (Cleveland)
1891-1893	52nd	D-235	R-88	9	R-47	D-39	2	R (B. Harrison)
1889-1891	51st	R-166	D-159	-	R-39	D-37	-	R (B. Harrison)
1887-1889	50th	D-169	R-152	4	R-39	D-37	-	D (Cleveland)
1885-1887	49th	D-183	R-140	2	R-43	D-34	-	D (Cleveland)
1883-1885	48th	D-197	R-118	10	R-38	D-36	2	R (Arthur)
1881-1883	47th	R-147	D-135	11	R-37	D-37	1	R (Arthur) R (Garfield)
1879-1881	46th	D-149	R-130	14	D-42	R-33	1	R (Hayes)

.. and the Presidency: 1789 to 1975

(Letter symbols for political parties: Ad—Administration; AM—Anti-Masonic; C—Coalition; D—Democratic; DR—Democratic-Republican; F—Federalist; J—Jacksonian; NR—National Republican; Op—Opposition; R—Republican; U—Unionist; W—Whig. Figures are for the beginning of the first session of each Congress.)

Year	Congress	HOUSE Majority party	HOUSE Principal minority party	HOUSE Other (except vacancies)	SENATE Majority party	SENATE Principal minority party	SENATE Other (except vacancies)	President
1877-1879	45th	D-153	R-140	-	R-39	D-36	1	R (Hayes)
1875-1877	44th	D-169	R-109	14	R-45	D-29	2	R (Grant)
1873-1875	43rd	R-194	D-92	14	R-49	D-19	5	R (Grant)
1871-1873	42nd	R-134	D-104	5	R-52	D-17	5	R (Grant)
1869-1871	41st	R-149	D-63	-	R-56	D-11	-	R (Grant)
1867-1869	40th	R-143	D-49	-	R-42	D-11	-	R (A. Johnson)
1865-1867	39th	U-149	D-42	-	U-42	D-10	-	R (A. Johnson) R (Lincoln)
1863-1865	38th	R-102	D-75	9	R-36	D-9	5	R (Lincoln)
1861-1863	37th	R-105	D-43	30	R-31	D-10	8	R (Lincoln)
1859-1861	36th	R-114	D-92	31	D-36	R-26	4	D (Buchanan)
1857-1859	35th	D-118	R-92	26	D-36	R-20	8	D (Buchanan)
1855-1857	34th	R-108	D-83	43	D-40	R-15	5	D (Pierce)
1853-1855	33rd	D-159	W-71	4	D-38	W-22	2	D (Pierce)
1851-1853	32nd	D-140	W-88	5	D-35	W-24	3	W (Fillmore)
1849-1851	31st	D-112	W-109	9	D-35	W-25	2	W (Fillmore) W (Taylor)
1847-1849	30th	W-115	D-108	4	D-36	W-21	1	D (Polk)
1845-1847	29th	D-143	W-77	6	D-31	W-25	-	D (Polk)
1843-1845	28th	D-142	W-79	1	W-28	D-25	1	W (Tyler)
1841-1843	27th	W-133	D-102	6	W-28	D-22	2	W (Tyler) W (W. Harrison)
1839-1841	26th	D-124	W-118	-	D-28	W-22	-	D (Van Buren)
1837-1839	25th	D-108	W-107	24	D-30	W-18	4	D (Van Buren)
1835-1837	24th	D-145	W-98	-	D-27	W-25	-	D (Jackson)
1833-1835	23rd	D-147	AM-53	60	D-20	NR-20	8	D (Jackson)
1831-1833	22nd	D-141	NR-58	14	D-25	NR-21	2	D (Jackson)
1829-1831	21st	D-139	NR-74	-	D-26	NR-22	-	D (Jackson)
1827-1829	20th	J-119	Ad-94	-	J-28	Ad-20	-	C (John Q. Adams)
1825-1827	19th	Ad-105	J-97	-	Ad-26	J-20	-	C (John Q. Adams)
1823-1825	18th	DR-187	F-26	-	DR-44	F-4	-	DR (Monroe)
1821-1823	17th	DR-158	F-25	-	DR-44	F-4	-	DR (Monroe)
1819-1821	16th	DR-156	F-27	-	DR-35	F-7	-	DR (Monroe)
1817-1819	15th	DR-141	F-42	-	DR-34	F-10	-	DR (Monroe)
1815-1817	14th	DR-117	F-65	-	DR-25	F-11	-	DR (Madison)
1813-1815	13th	DR-112	F-68	-	DR-27	F-9	-	DR (Madison)
1811-1813	12th	DR-108	F-36	-	DR-30	F-6	-	DR (Madison)
1809-1811	11th	DR-94	F-48	-	DR-28	F-6	-	DR (Madison)
1807-1809	10th	DR-118	F-24	-	DR-28	F-6	-	DR (Jefferson)
1805-1807	9th	DR-116	F-25	-	DR-27	F-7	-	DR (Jefferson)
1803-1805	8th	DR-102	F-39	-	DR-25	F-9	-	DR (Jefferson)
1801-1803	7th	DR-69	F-36	-	DR-18	F-13	-	DR (Jefferson)
1799-1801	6th	F-64	DR-42	-	F-19	DR-13	-	F (John Adams)
1797-1799	5th	F-58	DR-48	-	F-20	DR-12	-	F (John Adams)
1795-1797	4th	F-54	DR-52	-	F-19	DR-13	-	F (Washington)
1793-1795	3rd	DR-57	F-48	-	F-17	DR-13	-	F (Washington)
1791-1793	2nd	F-37	DR-33	-	F-16	DR-13	-	F (Washington)
1789-1791	1st	Ad-38	Op-26	-	Ad-17	Op-9	-	F (Washington)

Sources: *Historical Statistics of the United States, Colonial Times to 1957,* Bureau of the Census; *Statistical Abstract of the United States, 1975,* Bureau of the Census.

Leaders of the House and Senate

(For Presidents pro tempore of the Senate and Speakers of the House, see p. 173-A)

	Senate Floor Leaders		Senate Whips	
Congress	**Majority**	**Minority**	**Majority**	**Minority**
62nd (1911-1913)	Shelby M. Cullom (R Ill.)	Thomas S. Martin (D Va.)	None	None
63rd (1913-1915)	John W. Kern (D Ind.)	Jacob H. Gallinger (R N.H.)	J. Hamilton Lewis (D Ill.)	None
64th (1915-1917)	Kern	Gallinger	Lewis	James W. Wadsworth Jr. (R N.Y.)/Charles Curtis (R Kan.)[8]
65th (1917-1919)	Thomas S. Martin (D Va.)	Gallinger/Henry Cabot Lodge (R Mass.)[1]	Lewis	Curtis
66th (1919-1921)	Henry Cabot Lodge (R Mass.)	Martin/Oscar W. Underwood (D Ala.)[2]	Charles Curtis (R Kan.)	Peter G. Gerry (D R.I.)
67th (1921-1923)	Lodge	Underwood	Curtis	Gerry
68th (1923-1925)	Lodge/Charles Curtis (R Kan.)[3]	Joseph T. Robinson (D Ark.)	Curtis/Wesley L. Jones (R Wash.)[9]	Gerry
69th (1925-1927)	Curtis	Robinson	Jones	Gerry
70th (1927-1929)	Curtis	Robinson	Jones	Gerry
71st (1929-1931)	James E. Watson (R Ind.)	Robinson	Simeon D. Fess (R Ohio)	Morris Sheppard (D Texas)
72nd (1931-1933)	Watson	Robinson	Fess	Sheppard
73rd (1933-1935)	Joseph T. Robinson (D Ark.)	Charles L. McNary (R Ore.)	Lewis	Felix Hebert (R R.I.)
74th (1935-1937)	Robinson	McNary	Lewis	None
75th (1937-1939)	Robinson/Alben W. Barkley (D Ky.)[4]	McNary	Lewis	None
76th (1939-1941)	Barkley	McNary	Sherman Minton (D Ind.)	None
77th (1941-1943)	Barkley	McNary	Lister Hill (D Ala.)	None
78th (1943-1945)	Barkley	McNary	Hill	Kenneth Wherry (R Neb.)
79th (1945-1947)	Barkley	Wallace H. White Jr. (R Maine)	Hill	Wherry
80th (1947-1949)	Wallace H. White Jr. (R Maine)	Alben W. Barkley (D Ky.)	Kenneth Wherry (R Neb.)	Scott Lucas (D Ill.)
81st (1949-1951)	Scott W. Lucas (D Ill.)	Kenneth S. Wherry (R Neb.)	Francis Myers (D Pa.)	Leverett Saltonstall (R Mass.)
82nd (1951-1953)	Ernest W. McFarland (D Ariz.)	Wherry/Styles Bridges (R N.H.)[5]	Lyndon B. Johnson (D Texas)	Saltonstall
83rd (1953-1955)	Robert A. Taft (R Ohio)/William F. Knowland (R Calif.)[6]	Lyndon B. Johnson (D Texas)	Leverett Saltonstall (R Mass.)	Earle Clements (D Ky.)
84th (1955-1957)	Lyndon B. Johnson (D Texas)	William F. Knowland (R Calif.)	Earle Clements (D Ky.)	Saltonstall
85th (1957-1959)	Johnson	Knowland	Mike Mansfield (D Mont.)	Everett McKinley Dirksen (R Ill.)
86th (1959-1961)	Johnson	Everett McKinley Dirksen (R Ill.)	Mansfield	Thomas H. Kuchel (R Calif.)
87th (1961-1963)	Mike Mansfield (D Mont.)	Dirksen	Hubert H. Humphrey (D Minn.)	Kuchel
88th (1963-1965)	Mansfield	Dirksen	Humphrey	Kuchel
89th (1965-1967)	Mansfield	Dirksen	Russell Long (D La.)	Kuchel
90th (1967-1969)	Mansfield	Dirksen	Long	Kuchel
91st (1969-1971)	Mansfield	Dirksen/Hugh Scott (R Pa.)[7]	Edward M. Kennedy (D Mass.)	Hugh Scott (R Pa.)/Robert P. Griffin (R Mich.)[10]
92nd (1971-1973)	Mansfield	Scott	Robert C. Byrd (D W.Va.)	Griffin
93rd (1973-1975)	Mansfield	Scott	Byrd	Griffin
94th (1975-1977)	Mansfield	Scott	Byrd	Griffin

Senate Footnotes

1. Lodge became minority leader on Aug. 24, 1918, filling the vacancy caused by the death of Gallinger on Aug. 17, 1918.

2. Underwood became minority leader on April 27, 1920, filling the vacancy caused by the death of Martin on Nov. 12, 1919. Gilbert M. Hitchcock (D Neb.) served as acting minority leader in the interim.

3. Curtis became majority leader on Nov. 28, 1924, filling the vacancy caused by the death of Lodge on Nov. 9, 1924.

4. Barkley became majority leader on July 22, 1937, filling the vacancy caused by the death of Robinson on July 14, 1937.

5. Bridges became minority leader on Jan. 8, 1952, filling the vacancy caused by the death of Wherry on Nov. 29, 1951.

6. Knowland became majority leader on Aug. 4, 1953, filling the vacancy caused by the death of Taft on July 31, 1953. Taft's vacant seat was filled by a Democrat, Thomas Burke, on Nov. 10, 1953. The division of the Senate changed to 48 Democrats, 47 Republicans and 1 Independent, thus giving control of the Senate to the Democrats. However, Knowland remained as majority leader until the end of the 83rd Congress.

7. Scott became minority leader on Sept. 24, 1969, filling the vacancy caused by the death of Dirksen on Sept. 7, 1969.

8. Wadsworth served as minority whip for only one week, from Dec. 6 to Dec. 13, 1915.

9. Jones became majority whip filling the vacancy caused by the elevation of Curtis to the post of majority leader. *(Footnote 3)*

10. Griffin became minority whip on Sept. 24, 1969, filling the vacancy caused by the elevation of Scott to the post of minority leader. *(See footnote 7)*

House Floor Leaders

House Whips

Congress	Majority	Minority	Majority	Minority
56th (1899-1901)	Sereno E. Payne (R N.Y.)	James D. Richardson (D Tenn.)	James A. Tawney (R Minn.)	Oscar W. Underwood (D Ala.)[6]
57th (1901-1903)	Payne	Richardson	Tawney	James T. Lloyd (D Mo.)
58th (1903-1905)	Payne	John Sharp Williams (D Miss.)	Tawney	Lloyd
59th (1905-1907)	Payne	Williams	James E. Watson (R Ind.)	Lloyd
60th (1907-1909)	Payne	Williams/Champ Clark (D Mo.)[1]	Watson	Lloyd[7]
61st (1909-1911)	Payne	Clark	John W. Dwight (R N.Y.)	None
62nd (1911-1913)	Oscar W. Underwood (D Ala.)	James R. Mann (R Ill.)	None	John W. Dwight (R N.Y.)
63rd (1913-1915)	Underwood	Mann	Thomas M. Bell (D Ga.)	Charles H. Burke (R S.D.)
64th (1915-1917)	Claude Kitchin (D N.C.)	Mann	None	Charles M. Hamilton (R N.Y.)
65th (1917-1919)	Kitchin	Mann	None	Hamilton
66th (1919-1921)	Franklin W. Mondell (R Wyo.)	Clark	Harold Knutson (R Minn.)	None
67th (1921-1923)	Mondell	Claude Kitchin (D N.C.)	Knutson	William A. Oldfield (D Ark.)
68th (1923-1925)	Nicholas Longworth (R Ohio)	Finis J. Garrett (D Tenn.)	Albert H. Vestal (R Ind.)	Oldfield
69th (1925-1927)	John Q. Tilson (R Conn.)	Garrett	Vestal	Oldfield
70th (1927-1929)	Tilson	Garrett	Vestal	Oldfield/John McDuffie (D Ala.)[8]
71st (1929-1931)	Tilson	John N. Garner (D Texas)	Vestal	McDuffie
72nd (1931-1933)	Henry T. Rainey (D Ill.)	Bertrand H. Snell (R N.Y.)	John McDuffie (D Ala.)	Carl G. Bachmann (R W.Va.)
73rd (1933-1935)	Joseph W. Byrns (D Tenn.)	Snell	Arthur H. Greenwood (D Ind.)	Harry L. Englebright (R Calif.)
74th (1935-1937)	William B. Bankhead (D Ala.)[2]	Snell	Patrick J. Boland (D Pa.)	Englebright
75th (1937-1939)	Sam Rayburn (D Texas)	Snell	Boland	Englebright
76th (1939-1941)	Rayburn/John W. McCormack (D Mass.)[3]	Joseph W. Martin Jr. (R Mass.)	Boland	Englebright
77th (1941-1943)	McCormack	Martin	Boland/Robert Ramspeck (D Ga.)[9]	Englebright
78th (1943-1945)	McCormack	Martin	Ramspeck	Leslie C. Arends (R Ill.)
79th (1945-1947)	McCormack	Martin	Ramspeck/John J. Sparkman (D Ala.)[10]	Arends
80th (1947-1949)	Charles A. Halleck (R Ind.)	Sam Rayburn (D Texas)	Leslie C. Arends (R Ill.)	John W. McCormack (D Mass.)
81st (1949-1951)	McCormack	Martin	J. Percy Priest (D Tenn.)	Arends
82nd (1951-1953)	McCormack	Martin	Priest	Arends
83rd (1953-1955)	Halleck	Rayburn	Arends	McCormack
84th (1955-1957)	McCormack	Martin	Carl Albert (D Okla.)	Arends
85th (1957-1959)	McCormack	Martin	Albert	Arends
86th (1959-1961)	McCormack	Charles A. Halleck (R Ind.)	Albert	Arends
87th (1961-1963)	McCormack/Carl Albert (D Okla.)[4]	Halleck	Albert/Hale Boggs (D La.)[11]	Arends
88th (1963-1965)	Albert	Halleck	Boggs	Arends
89th (1965-1967)	Albert	Gerald R. Ford (R Mich.)	Boggs	Arends
90th (1967-1969)	Albert	Ford	Boggs	Arends
91st (1969-1971)	Albert	Ford	Boggs	Arends
92nd (1971-1973)	Hale Boggs (D La.)	Ford	Thomas P. O'Neill Jr. (D Mass.)	Arends
93rd (1973-1975)	Thomas P. O'Neill Jr. (D Mass.)	Ford/John J. Rhodes (R Ariz.)[5]	John J. McFall (D Calif.)	Arends
94th (1975-1977)	O'Neill	Rhodes	McFall	Robert H. Michel (R Ill.)

House Footnotes

1. Clark became minority leader in 1908.
2. Bankhead became Speaker of the House on June 4, 1936. The post of majority leader remained vacant until the next Congress.
3. McCormack became majority leader on Sept. 26, 1940, filling the vacancy caused by the elevation of Rayburn to the post of Speaker of the House on Sept. 16, 1940.
4. Albert became majority leader on Jan. 10, 1962, filling the vacancy caused by the elevation of McCormack to the post of Speaker of the House on Jan. 10, 1962.
5. Rhodes became minority leader on Dec. 7, 1973 filling the vacancy caused by the resignation of Ford on Dec. 6, 1973 to become Vice President.
6. Underwood did not become minority whip until 1901.

7. Lloyd resigned to become chairman of the Democratic Congressional Campaign Committee in 1908. The post of minority whip remained vacant until the beginning of the 62nd Congress.
8. John McDuffie became minority whip after the death of William Oldfield on Nov. 19, 1928.
9. Ramspeck became majority whip on June 8, 1942, filling the vacancy caused by the death of Boland on May 18, 1942.
10. Sparkman became majority whip on Jan. 14, 1946, filling the vacancy caused by the resignation of Ramspeck on Dec. 31, 1945.
11. Boggs became majority whip on Jan. 10, 1962, filling the vacancy caused by the elevation of Albert to the post of majority leader on Jan. 10, 1962.

Sources: U.S. Congress, Senate, *Majority and Minority Leaders of the Senate,* by Floyd M. Riddick, Senate Doc. 94-66, 94th Cong., 1st sess. (Government Printing Office, 1975). Walter J. Oleszek, "Party Whips in the United States Senate," *The Journal of Politics,* Vol. 33 (November 1971): pp. 955-79. Randall B. Ripley, *Party Leaders in the House of Representatives,* The Brookings Institution, 1967. U.S. Congress, Joint Committee on Printing, *Official Congressional Directory 1967-__* (Government Printing Office) and *Biographical Directory of the American Congress, 1774-1971,* compiled by Lawrence F. Kennedy, Senate Doc. 92-8, 92nd Cong., 1st sess. (Government Printing Office, 1971).

Chairmen of Senate, House, Joint Committees, 1947-76

Sources: Congressional Staff Directory, 1959-1976; Congressional Quarterly Almanac, 1947-1975; Official Congressional Directory, 1947-1976.

Following are the names and dates of terms of chairmen of standing committees of Congress from 1947 to 1976. Certain subcommittees and special committees are included because of their past importance or interest. The evolution of some committees also is indicated, such as the first one listed, the Senate Aeronautical and Space Sciences Committee, which originally was the Special Committee on Space and Astronautics.

Senate

Space and Astronautics, Special Committee on
Lyndon B. Johnson (D Texas-1957-1958)
Aeronautical and Space Sciences (renamed)
Lyndon B. Johnson (D Texas-1958-1961)
Robert S. Kerr (D Okla.-1961-1963)
Clinton P. Anderson (D N.M.-1963-1973)
Frank E. Moss (D Utah-1973-)

Agriculture and Forestry
Arthur Capper (R Kan.-1947-1949)
Elmer Thomas (D Okla.-1949-1951)
Allen J. Ellender (D La.-1951-1953)
George D. Aiken (R Vt.-1953-1955)
Allen J. Ellender (D La.-1955-1971)
Herman E. Talmadge (D Ga.-1971-)

Appropriations
Styles Bridges (R N.H.-1947-1949)
Kenneth McKellar (D Tenn.-1949-1953)
Styles Bridges (R N.H.-1953-1955)
Carl Hayden (D Ariz.-1955-1969)
Richard B. Russell (D Ga.-1969-1971)
Allen J. Ellender (D La.-1971-1972)
John L. McClellan (D Ark.-1972-)

Armed Services
Chan Gurney (R S.D.-1947-1949)
Millard E. Tydings (D Md.-1949-1951)
Richard B. Russell (D Ga.-1951-1953)
Leverett Saltonstall (R Mass.-1953-1955)
Richard B. Russell (D Ga.-1955-1969)
John C. Stennis (D Miss.-1969-)
Preparedness Investigating Subcommittee
Lyndon B. Johnson (D Texas-1950-1953)
[Seven special subcommittees were appointed by committee chairman Leverett Saltonstall (R Mass.) to investigate specific problems, 1953-1955.]
Lyndon B. Johnson (D Texas-1955-1961)
John C. Stennis (D Miss.-1961-)

Banking and Currency
Charles W. Tobey (R N.H.-1947-1949)
Burnet R. Maybank (D S.C.-1949-1953)
Homer E. Capehart (R Ind.-1953-1955)
J. W. Fulbright (D Ark.-1955-1959)
A. Willis Robertson (D Va.-1959-1967)
John J. Sparkman (D Ala.-1967-1970)
Banking, Housing and Urban Affairs (renamed)
John J. Sparkman (D Ala.-1971-1975)
William Proxmire (D Wis.-1975-)

Budget
Edmund S. Muskie (D Maine-1975-)

Interstate and Foreign Commerce
Wallace H. White (R Maine-1947-1949)
Edwin C. Johnson (D Colo.-1949-1953)
Charles W. Tobey (R N.H.-1953)
John W. Bricker (R Ohio-1953-1955)
Warren G. Magnuson (D Wash.-1955-1961)
Commerce (renamed)
Warren G. Magnuson (D Wash.-1962-)

District of Columbia
C. Douglass Buck (R Del.-1947-1949)
J. Howard McGrath (D R.I.-1949-1950)
Matthew M. Neely (D W.Va.-1950-1953)
Francis Case (R S.D.-1953-1955)
Matthew M. Neely (D W.Va.-1955-1959)
Alan Bible (D Nev.-1959-1969)
Joseph D. Tydings (D Md.-1969-1971)
Thomas F. Eagleton (D Mo.-1971-)

Finance
Eugene D. Millikin (R Colo.-1947-1949) .
Walter F. George (D Ga.-1949-1953)
Eugene D. Millikin (R Colo.-1953-1955)
Harry Flood Byrd (D Va.-1955-1965)
Russell B. Long (D La.-1965-)

Foreign Relations
Arthur H. Vandenberg (R Mich.-1947-1949)
Tom Connally (D Texas-1949-1953)
Alexander Wiley (R Wis.-1953-1955)
Walter F. George (D Ga.-1955-1957)
Theodore Francis Green (D R.I.-1957-1959)
J. W. Fulbright (D Ark.-1959-1975)
John J. Sparkman (D Ala.-1975-)

Expenditures in the Executive Departments
George D. Aiken (R Vt.-1947-1949)
John L. McClellan (D Ark.-1949-1952)
Government Operations (renamed)
John L. McClellan (D Ark.-1952-1953)
Joseph R. McCarthy (R Wis.- 1953-1955)
John L. McClellan (D Ark.-1955-1972)
Sam J. Ervin Jr. (D N.C.-1972-1974)
Abraham A. Ribicoff (D Conn.-1975-)
Permanent Investigations Subcommittee
Homer Ferguson (R Mich.-1948-1949)
Clyde R. Hoey (D N.C.-1949-1953)
Joseph R. McCarthy (R Wis.-1953-1955)
John L. McClellan (D Ark.-1955-1973)
Henry M. Jackson (D Wash.-1973-)

Interior and Insular Affairs
Hugh Butler (R Neb.-1947-1949)
Joseph C. O'Mahoney (D Wyo.-1949-1953)
Hugh Butler (R Neb.-1953-1954)
Guy Cordon (R Ore.-1954-1955)
James E. Murray (D Mont.-1955-1961)
Clinton P. Anderson (D N.M.-1961-1963)
Henry M. Jackson (D Wash.-1963-)

Judiciary
Alexander Wiley (R Wis.-1947-1949)
Pat McCarran (D Nev.-1949-1953)
William Langer (R N.D.-1953-1955)
Harley M. Kilgore (D W.Va.-1955-1956)

James O. Eastland (D Miss.-1956-)
Antitrust and Monopoly Subcommittee
Herbert R. O'Conor (D Md.-1951-1953)
William Langer (R N.D.-1953-1955)
Joseph C. O'Mahoney (D Wyo.-1955-1957)
Estes Kefauver (D Tenn.-1957-1963)
Philip A. Hart (D Mich.-1963-)
Internal Security Subcommittee
Pat McCarran (D Nev.-1950-1953)
William E. Jenner (R Ind.-1953-1955)
James O. Eastland (D Miss.-1955-)

Labor and Public Welfare
Robert A. Taft (R Ohio-1947-1949)
Elbert D. Thomas (D Utah-1949-1951)
James E. Murray (D Mont.-1951-1953)
H. Alexander Smith (R N.J.-1953-1955)
Lister Hill (D Ala.-1955-1969)
Ralph W. Yarborough (D Texas-1969-1971)
Harrison A. Williams Jr. (D N.J.-1971-)

Post Office and Civil Service
William Langer (R N.D.-1947-1949)
Olin D. Johnston (D S.C.-1949-1953)
Frank Carlson (R Kan.-1953-1955)
Olin D. Johnston (D S.C.-1955-1965)
A. S. Mike Monroney (D Okla.-1965-1969)
Gale W. McGee (D Wyo.-1969-)

Public Works
Chapman Revercomb (R W.Va.-1947-1949)
Dennis Chavez (D N.M.-1949-1953)
Edward Martin (R Pa.-1953-1955)
Dennis Chavez (D N.M.-1955-1962)
Pat McNamara (D Mich.-1963-1966)
Jennings Randolph (D W.Va.-1966-)

Rules and Administration
C. Wayland Brooks (R Ill.-1947-1949)
Carl Hayden (D Ariz.-1949-1953)
William E. Jenner (R Ind.-1953-1955)
Theodore Francis Green (D R.I.-1955-1957)
Thomas C. Hennings (D Mo.-1957-1960)
Mike Mansfield (D Mont.-1961-1963)
B. Everett Jordan (D N.C.-1963-1972)
Howard W. Cannon (D Nev.-1973-)

Veterans' Affairs
Vance Hartke (D Ind.-1971-)

Committees, Select Committee on
Adlai E. Stevenson III (D Ill. 1976-)

Defense Program, Select Committee to Investigate the National
Owen Brewster (R Maine-1947-1948)

Equal Educational Opportunity, Select Committee on
Walter F. Mondale (D Minn.-1970-1972)

Intelligence Activities, Select Committee to Study Governmental Operations With Respect to
Frank Church (D Idaho-1975-1976)

Intelligence Activities, Select Committee on
Daniel K. Inouye (D Hawaii 1976-)

Nutrition and Human Needs, Select Committee on
George McGovern (D S.D.-1969-)

Presidential Campaign Activities, Select Committee on
Sam J. Ervin Jr. (D N.C.-1973-1974)

Small Business, Special Committee to Study Problems of American
Kenneth S. Wherry (R Neb.-1947-1949)
Small Business, Select Committee on
John J. Sparkman (D Ala.-1950-1953)
Edward J. Thye (R Minn.-1953-1955)
John J. Sparkman (D Ala.-1955-1967)
George A. Smathers (D Fla.-1967-1969)
Alan Bible (D Nev.-1969-1975)
Gaylord Nelson (D Wis.-1975-)

Standards and Conduct, Select Committee on
John Stennis (D Miss.-1966-1975)
Howard W. Cannon (D Nev.-1975-)

Aged and Aging of Senate Labor and Public Welfare, Subcommittee on the
Lister Hill (D Ala.-1959-1960)
Aging, Special Committee on
Pat McNamara (D Mich.-1960-1963)
George A. Smathers (D Fla.-1963-1967)
Harrison A. Williams Jr. (D N.J.-1967-1971)
Frank Church (D Idaho-1971-)

National Emergency, Special Committee on the Termination of the
Frank Church (D Idaho) and Charles McC. Mathias Jr. (R Md.) (1973-1975)
National Emergencies and Delegated Emergency Powers, Special Committee on
Frank Church (D Idaho) and Charles McC. Mathias Jr. (R Md.) (1975-)

Democratic Policy and Steering Committees
Alben W. Barkley (D Ky.-1947-1949)
Scott W. Lucas (D Ill.-1949-1951)
Ernest W. McFarland (D Ariz.-1951-1953)
Lyndon B. Johnson (D Texas-1953-1961)
Mike Mansfield (D Mont.-1961-)

Democratic Senatorial Campaign Committee
Scott W. Lucas (D Ill.-1947-1949)
Clinton P. Anderson (D N.M.-1949-1951)
Earle C. Clements (D Ky.-1951-1955)
George A. Smathers (D Fla.- 1955-1961)
Vance Hartke (D Ind.-1961-1963)
Warren G. Magnuson (D Wash.-1963-1967)
Edmund S. Muskie (D Maine-1967-1969
Daniel K. Inouye (D Hawaii-1969-1971)
Ernest F. Hollings (D S.C.-1971-1973)
Lloyd Bentsen (D Texas-1973-1975)
J. Bennett Johnston Jr. (D La.-1975-)

Republican Policy Committee
Robert A. Taft (R Ohio-1947-1953)
William F. Knowland (R Calif.-1953)
Homer Ferguson (R Mich.-1953-1955)
Styles Bridges (R N.H.-1955-1961)
Bourke B. Hickenlooper (R Iowa-1962-1969)
Gordon Allott (R Colo.-1969-1972)
John G. Tower (R Texas-1973-)

Republican Senatorial Campaign Committee
John G. Townsend (Former Republican senator from Delaware, 1929-1941, Campaign Committee chairman, 1947-1949)
Owen Brewster (R Maine-1949-1951)
Everett McKinley Dirksen (R Ill.-1951-1955)
Barry Goldwater (R Ariz.-1955-1956)
Andrew F. Schoeppel (R Kan.-1956-1959)
Barry Goldwater (R Ariz.-1959-1963)
Thruston B. Morton (R Ky.-1963-1967)
George Murphy (R Calif.-1967-1969)
John G. Tower (R Texas-1969-1971)
Peter H. Dominick (R Colo.-1971-1973)
William E. Brock (R Tenn.-1973-1975)
Ted Stevens (R Alaska-1975-)

Republican Committee on Committees
Edward V. Robertson (R Wyo.-1947-1949)
Hugh A. Butler (R Neb.-1949-1954)
John W. Bricker (R Ohio-1954-1959)
Andrew F. Schoeppel (R Kan.-1959-1962)
Frank Carlson (R Kan.-1962-1969)
John J. Williams (R Del.-1969-1970)
Wallace F. Bennett (R Utah-1971-)
Jacob K. Javits (R N.Y.-1973-)

House

Agriculture
Clifford R. Hope (R Kan.-1947-1949)
Harold D. Cooley (D N.C.-1949-1953)
Clifford R. Hope (R Kan.-1953-1955)
Harold D. Cooley (D N.C.-1955-1967)
W. R. Poage (D Texas-1967-1975)
Thomas S. Foley (D Wash.-1975-)

Appropriations
John Taber (R N.Y.-1947-1949)
Clarence Cannon (D Mo.-1949-1953)
John Taber (R N.Y.-1953-1955)
Clarence Cannon (D Mo.-1955-1964)
George H. Mahon (D Texas-1964-)

Armed Services
Walter G. Andrews (R N.Y.-1947-1949)
Carl Vinson (D Ga.-1949-1953)
Dewey Short (R Mo.-1953-1955)
Carl Vinson (D Ga.-1955-1965)
L. Mendel Rivers (D S.C.-1965-1971)
F. Edward Hebert (D La.-1971-1975)
Melvin Price (D Ill.-1975-)
Special Investigations Subcommittee
F. Edward Hebert (D La.-1951-1953)
William E. Hess (R Ohio-1953-1955)
F. Edward Hebert (D La.-1955-1963)
Porter Hardy (D Va.-1963-1969)
Armed Services Investigations (renamed)
L. Mendel Rivers (D S.C.-1969-1971)
F. Edward Hebert (D La.-1971-)

Banking and Currency
Jesse P. Wolcott (R Mich.-1947-1949)
Brent Spence (D Ky.-1949-1953)
Jesse P. Wolcott (R Mich.-1953-1955)
Brent Spence (D Ky.-1955-1963)
Wright Patman (D Texas-1963-1975)
Banking, Currency and Housing (renamed)
Henry S. Reuss (D Wis.-1975-)

Budget
Brock Adams (D Wash.-1975-)

District of Columbia
Everett M. Dirksen (R Ill.-1947-1949)
John L. McMillan (D S.C.-1949-1953)
Sid Simpson (R Ill.-1953-1955)
John L. McMillan (D S.C.-1955-1973)
Charles C. Diggs Jr. (D Mich.-1973-)

Education and Labor
Fred A. Hartley (R N.J.-1947-1949)
John Lesinski (D Mich.-1949-1950)
Graham A. Barden (D N.C.-1950-1953)
Samuel K. McConnell (R Pa.-1953-1955)
Graham A. Barden (D N.C.-1955-1961)

Adam C. Powell Jr. (D N.Y.-1961-1967)
Carl D. Perkins (D Ky.-1967-)

Foreign Affairs
Charles A. Eaton (R N.J.-1947-1949)
John Kee (D W.Va.-1949-1951)
James P. Richards (D S.C.-1951-1953)
Robert B. Chiperfield (R Ill.-1953-1955)
James P. Richards (D S.C.-1955-1957)
Thomas S. Gordon (D Ill.-1957-1959)
Thomas E. Morgan (D Pa.-1959-1974)
International Relations (renamed)
Thomas E. Morgan (D Pa.-1975-)

Expenditures in the Executive Departments
Clare E. Hoffman (R Mich.-1947-1949)
William L. Dawson (D Ill.-1949-1952)
Government Operations (renamed)
William L. Dawson (D Ill.-1952-1953)
Clare E. Hoffman (R Mich.-1953-1955)
William L. Dawson (D Ill.-1955-1971)
Chet Holifield (D Calif.-1971-1975)
Jack Brooks (D Texas-1975-)

House Administration
Karl M. LeCompte (R Iowa-1947-1949)
Mary T. Norton (D N.J.-1949-1951)
Thomas B. Stanley (D Va.-1951-1953)
Karl M. LeCompte (R Iowa-1953-1955)
Omar Burleson (D Texas-1955-1968)
Samuel N. Friedel (D Md.-1968-1971)
Wayne L. Hays (D Ohio-1971-1976)
Frank Thompson Jr. (D N.J.-1976-)

Interstate and Foreign Commerce
Charles A. Wolverton (R N.J.-1947-1949)
Robert Crosser (D Ohio-1949-1953)
Charles A. Wolverton (R N.J.-1953-1955)
J. Percy Priest (D Tenn.-1955-1957)
Oren Harris (D Ark.-1957-1966)
Harley O. Staggers (D W.Va.-1966-)
Special Subcommittee on Legislative Oversight, 1957-1961
Morgan M. Moulder (D Mo.-1957-1958)
Oren Harris (D Ark.-1958-1961)
Special Subcommittee on Regulatory Agencies
Oren Harris (D Ark.-1961-1963)
Special Subcommittee on Investigations
Oren Harris (D Ark.-1963-1966)
Harley O. Staggers (D W.Va.-1966-1975)
Subcommittee on Oversight and Investigations (renamed)
John E. Moss (D Calif.-1975-)

Judiciary
Earl C. Michener (R Mich.-1947-1949)
Emanuel Celler (D N.Y.-1949-1953)
Chauncey W. Reed (R Ill.-1953-1955)
Emanuel Celler (D N.Y.-1955-1973)
Peter W. Rodino Jr. (D N.J.-1973-)

Merchant Marine and Fisheries
Fred Bradley (R Mich.-1947)
Alvin F. Weichel (R Ohio-1947-1949)
Schuyler Otis Bland (D Va.-1949-1950)
Edward J. Hart (D N.J.-1950-1953)
Alvin F. Weichel (R Ohio-1953-1955)
Herbert C. Bonner (D N.C.-1955-1966)
Edward A. Garmatz (D Md.-1966-1973)
Leonor K. Sullivan (D Mo.-1973-)

Public Lands
Richard J. Welch (R Calif.-1947-1949)
Andrew L. Somers (D N.Y.-1949)

J. Hardin Peterson (D Fla.-1949-1950)

Interior and Insular Affairs (renamed)
John R. Murdock (D Ariz.-1951-1953)
A. L. Miller (R Neb.-1953-1955)
Clair Engle (D Calif.-1955-1959)
Wayne N. Aspinall (D Colo.-1959-1973)
James A. Haley (D Fla.-1973-)

Post Office and Civil Service
Edward H. Rees (R Kan.-1947-1949)
Tom Murray (D Tenn.-1949-1953)
Edward H. Rees (R Kan.-1953-1955)
Tom Murray (D Tenn.-1955-1967)
Thaddeus J. Dulski (D N.Y.-1967-1975)
David N. Henderson (D N.C.-1975-)

Public Works
George A. Dondero (R Mich.-1947-1949)
William M. Whittington (D Miss.-1949-1951)
Charles A. Buckley (D N.Y.-1951-1953)
George A. Dondero (R Mich.-1953-1955)
Charles A. Buckley (D N.Y.-1955-1965)
George H. Fallon (D Md.-1965-1971)
John A. Blatnik (D Minn.-1971-1973)
Public Works and Transportation (renamed)
John A. Blatnik (D Minn.-1974-1975)
Robert E. Jones (D Ala.-1975-)

Rules
Leo E. Allen (R Ill.-1947-1949)
Adolph J. Sabath (D Ill.-1949-1953)
Leo E. Allen (R Ill.-1953-1955)
Howard W. Smith (D Va.-1955-1967)
William M. Colmer (D Miss.-1967-)

Astronautics and Space Exploration 1958, Select Committee
John W. McCormack (D Mass.-1958)
Science and Astronautics
Overton Brooks (D La.-1959-1961)
George P. Miller (D Calif.-1961-1973)
Olin E. Teague (D Texas-1973-)

Small Business, Select Committee to Conduct a Study and Investigation of the Problems of
Walter C. Ploeser (R Mo.-1947-1949)
Wright Patman (D Texas-1949-1953)
William S. Hill (R Colo.-1953-1955)
Wright Patman (D Texas-1955-1963)
Joe L. Evins (D Tenn.-1963-1966)
Small Business, Select Committee on
Joe L. Evins (D Tenn.-1967-1974)
Small Business
Joe L. Evins (D Tenn.-1975-)

Standards of Official Conduct
Melvin Price (D Ill.-1969-1975)
John J. Flynt Jr. (D Ga.-1975-)

Un-American Activities
J. Parnell Thomas (R N.J.-1947-1949)
John S. Wood (D Ga.-1949-1953)
Harold H. Velde (R Ill.-1953-1955)
Francis E. Walter (D Pa.-1955-1963)
Edwin E. Willis (D La.-1963-1969)
Internal Security (renamed)
Richard H. Ichord (D Mo.-1969-1974)

Veterans' Affairs
Edith Nourse Rogers (R Mass.-1947-1949)
John E. Rankin (D Miss.-1949-1953)
Edith Nourse Rogers (R Mass.-1953-1955)
Olin E. Teague (D Texas-1955-1973)
William Jennings Bryan Dorn (D S.C.-1973-1975)
Ray Roberts (D Texas-1975-)

Ways and Means
Harold Knutson (R Minn.-1947-1949)
Robert L. Doughton (D N.C.-1949-1953)
Daniel A. Reed (R N.Y.-1953-1955)
Jere Cooper (D Tenn.-1955-1957)
Wilbur D. Mills (D Ark.-1958-1975)
Al Ullman (D Ore.-1975-)

Committees of the House, Select Committee on
Richard Bolling (D Mo.-1973-1974)

Crime Investigation, Select Committee on
Claude Pepper (D Fla.-1969-1973)

Intelligence, Select Committee on
Lucien N. Nedzi (D Mich.-1975)
Otis G. Pike (D N.Y. 1975-1976)

Democratic Steering and Policy Committee
Carl Albert (D Okla.-1973-)

Democratic National Congressional Committee
Michael J. Kirwan (D Ohio-1947-1971)
Ed Edmondson (D Okla.) and Thomas P. O'Neill Jr. (D Mass.) 1971-1973
Wayne L. Hays (D Ohio-1973-1976)
James C. Corman (D Calif.-1976-)

Republican Policy Committee
Joseph W. Martin (R Mass.-1947-1959)
John W. Byrnes (R Wis.-1959-1965)
John J. Rhodes (R Ariz.-1965-1973)
Barber B. Conable Jr. (R N.Y.-1973-)

National Republican Congressional Committee
Leonard W. Hall (R N.Y.-1947-1953)
Richard M. Simpson (R Pa.-1953-1960)
William E. Miller (R N.Y.-1960-1961)
Bob Wilson (R Calif.-1961-1973)
Robert H. Michel (R Ill.-1973-1975)
Guy Vander Jagt (R Mich.-1975-)

Republican Committee on Committees
Joseph W. Martin (R Mass.-1947-1953)
Charles A. Halleck (R Ind.-1953-1955)
Joseph W. Martin (R Mass.-1955-1959)
Charles A. Halleck (R Ind.-1959-1965)
Gerald R. Ford (R Mich.-1965-1973)
John J. Rhodes (R Ariz.-1973-)

Joint Committees

Atomic Energy
Sen. Bourke B. Hickenlooper (R Iowa-1947-1949)
Sen. Brien McMahon (D Conn.-1949-1952)
Rep. W. Sterling Cole (R N.Y.-1953-1955)
Sen. Clinton P. Anderson (D N.M.-1955-1957)
Rep. Carl T. Durham (D N.C.-1957-1959)
Sen. Clinton P. Anderson (D N.M.-1959-1961)
Rep. Chet Holifield (D Calif.-1961-1963)
Sen. John O. Pastore (D R.I.-1963-1965)
Rep. Chet Holifield (D Calif.-1965-1967)
Sen. John O. Pastore (D R.I.-1967-1969)
Rep. Chet Holifield (D Calif.-1969-1971)
Sen. John O. Pastore (D R.I.-1971-1973)
Rep. Melvin Price (D Ill.-1973-1975)
Sen. John O. Pastore (D R.I.-1975-)

Congressional Operations
Rep. Jack Brooks (D Texas-1971-1973)
Sen. Lee Metcalf (D Mont.-1973-1975)
Rep. Jack Brooks (D Texas-1975-)

Defense Production
Sen. Burnet R. Maybank (D S.C.-1950-1953)
Sen. Homer E. Capehart (R Ind.-1953-1955)
Rep. Paul Brown (D Ga.-1955-1957)
Sen. A. Willis Robertson (D Va.-1957-1959)
Rep. Paul Brown (D Ga.-1959-1961)
Sen. A. Willis Robertson (D Va.-1961-1963)
Rep. Wright Patman (D Texas-1963-1965)
Sen. A. Willis Robertson (D Va.-1965-1967)
Rep. Wright Patman (D Texas-1967-1969)
Sen. John J. Sparkman (D Ala.-1969-1971)
Rep. Wright Patman (D Texas-1971-1973)
Sen. John J. Sparkman (D Ala.-1973-1975)
Rep. Wright Patman (D Texas-1975-)

Economic
Sen. Robert A. Taft (R Ohio-1947-1949)
Sen. Joseph C. O'Mahoney (D Wyo.-1949-1953)
Rep. Jesse P. Wolcott (R Mich.-1953-1955)
Sen. Paul H. Douglas (D Ill.-1955-1957)
Rep. Wright Patman (D Texas-1957-1959)
Sen. Paul H. Douglas (D Ill.-1959-1961)
Rep. Wright Patman (D Texas-1961-1963)
Sen. Paul H. Douglas (D Ill.-1963-1965)
Rep. Wright Patman (D Texas-1965-1967)
Sen. William Proxmire (D Wis.-1967-1969)
Rep. Wright Patman (D Texas-1969-1971)
Sen. William Proxmire (D Wis.-1971-1973)
Rep. Wright Patman (D Texas-1973-1975)
Sen. Hubert H. Humphrey (D Minn.-1975-)

Internal Revenue Taxation
Rep. Harold Knutson (R Minn.-1947-1948)
Sen. Eugene D. Millikin (R Colo.-1948-1949)
Rep. Robert L. Doughton (D N.C.-1949-1950)
Sen. Walter F. George (D Ga.-1950-1951)
Rep. Robert L. Doughton (D N.C.-1951-1952)
Sen. Walter F. George (D Ga.-1952-1953)
Rep. Daniel A. Reed (R N.Y.-1953-1954)
Sen. Eugene D. Millikin (R Colo.-1954-1955)
Rep. Jere Cooper (D Tenn.-1955-1956)
Sen. Harry Flood Byrd (D Va.-1956-1957)
Rep. Jere Cooper (D Tenn.-1957-1958)
Sen. Harry Flood Byrd (D Va.-1958-1959)

Rep. Wilbur D. Mills (D Ark.-1959-1960)
Sen. Harry Flood Byrd (D Va.-1960-1961)
Rep. Wilbur D. Mills (D Ark.-1961-1962)
Sen. Harry Flood Byrd (D Va.-1962-1963)
Rep. Wilbur D. Mills (D Ark.-1963-1964)
Sen. Harry Flood Byrd (D Va.-1964-1965)
Rep. Wilbur D. Mills (D Ark.-1965-1966)
Sen. Russell B. Long (D La.-1966-1967)
Rep. Wilbur D. Mills (D Ark.-1967-1968)
Sen. Russell B. Long (D La.-1968-1969)
Rep. Wilbur D. Mills (D Ark.-1969-1970)
Sen. Russell B. Long (D La.-1970-1971)
Rep. Wilbur D. Mills (D Ark.-1971-1972)
Sen. Russell B. Long (D La.-1972-1973)
Rep. Wilbur D. Mills (D Ark.-1973-1974)
Sen. Russell B. Long (D La.-1974-1975)
Rep. Al Ullman (D Ore.-1975-1976)
Sen. Russell B. Long (D La.-1976-)

Library
Rep. Samuel N. Friedel (D Md.-1969-1970)
Sen. B. Everett Jordan (D N.C.-1970-1971)
Rep. Wayne L. Hays (D Ohio-1971-1972)
Sen. B. Everett Jordan (D N.C.-1972-1973)
Rep. Lucien N. Nedzi (D Mich.-1973-1974)
Sen. Howard W. Cannon (D Nev.-1974-1975)
Rep. Lucien N. Nedzi (D Mich.-1975-1976)
Sen. Howard W. Cannon (D Nev.-1976-)

Printing
Sen. B. Everett Jordan (D N.C.-1969-1970)
Rep. Samuel N. Friedel (D Md.-1970-1971)
Sen. B. Everett Jordan (D N.C.-1971-1972)
Rep. Wayne L. Hays (D Ohio-1972-1973)
Sen. Howard W. Cannon (D Nev.-1973-1974)
Rep. Wayne L. Hays (D Ohio-1974-1975)
Sen. Howard W. Cannon (D Nev.-1975-1976)
Rep. Wayne L. Hays (D Ohio-1976-)

Reduction of Nonessential Federal Expenditures
Sen. Harry Flood Byrd (D Va.-1947-1965)
Rep. George H. Mahon (D Texas-1965-1968)
Reduction of Federal Expenditures (renamed)
Rep. George H. Mahon (D Texas-1969-1975)

Standing Rules of the Senate, 94th Congress

Sources: U.S. Congress, Senate, Committee on Rules and Administration, *Senate Manual*, Senate Doc. 94-1, 94th Congress, 1st sess. (Government Printing Office, 1975). Committee on Rules and Administration staff.

Rules adopted Jan. 11, 1884, effective Jan. 21, 1884. Includes amendments through Nov. 5, 1975. (Footnotes and citations to the *Senate Journal* have been deleted.)

RULE I

Appointment of a Senator to the Chair

1. In the absence of the Vice President, the Senate shall choose a President pro tempore.
On Mar. 12, 1890, the Senate agreed to the following:
Resolved, That it is competent for the Senate to elect a President pro tempore, who shall hold the office during the pleasure of the Senate and until another is elected, and shall execute the duties thereof during all future absences of the Vice President until the Senate otherwise order.
2. In the absence of the Vice President, and pending the election of a President pro tempore, the Secretary of the Senate, or in his absence the Assistant Secretary, shall perform the duties of the Chair.
3. The President pro tempore shall have the right to name in open Senate, or, if absent, in writing, a Senator to perform the duties of the Chair; but such substitution shall not extend beyond an adjournment, except by unanimous consent.
4. In event of a vacancy in the office of the Vice President, or whenever the powers and duties of the President shall devolve on the Vice President, the President pro tempore shall have the right to name, in writing, a Senator to perform the duties of the Chair during his absence; and the Senator so named shall have the right to name in open session, or, in writing, if absent, a Senator to perform the duties of the Chair, but such substitution shall not extend beyond adjournment, except by unanimous consent.
On Jan. 4, 1905, the Senate agreed to the following:
Resolved, That whenever a Senator shall be designated by the President pro tempore to perform the duties of the Chair during his temporary absence he shall be empowered to sign, as acting President pro tempore, the enrolled bills and joint resolutions coming from the House of Representatives for presentation to the President of the United States.

RULE II

Oaths, Etc.

The oaths or affirmations required by the Constitution and prescribed by law shall be taken and subscribed by each Senator, in open Senate, before entering upon his duties.

Oath Required by the Constitution and By Law To Be Taken By Senators Under Rule II

I, A B, do solemnly swear (or affirm) that I will support and defend the Constitution of the United States against all enemies, foreign and domestic; that I will bear true faith and allegiance to the same; that I take this obligation freely, without any mental reservation or purpose of evasion, and that I will well and faithfully discharge the duties of the office on which I am about to enter: So help me God.

RULE III

Commencement of Daily Sessions

1. The Presiding Officer having taken the chair, and a quorum being present, the Journal of the preceding day shall be read, and any mistake made in the entries corrected. The reading of the Journal shall not be suspended unless by unanimous consent; and when any motion shall be made to amend or correct the same, it shall be deemed a privileged question, and proceeded with until disposed of.
2. A quorum shall consist of a majority of the Senators duly chosen and sworn.
On Feb. 6, 1939, the Senate agreed to the following:
Resolved, That the Chaplain shall open each calendar day's session of the Senate with prayer.
On Feb. 29, 1960, the Senate agreed to the following:
Resolved, That during the session of the Senate when that body is in continuous session, the Presiding Officer shall temporarily suspend the business of the Senate at noon each day for the purpose of having the customary daily prayer by the Chaplain of the Senate.

RULE IV

Journal

1. The proceedings of the Senate shall be briefly and accurately stated on the Journal. Messages of the President in full; titles of bills and joint resolutions, and such parts as shall be affected by proposed amendments; every vote, and a brief statement of the contents of each petition, memorial, or paper presented to the Senate, shall be entered.
2. The legislative, the executive, the confidential legislative proceedings, and the proceedings when sitting as a Court of Impeachment, shall each be recorded in a separate book.

RULE V

Quorum—Absent Senators May Be Sent For

1. No Senator shall absent himself from the service of the Senate without leave.
2. If, at any time during the daily sessions of the Senate, a question shall be raised by any Senator as to the presence of a quorum, the Presiding Officer shall forthwith direct the Secretary to call the roll and shall announce the result, and these proceedings shall be without debate.
3. Whenever upon such roll call it shall be ascertained that a quorum is not present, a majority of the Senators present may direct the Sergeant at Arms to request, and, when necessary, to compel the attendance of the absent Senators, which order shall be determined without debate; and pending its execution, and until a quorum shall be present, no debate nor motion, except to adjourn, shall be in order.

RULE VI

Presentation of Credentials

1. The presentation of the credentials of Senators elect and other questions of privilege shall always be in order, except during the reading and correction of the Journal, while a question of order or a motion to adjourn is pending, or while the Senate is dividing; and all questions and motions arising or made upon the presentation of such credentials shall be proceeded with until disposed of.
2. The Secretary shall keep a record of the certificates of election of Senators by entering in a well-bound book kept for that purpose the date of the election, the name of the person elected and the vote given at the election, the date of the certificate, the name of the governor and the secretary of state signing and countersigning the same, and the State from which such Senator is elected.
On July 17, 1961, the Senate agreed to the following:
Resolved, That, in the opinion of the Senate, the following are convenient and sufficient forms of the certificates of election of a Senator for a six-year term, or an unexpired term, or for the appointment of a Senator to fill a vacancy, to be signed by the executive of any State in pursuance of the Constitution and the statutes of the United States:

"CERTIFICATE OF ELECTION FOR SIX-YEAR TERM

"To the President of the Senate of the United States:
"This is to certify that on the __ day of __, 19__, A__ B__ was duly chosen by the qualified electors of the State of __ a Senator from said State to represent said State in the Senate of the United States for the term of six years, beginning on the 3d day of January, 19__.
"Witness: His excellency our governor __, and our seal hereto affixed at __ this __ day of __, in the year of our Lord 19__.
"By the governor:

"C____ D____,
"*Governor.*

"E____ F____,
"*Secretary of State.*"

"CERTIFICATE OF ELECTION FOR UNEXPIRED TERM

"To the President of the Senate of the United States:

"This is to certify that on the __ day of __, 19__, A__ B__ was duly chosen by the qualified electors of the State of __ a Senator for the unexpired term ending at noon on the 3d day of January, 19__, to fill the vacancy in the representation from said State in the Senate of the United States caused by the __ of C__ D__.

"Witness: His excellency our governor __, and our seal hereto affixed at __ this __ day of __, in the year of our Lord 19__.

"By the governor:

"E____ F____,
"*Governor.*

"G____ H____,
"*Secretary of State."*

"CERTIFICATE OF APPOINTMENT

"To the President of the Senate of the United States:

"This is to certify that, pursuant to the power vested in me by the Constitution of the United States and the laws of the State of __, I, A__ B__, the governor of said State, do hereby appoint C__ D__ a Senator from said State to represent said State in the Senate of the United States until the vacancy therein, caused by the __ of E__ F__, is filled by election as provided by law.

"Witness: His excellency our governor __, and our seal hereto affixed at __ this __ day of __, in the year of our Lord 19__.

"By the governor:

"G____ H____,
"*Governor*

"I____ J____,
"*Secretary of State."*

Resolved, That the Secretary of the Senate shall send copies of these suggested forms and these resolutions to the executive and secretary of each State wherein an election is about to take place or an appointment is to be made in season that they may use such forms if they see fit.

RULE VII

Morning Business

1. After the Journal is read, the Presiding Officer shall lay before the Senate messages from the President, reports and communications from the heads of Departments, and other communications addressed to the Senate, and such bills, joint resolutions, and other messages from the House of Representatives as may remain upon his table from any previous day's session undisposed of. The Presiding Officer shall then call for, in the following order:

The presentation of petitions and memorials.
Reports of standing and select committees.
The introduction of bills and joint resolutions.
Concurrent and other resolutions

All of which shall be received and disposed of in such order, unless unanimous consent shall be otherwise given.

On Jan. 16, 1908, the Senate agreed to the following:

Resolved, That no communications from heads of departments, commissioners, chiefs of bureaus, or other executive officers, except when authorized or required by law, or when made in response to a resolution of the Senate, will be received by the Senate unless such communications shall be transmitted to the Senate by the President.

On Dec. 17, 1885, the Senate agreed to the following:

Ordered, That until otherwise ordered, the Chair shall proceed with the call for resolutions to be newly offered before laying before the Senate resolutions which came over from a former day.

2. Senators having petitions, memorials, pension bills, or bills for the payment of private claims to present after the morning hour may deliver them to the Secretary of the Senate, endorsing upon them their names and the reference or disposition to be made thereof, and said petitions, memorials, and bills shall, with the approval of the Presiding Officer, be entered on the Journal with the names of the Senators presenting them as having been read twice and referred to the appropriate committees, and the Secretary of the Senate shall furnish a transcript of such entries to the official reporter of debates for publication in the Record.

It shall not be in order to interrupt a Senator having the floor for the purpose of introducing any memorial, petition, report of a committee, resolution, or bill. It shall be the duty of the Chair to enforce this rule without any point of order hereunder being made by a Senator.

3. Until the morning business shall have been concluded, and so announced from the Chair, or until the hour of 1 o'clock has arrived, no motion to proceed to the consideration of any bill, resolution, report of a committee, or other subject upon the Calendar shall be entertained by the Presiding Officer, unless by unanimous consent; and if such consent be given, the motion shall not be subject to amendment, and shall be decided without debate upon the merits of the subject proposed to be taken up: *Provided, however,* Tha[t] on Mondays the Calendar shall be called under Rule VIII, and during th[e] morning hour no motion shall be entertained to proceed to the considerati[on] of any bill, resolution, report of a committee, or other subject upon the Calen[dar] except the motion to continue the consideration of a bill, resolutio[n,] report of a committee, or other subject against objection as provided in Ru[le] VIII.

4. Every petition or memorial shall be referred, without putting th[e] question, unless objection to such reference is made; in which case a[ny] motions for the reception or reference of such petition, memorial, or othe[r] paper shall be put in the order in which the same shall be made, and shall n[ot] be open to amendment, except to add instructions.

5. Every petition or memorial shall be signed by the petitioner [or] memorialist and have indorsed thereon a brief statement of its contents, an[d] shall be presented and referred without debate. But no petition or memoria[l] or other paper signed by citizens or subjects of a foreign power shall b[e] received, unless the same be transmitted to the Senate by the President.

6. Only a brief statement of the contents, as provided for in Rule VI[I,] paragraph five, of such communications as are presented under the order [of] business "Presentation of petitions and memorials" shall be printed in th[e] Congressional Record; and no other portion of such communications shall b[e] inserted in the Record unless specifically so ordered by vote of the Senate, a[s] provided for in Rule XXIX, paragraph one; except that communication[s] from the legislatures or conventions, lawfully called, of the respective States[,] Territories, and insular possessions shall be printed in full in the Recor[d] whenever presented, and the original copies of such communications shall b[e] retained in the files of the Secretary of the Senate.

On Feb. 7, 1887, the Senate agreed to the following:

Ordered, That when petitions and memorials are ordered printed in the Congressional Record the order shall be deemed to apply to the body of the petition only, and the names attached to said petition or memorial shall no[t] be printed unless specially ordered by the Senate.

7. The Presiding Officer may at any time lay, and it shall be in order a[t] any time for a Senator to move to lay, before the Senate, any bill or other matter sent to the Senate by the President or the House of Representatives[,] and any question pending at that time shall be suspended for this purpose. Any motion so made shall be determined without debate.

RULE VIII

Order of Business

1. At the conclusion of the morning business for each day, unless upon motion the Senate shall at any time otherwise order, the Senate will proceed to the consideration of the Calendar of Bills and Resolutions, and continue such consideration until 2 o'clock; and bills and resolutions that are not objected to shall be taken up in their order, and each Senator will be entitled to speak once and for five minutes only upon any question; and the objection may be interposed at any stage of the proceedings, but upon motion the Senate may continue such consideration; and this order shall commence immediately after the call for "concurrent and other resolutions," and shall take precedence of the unfinished business and other special orders. But if the Senate shall proceed with the consideration of any matter notwithstanding an objection, the foregoing provisions touching debate shall not apply.

2. All motions made before 2 o'clock to proceed to the consideration of any matter shall be determined without debate.

3. At the conclusion of the morning hour or after the unfinished business or pending business has first been laid before the Senate on any calendar day, and until after the duration of three hours, except as determined to the contrary by unanimous consent or on motion without debate, all debate shall be germane and confined to the specific question then pending before the Senate.

On August 10, 1888, the Senate agreed to the following:

Resolved, That after to-day, unless otherwise ordered, the morning hour shall terminate at the expiration of two hours after the meeting of the Senate.

RULE IX

Order of Business

Immediately after the consideration of cases not objected to upon the Calendar is completed, and not later than 2 o'clock if there shall be no special orders for that time, the Calendar of General Orders shall be taken up and proceeded with in its order, beginning with the first subject on the Calendar next after the last subject disposed of in proceeding with the Calendar; and in such case the following motions shall be in order at any time as privileged motions, save as against a motion to adjourn, or to proceed to the consideration of executive business, or questions of privilege, to wit:

First. A motion to proceed to the consideration of an appropriation or revenue bill.

Second. A motion to proceed to the consideration of any other bill on the Calendar, which motion shall not be open to amendment.

Third. A motion to pass over the pending subject, which if carried shall have the effect to leave such subject without prejudice in its place on the Calendar.

Fourth. A motion to place such subject at the foot of the Calendar.

Each of the foregoing motions shall be decided without debate and shall have precedence in the order above named, and may be submitted as in the nature and with all the rights of questions of order.

RULE X

Special Orders

1. Any subject may, by a vote of two-thirds of the Senators present, be made a special order; and when the time so fixed for its consideration arrives the Presiding Officer shall lay it before the Senate, unless there be unfinished business of the preceding day, and if it is not finally disposed of on that day it shall take its place on the Calendar of Special Orders in the order of time at which it was made special, unless it shall become by adjournment the unfinished business.

2. When two or more special orders have been made for the same time, they shall have precedence according to the order in which they were severally assigned, and that order shall only be changed by direction of the Senate.

And all motions to change such order, or to proceed to the consideration of other business, shall be decided without debate.

RULE XI

Objection to Reading a Paper

When the reading of a paper is called for, and objected to, it shall be determined by a vote of the Senate, without debate.

RULE XII

Voting, Etc.

1. When the yeas and nays are ordered, the names of Senators shall be called alphabetically; and each Senator shall, without debate, declare his assent or dissent to the question, unless excused by the Senate; and no Senator shall be permitted to vote after the decision shall have been announced by the Presiding Officer, but may for sufficient reasons, with unanimous consent, change or withdraw his vote. No motion to suspend this rule shall be in order, nor shall the Presiding Officer entertain any request to suspend it by unanimous consent.

2. When a Senator declines to vote on call of his name, he shall be required to assign his reasons therefor, and having assigned them, the Presiding Officer shall submit the question to the Senate: "Shall the Senator, for the reasons assigned by him, be excused from voting?" which shall be decided without debate; and these proceedings shall be had after the roll call and before the result is announced; and any further proceedings in reference thereto shall be after such announcement.

3. No request by a Senator for unanimous consent for the taking of a final vote on a specified date upon the passage of a bill or joint resolution shall be submitted to the Senate for agreement thereto until, upon a roll call ordered for the purpose by the Presiding Officer, it shall be disclosed that a quorum of the Senate is present; and when a unanimous consent is thus given the same shall operate as the order of the Senate, but any unanimous consent may be revoked by another unanimous consent granted in the manner prescribed above upon one day's notice.

RULE XIII

Reconsideration

1. When a question has been decided by the Senate, any Senator voting with the prevailing side or who has not voted may, on the same day or on either of the next two days of actual session thereafter, move a reconsideration; and if the Senate shall refuse to reconsider, or upon reconsideration shall affirm its first decision, no further motion to reconsider shall be in order unless by unanimous consent. Every motion to reconsider shall be decided by a majority vote, and may be laid on the table without affecting the question in reference to which the same is made, which shall be a final disposition of the motion.

2. When a bill, resolution, report, amendment, order, or message, upon which a vote has been taken, shall have gone out of the possession of the Senate and been communicated to the House of Representatives, the motion to reconsider shall be accompanied by a motion to request the House to return the same; which last motion shall be acted upon immediately, and without debate, and if determined in the negative shall be a final disposition of the motion to reconsider.

RULE XIV

Bills, Joint Resolutions, and Resolutions

1. Whenever a bill or joint resolution shall be offered, its introduction shall, if objected to, be postponed for one day.

2. Every bill and joint resolution shall receive three readings previous to its passage, which readings shall be on three different days, unless the Senate unanimously direct otherwise; and the Presiding Officer shall give notice at each reading whether it be the first, second, or third: *Provided,* That the first or second reading of each bill may be by title only, unless the Senate in any case shall otherwise order.

3. No bill or joint resolution shall be committed or amended until it shall have been twice read, after which it may be referred to a committee; bills and joint resolutions introduced on leave, and bills and joint resolutions from the House of Representatives, shall be read once, and may be read twice, on the same day, if not objected to, for reference, but shall not be considered on that day nor debated, except for reference, unless by unanimous consent.

4. Every bill and joint resolution reported from a committee, not having previously been read, shall be read once, and twice, if not objected to, on the same day, and placed on the Calendar in the order in which the same may be reported; and every bill and joint resolution introduced on leave, and every bill and joint resolution of the House of Representatives which shall have received a first and second reading without being referred to a committee, shall, if objection be made to further proceeding thereon, be placed on the Calendar.

5. The Secretary of the Senate shall examine all bills, amendments, and joint resolutions before they go out of the possession of the Senate, and shall examine all bills and joint resolutions which shall have passed both Houses, to see that the same are correctly enrolled, and, when signed by the Speaker of the House and the President of the Senate, shall forthwith present the same, when they shall have originated in the Senate, to the President of the United States and report the fact and date of such presentation to the Senate.

6. All resolutions shall lie over one day for consideration, unless by unanimous consent the Senate shall otherwise direct.

RULE XV

Bills

1. When a bill or resolution shall have been ordered to be read a third time, it shall not be in order to propose amendments, unless by unanimous consent, but it shall be in order at any time before the passage of any bill or resolution to move its commitment; and when the bill or resolution shall again be reported from the committee it shall be placed on the Calendar.

2. Whenever a private bill is under consideration, it shall be in order to move, as a substitute for it, a resolution of the Senate referring the case to the Court of Claims, under the provisions of the act approved March 3, 1883.

RULE XVI

Amendments to Appropriation Bills

1. All general appropriation bills shall be referred to the Committee on Appropriations, and no amendments shall be received to any general appropriation bill the effect of which will be to increase an appropriation already contained in the bill, or to add a new item of appropriation, unless it be made to carry out the provisions of some existing law, or treaty stipulation, or act, or resolution previously passed by the Senate during that session; or unless the same be moved by direction of a standing or select committee of the Senate, or proposed in pursuance of an estimate submitted in accordance with law.

2. The Committee on Appropriations shall not report an appropriation bill containing amendments proposing new or general legislation or any restriction on the expenditure of the funds appropriated which proposes a limitation not authorized by law if such restriction is to take effect or cease to be effective upon the happening of a contingency, and if an appropriation bill is reported to the Senate containing amendments proposing new or general legislation or any such restriction, a point of order may be made against the bill, and if the point is sustained, the bill shall be recommitted to the Committee on Appropriations.

3. All amendments to general appropriation bills moved by direction of a standing or select committee of the Senate, proposing to increase an appropriation already contained in the bill, or to add new items of appropriation, shall, at least one day before they are considered, be referred to the Committee on Appropriations, and when actually proposed to the bill no amendment proposing to increase the amount stated in such amendment shall be received; in like manner, amendments proposing new items of appropriation to river and harbor bills, establishing post roads, or proposing

new post roads, shall, before being considered, be referred to the Committee on Public Works.

4. No amendment which proposes general legislation shall be received to any general appropriation bill, nor shall any amendment not germane or relevant to the subject matter contained in the bill be received; nor shall any amendment to any item or clause of such bill be received which does not directly relate thereto; nor shall any restriction on the expenditure of the funds appropriated which proposes a limitation not authorized by law be received if such restriction is to take effect or cease to be effective upon the happening of a contingency; and all questions of relevancy of amendments under this rule, when raised, shall be submitted to the Senate and be decided without debate; and any such amendment or restriction to a general appropriation bill may be laid on the table without prejudice to the bill.

5. No amendment, the object of which is to provide for a private claim, shall be received to any general appropriation bill, unless it be to carry out the provisions of an existing law or a treaty stipulation, which shall be cited on the face of the amendment.

6. (a) Three members of the following-named committees, to be selected by their respective committees, shall be ex officio members of the Committee on Appropriations, to serve on said committee when the annual appropriation bill making appropriations for the purposes specified in the following table opposite the name of the committee is being considered by the Committee on Appropriations:

Name of committee	Purpose of appropriation
Committee on Agriculture and Forestry.	For the Department of Agriculture.
Committee on Post Office and Civil Service.	For the Post Office Department.
Committee on Armed Services.	For the Department of War; for the Department of the Navy.
Committee on the District of Columbia.	For the District of Columbia.
Committee on Public Works.	For Rivers and Harbors.
Committee on Foreign Relations.	For the Diplomatic and Consular Service.
Senate members of the Joint Committee on Atomic Energy (to be selected by said members).	For the development and utilization of atomic energy.
Committee on Aeronautical Space Sciences.	For aeronautical and space activities and matters relating to the scientific aspects thereof, except those peculiar to or primarily associated with the development of weapons systems or military operations.
Committee on Finance.	For the International Trade Commission.

(b) At least one member of each committee enumerated in subparagraph (a), to be selected by his or their respective committees, shall be a member of any conference committee appointed to confer with the House upon the annual appropriation bill making appropriations for the purposes specified in the foregoing table opposite the name of his or their respective committee.

7. When a point of order is made against any restriction on the expenditure of funds appropriated in a general appropriation bill on the ground that the restriction violates this rule, the rule shall be construed strictly and, in case of doubt, in favor of the point of order.

8. Every report on general appropriation bills filed by the Committee on Appropriations shall identify with particularity each recommended amendment which proposes an item of appropriation which is not made to carry out the provisions of an existing law, a treaty stipulation, or an act or resolution previously passed by the Senate during that session.

RULE XVII

Amendment May Be Laid on the Table Without Prejudice to the Bill

When an amendment proposed to any pending measure is laid on the table, it shall not carry with it, or prejudice, such measure.

RULE XVIII

Amendments—Division of a Question

If the question in debate contains several propositions, any Senator may have the same divided, except a motion to strike out and insert, which shall not be divided; but the rejection of a motion to strike out and insert one proposition shall not prevent a motion to strike out and insert a different

proposition; nor shall it prevent a motion simply to strike out; nor shall the rejection of a motion to strike out prevent a motion to strike out and insert. But pending a motion to strike out and insert, the part to be stricken out and the part to be inserted shall each be regarded for the purpose of amendment as a question; and motions to amend the part to be stricken out shall have precedence.

RULE XIX

Debate

1. When a Senator desires to speak, he shall rise and address the Presiding Officer, and shall not proceed until he is recognized, and the Presiding Officer shall recognize the Senator who shall first address him. No Senator shall interrupt another Senator in debate without his consent, and to obtain such consent he shall first address the Presiding Officer, and no Senator shall speak more than twice upon any one question in debate on the same day without leave of the Senate, which shall be determined without debate.

2. No Senator in debate shall, directly or indirectly, by any form of words impute to another Senator or to other Senators any conduct or motive unworthy or unbecoming a Senator.

3. No Senator in debate shall refer offensively to any State of the Union.

4. If any Senator, in speaking or otherwise, in the opinion of the Presiding Officer transgress the rules of the Senate the Presiding Officer shall, either on his own motion or at the request of any other Senator, call him to order; and when a Senator shall be called to order he shall take his seat, and may not proceed without leave of the Senate, which, if granted, shall be upon motion that he be allowed to proceed in order, which motion shall be determined without debate. Any Senator directed by the Presiding Officer to take his seat, and any Senator requesting the Presiding Officer to require a Senator to take his seat, may appeal from the ruling of the Chair, which appeal shall be open to debate.

5. If a Senator be called to order for words spoken in debate, upon the demand of the Senator or of any other Senator, the exceptionable words shall be taken down in writing, and read at the table for the information of the Senate.

6. Whenever confusion arises in the Chamber or the galleries, or demonstrations of approval or disapproval are indulged in by the occupants of the galleries, it shall be the duty of the Chair to enforce order on his own initiative and without any point of order being made by a Senator.

7. No Senator shall introduce to or bring to the attention of the Senate during its sessions any occupant in the galleries of the Senate. No motion to suspend this rule shall be in order, nor may the Presiding Officer entertain any request to suspend it by unanimous consent.

8. Former Presidents of the United States shall be entitled to address the Senate upon appropriate notice to the Presiding Officer who shall thereupon make the necessary arrangements.

RULE XX

Questions of Order

1. A question of order may be raised at any stage of the proceedings, except when the Senate is dividing, and, unless submitted to the Senate, shall be decided by the Presiding Officer without debate, subject to an appeal to the Senate. When an appeal is taken, any subsequent question of order which may arise before the decision of such appeal shall be decided by the Presiding Officer without debate; and every appeal therefrom shall be decided at once, and without debate; and any appeal may be laid on the table without prejudice to the pending proposition, and thereupon shall be held as affirming the decision of the Presiding Officer.

2. The Presiding Officer may submit any question of order for the decision of the Senate.

RULE XXI

Motions

1. All motions shall be reduced to writing, if desired by the Presiding Officer or by any Senator, and shall be read before the same shall be debated.

2. Any motion or resolution may be withdrawn or modified by the mover at any time before a decision, amendment, or ordering of the yeas and nays, except a motion to reconsider, which shall not be withdrawn without leave.

RULE XXII

Precedence of Motions

1. When a question is pending, no motion shall be received but—
To adjourn.
To adjourn to a day certain, or that when the

Senate adjourn it shall be to a day certain.
To take a recess.
To proceed to the consideration of executive business.
To lay on the table.
To postpone indefinitely.
To postpone to a day certain.
To commit.
To amend.

Which several motions shall have precedence as they stand arranged; and the motions relating to adjournment, to take a recess, to proceed to the consideration of executive business, to lay on the table, shall be decided without debate.

2. Notwithstanding the provisions of rule III or rule VI or any other rule of the Senate, at any time a motion signed by sixteen Senators, to bring to a close the debate upon any measure, motion, other matter pending before the Senate, or the unfinished business, is presented to the Senate, the Presiding Officer shall at once state the motion to the Senate, and one hour after the Senate meets on the following calendar day but one, he shall lay the motion before the Senate and direct that the Secretary call the roll, and upon the ascertainment that a quorum is present, the Presiding Officer shall, without debate, submit to the Senate by a yea-and-nay vote the question:
"Is it the sense of the Senate that the debate shall be brought to a close?"
And if that question shall be decided in the affirmative by three-fifths of the Senators duly chosen and sworn—except on a measure or motion to amend the Senate rules, in which case the necessary affirmative vote shall be two-thirds of the Senators present and voting—then said measure, motion, or other matter pending before the Senate, or the unfinished business, shall be the unfinished business to the exclusion of all other business until disposed of.

Thereafter no Senator shall be entitled to speak in all more than one hour on the measure, motion, or other matter pending before the Senate, or the unfinished business, the amendments thereto, and motions affecting the same, and it shall be the duty of the Presiding Officer to keep the time of each Senator who speaks. Except by unanimous consent, no amendment shall be in order after the vote to bring the debate to a close, unless the same has been presented and read prior to that time. No dilatory motion, or dilatory amendment, or amendment not germane shall be in order. Points of order, including questions of relevancy, and appeals from the decision of the Presiding Officer, shall be decided without debate.

3. The provisions of the last paragraph of rule VIII (prohibiting debate on motions made before 2 o'clock) [Refers to second paragraph of rule VIII, which rule has since been amended by the addition of a third paragraph.] shall not apply to any motion to proceed to the consideration of any motion, resolution, or proposal to change any of the Standing Rules of the Senate.

RULE XXIII

Preambles

When a bill or resolution is accompanied by a preamble, the question shall first be put on the bill or resolution and then on the preamble, which may be withdrawn by a mover before an amendment of the same, or ordering of the yeas and nays; or it may be laid on the table without prejudice to the bill or resolution, and shall be a final disposition of such preamble.

RULE XXIV

Appointment of Committees

1. In the appointment of the standing committees, the Senate, unless otherwise ordered, shall proceed by ballot to appoint severally the chairman of each committee, and then, by one ballot, the other members necessary to complete the same. A majority of the whole number of votes given shall be necessary to the choice of a chairman of a standing committee, but a plurality of votes shall elect the other members thereof. All other committees shall be appointed by ballot, unless otherwise ordered, and a plurality of votes shall appoint.

2. When a chairman of a committee shall resign or cease to serve on a committee, and the Presiding Officer be authorized by the Senate to fill the vacancy in such committee, unless specially otherwise ordered, it shall be only to fill up the number of the committee.

RULE XXV

Standing Committees

1. The following standing committees shall be appointed at the commencement of each Congress, with leave to report by bill or otherwise:

(a) (1) Committee on Aeronautical and Space Sciences, to which committee shall be referred all proposed legislation, messages, petitions, memorials, and other matters relating primarily to the following subjects:

(A) Aeronautical and space activities, as that term is defined in the National Aeronautics and Space Act of 1958, except those which are peculiar to or primarily associated with the development of weapons systems or military operations.

(B) Matters relating generally to the scientific aspects of such aeronautical and space activities, except those which are peculiar to or primarily associated with the development of weapons systems or military operations.

(C) National Aeronautics and Space Administration.

(2) Such committee also shall have jurisdiction to survey and review, and to prepare studies and reports upon, aeronautical and space activities of all agencies of the United States, including such activities which are peculiar to or primarily associated with the development of weapons systems or military operations.

(b) Committee on Agriculture and Forestry, to which committee shall be referred all proposed legislation, messages, petitions, memorials, and other matters relating to the following subjects:

1. Agriculture generally.
2. Inspection of livestock and meat products.
3. Animal industry and diseases of animals.
4. Adulteration of seeds, insect pests, and protection of birds and animals in forest reserves.
5. Agricultural colleges and experiment stations.
6. Forestry in general, and forest reserves other than those created from the public domain.
7. Agricultural economics and research.
8. Agricultural and industrial chemistry.
9. Dairy industry.
10. Entomology and plant quarantine.
11. Human nutrition and home economics.
12. Plant industry, soils, and agricultural engineering.
13. Agricultural educational extension services.
14. Extension of farm credit and farm security.
15. Rural electrification.
16. Agricultural production and marketing and stabilization of prices of agricultural products.
17. Crop insurance and soil conservation.

(c) Committee on Appropriations, to which committee shall be referred all proposed legislation, messages, petitions, memorials, and other matters relating to the following subjects:

1. Except as provided in subparagraph (r), appropriation of the revenue for the support of the Government.
2. Rescission of appropriations contained in appropriation Acts (referred to in section 105 of title 1, United States Code).
3. The amount of new spending authority described in section 401(c)(2) (A) and (B) of the Congressional Budget Act of 1974 provided in bills and resolutions referred to the committee under section 401(b)(2) of that Act (but subject to the provisions of section 401(b)(3) of that Act).
4. New advance spending authority described in section 401(c)(2)(C) of the Congressional Budget Act of 1974 provided in bills and resolutions referred to the committee under section 401(b)(2) of that Act (but subject to the provisions of section 401(b)(3) of that Act).

(d) Committee on Armed Services, to which committee shall be referred all proposed legislation, messages, petitions, memorials, and other matters relating to the following subjects:

1. Common defense generally.
2. The Department of Defense, the Department of the Army, the Department of the Navy, and the Department of the Air Force generally.
3. Soldiers' and sailors' homes.
4. Pay, promotion, retirement, and other benefits and privileges of members of the Armed Forces.
5. Selective service.
6. Size and composition of the Army, Navy, and Air Force.
7. Forts, arsenals, military reservations, and navy yards.
8. Ammunition depots.
9. Maintenance and operation of the Panama Canal, including the administration, sanitation, and government of the Canal Zone.
10. Conservation, development, and use of naval petroleum and oil shale reserves.
11. Strategic and critical materials necessary for the common defense.
12. Aeronautical and space activities peculiar to or primarily associated with the development of weapons systems or military operations.

(e) Committee on Banking, Housing and Urban Affairs, to which committee shall be referred all proposed legislation, messages, petitions, memorials, and other matters relating to the following subjects:

1. Banking and currency generally.
2. Financial aid to commerce and industry, other than matters relating to such aid which are specifically assigned to other committees under this rule.
3. Deposit insurance.
4. Public and private housing.
5. Federal Reserve System.

6. Gold and silver, including the coinage thereof.

7. Issuance of notes and redemption thereof.

8. Valuation and revaluation of the dollar.

9. Control of prices of commodities, rents, or services.

10. Urban affairs generally.

(f) Committee on Commerce, to which committee shall be referred all proposed legislation, messages, petitions, memorials, and other matters relating to the following subjects:

1. Interstate and foreign commerce generally.

2. Regulations of interstate railroads, busses, trucks, and pipe lines.

3. Communication by telephone, telegraph, radio, and television.

4. Civil aeronautics, except aeronautical and space activities of the National Aeronautics and Space Administration.

5. Merchant marine generally.

6. Registering and licensing of vessels and small boats.

7. Navigation and the laws relating thereto, including pilotage.

8. Rules and international arrangements to prevent collisions at sea.

9. Merchant marine officers and seamen.

10. Measures relating to the regulation of common carriers by water and to the inspection of merchant marine vessels, lights and signals, lifesaving equipment, and fire protection on such vessels.

11. Coast and Geodetic Survey.

12. The Coast Guard, including lifesaving service, lighthouses, lightships, and ocean derelicts.

13. The United States Coast Guard and Merchant Marine Academies.

14. Weather Bureau.

15. Except as provided in paragraph (d), the Panama Canal and interoceanic canals generally.

16. Inland waterways.

17. Fisheries and wildlife, including research, restoration, refuges, and conservation.

18. Bureau of Standards, including standardization of weights and measures and the metric system.

(g) Committee on the District of Columbia, to which committee shall be referred all proposed legislation, messages, petitions, memorials, and other matters relating to the following subjects:

1. All measures relating to the municipal affairs of the District of Columbia in general, other than appropriations therefor, including—

2. Public health and safety, sanitation, and quarantine regulations.

3. Regulation of sale of intoxicating liquors.

4. Adulteration of food and drugs.

5. Taxes and tax sales.

6. Insurance, executors, administrators, wills, and divorce.

7. Municipal and juvenile courts.

8. Incorporation and organization of societies.

9. Municipal code and amendments to the criminal and corporation laws.

(h) Committee on Finance, to which committee shall be referred all proposed legislation, messages, petitions, memorials, and other matters relating to the following subjects:

1. Except as provided in the Congressional Budget Act of 1974, revenue measures generally.

2. Except as provided in the Congressional Budget Act of 1974, the bonded debt of the United States.

3. The deposit of public moneys.

4. Customs, collection districts, and ports of entry and delivery.

5. Reciprocal trade agreements.

6. Transportation of dutiable goods.

7. Revenue measures relating to the insular possessions.

8. Tariffs and import quotas, and matters related thereto.

9. National social security.

(i) Committee on Foreign Relations, to which committee shall be referred all proposed legislation, messages, petitions, memorials, and other matters relating to the following subjects:

1. Relations of the United States with foreign nations generally.

2. Treaties.

3. Establishment of boundary lines between the United States and foreign nations.

4. Protection of American citizens abroad and expatriation.

5. Neutrality.

6. International conferences and congresses.

7. The American National Red Cross.

8. Intervention abroad and declarations of war.

9. Measures relating to the diplomatic service.

10. Acquisition of land and buildings for embassies and legations in foreign countries.

11. Measures to foster commercial intercourse with foreign nations and to safeguard American business interests abroad.

12. United Nations Organization and international financial and monetary organizations.

13. Foreign loans.

(j) (1) Committee on Government Operations, to which committee shall be referred all proposed legislation, messages, petitions, memorials, and other matters relating to the following subjects:

(A) Except as provided in the Congressional Budget Act of 1974, budget and accounting measures, other than appropriations.

(B) Reorganizations in the executive branch of the Government.

(2) Such committee shall have the duty of—

(A) receiving and examining reports of the Comptroller General of the United States and of submitting such recommendations to the Senate as it deems necessary or desirable in connection with the subject matter of such reports;

(B) studying the operation of Government activities at all levels with a view to determining its economy and efficiency;

(C) evaluating the effects of laws enacted to reorganize the legislative and executive branches of the Government;

(D) studying the intergovernmental relationships between the United States and the States and municipalities, and between the United States and international organizations of which the United States is a member.

(k) Committee on Interior and Insular Affairs, to which committee shall be referred all proposed legislation, messages, petitions, memorials, and other matters relating to the following subjects:

1. Public lands generally, including entry, easements, and grazing thereon.

2. Mineral resources of the public lands.

3. Forfeiture of land grants and alien ownership, including alien ownership of mineral lands.

4. Forest reserves and national parks created from the public domain.

5. Military parks and battlefields.

6. Preservation of prehistoric ruins and objects of interest on the public domain.

7. Measures relating generally to the insular possessions of the United States, except those affecting their revenue and appropriations.

8. Irrigation and reclamation, including water supply for reclamation projects, and easements of public lands for irrigation projects.

9. Interstate compacts relating to apportionment of waters for irrigation purposes.

10. Mining interests generally.

11. Mineral land laws and claims and entries thereunder.

12. Geological survey.

13. Mining schools and experimental stations.

14. Petroleum conservation and conservation of the radium supply in the United States.

15. Relations of the United States with the Indians and the Indian tribes.

16. Measures relating to the care, education, and management of Indians, including the care and allotment of Indian lands and general and special measures relating to claims which are paid out of Indian funds.

(l) Committee on the Judiciary, to which committee shall be referred all proposed legislation, messages, petitions, memorials, and other matters relating to the following subjects:

1. Judicial proceedings, civil and criminal, generally.

2. Constitutional amendments.

3. Federal courts and judges.

4. Local courts in the territories and possessions.

5. Revision and codification of the statutes of the United States.

6. National penitentiaries.

7. Protection of trade and commerce against unlawful restraints and monopolies.

8. Holidays and celebrations.

9. Bankruptcy, mutiny, espionage, and counterfeiting.

10. State and territorial boundary lines.

11. Meetings of Congress, attendance of Members, and their acceptance of incompatible offices.

12. Civil liberties.

13. Patents, copyrights, and trademarks.

14. Patent Office.

15. Immigration and naturalization.

16. Apportionment of Representatives.

17. Measures relating to claims against the United States.

18. Interstate compacts generally.

(m) Committee on Labor and Public Welfare, to which committee shall be referred all proposed legislation, messages, petitions, memorials, and other matters relating to the following subjects:

1. Measures relating to education, labor, or public welfare generally.

2. Mediation and arbitration of labor disputes.

3. Wages and hours of labor.

4. Convict labor and the entry of goods made by convicts into interstate commerce.

5. Regulation or prevention of importation of foreign laborers under contract.

6. Child labor.

7. Labor statistics.

8. Labor standards.

9. School-lunch program.

10. Vocational rehabilitation.

11. Railroad labor and railroad retirement and unemployment, except revenue measures relating thereto.

12. United States Employees' Compensation Commission.

13. Columbia Institution for the Deaf, Dumb, and Blind [now Gallaudet College]; Howard University; Freedmen's Hospital; and St. Elizabeths Hospital.

14. Public health and quarantine.

15. Welfare of miners.

(n) Committee on Post Office and Civil Service, to which committee shall be referred all proposed legislation, messages, petitions, memorials, and other matters relating to the following subjects:

1. The Federal civil service generally.

2. The status of officers and employees of the United States, including their compensation, classification, and retirement.

3. The postal service generally, including the railway mail service, and measures relating to ocean mail and pneumatic-tube service; but excluding post roads.

4. Postal-savings banks.

5. Census and the collection of statistics generally.

6. The National Archives.

(o) Committee on Public Works, to which committee shall be referred all proposed legislation, messages, petitions, memorials, and other matters relating to the following subjects:

1. Flood control and improvement of rivers and harbors.

2. Public works for the benefit of navigation, and bridges and dams (other than international bridges and dams).

3. Water power.

4. Oil and other pollution of navigable waters.

5. Public buildings and occupied or improved grounds of the United States generally.

6. Measures relating to the purchase of sites and construction of post offices, customhouses, Federal courthouses, and Government buildings within the District of Columbia.

7. Measures relating to the Capitol Building and the Senate and House Office Buildings.

8. Measures relating to the construction or reconstruction, maintenance, and care of the buildings and grounds of the Botanic Gardens, the Library of Congress, and the Smithsonian Institution.

9. Public reservations and parks within the District of Columbia, including Rock Creek Park and the Zoological Park.

10. Measures relating to the construction or maintenance of roads and post roads.

(p) (1) Committee on Rules and Administration, to which committee shall be referred all proposed legislation, messages, petitions, memorials, and other matters relating to the following subjects:

(A) Matters relating to the payment of money out of the contingent fund of the Senate or creating a charge upon the same; except that any resolution relating to substantive matter within the jurisdiction of any other standing committee of the Senate shall be first referred to such committee.

(B) Except as provided in paragraph (o) 8, matters relating to the Library of Congress and the Senate Library; statuary and pictures; acceptance or purchase of works of art for the Capitol; the Botanic Gardens; management of the Library of Congress; purchase of books and manuscripts; erection of monuments to the memory of individuals.

(C) Except as provided in paragraph (o) 8, matters relating to the Smithsonian Institution and the incorporation of similar institutions.

(D) Matters relating to the election of the President, Vice President, or Members of Congress; corrupt practices; contested elections; credentials and qualifications; Federal elections generally; Presidential succession.

(E) Matters relating to parliamentary rules; floor and gallery rules; Senate Restaurant; administration of the Senate Office Buildings and of the Senate wing of the Capitol; assignment of office space; and services to the Senate.

(F) Matters relating to printing and correction of the Congressional Record.

(2) Such committee shall also have the duty of assigning office space in the Senate wing of the Capitol and in the Senate Office Buildings.

(q) Committee on Veterans' Affairs, to which committee shall be referred all proposed legislation, messages, petitions, memorials, and other matters relating to the following subjects:

1. Veterans' measures generally.

2. Pensions of all wars of the United States, general and special.

3. Life insurance issued by the Government on account of service in the armed forces.

4. Compensation of veterans.

5. Vocational rehabilitation and education of veterans.

6. Veterans' hospitals, medical care and treatment of veterans.

7. Soldiers' and sailors' civil relief.

8. Readjustment of servicemen to civil life.

9. National cemeteries.

(r) (1) Committee on the Budget, to which committee shall be referred all concurrent resolutions on the budget (as defined in section 3(a)(4) of the Congressional Budget Act of 1974) and all other matters required to be referred to that committee under titles III and IV of that Act, and messages, petitions, memorials, and other matters relating thereto.

(2) Such committee shall have the duty—

(A) to report the matters required to be reported by it under titles III and IV of the Congressional Budget Act of 1974;

(B) to make continuing studies of the effect on budget outlays of **relevant existing and proposed legislation and to report the results of** such studies to the Senate on a recurring basis;

(C) to request and evaluate continuing studies of tax expenditures, to devise methods of coordinating tax expenditures, policies, and programs with direct budget outlays, and to report the results of such studies to the Senate on a recurring basis; and

(D) to review, on a continuing basis, the conduct by the Congressional Budget Office of its functions and duties.

2. Except as otherwise provided by paragraph 6 of this rule, each of the following standing committees shall consist of the number of Senators set forth in the following table on the line on which the name of that committee appears:

Committee	Members
Aeronautical and Space Sciences	10
Agriculture and Forestry	14
Appropriations	26
Armed Services	16
Banking, Housing and Urban Affairs	13
Budget	16
Commerce	20
Finance	18
Foreign Relations	16
Government Operations	14
Interior and Insular Affairs	14
Judiciary	15
Labor and Public Welfare	16
Public Works	14.

3. Except as otherwise provided by paragraph 6 of this rule, each of the following standing committees shall consist of the number of Senators set forth in the following table on the line on which the name of that committee appears:

Committee	Members
District of Columbia	7
Post Office and Civil Service	9
Rules and Administration	9
Veterans' Affairs	9.

4. The said committees shall continue and have the power to act until their successors are appointed.

5. (a) Except as provided in paragraph (b) of this subsection, each standing committee, and each subcommittee of any such committee, is authorized to fix the number of its members (but not less than one-third of its entire membership) who shall constitute a quorum thereof for the transaction of such business as may be considered by said committee, subject to the provisions of section 133(d) of the Legislative Reorganization Act of 1946.

(b) Each standing committee, and each subcommittee of any such committee, is authorized to fix a lesser number than one-third of its entire membership who shall constitute a quorum thereof for the purpose of taking sworn testimony.

6. (a) Except as otherwise provided by this paragraph, each Senator shall serve on two and no more of the standing committees named in paragraph 2. Except as otherwise provided by this paragraph, no Senator shall serve on more than one committee included within the following classes: standing committees named in paragraph 3; select and special committees of the Senate; and joint committees of the Congress.

(b) Each Senator who on the day preceding the effective date of section 132 of the Legislative Reorganization Act of 1970 was serving as a member of any standing committee shall be entitled to continue to serve on each such committee of which he was a member on that day as long as his service as a member of such committee remains continuous after that day. Each Senator who (1) on that day was serving as a member of the Committee on Aeronautical and Space Sciences or the Committee on Government Operations, (2) on that date was entitled, under the proviso contained in the first sentence of paragraph 4 of this rule as such rule existed on that day, to serve on three committees named in that sentence, and (3) on June 30, 1971, is serving on three such committees, of which at least one is the Committee on Aeronautical and Space Sciences or the Committee on Government Operations, shall be entitled to continue to serve on each of the committees of which he is a member on June 30, 1971, so long as his service as a member of each such committee remains continuous thereafter. Each Senator who on the day preceding the effective date of section 132 of the Legislative Reorganization Act of 1970, was a member of more than one committee of the classes described in the second sentence of subparagraph (a) shall be entitled to serve on each such committee of which he was a member on that day as long as his service as a member of that committee remains continuous after that day. Each Senator who on that day was a member of more than one committee of those classes may be assigned during the 92d Congress to other committees included within those classes, except that no Senator may serve on a number of committees of those classes greater than the number of such committees on which he was serving on the day preceding such effective date. Notwithstanding the provisions of paragraph 2 and 3, each committee of the Senate shall be temporarily increased in membership by such number as may be required to carry into effect the provisions of this subparagraph.

(c) By agreement entered into by the majority leader and the minority leader, the membership of one or more of the standing committees named in paragraph 2 or paragraph 3 of this rule may be increased temporarily from time to time by such number or numbers as may be required to accord to the majority party a majority of the membership of all standing committees. When any such temporary increase is necessary to accord to the majority party a majority of the membership of all standing committees, members of the majority party in such number as may be required for that purpose may serve as members of three standing committees named in paragraph 2. No such temporary increase in the membership of one or more standing committees under this subparagraph or subparagraph (b) shall be continued in effect after the need therefor has ended. No standing committee may be increased in membership under this subparagraph or subparagraph (b) by more than four members in excess of the number prescribed for that committee by paragraph 2 or paragraph 3 of this rule.

(d) Notwithstanding the limitations contained in subparagraph (a), a Senator may serve at any time on one additional committee included within the following classes: a temporary committee of the Senate or a temporary joint committee of the Congress which, by the terms of the measure by which it was established as initially agreed to, will not continue in existence for more than one Congress; or a joint committee of the Congress having jurisdiction with respect to a subject matter which is directly related to the jurisdiction of a committee named in paragraph 3 of which that Senator is a member.

(e) No Senator shall serve at any time on more than one of the following committees: Committee on Appropriations, Committee on Armed Services, Committee on Finance, and Committee on Foreign Relations. Notwithstanding the limitation contained in this subparagraph, a Senator who on the day preceding the effective date of section 132 of the Legislative Reorganization Act of 1970 was a member of more than one such committee may continue to serve as a member of each such committee of which he was a member on that day as long as his service on that committee remains continuous after that day.

(f) No Senator shall serve at any time as chairman of more than one committee included within the following classes: standing, select, and special committees of the Senate; and joint committees of the Congress except that—

(1) A Senator may serve as chairman of a joint committee of the Congress having jurisdiction with respect to a subject matter which is directly related to the jurisdiction of a committee named in paragraph 2 or paragraph 3 of which that Senator is the chairman;

(2) A Senator who on the day preceding the effective date of section 132 of the Legislative Reorganization Act of 1970 was serving as chairman of more than one committee included within the classes described in this subparagraph may continue to serve as chairman of each such committee of which he was chairman on that day as long as his service as chairman of that committee remains continuous after that day; and

(3) A Senator who is serving at any time as chairman of a committee included within the classes described in this subparagraph may at the same time serve also as chairman of one temporary committee of the Senate or temporary joint committee of the Congress which, by the terms of the measure by which it was established as originally agreed to, will not continue in existence for more than one Congress.

(g) No Senator shall serve at any time as chairman of more than one subcommittee of the same committee if that committee is named in paragraph 2. Notwithstanding the limitation contained in this subparagraph, a Senator who on the day preceding the effective date of section 132 of the Legislative Reorganization Act of 1970 was serving as chairman of more than one such subcommittee may continue to serve as chairman of each such subcommittee of which he was chairman on that day as long as his service as chairman of that subcommittee remains continuous after that day.

(h) For purposes of the first sentence of subparagraph (a), membership on the Committee on the Budget shall not be taken into account until that date occurring during the first session of the Ninety-fifth Congress, upon which the appointment of the majority and minority party members of the standing committees of the Senate is initially completed.

7. (a) No standing committee shall sit without special leave while the Senate is in session after (1) the conclusion of the morning hour, or (2) the Senate has proceeded to the consideration of unfinished business, pending business, or any other business except private bills and the routine morning business, whichever is earlier.

(b) Each meeting of a standing, select, or special committee of the Senate, or any subcommittee thereof, including meetings to conduct hearings, shall be open to the public, except that a meeting or series of meetings by a committee or subcommittee thereof on the same subject for a period of no more than fourteen calendar days may be closed to the public on a motion made and seconded to go into closed session to discuss only whether the matters enumerated in paragraphs (1) through (6) would require the meeting to be closed followed immediately by a record vote in open session by a majority of the members of the committee or subcommittee when it is determined that the matters to be discussed or the testimony to be taken at such meetings—

(1) will disclose matters necessary to be kept secret in the interests of national defense or the confidential conduct of the foreign relations of the United States;

(2) will relate solely to matters of committee staff personnel or internal staff management or procedure;

(3) will tend to charge an individual with crime or misconduct, to disgrace or injure the professional standing of an individual, or otherwise expose an individual to public contempt or obloquy, or will represent a clearly unwarranted invasion of the privacy of an individual;

(4) will disclose the identity of any informer or law enforcement agent or will disclose any information relating to the investigation or prosecution of a criminal offense that is required to be kept secret in the interests of effective law enforcement;

(5) will disclose information relating to the trade secrets of financial or commercial information pertaining specifically to a given person if—

(A) an Act of Congress requires the information to be kept confidential by Government officers and employees; or

(B) the information has been obtained by the Government on a confidential basis, other than through an application by such person for a specific Government financial or other benefit, and is required to be kept secret in order to prevent undue injury to the competitive position of such person; or

(6) may divulge matters required to be kept confidential under other provisions of law or Government regulations.

(c) Whenever any hearing conducted by any such committee or subcommittee is open to the public, that hearing may be broadcast by radio or television, or both, under such rules as the committee or subcommittee may adopt.

(d) Whenever disorder arises during a committee meeting that is open to the public, or any demonstration of approval or disapproval is indulged in by any person in attendance at any such meeting, it shall be the duty of the Chair to enforce order on his own initiative and without any point of order being made by a Senator. When the Chair finds it necessary to maintain order, he shall have the power to clear the room, and the committee may act in closed session for so long as there is doubt of the assurance of order.

(e) Each committee shall prepare and keep a complete transcript or electronic recording adequate to fully record the proceedings of each meeting or conference whether or not such meeting or any part thereof is closed under this paragraph, unless a majority of said members forgo such a record.

8. (a) Subject to the limitations contained in subparagraph (b) of this paragraph, each Senator serving on a committee is authorized to hire staff for the purpose of assisting him in connection with his membership on one or more committees on which he serves as follows:

(1) A Senator serving on one or more standing committees named in paragraph 2 shall receive, for each such committee as he designates, up to a maximum of two such committees, an amount equal to the amount referred to in section 105(e)(1) of the Legislative Appropriations Act, 1968, as amended and modified.

(2) A Senator serving on one or more standing committees named in paragraph 3 or, in the case of a Senator serving on more than two committees named in paragraph 2 but on none of the committees named in paragraph 3; select and special committees of the Senate; and joint committees of the Congress shall receive for one of such committees which he designates, an amount equal to the amount referred to in section 105(e)(1) of the Legislative Appropriations Act, 1968, as amended and modified.

(b) (1) The amounts referred to in subparagraph (a)(1) shall be reduced, in the case of a Senator who is—

(A) the chairman or ranking minority member of any of the two committees designated by the Senator under subsection (a)(1);

(B) the chairman or ranking minority member of any subcommittee of either of such committees that receives funding to employ staff assistance separately from the funding authority for staff of the committee; or

(C) authorized by the committee, a subcommittee thereof, or the chairman of the committee or subcommittee, as appropriate, to recommend or approve the appointment to the staff of such committee or subcommittee of one or more individuals for the purpose of assisting such Senator in his duties as a member of such committee or subcommittee,

by an amount equal to the total annual basic pay of all staff employees of that committee or subcommittee (i) whose appointment is made, approved, or recommended and (ii) whose continued employment is not disapproved by such Senator if such employees are employed for the purpose of assisting such

Senator in his duties as chairman, ranking minority member, or member of such committee or subcommittee thereof as the case may be, or to the amount referred to in section 105(e)(1) of such Act, whichever is less.

(2) The amount referred to in subsection (a)(2) shall be reduced in the case of any Senator by an amount equal to the total annual basic pay of all staff employees (i) whose appointment to the staff of any committee referred to in subsection (a)(2), or subcommittee thereof, is made, approved, or recommended and (ii) whose continued employment is not disapproved by such Senator if such employees are employed for the purpose of assisting such Senator in his duties as chairman, ranking minority member, or member of such committee or subcommittee thereof as the case may be, or an amount equal to the amount referred to in section 105(e)(1) of such Act, whichever is less.

(c) An employee appointed under this paragraph shall be designated as such and certified by the Senator who appoints him to the chairmen and ranking minority members of the appropriate committee or committees as designated if such Senator and shall be accorded all privileges of a professional staff member (whether permanent or investigatory) of such committee or committees including access to all committee sessions and files, except that any such committee may restrict access to its sessions to one staff member per Senator at a time and require, if classified material is being handled or discussed, that any staff member possess the appropriate security clearance before being allowed access to such material or to discussion of it.

(d) An employee appointed under this paragraph shall not receive compensation in excess of that provided for an employee under section 105(e)(1) of the Legislative Branch Appropriations Act, 1968, as amended and modified.

(e) Payments made with respect to individuals appointed to the office of a Senator under this paragraph shall be paid out of the contingent fund of the Senate.

(f) Individuals appointed as employees under this paragraph shall be in addition to employees otherwise authorized to be appointed to the office of a Senator.

RULE XXVI

Reference to Committees; Motions to Discharge, and Reports of Committees to Lie Over

1. When motions are made for reference of a subject to a select committee, or to a standing committee, the question of reference to a standing committee shall be put first; and a motion simply to refer shall not be opened to amendment, except to add instructions.

2. All reports of committees and motions to discharge a committee from the consideration of a subject, and all subjects from which a committee shall be discharged, shall lie over one day for consideration, unless by unanimous consent the Senate shall otherwise direct.

RULE XXVII

Conference Committees; Reports; Open Meetings

1. The presentation of reports of committees of conference shall always be in order, except when the Journal is being read or a question of order or a motion to adjourn is pending, or while the Senate is dividing; and when received the question of proceeding to the consideration of the report, if raised, shall be immediately put, and shall be determined without debate.

2. Conferees shall not insert in their report matter not committed to them by either House, nor shall they strike from the bill matter agreed to by both Houses. If new matter is inserted in the report, or if matter which was agreed to by both Houses is stricken from the bill, a point of order may be made against the report, and if the point of order is sustained, the report shall be recommitted to the committee of conference.

3. Each conference committee between the Senate and the House of Representatives shall be open to the public except when the managers of either the Senate or the House of Representatives in open session determine by a rollcall vote of a majority of those managers present, that all or part of the remainder of the meeting on the day of the vote shall be closed to the public.

RULE XXVIII

Messages

1. Messages from the President of the United States or from the House of Representatives may be received at any stage of proceedings, except while the Senate is dividing, or while the Journal is being read, or while a question of order or a motion to adjourn is pending.

2. Messages shall be sent to the House of Representatives by the Secretary, who shall previously certify the determination of the Senate upon all bills, joint resolutions, and other resolutions which may be communicated to the House, or in which its concurrence may be requested; and the Secretary shall also certify and deliver to the President of the United States all resolutions and other communications which may be directed to him by the Senate.

RULE XXIX

Printing of Papers, Etc.

1. Every motion to print documents, reports, and other matter transmitted by either of the executive departments, or to print memorials, petitions, accompanying documents, or any other paper, except bills of the Senate or House of Representatives, resolutions submitted by a Senator, communications from the legislatures or conventions, lawfully called, of the respective States, and motions to print by order of the standing or select committees of the Senate, shall, unless the Senate otherwise order, be referred to the Committee on Rules and Administration. When a motion is made to commit with instructions, it shall be in order to add thereto a motion to print.

2. Motions to print additional numbers shall also be referred to the Committee on Rules and Administration; and when the committee shall report favorably, the report shall be accompanied by an estimate of the probable cost thereof; and when the cost of printing such additional numbers shall exceed the sum of five hundred dollars, the concurrence of the House of Representatives shall be necessary for an order to print the same.

3. Every bill and joint resolution introduced on leave or reported from a committee, and all bills and joint resolutions received from the House of Representatives, and all reports of committees, shall be printed, unless, for the dispatch of the business of the Senate, such printing may be dispensed with.

4. Whenever a committee reports a bill or a joint resolution repealing or amending any statute or part thereof it shall make a report thereon and shall include in such report or in an accompanying document (to be prepared by the staff of such committee) (a) the text of the statute or part thereof which is proposed to be repealed; and (b) a comparative print of that part of the bill or joint resolution making the amendment and of the statute or part thereof proposed to be amended, showing by stricken-through type and italics, parallel columns, or other appropriate typographical devices the omissions and insertions which would be made by the bill or joint resolution if enacted in the form recommended by the committee. This subsection shall not apply to any such report in which it is stated that, in the opinion of the committee, it is necessary to dispense with the requirements of this subsection to expedite the business of the Senate.

RULE XXX

Withdrawal of Papers

1. No memorial or other paper presented to the Senate, except original treaties finally acted upon, shall be withdrawn from its files except by order of the Senate. But when an act may pass for the settlement of any private claim, the Secretary is authorized to transmit to the officer charged with the settlement the papers on file relating to the claim.

2. No memorial or other paper upon which an adverse report has been made shall be withdrawn from the files of the Senate unless copies thereof shall be left in the office of the Secretary.

RULE XXXI

Reference of Claims Adversely Reported

Whenever a committee of the Senate, to whom any claim has been referred, reports adversely, and the report is agreed to, it shall not be in order to move to take the papers from the files for the purpose of referring them at a subsequent session, unless the claimant shall present a petition therefor, stating that new evidence has been discovered since the report, and setting forth the substance of such new evidence. But when there has been no adverse report it shall be the duty of the Secretary to transmit all such papers to the committee in which such claims are pending.

RULE XXXII

Business Continued From Session to Session

1. At the second or any subsequent session of a Congress, the legislative business of the Senate which remained undetermined at the close of the next preceding session of that Congress shall be resumed and proceeded with in the same manner as if no adjournment of the Senate had taken place; and all papers referred to committees and not reported upon at the close of a session of Congress shall be returned to the office of the Secretary of the Senate, and be retained by him until the next succeeding session of that Congress, when they shall be returned to the several committees to which they had previously been referred.

2. The rules of the Senate shall continue from one Congress to the next Congress unless they are changed as provided in these rules.

RULE XXXIII

Privilege of the Floor

No person shall be admitted to the floor of the Senate while in session, except as follows:

The President of the United States and his private secretary.

The President elect and Vice President elect of the United States.

Ex-Presidents and ex-Vice Presidents of the United States.

Judges of the Supreme Court.

Ex-Senators and Senators elect.

The officers and employees of the Senate in the discharge of their official duties.

Ex-Secretaries and ex-Sergeants at Arms of the Senate.

Members of the House of Representatives and Members elect.

Ex-Speakers of the House of Representatives.

The Sergeant at Arms of the House and his chief deputy and the Clerk of the House and his deputy.

Heads of the Executive Departments.

Ambassadors and Ministers of the United States.

Governors of States and Territories.

The General Commanding the Army.

The Senior Admiral of the Navy on the active list.

Members of National Legislatures of foreign countries.

Judges of the Court of Claims.

The Commissioner of the District of Columbia.

The Librarian of Congress and the Assistant Librarian in charge of the Law Library.

The Architect of the Capitol.

The Chaplain of the House of Representatives.

The Secretary of the Smithsonian Institution.

The Parliamentarian Emeritus of the Senate.

Clerks to Senate committees and clerks to Senators when in the actual discharge of their official duties. Clerks to Senators, to be admitted to the floor, must be regularly appointed and borne upon the rolls of the Secretary of the Senate as such.

RULE XXXIV

Regulation of the Senate Wing of the Capitol

1. The Senate Chamber shall not be granted for any other purpose than for the use of the Senate; no smoking shall be permitted at any time on the floor of the Senate, or lighted cigars be brought into the Chamber.

2. It shall be the duty of the Committee on Rules and Administration to make all rules and regulations respecting such parts of the Capitol, its passages and galleries, including the restaurant and the Senate Office Building, as are or may be set apart for the use of the Senate and its officers, to be enforced under the direction of the Presiding Officer. They shall make such regulations respecting the reporters' galleries of the Senate, together with the adjoining rooms and facilities, as will confine their occupancy and use to bona fide reporters for daily newspapers and periodicals, to bona fide reporters of news or press associations requiring telegraph service to their membership, and to bona fide reporters for daily news dissemination through radio, wire, wireless, and similar media of transmission. These regulations shall so provide for the use of such space and facilities as fairly to distribute their use to all such media of news dissemination.

RULE XXXV

Session With Closed Doors

On a motion made and seconded to close the doors of the Senate, on the discussion of any business which may, in the opinion of a Senator, require secrecy, the Presiding Officer shall direct the galleries to be cleared; and during the discussion of such motion the doors shall remain closed.

RULE XXXVI

Executive Sessions

1. When the President of the United States shall meet the Senate in the Senate Chamber for the consideration of Executive business, he shall have a seat on the right of the Presiding Officer. When the Senate shall be convened by the President of the United States to any other place, the Presiding Officer of the Senate and the Senators shall attend at the place appointed, with the necessary officers of the Senate.

2. When acting upon confidential or Executive business, unless the same shall be considered in open Executive session, the Senate Chamber shall be cleared of all persons except the Secretary, the Chief Clerk, the Principal Legislative Clerk, the Executive Clerk, the Minute and Journal Clerk, the Sergeant at Arms, the Assistant Doorkeeper, and such other officers as the Presiding Officer shall think necessary; and all such officers shall be sworn to secrecy.

On May 2, 1892, the Senate agreed to the following:

Resolved, That until otherwise ordered there shall be admitted to the floor of the Senate during Executive sessions such clerks, not exceeding three in number, as may be assigned by the Secretary of the Senate to Executive duties.

3. All confidential communications made by the President of the United States to the Senate shall be by the Senators and the officers of the Senate kept secret; and all treaties which may be laid before the Senate, and all remarks, votes, and proceedings thereon shall also be kept secret, until the Senate shall, by their resolution, take off the injunction of secrecy, or unless the same shall be considered in open Executive session.

On Mar. 21, 1885, the Senate agreed to the following:

Ordered, That the injunction of secrecy be removed from the following report from the Committee on Rules, viz:

The Committee on Rules, to which was referred a question of order raised by the Senator from Maine (Mr. Frye) as to the operation of clause 3, Rule XXXVI, reported that it extends the injunction of secrecy to each step in the consideration of treaties, including the fact of ratification; that no modification of this clause of the rules ought to be made; that the secrecy as to the fact or ratification of a treaty may be of the utmost importance, and ought not to be removed except by order of the Senate, or until it has been made public by proclamation by the President.

On Feb. 8, 1900, the Senate agreed to the following:

Ordered, Whenever the injunction of secrecy shall be removed from any part of the proceedings of the Senate in Executive session, or secret legislative session, the order of the Senate removing the same shall be entered by the Secretary in the Legislative Journal as well as in the Executive Journal, and shall be published in the Record.

4. Any Senator or officer of the Senate who shall disclose the secret or confidential business or proceedings of the Senate shall be liable, if a Senator, to suffer expulsion from the body; and if an officer, to dismissal from the service of the Senate, and to punishment for contempt.

5. Whenever, by the request of the Senate or any committee thereof, any documents or papers shall be communicated to the Senate by the President or the head of any department relating to any matter pending in the Senate, the proceeding in regard to which are secret or confidential under the rules, said documents and papers shall be considered as confidential, and shall not be disclosed without leave of the Senate.

RULE XXXVII

Executive Session—Proceedings on Treaties

1. When a treaty shall be laid before the Senate for ratification, it shall be read a first time; and no motion in respect to it shall be in order, except to refer it to a committee, to print it in confidence for the use of the Senate, to remove the injunction of secrecy, or to consider it in open executive session.

When a treaty is reported from a committee with or without amendment, it shall, unless the Senate unanimously otherwise direct, lie one day for consideration; after which it may be read a second time and considered as in Committee of the Whole, when it shall be proceeded with by articles, and the amendments reported by the committee shall be first acted upon, after which other amendments may be proposed; and when through with, the proceedings had as in Committee of the Whole shall be reported to the Senate, when the question shall be, if the treaty be amended, "Will the Senate concur in the amendments made in Committee of the Whole?" And the amendments may be taken separately, or in gross, if no Senator shall object; after which new amendments may be proposed. At any stage of such proceedings the Senate may remove the injunction of secrecy from the treaty, or proceed with its consideration in open executive session.

The decisions thus made shall be reduced to the form of a resolution of ratification, with or without amendments, as the case may be, which shall be proposed on a subsequent day, unless, by unanimous consent, the Senate determine otherwise; at which stage no amendment shall be received unless by unanimous consent.

On the final question to advise and consent to the ratification in the form agreed to, the concurrence of two-thirds of the Senators present shall be necessary to determine it in the affirmative; but all other motions and questions upon a treaty shall be decided by a majority vote, except a motion to postpone indefinitely, which shall be decided by a vote of two-thirds.

2. Treaties transmitted by the President to the Senate for ratification shall be resumed at the second or any subsequent session of the same Congress at the stage in which they were left at the final adjournment of the session at which they were transmitted; but all proceedings on treaties shall terminate with the Congress, and they shall be resumed at the commence-

ent of the next Congress as if no proceedings had previously been had
.ereon.

3. All treaties concluded with Indian tribes shall be considered and
.ted upon by the Senate in its open or legislative session, unless the same
.all be transmitted by the President to the Senate in confidence, in which
.se they shall be acted upon with closed doors.

RULE XXXVIII

Executive Session—Proceedings on Nominations

1. When nominations shall be made by the President of the United
.tates to the Senate, they shall, unless otherwise ordered, be referred to
.ppropriate committees; and the final question on every nomination shall be,
.Will the Senate advise and consent to this nomination?'' which question
.all not be put on the same day on which the nomination is received, nor on
.ne day on which it may be reported by a committee, unless by unanimous
.onsent.

2. Hereafter all business in the Senate shall be transacted in open
.ession, unless the Senate in closed session by a majority vote shall determine
.nat a particular nomination, treaty, or other matter shall be considered in
.losed executive session, in which case all subsequent proceedings with
.espect to said nomination, treaty, or other matter shall be kept secret:
Provided, That the injunction of secrecy as to the whole or any part of
.roceedings in closed executive session may be removed on motion adopted
.y a majority vote of the Senate in closed executive session: *Provided further,*
.hat rule XXXV shall apply to open executive session: *And provided further,*
.hat any Senator may make public his vote in closed executive session.
Anything in the rules of the Senate inconsistent with the foregoing is
.ereby repealed.

3. When a nomination is confirmed or rejected, any Senator voting in
.he majority may move for a reconsideration on the same day on which the
.ote was taken, or on either of the next two days of actual executive session of
.he Senate; but if a notification of the confirmation or rejection of a nomina-
.ion shall have been sent to the President before the expiration of the time
.vithin which a motion to reconsider may be made, the motion to reconsider
.hall be accompanied by a motion to request the President to return such
.otification to the Senate. Any motion to reconsider the vote on a nomination
.nay be laid on the table without prejudice to the nomination, and shall be a
.inal disposition of such motion.

4. Nominations confirmed or rejected by the Senate shall not be
.eturned by the Secretary to the President until the expiration of the time
.imited for making a motion to reconsider the same, or while a motion to
.reconsider is pending unless otherwise ordered by the Senate.

5. When the Senate shall adjourn or take a recess for more than thirty
.days, all motions to reconsider a vote upon a nomination which has been con-
.firmed or rejected by the Senate, which shall be pending at the time of taking
.such adjournment or recess, shall fall; and the Secretary shall return all such
.nominations to the President as confirmed or rejected by the Senate, as the
.case may be.

6. Nominations neither confirmed nor rejected during the session at
.which they are made shall not be acted upon at any succeeding session
without being again made to the Senate by the President; and if the Senate
.shall adjourn or take a recess for more than thirty days, all nominations
pending and not fully acted upon at the time of taking such adjournment or
recess shall be returned by the Secretary to the President, and shall not again
be considered unless they shall again be made to the Senate by the President.

On Dec. 16, 1885, the Senate agreed to the following:
Resolved, All nominations to office shall be prepared for the printer by
the Official Reporter, and printed in the Record, after the proceedings of the
day in which they are received, also nominations recalled, and confirmed.

On Dec. 17, 1885, the Senate agreed to the following:
Ordered, The Secretary shall furnish the Official Reporters with a list of
nominations to office after the proceedings of the day on which they are
received, and a like list of all confirmations and rejections.

On May 2, 1894, the Senate agreed to the following:
Resolved, The Secretary shall furnish to the press, and to the public
upon request, the names of nominees confirmed or rejected on the day on
which a final vote shall be had, except when otherwise ordered by the Senate.

RULE XXXIX

The President Furnished With Copies of Records of Executive Sessions

The President of the United States shall, from time to time, be furnished
with an authenticated transcript of the executive records of the Senate, but
no further extract from the Executive Journal shall be furnished by the
Secretary, except by special order of the Senate; and no paper, except
original treaties transmitted to the Senate by the President of the United
States, and finally acted upon by the Senate, shall be delivered from the office of the Secretary without an order of the Senate for that purpose.

RULE XL

Suspension and Amendment of the Rules

No motion to suspend, modify, or amend any rule, or any part thereof,
shall be in order, except on one day's notice in writing, specifying precisely
the rule or part proposed to be suspended, modified, or amended, and the
purpose thereof. Any rule may be suspended without notice by the unanimous consent of the Senate, except as otherwise provided in clause 1, Rule
XII.

RULE XLI

Outside Business or Professional Activity or Employment by Officers or Employees

1. No officer or employee whose salary is paid by the Senate may engage
in any business or professional activity or employment for compensation unless—
(a) the activity or employment is not inconsistent nor in conflict
with the conscientious performance of his official duties; and
(b) he has reported in writing when this rule takes effect or when
his office or employment starts and on the 15th day of May in each year
thereafter the nature of any personal service activity or employment to
his supervisor. The supervisor shall then, in the discharge of his duties,
take such action as he considers necessary for the avoidance of conflict
of interest or interference with duties to the Senate.
2. For the purpose of this rule—
(a) a Senator or the Vice President is the supervisor of his administrative, clerical, or other assistants;
(b) a Senator who is the chairman of a committee is the supervisor of the professional, clerical, or other assistants to the committee except that minority staff members shall be under the supervision of the
ranking minority Senator on the committee;
(c) a Senator who is a chairman of a subcommittee which has its
own staff and financial authorization is the supervisor of the professional, clerical, or other assistants to the subcommittee except that
minority staff members shall be under the supervision of the ranking
minority Senator on the subcommittee;
(d) the President pro tempore is the supervisor of the Secretary of
the Senate, Sergeant at Arms and Doorkeeper, the Chaplain, and the
employees of the Office of the Legislative Counsel;
(e) the Secretary of the Senate is the supervisor of the employees
of his office;
(f) the Sergeant at Arms and Doorkeeper is the supervisor of the
employees of his office;
(g) the Majority and Minority Leaders and the Majority and
Minority Whips are the supervisors of the research, clerical, or other
assistants assigned to their respective offices;
(h) the Majority Leader is the supervisor of the Secretary for the
Majority. The Secretary for the Majority is the supervisor of the
employees of his office; and
(i) the Minority Leader is the supervisor of the Secretary for the
Minority. The Secretary for the Minority is the supervisor of the
employees of his office.
3. This rule shall take effect ninety days after adoption.

RULE XLII

Contributions

1. A Senator or person who has declared or otherwise made known his
intention to seek nomination or election, or who has filed papers or petitions
for nomination or election, or on whose behalf a declaration or nominating paper or petition has been made or filed, or who has otherwise, directly or indirectly, manifested his intention to seek nomination or election, pursuant to
State law, to the office of United States Senator, may accept a contribution
from—
(a) a fundraising event organized and held primarily in his behalf,
provided—
(1) he has expressly given his approval of the fundraising event
to the sponsors before any funds were raised; and
(2) he receives a complete and accurate accounting of the
source, amounts, and disposition of the funds raised; or
(b) an individual or an organization, provided the Senator makes
a complete and accurate accounting of the source, amount, and disposition of the funds received; or
(c) his political party when such contributions were from a
fundraising event sponsored by his party, without giving his express
approval for such fundraising event when such fundraising event is for
the purpose of providing contributions for candidates of his party and

such contributions are reported by the Senator or candidate for Senator as provided in paragraph (b).

2. The Senator may use the contribution only to influence his nomination for election, or his election, and shall not use, directly or indirectly, any part of any contribution for any other purpose, except as otherwise provided herein.

3. Nothing in this rule shall preclude the use of contributions to defray expenses for travel to and from each Senator's home State; for printing and other expenses in connection with the mailing of speeches, newsletters, and reports to a Senator's constituents; for expenses of radio, television, and news media methods of reporting to a Senator's constituents; for telephone, telegraph, postage, and stationery expenses in excess of allowance; and for newspaper subscriptions from his home State.

4. All gifts in the aggregate amount or value of $50 or more received by a Senator from any single source during a year, except a gift from his spouse, child, or parent, and except a contribution under sections 1 and 2, shall be reported under rule XLIV.

5. This rule shall take effect ninety days after adoption.

RULE XLIII

Political Fund Activity by Officers and Employees

1. No officer or employee whose salary is paid by the Senate may receive, solicit, be the custodian of, or distribute any funds in connection with any campaign for the nomination for election, or the election of any individual to be a Member of the Senate or to any other Federal office. This prohibition does not apply to any assistant to a Senator who has been designated by that Senator to perform any of the functions described in the first sentence of this paragraph and who is compensated at a rate in excess of $10,000 per annum if such designation has been made in writing and filed with the Secretary of the Senate. The Secretary of the Senate shall make the designation available for public inspection.

2. This rule shall take effect sixty days after adoption.

RULE XLIV

Disclosure of Financial Interests

1. Each Senator or person who has declared or otherwise made known his intention to seek nomination or election, or who has filed papers or petitions for nomination or election, or on whose behalf a declaration or nominating paper or petition has been made or filed, or who has otherwise, directly or indirectly, manifested his intention to seek nomination or election, pursuant to State law, to the office of United States Senator, and each officer or employee of the Senate who is compensated at a rate in excess of $15,000 a year, shall file with the Comptroller General of the United States, in a sealed envelope marked "Confidential Personal Financial Disclosure of _____(name)_____", before the 15th day of May in each year, the following reports of his personal financial interests:

(a) a copy of the returns of taxes, declarations, statements, or other documents which he, or he and his spouse jointly, made for the preceding year in compliance with the income tax provisions of the Internal Revenue Code;

(b) the amount or value and source of each fee or compensation of $1,000 or more received by him during the preceding year from a client;

(c) the name and address of each business or professional corporation, firm, or enterprise in which he was an officer, director, partner, proprietor, or employee who received compensation during the preceding year and the amount of such compensation;

(d) the identity of each interest in real or personal property having a value of $10,000 or more which he owned at any time during the preceding year;

(e) the identity of each trust or other fiduciary relation in which he held a beneficial interest having a value of $10,000 or more, and the identity if known of each interest of the trust or other fiduciary relation

in real or personal property in which the Senator, officer, or employe held a beneficial interest having a value of $10,000 or more, at any tim during the preceding year. If he cannot obtain the identity of th fiduciary interests, the Senator, officer, or employee shall request th fiduciary to report that information to the Comptroller General the same manner that reports are filed under this rule;

(f) the identity of each liability of $5,000 or more owed by him, by him and his spouse jointly, at any time during the preceding yea and

(g) the source and value of all gifts in the aggregate amount or val of $50 or more from any single source received by him during th preceding year.

2. Except as otherwise provided by this section, all papers filed und section 1 of this rule shall be kept by the Comptroller General for not le than seven years, and while so kept shall remain sealed. Upon receipt of resolution of the Select Committee on Standards and Conduct, adopted by recorded majority vote of the full committee, requesting the transmission the committee of any of the reports filed by any individual under section 1 this rule, the Comptroller General shall transmit to the committee th envelopes containing such reports. Within a reasonable time after suc recorded vote has been taken, the individual concerned shall be informed the vote to examine and audit, and shall be advised of the nature and scope such examination. When any sealed envelope containing any such report received by the committee, such envelope may be opened and the content thereof may be examined only by members of the committee in executiv session. If, upon such examination, the committee determines that furthe consideration by the committee is warranted and is within the jurisdiction the committee, it may make the contents of any such envelope available fo any use by any member of the committee, or any member of the staff of th committee, which is required for the discharge of his official duties. The com mittee may receive the papers as evidence, after giving to the individual con cerned due notice and opportunity for hearing in a closed session. Th Comptroller General shall report to the Select Committee on Standards and Conduct not later than the 1st day of June in each year the names o Senators, officers, and employees who have filed a report. Any paper which has been filed with the Comptroller General for longer than seven years, in accordance with the provisions of this section, shall be returned to the in dividual concerned or his legal representative. In the event of the death or termination of service of a Member of the Senate, an officer or employee, such papers shall be returned unopened to such individual, or to the surviv ing spouse or legal representative of such individual within one year of such death or termination of service.

3. Each Senator or person who has declared or otherwise made known his intention to seek nomination or election, or who has filed papers or petitions for nomination or election, or on whose behalf a declaration or nominating paper or petition has been made or filed, or who has otherwise, directly or indirectly, manifested his intention to seek nomination or election, pursuant to State law, to the office of United States Senator, and each officer or employee of the Senate who is compensated at a rate in excess of $15,000 a year, shall file with the Secretary of the Senate, before the 15th day of May in each year, the following reports of his personal financial interests:

(a) the accounting required by rule XLII for all contributions received by him during the preceding year, except that contributions in the aggregate amount or value of less than $50 received from any single source during the reporting period may be totaled without further itemization; and

(b) the amount or value and source of each honorarium of $300 or more received by him during the preceding year.

4. All papers filed under section 3 of this rule shall be kept by the Secretary of the Senate for not less than three years and shall be made available promptly for public inspection and copying.

5. This rule shall take effect on July 1, 1968. No reports shall be filed for any period before office or employment was held with the Senate, or during a period of office or employment with the Senate of less than ninety days in a year; except that the Senator, or officer or employee of the Senate, may file a copy of the return of taxes for the year 1968, or a report of substantially equivalent information for only the effective part of the year 1968.

Standing Orders of the Senate, 94th Congress

Sources: U.S. Congress, Senate, Committee on Rules and Administration, *Senate Manual*, S. Doc. 94-1, 94th Congress, 1st sess., 1975, pp. 101-26. Committee on Rules and Administration staff.

Includes nonstatutory standing orders not embraced in the Rules, and ~olutions affecting the business of the Senate. (Footnotes and citations to ~ *Senate Journal* have been deleted from the following.)

Committee Personnel and Expenditure Reports

Resolved, That the Senate shall not (1) authorize the payment from the ~ntingent fund of the Senate of the expenses, in excess of $5,000, of any in~iry or investigation hereafter authorized, or (2) increase the amount ~retofore authorized to be paid from the contingent fund of the Senate in ~nnection with any inquiry or investigation, unless, prior to adoption of the ~solution authorizing such payment or providing for such increase, the com~ittee or subcommittee thereof authorized to conduct such inquiry or in~stigation shall have submitted to the Committee on Rules and Administra~on a budget, in such form as the committee may require, setting forth its es~mates of expenses proposed to be incurred for personal services, hearings, ~d travel, and such other information as the committee may require.

Sec. 2. Whenever the head of any department or agency of the Govern~ent shall have detailed or assigned personnel of such department or agency ~ the staff of any Senate committee or subcommittee thereof, the ~ppropriations of such department or agency from which the personnel so ~ssigned or detailed is paid shall be reimbursed from funds available to the ~ommittee or subcommittee at the end of each quarterly period in the ~mount of the salaries of such personnel while on such detail or assignment; ~nd the services of any personnel so detailed or assigned shall not be accepted ~r utilized unless, at the time of such detail or assignment, funds are ~vailable to such committee or subcommittee for the reimbursement of ~ppropriations, as herein provided, for the period of such detail or ~ssignment.

Sec. 3. The foregoing provisions of this resolution shall become effective ~n April 1, 1946.

Sec. 4. The Committee on Rules and Administration of the Senate is ~uthorized to make such studies as may be necessary to enable it to prescribe ~niform requirements as to the form and content of budgets required to be ~ubmitted under the first section of this resolution and otherwise to carry out ~ts functions under such section.

Printing in Congressional Record

Resolved, That hereafter no written or printed matter shall be received ~or printing in the body of the Congressional Record as a part of the remarks ~f any Senator unless such matter (1) shall have been read orally by such Senator on the floor of the Senate, or (2) shall have been offered and received ~or printing in such manner as to indicate clearly that the contents thereof were not read orally by such Senator on the floor of the Senate. All such matter shall be printed in the Record in accordance with the rules prescribed by the Joint Committee on Printing. No request shall be entertained by the Presiding Officer to suspend by unanimous consent the requirements of this resolution.

Special Deputies

Resolved, That the Sergeant at Arms of the Senate is authorized and empowered from time to time to appoint such special deputies as he may think necessary to serve process or perform other duties devolved upon the Sergeant at Arms by law or the rules or orders of the Senate, or which may hereafter be devolved upon him, and in such case they shall be officers of the Senate; and any act done or return made by the deputies so appointed shall have like effect and be of the same validity as if performed or made by the Sergeant at Arms in person.

Persons Not Full-Time Employees of Senate

Resolved, That hereafter, standing or select committees employing the services of persons who are not full-time employees of the Senate or any committee thereof shall submit monthly reports to the Senate (or to the Secretary during a recess or adjournment) showing (1) the name and address of any such person; (2) the name and address of the department or organization by whom his salary is paid; and (3) the annual rate of compensation in each case.

Flowers in the Senate Chamber

Resolved, That until further orders the Sergeant at Arms is instructed not to permit flowers to be brought into the Senate Chamber.

Length of Service and Age of Senate Pages*

Resolved, That it shall be the duty of the Sergeant at Arms to classify the pages of the Senate, so that at the close of the present and each succeeding Congress, one-half the number shall be removed * * *

Resolved, * * * That in no case shall a page of the Senate be appointed for duty in the Senate Chamber who is younger than fourteen years of age and who has not completed the eighth grade of school, or is seventeen years of age or older, except that those enrolled in the Senate page school who attain age seventeen may serve as pages through the session of the Senate in which the page-school year terminates.

[* Superseded by the following section from the "General and Permanent Laws Relating to the Senate":

§ 88b-1. Congressional pages—Appointment conditions.

(a) A person shall not be appointed as a page of the Senate or House of Representatives—

(1) unless he agrees that, in the absence of unforeseen circumstances preventing his service as a page after his appointment, he will continue to serve as a page for a period of not less than two months; and

(2) until complete information in writing is transmitted to his parent or parents, his legal guardian, or other appropriate person or persons acting as his parent or parents, with respect to the nature of the work of pages, their pay, their working conditions (including hours and scheduling of work), and the housing accommodations available to pages.

(b) A person shall not serve as a page—

(1) of the Senate before he has attained the age of fourteen years; or

(2) of the House of Representatives before he has attained the age of sixteen years; or

(except in the case of a chief page, telephone page, or riding page) during any session of the Congress which begins after he has attained the age of eighteen years.

(c) The pay of pages of the Senate shall begin not more than five days before the convening or reconvening of a session of the Congress or of the Senate and shall continue until the end of the month during which the Congress or the Senate adjourns or recesses, or until the fourteenth day after such adjournment or recess, whichever is the later date, except that, in any case in which the Congress or the Senate adjourns or recesses on or before the last day of July for a period of at least thirty days but not more than forty-five days, such pay shall continue until the end of such period of adjournment or recess.

(d) The pay of pages of the House of Representatives shall begin not more than five days before the convening of a session of the Congress and shall continue until the end of the month during which the Congress adjourns sine die or recesses or until the fourteenth day after such adjournment or recess, whichever is the later date, except that, in any case in which the House adjourns or recesses on or before the last day of July in any year for a period of at least thirty days but not more than forty-five days, such pay shall continue until the end of such period of adjournment or recess. (Oct. 26, 1970, Pub.L. 91-510, § 491, 84 Stat. 1198.)]

Seal of the Senate

Resolved, That the Secretary shall have the custody of the seal, and shall use the same for the authentication of process transcripts, copies, and certificates whenever directed by the Senate; and may use the same to authenticate copies of such papers and documents in his office as he may lawfully give copies of.

Seal of President Pro Tempore

Resolved, That the President pro tempore of the Senate is authorized to adopt and use an official seal of his office.

Sec. 2. Expenses incident to the designing and procurement of such seal shall be paid from the contingent fund of the Senate upon vouchers signed by the President pro tempore of the Senate.

Sec. 3. A description and illustration of the seal adopted pursuant to this resolution shall be transmitted to the General Services Administration for publication in the Federal Register.

Marble Busts of Vice Presidents

Resolved, That marble busts of those who have been Vice Presidents of the United States shall be placed in the Senate wing of the Capitol from time to time, that the Architect of the Capitol is authorized, subject to the advice and approval of the Senate Committee on Rules and Administration, to carry into execution the object of this resolution, and the expenses incurred in doing so shall be paid out of the contingent fund of the Senate.

Reading of Washington's Farewell Address

Ordered, That, unless otherwise directed, on the twenty-second day of February in each year, or if that day shall be on Sunday, then on the day following, immediately after the reading of the Journal, Washington's Farewell Address shall be read to the Senate by a Senator to be designated for the purpose by the Presiding Officer; and that thereafter the Senate will proceed with its ordinary business.

Payment of Witnesses

Resolved, That witnesses summoned to appear before the Senate or any of its committees shall be entitled to a witness fee rated at not to exceed $35 for each full day spent in traveling to and from the place of examination and for each full day in attendance. A witness shall also be entitled to reimbursement of the actual and necessary transportation expenses incurred by him in traveling to and from the place of examination, in no case to exceed 35 cents a mile for the distance actually traveled by him for the purpose of appearing as a witness if such distance is not more than six hundred miles or 20 cents a mile if such distance is more than six hundred miles.

Select Committee on Small Business

Resolved, That there is hereby created a select committee to be known as the Committee on Small Business and to consist of seventeen Senators to be appointed in the same manner and at the same time as the chairmen and members of the standing committees of the Senate at the beginning of each Congress.

It shall be the duty of such committee to study and survey by means of research and investigation all problems of American small-business enterprises, and to obtain all facts possible in relation thereto which would not only be of public interest, but which would aid the Congress in enacting remedial legislation, and to report to the Senate from time to time the results of such studies and surveys. No proposed legislation shall be referred to such committee and such committee shall not have power to report by bill or otherwise have legislative jurisdiction.

Select Committee on Small Business—Additional Powers

Resolved, That the Select Committee on Small Business, created by Senate Resolution 58, agreed to February 20, 1950, or any duly authorized subcommittee thereof, is authorized to sit and act at such places and times during the sessions, recesses, and adjourned periods of the Senate, to require by subpena or otherwise the attendance of such witnesses and the production of such books, papers, and documents, to administer such oaths, to take such testimony, to procure such printing and binding, and to make such expenditures as it deems advisable. The cost of stenographic services to report such hearings shall not be in excess of 25 cents per 100 words.

Sec. 2. A majority of the members of the committee, or any subcommittee thereof, shall constitute a quorum for the transaction of business, except that a lesser number, to be fixed by the committee, shall constitute a quorum for the purpose of taking sworn testimony.

Sec. 3. The committee shall have power to employ and fix the compensation of such officers, experts, and employees as it deems necessary in the performance of its duties, but the compensation so fixed shall not exceed the compensation prescribed under the Classification Act of 1949 for comparable duties. The committee is authorized to utilize the services, information, facilities, and personnel of the various departments and agencies of the Government to the extent that such services, information, facilities, and personnel, in the opinion of the heads of such departments and agencies, can be furnished without undue interference with the performance of the work and duties of such departments and agencies.

Sec. 4. Until an appropriation shall be made for payment of expenses of the committee, such expenses, in an amount not to exceed $10,000, shall be paid from the contingent fund of the Senate upon vouchers approved by the chairman.

Pay of Clerical and Other Assistants as Affected by Resignation of Senators

Resolved, That in the case of the resignation of a Senator during his term of office, his clerical and other assistants on the payroll of the Senate on the date of such resignation shall be continued on such payroll at their respective salaries for a period of not to exceed thirty days, such sums to be paid from the contingent fund of the Senate: *Provided,* That any su assistants continued on the payroll, while so continued, shall perform th duties under the direction of the Secretary of the Senate, and he hereby authorized and directed to remove from such payroll any such assistants w are not attending to the duties for which their services are continued: *Prov ed further,* That this shall not operate to continue such assistants on su payroll beyond the expiration of their Senator's term of service.

Pay of Clerical and Other Assistants as Affected by Termination o Service of Appointed Senators

Resolved, That in any case in which (1) a Senator is appointed to fill a portion of an unexpired term, (2) an election is thereafter held to fill t remainder of such unexpired term, and (3) the Senator so appointed is not candidate or if a candidate is not elected at such election, his clerical ar other assistants on the payroll of the Senate on the date of termination of h service shall be continued on such roll at their respective salaries until the e piration of thirty days following such date or until they become otherwi gainfully employed, whichever is earlier, such sums to be paid from the co tingent fund of the Senate. A statement in writing by any such employee the he was not gainfully employed during such period or the portion thereof fo which payment is claimed shall be accepted as prima facie evidence that b was not so employed. The provisions of this resolution shall not apply to a employee of any such Senator if on or before the date of termination of hi service he notifies the Disbusing Office of the Senate in writing that he doe not wish the provisions of this resolution to apply to such employee.

Hearings Before Senate Members of Joint Committee on Atomic Energy

Resolved, That the Senate members of the Joint Committee on Atomi Energy, appointed by the President of the Senate as provided in Public Law 585, Seventy-ninth Congress, approved August 1, 1946, shall have the sam power and authority, in connection with the holding of hearings and the con duct of investigations and reporting to the Senate thereon, with reference to appointments under said Public Law 585 that require the advice and consen of the Senate, as are possessed by the standing committees of the Senate in other matters requiring the advice and consent of the Senate.

Printing of the Executive Journal

Resolved, That, beginning with the first session, Ninetieth Congress, the Secretary of the Senate is authorized to have printed not more than one hundred and fifty copies of the Executive Journal for a session of the Congress.

Loyalty Checks on Senate Employees

Resolved, That hereafter when any person is appointed as an employee of any committee of the Senate, of any Senator, or of any office of the Senate the committee, Senator, or officer having authority to make such appointment shall transmit the name of such person to the Federal Bureau of Investigation, together with a request that such committee, Senator, or officer be informed as to any derogatory and rebutting information in the possession of such agency concerning the loyalty and reliability for security purposes of such person, and in any case in which such derogatory information is revealed such committee, Senator, or officer shall make or cause to be made such further investigation as shall have been considered necessary to determine the loyalty and reliability for security purposes of such person.

Every such committee, Senator, and officer shall promptly transmit to the Federal Bureau of Investigation a list of the names of the incumbent employees of such committee, Senator, or officer together with a request that such committee, Senator, or officer be informed of any derogatory and rebutting information contained in the files of such agency concerning the loyalty and reliability for security purposes of such employee.

Authorizing Suit by Senate Committee

Resolved, That hereafter any committee of the Senate is hereby authorized to bring suit on behalf of and in the name of the United States in any court of competent jurisdiction if the committee is of the opinion that the suit is necessary to the adequate performance of the powers vested in it or the duties imposed upon it by the Constitution, resolution of the Senate, or other law. Such suit may be brought and prosecuted to final determination irrespective of whether or not the Senate is in session at the time the suit is brought or thereafter. The committee may be represented in the suit either by such attorneys as it may designate or by such officers of the Department of Justice as the Attorney General may designate upon the request of the committee. No expenditures shall be made in connection with any such suit in excess of the amount of funds available to the said committee. As used in this resolution, the term "committee" means any standing or special committee of the Senate, or any duly authorized subcommittee thereof, or the Senate members of any joint committee.

Senate Youth Program

Whereas by S. Res. 324 of the Eighty-seventh Congress, agreed to May 17, 1962, the Senate expressed its willingness to cooperate in a nationwide competitive Senate youth program supported by private funds, which would give representative high school students from each State a short indoctrination into the operation of the United States Senate and the Federal Government generally, and authorized the Senate Committee on Rules and Administration, if it should find such a program possible and advisable, to make the necessary arrangements therefor; and

Whereas the Committee on Rules and Administration, after appropriate investigation, having determined such a program to be not only possible but highly desirable, authorized its establishment and with the support of the leaders and other Members of the Senate and the cooperation of certain private institutions made the necessary arrangements therefor; and

Whereas, pursuant to such arrangements, and with the cooperation of and participation by the offices of every Member of the Senate and the Vice President, one hundred and two student leaders representing all States of the Union and the District of Columbia were privileged to spend the period from January 28, 1963, through February 2, 1963, in the Nation's Capitol, thereby broadening their knowledge and understanding of Congress and the legislative process and stimulating their appreciation of the importance of a freely elected legislature in the perpetuation of our democratic system of government; and

Whereas by S. Res 147 of the Eighty-eighth Congress, agreed to May 27, 1963, another group of student leaders from throughout the United States spent approximately one week in the Nation's Capitol, during January 1964; and

Whereas it is the consensus of all who participated that the above two programs were unqualifiedly successful, and in all respects worthy and deserving of continuance; and

Whereas the private foundation which financed the initial programs has graciously offered to support a similar program during the year ahead: Now, therefore, be it

Resolved, That, until otherwise directed by the Senate, the Senate Youth program authorized by S. Res. 324 of the Eighty-seventh Congress, agreed to May 17, 1962, and extended by S. Res. 147, agreed to May 27, 1963, may be continued at the discretion of and under such conditions as may be determined by the Committee on Rules and Administration.

Select Committee on Standards and Conduct

Resolved, That (a) there is hereby established a permanent select committee of the Senate to be known as the Select Committee on Standards and Conduct (referred to hereinafter as the "Select Committee") consisting of six Members of the Senate, of whom three shall be selected from members of the majority party and three shall be selected from members of the minority party. Members thereof shall be appointed by the President of the Senate. The Select Committee shall select a chairman and a vice chairman from among its members. For purposes of paragraph 6(f) of rule XXV of the Standing Rules of the Senate, service of a Senator as chairman of the Select Committee shall not be taken into account.

(b) Vacancies in the membership of the Select Committee shall not affect the authority of the remaining members to execute the functions of the committee, and shall be filled in the same manner as original appointments thereto are made.

(c) A majority of the members of the Select Committee shall constitute a quorum for the transaction of business, except that the Select Committee may fix a lesser number as a quorum for the purpose of taking sworn testimony. The Select Committee shall adopt rules of procedure not inconsistent with the rules of the Senate governing standing committees of the Senate.

Sec. 2. (a) It shall be the duty of the Select Committee to—

(1) receive complaints and investigate allegations of improper conduct which may reflect upon the Senate, violations of law, and violations of rules and regulations of the Senate, relating to the conduct of individuals in the performance of their duties as Members of the Senate, or as officers or employees of the Senate, and to make appropriate findings of fact and conclusions with respect thereto:

(2) recommend to the Senate by report or resolution by a majority vote of the full committee disciplinary action to be taken with respect to such violations which the Select Committee shall determine, after according to the individuals concerned due notice and opportunity for hearing, to have occurred;

(3) recommend to the Senate, by report or resolution, such additional rules or regulations as the Select Committee shall determine to be necessary or desirable to insure proper standards of conduct by Members of the Senate, and by officers or employees of the Senate, in

the performance of their duties and the discharge of their responsibilities; and

(4) report violations by a majority vote of the full committee of any law to the proper Federal and State authorities.

(b) The Select Committee from time to time shall transmit to the Senate its recommendation as to any legislative measures which it may consider to be necessary for the effective discharge of its duties.

Sec. 3. (a) The Select Committee is authorized to (1) make such expenditures; (2) hold such hearings; (3) sit and act at such times and places during the sessions, recesses, and adjournment periods of the Senate; (4) require by subpena or otherwise the attendance of such witnesses and the production of such correspondence, books, papers, and documents; (5) administer such oaths; (6) take such testimony orally or by deposition; and (7) employ and fix the compensation of such technical, clerical, and other assistants and consultants as it deems advisable.

(b) Upon request made by the members of the Select Committee selected from the minority party, the committee shall appoint one assistant or consultant designated by such members. No assistant or consultant appointed by the Select Committee may receive compensation at an annual gross rate which exceeds by more than $1,600 the annual gross rate of compensation of any individual so designated by the members of the committee who are members of the minority party.

(c) With the prior consent of the department or agency concerned, the Select Committee may (1) utilize the services, information, and facilities of the General Accounting Office or any department or agency in the executive branch of the Government, and (2) employ on a reimbursable basis or otherwise the services of such personnel of any such department or agency as it deems advisable. With the consent of any other committee of the Senate, or any subcommittee thereof, the Select Committee may utilize the facilities and the services of the staff of such other committee or subcommittee whenever the chairman of the Select Committee determines that such action is necessary and appropriate.

(d) Subpenas may be issued by the Select Committee over the signature of the chairman or any other member designated by him, and may be served by any person designated by such chairman or member. The chairman of the Select Committee or any member thereof may administer oaths to witnesses.

Sec. 4. The expenses of the Select Committee under this resolution shall be paid from the contingent fund of the Senate upon vouchers approved by the chairman of the Select Committee.

Sec. 5. As used in this resolution, the term "officer or employee of the Senate" means—

(1) an elected officer of the Senate who is not a Member of the Senate;

(2) an employee of the Senate, any committee or subcommittee of the Senate, or any Member of the Senate;

(3) the Legislative Counsel of the Senate or any employee of his office;

(4) an Official Reporter of Debates of the Senate and any person employed by the Official Reporters of Debates of the Senate in connection with the performance of their official duties;

(5) a member of the Capitol Police force whose compensation is disbursed by the Secretary of the Senate;

(6) an employee of the Vice President if such employee's compensation is disbursed by the Secretary of the Senate;

(7) an employee of a joint committee of the Congress whose compensation is disbursed by the Secretary of the Senate.

Award of Service Pins or Emblems to Employees in Legislative Branch

Resolved, That the Committee on Rules and Administration is hereby authorized to provide for the awarding of service pins or emblems to Members, officers, and employees of the Senate, and to promulgate regulations governing the awarding of such pins or emblems. Such pins or emblems shall be of a type appropriate to be attached to the lapel of the wearer, shall be of such appropriate material and design, and shall contain such characters, symbols, or other matter, as the committee shall select.

Sec. 2. The Secretary of the Senate, under direction of the committee and in accordance with regulations promulgated by the committee, shall procure such pins or emblems and award them to Members, officers, and employees of the Senate who are entitled thereto.

Sec. 3. The expenses incurred in procuring such pins or emblems shall be paid from the contingent fund of the Senate on vouchers signed by the chairman of the committee.

Acceptance of Decorations Tendered by Foreign Governments

Resolved, That the Committee on Rules and Administration is hereby authorized to grant approval, for the purposes of section 7342 of title 5, United States Code, and regulations prescribed thereunder, of the acceptance, retention, and wearing by a Member, officer, or employee of the

Senate of a decoration tendered by a foreign government in recognition of active field service in time of combat operations or awarded for other outstanding or unusually meritorious service.

Commission on Art and Antiquities of the United States Senate

Resolved, That (a) there is hereby established a Commission on Art and Antiquities of the United States Senate (hereinafter referred to as "the Commission") consisting of the President pro tempore of the Senate, the chairman and ranking minority member of the Committee on Rules and Administration of the Senate, and the majority and minority leaders of the Senate.

(b) The Commission shall elect a Chairman and a Vice Chairman at the beginning of each Congress. Three members of the Commission shall constitute a quorum for the transaction of business, except that the Commission may fix a lesser number which shall constitute a quorum for the taking of testimony.

(c) The Commission shall select a Curator of Art and Antiquities of the Senate who shall be appointed by and be an employee of the Secretary of the Senate. The Curator shall serve at the pleasure of the Commission, shall perform such duties as it may prescribe, and shall receive compensation at a gross rate, not to exceed $22,089 per annum to be fixed by the Commission. At the request of the Commission the Secretary of the Senate shall detail to the Commission such additional professional, clerical, and other assistants as, from time to time, it deems necessary.

(d) The Commission shall be empowered to hold hearings, summon witnesses, administer oaths, employ reporters, request the production of papers and records, take such testimony, and adopt such rules for the conduct of its hearings, and meetings, as it deems necessary.

Sec. 2. (a) The Commission is hereby authorized and, directed to supervise, hold, place, and protect all works of art, historical objects, and exhibits within the Senate wing of the Capitol, and in all rooms, spaces, and corridors thereof, which are the property of the United States, and in its judgment to accept any works of art, historical objects, or exhibits which may hereafter be offered, given, or devised to the Senate, its committees, and its officers for placement and exhibition in the Senate wing of the Capitol, the Senate Office Buildings, or in rooms, spaces, or corridors thereof.

(b) The Commission shall prescribe such regulations as it deems necessary for the care, protection, and placement of such works of art, exhibits, and historical objects in the Senate wing of the Capitol and the Senate Office Buildings and for their acceptance on behalf of the Senate, its committees, and officers. Such regulations shall be published in the Congressional Record at such times as the Commission may deem necessary for the information of the Members of the Senate and the Public.

(c) Regulations authorized by the provisions of section 1820 of the Revised Statutes (40 U.S.C. 193) to be issued by the Sergeant at Arms of the Senate for the protection of the Capitol, and any regulations issued, or activities undertaken, by the Committee on Rules and Administration of the Senate, or the Architect of the Capitol, in carrying out duties relating to the care, preservation, and protection of the Senate wing of the Capitol and the Senate Office Buildings, shall be consistent with such rules and regulations as the Commission may issue pursuant to subsection (b).

(d) The Committee on Rules and Administration of the Senate in consultation with the Architect of the Capitol and consistent with regulations prescribed by the Commission under subsection (b), shall have responsibility for the supervision, protection, and placement of all works of art, historical objects, and exhibits which shall have been accepted on behalf of the Senate by the Commission or acknowledged as United States property by inventory of the Commission, and which may be lodged in the Senate wing of the Capitol or the Senate Office Buildings by the Commission.

Sec. 3. The Commission shall have responsibility for the supervision and maintenance of the Old Senate Chamber on the principal floor of the Senate wing of the Capitol insofar as it is to be preserved as a patriotic shrine in the Capitol for the benefit of the people of the United States.

Sec. 4. The Commission shall, from time to time, but at least once every ten years, publish as a Senate document a list of all works of art, historical objects, and exhibits currently within the Senate wing of the Capitol and the Senate Office Buildings, together with their description, location, and with such notes as may be pertinent to their history.

Sec. 5. There is hereby authorized to be appropriated out of the contingent fund of the Senate for the expenses of the Commission the sum of $15,000 each fiscal year, to be disbursed by the Secretary of the Senate on vouchers signed by the Chairman or Vice Chairman of the Commission: *Provided,* That no payment shall be made from such appropriation as salary.

Commission on Art and Antiquities of the United States Senate—Additional Authority

Resolved, That (a) the Commission on Art and Antiquities of the United States Senate, in addition to any authority conferred upon it by Senate Resolution 382, Ninetieth Congress, agreed to October 1, 1968, is authorized to acquire any work of art, historical object, document or material relating to

historical matters, or exhibit for placement or exhibition in the Senate w of the Capitol, the Senate Office Buildings, or in rooms, spaces, or corrid thereof.

(b) This resolution shall be effective as of March 1, 1971.

Standards of Conduct for Members of the Senate and Officers and Employees of the Senate

Resolved, It is declared to be the policy of the Senate that—

(a) The ideal concept of public office, expressed by the words, "A pub office is a public trust", signifies that the officer has been entrusted w public power by the people; that the officer holds this power in trust to used only for their benefit and never for the benefit of himself or of a few; a that the officer must never conduct his own affairs so as to infringe on t public interest. All official conduct of Members of the Senate should guided by this paramount concept of public office.

(b) These rules, as the written expression of certain standards of co duct, complement the body of unwritten but generally accepted standar that continue to apply to the Senate.

Sec. 2. The Standing Rules of the Senate are amended by adding at t end thereof the following new rules:

* * * * * * *

Appointment for the Senate of Pages, Elevator Operators, Post Office Employees, or Capitol Policemen Without Discrimination on Account of Sex

Resolved, That no individual shall be denied appointment as a Sena page, elevator operator, or post office employee, or as a Capitol policema whose compensation is disbursed by the Secretary of the Senate, solely on th basis of sex. In the case of Senate pages, however, until such time as th fireproof building containing dormitory and classroom facilities, a authorized by section 492 of the Legislative Reorganization Act of 1970, constructed and the pages are living under appropriate supervision in suc building, the Sergeant at Arms of the Senate shall promulgate and have i effect regulations for the appointment of pages of the Senate requiring tha no female page shall be appointed by a Senator until the Senator files wit the Sergeant at Arms a written statement accompanying such appointmen that the Senator—

(1) will be responsible for the safe transportation of the femal page he appoints between the Senate and the page's place of loca abode and return; and

(2) will assume full responsibility for the safety, well-being, an strict supervision of such female page while such page is in her plac of local abode.

Designating the Old Senate Office Building and the New Senate Office Building as the "Richard Brevard Russell Office Building" and the "Everett McKinley Dirksen Office Building", Respectively

Resolved, That insofar as concerns the Senate—

(1) the Senate Office Building referred to as the Old Senate Office Building and constructed under authority of the Act of April 28, 1904 (33 Stat. 452, 481), is designated, and shall be known as, the "Richard Brevard Russell Office Building"; and

(2) The additional office building for the Senate referred to as the New Senate Office Building and constructed under the provisions of the Second Deficiency Appropriation Act of 1948 (62 Stat. 1928), including any extension to such building, is designated, and shall be known as, the "Everett McKinley Dirksen Office Building".

Sec. 2. Any rule, regulation, document, or record of the Senate, in which reference is made to either building referred to in the first section of this resolution, shall be held and considered to be a reference to such building by the name designated for such building by the first section of this resolution.

Sec. 3. The Committee on Rules and Administration shall place appropriate markers or inscriptions at suitable locations within the buildings referred to in the first section of this resolution to commemorate and designate such buildings as provided in this resolution. Expenses incurred under this resolution shall be paid from the contingent fund of the Senate upon vouchers approved by the chairman of the committee.

Printing of Memorial Tributes to Deceased Former Members of the Senate

Resolved, That when the Senate orders the printing as a Senate document of the legislative proceedings in the United States Congress relating to the death of a former United States Senator, such document shall be prepared, printed, bound, and distributed, except to the extent otherwise

⌐ided by the Joint Committee on Printing under chapter 1 of title 44, ╺ted States Code, in the same manner and under the same conditions as ⌐norial addresses on behalf of Members of Congress dying in office are ╺ted under sections 723 and 724 of such title.

Senate Parliamentarian Emeritus

⌐ereas the Senate has been advised of the retirement of its Parliamentarian, Floyd M. Riddick, at the end of this session: Therefore be it

Resolved, That, effective at the sine die adjournment of this session, as a ⌐en of the appreciation of the Senate for his long and faithful service, ⌐yd M. Riddick is hereby designated as Parliamentarian Emeritus of the ╺ted States Senate.

Committee-Related Senate Employees

[Section 1 of this resolution may be found as paragraph 8 of rule XXV of Standing Rules of the Senate....]

Sec. 2. Paragraph 8 of rule XXV of the Standing Rules of the Senate (as ╺led by the first section of this resolution) shall be suspended and shall ⌐ve no force or effect during any period during which, by law, a legislative ╺istance clerk-hire fund is established and funded to provide for legislative ╺istance for Senators serving on committees at rates not less than those ⌐vided in such paragraph 8, and subject to no more conditions and no ╺ater limitations than those provided in such paragraph.

Sec. 3. Each Senator and the chairman of each committee on which he serves shall, not later than five days (not including Saturdays, Sundays, or holidays) after the date on which this resolution is adopted certify to the Secretary of the Senate a list containing the names and the total aggregate annual compensation of any professional staff member on such committee whose appointment is made, approved, or recommended by such Senator. Whenever such certification has been made and is no longer applicable, the Senator and chairman of that committee shall jointly notify the Secretary of the Senate accordingly. Such certification shall be effective on the date received by the Secretary of the Senate.

Consultants for the Committee on Appropriations

Resolved, That within the limit of funds appropriated for expenses of inquiries and investigations for the Committee on Appropriations, the committee may expend such sums as it deems appropriate and necessary for the procurement of the services of individual consultants or organizations. Such services in the case of individuals or organizations may be procured by contract as independent contractors, or in the case of individuals by employment at daily rates of compensation not in excess of the per diem equivalent of the highest gross rate of compensation which may be paid to a regular employee of the committee. Such contracts may be made in the same manner and subject to the same conditions with respect to advertising as required of other standing committees of the Senate under section 202(i)(2) of the Legislative Reorganization Act of 1946, as amended.

Rules of the House of Representatives, 94th Congress

Sources: U.S. Congress, House, *Constitution, Jefferson's Manual and Rules of the House of Representatives*, by Wm. Holmes Brown, parliamentarian, H. Doc. 416, 93rd Congress, 2nd sess., 1975, pp. 319-650. Office of the Parliamentarian.

Includes amendments through June 30, 1976. (Lengthy notes and annotations have been deleted from the following.)

RULE I

Duties of the Speaker

1. The Speaker shall take the chair on every legislative day precisely at the hour to which the House shall have adjourned at the last sitting and immediately call the Members to order. On the appearance of a quorum, the Speaker, having examined the Journal of the proceedings of the last day's sitting and approved the same, shall announce to the House his approval of the Journal; whereupon, unless the Speaker, in his discretion, orders the reading of the Journal, the Journal shall be considered as read. However, it shall then be in order to offer one motion that the Journal be read and such motion is of the highest privilege and shall be determined without debate.

2. He shall preserve order and decorum, and, in case of disturbance or disorderly conduct in the galleries, or in the lobby, may cause the same to be cleared.

3. He shall have general control, except as provided by rule of law, of the Hall of the House, and of the corridors and passages and the disposal of the unappropriated rooms in that part of the Capitol assigned to the use of the House, until further order.

4. He shall sign all acts, addresses, joint resolutions, writs, warrants and subpenas of, or issued by order of, the House, and decide all questions of order, subject to an appeal by any Member, on which appeal no Member shall speak more than once, unless by permission of the House.

5. He shall rise to put a question, but may state it sitting; and shall put questions in this form, to wit: "As many as are in favor (as the question may be), say 'Aye'."; and after the affirmative voice is expressed, "As many as are opposed, say 'No'."; if he doubts, or a division is called for, the House shall divide; those in the affirmative of the question shall first rise from their seats, and then those in the negative, if he still doubts, or a count is required by at least one-fifth of a quorum, he shall name one or more from each side of the question to tell the Members in the affirmative and negative; which being reported, he shall rise and state the decision. However, if any Member requests a recorded vote and that request is supported by at least one-fifth of a quorum, such vote shall be taken by electronic device, unless the Speaker in his discretion orders clerks to tell the names of those voting on each side of the question, and such names shall be recorded by electronic device or by clerks, as the case may be, and shall be entered in the Journal, together with the names of those not voting. Members shall have not less than fifteen minutes to be counted from the ordering of the recorded vote or the ordering of clerks to tell the vote.

6. He shall not be required to vote in ordinary legislative proceedings, except where his vote would be decisive, or where the House is engaged in voting by ballot; and in cases of a tie vote the question shall be lost.

7. He shall have the right to name any Member to perform the duties of the Chair, but such substitution shall not extend beyond three legislative days: *Provided, however,* That in case of his illness, he may make such appointment for a period not exceeding ten days, with the approval of the House at the time the same is made; and in his absence and omission to make such appointment, the House shall proceed to elect a Speaker pro tempore to act during his absence.

8. He shall have the authority to designate any Member, officer or employee of the House of Representatives to travel on the business of the House of Representatives, as determined by him, within or without the United States, whether the House is meeting, has recessed or has adjourned, and all expenses for such travel may be paid for from the contingent fund of the House on vouchers solely approved and signed by the Speaker.

RULE II

Election of Officers

There shall be elected by a viva voce vote, at the commencement of each Congress, to continue in office until their successors are chosen and qualified, a Clerk, Sergeant-at-Arms, Doorkeeper, Postmaster, and Chaplain, each of whom shall take an oath to support the Constitution of the United States, and for the true and faithful discharge of the duties of his office to the best of his knowledge and ability, and to keep the secrets of the House; and each shall appoint all of the employees of his department provided for by law.

RULE III

Duties of the Clerk

1. The Clerk shall, at the commencement of the first session of ea[ch] Congress, call the Members to order, proceed to call the roll of Members [by] States in alphabetical order, and, pending the election of a Speaker [or] Speaker pro tempore, preserve order and decorum, and decide all questions [of] order subject to appeal by any Member.

2. He shall make and cause to be printed and delivered to each Memb[er] or mailed to his address, at the commencement of every regular session [of] Congress, a list of the report to which it is the duty of any officer or Depa[rt]ment to make to Congress, referring to the act or resolution and page of t[he] volume of the laws or Journal in which it may be contained, and placing u[n]der the name of each officer the list of reports required of him to be mad[e].

3. He shall note all questions of order, with the decisions thereon, t[he] record of which shall be printed as an appendix to the Journal of each sessio[n] and complete, as soon after the close of the session as possible, the printi[ng] and distribution to Members, Delegates, and the Resident Commission[er] from Puerto Rico of the Journal of the House, together with an accurate a[nd] complete index; retain in the library at his office, for the use of the Membe[rs], Delegates, the Resident Commissioner from Puerto Rico and officers of t[he] House, and not to be withdrawn therefrom, two copies of all the books a[nd] printed documents deposited there; send, at the end of each session, [a] printed copy of the Journal thereof to the executive and to each branch of t[he] legislature of every State; deliver or mail to any Member, Delegate, or t[he] Resident Commissioner from Puerto Rico an extra copy, in binding of go[od] quality, of each document requested by that Member, Delegate, or the Res[i]dent Commissioner which has been printed, by order of either House of t[he] Congress, in any Congress in which he served; attest and affix the seal of t[he] House to all writs, warrants, and subpenas issued by order of the House, ce[r]tify to the passage of all bills and joint resolutions, make or approve all co[n]tracts, bargains, or agreements relative to furnishing any matter or thing, [or] for the performance of any labor for the House of Representatives in pu[r]suance of law or order of the House, keep full and accurate accounts of t[he] disbursements out of the contingent fund of the House, keep the stationer[y] account of Members, Delegates, and the Resident Commissioner from Puer[to] Rico, and pay them as provided by law. He shall pay to the officers an[d] employees of the House of Representatives the amount of their salaries tha[t] shall be due them.

4. He shall, in case of temporary absence or disability, designate an o[f]ficial in his office to sign all papers that may require the official signature [of] the Clerk of the House, and to do all other acts, except such as are provide[d] for by statute, that may be required under the rules and practices of th[e] House to be done by the Clerk. Such official acts, when so done by th[e] designated official, shall be under the name of the Clerk of the House. Th[e] said designation shall be in writing, and shall be laid before the House an[d] entered on the Journal.

RULE IV

Duties of the Sergeant-at-Arms

1. It shall be the duty of the Sergeant-at-Arms to attend the House dur[]ing its sittings, to maintain order under the direction of the Speaker or Chair[]man, and, pending the election of a Speaker or Speaker pro tempore, under the direction of the Clerk, execute the commands of the House, and all processes issued by authority thereof, directed to him by the Speaker; and keep the accounts for the pay and mileage of Members, Delegates, and the Resident Commissioner from Puerto Rico, and pay them as provided by law.

2. The symbol of his office shall be the mace, which shall be borne by him while enforcing order on the floor.

RULE V

Duties of the Doorkeeper

1. The Doorkeeper shall enforce strictly the rules relating to the privileges of the Hall and be responsible to the House for the official conduct of his employees.

2. He shall allow no person to enter the room over the Hall of the House during its sittings; and fifteen minutes before the hour of the meeting of the

...use each day he shall see that the floor is cleared of all persons except those ...vileged to remain, and kept so until ten minutes after adjournment.

RULE VI

Duties of the Postmaster

The Postmaster shall superintend the post office in the Capitol and in ...e respective office buildings of the House for the accommodation of ...presentatives, Delegates, the Resident Commissioner from Puerto Rico, ...d officers of the House and shall be held responsible for the prompt and ...e delivery of their mail.

RULE VII

Duties of the Chaplain

The Chaplain shall attend at the commencement of each day's sitting of ...e House and open the same with prayer.

RULE VIII

Of the Members

1. Every Member shall be present within the Hall of the House during ...s sittings, unless excused or necessarily prevented; and shall vote on each ...uestion put, unless he has a direct personal or pecuniary interest in the ...ent of such question.

2. Pairs shall be announced by the Clerk immediately before the an-...ouncement by the Chair of the result of the vote, by the House or Com-...mittee of the Whole from a written list furnished him, and signed by the ...Member making the statement to the Clerk, which list shall be published in ...ne Record as a part of the proceedings, immediately following the names of ...hose not voting. However, pairs shall be announced but once during the ...ame legislative day.

RULE IX

Questions of Privilege

Questions of privilege shall be, first those affecting the rights of the ...House collectively, its safety, dignity, and the integrity of its proceedings; ...econd, the rights, reputation, and conduct of Members, individually, in ...heir representative capacity only; and shall have precedence of all other ...questions, except motions to adjourn.

RULE X

Establishment and Jurisdiction of Standing Committees
The Committees and Their Jurisdiction

1. There shall be in the House the following standing committees, each of which shall have the jurisdiction and related functions assigned to it by this clause and clauses 2, 3, and 4; and all bills, resolutions, and other matters relating to subjects within the jurisdiction of any standing com-mittee as listed in this clause shall (in accordance with and subject to clause 5) be referred to such committees, as follows:

(a) **Committee on Agriculture.**

(1) Adulteration of seeds, insect pests, and protection of birds and animals in forest reserves.

(2) Agriculture generally.

(3) Agricultural and industrial chemistry.

(4) Agricultural colleges and experiment stations.

(5) Agricultural economics and research.

(6) Agricultural education extension services.

(7) Agricultural production and marketing and stabilization of prices of agricultural products, and commodities (not including dis-tribution outside of the United States).

(8) Animal industry and diseases of animals.

(9) Crop insurance and soil conservation.

(10) Dairy industry.

(11) Entomology and plant quarantine.

(12) Extension of farm credit and farm security.

(13) Forestry in general, and forest reserves other than those created from the public domain.

(14) Human nutrition and home economics.

(15) Inspection of livestock and meat products.

(16) Plant industry, soils, and agricultural engineering.

(17) Rural electrification.

(18) Commodities exchanges.

(19) Rural development.

(b) **Committee on Appropriations.**

(1) Appropriation of the revenue for the support of the Government.

(2) Rescissions of appropriations contained in appropriation Acts.

(3) Transfers of unexpended balances.

(4) The amount of new spending authority (as described in the Congressional Budget Act of 1974) which is to be effective for a fiscal year, including bills and resolutions (reported by other committees) which provide new spending authority and are referred to the com-mittee under clause 4(a).

The committee shall include separate headings for "Rescissions" and "Transfers of Unexpected Balances" in any bill or resolution as reported from the committee under its jurisdiction specified in subparagraph (2) or (3), with all proposed rescissions and proposed transfers listed therein; and shall include a separate section with respect to such rescissions or transfers in the accompanying committee report. In addition to its jurisdiction under the preceding provisions of this paragraph, the committee shall have the fiscal oversight function provided for in clause 2(b) (3) and the budget hearing function provided for in clause 4(a).

(c) **Committee on Armed Services.**

(1) Common defense generally.

(2) The Department of Defense generally, including the Departments of the Army, Navy, and Air Force generally.

(3) Ammunition depots; forts; arsenals; Army, Navy, and Air Force reservations and establishments.

(4) Conservation, development, and use of naval petroleum and oil shale reserves.

(5) Pay, promotion, retirement, and other benefits and privileges of members of the armed forces.

(6) Scientific research and development in support of the armed services.

(7) Selective service.

(8) Size and composition of the Army, Navy, and Air Force.

(9) Soldiers' and sailors' homes.

(10) Strategic and critical materials necessary for the common defense.

In addition to its legislative jurisdiction under the preceding provisions of this paragraph (and its general oversight function under clause 2(b) (1)), the committee shall have the special oversight function provided for in clause 3(a) with respect to international arms control and disarmament, and military dependents education.

(d) **Committee on Banking, Currency and Housing.**

(1) Banks and banking, including deposit insurance and Federal monetary policy.

(2) Money and credit, including currency and the issuance of notes and redemption thereof; gold and silver, including the coinage thereof; valuation and revaluation of the dollar.

(3) Urban development.

(4) Public and private housing.

(5) Economic stabilization, defense production, renegotiation, and control of the price of commodities, rents, and services.

(6) International finance.

(7) Financial aid to commerce and industry (other than transpor-tation).

(8) International Financial and Monetary organizations.

(e) (1) **Committee on the Budget,** to consist of twenty-five Members as follows:

(A) five Members who are members of the Committee on Appropriations;

(B) five Members who are members of the Committee on Ways and Means;

(C) thirteen Members who are members of other standing com-mittees;

(D) one Member from the leadership of the majority party; and

(E) one Member from the leadership of the minority party.

No Member shall serve as a member of the Committee on the Budget during more than two Congresses in any period of five successive Congresses begin-ning after 1974 (disregarding for this purpose any service performed as a member of such committee for less than a full session in any Congress). All selections of Members to serve on the committee shall be made without regard to seniority.

(2) All concurrent resolutions on the budget (as defined in section 3(a) (4) of the Congressional Budget Act of 1974) and other matters re-quired to be referred to the committee under titles III and IV of that Act.

(3) The committee shall have the duty—

(A) to report the matters required to be reported by it under titles III and IV of the Congressional Budget Act of 1974;

(B) to make continuing studies of the effect on budget outlays of relevant existing and proposed legislation and to report the results of such studies to the House on a recurring basis;

(C) to request and evaluate continuing studies of tax expenditures, to devise methods of coordinating tax expenditures, policies, and programs with direct budget outlays, and to report the results of such studies to the House on a recurring basis; and

(D) to review, on a continuing basis, the conduct by the Congressional Budget Office of its functions and duties.

(f) Committee on the District of Columbia.

(1) All measures relating to the municipal affairs of the District of Columbia in general, other than appropriations therefor, including—

(2) Adulteration of foods and drugs.

(3) Incorporation and organization of societies.

(4) Insurance, executors, administrators, wills, and divorce.

(5) Municipal code and amendments to the criminal and corporation laws.

(6) Municipal and juvenile courts.

(7) Public health and safety, sanitation, and quarantine regulations.

(8) Regulation of sale of intoxicating liquors.

(9) Taxes and tax sales.

(10) Saint Elizabeth's hospital.

(g) Committee on Education and Labor.

(1) Measures relating to education or labor generally.

(2) Child labor.

(3) Columbia Institution for the Deaf, Dumb, and Blind [now Gallaudet College]; Howard University; Freedmen's Hospital.

(4) Convict labor and the entry of goods made by convicts into interstate commerce.

(5) Labor standards.

(6) Labor statistics.

(7) Mediation and arbitration of labor disputes.

(8) Regulation or prevention of importation of foreign laborers under contract.

(9) Food programs for children in schools.

(10) United States Employees' Compensation Commission.

(11) Vocational rehabilitation.

(12) Wages and hours of labor.

(13) Welfare of miners.

(14) Work incentive programs.

In addition to its legislative jurisdiction under the preceding provisions of this paragraph (and its general oversight function under clause 2(b) (1)), the committee shall have the special oversight function provided for in clause 3(c) with respect to domestic educational programs and institutions, and programs of student assistance, which are within the jurisdiction of other committees.

(h) Committee on Government Operations.

(1) Budget and accounting measures, other than appropriations.

(2) The overall economy and efficiency of Government operations and activities, including Federal procurement.

(3) Reorganizations in the executive branch of the Government.

(4) Intergovernmental relationships between the United States and the States and municipalities, and general revenue sharing.

(5) National archives.

In addition to its legislative jurisdiction under the preceding provisions of this paragraph (and its oversight functions under clause 2(b) (1) and (2)), the committee shall have the function of performing the activities and conducting the studies which are provided for in clause 4(c).

(i) Committee on House Administration.

(1) Appropriations from the contingent fund.

(2) Auditing and settling of all accounts which may be charged to the contingent fund.

(3) Employment of persons by the House, including clerks for Members and committees, and reporters of debates.

(4) Except as provided in clause 1(p) (4), matters relating to the Library of Congress and the House Library; statuary and pictures; acceptance or purchase of works of art for the Capitol; the Botanic Gardens; management of the Library of Congress; purchase of books and manuscripts; erection of monuments to the memory of individuals.

(5) Except as provided in clause 1(p) (4), matters relating to the Smithsonian Institution and the incorporation of similar institutions.

(6) Expenditure of contingent fund of the House.

(7) Matters relating to printing and correction of the Congressional Record.

(8) Measures relating to accounts of the House generally.

(9) Measures relating to assignment of office space for Members and committees.

(10) Measures relating to the disposition of useless executive papers.

(11) Measures relating to the election of the President, Vice President, or Members of Congress; corrupt practices; contested elections; credentials and qualifications; and Federal elections generally.

(12) Measures relating to services to the House, including House Restaurant, parking facilities and administration of the House Office Buildings and of the House wing of the Capitol.

(13) Measures relating to the travel of Members of the House.

(14) Measures relating to the raising, reporting and use of campaign contributions for candidates for office of Representative in the House of Representatives and of Resident Commissioner to the United States from Puerto Rico.

(15) Measures relating to the compensation, retirement and other benefits of the Members, officers, and employees of the Congress.

In addition to its legislative jurisdiction under the preceding provisions of this paragraph (and its general oversight function under clause 2(b) (1)), the committee shall have the function of performing the duties which are provided for in clause 4(d).

(j) Committee on Interior and Insular Affairs.

(1) Forest reserves and national parks created from the public domain.

(2) Forfeiture of land grants and alien ownership, including alien ownership of mineral lands.

(3) Geological Survey.

(4) Interstate compacts relating to apportionment of waters for irrigation purposes.

(5) Irrigation and reclamation, including water supply for reclamation projects, and easements of public lands for irrigation projects, and acquisition of private lands when necessary to complete irrigation projects.

(6) Measures relating to the care and management of Indians, including the care and allotment of Indian lands and general and special measures relating to claims which are paid out of Indian funds.

(7) Measures relating generally to the insular possessions of the United States, except those affecting the revenue and appropriations.

(8) Military parks and battlefields; national cemeteries administered by the Secretary of the Interior, and parks within the District of Columbia.

(9) Mineral land laws and claims and entries thereunder.

(10) Mineral resources of the public lands.

(11) Mining interests generally.

(12) Mining schools and experimental stations.

(13) Petroleum conservation on the public lands and conservation of the radium supply in the United States.

(14) Preservation of prehistoric ruins and objects of interest on the public domain.

(15) Public lands, generally, including entry, easements, and grazing thereon.

(16) Relations of the United States with the Indians and the Indian tribes.

In addition to its legislative jurisdiction under the preceding provisions of this paragraph (and its general oversight function under clause 2(b) (1)), the committee shall have the special oversight functions provided for in clause 3(e) with respect to all programs affecting Indians and nonmilitary nuclear energy and research and development including the disposal of nuclear waste.

(k) Committee on International Relations.

(1) Relations of the United States with foreign nations generally.

(2) Acquisition of land and buildings for embassies and legations in foreign countries.

(3) Establishment of boundary lines between the United States and foreign nations.

(4) Foreign loans.

(5) International conferences and congresses.

(6) Intervention abroad and declarations of war.

(7) Measures relating to the diplomatic service.

(8) Measures to foster commercial intercourse with foreign nations and to safeguard American business interests abroad.

(9) Neutrality.

(10) Protection of American citizens abroad and expatriation.

(11) The American National Red Cross.

(12) United Nations Organizations.

(13) Measures relating to international economic policy.

(14) Export controls.

(15) International commodity agreements (other than those involving sugar).

(16) Trading with the enemy.

(17) International education.

In addition to its legislative jurisdiction under the preceding provisions of this paragraph (and its general oversight function under clause 2(b) (1)), the committee shall have the special oversight functions provided for in clause 3(d) with respect to customs administration, intelligence activities relating to foreign policy, international financial and monetary organizations, and international fishing agreements.

(l) Committee on Interstate and Foreign Commerce.

(1) Interstate and foreign commerce generally.

(2) Inland waterways.

(3) Interstate oil compacts and petroleum and natural gas, except on the public lands.

(4) Railroads, including railroad labor, railroad retirement and unemployment, except revenue measures related thereto.

(5) Regulation of interstate and foreign communications.

(6) Regulation of interstate transmission of power, except the installation of connections between Government waterpower projects.

(7) Securities and exchanges.

(8) Consumer affairs and consumer protection.

(9) Travel and tourism.

(10) Public health and quarantine.

(11) Health and health facilities, except health care supported by payroll deductions.

(12) Biomedical research and development.

(m) Committee on the Judiciary.

(1) Judicial proceedings, civil and criminal generally.

(2) Apportionment of Representatives.

(3) Bankruptcy, mutiny, espionage, and counterfeiting.

(4) Civil liberties.

(5) Constitutional amendments.

(6) Federal courts and judges.

(7) Immigration and naturalization.

(8) Interstate compacts generally.

(9) Local courts in the Territories and possessions.

(10) Measures relating to claims against the United States.

(11) Meetings of Congress, attendance of Members and their acceptance of incompatible offices.

(12) National penitentiaries.

(13) Patent Office.

(14) Patents, copyrights, and trademarks.

(15) Presidential succession.

(16) Protection of trade and commerce against unlawful restraints and monopolies.

(17) Revision and codification of the Statutes of the United States.

(18) State and territorial boundary lines.

(19) Communist and other subversive activities affecting the internal security of the United States.

All property and records of the Committee on Internal Security are hereby transferred to the Committee on the Judiciary and shall be available for use by the latter committee to the same extent as if such property and records were originally that of the Committee on the Judiciary.

Such staff members of the Committee on Internal Security as the chairman of that committee for the 93rd Congress may designate after consultation and agreement with the chairman of the Committee on the Judiciary shall, without reduction in compensation, be transferred and appointed to the Committee on the Judiciary as additional members of the staff of the Committee on the Judiciary for the period of the 94th Congress, and shall be paid from the contingent fund of the House.

(n) Committee on Merchant Marine and Fisheries.

(1) Merchant marine generally.

(2) Oceanography and Marine Affairs, including coastal zone management.

(3) Coast Guard, including lifesaving service, lighthouses, lightships, and ocean derelicts.

(4) Fisheries and wildlife, including research, restoration, refuges, and conservation.

(5) Measures relating to the regulation of common carriers by water (except matters subject to the jurisdiction of the Interstate Commerce Commission) and to the inspection of merchant marine vessels, lights and signals, lifesaving equipment, and fire protection on such vessels.

(6) Merchant marine officers and seamen.

(7) Navigation and the laws relating thereto, including pilotage.

(8) Panama Canal and the maintenance and operation of the Panama Canal, including the administration, sanitation, and government of the Canal Zone; and interoceanic canals generally.

(9) Registering and licensing of vessels and small boats.

(10) Rules and international arrangements to prevent collisions at sea.

(11) United States Coast Guard and Merchant Marine Academies, and State Maritime Academies.

(12) International fishing agreements.

(o) Committee on Post Office and Civil Service.

(1) Census and the collection of statistics generally.

(2) All Federal Civil Service, including intergovernmental personnel.

(3) Postal-savings banks.

(4) Postal service generally, including the railway mail service, and measures relating to ocean mail and pneumatic-tube service; but excluding post roads.

(5) Status of officers and employees of the United States, including their compensation, classification, and retirement.

(6) Hatch Act.

(7) Holidays and celebrations.

(8) Population and demography.

(p) Committee on Public Works and Transportation.

(1) Flood control and improvement of rivers and harbors.

(2) Measures relating to the Capitol Building and the Senate and House Office Buildings.

(3) Measures relating to the construction or maintenance of roads and post roads, other than appropriations therefor; but it shall not be in order for any bill providing general legislation in relation to roads to contain any provision for any specific road, nor for any bill in relation to a specific road to embrace a provision in relation to any other specific road.

(4) Measures relating to the construction or reconstruction, maintenance, and care of the buildings and grounds of the Botanic Gardens, the Library of Congress, and the Smithsonian Institute.

(5) Measures relating to the purchase of sites and construction of post offices, customhouses, Federal courthouses, and Government buildings within the District of Columbia.

(6) Oil and other pollution of navigable waters.

(7) Public buildings and occupied or improved grounds of the United States generally.

(8) Public works for the benefit of navigation, including bridges and dams (other than international bridges and dams).

(9) Water power.

(10) Transportation, including civil aviation except railroads, railroad labor and pensions.

(11) Roads and the safety thereof.

(12) Water transportation subject to the jurisdiction of the Interstate Commerce Commission.

(13) Related transportation regulatory agencies, except (A) the Interstate Commerce Commission as it relates to railroads; (B) Federal Railroad Administration; and (C) Amtrak.

(q) Committee on Rules.

(1) The rules and joint rules (other than rules or joint rules relating to the Code of Official Conduct or relating to financial disclosure by a Member, officer, or employee of the House of Representatives), and order of business of the House.

(2) Emergency waivers (under the Congressional Budget Act of 1974) of the required reporting date for bills and resolutions authorizing new budget authority.

(3) Recesses and final adjournments of Congress.

(4) The Committee on Rules is authorized to sit and act whether or not the House is in session.

(r) Committee on Science and Technology.

(1) Astronautical research and development, including resources, personnel, equipment, and facilities.

(2) Bureau of Standards, standardization of weights and measures and the metric system.

(3) National Aeronautics and Space Administration.

(4) National Aeronautics and Space Council.

(5) National Science Foundation.

(6) Outer space, including exploration and control thereof.

(7) Science Scholarships.

(8) Scientific research and development.

(9) Civil aviation research and development.

(10) Environmental research and development.

(11) All energy research and development except nuclear research and development.

(12) National Weather Service.

In addition to its legislative jurisdiction under the preceding provisions of this paragraph (and its general oversight function under clause 2(b) (1)), the committee shall have the special oversight functions provided for in clause 3(f) with respect to all non-military research and development.

(s) Committee on Small Business.

(1) Assistance to and protection of small business, including financial aid.

(2) Participation of small-business enterprises in Federal procurement and Government contracts.

In addition to its legislative jurisdiction under the preceding provisions of this paragraph (and its general oversight function under clause 2(b) (1)), the committee shall have the special oversight function provided for in clause 3(g) with respect to the problems of small business.

(t) Committee on Standards of Official Conduct.

(1) Measures relating to the Code of Official Conduct.

(2) Measures relating to financial disclosure by Members, officers, and employees of the House of Representatives.

(3) Measures relating to activities designed to (1) assist in defeating, passing, or amending any legislation by the House or (2) influence, directly or indirectly, the passage or defeat of any legislation by the House.

In addition to its legislative jurisdiction under the preceding provisions of this paragraph (and its general oversight function under clause 2(b) (1)), the committee shall have the functions with respect to recommendations, studies, investigations, and reports which are provided for in clause 4(e).

(u) **Committee on Veterans' Affairs.**

(1) Veterans' measures generally.

(2) Cemeteries of the United States in which veterans of any war or conflict are or may be buried, whether in the United States or abroad, except cemeteries administered by the Secretary of the Interior.

(3) Compensation, vocational rehabilitation, and education of veterans.

(4) Life insurance issued by the Government on account of service in the Armed Forces.

(5) Pensions of all the wars of the United States, general and special.

(6) Readjustment of servicemen to civil life.

(7) Soldiers' and sailors' civil relief.

(8) Veterans' hospitals, medical care, and treatment of veterans.

(v) **Committee on Ways and Means.**

(1) Customs, collection districts, and ports of entry and delivery.

(2) Reciprocal trade agreements.

(3) Revenue measures generally.

(4) Revenue measures relating to the insular possessions.

(5) The bonded debt of the United States.

(6) The deposit of public moneys.

(7) Transportation of dutiable goods.

(8) Tax exempt foundations and charitable trusts.

(9) National social security, except (A) health care and facilities programs that are supported from general revenues as opposed to payroll deductions and (B) work incentive programs.

General Oversight Responsibilities

2. (a) In order to assist the House in—

(1) its analysis, appraisal, and evaluation of (A) the application, administration, execution, and effectiveness of the laws enacted by the Congress, or (B) conditions and circumstances which may indicate the necessity or desirability of enacting new or additional legislation, and

(2) its formulation, consideration, and enactment of such modifications of or changes in those laws, and of such additional legislation, as may be necessary or appropriate,

the various standing committees shall have oversight responsibilities as provided in paragraph (b).

(b) (1) Each standing committee (other than the Committee on Appropriations and the Committee on the Budget) shall review and study, on a continuing basis, the application, administration, execution, and effectiveness of those laws, or parts of laws, the subject matter of which is within the jurisdiction of that committee and the organization and operation of the Federal agencies and entities having responsibilities in or for the administration and execution thereof, in order to determine whether such laws and the programs thereunder are being implemented and carried out in accordance with the intent of the Congress and whether such programs should be continued, curtailed, or eliminated. In addition, each such committee shall review and study any conditions or circumstances which may indicate the necessity or desirability of enacting new or additional legislation within the jurisdiction of that committee (whether or not any bill or resolution has been introduced with respect thereto), and shall on a continuing basis undertake future research and forecasting on matters within the jurisdiction of that committee. Each such committee having more than twenty members shall establish an oversight subcommittee, or require its subcommittees, if any, to conduct oversight in the area of their respective jurisdiction, to assist in carrying out its reponsibilities under this subparagraph. This establishment of oversight subcommittees shall in no way limit the responsibility of the subcommittees with legislative jurisdiction from carrying out their oversight responsibilities.

(2) The Committee on Government Operations shall review and study, on a continuing basis, the operation of Government activities at all levels with a view to determining their economy and efficiency.

(3) The Committee on Appropriations shall conduct such studies and examinations of the organization and operation of executive departments and other executive agencies (including any agency the majority of the stock of which is owned by the Government of the United States) as it may deem necessary to assist it in the determination of matters within its jurisdiction.

(c) At the beginning of each Congress, an appropriate representative of the Committee on Government Operations shall meet with appropriate representatives of each of the other committees of the House to discuss the oversight plans of such committees and to assist in coordinating all of oversight activities of the House during such Congress. Within 60 days a the Congress convenes, the Committee on Government Operations s. report to the House the results of such meetings and discussions, and recommendations which it may have to assure the most effective coordi tion of such activities and otherwise achieve the objectives of this clau

(d) Each standing committee of the House shall have the functio reviewing and studying on a continuing basis the impact or probable imp of tax policies affecting subjects within its jurisdiction as described in clau 1 and 3.

Special Oversight Functions

3. (a) The Committee on Armed Services shall have the function reviewing and studying, on a continuing basis, all laws, programs, a Government activities dealing with or involving international arms cont and disarmament and the education of military dependents in schools.

(b) The Committee on the Budget shall have the function of—

(1) making continuing studies of the effect on budget outlays relevant existing and proposed legislation, and reporting the results such studies to the House on a recurring basis; and

(2) requesting and evaluating continuing studies of tax expe ditures, devising methods of coordinating tax expenditures, polici and programs with direct budget outlays, and reporting the results such studies to the House on a recurring basis.

(c) The Committee on Education and Labor shall have the function reviewing, studying, and coordinating, on a continuing basis, all law programs, and Government activities dealing with or involving domes educational programs and institutions, and programs of student assistanc which are within the jurisdiction of other committees.

(d) The Committee on International Relations shall have the function reviewing and studying, on a continuing basis, all laws, programs, a Government activities dealing with or involving customs administration, i telligence activities relating to foreign policy, international financial a monetary organizations, and international fishing agreements.

(e) The Committee on Interior and Insular Affairs shall have the fun tion of reviewing and studying, on a continuing basis, all laws, programs, an Government activities dealing with Indians and nonmilitary nuclear energ and research and development including the disposal of nuclear waste.

(f) The Committee on Science and Technology shall have the function reviewing and studying, on a continuing basis, all laws, programs, an Government activities dealing with or involving nonmilitary research an development.

(g) The Committee on Small Business shall have the function of study ing and investigating, on a continuing basis, the problems of all types of sma business.

Additional Functions of Committees

4. (a)(1)(A) The Committee on Appropriations shall, within thirty day after the transmittal of the Budget to the Congress each year, hold hearing on the Budget as a whole with particular reference to—

(i) the basic recommendations and budgetary policies of the Presi dent in the presentation of the Budget; and

(ii) the fiscal, financial, and economic assumptions used as base in arriving at total estimated expenditures and receipts.

(B) In holding hearings pursuant to subdivision (A), the com mittee shall receive testimony from the Secretary of the Treasury, the Director of the Office of Management and Budget, the Chairman of the Council of Economic Advisers, and such other persons as the committee may desire.

(C) Hearings pursuant to subdivision (A), or any part thereof, shall be held in open session, except when the committee, in open session and with a quorum present, determines by rollcall vote that the testimony to be taken at that hearing on that day may be related to a matter of national security: *Provided, however,* That the committee may by the same procedure close one subsequent day of hearing. A transcript of all such hearings shall be printed and a copy thereof furnished to each Member, Delegate, and the Resident Commissioner from Puerto Rico.

(D) Hearings pursuant to subdivision (A), or any part thereof, may be held before joint meetings of the committee and the Committee on Appropriations of the Senate in accordance with such procedures as the two committees jointly may determine.

(2) Whenever any bill or resolution which provides new spending authority described in section 401(c)(2)(C) of the Congressional Budget Act of 1974 is reported by a committee of the House and the amount of new budget authority which will be required for the fiscal year involved if such bill or resolution is enacted as so reported exceeds the appropriate allocation of new budget authority reported as described in clause 5(j) [*now clause 4 (g)*] in connection with the most recently agreed to concurrent resolution on the budget for such fiscal year, such

bill or resolution shall then be referred to the Committee on Appropriations with instructions to report it, with the committee's recommendations and (if the committee deems it desirable) with an amendment limiting the total amount of new spending authority provided in the bill or resolution, within 15 calendar days (not counting any day on which the House is not in session) beginning with the day following the day on which it is so referred. If the Committee on Appropriations fails to report the bill or resolution within such 15-day period, the committee shall be automatically discharged from further consideration of the bill or resolution and the bill or resolution shall be placed on the appropriate calendar.

(3) In addition, the Committee on Appropriations shall study on a continuing basis those provisions of law which (on the first day of the first fiscal year for which the congressional budget process is effective) provide spending authority or permanent budget authority, and shall report to the House from time to time its recommendations for terminating or modifying such provisions.

(b) The Committee on the Budget shall have the duty—

(1) to review on a continuing basis the conduct by the Congressional Budget Office of its functions and duties;

(2) to hold hearings, and receive testimony from Members of Congress and such appropriate representatives of Federal departments and agencies, the general public, and national organizations as it deems desirable, in developing the first concurrent resolution on the budget for each fiscal year;

(3) to make all reports required of it by the Congressional Budget Act of 1974, including the reporting of reconciliation bills and resolutions when so required;

(4) to study on a continuing basis those provisions of law which exempt Federal agencies or any of their activities or outlays from inclusion in the Budget of the United States Government, and to report to the House from time to time its recommendations for terminating or modifying such provisions; and

(5) to study on a continuing basis proposals designed to improve and facilitate methods of congressional budget-making, and to report to the House from time to time the results of such study together with its recommendations.

(c) (1) The Committee on Government Operations shall have the general function of—

(A) receiving and examining reports of the Comptroller General of the United States and of submitting such recommendations to the House as it deems necessary or desirable in connection with the subject matter of such reports;

(B) evaluating the effects of laws enacted to reorganize the legislative and executive branches of the Government; and

(C) studying intergovernmental relationships between the United States and the States and municipalities, and between the United States and international organizations of which the United States is a member.

(2) In addition to its duties under subparagraph (1), the Committee on Government Operations may at any time conduct investigations of any matter without regard to the provisions of clause 1, 2, or 3 (or this clause) conferring jurisdiction over such matter upon another standing committee. The committee's findings and recommendations in any such investigation shall be made available to the other standing committee or committees having jurisdiction over the matter involved (and included in the report of any such other committee when required by clause 2(l) (3) of Rule XI).

(d) The Committee on House Administration shall have the function of—

(1) examining all bills, amendments, and joint resolutions after passage by the House and, in cooperation with the Senate, examining all bills and joint resolutions which shall have passed both Houses to see that they are correctly enrolled, forthwith presenting those which originated in the House to the President of the United States in person after their signature by the Speaker of the House and the President of the Senate and reporting the fact and date of such presentation to the House;

(2) reporting to the Sergeant-at-Arms of the House concerning the travel of Members of the House; and

(3) providing, through the House Information Systems a scheduling service which may be used by all the committees and subcommittees of the House to eliminate, insofar as possible, any meeting and scheduling conflicts.

(e) (1) The Committee on Standards of Official Conduct is authorized; (A) to recommend to the House from time to time such administrative actions as it may deem appropriate to establish or enforce standards of official conduct for Members, officers, and employees of the House; (B) to investigate, subject to subparagraph (2) of this paragraph, any alleged violation, by a Member, officer, or employee of the House, of the Code of Official Conduct or of any law, rule, regulation, or other standard of conduct applicable to the conduct of such Member, officer, or employee in the performance of his duties or the discharge of his responsibilities, and after notice and hearing, to recommend to the House, by resolution or otherwise, such action as the committee may deem appropriate in the circumstances; (C) to report to the appropriate Federal or State authorities, with the approval of the House, any substantial evidence of a violation, by a Member, officer, or employee of the House, of any law applicable to the performance of his duties or the discharge of his responsibilities, which may have been disclosed in a committee investigation; and (D) to give consideration to the request of any Member, officer, or employee of the House for an advisory opinion with respect to the general propriety of any current or proposed conduct of such Member, officer, or employee and, with appropriate deletions to assure the privacy of the individual concerned, to publish such opinion for the guidance of other Members, officers, and employees of the House.

(2) (A) No resolution, report, recommendation, or advisory opinion relating to the official conduct of a Member, officer, or employee of the House shall be made by the Committee on Standards of Official Conduct, and no investigation of such conduct shall be undertaken by such committee, unless approved by the affirmative vote of a majority of the members of the committee.

(B) Except in the case of an investigation undertaken by the committee on its own initiative, the committee may undertake an investigation relating to the official conduct of an individual Member, officer, or employee of the House of Representatives only—

(i) upon receipt of a complaint, in writing and under oath, made by or submitted to a Member of the House and transmitted to the committee by such Member, or

(ii) upon receipt of a complaint, in writing and under oath, directly from an individual not a Member of the House if the committee finds that such complaint has been submitted by such individual to not less than three Members of the House who have refused, in writing, to transmit such complaint to the committee.

(C) No investigation shall be undertaken by the committee of any alleged violation of a law, rule, regulation, or standard of conduct not in effect at the time of the alleged violation.

(D) A member of the committee shall be ineligible to participate, as a member of the committee, in any committee proceeding relating to his or her official conduct. In any case in which a member of the committee is ineligible to act as a member of the committee under the preceding sentence, the Speaker of the House shall designate a Member of the House from the same political party as the ineligible member of the committee to act as a member of the committee in any committee proceeding relating to the official conduct of such ineligible member.

(f) (1) Each standing committee of the House shall, in its consideration of all bills and joint resolutions of a public character within its jurisdiction, insure that appropriation for continuing program and activities of the Federal Government and the District of Columbia government will be made annually to the maximum extent feasible and consistent with the nature, requirements, and objectives of the programs and activities involved. For the purposes of this paragraph a Government agency includes the organizational units of government listed in clause 7(d) of Rule XIII.

(2) Each standing committee of the House shall review, from time to time, each continuing program within its jurisdiction for which appropriations are not made annually in order to ascertain whether such program could be modified so that appropriations therefor would be made annually.

(g) Each standing committee of the House shall, on or before March 15 of each year, submit to the Committee on the Budget (1) its views and estimates with respect to all matters to be set forth in the concurrent resolution on the budget for the ensuing fiscal year which are within its jurisdiction or functions, and (2) an estimate of the total amounts of new budget authority, and budget outlays resulting therefrom, to be provided or authorized in all bills and resolutions within its jurisdiction which it intends to be effective during that fiscal year.

(h) As soon as practicable after a concurrent resolution on the budget for any fiscal year is agreed to, each standing committee of the House (after consulting with the appropriate committee or committees of the Senate) shall subdivide any allocations made to it in the joint explanatory statement accompanying the conference report on such resolution, and promptly report such subdivisions to the House, in the manner provided by section 302 of the Congressional Budget Act of 1974.

(i) Each standing committee of the House which is directed in a concurrent resolution on the budget to determine and recommend changes in laws, bills, or resolutions under the reconciliation process shall promptly make such determination and recommendations, and report a reconciliation bill or resolution (or both) to the House or submit such recommendations to the Committee on the Budget, in accordance with the Congressional Budget Act of 1974.

Referral of Bills, Resolutions, and Other Matters to Committees

5. (a) Each bill, resolution, or other matter which relates to a subject listed under any standing committee named in clause 1 shall be referred by the Speaker in accordance with the provisions of this clause.

(b) Every referral of any matter under paragraph (a) shall be made in such manner as to assure to the maximum extent feasible that each committee which has jurisdiction under clause 1 over the subject matter of any provision thereof will have responsibility for considering such provision and reporting to the House with respect thereto. Any precedents, rulings, and procedures in effect prior to the Ninety-Fourth Congress shall be applied with respect to referrals under this clause only to the extent that they will contribute to the achievement of the objectives of this clause.

(c) In carrying out paragraph (a) and (b) with respect to any matter, the Speaker may refer the matter simultaneously to two or more committees for concurrent consideration or for consideration in sequence (subject to appropriate time limitations in the case of any committee after the first), or divide the matter into two or more parts (reflecting different subjects and jurisdictions) and refer each such part to a different committee, or refer the matter to a special ad hoc committee appointed by the Speaker with the approval of the House (from the members of the committees having legislative jurisdiction) for the specific purpose of considering that matter and reporting to the House thereon, or make such other provision as may be considered appropriate.

(d) After the introduction in the House of each bill or resolution the Congressional Research Service of the Library of Congress shall prepare a factual description of the subject involved therein not to exceed one hundred words; such description shall be published in the Congressional Record and the Digest of Public General Bills and Resolutions as soon as possible after introduction.

Election and Membership of Committees; Chairmen; Vacancies; Select and Conference Committees

6. (a) (1) The standing committees specified in clause 1 shall be elected by the House at the commencement of each Congress, from nominations submitted by the respective party caucuses.

(2) One-half of the members of the Committee on Standards of Official Conduct shall be from the majority party and one-half shall be from the minority party.

(b) One of the Members of each standing committee shall be elected by the House, from nominations submitted by the majority party caucus, at the commencement of each Congress, as chairman thereof. In the temporary absence of the chairman, the Member next in rank in the order named in the election of the committee, and so on, as often as the case shall happen, shall act as chairman; and in case of a permanent vacancy in the chairmanship of any such committee the House shall elect another chairman.

(c) Each standing committee of the House of Representatives, except the Committee on the Budget, that has more than twenty members shall establish at least four subcommittees.

(d) All vacancies in standing committees shall be filled by election by the House.

(e) The Speaker shall appoint all select and conference committees which shall be ordered by the House from time to time. In appointing members to conference committees the Speaker shall appoint no less than a majority of members who generally supported the House position as determined by the Speaker.

(f) The Speaker may appoint the Resident Commissioner from Puerto Rico and the Delegate from the District of Columbia, Virgin Islands, and Guam to any conference committee that is considering legislation reported from a committee on which they serve.

(g) There shall be in the House the permanent Select Committee on Aging, which shall not have legislative jurisdiction but which shall have jurisdiction—

(1) to conduct a continuing comprehensive study and review of the problems of the older American, including but not limited to income maintenance, housing, health (including medical research), welfare, employment, education, recreation, and participation in family and community life as self-respecting citizens;

(2) to study the use of all practicable means and methods of encouraging the development of public and private programs and policies which will assist the older American in taking a full part in national life and which will encourage the utilization of the knowledge, skills, special aptitudes, and abilities of older Americans to contribute to a better quality of life for all Americans;

(3) to develop policies that would encourage the coordination of both governmental and private programs designed to deal with problems of aging; and

(4) to review any recommendations made by the President or by the White House Conference on Aging relating to programs or policies affecting older Americans.

RULE XI

Rules of Procedures for Committees
In General

1. (a) (1) The Rules of the House are the rules of its committees subcommittees so far as applicable, except that a motion to recess from to day is a motion of high privilege in committees and subcommittees.

(2) Each subcommittee of a committee is a part of that committee, and is subject to the authority and direction of that committee and to its rules so far as applicable.

(b) Each committee is authorized at any time to conduct such vestigations and studies as it may consider necessary or appropriate in the ercise of its responsibilities under Rule X, and (subject to the adoption of pense resolutions as required by clause 5) to incur expenses (including tra expenses) in connection therewith.

(c) Each committee is authorized to have printed and bound testimo and other data presented at hearings held by the committee. All costs stenographic services and transcripts in connection with any meeting or he ing of a committee shall be paid from the contingent fund of the House

(d) Each committee shall submit to the House, not later than January of each odd-numbered year, a report on the activities of that committee u der this rule and Rule X during the Congress ending at noon on January 3 such year.

Committee Rules

Adoption of written rules

2. (a) Each standing committee of the House shall adopt written rul governing its procedure. Such rules—

(1) shall be adopted in a meeting which is open to the public u less the committee, in open session and with a quorum present, dete mines by rollcall vote that all or part of the meeting on that day is to closed to the public;

(2) shall be not inconsistent with the Rules of the House or wit those provisions of law having the force and effect of Rules of the Hous and

(3) shall in any event incorporate all of the succeeding provision of this clause to the extent applicable.

Each committee's rules specifying its regular meeting days, and any othe rules of a committee which are in addition to the provisions of this clause shall be published in the Congressional Record not later than thirty day after the Congress convenes in each odd-numbered year. Each select or join committee shall comply with the provisions of this paragraph unles specifically prohibited by law.

Regular meeting days

(b) Each standing committee of the House shall adopt regular meetin days, which shall be not less frequent than monthly, for the conduct of it business. Each such committee shall meet, for the consideration of any bill o resolution pending before the committee or for the transaction of other com mittee business, on all regular meeting days fixed by the committee, unles otherwise provided by written rule adopted by the committee.

Additional and special meetings

(c) (1) The chairman of each standing committee may call and convene as he or she considers necessary, additional meetings of the committee for the consideration of any bill or resolution pending before the committee or for the conduct of other committee business. The committee shall meet for such purpose pursuant to that call of the chairman.

(2) If at least three members of any standing committee desire that a special meeting of the committee be called by the chairman, those members may file in the offices of the committee their written request to the chairman for that special meeting. Such request shall specify the measure or matter to be considered. Immediately upon the filing of the request, the clerk of the committee shall notify the chairman of the filing of the request. If, within three calendar days after the filing of the request, the chairman does not call the requested special meeting, to be held within seven calendar days after the filing of the request, a majority of the members of the committee may file in the offices of the committee their written notice that a special meeting of the committee will be held, specifying the date and hour of, and the measure or matter to be considered at, that special meeting. The committee shall meet on that date and hour. Immediately upon the filing of the notice, the clerk of the committee shall notify all members of the committee that such special meeting will be held and inform them of its date and hour and the measure or matter to be considered; and only the measure or matter specified in that notice may be considered at that special meeting.

Ranking majority Member to preside in absence of chairman

(d) If the chairman of any standing committee is not present at any meeting of the committee, the ranking member of the majority party on the committee who is present shall preside at that meeting.

Committee records

(e) (1) Each committee shall keep a complete record of all committee action which shall include a record of the votes on any question on which a rollcall vote is demanded. The result of each such rollcall vote shall be made available by the committee for inspection by the public at reasonable times in the offices of the committee. Information so available for public inspection shall include a description of the amendment, motion, order or other proposition and the name of each Member voting for and each Member voting against such amendment, motion, order, or proposition, and whether by proxy or in person, and the names of those Member present but not voting.

(2) All committee hearings, records, data, charts, and files shall be kept separate and distinct from the congressional office records of the Member serving as chairman of the committee; and such records shall be the property of the House and all Members of the House shall have access thereto.

(f) No vote by any Member of any Committee or subcommittee with ~spect to any measure or matter may be cast by proxy unless such com-.ittee, by written rule adopted by the committee, permits voting by proxy .d requires that the proxy authorization shall be in writing, shall assert that .e Member is absent on official business or is otherwise unable to be present the meeting of the committee, shall designate the person who is to execute .e proxy authorization, and shall be limited to a specific measure or matter .nd any amendments or motions pertaining thereto; except that a member .ay authorize a general proxy only for motions to recess, adjourn or other .rocedural matters. Each proxy to be effective shall be signed by the member ~ssigning his or her vote and shall contain the date and time of day that the roxy is signed. Proxies may not be counted for a quorum.

)pen meetings and hearings

(g) (1) Each meeting for the transaction of business, including the .arkup of legislation, of each standing committee or subcommittee thereof .hall be open to the public except when the committee or subcommittee, in .pen session and with a quorum present, determines by rollcall vote that all .r part of the remainder of the meeting on that day shall be closed to the ublic: *Provided, however,* That no person other than members of the com-.ittee and such congressional staff and such departmental representatives as .hey may authorize shall be present at any business or markup session which .as been closed to the public. This paragraph does not apply to open com-.ittee hearings which are provided for by clause 4(a) (3) [4(a) (1)] of Rule X .r by subparagraph (2) of this paragraph, or to any meeting that relates solely :o internal budget or personnel matters.

(2) Each hearing conducted by each committee or subcommittee thereof shall be open to the public except when the committee or subcommittee, in open session and with a quorum present, determines by rollcall vote that all or part of the remainder of that hearing on that day shall be closed to the public because disclosure of testimony, evidence, or other matter to be considered would endanger the national security or would violate any law or rule of the House of Representatives: *Provided, however,* That the committee or subcommittee may by the same procedure vote to close one subsequent day of hearing.

(3) Each committee of the House (except the Committee on Rules) shall make public announcement of the date, place and subject matter of any committee hearing at least one week before the commencement of the hearing. If the committee determines that there is good cause to begin the hearing sooner, it shall make the announcement at the earliest possible date. Any announcement made under this subparagraph shall be promptly published in the Daily Digest.

(4) Each committee shall, insofar as is practicable, require each witness who is to appear before it to file with the committee (in advance of his or her appearance) a written statement of the proposed testimony and to limit the oral presentation at such appearance to a brief summary of his or her argument.

(5) No point of order shall lie with respect to any measure reported by any committee on the ground that hearings on such measure were not conducted in accordance with the provisions of this clause; except that a point of order on that ground may be made by any member of the committee which reported the measure if, in the committee, such point of order was (A) timely made and (B) improperly overruled or not properly considered.

(6) The preceding provisions of this paragraph do not apply to the committee hearings which are provided for by clause 4(a) (1) of Rule X.

Quorum for taking testimony

(h) Each committee may fix the number of its members to constitute a quorum for taking testimony and receiving evidence, which shall be not less than two.

Prohibition against committee meetings during five-minute rule

(i) No committee of the House (except the Committee on Appropriations, the Committee on the Budget, and the Committee on Rules) may sit, without special leave, while the House is reading a measure for amendment under the five-minute rule.

Calling and interrogation of witnesses

(j) (1) Whenever any hearing is conducted by any committee upon any measure or matter, the minority party Members on the committee shall be entitled, upon request to the chairman by a majority of them before the co..pletion of the hearing, to call witnesses selected by the minority to testify with respect to that measure or matter during at least one day of hearing thereon.

(2) Each committee shall apply the five-minute rule in the interrogation of witnesses in any hearing until such time as each Member of the committee who so desires has had an opportunity to question each witness.

Investigative hearing procedures

(k) (1) The chairman at an investigative hearing shall announce in an opening statement the subject of the investigation.

(2) A copy of the committee rules and this clause shall be made available to each witness.

(3) Witnesses at investigative hearings may be accompanied by their own counsel for the purpose of advising them concerning their constitutional rights.

(4) The chairman may punish breaches of order and decorum, and of professional ethics on the part of counsel, by censure and exclusion from the hearings; and the committee may cite the offender to the House for contempt.

(5) If the committee determines that evidence or testimony at an investigative hearing may tend to defame, degrade, or incriminate any person, it shall—

(A) receive such evidence or testimony in executive session;

(B) afford such person an opportunity voluntarily to appear as a witness; and

(C) receive and dispose of requests from such person to subpena additional witnesses.

(6) Except as provided in subparagraph (5), the chairman shall receive and the committee shall dispose of requests to subpena additional witnesses.

(7) No evidence or testimony taken in executive session may be released or used in public sessions without the consent of the committee.

(8) In the discretion of the committee, witnesses may submit brief and pertinent sworn statements in writing for inclusion in the record. The committee is the sole judge of the pertinency of testimony and evidence adduced at its hearing.

(9) A witness may obtain a transcript copy of his testimony given at a public session or, if given at an executive session, when authorized by the committee.

Committee procedures for reporting bills and resolutions

(l) (1) (A) It shall be the duty of the chairman of each committee (except as provided in subdivision (C)) to report or cause to be reported promptly to the House any measure approved by the committee and to take or cause to be taken necessary steps to bring the matter to a vote.

(B) In any event, the report of any committee on a measure which has been approved by the committee shall be filed within seven calendar days (exclusive of days on which the House is not in session) after the day on which there has been filed with the clerk of the committee a written request, signed by a majority of the members of the committee, for the reporting of that measure. Upon the filing of any such request, the clerk of the committee shall transmit immediately to the chairman of the committee notice of the filing of that request. This subdivision does not apply to the reporting of a regular appropriation bill by the Committee on Appropriations prior to compliance with subdivision (C) and does not apply to a report of the Committee on Rules with respect to the rules, joint rules, or order of business of the House or to the reporting of a resolution of inquiry addressed to the head of an executive department.

(C) Before reporting the first regular appropriation bill for each fiscal year, the Committee on Appropriations shall, to the extent practicable and in accordance with section 307 of the Congressional Budget Act of 1974, complete subcommittee markup and full committee action on all regular appropriation bills for that year and submit to the House a summary report comparing the committee's recommendations with the appropriate levels of budget outlays and new budget authority as set forth in the most recently agreed to concurrent resolution on the budget for that year.

(2) (A) No measure or recommendation shall be reported from any committee unless a majority of the committee was actually present.

(B) With respect to each rollcall vote on a motion to report any bill or resolution of a public character, the total number of votes cast for, and the total number of votes cast against, the reporting of such bill or resolution shall be included in the committee report.

(3) The report of any committee on a measure which has been approved by the committee (A) shall include the oversight findings and recommendations required pursuant to the last sentence of clause 2(b)

(1) of Rule X separately set out and clearly identified; (B) the statement required by section 308(a) of the Congressional Budget Act of 1974, separately set out and clearly identified, if the measure provides new budget authority or new increased tax expenditures; (C) the estimate and comparison prepared by the Director of the Congressional Budget Office under section 403 of such Act, separately set out and clearly identified, whenever the Director (if timely submitted prior to the filing of the report) has submitted such estimate and comparison to the committee; and (D) a summary of the oversight findings and recommendations made by the Committee on Government Operations under clause 2(b) (2) of Rule X separately set out and clearly identified whenever such findings and recommendations have been submitted to the legislative committee in a timely fashion to allow an opportunity to consider such findings and recommendations during the committee's deliberations on the measure.

(4) Each report of a committee on each bill or joint resolution of a public character reported by such committee shall contain a detailed analytical statement as to whether the enactment of such bill or joint resolution into law may have an inflationary impact on prices and costs in the operation of the national economy.

(5) If, at the time of approval of any measure or matter by any committee, other than the Committee on Rules, any member of the committee gives notice of intention to file supplemental, minority, or additional views, that member shall be entitled to not less than three calendar days (excluding Saturdays, Sundays, and legal holidays) in which to file such views, in writing and signed by that member, with the clerk of the committee. All such views so filed by one or more members of the committee shall be included within, and shall be a part of, the report filed by the committee with respect to that measure or matter. The report of the committee upon that measure or matter shall be printed in a single volume which—

(A) shall include all supplemental, minority, or additional views which have been submitted by the time of the filing of the report, and

(B) shall bear upon its cover a recital that any such supplemental, minority, or additional views (and any material submitted under subdivisions (C) and (D) of subparagraph (3)) are included as part of the report.

This subparagraph does not preclude—

(i) the immediate filing or printing of a committee report unless timely request for the opportunity to file supplemental, minority, or additional views has been made as provided by this subparagraph; or

(ii) the filing by any such committee of any supplemental report upon any measure or matter which may be required for the correction of any technical error in a previous report made by that committee upon that measure or matter.

(6) A measure or matter reported by any committee (except the Committee on Rules in the case of a resolution making in order the consideration of a bill, resolution, or other order of business), shall not be considered in the House until the third calendar day (or the tenth calendar day in the case of a concurrent resolution on the budget), excluding Saturdays, Sundays, and legal holidays following the day on which the report of that committee upon that measure or matter has been available to the Members of the House. Nor shall it be in order to consider any measure or matter reported by any committee (except the Committee on Rules in the case of a resolution making in order the consideration of a bill, resolution, or other order of business, or any other committee in the case of a privileged resolution), unless copies of such report and the reported measure or matter have been available to the Members for at least two hours before the beginning of such consideration; *Provided, however,* That it shall always be in order to call up for consideration, notwithstanding the provisions of clause 4(b), rule XI, a report from the Committee on Rules specifically providing for the consideration of a reported measure or matter notwithstanding this restriction. If hearings have been held on any such measure or matter so reported, the committee reporting the measure or matter shall make every reasonable effort to have such hearings printed and available for distribution to the Members of the House prior to the consideration of such measure or matter in the House. This subparagraph shall not apply to—

(A) any measure for the declaration of war, or the declaration of a national emergency, by the Congress; or

(B) any executive decision, determination, or action which would become or continue to be, effective unless disapproved or otherwise invalidated by one or both Houses of Congress.

(7) If, within seven calendar days after a measure has, by resolution, been made in order for consideration by the House, no motion has been offered that the House consider that measure, any member of the committee which reported that measure may be recognized in the discretion of the Speaker to offer a motion that the House shall consider that measure, if that committee has duly authorized that member to offer that motion.

Power to sit and act; subpena power

(m) (1) For the purpose of carrying out any of its functions and duties under this rule and Rule X (including any matters referred to it under clause 5 of Rule X), any committee, or any subcommittee thereof, is authorized (subject to subparagraph (2) (A) of this paragraph)—

(A) to sit and act at such times and places within the United States, whether the House is in session, has recessed, or had adjourned, and to hold such hearings, and

(B) to require, by subpena or otherwise, the attendance and testimony of such witnesses and the production of such books, records, correspondence, memorandums, papers, and documents as it deems necessary. The chairman of the committee, or any member designated by such chairman, may administer oaths to any witness.

(2) (A) A subpena may be issued by a committee or subcommittee under subparagraph (1) (B) in the conduct of any investigation or activity or series of investigations or activities, only when authorized by a majority of the members of the committee, and authorized subpenas shall be signed by the chairman of the committee or by any member designated by the committee.

(B) Compliance with any subpena issued by a committee or subcommittee under subparagraph (1) (B) may be enforced only as authorized or directed by the House.

Use of committee funds for travel

(n) Funds authorized for a committee under clause 5 are for expenses incurred in the committee's activities within the United States; however, local currencies owned by the United States shall be made available to the committee and its employees engaged in carrying out their official duties outside the United States. No appropriated funds shall be expended for the purpose of defraying expenses of members of the committee or its employees in any country where local currencies are available for this purpose; and the following conditions shall apply with respect to their use of such currencies:

(1) No Member or employee of the committee shall receive or expend local currencies for subsistence in any country at a rate in excess of the maximum per diem rate set forth in applicable Federal law.

(2) Each Member or employee of the committee shall make to the chairman of the committee an itemized report showing the number of days visited in each country whose local currencies were spent, the amount of per diem furnished, and the cost of transportation if furnished by public carrier, or, if such transportation is furnished by an agency of the United States Government, the cost of such transportation and the identification of the agency. All such individual reports shall be filed by the chairman with the Committee on House Administration and shall be open to public inspection.

Broadcasting of Committee Hearings

3. (a) It is the purpose of this clause to provide a means, in conformity with acceptable standards of dignity, propriety, and decorum, by which committee hearings, or committee meetings, which are open to the public may be covered, by television broadcast, radio broadcast, and still photography, or by any of such methods of coverage—

(1) for the education, enlightenment, and information of the general public, on the basis of accurate and impartial news coverage, regarding the operations, procedures, and practices of the House as a legislative and representative body and regarding the measures, public issues, and other matters before the House and its committees, the consideration thereof, and the action taken thereon; and

(2) for the development of the perspective and understanding of the general public with respect to the role and function of the House under the Constitution of the United States as an organ of the Federal Government.

(b) In addition, it is the intent of this clause that radio and television tapes and television film of any coverage under this clause shall not be used, or made available for use, as partisan political campaign material to promote or oppose the candidacy of any person for elective public office.

(c) It is, further, the intent of this clause that the general conduct of each meeting (whether of a hearing or otherwise) covered, under authority of this clause, by television broadcast, radio broadcast, and still photograph, or by any of such methods of coverage, and the personal behavior of the committee members and staff, other Government officials and personnel, witnesses, television, radio, and press media personnel, and the general public at the hearing or other meeting shall be in strict conformity with and observance of the acceptable standards of dignity, propriety, courtesy, and decorum traditionally observed by the House in its operations and shall not be such as to—

(1) distort the objects and purposes of the hearing or other meeting or the activities of committee members in connection with that hearing or meeting or in connection with the general work of the committee or of the House; or

(2) cast discredit or dishonor on the House, the committee, or any Member or bring the House, the committee, or any Member into disrepute.

(d) The coverage of committee hearings and meetings by television broadcast, radio broadcast, or still photography is a privilege made available the House and shall be permitted and conducted only in strict conformity th the purposes, provisions, and requirements of this clause.

(e) Whenever any hearing or meeting conducted by any committee of e House is open to the public, that committee may permit, by majority vote the committee, that hearing or meeting to be covered, in whole or in part, television broadcast, radio broadcast, and still photography, or by any of ch methods of coverage, but only under such written rules as the committee ay adopt in accordance with the purposes, provisions, and requirements of is clause.

(f) The written rules which may be adopted by a committee under aragraph (e) of this clause shall contain provisions to the following effect:

(1) If the television or radio coverage of the hearing or meeting is to be presented to the public as live coverage, that coverage shall be conducted and presented without commercial sponsorship.

(2) No witness served with a subpena by the committee shall be required against his or her will to be photographed at any hearing or to give evidence or testimony while the broadcasting of that hearing, by radio or television, is being conducted. At the request of any such witness who does not wish to be subjected to radio, television, or still photography coverage, all lenses shall be covered and all microphones used for coverage turned off. This subparagraph is supplementary to clause 2(k) (5) of this rule, relating to the protection of the rights of witnesses.

(3) Not more than four television cameras, operating from fixed positions, shall be permitted in a hearing or meeting room. The allocation among the television media of the positions of the number of television cameras permitted in a hearing or meeting room shall be in accordance with fair and equitable procedures devised by the Executive Committee of the Radio and Television Correspondents' Galleries.

(4) Television cameras shall be placed so as not to obstruct in any way the space between any witness giving evidence or testimony and any member of the committee or the visibility of that witness and that member to each other.

(5) Television cameras shall not be placed in positions which obstruct unnecessarily the coverage of the hearing or meeting by the other media.

(6) Equipment necessary for coverage by the television and radio media shall not be installed in, or removed from, the hearing or meeting room while the committee is in session.

(7) Floodlights, spotlights, strobelights, and flashguns shall not be used in providing any method of coverage of the hearing or meeting, except that the television media may install additional lighting in the hearing or meeting room, without cost to the Government, in order to raise the ambient lighting level in the hearing or meeting room to the lowest level necessary to provide adequate television coverage of the hearing or meeting at the then current state of the art of television coverage.

(8) Not more than five press photographers shall be permitted to cover a hearing or meeting by still photography. In the selection of these photographers, preference shall be given to photographers from Associated Press Photos and United Press International Newspictures. If request is made by more than five of the media for coverage of the hearing or meeting by still photography, that coverage shall be made on the basis of a fair and equitable pool arrangement devised by the Standing Committee of Press Photographers.

(9) Photographers shall not position themselves, at any time during the course of the hearing or meeting, between the witness table and the members of the committee.

(10) Photographers shall not place themselves in positions which obstruct unnecessarily the coverage of the hearing by the other media.

(11) Personnel providing coverage by the television and radio media shall be then currently accredited to the Radio and Television Correspondents' Galleries.

(12) Personnel providing coverage by still photography shall be then currently accredited to the Press Photographers' Gallery.

(13) Personnel providing coverage by the television and radio media and by still photography shall conduct themselves and their coverage activities in an orderly and unobtrusive manner.

Privileged Reports and Amendments

4. (a) The following committees shall have leave to report at any time on the matters herein stated, namely: The Committee on Appropriations—on general appropriation bills; the Committee on the Budget—on the matters required to be reported by such committee under Titles III and IV of the Congressional Budget Act of 1974; the Committee on House Administration—on enrolled bills, contested elections, and all matters referred

to it of printing for the use of the House or the two Houses, and on all matters of expenditure of the contingent fund of the House; the Committee on Rules—on rules, joint rules, and the order of business; and the Committee on Standards of Official Conduct—on resolutions recommending action by the House of Representatives with respect to an individual Member, officer, or employee of the House of Representatives as a result of any investigation by the committee relating to the official conduct of such Member, officer, or employee of the House of Representatives.

(b) It shall always be in order to call up for consideration a report from the Committee on Rules on a rule, joint rule, or the order of business (except it shall not be called up for consideration on the same day it is presented to the House, unless so determined by a vote of not less than two-thirds of the Members voting, but this provision shall not apply during the last three days of the session), and, pending the consideration thereof, the Speaker may entertain one motion that the House adjourn; but after the result is announced the Speaker shall not entertain any other dilatory motion until the report shall have been fully disposed of. The Committee on Rules shall not report any rule or order which provides that business under clause 7 of Rule XXIV shall be set aside by a vote of less than two-thirds of the Members present; nor shall it report any rule or order which would prevent the motion to recommit from being made as provided in clause 4 of Rule XVI.

(c) The Committee on Rules shall present to the House reports concerning rules, joint rules, and order of business, within three legislative days of the time when the bill or resolution involved is ordered reported by the committee. If any such rule or order is not considered immediately, it shall be referred to the calendar and, if not called up by the Member making the report within seven legislative days thereafter, any member of the Rules Committee may call it up as a question of privilege and the Speaker shall recognize any member of the Rules Committee seeking recognition for that purpose. If the Committee on Rules makes an adverse report on any resolution pending before the committee, providing for an order of business for the consideration by the House of any public bill or joint resolution, on days when it shall be in order to call up motions to discharge committees it shall be in order for any Member of the House to call up for consideration by the House such adverse report, and it shall be in order to move the adoption by the House of such resolution adversely reported notwithstanding the adverse report of the Committee on Rules, and the Speaker shall recognize the Member seeking recognition for that purpose as a question of the highest privilege.

(d) Whenever the Committee on Rules reports a resolution repealing or amending any of the Rules of the House of Representatives or part thereof it shall include in its report or in an accompanying document—

(1) the text of any part of the Rules of the House of Representatives which is proposed to be repealed; and

(2) a comparative print of any part of the resolution making such an amendment and any part of the Rules of the House of Representatives to be amended, showing by an appropriate typographical device the omissions and insertions proposed to be made.

Committee Expenses

5. (a) Whenever any standing committee (except the Committee on Appropriations and the Committee on the Budget) is to be granted authorization for the payment, from the contingent fund of the House, of its expenses in any year, other than those expenses to be paid from appropriations provided by statute, such authorization initially shall be procured by one primary expense resolution for that committee providing funds for the payment of the expenses of the committee for that year from the contingent fund of the House. Any such primary expense resolution reported to the House shall not be considered in the House unless a printed report on that resolution has been available to the Members of the House for at least one calendar day prior to the consideration of that resolution in the House. Such report shall, for the information of the House—

(1) state the total amount of the funds to be provided to the committee under the primary expense resolution for all anticipated activities and programs of the committee; and

(2) to the extent practicable, contain such general statements regarding the estimated foreseeable expenditures for the respective anticipated activities and programs of the committee as may be appropriate to provide the House with basic estimates with respect to the expenditure generally of the funds to be provided to the committee under the primary expense resolution.

(b) After the date of adoption by the House of any such primary expense resolution for any such standing committee for any year, authorization for the payment from the contingent fund of additional expenses of such committee in that year, other than those expenses to be paid from appropriations provided by statute, may be procured by one or more additional expense resolutions for that committee, as necessary. Any such additional expense resolution reported to the House shall not be considered in the House unless a printed report on that resolution has been available to the Members of the House for at least one calendar day prior to the consideration of that resolution in the House. Such report shall, for the information of the House—

(1) state the total amount of additional funds to be provided to the committee under the additional expense resolution and the purpose or purposes for which those additional funds are to be used by the committee; and

(2) state the reason or reasons for the failure to procure the additional funds for the committee by means of the primary expense resolution.

(c) The preceding provisions of this clause do not apply to—

(1) any resolution providing for the payment from the contingent fund of the House of sums necessary to pay compensation for staff services performed for, or to pay other expenses of, any standing committee at any time from and after the beginning of any year and before the date of adoption by the House of the primary expense resolution providing funds to pay the expenses of that committee for that year; or

(2) any resolution providing in any Congress, for all of the standing committees of the House, additional office equipment, airmail and special delivery postage stamps, supplies, staff personnel, or any other specific item for the operation of the standing committees, and containing an authorization for the payment from the contingent fund of the House of the expenses of any of the foregoing items provided by that resolution, subject to and until enactment of the provisions of the resolution as permanent law.

(d) From the funds provided for the appointment of committee staff pursuant to primary and additional expense resolutions—

(1) The chairman of each standing subcommittee of a standing committee of the House is authorized to appoint one staff member who shall serve at the pleasure of the subcommittee chairman.

(2) The ranking minority party member of each standing subcommittee on each standing committee of the House is authorized to appoint one staff person who shall serve at the pleasure of the ranking minority party member.

(3) The staff members appointed pursuant to the provisions of subparagraphs (1) and (2) shall be compensated at a rate determined by the subcommittee chairman not to exceed (A) 75 per centum of the maximum established in paragraph (c) of clause 6 or (B) the rate paid the staff member appointed pursuant to subparagraph (1) of this paragraph.

(4) For the purpose of this paragraph, (A) there shall be no more than six standing subcommittees of each standing committee of the House, except for the Committee on Appropriations, and (B) no member shall appoint more than one person pursuant to the above provisions.

(5) The staff positions made available to the subcommittee chairman and ranking minority party members pursuant to subparagraphs (1) and (2) of this paragraph shall be made available from the staff positions provided under clause 6 of Rule XI unless such staff positions are made available pursuant to a primary or additional expense resolution.

Committee Staffs

6. (a) (1) Subject to subparagraph (2) of this paragraph and paragraph (f) of this clause, each standing committee may appoint, by majority vote of the committee, not more than eighteen professional staff members. Each professional staff member appointed under this subparagraph shall be assigned to the chairman and the ranking minority party member of such committee, as the committee considers advisable.

(2) Subject to paragraph (f) of this clause, whenever a majority of the minority party members of a standing committee (except the Committee on Standards of Official Conduct) so request, not more than six persons may be selected, by majority vote of the minority party members, for appointment by the committee as professional staff members from among the number authorized by subparagraph (1) of this paragraph. The committee shall appoint any persons so selected whose character and qualifications are acceptable to a majority of the committee. If the committee determines that the character and qualifications of any person so selected are unacceptable to the committee, a majority of the minority party members may select other persons for appointment by the committee to the professional staff until such appointment is made. Each professional staff member appointed under this subparagraph shall be assigned to such committee business as the minority party members of the committee consider advisable.

(3) The professional staff members of each standing committee—

(A) shall be appointed on a permanent basis, without regard to race, creed, sex, or age, and solely on the basis of fitness to perform the duties of their respective positions;

(B) shall not engage in any work other than committee business; and

(C) shall not be assigned any duties other than those pertaining to committee business.

(4) Services of the professional staff members of each standing committee may be terminated by majority vote of the committee.

(5) The foregoing provisions of this paragraph do not apply to Committee on Appropriations and to the Committee on the Budget.

(b) (1) The clerical staff of each standing committee shall consist of more than twelve clerks, to be attached to the office of the chairman, to ranking minority party member, and to the professional staff, as the committee considers advisable. Subject to subparagraph (2) of this paragraph and paragraph (f) of this clause, the clerical staff shall be appointed by majority vote of the committee, without regard to race, creed, sex, or age. Except as provided by subparagraph (2) of this paragraph, the clerical staff shall handle committee correspondence and stenographic work both for the committee staff and for the chairman and the ranking minority party member matters related to committee work.

(2) Subject to paragraph (f) of this clause, whenever a majority the minority party members of a standing committee (except the Committee on Standards of Official Conduct) so request, four persons may be selected, by majority vote of the minority party members, for appointment by the committee to positions on the clerical staff from among the number of clerks authorized by subparagraph (1) of this paragraph. The committee shall appoint to those positions any persons so selected whose character and qualifications are acceptable to a majority of the committee. If the committee determines that the character and qualifications of any person so selected are unacceptable to the committee, a majority of the minority party members may select other persons for appointment by the committee to the position involved on the clerical staff until such appointment is made. Each clerk appointed under this subparagraph shall handle committee correspondence and stenographic work for the minority party members of the committee and for any members of the professional staff appointed under subparagraph (2) of paragraph (a) of this clause on matters related to committee work.

(3) Services of the clerical staff members of each standing committee may be terminated by majority vote of the committee.

(4) The foregoing provisions of this paragraph do not apply to the Committee on Appropriations and to the Committee on the Budget.

(c) Each employee on the professional staff, and each employee on the clerical staff, of each standing committee, is entitled to pay at a single per annum gross rate, to be fixed by the chairman, which does not exceed the highest rate of basic pay, as in effect from time to time, of level V of the Executive schedule in section 5316 of title 5 United States Code.

(d) Subject to appropriations hereby authorized, the Committee on Appropriations and the Committee on the Budget may appoint such staff, in addition to the clerk thereof and assistants for the minority, as it determines by majority vote to be necessary, such personnel, other than minority assistants, to possess such qualifications as the committee may prescribe.

(e) No committee shall appoint to its staff any experts or other personnel detailed or assigned from any department or agency of the Government, except with the written permission of the Committee on House Administration.

(f) If a request for the appointment of a minority professional staff member under paragraph (a), or a minority clerical staff member under paragraph (b), is made when no vacancy exists to which that appointment may be made, the committee nevertheless shall appoint, under paragraph (a) or paragraph (b), as applicable, the person selected by the minority and acceptable to the committee. The person so appointed shall serve as an additional member of the professional staff or the clerical staff, as the case may be, of the committee, and shall be paid from the contingent fund, until such a vacancy (other than a vacancy in the position of head of the professional staff, by whatever title designated) occurs, at which time that person shall be deemed to have been appointed to that vacancy. If such vacancy occurs on the professional staff when seven or more persons have been so appointed who are eligible to fill that vacancy, a majority of the minority party members shall designate which of those persons shall fill that vacancy.

(g) Each staff member appointed pursuant to a request by minority party members under paragraph (a) or (b) of this clause, and each staff member appointed to assist minority party members of a committee pursuant to an expense resolution described in paragraph (a) or (b) of clause 5, shall be accorded equitable treatment with respect to the fixing of his or her rate of pay, the assignment to him or her of work facilities, and the accessibility to him or her of committee records.

(h) Paragraphs (a) and (b) of this clause shall not be construed to authorize the appointment of additional professional or clerical staff members of a committee pursuant to a request under either of such paragraphs by the minority party members of that committee if six or more professional staff members or four or more clerical staff members, provided for in paragraph (a) (1) or paragraph (b) (1) of this clause, as the case may be, who are satisfactory to a majority of the minority party members, are otherwise assigned to assist the minority party members.

(i) Notwithstanding paragraphs (a) (2) and (b) (2), a committee may employ nonpartisan staff, in lieu of or in addition to committee staff designated exclusively for the majority or minority party, upon an affirmative vote of a majority of the members of the majority party and a majority of the members of the minority party.

(j) Each committee shall report to the Clerk of the House within fifteen days after December 31 and June 30 of each year the name, profession, and total salary of each person employed by such committee or any subcommittee thereof during the period covered by such report, and shall make an accounting of funds made available to and expended by such committee or subcommittee during such period; and such information when reported shall be published in the Congressional Record.

RULE XII

Resident Commissioner From Puerto Rico and Delegate From the District of Columbia

1. The Resident Commissioner to the United States from Puerto Rico shall be elected to serve on standing committees in the same manner as Members of the House and shall possess in such committees the same powers and privileges as the other Members.

2. The Delegate from the District of Columbia shall be elected to serve as a member of the Committee on the District of Columbia and each Delegate to the House shall be elected to serve on standing committees of the House in the same manner as Members of the House and shall possess in all committees on which he serves the same powers and privileges as the other Members.

RULE XIII

Calendars and Reports of Committees

1. There shall be three calendars to which all business reported from committees shall be referred, viz.:

First. A Calendar of the Committee of the Whole House on the state of the Union, to which shall be referred bills raising revenue, general appropriation bills, and bills of a public character directly or indirectly appropriating money or property.

Second. A House Calendar, to which shall be referred all bills of a public character not raising revenue nor directly or indirectly appropriating money or property.

Third. A Calendar of the Committee of the Whole House, to which shall be referred all bills of a private character.

2. All reports of committees, except as provided in clause 4(a) of Rule XI, together with the views of the minority, shall be delivered to the Clerk for printing and reference to the proper calendar under the direction of the Speaker, in accordance with the foregoing clause, and the titles or subject thereof shall be entered on the Journal and printed in the Record: *Provided,* That bills reported adversely shall be laid on the table, unless the committee reporting a bill, at the time, or any Member within three days thereafter, shall request its reference to the calendar, when it shall be referred, as provided in clause 1 of this rule.

3. Whenever a committee reports a bill or a joint resolution repealing or amending any statute or part thereof it shall include in its report or in an accompanying document—

(1) The text of the statute or part thereof which is proposed to be repealed; and

(2) A comparative print of that part of the bill or joint resolution making the amendment and of the statute or part thereof proposed to be amended, showing by stricken-through type and italics, parallel columns, or other appropriate typographical devices the omissions and insertions proposed to be made: *Provided, however,* That if a committee reports such a bill or joint resolution with amendments or an amendment in the nature of a substitute for the entire bill, such report shall include a comparative print showing any changes in existing law proposed by the amendments or substitute instead of as in the bill as introduced.

(4). After a bill has been favorably reported and shall be upon either the House or Union Calendar any Member may file with the Clerk a notice that he desires such bill placed on a special calendar to be known as the "Consent Calendar." On the first and third Mondays of each month immediately after the reading of the Journal, the Speaker shall direct the Clerk to call the bills in numerical order, which have been for three legislative days upon the "Consent Calendar." Should objection be made to the consideration of any bill so called it shall be carried over on the calendar without prejudice to the next day when the "Consent Calendar" is again called, and if objected to by three or more Members it shall immediately be stricken from the Calendar, and shall not thereafter during the same session of that Congress be placed again thereon: *Provided,* That no bill shall be called twice on the same legislative day.

5. There shall also be a Calendar of Motions to Discharge Committees, as provided in clause 4 of Rule XXVII.

6. Calendars shall be printed daily.

7. (a) The report accompanying each bill or joint resolution of a public character reported by any committee shall contain—

(1) an estimate, made by such committee, of the costs which would be incurred in carrying out such bill or joint resolution in the fiscal year in which

it is reported and in each of the five fiscal years following such fiscal year (or for the authorized duration of any program authorized by such bill or joint resolution, if less than five years), except that, in the case of measures affecting the revenues, such reports shall require only an estimate of the gain or loss in revenues for a one-year period; and

(2) a comparison of the estimate of costs described in subparagraph (1) of this paragraph made by such committee with any estimate of such costs made by any Government agency and submitted to such committee.

(b) It shall not be in order to consider any such bill or joint resolution in the House if the report of the committee which reported that bill or joint resolution does not comply with paragraph (a) of this clause.

(c) For the purposes of this clause, the members of the Joint Committee on Atomic Energy who are Members of the House shall be deemed to be a committee of the House.

(d) For the purposes of subparagraph (2) of paragraph (a) of this clause, a Government agency includes any department, agency, establishment, wholly owned Government corporation, or instrumentality of the Federal Government or the government of the District of Columbia.

(e) The preceding provisions of this clause do not apply to the Committee on Appropriations, the Committee on House Administration, the Committee on Rules, and the Committee on Standards of Official Conduct.

RULE XIV

Of Decorum and Debate

1. When any Member desires to speak or deliver any matter to the House, he shall rise and respectfully address himself to "Mr. Speaker," and, on being recognized, may address the House from any place on the floor or from the Clerk's desk, and shall confine himself to the question under debate, avoiding personality.

2. When two or more Members rise at once, the Speaker shall name the Member who is first to speak; and no Member shall occupy more than one hour in debate on any question in the House or in committee, except as further provided in this rule.

3. The Member reporting the measure under consideration from a committee may open and close, where general debate has been had thereon; and if it shall extend beyond one day, he shall be entitled to one hour to close, notwithstanding he may have used an hour in opening.

4. If any Member, in speaking or otherwise, transgress the rules of the House, the Speaker shall, or any Member may, call him to order; in which case he shall immediately sit down, unless permitted, on motion of another Member, to explain, and the House shall, if appealed to, decide on the case without debate; if the decision is in favor of the Member called to order, he shall be at liberty to proceed, but not otherwise; and, if the case require it, he shall be liable to censure or such punishment as the House may deem proper.

5. If a Member is called to order for words spoken in debate, the Member calling him to order shall indicate the words excepted to, and they shall be taken down in writing at the Clerk's desk and read aloud to the House; but he shall not be held to answer, nor be subject to the censure of the House therefor, if further debate or other business has intervened.

6. No Member shall speak more than once to the same question without leave of the House, unless he be the mover, proposer, or introducer of the matter pending, in which case he shall be permitted to speak in reply, but not until every Member choosing to speak shall have spoken.

7. While the Speaker is putting a question or addressing the House no Member shall walk out of or across the hall, nor, when a Member is speaking, pass between him and the Chair; and during the session of the House no Member shall wear his hat, or remain by the Clerk's desk during the call of the roll or the counting of ballots, or smoke upon the floor of the House; and the Sergeant-at-Arms and Doorkeeper are charged with the strict enforcement of this clause. Neither shall any person be allowed to smoke upon the floor of the House at any time.

8. It shall not be in order for any Member to introduce to or to bring to the attention of the House during its sessions any occupant in the galleries of the House; nor may the Speaker entertain a request for the suspension of this rule by unanimous consent or otherwise.

RULE XV

On Calls of the Roll and House

1. Subject to clause 5 of this Rule, upon every roll call the names of the Members shall be called alphabetically by surname, except when two or more have the same surname, in which case the name of the State shall be added; and if there be two such Members from the same State, the whole name shall be called, and after the roll has been once called, the Clerk shall call in their alphabetical order the names of those not voting. Members appearing after the second call, but before the result is announced, may vote or announce a pair.

2. (a) In the absence of a quorum, fifteen Members, including the Speaker, if there is one, shall be authorized to compel the attendance of ab-

sent Members; and those for whom no sufficient excuse is made may, by order of a majority of those present, be sent for and arrested, wherever they may be found, by officers to be appointed by the Sergeant-at-Arms for that purpose, and their attendance secured and retained; and the House shall determine upon what condition they shall be discharged. Members who voluntarily appear shall, unless the House otherwise direct, be immediately admitted to the Hall of the House, and they shall report their names to the Clerk to be entered upon the Journal as present.

(b) Subject to clause 5 of this Rule, when a call of the House in the absence of a quorum is ordered, the Speaker shall name one or more clerks to tell the Members who are present. The names of those present shall be recorded by such clerks, and shall be entered in the Journal and the absentees noted, but the doors shall not be closed except when so ordered by the Speaker. Members shall have not less than fifteen minutes from the ordering of a call of the House to have their presence recorded.

3. On the demand of any Member, or at the suggestion of the Speaker, the names of Members sufficient to make a quorum in the Hall of the House who do not vote shall be noted by the Clerk and recorded in the Journal, and reported to the Speaker with the names of the Members voting, and be counted and announced in determining the presence of a quorum to do business.

4. Subject to clause 5 of this Rule, whenever a quorum fails to vote on any question, and a quorum is not present and objection is made for that cause, unless the House shall adjourn there shall be a call of the House, and the Sergeant-at-Arms shall forthwith proceed to bring in absent Members, and the yeas and nays on the pending question shall at the same time be considered as ordered. The Clerk shall call the roll, and each Member as he answers to his name may vote on the pending question, and, after the roll call is completed, each Member arrested shall be brought by the Sergeant-at-Arms before the House, whereupon he shall be noted as present, discharged from arrest, and given an opportunity to vote and his vote shall be recorded. If those voting on the question and those who are present and decline to vote shall together make a majority of the House, the Speaker shall declare that a quorum is constituted, and the pending question shall be decided as the majority of those voting shall appear. And thereupon further proceedings under the call shall be considered as dispensed with. At any time after the roll call has been completed, the Speaker may entertain a motion to adjourn, if seconded by a majority of those present, to be ascertained by actual count by the Speaker; and if the House adjourns, all proceedings under this section shall be vacated.

5. Unless, in his discretion, the Speaker orders the calling of the names of Members in the manner provided for under the preceding provisions of this rule, upon any roll call or quorum call the names of such Members voting or present shall be recorded by electronic device. In any such case, the Clerk shall enter in the Journal and publish in the Congressional Record, in alphabetical order in each category, a list of names of those Members recorded as voting in the affirmative, of those Members recorded as voting in the negative, and of those Members answering present, as the case may be, as if their names had been called in the manner provided for under such preceding provisions. Members shall have not less than fifteen minutes from the ordering of the roll call or quorum call to have their vote or presence recorded.

6. (a) It shall not be in order to make or entertain a point of order that a quorum is not present—

(1) before or during the offering of prayer;

(2) during the administration of the oath of office to the Speaker or Speaker pro tempore or a Member, Delegate, or Resident Commissioner;

(3) during the reception of any message from the President of the United States or the United States Senate, and

(4) during the offering, consideration, and disposition of any motion incidental to a call of the House.

(b) A quorum shall not be required in Committee of the Whole for agreement to a motion that the Committee rise.

(c) After the presence of a quorum is once ascertained on any day on which the House is meeting, a point of order of no quorum may not be made or entertained—

(1) during the reading of the Journal;

(2) during the period after a Committee of the Whole has risen after completing its consideration of a bill or resolution and before the Chairman of the Committee has reported the bill or resolution back to the House; and

(3) during any period of a legislative day when the Speaker is recognizing Members (including a Delegate or Resident Commissioner) to address the House under special orders, with no measure or matter then under consideration for disposition by the House.

(d) When the presence of a quorum is ascertained, a further point of order that a quorum is not present may not thereafter be made or entertained until additional business intervenes. For purposes of this paragraph, the term "business" does not include any matter, proceeding, or period referred to in paragraph (a), (b), or (c) of this clause for which a quorum is not required or a point of order of no quorum may not be made or entertained.

RULE XVI

On Motions, Their Precedence, Etc.

1. Every motion made to the House and entertained by the Speaker shall be reduced to writing on the demand of any Member, and shall be entered on the Journal with the name of the Member making it, unless it withdrawn the same day.

2. When a motion has been made, the Speaker shall state it or (if it be in writing) cause it to be read aloud by the Clerk before being debated, and shall then be in possession of the House, but may be withdrawn at any time before a decision or amendment.

3. When any motion or proposition is made, the question, Will the House now consider it? shall not be put unless demanded by a Member.

4. When a question is under debate, no motion shall be received but to adjourn, to lay on the table, for the previous question (which motions shall be decided without debate), to postpone to a day certain, to refer, or to amend or postpone indefinitely; which several motions shall have precedence in the foregoing order; and no motion to postpone to a day certain, to refer, or to postpone indefinitely, being decided, shall be again allowed on the same day at the same stage of the question. After the previous question shall have been ordered on the passage of a bill or joint resolution one motion to recommit shall be in order, and the Speaker shall give preference in recognition for such purpose to a Member who is opposed to the bill or joint resolution. However with respect to any motion to recommit with instructions after the previous question shall have been ordered, it always shall be in order to debate such motion for ten minutes before the vote is taken on that motion, one half of such time to be given to debate by the mover of the motion and one half to debate in opposition to the motion. It shall be in order at any time during a day for the Speaker, in his discretion, to entertain a motion that when the House adjourns it stand adjourned to a day and time certain. Such a motion shall be of equal privilege with the motion to adjourn provided for in this clause and shall be determined without debate.

5. The hour at which the House adjourns shall be entered on the Journal.

6. On the demand of any Member, before the question is put, a question shall be divided if it includes propositions so distinct in substance that one being taken away a substantive proposition shall remain: *Provided,* That any motion or resolution to elect the members or any portion of the members of the standing committees of the House and the joint standing committees shall not be divisible, nor shall any resolution or order reported by the Committee on Rules, providing a special order of business be divisible.

7. A motion to strike out and insert is indivisible, but a motion to strike out being lost shall neither preclude amendment nor motion to strike out and insert; and no motion or proposition on a subject different from that under consideration shall be admitted under color of amendment.

8. Pending a motion to suspend the rules, the Speaker may entertain one motion that the House adjourn; but after the result thereon is announced he shall not entertain any other motion till the vote is taken on suspension.

9. At any time after the reading of the Journal it shall be in order, by direction of the appropriate committees, to move that the House resolve itself into the Committee of the Whole House on the state of the Union for the purpose of considering bills raising revenue, or general appropriation bills.

10. No dilatory motion shall be entertained by the Speaker.

RULE XVII

Previous Question

1. There shall be a motion for the previous question, which, being ordered by a majority of Members voting, if a quorum be present, shall have the effect to cut off all debate and bring the House to a direct vote upon the immediate question or questions on which it has been asked and ordered. The previous question may be asked and ordered upon a single motion, a series of motions allowable under the rules, or an amendment or amendments, or may be made to embrace all authorized motions or amendments and include the bill to its passage or rejection. It shall be in order, pending the motion for, or after the previous question shall have been ordered on its passage, for the Speaker to entertain and submit a motion to commit, with or without instructions, to a standing or select committee.

2. A call of the House shall not be in order after the previous question is ordered, unless it shall appear upon an actual count by the Speaker that a quorum is not present.

3. All incidental questions of order arising after a motion is made for the previous question, and pending such motion, shall be decided, whether on appeal or otherwise, without debate.

RULE XVIII

Reconsideration

1. When a motion has been made and carried or lost, it shall be in order for any member of the majority, on the same or succeeding day, to move for

reconsideration thereof, and such motion shall take precedence of all
other questions except the consideration of a conference report or a motion to
adjourn, and shall not be withdrawn after the said succeeding day without
the consent of the House, and thereafter any Member may call it up for consideration: *Provided,* That such motion, if made during the last six days of a
session, shall be disposed of when made.

2. No bill, petition, memorial, or resolution referred to a committee, or
reported therefrom for printing and recommitment, shall be brought back
to the House on a motion to reconsider; and all bills, petitions, memorials,
and resolutions reported from a committee shall be accompanied by reports in
writing, which shall be printed.

RULE XIX

Of Amendments

When a motion or proposition is under consideration a motion to amend
and a motion to amend that amendment shall be in order, and it shall also be
in order to offer a further amendment by way of substitute, to which one
amendment may be offered, but which shall not be voted on until the original
matter is perfected, but either may be withdrawn before amendment or decision is had thereon. Amendments to the title of a bill or resolution shall not
be in order until after its passage, and shall be decided without debate.

RULE XX

Of Amendments of the Senate

1. Any amendment of the Senate to any House bill shall be subject to
the point of order that it shall first be considered in the Committee of the
Whole House on the state of the Union, if, originating in the House, it would
be subject to that point: *Provided, however,* That a motion to disagree with
the amendments of the Senate to a House bill or resolution and request or
agree to a conference with the Senate, or a motion to insist on the House
amendments to a Senate bill or resolution and request or agree to a conference with the Senate, shall always be in order if the Speaker, in his discretion, recognizes for that purpose and if the motion is made by direction of
the committee having jurisdiction of the subject matter of the bill or
resolution.

2. No amendment of the Senate to a general appropriation bill which
would be in violation of the provisions of clause 2 of Rule XXI, if said amendment originated in the House, nor any amendment of the Senate providing
for an appropriation upon any bill other than a general appropriation bill,
shall be agreed to by the managers on the part of the House unless specific
authority to agree to such amendment shall be first given by the House by a
separate vote on every such amendment.

RULE XXI

On Bills

1. Bills and joint resolutions on their passage shall be read the first time
by title and the second time in full, when, if the previous question is ordered,
the Speaker shall state the question to be: Shall the bill be engrossed and
read a third time? and, if decided in the affirmative, it shall be read the third
time by title, and the question shall then be put upon its passage.

2. No appropriation shall be reported in any general appropriation bill,
nor be in order as an amendment thereto, for any expenditure not previously
authorized by law, unless in continuation of appropriations for such public
works and objects as are already in progress. Nor shall any provision in any
such bill or amendment thereto changing existing law be in order, except
such as being germane to the subject matter of the bill shall retrench expenditures by the reduction of the number and salary of the officers of the United
States, by the reduction of the compensation of any person paid out of the
Treasury of the United States, or by the reduction of amounts of money
covered by the bill: *Provided,* That it shall be in order further to amend such
bill upon the report of the committee or any joint commission authorized by
law or the House Members of any such commission having jurisdiction of the
subject matter of such amendment, which amendment being germane to the
subject matter of the bill shall retrench expenditures.

3. A report from the Committee on Appropriations accompany any
general appropriation bill making an appropriation for any purpose shall contain a concise statement describing fully the effect of any provision of the accompanying bill which directly or indirectly changes the application of existing law.

4. No bill for the payment or adjudication of any private claim against
the Government shall be referred, except by unanimous consent, to any other
than the following committees, namely: To the Committee on International
Relations or to the Committee on the Judiciary.

5. No bill or joint resolution carrying appropriations shall be reported by
any committee not having jurisdiction to report appropriations, nor shall an
amendment proposing an appropriation be in order during the consideration

of a bill or joint resolution reported by a committee not having that jurisdiction. A question of order on an appropriation in any such bill, joint resolution,
or amendment thereto may be raised at any time.

6. No general appropriation bill or amendment thereto shall be received
or considered if it contains a provision reappropriating unexpended balances
of appropriations; except that this provision shall not apply to appropriations
in continuation of appropriations for public works on which work has commenced.

7. No general appropriation bill shall be considered in the House until
printed committee hearings and a committee report thereon have been
available for the Members of the House for at least three calendar days (excluding Saturdays, Sundays, and legal holidays).

RULE XXII

Of Petitions, Memorials, Bills, and Resolutions

1. Members having petitions or memorials or bills of a private nature to
present may deliver them to the Clerk, indorsing their names and the
reference or disposition to be made thereof; and said petitions and memorials
and bills of a private nature, except such as, in the judgment of the Speaker,
are of an obscene or insulting character, shall be entered on the Journal, with
the names of the Members presenting them, and the Clerk shall furnish a
transcript of such entry to the official reporters of debates for publication in
the Record.

2. No private bill or resolution (including so-called omnibus claims or
pension bills), and no amendment to any bill or resolution, authorizing or
directing (1) the payment of money for property damages, for personal injuries or death for which suit may be instituted under the Tort Claims
Procedure as provided in Title 28, United States Code, or for a pension (other
than to carry out a provision of law or treaty stipulation); (2) the construction
of a bridge across a navigable stream; or (3) the correction of a military or
naval record, shall be received or considered in the House.

3. Any petition or memorial or private bill excluded under this rule shall
be returned to the Member from whom it was received; and petitions and
private bills which have been inappropriately referred may, by the direction
of the committee having possession of the same, be properly referred in the
manner originally presented; and an erroneous reference of a petition or
private bill under this clause shall not confer jurisdiction upon the committee
to consider or report the same.

4. All other bills, memorials, and resolutions may, in like manner, be
delivered, indorsed with the names of Members introducing them, to the
Speaker, to be by him referred, and the titles and references thereof and of all
bills, resolutions, and documents referred under the rules shall be entered on
the Journal and printed in the Record of the next day, and correction in case
of error of reference may be made by the House, without debate, in accordance with Rule X on any day immediately after the reading of the Journal,
by unanimous consent, or on motion of a committee claiming jurisdiction, or
on the report of the committee to which the bill has been erroneously referred.
Two or more but not more than twenty-five Members may introduce jointly
any bill, memorial, or resolution to which this paragraph applies.

5. All resolutions of inquiry addressed to the heads of executive
departments shall be reported to the House within one week after presentation.

6. When a bill, resolution, or memorial is introduced "by request," these
words shall be entered upon the Journal and printed in the Record.

RULE XXIII

Of Committees of the Whole House

1. In all cases, in forming a Committee of the Whole House, the Speaker
shall leave his chair after appointing a Chairman to preside, who shall, in
case of disturbance or disorderly conduct in the galleries or lobby, have power
to cause the same to be cleared.

2. Whenever a Committee of the Whole finds itself without a quorum,
which shall consist of one hundred Members, the Chairman shall invoke the
procedure for the call of the roll under clause 5 of Rule XV, unless, in his discretion, he orders a call of the committee to be taken by the procedure set
forth in clause 2(b) of Rule XV; and thereupon the Committee shall rise, and
the Chairman shall report the names of the absentees to the House, which
shall be entered on the Journal; but if on such call a quorum shall appear, the
Committee shall thereupon resume its sitting without further order of the
House. If, at any time during the conduct of any quorum call in the Committee of the Whole, the Chairman determines that a quorum is present, he
may, in his discretion, declare that a quorum is constituted. Proceedings under the call then shall be considered as vacated, and the Committee shall not
rise but shall continue its sitting and resume its business.

3. All motions or propositions involving a tax or charge upon the people,
all proceedings touching appropriations of money, or bills making
appropriations of money or property, or requiring such appropriation to be
made, or authorizing payments out of appropriations already made, or releas-

ing any liability to the United States for money or property, or referring any claim to the Court of Claims, shall be first considered in a Committee of the Whole, and a point of order under this rule shall be good at any time before the consideration of a bill has commenced.

4. In Committees of the Whole House business on their calendars may be taken up in regular order, or in such order as the committee may determine, unless the bill to be considered was determined by the House at the time of going into committee, but bills for raising revenue, general appropriation bills, and bills for the improvement of rivers and harbors shall have precedence.

5. When general debate is closed by order of the House, any Member shall be allowed five minutes to explain any amendment he may offer, after which the Member who shall first obtain the floor shall be allowed to speak five minutes in opposition to it, and there shall be no further debate thereon, but the same privilege of debate shall be allowed in favor of and against any amendment that may be offered to an amendment; and neither an amendment nor an amendment to an amendment shall be withdrawn by the mover thereof unless by the unanimous consent of the committee. Upon the offering of any amendment by a Member, when the House is meeting in the Committee of the Whole, the Clerk shall promptly transmit to the majority committee table five copies of the amendment and five copies to the minority committee table. Further, the Clerk shall deliver at least one copy of the amendment to the majority cloak room and at least one copy to the minority cloak room.

6. The committee may, by the vote of a majority of the members present, at any time after the five minutes' debate has begun upon proposed amendments to any section or paragraph of a bill, close all debate upon such section or paragraph or, at its election, upon the pending amendments only (which motion shall be decided without debate); but this shall not preclude further amendment, to be decided without debate. However, if debate is closed on any section or paragraph under this clause before there has been debate on any amendment which any Member shall have caused to be printed in the Congressional Record after the reporting of the bill by the committee but at least one day prior to floor consideration of such amendment, the Member who caused such amendment to be printed in the Record shall be given five minutes in which to explain such amendment, after which the first person to obtain the floor shall be given five minutes in opposition to it, and there shall be no further debate thereon; but such time for debate shall not be allowed when the offering of such amendment is dilatory. Material placed in the Record pursuant to this provision shall indicate the full text of the proposed amendment, the name of the proponent Member, the number of the bill to which it will be offered and the point in the bill or amendment thereto where the amendment is intended to be offered, and shall appear in a portion of the Record designated for that purpose.

7. A motion to strike out the enacting words of a bill shall have precedence of a motion to amend, and, if carried, shall be considered equivalent to its rejection. Whenever a bill is reported from a Committee of the Whole with an adverse recommendation and such recommendation is disagreed to by the House, the bill shall stand recommitted to the said committee without further action by the House, but before the question of concurrence is submitted it is in order to entertain a motion to refer the bill to any committee, with or without instructions, and when the same is again reported to the House it shall be referred to the Committee of the Whole without debate.

8. The rules of proceeding in the House shall be observed in Committees of the Whole House so far as they may be applicable.

RULE XXIV

Order of Business

1. The daily order of business shall be as follows:
First. Prayer by the Chaplain.
Second. Reading and approval of the Journal.
Third. Correction of reference of public bills.
Fourth. Disposal of business on the Speaker's table.
Fifth. Unfinished business.
Sixth. The morning hour for the consideration of bills called up by committees.
Seventh. Motions to go into Committee of the Whole House on the State of the Union.
Eighth. Orders of the day.

2. Business on the Speaker's table shall be disposed of as follows:
Messages from the President shall be referred to the appropriate committees without debate. Reports and communications from heads of departments, and other communications addressed to the House, and bills, resolutions, and messages from the Senate may be referred to the appropriate committees in the same manner and with the same right of correction as public bills presented by Members; but House bills with Senate amendments which do not require consideration in a Committee of the Whole may be at once disposed of as the House may determine, as may also Senate bills substantially the same as House bills already favorably reported by a committee of the House, and not required to be considered in Committee of the Whole,

be disposed of in the same manner on motion directed to be made by su[c] committee.

3. The consideration of the unfinished business in which the House m[ay] be engaged at an adjournment, except business in the morning hour, shall [be] resumed as soon as the business on the Speaker's table is finished, and at t[he] same time each day thereafter until disposed of, and the consideration of [a] other unfinished business shall be resumed whenever the class of business [to] which it belongs shall be in order under the rules.

4. After the unfinished business has been disposed of, the Speaker sha[ll] call each standing committee in regular order, and then select committee[s,] and each committee when named may call up for consideration any bi[ll] reported by it on a previous day and on the House Calendar, and if th[e] Speaker shall not complete the call of the Committees before the Hous[e] passes to other business, he shall resume the next call where he left off, givin[g] preference to the last bill under consideration: *Provided*, That whenever an[y] committee shall have occupied the morning hour on two days, it shall not b[e] in order to call up any other bill until the other committees have been calle[d] in their turn.

5. After one hour shall have been devoted to the consideration of bill[s] called up by committees, it shall be in order, pending consideration or discus[s]sion thereof, to entertain a motion to go into Committee of the Whole Hous[e] on the state of the Union, or, when authorized by a committee, to go into th[e] Committee of the Whole House on the state of the Union to consider a par[t]ticular bill, to which motion one amendment only, designating another bil[l,] may be made; and if either motion be determined in the negative, it shall n[ot] be in order to make either motion again until the disposal of the matter und[er] consideration or discussion.

6. On the first Tuesday of each month after disposal of such business o[n] the Speaker's table as requires reference only, the Speaker shall direct th[e] Clerk to call the bills and resolutions on the Private Calendar. Should objec[c]tion be made by two or more Members to the consideration of any bill o[r] resolution so called, it shall be recommitted to the committee which reporte[d] the bill or resolution, and no reservation of objection shall be entertained b[y] the Speaker. Such bills and resolutions, if considered, shall be considered i[n] the House as in the Committee of the Whole. No other business shall be i[n] order on this day unless the House, by two-thirds vote on motion to dispens[e] therewith, shall otherwise determine. On such motion debate shall be limite[d] to five minutes for and five minutes against said motion.

On the third Tuesday of each month after the disposal of such business on the Speaker's table as requires reference only, the Speaker may direct the Clerk to call the bills and resolutions on the Private Calendar, preference t[o] be given to omnibus bills containing bills or resolutions which have previous[s]ly been objected to on a call of the Private Calendar. All bills and resolution[s] on the Private Calendar so called, if considered, shall be considered in the House as in the Committee of the Whole. Should objection be made by two or more members to the consideration of any bill or resolution other than an omnibus bill, it shall be recommitted to the committee which reported the bill or resolution and no reservation of objection shall be entertained by the Speaker.

Omnibus bills shall be read for amendment by paragraph, and no amendment shall be in order except to strike out or reduce amounts of money stated or to provide limitations. Any item or matter stricken from an omnibus bill shall not thereafter during the same session of Congress be included in any omnibus bill.

Upon passage of any such omnibus bill, said bill shall be resolved into the several bills and resolutions of which it is composed, and such original bills and resolutions, with any amendments adopted by the House, shall be engrossed, where necessary, and proceedings thereon had as if said bills and resolutions had been passed in the House severally.

In the consideration of any omnibus bill the proceedings as set forth above shall have the same force and effect as if each Senate and House bill or resolution therein contained or referred to were considered by the House as a separate and distinct bill or resolution.

7. On Wednesday of each week no business shall be in order except as provided by clause 4 of this rule unless the House by a two-thirds vote on motion to dispense therewith shall otherwise determine. On such a motion there may be debate not to exceed five minutes for and against. On a call of committees under this rule bills may be called up from either the House or the Union Calendar, excepting bills which are privileged under the rules; but bills called up from the Union Calendar shall be considered in Committee of the Whole House on the state of the Union. This rule shall not apply during the last two weeks of the session. It shall not be in order for the Speaker to entertain a motion for a recess on any Wednesday except during the last two weeks of the session: *Provided*, That not more than two hours of general debate shall be permitted on any measure called up on Calendar Wednesday, and all debate must be confined to the subject matter of the bill, the time to be equally divided between those for and against the bill: *Provided further*, That whenever any committee shall have occupied one Wednesday it shall not be in order, unless the House by a two-thirds vote shall otherwise determine, to consider any unfinished business previously called up by such committee, unless the previous question had been ordered thereon, upon any succeeding Wednesday until the other committees have been called in their

rn under this rule: *Provided,* That when, during any one session of ongress, all of the committees of the House are not called under the Calendar Wednesday rule, at the next session of Congress the call shall commence here it left off at the end of the preceding session.

8. The second and fourth Mondays in each month, after the disposition motions to discharge committees and after the disposal of such business on e Speaker's table as requires reference only, shall, when claimed by the ommittee on the District of Columbia, be set apart for the consideration of ich business as may be presented by said committee.

RULE XXV

Priority of Business

All questions relating to the priority of business shall be decided by a ajority without debate.

RULE XXVI

Unfinished Business of the Session

All business before committees of the House at the end of one session will e resumed at the commencement of the next session of the same Congress in ne same manner as if no adjournment had taken place.

RULE XXVII

Change or Suspension of Rules

1. No rule shall be suspended except by a vote of two-thirds of the Members voting, a quorum being present; nor shall the Speaker entertain a motion to suspend the rules except on the first and third Mondays of each month, and on the Tuesdays immediately following those days, and during the last six days of a session.

2. All motions to suspend the rules shall, before being submitted to the House, be seconded by a majority by tellers, if demanded.

3. (a) When a motion to suspend the rules has been seconded, it shall be in order, before the final vote is taken thereon, to debate the proposition to be voted upon for forty minutes, one-half of such time to be given to debate in favor of, and one-half to debate in opposition to, such proposition; and the same right of debate shall be allowed whenever the previous question has been ordered on any proposition on which there has been no debate.

(b) (1) On any legislative day (other than during the last six days of a session) on which the Speaker is authorized to entertain motions to suspend the Rules and pass bills or resolutions, he may announce to the House, in his discretion, before entertaining the first such motion, that he will postpone further proceedings on each of such motions on which a recorded vote or the yeas and nays is ordered or on which the vote is objected to under clause 4 of Rule XV, until all of such motions on that legislative day have been entertained and any debate thereon concluded, with the question having been put and determined on each such motion on which the taking of the vote will not be postponed.

(2) When the last of all motions on that legislative day to suspend the Rules and pass bills or resolutions has been entertained and any debate thereon concluded, with the question put and determined on each such motion on which further proceedings were not postponed, the Speaker shall put the question on each motion on which further proceedings were postponed, in the order in which that motion was entertained.

(3) At any time after the vote on the question has been taken on the first motion on which the Speaker has postponed further proceedings under this paragraph, the Speaker may, in his discretion, reduce to not less than five minutes the period of time within which a recorded vote on the question may be taken on any or all of the additional motions on which the Speaker has postponed further proceedings under this paragraph.

(4) If the House adjourns before the question is put and determined on all motions on which further proceedings were postponed under this paragraph, then, on the next following legislative day on which the Speaker is authorized to entertain motions to suspend the Rules and pass bills or resolutions, the first order of legislative business after the call of bills and resolutions on the Private Calendar as provided in clause 6 of Rule XXIV shall be the disposition of all such motions, previously undisposed of, in the order in which those motions were entertained.

4. A Member may present to the Clerk a motion in writing to discharge a committee from the consideration of a public bill or resolution which has been referred to it thirty days prior thereto (but only one motion may be presented for each bill or resolution). Under this rule it shall also be in order for a Member to file a motion·to discharge the Committee on Rules from further consideration of any resolution providing either a special order of business, or a special rule for the consideration of any public bill or resolution favorably reported by a standing committee, or a special rule for the consideration of a public bill or resolution which has remained in a standing committee thirty or more days without action: *Provided,* That said resolution from which it is moved to discharge the Committee on Rules has been referred to that committee at least seven days prior to the filing of the motion to discharge. The motion shall be placed in the custody of the Clerk, who shall arrange some convenient place for the signature of Members. A signature may be withdrawn by a Member in writing at any time before the motion is entered on the Journal. When a majority of the total membership of the House shall have signed the motion, it shall be entered on the Journal, printed with the signatures thereto in the Congressional Record, and referred to the Calendar of Motions to Discharge Committees.

On the second and fourth Mondays of each month except during the last six days of any session of Congress, immediately after the approval of the Journal, any Member who has signed a motion to discharge which has been on the calendar at least seven days prior thereto, and seeks recognition, shall be recognized for the purpose of calling up the motion, and the House shall proceed to its consideration in the manner herein provided without intervening motion except one motion to adjourn. Recognition for the motions shall be in the order in which they have been entered on the Journal.

When any motion under this rule shall be called up, the bill or resolution shall be read by title only. After twenty minutes' debate, one-half in favor of the proposition and one-half in opposition thereto, the House shall proceed to vote on the motion to discharge. If the motion prevails to discharge the Committee on Rules from any resolution pending before the committee, the House shall immediately vote on the adoption of said resolution, the Speaker not entertaining any dilatory or other intervening motion except one motion to adjourn, and, if said resolution is adopted, then the House shall immediately proceed to its execution. If the motion prevails to discharge one of the standing committees of the House from any public bill or resolution pending before the committee, it shall then be in order for any Member who signed the motion to move that the House proceed to the immediate consideration of such bill or resolution (such motion not being debatable), and such motion is hereby made of high privilege; and if it shall be decided in the affirmative, the bill shall be immediately considered under the general rules of the House, and if unfinished before adjournment of the day on which it is called up it shall remain the unfinished business until it is fully disposed of. Should the House by vote decide against the immediate consideration of such bill or resolution, it shall be referred to its proper calendar and be entitled to the same rights and privileges that it would have had had the committee to which it was referred duly reported same to the House for its consideration: *Provided,* That when any perfected motion to discharge a committee from the consideration of any public bill or resolution has once been acted upon by the House it shall not be in order to entertain during the same session of Congress any other motion for the discharge from that committee of said measure, or from any other committee of any other bill or resolution substantially the same, relating in substance to or dealing with the same subject matter, or from the Committee on Rules of a resolution providing a special order of business for the consideration of any other such bill or resolution, in order that such action by the House on a motion to discharge shall be res adjudicata for the remainder of that session: *Provided further,* That if before any one motion to discharge a committee has been acted upon by the House there are on the Calendar of Motions to Discharge Committees other motions to discharge committees from the consideration of bills or resolutions substantially the same, relating in substance to or dealing with the same subject matter, after the House shall have acted on one motion to discharge, the remaining said motions shall be stricken from the Calendar of Motions to Discharge Committees and not acted on during the remainder of that session of Congress.

RULE XXVIII

Conference Reports

1. (a) The presentation of reports of committees of conference shall always be in order, except when the Journal is being read, while the roll is being called, or the House is dividing on any proposition.

(b) After House conferees on any bill or resolution in conference between the House and Senate shall have been appointed for twenty calendar days and shall have failed to make a report, it is hereby declared to be a motion of the highest privilege to move to discharge said House conferees and to appoint new conferees, or to instruct said House conferees; and, further, during the last six days of any sessions of Congress, it shall be a privileged motion to move to discharge, appoint, or instruct, House conferees after House conferees shall have been appointed thirty-six hours without having made a report.

(c) Each report made by a committee of conference to the House shall be printed as a report of the House. As so printed, such report shall be accompanied by an explanatory statement prepared jointly by the conferees on the part of the House and the conferees on the part of the Senate. Such statement shall be sufficiently detailed and explicit to inform the House as to the effect which the amendments or propositions contained in such report will have upon the measure to which those amendments or propositions relate.

2. (a) It shall not be in order to consider the report of a committee of conference until the third calendar day (excluding any Saturday, Sunday, or legal holiday) after such report and the accompanying statement shall have been filed in the House, and such consideration then shall be in order only if such report and accompanying statement shall have been printed in the daily edition of the Congressional Record for the day on which such report and statement shall have been filed; but the preceding provisions of this sentence do not apply during the last six days of the session. Nor shall it be in order to consider any conference report unless copies of the report and accompanying statement have been available to Members for at least two hours before the beginning of such consideration; *Provided, however,* that it shall always be in order to call up for consideration, notwithstanding the provisions of clause 4(b), Rule XI, a report from the Committee on Rules only making in order the consideration of a conference report notwithstanding this restriction. The time allotted for debate in the consideration of any such report shall be equally divided between the majority party and the minority party.

(b) It shall not be in order to consider any amendment (including an amendment in the nature of a substitute) proposed by the Senate to any measure reported in disagreement between the two Houses, by a report of a committee of conference that the committee has been unable to agree, until the third calendar day (excluding any Saturday, Sunday, or legal holiday) after such report and accompanying statement shall have been filed in the House, and such consideration then shall be in order only if such report and accompanying statement shall have been printed in the daily edition of the Congressional Record for the day on which such report and statement shall have been filed; but the preceding provisions of this sentence do not apply during the last six days of the session. Nor shall it be in order to consider any such amendment unless copies of the report and accompanying statement, together with the text of such amendment, have been available to Members for at least two hours before the beginning of such consideration; *Provided, however,* that it shall always be in order to call up for consideration, notwithstanding the provisions of clause 4(b), Rule XI, a report from the Committee on Rules only making in order the consideration of such an amendment notwithstanding this restriction. The time allotted for debate on any such amendment shall be equally divided between the majority party and the minority party.

3. Whenever a disagreement to an amendment in the nature of a substitute has been committed to a conference committee it shall be in order for the Managers on the part of the House to propose a substitute which is a germane modification of the matter in disagreement, but the introduction of any language in that substitute presenting a specific additional topic, question, issue, or proposition not committed to the conference committee by either House shall not constitute a germane modification of the matter in disagreement. Moreover, their report shall not include matter not committed to the conference committee by either House, nor shall their report include a modification of any specific topic, question, issue, or proposition committed to the conference committee by either or both Houses if that modification is beyond the scope of that specific topic, question, issue, or proposition as so committed to the conference committee.

4. (a) With respect to any report of a committee of conference called up before the House containing any matter which would be in violation of the provisions of clause 7 of Rule XVI if such matter had been offered as an amendment in the House, and which—

(1) is contained in any Senate amendment to that measure (including a Senate amendment in the nature of a substitute for the text of that measure as passed by the House) accepted by the House conferees or agreed to by the conference committee with modification; or

(2) is contained in any substitute agreed to by the conference committee; it shall be in order, at any time after the reading of the report has been completed or dispensed with and before the reading of the statement, to make a point of order that such nongermane matter, as described above, which shall be specified in the point of order, is contained in the report.

For the purposes of this clause, matter which—

(A) is contained in any substitute agreed to by the conference committee;

(B) is not proposed by the House to be included in the measure concerned as passed by the House; and

(C) would be in violation of clause 7 of Rule XVI if such matter had been offered in the House as an amendment to the provisions of that measure as so proposed in the form passed by the House; shall be considered in violation of such clause 7.

(b) If such point of order is sustained, it then shall be in order for the Chair to entertain a motion, which is of high privilege, that the House reject the nongermane matter covered by the point of order. It shall be in order to debate such motion for forty minutes, one-half of such time to be given to debate in favor of, and one-half in opposition to, the motion.

(c) Notwithstanding the final disposition of any point of order made under paragraph (a), or of any motion to reject made pursuant to a point of order under paragraph (b), of this clause, it shall be in order to make further points of order on the ground stated in such paragraph (a), and motions to reject pursuant thereto under such paragraph (b), with respect to other nongermane matter in the report of the committee of conference not covered by any previous point of order which has been sustained.

(d) If any such motion to reject has been adopted, after final disposition of all points of order and motions to reject under the preceding provisions this clause, the conference report shall be considered as rejected and the question then pending before the House shall be—

(1) whether to recede and concur in the Senate amendment with a amendment which shall consist of that portion of the conference report rejected; or

(2) if the last sentence of paragraph (a) of this clause applies, whether insist further on the House amendment.

If all such motions to reject are defeated, then, after the allocation of time debate on the conference report as provided in clause 2(a) of this Rule, it sha be in order to move the previous question on the adoption of the conference report.

5. (a) (1) With respect to any amendment (including an amendment i the nature of a substitute) which—

(A) is proposed by the Senate to any measure and thereafter—
(i) is reported in disagreement between the two Houses by committee of conference; or
(ii) is before the House, the stage of disagreement having bee reached; and

(B) contains any matter which would be in violation of th provisions of clause 7 of Rule XVI if such matter had been offered as a amendment in the House;

it shall be in order, immediately after a motion is offered that the Hous recede from its disagreement to such amendment proposed by the Senate an concur therein and before debate is commenced on such motion, to make point of order that such nongermane matter, as described above, which sha be specified in the point of order, is contained in such amendment propose by the Senate.

(2) If such point of order is sustained, it then shall be in order for the Chair to entertain a motion, which is of high privilege, that the House reje the nongermane matter covered by the point of order. It shall be in order t debate such motion for forty minutes, one-half of such time to be given t debate in favor of, and one-half in opposition to, the motion.

(3) Notwithstanding the final disposition of any point of order made un der subparagraph (1), or of any motion to reject made pursuant to a point o order under subparagraph (2), of this paragraph, it shall be in order to make further points of order on the ground stated in such subparagraph (1), and motions to reject pursuant thereto under such subparagraph (2), with respect to other nongermane matter in the amendment proposed by the Senate not covered by any previous point of order which has been sustained.

(4) If any such motion to reject has been adopted, after final disposition of all points of order and motions to reject under the preceding provisions of this clause, the motion to recede and concur shall be considered as rejected, and further motions—

(A) to recede and concur in the Senate amendment with an amendment, where appropriate (but the offering of which is not in order unless copies of the language of the Senate amendment, as proposed to be amended by such motion, are then available on the floor when such motion is offered and is under consideration);

(B) to insist upon disagreement to the Senate amendment and request a further conference with the Senate; and

(C) to insist upon disagreement to the Senate amendment; shall remain of high privilege for consideration by the House. If all such motions to reject are defeated, then, after the allocation of time for debate on the motion to recede and concur as provided in clause 2(b) of this Rule, it shall be in order to move the previous question on such motion.

(b) (1) With respect to any such amendment proposed by the Senate as described in paragraph (a) of this clause, it shall not be in order to offer any motion that the House recede from its disagreement to such Senate amendment and concur therein with an amendment, unless copies of the language of the Senate amendment, as proposed to be amended by such motion, are then available on the floor when such motion is offered and is under consideration.

(2) Immediately after any such motion is offered and is in order and before debate is commenced on such motion, it shall be in order to make a point of order that nongermane matter, as described in subparagraph (1) of paragraph (a) of this clause, which shall be specified in the point of order, is contained in the language of the Senate amendment, as proposed to be amended by such motion, copies of which are then available on the floor.

(3) If such point of order is sustained, it then shall be in order for the Chair to entertain a motion, which is of high privilege, that the House reject the nongermane matter covered by the point of order. It shall be in order to debate such motion for forty minutes, one-half of such time to be given to debate in favor of, and one-half in opposition to, the motion.

(4) Notwithstanding the final disposition of any point of order under subparagraph (2), or of any motion to reject made pursuant to a point of order under subparagraph (3), of this paragraph, it shall be in order to make further points of order on the ground stated in subparagraph (1) of paragraph (a) of this clause, and motions to reject pursuant thereto under subparagraph (3) of this paragraph, with respect to other nongermane matter in the language of the Senate amendment, as proposed to be amended by the mo-

n described in subparagraph (1) of this paragraph, not covered by any evious point of order which has been sustained.

(5) If any such motion to reject has been adopted, after final disposition all points of order and motions to reject under the preceding provisions of is paragraph, the motion to recede and concur in the Senate amendment th an amendment shall be considered as rejected, and further motions—

(A) to recede and concur in the Senate amendment with an amendment, where appropriate (but the offering of which is not in order unless copies of the language of the Senate amendment, as proposed to be amended by such motion, are then available on the floor when such motion is offered and is under consideration);

(B) to insist upon disagreement to the Senate amendment and request a further conference with the Senate; and

(C) to insist upon disagreement to the Senate amendment; all remain of high privilege for consideration by the House. If all such otions to reject are defeated, then, after the allocation of time for debate on e motion to recede and concur in the Senate amendment with an amendent as provided in clause 2(b) of this Rule, it shall be in order to move the evious question on such motion.

(c) If, on a division of a motion that the House recede and concur, with without amendment, from its disagreement to any such Senate amendent as described in paragraph (a) (1) of this clause, the House agrees to ecede, then, before debate is commenced on concurring in such Senate mendment, or on concurring therein with an amendment, it shall be in order make and dispose of points of order and motions to reject with respect to uch Senate amendment in accordance with applicable provisions of this lause and to effect final determination of these matters in accordance with uch provisions.

6. Open Conference Meetings. Each conference committee meeting etween the House and Senate shall be open to the public except when the managers of either House or Senate, in open session, determine by a rollcall ote of a majority of those managers present, that all or part of the remainder f the meeting on the day of the vote shall be closed to the public: *Provided,* That this provision shall not become effective until a similar rule is adopted by the Senate.

RULE XXIX

Secret Session

Whenever confidential communications are received from the President of the United States, or whenever the Speaker or any Member shall inform the House that he has communications which he believes ought to be kept secret for the present, the House shall be cleared of all persons except the Members and officers thereof, and so continue during the readings of such communications, the debates and proceedings thereon. unless otherwise ordered by the House.

RULE XXX

Reading of Papers

When the reading of a paper other than one upon which the House is called to give a final vote is demanded, and the same is objected to by any Member, it shall be determined without debate by a vote of the House.

RULE XXXI

Hall of the House

The Hall of the House shall be used only for the legislative business of the House and for the caucus meetings of its Members, except upon occasions where the House by resolution agrees to take part in any ceremonies to be observed therein; and the Speaker shall not entertain a motion for the suspension of this rule.

RULE XXXII

Of Admission to the Floor

1. The persons hereinafter named, and none other, shall be admitted to the Hall of the House or rooms leading thereto, viz: The President and Vice President of the United States and their private secretaries, judges of the Supreme Court, Members of Congress and Members-elect, contestants in election cases during the pendency of their cases in the House, the Secretary and Sergeant-at-Arms of the Senate, heads of departments, foreign ministers, governors of States, the Architect of the Capitol, the Librarian of Congress and his assistant in charge of the Law Library, the Resident Commissioner to the United States from Puerto Rico, each Delegate to the House, such persons as have, by name, received the thanks of Congress, ex-Members of the House of Representatives who are not interested in any claim or direct-

ly in any bill pending before Congress, elected officers and elected minority employees of the House (other than Members), the Parliamentarian and former Parliamentarians of the House, former elected officers and former elected minority employees of the House (other than ex-Members) who are not interested in any claim or directly in any bill pending before Congress, and clerks of committees when business from their committee is under consideration; and it shall not be in order for the Speaker to entertain a request for the suspension of this rule or to present from the chair the request of any Member for unanimous consent.

2. There shall be excluded at all times from the Hall of the House of Representatives and the cloakrooms all persons not entitled to the privilege of the floor during the session, except that until fifteen minutes of the hour of the meeting of the House persons employed in its service, accredited members of the press entitled to admission to the press gallery, and other persons on request of Members, by card or in writing, may be admitted.

RULE XXXIII

Of Admission to the Galleries

The Speaker shall set aside a portion of the west gallery for the use of the President of the United States, the members of his Cabinet, justices of the Supreme Court, foreign ministers and suites, and the members of their respective families, and shall also set aside another portion of the same gallery for the accommodation of persons to be admitted on the card of Members. The southerly half of the east gallery shall be assigned exclusively for the use of the families of Members of Congress, in which the Speaker shall control one bench, and on request of a Member the Speaker shall issue a card of admission to his family, which shall include their visitors, and no other person shall be admitted to this section.

RULE XXXIV

Official and Other Reporters

1. The appointment and removal, for cause, of the official reporters of the House, including stenographers of committees, and the manner of the execution of their duties shall be vested in the Speaker.

2. Such portion of the gallery over the Speaker's chair as may be necessary to accommodate representatives of the press wishing to report debates and proceedings shall be set aside for their use, and reputable reporters and correspondents shall be admitted thereto under such regulations as the Speaker may from time to time prescribe; and the supervision of such gallery, including the designation of its employees, shall be vested in the standing committee of correspondents, subject to the direction and control of the Speaker; and the Speaker may assign one seat on the floor to Associated Press reporters and one to United Press International, and regulate the occupation of the same. And the Speaker may admit to the floor, under such regulations as he may prescribe, one additional representative of each press association.

3. Such portion of the gallery of the House of Representatives as may be necessary to accommodate reporters of news to be disseminated by radio, television, and similar means of transmission, wishing to report debates and proceedings, shall be set aside for their use, and reputable reporters thus engaged shall be admitted thereto under such regulations as the Speaker may from time to time prescribe; and the supervision of such gallery, including the designation of its employees, shall be vested in the Executive Committee of the Radio and Television Correspondents' Galleries, subject to the direction and control of the Speaker; and the Speaker may admit to the floor, under such regulations as he may prescribe, one representative of the National Broadcasting Company, one of the Columbia Broadcasting System, one of the Mutual Broadcasting System, and one of the American Broadcasting Company.

RULE XXXV

Pay of Witnesses

The rule for paying witnesses subpenaed to appear before the House or any of its committees shall be as follows: For each day a witness shall attend, the sum of twenty dollars; and actual expenses of travel in coming to or going from the place of examination, not to exceed twelve cents per mile; but nothing shall be paid for travel when the witness has been summoned at the place of examination.

RULE XXXVI

Papers

1. The clerks of the several committees of the House shall, within three days after the final adjournment of a Congress, deliver to the Clerk of the

House all bills, joint resolutions, petitions, and other papers referred to the committee, together with all evidence taken by such committee under the order of the House during the said Congress and not reported to the House; and in the event of the failure or neglect of any clerk of a committee to comply with this rule the Clerk of the House shall, within three days thereafter, take into his keeping all such papers and testimony.

2. At the close of each Congress the Clerk of the House shall obtain all noncurrent records of the House and each committee thereof and transfer them to the General Services Administration for preservation subject to the order of the House. In making the transfer, the Clerk may act jointly with the Secretary of the Senate.

RULE XXXVII

Withdrawal of Papers

No memorial or other paper presented to the House shall be withdrawn from its files without its leave, and if withdrawn therefrom certified copies thereof shall be left in the office of the Clerk; but when an act may pass for the settlement of a claim, the Clerk is authorized to transmit to the officer in charge with the settlement thereof the papers on file in his office relating to such claim, or may loan temporarily to an officer or bureau of the executive departments any papers on file in his office relating to any matter pending before such officer or bureau, taking proper receipt therefor.

RULE XXXVIII

Ballot

In all cases of ballot a majority of the votes given shall be necessary to an election, and where there shall not be such a majority on the first ballot the ballots shall be repeated until a majority be obtained; and in all balloting blanks shall be rejected and not taken into the count in enumeration of votes or reported by the tellers.

RULE XXXIX

Messages

Messages received from the Senate and the President of the United States, giving notice of bills passed or approved, shall be entered in the Journal and published in the Record of that day's proceedings.

RULE XL

Executive Communications

Estimates of appropriations and all other communications from the executive departments, intended for the consideration of any committees of the House, shall be addressed to the Speaker, and by him referred as provided by clause 2 of Rule XXIV.

RULE XLI

Qualifications of Officers and Employees

No person shall be an officer of the House, or continue in its employment, who shall be an agent for the prosecution of any claim against the Government, or be interested in such claim otherwise than as an original claimant; and it shall be the duty of the Committee on House Administration to inquire into and report to the House any violation of this rule.

RULE XLII

General Provisions

The rules of parliamentary practice comprised in Jefferson's Manual and the provisions of the Legislative Reorganization Act of 1946, as amended, shall govern the House in all cases to which they are applicable, and in which they are not inconsistent with the standing rules and orders of the House and joint rules of the Senate and House of Representatives.

RULE XLIII

Code of Official Conduct

There is hereby established by and for the House of Representatives the following code of conduct, to be known as the "Code of Official Conduct":

1. A Member, officer, or employee of the House of Representatives sh conduct himself at all times in a manner which shall reflect creditably on t House of Representatives.

2. A Member, officer, or employee of the House of Representatives sh adhere to the spirit and the letter of the Rules of the House of Representativ and to the rules of duly constituted committees thereof.

3. A Member, officer, or employee of the House of Representatives sh receive no compensation nor shall he permit any compensation to accrue his beneficial interest from any source, the receipt of which would occur virtue of influence improperly exerted from his position in the Congress.

4. A Member, officer, or employee of the House of Representatives sh accept no gift of substantial value, directly or indirectly, from any pers organization, or corporation having a direct interest in legislation before t Congress.

5. A Member, officer, or employee of the House of Representatives she accept no honorarium for a speech, writing for publication, or other simil activity, from any person, organization, or corporation in excess of the usu and customary value for such services.

6. A Member of the House of Representatives shall keep his campaig funds separate from his personal funds. Unless specifically provided by la he shall convert no campaign funds to personal use in excess of reimburs ment for legitimate and verifiable prior campaign expenditures and he sha expend no funds from his campaign account not attributable to bona fic campaign purposes.

7. A Member of the House of Representatives shall treat as campaig contributions all proceeds from testimonial dinners or other fund raisin events if the sponsors of such affairs do not give clear notice in advance to th donors or participants that the proceeds are intended for other purposes.

8. A Member of the House of Representatives shall retain no one fron his clerk hire allowance who does not perform duties commensurate with th compensation he receives.

9. A Member, officer or employee of the House of Representatives shal not discharge or refuse to hire any individual, or otherwise discriminat against any individual with respect to compensation, terms, conditions, or privileges of employment, because of such individual's race, color, religion, sex, or national origin.

As used in this Code of Official Conduct of the House of Represen tatives—(a) the terms "Member" and "Member of the House of Represen tatives" include the Resident Commissioner from Puerto Rico and each Delegate to the House; and (b) the term "officer or employee of the House of Representatives" means any individual whose compensation is disbursed by the Clerk of the House of Representatives.

10. A Member of the House of Representatives who has been convicted by a court of record for the commission of a crime for which a sentence of two or more years' imprisonment may be imposed should refrain from participation in the business of each committee of which he is a member and should refrain from voting on any question at a meeting of the House, or of the Committee of the Whole House, unless or until judicial or executive proceedings result in reinstatement of the presumption of his innocence or until he is reelected to the House after the date of such conviction.

RULE XLIV

Financial Disclosure

Members, officers, principal assistants to Members and officers, and professional staff members of committees shall, not later than April 30, 1969, and by April 30 of each year thereafter, file with the Committee on Standards of Official Conduct a report disclosing certain financial interests as provided in this rule. The interest of a spouse or any other party, if constructively controlled by the person reporting, shall be considered to be the same as the interest of the person reporting. The report shall be in two parts as follows:

PART A.

1. List the name, instrument of ownership, and any position of management held in any business entity doing a substantial business with the Federal Government or subject to Federal regulatory agencies, in which the ownership is in excess of $5,000 fair market value as of the date of filing or from which income of $1,000 or more was derived during the preceding calendar year. Do not list any time or demand deposit in a financial institution, or any debt instrument having a fixed yield unless it is convertible to an equity instrument.

2. List the name, address, and type of practice of any professional organization in which the person reporting, or his spouse, is an officer, director, or partner, or serves in any advisory capacity, from which income of $1,-000 or more was derived during the preceding calendar year.

3. List the source of each of the following items received during the preceding calendar year: (a) Any income for services rendered (other than from the United States Government) exceeding $5,000. (b) Any capital gain from a single source exceeding $5,000, other than from the sale of a residence occupied by the person reporting. (c) Reimbursement for expenditures (other than from the United States Government) exceeding $1,000 in each instance. (d) Honorariums from a single source aggregating $300 or more.

4. List each creditor to whom the person reporting was indebted for a period of ninety consecutive days or more during the preceding calendar year in an aggregate amount in excess of $10,000, excluding any indebtedness specifically secured by the pledge of assets of the person reporting of appropriate value.

Campaign receipts shall not be included in this report.

Information filed under part A shall be maintained by the Committee on Standards of Official Conduct and made available at reasonable hours to responsible public inquiry, subject to such regulations as the committee may prescribe including, but not limited to, regulations requiring identification by name, occupation, address, and telephone number of each person examining information filed under part A, and the reason for such inquiry.

The committee shall promptly notify each person required to file a report under this rule of each instance of an examination of his report. The committee shall also promptly notify a Member of each examination of the reports filed by his principal assistants and of each examination of the reports of professional staff members of committees who are responsible to such Member.

PART B.

1. List the fair market value (as of the date of filing) of each item listed under paragraph 1 of part A and the income derived therefrom during the preceding calendar year.

2. List the amount of income derived from each item listed under paragraphs 2 and 3 of part A, and the amount of indebtedness owed to each creditor listed under paragraph 4 of part A.

The information filed under this part B shall be sealed by the person filing and shall remain sealed unless the Committee on Standards of Official Conduct, pursuant to its investigative authority, determines by a vote of not less than seven members of the committee that the examination of such information is essential in an official investigation by the committee and promptly notifies the Member concerned of any such determination. The committee may, by a vote of not less than seven members of the committee, make public any portion of the information unsealed by the committee under the preceding sentence and which the committee deems to be in the public interest.

Any person required to file a report under this rule who has no interests covered by any of the provisions of this rule shall file a report, under part A only of this rule, so stating.

In any case in which a person required to file a sealed report under part B of this rule is no longer required to file such a report, the committee shall return to such person, or his legal representative, all sealed reports filed by such person under part B and remaining in the possession of the committee.

As used in this rule—(1) the term "Members" includes the Resident Commissioner from Puerto Rico and each Delegate to the House; and (2) the term "committees" includes any committee or subcommittee of the House of Representatives and any joint committee of Congress, the expenses of which are paid from the contingent fund of the House of Representatives.

House Democratic Caucus Rules

Following are the standing rules of the House Democratic Caucus, as revised Sept. 30, 1975:

R 1. Membership
a. All Democratic Members of the House of Representatives and the Resident Commissioner from Puerto Rico, the Delegate from the District of Columbia, the Delegate from Guam and the Delegate from the Virgin Islands who are members of the Democratic Party shall be prima facie members of the Democratic Caucus.

b. Any member of the Democratic Caucus of the House of Representatives failing to abide by the rules governing the same shall thereby automatically cease to be a member of the Caucus.

R 2. Meeting Dates
Meetings of the Democratic Caucus shall be called by the chairman upon his own motion or at the request of the Party Leader. Whenever fifty (50) members of the Caucus request the chairman, in writing, to hold a special meeting the chairman shall set the time and place of such special meeting and provide the members with the order of business of such special meeting at least 5 calendar days before the hour of convening; however, when the purpose of such special meeting is to consider a veto override or legislation that has been reported to the House, the chairman may waive the 5-day-notice requirement. In every instance, the chairman shall provide the members with reasonable notice of the time, place and order of business of all meetings. While the House is in session, the Democratic Caucus shall meet regularly at a time and place to be determined by the chairman, on the 3d Wednesday of each month, except January of odd numbered years. If the House not be in session on the 3d Wednesday, the monthly Caucus shall be held on the next succeeding Wednesday on which the House is in session. The chairman may cancel any monthly Caucus, but not two consecutive monthly Caucuses, provided members are given reasonable notice of such cancellation. Members of the Caucus shall not schedule committee meetings or hearings at times when the Caucus is to be in session.

R 3. Presiding Officer
The chairman shall have the right to name any member of the Caucus to perform the duties of the Chair during the temporary absence of the chairman.

R 4. Quorum
A quorum of the Caucus shall consist of a majority of the Democratic Members of the House. If the absence of a quorum is established, the chairman may continue the meeting for purposes of discussion only, but no motion of any kind, except a motion to adjourn, shall be in order at such continued meeting.

R 5. Agenda
At each such monthly Caucus, Members shall have the right to place before the Caucus any question, provided written notice of such intention is (1) delivered to the office of the chairman, and (2) transmitted to all members of the Caucus not later than 5 p.m. on the 9th day immediately preceding the day of such Caucus. The chairman shall prescribe the order of business and shall provide members with an agenda at least 5 days before the Caucus. Amendments to the agenda shall be in order only if submitted to Caucus members at least 48 hours before the hour of convening and if supported in writing by 50 members.

R 6. Rules
General parliamentary law, with such special rules as may be adopted, shall govern the meetings of the Caucus. The five-minute rule that governs the House of Representatives shall govern debate in the Democratic Caucus, unless suspended by a vote of the Caucus.

R 7. Elections
No Member shall be elected to serve as Chairman, Secretary, or Assistant Secretary of the Democratic Caucus for more than two consecutive terms.

With respect to voting in the House for Speaker and other officers of the House, for each committee chairman, and for membership of committees, a majority vote of those present and voting at a Democratic Caucus meeting shall bind all members of the Caucus.

R 8. Admittance to Caucus Meetings
All that portion of any Caucus meeting, regular or special, that involves action by the Caucus with respect to proposed legislation shall be open to the public, except when a majority determines by a rollcall vote, a quorum being present, that the portion of the Caucus meeting involving action by the Caucus with respect to proposed legislation shall be closed.

During the closed portion of any Caucus meeting, no persons, except Democratic Members of the House of Representatives, a Caucus Journal Clerk, and other necessary employees, shall be admitted to the meeting of the Caucus without the express permission of the chairman.

R 9. Journal and Notification of Policy Actions
The Caucus shall keep a journal of its proceedings, which shall be published after each meeting, and which shall be available for inspection by any member of the Caucus upon request. The yeas and nays on any question shall, at the desire of one-fifth of those present, be entered on the Journal, and a copy of each record vote shall be distributed to each Member of the Caucus. *Provided, however,* that a question shall be decided by secret ballot or other non-record vote if a majority so demand. *Provided, further,* that all votes involving the nomination or election of Members for office in the Caucus or in the House, including committee chairmanships, shall be by secret ballot unless a majority decide otherwise.

R 10. Manual of the House Democratic Caucus
There shall be a Manual of the House Democratic Caucus which shall contain all resolutions of continuing force and effect. Said Manual shall be kept current. Topical resolutions need not be included in the Manual but shall be published in the Journal. All matter included in the Manual shall have the same effect as if it were included in the Standing Rules.

Manual

M I. Standing Committee Memberships

A. *Committee Ratios.* Committee ratios should be established to create firm working majorities on each committee. In determining the ratio on the respective standing committees, the Speaker should provide for a *minimum* of three Democrats for each two Republicans.

B. *Seniority.* The Committee on Committees shall recommend to the Caucus nominees for chairman and membership of each committee other than the Committee on Rules for which the Democratic nominee for Speaker or Speaker as the case may be shall have exclusive nominating authority. Recommendations for committee posts need not necessarily follow seniority.

C. *Nominations for Committee Membership.* Upon a letter from a Member, signed by 50 percent or more of said Member's State Democratic Delegation, including said Member, said Member shall automatically be considered for nomination by the Committee on Committees for the committee membership position to which said Member aspires. The Chairman of the Committee on Committees shall see that such Member's name is placed in nomination. The provisions of this paragraph shall not apply with respect to nominations for the Committee on Rules.

D. *Procedures for Electing Committee Chairmen and Members.* The Democratic nominee for Speaker or Speaker as the case may be shall recommend to the Caucus nominees for chairman and membership of the Committee on Rules. Debate and balloting on any such nomination shall be subject to the same provisions as apply to the nominations of chairmen or Members of other committees. If a majority of those present and voting reject any nominee for chairman or membership of the Committee on Rules, the Democratic nominee for Speaker or Speaker as the case may be shall be entitled to submit new nominations until any such positions are filled. Chairmen: The Committee on Committees shall nominate one Member of each committee, other than the Committee on Rules, for the position of chairman and such nominations need not necessarily follow seniority. The Caucus shall vote on each nominee. If a secret ballot is demanded on any chairman nominated by the Committee on Committees, such vote will be taken by secret ballot if the demand for the same is supported by one-fifth of those present. No debate shall be allowed unless requested by a nominee or a Member who wishes to speak in opposition to a nomination provided that the request to speak in opposition is supported by three or more Members. Debate on any nomination shall be limited to 30 minutes equally divided between proponents and opponents of that nominee, such time to be further extended only by majority vote of the Caucus. If a majority of those present and voting reject its nominee for chairman, the Committee on Committees shall make a new nomination within 5 days. Five to ten days after the Committee on Committees reports such new nominations, the Caucus shall meet to consider the new nominee of the Committee on Committees and any additional nominations offered from the floor. Only Members who have been recommended for membership on the committee shall be eligible for nomination as chairman. Should additional nominations be made from the floor, debate shall be limited to 15 minutes per nominee, unless extended by majority vote of the Caucus; election shall be by secret ballot; and a majority of those present and voting a quorum being present, shall be required to elect.

The Committee on Committees shall make recommendations to the Caucus regarding the assignment of Members to each committee other than the Committee on Rules, one committee at a time. Upon a demand supported by 10 or more Members, a separate vote shall be had on any member of the committee. If any such motion prevails, the committee list of that particular committee shall be considered recommitted to the Committee on Committees for the sole purpose of implementing the direction of the Caucus. Also, such demand, if made and properly supported, shall be debated for no more than 30 minutes with the time equally divided between proponents and opponents. If the Caucus and the Committee on Committees be in disagreement after completion of the procedure herein provided, the Caucus may make final and complete disposition of the matter.

In making nominations for committee assignments the Committee on Committees shall not discriminate on the basis of prior occupation or profession in making such nominations.

E. *Rules for Making Committee Assignments.* For the purposes of this section the following committee designations shall apply:

(1) Appropriations; Ways and Means; and Rules Committee shall be "exclusive" committees.

(2) Agriculture; Armed Services; Banking, Currency and Housing; Education and Labor; International Relations; Interstate and Foreign Commerce; Judiciary; and Public Works and Transportation shall be considered "major" committees.

(3) Budget; District of Columbia; Government Operations; House Administration; Interior and Insular Affairs; Merchant Marine and Fisheries; Post Office and Civil Service; Science and Technology; Small Business; and Veterans' Affairs shall be considered "nonmajor" committees.

a. No Democratic Member of an exclusive committee shall also serve on another exclusive, major, or nonmajor committee.

b. Each Democratic Member shall be entitled to serve on one b᷒ only one exclusive or one major committee.

c. No Democratic Member shall serve on more than one major an one nonmajor committee or two nonmajor committees.

d. No chairman of an exclusive or major committee may serve c another exclusive, major or nonmajor committee.

e. Members who served as members of the Select Committee c Small Business or the Small Business Subcommittee of the Committe on Banking and Currency on October 8, 1974, shall not be deemed to b in violation of the provisions of this clause by reason of membership c the Small Business Committee.

f. Members of the Budget Committee as of December 1, 197᷄ shall not be deemed to be in violation of the provisions of this clause b reason of their Budget Committee membership and Members of th Appropriations and Ways and Means Committees shall be eligible fo membership on the Budget Committee as provided by law, no withstanding the provisions of subsection a. Any Member of the Budge Committee shall be entitled to take a leave of absence from service o᷒ any committee or subcommittee during the period he or she serves o᷒ the Budget Committee and seniority rights of such Member on suc᷄ committee and on each subcommittee to which such Member wa assigned at the time shall be fully protected as if such Member had con tinued to so serve during the period of the leave of absence. An᷒ Member on such leave of absence shall not be deemed to be in violatio᷒ of the provisions of this clause by reason of their membership on th᷐ committee from which they are on a leave of absence.

M II. Standing Full Committee and Subcommittee Chairmanships

A. The chairman of a full committee shall not be the chairman of mor᷐ than one subcommittee on such full committee and shall insofar as prac ticable permit subcommittee chairmen of other subcommittees to handl᷐ legislation on the floor which has been reported by their subcommittee.

B. No Member shall be chairman of more than one legislative subcom mittee. A subcommittee chairman shall be entitled to select and designate at least one staff member for said subcommittee, subject to the approval of ᷐ majority of the Democratic Members of said full committee. Said staff member shall be compensated at a salary commensurate with the respon sibilities prescribed by said subcommittee chairman. The staff members' compensation shall be provided out of appropriated amounts, if any, rather than statutory amounts allowed each committee.

C. No Member shall be a member of more than two committees with legislative jurisdiction.

D. The following committees shall be exempt from the three immediately preceding provisions: House Administration; Standards of Official Conduct; House Recording; House Beauty Shop; and Joint Committees.

E. A Member who served as chairman or subcommittee chairman of the Select Committee on Small Business or as subcommittee chairman of the Small Business Subcommittee of the Banking and Currency Committee as of October 8, 1974, shall not be deemed to be in violation of the provisions of this clause because of service as chairman or subcommittee chairman on the Small Business Committee. The chairman of a major or exclusive full committee shall not serve simultaneously as the chairman of any other full, select or joint committee; *Provided, however,* the chairman of the Ways and Means Committee may also serve as chairman of the Joint Committee on Internal Revenue Taxation.

F. Members of the Budget Committee shall be eligible for subcommittee chairmanships on such committee without regard to the first sentence of section B.

M III. Committee and Subcommittee Organization and Procedure

A. At the start of each Congress, the chairman of each standing committee or other committee with legislative jurisdiction shall call a meeting of all of the Democratic Members of the committee, giving at least 3 days notice to all Democratic Members of the committee. Said meeting shall be called subsequent to the House Democratic Caucus approval of the committee lists but prior to any organizational meeting of the full committee. Such Caucus shall fill the positions of subcommittee chairmen and subcommittee members in accordance with procedures described in sections M. V. A and M. V. B and shall approve and secure adoption of committee rules incorporating the following principles:

(1) *Jurisdiction and number of subcommittees.* The Democratic Caucus of each committee shall establish the number of subcommittees and shall fix the jurisdiction of each subcommittee.

(2) *Powers and duties of subcommittees.* Each subcommittee is authorized to meet, hold hearings, receive evidence and report to the committee on all matters referred to it. Subcommittee chairmen shall set meeting dates after consultation with the chairman and other subcommittee chairmen with a view toward avoiding simultaneous scheduling of committee and subcommittee meetings or hearings wherever possible.

(3) *Reference of legislation and other matters.* All legislation and other matters referred to a committee shall be referred to the subcom-

mittee of appropriate jurisdiction within 2 weeks unless, by majority vote of the Democratic Members of the full committee, consideration is to be by the full committee.

(4) *Party ratios.* The Democratic Caucus of each committee shall determine an appropriate ratio of Democratic to minority party members for each subcommittee and shall authorize a Member or Members to negotiate that ratio with the minority party; *Provided, however,* That party representation on each subcommittee, including any ex-officio members, shall be no less favorable to the Democratic Party than the ratio for the full committee. *Provided, further,* That Democratic Party representation on conference committees also shall be no less favorable to the Democratic Party than the ratio for the full House committee.

(5) *Subcommittee budget and staffing.* Subject to overall control of a majority of the Democratic Caucus on the committee, each subcommittee shall have an adequate budget to discharge its responsibilities for legislation and oversight. All subcommittee staff shall be selected in the manner provided in M II. B of this Manual.

M IV. Periodic Committee Caucuses

A. There shall be a Democratic Caucus of each standing committee and any other committee with legislative jurisdiction consisting of all Democratic Members of the committee. Meetings of the Caucus may be called by the chairman or a majority of the Democratic Members of the committee with due notice to all Caucus Members. A quorum of the Democratic Caucus on each committee shall consist of a majority of the Democratic Members assigned thereto. All actions by the Democratic Caucus of said committees shall require a majority of those voting, a quorum being present. Upon written request of 10 Democratic Members of any committee or upon the written request of a majority of the Democratic Members, whichever is less, addressed to the chairman thereof to hold a Caucus of the Democratic Members, said chairman shall call such Caucus within 10 days of such request. Said request shall contain the subject matter for discussion at such Caucus.

M V. Rules for Making Subcommittee Assignments

A. *Subcommittee Chairmen.* At the Democratic Caucus described in section M III. A, Democratic Members of the committee shall have the right, in order of full committee seniority, or seniority on the subcommittee concerned, as the Democratic Caucus on the committee may determine, to bid for subcommittee chairmanships. Any such request shall be subject to approval by a majority of those present and voting in the Democratic Caucus on the committee. If the committee Caucus rejects a subcommittee chairmanship bid, the next senior Democratic Member may bid for the position as in the first instance. *Provided however,* That the full Democratic Caucus also shall vote on each Member nominated to serve as chairman of an Appropriations subcommittee following the same procedure set forth in Caucus Rules for the election of standing committee chairmen.

B. *Subcommittee Membership.* All Democratic subcommittee positions on House standing committees shall be filled at the Democratic Committee Caucus described in section M III. A in the following manner:

(1) Step One—Members who served on the committee in the preceding Congress shall be entitled to retain not more than two subcommittee assignments held on that committee in the preceding Congress. Members chosen as subcommittee chairmen in accord with the procedure set forth in section M V. A shall be entitled to retain only one other subcommittee assignment held on that committee in the preceding Congress.

(2) Step Two—Members who retain no subcommittee assignments in Step One and new Members shall be entitled, in order of their ranking on the full committee, to select one subcommittee position each.

(3) Step Three—Members who have selected only one subcommittee assignment shall be entitled, in order of their ranking on the full committee, to select a second subcommittee assignment, to the extent that subcommittee size permits.

(4) Step Four—Any remaining subcommittee vacancies shall be filled by additional rounds of selection in order of Members' ranking on the full committee.

(5) If a committee Caucus determines, as described in section M V. A, that Members may bid for subcommittee chairmanships by subcommittee rather than full committee seniority, the ranking Members on each subcommittee shall be determined by the order in which Members elect to go on the subcommittee.

M VI. Appointments to Joint and Select Committees, Boards, and Commissions

In those instances where the Speaker has the power to appoint Members to joint and select committees, boards, and commissions, due consideration should be given to sharing the workload and responsibility among qualified Members of the House who have indicated an interest in the subject matter of the committee, board, or commission, and have expressed a willingness to

actively participate in its deliberations and operations. All Members serving on joint and select committees, boards, and commissions by virtue of appointment by the Speaker shall be considered to have completed their tenure and their positions deemed to be vacant until filled by appointment or reappointment by the Speaker.

M VII. House Democratic Policy and Steering Committee

There should be a House Democratic Steering and Policy Committee constituted as follows:

a. *Membership.* The Democratic Steering and Policy Committee shall consist of the elected Democratic leadership (the Speaker, Majority Leader, and Caucus Chairman), 12 Members who shall be elected from 12 equal regions as set forth below, and not to exceed eight Members who shall be appointed by the Speaker. (*Provided,* that in the 93d and 94th Congresses, five of the eight appointees shall be the Whip and the four Deputy Whips) And the Speaker is authorized to appoint one additional Member for the 94th Congress only. The size of the committee shall be reviewed at the start of the 94th Congress and consideration shall be given to reducing the number of appointive Members thereto.

b. *Organization and Procedure.* The Speaker shall serve as Chairman of the committee, the Majority Leader as Vice Chairman, and the Caucus Chairman as Second Vice Chairman. The committee shall adopt its own rules which shall be in writing; shall keep a journal of its proceedings; and shall meet at least once each month while the House is in session and upon the call of the Chairman or whenever requested in writing by four of its Members. In addition, the committee may authorize the Chairman to appoint ad hoc committees from among the entire membership of the Caucus to conduct special studies or investigations whenever necessary.

c. *Functions.* The committee shall make recommendations regarding party policy, legislative priorities, scheduling of matters for House or Caucus action, and other matters as appropriate to further Democratic programs and policies.

d. *Regions.* The 50 States (and other areas represented in the House) shall be divided into 12 compact and contiguous regions, each containing approximately one-twelfth of the Members of the Democratic Caucus. At the beginning of each Congress, the Speaker (or Minority Leader if Democrats are in the minority) shall submit to the Caucus for its approval changes necessary to maintain, as near as practicable, an equal number of Members in each region. The proposed changes and a list of Members in each region indicating the total years of service for each as of the start of that Congress shall be made available to Members of the Caucus at least 10 days before a Caucus which shall meet no later than March 1 of odd-numbered years to approve or amend the regions.

e. *Regional Elections.* Each region shall meet no later than March 30 in odd-numbered years to elect its representatives to the committee. Such regional elections shall be held at a time determined by the Chairman of the Steering and Policy Committee and announced by written notice at least 10 days in advance. The Chairman shall also designate a Member from each region to call that region's election meeting to order and to preside until a permanent presiding officer is elected, which shall be the first order of business. If at such meeting, the election of a Member to the Steering and Policy Committee does not take place due to lack of a quorum, the Chairman shall reschedule the meeting as soon as practicable, provided Members are given at least 48 hours notice in writing of when and where the rescheduled meeting will be held. Nominations may be made from the floor or in advance of the election meeting by written notice signed by two Members from the region other than the nominee. Written nominations must be delivered to the Steering and Policy Committee office not later than 5 p.m. on the second day immediately preceding the day of the election meeting and mailed to all Members of the Caucus in that region not later than midnight of the second day immediately preceding the day of the election meeting. Following the close of advance nominations, a ballot shall be prepared for each region containing the names of candidates nominated in advance for election from the region. Candidates shall be listed in alphabetical order and all ballots shall contain space to write in the names of Members nominated from the floor. One-half of the Members of a region shall constitute a quorum for an election and a majority of those present and voting shall be required to elect. If more than one ballot be required, the candidate receiving the fewest votes on each ballot shall be eliminated from all succeeding votes until one candidate receives a majority of the votes cast. If a region's representative in the preceding Congress had completed 12 or more years service at the start of said Congress, he or she shall be succeeded by a Member who has less than 12 years service. This provision shall not apply to the re-election of an incumbent Member of the committee who is entitled to seek another term.

f. *Terms of Service.* Each regionally elected Member of the committee shall serve for a term of two years, or until his successor is elected. In the event of a vacancy the region shall elect a successor to fill the unexpired term. No Member shall be elected or appointed to more than two consecutive full terms. However, six of the 12 members elected in the 93d Congress—as determined by lot at the first meeting of the committee—shall not be eligible for re-election in the 94th Congress.

M VIII. Committee on Organization, Study and Review

The Caucus Chairman shall appoint a committee on Organization, Study and Review for the purposes of review of the Caucus Rules and Manual as circumstances may indicate, with no powers other than those recommending action to the Caucus.

M IX. Closed Rule Restriction

(a) It shall be the policy of the Democratic Caucus that no committee chairman or designee shall seek, and the Democratic Members of the Rules Committee shall not support, any rule or order prohibiting any germane amendment to any bill reported from committee until four (4) legislative days have elapsed following notice in the Congressional Record of an intention to do so.

(b) If, within the four (4) legislative days following said notice in the Congressional Record, 50 or more Democratic Members give written notice to the chairman of the committee seeking the rule and to the chairman of the Rules Committee that they wish to offer a particular germane amendment, the chairman or designee shall not seek and the Democratic Members of the Rules Committee shall not support, any rule or order relating to the bill or resolution involved until the Democratic Caucus has met and decided whether the proposed amendment should be allowed to be considered in the House.

(c) If 50 or more Democratic Members give notice as provided in subsection (b) above, then, notwithstanding the provisions of Caucus Rule No. 5, the Caucus shall meet for such purpose within three (3) legislative days following a request for such a Caucus to the Speaker and the chairman of the Democratic Caucus by said committee chairman or designee.

(d) *Provided, further,* that notices referred to above also shall be submitted to the Speaker, the Majority Leader, and the chairman of the Democratic Caucus.

M X. Budget Committee

The Democratic Caucus shall elect the Democratic Members of the Budget Committee at the start of each Congress in accord with the following provisions:

A. *Party Ratio.* The party ratio on the Budget Committee shall be determined by the Caucus at the start of each Congress; *Provided, however,* that the ratio shall not be less than three Democrats for each two Republicans.

B. *Leadership Member.* The Speaker shall appoint the leadership member of the committee.

C. *Nomination of Other Members.* The chairman of the Appropriations Committee shall nominate three of the Democratic Members of that committee, the chairman of the Ways and Means Committee shall nominate three of the Democratic Members of that committee, and the chairman of the Steering and Policy Committee shall nominate Members from other committees to fill all remaining vacancies. A list of said nominees shall be distributed to all Members of the Caucus at least 9 days prior to the election meeting. Members shall then have at least 7 days to nominate additional candidates by written notice signed by five Members other than the nominee. Written nominations must be delivered to the offices of the Caucus chairman and the Caucus secretary not later than noon on the second day immediately preceding the election meeting, and the Caucus chairman or secretary shall mail a list of all nominees to Members of the Caucus that same day.

D. *Election Procedure.* Election shall be by ballot which lists all candidates by category (Appropriations, Ways and Means, other committees) the order they were nominated, and a majority shall be required to elect.

E. *Election of Chairman.* Following election of all Democratic Members the Caucus shall elect one of said Members to serve as chairman. Nomination speeches shall not exceed 3 minutes per nominee and seconding speeches shall not exceed 1 minute and shall be limited to two per nominee. Election shall be by ballot and a majority shall be required to elect.

F. *Service Limitations.* The following limitations shall apply to Members of the Budget Committee:

(1) The Democratic Members elected in 1974 shall serve on an interim basis for the remainder of the 93d Congress only. A new election shall be held at the start of the 94th Congress and half of the Members elected at that time (to be determined by lot at the first meeting following that election) shall not be eligible for reelection at the start of the 95th Congress.

(2) The chairman of the Budget Committee shall not serve simultaneously as chairman of any other standing committee.

(3) No Member shall serve as a Member of the Committee on the Budget during more than two Congresses in any period of five successive Congresses beginning after 1974 (disregarding for this purpose any service performed as a Member of such committee for less than a full session in any Congress). All selections of Members to serve on the committee shall be made without regard to seniority.

M XI. Election Procedure for Ways and Means Vacancies

Resolved, That for the 94th Congress the Democratic Caucus shall elect Democratic Members to fill vacancies on the Ways and Means Committee in accord with the following procedure:

(1) *Nominations.* The Democratic Committee on Committees shall nominate one Member for each Democratic vacancy to be filled on the Ways and Means Committee and shall distribute the name(s) of such nominee(s) to all Members of the Democratic Caucus at least 9 days prior to the election meeting. Members shall then have 7 days to nominate additional candidates by written notice signed by 5 Democratic Members other than the nominee. Written nominations must be delivered to the offices of the Caucus chairman and the Caucus secretary not later than noon at the second day immediately preceding the election meeting, and the Caucus chairman or secretary shall mail a list of all nominees to Members of the Caucus that same day.

(2) *Election Procedure.* Election shall be by ballot which lists all candidates in the order they were nominated, and a majority shall be required to elect; *Provided, however,* that any ballot which contains votes for more or fewer candidates than there are vacancies to be filled shall not be counted.

(3) *Previous Members.* The nomination of any Member who served on the committee in the preceding Congress shall be reported by the Committee on Committees for action by the Caucus in the same manner as is provided for nomination of Members to other standing committees.

Highlights of House GOP Conference Rules

Following are highlights of the rules governing the House Republican Conference for the 94th Congress.

Open Meetings

Resolved, that each meeting of the conference for the 1st session of the 94th Congress shall be open to the public except when the conference, in open session and with a quorum present, determines by vote that all or part of the remainder of the meeting on that day shall be closed.

Secret Ballots

Resolved further, that all elections, where contested, shall be decided by secret ballot, and that no proxy voting shall be allowed. Balloting shall continue until a majority of the votes of the members present are cast for one candidate.

Resolved further, that on demand the vote on any matter properly pending before the Conference shall be taken by secret ballot.

Resolved further, that the rules of the House of Representatives of the 93rd Congress insofar as they are applicable shall govern the proceedings of this Republican Conference.

Establishment of the Committee on Policy

Resolved, that there is hereby created a Committee on Policy which shall be an advisory committee to the membership of the House Republican Conference. The Committee on Policy shall meet at the call of the chairman of the Committee on Policy or the Republican leader, and shall discuss legislative proposals with Republican members of the appropriate standing and special committees and with such other Republican members as the chairman may invite to the meetings. The Committee on Policy shall report its suggestions for Republican action and policy to the Republican members of the House. The chairman of the Committee on Policy may appoint, in consultation with the Republican leader, such subcommittees from the Republican members of the House for such purposes as may be deemed appropriate.

Resolved further, that the Committee on Policy shall be composed of:

I. One member from each of eight regions apportioned by the Conference as equally as possible. The Republican members of Congress from the states of each region shall meet in caucus and shall select from their number, by secret ballot, the member of the Committee on Policy and shall report their selection to the chairman of said committee.

[A list of the regions and the states composing each for the 94th Congress followed.]

II. From each of the two latest congressional clubs, one member for each twenty-five members of each club and one member for each majority fraction of twenty-five of each club,

III. The House Republican leadership, as designated by the House Republican Conference, and

IV. A maximum of seven members-at-large appointed by the Republican leader.

Resolved further, that the traditions and privileges of seniority shall not apply to membership of the Committee on Policy and that the committee may, at its discretion, make such rules as are necessary for the conduct of its business.

Establishment of the Committee on Research

Resolved, that there is hereby created a Committee on Research which shall be an advisory committee to the members of the House Republican Conference.

Its function shall be to perform and supervise research for Republican members of the House, and to assist in preparing research and information for their use.

The committee shall have a maximum of seventeen members including the members of the House Republican leadership.

The chairman of the committee shall be elected by members of the House Republican Conference. The remaining members shall be selected by the House Republican leadership, which selection shall be subject to confirmation by the House Republican Conference.

Subject to the approval of the House Republican leadership, which shall consult with the ranking members of the various standing committees, the committee on Research may appoint task forces comprised of any Republican members of the House and may make such rules as are necessary for the conduct of the committee and its task forces.

National Republican Congressional Committee

Resolved, that there is hereby created a National Republican Congressional Committee to be composed of members selected by the Republican delegation from the several states.

Resolved further, that the voting strength of each member shall be equal to the number of Republican members of the House of Representatives elected to the 94th Congress from his state.

Resolved further, that the duties of the National Republican Congressional Committee shall be to:

act as counsel and adviser to the members of the House Republican Conference, furnish support services and have oversight in election campaigns in all general and special elections for membership in the House of Representatives.

Resolved further, that the minority leader shall serve as an ex officio member of the National Republican Congressional Committee.

Resolved further, that the secretary of the conference shall call the roll by states, and each state shall report its member of the National Republican Congressional Committee.

Committee on Committees

Resolved, that there is hereby created a House Republican Committee on Committees to be composed of members selected by the Republican delegations from the several states.

Resolved further, that the voting strength of each member shall be equal to the number of Republican members of the House of Representatives elected to the 94th Congress from his state.

Resolved further, that the duties of the House Republican Committee on Committees shall be to:

1. Recommend the Republican members of the standing committees of the House of Representatives,

2. Recommend the Republican members who shall serve as ranking minority members of said standing committees, and

3. Recommend directly to the House of Representatives the Republican members to fill vacancies on standing committees which occur following the initial organization of the 94th Congress.

Resolved further, that the member recommended by the House Republican Committee on Committees for ranking minority member need not be the member with the longest consecutive service on that committee.

Resolved further, that nomination for such positions shall be out of order except as contained in the report of the committee.

Resolved further, that the conference shall vote by secret ballot on each recommendation of the House Republican Committee on Committees for the position of ranking minority member. The call of the conference at which such balloting will take place shall name and list the individuals recommended by the committee.

Resolved further, that if the Republican Conference fails to approve a recommendation of the House Republican Committee on Committees, the matter shall be automatically recommitted without instructions to that committee.

Resolved further, that the House Republican leader shall serve as ex officio chairman of the Committee on Committees; and

Resolved further, that the secretary of the conference shall call the roll by states, and each state shall report its member of the Committee on Committees.

Leadership Committee Assignment Limits

Resolved, that the Republican leader and whip, and the chairmen of the Republican Conference, Committee on Policy, Committee on Research, and the National Republican Congressional Committee shall not serve on more than one standing committee of the House of Representatives and in no case shall any of these individuals serve as ranking Republican member of a standing committee of the House of Representatives other than the Committee on Budget.

Resolved further, that if a member shall, at any time, cease to serve in any of the leadership positions named above, he may resume his position on the standing committee on which he previously served.

Resolved further, that no individual shall serve as ranking Republican member of more than one standing committee.

Call of the Conference

Resolved, that future meetings of the Republican Conference for the 94th Congress may be called by the chairman of the conference, after consultation with the Republican leader, at any time and shall be called upon the written request of 50 members, addressed and delivered to the chairman.

Articles of Impeachment Against President Andrew Johnso

Source: Asher C. Hinds, *Hinds' Precedents of the House of Representatives of the United States*, Vol. 3 (Government Printing Office, 1907), pp. 863-69.

Following is the complete text of the articles of impeachment against President Andrew Johnson adopted by the House of Representatives on Feb. 24, 1868.

Articles exhibited by the House of Representatives of the United States, in the name of themselves and all the people of the United States, against Andrew Johnson, President of the United States, in maintenance and support of their impeachment against him for high crimes and misdemeanors in office.

Article I.

That said Andrew Johnson, President of the United States, on the 21st day of February, in the year of our Lord 1868, at Washington, in the District of Columbia, unmindful of the high duties of his office, of his oath of office, and of the requirement of the Constitution that he should take care that the laws be faithfully executed, did unlawfully, and in violation of the Constitution and laws of the United States, issue an order in writing for the removal of Edwin M. Stanton from the office of Secretary for the Department of War, said Edwin M. Stanton having been theretofore duly appointed and commissioned, by and with the advice and consent of the Senate of the United States, as such Secretary, and said Andrew Johnson, President of the United States, on the 12th day of August, in the year of our Lord 1867, and during the recess of said Senate, having suspended by his order Edwin M. Stanton from said office, and within twenty days after the first day of the next meeting of said Senate—that is to say, on the 12th day of December, in the year last aforesaid—having reported to said Senate such suspension, with the evidence and reasons for his action in the case and the name of the person designated to perform the duties of such office temporarily until the next meeting of the Senate, and said Senate thereafterwards, on the 13th day of January, in the year of our Lord 1868, having duly considered the evidence and reasons reported by said Andrew Johnson for said suspension, and having refused to concur in said suspension, whereby and by force of the provisions of an act entitled "An act regulating the tenure of certain civil offices," passed March 2, 1867, said Edwin M. Stanton did forthwith resume the functions of his office, whereof the said Andrew Johnson had then and there due notice, and said Edwin M. Stanton, by reason of the premises, on said 21st day of February, being lawfully entitled to hold said office of Secretary for the Department of War, which said order for the removal of said Edwin M. Stanton is, in substance, as follows, that is to say:

> "Executive Mansion,
> *"Washington, D.C., February 21, 1868.*
> "Sir: By virtue of the power and authority vested in me as President by the Constitution and laws of the United States you are hereby removed from office as Secretary for the Department of War, and your functions as such will terminate upon receipt of this communication.
> "You will transfer to Brevet Maj. Gen. Lorenzo Thomas, Adjutant-General of the Army, who has this day been authorized and empowered to act as Secretary of War ad interim, all records, books, papers, and other public property now in your custody and charge.
> "Respectfully yours,
>
> ANDREW JOHNSON.
>
> "Hon. Edwin M. Stanton, *Washington, D.C.*"

Which order was unlawfully issued with intent then and there to violate the act entitled "An act regulating the tenure of certain civil offices," passed March 2, 1867; and with the further intent, contrary to the provisions of said act, in violation thereof, and contrary to the provisions of the Constitution of the United States, and without the advice and consent of the Senate of the United States, the said Senate then and there being in session, to remove said Edwin M. Stanton from the office of Secretary for the Department of War, the said Edwin M. Stanton being then and there Secretary of War, and being then and there in the due and lawful execution and discharge of the duties of said office, whereby said Andrew Johnson, President of the United States, did then and there commit, and was guilty of a high misdemeanor in office.

Article II.

That on said 21st day of February, in the year of our Lord 1868, at Washington, in the District of Columbia, said Andrew Johnson, President of the United States, unmindful of the high duties of his office, of his oath of office, and in violation of the Constitution of the United States, and contrary to the provisions of an act entitled "An act regulating the tenure of certain civil offices," passed March 2, 1867, without the advice and consent of the Senate of the United States, said Senate then and there being in session, and without

authority of law, did, with intent to violate the Constitution of the United States and the act aforesaid, issue and deliver to one Lorenzo Thomas a letter of authority in substance as follows, that is to say:

> "Executive Mansion,
> *"Washington, D.C., February 21, 1868.*
> "Sir: Hon. Edwin M. Stanton having been this day removed from office as Secretary for the Department of War, you are hereby authorized and empowered to act as Secretary of War ad interim, and will immediately enter upon the discharge of the duties pertaining to that office.
> "Mr. Stanton has been instructed to transfer to you all the records, books, papers, and other public property now in his custody and charge.
> "Respectfully, yours,
>
> ANDREW JOHNSON
>
> "To Brevet Maj. Gen. Lorenzo Thomas,
> *"Adjutant-General United States Army, Washington, D.C."*

Then and there being no vacancy in said office of Secretary for the Department of War, whereby said Andrew Johnson, President of the United States, did then and there commit, and was guilty of a high misdemeanor in office.

Article III.

That said Andrew Johnson, President of the United States, on the 21 day of February, in the year of our Lord 1868, at Washington, in the District of Columbia, did commit and was guilty of a high misdemeanor in office in this, that, without authority of law, while the Senate of the United States was then and there in session, he did appoint one Lorenzo Thomas to be Secretary for the Department of War ad interim, without the advice and consent of the Senate and with intent to violate the Constitution of the United States, no vacancy having happened in said office of Secretary for the Department of War during the recess of the Senate, and no vacancy existing in said office at the time, and which said appointment, so made by said Andrew Johnson, of said Lorenzo Thomas, is in substance as follows, that is to say:

> "Executive Mansion
> *"Washington, D.C., February 21, 1868*
> "Sir: Hon. Edwin M. Stanton having been this day removed from office as Secretary for the Department of War, you are hereby authorized and empowered to act as Secretary of War ad interim, and will immediately enter upon the discharge of the duties pertaining to that office.
> "Mr. Stanton has been instructed to transfer to you all the records, books, papers, and other public property now in his custody and charge.
> "Respectfully, yours,
>
> ANDREW JOHNSON
>
> "To Brevet Maj. Gen. Lorenzo Thomas,
> *"Adjutant-General United States Army, Washington, D.C."*

Article IV.

That said Andrew Johnson, President of the United States, unmindful of the high duties of his office and of his oath of office, in violation of the Constitution and laws of the United States, on the 21st day of February, in the year of our Lord 1868, at Washington, in the District of Columbia, did unlawfully conspire with one Lorenzo Thomas, and with other persons to the House of Representatives unknown, with intent, by intimidation and threats, unlawfully to hinder and prevent Edwin M. Stanton, then and there the Secretary for the Department of War, duly appointed under the laws of the United States, from holding said office of Secretary for the Department of War, contrary to and in violation of the Constitution of the United States and of the provisions of an act entitled "An act to define and punish certain conspiracies," approved July 31, 1861, whereby said Andrew Johnson, President of the United States, did then and there commit, and was guilty of a high crime in office.

Article V.

That said Andrew Johnson, President of the United States, unmindful of the high duties of his office and of his oath of office, on the 21st day of February, in the year of our Lord 1868, and on divers other days and times in said year, before the 2d day of March, A.D. 1868, at Washington, in the District of Columbia, did unlawfully conspire with one Lorenzo Thomas, and with other persons to the House of Representatives unknown, to prevent and hinder the execution of an act entitled "An act regulating the tenure of certain civil offices," passed March 2, 1867, and in pursuance of said conspiracy unlawfully attempt to prevent Edwin M. Stanton, then and there being ...retary for the Department of War, duly appointed and commissioned un-... the laws of the United States, from holding said office, whereby the said ...drew Johnson, President of the United States, did then and there commit ... was guilty of a high misdemeanor in office.

Article VI.

That said Andrew Johnson, President of the United States, unmindful of ... high duties of his office and of his oath of office, on the 21st day of ...bruary, in the year of our Lord 1868, at Washington, in the District of ...lumbia, did unlawfully conspire with one Lorenzo Thomas, by force to ...ze, take, and possess the property of the United States in the Department ... War, and then and there in the custody and charge of Edwin M. Stanton, ...cretary for said Department, contrary to the provisions of an act entitled ...n act to define and punish certain conspiracies," approved July 31, 1861, ...d with intent to violate and disregard an act entitled "An act regulating ...e tenure of certain civil offices," passed March 2, 1867, whereby said ...ndrew Johnson, President of the United States, did then and there commit ... high crime in office.

Article VII.

That said Andrew Johnson, President of the United States, unmindful of ... high duties of his office and of his oath of office, on the 21st day of ...ebruary, in the year of our Lord 1868, at Washington, in the District of ...olumbia, did unlawfully conspire with one Lorenzo Thomas with intent un-...wfully to seize, take, and possess the property of the United States in the ...epartment of War, in the custody and charge of Edwin M. Stanton, ...ecretary for said Department, with intent to violate and disregard the act ...ntitled "An act regulating the tenure of certain civil offices," passed March ... 1867, whereby said Andrew Johnson, President of the United States, did ...en and there commit a high misdemeanor in office.

Article VIII.

That said Andrew Johnson, President of the United States, unmindful of ...he high duties of his office and of his oath of office, with intent unlawfully to ...control the disbursements of the moneys appropriated for the military service ...and for the Department of War, on the 21st day of February, in the year of our ...Lord 1868, at Washington, in the District of Columbia, did unlawfully and ...contrary to the provisions of an act entitled "An act regulating the tenure of ...certain civil offices," passed March 2, 1867, and in violation of the Constitu-...tion of the United States, and without the advice and consent of the Senate of ...the United States, and while the Senate was then and there in session, there ...being no vacancy in the office of Secretary for the Department of War, with ...intent to violate and disregard the act aforesaid, then and there issue and ...deliver to one Lorenzo Thomas a letter of authority in writing, in substance as follows, that is to say:

"Executive Mansion,
"Washington, D.C., February 21, 1868.
"Sir: Hon. Edwin M. Stanton having been this day removed from office as Secretary for the Department of War, you are hereby authorized and empowered to act as Secretary of War ad interim, and will immediately enter upon the discharge of the duties pertaining to that office.

"Mr. Stanton has been instructed to transfer to you all the records, books, papers, and other public property now in his custody and charge.

"Respectfully yours,

ANDREW JOHNSON.

"Brevet Maj. Gen. Lorenzo Thomas,
"Adjutant-General United States Army, Washington, D.C."
whereby said Andrew Johnson, President of the United States, did then and there commit and was guilty of a high misdemeanor in office.

Article IX

That said Andrew Johnson, President of the United States, on the 22d day of February, in the year of our Lord 1868, at Washington, in the District of Columbia, in disregard of the Constitution and the laws of the United States, duly enacted, as Commander in Chief of the Army of the United States, did bring before himself then and there William H. Emory, a major-general by brevet in the Army of the United States, actually in command of the Department of Washington and the military forces thereof, and did then and there, as such Commander in Chief, declare to and instruct said Emory that part of a law of the United States, passed March 2, 1867, entitled "An act making appropriations for the support of the Army for the year ending June 30, 1868, and for other purposes," especially the second section thereof which provides among other things, that "all orders and instructions relating to military operations issued by the President or Secretary of War shall be issued through the General of the Army, and, in case of his inability, through the next in rank," was unconstitutional and in contravention of the commission of said Emory, and which said provision of law had been therefore duly and legally promulgated by general order for the government and direction of

the Army of the United States, as the said Andrew Johnson then and there well knew, with intent thereby to induce said Emory, in his official capacity as commander of the Department of Washington, to violate the provisions of said act, and to take and receive, act upon, and obey such orders as he, the said Andrew Johnson, might make and give, and which should not be issued through the General of the Army of the United States, according to the provisions of said act, and with the further intent thereby to enable him, the said Andrew Johnson, to prevent the execution of an act entitled "An act regulating the tenure of certain civil offices," passed March 2, 1867, and to unlawfully prevent Edwin M. Stanton, then being Secretary for the Department of War, from holding said office and discharging the duties thereof, whereby said Andrew Johnson, President of the United States, did then and there commit and was guilty of a high misdemeanor in office.

Article X

That said Andrew Johnson, President of the United States, unmindful of the high duties of his office and the dignity and proprieties thereof, and of the harmony and courtesies which ought to exist and be maintained between the executive and legislative branches of the Government of the United States, designing and intending to set aside the rightful authority and powers of Congress, did attempt to bring into disgrace, ridicule, hatred, contempt, and reproach the Congress of the United States and the several branches thereof, to impair and destroy the regard and respect of all the good people of the United States for the Congress and legislative power thereof(which all officers of the Government ought inviolably to preserve and maintain), and to excite the odium and resentment of all the good people of the United States against Congress and the laws by it duly and constitutionally enacted; and in pursuance of his said design and intent, openly and publicly, and before divers assemblages of the citizens of the United States convened in divers parts thereof to meet and receive said Andrew Johnson as the Chief Magistrate of the United States, did, on the 18th day of August, in the year of our Lord 1866, and on divers other days and times, as well before as afterwards, make and deliver with a loud voice certain intemperate, inflammatory, and scandalous harangues, and did therein utter loud threats and bitter menaces as well against Congress as the laws of the United States duly enacted thereby, amid the cries, jeers, and laughter of the multitudes then assembled and within hearing, which are set forth in the several specifications hereinafter written, in substance and effect, that is to say:

Specification first.—In this, that at Washington, in the District of Columbia, in the Executive Mansion, to a committee of citizens who called upon the President of the United States, speaking of and concerning the Congress of the United States, said Andrew Johnson, President of the United States, heretofore, to wit, on the 18th day of August, in the year of our Lord 1866, did, in a loud voice, declare in substance and effect, among other things, that is to say:

"So far as the executive department of the Government is concerned, the effort has been made to restore the Union, to heal the breach, to pour oil into the wounds which were consequent upon the struggle, and (to speak in common phrase) to prepare, as the learned and wise physician would, a plaster healing in character and coextensive with the wound. We thought, and we think, that we had partially succeeded; but as the work progresses, as reconstruction seemed to be taking place and the country was becoming reunited, we found a disturbing and marring element opposing us. In alluding to that element, I shall go no further than your convention and the distinguished gentleman who has delivered to me the report of its proceedings. I shall make no reference to it that I do not believe the time and the occasion justify.

"We have witnessed in one department of the Government every endeavor to prevent the restoration of peace, harmony, and union. We have seen hanging upon the verge of the Government, as it were, a body called, or which assumes to be, the Congress of the United States, while in fact it is a Congress of only a part of the States. We have seen this Congress pretend to be for the Union when its every step and act tended to perpetrate disunion and make a disruption of the States inevitable.***We have seen Congress gradually encroach step by step upon constitutional rights and violate, day after day and month after month, fundamental principles of the Government. We have seen a Congress that seemed to forget that there was a limit to the sphere and scope of legislation. We have seen a Congress in a minority assume to exercise power which, allowed to be consummated, would result in despotism or monarchy itself."

Specification second.—In this, that at Cleveland, in the State of Ohio, heretofore, to wit, on the 3d day of September, in the year of our Lord 1866, before a public assemblage of citizens and others, said Andrew Johnson, President of the United States, speaking of and concerning the Congress of the United States did, in a loud voice, declare in substance and effect among other things, that is to say:

"I will tell you what I did do. I called upon your Congress that is trying to break up the Government...

"In conclusion, beside that, Congress had taken much pains to poison their constituents against him. But what had Congress done? Have they done anything to restore the union of these States? No; on the contrary, they had done everything to prevent it; and because he stood now where he did when the rebellion commenced he had been denounced as a traitor. Who had run greater risks or made greater sacrifices than himself? But Congress, factious and domineering, had undertaken to poison the minds of the American people."

Specification third.—In this, that at St. Louis, in the State of Missouri, heretofore, to wit, on the 8th day of September, in the year of our Lord 1866, before a public assemblage of citizens and others, said Andrew Johnson, President of the United States, speaking of and concerning the Congress of the United States, did in a loud voice, declare, in substance and effect, among other things, that is to say:

"Go on. Perhaps if you had a word or two on the subject of New Orleans you might understand more about it than you do. And if you will go back—if you will go back and ascertain the cause of the riot at New Orleans, perhaps you will not be so prompt in calling out 'New Orleans.' If you will take up the riot at New Orleans and trace it back to its source or its immediate cause, you will find out who was responsible for the blood that was shed there. If you will take up the riot at New Orleans and trace it back to the Radical Congress, you will find that the riot at New Orleans was substantially planned. If you will take up the proceedings in their caucuses you will understand that they there knew that a convention was to be called which was extinct by its power having expired; that it was said that the intention was that a new government was to be organized, and on the organization of that government the intention was to enfranchise one portion of the population, called the colored population, who had just been emancipated, and at the same time disenfranchise white men. When you design to talk about New Orleans you ought to understand what you are talking about. When you read the speeches that were made, and take up the facts on the Friday and Saturday before that convention sat, you will there find that speeches were made incendiary in their character, exciting that portion of the population, the black population, to arm themselves and prepare for the shedding of blood. You will also find that the convention did assemble in violation of law, and the intention of that convention was to supersede the reorganized authorities in the State government of Louisiana, which had been recognized by the Government of the United States; and every man engaged in that convention, with the intention of superseding and upturning the civil government which had been recognized by the Government of the United States, I say that he was a traitor to the Constitution of the United States, and hence you find that another rebellion was commenced having its origin in the Radical Congress....

"So much for the New Orleans riot. And there was the cause and the origin of the blood that was shed; and every drop of blood that was shed is upon their skirts, and they are responsible for it. I could test this thing a little closer, but will not do it here tonight. But when you talk about the causes and consequences that resulted from proceedings of that kind, perhaps as I have been introduced here and you have provoked questions of this kind, though it does not provoke me, I will tell you a few wholesome things that have been done by this Radical Congress in connection with New Orleans and the extension of the elective franchise.

"I know that I have been traduced and abused. I know it has come in advance of me here, as elsewhere, that I have attempted to exercise an arbitrary power in resisting laws that were intended to be forced upon the Government; that I had exercised that power; that I had abandoned the party that elected me, and that I was a traitor because I exercised the veto power in attempting and did arrest for a time a bill that was called a 'Freedman's Bureau' bill; yes, that I was a traitor. And I have been traduced, I have been slandered, I have been maligned, I have been called Judas Iscariot, and all that. Now, my countrymen here to-night, it is very easy to indulge in epithets; it is easy to call a man a Judas and cry out traitor; but when he is called upon to give arguments and facts he is very often found wanting. Judas Iscariot—Judas. There was a Judas, and he was one of the twelve apostles. Oh yes; the twelve apostles had a Christ. The twelve apostles had a Christ, and he never could have had a Judas unless he had had twelve apostles. If I have played the Judas, who has been my Christ that I have played the Judas with? Was it Thad. Stevens? Was it Wendell Phillips? Was it Charles Sumner? These are the men that stop and compare themselves with the Savior; and everybody that differs with them in opinion, and to try and stay and arrest the diabolical and nefarious policy, is to be denounced as a Judas...."

"Well, let me say to you, if you will stand by me in this action; if you w stand by me in trying to give the people a fair chance, soldiers and citizens, participate in these offices, God being willing, I will kick them out. I will ki them out just as fast as I can.

"Let me say to you, in concluding, that what I have said I intended say. I was not provoked into this, and I care not for their menaces, the taun and the jeers. I care not for threats. I do not intend to be bullied by n enemies nor overawed by my friends. But, God willing, with your help I w veto their measures whenever any of them come to me."

Which said utterances, declarations, threats and harangues, highly cer surable in any, are peculiarly indecent and unbecoming in the Chi Magistrate of the United States, by means whereof said Andrew Johnson h brought the high office of the President of the United States into contemp ridicule, and disgrace, to the great scandal of all good citizens, whereby sa Andrew Johnson, President of the United States, did commit, and was the and there guilty of, a high misdemeanor in office.

Article XI.

That said Andrew Johnson, President of the United States, unmindful the high duties of his office and of his oath of office, and in disregard of th Constitution and laws of the United States, did heretofore, to wit, on the 18t day of August, 1866, at the city of Washington, and the District of Columbia by public speech, declare and affirm, in substance, that the Thirty-ninth Congress of the United States was not a Congress of the United State authorized by the Constitution to exercise legislative power under the same but, on the contrary, was a Congress of only part of the States, thereby deny ing and intending to deny that the legislation of said Congress was valid o obligatory upon him, the said Andrew Johnson, except in so far as he saw fit to approve the same, and also thereby denying and intending to deny the power of the said Thirty-ninth Congress to propose amendments to the Constitution of the United States; and, in pursuance of said declaration, the said Andrew Johnson, President of the United States, afterwards, to wit, on the 21st day of February, 1868, at the city of Washington, in the District of Columbia, did unlawfully and in disregard of the requirements of the Constitution, that he should take care that the laws be faithfully executed, attempt to prevent the execution of an act entitled "An act regulating the tenure of certain civil offices," passed March 2, 1867, by unlawfully devising and contriving, and attempting to devise and contrive, means by which he should prevent Edwin M. Stanton from forthwith resuming the functions of the office of Secretary for the Department of War, notwithstanding the refusal of the Senate to concur in the suspension theretofore made by said Andrew Johnson, of said Edwin M. Stanton from said office of Secretary for the Department of War, and also by further unlawfully devising and contriving, and attempting to devise and contrive, means then and there to prevent the execution of an act entitled "An act making appropriations for the support of the Army for the fiscal year ending June 30, 1868, and for other purposes," approved March 2, 1867, and also to prevent the execution of an act entitled "An act to provide for the more efficient government of the rebel States," passed March 2, 1867; whereby the said Andrew Johnson, President of the United States, did then, to wit, on the 21st day of February, 1868, at the city of Washington, commit and was guilty of a high misdemeanor in office.

And the House of Representatives, by protestation, saving to themselves the liberty of exhibiting at any time hereafter any further articles or other accusation or impeachment against the said Andrew Johnson, President of the United States, and also of replying to his answers which he shall make unto the articles herein preferred against him, and of offering proof to the same and every part thereof, and to all and every other article, accusation, or impeachment which shall be exhibited by them, as the case shall require, do demand that the said Andrew Johnson may be put to answer the high crimes and misdemeanors in office herein charged against him, and that such proceedings, examinations, trials, and judgments may be thereupon had and given as may be agreeable to law and justice.

SCHUYLER COLFAX,
Speaker of the House of Representatives.

Attest:
Edward McPherson,
Clerk of the House of Representatives.

roposed Articles of Impeachment Against President Nixon

Source: U.S. Congress, House, Committee on the Judiciary, *Impeachment of Richard M. Nixon, President of the United States*, S Rept 93-1305, 93rd Cong. 2d sess., 1974, pp. 1-4.

Following is the complete text of the proposed articles of impeachment inst President Richard M. Nixon. The House Judiciary Committee pted Article I on July 27, 1974, Article II on July 29, 1974 and Article III July 30, 1974.

RESOLUTION

Impeaching Richard M. Nixon, President of the United States, of high nes and misdemeanors.

Resolved, That Richard M. Nixon, President of the United States, is im- ched for high crimes and misdemeanors, and that the following articles of peachment be exhibited to the Senate:

Articles of impeachment exhibited by the House of Representatives of United States of America in the name of itself and of all of the people of United States of America, against Richard M. Nixon, President of the ited States of America, in maintenance and support of its impeachment inst him for high crimes and misdemeanors.

Article I

In his conduct of the office of President of the United States, Richard M. xon, in violation of his constitutional oath faithfully to execute the office of esident of the United States and, to the best of his ability, preserve, protect, d defend the Constitution of the United States, and in violation of his con- tutional duty to take care that the laws be faithfully executed, has evented, obstructed, and impeded the administration of justice, in that:

On June 17, 1972, and prior thereto, agents of the Committee for the Re- ection of the President committed unlawful entry of the headquarters of the mocratic National Committee in Washington, District of Columbia, for e purpose of securing political intelligence. Subsequent thereto, Richard . Nixon, using the powers of his high office, engaged personally and through subordinates and agents, in a course of conduct or plan designed to delay, pede, and obstruct the investigation of such unlawful entry; to cover up, nceal and protect those responsible; and to conceal the existence and scope other unlawful covert activities.

The means used to implement this course of conduct or plan included e or more of the following:

(1) making or causing to be made false or misleading statements to law- lly authorized investigative officers and employees of the United States;

(2) withholding relevant and material evidence or information from law- lly authorized investigative officers and employees of the United States;

(3) approving, condoning, acquiescing in, and counseling witnesses with spect to the giving of false or misleading statements to lawfully authorized vestigative officers and employees of the United States and false or mis- ading testimony in duly instituted judicial and congressional proceedings;

(4) interfering or endeavoring to interfere with the conduct of in- estigations by the Department of Justice of the United States, the Federal ureau of Investigation, the Office of Watergate Special Prosecution Force, nd Congressional Committees;

(5) approving, condoning, and acquiescing in, the surreptitious payment f substantial sums of money for the purpose of obtaining the silence or in- uencing the testimony of witnesses, potential witnesses or individuals who articipated in such unlawful entry and other illegal activities;

(6) endeavoring to misuse the Central Intelligence Agency, an agency of he United States;

(7) disseminating information received from officers of the Department f Justice of the United States to subjects of investigations conducted by law- ully authorized investigative officers and employees of the United States, for he purpose of aiding and assisting such subjects in their attempts to avoid criminal liability;

(8) making false or misleading public statements for the purpose of deceiving the people of the United States into believing that a thorough and complete investigation had been conducted with respect to allegations of mis- conduct on the part of personnel of the executive branch of the United States and personnel of the Committee for the Re-election of the President, and that there was no involvement of such personnel in such misconduct; or

(9) endeavoring to cause prospective defendants, and individuals duly tried and convicted, to expect favored treatment and consideration in return for their silence or false testimony, or rewarding individuals for their silence or false testimony.

In all of this, Richard M. Nixon has acted in a manner contrary to his trust as President and subversive of constitutional government, to the great prejudice of the cause of law and justice and to the manifest injury of the peo- ple of the United States.

Wherefore Richard M. Nixon, by such conduct, warrants impeachment and trial, and removal from office.

Article II

Using the powers of the office of President of the United States, Richard M. Nixon, in violation of his constitutional oath faithfully to execute the of- fice of President of the United States and, to the best of his ability, preserve, protect, and defend the Constitution of the United States, and in disregard of his constitutional duty to take care that the laws be faithfully executed, has repeatedly engaged in conduct violating the constitutional rights of citizens, impairing the due and proper administration of justice and the conduct of lawful inquiries, or contravening the laws governing agencies of the executive branch and the purposes of these agencies.

This conduct has included one or more of the following:

(1) He has, acting personally and through his subordinates and agents, endeavored to obtain from the Internal Revenue Service, in violation of the constitutional rights of citizens, confidential information contained in in- come tax returns for purposes not authorized by law, and to cause, in viola- tion of the constitutional rights of citizens, income tax audits or other income tax investigations to be initiated or conducted in a discriminatory manner.

(2) He misused the Federal Bureau of Investigation, the Secret Service, and other executive personnel, in violation or disregard of the constitutional rights of citizens, by directing or authorizing such agencies or personnel to conduct or continue electronic surveillance or other investigations for pur- poses unrelated to national security, the enforcement of laws, or any other lawful function of his office; he did direct, authorize, or permit the use of in- formation obtained thereby for purposes unrelated to national security, the enforcement of laws, or any other lawful function of his office; and he did direct the concealment of certain records made by the Federal Bureau of Investigation of electronic surveillance.

(3) He has, acting personally and through his subordinates and agents, in violation or disregard of the constitutional rights of citizens, authorized and permitted to be maintained a secret investigative unit within the office of the President, financed in part with money derived from campaign con- tributions, which unlawfully utilized the resources of the Central Intelligence Agency, engaged in covert and unlawful activities, and attempted to prej- udice the constitutional right of an accused to a fair trial.

(4) He has failed to take care that the laws were faithfully executed by failing to act when he knew or had reason to know that his close subordinates endeavored to impede and frustrate lawful inquiries by duly constituted ex- ecutive, judicial, and legislative entities concerning the unlawful entry into the headquarters of the Democratic National Committee, and the cover-up thereof, and concerning other unlawful activities, including those relating to the confirmation of Richard Kleindienst as Attorney General of the United States, the electronic surveillance of private citizens, the break-in into the of- fices of Dr. Lewis Fielding, and the campaign financing practices of the Com- mittee to Re-elect the President.

(5) In disregard of the rule of law, he knowingly misused the executive power by interfering with agencies of the executive branch, including the Federal Bureau of Investigation, the Criminal Division, and the Office of Watergate Special Prosecution Force, of the Department of Justice, and the Central Intelligence Agency, in violation of his duty to take care that the laws be faithfully executed.

In all of this, Richard M. Nixon has acted in a manner contrary to his trust as President and subversive of constitutional government, to the great prejudice of the cause of law and justice and to the manifest injury of the people of the United States.

Wherefore Richard M. Nixon, by such conduct, warrants impeachment and trial, and removal from office.

Article III

In his conduct of the office of President of the United States, Richard M. Nixon, contrary to his oath faithfully to execute the office of President of the United States and, to the best of his ability, preserve, protect, and defend the Constitution of the United States, and in violation of his constitutional duty to take care that the laws be faithfully executed, has failed without lawful cause or excuse to produce papers and things as directed by duly authorized subpoenas issued by the Committee on the Judiciary of the House of Representatives on April 11, 1974, May 15, 1974, May 30, 1974, and June 24, 1974, and willfully disobeyed such subpoenas. The subpoenaed papers and things were deemed necessary by the Committee in order to resolve by direct evidence fundamental, factual questions relating to Presidential direction, knowledge, or approval of actions demonstrated by other evidence to be substantial grounds for impeachment of the President. In refusing to produce these papers and things, Richard M. Nixon, substituting his judgment as to what materials were necessary for the inquiry, interposed the powers of the Presidency against the lawful subpoenas of the House of Representatives, thereby assuming to himself functions and judgments necessary to the exercise of the sole power of impeachment vested by the Constitution in the House of Representatives.

In all of this, Richard M. Nixon has acted in a manner contrary to trust as President and subversive of constitutional government, to the great prejudice of the cause of law and justice, and to the manifest injury of the people of the United States.

Wherefore Richard M. Nixon, by such conduct, warrants impeachment and trial, and removal from office.

Excerpts From Chief Justice John Marshall's Opinion in
Marbury v. Madison, 1803
(1 Cranch 137)

Following is the part of Marshall's opinion dealing with the question of power of the courts to invalidate an act of Congress:

...The authority, therefore, given to the Supreme Court, by the act establishing the judicial courts of the United States, to issue writs of mandamus to public officers, appears not to be warranted by the constitution; and it becomes necessary to inquire whether a jurisdiction so conferred can be exercised.

The question, whether an act, repugnant to the constitution, can become the law of the land, is a question deeply interesting to the United States; but, happily, not of an intricacy proportioned to its interest. It seems only necessary to recognize certain principles, supposed to have been long and well established, to decide it.

That the people have an original right to establish, for their future government, such principles, as, in their opinion, shall most conduce to their own happiness is the basis on which the whole American fabric has been erected. The exercise of this original right is a very great exertion; nor can it, nor ought it, to be frequently repeated. The principles, therefore, so established, are deemed fundamental. And as the authority from which they proceed is supreme, and can seldom act, they are designed to be permanent.

This original and supreme will organizes the government, and assigns to different departments their respective powers. It may either stop here, or establish certain limits not to be transcended by those departments.

The government of the United States is of the latter description. The powers of the legislature are defined and limited; and that those limits may not be mistaken, or forgotten, the constitution is written. To what purpose are powers limited, and to what purpose is that limitation committed to writing, if these limits may, at any time, be passed by those intended to be restrained? The distinction between a government with limited and unlimited powers is abolished, if those limits do not confine the persons on whom they are imposed, and if acts prohibited and acts allowed, are of equal obligation. It is a proposition too plain to be contested, that the constitution controls any legislative act repugnant to it; or, that the legislature may alter the constitution by an ordinary act.

Between these alternatives there is no middle ground. The constitution is either a superior paramount law, unchangeable by ordinary means, or it is on a level with ordinary legislative acts, and, like other acts, is alterable when the legislature shall please to alter it.

If the former part of the alternative be true, then a legislative act contrary to the constitution is not law: if the latter part be true, then written constitutions are absurd attempts, on the part of the people, to limit a power in its own nature illimitable.

Certainly all those who have framed written constitutions contemplate them as forming the fundamental and paramount law of the nation, and consequently, the theory of every such government must be that an act of the legislature, repugnant to the constitution, is void.

This theory is essentially attached to a written constitution, and is, consequently, to be considered, by this court, as one of the fundamental principles of our society. It is not therefore to be lost sight of in the further consideration of this subject.

If an act of the legislature, repugnant to the constitution, is void, does it, notwithstanding its invalidity, bind the courts, and oblige them to give it effect? Or, in other words, though it be not law, does it constitute a rule as operative as if it was a law? This would be to overthrow in fact what was established in theory; and would seem, at first view, an absurdity too gross to be insisted on. It shall, however, receive a more attentive consideration.

It is emphatically the province and duty of the judicial department to say what the law is. Those who apply the rule to particular cases, must of necessity expound and interpret that rule. If two laws conflict with each other, the courts must decide on the operation of each.

So if a law be in opposition to the constitution; if both the law and the constitution apply to a particular case, so that the court must either decide that case conformably to the law, disregarding the constitution; or conformably to the constitution, disregarding the law; the court must determine which of these conflicting rules governs the case. This is of the very essence of judicial duty.

If, then, the courts are to regard the constitution, and the constitution is superior to any ordinary act of the legislature, the constitution, and not such ordinary act, must govern the case to which they both apply.

Those, then, who controvert the principle that the constitution is to be considered, in court, as a paramount law, are reduced to the necessity of maintaining that courts must close their eyes on the constitution, and see only the law.

This doctrine would subvert the very foundation of all written constitutions. It would declare that an act which, according to the principles and theory of our government, is entirely void, is yet, in practice, completely obligatory. It would declare that if the legislature shall do what is expressly forbidden, such act, notwithstanding the express prohibition, is in reality effectual. It would be giving to the legislature a practical and real omnipotence, with the same breath which professes to restrict their powers within narrow limits. It is prescribing limits, and declaring that those limits may be passed at pleasure.

That it thus reduces to nothing what we have deemed the greatest improvement on political institutions—a written constitution—would of itself be sufficient, in America, where written constitutions have been viewed with so much reverence, for rejecting the construction. But the peculiar expressions of the constitution of the United States furnish additional arguments in favour of its rejection.

The judicial power of the United States is extended to all cases arising under the constitution.

Could it be the intention of those who gave this power, to say that in using it the constitution should not be looked into? That a case arising under the constitution should be decided without examining the instrument under which it arises?

This is too extravagant to be maintained.

In some cases, then, the constitution must be looked into by the judges. And if they can open it at all, what part of it are they forbidden to read or to obey?

There are many other parts of the constitution which serve to illustrate this subject. It is declared, that "no tax or duty shall be laid on articles exported from any state." Suppose, a duty on the export of cotton, of tobacco or of flour; and a suit instituted to recover it. Ought judgment to be rendered in such a case? Ought the judges to close their eyes on the constitution, and only see the law?

The constitution declares "that no bill of attainder or ex post facto law shall be passed."

If, however, such a bill should be passed, and a person should be prosecuted under it; must the court condemn to death those victims whom the constitution endeavors to preserve?

"No person," says the constitution, "shall be convicted of treason unless on the testimony of two witnesses to the same overt act, or on confession in open court."

Here the language of the constitution is addressed especially to the courts. It prescribes, directly for them, a rule of evidence not to be departed from. If the legislature should change that rule, and declare *one* witness, or a confession *out* of court, sufficient for conviction, must the constitutional principle yield to the legislative act?

From these, and many other selections which might be made, it is apparent, that the framers of the constitution contemplated that instrument as a rule for the government of *courts,* as well as of the legislature.

Why otherwise does it direct the judges to take an oath to support it? This oath certainly applies in an especial manner, to their conduct in their official character. How immoral to impose it on them, if they were to be used as the instruments, and the knowing instruments, for violating what they swear to support!

The oath of office, too, imposed by the legislature, is completely demonstrative of the legislative opinion on this subject. It is in these words: "I do solemnly swear that I will administer justice without respect to persons, and do equal right to the poor and to the rich; and that I will faithfully and impartially discharge all the duties incumbent on me as—, according to the best of my abilities and understanding agreeably to the *constitution* and laws of the United States."

Why does a judge swear to discharge his duties agreeably to the constitution of the United States, if that constitution forms no rule for his government? If it is closed upon him, and cannot be inspected by him?

If such be the real state of things, this is worse than solemn mockery. To prescribe, or to take this oath, becomes equally a crime.

It is also not entirely unworthy of observation, that in declaring what shall be the *supreme* law of the land, the *constitution* itself is first mentioned; and not the laws of the United States generally, but those only which shall be made in *pursuance* of the constitution, have that rank.

Thus, the particular phraseology of the constitution of the United States confirms and strengthens the principle, supposed to be essential to all written constitutions, that a law repugnant to the constitution is void; and that *courts,* as well as other departments, are bound by that instrument.

The rule must be discharged.

Acts of Congress Held Unconstitutional in Whole or in Part by the Supreme Court

Sources: Library of Congress, *The Constitution of the United States of America: Analysis and Interpretation*, S. Doc. 92-82, 92d Cong., 2d sess., 1973; 1974 Supplement, S. Doc. 93-134, 93d Cong., 2d sess., 1974; Library of Congress, Congressional Research Service.

1. Act of September 24, 1789 (1 Stat. 81, § 13, in part).

   Provision that "...[the Supreme Court] shall have power to issue...writs of mandamus, in cases warranted by the principles and usages of law, to any...persons holding office, under authority of the United States" as applied to the issue of mandamus to the Secretary of State requiring him to deliver to plaintiff a commission (duly signed by the President) as justice of the peace in the District of Columbia, *held* an attempt to enlarge the original jurisdiction of the Supreme Court, fixed by Article III, § 2.

   Marbury v. *Madison,* 1 Cr. (5 U.S.) 137 (1803).

2. Act of February 20, 1812 (2 Stat. 677).

   Provisions establishing board of revision to annul titles conferred many years previously by governors of the Northwest Territory were *held* violative of the due process clause of the Fifth Amendment.

   Reichart v. *Felps,* 6 Wall. (73 U.S.) 160 (1868).

3. Act of March 6, 1820 (3 Stat. 548, § 8, proviso).

   The Missouri Compromise, prohibiting slavery within the Louisiana Territory north of 36° 30′, except Missouri, *held* not warranted as a regulation of Territory belonging to the United States under Article IV, § 3, clause 2 (and *see* Fifth Amendment).

   Scott v. *Sandford,* 19 How. (60 U.S.) 393 (1857).

4. Act of February 25, 1862 (12 Stat. 345, § 1); July 11, 1862 (12 Stat. 532, § 1); March 3, 1863 (12 Stat. 711, § 3), each in part only.

   "Legal tender clauses," making noninterest-bearing United States notes legal tender in payment of "all debts, public and private," so far as applied to debts contracted before passage of the act, *held* not within express or implied powers of Congress under Article I, § 8, and inconsistent with Article I, § 10, and Fifth Amendment.

   Hepburn v. *Griswold,* 8 Wall. (75 U.S.) 603 (1870); overruled in *Knox* v. *Lee (Legal Tender Cases),* 12 Wall. (79 U.S.) 457 (1871).

5. Act of March 3, 1863 (12 Stat. 756, § 5).

   "So much of the fifth section...as provides for the removal of a judgment in a State court, and in which the cause was tried by a jury to the circuit court of the United States for a retrial on the facts and law, is not in pursuance of the Constitution, and is void" under the Seventh Amendment.

   The Justices v. *Murray,* 9 Wall. (76 U.S.) 274 (1870).

6. Act of March 3, 1863 (12 Stat. 766, § 5).

   Provision for an appeal from the Court of Claims to the Supreme Court—there being, at the time, a further provision (§ 14) requiring an estimate by the Secretary of the Treasury before payment of final judgments, *held* to contravene the judicial finality intended by the Constitution, Article III.

   Gordon v. *United States,* 2 Wall. (69 U.S.) 561 (1865). (Case was dismissed without opinion; the grounds upon which this decision was made were stated in a posthumous opinion by Chief Justice Taney printed in the appendix to volume 117 U.S. 697.)

7. Act of June 30, 1864 (13 Stat. 311, § 13).

   Provision that "any prize cause now pending in any circuit court shall, on the application of all parties in interest...be transferred by that court to the Supreme Court...," as applied in a case where no action had been taken in the Circuit Court on the appeal from the district court, *held* to propose an appeal procedure not within Article III, § 2.

   The Alicia, 7 Wall. (74 U.S.) 571 (1869).

8. Act of January 24, 1865 (13 Stat. 424).

   Requirement of a test oath (disavowing actions in hostility to the United States) before admission to appear as attorney in a federal court by virtue of any previous admission, *held* invalid as applied to an attorney who had been pardoned by the President for all offenses during the Rebellion—as *ex post facto* (Article I, § 9, clause 3) and an interference with the pardoning power (Article II, § 2, clause 1).

   Ex parte Garland, 4 Wall. (71 U.S.) 333 (1867).

9. Act of March 2, 1867 (14 Stat. 484, § 29).

   General prohibition on sale of naphtha, etc., for illuminating purposes, if inflammable at less temperature than 110° F., *held* invalid "except so far as the section named operates within the United

States, but without the limits of any State," as being a mere po... regulation.

   United States v. *Dewitt,* 9 Wall. (76 U.S.) 41 (1870).

10. Act of May 31, 1870 (16 Stat. 140, §§ 3, 4).

   Provisions penalizing (1) refusal of local election officials to p... mit voting by persons offering to qualify under State laws, applica... to any citizens; and (2) hindering of any person from qualifying... voting, *held* invalid under Fifteenth Amendment.

   United States v. *Reese,* 92 U.S. 214 (1876).

11. Act of July 12, 1870 (16 Stat. 235).

   Provision making Presidential pardons inadmissible in evider... in Court of Claims, prohibiting their use by that court in decidi... claims or appeals, and requiring dismissal of appeals by the Supre... Court in cases where proof of loyalty had been made otherwise than... prescribed by law, *held* an interference with judicial power under *A*... ticle III, § 1, and with the pardoning power under Article II, § ... clause 1.

   United States v. *Klein,* 13 Wall. (80 U.S.) 128 (1872).

12. Act of June 22, 1874 (18 Stat. 1878, § 4).

   Provision authorizing federal courts, in suits for forfeitures und... revenue and custom laws, to require production of documents, wi... allegations expected to be proved therein to be taken as proved ... failure to produce such documents, was *held* violative of the sear... and seizure provision of the Fourth Amendment and the sel... incrimination clause of the Fifth Amendment.

   Boyd v. *United States,* 116 U.S. 616 (1886).

13. Revised Statutes 1977 (Act of May 31, 1870, 16 Stat. 144).

   Provision that "all persons within the jurisdiction of the Unite... States shall have the same right in every State and Territory to mak... and enforce contracts...as is enjoyed by white citizens...," *held* ir... valid under the Thirteenth Amendment.

   Hodges v. *United States,* 203 U.S. 1 (1906).

14. Revised Statutes 4937-4947 (Act of July 8, 1870, 16 Stat. 210), and Act o... August 14, 1876 (19 Stat. 141).

   Original trademark law, applying to marks "for exclusive us... within the United States," and a penal act designed solely for th... protection of rights defined in the earlier measure, *held* not suppor... table by Article I, § 8, clause 8 (copyright clause), nor Article I, § ... clause 3, by reason of its application to intrastate as well as interstat... commerce.

   Trade-Mark Cases, 100 U.S. 82 (1879).

15. Revised Statutes 5132, subdivision 9 (Act of March 2, 1867, 14 Stat. 539)...

   Provision penalizing "any person respecting whom bankruptc... proceedings are commenced...who, within 3 months before the com... mencement of proceedings in bankruptcy, under the false color and... pretense of carrying on business and dealing in the ordinary course o... trade, obtains on credit from any person any goods or chattels with in... tent to defraud...," *held* a police regulation not within the bankruptc... power (Article I, § 4, clause 4).

   United States v. *Fox,* 95 U.S. 670 (1878).

16. Revised Statutes 5507 (Act of May 31, 1870, 16 Stat. 141, § 4).

   Provision penalizing "every person who prevents, hinders, con... trols, or intimidates another from exercising...the right of suffrage, to... whom that right is guaranteed by the Fifteenth Amendment to the... Constitution of the United States, by means of bribery...," *held* not... authorized by the Fifteenth Amendment.

   James v. *Bowman,* 190 U.S. 127 (1903).

17. Revised Statutes 5519 (Act of April 20, 1871, 17 Stat. 13, § 2).

   Section providing punishment in case "two or more persons in... any State...conspire...for the purpose of depriving...any person...of... the equal protection of the laws...or for the purpose of preventing or... hindering the constituted authorities of any State...from giving or... securing to all persons within such State...the equal protection of the... laws...," *held* invalid as not being directed at state action proscribed... by the Fourteenth Amendment.

   United States v. *Harris,* 106 U.S. 629 (1883).

   In *Baldwin* v. *Franks,* 120 U.S. 678 (1887), an attempt was made... to distinguish the *Harris* case and to apply the statute to a con...

spiracy directed at aliens within a State, but the provision was *held* not enforceable in such limited manner.

Revised Statutes of the District of Columbia, § 1064 (Act of June 17, 1870, 16 Stat. 154, § 3).

Provision that "prosecutions in the police court [of the District of Columbia] shall be by information under oath, without indictment by grand jury or trial by petit jury," as applied to punishment for conspiracy held to contravene Article III, § 2, clause 3, requiring jury trial of all crimes.

Callan v. *Wilson,* 127 U.S. 540 (1888).

Act of March 1, 1875 (18 Stat. 336, §§ 1, 2).

Provision "That all persons within the jurisdiction of the United States shall be entitled to the full and equal enjoyment of the accommodations...of inns, public conveyances on land or water, theaters, and other places of public amusement; subject only to the conditions and limitations established by law, and applicable alike to citizens of every race and color, regardless of any previous condition of servitude"—subject to penalty, *held* not to be supported by the Thirteenth or Fourteenth Amendments.

Civil Rights Cases, 109 U.S. 3 (1883), as to operation within States.

Act of March 3, 1875 (18 Stat. 479, § 2).

Provision that "if the party [i.e., a person stealing property from the United States] has been convicted, then the judgment against him shall be conclusive evidence in the prosecution against [the] receiver that the property of the United States therein described has been embezzled, stolen, or purloined," *held* to contravene the Sixth Amendment.

Kirby v. *United States,* 174 U.S. 47 (1899).

Act of July 12, 1876 (19 Stat. 80, sec. 6, in part).

Provision that "postmasters of the first, second, and third classes...may be removed by the President by and with the advice and consent of the Senate," *held* to infringe the executive power under Article II, § 1, clause 1.

Myers v. *United States,* 272 U.S. 52 (1926).

Act of August 14, 1876 (19 Stat. 141, Trademark Act). *See* Revised Statutes 4937, above, No. 14.

Act of August 11, 1888 (25 Stat. 411).

Clause, in a provision for the purchase or condemnation of a certain lock and dam in the Monongahela River, that "...in estimating the sums to be paid by the United States, the franchise of said corporation to collect tolls shall not be considered or estimated...," *held* to contravene the Fifth Amendment.

Monongahela Navigation Co. v. *United States,* 148 U.S. 312 (1893).

Act of May 5, 1892 (27 Stat. 25, § 4).

Provision of a Chinese exclusion act, that Chinese persons "convicted and adjudged to be not lawfully entitled to be or remain in the United States shall be imprisoned at hard labor for a period not exceeding 1 year and thereafter removed from the United States...(such conviction and judgment being had before a justice, judge, or commissioner upon a summary hearing), *held* to contravene the Fifth and Sixth Amendments.

Wong Wing v. *United States,* 163 U.S. 228 (1896).

Joint Resolution of August 4, 1894 (28 Stat. 1018, No. 41).

Provision authorizing the Secretary of the Interior to approve a second lease of certain land by an Indian chief in Minnesota (granted to lessor's ancestor by art. 9 of a treaty with the Chippewa Indians), *held* an interference with judicial interpretation of treaties under Article III, § 2, clause 1 (and repugnant to the Fifth Amendment).

Jones v. *Meehan,* 175 U.S. 1 (1899).

26. Act of August 27, 1894 (28 Stat. 553-560, §§ 27-37).

Income tax provisions of the tariff act of 1894. "The tax imposed by §§ 27 and 37, inclusive...so far as it falls on the income of real estate and of personal property, being a direct tax within the meaning of the Constitution, and, therefore, unconstitutional and void because not apportioned according to representation [Article I, § 2, clause 3], all those sections, constituting one entire scheme of taxation, are necessarily invalid" (158 U.S. 601, 637).

Pollock v. *Farmers' Loan & Trust Co.,* 157 U.S. 429 (1895), and rehearing, 158 U.S. 601 (1895).

27. Act of January 30, 1897 (29 Stat. 506).

Prohibition on sale of liquor "...to any Indian to whom allotment of land has been made while the title to the same shall be held in trust by the Government...," *held* a police regulation infringing state powers, and not warranted by the commerce clause, Article I, § 8, clause 3.

Matter of Heff, 197 U.S. 488 (1905), overruled in *United States* v. *Nice,* 241 U.S. 591 (1916).

28. Act of June 1, 1898 (30 Stat. 428).

Section 10, penalizing "any employer subject to the provisions of this act" who should "threaten any employee with loss of employment...because of his membership in...a labor corporation, association, or organization" (the act being applicable "to any common carrier...engaged in the transportation of passengers or property...from one State...to another State...," etc.), *held* an infringement of the Fifth Amendment and not supported by the commerce clause.

Adair v. *United States,* 208 U.S. 161 (1908).

29. Act of June 13, 1898 (30 Stat. 451, 459).

Stamp tax on foreign bills of lading, *held* a tax on exports in violation of Article I, § 9.

Fairbank v. *United States,* 181 U.S. 283 (1901).

30. Same (30 Stat. 451, 460).

Tax on charter parties, as applied to shipments exclusively from ports in United States to foreign ports, *held* a tax on exports in violation of Article I, § 9.

United States v. *Hvoslef,* 237 U.S. 1 (1915).

31. Act of June 6, 1900 (31 Stat. 359, § 171).

Section of the Alaska Code providing for a six-person jury in trials for misdemeanors, *held* repugnant to the Sixth Amendment, requiring "jury" trial of crimes.

Rassmussen v. *United States,* 197 U.S. 516 (1905).

32. Act of March 3, 1901 (31 Stat. 1341, § 935).

Section of the District of Columbia Code granting the same right of appeal, in criminal cases, to the United States or the District of Columbia as to the defendant, but providing that a verdict was not to be set aside for error bound in rulings during trial, *held* an attempt to take an advisory opinion, contrary to Article III, § 2.

United States v. *Evans,* 213 U.S. 297 (1909).

33. Act of June 11, 1906 (34 Stat. 232).

Act providing that "every common carrier engaged in trade or commerce in the District of Columbia...or between the several States...shall be liable to any of its employees...for all damages which may result from the negligence of any of its officers...or by reason of any defect...due to its negligence in its cars, engines...roadbed," etc., *held* not supportable under Article I, § 8, clause 3 because it extended to intrastate as well as interstate commercial activities.

The Employers' Liability Cases, 207 U.S. 463 (1908). (The act was upheld as to the District of Columbia in *Hyde* v. *Southern R. Co.,* 31 App. D.C. 466 (1908); and as to the Territories, in *El Paso & N.E. Ry.* v. *Gutierrez,* 215 U.S. 87 (1909).)

34. Act of June 16, 1906 (34 Stat. 269, § 2).

Provision of Oklahoma Enabling Act restricting relocation of the State capital prior to 1913, *held* not supportable by Article IV, § 3, authorizing admission of new States.

Coyle v. *Smith,* 221 U.S. 559 (1911).

35. Act of February 20, 1907 (34 Stat. 889, § 3).

Provision in the Immigration Act of 1907 penalizing "whoever...shall keep, maintain, control, support, or harbor in any house or other place, for the purpose of prostitution...any alien woman or girl, within 3 years after she shall have entered the United States," *held* an exercise of police power not within the control of Congress over immigration (whether drawn from the commerce clause or based on inherent sovereignty).

Keller v. *United States,* 213 U.S. 138 (1909).

36. Act of March 1, 1907 (34 Stat. 1028).

Provisions authorizing certain Indians "to institute their suits in the Court of Claims to determine the validity of any acts of Congress passed since...1902, insofar as said acts...attempt to increase or extend the restrictions upon alienation...of allotments of lands of Cherokee citizens...," and giving a right of appeal to the Supreme Court, *held* an attempt to enlarge the judicial power restricted by Article III, § 2, to cases and controversies.

Muskrat v. *United States,* 219 U.S. 346 (1911).

37. Act of May 27, 1908 (35 Stat. 313, § 4).

Provision making locally taxable "all land [of Indians of the Five Civilized Tribes] from which restrictions have been or shall be removed," *held* a violation of the Fifth Amendment, in view of the Atoka Agreement, embodied in the Curtis Act of June 28, 1898, providing tax-exemption for allotted lands while title in original allottee, not exceeding 21 years.

Choate v. *Trapp,* 224 U.S. 665 (1912).

38. Act of February 9, 1909, § 2, 35 Stat. 614, as amended.

Provision of Narcotic Drugs Import and Export Act creating a presumption that possessor of cocaine knew of its illegal importation into the United States *held,* in light of the fact that more cocaine is produced domestically than is brought into the country and in absence of any showing that defendant could have known his cocaine was imported, if it was, inapplicable to support conviction from mere possession of cocaine.

Turner v. *United States,* 396 U.S. 398 (1970).

39. Act of August 19, 1911 (37 Stat. 28).

A proviso in § 8 of the Federal Corrupt Practices Act fixing a maximum authorized expenditure by a candidate for Senator "in any campaign for his nomination and election," as applied to a primary election, *held* not supported by Article I, § 4, giving Congress power to regulate the manner of holding elections for Senators and Representatives.

Newberry v. *United States*, 256 U.S. 232 (1921), overruled in *United States* v. *Classic*, 313 U.S. 299 (1941).

40. Act of June 18, 1912 (37 Stat. 136, § 8).

Part of § 8 giving the Juvenile Court of the District of Columbia (proceeding upon information) concurrent jurisdiction of desertion cases (which were, by law, punishable by fine or imprisonment in the workhouse at hard labor for 1 year), *held* invalid under the Fifth Amendment, which gives right to presentment by a grand jury in case of infamous crimes.

United States v. *Moreland*, 258 U.S. 433 (1922).

41. Act of March 4, 1913 (37 Stat. 988, part of par. 64).

Provision of the District of Columbia Public Utility Commission Act authorizing appeal to the United States Supreme Court from decrees of the District of Columbia Court of Appeals modifying valuation decisions of the Utilities Commission, *held* an attempt to extend the appellate jurisdiction of the Supreme Court to cases not strictly judicial within the meaning of Article III, § 2.

Keller v. *Potomac Elec. Co.*, 261 U.S. 428 (1923).

42. Act of September 1, 1916 (39 Stat. 675).

The original Child Labor Law, providing "that no producer...shall ship...in interstate commerce...any article or commodity the product of any mill...in which within 30 days prior to the removal of such product therefrom children under the age of 14 years have been employed or permitted to work more than 8 hours in any day or more than 6 days in any week...," *held* not within the commerce power of Congress.

Hammer v. *Dagenhart*, 247 U.S. 251 (1918).

43. Act of September 8, 1916 (39 Stat. 757, § 2(a), in part).

Provision of the income tax law of 1916, that a "stock dividend shall be considered income, to the amount of its cash value," *held* invalid (in spite of the Sixteenth Amendment) as an attempt to tax something not actually income, without regard to apportionment under Article I, § 2, clause 3.

Eisner v. *Macomber*, 252 U.S. 189 (1920).

44. Act of October 6, 1917 (40 Stat. 395).

The amendment of §§ 24 and 256 of the Judicial Code (which prescribe the jurisdiction of district courts) "saving...to claimants the rights and remedies under the workmen's compensation law of any State," *held* an attempt to transfer federal legislative powers to the States—the Constitution, by Article III, § 2, and Article I, § 8, having adopted rules of general maritime law.

Knickerbocker Ice Co. v. *Stewart*, 253 U.S. 149 (1920).

45. Act of September 19, 1918 (40 Stat. 960).

Specifically, that part of the Minimum Wage Law of the District of Columbia which authorized the Wage Board "to ascertain and declare...(a) Standards of minimum wages for women in any occupation within the District of Columbia, and what wages are inadequate to supply the necessary cost of living to any such women workers to maintain them in good health and to protect their morals...," *held* to interfere with freedom of contract under the Fifth Amendment.

Adkins v. *Children's Hospital*, 261 U.S. 525 (1923), overruled in *West Coast Hotel Co.* v. *Parrish*, 300 U.S. 379 (1937).

46. Act of February 24, 1919 (40 Stat. 1065, § 213, in part).

That part of § 213 of the Revenue Act of 1918 which provided that "...for the purposes of this title...the term 'gross income'...includes gains, profits, and income derived from salaries, wages, or compensation for personal service (including in the case of...judges of the Supreme and inferior courts of the United States...the compensation received as such)..." as applied to a judge in office when the act was passed, *held* a violation of the guaranty of judges' salaries, in Article III, § 1.

Evans v. *Gore*, 253 U.S. 245 (1920).
Miles v. *Graham*, 268 U.S. 501 (1925), held it invalid as applied to a judge taking office subsequent to the date of the act.

47. Act of February 24, 1919 (40 Stat. 1097, § 402(c)).

That part of the estate tax law providing that "gross estate" of a decedent should include value of all property "to the extent of any interest therein of which the decedent has at any time made a transfer or with respect to which he had at any time created a trust, in contemplation of or intended to take effect in possession or enjoyment at or after his death (whether such transfer or trust is made or created before or after the passage of this act), except in case of a *bona fide* sale..." as applied to a transfer of property made prior to the act and intended to take effect "in possession or enjoyment" at death of grantor, but not in fact testamentary or designed to evade taxation, *held* confiscatory, contrary to Fifth Amendment.

Nicholds v. *Coolidge*, 274 U.S. 531 (1927).

48. Act of February 24, 1919, title XII (40 Stat. 1138, entire title).

The Child Labor Tax Act, providing that "e[ach] person...operating...any...factory...in which children under the a[ge of] 14 years have been employed or permitted to work...shall pay...i[n ad]dition to all other taxes imposed by law, an excise tax equivalent [to 10] percent of the entire net profits received...for such year from [the] sale...of the product of such...factory...," *held* beyond the ta[xing] power under Article I, § 8, clause 1, and an infringement of [state] authority.

Bailey v. *Drexel Furniture Co. (Child Labor Tax Case)*, 259 [U.S.] 20 (1922).

49. An Act of October 22, 1919 (41 Stat. 298, § 2), amending Act of Augus[t 10,] 1917 (40 Stat. 277, § 4).

(a) § 4 of the Lever Act, providing in part "that it is hereby m[ade] unlawful for any person willfully...to make any unjust or [un]reasonable rate or charge in handling or dealing in or with [any] necessaries...and fixing a penalty, *held* invalid to support an in[dict]ment for charging an unreasonable price on sale—as not setting u[p an] ascertainable standard of guilt within the requirement of the S[ixth] Amendment.

United States v. *Cohen Grocery Co.*, 255 U.S. 81 (1921).

(b) That provision of § 4 making it unlawful "to conspire, c[om]bine, agree, or arrange with any other person to...exact exces[sive] prices for any necessaries" and fixing a penalty, *held* invalid to s[up]port an indictment, on the reasoning of the *Cohen Grocery* case.

Weeds, Inc. v. *United States*, 255 U.S. 109 (1921).

50. Act of August 24, 1921 (42 Stat. 187, Future Trading Act).

(a) § 4 (and interwoven regulations) providing a "tax of 20 ce[nts] a bushel on every bushel involved therein, upon each contract of s[ale] of grain for future delivery, except...where such contracts are made [in] or through a member of a board of trade which has been designa[ted] by the Secretary of Agriculture as a 'contract market'...," *held* [not] within the taxing power under Article I, § 8.

Hill v. *Wallace*, 259 U.S. 44 (1922).

(b) § 3, providing "That in addition to the taxes now imposed [by] law there is hereby levied a tax amounting to 20 cents per bushel [on] each bushel involved therein, whether the actual commodity is in[tended] to be delivered or only nominally referred to, upon each...[op]tion for a contract either of purchase or sale of grain...," *held* inva[lid] on the same reasoning.

Trusler v. *Crooks*, 269 U.S. 475 (1926).

51. Act of November 23, 1921 (42 Stat. 261, § 245, in part).

Provision of Revenue Act of 1921 abating the deduction (4 p[er] cent of mean reserves) allowed from taxable income of life insuran[ce] companies in general by the amount of interest on their tax-exempt [bonds] and so according no relative advantage to the owners of the ta[x-] exempt securities, *held* to destroy a guaranteed exemption.

National Life Ins. v. *United States*, 277 U.S. 508 (1928).

52. Act of June 10, 1922 (42 Stat. 634).

A second attempt to amend §§ 24 and 256 of the Judicial Cod[e,] relating to jurisdiction of district courts, by saving "to claimants f[or] compensation for injuries to or death of persons other than the mast[er] or members of the crew of a vessel, their rights and remedies und[er] the workmen's compensation law of any State..." *held* invalid o[n the] authority of *Knickerbocker Ice Co.* v. *Stewart*.

Washington v. *Dawson & Co.*, 264 U.S. 219 (1924).

53. Act of June 2, 1924 (43 Stat. 313).

The gift tax provisions of the Revenue Act of 1924, applicable t[o] gifts made during the calendar year, were *held* invalid under the Fift[h] Amendment insofar as they applied to gifts made before passage o[f] the act.

Untermeyer v. *Anderson*, 276 U.S. 440 (1928).

54. Act of February 26, 1926 (44 Stat. 70, § 302, in part).

Stipulation creating a conclusive presumption that gifts mad[e] within two years prior to the death of the donor were made in con[templation of death of donor and requiring the value thereof to be in[cluded] in computing the death transfer tax on decedent's estate wa[s] *held* to effect an invalid deprivation of property without due process.

Heiner v. *Donnan*, 285 U.S. 312 (1932).

55. Act of February 26, 1926 (44 Stat. 95, § 701).

Provision imposing a special excise tax of $1,000 on liquor dealer[s] operating in States where such business is illegal, was *held* a penalty without constitutional support following repeal of the Eighteenth Amendment.

United States v. *Constantine*, 296 U.S. 287 (1935).

56. Act of March 20, 1933 (48 Stat. 11, § 17, in part).

Clause in the Economy Act of 1933 providing "...all laws granting or pertaining to yearly renewable term war risk insurance are hereby repealed," *held* invalid to abrogate an outstanding contract of insurance, which is a vested right protected by the Fifth Amendment.

Lynch v. *United States*, 292 U.S. 571 (1934).

Act of May 12, 1933 (48 Stat. 31).

Agricultural Adjustment Act providing for processing taxes on agricultural commodities and benefit payments therefrom to farmers, *held* not within the taxing power under Article I, § 8, clause 1.

United States v. *Butler,* 297 U.S. 1 (1936).

Joint Resolution of June 5, 1933 (48 Stat. 113, § 1).

Abrogation of gold clause in Government obligations, *held* a repudiation of the pledge implicit in the power to borrow money (Article I, § 8, clause 2), and within the prohibition of the Fourteenth Amendment, against questioning the validity of the public debt. (The majority of the Court, however, held plaintiff not entitled to recover under the circumstances.)

Perry v. *United States,* 294 U.S. 330 (1935).

Act of June 16, 1933 (48 Stat. 195, the National Industrial Recovery Act).

(a) Title I, except § 9.

Provisions relating to codes of fair competition, authorized to be approved by the President in his discretion "to effectuate the policy" of the act, *held* invalid as a delegation of legislative power (Article I, § 1) and not within the commerce power (Article I, § 8, clause 3).

Schechter Corp. v. *United States,* 295 U.S. 495 (1935).

(b) § 9(c).

Clause of the oil regulation section authorizing the President "to prohibit the transportation in interstate...commerce of petroleum...produced or withdrawn from storage in excess of the amount permitted...by any State law..." and prescribing a penalty for violation of orders issued thereunder, *held* invalid as a delegation of legislative power.

Panama Refining Co. v. *Ryan,* 293 U.S. 388 (1935).

Act of June 16, 1933 (48 Stat. 307, § 13).

Temporary reduction of 15 percent in retired pay of judges, retired from service but subject to performance of judicial duties under the Act March 1, 1929 (45 Stat. 1422), was *held* a violation of the guaranty of judges' salaries in Article III, § 1.

Booth v. *United States,* 291 U.S. 339 (1934).

Act of April 27, 1934 (48 Stat. 646, § 6), amending § 5(i) of Home Owners' Loan Act of 1933.

Provision for conversion of state building and loan associations into federal associations, upon vote of 51 percent of the votes cast at a meeting of stockholders called to consider such action, *held* an encroachment on reserved powers of State.

Hopkins Savings Assn. v. *Cleary,* 296 U.S. 315 (1935).

2. Act of May 24, 1934 (48 Stat. 798).

Provision for readjustment of municipal indebtedness, though "adequately related" to the bankruptcy power, was *held* invalid as an interference with state sovereignty.

Ashton v. *Cameron County Dist.,* 298 U.S. 513 (1936).

3. Act of June 27, 1934 (48 Stat. 1283).

The Railroad Retirement Act, establishing a detailed compulsory retirement system for employees of carriers subject to the Interstate Commerce Act, *held,* not a regulation of commerce within the meaning of Article I, § 8, clause 3, and violative of the due process clause (Fifth Amendment).

Railroad Retirement Board v. *Alton R. Co.,* 295 U.S. 330 (1935).

34. Act of June 28, 1934 (48 Stat. 1289, ch. 869).

The Frazier-Lemke Act, adding subsection (s) to § 75 of the Bankruptcy Act, designed to preserve to mortgagors the ownership and enjoyment of their farm property and providing specifically, in paragraph 7, that a bankrupt left in possession has the option at any time within 5 years of buying at the appraised value—subject meanwhile to no monetary obligation other than payment of reasonable rental, *held* a violation of property rights, under the Fifth Amendment.

Louisville Bank v. *Radford,* 295 U.S. 555 (1935).

65. Act of August 24, 1935 (49 Stat. 750).

Amendments of Agricultural Adjustment Act *held* not within the taxing power.

Rickert Rice Mills v. *Fontenot,* 297 U.S. 110 (1936).

66. Act of August 30, 1935 (49 Stat. 991).

Bituminous Coal Conservation Act of 1935, *held* to impose, not a tax within Article I, § 8, but a penalty not sustained by the commerce clause (Article I, § 8, clause 3).

Carter v. *Carter Coal Co.,* 298 U.S. 238 (1936).

67. Act of June 25, 1938 (52 Stat. 1040).

Federal Food, Drug, and Cosmetic Act of 1938, § 301(f), prohibiting the refusal to permit entry or inspection of premises by federal officers *held* void for vagueness and as violative of the due process clause of the Fifth Amendment.

United States v. *Cardiff,* 344 U.S. 174 (1952).

68. Act of June 30, 1938 (52 Stat. 1251).

Federal Firearms Act, § 2(f), establishing a presumption of guilt based on a prior conviction and present possession of a firearm, *held* to violate the test of due process under the Fifth Amendment.

Tot v. *United States,* 319 U.S. 463 (1943).

69. Act of October 14, 1940 (54 Stat. 1169, § 401(g)); as amended by Act of January 20, 1944 (58 Stat. 4, § 1).

Provision of Aliens and Nationality Code (8 U.S.C. § 1481(a) (8)), derived from the Nationality Act of 1940, as amended, that citizenship shall be lost upon conviction by court martial and dishonorable discharge for deserting the armed services in time of war, *held* invalid as imposing a cruel and unusual punishment barred by the Eighth Amendment and not authorized by the war powers conferred by Article I, § 8, clauses 11 to 14.

Trop v. *Dulles,* 356 U.S. 86 (1958).

70. Act of November 15, 1943 (57 Stat. 450).

Urgent Deficiency Appropriation Act of 1943, § 304, providing that no salary should be paid to certain named federal employees out of moneys appropriated, *held* to violate Article I, § 9, clause 3, forbidding enactment of bill of attainder or *ex post facto* law.

United States v. *Lovett,* 328 U.S. 303 (1946).

71. Act of September 27, 1944 (58 Stat. 746, § 401 (J)); and Act of June 27, 1952 (66 Stat. 163, 267-268, § 349(a) (10)).

§ 401 (J) of Immigration and Nationality Act of 1940, added in 1944, and § 49(a) (10) of the Immigration and Nationality Act of 1952 depriving one of citizenship, without the procedural safeguards guaranteed by the Fifth and Sixth Amendments, for the offense of leaving or remaining outside the country, in time of war or national emergency, to evade military service *held* invalid.

Kennedy v. *Mendoza-Martinez,* 372 U.S. 144 (1963).

72. Act of June 25, 1948 (62 Stat. 760).

Provision of Lindbergh Kidnapping Act which provided for the imposition of the death penalty only if recommended by the jury *held* unconstitutional inasmuch as it penalized the assertion of a defendant's assertion of his Sixth Amendment right to a jury trial.

United States v. *Jackson,* 390 U.S. 570 (1968).

73. Act of May 5, 1950 (64 Stat. 107).

Article 3(a) of the Uniform Code of Military Justice subjecting civilian ex-servicemen to court martial for crime committed while in military service *held* to violate Article III, § 2, and the Fifth and Sixth Amendments.

Toth v. *Quarles,* 350 U.S. 11 (1955).

74. Act of May 5, 1950 (64 Stat. 107).

Insofar as Article 2(11) of the Uniform Code of Military Justice subjects civilian dependents accompanying members of the armed forces overseas in time of peace to trial, in capital cases, by court martial, it is violative of Article III, § 2, and the Fifth and Sixth Amendments.

Reid v. *Covert,* 354 U.S. 1 (1957).

Insofar as the aforementioned provision is invoked in time of peace for the trial of noncapital offenses committed on land bases overseas by employees of the armed forces who have not been inducted or who have not voluntarily enlisted therein, it is violative of the Sixth Amendment.

McElroy v. *United States,* 361 U.S. 281 (1960).

Insofar as the aforementioned provision is invoked in time of peace for the trial of noncapital offenses committed by civilian dependents accompanying members of the armed forces overseas, it is violative of Article III, § 2, and the Fifth and Sixth Amendments.

Kinsella v. *United States,* 361 U.S. 234 (1960).

Insofar as the aforementioned provision is invoked in time of peace for the trial of a capital offense committed by a civilian employee of the armed forces overseas, it is violative of Article III, § 2, and the Fifth and Sixth Amendments.

Grisham v. *Hagan,* 361 U.S. 278 (1960).

75. Act of August 16, 1950 (64 Stat. 451, as amended).

Statutory scheme authorizing the Postmaster General to close the mails to distributors of obscene materials *held* unconstitutional in the absence of procedural provisions which would assure prompt judicial determination that protected materials were not being restrained.

Blount v. *Rizzi,* 400 U.S. 410 (1971).

76. Act of September 23, 1950 (Title I, § 5, 64 Stat. 992).

Provision of Subversive Activities Control Act making it unlawful for member of Communist front organization to work in a defense plant *held* to be an overbroad infringement of the right of association protected by the First Amendment.

United States v. *Robel,* 389 U.S. 258 (1967).

77. Act of September 23, 1950 (64 Stat. 993, § 6).

Subversive Activities Control Act of 1950, § 6, providing that any member of a Communist organization, which has registered or has been ordered to register, commits a crime if he attempts to obtain or use a passport, *held* violative of due process under the Fifth Amendment.

Aptheker v. *Secretary of State,* 378 U.S. 500 (1964).

78. Act of September 23, 1950 (Title I, §§ 7, 8, 64 Stat. 993).

Provisions of Subversive Activities Control Act of 1950 requiring in lieu of registration by the Communist Party registration by Party members may not be applied to compel registration or to prosecute for refusal to register of alleged members who have asserted their privilege against self-incrimination inasmuch as registration would expose such persons to criminal prosecution under other laws.

Albertson v. *Subversive Activities Control Board,* 382 U.S. 70 (1965).

79. Act of June 27, 1952 (Title III, § 349, 66 Stat. 267).

Provision of Immigration and Nationality Act of 1952 providing for revocation of United States citizenship of one who votes in a foreign election *held* unconstitutional under § 1 of the Fourteenth Amendment.

Afroyim v. *Rusk,* 387 U.S. 253 (1967).

80. Act of June 27, 1952 (66 Stat. 163, 269, § 352(a) (1)).

§ 352(a) (1) of the Immigration and Nationality Act of 1952 depriving a naturalized person of citizenship for "having a continuous residence for three years" in state of his birth or prior nationality *held* violative of the due process clause of the Fifth Amendment.

Schneider v. *Rusk,* 377 U.S. 163 (1964).

81. Act of August 26, 1954 (68A Stat. 525, Int. Rev. Code of 1954, §§ 4401-4423).

Provisions of tax laws requiring gamblers to pay occupational and excise taxes may not be used over an assertion of one's privilege against self-incrimination either to compel extensive reporting of activities, leaving the registrant subject to prosecution under the laws of all the States with the possible exception of Nevada, or to prosecute for failure to register and report, because the scheme abridged the Fifth Amendment privilege.

Marchetti v. *United States,* 390 U.S. 39 (1968), and *Grosso* v. *United States,* 390 U.S. 62 (1968).

82. Act of August 16, 1954 (68A Stat. 560, Marijuana Tax Act, §§ 4741, 4744, 4751, 4753).

Provisions of tax laws requiring possessors of marijuana to register and to pay a transfer tax may not be used over an assertion of the privilege against self-incrimination to compel registration or to prosecute for failure to register.

Leary v. *United States,* 395 U.S. 6 (1969).

83. Act of August 16, 1954 (68A Stat. 728, Int. Rev. Code of 1954, §§ 5841, 5851).

Provisions of tax laws requiring the possessor of certain firearms, which it is made illegal to receive or to possess, to register with the Treasury Department may not be used over an assertion of the privilege against self-incrimination to prosecute one for failure to register or for possession of an unregistered firearm since the statutory scheme abridges the Fifth Amendment privilege.

Haynes v. *United States,* 390 U.S. 85 (1968).

84. Act of August 16, 1954 (68A Stat. 867, Int. Rev. Code of 1954, § 7302).

Provisions of tax laws providing for forfeiture of property used in violating internal revenue laws may not be constitutionally used in face of invocation of privilege against self-incrimination to condemn money in possession of gambler who had failed to comply with the registration and reporting scheme held void in *Marchetti* v. *United States,* 390 U.S. 39 (1968).

United States v. *United States Coin & Currency,* 401 U.S. 715 (1971).

85. Act of July 18, 1956 (§ 106, Stat. 570).

Provision of Narcotic Drugs Import and Export Act creating a presumption that possessor of marijuana knew of its illegal importation into the United States *held,* in absence of showing that all marijuana in United States was of foreign origin and that domestic users could know that their marijuana was more likely than not of foreign origin, unconstitutional under the due process clause of the Fifth Amendment.

Leary v. *United States,* 395 U.S. 6 (1969).

86. Act of August 10, 1956 (70A Stat. 65, Uniform Code of Military Justice, Articles 80, 130, 134).

Servicemen may not be charged under the Act and tried in military courts because of the commission of non-service connected crimes committed off-post and off-duty which are subject to civilian court jurisdiction where the guarantees of the Bill of Rights are applicable.

O'Callahan v. *Parker,* 395 U.S. 258 (1969).

87. Act of August 10, 1956 (70A Stat. 35, § 772(f)).

Proviso of statute permitting the wearing of United States military apparel in theatrical productions only if the portrayal does not tend to discredit the armed force imposes an unconstitutional restraint upon First Amendment freedoms and precludes a prosecution under 18 U.S.C. § 702 for unauthorized wearing of uniform in a street skit disrespectful of the military.

Schacht v. *United Statees,* 398 U.S. 58 (1970).

87a. Act of September 2, 1958 (§ 5601(b) (1), 72 Stat. 1399).

Provision of Internal Revenue Code creating a presumption that one's presence at the site of an unregistered still shall be sufficient for conviction under a statute punishing possession, custody, or c⦁ of an unregistered still unless defendant otherwise explaine⦁ presence at the site to the jury is unconstitutional becaus⦁ presumption is not a legitimate, rational, or reasonable infe⦁ that defendant was engaged in one of the specialized func⦁ proscribed by the statute.

United States v. *Romano,* 382 U.S. 136 (1965).

88. Act of September 14, 1959 (§ 504, 73 Stat. 536).

Provision of Labor-Management Reporting and Disclosure A⦁ 1959 making it a crime for a member of the Communist Party to ⦁ as an officer or, with the exception of clerical or custodial positio⦁ an employee of a labor union *held* to be a bill of attainder and u⦁ stitutional.

United States v. *Brown,* 381 U.S. 437 (1965).

89. Act of October 11, 1962 (§ 305, 76 Stat. 840).

Provision of Postal Services and Federal Employees Salary A⦁ 1962 authorizing Post Office Department to detain material d⦁ mined to be "communist political propaganda" and to forward the addressee only if he requested it after notification by Department, the material to be destroyed otherwise, *held* to im⦁ on the addressee an affirmative obligation which amounted t⦁ abridgment of First Amendment rights.

Lamont v. *Postmaster General,* 381 U.S. 301 (1965).

90. Act of October 15, 1962 (76 Stat. 914).

Provision of District of Columbia laws requiring that a perso⦁ be eligible to receive welfare assistance must have resided in District for at least one year impermissibly classified persons on basis of an assertion of the right to travel interstate and therefore ⦁ to violate the due process clause of the Fifth Amendment.

Shapiro v. *Thompson,* 394 U.S. 618 (1969).

91. Act of December 16, 1963 (77 Stat. 378, 20 U.S.C. § 754).

Provision of Higher Education Facilities Act of 1963 whic⦁ effect removed restriction against religious use of facilities c⦁ structed with federal funds after 20 years *held* to violate the establi⦁ ment clause of the First Amendment inasmuch as the property ⦁ still be of considerable value at the end of the period and remova⦁ the restriction would constitute a substantial governmental contri⦁ tion to religion.

Tilton v. *Richardson,* 403 U.S. 672 (1971).

92. Act of June 22, 1970 (ch III, 84 Stat. 318).

Provision of Voting Rights Act Amendments of 1970 which se⦁ minimum voting age qualification of 18 in state and local electi⦁ *held* to be unconstitutional because beyond the powers of Congress legislate.

Oregon v. *Mitchell,* 400 U.S. 223 (1970).

93. Act of July 31, 1946 (ch. 707, § 7, 60 Stat. 719).

District court decision holding invalid under First and Fif⦁ Amendments of statute prohibiting parades or assemblages ⦁ United States Capitol grounds is summarily affirmed.

Chief of Capitol Police v. *Jeannette Rankin Brigade,* 409 U.⦁ 972 (1972).

94. Act of September 2, 1958 (§ 1(25) (B), 72 Stat. 1446), and Act ⦁ September 7, 1962 (§401, 76 Stat. 469).

Federal statutes providing that spouses of female members of th⦁ Armed Services must be dependent in fact in order to qualify for ce⦁ tain dependent's benefits whereas spouses of male members a⦁ statutorily deemed dependent and automatically qualify fo⦁ allowances, whatever their actual status, is invalid under the equa⦁ protection principles of the Fifth Amendment's due process clause⦁

Frontiero v. *Richardson,* 411 U.S. 677 (1973).

95. Act of July 30, 1965 (§ 339, 79 Stat. 409).

Section of Social Security Act qualifying certain illegitimat⦁ children for disability insurance benefits but disqualifying children i⦁ the disabled wage earner parent did not contribute to the child's sup⦁ port before the onset of the disability or if the child did not live wit⦁ the parent before the onset of disability denies such children equa⦁ protection guaranteed by the due process clause of the Fifth Amendment.

Jiminez v. *Weinberger,* 417 U.S. 628 (1974).

96. Act of January 2, 1968 (§ 163(a) (2), 81 Stat. 872).

District court decisions holding unconstitutional under Fifth Amendment's due process clause section of Social Security Act that reduced, perhaps to zero, benefits coming to illegitimate children upon death of parent in order to satisfy the maximum payment due the wife and legitimate children are summarily affirmed.

Richardson v. *Davis,* 409 U.S. 1069 (1972).
Richardson v. *Griffin,* 409 U.S. 1069 (1972).

97. Act of January 11, 1971 (§ 2, 84 Stat. 2048).

Provision of Food Stamp Act disqualifying from participation in program any household containing an individual unrelated by birth, marriage, or adoption to any other member of the household violates the due process clause of the Fifth Amendment.

Department of Agriculture v. *Moreno,* 413 U.S. 528 (1973).

ct of January 11, 1971 (§ 4, 84 Stat. 2049).

    Provision of Food Stamp Act disqualifying from participation in program any household containing a person 18 or older who had been claimed as a dependent child for income tax purposes in the present or preceding tax year by a taxpayer not a member of the household violates the due process clause of the Fifth Amendment.

    Department of Agriculture v. *Murry,* 413 U.S. 508 (1972).

Weinberger v. *Wiesenfeld*
Decided 1975
Vol. 420, U.S. Code
Title 42, Sec. 402G
Widows (and not widowers) entitled to survivor benefits.

100. *Buckley* v. *Valeo*
    Decided 1976
    Vol. 424, U.S. Code
    Title 2 et al.
    Declared certain parts of the Campaign Reform Act of 1974 unconstitutional.

Legislative Reorganization Act of 1946
Title III—Regulation of Lobbying Act

Short Title

Sec. 301. This title may be cited as the "Federal Regulation of Lobbying ".

Definitions

Sec. 302. When used in this title—

(a) The term "contribution" includes a gift, subscription, loan, ad-ce, or deposit of money or anything of value and includes a contract, mise, or agreement, whether or not legally enforceable, to make a con-ution.

(b) The term "expenditure" includes a payment, distribution, loan, ad-ce, deposit, or gift of money or anything of value, and includes a contract, mise, or agreement, whether or not legally enforceable, to make an expen-ure.

(c) The term "person" includes an individual, partnership, committee, sociation, corporation, and any other organization or group of persons.

(d) The term "Clerk" means the Clerk of the House of Representatives the United States.

(e) The term "legislation" means bills, resolutions, amendments, minations, and other matters pending or proposed in either House of ongress, and includes any other matter which may be the subject of action either House.

Detailed Accounts of Contributions

Sec. 303. (a) It shall be the duty of every person who shall in any anner solicit or receive a contribution to any organization or fund for the urposes hereinafter designated to keep a detailed and exact account of—

(1) all contributions of any amount or of any value whatsoever;

(2) the name and address of every person making any such contribution $500 or more and the date thereof;

(3) all expenditures made by or on behalf of such organization or fund; nd

(4) the name and address of every person to whom any such expenditure made and the date thereof.

(b) It shall be the duty of such person to obtain and keep a receipted ill, stating the particulars, for every expenditure of such funds exceeding $10 n amount, and to preserve all receipted bills and accounts required to be ept by this section for a period of at least two years from the date of the filing f the statement containing such items.

Receipts for Contributions

Sec. 304. Every individual who receives a contribution of $500 or more for any of the purposes hereinafter designated shall within five days after receipt thereof render to the person or organization for which such contribu-tion was received a detailed account thereof, including the name and address of the person making such contribution and the date on which received.

Statements to be Filed With Clerk of House

Sec. 305. (a) Every person receiving any contributions or expending any money for the purposes designated in subparagraph (a) or (b) of section 307 shall file with the Clerk between the first and tenth day of each calendar quarter, a statement containing complete as of the day next preceding the date of filing—

(1) the name and address of each person who has made a contribution of $500 or more not mentioned in the preceding report; except that the first report filed pursuant to this title shall contain the name and address of each person who has made any contribution of $500 or more to such person since the effective date of this title;

(2) the total sum of the contributions made to or for such person during the calendar year and not stated under paragraph (1);

(3) the total sum of all contributions made to or for such person during the calendar year;

(4) the name and address of each person to whom an expenditure in one or more items of the aggregate amount of value, within the calendar year, of $10 or more has been made by or on behalf of such person, and the amount, date, and purpose of such expenditure;

(5) the total sum of all expenditures made by or on behalf of such person during the calendar year and not stated under paragraph (4);

(6) the total sum of expenditures made by or on behalf of such person during the calendar year.

(b) The statements required to be filed by subsection (a) shall be cumulative during the calendar year to which they relate, but where there has been no change in an item reported in a previous statement only the amount need be carried forward.

Statement Preserved for Two Years

Sec. 306. A statement required by this title to be filed with the Clerk—

(a) shall be deemed properly filed when deposited in an es-tablished post office within the prescribed time, duly stamped, registered, and directed to the Clerk of the House of Representatives of the United States, Washington, District of Columbia, but in the event it is not received, a duplicate of such statement shall be promptly filed upon notice by the Clerk of its nonreceipt;

(b) shall be preserved by the Clerk for a period of two years from the date of filing, shall constitute part of the public records of his office, and shall be open to public inspection.

Persons to Whom Applicable

Sec. 307. The provisions of this title shall apply to any person (except a political committee as defined in the Federal Corrupt Practices Act, and duly organized State or local committees of a political party), who by himself, or through any agent or employee or other persons in any manner whatsoever, directly or indirectly, solicits, collects, or receives money or any other thing of value to be used principally to aid, or the principal purpose of which person is to aid, in the accomplishment of any of the following purposes:

(a) The passage or defeat of any legislation by the Congress of the United States.

Registration With Secretary of the Senate and Clerk of the House

Sec. 308. (a) Any person who shall engage himself for pay or for any con-sideration for the purpose of attempting to influence the passage or defeat of any legislation by the Congress of the United States shall, before doing anything in furtherance of such object, register with the Clerk of the House of Representatives and the Secretary of the Senate and shall give to those of-ficers in writing and under oath, his name and business address, the name and address of the person by whom he is employed, and in whose interest he appears or works, the duration of such employment, how much he is paid and is to receive, by whom he is paid or is to be paid, how much he is to be paid for expenses, and what expenses are to be included. Each such person so registering shall, between the first and tenth day of each calendar quarter, so long as his activity continues, file with the Clerk and Secretary a detailed report under oath of all money received and expended by him during the preceding calendar quarter in carrying on his work; to whom paid; for what purposes; and the names of any papers, periodicals, magazines, or other publications in which he has caused to be published any articles or editorials; and the proposed legislation he is employed to support or oppose. The provisions of this section shall not apply to any person who merely appears before a committee of the Congress of the United States in support of or opposition to legislation; nor to any public official acting in his official capacity; nor in the case of any newspaper or other regularly published periodical (including any individual who owns, publishes, or is employed by any such newspaper or periodical) which in the ordinary course of business publishes news items, editorials, or other comments, or paid advertisements, which directly or indirectly urge the passage or defeat of legislation, if such newspaper, periodical, or individual, engages in no further or other activities in connection with the passage or defeat of such legislation, other than to appear before a committee of the Congress of the United States in support of or in opposition to such legislation.

(b) All information required to be filed under the provisions of this section with the Clerk of the House of Representatives and the Secretary of the Senate shall be compiled by said Clerk and Secretary, acting jointly, as soon as practicable after the close of the calendar quarter with respect to which such information is filed and shall be printed in the Congressional Record.

Reports and Statements to be Made Under Oath

Sec. 309. All reports and statements required under this title sh made under oath, before an officer authorized by law to administer c

Penalties

Sec. 310. (a) Any person who violates any of the provisions of this shall, upon conviction, be guilty of a misdemeanor, and shall be punish a fine of not more than $5,000 or imprisonment for not more than t months, or by both such fine and imprisonment.

(b) In addition to the penalties provided for in subsection (a), person convicted of the misdemeanor specified therein is prohibited, period of three years from the date of such conviction, from attempting t fluence, directly or indirectly, the passage or defeat of any proposed leg tion or from appearing before a committee of the Congress in support of o position to proposed legislation; and any person who violates any provisi this subsection shall, upon conviction thereof, be guilty of a felony, and s be punished by a fine of not more than $10,000, or imprisonment for not r than five years, or by both such fine and imprisonment.

Exemption

Sec. 311. The provisions of this title shall not apply to practices or tivities regulated by the Federal Corrupt Practices Act nor be construe repealing any portion of said Federal Corrupt Practices Act.

Text of Supreme Court Lobby Law Ruling and Dissents
United States v. Harriss

June 7, 1954
(347 U.S. 612, 74 S.Ct. 808)

Mr. Chief Justice WARREN delivered the opinion of the Court.

The appellees were charged by information with violation of the Federal Regulation of Lobbying Act, 60 Stat. 812, 839, 2 U.S.C. §§ 261-270, 2 U.S.C.A. §§ 261-270. Relying on its previous decision in National Association of Manufacturers v. McGrath, D.C., 103 F.Supp. 510, vacated as moot, 344 U.S. 804, 73 S.Ct. 313, 97 L.Ed. 627, the District Court dismissed the information on the ground that the Act is unconstitutional. The case is here on direct appeal under the Criminal Appeals Act, 18 U.S.C. § 3731, 18 U.S.C.A. § 3731.

Seven counts of the information are laid under § 305, which requires designated reports to Congress from every person "receiving any contributions or expending any money" for the purpose of influencing the passage or defeat of any legislation by Congress. One such count charges the National Farm Committee, a Texas corporation, with failure to report the solicitation and receipt of contributions to influence the passage of legislation which would cause a rise in the price of agricultural commodities and commodity futures and the defeat of legislation which would cause a decline in those prices. The remaining six counts under § 305 charge defendants Moore and Harriss with failure to report expenditures having the same single purpose. Some of the alleged expenditures consist of the payment of compensation to others to communicate face-to-face with members of Congress, at public functions and committee hearings, concerning legislation affecting agricultural prices; the other alleged expenditures relate largely to the costs of a campaign to induce various interested groups and individuals to communicate by letter with members of Congress on such legislation.

The other two counts in the information are laid under § 308, which requires any person "who shall engage himself for pay or for any consideration for the purpose of attempting to influence the passage or defeat of any legislation" to register with Congress and to make specified disclosures. These two counts allege in considerable detail that defendants Moore and Linder were hired to express certain views to Congress as to agricultural prices or to cause others to do so, for the purpose of attempting to influence the passage of legislation which would cause a rise in the price of agricultural commodities and commodity futures and a defeat of legislation which would cause a decline in such prices; and that pursuant to this undertaking, without having registered as required by § 308, they arranged to have members of Congress contacted on behalf of these views, either directly by their own emissaries or through an artificially stimulated letter campaign.

We are not concerned here with the sufficiency of the information as a criminal pleading. Our review under the Criminal Appeals Act is limited to a decision on the alleged "invalidity" of the statute on which the information

is based. In making this decision, we judge the statute on its face. See Unit States v. Petrillo, 332 U.S. 1, 6, 12, 67 S.Ct. 1538, 1541, 1544, 91 L.Ed. 18 The "invalidity" of the Lobbying Act is asserted on three grounds: (1) th §§ 305, 307, and 308 are too vague and indefinite to meet the requirements due process; (2) that §§ 305 and 308 violate the First Amendment guarante of freedom of speech, freedom of the press, and the right to petition t Government; (3) that the penalty provision of § 310 (b) violates the right the people under the First Amendment to petition the Government.

I.

The constitutional requirement of definiteness is violated by a crimin statute that fails to give a person of ordinary intelligence fair notice that h contemplated conduct is forbidden by the statute. The underlying princip is that no man shall be held criminally responsible for conduct which h could not reasonably understand to be proscribed.

On the other hand, if the general class of offenses to which the statute directed is plainly within its terms, the statute will not be struck down vague even though marginal cases could be put where doubts might aris United States v. Petrillo, 332 U.S. 1, 7, 67 S.Ct. 1538, 1541. Cf. Jordan v. D George, 341 U.S. 223, 231, 71 S.Ct. 703, 707, 95 L.Ed. 886. And if this genera class of offenses can be made constitutionally definite by a reasonable con struction of the statute, this Court is under a duty to give the statute tha construction. This was the course adopted in Screws v. United States, 32 U.S. 91, 65 S.Ct. 1031, 89 L.Ed. 1495, upholding the definiteness of the Civi Rights Act.

The same course is appropriate here. The key section of the Lobbying Act is § 307 entitled "Persons to Whom Applicable". Section 307 provides:

"The provisions of this title shall apply to any person (except a political committee as defined in the Federal Corrupt Practices Act and duly organized State or local committees of a political party) who by himself, or through any agent or employee or other persons in any manner whatsoever, directly or indirectly, solicits, collects, or receives money or any other thing of value to be used principally to aid, or the principal purpose of which person is to aid, in the accomplishment of any of the following purposes:

"(a) The passage or defeat of any legislation by the Congress of the United States.

"(b) To influence, directly or indirectly, the passage or defeat of any legislation by the Congress of the United States."

This section modifies the substantive provisions of the Act, including § 305 and § 308. In other words, unless a "person" falls within the category es-shed by § 307, the disclosure requirements of § 305 and § 308 are in-cable. Thus coverage under the Act is limited to those persons (except he specified political committees) who solicit, collect, or receive con-tions of money or other thing of value, and then only if the principal ose of either the persons or the contributions is to aid in the accomplish-t of the aims set forth in § 307(a) and (b). In any event, the solicitation, ction, or receipt of money or other thing of value is a prerequisite to rage under the Act.

The Government urges a much broader construction—namely, that un-305 a person must report his expenditures to influence legislation even gh he does not solicit, collect, or receive contributions as provided in § Such a construction, we believe, would do violence to the title and uage of § 307 as well as its legislative history. If the construction urged he Government is to become law, that is for Congress to accomplish by her legislation.

We now turn to the alleged vagueness of the purposes set forth in § a) and (b). As in United States v. Rumely, 345 U.S. 41, 47, 73 S.Ct. 543, 97 L.Ed. 770, which involved the interpretation of similar language, we eve this language should be construed to refer only to " 'lobbying in its monly accepted sense' "—to direct communication with members of gress on pending or proposed federal legislation. The legislative history he Act makes clear that, at the very least, Congress sought disclosure of h direct pressures, exerted by the lobbyists themselves or through their lings or through an artificially stimulated letter campaign. It is likewise ar that Congress would have intended the Act to operate on this narrower is, even if a broader application to organizations seeking to propagandize general public were not permissible.

There remains for our consideration the meaning of "the principal pur-e" and "to be used principally to aid." The legislative history of the Act licates that the term "principal" was adopted merely to exclude from the pe of § 307 those contributions and persons having only an "incidental" rpose of influencing legislation. Conversely, the "principal purpose" re-irement does not exclude a contribution which in substantial part is to be d to influence legislation through direct communication with Congress or person whose activities in substantial part are directed to influencing islation through direct communication with Congress. If it were erwise—if an organization, for example, were exempted because lobbying s only one of its main activities—[the Act would in large measure be luced to a mere exhortation against abuse of the legislative process.] In con-ruing the Act narrowly to avoid constitutional doubts, we must also avoid a nstruction that would seriously impair the effectiveness of the Act in cop-g with the problem it was designed to alleviate.

To summarize, therefore, there are three prerequisites to coverage under 307: (1) the "person" must have solicited, collected, or received con-ibutions; (2) one of the main purposes of such "person," or one of the main rposes of such contributions, must have been to influence the passage or efeat of legislation by Congress; (3) the intended method of accomplishing is purpose must have been through direct communication with members of ongress. And since § 307 modifies the substantive provisions of the Act, our nstruction of § 307 will of necessity also narrow the scope of § 305 and §)8, the substantive provisions underlying the information in this case. Thus 305 is limited to those persons who are covered by § 307; and when so overed, they must report all contributions and expenditures having the pur-ose of attempting to influence legislation through direct communication vith Congress. Similarly, § 308 is limited to those persons (with the stated xceptions) who are covered by § 307 and who, in addition, engage hemselves for pay or for any other valuable consideration for the purpose of attempting to influence legislation through direct communication with Congress. Construed this way, the Lobbying Act meets the constitutional re-uirement of definiteness.

II.

Thus construed, §§ 305 and 308 also do not violate the freedoms guaranteed by the First Amendment—freedom to speak, publish, and peti-tion the Government.

Present-day legislative complexities are such that individual members of Congress cannot be expected to explore the myriad pressures to which they are regularly subjected. Yet full realization of the American ideal of govern-ment by elected representatives depends to no small extent on their ability to properly evaluate such pressures. Otherwise the voice of the people may all too easily be drowned out by the voice of special interest groups seeking favored treatment while masquerading as proponents of the public weal. This is the evil which the Lobbying Act was designed to help prevent.

Toward that end, Congress has not sought to prohibit these pressures. It has merely provided for a modicum of information from those who for hire attempt to influence legislation or who collect or spend funds for that pur-pose. It wants only to know who is being hired, who is putting up the money, and how much. It acted in the same spirit and for a similar purpose in pass-ing the Federal Corrupt Practices Act—to maintain the integrity of a basic governmental process. See Burroughs v. United States, 290 U.S. 534, 545, 54 S.Ct. 287, 290, 78 L.Ed. 484.

Under these circumstances, we believe that Congress, at least within the bounds of the Act as we have construed it, is not constitutionally forbidden to require the disclosure of lobbying activities. To do so would be to deny Congress in large measure the power of self-protection. And here Congress has used that power in a manner restricted to its appropriate end. We con-clude that §§ 305 and 308, as applied to persons defined in § 307, do not of-fend the First Amendment.

It is suggested, however, that the Lobbying Act, with respect to persons other than those defined in § 307, may as a practical matter act as a deterrent to their exercise of First Amendment rights. Hypothetical borderline situations are conjured up in which such persons choose to remain silent because of fear of possible prosecution for failure to comply with the Act. Our narrow construction of the Act, precluding as it does reasonable fears, is calculated to avoid such restraint. But, even assuming some such deterrent effect, the restraint is at most an indirect one resulting from self-censorship, comparable in many ways to the restraint resulting from criminal libel laws. The hazard of such restraint is too remote to require striking down a statute which on its face is otherwise plainly within the area of congressional power and is designed to safeguard a vital national interest.

III.

The appellees further attack the statute on the ground that the penalty provided in § 310(b) is unconstitutional. That section provides:

"(b) In addition to the penalties provided for in subsection (a), any person convicted of the misdemeanor specified therein is prohibited, for a period of three years from the date of such convic-tion, from attempting to influence, directly or indirectly, the passage or defeat of any proposed legislation or from appearing before a com-mittee of the Congress in support of or opposition to proposed legislation; and any person who violates any provision of this subsec-tion shall, upon conviction thereof, be guilty of a felony, and shall be punished by a fine of not more than $10,000, or imprisonment for not more than five years, or by both such fine and imprisonment."

This section, the appellees argue, is a patent violation of the First Amend-ment guarantees of freedom of speech and the right to petition the Government.

We find it unnecessary to pass on this contention. Unlike §§ 305, 307, and 308 which we have judged on their face, § 310 (b) has not yet been applied to the appellees, and it will never be so applied if the appellees are found innocent of the charges against them. See United States v. Wurzbach, 280 U.S. 396, 399, 50 S.Ct. 167, 168, 74 L.Ed. 508; United States v. Petrillo, 332 U.S. 1, 9-12, 67 S.Ct. 1538, 1542, 1544, 91 L.Ed. 1877.

Moreover, the Act provides for the separability of any provision found invalid. If § 310(b) should ultimately be declared unconstitutional, its elimination would still leave a statute defining specific duties and providing a specific penalty for violation of any such duty. The prohibition of § 310(b) is expressly stated to be "In addition to the penalties provided for in subsec-tion (a) * * *"; subsection (a) makes a violation of § 305 or § 308 a mis-demeanor, punishable by fine or imprisonment or both. Consequently, there would seem to be no obstacle to giving effect to the separability clause as to § 310 (b), if this should ever prove necessary. Compare Electric Bond & Share Co. v. Securities & Exchange Commission, 303 U.S. 419, 433-437, 58 S.Ct. 678, 682-684, 82 L.Ed. 936.

The judgment below is reversed and the cause is remanded to the District Court for further proceedings not inconsistent with this opinion.

Reversed.

Mr. Justice CLARK took no part in the consideration or decision of this case.

Mr. Justice DOUGLAS, with whom Mr. Justice BLACK concurs, dis-senting.

I am in sympathy with the effort of the Court to save this statute from the charge that it is so vague and indefinite as to be unconstitutional. My in-clinations were that way at the end of the oral argument. But further study changed my mind. I am now convinced that the formula adopted to save this Act is too dangerous for use. It can easily ensnare people who have done no more than exercise their constitutional rights of speech, assembly, and press.

We deal here with the validity of a criminal statute. To use the test of Connally v. General Construction Co., 269 U.S. 385, 391, 46 S.Ct. 126, 127, 70 L.Ed. 322, the question is whether this statute "either forbids or requires the doing of an act in terms so vague that men of common intelligence must necessarily guess at its meaning and differ as to its application". If it is so vague, as I think this one is, then it fails to meet the standards required by due process of law. See United States v. Petrillo, 332 U.S. 1, 67 S.Ct. 1538, 91 L.Ed. 1877. In determining that question we consider the statute on its face. As stated in Lanzetta v. New Jersey, 306 U.S. 451, 453, 59 S.Ct. 618, 619, 83 L.Ed. 888:

"If on its face the challenged provision is repugnant to the due process clause, specification of details of the offense intended to be charged would not serve to validate it. * * * It is the statute, not the accusation under it, that prescribes the rule to govern conduct and warns against transgression. * * * No one may be required at peril of life, liberty or property to speculate as to the meaning of penal statutes. All are entitled to be informed as to what the State commands or forbids."

And see Winters v. New York, 333 U.S. 507, 515, 68 S.Ct. 665, 670, 92 L.Ed. 840.

The question therefore is not what the information charges nor what the proof might be. It is whether the statute itself is sufficiently narrow and precise as to give fair warning.

It is contended that the Act plainly applies

—to persons who pay others to present views to Congress either in committee hearings or by letters or other communications to Congress or Congressmen and

—to persons who spend money to induce others to communicate with Congress.

The Court adopts that view, with one minor limitation which the Court places on the Act—that only persons who solicit, collect, or receive money are included.

The difficulty is that the Act has to be rewritten and words actually added and subtracted to produce that result.

Section 307 makes the Act applicable to anyone who "directly or indirectly" solicits, collects, or receives contributions "to be used principally to aid, or the principal purpose of which person is to aid" in either.

—the "passage or defeat of any legislation" by Congress, or "to influence, directly or indirectly, the passage or defeat of any legislation" by Congress.

We start with an all-inclusive definition of "legislation" contained in § 302(e). It means, "bills, resolutions, amendments, nominations, and other matters pending or proposed in either House of Congress, and includes any other matter which may be the subject of action by either House." What is the scope of "any other matter which may be the subject of action" by Congress? It would seem to include not only pending or proposed legislation but any matter within the legitimate domain of Congress.

What contributions might be used "principally to aid" in influencing "directly or indirectly, the passage or defeat" of any such measure by Congress? When is one retained for the purpose of influencing the "passage or defeat of any legislation"?

(1) One who addresses a trade union for repeal of a labor law certainly hopes to influence legislation.

(2) So does a manufacturers' association which runs ads in newspapers for a sales tax.

(3) So does a farm group which undertakes to raise money for an educational program to be conducted in newspapers, magazines, and on radio and television, showing the need for revision of our attitude on world trade.

(4) So does a group of oil companies which puts agents in the Nation's capital to sound the alarm at hostile legislation, to exert influence on Congressmen to defeat it, to work on the Hill for the passage of laws favorable to the oil interests.

(5) So does a business, labor, farm, religious, social, racial, or other group which raises money to contact people with the request that they write their Congressman to get a law repealed or modified, to get a proposed law passed, or themselves to propose a law.

Are all of these activities covered by the Act? If one is included why are not the others? The Court apparently excludes the kind of activities listed in categories (1), (2), and (3) and includes part of the activities in (4) and (5)—those which entail contacts with the Congress.

There is, however, difficulty in that course, a difficulty which seems to me to be insuperable. I find no warrant in the Act for drawing the line, as the Court does, between "direct communication with Congress" and other pressures on Congress. The Act is as much concerned with one, as with the other.

The words "direct communication with Congress" are not in the Act. Congress was concerned with the raising of money to aid in the passage or defeat of legislation, whatever tactics were used. But the Court not only strikes out one whole group of activities—to influence "indirectly—but substitutes a new concept for the remaining group—to influence "directly." To influence "directly" the passage or defeat of legislation includes any number of methods—for example, nationwide radio, television or advertising programs promoting a particular measure, as well as the "button holing" of Congressmen. To include the latter while excluding the former is to rewrite the Act.

This is not a case where one or more distinct types of "lobbying" are specifically proscribed and another and different group defined in such loose, broad terms as to make its definition vague and uncertain. Here if we give the words of the Act their ordinary meaning, we do not know what the terminal points are. Judging from the words Congress used, one type of activity which I have enumerated is as much proscribed as another.

The importance of the problem is emphasized by reason of the fact that this legislation is in the domain of the First Amendment. That Amendment provides that "Congress shall make no law * * * abridging the freedom of speech, or of the press; or the right of the people * * * to petition Government for a redress of grievances."

Can Congress require one to register before he writes an article, makes a speech, files an advertisement, appears on radio or television, or writes a letter seeking to influence existing, pending, or proposed legislation? That would pose a considerable question under the First Amendment, as Thomas v. Collins, 323 U.S. 516, 65 S.Ct. 315, 89 L.Ed. 430, indicates. I do not mean to intimate that Congress is without power to require disclosure of the real principals behind those who come to Congress (or get others to do so) and speak as though they represent the public interest, when in fact they are undisclosed agents of special groups. I mention the First Amendment to emphasize why statutes touching this field should be "narrowly drawn to prevent the supposed evil," see Cantwell v. Connecticut, 310 U.S. 296, 60 S.Ct. 900, 905, 84 L.Ed. 1213, and not be cast in such vague and indefinite terms as to cast a cloud on the exercise of constitutional rights. Stromberg v. California, 282 U.S. 359, 369, 51 S.Ct. 532, 535, 75 L.Ed. 1117; Thornhill v. Alabama, 310 U.S. 88, 97-98, 60 S.Ct. 736, 741-742, 84 L.Ed. 1093; Winters v. New York, 333 U.S. 507, 509, 68 S.Ct. 665, 667, 92 L.Ed. 840; Joseph Burstyn, Inc., v. Wilson, 343 U.S. 495, 504-505, 72 S.Ct. 777, 781-782, 96 L.Ed. 1098.

If that rule were relaxed, if Congress could impose registration requirements on the exercise of First Amendment rights, saving to the courts the salvage of the good from the bad, and meanwhile causing all who might possibly be covered to act at their peril, the law would in practical effect be a deterrent to the exercise of First Amendment rights. The Court seeks to avoid that consequence by construing the law narrowly as applying only to those who are paid to "button hole" Congressmen or who collect and expend moneys to get others to do so. It may be appropriate in some cases to read a statute with the gloss a court has placed on it in order to save it from the charge of vagueness. See Fox v. Washington, 236 U.S. 273, 277, 35 S.Ct. 383, 384, 59 L.Ed. 573. But I do not think that course is appropriate here.

The language of the Act is so broad that one who writes a letter or makes a speech or publishes an article or distributes literature or does many of the other things with which appellees are charged has no fair notice when he is close to the prohibited line. No construction we give it today will make clear retroactively the vague standards that confronted appellees when they did the acts now charged against them as criminal. Cf. Pierce v. United States, 314 U.S. 306, 311, 62 S.Ct. 237, 239, 86 L.Ed. 226. Since the Act touches the exercise of First Amendment rights, and is not narrowly drawn to meet precise evils, its vagueness has some of the evils of a continuous and effective restraint.

Mr. Justice JACKSON, dissenting.

Several reasons lead me to withhold my assent from this decision.

The clearest feature of this case is that it begins with an Act so mischievously vague that the Government charged with its enforcement does not understand it, for some of its important assumptions are rejected by the Court's interpretation. The clearest feature of the Court's decision is that it leaves the country under an Act which is not much like any Act passed by Congress. Of course, when such a question is before us, it is easy to differ as to whether it is more appropriate to strike out or to strike down. But I recall few cases in which the Court has gone so far in rewriting an Act.

The Act passed by Congress would appear to apply to all persons who (1) solicit or receive funds for the purpose of lobbying, (2) receive and expend funds for the purpose of lobbying, or (3) merely expend funds for the purpose of lobbying. The Court at least eliminates this last category from coverage of the Act, though I should suppose that more serious evils affecting the public interest are to be found in the way lobbyists spend their money than in the ways they obtain it. In the present indictments, six counts relate exclusively to failures to report expenditures while only one appears to rest exclusively on failure to report receipts.

Also, Congress enacted a statute to reach the raising and spending of funds for the purpose of influencing congressional action *directly or indirectly*. The Court entirely deletes "indirectly" and narrows "directly" to mean "direct communication with members of Congress." These two constructions leave the Act touching only a part of the practices Congress deemed sinister.

Finally, as if to compensate for its deletions from the Act, the Court expands the phrase "the principal purpose" so that it now refers to any contribution which "in substantial part" is used to influence legislation.

I agree, of course, that we should make liberal interpretations to save legislative Acts, including penal statutes which punish conduct traditionally recognized as morally "wrong." Whoever kidnaps, steals, kills, or commits similar acts of violence upon another is bound to know that he is inviting retribution by society, and many of the statutes which define these long-established crimes are traditionally and perhaps necessarily vague. But we are dealing with a novel offense that has no established bounds and no such moral basis. The criminality of the conduct dealt with here depends entirely

a purpose to influence legislation. Though there may be many abuses
pursuit of this purpose, this Act does not deal with corruption. These
ndants, for example, are indicted for failing to report their activities in
ng and spending money to influence legislation in support of farm prices,
no charge of corruption, bribery, deception, or other improper action.
may be a selfish business and against the best interests of the nation as
ole, but it is in an area where legal penalties should be applied only by
ulae as precise and clear as our language will permit.

The First Amendment forbids Congress to abridge the right of the
le "to petition the Government for a redress of grievances." If this right
have an interpretation consistent with that given to other First Amend-
t rights, it confers a large immunity upon activities of persons,
nizations, groups and classes to obtain what they think is due them from
ernment. Of course, their conflicting claims and propaganda are con-
ng, annoying and at times, no doubt, deceiving and corrupting. But we
not forget that our constitutional system is to allow the greatest freedom
ccess to Congress, so that the people may press for their selfish interests,
n Congress acting as arbiter of their demands and conflicts.

In matters of this nature, it does not seem wise to leave the scope of a
ninal Act, close to impinging on the right of petition, dependent upon
icial construction for its limitations. Judicial construction, constitutional
tatutory, always is subject to hazards of judicial reconstruction. One may
on today's narrow interpretation only at his peril, for some later Court
y expand the Act to include, in accordance with its terms, what today the

Court excludes. This recently happened with the anti-trust laws, which the
Court cites as being similarly vague. This Court, in a criminal case,
sustained an indictment by admittedly changing repeated and long-
established constitutional and statutory interpretations. United States v.
South-Eastern Underwriters Ass'n, 322 U.S. 533, 64 S.Ct. 1162, 88 L.Ed.
1440. The *ex post facto* provision of our Constitution has not been held to
protect the citizen against a retroactive change in decisional law, but it does
against such a prejudicial change in legislation. As long as this statute stands
on the books, its vagueness will be a contingent threat to activities which the
Court today rules out, the contingency being a change of views by the Court
as hereafter constituted.

The Court's opinion presupposes, and I do not disagree, that Congress
has power to regulate lobbying for hire as a business or profession and to require such agents to disclose their principals, their activities, and their
receipts. However, to reach the real evils of lobbying without cutting into the
constitutional right of petition is a difficult and delicate task for which the
Court's action today gives little guidance. I am in doubt whether the Act as
construed does not permit applications which would abridge the right of
petition, for which clear, safe and workable channels must be maintained. I
think we should point out the defects and limitations which condemn this
Act so clearly that the Court cannot sustain it as written, and leave its
rewriting to Congress. After all, it is Congress that should know from experience both the good in the right of petition and the evils of professional
lobbying.

Major Provisions of the 1970 Legislative Reorganization Act

Following are major provisions of the Legislative Reorganization Act of 1970 (HR 17654—PL 91-510) which Congress cleared Oct. 8, 1970:

Title I—The Committee System

The bill recognized the right of both the House and the Senate to change their own rules of procedure at any time. (The Constitution, Article I, Section 5, states: "Each House may determine the Rules of its Proceedings.")

HOUSE

It amended the rules of the House to:

• Provide that the ranking majority member of the committee preside at any meeting from which the chairman is absent. (This was already the custom in most committees.)

• Provide that committee business meetings and hearings be open to the public unless the committee by majority vote decides otherwise. *(Open and Closed Committee Meetings box, p. 370)*

• Require that all roll-call votes taken in committee—and each member's vote—be made public and that committee reports on bills contain the vote by which the committee ordered the bill reported. (Under existing rules, such votes were not necessarily made public.)

• Provide that committee reports on bills be filed within seven calendar days (excluding days the House was not in session) after a majority of the committee filed a written request that the report be submitted. This provision did not apply to the House Rules Committee with regard to House rules and House business. (Under existing rules, the chairman had the duty to report a bill and act to bring it to a vote on the floor.)

• Prohibit proxy voting in committee except when the committee's written rules permit it, when the proxy is limited to a specific matter, and is in writing, designating the person to whom it is given. (Proxy votes were not mentioned in existing House rules; different committees allowed them in different circumstances.)

• Allow committee members (who indicate this intention) three days (excluding (Saturday, Sunday and legal holidays) to file supplementary, minority or additional views to be included with the committee report on a bill or other matter. This provision did not apply to the House Rules Committee. (There was no similar provision in existing rules; generally, time was allowed for the filing of such views.)

• Prohibit the House from considering any bill or other matter (except from the Appropriations, House Administration, Standards, or Rules Committees) unless the committee report on the measure has been available for at least three days (excluding Saturday, Sunday and legal holidays) prior to consideration. This rule did not apply to declarations of war or emergency, or to legislative veto procedures, or executive reorganization plans. (There was no such provision in existing rules.)

• Prohibit the House from considering any general appropriations bill until printed committee hearings and the report on the bill have been available for at least three days (excluding Saturday, Sunday and legal holidays) prior to consideration. (A similar provision in existing House rules did not exclude Saturdays, Sundays and holidays.

• Authorize the Speaker—if no motion is offered House consideration of a bill within seven days after a r for its consideration has been granted—to recognize member of the committee that reported the bill to move consideration, if so authorized by the committee.

• Specify procedures by which funds are provided meet committee expenses. (Existing rules did not conta such provisions, but the procedures set forth were genera followed.)

• Require that no less than one-third of a committee funds be used for minority staff. (There was no such prov sion in existing rules.)

• Require committees to announce hearings at least o week in advance unless there is good reason that they beg earlier. This provision did not apply to the House Rul Committee. (There was no such provision in existing rules

• Provide that a majority of the minority party membe of a committee are entitled to call witnesses during at lea one day of hearings on a matter. (Many committees custom allowed minority members this opportunity.)

• Allow any open hearing to be broadcast over radio television if a majority of the committee involved so vote and if the broadcast is carried out in accordance with rule specifying that coverage shall be live, without commercia sponsorship; no subpoenaed witness be photographed, the testimony broadcast, without his consent; and equip ment be limited so as not to obstruct the hearings. (Broad casting was not permitted under existing House rules.)

• Provide that all committees could sit without specia leave while the House was in session except when a bill wa being read for amendment under the five-minute rule. Th five-minute rule limitation would not apply to th Appropriations, Government Operations, Internal Security Rules, and Standards Committees. (Under existing rules only the Government Operations, Rules, Standards, an Internal Security Committees could sit without specia leave while the House was in session.)

• Require each standing committee (except the Appropriations, House Administration, Rules, and Standards Committees) to report annually on its review of the execution of laws enacted within its jurisdiction. (Committees already had this review function but had not been required to report on its exercise.)

• Allow 10 minutes' debate on any amendment offered on the floor—even if debate has been closed on the section to which the amendment is proposed—so long as the amendment has been printed in the *Congressional Record* at least one day before consideration. (Under existing rules, an amendment received no explanation at all during consideration of a bill when a majority of the Committee of the Whole agreed to cut off debate on a section before there had been any debate on the amendment.)

• Provide that, upon request of one-fifth of a quorum, a teller vote be recorded by clerks or electronic devices; that members be given not less than 12 minutes to be counted; and that the record include the names of members voting for, against and not voting on the question. (Under existing rules, only the outcome of such votes was recorded, not the positions of members voting. All amendments were

epted or rejected in the Committee of the Whole by
ce, standing, or teller votes, on which members' positions
ained unknown.)

● Provide that once a quorum is obtained, the call of the
use for a quorum can be ended; that for 30 minutes from
beginning of the call members may register their
sence by signing in on tally sheets. (Under existing rules,
ce the call of the House for a quorum was begun, the en-
roll had to be called, which took at least 30-35 minutes.)

● Provide for 10 minutes' debate on a motion to send a
l back to committee with instructions, with the time
vided evenly between the person making the motion and
e persons opposed. (In existing practice, a resolution
ued by the Rules Committee for consideration of a bill
ually specified that there would be no debate on a motion
recommit.)

● Require that every conference report be printed as a
ouse report and be accompanied by an explanatory state-
ent prepared jointly by House and Senate conferees. (In
isting practice, the report was printed as a House report
it only House conferees prepared such a statement.)

● Divide debate on a conference report evenly between
ajority and minority. (In existing practice, such time was
ot formally divided and was controlled by the chairman of
he conferees.)

● Forbid conferees to include any language in a con-
erence version of a bill which concerns a topic which neither
hamber sent to conference; or to modify any topic beyond
he scope of the differing versions of the bill sent to con-
erence. (Existing rules stated that a conference report
hould not include matter not sent to conference by either
hamber.)

● Prohibit the House from considering a conference
eport unless the report and accompanying statement have
been printed in the *Congressional Record* three calendar
days (excluding Saturday, Sunday and legal holidays) prior
o consideration and copies are available on the floor. This
ule would not apply during the last six days of a session.
Existing rules provided only that the House might not consider a conference report—except in the last six days of a
session—until it had been printed in the *Congressional
Record,* and conference reports were often brought up for a
vote with little or no notice.)

● Allow a separate House vote, upon the request of any
member, on any nongermane amendment added by the
Senate to a House-passed bill (requiring only a majority
vote to approve the amendment); prohibit House conferees
from agreeing to a nongermane Senate amendment unless
authorized to do so by a vote on that amendment by the
House. (In existing practice, the House had often been
forced to vote on the bill as a whole, having to defeat the bill
or accept the nongermane amendment. This new rule
applied the same rules to nongermane Senate amendments
as were already applied to legislative amendments to
appropriations bills. In existing practice, conferees reported
such amendments in disagreement and moved for a House
vote to agree to them.)

● Direct that the Journal not be read daily unless the
Speaker or a motion supported by a majority of the
members present so orders. (Such reading was routinely
omitted by unanimous consent under existing practice, but
the objection of one member was enough to require that the
Journal be read in full, a tactic occasionally used to delay or
to force action on some measure.)

● Provide that the resident commissioner from Puerto
Rico be elected to standing committees just as any elected
member of the House and that he be allowed to vote in committee. (Under existing rules, the commissioner was an additional, nonvoting member of the Agriculture, Armed Services and Interior Committee.)

SENATE

Amended the Legislative Reorganization Act of 1946 to
amend the rules of the Senate to:

● Allow a majority of a committee to call a meeting when
the chairman does not call a meeting on request. (The
House, but not the Senate, had this procedure available.)

● Provide that the ranking majority member of the committee preside at any meeting from which the chairman is
absent. (This was already the custom in most committees.)

● Require that Senate committees adopt and publish
rules of committee procedure. (Under existing rules, there
was no such requirement.)

● Provide that committee business meetings be open to
the public except during sessions to mark up bills, to vote or
when the committee by majority vote decides otherwise.
(Open and Closed Committee Meetings box p. 370)

● Provide that committee hearings be open to the public
except when the committee decides that the testimony may
relate to national security, may reflect adversely on an individual's character or reputation or may contain confidential information.

● Require that all roll-call votes taken in committee on a
measure or amendment—and the positions of senators
voting—be announced in the committee report on that
measure unless previously made public.

● Provide that committee reports on bills be filed within
seven calendar days (excluding days the Senate is not in
session) after a majority of the committee files a written request that the report be filed.

● Provide that no proxy vote may be cast on a motion to
report a bill if committee rules forbid the use of a proxy on
such a motion; prescribe that proxies be voted only on such
a motion upon the affirmative request of an absent member.

● Allow committee members (who indicate this intention) three days to file supplementary, minority or additional views to be included with the committee report on a
bill or other matter. (There was no similar provision in existing rules; generally, time was allowed for the filing of such
views.)

● Prohibit the Senate from considering any bill or other
matter reported from a standing committee unless the committee report on the measure has been available for at least
three days (excluding Saturday, Sunday and legal holidays)
prior to consideration. This rule did not apply to
declarations of war or emergency, to legislative veto
procedures or to executive reorganization plans, and could
be waived by agreement of the Senate majority and minority leaders. (There was no such provision in existing rules.)

● Specify procedures to govern procurement of funds for
committees in excess of the annual $10,000 limit.

● Require committees (except the Senate Appropriations
Committee) to announce hearings at least one week in ad-
vance unless there is good reason that they begin earlier.
(There was no such provision in existing rules.)

● Provide that a majority of the minority party members
of a committee (except the Senate Appropriations Committee) are entitled to call witnesses during at least one day
of hearings on a matter. (Many committees by custom
allowed minority members this opportunity.)

● Allow any open hearing to be broadcast over radio or
television under whatever rules the committee may adopt.

● Forbid Senate committees (except the Appropriations Committee) to sit while the Senate is in session unless special leave has been obtained from the Senate majority and minority leaders.

● Require each standing committee (except the Senate Appropriations Committee) to report annually on its activities reviewing the execution of laws enacted within its jurisdiction. (Committees already possessed this review function but had not been required to make reports.)

● Require that every conference report be printed as a Senate report and be accompanied by an explanatory statement prepared jointly by House and Senate conferees. (By existing custom, only House conferees prepared such a statement and conference reports were usually only printed as House reports.)

● Divide debate on a conference report evenly between majority and minority. (By existing custom, such time was not formally divided and was controlled by the chairman of the conferees.)

● Require a quorum of the Senate Appropriations Committee to be present for a vote to report an appropriations bill from committee. (This was committee practice but existing rules exempted the Appropriations Committee from the requirement.)

● Rename the Senate Banking and Currency Committee the Senate Banking, Housing and Urban Affairs Committee.

● Reduce the size of certain Senate committees; provide that, in the future, senators may be members of only two major committees and one minor, select, or joint committee; that no senator may serve on more than one of the Armed Services, Appropriations, Finance or Foreign Relations Committees; that no senator may hold the chairmanship of more than one full committee and one subcommittee of a major committee. (This provision would not deprive any senator of any committee position or chairmanship currently held, but would apply to all future assignments.)

● Create a Senate Committee on Veterans' Affairs.

Title II—Fiscal Controls

● Directed the Secretary of the Treasury and the director of the Office of Management and Budget to set up and maintain a standardized data processing system for federal budgetary and fiscal data.

● Directed the Secretary and director to furnish to congressional committees, upon request, information on the location and nature of available data on federal programs, activities, receipts and expenditures.

● Directed the comptroller general to review and analyze the results of government programs; to make cost benefit studies of the programs at the direction of Congress or on his own initiative or upon request of any congressional committee; to assist congressional committees in analyzing cost-benefit studies furnished by any federal agencies or in conducting such studies.

● Required that the President send Congress—as part of the budget—five-year forecasts of the costs of every new or expanded federal program.

● Required that the President update the budget for the next fiscal year and the five-year cost forecasts at midyear, beginning with 1972, and transmit to Congress a supplementary summary of those revisions by June 1 each year.

● Required the comptroller general (or a designated employee of the General Accounting Office (GAO)) to ex-plain to any congressional committee so requesting a GAO report relevant to legislation, appropriations programs within the committee's jurisdiction.

● Directed the comptroller general to deliver copies GAO reports to the Appropriations and Governme Operations Committees and to any other committees r questing them.

● Limited to one year the period of time for which t GAO employee could be assigned fulltime to work with a congressional committee.

● Required federal agencies to report to the Governme Operations Committees—no later than 60 days after a GA report made recommendations concerning that age cy—what action has been taken with respect to tho recommendations.

● Required the House Appropriations Committee, withi 30 days after the President sent the budget to Congress, t hold hearings on the budget and receive testimony from th director of the Office of Management and Budget, th Secretary of the Treasury, and the chairman of the Counc of Economic Advisers; and that such hearings be open ex cept when the national security requires otherwise.

● Required that committee reports on all measures—ex cept revenue bills—include cost estimates for the program affected for that year and the next five years. This provisio did not apply to the House Appropriations, Administration Rules, and Standards Committees or the Senat Appropriations Committee.

Title III—Sources of Information

● Increased to six from four the number of permanent professional staff for each congressional standing committee, two of whom, in addition to one of the six permanent clerical staff members, might be selected by a majority of the committee's minority party members. This provision did not apply to the House and Senate Appropriations Committees or to the House Standards Committee.

● Authorized standing committees—with the approval of the Senate Rules or House Administration Committee—to provide staff members with specialized training.

● Authorized salaries of Senate committee staff personnel comparable to those of House committee staff personnel.

● Redesignated the Legislative Reference Service the Congressional Research Service, redefining its duties to assist congressional committees by providing research and analytical services, records, documents and other information and data, including memoranda on proposed legislation; and expanding its staff resources.

● Directed the House parliamentarian, after the compilation of parliamentary precedents of the House currently under way (the first since 1936) was completed, to compile such precedents every five years.

Title IV—Congress as an Institution

● Created a Joint Committee on Congressional Operations to continue the study of the operations and organization of Congress and to recommend improvements, including possible uses of automatic data processing systems.

● Abolished the Joint Committee on Immigration and Nationality Policy, which, established in 1952, had never met.

● Created a Capitol Guide Service to provide free tours of the Capitol.

● Provided that Congress take a 30-day recess in August every nonelection year, unless it had already adjourned or state of war existed.

● Converted the House payroll system from the base pay standard using 1945 figures to a gross pay standard reflecting the 17 pay raises since 1945 and showing the actual amounts paid to House employees.

● Provided that Senate pages be between 14 and 18 years old and that House pages be between 16 and 18; and authorized the construction of the John W. McCormack Residential Page School.

● Authorized the Speaker of the House to appoint a commission to plan and oversee the modernization of the House galleries, including the enclosure of the galleries with soundproof glass.

Title V—Office of the Legislative Counsel, House of Representatives

● Established the Office of Legislative Counsel for the House of Representatives, expanding and defining its duties.

Title VI—Effective Dates

● Provided that most of the provisions, with a few exceptions, would become effective immediately before noon Jan. 3, 1971.

Provisions of the 1974 House Committee Reform

Following are provisions of H Res 988 which the House approved Oct. 8, 1974:

Procedural

● Increased each committee's permanent staff from six professional and six clerical employees to 18 professionals and 12 clerks, and granted the minority party control of one-third (10) of those employees. The minority would also control one-third of the investigative funds committees use to supplement their staffs, with the ranking minority member of each subcommittee (up to six) permitted to appoint one professional using investigative funds. *[However, in connection with minority staffing, see p. 393]*

● Banned voting by proxy in committee.

● Required that committees with over 15 members establish at least four subcommittees.

● Required the House to return between Dec. 1 and 20 in election years to organize the next Congress in advance, effective in 1974.

● Authorized the speaker to refer bills to more than one committee at a time or to several committees in sequence. He could also split bills up and send the parts to different committees.

● Required all committee reports to include a statement of the bill's impact on inflation, and required all reports on appropriations bills to include statements on changes in law made in the accompanying bill.

● Required a one-hundred word summary of the contents of each House bill introduced to be filed for public inspection.

● Gave all standing committees across-the-board subpoena authority without the necessity for individually approved House resolutions, and required that all subpoenas be authorized by a majority of a committee.

● Directed the speaker to complete compilation of House precedents by January 1, 1977, and to update them every two years after that.

● Established a Commission on Information and Facilities, controlled by the House members of the Joint Committee on Congressional Operations.

● Established a Legislative Classification Office to develop a system linking federal programs and expenditures to the authorizing statutes, and showing the committee jurisdiction for each authorization.

● Allowed resident commissioners and delegates to sit on conference committees and required that a majority of House conferees support the House position on the bill in question.

Jurisdictional

● Consolidating most transportation matters in the Public Works Committee, to be renamed Public Works and Transportation. The panel, which already had jurisdiction over highways, would gain urban mass transit from Banking and Currency, and civil aviation and surface transit from Interstate and Foreign Commerce. Commerce would keep railroads.

● Giving the Interstate and Foreign Commerce Committee, to be renamed Commerce and Health, jurisdiction over biomedical research (from Science and Astronautics), nursing home construction (from Banking) and health care programs except those financed through payroll taxes (from Ways and Means). [Name change did not take place.]

● Giving Banking and Currency, to be renamed Banking, Currency and Housing, jurisdiction over renegotiation (from Ways and Means) and international financial organizations (from Foreign Affairs).

● Giving Science and Astronautics, to be renamed Science and Technology, jurisdiction over civil aviation research and development (from Commerce), environmental research and development (from several committees) and all energy research and development except nuclear (from several committees).

● Giving the Foreign Affairs Committee authority over some international trade matters (from Banking and Currency), the Food for Peace Program (PL 480) except domestic production (from Agriculture), international commodity agreements and export controls (from Banking and Ways and Means).

● Transferring revenue sharing from Ways and Means to Government Operations.

● Moving legal services from Education and Labor to Judiciary.

● Setting up a new Select Committee on Aging.

● Making the Select Committee on Small Business a legislative committee with the jurisdiction of the Banking and Currency Committee's Small Business Subcommittee.

Index

> **Note:** Pages in the Appendix are numbered 1-A, 2-A, 3-A, etc. The word "box" indicates that the entry contains detailed information.

Q

R

W